CHAM

ANAGRAMS

for crosswords and all word games

New edition

CHAMBERS

CHAMBERS
An imprint of Chambers Harrap Publishers Ltd
7 Hopetoun Crescent
Edinburgh EH7 4AY

www.chambers.co.uk

This edition first published Chambers 2001
First edition W & R Chambers 1985
Second edition Chambers 1994

A CIP catalogue record for this book is available from the British Library.

ISBN 0550 12005 X

Designed and typeset in Great Britain by Chambers Harrap Publishers Ltd
Printed and bound in Great Britain by Cox & Wyman Ltd, Reading, Berkshire

Contents

Contributors

Editor
Marc Oven-Gnu

Consultant Editor
Sarah Czech-Winter

Computerization
Zac Wherpster

Prepress
Naomi I Caravan-Park

The editors would also like to acknowledge the valuable contribution made to the planning of this book by Elaine Higgleton

Introduction

This new edition of *Chambers Anagrams* lists 110,000 solutions to anagrams, and is based on *Chambers Crossword Dictionary.* It includes not only single words and abbreviations, but also phrases and many proper nouns, and is an essential addition to the library of every word-puzzler.

Letter groupings are listed according to length, that is by the total number of letters in each word or phrase (from 3 to 15 letters), and then alphabetically within each length, all possible anagram solutions being clearly presented beside them. For quick reference, each page of *Anagrams* is clearly marked with the letter lengths and a guide to the letter combinations.

All you have to do to find an anagram solution is to decide which letters make up the anagram, put these letters into alphabetical order — hyphens, accents, capital letters, etc should be ignored — and look up this combination of letters in the book.

For example, if the anagram you wish to solve is OPEN A RIOT (9 letters), arrange these letters into alphabetical order to give AEINOOPRT, then look for this combination in the 9-letter section where you will find the answer: OPERATION. Or if you wish to solve the anagram CAN'T EASE ALL (1, 5, 5 or 11 letters in total) arrange the letters to AAACEELLNST, and in the 11-letter section you'll find the answer: A CLEAN SLATE. Sometimes more than one solution is given under a letter combination, for example AACEIRV = AVARICE or CAVIARE, but in these cases the correct answer should be obvious from the wording of the clue and the letters already filled in on the crossword grid.

To retain information which may help with crossword clues, the solution words are listed as they appear in *Chambers Crossword Dictionary* (not in capitals, as in some word-books); words genuinely beginning with a capital can therefore be recognized. Where a word can be spelled with or without an initial capital letter, often with different meanings, this is shown by the symbol ▫ (eg 'Moor' and 'moor'). Accents have been retained since they often point to separate meanings (eg 'pate' and 'pâté') or to the foreign origin of a word.

Summary of common anagram indicators

The following list includes words regularly used to indicate an anagram in cryptic crossword clues. No such list could be comprehensive. Almost any word or phrase meaning or suggesting disturbance or an abnormal state may be used as or as part of an anagram indicator in a cryptic clue. The list shows base forms of common anagram indicators; full inflected forms are not shown. Verbs in the list may appear in clues in any of their inflected forms; derivative nouns may be used; and adjectives may be found in their adverbial forms. For example, the list includes **annoy**, **arrange**, **awkward** and **random**, but omits **annoys**, **arrangement**, **awkwardly** and **at random**.

about
abroad
adjust
adrift
afresh
all over the place
alter
amend
amiss
annoy
another: in another way
anyhow
anyway
appal
around
arrange
awful
awkward
bad
baffle
bastard
bats
batting
beat up
become
bedevil
bend
bewilder
blend
boil
bottle
break
brew
buckle
bust
camouflage
capriccioso
careless
change
chaotic
chip
chop
circulate
clumsy
cocktail
collapse
complicate
compose
confound
confuse
construe
contrive
conversion
convert
cook
correct
could be
crack
crash
crazy
criminal
cripple
crooked
cruel
cuckoo
curious
cut
damage
dance
deform
deploy
derange
desecrate
destroy
detour
develop
dicky
different
disconcert
discord
discordant
diseased
disfigure
disgruntled
disguise
dishevel
disorder
dispose
disrupt
dissipate
dissolute
distort
distract
distress
distribute
disturb
divert
do
doctor
dreadful
dress
drunk
dubious
eccentric
edit

effervescent
embarrass
enigmatic
entangle
erratic
erroneous
error
erupt
evolve
explode
explosive
false
fancy
flap: in a flap
flash
flexible
flighty
flounder
fluid
form of
foul
free
fresh
frilly
fuddle
garble
gauche
ground
hammer
hammy
haphazard
hash
havoc
hit
ill
ill-
ill-composed
improper
injure
inordinate
involve
irregular
irritate
jockey
jolt
jumble
kink
knock out
labyrinthine
lax
light
loose
lost
lunatic
mad
malleable
mangle
manipulate
manoeuvre
maybe
medley
mend
mess
metamorphose
mis-
misdeliver
misguided
mislead
misshape
mistake
misuse
mix
mixture
model
mongrel
move
muddle
mutate
mutilate
mysterious
neglect
nervous
new
nobble
nonconformist
novel
nuts
oblique
obscure
obtainable
odd
off
off-
off-colour
on
order
order: out of order
organize
out
outlandish
out of
outrageous
part
peculiar
perhaps
pervert
phony
pickled
pie
place: all over the place
place: out of place
plastic
play
ply
poorly
pop
possible
potential
prepare
process
produce
pummel
punish
put off
queer
ragged
random
rearrange
recast
reckless
recollect
redevelop
rediscover
reel
reform
refurbish
relay
repair
represent
reproduce
resolve
resort
restless
restraint: without restraint
review
revise
revolt: in revolt
revolution
rewrite
rickety
rig
riotous
ripple
rocky
rollicking
rotten
rough
ruin
run
runny
sad
scramble

scratch
scuffle
sea: at sea
seethe
set off
set out
shake
shell
shift
shimmer
shiver
shock
shower
shuffle
silly: look silly
slipshod
sloppy
solution: in solution
solve
somehow
sorry
sorts: out of sorts
soup
spasmodic
spill
spray
spread
spurious
stagger
stew
stir
storm
strange
struggle
supple
suspect
swill
swim
swirl
switch
tangle
terrible
throb
throw
tipsy
tortuous
torture
train
trammel
transfer
transform
translate
transpose
treat
trip
trouble
tumble
turbulent
turnover
twirl
twist
un-
unconventional
undulate
unfit
unhappy
unnatural
unordered
unorthodox
unruly
unsettled
unsound
unstuck
untidy
unusual
unwind
upset
vague
vary
variety
version
vigorous
wander
warp
waste
wave
way: in another way
whirl: in a whirl
whisk
wicked
wild
work
worry
worsted
wreck
wrestle
wretched
writhe
wrong
wry
yank

3 letters

A

AAB aba
BAA
baa
AAC caa'
AAD Ada
AAE AEA
AAG aga□
AAH aha
AAK AKA
aka
Kaa
AAL à la
AAM maa
AAN ana
AAR Ara
AAS ASA
Asa
AAV AVA
ava
ava'
ABB Bab
ABC ABC
BAC
cab
ABD bad
BDA
dab
ABE Abe
BAe
Bea
ABF BAF
fab
FBA
ABG bag
gab
GBA
ABH ABH
bah
ABI IBA
ABJ jab
ABL alb
lab□
ABM ABM
bam
BMA
MBA
ABN ban
nab
NBA
ABO Åbo
AOB
BOA
boa
ABP Abp
bap
ABR bar
bra
Rab
ABS ABS
BAS
ABT BAT
bat
BTA
TAB
tab
ABW WBA
ABX Bax
ABY bay
ABZ Baz
ACD ADC
CAD
cad
ACE ace
CAE
ACF AFC
ACG GCA
ACH ach
ACI ICA
ACL lac
ACM CAM
cam
mac
ACN ANC
can
ACO AOC
ACP CAP
cap
ACR ARC
arc
car
RAC
RCA
ACS CSA
sac
ACT ACT
act
ATC
CAT
cat
ACV CVA
vac□
ACW caw
ACY cay
ADD add
dad
ADE dae
ADF fad
ADG dag
gad□
ADH had
ADI aid
dai□
IDA
Ida
ADL dal
lad
ADM dam
mad
ADN ADN
AND
and
dan□
DNA
ADO ado
Dao
DOA
ODA
ADP ADP
dap
DPA
pad
ADR RDA
ADS SAD
sad
SDA
ADT tad
ADU UDA
ADV VAD
ADW daw
wad
ADY day□
AEG aeg
age
AEH hae
AEI EIA
AEK EAK
kea
AEL ale
Lae
LEA
lea
AEM Mae
AEN ean
Ena
nae
AEP ape
pea
AER are
ear
era
Rae
Rea
AES ASE
ESA
SAE
sae
sea
AET ate
EAT
eat
ETA
eta
tea
AEU AEU
EAU
UAE
AEV Eva
AEW awe
wae
WEA
AEX axe
AEY aye
AEZ EAZ
zea
AFG AFG
fag
AFH fah
AFK kaf
AFL Alf
AFM AFM
AFN fan
AFO FAO
oaf
AFP AFP
fap
FPA
AFQ FAQ
qaf
AFR far
RAF
AFS FAS
SFA
AFT aft
fat
AFU Ufa
AFX fax
AFY fay□
AGG gag
AGH hag
AGJ jag
AGL gal□
lag
AGM AGM
gam
mag□
AGN nag
NGA
AGO ago
Gao
goa□
AGP gap
PGA
AGR AGR
gar
rag
AGS gas
sag
AGT gat
tag
AGV VGA
AGW wag
AGY gay□
AGZ Gaz
zag
AHH hah
AHI AIH
AHK kha
AHL Hal
lah
AHM ham□
AHO hao
hoa
AHP hap
pah
AHR rah
RHA
AHS ash
has
AHT hat
tha
AHW haw
AHY hay
yah
YHA
AIK kai
AIL ail
Ali
AIM aim
Mia
AIN ani
Ian
AIP IPA
AIR air
IRA
Ira
rai
RIA
ria
AIS sai
AIT i.t.a.
ITA
ita
Tai
Taï
AIV via
viâ
AIZ Zia
AJM jam□
AJN Jan
AJR jar
raj
AJS JSA
AJW jaw
AJY jay□
AKM kam
AKO koa
oak
AKP PAK
AKR ark
AKS ask
ska
AKT kat
AKU auk
AKY Kay
yak
ALL all
ALM lam
MAL
MLA
ALN LANtw
ALP ALP
alp
lap
PAL
pal
ALS ASL
sal□
ALT alt
Tal
ALU ALU
ULA
ula
ALV lav
Val
ALW awl
law□
WAL
ALX lax
ALY lay
AMM mam
AMN man
MNA
AMO moa
AMP amp
map
AMR arm
mar
r.a.m.
RAM
ram□
RMA
AMS ASM
Sam
AMT amt

Words marked □ can also be spelled with an initial capital letter

ATM
mat❑
Tam
AMV AVM
AMW maw
AMX max❑
AMY Amy
may❑
yam
ANN Ann
nan❑
ANP nap
NPA
pan❑
ANR RAN
ran❑
RNA
ANS San
ANT ant
nat❑
NTA
tan
ANU ANU
Anu
Una
ANV NAV
van❑
ANW awn
WAN
wan
ANY any
ayn
nay
AOP Apo
OAP
poa
AOR oar
Rao
AOS OAS
AOT oat
AOU OAU
AOV ova
AOZ zoa
APP pap
APR APR
Apr
ARP
Arp
par
rap
APS asp
pas
PSA
sap
spa
APT apt
ATP
pat❑
PTA
tap
APU Pau
APW paw
PWA
wap
APX pax
APY pay
pya
yap
APZ Paz
zap
AQT qat
AQU qua
ARR arr
ARS RAS
RSA
ART art
rat
tar
ARU Rau
UAR
ARW raw
RWA
war
ARX rax
ARY Ayr
ray❑
rya
ASS ass
SAS
AST sat
ASU AUS
USA
ASV vas
ASW saw
was
ASX sax
ASY say
ATT tat
ATU AUT
tau
ATV ATV
tav
VAT
vat❑
ATW taw
TWA
wat❑
ATX tax
ATY Tay
ATZ AZT
AUV UVA
UV-A
AVW vaw
AWW waw
AWX wax❑
AWY way
yaw
AYZ zay

B

BBB BBB
BBC BBC
BBE ebb
BBI bib
BBO bob❑
BCC BCC
CBC
BCD BCD
BCE BCE
CBE
BCG BCG
bcg
GCB
BCH ChB
BCI CBI
CIB
BCJ JCB
BCK KCB
BCL BCL
BCN NBC
BCO cob
BCP PCB
BCR RCB
BCS BSc
CBS
ScB
BCU cub
BCW WBC
BDE BEd
bed
DBE
deb❑
BDI BDI
bid
dib
BDN DNB
BDO bod
dob
BDS BDS
DBS
BDU bud
dub
BEE bee❑
BEF BEF
BEG beg
GBE
Geb
BEK KBE
keb
BEL bel❑
BEM BEM
MBE
BEN ben❑
NEB
neb
BEO OBE
BER BRE
BES BSE
BET bet❑
BEU EBU
BEV BeV
BEW web❑
BEY bye
BFI FBI
fib
BFO fob
BFR FBR
BFS FSB
BGG GBG
BGH GBH
gbh
BGI big
gib❑
BGJ GBJ
BGK KGB
BGM GBM
GMB
BGO bog
gob
BGU bug
BGZ GBZ
BHM HBM
BHO boh
hob
BHP bhp
BHS BHS
Bhs
BHU hub
BIJ jib
BIL lib
BIM BIM
BMI
BIN bin
nib
BIO Ibo
IOB
obi
BIP bpi
BIR rib
BIS bis
BSI
IBS
SIB
BIT bit
Tib
BJM BMJ
BJO job❑
BLL LLB
BLO lob
BLW lbw
BMO MBO
mob
BMP BPM
bpm
BMS BSM
BMU bum
BMV BVM
BMW BMW
BMW®
BMX BMX
BNO Bon
nob
BNR BRN
BNS NSB
SBN
BNU bun
nub
BOO boo
BOP bop
BOR Bor
orb
rob❑
BOS bos
sob
BOT bot
BOW bow❑
WBO
BOX box
BOY boy
BYO
yob
BPR RPB
BPS bps
BPU pub
BPW wpb
BPX PBX
BRS BRS
BRU BRU
BUR
bur
rub
UBR
BST BST
TSB
BSU bus
sub
BSY bys
BTU BTU
but
tub
BUV UVB
UV-B
BUY buy

C

CCD CCD
DCC
CCF CFC
CCM MCC
CCN NCC
CCW WCC
CDE EDC
CDF DFC
CDI CDI
CID
Cid
ICD
CDJ CJD
CDL DCL
LCD
CDM DCM
CDN CDN
CND
CDO cod
DOC
doc
CDR Cdr
CDS DSC
DSc
ScD
CDT CDT
TCD
CDU cud
CEE ECE
EEC
CEG ECG
GCE
GEC
CEH che
ech
CEI ice
CEK Eck
CEN NEC
CEO CEO
Coe
Eco
EOC
CEP cep
PEC
pec
CER rec
CES CSE
SCE
SEC
sec❑
CET ECT
etc
tec
CEU cue
ecu❑
CFH HCF
CFI IFC
CFO FCO
FOC
foc
CFR RFC
CFS SCF
CFU UFC
CGI CGI
cig
IGC
CGL GLC
CGM CMG
GMC
Gmc
CGO cog
CHI chi
ch'i
hic
ich
CHM HCM
CHN HNC
CHO hoc
och
CHR RCH
CII CII

Words marked ❑ can also be spelled with an initial capital letter

ICI
CIL ICL
CIN NIC
CIO IOC
CIP IPC
pic
CIR ICR
RIC
CIS CIS
Cis
sic
CIT ITC
tic
CIU ICU
CIV Vic
CIY icy
CJR JCR
CLM LCM
lcm
MLC
CLO col
CLP PLC
plc
CLR RLC
CLT TLC
CLY cly
CMM MMC
CMP MCP
pcm
CMR MRC
RCM
CMS MSc
SCM
CMT TCM
CMU cum
CMW cwm
CNN CNN
CNO con□
NCO
NOC
ONC
CNP NCP
PCN
CNR CNR
RCN
CNS NSC
CNT NCT
CNY NYC
COO coo
COP cop
CPO
COR cor
OCR
orc
ROC
roc
COS cos□
Soc
COT cot
OTC
COV CVO
COW cow
COX cox
COY coy
CPP PCP
CPR CPR
RCP
CPS CSP
CPT TCP
CPU CPU
cup□
CPV PVC
CPW WPC
CRR RCR
CRS RCS
RSC
SCR
SRC
CRT CRT
RCT
CRU cur
RUC
CRV VCR
CRY cry
CSU CSU
CSV CSV
CVS
CSW CWS
CTU cut
TUC
UTC
CTW cwt

D

DDI did
IDD
DDO dod
odd
DDR DDR
DDS DDS
DDT DDT
DDU dud
DEE Dee
DEF EDF
fed
DEH he'd
DEI dei
die
Eid
DEL del□
LED
DEN den□
end
ned□
DEO DoE
doe
ode
OED
DEP EDP
DEQ QED
DER red□
DES DES
SED
DET ETD
ted□
DEU due
DEW dew
wed
DEY dye
Edy
DEZ zed
DFI fid
DFM DFM
DFR RDF
DFU UDF
DFW fwd
DGI dig
DGO dog
god□
DGP GDP
DGR GDR
DGU dug
DHI hid
DHL LHD
lhd
DHN HND
DHO doh
hod
DHP DPh
PhD
DIK kid
DIL lid
DIM dim
mid
DIN DIN
din
IND
nid
DIO DoI
DIP dip
IDP
PID
DIR rid
DIS Dis
DIT dit
DTI
DIU IUD
UDI
DIV div
vid
DIX Dix
DIY DIY
DKO KO'd
DKY Kyd
DLL LLD
DLO old
DLP PDL
DLS LSD
DLT Ltd
DMO DOM
MOD
MoD
mod□
DMS DMs
DSM
MDS
DMU mud
UDM
DMZ DMZ
DNO don□
nod
OND
DNU dun
DNV nvd
DOP pod
DOR dor
rod□
DOS DOS
dos
do's
DSO
sod
DOT dot□
tod
DOU duo
DOV VOD
DOY yod
DPP DPP
DPQ PDQ
pdq
DPS SDP
DPT dpt
DTP
DPU dup
pud
DRS SDR
DRU rud
UDR
DRY dry
DSS DSS
SSD
DST STD
DSY yds
DUV VDU
DUX dux

E

EEF fee
fée
EEG EEG
gee
EEK eek
eke
Kee
EEL eel
lee□
EEM Mee
EEN een
ENE
née
EEP pee
EER e'er
ere
EES ESE
see
EET EET
tee
EEV eve□
vee
EEW ewe
wee
EEY eye
EEZ zee
EFF eff
EFI fie
EFK kef
EFL EFL
elf
EFM EMF
fem
EFN fen
NEF
EFO foe
EFR erf
ref
EFS Fès
EFT eft
tef
EFU feu
EFW few
wef
EFY fey
EFZ fez□
EGG egg
EGI gie
EGK keg
EGL gel
leg
EGM gem
Meg
EGN ENG
gen
EGO ego
EGP peg□
EGR erg
Reg
EGT get
teg
EGV GeV
veg
EHI hie
EHL Hel
EHM hem
EHN hen
EHO EHO
hoe
EHP hep
EHR her
HRE
EHS hes
he's
HSE
Hse
she□
she-
EHT ETH
het
the
EHU hue
Hué
EHW hew□
EHX hex
EHY hey
EIK eik
Ike
EIL lei
lie□
EIP PEI
pie
EIR ire
rei
EIS EIS
EIT tie
EIV I've
vie
EJM Jem
EJN Jen
EJO Joe
EJR RJE
EJT jet
EJW Jew
EKL elk
lek
EKN ken□
EKO oke
EKP kep
EKS Kes
EKU uke
EKY key
kye
EKZ zek
ELM elm
LEM
lem
ELN Len
ELO Leo
olé
ELP lep
ELS ESL
les
LSE
ELT ELT
elt
let
tel
ELU leu
ELV lev
ELW Lew
ELY Ely
ley
lye
ELZ lez
EMM Emm
mem
Mme
EMN men

EMP MEP
EMR ERM
REM
rem
EMS EMS
Ems
SEM
EMT met
EMU EMU
emu
EMV MeV
EMW mew
EMX MEX
EMZ MEZ
ENN NNE
ENO ENO
Eno
eon
one
ENP PEN
pen□
ENR ren
ENS ESN
NES
SEN
sen
ENT ENT
net□
ten
ENW new
wen
ENY Ney
nye□
yen
ENZ Zen
EOP ope
Poe
EOR ore
o’re
öre
roe
EOS Eos
oes□
EOT OTE
toe
EOV voe
EOW owe
woe
EOY Yeo
EOZ Zoe
Zoë
EPP EPP
PEP
pep
PPE
EPR per
Pré
rep
EPS ESP
pes
EPT PET
pet
Pte
EPW pew
EPY Pye
yep
EQS esq.□
ERR err
ERS res
ERT ret
RTE
ERU rue
ERV rev□
ERX Rex
ERY rye
ERZ ZRE
ESS SSE
EST est
set
Ste
ESU ESU
sue□
use
ESW sew
ESX ex’s
sex
ESY sye
yes□
ETU ute□
ETV vet
ETW Tew
wet□
ETY tye
yet
EUY uey
EVX vex
EWY Wye
yew
EXY yex

F

FFI iff
FFO off
FGI fig
FGO fog
FGR FRG
FGU fug
FHM FHM
FHO foh
Hof
FHS FSH
SHF
shf
FHU UHF
FHV VHF
FIK kif
FIM IMF
FIN fin
FIR fir
Fri
FIS Sif
FIT fit
FIV IVF
FIX fix
FIZ fiz
FJK JFK
FLO Flo
FLU flu
FLV VLF
FLY fly□
FMS MSF
FNS NFS
FNT NFT
FNU fun
NFU
FNY Fyn
FOO oof
FOP fop
FOR for
fro
FOT OFT
oft
FOU UFO
ufo
FOX fox□
FPP PFP
FPS SPF
FPT FTP
FRS FRS
FRU fur
RFU
FRY fry□
FSX sfx
FUV UVF
FWW WWF

G

GGI gig
GHH HGH
GHI ghi
GHM HMG
GHO hog
OHG
GHQ GHQ
GHR RHG
GHU hug
ugh
GHV HGV
GHZ GHz
GIJ jig
GIL Gil
lig
GIM mig
GIN gin
GIP pig
GIR rig
GIT git
GTi
tig
GIU GUI
GIW wig
GIZ zig
GJO jog
GJU jug
GKP kpg
GKY kGy
GLN LNG
GLO log
GLP LPG
GLU LGU
lug□
GMO GOM
mog
GMP mpg
PMG
GMQ QMG
GMR Mgr
GMS MSG
GMT GMT
GMU gum
mug
GMY gym
GNO NGO
nog
GNP GNP
PNG
GNR RGN
GNU gnu
gun
GOO goo
GOP GPO
GOS sog
GOT got
tog
GOW Gow
GOY goy
GOZ Zog
GPR RPG
GPS GPS
GPU gup
pug
GPY gyp
GPZ ZPG
GRS RGS
GRU rug
GRV RGV
GST Sgt
stg
GSU Gus
GTU gut
tug
GUV guv
GUY GUY
guy□
GUZ Zug

H

HHI HIH
HHO hoh
HHR HRH
HHS HSH
HHU huh
HIM HIM
him
HMI
HIN NHI
HIO hoi
HIP hip
phi
HIS his□
IHS
HIT hit
HIU hui
HIV HIV
HKP kph
HKW kWh
HKZ kHz
HMO Hom
MOH
ohm□
HMP mph
HMR MHR
HMS HMS
HSM
shm
HMT mth
HMU hum
HMV VMH
HMW HWM
HMZ MHz
HNO noh□
HNS NHS
HNT nth□
HOO hoo
oho
ooh
HOP hop
OHP
pho
poh
HOR rho
HOS hos
soh
HOT hot
tho
tho’
HOW how
WHO
who
HOX hox
HOY hoy
HPU hup
puh
HRS RHS
HRT HRT
TRH
HSS sh’s
HSU Hus
HSV VHS
HSY shy
HTU hut
UHT
HUW Huw
HWY why

I

IJM jim□
IJO IoJ
IJT JIT
IKL ilk
IKM Kim
IKN ink
kin
IKO koi
oik
IKP kip
IKR irk
kir
IKS ski
IKT kit□
ILL ill
I’ll
ILM mil
ILN lin
nil
ILO ILO
oil
ILP lip
ILR IRL
ILS lis
ILT lit
ILV Liv
ILZ Liz
IMM mim
IMN nim
IMO IOM
Moi
IMP imp
IPM
IMR MIR
MRI
RIM
rim
IMS ism
Sim
IMT MIT
Tim
IMV vim
IMX mix
INN inn
INO ion
INP nip□
PIN
pin
INR rin
INS INS
Nis
sin
sin’
INT ITN
nit
tin
INU uni
INW win
INY yin

IOP poi
IOR IRO
IOS Ios
ISO
IOT ITO
IOU IOU
IOV Ivo
IOW IOW
IPP pip□
IPR pir□
RIP
rip
RPI
IPS ISP
psi
sip
IPT pit
tip
TPI
IPU più
UPI
IPV VIP
IPX pix
IPY yip
IPZ zip
IQR IRQ
IRS IRS
RSI
sir
Sri
IRT rit
TIR
IRV IVR
VRI
ISS sis
IST it's
sit
ISV vis□
ISX six
ITT ITT
tit
ITU ITU
tui
ITV ITV
ITW wit
ITZ tiz
zit
IVV Viv
IVY ivy□
IVZ viz□
IZZ ziz

J

JNO Jon
JNR jnr□
JNU NUJ
JOT jot
JOW jow
JOY joy□
JSU jus
JTU jut

K

KKO Kok
KLM KLM
KMS MKS
mks
KOP kop
KOR ROK
KOS k.o.'s
Kos
KO's
OKs
OK's
KOT TKO
KOW wok
KOY yok
KSU suk
KSY sky
KTW KWT
KUY kyu
yuk

L

LLU Ull
LMO Lom
olm
LMR MLR
LMS LMS
LMU lum
Ulm
LMY lym
LOO loo
LOP lop
PLO
LOS LSO
sol□
LOT lot□
LOU Lou
LOV vol
LOW low
owl
LOX lox
LOY Loy
LPP PLP
LPR PLR
LPU pul
LPV VPL
LPY ply
LQS SQL
LRS RSL
SLR
LRT TLR
LRY rly
LST TLS
LSY sly□
LUX lux
LUZ luz

M

MMO mom
MMR MMR
RMM
MMU mum
MNO mon
MNR NMR
MNU mun
NUM
MNY Nym
MOO moo
Omo
MOP mop
Pom
MOQ Qom
MOR MOR
RMO
ROM
rom□
MOS som
MOT MOT
MoT
mot
tom□
MOV MVO
MOW mow
WMO
MOY moy
MPP ppm
MPQ QPM
MPR RMP
RPM
rpm
MPS PMS
MPT PMT
MPW wpm
MPY Pym
MQS QMS
MRS Mrs
rms
RSM
MRT RMT
MRU rum□
MSS SSM
MST Mts
MSU sum
USM
MTU tum
MTV MTV
MUV vum
MUX mux

N

NNU nun
NNW NNW
NOO Ono
NOP NOP
NOR nor
nor'
NOS nos□
SNO
son
NOT not
ton
NOU UNO
NOW now
own
won
NOY NYO
yon
NPS SNP
NPT NTP
ntp
NPU pun
NPW WNP
NQS sqn
NQV NVQ
NRR RNR
NRS snr□
SRN
NRT RNT
NRU NUR
run
urn
NRV NRV
NST NTS
NSU NSU
NUS
sun
USN
NSW NSW
NTT TNT
NTU NUT
nut□
tun
NTW NWT
NUU U Nu
NWW WNW
NWY wyn□

O

OOP oop
poo
OOR roo□
OOT too
OOW woo
OOZ zoo
OPP pop□
OPR PRO
pro
RPO
OPS Ops
osp
POS
SOP
sop
OPT opt
pot
PTO
pto
top
OPU oup
OPW POW
pow
OPX pox
OQS QSO
OQT qto
OQU quo'
ORS Ros
SRO
ORT ORT
Otr
rot
tor□
ORU our
ROU
ORV Vor
ORW row
ORY Ory
Roy
ORZ Roz
OSS SOS
OST sot
OSU sou
OSV sov
VSO
OSW sow
wos
OSY soy
yos
OSZ ozs
OTT OTT
Ott
tot
OTU out
OTW tow
two
wot
OTY toy
OUY you
OVW vow
OWW wow

P

PPS PPS
spp
PPU pup
PQR QPR
PRR RRP
PRS PRS
RPS
rps
PRT tpr
PRU pur
PRV RPV
PRW WRP
PRY pry
PSS SSP
PST STP
tsp
PSU pus
sup
PSV PSV
PVS
PSW SWP
PSY spy
PTU put
tup
PTV TVP
PTY pty□
PUU UPU
PXY pyx

Q

QQV qqv
QSU suq
QSV SVQ
QTY qty

R

RSS SSR
RST TSR
RSU SRU
sur
RSV RSV
RTU rut
RTV VTR
RTY try
Tyr
RWY wry

S

SST SST
st's
TSS
SSU sus
USS
SSW SSW
STV STV
STY sty
YTS
SUW USW
SVW WVS
SWW WSW

T

TTU tut

W

WWW WWW
www

4 letters

A

AABB	abba□
	baba
AABH	Ahab
AABK	Kaba
AABL	Baal
AABR	Arab
AABS	à bas
AABT	ABTA
AACN	CNAA
AACP	Capa
	paca
AACR	Cara
AACS	ACAS
AACV	Cava
AACW	WAAC
	Waac
AADD	Dada
AADI	Aida
AADL	Lada®
AADM	Adam
AADN	Dana
AADR	Adar
	RADA
AADT	data
AADY	Daya
AAEG	Gaea
AAEI	IAEA
AAEL	alae
AAER	Aare
	area
AAFI	IAAF
AAFR	afar
	Afra
	RAAF
AAFW	WAAF
AAGG	gaga
AAGI	Gaia
AAGL	alga
	gala
AAGM	Gama
AAGR	agar
	Agra
	raga
AAGS	saga
AAHH	ha-ha
AAHK	haka
AAHN	Naha
AAHR	haar
AAHS	Saha
AAHT	taha
AAHY	ayah
AAIM	Maia
AAIP	Apia
AAIR	aria
AAIS	Asia
AAIT	IATA
AAJR	ajar
	raja
AAJV	Java
AAJX	Ajax
AAKK	kaka
AAKM	Kama
AAKN	kana
AAKR	arak
	kara□
AAKT	kata
	taka
AAKV	kava
AALL	la-la
AALM	Alma
AALN	Alan
AALR	Aral
	Lara
AALS	alas
AALT	Taal
	tala
AALV	lava
	Vaal
AAMM	ma'am
	mama
AAMR	Aram
	Rama
AAMT	Maat
AAMY	Maya
AAMZ	Zama
AANN	anna□
	naan
	nana□
AANP	napa
AANR	Aran
	Nara
	Rana
AANS	anas
	ana's
	San'a
AANT	Tana
AANZ	azan
AAPP	papa□
AAPR	para
AAPS	ASAP
	asap
AAPT	atap
AARS	åsar
	Saar
	Sara
AARU	aura
AARZ	Zara
AASS	sa sa
	sasa
AAST	asta
AASV	Vasa
AATT	ta-ta
AATX	taxa
AAWY	away
ABBE	Abbe
	abbé□
	babe□
	BEAB
ABBL	blab
ABBR	barb□
ABBS	Babs
ABBY	Abby
	baby
ABCH	Bach
ABCI	Ciba
ABCK	back
ABCO	AOCB
ABCR	crab□
ABCS	scab
ABCU	Cuba
ABDE	abed
	bead
ABDL	bald
ABDN	band
ABDO	doab
ABDR	bard
	brad
	drab
ABDU	baud
	daub
ABDW	bawd
ABEK	bake
	beak
ABEL	Abel
	able
	bale
	blae
	Elba
ABEM	beam
ABEN	bane
	bean□
ABER	Baer
	bare
	bear
	brae
ABES	base
ABET	abet
	bate
	beat
	beta
ABEU	beau
ABEZ	Baez
ABFF	baff
ABFL	flab
ABFR	barf
	frab
ABFS	BASF
ABFT	baft
ABGI	Gabi
ABGL	blag
ABGN	bang
ABGO	Gabo
ABGR	BAgr
	brag
	garb
	grab
ABGS	bags
ABHL	blah
ABHS	bash
ABHT	baht
	bath□
ABIL	bail
	Bali
ABIM	iamb
ABIN	Bain
	bani
ABIR	Bari
	rabi□
	RIBA
ABIS	bias□
ABIT	a bit
	bait
ABIW	Biwa
ABJM	jamb
ABKL	balk
ABKN	bank
ABKO	boak
ABKR	bark
ABKS	bask
ABKU	Baku
ABLL	ball□
ABLM	balm
	lamb□
ABLS	slab
ABLT	blat
ABLW	bawl
ABLY	ably
ABMO	ambo
ABMR	barm
	Bram
ABNN	Bann
ABNO	Oban
ABNR	barn
	bran□
ABNS	snab
ABNT	bant
ABOR	BAOR
	boar
	bora
ABOS	Abos
ABOT	boat
ABPS	SPAB
ABPU	BUPA
ABPX	PABX
ABRS	bars
ABRT	Bart
	brat
ABRW	braw
ABRY	bray
ABSS	bass
ABST	bast□
	bats
	SATB
	stab
ABSW	BASW
	swab
ABSY	bays
ABTU	abut
	tabu
	tuba
ACCD	AC/DC
ACCE	ceca
ACCO	coca
ACCU	UCCA
ACDE	Cade
	dace
	ecad
ACDH	Chad
ACDI	acid
	cadi
ACDL	clad
ACDO	coda
ACDR	card
	crad
	RADC
ACDS	scad
ACEF	cafe
	café
	face
ACEG	cage□
ACEH	ache
	each
ACEK	cake
ACEL	Alec
	lace
ACEM	acme
	came
	mace□
ACEN	acne
	Caen
	cane
ACEP	cape
	pace
ACER	acer
	acre□
	care
	race
	RAEC

ACES	case
ACEV	cave
ACFL	calf
ACFR	RCAF
ACFT	fact
ACGL	clag
ACGP	CPAG
ACGR	crag
ACGS	scag
ACGY	cagy
ACHK	hack
ACHM	Mach
ACHN	Cahn
	Chan
ACHP	chap
ACHR	arch
	char
ACHS	cash□
ACHT	chat□
ACHY	achy
	Chay
ACHZ	Zach
ACIL	Cali
	laic
ACIM	mica
ACIN	Cain
	Inca
ACIO	ciao
	ICAO
ACIP	capi
	CIPA
	pica
ACIS	asci
ACJK	jack□
ACKL	calk
	kcal
	lack
ACKM	mack□
ACKP	pack
ACKR	rack
ACKS	cask
	sack
ACKT	tack
ACKW	KWAC
ACKY	yack
ACKZ	Zack
ACLL	call
ACLM	calm
	clam
ACLN	clan
ACLO	coal
	cola
ACLP	clap
ACLR	Carl
ACLT	talc
ACLU	caul
ACLW	claw
ACLX	calx
ACLY	clay□
	lacy
ACMO	coma
ACMP	camp□
ACMR	cram□
	marc□
	RAMC
ACMS	scam
ACMY	cyma
	YMCA
ACNO	Cano
ACNS	scan
ACNT	cant
	can't
ACNY	cyan
ACOR	arco
	Caro
	Cora
	RAOC
ACOS	soca
ACOT	Cato
	coat
	taco
ACOW	Waco
ACOX	coax
	coxa
ACPR	carp
	crap
ACPS	CPSA
	PCAS
ACPT	pact
ACPY	pacy
ACRS	cars
	scar
ACRT	cart
ACRW	craw
	WRAC
ACRY	Cary
	Cray
	racy
ACRZ	czar
ACSS	Cass
ACST	acts
	cast
	Cats
	scat
ACSU	UCAS
ACTT	ACTT
	tact
ACVY	cavy
ACWY	YWCA
ADDE	dead□
	Edda
ADDO	dado
ADDU	daud
ADDW	dawd
	wadd
ADDY	Addy
	D-Day
ADEF	deaf
	fade
ADEG	aged
ADEH	hade
	head
ADEI	Adie
	aide
	idea
ADEJ	jade□
ADEL	Aled
	dale
	deal□
	lade
	lead
	Leda
ADEM	dame
	Edam
	made
	mead□
ADEN	Aden
	Dane
	dean□
	Edna
ADEO	odea
ADER	dare
	dear
	read□
ADES	Eads
	sade□
ADET	date
ADEU	a due
ADEV	Dave
	Veda
ADEW	awed
	wade□
ADEX	axed
ADEZ	adze
	daze
ADFF	daff
ADFH	Fahd
ADFI	IFAD
ADFR	fard
ADFS	DAFS
ADFT	daft
ADGL	glad
ADGN	dang
ADGO	goad
ADGR	drag
ADGU	gaud
ADGW	gawd
ADHI	dhai
ADHJ	hadj
ADHL	dahl□
	dhal
ADHN	hand
ADHO	Doha
	Hoad
ADHR	hard
ADHS	dash
	shad
ADHU	haud
ADIK	kadi
ADIL	Dáil
	Dali
	dial
	laid
ADIM	amid
	maid
ADIN	Dian
ADIP	paid
ADIQ	qadi
ADIR	arid
	raid
ADIS	AIDS
	Aids
	dais
	said
ADIU	Audi®
ADIV	avid
	diva□
ADIW	wadi
ADIZ	Diaz
	Díaz
ADJO	Joad
ADKN	dank
ADKR	dark
ADLN	land□
ADLO	load
ADLR	lard
ADLU	auld
	dual
	laud□
	Lüda
ADLV	DVLA
ADLW	wald
ADLY	Daly
	lady
ADMM	MDMA
ADMN	damn
ADMP	damp
ADMR	dram
ADMU	Duma
	Maud
ADMW	dwam
ADNO	Doña
ADNR	darn
	nard
	rand□
ADNS	sand□
ADNU	Danu
ADNW	dawn□
	wand
ADNY	Andy
ADOP	dopa
ADOR	Dora
	road
ADOS	ados
	soda
ADOT	doat
	toad□
ADOW	woad
ADPR	drap
	pard
ADPS	PDSA
ADQU	quad
ADRS	sard
ADRT	dart
	d'art
	drat
	trad
ADRW	draw
	ward□
ADRY	dray
	yard
ADSW	swad
	wads
ADSY	days□
ADTU	daut
ADTV	advt
ADTW	dawt
ADVY	Davy
ADWY	wady
AEEG	agee
AEEJ	ajee
AEEL	alee
AEES	ease
AEFK	fake
AEFL	alef
	flea
	leaf
AEFM	fame
AEFN	fane
AEFR	fare
	fear
AEFS	safe
AEFT	EFTA
	Efta
	fate
	feat
	feta□
	Tafe
AEFU	UEFA
AEFW	a few
AEFY	Faye
AEFZ	faze
AEGG	gage
AEGL	egal
	Gael
	gale□
AEGM	game
	mage
	mega
AEGN	gean
AEGP	gape
	page□
AEGR	areg
	gear
	rage
AEGS	ages
	sage
AEGT	gate
	geta
AEGU	ague
AEGV	gave
	Vega
AEGW	wage
AEGY	Gaye
AEGZ	gaze

AEHK hake
AEHL hale□
heal
Leah
AEHM ahem
haem
hame
Mahe
AEHP heap
AEHR hare□
hear
Hera
rhea□
AEHS Ashe
shea
AEHT hate
heat
Thea
AEHV have
AEHY yeah
AEHZ haze
AEIL ilea
AEIN aîné
AEJK Jake
AEJN Jane
jean□
AEJP jape
AEKL kale
lake
leak
AEKM kame
make
AEKN Kean
AEKO EOKA
AEKP peak
AEKR rake
AEKS sake
AEKT Kate
keta
take
teak
AEKW wake
weak
AEKY Kaye
AELL Ella
AELM Elma
lame
lamé
leam
male
Malé
meal
AELN élan
lane
lean□
Lena
Neal
AELO aloe
AELP leap
pale
peal
plea
AELR earl
Lear
rale
râle
real
AELS sale
seal
AELT Elat
et al
late
tale
teal
AELU Laue
AELV lave
leva
vale
veal
Vela
AELW wale
weal
AELX Alex
axel
axle
AELY Yale
AELZ laze
zeal
AEMM Emma
AEMN amen
mane
mean
name
AEMR mare
AEMS Ames
mase
mesa
same
seam
AEMT mate
meat
tame
team
Tema
AEMV Maev
AEMX Amex
exam
AEMZ maze
AENN Anne
AENO a one
aeon
eaon
AENP nape
neap
pane
AENR Arne
earn
near
AENS ENSA
sane
Sean
AENT ante
Aten
neat
tane
AENV Evan
nave
Neva
vane
vena
AENW anew
Ewan
wane
wean
AENZ naze
Zena
AEPR pare
pear
rape
reap
AEPS apse
peas
spae
AEPT pate
paté
pâté
peat
tape
AEPV pave
AEPX APEX
apex
AEQS SEAQ
AERR rare
rear
AERS Ares
arse
RAeS
rase
sear
sera
AERT aret
rate
tear
AERU urea
AERV aver
rave
Vera
AERW AWRE
ware
wear
AERY Ayer
yare
year
AERZ Ezra
raze
AESS seas
AEST east
eats
sate
seat
seta
AESU Esau
AESV aves
save
vase
AESX axes
AESY easy
eyas
SAYE
AETT Tate
teat
AETZ ZETA
zeta□
AEUW AUEW
AEVW wave
AFFF faff
AFFI FIFA
AFFM MAFF
AFFN naff
AFFO Offa
AFFT Taff
AFFY yaff
AFGL flag□
AFGN fang
AFGR frag
Graf
AFHL half
AFHS fash
AFHT haft
AFIK faik
AFIL alif
fail
AFIN fain
naif
naïf
AFIP Piaf
AFIR fair
fiar
AFIS as if
Safi
AFIT fiat
Fiat®
AFIW waif
AFIX faix
AFKL flak
AFKN fank
AFLL fall
AFLN flan
AFLO foal
loaf
AFLP flap
AFLT flat
AFLW flaw
AFLX flax
AFLY flay
AFMO foam
AFMR farm
AFNP NPFA
AFNS fans
AFNU faun
AFNW fawn
AFOR Afro
faro□
fora
AFOS as of
oafs
sofa
AFPR frap
AFRT raft
AFRU Frau
AFRW WRAF
AFRY fray
AFST fast
AFSU USAF
AFSX Sfax
AFTT Taft
AFTU tufa
AFTW waft
AGGI giga
AGGN gang
AGGO agog
AGGR ragg
AGGS gags
AGGY Aggy
AGHI Haig
AGHN hang
AGHS gash
shag
AGHT ghat
AGIL Gail
gila
glia
AGIM magi
AGIN agin
Agni
gain
Gina
Inga
AGIO Iago
AGIR Riga
AGIT gait
Gita
AGIV vagi
AGJU juga
AGKN knag
AGKS skag
AGKU kagu
AGKW gawk
AGLL gall□
AGLM glam
AGLN Lang
AGLO Algo
gaol
goal
Olga
AGLS slag
AGLU Gaul
AGLY Algy
AGMN G-man
AGMO ogam
Ogma
AGMP gamp
AGMR gram□
marg
AGMU gaum

	Guam
AGMY	gamy
AGNP	pang
AGNR	gnar
	gran
	rang
AGNS	sang
	snag
AGNT	gant
	gnat
	tang
AGNU	guan
AGNV	vang
AGNW	gnaw
	Wang
AGNY	Angy
	Nagy
AGOR	Argo
AGOS	sago
AGOT	go at
	goat❑
	toga
AGOY	Goya
	yoga
AGPS	gasp
AGPU	gaup
AGPW	gawp
AGQU	quag
AGRS	GRAS
AGRY	Gary
	Gray
AGRZ	Graz
AGST	stag
AGSW	swag
AGTT	GATT
AHHS	hash
	shah❑
AHHT	hath
AHIJ	haji
AHIK	haik
AHIL	hail
	hila
AHIN	hain
AHIR	hair❑
AHIS	Shia
	Shi'a
AHIT	Thai
AHIY	hiya
AHJJ	hajj
AHKN	ankh
	hank❑
	khan❑
AHKP	kaph
AHKR	hark
AHKT	Kath
	khat
AHKW	hawk
AHLL	hall❑
AHLM	halm
AHLO	halo
AHLR	harl

AHLS	Hals
	lash
AHLT	halt
	lath
AHLU	haul
	hula
AHMR	harm
AHMS	mash
	sham
AHMW	hawm
	wham❑
AHNO	Noah
AHNS	Nash
AHNT	NAHT
	tanh
	than
AHNW	Hawn
AHOP	opah
AHOR	haro
	hoar
AHOS	hoas
AHOT	oath
AHOU	Oahu
AHOV	Hova
AHOW	whoa
AHOX	hoax
AHOY	ahoy
AHPR	harp❑
AHPS	hasp
	pash
AHPT	path
	Ptah
AHPW	whap
AHRS	rash
AHRT	hart
	Thar
AHSS	sash
AHST	hast
	tash
AHSW	Shaw
	shwa
	wash
AHSY	ashy
	SYHA
AHTT	tath
	that
AHTU	Utah
AHTW	thaw
	what
AHYZ	hazy
AIIL	ilia
AIIN	Iain
	inia
AIIS	Iasi
AIIX	ixia
AIJL	jail
AIJM	Jima
AIJN	Jain
AIJO	jiao
AIKK	kaki
AIKL	kail

	kali❑
AIKN	akin
	kina
AIKP	paik
	pika
AIKR	raik
	raki
AIKS	saki❑
	sika
AIKT	ikat
AIKZ	kazi
AILM	Liam
	Lima
	mail
	Mali
AILN	anil❑
	INLA
	lain
	Lian
	nail
AILP	pail
	Pali
	pila
AILR	lair
	lari
	liar
	lira
	rail
	rial
AILS	Isla
	Lias
	Lisa
	sail
	sial
AILT	tail
	tali
AILV	vial
AILW	wail
AILX	axil
AILZ	Liza
AIMM	imam
	maim
AIMN	Amin
	main
	mina
AIMR	Irma
	Mira
	ram i
	RIAM
AIMS	aims
	Amis
	sima
AIMU	Maui
AIMX	maxi
AINN	Nina
AINO	Iona
AINP	nipa
	pain
AINR	Iran
	rain
	rani

AINS	anis
	Sian
AINT	ain't
	anti
	Nita
	Tina
AINV	Ivan
	vain
	vina
AINW	wain❑
AINX	Xi'an
AINY	ayin
AINZ	Nazi
AIOT	iota
	Oita
AIOW	Iowa
AIPP	pipa
AIPR	pair
	RIPA
AIPS	Apis
	Pisa
AIPT	pita
AIQR	Iraq
AIRS	airs
	Rais
	sari
AIRT	airt
	rait
	Rita
AIRV	Ravi
AIRY	airy
	Iyar
AIRZ	riza
AISS	as is
AIST	Asti
	sati
	Sita
AISU	USIA
AISV	Siva
	visa
AISX	axis
AISY	I say!
AITT	at it
	Tait
	Tati
AITV	Vita
AITW	wait
AITX	taxi
AITZ	zati
AIVV	viva
AIZZ	Aziz
AJNN	jann
AJNO	Joan
AJOT	jato
AJPU	jaup
AJRU	Jura
AJSW	jaws❑
AJZZ	jazz
AKKR	kark
AKLN	lank
AKLO	kola

AKLR	Karl
	lark
AKLT	talk
AKLW	lawk
	walk
AKMO	amok
	mako
AKMR	mark❑
AKMS	mask
AKNO	Kano
	kaon
	koan
AKNP	knap
AKNR	knar
	nark
	rank
AKNS	sank
AKNT	Kant
	tank
AKNU	KANU
	kuna
AKNW	wank
AKNY	yank❑
AKOR	kora
	okra
AKOS	Oaks
	soak
AKOT	Kota
AKOY	kayo
	okay
AKPR	park❑
AKRS	Sark
AKRT	kart
AKRU	raku
AKRW	Wark
AKRY	Kray
AKST	skat
	task
AKSU	skua
AKTY	Katy
	kyat
AKTZ	Katz
AKUW	wauk
ALLM	mall
ALLO	Lola
	olla
ALLP	pall
ALLT	tall
ALLW	wall
ALLY	ally❑
ALMM	malm
ALMO	loam
ALMP	lamp
	palm
ALMR	LRAM
	marl
ALMS	alms
	slam
ALMT	malt
ALMU	alum
	maul

ALMY	lyam
ALNO	loan
ALNP	plan
ALNR	larn
ALNU	Alun
	ulna
ALNV	NVLA
ALNW	lawn
ALOP	opal
ALOR	oral
ALOS	also
	Laos
	sola
ALOT	a lot
	alto
ALOV	Olav
	oval
ALOW	alow
	AWOL
ALOZ	Ozal
	Zola
ALPP	Lapp
	palp
	plap
ALPS	Alps
	slap
ALPU	Paul
	pula□
ALPW	pawl
ALPY	play
ALRY	aryl
	Lyra
ALSS	lass
ALST	last
	lats
	SALT
	salt
	slat
ALSU	Saul
ALSV	Slav
ALSW	laws
ALSY	slay
ALTU	Tula
ALTW	Walt
ALUU	luau
ALUW	waul
ALUY	Yalu
ALWW	wawl
ALWY	waly
	yawl
ALYZ	lazy
AMMO	ammo
AMMR	marm
AMNN	Mann
AMNO	moan
	mona□
	Noam
	noma
	Oman
AMNR	mRNA
AMNU	maun
AMNX	Manx
AMNY	many
	myna
AMOR	mora
	Omar
	roam
	roma
AMOS	Amos
	soma□
AMOT	atom
	moat
AMOX	moxa
AMOY	Mayo
AMPR	pram
	ramp
AMPS	spam□
AMPT	tamp
AMPU	puma
AMPV	vamp
AMRS	arms
	Mars
	Rams
AMRT	mart
	tram
AMRU	Amur
	arum
AMRV	VRAM
AMRW	warm
AMRX	Marx
AMRY	army
	Mary
	Mayr
	Myra
AMSS	mass□
AMST	mast
AMSW	swam
AMSX	Xmas
AMTT	matt□
AMTY	maty
AMWY	M-way
AMYZ	azym
	mazy
ANOR	Nora
	Oran
	roan
	Rona
ANOT	NATO
	Nato
ANOV	Avon
	nova
ANOX	axon
ANPS	snap
	span
ANPT	pant
ANPW	pawn
ANRS	RNAS
ANRT	rant
	tarn
	tRNA
ANRU	Arun
ANRW	warn
ANRY	nary
	Ryan
	yarn
ANSS	sans
ANSU	anus
ANSW	sawn
	swan□
ANTU	aunt
	tuna
ANTV	vant
ANTW	want
ANUU	unau
ANUY	yuan
ANUZ	ZANU
ANVY	navy
ANWY	wany
	yawn
ANYZ	zany
AOPR	proa
AOPS	OAPs
	soap
AOPT	atop
AOPV	Pavo
AORR	roar
AORS	Rosa
	soar
AORT	rota
	taro
AORV	arvo
AORW	arow
	a-row
AOSS	ossa
	so as
AOST	as to
	oast
	oats
	stoa
AOSY	Soay
	soya
AOTT	to a T
AOTU	auto
AOUY	ou ay
AOVW	avow
AOVZ	Azov
APPR	parp
APPU	pupa
APPY	yapp
APRR	parr□
APRS	rasp
	spar
APRT	part
	prat
	rapt
	trap
APRU	prau
APRW	warp
	wrap
APRY	pray
APSS	pass
APST	past
	spat
APSU	Apus
APSW	swap
	wasp
APSY	spay
APTU	up at
APUZ	ZAPU
APWY	yawp
AQTU	quat
AQUY	quay
ARSS	RSSA
ARST	arts
	rats
	star
	tsar
ARSU	rusa
	sura
ARSY	rays
ARTT	tart
ARTW	wart
ARTY	arty
	tray
ARVY	vary
ARWY	awry
	wary
ARXY	X-ray
ARZZ	razz
ASSS	sass
ASST	Tass
ASSU	Susa
ASTT	tats
ASTV	vast
ASTW	swat
	taws
	wast
ASTY	stay
ASUV	Suva
ASWY	sway
	ways
	yaws
ATTT	tatt
ATTU	taut
ATTW	watt□
ATUV	vatu
AVWY	wavy
AWXY	waxy

B

BBBC	BBBC
BBCF	BBFC
BBCO	Cobb
BBEL	bleb
BBEW	Webb
BBLO	blob
BBLU	blub
	bulb
BBMO	bomb
BBOO	boob
BBOU	bubo
BBOY	BYOB
BCCI	CICB
BCEG	CEGB
BCEK	beck□
BCET	BTEC
BCEU	Cebu
	cube
BCHU	chub
BCIM	ICBM
BCIO	CIOB
BCIR	crib
BCKU	buck□
BCLO	bloc
BCLU	club
BCMO	BCom
	comb
BCNZ	NZBC
BCOS	CBSO
BCRS	BRCS
BCRU	curb
BDDU	Budd
BDEE	Bede
BDEI	Bedi
	bide
BDEL	bled□
BDEN	bend
BDEO	bode
BDES	Debs
BDET	debt
BDII	ibid
BDIN	bind
BDIR	bird□
	IBRD
BDLO	bold
BDLV	blvd
BDMU	dumb
BDNO	bond□
BDNP	PNdB
BDNU	bund
BDOY	body
	do by
BDRU	drub
BDRY	Byrd
BEEF	beef
BEEH	hebe□
BEEL	Elbe
BEEN	been
BEEP	beep
BEER	beer□
BEET	beet
BEGI	gibe
BEGN	BEng
BEGR	berg□
BEGY	gybe
BEHN	Behn
BEHR	herb
BEHT	Beth
BEIJ	jibe
BEIK	bike
	kibe
BEIL	bile
BEIN	bein
	bien
BEIR	bier

	Brie
BEIS	bise
BEIT	bite
BEIX	ibex
BEJO	jobe
BEJU	jube
BEKO	boke
	Kobe
BEKR	berk
	kerb
BELL	bell□
BELO	Belo
	bole
	lobe
BELP	pleb
BELT	belt
	blet
BELU	blue
BELW	blew
BEMR	berm
BENN	Benn
BENO	bone
BENR	Bern
	bren
BENT	bent
BENU	unbe
BENZ	Benz
BEOO	oboe
BEOR	Boer
	bore
	Ebro
	robe
BEOS	Bose
BEOT	to be
BEOY	obey
BERS	Serb
BERT	Bert
BERV	verb
BERW	brew
BERY	byre
BESS	Bess
BEST	best□
BESY	byes
BETU	tube
BETY	byte
BEUZ	zebu
BEVY	bevy
BFFI	biff
BFFO	boff
BFFU	buff
BFIS	fibs
BFIU	BIFU
BFLN	BNFL
BFMU	bumf
BFOP	BFPO
BGHM	GmbH
BGIL	glib
BGIO	Gobi
BGIR	brig
BGLO	glob
BGNO	bong

BGNU	bung
BGNY	Byng
BGOR	Borg
	brog
BGOY	bogy
	go by
	goby
	go-by
BGRU	grub
BGSU	bugs
BHLU	buhl
BHMO	Böhm
BHOO	hobo
BHOR	Bohr
BHOS	bosh
BHOT	both
BHSU	bush□
BIIS	ibis
BIKL	bilk
BIKO	Biko
BILL	bill□
BILM	limb
BILO	boil
	lobi
BILP	blip
BILR	birl
BIMR	brim
	IRBM
BINR	RNIB
BINS	ISBN
	snib
BINT	bint
BINY	inby
BIOR	Biro
	Biro®
	brio
BIOS	Ibos
BIOT	Biot
BIOZ	Zibo
BIRR	birr
BIRT	Birt
	brit□
BIST	bits
BITT	bitt
BJOS	Jobs
BKLO	Blok
BKLU	bulk
BKNO	knob
BKNU	bunk
	knub
BKOO	boko
	book
BKRU	burk
BKSU	busk
BLLO	boll
	Böll
BLLU	bull□
BLMU	Blum
BLOO	lobo
	obol
BLOS	slob

BLOT	blot
	bolt□
BLOW	blow
	bowl
BLRU	blur□
	burl
BLSU	slub
BMNU	numb
BMOO	boom
BMOT	tomb
BMOU	umbo
BMOW	womb
BMPU	bump
BMSU	BMus
	MusB
BNNO	Bonn
BNOO	boon
	Obon
BNOR	born□
	Brno
BNOS	nobs
	snob
BNOU	boun
BNOY	bony
BNRU	burn
BNRY	Bryn
BNSU	snub
BNTU	bunt
BOOR	boor
	Boro
BOOS	obos
BOOT	boot□
BOOY	boyo
BOPP	Bopp
BOPR	prob
BORS	Bors
	Bros
	sorb
BORW	brow
BOSS	boss
BOSW	bows
BOTT	bott
BOTU	bout
BOTY	Toby
BOUY	buoy
BPRS	PSBR
	RSPB
BPRU	burp
BPST	tbsp
BPUY	upby
BRRR	brrr
BRRU	burr
BRTU	brut
BRUY	bury□
	ruby□
BSTU	bust
	stub
BSUY	busy
BTTU	butt□
BUZZ	buzz

C

CCEE	ecce
CCES	ECSC
CCHI	chic□
CCHO	choc
CCIN	C-in-C
CCIP	IPCC
CCKO	cock
CCLN	NCCL
CCLS	SCCL
CCOO	coco
CCTV	CCTV
CDEE	cede
CDEI	cedi
	cide
	dice
	iced
CDEK	deck
CDEN	NEDC
CDEO	code
	OECD
CDER	cred
CDEU	duce
CDGM	DCMG
CDGO	DOCG
CDHI	dich
CDIK	dick□
CDIS	disc
	SCID
CDIU	IUCD
CDKO	dock
CDKU	duck
CDLO	clod
	cold
CDOR	cord
CDOU	douc
CDOV	DCVO
CDRU	crud
	curd
CDSU	scud□
CDTU	duct
CEEH	eche
	eech
CEEO	OEEC
CEER	cere
	Cree
CEET	cete
CEFH	chef
CEFL	clef
CEFO	C of E
CEGK	geck
CEGS	GCSE
CEHH	hech
CEHK	heck
CEHL	lech
CEHO	echo□
	oche
CEHP	pech
CEHR	Cher
CEHS	sech

CEHT	echt
	etch
	tech
CEHW	chew
CEHY	yech
CEHZ	chez
CEIL	ceil
	Icel
	lice
CEIM	mice
CEIN	cine
	nice□
CEIP	epic
	pice
CEIR	Ceri
	Eric
	rice□
CEIT	cite
	tice
CEIV	vice
CEKK	keck
CEKN	neck
CEKO	coke
	Coke®
CEKP	peck□
CEKR	reck
CEKY	Eyck
CELL	cell
CELM	Clem
CELO	Cleo
	cole□
CELT	Celt
CELU	clue
	Luce
CELW	clew□
CEMO	come
CEMR	merc
	Merc®
CEMY	cyme
CENO	cone
	once
CENR	NERC
CENT	cent
CEOP	cope□
	OPEC
CEOR	core
CEOS	OSCE
CEOT	cote
CEOV	cove
CEOZ	coze
CEPR	CPRE
CEPS	Pécs
	spec
CEPU	puce
CERS	ESRC
	SERC
CERT	cert
CERU	cure□
	curé
	ecru
CERW	crew

CEST	sect
CESU	CSEU
CETU	cute
CFFO	coff
CFFU	cuff
CFHO	Foch
CFIL	flic
CFIO	coif
	fico
	foci
CFIU	fuci
CFNS	NFSC
	SNCF
CFPR	FRCP
CFRS	FRCS
CGGM	GCMG
CGHQ	GCHQ
CGHU	chug
CGIL	CGLI
CGKM	KCMG
CGLO	clog
CGOR	RCOG
CGOV	GCVO
CHIK	hick❑
CHIN	chin
	inch
CHIP	chip
CHIR	rich❑
CHIT	chit
	itch
	tich
CHIV	chiv
CHKO	hock
	Koch
CHKU	huck
CHLO	loch
CHMU	chum
	much
CHNO	chon
	Cohn
CHOP	chop
CHOS	cosh
CHOU	ouch
CHOW	chow
CHRS	SRCh
CHSU	cush
	such
CHTU	chut
CIIX	Ci-xi
CIKK	kick
CIKL	lick
CIKM	Mick
CIKN	nick❑
CIKP	pick
CIKR	rick❑
CIKS	sick
CIKT	tick
CIKW	KWIC
	wick❑
CIKX	Ickx
CILO	Clio
	coil
	loci
CILP	clip
CIMO	mico
CIMR	MICR
CINO	coin
	icon
CINR	NIRC
CINU	unci
CINZ	zinc
CIOR	coir
CIOT	cito
	otic
CIOZ	zoic
CIPS	IPCS
	pics
CIPT	Pict
CIRS	RICS
	RISC
CIRT	crit
CIRU	uric
CIRY	ricy
CIST	cist
CITY	city
CJKO	Jock
CKLO	lock❑
CKLU	luck
CKMO	mock
CKMU	muck❑
CKNO	conk
	nock
CKOO	cook❑
CKOP	pock
CKOR	cork❑
	rock
CKOS	sock
CKOT	tock
CKOV	KCVO
CKOW	KWOC
CKPS	SPCK
CKPU	puck❑
CKRU	ruck
CKSU	suck
CKTU	tuck❑
CKUY	yuck
CLLO	Coll
CLLU	cull
CLMO	Colm
CLMU	culm
CLOO	cool
CLOP	clop
CLOT	clot
	colt❑
	Colt®
	CTOL
CLOW	cowl
CLOY	cloy
CLPR	LRCP
CLRS	LRCS
CLRU	curl
CLTU	cult
CLUY	Lucy
CMNR	RNCM
CMOO	Como
	coom
CMOP	comp
CMOR	corm
CMPR	MRCP
	RCMP
CMSU	scum
CNNO	conn
CNOO	Cono
CNOR	corn
CNOU	unco
CNOY	cony
CNQV	NCVQ
CNRS	RSNC
CNSY	sync
COOP	coop
	co-op
	poco
COOT	coot
COPR	crop
COPS	cops
COPT	Copt
COPU	coup
COPY	copy
CORT	torc
CORW	crow❑
COST	cost
	Scot
COSW	cows
	scow
COSY	cosy
CPSS	SCPS
CPSU	cusp
	SPUC
CPUV	uPVC
CRRU	curr
CRSU	crus
	scur
CRSV	RCVS
CRTU	curt
CRUX	crux❑
CSSU	cuss
CSSY	CSYS
CSTU	scut
	STUC
CSTY	cyst

D

DDDO	Dodd
DDEE	deed
DDEI	died
DDER	redd
DDEU	dude
DDEY	eddy❑
DDII	Didi
DDIK	Kidd
DDIO	dido❑
DDOO	dodo
DDOS	odds
DDOT	Todd
DDRU	rudd
DDSU	duds
DEEF	feed
DEEG	edge
DEEH	heed
DEEI	Edie
DEEK	deek
DEEL	dele
DEEM	deem
	deme
DEEN	Eden
	need
DEEP	deep
DEER	deer
	dree
	reed❑
DEES	seed
DEEW	weed
DEFI	FIDE
DEFL	delf
DEFN	fend
DEFR	Fred
DEFT	deft
DEFU	feud
DEFY	defy
DEGI	Gide
DEGL	geld
DEGO	doge
DEGY	edgy
DEHI	hide
DEHL	held
DEHR	herd
DEHS	shed
	she'd
DEHU	hued
DEIK	dike
DEIL	deli
	idle❑
	lied
DEIM	dime
	idem
DEIN	dine
	Enid
DEIO	Odie
DEIP	pied
DEIR	dire
	ride❑
DEIS	dies
	Ides
	side
DEIT	diet❑
	dite
	edit
	tide
	tied
DEIV	Devi
	dive
	vide
DEIW	wide
DEJU	Jude
DEKS	desk
DEKU	duke
DEKY	dyke
DELL	dell
DELM	meld
DELN	lend
DELO	dole❑
	lode
DELS	sled
DELU	duel
DELV	veld
DELW	lewd
	weld
DEMN	mend
DEMO	demo
	dome
	mode
DEMY	demy
DENO	done
	node
DENR	Dern
	nerd
	rend
DENS	send
	sned
DENT	dent
	tend
DENU	dune
	nude
DENV	vend
DENW	wend
DENY	deny
	dyne
DEOP	dope
DEOR	doer
	Doré
	Oder
	redo
	rode
	roed
DEOS	dose
	Odes
DEOT	dote
DEOV	Devo
	dove❑
DEOW	owed
DEOZ	doze
DEPP	Depp
DEPU	dupe
DERS	Reds
DERT	retd
DERU	Edur
	rude❑
DERV	derv
	Revd
DERW	drew❑
DERY	drey
	Ryde
DESU	dues
	Duse
	used

DETU	duet
	Udet
DEUV	Duve
DEWY	dewy
DFFO	doff
DFFU	duff
DFIN	find
DFLO	fold
DFNO	fond
DFNU	fund
DFOO	food
DFOR	ford□
	Ford®
DFUY	Dufy
DGIL	gild
DGIN	DIng
	ding
DGIR	gird
	grid
DGIS	digs
DGLO	gold□
DGNO	dong
DGNS	Gdns
DGNU	dung
DGOO	good
DGOS	gods
DGOU	Doug
DGRU	drug
DHIN	hind
DHIS	dish
DHIW	whid
DHLO	hold
DHOO	hood□
DHOS	dohs
	dosh
DHOT	doth
DHOW	dhow
	who'd
DHOY	yodh
DHRU	Hurd
DHSS	DHSS
DHSU	dush
DHTU	thud
DHTV	HDTV
DIIM	MIDI
	midi
DIIN	Dini
	nidi
DIJO	Jodi
DIKN	dink
	kind
DIKR	dirk□
DIKS	disk
	kids
	skid
DILL	dill
DILM	mild
DILN	Lind
DILO	idol
	lido
	loid
DILR	dirl
DILS	sild
	slid
DILW	wild
DILY	idly
	idyl
DIMN	mind□
DIMO	modi
DINO	Dion
	do in
	nodi
	Odin
DINR	rind
	RNID
DINS	ISDN
	sind
DINT	dint
	tind
DINW	wind
DINY	Indy
DIOR	Dior
DIOV	Ovid
	void
DIPR	drip
DIQU	quid
DIRT	dirt
DIRY	yird
DISS	diss
	SIDS
DITY	tidy
DJLO	Jodl
DJOU	judo
DJOY	Jody
DJUY	Judy
DKNU	dunk
DKOR	dork
DKRU	Kurd
DKSU	dusk
DKUU	kudu
DLLO	doll
DLLU	dull□
DLMO	Mold
DLNU	Lund
DLOP	plod
DLOR	lord□
DLOS	sold
DLOT	dolt
	told
DLOU	loud
	ludo
DLOW	dowl
	wold
DLOZ	Lódz
DLPS	SDLP
DLUY	duly
DMNO	Mond
DMOO	doom
	mood
DMOR	dorm
DMPU	dump
DMRU	drum
DMSU	DMus
	MusD
DNNU	Dunn
DNOP	pond
DNOS	Dons
	snod
DNOT	don't
DNOU	undo
DNOW	down
DNRU	nurd
DNSY	synd
DNTU	dunt
DNTY	tynd
	tyn'd
DNWY	wynd
DOOR	door
	rood
DOOT	do to
	to-do
DOOW	wood□
DOPR	dorp
	drop
	drop-
	prod□
DOPS	pods
DOPU	do up
DOPY	dopy
DOQU	quod
DORS	Dors
DORT	dort
	trod
DORU	dour
DORW	word
DORY	dory
DOSS	doss
DOST	dost
DOSU	duos
	udos
DOTU	dout
DOTY	tody
DOUY	you'd
DOYZ	dozy
DPSU	spud
DQSV	VDQS
DRSU	surd
DRTU	turd
DRUU	Urdu
DRUY	Dury
DRUZ	Druz
DSSU	suds
DSTU	dust
	stud
DTUY	duty

E

EEEP	épée
EEFL	feel
	flee
EEFR	free
	reef
EEFS	fees
EEFT	feet
	fête
EEGH	ghee
EEGK	geek
EEGL	glee
EEGN	gene□
EEGO	ogee
EEGP	geep
EEGR	Gere
	gree
EEGU	euge
EEHH	he-he
EEHL	heel
	hele
EEHM	heme
EEHR	here
	Rhee
EEHT	thee
EEHW	whee
EEIR	Eire
	Erie
EEIV	Evie
EEJL	jeel
EEJP	jeep□
EEJR	jeer
EEJT	jeté
EEJZ	Jeez
EEKK	keek
EEKL	keel
	Klee
	leek
EEKM	meek
EEKN	keen
	knee
EEKP	keep
	peek
	Peke
EEKR	reek
EEKS	seek
EEKW	week
EELL	Elle
EELP	leep
	peel□
	Pele
EELR	leer
	reel
EELS	else
	lees
	seel
EELT	leet
EELV	leve
EELW	weel
EEMN	mene
EEMR	mere
	REME
EEMS	seem
	smee□
EEMT	meet
	mete
	teem
EENP	neep
	peen
EENR	erne
	ne'er
	Rene
	René
EENS	seen
EENT	teen
EENV	even
	névé
EENW	enew
	Ewen
EEOV	evoe
EEPP	peep
EEPR	peer
	pree
EEPS	seep
	Spee
EEPT	Pete
EEPW	weep
EERS	Erse
	seer
	sere
EERT	rete
	teer
	tree
EERV	ever
	veer
EERW	ewer
	were
	we're
EERY	Eyre
EESS	esse
EEST	Tees
EESW	swee
EESX	exes
EESY	eyes
EETW	twee
	weet
EEUW	Euwe
EEVW	we've
EFFI	fief
	fife□
EFFJ	Jeff
EFFT	teff
EFGL	fleg
EFGS	fegs
EFHT	heft
EFIK	fike
EFIL	file
	life
EFIN	feni
	fine
EFIR	fire
	rife
EFIV	five
EFIW	wife
EFKR	kerf
EFLL	fell□
EFLO	floe
EFLP	pelf
EFLS	self

EFLT	felt
	left
	TEFL
EFLU	flue
	fuel
EFLW	flew
EFLX	flex
EFLY	fley
EFMU	fume
EFNR	fern
	NFER
EFNS	NFSE
EFOR	fore
EFOS	foes
EFPT	PTFE
EFRS	FRSE
	serf
EFRT	fret
	tref
EFRY	Frey
EFSS	fess
EFST	EFTS
	fest
EFSU	fuse
EFTW	weft
EGGI	Eigg
EGGS	eggs
EGGY	eggy
EGHP	pegh
EGHU	huge
EGIL	glei
EGIN	Inge
EGIT	gite
	gîte
EGIV	give
EGLN	glen□
	Leng
EGLO	loge
	ogle
EGLS	legs
EGLT	gelt
EGLU	glue
	luge
EGLY	gley
EGMR	germ
EGMS	gems□
EGMU	geum
EGNO	Egon
	gone
EGNT	gent□
EGNW	Gwen
EGOR	ergo
	goer
	gore□
	ogre
	Roeg
EGOS	geos
	goes
	sego
EGOY	goey
EGPU	Pegu
EGRS	ergs
	Gers
EGRT	Gert
	regt
EGRU	grue
	urge
EGRW	grew
EGRY	grey□
	gyre
EGTZ	Getz
EGVY	gyve
EHHT	heth
EHIK	hike
EHIL	heil!
EHIR	heir
	hire
EHIT	Hite
EHIV	hive
EHJU	Jehu
EHKO	hoke
EHKS	kesh
EHLL	hell□
	he'll
EHLM	helm
EHLO	hole
EHLP	help
EHLR	herl
EHMO	home□
EHMP	hemp
EHMS	mesh
	Shem
EHMT	them
EHMU	Hume
EHNO	hone
EHNR	Hern
EHNT	then
EHNW	when
EHNY	hyen
EHOP	hope□
EHOR	hero□
EHOS	hose
	shoe
EHOT	Theo
EHOV	Hove
EHOW	Howe
EHPS	Shep
EHPW	phew
EHPY	hype
EHRS	hers
	resh
EHRW	whe'r
EHSS	Hess
	shes
	she's
EHST	Seth
EHTT	teth
EHTW	thew
	whet
EHTY	they
EHUY	Huey
EHWW	whew
EHWY	whey
EIJV	jive
EIKL	Kiel
	like
EIKM	Kemi
	mike□
EIKN	kine
	Nike
EIKP	kepi
	pike
EIKR	kier
EIKT	kite
EIKV	Kiev
EIKY	yike
EILM	lime
	mile
EILN	lien
	line
	Neil
	Nile
EILP	pile
	plié
EILR	lire
	riel
	rile
EILS	isle
	lies
	Lise
	seil
	sile
EILT	lite
	tile
EILU	lieu
EILV	evil
	Levi
	live
	veil
	vile
EILW	lwei
	Weil
	wile
EILX	ilex
	Leix
EIMM	mime
EIMN	mein
	mien
	mine
EIMR	emir
	Meir
	mire
	rime
EIMS	semi
	semi-
EIMT	emit
	item
	mite
	time□
EINN	nine
EINP	pein
	pine□
EINR	Erin
	in re
	rein
EINS	Ines
	sien
	sine
EINT	tine
EINV	vein
	vine
EINW	Wien
	wine
EINZ	Inez
	zein
	zine
EIPP	pipe
EIPR	peri
	pier
	ripe
EIPS	sipe
EIPW	wipe
EIRS	rise
	sire
EIRT	rite
	tier
	tire
EIRU	iure
EIRV	rive
	vier
	vire
EIRW	weir
	wire
EIST	Seti
	site
	ties
EISV	Ives
EISW	wise□
EISZ	size
EITV	TVEI
	vite
EITW	wite
EITX	exit
EITY	yeti
EIVV	vive
EIVW	view
EJKO	joke
EJKR	jerk
EJKU	juke
EJLL	jell
EJLO	Joel
EJNU	June
EJOS	joes
EJOV	Jove
EJOY	joey□
EJRU	jure
EJSS	jess□
EJST	jest
EJTU	jute□
EKKS	keks
EKLP	kelp
EKLT	kelt□
EKLU	Luke
EKLW	welk
EKLY	kyle
EKMO	moke
EKMP	Kemp
EKNR	kern□
EKNT	Kent
EKNW	knew
EKOP	poke
EKOR	roke
EKOT	toke
EKOW	woke
EKOY	yoke
EKPR	perk
EKPS	skep
EKPT	kept
EKPU	puke
EKRS	sker
EKRT	trek
EKRY	yerk
EKST	Sekt
EKSU	Suke
EKSW	skew
EKSY	Skye
EKTT	Kett
EKTY	tyke
EKUY	yuke
ELLM	mell
	Mlle
ELLN	Nell
ELLS	sell
ELLT	tell
ELLU	Elul
ELLW	well□
	we'll
ELLY	Lyle
	yell
ELMO	Lomé
	mole□
ELMT	melt
ELMU	mule
ELMW	mewl
ELMY	Lyme
	yelm
	ylem
ELNO	León
	lone
	noel□
	Noël
	nole
ELNS	lens
ELNT	lent□
ELNZ	Lenz
ELOO	oleo
ELOP	lope
	Opel®
	pole□
ELOR	lore
	orle
	role
	rôle
ELOS	lose
	sloe

	sole□
ELOT	Leto
	tole
ELOV	love
	vole
ELPT	pelt
ELPU	pule
ELPY	yelp
ELRU	lure
	rule
ELRY	lyre
	rely
	Ryle
ELSS	less
ELST	lest
	LETS
	TESL
ELSU	lues
	slue
ELSW	slew
ELSY	lyse
ELTU	lute
ELTW	welt
ELUY	Yule
ELVY	levy
ELZZ	lezz
EMMO	memo
EMMS	Mmes
EMMY	Emmy
EMNO	omen
EMNU	menu
	neum
EMOP	mope
	poem
	pome
EMOR	more□
	Rome
EMOS	mose
	some
EMOT	tome
EMOU	moue
EMOV	move
EMOW	meow
EMOZ	moze
EMPR	perm□
EMPT	temp
EMRT	term
EMRU	mure
	rume
EMSS	mess
EMST	stem
EMSU	muse□
EMSW	mews
	smew
EMTU	mute
EMTZ	Metz
ENNO	neon
	none
ENNP	Penn
ENNV	Venn
ENOP	nope
	open
	peon
	pone
ENOR	Nero
	Reno
	rone
ENOS	noes
	nose
ENOT	Eton
	note
	tone
ENOV	oven
ENOW	enow
	Owen
ENOX	exon
	oxen
ENOZ	zone
ENPS	EPNS
ENPU	NUPE
ENRT	rent□
	tern
ENRU	rune
ENRW	wren□
ENSS	ness
ENST	nest
	sent
ENSW	news
	sewn
ENSY	syen
	syne
ENTT	nett
	tent
ENTU	tune
ENTV	vent
ENTW	newt
	went
ENTX	next
ENTY	Tyne
ENVY	envy
EOOZ	ooze
EOPP	pepo
	pope□
EOPR	pore
	repo
	rope
EOPS	EPOS
	epos
	peso
	pose
EOPT	poet
	pote
	tope
EOPX	expo
EORR	rore
EORS	Eros
	rose□
	rosé
	sore
EORT	rote
	tore
EORU	euro□
	roué
EORV	over
	rove
EORW	ower
	owre
	Rowe
	wore
EORX	exor
EORZ	zero
EOSS	Esso
EOST	tose
EOSU	Ouse
EOSY	oyes
EOTT	tote
EOTV	veto
	vote
EOTY	eyot
EOTZ	toze
EOYZ	oyez
EPPR	prep
	repp
EPQU	quep
EPRT	PERT
	pert
	rept
EPRU	Peru
	Prue
	puer
	pure
EPRV	perv
EPRY	prey
	pyre
EPST	pest
	sept
	step□
EPSW	spew
EPSY	espy
	Spey
	sype
EPTW	wept
EPTY	type
EQQS	seqq
ERRS	serr
ERST	erst
	rest
	très
ERSU	ruse□
	suer
	sure
	user
ERTU	true
ERTX	T Rex
ERTY	trey
	tyre□
ERUY	Urey
ERVY	very
ESST	Tess
ESSY	yes's
ESTT	sett
	stet
	test
ESTU	suet
	Utes
ESTV	vest
ESTW	stew
	west□
ESTX	sext
ESTY	stye
ESTZ	zest
ESUZ	Suez
	Zeus
	Zuse
ESVY	Yves
ESXY	sexy
ETTX	text

F

FFFU	fuff
FFGU	guff
FFHU	huff
FFIJ	jiff
FFIM	miff
FFIN	niff
FFIO	FIFO
FFIR	riff
FFIT	tiff
FFIY	iffy
FFIZ	ziff
FFLU	luff
FFMU	muff
FFOR	Orff
FFOT	toff
FFPU	puff
FFRU	ruff
FFTU	tuff
FGIO	figo
FGIR	frig
FGIT	GIFT
	gift
FGIU	Gifu
FGLO	flog
	golf□
FGLU	gulf
FGOO	goof
FGOR	frog□
FGOW	gowf
FGOY	fogy
FHII	hi-fi
FHIS	fish□
FHMT	fthm
FHNO	föhn
FHOO	hoof
FHOW	howf
FIIJ	Fiji
FIJU	Fuji®
FIKN	fink
FIKR	firk
FILL	fill
FILM	film
FILO	filo
	foil
	LIFO
FILP	flip
FILS	fils
FILT	flit
	lift
FIMR	firm
FINN	Finn
FINO	fino
	info
FINW	NFWI
FIOR	Ifor
FIPP	IPPF
FIRT	frit
	rift
FIRZ	friz
FIST	fist
	sift
FISU	Sufi
FITT	tift
FITZ	ZIFT
	Zift
FIZZ	fizz
FKLO	folk
FKNU	funk
FKOR	fork
FLLU	full
FLOO	fool□
FLOP	flop
FLOR	flor
	Rolf
FLOT	loft
FLOU	foul
FLOW	flow
	fowl
	wolf□
FLRU	furl
FLUX	flux
FMOR	form
	from
FMRS	mfrs
FMUY	fumy
FNOT	font
FOOP	poof
FOOR	roof
FOOT	foot□
FOOW	woof
FOPR	prof
FOPU	pouf
FORT	fort
FORU	four
FOSS	foss
	S. of S.
FOST	soft
FOSU	UFOs
FOSW	sowf
FOTU	tofu
FOXY	foxy
FRSU	surf
FRTU	turf
FRUY	fury□
FSSU	fuss
FSTU	fust

FTTU	tuft
FTUW	WFTU
FUZZ	fuzz

G

GGHO	Hogg
GGII	Gigi
GGIO	GIGO
GGIR	grig
	Rigg
GGIT	Tigg
GGLU	glug
GGNO	gong
GGOR	grog
GHHI	high
GHHU	Hugh
GHIN	nigh
GHIS	Gish
	sigh
GHIT	thig
GHIW	Whig
GHLU	Lugh
GHNU	hung
GHOS	gosh
	shog
GHOT	Goth
GHOU	Hugo
GHOY	yogh
GHSU	gush
GHTU	thug
GIKN	gink
	king❑
GILL	gill❑
GILN	ling
GILO	Logi
GILR	girl
GILT	gilt
GIMN	Ming
GIMP	gimp
GIMR	grim
GINO	go in
GINP	ping
GINR	girn
	grin
	ring
GINS	sign
	sing
	snig
GINT	ting
GINW	wing
GINZ	zing
GIOR	giro
GIOS	gios
GIOT	go it
GIOV	Vigo
GIOY	yogi
GIPR	grip
	prig
GIPS	pigs❑
GIRS	Gris
GIRT	girt
	grit
	trig
GIST	gist
GISW	swig
GITW	twig
GJNU	Jung
GKNU	gunk
GKSU	skug
GLLU	gull
GLMO	glom
GLMU	glum
GLNO	long❑
GLNU	lung
GLNY	Glyn
GLOO	logo
GLOP	glop
GLOS	slog
GLOW	glow
	gowl
GLPU	gulp
	plug
GLRU	gurl
GLSU	slug
GLTU	glut
GLUY	ugly
GMOO	Moog®
GMOR	gorm
GMOS	smog
GMPU	gump
GMPY	gymp
GMRS	Msgr
GMSU	smug
GMUW	GMWU
GNNO	nong
GNNU	Gunn
GNOO	go on
	no go
GNOP	pong
GNOS	snog
	song
GNOT	tong
GNOW	gown
GNQV	GNVQ
GNRU	rung
GNSU	gnus
	guns
	snug❑
	sung
GNWY	Gwyn
GOOP	goop
	pogo
GOOT	go to
	Togo
GOOZ	Gozo
GOPR	prog
GOPU	go up
GORT	grot
	trog
GORW	grow
GORY	gory
	Györ
	orgy
GOST	togs
GOSY	goys
GOTU	gout
GOTV	Govt
GRSU	Grus
GRTU	trug
GRUU	guru
GSTU	gust
	guts
GTUW	TGWU

H

HHOS	hohs
HHSU	hush
HIIL	hili
HIKO	hoik
HIKS	Sikh
HILL	hill❑
HILO	Holi
HILP	Phil
HILT	hilt
HIMS	mish
	shim
HIMW	whim
HINS	hisn
	his'n
	shin
HINT	hint
	thin
HINW	whin
HIOO	Ohio
HIOP	Hopi
	Ipoh
HIPS	hips
	pish
	ship
HIPT	pith
HIPW	whip
HIPZ	phiz
HIRS	Shri
HIRW	whir
HISS	hiss❑
HIST	hist
	hits
	shit
	sith
	this
HISU	huis
HISW	wish
HITW	whit❑
	with
HIWZ	whiz
HIZZ	hizz
HJNO	john❑
HJOS	josh❑
HKLO	kohl❑
HKLU	hulk
HKNO	honk
HKNU	hunk
	Kuhn
HKOO	hook❑
HKOP	koph
HKOW	howk
HKSU	husk
	sukh
HLLU	hull❑
HLMO	holm
HLMT	HTML
HLOS	hols
HLOT	holt
	loth
HLOW	howl❑
HLOY	holy
HLPY	Phyl
HLRU	hurl
HLRY	Rhyl
HLSU	lush
	shul
HLTV	HTLV
HMNY	hymn
HMOO	homo
HMOR	Röhm
HMOS	HMSO
	Homs
	mhos
	OHMS
HMOT	moth❑
HMOW	whom
HMOY	homy
HMPU	hump
HMSU	mush
HMTY	myth
HNOP	phon
HNOR	horn
HNOS	nosh
HNRU	Rhun
HNSU	shun
HNTU	hunt❑
	Thun
HOOP	hoop
	pooh❑
HOOS	ohos
	shoo
	soho
	so-ho
HOOT	hoot
	Otho
	toho
HOOY	yo-ho
HOPQ	qoph
HOPS	posh
	shop
HOPU	ouph
HOPW	whop
HOPY	hypo
HORS	hors
	rhos
HORT	Roth
	Thor
	thro
	thro'
HORU	hour
HOST	host
	shot
	tosh
HOSW	show
	who's
HOTU	thou
HOWW	whow
HPRU	pruh
HPSU	push
HPTT	http
HPTU	phut
HRRU	Ruhr
HRSU	rush❑
HRSY	Rhys
HRTU	hurt❑
	Ruth
HSSU	Huss
HSTU	shut
	thus
	tush
HUUW	Wuhu

I

IIJX	Jixi
IIKW	kiwi
IILP	pili
IIMN	mini
	Mini®
IIMR	miri
IINS	nisi
IINT	in it
IIRS	iris❑
IISS	ISIS
	Isis
IITT	titi
IITZ	ziti
IJKN	jink
IJLL	jill❑
IJLT	jilt
IJNN	jinn
IJNO	join
	Joni
IJNX	jinx
IJZZ	jizz
IKKN	kink
IKKR	kirk❑
IKLL	kill
IKLM	milk
IKLN	kiln
	link
IKLO	kilo❑
	Loki
IKLR	lirk
IKLS	silk
IKLT	kilt
IKMN	mink
IKMR	mirk
IKMS	skim
IKNO	ikon
	kino

	oink
IKNP	pink
IKNR	rink
IKNS	sink
	skin
IKNT	knit
	tink
IKNW	wink
IKNY	inky
IKPS	skip
IKRS	kris
	risk
IKRU	kuri
IKSS	kiss❑
	skis
IKST	kist
	skit
IKUV	Kivu
ILLL	lill
ILLM	mill❑
ILLO	lilo❑
ILLP	pill
ILLR	rill
ILLS	sill
ILLT	it'll
	lilt
	till
ILLW	will❑
ILLY	lily❑
ILMN	limn
ILMO	limo
ILMP	limp
	plim
ILMS	slim
ILMT	milt
ILMY	limy
ILNN	linn
ILNO	lino
	lion❑
	loin
ILNR	nirl
	RNLI
ILNT	lint
ILNY	inly
ILNZ	Linz
ILOO	olio
ILOR	roil
ILOS	Lois
	oils
	silo
	soil
	soli
ILOT	loti
	toil
ILOV	viol
ILOY	oily
ILPS	lips
	LISP
	lisp
	Pils
	slip

ILRT	tirl
ILST	list
	silt
	slit
ILTT	tilt
ILTW	wilt
ILVY	Livy
ILWY	wily
IMNT	mint
IMNX	minx
IMOR	IMRO
	Miró
	MORI
IMOS	miso
IMOT	omit
IMPP	pimp
IMPR	prim
IMPS	MIPS
	mips
IMPW	WIMP
	wimp
IMRS	mirs
IMRT	trim❑
IMRU	Muir
	rimu
IMRV	MIRV
IMRY	miry
	rimy
IMSS	miss
	Sims
IMST	mist
IMSW	swim
IMTT	mitt
IMTU	muti
INNO	in on
INOP	pion
INOR	inro
	iron
	nori
INOS	Sion
INOT	into
	oint
	Toni
INOV	Ivon
	vino
INOW	wino
INOZ	Zion
INPS	pins
	snip
	spin
INPT	pint
	pint-
INPY	piny
INQU	quin
INRU	ruin
INST	inst
	isn't
INTT	tint
INTU	unit
INTV	vint
INTW	twin

INTY	tiny
INUX	UNIX
	Unix
	UNIX®
INUZ	Zuni
	Zuñi
INVY	viny
INWY	winy
IOPT	topi
IOPY	pioy
IORS	sori
IORT	riot
	roti
	tiro
	tori
	trio
IORV	Ivor
	rivo
IOST	Otis
IOTT	Tito
IPPY	pipy
IPQU	quip
IPRS	risp
IPRT	trip
IPRU	puri
IPST	spit
	tips
IPSU	Pius
IPSV	spiv
IPSW	wisp
IPSY	I-spy
IPTT	Pitt
IPTU	Tupí
IPTY	pity
IPUY	Pu Yi
IPXY	pixy
IQTU	quit
IQUZ	quiz
IRRT	tirr
IRST	stir
IRSW	SWRI
IRTT	ritt
IRTW	writ
IRTX	Trix
IRWY	wiry
ISSS	SSSI
ISST	sist
ISTT	tits
ISTU	suit
	utis
ISTW	wist
	wits
ISUZ	Uzis
ISWZ	swiz
ITTW	twit
	Witt
ITZZ	tizz
IUWX	Wuxi
IZZZ	zizz

J

JJUU	juju
	ju-ju
JKNU	junk
JKOO	jook
JKOU	jouk
JLOT	jolt
JLOW	jowl
JLUY	July
JMOO	Mojo
JMPU	jump
JNOU	Juno
JOOT	Tojo
JOSS	Joss
JOUY	Jouy
JRUY	jury
JSTU	just

K

KKOO	kook
KLNO	Köln
KLOO	look
KLOP	Polk
KLOS	skol
KLOY	yolk
KLRU	lurk
KLSU	sulk
KMNO	monk❑
KMOS	Omsk
KMRU	murk
KMSU	musk
KNOO	nook
KNOT	knot
	tonk
KNOW	know
KNOX	Knox
KNOZ	zonk
KNPU	punk
KNRU	knur
KNSU	sunk
KNTU	Knut
KOOP	pook
KOOR	rook❑
KOOS	sook
KOOT	koto
	took
KOPR	pork
KOPU	pouk
KOPY	poky
KORW	work
KORY	York
KOSU	souk
KOUY	yuko
KOUZ	zouk
KRSU	rusk❑
KRTU	Kurt
	Turk
KRUU	Uruk
KSTU	tusk
KSUY	Suky

L

LLLO	loll
LLLU	lull
LLMO	moll❑
LLMU	mull❑
LLNU	null
LLOP	poll❑
LLOR	roll
LLOT	toll
LLPU	pull
LLTU	Tull
LLUU	Lulu
LLUW	wull
LLVV	vvll
LMOO	Lomo
	loom
LMPU	lump
	plum
LMRU	murl
LMSU	slum
LNNY	Lynn
LNOO	loon
LNOW	lown
	nowl
LNOY	only
LNRU	nurl
LNTU	lunt
LNUV	vuln
LNXY	lynx❑
LOOP	loop
	polo❑
	Polo®
	pool
LOOS	Loos
	Oslo
	solo
LOOT	loot❑
	tool
LOOW	wool
LOPP	plop
LOPS	slop
LOPT	plot
LOPU	loup
LOPY	ploy
	poly
LORU	lour
LORY	lory
LOSS	loss
	sols
LOST	lost
	lots
	slot
	St-Lô
	STOL
LOSU	soul❑
LOSW	Owls
	slow
LOTU	lout
	tolu
LOTV	volt

VTOL
LOUU Oulu
LOVV Lvov
LOWY yowl
LPPU pulp❑
LPRU purl
LPSU plus
LPUY puly
LRSU slur
LRUY ruly
LSTU lust
slut
LSUU sulu
LTUZ lutz
LUUZ Zulu

M

MMPU mump
MMST SMMT
MNOO mono
moon
MNOR morn
norm
MNOS Mons
MNOU muon
MOOP moop
MOOR moor❑
Moro
room
MOOT moot
toom
MOOZ zoom
MOPP pomp
MOPR PROM
prom
romp
MOPU moup
MOPY mopy
yomp
MORW WORM
worm
MOSS moss❑
MOST most
MOSU muso
soum
sumo
MOTT Mott
MOTU motu
MOUV ovum
MPPU pump
MPRU rump
MPSU sump
MPTU tump
MPUY yump
MRSU smur
MSSU muss
MSTU must
smut
stum
MSUW swum
MTTU mutt

N

NNNU Nunn
NNOO no-no
noon
NNOU non-U
noun
NNWY wynn
NOOS soon
NOOT on to
onto
NOPR porn
NOPS pons
NOPU up on
upon
NOPY pony
NORS RSNO
sorn
NORT torn
NORW worn
NOST onst
snot
tons
NOSU nous
onus
NOSW snow❑
sown
NOSY nosy
NOTW nowt
town
wont
won't
NOTY Tony
yont
NOXY onyx
NPSU puns
spun
NPTU punt
NPUY puny
NRRV RNVR
NRSU runs
NRSW WRNS
NRTU runt
turn
NSTU nuts
stun

O

OOPP oppo
poop
OOPR poor
proo
roop
OOPS oops
soop
OOPY yoop
OORR ro-ro
OORS or so
OORT Oort
root
OOSS so so
so-so
OOST soot
Soto
OOTT otto❑
toot
Toto
OOTW woot
woo't
OOUZ ouzo
OOYY yo-yo
OOYZ oozy
OPPP Popp
OPPR prop
OPRS pros
OPRT port
OPRU pour
roup
OPRW prow
OPRY ropy
OPST post
pots
spot
stop
tops
OPSU opus
soup
OPSV VSOP
OPSW swop
OPSY posy
OPTT pott
OPTU pout
up to
OPTY typo
OPUZ Puzo
OPXY poxy
ORRT rort
torr
ORRY Rory
ORSS Ross
ORST sort
ORSU Rous
sour
ORSW rows
ORSY rosy
ORTT tort
trot❑
ORTU rout
tour
ORTW trow
wort
ORTY ryot
Tory
troy❑
tyro
ORUX roux❑
ORUY your
ORXY oryx
OSSS soss
OSST toss
OSSV Voss
OSTT stot
OSTU oust
OSTW stow
swot
OSUX Oxus
OSVW vows
OTTU tout
OTWY towy❑
OYZZ Ozzy

P

PRRU purr
rurp
PRSU spur
PRSV RSVP
PRSY spry❑
PSST psst
tsps
PSSU puss
PTTU putt

R

RSSU USSR
RSTU rust❑
RSVW WRVS
RTUY yurt

S

SSSU suss
SSUW wuss
SSUY Susy
SUYZ Suzy

T

TTUU tutu❑

5 letters

A

AAABC abaca
AAABK Ka'aba
AAABQ Aqaba
AAABY abaya
AAADN Adana
AAAGN Agana
AAANS asana
AAASV Vaasa
AABCI abaci
AABCK aback
AABCL cabal
AABDE Baade
AABDN Banda
AABEM abeam
AABES abase
AABET abate
AABFT abaft
BAFTA
Bafta
AABGL Galba
AABHI Bahai
Baha'i
AABHS abash
AABJN Bajan
AABJR bajra
AABJU Abuja
AABKR Akbar
Barak
AABKS abask
AABLN Alban
banal
Laban
nabla
AABLR labra
AABLS balsa
basal
Sabal
AABLT tabla
AABMM mamba
AABMR Abram
AABMS samba
AABNW nawab
AABNY Bayan
AABRR Barra
AABRS Basra
sabra
AABRT Rabat
AABRZ zabra

AABST basta
AABZZ Bazza
AACCD Dacca
AACCE caeca
AACCO cacao
AACCR Accra
AACDH dacha
AACEI aecia
AACEP apace
AACER areca
AACFI facia
AACHM Macha
AACHS Sacha
AACIR acari
Arica
AACIS Isaac
AACLL calla
AACLN canal
AACLR Carla
Clara
AACMO Macao
AACMR CAMRA
AACMS camas
AACMW macaw
AACNV Cavan
AACNZ Anzac
AACPR Capra
AACPS scapa
AACRS sacra
AACRT carat
AACST act as
AACSW AWACS
AACUV vacua
AADDG Dagda
AADEG adage
AADEH ahead
AADEL Adela
AADEN Danae
AADFR farad
AADGG dagga
AADGM Magda
AADGR darga
garda□
AADHK Dhaka
AADHM Ahmad
Hamad
AADIN Aidan
Diana
Nadia
naiad
AADKR Dakar
AADLM LAMDA
AADLN Åland
AADLS salad
AADLU Duala
Lauda
AADMM madam
AADMN adman
daman
AADMR drama
AADMS Adams
AADNN Adnan
AADNP panda
AADNU Nuada
AADNV V and A
AADNW Wanda
AADNY Dayan
AADOR A-road
AADOV Davao
AADPT adapt
AADPU Padua
AADRR radar
AADRW award
AADSS Assad
AADST Sadat
AADTY adyta
AAEGL algae
AAEGP agape
apage
AAEGT agate
AAEGV agave
AAEKL Akela
AAEKP apeak
AAEKU UKAEA
AAEKW awake
AAELT alate
AAEMS Saame
AAEMT amate
AAEMZ amaze
AAENP paean
AAENR arena
AAENS ASEAN
Asean
AAENT antae
AAERU aurae
AAERW aware
AAEST at sea
AAFFJ Jaffa
AAFHI Haifa
AAFHR Farah
AAFIM Mafia
AAFIN NAAFI
AAFIT tafia
AAFJL aflaj
AAFKK Kafka
AAFKN nakfa
AAFLL Falla
AAFLN fanal
AAFLT fatal
AAFNT NAFTA
Nafta
AAFNU fauna□
AAFTW fatwa
AAGGR ragga
AAGHL galah
AAGHN Ghana
AAGIM agami
AAGIN again
AAGIS saiga
AAGIT taiga
AAGJN ganja
AAGKN kanga□
AAGLR argal
AAGLV vagal
AAGMM gamma
magma
AAGMN Manga
AAGNP pagan
AAGNS Sagan
AAGNT tanga□
AAGNU guana
AAGOR agora
AAGRZ gazar
AAGUV guava
AAGZZ Gazza
AAHIS Aisha
AAHJR rajah
AAHKM hakam
AAHKS kasha
AAHLL Allah
halal
AAHLM halma
AAHLO aloha
AAHLP alpha□
AAHLS Halas
Lhasa
AAHLV halva
AAHMO Omaha
AAHNS Hasan
AAHOR O'Hara
AAHPR Aphra
AAHPS pasha
AAHRR arrah
AAHRS Sarah
AAHRT Hatra
AAHSS Sasha
AAHST hasta
AAHSU Hausa
AAHSW awash□
AAHSY Aysha
AAHVZ Ahvaz
AAIKL Laika
AAIKS Sakai
AAILM lamia□
AAILN Lanai
liana□
AAILS Ailsa
alias
AAILV avail
Ávila
AAILX axial
AAIMN amnia
anima
mania
AAIMR Maria
AAIMS Masai
AAIMT aim at
Amati
AAINP apian
AAINR Arian
naira
AAINS Anaïs
Asian
AAINT Anita
Tania
AAINV avian
Ivana
AAIPR Praia
AAIPV Pavia
AAIRT Arita
atria
raita
tiara
AAISS assai
AAITW await
AAJKR Karaj
AAJLM Jamal
AAJNP japan□
AAJNZ zanja
AAKKN Kanak
AAKKR Kraak
AAKKY kayak
AAKKZ Kazak
AAKLM Kamal
AAKLO koala
AAKLR Karla
kraal
AAKMR Akram
karma
marka
AAKNR Karan
AAKNT tanka
AAKNZ Kazan
AAKOS Osaka
AAKPP kappa
AAKPR parka
AAKRT Tarka
AAKTY Katya
AAKTZ zakat
AALLL Lalla
AALLM llama
AALLN Allan
AALLT at all
AALLU alula
AALLW walla
AALLY allay
Layla
AALMO Alamo
AALMP Palma
AALMR alarm
ramal
AALMS Salam
AALMT Malta
AALMX malax
AALMY Malay
AALNS Aslan
nasal
AALNT natal□
AALNU Nuala
AALNV naval
NVALA
AALNY Al Ayn
nyala
AALNZ Lanza
AALOT Aalto
AALPP appal
papal
AALPU Palau
Paula
AALPY playa
AALPZ La Paz
plaza
AALRT altar□
artal
tra-la
AALRU aural
Laura
AALRV larva
AALRZ lazar
AALSS salsa
AALST atlas□
AALSV lavas
vasal
AAMMM mamma
AAMMN Amman
AAMNN manna
AAMNR Raman
AAMNS Masan
AAMNT atman
manat
manta
AAMNY many a
AAMOR aroma
AAMOS omasa
Samoa
AAMPR Parma
AAMPT Tampa
AAMRT Marat
AAMSS a mass
amass
Assam
AANNN Nanna
AANOR Aaron
AANOX xoana
AANPP nappa
AANPR prana
AANPT Patna
AANPV pavan
AANRR Arran
AANRT antar
antra
ratan
AANRV Varna
AANRW Anwar
AANRY Aryan
nary a
AANST Satan
AANSU sauna
AANSW Aswan
AANSY Nyasa
AANTY Tanya
AANUW NUAAW
AAORT aorta
AAOST Aosta
AAPPW papaw

AAPPZ	Zappa
AAPRT	apart
	at par
AAPST	pasta
	tapas
AAPWW	pawaw
AAQRT	Qatar
AAQRZ	Zarqa
AARRS	arras□
AARRY	array
AARST	Astra®
AARSU	auras
AARTT	attar
	Tatar
AARTW	at war
AARUW	Urawa
AASSW	as was
AASSY	assay
AASTV	avast
AASTY	satay
AASWY	asway
AATXY	ataxy
ABBCY	cabby
ABBDN	b and b
ABBEK	kebab
ABBEL	babel□
ABBEY	abbey
ABBGY	gabby□
ABBIM	Bambi
ABBIR	rabbi
ABBKU	Bubka
ABBNO	nabob
ABBOT	abbot
ABBQR	bar-b-q
ABBRU	Babur
ABBTY	tabby
ABCCO	Caboc
ABCCY	baccy
ABCEH	beach
ABCEL	cable
ABCER	brace
	caber
ABCHI	Chiba
ABCHR	BArch
ABCHT	batch
ABCIN	cabin
ABCIR	Carib
ABCIS	BASIC
	basic□
ABCJO	Jacob
ABCKL	black□
ABCLN	Blanc
ABCNO	bacon□
ABCNU	Cuban
ABCOR	Broca
	carob
	cobra
ABCOT	Cabot
ABCOV	vocab
ABCRT	bract
ABCSU	scuba
ABDDE	bedad
ABDDY	baddy
ABDEG	badge
	begad
	debag
ABDEI	abide
ABDEK	baked
ABDEL	blade
ABDEN	Baden
	Bände
ABDEO	abode
	adobe
ABDER	Bader
	beard
	bread
	Breda
	debar
	Debra
ABDES	based
	beads
ABDEU	daube
ABDEY	beady
ABDGO	go bad
ABDIL	ad lib
	ad-lib
ABDIR	Baird
	braid□
	rabid
ABDIU	Dubai
ABDLN	bland
ABDLU	Abdul
	blaud
ABDLY	badly
ABDNR	brand
	R and B
ABDNY	bandy
ABDOR	abord
	board
	broad
	dobra
ABDOY	a'body
ABDRY	Brady
	Darby
ABDWY	bawdy
ABEEL	Albee
ABEFL	fable
ABEFR	Fabre
ABEGI	bigae
ABEGL	bagel
	gable□
ABEGN	began
ABEGR	barge
	begar
ABEHJ	hejab
ABEHN	Behan
ABEHO	obeah
ABEHR	Behar
	Brahe
	Haber
	rehab
ABEHS	Sheba
ABEHT	bathe
ABEIM	I-beam
ABEIR	Beira
ABEIS	Basie
ABEIZ	baize
ABEKL	Blake
	bleak
ABEKR	baker□
	brake
	break
ABEKY	beaky
ABELL	Bella
	label
ABELM	amble
	blame
	Mabel
	Melba
ABELR	baler
	blare
	blear
ABELS	Basle
	blasé
	sable
ABELT	bleat
	table□
ABELY	Bayle
	belay
ABELZ	blaze
ABEMR	amber□
	bream□
	embar
ABEMS	beams
ABEMY	embay
	maybe
ABENO	beano
ABENV	Bevan
ABEOV	above
ABERR	barre
	Berra
	re-bar
ABERS	sabre
ABERV	brave
ABERY	yerba
ABERZ	braze
	zebra
ABESS	bases
ABEST	baste
	Bates
	beast
	tabes
ABESU	abuse
ABESY	by sea
ABETU	beaut
	tubae
ABEUX	beaux
ABFFN	Banff
ABFFU	buffa
ABFRY	by far
ABGGR	Bragg
ABGGY	baggy
ABGHN	bhang
ABGIS	bags I
ABGNO	Gabon
ABGNS	bangs
ABGNU	unbag
ABGOR	Gabor
	garbo□
ABHIJ	hijab
ABHIR	Bihar
ABHIS	sahib
ABHIT	habit
ABHOR	abhor
ABHOS	basho□
ABHOT	Botha
ABHRS	brash
ABHRT	Barth
ABHST	baths
ABIIL	alibi
ABIIM	iambi
ABIIT	tibia
ABIIZ	Ibiza
ABIJO	Baoji
ABIKT	batik
ABILN	binal
	blain
ABILO	aboil
ABILQ	qibla
ABILR	Blair
	brail
	Libra
ABILS	basil□
ABILT	balti
ABILY	Baily
	Libya
ABIMN	Namib
ABIMR	abrim
ABIMT	ambit
ABINR	abrin
	bairn
	brain
	Brian
	Rabin
ABINS	basin
ABIOT	biota
ABIRR	briar
ABIRY	by air
ABISS	basis
	bassi
ABJMO	jambo
ABJNO	banjo
ABJOT	jabot
ABKLN	blank
ABKLU	baulk
	Kabul
ABKNS	Banks
ABKOR	borak
ABKST	Bakst
ABLLS	balls
ABLLU	bulla
ABLLY	bally
ABLMU	album
ABLMY	balmy
ABLNO	Bolan
ABLOO	Baloo
ABLOR	Balor
	lobar
ABLOS	bolas
ABLOT	bloat
ABLOW	ablow
ABLRW	brawl
ABLST	blast
ABLTU	tubal
ABLWY	by law
	by-law
ABLYY	lay by
ABMMO	mambo
ABMOS	ambos
	sambo
ABMOT	Tambo
	Tomba
ABMRU	Burma
	rumba
	umbra
ABMRY	barmy
ABNNO	Boann
ABNNS	banns
ABNOR	baron
ABNOT	baton
ABNRU	Braun
	buran
	unbar
	urban□
ABNRW	brawn
ABNRY	Bryan
ABNSU	Busan
ABNTU	Bantu
ABOOT	taboo
ABOOV	ab ovo
ABOQT	Q-boat
ABORR	arbor
ABORS	Bosra
ABORT	abort
	tabor
ABORV	bravo□
ABORX	borax
ABORZ	Zorba
ABOST	boast
	sabot
ABOTU	about
	U-boat
ABOUY	bayou
ABQSU	squab
ABRRU	Burra
ABRRY	Barry
ABRSS	brass
ABRSU	Arbus
	bursa□
ABSSW	swabs
ABSSY	abyss
ABSTT	batts
ABSTU	tabus
	tubas
ABTTU	battu

ABTTY batty□
Byatt
ABUZZ abuzz
ABWYY byway
ACCDY cycad
ACCEH cache
ACCEM mecca□
ACCHI chica
ACCHK chack
ACCHO coach
ACCHT catch
ACCIR circa
ACCIT cacti
ACCKL clack
ACCKO acock
ACCKR crack
ACCMO OCCAM
occam
ACCOO cocoa
ACCOT coact
ACCUY yucca
ACDDN D and C
ACDDY caddy
ACDEF faced
ACDEG cadge
caged
ACDEL laced
ACDEN dance
ACDER cadre
cedar
ACDET cadet
ACDEY decay
ACDFO CAFOD
ACDHN h and c
ACDHO ad hoc
ACDHR chard
ACDIN nicad
ACDIR acrid
Dirac
ACDIS asdic□
ACDIT dicta
ACDIY acidy
ACDIZ Cádiz
ACDLO acold
ACDLS scald
ACDLU Claud
ducal
ACDNO can do
ACDNW C and W
ACDNY candy□
ACDOR Draco
ACDOT octad
ACDRY Darcy
ACDSS scads
ACDTU ducat
ACEEP peace
ACEES cease
ACEFH chafe
ACEFR facer
farce
ACEFT facet
ACEGL glacé
ACEGR GRACE
grace□
ACEGY cagey
ACEHL chela
leach
ACEHN nache
ACEHP cheap
peach
ACEHR reach
ACEHS chase□
ACEHT cheat
tache
teach□
theca
ACEIL Alice
Celia
ileac
Leica®
ACEIN Caine
ACEIR erica□
ACEKR crake
creak
ACELM camel
ACELN clean
lance□
ACELP place
ACELR Clare
clear
recal
ACELS scale
ACELT cleat
éclat
ACELV calve
ACEMO cameo
comae
ACEMR cream
ACEMS SECAM
ACENN Nance
ACENO canoe
ocean
ACENP pecan
ACENR Carné
crane□
nacre
rance
ACENS scena
ACENT enact
ACENV Vance
ACEOR Corea
ocrea
ACEOT coate
ACEOX coxae
ACEPR caper
crape
pacer
recap
ACEPS scape
space
ACEPT Capet
epact
ACEPY pacey
ACERR carer
Carré
racer
ACERS acres
races
scare
ACERT caret
cater
crate
react
recta
trace
ACERV carve
caver
crave
varec
ACERY Carey
ACERZ craze
ACESS cases
ACEST caste
ACESU cause
sauce
ACETT tacet
ACETU acute
ACETX exact
ACETZ Aztec
ACFFH chaff
ACFIL calif
ACFIP CIPFA
ACFIS fasci
ACFKL Flack
ACFLO focal
ACFLS calfs
ACFNR franc
ACFNY fancy
ACFRS scarf
ACFRT craft
fract
ACFST facts
ACGHN ganch
ACGIM magic
ACGIR cigar□
Craig
ACGLN clang
ACGNO conga
ACGOR cargo
ACGRS scrag
ACGSS CS gas
ACHHT hatch
ACHIM Chaim
Micah
ACHIN chain□
china□
ACHIO chiao
ACHIR chair
ACHIT aitch
Chita
ACHKL chalk
ACHKR chark
ACHKS hacks
shack
ACHKW whack
ACHLO loach
ACHLR larch
ACHLS clash□
ACHLT latch
ACHMO macho
mocha
ACHMP champ
ACHMR charm
march□
ACHMS chasm
ACHMT match
ACHMU Mucha
ACHNO Cohan
ACHNR ranch
ACHNT chant
natch
ACHNU nucha
ACHOP poach
ACHOR roach□
ACHOS chaos
ACHOV havoc
ACHPR parch
ACHPS chaps
Pasch
ACHPT patch
ACHRR charr
ACHRS crash□
ACHRT chart
ACHRY Archy
chary
ACHSS Sachs
ACHSW schwa
ACHTW watch
ACHTY Cathy
yacht
ACIIL cilia
iliac
ACIIM amici
ACIIN acini
ACIIS ASCII
ACILL lilac
ACILM claim
ACILS Alcis
Salic
scail
ACILU Lucia
ACILV cavil
ACIMN manic
Nicam
ACIMR micra
ACIMS micas
ACINN Incan
ACINP panic
ACINR cairn
in-car
ACINT actin
antic
ACIOR Cairo
ACIOS ciaos
ACIOT coati
ACIOZ azoic
ACIPR Capri
carpi
ACIPS aspic
scapi
spica□
ACIRT artic
ACIRU auric
ACIRV vicar
vraic
ACITT attic□
tacit
ACITU Utica
ACITV vatic
ACJKS jacks
ACKKN knack
ACKLN clank
ACKLO cloak
ACKLR Clark
ACKLS slack
ACKLU caulk
ACKMS smack
ACKMU amuck
ACKNR crank
ACKNS snack
ACKOR croak
ACKOW wacko
ACKQU quack
ACKRT track
ACKRW wrack
ACKST stack
ACKTY tacky
ACKWY wacky
ACLLO local
ACLMP clamp
ACLMU Calum
ACLNU Lucan
ACLOR carol□
coral□
Lorca
ACLOS COSLA
ACLOT octal
ACLOV vocal
ACLPS clasp
scalp
ACLRT clart
ACLRW crawl
ACLRY Carly
clary
Lycra®
ACLSS class
ACLSU Lucas
ACLSW claws
ACLSY scaly
ACLTU claut
ACLXY calyx
ACMMO comma
ACMNO Mâcon
ACMNY -mancy
ACMOR coram

	macro
ACMOS	Mosca
ACMPR	cramp
ACMPS	scamp
ACMPY	campy
ACMRS	scram
ACMSU	Camus
	Musca
	sumac
ACNNO	ancon
	canon
	Canon®
ACNNY	canny
	nancy□
ACNOP	capon
	Copán
ACNOR	acorn
	NACRO
	Nacro
	narco
	racon
ACNOT	act on
	canto
ACNPU	uncap
ACNRS	narcs
ACNRY	carny
ACNST	canst
	scant
ACOPR	copra
ACOPS	capos
	pacos
ACOPT	capot
	coapt
ACORS	oscar□
ACORT	actor
	Croat
ACORY	oracy
ACOST	Ascot
	coast
	costa
	tacos
	Tosca
ACOTT	cotta
ACPPR	PPARC
ACPPU	cuppa
ACPRS	craps
	RSPCA
	scarp
	scrap
ACPSU	scaup
ACPTU	act up
	caput
ACRRY	carry
ACRSS	crass
ACRST	scart
ACRSU	scaur
ACRSY	scary
ACRTT	tract
ACRTY	Tracy
ACRYZ	crazy
ACSST	scats
ACSSU	ascus
ACSTU	actus
	scuta
ACSTY	Stacy
ACSUY	saucy
ACTTU	UCATT
ACTTY	catty
ADDDE	added
ADDDY	daddy
ADDEF	faded
ADDEI	Addie
ADDEJ	jaded
	Jedda
ADDEL	addle
ADDER	adder
	dread
ADDET	dated
ADDEV	Vedda
ADDEZ	dazed
ADDFY	faddy
ADDIN	add in
ADDIO	addio
ADDIV	David
ADDNO	add-on
ADDNY	dandy
ADDOS	dados
ADDOT	add to
ADDPU	add up
ADDPY	paddy□
ADDRY	dryad
ADDWY	waddy
ADEEL	Adèle
ADEEM	adeem
	Meade
	Medea
ADEEO	Aoede
ADEER	eared
ADEEV	deave
	evade
ADEFK	faked
ADEFM	famed
ADEFR	Freda
ADEFT	defat
	fated
ADEFZ	fazed
ADEGI	Adige
ADEGL	glade
ADEGM	Madge
ADEGR	Edgar
	Gerda
	grade□
	ragde
ADEGS	degas□
ADEGT	gated
ADEGW	waged
ADEHJ	jehad
ADEHL	heald
ADEHM	Ahmed
ADEHR	heard
ADEHS	Hades
	sadhe
	shade
ADEHT	death
	hated
ADEHX	hexad
ADEHY	heady
ADEIL	Delia
	eliad
	ideal
ADEIM	amide
	media
ADEIN	Aiden
	Diane
ADEIR	irade
ADEIS	aides
	aside
	A-side
	Desai
	ideas
	Sadie
ADEIU	adieu
ADEIV	Davie
ADEIZ	azide
ADEJR	Jared
ADEKL	Dalek
ADEKN	knead
	naked
ADEKR	daker
	drake□
ADELL	Della
	ladle
ADELM	medal
ADELN	eland
	laden
ADELP	pedal
	plead
ADELR	Adler
	alder
ADELS	Dales
	slade□
ADELT	dealt
	delta□
	lated
ADELW	dwale
	weald
ADELY	delay
ADELZ	Zelda
ADEMM	damme
ADEMN	amend
	deman
	maned
	Medan
	named
ADEMR	ad rem
	armed
	derma
	dream
ADEMS	Meads
ADEMT	mated
	tamed
ADEMU	Maude
ADENN	an-end
ADENO	anode
ADENP	Penda
ADENR	Andre
	Arden
	Enard
	Nader
ADENS	Andes
	sedan□
	Snead
ADENT	Dante
ADENU	Auden
	Duane
ADENV	daven
	vaned
ADENW	awned
	Dwane
ADEOR	adore
	oared
	oread
ADEPR	drape
	padre
ADEPS	sepad
	spade□
ADEPT	adept
ADEPV	paved
ADERR	drear
ADERT	trade
	tread
ADERW	Dewar
	wader
ADERY	ready
ADEST	sated
	stead□
ADESV	saved
	Vedas
ADESW	sawed
ADETX	taxed
ADEUX	à deux
ADEVW	waved
ADEVY	VE day
ADEWX	waxed
ADFFR	draff
ADFFY	daffy
ADFLO	Adolf
	Faldo
ADFNO	Fonda
ADFOS	fados
ADFRT	draft
ADFRU	fraud
ADFRW	dwarf
ADGGY	daggy
ADGIL	algid
ADGIU	Gaudí
ADGLN	gland
ADGLO	Golda
ADGMO	dogma
	go mad
ADGNO	donga
	go and
	gonad
ADGNR	grand
ADGNT	G and T
ADGOO	agood
ADGOS	dagos
ADGOT	toga'd
ADGOU	Gouda
ADGRU	Durga
	guard
ADGSU	gauds
ADGUY	gaudy
ADHIJ	hadji
	jihad
ADHIK	khadi
ADHIL	Hilda
ADHIM	Mahdi
ADHIN	ahind
	Dinah
ADHIO	Idaho
ADHIP	aphid
ADHIS	Hasid
ADHJU	Judah
ADHLO	ahold
ADHNO	Honda
ADHNS	hands
ADHNT	hadn't
ADHNY	handy
	Haydn
ADHOR	hoard
	Rhoda
ADHRS	shard
ADHRY	hardy□
	hydra□
ADHST	hadst
ADHSU	sadhu
ADHSY	Hyads
	shady
ADIIN	I-and-I
	India
ADIIO	oidia
ADIIR	radii
ADIIT	Aditi
ADIKN	kinda
ADILN	Linda
	nidal
ADILO	dolia
	Idola
ADILP	plaid
ADILR	drail
	laird
ADILS	dials
ADILT	Dalit
	tidal
ADILV	valid
	Vidal
ADILY	daily
	Lydia
ADIMN	admin
ADIMS	Midas
ADIMT	admit
ADIMV	Vadim
ADIMX	admix
ADINR	dinar

	drain
	Indra
	nadir
ADINS	NSAID
ADINV	divan
ADIOP	podia
ADIOR	Doria
	radio
ADIOS	adios
	adiós
ADIOU	audio
ADIOV	avoid
ADIPR	pardi
	rapid
ADIPS	sapid
ADIPV	vapid
ADIRT	triad
ADIRV	Vidar
ADIRX	radix
ADIRY	dairy
	diary
ADIST	staid
ADISV	Davis
ADISY	daisy□
	sayid
ADITU	audit
ADITV	davit
ADJOU	Oujda
ADJSU	Judas
ADKKO	Kodak®
ADKLS	skald
ADKMR	D-mark
ADKNR	drank
ADKNY	Kandy
ADKOR	Korda
ADKOV	vodka
ADKSU	Dukas
ADLLO	do-all
ADLLY	dally
ADLMO	dolma
	domal
	modal
ADLMY	madly
ADLNO	Donal
	Lando
	Ndola
	nodal
ADLNS	lands
ADLNU	laund
ADLNY	Dylan
	Lynda
ADLOR	Roald
ADLOS	loads
ADLOU	aloud
ADLOW	Waldo
ADLRW	drawl
ADLRY	lardy
ADLSU	lauds
ADLSY	sadly
ADLTU	adult
ADMNO	Damon
	mad on
	monad
	nomad
ADMNS	S and M
ADMNY	Mandy
ADMPU	dam up
ADMRS	DRAMs
ADMRU	Murad
ADMRY	mardy
ADMSU	Dumas
ADMTU	datum
ADNNO	Donna
ADNNY	Danny
ADNOO	doona
ADNOR	adorn
	radon
ADNOU	Donau
ADNOZ	zonda
ADNPY	pandy
ADNRS	rands
ADNRT	drant
ADNRW	drawn
ADNRY	randy□
ADNSS	sands□
ADNST	stand
ADNSY	sandy□
ADNTU	daunt
ADOPR	Prado
ADOPT	adopt
ADORS	dorsa
	roads
	sarod
ADOSV	Davos
ADOTY	toady
	today
ADPRY	pardy
ADQSU	squad
ADRST	darts
	strad
ADRSW	sward
	-wards
ADRTY	tardy
ADSUW	USDAW
ADUVZ	Vaduz
AEEFN	neafe
AEEGL	aglee
	eagle□
AEEGR	agree
	eager
	eagre
AEEGT	Geeta
AEEHV	heave
AEEIN	aînée
AEEKN	Keane
AEEKP	apeek
	Peake
AEEKR	rakee
AEEKW	a-week
AEELN	anele
	Neale
AEELS	easel
	lease
AEELT	elate
	telae
AEELV	leave
AEELW	aweel
AEELY	aleye
AEEMN	enema
	meane
AEEMS	seame
AEEMV	Maeve
AEENR	ranee
AEENT	eaten
AEENV	venae
AEEPY	payee
AEERS	erase
	saree
AEERT	arête
	eater
AEERZ	razee
AEESS	sease
	see as
AEEST	setae
	tease
AEESV	eaves
AEESZ	seaze
AEETX	exeat
AEEVW	weave
AEFFG	gaffe
AEFGO	of age
AEFHS	Shaef
	sheaf
AEFIL	Alfie
AEFIR	afire
AEFKL	flake
AEFKN	kenaf
AEFKR	faker
	freak
AEFLL	fella
AEFLM	flame
AEFLO	Foale
AEFLR	feral
	flare
AEFLS	ASLEF
	false□
AEFLT	aleft
	fetal
AEFLY	leafy
AEFMR	frame
AEFNR	frena
AEFOV	fovea
AEFRS	farse
AEFRT	after
	trefa
AEFRU	Fauré
AEFRW	wafer
AEFRY	Freya
AEFST	feast
	feats
AEFTT	fetta
AEFTW	fetwa
AEGGI	Aggie
AEGGR	eggar
AEGGU	gauge
AEGHL	Helga
AEGHN	Hagen
AEGHP	phage
AEGHU	Hague
AEGIL	agile
AEGIM	image
AEGIN	Angie
AEGIP	Paige
AEGIR	Aegir
AEGIS	aegis
AEGJR	jäger
AEGLL	Galle
	legal
AEGLM	gleam
AEGLN	angel□
	angle□
	Galen
	glean
	Lange
AEGLR	Elgar
	glare
	lager
	large
	regal
AEGLT	aglet
AEGLV	gavel
	Gavle
AEGLY	agley
	Gayle
AEGLZ	glaze
AEGMM	gemma□
AEGMN	mange
	Megan
AEGMO	omega
AEGMR	marge
AEGMS	games
AEGMY	gamey
AEGNO	genoa□
	Onega
AEGNR	anger
	range
	Regan
AEGNS	Agnes
AEGNT	agent
AEGNV	vegan
AEGNW	Agnew
AEGNY	geyan
AEGOP	go ape
AEGPR	gaper
	grape
	pager
	parge
AEGPT	Paget
AEGRR	rager
AEGRS	gears
	sarge
AEGRT	grate
	great□
	Greta
	targe
	terga
AEGRU	argue
	auger
AEGRV	grave
AEGRW	wager
AEGRY	aygre
AEGRZ	graze
AEGSS	gases
AEGST	Gates
	getas
	stage
AEGSU	usage
AEGSW	swage
	wages
AEGTT	get at
AEGTU	Taegu
AEGUV	vague
AEGUZ	gauze
AEHHT	heath□
AEHKL	Hekla
AEHKS	shake
AEHKW	Hawke
AEHLL	Halle
	Hallé
AEHLM	hemal
AEHLP	aleph
AEHLS	halse
	leash
	shale
	sheal
AEHLT	lathe
AEHLV	halve
	Havel
AEHLW	whale□
AEHLY	Haley
AEHLZ	hazel□
AEHMN	he-man
AEHMR	harem
AEHMS	shame
AEHMT	Meath
AEHNN	henna
AEHNR	Ahern
AEHNS	ashen
	Nashe
	ne has
	Shane
AEHNT	neath
	thane□
AEHNV	haven
AEHNY	hyena
AEHOR	O'Hare
AEHOS	Hosea
AEHPS	heaps
	Pesah
	phase
	shape□
AEHRS	Asher
	share
	shear
AEHRT	earth□

	Harte
	heart
	Thera
AEHRV	haver
AEHSS	ashes
AEHST	ashet
	haste
AEHSV	haves
	shave
AEHSY	Hayes
AEHTT	theta
AEHTW	wheat
AEHVY	heavy
AEIJM	Jamie
AEIKL	alike
	alkie
AEIKR	Kiera
AEIKT	Katie
AEILL	Allie
	Leila
AEILM	email
	e-mail□
AEILN	alien□
	aline
	liane
AEILP	pilea
AEILR	ariel□
AEILS	aisle
AEILT	Eilat
	telia
AEILV	alive
AEILX	axile
AEILZ	Eliza
AEIMM	Mamie
AEIMN	amine
	Maine
AEIMR	Marie
	ramie
	rimae
AEIMZ	maize
AEINN	Annie
	inane
AEINP	Paine
AEINR	Irena
	Raine
AEINS	anise
	Siena
AEINT	eat in
	entia
	tinea
AEINU	Ieuan
AEINV	avine
	naevi
	naive
	naïve
AEINX	xenia
AEINZ	azine
AEIPR	paire
AEIPS	sepia
AEIPT	pieta□
	pietà□
AEIRR	airer
AEIRS	aesir
	Aries
	arise
	raise
AEIRT	irate
AEIRU	aurei
AEIRZ	zaire□
AEIST	Satie
AEITV	Evita
AEITW	Waite
AEITZ	Taizé
AEIVW	waive
AEJKS	jakes
AEJMM	Jemma
AEJMS	James
AEJNN	Jenna
AEJNS	jeans□
AEJNT	Janet
AEJPR	japer
AEJPS	jaspe
AEKLN	ankle
AEKLR	Arkle
	Laker
AEKLS	slake
AEKLY	leaky
AEKMM	kamme
AEKMR	maker□
	Merak
AEKNO	oaken
AEKNP	pekan
AEKNR	Karen
	nerka
	Ranke
AEKNS	skean
	snake
	sneak
AEKNT	taken
AEKNV	knave
AEKNW	waken
AEKNY	Kenya
AEKOP	poake
AEKPS	speak
AEKPY	peaky
AEKQU	quake
AEKRR	raker
AEKRS	reaks
	saker
AEKRT	taker
AEKRW	wreak
AEKST	Keats
	skate
	Skeat
	stake
	steak
AEKSU	ukase
AEKSW	askew
AEKTW	tweak
AELLM	Malle
AELLN	Allen
AELLP	lapel
AELLS	Sella
AELLY	alley
AELMM	lemma
AELMN	leman
AELMP	ample
	maple
AELMR	realm
AELMS	meals
	Salem
AELMT	metal
AELMU	ulema
AELMY	mealy
AELNO	alone
	Leona
AELNP	Nepal
	panel
	penal
	plane
AELNR	Larne
	learn
	renal
AELNT	laten
AELNU	ulnae
AELNV	elvan
	navel
	venal
AELNY	Lenya
AELOV	loave
	volae
AELOW	alowe
AELPP	apple
AELPR	pearl□
	repla
AELPS	lapse
	sepal
AELPT	lepta
	petal
	plate
	pleat
AELPY	ayelp
	Paley
AELQU	equal
AELRS	Arles
	Lares
	laser
AELRT	alert
	alter
	later
	ratel
AELRU	ureal
AELRV	laver□
	ravel□
	velar
AELRW	Waler
AELRX	relax□
AELRY	early
	layer
	relay
AELST	least
	slate
	Staël
	stale
	steal
	tales
	teals
	tesla□
AELSV	salve
	selva
	slave
	valse
AELSW	Lawes
	swale
	sweal
	Wales
AELSY	Sayle
AELTT	latte
AELTV	valet
AELTX	exalt
	latex
AELUV	value
AELVV	valve
AELWY	Elway
AEMMT	Mamet
AEMNN	Neman
AEMNR	Marne
	ramen
AEMNS	Manes
	manse
	means
	Mensa
AEMNT	Manet
	meant
AEMNV	maven
AEMNY	meany
AEMOV	amove
AEMRR	rearm
AEMRS	maser
	smear
AEMRT	mater
	tamer
AEMRY	Marey
	Mayer
	Yerma
AEMSS	massé
AEMST	steam
AEMSU	amuse
AEMSY	samey
	seamy
AEMTY	etyma
	matey
	meaty
AEMUV	mauve
AEMYZ	azyme
AENNP	panne
	penna
AENNR	Renan
AENNS	senna□
AENNT	anent
AENNX	annex
AENOP	Epona
	paeon
	Peano
AENOS	as one
	Soane
AENOT	at one
	atone
	oaten
AENOV	novae
AENOZ	zonae
AENPP	nappe
AENPS	aspen□
	sneap
	spane
	spean
AENPT	paten
AENPZ	Penza
AENRS	nares
	snare
AENRT	aren't
AENRV	Nerva
	raven
AENRW	Warne
AENRY	yearn
AENSS	sensa
AENST	nates
	Nesta
	stean
AENSV	Evans
AENSW	as new
	ne was
AENSZ	senza
AENTT	Netta
AENWX	waxen
AENWY	waney
	Wayne
AEOPR	opera
	pareo
AEOPS	Aesop
AEORT	Erato
	orate
	roate
AEOSS	oases
AEOST	Oates
	SEATO
	stoae
AEOSV	oaves
	Soave
AEOTV	ovate
AEOTZ	toaze
AEPPR	paper
AEPPU	pupae
AEPRS	après
	as per
	parse
	Pears
	spare
	spear
AEPRT	pater□
	petar
	Petra
	prate
	taper
	trape

AEPRU	pareu
AEPRY	apery
	payer
	Peary
	repay
AEPSS	passé
AEPST	paste
	spate
	tapes
AEPSU	pause
AEPTU	eat up
	taupe
AEPTX	expat
	ex-pat
AEPTY	peaty
AEPVY	peavy
AERRV	raver
AERST	aster
	rates
	reast
	stare
	tears
	teras
AERSV	saver
AERSW	swear
	wares
AERSY	resay
	sayer
	years
AERTT	arett
	tetra
	treat
AERTU	urate
AERTV	avert
AERTW	tawer
	water
AERTX	extra
AERTY	teary
AERUZ	azure
AERVV	varve
AERVW	waver
AERVY	Avery
AERWY	weary
AESSS	asses
	sessa
AESST	asset
	seats
	TESSA
	Tessa
AESSY	essay
AESTT	state
	taste
	testa
AESTU	sauté
AESTV	stave
	vesta□
AESTW	sweat
	tawse
	waste
AESTX	taxes
	Texas
AESTY	as yet
	as-yet
	Yates
	yeast
	Yeats
AESUV	suave
AESVW	waves
AESVY	savey
AETZZ	tazze
AFFFL	flaff
AFFGR	graff
AFFIX	affix
AFFLO	offal
AFFLU	luffa
AFFNY	nyaff
AFFQU	quaff
AFFST	staff
AFFTY	Taffy
AFGHU	faugh
AFGLU	fugal
AFGOR	go far
AFGOS	OFGAS
	Ofgas
AFGRT	graft
AFHIR	Farhi
AFHIT	faith□
AFHLS	flash
	halfs
AFHRW	wharf
AFHST	shaft
AFIKL	kalif
AFIKR	fakir
AFILL	flail
AFILN	final
AFILO	folia
AFILR	filar
	flair
	frail
	Lifar
AFIMO	ma foi
AFINO	Fiona
AFINR	infra
AFINS	fains
	Safin
AFINT	faint
AFIOS	Sofia
AFIRR	friar
AFIRS	Farsi
AFIRT	afrit
	frati
AFIRY	fairy
AFKLN	flank
AFKLS	flask
AFKLY	flaky
AFKNR	frank□
AFKOT	kofta
AFKRT	kraft
AFLLO	all of
AFLLS	falls
AFLOO	aloof
	loofa
AFLOR	flora□
AFLOS	sol-fa
AFLOT	aloft
	float
AFLOU	afoul
AFLTU	fault
AFLTY	fatly
	fly at
AFLUW	awful
AFMOX	OXFAM
AFMOY	foamy
AFMSU	samfu
AFNNO	Fanon
AFNNY	Fanny
AFNSU	snafu
AFOOT	afoot
AFORS	as for
	so far
AFORY	foray
AFOSS	fossa
AFOST	fatso
AFOTW	OFWAT
	Ofwat
AFQRU	Faruq
AFRSS	frass
AFRSW	swarf
AFSTU	Faust
AFTTY	fatty
AGGIN	aging
AGGJY	jaggy
AGGLU	gulag
AGGOR	aggro
AGGRY	raggy
AGGSY	saggy
AGHIL	laigh
AGHLU	laugh
AGHMO	ogham
	Omagh
AGHNO	Hogan
AGHNP	phang
AGHNS	gnash
AGHNW	whang
AGHNY	ghayn
AGHPR	graph
AGHST	Ghats
AGHTU	aught
AGHUW	Waugh
AGIKN	kiang
AGILL	glial
AGILN	align
	Laing
AGILR	argil
	glair
	grail□
AGILS	sigla
AGILY	gaily
AGIMN	gamin
AGIMO	amigo
	imago
AGIMS	sigma
AGINO	gonia
	ngaio□
AGINP	aping
AGINR	garni
	grain
AGINS	gains
AGINT	giant□
AGINV	Gavin
AGINW	a-wing
	Wigan
AGIOR	orgia
AGIOS	agios
AGIRT	tragi
AGIRU	Gauri
AGIRV	virga
AGIST	agist
AGITU	aguti
AGJOS	gajos
AGKLN	klang
AGKOP	gopak
AGKOS	kagos
AGKWY	gawky
AGLLO	ALGOL
	Algol
AGLLY	gally
AGLMU	glaum
AGLNO	along
	NALGO
AGLNR	gnarl
AGLNS	slang
AGLOP	galop
	Gopal
AGLOR	argol
	largo
AGLOS	goals
	Lagos
AGLOT	gloat
AGLOV	Volga
AGLOW	aglow
AGLPY	pygal
AGLRU	glaur
AGLRY	gyral
AGLSS	glass□
AGMMY	gammy
AGMNO	among
	mango
AGMNY	mangy
AGMOR	Margo
	Morag
AGMOT	magot
AGMOW	Gamow
AGMRU	garum
AGMSU	magus
AGMTU	gamut
AGNNO	gonna
AGNOR	argon
	groan
	organ
AGNOT	tango□
	Tonga
AGNOU	guano
AGNOW	wagon
	wonga
AGNOY	agony
AGNPR	prang
AGNPS	pangs
	spang
AGNRR	gnarr
AGNRT	grant□
AGNRU	Argun
AGNRY	angry
	rangy
AGNSS	snags
AGNST	angst
AGNSU	Angus
AGNTU	gaunt
AGNTW	twang
AGNTY	tangy
AGOPR	GRAPO
	Grapo
AGOPS	gapós
AGORS	Argos
AGORT	argot
	groat
	Torga
AGOST	SOGAT
AGOTT	gotta
AGPPY	gappy
AGPRS	grasp
	sprag
AGRRY	Garry
AGRSS	grass□
AGRSU	Argus
	sugar□
AGRUU	augur
AGRVY	gravy
AGSSU	gauss□
AGSSY	gassy
AGSTU	Tagus
AGSTY	stagy
AGTTU	gutta
AGUYZ	gauzy
AHHIS	Shiah
AHHIT	haith
	hi-hat
AHHOO	hoo-ha
AHHOX	Hoxha
AHHPY	hypha
AHHRS	harsh
AHIIT	Haiti
AHIJJ	hajji
AHIKK	khaki
AHIKM	hakim
AHIKU	haiku
AHILP	phial
AHILT	lathi
AHIMN	Niamh
AHIMS	Amish
AHIMT	ham it
AHINO	Hanoi
AHINR	Rhian
AHINT	ahint
AHIPS	aphis

apish
spahi
AHIRT Thira
AHIRU Huari
AHIRY hairy
AHIST saith
AHISV shiva□
AHITT hit at
AHJNO Jonah
AHKLO Kahlo
AHKNS Hanks
shank
AHKNT thank
AHKNY hanky
AHKOO hooka
AHKOS shako
AHKRS shark□
AHKSW Hawks
AHKSY shaky
AHKTY Kathy
AHLLO hallo
holla
AHLLS shall
AHLLU ahull
AHLMU haulm
AHLNO halon
AHLNU uhlan
AHLOS halos
shoal
AHLOT loath
AHLPR Ralph
AHLPS plash
AHLPT Plath
AHLPY haply
phyla
AHLSS slash
AHLST laths
AHLSU Shula
AHLSW shawl
AHLSY shaly
AHMMY hammy
AHMNU human
Nahum
AHMNY mynah
AHMPS pashm
AHMPU ham up
AHMRS marsh□
AHMSS smash
AHMST maths
AHMSU musha
AHMSW shawm
AHMTY my hat!
AHNNO Hanno
Honan
AHNOR Norah
Rhona
Rohan
AHNOS Shona
AHNSS snash
AHNST Hants
hasn't
shan't
AHNSU Shaun
AHNSW Shawn
AHNTU haunt
unhat
AHNUW Wuhan
AHOOT a hoot
AHOOW wahoo
AHOOY yahoo
AHOPR Oprah
AHORS haros
AHORT Thora
Torah
AHORY hoary
AHORZ Zohar
AHOST Athos
hoast
hosta
oaths
AHOSV Hovas
AHOSW as how
AHOSX Xhosa
AHPPY happy
AHPRS sharp□
AHPRT Tharp
AHPRU prahu
AHPRY harpy
AHPST paths
AHPSW pshaw
AHPUW whaup
AHQSU quash
AHRRU hurra
AHRRY harry□
AHRST trash
AHRSU Århus
surah
AHRSY Syrah
AHRTW thraw
wrath
AHRTY rhyta
AHRXY hyrax
AHSST stash
AHSSW swash
AHSTW swath
AHSTY hasty
AHSWY washy
AHTTY Hatty
AHUZZ huzza
AIIKW Iwaki
AIILO aioli
aïoli
AIILV Livia
AIIMM Miami
AIIMR Imari
AIIQR Iraqi
AIJKN kanji
AIJKT Kitaj
AIJLM Jamil
AIJLU Julia
AIJNN Jinan
ninja
AIJNS Janis
AIJOR rioja□
AIJRV Rajiv
AIJVY Vijay
AIKKM kamik
AIKKT tikka
AIKLN lakin
AIKLS Laski
skail
AIKLT Tikal
AIKMO maiko
AIKMR mikra
AIKMS Kasim
AIKMU umiak
AIKNR Karin
AIKNU nikau
AIKOP okapi
AIKRR karri
AIKRT krait
traik
AIKRU kauri
AIKRV Kavir
AIKST Sakti
AILLN all in
all-in
in all
Niall
AILLV villa□
AILMN Malin
Milan
AILMO Imola
AILMS Islam
salmi
AILMT Mitla
Tamil
AILMU miaul
AILMW Wilma
AILNO Ilona
AILNP Palin
plain
AILNS slain
snail
AILNT in alt
Latin
AILNV anvil
AILNY inlay
lay in
AILOP paoli
Pilao
AILOS Laois
AILOU auloi
AILOV viola□
voila
voilà
AILOZ Lao Zi
AILPP palpi
pipal
AILPR April
prial
AILPS lapis
AILPT plait
AILPU Pauli
pilau
AILPW pilaw
AILQU quail
AILRS liras
rails
AILRT trail
trial
AILRU urial
AILRV Avril
rival
viral
AILRY riyal
AILSS Sails
Silas
sisal
AILST litas
AILSU Laius
AILSY Islay
AILTT atilt
AILTV vital
AILTY Italy
laity
AILZZ lazzi
AIMMX maxim□
AIMNN Inman
AIMNO amino
amnio
AIMNR inarm
minar
ramin
AIMNS minas
AIMNV mavin
AIMNZ Mainz
nizam
AIMOR Maori
Moira
Moria
AIMOW miaow
AIMOX axiom
AIMOY Omiya
AIMPR Priam
Prima
AIMRS MIRAS
AIMSS amiss□
AIMST Samit
AIMSV mavis□
AIMSW swami
Wasim
AIMTY amity
AINNO anion
AINNP pinna
AINNS Nisan
AINOP piano□
AINOR noria
AINOS Sonia
AINOT Taino
AINOZ Anzio
AINPS a snip
pains
Spain
AINPT inapt
paint
pinta□
AINPY pay in
AINPZ Pinza
AINRT train
Trina
AINRV Invar®
ravin
AINRY rainy
AINRZ zirna
AINST saint
satin
stain
AINSV savin
Sivan
AINSW swain
AINTT taint
titan□
AINTU Uniat
UNITA
AINTW Twain
AINUX auxin
AINWY way in
AINYZ zayin
AIOPT patio
AIORT ariot
ratio
AIOSS oasis□
ossia
AIOST Ostia
stoai
AIPPP Pippa
AIPPU appui
AIPRS pairs
Paris
Parsi
Sapir
AIPRT atrip
tapir
AIPSS apsis
AIPTT Patti
pitta
AIPZZ pizza
AIQRT Tariq
AIQSU quasi
quasi-
AIRRS arris
AIRST astir
sitar
Sitra
stair
stria
tarsi
AIRSU Arius
AIRSY Syria
AIRTT trait
AIRVX varix
AIRWZ wazir
AISSY says I
AISTT sit at

AISTU	Suita
AISTV	vista
	vitas
AISTW	waist
	Waits
AISTX	taxis
AISWZ	Swazi
AISXX	x-axis
AISXY	y-axis
AITTV	vitta
AITVV	vivat
AJMMY	jammy
AJMNU	Jumna
AJMOR	major□
AJMRU	jumar
AJNOS	Jason
AJNSU	Janus
AJNTU	jaunt
	junta
AJOST	jatos
AJOSU	sajou
AJRTU	jurat
AJYZZ	jazzy
AKKLU	kulak
AKKNS	skank
AKKOP	kapok
AKKPU	pukka
AKLNP	plank
AKLNY	lanky
AKLOP	polka
AKLOS	skoal
AKLRS	larks
AKLST	stalk
	talks
AKLSW	lawks
	SWALK
AKLUW	waulk
AKMNY	manky
AKMOR	korma
AKMOS	makos
AKMOU	oakum
AKMRS	marks□
AKMRU	Kumar
AKMSU	Aksum
AKNOR	Koran
	krona
AKNOY	Konya
AKNPR	prank
AKNPS	spank
AKNPU	punka
AKNRS	krans
AKNRU	kunar
AKNRY	narky
AKNRZ	kranz
AKNSW	swank
AKNSY	snaky
AKOOP	pooka
AKOOR	Karoo
AKOOZ	kazoo
AKOSY	kayos
	okays
AKPRS	spark□
AKPRY	parky
AKPTU	kaput
AKPWY	pawky
AKQRU	quark
AKQUY	quaky
AKRST	karst
	stark
AKRSY	karsy
	sarky
AKRYZ	karzy
AKSSV	kvass
AKTUY	Yakut
ALLMO	molal
ALLMS	small
ALLOT	all to
	allot
	all-to
	atoll
ALLOW	allow
ALLOY	alloy
	loyal
ALLPS	spall
ALLPY	pally
ALLRY	rally
ALLST	stall
ALLSU	Sulla
ALLSY	sally□
ALLTY	tally
ALLWY	wally□
ALLXY	laxly
ALMMO	Malmo
	Malmö
ALMNO	Loman
ALMNY	manly
ALMOR	molar
	moral
ALMOS	molas
ALMOT	matlo
ALMOY	loamy
ALMPS	plasm
	psalm
ALMPY	amply
	palmy
ALMQU	qualm
ALMRU	mural
ALMRY	marly
ALMST	smalt
ALMTY	malty
ALMUX	Uxmal
ALNNU	annul
ALNOR	loran□
	Lorna
ALNOS	salon
ALNOT	talon
	tonal
ALNOY	lay on
ALNOZ	zonal
ALNPS	plans
ALNPT	plant
ALNRS	snarl
ALNRU	lunar
	ulnar
ALNST	slant
ALNSU	Ulsan
ALNUY	unlay
ALNWY	wanly
ALOPR	polar
ALOPT	Plato
ALORR	roral
ALORS	solar
ALORT	tolar
ALORV	volar
ALORY	royal
ALOSS	lasso
ALOST	altos
	salto
ALOSV	salvo
ALOTT	total
ALOTV	lovat
	Volta
ALOWY	Yalow
ALPPU	lap up
	pupal
ALPPY	apply
ALPST	spalt
	splat
ALPSY	palsy
	splay
ALPTY	aptly
	patly
ALPUY	lay up
	uplay
ALRRU	rural
ALRRY	Larry
ALRSU	sural
	Urals
ALRTU	ultra
	ultra-
ALRTW	trawl
ALRWY	rawly
ALSST	salts
ALSTU	talus
	Tulsa
ALSTY	salty
	slaty
ALSUU	usual
ALSWY	swayl
ALTUV	vault
ALTWZ	waltz
ALUUV	uvula
ALUVV	vulva
AMMMO	momma
AMMNO	ammon
AMMRS	smarm
AMMSY	Sammy
AMMTY	tammy□
AMNNU	unman
AMNNY	Manny
AMNOP	Nampo
AMNOR	manor
	Morna
	Norma
	roman□
AMNOS	manos
	mason□
AMNOW	woman□
AMNOY	anomy
	Mayon
AMNOZ	Monza
AMNRU	Namur
	unarm
	urman
AMNRY	Myrna
AMNSU	manus
AMNUZ	Manzú
AMOPR	pro-am
AMORS	Ramos
	romas
AMORU	amour
AMORY	mayor
	moray□
AMOSS	Samos
	somas
AMOST	stoma
AMOTY	atomy
AMOTZ	matzo
AMOWY	Mayow
AMPRT	tramp
AMPSS	spasm
AMPST	stamp
AMPSU	pumas
AMPSW	swamp
AMRRY	marry
AMRST	smart□
AMRSU	ramus
AMRSW	swarm
AMRTU	Murat
AMRTY	Marty
AMTTU	Tatum
ANNNY	nanny
ANNOY	annoy
ANNSU	Sunna
ANOOP	napoo
	Poona
ANOPR	apron
ANOPT	on tap
	panto
ANOQR	Qoran
ANORR	Arnor
ANORS	arson
	sonar
ANORT	rat on
ANORW	rowan□
ANORY	rayon
ANOSV	novas
ANOSW	as now
ANOSX	Naxos
	Saxon
ANOSY	say no
	Sonya
ANOTT	tanto
ANOTW	Wotan
ANOTX	taxon
ANOTY	atony
	ayont
ANOWY	no way
	noway
ANPPY	nappy
ANPRW	prawn
ANPST	pants
ANPSU	Pusan
ANPSW	spawn
ANPSY	pansy□
ANPTU	unapt
ANPUY	unpay
ANQRU	Quran
	Qur'an
ANQTU	quant□
ANRSU	Sun Ra
ANRTT	trant
ANRUU	Nauru
ANRUW	UNRWA
ANRUZ	zurna
ANSSU	Susan
ANSTU	tunas
ANSTY	nasty
	tansy
ANSUY	unsay
ANTTU	taunt
ANTTY	natty
ANTUV	vaunt
ANTUX	untax
ANTUY	aunty
ANTWY	tawny
ANVVY	navvy
AOOPP	apoop
AOORZ	razoo
AOPPR	appro
AOPRS	Paros
	RoSPA
	sapor
	sopra
AOPRT	aport
	Op Art
AOPSS	psoas
AOPST	Patos
AOPSW	SWAPO
	Swapo
AOPSY	soapy
AOPTT	apt to
AOPTZ	topaz
AOQTU	quota
AORRW	arrow□
AORRZ	razor
AORSS	saros
AORST	Astor
	roast
	Sarto
	taros
AORSV	arvos
AORTT	tarot
	troat
AORVY	ovary

AOSST stoas
Tasso
AOSSU Sousa
AOSSY say-so
AOSTT stoat
toast
AOSTU autos
AOSVY savoy
APPPY pappy
APPSU pupas
APPSY sappy
APPUY appuy
pay up
APPUZ zap up
APPYY yappy
APPYZ zappy
APRRY parry□
APRST parts
sprat
strap
APRSU supra
APRSY raspy
spray
APRTY party
APSTU sputa
stupa
APSTY pasty
patsy□
APSWY waspy
APSZZ spazz
APTTY patty□
APTVY pay TV
APUWX wax up
AQRTU quart
AQSTU squat
AQSUW squaw
ARRST Starr
ARRSU surra
ARRTY tarry
ARSST stars
ARSTT START
start
ARSTU Surat
sutra
ARSTW straw□
ARSTY satyr
stray
ARSUV varus
ARSUY saury
Surya
ARTTY ratty□
tarty
ARTWY warty
ASSSY sassy
ASSTY stays
ASTTY tasty
ASVVY savvy
ATTTY tatty

B

BBBOY bobby□
BBDEY debby□
BBEEE Beebe
BBEIL bible□
BBEIR bribe
BBEMO bombe
BBEOP bebop
BBERU Buber
BBGIO gobbi
BBGOO Gobbo
BBHMO H-bomb
BBHOS Hobbs
BBHOY hobby
BBHUY hubby
BBILY Libby
BBIMO bimbo
BBITY Tibby
BBLOY lobby
BBLRU blurb
BBLSU slubb
BBMOS bombs
BBOOS boobs
BBOOY booby
yobbo
BBOPU bob up
BBSTU Stubb
BBSUY busby□
BBTUY tubby
BCCIU cubic
BCEEH beech
BCEER rebec
BCEEX xebec
BCEHL belch□
BCEHN bench□
BCEHO Boche
BCEKY Becky
BCEMO combe
BCENO bonce
BCENU bunce
BCERU Bruce
BCHIR birch
BCHIT bitch
BCHLO Bloch
BCHNR NHBRC
BCHNU bunch
BCHOR broch
BCHOS Bosch
BCHOT botch
BCHTU butch□
BCIKR brick
BCIKU Buick®
BCILM climb
BCIOR boric
BCITU cubit
BCKLO block
BCKSU Buck's
BCLOO COBOL
BCLSU clubs
BCMMO BComm
BCMOO combo
coomb
BCMRU crumb
BCNOU bunco
BCOSY Cosby
BCRSU curbs
scrub
BDDIY biddy□
BDDUY buddy
BDEEL bedel
bleed
BDEEM embed
BDEEN Deneb
BDEER breed
BDEEW bedew
BDEEY bedye
Debye
BDEGO bodge
BDEGU budge□
debug
BDEIL bield
BDEIM bedim
imbed
BDEIP biped
BDEIR bride
rebid
BDEIT bidet
debit
BDELN blend
BDELO lobed
BDEMO demob
BDENO boned
BDENU U-bend
unbed
BDENY bendy
BDEOR bored
BDEOW bowed
BDERY derby□
BDEST debts
BDESU debus
BDETU debut
début
tubed
BDFII bifid
BDHIO dhobi
BDIIN bid in
BDILN blind□
BDILU build
BDINO Bondi
BDINU in bud
BDIPU bid up
BDIRS birds
BDLNO blond
BDLOO blood□
BDMOU dumbo□
BDNOS bonds
BDNOU bound
BDOOR brood
BDOOY boody
BDOSU budos
BDOTU doubt
BDRSY Byrds
BEEEL belee
BEEFS beefs
BEEFY beefy
BEEGI beige
BEEGL glebe
BEEGM begem
BEEGR gerbe
grebe
BEEGT beget
BEEHT Bethe
BEEIL belie
BEELL belle□
BEELM Belém
BEELP bleep
BEELR rebel
BEELT betel
let be
BEELV bevel
BEELZ bezel
BEEMR ember
BEENR Berne
BEENT benet
Benét
BEEOS obese
BEERT beret
BEERV breve
BEERW weber□
BEERY beery
BEEST beset
BEETW bewet
BEFFO be off
BEFFU buffe
BEFGO befog
BEFIR brief
fibre
BEFIT befit
BEGIL bilge
BEGIN begin□
being
binge
BEGIO bogie
BEGIR giber
BEGIW bewig
BEGLO globe
BEGLU bugle
bulge□
BEGMO embog
BEGMU begum
BEGNU begun
BEGOU bouge
BEGOY bogey
BEGTY get by
BEHLU Hubel
BEHRS herbs
BEHRT berth
BEIKM Mbeki
BEIKR biker
BEILL libel
BEILO obeli
BEIMO biome
BEIMU imbue
BEINN Benin
BEINO Niobe
BEINR brine
BEINS Ibsen
BEINT Binet
BEINV Bevin
BEINX Benxi
BEINY inbye
BEINZ zineb
BEIOS Boise
BEIOW Bowie
BEIRR brier
BEIRT biter
Tiber
tribe
BEISV vibes
BEITT bitte
BEITZ Bizet
BEIVX vibex
BEJOT objet
BEKLO bloke
BEKOR broke
BEKRS Krebs
BEKRU Buerk
Burke
BEKTY kbyte
BEKUZ Uzbek
BELLS bells
BELLY belly
BELMU umbel
BELNO Nobel
noble
BELOO Boole
BELOS lesbo
BELOW below
bowel
elbow
BELOY Boyle
BELPS plebs
BELRU brûlé
BELRY beryl□
BELSS bless
BELSU blues□
BELUY bluey
BEMOR ombre
ombré
BEMOS besom
BEMOX embox
BEMRU umber
BEMSU embus
sebum
BEMSW BMEWS
BENNY benny□
BENOO Boone
BENOR boner
borne
BENOS bones□
BENOT bet on
BENOU Bueno
BENOW bowne
BENOY Boyne
ebony
BENRT Brent

BENWY Newby
BEOOT Obote
BEOOZ booze
BEOPR probe
BEORR borer
BEORS brose
robes
sober
BEORW bower
BEORX boxer□
BEORY o'erby
Robey
BEOST besot
BEOSU bouse
BEOTW be two
BEPUY upbye
BERRY berry□
BERST Brest
BERSU rebus
suber
BERTT Brett
BERTU brute
rebut
tuber
BERUX exurb
BERUY buyer
BESSU buses
BESSY Bessy
BESTY Betsy
set by
BESUY Beuys
BETTU butte
BETTY Betty
BEVVY bevvy
BFFIU buffi
BFFLU bluff
BFFOU buffo
BFIOR fibro
BFLYY fly-by
BFORY forby
BGGIS Biggs
BGGIY biggy
BGGOS Boggs
BGGOY boggy
BGGUY buggy
BGHIL Bligh
BGHIT bight
BGHOU bough
BGHRU burgh□
BGIMR Mr Big
BGINO bingo
boing
BGINR bring
BGIOT bigot
BGLUY bulgy
BGMOU gumbo
BGNOO bongo
BGOOS gobos
BGOSU bogus
BGRUY rugby□
BHILP BPhil

BHIRT birth
BHLSU blush
BHLTY Blyth
BHMOR rhomb
BHMPU bumph
BHMRU rhumb
BHMTU thumb
BHOOS hobos
BHOOT booth□
BHOOY oh boy!
BHORT broth
throb
BHOTY bothy
BHRSU brush
shrub
BHSUY bushy
BIILM Limbi
BIILN blini
BIIMN nimbi
BIIOR oribi
BIJOU bijou
BIKLN blink
BIKMO kimbo
BIKNR brink□
BIKRS brisk
BILLR brill
BILLS bills
BILLY billy□
BILMO limbo□
BILMP blimp□
BILMY blimy
BILOO oboli
BILOR broil
BILSS bliss□
BILST stilb
BILSY sibyl□
Sybil
BILTT BLitt
BILTU built
BILTZ blitz
BIMNY NIMBY
Nimby
BIMOZ zombi
BINNU Bunin
BINOR inorb
robin□
BINOS bison
BINOT Tobin
BINOW bow in
BINOX box in
BINRU burin
rub in
BINRY briny
BINUY buy in
BIORS Biros
Boris
BIORT orbit
BIORX Ibrox
BIOST bitos
BIOTT Tobit

BIPSU pubis
BIQSU squib
BIRTU bruit
BISTU buist
BISTY sit by
BITTY bitty
BIVVY bivvy
BJMOU jumbo
BKLNU blunk
BKLUY bulky
BKMOU kombu
BKNOS knobs
BKNOU bunko
BKOOR brook□
BKOOS bokos
books
BKOSY bosky
BLLSU bulls
BLLUY bully
BLMOO bloom□
BLMPU plumb
BLNOW blown
BLNOY nobly
BLNTU blunt□
BLOOP bloop
BLOOS bolos
BLOST bolts
BLOSU bolus
BLOSW blows
bowls
BLOTU boult□
BLOUW Bülow
BLOWY blowy
BLRTU blurt
BLRUY burly
BMOOR broom
BMOOS bosom
BMOST tombs
BMOSU ombus
ombús
umbos
BMOUX buxom
BMOWY womby
BMPUY bumpy
BNNOY bonny□
BNNUY bunny
BNOOR boron
BNOOS boson
BNORU bourn
Bruno
BNORW brown□
BNORY Byron
Robyn
BNOSU bonus
bosun
BNOUX unbox
BNOWY by now
BNRSU Burns
BNRTU brunt
burnt
BNTUY Bunty

BOORT robot
BOOST boost
boots
BOOSZ bozos
zobos
BOOTW bow to
BOOTY booty
BOOYZ boozy
BORRU burro
BORTU turbo
BOSSY bossy
BOTUY outby
BPRUU rub up
BPSST tbsps
BPTUY put by
BPUUY buy up
BRSTU burst
BSSUU bussu
BSTUY busty
BTTUU butut
BTTUY butty

C

CCCIO cocci
CCEER recce
CCEHK check
CCEHZ Czech
CCEIL Cecil
CCEIR cerci
Circe
CCEKL cleck
CCELY cycle
CCEOP copec
CCEOR Croce
CCERY Crécy
reccy
CCHIK chick
CCHIN cinch
CCHKO chock
CCHKU chuck□
CCHNO conch
CCHOU couch□
CCIIR Ricci
CCIIV civic
CCIKL click
CCIKR crick□
CCILO colic
CCIMO comic
CCINO conic
CCINY cynic
CCIPU Pucci
CCIPY piccy
CCISU succi
CCKLO clock□
CCKLU cluck
CCKOR crock
CCKOY cocky
CCMOY McCoy
CCNPS NSPCC
CCOOS cocos
CCORU occur

CCOUZ Cuzco
CDEEI de-ice
CDEER creed
CDEEU deuce
educe
CDEHI chide
CDEHN Dench
CDEIL El Cid
Le Cid
CDEIM medic
CDEIR cider
CDEIS cedis
CDEIT cited
edict
CDEIV Vedic
CDEIY dicey
CDEKO decko
CDELO dolce
CDELY Clyde
CDEMO Médoc
CDENU dunce
CDEOR cored
credo
décor
CDEOW cowed
CDEOX codex
CDEOY decoy
CDERU crude
cured
CDERY cyder
decry
CDHIL child
CDHIT dicht
ditch
CDHNU dunch
CDHOR chord
CDHTU Dutch
CDHUY duchy
CDIIN dinic
Indic
CDIKY dicky□
CDILU lucid
ludic
CDIMU mucid
CDINY Cindy
CDIOR Doric
CDIOS disco
CDIPU cupid□
CDISU scudi
CDLOS scold
CDLOU cloud
CDLWY Clwyd
CDMOR CD-ROM
CDNOO codon
CDNOT contd
CDORS cords
CDORU Duroc
CDORW crowd
CDRUY crudy
CEEEM emcee
CEEFN fence

CEEGR	cerge
CEEHK	cheek
	keech
CEEHL	leech
CEEHN	hence
CEEHP	cheep
CEEHR	cheer
CEEIN	niece
CEEIP	piece
CEEJT	eject
CEEKL	cleek
CEEKP	pecke
CEEKR	creek□
CEELR	creel
CEELT	elect
CEELX	excel
CEEMR	crème
CEENP	pence
CEENR	cerne
CEENS	cense
	scene
CEEOO	cooee
CEEPR	creep
	crepe
	crèpe
	crêpe
CEERS	Ceres
	scree
CEERT	Crete
	erect
	terce
CEERW	Crewe
CEESS	cesse
CEFGL	G-clef
CEFHI	chief
	fiche
CEFHT	fetch
CEFKL	fleck
CEFLT	cleft
CEFOR	force
CEGIN	genic
CEGIR	grice
CEGKO	gecko
CEGNO	congé
CEGOR	Greco
CEHHT	hecht
CEHIL	Chile
CEHIM	chime
	miche
CEHIN	chine
	niche
CEHIR	Reich
CEHIT	ethic
	hi-tec
CEHIV	chive
CEHKO	choke
CEHKT	ketch
CEHLO	Chloe
CEHLT	letch
CEHLW	Welch
CEHLY	chyle
CEHMO	Moche
CEHMY	chyme
CEHNO	Cohen
	Enoch
CEHNT	tench
CEHNW	wench
CEHOP	epoch
CEHOR	chore
	ochre
CEHOS	chose
	COHSE
CEHPR	perch
CEHRT	chert
	retch
CEHRU	ruche
CEHSS	chess□
CEHST	chest
CEHTU	chute
CEHTV	vetch
CEHVY	chevy
CEHWY	chewy
CEIIL	ceili
CEIJU	juice
CEILM	clime
CEILN	cline
CEILO	E. coli
	oleic
CEILP	clipe
CEILR	relic
CEILS	slice
CEILV	Clive
CEIMN	mince
CEIMR	crime
CEINO	on ice
CEINR	crine
	nicer
CEINS	since
CEINW	wince
CEIOV	voice
CEIPR	price□
CEIPS	spice
CEIPU	ice up
CEIRR	crier
CEIRS	cries
CEIRT	récit
	recti
	trice
CEIRU	curie□
	ureic
CEIRX	xeric
CEIRY	ricey
CEIST	CITES
CEITV	civet
	evict
CEITW	twice
CEJOY	Joyce
CEKKS	kecks
CEKLO	Locke
CEKLR	clerk
CEKNS	sneck
CEKOO	Cooke
CEKOR	ocker
CEKPS	speck
CEKRW	wreck
CELLO	cello
CELLT	t-cell
CELMO	celom
CELNO	Cleon
	clone
CELNU	uncle
CELOS	close□
	socle
CELOY	cloye
	coley
CELPU	cupel
CELPY	clype
CELRU	cruel
	lucre
	ulcer
CELSU	clues
	luces
CEMOR	comer
	crome
CEMOT	comet□
	Comte
CEMRY	mercy□
CENNO	nonce
CENOP	ponce
CENOR	Creon
	crone
	oncer
CENOS	scone
CENOU	on cue
	ounce
CENOV	coven
CENOY	coney
CENOZ	cozen
CENST	scent
CEOPR	coper
CEOPS	copse
	Pecos
	scope
CEOPU	coupe
	coupé
CEORR	corer
CEORS	score
CEORT	recto
CEORV	cover
CEORW	cower
CEORY	Royce
CEOST	escot
CEOSU	souce
CEOSV	voces
CEOSW	Cowes
CEOTT	octet
CEOTV	covet
CEOVY	covey
CEPRS	EPSRC
CEPRT	crept
	recpt
CEPRY	crêpy
	Percy
CEPSS	specs
CERRU	recur
CERSS	cress
CERST	crest
CERSU	curse
	sucre□
CERSW	screw
CERTU	cruet
	eruct
	truce
CERUV	curve
CESSU	scuse
CESTU	Cetus
	scute
CFFHU	chuff
CFFIL	cliff
CFFOS	scoff
CFFOU	cuffo
CFFSU	cuffs
	scuff
CFHIL	filch
CFHIN	finch
CFHIT	fitch
CFHOO	choof
CFHSU	Fuchs
CFIIS	sci-fi
CFIKL	flick
CFIKU	Kufic
CFILO	folic
CFILT	Clift
CFIOS	ficos
CFITU	ICFTU
CFKLO	flock
CFKOR	frock
CFMOY	comfy
CFORT	croft
CFORU	Corfu
CFOSU	focus
CFRSU	scurf
CFSUU	fucus
CGGIY	ciggy
CGHLU	gulch
CGHOO	Gooch
CGHOU	cough
CGIIN	icing
CGILN	cling
CGILO	logic
CGIMO	ogmic
CGIOR	CORGI
	corgi
CGIOY	yogic
CGKLU	Gluck
CGNOO	Congo
CHHIL	hilch
CHHIT	hitch
CHHIW	which
	Which?
CHHNU	hunch
CHHOO	hooch
CHHOT	hotch
CHHTU	hutch
CHIKN	chink□
CHIKO	hoick
	Kochi
CHIKR	chirk
CHIKS	Hicks
CHIKT	thick
CHILL	chill
CHILM	milch
CHILR	chirl
CHILZ	zilch
CHIMO	chimo
CHIMR	chirm
CHIMT	mitch
CHIMU	humic
CHINO	chino
CHINP	pinch
CHINW	winch
CHIOR	choir
CHIOS	Chios
	Sochi
CHIPR	chirp
CHIPT	pitch
CHIRR	chirr
CHIRS	Chris
CHIRT	chirt
CHIST	stich
CHITT	titch
CHITW	witch
CHITY	itchy
CHIVY	chivy
CHIZZ	chizz
CHKNU	chunk
CHKOO	choko
CHKOS	shock
CHKOY	choky
CHKSU	hucks
	shuck
CHLMU	mulch
CHLNU	lunch
CHLNY	lynch□
CHLOT	cloth
CHLRU	churl
	lurch
CHMNU	munch□
CHMOO	mooch
CHMOP	chomp
CHMOU	mouch
CHMPU	chump
CHNOT	notch
CHNPU	punch□
CHNRU	churn
	UNHCR
CHNSY	synch
CHOOP	pooch
CHOOS	cohos
CHOPR	porch
CHOPS	chops
CHOPU	pouch
CHORT	torch
CHORY	ochry
CHOSU	hocus

CHOTU touch
CHOUV vouch
CHOUX choux
CHPSY psych
CHRRU churr
CHRSU crush
CHSUY cushy
CIILT licit
CIILV civil
CIILY icily
CIIMM mimic
CIINO ionic□
CIIOV voici
CIIPP cippi
CIIRR cirri
CIJUY juicy
CIKKS kicks
CIKLN clink
CIKLS slick
CIKMY Micky
CIKNS snick
CIKNY Nicky
CIKOY yoick
CIKPR prick
CIKPS spick
CIKPY picky
CIKQU quick
CIKRT trick
CIKRW wrick
CIKRY Ricky
CIKST stick
CILNO Colin
CILNT clint□
CILOU oculi
CILOW wilco
CILRY Cyril
lyric
CILSU sulci
CIMNO Cimon
CIMNU cumin
CIMOR micro
CIMOS micos
CIMPR crimp
CIMRS scrim
CIMSU music
CINOR Corin
corni
CINOS coins
scion
sonic
CINOT tonic
CINOZ zinco
CINPU Punic
CINRU incur
runic
CINSU incus
CINTT tinct
CINTU cut in
tunic
CIOPT optic□
picot
topic
CIORR roric
CIORT toric□
CIORU curio
CIOST stoic
Ticos
CIOTX toxic
CIPRS crisp
scrip
CIPRY pricy
CIPSY spicy
CIRSU cursi
CISSY cissy□
CISTU cutis
ictus
CITTU cut it
CIVVY civvy
CKKNO knock
CKLNO clonk
CKLNU clunk
CKLOS locks
CKLPU pluck
CKLUY lucky□
CKMNO Monck
CKMOS smock
CKMUY mucky
CKOOR crook
CKORS rocks
CKORU Cukor
CKORY corky
rocky□
CKOSS socks
CKOST stock
CKRTU truck
CKSSU sucks!
CKSTU stuck
CKUYY yucky
CLLOY colly
CLLSU scull
CLMOP clomp
CLMOU Colum
locum
CLMPU clump
CLMTU mulct
CLNOO colon
Colón
CLNOW clown
CLOOS locos
CLOOT cloot
CLORU clour
CLOSU locus
CLOSW scowl
CLOTU clout
CLOYY coyly
CLRUY curly
CMOOS Cosmo
CMORS corms
CMOSU Comus
CMPRU crump
CMRSU scrum
CMSUU mucus
CNNOY Cynon
CNOOR Conor
croon
CNOPY poncy
CNORS scorn
CNORW crown
CNORY corny
crony
cry on
CNOSU uncos
CNOTU count
CNOWY Conwy
CNPSU NUCPS
CNTUU uncut
COOPS scoop□
COOPT coopt
co-opt
COORT Corot
COOST scoot
tocos
COPRS corps
COPRU croup
COPSU scoup
COPSW scowp
COPUY coypu
CORRU cruor
CORSS cross
CORSU scour
CORTU court□
CORWY cowry
COSST costs
Scots
COSTT Scott
COSTU scout
souct
CPRTY crypt
CPRUY cry up
CPTUU cut up
CRRUY curry□
CRSTU crust
CRSUY Cyrus
CRUVY curvy

D

DDDIY diddy
DDEEG edged
DDEEI Eddie
DDEEN ended
DDEER Edred
DDEES deeds
DDEFY Dyfed
DDEGO dodge
DDEIO diode
Oddie
DDEIR dried
DDEIS sided
DDEMO domed
DDENY neddy□
DDEOP doped
DDEPU duped
DDERU udder
DDERY reddy
DDETY teddy□
DDGIY giddy
DDGOY dodgy
DDIKY kiddy
DDIMX Middx
DDIMY middy
DDINU undid
DDIOS didos
DDIRU druid□
DDIWY widdy
DDLOY oddly
DDMUY muddy
DDNOY noddy
DDOOR Drood
DDOOS dodos
DDORY Roddy
DDOSY Soddy
DDOTY toddy
DDOWY dowdy
DDRUY ruddy
DEEEM Médée
DEEEV deeve
DEEFO Defoe
DEEFR defer
freed
DEEGH hedge
DEEGK kedge
DEEGL ledge
DEEGO geode
DEEGR edger
greed□
DEEGS edges
sedge
DEEGW wedge
DEEIL elide
DEEIN diene
DEEIR eider
DEEKN kneed
knee'd
DEEKR Derek
DEEKY keyed
DEELR elder
DEELS Leeds
DEELU elude
DEELV delve
DEEMN Emden
emend
DEENO donee
DEENR Ender
DEENS dense
needs
DEENT denet
teend
DEENU endue
DEENY needy
DEENZ Enzed
DEEOP epode
DEEOR erode
DEEPS speed
DEERS Seder
DEERT deter
DEERY reedy
DEEST steed
DEESU suede
DEESW sewed
swede□
DEESX desex
sexed
DEESY seedy
DEETU étude
DEETW tweed□
DEEUX exude
DEEVX vexed
DEEWY weedy
DEFGI fidge
DEFGU fudge
DEFIL field□
filed
DEFIN fiend
DEFIO die of
DEFIR fired
fried
DEFIS Fides
DEFIT fetid
DEFIX fixed
DEFIY deify
edify
DEFLS delfs
DEFLT delft□
DEFOX foxed
DEFPU fed up
DEFRU Freud
DEFSU fused
DEGIL gelid
glide
DEGIM midge
DEGIN deign
dinge
DEGIO geoid
DEGIR derig
dirge
ridge
DEGIU guide
DEGJU judge□
DEGLO Gödel
lodge□
DEGLU glued
DEGMU degum
DEGNU nudge
DEGOR go red
DEGOW wodge
DEGRS dregs
DEGRU Rudge
DEGSY sedgy
DEGWY wedgy
DEHII Heidi
DEHIL Delhi
DEHIR hired
DEHIT Edith
DEHLO holed
DEHLP delph

DEHOP	ephod
DEHOR	Herod
	horde
DEHPT	depth
DEHRS	herds
	sherd
	shred
DEHTY	they'd
DEHUZ	Zhu De
DEIIN	indie
DEIIX	dixie
DEIJO	Jodie
DEIKL	liked
DEIKR	irked
DEILN	lined
DEILO	oiled
	oldie
DEILP	lepid
	piel'd
	piled
DEILR	idler
	riled
DEILS	sidle
	slide
DEILT	tilde
	tiled
DEILV	devil
DEILW	wield
	Wilde
DEILY	yield
DEIMN	denim
DEIMR	dimer
DEIMS	deism
	disme
DEIMT	demit
DEIMX	mixed
DEINR	diner
DEINS	Denis
	snide
DEINT	teind
	tined
DEINU	indue
	nudie
DEINW	dwine
	Edwin
	w iden
	widen
DEINX	index
DEIOV	video
DEIOX	oxide
DEIPR	pride❑
DEIPT	tepid
DEIRR	drier
	rider
DEIRT	tired
	tried
DEIRV	diver
	drive
	Verdi
DEIRW	weird
	wired❑
DEIRY	DIYer
DEIST	deist
DEISV	Dives
DEISZ	sized
DEITY	deity❑
DEIVW	wived
DEKKO	dekko
DEKMU	ek dum
DEKNO	kendo
DEKOY	yoked
DEKYY	dykey
DELLN	Lendl
DELLW	dwell
DELMO	model
DELNO	loden
	olden
DELOR	older
DELOS	Delos
DELOV	loved
DELOW	dowel
	dowle
DELOY	Doyle
	yodel
	yodle
DELPS	speld
DELPU	duple
DELRU	ruled
DELRY	redly
DELSU	dulse
DELTV	veldt
DEMMO	modem
DEMNO	demon
DEMOP	moped
DEMOS	demos
DEMOV	moved
DEMRU	demur
DEMSU	sedum
DEMTU	muted
DENNO	Donne
	end-on
	no end
	on end
DENNY	Denny
DENOO	Doone
	odeon
DENOR	drone
DENOS	nosed
	sonde
DENOT	noted
DENOV	Devon
DENOW	endow
	Woden
DENOY	doyen
DENOZ	dozen
DENPS	spend
DENPU	end up
	upend
	up-end
DENRT	trend
DENRU	under
DENRY	nerdy
DENST	stend
DENSY	Denys
DENTU	tuned
DENTY	tynde
	tyned
DENUU	undue
DENUW	unwed
DENWY	Wendy
DEOOR	rodeo❑
DEOPR	Pedro
	roped
DEOPS	posed
	spode❑
DEOPT	depot
DEOPY	dopey
DEORR	order
DEORV	Dover
	drove
DEORW	dower
DEOST	Odets
DEOSU	douse
DEOSW	dowse
	sowed
DEOTU	due to
DEOTX	detox
DEPRU	drupe
	prude
DEPRY	perdy
	predy
DEPSU	pseud
DERRU	Dürer
DERRY	dryer
	Ryder
DERSS	dress
DERSU	Druse
DERUZ	Druze
DESTU	duets
DETTU	duett
DETUV	duvet
DFFUY	Duffy
DFILU	fluid
DFINU	fundi
DFIOR	fiord
DFIRT	drift
DFJOR	fjord
DFLOO	flood
	of old
DFLOY	Floyd
DFNOR	frond
DFNOU	found
DFNSU	funds
DFNUY	Fundy
DFOOR	do for
DGGOO	doggo
DGGOY	doggy
DGHOU	dough
DGIIN	dig in
DGIIR	rigid
DGIIT	digit
DGILU	guild
DGINO	dingo
	doing
DGINR	grind
DGINY	dingy
	dying
DGIPU	dig up
DGLOU	Gould
DGLOY	godly
DGNOO	Ogdon
DGNOU	ungod
DGOOO	good-o
DGOOS	goods
DGOOY	goody
DGOPY	podgy
DGORU	gourd
DGORY	go dry
DGPUY	pudgy
DGRSU	drugs
DHIIN	Hindi
DHIMU	humid
DHINU	Hindu
DHIOR	Ohrid
DHIOT	dhoti
DHIOY	hyoid
DHIRT	third
DHISY	dishy
DHITW	width
DHNOU	hound
DHNSU	dunsh
DHORY	hydro
	rhody
DIILP	Dilip
	lipid
DIILV	livid
DIIMO	idiom
	modii
DIIMT	timid
DIINP	dip in
DIINR	indri
DIINT	nitid
DIIOT	idiot
DIIRS	Idris
DIIRV	virid
DIIVV	vivid
DIJNN	djinn
DIJNO	Dijon
DIKNR	drink
DIKNY	dinky❑
	kindy
DILLR	drill
DILLY	dilly
	idyll
DILMY	dimly
DILNO	Dolin
DILNU	unlid
DILNY	Lindy
DILOS	Isold
	lidos
	soldi
	solid
DILOY	doily
DILRU	lurid
DILRY	drily
DILSW	wilds
DILSY	Dilys
DILTT	DLitt
DIMNO	mid-on
DIMOS	misdo
DIMOU	duomi
	Iomud
	odium
DIMST	midst
DIMTU	tumid
DINNU	Idunn
DINOP	poind
DINOR	Rodin
DINOS	Sidon
DINOT	tondi
DINOU	UNIDO
DINPU	Dupin
DINSU	Indus
DINSY	Sindy
	Sindy®
DINWY	windy
DIOOV	ovoid
DIOPR	Prodi
DIOPS	dipso
DIORR	rorid
DIORS	Doris
DIORT	droit
DIOSY	Doisy
DIOTT	ditto
DIOTV	divot
DIOWW	widow
DIPPY	dippy
DIQSU	quids
	squid
DIRTY	dirty
DISTY	ditsy
DITTY	ditty
DITYZ	ditzy
DIVVY	divvy
DIYZZ	dizzy
DJNOR	Njord
DJOOS	dojos
DKMUY	dumky
DKNRU	drunk
DKOOR	drook
DKORU	drouk
DKOSU	kudos
DKOUU	Dukou
DKSUY	dusky
DKUUZ	kudzu
DLLOR	droll
DLLOY	dolly❑
	Lloyd
DLLUY	dully
DLMOU	mould
DLNUY	Lundy
DLOOR	drool
DLOOW	woold
DLORS	lords❑
DLORW	world❑

DLOSU	ludos
DLOUW	would
DLPUY	duply
DLRYY	dryly
DMMUY	dummy
DMNOO	mondo
	Monod
DMNOU	mound
DMOOS	dooms
	Sodom
DMOOU	duomo
DMOOY	moody❑
DMORU	Murdo
DMORY	dormy
DMOSS	MSDOS
	MS-DOS
DMPSU	dumps
DMPUY	dumpy
DMRUU	durum
DNOOR	donor
	rondo
DNOOS	snood
DNOOT	nod to
	tondo
DNOPU	pound❑
DNORU	round
DNORW	drown
DNOSU	sound
DNOSW	downs❑
DNOSY	synod
DNOUW	wound
DNOWY	downy
DOOPR	droop
DOORS	Doors
	Ordos
DOORU	Douro
	odour
DOOSS	odsos
DOOST	stood
	to-dos
DOOSW	woods❑
DOOTU	do out
	outdo
DOOWY	woody
DOPRU	proud
DORSS	dross
DORSU	duros
	sudor
DORSW	sword
	words
DORTU	Tudor
DORWY	dowry
	rowdy
	wordy
DOTTY	dotty
DPRUY	dry up
	dry-up
DRTUY	Trudy
DSSUY	sudsy
DSTUY	dusty
	study

E

EEEFS	feese
EEEFZ	feeze
EEEGS	geese
EEEHT	te-hee
EEEHZ	heeze
EEEIR	eerie
EEEJZ	Jeeze
EEEKV	keeve
EEELM	melee
	mêlée
EEELS	leese
EEELV	levee
EEENR	Renée
EEENS	neese
EEENZ	neeze
EEEPP	peepe
EEEPT	tepee
EEEPV	peeve
EEERV	reeve❑
EEFFI	Effie
EEFGR	Frege
EEFHI	Hefei
EEFLM	fleme
EEFLR	fleer
EEFLT	fleet❑
EEFMM	femme
EEFRR	freer
	frère
	refer
EEFRV	fever❑
EEFRW	fewer
EEFSS	fesse
EEFST	Feste
EEFSU	fusee
EEFSZ	fezes
EEGGL	legge
EEGGR	egger
EEGHL	Hegel
EEGHN	henge
EEGIL	liege
	Liège
EEGIN	eigne
	genie
EEGIR	Eiger
EEGIS	siege
EEGIV	vegie
EEGKL	gleek
EEGKR	Greek
EEGKY	geeky
EEGLR	Léger
EEGLT	gleet
EEGLY	elegy
EEGMR	merge
EEGNR	genre
	green❑
EEGNT	genet❑
	tenge
EEGNV	venge
EEGNW	ngwee
EEGPU	gee up
EEGRR	Greer
EEGRS	Segrè
	serge
EEGRT	egret
	greet
EEGRV	verge
EEGST	egest
EEGSU	segue
EEHIN	Heine
EEHLN	Helen
EEHLS	sheel
EEHLT	Ethel
EEHLV	helve
EEHLW	wheel
EEHMT	theme
EEHNS	sheen❑
EEHOR	heroe
EEHPS	phese
	sheep
EEHRS	sheer
EEHRT	ether
	there
	three
EEHRW	where
EEHRY	Heyer
EEHSS	Hesse
EEHST	sheet
	these
EEHTT	teeth
EEILL	Ellie
EEILM	elemi
EEILS	Elsie
EEILT	elite
	élite
EEILV	lieve
EEILX	exile
EEIMM	Emmie
EEINR	Ernie
	Irene
EEINS	seine❑
EEIRT	Tiree
EEIRV	Revie
EEIRY	eyrie
EEISS	Essie
EEISV	sieve
EEISZ	seize
EEITY	Eyeti
	Eytie
EEJLW	jewel
EEJSS	Jesse
EEKLN	kneel
EEKLS	sleek
EEKMP	Kempe
EEKOP	pekoe
EEKOV	evoke
EEKPS	Speke
EEKRS	esker
EEKST	skeet
	steek
EEKSY	Kesey
EELLN	Ellen
EELLV	level
EELMU	emule
EELNO	leone
EELNS	lenes
EELNV	nevel
EELNW	newel
EELOP	elope
EELOW	Loewe
EELPR	leper
	repel
EELPS	sleep
	speel
EELPX	expel
EELRU	Euler
EELRV	elver
	lever
	revel
EELRY	leery
EELSS	Seles
EELST	sleet
	steel❑
	stele
EELSV	elves
EELSW	Lewes
	sweel
EELTT	ettle
EELTU	elute
EELTX	telex
	Texel
EEMMN	Menem
	Mneme
EEMMR	emmer
EEMMW	emmew
EEMNS	mense
	semen
EEMNU	neume
EEMNW	enmew
EEMNY	enemy
	Yemen
EEMOT	emote
EEMRT	meter
	metre
EEMRU	emure
EEMRX	remex
EEMRY	emery❑
	Meyer
EEMST	temse
EEMSU	Meuse
EEMSW	Weems
EENNP	penne
EENPR	preen
EENQU	queen❑
EENRS	sneer
EENRT	enter
	terne
	treen
EENRV	erven
	nerve
	never
	Verne
EENRW	renew
EENSS	Essen
	sense
EENST	steen
	teens
	tense
EENSU	ensue
EENSV	evens
	seven
EENSY	seyen
EENTT	tenet
EENTV	event
EENTY	teeny
EENUV	venue
EENVY	veney
EENWY	weeny
EEOPT	topee
EEOPY	peeoy
EEORS	erose
EEOST	see to
EEOWW	wowee
EEPRS	peers
	Peres
	perse
	prese
	Speer
	spree
EEPRT	peter❑
EEPRU	purée
	rupee
EEPRV	perve
EEPRY	peery
EEPST	steep
EEPSW	sweep
EEPSY	seepy
EEPTU	tee up
EEPUY	eye up
EEPWY	weepy
EEQRU	queer
EEQUU	queue
EERRS	serre
EERST	ester
	reest
	reset
	steer
	stere
	terse
	trees
EERSU	reuse
	re-use
EERSV	serve
	sever
	verse
EERSW	sewer
	Weser
EERSY	Reyes
EERTV	evert❑
	revet
EERTW	tweer
EERTX	exert
EERUV	revue

EERVV verve
EERVY every□
EESSX Essex
EESSY sesey
yeses
EESTV Steve
EESTW ewest
sweet
EETTU tutee
EETTV Tevet
EETTW tweet
EFFFO feoff
EFFGO Geoff
EFFIL LIFFE
EFFIR fifer
EFFOR offer
EFFTU tuffe
EFGIN feign
EFGIR grief
EFGLU fugle
EFGOR forge
gofer
EFGOY fogey
EFGUU fugue
EFHIT thief
EFHLS flesh
shelf
EFHNO foehn
EFHRS fresh
EFHTT theft
EFHTY hefty
EFIKN knife
EFILN elfin
EFILR filer
flier
lifer
rifle
EFILS files
flies
EFILT filet
flite
EFILX Felix
EFIMR fermi□
EFIMT metif
EFIMU Fiume
EFINR finer
infer
EFINS fines
EFINT feint
EFINW in few
EFINX enfix
EFIRR firer
frier
EFIRS serif
EFIRT refit
EFIRV fiver
EFIRX fixer
EFIRY fiery
reify
EFISV fives
EFKLU fluke
EFKNS fenks
EFLLY felly
EFLMU flume
EFLNO felon
EFLOT OFTEL
Oftel
EFLOW Wolfe
EFLPY flype
EFLRU Fleur
EFLRY ferly
flyer
EFLSS selfs
EFLTU flute□
EFLTY flyte
EFMOR forme
Frome
EFMRU femur
EFMSU fumes
EFMTU fumet
EFNNU Funen
EFNNY fenny
EFNOT often
EFNRY ferny
EFORR frore
EFORT fetor
forte□
EFORY foyer
EFORZ froze
EFOSS fosse
EFOSU of use
EFOSX Foxes
EFRRY ferry□
fryer
EFRSS serfs
EFRSW swerf
EFRUZ furze
EFSTU fetus
EGGIR Greig
Grieg
EGGIU gigue
EGGLY leggy
EGGNO egg on
EGGNU gunge
EGGOR gorge
EGGOU gouge
EGGPY Peggy
EGHHI heigh
EGHHW hewgh
EGHIL Leigh
EGHIN hinge
neigh
EGHIT eight
EGHIW weigh
EGHNT Ghent
EGIIN genii
EGIJR rejig
re-jig
EGIKL glike
EGIKR grike
EGILM gimel
EGILN Nigel
EGILR liger
EGILS Giles
EGILT gilet
leg it
legit
EGILU guile
EGIMM gimme
EGIMR grime
EGINR Niger
reign
renig
EGINS singe
EGINT get in
tinge
EGINV given
EGIOV ogive
EGIPR gripe
EGIRS grise
EGIRT tiger
EGIRV giver
EGISU guise
EGITT get it
EGLLY gelly
EGLMO golem
Gomel
EGLMU glume
EGLNN Glenn
EGLNT glent
EGLNU lunge
EGLOT let go
EGLOV glove
Vogel
EGLPU leg-up
EGLRU gruel
Luger
Luger®
EGLSU gules
EGLUY gluey
EGMNO gnome
EGMOT gemot
EGMRS germs
EGMRU grume
EGNOR goner
Negro
EGNOT get on
EGNOY Yonge
EGNPU gen up
EGNST gents
EGNSU genus
EGNSY Synge
EGNTU unget
EGNTW Gwent
EGOOS goose
EGOOY gooey
EGOPR grope
porge
EGORR Roger
EGORS gorse
EGORT ergot
EGORU rogue
rouge
EGORV grove□
EGORW Gower
EGOSS gesso
gosse
segos
EGOTT get to
EGOUV vogue□
EGPRU purge
EGPTU get up
get-up
EGPTY Egypt
EGRRU urger
EGRRY Gerry
EGRSU surge
EGSSU guess
EGSTU guest
EGSVY gyves
EGTTY Getty
EHHIT hithe
EHIKR hiker
EHIKS sheik
EHIKT Keith
kithe
EHILS shiel
EHILT Leith
lithe
EHILW while
EHILX helix
EHIMN hem in
EHIMS hiems
EHINR Henri
Rhine
EHINS Hines
shine
EHINW whine
EHINZ Heinz
EHIOP I hope
EHIRR hirer
EHIRS heirs
shire□
EHIRT Reith
their
EHISS shies
EHIST heist
sieth
sithe
EHISV hives
EHITT tithe
EHITW white□
withe
EHKLW whelk
EHKMR Khmer
EHKNU Kühne
EHKOO Hooke
EHKTY kythe
EHLLO hello□
EHLLS shell
she'll
EHLMO mohel
EHLOT helot
hotel□
thole
EHLOV hovel
EHLOW whole
EHLOY holey
Hoyle
EHLPS shlep
EHLPW whelp
EHLSU shule
EHLSW welsh□
EHLTU Thule
EHLTY ethyl
EHLWY Hywel
EHMNY hymen
EHMOR Homer
EHMOS homes
Moshe
EHMOY homey
EHMRS herms
EHMRT therm
EHMRU rheum
EHMRY rhyme
EHMST meths
EHMTY thyme
EHNOO ohone
EHNOP phone
EHNOR heron
Rhône
EHNOS hosen
shone
EHNOY honey
EHNRU Nehru
EHNRY henry□
EHNTT tenth
EHNTU uneth
EHOOY hooey
EHOPU ouphe
EHORS horse
shore
EHORT other
throe
EHORV hover
EHORW whore
EHOSS hoses
shoes
EHOST ethos
those
EHOSU house□
EHOSV shove
EHOSW whose
EHOWW ewhow
EHPRT Perth
EHPRY hyper
EHPTU het up
EHRSU usher
EHRSW shrew
EHRTW threw
EHRTZ hertz□
EHSTU Shute
EHTTY Hetty
EIILP pilei
EIINS nisei

EIINT	tie in
	tie-in
EIINX	nixie
EIIPX	pixie
EIISV	visie
EIJLU	Julie
EIJOS	Josie
EIJRV	jiver
EIKLM	kelim
EIKLN	inkle
	Klein
	Kline
	liken
EIKLR	Rilke
EIKLY	kiley
	kylie□
EIKMS	Smike
EIKNO	koine□
EIKNS	skein
EIKNV	Kevin
EIKNY	key in
EIKPS	spike
EIKRS	skier
EIKSS	Sikes
	skies
EIKST	skite
EIKSU	Sukie
EIKSV	skive
EIKSY	yikes
EIKTW	Kitwe
EILLL	Lille
EILLO	Ollie
EILLS	Ellis
	lisle
EILLW	Weill
EILMN	Milne
	n mile
EILMP	impel
EILMR	miler
EILMS	miles□
	Selim
	slime
	smile
EILMU	ileum
EILMY	Emily
	limey
EILNN	Lenin
	linen
EILNO	olein
EILNR	liner
EILNS	lenis
	lines
	nelis
EILNT	inlet
	lenti
	let in
EILNV	Levin
	liven
EILOR	Loire
	oiler
	oriel
EILOT	Eliot
	toile
EILOU	Louie
EILOV	olive□
	voile
EILPR	peril
	plier
EILPS	piles
	plies
	spiel
	spile
EILPX	pixel
EILRT	litre
	tiler
EILRV	liver
	rivel
EILRY	Riley
EILST	islet
	istle
	stile
EILSV	Elvis
	Levis®
	lives
	slive
EILSW	lewis□
	wiles
EILSX	lexis
	silex
EILTT	title
EILTU	utile
EILTX	ixtle
EILVY	veily
EIMMR	mimer
EIMMW	immew
EIMNR	in rem
	miner
EIMNS	Nîmes
EIMNU	IMunE
EIMOR	moire
	moiré
EIMOV	movie
EIMPR	prime
EIMPT	tempi
EIMRS	miser
	Reims
EIMRT	merit
	mitre
	remit
	timer
EIMRX	mixer
EIMSS	seism
EIMST	items
	Métis
	smite
	times
EINNO	in one
EINNP	pen in
EINNR	inner
	renin
EINNS	Innes
EINNU	ennui
EINNV	Niven
EINOP	opine
EINOS	eosin
	noise
EINOV	ovine
EINPP	Pepin
EINPR	ripen
EINPS	penis
	snipe
	spine
EINPT	inept
EINRS	reins
	resin
	rinse
	serin
	siren□
EINRT	inert
	inter
	nitre
	trine
EINRU	inure
	urine
EINRV	Nervi
EINRX	NIREX
EINST	INSET
	inset
	set in
	stein□
EINSU	in use
EINSW	sinew
	swine
EINTU	unite
	untie
EINTW	twine
EINVW	vinew
EINVX	vixen□
EINVY	veiny
EINWY	winey
EINWZ	winze
	wizen
EIOPS	poise
EIORS	osier
	Rosie
EIORV	vireo
EIOWZ	zowie
EIOZZ	Ozzie
EIPPR	piper□
EIPPS	Pepsi®
	pipes
EIPQU	equip
	pique
	piqué
EIPRS	Piers
	prise
	speir
	spire
EIPRT	tripe
EIPRV	vipèr
EIPRW	wiper
EIPRZ	prize
EIPSS	spies
EIPST	piste
	spite
	stipe
EIPSW	swipe
EIPTU	tie up
	tie-up
	uptie
EIPTW	pewit
EIPTY	piety
EIQRU	quire
EIQTU	quiet
	quite
EIRRS	riser
EIRRT	trier□
EIRRV	river
EIRRW	wirer
EIRST	reist
	resit
EIRSV	vires
EIRSX	sixer
EIRSZ	sizer
EIRTT	trite
EIRTU	uteri
EIRTV	rivet
EIRTW	twire
	write
EISST	sties
EISSU	issue
	Susie
EISSZ	Zeiss
EISTU	suite
EISTV	stive
EISTX	exist
	exits
	sixte
EISVW	wives
EITTW	twite
EJKOP	kopje
EJKOR	joker
EJKOS	jokes
EJKOY	jokey
EJKRY	jerky
EJLLY	jelly
EJLOU	joule□
EJLOY	Joely
EJLPU	julep
EJMMY	jemmy
EJNNY	jenny□
EJNOR	rejón
EJNOS	Jones
EJNOT	jeton
EJNOY	enjoy
EJPTU	upjet
EJRRY	jerry□
EJRWY	Jewry
EJSSU	Jesus
	jésus
EJSSY	Jessy
EJTTY	jetty
EKKLR	Klerk
EKKOP	kopek
EKLLN	knell
EKLLY	Kelly
EKLNT	knelt
EKLOS	Kelso
EKLOY	kyloe
	yokel
EKLPS	skelp
EKLPY	kelpy
EKLTU	Klute
EKLTW	welkt
EKMOS	smoke
EKMPT	kempt
EKNNY	Kenny
EKNOR	Kreon
	krone
EKNOS	snoek
	snoke
EKNOT	token
EKNOW	knowe
	woken
EKNOZ	Kenzo
EKNRZ	Krenz
EKNSY	ensky
EKOPR	poker
	proke
EKOPS	spoke
EKOPU	pouke
EKOSS	skeos
EKOST	stoke
EKPRY	perky
EKPSY	pesky
EKRRY	Kerry
EKRSY	skyer
	skyre
EKSTY	skyte
ELLMS	Mlles
	smell
ELLNY	nelly□
ELLPS	spell
ELLQU	quell
ELLSS	sells
ELLST	stell
ELLSW	swell
	Wells
ELLTU	tulle
ELLTY	telly
ELLWY	welly
ELMMU	lumme
ELMNO	lemon
	melon
ELMNU	lumen
ELMNY	Emlyn
ELMOR	morel
ELMOS	Melos
	Mosel
ELMOT	metol□
	motel
ELMOU	oleum
ELMPU	plume
ELMRU	lemur
ELMRY	Meryl

ELMST	smelt
ELMSY	Myles
ELMUV	velum
ELMXY	xylem
ELNNY	Lenny
	Lynne
ELNOR	enrol
	loner
	Loren
ELNOS	lenos
	Olsen
ELNOT	Elton
	lento
	let on
ELNOV	novel
ELNOW	lowne
	Olwen
ELNWY	Elwyn
	newly
ELOOP	Poole
ELOOS	loose
	oleos
ELOPR	prole
ELOPS	slope□
ELOPU	loupe
ELORR	Errol
	Lorre
ELORS	loser
ELORV	lover
ELORW	lower
	rowel
ELORY	Elroy
	Leroy
ELOSS	loess
	soles
ELOST	stole
ELOSU	louse
	ousel
	Seoul
ELOSV	solve
ELOSW	lowse
ELOTT	to let
ELOTV	volte
ELOTW	owlet
	towel
ELOTX	extol
ELOTY	Otley
ELOUV	ovule
ELOUZ	ouzel
ELOVW	vowel
ELPRU	puler
ELPRY	reply
ELPST	slept
	spelt
ELPSU	Lepus
	pulse
ELPSY	slype
ELPTU	let up
	let-up
ELRRU	ruler
ELRSU	rules
ELRTY	Tyler
ELRUX	Lurex®
ELRWY	Wyler
ELSTY	style
ELSUX	luxes
ELTTY	Letty
ELTUX	exult
ELTWY	wetly
ELYZZ	lezzy
EMMOS	memos
	Somme
EMMSY	Emmys
EMNNU	numen
EMNOS	meson
EMNOT	Monet
	monte
	moten
EMNOV	venom
EMNOW	women
EMNOY	money□
EMNRU	rumen
EMNTU	unmet
EMNUW	unmew
EMOOR	Moore
	romeo□
EMOOS	moose
EMOOT	me-too
EMOPR	EPROM
	moper
	proem
EMOPS	Epsom
	poems
EMOPT	tempo
EMORR	ormer
EMORS	mores
	Morse
	smore
EMORT	metro
EMORV	mover
	vomer
EMORW	mower
EMOSS	Moses
EMOSU	mouse
EMOSV	moves
EMOSY	mosey
EMOTT	motet
	motte
	totem
EMOZZ	mezzo
EMPRS	sperm
EMPSU	spume
EMPTT	tempt
EMPTY	empty
EMRRY	merry
EMRST	RMetS
	terms
EMRSU	Remus
	serum
EMRSY	Emrys
EMSSY	messy
EMSTY	styme
ENNOO	no one
	no-one
ENNOS	nones
ENNOT	nonet
	tenon
	tonne
ENNOX	xenon
ENNPU	unpen
ENNPY	penny□
ENNWY	Wynne
ENOOR	roneo
ENOOS	noose
ENOOZ	ozone
ENOPR	Perón
	prone
ENOPS	Nepos
ENOPU	one up
ENOPY	peony
ENORS	Ensor
	Norse
	Señor
	snore
ENORT	tenor
ENORU	Rouen
ENORW	owner
ENORY	royne
ENOST	notes
	onset
	set on
	Steno
	stone□
ENOSW	Owens
ENOSY	nosey
ENOVY	envoy
ENPRU	prune
ENPST	spent
ENPSU	Nupes
ENQRU	quern
ENRRU	rerun
ENRST	Ernst
	stern□
ENRSU	nurse□
	Unser
ENRTT	Trent
ENRTU	tuner
	urent
ENRTY	entry
ENRVY	nervy
ENSTT	stent
	tents
ENSTU	unset
ENSUV	Venus
ENSUW	unsew
ENSUX	nexus
	unsex
ENSWY	newsy
ENTTY	Netty
EOORS	roose
EOORW	wooer
EOPPS	pepos
EOPPU	poupe
EOPRR	prore
	repro
EOPRS	poser
	prose
	repos
	Soper
	spore
EOPRT	repot
	toper
	trope
EOPRV	prove
EOPRW	power
EOPRY	ropey
EOPSS	pesos
EOPST	estop
	pesto
	stoep
	stope
EOPSX	expos
EOPSY	poesy
	sepoy
EOPXY	epoxy
EOQTU	quote
	toque
EORRR	error
EORRT	retro
EORRV	rover
EORRW	rower
EORSS	Roses
EORST	roset
	Soter
	store
EORSU	euros
	rouse
EORSV	servo
	verso
EORSW	worse
EORSY	Soyer
EORSZ	zeros
EORTT	otter
	torte
EORTU	outer
	outré
	route
EORTV	overt
	voter
EORTW	tower
	wrote
EORTX	oxter
EORTY	toyer
EORUY	you're
EORXX	xerox
	Xerox®
EOSSU	souse
EOSSW	sowse
EOSTT	set to
	set-to
EOSTU	touse
EOSTV	stove
EOSTW	Stowe
	towse
EOTTV	Ovett
EOTUZ	touze
EOTWZ	towze
EOUVY	you've
EPPPU	pep up
EPPPY	peppy
EPPRU	upper
EPPSY	Pepys
EPRRY	perry□
	ryper
EPRSS	press
	SERPS
	Serps
EPRST	strep
EPRSU	purse
	sprue
	super
EPRSY	Ypres
EPRTU	erupt
EPRTW	twerp
EPSST	steps
EPSTU	set up
	set-up
	stupe
	upset
EPSTW	swept
EPSUU	use up
EPSUW	sew up
EPSUY	Pusey
EPTTY	petty
EQRUY	query
EQSTU	quest
EQSUU	Equus
EQTUU	tuque
ERRSY	serry
ERRTY	retry
	terry□
ERSST	tress
ERSSU	users
ERSTW	strew
	trews
	wrest
ERSTY	styre
ERSUU	usure
ERTTU	utter
ERTUV	vertu
ERTWY	twyer
ESSTT	tests
ESSTY	styes
	Tysse
ESTTY	styte
	testy
ESTWY	stewy
ESTYZ	zesty

F

FFFLU	fluff
FFGIR	griff
FFGOO	go off
FFGRU	gruff
FFHIT	fifth

FFHIW	whiff
FFHUY	huffy
FFIJY	jiffy
FFIKS	skiff
FFIMY	miffy
FFINO	Ffion
	in-off
FFINS	sniff
FFINY	niffy
FFIQU	quiff
FFIST	stiff
FFITY	fifty
FFLPU	pluff
FFNOO	on-off
FFNSU	snuff
FFOOT	off to
FFOST	toffs
FFOSW	sowff
FFPUY	puffy
FFSTU	stuff
FGGIR	Frigg
FGGOY	foggy
FGGUY	fuggy
FGHIT	fight
FGIIN	fingi
FGILN	fling
FGINU	fungi
FGIOS	figos
FGIST	gifts
FGLNO	flong
FGOOR	forgo
	go for
FGOOY	goofy❑
FGOPU	fog up
FHILT	filth
FHIRT	firth
FHIST	shift
FHISY	fishy
FHLSU	flush
FHOOS	hoofs
FHORT	forth❑
	froth
FHRSU	frush
FHRTU	furth
FIINS	finis
FIINT	fit in
FIINX	infix
FIKLS	flisk
FIKNO	of kin
FIKNR	Frink
FIKRS	frisk
FILLR	frill
FILLY	filly
FILMP	flimp
FILMS	films
FILMY	filmy
FILNT	flint
FILOO	folio
FILRT	flirt
FILSU	fusil
FILTY	fitly

FIMOT	motif
FIMTU	mufti
FINNU	in fun
FINNY	finny
FINOR	in for
FINOS	finos
FINOT	fit on
	if not
FINOX	fix on
FINST	snift
FINTU	unfit
FINTY	nifty
FINUX	Fuxin
	unfix
FINUY	unify
FIOST	foist
FIOTU	Fitou
FIPTU	fit up
	fit-up
FIPUX	fix up
FIRST	first
FIRTU	fruit
FIRTZ	fritz
FIRZZ	frizz
FISSU	Sufis
FISTW	swift❑
FIYZZ	fizzy
FJLOO	Flo-Jo
FKLNU	flunk
FKLOO	kloof
FKLOS	folks
FKLUY	fluky
FKNUY	funky
FLLOY	folly
FLLUY	fully
FLMPU	flump
FLNNY	Flynn
FLNOW	flown
FLNOY	fonly
FLOOR	floor
FLOOS	loofs
FLOOT	OFLOT
	Oflot
FLOOW	Woolf
FLORU	flour
	fluor
FLOSS	floss
FLOSW	fowls
FLOTU	flout
FLOTY	lofty
FLPUY	fly up
FLTUY	fluty
FMORU	forum❑
FMPRU	frump
FNNUY	funny
FNOOS	son of
FNORT	front
FNORW	frown
FNOTU	fount
	futon
FOOPR	proof

FOOPS	spoof
FOORS	roofs
FOOST	foots
FOOTU	out of
FOOTY	footy
FOPRU	up for
FORST	frost❑
FORTY	forty
FOSTU	Fouts
FOSTY	softy
FPRUY	fry-up
FRRSS	RSFSR
FRRUY	furry
FRSTU	turfs
FRSUU	Rufus
FRSUY	surfy
FRTUY	turfy
FSSUY	fussy
FSTUY	fusty
FTTUY	tufty
FUYZZ	fuzzy

G

GGGIS	Giggs
GGHOU	Gough
GGIIL	Gigli
GGILO	Golgi
GGINO	going
	oggin
GGIOT	gigot
GGIPY	piggy❑
GGLOO	Gogol
GGMOY	moggy
GGMUY	muggy
GGNUY	gungy
GGOSY	soggy
GHHIT	hight
	thigh
GHILT	light
GHIMT	might
GHINT	night
	thing
GHIOS	shogi
GHIOT	hog it
GHIRT	girth
	right
GHIST	sight
GHITT	tight
GHITW	Wight
GHLLY	ghyll
GHLOU	ghoul
	lough
GHLPY	glyph
GHNOT	thong
GHORU	rough
GHOST	ghost❑
GHOSU	sough
GHOTU	ought
	tough
GHRSU	shrug
GHSUY	gushy

GIILV	vigil
GIINO	Inigo
GIJNO	jingo❑
GIKNS	Kings
GILLR	grill
GILNO	lingo
GILNS	sling
GILNT	glint
GILNU	lug in
	Luing
	lungi
GILNY	lying
GILOO	igloo
GILOS	Sligo
GILRU	lurgi
GILRY	girly
GILTU	guilt
GILTZ	glitz
GIMNY	mingy
GIMOS	gismo
GIMOY	goyim
GIMOZ	gizmo
GIMPU	guimp
GIMPY	pigmy
GIMRY	grimy
GINNU	Nguni
GINNY	Ginny
GINOP	pingo
GINOR	groin
GINOT	ingot
	tigon
GINOW	owing
	wongi
GINOY	yogin
GINPU	Pugin
GINRS	rings
GINRU	unrig
GINRW	wring
GINSS	signs
GINST	sting
GINSU	using
GINSV	V-sign
GINSW	swing
	wings❑
GINVY	vying
GINYZ	zingy
GIORS	giros
GIORV	Virgo
GIPRS	sprig
GIPRU	rig up
GIPSY	Gipsy
GIRST	grist
	grits
	strig
GISTU	g-suit❑
GKORY	Gorky
GLLOY	golly
GLLUY	gully
GLMOO	gloom
GLMOU	mogul
GLNOU	gluon

GLOOP	gloop
GLOOS	logos
GLOOY	ology
GLORW	growl
GLORY	glory
GLOSS	gloss
GLOUV	vulgo
GLRUY	lurgy
GLSSU	slugs
GMMUY	gummy
GMNOU	Mungo
GMNUU	ungum
GMNUW	NUGMW
GMOOR	groom
GMPRU	grump
GMPUU	gum up
	mug up
GMPYY	pygmy
GNNUY	gunny
GNNYY	gynny
GNOOP	pongo❑
GNOOZ	gonzo
GNOPR	prong
GNOPY	pongy
GNORU	Rogun
GNORW	grown
	wrong
GNOST	tongs
GNOUY	young❑
GNRTU	grunt
GNSTU	stung
GNSUW	swung
GOOTU	go out
	outgo
GOPRS	sprog
GOPRU	group
GOPRY	Porgy
GOPST	g-spot
GOPTU	tog up
GORSS	gross
GORSY	gorsy
GORSZ	Grosz
GORTU	grout
GOSTU	gusto
GOTUY	gouty
GPPUY	guppy
GPSYY	gypsy❑
GRSUY	gyrus
GSTUY	gusty
	gutsy

H

HHHUU	uh-huh
HHIPR	RIPHH
HHISW	whish
HHMOU	ho-hum
HHMPU	humph❑
HHOOS	hoosh
HHOOT	Hohot
HHOTT	Thoth
HHSSU	shush

HIIMS	imshi
HIIRS	Irish
HIITT	hit it
HIJOS	shoji
HIKLT	thilk
HIKNS	knish
HIKNT	think❑
HIKRS	shirk
HIKSW	whisk
HILLS	shill
HILLY	hilly
HILMP	MPhil
HILMU	hilum
HILOT	litho
	tholi
HILRT	thirl
HILRW	whirl
HILSS	slish
HILSY	shily
HILTT	tilth
HIMRT	mirth
HIMST	smith❑
HIMSY	imshy
HIMTY	thymi
HINNT	ninth
HINNY	hinny
HINOR	rhino
HINOT	hit on
HINPU	unhip
HINST	hints
HINSU	Husni
HINSY	shiny
HINWY	whiny
HIOPP	hippo
HIOPT	hop it
	tophi
HIORU	houri
HIOST	hoist
HIPPY	hippy
HIPQS	Q-ship
HIPRT	thrip
HIPSS	ships
HIPSW	whisp
HIPTY	pithy
HIRRS	shirr
HIRRW	whirr
HIRST	Hirst
	shirt
	Trish
HISSU	sushi
HISSW	swish
	whiss
HISTW	whist
HISTX	sixth
HITWY	withy
HIWZZ	whizz
HJNOS	Johns
HKKOU	hokku
HKNUY	hunky
HKOOS	shook
HKOOY	hooky
HKSSU	husks
HKSUY	husky
HLLOO	hollo
HLLOU	hullo
HLLOY	holly❑
HLMPY	lymph
HLNSU	shuln
HLOOS	shool
HLOOT	HOTOL
HLOOY	hooly
HLOPX	phlox
HLORW	whorl
HLOSS	slosh
HLOST	Holst
	sloth❑
HLOTU	Louth
HLOTY	hotly
HLPSU	plush
HLPSY	sylph
HLSSU	shuls
	slush
HLSYY	shyly
HMNOT	month
HMNPY	nymph
HMOOP	oomph
HMOPR	morph
HMOST	moths
HMOTU	mouth
HMPTU	thump
HMPUY	humpy
HMRRY	myrrh
HMRTU	thrum
HMSTU	musth
	shtum
HMSTY	myths
HMSUU	humus
HMSUY	mushy
HNOOR	Honor
HNOOT	hot on
HNORS	shorn
HNORT	north❑
	thorn
HNORU	Huron
HNORY	horny
HNOSW	shown
HNSTU	shunt
HNSTY	synth
HOOOO	hoo-oo
HOOPS	Hoops
HOOPT	photo
HOOPW	whoop
HOOST	shoot
	sooth
	tohos
HOOSW	woosh
HOOTT	tooth
HOPPY	hoppy
HOPSY	hypos
	Sophy
HOPTU	hot up
HORST	horst
	short❑
HORSU	Horus
HORSW	shrow
HORSY	horsy
HORTT	troth
HORTW	throw
	worth
	wroth
HOSST	hosts
HOSSU	husos
HOSTU	shout
	south❑
	thous
HOSTW	sowth
HOSUY	shoyu
HOSWY	showy
HOTUY	youth
HPSTU	shtup
HPSUY	pushy
HRRUY	hurry
HRSTU	hurst❑
HRTTU	truth
HRUUU	uhuru
HSSUY	hussy

I

IIJLN	Jilin
IIJNN	jinni
IIKLM	kilim
IIKNN	ink in
	kinin
IILLV	villi
IILMT	limit
IILMU	ilium
IILNT	intil
IILPP	Lippi
IIMMN	minim
IIMMR	Mimir
IIMNR	mirin
IIMNX	mix in
IIMPS	impis
IIMRZ	Izmir
IIMTX	mix it
IINOS	Oisin
IINST	sit in
	sit-in
IINTU	Inuit
IIORT	torii
IIPPT	pipit
IISTV	visit
IJMMY	Jimmy
IJNNY	Jinny
IJNOT	joint
IJOST	joist
IKKNS	Kinks
	skink
IKKNY	kinky
IKKOS	kiosk
IKKRU	kukri
IKLLR	krill
IKLLS	skill
IKLLY	Killy
IKLMT	Klimt
IKLMY	milky
IKLNP	plink
IKLNS	links
	slink
IKLOS	kilos
IKLRS	skirl
IKLSY	silky
IKLTY	kilty
IKMNS	Minsk
IKMPS	skimp
IKMRS	smirk
IKNNO	Nikon®
IKNOS	kinos
IKNOW	I know
IKNPR	prink
IKNST	skint
	stink
IKNTW	twink
IKOOR	koori
IKORV	Kirov
IKOSS	skios
IKPPS	Kipps
IKPSY	spiky
IKPTU	tupik
IKQRU	quirk
IKRRS	skirr
IKRST	skirt
IKRSY	risky
IKRTU	Turki
IKTTY	kitty❑
ILLMS	Mills
ILLOR	Rolli
ILLPR	prill
ILLPS	spill
ILLQU	quill
ILLRT	trill
ILLST	still
ILLSW	swill
	Wills
ILLSY	silly
	slily
ILLTW	twill
ILLTY	Tilly
ILLWY	willy❑
ILMOO	mooli
ILMOS	milos
ILMPY	imply
ILMSY	slimy
ILNOS	linos
ILNOT	Nilot
ILNOW	Olwin
ILNPU	lupin
ILNSU	Linus
	Sunil
ILNTU	unlit
	until
ILNTY	linty
ILNVY	vinyl
ILOOP	polio
ILOOS	olios
ILOOV	ovoli
ILOPS	spoil
ILOPT	pilot
ILOPW	pilow
ILOPX	oxlip
ILORS	loris
ILOSS	silos
ILOST	Solti
ILOSU	louis❑
ILPPU	pipul
	pupil
ILPPY	lippy
ILPQU	Quilp
ILPST	spilt
	split❑
ILPTU	lit up
	tulip
ILQTU	quilt
ILRSW	swirl
ILRTW	twirl
ILSSY	lysis
ILSTT	stilt
ILSTY	styli
ILSTZ	Liszt
IMMTY	Timmy
IMNOO	nomoi
IMNOR	minor
IMNOS	Minos
	Simon
IMNOT	Timon
IMNOY	Nimoy
IMNRU	Nurmi
IMNSU	in sum
	minus
IMOPR	primo
IMOPT	Mopti
IMOPU	opium
IMORT	Timor
IMOSS	misos
IMOST	moist
IMOTV	vomit
IMPPR	primp
IMPRS	prism
IMPRU	Purim
IMPRY	primy
IMPST	timps
IMPUX	mix up
	mix-up
IMPWY	Wimpy
IMRTU	Timur
IMSSY	missy
IMSTU	musit
	UMIST
IMSTY	misty
IMTTY	Mitty
INNNO	ninon
INNNY	ninny
INNOO	onion
INNOP	pin on
INNOU	Inönü

	union
INNOW	win on
INNOX	Nixon
INNPU	unpin
INNRU	inurn
	run in
	run-in
INNSU	Sunni
INNTU	untin
INNTY	tinny
INOOR	Orion
INOPP	pop in
INOPR	orpin
	Ripon
INOPT	pinto□
	piton
	point
	potin
INOQU	quoin
INORS	irons□
	rosin
INORT	intro
INORY	irony
INOST	sit on
INOSV	vinos
INOSW	winos
INOSY	noisy
INOTW	in tow
	in two
INOTX	toxin
INPPU	in pup
	pin up
	pin-up
INPPY	nippy
INPRT	print
INPRU	purin
	unrip
INPRY	pry in
INPSS	snips
INPSY	spiny
INPTU	input
	put in
	Putin
INPUZ	unzip
INQTU	quint
INRSU	ruins
INRTU	Turin
INSSU	sinus
INSTT	stint
INSTU	Tunis
	units
INSTW	twins□
INTTY	nitty
INTUW	unwit
INTUY	unity□
INTWY	twiny
IOOPT	topoi
IOPRR	prior
IOPST	posit
IOPSU	pious
IOPTV	pivot
IOPTZ	Opitz
IOQTU	Quito
	quoit
IORRS	orris
IORST	roist
	rotis
	trios
IORSV	rivos
	visor
IORSZ	zoris
IORVY	ivory□
IORVZ	vizor
IOSSS	Ossis
IOSTT	stoit
IOSUX	Sioux
IOTTV	Titov
IOTTW	to wit
IPPPY	pippy
IPPRU	rip up
IPPUZ	zip up
IPPYZ	zippy
IPRST	spirt
	sprit
	strip
IPRTW	twirp
IPRVY	privy
IPSTU	sit up
IPSTY	tipsy
IPSTZ	spitz□
IPSWY	wispy
IPSXY	pyxis□
IPTTU	putti
	titup
IQRTU	quirt
IQSTU	quits
	squit
IRSTW	wrist
IRSUV	virus
IRTUV	virtu
IRTXY	Trixy
IRTYZ	ritzy
ISSSU	Issus
ISSSW	Swiss
ISSSY	sissy
ISSTU	situs
ISSTW	swits
ISTTU	Titus
ISTTW	twist□
ISTUV	Vitus
ISTUW	UWIST
ISTXY	sixty
	xyst i
ITTTU	tutti
ITTWY	witty
ITYZZ	tizzy

J

JKNUY	junky
JLLOY	jolly
JLOOS	Jools
JLOWY	jowly
JMOOS	mojos
JMPUY	jumpy
JNOPU	jupon
JNORU	Junor
JNOTU	junto
JOOSS	Jooss
JORRU	juror
JOSTU	joust
JTTUY	jutty

K

KKLSU	skulk
KKNSU	skunk
KKOOY	kooky
KKORY	Korky
KKRSU	Kursk
KKUYY	yukky
KLLNO	knoll
KLLSU	skull
KLNOP	plonk
KLNPU	plunk
KLNRU	knurl
KLOOP	plook
KLOOS	kolos
	looks
KLOPU	plouk
KLOUY	yokul
KLSSU	sulks
KLSUY	sulky
KMNOO	Nkomo
KMOOS	mokos
KMOST	Tomsk
KMOSY	smoky
KMRUY	murky
KMSUY	musky
KNNOW	known
KNOOR	kroon
KNOOS	snook
KNOPR	pronk
KNOPS	knosp
KNOQU	quonk
KNOST	stonk
KNOSW	snowk
KNOSY	yonks
KNOTT	Knott
KNOTU	knout
KNOUY	Yukon
KNOWY	wonky
KNPSU	spunk
KNRRU	knurr
KNRTU	trunk
KOOPS	spook
KOORR	Koror
KOORY	rooky
KOOST	kotos
	stook
	tokos
KOOTW	kotow
KOOTY	Kyoto
	Tokyo
KOPRY	porky
KORST	stork
KORSW	works
KPPRU	Krupp
KRTUU	Turku
KSTUY	tusky

L

LLLOY	lolly
LLLUY	Lully
LLMOY	Molly
LLOPY	Polly
LLORS	Rolls
	Rolls®
LLORT	troll
LLOSY	Solly
LLOUY	you'll
LLOWY	lowly
LLOXY	xylol
LLPWY	Pwyll
LLSUY	sully□
LLSYY	slyly
LMMUY	lummy
LMOOS	sloom
LMOOT	molto
LMOST	smolt
LMOSU	Mosul
LMOTU	moult
LMPPU	plump
LMPSU	slump
LMPUY	lumpy
	plumy
LMRUY	rumly
LNNOY	nylon
LNOOS	snool
	Solon
LNOOW	low on
LNOOY	loony
LNOPY	pylon
LNOSY	Lyons
LNOTU	Luton
LNOUZ	Luzon
LNOWY	Olwyn
LOOOV	ovolo
LOOPR	orlop
LOOPS	polos
	sloop
	spool
LOOPY	loopy
LOORY	Oryol
LOOSS	solos
LOOST	lotos
	stool
	tools
LOOSW	Solow
LOOTT	lotto
LOOVV	Volvo®
LOPPY	polyp
LOPRW	prowl
LOPSS	slops
LOPSY	polys
	slopy
LOPTU	Pluto
	poult
LORRY	lorry
LORST	rotls
LORTY	Tylor
LORUX	Luxor
LORWY	Lowry
LOSTU	lotus
LOSUY	lousy
LOTYZ	zloty
LPPUY	pulpy
LPRSU	slurp
LPSUU	lupus□
LRSUY	surly
LRTUY	truly
LRUUU	Uluru
LRWYY	wryly
LSTUY	lusty
LUVVY	luvvy

M

MMMOY	mommy
MMMUY	mummy
MMOTY	tommy□
MMPSU	mumps
MMRUY	rummy
MMSTU	stumm
MMSUY	mumsy
MMTUY	tummy
MMUYY	yummy
MNOOR	Monro
	moron
MNOOS	monos
MNOOY	moony
MNORU	mourn
	Munro
MNORY	Myron
MNOTU	mount
MNOUV	novum
MNTUZ	Muntz
MOOPR	promo
MOOPS	spoom
MOORS	Moros
	rooms
	smoor
MOORT	motor
MOORV	vroom
MOORY	roomy
MOOST	smoot
MOOTT	motto
MOPPU	mop up
	mop-up
MOPRT	tromp
MOPST	stomp
MORST	storm
MORSW	Worms
MORWY	wormy
MOSSU	musos
	sumos
MOSSY	mossy
MOSTU	Motus

MOSUY	mousy
MPRTU	trump
MPSTU	stump
MPSUU	sum up
MPSUY	spumy
MRSTU	strum
MSSTU	Smuts
MSSUY	mussy
MSTUY	musty
MUYZZ	muzzy

N

NNOOS	no-nos
	no-no's
NNOOT	not on
NNORU	run on
NNOSY	sonny
NNOUY	nouny
NNRUY	runny
NNSUY	sunny
NNTUY	tunny
NOOPR	porno
NOOPS	snoop
	spoon
NOOPT	pot on
NOORS	Orson
NOORT	Orton
	Troon
NOOST	snoot
NOOSW	swoon
NOOSZ	zoons
NOPSY	spy on
NOPTU	not up
	put on
	put-on
	ton-up
NOPUW	own up
NORST	snort
NORSW	sworn
NORTU	run to
NORTY	try on
	try-on
NOSSY	sonsy
NOSTU	snout□
NOSTY	stony
	Tonys
	Tyson
NOSUW	Suwon
NOSWY	snowy□
NOTWY	towny
NPRSU	spurn
NPRUU	run up
	run-up
NPSUU	sun-up
NRTUU	U-turn
NSTTU	stunt
NTTUY	nutty

O

OOOPP	Poopó
OOOPT	potoo
OOPPS	oppos
OOPRS	sopor
	spoor
OOPRT	troop
OOPRV	Provo
OOPST	stoop
OOPSW	swoop
OOPTT	potto
OOPZZ	Pozzo
OORRS	ro-ros
OORRT	rotor
OORST	roost
	roots□
	torso□
OOSTY	sooty
OOSUZ	ouzos
OOTTU	out to
OOWYZ	woozy
OPPPU	pop up
	pop-up
OPPPY	poppy
OPPSY	popsy
	soppy
OPPTU	pot up
	poupt
	top up
	up top
OPRRY	Pryor
OPRST	Prost
	sport
	strop
OPRSY	prosy
OPRTU	Prout
OPRXY	proxy
OPSST	spots
OPSTU	spout
	stoup
OPSTY	Topsy
	typos
OPSUY	soupy
OPSWY	Powys
OPTTU	put to
	putto
	tot up
OPTTY	potty
	typto
OPTUW	two-up
OPTUY	pouty
OPTZZ	ZZ Top
ORRSY	sorry
ORRTU	Truro
ORRTY	rorty
ORRWY	worry
ORSSU	sorus
ORSTU	roust
	torus
	Tours
ORSTW	worst
ORSTY	royst
	story
ORSUY	yours
ORTTU	trout
	tutor
OSSTY	tossy
OSTTU	stout

P

PPPUY	puppy
PPTUU	put up
PPUYY	yuppy
PRSSU	Spurs
PRSTU	spurt
PRSUU	usurp
PRSUY	pursy
	syrup
PSSUY	pussy
PTTUY	putty

R

RSSTU	truss
RSTTU	strut
	Sturt
	trust
RSTTY	tryst
RSTUW	wurst
RSTUY	rusty
RSUUY	usury
RTTUY	rutty

S

TTTUY	tutty

6 letters

A

AAABCH	Abacha
AAABCL	cabala
AAABDN	Abadan
AAABKL	kabala
AAABNN	Annaba
	banana
AAABNS	anabas
AAABRZ	bazaar
AAACCI	acacia
AAACDN	Canada
AAACJN	jacana
AAACLN	Nacala
AAACLP	alpaca
AAACMR	maraca
AAACNR	arcana
AAACPT	pataca
AAADMN	Amanda
AAADMR	armada
AAADNN	Danaan
AAADNP	panada
AAAEGP	agapae
AAAELZ	azalea
AAAFLL	fa la la
AAAFRT	Arafat
AAAGHT	Agatha
AAAGIL	Aglaia
AAAGLM	Malaga
AAAGNN	nagana
AAAGNP	pa'anga
AAAHNV	Havana
AAAHRS	Sahara
AAAILR	aralia
AAAIMS	Saimaa
AAAITX	ataxia
AAAJKT	jataka
AAAKKN	Kanaka
AAAKLM	kamala□
AAAKLS	Alaska
AAAKNR	Ankara
AAAKNT	katana
AAALLS	Salala
AAALMS	masala
	salaam
AAAMMN	Manama
AAAMNN	mañana
AAAMNP	panama□
AAAMNT	ataman
AAAMRS	Asmara
	samara□
AAAMRT	Tamara
AAAMRY	Aymara
AAANPR	Paraná
AAAPPY	papaya
AAAPTZ	Zapata
AAARTV	avatar
AAARTW	Tarawa
AAARUV	Avarua
AABBBO	baobab
AABBCY	abbacy
AABBDO	Abbado
AABBDS	abdabs
AABBLO	balboa□
AABCHS	casbah□
AABCIM	cambia
AABCIN	Bianca
AABCIR	arabic□
AABCLL	Bacall
AABCLZ	Balzac
AABCMT	tambac
AABCRS	scarab
AABCSU	abacus
AABDER	abrade
	Baader
AABDES	abased
AABDEU	aubade
AABDGO	dagoba
AABDIN	Ibadan
	indaba
AABDIR	abraid
AABDLL	ballad
AABDLM	lambda
AABDLN	Blanda
AABDNR	bandar
AABDOR	aboard
	abroad
AABDRT	tabard
AABDSS	badass
AABEGT	tea bag
AABELM	Amabel
AABELR	arable

AABELT	ablate
AABELZ	ablaze
AABEMO	amoeba
AABERZ	zareba
AABESS	Bassae
AABETU	bateau
AABFIN	Fabian
AABGGR	ragbag
AABGGS	gasbag
AABGIR	air bag
	airbag
AABGRT	grab at
	ratbag
AABHKS	kasbah❑
AABHLR	bharal
AABHMR	Brahma
AABHSW	Wabash
AABIKL	Baikal
AABIKR	Kariba
AABILL	labial
AABILM	Baalim
AABILU	abulia
AABIMR	Bairam
AABIMZ	Zambia
AABINN	banian
AABINS	Sabina
AABINZ	banzai
	Zainab
AABIST	abatis
AABJNX	banjax
AABKLT	balk at
AABKMO	Bamako
AABKRT	bark at
AABLMO	Malabo
AABLMS	balsam
AABLNY	Albany
AABLST	basalt
AABLTU	ablaut
AABMNR	barman
AABMNT	bantam
	batman
AABMRS	sambar
AABNNY	banyan
AABNUV	Vauban
AABNYZ	Zaynab
AABRSX	braxas
AACCDI	cicada
AACCEL	caecal
AACCHH	cha-cha
AACCHK	kaccha
AACCIL	cicala
AACCKK	ack-ack
AACCLO	cloaca
AACCNN	cancan
	can-can
AACCRT	caract
AACDEF	facade
	façade❑
AACDEI	acedia
AACDER	arcade
AACDHR	chadar
AACDLU	caudal
AACDMM	McAdam
AACDMP	madcap
AACDNR	canard
AACDOP	da capo
AACEFL	faecal
AACEFR	carafe
AACEHN	Aachen
AACEHP	apache❑
AACELP	palace
AACELS	Alsace
	scalae
AACEMR	camera
	macera
AACENN	Cannae
AACENP	canapé
AACENR	arcane
AACEPR	Parcae
AACEPS	sea cap
AACERS	caesar❑
AACETV	caveat
	vacate
AACFIL	facial
AACFIR	Africa
AACFIS	fascia
AACFNT	caftan
AACFRS	fracas
AACFTT	fat cat
AACGIR	agaric
	Garcia
AACGUY	Cayuga
AACHKR	chakra
	charka
AACHKW	kwacha
AACHLN	chalan
AACHMS	camash
AACHTT	attach
AACIIL	Alicia
AACIIR	Icaria
AACILM	calami
AACILP	apical
AACILR	Alaric
	racial
AACILS	Calais
AACILT	Altaic
AACIMN	caiman
	maniac
AACIMR	Marcia
AACINR	arnica
	crania
AACIOT	atocia
	coaita
AACIPT	capita
AACIRV	caviar
AACISS	Isaacs
AACJKL	jackal
AACKMY	Mackay
AACKRR	arrack
AACKTT	attack
AACLLO	Callao
AACLLS	Callas
AACLMU	macula
AACLNR	carnal
AACLNU	lacuna
AACLOR	Carola
AACLPR	carpal
AACLPS	PASCAL
	pascal❑
AACLRS	lascar
	rascal
	sacral
	scalar
AACLRW	acrawl
AACLSS	Casals
AACLSU	casual
	causal
AACLTU	actual
AACMNY	cayman
AACMOT	Tacoma
AACMRT	tarmac
AACMSS	camass
AACNNO	Ancona
AACNOR	ancora
AACNOV	Canova
AACNPR	Carnap
AACNPT	catnap
AACNQR	QARANC
AACNRY	canary
AACNSV	canvas
AACNTV	vacant
AACORR	Arcaro
AACPPY	papacy
AACPRS	Caspar
	scarpa
AACRTV	cravat
AACSST	Cassat
AADDIL	la-di-da
AADDOU	aoudad
AADEFR	afeard
AADEGM	damage
AADEGN	agenda
AADEGZ	agazed
AADEHN	Hadean
AADEHS	a shade
AADEMM	Madame
AADEMN	maenad
AADEMZ	amazed
AADENN	Deanna
AADENR	Andrea
AADENV	Nevada
AADEPR	parade❑
AADFIR	afraid
AADGIM	agamid
AADGIO	adagio
AADGIR	Agadir
	Gaidar
	gardai
AADGLO	Ladoga
AADGNP	Padang
AADGNU	Uganda
AADGOP	pagoda
AADGRS	Asgard
AADHIL	dahlia
AADHLM	Amdahl
AADHLR	Harald
AADHMR	dharma
AADHNN	Handan
AADHNT	at hand
AADHRZ	hazard
AADIJN	Adjani
AADILN	Dalian
AADILR	radial
AADILS	dalasi
AADIMN	Damian
AADINR	Adrian
	radian
AADINS	Naiads
AADINV	Davina
AADIST	stadia
AADKLN	Kandla
AADKMS	damask
AADKNU	Kaunda
AADKOT	Dakota
AADKPU	padauk
AADLLN	and all
AADLLS	Dallas
AADLMY	malady
AADLNO	anodal
AADLNR	Randal
AADLNS	sandal
AADLNU	landau
	Luanda
AADLNV	vandal❑
AADLOP	apodal
AADLOU	Douala
AADLRU	radula
AADLRY	Layard
AADMMM	Dammam
AADMMN	madman
AADMMS	madams
AADMMX	Mad Max
AADMNW	Wadman
AADMNY	man-day
AADMOR	Armado
AADMRS	madras❑
AADMRU	maraud
AADMYY	May Day
	mayday❑
AADNRS	Sandra
AADNRW	Rwanda
AADNTW	at dawn
	want ad
AADNUX	Xanadu
AADNYY	any day
AADPRS	Prasad
AADRTU	Artaud
	datura
AADRVW	vaward
AAEEGN	Aegean
AAEELP	paleae
AAEELT	taleae
AAEENS	Aeneas
AAEERT	aerate

AAEEST	at ease
AAEEYY	aye-aye
AAEFLM	aflame
AAEFLR	rafale
AAEFLV	favela
AAEFNR	fraena
AAEFNU	faunae
AAEGGR	garage
AAEGLM	agleam
AAEGLN	Angela
	anlage
	galena
AAEGLR	laager
AAEGMN	manage
AAEGMR	Gemara
	Megara
AAEGNP	Pangea
AAEGNR	Reagan
AAEGNS	Ganesa
AAEGNT	agnate
AAEGPT	gape at
AAEGRV	ravage
AAEGSV	savage
AAEGTU	gateau
	gâteau
AAEGTZ	gaze at
AAEHKT	takahe
AAEHLM	haemal
AAEHLT	Althea
AAEHMT	hamate
AAEHNT	aneath
	Anthea
AAEHNY	hyaena
AAEHRR	Harare
AAEHRT	Aretha
	Eartha
AAEHSY	Ayesha
AAEHTV	have at
AAEILM	Amelia
AAEILR	aerial
AAEILX	alexia❑
AAEINT	taenia
AAEIRS	araise
AAEIRV	Aveira
AAEITV	aviate
AAEKLN	alkane
AAEKLR	Kerala
AAEKMT	make at
AAEKNN	Anneka
AAEKNW	awaken
AAEKRT	karate
AAELLP	paella
	pallae
AAELMP	Pamela
AAELMT	tamale❑
AAELNN	anneal
AAELNT	lanate
AAELOR	areola
AAELPP	appeal
AAELPS	salpae
AAELPT	leap at
	palate
AAELRV	larvae
	Valera
AAELST	a steal
AAELSW	Walesa
AAELTV	valeta
AAEMMM	mammae
AAEMNP	apeman
AAEMNS	seaman❑
AAEMNT	amenta
AAEMNX	axeman
AAEMRT	ramate
AAEMRU	Rameau
AAEMSS	Seamas
AAENNZ	zenana
AAENOP	apnoea
AAENPV	pavane
AAENRT	Renata
AAENST	ansate
AAENSU	nausea❑
AAEPPR	appear
AAEPRS	pasear
AAEPTT	tapeta
AAERRR	arrear
AAERRT	errata
AAERST	sea rat
AAERSY	arayse
AAERTT	tear at
	terata
AAESTV	Avesta
	savate
AAFFIR	affair
	raffia
AAFFJN	Jaffna
AAFFNO	a fan of
AAFFRY	affray
AAFFST	Staffa
AAFGHN	Afghan
AAFHTW	fatwah
AAFILS	Faisal
AAFILV	Flavia
AAFIMT	Fatima
AAFINR	farina
AAFIRS	safari
AAFIST	fatsia
AAFITU	au fait
AAFKNT	kaftan
AAFLLL	fallal
AAFLNU	faunal
AAFLOT	afloat
AAFLSY	Faysal
AAFNSU	faunas
AAGGHI	Haggai
AAGGLO	galago
AAGGQU	quagga
AAGGRS	saggar
AAGGRT	ragtag
AAGHKN	kangha
	khanga
AAGHMR	Armagh
	Graham
AAGHNP	Pahang
AAGHNR	hangar
AAGHOT	Agatho
AAGHST	aghast
AAGILN	agnail
AAGILR	argali
	garial
AAGILV	gavial
AAGIMN	magian
AAGINN	angina
AAGINR	nagari
AAGINU	iguana
AAGINV	vagina
AAGINW	Gawain
AAGIRU	Auriga
AAGISS	Agassi
AAGJRS	gas jar
AAGJRU	jaguar
	Jaguar®
AAGKLU	Kaluga
AAGLLP	plagal
AAGLMM	malmag
AAGLMN	Malang
AAGLNO	Angola
AAGLNR	raglan❑
AAGLST	stalag
AAGLWY	Galway
AAGLXY	galaxy
AAGMMS	magmas
AAGMRW	Wagram
AAGMRY	Magyar
AAGNNO	Nagano
AAGNNW	An Wang
AAGNOR	angora❑
	Aragon
	organa
AAGNOY	Nagoya
AAGNRR	garran
AAGNRT	Granta
AAGNST	satang
AAGNSY	Sangay
AAGNTW	gnaw at
AAGNUY	Guyana
AAGOWY	go away
AAGPPR	grappa
AAGRSV	Vargas
AAGRSW	Swarga
AAGRVY	vagary
AAHHNN	Hannah
AAHHPT	aphtha
AAHHWW	haw-haw
	wah-wah
AAHIIS	Isaiah
AAHIIW	Hawaii
AAHILT	Thalia
AAHIMS	ahimsa
AAHINN	Hainan
AAHIPR	pariah
	raphia❑
AAHIRS	sharia
AAHIRV	vihara
AAHKKZ	Kazakh
AAHKLS	Khalsa
AAHLLL	hallal
AAHLLO	halloa
AAHLLW	wallah
AAHLRS	ashlar
AAHLRT	hartal
AAHMMN	hamman
AAHMNR	Harman
	Rahman
AAHMNS	shaman
AAHMNT	Namath
AAHMRS	ashram
	Marsha
AAHMRT	Martha
AAHMST	asthma
AAHNNS	Anshan
AAHNNT	Nathan
AAHNNY	Hannay
AAHNOV	Navaho
AAHNPT	Pathan
AAHNSS	Hassan
AAHPPR	paraph
AAHPRY	yarpha
AAHPTY	apathy
AAHRSS	harass
AAHRSU	Aarhus
AAHSSY	sashay
AAHTTT	at that
AAIJLM	Jamila
AAIJMN	in a jam
	Jamnia
AAIJNN	Janina
AAIKLL	alkali
AAIKLM	kalmia
AAIKLN	kalian
AAIKNN	Annika
AAIKNO	aikona
AAIKNR	Karina
AAIKOR	kia-ora
AAIKRU	uakari
AAIKSS	Saskia
AAILLP	pallia
AAILMN	animal
	lamina
	Malian
	manila❑
AAILMP	impala
AAILMS	salami
AAILMW	Malawi
AAILNN	Lianna
AAILNR	narial
AAILNS	Salian
	salina
AAILNT	Antlia
	Latina
AAILQU	Aquila
	qualia
AAILRT	atrial
	lariat
	rail at

AAILSS	assail
AAILSV	saliva
	salvia
AAILTT	Attila
AAILTV	Latvia
AAIMMS	miasma
AAIMMX	maxima
AAIMNR	airman
	Armani
	Marian
	marina□
AAIMNS	Samian
AAIMNV	vimana
AAIMRS	Aramis
AAIMRT	amrita
	tamari
AAINNR	Narnia
AAINNT	Tainan
AAINOR	Oriana
AAINOX	anoxia
AAINPP	papain
AAINPR	Parian
	piraña
AAINPT	patina
	taipan
AAINRR	Arrian
AAINRT	Tirana
AAINRU	anuria
	Urania
AAINTT	attain
AAINTV	avanti
AAINTW	Taiwan
AAINWY	in a way
AAIOTU	Aouita
AAIPRU	au pair
AAIPRY	apiary
AAIPZZ	piazza
AAIRST	arista
AAIRVY	aviary
AAIRWY	airway
AAJKRT	Rajkat
AAJMNP	jampan
AAJMNR	Jarman
AAJNNO	Joanna
AAJNNY	Nyanja
AAJNOV	Navajo
AAJNRT	Trajan
AAJNSY	Sanjay
AAKKLP	kalpak
AAKKMR	markka
AAKKOP	kakapo
AAKLMO	Akmola
AAKLMU	Makalu
AAKLNR	Lanark
AAKLOT	Lakota
AAKLSU	Lusaka
AAKLTT	talk at
AAKMNU	manuka
AAKMRU	kumara
AAKNOR	anorak
AAKNRT	nark at
AAKNSS	Kansas
AAKNST	askant
	tankas
AAKNSU	Kaunas
AAKNWZ	kwanza
AAKOPR	pakora
AAKPRS	Kaspar
AAKUYZ	yakuza
AALLMY	Mayall
AALLNY	anally
AALLPP	palpal
AALLRV	larval
AALMMM	mammal
AALMMS	Lammas
AALMNP	napalm
AALMNT	Altman
AALMNU	alumna
	manual
AALMNY	layman
AALMOP	Paloma
AALMOR	amoral
AALMPR	palmar
AALMPS	plasma
AALNNS	annals
AALNNU	annual
AALNOT	atonal
AALNOV	Avalon
AALNOZ	azonal
AALNPR	planar
AALNPT	platan
AALNRT	tarnal
AALNST	aslant
AALNSY	nyalas
AALOPY	payola
AALOSS	as also
AALOVW	avowal
AALPPU	papula
AALPRY	parlay
AALPSS	salpas
AALPTU	Laputa
AALPTY	play at
AALQWW	qawwal
AALRST	astral
	tarsal
AALRSY	salary
AALSSV	vassal
AALSTT	at last
AALSWY	always
AALTUV	valuta
AALWYY	waylay
AAMMRR	marram
AAMMTT	tam-tam
AAMNOT	to a man
AAMNOZ	amazon□
AAMNPS	sampan
AAMNPX	Paxman
AAMNRT	mantra
AAMNRY	Man Ray
AAMNST	Tasman
AAMNSU	Manaus
AAMNTU	mantua□
AAMNTV	Vatman
AAMOSS	samosa
AAMOST	somata
AAMOTY	Toyama
AAMPPS	pampas
AAMQSU	squama
AAMRSW	aswarm
AAMRSY	Ramsay
AAMRTU	trauma
AANNPS	sanpan
AANOPR	on a par
AANORX	Roxana
AANOST	sonata
AANOTT	anatto
AANPRY	panary
AANQST	QANTAS
	Qantas
AANQTU	quanta
AANRRT	arrant
AANRTT	rattan
	tantra□
	tartan
AANRTZ	Tarzan
AANRUV	Varuna
AANSSU	Nassau
AANSTV	savant
AANSTW	Tswana
AANSTZ	stanza
AANTUV	avaunt
AANWYY	anyway
AAORRU	aurora□
AAOTTW	Ottawa
AAPPWW	pawpaw
AAPQUW	Quapaw
AAPRST	satrap
	Sparta
AAPSSS	pass as
AAPZZZ	pazazz
AAQRSU	quasar
AARRTT	tartar□
AARSST	assart
AARSTT	strata
AARSTY	astray
AARSWW	Warsaw
AASTTY	stay at
AASTZZ	tazzas
ABBBEL	babble
ABBCEI	cabbie
ABBCER	Crabbe
ABBCOT	bobcat
ABBCRY	crabby
ABBCSY	scabby
ABBDEL	dabble
ABBDER	barbed
	rabbed
ABBDET	tabbed
ABBDEU	bedaub
ABBEGL	gabble
ABBEGR	gabber
ABBEIR	barbie□
	Barbie®
ABBEIS	babies
ABBEJL	jabble
ABBEJR	jabber
ABBELR	barbel
	rabble
ABBELU	bauble
ABBENR	nabber
ABBERR	barber□
ABBERT	barbet
	rabbet
ABBERY	yabber
ABBESS	abbess
ABBESY	abbeys
ABBFLY	flabby
ABBGIN	bin-bag
ABBGMU	bum bag
ABBGOR	gabbro
ABBGRY	grabby
ABBHSY	shabby
ABBILO	Bilbao
ABBIRS	rabbis
ABBIRT	rabbit□
ABBMOO	bamboo
ABBMOY	Bombay
ABBNOO	baboon
ABBORS	absorb
ABBOTT	Abbott
ABBRRU	Rubbra
ABBRTY	Bratby
ABCCLU	buccal
ABCDER	decarb
ABCDEU	abduce
ABCDIR	bardic
ABCDTU	abduct
ABCEEH	Achebe
ABCEEL	belace
ABCEEM	became
ABCEHL	bleach
ABCEHR	breach
ABCEHU	Hecuba
ABCEJT	abject
ABCEKR	backer
	reback
ABCELL	becall
ABCELM	becalm
ABCEMN	McBean
ABCEMR	camber
ABCEMX	excamb
ABCENO	beacon
ABCERR	bracer
ABCERS	braces
ABCFIR	fabric
ABCFKO	back of
ABCFNO	confab
ABCGIR	BAgric
ABCGIT	act big
	big cat
ABCGKO	go back
ABCHIT	Bichat
ABCHLN	blanch□
ABCHNR	branch

ABCHNU	Buchan
ABCHOR	broach
ABCHPU	hub-cap
ABCHRU	Baruch
ABCIIM	iambic
ABCIJO	Jacobi
ABCILT	Baltic
ABCINN	in banc
ABCISS	basics
ABCISU	Baucis
ABCISY	Biscay
ABCKPU	back up
	backup
	back-up
ABCKSU	Backus
ABCLLY	call by
ABCLMY	cymbal
ABCLNO	Blanco
ABCLOT	cobalt
ABCMOP	mob-cap
ABCMOT	combat
	tombac
ABCNOR	carbon
ABCORY	carboy
ABCSTU	subact
ABDDEE	beaded
ABDDEN	banded
ABDDEY	day bed
	daybed
ABDDHU	Buddha
ABDEEH	behead
ABDEEK	beaked
ABDEEL	beadle❑
ABDEEM	be made
ABDEES	debase
ABDEET	debate
ABDEEZ	bedaze
ABDEFL	fabled
ABDEGL	gabled
ABDEGO	bodega
ABDEGR	badger❑
ABDEHS	bedash
ABDEIR	braide
ABDEIS	biased
ABDEKR	debark
ABDELM	bedlam
ABDELO	doable
ABDELR	Balder
ABDELU	belaud
ABDENN	banned
ABDENP	bedpan
ABDENR	Brenda
ABDENU	Benaud
	Danube
ABDEPY	pay bed
ABDERR	barred
ABDERU	dauber
ABDERV	adverb
ABDESU	abused
ABDGNO	bandog
ABDGRY	drag by
ABDHNY	by hand
ABDHOY	hobday
ABDILR	bridal
	ribald
ABDINR	riband
ABDINT	bandit
ABDIRR	braird
	briard
ABDIRS	disbar
ABDLLY	baldly
ABDLRY	drably
ABDNOR	Brando
ABDNOT	not bad
ABDNOU	abound
ABDNRT	Brandt
ABDNRU	Dunbar
	Durban
ABDNRY	brandy
ABDOOT	too bad
ABDORS	adsorb
	boards
	broads
ABDORT	Bardot
ABDORY	by road
	byroad
ABDOYY	day-boy
ABDRSU	absurd
ABDRWY	dawbry
ABEEGH	bhagee
ABEEGL	beagle❑
ABEEGR	abrégé
	bargee
ABEEHV	behave
ABEEIN	beanie
ABEEKR	beaker
ABEEKT	betake
ABEELM	embale
ABEELN	baleen
	enable
ABEELT	let-a-be
ABEEMN	bemean
	bename
ABEEMR	beamer
ABEEMS	embase
ABEENT	beaten
ABEENU	Beaune
ABEEOR	aerobe
ABEEOU	Euboea
ABEERR	bearer
ABEERT	beater
	berate
	rebate
ABEERV	beaver
ABEERW	beware
ABEERY	Baeyer
ABEESY	be easy
ABEFFL	baffle
ABEFHL	behalf
ABEFLL	befall
ABEFLM	flambé
ABEFLR	fabler
ABEFLS	fables
ABEFPR	prefab
ABEFTY	tabefy
ABEGGR	beggar
ABEGHI	abeigh
ABEGLM	gamble
ABEGLN	bangle
	Bengal
ABEGLR	garble
ABEGLU	beluga
ABEGMU	Mugabe
ABEGNR	banger
ABEGNW	begnaw
ABEGOR	borage
ABEGOZ	gazebo
ABEGRZ	Zagreb
ABEHLM	hamble
ABEHLR	herbal
ABEHNO	hebona
ABEHRS	basher
ABEHRT	bather
	bertha❑
	breath
ABEIIT	tibiae
ABEILL	Belial
	labile
	liable
ABEILR	bailer
ABEILS	abseil
	Blaise
	Isabel
ABEILT	albeit
ABEILV	viable
ABEILW	bewail
ABEILY	bailey❑
ABEIMS	imbase
ABEINR	Braine
	Ribena®
ABEINS	Sabine
ABEINT	binate
ABEIOT	boatie
ABEIRR	Barrie
ABEIRS	braise
	rabies
ABEIRT	barite
ABEITT	beat it
ABEJMN	enjamb
ABEJOR	jerboa
ABEJRT	Béjart
ABEJRU	abjure
ABEJTU	jubate
ABEKLY	Blakey
	Kabyle
ABEKMN	embank
ABEKMR	embark
ABEKNR	banker
ABEKNU	Eubank
ABEKRR	barker❑
ABEKRY	bakery
ABEKST	basket
ABELLM	emball
ABELLT	ballet
ABELLU	bullae
ABELMM	embalm
ABELMR	marble
	ramble
ABELMW	wamble
ABELNU	nebula
	unable
ABELOR	boreal
ABELOT	lobate
	oblate
ABELPU	Puebla
ABELRR	barrel
ABELRT	Albert
ABELRV	verbal
ABELRW	warble
ABELRY	barely
	barley
	bleary
ABELRZ	blazer
ABELST	stable
ABELSU	suable
	usable
ABELSY	basely
ABELSZ	blazes
ABELTT	battel
	battle
	tablet
ABELWY	bye-law
ABEMNO	Beamon
	bemoan
ABEMNY	byname
ABEMOY	Abomey
ABEMRU	umbrae
ABEMSU	Mabuse
ABENNR	banner
ABENOR	bear on
ABENOS	beanos
ABENOT	Beaton
ABENRR	barren
ABENRS	Barnes
ABENRT	banter
	Barnet
ABENRU	unbare
	unbear
	urbane
ABENRY	barney❑
	near by
	nearby
	near-by
ABENRZ	brazen
ABENST	absent
	Besant
ABENSY	Naseby
ABENTT	batten
ABENTU	butane
ABENTZ	bezant
ABEORS	Boreas
ABEORT	boater
	borate
	rebato

ABEOSS	Sasebo
ABEOSY	sea boy
ABEPRU	bear up
	upbear
ABEPTU	beat up
	beat-up
	upbeat
ABEQRU	barque
	Braque
ABEQSU	basque□
ABERRT	barter
ABERST	baster
	breast
ABERSU	abuser
	bursae
ABERTT	batter
ABERTY	betray
ABERUU	bureau
ABERUY	Aubrey
ABERWY	bewray
ABESST	basset
	beasts
ABESSU	subsea
ABESSY	Bassey
ABESTT	at best
ABETTU	tubate
ABETTY	Beatty
ABETUY	beauty
ABFFIN	Baffin
ABFGLU	bagful
ABFGOS	bags of
ABFHLY	by half
ABFILU	fibula
ABFINR	Finbar
ABFIOT	a bit of
ABFISU	Fabius
ABFOTX	fox-bat
ABGGIO	Baggio
ABGGNO	go bang
ABGIKN	baking
ABGIKT	kitbag
ABGILO	go bail
ABGIMR	gambir
ABGIMT	gambit
ABGIMY	bigamy
ABGINO	bagnio
ABGINT	bating
ABGINU	Bangui
	Ubangi
ABGIOR	Borgia
ABGIOS	biogas
ABGLLO	global
ABGLMO	gambol
ABGLOR	brolga
ABGMNO	bogman
ABGMUY	may bug
ABGNNO	bang on
ABGNOR	Bangor
ABGNPU	bang up
ABGOOT	Bogotá
	Tobago
ABGORS	garbos
ABGORT	Bogart
ABGSTY	Gatsby
ABHIKL	kiblah
ABHIKT	bhakti
ABHIMR	mihrab
ABHINR	Harbin
ABHINS	banish
ABHIOP	phobia
ABHIST	habits
ABHLOP	Bhopal
ABHLSU	ablush
ABHMOT	Botham
ABHMRS	Brahms
ABHMRU	rhumba
ABHMSU	ambush
ABHNOS	bash on
ABHNTU	Bhutan
ABHORT	athrob
	Hobart
ABHOST	bathos
ABHOTX	hatbox
ABHOXY	haybox
ABHPTY	bypath
ABIILT	tibial
ABIIST	tibias
ABIJOW	Ojibwa
ABIJRU	jabiru
ABIKKU	kabuki
ABIKMO	akimbo
ABIKMR	imbark
ABIKRS	Barkis
ABILMU	labium
ABILNO	albino
	Albion
ABILNS	ablins
ABILNY	Libyan
ABILRT	tribal
ABILRU	burial
ABILRY	by rail
ABILRZ	Brazil
ABILSS	Blasis
ABIMNN	binman
ABIMNR	Birman
ABIMRU	barium
ABIMSU	iambus
ABIMTU	Batumi
ABINNU	Nubian
ABINOS	bonsai
ABINOT	obtain
ABINRS	brains
ABINRU	Rubina
ABINRY	binary
	brainy
ABINSU	Anubis
	unbias
ABIORS	isobar
ABIOST	Tobias
ABIRRS	briars
ABIRSU	Airbus®
ABIRTU	rubati
ABIRTZ	Tabriz
ABISSU	Bissau
ABISSW	Biswas
ABISTU	Ubasti
ABJJOO	jojoba
ABJKMO	jambok
ABJLNU	Banjul
ABJMOS	jambos
ABJNOS	banjos
ABJNPU	Punjab
ABKLNY	blanky
ABKLSY	Skylab
ABKMOT	tombak
ABKNNO	bank on
ABKNRU	unbark
ABKORT	Bartók
ABKRST	Bratsk
ABLLNO	ballon
	no ball
ABLLOT	ballot
ABLLOW	ballow
ABLLPU	ball up
ABLLTU	all but
ABLMOO	abloom
ABLMOP	aplomb
ABLMOU	bumalo
ABLMRU	brumal
	lumbar
	umbral
ABLMRY	marbly
ABLMSU	albums
ABLNOZ	blazon
ABLNSU	Nablus
ABLOOR	Barolo
ABLORU	labour
ABLOST	oblast
ABLOTT	Talbot
ABLPRU	burlap
ABLPYY	by-play
ABLRTU	brutal
ABLRWY	brawly
ABLSTY	stably
ABLSUY	suably
	usably
ABLSYY	lay-bys
ABLTTY	Tybalt
ABMMOS	mambos
ABMNTU	numbat
	Tubman
ABMOSS	sambos
ABMOSZ	zambos
ABMOTV	Tambov
ABMOTW	wombat
ABMRSU	sambur
	umbras
ABNNRY	branny
ABNNUY	Bunyan
ABNOQU	Banquo
ABNORY	barony
	baryon
ABNOTY	botany□
ABNRTU	turban
ABNRTY	Bantry
ABNRUU	auburn
ABNRWY	brawny
ABOOST	taboos
ABOOTU	Baotou
ABORRU	arbour
ABORRW	barrow□
ABORST	Strabo
ABORSV	Brasov
	bravos
ABORTU	rubato
ABORTW	towbar
ABORTY	Tor Bay
	Torbay
ABORUY	Yoruba
ABORVY	Bovary
ABOSSS	bassos
ABOSST	bastos
ABOUXY	boyaux
ABPRTU	abrupt
ABPSSY	bypass
	pass by
ABRRSU	bursar
ABRSSY	brassy
ABRSTU	aburst
ABRTTY	bratty
ABSUWY	subway
ACCDEE	accede
ACCDEN	Deccan
ACCDHI	Chadic
ACCDII	acidic
ACCDKO	Adcock
ACCDOR	accord
ACCEHN	chance
ACCEHT	cachet
ACCEIP	icecap
ACCEIT	accite
	acetic
ACCEKL	cackle
ACCELN	cancel
ACCELR	cercal
ACCELS	calces
ACCEMU	caecum
ACCENR	cancer□
ACCENT	accent
ACCEPT	accept
ACCERS	scarce
ACCERU	accrue
ACCESS	access
ACCESU	accuse
ACCGNO	cognac
ACCHIK	chiack
ACCHIN	a cinch
ACCHIR	Chirac
ACCHKY	chyack
ACCHLT	clatch
ACCHNO	concha
ACCHNR	cranch
ACCHNY	chancy
ACCHTY	catchy

ACCILO	calico
ACCILT	lactic
ACCIRR	ric-rac
ACCIRT	arctic□
ACCITT	tactic
ACCKLO	Alcock
ACCLNY	Clancy
ACCMOY	occamy
ACCORW	Cracow
ACCOSS	cascos
ACCOST	accost
ACCRUY	curacy
ACCSTU	cactus
ACCSUU	caucus
ACDDEE	decade
ACDDEI	caddie
ACDDEU	adduce
ACDDII	diacid
ACDDIN	candid
ACDDIS	caddis
ACDDIT	addict
ACDDTU	adduct
ACDEEF	deface
ACDEEN	decane
ACDEFF	decaff
ACDEFH	chafed
ACDEGR	cadger
	graced
ACDEHR	arched
ACDEHT	detach
ACDEIN	cnidae
ACDEIS	De Sica
ACDEIV	advice
ACDEKP	packed
ACDEKR	dacker
	racked
ACDEKS	sacked
ACDELL	called
ACDELN	candle
	Declan
ACDELR	Calder
	cradle
	credal
ACDELU	caudle
	Claude
ACDEMN	Camden
ACDEMP	decamp
ACDENN	canned
ACDENO	deacon□
ACDENR	dancer□
ACDENS	ascend
ACDENT	cadent
	decant
ACDEOT	coated
ACDEPR	redcap
	red-cap
ACDEPS	spaced
ACDERR	Redcar
ACDERS	sacred
	scared
ACDERT	redact
ACDERZ	crazed
ACDEST	casted
ACDHIS	Chasid
ACDHMR	drachm
ACDHOR	chador
ACDIJU	Judaic
ACDILL	callid
ACDILP	placid
ACDILY	acidly
ACDINO	anodic
ACDINR	Cardin
	rancid
ACDIOT	dacoit
ACDIOZ	zodiac□
ACDLNU	unclad
ACDLTY	dactyl
ACDMSU	Cadmus
ACDNNU	Duncan
ACDNOR	Conrad
	Dacron®
ACDNRU	Cunard
ACDNTU	UNCTAD
ACDORW	coward□
ACDORY	Corday
ACDRSY	darcys
ACEEFF	efface
ACEEFN	enface
ACEEFS	faeces
ACEEGI	ice age
ACEEGN	encage
ACEEHL	chelae
ACEEHT	Hecate
	thecae
ACEEIP	a piece
	apiece
ACEEIX	ice axe
ACEELL	cellae
ACEELN	elance
	enlace
ACEELR	cereal
ACEELV	cleave
ACEEMN	menace
ACEEMR	amerce
	raceme
ACEEMZ	eczema
ACEENS	encase
	séance
	Seneca
ACEENT	cetane
ACEENV	encave
ACEEOR	ocreae
ACEEPR	Pearce
ACEEPS	escape
ACEERR	career
ACEERS	crease
ACEERT	create
	écarté
ACEFFT	affect
ACEFHR	chafer
ACEFIL	facile
ACEFIN	fiancé
ACEFIR	fiacre
ACEFIS	facies
ACEFLS	falces
ACEFLY	calefy
ACEFNR	France
ACEFOR	care of
ACEFRS	Scarfe
ACEFSS	fasces
ACEFSU	fauces
ACEFTU	faucet
ACEGHN	change
ACEGHR	charge
ACEGHU	gauche
ACEGIL	Gaelic
ACEGIN	cage in
ACEGIR	Gracie
ACEGLN	cangle
	glance
ACEGLY	legacy
ACEGNU	uncage
ACEGNY	agency
	Cagney
ACEHIM	haemic
	heamic
ACEHIR	Archie
ACEHIS	chaise
ACEHKL	hackle
ACEHKR	hacker
ACEHLN	Chanel
ACEHLP	chapel
	pleach
ACEHLR	Rachel
ACEHLS	laches
ACEHLT	chalet
	thecal
ACEHMS	sachem
	schema
ACEHNR	enarch
ACEHNS	encash
ACEHNU	nuchae
ACEHNY	Chaney
ACEHOP	cheapo
	phocae
ACEHOR	chorea
	Horace
	ochrea
ACEHPR	eparch
	preach
ACEHPS	Pesach
ACEHRR	archer□
ACEHRS	chaser
	search
ACEHRT	Cather
ACEHRV	varech
ACEHSS	chassé
ACEHST	chaste
	sachet
	scathe
ACEHSW	cashew
ACEIJN	Janice
ACEILM	malice
ACEILN	Celina
ACEILP	plaice
	plicae
ACEILR	Claire
	éclair
ACEIMN	cinema
ACEIMO	Maceio
ACEIMT	micate
ACEINN	canine
	neanic
ACEINR	in care
	Racine
ACEINS	casein
	incase
ACEINT	anetic
ACEINV	cave in
	cave-in
	incave
ACEIPS	apices
	spicae
ACEIQU	caique
ACEIRR	Carrie
ACEIRS	caries
ACEISS	Cassie
ACEISV	vesica
ACEITV	active
ACEIVV	vivace
ACEJKT	jacket
ACEJLO	cajole
ACEJNU	jaunce
ACEKLM	mackle
ACEKLR	Clarke
ACEKLT	tackle
ACEKLY	lackey
ACEKNR	canker
ACEKPR	packer□
ACEKPT	packet
ACEKRR	racker
ACEKRS	screak
ACEKRT	racket
ACEKRY	creaky
ACEKST	casket
ACELLO	locale
ACELLR	caller
	cellar
	recall
ACELLT	callet
ACELLV	Cavell
ACELMR	Carmel
	Marcel
ACELMS	mescal
	scamel
ACELMY	Mycale
ACELNR	lancer
ACELNS	lances
ACELNT	cantle
	lancet□
ACELNU	launce
	unlace
ACELOR	Carole
	coaler

Words marked □ can also be spelled with an initial capital letter

	oracle❑
ACELOS	solace
ACELOT	locate
ACELOV	alcove
	coeval
ACELPR	carpel
	parcel
	placer
ACELPS	places
ACELPT	placet
ACELPU	lace-up
ACELQU	calque
	claque
ACELRR	carrel❑
ACELRS	sclera
ACELRT	cartel
	claret
	rectal
ACELRV	calver
	carvel
	claver
ACELSS	scales❑
ACELST	castle❑
ACELSU	caules
	clause
ACELSV	calves
	claves
ACELSX	calxes
ACELTT	cattle
ACELTU	cautel
ACELTY	acetyl
ACELWY	Cawley
ACELYY	clayey
ACEMNP	encamp
ACEMNR	Carmen
ACEMNU	acumen
ACEMNW	McEwan
ACEMOP	pomace
ACEMOS	cameos
ACEMOT	came to
	come at
ACEMPR	camper
ACEMRS	scream
ACEMRY	creamy
ACENNS	Cannes
ACENNU	nuance
ACENNY	Annecy
ACENOP	Capone
ACENOR	cornea
	earcon
ACENOS	oceans
ACENOT	at once
	octane
ACENPR	prance
ACENPU	uncape
ACENRS	casern
ACENRT	canter
	centra
	nectar
	recant
	trance
ACENRV	cavern
	craven
ACENRY	carney
ACENST	ascent
	secant
	stance
ACENSU	uncase
	usance
ACENTU	Canute
	uncate
ACEOPS	scopae
ACEOPT	Capote
	toecap
ACEOPW	cowpea
ACEORS	coarse
	rosace
ACEORX	coaxer
ACEOST	Coates
	costae
ACEOSW	sea cow
ACEOSY	O'Casey
ACEOTV	avocet
	octave
ACEPRR	carper
ACEPRS	capers
	escarp
	parsec
	scrape
	spacer
ACEPRT	carpet
ACEPST	aspect
ACEPTU	teacup
ACERRS	scarer
ACERRT	Carter
	crater❑
	tracer
ACERRU	curare
ACERRV	carver❑
ACERSS	caress
	crases
ACERST	caster
	recast
	traces
ACERSU	cesura
	saucer
ACERSY	creasy
ACERTU	acture
	curate
ACERTY	Tracey
ACESTY	Stacey
ACESUV	cauves
ACFFLS	sclaff
ACFGIN	facing
ACFILN	in calf
ACFILS	fiscal
ACFINT	in fact
ACFIOS	fiasco
ACFIPY	pacify
ACFKNR	Franck
ACFLNO	falcon
	flacon
ACFLOT	olfact
ACFLRU	fulcra
	furcal
ACFNOR	Franco
ACFORT	act for
	factor
ACFRRY	far cry
ACFRSS	scarfs
ACFRTY	crafty
ACGGNO	Coggan
ACGGRY	craggy
ACGHIN	aching
	Changi
ACGHNU	gaunch
ACGHOU	gaucho
ACGHTU	caught
ACGIKN	caking
ACGILL	Gallic
ACGILN	lacing
ACGILR	garlic
ACGILS	glacis
ACGILY	cagily
ACGIMO	ogamic
ACGINN	caning
ACGINR	caring
	racing
ACGINS	casing
ACGINT	acting
ACGINV	caving
ACGIRT	tragic
ACGNOR	garçon
ACGNOS	gascon
ACGORT	go-cart
ACGORU	cougar
ACGOSU	guacos
ACGTTU	catgut
ACHHNU	haunch
ACHHTT	thatch
ACHIIS	ischia
ACHIJK	hijack
ACHIKT	hack it
ACHILP	caliph
ACHILR	archil
ACHINR	Ranchi
ACHINS	cash in
	chains
	in cash
ACHINT	canthi
ACHIOR	choria
ACHIPT	haptic
ACHIQU	quaich
ACHIRS	chairs
	rachis
	Sirach
ACHIST	scaith
ACHKKU	chukka
ACHKLY	chalky
	hackly
ACHKOW	whacko
ACHKPU	hack up
ACHKTW	thwack
ACHLNO	lochan
ACHLNP	planch
ACHLNU	launch
	nuchal
ACHLOR	choral
ACHLRY	archly
ACHMOS	machos
ACHMSU	as much
	much as
	sumach
ACHNOR	anchor
	Charon
ACHNOS	nachos
ACHNPU	paunch
ACHNRU	raunch
ACHNST	snatch
	stanch
ACHOPS	phocas
ACHOPT	chop at
ACHOTU	a touch
ACHOUV	avouch
ACHPSU	cash up
ACHPTU	chat up
ACHPTY	patchy
ACHRST	starch
ACHSSU	as such
	such as
ACHSTU	cushat
ACHSTW	swatch
ACHTTY	chatty
ACIILS	silica
ACIILT	italic
ACIINN	niacin
ACIINV	incavi
ACIIRT	Tricia
ACIJKN	jack in
ACIJNS	Jancis
ACIKMR	karmic
ACIKNO	Konica®
ACIKNP	ink cap
	ink-cap
	pack in
ACIKNT	catkin
ACIKOP	paiock
ACIKPS	aspick
ACIKPT	pick at
ACILLL	Callil
ACILLN	call in
ACILLS	scilla
ACILMX	climax
ACILNO	Nicola
ACILNR	crinal
ACILNU	Alcuin
	Lucian
	uncial
ACILNV	Calvin
ACILOR	caroli
ACILOS	scolia
	social
ACILOT	coital
ACILOX	oxalic

ACILRT	rictal
ACILRU	Ulrica
	uracil
	Uralic
ACILRY	racily
ACILSV	Slavic
ACIMNO	manioc
	Monica
ACIMNR	cram in
ACIMNT	mantic
ACIMOO	oomiac
ACIMOS	mosaic□
ACIMOT	atomic
ACIMPS	scampi
ACIMPT	impact
ACIMRS	racism
ACIMRU	Murcia
ACIMST	mastic
ACIMTU	Actium
ACINNT	tannic
ACINNY	cyanin
ACINOP	Pacino
ACINOS	casino
ACINOT	action
	cation
ACINOX	anoxic
ACINPT	catnip
ACINRS	Cairns
ACINRU	uranic
ACINST	antics
ACINSU	acinus
ACINTT	intact
ACINUV	vicuna
	vicuña
ACIORS	scoria
ACIORT	aortic
ACIOSS	Cassio
ACIPRS	Prisca
ACIPRY	piracy
ACIPSS	spicas
ACIQTU	acquit
ACIRSS	crissa
ACIRST	racist
ACIRSU	Icarus
ACIRSY	Syriac
ACIRTU	urtica
ACISSS	cassis
ACISTT	static
ACITUY	acuity
ACITVY	cavity
ACJKOP	pajock
ACJKPU	jack up
ACJKSY	jacksy
ACKLNP	Planck
ACKLSS	slacks
ACKLSU	Lukacs
	Lukács
ACKNOR	Cranko
ACKNOT	tack on
ACKNPU	unpack
ACKNRY	cranky
ACKNSS	snacks
ACKNTU	untack
ACKNUZ	Zanuck
ACKORY	croaky
ACKPPU	pack up
ACKRST	tracks
ACKSST	stacks
ACLLMU	Callum
ACLLMY	calmly
ACLLNO	call on
	clonal
	on call
ACLLOR	collar
ACLLOS	Laclos
ACLLOW	callow
ACLLPU	call up
	call-up
ACLLSU	callus
	sulcal
ACLLSY	Scylla
ACLMMY	clammy
ACLMPU	clam up
ACLMPY	camply
ACLMTU	talcum
ACLNOP	clap on
ACLNUV	Vulcan
ACLNUY	lunacy
ACLOPU	copula
	cupola
ACLORR	corral
ACLORS	claros
ACLORT	carlot
ACLORU	ocular
ACLORW	Carlow
ACLOST	costal
ACLOSU	oscula
ACLOTT	Alcott
ACLRRU	crural
ACLRSW	scrawl
ACLSSY	classy
ACLSTU	scutal
ACMNNO	con man
ACMNOO	Monaco
ACMNOP	camp on
ACMNOR	Corman
	macron
ACMNOW	cowman
ACMOPS	Campos
ACMORS	macros
	Marcos
ACMORT	comart
ACMOSS	Cosmas
ACMOST	mascot
ACMOSU	mucosa
ACMOTT	tomcat
ACMPSU	campus
ACMRSU	Marcus
	sacrum
ACMRSW	scrawm
ACMSTU	muscat□
ACMSTY	McStay
ACMUUV	vacuum
ACNNNO	cannon□
ACNNOR	Conran
ACNNOT	cannot
	canton□
ACNNOY	canyon
ACNNRY	cranny
ACNOOR	corona
	racoon
ACNOPY	canopy
ACNORS	Carson
	narcos
ACNORT	cantor
	carton
	contra
	craton
ACNORU	cornua
ACNORY	crayon
ACNOSS	Casson
ACNOST	cantos
	cast on
	Octans
ACNOTT	octant□
ACNOTU	toucan
ACNPTU	puncta
ACNRST	crants
ACNSTU	cantus
	Tuscan
ACNSTY	scanty
ACOOSS	Osasco
ACOOTV	octavo
ACOPRT	captor
ACOPSS	Scopas
ACOPTT	Top Cat
ACOPTW	cowpat
ACORRT	carrot
	trocar
ACORSS	across
ACORST	actors
	castor□
	Castro
	co-star
ACORSU	Caruso
ACORTT	cottar
ACORTU	turaco
ACORTV	cavort
ACORVY	covary
ACOTTU	act out
ACPPRY	crappy
ACPRSS	scraps
ACPRSU	carpus
ACPSTU	cast up
	upcast
ACRRWY	War Cry
	war cry
	warcry
ACSTTY	scatty
ADDDEL	addled
	daddle
ADDDEP	padded
ADDDFY	Dafydd
ADDEEH	headed
ADDEEI	Aideed
ADDEEN	deaden
ADDEFL	faddle
ADDEGO	goaded
ADDEHJ	Jeddah
ADDEHN	handed
ADDEHS	dashed
	shaded
ADDEIL	daidle
	laddie
ADDEIM	diadem
ADDELN	dandle
	landed
ADDELO	loaded□
ADDELP	paddle
ADDELR	ladder
	raddle
ADDELS	saddle
ADDELW	dawdle
	waddle
ADDELY	deadly
ADDEMN	damned□
	demand
	madden
ADDEMR	madder
ADDENO	dead on
	dead-on
ADDENR	dander
	darned
ADDENS	sadden
	sanded
ADDENU	undead
ADDEOR	adored
	deodar
ADDEOS	dadoes
ADDERW	Edward
ADDGIN	adding
ADDGIO	gadoid
ADDGIP	giddap
ADDGMO	goddam
ADDGOR	Godard
ADDHIJ	Jiddah
ADDHOO	doodah
ADDHOS	Ashdod
ADDHSU	saddhu
ADDIMR	Madrid
ADDIMY	midday
ADDINS	add-ins
ADDIOS	addios
ADDLNO	Donald
ADDLOY	day-old
ADDMOO	Dodoma
ADDNOS	add-ons
ADDOOR	dorado
ADDORT	dotard
ADDOST	at odds
ADDRSY	Dryads
ADDSWY	swaddy
ADEEFL	leafed
ADEEFM	defame

ADEEFN	deafen
ADEEFR	feared
ADEEFT	defeat
ADEEGR	agreed
	dragée
ADEEHL	Hadlee
	healed
ADEEHP	heaped
ADEEHR	adhere
	header
ADEEHT	heated
ADEEIL	aedile
	Eliade
ADEEIM	mediae
ADEEIR	rediae
ADEEIT	ideate
ADEEJY	deejay
	dee-jay
ADEEKP	peaked
ADEELN	leaden
ADEELR	dealer
	leader
ADEELS	sealed
ADEELT	delate
	elated
	tele-ad
ADEELV	leaved
ADEEMN	demean
ADEEMO	oedema
ADEEMR	dear me
ADEENN	Deanne
ADEENR	earned
	endear
ADEENV	Evadne
ADEEPS	pesade
ADEEPT	pedate
ADEERR	reader
	reread
ADEERS	Red Sea
	seared
ADEERT	derate
ADEERV	evader
ADEEST	seated
	sedate
ADEFGG	fagged
ADEFGN	fag end
	fag-end
	fanged
ADEFGR	defrag
ADEFIL	afield
	failed
ADEFIN	fade in
	fade-in
ADEFIR	Frieda
ADEFIT	daftie
ADEFLR	Alfred
	flared
ADEFLU	feudal
ADEFLW	flawed
ADEFLY	deafly
ADEFMR	farmed
ADEFNR	far end
ADEFNU	undeaf
ADEFOR	fedora❑
ADEFPU	fade up
ADEFRY	defray
	frayed
ADEGGJ	jagged
ADEGGL	daggle
ADEGGR	dagger
	ragged
ADEGGT	gadget
ADEGIM	mid-age
ADEGLL	galled
ADEGLN	angled
	dangle
	Glenda
	lag-end
ADEGLO	age-old
	old age
ADEGLR	Gerald
ADEGLZ	glazed
ADEGNR	danger
	gander
	garden❑
ADEGNW	Gwenda
ADEGOR	O-grade
ADEGOS	dosage
	sea dog
ADEGOT	dotage
	togaed
ADEGRR	Gerard
	grader
	red rag
	regard
ADEGRZ	grazed
ADEGST	staged
ADEHIL	halide
ADEHIR	haired
	Hardie
ADEHLM	lamedh
ADEHLN	Handel
	handle
ADEHLR	hareld
	herald
ADEHLS	lashed
ADEHLT	daleth
	halted
ADEHLV	halved
ADEHMR	harmed
ADEHMS	shamed
ADEHNO	head-on
ADEHNP	daphne❑
ADEHNR	harden
ADEHNU	unhead
ADEHNY	Hayden
ADEHOR	oh dear!
ADEHPS	shaped
ADEHPT	heptad
ADEHPU	head up
ADEHRR	Erhard
ADEHRS	Dasher
	shared
ADEHRT	dearth
	hatred
	thread
ADEHSV	shaved
ADEHSW	washed
ADEHSY	Hyades
ADEHTW	thawed
ADEHTY	the day
ADEHYY	heyday
ADEIJL	jailed
ADEIKR	daiker
ADEILL	allied
ADEILM	Imelda
	mailed
	medial
ADEILN	Daniel
	deal in
	denial
	lead in
	lead-in
ADEILO	eidola
ADEILP	pleiad
ADEILR	derail
ADEILS	deasil
	ideals
	ladies
	sailed
ADEILT	detail
	dilate
	tailed
ADEILU	audile
ADEIMM	maimed
ADEIMN	Damien
	maiden
	median
	Medina
ADEIMR	admire
ADEINN	Dianne
	Nadine
ADEINP	pained
ADEINR	Darién
	Derain
	read in
ADEINS	Sendai
	Sinéad
ADEINT	detain
ADEINV	invade
ADEINW	Edwina
	wade in
ADEINZ	Zidane
ADEIOR	roadie
ADEIPR	diaper
	paired
	pardie
ADEIRR	raider
ADEIRS	raised
ADEIRT	tirade
ADEIRU	uredia
ADEIRV	varied
ADEIRY	Yardie
ADEISS	dassie
ADEISU	adieus
ADEISV	advise
	Davies
ADEITV	dative
ADEIUX	adieux
ADEJMM	jammed
ADEJRU	adjure
ADEJUV	déjà vu
ADEKLN	Kendal
ADEKLR	darkle
ADEKLW	wealk'd
ADEKMO	make do
	make-do
ADEKMR	demark
	marked
ADEKMS	masked
ADEKNR	darken
	narked
ADEKOS	soaked
ADEKOY	kayoed
ADEKPR	parked
ADEKPY	keypad
ADEKRS	Drake's
ADELLU	allude
ADELLV	devall
ADELLW	walled
ADELMR	dermal
	medlar
ADELMS	damsel
ADELMT	malted
ADELNO	lead on
ADELNR	darnel
	enlard
	Länder
ADELNT	dental
ADELNU	unlade
	unlead
ADELNW	Walden
	Weland
ADELOP	pedalo
ADELOR	loader
	ordeal
	reload
ADELOT	lead to
ADELPP	dapple
ADELPR	pedlar
ADELPS	lapsed
ADELPT	plated
ADELPU	uplead
ADELPW	dewlap
ADELPY	played
ADELRR	larder
ADELRU	Eluard
	Lauder
ADELRV	Dervla
ADELRY	dearly
ADELST	desalt
	salted
	slated
ADELSU	salued

Words marked ❑ can also be spelled with an initial capital letter

ADELUV	valued
ADELVV	valved
ADELZZ	dazzle
ADEMNN	manned
ADEMNO	daemon
ADEMNP	dampen
ADEMNR	randem
	remand
ADEMNS	amends
ADEMNT	tandem
ADEMNU	unmade
ADEMOP	pomade
ADEMOR	radome
ADEMOT	moated
ADEMOW	meadow
ADEMPR	damper
ADEMPU	made up
	made-up
ADEMRR	marred
ADEMRT	dreamt
ADEMRY	dreamy
ADEMSS	massed
ADEMST	masted
ADEMSU	amused
	medusa□
ADEMTT	matted
ADENNT	tanned
ADENNU	duenna
ADENOT	donate
ADENOY	day one
	one day
ADENPP	append
	napped
ADENPR	pander
	repand
ADENPT	pedant
	pentad
ADENPX	expand
ADENRR	darner
	Darren
	errand
ADENRS	sander
	snared
ADENRT	ardent
	endart
ADENRU	dauner
	Neruda
	unread
ADENRV	Varden
ADENRW	Andrew
	dawner
	wander
	warden
ADENRY	denary
ADENSU	sundae
ADENSW	new-sad
ADENTT	attend
ADENTU	undate
ADENTV	advent□
ADENTW	wanted
ADEOPP	peapod
ADEORR	adorer
ADEORS	Oreads
ADEOSS	Odessa
ADEOTT	to date
ADEOVW	avowed
ADEPPR	dapper
ADEPPS	sapped
ADEPRR	draper
ADEPRS	spader
	spared
	spread
ADEPRT	depart
	parted
	petard
ADEPRU	read up
ADEPRW	warped
ADEPTU	update
ADERRT	darter
	retard
	trader
ADERRW	drawer
	reward
	warder
ADERRY	dreary
ADERSS	Esdras
ADERSW	sawder
ADERTT	tetrad
ADERTV	advert
ADERUY	Audrey
ADERWX	wax-red
ADESTT	stated
ADESTU	sudate
ADESTW	wadset
	wasted
ADESTY	steady
ADESWY	swayed
ADETUV	veduta
ADFFOR	afford
ADFFOY	day off
ADFGIN	fading
ADFGLO	glad of
ADFGLY	gadfly
ADFHSU	shaduf
ADFILU	Faludi
ADFILY	ladify
ADFIRT	adrift
ADFIRY	Friday
ADFLTY	daftly
ADFLYY	ladyfy
ADFNOT	daft on
ADFORR	forrad
ADFRSW	dwarfs
ADGHIN	Gandhi
ADGHOR	go hard
ADGIIN	aiding
ADGILN	lading
	ligand
ADGINO	ganoid
ADGINQ	Daqing
ADGINR	daring
ADGINT	dating
ADGINY	Gdynia
ADGINZ	Danzig
ADGIRV	gravid
ADGKNS	Gdansk
ADGLLO	old lag
ADGLLY	gladly
ADGLOS	Galdós
ADGLOU	Dougal
ADGLOY	dayglo
ADGLSY	Gladys
ADGNOR	drag on
	dragon□
ADGNOT	Datong
ADGORR	Garrod
ADGORW	wardog
ADGOSS	gadsos
ADGPRU	drag up
ADGRTU	Utgard
ADHHIT	Hadith
ADHHIW	whidah
ADHHOU	houdah
ADHHOW	howdah
ADHHWY	whydah
ADHIKL	Khalid
ADHILO	haloid
ADHIMR	dirham
ADHINN	hand in
	in hand
ADHINS	Danish
ADHIOR	hairdo
ADHIPS	aphids
ADHIRS	radish
ADHIRY	hydria
	Riyadh
ADHISS	Hassid
ADHLMO	Oldham
ADHLOR	Harold
ADHLOT	old hat
	old-hat
ADHLRY	hardly
ADHMMU	Mahmud
ADHMRU	Durham
	Madhur
ADHNNO	hand on
	on hand
ADHNNU	unhand
ADHNOR	hadron
	Rhonda
ADHNOT	to hand
ADHNOU	houdan
ADHNOW	and how
ADHNOY	Haydon
ADHNSY	shandy□
ADHORW	Howard
ADHOSW	shadow
ADHPRU	hard up
	hard-up
	purdah
ADHPUU	uphaud
ADIIKO	aikido
ADIILL	illiad
ADIILN	inlaid
ADIILV	Divali
ADIILW	Diwali
ADIINN	Indian
ADIINR	Indira
ADIINV	avidin
ADIJNO	adjoin
ADIKKO	Kodiak
ADIKMN	Kidman
ADIKMO	mikado□
ADIKNP	kidnap
ADIKOT	dakoit
ADIKTT	diktat
ADILLP	pallid
ADILMS	dismal
ADILMY	milady
ADILNN	inland
ADILNR	aldrin□
ADILNS	island
ADILOS	Isolda
ADILOZ	Ozalid®
ADILPU	laid up
ADILRY	aridly
ADILRZ	lizard□
ADILSS	Aldiss
ADILST	distal
ADILVY	avidly
ADIMMT	dammit
ADIMNO	daimon
	domain
ADIMNS	disman
ADIMOT	diatom
ADIMRS	disarm
ADIMRU	radium
ADIMRY	myriad
ADIMSS	sadism
ADIMST	amidst
ADIMSY	dismay
ADIMWY	midway□
ADINOR	inroad
	ordain
ADINOS	Adonis
	danios
ADINPR	Pindar
ADINPU	unpaid
ADINRT	indart
ADINRW	Darwin
	draw in
	inward
ADINSU	unsaid
ADINSV	viands
ADINTY	dainty
ADIORS	radios
ADIORT	adroit
ADIOSU	audios
ADIOSZ	diazos
ADIPPU	paid-up
ADIPRS	rapids
ADIPSX	spadix
ADIRRY	air-dry
ADIRSS	Sardis

ADIRST	Astrid
ADIRSU	Darius
	radius
ADIRVZ	vizard
ADIRWY	rid way
ADIRWZ	wizard
ADISST	sadist
ADISYY	sayyid
ADJNOR	Jordan
ADJSTU	adjust
ADKLRY	darkly
ADKORV	Dvorák
ADLLOR	dollar
ADLLOS	sod all
ADLLUY	dually
ADLMNO	almond
	old man
ADLMOS	dolmas
ADLMPY	damply
ADLMRY	Myrdal
ADLMTU	Talmud
ADLMYY	my lady
ADLNOP	Poland
ADLNOR	Arnold
	Dralon®
	lardon
	Roland
	Ronald
ADLNOT	dalton❑
ADLNOU	unload
ADLNOY	any old
ADLNPU	upland
ADLOPU	upload
ADLORS	dorsal
ADLOSS	dossal
ADLOSW	Oswald
ADMNOR	random❑
	rodman
ADMNOS	damson
ADMNOW	woman'd
ADMNOY	dynamo
	Monday
ADMNUY	maundy
ADMORR	ramrod
ADMOSS	MOSSAD
ADNNOR	randon
ADNNOT	Danton
ADNNOW	dawn on
ADNOOR	nardoo
ADNOOW	wandoo
ADNOPR	pardon
	pardon?
ADNORS	Andros
ADNORU	around
ADNORV	Vardon
ADNORW	draw on
	onward
ADNOSW	Dawson
ADNOTT	dotant
ADNOTY	Dayton
ADNRST	strand
ADNRTU	draunt
	tundra
ADNRTY	try and
ADNRUW	undraw
ADNSTY	dynast
ADNSUY	Sunday
ADOOTW	Atwood
ADOOUV	vaudoo
ADOPRU	road up
ADOPRY	parody
ADOPSS	spados
ADOPTU	pad out
ADORRU	ardour
ADORRW	Darrow
ADORWY	ayword
ADOSTY	today's
ADOTUY	day out
ADPRUW	draw up
	upward
ADRSUW	usward
ADRTWY	tawdry
ADSTTU	at stud
AEEFFN	neaffe
AEEFLM	female
AEEFOV	foveae
AEEGGN	engage
	engagé
AEEGGR	reggae
AEEGKN	Keegan
AEEGLL	allege
AEEGLP	pelage
AEEGLR	regale
AEEGLS	Eagles
AEEGLT	eaglet
	legate
	teagle
AEEGLU	league
AEEGMM	gemmae
AEEGMN	manège
	ménage
AEEGMR	Graeme
	meagre
AEEGMT	gamete
	metage
AEEGNR	enrage
	genera
AEEGNT	negate
AEEGNV	avenge
	Geneva
AEEGNW	New Age
AEEGOP	apogee
AEEGOT	goatee
AEEGRS	grease❑
AEEGRV	greave
AEEGRY	Yeager
AEEGST	egesta
AEEGSW	sewage
AEEHHW	heehaw
AEEHLN	Helena
AEEHLR	healer
AEEHLS	Sheela
AEEHLW	awheel
AEEHLX	exhale
AEEHLY	Healey
AEEHMR	hareem
	hermae
AEEHNN	Heenan
AEEHNP	peahen
AEEHNS	Sheena
AEEHNT	Athene
	ethane
AEEHNV	heaven❑
AEEHNW	a wheen
AEEHNX	hexane
AEEHNY	Heaney
AEEHRR	hearer
	rehear
AEEHRS	hearse
AEEHRT	aether
	heater
	reheat
AEEHRV	heaver
AEEHRW	a'where
AEEHSV	sheave
AEEHTX	the axe
AEEIJN	Jeanie
AEEILM	mealie
AEEILN	Aileen
	Elaine
AEEILS	Elaeis
AEEILX	Alexei
AEEIMN	meanie
AEEIMS	semeia
AEEINS	ease in
AEEIPR	pereia
AEEJRT	jeer at
AEEKLN	alkene
AEEKLY	Leakey
AEEKMR	remake
	re-make
AEEKMZ	kameez
AEEKNW	weaken
AEEKNY	Yankee
AEEKPT	keep at
AEEKRT	retake
AEEKRU	eureka
AEELLL	allele
AEELMN	enamel
AEELMP	empale
AEELMS	measle
AEELNN	Leanne
AEELNP	alpeen
AEELNT	lateen
AEELNV	leaven
AEELOT	oleate
AEELPR	repeal
AEELPS	asleep
	elapse
	please
	sapele
AEELRS	leaser
	resale
	sealer
	Searle
AEELRT	relate
	Tralee
AEELRV	reveal
AEELRY	E-layer
AEELSS	eassel
AEELST	stelae
	teasel
AEELSV	leaves
	sleave
AEELSW	weasel
AEELSZ	sleaze
AEELTT	Attlee
AEELTU	eluate
AEELTV	veleta
AEELTW	atweel
AEELTZ	teazel
	teazle
AEELWY	leeway
AEEMNR	rename
AEEMNS	enemas
	enseam
AEEMNT	entame
AEEMOR	Moerae
AEEMPR	ampere
	Ampère
AEEMRS	seamer
AEEMSS	sesame
AEENNP	pennae
AEENNT	neaten
AEENNX	annexe
AEENPW	pawnee❑
AEENRR	earner
AEENRS	ensear
	Serena
AEENRT	entera
AEENRV	never a
AEENRW	weaner
AEENST	sateen
	senate❑
AEENSU	unease
AEENSV	even as
AEENUV	avenue
AEEOTT	to a tee
AEEPRR	reaper
AEEPRS	Parsee
	serape
AEEPRT	peer at
	repeat
AEEPST	peseta
AEEPSU	ease up
AEEPSW	pesewa
AEEPSX	apexes
AEEPVY	peavey
AEEQRU	quaere
AEEQTU	equate
AEERRS	eraser
	serrae
AEERRT	terrae
AEERRW	wearer

AEERST	Easter
	teaser
	Teresa
AEERSV	averse
	Varèse
AEERTY	eatery
AEERVW	weaver❑
AEESSW	seesaw
AEESTT	estate
AEFFGR	gaffer
AEFFIP	piaffe
AEFFKR	Kaffer
AEFFLR	raffle
AEFFLW	waffle
AEFFLY	yaffle
AEFFOT	eat off
AEFFRZ	zaffer
	zaffre
AEFGLN	flange
AEFGLR	reflag
AEFGOR	forage
AEFHLL	fellah
AEFHNT	fat hen
AEFHRS	afresh
AEFHRT	father❑
AEFILN	al fine
	finale
AEFILR	ferial
AEFIMN	famine
	infame
AEFINN	Fenian
AEFIRS	fraise
AEFIRT	fire at
AEFIST	fiesta
	Fiesta®
AEFITX	fixate
AEFJNT	fan-jet
AEFJRY	Freyja
AEFKLN	fankle
AEFKMO	make of
AEFKRY	freaky
AEFKSW	Fawkes
AEFLLN	fallen
AEFLMS	flames
AEFLNX	flaxen
AEFLOR	florae
	loafer
AEFLOT	foetal
	folate
	of late
AEFLOV	foveal
AEFLRS	flares
AEFLRT	falter
AEFLRU	earful
AEFLRY	flayer
	F-layer
AEFLST	festal
AEFLSY	safely
AEFLTY	fealty
	featly
AEFMNN	fenman
AEFMOR	femora
AEFMRR	farmer
	framer
AEFMRT	Fermat
AEFNOR	no fear
AEFNRW	fawner
AEFNST	fasten
AEFNSU	unsafe
AEFNTT	fatten
AEFORS	Faroes
AEFORY	for aye
AEFOSS	fossae
AEFPPR	frappé
AEFRRS	Fraser
	Frears
AEFRRT	frater
	rafter
AEFRRY	rarefy
AEFRRZ	Frazer
AEFRST	afters
	strafe
AEFRWY	wafery
AEFSTY	safety
AEGGGL	gaggle
AEGGHL	haggle
AEGGHN	Hegang
AEGGIM	Maggie
AEGGIN	ageing
AEGGLR	gargle
	raggle
AEGGLW	waggle
AEGGNR	ganger
	grange❑
AEGGNS	Ganges
AEGGNU	gangue
AEGGRS	sagger
AEGGRY	yagger
AEGGWW	gewgaw
AEGHIR	hegira❑
AEGHIS	geisha
AEGHIW	aweigh
AEGHMO	homage
	ohmage
AEGHNR	hanger
AEGHOR	gherao
AEGHRT	Gareth
	gather
AEGILN	Ealing
	genial
	Nägeli
AEGILO	goalie
AEGILS	ligase
	silage
AEGILT	gelati
	ligate
	taigle
AEGILZ	El Giza
AEGIMN	enigma
	gamine
AEGIMP	magpie
AEGIMR	maigre
	mirage
AEGIMS	ageism
AEGINR	regain
	Regina
AEGINS	easing
AEGINT	eating
AEGINU	guinea❑
AEGIPT	Piaget
AEGIRT	gaiter
AEGIRW	earwig
AEGIST	ageist
AEGISV	visage
AEGITY	gaiety
AEGJLN	jangle
AEGJLT	jet-lag
AEGJST	gas jet
AEGJTU	jugate
AEGKMO	make go
AEGKST	gasket
AEGLLT	gallet
AEGLLU	Gaulle
	ullage
AEGLLY	galley
AEGLMN	leg-man
	mangle
AEGLMR	mal gré
	malgré
AEGLMV	maglev
AEGLMY	gamely
	mygale
AEGLNO	Angelo
	engaol
AEGLNR	angler
	largen
	regnal
AEGLNT	tangle
AEGLNU	langue
AEGLNW	wangle
AEGLOR	Al Gore
	galore
	gaoler
AEGLOT	legato
AEGLOV	lovage
AEGLPU	a leg up
	plague
AEGLRR	larger
AEGLRS	Glaser
AEGLRV	gravel
AEGLRY	argyle
AEGLSY	sagely
AEGMMR	gramme
AEGMMS	smegma
AEGMNO	gnomae
AEGMNR	german❑
	manger
AEGMNT	magnet
AEGMNY	mangey
AEGMOR	romage
AEGMUZ	zeugma
AEGNNO	nonage
AEGNNP	Penang
AEGNNT	gannet
AEGNOR	onager
	orange❑
AEGNRR	garner❑
	ranger
AEGNRS	Sanger
AEGNRT	garnet
AEGNRU	ungear
AEGNRV	graven
AEGNRW	Wagner
AEGNSY	gansey
AEGOPS	sapego
AEGOPT	potage
AEGORT	Ortega
	Tagore
	toerag
AEGOSY	go easy
AEGOTU	outage
AEGOTW	towage
AEGOVY	voyage
AEGPRS	gasper
	sparge
AEGPRT	parget
AEGPRU	gear up
	Prague
AEGPRW	gawper
AEGRRT	garret
	garter
	grater
AEGRRU	arguer
AEGRRV	graver
AEGRRZ	grazer
AEGRST	stager
AEGRSV	graves❑
AEGRSY	greasy
AEGRTT	target
AEGRTU	rugate
	Tuareg
AEGRTY	gyrate
AEGRVY	Garvey
AEGSTY	stagey
AEGTTU	guttae
AEHHLT	health
AEHHPY	hyphae
AEHHRS	rehash
AEHHRT	hearth
AEHHST	sheath
AEHHTY	heathy
AEHHWY	Yahweh
AEHIJL	Elijah
AEHIJR	Hejira
AEHIKN	hankie
AEHILM	hiemal
AEHILN	inhale
AEHILS	Elisha
	sheila❑
AEHILT	halite
AEHILW	a while
AEHIMR	Hermia
AEHIMS	mashie
AEHIMT	Heimat

AEHINR	hernia
AEHINW	wahine
AEHITT	Hattie
AEHITV	have it
AEHKMS	samekh
AEHKNR	hanker
	harken
AEHKNS	shaken
AEHKRS	shaker
AEHKRW	hawker
AEHKSS	shakes
AEHLLR	Haller
AEHLLS	Hellas
AEHLLT	lethal
AEHLLY	Halley
AEHLMP	pelham□
AEHLMR	Harlem
	Mahler
AEHLMT	hamlet□
	Thelma
AEHLNO	enhalo
AEHLOR	Lahore
AEHLOS	haloes
AEHLOT	loathe
AEHLRS	ashler
AEHLRT	halter
	lather
	thaler
AEHLRW	whaler
AEHLSS	hassle
AEHLST	haslet
	Shelta
	Thales
AEHLSV	halves
AEHLSY	Ashley
AEHLTW	the Law
	wealth
AEHLTY	eathly
	hyetal
AEHLYY	Hayley
AEHMMR	hammer□
AEHMMY	mayhem
AEHMNN	Henman
AEHMNR	Arnhem
	Herman
AEHMNT	anthem
	hetman
AEHMNU	humane
AEHMNW	Newham
AEHMOS	hamose
AEHMOT	at home
	at-home
AEHMPR	hamper
AEHMRS	masher
AEHMRT	Mather
AEHMST	smeath
	Thames
AEHNOV	have on
AEHNPP	happen
AEHNRT	anther
	Tehran
	thenar
AEHNST	as then
	Athens
	hasten
AEHNSV	shaven
AEHNSW	whenas
AEHNTU	uneath
AEHNTV	haven't
AEHNTX	Xanthe
AEHORS	ashore
	hoarse
AEHORX	hoaxer
AEHOTV	have to
AEHPPU	heap up
AEHPRR	harper
AEHPRS	phrase
	seraph
	shaper
	Sharpe
	Sherpa
AEHPRT	tephra
	threap
AEHPSS	phases
AEHPST	spathe
AEHPSW	peshwa
AEHPTU	heat up
AEHPUV	have up
AEHRRS	rasher
	sharer
AEHRRT	rather
AEHRSS	shares
	shears
AEHRSV	shaver
AEHRSW	hawser
	washer
AEHRTT	hatter
	threat
AEHRTW	wreath
AEHRTY	earthy
	hearty
AEHRVY	Harvey
AEHSSY	says he
AEHSTV	Shevat
AEHSTW	swathe
AEIILM	Emilia
AEIILS	liaise
AEIIMS	Maisie
AEIIPT	Taipei
AEIJKR	Rijeka
AEIJLR	jailer
AEIJMM	Jemima
AEIJNN	Janine
AEIJNO	Joanie
AEIJNR	injera
AEIKLT	talkie
AEIKMN	kinema
AEIKMT	make it
AEIKMY	Miyake
AEIKNR	Kieran
	rake in
AEIKNT	intake
	kentia
	take in
AEIKPR	parkie
AEIKRR	kerria
AEIKRS	kaiser□
AEIKTT	take it
AEILLN	lineal
AEILLS	allies
AEILMN	menial
AEILMP	impale
AEILMR	Mailer
AEILMS	mesial
	samiel
AEILNN	Lianne
AEILNP	alpine
	Nepali
AEILNR	linear
	nailer
AEILNS	saline
	Selina
AEILNT	entail
AEILNV	alevin
	valine
	venial
AEILNX	xenial
AEILOS	Eloisa
AEILPT	Pilate
AEILRR	rerail
AEILRS	Israel
	sailer□
	serial
AEILRT	retail
	retial
AEILRU	Auriel
	Laurie
AEILRV	Averil
	Elvira
AEILRW	Lawrie
	wailer
AEILSS	Alessi
	eassil
	lassie□
AEILSV	Aviles
	Leavis
	valise
AEILSX	Alexis
AEILSY	easily
AEIMNN	in name
AEIMNO	anomie
AEIMNR	marine
	remain
AEIMNS	Amiens
AEIMNT	inmate
AEIMNX	Maxine
	Xiamen
AEIMNY	Niamey
AEIMPV	impave
AEIMPY	pyemia
AEIMRS	armies
AEIMRW	Weimar
AEIMTT	Mattie
AEINNP	pinnae
AEINNR	Nairne
	narine
AEINNS	insane
	sienna
AEINNT	innate
AEINNV	Vienna
AEINPR	Napier
	rapine
AEINPT	Pétain
	pineta
AEINRS	arsine
	sarnie
AEINRT	retain
	retina
	tear in
AEINRV	ravine
AEINSS	sanies
AEINST	tisane
AEINSV	navies
	savine
AEINTU	auntie□
	Uniate
AEINTV	native
AEIOPT	opiate
AEIOPZ	epizoa
AEIPPT	Petipa
AEIPRR	rapier
	repair
AEIPRS	aspire
	praise
	spirea
AEIPRT	pirate
	pteria
AEIRRS	raiser
	sierra□
AEIRRV	arrive
	Rivera
AEIRST	satire
	striae
AEIRTT	attire
AEIRTW	waiter
AEIRVW	waiver
AEIRVX	Xavier
AEISST	siesta
AEISSU	Aussie
AEISSX	axises
AEISSZ	assize
AEISTX	taxies
AEISVW	view as
AEITTT	tattie
AEITTV	vittae
AEJMRT	ramjet
AEJMST	jetsam
AEJNNO	Joanne
AEJNNS	Jansen
AEJNOT	Taejon
AEJNST	sejant
AEJNSU	jaunse
AEJNUU	Juneau
AEJPRS	jasper□

AEJQSU	Jaques
AEJRUZ	Juárez
AEKKNR	kraken
AEKLMN	Kelman
AEKLNO	Ankole
AEKLNR	rankle
AEKLNT	anklet
AEKLNW	Wankel
AEKLNY	alkyne
AEKLRS	Lasker
AEKLRT	talker
AEKLRW	walker□
AEKLSS	Kassel
AEKLWY	weakly
AEKMNO	make on
AEKMNU	unmake
AEKMNY	key man
AEKMPU	make up
	make-up
AEKMRR	marker
	remark
AEKMRS	masker
AEKMRT	market
AEKNOT	Keaton
	take on
AEKNRR	ranker
AEKNRT	tanker
AEKNRU	unrake
AEKNRW	Newark
AEKNSY	sneaky
AEKOPT	Topeka
AEKORS	arkose
	soaker
AEKOSY	kayoes
AEKOTT	take to
AEKOTW	wake to
AEKPRR	Parker
AEKPRU	rake up
AEKPTU	take up
	take-up
	uptake
AEKPUW	wake up
AEKQRU	Quaker
AEKQSU	squeak
AEKRRT	karter
AEKRRY	rakery
AEKRST	skater
	strake
	streak
AEKRSY	karsey
AEKSST	stakes
AEKWYY	keyway
AELLLY	leally
AELLMT	mallet
AELLMY	lamely
AELLNO	all one
AELLNW	enwall
AELLNY	Alleyn
	leanly
AELLPT	L-plate
	pallet
AELLPY	palely
AELLRU	allure
	laurel□
AELLRW	Waller
AELLRY	really
AELLST	all set
	Stella
AELLSW	as well
AELLSY	alleys
AELLTW	wallet
AELLTY	lately
	yell at
AELLVY	valley
AELMMS	lemmas
AELMNS	Anselm
	Le Mans
	lemans
AELMNT	lament
	mantel
	mantle□
	mental
AELMNY	Manley
	meanly
	namely
AELMOR	morale
AELMOS	Salome
AELMPR	Marple
	palmer□
AELMPS	sample
AELMRS	realms
AELMRT	armlet
	martel
AELMRV	marvel
AELMRY	Marley
AELMSU	Samuel
AELMSY	measly
AELMTU	amulet
AELMTY	tamely
AELNNO	lean on
AELNOS	on sale
	Sloane
AELNOT	etalon
	lean-to
AELNPP	pen-pal
AELNPR	planer
AELNPS	Naples
AELNPT	planet
	platen
AELNRT	antler
	rental
AELNRU	Lauren
	neural
	unreal
AELNRV	vernal
AELNRY	nearly
AELNSU	unseal
AELNSY	sanely
AELNTT	latent
	latten
	talent
AELNTU	eluant
	lunate
AELNTV	levant□
AELNTY	neatly
AELOPP	Aleppo
AELOPR	parole
AELOPS	aslope
	El Paso
AELOPT	pelota
AELORS	realos
AELOST	osteal
AELOSU	Aeolus
AELOSV	loaves
AELOSW	leasow
AELOTZ	zealot
AELPPR	lapper
	rappel
AELPPS	apples
	sapple
AELPPT	lappet
AELPPU	leap up
	papule
AELPQU	plaque
AELPRS	pearls
AELPRT	palter
	plater
AELPRU	pleura
AELPRW	prawle
AELPRY	parley
	pearly
	player□
	replay
AELPST	pastel
	plates
	staple
AELPTU	Petula
AELQRU	Raquel
AELQSU	squeal
AELQUY	Quayle
AELRRY	rarely
	rearly
AELRST	stelar
AELRSV	salver
	serval
	slaver
AELRSY	slayer
AELRTT	Lartet
	latter
	rattle□
	tatler
AELRTV	travel
AELRTW	Walter
AELRTY	elytra
	lyrate
AELRUV	valuer
AELRVY	Valéry
AELRWX	wraxle
AELRWY	lawyer
AELRYY	yearly
AELRZZ	razzle
AELSST	tassel
AELSSV	selvas
AELSTT	latest
AELSTU	salute
AELSTV	vestal
AELSUV	avulse
	values
AELSUX	sexual
AELSVY	sylvae
AELSYZ	sleazy
AELTTT	tattle
AELTTW	wattle
AELTUX	luxate
AELUUV	uvulae
AEMMMR	mammer
AEMMMT	mammet
AEMMNR	merman
AEMMNT	met man
AEMMRR	rammer
AEMMRY	yammer
AEMMST	stemma
AEMMSU	summae
AEMNNO	Eamonn
	one-man
AEMNNP	penman
AEMNNR	manner
AEMNNW	new man
	Newman
AEMNOR	moaner
	monera
AEMNOT	omenta
AEMNOU	Nouméa
AEMNOY	yeoman
AEMNPU	pneuma
AEMNQU	manqué
AEMNRR	Marner
AEMNRT	marten
AEMNRU	Amun-Re
	manure
AEMNST	stamen
AEMNSU	unseam
AEMNSY	yes-man
AEMNTU	untame
	unteam
AEMOPT	a tempo
AEMOPZ	apozem
AEMORR	remora
	roamer
AEMORS	ramose
AEMORT	omertà
AEMORU	Moreau
AEMORW	womera
AEMOSV	vamose
AEMPPR	mapper
	pamper
AEMPRR	ramper
AEMPRT	tamper
AEMPRV	revamp
AEMPTU	team up
AEMQRU	marque
AEMQSU	masque
AEMRRV	marver
AEMRST	master

	stream
AEMRSU	Maseru
	Mauser
AEMRSY	smeary
AEMRTT	matter
AEMRTU	mature
AEMRUU	Uemura
AEMSSS	masses
AEMSSU	assume
	Seamus
	Seumas
AEMSTU	meatus
AEMSTY	steamy
AEMSYZ	zymase
AEMTTU	mutate
AENNNO	nonane
AENNNS	Nansen
AENNOV	novena
AENNOY	any one
	anyone
AENNRT	tanner
AENNRV	Vänern
AENNST	Nantes
AENNTT	tenant
AENOPS	peason
AENOPW	weapon
AENOPY	paeony
AENORS	reason
	Señora
AENORT	ornate
AENORV	Verona
AENORW	Rowena
	wear on
AENORX	Roxane
AENOSS	season
AENOTT	notate
AENOWY	one-way
AENPPR	parpen
AENPRT	enrapt
	entrap
	parent
	trepan
AENPRW	enwrap
	pawner
AENPRY	napery
AENPRZ	panzer
AENPTT	patent
	patten□
AENPTU	peanut
AENPTX	Pentax®
AENPTY	net pay
AENRRS	snarer
AENRRT	errant
	ranter
	Ratner
AENRRW	warner□
	warren□
AENRSS	Nasser
	sarsen
AENRST	astern
AENRSW	answer
AENRTT	natter
	ratten
AENRTU	nature□
AENRTV	tavern
AENRTW	wanter
AENRUW	unware
AENSST	assent
AENSTU	Austen
	unseat
AENSTZ	stanze
AENSUV	naevus
AENSUY	uneasy
AENTTT	attent
AENTTU	attune
	nutate
	tauten
AENTTX	extant
AENTWY	Tawney
AEOPPS	appose
AEOPQU	opaque
AEOPRT	protea
AEOPRU	Europa
AEOPSS	pose as
AEOPTT	teapot
AEORRR	roarer
AEORRU	Aurore
AEORSU	arouse
	Roseau
AEORSZ	Azores
AEORTT	rotate
	to-tear
AEORVW	avower
AEORZZ	Arezzo
AEOSTW	awetos
AEOTTU	eat out
AEOTVW	wave to
AEPPRR	rapper
AEPPRS	papers
	sapper□
AEPPRU	pauper
AEPPRW	wapper
AEPPRY	papery
	prepay
	yapper
AEPPRZ	zapper
AEPPTT	tappet
AEPPTU	pupate
AEPRRS	parser
AEPRRU	uprear
AEPRRW	warper
AEPRRY	prayer
AEPRSS	repass
	sparse
AEPRST	repast
	trapes
AEPRSU	pauser
AEPRTT	patter
AEPRTU	tear up
	uprate
	uptear
AEPRTX	pre-tax
AEPRUV	rave-up
AEPSST	stapes
AEPSUV	save up
AEQRSU	square
AEQRTU	quarte
AEQRUV	quaver
AEQSUY	queasy
AERRSS	serras
AERRST	arrest
	raster
	Sartre
AERRTT	ratter
AERRTY	artery
AERRWY	warrey
AERSST	assert
AERSSU	assure
AERSSW	wrasse
AERSSY	Sayers
AERSTT	at rest
	stater
	taster
AERSTU	Atreus
	Seurat
AERSTV	starve
AERSTW	waster
	Waters
AERSTX	extras
AERSTY	estray
	stayer
AERSTZ	ersatz
AERSUU	aureus
AERSVW	swarve
AERSVY	Savery
AERSWY	sawyer□
AERTTT	tatter
AERTTY	treaty
	yatter
AERTUU	auteur
AERTWY	watery
AESSSS	assess
AESSST	assets
AESSTU	sautés
AESSTV	staves
	vestas
AESSUV	save us
AESTTT	attest
AESTTU	astute
	statue
AESTWY	sweaty
AESTYY	yeasty
AESVVY	savvey
AESWYZ	Swayze
AFFFOR	far-off
AFFGUW	guffaw
AFFILP	pilaff
AFFIMO	aim off
AFFIMR	affirm
AFFINR	Fafnir
AFFIRT	tariff
AFFLNY	naffly
AFFLOY	lay off
	lay-off
	Offaly
AFFOPT	off pat
AFFOPY	pay off
	pay-off
AFFRST	straff
AFFSST	Staffs
AFGGOT	faggot
AFGIKN	faking
AFGILN	Fingal
AFGINO	Fangio
AFGISY	gasify
AFGLNO	flagon
AFGLNU	fungal
AFGLRU	frugal
AFGNOS	fangos
AFGOST	go fast
AFGOTU	fag out
	fugato
AFGRUY	argufy
AFHIKL	khalif
AFHIMS	famish
AFHIOS	oafish
AFHIRS	Sharif
AFHITW	what if
AFHLOO	loofah
AFHLSY	flashy
	fly ash
AFHMOT	fathom
AFHOTW	what of
AFHRSW	wharfs
AFIILL	filial
AFIILN	fail in
	finial
AFIINX	in a fix
AFILLN	fall in
AFILMY	family
AFILNO	in foal
AFILNV	flavin
AFILNY	fainly
	Finlay
AFILOR	foliar
AFILRY	fairly
AFILRZ	frazil
AFILSY	salify
AFIMNR	firman
AFIMNY	infamy
AFIMOR	aim for
AFIMRY	ramify
AFIMSS	massif
AFINNN	finnan
AFINNO	fanion
AFINNT	Fintan
	infant
AFINRU	unfair
AFINSY	sanify
AFINYZ	Nazify
AFIRRY	friary
AFIRTY	ratify
AFIRUY	aurify
AFKLOT	talk of

AFKLSU	Faulks
AFKORS	ask for
AFKORU	Farouk
AFKOUX	Koufax
AFLLNO	fall on
	Fallon
	onfall
AFLLOR	all for
	floral
	for all
AFLLOT	fall to
AFLLOW	fallow
AFLLTY	flatly
AFLLUW	lawful
AFLMNU	manful
AFLMOR	formal
AFLMRU	armful
	fulmar
AFLMYY	mayfly
AFLNOT	fontal
AFLNPU	panful
AFLNRU	Ranulf
AFLNTU	flaunt
AFLOOT	a lot of
AFLORS	floras
AFLOST	floats
AFLOTY	floaty
AFLPPY	flappy
AFLRTU	artful
AFLSTU	flatus
AFLSWY	sawfly
AFLTUY	faulty
AFLWYY	flyway
AFMNOR	Forman
AFMOOS	samfoo
AFMORS	as from
AFMORT	format
AFMOSU	famous
AFNNOT	non-fat
AFNNOW	fawn on
AFNORT	afront
	not far
AFNORW	warn of
AFNOTU	fan out
AFNSUU	Faunus
AFOOPX	a pox of
AFOORT	footra
AFOPRT	part of
AFOPRY	pay for
AFORRW	farrow□
AFORTU	far out
	far-out
	foutra
AFORUV	favour
AFORWY	wary of
AFOSST	fatsos
AFRSTU	frusta
AGGHIS	haggis
AGGHNO	go hang
AGGHOR	Hoggar
AGGHSY	shaggy
AGGILO	loggia
AGGIMN	gaming
AGGINP	gaping
AGGINR	raging
AGGINT	gating
AGGINZ	gazing
AGGIWW	wigwag
AGGIZZ	zigzag
AGGKNY	knaggy
AGGLLO	Glagol
AGGLNY	gangly
AGGLWY	waggly
AGGMOT	maggot
AGGNOW	waggon
AGGNSY	snaggy
AGGQUY	quaggy
AGHILT	alight
AGHINN	hang in
AGHINT	anight
	a'thing
AGHINV	having
AGHIRS	garish
AGHIRT	aright
	graith
AGHKRU	Gurkha
AGHLOS	galosh
AGHLSU	laughs
AGHLSY	gashly
AGHNNO	hang on
AGHNPU	hang up
	hang-up
AGHNRT	Granth
AGHNTU	naught
AGHNUY	gunyah
AGHOQU	quahog
AGHTTU	taught
AGHTUW	waught
AGIIJN	gaijin
AGIIKL	Kigali
AGIILN	ailing
	nilgai
AGIINR	airing
AGIJNP	japing
AGIJSW	jigsaw
	jig-saw
AGIKLN	Glinka
AGIKMN	making
AGIKNT	taking
AGIKNW	waking
AGILMN	Gilman
	malign
AGILMO	glioma
AGILMP	magilp
AGILNO	Ginola
AGILNP	paling
AGILNS	signal
AGILNU	nilgau
AGILNY	gainly
AGILNZ	lazing
AGILOR	gloria□
AGILOS	Galois
	golias
AGILOT	galiot
AGILOV	ogival
AGILRS	slairg
AGILRU	arguli
AGIMNN	naming
AGIMNR	margin
AGIMNT	mating
AGIMNW	Wigman
AGIMOS	amigos
	imagos
AGIMST	stigma
AGIMWW	wigwam
AGINNN	Anning
AGINNO	gain on
AGINNW	awning
	waning
AGINOS	ngaios
	sagoin
	Saigon
AGINPR	paring
AGINPV	paving
AGINPY	paying
AGINRR	raring
AGINRS	grains
	in rags
AGINRT	gratin
	rating
AGINRU	airgun
AGINRV	raving
AGINRY	grainy
AGINRZ	razing
AGINSS	assign
AGINST	gainst
AGINSU	saguin
AGINSV	saving
AGINSY	saying
AGINTX	taxing
AGINVW	waving
AGIORV	virago
AGIOTU	agouti
AGIRST	gratis
	striga
AGIRTU	guitar
	Ugarit
AGJLMO	log-jam
AGJLNY	jangly
AGJNOR	jargon
AGJRTU	Gujrat
AGKLNO	kalong
AGKLOT	kgotla
AGKNOU	nogaku
AGKNRU	Kurgan
AGKORT	go-kart
AGLLNO	gallon
AGLLOP	gallop
AGLLOR	gollar
AGLLOW	gallow
AGLLPU	Gallup
AGLLSU	gallus
AGLNOO	lagoon
AGLNOS	Anglos
	slogan
AGLNOT	Galton
AGLNOU	lanugo
	Lugano
AGLNRU	langur
AGLNRY	gnarly
AGLNSY	slangy
AGLNTY	tangly
AGLNUU	ungual
	ungula
AGLOOT	galoot
AGLOOW	go AWOL
AGLOPR	Polgar
AGLORS	largos
AGLOST	slog at
AGLRUV	vulgar
AGLRUY	glaury
AGLSSY	glassy
AGMMNO	gammon
AGMMNU	magnum
AGMMRY	Grammy
AGMNNU	gunman
AGMNOR	Morgan
AGMNSU	Magnus
AGMOOY	oogamy
AGMORS	orgasm
AGMORV	vagrom
AGMPUZ	gazump
AGMRTU	targum□
AGNNOY	Yangon
AGNNRY	granny
AGNOOT	go on at
AGNOQU	quango
AGNORR	garron
AGNORS	organs
	Sargon
	sarong
AGNORY	Gaynor
AGNOST	Sontag
	tangos
AGNOSU	guanos
AGNOTU	nougat
AGNPRU	Nagpur
AGNRTY	gantry
AGNTUY	Tanguy
AGOORT	agorot
AGOPST	go past
AGORRT	garrot
AGORST	groats
AGORTU	ragout
AGORWY	go awry
AGOSTU	outgas
AGRSSY	grassy
AGRSTU	tragus
AGRSUY	sugary
AGRUUY	augury
AGSTUU	august□
AHHHOO	hoo-hah
AHHIMS	Hamish
AHHKOO	hookah

AHHLPY	hyphal
AHHOOW	wo ha ho
AHHORT	Hathor
AHHORW	Howrah
AHHOTW	what ho
AHHRRU	hurrah
AHHRST	thrash
AHIILT	lithia
AHIINT	tahini
AHIITT	Tahiti
AHIJNN	Jinnah
AHIKNS	naskhi
AHIKOW	kowhai
AHIKRS	rakish
AHIKST	Shakti
	skaith
AHILLT	thalli
AHILMU	hamuli
AHILNR	rhinal
AHILPS	palish
AHILRY	Hilary
AHILST	latish
AHILSV	lavish
AHILYZ	hazily
AHIMNS	Mishna
AHIMNT	hit man
	hit-man
AHIMOR	mohair
AHIMPS	mishap
AHIMRS	Shamir
AHINPT	hatpin
AHINRS	Sirhan
AHINRU	unhair
AHINSU	Husain
AHINSV	vanish
AHINTT	hint at
	in that
	tin hat
AHIOPS	Sophia
AHIORT	hot air
AHIPRS	parish
AHIPRU	rupiah
AHIPTY	Pythia
AHIRRS	Harris
AHIRST	Trisha
AHIRSV	ravish
AHIRSZ	Shiraz
AHIRTW	wraith
AHISTT	that is
AHISTU	hiatus
AHJNSU	Jan Hus
AHJOSU	Joshua
AHKLNU	Khulna
AHKMOW	Mohawk
AHKNPU	punkah
AHKNRS	shrank
AHKNST	thanks
AHKOSS	shakos
AHLLMU	mullah
AHLLOO	halloo
AHLLOS	hallos
AHLLOW	hallow
AHLLRT	thrall
AHLLUX	hallux
AHLMNY	hymnal
AHLMOO	moolah
AHLMOS	shalom
AHLNSU	unlash
AHLOOP	hoop-la
AHLORT	harlot
AHLORW	Harlow
	Warhol
AHLOSS	shoals
AHLOST	shalot
AHLPSS	splash
AHLPSU	sulpha
AHLPUU	haul up
AHLRSY	rashly
AHMMSY	shammy
AHMMWY	whammy
AHMNOS	hansom
AHMNSU	Hamsun
	humans
AHMOOP	oompah
AHMORZ	mahzor
AHMOST	Thomas
AHMOSU	hamous
AHMOSV	moshav
AHMOTU	mahout
AHMOWY	haymow
AHMRSY	marshy
AHMRTW	warmth
AHMSSU	shamus❑
AHNNSU	Sunnah
AHNNSY	shanny
AHNOOR	Honora
AHNOOT	on oath
AHNOPR	harp on
	orphan
AHNORS	Sharon
	shoran
AHNORU	Haroun
AHNOST	Ashton
AHNOSX	Xhosan
AHNOWY	anyhow
AHNPRU	Nuphar
AHNPSU	unhasp
AHNRTW	thrawn
AHNRVY	hryvna
AHNSTU	sunhat
AHNSTY	shanty
AHNTUW	unthaw
AHOORY	hooray
AHOOSY	Yahoos
AHOPPS	Paphos
	Sappho
AHOPRS	pharos
AHOPST	Pashto
	pathos
	potash
	shop at
AHOPTT	top hat
	top-hat
AHOQTU	quotha
AHORRW	harrow❑
AHORTT	throat
AHORTU	author
AHORTW	hot war
	wroath
AHORTX	thorax
AHOSTT	so that
AHOSTW	so what?
	whatso
AHOTWZ	howzat
AHPSUW	wash up
AHQSSU	squash
AHRRTU	Arthur
AHRRUY	hurray
AHRSSU	hussar
AHRSTT	strath
AHRSTU	rush at
AHRSTY	trashy
AHRTTW	thwart
AHSWYY	say why
AIILLN	Lilian
AIILLR	arilli
AIILMS	Ismail
AIILOV	Olivia
AIILRY	airily
AIILSV	Silvia
AIIMMN	minima
AIIMMR	Miriam
AIIMMS	misaim
AIIMNR	Marini
AIIMNS	simian
AIIMOR	Moirai
AIIMPR	impair
AIINNN	Ninian
AIINNO	Ionian
AIINNP	in pain
AIINNR	rain in
AIINNV	in vain
AIINNZ	zinnia
AIINRS	raisin
AIINRX	in rixa
AIINTT	titian❑
AIINVV	Vivian
AIIORS	ariosi
AIIPTU	Itaipu
AIIPTW	wapiti
AIIRTV	trivia
AIJKNS	kanjis
AIJLMS	Majlis
AIJLNU	Julian
AIJLOR	jailor
AIJLOV	jovial
AIJMOR	romaji
AIJNNS	ninjas
AIJPRU	Jaipur
AIJPTU	jupati
AIJRSV	Jarvis
AIKLNO	kaolin
AIKLNR	Larkin
AIKLOS	skolia
AIKLSU	saluki
AIKLTW	walk it
AIKMMS	immask
AIKMOO	oomiak
AIKMOS	maikos
AIKMRV	Vikram
AIKNNP	napkin
AIKNNR	Rankin
AIKNPR	kirpan
	parkin
AIKNRT	nark it!
AIKNRV	Narvik
AIKNRW	Kirwan
AIKNTW	wink at
AIKOPS	okapis
AIKOPT	katipo
AIKORT	troika
AIKRST	at risk
	straik
AIKTUW	Kuwait
AILLMU	allium
AILLMY	Millay
AILLNW	inwall
	wall in
AILLOT	Lolita
AILLPR	pillar
AILLSW	Wallis
AILLSY	I'll say!
AILLYZ	lazily
AILMNO	oilman
AILMNR	marlin
AILMNT	Tilman
AILMNU	alumni
	lumina
AILMNY	mainly
AILMOS	Somali
AILMPR	primal
AILMRU	ramuli
AILMSS	missal
	salmis
AILMST	smalti
AILMSX	smilax
AILMSY	mislay
AILMTU	ultima
AILMTY	matily
AILMUV	Valium®
AILMYZ	mazily
AILNNU	annuli
	unnail
AILNOS	Alison
AILNOT	talion
AILNPS	spinal
AILNPT	plaint
	pliant❑
AILNPU	nail up
AILNPY	in play
AILNRT	trinal
AILNRU	urinal
AILNST	Stalin
AILNSV	silvan

AILNSW	in-laws
AILNTY	litany
AILNVY	vainly
AILOOR	oorial
AILORS	sailor
AILORT	tailor
AILORU	Auriol
AILOSS	assoil
AILOSU	Louisa
AILOSX	oxalis
AILOTX	oxtail
AILPRS	spiral
AILPTY	play it
AILQSU	squail
AILRST	trials
AILRSV	rivals
AILRSW	aswirl
AILRTU	ritual
AILRWY	warily
AILSTV	vitals
AILSUV	visual
AILSVW	Walvis
AILSVY	Sylvia
AILSVZ	vizsla
AILTXY	laxity
AILVWY	wavily
AILWXY	waxily
AIMMNT	Timman
AIMMOS	Maoism
	mimosa
AIMMRY	Myriam
AIMMSS	miasms
AIMNNO	amnion
	Minoan
	nomina
AIMNNU	numina
AIMNOR	Marino
	Marion
	Romani
AIMNPT	pitman□
AIMNRS	in arms
AIMNRT	martin□
AIMNRU	rumina
AIMNRV	Marvin
AIMNSS	in mass
AIMNST	mantis
	matins
	Tamsin
AIMNSU	animus
AIMNSY	Yasmin
AIMNSZ	Nazism
AIMNUV	mauvin
AIMOPT	optima
AIMOPY	myopia
AIMORS	Maoris
AIMOST	Maoist
	Taoism
AIMOSV	Asimov
AIMPRT	armpit
	impart
	partim
AIMPSS	passim
AIMQSU	maquis
AIMRSU	Marius
AIMRTU	atrium
	Timaru
AIMRTX	matrix
AIMRTY	Taimyr
AIMSTT	statim
AIMSTU	autism
AINNNT	tannin
AINNOT	anoint
	nation
AINNOW	wanion
	Winona
AINNPS	inspan
AINNSW	swan in
AINNTW	in want
	want in
AINOPR	Oparin
AINOPS	pianos
	Pisano
AINOQU	Aquino
AINORT	aroint
	ration
AINORW	in a row
AINOSS	Ossian
AINOST	Tainos
AINOTW	wait on
AINPRS	sprain
AINPRT	in part
AINPRW	inwrap
AINPSV	spavin
AINPTY	painty
AINQTU	quaint
	quinta
AINRST	instar
	strain
AINRSY	Syrian
AINRTU	in a rut
	nutria
AINRTY	in-tray
	Tyrian
AINSST	Saints
AINSTT	Titans
AINSTU	Austin
	Unitas
AINSTY	sanity
	satiny
	stay in
AINTVY	vanity
AIOORS	arioso
AIOPRT	Portia
AIOPRV	pavior
AIOPST	patios
	patois
AIOPTU	utopia□
AIORSS	Orissa
AIORST	aorist
	ratios
	satori
AIOSSV	avisos
AIOSTT	Taoist
AIPPRU	pair up
AIPPRY	papyri
AIPPTT	pit-pat
AIPRRU	Raipur
AIPRST	rapist
AIPRSV	parvis
AIPRSW	ripsaw
AIPRSX	praxis
AIPRTY	parity
AIPSST	pastis
AIPSTT	past it
AIPTUW	wait up
AIPZZZ	pizazz
AIRRTY	rarity
AIRRZZ	rizzar
AIRSST	sistra
	stairs
AIRSSU	Russia
AIRSTT	artist
	strait
	traits
AISSST	assist
	stasis
AISSTY	it says
AITTWX	atwixt
AJKNSY	Jansky
AJLOPY	jalopy
AJMORU	Majuro
AJMPTU	jump at
AJNORT	Trojan
AJNTUY	jaunty
AJORRW	Jarrow
AJPRTU	Rajput
AJPUZZ	jazz up
AKKOQU	quokka
AKKORW	Kraków
AKLLNY	lankly
AKLMOY	Kolyma
AKLNOW	walk on
	walk-on
AKLNOX	klaxon
AKLNPS	planks
AKLNRY	rankly
AKLOOT	look at
AKLOSV	Slovak
AKLOTT	talk to
AKLPTU	talk up
AKMNSU	unmask
AKMPRU	mark up
	mark-up
AKNOOT	Nootka
AKNORU	koruna
AKNORY	ryokan
AKNOSS	sankos
AKNOSW	know as
AKNPRS	pranks
AKNPRU	Kanpur
AKNPTU	tank up
AKNRTZ	krantz
AKNSWY	swanky
AKOOPR	Kapoor
AKOORR	Karroo
AKOPRV	Karpov
AKOPSU	soak up
	soakup
AKORSS	kaross
AKORSW	work as
AKORSZ	Ozarks
AKORTW	at work
	work at
AKOSTU	out-ask
AKPPRU	park up
AKPRSS	sparks
AKPRSY	sparky
AKQSUW	squawk
ALLMNO	Mallon
ALLMNU	Ullman
ALLMOR	morall
ALLMOS	slalom
ALLMOW	mallow
ALLMSS	smalls
ALLMUV	vallum
ALLNOP	pall on
	pollan
ALLNOS	allons
	llanos
ALLNUU	lunula
ALLOOP	apollo□
	palolo
ALLOPR	pallor
ALLOPW	wallop
ALLORY	orally
ALLOSW	sallow
ALLOTU	all out
	all-out
ALLOTV	lavolt
ALLOTW	tallow
ALLOVY	ovally
ALLOWW	wallow
ALLOWY	lay low
ALLOYY	Y-alloy
ALLPRU	plural
ALLPUW	wall up
ALLQSU	squall
ALLSST	stalls
ALLSTY	lastly
	saltly
ALMMOW	Mowlam
ALMNOR	Marlon
	normal
ALMNOS	salmon
ALMNOT	Lamont
ALMNTU	Multan
ALMORS	morals
	morsal
ALMORT	mortal
ALMOST	almost
	matlos
	St-Malo
ALMOTW	matlow
ALMPSS	Psalms

ALMQSU	qualms
ALMRWY	warmly
ALMSUY	asylum
ALMTUU	mutual
	umlaut
ALNNOU	nounal
ALNOOS	Alonso
	saloon
ALNOPY	play on
ALNOSW	Lawson
ALNOTV	volant
ALNOTW	Walton
ALNPST	plants
ALNRSY	snarly
ALNRXY	larynx
ALNSTU	sultan
	unlast
ALNSVY	sylvan
ALNTUW	walnut
ALOPPR	poplar
ALOPPT	laptop
ALOPRT	patrol
	portal
ALOPST	postal
ALOPVV	Pavlov
ALOQTU	loquat
ALORTU	LAUTRO
ALORTW	low-tar
ALORTY	Taylor
ALORUV	ovular
	valour
ALOSSS	lassos
ALOSST	saltos
ALOSSV	salvos
ALOTUW	outlaw
ALOTUY	lay out
	layout
	outlay
ALOTUZ	Lao-tzu
ALPPSU	palpus
	slap-up
ALPPUY	play up
ALPRRU	larrup
ALPRSU	pulsar
ALPRSW	sprawl
ALPRTY	paltry
	partly
	raptly
ALPSTU	St Paul
ALRSTU	lustra
ALRSUU	Ursula
ALRSUW	walrus
ALRTTY	tartly
ALRTUW	tulwar
ALRUUV	uvular
ALSSTU	saltus
ALSTVY	vastly
ALSUUV	uvulas
ALTTUY	tautly
ALTUUV	Tuvalu
AMMMNO	mammon
AMMORT	marmot
AMMOSU	omasum
AMMOXY	myxoma
AMMRSY	smarmy
AMMTUZ	Tammuz
AMNNOR	Norman
AMNNOS	Manson
AMNNOY	anonym
AMNOOP	Pomona
AMNOOR	maroon
AMNOPT	tampon
AMNORS	ransom
	Romans
AMNORT	matron
AMNORY	mornay❑
	Romany
AMNOSS	Samson
AMNOST	mantos
AMNOSY	so many
AMNOTU	amount
	outman
AMNPTY	tympan
AMNRSY	Smyrna
AMNRTU	antrum
	Truman
AMNRTY	Martyn
AMNSSU	Samsun
AMNTTU	mutant
AMNTUU	autumn
AMOOSZ	Somoza
AMOOTT	tomato
AMOOYY	Yo-Yo Ma
AMOPST	Patmos
AMOPTU	map out
	Maputo
AMORRT	mortar
AMORRU	armour
AMORRW	marrow
AMORSS	morass
AMORST	stroam
	stroma
AMORSU	ramous
AMORTW	warm to
AMORTZ	Mozart
AMOSTT	at most
AMOSTZ	matzos
AMPRST	stramp
	tramps
AMPRUW	warm up
	warm-up
AMPSWY	swampy
AMRRTY	martyr
AMRRUY	Murray
AMRSSW	swarms
AMRSTU	struma
AMRSTY	smarty
AMRTYY	Taymyr
AMSSSY	Massys
ANNOPT	panton
ANNOPZ	Poznan
ANNORT	natron
ANNORY	nonary
ANNOST	sonant
ANNOTW	wanton
ANNOTY	Antony
	not any
	tannoy❑
ANNPSU	pannus
ANNQRS	QARNNS
ANNRTY	tranny
ANNSTU	suntan
ANNTTU	nutant
ANOOPX	a pox on
ANOORT	ratoon
ANOOST	soon at
ANOPRS	parson
ANOPRT	patron
ANOPSS	pass on
ANOPST	pantos
ANOPTT	Patton
ANOPTU	pan out
ANOPTX	Paxton
ANOPTY	Payton
ANORRW	narrow
ANORTT	attorn
ANORTW	Warton
ANORTY	aroynt
	notary
ANORWY	Norway
ANOSST	Santos
ANOSTW	Watson
ANOSTY	stay on
ANOSTZ	stanzo
ANOSWY	noways
ANPPSU	snap up
ANPPSY	snappy
ANPRSU	unspar
ANPRTY	pantry
ANPRUW	unwrap
ANPRUY	unpray
ANPSUW	swan up
ANPTUW	want up
ANRSTU	Saturn
ANRSUU	Uranus
ANRTTU	truant
ANRTTY	tyrant
ANRUWY	runway
	unwary
ANSTTU	tutsan
ANSTUW	NAS/UWT
ANSTXY	syntax
ANSYZZ	snazzy
AOOPTT	potato
AOORRT	orator
AOOSST	so as to
AOOTTT	tattoo
AOOTTY	Toyota
	Toyota®
AOPPRT	Pop Art
AOPRRT	parrot
	raptor
AOPRRU	uproar
AOPRST	pastor
AOPRTY	pray to
AOPRUV	vapour
AOPSTT	stop at
AOPTUY	pay out
AOPWWW	powwaw
AOQRTU	quarto
AOQSTU	quotas
AORRST	rostra
	sartor
AORRSY	rosary
AORRTY	rotary
AORRWY	yarrow
AORSST	assort
AORSTT	stator
	Strato
AORSTX	storax
AORSUU	aurous
AORSUV	savour
AORTVY	votary
AOSTTU	at outs
AOTUWY	way out
	way-out
AOTWWY	two-way
APPPSU	pappus
APPRUW	wrap up
APPSSU	pass up
APRRSY	sparry
APRSST	straps
APRSTT	Pratt's
APRSTY	pastry
APRTTU	tart up
APSUWY	upsway
AQRRUY	quarry
AQRTUZ	quartz
ARRSTY	starry
ARSSTU	tarsus❑
ARSSTY	Satyrs
ARSTTU	astrut
	Stuart
ARSTUU	Taurus
ARSTUX	surtax
ARSTWY	strawy
ASSTTU	status

B

BBBEIR	bibber
BBBELO	bobble
BBBELU	bubble
BBBHUU	hubbub
BBBINO	bobbin
BBBLOY	bobbly
BBBLUY	bubbly
BBCEIR	Cibber
BBCELO	cobble
BBCEOR	cobber
BBCEOW	cobweb❑
BBCHUY	chubby
BBCOTY	Ty Cobb
BBDDEU	dubbed
BBDEEI	Debbie

BBDEEW	webbed
BBDEGU	bedbug
BBDEIL	dibble
BBDEIR	dibber
	ribbed
BBDEMO	bombed
	mobbed
BBDEOR	dobber
	robbed
BBDINO	dobbin
BBDINU	dubbin
BBDKUY	dybbuk
BBEELP	pebble
BBEERR	Berber
BBEEYY	bye-bye
BBEFIR	fibber
BBEGIN	ebbing
BBEGIR	gibber
BBEGIT	gibbet
BBEGLO	gobble
BBEGOT	gobbet
BBEHIU	hubbie
BBEHLO	hobble
BBEHLU	Hubble
BBEHOS	Hobbes
BBEIIM	imbibe
BBEIKL	kibble
BBEILN	nibble
BBEILR	libber
	Ribble
BBEIOR	Robbie
BBEIRR	briber
BBEITT	Tebbit
BBEJOR	jobber
BBELMU	bumble□
BBELNO	nobble
BBELNU	nubble
BBELOW	wobble
BBELPY	pebbly
	plebby
BBELRU	burble
	lubber
	rubble
BBEMNU	benumb
BBEMOR	bomber
BBENOW	Benbow
BBEORR	robber
BBEOSU	buboes
BBERRU	rubber
BBERTU	tubber
BBGIKN	B B King
BBGINO	gibbon□
BBGRUY	grubby
BBHIOT	hobbit
BBHJOO	hobjob
BBHNOO	hobnob
BBIKOS	skibob
BBILOS	bilbos
BBIMOS	bimbos
BBINOR	ribbon□
BBKNOY	knobby
BBLLUU	bulbul
BBLOSY	Byblos
	slobby
BBLOWY	Bowlby
	wobbly
BBLSUY	slubby
BBMOOS	bombos
BBMOSU	bumbos
BBMRUY	Brumby
BBNNOO	bonbon
BBNOSY	snobby
BBNOTU	nobbut
BBNSUY	snubby
BBOOOO	booboo
	boo-boo
BBOOSY	yobbos
BBOOWY	bow-boy
BBORTU	burbot
BBRSUU	suburb
BBSSTU	Stubbs
BBSTUY	stubby
BCCDEI	EBCDIC
BCDEEK	bedeck
BCDEIO	bodice
BCDEKU	beduck
	Dubcek
BCDENO	Cobden
BCDERU	curbed
BCDIOU	cuboid
BCEEHO	obeche
BCEEHR	breech
BCEEHT	Bechet
BCEEIR	Bierce
BCEEKR	Becker
BCEEKT	Becket
BCEELY	Cybele
BCEEMO	become
BCEEOS	Seb Coe
BCEEQU	Quebec
BCEHLN	blench
BCEHRT	Brecht
BCEHRU	cherub
BCEIIS	ibices
BCEIKR	bicker
BCEIKS	be sick
BCEIOR	corbie
BCEIPS	biceps
BCEIRS	scribe
BCEIST	bisect
BCEJOT	object
BCEKLU	buckle
	Lübeck
BCEKNO	beckon
BCEKOZ	Ozbeck
BCEKTU	bucket
BCELLO	Belloc
BCELNO	en bloc
BCELOR	corbel
BCELOU	bouclé
BCELRU	becurl
BCEMOO	coombe
BCEMOR	comber
BCEMOY	come by
BCEMRU	cumber
BCENOU	bounce
BCHINY	Binchy
BCHIOP	phobic
BCHITY	bitchy
BCHLOT	blotch
BCHMOU	Bochum
BCHNRU	brunch
BCHNUY	bunchy
BCHOOR	brooch
BCHORS	borsch
BCHOTY	botchy
BCIINO	bionic
BCIIOP	biopic
BCIIOT	biotic
BCILMO	Imbolc
BCILOO	colobi
BCILPU	public
BCIMSU	Cubism
BCIRRU	rubric
BCISTU	Cubist
BCKPUU	buck up
BCMOOS	combos
BCMORY	corymb
BCMRSU	crumbs
BCMRUY	crumby
BCNOOR	bronco
BCNORU	Coburn
BCNOSU	buncos
BCNOTU	cobnut
BCNOUY	bouncy
BCOOWY	cowboy
BCORSY	Crosby
BDDDOO	odd bod
BDDEEN	bended
BDDEET	debted
BDDEIR	bidder
BDDELU	buddle
BDDIOR	do bird
BDDISU	disbud
BDEEET	debtee
BDEEGR	Edberg
BDEEIL	edible
BDEEIS	beside
BDEEIT	betide
BDEELN	blende
BDEELT	belted
BDEENO	be done
BDEENR	bender
BDEERU	Debreu
BDEERW	brewed
BDEFIR	fibred
BDEGGU	bugged
BDEGIL	begild
BDEGIN	big end
BDEGIR	bridge
BDEGIU	budgie
BDEGLU	bludge
BDEGNU	bedung
BDEGTU	budget
BDEHIN	behind
BDEHLO	behold
BDEHOT	hotbed
BDEHSU	bushed
BDEIIM	ibidem
BDEIIR	birdie
	Bridie
BDEILO	boiled
	bolide
BDEILR	bridle
BDEIMU	imbued
BDEINR	binder
	inbred
	rebind
BDEINT	in debt
BDEIOR	Brodie
BDEIOS	bodies
BDEIRR	birder
BDEIRS	debris
	débris
BDEIRU	buried
BDEIST	bedsit
	bed-sit
BDEKNU	debunk
BDEKOO	booked
BDELMO	mobled
BDELNO	blonde
BDELNU	bundle
BDELOO	boodle
BDELOU	double
	double-
BDELOW	bowled
BDELRU	de-blur
BDEMNU	numbed
BDEMOY	Dombey
	embody
BDENNU	unbend
BDENOO	De Bono
BDENOR	Borden
BDENOY	beyond
BDENRU	burden
	burned
BDENSU	sunbed
BDEOPR	bedrop
BDEORR	border□
BDEORS	desorb
BDEORT	Bordet
	debtor
BDEOSS	bossed
	deboss
BDEOTU	bed out
BDESTU	bedust
	bestud
BDESUU	subdue
BDFIOR	forbid
BDGIIR	Brigid
BDGINO	Gobind
BDHIIN	bhindi
BDHIRY	hybrid
BDHLOY	hold by

BDIILO	libido
BDIIMR	midrib
BDIINR	in bird
BDIITT	tidbit
BDIKNO	bodkin
BDILNS	blinds
BDILNU	Dublin
BDILOY	bodily
BDIMOR	morbid
BDINNU	unbind
BDINPU	bind up
	upbind
BDIOSU	Du Bois
BDIOTU	outbid
BDIRTU	turbid
BDKLOO	kobold
BDLLOY	boldly
BDLMUY	dumbly
BDLOOY	bloody
	old boy
BDLOUY	doubly
BDNOOS	Dobson
BDNOOY	nobody
BDNOSU	bounds
BDOORY	broody
BDOPRY	drop by
BDORWY	byword
BEEEFL	feeble
BEEELT	beetle
	Beetle®
BEEEMS	beseem
BEEEMT	beteem
BEEEPR	beeper
BEEEPW	beweep
BEEERZ	breeze
BEEESV	beeves
BEEFIL	belief
BEEFLY	feebly
BEEFOR	before
BEEFPU	beef up
BEEFRT	bereft
BEEGIL	beigel
BEEGLY	leg bye
BEEGNO	begone
BEEGNR	Bergen
BEEGRR	Berger
BEEGRT	Egbert
BEEGRU	burgee
BEEHIP	ephebi
BEEHIR	Herbie
BEEHIS	Hibees
BEEHLT	bethel
BEEHOP	phoebe□
BEEHOV	behove
BEEHRW	Hebrew
BEEHRY	hereby
BEEHST	behest
	Thebes
BEEHTW	the Web
BEEILZ	Belize
BEEIMT	betime
BEEINR	Bernie
BEEIRT	Bertie
	rebite
BEEISS	Bessie
BEEISX	ibexes
BEEKLM	Kemble
BEEKOR	reebok
BEEKRU	rebuke
BEELMM	emblem
BEELMR	remble
BEELMS	semble
BEELRT	belter
	treble
BEELRY	berley
BEELXY	Bexley
BEEMMR	member
BEEMNR	Bremen
BEEMRS	embers
BEEMRU	embrue
BEEMSU	bemuse
BEENNR	brenne
BEENNT	Bennet
BEENOR	enrobe
BEENOT	Beeton
BEENRU	Reuben
BEENRW	Webern
BEEOOT	bootee
BEEORR	rebore
BEEORT	bo tree
BEEPRU	beer-up
BEERRV	reverb
BEERRW	brewer□
BEERSU	be sure
BEERTT	better
BEERYZ	breezy
BEFFRU	buffer
	rebuff
BEFFTU	buffet
BEFGIT	begift
BEFILO	foible
BEFIRS	briefs
BEFLMU	beflum
	fumble
BEFLOO	befool
BEFLOU	befoul
BEFLRY	belfry
BEFORS	Forbes
BEFORY	forbye
BEFRUY	rubefy
BEFSUU	subfeu
BEGGII	biggie
BEGGIR	bigger
BEGGLO	boggle
BEGGRU	Brugge
	bugger
BEGIIL	Liebig
BEGILN	bingle
BEGILO	oblige
BEGILR	gerbil
BEGINN	benign
BEGINO	Boeing
BEGINR	Bering
BEGINU	beguin
BEGIOO	boogie
BEGIOS	bogies
BEGIOU	bougie
BEGIRU	brigue
BEGKNU	begunk
BEGLNO	belong
BEGLNU	blunge
	bungle
BEGLOT	goblet
BEGLRU	bugler
	burgle
BEGNOR	bon gré
BEGNOY	bygone
	gone by
BEGNPU	Bengpu
BEGOOR	bog-ore
BEGOOS	goboes
BEGORS	Borges
BEGORU	brogue
BEGOSY	bogeys
BEGRRU	burger
BEGRSU	Bruges
BEHILS	Ishbel
BEHILT	blithe
BEHINS	nebish
BEHIST	Thisbe
BEHKOR	rhebok
BEHLMU	humble
BEHLOW	behowl
BEHLRU	burhel
BEHLSU	bushel
BEHMOT	the mob
BEHMRU	Humber
BEHNOR	Hebron
BEHNRU	Ben-Hur
BEHNTY	by then
BEHOOS	hoboes
BEHORT	bother
BEHOTX	the box
BEHRTU	Hubert
BEHSSU	bushes
BEIINT	be in it
	bite in
BEIJLR	jirble
BEIKLN	libken
BEIKLR	bilker
BEIKOO	bookie
BEIKSS	bekiss
BEILLT	billet
BEILMN	nimble
BEILMO	bemoil
	mobile□
BEILMR	limber
BEILMW	wimble
BEILMY	blimey
BEILNR	Berlin
BEILNU	nubile
BEILNX	Blixen
BEILNY	byline
BEILOR	boiler
	libero
BEILOS	Isobel
BEILOT	betoil
	boleti
BEILRS	birsle
BEILRU	Breuil
BEILST	Lisbet
BEILSY	Sibley
BEILVY	live by
BEIMOV	B-movie
BEIMOZ	zombie
BEIMRT	betrim
	timber
	timbre
BEIMRU	erbium
	imbrue
BEINNO	Bonnie
BEINOR	O'Brien
BEINOT	Benoît
BEINOV	bovine
BEINPU	be up in
BEINRU	Brunei
BEINST	Nesbit
BEINTT	bitten
BEIORS	ribose
BEIORT	obiter
BEIORV	Boveri
BEIOST	so be it
BEIOTW	bow-tie
BEIQSU	bisque
BEIQUU	ubique
BEIRRY	briery
BEIRST	bestir
	bister
	bistre
BEIRSU	bruise
BEIRTT	bitter
BEIRTU	Beirut
BEISST	Bisset
BEITUY	ubiety
BEJJUU	jujube
BEJLMU	jumble
BEJORU	objure
BEJOST	objets
BEJOVY	by Jove
BEKLOY	blokey
BEKNOR	broken
BEKNRU	bunker
BEKOOR	Brooke
BEKORR	broker
BEKRSU	busker
BELLOU	boulle
	lobule
BELLOW	bellow□
BELLRU	buller
BELLTU	bullet
BELLUY	bluely
BELMMU	bummle
	mumble
BELMRU	lumber

	rumble
BELMSU	umbles
BELMTU	tumble
BELNNY	blenny
BELNOS	nobles
BELNOY	Boleyn
BELNRU	Brunel
BELNTU	unbelt
BELNUU	Buñuel
BELOOR	bolero□
	Boléro
BELOOT	Bootle
BELOPU	pueblo□
BELORS	Olbers
BELORU	rouble
BELORW	blower
	bowler
BELOSS	Lesbos
BELOSU	blouse
	boules
	obelus
BELOSW	bowels
BELOTT	bottle
BELOUZ	Boulez
BELPTU	belt up
BELRRU	burrel
BELRTU	butler□
BELRTY	beltry
	trebly
BELRUY	burley
BELSTU	bustle
	sublet
	subtle□
BELSUY	bluesy
BELTTU	buttle
BELTUU	tubule
BEMMRU	bummer
BEMNOT	entomb
BEMNOW	enwomb
BEMNRU	number
BEMORS	sombre
BEMORY	embryo
BEMOSS	emboss
BEMPRU	bumper
BEMSTU	besmut
BENNOT	bent on
	Benton
	bonnet
BENNOY	Bonney
BENNSU	Bunsen
BENNTU	unbent
BENOOR	Borneo
	Oberon
BENOPU	bone up
BENORR	reborn
BENORT	Breton
	Brontë
BENORU	unrobe
BENORW	Browne
BENORZ	bronze
BENOSS	Besson

BENRSU	Rubens
BENRTU	Bunter
	burnet□
BENRUY	Burney
BEOORT	reboot
BEOORZ	boozer
BEOOST	Boötes
BEOPPR	bopper
BEOPRR	prober
BEOPST	bespot
BEORRS	resorb
BEORRT	Robert
BEORSS	Sobers
BEORST	besort
	Osbert
	sorbet
	strobe
BEORSU	bourse
BEORSW	bowser
	browse
BEORTT	bettor
BEORTV	obvert
BEORTY	by rote
BEORVV	bovver
BEORVY	overby
BEORWY	bowery
	owerby
BEOSSS	bosses
	obsess
BEOSST	betoss
BEOSSY	syboes
BEOSTT	obtest
BEOSTU	obtuse
BEOSTW	bestow
BEOTUY	outbye
	you bet
BEPRSU	superb
BEPRUW	brew up
BERSUY	buyers
BERTTU	butter
BERUZZ	buzzer
BESSSU	busses
BESSTU	subset
BFFFOO	fob off
BFFFOU	fub off
BFFINO	boffin
BFFNOU	Buffon
BFFOUY	buy off
BFFPUU	buff up
BFIILR	fibril
BFIINR	fibrin
BFIORS	fibros
BFLOTY	botfly
BFLTUU	tubful
BFORSU	sub for
BFORTU	but for
BFORUY	buy for
BGGIIN	gibing
BGGIIW	bigwig
BGGINU	big gun
BGGIRS	Briggs

BGHIIT	big hit
BGHILT	blight
BGHIRT	bright□
BGHMUU	humbug
BGHOSU	go bush
BGHOTU	bought
BGIIKN	biking
BGIINT	biting
BGIIRT	Brigit
BGILLY	glibly
BGILNO	globin
	goblin
BGINNO	Ningbo
BGINOR	boring
BGINOS	bingos
	Gibson
	obsign
BGINOX	boxing
BGINTU	tubing
BGINUY	buying
BGIOPT	big pot
	big top
BGIORV	Viborg
BGLNOO	oblong
BGLRUU	bulgur
BGMOSU	gumbos
BGNOOS	bongos
BGNORY	Nyborg
BGNPUU	bung up
BGOORS	borgos
BGORSU	Burgos
BGOSTU	go bust
BHIKOS	kibosh
BHILPY	Philby
BHILSU	bluish
BHIMOR	rhombi
BHIMOS	himbos
BHIOPS	bishop□
BHIOSY	boyish
BHIRSU	hubris
BHITWY	Whitby
BHKOSY	kybosh
BHLMUY	humbly
BHLOTY	Holtby
BHNORY	Hornby
BHOOOO	boohoo
	boo-hoo
BHOTTU	Bhutto
BHRSSU	shrubs
BIIIKN	bikini□
BIILNS	blinis
BIILOX	Biloxi
BIINOT	biotin
BIINST	in bits
BIIRRS	sbirri
BIITTT	titbit
BIJOUX	bijoux
BIKKRY	Kirkby
BIKNOO	book in
BIKRSY	brisky
BILLNU	Lublin

BILLOU	lobuli
BILLOW	billow
BILLOY	billy-o
BILMNY	nimbly
BILMOS	limbos
BILNOS	Lisbon
BILNOW	blow in
BILNTU	Butlin
BILOOT	Lobito
BILOTW	blow it
BILPSY	slip by
BILRTY	trilby□
BILSUY	busily
BIMNSU	nimbus
BIMOST	timbós
BIMOSU	Möbius
BIMSTU	submit
BINNOR	born in
	inborn
BINNOU	bunion
BINNOY	Binyon
BINNRU	burn in
BINORT	Briton
BINORY	Briony
BINOSS	bisson
BINPUY	bunyip
BINTTU	butt in
	unbitt
BIOORZ	borzoi
BIOOST	oboist
BIOPSY	biopsy
BIORST	bistro
BIOSTT	to bits
BIOSTU	subito
BIOTTW	two-bit
BIRTTU	turbit
BJLOOT	job-lot
BJMOSU	jumbos
BKMNUU	bunkum
BKNOSU	bunkos
BKOORS	Brooks
BKORTU	Korbut
	Tobruk
BKSTUU	Butkus
BLLORY	brolly
BLMNUY	numbly
BLMOSY	symbol
BLNOOT	Bolton
BLNOTU	unbolt
BLNOTY	Blyton
BLOOSU	obolus
BLOOTT	blotto
BLOOWY	lowboy
BLOPTU	blot up
BLOPUW	blow up
	Blow-Up
	blow-up
	upblow
BLOSWY	blowsy
BLOWYZ	blowzy
BLRRUY	blurry

BLSTUY	subtly
BMNOOT	bon mot
BMNOTU	untomb
BMOORY	byroom
BMOOSY	bosomy
BMOOTT	bottom□
BMOOTY	tomboy
BMOPPU	Bumppo
BMORSU	rumbos
BMOTUU	Mobutu
BMPPUU	bump up
BNNOOT	bon ton
BNNORU	unborn
BNOORS	Robson
BNOOST	Boston
BNOOSY	Boyson
BNORSU	suborn
BNORSY	Bryson
BNORTU	Bruton
	burton□
BNORWY	browny
BNORYY	bryony□
BNORYZ	bronzy
BNOSUW	sunbow
BNOTTU	button
BNOTUX	Buxton
BNOTUY	bounty□
BNPRUU	burn up
BNRUUY	unbury
BOOOTT	to boot
BOORRW	borrow
BOORRY	Rob Roy
BOOTUW	bow out
BOOTYY	toy boy
	toyboy
BOPSTY	stop by
BOPUUY	buoy up
BORRSU	burros
BORRUW	burrow
BORSTU	robust
	turbos
BORTTU	turbot
BORTUU	rub out
BOSSWY	sybows
BOTUUY	buy out
	buyout
	buy-out
BPSTUU	bust up
	bust-up
BQRTUU	Tubruq
BRSTUU	Brutus

C

CCCILY	cyclic
CCCOOS	coccos
CCCOSU	coccus
CCCOXY	coccyx
CCDEIR	Cedric
CCDEOT	decoct
CCEEHR	crèche
CCEEOR	coerce
CCEERS	recces
CCEHIL	cliché
CCEHIM	chemic
CCEHIO	choice
	echoic
CCEHIT	hectic
CCEHKS	checks
CCEHLN	clench
CCEHLO	cloche
CCEHNO	conche
CCEIIL	icicle
CCEILR	circle
	cleric
CCEILT	Celtic
CCEILY	Cecily
	cicely□
CCEINS	scenic
CCEIOR	Cicero
CCEKLO	cockle
CCEKOP	copeck
CCEKOR	cocker
CCENOS	sconce
CCEORS	reccos
	soccer
CCEOSS	seccos
CCERSU	cruces
CCFILO	flocci
CCHHII	chichi
CCHHRU	church□
CCHIKS	chicks
	Schick
CCHIKT	tchick
CCHILN	clinch
CCHILY	chicly
CCHINO	Cochin
CCHIPU	hiccup
CCHLTU	clutch
CCHNOS	conchs
CCHNOY	conchy
CCHNRU	crunch
CCHORS	scorch
CCHORT	crotch
CCHORU	crouch
CCHOST	scotch□
CCHRTU	crutch
CCHSTU	scutch
CCIILN	clinic
CCIINO	iconic
CCIINP	picnic
CCIIRT	citric
	critic
CCIISV	civics
CCIKRY	cricky
CCILTU	cultic
CCIMOS	cosmic
CCIMRY	Cymric
CCIOPT	Coptic
CCIOSS	ciscos
CCIPRU	cupric
CCIRSU	circus
CCISTY	cystic
CCKLOO	o'clock
CCKNOU	uncock
CCKOOU	cuckoo
CCKOPU	cock up
	cock-up
CCLOSY	cyclos
CCLOTU	occult
CCNOOO	cocoon
CCNORU	concur
CCOOOR	rococo□
CCOOSZ	zoccos
CCOPUY	occupy
CCORSU	crocus
CCOSTU	stucco
CCPRSS	RSSPCC
CCSSUU	cuscus
CDDEEI	decide
CDDEEK	decked
CDDEEO	decode
CDDEEU	deduce
	deuced
CDDELO	coddle
CDDELU	cuddle
CDDEOR	corded
CDDETU	deduct
CDDLUY	cuddly
CDDRUY	cruddy
CDEEER	decree
	recede
	re-cede
CDEEES	secede
CDEEEX	exceed
CDEEFT	defect
CDEEIN	Edenic
CDEEIR	de-icer
CDEEIT	deceit
CDEEIV	device
CDEEJT	deject
CDEEKL	deckle
CDEEKO	decoke
CDEELU	Culdee
CDEENO	encode
CDEENR	decern
CDEENT	decent
CDEERS	screed
CDEERU	reduce
CDEESU	seduce
CDEETT	detect
CDEFII	deific
CDEFNU	fecund
CDEFOR	forced
CDEGIN	ceding
CDEGLU	cudgel
CDEGOR	codger
CDEHIN	niched
CDEHIR	chider
	Edrich
CDEHKO	choked
	Ed Koch
CDEHNR	drench
CDEHOU	douche
CDEIIK	dickie□
CDEIIM	Medici
CDEIKN	Dicken
	nicked
CDEIKP	picked
CDEIKR	dicker
CDEIKW	wicked
CDEIKY	dickey
CDEILO	coiled
	docile
CDEILU	Dulcie
	Euclid
CDEIMO	medico
CDEIMR	dermic
CDEINR	cinder
CDEINU	induce
CDEIOP	copied
CDEIOV	voiced
CDEIPS	spiced
CDEIPT	depict
CDEIRT	credit
	direct
CDEIRY	dry ice
CDEKLO	locked
CDEKNU	undeck
CDEKOO	cooked
CDEKOR	corked
CDEKOS	deckos
CDEKOT	docket
CDEKRU	rucked
CDEKTU	tucked
CDELNO	cloned
CDELOS	closed
CDELOU	Cluedo®
CDELRU	curdle
	curled
CDELTU	dulcet
CDEMOO	comedo
CDEMOY	comedy
CDENOR	corned
CDENOS	second
CDENSU	secund
CDEORR	record
CDEORS	credos
	scored
CDEOSU	escudo
CDEPPU	cupped
CDERSU	cursed
CDERSY	descry
CDERUV	curved
CDESSU	cussed
CDFINO	fi donc!
CDFIOU	fucoid
CDFIOY	codify
CDGLOO	go cold
CDHIOR	orchid
CDHIRY	hydric
CDIINT	indict
CDIIOY	idiocy
CDIISV	viscid
CDIKNO	Dickon

CDILOV	Old Vic
CDIMTU	dictum
CDINOR	Nordic
CDINSY	syndic
CDINTU	induct
CDIORS	roscid
CDIOSS	discos
CDIOTY	cytoid
CDISSU	discus
CDJNOU	jocund
CDKNOU	undock
CDLLOY	clodly
	coldly
CDLOUY	cloudy
CDMNOO	condom
	mod con
CDNOOR	condor
	con-rod
	cordon
CDNORU	uncord
CDNSTU	UNCSTD
CDOORT	doctor
CDORSW	crowds
CEEEFL	fleece
CEEEGR	Greece
CEEEHS	cheese
CEEELS	Cleese
CEEENO	Eocene
CEEERS	creese
CEEFFO	coffee
CEEFFT	effect
CEEFHL	flèche
	fleech
CEEFIR	fierce
	Recife
CEEFLY	fleecy
CEEFNN	fennec
CEEFNR	fencer
CEEFRT	refect
CEEFSU	fescue
CEEHHW	wheech
CEEHIL	lichee
CEEHIR	Cherie
	rechie
CEEHKL	heckle
CEEHKY	cheeky
CEEHLR	lecher
CEEHLW	lechwe
CEEHLY	lychee
CEEHMS	scheme
CEEHNT	thence
CEEHNW	whence
CEEHOR	cohere
	re-echo
CEEHOS	echoes
CEEHPS	speech
CEEHQU	cheque
CEEHRS	cheers
	creesh
	Escher
CEEHRT	etcher

CEEHRU	euchre
CEEHRY	cheery
CEEHSW	eschew
CEEHSY	cheesy
CEEIMR	eremic
CEEIMT	emetic
CEEINP	Niepce
	picene
	piecen
CEEINT	entice
CEEINU	Eunice
CEEINV	evince
	Venice
CEEIPR	pierce❑
	recipe
CEEIPS	pieces
	specie
CEEIRS	cerise
CEEIRT	recite
	tierce
CEEISX	excise
CEEITX	excite
CEEJNO	conjee
CEEJRT	reject
CEEKKL	keckle
CEEKNR	Necker
CEEKPR	pecker
CEEKRT	Eckert
CEELNR	crenel
CEELOR	creole❑
CEELOS	eclose
CEELOV	veloce
CEELRT	tercel
CEELRV	clever
CEELRW	crewel
CEELRY	celery
CEELST	select
CEEMNT	cement
CEEMRR	mercer❑
CEEMRT	cermet
CEENOR	encore
CEENPT	pecten
CEENRS	censer
	screen
	secern
CEENRT	centre
	recent
	tenrec
CEENRY	Cyrene
CEENSS	scenes
CEEOTX	Exocet®
CEEPRS	creeps
CEEPRY	creepy
CEEPTX	except
	expect
CEERRU	recure
CEERSS	recess
CEERST	resect
	secret
CEERSU	recuse
	rescue

	secure
CEERTT	tercet
CEESSX	excess
CEESSY	cyeses
CEESTX	exsect
CEESUX	excuse
CEFFIO	office
CEFFOR	coffer
CEFHIT	Fichte
CEFHLN	flench
CEFHLT	fletch
CEFHNR	French
CEFIKL	fickle
CEFINT	infect
CEFINU	UNICEF
CEFIRR	ferric
CEFLOS	fo'c'sle
CEFMOO	come of
CEFNOR	confer
CEFORR	forcer
CEFORS	forces
	fresco
CEFRUW	curfew
CEGGLO	coggle
CEGGPU	eggcup
CEGHIO	chigoe
CEGINR	cringe
CEGIRS	grices
CEGKOS	geckos
CEGLRY	clergy
CEGNOR	conger
CEGNOT	cogent
CEGNSU	scunge
CEGNTY	cygnet
CEGORR	grocer
CEHHIT	hi-tech
CEHHSU	sheuch
CEHIIM	Michie
CEHIIR	Richie
CEHIKR	hicker
CEHILN	lichen
CEHILS	chesil
	chisel
CEHINR	enrich
	richen
CEHINT	ethnic
CEHIOR	co-heir
	heroic
CEHIPR	cipher
CEHIQU	quiche
CEHIRR	chirre
CEHIRS	riches
CEHIRT	cither
	thrice
CEHIST	ethics
CEHISV	chives
CEHKLO	Köchel
CEHKLU	huckle
CEHKOR	choker
CEHKOY	hockey
CEHKST	sketch

CEHKTV	kvetch
CEHLOR	choler
	orchel
CEHLOT	clothe
CEHLPS	schlep
CEHLQU	quelch
CEHMOR	chrome
CEHMTU	humect
CEHNOO	ochone
CEHNOS	chosen
CEHNOT	techno
CEHNOU	cohune
CEHNQU	quench
CEHNRT	trench
CEHNRW	wrench
CEHNST	stench
CEHNUU	eunuch
CEHOOS	choose
	cohoes
CEHOPT	potche
CEHORS	cosher
CEHORT	hector❑
	rochet
	tocher
	troche
CEHOSU	chouse
CEHOTU	touché
CEHPRY	cypher
CEHPSY	psyche
CEHPUW	chew up
CEHRRY	cherry❑
CEHRTW	wretch
CEHSTU	tusche
CEHSTY	chesty
	scythe
CEHTTY	tetchy
CEIIKS	sickie
CEIILS	ilices
CEIILT	elicit
CEIINR	irenic
CEIINS	incise
CEIINT	incite
CEIISS	Cissie
CEIIST	cities
CEIJNT	inject
CEIKKR	kicker
CEIKLN	nickel
CEIKLP	pickle❑
CEIKLS	sickle
CEIKLT	Keltic
	tickle
CEIKNR	nicker
CEIKNS	sicken
CEIKOO	cookie
CEIKOS	Kosice
CEIKPR	picker
CEIKPT	picket
CEIKRR	ricker
CEIKRT	ticker
CEIKRW	wicker
CEIKRY	crikey

CEIKTT	ticket
CEIKTW	wicket
CEILLO	collie
	ocelli
CEILNO	Nicole
CEILNP	pencil
CEILNT	client
	lectin
	lentic
CEILNU	clue in
	leucin
	nuclei
CEILNY	nicely
CEILOP	police□
CEILOR	recoil
CEILPS	splice
CEILPV	pelvic
CEILQU	clique
CEILRS	relics
	slicer
CEILRT	relict
CEILSU	sluice
CEILTU	luetic
CEIMMO	commie
CEIMNO	come in
	income
CEIMNR	mincer
CEIMOX	Mexico
CEIMPU	pumice
CEIMRT	metric
CEIMRU	cerium
CEIMSU	miscue
CEINNO	Connie
CEINOR	coiner
	orcein
	recoin
CEINOS	cosine
	oscine
CEINOT	noetic
	notice
CEINOV	novice
CEINPR	pincer
	prince□
CEINPT	incept
	pectin
CEINQU	quince□
CEINRT	cretin
CEINRU	Runcie
CEINRW	wincer
CEINST	insect
CEINSU	incuse
CEINTY	nicety
CEIOPR	copier
CEIOPT	poetic
CEIORR	corrie
CEIORS	cosier
CEIORT	erotic
CEIORW	cowrie
CEIORZ	cozier
CEIOST	cotise
CEIOTU	ice out
CEIOTX	exotic
CEIOTZ	zoetic
CEIPPT	peptic
CEIPRS	cripes
	précis
	prices
CEIPRY	pricey
CEIPSS	Pisces
CEIPST	septic
CEIQRU	cirque
CEIRSS	crises
CEIRST	steric
CEIRSU	cruise□
CEIRSV	scrive
CEIRSZ	cizers
CEIRTU	cuiter
CEIRUV	Cuvier
CEIRVX	cervix
CEJKOY	jockey
CEJNOU	jounce
CEJOOS	jocose
CEJRUV	J-curve
CEKKOP	kopeck
CEKLMU	muckle
CEKLNO	enlock
CEKLOR	locker
CEKLOT	locket
CEKLRU	ruckle
CEKLSU	suckle
CEKMOR	mocker
CEKMRU	mucker
CEKMRX	Merckx
CEKNOR	conker
	reckon
CEKOOR	cooker
CEKOPT	pocket
CEKORR	corker
	rocker
CEKORT	rocket
CEKOST	socket
CEKPRU	pucker
CEKPSY	specky
CEKRSU	sucker
CEKTTU	tucket
CELLOS	cellos
CELMOO	coelom
CELMOP	compel
CELMOY	comely
CELMSU	muscle
CELMUY	lyceum
CELNNU	nuncle
CELNOT	Cloten
CELNOV	cloven
CELNOY	Ceylon
CELNTU	lucent
CELOOR	cooler
CELOOT	ocelot
CELOPU	couple
CELORT	lector
CELORV	clover
	Velcro®
CELOST	closet
CELOSU	coleus
CELOSV	cloves
CELPUU	clue up
CELPUW	clew up
CELRRU	curler
CELRTU	cutler
CELRUW	curlew
CELSSU	Celsus
CELTTU	cutlet
CELTUY	cutely
CEMNNO	nem con
CEMNOO	come on
	come-on
CEMOOT	come to
	to come
	to-come
CEMOPU	come up
CEMOSY	cymose
CEMRTU	rectum
CENOPS	on spec
CENOPU	pounce
	uncope
CENORR	corner
CENORS	censor
CENORT	cornet
CENOST	centos
CENOSU	UNESCO
CENOTU	econut
CENOVX	convex
CENOVY	convey
CENSSU	census
CENSTY	encyst
CEOOPR	cooper□
CEOOTY	coyote
	oocyte
CEOPPR	copper
CEOPRS	corpse
CEOPRU	recoup
CEOPRW	Cowper
CEOPTY	ectopy
CEOQTU	coquet
CEORRS	scorer
CEORRT	rector
CEORSS	crosse
	scores
	scorse
CEORST	corset
	Cortes
	Cortés
	coster
	escort
	Escort®
	rectos
	scoter
	sector
CEORSU	course
	crouse
	Crusoe
	source
CEORSV	corves
	covers
CEORSW	escrow
CEORTT	cotter
CEORTV	covert
	vector
CEORTX	cortex
CEOSST	cosset
CEOSSU	Scouse
CEPRSU	spruce
CERSSW	screws
CERSTU	Custer
	rectus
CERSUX	cruxes
CERSWY	screwy
CERTTU	cutter
CERTUV	curvet
CESSTU	cestus
CFFINO	coffin
CFFORY	cry off
CFFOTU	cut off
	cut-off
	offcut
CFFRSU	scruff
CFFRUY	Cruyff
CFHILN	flinch
CFHILT	flitch
CFHIRS	Frisch
CFHIRT	fricht
CFIILM	filmic
CFIINU	unific
CFIITY	citify
CFIKLS	flicks
CFIKOS	sick of
CFILOR	frolic
CFIMOR	formic
CFIMOT	comfit
CFINOT	confit
CFINOX	confix
CFISTU	fustic
CFITYY	cityfy
CFKLOS	flocks
CFKPUU	fuck up
CFLPUU	cupful
CFRSUY	scurfy
CGGLOY	cloggy
	coggly
CGHHOU	chough
CGHIIN	I Ching
CGHILT	glitch
CGHIOT	Gothic
CGHLOU	Clough
CGHORU	grouch
CGILNY	clingy
CGIMNO	coming
	gnomic
CGINOP	coping
CGINOV	coving
CGINRU	curing
CGINRY	crying
CGLLOY	glycol
CGLNOU	unclog

CGLOOU	colugo
CGLOPU	clog up
CGNSUY	Cygnus
CHHNOO	honcho
CHHOOT	hootch
CHIIKM	kimchi
CHIILL	chilli
CHIILT	litchi
	lithic
CHIINP	chip in
CHIINT	chitin
CHIIPP	hippic
CHIKNS	chinks
CHIKOS	hoicks
CHIKRS	kirsch
CHIKST	kitsch
CHILLY	chilly
CHILNO	Chilon
	Nichol
CHILOR	orchil
CHILRY	richly
CHIMNU	Munich
CHIMRS	chrism
	smirch
CHIMSS	schism
CHIMTY	mythic
CHINNO	Inchon
CHINOP	chop in
	Chopin
	phonic
CHINOR	Chiron
CHINOS	chinos
CHINPU	chin up
CHINPY	hypnic
CHINRU	urchin
CHINST	snitch
CHINTZ	chintz
CHINUY	Yichun
CHIOPR	Orphic
CHIOPT	photic
CHIOSZ	schizo
CHIPPY	chippy
CHIPRY	chirpy
CHIPSY	physic
	scyphi
CHIPTY	pitchy
CHIRST	Christ
CHIRUZ	Zurich
CHISST	schist
CHISTT	stitch
CHISTW	switch ❑
CHITTW	twitch
CHITTY	chitty
	titchy
CHIVVY	chivvy
CHJNOU	Chonju
CHKNUY	chunky
CHKOOS	chokos
CHKSSU	shucks
CHLOOS	school
CHLOST	cloths
CHLOSU	slouch
CHMMUY	chummy
CHMOOS	smooch
CHMOSU	smouch
	so much
CHMSTU	smutch
CHNOOP	poncho
CHNOTY	notchy
CHNPUY	punchy
CHOORT	cohort
CHOOST	co-host
CHOOSY	choosy
CHOPPU	chop up
CHOPPY	choppy
CHOPSY	psycho
CHOPUY	pouchy
CHORSU	chorus
CHOTUY	touchy
CHPSTU	putsch
CHSSSU	schuss
CIIKKN	kick in
CIIKNW	inwick
CIIKST	tisick
CIILMU	cilium
CIILSY	Sicily
CIIMTV	victim
CIINNU	uncini
CIINOR	ironic
CIINOT	coin it
CIINRT	citrin
	nitric
CIIOPS	Scipio
CIIRSS	crisis
CIISTY	cytisi
CIJNOO	cojoin
CIKLNO	inlock
	lock in
CIKLNU	Culkin
	in luck
CIKLSY	sickly
CIKMNU	muck in
CIKNOP	pick on
CIKNOT	on tick
CIKNPU	unpick
CIKNPY	pyknic
CIKNSU	suck in
CIKNTU	tuck in
CIKORR	corkir
CIKORY	Yorick
CIKOSS	sickos
CIKOSY	yoicks
CIKPPU	pick up
	pick-up
CIKRST	tricks
CIKRTU	Turkic
CIKRTY	tricky
CIKSST	sticks
CIKSTY	sticky
CILLOU	loculi
CILMUU	cumuli
CILNOU	uncoil
CILNSY	Lyncis
CILOOT	cool it
CILOPU	upcoil
CILOPY	policy
CILORT	lictor
CILOSU	coulis
CILOSV	Clovis
CILOSY	cosily
CILRSY	lyrics
CILSUU	Lucius
CIMMNU	cummin
CIMMOS	commis
CIMMOT	commit
CIMMOX	commix
CIMNOO	Comino
CIMNOR	micron
CIMNOU	muonic
CIMNRU	crinum
CIMOPY	myopic
CIMORS	micros
CIMORU	corium
CIMOST	sitcom
CIMOTY	comity
CIMPRS	scrimp
CIMRUU	curium
CIMSTY	mystic
CINNOR	Cronin
CINNOU	nuncio
CINNOY	incony
CINNSY	in sync
CINORT	citron
CINORZ	zircon
CINOSS	scions
	sonics
CINOST	tocsin
CINOSU	cousin
CINOSZ	zincos
CINPSU	Pincus
CIOOPT	octopi
CIOORT	octroi
CIOPRT	Pictor
	tropic
CIOPST	optics
CIORSU	curios
CIORTT	tricot
CIORTV	victor ❑
CIOSTU	coitus
CIPPRS	Cripps
CIPPSU	cippus
CIPRST	script
CIPRSY	crispy
CIRRSU	cirrus
CIRSTT	strict
CIRSTU	citrus
	Curtis
	rictus
	rustic
CISSUV	viscus
CJKOOS	jockos
CJNOSU	juncos
CKLNOO	lock on
CKLNOU	unlock
CKLNUY	clunky
CKLOPU	lock up
	lock-up
	uplock
CKLPUY	plucky
CKMOPU	mock up
	mock-up
CKMPUU	muck up
CKNORU	uncork
CKNTUU	untuck
CKOOPU	cook up
CKOSST	stocks
CKOSTY	stocky
CKPSUU	suck up
CKPTUU	tuck up
CKRSTU	struck
CKRSUU	ruckus
CLLOOY	coolly
CLLORS	scroll
CLMNOU	column
CLMOPY	comply
CLMOSU	locums
CLMPUY	clumpy
CLMSUY	clumsy
	muscly
CLNOOS	colons
CLNOOU	uncool
CLNOOY	colony
CLNOSU	consul
	SCONUL
CLNOTU	uncolt
CLNOUW	uncowl
CLNOWY	Colwyn
CLNRUU	uncurl
CLOORU	colour
CLOOTT	Olcott
CLOSTU	clouts
	locust
CLOSTY	costly
CLOSUU	oculus
CLOTUW	low-cut
CLPRUU	curl up
CLPSTU	sculpt
CLRTUY	curtly
CLSSUU	sulcus
CMMNOO	common
CMMOOS	commos
CMMRUY	crummy
CMMSUY	scummy
CMNNOO	non-com
CMOOPS	compos
CMOOSS	cosmos
CMOOSW	Moscow
CMORSU	mucros
CMOSTU	custom
CMOSUU	mucous
CMPRSU	scrump
CMSTUU	scutum
CNNOOR	Connor
CNOOPU	coupon

Words marked ❑ can also be spelled with an initial capital letter

CNOOST	contos
	nostoc
	oncost
CNOOTT	cotton
CNOOTY	tycoon
CNOOVY	convoy
CNOPSW	C P Snow
CNORSU	Cronus
CNORSY	synroc
CNORUZ	Curzon
CNOSTU	Tucson
CNOTUY	county
COOORZ	corozo
COOPPU	coop up
COOPRS	scroop
COOPTU	cop out
	cop-out
COOPWX	cowpox
COORSS	corsos
COORUU	roucou
COPPRU	crop up
COPPUY	copy up
COPRSU	corpus
COPRUY	croupy
COPSUY	cosy up
CORRSU	cursor
CORSSY	Y-cross
CORSTU	courts
	scruto
	Turcos
CORSUV	Corvus
CORTUY	cry out
	outcry
COTTUU	cut out
	cut-out
CPRSUY	Cyprus
CRRSUY	scurry
CRSSTU	crusts
CRSTUY	crusty
	curtsy
CRSUVY	scurvy
CSUYZZ	scuzzy

D

DDDEEW	wedded
DDDEIL	diddle
	lidded
DDDEIR	didder
DDDELO	doddle
DDDEOR	dodder
DDEEEN	needed
DDEEES	Deedes
	seeded
DDEEFN	defend
DDEEGR	dredge
DDEEGW	wedged
DDEEHL	heddle
DDEEIN	in deed
	indeed
DDEEIR	Deidre
	deride
DDEELM	meddle
DDEELP	peddle
DDEELR	reddle
DDEELS	sleded
DDEELU	delude
DDEEMN	mended
DDEEMO	démodé
DDEENP	depend
DDEENR	redden
DDEENT	dented
DDEENU	denude
	dudeen
	Dundee
DDEEOR	eroded
DDEERT	tedder
DDEERY	Eddery
DDEFIL	fiddle
DDEFLO	folded
DDEFLU	fuddle
DDEFNU	funded
DDEFOR	fodder
DDEFRY	Freddy
DDEGGO	dogged
DDEGIL	gilded
DDEGIR	ridged
DDEGIT	geddit
DDEGJU	judged
DDEGLU	guddle
DDEGNO	dog end
	dog-end
	Godden
DDEGOR	dodger
DDEGRU	drudge
DDEHIN	hidden
DDEHIS	dished
DDEHLO	Hoddle
DDEHLU	huddle
DDEHOO	hooded
DDEIIO	iodide
DDEIIV	divide
DDEIKR	kidder
DDEILM	middle
DDEILP	piddle
DDEILR	riddle
DDEILT	tiddle
DDEILW	widdle
DDEIMN	midden
	minded
DDEIMS	desmid
DDEINR	ridden
	rinded
DDEINW	winded
DDEIOS	didoes
DDEIOV	devoid
DDEJRU	judder
DDELLU	dulled
DDELMU	muddle
DDELNO	noddle
DDELOO	doodle
DDELOT	toddle
DDELPU	puddle
DDELRU	ruddle
DDELUY	Dudley
DDEMNU	Edmund
DDEMOO	doomed
DDEMOR	Modred
DDEMPU	dumped
DDEMRU	red mud
DDENOR	donder
DDENOS	sodden
DDENRY	Dryden
DDENSU	sudden
DDEOOS	dodoes
DDEOOW	wooded
DDEOSU	doused
DDEOTT	dotted
DDEPUU	dude up
DDERRU	rudder
DDFILY	fiddly
DDGIPU	giddup
DDHIOS	oddish
DDHOSY	shoddy
DDHPUU	huddup
DDIIKK	dik-dik
DDIKSY	skiddy
DDILNR	dirndl
DDILTY	tiddly
DDINNO	nid-nod
DDIORS	sordid
DDIOTY	oddity
DDLOOT	odd lot
DDMMUU	dumdum
DDMORV	DVD-ROM
DDNOOS	odds-on
DDNOOW	do down
DEEEFR	feeder
DEEEGR	degree
DEEEHL	heeled
DEEEKL	keeled
DEEELN	needle
DEEELT	delete
DEEEMR	redeem
DEEENP	deepen
DEEENV	vendee
DEEEPV	peeved
DEEERS	see red
DEEERW	weeder
DEEERY	red-eye
DEEFGL	fledge
DEEFIL	defile
DEEFIN	define
	feed in
DEEFIR	defier
DEEFLW	flewed
DEEFLX	deflex
DEEFNO	feed on
DEEFNR	fender□
DEEFPU	feed up
DEEFSU	defuse
DEEGGL	gledge
	legged
DEEGHR	hedger
DEEGLN	legend
DEEGLP	pledge
DEEGLR	ledger
DEEGLS	sledge
DEEGLU	deluge
DEEGLY	gleyed
DEEGMR	merged
DEEGNO	on edge
DEEGNR	gender
DEEGNU	dengue
	unedge
DEEGRY	greedy
DEEGSZ	Szeged
DEEHMS	meshed□
DEEHNT	the end
DEEHPR	Phèdre
DEEHRR	herder□
DEEHRT	the red
DEEILN	Leiden
DEEILR	lieder
DEEILS	diesel□
	sedile
DEEILV	veiled
DEEILX	exiled
DEEIMP	impede
DEEIMS	demies
	demise
	Medise
DEEIMZ	Medize
DEEINN	in need
DEEINR	denier
	nereid
DEEINS	Denise
DEEINV	endive
	veined
DEEIPP	Dieppe
DEEIPR	perdie
DEEIRS	desire
	reside
DEEIRT	dieter
DEEIRU	ureide
DEEIRV	derive
DEEISS	dieses
DEEISV	devise
DEEJRU	de jure
DEEJSS	jessed
DEEKKR	Dekker
DEEKSW	skewed
DEELMN	Mendel
DEELMT	melted
DEELMY	medley
DEELNR	lender
DEELNW	wedeln
DEELNY	Leyden
	needly
DEELOP	delope
DEELPY	deeply
DEELRW	welder
DEELST	eldest
DEELSV	delves
DEELUX	de luxe

	deluxe
	de-luxe
DEELVV	devvel
DEEMNO	omened
DEEMNR	mender
DEEMNT	dement
DEEMOT	demote
DEEMPR	permed
	premed
DEEMRT	termed
DEEMRU	demure
DEEMRY	remedy
DEEMSY	emydes
DEEMTU	Te Deum
DEENNP	penned
DEENOP	depone
	opened
DEENOR	Doreen
DEENOS	Odense
DEENOT	denote
DEENPX	expend
DEENRR	render
DEENRS	Enders
	sender
DEENRT	tender
DEENRU	endure
DEENRV	Denver
	nerved
	vender
DEENST	tensed
DEENSU	Eusden
DEENSW	Sweden
DEENTT	netted
DEENTU	detune
DEENTX	extend
DEEOPS	depose
	speedo
DEEORT	teredo
DEEOTT	Odette
DEEOTV	devote
	vetoed
DEEOXY	ox-eyed
DEEPSY	speedy
DEEPTT	petted
DEEPTU	depute
DEERSS	des res
DEERST	desert
	rested
DEERSV	versed
DEERTX	dexter□
DEESTT	detest
	tested
DEESTU	Études
DEESTV	devest
	vested
DEESTW	stewed
DEETUV	vedute
DEETWY	tweedy
DEFFIM	miffed
DEFFIO	die off
DEFFIR	differ
DEFFLU	duffel
	duffle
DEFFNO	offend
DEFFPU	puffed
DEFFRU	duffer
	ruffed
DEFGIR	fridge
DEFGIT	fidget
	gifted
DEFGOR	forged
DEFHOO	hoofed
DEFILL	filled
DEFILO	foiled
DEFILS	fields□
DEFILT	lifted
DEFINN	finned
DEFINR	finder
	friend
DEFIOO	foodie
DEFIOR	die for
DEFIOT	foetid
DEFIOW	wide of
DEFIRV	fervid
DEFITT	fitted
DEFKOR	forked
DEFLNO	enfold
	fondle
DEFLOR	folder
DEFLOT	lofted
DEFLTU	fluted
DEFLTY	deftly
DEFMOR	deform
	formed
DEFNOU	fondue
DEFNRU	Freund
	funder
	refund
DEFOOR	roofed
DEFOOT	footed
DEFOST	OFSTED
	Ofsted
DEFRTU	turfed
DEFTTU	tufted
DEGGIN	edging
DEGGIR	digger
DEGGIU	Duggie
DEGGIW	wigged
DEGGLO	dog-leg
DEGGOR	dogger□
	gorged
DEGGRU	grudge
	rugged
DEGHIN	hinged
DEGILM	mid-leg
DEGILN	dingle
	engild
DEGILO	Goidel
	Goldie
DEGILR	gilder
	girdle
	glider
DEGIMT	midget
DEGINN	ending
DEGINO	Gideon
DEGINR	engird
	ringed
DEGINS	design
	dinges
DEGINW	winged
DEGIRR	girder
DEGIST	digest
DEGITW	widget
DEGJSU	Judges
DEGKLU	kludge
DEGLNO	golden
DEGLNU	gulden
DEGLOR	lodger
DEGLSU	sludge
DEGMMU	gummed
DEGMSU	smudge
DEGNOO	Gooden
DEGNRU	gerund
DEGNSU	snudge
DEGOPY	pye-dog
DEGORU	drogue
	gourde
DEGOST	stodge
DEGRTU	trudge
DEGTTU	gutted
DEHHSU	hushed
DEHIKT	The Kid
DEHILN	held in
DEHILS	shield
DEHINO	honied
DEHINR	hinder
DEHINT	hinted
DEHIOR	rhodie
DEHIOS	Hesiod
DEHIPP	hipped
DEHIRT	dither
DEHISS	dishes
DEHITW	wideth
DEHKOO	hooked
DEHLOR	holder
DEHLPS	delphs
DEHLRU	hurdle
DEHMOT	method
DEHMPU	humped
DEHMRY	rhymed
DEHNOR	dehorn
	horned
DEHNOY	hoyden
DEHNRY	Hendry
DEHORS	hordes
	Rhodes
DEHORT	dehort
	red hot
	red-hot
DEHORW	Howerd
DEHOSW	showed
DEHPST	depths
DEHPSU	pushed
DEHRSS	shreds
DEHRSU	rushed
DEHRSW	shrewd
DEHRTY	the dry
DEIINO	iodine
DEIINS	inside
DEIINV	divine
DEIIOS	iodise
DEIIOZ	iodize
DEIIRS	irides
	irised
DEIISS	diesis
DEIJLT	jilted
DEIJNO	joined
DEIJNX	jinxed
DEIKLL	killed
DEIKLN	kindle
	linked
DEIKLO	keloid
DEIKLT	kilted
DEIKNP	pinked
DEIKNY	kidney
DEIKPS	spiked
DEIKPU	Updike
DEIKRU	duiker
DEILLU	illude
DEILLW	willed
DEILMN	milden
DEILMP	dimple
DEILMR	Midler
DEILMS	misled
DEILMW	mildew
DEILNN	dinnle
	linden
DEILNT	dentil
DEILNZ	Denzil
DEILOP	dipole
DEILOS	Isolde
	oldies
	soiled
DEILPP	lipped
DEILPS	dispel
DEILRS	slider
DEILRV	drivel
DEILRW	Wilder
DEILRY	Ridley
DEILSU	Delius
DEILTT	tilted
	titled
DEILTU	dilute
DEILTW	wilted
DEILWY	dewily
	widely
	wieldy
DEIMMR	dimmer
	rimmed
DEIMMU	medium
DEIMNO	monied
DEIMNP	impend
DEIMNR	minder
	remind

DEIMNS	denims
DEIMOR	dormie
	moider
DEIMOT	do time
DEIMPR	primed
DEIMRS	dermis
DEIMSS	missed
DEIMST	demist
DEIMTU	tedium
DEINNO	dine on
	Dionne
	done in
	Donnie
	Ondine
DEINNR	dinner
DEINNS	Dennis
	Sinden
DEINNT	dentin
	indent
	intend
	tinned
DEINNU	undine
DEINNW	enwind
DEINOP	pioned
DEINOR	De Niro
	Indore
	ride on
DEINOS	Edison
	no-side
	onside
	side-on
DEINOV	dive on
DEINPU	uniped
DEINRT	tinder
DEINRU	inured
	ruined
DEINRV	driven
DEINRW	winder
DEINRZ	Zinder
DEINSU	undies
DEINSW	Widnes
DEINSY	Disney
	Sidney
DEINTU	united□
	untied
DEINTW	twined
DEIOOR	oroide
DEIOOV	Oviedo
DEIOPR	period
DEIOPS	poised
DEIORS	dorise
DEIORT	editor
	triode
DEIORW	weirdo
DEIORZ	dorize
DEIOSV	videos
DEIOTT	Dottie
DEIOTU	die out
DEIOTV	DeVito
DEIPPR	dipper
	ripped
DEIPPT	tipped
DEIPQU	piqued
DEIPRS	spider
DEIPRU	ride up
DEIPRZ	prized
DEIPSS	pissed
DEIPSU	upside
DEIPTT	pitted
DEIPTU	tied up
DEIRRS	derris
DEIRRV	driver
DEIRST	stride
DEIRSV	divers
DEIRTV	divert
DEISST	desist
DEISSU	disuse
DEISTU	duties
	suited
DEISTV	divest
	Vedist
DEITTU	duetti
DEITTW	dewitt
DEITUV	veduti
DEJLOW	jowled
DEKKOS	dekkos
DEKMNU	Mukden
DEKMOS	smoked
DEKNOT	token'd
DEKNOY	donkey
DEKNOZ	zonked
DEKNSU	dusken
DEKORW	worked
DELLOR	rolled
DELLOW	do well
	Dowell
DELLSU	Dulles
DELLWY	lewdly
DELMNO	dolmen
DELMOS	seldom
DELMOU	module
DELMOY	melody□
DELMPU	plumed
DELNNO	on-lend
DELNOO	noodle
DELNOR	rondel
DELNOU	louden
	nodule
DELNOW	Weldon
DELNRU	nurdle
DELNRY	dernly
DELNUY	nudely
DELOOP	looped
	poodle
	pooled
DELOOS	oodles
DELOOT	Toledo
DELOPR	polder
DELOPY	deploy
DELORS	solder
DELORW	weldor
DELORY	Delroy
DELOSS	dossel
DELOST	oldest
DELPUX	duplex
DELRUY	rudely
DELSTY	styled
DEMNOR	modern
DEMOOR	moored
	roomed
DEMORR	dormer
DEMORT	Dermot
DEMOST	modest
DEMOSU	dumose
	odeums
DEMPRU	dumper
DEMRRU	murder
	Red Rum
DENNOR	Donner
DENNOS	donnés
	send on
DENNOT	tendon
DENNOU	undone
DENOOS	nodose
DENOOT	dote on
DENOOV	de novo
DENOOW	wooden
DENOPR	ponder
DENOPU	done up
DENORT	rodent
DENORV	vendor
DENORW	downer
	wonder□
DENORY	Rodney
	yonder
DENOST	Ostend
	stoned
DENOSZ	dozens
DENOTW	wonted
DENPSU	send up
	send-up
DENRST	Dnestr
DENRSU	sunder
DENRTU	retund
	turned
DENRTY	trendy
DENRUV	Verdun
DENSUU	unused
DENSUW	sundew
DENSYY	Sydney
DEOOPP	pooped
DEOORS	rodeos
DEOORT	rooted
DEOORV	do over
	overdo
DEOPQU	Pequod
DEOPRT	de trop
	deport
DEOPRV	proved
DEOPRW	powder
DEOPST	despot
	posted
DEOPSU	pseudo
DEOPTT	potted
DEOQTU	quoted
DEORRS	orders
DEORRU	ordure
DEORRV	drover
DEORRW	reword
DEORSS	dosser
DEORST	Dorset
	sorted
	stored
DEORSU	roused
	soured
DEORSV	droves
DEORSW	dowser
	drowse
DEORSY	Dorsey
DEORTU	detour
	outred
	red out
	routed
DEORUV	devour
DEOSSU	soused
DEOSTU	used to
DEOSUX	exodus□
DEOTUV	devout
DEPSUU	used up
DEPTUY	deputy
DERRSU	Durres
DERRUY	rudery
DERSSU	duress
DERSSY	dressy
DERSTU	duster
	rusted
DERTTU	rutted
DESTTU	duetts
DESTUV	duvets
DFFIMO	mid-off
DFFNOO	fond of
	nod off
DFGIIR	frigid
DFGIOR	dig for
DFHLOO	hold of
DFIINY	nidify
DFIIRT	trifid
DFIKNO	kind of
DFIKOX	kid-fox
DFILNO	fold in
	infold
DFILOR	florid
DFILUV	fulvid
DFIMOY	modify
DFLNOU	unfold
DFLNOY	fondly
DFLOOS	floods
DFLOPU	fold up
DFLORU	Rudolf
DFLORY	dor-fly
DFLRYY	dry-fly
DFNSUU	fundus
DFOORX	Oxford
DGGNOU	dugong

	gun dog
DGGRUY	druggy
DGHIIN	hiding
DGHINY	dinghy
DGHOOO	good-oh
DGHOOT	hot dog
	hot-dog
DGHOUY	doughy
DGIINO	indigo
DGIINP	pidgin
DGIINR	Ingrid
	riding□
DGIINS	siding
DGIINV	diving
DGIJOU	judogi
DGINNO	doning
DGINOP	doping
DGINOS	doings
DGINOT	doting
	tin god
DGINOV	Govind
DGINOW	Godwin
DGINOZ	dozing
DGINPU	duping
DGINRU	during
	ungird
DGINRY	drying
DGIOTU	dig out
DGIOTW	godwit
DGIRTU	turgid
DGLOOY	goodly
DGLSUY	sludgy
DGMSUY	smudgy
DGNOOO	no good
	no-good
DGNOOR	drongo
	Gondor
	Gordon
DGNOOS	godson
DGNOOU	Gounod
DGNOOW	go down
	godown
DGNORU	ground
	ungord
DGNOSU	sun-god
DGNRUU	Gudrun
DGOOPT	top dog
DGOORW	word go
DGOSTY	stodgy
DGOTUU	dugout
DHIIPS	hispid
DHIISW	widish
DHIJTU	Judith
DHILNO	hold in
DHILOS	oldish
DHILOT	hold it!
DHIMOS	modish
DHINSY	shindy
DHIOOT	dhooti
DHIOPY	hypoid
DHIORR	horrid
DHIOSV	dovish
DHIOTW	do with
DHIPSU	dish up
DHLNOO	hold on
	on hold
DHLOOT	hold to
DHLOPU	hold up
	hold-up
	uphold
DHLOSU	should
DHLTUU	Duluth
DHNOSU	Hudson
	unshod
DHOOOO	hoodoo
DHOORT	hot rod
DHORSU	shroud
DHORSW	shrowd
DHORSY	hydros
DHORTU	drouth
DHRSUY	Hydrus
DIIJNN	djinni
DIIKNN	in kind
DIIKWZ	wiz kid
DIILMP	limpid
DIILOP	lipoid
DIILOS	solidi
DIILQU	liquid
DIILST	distil
DIILTY	tidily
DIIMNU	indium
DIIMTW	dimwit
DIIMTY	dimity
DIINNW	inwind
DIINOX	dioxin
DIINRS	indris
DIINSV	invis'd
DIKLNY	kindly
DIKMNU	dinkum
DIKNNU	unkind
DIKNRS	drinks
DIKOOS	skidoo
DIKORY	Kid Ory
DILLMY	mildly
DILLNO	Dillon
DILLOW	will do
DILLVY	vildly
DILLWY	wildly
DILMOR	milord
DILMOU	moduli
DILNNU	dunlin
DILOPY	ploidy
DILOST	stolid
DILOXY	xyloid
DIMMSU	dim sum
DIMNOO	domino□
DIMNSU	nudism
DIMOOR	Dromio
	dromoi
DIMOPU	podium
DIMOSU	sodium
DIMOSW	wisdom□
DIMOTU	dim out
	dim-out
DINNUW	unwind
DINOOR	indoor
DINOPR	drop in
	drop-in
DINOPU	unipod
DINORW	in word
DINOST	on-dits
DINOSW	disown
DINOTZ	Dönitz
DINOWW	window
DINPTU	pundit
DINPUW	upwind
	up-wind
	wind up
	wind-up
DINSTU	Dustin
	nudist
DINTUY	nudity
	untidy
DIOORT	toroid
DIOOSU	odious
DIOOTX	toxoid
DIOPRT	torpid
	tripod
DIOPSS	dipsos
DIORRT	Dorrit
	torrid
DIOSTT	dittos
DIOSTU	studio
DIPRTU	putrid
DIPSTU	stupid
DIPTUY	tidy up
	tidyup
DIQSSU	squids
DJLMOY	jymold
DJNNOO	donjon
DKLSUY	duskly
DKMOOO	Komodo
DKNOOP	pondok
DKOOOO	koodoo
DLLOOP	dollop
DLLOPU	doll up
DLLORY	drolly
	lordly
DLLOUW	Ludlow
DLLOUY	loudly
DLMOOU	modulo
DLMORY	My Lord
DLMOUY	mouldy
DLNNOO	London
DLNOOP	plod on
DLNOOS	sold on
DLNOPU	Dunlop
DLNORU	unlord
DLNOTU	untold
DLNUUY	unduly
DLOOPS	podsol
DLOOPZ	podzol
DLOORU	dolour
DLORSW	worlds
DLORUY	dourly
DLORWY	wordly
DMNOOY	monody
DMNOPU	dump on
DMOORR	Mordor
DMOOSU	duomos
DMORSU	dorsum
DMORWY	my word
DMOSUU	dumous
DMPRUU	drum up
DNOOPR	drop on
DNOORS	rondos
DNOOST	tondos
DNOOSU	nodous
DNOPSU	pounds
DNOPTU	Du Pont
DNORST	strond
DNORSU	rounds
DNORTU	rotund
DNOSTU	stound
DNOTUY	on duty
DNRRUY	dry run
	run dry
DNRSUY	sundry
DOOOOV	voodoo
DOOOPW	doo-wop
DOOPRY	droopy□
DOPRSY	dropsy
DORSSY	drossy
DORSTU	Stroud
DORSWY	drowsy
DORTUY	dry out
DPSTUU	dust-up
DRSTUY	sturdy

E

EEEEGG	gee-gee
EEEEHT	tee-hee
EEEEPT	teepee
EEEEWW	wee-wee
EEEFFT	effete
EEEFKO	O'Keefe
EEEFLR	feeler
EEEFNR	enfree
EEEFNT	en fête
EEEFRR	reefer
EEEFRZ	freeze
EEEGLR	Legree
EEEGMR	emerge
EEEGNP	peenge
EEEGNR	Greene
	renege
EEEGNU	Eugene
EEEGRS	Seeger
EEEGRZ	geezer
EEEHLT	lethee
EEEHNS	Sheene
EEEHNT	ethene
EEEHPS	pheese
EEEHPZ	pheeze

EEEHST	seethe
EEEHTT	teethe
EEEHWZ	wheeze
EEEIJL	jeelie
EEEIKL	keelie
EEEILN	Eileen
EEEIPW	weepie
EEEITY	Eyetie
EEEJRR	jeerer
EEEJSV	Jeeves
EEEKLU	ekuele
EEEKMN	meeken
EEEKNR	keener
EEEKPR	keeper
EEEKRS	kreese
	seeker
EEELMS	Semele
EEELMT	Melete
EEELMX	lexeme
EEELNS	Selene
EEELNV	eleven
EEELPR	peeler
EEELSS	lessee
EEELST	Steele
EEELSV	sleeve
EEELTY	eyelet
EEEMMS	sememe
EEEMNR	meneer
EEEMST	esteem
	mestee
EEENRS	serene
EEENRT	entrée
EEENRV	veneer
EEENSS	Essene
EEENSZ	sneeze
EEENTT	entêté
EEENVW	venewe
EEEOPP	epopee
EEEORY	Eeyore
EEEPRW	weeper
EEERRV	revere□
EEERSV	Reeves
	severe
EEERTT	teeter
EEERTX	Exeter
EEERVW	weever
EEESTT	settee
	testee
EEESTV	steeve
EEETWZ	tweeze
EEFFIL	Eiffel
EEFFKL	keffel
EEFFOT	toffee
EEFFSU	effuse
EEFGRU	refuge
EEFHIR	heifer
EEFHOR	hereof
EEFHTW	the few
EEFILN	feline
EEFILR	relief
EEFILT	leftie
EEFINR	ferine
	in fere
	refine
EEFINV	even if
EEFIRZ	frieze
EEFIST	see fit
EEFLLR	feller
EEFLNN	fennel
EEFLNS	flense
EEFLRT	reflet
EEFLRU	ferule
EEFLRX	reflex
EEFLRY	freely
EEFLTT	fettle
EEFLUY	eyeful
EEFPRR	prefer
EEFPTY	tepefy
EEFQRV	Q-fever
EEFRRT	ferret
EEFRST	fester
EEFRSU	refuse
EEFRTT	fetter
EEFRTU	refute
EEFSTT	eftest
EEFSTW	fewest
EEFSZZ	fezzes
EEGGIR	Geiger
	greige
	Reggie
EEGGOR	George
EEGHLT	the leg
EEGHOT	Goethe
EEGIMR	émigré
	regime
	régime
EEGIMV	give me
EEGINN	engine
EEGINS	seeing
EEGIRT	Gertie
EEGIRV	grieve
EEGLMU	legume
EEGLNS	Engels
EEGLNT	gentle
EEGLRT	reglet
EEGMMN	gemmen
EEGMNO	genome
EEGMNT	tegmen
EEGMOR	Göreme
EEGMRR	merger
EEGNOP	pongee
EEGNOR	engore
EEGNRS	greens
EEGNRT	regent
EEGNRW	Wenger
EEGNRY	energy
	greeny
EEGNST	gentes
EEGOOS	soogee
EEGRRT	regret
EEGRRV	verger
EEGRSS	egress
EEGRSY	geyser
EEGRTT	getter
EEHILN	heel in
	hele in
EEHINR	herein
	inhere
EEHINT	theine
EEHIRT	either
EEHITV	thieve
EEHKLS	shekel
EEHLLR	Heller
EEHLMT	helmet
EEHLNU	unhele
EEHLNY	Henley
EEHLPR	helper
EEHLSV	shelve
EEHLSW	wheels
EEHMMS	emmesh
EEHMMT	Mehmet
EEHMNP	hempen
EEHMNS	enmesh
EEHMRS	Hermes
EEHMST	smeeth
EEHMTT	the Met
EEHMUX	exhume
EEHNOR	hereon
EEHNOT	the one
EEHNPW	nephew
EEHNRR	Herren
EEHNRT	nether
	threne
EEHNSY	sheeny
EEHNTT	the Net
	the net
EEHNTY	ethyne
EEHORS	heroes
EEHORT	hereto
	hetero
EEHOSX	hexose
EEHPRS	herpes
	sphere
EEHPRT	threep
EEHRST	Esther
	Hester
EEHRSY	heresy
EEHRTT	tether
EEHRTW	wether
EEHRTY	they're
EEHSST	sheets
	theses
EEHSVY	Hevesy
EEHTVY	they've
EEHWYZ	wheezy
EEIJNN	jinnee
EEIJSS	jessie□
EEIKLP	kelpie
EEIKNP	keep in
EEILLS	Leslie
EEILLW	wellie
EEILMR	Meriel
EEILNO	Leonie
EEILNP	penile
EEILNR	reline
EEILNS	enisle
	ensile
	nelies
	senile
EEILOS	Eloise
EEILPT	pelite
EEILRR	relier
EEILRS	resile
EEILRV	relive
	revile
EEILRY	eerily
EEILSW	Wiesel
EEILSX	ilexes
EEILTT	Lettie
EEILVW	weevil
EEIMMS	Emmies
EEIMNR	ermine
EEIMNS	inseem
EEIMPR	empire□
EEIMRS	misère
	remise
EEIMRT	métier
EEIMSS	emesis
	missee
EEINNR	nerine
	Rennie
EEINPR	repine
EEINQU	equine
EEINRS	serine
EEINRT	entire
EEINRW	Wiener
EEINSS	in esse
EEINTV	venite
EEIORS	soirée
EEIPPY	yippee
EEIPQU	équipe
EEIPRR	Pierre
EEIPRT	Petrie
EEIPRV	prieve
EEIPRX	expire
EEIPTT	petite
EEIPTW	peewit
EEIRRT	retire
EEIRSS	series
EEIRSV	revise
EEIRVV	revive
EEIRVW	review
	viewer
EEISTW	Westie
EEJJNU	jejune
EEJLLO	Joelle
EEJLNO	Joleen
	Jolene
EEJLSW	jewels
EEJMOR	Jerome
EEJMRY	Jeremy
EEJNNR	Jenner
EEJNNT	jennet
EEJQRU	jerque

EEJRST	jester
EEJRSY	jersey□
EEJSTT	jet set
EEKLMY	meekly
EEKLNN	kennel
EEKLNR	kernel
EEKLNY	keenly
EEKLPR	kelper□
	Kepler
EEKLRT	kelter
	Terkel
EEKLTT	kettle
EEKLWY	weekly
EEKMNS	Meknès
EEKMPR	kemper
EEKMRS	kermes
EEKNNO	keen on
EEKNOP	keep on
EEKNOT	keen to
	ketone
EEKNSY	Keynes
EEKOPT	keep to
EEKORV	revoke
EEKOST	seek to
	to seek
EEKOTU	eke out
EEKPPU	keep up
	upkeep
EEKPRU	peruke
EEKRST	streek
EEKRSW	skewer
	Wesker
EEKRSY	kersey
EELLNO	Noelle
EELLPT	pellet
EELLRS	seller
EELLRT	retell
	teller□
EELLRW	Weller
EELLSW	Sewell
	Welles
EELLSY	Lesley
EELMPT	pelmet
	temple□
EELMRY	merely
EELMSY	seemly
EELMTT	mettle
EELMTY	meetly
EELNNT	Lenten
EELNPS	spleen
EELNRR	Lerner
EELNRT	relent
EELNRU	unreel
EELNSS	lenses
	lessen
EELNST	nestle
EELNSU	unseel
EELNSV	Velsen
EELNTT	nettle
EELNTU	eluent
EELNUV	Leuven
	venule
EELNVY	Evelyn
	evenly
EELNXY	xylene
EELOPP	people
EELOPR	eloper
EELORS	or else
EELOVV	evolve
EELPPU	peepul
EELPRT	petrel
EELPRY	yelper
EELPST	Elspet
	pestle
EELPSV	pelves
EELPSY	sleepy
EELPTT	pettle
EELQSU	sequel
EELRSS	lesser
EELRST	Lester
	streel
EELRSV	levers
	revels
EELRTT	letter
EELRTW	welter
EELRUV	velure
EELSSV	selves
	vessel
EELSTT	settle
EELSTV	svelte
EELSTY	sleety
	steely
EELSUV	evulse
EELSWY	Wesley
EELTVV	velvet
EELTVW	twelve
EELTWY	tweely
EEMMRS	Mesmer
EEMMST	stemme
EEMNOT	toneme
EEMNOY	yeomen
EEMNSS	menses
EEMNYZ	enzyme
EEMOPR	EEPROM
EEMOPT	metope
EEMORT	meteor
	remote
EEMORV	remove
EEMPRS	Semper
	sempre
EEMPRT	temper
EEMPTU	meet up
EEMPTX	exempt
EEMRST	restem
EEMRSU	resume
	résumé
EEMRSV	vermes
EEMRSY	Mersey
EEMRTU	Meerut
EEMSST	tmeses
EEMSSW	mewses
EEMSTX	Semtex®
EEMTXX	Tex-Mex
EENNOR	Noreen
EENNOS	Neeson
EENNOV	even on
	Evonne
EENNOZ	enzone
EENNRS	Rennes
EENNRT	rennet
	tenner
EENNST	sennet
EENNSU	unseen
EENNUV	uneven
EENNUY	ennuyé
EENOPR	opener
	reopen
	repone
EENOPT	poteen
EENORS	or snee
EENORW	ere now
	erenow
EENORY	oneyer
	oneyre
EENORZ	rezone
EENOSS	enoses
EENOST	not see
EENOSV	even so
	venose
EENOTW	townee
EENPRT	repent
EENPRY	pyrene
EENPUV	even up
EENQSU	Queens
EENRRT	renter
EENRST	Ernest
	resent
	Sterne
EENRSU	ensure
EENRSV	nerves
	Severn
EENRTT	tenter
EENRTU	neuter
	tenure
	tureen
EENRTV	venter
EENSSS	senses
EENSTT	tenets
EENSTU	tenues
EENSTV	events
	Steven
EENSTW	newest
EENSTY	teensy
EENSYZ	sneezy
EENTTX	extent
EENTUX	exeunt
EEOPRS	repose
EEOPRU	Europe
EEOPSS	eposes
EEOPSX	expose
	exposé
EEOPTU	toupee
EEOPTY	peyote
EEORRV	Rovere
EEORST	stereo
EEORSV	ever so
	soever
EEORUV	oeuvre
EEOSST	setose
EEOSTV	vetoes
EEOSUY	see you
EEPPPR	pepper
EEPPST	steppe
EEPRRS	sperre
EEPRRU	repure
EEPRSS	preses
EEPRST	pester
	Peters
	preset
	Streep
EEPRSU	peruse
EEPRSW	spewer
EEPRTU	repute
EEPRTW	pewter
EEPRTX	expert
EEPSSS	sepses
EEPSTT	septet
EEPTTU	puttee
EERRST	rester
EERRSV	revers
	server
	verser
EERRTU	Reuter
	ureter
EERRTV	revert
EERSSV	Sèvres
EERSTT	setter
	street
	tester
EERSTU	retuse
EERSTV	revest
	Treves
EERSTW	wester
EERSTX	exsert
EERSTZ	zester
EERSVW	swerve
EERSXX	Xerxes
EERTTT	tetter
EERTUY	tuyère
EERTVV	vervet
EERTVX	vertex
EERUVX	Evreux
EESSSY	yesses
EESSTT	sestet
	tsetse
EESSTW	sweets
EESTTU	suttee
EESTTX	sextet
EESTWY	sweety
EETTVY	Yvette
EFFGIR	griffe
EFFGIY	effigy
EFFGOR	goffer
EFFGOT	get off

EFFILP	piffle
EFFILS	siffle
EFFILY	Liffey
EFFINR	niffer
EFFINT	infeft
EFFKOY	off-key
EFFLMU	muffle
EFFLOT	let off
	let-off
EFFLRU	ruffle
EFFLUX	efflux
EFFNOO	one-off
EFFOPU	pouffe
EFFORS	reffos
EFFORT	effort
EFFORX	forfex
EFFOST	offset
	set off
	set-off
EFFPRU	puffer
EFFRSU	suffer
EFFTTU	tuffet
EFGGRU	Fugger
EFGINR	finger □
	fringe
EFGIOS	fogies
EFGIRU	figure
EFGLNU	engulf
EFGLOR	golfer
EFGOOR	forego
EFGORR	forger
EFGORT	forget
EFGOSY	fogeys
EFGRSU	Fergus
EFHILS	elfish
EFHIRS	fisher □
	sherif
EFHISS	Fishes
EFHIST	fetish
EFHLSY	fleshy
EFHLTY	The Fly
EFHOOR	hoofer
EFHORT	fother
EFHORY	hey for
EFHRRU	Führer
EFIINT	finite
EFIKLO	folkie
EFIKNO	Fokine
EFILLR	filler
	refill
EFILLT	fillet
EFILNO	olefin
	on file
EFILNY	finely
	Finley
	lenify
EFILPP	fipple
EFILPR	pilfer
EFILRR	rifler
EFILRT	filter
	trifle
EFILRU	ireful
EFILSS	fissle
EFILST	itself
	stifle
EFILSU	Fuseli
EFILTU	futile
EFILWY	wifely
EFILZZ	fizzle
EFINNY	Finney
EFINOR	fire on
	on fire
EFINRY	finery
EFINST	finest
	infest
EFINSU	infuse
EFIOOT	footie
EFIORT	trofie
EFIORX	orifex
EFIOST	softie
EFIPRU	fire up
EFIPRX	prefix
EFIRST	sifter
	strife
EFIRSU	Furies
EFIRTT	fitter
	titfer
EFIRTY	ferity
EFIRUX	fixure
EFIRVY	verify
EFIRZZ	fizzer
EFISTY	feisty
EFKKOR	Fokker
EFKLUY	flukey
EFKORR	forker
EFLLOT	flotel
EFLLOW	fellow
EFLLRU	Fuller
EFLLTY	let fly
EFLMSY	myself
EFLNNU	funnel
EFLNOT	Teflon®
EFLNOY	felony
EFLNSU	unself
EFLNTU	fluent
EFLOOT	footle
EFLOOZ	foozle
EFLORS	Flores
EFLORT	floret
EFLORW	flower
	fowler □
	reflow
EFLORX	flexor
EFLOSU	flouse
EFLOSW	Fowles
EFLOUW	woeful
EFLPRU	purfle
EFLRUU	rueful
EFLRUX	reflux
EFLSUU	useful
EFLUZZ	fuzzle
EFMNOT	foment
EFMNRU	frenum
EFMORR	former
	reform
	re-form
EFMRSU	femurs
EFMTUY	tumefy
EFNOOR	for one
EFNOOT	of note
EFNORS	Fresno
EFNORY	yen for
EFNORZ	frozen
EFNOST	soften
EFNRYZ	frenzy
EFOORR	roofer
EFOORT	footer
	tofore
EFOORY	of yore
EFOOTW	too few
EFOPST	EFTPOS
EFORRU	furore
EFORST	forest
	fortes
	foster □
EFORSU	fueros
	sure of
EFORTU	fouter
EFOSTU	foetus
EFRRSU	surfer
EFRRUU	fureur
EFRSSU	fusser
EFRTUU	future
EGGGIL	giggle
EGGGLO	goggle
EGGGLU	guggle
EGGGNO	eggnog
EGGHIL	higgle
EGGHIR	Gehrig
EGGHOT	hogget
EGGIIP	piggie
EGGIJL	jiggle
EGGIJR	jigger
EGGILN	niggle
EGGILO	loggie
EGGILR	ligger
EGGILW	wiggle
EGGIMO	moggie
EGGINR	ginger □
EGGIOR	Reggio
EGGIRR	rigger
EGGIRT	Tigger
EGGJLO	joggle
EGGJLU	juggle
EGGJOR	jogger
EGGLOO	google
EGGLOT	toggle
EGGLOW	woggle
EGGLPU	puggle
EGGLRU	gurgle
	lugger
EGGMRU	mugger
EGGNRU	grunge
EGGNTU	nugget
EGGORR	gorger
EGGORS	gregos
EGGORT	gorget
EGGRRU	rugger
EGGRTU	tugger
EGHHIR	higher □
EGHHIT	eighth
	height
EGHHIU	Hughie
EGHHSU	Hughes
EGHHUW	wheugh
EGHILS	sleigh
EGHINW	whinge
EGHITW	weight
EGHITY	eighty
EGHLMP	phlegm
EGHLNT	length
EGHLPU	Guelph
EGHLUY	hugely
EGHMOO	go home
EGHNOU	enough
EGHNRU	hunger
EGHOPR	gopher
EGHORZ	Herzog
EGHOTT	ghetto
EGHRSU	gusher
EGIILL	gillie
EGIILR	girlie
EGIILT	Ligeti
EGIIMN	Gemini
EGIINT	ignite
EGIINV	give in
EGIITV	give it
EGIJLN	jingle
EGIKNP	Peking
EGILLR	grille
EGILLT	gillet
EGILMN	mingle
EGILMP	megilp
EGILMT	gimlet
EGILNO	legion
EGILNP	pingle
EGILNR	linger
EGILNS	single
EGILNT	tingle
EGILOO	goolie
EGILOV	go live
EGILPR	Pilger
EGILPT	piglet □
EGILRS	grilse
EGILTU	glutei
EGIMMR	megrim
EGIMNO	Imogen
EGIMNY	geminy
EGIMOS	egoism
EGINNO	Onegin
EGINNR	enring
EGINNS	ensign
EGINOP	pigeon
EGINOR	ignore

	Origen
	region
EGINOS	ingoes
	soigné
EGINOV	give on
EGINOW	wigeon
EGINPR	pinger
EGINRR	erring
	girner
	ringer
EGINRS	Ingres
	resign
	re-sign
	signer
	singer□
EGINRW	winger
EGINRZ	zinger
EGINSS	gneiss
EGINST	ingest
	signet
EGINSU	genius□
EGINSW	sewing
	swinge
EGINTW	twinge
EGINVX	vexing
EGINZZ	gizzen
EGIORT	goitre
EGIOST	egoist
EGIPUV	give up
EGIRSU	guiser
EGIRTV	grivet
EGISSU	Gussie
EGJLNU	jungle
EGKMNO	Mekong
EGKRRU	Kruger
EGLLOW	go well
EGLLTU	gullet
EGLLUY	gulley
EGLNNU	gunnel
EGLNOR	longer
EGLNOU	lounge
EGLNPU	plunge
EGLNSY	Glenys
EGLNTU	englut
	gluten
EGLNTY	gently
EGLNUU	unglue
EGLOPS	gospel
EGLORV	glover
	grovel
EGLORW	glower
EGLOSV	gloves
EGLOUY	eulogy
EGLRYY	greyly
EGLTTU	guttle
EGLTUU	Telugu
EGLUZZ	guzzle
EGMMRU	Gummer
EGMNOR	monger
EGMNOS	gnomes
EGMNOT	Egmont
EGMNTU	nutmeg
EGMORU	morgue
EGMRTU	tergum
EGNNOO	non-ego
EGNNOU	guenon
EGNNRU	gunner
EGNNYY	gynney
EGNOOR	Oregon
	orogen
EGNOOT	gentoo
EGNOPS	sponge
EGNORV	govern
EGNORY	groyne
EGNOSS	gnoses
	segnos
EGNOTU	tongue
EGNOXY	oxygen
EGNPRU	repugn
EGNPUX	expugn
EGNRTU	urgent
EGNRTY	gentry
EGNRUY	Gurney
EGNSUU	ungues
EGOORV	go over
	groove
EGOOSS	gooses
EGOOST	stooge
EGOPRR	groper
EGOPSU	Pogues
EGOPTU	peg out
EGORRS	Rogers
EGORRW	grower
EGORSS	ogress
EGORSU	grouse
	rugose
EGOSSV	Vosges
EGOSTW	go west
EGOTTU	get out
	get-out
	goutte
EGOTYZ	zygote
EGPRSU	spurge
EGRTTU	gutter
EGSSTU	guests
	gusset
EHHIKS	sheikh
EHHIRT	hither
EHHISW	Hewish
EHHNPY	hyphen
EHHOTW	The Who
EHHRST	thresh
EHIIJM	Himeji
EHIIPP	hippie
EHIIST	Shiite
EHIJSW	Jewish
EHIKNO	honkie
EHIKPU	hike up
EHIKRS	shriek
	shrike
EHILLL	Hillel
EHILMU	helium
EHILOS	Helios
	isohel
EHILOT	eolith
EHILPR	hirple
EHILRS	hirsel
	hirsle
	relish
EHILRT	Hitler
	lither
EHILSV	elvish
EHILSW	whiles
EHIMMS	immesh
EHIMNO	home in
EHIMNR	menhir
EHIMNS	inmesh
EHIMNU	inhume
EHIMRS	Rheims
EHIMRT	hermit
	mither
EHIMRU	humeri
EHIMST	theism
EHINOR	heroin
	on hire
EHINRS	shiner
	shrine
EHINRW	whiner
EHINST	sithen
EHINSW	newish
EHINTW	whiten
EHINTZ	zenith
EHINUV	unhive
EHIOPS	Sophie
EHIOPT	ophite
EHIORS	hosier
EHIPRS	perish
EHIRST	theirs
EHIRSV	shiver
	shrive
EHIRSW	wisher
EHIRTV	thrive
EHIRTW	wither
	writhe
EHIRTZ	zither
EHISST	sithes
	thesis
EHISTT	theist
EHISTW	whites
	White's
EHITWZ	The Wiz
EHJOPS	Joseph
EHJORS	josher
EHJORT	Jethro
EHKMNO	Ken Hom
EHKOOR	hooker□
EHKORS	kosher
EHKPTU	Phuket
EHLLOR	holler
EHLLOS	hellos
EHLLOW	Howell
EHLLSS	shells
EHLLTY	they'll
EHLMMU	hummel
EHLMNU	unhelm
EHLMOP	phloem
EHLMOS	Holmes
EHLMOY	homely
EHLNOP	phenol
EHLNPY	phenyl
EHLOOS	shoole
EHLOOY	hooley
EHLOPP	hopple
EHLOPU	hole up
EHLORW	howler
EHLOST	hostel
	Lhotse
EHLOSU	housel
EHLOSV	shovel
EHLOTT	the lot
EHLPPS	Phelps
EHLRSY	Sheryl
EHLRTU	hurtle
	Luther
EHLRUY	hurley
EHLSTU	hustle
	sleuth
EHLSTY	shelty
EHLUXY	Huxley
EHMORT	mother
EHMOSS	shmoes
EHMRRY	rhymer
EHMRUY	rheumy
EHMSTU	the sum
EHNNSU	Hun Sen
EHNOPY	phoney
EHNORT	hornet
	throne
EHNOST	Heston
	honest
	so then
	the Son
EHNOSU	unshoe
EHNOTW	the now
	whet on
EHNRSY	henrys
EHNRTU	hunter□
EHNRVY	Henry V
EHNSTU	The Sun
EHOOOP	hoopoe
EHOOPY	phooey
EHOORT	hooter
EHOORV	Hoover®
	hoover
EHOOST	soothe
EHOOSV	hooves
EHOPPR	hopper□
EHOPRT	pother
	Thorpe
EHOPTT	Tophet
EHORRR	Rohrer
EHORRT	rother
EHORSS	horses
EHORST	others

	throes
EHORSV	shover
EHORSW	reshow
	shower
EHORSY	horsey
EHORTT	hotter
	tother
	t'other
EHORTX	exhort
EHORTY	theory
EHORTZ	zeroth
EHOSSU	houses
EHOTTW	the two
EHPRSU	pusher
EHPRSY	sypher
EHPRYZ	zephyr
EHRRSY	sherry □
EHRRWY	wherry
EHRSSU	rhesus
	Ussher
EHRTTU	Hutter
EHRTUW	wuther
EHSSTY	sythes
EIIKLL	Killie
EIIKLT	kiltie
EIIKLW	Wilkie
EIIKNP	Pinkie
EIILLL	Lillie
EIILLM	Millie
EIILLN	nielli
EIILLW	Willie
EIILMS	simile
EIILMU	milieu
EIILNN	in line
EIILNS	inisle
	Sileni
EIILNV	live in
	live-in
EIILRV	virile
EIILRX	elixir
EIILZZ	Lizzie
EIIMMT	Timmie
EIIMNN	Minnie
EIIMNT	in time
EIIMPS	impies
EIINNR	rein in
EIINNW	Winnie
EIINOS	ionise
EIINOZ	ionize
EIINPT	tiepin
EIINRV	Irvine
EIINRW	wire in
EIINTV	invite
EIINVV	Vivien
EIINVW	in view
EIIPRT	periti
EIIRSS	irises
EIIRTX	Trixie
EIIRVZ	vizier
EIJKNO	in-joke
EIJKNR	jerkin
EIJKNU	junkie
EIJLTU	Juliet
EIJNNO	enjoin
EIJNOR	joiner
	rejoin
EIJNRU	injure
EIJNST	in jest
EIJRSV	Jervis
EIJRTT	jitter
EIJSTU	Jesuit
EIKKOO	kookie
EIKKRY	yikker
EIKLLR	killer
EIKLLY	likely
EIKLMR	milker
EIKLNN	enlink
EIKLNS	silken
EIKLNT	tinkle
EIKLNU	unlike
EIKLNV	kelvin □
EIKLNW	welkin
	winkle
EIKLRT	kilter
	kirtle
EIKLSV	Kislev
EIKLSW	Wilkes
EIKLTT	kittle
EIKMNS	misken
EIKMOS	Eskimo
EIKMPS	Kempis
EIKMRS	kermis
EIKMST	kismet □
EIKMSY	miskey
EIKNOO	nookie
EIKNOR	Kieron
EIKNOV	invoke
EIKNPR	perkin
EIKNRS	sinker
	Sir Ken
EIKNRT	tinker
EIKNRW	winker
EIKNSV	knives
EIKNSY	Kinsey
EIKNTT	kitten
EIKOOR	rookie
EIKOPP	koppie
EIKOPS	pokies
EIKORY	yorkie □
EIKPPR	kipper
EIKPRU	Kuiper
EIKRSS	kisser
	krises
EIKRST	strike
EIKRSV	skiver
EILLLY	Lilley
EILLMR	miller □
EILLMT	millet □
EILLMU	illume
EILLNO	Lionel
	niello
	O'Neill
EILLNT	lentil
	lintel
EILLOW	lie low
EILLPU	pilule
EILLRT	rillet
	tiller
EILLSU	ill-use
EILLTT	little
EILLTW	willet
EILLVY	evilly
	lively □
	vilely
EILMNR	limner
	merlin □
EILMNS	simnel
EILMNU	lumine
	unlime
EILMNV	Melvin
EILMNY	myelin
EILMOR	Ormeli
EILMOT	motile
EILMPP	pimple
EILMPR	prelim
EILMPS	simple
EILMPT	limpet
EILMPU	pileum
EILMPW	wimple
EILMRS	smiler
EILMRU	Muriel
EILMRV	vermil
EILMST	smilet
EILMSU	muesli
EILMSY	smiley
EILMTY	timely
EILMZZ	mizzle
EILNNO	El Niño
	on-line
EILNNS	Nilsen
EILNNT	linnet □
EILNNU	unline
EILNOP	loipen
	pinole
EILNOR	Elinor
	Lorien
	neroli
EILNOS	insole
	lesion
EILNOT	entoil
	lionet
	Nilote
EILNOV	in love
	live on
EILNPP	lippen
	nipple
EILNPS	Pilsen
	spinel
	spline
EILNPT	pintle
EILNPU	line up
	line-up
	lupine
EILNST	enlist
	listen
	silent
	tinsel
EILNSV	snivel
EILNSY	lysine
EILNTU	lutein
	untile
EILNTV	ventil
EILNTW	wintle
EILNTY	lenity
EILNUV	unlive
	unveil
EILOOR	oriole
EILOOT	oolite
EILOPS	pilose
EILOPT	polite
EILORS	Serlio
EILORT	loiter
	toiler
EILORV	Oliver
EILOSU	Louise
EILOTT	Lottie
	toilet
EILOTV	live to
	violet □
EILOVY	Yeovil
EILPPR	ripple
EILPPS	sipple
EILPPT	tipple
EILPPU	pile up
	pile-up
EILPRS	lisper
	pliers
EILPRT	let rip
	triple
EILPRY	ripely
EILPSS	plissé
EILPST	stipel
EILPSU	pileus
EILPSV	pelvis
EILRST	Lister
EILRSV	silver □
	sliver
EILRTT	litter
EILRTU	rutile
EILRVY	livery
	verily
EILSSS	lisses
EILSSY	Sisley
EILSTU	Iseult
EILSVW	swivel
EILSWY	wisely
EILSZZ	sizzle
EILTTT	tittle
EILTTU	titule
EILTVY	levity
EILUVV	luvvie
EILVVY	vively
EIMMNU	immune
EIMMOR	memoir

EIMMRS	simmer
EIMMRU	immure
EIMNOP	impone
EIMNOR	merino
EIMNOS	eonism
	monies
	Simeon
	Simone
EIMNOT	no time
	on time
EIMNOV	move in
EIMNRR	Mirren
EIMNRS	Mersin
EIMNRU	murine
EIMNRV	vermin
EIMNTT	mitten
EIMNTU	minuet
	minute
	munite
	mutine
EIMNTY	enmity
EIMNZZ	mizzen
EIMOPS	impose
EIMORS	isomer
EIMOSS	mossie
EIMOSV	movies
EIMOTV	motive
EIMOTY	moiety
	Tim Yeo
EIMOZZ	mozzie
EIMPRR	primer
EIMPRS	simper
EIMPRT	permit
EIMPRU	impure
	umpire
EIMPTU	impute
EIMRRT	trimer
EIMRSS	remiss
EIMRST	merits
	mister
	smiter
EIMRSV	verism
	vermis
EIMRSY	misery
EIMRTU	iterum
EIMSSS	misses
EIMSST	misset
EIMSSU	misuse
EIMSSX	sexism
EIMSTY	stymie
EIMSWY	Wimsey
EINNNR	rennin
EINNOT	intone
EINNPT	tenpin
EINNRS	sinner
EINNRT	intern
EINNRU	unrein
EINNRW	winner
EINNST	tennis
EINNSU	Ennius
EINNTT	intent
EINNTU	in tune
	tune in
EINNTV	invent
EINNTY	ninety
EINOPP	pepino
EINOPR	orpine
	Pinero
	pioner
	rope in
EINORR	Renoir
EINORS	senior
EINORT	orient
EINORZ	zero in
EINOSS	enosis
	noesis
EINOST	on-site
	Tonies
EINOSW	nowise
EINOTV	vote in
EINOTW	townie
EINOVW	on view
EINPPR	nipper❑
EINPPS	pepsin
EINPRS	sniper
EINPRT	Pinter
EINPRU	pruine
	purine
	unripe
EINPRV	Previn
EINPSS	snipes
EINPST	in step
	instep
	spinet
	step in
EINPSU	puisne
	supine
EINPTY	Pitney
EINQSU	sequin
EINQTU	quinte
EINQUU	unique
EINRRS	rinser
EINRRU	ruiner
EINRSS	Sirens
EINRST	insert
	sinter
EINRSU	insure
	ursine
EINRSY	Erinys
EINRTU	triune
	uniter
EINRTV	invert
	virent
EINRTW	twiner
	winter
EINRTY	nitery
EINRUW	unwire
EINRVW	wivern
EINRVY	vinery
EINRWY	winery
EINSSS	nisses
EINSSW	sinews
EINSTV	invest
EINSUW	unwise
EINSUX	unisex
EINSWY	sinewy
EINTTY	entity
EINUVW	unwive
EIOOST	otiose
EIOPST	postie
EIOPTT	tiptoe
EIORRT	rioter
EIORST	sortie
EIORSV	vireos
EIOSTV	soviet❑
EIOSTW	wise to
EIOTVV	votive
EIPPPU	pipe up
EIPPRS	sipper
EIPPRZ	zipper
EIPPST	sippet
EIPPTT	tippet
EIPPUW	wipe up
EIPPUY	yuppie
EIPQTU	piquet❑
EIPRST	esprit
	priest
	sprite
	stripe
EIPRSU	rise up
	uprise
EIPRSZ	prizes
EIPRTT	pitter
EIPRTV	privet
EIPRTY	pyrite
EIPRXY	expiry
EIPSSS	sepsis
	speiss
EIPSST	stipes
EIPSTT	pet-sit
EIPSUW	wise up
EIPSUZ	size up
EIQRSU	risqué
	squier
	squire
EIQRTU	requit
EIQRUV	quiver
EIQTUY	equity
EIRRTW	writer
EIRRVY	rivery
EIRRZZ	rizzer
EIRSST	resist
	sister
EIRSTT	sitter
EIRSTV	strive
	verist
EIRTTT	titter
EIRTTV	trivet
EIRTTW	witter
EIRTUV	virtue
EIRTVY	verity❑
EISSSW	Wessis
EISSTU	tissue
EISSTV	St Ives
EISSTW	wisest
EISSTX	sexist
EISTTW	Sittwe
EJKLLY	Jekyll
EJKNOO	no joke
EJKNTU	junket
EJKOPS	Skopje
EJLLOS	jellos
EJLLOW	Jowell
EJLOST	jostle
EJLSTU	justle
EJMOOS	mojoes
EJMPRU	jumper
EJNOTT	jetton
EJORTT	jotter
EJOTUV	Jouvet
EKKOPU	pukeko
EKLLSY	skelly
EKLMMU	kümmel
EKLMOT	Moltke
EKLNOS	kelson
	sloken
EKLNRU	runkle
EKLOOR	looker
EKLORU	rule OK
EKLOWY	low-key
EKMNOY	monkey
EKMORS	smoker
EKMSTU	musket
EKNNOR	kronen
EKNNOT	Kenton
	nekton
EKNNSU	sunken
EKNOPS	spoken
EKNORR	kroner
EKNORY	Orkney
EKNOUY	unyoke
EKOPRR	porker
EKOPSY	pokeys
EKORRW	rework
	worker
EKORRY	yorker
EKORST	stoker❑
	stroke
EKOSST	stokes❑
EKPPRU	perk up
EKRRSY	skerry
EKRSTU	tusker
EKRSTY	Tersky
EKRTUY	turkey❑
ELLLOR	loller
ELLLOV	Lovell
ELLLOW	Lowell
ELLMNO	Mellon
ELLMOR	Mellor
ELLMOW	mellow
ELLMRU	Muller
	Müller
ELLMSY	smelly
ELLMTU	mullet

ELLMUV	vellum
ELLMUY	Lumley
ELLNOP	pollen
ELLNOT	tell on
ELLNOY	lonely
ELLNSU	sullen
ELLNSY	snelly
ELLNUW	unwell
ELLOOT	Otello
ELLOPW	Powell
ELLOPX	pollex
ELLORR	roller □
ELLORW	Orwell
ELLOST	to sell
ELLOSY	solely
ELLOVY	lovely
	volley
ELLOWY	yellow □
ELLPSU	sell up
ELLPTU	pullet
ELLPUW	well up
ELLPUY	pulley
ELLSSW	swells
ELMMNO	Lemmon
ELMMOR	Rommel
ELMMOS	Moslem
ELMMPU	pummel
ELMNOR	merlon
ELMNOS	Lemnos
	solemn
ELMNOT	molten
ELMNOY	lemony
ELMNPU	lumpen
	plenum
ELMNSU	lumens
ELMNVY	Melvyn
ELMOOP	pomelo
ELMOPY	employ
ELMORS	morsel
ELMORT	Merlot
ELMOST	molest
ELMOSU	mousle
ELMOSY	Mosley
ELMOTT	Mel Ott
	mottle
ELMOTY	motley
ELMOUV	volume
ELMPPU	peplum
ELMPRU	rumple
ELMRSU	lemurs
ELMRTY	Myrtle
	termly
ELMSSU	mussel
ELMTUY	mutely
ELMUZZ	muzzle
ELNNNO	Lennon
ELNNOS	nelson □
ELNNRU	runnel
ELNNTU	tunnel
ELNOOS	loosen
ELNOPT	lepton
ELNOPY	openly
ELNORY	rely on
ELNORZ	Lorenz
ELNOSS	lesson
	no less
ELNOST	lentos
	stolen
	telson
ELNOSU	ensoul
	nousle
ELNOSV	novels
	sloven
ELNOSW	new sol
ELNOTT	not let
ELNOUV	unlove
ELNOWY	Olwyne
ELNOZZ	nozzle
ELNPTU	penult
ELNPTY	plenty □
ELNRSU	nursle
ELNRUU	unrule
ELNSSU	unless
ELNSXY	lynxes
ELNSYY	Lynsey
ELNTXY	nextly
ELNUZZ	nuzzle
ELOOOT	O'Toole
ELOOPR	looper
ELOORT	looter
ELOOSV	looves
ELOOSW	woosel
ELOOSZ	zeloso
ELOOTT	tootle
ELOPPP	popple
ELOPPR	lopper
	propel
ELOPPT	topple
ELOPRS	proles
ELOPRT	petrol
ELOPRV	plover
ELOPRX	plexor
ELOPSU	poules
	souple
ELOPSW	Wopsle
ELOPTU	tupelo
ELORRS	sorrel
ELORSS	lessor
ELORST	ostler
	sterol
ELORSV	lovers
	solver
ELORSY	sorely
	Sorley
ELORTT	tolter
ELORTV	revolt
ELORTW	trowel
ELORTY	troely
ELORUV	louvre □
	velour
ELORVY	overly
ELOSSU	louses
	soleus
ELOSTU	solute
	tousle
ELOSTW	lowest
ELOSVW	wolves
ELOSWY	Wolsey
ELOSZZ	sozzle
ELOTTU	let out
	let-out
	outlet
ELOTUV	volute
ELOTUZ	touzle
ELPPRU	purple
ELPPSU	supple
ELPQUU	pulque
ELPRRU	purler
ELPRTY	peltry
	pertly
ELPRUY	purely
ELPSSU	pluses
	pussel
ELPSUX	plexus
ELPUZZ	puzzle
ELRSTU	lustre
	result
	rustle
	ulster
ELRSUY	surely
ELRTTU	turtle
ELSSTU	tussle
ELSTTU	suttle
ELUWZZ	wuzzle
EMMMRU	mummer
EMMNNO	Memnon
EMMNOT	moment
EMMORY	memory
EMMRRU	rummer
EMMRSU	summer □
EMMSUU	museum
EMNOOR	Monroe
	mooner
	no more
EMNOOV	move on
EMNOPS	Empson
EMNOPY	eponym
EMNORS	sermon
EMNORT	mentor
	Merton
EMNOST	mentos
EMNOSU	muse on
EMNOSY	moneys
EMNOTY	etymon
EMNRRU	Murner
EMNRVY	Mervyn
EMOORR	roomer
EMOORS	more so
	morose
	Romeos
EMOORX	Exmoor
EMOOSS	osmose
EMOPPR	mopper
EMOPPT	moppet
EMOPPY	Pompey
EMOPRR	romper
EMOPRT	emptor
	pro tem
	trompe
EMOPRU	Euro-MP
EMOPST	tempos
EMOPUV	move up
	move-up
EMOQSU	mosque
EMORRT	tremor
EMORRW	wormer
EMORST	métros
EMORSU	mouser
EMORSY	Mysore
EMOSSU	mousse
EMOSUY	mousey
EMOSZZ	mezzos
EMPSSU	mess up
EMPSTU	septum
EMRSSS	Messrs
EMRSSU	serums
EMRSTU	muster
EMRTTU	mutter
EMSSTY	system
ENNNOP	pennon
ENNOOS	no-noes
ENNOOT	not one
ENNORU	neuron
ENNORV	Vernon
ENNORW	renown □
ENNOST	sonnet
ENNOTW	newton □
ENNOVY	Yvonne
ENNPTU	punnet
ENNRRU	runner
ENNRST	Nernst
ENNSTU	unnest
ENNTTU	untent
ENNTUU	untune
ENOORS	sooner
ENOORT	enroot
ENOORY	Rooney
ENOOSZ	snooze
ENOOTW	one-two
ENOPPU	open up
	unpope
ENOPRR	perron
ENOPRS	person
ENOPRU	unrope
ENOPRV	proven
ENOPRY	prey on
	pyoner
ENOPST	pontes
	step on
ENOPSU	nose up
ENOPTT	potent
ENOPTU	tone up
ENORRS	snorer
ENORSS	sensor

ENORST	Nestor
	rest on
	stoner
ENORSW	owners
	worsen
ENORTT	Retton
	rotten
	torten
	Trento
ENORTY	nor yet
	Tyrone
ENOSST	stones
ENOSTT	ostent
ENOSTX	sexton
ENOSUV	venous
ENOTTU	tenuto
	Teuton
ENOTTX	next to
ENPPTU	pent-up
ENPRRU	pruner
ENPRTU	punter
ENPRUY	penury
ENPRWY	prewyn
ENPSTU	unstep
ENPSUW	sewn up
ENPTUU	tune up
ENPTUW	unwept
ENRRTU	return
	re-turn
	turner□
ENRSTU	unrest
ENRSTY	sentry
ENRSUU	unsure
ENRTTU	nutter
ENRTUU	untrue
ENRVWY	wyvern
ENSSTU	sunset
ENTTWY	twenty
EOOPPS	oppose
EOOPST	stoope
EOORRT	rooter
	torero
EOOSTW	Soweto
EOPPPR	popper□
EOPPPT	poppet
EOPPRR	proper
EOPPRT	topper
EOPPRY	pyrope
EOPRRS	repros
EOPRRT	porter□
	report
EOPRRU	pourer
EOPRST	poster
	presto
EOPRSU	poseur
	uprose
EOPRSW	powers
EOPRSY	osprey
EOPRTT	potter
EOPRTU	pouter
	troupe
EOPRTW	powter
EOPRTX	export
EOPRTY	poetry
EOPSST	posset
	ptoses
	Stopes
EOPSSU	opuses
	spouse
EOPSTX	sexpot
EOQRTU	roquet
	torque
EORRRT	rorter
	terror
EORRRY	orrery
EORRST	resort
	retros
	roster
	sorter
EORRSU	rouser
EORRSW	worser
EORRTT	retort
	rotter
EORRTU	retour
	tourer
EORRTV	Trevor
EORRZZ	rozzer
EORSST	stores
EORSSU	serous
EORSSV	versos
EORSTT	tortes
EORSTU	ouster
	souter
EORSTV	voters
EORSTW	stower
EORSTY	oyster
	storey
EORSTZ	zoster
EORSWW	wowser
EORTTT	totter
EORTTU	touter
	true to
EORTTW	wet rot
EORTTX	extort
EORTVX	vortex
EORUVY	voyeur
EOSSSU	souses
	Sousse
EOSSSW	sowsse
EOSSTT	set-tos
	set-to's
EOSSVW	vowess
EOSTTU	outset
	set out
EOTTUW	wet out
EPPPRY	preppy
EPPPTU	puppet
EPPRSU	supper
EPPSTU	step up
	step-up
EPRRSU	purser
EPRRTU	Rupert
EPRSUU	pursue
EPRTTU	putter
EPRTTY	pretty
EPRTUZ	Perutz
EPRUVY	purvey
EPSTUZ	putzes
EQRTWY	QWERTY
	qwerty
ERRSUU	usurer
ERRSUY	surrey□
ERRTTU	turret
ERSSST	stress
ERSSTU	russet
	tusser
ERSSTY	syrtes
	tressy
ERSSUU	uruses
ERSSUV	versus
ERSTUU	suture
	uterus
ERSTUV	turves
ERSTUY	surety
ERSTVY	vestry
ERSUVY	survey

F

FFFLUY	fluffy
FFGINO	offing
FFHIOS	offish
FFHIOT	hit off
FFHIWY	whiffy
FFHORS	shroff
FFIINT	tiffin
FFIIUZ	Uffizi
FFILLO	ill off
FFILLU	fulfil
FFILPS	spliff
FFILTU	fitful
FFIMNU	muffin
FFINPU	puffin
FFINSY	sniffy
FFIOPR	rip off
	rip-off
FFIOPT	tip off
	tip-off
FFIOST	soffit
FFIQSU	squiff
FFISTY	stiffy
FFISUX	suffix
FFLLOU	full of
FFLOOP	lop off
FFLOTY	fylfot
FFNOPU	puff on
FFNORU	for fun
	run off
	run-off
FFNSUY	snuffy
FFOOPP	pop off
FFOOPT	top off
FFOPTU	put off
	put-off
FFPPUU	puff up
FFRRUU	furfur
FFSTUY	stuffy
FGGIIS	fisgig
FGGIIZ	fizgig
FGGORY	froggy□
FGHILT	flight
FGHIRT	fright
FGHOTU	fought
FGIIIN	Figini
FGIILN	filing
FGIINR	firing
FGIINX	fixing
FGILNU	ingulf
FGILNY	flying
FGILUY	uglify
FGIMNU	fuming
FGINOS	sign of
FGINOX	foxing
FGINRY	fringy
FGINSU	fusing
FGIOOT	goof it
FGJLUU	jugful
FGKNUU	kung fu
FGLMUU	mugful
FGNORU	gun for
FGNSUU	fungus
FGNUUY	fu yung
FGOORT	forgot
FHIINS	finish
FHILTY	filthy
FHIMUY	humify
FHIOOT	hoof it
FHIPSU	fish up
FHIRST	shrift
FHIRTT	thrift
FHISTU	shufti
FHISTY	shifty
FHLOSU	floush
FHNSUU	Fushun
FHOORW	forhow
FHORTU	fourth
FHORTY	frothy
FHOUUZ	Fuzhou
FHSTUY	shufty
FIIKNR	firkin
FIILLN	fill in
	fill-in
	infill
FIILLP	fillip
FIILVY	vilify
FIIMNR	infirm
FIIMNY	minify
FIIMST	misfit
FIITXY	fixity
FIIVVY	vivify
FIJLOR	frijol
FIKNNO	fink on
FIKRSY	frisky
FILLNU	in full
FILLPU	fill up

FILLRS	frills
FILLRY	frilly
FILLUW	wilful
FILMRY	firmly
FILMSY	flimsy
FILNOR	florin
FILNOW	inflow
FILNOY	if only
FILNSU	sinful
FILNTU	tinful
FILNTY	flinty
FILNUX	influx
FILOOS	folios
FILORV	frivol
FILOSS	fossil
FILOTW	Wolfit
FILOUZ	zufoli
FILPTU	lift up
	uplift
FILRTY	flirty
FIMNOR	inform
FIMNUY	munify
FIMPRU	firm up
FIMSSU	Sufism
FIMSTU	Muftis
FINORT	forint
FINOSU	fusion
FINOTY	notify
FIOOTT	foot it
FIOPRT	profit
FIORRT	forrit
FIORST	fortis
FIORTY	Torify
FIOSSY	ossify
FIOTTU	fit out
	outfit
FIPRUY	purify
FIPTYY	typify
FIRSTU	fruits
FIRTUY	fruity
FIRYZZ	frizzy
FJLOUY	joyful
FKLNUY	flunky
FKLOSY	folksy
FKOPRU	fork up
FLLOOW	follow
FLLOUY	foully
FLLPUU	full up
FLMNOU	muflon
FLNOOU	unfool
FLNOOW	onflow
FLNRUU	unfurl
FLOOST	lots of
FLOOYZ	floozy
FLOPPY	floppy
FLOPTU	potful
FLOPUU	foul up
	foul-up
FLOPUW	upflow
FLORUY	floury
FLOSSY	flossy
FLOSTY	softly
FLOTUY	fly out
FLRRUY	flurry
FMNORU	unform
FMOOTY	my foot!
FMORSU	forums
FMOSUU	fumous
FMPRUY	frumpy
FNNRUU	fun run
FNOOOT	on foot
FNOORU	unroof
FNOORW	for now
FNOOST	soft on
	tons of
FNRTUU	unturf
FOOPRS	proofs
FOOPRT	opt for
FOORSS	fossor
FOORST	sort of
FOORTU	out for
FOOSST	toss of
FOOTUX	outfox
FOPRTU	put for
FORRTY	try for
FORRUW	furrow
FORSTW	frowst
FORSTY	frosty
FORSUU	rufous
FORSWY	frowsy
FORTYY	Toryfy
FORWYZ	frowzy
FOSTUY	fousty

G

GGGIIT	giggit
GGGILY	giggly
GGGORY	groggy
GGHNOU	gung-ho
GGIINP	piggin
GGIINV	giving
GGIJJO	jig-jog
GGIKNO	gingko
	ginkgo
GGILOO	gigolo
GGILWY	wiggly
GGINNO	noggin
GGINOQ	qi gong
GGINRU	urging
GGIOOR	gorgio
GGITWY	twiggy
GGLLOO	loglog
GGLOOO	googol
GGLOOY	googly
GGMOSY	smoggy
GGNOOR	gorgon□
GGNRUY	grungy
GGORST	troggs
GGRRUU	gru-gru
GHHILY	highly
GHHINO	on high
GHHIPU	high up
	high-up
GHHIST	thighs
GHHOTU	though
GHIINR	hiring
GHIINS	Hingis
GHIKNT	knight□
GHILNO	holing
GHILNY	nighly
GHILPT	plight
GHILST	lights
	slight
GHIMNO	homing
GHIMTY	mighty
GHINNO	nigh on
GHINOP	hoping
GHINST	nights
	things
GHINTY	nighty
	thingy
GHIOPZ	phizog
GHIORS	ogrish
GHIORT	righto
GHIOSY	goyish
GHIOTW	go with
GHIPST	spight
GHIRST	rights
GHIRTW	wright□
GHISTT	tights
GHLOOS	golosh
GHLOPU	plough
GHLOSU	slough□
GHMPRU	grumph
GHNORT	throng
GHNOSU	shogun
GHNOTU	nought
GHNPUU	hung up
	hung-up
GHNRUY	hungry
GHNSUY	gun-shy
GHORTU	trough
GHORTW	growth
GIIKLN	liking
GIIKNR	irking
GIIKNS	skiing
GIIKNT	king it
	kiting
GIIKNV	viking□
GIILMN	liming
GIILNN	lignin
	lining
GIILNP	piling
GIILNT	tiling
GIILNV	living
GIILOR	oil rig
GIILRV	Virgil
GIIMNT	timing
GIIMNX	mixing
GIINNP	pining
GIINNR	ring in
GIINNX	Xining
GIINOR	origin
GIINOY	yogini
GIINPP	piping
GIINRS	rising
GIINRT	tiring
GIINRV	Irving
	virgin□
GIINRW	wiring
GIINST	siting
GIINSZ	sizing
GIINTW	wing it
GIIRST	Tigris
GIISTU	Giusti
GIJKNO	joking
GIJLNY	jingly
GIKLNY	kingly
GIKNNU	unking
GIKNOW	Woking
GIKNPU	puking
GIKRTU	tugrik
GILLTU	Gullit
GILLUY	uglily
GILMNU	lignum
GILMOW	Mowgli
GILMRY	grimly
GILNOS	losing
GILNOT	tiglon
GILNOV	loving
GILNOW	lowing
GILNPU	plug in
	puling
GILNRU	luring
	ruling
GILNSY	Glynis
	singly
GILORY	gorily
GILOSU	Lugosi
GILRSY	grisly
GILRTY	trigly
GILTUY	guilty
GILTYZ	glitzy
GIMMOR	gimmor
GIMNNO	mignon
GIMNOP	moping
GIMNOV	moving
GIMNOY	ignomy
GIMNPU	impugn
GIMNSU	Mingus
	musing
GIMOOS	Ogmios
GIMORT	Gromit
GIMOSS	gismos
GIMOSZ	gizmos
GIMOTU	gomuti
GINNOS	nosing
	sign on
GINNOT	noting
GINNSU	Ngunis
GINNTU	tuning
GINOOT	go in to
	go into
GINOOW	wooing

GINOOZ	oozing
GINOPS	pingos
	posing
GINOPT	opting
GINORS	Signor
GINORT	trigon
GINORV	roving
GINORW	rowing
GINOTU	outing
GINOTV	voting
GINOTW	towing
GINOTY	toying
GINPPU	upping
GINPRS	spring□
GINPRU	ring up
GINPRY	prying
GINPSU	sign up
GINPSY	spying
GINPTU	pignut
GINPTY	typing
GINRRU	Runrig
GINRST	string
GINRTU	Turing
GINRTY	trying
GINSTY	stingy
GINSUU	unguis
GINSUX	six-gun
GIOORV	vigoro
GIOOTT	Giotto
GIOPPS	gippos
GIOPSS	gossip
GIOPST	spigot
GIOPTU	pig out
GIORRU	rigour
GIORSU	guiros
GIORTU	rig out
	rig-out
GIORUV	vigour
GIOSTU	giusto
GIPSTY	pigsty
GIRTTY	gritty
GJLNUY	jungly
GLLMUY	glumly
GLLNOY	longly
GLLOOP	gollop
GLMOOY	gloomy
GLMRUY	grumly
GLMSUY	smugly
GLNNOO	long on
GLNOOO	oolong
GLNOOS	so long
	so long!
	so-long
GLNOOU	oulong
GLNPUU	unplug
GLNSUY	snugly
GLOOOY	oology
GLOOPR	PROLOG
GLOOSW	go slow
	go-slow
GLORWY	growly
GLOSSY	glossy
GMNNOO	gnomon
GMNOSU	mungos
GMOOPR	pogrom
GMPRSU	grumps
GMPRUY	grumpy
GMPSUY	gypsum
GNNOOS	on song
GNNOUW	ungown
GNNSUU	unsung
GNOOPS	pongos
GNOORT	trogon
GNOORW	grow on
GNOPPU	oppugn
GNOPSY	spongy
GNOPTU	Top Gun
GNORST	strong□
GNORYZ	Grozny
GNOTUU	outgun
GNPRSU	sprung
GNRSTU	strung
GNSTUU	Tungus
GOOPST	stop-go
GOOPTU	go up to
GOORSS	sorgos
GOORSU	go sour
GOORTT	grotto
GOORTW	grow to
GOORVY	groovy
GOPRUW	grow up
	upgrow
GORRTU	turgor
GORSUU	rugous
GORTTU	gutrot
	rotgut
GORTTY	grotty
GORTUY	yogurt

H

HHILOS	Shiloh
HHIOPP	hip-hop
HHISTW	whisht
HHMRTY	rhythm
HHNOSU	Honshu
HHOOOY	yo-ho-ho
HHOOSW	whoosh
HHORTY	Horthy
HHPSUU	hush up
HHRSTU	thrush
HIILLT	Lilith
HIILNS	linish
HIILPP	Philip
HIIMPS	impish
HIIMSS	Shiism
HIIMST	mishit
HIINPS	inship
HIINPW	whip in
HIINTW	in with
	inwith
	within
HIIOPT	pithoi
HIIRST	Tishri
HIITTW	with it
HIJOSS	shojis
HIKNRS	shrink
HIKOOT	hook it
HIKSSY	skyish
HIKSTY	tykish
HIKSWY	whisky
HILLOY	holily
HILLPU	uphill
HILLRS	shrill
HILLRT	thrill
HILLWY	whilly
HILMOS	holism
HILMOY	homily
HILMSU	mulish
HILNOT	Hilton
HILNPT	plinth
HILNTY	thinly
HILOOT	tholoi
HILOPS	Hislop
	polish□
HILOST	holist
	lithos
HILOSW	owlish
HILPST	spilth
HILSTW	whilst
HIMORS	morish
	Romish
HIMPRS	shrimp
HIMSST	Smiths
HIMSTY	smithy
HIMSWY	whimsy
HINNOR	horn in
HINNSY	shinny
HINNTU	hunt in
HINNWY	whinny
HINOOP	inhoop
HINOOS	shoo-in
HINOPS	siphon
HINORS	rhinos
HINOST	Shinto
HINOSW	wish on
HINPSU	punish
	push in
	shin up
	unship
HINPSX	sphinx□
HINRSU	inrush
HINSTU	shut in
	shut-in
HINSTY	shinty
HINSUV	Vishnu
HINSUW	unwish
HIOPPS	hippos
HIOPSY	physio
HIOTTU	hit out
HIPPSU	uppish
HIPPUW	whip up
HIPPWY	whippy
HIPRST	thrips
HIPTUW	up with
HIQSSU	squish
HIRRWY	whirry
HIRSTT	thirst
	T-shirt
HIRSTY	Irtysh
	shirty
	thyrsi
HIRTTY	thirty
HJNOST	St John
HKNOOU	unhook
HKNRSU	shrunk
HKNSUU	unhusk
HKOOPU	hook up
	hook-up
HKOORT	Rothko
HKOOSS	skoosh
HKOOST	shtook
HKOUVZ	Zhukov
HKSUUY	Kyushu
HLLOOS	hollos
HLLOOW	hollow
HLLOPY	phyllo
HLLOSU	hullos
HLLOWY	wholly
HLLSUY	lushly
HLMOTY	thymol
HLMPUY	phylum
HLNOUY	unholy
HLOOSS	sloosh
HLOPSS	splosh
HLOPSU	Ophuls
HLOPSY	poshly
HLORUY	hourly
HLPSUY	plushy
HLSSUY	slushy
HMMSTU	shtumm
HMMSUU	hummus
HMNPSY	Nymphs
HMOOST	shtoom
	smooth
HMORUU	humour
HMOSTU	mouths
HMOSUU	houmus
	humous
HMOTUY	mouthy
HMPRUY	Murphy
HMSTUY	thymus
HNOOPT	photon
HNOOPU	unhoop
HNOORS	horson
HNOORU	honour□
HNOOSW	no-show
	on show
HNOOWW	how now
HNOPSU	nosh-up
HNOPSY	syphon
HNOPTY	python
	Typhon
HNORSU	onrush
HNORTW	thrown

Words marked □ can also be spelled with an initial capital letter

HNORTY	thorny
HNOSTU	Huston
HNOTTU	Hutton
HNPTUU	hunt up
HNRTUU	unhurt
HNSTUU	unshut
HOOOOR	hooroo
HOOOOY	yoo-hoo
HOOPST	photos
HOOPSW	whoops
HOOPTT	hotpot
HOORRR	horror
HOORST	orthos
HOOSSW	swoosh
HOOTTY	toothy
HOOTUW	tu-whoo
HOPRRY	Pyrrho
HOPRTY	trophy
HOPSSY	hyssop
HOPSTU	Pushto
	upshot
HOPSUW	show up
HORSST	shorts
HORSTU	Thurso
HORSTY	shorty
HORTWY	worthy
HOSSTU	stoush
HOSTUY	youths
HOSUUZ	Suzhou
HOUUXZ	Xuzhou
HPPSUU	push up
HPRSSU	sprush
HPSTUU	Pushtu
	shut up
HPSTUY	typhus
HRSTTU	thrust

I

IIIMNR	Rimini
IIIMRT	miriti
IIJNNO	join in
IIKKMS	Sikkim
IIKNNS	sink in
IIKNPP	pipkin
IIKNSS	siskin
IIKPST	skip it!
IILLOY	oilily
IILLSW	Willis
IILLWY	wilily
IILMST	limits
IILNNU	inulin
IILNOV	violin
IILNPS	slip in
IILNST	instil
IILNTY	tinily
IILPST	pistil
IILRWY	wirily
IILSTT	Tilsit
IILTTW	twilit
IIMNNO	minion
IIMNRT	in trim
IIMNTZ	Nimitz
IIMSSS	missis
IIMSSZ	sizism
IINNOP	pinion
IINNPY	Pinyin
IINNTU	Innuit
IINORS	Roisin
IINOSV	vision
IINOVV	in vivo
IINPPP	pippin
IINSST	insist
IINSTU	in situ
	SI unit
IINTTU	intuit
IINTTW	nitwit
IIORSS	Osiris
IIORZZ	Rizzio
IIOSTT	otitis
IIPPUU	piupiu
IIPRST	spirit
IIPTTU	Titipu
IIRRTT	tirrit
IIRSSU	Sirius
IJLMPY	jimply
IJLNOP	Joplin
IJLSUU	Julius
IJMOSS	jissom
IJNOPS	Jospin
IJNOPU	join up
IJNORU	junior
IJNRUY	injury
IJNSTU	Justin
IKKKRU	Kirkuk
IKKMOW	Wim Kok
IKKORR	korkir
IKLLPU	kill up
IKLLSY	skilly
IKLNNU	unlink
IKLNOO	look in
	look-in
IKLNPU	link up
	link-up
IKLNSY	slinky
IKLNTY	tinkly
IKLSSU	suslik
IKLTTU	kittul
IKMNOO	kimono
IKMPRS	skrimp
IKMPSY	skimpy
IKMSSU	kumiss
IKNNSY	skinny
IKNNTU	unknit
IKNOPS	pinkos
IKNORW	in work
	inwork
	work in
	work-in
IKNPSS	Spinks
IKNPSU	skin up
IKNPTU	upknit
IKNRSU	Ruskin
IKNSSU	unkiss
IKOORS	irokos
IKORSS	Skiros
IKOTTU	kit out
IKPRSU	spruik
IKQRUY	quirky
IKRSSU	Russki
IKRSTY	Kirsty
IKSVVY	skivvy
ILLMPY	limply
ILLMSY	slimly
ILLNOR	roll in
ILLNOV	Villon
ILLNPU	pull in
ILLNUW	unwill
ILLOPW	pillow
ILLOWW	willow
ILLPUV	pulvil
ILLQSU	squill
ILLSUV	villus
ILMMSU	Muslim
ILMNOT	Milton
ILMNSU	muslin
ILMOSS	lissom
ILMOSZ	Milosz
ILMOTU	ultimo
ILMPPY	pimply
ILMPRY	primly
ILMPSY	simply
ILMRTY	trimly
ILMSTU	litmus
ILMTUU	tumuli
ILNOOT	lotion
ILNOPP	poplin
ILNOPS	slip on
	slip-on
ILNOQU	quinol
ILNOST	Liston
	tonsil
ILNOSU	insoul
ILNOSW	Wilson
ILNOSY	nosily
ILNOTU	nut oil
	ultion
ILNOTW	Wilton
ILNPRU	purlin
ILNPST	splint
ILNPUY	punily
ILNSTU	insult
	sunlit
ILOOPS	polios
ILOOST	solito
ILOOYZ	oozily
ILOPPY	polypi
ILOPRX	prolix
ILOPRY	ropily
ILOPSS	spoils
ILOPST	pistol❑
	postil
	spoilt
ILOPSX	oxslip
ILOPTY	polity
ILOQRU	liquor
ILORSY	rosily
ILORTU	toruli
ILPPRY	ripply
ILPPSU	pupils
	slip up
	slip-up
ILPPSY	slippy
ILPPTU	pulpit
ILPRTY	triply
ILPSST	splits
ILPSTU	silt up
ILRTWY	twirly
ILSTTU	lutist
ILSTWY	wistly
IMMNOS	monism
IMMNOU	omnium❑
IMMOOS	simoom
IMMOSU	osmium
IMMSTU	mutism
	summit
IMNNOT	Minton
IMNNOW	minnow
IMNNTU	muntin
IMNOOR	Moroni
IMNOOS	simoon
IMNOOT	motion❑
IMNOOZ	zoom in
IMNOST	inmost
	monist
IMNOSY	myosin
	simony
IMNRTU	untrim
IMNTUY	mutiny
IMOPRS	primos
IMOPRT	import
IMOPST	impost
IMORRR	mirror
IMORRS	Morris
	Morris®
IMOTTT	tomtit
	tom-tit
IMPRSU	Primus
	purism❑
IMPSTU	mist up
IMQRSU	squirm
IMQRUU	Urumqi
IMRSTU	truism
IMSSSU	missus
IMSTTU	Titmus
INNOOS	Onions
INNOOT	notion
INNOOY	oniony
INNOPP	Nippon
INNORT	intron
INNOSU	UNISON
	unison
INNOWW	winnow
INNRTU	in turn
	turn in

Words marked ❑ can also be spelled with an initial capital letter

INOOPS	poison
INOOPT	option
	potion
INOORS	orison
	Orsino
INOOTT	in toto
INOPPR	poprin
	Rippon
INOPRS	prison
INOPST	pintos
	piston
	points
	stop in
INOPTT	tinpot
INORRS	Norris
INORST	in sort
	intros
INORSY	rosiny
INORTT	triton□
INORTU	turion
INOSTW	in twos
INOSUV	vinous
INOTUW	win out
INPPRU	Nippur
INPRST	sprint
INPRTU	turnip
	Turpin
INQSTU	squint
INQSUY	quinsy
	squiny
INRSXY	syrinx□
INRTWY	wintry
INSTUU	unsuit
IOOPRT	Poirot
IOOPST	Potosí
IOPPTT	tiptop
IOPRRY	priory
IOPRST	prosit
	tripos
IOPTTU	tip out
	up to it
IOQSTU	quoits
IORRTW	worrit
IORRZZ	rizzor
IORSTU	suitor
IOSTTU	outsit
	sit out
IOTTUW	outwit
IPPRTU	trip up
IPPRTY	trippy
IPPTUY	uppity
IPRRTU	irrupt
IPRSST	stirps
IPRSSY	prissy
IPRSTU	purist
	stir up
	uprist
IPRSTY	stripy
IPRSTZ	spritz
IPRTUY	purity
IPSTTY	typist
IPSVVY	spivvy
IPTTTU	tittup
IQRRSU	squirr
IQRSTU	squirt
IRSTWY	wristy
ISSSTU	tussis
ISSTUX	Sixtus
ISTTWY	twisty

J

JLNOOS	Jolson
JLNOOY	Jolyon
JLSTUY	justly
JMNOPU	jump on
JMPPUU	jump up
	jump-up
JNNOOS	Jonson
JNOORU	journo
JNOSTU	juntos
JNSTUU	unjust
JOOPPY	joy-pop
	popjoy
JOOSUY	joyous
JORRSU	jurors
JOSSTU	just so
JOTTUU	jut out

K

KKOSTU	Sukkot
KLNOOO	look on
KLNRUY	knurly
KLOOOT	look to
KLOOPU	look up
	uplook
KLORVY	Krylov
KMOOSS	smokos
KMOSUX	musk ox
KMPRSU	skrump
KNNOTU	unknot
KNOORR	kronor
KNOORS	Kronos
KNOORW	work on
KNORRU	krónur
KNORUW	unwork
KNOTTY	knotty
KNPSUY	spunky
KNRSTU	trunks
KOOOSV	Kosovo
KOOPSY	spooky
KOOTWW	kowtow
KOPRUW	work up
KRSSUY	Russky

L

LLLOOP	lollop
LLNOOR	roll on
	roll-on
LLNOPU	pull on
LLNORU	unroll
LLOOWY	woolly
LLOPRU	roll up
	roll-up
	uproll
LLOPUX	Pollux
LLORST	stroll
LLORTY	trolly
LLOSWY	slowly
LLPPUU	pull up
LMMOUX	lummox
LMMPUY	plummy
LMMSUY	slummy
LMOOPU	loom up
LMOORU	ormolu
LMOSTY	mostly
LMPSUY	slumpy
LMTTUU	tumult
LNOOPY	polony
LNOOST	stolon
LNOOTU	Toulon
LNOPSY	pylons
LNORUW	run low
LNOSUU	unsoul
LNRUUY	unruly
LOOPPT	Pol Pot
LOOPRY	poorly
LOOSST	stools
LOOSTT	lost to
	lottos
LOPPRY	propyl
LOPPSY	polyps
	sloppy
LOPRTY	portly
LOPRUX	Proulx
LOPSUW	slow up
LOPTWY	two-ply
LORSUY	sourly
LOSSTY	stylos
LOSTYZ	zlotys
LPPSUY	supply
LPRSYY	spryly
LRRSUY	slurry
LRSTUY	sultry
LRUUXY	luxury
LSSTUY	stylus
LSTTUY	suttly

M

MMNOOR	Mormon
MMNOSU	summon
MMOOPP	pompom
MMOOTT	motmot
	tom-tom
MMOPRS	Mrs Mop
MMRRUU	murmur
MMTTUU	tum-tum
MMUUUU	muu-muu
MMUUYY	yum-yum
MNOORT	Morton
MNOORU	unmoor
MNORSU	Munros
MNOTTU	mutton
MNOTUY	mounty□
MOOPRS	promos
MOORRS	morros
MOPPRT	prompt
MOPSSU	possum
MOPSTU	upmost
MOQRUU	quorum
MORRUU	rumour
MORSST	storms
MORSTY	stormy
MORTUU	tumour
MOSTTU	utmost
MOSTUU	outsum
MPPPUU	pump up
MPRSUU	rumpus
MPSSTU	stumps
MPSTUU	sputum
MPSTUY	stumpy
MSTTUY	smutty

N

NNOORY	ronyon
NNORTU	turn on
	turn-on
NNOSTU	nuts on
NNOSUW	unsown
NNRTUU	unturn
NOOOSS	so soon
NOOOST	soon to
NOOPRT	pronto
	proton
NOOPST	spot on
	spot-on
NOOPSY	snoopy□
NOORTU	unroot
NOOSTY	snooty
NOOSYZ	snoozy
NOOTTU	not out
	not-out
NOOTTW	wont to
NOPRSU	spur on
NOPSTU	puntos
	unstop
NOPTUW	up town
	uptown
NORTTU	turn to
NORTUU	outrun
	run out
NOSTTU	Sutton
NOSTTY	snotty
NOSTUW	unstow
NOSTUY	snouty
NPRTUU	turn up
	turn-up
	upturn
NRSTTU	strunt
NSSTTU	stunts

O

OOOOPP	poo-poo
OOOOTT	too-too
OOOOZZ	zoozoo

OOOPRT	Oporto
OOPPRS	Proops
OOPPRT	troppo
OOPPVX	vox pop
OOPRRT	torpor
OOPRST	troops
OOPRSU	porous
OOPRSV	Provos
OOPRTU	uproot
OOPSTT	pottos
OOPTTU	opt out
	opt-out
	outtop
	top out
OOPWWW	powwow
OORRSW	sorrow
OORRSZ	zorros
OORSST	torsos
OORSTY	rootsy
OOSTTY	tootsy
OPPPRU	prop up
OPPSTU	stop up
OPPSUU	soup up
OPRSST	sports
OPRSTU	Proust
	sprout
	stupor
OPRSTY	sporty
OPRTUY	pry out
OPSSTU	toss up
	toss-up
OPSTTY	spotty
OPSTUW	swot up
OPSTUY	spy out
OPTTUU	output
	put out
ORSSTY	storys
ORSTTU	strout
	trouts
ORTTUY	try out
	try-out
OSSTUU	sus out

P

PPTTUU	put-put
PRRSUY	spurry
PRSUYY	syrupy

R

RSTTUU	Ust'-Urt
RSTTUY	trusty

T

TTTTUU	tut-tut

7 letters

A

AAAABLM	Alabama
AAAACMT	Atacama
AAAALMT	Alma-Ata
AAABBCL	cabbala
AAABBKL	kabbala
AAABBRR	Barbara
AAABCIR	arabica
AAABCLR	Calabar
AAABCLV	baclava
AAABCMR	caramba
AAABDHT	a bad hat
AAABDLM	lambada
AAABDNN	bandana
AAABDYY	Daya Bay
AAABFLL	falbala
AAABGMR	Garamba
AAABHMR	Abraham
AAABHMS	Bahamas
AAABHNS	Sabahan
AAABILN	Albania
AAABINR	Arabian
AAABKLV	baklava
AAABLLU	Lualaba
AAABMOS	abomasa
AAABMST	mastaba
AAABNNS	bananas
AAABNPR	pan-Arab
AAABRSX	abraxas
AAACCIS	acacias
AAACCLR	caracal
AAACCRS	Caracas
AAACCTT	attacca
AAACDIN	Acadian
AAACDIR	Arcadia
AAACDMM	macadam
AAACENP	panacea
AAACHHL	Halacha
AAACHLP	Chapala
AAACHLZ	chalaza
AAACHNT	acantha
AAACIJM	Jamaica
AAACIMR	Aramaic
AAACINT	Catania
AAACJMR	jacamar
AAACLMN	almanac
AAACLNR	Larnaca
AAACLNT	Catalan
AAACMRS	maracas
	mascara
AAACMRY	Maracay
AAACNRV	caravan
AAACNST	canasta
AAACNTT	cantata
AAACRWY	caraway
AAACSSV	cassava
AAADFRY	faraday □
AAADGHL	Galahad
AAADGLY	gala day
AAADGNR	Granada
AAADINR	Adriana
AAADLMN	mandala
AAADMNN	Andaman
AAADMNR	Ramadan
AAADMNT	adamant
AAAEGLT	Galatea
AAAEGNP	apanage
	Pangaea
AAAEHLT	althaea
AAAEIMN	anaemia
AAAEJSV	Java Sea
AAAEKRS	Kara Sea
AAAELMP	palamae
AAAELRS	Aral Sea
AAAEMST	as a team
AAAETWY	eat away
AAAFFLL	alfalfa
AAAFIRT	ratafia
AAAFRSS	as far as
AAAFRWY	faraway
	far-away
AAAGHIP	aphagia
AAAGHKN	Aga Khan
AAAGHPR	agrapha
AAAGIPT	patagia
AAAGISS	assagai
AAAGLMM	amalgam
AAAGLNS	lasagna
AAAGMMT	magmata
AAAGMNR	anagram
AAAGMNU	Managua
AAAGMTT	tagmata
AAAGNRY	yaranga
AAAGNTY	yatagan
AAAGRSY	Asa Gray
AAAHHKL	Halakah
AAAHILT	Athalia
AAAHIPS	aphasia
AAAHLNS	Alashan
AAAHLRZ	al-Azhar
AAAHLTT	at a halt
AAAHMMT	mahatma □
AAAHNRS	Saharan
AAAHNST	Natasha

AAAHOPR	Arapaho
AAAHPRT	paratha
AAAHRTW	waratah
AAAIKLT	Latakia
AAAILMR	malaria
AAAILNT	Natalia
AAAIMNR	Mariana
AAAIMNT	amanita
AAAIMRS	Samaria
AAAIPRX	apraxia
AAAIQRU	aquaria
AAAJKNR	Karajan
AAAJKRT	Jakarta
AAAJMNV	Java Man
AAAKKMR	markkaa
AAAKLMP	Kampala
AAAKMOY	Okayama
AAAKNRS	Sankara
AAALLPT	La Plata
	palatal
AAALMRS	Marsala
AAALNTT	Atlanta
AAALSSV	Savalas
AAAMMRR	Marmara
AAAMNST	atamans
AAAMRSY	Aymaras
AAANNSV	savanna
AAANRTT	tantara
AAAOPRZ	Parazoa
AAAPSST	passata
AAARTTU	tuatara
AAARTXY	ataraxy
AABBBEG	Babbage
AABBCEG	cabbage
AABBDHS	habdabs
AABBEGN	beanbag
	bean-bag
AABBEKL	Baalbek
AABBEMN	Mbabane
AABBEWY	ebb away
AABBHMR	Brabham
AABBHST	Sabbath
AABBMRU	rum baba
AABBNRY	Barnaby
AABBRWY	war baby
AABBSSU	babassu
AABCCER	baccare
AABCDIN	Cabinda
AABCDIR	carabid
AABCEKR	backare
AABCELL	Caballé
AABCELN	balance
AABCELP	capable
AABCELT	actable
AABCEMR	macabre
AABCERT	abreact
	cabaret❑
AABCIIP	Picabia
AABCILN	Caliban
AABCIMR	Cambrai
AABCITX	taxicab
AABCKPY	pay back
AABCKRR	barrack
AABCLPY	capably
AABCLRY	Barclay
AABCLSY	scybala
AABCNOS	cabanos
AABCORT	acrobat
AABCOST	Tabasco®
AABCOTT	catboat
AABDDER	abraded
AABDDGH	Baghdad
AABDDHN	dab hand
AABDDIN	Band-aid®
AABDDNO	Abaddon
AABDEGG	a bad egg
AABDEGN	bandage
AABDEHS	abashed
AABDELL	ballade
AABDELR	Abelard
AABDELT	datable
AABDENU	bandeau
AABDGHN	handbag
AABDGLY	bag lady
AABDGNS	sandbag
AABDHIO	Obadiah
AABDHNT	hatband
AABDIIS	basidia
AABDIJN	Abidjan
AABDIMR	barmaid
AABDJOZ	Badajoz
AABDLLR	Ballard
AABDLRW	bradawl
AABDMNR	armband
	Bradman
AABDNNO	abandon
AABDNRR	Barnard
AABDNRS	sand bar
	sandbar
AABDNSW	band-saw
AABDORV	bravado
AABDRST	bastard
AABEELT	eatable
AABEEMO	amoebae
AABEFFL	affable
AABEFGL	flea-bag
AABEFNR	Aberfan
AABEGGG	baggage
AABEGGR	garbage
AABEGLR	algebra
AABEGMR	Bergama
AABEGRR	barrage
AABEHLT	hatable
AABEIKN	ikebana
AABEILM	amiable
AABEILT	labiate
AABEIRS	arabise
AABEIRZ	arabize
AABEKLM	makable
AABELLL	labella
AABELLN	balneal
AABELMN	namable
AABELMT	tamable
AABELNN	Annabel
AABELNO	abalone
AABELPR	parable
AABELPY	payable
AABELRT	Alberta
	ratable
AABELRY	lay bare
AABELSV	savable
AABELSY	sayable
AABELTT	at table
AABELTU	tableau
	tabulae
AABELTX	taxable
AABEMNU	Abu Mena
AABEMOS	amoebas
AABENNW	wannabe
AABENRS	Banares
AABENRT	ant-bear
AABENWX	wax bean
AABERST	abreast
AABERTT	rabatte
	tabaret
AABERTU	abature
AABESSS	sea bass
AABETUX	bateaux
AABFFLY	affably
AABGHNR	bhangra
	Branagh
AABGHNS	gabnash
AABGIIL	abigail❑
AABGINR	bargain
AABGINT	abating
AABGLOR	Aalborg
AABGLOY	Algo Bay
AABHIMS	Bahaism
	Baha'ism
AABHINR	Bahrain
AABHIST	Bahaist
AABHITT	habitat
	Tabitha
AABHMNR	Brahman
AABIILX	biaxial
AABIIMN	Namibia
AABIJMY	jambiya
AABIJNP	Panjabi
AABIKNS	banksia
AABILMY	amiably
AABILNY	Aly Bain
AABILOU	aboulia
AABILRS	basilar
AABIMMR	marimba
AABIMNZ	Zambian
AABINRS	Sabrina
AABINST	abstain
AABIPUX	paxiuba
AABIRSS	Brassai
AABIRST	Arabist
AABIRSV	Vasarib
AABISTT	abattis
	Batista

Words marked ❑ can also be spelled with an initial capital letter

AABKMRU	Mubarak
AABKOOZ	bazooka
AABLLNY	banally
AABLLST	ballast
AABLLSY	salably
AABLLWY	wallaby
AABLMOS	Absalom
AABLMRU	labarum
AABLMST	lambast
AABLMSY	abysmal
AABLNOT	Balaton
AABLNTT	blatant
AABLOSV	lavabos
AABLOTW	at a blow
AABLRTU	tabular
AABLRTY	ratably
AABLTXY	taxably
AABMMOS	Mombasa
AABMNOT	boatman
AABMNST	batsman
AABMORU	marabou
AABMRRT	Bartram
AABMRTU	tambura
AABNNOZ	bonanza
AABNOSY	sabayon
AABORSZ	abrazos
AABOTTY	attaboy
AABQSUU	subaqua
AABRRUV	bravura
AABRUWY	rub away
AABSSSY	sassaby
AABSTTY	A S Byatt
AACCCIO	Iacocca
AACCDEN	Candace
AACCDES	cascade
	saccade
AACCDIR	cardiac
AACCELO	cloacae
AACCERS	carcase
AACCEST	saccate
AACCGIM	MacCaig
AACCHIR	archaic
AACCHNR	Cranach
AACCHTT	catch at
AACCIJO	Ajaccio
AACCILM	acclaim
AACCJKR	carjack
AACCLLO	cloacal
AACCLLT	catcall
AACCLOR	caracol
AACCLRU	accrual
	caracul
AACCMOS	macacos
AACCNNY	ca' canny
AACCNVY	vacancy
AACCORU	curaçao □
AACCOST	accoast
AACCOTT	toccata
AACCRSS	carcass
AACDDIN	candida □
AACDEEM	academe

AACDEFL	Cadfael
AACDEHR	charade
AACDEII	aecidia
AACDELN	candela
	decanal
AACDELR	caldera □
AACDEMY	academy
AACDENV	advance
AACDENZ	cadenza
AACDERV	cadaver
AACDERY	day care
AACDETU	caudate
AACDEUX	cadeaux
AACDFIR	faradic
AACDHMR	drachma
AACDHNR	Chandra
AACDIIS	ascidia
AACDILR	radical
AACDILU	Claudia
AACDINT	antacid
AACDIRS	ascarid
AACDJKW	jackdaw
AACDLNN	Clannad
AACDLNO	calando
AACDLNS	scandal
AACDLPR	placard
AACDLRU	Dracula
AACDNOR	Cardano
AACDOOV	avocado
AACEEGR	acreage
AACEEHT	chaetae
AACEEKT	teacake
AACEELS	sea lace
AACEEMR	camerae
AACEENT	catenae
AACEEPT	at peace
AACEETT	acetate
AACEFLT	falcate
AACEFLU	faculae
AACEGKP	package
AACEGNR	carnage
AACEHLR	Rachael
AACEHLV	à cheval
AACEHNO	choanae
AACEHNP	panache
AACEHNR	Arachne
AACEHPP	appeach
AACEHRT	trachea
AACEHTT	attaché
AACEHTU	chateau
	château
AACEHWY	each way
AACEILN	Caelian
AACEIMN	anaemic
AACEIPP	cap-a-pie
	cap-à-pie
AACEIRV	avarice
	caviare
AACEJKN	Janácek
AACEKMM	ack-emma
AACEKNP	pancake

AACEKNS	askance
AACEKOT	oatcake
AACELLP	Capella
	Laplace
AACELLS	sacella
AACELLT	lacteal
AACELLW	Wallace
AACELMN	MacLean
	Maclean
	manacle
AACELMR	caramel
AACELMU	maculae
AACELNU	lacunae
AACELNV	valance
AACELPS	Pascale
AACELPT	placate
AACELRT	Lacerta
AACELRV	caravel
AACELTT	lactate
AACEMMR	macramé
AACEMNV	caveman
AACEMPR	paracme
AACEMQU	macaque
AACEMRS	a scream
	cameras
AACEMRU	Marceau
AACENOT	Actaeon
AACENRS	Saracen
AACENRT	cane rat
AACENST	catenas
AACEPRT	rate-cap
AACERRT	rat race
AACERSU	caesura
AACERSZ	Sazerac®
AACERTU	arcuate
AACERTV	cave art
AACETTU	actuate
AACFHLP	half-cap
AACFILS	fascial
AACFINR	African
AACFINT	fanatic
AACFLLY	fallacy
AACFLPT	flat cap
	flat-cap
AACFLRT	fractal
AACFLTU	factual
AACFRRY	a far cry
AACGHLL	Chagall
AACGILL	glacial
AACGILM	magical
AACGLOS	coal gas
AACGLRY	Calgary
AACGNOU	guanaco
AACHHLL	challah
AACHIKR	Karachi
AACHILM	Malachi
AACHILT	calathi
AACHIMR	Amharic
AACHIMS	chiasma
AACHIPS	aphasic
AACHIPT	chapati

AACHIRT	Cathari
AACHITY	cyathia
AACHKMR	Rackham
AACHKSW	hacksaw
AACHLLN	Lachlan
AACHLNT	Chantal
AACHLPS	paschal❑
AACHMMN	Mancham
AACHMNP	chapman❑
AACHNOP	panocha
AACHNPX	panchax
AACHNRY	anarchy
AACHPST	Pat Cash
AACHRRT	catarrh
AACHRST	Cathars
AACHRWY	archway
AACHRYZ	Zachary
AACIIST	Asiatic
AACIITV	viatica
AACIJNT	Jacinta
AACIKNN	canakin
AACILLM	Camilla
AACILNR	cranial
AACILNZ	Zincala
AACILOS	asocial
AACILOX	coaxial
AACILPS	spacial
AACILPT	capital❑
	placita
AACILUY	Ucayali
AACIMNO	in a coma
AACIMNR	Marcian
AACIMOR	acromia
AACIMRU	Mauriac
AACINOR	Aaronic
	conaria
	ocarina
AACINPS	Caspian
AACINPT	captain
AACINPY	pay cain
AACINRZ	czarina
AACINST	satanic
AACINTV	Vatican
AACIOPT	tapioca
AACIORT	Croatia
AACIOTV	Octavia
AACIQTU	aquatic
AACIRST	caritas
AACISTT	astatic
AACJKMN	man jack
	manjack
AACJKRT	Jack Tar
	Jack tar
AACJKSS	jackass
AACJMOR	Majorca
AACJOST	Jocasta
AACKLMR	Lamarck
AACKLMS	Almack's
AACKLTW	catwalk
AACKMNP	packman
AACKNRS	ransack
AACKPRT	pack rat
	pack-rat
	ratpack
AACLLOR	coralla
AACLLSU	clausal
AACLMNT	calmant
	clamant
AACLMRU	macular
AACLMSU	calamus
AACLNNU	cannula
AACLORT	crotala
AACLOST	coastal
AACLPSU	scapula
AACLPTY	play-act
AACLRVY	cavalry
AACLSTT	last act
AACLSUV	vascula
AACMNOR	camaron
AACMNRS	Scarman
AACMNSY	caymans
AACMNTX	Manx cat
AACMORS	sarcoma
AACMORT	marcato
AACMRSS	sarcasm
AACNNOT	Cantona
AACNPST	capstan
AACNSSV	canvass
AACNSTU	ascaunt
AACORST	ostraca
AACPSTW	cat's paw
	cat's-paw
AACRTTT	attract
AACRTUY	actuary
AACTUWY	cutaway
AADDDEN	addenda
AADDEES	Dead Sea
AADDEGM	damaged
AADDENP	deadpan
	dead-pan
AADDEPT	adapted
AADDFGI	Gaddafi
AADDGNR	graddan
	grandad
AADDHKR	khaddar
AADDIMS	Dadaism
AADDIMY	may I add
AADDIST	Dadaist
AADDLYY	Lady Day
AADDRST	dastard
AADEERT	aerated
AADEFFR	affeard
AADEFHO	ahead of
AADEFHT	fat head
	fathead
	fat-head
AADEFNZ	fazenda
AADEGGR	aggrade
AADEGHO	go ahead
	go-ahead
AADEGMS	damages
AADEGNR	Grenada
AADEGRT	at grade
	gradate
AADEGRV	ravaged
AADEGRY	yardage
AADEHLN	Haldane
AADEHMN	headman
AADEHMS	ashamed
AADEHNX	handaxe
AADEHPR	Phaedra
AADEHRW	warhead
AADEHWY	headway
AADEILN	Daniela
AADEILR	radiale
AADEILV	vedalia
AADEIMR	Madeira
AADEIMS	seamaid
AADEINR	araneid
	Ariadne
AADEINS	naiades
AADEINZ	in a daze
AADEIRT	radiate
AADEITW	awaited
AADEIWY	die away
	die-away
AADEKMR	kamerad
AADELMN	Mandela
AADELMO	à la mode
	alamode
AADELMP	De Palma
AADELMR	alarmed
AADELNR	adrenal
AADELNW	Danelaw
AADELNZ	Zealand
AADELRU	radulae
AADELRY	already
AADELTU	adulate
AADEMMN	man-made
AADEMNS	Maenads
AADEMNT	mandate
AADEMRW	Medawar
AADEMSU	Amadeus
AADENNP	Pandean
AADENNT	andante
	at an end
	Dantean
AADENRV	veranda
AADENSW	weasand
AADENTV	Vedanta
AADEPRR	para-red
AADEPRT	adapter
AADEPSS	passade
AADERRY	arrayed
AADERSW	seaward
AADFGLN	Gandalf
AADFHLY	half-day
AADFLOO	a load of
AADFLTW	twafald
AADGGHR	haggard❑
AADGGLR	laggard
AADGHIL	hidalga
AADGIMR	diagram

AADGINO	do again
AADGIOS	adagios
AADGLLW	gadwall
AADGLNO	Lagonda®
AADGLNR	garland□
AADGLRU	gradual
AADGMNR	grandma
AADGNPR	grandpa
AADGNRY	yardang
AADGOPR	podagra
AADHHMS	Mashhad
AADHHRT	hard hat
AADHINP	daphnia
AADHINR	Hadrian
AADHLRY	halyard
AADHNRS	darshan
	Hansard
AADHNSW	handsaw
AADHNTT	and that
AADHOSS	soda ash
AADHRRV	Harvard
AADHRST	Harstad
AADHSWY	washday
AADIINN	Indiana
AADIIPS	aspidia
AADIIRR	air raid
AADIKLY	ilkaday
AADILMR	admiral
AADILMT	Matilda
AADILNP	paladin
AADILNR	laniard
AADIMNR	Miranda
AADIMOR	diorama
AADIMOT	domatia
AADIMRR	ram-raid
AADIMRU	Madurai
AADIMST	Amistad
AADINRT	radiant
AADIORS	Isadora
AADIPPR	Paradip
AADIRRW	airward
AADKLNO	Oakland
AADKNRT	tankard
AADKRWW	awkward
AADLLMN	damn all
AADLLMR	mallard
AADLLNR	Randall
AADLLPU	paludal
AADLMMU	Malamud
AADLNOY	Yolanda
AADLNRY	lanyard
AADLNWY	Wayland
AADLOPY	payload
	pay-load
AADLPPU	applaud
AADLRRU	radular
AADLRWY	Aylward
AADMNNO	Madonna
AADMNOR	roadman
AADMNOS	Adamson
AADMNRS	mansard

AADMNSY	man-days
AADMNTU	mutanda
AADMOPR	road-map
AADMORT	matador
AADMRRY	yard-arm
AADMSSU	Damasus
AADNNOT	notanda
AADNOPR	Pandora
AADNORR	Andorra
AADNORT	ondatra
AADNORY	anyroad
AADNOTY	Daytona
AADNRST	astrand
AADNRVW	vanward
AADNRWY	nayward
AADOPRS	parados
AADOPRT	adaptor
AADOPRX	paradox
AADORTW	at a word
AADORTX	road tax
AADORWY	roadway
AADOSTT	tostada
AADQRTU	quadrat
AADRSTY	daystar
AADRWWY	wayward
AAEEFGL	leafage
AAEEFLT	tea leaf
AAEEGKL	leakage
AAEEGRV	average
AAEEHRT	hetaera
AAEEHSY	Ayeesha
AAEEINT	taeniae
AAEELLP	pale ale
AAEELLR	real ale
AAEELOR	areolae
AAEEMNT	emanate
	enemata
	manatee
AAEENRT	e re nata
AAEEPPS	appease
AAEEPRT	paterae
AAEERSW	seaware
AAEERTU	aureate
AAEERTX	exarate
AAEFFLL	falafel
AAEFFNR	fanfare
AAEFFTT	taffeta
AAEFGLR	Feargal
AAEFHMR	Fareham
AAEFMRT	fermata
AAEFNST	Santa Fe
AAEFORW	aware of
AAEFRRR	Ferrara
AAEFRRW	warfare
AAEGHLU	haulage
AAEGHMR	Grahame
AAEGHNS	Ganesha
AAEGHOV	have a go
	have-a-go
AAEGILR	Algeria
	regalia

AAEGISS	assegai
AAEGITT	agitate
AAEGKOS	soakage
AAEGLLT	tallage
AAEGLNS	lasagne
AAEGLRR	realgar
AAEGLRT	at large
AAEGLSV	salvage
AAEGMNR	manager
AAEGMNT	magenta
	magnate
AAEGMPR	rampage
AAEGMRT	Margate
	regmata
AAEGMRW	war game
AAEGMSS	massage
AAEGNPT	pageant
AAEGNRR	arrange
AAEGNRT	tanager
AAEGNTV	vantage
AAEGOST	Sea Goat
AAEGPRR	parerga
AAEGPSS	passage
AAEGPSY	paysage
AAEGPWY	peg away
AAEGQUY	quayage
AAEGRRS	rare gas
AAEGRRV	ravager
AAEGRST	tear gas
	tear-gas
AAEGRSV	ravages
AAEGRTT	regatta
AAEGRUV	Guevara
AAEGRWW	wage war
AAEGSSU	assuage
	sausage
AAEGSTU	gateaus
AAEGSTW	wastage
AAEGTTW	wattage
AAEGTUX	gâteaux
AAEGTWY	gateway
	get away
	getaway
AAEHHPT	aphthae
AAEHHSY	Ayeshah
AAEHILP	aphelia
AAEHINZ	in a haze
AAEHIRT	hetaira
AAEHLNZ	Alhazen
AAEHLPR	Raphael
AAEHMST	Eastham
AAEHMTT	themata
AAEHNPS	saphena
AAEHRRT	Earhart
AAEHRSY	hearsay
AAEHRTT	at heart
AAEHSTT	hastate
AAEHVWY	have way
AAEIKLU	Kilauea
AAEIKMT	take aim
AAEIKRT	take air

Words marked □ can also be spelled with an initial capital letter

AAEILLX	axillae
AAEILMN	A A Milne
	laminae
AAEILMR	Almeria
AAEILMS	malaise
AAEILNN	alanine
AAEILNO	aeolian
AAEILNT	antliae
	Natalie
AAEILOR	olearia
AAEILRV	velaria
AAEILSS	aliases
AAEIMMT	imamate
AAEIMNR	Armenia
AAEIMNS	amnesia
AAEIMNT	amentia
	animate
AAEIMPY	pyaemia
AAEIMRU	uraemia
AAEIMTV	amative
AAEINRZ	Zairean
AAEINST	taenias
AAEIPRS	spiraea
AAEIPRT	apteria
	Tarpeia
AAEIPTT	apatite
AAEIRST	Astaire
AAEIRTT	arietta
AAEIRTV	variate
AAEISTT	satiate
AAEJKOS	as a joke
AAEJNPR	Jean Arp
AAEJNRT	naartje
AAEJNTT	Janetta
AAEKKOR	karaoke
AAEKLMW	make law
AAEKLNT	alkanet
AAEKLNV	Lake Van
AAEKMRR	earmark
AAEKMRW	make war
AAEKMWY	make way
AAEKPRT	partake
AAELLLM	lamella
AAELLNV	avellan
AAELLPT	patella
AAELLRS	all ears
AAELLRT	lateral
AAELMMT	lemmata
AAELMNS	Ameslan
AAELMNU	alumnae
AAELMOT	oatmeal
AAELMPT	palmate
AAELMST	maltase
AAELMSY	amylase
AAELNNO	Oleanna
AAELNPT	platane
AAELNRS	arsenal
AAELNST	sealant
AAELNSY	analyse
AAELORU	aureola
AAELPPR	apparel
AAELPPT	palpate
AAELPPU	papulae
AAELPRV	palaver
AAELPTU	plateau
AAELRST	tar-seal
AAELRSU	as a rule
AAELRTZ	lazaret
AAELRVZ	Alvarez
AAELSST	atlases
	sea-salt
AAELSTT	at least
	saltate
AAELSUX	asexual
AAELTTV	Valetta
AAELTUV	valuate
AAELTVV	valvate
AAEMMOT	ommatea
AAEMNNT	emanant
AAEMNPS	spaeman
AAEMNRT	ramenta
AAEMNST	Eastman
	Smetana
AAEMPPZ	Mazeppa
AAEMQSU	squamae
AAEMRTU	amateur
AAEMSTX	Metaxas
AAENNNT	antenna
AAENNRV	Ravenna
AAENPST	peasant
AAENRRT	narrate
AAENRST	Antares
AAENRSZ	Sarazen
AAENRTT	tartane
AAENRTU	Taurean
AAENRTV	taverna
AAENRUW	unaware
AAENSST	Nastase
AAENSSV	Vanessa
AAENSSW	Swansea
AAENSTV	Avestan
AAENVYY	Yanayev
AAEORRU	aurorae
AAEOSVZ	Azov Sea
AAEPPRT	parapet
AAERRRS	arrears
AAERSSY	assayer
AAERSTT	stare at
AAERSTW	swear at
AAERTTY	tea tray
AAETTUW	Watteau
AAFFINS	saffian
AAFFIRS	affairs
AAFFIRX	Fairfax
AAFGHIN	Afghani
AAFGORR	farrago
AAFHILX	Halifax
AAFHINS	Isfahan
AAFHLWY	halfway
AAFIILR	filaria
AAFIJST	fajitas
AAFILNP	in a flap
AAFILNT	fantail
AAFIMRY	Mayfair
AAFIMUX	faux ami
AAFINNT	infanta
AAFIPRT	parfait
AAFIRUY	rufiyaa
AAFIRWY	fairway
AAFKMNU	Kaufman
AAFLLTY	fatally
AAFLTTU	at fault
AAFMSTU	Mustafa
AAFNSTY	fantasy
AAFOPRT	a part of
AAFPSUX	faux pas
AAGGHNU	Gaughan
AAGGILN	ganglia
AAGGINR	Gagarin
AAGGLOS	galagos
AAGGLOT	Tagálog
AAGGNOY	anagogy
AAGGNST	gangsta
AAGGNSW	gang saw
AAGGNWY	gangway
AAGHILR	Aligarh
	gharial
AAGHLNT	gnathal
AAGHLTU	laugh at
AAGHMMU	Maugham
AAGHMNN	hangman
AAGHNUV	Vaughan
AAGHQUU	quahaug
AAGIINO	Goiânia
AAGIKNW	awaking
AAGILMR	Alamgir
AAGILMY	myalgia
AAGILNV	Galvani
AAGILOT	otalgia
AAGILTW	wagtail
AAGIMNO	angioma
AAGIMNS	gas main
	siamang
AAGIMNZ	amazing
AAGINRR	arraign
AAGINRS	sangria
AAGINRU	guarani
	Guaraní
AAGINRZ	Zingara
AAGINST	against
AAGINSY	gainsay
AAGIOTT	agitato
AAGIPPR	Agrippa
AAGISSZ	Agassiz
AAGISTT	Sagitta
AAGJRTU	Gujarat
AAGKLLO	oak-gall
AAGKMSS	gas mask
AAGKNST	gas tank
AAGLLNT	gallant
AAGLNOY	analogy
AAGLNPS	lapsang
AAGLNRU	angular

AAGLRUU augural
AAGLRVX gravlax
AAGMMRR grammar
AAGMMTU gummata
AAGMNPR pangram
AAGMNRT tangram
AAGMNSW swagman
AAGMOPY apogamy
AAGMRUX Margaux
AAGNOPR paragon
AAGNORZ organza
AAGNRRY granary
AAGNRTV vagrant
AAGNRTY angry at
AAGORSU saguaro
AAGSTUU Augusta
AAHHIRS Shari'ah
AAHHNPT naphtha
AAHHOPR pharaoh❑
AAHIINT Haitian
AAHIKMT Khatami
AAHIKNT Inkatha
AAHILMT thalami
AAHIMNS Samhain
AAHINNU Huainan
AAHINOP aphonia
AAHINOR Honiara
AAHINPR piranha
AAHIORT to a hair
AAHIPTY Hypatia
AAHIRST shariat
AAHKMSY yashmak
AAHKNOR Khorana
AAHKNRS Shankar
AAHKNSU Anushka
AAHKRSS rakshas
AAHLLTT all that
AAHLLWY hallway
AAHLMRS marshal
AAHLMRU hamular
AAHLNPX phalanx
AAHLNRW narwhal
AAHLPPR Pharlap
AAHLPRS phrasal
AAHLPST asphalt
AAHMNNU hanuman❑
AAHMNRS Sharman
AAHMNSS shamans
AAHMOPR amphora
AAHMQSU quamash
AAHMSTZ matzahs
AAHMTTU Matthau
AAHNNOS hosanna
AAHNOSV Navahos
AAHNPRS Hans Arp
AAHNRTX anthrax
AAHNRTY rhatany
AAHPRTW warpath
AAHPSTU at a push
AAHPTWY pathway
AAHRTTW athwart

AAHSWYY shy away
AAIILMR airmail
AAIILNT Italian
AAIILNV Lavinia
AAIINNR Iranian
AAIINTT Titania
AAIIRVV vivaria
AAIJLNU Juliana
AAIJMNP jampani
AAIJNTU Tijuana
AAIKLLS alkalis
AAIKMNN manakin
AAIKMNR ramakin
AAIKMSY may I ask
AAIKNNT Kantian
AAIKNOW Okinawa
AAIKNRT Katrina
AAIKOSY sokaiya
AAIKPPR paprika
AAIKRSS askaris
AAILLMM mamilla
AAILLMN manilla
AAILLMX maxilla
AAILLNV vanilla
AAILLPP papilla
AAILLRX axillar
AAILLUV alluvia
AAILLXY axially
AAILMMN mailman
AAILMMS Lamaism
miasmal
AAILMMX maximal
AAILMNR laminar
AAILMNS animals❑
AAILMNT matinal
AAILMNU alumina
AAILMOS Somalia
AAILMPS impalas
AAILMRT marital
martial❑
AAILMSS Salamis
AAILMST Lamaist
AAILNOP Pianola®
AAILNOV valonia
AAILNPU Naipaul
Paulina
AAILNRU ulnaria
Uralian
AAILNSV Silvana
AAILNTV Latvian
valiant
AAILORV variola
AAILOST solatia
AAILPPT appalti
AAILPRT partial
patrial
AAILPST spatial
AAILPTT talipat
AAILPZZ palazzi
AAILQWW qawwali
AAILRRV arrival

AAILRTV travail
AAILRWY railway
AAILSSW wassail
AAIMMNO ammonia
AAIMNNR Rain Man
AAIMNOR Romania
AAIMNOS anosmia
AAIMNOT animato
AAIMNRT Martian
Martina
tamarin
AAIMNRZ Mazarin
AAIMNST stamina
AAIMORV Moravia
AAIMRSU samurai
AAIMSST stasima
AAIMSTV atavism
AAINNOT Antonia
AAINNRU Uranian
AAINNRV navarin
nirvana❑
AAINOPS paisano
AAINORR orarian
AAINORV ovarian
AAINORZ Arizona
AAINPST at pains
AAINQSU Aquinas
AAINRST artisan
Sinatra
tsarina
AAINRSU saurian
AAINRTV variant
AAINSTV vanitas
AAINTTT attaint
AAINTTU tutania
AAINTUY Taiyuan
AAIORRS Rosaria
AAIORTV aviator
AAIPPRU puparia
AAIPPTT pitapat
AAIPRTT partita
AAIPRTV Parvati
AAIQSSU quassia
AAIQTUV aquavit
AAIRSTU Austria
AAJKLWY jaywalk
AAJMPSY pyjamas
AAJMRTT jam tart
AAJNNSU San Juan
AAJNNSY Nyanjas
AAJNOSV Navajos
AAJNRUY January
AAJOPSU sapajou
AAKKLRU karakul
AAKKMOT tokamak
AAKKMRS markkas
AAKKMRU Kara Kum
AAKKOPS kakapos
AAKLMRY malarky
AAKLOOP palooka
AAKLRSU rusalka

AAKLWWY	walkway
AAKMNSW	Waksman
AAKMORV	Markova
AAKMRUZ	mazurka
AAKMRWY	waymark
AAKNRTU	Turkana
AAKOOPP	pakapoo
AAKORST	ostraka
AAKRTTU	Ataturk
	Atatürk
AAKRTUY	autarky
AALLLNS	Lallans
AALLLSW	Walsall
AALLMPU	ampulla
AALLNSY	nasally
AALLOTV	lavolta
AALLPPY	papally
AALLRST	all-star
AALLRUY	aurally
AALMMMS	mammals
AALMNOY	anomaly
	Layamon
AALMNST	last man
AALMORY	mayoral
AALMPRY	palmyra
AALMPWX	wax palm
AALMRUX	Malraux
AALMTTU	mulatta
AALNNRU	annular
AALNORS	also-ran
AALNOUV	Ulanova
AALNPRT	plantar
AALNPST	salt pan
AALNPSV	pan-Slav
AALNRST	snarl at
AALNRTU	natural
AALNSTT	saltant
AALNSTU	sultana
AALNSTY	analyst
AALOPRS	parasol
AALOPTV	Poltava
AALOPVV	pavlova□
AALOPZZ	palazzo
AALORSU	arousal
AALOSST	at a loss
AALOSTT	saltato
AALPPRU	papular
AALPPSU	Uppsala
AALPSTU	spatula
AALRSTU	austral
AALRSUZ	Lazarus
AALRWYY	lyra-way
AALSSTU	assault
AALSSUU	as usual
AAMMMRY	mammary
AAMMNNX	Manxman
AAMMNRT	mantram
AAMMNRY	Myanmar
AAMMRST	ramstam
AAMNNOT	Montana
AAMNOOS	manoaos
AAMNORS	oarsman
AAMNORW	man-o'-war
AAMNOTY	anatomy
AAMNPRT	mantrap
	rampant
AAMNPRY	paranym
AAMNPTY	tympana
AAMNRTY	army ant
AAMOPRS	paramos
AAMORSV	samovar
AAMORTY	amatory
AAMOSSS	samosas
AAMOSTT	stomata
AAMPRRT	rampart
AAMPRSS	Sampras
AAMRRTY	Marryat
AAMRSST	matrass
AAMRSTU	Sumatra
	traumas
AAMRTWY	tramway
AAMSSTU	satsuma□
AANNORS	Rosanna
AANNOTT	annatto
AANNSSU	Susanna
AANORTT	Taranto
AANOSTT	anattos
AANPRST	spartan□
AANPRSU	Puranas
AANPSST	passant
AANQRTU	quartan
AANRRTW	warrant
AANRUWY	run away
	runaway
AANSSTW	Tswanas
AANSTTT	statant
AANTUUV	Vanuatu
AAOPRRT	pro rata
AAORRSU	auroras
AAORSTV	Saratov
AAPQSUW	Quapaws
AAPRSTY	satrapy
AAPRTWY	part way
AAPTUWY	put away
AAPZZZZ	pazzazz
ABBBELR	babbler
	blabber
ABBBITT	Babbitt
ABBCCKO	Babcock
ABBCDER	crabbed
ABBCELS	scabble
ABBCKUY	buy back
	buy-back
ABBCMOR	car bomb
ABBCRYY	crybaby
	cry-baby
ABBDDET	bad debt
ABBDEGR	grabbed
ABBDEIY	abide by
ABBDELR	dabbler
	Drabble
ABBDELS	slabbed
ABBDHRU	Hubbard
ABBDINR	ribband
ABBDMOR	bombard
ABBDNYY	by and by
	by-and-by
ABBEERR	Berbera
ABBEGLR	gabbler
	grabble
ABBEGRU	bugbear
	Burbage
ABBEHII	Habibie
ABBEHMO	Hobbema
ABBELMR	bramble□
ABBELPR	prabble
ABBELRS	slabber
ABBELRU	barbule
ABBELSU	baubles
ABBELUY	buyable
ABBEMUZ	bumbaze
ABBEOTU	be about
ABBEOTX	beat box
ABBERST	stabber
ABBERSW	swabber
ABBGGIN	Big Bang
ABBGINN	nabbing
ABBGINU	bubinga
ABBGOOU	bugaboo
ABBGORS	gabbros
ABBHISY	babyish
ABBHNTU	Bath bun
ABBHRRU	rhubarb
ABBHTTU	bathtub
ABBIIMN	bambini
ABBILOT	bobtail
ABBINRS	rabbins
ABBIRSU	Babrius
ABBIRTY	rabbity
ABBISTY	babysit
	baby-sit
ABBKNRU	Burbank
ABBLLOY	ball-boy
ABBLMRY	brambly
ABBLNOY	Babylon
ABBMOOR	bombora
ABBMOST	bombast
ABBMOTU	bum-boat
ABBNRUY	Banbury
ABBOORR	Roobarb
ABBOSTY	bobstay
ABBQSUY	squabby
ABCCEER	Rebecca
ABCCEIR	acerbic
	breccia
ABCCHII	bacchii
ABCCHSU	Bacchus
ABCCILU	cubical
ABCCIMR	cambric
ABCCINU	buccina
ABCCIOR	boracic
ABCCKTU	cut back
	cutback

Words marked □ can also be spelled with an initial capital letter

ABCCNOU	Nabucco
ABCCOOT	tobacco
ABCDEEH	beached
ABCDEEL	debacle
	débâcle
ABCDEHU	debauch
ABCDEIK	die back
	dieback
ABCDEIP	pedicab
ABCDEIR	carbide
ABCDEKR	redback
ABCDEMP	camp-bed
ABCDEOR	bar code
	brocade
ABCDERU	cudbear
ABCDHIO	ichabod
ABCDIIS	dibasic
ABCDILR	baldric
ABCDINS	abscind
ABCDIRS	scabrid
ABCDKLU	bad luck
ABCDNOS	abscond
ABCDOOR	cordoba
	Córdoba
ABCDRUY	Cadbury
ABCEEHM	Beecham
ABCEEHU	ébauche
ABCEEMR	embrace
ABCEENS	absence
ABCEERR	cerebra
ABCEESU	because
ABCEGIR	ribcage
ABCEGKP	peg back
ABCEGKT	get back
ABCEGOS	boscage
ABCEHIR	Hebraic
ABCEHKM	Beckham
ABCEHLN	Blanche
ABCEHLU	bauchle
ABCEHMR	becharm
	chamber
	chambré
ABCEHMT	Macbeth
ABCEIKL	lie back
ABCEILM	cembali
ABCEILR	calibre
ABCEILT	citable
ABCEIMO	amoebic
ABCEIMU	Cimabué
ABCEINR	carbine
ABCEINT	cabinet
ABCEIOR	aerobic
ABCEIRS	ascribe
	Brescia
ABCEISS	abscise
	scabies
ABCEKLN	blacken
ABCEKLY	Backley
ABCEKNR	bracken
ABCEKRS	backers
ABCEKRT	bracket
ABCEKST	set back
	setback
ABCELMR	clamber
ABCELMS	scamble
ABCELOP	placebo
ABCELOV	vocable
ABCELPU	bluecap
ABCELRU	curable
ABCELSU	bascule
ABCELTV	cable TV
ABCELUY	Luce Bay
ABCELWY	Clew Bay
ABCENOW	cowbane
ABCENRU	unbrace
ABCESSS	abscess
ABCESTY	Catesby
ABCFFKO	back off
ABCFIKN	finback
ABCFILO	bifocal
ABCGHKO	hogback
ABCGIKN	backing
ABCGINR	bracing
ABCGIST	big cats
ABCGKLO	backlog
ABCGLOO	cool bag
ABCGMSU	scumbag
ABCGORY	go by car
ABCHHII	hibachi
ABCHIKT	hit back
ABCHILS	Chablis
ABCHIOT	cohabit
ABCHLOR	Chabrol
ABCHNRY	branchy
ABCHOSX	cash box
ABCIILL	bacilli
ABCIIMN	minicab
ABCIIMS	iambics
ABCIIOR	ciboria
ABCIKNW	win back
ABCIKST	sit back
ABCIKSY	sick bay
ABCILRS	scribal
ABCIMMU	cambium
ABCIMOR	Coimbra
ABCIMRU	Cumbria
ABCINNO	in banco
ABCINOT	botanic
ABCIORU	caribou
ABCIOUV	bivouac
ABCKLLY	blackly
ABCKMRU	buckram
ABCKNNO	bannock
ABCKOTU	back out
	outback
ABCKPTU	put back
ABCKRTU	Tarbuck
ABCKRTY	try back
ABCKSTU	sackbut
ABCLMNU	clubman
ABCLMOU	Columba
ABCLNOY	balcony
ABCORRW	crowbar
ABDDEER	bearded
ABDDEES	debased
ABDDEET	debated
ABDDEIR	braided
ABDDELR	bladder
ABDDEMR	mad-bred
ABDDENR	branded
ABDDERW	bedward
ABDDINS	disband
ABDDLLO	oddball
ABDDLOY	do badly
ABDDMOO	bad mood
ABDEEFL	feel-bad
ABDEEGR	rebadge
ABDEELM	bemedal
ABDEELR	Bradlee
ABDEELT	belated
ABDEERS	debaser
ABDEERT	betread
	debater
ABDEEST	bestead
ABDEFFL	baffled
ABDEFOR	forbade
ABDEFOS	sofa bed
ABDEFRW	bedwarf
ABDEGHI	bighead
ABDEGIN	beading
ABDEGIR	abridge
	brigade
ABDEGLR	garbled
ABDEGNO	bondage
ABDEGOR	Bogarde
ABDEHLR	halberd
ABDEHOR	Deborah
ABDEHOT	to be had
ABDEHOY	head boy
ABDEHRT	breadth
	the Bard
ABDEHST	had best
ABDEILN	Belinda
	nail-bed
ABDEILP	piebald
ABDEILS	disable
ABDEILU	audible
ABDEINR	brained
ABDEIRS	darbies
ABDEIRT	tribade
ABDEJOU	j'adoube
ABDELMR	marbled
ABDELNO	old bean
ABDELOS	albedos
ABDELOT	bloated
ABDELPU	dupable
ABDELRU	durable
ABDELRY	Bradley
ABDELST	blasted
ABDEMNO	abdomen
ABDEMRU	Bermuda
ABDENNR	Brendan
ABDENOR	broaden

ABDENOS	based on
ABDENRR	Bernard
	brander
ABDENSS	badness
ABDENSW	bad news
ABDEORR	boarder
ABDERTY	drybeat
ABDFIIR	bid fair
ABDFMOR	bad form
ABDGHOO	Habgood
ABDGHOT	Godthab
ABDGIIN	abiding
ABDGILN	balding
ABDGINR	brigand
ABDGINT	dingbat
ABDGINW	windbag
ABDGNNU	Bandung
ABDHIIT	adhibit
ABDHMTU	mudbath
ABDHNOR	bodhran
ABDHNSU	husband
ABDIKRS	disbark
ABDILNW	Baldwin
ABDILOO	diabolo
ABDILOT	tabloid
ABDILRY	rabidly
ABDILUY	audibly
ABDILWY	bawdily
ABDIMOR	ambroid
ABDIMRU	Rimbaud
ABDINOR	inboard
ABDINOY	in a body
ABDINRT	antbird
ABDINST	bandits
ABDIPRT	bad trip
ABDIPRU	upbraid
ABDIRTY	tribady
ABDKNOU	do a bunk
ABDKOOY	daybook
	day-book
ABDLLNY	blandly
ABDLLOR	bollard
ABDLMOR	Lombard
ABDLORY	broadly
ABDLRUY	durably
ABDLSUU	subdual
ABDMNNO	bondman
ABDNNOR	Bonnard
ABDNOOR	on board
ABDNOPR	proband
ABDNOSX	sandbox
ABDNOSY	sandboy
ABDNOUU	Audubon
ABDNOYY	anybody
ABDNRTU	bad turn
	turband
ABDNSTY	stand by
	stand-by
ABDOORW	barwood
ABDOPRU	board up
ABDRSTU	bustard❑
ABDRUZZ	buzzard
ABEEELM	lee beam
ABEEERV	bereave
ABEEFLO	beefalo
ABEEFST	safe bet
ABEEGHR	herbage
ABEEGLR	beagler
ABEEGPW	Web page
ABEEHKR	Rebekah
ABEEHNN	henbane
ABEEHNS	banshee
	has-been
ABEEHNT	beneath
ABEEHRT	breathe
ABEEHST	H E Bates
ABEEIMT	tie beam
ABEEIST	beastie
ABEEKNV	beknave
ABEEKPS	bespeak
ABEEKRR	breaker
ABEELLY	eyeball
ABEELMM	emblema
ABEELMZ	emblaze
ABEELNP	plebean
ABEELNR	enabler
ABEELNT	Beltane
	tenable
ABEELNU	nebulae
ABEELQU	equable
ABEELRT	retable
ABEELST	Beatles
ABEELSV	beslave
ABEEMRS	besmear
ABEEMRT	beer-mat
ABEENRS	Benares
ABEENRV	verbena
ABEERTT	abetter
ABEESTY	Tees Bay
ABEESWX	beeswax
ABEFFMO	off beam
ABEFFOS	off base
ABEFFOT	beat off
	off beat
	offbeat
	off-beat
ABEFGST	gabfest
ABEFILN	finable
ABEFILR	friable
ABEFIRT	far be it
ABEFITY	beatify
ABEFLLU	baleful
ABEFLNT	fan belt
ABEFLNU	baneful
ABEFLST	Belfast
ABEFORR	forbear
ABEGGIM	big game
ABEGGLR	blagger
ABEGGMO	gamboge
ABEGGRY	beggary
ABEGHNS	shebang
ABEGHOT	Bagehot
ABEGILN	Belgian
	Bengali
ABEGILR	Gabriel
ABEGIMN	beaming
	big name
ABEGIMR	gambier
ABEGINO	begonia
ABEGINR	barge in
	bearing
ABEGINT	beating
ABEGINW	wine-bag
ABEGIPP	bagpipe
ABEGLMR	gambler
	gambrel
ABEGLOT	globate
ABEGMNR	Bergman
ABEGMOR	Bergamo
	embargo
ABEGMRU	umbrage
ABEGNOS	nosebag
ABEGNOT	Boateng
ABEGOPY	pageboy
ABEGORR	begorra
ABEGORS	Seaborg
ABEGORX	gearbox
ABEGOSZ	gazebos
ABEGOTT	tote bag
ABEHILR	hirable
ABEHILS	Belisha
ABEHIRS	bearish
ABEHITU	habitué
ABEHKRU	hauberk
ABEHKTU	Ketubah
ABEHLMS	shamble
ABEHLMT	Lambeth
	the Lamb
ABEHLRT	blather
	halbert
ABEHMNT	Bentham
ABEHNTY	Bethany
ABEHOTT	The Boat
ABEHRST	Barthes
ABEHRSY	Ashbery
ABEHRTY	breathy
	by heart
ABEIILR	Liberia
ABEIINR	Iberian
ABEIKLL	likable
ABEIKLS	skiable
ABEIKLY	Kiel Bay
ABEIKNR	break in
	break-in
ABEIKNT	beatnik
ABEIKWY	bikeway
ABEILLO	lobelia
ABEILLP	pliable
ABEILLR	braille❑
	liberal
ABEILMT	timbale
ABEILMX	mixable
ABEILMY	beamily

Words marked ❑ can also be spelled with an initial capital letter

ABEILNP	biplane
ABEILNS	lesbian
ABEILNZ	Albéniz
ABEILRT	Alberti
	librate
	triable
ABEILST	bestial
ABEILSZ	sizable
ABEILVV	bivalve
ABEIMNT	ambient
ABEIMZZ	Zambezi
ABEINOZ	Zenobia
ABEINRS	Serbian
ABEINRT	atebrin
ABEINRW	wine bar
ABEINST	Antibes
ABEINTT	Bettina
	Tibetan
ABEIOTV	obviate
ABEIPST	baptise
ABEIPTZ	baptize
ABEIRRR	barrier
ABEIRRT	arbiter
	rarebit
ABEIRRZ	bizarre
	brazier
ABEIRSS	brassie
ABEIRTT	biretta
ABEIRTV	vibrate
ABEIRTX	Beatrix
ABEIRTZ	Bizerta
ABEIRUX	exurbia
ABEISUV	abusive
ABEITUX	bauxite
ABEJLUY	blue jay
ABEJMUX	jambeux
ABEJNOS	banjoes
ABEJNOW	jawbone
ABEKLLY	bleakly
ABEKLNT	blanket
ABEKLTU	Blue-tak®
ABEKNSU	sunbake
ABEKOOR	abrooke
ABEKPRU	break up
	break-up
	upbreak
ABELLMY	Bellamy
ABELLNO	Bellona
ABELLNT	netball
ABELLNY	Allenby
ABELLOV	lovable
	volable
ABELLRU	rubella
	rulable
ABELMMR	membral
ABELMNT	beltman
	lambent
ABELMNU	albumen
ABELMOT	to blame
ABELMOV	movable
ABELMRR	rambler
ABELMRS	marbles
ABELMRT	lambert □
ABELMRY	Bramley
ABELMTU	mutable
ABELMYY	Lyme Bay
ABELNNO	Lebanon
ABELNOT	notable
ABELNOY	baloney
ABELNRT	brantle
ABELNRU	nebular
ABELNRY	blarney □
ABELNSU	bus lane
	nebulas
ABELNTU	tunable
ABELOPR	ropable
ABELOPT	potable
ABELORS	Rosabel
ABELORT	bloater
ABELORU	rubeola
ABELOSV	absolve
ABELOTU	bale out
ABELOTW	towable
ABELPUZ	blaze up
ABELQUY	equably
ABELRRW	brawler
	warbler
ABELRSS	braless
ABELRST	blaster
ABELRSU	Belarus
ABELRTT	battler
	blatter
	brattle
ABELRVY	bravely
ABELSTT	battles
ABELSTU	sublate
ABELSTY	beastly
ABEMNNN	Ben Mann
ABEMNOS	ambones
ABEMNST	best man
ABEMNSU	sunbeam
ABEMORS	Ambrose
ABEMRRT	Bertram
	Rambert
ABEMRUZ	Merzbau
ABEMSSY	embassy
ABENNNR	Brennan
ABENNOR	bar none
ABENNRW	Branwen
ABENORT	baronet
ABENORU	Auberon
ABENOST	Bateson
ABENOSY	by a nose
	soy bean
ABENOTY	bayonet
ABENQTU	banquet
ABENRRU	Raeburn
ABENRST	Barents
ABENRTZ	Barentz
ABENRUX	exurban
ABEOOTV	obovate
ABEOPRT	probate
ABEOPUV	up above
ABEOQRU	baroque □
ABEORRT	Roberta
ABEORST	boaster
ABEORSV	bravoes
ABEORTT	abettor
ABEORTU	bear out
ABEOSTU	base out
ABEOTTU	beat out
ABERRVY	bravery
ABERSST	breasts
ABERSSU	surbase
ABERSTY	barytes
ABERSUU	bureaus
ABERSWY	swear by
ABERTTY	battery
ABERTWY	by water
ABERUUX	bureaux
ABERUVY	Avebury
ABESTWY	W B Yeats
ABFFGNO	bang off
ABFFIIL	bailiff
ABFFIOT	a bit off
ABFFLOU	buffalo □
ABFGGLO	golf bag
ABFGINR	barfing
ABFGLSU	bagfuls
ABFHLSU	bashful
ABFIIMR	fimbria
ABFILRU	fibular
ABFINRR	Finbarr
ABFLORU	Balfour
ABFLOTY	flyboat
ABFOOST	boast of
ABFOWYY	by way of
ABGGILY	baggily
ABGGINN	banging
ABGGINS	Baggins
ABGHHIR	high bar
ABGHINS	bashing
ABGHMRU	Hamburg
ABGHNOR	Bronagh
ABGIINT	baiting
ABGIKLN	balking
ABGIKLT	talk big
ABGIKNN	banking
ABGIKNS	basking
ABGILNR	blaring
ABGILNT	tabling
ABGILNZ	blazing
ABGINNT	Banting
ABGINOS	bagnios
ABGINOT	boating
ABGINRR	barring
ABGINST	basting
ABGINTT	batting
ABGIOSU	baguios
ABGITTU	Bugatti
ABGKKNO	Bangkok
ABGKLNO	go blank
ABGKOOR	rag-book

ABGKORW	workbag
ABGLMOU	lumbago
ABGLNOO	Bologna
ABGLOOT	toolbag
ABGLORT	ragbolt
ABGLOSU	albugos
ABGLRRU	burglar
ABGMRRU	Marburg
ABGNOPR	probang
ABGNOTU	bang out
	gunboat
ABGOOTU	go about
ABGORTU	outbrag
ABGPSSU	Bagpuss
ABGRRUW	Warburg
ABHHKTU	khutbah
ABHHSUY	hushaby
ABHIIMR	Ibrahim
ABHIINT	inhabit
ABHILNO	hobnail
ABHILOS	abolish
ABHILTU	halibut
ABHINOS	Siobhán
ABHINST	absinth
ABHKRSU	kurbash
ABHMNSU	bushman
ABHOPTW	P W Botha
ABHORRU	harbour
ABHOTUY	hautboy
ABHTTTU	but that
ABIILMU	bulimia
ABIILNS	aiblins
ABIILOV	Bolivia
ABIILRY	biliary
ABIILTY	ability
ABIIMSV	Savimbi
ABIINOR	Nairobi
	robinia
ABIINRT	Britain
ABIINRY	biryani
ABIJLNR	brinjal
ABIJNOT	abjoint
ABIJNPU	Punjabi
ABIJOSW	Ojibwas
ABIKNNU	Bakunin
ABIKORU	Aboukir
ABIKOUZ	bazouki
ABILLMY	balmily
ABILLNP	pinball
ABILLPY	pliably
ABILLSY	Sibylla
	Sybilla
	syllabi
ABILLWX	waxbill
ABILLWY	waybill
ABILMNU	albumin
ABILNOS	albinos
ABILNOT	bitonal
ABILOPR	bipolar
	parboil
ABILORT	orbital
ABILORV	bolivar
	Bolívar
ABILOTU	bail out
ABILRRY	library
ABIMNRU	Umbrian
ABIMOSS	biomass
ABIMPST	baptism
ABINORW	rainbow
ABINOST	bastion
ABINOTT	not a bit
ABINRTT	Brittan
ABINRTV	vibrant
ABIORRS	barrios
ABIORTV	vibrato
ABIPRTT	bit-part
ABIPSTT	baptist
ABIRSSY	Sybaris
ABISSST	bassist
ABJKMOS	sjambok
ABKLLNY	blankly
ABKLRUW	bulwark
ABKNOOV	Nabokov
ABLLLUY	lullaby
ABLLNOO	balloon
ABLLOPR	proball
ABLLORR	roll-bar
ABLLOTY	tallboy
ABLLPSU	balls up
	balls-up
ABLMMOU	bummalo
ABLMNOU	umbonal
ABLMOOT	tombola
ABLMOVY	movably
ABLMPUU	pabulum
ABLMTUY	mutably
ABLNORW	barn owl
ABLNOTY	notably
ABLNTUY	tunably
ABLOORS	robalos
ABLOORT	toolbar
ABLOORY	obolary
ABLOPYY	playboy□
ABLORST	borstal
ABLORTT	Rotblat
ABLOTUW	bawl out
ABLRTUU	tubular
ABMNNOR	Bormann
ABMNOOR	Boorman
ABMNORX	Max Born
ABMOORR	bar-room
ABMORTU	tambour
ABNNORS	Branson
ABNOOSS	bassoon
ABNOTUY	buoyant
ABOOPSX	soapbox
ABORSSU	sub rosa
ABORSTU	robusta
	rubatos
ABPPUUY	buy a pup
ABRRSUY	bursary
ABRRTUY	turbary
ABRUWXY	Ruby Wax
ACCDDOR	d'accord
ACCDEEN	cadence
ACCDEII	accidie
ACCDEIN	Candice
ACCDEIU	caducei
ACCDEKO	cockade
ACCDEKR	cracked
ACCDESU	accused
ACCDFIL	flaccid
ACCDILS	scaldic
ACCDIOT	octadic
ACCDIPR	Piccard
ACCDKNO	candock
ACCDKOR	Cradock
ACCDKOW	dawcock
ACCEERT	accrete
ACCEFLU	felucca
ACCEGIN	accinge
ACCEHIL	chalice
ACCEHIN	chicane
ACCEHLN	chancel
ACCEHLO	cochlea
ACCEHMT	catch me
ACCEHNO	conchae
ACCEHNR	chancer
	chancre
ACCEHNS	chances
ACCEHPU	capuche
ACCEHRT	catcher
ACCEHRU	Chaucer
ACCEHST	catches
ACCEIIL	Cecilia
ACCEIKP	pack ice
ACCEILN	calcine
ACCEILO	coeliac
ACCEILR	Clarice
ACCEILS	calices
ACCEILT	calcite
ACCEIMR	ceramic
	racemic
ACCEINO	cocaine
	oceanic
ACCEINV	vaccine
ACCEIPR	caprice
ACCEIPV	peccavi
ACCEIRS	carices
ACCEIST	ascetic
ACCEKLR	crackle
ACCEKMO	meacock
ACCEKOP	peacock□
ACCEKRR	cracker
ACCELNO	conceal
ACCELOR	coracle
ACCELSU	saccule
ACCELSY	calyces
ACCENOR	conacre
ACCENOS	a sconce
ACCENOV	concave
ACCENPT	peccant
ACCEOTU	Cocteau

ACCEPRY	peccary
ACCERSU	accurse
	accuser
ACCFIIP	pacific❑
ACCFILY	calcify
ACCGHIO	Chicago
ACCHIOT	chaotic
ACCHIRS	scraich
ACCHITT	catch it
ACCHKNO	Hancock
ACCHKOY	haycock
ACCHLTU	claucht
ACCHNOR	Cochran
ACCHNOT	catch on
ACCHNRS	scranch
ACCHOTW	Choctaw
ACCHPTU	catch up
	upcatch
ACCHRRU	currach
ACCHRST	scratch
ACCIIST	sciatic
ACCIKRS	carsick
	car-sick
ACCIKRT	crack it
	Crackit
ACCILLU	calculi
ACCILMO	comical
ACCILMU	calcium
ACCILNO	conical
	laconic
ACCILNY	cynical
ACCILOS	calicos
ACCILOV	vocalic
ACCILRU	crucial
ACCILRY	acrylic
ACCILSS	classic
ACCILST	clastic
ACCILSU	sacculi
ACCILTU	Calicut
ACCIMOR	CARICOM
ACCIORS	Corsica
ACCISTT	tactics
ACCISTU	caustic
ACCKLLO	Allcock
ACCKLRY	crackly
ACCKNOR	crack on
ACCKOSS	cassock
	Cossack
ACCKPRU	crack up
ACCLLMO	MacColl
ACCMOPT	compact
ACCNOOR	raccoon
ACCNOTT	contact
ACCNOTU	account
ACCOPTY	copycat
	copy-cat
ACCOQSU	squacco
ACDDEEF	defaced
ACDDEEY	decayed
ACDDEHR	Cheddar
ACDDEIN	Candide
	candied
ACDDEMU	ducdame
ACDDEOP	decapod
ACDDERR	red card
ACDDETU	cut dead
ACDDHIS	caddish
ACDDHKO	haddock
ACDDHRU	chuddar
ACDDIOT	act dido
ACDDIRS	discard
ACDDKOP	paddock
ACDDSSY	caddyss
ACDEEES	decease
ACDEEFR	defacer
ACDEEGN	encaged
ACDEEHL	Chaldee
	Cheadle
ACDEELL	cadelle
ACDEELR	cleared
	creedal
	declare
ACDEELS	descale
ACDEEMR	racemed
ACDEENV	vendace
ACDEEOT	Docetae
ACDEEPS	escaped
ACDEERS	creased
ACDEEST	tedesca
ACDEETU	educate
ACDEFIN	fancied
ACDEFOP	po-faced
ACDEFOT	de facto
ACDEGGR	cragged
ACDEGHN	changed
ACDEGHR	charged
ACDEGIS	discage
ACDEGNO	decagon
ACDEGOR	cordage
ACDEHIN	chained
	echidna
ACDEHIP	edaphic
ACDEHKW	whacked
ACDEHMR	charmed
ACDEHMT	matched
ACDEHOR	chordae
ACDEHOT	cathode
ACDEHPP	chapped
ACDEHPR	parched
ACDEHRR	charred
ACDEHRS	crashed
ACDEHRT	charted
ACDEHTW	watched
ACDEILL	cedilla
ACDEILM	claimed
	decimal
	declaim
	medical
ACDEILN	Iceland
ACDEILR	decrial
	radicle
ACDEILT	citadel
	deltaic
	dialect
	edictal
ACDEINN	nice and
ACDEINS	candies
ACDEINV	caved-in
ACDEINY	cyanide
ACDEIRS	darcies
	radices
	sidecar
ACDEISS	discase
ACDEITT	dictate
ACDEITY	edacity
ACDEKLO	cloaked
ACDEKRW	wracked
ACDEKRY	key card
ACDEKST	stacked
ACDELLN	Cleland
ACDELMO	MacLeod
	Macleod
ACDELMP	clamped
ACDELNO	celadon
ACDELNS	calends
ACDELNU	unlaced
ACDELOT	located
ACDELRS	scalder
ACDELSS	declass
ACDEMMR	crammed
ACDEMNO	Caedmon
ACDEMOR	comrade
ACDEMPR	cramped
ACDENRT	Tancred
	tranced
ACDENST	descant
ACDEORR	corrade
ACDEORT	Art Deco
	cordate
	redcoat
ACDEORU	Ecuador
ACDEPRS	scraped
ACDERRS	scarred
ACDERSU	crusade
ACDERTT	detract
ACDERTU	traduce
ACDFFIR	Cardiff
ACDFFMU	Macduff
ACDFIIY	acidify
ACDFIOT	factoid
ACDFMOR	Camford
ACDGGIN	cadging
ACDGIMO	do magic
ACDGINN	dancing
ACDGINR	carding
ACDGORT	dogcart
	dog-cart
ACDHIIS	Hasidic
ACDHIKU	haiduck
ACDHILR	Aldrich
ACDHIOP	phacoid
ACDHIRR	Richard
ACDHIRY	diarchy

ACDHISS	Chassid
ACDHMPU	Duchamp
ACDHNOW	cowhand
ACDHOPR	pochard
ACDHORR	orchard
ACDIINO	conidia
	DiCanio
ACDIIRT	triacid
	triadic
ACDIITY	acidity
ACDIKLS	skaldic
ACDILNU	Lucinda
ACDILOP	placoid
ACDILOR	cordial
ACDILOU	Claudio
ACDILSY	Lycidas
ACDILTW	wildcat
ACDIMMU	cadmium
ACDIMNO	mandioc
	monadic
	nomadic
ACDIMNY	dynamic
ACDINRU	iracund
ACDINSU	Sudanic
ACDIOPR	parodic
	picador
ACDIORR	Ricardo
ACDIORT	arctoid
	carotid
ACDIOTY	dacoity
ACDIQRU	quadric
ACDIRST	drastic
ACDISTX	tax disc
ACDITUV	viaduct
ACDJNTU	adjunct
ACDKLOP	padlock
ACDKMPU	mudpack
ACDKORY	Ackroyd
ACDLLUY	ducally
ACDLNOP	Copland
ACDLNOR	caldron
ACDLORW	cold war
ACDMMNO	command
ACDMNOP	compand
ACDMOOW	camwood
ACDNNOO	no can do
ACDNORU	candour
ACDORST	Costard
ACDRSTU	custard ❑
ACDRSUU	carduus
ACEEEPS	escapee
ACEEEUV	evacuee
ACEEFFH	Chaffee
ACEEFHT	The Face
ACEEFIN	faience
	faïence
	fiancée
ACEEFLN	Fleance
ACEEFPR	preface
ACEEGIL	elegiac
ACEEGNR	engrace
ACEEHHT	cheetah
ACEEHIV	achieve
ACEEHKL	Haeckel
ACEEHLS	Chelsea
ACEEHLT	chelate
ACEEHMR	Meacher
ACEEHMT	machete
ACEEHNN	enhance
ACEEHNO	each one
ACEEHNP	cheapen
ACEEHNS	enchase
ACEEHNT	the cane
ACEEHOR	ochreae
ACEEHPP	échappé
ACEEHRS	reaches
ACEEHRT	cheater
	hectare
	rechate
	recheat
	teacher
ACEEHST	escheat
ACEEILP	calipee
ACEEIMT	emicate
ACEEINP	in peace
ACEEISV	vesicae
ACEEKNP	kneecap
	knee-cap
ACEELLN	nacelle
ACEELMP	emplace
ACEELNR	cleaner
ACEELNS	cleanse
	scalene
ACEELNV	enclave
ACEELOS	Seacole
ACEELPR	replace
ACEELRR	Le Carré
ACEELRS	cereals
	rescale
	re-scale
ACEELRT	Electra
	treacle
ACEELRV	cleaver
ACEELST	celesta
ACEELVX	exclave
ACEEMNR	menacer
ACEEMNS	menaces
ACEEMNY	Mycenae
ACEEMPS	Campese
ACEEMRT	cremate
	meercat
ACEENNP	penance
ACEENNT	canteen
ACEENNY	cayenne ❑
ACEENNZ	Cézanne
ACEENOT	acetone
ACEENRT	crenate
	re-enact
ACEEOTV	evocate
ACEEPRS	escaper
ACEERRS	creaser
ACEERRT	caterer
	retrace
	terrace
ACEERSV	Versace
ACEERTX	excreta
ACEESST	ectases
ACEESTU	Eustace
ACEESTY	cat's eye
ACEFFFO	face-off
ACEFFHR	chaffer
ACEFFIS	scaffie
ACEFFOR	afforce
ACEFHMR	chamfer
ACEFHOP	cheap of
ACEFHOR	ache for
ACEFIIL	felicia ❑
ACEFINN	finance
ACEFINR	fancier
ACEFINS	fascine
ACEFITV	factive
ACEFITY	acetify
ACEFKLR	flacker
ACEFKLT	flacket
ACEFLLS	Scafell
ACEFLOR	clear of
ACEFLRU	careful
ACEFNRS	Frances
ACEFNRU	furnace
ACEFOPR	proface
ACEFORR	care for
ACEFOTU	face out
	outface
ACEFRRT	refract
ACEFRRU	farceur
ACEFRSU	surface ❑
ACEFRTU	furcate
ACEFTTW	Fawcett
ACEGGRW	W G Grace
ACEGHNR	changer
ACEGHNS	changes
ACEGHOU	gouache
ACEGHRR	charger
ACEGHRS	charges
ACEGHRT	gertcha
ACEGIIR	Craigie
ACEGILL	Gallice
ACEGILN	angelic
	Anglice
ACEGILP	pelagic
ACEGILR	glacier
ACEGIMR	grimace
ACEGIMT	gametic
ACEGINO	coinage
ACEGINR	Grecian
ACEGINS	ceasing
ACEGKLO	lockage
ACEGKLR	grackle
ACEGKOR	corkage
ACEGLLO	collage
ACEGLNO	congeal
ACEGLNR	clanger
ACEGLOU	cagoule

ACEGNOT	cognate
ACEGORS	cargoes
	corsage
ACEGORU	courage
ACEGOTT	cottage
ACEHHLT	hatchel
ACEHHRU	hachure
ACEHHTT	hatchet
ACEHILL	helical
ACEHILM	Michael
ACEHILN	Chilean
ACEHILR	charlie□
ACEHILT	ethical
ACEHIMN	machine
ACEHIMP	impeach
ACEHIMR	chimera□
ACEHINN	enchain
ACEHINT	teach-in
ACEHIPT	aphetic
	hepatic
ACEHIRS	cashier
ACEHIRT	theriac
ACEHIRV	archive
ACEHKLR	hackler
ACEHKLS	shackle
ACEHKNY	hackney□
ACEHKRT	Eckhart
ACEHKRW	whacker
ACEHKRY	hackery
ACEHKST	the sack
ACEHLLS	shellac
ACEHLLT	hell-cat
ACEHLMY	alchemy
ACEHLNN	channel
ACEHLOP	epochal
ACEHLOR	cholera
	chorale
	Laroche
ACEHLOS	sea-loch
ACEHLPT	chaplet
ACEHLPY	cheaply
ACEHLRS	Charles
ACEHLRY	Charley
ACEHLST	satchel
ACEHLTT	chattel
ACEHMNT	manchet
ACEHMPU	Peachum
ACEHMRR	charmer
	marcher
ACEHMRS	marches
ACEHMRT	rematch
ACEHMST	matches
ACEHNNT	enchant
ACEHNOR	Acheron
ACEHNOS	Acheson
ACEHNOT	cheat on
ACEHNRR	rancher
ACEHNRT	chanter
	tranche
ACEHNST	chasten
ACEHNTU	unteach
ACEHNTZ	Natchez
ACEHOPR	Pechora
	poacher
ACEHPPS	schappe
ACEHPRT	chapter
ACEHPRY	preachy
ACEHQUU	Quechua
ACEHRRT	charter
ACEHRRY	archery
ACEHRSY	hyraces
ACEHRTT	chatter
	ratchet
ACEHRTW	watcher
ACEIILT	ciliate
ACEIITV	viciate
ACEIJSS	Jessica
ACEIKLT	catlike
ACEIKOP	paiocke
ACEIKPX	pickaxe
	pick-axe
ACEIKSS	seasick
ACEILLX	lexical
ACEILMR	claimer
	miracle
	reclaim
ACEILMS	limaces
ACEILMT	climate
	metical
ACEILMX	exclaim
ACEILMY	mycelia
ACEILNP	in place
	panicle
	pelican□
ACEILNS	scaleni
ACEILNU	cauline
ACEILOR	calorie
	loricae
ACEILOS	coalise
ACEILOZ	coalize
ACEILPP	pile-cap
ACEILPR	replica
ACEILPS	special
ACEILPT	plicate
ACEILRT	article
	recital
ACEILRU	auricle
ACEILRV	caliver
ACEILSS	salices
ACEILST	elastic
	latices
ACEILSV	vesical
ACEILTT	lattice
	tactile
ACEIMNO	encomia
ACEIMNP	pemican
ACEIMNR	carmine
ACEIMNS	amnesic
ACEIMNX	Mexican
ACEIMRU	Maurice
	uraemic
ACEIMST	sematic
ACEIMSU	caesium
ACEINNP	pinnace
ACEINNS	Nancies
ACEINNT	ancient
ACEINOT	aconite
ACEINPR	caprine
ACEINPS	in space
ACEINRS	arsenic
ACEINRT	certain
	creatin
	crinate
ACEINST	cineast
	Insecta
ACEINSY	cyanise
ACEINTT	Canetti
	nictate
ACEINTV	Vectian
ACEINTX	inexact
ACEINTY	cyanite
ACEINVZ	Vicenza
ACEINYZ	cyanize
ACEIOOZ	zooecia
ACEIOPT	ectopia
ACEIORS	scoriae
ACEIORT	erotica
ACEIOTX	exotica
ACEIPPR	epicarp
ACEIPPT	tappice
ACEIPRS	scrapie
ACEIPRT	paretic
ACEIPST	aseptic
	spicate
ACEIPSU	auspice
ACEIPSZ	capsize
ACEIPTV	captive
ACEIQRU	acquire
ACEIRRR	carrier
ACEIRRT	erratic
ACEIRRW	aircrew
ACEIRST	cristae
	stearic
ACEIRSV	varices
	viscera
ACEIRSZ	crazies
ACEIRTT	citrate
ACEISSS	ascesis
ACEISTV	Avestic
ACEISUX	ciseaux
ACEITTV	cavetti
ACEITTW	at twice
ACEJKOP	pajocke
ACEJLOR	cajoler
ACEJNOT	jaconet
ACEJQSU	Jacques
ACEJRTT	traject
ACEKKNR	knacker
ACEKLNR	crankle
ACEKLNS	slacken
ACEKLPT	placket
ACEKLQU	quackle
ACEKLRS	slacker

ACEKLRT	tackler
ACEKLSY	lackeys
ACEKMRS	smacker
ACEKNVY	Van Eyck
ACEKORT	a rocket
ACEKORU	Kerouac
ACEKPPR	prepack
ACEKPST	packets
ACEKPTW	wet pack
ACEKQRU	quacker
ACEKRRT	tracker
ACEKRST	rackets
	stacker
ACELLLV	Clavell
ACELLNY	cleanly
ACELLOR	ocellar
ACELLOT	collate
ACELLPS	scalpel
ACELLRR	carrell
ACELLRS	callers
ACELLRU	cure-all
ACELLRY	Carlyle
	clearly
ACELMNO	Coleman
ACELMNR	McLaren
ACELMOT	Camelot
ACELMOU	leucoma
ACELMPR	clamper
ACELMTU	calumet
ACELNNU	unclean
ACELNOP	place on
ACELNOR	corneal
ACELNOZ	calzone
ACELNPS	enclasp
	spancel
ACELNPU	clean up
	clean-up
	unplace
ACELNRS	lancers □
ACELNRT	central
ACELNRU	lucarne
	nuclear
	unclear
ACELNRY	larceny
ACELNST	scantle
ACELNSU	censual
	unscale
ACELNTY	latency
ACELNVY	valency
ACELOPT	polecat
ACELOPU	a couple
ACELOQU	coequal
ACELORS	claroes
ACELOST	LaCoste
	lactose
ACELOTU	oculate
ACELOTY	acolyte
	cotylae
ACELOUV	vacuole
ACELPPR	clapper
ACELPPS	scapple
ACELPRS	parcels
ACELPRT	plectra
ACELPRU	clear up
ACELPRY	prelacy
ACELPSU	capsule
	scale up
	specula
	upscale
ACELPTU	Capulet
ACELQRU	lacquer
ACELRRW	crawler
ACELRST	scarlet □
ACELRSU	secular
ACELRTT	clatter
ACELRTU	Leuctra
ACELRTY	treacly
ACELRWY	Crawley
ACELSSS	classes
ACELSSU	clauses
ACELSTU	sulcate
ACELSUX	excusal
ACELSUY	Causley
ACELSXY	calyxes
ACELTUY	acutely
ACELTXY	exactly
ACEMMRR	crammer
ACEMNOR	Cameron
	Menorca
	romance
ACEMNRR	Cranmer
ACEMNRW	crewman
ACEMOPR	compare
	compear
ACEMOSU	mucosae
ACEMPRS	scamper
ACEMRSU	Marcuse
ACENNOS	ancones
	sonance
ACENNOT	connate
ACENNOY	noyance
ACENNRS	scanner
ACENNST	nascent
ACENNTY	tenancy
ACENOOR	coronae
ACENOPU	ponceau
ACENORS	carnose
	coarsen
ACENORT	e contra
ACENOST	costean
ACENOSU	Oceanus
ACENOTV	centavo
ACENOUV	una voce
ACENPRR	Prancer
ACENRSS	ancress
ACENRSU	surance
ACENRSY	carneys
ACENRTT	tranect
ACENRTU	centaur □
	untrace
ACENRTY	encraty
	nectary
ACENSTU	nutcase
ACEOOPP	apocope
ACEOOTZ	ectozoa
ACEOPRX	exocarp
ACEOPTU	outpace
	pace out
ACEORRT	creator □
ACEORST	coaster
ACEORSU	carouse
ACEORTT	cater to
	react to
ACEORTV	overact
ACEORTW	eat crow
ACEOSSU	caseous
ACEOSTU	acetous
ACEOSTY	tea cosy
ACEOTTV	cavetto
ACEOTUU	Autocue
ACEOTUX	coteaux
ACEPRRS	scarper
	scraper
ACEPRST	precast
	spectra
ACEPRSU	scare up
ACEPRTU	capture
ACEPRUV	carve up
	carve-up
ACEPSTU	cuspate
	put case
ACEQRTU	racquet
ACERRTT	retract
ACERRTY	tracery
ACERRUV	verruca
ACERRVY	carvery
ACERSST	actress
ACERSSV	scarves
ACERSTT	scatter
ACERSTU	crustae
ACERSTY	sectary
ACERTTU	cut-rate
ACERTTX	extract
ACERTTY	cattery
ACESSTY	ecstasy □
ACESTTU	scutate
ACFFHKO	hack off
ACFFIIT	caitiff
ACFFIKM	maffick
ACFFILT	afflict
ACFFIRT	traffic
ACFFIRY	farcify
ACFFJKO	jack off
ACFFKOP	pack off
ACFFLLO	call off
ACFFLOW	claw off
ACFFORT	cart off
ACFFOST	cast off
	cast-off
	scoff at
ACFGHIN	chafing
ACFHIST	catfish
ACFHISU	fuchsia

Words marked □ can also be spelled with an initial capital letter

ACFHLNU	Funchal
ACFHLTU	half-cut
ACFIILN	finical
ACFILRY	clarify
ACFIMSS	fascism
ACFINNY	infancy
ACFINOT	faction
ACFINRS	Francis
ACFINRT	frantic
	infract
ACFINRY	carnify
ACFIOSS	fiascos
ACFIPRY	caprify
ACFIRSY	scarify
ACFISST	fascist
ACFKLSU	sackful
ACFLLOR	call for
ACFLLOY	focally
ACFLNSU	canfuls
ACFLRUU	furcula
ACFLTTU	tactful
ACFLTUY	faculty
ACFORST	factors
ACFORTY	factory
ACGGRSY	scraggy
ACGHIKN	hacking
ACGHIMO	oghamic
ACGHINR	chagrin
ACGHINS	chasing
ACGHINT	gnathic
ACGHINW	chinwag
ACGHIPR	graphic
ACGHIRS	scraigh
ACGHLTU	claught
ACGHNRU	graunch
ACGHOSU	gauchos
ACGHRRU	curragh
ACGHRSU	scraugh
ACGIKLN	lacking
ACGIKNP	packing
ACGIKNR	racking
ACGIKNS	sacking
ACGIKRR	Garrick
ACGIKTW	Gatwick
ACGILLN	calling
ACGILLO	logical
ACGILMN	calming
ACGILMY	myalgic
ACGILNP	placing
ACGILNR	Carling
ACGILNS	scaling
ACGIMNO	coaming
ACGINNN	Canning
ACGINNT	canting
ACGINOR	organic
ACGINOS	angicos
ACGINOT	coating
	cotinga
ACGINOX	coaxing
ACGINPP	capping
ACGINPR	carping
ACGINPS	spacing
ACGINRS	scaring
ACGINRT	tracing
ACGINRV	carving
	craving
ACGINRZ	crazing
ACGINST	casting
ACGINSU	causing
ACGIRST	gastric
ACGKMMO	gammock
ACGNOOT	octagon
ACGORYZ	go crazy
ACHHIRS	rhachis
ACHHIRW	Harwich
ACHIIMS	chiasmi
ACHIIMT	Hamitic
ACHIINT	Chianti
ACHIIPS	pachisi
ACHIITW	Wichita
ACHIJNT	jacinth□
ACHIKMW	Wickham
ACHIKRS	ricksha
ACHIKRY	hayrick
ACHILLO	lochial
ACHILMO	malicho
ACHILNO	Nichola
ACHILNP	Chaplin
ACHILOS	scholia
ACHILRY	charily
ACHIMNO	manihoc
	mohican□
ACHIMNR	rich man
ACHIMOS	chamois
ACHIMSS	chiasms
ACHIMST	tachism
ACHINNU	unchain
ACHINOT	Antioch
ACHINPS	spinach
ACHINTW	Chatwin
	watch in
ACHINTX	xanthic
ACHINTY	Cynthia
ACHIOPT	aphotic
ACHIORT	chariot
	haricot
ACHIPPS	Sapphic
ACHIPST	spathic
ACHIRTU	haircut
ACHIRTY	charity□
ACHISSS	chassis
ACHISTT	tachist
ACHITTW	watch it!
ACHJMOR	Jo March
ACHKLPU	chalk up
ACHKMMO	hammock
ACHKOSS	hassock
ACHKOST	Toshack
ACHKOSW	whackos
ACHKPSU	shack up
ACHLLOO	alcohol
ACHLLOR	chloral
ACHLMUY	Mauchly
ACHLNOY	halcyon
ACHLNTU	unlatch
ACHLORS	scholar
ACHLORT	trochal
ACHLOSW	salchow
ACHLPST	splatch
ACHMNOR	monarch
ACHMNRU	uncharm
ACHMOPR	camphor
ACHMOST	Satchmo
	stomach
ACHMPTU	match up
ACHNNOO	hoc anno
ACHNNOR	Rannoch
ACHNNOS	chanson
ACHNNSW	Schwann
ACHNORS	ranchos
ACHNOSS	sanchos
ACHNOVY	anchovy
ACHNPSS	schnaps
ACHNPUY	paunchy
ACHNRTY	chantry
ACHNRUY	raunchy
ACHNSTU	staunch
ACHNSTY	snatchy
ACHOOST	cahoots
ACHOPRY	Corypha
ACHORSU	aurochs
ACHPPTU	patch up
	patch-up
ACHPTUW	watch up
ACHRSTY	starchy
ACIIKNN	canikin
ACIIKNT	in a tick
ACIIKRS	airsick
ACIILMS	Islamic
ACIILNR	clarini
ACIILNS	salicin
ACIILNT	Caitlín
ACIILNV	vicinal
ACIILNZ	Zincali
ACIILSS	Liassic
ACIIMMN	minicam
ACIIMMS	miasmic
ACIIMNN	Mancini
ACIIMNR	crimina
ACIINNO	anionic
ACIINOS	asinico
	Nicosia
ACIINPS	piscina
ACIINSS	Cassini
ACIINTT	titanic□
ACIIPRT	piratic
ACIIRST	satiric
ACIJKLN	Jacklin
ACIJUZZ	Jacuzzi®
ACIKLNW	Alnwick
ACIKLOR	airlock
ACIKLTY	tackily
ACIKMOO	oomiack

ACIKNOR	Koranic
ACIKNPY	panicky
ACIKPRT	Patrick
ACIKPSX	six-pack
ACIKPSY	sick pay
ACIKRWW	Warwick
ACIKSTT	stick at
ACIKUWZ	Zwickau
ACILLLU	Lucilla
ACILLMS	miscall
ACILLRY	lyrical
ACILMOT	comital
ACILMSU	musical
ACILNNY	cannily
ACILNOR	clarion
ACILNOS	Nicolas
ACILNOU	Luciano
ACILNOV	Calvino
ACILNOZ	calzoni
	Zincalo
ACILNPY	pliancy
ACILNTU	lunatic
ACILNUV	vincula
ACILOOR	air-cool
ACILOPT	optical
	topical
ACILORX	Lacroix
ACILOST	stoical
ACILOTT	coal tit
	coal-tit
ACILPST	plastic
ACILPSU	spicula
ACILPTY	typical
ACILRTU	curtail
ACILRTY	clarity
ACILRYZ	crazily
ACILSTU	St Lucia
ACILSUY	saucily
ACILTTY	cattily
	tacitly
ACILTUV	victual
ACIMNOP	campion□
ACIMNOR	Marconi
	Minorca
ACIMNOS	masonic□
ACIMNRU	cranium
ACIMNTT	catmint
ACIMOPT	potamic
	Tampico
ACIMOST	maticos
	somatic
ACIMPRY	primacy
ACIMRSU	muscari
ACIMSST	miscast
ACINNOR	Corinna
ACINNOT	contain
ACINNOZ	canzoni
ACINNST	stannic
ACINOPT	caption
	paction
ACINORR	carrion
ACINORT	carotin
	Cortina®
ACINOSS	caisson
	casinos
ACINOST	actions
ACINOTU	auction
	caution
ACINPRY	Cyprian
ACINQTU	quantic
ACINRTT	Tantric
ACINRTU	curtain
ACIOPRS	prosaic
ACIOPRT	apricot
ACIOPSS	Picasso
ACIOPTY	opacity
ACIORRS	corsair
ACIORSU	carious
ACIORTT	ricotta
	Riot Act
ACIPRVY	privacy
ACIPSST	spastic
ACIPTUY	paucity
ACIQRTU	quartic
ACIRRTY	carry it
ACIRSST	sacrist
ACIRSSU	cuirass
ACIRSTT	astrict
ACIRSTU	Scutari
ACIRSTY	satyric
ACISSSU	Cassius
ACISSTT	statics
ACISSTU	casuist
ACISSTV	sits vac
ACISTTU	catsuit
	Tacitus
ACITUVY	vacuity
ACJKKSY	skyjack
ACJKLOW	lockjaw
ACJKNNO	jannock
ACJKNOS	Jackson
ACJKOPT	jackpot
ACJLORU	jocular
ACJMNTU	muntjac
ACKKOOR	cork oak
ACKLLOP	pollack□
ACKLLOR	Rockall
ACKLLSY	slackly
ACKLMOR	armlock
ACKLMOT	Matlock
ACKLNOU	uncloak
ACKLORW	warlock
ACKLPSU	slack up
ACKMOTT	mattock
ACKNNOS	snack on
ACKNORY	Conakry
ACKNSTU	unstack
ACKOPRR	parrock
ACKORRT	rock art
ACKPSTU	stack up
ACLLLOY	locally
ACLLMMO	Malcolm
ACLLOOR	corolla
ACLLOPS	scallop
ACLLORR	Carroll
ACLLORU	locular
ACLLOSU	callous
ACLLOTU	call out
ACLLOVY	vocally
ACLMNUY	calumny
ACLMORU	clamour
ACLNOOO	Laocoon
ACLNOOR	coronal
ACLNOOT	coolant
ACLNOOV	volcano□
ACLNOPT	Clapton
ACLNORY	Carolyn
ACLNOUV	Vulcano
ACLNPSU	unclasp
ACLNSTY	scantly
ACLOOPP	Coppola
ACLOPSY	calypso□
ACLORSU	oscular
ACLORWW	Wroclaw
ACLOTTW	Walcott
ACLPRTY	cryptal
ACLRSSY	crassly
ACLRSTY	crystal□
ACLRSWY	scrawly
ACLSSTU	cutlass
ACMNOPR	crampon
ACMNOPY	company□
ACMNORY	acronym
ACMNSTU	sanctum
ACMOOPT	Potomac
ACMOOST	scotoma
ACMOPSS	compass
ACMOPTU	camp out
ACMQTUU	cumquat
ACMSUUV	vacuums
ACNNNOS	cannons
ACNNNOY	no' canny
ACNNNUY	uncanny
ACNNORU	Corunna
ACNOORS	coronas
ACNOORT	cartoon
ACNOPSU	Canopus
ACNOPSW	snowcap
ACNOPTU	act upon
ACNORRU	rancour
ACNORRY	carry on
	carry-on□
ACNOSSZ	scazons
ACNOSTU	conatus
ACNRRTU	currant
ACNRSWY	scrawny
ACNRTUY	truancy
ACNSSTU	Sanctus
ACOOPRR	corpora
ACOOPTT	topcoat
ACOORTU	touraco
ACOOSTV	octavos
ACOPRRT	car port

Words marked □ can also be spelled with an initial capital letter

	carport
ACOPRTU	crap out
ACOPSTU	upcoast
ACOPTTU	act up to
ACORRTT	Carrott
	tractor
ACORRTU	curator
ACORRTY	carroty
ACORSSU	sarcous
ACORSTU	turacos
ACORSUU	raucous
ACORSXY	Sycorax
ACOSTTU	cast out
	outcast
ACOSUUV	vacuous
ACPPRSY	scrappy
ACPRRUY	carry up
ACPRSUY	carpyus
ACPSTUU	usucapt
ACRSSSU	Crassus
ADDDEEN	dead end
ADDDEER	dreaded
ADDDELO	a doddle
ADDDELR	raddled
ADDDEOT	added to
ADDDGOR	Goddard
ADDEEEY	dead-eye
ADDEEFM	defamed
ADDEEGR	degrade
ADDEEHR	redhead
ADDEEHT	the dead
ADDEELR	red lead
ADDEELY	delayed
ADDEEMR	dreamed
ADDEEST	dead set
ADDEFLY	fadedly
ADDEFNU	unfaded
ADDEFRU	defraud
ADDEFRW	dwarfed
ADDEGHO	godhead □
ADDEGJU	adjudge
ADDEGLN	gladden
ADDEGRU	guarded
ADDEHIO	Hodeida
ADDEHIR	Die Hard
	diehard
	die-hard
ADDEHLN	handled
ADDEILT	dilated
ADDEIMR	admired
ADDEINR	drained
	in dread
ADDEINU	unaided
ADDEINV	videnda
ADDEIOV	avoided
ADDEIRR	Derrida
ADDEISV	advised
ADDEJLY	jadedly
ADDELOR	old dear
ADDELPP	dappled
ADDELRS	saddler
ADDELRW	dawdler
	waddler
ADDELRY	dreadly
ADDELSU	Dedalus
ADDELSW	swaddle
ADDELTW	twaddle
ADDELYZ	dazedly
ADDELZZ	dazzled
ADDENOR	adorned
	Deronda
ADDENOU	duodena
ADDENPU	pudenda
ADDENRU	daunder
ADDENTU	daunted
ADDEOPT	adopted
ADDERSS	address
ADDERSW	Edwards
	swarded
ADDERSY	dryades
ADDERTT	dratted
ADDFHIS	faddish
ADDFINY	dandify
ADDGINP	padding
ADDGINW	wadding
ADDGNOO	good and
ADDGOOY	good-day
ADDGORW	godward
ADDHIKS	Kaddish
ADDHILS	laddish
ADDHIQS	Qaddish
ADDHITY	hydatid
ADDHLNO	old hand
ADDHNOR	Rhondda
ADDIINS	disdain
ADDIKSW	Skiddaw
ADDIKSZ	zaddiks
ADDILMN	midland
ADDILMO	old maid
ADDILNY	dandily
ADDILOS	disload
ADDIMNO	diamond □
ADDINOR	android
ADDINOS	Addison
ADDKLNU	Dundalk
ADDLLOY	old lady
ADDLLRU	dullard
ADDLNOW	Dowland
ADDLNRY	dry land
ADDLOSY	lay odds
ADDLTWY	twaddly
ADDOORS	dorados
ADDOPTU	add up to
ADDQSUY	squaddy
ADEEEFY	fedayee
ADEEEHN	Dehaene
ADEEEPS	deep-sea
ADEEERX	exedrae
ADEEESW	seaweed
ADEEFIR	fedarie
ADEEFLR	federal
ADEEFLS	feel sad
ADEEFLT	deflate
ADEEFMR	defamer
ADEEFPR	prefade
ADEEFRT	draftee
ADEEGGH	egghead
ADEEGGN	engaged
ADEEGIM	die game
ADEEGLL	alleged
ADEEGLY	glad eye
ADEEGMN	endgame □
ADEEGNR	angered
	derange
	en garde
	enraged
	grandee
	grenade
ADEEGRW	ragweed
ADEEHLT	the lead
ADEEHNS	dasheen
ADEEHPR	per head
ADEEHPY	pay heed
ADEEHRT	hearted
	red heat
ADEEHST	headset
ADEEHSV	sheaved
ADEEHSY	hayseed
ADEEIJT	jadeite
ADEEILM	limeade
ADEEILS	deiseal
ADEEIMT	mediate
ADEEINN	adenine
ADEEINS	aniseed
	Sedaine
ADEEIRS	readies
ADEEIRW	wearied
ADEEISS	disease
	dis-ease
	seaside
ADEEITV	deviate
ADEEKNR	kneader
ADEEKNW	wakened
ADEEKWY	weekday
ADEELLN	Allende
ADEELMN	Edelman
ADEELMR	emerald □
ADEELNP	deplane
ADEELNR	Laender
	learned
ADEELNS	sand eel
ADEELNT	al dente
ADEELPR	pearled
	pleader
ADEELPS	elapsed
	pleased
ADEELPT	pleated
ADEELRS	leaders
ADEELRT	altered
	related
	treadle
ADEELRW	leeward
ADEELRX	relaxed

ADEELRY	delayer
	layered
ADEELTX	exalted
ADEELUV	devalue
ADEEMNR	meander
ADEEMRR	dreamer
ADEEMRT	red meat
ADEEMRY	deary me
ADEEMST	steamed
ADEEMSU	medusae
ADEEMWY	mayweed
ADEENOR	dear one
	Roedean
ADEENRR	rear end
ADEENRY	deanery
ADEENST	East End
ADEENTT	dentate
ADEEORS	oreades
ADEEORW	oarweed
ADEEPRS	speared
ADEEPRT	predate
	red tape
	tapered
ADEEPRV	deprave
	pervade
ADEERRT	retread
	treader
ADEERRW	redware
ADEERST	dearest
ADEERSV	adverse
ADEERTT	treated
ADEERTW	dewater
	watered
ADEETUX	exudate
ADEFFHO	head off
ADEFFLO	lead off
ADEFFOR	read off
ADEFGLN	fangled
	flanged
ADEFGLR	red flag
ADEFHOR	head for
ADEFILN	Anfield
ADEFILS	disleaf
ADEFINR	Friedan
ADEFINT	defiant
	fainted
ADEFITX	fixated
ADEFLLU	fall due
ADEFLMN	Feldman
ADEFLRU	dareful
ADEFLTU	default
ADEFMOR	dream of
ADEFNUZ	unfazed
ADEFOOS	seafood
ADEFOTU	fade out
	fade-out
ADEFRRT	redraft
ADEGGLR	draggle
ADEGGNS	snagged
ADEGGRS	daggers
ADEGGRY	raggedy
ADEGHIN	heading
ADEGHIR	hag-ride
ADEGILN	aligned
	dealing
	leading
ADEGINR	grained
	reading❑
ADEGINW	windage
ADEGIOS	go aside
ADEGIOT	godetia
ADEGIPT	get paid
ADEGLMN	mangled
ADEGLMO	Gaeldom
ADEGLNN	endlang
	England
ADEGLNO	Donegal
ADEGLNR	gnarled
ADEGLNS	glandes
ADEGLNT	tangled
ADEGLOR	L'Age d'Or
ADEGLPU	plagued
ADEGLRY	gradely
ADEGNNO	Donegan
ADEGNPU	unpaged
ADEGNRR	Gardner
ADEGNRS	gardens
ADEGNRT	dragnet
	granted
ADEGNRU	enguard
ADEGNUW	unwaged
ADEGORS	dog's-ear
ADEGORW	dowager
	wordage
ADEGPRS	spadger
ADEGPRU	upgrade
ADEGRRS	regards
ADEGRSU	sugared
ADEGRTY	tragedy
ADEGRUY	gaudery
ADEGSSU	degauss
ADEHHOT	hothead
ADEHIKS	dasheki
ADEHIKV	khediva
ADEHILL	Delilah
ADEHILM	El Mahdi
ADEHILP	helipad
ADEHILY	headily
ADEHINP	pinhead
ADEHIPS	aphides
ADEHIPT	pithead
ADEHIRR	harried
ADEHIRW	rawhide
ADEHKOR	hardoke
ADEHLNR	handler
ADEHLNS	handsel
ADEHLNY	Handley
ADEHLSS	hassled
	slashed
ADEHLTY	deathly
	The Lady
ADEHMSS	smashed
ADEHNOT	death on
ADEHNRU	unheard
ADEHNST	handset
ADEHNTU	haunted
ADEHNUW	W H Auden
ADEHOPX	hexapod
ADEHORR	hoarder
ADEHORW	draw hoe
ADEHOTT	to death
ADEHPRS	Shepard
ADEHPST	spathed
ADEHPSV	V-shaped
ADEHPSY	Y-shaped
ADEHQSU	quashed
ADEHRST	hardest
ADEHRTY	hydrate
	thready
ADEHSTW	swathed
ADEIILR	deliria
ADEIINR	denarii
ADEIIRR	Airdrie
ADEIIRS	airside
	diaries
	diarise
ADEIIRZ	diarize
ADEIJLM	Djemila
ADEIJNR	Jardine
ADEIJSU	Judaise
ADEIJUZ	Judaize
ADEIKLM	like mad
ADEIKLR	Kildare
ADEIKMV	Kiev Dam
ADEILLM	ill-made
ADEILLR	dallier
	dialler
ADEILLY	ideally
ADEILMM	dilemma
ADEILMP	impaled
ADEILMR	Daimler
	Daimler®
ADEILMS	misdeal
	mislead
ADEILNN	annelid
ADEILNR	Ireland
ADEILNS	Ladenis
ADEILNT	tail end
	tail-end
ADEILNU	aliunde
ADEILNW	new-laid
	Weiland
ADEILOP	oedipal❑
ADEILOR	dariole
ADEILOS	deasoil
ADEILPP	applied
ADEILPR	lip-read
ADEILPS	palsied
ADEILPT	plaited
ADEILRY	readily
ADEILST	details
ADEILSU	deasiul
ADEILSV	devisal

Words marked ❑ can also be spelled with an initial capital letter

ADEILSY	dialyse
ADEILYZ	dialyze
ADEIMMR	mermaid
ADEIMNT	mediant
ADEIMPR	Dampier
ADEIMRR	admirer
	married
ADEIMRS	misread
	sidearm
ADEIMRU	Daumier
ADEIMST	misdate
ADEIMTY	daytime
ADEINOR	aneroid
ADEINOS	adonise
	anodise
ADEINOV	naevoid
ADEINOZ	adonize
	anodize
ADEINPT	painted
ADEINRR	drainer
ADEINRS	sardine
ADEINRT	detrain
	trade in
	trade-in
	trained
ADEINRV	invader
ADEINST	instead
	sainted
	stained
ADEINTT	tainted
ADEINTV	deviant
ADEIOPS	adipose
ADEIORS	Isadore
	soredia
ADEIORV	avoider
ADEIORX	exordia
ADEIOSX	oxidase
ADEIOSZ	diazoes
ADEIOTX	oxidate
ADEIPPR	prepaid
ADEIPRS	despair □
ADEIPRT	diptera
	Perdita
ADEIPSS	apsides
ADEIRST	astride
	disrate
ADEIRSU	residua
ADEIRSV	adviser
ADEIRTT	attired
	eat dirt
ADEIRTV	drive at
ADEIRTY	dietary
ADEISST	disseat
ADEISTW	waisted
ADEISTY	Tayside
ADEISWY	wayside
ADEITUZ	deutzia
ADEITWY	tideway
ADEJMPS	P D James
ADEKLNR	rankled
ADEKLNS	kalends
ADEKLNY	nakedly
ADEKLST	stalked
ADEKMNR	Denmark
ADEKNRS	Dansker
ADEKNRU	Kundera
ADEKNSU	unasked
ADEKNVY	vandyke □
ADELLLY	Dalyell
ADELLMU	medulla
ADELLNO	all done
ADELLOW	allowed
ADELLOY	alloyed
ADELMNO	Mondale
ADELMNR	mandrel
ADELMOR	earldom
ADELNNP	planned
ADELNOR	Leonard
ADELNRR	Lardner
ADELNRS	slander
	snarled
ADELNRU	Arundel
	launder
ADELNRY	dearnly
ADELNST	slanted
ADELNTU	lunated
ADELNTW	wetland
ADELNTY	Tyndale
ADELOPR	leopard
ADELOPS	pedalos
ADELOPT	tadpole
ADELORT	do later
	leotard
ADELORU	roulade
ADELORX	Axelrod
ADELOTU	deal out
	lead out
ADELOVY	love-day
ADELPTY	adeptly
ADELRRU	ruderal
ADELRTX	dextral
ADELRZZ	dazzler
ADELTTW	wattled
ADELUVX	Delvaux
ADEMMOP	memo pad
ADEMNNU	mundane
	unnamed
ADEMNOZ	Mendoza
ADEMNRU	maunder
	unarmed
ADEMNSS	madness
ADEMNTU	untamed
ADEMOSW	meadows
ADEMOSY	Samoyed
	someday
ADEMOWY	meadowy
ADEMPRU	dream up
ADEMPST	stamped
ADEMPSW	swamped
ADEMRRU	eardrum
ADEMSSU	assumed
	medusas
ADENNOY	annoyed
	anodyne
ADENNPT	pendant
ADENNWW	new dawn
ADENOOZ	endozoa
ADENOPR	operand
	padrone
ADENOPT	notepad
	tonepad
ADENOPY	open day
ADENORR	Reardon
ADENORT	trade on
ADENORU	rondeau
ADENOUY	Yaoundé
ADENPPW	wappend
ADENPSX	spandex □
ADENPSY	dyspnea
ADENRRY	reynard □
ADENRSS	Andress
ADENRSU	asunder
	danseur
ADENRSV	Danvers
ADENRSW	Andrews
ADENRTU	untread
ADENRTV	verdant
ADENRTX	dextran
ADENRUY	unready
ADENSSS	sadness
ADENSWY	endways
	Newsday
ADENTTU	attuned
ADEOPSS	spadoes
ADEORST	roasted
ADEORSU	aroused
ADEORTU	outdare
	read out
ADEORTY	ready to
ADEORWY	rodeway
ADEORYZ	zedoary
ADEOSTT	toasted
ADEOTTU	outdate
ADEPPRT	trapped
ADEPPRW	wrapped
ADEPRRY	drapery
ADEPRSS	adpress
ADEPRSU	Persaud
ADEPRTU	trade up
ADERRSW	drawers
	rewards
ADERSSU	assured
ADERSTT	started
ADERSTV	starved
ADERSTW	steward
ADERSTY	strayed
ADERSVW	dwarves
ADERTUU	Trudeau
ADESTUY	Tuesday
ADFFHNO	offhand
	off-hand
ADFFHOS	dash off
ADFFILO	laid off

ADFFIST distaff
ADFFLNO fanfold
ADFFLOO offload
ADFFOOR off-road
ADFFORW draw off
off-ward
ward off
ADFHLNU handful
ADFHOOS shadoof
ADFHORS Ashford
ADFIINO in aid of
ADFIKNO of a kind
ADFILNN Finland
ADFILOR Florida
ADFIMNO of a mind
ADFIMNY damnify
ADFINRT indraft
ADFIOOR Dario Fo
ADFIORS fair do's
ADFLMOO damfool
ADFLMPU mudflap
ADFLMTU mudflat
ADFLNOP plafond
ADFLNOR Randolf
ADFLNSY sandfly
ADFLORS Salford
ADFLORU foulard
ADFMOSU fumados
ADFNNOT fondant
ADFOOPT footpad
ADFORRW forward
froward
ADFORTW Watford
ADGGHNO hangdog
ADGGINO goading
ADGGINR grading
niggard
ADGHINR Harding
ADGHINS dashing
shading
ADGHIPR digraph
ADGHNNU handgun
ADGHOOR road-hog
ADGHRTU draught
ADGIILN gliadin
ADGIILT digital
ADGIINO gonidia
ADGIINR gradini
raiding
ADGIKRS Riksdag
ADGILNN landing
ADGILNR darling□
R D Laing
ADGILNU languid
ADGILRY day-girl
ADGILUY gaudily
ADGIMNN damning
ADGIMRU Guri Dam
ADGINNR darning
ADGINNW dawning
ADGINOR adoring
Gordian
ADGINPR draping
ADGINRT trading
ADGINRW drawing
ADGIRZZ gizzard
ADGLLOR rag-doll
ADGLMNO Goldman
ADGLNOO gondola
ADGLNOR goldarn
ADGLNOT Gotland
ADGLNOY daylong
ADGLNRY grandly
ADGLOSU Douglas
ADGMNOO Goodman
ADGNOOR dragoon
gadroon
ADGNORU aground
on guard
ADGNRRU gurnard
ADGNRUU unguard
ADGORST Dog Star
ADGORTU drag out
ADHHIRT hard-hit
ADHIIKS dashiki
ADHIIMS Hasidim
ADHIIPS Phidias
ADHIKNS dankish
ADHIKRS darkish
ADHILNY handily
ADHILOP haploid
ADHILOY holiday□
hyaloid
ADHILRY hardily
ADHILSY shadily
ADHIMPS dampish
ADHIMST Mahdist
ADHINPS Daphnis
ADHIORS hairdos
ADHISTY this day
ADHKOSU shakudo
ADHLLLO holdall
hold-all
ADHLLNO holland□
ADHLMOY holydam
ADHLMPY lymphad
ADHLOYY holy day
ADHMMNO Hammond
ADHMNOO manhood
ADHMNWY Wyndham
ADHNNOS hands on
hands-on
ADHNNUY unhandy
ADHNORU unhoard
ADHNOSW Ashdown
ADHNOTU hand out
handout
hand-out
ADHNOTW two-hand
ADHNOVZ Zhdanov
ADHNPSU hands up
ADHNRRU run hard
ADHNRTY hydrant
ADHOORW Harwood
ADHOPRU hoard up
uphoard
ADHOSSW shadows□
ADHOSTU dash out
ADHOSWY shadowy
ADHPRTU hard put
ADHRRTY try hard
ADIIIMN Idi Amin
ADIILMS misdial
mislaid
ADIILNV invalid
ADIILVV Vivaldi
ADIIMOS daimios
ADIINNN in-and-in
ADIINSU indusia
ADIIORS Isidora
ADIIPXY pyxidia
ADIIRST diarist
ADIIRTY aridity
ADIITVY avidity
ADIJMSU Judaism
ADIKLOS odalisk
ADIKLST St Kilda
ADIKMNN mankind
ADIKMOS mikados
ADIKMSS dismask
ADIKNPS skid pan
ADIKNRS disrank
ADIKNSW Dawkins
ADIKPRS dispark
ADILLOW laid low
ADILLPY lily pad
ADILLSY disally
ADILLVY validly
ADILLYY day-lily
ADILMNO mondial
ADILMNR mandril
ADILMNU maudlin
ADILMNW wild man
ADILMOP diploma
ADILMPS plasmid
ADILMSU dualism
ADILNOR ordinal
ADILNOS Ladinos
oil sand
ADILNRU diurnal
ADILNSU sundial
ADILNSY Lindsay
ADILOOV ovoidal
ADILOPR dipolar
ADILORV Rivaldo
ADILOTW wild oat
ADILPRY rapidly
ADILPST plastid
ADILPSY display
ADILPTU plaudit
ADILPVY vapidly
ADILQSU squalid
ADILRSZ Szilard

Words marked □ can also be spelled with an initial capital letter

ADILRTY	tardily
ADILSSW	wild ass
ADILSTY	staidly
ADILTUY	duality
ADIMNOO	in a mood
ADIMNOS	Madison
ADIMOOS	isodoma
ADIMORR	mirador
ADIMOST	mastoid
ADIMPRY	pyramid
ADIMQSU	quidams
ADIMRSW	misdraw
ADIMRSY	myriads
ADIMSST	dismast
ADIMSTU	stadium
ADINNOR	andiron
	Rodnina
ADINNOS	Sandino
ADINNRS	innards
ADINNRW	indrawn
ADINNST	stand in
	stand-in
ADINOPP	oppidan
ADINOPR	padroni
	poniard
ADINORS	inroads
ADINORW	in a word
ADINOSV	Davison
	Novi Sad
ADINOTX	oxidant
ADINPRY	Prydain
ADINPST	sandpit
ADINRSW	inwards
ADINRTU	unitard
ADINRUY	Ian Dury
ADINSTT	distant
ADINSUW	unswai'd
ADIOPRR	air-drop
ADIOPRT	parotid
ADIORSV	advisor
ADIORTU	auditor
ADIOSUV	Vaudois
ADIOSVW	disavow
ADIPRST	dispart
ADIPRTY	day trip
ADIRSSU	sardius
ADIRSTY	satyrid
ADJLNTU	Jutland
ADJMNTU	Tudjman
ADJNNOU	Don Juan
ADJNORU	adjourn
ADKLMRU	mudlark
ADKNNSU	unskan'd
ADKORWY	work-day
ADKORYY	Aykroyd
ADKRSWY	skyward
ADLLLOT	all told
ADLLMOY	modally
ADLLNOW	lowland
ADLLNOY	nodally
ADLLOPR	pollard
ADLLORW	Law Lord
ADLMNOS	Salmond
ADLMOOV	Moldova
ADLMORU	modular
ADLNOOR	lardoon
	Orlando
	Ronaldo
ADLNOPU	poundal
ADLNORU	nodular
ADLNORW	Rowland
ADLNOTY	Toyland
ADLNOWY	lay down
ADLNPSU	Asplund
ADLNRUY	laundry
ADLNTWY	Tynwald
ADLOORW	Larwood
ADLOPRU	poulard
ADLORRW	warlord
ADLORUY	Our Lady
ADLOSSW	Sod's law
ADLRSTY	dry-salt
ADMNOOR	doorman
ADMNOOW	woodman
ADMNOQU	quondam
ADMNORS	rodsman
ADMNORT	dormant
	mordant
ADMNORY	Raymond
ADMNOSY	dynamos
ADMNSTU	dustman
ADMOORT	doormat
ADMOORY	day room
	day-room
ADMOPST	Potsdam
ADMORST	stardom
	tsardom
ADMOSTU	Matsudo
ADMRSTU	mustard
ADNNNOO	on and on
ADNNOOS	and so on
ADNNOOY	noonday
ADNNOST	stand on
ADNNOSW	Sandown
ADNNOTU	daunton
ADNNRUW	Dawn Run
ADNNSTU	Dunstan
ADNOORT	donator
	tornado❑
ADNOOSS	so and so
	so-and-so
ADNORRS	Ronsard
ADNORRW	norward
	nor'ward
ADNORST	Rostand
ADNORSW	onwards
ADNORTU	rotunda
ADNORTW	drawn to
ADNORWY	nayword
ADNOSTT	stand to
ADNOSTU	astound
ADNOSTY	don't say
ADNPQSS	p's and q's
ADNPRUW	drawn up
ADNPSTU	stand up
	stand-up
ADNRSUW	sunward
ADNSTYY	dynasty
ADOOPSU	apodous
ADOOPSW	sapwood
ADOORTW	wood tar
ADOORWY	doorway
ADOOTTY	toady to
ADORSTW	towards
ADORSUU	arduous
ADORTUW	draw out
	outward
ADOUUVX	vaudoux
ADPRSUW	upwards
AEEEGGL	lee-gage
AEEEGLT	legatee
AEEEGNT	teenage
AEEEGPR	peerage
AEEEGPS	seepage
AEEELRS	release
AEEELTV	elevate
AEEEPPT	Papeete
AEEFFLL	felafel
AEEFFMR	fee-farm
AEEFFOS	ease off
AEEFHRT	feather
AEEFILW	alewife
AEEFIRS	freesia
AEEFLLN	Fenella
AEEFLLT	fellate
	leaflet
AEEFLNW	new leaf
AEEFLRT	reflate
AEEFLRW	welfare
AEEFLSU	easeful
AEEFLTX	telefax
AEEFMNR	enframe
	freeman
AEEFMRT	fermate
AEEFNRS	Farnese
AEEFOTV	foveate
AEEFRRT	ferrate
AEEFRST	feaster
AEEFRTU	feature
AEEFRTX	tax-free
AEEFSTW	sweet FA
AEEGGLR	gregale
AEEGHMT	the game
AEEGHNN	Gehenna
AEEGHNW	whangee
AEEGHRT	the rage
AEEGILL	Galilee
AEEGILM	mileage
AEEGILN	lineage
AEEGILW	weigela
AEEGINU	Eugenia
AEEGIRR	Egreria
AEEGIRT	Reigate

AEEGIRV	give ear
AEEGLLZ	gazelle
AEEGLMN	melange
	mélange
AEEGLMY	Gemayel
AEEGLNR	Al Green
	enlarge
	general
	gleaner
AEEGLNS	Selenga
	Senegal
	Sénégal
AEEGLNT	elegant
AEEGLNU	euglena
AEEGLNV	evangel
AEEGLRT	get real
AEEGLRU	glue ear
	leaguer
	regulae
AEEGLRY	eagerly
AEEGLSS	ageless
	sea legs
AEEGLSV	selvage
AEEGLTT	galette
AEEGLTU	tegulae
AEEGLTV	vegetal
AEEGMNR	germane
AEEGMNT	net game
AEEGMRU	remuage
AEEGMSS	message
AEEGNNV	Genevan
AEEGNOP	peonage
AEEGNOR	agree on
AEEGNRT	grantee
	greaten
	reagent
AEEGNRU	renague
AEEGNRV	avenger
	engrave
AEEGNTV	ventage
AEEGORT	agree to
	eager to
AEEGORV	over age
	over-age
AEEGPRS	asperge
	presage
AEEGRRT	greater
	regrate
AEEGRRW	wagerer
AEEGRSV	Gervase
	Greaves
	Segrave
AEEGRUZ	guereza
AEEGSTT	gestate
	tagetes
AEEGTTZ	gazette
AEEHHNT	heathen
AEEHHOV	heave ho!
AEEHHRT	heather□
AEEHHST	sheathe
AEEHIST	atheise
AEEHITZ	atheize
AEEHKNR	hearken
AEEHKNT	thankee
AEEHKRU	heureka
AEEHLNT	lethean
AEEHLRT	leather
AEEHLRV	Le Havre
AEEHLSY	eyelash
AEEHLTT	athlete
AEEHMNT	methane
AEEHMRT	thermae
AEEHMST	the same
AEEHMSV	Evesham
AEEHNPT	heptane
AEEHNRT	earthen
	hearten
	Teheran
AEEHNSV	heavens
AEEHNSW	Shawnee
AEEHNTW	wheaten
AEEHOTV	heave to
AEEHPRS	reshape
AEEHPTT	pet hate
AEEHPUV	heave up
	upheave
AEEHRRS	shearer□
AEEHRRV	haverer
AEEHRST	Theresa
AEEHRSW	whereas
AEEHRTT	theatre
	thereat
AEEHRTW	weather
	whateer
	whereat
	wreathe
AEEHSSV	sheaves
AEEHSTT	the East
AEEHSVX	have sex
AEEHSWY	eyewash
AEEIJNN	Jeannie
AEEIKLS	sea-like
AEEILMN	Melanie
AEEILPT	epilate
	pileate
AEEILRR	earlier
AEEILRS	realise
AEEILRT	atelier
AEEILRV	Valerie
AEEILRZ	realize
AEEIMNS	nemesia
AEEIMNT	matinee
	matinée
AEEIMNX	examine
AEEIMRT	emirate
AEEIMSS	Siamese
AEEIMST	steamie
AEEINRT	Aintree
	retinae
	trainee
AEEINST	etesian
AEEINTV	naïveté
	Venetia
AEEINVW	inweave
AEEIOPP	epopeia
AEEIPRR	pereira
AEEIPTX	expiate
AEEIRRT	Eritrea
AEEIRST	seriate
AEEIRTT	ariette
	iterate
AEEIRTV	evirate
AEEISVV	evasive
AEEITTV	evitate
AEEIUVX	exuviae
AEEJNTT	Janette
AEEKMRT	meerkat
AEEKMTW	make wet
AEEKNNN	nankeen
AEEKNRS	sneaker
AEEKPRS	respeak
	speaker
AEEKPRT	pertake
AEEKRRT	retaker
AEEKRRW	wreaker
AEEKRST	sakeret
AEELLRS	all-seer
AEELLST	Estella
AEELLTV	level at
AEELMNP	empanel
	emplane
AEELMNR	Marlene
AEELMNU	Emanuel
AEELMNV	velamen
AEELMPX	example
	exempla
AEELMSS	measles
AEELMST	Maltese
AEELMTU	emulate
AEELNNP	enplane
AEELNOR	Eleanor
AEELNPS	spelean
AEELNRR	learner
	relearn
AEELNRT	enteral
	eternal□
AEELNRW	renewal
AEELNSV	enslave
AEELNSW	Salween
AEELNTY	entayle
AEELOPX	pole-axe
AEELORU	aureole
AEELPRR	pearler
AEELPRS	relapse
AEELPRT	prelate
AEELPRU	pleurae
AEELPTT	palette
	peltate
AEELQSU	sequela
AEELRRT	relater
AEELRST	Laertes
	stealer
AEELRSV	several

Words marked □ can also be spelled with an initial capital letter

AEELRUV	revalue
AEELSSU	Auslese
AEELSTT	Seattle
AEELSTV	salvete
AEELSTX	latexes
AEELTTY	layette
AEELTVW	wavelet
AEEMMPY	empyema
AEEMMRT	ammeter
AEEMNNO	anemone
AEEMNNP	pen name
	pen-name
AEEMNPT	pet name
	pet-name
AEEMNRS	mens rea
AEEMNRU	Maureen
AEEMNSS	en masse
AEEMOSW	awesome
AEEMPRT	tempera
AEEMPTU	amputee
AEEMQRU	marquee
AEEMRRS	smearer
AEEMRST	steamer
AEEMRSU	measure
AEEMSTW	Mae West
AEEMUWX	Max Euwe
AEENNOT	neonate
AEENNPT	pennate
	pentane
AEENNRS	ensnare
AEENNTT	Annette
	Nanette
AEENNTU	uneaten
AEENOSS	anoeses
AEENPST	Penates
	pesante
AEENPSX	expanse
AEENRRY	yearner
AEENRST	earnest
	eastern□
	nearest
	sneer at
AEENRTT	entreat
	ternate
AEENRTV	Tavener
	veteran
AEENRUV	unreave
AEENRVY	Yerevan
AEENRWY	New Year
AEENUVW	unweave
AEENVWW	new wave
AEEOPRT	operate
AEEORSS	serosae
AEEORST	roseate
	tea rose
AEEORTV	overeat
AEEORVW	overawe
AEEOSTT	to tease
AEEPPRR	paperer
	prepare
AEEPRRY	per year

AEEPRSS	asperse
	praeses
AEEPRTU	epurate
	up a tree
AEEPRTZ	trapeze
AEEPSSS	asepses
AEEPSSW	pesewas
AEERRST	serrate
AEERRSU	erasure
AEERRSW	swearer
AEERRTT	retrate
	retreat
	treater
AEERRTW	waterer
AEERRUX	Auxerre
AEERRVW	waverer
AEERSST	tessera
AEERSSU	réseaus
AEERSSV	serve as
AEERSTT	estreat
	restate
AEERSTU	austere
AEERSTW	sweater
AEERSUX	réseaux
AEERTWX	wax tree
AEESSTU	sautées
AEESTTT	testate
AEFFFLR	flaffer
AEFFGIR	giraffe□
AEFFGRU	gauffer
AEFFHRS	Shaffer
AEFFIPR	piaffer
AEFFJRY	Jaffrey
AEFFKMO	make off
AEFFKOP	off-peak
AEFFKOR	rake-off
AEFFKOT	take off
	take-off
AEFFLLY	flyleaf
AEFFLMW	flamfew
AEFFLNS	snaffle
AEFFLOS	seal off
AEFFLRR	raffler
AEFFLRS	Raffles
AEFFLRU	fearful
AEFFLTU	fateful
AEFFORR	for fear
AEFFORT	tear off
AEFFORW	wear off
AEFFOVW	wave off
AEFFQRU	quaffer
AEFFRST	staffer
AEFGGGO	foggage
AEFGILN	finagle
AEFGILO	foliage
AEFGILR	fragile
AEFGIRT	frigate
AEFGIRU	refugia
AEFGITU	fatigue
AEFGLOT	flotage
AEFGNOR	far gone

AEFGNRT	engraft
AEFGOOT	footage
AEFGORR	forager
AEFGORT	go after
AEFGORV	forgave
AEFGRRT	grafter
AEFHILM	Alfheim
AEFHIRT	the fair
AEFHLLS	fellahs
AEFHLLT	The Fall
AEFHLNO	half one
AEFHLOO	ale hoof
AEFHLOP	hop-flea
AEFHLRS	flasher
AEFHLTT	the flat
AEFHLTU	hateful
AEFHNUV	have fun
AEFHOPS	heaps of
AEFHRRT	farther
AEFIIMN	infimae
AEFIKNR	Frankie
AEFILLM	ill fame
AEFILMN	inflame
AEFILNT	inflate
AEFILNU	infulae
AEFILNV	flavine
AEFILOT	foliate
AEFILPT	fleapit
AEFILRT	a trifle
AEFILRU	failure
AEFILSS	falsies
AEFILTT	Lafitte
AEFIMNR	fireman
AEFIMRR	firearm
AEFINNT	infante
AEFINNZ	fanzine
AEFINRR	refrain
AEFINRT	fine art
AEFINSW	fanwise
AEFINTX	antefix
AEFIOSZ	of a size
AEFIQRU	aquifer
AEFIRRR	farrier
	Ferrari
	Ferrari®
AEFIRRZ	Frazier
AEFIRST	set fair
AEFKLNR	flanker
AEFKLRT	fartlek
AEFKLUW	wakeful
AEFKMOR	make for
AEFKOPS	speak of
AEFKORS	forsake
AEFKORT	take for
AEFLLLO	Floella
AEFLLLT	let fall
AEFLLLW	Falwell
AEFLLNN	flannel
AEFLLOT	floatel
AEFLLSY	falsely
AEFLLTT	flatlet

AEFLMOR	femoral
AEFLNRU	frenula
	funeral
AEFLNTT	flatten
AEFLOPW	peafowl
AEFLORR	for real
AEFLORS	for sale
AEFLORT	floater
AEFLORY	forelay
AEFLOSW	sea wolf
	sea-wolf
AEFLPPR	flapper
AEFLPRS	felspar
AEFLPRU	flare up
	flare-up
AEFLRSU	fur seal
	refusal
AEFLRTT	flatter
AEFLRTU	tearful
AEFLRZZ	frazzle
AEFMNNY	Feynman
AEFMNOR	foramen
	foreman□
	name for
AEFMNRU	fraenum
AEFMORR	forearm
AEFMORT	formate
AEFMPRU	frame-up
AEFNOOR	a one for
AEFNOPR	profane
AEFNORR	foreran
AEFNORT	Torfaen
AEFNOST	fast one
	feast on
AEFNRSS	farness
AEFNSST	fatness
AEFNSTT	Fastnet
AEFORRV	overfar
AEFORRY	forayer
AEFOSST	fatsoes
AEFRRST	rafters
AEFRSTW	fretsaw
AEFRTUW	wafture
AEGGGLU	luggage
AEGGHLR	haggler
AEGGHSW	eggwash
AEGGINR	gearing
AEGGIOR	Georgia
AEGGISW	swaggie
AEGGJRS	Jaggers
AEGGLNR	gangrel
AEGGNOR	o'ergang
AEGGORT	great go
AEGGRRY	Gargery
AEGGRSS	aggress
AEGGRST	gagster
	stagger
AEGGRSW	swagger
AEGGRWY	waggery
AEGGSWW	gewgaws
AEGHHIT	high tea
	high-tea
AEGHHLS	Shelagh
AEGHHNT	the hang
AEGHHUY	Haughey
AEGHILN	healing
AEGHILR	Raleigh
	Raleigh®
AEGHINR	hearing
AEGHINT	heating
AEGHINV	heaving
AEGHISS	geishas
AEGHLNO	halogen
AEGHLNT	alength
AEGHNOX	hexagon
AEGHNRS	Gnasher
AEGHOPY	hypogea
AEGHORS	gheraos
AEGHOST	hostage
AEGHOTV	have got
AEGHRRS	Shergar
AEGIILL	Galilei
AEGIIMN	imagine□
AEGIINR	Igraine
	Nigeria
AEGIKLN	leaking
	linkage
AEGIKNT	Keating
AEGIKPR	garpike
AEGILLL	illegal
AEGILLN	nigella□
AEGILLO	Galileo
AEGILLP	pillage
AEGILLS	gallise
AEGILLT	tillage
AEGILLV	village
AEGILLY	agilely
AEGILLZ	gallize
AEGILMR	gremial
AEGILMT	time lag
AEGILNN	Gin Lane
	leaning
AEGILNR	engrail
	nargile
	realign
AEGILNS	leasing
AEGILNT	atingle
	gelatin
	genital
AEGILNV	leaving
AEGILOU	eulogia
AEGILRS	Algiers
AEGILRZ	glazier
AEGILTU	glutaei
AEGIMNN	meaning
AEGIMNT	mintage
	tegmina
AEGIMOS	imagoes
AEGIMPR	epigram
AEGIMPS	Magpies
AEGIMRR	armiger
AEGIMRT	Maigret
	migrate
	ragtime
AEGIMRY	imagery
AEGIMST	sigmate
AEGINNR	earning
	engrain
	grannie
	nearing
AEGINNT	antigen
	gentian
AEGINNU	guanine
AEGINOR	Iron Age
AEGINOS	agonies
	agonise
AEGINOZ	agonize
AEGINPR	reaping
AEGINRR	earring
	rearing
AEGINRS	searing
AEGINRT	Geraint
	granite
	gratiné
	Tangier
AEGINRV	vinegar
AEGINRW	wearing□
AEGINRZ	Zingare
AEGINST	easting
	genista
	seating
	teasing
AEGINTV	vintage
AEGINVW	weaving
AEGIOSV	Segovia
AEGIPRS	spairge
AEGIPRU	Perugia
AEGIPST	gap site
AEGIRRZ	grazier
AEGIRST	sea-girt
	strigae
AEGIRTU	Gautier
AEGIVWY	give way
AEGKKNO	angekok
AEGKLLS	Gaskell
AEGKLOU	kagoule
AEGKMRY	kerygma
AEGLLLY	legally
AEGLLNO	allonge
	galleon
AEGLLNY	Langley
AEGLLOR	allegro
AEGLLRY	allergy
	gallery
	largely
	regally
AEGLLSU	seagull
	sullage
AEGLLTU	gluteal
AEGLMNR	mangler
AEGLMPU	plumage
AEGLNOS	al segno
AEGLNOT	tangelo

AEGLNOU	Angelou
AEGLNPR	grapnel
AEGLNPS	spangle
AEGLNRU	granule
AEGLNRW	wangler
	wrangle
AEGLNSU	angelus
AEGLNTU	lunge at
AEGLNUU	ungulae
AEGLNUW	gunwale
AEGLOPR	pergola
AEGLOST	go stale
	legatos
AEGLOTV	voltage
AEGLPPR	grapple
AEGLRRU	regular
AEGLRSS	largess
AEGLRST	largest
AEGLRSV	verglas
AEGLRTY	greatly
AEGLRVY	gravely
AEGLSSU	sea slug
AEGLSTT	gestalt□
AEGLTUV	Vulgate
AEGLUVY	vaguely
AEGMMRU	rummage
AEGMNOR	Marengo
AEGMNOS	mangoes
AEGMNOT	magneto
	megaton
	montage
AEGMNPY	pygmean
AEGMNRS	Germans
AEGMNRT	garment
AEGMNRY	Germany
	Meg Ryan
AEGMNTU	augment
	mutagen
AEGMOXY	exogamy
AEGMRRY	Margery
AEGNNOR	Garonne
AEGNNOT	tonnage
AEGNNRT	regnant
AEGNNTT	tangent
AEGNOOR	oregano
AEGNOOT	at one go
AEGNORR	groaner
AEGNORW	wagoner
AEGNORY	orangey
AEGNOST	on stage
	on-stage
AEGNOSW	sea gown
AEGNOSY	nosegay
AEGNOWY	waygone
AEGNPRT	trepang
AEGNRST	Sargent
	strange
AEGNSSY	gayness
AEGNTTU	tutenag
AEGNTYZ	Yangtze
AEGOOST	go to sea
AEGOPPR	propage
AEGOPRS	go spare
AEGOPRT	portage
	top gear
AEGOPST	Gestapo
	postage
AEGOPTT	pottage
AEGORST	storage
AEGORTT	garotte
AEGORTU	outrage
AEGORVY	voyager
AEGOSSU	gaseous
AEGOSTW	stowage
AEGOTTV	gavotte
AEGPSSU	Pegasus
AEGPSTT	get past
AEGPSTU	upstage
AEGRRUU	augurer
AEGRRUV	gravure
AEGRSSU	arguses
AEGRSTT	Targets
AEGTTTU	guttate
AEHHJOV	Jehovah
AEHHJPT	Japheth
	Jephtha
AEHHLTY	healthy
AEHHNRS	harshen
AEHHNSV	Heshvan
AEHHSST	sheaths
AEHIITV	I have it
AEHILMS	Ishmael
AEHILNO	in a hole
AEHILNR	hernial
	inhaler
AEHILNY	hyaline
AEHILOP	Ophelia
AEHILOR	airhole
AEHILPR	hare lip
AEHILRU	haulier
AEHILSW	whaisle
AEHILTY	hyalite
AEHILVY	heavily
AEHILWZ	whaizle
AEHIMPR	Ephraim
AEHIMRS	mishear
AEHIMSS	Messiah
AEHIMST	atheism
AEHINOV	Ivanhoe
AEHINPR	heparin
AEHINPS	in phase
	in shape
	phase in
AEHINRS	share in
AEHINRT	hairnet
	inearth
AEHINSS	hessian
AEHINST	in haste
	shine at
AEHINSV	evanish
AEHIPPT	epitaph
AEHIPRS	Harpies
AEHIPRT	the pair
AEHIPSS	aphesis
AEHIRRR	harrier
AEHIRRT	Harriet
AEHIRWY	haywire
AEHISTT	atheist
AEHISVY	yeshiva
AEHKLNT	the Klan
AEHKOSS	shakoes
AEHKOST	the Oaks
AEHKPSU	shake up
	shake-up
AEHLLNW	New Hall
AEHLLOV	hellova
AEHLLTW	The Wall
AEHLMNN	Lehmann
AEHLMNO	manhole
AEHLMNY	hymenal
AEHLMOR	armhole
AEHLMRT	thermal
AEHLMRU	humeral
AEHLNOT	ethanol
AEHLNRT	enthral
AEHLNSU	unleash
	unshale
AEHLORW	Harlowe
AEHLOTV	The Oval
AEHLPRS	spheral
AEHLPSS	hapless
AEHLPSY	shapely
	Shapley
AEHLPTY	the play
AEHLPUV	pH value
AEHLRSS	slasher
AEHLRST	slather
AEHLRSV	halvers
AEHLRTY	earthly
	Hartley
	heartly
	lathery
AEHLSST	hatless
AEHLSTT	stealth□
AEHLTWY	wealthy
AEHMMOT	Mahomet
AEHMMRS	Hammers
AEHMMTT	Hammett
AEHMNOR	menorah
AEHMNRS	Sherman
AEHMNST	hetmans
AEHMNTT	Hamnett
AEHMNTY	the many
AEHMOPT	apothem
AEHMOPY	pay home
AEHMOTT	moth-eat
AEHMPTY	empathy
AEHMRSS	smasher
AEHMRST	hamster
AEHMRWX	Wrexham
AEHMTTW	Matthew
AEHMUZZ	mezuzah
AEHNNPY	ha'penny

AEHNNTU	unneath
AEHNNWY	anywhen
AEHNOPR	Orphean
AEHNOPT	phaeton
	phonate
AEHNORS	hoarsen
AEHNORT	another
	on earth
AEHNORV	Hanover
AEHNOTV	have-not
	not have
AEHNPRS	sharpen
AEHNPRT	panther
AEHNPSU	unshape
AEHNRSS	harness
AEHNRST	Shatner
AEHNRSW	Renshaw
AEHNRTU	haunter
	unearth
	unheart
AEHNRTX	narthex
AEHNSWY	say when
AEHOPST	tea shop
AEHORST	earshot
AEHORTU	hear out
	Thoreau
AEHPPRS	perhaps
AEHPPSU	shape up
AEHPRRS	phraser
	sharper
AEHPRSS	seraphs
	Sherpas
AEHPRSW	pre-wash
AEHPRTY	therapy
AEHPRUU	Ruapehu
AEHPSTY	Pytheas
AEHRRTU	urethra
AEHRSSW	swasher
AEHRSTT	shatter
	the arts
	The Star
	threats
AEHRSTV	harvest
AEHRSTW	wreaths
AEHRSVW	wharves
AEHRSXY	hyraxes
AEHRTUU	hauteur
AEHSTUX	exhaust
AEHSTYY	they say
AEIIKNT	kainite
AEIILNN	aniline
AEIILNR	airline
AEIILRS	Israeli
	Salieri
AEIILSW	lewisia
AEIILTT	Letitia
AEIIMNT	intimae
	miniate
AEIIMPR	imperia
AEIIMRT	airtime
AEIIMTT	imitate
AEIINNS	asinine
AEIINRR	Rainier
AEIINRS	senarii
AEIINRT	inertia
AEIIPRR	prairie
AEIIRRV	riviera
AEIIRST	irisate
AEIITTV	vitiate
AEIJLNV	javelin
AEIJMNS	jasmine□
AEIJNRT	nartjie
AEIKLMN	manlike
	man-like
AEIKLNO	kaoline
AEIKLRW	warlike
AEIKLSW	sawlike
AEIKLUZ	Zuleika
AEIKMMS	mismake
AEIKMNR	ramekin
AEIKMST	mistake
AEIKNNR	Rankine
AEIKNNS	sneak in
AEIKNNT	taken in
AEIKNPS	sea pink
AEIKNRT	Kenitra
	keratin
AEIKNRU	Ukraine
AEIKNSX	Xenakis
AEIKNSY	kyanise
AEIKNTY	kyanite
AEIKNYZ	kyanize
AEIKRSY	Kayseri
AEILLMT	all-time
AEILLOV	alveoli
AEILLPS	illapse
AEILLRR	rallier
AEILLRT	literal
AEILLST	tailles
	tallies
AEILLSW	all-wise
	wallies
AEILLTT	a little
AEILLVX	vexilla
AEILLVY	Viyella®
AEILMNN	melanin
AEILMNR	marline
	mineral
AEILMNS	seminal
AEILMNT	ailment
	aliment
AEILMPR	impearl
	lempira
AEILMPT	implate
AEILMRS	realism□
AEILMRT	Latimer
AEILMRU	Lemuria
AEILMSS	aimless
	Melissa
	seismal
AEILMST	smile at
AEILMTY	meatily
AEILNNY	inanely
AEILNOP	opaline
AEILNOR	aileron
AEILNOS	sea lion
AEILNOT	elation
	toenail
AEILNOZ	Zoilean
AEILNPR	pearlin
	praline
AEILNPS	Nepalis
	spaniel
AEILNPT	pantile
AEILNPU	Pauline
AEILNPX	explain
AEILNRT	latrine
	reliant
	retinal
	trenail
AEILNRV	ravelin
AEILNRX	relax in
	relaxin
AEILNRY	nailery
AEILNST	elastin
	salient
	slàinte
AEILNSY	elysian□
AEILNVY	naively
	naïvely
AEILORS	Rosalie
AEILOST	isolate
AEILOTV	alive to
	violate
AEILPPR	apperil
	aripple
AEILPRT	plaiter
AEILPRV	prevail
AEILPST	talipes
AEILPSY	paisley□
AEILQTU	liquate
	tequila
AEILRRT	retiral
	retrial
	trailer
AEILRSS	airless
AEILRST	realist
	saltier
	saltire□
AEILRSV	revisal
AEILRTY	irately
	reality
AEILRVV	revival
AEILRVY	virelay
AEILRWY	wearily
AEILSST	set sail
AEILSTU	situlae
AEILSUX	Alexius
AEILTVV	Tel Aviv
AEILUVX	exuvial
AEIMMNS	misname
AEIMMPP	pip emma
AEIMMRT	marmite□

AEIMMST	mismate
AEIMNNR	Riemann
AEIMNOR	moraine
AEIMNOT	on a time
AEIMNPR	Permian
AEIMNRR	mariner
AEIMNRS	remains
	seminar
AEIMNRT	Martine
	minaret
	raiment
	Tremain
AEIMNRV	Minerva
	vermian
AEIMNSS	in a mess
	Massine
	Messina
	samisen
AEIMNSW	wise man
	Wiseman
AEIMNSZ	man-size
AEIMNTV	Vietnam
AEIMNTY	amenity
	anytime
AEIMNUV	mauvein
	mauvine
AEIMNWZ	Weizman
AEIMOPR	emporia
AEIMORR	armoire
AEIMOST	atomise
AEIMOTZ	atomize
AEIMPRT	primate
AEIMPRV	vampire
AEIMPSS	impasse
	pessima
AEIMPST	impaste
	pastime
AEIMPSW	mapwise
AEIMRST	Artemis
	maestri
	misrate
	smartie
AEIMRTW	wartime
AEIMSST	Matisse
AEIMSSV	massive
AEIMSTT	at times
AEIMSTW	time was
AEIMSTZ	mestiza
AEINNNS	nannies
AEINNOT	Etonian
AEINNOZ	Neo-Nazi
AEINNPR	pannier
AEINNPT	pinnate
AEINNRT	entrain
	trannie
AEINNRU	Aneurin
AEINOPR	open-air
AEINOPT	à pointe
AEINOPZ	epizoan
AEINORT	Aretino
AEINOST	Estonia
AEINOSV	evasion
AEINOTT	eat into
AEINPPS	nappies
AEINPRS	Persian
AEINPRT	painter
	pertain
	pine tar
	repaint
AEINPST	panties
	sapient
	snipe at
AEINPSZ	Penzias
AEINPTT	patient
AEINPTU	petunia
AEINQTU	antique
	quinate
AEINRRT	terrain
	trainer
AEINRSS	Resnais
AEINRST	in tears
	retinas
	retsina
	stainer
	stearin
AEINRSW	swear in
AEINRTT	nitrate
AEINRTU	ruinate
	uranite
	urinate
AEINRUZ	azurine
AEINRVV	vervain
AEINSST	entasis
	sestina
	Staines
AEINSTT	instate
	satinet
AEINSTU	sinuate
AEINSTV	natives
AEINSTW	in a stew
AEINSWY	anywise
AEINTVY	naivety
	naïvety
AEINTXY	anxiety
AEIOQSU	sequoia
AEIORST	otaries
AEIOSTT	toastie
AEIOSTZ	azotise
AEIOTZZ	azotize
AEIPPRS	apprise
AEIPPRT	periapt
AEIPRRS	repairs
AEIPRSS	paresis
	praises
AEIPRST	parties
	piastre
	traipse
AEIPRSU	Piraeus
	upraise
AEIPRSV	parvise
AEIPRTT	partite
AEIPRTV	private
AEIPRTW	wiretap
	wire-tap
AEIPRXY	pyrexia
AEIPSSS	asepsis
AEIPSSV	passive
AEIPTXY	epitaxy
AEIQRUV	aquiver
AEIRRRT	tarrier
AEIRRST	tarsier
AEIRRTY	retiary
AEIRSTT	artiste
	striate
AEIRTTT	attrite
	titrate
AEIRTVY	variety
AEISSSZ	assizes
AEISSTU	at issue
AEISSUX	auxesis
AEISTTU	situate
AEISTTV	stative
AEISTTY	satiety
AEITTTU	attuite
AEITTTV	vittate
AEJKNRS	jankers
AEJLNUV	Juvenal
AEJLOSU	jalouse
	jealous
AEJMNOS	Jameson
AEJMSTY	majesty
AEJNOSS	San José
AEJPRSS	Jaspers
AEJRRTT	Jarrett
AEKLLMS	Maskell
AEKLMMR	Klammer
AEKLNPP	knapple
AEKLNST	asklent
AEKLOTU	leak out
AEKLPPT	pep talk
AEKLPRS	sparkle
AEKMOTU	make out
AEKNNNY	Nykanen
AEKNNTU	untaken
AEKNOOR	Roanoke
AEKNOPS	Spokane
AEKNOTW	waken to
AEKNPRS	spanker
AEKNPSU	unspeak
AEKNPTU	taken up
AEKNRST	starken
AEKNRSW	swanker
AEKNRVY	knavery
AEKOPST	speak to
AEKORSV	ask over
AEKOTTU	take out
AEKPPSU	speak up
	upspeak
AEKPSSY	passkey
AEKQRSU	Quakers
AEKQSUY	squeaky
AEKRSTY	streaky
AELLLLT	tell all

AELLMNN	Ellmann
AELLMNS	Mansell
AELLMNT	Mantell
AELLMRS	smaller
AELLMRV	Marvell
AELLMST	smell at
AELLMSU	malleus
AELLMSY	mesally
AELLMWX	maxwell❑
AELLNOS	all's one
AELLNOV	novella
AELLNOY	alonely
AELLNPR	Parnell
AELLNPY	penally
AELLNTT	tallent
AELLNVY	venally
AELLOPW	Walpole
AELLORS	rosella
AELLORV	all over
	all-over
	overall
	over-all
AELLPRU	pleural
AELLQUY	equally
AELLRST	stellar
AELLRSU	laurels
AELLRTY	alertly
AELLSSW	lawless
AELLSTY	stalely
AELLSVY	valleys
AELLTTW	Attwell
AELLTUU	ululate
AELMMOY	myeloma
AELMMRS	slammer
AELMMRT	trammel
AELMMSY	malmsey
AELMNOR	almoner
	nemoral
AELMNOS	melanos
AELMNOT	lomenta
	telamon
AELMNPR	Perlman
AELMNRU	numeral
AELMNRV	Malvern
AELMOPR	Palermo
	pleroma
AELMOPU	ampoule
AELMOPY	maypole
AELMORT	mole rat
AELMORV	removal
AELMORW	Marlowe
AELMOST	maltose
AELMOTT	matelot
AELMPRS	sampler
AELMPRT	trample
AELMPRY	lamprey
AELMPTU	plumate
AELMRSS	armless
AELMRSV	marvels
AELMRTT	martlet
AELNNPR	planner
AELNNPU	unpanel
AELNNRT	lantern
AELNNRU	unlearn
AELNNTU	annulet
AELNOOR	Leonora
AELNOPT	Lepanto
	polenta
AELNOPY	lay open
AELNORS	orleans❑
	Orléans
	Salerno
AELNORT	later on
AELNOST	lean-tos
AELNPPY	playpen
AELNPRT	pantler
	planter
	replant
AELNPRY	plenary
AELNPTX	explant
AELNPTY	penalty
AELNQUU	unequal
AELNRRS	snarler
AELNRST	sternal
AELNRSU	Al Unser
AELNRTU	neutral
	Renault
AELNRTV	ventral
AELNRUV	unravel
AELNSSU	sensual
AELNSSW	awnless
AELNSSX	laxness❑
AELNSTU	unlaste
AELNSTY	Stanley
AELOORS	aerosol
	roseola
AELOPRV	overlap
AELOPST	apostle
AELOPSX	exposal
AELOPTU	outleap
AELOQTU	equal to
AELORRT	realtor
AELORSS	oarless
AELORST	oestral
AELORTT	alert to
	Loretta
AELORTU	torulae
AELORTV	levator
AELORVY	overlay
AELOSSS	lassoes
AELOSSV	salvoes
AELOSTV	solvate
AELOSUZ	zealous
AELOSVY	saveloy
AELOSWY	lose way
AELOTUV	ovulate
AELPPSU	papules
AELPRST	plaster
	psalter
	stapler
AELPRSU	perusal
AELPRSY	parsley
	players
	sparely
AELPRTT	platter
	prattle
AELPRTY	peartly
AELPSST	let pass
	pastels
AELPSSU	pas seul
AELPSSY	Plassey
AELPSTU	pulsate
AELPUUV	upvalue
AELQRRU	quarrel
AELQTUZ	quetzal
AELRRSU	surreal
AELRRTW	trawler
AELRSST	artless
AELRSTT	slatter
	starlet
	startle
AELRSTU	saluter
AELRSTV	travels
	vestral
AELRSTW	wastrel
AELRSVY	slavery
AELRSWY	lawyers
AELRTTT	tartlet
	tattler
AELRTTU	tutelar
AELRTWZ	waltzer
AELSTTY	stately
AELSUVY	suavely
AELTTTW	twattle
AELTTUX	textual
AEMMNOT	a moment
	momenta
AEMMRST	stammer
AEMMRSZ	mamzers
AEMMSTU	summate
AEMNNOU	noumena
AEMNNRS	manners
AEMNNRT	remnant
AEMNNSW	newsman
AEMNOPZ	zampone
AEMNORS	Ransome
	San Remo
AEMNORU	enamour
AEMNORV	overman
AEMNORW	men-o'-war
AEMNORY	any more
	romneya
AEMNOST	mantoes
AEMNOTT	meant to
AEMNOTU	outname
AEMNPST	enstamp
AEMNPTY	payment
AEMNRRU	manurer
AEMNRST	smarten
AEMNRSU	surname
AEMNRTU	Trueman
AEMNSST	stamens
AEMNSTY	amnesty

AEMOORT	tea room
AEMOORW	woomera
AEMOOST	osteoma
	Sao Tomé
	São Tomé
AEMOOSV	vamoose
AEMOPPR	pampero
AEMORRV	overarm
AEMORST	maestro
AEMORSX	xeromas
AEMORTU	Euratom
AEMOSSS	sea moss
AEMOSWY	someway
AEMPPRY	mappery
AEMPRST	stamper
AEMPRTT	trampet
AEMPRTU	tempura
AEMPSTU	steam up
AEMPTTT	attempt
AEMPTTU	tapetum
AEMQRUZ	Márquez
AEMRRTU	erratum
AEMRRUU	Réaumur
AEMRSSU	Erasmus
	masseur
AEMRSTT	matters
	smatter
AEMRSTU	strumae
AEMRSTY	mastery
	streamy
AEMRTTX	Martext
AEMRTUU	trumeau
AEMSTVZ	zemstva
AENNNPT	pennant
AENNNTT	Tennant
AENNOPS	pannose
AENNORT	norteña
AENNORX	Roxanne
AENNPRS	spanner
AENNRTT	entrant
AENNRTY	tannery
AENNSSW	wanness
AENOOTZ	entozoa
AENOPPR	on paper
	propane
AENOPRS	Pearson
	persona
AENOPRT	operant
	pronate
	protean □
AENOPSW	weapons
AENORSS	reasons
AENORST	nor'-east
	senator
	treason
AENORTU	earn out
AENORTV	venator
AENORWZ	war zone
AENOSTU	soutane
AENOSTW	no sweat
AENPPRS	snapper
AENPPRU	unpaper
AENPRRT	partner
AENPRST	parents
	pastern
AENPRSW	spawner
AENPRTT	pattern
	reptant
AENPRTW	Antwerp
AENPRUV	parvenu
AENPSST	aptness
AENPSSY	synapse
AENPSTU	peanuts
AENQUWY	Newquay
AENRSSW	rawness
AENRSTU	saunter
AENRSTV	servant
	versant
AENRSUW	unswear
	unwares
AENRTUV	vaunter
AENRTUW	unwater
AENSSTX	Sextans
AENSTTU	tetanus
	unstate
AENSTTX	sextant □
AEOOPPS	papoose
AEOPPPS	pappose
AEOPPRV	approve
AEOPRRT	praetor
	prorate
AEOPRST	esparto
	seaport
	to spare
AEOPRVY	overpay
AEOPRWY	ropeway
AEOQRTU	equator
	quorate
AEOQRUV	vaquero
AEOQSUU	aqueous
AEORRST	roaster
AEORSSS	Ross Sea
	serosas
AEORSTT	Rosetta
	toaster
AEORSTW	swear to
AEORTTU	outrate
	tear out
AEORTUW	outwear
	wear out
AEORTVX	overtax
AEOSUVY	save you
AEPPRRT	trapper
AEPPRRW	wrapper
AEPPRSU	upspear
AEPPRSW	swapper
AEPPSTU	paste-up
AEPQRTU	parquet
AEPRRRS	sparrer
AEPRRSY	prayers
	respray
	sprayer
AEPRRTU	rapture
AEPRSST	at press
AEPRSSY	pessary
AEPRSTT	spatter
AEPRSTU	Pasteur
	pasture
	upstare
AEPRTXY	apteryx
AEPSTTU	upstate
AEQRRSU	squarer
AEQRRTU	quarter
AEQRSTU	T-square
AEQRTTU	quartet
AEQRUVY	quavery
AERRSSU	assurer
AERRSTT	restart
	starter
AERRSTY	strayer
AERSTTT	tatters
AERSTTU	stature
AERSTTW	Stewart
	swatter
AERSTUY	estuary
AESSTUY	eustasy
AESTTTU	statute
AFFFLLO	fall off
	fall-off
AFFGHNO	hang off
AFFGINN	naffing
AFFGLOS	slag off
AFFHINU	in a huff
AFFHIRS	raffish
AFFHLOU	haul off
AFFHMNO	Hoffman
AFFILOT	tail off
AFFILOX	Filofax®
AFFILSY	falsify
AFFIMST	mastiff
AFFINRU	funfair
	ruffian
AFFINST	sniff at
AFFINTY	tiffany □
AFFIOPR	a rip-off
	pair off
AFFIOTW	wait off
AFFKLOR	Karloff
AFFKLOW	walk off
AFFKMOR	mark off
AFFLLOR	fall for
AFFLLOW	wall off
AFFLMOP	palm off
AFFLOPY	play off
	play-off
AFFNOPS	snap off
AFFNORS	saffron □
AFFNORT	affront
AFFNORW	warn off
AFFNOSW	swan off
AFFOPRT	part-off
AFFOPSS	pass off
AFFOSTY	stay off

AFGHHIS	hagfish
AFGHIRS	garfish
AFGHLTU	flaught
AFGHRTU	fraught
AFGIILN	failing
AFGIINR	fairing
AFGILLN	falling
AFGILMN	flaming
AFGILNO	loafing
AFGILNU	gainful
AFGILNY	flaying
AFGIMNO	foaming
AFGIMNR	farming
	framing
AFGIMNY	magnify
AFGINNW	fawning
AFGINOS	a sign of
AFGINOT	go Fanti
AFGINRT	farting
AFGINST	fasting
AFGINTW	wafting
AFGIOTT	fagotti
AFGIRTY	gratify
AFGLLUY	fall guy
	fugally
AFGLMOP	fog lamp
AFGLRUW	Gulf War
AFGMNOR	frogman
AFGOORS	go so far
AFGOSTU	fugatos
AFHIIRS	fairish
AFHIKUY	kufiyah
AFHILOS	loafish
AFHILTW	halfwit
	half-wit
AFHIMNU	hafnium
AFHINOS	fashion
AFHISST	fastish
AFHISTT	fattish
AFHKORY	hay fork
	hayfork
AFHKRTU	futhark
AFHLMRU	harmful
AFHLNOT	not half
AFHLOTW	half two
AFHLSTU	hatfuls
AFHMOST	fathoms
AFHMOUZ	Mahfouz
AFHORSS	shofars
AFHORTW	what for
AFHRSTU	thus far
AFIILNT	tail fin
AFIILRT	airlift
AFIILRY	fairily
AFIIMOS	Mafiosi
AFIINRS	Frisian
AFIKKLR	Falkirk
AFIKLOT	flokati
AFILLMO	a mill of
AFILLNY	finally
AFILLPT	pitfall
AFILLPU	pailful
AFILLRY	frailly
AFILLUV	fluvial
AFILMOY	foamily
AFILMPY	amplify
AFILNPU	painful
AFILNTY	faintly
AFILQUY	qualify
AFILRTY	frailty
AFILSSY	salsify
AFILSTU	fistula
AFILSTY	falsity
AFILSVY	Slavify
AFIMOOS	mafioso□
AFIMSUV	Fauvism
AFINORV	for vain
AFINSTU	fustian
AFIORTW	wait for
AFIRSTT	at first
AFISSTY	satisfy
AFISTUV	Fauvist
AFITTUY	fatuity
AFJLRSU	jarfuls
AFKKOUU	Fukuoka
AFKLNRY	frankly
AFKLNTU	tankful
AFKLORT	folk art
AFLLOOY	aloofly
AFLLOTU	fall out
	fallout
	outfall
AFLLPUY	playful
AFLLUWY	awfully
AFLMMOR	malform
AFLMNOU	moanful
AFLMORU	formula
AFLMORW	wolfram
AFLMOST	flotsam
AFLMRSU	armfuls
AFLNOOS	Alfonso
AFLNOPR	plan for
AFLNORT	frontal
AFLNPSU	panfuls
AFLNTUY	flaunty
AFLOPTU	float up
AFLORUV	flavour
AFLOTTU	flat out
AFLPRTY	flytrap
AFLRTUY	trayful
AFLSTUV	vatfuls
AFMNOOT	footman
AFMNORT	formant
AFMNWYY	Myfanwy
AFMORST	farmost
AFMORTU	farm out
AFMOSTU	sfumato
AFNOOSW	as of now
AFNOPRT	pant for
AFNORRT	FORTRAN
AFNORRW	forwarn
AFNORTU	Fortuna
AFNSSTU	sunfast
AFOORST	of a sort
AFOOTWY	footway
AFOPRSS	pass for
AFOSTUU	fatuous
AGGGGIN	gagging
AGGGILN	lagging
AGGGINN	nagging
AGGGINR	ragging
AGGGINS	sagging
AGGGINU	gauging
AGGHHIS	haggish
AGGHIMN	gingham
AGGHINN	hanging
AGGHISW	waggish
AGGHNOV	Van Gogh
AGGHORT	Hoggart
AGGIIJJ	jig-a-jig
AGGIIMN	imaging
AGGIINN	gaining
AGGILLN	galling
AGGILNN	angling
AGGILNR	glaring
AGGILNZ	glazing
AGGILOS	loggias
AGGINNP	panging
AGGINNR	ranging
AGGINNW	gnawing
AGGINPS	gasping
AGGINRS	gas ring
AGGINRT	grating
AGGINRU	arguing
AGGINRZ	grazing
AGGINSS	gassing
AGGINST	staging
AGGINTT	Gatting
AGGINUU	Gauguin
AGGINUY	Guiyang
AGGIORS	Gorgias
AGGJNUW	Gwangju
AGGLNOO	go along
	long ago
AGGLOSW	Glasgow
AGGMORR	grogram
AGGMOTY	maggoty
AGGNOSU	guangos
AGHHHIT	high-hat
AGHHIRT	high-tar
AGHHIWY	highway
AGHHMNU	Hamhung
AGHHNOU	Huang Ho
AGHHORT	Hogarth
AGHHOSW	hogwash
AGHHTUY	haughty
AGHIKNS	shaking
AGHIKNW	hawking□
AGHILNS	lashing
AGHILNT	halting
AGHILNW	whaling
AGHILOT	goliath□
AGHILRS	largish

Words marked □ can also be spelled with an initial capital letter

AGHILRT alright
AGHILSU Gaulish
AGHIMNS shaming
AGHIMRS Grisham
AGHINPS shaping
AGHINRS garnish
sharing
AGHINRU nuraghi
AGHINSU anguish
AGHINSV shaving
AGHINSW washing
AGHINTW thawing
AGHIOST goatish
AGHJMNO mah-jong
AGHJNOY John Gay
AGHKOSW goshawk
AGHLMPU galumph
AGHLOOS gasohol
AGHLOSU goulash
AGHLOSW Glashow
AGHLSTY ghastly
AGHNOTU hang out
hangout
hang-out
AGHNRSU nurhags
AGHNRUY Hungary
AGHNTUY naughty
AGHORTW warthog
AGIILLM Gilliam
AGIILLN Gillian
AGIILNR railing
AGIILNS sailing
AGIILNT tailing
AGIILNW wailing
AGIILPT pigtail
AGIILTY agility
AGIIMMN maiming
AGIIMOR origami
AGIINNR in grain
ingrain
raining
AGIINPR pairing
AGIINRS arising
raising
AGIINRZ Zingari
AGIINTW waiting
AGIINVW waiving
AGIJNNN Nanjing
AGIJNNU Jungian
AGIJNRR jarring
AGIKLNT talking
AGIKLNW walking
AGIKMNR marking
AGIKNNN Nanking
AGIKNNR ranking
AGIKNNS snaking
AGIKNNU unaking
AGIKNNW wanking
AGIKNOS soaking
AGIKNOY kayoing
AGIKNQU quaking
AGIKNRS sarking
AGIKNRT karting
AGIKNST skating
takings
AGILLMU gallium
AGILLNU lingual
AGILLOR gorilla
AGILLOS Gallios
AGILLOT galliot
AGILLSU lugsail
AGILMMN lamming
AGILMNT malting
AGILMNU mauling
AGILMOS gliomas
AGILNNU nail gun
AGILNPP lapping
AGILNPS sapling
AGILNPU Pauling
AGILNPW lapwing
AGILNPY playing
AGILNRY angrily
AGILNST lasting
salting
slating
AGILNSV slaving
AGILNSY slaying
AGILNUV valuing
AGILORS girasol
AGILORW Gwalior
AGILSTY stagily
AGIMNNN Manning
AGIMNNO moaning
AGIMNOR roaming
AGIMNPP mapping
AGIMNPR ramping
AGIMNRS Ingrams
margins
AGIMNRT migrant
AGIMNSU amusing
AGIMNTT matting
AGIMOSS go amiss
AGIMRRT trigram
AGIMSST stigmas
AGINNNN Nanning
AGINNNT tanning
AGINNOT atoning
AGINNOV Avignon
AGINNOY in agony
AGINNPP napping
AGINNPT panting
AGINNRS snaring
AGINNRT ranting
AGINNRW warning
AGINNTW wanting
AGINNWY yawning
AGINOOO oogonia
AGINORR roaring
AGINORS ignaros
Signora
soaring
AGINORV Virgoan
AGINORZ Zingaro
AGINOST gitanos
AGINOSU sagouin
AGINPPS sapping
AGINPPT tapping
AGINPRS rasping
sparing
AGINPRT parting
prating
AGINPSS passing
AGINPST pasting
AGINPSU pausing
AGINRRW warring
AGINRST gastrin
ratings
staring
AGINRSY syringa
AGINRUV Virunga
AGINRVY varying
AGINSSV savings
AGINSSY sayings
AGINSTT tasting
AGINSTW wasting
AGINSTY Stygian
AGINSWY swaying
AGINTTT tatting
AGINTYZ tzigany
AGINWWX waxwing
AGIORSV viragos
AGIOUUY ouguiya
AGIRTVY gravity
AGJLRUU jugular
AGJNOOR jargoon
AGKMNOP kampong
AGKOPTU go kaput
AGKORRW ragwork
AGLLNOO galloon
AGLLNTU gallnut
nutgall
AGLLOSW gallows
AGLLOTT glottal
AGLLRYY gyrally
AGLMORU glamour
AGLNNOT Langton
AGLNOOW own goal
AGLNOOZ Gonzalo
AGLNOPU up-along
AGLNORU langour
languor
AGLNOSU lanugos
AGLNOUY Luoyang
AGLNPSY spangly
AGLNRTY Langtry
AGLNTUY gauntly
AGLOOPY apology
AGLORTW growl at
AGMMNSU magnums
AGMMPRS Mrs Gamp
AGMNNOS songman
Songnam
AGMNOST amongst

AGMNOTU	Gaumont
	Montagu
AGMNRUY	gymnura
AGMNSTU	mustang ❑
AGMNSTY	gymnast
AGMOPRR	program
AGMORRW	ragworm
AGMOSYZ	zygomas
AGMPRSU	grampus
AGMRSTU	Targums
AGNNNOO	nonagon
AGNNOOR	Rangoon
AGNOQSU	quangos
AGNORRT	grantor
AGNORSS	grass on
AGNORSW	war song
	war-song
AGNOSTW	town gas
AGOORTW	go to war
AGOPPST	stopgap
	stop-gap
AGORRTW	ragwort
AGOSUYZ	azygous
AGPRSSU	grass up
AGRUUUY	Uruguay
AHHHISS	hashish
AHHIKSW	hawkish
AHHIMNS	Mishnah
AHHIMNU	hahnium
AHHLLOO	holla-ho!
AHHLRSY	harshly
AHHOPRT	hap'orth
AHHRRSU	hurrahs
AHIIKNT	Haitink
AHIIKOT	Akihito
AHIILPS	silphia
AHIILSW	Swahili
AHIIMMS	Mishima
AHIIMNT	thiamin
AHIIMSS	sashimi
AHIINOR	Honiari
AHIINPR	hairpin
AHIIPRS	airship
AHIKLMS	Lakshmi
AHIKLSY	shakily
AHIKMNS	khamsin
AHIKMSW	mawkish
AHIKNRS	Krishna
AHIKNSV	knavish
AHIKNSW	Hawkins
AHILLRY	Hillary
AHILLTT	tallith
AHILMMY	hammily
AHILMTW	Whitlam
AHILNOT	Lothian
AHILNOU	Anouilh
AHILNPS	planish
AHILNTU	Hinault
AHILORT	Lothair
AHILORY	hoarily
AHILPPS	shiplap
AHILPPY	happily
AHILPST	Lapiths
AHILPSY	apishly
AHILRSU	Hilarus
AHILSST	saltish
AHILSSV	slavish
AHILSTY	hastily
AHILTTZ	Hazlitt
AHIMNNS	mannish
AHIMNNU	inhuman
AHIMNPS	Shipman
AHIMNTW	Whitman
AHIMPSV	vampish
AHIMPSW	wampish
AHIMRST	Mithras
AHIMRSW	warmish
AHIMTUZ	azimuth
AHINOPS	Hispano
AHINOTZ	hoatzin
AHINPSS	Spanish
AHINRST	tarnish
AHINRSU	Ian Rush
AHINRSV	varnish
AHINSSU	Hussain
AHIOORT	Horatio
AHIOOST	atishoo
AHIOPXY	hypoxia
AHIORST	air shot
AHIPRST	harpist
AHIPRSU	rupiahs
AHIPRSW	warship
AHIPSSW	waspish
AHIPSWW	whipsaw
AHIQSTU	Asquith
AHIRSTW	trishaw
AHISSTU	shiatsu
AHISTTW	whatsit
AHISTUZ	shiatzu
AHJNORY	John Ray
AHJOTZZ	hot jazz
AHKKORV	Kharkov
AHKLNSY	Shankly
AHKLTUY	Hakluyt
AHKMNRU	Nkrumah
AHKNRTY	Kathryn
AHKNSWY	Hawkyns
AHKRSSU	kashrus ❑
AHKRSTU	kashrut ❑
AHLLOPS	shallop
AHLLOST	shallot
AHLLOSW	shallow
AHLLOTY	tally-ho
AHLLPSU	phallus
AHLLPYY	aphylly
AHLLSTU	thallus
AHLMNPY	nymphal
AHLMNUY	humanly
AHLMORU	humoral
AHLMOSW	Ohm's law
AHLMSTU	Malthus
AHLMSUU	hamulus
AHLNOPR	alphorn
AHLNORT	althorn
AHLNOUZ	Lanzhou
AHLNPRU	Ranulph
AHLORWY	holy war
AHLOSTT	Shalott
AHLOSTU	lash out
AHLOTUU	haul out
AHLPRSY	sharply
AHLPSSY	splashy
AHMMMOT	mammoth
AHMNNTU	manhunt
AHMNOPT	Hampton
	phantom
AHMNORT	not harm
AHMNORU	man-hour
AHMNORY	harmony
AHMNOSU	Housman
AHMNOSW	showman
AHMNSTY	Nasmyth
AHMOOPS	shampoo
AHMOTTZ	matzoth
AHMPSSU	smash up
	smash-up
AHNNNOS	Shannon
AHNNOTY	Anthony
AHNOOPR	harpoon
AHNORSX	saxhorn
AHNORTW	Wharton
AHNOTTT	not that
AHNOTTW	what not
	whatnot
AHNOTWW	what now?
AHNPPUU	pupunha
AHNPPUY	unhappy
AHNPRXY	pharynx
AHNSTUY	unhasty
AHOOSTT	shoot at
AHOPRTY	atrophy
AHOPTTW	towpath
AHORSTU	Suharto
AHORTTY	throaty
AHOSTUV	Shavuot
AHOSTUW	wash out
	washout
	wash-out
AHOTTUW	thaw out
AHPSSTU	Thapsus
AHPSTUW	what's up?
AHQSSUY	squashy
AHRSSSU	hussars
AHRSTWY	swarthy
AIIILMT	militia
AIIILNT	initial
AIIIMRS	saimiri
AIIJLLN	Jillian
AIIJMNS	Jainism
AIIJMOW	Iwo Jima
AIIJNNT	Tianjin
AIIKLLN	Killian
AIIKLNN	Kalinin

AIIKLPR Palikir
AIIKMMS skimmia
AIIKMNN manikin
AIILLLN Lillian
AIILLMS Millais
AIILLMW William
AIILLNV villain
AIILMMN minimal
AIILMNV Viminal
AIILMRS similar
AIILNOS liaison
AIILNPT pintail
AIILNPU nauplii
AIILNTU nautili
AIILNTY anility
AIILORV ravioli
AIILRTV trivial
AIIMMNS animism
AIIMMNX maximin
minimax
AIIMNOR amorini
AIIMNPT impaint
timpani
AIIMNRT martini
AIIMNST animist
AIIMNTV vitamin
AIINNRT in train
AIINNST in antis
AIINNTW in twain
AIINNTY inanity
AIINOPS sinopia
AIINPRS aspirin
AIINPST pianist
AIINSTU Tunisia
AIINTZZ in a tizz
AIIOPRR a priori
AIIOPST Pistoia
AIIORTV Vitoria
AIISSVV vis-à-vis
AIJJMMS jimjams
AIJLYZZ jazzily
AIJMNOR major in
AIJNORT janitor
AIJNSTU Justina
AIKKMOT komatik
AIKKSUZ zakuski
AIKLLNY lankily
AIKLMMN milkman
AIKLMNN link man
linkman
AIKLMNP milk pan
AIKLMNS silk-man
AIKLNSU in a sulk
AIKLNSY snakily
AIKLPWY pawkily
AIKLRTT titlark
AIKLSSY skysail
AIKMNNS kinsman
AIKMNST Kantism
AIKNNPS napkins
AIKNOSY Soyinka
AIKNSTT Kantist
AIKOSUY I ask you!
AIKPRRT Prakrit
AILLMNS in small
AILLMOP oil-palm
AILLMPU pallium
AILLMSY misally
AILLMYY may-lily
AILLNNO lanolin
AILLNNT Tallinn
AILLNPY plainly
AILLNST install
AILLPRU pilular
AILLPUV pluvial
AILLSTY saltily
AILLTVY vitally
AILMMOR immoral
AILMNNO nominal
AILMNOS malison
Osmanli
AILMNOT Minolta®
AILMNOY alimony
Mina Loy
AILMNPS plasmin
AILMNPT implant
AILMNRY Marilyn
AILMOPT optimal
AILMOPY Olympia
AILMPRU primula
AILMPST palmist
AILMPSY misplay
AILMRST mistral
AILNOQU Aquilon
AILNOSV Novalis
AILNOTT in total
AILNOTY lay into
lay it on
AILNOUV Louvain
AILNPRS Praslin
AILNPSX salpinx
AILNPTU nuptial
AILNPTY inaptly
ptyalin
AILNQTU quintal
AILNRSU insular
AILNSTU Latinus
AILNSTY nastily
saintly
AILNTTY nattily
AILOPRS Polaris
AILOPST topsail
AILOPSY soapily
AILOPTT talipot
AILOPTV pivotal
AILOQTU aliquot
AILORUX uxorial
AILOSSU São Luis
AILOSTU outsail
AILOVVV Vavilov
AILPQSU Pasquil
AILPSWY slipway
AILQTTU quittal
AILQTUY quality
AILRRVY rivalry
AILRSTT starlit
AILRSTY trysail
AILRTTU titular
AILRTUV virtual
AILSTTY tastily
AILSTUV Vistula
AILSTUW lawsuit
AILTTTY tattily
AIMMMUX maximum
AIMMNOR Marmion
AIMMNTU manumit
AIMMOST atomism
AIMMRSX Marxism
AIMNNOS mansion
onanism
AIMNNOZ Manzoni
AIMNNSY minyans
AIMNOPR rampion
AIMNOPT tampion
AIMNOPZ zamponi
AIMNOST stamnoi
AIMNOTU tinamou
AIMNPRU Manipur
AIMNPTY tympani
AIMNRRU murrain
AIMNRSU Marinus
AIMNRUU uranium
AIMNSTU tsunami
AIMNSYZ zanyism
AIMNWYY in my way
AIMOPST impasto
AIMORST amorist
AIMORTT Tritoma
AIMPPRU Air Pump
AIMPRRY primary
AIMPRSY pyramis
AIMQRSU marquis
AIMRSST tsarism
AIMRSTU atriums
AIMRSTX Marxist
AINNOOT Antonio
AINNOOX Oxonian
AINNOPS saponin
AINNOPT Pontian
AINNORT train on
AINNOST nations
onanist
AINNOWY in no way
AINNPTU unpaint
AINNQTU quintan
AINNRTU urinant
AINNSTT instant
AINNSTU unsaint
AINNTUY annuity
AINOOPR pronaoi
AINOORT Ontario
oration
AINOOTV ovation

AINOPPT	appoint
AINOPRS	parison
	soprani
AINOPRT	atropin
	on a trip
AINOPSS	passion□
AINOPST	in a spot
AINOPSZ	Spinoza
AINOPTT	at point
AINOPTU	opuntia
	utopian□
AINORSS	San Siro
AINORST	in a sort
	rations
AINORTU	Tournai
AINOSSS	Onassis
AINOSSU	sanious
AINOSTT	station
AINOSUX	anxious
AINOSVY	synovia
AINPPRS	parsnip
AINPQTU	piquant
AINPRST	spraint
AINPRTU	puritan
	uptrain
AINQRTU	Tarquin
AINQRUY	quinary
AINQSTU	asquint
AINRRTY	trinary
AINRRUY	urinary
AINRSSU	Russian
AINRSTT	start in
	transit
	Tristan
AINRTUY	unitary
AINSSTU	sustain
AIOORRS	Rosario
AIOORSS	ariosos
AIOORST	Ariosto
AIOPRRT	airport
	paritor
AIOPRRZ	Pizarro
AIOPRTT	patriot
AIOPRTY	topiary
AIORRRW	warrior
AIORRTT	traitor
AIORSST	aristos
AIORSTY	ostiary
AIORSUV	saviour□
	various
AIOTUWY	you wait!
AIPPTUZ	zap it up
AIPRRTU	Tripura
AIPZZZZ	pizzazz
AIRSSTT	straits
	tsarist
AIRSTVY	varsity
AIRTUVX	vitraux
AISTUVY	suavity
AJKMNTU	muntjak
AJKNSSY	janskys

AJLLMOR	jam roll
AJLLRUY	jurally
AJLNORU	journal
AJLOPPY	jaloppy
AJMNRUY	juryman
AJMORRY	Marjory
AJOOPRT	Rajpoot
AKKKORU	rokkaku
AKKLRSY	skylark
AKLLNOW	know-all
AKLOPUV	Volapük
AKLOTTU	talk out
AKLOTUW	walk out
	walk-out
AKLPRSY	sparkly
AKLRSTY	starkly
AKMNORT	Art Monk
AKMNORU	run amok
AKMNORW	workman
AKMOOSS	oak moss
AKMORST	Ostmark
AKMORTU	mark out
AKMQTUU	kumquat
AKMRSTU	muskrat
AKNNOSW	known as
AKNOPRT	top-rank
AKNOPTT	tank top
AKNORSU	Sukarno
AKNORTU	outrank
AKORRTW	artwork
AKORWWX	waxwork
AKPSSSY	Spassky
AKQSUWY	squawky
ALLLOYY	loyally
ALLMNNU	Ullmann
ALLMNOY	allonym
ALLMNPU	Pullman
ALLMORY	Mallory
	morally
ALLMPUU	plumula
ALLNOOR	on a roll
ALLNOOW	Walloon
ALLNOTT	not tall
ALLNOTY	tonally
ALLNRUU	lunular
ALLNSTY	slantly
ALLNTUU	ululant
ALLOOPS	apollos
	palolos
ALLOOTX	axolotl
ALLOPRY	payroll
ALLOPTX	poll tax
ALLORYY	royally
ALLOSWW	swallow
ALLOSWY	sallowy
ALLOTTY	totally
ALLOTYY	loyalty
ALLQSUY	squally
ALLRRUY	rurally
ALLRSTU	lustral
ALLSSTU	Sallust

ALLSUUY	usually
ALMNNUY	unmanly
ALMNOOP	lampoon
ALMNORU	unmoral
ALMNORY	almonry
ALMNOSS	salmons
ALMNOWY	womanly
ALMNSUU	alumnus
ALMOPPT	palmtop
ALMORST	mortals
ALMOSST	smaltos
ALMOSTW	matlows
ALMOSXY	xylomas
ALMOTTU	mulatto
ALMRSTY	smartly
ALMRSUU	ramulus
ALMRTUU	tumular
ALMSSUY	alyssum
	asylums
ALNNRSU	unsnarl
ALNNSUU	annulus
ALNOOPT	platoon□
ALNOORT	ortolan
ALNOOSS	solanos
ALNOPPY	panoply
ALNPRSU	snarl up
	snarl-up
ALNPTUY	unaptly
ALNSUUU	unusual
ALOOPRW	poor law
ALOORRS	sororal
ALOPPRU	popular
ALOPPRY	propyla
ALOPPTY	apply to
ALOPRRU	parlour
ALOPRSU	parlous
ALOPSSU	spousal
ALOPTUY	outplay
	play out
ALOQRRU	rorqual
ALOQRSU	squalor
ALORRST	rostral
ALORTYY	royalty
ALOSTTU	last out
	outlast
	salt out
ALPPRUY	Paul Pry
ALPSSTU	St Paul's
ALPSTUU	Plautus
ALRUUWZ	Zulu War
AMMNRUY	nummary
AMMRSUY	summary
AMNNORS	Normans
AMNNOSW	snowman
AMNNOTY	antonym
	not many
AMNNOUW	unwoman
AMNOOPP	pompano
AMNOOSW	Woosnam
AMNOOTT	ottoman□
AMNOPRY	paronym

Words marked □ can also be spelled with an initial capital letter

AMNOPST	postman
AMNORST	Marston
	transom
AMNORSU	Romanus
AMNORSY	masonry
AMNQTUU	quantum
AMNRRUY	unmarry
AMNRTTU	tantrum
AMOOORS	amoroso
AMOOPRT	taproom
AMOORSU	amorous
AMORRUY	armoury
AMORRWY	marrowy
AMORSSY	morassy
AMPRSUW	up-swarm
AMPRSUY	Pyramus
AMRRTYY	martyry
AMRSTTU	stratum
ANNOORS	Sonoran
ANNOOTV	Novotna
ANNOTTU	Taunton
ANNRTYY	tyranny
ANOOPPR	on appro
ANOOPRS	soprano
ANOOPRT	pronota
ANOOSSS	Sassoon
ANOOSTY	say no to
ANOPRRS	sporran
ANOPRSS	Parsons
ANOPRST	patrons
ANOPRSY	spray-on
ANOPSTU	outspan
ANORRSW	narrows
ANORRTW	war-torn
ANORRWW	war-worn
ANORSTT	start on
ANORTTU	to a turn
ANORWWY	wayworn
ANOTTUW	want out
ANPRSTU	run past
	suntrap
	unstrap
AOOPPRS	apropos
	Sapporo
AOORRSY	arroyos
AOORRTT	rotator
AOORRTY	oratory
AOOSSTY	so to say
AOPPPSU	pappous
AOPPRRT	rapport
AOPPRST	pop star
AOPPRTU	up to par
AOPRRSW	sparrow
AOPRRTY	portray
AOPRSTW	postwar
AOPRTTY	party to
AOPRTUY	outpray
AOPRUVY	vapoury
AOPSSTU	pass out
AOPSTUY	autopsy
AOPSTWY	waypost

AOQRSTU	quartos
AOQRTUY	Torquay
AORSSUY	ossuary
AORSTTW	at worst
AORSUVY	savoury
AORUVVY	Vouvray
AOSSSST	Sotsass
AOSSUYY	says you
AOSTTUY	outstay
	stay out
APPRSTY	strappy
APPRSUY	papyrus
APRSSSU	surpass
APRSTTU	start up
	start-up
	upstart
APSTTUY	stay put
ARSSSTU	Strauss
ARSSTTU	stratus

B

BBBELRU	blubber
BBBELSU	bubbles ❑
BBBGINO	bobbing
BBBIOTT	bobbitt
BBCDEIR	cribbed
BBCDELU	clubbed
BBCEHIN	nebbich
BBCEILR	cribble
BBCEKRU	Brubeck
BBCELOR	clobber
	cobbler
BBCELRU	clubber
BBCEOTT	Cobbett
BBCINOU	bubonic
BBCKLOU	Lubbock
BBDEEIT	ebb tide
	ebbtide
BBDEELP	pebbled
BBDEILO	bilobed
BBDEILR	dribble
BBDELOO	Bob Dole
BBDELOS	bobsled
BBDELSU	slubbed
BBDESTU	stubbed
BBEEENT	Entebbe
BBEELPS	pebbles
BBEESYY	bye-byes
BBEGINO	be big on
BBEGINW	webbing
BBEGLOR	gobbler
BBEGRRU	grubber
BBEHINS	nebbish
BBEHMTU	bethumb
BBEHOOP	Bob Hope
BBEHTYY	by the by
BBEIIMR	imbiber
BBEILNR	nibbler
BBEILNS	nibbles
BBEILOS	bilboes
BBEILOT	bibelot

BBEILQU	quibble
BBEILSY	yibbles
BBEIRRY	bribery
BBEKLNO	knobble
BBEKLNU	knubble
BBEKLOS	blesbok
BBEKLUU	bubukle
BBELLOY	bell-boy
BBELMRU	bumbler
BBELNOR	nobbler
BBELORS	slobber
BBELORW	wobbler
BBELRSU	Lubbers
	slubber
BBELSTU	stubble
BBEMOSX	sex bomb
BBEOOSY	yobboes
BBEORRY	robbery
BBEOSTY	best boy
BBERRUY	rubbery
BBFGIIN	fibbing
BBGIINR	ribbing
BBGIMNO	bombing
BBGINOR	robbing
BBGINOS	Gibbons
	sobbing
BBGINRU	rubbing
BBGINSU	gubbins
BBGIOSU	gibbous
BBHIOSY	yobbish
BBHIRSU	rubbish
BBHIRTY	by birth
BBHOOUW	whoobub
BBHRSUY	shrubby
BBIKTUZ	kibbutz
BBILNOY	nobbily
BBINORS	Robbins
BBKLNOY	knobbly
BBLOSUU	bulbous
BBLSTUY	stubbly
BBNOORU	bourbon ❑
BBNRUUY	Bunbury
BBRSSUU	suburbs
BCCEEIU	ice cube
BCCEIIS	biccies
BCCEILU	cubicle
BCCEILY	bicycle
BCCILOU	bucolic
BCCINOO	obconic
BCCMOOX	coxcomb
BCCMSUU	succumb
BCDEEIL	decibel
BCDEHNU	bunched
BCDEHOT	botched
BCDEHOU	debouch
BCDEIKS	sickbed
BCDEIMR	McBride
BCDEKLO	blocked
BCDEKLU	buckled
BCDEKOR	bedrock
BCDELOU	becloud

	could be
BCDIORW	cowbird
BCDKORU	burdock
BCDSTUU	subduct
BCEEEHS	beseech
BCEEELS	Celebes
BCEEGIR	iceberg
BCEEHIP	ephebic
BCEEHNR	bencher
BCEEINR	Bernice
BCEEIPS	bespice
BCEEIRS	escribe
BCEEKTT	Beckett
BCEEMOS	Secombe
BCEENOS	obscene
BCEFORY	by force
BCEHINT	benthic
BCEHIOR	brioche
BCEHITW	bewitch
BCEHLRU	Blücher
BCEHNRU	Buchner
	Büchner
BCEHORT	botcher
BCEHORU	Boucher
BCEHRSU	cherubs
BCEHRTU	butcher
BCEIISV	vibices
BCEIKLM	limbeck
BCEIKST	bestick
BCEILMR	climber
BCEIMNO	combine
BCEIMOR	microbe
BCEINOZ	benzoic
BCEIRRS	scriber
BCEIRSU	suberic
BCEJOST	objects
BCEJSTU	subject
BCEKLOR	blocker
BCEKLRU	buckler
BCEKLUY	Buckley
BCEKOSU	buckoes
BCELLOW	cowbell
BCELMRU	crumble
BCELMSU	scumble
BCELNOZ	Coblenz
BCELORT	Colbert
BCELOSY	close by
BCENORU	bouncer
BCEOORT	October
BCEORSU	obscure
BCEORTT	Corbett
BCEORTU	Courbet
BCFSSUU	subfusc
BCGINRU	curbing
BCHIMOR	rhombic
BCHINOR	bronchi
BCHIOPR	pibroch
BCHLOTY	blotchy
BCHNOOR	broncho
BCHOPTU	botch up
	botch-up
BCHORST	borscht
	bortsch
BCIIKLN	niblick
BCIILMU	bulimic
BCIINOS	bionics
BCIISTU	biscuit
BCIKKRU	Kubrick
BCIKLNO	block in
BCIKLSU	Ski Club
BCIKSTY	stick by
BCILMNO	climb on
BCILMPU	climb up
BCINOOR	con brio
BCINOOX	coin box
BCINORU	rubicon□
BCINSTU	NBC suit
BCINSUU	incubus
BCIOORT	robotic
BCIORST	strobic
BCJKMUU	jumbuck
BCKLLOO	bollock
BCKLLOU	bullock□
BCKLNOU	unblock
BCKLOPU	block up
BCKOTTU	buttock
BCLMOOO	Colombo
BCLMOOU	Columbo
	coulomb□
BCLMRUY	crumbly
BCLOOOX	cool box
BCLOOSU	colobus
BCMOOTU	comb out
BCMOSTU	combust
BCNOORS	broncos
BCOOOPR	Robocop
BCOOTTY	boycott□
BCPRSUU	scrub up
BDDEEES	seedbed
BDDEEIR	débride
BDDEEIS	bedside
BDDEELN	blended
BDDEEOS	Beddoes
BDDEFOR	Bedford
BDDEGIN	bedding
BDDEILL	Biddell
BDDEILN	blinded
BDDEILR	bridled
BDDEINR	brinded
BDDELOO	blooded
BDDELOU	doubled
BDDENOU	bounded
BDDENOW	bed down
BDDESUU	subdued
BDDGIIN	bidding
BDDGINU	budding
BDEEELR	bleeder
BDEEERR	breeder
BDEEFIR	briefed
	debrief
BDEEILS	Delibes
	edibles
BDEEILV	bedevil
BDEEIMT	bedtime
BDEEINR	inbreed
BDEEINZ	bedizen
BDEEISS	besides
BDEEIVV	bevvied
BDEELNR	blender
BDEELOV	beloved□
BDEELRU	be ruled
BDEELSS	blessed
BDEEMSU	bemused
BDEENPR	prebend
BDEEORS	bedsore
BDEEOTW	web-toed
BDEERST	bed-rest
BDEGHIT	bedight
BDEGIIR	GI bride
BDEGILO	obliged
BDEGINN	bending
BDEGINO	Bendigo
BDEGIOT	bigoted
BDEGIRS	Bridges
BDEGIRT	Bridget
BDEGLRU	bludger
BDEGOOT	go to bed
BDEGOOY	goodbye
	good-bye
BDEGPUU	budge up
BDEHLMU	humbled
BDEHORY	herdboy
BDEHRSU	brushed
BDEIKSS	Beskids
BDEILLR	ill-bred
BDEILLU	bullied
BDEILNO	Blondie
BDEILNR	blinder
	brindle
BDEILRT	driblet
BDEILRU	builder
	rebuild
BDEILTZ	blitzed
BDEIMOR	bromide
BDEINOU	Bedouin
BDEINRY	bindery
BDEIORS	disrobe
BDEIORT	debitor
BDEIORV	overbid
BDEIORZ	zebroid
BDEIOSY	disobey
BDEIOWY	wide boy
BDEIRSU	bruised
BDEISSU	subside
BDEISTU	subedit
BDEITUY	dubiety
BDEJLMU	jumbled
BDEKORW	bed-work
BDELLNO	Blondel
BDELMMU	mumbled
BDELMRU	drumble
BDELMTU	tumbled
BDELNNU	Blunden

BDELNRU	blunder
	Brundle
BDELOOS	Boodle's
BDELORU	boulder❑
BDELORW	low-bred
BDELOTT	bottled
BDELOTU	doublet
BDELOUW	would-be
BDELRRU	blurred
BDELRUY	ruled by
BDEMNOU	embound
BDEMOOR	bedroom
	boredom
BDEMOVY	moved by
BDENNOU	bounden
BDENORU	bounder
	rebound
BDENORW	browned
BDENORY	bone-dry
BDENORZ	bronzed
BDENOUW	unbowed
BDENOWY	owned by
BDENRSU	burdens
BDENSTU	subtend
BDENTTU	butt end
BDEOORR	brooder
BDEOPST	bedpost
BDEORRS	borders❑
BDEORRU	bordure
BDEORTU	doubter
	obtrude
	redoubt
BDERSUY	rudesby
BDESSUY	Debussy
BDFIIOR	fibroid
BDGHIIR	Brighid
BDGIINN	binding
BDGIINR	birding
BDGILOO	globoid
BDGINNO	bonding
BDGLLOU	bulldog
BDGNOOW	bog down
BDGOOUY	good buy
BDHOOOY	boyhood
BDIILMS	dislimb
BDIILNU	build in
BDIILOS	libidos
BDILLNY	blindly
BDILNNO	Blondin
BDILNNU	unblind
BDILNOO	in blood
BDILNOU	build on
BDILNUU	unbuild
BDILPUU	build up
	build-up
	upbuild
BDIMNPU	dumpbin
BDINNOU	inbound
BDINOOR	Borodin
BDINOTU	in doubt
BDINRSU	sunbird
BDINRUU	Burundi
BDINSTU	dustbin
BDIOORU	boudoir
BDIOSUU	dubious
BDIOSUV	sub divo
BDIRSTU	disturb
BDISSUY	subsidy
BDKNOOU	bundook
BDKORSY	Brodsky
BDLOOOX	oxblood
BDNNOUU	unbound
BDNOOOR	brood on
BDNOORU	bourdon
BDNOORW	do brown
BDNOOTU	bound to
	no doubt
BDNOOWW	bow down
BDNORTU	turbond
BDNORUW	rub down
	rub-down
BDOOOWX	boxwood
BDRSUUY	Sudbury
BEEEEFR	freebee
BEEEEGS	Bee Gees
BEEEEMT	beteeme
BEEEFIR	freebie
BEEEGIS	besiege
BEEEGKR	keg beer
BEEEHIV	beehive
BEEEHNS	shebeen
BEEEHPS	ephebes
BEEEHRT	be there
BEEEILN	beeline
BEEEILV	believe
BEEEJLW	bejewel
BEEEJLZ	Jezebel
BEEEKLL	Belleek
BEEELPR	bleeper
BEEELPS	Peebles
BEEEMOS	beesome
BEEENNZ	benzene
BEEENTW	between
BEEFGIN	beefing
BEEFILR	febrile
BEEFILS	beliefs
BEEFINT	benefit
BEEGILL	legible
BEEGILU	beguile
BEEGIMR	begrime
BEEGINU	beguine
BEEGJRS	Esbjerg
BEEGLNO	englobe
BEEGMOU	embogue
BEEGNTU	unbeget
BEEHLLT	The Bell
BEEHLRT	blether
	herblet
BEEHLTU	the blue
BEEHNNO	hebenon
BEEHNRS	Behrens
BEEHORT	The Robe
BEEHORW	bewhore
BEEHRRT	Herbert
BEEHRST	sherbet
BEEHRSW	Hebrews
BEEHRTY	thereby
BEEHRWY	whereby
BEEHTTU	the tube
BEEIJLU	jubilee
BEEILOS	obelise
BEEILOZ	obelize
BEEILTT	betitle
BEEIMST	betimes
BEEINNT	Bentine
BEEINNZ	benzine
BEEINOS	ebonise
BEEINOT	ebonite
BEEINOZ	ebonize
BEEINST	E Nesbit
BEEIOSU	Eusebio
BEEIQTU	be quiet
BEEIQUZ	bezique
BEEISTW	Web site
BEEKNOT	betoken
BEEKOPS	bespoke
BEEKRRS	berserk
BEEKRRU	rebuker
BEELMOW	embowel
BEELMRT	tremble
BEELMSS	bless me!
BEELNNO	ennoble
BEELNTY	Bentley®
BEELNUX	Benelux
BEEMMRS	members
BEEMNRR	Bremner
BEEMORW	embower
BEEMRSU	Burmese
BEENNTT	Bennett
BEENOST	Beeston
BEENOTY	Toynbee
BEEORRU	bourrée
BEEORSV	observe
	obverse
	verbose
BEEQSTU	bequest
BEERRWY	brewery
BEERSSU	rebuses
BEERSTW	bestrew
	Webster
BEERTTU	burette
BEFFHTU	the buff
BEFFLRU	bluffer
BEFGIIL	filibeg
BEFGIRU	firebug
	fire-bug
BEFIINR	in brief
BEFILPY	plebify
BEFILRT	filbert
BEFILRY	briefly
BEFILSU	fusible
BEFINOR	bonfire
BEFIORS	fibrose

BEFIORT	be for it
BEFIRVY	verbify
BEFLMRU	fumbler
BEFLOUW	Beowulf
BEFMNRU	f-number
BEFOOTW	webfoot
BEFORRX	Brer Fox
BEFOSUX	fuse box
BEGGGIN	begging
BEGGILS	Biggles
BEGGIST	biggest
BEGHINR	Behring
BEGHINT	benight
BEGHRRU	burgher
BEGIIJN	Beijing
BEGIIMT	big time
BEGILLY	legibly
BEGILMU	Belgium
BEGILNO	ignoble
BEGILNT	belting
BEGILOR	Broglie
BEGILRT	Gilbert
BEGILST	giblets
BEGINNU	unbeing
BEGINOT	big-note
BEGINRR	bringer
BEGINRW	brewing
BEGINSS	bigness
BEGINTT	betting
BEGIRSU	Bergius
BEGKMOS	gemsbok
BEGKOOR	go broke
BEGLLOU	globule
BEGLMOO	begloom
BEGLMRU	grumble
BEGLMUU	blue gum
BEGLNRU	bungler
BEGLOOS	globose
BEGLOOT	bootleg
BEGLORY	glory be
BEGMORR	Romberg
BEGNNNU	Ben Gunn
BEGNNRU	bren gun❑
BEGNORU	burgeon
BEGORSU	rose-bug
BEGRSSU	Burgess
BEHIITX	exhibit
BEHIKKS	Bishkek
BEHIKNT	bethink
BEHILLT	the Bill
BEHILLX	Bexhill
BEHILMS	blemish
BEHILMT	thimble
BEHILNO	Holbein
BEHILOS	bolshie
BEHILRT	blither
	Hilbert
BEHILST	Lisbeth
BEHILTZ	Lizbeth
BEHINOP	hip-bone
BEHINRS	her nibs
BEHIOTW	howbeit
BEHIRRT	rebirth
BEHIRST	herbist
BEHLLOP	bell-hop
BEHLORT	brothel
BEHLRRU	burrhel
BEHLRSU	blusher
BEHLSSU	blushes
BEHMPTU	bethump
BEHMRTU	Humbert
BEHNOST	benthos
BEHNPRU	Hepburn
BEHOORT	theorbo
BEHOOTT	the boot
BEHORRT	brother
BEHORTT	betroth
BEHOSST	the boss
BEHOSTY	Sotheby
BEHRRSU	brusher
BEHRRTU	Thurber
BEIILLN	Bellini
BEIILLS	billies
BEIILNZ	Leibniz
BEIILRS	risible
BEIILSV	visible
BEIINNR	Bernini
BEIINST	stibine
BEIKLNR	blinker
BEIKLOS	obelisk
BEIKNRS	brisken
BEIKRST	brisket
BEIKSTV	Vitebsk
BEILMOR	embroil
BEILMRT	timbrel
	Trimble
BEILMSU	sublime
BEILNOW	bowline
BEILNTZ	Blitzen
BEILOQU	oblique
BEILORR	broiler
BEILORS	liberos
BEILORT	Blériot
BEILORZ	Berlioz
BEILRSS	ribless
BEILRST	blister
	bristle
BEILRTT	brittle
BEILRTU	rebuilt
BEILRTY	liberty
BEILSTW	blewits
BEILTTU	blue tit
	bluetit
BEIMMRU	Brummie
BEIMNOR	bromine
BEIMNTU	bitumen
BEIMORW	imbower
BEIMRTU	terbium
BEIMSTY	by times
BEINNOS	benison
BEINNOZ	benzoin
BEINOOS	boonies
BEINORT	bornite
BEINORW	brownie❑
BEINRSU	suberin
BEINRTT	bittern
	Britten
BEINRTU	tribune❑
	turbine
BEIORRT	orbiter
BEIOSSU	soubise
BEIOSTY	obesity
BEIQRTU	briquet
BEIRRSU	bruiser
BEIRRTU	true rib
BEIRSTT	bitters
BEIRSTU	bustier
BEIRTTU	tribute
BEIRTVY	brevity
BEJLLYY	Jellyby
BEJLOOW	Joe Blow
BEJLOSS	jobless
BEJNOOS	nose job
BEJOSUV	sub Jove
BEKLNOZ	Koblenz
BEKLOOT	booklet
BEKLSUY	blue-sky
	sky-blue
BEKNORS	bonkers
BEKOORS	Brookes
BEKOOST	set book
BELLOSU	soluble
BELLOSW	bellows
	Boswell
BELLOUV	voluble
BELLRRU	burrell
BELLSSU	Bussell
BELLSTU	bullets
BELMMOO	embloom
BELMMRU	mumbler
BELMOOR	bloomer
BELMOPR	problem
BELMORU	mob rule
	mob-rule
BELMORY	Bromley
BELMOSU	embolus
BELMPRU	plumber
BELMRSU	slumber
BELMRTU	tumbler
	tumbrel
BELMRTY	trembly
BELMSTU	stumble
BELNNOU	unnoble
BELNOOY	boloney
BELNRUY	Burnley
BELNSSU	unbless
BELNSTU	sunbelt
BELNUUZ	Zebulun
BELOOPR	blooper
BELOORS	boleros
BELOOSS	soboles
BELOPSU	pueblos
BELORST	bolster

	lobster
BELORSY	soberly
BELORTT	blotter
BELORTU	trouble
BELOSSU	boluses
BELOSTU	boletus
BELOTTU	belt out
BELRSTU	bluster
	bustler
BELRTUY	butlery
BEMMOOS	embosom
BEMNORW	embrown
BEMNOSU	umbones
BEMNRSU	numbers□
BEMORST	mobster
BEMORSU	umbrose
BEMORSY	embryos
BEMSSUU	subsume
BENNORW	Bronwen
	newborn
BENNRRY	Brynner
BENOORS	Osborne
	Robeson
BENOOYZ	Boyzone
BENORTY	rent-boy
BENOTTX	box tent
BENRTTU	Burnett
BENRUWY	Newbury
BEOOPUZ	booze-up
BEOORST	booster
BEOPRRV	proverb
BEOPRST	besport
BEOPSTU	bespout
BEOQSUY	obsequy
BEOQTUU	bouquet
BEORRST	Roberts
BEORRSW	browser
BEORSUY	be yours
BEORSUZ	subzero
BEORUVY	buy over
	overbuy
BEPRRTU	perturb
BEPRTUY	puberty
BEPSTUY	upset by
BEQRSUU	brusque
BERSTUV	subvert
BERTTUY	buttery
BESTTUX	subtext
BFFILOO	boil off
BFFIPTU	buff-tip
BFFKNOU	bunk off
BFFLLUY	bluffly
BFFMOPU	bump off
BFFNOOU	buffoon
BFFOUZZ	buzz off
BFGIOOT	Bigfoot
BFHIRSU	furbish
BFILMRU	brimful
BFIMOYZ	zombify
BFIORSU	fibrous
BFIRTUY	brutify
BFKLOOY	flybook
BFLLOUW	bowlful
BFLOSUX	boxfuls
BFLSTUU	tubfuls
BFMORUY	buy from
BFNORRU	burn for
BFORSUY	Fosbury
BGGGINU	bugging
BGGHIIS	biggish
BGGILNU	bulging
BGGINSU	big guns
BGHINOR	bighorn
BGHIOST	big shot
BGHIRTY	by right
BGHLRUU	bulghur
BGHMORU	Homburg
BGHNORU	horn-bug
BGHOORU	borough
BGHORTU	brought
BGIILNO	boiling
BGIILNS	sibling
BGIIMNU	imbuing
BGIINNR	bring in
BGIKNOO	booking
BGIKNOR	broking
BGILMOU	gumboil
BGILMRU	Limburg
BGILNOW	blowing
	bowling
BGILNOY	ignobly
BGILOOY	biology
BGIMNNU	numbing
BGIMNOO	booming
BGIMRSY	Grimsby
BGINNOR	bring on
BGINNRU	burning
BGINNTU	bunting
BGINOOR	bog-iron
BGINOPR	probing
BGINORT	bring to
BGINPRU	bring up
BGINRTU	bruting
BGINRUY	burying
BGINUZZ	buzzing
BGIORTY	bigotry
BGJOTUY	Toby jug
BGKLOOO	logbook
BGLMRUY	grumbly
BGLNOOW	longbow
BGLOSSU	bugloss
BGMOOTU	gumboot
BGNOORW	go brown
BHIIINT	inhibit
BHIINRS	brinish
BHIINSS	his nibs
BHIIRST	British
BHIKOOS	bookish
BHILLOY	billy-oh
BHILLSU	bullish
BHILPSU	publish
BHIMOOR	rhomboi
BHIMORT	thrombi
BHIMSTU	bismuth
BHINRSU	burnish
BHIOORS	boorish
BHIOSWZ	show biz
	showbiz
BHIRSTU	brutish
BHJORSU	rush job
BHLRSUU	bulrush
BHMORSU	rhombus
BHOOPSY	shop-boy
BHPRSUU	brush up
	brush-up
BIIILST	Tbilisi
BIIKLOT	kilobit
BIILLNO	billion
BIILLTW	twibill
BIILMNO	in limbo
BIILNTU	built-in
	inbuilt
	in-built
BIILOSU	bilious
BIILSVY	visibly
BIIMNOU	niobium
BIIMNSU	minibus
BIINRTU	rub it in
BIIORSV	vibrios
BIISTTT	titbits
BIISTTZ	Stibitz
BIJNOOV	Bon Jovi
BIJNOSU	subjoin
BIKLLUY	bulkily
BIKLRSY	briskly
BIKMNPU	bumpkin
BIKRTTU	Burkitt
BILLNOU	bullion
BILLOPX	pill-box
BILLOWY	billowy
BILLRWY	wrybill
BILMNOO	in bloom
BILMNRU	Milburn
BILMPUY	bumpily
BILMRTU	tumbril
BILNNOY	bonnily
BILNTUU	tubulin
BILOOYZ	boozily
BILORST	bristol□
BILOSSU	subsoil
BILOSSY	bossily
BILPTUU	built-up
BILRSTY	bristly
	trilbys
BILRTTY	brittly
BILRTUY	Tilbury
BIMMOOS	imbosom
	miombos
BIMNORW	imbrown
BIMNOSU	omnibus
BINOORS	Orbison
BINOOST	bonitos
BINORSU	Boursin

BINOTUY	buy into
BINRSTU	burst in
BIOOSUV	obvious
BIOPPRT	Britpop
BIOPRTY	probity
BIORRTU	burrito
BIORRTW	ribwort
BIORSST	bistros
BIORSTT	bistort
BIORSTW	Bristow
BIOSTTW	two bits
BISSSTU	subsist
BJLMOPU	plum job
BKLOTUU	bulk out
BKNOOTW	bowknot
BKOOOTU	book out
BKOORSS	Brooks's
BKOORWX	workbox
BLLNRUU	Bull Run
BLLNTUY	bluntly
BLLOUVY	volubly
BLMNPUU	unplumb
BLMOORW	lobworm
BLMOOSS	blossom
BLMOSSY	symbols
BLNNOUW	unblown
BLNOORW	low-born
BLNOOSU	blouson
BLNOPUW	blown up
BLOOOTX	toolbox
BLOOQUY	obloquy
BLOORWW	lowbrow
BLOOTTU	blot out
BLOOTUW	blow out
	blow-out
BLOPSTU	subplot
BMNOOSU	unbosom
BMOOOTU	boom out
BMORSUU	brumous
	umbrous
BNNOORS	Bronson
BNNRSUU	sunburn
BNORSUU	burnous
BNOSTTU	buttons
BNRSTUY	by turns
BOOOTTU	boot out
BOOPPST	post-bop
BOPSSTU	bus stop
BOSTTUU	stub out
BPRSTUU	upburst

C

CCCNOOT	concoct
CCCOORU	co-occur
CCDEEHK	checked
CCDEEIO	ecocide
CCDEENO	concede
CCDEENY	decency
CCDEEOR	coerced
CCDEESU	succeed
CCDEHIL	clichéd
	cliché'd
CCDEILO	ice-cold
CCDEIOS	codices
CCDELOU	occlude
CCDENOO	concedo
CCDENOU	conduce
CCDIILO	codicil
CCDIIOR	cricoid
CCDILOY	cycloid
CCDKLOU	cuckold
CCDNOOR	concord □
CCDNOTU	conduct
CCEEHKR	checker
CCEEHRS	screech
CCEEILN	licence
CCEEINR	eccrine
CCEEINS	science □
CCEEIRV	crevice
CCEELRU	Lucrece
CCEELRY	recycle
CCEENRY	recency
CCEERSY	secrecy
CCEFNOT	confect
CCEGNOY	cogency
CCEHIKN	check in
	check-in
	chicken
CCEHINT	technic
CCEHKLU	chuckle
CCEHKNU	uncheck
CCEHKPU	check up
	check-up
CCEHNOS	conches
CCEHORT	crochet
CCEIIKP	ice pick
CCEIIMS	cimices
CCEIIPS	piccies
CCEIKLT	clicket
CCEIKRT	cricket
CCEIKRY	crickey
CCEILNU	nucleic
CCEILRR	circler
CCEILRS	clerics
CCEILRT	circlet
CCEILSU	culices
CCEILSY	cylices
CCEILTU	cuticle
CCEIMST	smectic
CCEINOR	cornice
CCEINOS	concise
CCEINOT	conceit
CCEIOPP	coppice
CCEIOPT	ectopic
CCEIOSS	ciscoes
CCEIOST	Scotice
CCEIPST	sceptic
CCEJNOT	conject
CCEKNOY	cockney
CCEKORT	crocket
CCELLOT	collect
CCELLOU	Uccello
CCELNOY	cyclone
CCENNOR	concern
CCENNOT	connect
CCENOOS	Conseco
CCENOPT	concept
CCENORT	concert
CCEOOTT	cocotte
CCEORRT	correct
CCEOSTV	SCOTVEC
	Scotvec
CCERTUW	crewcut
	crew-cut
CCESSSU	success
CCFIRUY	crucify
CCFLOSU	floccus
CCGHINO	gnocchi
CCHHILS	schlich
CCHHOOS	chochos
CCHIIST	stichic
CCHIKNU	chuck in
CCHILOR	chloric
CCHINOR	chronic
CCHIORY	chicory
CCHIPSY	psychic
CCHIRST	scritch
CCHKLOS	schlock
CCHKMSU	schmuck
CCHKPUU	upchuck
CCHLOOO	hoc loco
CCHNRSU	scrunch
CCHNRUY	crunchy
CCHOSTU	Succoth
CCIIILS	silicic
CCIINPU	Puccini
CCIIRTU	circuit
CCIKLNO	clock in
CCIKLOW	cowlick
CCIKLOY	cockily
	colicky
CCIKOPT	cockpit
CCILNOO	colonic
CCILNOU	council
CCILOOP	piccolo
CCILSTY	cyclist
CCIMOST	McCoist
CCIMOTY	mycotic
CCINOTV	convict
CCIOORS	sirocco
CCIOPTU	occiput
CCIPRTY	cryptic
CCKLNOO	clock on
CCKLOPU	clock up
CCLOPSY	cyclops □
CCMOOOR	morocco □
CCNOOTU	coconut
CCNOPUY	concupy
CCNOSSU	concuss
CCOOORS	rococos
CCOORTU	occur to
CCORSUU	succour
CCOSSTU	stuccos

CCSSSUU	succuss
CDDDEEI	decided
CDDDEEU	deduced
CDDDELO	coddled
CDDEEER	decreed
CDDEEIR	decider
CDDEENS	descend
CDDEEOR	decoder
CDDEERU	reduced
CDDEHIL	childed
CDDEHIT	ditched
CDDEILM	middle C
CDDELOU	clouded
CDDELRU	curdled
CDDELSU	scuddle
CDDEORW	crowded
CDDERSU	scudder
CDDGINO	codding
CDDIIIO	didicoi
CDDIIOS	discoid
CDDIIOY	didicoy
CDDIIRU	druidic
CDDIKOR	Roddick
CDDIORS	discord
CDDKORU	ruddock
CDEEEFN	defence
CDEEEIV	deceive
CDEEELT	elected
CDEEEPR	precede
CDEEERS	seceder
CDEEFII	edifice
CDEEFKL	flecked
CDEEFLT	deflect
CDEEFOR	deforce
CDEEHIS	dehisce
CDEEIIT	eidetic
CDEEILN	decline
CDEEILP	pedicel
	pedicle
CDEEIMN	endemic
CDEEIMS	demi-sec
CDEEINO	codeine
CDEEINT	enticed
CDEEIOS	diocese
CDEEIOV	devoice
CDEEIPR	pierced
CDEEIRR	decrier
CDEEIRT	tierced
CDEEITV	evicted
CDEEITX	excited
CDEEKNR	redneck
CDEEKRW	wrecked
CDEELPU	decuple
CDEELRU	ulcered
CDEELSU	seclude
CDEELUX	exclude
CDEENOS	seconde
CDEENRT	red cent
CDEENST	descent
	scented
CDEEOPR	proceed
CDEEORV	covered
CDEERRU	reducer
CDEERST	crested
CDEERSU	secured
	seducer
CDEERUV	decurve
CDEESUX	excused
CDEFFHU	chuffed
CDEFIIT	deficit
CDEFINO	confide
CDEFKOR	defrock
CDEFNTU	defunct
CDEFOSU	focused
CDEGGLO	clogged
CDEGHNU	Chengdu
CDEGIKN	decking
CDEGKNU	gun deck
CDEGLOT	get cold
CDEHHIT	hitched
CDEHHNU	hunched
CDEHIIL	ceilidh
CDEHILL	chilled
CDEHILO	cheloid
	helcoid
CDEHILP	Delphic
CDEHINO	hedonic
CDEHINP	pinched
CDEHIOW	cowhide
CDEHIPP	chipped
CDEHKOS	shocked
CDEHLOT	clothed
CDEHNOT	notched
CDEHNPU	punched
CDEHOPU	pouched
CDEHORW	chowder
	cowherd
CDEHOSW	cowshed
CDEHOTU	touched
CDEHRSU	crushed
CDEHSSU	duchess
CDEIIMR	dimeric
CDEIINS	indices
CDEIIST	deistic
CDEIISU	suicide
CDEIJST	disject
CDEIKLP	pickled
CDEIKNS	dickens ❑
CDEIKRR	derrick ❑
CDEIKRT	tricked
CDEILLO	collide
CDEILMO	melodic
CDEILNU	include
	nuclide
CDEILPP	clipped
CDEILPS	spliced
CDEILTU	ductile
CDEIMNO	demonic
CDEIMOR	dormice
CDEIMOS	medicos
CDEIMOT	demotic
CDEIMPR	crimped
CDEINOS	secondi
CDEINOT	deontic
	D-notice
	noticed
CDEINRS	cinders
	discern
	rescind
CDEINRY	cindery
CDEINSU	incudes
CDEINSX	exscind
CDEIOPR	percoid
CDEIOPZ	zip code
CDEIORT	cordite
CDEIORV	divorce
CDEIPRT	predict
CDEIPST	discept
CDEIPTU	cup-tied
CDEIRST	credits
CDEIRTV	verdict
CDEISST	dissect
CDEISSY	ecdysis
CDEKLOW	wedlock
CDEKLOY	key-cold
CDEKLRU	ruckled
CDEKNSU	sundeck
CDEKOOR	crooked
CDEKOPT	top deck
CDEKOTU	deck out
CDELLOU	collude
CDELNOO	condole
CDELNOU	encloud
CDELOOR	croodle
	decolor
CDELOPU	coupled
CDELORS	scolder
CDELOTT	clotted
CDELOUY	doucely
CDELPUU	clued up
	clued-up
CDELRUY	crudely
CDEMMNO	commend
CDEMMOO	commode
CDEMNNO	condemn
CDEMOOS	comedos
CDEMORU	decorum
CDENNOO	condone
CDENNOT	contend
CDENORW	decrown
CDENPUY	pudency
CDENRUU	uncured
CDEOOPS	scooped
CDEOORR	corrode
CDEOORV	vocoder
CDEOOTV	dovecot
CDEOPPR	cropped
CDEOPRU	produce
CDEOQTU	docquet
CDEORRS	records
CDEORSW	scowder
CDEORUU	douceur
CDEORWY	Cowdrey

Words marked ❑ can also be spelled with an initial capital letter

CDEOSSU	escudos
CDEPRTY	decrypt
CDERRUY	dry-cure
CDFIILU	fluidic
CDGHIIN	chiding
CDGHOTU	go Dutch
CDGIKNO	docking
CDGIKNU	ducking
CDGILNO	codling
CDGINNO	condign
CDGLOPU	goldcup
CDHIIMW	Midwich
CDHIKMO	hickdom
CDHILNU	unchild
CDHIMST	Schmidt
CDHINOR	chondri
CDHIOOR	choroid
CDHIPTY	diptych
CDHMORU	Murdoch
CDIIIOT	idiotic
CDIIJRU	juridic
CDIILLY	idyllic
CDIIMNO	Dominic
CDIINOR	crinoid
CDIINOT	diction
CDIIOSV	viscoid
CDIKLNO	Old Nick
CDILLOO	colloid
CDILLUY	lucidly
CDILOUV	Ludovic
CDIMMOU	modicum
CDIMNOO	monodic
CDINORW	in-crowd
CDINOTU	conduit
CDIOTUV	oviduct
CDIRTUY	crudity
CDISSSU	discuss
CDKNNOU	dunnock
CDKRSUY	suck dry
CDLNOUU	uncloud
CDLOOTU	out cold
CDMMOOO	commodo
CDNOORY	Croydon
CDNORWY	cry down
CDNOTUW	cut down
CDOORST	doctor's
CDOOTUW	woodcut
CDOPRTU	product
CDOSTUY	custody
CEEEFLR	fleecer
CEEEHIR	reechie
CEEEHLS	Scheele
CEEEINP	epicene
CEEEIRV	receive
CEEELRT	re-elect
CEEELST	celeste
CEEENRS	recense
CEEENRT	Terence
CEEENSS	essence
CEEEOTZ	Coetzee
CEEEPRR	creeper
CEEERRT	erecter
CEEERST	secrete
CEEERSV	screeve
CEEERTX	excrete
CEEETUX	execute
CEEFFNO	offence
CEEFFST	effects
CEEFILO	ice floe
CEEFINN	fence in
CEEFKLR	flecker
	freckle
CEEFLRT	reflect
CEEFNOR	enforce
CEEFPRT	perfect
	prefect
CEEGINR	generic
CEEGINT	genetic
CEEGINU	eugenic
CEEGIRZ	Grecize
CEEGKOS	geckoes
CEEGLLO	college
CEEGLNT	neglect
CEEGLOR	El Greco
CEEGLOU	eclogue
CEEGNRY	regency ❑
CEEGORT	cortège
CEEHILN	elenchi
CEEHILS	helices
	Schiele
CEEHILV	vehicle
CEEHIMS	chemise
CEEHINR	inherce
CEEHINS	Chinese
CEEHIOR	cheerio
CEEHIOS	echoise
CEEHIOZ	echoize
CEEHIRT	heretic
CEEHKLR	heckler
CEEHKNP	henpeck
CEEHLNO	echelon
CEEHLRY	lechery
CEEHLSY	Chelsey
CEEHMRS	schemer
CEEHNOR	cheer on
CEEHORR	coherer
CEEHORT	trochee
CEEHPRU	cheer up
	upcheer
CEEHPSU	Cepheus
CEEHQRU	chequer
CEEHRST	Chester
CEEIJOR	rejoice
CEEIKNT	necktie
CEEIKPR	pickeer
CEEILNR	recline
CEEILNS	license
	selenic
	silence
CEEILNU	leucine
CEEILPS	eclipse ❑
CEEILRT	reticle
	tiercel
CEEILSV	vesicle
CEEILTT	Lettice
CEEIMNO	Miocene
CEEIMNT	centime
CEEINNS	incense
CEEINRS	sincere
CEEINRT	enteric
	enticer
CEEINRV	cervine
CEEINTV	Vicente
CEEIOPT	picotee
CEEIORT	coterie
CEEIORV	ice over
CEEIPRS	precise
	recipes
CEEIPRT	receipt
CEEIPRU	epicure
CEEIPSS	species
CEEIPST	pectise
CEEIPTZ	pectize
CEEIQSU	quiesce
CEEIRRT	reciter
CEEIRSV	scrieve
	service
CEEIRTX	exciter
CEEITTZ	zetetic
CEEJORT	ejector
CEEKLNT	necklet
CEEKLPS	speckle
CEEKMNN	Mencken
CEEKNSY	Eysenck
CEEKOSY	sockeye
CEEKRRW	wrecker
CEELLLU	cellule
CEELLNO	colleen ❑
CEELMNT	clement ❑
CEELMOW	welcome
CEELNOS	enclose
CEELNRT	lectern
CEELNRU	lucerne ❑
CEELORT	elector
	electro
CEELOTT	Colette
CEELOTU	elocute
CEELPRT	prelect
CEELRSU	recluse
CEELRTU	lecture
CEELRTY	erectly
CEELTTU	lettuce
CEEMNOR	McEnroe
CEEMNQU	McQueen
CEEMNRU	cerumen
CEEMOPR	compeer
	compère
CEEMOPT	compete
CEEMSTU	tumesce
CEENNOU	enounce
CEENNOV	convene
CEENORS	necrose
CEENORZ	cozener

CEENPRS	spencer□
CEENPRT	per cent
CEENRSU	censure
CEENRSY	scenery
CEEOPST	pectose
CEEOPTY	ecotype
CEEORRS	rescore
CEEORRT	erector
CEEORRV	recover
	re-cover
CEEORSU	cereous
CEEOTTT	octette
CEEPPRT	percept
	precept
CEEPRSS	precess
CEEPRST	respect
	sceptre□
	spectre
CEEPRTX	excerpt
CEERRSU	rescuer
	securer
CEERRSW	screwer
CEERRUV	recurve
CEERSST	cresset
CEERTTU	curette
CEFFIOR	officer
CEFFISU	suffice
CEFFLSU	scuffle
CEFFMOO	come off
CEFFNOO	cone off
CEFFORS	coffers
	scoffer
CEFFORT	coffret
CEFGINN	fencing
CEFHIIN	in chief
CEFHILR	filcher
CEFHILY	chiefly
CEFHIRS	Fischer
CEFHNRY	Frenchy
CEFHPTU	fetch up
CEFIILT	fictile
CEFIIOR	orifice
CEFIKLR	flicker
CEFILNT	inflect
CEFILRU	Lucifer
CEFIMRY	mercify
CEFINNO	confine
CEFINOR	conifer
	in force
CEFIPSY	specify
CEFIRTY	certify
	rectify
CEFKLOT	fetlock
CEFKLRY	freckly
CEFLNOU	flounce
CEFLNUY	fluency
CEFMOOR	come for
CEFMORY	comfrey
CEFNOOR	for once
CEFNORU	frounce
CEFNOSS	confess
CEFNOSU	confuse
CEFNOTU	confute
CEFOPRS	forceps
CEFORRT	crofter
CEFORSS	frescos
CEFOSSU	focuses
CEFSSUU	fucuses
CEGGHIR	chigger
CEGGIOR	georgic
CEGGOSY	egg-cosy
CEGHINO	echoing
CEGHINT	etching
CEGHNTU	Cheng-tu
CEGIILN	ceiling
CEGIKNN	necking
CEGILNR	clinger
	cringle
CEGILNY	glycine
CEGINOS	cognise
CEGINOZ	cognize
CEGINRR	cringer
CEGKLOR	grockle
CEGLNOO	cologne□
CEGLOOY	ecology
CEGLOSU	glucose
CEGNOST	congest
CEGNRUY	urgency
CEGOORS	Scrooge
CEGORRY	grocery
CEGORSU	scourge
	scrouge
CEHHILR	Ehrlich
CEHHIRS	cherish
CEHHIRT	hitcher
CEHHKOV	Chekhov
CEHHOPT	the chop
CEHIIKN	chinkie□
CEHIIMN	chime in
CEHIJOR	Jericho
CEHIKNT	kitchen
	thicken
CEHIKPS	peckish
CEHIKRR	Herrick
CEHIKRW	whicker
CEHIKTT	thicket
CEHILMN	Mechlin
CEHILMY	chimley
CEHILNO	choline
CEHILPR	pilcher
CEHILRR	Richler
CEHILRV	chervil
CEHILTY	techily
CEHIMNY	chimney
CEHIMOR	Homeric
	moriche
CEHIMST	chemist
CEHINOT	henotic
CEHINPR	phrenic
CEHINRT	cithern
CEHINRW	new rich
CEHINST	sthenic
CEHINSU	echinus
CEHIOPS	hospice
CEHIOTV	Cheviot
CEHIPPR	chipper
CEHIPRS	spheric
CEHIPRT	pitcher
CEHIRRT	Richter
CEHIRSZ	scherzi
CEHIRTT	chitter
CEHKKRU	chukker
CEHKLMO	hemlock
CEHKLSU	huckles
CEHKNOY	Hockney
CEHKOPU	choke up
CEHKORS	shocker
CEHKORT	the Rock
CEHKPTU	ketchup
CEHKSTY	sketchy
CEHLLNS	schnell
CEHLLOY	yelloch
CEHLMOR	chromel
CEHLMUY	chumley
CEHLMWY	wych-elm
CEHLNNU	Chunnel
CEHLNOT	notchel
CEHLOOS	schoole
CEHLORT	chortle
CEHLOST	clothes
CEHLOTW	low-tech
CEHLPPS	schlepp
CEHLQSU	squelch
CEHLRRU	lurcher
CEHMNRU	muncher
CEHMNUW	new chum
CEHMOOR	moocher
CEHMOOW	how come?
CEHMOSS	schmoes
CEHNORV	chevron
CEHNPRU	unperch
CEHNRTU	chunter
CEHNTUY	chutney
CEHOORT	cheroot
CEHOPPR	chopper
CEHOPRS	Porsche
	Porsche®
CEHORRT	torcher
CEHORSZ	scherzo
CEHORTU	retouch
CEHORTW	wotcher
CEHORUV	voucher
CEHOTUW	chew out
CEHRRSU	crusher
CEHRSTT	stretch
CEHRTTU	Utrecht
CEIIKLS	siclike
CEIIKNT	kinetic
CEIIKQU	quickie
CEIILLN	Cellini
CEIILNN	incline
CEIILPT	pelitic
	tie clip

CEIILSU	Iliescu
CEIIMMT	mimetic
CEIIMNS	menisci
CEIIMOT	meiotic
CEIIMPR	empiric
CEIIMRT	Tim Rice
CEIIMSS	seismic
CEIIMST	Semitic
CEIIMTT	titmice
CEIINNO	inconie
CEIINOS	iconise
CEIINOV	invoice
CEIINOZ	iconize
CEIINPS	piscine
CEIINRS	sericin
CEIINRT	citrine
	crinite
	inciter
CEIINSS	iciness
CEIINSU	cuisine
CEIINTZ	citizen
	zincite
CEIIOPZ	epizoic
CEIIRST	eristic
CEIISVV	civvies
CEIJLNO	Jocelin
CEIJSTU	justice
CEIKKSW	Keswick
CEIKLNR	clinker ❑
	crinkle
CEIKLNS	slicken
CEIKLOW	cowlike
CEIKLPR	pickler
	prickle
CEIKLRS	slicker
CEIKLRT	trickle
CEIKLRW	Lerwick
CEIKLST	stickle
CEIKMMW	Wemmick
CEIKNQU	quicken
CEIKNRS	snicker
CEIKORS	Rockies
CEIKPTT	Pickett
CEIKRRT	tricker
CEIKRST	rickets
	Sickert
	sticker
CEIKRTY	rickety
CEILLLU	Lucille
CEILLMN	McNeill
CEILLNU	nucelli
CEILLOR	collier
	Corelli
CEILLST	cellist
CEILMOP	compile
	polemic
CEILMPR	crimple
CEILNOP	pinocle
CEILNOS	close in
	inclose
CEILNOT	lection
CEILNOX	lexicon
CEILNST	clients
	stencil
CEILNTU	tunicle
CEILOSS	ossicle
CEILPPR	clipper
	cripple
CEILPRS	splicer
CEILPSU	slice up
	spicule
CEILQUY	cliquey
CEILRTT	clitter
CEILRTU	utricle
CEILSSU	Celsius
CEILSSW	C S Lewis
CEILTTU	cuittle
CEIMNOR	incomer
CEIMNOT	centimo
	tonemic
CEIMNRU	numeric
CEIMNSU	Mencius
CEIMNYZ	enzymic
CEIMOPT	metopic
CEIMORT	mortice
CEIMOTT	totemic
CEIMPRR	crimper
CEIMRSU	murices
CEINNOR	Corinne
CEINNOV	connive
CEINNTV	Vincent
CEINOOS	Ionesco
CEINOOZ	Neozoic
CEINOPR	porcine
CEINOPT	nepotic
CEINORS	crinose
CEINORT	Citroën
CEINORV	corvine
	cover in
CEINOSS	cession
CEINOST	section
CEINOTX	exciton
CEINOUV	unvoice
CEINPPR	Crippen
CEINPRS	pincers
CEINPST	inspect
CEINRST	cistern
CEINRSV	crivens
CEINRTT	cittern
CEINRUV	incurve
CEINSTY	cystine
CEINTTX	extinct
CEIOPSU	piceous
CEIORRS	crosier
CEIORRU	courier
CEIORRZ	crozier
CEIORST	tercios
CEIORTW	co-write
CEIORTX	excitor
CEIORVY	viceroy
CEIOSSV	viscose
CEIOSTT	Scottie
CEIOSTV	costive
CEIOSTX	coexist
CEIOSTY	society
CEIPPSU	spice up
CEIPQTU	picquet
CEIPRST	triceps
CEIPRTU	cuprite
	picture
CEIPRTY	pyretic
CEIPSST	cesspit
CEIRRSU	cruiser
CEIRRTU	recruit
CEIRRTX	rectrix
CEIRSTT	trisect
CEIRSTW	screw it
CEIRSUV	cursive
CEIRTTX	tectrix
CEISSTU	ictuses
CEJLNOY	Jocelyn
CEJNORU	conjure
CEJNOSU	juncoes
CEJOPRT	project
CEKKLNU	knuckle
CEKKNOR	knocker
CEKLNOS	slocken
CEKLNRU	crunkle
CEKLORY	Lockyer
CEKLRSU	suckler
CEKLRTU	truckle
CEKMORY	mockery
CEKNOOV	convoke
CEKNPSU	sneck up
CEKNRWY	wryneck
CEKOOPR	precook
CEKOOPW	cowpoke
CEKOORY	cookery
CEKORRY	rockery
CEKORST	restock
	rockets
CEKOWZZ	Wozzeck
CEKRRTU	trucker
CELLNOO	colonel
CELLNOR	Cornell
CELLNOS	Lenclos
CELLOSU	locules
	ocellus
CELLOSY	closely
CELLPRU	Purcell
CELLRSU	sculler
CELLRUY	cruelly
CELMNOO	monocle
CELMNSU	mesclun
CELMOOW	come low
CELMOPX	complex
CELMPRU	crumple
CELMSSU	muscles
CELMSUY	lyceums
CELNNOU	nucleon
CELNOOS	close on
	Colenso
	colones

	console
CELNOPU	Poulenc
CELNOSU	counsel
	unclose
CELNOTU	noctule
CELNSUU	nucleus
CELOOST	close to
CELOPSU	close up
	close-up
CELOPTU	couplet
	octuple
CELORST	corslet
CELORSU	closure
CELORTT	clotter
CELORTU	cloture
CELORWY	Crowley
CELOSST	closest
CELOSTY	cotyles
CELPRSU	scruple
CELRSTU	cluster
CELRTTU	clutter
CELRTUU	culture
CELRTUV	culvert
CELRTUY	cruelty
	cutlery
CELSTTU	scuttle
CEMMNOT	comment
CEMMNOU	commune
CEMMOTU	commute
CEMMRSU	scummer
CEMNNOO	non-come
CEMNNOT	contemn
CEMNOOY	economy
CEMNOSU	consume
CEMOOPS	compose
CEMOOPT	compote
CEMOOTU	come out
	outcome
CEMOPTU	compute
CEMOSTU	costume
CEMPRTU	crumpet
CEMRRUY	mercury □
CEMRSTU	rectums
CENNOOT	connote
CENNORY	Connery
CENNOST	consent
CENNOTT	content
CENNOTV	convent
CENNRSU	scunner
CENOORR	coroner
	crooner
CENOORT	coronet
CENOPSY	syncope
CENOPTU	cut open
CENOPTY	potency
CENOQRU	conquer
CENORRS	scorner
CENORSS	Cresson
CENORST	conster
	Costner
CENORTU	counter
	recount
	trounce
CENORTV	convert
CENORUV	uncover
CENOSSY	coyness
CENOSTT	contest
CENOSTU	contuse
CENOTTX	context
CENPRTY	encrypt
CENRRTU	current
CENRSTU	encrust
CENRSUU	uncurse
CENRSUW	unscrew
CENRTUY	century
CEOOPRS	scooper
CEOORST	scooter
CEOOSTY	coyotes
CEOPPRR	cropper
CEOPPRS	coppers
CEOPPRY	coppery
CEOPRRT	porrect
CEOPRRU	procure
CEOPRSS	process
CEOPRTT	protect
CEOPRUV	cover up
	cover-up
CEOQRTU	croquet
CEORRSU	courser
	cruores
	scourer
CEORRSY	sorcery
CEORRTY	rectory
CEORRVY	cry over
CEORSSU	courses
	Croesus
	sucrose
CEORSTU	Scouter
CEORTUU	couture
CEOSTTU	cuttoes
CEPPRSU	scupper
CEPRSSU	percuss
CEPRSSY	cypress
CEPRSUW	screw up
	screw-up
CEPSSTU	suspect
CERSTTU	scutter
CERSTUY	curtsey
CFFHINO	chiffon
CFFHIOP	chip off
CFFHOOP	chop off
CFFIKKO	kick off
	kick-off
CFFIKOP	pick off
CFFIKOT	tick off
CFFKOOO	cook off
CFFKOSU	suck off
CFFLOOO	cool off
CFFMOSU	offscum
CFFRSUY	scruffy
CFGIKNU	fucking
CFHILYY	chylify
CFHIMYY	chymify
CFHIORT	itch for
CFHOOOW	Foochow
CFIIKNY	finicky
CFIILNT	inflict
CFIIMNO	omnific
CFIINOT	fiction
CFIINOY	iconify
CFIINYZ	zincify
CFIKOSS	fossick
CFILORS	frolics
CFIMNOR	confirm
CFINOSU	in focus
CFIORSY	scorify
CFIOSTY	Scotify
CFKNORU	unfrock
CFKOTTU	futtock
CFLMRUU	fulcrum
CFLNOUX	conflux
CFLORWY	cry wolf
CFLPSUU	cupfuls
CFMNOOR	conform
CFMOORT	comfort
CFNOOSU	focus on
CGGHMOU	McGough
CGHHNOU	Chungho
CGHIINT	itching
CGHIKNO	choking
CGHIKNU	chi kung
	Kuching
CGHINNO	chignon
CGHINRU	ruching
CGHINSU	Cushing
CGHIOSY	goyisch
CGHOPUU	cough up
CGHORUY	grouchy
CGIIKLN	licking
CGIIKMM	gimmick
CGIIKNN	nicking
CGIIKNP	picking
CGIIKNT	ticking
CGIILNO	coiling
CGIILNS	slicing
CGIIMNN	mincing
CGIINOV	voicing
CGIKMNO	mocking
CGIKNOO	cooking
CGIKNOR	rocking
CGIKNPU	kingcup
CGILNNO	cloning
CGILNOO	cooling
CGILNOS	closing
CGILNOT	cling to
CGILNOW	cowling
CGILNOY	cloying
	Coligny
CGILNRU	curling
CGILORW	cowgirl
CGILOSS	Glossic
CGILOTT	glottic
CGILPTY	glyptic

CGINNNU cunning
CGINNOS consign
CGINOPY copying
CGINORW crowing
CGINOST gnostic
CGINPPU cupping
CGINRSU cursing
CGINRUV curving
CGINSSU cussing
CGINTTU cutting
CGIOOOS giocoso
CGIOTYZ zygotic
CGKLNOU gunlock
CGKOOOR go crook
CGLOOSU colugos
CGNOUYY Cy Young
CGOSTTU Guscott
CHHINOR rhonchi
CHHINTU unhitch
CHHIPTU hitch up
CHHNOOS honchos
CHHRTTU thrutch
CHIIIST Shiitic
CHIILLS chillis
CHIILLT Tillich
CHIIMSU ischium
CHIINPT pitch in
CHIIOPT ophitic
CHIIOST stichoi
CHIIPST Pictish
CHIIPSW Ipswich
CHIKLLO hillock
CHIKLTY thickly
CHIKNOO chinook□
CHIKNOS in shock
CHIKORY hickory
CHIKOST thickos
CHIKPSU puckish
CHIKSTY kitschy
CHILOPS Schipol
CHILOST coltish
CHILSTU cultish
CHIMMTU Mitchum
CHIMORS chrisom
CHINOOR chorion
CHINOPS phonics
CHINOPT to-pinch
CHINORS Cornish
CHINORT Corinth
CHINORW Norwich
CHINOSU cushion
CHINOTU in touch
CHINPUW winch up
CHINQSU squinch
CHINTUW unwitch
CHINTYZ chintzy
CHIOOPR pochoir
CHIOORZ chorizo
CHIOPRT trophic
CHIOPXY hypoxic
CHIORST Christo
ostrich
CHIOSSZ schizos
CHIPRRU chirrup
CHIPRRY pyrrhic□
CHIPSSY physics
CHIRSTY Christy
CHITTWY twitchy
CHKLOSY Shylock
CHKMMOU hummock
CHKMOSY Chomsky
CHKOOST schtook
CHLOOSS schools
CHLOPST splotch
CHLOSSS schloss□
CHMNOTU not much
CHMOORS chromos
CHMOOST schtoom
CHMOOTU too much
CHNNOPY Pynchon
CHNNOSU nonsuch
CHNOOPS ponchos
CHNOORT torchon
CHNOOTU touch on
CHNOPTU notch up
CHNORRS schnorr
CHNORSY synchro
CHNOTUU uncouth
CHNPPUU punch-up
CHOORST cohorts
CHOORSU ochrous
CHOPSSY psychos
CHOPTUU touch up
CHPPSUY psych up
CIIILLT illicit
CIIKKLL killick
CIIKMNN minnick
CIIKNPT nit-pick
CIIKNST stick in
CIILLTY licitly
CIILLVY civilly
CIILNOS silicon
CIILNOT Nilotic
CIILNUV uncivil
CIILOOT oolitic
CIILOPT politic
CIILORT cortili
CIILOST colitis
solicit
CIILPSY spicily
CIIMMRY mimicry
CIIMOST mistico
CIIMOTT mitotic
CIINOOT coition
CIINORS incisor
CIINPPR Princip
CIINPRS Crispin
CIINSTU Ictinus
CIIOSUV vicious
CIIRSTV vitrics
CIJNNOO conjoin
CIJNNTU injunct
CIKKLLO killock
CIKKNNO Kinnock
CIKKOTU kick out
CIKLLLU ill luck
ill-luck
CIKLLOP pillock
CIKLLOR rollick
CIKLLSY slickly
CIKLLUY luckily
CIKLMOR rim-lock
CIKLMSU misluck
CIKLMSY smickly
CIKLNRY crinkly
CIKLORY rockily
CIKLOWW Wicklow
CIKLPRY prickly
CIKLQUY quickly□
CIKNOST in stock
stick-on
CIKNPSU snick up
CIKNPTU pin tuck
CIKNSTU unstick
CIKOPPT pockpit
CIKOPTU pick out
CIKOSTT stick to
CIKOTUW outwick
CIKPSTU stick up
stick-up
CIKRSTY tricksy
CILLNNO Lincoln
CILLNOS Collins
CILMNOP complin
CILMOPY Olympic
CILMSTU cultism
CILNNOT Clinton
CILNOTU linocut
CILNPSU insculp
CILNPSY lip-sync
CILNSTU linctus
CILOOPT co-pilot
CILOOSS colossi
CILOOST sciolto
CILOPRY pyloric
CILOPSW cowslip
CILOSTU oculist
CILPRSY crisply
CILPRTU culprit
CILSTTU cultist
CIMNOOR moronic
omicron
CIMNORS crimson
microns
CIMOOST osmotic
CIMOPSY miscopy
CIMOSSY mycosis
CIMOTYZ zymotic
CIMPRSY scrimpy
CINNORU unicorn□
CINNOSU nuncios
CINNOTU unction
CINOOOR Orinoco

CINOORT	Corinto
CINOPRX	princox
CINORRT	tricorn
CINORSS	incross
CINORST	cistron
CINORTU	ruction
CINOSST	consist
CINOSSU	cousins ❑
CINOSTU	suction
CINOTTU	cut into
CINRSTU	incrust
CIOOPRS	Scorpio
CIOOPRT	portico
CIOOPSU	copious
CIOOQTU	coquito
CIOORSU	corious
CIOPRTY	Cypriot
CIOPSTY	copyist
CIOQRSU	croquis
CIORSSS	scissor
CIORSSU	Roscius
CIORSUU	curious
CIORTVY	victory ❑
CIOSSUV	viscous
CIPRSSU	prussic
CIPRTTY	tryptic
CIPRUVY	pyruvic
CIPSTTY	styptic
CKKNNOO	knock on
	knock-on
CKKNOPU	knock up
	knock-up
CKLLMOU	mullock
CKLLOOP	pollock ❑
CKLNOUW	Lucknow
CKLNUUY	unlucky
CKLOORW	rowlock
CKLOOTU	lock out
	lockout
CKLOPTU	pot luck
CKLOTUU	luck out
CKLPPUU	pluck up
CKNOOOS	Cookson
CKNOOTU	conk out
CKNOSTU	stuck on
	unstock
CKNSTUU	unstuck
CKOORST	Rostock
CKOPSTU	stock up
CKOSSTU	tussock
CKPSTUU	stuck up
	stuck-up
CLLMOSU	mollusc
CLLOSUU	loculus
CLMOOPT	complot
CLMOSUU	lucumos
	osculum
CLMSUUU	cumulus
CLNOORT	control
CLNOOSS	consols
CLNOSTU	consult

CLOOOSU	suo loco
CLOORSU	colours
CLOOSTW	low-cost
CLOPRSU	Proclus
CLORSSY	crossly
CLORTUY	courtly
CMMNOOS	commons ❑
CMMRSUY	scrummy
CMNOOOT	con moto
CMNOOPT	Compton
CMOOORS	Comoros
CMOOPRT	comport
CMOOPST	compost
CMORSTU	scrotum
CMOSSTU	customs
CMOSUVY	muscovy
CMPRSUY	scrumpy
CNNOOOR	O'Connor
CNNOORS	Connors
CNNOOTU	count on
CNNORRU	Runcorn
CNNORUW	uncrown
CNOOPPR	popcorn
CNOOPSU	soupçon
CNOORST	consort
CNOORTT	contort
CNOORTU	contour
	croûton
CNOOSST	oncosts
CNOOTTY	cottony
CNOPSTU	punctos
CNOPTUU	count up
CNORSSU	uncross
CNORTUY	country
COOORSZ	corozos
COOPPSU	scoop up
COOPRRT	proctor
COOPRTU	outcrop
COOPSTU	octopus
COOPTUY	copy out
COOSTTU	cost out
COPRRTU	corrupt
COPRSTY	cryptos
COPRSUU	cuprous
CORRSUY	cursory
CORSSTU	scrutos

D

DDDEELU	deluded
DDDEEMO	demoded
DDDEENU	denuded
DDDEFLU	fuddled
DDDEHLU	huddled
DDDEIIV	divided
DDDEILR	diddler
DDDEILY	Diddley
DDDEIMU	muddied
DDDEKNO	Ken Dodd
DDDELMU	muddled
DDDEORY	doddery
DDDERUY	duddery

DDDESTU	studded
DDEEELN	needled
DDEEERR	red deer
DDEEFGL	fledged
DDEEFIL	defiled
	fielded
DDEEFIN	defined
DDEEFIR	Freddie
DDEEGLP	pledged
DDEEGRR	dredger
DDEEHRS	shedder
DDEEILS	sleided
DDEEILY	deedily
DDEEIMO	Diomede
DDEEIMS	misdeed
DDEEIRR	Deirdre
	derider
DDEEIRS	desired
DDEEIRV	derived
DDEELLW	Weddell
DDEELMR	meddler
DDEELPR	peddler
DDEELRU	deluder
DDEENOV	odd-even
DDEENOW	endowed
DDEENPU	up-ended
DDEENRS	Dresden
DDEENSU	duendes
DDEEORR	ordered
DDEEOTV	devoted
DDEEPTU	deputed
DDEERSS	dressed
DDEERTU	detrude
DDEERYY	dry-eyed
DDEESTU	Deus det
DDEFILR	fiddler
DDEFLNO	Flodden
DDEFLOO	flooded
DDEFORR	Redford
DDEGGRU	drugged
DDEGILR	griddle
DDEGIMO	demigod
DDEGINR	Redding
DDEGINW	wedding
DDEGNOO	good-den
DDEGNOS	godsend
DDEGNOU	dudgeon
DDEGNWY	Gwynedd
DDEGORS	gorsedd
DDEGOSS	goddess
DDEHIRS	reddish
DDEHIRW	whidder
DDEHIRY	hydride
DDEHNOU	hounded
DDEHNRU	hundred
DDEHRSU	shudder
DDEIIKS	kiddies
DDEIIOX	dioxide
DDEIIRT	dirtied
DDEIIRV	divider
DDEIKNR	kindred

DDEILLL	Liddell
DDEILLR	drilled
DDEILMP	dimpled
DDEILMR	Mildred
DDEILNW	dwindle
DDEILOT	deltoid
DDEILPR	piddler
DDEILQU	quiddle
DDEILRR	riddler
DDEILRS	slidder
DDEILRT	tiddler
DDEILTU	diluted
	Luddite
DDEILTW	twiddle
DDEINNU	Dunedin
DDEINOW	die down
DDEINRU	undried
DDEINST	distend
DDEIOOR	do or die
	do-or-die
DDEIORT	Diderot
DDEIOTU	died out
DDEIOWW	widowed
DDEIPRU	dried up
	dried-up
DDEISSU	disused
DDEISTU	studied
DDEKMOU	dukedom
DDELMRU	muddler
DDELOOR	doodler
DDELOPR	plodder
DDELORT	toddler
DDEMNOS	Desmond
DDEMNOT	oddment
DDENNOR	dendron
DDENOPS	despond
DDENOPW	dew-pond
DDENORT	trodden
DDENORU	redound
	rounded
	underdo
DDENORW	drowned
DDENOSS	oddness
DDENOUW	wounded
DDEOORW	redwood□
DDEOPPR	dropped
DDFHIOS	odd fish
DDGGINO	dodging
DDGIIKN	kidding
DDGIILY	giddily
DDGILOW	wild dog
DDGINNO	nodding
DDGINPU	pudding
DDGIPUY	giddy-up
DDGLLOO	old gold
DDGNOOS	Dodgson
DDGOOOW	dogwood
DDHIISY	Yiddish
DDHIKSU	kiddush
DDHIORY	hydroid
DDHOOWY	howdy-do
DDHORSY	dry-shod
DDIIKLS	skid lid
DDIILOP	diploid
DDILMUY	muddily
DDILOWY	dowdily
DDILRUY	ruddily
DDILTWY	twiddly
DDINOSS	Siddons
DDIOOSS	dosi-dos
DDIPRRY	drip-dry
DDMNOOR	dromond
DDOORST	odd sort
DEEEFPT	deep-fet
DEEEFRV	fevered
DEEEGLP	pledgee
DEEEGMR	demerge
DEEEGRT	deterge
DEEEHLW	wheedle
DEEEHPT	the deep
DEEEIPY	pie-eyed
DEEEIRS	Désirée
DEEEISV	devisee
DEEEKLN	kneeled
DEEEKNW	weekend
DEEELPT	deplete
DEEELSV	sleeved
DEEELTW	tweedle
DEEEMRT	Demeter
DEEENNV	end even
DEEENRW	renewed
DEEENTT	détente
DEEENUV	Deneuve
DEEEORR	roe deer
DEEEOTV	devotee
DEEEPRS	speeder
DEEEPST	deepest
	deep-set
	steeped
DEEERRV	revered
DEEERSV	deserve
	severed
DEEFFIN	effendi
DEEFGIN	feeding
	feigned
DEEFGOR	Godfree
DEEFHLU	heedful
DEEFILN	Enfield
DEEFILR	fielder
DEEFIMS	misfeed
DEEFINR	definer
	refined
DEEFIRY	re-edify
DEEFLNU	needful
DEEFMOR	freedom
DEEFORT	defer to
DEEFORV	overfed
DEEFPRY	deep-fry
DEEGHIN	hedge in
	heeding
DEEGHOW	hogweed
DEEGILS	leg side
DEEGINN	needing
DEEGINW	weeding
DEEGIOR	Geordie
DEEGIRV	diverge
	grieved
DEEGLNR	Grendel
DEEGLNS	legends
DEEGLPR	pledger
DEEGLPT	pledget
DEEGLRS	ledgers
	sledger
DEEGNOO	good-e'en
DEEGOSY	geodesy
DEEGOTU	edge out
DEEGSSU	guessed
DEEGSTU	get used
DEEHHRT	the herd
DEEHIKV	khedive
DEEHILT	lethied
DEEHJNO	John Dee
DEEHJUY	Hey Jude
DEEHLSV	shelved
DEEHMRU	rheumed
DEEHNOY	honeyed
DEEHNPR	prehend
DEEHPRS	sphered
DEEHRSS	herdess
DEEIIRW	weirdie
DEEIJLL	jellied
DEEILLM	de Mille□
DEEILMR	Demirel
DEEILNR	red-line
DEEILNS	linseed
DEEILNY	needily
DEEILRT	let ride
DEEILRV	deliver
DEEILRW	wielder
DEEILRY	yielder
DEEILSY	seedily
DEEIMNS	sidemen
DEEIMPT	emptied
DEEIMRT	merited
DEEINNT	dentine
DEEINNU	ennuied
DEEINNZ	denizen
DEEINPR	Dnieper
	ripened
DEEINRS	Nereids
DEEINRW	red wine
	widener
DEEINRX	indexer
DEEINST	destine
DEEINSW	endwise
DEEINSX	indexes
DEEINTT	dinette
DEEINTV	evident
DEEINWZ	wizened
DEEIOPS	episode
DEEIPPT	peptide
DEEIPRS	preside
DEEIPRV	deprive

DEEIPRX expired
DEEIPSS despise
DEEIPST despite
DEEIRRS resider
serried
DEEIRRT retired
DEEIRRV rivered
DEEIRSU residue
DEEIRSV De Vries
deviser
diverse
DEEIRTU erudite
DEEIRTV riveted
DEEIRVV revived
DEEISVZ Devizes
DEEKKLR De Klerk
DEEKLRS skelder
DEEKMOR Kermode
DEEKNNY Kennedy
DEEKORV revoked
DEEKPUY keyed up
keyed-up
DEELLMS smelled
DEELLNR Rendell
DEELLPS spelled
DEELLRU dueller
DEELLRW dweller
DEELLRY elderly
DEELLSW swelled
DEELMNO Mole End
DEELMOR remodel
DEELMPU deplume
DEELNRS slender
DEELNSS endless
DEELNSY densely
DEELNTT nettled
DEELOPP peopled
DEELOPR deplore
DEELOPV develop
DEELOPX explode
DEELORU Lou Reed
DEELORV lovered
DEELORW lowered
DEELOSU delouse
DEELOVV devolve
DEELPRS spelder
DEELPRU prelude
DEELSTT settled
DEELTUX exulted
DEELVXY vexedly
DEEMMST stemmed
DEEMNOV venomed
DEEMNOY moneyed
DEEMORV removed
DEEMORX exoderm
DEEMOSS Ed Moses
DEENNOS données
DEENNOT not need
DEENNOY doyenne
DEENNPT pendent
DEENOPS spondee
DEENOPT not deep
DEENORS endorse
DEENORT erodent
DEENPPR perpend
DEENPRS spender❑
DEENPRT pretend
DEENRSS redness
DEENRSU end-user
ensured
DEENRSW Wenders
DEENRTU denture
tenured
DEENSUX unsexed
DEEOPPY pop-eyed
DEEOPRS deposer
reposed
DEEOPRW powered
DEEOPRY eye-drop
DEEOPSS speedos
DEEOPSX exposed
DEEOPTW two deep
DEEORRR reorder
DEEORRS reredos
rose-red
DEEORRV overred
DEEORST oersted
teredos
DEEORTW towered
DEEORUV overdue
DEEOTUW weed out
DEEPPSU speed up
DEEPRRU perdure
DEEPRSS depress
pressed
DEEPRTU reputed
DEERRSS dresser
redress
re-dress
DEERRUV verdure
DEERSST deserts
dessert
tressed
DEERTTU uttered
DEERTUX extrude
DEFFFNO fend off
DEFFIMO fiefdom
DEFFINO dine off
DEFFIOS offside
DEFFISU diffuse
DEFFLMU muffled
DEFFLRU ruffled
DEFFNOS send off
send-off
DEFFOOZ doze off
DEFFSTU stuffed
DEFGHHI high-fed
DEFGINR fringed
DEFGINU feuding
DEFGINY defying
DEFGIOR firedog
DEFGIRU figured
DEFGIST fidgets
DEFGITY fidgety
DEFGORY Godfrey
DEFHLSU flushed
DEFIILN infidel
infield
DEFIILO Fidelio
DEFIIMW midwife
DEFIINU unified
DEFILLR frilled
DEFILRU direful
DEFILRW Wilfred
DEFILST stifled
DEFILXY fixedly
DEFIMMO Femidom®
DEFIMOR deiform
DEFINOX fixed on
DEFINSY densify
DEFINTX FT Index
DEFINUX unfixed
DEFINUY undeify
DEFIPRU fired up
DEFIPRY perfidy
DEFIRRT drifter
DEFIRZZ frizzed
DEFLLOU doleful
DEFLNOP penfold
DEFLNOR fondler
DEFLNOT tenfold
DEFLOOR floored
DEFLORT Telford
DEFMORS serfdom
DEFMPRU rump-fed
DEFNOOR done for
DEFNORS send for
DEFNORT fronted
DEFNORU founder
DEFOOPR proofed
DEFORST defrost
frosted
DEFORWX Wexford
DEFRSUY Dreyfus
DEGGGOO good egg
DEGGHIN hedging
DEGGILU Gielgud
DEGGIRU druggie
DEGGLPU plugged
DEGGNOO doggone
DEGGNOU gudgeon
DEGGRTU drugget
DEGHILT delight
lighted
DEGHINR herding
DEGHIST sighted
DEGHOST the gods
DEGIINT editing
ignited
DEGIKLO godlike
DEGILLY gelidly
DEGILMN mingled
DEGILNN lending

DEGILNU indulge
DEGILNW welding
wing-led
DEGILRU guilder
DEGILUV divulge
DEGIMNN mending
DEGIMNS smidgen
DEGINNN Denning
DEGINNP pending
DEGINNR rending
DEGINNS sending
DEGINNT tending
DEGINNV vending
DEGINNY denying
DEGINOR Dorigen
groined
ignored
Negroid
DEGINOS dingoes
DEGINOW widgeon
DEGINRR grinder
DEGINRW redwing
DEGINST stinged
DEGINSW swindge
DEGINUX exuding
DEGIPPR gripped
DEGIQSU squidge
DEGIRSS digress
DEGLMOU moguled
DEGLNNO endlong
DEGLOPR pledgor
DEGLOPS splodge
DEGLOSS godless
DEGLTTU glutted
DEGMRSU smudger
DEGNNOU dungeon
DEGNOPR pronged
DEGNOPW peg down
DEGNORU go under
guerdon
undergo
DEGNORW wronged
DEGNOTW get down
DEGOORS dog rose
DEGOORV grooved
DEGOPRU grouped
DEGORRS Rodgers
DEHIKSW whisked
DEHILMS dishelm
DEHILNY Hindley
DEHILTY diethyl
DEHIMOS dishome
DEHIMOT ethmoid
DEHINOR hordein
DEHINPT in depth
in-depth
DEHINRX Hendrix
DEHIOST hoisted
DEHIOSU hideous
DEHIOTU hide out
hideout
DEHIPPW whipped
DEHIRRU hurried
DEHIRSU Rushdie
DEHIRSV dervish
DEHIRTY dithery
DEHISSW Swedish
DEHLNOS Sheldon
DEHLOOT toehold
DEHLORW whorled
DEHLORY dry hole
DEHLOSS sloshed
DEHLRRU hurdler
DEHLRSU hurdles
DEHMOST methods
DEHNNSU shunned
DEHNOOW hoe-down
DEHNORR Hordern
DEHNOTZ dozenth
DEHNRTU thunder□
DEHOOTT toothed
DEHORTW the Word
DEHPPUY hyped up
DEIIIRS iridise
DEIIIRZ iridize
DEIIKLS dislike
DEIIKNS dinkies
DEIILMP implied
DEIILMT delimit
limited
DEIILNS slide in
DEIILNV lived-in
DEIILOS idolise
DEIILOZ idolize
DEIIMNO dominie
DEIINOS Sidonie
DEIINOT edition
DEIINRS insider
DEIINRT nitride
DEIINRU uridine
DEIINRV diviner
drive-in
DEIINSS insides
DEIIORS Isidore
DEIIOSX oxidise
DEIIOXZ oxidize
DEIJNOT jointed
DEIJNRU injured
DEIJORY joy-ride
DEIKLLS deskill
skilled
DEIKLNR kindler
DEIKLOR rodlike
DEIKNNS skinned
DEIKNRR drinker
DEIKOSY disyoke
DEIKRST skirted
DEILLMO modelli
DEILLNW dwell in
indwell
DEILLPS spilled
DEILLSS lidless
DEILLSU ill-used
sullied
DEILLTW twilled
DEILMNO Mindelo
DEILMOP implode
DEILMOT old-time
DEILMOY myeloid
DEILMPP pimpled
DEILMWY mildewy
DEILMXY mixedly
DEILNNU unlined
DEILNOU unoiled
DEILNOW lie down
lie-down
DEILNPS spindle
DEILNRT tendril
trindle
DEILNSW swindle
DEILNSY Lindsey
DEILNTU diluent
DEILOPS despoil
spoiled
DEILORS soldier
DEILOTW low tide
DEILOTY yield to
DEILPPR rippled
DEILPRU preludi
DEILPSU Lepidus
DEILPTY tepidly
DEILQTU quilted
DEILRRV L-driver
DEILRTY tiredly
DEILRVY devilry
DEILRWY weirdly
DEILRZZ drizzle
DEILSTT stilted
DEIMMRT midterm
trimmed
DEIMMRU immured
DEIMMSU mediums
DEIMNNU minuend
DEIMNSS dimness
missend
DEIMNST mindset
DEIMNUX unmixed
DEIMOOR moidore
DEIMOPS imposed
DEIMOST modiste
DEIMOTT omitted
DEIMPRT dirempt
DEIMPUX mixed up
mixed-up
DEIMSSU misused
DEIMSTY stymied
DEINNOS dies non
Dineson
DEINNTW twinned
DEINOPS dispone
DEINOPT pointed
DEINORR Dornier
in order

Words marked □ can also be spelled with an initial capital letter

DEINORS	indorse
DEINORV	on-drive
DEINOTU	dine out
DEINOTW	tie down
DEINPRT	printed
DEINPST	stipend
DEINRSS	dress in
DEINRSU	insured
DEINRTT	trident
DEINRTU	intrude
	untride
	untried
DEINRTX	dextrin
DEINSST	disnest
	dissent
	St Denis
DEINSTT	dentist
	stinted
DEINSTY	density
	destiny
DEIOPRT	dioptre
	peridot
DEIOPRU	Proudie
DEIOPRV	provide
DEIOPSS	dispose
DEIOPST	deposit
	posited
	topside
DEIOPSU	Oedipus
	Opus Dei
DEIORRW	worried
DEIORSS	dossier
DEIORST	steroid
	storied
DEIORSV	devisor
	devoirs
DEIORSW	weirdos
DEIORTT	Detroit
	Dettori
DEIORTU	outride
	ride out
DEIORWW	widower
DEIOSTU	outside
	tedious
DEIOSUV	devious
DEIOTTU	edit out
DEIPRSS	Spiders
DEIPRST	striped
DEIPRSY	spidery
DEIPSSU	upsides
DEIPSTU	dispute
DEIPSUW	wised up
DEIPSXY	pyxides
DEIRRST	stirred
DEISSTU	studies
DEISTTW	twisted
DEKLNRU	knurled
DEKNNRU	drunken
DEKNOST	Donetsk
DEKNOSY	donkeys
DEKNOTT	knotted
DEKOPST	desktop
DEKORWY	keyword
DELLMOO	modello
DELLNOW	dwell on
DELLOOP	Leopold
DELLOPR	Red Poll
	redpoll
DELLORR	Dorrell
DELLOSU	duellos
DELLRRU	Durrell
DELMORU	moulder
	remould
DELMOST	Olmsted
DELMOTT	mottled
DELMPRU	rumpled
DELNORU	lounder
	roundel
DELNORY	Reynold
DELNOSS	oldness
DELNOTW	let down
	let-down
DELNOTY	notedly
DELNOUV	unloved
DELNPRU	plunder
DELNRTU	rundlet
	trundle
DELOORS	Dolores
	old rose
DELOOST	Toledos
DELOOTU	dole out
DELOPPR	Doppler
DELOPRT	droplet
	let drop
DELORRY	orderly
DELORSS	rodless
DELORST	oldster
DELORTT	dottrel
DELORUV	louvred
DELOSTU	tousled
DELOSZZ	sozzled
DELOTUV	voluted
DELPUZZ	puzzled
DELRRSU	slurred
DELRSTU	strudel
DEMMRRU	drummer
DEMNOOR	morendo
DEMNORT	mordent
DEMNOST	endmost
DEMNOTU	demount
	mounted
DEMNOUV	unmoved
DEMOOPP	popedom
DEMOOTU	outmode
DEMOSTY	modesty
DEMPSTU	stumped
DENNORT	tendron
DENNORU	enround
DENNOTU	unnoted
DENNSTU	stunned
DENNTUU	untuned
DENOORR	on order
DENOPPR	propend
DENOPRS	respond
DENOPRT	drop-net
	portend
DENOPUX	expound
DENORRU	rondure
	rounder
	unorder
DENORSU	resound
DENORSW	wonders
DENORWW	new word
DENOSTU	send out
	snouted
DENOSTW	set down
DENPRSU	spurned
DENPRTU	prudent
DENPSSU	suspend
DENRRTU	turn red
DENRSSU	undress
DENRSSY	dryness
DENRSUU	unsured
DENSTTU	student
	stunted
DEOOPPS	opposed
DEOOPRT	torpedo
DEOOPST	stooped
DEOORRT	to order
DEOPPRR	dropper
DEOPRWY	powdery
DEOPSTT	spotted
DEORRST	rodster
DEORSSS	dossers
DEORSTW	worsted
DEORSTY	destroy
DEORTTU	tutored
DEOSSYY	odyssey
DEOSTTU	duettos
DEOSTUU	duteous
DEOSTUX	tuxedos
DEPRRUY	prudery
DEPRSSU	dress up
DERSSTU	trussed
DERSTTU	trusted
DFFGIOR	Gifford
DFFHLOO	hold off
DFFIIMR	midriff
DFFIMOR	difform
DFFOOPR	drop off
DFFOTUY	off duty
	off-duty
DFGGINU	fudging
DFGHIOS	dogfish
DFGIINN	finding
DFGIINY	dignify
DFGILNO	folding
DFGINNU	funding
DFGINOU	fungoid
DFGOOOR	for good
DFIIKNR	Rifkind
DFIILRW	Wilfrid
DFILMNU	mindful

DFILNOP	pinfold
DFILOSX	sixfold
DFILTUU	dutiful
DFIMNUY	mundify
DFIMOOS	foodism
DFIMORS	disform
DFIMORT	Mitford
DFINNOT	not find
DFINOTU	find out
DFIORST	do first
DFLOOTW	twofold
DFNORUY	foundry
DFOOOTU	do out of
DFOORTY	dry-foot
DGGHIOS	doggish
DGGIILN	gilding
	gliding
DGGIINR	ridging
DGGIINU	guiding
DGGILNO	Golding
	lodging
DGHIILN	hidling
DGHIINS	shindig
DGHIKNO	Hodgkin
DGHILNO	holding❑
DGHORTU	drought
DGHOTUY	doughty
DGIILNS	sliding
DGIILRY	rigidly
DGIIMMN	dimming
DGIIMNN	minding
DGIIMNS	smidgin
DGIINNW	winding
DGIINOS	indigos
DGIINOT	dig into
DGIINOV	voiding
DGIINOW	windigo
DGIINPP	dipping
DGIINPU	pinguid
DGIINRV	driving
DGIINST	tidings
DGIINTY	dignity
DGIKMNO	kingdom
DGIKNNO	Don King
DGIKNNU	dunking
DGIKNOR	Dorking
DGILLNU	dulling
DGILLOR	old girl
DGILNYY	dyingly
DGIMNOO	Domingo
DGIMNOR	Grimond
DGINNOR	droning
DGINNOU	undoing
DGINNUY	undying
DGINORW	wording
DGINOSS	dossing
DGINOSU	dousing
DGINOSW	disgown
DGINSTU	dusting
DGIOPRY	prodigy
DGIQSUY	squidgy
DGISSTU	disgust
DGLNOUY	ungodly
DGLNOWY	Goldwyn
DGLOORW	grow old
DGLOOST	God slot
DGLOPSY	splodgy
DGMOPRU	gumdrop
DGNNOUW	gun down
DGNOOOR	godroon
DGNOOOT	not good
DGNOORS	drongos
DGNOORU	go round
DGNOORW	do wrong
DGNORSU	grounds
DGOORTT	dogtrot
DHIIKWZ	whiz kid
DHIILNS	hidlins
DHIILSW	wildish
DHIIMMS	dimmish
DHIIMNO	hominid
DHIIORZ	rhizoid
DHIKRSU	Kurdish
DHILMUY	humidly
DHILNOP	dolphin❑
DHILOST	doltish
DHILOSU	loudish
DHILRTY	thirdly
DHIMORU	humidor
	rhodium
DHINNOS	donnish
DHINOPY	hypnoid
DHINORS	dishorn
DHINSTU	tun-dish
DHIOPTY	typhoid
DHIORTY	thyroid
DHIOSTU	dish out
DHIPRSU	prudish
DHJNNOO	Don John
DHJOPRU	Jodhpur
DHLMOOU	hoodlum
DHLOORY	Holroyd
DHLOOTU	hold out
DHLOPRU	Rudolph
DHMMRUU	humdrum
DHMNOYY	hymnody
DHNNSUU	unshun'd
DHNOSSU	Hudson's
DHOOPRU	uphoord
DHOORTY	Dorothy
DHOPRSU	push-rod
DHORSUY	hydrous
DIIIMRU	iridium
DIIIMSV	divisim
DIIINPS	insipid
DIIJNOS	disjoin
DIIKKNS	kidskin
DIIKLNS	dislink
DIIKNNR	drink in
DIILLVY	lividly
DIILMNS	dislimn
DIILMOS	idolism
DIILMTY	timidly
DIILNWY	windily
DIILOST	idolist
DIILRTY	dirtily
DIILVVY	vividly
DIILYZZ	dizzily
DIIMNOR	midiron
DIIMSSS	dismiss
DIIMSUV	vidimus
DIINNOT	din into
	tondini
DIINOPT	dip into
DIINORS	sordini
DIINQSU	quids in
DIIORSV	divisor
DIJLMOR	Lord Jim
DIKKNRU	Dunkirk
DIKLNRY	kiln-dry
DIKLSUY	duskily
DIKNNOS	non-skid
DIKNOPW	kip down
DIKNORT	drink to
DIKNPRU	drink up
DIKOORT	drookit
DIKORSW	skid row
DILLOSY	solidly
DILLRUY	luridly
DILMNRU	drumlin
DILMOOY	moodily
DILMTUY	tumidly
DILNNSU	dunlins
DILNPSY	spindly
DILNRUW	run wild
DILOPVV	Plovdiv
DILORWY	rowdily
	wordily
DILOSSU	dulosis
	solidus
DILRYZZ	drizzly
DILSTUY	dustily
DIMMOST	midmost
DIMNNOS	donnism
DIMNNOT	not mind
DIMNOOR	Mindoro
DIMNOOS	dominos
DIMNOPU	impound
DIMNOTU	mind out
DIMNOUY	mind you
DIMORSW	misword
DIMSTUY	tidy sum
DINNOPR	non-drip
DINNOPW	pin down
DINNOSW	Swindon
DINOORS	indoors
	sordino
DINORSW	Windsor
DINORWW	windrow
DINOSTW	sit down
	sit-down
DINOSWW	Windows®
DINPRSY	spin-dry

Words marked ❑ can also be spelled with an initial capital letter

DIOORST	disroot
DIOOTTW	do to wit
DIOOTTX	Otto Dix
DIOPRST	disport
DIOPSST	dispost
DIORRST	stridor
DIORSTT	distort
DIOSSTU	studios
DIPRSTU	disrupt
DIPUVVY	divvy up
DJNOOTW	jot down
DLLORWY	worldly
DLMNOOO	old moon
DLMNOOU	Muldoon
DLMNOUU	unmould
DLMOSUU	modulus
DLNOOWW	lowdown
	low-down
DLNORUY	roundly
DLNOSUY	soundly
DLOOPST	Old Spot
DLOOPTY	tylopod
DLOOPUY	duopoly
DLOOPWY	plywood
DLOOTUU	out loud
DLOPRUY	proudly
DMNOOSS	Osmonds
DMNOOWW	mow down
DMORTUU	drum out
DNNOORU	round on
DNNOOSW	Snowdon
DNNORUW	run down
	rundown
	run-down
DNNOSUU	unsound
DNNOSUW	sundown
DNOORTU	orotund
DNOOTWW	two-down
DNOPRUU	round up
	round-up
DNOPTUW	put down
	putdown
	put-down
DNOPUUW	wound up
DOOORSU	odorous
DOOORTU	outdoor
DOOPRSY	prosody
DOOPRTU	drop out
	dropout
	drop-out

E

EEEEFRR	referee
EEEEGTX	exegete
EEEELMZ	leeze me
EEEENTT	entêtée
EEEFFFO	feoffee
EEEFGRU	refugee
EEEFHRS	shereef
EEEFILS	see life
EEEFLRV	Le Fever
EEEFMNR	freemen
EEEFORS	foresee
EEEFRRZ	freezer
EEEFRST	set free
EEEGHNW	wheenge
EEEGHRT	get here
EEEGILS	elegise
EEEGILZ	elegize
EEEGINP	epigene
EEEGINU	Eugenie
	Eugénie
EEEGIPR	perigee
EEEGLNR	en règle
EEEGLNT	genteel
EEEGMRR	remerge
EEEGNOS	Genoese
EEEGNRR	reneger
EEEGNRU	renegue
EEEGNRV	revenge
EEEGNSS	geneses
EEEGNTT	genette
EEEGNTV	get even
EEEGRRT	regreet
EEEHILW	wheelie
EEEHLLN	Hellene
EEEHLNW	enwheel
EEEHLPW	wheeple
EEEHLRW	Wheeler
EEEHLWZ	wheezle
EEEHNRW	whene'er
EEEHRRW	whereer
EEEIKLZ	Ezekiel
EEEILRV	relieve
EEEILVY	evil eye
EEEIMRT	eremite
EEEINQU	Queenie
EEEIRRV	reverie
EEEISTW	sweetie
EEEJPRS	jeepers
EEEKLLU	ukelele
EEEKLNR	kneeler
EEEKLNS	sleeken
EEEKLNX	Kleenex®
EEEKNPT	keepnet
EEELLST	Estelle
EEELMNT	element
EEELPRS	sleeper
EEELPRT	replete
EEELPST	steeple
EEELRTV	leveret
EEELSSY	eyeless
EEEMNSS	Nemeses
EEEMRRV	Vermeer
EEEMRTX	extreme
EEENNTT	entente
EEENPRT	terpene
EEENPRV	prevene
EEENPST	ensteep
	steepen
EEENPSX	expense
EEENRRS	sneerer
EEENRRT	enterer
	re-enter
EEENRRV	venerer
EEENRRW	renewer
EEENRRY	Nyerere
EEENRSZ	sneezer
EEENRTV	eventer
EEENRUV	revenue
	unreeve
EEENSSS	Essenes
EEENSTW	sweeten
EEEORSV	oversee
	see over
EEEORSY	eyesore
EEEPRSS	peeress
EEEPRST	estrepe
EEEPRSW	sweeper
EEEPRTU	Euterpe
EEEQSUZ	squeeze
EEERRRV	reverer
EEERRST	steerer
EEERRSV	reserve
	reverse
EEERSSS	seeress
EEERTTV	Everett
EEERTTW	tweeter
EEFFFNO	enfeoff
EEFFFOR	feoffer
EEFFGLU	effulge
EEFFINT	fifteen
EEFFJRY	Jeffrey
EEFFKOP	keep off
EEFFLOP	peel off
EEFFLOR	feel for
	reel off
EEFFORR	for free
	offerer
EEFFOST	toffees❑
EEFGILN	feeling
	fine leg
	fleeing
EEFGINR	feigner
	freeing
EEFGLLU	gleeful
EEFGLOR	foreleg
EEFHITZ	Heifetz
EEFHLNS	enflesh
EEFHLRS	herself
EEFHNRS	freshen
EEFHORT	thereof
EEFHORW	whereof
EEFHRRS	fresher
	refresh
EEFHRST	freshet
EEFIKLL	elflike
EEFIKPT	keep fit
	keep-fit
EEFILLX	flexile
EEFILOR	forelie
EEFILRT	fertile
EEFINNS	Fiennes

EEFINRR refiner
EEFINSS finesse
EEFIOSS seise of
EEFIOSZ seize of
EEFIRRR Ferrier
EEFIRRT ferrite
EEFIRSS Seferis
EEFIRST Seifert
EEFISTV festive
EEFKORS seek for
EEFLLRU fueller
EEFLLTY fleetly
EEFLNNO Fénelon
EEFLNOS one self
oneself
EEFLNRS Fresnel
EEFLNTW New Left
EEFLRRU ferrule
EEFLRTT fettler
EEFLRUX flexure
EEFMNOR foremen
EEFMNRT ferment
EEFMOSW some few
EEFMPRU perfume
EEFMTTU fumette
EEFNRTV fervent
EEFNSSW fewness
EEFOPRW weep for
EEFORRT refer to
EEFORRV for ever
forever
EEFOTTU fouetté
EEFPRSU perfuse
EEFRRTU refuter
EEFRSTT fetters
EEFRSTY Seyfert
EEGGIOR Georgie
EEGGLNO Geelong
EEGGNOR engorge
EEGGNST nest egg
EEGGORR regorge
EEGGORU gougère
EEGHINY hygiene
EEGHIRW weigher
EEGHIWZ gee whiz
EEGIJNR jeering
EEGIKNN keening
EEGIKNP keeping
EEGIKNR reeking
EEGIKNS seeking
EEGILLS Giselle
EEGILMN Leeming
EEGILNN Glennie
EEGILNP peeling
EEGILNR leering
reeling
EEGILNT gentile
EEGILST elegist
EEGIMMR immerge
EEGIMNR regimen
EEGIMNS seeming
EEGIMNT meeting
teeming
EEGIMRS remiges
EEGINNR enginer
ingener
EEGINNU genuine
ingénue
EEGINNV evening
V-engine
EEGINOP epigone
EEGINOR E-region
EEGINOS soignée
EEGINPP peeping
EEGINPR peering
EEGINPS seeping
EEGINPW weeping
EEGINRR Régnier
EEGINRT integer
EEGINRV veering
EEGINSS genesis❑
EEGINTV ventige
EEGINTX exigent
EEGIOST egotise
EEGIOTZ egotize
EEGIRRV griever
EEGIRST Steiger
EEGISTV vestige
EEGISTW get wise
EEGLLNN Lenglen
EEGLLSS legless
EEGLLTW get well
EEGLNOR ere long
erelong
EEGLNOZ lozenge
EEGLNRY greenly
EEGLNST Stengel
EEGLRST leg-rest
St Leger
EEGLSST get less
EEGMMRY gemmery
EEGMNST segment
EEGNORS Negroes
EEGNORV verge on
EEGNPUX expunge
EEGNSSU genuses
EEGOPRT protégé
EEGORTV get over
overget
EEGOSSS gessoes
EEGPRUX expurge
EEGRRSS regress
EEGRRST regrets
EEGRRUY Gruyère
EEGRSSU guesser
EEGRSTU gesture
EEHHRSY Hershey
EEHHRTW whether
EEHHSTW wheesht
EEHIKLT the like
EEHILOS Heloise
EEHILST sheltie
EEHILSX helixes
EEHIMPT epithem
EEHINNV Nineveh
EEHINOR heroine
EEHINRS henries
EEHINRT neither
therein
EEHINRW wherein
EEHIORS heroise
EEHIORZ heroize
EEHIPSV peevish
EEHIPTT epithet
EEHIRSS heiress
EEHIRST heister
EEHISTV thieves
EEHKLOY keyhole
EEHKLSS shekels
EEHKMST Sekhmet
EEHKNNT Kenneth
EEHKORT Roethke
EEHLLMP phellem
EEHLLSY Shelley
EEHLMMW whemmle
EEHLPRS helpers
EEHLPRT telpher
EEHLPST Elspeth
EEHLRST shelter
EEHLRSY sheerly
EEHLSSU hueless
EEHLSSV shelves
EEHMNOP phoneme
EEHMNOT The Omen
EEHMNRY mynheer
EEHMNTY Metheny
EEHMORT theorem
EEHNNOT none the
EEHNOPT potheen
EEHNORT not here
EEHNORW Erewhon
nowhere
EEHNOSW Wheeson
EEHNPST Stephen
EEHNSTU enthuse
EEHNSTV seventh
EEHOOPW whoopee
EEHOPRT the rope
EEHOPSS sheepos
EEHORRS Hereros
EEHORST here's to
heteros
so there
EEHORSU rehouse
EEHORSW whereso
EEHORTT thereto
EEHORTW whereto
EEHORVW however
whoever
EEHPRTU up there
EEHPSSU Ephesus
EEHRRTW Werther
wherret

EEHRTTW	whetter
EEHRVWY	whyever
EEHSSTU	Theseus
EEHSTUY	shut-eye
EEIIMRT	emeriti
EEIIMST	itemise
EEIIMTZ	itemize
EEIINRT	niterie
EEIINSY	Yenisei
EEIIRRV	rivière
EEIJMNZ	Jiménez
EEIKLLS	skellie
EEIKLNR	Lineker
EEIKNRS	Erskine
EEIKNWY	eye-wink
EEIKRST	keister
EEIKTTT	tektite
EEILLNV	Neville
EEILLOR	lorelei□
EEILLPS	ellipse
EEILLSV	Seville
EEILMMT	meltemi
EEILMOR	Molière
EEILMRU	Lumière
EEILMRV	vermeil
EEILNNO	leonine
EEILNNS	Nielsen
EEILNNT	lenient
	Tenniel
EEILNNV	enliven
EEILNOV	Evil One
EEILNPS	pensile
	sleep in
EEILNRV	revel in
EEILNST	setline
	tensile
EEILNTT	entitle
	Linette
EEILNTV	veinlet
EEILOPT	petiole
EEILORT	troelie
EEILORV	overlie
	relievo
EEILOTZ	zeolite
EEILPRR	replier
EEILPRS	spieler
EEILPRT	perlite
	reptile
EEILPRU	puerile
EEILPSS	pelisse
EEILPST	epistle
EEILRRV	reliver
	reviler
EEILRST	leister
	sterile
EEILRSU	leisure
EEILRSV	servile
EEILSSS	sessile
EEILSSU	ileuses
EEILSTT	Lisette
EEILSUV	elusive
EEILTTX	textile
EEILVWY	weevily
EEIMMNS	immense
EEIMMRS	immerse
EEIMNNO	nominee
EEIMNNT	eminent
EEIMNOT	one time
	one-time
EEIMNRT	Meitner
EEIMNRV	minever
EEIMNSS	Meissen
	nemesis□
	siemens□
EEIMNST	Steinem
EEIMNSX	Ximenes
EEIMOPT	epitome
EEIMOSS	meioses
EEIMOTV	emotive
EEIMPRR	premier
EEIMPRS	premise
EEIMPST	empties
	septime
EEIMQRU	requiem□
EEIMRRT	trireme
EEIMRST	meister
EEIMRTT	termite
EEIMSST	it seems
	Métisse
EEINNNP	pennine
EEINNPS	pennies
EEINNRT	interne
EEINNRV	innerve
EEINNST	intense
EEINNTT	Ninette
EEINNTW	entwine
EEINOPR	pioneer
EEINPRS	erepsin
EEINPRT	Petrine
EEINPRZ	prenzie
EEINPST	Epstein
EEINPSV	pensive
EEINQRU	enquire
EEINQTU	quieten
EEINRRT	terrine
EEINRRV	vernier□
EEINRST	Steiner
EEINRSV	inverse
EEINRSY	Erinyes
EEINRTU	retinue
	reunite
	uterine
EEINSTU	en suite
EEINSTX	sixteen
EEIOPST	poetise
EEIOPTZ	poetize
EEIORSV	erosive
EEIOSST	isoetes
EEIPPST	peptise
EEIPPTT	pipette
EEIPPTZ	peptize
EEIPQRU	perique
	re-equip
	repique
EEIPRRR	Perrier®
EEIPRRS	reprise
	respire
EEIPRSS	pressie
EEIPRST	respite
EEIPRSV	previse
EEIPRVW	preview
EEIPRZZ	prezzie
EEIPSUZ	seize up
EEIQRRU	require
EEIQRSU	esquire□
EEIQRTU	requite
EEIRRRT	terrier
EEIRRSV	reviser
EEIRRTW	rewrite
EEIRRVV	reviver
EEIRSTT	Trieste
EEIRSTV	restive
	sievert
EEIRSUZ	seizure
EEIRSVW	reviews
	viewers
EEJNORS	rejones
EEJOSTT	Josette
EEJPRRU	perjure
EEKKRRT	trekker
EEKLLSY	sleekly
EEKLLUU	ukulele
EEKLMRZ	klezmer
EEKLNOS	keelson
EEKLOOS	look-see
EEKLRST	kestrel
	skelter
EEKLSSY	keyless
EEKMMPU	keep mum
EEKMNOS	Monkees
EEKNOTY	keynote
EEKNPSU	knees-up
EEKNSST	Knesset
EEKNSTU	netsuke
EEKOPTU	keep out
EEKOSTU	seek out
EELLMOS	moselle□
EELLMRS	smeller
EELLNOV	novelle
EELLPRS	pre-sell
EELLPST	pellets
EELLPUV	level up
EELLQRU	queller
EELLRSS	Sellers
EELMOPP	M People
EELMORW	eelworm
EELMPST	temples
EELMPTT	templet
EELMRSU	Lemures
EELMSTT	stemlet
EELNOPS	on sleep
	sleep on
EELNOPV	envelop

EELNOST	Leontes
EELNOSV	Slovene
EELNOTT	notelet
EELNOTU	toluene
EELNPSY	spleeny
EELNQUY	queenly
EELNSTU	unsteel
EELNSTY	tensely
EELNTTU	lunette
EELNTTY	Lynette
EELOPPS	peoples
EELOPRX	explore
EELOPTU	eelpout
EELORSS	Loesser
EELORSV	resolve
EELORTT	lorette
EELORVV	revolve
EELOTUV	evolute
	velouté
EELPPRX	perplex
EELPQRU	prequel
EELPRST	Prestel®
	spelter
EELPRSU	repulse□
EELPRSY	Presley
EELPRTZ	pretzel
EELPRVY	replevy
EELPSSS	Lesseps
EELPSTY	steeply
EELQRUY	queerly
EELRRVY	revelry
EELRSTT	letters
	settler
	trestle
EELRSTW	swelter
	wrestle
EELRSTY	restyle
	tersely
EELRSTZ	seltzer
EELSSSU	use less
	useless
EELSSSX	sexless
EELSTWY	sweetly
EELTVVY	velvety
EEMMNOT	memento
EEMNNOV	envenom
EEMNOOS	someone
EEMNORS	Emerson
EEMNOST	stone me!
EEMNOSW	Newsome
EEMNPTU	umpteen
EEMOOSW	woesome
EEMOPRR	emperor
EEMOPRV	premove
EEMOPRW	empower
EEMORRS	remorse
EEMORRT	remoter
EEMORRV	remover
EEMOTTU	mete out
EEMPPRT	pre-empt
EEMPRRT	preterm
EEMPRSS	empress
EEMPRSU	presume
	supreme
	suprême
EEMPRTT	tempter
EEMPRTU	permute
EEMPSTT	tempest
EEMRRUU	remueur
EEMRSUX	murexes
EENNORT	enter on
EENNORU	neurone
EENNOSS	oneness
EENNOTY	neoteny
EENNOVW	even now
EENNPTU	Neptune
EENNQUU	unqueen
EENNRUV	unnerve
EENNSSU	unsense
EENNSSW	newness
EENNSTT	Sennett
EENOPPR	prepone
EENOPRS	Penrose
EENOPST	en poste
	one-step
	pentose
EENORRV	overren
EENORTU	en route
EENORTV	not ever
	overnet
EENOSTV	ventose
EENOSTW	sweet on
EENOTUV	even out
EENPRSS	Serpens
	Spenser
EENPRST	present
	serpent□
EENPRSV	Pevsner
EENPRTV	prevent
EENPSTU	tense up
EENQSTU	sequent
EENRRTY	re-entry
EENRRUV	nervure
EENRSTT	testern
EENRSTW	western
EENRSTY	styrene
EENRTTU	nut-tree
EENRTUV	venture
EENRUVY	Nureyev
EENSSTV	Stevens
EENSSTW	wetness
EENSTVY	seventy
EEOPPRS	prepose
EEOPRRV	reprove
EEOPRTT	treetop
EEOPRTU	outpeer
EEOPSSS	speoses
EEOPSST	poetess
EEOPSSU	espouse
	poseuse
EEOPSTU	seep out
EEOPTUW	outweep
EEORRST	restore
EEORRTU	reroute
EEORSST	Orestes
	stereos
EEORSTT	rosette
EEORSTV	overset
EEORSUV	overuse
EEORSVW	oversew
EEPPPRY	peppery
EEPPRST	stepper
EEPPRSX	Perspex®
EEPPSUY	eupepsy
EEPQUUU	queue up
EEPRRSS	repress
	re-press
EEPRRSU	peruser
EEPRRTV	pervert
EEPRSSU	Perseus
EEPRSSV	vespers
EEPRSSX	express
EEPRSTU	pertuse
EEPRSTX	sexpert
EEPRSUV	serve up
EEPRTTX	pretext
EEPSTTY	typeset
EEQRRUY	equerry
EEQRSSU	Squeers
EEQRSTU	quester
	request
EEQSUYZ	squeezy
EERRSTW	strewer
	wrester
EERRSVW	swerver
EERSSST	tresses
EERSSTU	Surtees
EERSSUV	Severus
EERSSUY	seysure
EERSTTT	strette
EERSTTU	trustee
EERSTUV	vesture
EERTTUX	texture
EFFFILO	file off
EFFFIOR	fire off
EFFFOOR	feoffor
EFFGIOV	give off
EFFGNOO	gone off
EFFHILW	whiffle
EFFHIOV	hive off
EFFHIRS	sheriff
EFFHLSU	shuffle
EFFIIST	fifties
	stiffie
EFFIKLS	skiffle
EFFILNO	off line
	off-line
EFFILNS	sniffle
EFFILOR	for life
EFFILOV	live off
EFFILRY	firefly
EFFIMOT	time off
EFFINRS	sniffer

EFFINST	stiffen
EFFIORT	forfeit
EFFIOST	off-site
EFFJKOR	jerk off
EFFLLOS	sell off
EFFLLOT	tell off
EFFLLOW	well off
	well-off
EFFLMRU	muffler
EFFLNSU	snuffle
EFFLOSU	souffle
	soufflé
EFFLRTU	fretful
	truffle
EFFNOOR	on offer
EFFNRSU	snuffer
EFFNRUU	unruffe
EFFOORR	offeror
EFFOPRR	proffer
EFFOPRU	offer up
EFFOPST	step off
EFFSSUU	suffuse
EFGGILP	egg-flip
EFGGIRY	figgery
EFGHIRT	fighter
	freight
EFGILMN	Fleming
EFGIMNT	figment
EFGINNP	pfennig□
EFGINOR	foreign
EFGINRS	fringes
EFGINRU	gunfire
EFGIORV	forgive
EFGIRSU	figures
EFGLNTU	fulgent
EFGLOOT	let go of
EFGLOSS	fogless
EFGORRY	forgery
EFHILMS	Flemish
	himself
EFHILNS	in flesh
EFHILSS	selfish
EFHILTY	heftily
EFHIMNO	Meinhof
EFHINNS	fennish
EFHINST	fishnet
EFHIOTV	Hot Five
EFHIRSY	fishery
EFHLLPU	helpful
EFHLLSY	fleshly
EFHLNSU	unflesh
EFHLOOT	The Fool
EFHLOOX	foxhole
EFHLOPU	hopeful□
EFHLRSY	freshly
EFHLTTW	twelfth
EFHNORT	forhent
EFHOOPR	hope for
EFHRRTU	further
EFHTUZZ	the fuzz
EFIIINR	in fieri
EFIILLN	Fellini
EFIILMS	misfile
EFIILRY	fierily
EFIILSS	fissile
EFIIMRS	misfire
EFIINRU	unifier
EFIISSV	fissive
EFIJLLY	jellify
EFIKLNU	like fun
EFIKRRS	frisker
EFILLOO	foliole
EFILLOS	Follies
EFILMST	film set
	filmset
	leftism
EFILNOX	flexion
EFILNSS	finless
EFILOOS	floosie
	foliose
EFILOOZ	floozie
EFILOPR	profile
	pro-life
EFILORR	Florrie
EFILORT	loftier
	trefoil
EFILORV	live for
EFILOSS	Flossie
EFILPPR	flipper
EFILPPU	pipeful
EFILPTT	felt-tip
EFILQUY	liquefy
EFILRRT	trifler
EFILRST	stifler
	trifles
EFILRTT	flitter
EFILRZZ	frizzle
EFILSTT	leftist
EFILUVX	fluxive
EFIMMRU	fermium
EFIMNOR	fermion
EFIMNTT	fitment
EFIMOST	fomites
EFIMTTU	fumetti
EFINNOR	inferno
EFINNRU	funnier
EFINNSU	funnies
EFINOPR	pine for
EFINOPU	fie upon
EFINSST	fitness
EFIOOST	footsie□
EFIOPST	spite of
EFIORRT	rotifer
EFIORRU	Fourier
EFIORST	forties□
EFIORTU	fire out
EFIPRTY	petrify
EFIRRRU	furrier
EFIRRSU	friseur
EFIRRTT	fritter
EFIRRTU	friture
	fruiter
EFIRRTY	terrify
EFIRSSU	fissure
EFIRSTU	surfeit
EFIRSVY	versify
EFIRTUV	furtive
EFIRTUX	fixture
EFISTTY	testify
EFJLSTU	jestful
EFKLMNO	menfolk
EFKLNUY	flunkey
EFKLPSU	skepful
EFKNOPU	poke fun
EFLLMOS	smell of
EFLLORS	sell for
EFLLOSW	fellows
EFLMOSU	fulsome
EFLMPRU	frumple
EFLMSUU	museful
EFLNOPY	fly open
EFLNSSU	fulness
EFLNTUU	tuneful
EFLOORR	floorer
EFLOORV	for love
EFLOORY	foolery
EFLORSW	flowers
EFLORTU	flouter
EFLORVY	flyover
	overfly
EFLORWY	flowery
EFLOSSW	self-sow
EFLPRUY	preyful
EFLRSTU	fluster
	restful
EFLRTTU	flutter
EFLSTTY	test-fly
EFLSTUZ	zestful
EFMNOOT	footmen
EFMOPRR	perform
	preform
EFMOPRT	pomfret
EFMPRUY	perfumy
EFNNORT	fornent
EFNNOTU	unoften
EFNNOTY	Fonteyn
EFNOOST	festoon
EFNOOSU	one of us
EFNORRU	forerun
EFNORTU	fortune□
EFOOPRR	reproof
EFOOPRS	spoofer
EFOOPRT	foretop
EFOORTV	vote for
EFOORTW	woofter
EFOOSTU	of use to
EFOPPRY	foppery
EFOPRSS	profess
EFOPRSU	profuse
EFOPRTU	poufter
EFOPRTY	torpefy
EFORRST	Forrest
	Forster

EFORRSU	ferrous
	for sure
EFORRTY	torrefy
EFORRUV	fervour
EFOSSTT	Fossett
EFPRTUY	putrefy
EFPSTUY	stupefy
EGGGILR	giggler
EGGGLOS	goggles
EGGHLOS	shoggle
EGGILNR	niggler
EGGILNS	sniggle
EGGILRW	wiggler
	wriggle
EGGIMNR	merging
EGGINNS	ginseng
EGGINOR	Goering
EGGINRS	snigger
EGGINRV	verging
EGGINRY	gingery
	greying
EGGINTT	getting
EGGINTW	twiggen
EGGIPRY	piggery
EGGIRRT	trigger
EGGJLRU	juggler
EGGLLNO	long leg
EGGLMSU	smuggle
EGGLNSU	snuggle
EGGLOOY	geology
EGGLORS	slogger
EGGLPRU	plugger
EGGNTUY	nuggety
EGGORRY	Gregory
EGGSSTU	suggest
EGHHHIO	heigh-ho
EGHHIKY	high-key
EGHHIMN	highmen
EGHHIST	highest
EGHHOSW	showghe
EGHIILL	ghillie
EGHIINT	nightie
EGHIINV	inveigh
EGHIINW	weigh in
	weigh-in
EGHIKNR	gherkin
EGHIKRS	skreigh
EGHILNP	helping
EGHILNS	English
	shingle
EGHILNT	lighten
EGHILRT	lighter
EGHILST	sleight
EGHINNO	hinge on
EGHINNU	unhinge
EGHINRR	herring
EGHINRT	The Ring
	the ring
EGHINRW	whinger
EGHINTT	tighten
EGHIOOS	shoogie
EGHIORS	ogreish
EGHIOTU	toughie
EGHIOTW	go white
EGHIPUW	weigh up
EGHIRSY	greyish
EGHIRTU	Guthrie
EGHITWY	weighty
EGHLLSW	H G Wells
EGHLMPY	phlegmy
EGHLNOR	leghorn□
EGHLNST	lengths
EGHLNTY	lengthy
EGHLOOS	shoogle
EGHMOSU	gumshoe
EGHMOSY	gym shoe
EGHNOOT	on the go
EGHNORU	roughen
EGHNOTU	toughen
EGHNSUY	Huygens
EGHNTWY	Gwenyth
	Gwyneth
EGHOSTT	ghettos
EGHRTUY	theurgy
EGIILNT	lignite
EGIILNV	veiling
EGIILPZ	Leipzig
EGIIMNP	impinge
EGIIMNS	Geminis
EGIIMSV	misgive
EGIINOP	epigoni
EGIINRT	igniter
EGIINSZ	seizing
EGIINVW	viewing
EGIIPRW	periwig
EGIJLNR	jingler
EGIJNOS	jingoes
EGIJNST	jesting
EGILLMU	Guillem
EGILLNS	selling
EGILLNT	telling
EGILLNW	welling
EGILLNY	yelling
EGILLPS	leg slip
EGILLSU	gullies
EGILMMN	lemming
EGILMMR	glimmer
EGILMNR	gremlin
	mingler
EGILMNT	melting
EGILMOS	Limoges
EGILMOV	Mogilev
EGILMPS	glimpse
EGILNOR	Goneril
	leg-iron
EGILNOS	legions
	lingoes
	sloe gin
EGILNOW	Niel Gow
EGILNPS	leg spin
EGILNRT	ringlet
EGILNSS	Lessing
EGILNST	glisten
	singlet
EGILNSW	swingle
EGILNVY	levying
EGILOOS	goolies
EGILOTT	let it go
EGILRST	gristle
EGILRTT	glitter
EGILRUV	virgule
EGILRZZ	grizzle
EGILSSW	wigless
EGIMNOU	Minogue
EGIMNPT	pigment
EGIMOST	egotism
EGINNOP	opening
EGINNOT	get in on
EGINNPU	penguin
EGINNRT	renting
EGINNST	tensing
EGINNSU	ensuing
EGINNTT	netting
EGINNTV	venting
EGINNTZ	Tenzing
EGINOPS	pingoes
EGINORR	ignorer
EGINORS	Signore
EGINORT	Negrito
EGINOSU	igneous
EGINOTT	get in to
	get into
	get it on
EGINOTV	given to
EGINOUV	in vogue
EGINPRS	springe
EGINPRY	preying
EGINPSW	spewing
EGINPTT	petting
EGINRRW	wringer
EGINRSS	ingress
	singers
EGINRST	resting
	stinger
EGINRSV	serving
	versing
EGINRSW	swinger
EGINRSY	syringe
EGINRTT	gittern
EGINSTT	setting
	testing
EGINTTV	vetting
EGIOPRT	ego-trip
EGIOPRU	groupie
EGIORTV	vertigo
EGIOSTT	egotist
EGIOTUV	give out
EGIPPRR	gripper
EGIPPSU	guppies
EGIPRUU	guipure
EGIRRTT	gritter
EGIRSST	tigress
EGIRSSU	Sergius

EGISUWY	wise guy
EGKLORW	legwork
EGKRTYZ	Gretzky
EGLLLPU	leg-pull
EGLLNNU	Gunnell
EGLLSUY	gulleys
EGLMNOO	engloom
EGLMNOR	mongrel
EGLMOOR	legroom
EGLMORY	Gormley
EGLNORU	lounger
EGLNPRU	plunger
EGLNRTU	gruntle
EGLOORW	go lower
EGLOPSS	Gospels
EGLORRW	growler
EGLORSS	glosser
EGLOSTT	get lost
	get lost!
EGLPRSU	splurge
EGLRSUU	regulus
EGLRUZZ	guzzler
EGLSSTU	gutless
EGLSTUU	gluteus
	Telugus
EGMMORT	grommet
EGMMRTU	grummet
EGMNOOT	Montego
EGMNORU	murgeon
EGMORTU	gourmet
EGNNOPU	gen up on
EGNNORT	röntgen□
EGNNPTU	pungent
EGNNRSU	Gunners
EGNNRUY	gunnery
EGNNSTU	sten gun□
EGNNTUU	unguent
EGNOOPS	pongoes
EGNOORY	orogeny
EGNOOTT	get onto
EGNOPRS	sponger
EGNOPRY	progeny
	pyrogen
EGNORRW	wronger
EGNORSS	engross
EGNORSU	surgeon
EGNORSY	eryngos
EGNORUY	younger
EGNRRTU	grunter
EGNRSYY	synergy
EGOOSTU	outgoes
EGOPRRS	gropers
EGOPRRU	grouper
	regroup
EGOPRUY	guy-rope
EGOPTTU	get up to
EGORRSU	grouser
EGORRUY	roguery
EGPRSUU	upsurge
EGRRSUY	surgery
EHHILLS	hellish
EHHINRS	Rhenish
EHHIRTW	whither
EHHITTW	T H White
EHHOSTT	the hots
EHHPSTU	the push
EHHRSTU	the rush
EHIINRT	inherit
EHIITVW	vie with
EHIJNNO	johnnie□
EHIKNRT	rethink
	thinker
EHIKNST	Kentish
EHIKRRS	shirker
EHIKRSW	whisker
EHIKSST	The Kiss
EHIKSVZ	Izhevsk
EHIKSWY	whiskey
EHILLNO	hellion
EHILLNS	inshell
EHILLOS	Hollies
EHILLTY	lithely
EHILNOP	pinhole
EHILNOS	in holes
EHILNOT	hot line
	neolith
EHILOST	hostile
	Sithole
EHILPPW	Whipple
EHILPRT	philtre
EHILRRW	whirler
EHILRST	slither
EHILRSV	shrivel
EHILRSY	Shirley
EHILSTT	thistle
EHILSTW	whistle
EHILTTW	whittle□
EHIMMPS	Memphis
EHIMMRS	shimmer
EHIMNNU	Menuhin
EHIMNPS	shipmen
EHIMNRU	rhenium
EHIMNTY	thymine
EHIMOPT	Imhotep
EHIMORS	heroism
	moreish
EHIMORT	moither
EHIMORZ	rhizome
EHIMPRW	whimper
EHIMSTY	mythise
EHIMSWY	whimsey
EHIMTYZ	mythize
EHINNOS	shine on
EHINNOT	on the in
EHINNRT	thinner
EHINOPX	phoenix□
EHINORS	inshore
EHINOST	histone
EHINOSU	heinous
	in-house
EHINPRT	Penrith
EHINRSU	usher in
EHINRVY	Henry IV
	Henry VI
EHINSST	sithens
EHINSSU	Hussein
EHIORRT	heritor
EHIORST	hoister
	shortie
EHIORSY	hosiery
EHIORTU	hire out
	outhire
EHIORTV	overhit
EHIORTW	hot-wire
EHIOSTY	isohyet
EHIPPRW	whipper
EHIPPTW	whippet
EHIPRSW	whisper
EHIPSTT	pettish
	the pits
EHIRSSV	shivers
EHIRSTU	hirsute
EHIRSTW	swither
	withers
EHIRSVY	shivery
EHIRTTW	whitter
EHISSTU	Hussite
	stushie
EHISTTW	wettish
EHJLOOY	holy Joe
EHKNORS	Kherson
EHKNRSU	hunkers
EHLLNSU	unshell
EHLLOOS	holloes
EHLLOOT	Othello
EHLMNOT	menthol
EHLMOTT	hot melt
EHLMPTU	the lump
EHLNOOY	Holy One
EHLNTTY	tenthly
EHLOOPT	pothole
	top-hole
EHLOOST	Lesotho
EHLOOTU	hole out
EHLOPSX	phloxes
EHLOPSY	spyhole
EHLOPTU	help out
EHLORST	holster
EHLRSSU	Husserl
EHLRSTU	hustler□
EHLSSTT	shtetls
EHLSTTU	shuttle
EHMNOOR	hormone
	moorhen
EHMNORT	the morn
EHMNOST	Thomsen
EHMNPTY	nymphet
EHMNTTU	hutment
EHMOOSS	shmoose
EHMOOSW	somehow
EHMOOSZ	shmooze
EHMOPRT	Morpeth
EHMORST	smother

EHMOTUX	Exmouth
EHMPRWY	Whymper
EHMRSUU	humerus
EHNNOPR	nephron
EHNNOTW	now then!
EHNOOPR	no-hoper
EHNOORS	onshore
	on-shore
EHNOPPU	phone up
EHNOPRY	hyperon
EHNOPTU	on the up
EHNOPUY	euphony
EHNOQTT	on the QT
EHNORRT	norther
EHNORRY	heronry
EHNORST	Hornets
	shorten
	threnos
EHNORSU	unhorse
EHNOSST	hotness
EHNOSTY	honesty
EHNOSUU	unhouse
EHNRSTU	Nerthus
	shunter
	the runs
	unherst
EHNSSSY	shyness
EHOOPRW	whooper
EHOORST	shooter
	soother
EHOPPRS	shopper
EHOPPRT	prophet
EHOPPRW	whopper
EHOPRRY	orphrey
EHOPRST	strophe
EHOPRSU	Orpheus
	shore up
EHOPSTT	the tops
EHOPSTU	the soup
EHORRST	Shorter
EHORSTU	shouter
	souther
EHORSWY	showery
EHORTUX	Theroux
EHOSSST	hostess
EHOSTUY	Southey
EHPPRTU	Huppert
EHPRTTU	turpeth
EHRSSTY	shyster
	thyrses
EHRSTTU	shutter
EHRSTTW	strewth
EIIILRV	rilievi
EIIINPR	ripieni
EIIKNSS	kinesis
EIILLNV	villein
EIILLSW	willies
EIILLTV	vitelli
EIILMNT	Minitel
EIILMPR	imperil
EIILMRS	milreis

EIILMRT	Leitrim
	limiter
EIILMSS	missile
	similes
EIILMST	elitism
	limites
EIILMSU	milieus
EIILMUX	milieux
EIILNOS	elision
	lionise
EIILNOT	etiolin
EIILNOV	olivine
EIILNOZ	lionize
EIILORV	Olivier
	rilievo
EIILSTT	elitist
	élitist
EIILSTU	utilise
EIILTUZ	utilize
EIIMMSS	mimesis
EIIMMST	mistime
EIIMNRT	interim
	termini
EIIMNRV	miniver
EIIMOPP	Pompeii
EIIMOSS	meiosis
EIIMPST	pietism
EIIMPTY	impiety
EIIMSSV	missive
EIIMSSZ	sizeism
EIINNQU	quinine
EIINNSW	insinew
EIINNTW	intwine
EIINOPR	ripieno
EIINORS	ioniser
	ironise
EIINORZ	ionizer
	ironize
EIINPRS	inspire
EIINQRU	inquire
EIINRTT	nitrite
EIINRTW	write in
EIINSTT	tiniest
EIINSTU	unitise
EIINTUV	unitive
EIINTUZ	unitize
EIIOPRT	Poitier
EIIPSTT	pietist
EIIQQUU	Iquique
EIIRSTV	revisit
EIISSTX	sixties
EIISSTZ	sizeist
EIJKLRY	jerkily
EIJKNNS	Jenkins
EIJLLNY	injelly
EIJNORY	joinery
EIJNPRU	juniper
EIJNSTU	Justine
EIJPRTU	Jupiter
EIJRSTT	jitters
EIJRTTY	jittery

EIJSSTU	Jesuits
EIKKLNR	klinker
EIKKLRS	Selkirk
EIKLLNW	inkwell
EIKLLOW	owl-like
EIKLLRS	reskill
EIKLLST	skillet
EIKLMNR	kremlin
EIKLNOT	liken to
	Tolkien
EIKLNRW	Winkler
	wrinkle
EIKLNSU	sunlike
EIKLNSY	skyline
EIKLNTW	twinkle
EIKLPRY	perkily
EIKLPSY	peskily
EIKLSTT	skittle
EIKMMRR	krimmer
EIKMMRS	skimmer
EIKMNNS	kinsmen
EIKMNOR	moniker
EIKMORS	irksome
EIKMOSS	Eskimos
EIKMOSY	misyoke
EIKMRSS	kirmess
EIKNNRS	Skinner
EIKNOPS	pinkoes
EIKNPRS	Perkins
EIKNRST	stinker
EIKNRTT	knitter
	trinket
EIKOPRS	porkies
EIKOSST	ketosis
EIKPPRS	skipper
EIKPPST	skippet
EIKRRST	striker
EIKRSTT	skitter
EIKRSTU	turkies
EILLLOW	oil well
EILLLTW	well-lit
EILLMNU	mullein
EILLMST	mistell
EILLNNP	pennill
EILLNOS	niellos
EILLNSS	illness
EILLORU	rouille
EILLORY	O'Reilly
EILLOSV	villose
EILLPPP	pep pill
EILLPST	let slip
EILLRST	trellis
EILLSTW	Sitwell
EILMMRS	slimmer
EILMNOS	smile on
EILMOPR	implore
EILMOSS	lissome
EILMPPU	plum pie
EILMPRS	prelims
EILMPRY	primely
EILMPSU	impulse

EILMPTY	emptily	EILPSTU	stipule	EIMOTTW	two-time
EILMRRY	merrily	EILPSUZ	spulzie	EIMOTVV	TV movie
EILMRSS	rimless	EILPTTY	pettily	EIMPRSS	impress
EILMRSU	misrule	EILQRTU	quilter		premiss
EILMRSY	miserly	EILQRUU	liqueur	EIMPRST	imprest
EILMSSY	messily	EILQTUY	quietly	EIMPSST	misstep
EILMSTU	Miletus	EILRRTW	twirler	EIMPSTU	impetus
EILMSUY	Elysium	EILRSTT	slitter	EIMRSSU	misuser
EILNNOT	let in on	EILRSUW	wurlies		surmise
EILNNPU	pinnule	EILRSVY	silvery	EIMRTUX	mixture
EILNOOR	loonier		silver-Y	EIMSTTV	TV Times
EILNOOS	loonies	EILRSZZ	sizzler	EINNOPS	pension
EILNOPR	proline	EILRTTY	tritely	EINNOQU	quinone
EILNOPS	epsilon	EILRTUV	rivulet	EINNORU	reunion
EILNOPT	topline	EILSSTW	witless		Réunion
EILNORT	retinol	EILSSTY	stylise	EINNORV	environ
EILNOSS	lioness	EILSTTY	stylite	EINNOST	tension
EILNOST	Nilotes		testily	EINNOSV	venison
EILNOTT	let into	EILSTYZ	stylize	EINNOTT	nonetti
EILNOTU	outline	EILSWZZ	swizzle		tontine
EILNOTV	violent	EILTWZZ	twizzle	EINNPRS	spinner
EILNOTW	towline	EIMMORS	memoirs	EINNPRT	enprint
EILNOVV	involve	EIMMPRU	premium	EINNPSY	spinney
EILNPRS	Pilsner	EIMMRRT	trimmer	EINNQTU	Quentin
EILNPRU	purline	EIMMRST	misterm	EINNRTV	vintner
EILNPSU	spinule	EIMMRSW	swimmer	EINNSSY	sinsyne
EILNPTY	ineptly	EIMMSTZ	tzimmes	EINNSUW	unsinew
EILNPUV	liven up	EIMNNOS	Simenon	EINNTUW	untwine
	vulpine	EIMNNOT	mention	EINOOPZ	epizoon
EILNRST	snirtle	EIMNOOR	ionomer	EINOORR	iron ore
EILNRTY	inertly	EIMNOOS	Moonies	EINOORS	erosion
EILNRVY	nervily		noisome	EINOOSZ	ozonise
EILNSSS	sinless	EIMNOOT	emotion	EINOOZZ	ozonize
EILNSSU	silenus ❑	EIMNOPS	peonism	EINOPRT	pointer
EILNSTU	utensil	EIMNOPT	emption		protein
EILNSTY	in style		pimento		repoint
	Yeltsin	EIMNORS	merinos	EINOPRV	provine
EILNTUX	exult in	EIMNOST	moisten	EINOPRW	in power
EILNVXY	vixenly	EIMNOSW	winsome	EINOPSS	in posse
EILOORT	troolie	EIMNOTT	Menotti		spinose
EILOPRS	spoiler	EIMNOTU	mountie ❑	EINOPST	pointes
EILOPST	pistole	EIMNPTU	Pentium®	EINOQUX	equinox
EILOPSU	pileous	EIMNRST	entrism	EINORRR	in error
EILOPSV	plosive		minster	EINORST	in store
EILOPTX	exploit	EIMNRTU	run time		in-store
EILORSS	rissole	EIMNSTT	mist-net	EINORSV	version
EILORTT	triolet		smitten	EINORTT	tritone
EILORTU	outlier	EIMNSTU	minutes	EINORTU	in utero
EILOSTT	litotes		mistune		routine
	T S Eliot	EIMNUZZ	muezzin	EINORTV	Trevino
EILOTUV	live out	EIMOPRS	imposer	EINORVW	win over
	outlive		promise	EINOSSS	session
EILPPRS	slipper	EIMOPRV	improve	EINOSST	sonties
EILPPRT	ripplet	EIMOPST	imposte	EINOSUV	envious
	tippler	EIMORST	mortise		niveous
	tripple	EIMOSST	mitoses	EINPPRS	nippers
EILPPST	stipple	EIMOSTV	motives		snipper
EILPRST	spirtle	EIMOSTZ	mestizo	EINPPST	snippet
EILPRTT	triplet	EIMOTTU	Time Out	EINPRRT	printer
EILPRUU	purlieu		time out		reprint
EILPSTT	spittle		time-out	EINPRRZ	Prizren

EINQRUY	enquiry
EINQSTU	inquest
EINQTTU	quintet
EINQTUU	unquiet
EINRRSU	insurer
EINRSSU	sunrise
EINRSTT	entrist
	stinter
EINRSTV	Ventris
EINRTTW	written
EINRTUV	unrivet
	Venturi
EINRTUW	unwrite
EINRTWY	wintery
EINSSSU	Senussi
	sinuses
EINSSTW	witness
EINSSUW	sunwise
EINSTTW	entwist
	twin-set
EINTTUY	tenuity
EIOOPST	isotope
EIOORTV	Orvieto
EIOOSTT	tootsie□
EIOPRRT	pierrot□
EIOPRST	reposit
	riposte
EIOPRTV	tip over
EIOPSTU	piteous
EIOPTUW	wipe out
	wipeout
EIOQRTU	quoiter
EIOQSTU	quite so
EIORRRW	worrier
EIORRST	roister
EIORRSW	worries
EIORSST	stories
EIORSSU	serious
EIORSTT	stoiter
EIORTTU	tire out
EIORTTV	tortive
EIORTTW	write to
EIOSSTV	stovies
EIOSTUZ	outsize
EIPPRRT	tripper
EIPPTTT	Tippett
EIPRSST	persist
	stirpes
EIPRSSU	Persius
	suspire
EIPRSTT	spitter
	tipster
EIPRSTY	pyrites
EIPRTUW	write up
	write-up
EIPRUVW	purview
EIPSTUW	put wise
EIQRSTU	querist
EIQRTTU	quitter
EIQRUVY	quivery
EIQRUZZ	quizzer
EIQSTUU	quietus
EIQSUZZ	quizzes
EIRRRST	stirrer
EIRSSUV	viruses
EIRSTTT	stretti
EIRSTTW	twister
EIRSUVV	survive
EIRSUVW	surview
EIRTTTW	twitter
EISSSSW	Swisses
EISSTUV	tussive
EISTTUW	wet suit
EJJMNUU	jejunum
EJJMPTU	jump-jet
EJLOSSY	joyless
EJMNRUY	jurymen
EJNORRU	rejourn
EJNORUY	journey
EJOORVY	overjoy
EJORSTU	jouster
EJORSUU	suo jure
EJOSTTU	outjest
EJPRRUY	perjury
EKKLRSU	skulker
EKKOPSU	pukekos
EKLMSUY	Slumkey
EKLNOOW	new look
EKLNOPR	plonker
EKLNORS	snorkel
EKLNOST	Skelton
EKLNOSY	Lysenko
EKLNOTW	let know
EKLORSU	rules OK
EKMNORW	workmen
EKMNOSY	monkeys
	monkey's
EKMNPTU	unkempt
EKMNRTU	Turkmen
EKNOORS	snooker
EKNORST	stonker
EKNORSY	Yonkers
EKNORTW	network
EKNORWY	New York
EKNRTUY	turnkey
EKNSTUZ	Kuznets
EKOOPRV	provoke
EKOOPTU	poke out
EKOORRY	rookery
EKOORST	stooker
EKOPRUY	kouprey
EKOPSTU	stoke up
EKORRSW	workers
EKPPSUU	seppuku
ELLMOOR	morello
ELLMORS	Mellors
ELLMPUU	plumule
ELLNOOV	Novello
ELLNOOW	woollen
ELLNOST	stollen
ELLNOSU	nousell
ELLNOSW	swollen
ELLNPSU	unspell
ELLNRUW	well-run
ELLOOSW	woosell
ELLOOSY	loosely
ELLOOWY	Woolley
ELLOPTU	pollute
ELLORTY	trolley
ELLOSTU	outsell
	sell out
	sell-out
ELLOSVY	volleys
ELLOWYY	yellowy
ELLPSUY	pulleys
ELLRSSU	Russell
ELMMORT	trommel
ELMMPTU	plummet
ELMNNOY	Men Only
ELMNPUU	unplume
ELMOOPS	pomelos
ELMOORT	tremolo
ELMOPRY	polymer
ELMOPSU	plumose
ELMOPTY	Ptolemy
ELMOSUU	emulous
ELMRTUU	multure
ELMRTUY	elytrum
ELNOORZ	Lorenzo
ELNOOSU	unloose
ELNOOSZ	snoozle
ELNOPRY	pronely
ELNOPST	leptons
ELNOPTU	let up on
	opulent
ELNORTY	elytron
ELNORTZ	Lorentz
ELNOSSS	lessons
ELNOSSW	lowness
ELNOSTV	solvent
ELNOTVY	novelty
ELNRSTY	sternly
ELNSSSU	sunless
ELNSSSY	slyness
ELNSTUY	Lutyens
ELNSUZZ	snuzzle
ELOOPST	Spoleto
ELOORTT	rootlet
ELOOSTU	lose out
ELOOSWY	woolsey
ELOPPST	stopple
ELOPPSU	slope up
ELOPPSY	polypes
ELOPRRW	prowler
ELOPRRY	pyrrole
ELOPRSS	plessor
ELOPRSU	leprous
	pelorus
	sporule
ELOPRSY	leprosy
ELOPRTT	plotter
ELOPRTU	plouter
ELOPRTW	plowter

ELOPRTY	reply to	ENNOTWW	new town	ENRSTTU	entrust
ELOPRVY	overply	ENNPSTU	unspent	EOOOPRS	oospore
ELOPSST	topless	ENNRRSU	runners	EOOPPRS	opposer
ELOPSTU	tupelos	ENNRSTU	stunner		propose
ELOPSUU	louse up	ENOOPPR	propone	EOOPRRT	trooper
ELOPTUV	Tupolev	ENOOPPT	open-top	EOOPRSS	poroses
ELORSUV	velours	ENOOPRS	snooper	EOOPRST	poorest
ELORTTY	lottery		Spooner	EOOPRTV	overtop
ELORTUU	rule out	ENOOPRT	prone to		prove to
ELORTVY	overtly	ENOOPST	one-stop	EOOPRTW	towrope
ELOSSTY	systole	ENOOPTU	open out	EOORRST	rooster
	tyloses	ENOORSU	onerous		toreros
ELPRSTU	spurtle		rouse on	EOORSTW	Wooster
ELPRUZZ	puzzler	ENOORSZ	snoozer	EOORSVW	oversow
ELPSSSU	plusses	ENOORUY	you're on!	EOORTUV	out-over
ELPSTUU	pustule	ENOORVW	won over	EOORTUW	out-owre
ELRRSTU	rustler	ENOOSST	soonest	EOOSSSU	osseous
ELRSSTU	lustres	ENOOSTU	nose out	EOOTTUV	outvote
	results	ENOOTTV	not vote	EOPPRRS	prosper
ELRSUWY	wurleys	ENOOTTW	two-tone	EOPPRSS	oppress
ELRTTUY	utterly	ENOOTUW	woe unto	EOPPRST	stopper
ELRTUUV	vulture	ENOOTXY	oxytone	EOPPRSU	purpose
ELSSSUY	Ulysses	ENOPRSS	persons	EOPPSSU	suppose
EMMMNOS	Mommsen		press on	EOPRRST	reports
EMMMRUY	mummery	ENOPRST	postern	EOPRRTU	trouper
EMMNOOR	monomer		Preston	EOPRSST	prestos
EMMNOTU	omentum	ENOPRTT	portent	EOPRSSW	prowess
EMMRSUY	summery	ENOPRTW	Newport	EOPRSTT	protest
EMMSSUU	museums	ENOPRTY	entropy		spotter
EMNNOOW	new moon	ENOPSTU	set upon	EOPRSTU	petrous
EMNOORT	montero	ENOQTUU	unquote		posture
EMNORRU	mourner	ENORRST	snorter		Proteus
EMNORSS	sermons		Torrens		store up
EMNORST	monster	ENORRTT	torrent	EOPRSTV	Prévost
EMNORTT	torment	ENORRUV	overrun	EOPRSUU	poursue
EMNORTU	remount		run over	EOPRSUW	poursew
EMNORTV	Vermont	ENORSSY	sensory	EOPRTTY	pottery
EMNOSST	stemson	ENORSTT	snotter	EOPRTUV	put over
EMNOSTY	etymons	ENORSTU	tonsure	EOPRTVY	poverty
EMNRSTU	Munster	ENORSTW	nor'-west	EOPSSSS	possess
	Münster	ENORSTY	tyrones	EOPSTTU	outstep
	sternum	ENORSUV	nervous		step out
EMOOPRT	promote	ENORTTU	rent out	EOPSTTW	two-step
EMOOSTT	mottoes	ENORTUY	tourney	EOPSTUW	spew out
EMOOSTW	twosome	ENORTVY	not very	EOQRSTU	questor
EMOOTUV	move out	ENOSSSU	Souness	EORRSTU	trouser
	outmove	ENOSSTT	stetson	EORRSTV	Vorster
EMOPPTU	up-tempo	ENOSTTU	stouten	EORRSZZ	rozzers
EMOPRSU	supremo		tenutos	EORRTTT	trotter
EMORSUY	Seymour	ENOSTUU	tenuous	EORRTTU	torture
EMORWZZ	Mezzrow	ENOSTWW	wet snow	EORSSTU	oestrus
EMPRSTU	stumper	ENOTTUU	tune out		tussore
EMPRTTU	trumpet	ENOTTUW	outwent	EORSSTY	storeys
EMRRSTU	sturmer ❑	ENPRSTU	pre-stun	EORSTTT	stotter
EMRSTYY	mystery		punster		stretto
ENNNRUY	nunnery		punters	EORTTTY	tottery
ENNOOOT	none too	ENPRSUU	unpurse	EPPRSSU	press-up
ENNOPST	spent on	ENRRSTU	returns	EPRRSUU	pursuer
ENNORTT	Trenton	ENRRSUY	nursery		usurper
ENNORTU	neutron	ENRRTUU	nurture	EPRRSUY	spurrey
ENNORTV	Ventnor	ENRSSWY	wryness	EPRRTUU	rupture

EPRSTTU sputter
ERRSSTU trusser
ERRSTTU truster
ERSSTTU tutress
ERSSTUY russety
Surtsey
ERSTTTU stutter

F

FFFGIOR frig off
FFFILOT lift off
lift-off
FFFMOOR from off
off form
FFGIINR griffin□
FFGINOR griffon
FFGINPU puffing
FFGLNOO long off
FFGLRUY gruffly
FFHHISU huffish
FFHIISY fishify
FFHILSY fly-fish
FFHILTY fifthly
FFHILUY huffily
FFHIOTW off with
FFHOOSW show off
show-off
FFHOPSU push off
FFHOSTU shut off
shut-off
FFIILMY miffily
FFIKLLO kill off
FFIKOSS kiss off
kiss-off
FFILOPS slip off
FFILOUZ zuffoli
FFILPUY puffily
FFILSTU fistful
FFILSTY stiffly
FFINOPS off-spin
spin-off
FFINOPT pontiff
FFINSTU snuff it
FFIOPSS piss off
FFIORTY fortify
FFIQSUY squiffy
FFIRTUY frutify
FFISTTU stuff it
FFJMOPU jump off
jump-off
FFKLORU forkful
FFKLOSU Suffolk
FFKOORW off work
work off
FFLLOPU pull off
FFMOPPU pump off
FFNORTU turn off
turn-off
FFOOPST stop off
stop-off
FFOOSST toss off
FFOPTUU puff out
FGGHIIS fishgig
FGGILOY foggily
FGGINOR forging
FGHHILY fly high
FGHIINS fishing
FGHILTY flighty
FGHIORS sigh for
FGHIOSY fogyish
FGHNOOR foghorn
FGIIKNN knifing
FGIILLN filling
FGIILNO foiling
FGIILNR rifling
FGIILNT lifting
FGIILNY lignify
FGIINRY nigrify
FGIINST sifting
FGIINSX fixings
FGIINSY signify
FGIINTT fitting
FGIINZZ fizzing
FGIKNOR forking
FGILNOO fooling
FGILNOR Rolfing
FGILNOU fouling
FGILNOW flowing
fowling
FGILNTU fluting
FGILOOY goofily
FGILORY glorify
FGIMNOR forming
FGINOOR go in for
roofing
FGINOOT footing
FGINRRU furring
FGINRSU surfing
FGINTTU tufting
FGIOORT go for it
FGIORST go first
FGJLSUU jugfuls
FGLMSUU mugfuls
FGLNOOR long for
FGLNORU furlong
FGLOOUY ufology
FGNOSUU fungous
FHIINNS Finnish
FHIKNOT think of
FHILOOS foolish
FHILOSW wolfish
FHILSUW wishful
FHINRSU furnish
FHINSSU sunfish
FHIOOPR hip roof
FHIOPPS foppish
FHIOPSX foxship
FHIORRY horrify
FHIORSW wish for
FHIOSTU fish out
FHIPSTU shift up
FHIRTTY thrifty
FHIRTUY thurify
FHKORTU futhork
FHLLOTU full-hot
FHLNSUU unflush
FHLRTUU hurtful
FHNORTU hunt for
FHOOOTT hotfoot
FHOOPRS shop for
FHOORST short of
FHOPRSU push for
FHORSTY Forsyth
FIIKLST ski lift
FIIKNYZ zinkify
FIILLSU fusilli
FIILNOO in folio
FIILNOT tinfoil
FIILNTY niftily
FIILPTU pitiful
FIINORT in for it
FIINOSS fission
FIINRST first in
FIINRTY nitrify
FIIPSTY tipsify
FIIRTVY vitrify
FIJLLOY jollify
FIJSTUY justify
FIKLLSU skilful
FIKLNSU skinful
FIKRTUY Turkify
FILLMOY mollify
FILLNUY nullify
FILLOTU fill out
FILLOTY loftily
FILNNUY funnily
FILNSTU tinfuls
FILNTUY unfitly
FILOPTU flip out
FILORST florist
FILORTU floruit
FILOSSS fossils
FILPPUY pulpify
FILRSTY firstly
FILSSUY fussily
FILSTUW wistful
FILSTUY fustily
FILSTWY swiftly
FILUYZZ fuzzily
FIMMMUY mummify
FIMMORS misform
FIMNORU uniform□
FIMOORV oviform
FIMORRT triform
FIMORTY mortify
FIMSTYY mystify
FINNORT in front
FINOPTY pontify
FINORSS frisson
FIOORSU furioso□
FIOOTTU out of it
FIOPRST profits
FIOPRSY prosify

FIOPSTX postfix
FIORSUU furious
FIPPUYY yuppify
FIRRSTY stir-fry
FIRSSUY Russify
FKLNOOR Norfolk
FKLOOOR look for
FKOORRW work for
FKOORTU fork out
FLLOPRU pull for
FLLOPTU topfull
FLLOSUU soulful
FLLOSWY fly-slow
FLLOTUU full-out
FLLOUWY wofully
FLLSTUU lustful
FLMMOUX flummox
FLMNOOU mouflon
FLMOOOT tomfool
FLMOORU roomful
FLNOORR forlorn
FLNOPUY fly upon
FLNRSUU urnfuls
FLOORSW forslow
FLOOTUW flow out
outflow
FLOPSTU potfuls
FLOSUUV fulvous
FMOOPRU Profumo
FMOORTU from out
FMRSTUU frustum
FNNOORT front on
fronton
FNNOORW frown on
FNOOOPT on top of
FNOORSU sunroof
FNOPRTU up front
upfront
up-front
FNORRTU turn for
FNORSTY Y-fronts
FNSSUUY unfussy
FOOOPRT rooftop
FOOORRT root for
FOOOTTU outfoot
FOOPSTT soft top
FOORSST of sorts
FOORTTX foxtrot□
fox-trot
FOPSSTU fusspot
fuss-pot
FORSTWY frowsty
FORTTUU turf out

G

GGGHINO hogging
GGGIINR rigging
GGGIINW wigging
GGGIJNO jogging
GGGIMNU mugging
GGGINNO nogging
GGGINPU pugging
GGGINSU sugging
GGGINTU tugging
GGHHIOS hoggish
GGHIINS Higgins
sighing
GGHIIPS piggish
GGHIIRS riggish
GGHINSU gushing
GGHOSTU thuggos
GGIIILN gingili
GGIINNO ingoing
GGIINNR ringing
GGIINNS singing
GGIINNW winging
GGIINPR griping
GGIINRT ringgit
GGIINSS Gissing
GGIJNSU juggins
GGILNNO longing
GGILNOS gosling
GGILNOW glowing
GGILOOS gigolos
GGILOSY soggily
GGILRWY wriggly
GGIMNSU muggins
GGINNOO going on
ongoing
GGINOOT going to
GGINORS Grigson
GGINORU roguing
GGINORW growing
GGINPRU purging
GGINRST G-string
GGINRSU surging
GGIOORS gorgios
GGIOPPY Iggy Pop
GGIOPTT Piggott
GGNOORS Gorgons
GGNOORW go wrong
GHHIKSY sky-high
GHHIOPT high-top
GHHIORT right-oh
GHHORTU through
GHHOTTU thought
GHIIKNT king-hit
GHIILRS girlish
GHIINNS shining
GHIINNT in thing
in-thing
GHIINNW whining
GHIINSS hissing
GHIINST in sight
insight
GHIINSW wishing
GHIINTT hitting
GHIINTW whiting
GHIKLNU hulking
GHILLTY lightly
GHILNOT light on
GHILNOW howling
GHILNRU hurling
GHILNSY shingly
GHILNTY nightly
GHILPTU light up
GHILRTY rightly
GHILSTY sightly
GHILTTY tightly
GHILTWY wightly
GHIMMNU humming
GHIMNOS moshing
GHIMNRY rhyming
GHIMRRT Mr Right
GHINNOT nothing
GHINNTU hunting
GHINOPP hopping
GHINORS shoring
GHINORT right on
right-on
GHINORU rough in
GHINORW whoring
GHINOSU housing
GHINOSW showing
GHINOTT hotting
tonight
GHINPSU pushing
GHINRSU rushing
GHINRTU hurting
ungirth
GHIORST rightos
GHIORSU roguish
GHIORTU rough it
GHIOSUV voguish
GHIPRTU upright
GHIPTTU uptight
GHLNOOP long hop
GHLORUY roughly
GHLOSTY ghostly
GHLOTUY toughly
GHMORSU sorghum
GHMOSTU mug shot
mugshot
GHNOORU rough on
GHNOPRY gryphon□
GHNOSTU gunshot
shotgun
GHOOOSW hoosgow
GHOORSS sorghos
GHOPRUU rough up
GHORTUW wrought
GHORTUY yoghurt
GIIJLNT jilting
GIIJNNO joining
GIIKKNR kirking
GIIKLLN killing
GIIKLMN milking
GIIKLNN inkling
linking
GIIKLNP Kipling
GIIKNNP kingpin
pink gin
GIIKNNS sinking

GIIKNNW	winking
GIIKNPS	pigskin
GIIKNSV	skiving
GIILLMN	milling
GIILLNT	lilting
	tilling
GIILLNW	willing
GIILMNP	limping
GIILMNS	smiling
GIILMPR	pilgrim
GIILMRY	grimily
GIILNNY	lying-in
GIILNOS	soiling
GIILNOT	toiling
GIILNPS	lisping
GIILNST	listing
GIILNTT	tilting
	Tlingit
GIILNTW	wilting
GIILNWZ	Zwingli
GIILOSS	gliosis
GIILOST	oligist
GIILRST	strigil
GIIMNPR	priming
GIIMNSS	missing
GIINNNS	sinning
GIINNNW	winning
GIINNOR	ironing
GIINNPP	nipping
GIINNPS	sniping
GIINNRS	rinsing
GIINNTU	uniting
GIINNTW	twining
GIINORS	origins
	signori
GIINORT	rioting
GIINPPR	ripping
GIINPSW	swiping
GIINPTY	pitying
GIINRTW	writing
GIINSTT	sitting
GIINSTU	suiting
GIINSTW	swing it
GIINTTW	witting
GIJLNOT	jolting
GIJMPPU	pig-jump
GIJNOTT	jotting
GIJNTTU	jutting
GIJRRUY	jury rig
GIKLNOO	looking
GIKLNRU	lurking
GIKMNNU	Kunming
GIKMNOS	smoking
GIKNNOW	knowing
GIKNORW	working
GIKNOSY	Kosygin
GILLLNU	lulling
GILLMNU	mulling
GILLMWY	Gwillym
GILLNOO	long-oil
GILLNOP	polling
GILLNOR	rolling
GILLNPU	pulling
GILLNYY	lyingly
GILMNOO	looming
GILMPSY	gym slip
GILNNSU	unsling
GILNOOP	looping
GILNOOS	loosing
GILNOOT	looting
GILNOPS	sloping
GILNORU	louring
GILNORW	Rowling
GILNORY	glory in
GILNOSV	solving
GILNOSW	slowing
GILNOWY	yowling
GILNPSU	pulsing
GILNVYY	vyingly
GILORTY	trilogy
GILOSTT	glottis
GILRSTY	gristly
GILRTUY	liturgy
GILRYZZ	grizzly
GIMMMNU	mumming
GIMNNOR	morning
GIMNNTU	munting
GIMNOOR	mooring
GIMNOPR	romping
GIMNOSU	mousing
GIMNOWY	Wyoming
GIMNPPU	pumping
GIMORSS	Grissom
GINNNPU	punning
GINNNRU	running
GINNORW	ingrown
GINNOST	stoning
GINNOSW	on wings
GINNPRU	pruning
GINNRSU	nursing
GINNRTU	turning
GINNTTU	nutting
GINNTUW	wing nut
GINOOTW	owing to
GINOPPP	popping
GINOPPS	sopping
GINOPPT	topping
GINOPRU	pouring
GINOPST	stoping
GINOQTU	quoting
GINORSS	in gross
	signors
GINORST	sorting
GINORSU	rousing
	souring
GINORTT	rotting
GINORTU	ring out
	touring
GINOSST	stingos
	tossing
GINOSTU	ousting
	sing out
GINOSTW	stowing
GINOTUW	outwing
GINPRRU	purring
GINPRSY	springy
GINPSUU	using-up
GINPSUW	upswing
GINPTTU	putting
GINRSST	strings
GINRSTU	rusting
GINRSTY	stringy
GINRSUU	usuring
GIOPRRU	prurigo
GIOPRSU	Gropius
GIOPSSY	gossipy
GIORSTU	Grotius
GISWWYY	WYSIWYG
GJNOOSU	goujons
GJOORTT	jogtrot
GKMOORY	Gromyko
GLMORUW	lugworm
GLNOOPR	prolong
GLNOOPY	polygon
GLNORWY	wrongly
GLNOTTU	glutton
GLOOORY	orology
GLOOOTY	otology
GLOOOYZ	zoology
GLOORUY	urology
GLORSSY	grossly
GLPRSUY	splurgy
GMNOORU	gunroom
GNNORUW	wrong 'un
GNNOUUY	young'un
GNNSTUU	stun gun
GNOOOTT	not go to
GNOOPPS	pop song
GNOPRUW	grown-up
GOOOPTT	go to pot
GOOPRST	Gosport
GOORSTT	grottos
GOORTUW	outgrow
GOPRSSU	gross up
GPSSUUY	gussy up

H

HHIISTW	whitish
HHIMPTU	Thimphu
HHIMTUW	hum with
HHIOSTT	shit-hot
HHISTUZ	shih tzu
HHMPRUY	Humphry
HHOOSTT	hotshot
HHOOSWW	who's who
HIIIKRS	rikishi
HIIKMSS	Sikhism
HIIKNPS	kinship
HIILLPP	Phillip
HIILMTU	lithium
HIILPTY	pithily
HIILSTT	hit list
HIIMPSW	wimpish

HIIMSSS	missish
HIIMSUZ	Shimizu
HIIMTWX	mix with
HIINSSW	swinish
HIINSTW	Swithin
HIIPTTU	hit it up
HIJNOUZ	Jinzhou
HIKLSUY	huskily
HIKMNOS	monkish
HIKNNTU	unthink
HIKNOPS	Hopkins
HIKNPSU	Pushkin
HIKNPTU	think up
HIKORSU	Kushiro
HIKOVVZ	Zhivkov
HIKRSTU	Turkish
HILLOPT	hill top
	hilltop
HILLPSY	Phyllis
HILLRSY	shrilly
HILMMOU	holmium
HILMOPS	phlomis
HILMPSU	lumpish
HILMSUY	mushily
HILMTUU	thulium
HILNNTY	ninthly
HILNOST	Shilton
HILOOTT	otolith
HILOSTU	loutish
HILOSVW	wolvish
HILOSWY	showily
HILOTWW	whitlow
HILOUUZ	Liuzhou
HILSSTY	stylish
HILSTTY	thistly
HILSTXY	sixthly
HIMNSTY	hymnist
HIMOORS	Moorish
HIMOPSS	sophism
HIMORTU	thorium
HIMOTTY	Timothy
HIMPRTU	triumph
	Triumph®
HIMRSTY	rhymist
HIMSSTU	isthmus
HINNNSU	nunnish
HINNOOT	Honiton
HINNORT	tinhorn
HINOORZ	horizon
HINOPST	Shipton
HINOPTU	hit upon
HINORST	in short
HINORSU	nourish
HINORSY	roynish
HINORTW	throw in
	throw-in
HINOTTU	thin out
HINRSTU	runtish
HINRTTU	in truth
HINRTUW	run with
HINSTUW	Whitsun
HIOPPRT	trip hop
HIOPRSW	worship
HIOPSST	sophist
HIOPSSY	physios
HIOPSTU	Photius
HIOPSTW	Sopwith
HIORSSU	sourish
HIORSTY	history
HIORTTW	worth it
HIOSSTT	sottish
HIOTTUW	out with
	outwith
	without
HIOTTWY	toy with
HIQSSUY	squishy
HIRSTTU	ruttish
HIRSTTY	thirsty
HJMNOPY	John Pym
HJNNOOS	Johnson
HJNOSST	St John's
HKKLOOZ	kolkhoz
HKKOOST	Okhotsk
HKKOSTU	Sukkoth
HKNOOWW	know-how
HKORSWY	workshy
	work-shy
HLMNOTY	monthly
HLOOSTY	soothly
HLORSTY	shortly
HLPRSUU	sulphur
HMMNOOY	homonym
HMMOOSU	hoummos
HMNOOST	Thomson
HMNOPYY	hyponym
HMOOPRS	morphos
HMOOSTY	smoothy
HNNORSU	unshorn
HNOOPTY	typhoon
HNOORST	short on
HNOORSU	honours
HNOORTW	throw on
HNOOSTU	Houston
	unshoot
HNOPSUW	shown up
HNOSTUU	unshout
HNOTTUU	hunt out
HNPSTUU	hunt's-up
HNRTTUU	untruth
HOOPPPS	pop-shop
HOOPRST	Porthos
HOOPSTT	hot spot
	pot shot
HOOPSTU	shoot up
	upshoot
HOPRSTU	hotspur □
HOPRTUW	throw up
	upthrow
HOPSTTU	shotput
HOPSTUU	push out
HOPSTUY	typhous
HORSTUU	outrush
HOSTTUU	shut out
	shut-out
HPRRUUY	hurry up

I

IIIKMNN	minikin
IIJMNOS	misjoin
IIJNNOT	injoint
IIKKLNY	kinkily
IIKLLMY	milkily
IIKLLSY	silkily
IIKLMNP	limpkin
IIKLNOS	oilskin
IIKLPSY	spikily
IIKLRSY	riskily
IIKMNPS	Simpkin
IIKNRST	Kirstin
IILLLLW	ill will
	ill-will
IILLLSY	sillily
IILLMNO	million
IILLMSY	slimily
IILLNOP	pillion
IILLNOZ	zillion
IILMORS	similor
IILMSTU	stimuli
IILMSTY	mistily
IILNNSU	insulin
IILNORS	sirloin
IILNOSY	noisily
IILNPPY	nippily
IILNPUV	pulvini
IILNSUV	Vilnius
IILOPRT	Tripoli
IILORTV	vitriol
IILOSTV	violist
IILPRVY	privily
IILPSTY	tipsily
IILTTUY	utility
IILTTWY	wittily
IIMMMNU	minimum
IIMNOSS	mission
IIMNOSZ	Zionism
IIMNPRT	imprint
IIMNTTY	Tiny Tim
IIMOPSU	impious
IIMOSST	mitosis
IIMOSTT	Titoism
IIMRTTU	tritium
IIMRTUV	trivium
IIMSSTU	missuit
IINNOOP	opinion
IINNOPT	in point
	pin it on
IINNPRT	in print
IINNQTU	Quintin
IINNRSU	in ruins
IINOPRT	rip into
IINORSS	Rossini
IINORTT	introit
IINORTV	in vitro

IINOSTZ	Zionist
IINOTTU	tuition
IINPRST	strip in
IINQRUY	inquiry
IINRTTY	trinity□
IINSTTW	intwist
IIOPRSS	pissoir
IIOQSTU	Iquitos
IIORRSV	Sir Ivor
IIORSTV	visitor
IIPRSST	spirits
IIPRTTZ	Tirpitz
IIPRTVY	privity
IJJSTUU	jujitsu
	ju-jitsu
IJKLLOY	killjoy
IJLLLOY	jollily
IJLLOTY	jollity
IJLMPUY	jumpily
IJLNOQU	jonquil□
IJLNOTY	jointly
IJNNOTU	unjoint
IKKRSTU	Irkutsk
IKLLSUY	sulkily
IKLMOPS	milksop
IKLMOSY	smokily
IKLMRUY	murkily
IKLMSUY	muskily
IKLNOOT	kiloton
IKLNRWY	wrinkly
IKLOOTT	toolkit
IKLOSSU	souslik
IKMNOOS	kimonos
	Mikonos
	mono-ski
IKMNOPS	skimp on
IKMNORS	mikrons
IKMNOSW	misknow
IKMNPPU	pumpkin
IKMOOST	mistook
IKMOSSU	koumiss
IKNNPTU	unpinkt
IKNPSTU	sputnik□
IKORSTY	Yorkist
ILLLOWY	lowlily
ILLMNOU	mullion
ILLMPUY	lumpily
ILLNORS	Rollins
ILLNOTW	till now
ILLNTUY	nullity
ILLOPRY	pillory
ILLORTU	Utrillo
ILLORTV	Torvill
ILLOSUV	villous
ILLOSUY	lousily
ILLOWWY	willowy
ILLPPUY	pulpily
ILLRSUY	surlily
ILLSTUY	lustily
ILMMRUY	rummily
ILMNOOT	moonlit
ILMOOPP	Limpopo
ILMOORY	roomily
ILMOOSS	molossi
ILMOPPU	oil pump
ILMORTU	turmoil
ILMOSTY	moistly
ILMSTUY	mustily
ILMUYZZ	muzzily
ILNNOPS	non-slip
ILNNOSS	Nilsson
ILNNSUY	sunnily
ILNOORV	Livorno
ILNOPRU	purloin
ILNOPST	split on
ILNOPSU	upsilon
ILNORST	nostril
ILNOSTT	Stilton
ILNOSTY	stonily
ILNOSWY	snowily
ILNSSTU	insults
ILNTTUY	nuttily
ILOOORS	rosolio
ILOOPST	topsoil
ILOOSST	soloist
ILOOSTY	sootily
ILOOWYZ	woozily
ILOPPSY	soppily
ILOPRSY	prosily
ILOPSUY	piously
ILORRSY	sorrily
ILORSTU	Troilus
ILOSSTU	St Louis
ILOSSTY	tossily
ILPPSTU	split up
	split-up
ILRSTUY	rustily
ILSSTTY	stylist
IMMOPTU	optimum
IMNNSSU	Sunnism
IMNOOPT	tompion
IMNOORT	monitor
IMNOOSU	ominous
IMNOOSY	isonomy
IMNOPRW	pinworm
IMNOPSS	Simpson
IMNORRU	murrion
IMNOSST	not miss
IMNOSVY	visnomy
IMOOPRX	proximo
IMOORST	Morisot
IMOOSSS	osmosis
IMOPRST	tropism
IMOPTUW	wimp out
IMORSTU	tourism
IMORSTY	Toryism
	trisomy
IMOSSTU	miss out
IMOSSUZ	Zosimus
IMQRSUY	squirmy
IMRSSTU	sistrum
IMRTTUY	yttrium
INNNORU	runnion
INNOPUW	win upon
INNOQTU	Quinton
INNORTU	run into
INNOSTU	nonsuit
INNOSTW	Winston
INNQSUY	squinny
INNRSTU	in turns
INOOPRT	portion
INOOPSS	Poisson
INOOPTT	point to
	to point
INOORST	torsion
INOORSZ	zorinos
INOORTU	iron out
INOOSUX	noxious
INOPPST	topspin
INOPPTU	point up
INOPSSU	poussin□
	spinous
INOPSTU	sit upon
	spin out
INOPTTU	put it on
INORRTU	run riot
INORSTU	nitrous
INORSUU	ruinous
	urinous
INORSUV	unvisor
INORTTY	try it on
INOSSUU	sinuous
INOSTUV	Ustinov
INOTTTY	tiny tot
INPRSTU	unstrip
INPRSTY	trypsin
INRSSUU	Ursinus
INRSTTU	intrust
	trust in
INSTTUW	untwist
IOOPRRT	prior to
IOOPRSV	proviso
IOOPSTY	isotopy
IOORSSS	sorosis
IOORSTT	risotto
IOORSTU	riotous
IOPRSSY	pyrosis
IOPRSTT	protist
IOPRTTU	trip out
IOPRTVY	privy to
IOPSSTX	six-spot
IOPSTTU	spit out
IOPTTTU	put to it
IORSTTU	stir out
	tourist
IPRRSTU	stirrup
IPRSTUU	pursuit

J

JNOORSU	journos
	sojourn
JNOSTUW	just now

K

KLNOOOW Kowloon
KLOOOTU look out
lookout
outlook
KNNNOUW unknown
KNNOOTW not know
KNOOPTT topknot
KNOORTW not work
KNOOUWY you know
KNOPRTY krypton
KOOPRTW worktop
KOORTUW outwork
work out
workout
work-out
KOOSSUU soukous
KORSTTY Trotsky
KOTUUVZ Kutuzov

L

LLLOOOR loo roll
LLMOOPR rollmop
LLMPPUY plumply
LLOOPRT trollop
LLOPTUU pull out
pull-out
LLORSWY L S Lowry
LMMPSUU lump sum
LMNOOOS Solomon
LMOOOTV Molotov
LMOPSUU plumous
LMOPSUY Olympus
Olympus®
LMORSUU Romulus
LMSTUUU tumulus
LNNOPSU nonplus
LNOOOTY only too
LNRTUUY untruly
LOOOORS oloroso
LOOPSTU slop out
LOOSTTY Tolstoy
LOPPSUU pulpous
LOPRSUY pylorus
LOPRTUY poultry
LOSTTUY stoutly
LPRSSUU surplus

M

MMNOSSU summons
MMOPPRS Mrs Mopp
MMOPSTY symptom
MNNOOOS monsoon
MNNOSYY synonym
MNNOTUU unmount
MNOOPTY toponym
MNOPRTU no-trump
MNOPTUU mount up
MNORSTU nostrum
MOOOTYZ zootomy
MOOPPSU pompous
MOOPSSU opossum
MOOPSTT topmost
MOORTUW worm out
MOOSTTU outmost
MOPPTUU pump out
MOPSSUU spumous
MOPSTUU to sum up
MORRSTU rostrum
MORRSUU rumours
MPPRTUU trump up
MPPSTUU stump up

N

NNOOOPT pontoon
NNOOPRU pronoun
NNOOPSS sponson
NNOOPST non-stop
NOOOOST too soon
NOOOPSW swoop on
NOOORTT Toronto
NOOPRSS sponsor
NOOPSTT not spot
not stop
NOOPTTU not up to
put on to
NOOPTUW own up to
up to now
NOORSTU unroost
NOORTUW outworn
worn out
worn-out
NOPPTUU put upon
put-upon
NOPSSTU sunspot
NOPSTUU spun out
NORTTUU outturn
turn out
turnout
turn-out
NRSSTUU untruss

O

OOOOPRT potoroo
OOORTTU root out
OOPRSSU soursop
OOPRSTV provost
OOPRTUU outpour
pour out
OOPSSTT tosspot
OOPSTTU outpost
OOPTTTU tot up to
OORSTTU sort out
OORTTTU trot out
OOSSTTU toss out
OPPRRTU purport
OPPRSTU support
OPPRSTY stroppy
OPPTTUU put up to
OPTTTUU putt out
OSSSTUU suss out

8 letters

A

AAAACNPR pacarana
AAAADMTV amadavat
AAAADTVV avadavat
AAAAGGRR agar-agar
AAAAGMTY Yamagata
AAAAHJMR maharaja
AAAAHMNY Mahayana
AAAAINPY Ayia Napa
AAAAIRTX ataraxia
AAAAJNRT Nataraja
AAAAKKNT katakana
AAAAKLRZ kala-azar
AAAALNTT Atalanta
AAAAMNRY Ramayana
AAAANNST Santa Ana
AAABBBRS Barabbas
AAABBNRS Barnabas
AAABCCRT baccarat
AAABCHLS calabash
AAABCITT ciabatta
AAABCKWY back away
AAABCNRU carnauba
AAABCPRY capybara
AAABDEST database
AAABDKNT databank
AAABDNNN bandanna
AAABDNRS saraband
AAABEFNV fava bean
AAABEHNR habanera
AAABEHRT barathea
AAABELLR Arabella
AAABELNN Alan Bean
AAABERWY bear away
AAABGNRZ Braganza
AAABHJLV Jhabvala
AAABHKKR Karabakh
AAABHLMR Alhambra
AAABHRST Sabratha
AAABIKRR Karabair
AAABILNN Albanian
AAABIPSS piassaba
AAABLLOZ Olazabal
AAABLOPR parabola

AAABRSUY	Surabaya
AAABTTTU	a battuta
AAACCELN	calcanea
AAACCEPR	carapace
AAACCILR	calcaria
AAACCRTT	cataract
AAACCTTU	tac-au-tac
AAACDEIM	academia
AAACDILR	caldaria
AAACDINN	Canadian
AAACDINR	Arcadian
AAACDNNO	anaconda
AAACDNRS	sandarac
AAACDOTV	advocaat
AAACEHLZ	chalazae
AAACEHNR	Archaean
AAACELRT	à la carte
AAACENVV	vena cava
AAACGMNR	Armagnac
AAACHIPS	Caiaphas
AAACHLSZ	chalazas
AAACIJMN	Jamaican ❑
AAACILMN	maniacal
AAACILMR	calamari
AAACINSU	Nausicaa
AAACIRRS	sacraria
AAACIRTX	ataraxic
AAACKPWY	pack away
AAACLLPY	pay a call
AAACLLWY	call away
AAACLMRR	car alarm
AAACLMUY	Macaulay
AAACLSSS	Las Casas
AAACMMNR	McNamara
AAACNOSV	Casanova
AAACSTWY	cast away
	castaway
AAADDORV	Vadodara
AAADEFHR	far ahead
AAADEFWY	fade away
AAADELRW	a raw deal
AAADENPS	Pasadena
AAADGGHH	Haggadah
AAADGIMM	gammadia
AAADGLMY	amygdala
AAADGLNN	Nagaland
AAADHKNR	Kandahar
AAADHMNR	Ramadhan
AAADIILR	radialia
AAADILRS	Alasdair
AAADIMMR	Mad Maria
AAADJKRT	Djakarta
AAADKRRV	aardvark
AAADLMNY	Mandalay
AAADMNOR	Maradona
AAADMNSW	Aswan Dam
AAADRWWY	draw away
AAAEEGMR	game area
AAAEGNPP	appanage
AAAEHMNT	anathema
AAAEHNPS	anaphase
AAAEIMRV	Ave Maria
AAAEKKRT	karateka
AAAEKLLV	Kalevala
AAAEKLNT	Lake Tana
AAAEKMNU	Mauna Kea
AAAEKMWY	make away
AAAEKNPT	take a nap
AAAEKNTW	Te Kanawa
AAAEKTWY	take away
	takeaway
	take-away
AAAELLST	all at sea
AAAELMTX	malaxate
AAAELPRY	play area
AAAENPRV	paravane
AAAENPST	anapaest
AAAEPPRS	appear as
AAAERSST	Sarasate
AAAERTWY	tearaway
AAAERWWY	wear away
AAAFGLNO	Fanagalo
AAAFINST	fantasia ❑
AAAFINUV	avifauna
AAAFLLWY	fall away
AAAGHINN	Ghanaian
AAAGHINR	hiragana
AAAGIKNS	Nagasaki
AAAGINRR	agrarian
AAAGINSY	say again
AAAGKRSV	Gavaskar
AAAGLMSY	Malagasy
AAAGLNRS	Sangraal
AAAGLRRW	warragal
AAAGLRST	astragal
AAAGMMRY	gamma ray
AAAGMORS	Saramago
AAAGNRTU	Tauranga
AAAGORST	Saratoga
AAAGPRUY	Paraguay
AAAHHHKL	Halakhah
AAAHHITW	Hiawatha
AAAHHNNR	Hanrahan
AAAHIINW	Hawaiian
AAAHIKLR	Kalahari
AAAHIMNR	maharani
AAAHIMRT	Mata Hari
AAAHIMRV	Mahavira
AAAHINNY	Hinayana
AAAHJLMT	Taj Mahal
AAAHKRWY	hark away
AAAHLLLV	Valhalla
AAAHLPRY	alpha ray
AAAHMNRT	amaranth
AAAHMNST	Samantha
AAAHNNSV	savannah ❑
AAAHNOPR	anaphora
AAAHSWWY	wash away
AAAHTTWY	thataway
AAAIIMRT	Tia Maria®
AAAIINPR	apiarian
AAAIKKSW	Kawasaki
AAAIKLTT	Lattakia
AAAILLMR	malarial
AAAILLPT	palatial
AAAILMRT	Altamira
AAAILMSV	Malvasia
AAAILMSY	Malaysia
AAAILNST	Alsatian
AAAILNTT	Alan Tait
AAAILRST	Alastair
AAAILRSU	Laurasia
AAAIMNOZ	Amazonia
AAAIMNST	Tasmania
AAAINNTZ	Tanzania
AAAINOPR	paranoia
AAAINQRU	Aquarian
AAAINRSV	Varanasi
AAAIPSSV	piassava
AAAKKORT	Krakatoa
AAAKMRSS	Makassar
AAAKNRSS	Arkansas
AAAKOSWY	soakaway
AAALLPRX	parallax
AAALMNOU	Mauna Loa
AAALNRTT	tarlatan
AAALNSTT	at a slant
AAALPRST	satrapal
AAALSTWY	salt away
AAAMNNNN	Manannan
AAAMNOPR	panorama
AAAMNRST	Rastaman
AAAMNSSY	as many as
AAAMOTTU	automata
AAAMRRSZ	zamarras
AAAMRTTU	traumata
AAANOPRZ	parazoan
AAANORSY	sayonara
AAAPSSST	passatas
AAAPSSWY	pass away
AABBCDRS	scabbard
AABBCEKR	bareback
AABBCEKT	backbeat
	beat back
AABBCINR	barbican
AABBCIRR	barbaric
AABBCOOR	Carabobo
AABBDEKR	bad break
AABBDHIT	bad habit
AABBDHIU	Abu Dhabi
AABBDORS	Barbados
AABBEEKL	Lake Abbe
AABBEELR	bearable
AABBEELT	beatable
AABBELLM	blamable
AABBELLS	baseball
AABBELRY	bearably
AABBELTY	Table Bay
AABBHKKU	Habbakuk
AABBHKSU	babushka
AABBIILL	bilabial
AABBLLMY	blamably
AABCCEHK	backache

Words marked ❑ can also be spelled with an initial capital letter

AABCCHKT	backchat
AABCCKKP	backpack
AABCCKLL	call back
AABCCKLP	black cap
	blackcap
AABCCKLW	claw back
	clawback
AABCCKST	cast back
AABCCMOT	catacomb
AABCDEIO	Boadicea
AABCDEIT	abdicate
AABCDEKT	back-date
AABCDELN	balanced
AABCDHKN	backhand
	hand back
AABCDHKR	hardback
AABCDIKL	laid back
	laid-back
AABCDIMO	Cambodia
AABCDKLO	back-load
AABCDKRW	backward
	draw back
	drawback
AABCDKRY	backyard
AABCEENY	abeyance
AABCEERT	acerbate
AABCEHRU	Auerbach
AABCEILM	amicable
AABCEIMN	ambiance
AABCEIRT	bacteria
AABCEJNO	Jacobean
AABCEKKT	take back
AABCEKLN	lean back
AABCEKLS	Black Sea
AABCEKMR	barm cake
AABCEKPR	pare back
AABCELLP	placable
AABCELNR	balancer
	barnacle
AABCELRT	bracteal
AABCEMPS	base camp
AABCENRR	Canberra
AABCENRT	can't bear
AABCEORT	Boat Race
	boat race
AABCESSU	abacuses
AABCFKLL	fall back
	fall-back
AABCFKLT	flatback
AABCFKST	fastback
AABCGHKN	hang back
AABCHILR	brachial
AABCHKKR	hark back
AABCHKLS	backlash
AABCHKSW	backwash
AABCHMRY	chambray
AABCHNNU	Buchanan
AABCHRRT	bar chart
AABCIILS	basilica
AABCIKLT	tailback
AABCILMS	balsamic
AABCILMY	amicably
AABCILNN	cannibal
AABCILNO	anabolic
AABCILST	basaltic
AABCIMNR	Cambrian
AABCINNR	cinnabar
AABCINNS	cannabis
AABCINSU	banausic
AABCIRSS	brassica
AABCISSS	abscissa
AABCKKLT	talk back
AABCKLPY	play back
	playback
AABCKLRT	black art
	black rat
AABCKNRS	snackbar
AABCKPRT	brat pack
AABCKPSS	pass-back
AABCKRRS	barracks
AABCKSWY	sway-back
AABCLLPY	placably
AABCNOSU	Casaubon
AABCRSTT	abstract
AABDDEEM	Adam Bede
AABDDEET	dead beat
	dead-beat
AABDDEGN	bandaged
AABDDEHN	headband
AABDDEMR	bad dream
AABDDYYY	day by day
AABDEEKM	make a bed
AABDEELR	readable
AABDEELT	dateable
AABDEELV	evadable
AABDEERT	tea bread
AABDEGIN	badinage
AABDEHHI	dahabieh
AABDEHKN	Bankhead
AABDEHRR	bear hard
AABDEILR	laid bare
AABDEKPR	brake pad
AABDEKRY	daybreak
AABDELLS	Ballades
AABDELLU	laudable
AABDELMN	damnable
AABDELOR	adorable
AABDELPT	baldpate
AABDELRT	Adalbert
AABDELRY	readably
AABDEMOV	a bad move
AABDENRY	Enard Bay
AABDENTU	unabated
AABDENUX	bandeaux
AABDENVW	waveband
AABDEORS	seaboard
AABDESTT	bad taste
AABDFHIT	bad faith
AABDGHIN	a big hand
AABDGHOT	Godthaab
AABDGINR	abrading
AABDGMOS	gambados
AABDGNOV	vagabond
AABDGOOR	go aboard
	go abroad
AABDGOTU	gad about
	gadabout
AABDHINR	hair-band
AABDHLLN	handball
AABDHLLR	hardball
AABDILNT	tailband
AABDILNU	Abu Nidal
AABDINNU	Danubian
AABDINRY	Ian Brady
AABDISSY	as said by
AABDKLNN	land bank
AABDKLRS	Karlsbad
AABDKNNS	sandbank
AABDLLUY	laudably
AABDLMNY	damnably
AABDLNNO	Alan Bond
AABDLORR	Labrador
AABDLORY	adorably
AABDMNNS	bandsman
AABDMNOR	Boardman
AABDMOTU	mad about
AABDNNTU	abundant
AABDNRRY	barnyard
AABDNRTU	a bad turn
AABDORSV	bravados
AABDORTY	boat-yard
AABDOTUY	day about
AABEEFLS	leaf-base
AABEEGHR	Bagheera
AABEEGKR	breakage
AABEEGNT	abnegate
AABEEHLR	hearable
AABEEHLT	hateable
AABEEHMR	harambee
AABEEKMT	makebate
AABEEKRT	tea break
AABEELLS	leasable
	saleable
AABEELMN	amenable
	nameable
AABEELMT	tameable
AABEELRS	erasable
AABEELRT	rateable
AABEELRW	wearable
AABEELST	eatables
AABEEMRS	sea bream
AABEENNW	wannabee
AABEENOR	anaerobe
AABEERRT	aberrate
AABEERST	base rate
AABEFIRT	a fair bet
AABEFLMU	flambeau
AABEFLSY	False Bay
AABEGLLL	glabella
AABEGLRT	glabrate
AABEGLRU	arguable
AABEGMNY	mangabey
AABEGMRT	bregmata

AABEGORT	abrogate
AABEGOST	sabotage
AABEGRTW	water bag
AABEHIRR	herbaria
AABEHJOV	have a job
AABEHKLS	shakable
AABEHKWY	Hawke Bay
AABEHLOT	oathable
AABEHLPS	shapable
AABEHLPT	alphabet
AABEHLSW	washable
AABEHRTT	at the bar
AABEIKLW	Lake Biwa
AABEIKRR	air brake
AABEILLS	Isabella
	sailable
AABEILMN	lima bean
AABEILNS	banalise
AABEILNZ	banalize
AABEILRS	Rabelais
	raisable
AABEILRV	variable
AABEILST	satiable
AABEILTV	ablative
AABEIMRU	Mirabeau
AABEIRSV	abrasive
AABEISUV	Beauvais
AABEJMUX	jambeaux
AABEJNOZ	Joan Baez
AABEKNRS	Nebraska
AABEKOTW	take a bow
AABELLMR	Marbella
AABELLMT	meatball
AABELLOV	above all
AABELLPP	palpable
AABELLPY	playable
AABELLSY	saleably
AABELLUV	valuable
AABELMNY	amenably
AABELMST	lambaste
AABELMTT	table mat
AABELMTU	ambulate
AABELNPS	anableps
AABELNPT	pantable
AABELNRY	balneary
AABELOPR	parabole
AABELORR	arboreal
AABELOSV	lavaboes
AABELOVW	avowable
AABELPRS	sparable
AABELPSS	passable
AABELRTY	betrayal❑
	rateably
AABELSTT	statable
	tastable
AABELTTU	tabulate
AABELTUX	tableaux
AABEMNRT	Bramante
AABENNPS	snap bean
AABENOSY	soya bean
AABENRRT	aberrant
AABENRST	Strabane
AABENSVY	Evans Bay
AABEOPRV	above par
AABEORRT	arboreta
AABFILUX	fabliaux
AABFLLST	fastball
AABFLOTT	faltboat
	flatboat
AABGGRRT	braggart
AABGHPRR	bar graph
AABGILRU	Bulgaria
AABGLLRY	ballyrag
AABGLMNS	slam-bang
AABGLNPS	slap bang
	slap-bang
AABGLRUY	arguably
AABGMNOU	Naum Gabo
AABHHKLS	Balkhash
AABHHORU	brouhaha
AABHILNN	Hannibal
AABHILTU	habitual
AABHINST	habitans
AABHINTT	habitant
AABHKKKU	Habakkuk
AABHKLOS	Lok Sabha
AABHKNUY	Ayub Khan
AABHKRSY	Shark Bay
AABHNOTU	autobahn
AABHORRT	Arbroath
AABHQSSU	squabash
AABHRRSU	surbahar
AABHRSST	brass hat
AABIILRS	Brasília
AABIINST	Sabatini
AABIKLNU	Kinabalu
AABILLLY	labially
AABILMNS	bailsman
AABILMNU	bimanual
AABILNNU	biannual
AABILNOR	baronial
AABILNOT	ablation
AABILNRU	binaural
AABILNTY	banality
AABILOWY	boil away
AABILRVY	variably
AABIMNNO	bonamani
AABIMNOT	Manitoba
AABIMNRU	manubria
AABIMORS	ambrosia
AABINORS	abrasion
AABINOSS	Bassanio
AABINRZZ	Zanzibar
AABIORTT	abattoir
AABIOSSY	bioassay
AABIQRST	Istabraq
AABIRTUY	rubaiyat
AABJLPRU	Jabalpur
AABKLLPR	ball park
	ballpark
AABKOSTU	ask about
AABLLLPY	play ball
AABLLMOR	balmoral
AABLLOTU	all about
AABLLPPY	palpably
AABLLRSW	wall bars
AABLLSTU	blastula
AABLLUVY	valuably
AABLMNOR	abnormal
AABLMNTU	ambulant
AABLNORW	Bonar Law
AABLNSST	St Albans
AABLORTY	altar boy
AABLOTUX	lax about
AABLOTUY	layabout
AABLOUWY	Bulawayo
AABLOWWY	blow away
AABLPSSY	passably
AABLRRTU	Barrault
AABMMOSU	abomasum
AABMNRTU	rambutan
AABMORTU	marabout
AABNOSSU	as a bonus
AABNOSTW	Botswana
AABORSTT	barostat
AACCCDIS	saccadic
AACCCFIO	focaccia
AACCCLOO	Coca Cola®
AACCCRUY	accuracy
AACCDEIM	academic
AACCDEJK	Jack Cade
AACCDELO	accolade
AACCDHRS	cash card
AACCDILL	Cadillac®
AACCDOVY	advocacy
AACCEEFH	face-ache
AACCEELT	calceate
AACCEENT	cetacean
AACCEFKP	face pack
AACCEFLO	coalface
AACCEILN	calcanei
AACCENRT	carcanet
AACCERTU	accurate
AACCFILR	farcical
AACCGILT	galactic
AACCHINR	anarchic
AACCHISV	viscacha
AACCHIVZ	vizcacha
AACCHLLT	catch-all
AACCHLOR	charcoal
AACCHLRS	clarsach
AACCHMNO	coachman
AACCHORW	Chaco War
AACCIINV	vaccinia
AACCIIST	sciatica
AACCIITT	Titicaca
AACCILNV	vaccinal
AACCILRU	acicular
AACCILTT	tactical
AACCIMOS	Masaccio
AACCIPTY	capacity
AACCLOPU	Acapulco
AACCLTTU	Calcutta

AACCOSTT	staccato
AACCSSUU	Caucasus
AACDDEHI	acid-head
AACDDENV	advanced
AACDDETU	caudated
AACDDETY	tea caddy
AACDDHRR	hard card
AACDEEHH	headache
AACDEEHR	headrace
AACDEEHS	headcase
AACDEELS	escalade
AACDEENT	tea dance
AACDEEPS	escapade
AACDEFLT	falcated
AACDEFNN	fan dance
AACDEGRR	drag race
AACDEHHY	headachy
AACDEHIN	hacienda
AACDEHKL	Lake Chad
AACDEHMR	drachmae
AACDEHPT	death cap
AACDEHRS	charades
	hard case
AACDEHTT	attached
AACDEILS	sidalcea
AACDEIMN	maenadic
AACDEINR	radiance
AACDEIRT	radicate
AACDEJNT	adjacent
AACDEKST	stackade
AACDELNR	calendar
	landrace
AACDELNV	valanced
AACDEMRY	Macready
AACDENPT	tap-dance
AACDENRW	war dance
AACDENSV	advances
AACDEOTV	advocate
AACDEQUY	adequacy
AACDGGHI	Haggadic
AACDGINR	cardigan□
AACDHHRS	hard cash
AACDHIIS	dichasia
AACDHIMR	drachmai
AACDHINP	handicap
AACDHINR	arachnid
AACDHKRT	hardtack
AACDHLNP	handclap
AACDHLRY	charlady
AACDHMRS	drachmas
AACDHNRT	handcart
AACDHSTU	cut a dash
AACDIINR	acid rain
AACDIIRT	Adriatic
AACDIJZZ	acid jazz
AACDIKRZ	Karadzic
AACDILMT	dalmatic
AACDILNO	diaconal
AACDILNR	cardinal
	Clarinda
AACDILNU	Claudian
AACDILOZ	zodiacal
AACDILRR	railcard
AACDIMNO	mandioca
AACDIMRT	dramatic
AACDINOR	Orcadian
AACDINRY	radiancy
AACDIORR	car radio
AACDIOTU	autacoid
AACDIRTY	caryatid
AACDITUY	audacity
AACDJQRU	jacquard
AACDKLNU	Auckland
AACDKLOP	pack-load
AACDLNRT	Cartland
AACDLOSS	scalados
AACDLOSV	Calvados
AACDMMOR	cardamom
AACDMMRU	cardamum
AACDMNNO	mancando
AACDMNOR	cardamon
AACDMSSU	Damascus
AACDNORU	una corda
AACDNSST	sand-cast
AACDOOSV	avocados
AACDQRSU	squad car
AACEEFIT	facetiae
AACEEGLV	cleavage
AACEEGPS	space age
AACEEHRT	tracheae
AACEEIMT	emaciate
AACEEIRT	acierate
AACEEKRT	caretake
	take care
AACEELRT	lacerate
AACEELST	escalate
AACEELTU	aculeate
AACEEMRT	cream-tea
	macerate
	racemate
AACEENRS	Canarese
AACEENTT	catenate
AACEEPSS	seascape
AACEERSU	caesurae
AACEERSY	easy-care
AACEETUV	evacuate
AACEETVX	excavate
AACEFFIN	affiance
AACEFLRT	flat race
AACEFRTT	artefact
AACEGHNT	chantage
AACEGHRT	Carthage
AACEGILN	angelica□
AACEGILT	glaciate
AACEGIRR	carriage
AACEGIRV	vicarage
AACEGKPR	packager
AACEGKPS	packages
AACEGLNT	glance at
AACEGRSV	scavager
AACEHHMT	MacHeath
AACEHILL	heliacal
AACEHILM	Michaela
AACEHIMR	chimaera□
AACEHIMT	haematic
AACEHINT	China tea
AACEHIPT	hepatica
AACEHIRS	archaise
AACEHIRZ	archaize
AACEHLRT	tracheal
AACEHMST	schemata
AACEHPUX	chapeaux
AACEHTUX	châteaux
AACEIILN	laciniae
AACEIINT	actiniae
AACEIIRV	caviarie
AACEILLM	camellia
AACEILLN	alliance
	canaille
AACEILMN	calamine
	MacLaine
AACEILNS	canalise
AACEILNT	Alicante
AACEILNV	Valencia
	valiance
AACEILNZ	canalize
AACEILOP	alopecia
AACEILRV	cavalier
AACEILST	saliceta
AACEIMNR	American
	in camera
AACEIMNS	amnesiac
AACEIMRS	macarise
AACEIMRZ	macarize
AACEIMUX	camaïeux
AACEINNO	Oceanian
AACEINNV	Avicenna
AACEINPZ	Piacenza
AACEINRV	variance
AACEINST	estancia
AACEIPRS	airspace
AACEIPRT	at a price
AACEIPTT	apatetic
AACEITTV	activate
	cavitate
AACEJLTU	jaculate
AACEKKLW	cakewalk
AACEKRSW	sea wrack
AACEKRTT	attacker
AACELLMN	Lac Léman
AACELLOT	allocate
AACELMNO	Alcmaeon
AACELMNP	placeman
AACELMNS	manacles
AACELMPP	Applemac®
AACELMPT	place mat
AACELMPU	mea culpa
AACELMTU	maculate
AACELNNU	cannulae
AACELNOP	Al Capone
AACELNOR	lecanora
AACELNPR	parlance
AACELNPT	placenta

Words marked □ can also be spelled with an initial capital letter

AACELNRY	arcanely
AACELNTU	tenacula
AACELORS	Coral Sea
AACELPSU	scapulae
AACELRWY	clearway
AACELSTY	catalyse
AACELTTY	cattleya
AACEMNOR	on camera
AACEMNPS	spaceman□
AACEMORT	to camera
AACEMOWY	come away
AACEMRSS	massacre
AACENNOR	Anacreon
AACENPRS	pancreas
AACENPSU	saucepan
AACENRTY	catenary
AACENRVZ	czarevna
AACENTUV	evacuant
AACERRRS	Carreras
AACERSSU	caesuras
AACERSTT	castrate
AACESSTT	sceattas
AACESUWY	causeway
AACFFGHR	Chargaff
AACFFHLL	half-calf
AACFHMST	camshaft
AACFILLY	facially
AACFILNT	final act
AACFIRRT	aircraft
AACFIRST	Frascati
AACFIRTT	artifact
AACFJKLP	flapjack
AACFMNNY	fancy man
AACGHHNS	Changsha
AACGHNNN	Nanchang
AACGHOPZ	gazpacho
AACGIILR	Cagliari
AACGIIMN	magician
AACGILLU	Caligula
AACGILNN	Anglican
AACGILNV	galvanic
AACGILOR	Agricola
AACGILRT	tragical
AACGIMMT	magmatic
AACGIMNP	campaign
AACGINTV	vacating
AACGISTY	sagacity
AACGLMOU	glaucoma
AACGLORS	calor gas®
AACGNRVY	vagrancy
AACHHLOR	Hal Roach
AACHHTWY	hatchway
AACHIJNT	Jacintha
AACHILNP	chaplain
AACHILPS	calipash
AACHILRV	archival
AACHIMNN	Chinaman
AACHIMNR	chairman
AACHIMRR	armchair
AACHIMRS	archaism
	charisma
AACHINNT	at an inch
AACHINPT	at a pinch
AACHINRT	canthari
AACHINSW	chainsaw
AACHIPTT	chapatti
AACHIRSS	Issachar
AACHKSTY	haystack
AACHLMPT	palmchat
AACHMMRY	Amy March
AACHMNTW	watchman
AACHMORT	achromat
	trachoma
AACHMORX	Max Roach
AACHMPRY	pharmacy
AACHMSSU	as much as
AACHNORT	at anchor
AACHNOSU	huanacos
AACHNSTT	snatch at
AACHNSTU	acanthus
AACHOPPR	approach
AACHOTTT	attach to
AACHRTUY	autarchy
AACIILMN	animalic
AACIILMO	maiolica
AACIILRV	vicarial
AACIINNP	in a panic
AACIINPT	capitani
AACIINST	actinias
AACIIPRT	Patricia
AACIJLMO	majolica
AACIJNOP	japonica
AACIKMNW	mackinaw
AACIKPRT	Praktica®
AACIKRTU	autarkic
AACIKTWY	tick away
AACILLPU	Pauillac
AACILLPY	apically
AACILLRY	racially
AACILMNT	claimant
AACILMTY	calamity
AACILNOP	Al Pacino
AACILNOS	Salonica
AACILNRV	carnival□
AACILNTT	Atlantic
AACILNTU	nautical
AACILNTY	analytic
AACILPRU	piacular
AACILPST	aplastic
AACILPTU	capitula
AACILPTY	atypical
AACILRSS	Clarissa
AACILRTY	alacrity
AACILSTY	salacity
AACIMMRS	marasmic
AACIMNOR	macaroni
	Marciano
AACIMORT	aromatic
AACIMRST	Sarmatic
AACIMTVY	Macavity
AACINOPR	paranoic
AACINORT	Catriona
	Croatian
	raincoat
AACINOTV	vacation
AACINPST	captain's
AACINQTU	acquaint
AACINSTZ	stanzaic
AACIPRTY	rapacity
AACIRRTT	tartaric
AACIRSTT	castrati
AACJKOOR	jackaroo
AACKKNPS	knapsack
AACKLOWY	lock away
AACKTUWY	tuck away
AACLLNRY	carnally
AACLLOWY	Calloway
AACLLRSY	rascally
AACLLSUY	casually
	causally
AACLLTUY	actually
AACLMNNS	clansman
AACLNNOW	canon law
AACLNNSU	cannulas
AACLNORU	La Coruna
AACLNOTT	octantal
AACLNRSU	lacunars
AACLNRUY	lacunary
AACLNTVY	vacantly
AACLOPTU	tapaculo
AACLORRU	oracular
AACLORSU	carousal
AACLORUV	vacuolar
AACLOSTT	cattalos
AACLPPRT	claptrap
AACLPRSU	capsular
	scapular
AACLPSSU	scapulas
AACLPTTU	catapult
AACLRSSW	class war
AACLRSTU	claustra
AACLRSUV	vascular
AACLSTTY	catalyst
AACLSTUY	casualty
AACMNOOR	macaroon
AACMNPRY	rampancy
AACMORSS	sarcomas
AACNNOSZ	canzonas
AACNRSTT	transact
AACOORTX	toxocara
AACORRTV	varactor
AACORSTT	castrato
AACORTTU	autocrat
AADDDEEH	deadhead
	dead-head
AADDDGNR	granddad
AADDEEHT	dead heat
	dead-heat
AADDEEIL	Adelaide
AADDEELP	pale-dead
AADDEHLN	headland
AADDEHMN	handmade
AADDEILR	Daladier

AADDELSU	Daedalus
AADDEMRY	daydream
AADDGGOO	gado-gado
AADDGHLN	glad hand
AADDGNRU	graduand
AADDHHIL	lah-di-dah
AADDINPY	in a paddy
AADDINRW	dawn raid
AADDLLNY	landlady
AADDLNRW	landward
AADDMMQU	muqaddam
AADDNRST	standard
AADDOTYY	day-to-day
AADEEGHR	headgear
AADEEGHT	get ahead
AADEEGMN	endamage
AADEEGNR	Gadarene
AADEEHLR	hard-a-lee
AADEEIKT	Kate Adie
AADEEILR	Airedale
AADEEIRT	eradiate
AADEELLM	male lead
AADEELMR	De La Mare
AADEELRV	de Valera
AADEELRW	Delaware
AADEEMRR	demerara
AADEENRU	Adenauer
AADEENTT	antedate
AADEEPRT	date rape
AADEEQTU	adequate
AADEFHLT	flathead
AADEFILM	mala fide
AADEFIRS	faradise
AADEFIRZ	faradize
AADEFLLR	falderal
AADEFLNS	sand flea
AADEFLRY	defrayal
AADEFOTU	auto-da-fé
AADEFSTY	feast day
AADEGGRU	guardage
AADEGHRS	rhagades
AADEGILL	legal aid
AADEGILS	ideal gas
AADEGINR	drainage
	gardenia
AADEGITT	agitated
AADEGITV	divagate
AADEGLMN	Magdalen
AADEGLMY	amygdale
AADEGNRR	arranged
AADEGORR	road rage
AADEGPRT	trade gap
AADEGRRS	regard as
AADEGRRT	rag trade
AADEGRTU	graduate
AADEHILN	nail-head
AADEHILR	railhead
AADEHILS	headsail
AADEHIWY	hide away
	hideaway
	hide-away
AADEHKMR	make hard
AADEHLMP	headlamp
AADEHMNS	headsman
AADEHMST	masthead
AADEHNNR	near-hand
AADEHNRV	verandah
AADEHRRW	hardware
AADEHRSS	harassed
AADEIKPT	take a dip
AADEILLN	Daniella
AADEILMP	maid-pale
AADEILNT	dentalia
AADEILPR	praedial
AADEILPS	palisade
AADEILRS	salaried
AADEILSY	lay aside
AADEILTV	validate
AADEIMNN	amandine
AADEIMNR	marinade
AADEIMNT	animated
	diamanté
AADEIMPZ	diazepam
AADEINNR	Adrianne
AADEIPRS	paradise ❑
AADEIPSU	diapause
AADEIPTV	adaptive
AADEIRSY	I dare say
	I daresay
AADEISST	diastase
AADEISTT	satiated
AADEITVW	viewdata
AADEJMNN	Ndjamena
AADEJMNU	Maja Nude
AADEJNOT	Ondaatje
AADEKMNR	mandrake
AADEKMRT	dark meat
AADELLPP	appalled
AADELMNR	alderman
AADELMNS	dalesman
AADELMPT	date palm
	date-palm
	palmated
AADELMYZ	amazedly
AADELNRU	red lauan
AADELNUY	Delaunay
AADELRTU	radulate
AADELTUV	valued at
AADEMMNV	Van Damme
AADEMNOS	adenomas
AADEMPSS	Sam Spade
AADEMRRU	marauder
AADEMRRY	Mary Read
AADENNTV	Davenant
AADENRRW	draw near
AADENSWY	send away
AADEQRTU	quadrate
AADERRRW	rearward
AADERRTW	trade war
AADERSSW	seawards
AADERSTW	eastward
	radwaste
AADERUVY	ayurveda
AADFFIOR	afraid of
AADFGNNO	fandango
AADFHITW	Haft Wadi
AADFHMNR	farm-hand
AADFINRU	unafraid
AADFINWY	find a way
AADFLLLN	landfall
AADFLLNT	flatland
AADFLMNR	farmland
AADFLORW	aardwolf
AADFLOTX	toadflax
AADFLOWY	foldaway
AADFMRRY	farmyard
AADFNNOR	Anna Ford
AADGGIMN	damaging
AADGGLNN	gangland
AADGGLRS	glad rags
AADGHILS	hidalgas
AADGILLR	galliard
AADGILMR	madrigal
AADGILNO	diagonal
AADGIMPR	paradigm
AADGIMRT	gradatim
AADGINPR	parading
AADGINRU	guardian
AADGLLNN	Langland
AADGLMNR	grand mal
AADGLOPR	podagral
AADGMNOR	dragoman
AADGNNOW	Gondwana
AADGNNQU	quandang
AADGNRUV	vanguard
AADGOORV	Avogadro
AADGOOSS	as good as
AADGOOWY	a good way
AADGRRUW	gurdwara
AADHHMNU	hum and ha
AADHILLR	halliard
AADHILNR	handrail
AADHILNT	Thailand
AADHILRV	havildar
AADHINRR	harridan
AADHIRTT	hard at it
AADHLLNU	land-haul
AADHLLOT	Toad Hall
AADHLMST	Halmstad
AADHLPSS	slapdash
	slap-dash
AADHMMMU	Muhammad
AADHMNNY	handyman
AADHNSTT	hatstand
AADIILNT	Aldaniti
AADIILPV	Dipavali
AADIIMNN	Indiaman
AADIINRS	Sardinia
AADIKLLO	alkaloid
AADIKLRY	kailyard
AADIKMNS	damaskin
AADILLNR	landrail
AADILLOP	Palladio

Words marked ❑ can also be spelled with an initial capital letter

AADILLRY	radially
AADILLSW	Ladislaw
AADILMNN	mainland
AADILMNO	domainal
AADILNOV	Danilova
AADILNPR	prandial
AADILOPS	palisado
AADILORR	railroad
AADILPRY	lapidary
AADILRTY	trial-day
AADIMNNO	Mindanao
AADIMNNR	mandarin❑
AADIMNRT	tamarind
AADIMNRY	dairyman
AADIMNUV	vanadium
AADIMSTZ	samizdat
AADINOPR	paranoid
AADINOPS	diapason
AADINPRS	Spaniard
AADIOPRS	diaspora
AADIORRT	radiator
AADIRRSW	airwards
AADIRRSY	disarray
AADITWYY	tidy away
AADJNTTU	adjutant
AADJNTUV	adjuvant
AADKLMNR	landmark
AADKLNPR	parkland
AADKORWY	workaday
AADKPRRW	parkward
AADLMNRY	Maryland
AADLMNSS	landmass
AADLMNSY	lady's man
AADLMNUU	laudanum
AADLMRYY	Mary Daly
AADLNOPR	parlando
AADLNOST	saltando
AADLORST	loadstar
AADLORSV	Salvador
AADLORTU	adulator
AADLOSUY	say aloud
AADMMNOW	madwoman
AADMMNSU	mandamus
AADMNORT	at random
AADMNOWY	day-woman
AADMOPPP	pappadom
AADNOSWY	nowadays
AADNPSTT	stand pat
AADNQRTU	quadrant
AADNQRUY	quandary
AADNRVYY	navy yard
AADOPRWY	drop away
AADOPRXY	paradoxy
AADOPSSS	passados
AADORSVY	Savoyard
AADOSSTY	sad to say
AADOSTUY	USA Today
AADRSTUY	Saturday
AAEEEGLS	sea eagle
AAEEEHRT	hetaerae
AAEEFKMS	make safe
AAEEFRRS	seafarer
AAEEFSST	safe seat
AAEEGGLL	legal age
AAEEGMPR	amperage
AAEEGMSY	easy game
AAEEGPRS	a presage
AAEEGPRT	great ape
AAEEGRRY	grey area
AAEEHHRR	hear, hear!
AAEEHIMR	haeremai
AAEEHRST	Earthsea
AAEEHRTW	a-weather
	wheatear
AAEEHRWY	hereaway
AAEEILNT	alienate
AAEEINTT	taeniate
AAEEJMNP	jampanee
AAEEJNPS	Japanese
AAEEKLMP	make pale
AAEEKLMT	make late
AAEEKMNS	namesake
AAEEKMNT	make neat
AAEEKMSY	make easy
AAEEKNRS	Kanarese
AAEEKNRW	reawaken
AAEEKPRT	parakeet
AAEEKPWY	keep away
AAEELLLM	lamellae
AAEELLMT	malleate
AAEELLPT	patellae
AAEELNPS	seaplane
	sea-plane
	spelaean
AAEELORV	aloe vera
AAEELPRY	leap year
AAEELRTU	laureate
AAEELSST	elastase
AAEELTUV	evaluate
AAEELVWY	wayleave
AAEEMMTT	team-mate
AAEEMNPT	nametape
AAEEMNRT	man-eater
AAEEMSTY	easy meat
AAEENNNT	antennae
AAEENNRZ	Nazarene
AAEENRST	Near East
AAEENRTT	anteater
AAEENSTU	nauseate
AAEEPPRR	reappear
AAEEPPRS	appeaser
AAEEPRST	asperate
	separate
AAEERRWW	rewarewa
AAEERSTT	stearate
AAEERSTW	seawater
AAEFFILS	fail-safe
AAEFFLLL	leaf-fall
AAEFGHRW	wharfage
AAEFGIMR	fair game
AAEFGITT	fatigate
AAEFGLLL	flagella
AAEFGLOT	floatage
AAEFGRTU	frautage
AAEFIKMS	make as if
AAEFILLX	leaf axil
AAEFIMRR	airframe
AAEFINNT	fainéant
AAEFINTX	antefixa
AAEFIRWY	fire away
AAEFKLMT	make flat
AAEFKMST	make fast
AAEFLLRT	after all
AAEFLMOT	meat loaf
AAEFLMTT	flatmate
AAEFLPSY	play safe
AAEFLRTT	flat rate
AAEFMRST	fermatas
AAEFMRSW	frame-saw
AAEFRRWY	wayfarer
AAEFRTTX	after tax
	after-tax
AAEGGLNR	Lagrange
AAEGGLNU	language
AAEGGLNY	lay an egg
AAEGGNPR	gang rape
AAEGGNRY	garganey
AAEGHLNP	phalange
AAEGHLPS	slag heap
AAEGHMRX	hexagram
AAEGHNRU	harangue
AAEGHOPY	hypogaea
AAEGILLN	Galilean
AAEGILLR	galleria
AAEGILNN	Angelina
AAEGILNT	alginate
AAEGILTT	tailgate
AAEGIMNO	egomania
AAEGIMNS	magnesia
AAEGIMNZ	magazine
AAEGIMRR	marriage
AAEGINPS	paganise
AAEGINPT	paginate
AAEGINPZ	paganize
AAEGINST	saginate
AAEGINTV	navigate
AAEGINTY	yet again
AAEGIRSV	vagaries
AAEGIRTX	ex gratia
AAEGIVWY	give away
	giveaway
	give-away
AAEGKRTU	great auk
AAEGLLMN	Magellan
AAEGLLPR	pellagra
AAEGLMNP	game plan
AAEGLMSW	game laws
AAEGLNOU	analogue
AAEGLNPT	plantage
AAEGLNRS	Sangreal
AAEGLOSV	aasvogel
AAEGLPRV	Palgrave
AAEGLRTY	legatary

Words marked ❑ can also be spelled with an initial capital letter

AAEGLSSV	Las Vegas
AAEGLSVY	savagely
AAEGMNNT	Mantegna
AAEGMNPY	pygmaean
AAEGMNRS	managers
AAEGMNRV	gravamen
AAEGMORR	aerogram
AAEGMORS	sagamore
AAEGMRRT	Margaret
AAEGMRST	Ramsgate
AAEGNOOR	no-go area
AAEGNRRR	arranger
AAEGNSTT	stagnate
AAEGORRT	arrogate
AAEGPRSU	sugar pea
AAEGPSTU	Agapetus
AAEGRSTW	water gas
AAEGRSTZ	star-gaze
AAEGRSVY	savagery
AAEHHRST	heat rash
AAEHIIRT	hetairai
AAEHILMT	hate mail
AAEHILNT	anthelia
AAEHILPR	parhelia
AAEHILPT	Lapithae
AAEHIMNT	anthemia
	haematin
AAEHIMNV	Vanaheim
AAEHIMRT	Mithraea
AAEHINNT	Athenian
AAEHINRT	Rhaetian
AAEHINST	asthenia
AAEHIPPS	Pasiphae
AAEHIPSS	ship a sea
AAEHIRST	hetairas
AAEHKMRY	haymaker
AAEHKTTT	Take That
AAEHLMNT	methanal
AAEHLMOT	The Alamo
AAEHLMSY	Sealyham
AAEHLMTU	hamulate
AAEHLNNV	Van Halen
AAEHLOSW	as a whole
AAEHLPRS	harp seal
	harp-seal
AAEHLPUV	upheaval
AAEHMNRT	Earthman
AAEHMNSS	Manasseh
AAEHMOPR	amphorae
AAEHMORT	atheroma
AAEHNPST	pheasant
AAEHNRTU	Rathenau
AAEHNRTZ	Nazareth
AAEHNTVX	tax haven
AAEHORVW	have a row
AAEHPRSW	Peshawar
AAEHRSTU	Arethusa
AAEHRTVY	have a try
AAEIINRS	Arianise
AAEIINRZ	Arianize
AAEIJNPS	Japanise
AAEIJNPZ	Japanize
AAEIKKMZ	kamikaze
AAEIKLLN	alkaline
AAEIKLLS	alkalies
	alkalise
AAEIKLLZ	alkalize
AAEIKLMP	make a lip
AAEIKLMS	make sail
AAEIKNRT	Katerina
AAEILLLU	alleluia
AAEILLMM	mamillae
AAEILLMX	maxillae
AAEILLPP	papillae
AAEILLPT	palliate
AAEILLRV	Vila Real
AAEILLRY	aerially
AAEILLTT	talliate
AAEILMMN	main meal
AAEILMNT	laminate
AAEILMNV	velamina
AAEILMRT	material
AAEILNNN	Linnaean
AAEILNNS	annalise
AAEILNNZ	annalize
AAEILNPR	airplane
AAEILNPT	palatine □
AAEILNRV	valerian □
AAEILNSS	nasalise
AAEILNSZ	nasalize
AAEILNTT	Latinate
AAEILPPS	papalise
AAEILPPZ	papalize
AAEILPRT	parietal
AAEILRRT	arterial
AAEILRSS	assailer
AAEILRTT	retail at
AAEILSTV	aestival
	salivate
AAEILTVX	laxative
AAEIMNNR	Armenian
AAEIMNPR	pearmain
AAEIMNRT	marinate
AAEIMOPR	paroemia
AAEIMOTX	toxaemia
AAEIMPRT	pia mater
AAEIMRST	Maserati®
AAEINORT	aeration
AAEINORX	anorexia
AAEINPWY	pine away
AAEINRST	anti-sera
AAEINRSU	Eurasian
AAEINRSY	Aryanise
AAEINRTZ	Nazarite
AAEINRYZ	Aryanize
AAEINSTT	astatine
	in a state
	sanitate
AAEINSTV	sanative
AAEINSTW	in a sweat
AAEIPPRS	appraise
AAEIPRST	aspirate
	parasite
	septaria
AAEIPRTT	patriate
AAEIPRTZ	trapezia
AAEIRRRT	terraria
AAEIRRTV	arrive at
AAEIRWWY	wire away
AAEIVWWY	view away
AAEJLNOP	jalapeño
AAEJORSV	Sarajevo
AAEKLLST	salt lake
AAEKLMPY	make play
AAEKLMRW	law-maker
AAEKLMRY	malarkey
AAEKLNRS	larnakes
AAEKLNSW	Swan Lake
AAEKMMRW	make warm
AAEKNNOS	Nakasone
AAEKNOPZ	Zakopane
AAEKNTTY	Kenyatta
AAEKPRTT	take part
AAELLLPR	parallel
AAELLMMR	Mallarmé
AAELLMPU	ampullae
AAELLNNV	Van Allen
AAELLNPU	planulae
AAELLORV	alveolar
AAELLPST	patellas
AAELLSSW	as well as
AAELLSWY	Wallasey
AAELLTTV	Valletta
AAELLUVV	valvu-lae
AAELLWYY	alleyway
AAELMMNO	melanoma
AAELMNRT	maternal
AAELMNSS	salesman
AAELMNSW	wealsman
AAELMNSY	seamanly
AAELMPSS	lampasse
AAELMPTY	playmate
AAELMRTT	maltreat
AAELMTWY	melt away
AAELNNOT	neonatal
AAELNNSU	Lausanne
AAELNOSS	seasonal
AAELNPRT	parental
	paternal
	prenatal
AAELNPRW	warplane
AAELNPST	pleasant
AAELNPSW	panel saw
AAELNRSY	analyser
AAELNRTX	relaxant
AAELNSSY	analyses
AAELNSTT	Atlantes
AAELOPPT	appeal to
AAELORTY	aleatory
AAELPPSU	applause
AAELPRSY	paralyse
AAELPRUV	par value
AAELPSTU	plateaus

AAELPTUV	vapulate
AAELPTUX	plateaux
AAELRSSS	Rasselas
AAELRSTU	australe
AAELRTTU	Lauretta
AAELRTTV	travel at
AAELRUZZ	zarzuela
AAELRWYY	waylayer
AAELSSTX	sales tax
AAELSTWY	lay waste
AAEMMNRT	armament
AAEMMSTT	stemmata
AAEMNNOS	as one man
AAEMNOTZ	metazoan
AAEMNPRS	Parmesan
AAEMNRST	sarmenta
	semantra
AAEMNRSY	man-years
AAEMNRTW	waterman
AAEMNSTU	manteaus
AAEMNTUX	manteaux
AAEMORTT	amaretto
	teratoma
AAEMORTX	xeromata
AAEMOTTU	automate
AAEMOVWY	move away
AAEMPTTU	amputate
AAEMRRTU	armature
AAEMRTTU	maturate
AAENNNST	antennas
AAENNORS	Roseanna
AAENNOTT	annotate
AAENOSST	assonate
AAENPPRT	apparent
AAENPRTY	prytanea
AAENPSTY	peasanty
AAENRSTV	tsarevna
AAENRSUW	unawares
AAENRSYY	nay-sayer
AAEOPSTT	apostate
AAEORTTV	rotavate
AAEPPRWX	wax paper
AAEPRRTY	at prayer
AAEPRSTT	set apart
AAEPRTTY	tea-party
AAEPRTXY	taxpayer
AAERRTTW	water rat
AAERSTTU	saturate
AAERTWWY	waterway
AAFFFLST	Falstaff
AAFFGILS	gaff sail
AAFFILLR	fair fall
AAFFILRT	taffrail
AAFFINPR	paraffin
AAFFLLLT	fall flat
AAFFNNOR	fanfaron
AAFFNOST	Atansoff
AAFGILNO	golfiana
AAFGLLNU	langlauf
AAFGLNRT	flagrant
AAFGNRRT	fragrant
AAFGORRS	farragos
AAFGORRT	Agra Fort
AAFHILNS	in a flash
AAFHINTW	what an if
AAFHLMNS	Flashman
AAFHLMST	half-mast
AAFHRSUU	hausfrau
AAFIILLM	familial
AAFIILLR	filarial
AAFIILMR	familiar
AAFIINST	fistiana
AAFIKLLY	alkalify
AAFILLNR	rainfall
AAFILMST	fatalism
AAFILNSY	final say
AAFILPRS	Parsifal
AAFILPRY	fair play
	play fair
AAFILSTT	fatalist
AAFILTTY	fatality
AAFIMNOR	foramina
AAFINNRS	safranin
AAFINRRW	warfarin
AAFINSTU	Faustina
AAFKLSTT	fast-talk
AAFKMUUY	Fukuyama
AAFLLMOT	malt loaf
AAFLLPRT	pratfall
AAFLLRTY	try a fall
AAFLLSTT	salt flat
AAFLOOWY	fool away
AAFLOTTU	to a fault
AAFLSTWY	flatways
AAFMNORW	man-of-war
AAFMORWY	away from
AAGGGINR	garaging
AAGGILNR	gangliar
AAGGIMNN	managing
AAGGINRV	ravaging
AAGGLLLY	lallygag
AAGGLNOT	tag along
AAGGNORT	Taganrog
AAGGOOPP	Pago Pago
AAGHHINS	shanghai ❑
AAGHIJNR	Jahangir
AAGHILNN	hangnail
AAGHILPY	hypalgia
AAGHIMRT	taghairm
AAGHKMNY	gymkhana
AAGHLNNS	Langshan
AAGHLNOT	Loaghtan
AAGHLNPY	anaglyph
AAGHMNNO	Monaghan
AAGHMNOY	Hogmanay
	mahogany
AAGHMNRS	Hans Gram
AAGHMNRT	Grantham
AAGHMRSS	marsh gas
AAGHNNST	Tangshan
AAGIILNS	aliasing
AAGIINNP	Paganini
AAGIINTT	Itatinga
AAGIINTW	awaiting
AAGILLNO	Galliano
AAGILLNU	Anguilla
AAGILLNY	allaying
AAGILLTV	gallivat
AAGILMNO	magnolia
AAGILMNR	alarming
	marginal
AAGILMOT	gliomata
AAGILNOR	Gloriana
AAGILNOT	galtonia
AAGILNRS	Sangrail
AAGILOOP	apologia
AAGILRRW	warrigal
AAGILSTT	sagittal
AAGIMNOS	angiomas
AAGIMNPR	Grampian
AAGIMNPS	paganism
AAGIMNSY	gymnasia
AAGIMSTT	stigmata
AAGINNUW	Wanganui
AAGINOST	Santiago
AAGINRRS	Srinagar
AAGINRTT	Rattigan
AAGINRTU	au gratin
AAGINSSU	Gaussian
AAGINSWY	sign away
AAGIORTT	agitator
AAGIRSTV	gravitas
	stravaig
AAGKNOOR	kangaroo
AAGKNOOV	Okavango
AAGKNORR	Ragnarok
AAGKOTUW	Tokugawa
AAGKPPRS	spark gap
AAGLLLNO	all along
AAGLLOWY	galloway ❑
AAGLMOPS	sago-palm
AAGLNOSS	as long as
AAGLNOWY	a long way
AAGLNQUU	aqualung
AAGLNRRU	granular
AAGLOSWY	slog away
AAGLPRUW	Walpurga
AAGLPSST	last-gasp
AAGLPUWY	plug away
AAGMNOOT	Tomonaga
AAGMNORT	martagon
AAGMNRTU	armgaunt
AAGMOTUY	autogamy
AAGMOTYZ	zygomata
AAGNNSTT	stagnant
AAGNOPRT	tragopan
AAGNORRT	arrogant
	tarragon
AAGNRSTV	vagrants
AAGNRTUY	guaranty
AAGNSTUU	Augustan
AAGOPPST	stop a gap
AAGOPRSU	as a group

AAGOPSSS	sapsagos
AAGORSSS	sargasso□
AAGORSSU	saguaros
AAGORSTY	go astray
AAGRSSTU	sastruga
AAHHILMS	Hailsham
AAHHIMRT	Mahathir
AAHHIMSV	Havisham
AAHHKKNU	Hanukkah
AAHHLLOO	holla-hoa!
AAHHLLUU	hula-hula
AAHIIKRR	hara-kiri
	hari-kari
AAHIINTT	Tahitian
AAHIJPRS	rajaship
AAHIKLNS	Sakhalin
AAHIKNSS	Kinshasa
AAHILMRY	hail Mary□
AAHILNNT	inhalant
AAHILNOT	halation
AAHIMSTT	Matthias
AAHINORT	Horatian
AAHINPRT	Parthian
AAHIPSXY	asphyxia
AAHITWWY	away with
AAHJNNOT	Jonathan
AAHKLLMR	hallmark
AAHKLMOO	Oklahoma
AAHKMOOY	Yokohama
AAHKMOTW	tomahawk
AAHKORSV	Sakharov
AAHLLMRS	Marshall
AAHLMOOS	masoolah
AAHLMSTU	thalamus
AAHLNPSU	Paul Nash
AAHMMRRU	Muharram
AAHMNORT	marathon□
AAHMNOTX	xanthoma
AAHMNPST	phantasm
AAHMRSST	stramash
AAHMSTTU	Matthaus
AAHNNSSU	Susannah
AAHNOSTT	Thanatos
AAHNPSTY	phantasy
AAHNRTTY	Hanratty
AAHOPRTU	autoharp
AAHRSTTW	straw hat
AAHSSTTU	Hattusas
AAHSTUWY	shut away
AAIILMNS	mainsail
AAIILNUX	uniaxial
AAIILPRR	riparial
AAIILRST	Alistair
AAIILTXY	axiality
AAIIMMNX	Maximian
AAIIMNNT	maintain
AAIINOTV	aviation
AAIINPRR	riparian
AAIINPRS	Parisian
AAIINRST	intarsia
AAIIORRT	air-to-air
AAIIPRST	apiarist
AAIIRSTV	aviarist
AAIIRSTW	wistaria
AAIKLNOS	Salonika
AAIKLNRS	Sri Lanka
AAIKLOSV	Slovakia
AAIKMORS	Makarios
AAIKMOSY	Kismaayo
AAIKMRST	tamarisk
AAIKNPST	Pakistan
AAIKNRTX	taxi rank
AAIKSSTW	swastika
AAILLLLN	all in all
AAILLLUV	alluvial
AAILLMNT	mantilla
AAILLMNY	animally
AAILLMOR	Amarillo
AAILLRXY	axillary
AAILMMRS	alarmism
AAILMNOP	palamino
AAILMNOR	manorial
	morainal
AAILMNOS	Mona Lisa
AAILMNPS	Panislam
AAILMNST	talisman
AAILMOPT	lipomata
AAILMORR	armorial
AAILMPPS	papalism
AAILMRSS	Marsalis
AAILMRST	alarmist
AAILMRSY	amarylis
AAILMSWW	Mawlawis
AAILMTTU	ultimata
AAILNNOT	national
AAILNNPT	plantain
AAILNNST	annalist
AAILNNTY	Latynina
AAILNOPS	Salopian
AAILNOPT	talapoin
AAILNORT	notarial
	rational
AAILNOST	ailantos
AAILNSSY	analysis
AAILNSTT	Atlantis
AAILNSTY	nasality
AAILNSVY	Sylvania
AAILORRV	variolar
AAILPPRS	apprisal
AAILPPST	papalist
AAILPSWY	slip away
AAILQRSU	squarial
AAILRSVY	salivary
AAILSSTY	staysail
AAIMMNRR	arm-in-arm
AAIMMNST	mainmast
AAIMMRSU	samarium
AAIMNNOR	Romanian
AAIMNNRU	Rumanian
AAIMNORT	animator
AAIMNORV	Moravian
AAIMNORW	airwoman
AAIMNOST	Tomasina
AAIMNPRT	main part
AAIMNPRZ	marzipan
AAIMNPTU	putamina
AAIMNRRT	trimaran
AAIMNSST	mantissa
	Satanism
AAIMNSTU	amiantus
AAIMNSTY	mainstay
AAIMPRST	pastrami
AAIMQRUU	aquarium
AAIMRRST	Amritsar
AAIMRRTY	martyria
AAINNOST	sonatina
AAINNOTT	natation
AAINNOTV	Novatian
AAINNSST	naissant
AAINOPRV	par avion
AAINOPSS	paisanos
AAINOPTT	at a point
AAINORRS	rosarian
AAINORRT	Rotarian
AAINOTTX	taxation
AAINPRST	aspirant
	partisan
AAINPRTW	war paint
AAINQRTU	quatrain
AAINQTTU	aquatint
AAINRSSY	Assyrian
AAINRSTU	Austrian
AAINRSTY	sanitary
AAINSSSS	assassin
AAINSSTT	Satanist
AAIOPRRT	troparia
AAIOPRSU	parousia
AAIPRSSX	sparaxis
AAIQRSUU	Aquarius
AAIRRSST	Stari Ras
AAIRSSTT	ITAR-Tass
	Itar-Tass
AAIRSSTU	Asturias
AAIRSTWY	stairway
AAJMMORR	marjoram
AAJMPUWY	jump away
AAKLLLTT	talk tall
AAKLLLTW	walk tall
AAKLMNNS	Klansman
AAKLMNSW	Walkmans
AAKLMRRX	Karl Marx
AAKLMRUY	yarmulka
AAKLORRY	Ark Royal
AAKMMNRS	marksman
AAKMOSSU	moussaka
AAKNNSTU	nunataks
AAKOPRSV	Kasparov
AAKORSUW	Kurosawa
AAKORWWY	work away
AALLMNTY	tallyman
AALLMNUY	manually
AALLNNUY	annually
AALLNOTT	not at all

AALLNRTY	tarnally
AALLOORW	wallaroo
AALLPRST	plastral
AALLPUWY	pull away
AALLRSST	All Stars
AALLRUVV	valvular
AALMNOPP	Pamplona
AALMNORU	monaural
AALMNOWY	laywoman
AALMNTTU	tantalum
AALMOOSS	massoola
AALMOPPR	Malaprop
AALMOSTT	stomatal
AALMOTXY	xylomata
AALNOPRT	patronal
AALNPTWX	wax plant
AALNRRTY	arrantly
AALNSTTU	tantalus □
AALOOPSU	São Paulo
AALOPPRV	approval
AALOPRST	pastoral
AALORTTV	Travolta
AALORTTW	total war
AALORTVY	lavatory
AALPRSTU	pastural
	spatular
AALRSTTW	stalwart
AALRSTUY	salutary
AAMMNNOT	man to man
	man-to-man
AAMMOOTY	Yamamoto
AAMMOTXY	myxomata
AAMMRSSU	marasmus
AAMNNOPR	apron-man
AAMNORRS	Marranos
AAMNPRTY	party man
AAMNQSUW	squawman
AAMOPRRU	paramour
AAMORRSZ	zamarros
AAMORSTT	stromata
AAMRSSST	smart ass
	smart-ass
AAMRTTTU	Art Tatum
AANNOSTT	annattos
AANNRSTY	stannary
AANOOSSS	as soon as
AANORRRT	narrator
AANORTTY	natatory
AANRRTWY	warranty
AANRSTTU	saturant
AANRTUWY	turn away
AAOPSSTY	apostasy
AAORSUVV	vavasour
AAOSTWWY	stow away
	stowaway
AARRSSTW	Star Wars
AARRSTTU	Tartarus
AARSTTUY	statuary
ABBBDEEL	bedabble
ABBBEILR	bribable
ABBBELUY	blue baby
ABBBGILN	babbling
	blabbing
ABBBHSUY	bushbaby
	bush-baby
ABBCCKMO	back-comb
ABBCEERU	barbecue
ABBCEGIR	cribbage
ABBCEHTU	bathcube
ABBCEIKT	backbite □
	bite back
ABBCEKNO	backbone
ABBCELRS	scrabble □
	Scrabble®
ABBCIILL	biblical
ABBCIINR	rabbinic
ABBCIKRT	brickbat
ABBCILRY	crabbily
ABBCINOY	cabin boy
ABBCKLOX	black box
ABBDDEEL	beddable
ABBDDEIL	biddable
ABBDDLOO	bad blood
ABBDEELN	bendable
ABBDEERT	rabbeted
ABBDEILN	dabble in
ABBDEILR	ad-libber
ABBDEINR	breadbin
ABBDEISV	bad vibes
ABBDEORS	absorbed
ABBDGILN	dabbling
ABBDHIRT	birdbath
ABBDHOOY	babyhood
ABBDILNY	Blind Bay
ABBDLLOY	baby doll
ABBDLNOY	Bob Dylan
ABBDNORW	bawd-born
ABBDRRUY	Bradbury
ABBEEJRR	jabberer
ABBEEJRS	bejabers
ABBEELVW	Ebbw Vale
ABBEENOR	barebone
ABBEEQRU	barbeque
ABBEHORT	bathrobe
ABBEHRTU	Babe Ruth
ABBEILOT	bilobate
ABBEILST	bistable
ABBEIMWZ	Zimbabwe
ABBEINRS	Brisbane
ABBEIRRT	rabbiter
ABBEKLOO	bookable
ABBELMRS	brambles
ABBELNRU	burnable
ABBELOOT	bootable
ABBELOPR	probable
ABBELORU	belabour
ABBELQSU	squabble
ABBEORTW	browbeat
ABBERRRY	barberry
ABBERSSU	Barbusse
ABBFILLY	flabbily
ABBGGILN	gabbling
ABBGGINR	grabbing
ABBGILNU	baubling
ABBGINST	stabbing
ABBGNORW	brown-bag
ABBGORSY	Babygros
ABBHILSY	shabbily
ABBILLSU	sillabub
ABBIMNOS	bambinos
ABBINORT	rabbit on
ABBINORX	brainbox
ABBINORZ	Barbizon
ABBIRRTY	rabbitry
ABBIRSUU	suburbia
ABBLLSUY	syllabub
ABBLOPRY	probably
ABBMMOOT	atom bomb
ABBNRSUU	suburban
ABBOSSTY	bobstays
ABCCDEHO	caboched
ABCCDHIK	dabchick
ABCCDIOU	Boudicca
ABCCEEHN	bechance
ABCCEELP	peccable
ABCCEHNY	by chance
ABCCEIKL	black ice
ABCCEILY	celibacy
ABCCEKMO	come back
	comeback
ABCCESUU	succubae
ABCCHNOO	cabochon
ABCCIKKK	kick back
	kickback
ABCCILOR	carbolic
ABCCILOT	cobaltic
ABCCINOR	carbonic
ABCCIORS	ascorbic
ABCCKLLO	ballcock
ABCCKOOT	cockboat
ABCCOOST	tobaccos
ABCDDEOR	bar-coded
	brocaded
ABCDEEFK	feedback
ABCDEEHL	bleached
ABCDEELM	becalmed
ABCDEELU	educable
ABCDEFLO	bold face
ABCDEGIR	birdcage
	cagebird
ABCDEHLN	blanched
ABCDEHNR	branched
ABCDEIIT	diabetic
ABCDEIKS	backside
ABCDEKLO	blockade
ABCDEKLV	backveld
ABCDEKNN	neckband
ABCDEKNS	send back
ABCDEKNU	unbacked
ABCDEKOT	boat deck
ABCDELOO	caboodle
ABCDESUY	caused by
ABCDGKLO	Black Dog

Words marked □ can also be spelled with an initial capital letter

ABCDHKLO	hold back
ABCDIILO	diabolic
ABCDIIMY	cymbidia
ABCDIIRT	tribadic
ABCDIKLR	baldrick
ABCDILLR	bird call
	birdcall
ABCDKLOR	Black Rod
ABCDKNOW	back down
ABCDKOOR	back-door
ABCDKOPR	backdrop
	drop back
ABCDLOSU	club soda
ABCDOPRU	cupboard
ABCDORTU	abductor
ABCDORUY	obduracy
ABCEEEFK	beefcake
ABCEEFNT	benefact
ABCEEGRR	Bergerac
ABCEEHKL	back-heel
ABCEEHLM	béchamel
ABCEEHLR	bleacher
ABCEEILR	Liberace
ABCEEILT	celibate
ABCEEIMN	ambience
ABCEEIRT	Beatrice
ABCEEKKP	keep back
ABCEEKLY	black eye
ABCEELLO	eco-label
ABCEELRR	cerebral
ABCEELRT	bracelet
ABCEERUX	berceaux
ABCEFIIT	beatific
ABCEFIKR	backfire
ABCEFINO	Boniface
ABCEFLSS	bass clef
ABCEGIKV	give back
ABCEGKLL	blackleg
ABCEGKLO	blockage
ABCEGKMU	megabuck
ABCEHHTU	beach-hut
ABCEHITT	bathetic
ABCEHKTW	bethwack
ABCEHLOR	bachelor
ABCEHLSU	chasuble
ABCEHMOT	hecatomb
ABCEHMRS	Chambers
ABCEHNSW	bench saw
ABCEHOOT	cohobate
ABCEHOPU	pabouche
ABCEHORU	barouche
ABCEIJOT	Jacobite
ABCEIKLT	black tie
ABCEIKNR	rein back
ABCEIKWZ	Zwieback
ABCEILLR	cribella
ABCEILLT	balletic
ABCEILNN	binnacle
ABCEILOR	cabriole
ABCEILOS	sociable
ABCEIMRW	Micawber
ABCEINOO	coenobia
ABCEINTU	incubate
ABCEIORS	aerobics
ABCEIRRT	cribrate
ABCEIRSW	crabwise
ABCEIRTT	brattice
ABCEIRTY	acerbity
ABCEJKLT	jet-black
ABCEJLTY	abjectly
ABCEJNOS	Jacobsen
ABCEKLLO	lockable
ABCEKMOV	move back
ABCEKOOS	bookcase
ABCEKPST	step back
ABCELLMP	Campbell
ABCELLPU	culpable
ABCELMNY	lambency
ABCELMOS	cembalos
ABCELMRS	scramble
ABCELNOT	bel canto
ABCELOOT	bootlace
ABCELOPS	placebos
ABCELOST	obstacle
ABCELOTU	Bluecoat
ABCEMORS	cramboes
ABCENNOS	Besançon
ABCENOUY	buoyance
ABCEPRSY	scrape by
ABCERRTU	carburet
ABCFIKLL	backfill
ABCFIKNO	in back of
ABCFILOS	bifocals
ABCFKLLU	fullback
ABCFKLLY	blackfly
ABCFKLOW	flow back
ABCFKOST	softback
ABCFKSTU	fast buck
ABCFNORT	Bancroft
ABCGHKOS	hog's back
	hog's-back
ABCGIKLN	blacking
ABCGILNO	log cabin
ABCGKMOS	gobsmack
ABCGKNOO	go back on
ABCHHIIS	hibachis
ABCHIKRS	brackish
ABCHIMOR	choriamb
ABCHIMRU	brachium
ABCHIMTU	a bit much
ABCHIRRT	tribrach
ABCHKMPU	humpback
ABCHKPSU	push back
ABCHLLUU	club-haul
ABCHMOTX	matchbox
ABCHOORT	broach to
ABCIINRS	Scriabin
ABCIINTU	bucatini
ABCIIORS	isobaric
ABCIIRTU	Curitiba
ABCIKLST	backlist
ABCIKMRS	Bismarck
ABCIKNPS	backspin
ABCILLSU	bacillus
ABCILLSY	syllabic
ABCILMMO	cimbalom
ABCILMOO	Colombia
ABCILMOU	Columbia
ABCILNPU	publican
ABCILOSY	sociably
ABCIMMSU	cambiums
ABCINPUY	panic-buy
ABCINRSU	Brancusi
ABCINRVY	vibrancy
ABCIORRS	barricos
ABCIOSSU	scabious
ABCIRSTT	abstrict
ABCJKMPU	jump back
ABCJKOOT	boot-jack
	jackboot
ABCKKLOO	look back
ABCKKORW	work back
ABCKLLOS	ballocks
ABCKLLPU	pull back
ABCKLOTU	black out
	blackout
ABCKMOOR	backroom
ABCKNRTU	turn back
ABCKOORU	buckaroo
ABCKOPST	backstop
ABCKRSTU	Starbuck
ABCLLPUY	culpably
ABCLMOSY	cymbalos
ABCLPRUW	pub-crawl
ABCLRSTU	Arts Club
ABCNOUYY	buoyancy
ABCORRSS	crossbar
ABCORSSU	scabrous
ABCRSTTU	subtract
ABDDDEOY	dead body
ABDDEEGR	badgered
ABDDEERR	debarred
	Redbeard
ABDDEEST	bedstead
ABDDEGIR	abridged
ABDDEILS	disabled
ABDDEILU	buddleia
ABDDEINR	brandied
ABDDEINS	sideband
ABDDELOT	dead bolt
ABDDERSW	bedwards
ABDDFORR	Bradford
ABDDHIOR	rhabdoid
ABDDILRY	ladybird
ABDDIMNO	bondmaid
ABDDINNW	wind band
ABDDIRRY	yardbird
ABDDLOUZ	Zola Budd
ABDEEEFN	bedeafen
ABDEEEKR	Baedeker
ABDEEENR	Aberdeen
ABDEEERV	bereaved
ABDEEGGL	bedaggle

ABDEEGGR	beggared
ABDEEGLR	Belgrade
ABDEEHNO	bonehead
ABDEEILN	deniable
ABDEEIST	diabetes
ABDEEKLL	Lake Bled
ABDEEKNR	bedarken
ABDEELLL	labelled
ABDEELLW	weldable
ABDEELOR	lee-board
ABDEELRZ	blazered
ABDEELZZ	bedazzle
ABDEEPRS	bespread
ABDEERTT	battered
ABDEERTW	water-bed
ABDEERTY	betrayed
ABDEFHLR	half-bred
ABDEFILR	leafbird
ABDEFINO	bona fide
ABDEFLLO	foldable
ABDEFLOR	fordable
ABDEFMRY	framed by
ABDEGGIL	diggable
ABDEGIMX	mixed bag
ABDEGINS	debasing
ABDEGOOT	a good bet
ABDEGRSU	subgrade
ABDEHINS	banished
ABDEHKLU	bulkhead
ABDEHLLN	handbell
ABDEHLLU	bullhead
ABDEHMSU	ambushed
ABDEHNSU	Dushanbe
ABDEHOTT	to the bad
ABDEHTTU	head-butt
ABDEIIRT	diatribe
ABDEILMN	mandible
ABDEILNY	deniably
ABDEILOV	voidable
ABDEILRT	bridle at
ABDEILRV	drivable
ABDEILTU	dutiable
ABDEIMOR	amberoid
ABDEIMRU	Drambuie®
ABDEINOR	debonair
ABDEINOT	obtained
ABDEINSU	unbiased
ABDEIOPT	to be paid
ABDEIPTZ	baptized
ABDEIRRR	rare bird
ABDEIRRW	war bride
ABDEISSU	disabuse
ABDEITTU	dubitate
ABDEKLMO	make bold
ABDEKLRU	dark-blue
ABDEKLSW	skewbald
ABDEKORY	keyboard
ABDELLMS	bad smell
ABDELNOR	banderol
ABDELNSS	baldness
ABDELORU	laboured
ABDELOSV	absolved
ABDELOTT	do battle
ABDEMNOR	Doberman
ABDEMNRU	Bermudan
ABDEMRSU	Bermudas
ABDEMRTU	drumbeat
ABDENNOS	noseband
ABDENNRW	brand-new
ABDENORR	Dearborn
ABDENORW	bear down
	rawboned
	raw-boned
ABDENOTW	beat down
	downbeat
	down-beat
ABDENRRU	unbarred
ABDENRSS	drabness
ABDENRTU	turbaned
ABDENTTU	débutant
ABDEORRW	wardrobe
ABDEORTU	obdurate
ABDEORUX	Bordeaux
ABDEPRSS	bad press
ABDEPSTU	Budapest
ABDERSTW	bedstraw
ABDESTTU	taste bud
ABDFFLOY	badly off
ABDFLOOT	foldboat
ABDGGGOY	doggy-bag
ABDGGINO	going bad
ABDGILOO	Badoglio
ABDGINOR	boarding
ABDGINST	dingbats
ABDGNRSU	Sandburg
ABDGOOUY	a good buy
ABDHIIST	dishabit
ABDHILLN	handbill
ABDHILNS	blandish
ABDHINRS	brandish
ABDHIRSU	Hudibras
ABDHIRTY	birthday
ABDHKNOO	handbook
ABDHLOPR	Bardolph
ABDHMOTU	badmouth
	bad-mouth
ABDIIJLR	jailbird
ABDIILLR	billiard
ABDIIMNR	midbrain
ABDIIMSU	basidium
ABDIINOS	obsidian
ABDIINRR	rainbird
ABDIINTT	banditti
ABDIIRTY	rabidity
ABDILLTY	badly lit
ABDILMOR	Lombardi
ABDILORW	wild boar
ABDILRRY	ribaldry
ABDILRZZ	blizzard
ABDIMNRY	myna bird
ABDINNOU	abound in
ABDINORY	Robin Day
ABDINOTY	antibody
ABDINRTY	banditry
ABDIPRTT	Brad Pitt
ABDLRSUY	absurdly
ABDMNNOS	bondsman
ABDMRSSU	bass drum
ABDNORUY	boundary
ABDNOSWW	swab down
ABDOORTU	board out
	outboard
ABDOOSSW	basswood
ABDOOSTU	sod about
ABDOOTTU	dot about
ABEEEERT	bee-eater
ABEEEFRS	freebase
ABEEEGRS	bargeese
ABEEEGRV	beverage
ABEEEHTT	hebetate
ABEEELPS	Bel Paese
	bel paese
ABEEENRR	near beer
ABEEENST	absentee
ABEEERRT	terebrae
ABEEFILS	feasible
ABEEFILT	flea-bite
ABEEFLOS	beefalos
ABEEFORR	forebear
ABEEGIRV	verbiage
ABEEGKLR	leg break
ABEEGMTY	megabyte
ABEEGNRR	Berengar
ABEEGOSZ	gazeboes
ABEEGRST	absterge
ABEEGTTU	baguette
ABEEHILR	hireable
ABEEHINT	thebaine
ABEEHIRS	Hebraise
ABEEHIRZ	Hebraize
ABEEHLLP	helpable
ABEEHLLR	harebell
ABEEHLMO	La Bohème
ABEEHNOT	The Beano
ABEEHNSS	has-beens
ABEEHNTT	hebetant
ABEEHOTV	have to be
ABEEHQTU	bequeath
ABEEHRRT	breather
ABEEHSTT	the Beast
ABEEIKLL	likeable
ABEEIKLT	Bakelite®
ABEEIKRT	tie-break
ABEEILLR	reliable
ABEEILLV	liveable
ABEEILNP	plebeian
ABEEILNV	enviable
ABEEILPX	expiable
ABEEILRT	liberate
ABEEILSZ	seizable
	sizeable
ABEEILVW	viewable
ABEEIRTT	batterie

ABEEISTU	beauties
ABEEJMNT	Betjeman
ABEEJMOR	jamboree
ABEEKLLW	Bakewell
ABEEKLOT	keelboat
ABEEKRST	bestreak
ABEELLLS	sellable
ABEELLOV	loveable
ABEELLTT	lettable
ABEELMMR	embalmer
	emmarble
ABEELMNO	bone meal
ABEELMOV	moveable
ABEELMPR	preamble
ABEELMSS	assemble
ABEELMTT	embattle
ABEELNOP	beanpole
	openable
ABEELNTU	tuneable
ABEELOPR	operable
	ropeable
ABEELSSS	baseless
ABEELSST	bateless
ABEELSSU	sublease
ABEELSTT	seat belt
	testable
ABEEMMNR	membrane
ABEEMNQU	Queen Mab
ABEEMNST	basement
ABEEMNTT	abetment
ABEENNOT	nota bene
ABEENNRT	banneret
ABEENNRU	eburnean
ABEENNTU	unbeaten
ABEENORS	seaborne
ABEENRRT	banterer
ABEENRSS	bareness
ABEENSSS	baseness
ABEEORRV	overbear
ABEEORST	rebatoes
ABEEOSTU	see about
ABEERRRT	barterer
ABEERRST	terebras
ABEERRTV	vertebra
ABEERRTY	betrayer
ABEERSTU	suberate
ABEESTTT	beta test
	beta-test
ABEFFKOR	break off
	off-break
ABEFGLLU	blue flag
ABEFILLL	fallible
ABEFILLM	filmable
ABEFILLR	fireball
ABEFILOT	lifeboat
ABEFILRS	false rib
ABEFILSU	fabulise
ABEFILSY	feasibly
ABEFILUZ	fabulize
ABEFITUY	beautify
ABEFLMOR	formable
ABEFLNRU	funebral
ABEFLRTU	Flaubert
ABEFMRSU	subframe
ABEFOORT	barefoot
ABEFORTU	Beaufort
ABEFORWY	be wary of
ABEFRRUY	February
ABEGGHLU	huggable
ABEGGILN	beagling
ABEGGIRT	great big
ABEGGITY	gigabyte
ABEGGLRY	beggarly
ABEGGNOS	bang goes
ABEGHILR	alberghi
ABEGHINT	in the bag
ABEGHINZ	Benghazi
ABEGHNNO	Ben Hogan
ABEGHORR	begorrah
ABEGHOUZ	Gezhouba
ABEGHRRY	hagberry
ABEGIILV	give bail
ABEGIKNR	breaking
ABEGILNT	bleating
	tangible
ABEGILOT	obligate
ABEGINRS	Basinger
	bearings
ABEGINRT	berating
ABEGINTT	abetting
ABEGINTW	wingbeat
ABEGIPPR	bagpiper
ABEGIPPS	bagpipes
ABEGJLLY	jelly bag
ABEGKMPR	Bergkamp
ABEGKORS	grosbeak
ABEGLLOR	Bargello
ABEGLLRY	Llaregyb
ABEGLNOS	noble gas
ABEGLPRU	Paul Berg
ABEGMNNU	mung bean
ABEGMNOY	bogeyman
	money-bag
ABEGMORT	bergamot
ABEGNOOR	Gaborone
ABEGOTTU	get about
ABEHILNR	hibernal
ABEHILTT	tithable
ABEHIMNO	bohemian□
ABEHINRT	breath in
ABEHINST	absinthe
ABEHIRTW	bear with
ABEHJLNO	John Abel
ABEHKNST	thanks be
ABEHKSTU	Kate Bush
ABEHLMMU	hummable
ABEHLMSS	shambles
ABEHLSVY	by halves
ABEHMNOR	hornbeam
ABEHMOOR	rehoboam
ABEHNOTT	on the tab
ABEHNSTU	sunbathe
ABEHOSTU	house bat
ABEHRSST	the brass
ABEHRTUY	Bayreuth
ABEHTWYY	by the way
ABEIILMT	imitable
ABEIILNN	biennial
ABEIILPT	pitiable
ABEIILST	albitise
	sibilate
ABEIILTZ	albitize
ABEIINRS	Siberian
ABEIIRST	Tiberias
ABEIJLTU	jubilate
ABEIJMNN	Benjamin
ABEIKLSS	kissable
ABEIKMRR	rim-brake
ABEIKNRS	bearskin
ABEILLLT	tillable
ABEILLMM	limbmeal
ABEILLNV	Banville
ABEILLOT	liable to
ABEILLOV	violable
ABEILLRR	brailler
ABEILLRY	Bareilly
	blearily
	reliably
ABEILLST	bastille□
ABEILMSS	missable
ABEILNNW	winnable
ABEILNST	instable
ABEILNTV	bivalent
ABEILNUV	unviable
ABEILNVY	enviably
ABEILOTU	lie about
ABEILPRT	partible
ABEILPSS	passible
ABEILPST	epiblast
ABEILRYY	bi-yearly
ABEILSTU	suitable
ABEILSTY	beastily
ABEILSUX	bisexual
ABEIMRTV	verbatim
ABEIMSSU	iambuses
ABEINNOR	Brian Eno
ABEINORR	airborne
ABEINORT	baritone
	obtainer
ABEINOST	botanise
	obeisant
ABEINOTZ	botanize
ABEINRST	banister
ABEINRSU	urbanise
ABEINRTU	urbanite
ABEINRUZ	urbanize
ABEINSST	bassinet
ABEINSTW	waste bin
ABEINTTU	intubate
ABEIORTV	abortive
ABEIORUV	Beauvoir
ABEIOTTT	beat to it
ABEIPRRS	spare rib

Words marked □ can also be spelled with an initial capital letter

	spare-rib
ABEIRRVY	breviary
ABEIRSTY	bestiary
	sybarite□
ABEITTTU	titubate
ABEJMOOR	jeroboam
ABEKLMOS	smokable
ABEKLNOW	knowable
ABEKLNRZ	Karl Benz
ABEKLNST	blankets
ABEKLNTY	blankety
ABEKLORW	workable
ABEKMNOR	embark on
ABEKMOOT	book-mate
ABEKNNOT	banknote
ABEKOORY	yearbook
	year-book
ABEKORTU	break out
	breakout
	outbreak
ABEKORVW	break-vow
ABEKRSTY	basketry
ABELLLSY	syllable
ABELLMRU	umbellar
	umbrella
ABELLOSV	solvable
ABELLRVY	verbally
ABELMNNO	nobleman
ABELMNOP	Belmopan
ABELMNOR	ramble on
ABELMNOZ	emblazon
ABELMOSV	movables
ABELMOVY	moveably
ABELMSSY	assembly□
ABELNNRU	runnable
ABELNORW	brown ale
ABELNRSY	Barnsley
ABELNRTY	Blantyre
ABELNRUY	urbanely
ABELNRYZ	brazenly
ABELNSTU	unstable
ABELNSTY	absently
ABELNSUU	unusable
ABELNUVY	navy blue
ABELOOST	boot sale
ABELOPRT	portable
ABELOPRV	provable
ABELOPRW	below par
ABELOQTU	quotable
ABELORRU	labourer
ABELORST	sortable
	storable
ABELORTU	blare out
ABELOSSU	sabulose
ABELOSTU	absolute□
ABELOSTW	bestowal
ABELRSTU	baluster
ABELRTTU	rebuttal
ABELSTUU	subulate
ABELTTUU	tubulate
ABEMMNOO	moonbeam

ABEMNNOR	mean-born
ABEMNORT	rent-a-mob
ABEMNOTU	Beaumont
	umbonate
ABEMNPRU	penumbra
ABEMNRRY	Berryman
ABEMNTTU	abutment
ABEMRRUW	raw umber
ABENNORT	Brentano
ABENNRUV	Van Buren
ABENOPRU	bear upon
ABENOPSU	subpoena
ABENOPTU	beat up on
ABENORSS	baroness
ABENORTT	betatron
ABENORTV	bevatron
ABENORTW	banewort
ABEORRSS	braseros
ABEORRSW	Boer Wars
ABEORRTU	outer bar
ABEORSTU	saboteur
ABEORTTU	obturate
	tabouret
ABEORTUV	outbrave
ABEOSSST	asbestos
ABEOSTTU	set about
ABEPRSSY	passer-by
ABEPRSTT	best part
ABEQRSUU	arquebus
ABERRWXY	waxberry
ABERSSTU	abstruse
ABERSTUW	water bus
ABFFGIJY	Jiffy bag®
ABFFGILN	baffling
ABFFLLPU	puffball
ABFFLOST	blast off
	blast-off
ABFFNOTU	bouffant
ABFFORSS	brass off
ABFGLLLO	golf ball
ABFGORUU	faubourg
ABFHLOOT	half-boot
ABFHLSUX	flax-bush
ABFHLTTU	half-butt
ABFILLLY	fallibly
ABFILNSU	basinful
ABFILSTU	fabulist
ABFIMORS	fibromas
ABFIRTTU	fruit bat
ABFJORSU	frabjous
ABFKLLOR	korfball
ABFLLOOT	football
ABFLOSTU	boastful
ABFLOSUU	fabulous
ABFMOORT	from A to B
ABFNORTU	turbofan
ABFNORTW	brown fat
ABGGGINR	bragging
ABGGILMN	gambling
ABGGILNR	garbling
ABGGNOOT	toboggan

ABGGRSUU	Augsburg
ABGHHIKN	bank-high
ABGHHILL	highball
ABGHHMRU	Hamburgh
ABGHILRT	Albright
ABGHINWZ	whizbang
ABGHIOPR	biograph
ABGHMORU	brougham
ABGHMOTU	Tombaugh
ABGHNRUV	Vanbrugh
ABGIILOT	obligati
ABGIIMST	bigamist
ABGIKNRR	ring-bark
ABGILLLR	ball-girl
ABGILMNR	marbling
	rambling
ABGILNNU	Bulganin
ABGILNOT	bloating
ABGILNRW	brawling
ABGILNST	blasting
ABGILNTY	tangibly
ABGILOOT	obligato
ABGIMOSU	bigamous
ABGINNOR	aborning
ABGINORT	aborting
ABGINOST	boasting
ABGINTTU	abutting
ABGKLOUV	Bulgakov
ABGLLLOY	globally
ABGLLORU	globular
ABGLLRUY	bullyrag
ABGLMOPU	plumbago
ABGLMOSU	lumbagos
ABGLNOOT	longboat
ABGLNORU	rub along
ABGLNOUW	bungalow
ABGLORSU	glabrous
ABGLRRUY	burglary
ABGLRSUZ	Salzburg
ABGOORST	botargos
ABGORSSX	grass box
ABGSTTUU	bust a gut
ABHHOSTU	Shabuoth
ABHIINRS	brainish
ABHIIORZ	rhizobia
ABHIJOTW	with a job
ABHIKLOR	kohlrabi
ABHIKNRU	Bukharin
ABHILNOT	biathlon
ABHILOTT	hit a blot
ABHIRRSU	air-brush
ABHIRSTT	brattish
ABHKLMOR	Karl Böhm
ABHKLSUW	bushwalk
ABHLLMOT	mothball
ABHLLNTU	hunt ball
ABHLLOOY	ballyhoo
ABHLOSST	sash bolt
ABHLSSTU	saltbush
ABHMNSUU	subhuman
ABHMOORT	bathroom

ABHOORST	tarboosh
ABHOOSST	Basothos
ABHOOSTW	Show Boat
ABHOOTUW	how about
ABHOPSTT	stop bath
ABHRSTTU	Bathurst
ABIIIKRT	Kiribati
ABIIINOT	ab initio
ABIIINRY	biriyani
ABIIKLSS	basilisk ❑
ABIILLMR	millibar
ABIILMNO	binomial
ABIILMNS	albinism
ABIILNOT	libation
ABIILNST	sibilant
ABIILPTY	pitiably
ABIIMNOT	ambition
ABIINRTT	Brittain
ABIIRRTZ	Biarritz
ABIIRSSV	vibrissa
ABIJLMPU	jump bail
ABIJLNTU	jubilant
ABIJNOST	banjoist
ABIKLMNS	lambskin
ABILLLPY	playbill
ABILLOVY	violably
ABILLRTY	tribally
ABILMNOU	olibanum
ABILNOOT	oblation
ABILNOTU	ablution
ABILNRTU	tribunal
	turbinal
ABILNSTU	Istanbul
ABILPSSY	passibly
ABILRSSY	brassily
ABILRSUV	subviral
ABILSSUY	issuably
ABILSTUY	suitably
ABIMRSST	strabism
ABINOORT	abortion
ABINOPTU	Pinatubo
ABINORWY	rainbowy
ABINOSTT	botanist
ABINRTUY	urbanity
ABIOPSTU	subtopia
ABIORRTV	vibrator
ABIORSTV	vibratos
ABIORTUY	obituary
ABIPSSTT	Baptists
ABKKMOOR	bookmark
ABKLLNOR	bankroll
ABKLNOTU	blank out
ABKLRSUW	bulwarks
ABKMOOOS	Akosombo
ABKMOOSS	mass-book
ABKNPRTU	bankrupt
ABLLMNOO	moon-ball
ABLLMOOR	ballroom
ABLLNOSW	snowball ❑
ABLLOORT	root-ball
ABLLRTUY	brutally
ABLLSSUY	syllabus
ABLMNNTU	Bultmann
ABLMNRUU	laburnum
ABLNORYZ	blazonry
ABLNRSUU	sublunar
ABLNRSUY	Lansbury
ABLOORTY	oblatory
ABLOPRVY	provably
ABLOQTUY	quotably
ABLORSSU	subsolar
ABLOSSUU	sabulous
ABLOSTTU	blast out
	subtotal
ABLPRTUY	abruptly
ABMOORTW	warm-boot
ABMOOTTT	at bottom
ABNOORRT	roborant
ABNORRTW	brown rat
ABNORTUU	runabout
ABNOSSUU	Aubusson
ABOPRSST	top brass
ABOPTTUU	put about
ABRRSTUY	star ruby
ACCCDIIO	coccidia
ACCCENPY	peccancy
ACCCHILO	colchica
ACCCIIPR	capricci
ACCCILLY	cyclical
ACCDDIIT	didactic
ACCDEEIN	ice dance
ACCDEEOT	accede to
ACCDEEPT	accepted
ACCDEGIN	acceding
ACCDEILY	delicacy
ACCDEINT	accident
ACCDEIRT	accredit
ACCDEISU	caudices
ACCDELSU	cul-de-sac
ACCDELSY	Cyclades
ACCDERSU	accursed
ACCDHIKW	Chadwick
ACCDIIRU	uric acid
ACCDIITY	dicacity
ACCDIKOR	acid rock
ACCDILTY	dactylic
ACCDINOR	draconic
	in accord
ACCDITUY	caducity
ACCDOSUU	caducous
ACCEEHLO	cochleae
ACCEEILR	celeriac
ACCEEIMN	MacNeice
ACCEEIMR	ice cream
ACCEEKLN	necklace
ACCEELNR	Clarence
ACCEELOS	coalesce
ACCEFFIY	efficacy
ACCEFILS	fascicle
ACCEFKOR	rock-face
ACCEFOSU	accuse of
ACCEGKMO	gamecock
ACCEHIKP	chick pea
	chickpea
ACCEHILM	chemical
ACCEHILP	cephalic
ACCEHIMN	mechanic
ACCEHINO	anechoic
ACCEHINT	chance it
ACCEHLOR	cochlear
ACCEHMNO	Comanche
ACCEHNNO	chaconne
	chance on
	no chance
ACCEHNOR	encroach
ACCEHNRY	chancery
ACCEILLR	clerical
ACCEILLV	clavicle
ACCEILNT	canticle
ACCEILOS	calicoes
ACCEILRV	cervical
ACCEIMNO	Comaneci
ACCEIMRS	ceramics
ACCEINRT	Nearctic
ACCEIOTV	coactive
ACCEIPRS	Caprices
ACCEIPRT	practice
ACCEIPSV	peccavis
ACCEISTT	ecstatic
ACCEKKOR	rock cake
ACCEKLNR	cracknel
ACCEKRRS	crackers
ACCELMNY	cyclamen
ACCELNOV	conclave
ACCELNRU	caruncle
ACCELNTU	clean-cut
ACCELRSY	scarcely
ACCELRTU	clear-cut
ACCELSSU	saccules
ACCELWYY	cycleway
ACCENNSY	nascency
ACCENORT	accentor
ACCENOST	cosecant
ACCEOPRT	acceptor
ACCEORTU	accouter
	accoutre
ACCESSTU	cactuses
ACCFHKLO	half-cock
ACCGHINO	coaching
ACCGHINT	catching
ACCGIKLN	cackling
ACCGIKMR	gimcrack
ACCGIKNR	cracking
ACCGINSU	accusing
ACCGLOOY	cacology
ACCHHIMT	catch him
ACCHHITT	chitchat
	chit-chat
ACCHIIRT	rachitic
ACCHILOR	orichalc
ACCHILOT	catholic
ACCHINNO	cinchona
ACCHINPU	capuchin ❑

Words marked ❑ can also be spelled with an initial capital letter

ACCHIORT	thoracic
	trochaic
ACCHIRTT	Cratchit
ACCHKLOR	charlock
ACCHKMOR	arch-mock
ACCHLOPT	cloth cap
ACCHMRTY	McCarthy
ACCHNNOT	Connacht
ACCHNOOR	coronach
ACCHNOTU	couchant
ACCHOPRS	cash crop
ACCHOSTY	cosy chat
ACCHOTTU	catch out
ACCHRSTY	scratchy
ACCIILLN	clinical
ACCIILMT	climatic
ACCIILRT	critical
ACCIINNO	aniconic
ACCIIRTX	cicatrix
ACCIKKNN	nick-nack
ACCIKKRR	rick-rack
ACCIKKTT	tick-tack
ACCIKLOT	cocktail
ACCIKNST	canstick
ACCILNOV	volcanic
ACCILORT	cortical
ACCILRRU	circular
ACCIMNOS	moccasin
ACCIMPSU	capsicum
ACCINOOS	occasion
ACCINOOT	coaction
ACCINORT	narcotic
ACCINOTY	cyanotic
ACCIOPST	spiccato
ACCIORST	acrostic
	Socratic
ACCIORSY	isocracy
ACCIOSTU	acoustic
ACCIRSTY	scarcity
ACCKKRSU	rucksack
ACCKOOOT	cockatoo
ACCKOPRT	crackpot
ACCKORST	stock car
ACCLLSUU	calculus
ACCLMOOP	coco-palm
ACCLMOSU	Moluccas
ACCLSSUU	sacculus
ACCMOSTU	accustom
ACCNOPTU	occupant
ACCNORTT	contract
ACCNOSTT	contacts
ACCNOSTU	accounts
ACCOQSSU	squaccos
ACCORRTY	carrycot
	carry-cot
ACDDDEIT	addicted
ACDDDEKU	dead duck
ACDDEEES	deceased
ACDDEEFR	red-faced
ACDDEEHT	detached
ACDDEEIT	dedicate
ACDDEEIU	deciduae
ACDDEELR	declared
ACDDEENR	credenda
ACDDEENT	decadent
ACDDEERR	red cedar
ACDDEERT	dead cert
ACDDEESU	Sadducee
ACDDEETU	educated
ACDDEHKN	deck hand
	deckhand
ACDDEHLO	head cold
ACDDEINR	riddance
ACDDEISU	deciduas
ACDDEITT	dictated
ACDDEKLO	deadlock
ACDDEKMU	mud-caked
ACDDGILN	cladding
ACDDGLOR	gold card
ACDDILNY	candidly
ACDDILRW	wild card
ACDDINNU	uncandid
ACDDINSY	discandy
ACDDIOPR	acid drop
ACDDKORY	dockyard
ACDDLMNO	McDonald
ACDEEEFT	defecate
ACDEEEKS	seedcake
ACDEEENT	antecede
ACDEEERS	decrease
ACDEEFFT	affected
ACDEEFIN	defiance
ACDEEFRY	federacy
ACDEEGLY	delegacy
ACDEEHIV	achieved
ACDEEHKO	coke-head
ACDEEHMR	démarche
ACDEEHNS	enchased
ACDEEIIP	epicedia
ACDEEILR	I declare!
ACDEEILT	delicate
ACDEEIMT	decimate
	medicate
ACDEEINU	audience
ACDEEINV	deviance
ACDEEKPT	tape deck
ACDEELNR	calender
	encradle
ACDEELNS	cleansed
ACDEELRR	declarer
ACDEELRT	decretal
ACDEENOT	anecdote
	toe-dance
ACDEENRS	ascender
	reascend
ACDEENRT	decanter
ACDEEORT	decorate
ACDEERRT	terraced
ACDEERSU	red sauce
ACDEESUX	caudexes
ACDEFIIL	deifical
ACDEFIIP	pacified
ACDEFILR	fricadel
ACDEFNOW	face down
ACDEFORS	scared of
ACDEFOTW	two-faced
ACDEFRSU	surfaced
ACDEGINU	guidance
ACDEGINY	decaying
ACDEGIRS	disgrace
ACDEGORS	God's acre
ACDEHILL	Helladic
ACDEHILR	heraldic
ACDEHIRS	rachides
ACDEHKLS	shackled
ACDEHKRU	archduke
ACDEHKSS	cash desk
ACDEHLNP	planched
ACDEHLNR	chandler❑
ACDEHLNU	launched
ACDEHLOR	hole card
	Rochdale
ACDEHNOR	anchored
ACDEHORR	hard core
	hard-core
ACDEHORY	ad hocery
ACDEHPST	despatch
ACDEHRST	starched
ACDEIINT	actinide
	indicate
ACDEIJNU	jaundice
ACDEIKMN	main deck
ACDEILMT	maledict
ACDEILNU	Claudine
ACDEILOR	Cordelia
ACDEILPS	displace
ACDEILRT	articled
ACDEIMNO	comedian
	daemonic
	demoniac
ACDEIMNP	pandemic
ACDEIMOR	Mordecai
ACDEINNR	crannied
ACDEINOS	diocesan
	oceanids
ACDEINOV	voidance
ACDEINPT	pedantic
ACDEINST	disenact
	distance
ACDEINTV	ci-devant
	Vedantic
ACDEINVY	deviancy
ACDEIORT	ceratoid
ACDEIOSU	edacious
ACDEIPRT	priced at
ACDEIPSS	spadices
ACDEIPST	spicated
ACDEIQRU	acquired
ACDEIRSS	Cressida
ACDEIRTT	direct at
ACDEJNRY	Jarndyce
ACDEKLMO	make cold
ACDEKLMU	lame duck

Words marked ❑ can also be spelled with an initial capital letter

ACDEKOST	stockade
ACDELLMO	cold meal
ACDELLNO	Candolle
ACDELLOR	collared
ACDELLOS	so-called
ACDELMSU	muscadel
ACDELNOO	canoodle
ACDELNOR	colander
ACDELNPU	unplaced
ACDELNRY	dry-clean
ACDELOTU	oculated
ACDELOUZ	Lucozade®
ACDELRSW	scrawled
ACDELRSY	sacredly
ACDELSTU	sulcated
ACDEMORS	comrades
ACDEMORT	democrat
	Tremadoc
ACDEMSTU	Muscadet
ACDENNOR	ordnance
ACDENOPR	endocarp
ACDENOSY	cyanosed
ACDENRTU	under-act
ACDENRVY	verdancy
ACDEOPRY	copyread
ACDEORRT	redactor
ACDEORTU	educator
ACDEPPRS	scrapped
ACDEQTUU	aqueduct
ACDERRSU	crusader
	sure card
ACDERRTU	traducer
ACDERSSU	Crusades
ACDERTTU	tear duct
ACDFFHNU	handcuff
ACDFFIRT	diffract
ACDFFLOS	scaffold
ACDFGOOT	act of God
ACDFIILU	fiducial
ACDFORRW	Crawford
ACDGHOTW	watchdog
ACDGILNS	scalding
ACDGIMOT	dogmatic
ACDHHNTU	unhatch'd
ACDHIKNP	hand-pick
ACDHILPR	pilchard
ACDHINOR	hadronic
ACDHINSW	sandwich□
ACDHIOPS	scaphoid
ACDHIPST	dispatch
ACDHIRRS	Richards
ACDHKLRU	hard luck
ACDHKORR	hard rock
ACDHMNTU	Dutchman
ACDHNORW	chawdron
ACDHNOSW	cash down
ACDHOPRY	hard copy
ACDHORSY	dyschroa
ACDIIJLU	judicial
ACDIILMS	disclaim
ACDIILNS	scaldini
ACDIILSU	suicidal
ACDIIMNO	daimonic
	Dominica
ACDIIMOT	diatomic
ACDIINNT	indicant
ACDIINOT	diatonic
ACDIINPR	Pindaric
ACDIIOSS	acidosis
ACDIIRTY	acridity
ACDIISST	sadistic
ACDILLPY	placidly
ACDILMTU	Talmudic
ACDILNOR	ironclad
	iron-clad
ACDILOUV	oviducal
ACDILSUU	Claudius
ACDIMNSU	muscadin
	scandium
ACDIMNSY	dynamics
ACDINOPS	spondaic
ACDINORS	sardonic
ACDINSTY	dynastic
ACDIOPRS	sporadic
ACDIORTT	dictator
ACDIOSUU	aciduous
ACDIRSTT	distract
ACDKNOPW	pack down
ACDKORRT	track rod
ACDLLNOW	call down
ACDLMNOW	calm down
ACDLNOPS	cold snap
ACDLNORU	cauldron
ACDLNOST	Scotland
ACDLOOOR	Colorado
ACDLOORT	doctoral
ACDLORWY	cowardly
ACDMMNOO	commando
ACDMNORY	dormancy
	mordancy
ACDMOOPR	macropod
ACDNOOTU	ducatoon
ACDNOSTW	cast down
	cast-down
	downcast
ACDOPRST	postcard
ACDORSSU	crusados
ACDORSUZ	cruzados
ACDRSTTU	dustcart
ACEEEFRR	carefree
ACEEEGLN	elegance
ACEEEGRS	cargeese
ACEEEKPP	keep pace
ACEEELMR	cameleer
ACEEELMS	McAleese
ACEEENSV	evanesce
ACEEERRT	recreate
ACEEERTT	et cetera
	etcetera
ACEEERTX	execrate
ACEEFFIN	caffeine
ACEEFFLT	left face!
ACEEFIOP	a piece of
	of a piece
ACEEFKOR	ecofreak
ACEEFLNV	Van Cleef
ACEEFLOS	lose face
ACEEFLPU	peaceful
ACEEFLRT	tree calf
ACEEFLSS	faceless
ACEEFPRT	perfecta
	praefect
ACEEFPTY	typeface
ACEEFRSU	farceuse
ACEEGHNR	Grenache
ACEEGHNX	exchange
ACEEGHOR	ogee arch
ACEEGHRR	recharge
ACEEGIMY	magic eye
ACEEGINR	Carnegie
ACEEGIRS	Graecise
ACEEGIRZ	Graecize
ACEEGKRW	wreckage
ACEEGLNY	elegancy
ACEEGLRT	get clear
ACEEGNRY	reagency
ACEEGNSV	scavenge
ACEEGORV	coverage
ACEEHIPT	petechia
ACEEHIRV	achiever
	chivaree
ACEEHKLO	cakehole
ACEEHKLR	keel arch
ACEEHKTT	hackette
ACEEHLMP	empleach
ACEEHLNR	Charlene
ACEEHLOS	shoelace
ACEEHLRS	Heracles
ACEEHLSW	eschewal
ACEEHMNP	camphene
ACEEHMNR	menarche
ACEEHMRS	cashmere
ACEEHORT	ochreate
ACEEHPRR	preacher
ACEEHRRS	research
	searcher
ACEEHRST	teachers
ACEEHRTT	catheter
ACEEHRTZ	the craze
ACEEHSTT	tea chest
ACEEHSTX	cathexes
ACEEIKST	ice skate
ACEEILMT	emetical
ACEEILNP	capeline
ACEEILNR	reliance
ACEEILNS	salience
ACEEILPS	especial
ACEEIMRR	rearmice
ACEEIMRS	racemise
ACEEIMRZ	racemize
ACEEINPS	sapience
ACEEINPT	patience□
ACEEINRS	increase

Words marked □ can also be spelled with an initial capital letter

ACEEINRT	creatine
	iterance
ACEEINST	cineaste
ACEEIPST	speciate
ACEEIRSW	wiseacre
ACEEIRTV	creative
	reactive
ACEEIRTW	water ice
ACEEISTV	vesicate
ACEEKLMP	keep calm
ACEEKLMR	mackerel
ACEEKLRW	eelwrack
ACEEKMPT	empacket
ACEEKNRW	neckwear
ACEELLOT	ocellate
ACEELLOV	Lovelace
ACEELMNP	placemen
ACEELNPT	pentacle
ACEELNRS	cleanser
ACEELNRU	cerulean
	Laurence
ACEELNRW	Lawrence
ACEELNSU	nuclease
ACEELNTT	tentacle
ACEELNTU	nucleate
ACEELOPS	escalope
ACEELORT	relocate
ACEELOTV	cleave to
ACEELPRR	replacer
ACEELPRV	Perceval
ACEELPTU	peculate
ACEELRSS	careless
ACEELRTT	raclette
ACEELRTU	ulcerate
ACEELRTV	cervelat
ACEELSTT	telecast
ACEEMNOR	come near
ACEEMNST	casement
ACEEMORS	racemose
ACEEMRRS	screamer
ACEEMRRY	creamery
ACEENNPZ	Penzance
ACEENNRT	entrance
ACEENORT	carotene
ACEENOST	notecase
ACEENPRR	parcener
ACEENRRS	Sancerre
ACEENRRT	recanter
	recreant
	Terrance
ACEENRST	sarcenet
ACEENRTT	entr'acte
ACEENRTU	enacture
	uncreate
ACEEPRSU	crease up
ACEEPSTT	spectate
ACEERRTU	creature
ACEERRUV	verrucae
ACEERSST	cerastes
ACEERSSV	crevasse
ACEERTTU	eructate
ACEESSTT	cassette
	test case
ACEFFILT	facelift
ACEFFLLU	full-face
ACEFFLOR	clear off
ACEFFORS	scare off
ACEFGLNO	long face
ACEFGLRU	graceful
ACEFHIKS	fishcake
ACEFHIRT	car-thief
ACEFHNTY	the fancy
ACEFHORU	farouche
ACEFIIPR	pacifier
ACEFIIRT	artifice
ACEFILLY	facilely
ACEFILOS	focalise
ACEFILOZ	focalize
ACEFINNR	Francine
ACEFINNS	finances
ACEFINOR	café noir
	in care of
ACEFINOS	in case of
ACEFIORR	air force
ACEFIOSS	fiascoes
ACEFIRTT	trifecta
ACEFIRTY	feracity
ACEFLLOT	alto clef
ACEFLLRU	leaf-curl
ACEFLMNO	flamenco
ACEFLNOR	falconer
ACEFLNOT	conflate
ACEFLNRY	cranefly
ACEFLORS	alfresco
ACEFMNOO	moonface
ACEFNORV	conferva
ACEFOPTU	cup of tea
	face up to
ACEFORRT	cater for
ACEFORST	forecast
ACEFRRRY	car ferry
ACEFRRSU	surfacer
ACEFRRTU	fracture
ACEGHILT	lichgate
ACEGHINR	in charge
	reaching
ACEGHINT	cheating
	teaching
ACEGHJNO	John Cage
ACEGHLTY	lychgate
ACEGHLUY	Caughley
ACEGHMMR	Meg March
ACEGHNPU	change up
ACEGHNRU	uncharge
ACEGIINV	vicinage
ACEGIKNR	creaking
ACEGILLO	collegia
ACEGILLR	allergic
ACEGILMU	mucilage
ACEGILNN	cleaning
ACEGILNO	Angelico
ACEGILNR	clearing
ACEGILNW	lacewing
ACEGILSS	glacises
ACEGILST	gelastic
ACEGIMNN	menacing
ACEGIMNR	Germanic
ACEGIMNT	magnetic
ACEGIMOX	exogamic
ACEGINNO	canoeing
ACEGINRT	catering
	creating
	cringe at
ACEGINRU	Guernica
ACEGINSS	caginess
ACEGINSW	wing case
ACEGINTX	exacting
ACEGIOTT	cogitate
ACEGIPRT	price tag
ACEGIRST	agrestic
ACEGKLOT	lock gate
ACEGLLNO	collagen
ACEGLOPS	go places
ACEGMOPS	compages
ACEGNNOY	cyanogen
ACEGORST	escargot
ACEGORSV	Cosgrave
ACEGORTY	category
ACEHHIRR	hierarch
ACEHHKLT	the Chalk
ACEHHLSU	shauchle
ACEHHMNN	henchman
ACEHHNSU	haunches
ACEHHPRT	heptarch
ACEHHRTT	thatcher ❑
ACEHHRTY	thearchy
ACEHIIMS	ischemia
ACEHIINR	Reichian
ACEHIIRT	hieratic
ACEHIJKR	hijacker
ACEHIJNT	Jacinthe
ACEHILLS	Achilles
ACEHILMN	inchmeal
ACEHILMP	impleach
ACEHILMS	MacLeish
ACEHILPR	parhelic
ACEHILTT	athletic
ACEHIMNN	Eichmann
ACEHIMPT	empathic
	emphatic
ACEHIMSS	chamises
ACEHIMST	misteach
	tachisme
ACEHIMTT	thematic
ACEHINOT	ethanoic
	inchoate
ACEHINRV	vacherin
ACEHINST	asthenic
ACEHIPRS	seraphic
ACEHIPRT	phreatic
	pie chart
ACEHIPST	pastiche
ACEHIPTT	pathetic

ACEHIRRS	Chris Rea
ACEHIRSS	rachises
ACEHIRSV	archives
ACEHIRSW	archwise
ACEHISST	chastise
ACEHISTT	tachiste
ACEHISTX	cathexis
ACEHKKNT	the knack
ACEHKLOV	havelock
ACEHKLSS	shackles
ACEHKMPU	muckheap
ACEHKOSW	whackoes
ACEHKRSW	skew arch
ACEHKRTW	what reck?
ACEHLLMO	mallecho
ACEHLLOR	orchella
ACEHLLPP	Chappell
ACEHLLSU	halluces
ACEHLNNS	channels
ACEHLNOR	Loch Earn
ACEHLNPT	planchet
ACEHLNRU	launcher
	relaunch
ACEHLNRY	Charnley
ACEHLNST	stanchel
ACEHLORT	chlorate
	trochlea
ACEHLOSU	Achelous
ACEHLOTT	tea cloth
ACEHLRTU	trauchle
ACEHLSSS	cashless
ACEHLSTT	chattels
ACEHLSTY	chastely
ACEHMNRT	merchant ❑
ACEHMNSS	chessman
ACEHMPRS	champers
ACEHNNOP	pancheon
ACEHNNPT	penchant
ACEHNOPR	car phone
	chaperon
ACEHNOPT	cenotaph ❑
	not cheap
ACEHNORR	ranchero
ACEHNORT	anchoret
ACEHNRST	snatcher
	stancher
ACEHNSTU	unchaste
ACEHOPRR	reproach
ACEHORRV	overarch
ACEHORST	thoraces
ACEHORTT	theocrat
ACEHORTU	outreach
	reach out
ACEHOSSW	showcase
ACEHOSTU	cathouse
	cat-house
	soutache
ACEHPRRT	Petrarch
ACEHPRSU	purchase
ACEHPRTY	patchery
ACEHRRST	Chartres
	starcher
ACEHRSSU	chasseur
ACEHRSTY	Strachey
ACEHRTTY	trachyte
ACEIILNR	irenical
ACEIILNT	Catiline
ACEIILST	silicate
ACEIIMSS	aseismic
ACEIINPS	piscinae
ACEIINRT	in a trice
ACEIINTV	inactive
ACEIIRRT	criteria
ACEIISTT	Atticise
ACEIITTZ	Atticize
ACEIJMST	majestic
ACEIKKMS	make sick
ACEIKLMR	Milk Race
ACEIKLRY	creakily
ACEIKMNN	nickname
ACEIKMRV	maverick
ACEIKNRS	skincare
ACEIKNRW	wine rack
ACEIKOTW	Katowice
ACEILLLT	clitella
ACEILLMT	metallic
ACEILLMY	mycelial
ACEILLOP	calliope ❑
ACEILLOR	rocaille
ACEILLOS	localise
ACEILLOZ	localize
ACEILLPR	calliper
ACEILLPS	allspice
ACEILLPY	epically
ACEILLRS	Carlisle
ACEILLRV	caviller
ACEILMMO	camomile
ACEILMNO	coalmine
ACEILMNP	manciple
ACEILMNS	mescalin
ACEILMOS	camisole
ACEILMPS	misplace
ACEILMRT	metrical
ACEILMST	clematis
ACEILNNP	pinnacle
ACEILNOR	Caroline
ACEILNRT	clarinet
ACEILNSY	saliency
ACEILOPP	Coppélia
ACEILOPR	capriole
ACEILOPT	poetical
ACEILORT	loricate
ACEILOST	societal
ACEILOSV	vocalise
ACEILOTV	locative
ACEILOVZ	vocalize
ACEILPPY	claypipe
	pipeclay
ACEILPRS	spiracle
ACEILPRT	particle
	prelatic
ACEILPRU	peculiar
ACEILPRV	Percival
ACEILPSS	slipcase
ACEILPXY	epicalyx
ACEILRST	articles
ACEILRSV	visceral
ACEILRTT	tractile
ACEILRTU	Lucretia
ACEILRTV	vertical
ACEILRTY	literacy
ACEILSST	Alcestis
ACEILSUV	vesicula
ACEILTVY	actively
ACEIMMNP	pemmican
ACEIMMRS	racemism
ACEIMNNS	MacInnes
ACEIMNRU	manicure
ACEIMNST	semantic
ACEIMOTX	toxaemic
ACEIMPSS	escapism
ACEIMPST	campsite
ACEIMRRW	war crime
ACEIMRST	matrices
ACEIMSST	ascetism
ACEINNOS	canonise
ACEINNOZ	canonize
ACEINNST	instance
ACEINNSU	nuisance
ACEINNTU	uncinate
ACEINOPR	apocrine
	Poincaré
	procaine
ACEINOPS	caponise
ACEINOPZ	caponize
ACEINORS	scenario
ACEINORT	creation ❑
	reaction
ACEINORV	veronica ❑
ACEINORX	anorexic
ACEINOST	canoeist
ACEINOTX	exaction
ACEINPTT	pittance
ACEINPUY	picayune
ACEINRRY	cinerary
ACEINRSS	raciness
ACEINRST	canister
ACEINRTT	interact
ACEINSSU	issuance
ACEINSTV	vesicant
ACEINTTX	excitant
ACEINTTY	tenacity
ACEIOPRT	operatic
ACEIORRT	race riot
ACEIORSV	varicose
ACEIOSTT	oscitate
ACEIOTVV	vocative
ACEIOVVV	viva voce
ACEIPPRR	pericarp
ACEIPRRW	price war
ACEIPRST	practise
ACEIPSST	escapist
ACEIPSSU	auspices

ACEIRRSU	curarise
ACEIRRUZ	curarize
ACEIRSST	Castries
ACEIRSTU	suricate
ACEIRTTU	urticate
ACEIRTTV	tractive
ACEIRTUV	curative
ACEIRTVY	veracity
ACEISSTU	suitcase
ACEISTTU	eustatic
ACEJKOOR	jackeroo
ACEJLORY	cajolery
ACEJMRST	scramjet
ACEJNRRY	jerrycan
ACEKKMRU	muck-rake
ACEKLLOY	Yale lock
	Yale® lock
ACEKLMOO	Lake Como
ACEKLNTU	untackle
ACEKLORV	laverock
ACEKLORW	lacework
ACEKLPRS	sprackle
ACEKMSTU	make cuts
ACEKNNOW	acknowne
ACEKNORT	one-track
ACEKNPSU	sneak-cup
ACEKNRRT	rack-rent
ACEKORRV	overrack
ACEKQRUY	quackery
ACEKSSUW	waesucks
ACELLLRU	cellular
ACELLNOT	Lancelot
ACELLOPS	collapse
	escallop
ACELLORV	call over
	coverall
	overcall
ACELLOSW	coleslaw
ACELLPRU	Lupercal
ACELLRTY	rectally
ACELLSTU	scutella
ACELMNOR	amelcorn
	Calormen
ACELMNSS	calmness
ACELMNSU	Uncle Sam
ACELMORS	scleroma
ACELMORY	claymore
ACELMSTU	muscatel
ACELMTUU	cumulate
ACELNOPT	not place
ACELNORT	Coltrane
ACELNOSZ	calzones
ACELNOTU	clean out
ACELNRVY	cravenly
ACELNSSU	scalenus
ACELNSTY	secantly
ACELOPPU	populace
ACELOPRT	pectoral
ACELOPRU	opercula
ACELOPTU	copulate
	outplace
ACELORSS	lacrosse
ACELORST	sectoral
ACELORSU	carousel□
ACELORSY	coarsely
ACELORTU	clear out
ACELOSTU	locustae
	osculate
ACELPPRS	clappers
ACELPPRU	parcel up
ACELPRST	spectral
ACELPRSU	specular
	sur place
ACELQSUY	lacqueys
ACELRRSW	scrawler
ACELRSTT	Scarlett
	scrattle
ACELSSTT	tactless
ACEMNOOR	Cameroon
	con amore
ACEMNORR	romancer
ACEMNRSU	sun cream
ACEMNRUY	numeracy
ACEMNSSU	mancuses
ACEMOOST	comatose
ACEMORRT	Mercator
ACEMORSY	sycamore
ACEMORUX	morceaux
ACEMPSSU	campuses
ACENNNOU	announce
ACENNOSS	canoness
ACENNOTV	covenant
ACENNOTZ	canzonet
ACENOPST	capstone
	open-cast
ACENOPTW	Cape Town
ACENOPUX	ponceaux
ACENORRT	Torrance
ACENORRW	careworn
ACENORST	ancestor
	sortance
ACENORSU	carneous
	nacreous
ACENORTU	courante
ACENOSTT	constate
ACENOSTV	centavos
ACENRSTT	transect
ACENRSTU	Centaurs
	recusant
ACENRSTY	ancestry
ACENRTTU	truncate
ACENSSTW	newscast
ACEOORTV	overcoat
ACEOPSTU	space out
ACEORRSU	carouser
ACEORRTT	retroact
ACEORRTU	Eurocrat
ACEORSST	Socrates
ACEORSTV	overcast
ACEORTTV	overt act
ACEORTUV	à couvert
	carve out
ACEOSSTU	Sea Scout
ACEOSSUY	soy sauce
ACEOSTTU	outcaste
ACEOSTUU	Cousteau
ACEPRRTU	capturer
ACEPSTTY	typecast
ACERRSUV	verrucas
ACERRUVZ	Veracruz
ACERSSUY	Syracuse
ACERTTUW	cut-water
ACFFGHIN	chaffing
ACFFIILO	official
ACFFILNU	fanciful
ACFFKLOS	slack off
ACFFLORR	Carl Orff
ACFFORRY	carry off
ACFFOSST	cast-offs
ACFGITUY	fugacity
ACFHHILN	half-inch
ACFHHINW	hawfinch
ACFHILTW	with calf
ACFHIRSW	crawfish
ACFHIRSY	crayfish
ACFHLOSW	cash flow
ACFHLTUW	watchful
ACFHORST	Ashcroft
ACFHORTW	watch for
ACFIILTY	facility
ACFIIMPS	pacifism
ACFIIPST	pacifist
ACFIISST	Fascisti
ACFIKLNS	calfskin
ACFILLSY	fiscally
ACFILORT	trifocal
ACFILRTY	craftily
ACFILSSY	classify
ACFIMNRU	francium
ACFINORT	fraction
ACFINSTY	sanctify
ACFIOPRY	fair copy
ACFIOSTU	factious
ACFISSST	Fascists
ACFKLLOR	rockfall
ACFKLOPW	wolf pack
ACFKLSSU	sackfuls
ACFKOORR	roof rack
ACFKOSST	stacks of
ACFLNORY	falconry
ACFLOOPS	fool's cap
	foolscap
ACFLORSU	scrofula
ACFLOTUU	Foucault
ACFLRRUU	furcular
ACFMOTTU	factotum
ACGGHINN	changing
ACGGIINT	gigantic
ACGGIIOS	isagogic
ACGGILNN	glancing
ACGGIMNU	McGuigan
ACGGINNU	uncaging
ACGGIOOR	coraggio

ACGGLNOU	glucagon
ACGHHIJK	highjack
	jack-high
ACGHHINT	hatching
ACGHIIMN	Michigan
ACGHIKNW	whacking
ACGHILNS	clashing
ACGHILNY	achingly
ACGHILOR	oligarch
ACGHIMNR	charming
ACGHIMNT	matching
ACGHIMTW	Magwitch
ACGHINOP	poaching
ACGHINPR	parching
ACGHINPT	nightcap
ACGHINRS	crashing
ACGHINST	scathing
ACGHINTU	Taichung
ACGHINTW	watching
ACGHINTY	yachting
ACGHIPRS	graphics
ACGHLLOR	gralloch
ACGHPTUU	caught up
ACGIILNO	logician
ACGIINRT	granitic
ACGIKKLO	goal kick
ACGIKLNS	slacking
ACGIKLRY	garlicky
ACGIKMNS	smacking
ACGIKNOR	croaking
ACGIKNRT	tracking
ACGILLLR	call girl
	callgirl
	call-girl
ACGILLNS	call sign
ACGILNOP	Polignac
ACGILNOT	locating
ACGILNPP	clapping
ACGILNRW	crawling
ACGILNSS	classing
ACGILRSU	surgical
ACGIMMNR	cramming
ACGIMNOR	G Marconi
ACGINNNS	scanning
ACGINNPR	prancing
ACGINNRU	uncaring
ACGINOST	agnostic
ACGINPRS	scraping
ACGINRRY	carrying
ACGIORST	orgastic
ACGIORSU	gracious
ACGJLNOU	conjugal
ACGJLNRU	Carl Jung
ACGKLMOR	glam rock
ACGLMOUU	coagulum
ACGLNORU	clangour
ACGLNOTU	cut along
ACGLOSUU	glaucous
ACGLSSTU	cut glass
ACGNNOOT	contango
ACGNORST	congrats
ACGOORSS	go across
ACHHINTY	hyacinth
ACHHLNOR	rhonchal
ACHHNTTU	nuthatch
	unthatch
ACHHOSTW	chat show
ACHHPTUZ	chutzpah
ACHHSTTU	such that
ACHIIMNS	Mishnaic
ACHIINRT	trichina
ACHIINSU	Chisinau
ACHIIRST	rachitis
ACHIKKSW	kickshaw
ACHIKNOP	pachinko
ACHIKRSW	rickshaw
ACHIKRTT	hat trick
ACHILLOR	orchilla
ACHILLTY	city hall
ACHILMRS	chrismal
ACHILMTY	mythical
ACHILNNS	clannish
ACHILNNU	launch in
ACHILNOS	Nicholas
ACHILPSY	physical
ACHILPTY	patchily
ACHILRVY	chivalry
ACHIMMOS	machismo
ACHIMMST	mismatch
ACHIMNOP	champion❑
ACHIMNOR	harmonic
ACHIMOPR	amphoric
ACHIMOSS	chamisos
ACHIMPSS	scampish
ACHIMRST	Chartism
ACHIMSSU	chiasmus
ACHINNOS	cash in on
ACHINOTZ	hoactzin
ACHIORTV	tovarich
ACHIRSTT	Chartist
ACHISTTY	chastity
ACHJNORY	John Cary
ACHKKORW	hack-work
ACHKKRUV	Kravchuk
ACHKLOTU	chalk out
ACHKLSTU	stulchak
ACHKMORS	shamrock
ACHKNNUU	nunchaku
ACHLLNWY	lynch law
ACHLLORY	chorally
ACHLMSTZ	schmaltz
ACHLNORT	Charlton
ACHLNSTY	stanchly
ACHLOPTT	potlatch
ACHLOTWX	waxcloth
ACHLPRTU	Plutarch
ACHMNNSU	Schumann
ACHMNORY	monarchy
ACHMNOTT	not match
ACHMOORR	Chamorro
ACHMOORT	chat room
ACHMOSSU	so much as
ACHNNORU	unanchor
ACHNOPRU	up-anchor
ACHNPPSS	schnapps
ACHNRSTU	unstarch
ACHOPSST	spot cash
ACHORSTU	crash out
ACHOTTUW	outwatch
	watch out
ACHRSTTU	straucht
ACIIILMN	inimical
ACIIILNV	civilian
ACIIKNNN	cannikin
ACIIKNPT	pack it in
ACIILLVW	civil law
ACIILMNR	criminal
ACIILNOR	ironical
ACIILNPT	platinic
ACIILNRS	Sinclair
ACIILRVW	civil war
ACIIMNOP	Ciampino
ACIIMNOR	morainic
ACIIMNSU	musician
ACIIMNTU	actinium
ACIIMNTY	intimacy
	main city
ACIIMOTT	amitotic
ACIIMPRV	vampiric
ACIIMRST	scimitar
ACIIMSTT	Atticism
ACIIMSTV	activism
ACIIMTUV	viaticum
ACIINNOT	in action
	inaction
ACIINNQU	cinquain
ACIINOPT	optician
ACIINOSV	avionics
ACIINOTT	citation
ACIINPRS	Crispian
ACIINPRT	Pitcairn
ACIINPSS	piscinas
ACIINRSS	narcissi
ACIIORST	aoristic
ACIIORTV	victoria❑
ACIIOTWY	Iowa City
ACIIRSST	Triassic
ACIIRSTT	artistic
ACIISTTU	autistic
ACIISTTV	activist
ACIITTVY	activity
ACIITVVY	vivacity
ACIJKKPS	skipjack
ACIJKLMR	Jim Clark
ACIJNNOR	A J Cronin
ACIJRSSU	Jurassic
ACIKLLST	salt lick
ACIKLMNV	Vlaminck
ACIKLNOT	anti-lock
ACIKLNRY	crankily
ACIKLNSU	Nicklaus
ACIKLORY	croakily
ACIKPPTU	pack it up

ACILLMMY	clammily
ACILLMOS	localism
ACILLNOO	colonial□
ACILLNOR	carillon
ACILLNOS	scallion
ACILLORT	clitoral
ACILLORY	collyria
ACILLOSY	socially
ACILLOTY	locality
ACILMNNO	non-claim
ACILMNOP	complain
ACILMNOS	laconism
ACILMOPR	proclaim
ACILMOSV	vocalism
ACILMSTY	mystical
ACILMTUY	ultimacy
ACILNOOT	location
ACILNOPT	platonic□
ACILNORS	clarinos
ACILNOSU	unsocial
ACILNOSV	Slavonic
ACILNOUV	univocal
ACILNRUY	culinary
ACILNSTU	sultanic
ACILNSTY	scantily
ACILOPRT	tropical
ACILORTV	vortical
ACILORYZ	zircaloy
ACILOSTV	vocalist
ACILPRSU	spicular
ACILPSST	plastics
	slip-cast
ACILRTUV	cultivar
ACILSTUV	victuals
ACILSTUX	Calixtus
ACIMMTUY	cymatium
ACIMNNNO	cinnamon
ACIMNOPT	impact on
ACIMNORT	romantic
ACIMNORY	acrimony
ACIMNOST	monastic
ACIMNPTY	tympanic
ACIMNRSU	craniums
ACIMOSTT	stomatic
ACIMPPTU	camp it up
ACIMRRSY	miscarry
ACINNOSS	scansion
ACINNOST	sanction
ACINNOSU	Asunción
ACINNOTU	continua
ACINNRTY	tyrannic
ACINNSTY	instancy
ACINOOPR	picaroon
ACINOOTV	vocation
ACINOPPT	panoptic
ACINOQUV	coq au vin
ACINORSS	narcosis
ACINORST	cast iron
	cast-iron
ACINORTT	traction
ACINOSSS	cassinos
ACINOSSY	cyanosis
ACINOSTT	oscitant
ACINOSTW	wainscot
ACINOSWX	coxswain
ACINOTTX	toxicant
ACINPQUY	piquancy
ACINPSTY	synaptic
ACINRSTU	curtains
ACINRTTU	taciturn
	urticant
ACINSTTY	sanctity
ACINSTYY	syncytia
ACIOOPTX	Cotopaxi
ACIOOTYZ	zoocytia
ACIOPRST	piscator□
ACIOPSSU	spacious
ACIOPSTU	captious
ACIORTTY	atrocity
ACIORTVY	voracity
ACIOSTUU	cautious
ACIPSTTU	Pittacus
ACIRSSTY	sacristy
ACISTTUY	astucity
ACKKMOPR	pockmark
ACKLLPSU	skullcap
ACKLOOSW	woolsack
ACKLORST	rock salt
	rock-salt
ACKMNOST	stockman
ACKPRSTU	Turk's cap
ACLLLLOR	roll-call
ACLLLNOY	clonally
ACLLMNOU	columnal
ACLLNOPU	call upon
ACLLNORW	Cornwall
ACLLOORT	collator
ACLLOOSS	colossal
ACLLORUY	ocularly
ACLLRTUU	cultural
ACLLSTUU	Catullus
ACLMMNOU	communal
ACLMNORU	columnar
ACLMRSUU	muscular
ACLNOORT	colorant
ACLNORSU	consular
ACLNPTUU	punctual
ACLOOPRR	corporal
ACLOOPRT	Coalport
ACLOOSTY	stay cool
ACLOPPRY	Polycarp
ACLOPSST	top-class
ACLOPSSY	calypsos
ACLOPSUU	opuscula
ACLORTUW	lawcourt
ACLOSSTT	cast lots
ACLOSSTU	outclass
ACMNOOPR	monocarp
ACMNOORT	monocrat
ACMNOSST	Scotsman
ACMOORRT	motor car
ACMOOSST	scotomas
ACMORRTY	Cromarty
ACMORSTW	wormcast
ACNNNORY	cannonry
ACNNOSST	Constans
ACNNOSTT	constant□
ACNOOORT	octaroon
ACNOORRY	coronary
ACNOORST	corantos
ACNOORSU	canorous
ACNOOSTT	at no cost
ACNORRSY	carry-ons
ACNORRTY	contrary
ACNORSTT	contrast
ACNORTTU	turncoat
ACOORSTU	touracos
ACOPRRTT	protract
ACOPRTUY	pay court
ACORRSUW	currasow
ACORRTUY	carry out
	carry-out
ACORRTUZ	razor-cut
ACORSSTU	tau cross
ACORSTTY	cryostat
ACOSSTTU	outcasts
ACPSSTUY	pussy cat
ACRRSTUU	Arcturus
ADDDEEEN	deadened
ADDDEEGR	degraded
ADDDEELR	laddered
ADDDEEMN	demanded
	maddened
ADDDEENR	reddenda
ADDDEENS	saddened
ADDDEMNU	addendum
ADDDEOOW	dead wood
ADDDEOPR	drop-dead
ADDEEEFT	defeated
ADDEEENR	deadener
ADDEEFIL	defilade
ADDEEFLT	deflated
ADDEEGHR	hard edge
ADDEEGNR	deranged
ADDEEGOR	dog-eared
ADDEEGRR	regarded
ADDEEGSW	saw-edged
ADDEEHLY	aldehyde
ADDEEHNR	hardened
ADDEEILN	deadline
ADDEEILP	deep-laid
ADDEEILT	detailed
ADDEEINT	detained
ADDEEISS	diseased
ADDEEKNR	darkened
ADDEELNU	unleaded
ADDEELRY	Adderley
ADDEELUV	devalued
ADDEEMNP	dampened
ADDEEMNR	demander
ADDEENPX	expanded
ADDEENSS	deadness
ADDEENTT	attended

ADDEEPRT departed
ADDEEPRV depraved
pervaded
ADDEERRT retarded
ADDEFILY field day
ADDEFLRU dreadful
ADDEFNOW fade down
ADDEFRRW red dwarf
ADDEGHOR Drogheda
ADDEGRRU Red Guard
ADDEHHSY Eddy Shah
ADDEHILR dihedral
ADDEHLOR hold dear
ADDEHMRU drumhead
ADDEHNTY The Dandy
ADDEHORW headword
ADDEHOST dead shot
ADDEHSTU Thaddeus
ADDEIITV additive
ADDEIJOV Joe David
ADDEILNS landside
ADDEIMNN in demand
ADDEIMRS disarmed
misdread
ADDEIMRV drive mad
ADDEIMSY dismayed
ADDEIMTT admitted
ADDEINOR ordained
ADDEIORS roadside
ADDEIPRS dispread
ADDEIPSS dipsades
ADDEIPST dead spit
ADDEIQSU squaddie
ADDEIRSW sideward
ADDEIRWW wideward
ADDEISSU dissuade
ADDEJSTU adjusted
ADDELMOS dolmades
ADDELNOU duodenal
ADDELNSU unsaddle
ADDELOOR El Dorado
ADDELOSS dead loss
ADDELRST straddle
ADDELRSY saddlery
ADDELRTW twaddler
ADDEMNNO on demand
ADDENNSU sand-dune
ADDENPRU undraped
ADDENRST stranded
ADDEOPST dead stop
ADDEOTTU outdated
ADDEPRSU superadd
ADDFFILO daffodil
ADDFFNRU dandruff
ADDFORRT Dartford
ADDGGORU guard dog
ADDGILNW dawdling
waddling
ADDGLORU old guard
ADDGMRUU mudguard
ADDGORSW godwards
ADDHHLOR hold hard
hold hard!
ADDHIKRS hard disk
ADDHINRW hindward
ADDHINSY dandyish
ADDHNNOW hand down
ADDHOORW hardwood
ADDIIKMZ zaddikim
ADDIINOT addition
ADDIINRT Trinidad
ADDIINTV dividant
ADDIKORS skid road
ADDILNOW laid down
ADDIMNSY dandyism
ADDINNOR ordinand
ADDISSTV St David's
ADDKMORT Mark Todd
ADDKNRRU drunkard
ADDLLNOR landlord
ADDLNOOW woodland
ADDLOOSS soldados
ADDMMOOY moody-mad
ADDMNOPW damp down
ADDMOOSY doomsday
ADDNORWW downward
ADDOORWW Woodward
ADEEEFNY fedayeen
ADEEEFRT federate
ADEEEGLT delegate
ADEEEGNR renegade
ADEEEGNT teenaged
ADEEEGRS degrease
ADEEEHKT take heed
ADEEEHRX exhedrae
ADEEEIMR dearie me
ADEEEINT detainee
ADEEEIUV eau de vie
ADEEEKNW weakened
ADEEELNV leavened
ADEEELRS released
ADEEELRV revealed
ADEEELTV elevated
ADEEEMNT emendate
ADEEENRS serenade
ADEEENTT edentate
ADEEEPRT repeated
ADEEERTT date-tree
ADEEFHNR free hand
freehand
ADEEFHOR forehead
ADEEFILN enfilade
ADEEFIOR foedarie
ADEEFIRR rarefied
ADEEFLMS self-made
ADEEFLOR freeload
ADEEFLRR deferral
ADEEFLRT deflater
ADEEFLSS fadeless
ADEEFMNR freedman
ADEEFMTU deaf-mute
ADEEFNOT tone-deaf
ADEEFNSS deafness
ADEEFNST fastened
ADEEFORR foreread
ADEEFORT foredate
ADEEFRRT raftered
ADEEFRRY defrayer
federary
ADEEGGHS eggheads
ADEEGHIV give head
ADEEGHRT gathered
ADEEGILO ego ideal
ADEEGIRS disagree
ADEEGIST get ideas
ADEEGLNR enlarged
ADEEGMNR gendarme
ADEEGMNY Ganymede
ADEEGMOP megapode
ADEEGNNR endanger
ADEEGNOS go and see
ADEEGNRR gardener
ADEEGNRS grenades
ADEEGNRU under age
under-age
ADEEGNSS agedness
ADEEGORT derogate
ADEEGPRU geared up
ADEEGRRR regarder
ADEEGRRU Daguerre
ADEEGRRV Redgrave
ADEEGRSS dressage
ADEEGRTY get ready
ADEEGSWY edgeways
ADEEHHRS rehashed
ADEEHILN headline
ADEEHILS deisheal
ADEEHIMT the media
ADEEHISV adhesive
ADEEHKWW hawkweed
ADEEHKWY hawk-eyed
ADEEHLLW wellhead
well-head
ADEEHLSS headless
ADEEHMMO home-made
ADEEHMMR hammered
ADEEHMPR hampered
ADEEHNOV have done
ADEEHNRR hardener
ADEEHNRT adherent
threaden
ADEEHNTT at the end
ADEEHNTU unheated
ADEEHORT adhere to
ADEEHORV overhead
ADEEHRRW Hereward
ADEEHRST headrest
ADEEIILS idealise
ADEEIILZ idealize
ADEEIIRS dies irae
ADEEIJMR jeremiad
ADEEIKLS lakeside
ADEEIKSW weak side

ADEEILLN	Danielle
ADEEILMN	Madeline
ADEEILMR	remedial
ADEEILMT	lead time
ADEEILMV	medieval
ADEEILNU	eau de nil
ADEEILPS	Pleiades
ADEEILPT	depilate
	pileated
ADEEILRS	sidereal
ADEEILRZ	realized
ADEEILSV	disleave
ADEEIMNT	dementia
ADEEIMRS	maderise
ADEEIMRT	diameter
ADEEIMRZ	maderize
ADEEIMTT	meditate
ADEEINNR	Adrienne
ADEEINOP	Oedipean
ADEEINRS	arsenide
	draisene
	nearside
ADEEINRT	retained
ADEEIPRS	airspeed
ADEEIRST	siderate
ADEEISST	set aside
	set-aside
ADEEISTV	sedative
ADEEJNOT	Joe Dante
ADEEKKPR	keep dark
ADEEKMRR	remarked
ADEEKNPW	knapweed
ADEEKRST	streaked
ADEELLLP	lapelled
ADEELLMU	medullae
ADEELLMW	well-made
ADEELLNY	leadenly
ADEELLPR	predella
ADEELLRV	ravelled
ADEELLRW	well-read
ADEELLTY	elatedly
ADEELMMR	mal de mer
ADEELMNO	lemonade
ADEELMNR	aldermen
ADEELMNT	lamented
ADEELMRS	demersal
ADEELNOR	oleander
ADEELNRS	Landseer
ADEELNRT	antlered
ADEELNRV	lavender
ADEELNRY	Alderney
ADEELNSU	unsealed
ADEELNSV	enslaved
ADEELNTT	talented
ADEELOPR	lop-eared
ADEELOPS	pedaloes
ADEELORV	overlade
ADEELOST	desolate
ADEELPRS	relapsed
ADEELPST	pedestal
ADEELPTY	pedately
ADEELRRT	red alert
ADEELRST	Lestrade
ADEELSST	dateless
ADEELSTY	sedately
ADEEMMSS	Mesdames
ADEEMNNR	mannered
	Menander
ADEEMNOT	nematode
ADEEMNPR	dampener
ADEEMORT	moderate
ADEEMORV	made over
ADEEMPPR	pampered
ADEEMPST	stampede
ADEEMRSU	measured
ADEENNRS	Andersen
	ensnared
ADEENNRU	unearned
ADEENNTT	tenanted
ADEENOPW	weaponed
ADEENORS	reasoned
ADEENOSS	seasoned
ADEENOTT	detonate
ADEENPPR	endpaper
ADEENPRR	panderer
ADEENPRX	expander
ADEENRRW	wanderer
ADEENRSS	dearness
ADEENRSU	undersea
ADEENRSW	Andrewes
ADEENRTT	attender
ADEENRTU	denature
ADEENSSU	danseuse
	Sudanese
ADEENTTV	vendetta
ADEEORRV	overread
ADEEORVW	overawed
ADEEPPRR	prepared
ADEEPRRS	spreader
ADEEPRST	pederast
ADEEPRSU	persuade
ADEEPRTU	depurate
ADEEPSST	stapedes
ADEEPSWY	speedway
ADEERRRT	retarder
ADEERRRW	rewarder
ADEERRST	serrated
ADEERTTT	tattered
ADEERVYY	every day
	everyday
ADEESTTT	attested
ADEFFORT	trade off
	trade-off
ADEFGILR	Garfield
ADEFGILS	gasfield
ADEFGITU	fatigued
ADEFGLLO	gold leaf
ADEFGLOT	gatefold
ADEFGOOW	a good few
ADEFHIMS	famished
ADEFHLNO	half-done
ADEFHLNT	left-hand
ADEFHNOR	forehand
ADEFHOST	softhead
	soft-head
ADEFIILR	airfield
ADEFIIMR	ramified
ADEFIIRT	ratified
ADEFILLM	ill-famed
ADEFILLT	ill-fated
ADEFILMN	inflamed
ADEFILNT	inflated
ADEFIMNR	Friedman
ADEFIMPR	fire damp
	firedamp
ADEFINRR	infrared
ADEFINRU	Freudian
ADEFINRW	fine-draw
ADEFINYZ	denazify
ADEFIORS	foresaid
ADEFKORS	asked for
ADEFLLLU	ladleful
ADEFLLMO	old flame
ADEFLLUY	feudally
ADEFLNOR	foreland
ADEFLNRS	Flanders
ADEFLNUW	unflawed
ADEFLOPR	drop-leaf
	plead for
ADEFLORT	deflator
ADEFLPRS	feldspar
ADEFLPSU	spadeful
ADEFLRTW	leftward
ADEFMNRU	unframed
ADEFMOPU	made up of
ADEFMOSU	fumadoes
ADEFNSST	daftness
ADEFORUV	favoured
ADEGGJLY	jaggedly
ADEGGLRU	leg guard
ADEGGLRY	raggedly
ADEGGMOY	demagogy
ADEGGNOT	go and get
ADEGGOPY	pedagogy
ADEGGORT	Great Dog
ADEGGORU	gauge rod
ADEGGRTY	gadgetry
ADEGHHOS	hogshead
ADEGHILR	head girl
ADEGHINR	adhering
ADEGHINS	sheading
ADEGHLNO	headlong
ADEGHMOY	hey-go-mad
ADEGHORT	goatherd
ADEGHRTU	daughter
ADEGIIMN	imagined
ADEGIITT	digitate
ADEGIKNN	kneading
ADEGIKOR	Oak Ridge
ADEGILMN	maligned
ADEGILNP	pleading
ADEGILNR	dragline
	Reginald

ADEGILNS	dealings
ADEGILNY	delaying
ADEGILOU	dialogue
ADEGILRS	Griselda
ADEGILSS	glissade
ADEGILSV	disgavel
ADEGIMNR	dreaming
	margined
ADEGIMOR	ideogram
ADEGINOR	organdie
ADEGINOS	diagnose
	San Diego
ADEGINOZ	agonized
ADEGINRR	Gardiner
ADEGINRT	gradient
	red giant
	treading
ADEGINSS	assigned
ADEGINST	steading
ADEGINSU	Agnus Dei
ADEGIRWY	ridgeway
ADEGJKSU	Gajdusek
ADEGKMOO	make good
ADEGLLNO	Legoland
ADEGLMOS	gladsome
ADEGLMUY	amygdule
ADEGLNOS	dal segno
ADEGLNPS	spangled
ADEGLNRS	glanders
ADEGLNSS	gladness
ADEGLORW	low-grade
ADEGMNOO	good name
ADEGMNOY	endogamy
ADEGMORW	word game
	wordgame
ADEGNNOR	androgen
	end organ
ADEGNOPU	poundage
ADEGNORW	gear down
ADEGNRRU	grandeur
ADEGNRUZ	gazunder
ADEGOORY	Goodyear
ADEGOPRR	dragrope
	prograde
ADEGOPRT	top-grade
ADEGORTU	outraged
ADEGORWY	dog-weary
ADEGOSTY	go steady
ADEGRRST	dragster
ADEGTTTU	guttated
ADEHHIPS	headship
ADEHHLOY	Holyhead
ADEHHNTU	headhunt
ADEHHPRS	Shephard
ADEHIILT	The Iliad
ADEHIIPS	Pheidias
ADEHIKLV	khedival
ADEHIKNS	skinhead
ADEHILLM	Heimdall
ADEHILLP	pillhead
ADEHILMW	Waldheim
ADEHILNN	hand line
ADEHILNR	hard line
	hardline
	hard-line
ADEHILNU	unhailed
ADEHILTW	deal with
ADEHIMRS	misheard
ADEHINOS	adhesion
ADEHINRS	Sheridan
ADEHINSV	vanished
ADEHIORS	Rhodesia
ADEHIPRS	raphides
ADEHIRSV	ravished
ADEHIRVW	hiveward
ADEHKNRS	redshank
ADEHKORW	headwork
ADEHLLOW	hallowed
ADEHLLRW	hellward
ADEHLLSW	Shadwell
ADEHLMNO	homeland
ADEHLMOY	holydame
ADEHLNSS	handless
ADEHLNST	Shetland
	Stendhal
ADEHLOPS	asphodel
	pholades
ADEHLRRY	heraldry
ADEHMMMO	Mohammed
ADEHMNOS	handsome
ADEHMNRS	herdsman □
ADEHMNRU	unharmed
ADEHMNUY	many-hued
ADEHMOOR	headroom
ADEHMORW	homeward
ADEHMOSU	madhouse
ADEHNOPR	orphaned
ADEHNORV	hand over
	handover
	overhand
ADEHNOSS	sandshoe
ADEHNPRS	sharp end
ADEHNPSU	unshaped
ADEHNRSS	hardness
ADEHNRSU	unshared
ADEHNRTU	unthread
ADEHNSSU	sunshade
ADEHNSTU	The Sudan
ADEHNSUW	unwashed
ADEHOORT	Dorothea
	Theodora
ADEHORRW	harrowed
ADEHPPRS	Sheppard
ADEHPRSU	Phaedrus
ADEHPSUW	washed-up
ADEHQSSU	squashed
ADEHRTTW	thwarted
ADEIILMS	idealism
ADEIILNT	in detail
ADEIILRS	Disraeli
ADEIILST	idealist
ADEIIMNR	meridian
ADEIIMNT	miniated
ADEIIMPR	impaired
ADEIIMTT	imitated
ADEIIMVW	a dim view
ADEIINOT	taenioid
ADEIINRS	draisine
ADEIINRU	uredinia
ADEIIPRR	perradii
ADEIIPRS	presidia
ADEIIRST	Aristide
	irisated
ADEIITTV	tidivate
	vitiated
ADEIJMSS	Sid James
ADEIKLLO	keloidal
ADEIKLLT	idle talk
ADEIKLLY	ladylike
ADEIKLPV	Kapil Dev
ADEIKLSW	sidewalk
ADEIKMRT	tidemark
ADEIKMTY	make tidy
ADEIKORT	keratoid
ADEILLMY	medially
ADEILLNW	walled in
ADEILLPW	well-paid
ADEILLSW	sidewall
ADEILMNN	land mine
	land-mine
ADEILMNY	maidenly
ADEILMOS	soda lime
ADEILMPS	misplead
ADEILMRY	dreamily
ADEILMSV	Maldives
ADEILNNO	nailed on
ADEILNOS	Leonidas
	nodalise
ADEILNOT	delation
	dilate on
	lead into
ADEILNOZ	nodalize
ADEILNPT	pantiled
ADEILNPU	paludine
ADEILNRS	islander
ADEILNTV	divalent
ADEILOPR	Leopardi
ADEILORS	solidare
ADEILORT	idolater
	tailored
ADEILORX	exordial
ADEILOST	diastole
	isolated
	sodalite
ADEILOSV	de Valois □
ADEILOTV	dovetail
ADEILPRT	dipteral
ADEILPRU	epidural
ADEILRRY	drearily
ADEILRSU	residual
	Ruisdael
ADEILRSY	dialyser
ADEILRTT	detrital

ADEILRUV	Duvalier
ADEILRVY	variedly
ADEILSSY	dialyses
ADEILSTY	steadily
ADEILSWY	Day-Lewis
ADEILSXY	dyslexia
ADEILTTU	altitude
	latitude
ADEIMMST	mismated
ADEIMNNT	in tandem
ADEIMNOP	dopamine
ADEIMNOS	nomadise
ADEIMNOT	dominate
ADEIMNOZ	nomadize
ADEIMNSS	sidesman
ADEIMNSY	dynamise
ADEIMNSZ	man-sized
ADEIMNTY	dynamite
ADEIMNYZ	dynamize
ADEIMORT	mediator□
ADEIMOSS	sesamoid
ADEIMRRS	admirers
ADEINNOT	antinode
ADEINNOV	Devonian
ADEINNRZ	rendzina
ADEINNSX	disannex
ADEINNTU	inundate
ADEINORR	ordainer
ADEINORT	deration
	ordinate
	read into
ADEINOST	sedation
ADEINOTT	antidote
ADEINOTW	wade into
ADEINPPX	appendix
ADEINPRU	unpaired
ADEINRRW	draw rein
ADEINRSS	aridness
	sardines
ADEINRST	strained
ADEINRSU	denarius
	Eridanus
ADEINRSY	synedria
ADEINRTT	Andretti
ADEINRTU	indurate
ADEINRUV	unvaried
ADEINRVY	vineyard
ADEINSTU	sinuated
ADEINSTW	east wind
ADEIOPTV	adoptive
ADEIORST	asteroid
ADEIORTT	teratoid
ADEIPPRS	apprised
ADEIPRST	spirated
ADEIPRTU	eupatrid
ADEIPSTU	put aside
ADEIPTTU	aptitude
ADEIQSUY	quayside
ADEIRRWW	wiredraw
ADEIRSST	disaster
ADEIRSSU	radiuses
ADEIRSSV	advisers
ADEIRSTT	striated
ADEIRVWY	driveway
ADEISSTT	distaste
ADEISSWY	sideways
ADEISTTU	situated
ADEISWWY	wideways
ADEITTTU	attitude
ADEJLMPU	jump lead
ADEJOPRY	jeopardy
ADEJRSTU	adjuster
ADEKLMRY	markedly
ADEKMNOW	make down
ADEKMNRU	unmarked
ADEKNNSS	dankness
ADEKNOTW	take down
ADEKNPTU	tanked up
ADEKNRSS	darkness
ADEKNRSU	Dean Rusk
ADELLMRU	medullar
ADELLMSU	medullas
ADELLNNU	annulled
ADELLNOS	Lonsdale
ADELLNPS	spendall
ADELLNSW	Wallsend
ADELLOTT	allotted
ADELLOTU	allude to
	ladle out
ADELLOVY	lady love
	lady-love
ADELMOTU	modulate
ADELMPRT	trampled
ADELMRRU	demurral
ADELMSUY	amusedly
ADELNNNU	unnaneld
ADELNNOT	lentando
ADELNOOR	Leonardo
ADELNORU	unloader
ADELNORV	overland
	rondavel
ADELNOVY	Donleavy
ADELNPRS	spandrel
ADELNPRU	pendular
	underlap
ADELNPRY	panderly
ADELNRSY	Lysander
ADELNRTY	ardently
ADELNRUY	Dunleary
	underlay
ADELNSTW	wetlands
ADELNTUU	undulate
ADELNUUV	unvalued
ADELNUZZ	undazzle
ADELOORV	overload
ADELOPTU	lead up to
ADELORRV	overlard
	Rod Laver
ADELORSS	roadless
ADELORST	lodestar
ADELOTUW	outlawed
ADELOVWY	avowedly
ADELPPRY	dapperly
ADELPRTY	dry-plate
ADELRSTT	startled
ADELRSUY	Ruysdael
ADELRTUY	adultery
ADELSTTY	statedly
ADEMNNNU	unmanned
ADEMNNOR	on remand
ADEMNNRU	underman
ADEMNNSU	Amundsen
ADEMNOOR	marooned
ADEMNOPR	name-drop
	pardon me
	pomander
ADEMNOTW	team down
ADEMNPSS	dampness
ADEMNPUU	unmade-up
ADEMNRRU	underarm
	unmarred
ADEMNRTU	undreamt
ADEMOORT	moderato
ADEMORRU	armoured
ADEMORRW	Romeward
ADENNOPX	expand on
ADENNORS	Anderson
ADENNOTT	attend on
ADENNTUW	unwanted
ADENOORW	wanderoo
ADENOPRR	pardoner
ADENOPRS	San Pedro
	spread on
ADENOPRT	pander to
ADENOPRU	read up on
ADENOPRW	pare down
ADENOPSS	spadones
ADENOPSY	dyspnoea
ADENOPTT	not-pated
ADENORRW	narrowed
ADENORTW	tear down
	wonder at
ADENORUX	rondeaux
ADENORWW	wear down
ADENOSSY	Odyssean
ADENOSTY	steady on!
ADENOTTT	attend to
ADENOTUY	autodyne
ADENOVWW	wave down
ADENPPTU	untapped
ADENPRRU	under par
ADENPRTY	pedantry
ADENPRUY	underpay
ADENQRSU	squander
ADENRSSU	Saunders
ADENRSTU	transude
ADENRUWY	under way
ADENSTTU	unstated
ADENSTUY	unsteady
ADEOORRT	toreador
ADEOOSTW	Eastwood
ADEOPPRR	pear drop
ADEOPPRV	approved

ADEOPRRS	ear drops
ADEOPRRT	predator
ADEOPRST	spread to
ADEOPRTT	tetrapod
ADEOPSTT	postdate
ADEOPTTU	up to date
	up-to-date
ADEORRST	roadster
ADEORRVW	overdraw
ADEORSST	assorted
ADEORSTT	road-test
ADEORSTX	extrados
ADEORSUV	savoured
ADEPPRST	strapped
ADERRSSW	wardress
ADERRSTT	redstart
ADERSTWW	westward
ADFFGORU	off guard
ADFFHNOS	hands off
	hands-off
ADFFNNOO	off and on
	on and off
ADFFNOST	stand off
	stand-off
ADFFNSTU	and stuff
ADFFOOST	fast food
ADFFORST	Stafford
ADFFORSW	off-wards
ADFGIINR	infra dig
ADFGINNU	unfading
ADFGINRT	drafting
ADFGLNOW	flag down
ADFGLOUW	god-awful
ADFGMNOO	man of God
ADFHILNS	land-fish
ADFHIORV	VHF radio
ADFHIRSW	dwarfish
ADFHLLNU	full hand
ADFHLNSU	handfuls
ADFHLOST	hold fast
	holdfast
ADFHORRT	Hartford
ADFIILRT	Id al-Fitr
ADFILLLN	landfill
ADFILLNW	windfall
ADFILMNO	manifold
ADFIMNRW	wind farm
ADFIMRSW	dwarfism
ADFLLNOU	all found
ADFLLNOW	downfall
	fall down
ADFLMNOY	manyfold
ADFLOOWY	floodway
ADFMORST	Stamford
ADFNOORT	to and fro
ADFNORST	stand for
ADFNOSTU	Dan Fouts
ADFORRSW	forwards
ADGGGINR	dragging
ADGGGINS	daggings
ADGGIIMO	DiMaggio

ADGGILNN	dangling
ADGGINNU	Gunga Din
ADGGINRU	guarding
ADGGLRSU	sluggard
ADGHHILN	highland □
ADGHHINN	nigh-hand
ADGHILLS	Dalglish
ADGHILNN	handling
ADGHILOS	hidalgos
ADGHILTY	daylight
ADGHINOR	hoarding
ADGHINPR	handgrip
ADGHITTW	tightwad
ADGHLNNO	longhand
ADGHNNOW	hang down
ADGHRSTU	draughts
ADGHRTUY	draughty
ADGIILLO	gladioli
ADGIILMR	Grimaldi
ADGIIMNR	admiring
ADGIINNR	draining
ADGIINNT	gin and it
ADGIINRR	Girardin
ADGIINRY	dairying
ADGIINSV	advising
ADGIKLNR	darkling
ADGILLNR	land-girl
ADGILLNY	dallying
ADGILMNU	Maudling
ADGILMOR	marigold □
ADGILNRY	daringly
ADGILNZZ	dazzling
ADGILOPR	prodigal
ADGINNOR	adorning
ADGINNOT	donating
ADGINNST	standing
ADGINNTU	daunting
ADGINOOR	rigadoon
ADGINORR	ring road
ADGINORS	road sign
ADGINOTY	toadying
ADGINPTU	updating
ADGINRTT	dratting
ADGIORTT	Titograd
ADGLOORY	gardyloo
ADGMNORU	gourmand
ADGNNOQU	quandong
ADGNNORS	grandson
ADGNOORS	dragoons
ADGNOORU	go around
ADHHINPW	whip hand
ADHHIPRS	hardship
ADHHNORU	hour hand
ADHIILLR	Hilliard
ADHIIMSS	Hasidism
ADHIINOP	ophidian
ADHIISST	Hasidist
ADHIKKOO	Hokkaido
ADHIKNNT	hand-knit
ADHILLMO	hollidam
ADHILLNS	sandhill

ADHILLOT	thalloid
ADHILNTW	land with
ADHILOPS	shipload
ADHILOPY	haploidy
ADHILPSY	Ladyship
ADHIMNOS	admonish
ADHIMNOU	humanoid
ADHIMNRT	third man
ADHIMOPP	amphipod
ADHINNOR	iron hand
ADHINPRT	hind part
ADHINSST	Standish
ADHINSTU	dianthus
ADHIOSTY	toadyish
ADHIPRSW	wardship
ADHIPRSY	shipyard
ADHIRTWW	withdraw
ADHKNORW	handwork
ADHKORRW	hard work
	work hard
ADHLMORT	thraldom
ADHLNOPR	Randolph
ADHLORRY	Old Harry
ADHLOSWY	hold sway
ADHMOPRU	road hump
ADHNNOOR	honorand
ADHNOPRR	hard porn
ADHNOPST	handpost
ADHNORSU	Honduras
ADHNOSTU	hand-outs
	thousand
ADHNOSUW	unshadow
ADHNOSWW	wash down
ADHOORYZ	hydrozoa
ADHOPRSY	rhapsody
ADHPSTYY	dyspathy
ADHRSTUY	Thursday
ADIIINRV	viridian
ADIIIQRU	daiquiri
ADIIISST	it is said
ADIIKLMM	milkmaid
ADIILLMR	milliard
ADIILLUV	diluvial
ADIILMRV	Vladimir
ADIILNOT	dilation
ADIILNTW	tail wind
ADIILNTY	daintily
ADIILNUV	diluvian
ADIILSSY	dialysis
ADIILTVY	validity
ADIIMNOT	Domitian
ADIINNRU	Indurain
ADIINOTU	audition
ADIINRST	distrain
ADIIOPRS	sporidia
ADIIPRTY	rapidity
ADIIPSTY	sapidity
ADIIPTVY	vapidity
ADIIRSTT	distrait
ADIKKLRY	Kirkaldy
ADIKKRRW	kirkward

Words marked □ can also be spelled with an initial capital letter

ADIKNNST	inkstand
ADILLLPY	pallidly
ADILLMNR	mandrill
ADILLMSY	dismally
ADILLNPS	landslip
ADILLOSW	disallow
ADILLOSY	disloyal
ADILLSTY	distally
ADILMNNO	mandolin
ADILMOPT	diplomat
ADILMOPY	Olympiad
ADILMOTY	modality
ADILMRUW	wild arum
ADILNNNU	nundinal
ADILNNOW	nail down
ADILNNSU	disannul
ADILNOOV	vindaloo
ADILNORS	Rosalind
ADILNPRS	spandril
ADILNPST	displant
ADILNRWY	inwardly
ADILNSSW	windlass
ADILOOPR	Polaroid®
ADILOOPZ	diplozoa
ADILOORT	toroidal
ADILOPRS	slip road
ADILOPRT	tripodal
ADILOPSS	disposal
ADILORTY	adroitly
	dilatory
	idolatry
ADILOSTY	sodality
ADILPPSY	disapply
ADILPSTU	plaudits
ADILRTWY	tawdrily
ADILRWYZ	wizardly
ADIMMNOS	nomadism
ADIMMNSY	dynamism
ADIMMOST	amidmost
ADIMNNOR	Mondrian
ADIMNNOT	dominant
ADIMOPRY	myriapod
ADIMOPST	impasto'd
ADIMOPSY	sympodia
ADIMOSTY	toadyism
ADIMPRSY	Pyramids
ADIMRSUU	sudarium
ADIMSSTU	stadiums
ADINNNTU	inundant
ADINNOOT	donation
ADINNORY	non-dairy
ADINOOPT	adoption
ADINOORT	tandoori
ADINOPRR	raindrop
ADINOPST	pintados
ADINORRY	ordinary
ADINORST	intrados
ADINORSU	dinosaur
ADINORTU	duration
ADINORTW	draw into
ADINORWZ	Zionward
ADINRUVZ	unvizard
ADIOOPSS	apodosis
ADIOPRST	parodist
	Port Said
ADIOPRSV	privados
ADIOPRTY	podiatry
ADIORSVY	advisory
ADIORTUY	auditory
ADIRRWYZ	wizardry
ADJKNRUY	junkyard
ADKLNOTW	talk down
ADKLOOPT	polka-dot
ADKLOORW	woodlark
	workload
ADKMNORW	mark down
	mark-down
ADKMOORR	darkroom
ADKNORSU	ask round
ADKRSSWY	skywards
ADLLLOOY	doolally
ADLLNORU	all round
	all-round
ADLLORSU	US dollar
ADLLORSY	dorsally
ADLMNOOR	moorland
ADLMNOOW	old woman
ADLMNORY	randomly
ADLMOOOR	Aldo Moro
ADLMOORU	malodour
ADLMOPSY	psalmody
ADLNNTUU	undulant
ADLNOORW	loan-word
ADLNOPRT	Portland
ADLNOPWY	downplay
	play down
ADLNOSTW	salt down
	stand low
ADLOPRWY	word play
	wordplay
	word-play
ADLORRWW	world war
ADLORSTW	draw lots
	last word
ADLPRUWY	upwardly
ADMMNORU	Omdurman
ADMMRSSU	Drum Mass
ADMNNORY	monandry
ADMNOORS	madroños
	Rosamond
ADMNOOST	mastodon
ADMNOOSW	woodsman
ADMNOPTW	tamp down
ADMNORSU	Rosamund
ADMOORRT	Dartmoor
ADMOORRW	wardroom
ADMOPPPU	poppadum
ADNNOSTT	not stand
ADNNOTWW	want down
ADNOOPRV	Andropov
ADNOOQRU	quadroon
ADNOORST	tornados
ADNOPRUW	draw upon
ADNOPRUY	pay round
ADNOPSSW	pass down
ADNOQRSU	squadron
ADNORSSV	Vandross
ADNORSXY	sardonyx
ADNORTTU	Turandot
ADNORTUU	do a U-turn
ADNORTUW	drawn-out
	untoward
ADNOSTTU	outstand
	stand out
	standout
ADNRSSUW	sunwards
ADOOPRRT	trapdoor
ADOOPRSU	Sauropod
ADOPPRST	Stoppard
ADOPRSSW	password
ADOPSSSU	soapsuds
ADORRSTW	Wordstar®
ADORSTUW	outwards
ADORSTUY	sudatory
ADRSSTTU	stardust
AEEEFKPS	keep safe
AEEEFRRW	freeware
AEEEFRTY	aftereye
AEEEGGLU	lee-gauge
AEEEGHLT	The Eagle
AEEEGLLS	legalese
AEEEGLMR	Meleager
AEEEGLRT	regelate
	relegate
AEEEGLRV	leverage
AEEEGNPR	pea-green
AEEEGNRT	generate
	green tea
	renegate
	teenager
AEEEGRST	steerage
AEEEGTTV	vegetate
AEEEHLRT	ethereal
AEEEHMPR	ephemera
AEEEHMRS	same here
AEEEHNRS	enhearse
AEEEHRRS	rehearse
AEEEHRRT	reheater
AEEEHSTT	aesthete
AEEEIKLR	Lake Erie
AEEEIMNX	examinee
AEEEJNRY	Jane Eyre
AEEEJNTT	Jeanette
AEEEKKPS	keepsake
AEEEKLRY	Lake Eyre
AEEEKMNV	make even
AEEEKNRW	weakener
AEEELLSV	sea level
	sea-level
AEEELNOR	Eleanore
AEEELNPS	Nepalese
AEEELNRV	venereal
AEEELPRR	repealer

AEEELQSU	sequelae
AEEELRRV	revealer
AEEELSTW	wet lease
AEEEMNST	easement
AEEEMPRT	permeate
AEEENPTT	patentee
AEEENRTV	enervate
	venerate
AEEEPRRT	repartee
	repeater
AEEEPSTW	sweet pea
AEEERSST	tesserae
AEEFFLLR	free fall
	free-fall
AEEFFLOV	leave off
AEEFFNRT	afferent
AEEFGILR	filagree
AEEFGILT	get a life
AEEFGIRR	ferriage
AEEFGLSU	fuselage
AEEFGORR	eager for
AEEFGPRS	Graf Spee
AEEFHILV	have life
AEEFHLLS	self-heal
AEEFHRTY	feathery
AEEFHRVY	hay fever
AEEFIKRT	take fire
AEEFIKTV	take five
AEEFILLR	real life
	real-life
AEEFILMN	filename
AEEFILNP	feel pain
AEEFINPR	pain-free
AEEFIPSW	spaewife
AEEFLLMR	femerall
AEEFLLRW	farewell
AEEFLLSS	leafless
AEEFLLST	leaflets
AEEFLMSS	selfsame
	self-same
AEEFLNRU	funereal
AEEFLORV	overleaf
AEEFLOSW	see a wolf
AEEFLRRR	referral
AEEFLRSS	fearless
AEEFMNOR	forename
AEEFMORS	fearsome
AEEFNRST	fastener
	fenestra
AEEFNRTT	fattener
AEEFNSSS	safeness
AEEFRSTU	features
AEEGGINN	engage in
AEEGGINR	agreeing
AEEGGIRV	aggrieve
AEEGGNNR	gangrene
AEEGHHTU	The Hague
AEEGHILN	Hegelian
AEEGHIRT	heritage
AEEGHMOP	home page
AEEGHMPR	grapheme
AEEGHNRS	shagreen
AEEGHRRT	gatherer
AEEGHRTV	the grave
AEEGHSTT	the stage
AEEGILLS	legalise
AEEGILLZ	legalize
AEEGILMN	liegeman
AEEGILNS	ensilage
AEEGILNT	gelatine
AEEGILNU	in league
AEEGILTV	levigate
AEEGIMNR	Germaine
AEEGIMNT	geminate
AEEGIMRT	emigrate
AEEGINRR	regainer
AEEGINRT	gratinée
AEEGINSS	assignee
	seeing as
AEEGINSV	envisage
AEEGINTV	negative
AEEGIPQU	equipage
AEEGIRSS	greasies
AEEGIRTT	aigrette
AEEGJNRY	Jane Grey
AEEGKSTY	key stage
AEEGLLNR	allergen
AEEGLMRT	telegram
AEEGLMRY	meagrely
AEEGLNNT	entangle
AEEGLNOT	elongate
AEEGLNRR	enlarger
AEEGLNSY	Anglesey
AEEGLRRY	Earl Grey
AEEGLRSS	eelgrass
	largesse
AEEGLRSY	grey seal
AEEGLRTU	regulate
AEEGLSSY	eyeglass
	glass eye
AEEGLTTU	tutelage
AEEGLTUV	evulgate
AEEGMMOS	gamesome
AEEGMNSS	gameness
AEEGMNTT	tegmenta
AEEGMOST	somegate
AEEGMRRS	Grasmere
AEEGMRST	gamester
	gas meter
AEEGNNRU	enraunge
AEEGNOST	Stone Age
AEEGNRRV	engraver
AEEGNRST	estrange
	sergeant
	sternage
AEEGNRSV	nerve gas
AEEGNRYZ	Zane Grey
AEEGOPRV	overpage
AEEGPRRS	presager
AEEGRSTT	greatest
AEEHHHSS	hasheesh
AEEHHIKZ	Hezekiah
AEEHHIMN	Nehemiah
AEEHHNST	ensheath
	heathens
AEEHHOOP	pahoehoe
AEEHIJMR	Jeremiah
AEEHIKLN	Alekhine
AEEHIKMN	Khamenei
AEEHIMTT	hematite
AEEHINRS	an-heires
	inhearse
AEEHIPRS	Pharisee
AEEHIPST	aphetise
	hepatise
AEEHIPTZ	aphetize
	hepatize
AEEHISTT	athetise
	hesitate
AEEHISTW	White Sea
	with ease
AEEHITTZ	athetize
AEEHKLLR	rakehell
AEEHKLLU	keel-haul
AEEHKLNT	Kathleen
AEEHKMOT	take home
	take-home
AEEHLLRT	all there
AEEHLLSS	seashell
AEEHLMNY	hymeneal
AEEHLMPT	helpmate
AEEHLNPT	elephant
AEEHLNRT	leathern
AEEHLNSS	haleness
AEEHLNVY	heavenly
AEEHLOSU	alehouse
AEEHLPPT	the Apple
AEEHLPRT	The Pearl
AEEHLPTT	telepath
AEEHLRST	halteres
AEEHLRTY	leathery
AEEHLSTW	what else?
AEEHLTTY	ethylate
AEEHMNNY	hymenean
AEEHMNRT	three-man
AEEHMPSS	emphases
AEEHMRTY	erythema
AEEHMTUX	exhumate
AEEHNNTX	xanthene
AEEHNNVW	New Haven
	Newhaven
AEEHNRSU	unhearse
AEEHNRTT	threaten
AEEHNRTU	urethane
AEEHNRTW	water-hen
AEEHNRWY	anywhere
AEEHNSTU	uneathes
AEEHNSTW	enswathe
AEEHORRV	overhear
AEEHORSS	seahorse
	seashore
AEEHORTV	overheat
AEEHORVV	have over

AEEHPRRS	rephrase
AEEHRRTU	urethrae
AEEHRTVW	whatever
AEEHRTWY	three-way
AEEHSTVW	The Waves
AEEIILLV	live a lie
AEEIKKLM	make like
AEEIKLMZ	mazelike
AEEIKMMT	make time
AEEIKMNT	ketamine
AEEIKPTT	keep at it
AEEIKRST	take rise
AEEIKRTU	Kaieteur
AEEILLLT	tell a lie
AEEILLRV	real live
AEEILMMN	melamine
AEEILMRT	Lemaître
	matériel
AEEILMTZ	metalize
AEEILNPR	perineal
AEEILNPS	penalise
AEEILNPZ	penalize
AEEILNRT	treenail
AEEILNRV	Verlaine
AEEILORT	aerolite
AEEILOTT	etiolate
AEEILPPP	apple pie
AEEILPRS	espalier
	pearlies
AEEILPRT	pearlite
AEEILPST	please it
AEEILPSW	palewise
AEEILQSU	equalise
AEEILQUX	exequial
AEEILQUZ	equalize
AEEILRRT	retailer
AEEILRRZ	realizer
AEEILRST	earliest
AEEILRSV	velarise
AEEILRTT	laterite
	literate
AEEILRTV	relative
AEEILRVW	liveware
	reviewal
AEEILRVZ	velarize
AEEILSSS	Selassie
AEEILSVW	alewives
AEEILTTV	levitate
AEEILTXX	tax exile
AEEIMMNT	meantime
AEEIMNRX	examiner
AEEIMNSS	Messiaen
AEEIMNST	seminate
AEEIMNUV	mauveine
AEEIMORV	Aviemore
AEEIMRTT	Mariette
AEEIMSTT	estimate
AEEIMSTW	teamwise
AEEINNRR	inner ear
AEEINNRS	anserine
AEEINNSS	in a sense
AEEINNTV	Aventine
	Venetian
AEEINPRT	aperient
AEEINQUU	in a queue
AEEINRRT	rain-tree
	retainer
AEEINRST	arsenite
	resinate
	stearine
	Teresina
AEEINRSU	Irenaeus
AEEINSSS	easiness
AEEINSTT	tetanise
AEEINSVW	sine wave
AEEINTTZ	tetanize
AEEIORST	etaerios
	Oresteia
AEEIPPST	appetise
AEEIPPSU	eupepsia
AEEIPPTT	appetite
AEEIPPTZ	appetize
AEEIPRTV	perviate
AEEIPSST	epitases
AEEIRRST	arteries
AEEIRSTT	treaties
	treatise
AEEIRSTW	as it were
AEEISTTT	steatite
AEEITUVX	exuviate
AEEJNRST	serjeant
AEEJOPRT	pejorate
AEEKLLMW	make well
AEEKLLNY	Keneally
AEEKLLPU	Paul Klee
AEEKLLST	skeletal
AEEKLMOV	make love
AEEKLMRT	telemark
AEEKLMSS	make less
AEEKMNSW	man-weeks
AEEKMORV	make over
	makeover
AEEKMPRW	keep warm
AEEKMRRR	remarker
AEEKMRRT	marketer
AEEKMRSU	make sure
AEEKNOPT	keep on at
AEEKNOTT	take note
AEEKNPSW	newspeak
AEEKNSSW	weakness
AEEKORRV	overrake
AEEKORST	keratose
AEEKORTV	overtake
	take over
	takeover
AEEKQRSU	squeaker
AEEKRRST	streaker
AEELLLTT	telltale
	tell-tale
AEELLNOT	let alone
	let-alone
AEELLNOV	novellae
AEELLPTT	platelet
AEELLSTT	stellate
AEELLSWY	weaselly
AEELMMNT	Emmental
AEELMMNU	Emmanuel
AEELMNNT	Telemann
AEELMNOT	lemon tea
AEELMNSS	lameness
	maleness
	maneless
	nameless
AEELMNSU	Menelaus
AEELMORY	Moray eel
AEELMPRX	exemplar
AEELMPRY	empyreal
AEELMPTT	palmette
	template
AEELMSSS	seamless
AEELMSST	meatless
AEELNNRT	lanneret
AEELNNSS	leanness
AEELNOPR	peroneal
AEELNOPT	antelope
AEELNORU	aleurone
AEELNORV	lean over
AEELNPQU	Palenque
AEELNPSS	paleness
AEELNRSS	realness
AEELNRTV	relevant
AEELNRTX	external
AEELNSST	lateness
AEELNSSV	vaneless
AEELNSWY	Wesleyan
AEELNTUV	eventual
AEELOPRV	leap over
	overleap
AEELOPST	please to
AEELORST	oleaster
AEELORTT	relate to
	tolerate
AEELORTV	elevator
AEELOTTT	teetotal
AEELOTTW	tea towel
AEELOTUV	leave out
AEELPRRS	relapser
AEELPRRY	parleyer
AEELPRSU	pleasure
	serpulae
AEELPRTU	tape-lure
AEELPRTY	pterylae
AEELPSST	Spätlese
AEELPTTU	Paulette
AEELPTTW	wet-plate
AEELQRSU	squealer
AEELRRSV	reversal
	slaverer
AEELRRTU	ureteral
AEELRSST	tearless
AEELRSTY	easterly
AEELRSVY	aversely
AEELRVWY	Waverley

AEELSSVW	waveless
AEEMNNRT	remanent
AEEMNNSS	meanness
AEEMNORV	overname
AEEMNPRY	empyrean
AEEMNPTV	pavement
AEEMNQUY	May queen
AEEMNRSU	user name
AEEMNRSW	menswear
AEEMNRTU	numerate
AEEMNRTV	averment
AEEMNRVY	Everyman
AEEMNSSS	sameness
AEEMNSST	Massenet
	tameness
AEEMOSSU	sea mouse
AEEMPPRR	pamperer
AEEMPRRT	tamperer
AEEMQRRU	remarque□
AEEMQTTU	maquette
AEEMRRST	remaster
	streamer
AEEMRSSS	Ramesses
AEEMRSST	seamster
AEEMRSSU	measures
AEEMSSSU	masseuse
AEEMSSTU	meatuses
AEENNORS	Roseanne
AEENNRSS	nearness
AEENNRTV	renevant
	revenant
AEENNSSS	saneness
AEENNSST	neatness
AEENOPPT	not a peep
AEENOPRS	personae
AEENOPRU	European
AEENOPRV	Eva Perón
AEENORSS	seasoner
AEENORST	resonate
AEENORTV	renovate
AEENORVW	ovenware
AEENPPRT	Peter Pan
AEENPPTT	appetent
AEENPQTU	pétanque
AEENPRUV	parvenue
AEENRRSS	rareness
AEENRRSW	reanswer
AEENRRTT	natterer
AEENRRTV	taverner
AEENRSST	sarsenet
AEENRSTU	Sauterne
AEENRTTV	antevert
AEENRTTY	entreaty
AEEOPRRT	perorate
AEEOPRST	protease
AEEOPRTT	operetta
AEEORRST	ore-stare
AEEORRSV	Averroës
	sea rover
	sea-rover
AEEORRTV	overrate
AEEORRTZ	zero-rate
AEEORRVV	rave over
AEEORRVW	overwear
AEEORSSV	overseas
AEEORSTT	sea otter
AEEORSVY	easy over
AEEPRRSS	asperser
AEEPRRTU	aperture
AEEQRRUV	quaverer
AEERRRST	arrester
AEERRSSU	reassure
AEERRSTU	treasure
AEERRSTV	traverse
AEERRSTW	sewer rat
	sewer-rat
AEERSSSS	reassess
AEERVWYY	everyway
AEFFFKLO	flake off
AEFFGOST	off-stage
AEFFGRSU	suffrage
AEFFHIKY	kaffiyeh
AEFFHILL	half-life
AEFFHKOS	off-shake
	shake off
AEFFILUV	effluvia
AEFFIMRR	reaffirm
AEFFKNOS	sneak off
AEFFKOST	stake off
AEFFLNTU	affluent
AEFFLOSS	off-sales
AEFFMORS	safe from
AEFFMRSU	earmuffs
AEFFOPRT	taper off
AEFFORST	afforest
AEFFORSW	swear off
AEFFOSTV	stave off
AEFFRRTY	Rafferty
AEFFRTTU	Tartuffe
AEFGHINR	hang fire
AEFGIKMN	Mafeking
AEFGIMTU	fumigate
AEFGINST	feasting
AEFGIORS	foie gras
AEFGIRTU	fruitage
AEFGLLPU	full-page
AEFGLMNU	fugleman
AEFGLMOP	megaflop
AEFGLNOR	angle for
AEFGLNSS	fangless
AEFGLOPR	leap-frog
AEFGLORU	Laforgue
AEFGLRTU	grateful
AEFGMNRT	fragment
AEFGNORT	frontage
AEFGORRU	argue for
AEFGORST	go faster
AEFGORTT	frottage
AEFHIINR	fine hair
AEFHIKRS	freakish
AEFHILLN	fellahin
AEFHILMT	half-time
AEFHILNW	fin whale
AEFHILSZ	half-size
AEFHIRRS	fresh air
AEFHIRRT	The Friar
AEFHLLOS	half-sole
AEFHLMRT	half-term
AEFHLMSU	shameful
AEFHLNOT	half-tone
AEFHLPST	half-step
AEFHLRTY	fatherly
AEFHMNOZ	Zamenhof
AEFHMNRS	freshman
AEFHRSTT	farthest
AEFIILNS	finalise
AEFIILNZ	finalize
AEFIILRR	air rifle
AEFIILRS	Fair Isle
AEFIIMNS	infamise
AEFIIMNZ	infamize
AEFIINRS	Friesian
AEFIINST	fainites
AEFIIPRT	aperitif
AEFIITVX	fixative
AEFIKLPR	Parklife
AEFIKLTY	fly a kite
AEFILLRW	firewall
AEFILMNR	rifleman
AEFILMNS	in flames
AEFILMNT	filament
AEFILNNR	infernal
AEFILNPS	lifespan
AEFILNPY	play fine
AEFILNRU	Fräulein
AEFILOOR	aerofoil
AEFILOPR	fire opal
AEFILORS	foresail
AEFILPST	file past
AEFILRSV	F R Leavis
AEFILRTT	filtrate
AEFILSTU	fistulae
AEFILSTV	festival
AEFILSTW	flatwise
AEFILTUU	fauteuil
AEFIMNST	manifest
AEFIMORT	for a time
AEFIMRRS	firearms
AEFIMRRW	firmware
AEFINNNS	Anfinsen
AEFINOPR	pinafore
AEFINRRT	Ferranti
AEFINRSS	fairness
	sanserif
AEFINSTT	faintest
AEFIOTTT	fit to eat
AEFIRRRY	farriery
AEFIRTTU	fruit tea
AEFJMOSX	James Fox
AEFKLLMU	make full
AEFKLLOT	folk tale
	folk-tale
AEFKLMOW	make flow

Words marked □ can also be spelled with an initial capital letter

AEFKLNRU	Faulkner
AEFKLOTU	flake out
AEFKNORS	forsaken
AEFKOPRS	forspeak
	speak for
AEFKORRW	workfare
AEFKORTU	freak out
	freak-out
AEFLLNNS	flannels
AEFLLORV	fall over
	overfall
AEFLLPTU	plateful
AEFLLRUX	flexural
AEFLLSSW	flawless
AEFLLSTY	festally
AEFLLTTY	let fly at
AEFLMORU	formulae
	fumarole
AEFLMOSS	foamless
AEFLMOTU	flame out
AEFLNNOT	fontanel
AEFLNOPR	foreplan
AEFLNOPT	pantofle
AEFLNRTU	flaunter
AEFLNSST	flatness
AEFLNSUY	unsafely
AEFLOPRV	flap over
AEFLOPRY	foreplay
AEFLORST	forestal
AEFLORTU	flare out
AEFLORTW	fleawort
AEFLOSTT	falsetto
AEFLPPRY	flypaper
AEFLRTTU	aflutter
AEFLRTTY	flat tyre
	flattery
AEFLSSTU	flatuses
AEFLSTTU	tasteful
AEFLSTUW	wasteful
AEFMNORW	men-of-war
AEFMNRRY	ferryman
AEFMORST	foremast
AEFMORVW	waveform
AEFNNOST	fasten on
AEFNNSTU	unfasten
AEFNOORT	atone for
AEFNORRW	forewarn
AEFNORRY	yearn for
AEFNORST	seafront
AEFNOSTW	feast-won
AEFNRRST	transfer
AEFNRRTU	run after
AEFNRRUY	funerary
AEFNSSST	fastness
AEFNSTUY	unsafety
AEFOORTW	footwear
AEFOPRRT	forepart
AEFOPRST	forepast
AEFOPTUU	pot-au-feu
AEFORRSW	forswear
AEFORRUV	favourer

AEFORSTW	software
AEFRSTVY	very fast
AEGGGINN	engaging
AEGGHHIR	high gear
AEGGHORU	roughage
AEGGILMN	gleaming
AEGGILNN	gleaning
AEGGILOU	oil gauge
AEGGIMOR	Maggiore
AEGGIMRT	gregatim
AEGGINNR	angering
	enraging
AEGGINNV	avenging
AEGGINOR	Georgian
	Georgina
AEGGINOS	seagoing
	sea-going
AEGGINRR	Grainger
AEGGINST	Gigantes
AEGGIOPR	arpeggio
AEGGLNOT	get along
AEGGLNPT	eggplant
AEGGLORY	gargoyle
AEGGLRST	straggle
AEGGMORT	mortgage
AEGGNORV	overgang
AEGGNRST	gangster
AEGGNRTY	get angry
AEGGOPRU	age group
AEGGRSST	staggers
AEGHHISS	high seas
AEGHILLS	shigella
AEGHILLT	light ale
AEGHILMT	megalith
AEGHILNR	narghile
	nargileh
AEGHILRT	litharge
AEGHINRT	gather in
	ingather
AEGHINRV	havering □
AEGHINRY	Haringey
AEGHINTU	Naughtie
AEGHIPPR	epigraph
AEGHIPRT	graphite
AEGHLNTT	at length
AEGHLOPY	hypogeal
AEGHLOSV	go halves
AEGHLOSW	show a leg
AEGHLRTU	laughter
AEGHLRTY	lethargy
AEGHMOPT	apothegm
AEGHMOSW	game show
AEGHNNOR	hanger-on
AEGHNNSY	Shenyang
AEGHNOPT	heptagon
	pathogen
AEGHNOPY	hypogean
AEGHNORV	hang over
	hangover
	overhang
AEGHOORS	go ashore

AEGHOPPY	apophyge
AEGHOPXY	exophagy
AEGHORSS	go shares
AEGHORST	shortage
AEGHOSTT	Tashtego
AEGHPRTU	upgather
AEGIILLU	aiguille
AEGIILMR	remigial
AEGIILRT	Galtieri
AEGIILTT	litigate
AEGIIMNR	imaginer
	migraine
AEGIIMNS	imagines
AEGIIMNT	gain time
AEGIIMTT	mitigate
AEGIINNR	arginine
AEGIIRRT	irrigate
AEGIISTV	vestigia
AEGIKLNR	King Lear
AEGIKLNW	weakling
AEGIKMNW	make wing
AEGIKNNS	sneaking
AEGIKNNW	wakening
AEGIKNPS	speaking
AEGIKNRR	Kerrigan
AEGIKNRW	wreaking
AEGIKNTW	take wing
AEGILLMS	legalism
AEGILLNO	goal line
AEGILLNY	genially
AEGILLPR	pillager
AEGILLPS	spillage
AEGILLRU	guerilla
AEGILLRV	villager
AEGILLST	legalist
	stillage
AEGILLSU	ill-usage
AEGILLTY	legality
AEGILMMR	aglimmer
AEGILMNR	germinal □
	maligner
	malinger
AEGILMNT	ligament
AEGILMRX	lexigram
AEGILNNR	learning
AEGILNNT	gantline
AEGILNNV	Langevin
AEGILNNW	weanling
AEGILNOR	regional
AEGILNOS	gasoline
AEGILNOT	gelation
	legation
	Lion Gate
AEGILNPS	pleasing
AEGILNRS	Salinger
	seal ring
AEGILNRT	integral
	relating
	triangle □
AEGILNRX	relaxing
AEGILNRY	relaying

	yearling
AEGILNSS	gainless
	glassine
AEGILNST	genitals
	stealing
AEGILNSV	Gil Evans
	leavings
	Svengali
AEGILNTX	exalting
AEGILNUV	vaginule
AEGILOPS	spoilage
AEGILOPT	pilotage
AEGILORS	girasole
	seraglio
AEGILPPS	slippage
AEGILPSU	Pelagius
AEGILRSU	Galerius
AEGILRSY	greasily
AEGILRTT	aglitter
AEGILRTU	Gaultier
	ligature
AEGILRTY	regality
AEGILRVW	law-giver
AEGILSSU	Gelasius
AEGIMNRT	emigrant
AEGIMNRU	geranium
AEGIMNRY	Imre Nagy
AEGIMNSS	gaminess
AEGIMNST	steaming
AEGIMNSV	veganism
AEGIMOPT	magot-pie
AEGIMQRU	quagmire
AEGIMRTT	Magritte
AEGIMSTY	Gay Times
AEGINNOT	Antigone
	negation
AEGINNPS	sneaping
AEGINNRS	earnings
AEGINNRV	ravening
AEGINNRY	yearning
AEGINNSU	sanguine
AEGINOPT	Pinotage
AEGINORS	ignaroes
	organise
AEGINORZ	organize
AEGINOTV	go native
AEGINPPR	papering
AEGINPRT	tapering
AEGINPTY	Egyptian
AEGINRST	astringe
	ganister
	inert gas
AEGINRSW	swearing
AEGINRTT	treating
AEGINRVW	wavering
AEGINRVY	vinegary
AEGINRWY	wearying
AEGINSST	giantess
	in stages
AEGINSTW	sweating
AEGIORSV	viragoes
AEGIPRTY	pterygia
AEGIRTTT	great tit
AEGJLTUU	jugulate
AEGKKKNO	angekkok
AEGKLMUY	make ugly
AEGKLORY	Key Largo
AEGKMNSU	make snug
AEGKOPRS	gas poker
AEGLLMNN	Gell-Mann
AEGLLNST	St Gallen
AEGLLOPR	galloper
AEGLLORS	allegros
AEGLLORV	overgall
AEGLLORY	allegory
AEGLLOSS	goalless
AEGLLRVY	gravelly
AEGLLSSU	galluses
AEGLMNOW	leg-woman
AEGLMNTU	gunmetal
AEGLNNOR	Algernon
AEGLNNPT	plangent
AEGLNNSY	lang syne
AEGLNNTU	untangle
AEGLNORV	Lavengro
AEGLNORY	yearlong
AEGLNOST	tangelos
AEGLNOSZ	Gonzales
AEGLNOZZ	González
AEGLNPRS	sprangle
AEGLNRRW	wrangler
AEGLNRST	strangle
AEGLNRSY	larynges
AEGLNRTU	Regnault
AEGLNTTU	gauntlet
AEGLNTUU	ungulate
AEGLOOPU	apologue
AEGLOPRW	grow pale
AEGLORSU	glareous
AEGLORTU	outglare
AEGLORTW	waterlog
AEGLOSSW	galowses
AEGLRRSU	regulars
AEGLRSTU	gestural
AEGLRTUY	argutely
AEGMMPRU	Pergamum
AEGMMRRU	rummager
AEGMNOPR	Pergamon
AEGMNORV	mangrove
AEGMNOST	magnetos
AEGMNOTU	Montague
AEGMNRST	garments
AEGMNRTU	argument
AEGMORRW	worm gear
AEGMORSS	gossamer
AEGNNOPT	pentagon
AEGNNPRT	pregnant
AEGNNRTY	gannetry
AEGNOORS	oreganos
AEGNOOSY	go easy on
AEGNORRY	orangery
AEGNORST	Estragon
	ragstone
AEGNORTT	on target
	tetragon
AEGNPRYY	panegyry
AEGNRRST	stranger
AEGNRSST	Sangster
AEGNRSYY	asynergy
AEGNSSST	gastness
AEGNSTTZ	Stan Getz
AEGOORSV	voragoes
AEGOPPST	stoppage
AEGOPPSU	sup-peago
AEGOPSST	gestapos
AEGOPSSU	spousage
AEGOPSTT	gatepost
AEGORRTT	garrotte
AEGORTTU	tutorage
AEGORUVY	voyageur
AEGPRRSU	spur gear
AEGRRSSY	ryegrass
AEGRRSUV	verrugas
AEGRRTUW	water rug
AEGRSTTY	strategy
AEHHIMTW	hamewith
AEHHISVY	yeshivah
AEHHLLST	the halls
AEHHNOPT	Phaethon
AEHHNRSW	hernshaw
AEHHNTTW	what then?
AEHHORTW	Heathrow
AEHHRRST	thrasher
AEHIIKLR	hairlike
AEHIIKST	shiitake
AEHIILNR	hairline
AEHIILNW	in a while
AEHIIMNT	thiamine
AEHIINRT	in the air
AEHIIOPT	Ethiopia
AEHIIRSS	Irish Sea
AEHIKKLW	hawklike
AEHIKKNN	Hakkinen
AEHIKLTT	like that
AEHIKMNT	make thin
AEHIKMTW	make with
AEHIKPST	take ship
AEHILLOS	oil shale
AEHILLOW	whale oil
AEHILMSW	Lewisham
AEHILNOP	aphelion
AEHILNOT	Iolanthe
AEHILORT	aerolith
AEHILRSS	hairless
AEHILRSV	shrieval
AEHILRTT	The Trial
AEHILRTY	heartily
AEHILTWW	Whitelaw
AEHIMMNN	Mannheim
AEHIMNNU	inhumane
AEHIMNRT	theramin
AEHIMNSU	humanise
AEHIMNTU	inhumate

AEHIMNUZ	humanize
AEHIMPRS	samphire
	seraphim
AEHIMPRT	teraphim
AEHIMPSS	emphasis
	misshape
AEHIMPST	mateship
	shipmate
AEHINOPT	The Piano
AEHINORT	on the air
AEHINPPY	epiphany □
AEHINPRS	seraphin
	shear pin
AEHINPRT	perianth
AEHINPST	thespian □
AEHINRSV	enravish
AEHINRTW	in the raw
	wear thin
AEHINRWY	in her way
AEHINSST	anthesis
AEHINSSZ	haziness
AEHINSTT	hesitant
AEHINSTW	inswathe
AEHINTTW	white ant
AEHINTWY	in the way
AEHIOPRS	aphorise
AEHIOPRU	euphoria
AEHIOPRZ	aphorize
AEHIPPRS	sapphire
AEHIPTVY	Have Pity
AEHIRRSY	Ayrshire
AEHIRSTU	thesauri
AEHIRSTY	hysteria
AEHISSTU	hiatuses
AEHJNRSY	Jean Rhys
AEHJPRSW	jew's harp □
AEHKLMOY	make holy
AEHKNNSU	unshaken
AEHKNRST	the narks
AEHKNSTT	Tashkent
AEHKOSTU	shake out
	shake-out
AEHLLLTY	lethally
AEHLLOSY	sea holly
AEHLMMNS	helmsman
AEHLMNNP	Helpmann
AEHLMNOO	home loan
AEHLMNOT	methanol
AEHLMNSW	Welshman
AEHLMNUY	humanely
AEHLMPPT	pamphlet
AEHLMRSS	harmless
AEHLNPRS	shrapnel
AEHLNPTY	enthalpy
AEHLNRTU	Lutheran
AEHLNSST	less than
AEHLNTUZ	hazelnut
AEHLOPRT	plethora
	traphole
AEHLORSY	hoarsely
AEHLORUV	overhaul

AEHLOTTT	the total
AEHLPPRT	thrapple
AEHLPSST	pathless
AEHLPSTU	sulphate
AEHLRRTU	urethral
AEHLSTTY	stealthy
AEHLSTUU	the usual
AEHMNNPY	nymphean
AEHMNOPT	on the map
AEHMNORS	horseman
AEHMNORT	more than
	other man
AEHMNOSU	houseman
AEHMNOTT	on the mat
AEHMNSTW	new maths
AEHMOPRT	metaphor
AEHMOSTW	somewhat
AEHMPPTU	heat pump
AEHMRSSY	Myra Hess
AEHMSSSU	shamuses
AEHMSTTW	Matthews
AEHMSTTY	amethyst
AEHMSTUV	must-have
AEHMSUZZ	mezuzahs
AEHNNOPP	happen on
AEHNNOPT	pantheon □
AEHNNORV	Hannover
AEHNNPRU	nenuphar
AEHNNPSU	unshapen
AEHNNSUV	unshaven
AEHNOOPT	hanepoot
	not a hope
AEHNOPPT	happen to
	phone-tap
AEHNOPST	stanhope □
	Stephano
AEHNORST	North Sea
	Sheraton
AEHNORTT	Atherton
AEHNOSTV	have-nots
AEHNOTWY	on the way
AEHNRSSS	rashness
AEHNSTUW	unswathe
AEHNSTWW	what's new?
AEHNTTWX	what next?
AEHOPPRS	prophase
AEHOPSST	spathose
AEHOPSTU	phase out
	tap-house
AEHOPTVY	top-heavy
AEHORRSW	warhorse
AEHORSTT	rheostat
AEHORSTU	share out
	share-out
AEHORSTX	thoraxes
AEHORTTW	hot water
AEHPRSST	sharp-set
AEHPRSTT	the strap
AEHPRSUX	haruspex
AEHPRSUY	euphrasy
AEHPSSTW	The Wasps

AEHRRSTU	urethras
AEHRSSTT	the stars
AEHRSTTY	shattery
AEIIINTT	initiate
AEIIKRTY	teriyaki
AEIILMNN	main line
	mainline
AEIILMPR	imperial
AEIILMSS	Islamise
AEIILMSZ	Islamize
AEIILMTT	militate
AEIILNQU	aquiline
AEIILNRR	airliner
AEIILNRT	air inlet
	inertial
AEIILNST	Latinise
	Taliesin
AEIILNTZ	Latinize
AEIILPPT	tailpipe
AEIILRST	listeria
AEIILRSV	rivalise
AEIILRTT	literati
AEIILRVZ	rivalize
AEIILSTV	vitalise
AEIILTVZ	vitalize
AEIIMMRT	maritime
AEIIMMSX	maximise
AEIIMMXZ	maximize
AEIIMNTT	intimate
AEIIMNTU	minutiae
AEIIMRST	seriatim
AEIINPRS	Piranesi
AEIINRSS	airiness
AEIINSST	sanitise
AEIINSTZ	sanitize
AEIINSVV	invasive
AEIIPRSW	pairwise
AEIIPRZZ	pizzeria
AEIIRRTT	irritate
AEIIRSST	satirise
	Tiresias
AEIIRSTW	wisteria
AEIIRSTZ	satirize
AEIIRTTT	tritiate
AEIITTTV	titivate
AEIJKLMR	Jim Laker
AEIJLOSU	jalousie
AEIJMNRU	Jean Muir
AEIJMORR	Marjorie
AEIKKLUV	Lake Kivu
AEIKKMNO	kakiemon □
AEIKKMRT	kite mark □
AEIKLNSW	swanlike
AEIKLNSY	sneakily
AEIKLRST	starlike
AEIKLRVY	Valkyrie
AEIKMMRT	mark time
AEIKMNST	mistaken
AEIKMOTT	make it to
AEIKMPSS	misspeak
AEIKNRTW	knitwear

AEIKPRSS	après-ski	AEILNRST	entrails	AEIMNOTT	at no time
AEIKRSST	asterisk	AEILNRTU	tenurial	AEIMNOWZ	womanize
AEIKRSTT	strike at	AEILNRTV	interval	AEIMNPRZ	prizeman
AEIKRSTW	water-ski	AEILNRTY	interlay	AEIMNPST	time span
AEILLLNY	lineally	AEILNSST	eastlins	AEIMNQRU	ramequin
AEILLMSY	mesially	AEILNSSZ	laziness	AEIMNRSS	near miss
AEILLNNO	all in one	AEILNSTT	Intelsat	AEIMNRSU	aneurism
AEILLNPS	Spillane	AEILNSTU	insulate		Sumerian
	splenial	AEILNSUY	uneasily		Suriname
AEILLNQU	quinella	AEILNTVY	natively	AEIMNRSY	seminary
AEILLNRY	linearly		venality	AEIMNRTT	martinet
AEILLNSS	sensilla	AEILNUVV	univalve	AEIMNRTU	ruminate
AEILLNVY	venially	AEILOPPT	oppilate	AEIMNSST	matiness
AEILLOTV	volatile	AEILOPRS	polarise	AEIMNTVZ	vizament
AEILLPPR	apperill	AEILOPRT	epilator	AEIMOPTT	optimate
AEILLPST	pastille	AEILOPRZ	polarize	AEIMORST	amortise
AEILLRRY	raillery	AEILOPST	spoliate		atomiser
AEILLRSW	Walliser	AEILORSS	solarise		Timor Sea
AEILLRSY	serially	AEILORST	soterial	AEIMORTT	amoretti
AEILLRTT	ill-treat	AEILORSV	oversail		Mariotte
AEILLSST	tailless		valorise	AEIMORTZ	amortize
AEILLSUV	allusive	AEILORSZ	solarize		atomizer
AEILLSYZ	sleazily	AEILORTV	Voltaire	AEIMOTTV	motivate
AEILMMNT	immantle	AEILORVZ	valorize	AEIMPRTT	part-time
AEILMMNY	immanely	AEILOSTT	totalise	AEIMPRTW	time warp
AEILMMOR	memorial	AEILOTTV	volitate	AEIMPRTX	mixer tap
AEILMMOT	immolate	AEILOTTZ	totalize	AEIMQRSU	marquise
AEILMMSS	melismas	AEILPPQU	appliqué	AEIMRSSY	emissary
AEILMNNO	minneola	AEILPPST	split pea	AEIMRSTT	mistreat
AEILMNNS	linesman	AEILPRRS	reprisal		teratism
AEILMNOS	semolina	AEILPRST	pilaster	AEIMRSTX	matrixes
AEILMNRT	terminal	AEILPRSW	slipware	AEIMSSTT	misstate
AEILMOPR	proemial	AEILPSTY	ptyalise	AEIMSSTZ	mestizas
AEILMORS	moralise	AEILPSUU	Apuleius	AEINNNOR	Neronian
AEILMORZ	moralize	AEILPTYZ	ptyalize	AEINNNOX	annexion
AEILMPRS	pile arms	AEILQRTU	quartile	AEINNORS	in reason
AEILMPRV	primeval		requital	AEINNORT	anointer
AEILMPTT	petit mal	AEILQSUY	queasily		inornate
AEILMPTY	playtime	AEILQTUY	equality	AEINNOSS	in season
AEILMRSY	smearily	AEILRRSU	ruralise	AEINNOST	Estonian
AEILMRTT	remittal	AEILRRTY	literary	AEINNOTT	intonate
AEILMSTU	simulate	AEILRRUZ	ruralize	AEINNOTV	innovate
AEILMSTY	steamily	AEILRSST	slaister		venation
AEILMTTU	mutilate	AEILRSUU	Aurelius	AEINNSSV	vainness
	ultimate	AEILRSWY	lyra-wise	AEINNSSZ	zaniness
AEILNNPP	panel pin	AEILRTVY	at livery	AEINNSTT	stannite
AEILNNRT	internal	AEILSSUV	Vesalius	AEINNSUV	Venusian
AEILNNSU	Linnaeus	AEILSSUW	Sulawesi	AEINOPPT	antipope
AEILNNSY	insanely	AEIMMNNT	immanent	AEINOPRT	atropine
AEILNNTW	New Latin	AEIMMNOT	ammonite	AEINOQTU	equation
AEILNNTY	innately	AEIMMRTU	immature	AEINORRT	anterior
AEILNORR	Lorraine	AEIMNNNR	inner man	AEINORSS	sensoria
AEILNORS	Rosaline	AEIMNNOT	nominate	AEINORST	notarise
AEILNORT	oriental	AEIMNNSW	Weismann		Señorita
	relation	AEIMNNWZ	Weizmann	AEINORSV	aversion
AEILNOST	insolate	AEIMNOPT	ptomaine	AEINORTT	tear into
AEILNOSV	Slovenia		Tom Paine	AEINORTZ	notarize
AEILNOTV	Ovaltine®	AEIMNORS	Romanise	AEINOSSX	Saxonise
AEILNPSS	painless	AEIMNORZ	Romanize	AEINOSXZ	Saxonize
AEILNPTT	tinplate	AEIMNOST	somniate	AEINOTVX	vexation
AEILNRSS	rainless	AEIMNOSW	womanise	AEINPPPS	Pan-pipes

AEINPPTZ Zantippe
AEINPRRT terrapin
AEINPRSU unpraise
AEINPRTT triptane
AEINPRUV Peruvian
AEINPSTU supinate
AEINPSTY epinasty
AEINQSTU antiques
quantise
AEINQTUZ quantize
AEINRRST restrain
strainer
AEINRSSW wariness
AEINRSSX xeransis
AEINRSTT straiten
AEINRSUZ suzerain
AEINSSVW waviness
AEINSSWX waxiness
AEINSTWY Steinway
AEINTTUU autunite
AEIOPPST apposite
AEIOPRRT Pretoria
AEIOPRST aspire to
AEIOPRSV vaporise
AEIOPRTX expiator
AEIOPRVZ vaporize
AEIOPTTV optative
AEIORRRS arrieros
AEIORRUV au revoir
AEIPRSTV privates
AEIPRSTY asperity
AEIPRSVY vespiary
AEIPTTUV putative
AEIRRTTY tertiary❑
AEIRSSTW waitress
AEIRTTTW atwitter
AEISSSTY essayist
AEJKNOOR Jean Rook
AEJLOSUY jealousy
AEJLOSUZ azulejos
AEJNORSZ zanjeros
AEKKMNOO kakemono
AEKLMNOV Malenkov
AEKLMRUW lukewarm
AEKLMRUY yarmulke
AEKLNNSS lankness
AEKLNOSY ankylose
AEKLNOTW wale knot
AEKLOPRW rope-walk
AEKLORTV overtalk
talk over
AEKLORVW walk over
walkover
walk-over
AEKLOSST stalkoes
AEKLPRRS sparkler
AEKLQRUY Quakerly
AEKMNORR remark on
AEKMNRST Stenmark
AEKMNRSU unmasker
AEKMOPTU make up to
AEKMORTW teamwork
workmate
AEKMPRTU up-market
AEKNNRSS rankness
AEKOORTT take root
AEKOPSTU speak out
AEKOPSTW weak spot
AEKOPTUW wake up to
AEKORRTW work rate
AEKORRWW workwear
AEKORSTV overtask
AEKOSTTU stake out
stake-out
AEKQRSUW squawker
AEKRRSST starkers
AELLMNTY mentally
AELLMORT martello
AELLMPUU plumulae
AELLMSST smallest
AELLNOPV volplane
AELLNORS llaneros
AELLNOST Stallone
AELLNOSV novellas
AELLNPRU prunella❑
AELLNRUY neurally
unreally
AELLNRVY vernally
AELLNSST tallness
AELLNTTY latently
AELLOPRS reposall
AELLOPRW walloper
AELLOPRY role-play
AELLORSV overalls
AELLORWW wallower
AELLOSUV alveolus
AELLPPSU sell a pup
AELLQRSU squaller
AELLRRTY retrally
AELLRTTY latterly
AELLRTVY trevally
AELLSSST saltless
AELLSSTY tasselly
AELLSUXY sexually
AELMMRST trammels
AELMNNOP neon lamp
AELMNNOT non-metal
AELMNNRY mannerly
AELMNNTU unmantle
AELMNOPS neoplasm
pleonasm
AELMNORT Montreal
AELMNOYY yeomanly
AELMNRSU mensural
AELMNSUY Süleyman
AELMOORS saleroom
AELMOPRR premolar
AELMOPRT temporal
AELMOPTT metaplot
pot metal
AELMORTU emulator
AELMOSSS molasses
AELMOSTU soul mate
AELMOSTY atmolyse
AELMOTVZ mazel tov
mazeltov
AELMOTYZ atmolyze
AELMPRRT trampler
AELMPRSY lampreys
AELMPSUX amplexus
AELMRSTY masterly
AELMRTUY maturely
AELNNNPU unpannel
AELNNOOP napoleon❑
AELNNOPP open-plan
AELNOPPT Appleton
AELNOPRS personal
AELNOQSU squeal on
AELNORTT rattle on
tolerant
AELNORTU outlearn
AELNORTY ornately
Tyrolean
AELNPPSY spy plane
AELNPRSU supernal
AELNPRTU turn pale
AELNPTTU petulant
AELNPTTY patently
AELNRRTY errantly
AELNRSTT slattern
AELNRSXY larynxes
AELNRUWY unwarely
AELNSUUX unsexual
AELNTTUX exultant
AELOORTW Waterloo
AELOORTY too early
AELOPPRS prolapse
AELOPPSU papulose
AELOPPTU populate
AELOPPXY apoplexy
AELOPQUY opaquely
AELOPRST Pole Star
AELOPRVY overplay
play over
AELOPSSU espousal
AELORRSS Rosslare
AELORSSU Larousse
AELORSUU rouleaus
AELORTTV varletto
AELORTWW low water
AELORTYZ zealotry
AELORUUV au voleur
AELORUUX rouleaux
AELOSSTY asystole
AELOSTUY autolyse
AELOTUYZ autolyze
AELPRRTT prattler
AELPRSSY sparsely
AELPRSTT splatter
sprattle
AELPRSTY plastery
psaltery
AELQRRSU quarrels

AELQRSUY	squarely
AELQSTTU	squattle
AELRRSTT	startler
AELRRTVY	varletry
AELRSSST	starless
AELRSTTU	lustrate
AELRSTTY	Slattery
AELRTTUX	textural
AELRTTUY	tutelary
AELRTTWY	Wat Tyler
AELSSSTU	saltuses
AELSTTUY	astutely
AEMMMOTU	ommateum
AEMMNNOY	moneyman
AEMMNRRY	merryman
AEMMORST	marmoset
AEMMOSTU	mouse mat
AEMNNOPW	penwoman
AEMNNORS	Norseman
AEMNNORT	ornament
AEMNNORW	Morwenna
AEMNNPRU	per annum
AEMNNRST	remnants
AEMNOORT	anteroom
AEMNOPRT	empatron
AEMNOPRW	manpower
AEMNORRS	ransomer
AEMNORST	monstera
	on stream
	on-stream
	storeman
AEMNORSU	neuromas
AEMNORTT	no matter
AEMNORTU	routeman
AEMNORTY	monetary
AEMNORYY	yeomanry
AEMNPRSS	pressman
AEMNPRSU	superman
AEMNPSTU	spumante□
AEMNRSSW	warmness
AEMNRSTU	menstrua
	transume
AEMNRSTX	Max Ernst
AEMNRSUY	aneurysm
AEMNRVYY	very many
AEMNSTUW	mute swan
AEMOOPST	pomatoes
AEMOOSST	maestoso
AEMOOSTT	tomatoes
AEMOOSTU	autosome
AEMOPPRS	pamperos
AEMOPRTW	pomwater
	tapeworm
AEMOPSTV	move past
AEMOQSSU	squamose
AEMORRRU	armourer
AEMORRST	rearmost
AEMORRSY	Mary Rose
	rosemary□
AEMORSST	maestros
AEMORSSY	mayoress
AEMORSTV	overmast
AEMOSSWY	someways
AEMPRRSY	spermary
AEMPRSTU	upstream
AEMQRSSU	marquess
AEMRSSTT	mattress
AEMRSSUU	Sarum use
AEMRSTUX	extra sum
AEMRTUUX	trumeaux
AENNNOST	an sonnet
AENNNOTU	Nuneaton
AENNNTTU	untenant
AENNOPRY	non-payer
AENNOPUW	unweapon
AENNORST	norteñas
	resonant
AENNORSU	unreason
AENNORWY	Norweyan
AENNOSTU	tonneaus
AENNOSTW	tenon saw
	tenon-saw
AENNOTUX	tonneaux
AENNRSTT	entrants
AENNRSWY	swannery
AENNRTTY	tenantry
AENOOPST	teaspoon
AENOPRRY	rope-yarn
AENOPRSS	personas
AENOPRST	Paterson
AENOPRTT	patentor
AENOPRTY	one-party
AENOPRWY	weaponry
AENOPSTT	ante-post
AENORRST	antrorse
AENORSTW	answer to
AENORSUV	ravenous
AENORTTY	attorney
AENOSSTT	assent to
AENOSSUU	nauseous
AENPRRST	partners
AENPRSTT	transept
AENPSSSY	synapses
AENQSTTU	questant
AENRRRTY	errantry
AENRSSTT	tartness
AENRSSTV	servants
AENRTUVY	vauntery
AENSSSTV	vastness
AENSSTTU	tautness
AEOOPRRT	operator
AEOOPSTT	potatoes
AEOORTTV	rotovate
AEOPRRRT	parroter
AEOPRRTV	overpart
AEOPRSST	espartos
	protases
AEOPRSSV	overpass
	pass over
	Passover
AEOPRSTT	prostate
AEOPRSTU	apterous
AEOPSTTU	put to sea
AEOPTTUY	autotype
AEOQRSUV	vaqueros
AEOQRTUZ	quatorze
AEORRTZZ	terrazzo
AEORSSSS	assessor
AEORSSTT	stratose
AEORSSUU	Rousseau
AEORSTTU	outstare
	sea trout
	stare out
AEORSTUW	outswear
AEORSTVY	overstay
	stay over
AEORTUWY	outweary
	weary out
AEOSSTYY	say yes to
AEOSTTTT	attest to
AEPPRRST	strapper
AEPPRRSW	wrappers
AEPQRSUU	square up
AEPRSSST	trespass
AEPRSTTY	tapestry
AEPRSTUX	supertax
AEQRRSTU	quarters
AEQRSTTU	squatter
AERRSSTT	starters
AERRSTUY	treasury
AERSSSUU	Saussure
AERSTTVY	travesty
AESSSTTU	statuses
AESSTTTU	statutes
AFFFFINN	niffnaff
AFFFFIRR	riff-raff
AFFGHIRT	affright
AFFGHLOU	laugh off
AFFGIIRT	graffiti
AFFGILNW	waffling
AFFGIMRS	misgraff
AFFGIORT	graffito
AFFGLNRU	far-flung
AFFHILST	flatfish
AFFHILTU	faithful□
AFFHMNNO	Hoffmann
AFFIIJNY	in a jiffy
AFFIINTY	affinity
AFFILLMM	flim-flam
AFFILLPP	flip-flap
AFFILORT	trail off
AFFINOSU	affusion
AFFIPSTT	tipstaff
AFFKOPRS	spark off
AFFLLOOT	footfall
AFFLLTUU	faultful
AFFLOORT	flat roof
AFFLOOTT	flatfoot
AFFMORRY	marry off
AFFNORSY	saffrony
AFFORSTT	start off
AFFRTTUU	Truffaut
AFGGGILN	flagging

AFGGINRT	grafting
AFGHILNS	flashing
AFGHILNT	fanlight
AFGHILPS	flagship
AFGHINOT	of a night
AFGHINRT	farthing
AFGHLNSU	flashgun
AFGIINNT	fainting
AFGIKLNN	flanking
AFGILLNT	flatling
AFGILMNO	flamingo
AFGILNOT	floating
AFGILNPP	flapping
AFGILSSY	glassify
AFGIMNTU	fumigant
AFGIMRST	misgraft
AFGINNNS	fannings
AFGINRTU	figurant
AFGINSUY	sanguify
AFGIPRTW	gift-wrap
AFGJNRUU	Jungfrau
AFGLLNOT	flatlong
AFGLLRUU	fulgural
AFGLLRUY	frugally
AFGLNNOO	gonfalon
AFGOOORT	go too far
AFGORTUW	tug of war
	tug-of-war
AFHHIKSW	fish-hawk
AFHHLORU	half-hour
AFHIILSS	sailfish
AFHIILST	fish-tail
AFHIKLPS	hip flask
AFHIKNRS	Frankish
AFHILLNS	halflins
AFHILLPS	half-slip
AFHILLSY	flashily
AFHILMOR	hail from
AFHILNPT	half-pint
AFHILOTW	with foal
AFHILSTT	flattish
AFHIOTTW	what of it?
AFHIRSST	starfish
AFHKLNTU	thankful
AFHLLOTU	loathful
AFHLMNOO	half-moon
AFHLMOTU	Falmouth
AFHLRTUW	wrathful
AFHNORRT	far north
AFHOOPTT	footpath
AFHORTTU	of a truth
AFIILLLY	filially
AFIILLNU	unfilial
AFIILNST	finalist
AFIILNTY	finality
AFIINNOS	sainfoin
	sinfonia
AFIINOTX	fixation
AFIIORRT	triforia
AFIKLNNR	Franklin
AFIKORST	ask for it
AFIKRSTY	karstify
AFILLLOT	flotilla
AFILLLSU	full-sail
AFILLLXY	flax-lily
AFILLTUY	faultily
AFILMNOR	formalin
	informal
AFILMRST	film star
AFILNORT	flatiron
AFILNPPT	flippant
AFILNPST	flat spin
AFILNRUY	unfairly
AFILRSTU	fistular
AFILSSTU	fistulas
AFILSTTU	flautist
AFIMMORR	ramiform
AFIMNNOS	man of sin
AFIMNORT	farm into
AFIMNOSU	infamous
AFIMORRV	variform
AFIMORSV	vasiform
AFINNOOP	on pain of
AFINNOTU	fountain
AFINNRTY	infantry
AFINOPSY	saponify
AFINORUV	in favour
AFINQTUY	quantify
AFINRSTX	transfix
AFIORRST	air frost
AFIORSTZ	sforzati
AFIRSTTY	stratify
AFJKNUZZ	jazz-funk
AFKLNOTT	flat knot
AFKLNOTU	outflank
AFKLNSTU	tankfuls
AFKMOORT	footmark
AFKNOPSY	Panofsky
AFKNOSYY	Yanofsky
AFLLLORY	florally
AFLLLPUY	play full
AFLLLUWY	lawfully
AFLLMNUY	manfully
AFLLMORY	formally
AFLLMRSY	small fry
AFLLNOPU	fall upon
AFLLNOSW	snowfall
AFLLNUUW	unlawful
AFLLOORW	allow for
AFLLOPUY	foul play
AFLLRTUY	artfully
AFLMOPRT	platform
AFLMORSU	formulas
AFLMORTW	flatworm
AFLMOSUY	famously
AFLNOOST	soft loan
AFLOPPRY	apply for
AFLRSTUY	trayfuls
AFMNNNUY	funny man
AFMNNOOS	Son of Man
AFMNNORT	front man
	frontman
AFMNOOSS	Son of Sam
AFMOOPRR	pro forma
AFMOORTZ	from A to Z
AFMORTUY	fumatory
AFMOSSTU	sfumatos
AFNOOPRT	patron of
AFOOPSST	soft soap
	soft-soap
AFOORSTZ	sforzato
AFOORSUV	savour of
AGGGHILN	haggling
AGGGILNN	gangling
AGGGIYZZ	zigzaggy
AGGGLNPU	gang plug
AGGHILNU	laughing
AGGHILST	gaslight
AGGHILSY	shaggily
AGGHINNS	hangings
AGGHJMNO	mah-jongg
AGGIILNV	gingival
AGGIINNR	graining
AGGIJLNN	jangling
AGGILMNO	gloaming
AGGILNNO	ganglion
AGGILNNS	slanging
AGGILNOT	gloating
	goatling
AGGILNPU	plaguing
AGGILNPY	gapingly
AGGILNRY	grayling
	ragingly
AGGINNOR	groaning
AGGINNRT	granting
AGGINOVY	voyaging
AGGINPRS	grasping
AGGINRSU	sugaring
AGGINRTY	gyrating
AGGIRTUZ	ziggurat
AGGLLLOY	lollygag
AGGLMOOR	logogram
AGGLRSTY	straggly
AGGMRSUU	sugar gum
AGGNNOPU	gang up on
AGGNUWZZ	zugzwang
AGHHIILT	hightail
AGHHIMSS	High Mass
AGHHINOP	Haiphong
AGHHLOTU	although
AGHHNOUZ	Hangzhou
AGHHORRT	Hrothgar
AGHHOSTU	as though
AGHIILMP	Malpighi
AGHIILNN	inhaling
AGHIILOS	Laoighis
AGHIIPRR	hairgrip
AGHIIRTT	airtight
AGHIJNRT	nightjar
AGHIKLRU	Gurkhali
AGHILLNT	all-thing
AGHILLRT	all right
	all-right

AGHILMTY	almighty □
AGHILNOO	hooligan
AGHILNOT	loathing
AGHILNRS	ringhals
AGHILNSS	lashings
	slashing
AGHILNSU	languish
AGHILRSY	garishly
AGHILRTY	graithly
AGHILSUY	aguishly
AGHILTWX	wax-light
AGHIMNRS	Ram Singh
AGHIMNSS	smashing
AGHIMNTY	thingamy
AGHIMPRU	graphium
AGHIMRRT	right arm
AGHINNTU	haunting
AGHINNTY	anything
AGHINPRS	phrasing
AGHINPRY	Phrygian
AGHINQSU	quashing
AGHINRRY	harrying
AGHINSST	Hastings
AGHIPRRT	trigraph
AGHIRSTT	straight
AGHLLMPU	gallumph
AGHLLNOU	long haul
AGHLMOOR	hologram
AGHLNOSU	shogunal
AGHLNOTU	Laughton
AGHLNSUY	nylghaus
AGHMMOOY	homogamy
AGHMNPSU	sphagnum
AGHNNOOT	hang on to
AGHNNSTU	shantung
AGHNTTUU	untaught
AGHRSTTU	straught
AGIIINNS	insignia
AGIIINRV	Virginia
AGIIIRSY	Sigiriya
AGIIKNNT	taking-in
AGIILLMN	Milligan
AGIILLOV	villiago
AGIILMNS	misalign
AGIILNNP	plaining
AGIILNNU	inguinal
AGIILNNY	inlaying
AGIILNOR	original
AGIILNOT	intaglio
	ligation
AGIILNOX	gloxinia
AGIILNRT	ringtail
	trailing
AGIILNRU	Ligurian
AGIILNRV	virginal
AGIILNTT	litigant
AGIILNTV	vigilant
AGIIMNNR	ring main
AGIINNPT	painting
AGIINNRT	training
AGIINNST	staining
AGIINNTT	tainting
AGIINORT	rigatoni
AGIINOST	Agostini
AGIINPRS	aspiring
	praising
AGIINRRV	arriving
AGIINSTU	Ignatius
AGIJNRSU	Juan Gris
AGIKLMOR	kilogram
AGIKLNNO	Algonkin
AGIKLNNP	planking
AGIKLNNR	rankling
AGIKLNST	stalking
AGIKLNTY	takingly
AGIKLORY	kilogray
AGIKMNRS	markings
AGIKNNOT	taking on
	taking-on
AGIKNNPS	spanking
AGIKNNSW	swanking
AGIKNPTU	taking up
	taking-up
AGILLMNU	Mulligan
AGILLMNY	malignly
AGILLMSU	Gaullism
AGILLNOW	allowing
AGILLNPR	grill pan
AGILLNRU	alluring
AGILLNRY	rallying
AGILLNST	stalling
AGILLNSY	signally
	slangily
AGILLPUY	plaguily
AGILLSSY	glassily
AGILLSTU	Gaullist
AGILMMNS	slamming
AGILMNOO	Mongolia
AGILMNPR	Rampling
AGILMNPS	sampling
AGILMNRU	Langmuir
AGILMOPR	lipogram
AGILNNNP	planning
AGILNNOP	pangolin
AGILNNRS	snarling
AGILNNST	slanting
AGILNNUY	ungainly
AGILNORT	trigonal
AGILNOST	signal to
AGILNOTW	wagon-lit
AGILNPPS	slapping
AGILNRST	starling
AGILNRSU	singular
AGILNRSW	Rawlings
AGILNRTT	rattling
AGILNRTW	trawling
AGILNRVY	ravingly
AGILNSTU	saluting
AGILNSVY	savingly
AGILNTUV	vaulting
AGILOOXY	axiology
AGILQUUY	Guyaquil
AGIMMOSY	misogamy
AGIMNNRU	manuring
AGIMNORR	Morrigan
AGIMNORS	organism
AGIMNORU	origanum
AGIMNORY	agrimony
AGIMNPST	stamping
AGIMNRRY	marrying
AGIMNRST	smarting
AGIMNRSW	swarming
AGIMNSSU	assuming
AGIMORRT	migrator
AGINNNOY	annoying
AGINNOPT	poignant
AGINNOPU	gain upon
AGINNORT	ignorant
	Tir nan-Og
AGINNPPS	snapping
AGINNPSW	spawning
	wingspan
AGINNTTU	taunting
AGINNTUV	vaunting
AGINNTUX	untaxing
AGINOORT	rogation
AGINORRS	garrison
AGINORSS	assignor
AGINORST	organist
	roasting
AGINORSU	arousing
AGINORTT	rotating
AGINORTY	gyration
AGINPPRT	trapping
AGINPPRW	wrapping
AGINPPSW	swapping
AGINPRRS	sparring
AGINPRTY	partying
AGINQRSU	squaring
AGINRRTY	tarrying
AGINRSTT	starting
AGINRSTV	starving
AGINRSTY	stingray
	straying
AGIOORSZ	grazioso
AGIOORTU	autogiro
AGIOPPRT	agitprop
AGIRSSTU	sastrugi
AGIRSTUZ	zastrugi
AGIRTTUY	gratuity
AGJNOPST	jog pants
AGKMMORY	kymogram
AGKNSTUU	Tunguska
AGLLOOTU	go all out
AGLLPRSU	spur-gall
AGLLRUVY	vulgarly
AGLMOPYY	polygamy
AGLNNORU	run along
AGLNOOSS	so long as
AGLNOSST	glasnost
AGLNOSWY	longways
AGLOOPST	goalpost
AGLOPRTU	Portugal

AGLORSSY	glossary
AGLOSUVY	Yugoslav
AGLPSSSY	spyglass
AGLRTTUU	guttural
AGLSTUUY	augustly
AGMMNOOR	monogram
	nomogram
AGMMNOOY	monogamy
AGMNNOUY	young man
AGMNOORS	sonogram
AGMNOORY	agronomy
AGMNORST	angstrom
	Ångström
AGMOOOSU	oogamous
AGMRSTUY	smart guy
AGNNOQTU	quantong
AGNNOSSW	swan song
AGNORTUY	nugatory
AGNPRSUY	spraygun
AGOORTUY	autogyro
AGOPRSSY	gross pay
AGORRTYY	gyratory
AGSSTUUU	Augustus
AHHHOOOW	whoa-ho-ho
AHHILPSW	whiplash
AHHIMMSS	mishmash
	mish-mash
AHHIMMWW	whim-wham
AHHIMSST	smash hit
	smash-hit
AHHIPRSS	sharpish
AHHITTTW	with that
AHHITTWW	what with
AHHJNNOS	John Nash
AHHKRSTU	Kashruth
AHHMPRRU	harrumph
AHHNORTW	hawthorn
AHHORTWY	Hayworth
AHHOSTTW	how's that
AHHOSTUV	Shavuoth
AHIIKMRS	Kashmiri
AHIILOST	haliotis
AHIILPPP	Philippa
AHIILRTY	hilarity
AHIIMNRS	Irishman
AHIIMNST	Ian Smith
AHIINSWY	in his way
AHIIOPST	hospitia
AHIIPRTW	pair with
AHIJNNOW	John Wain
AHIKLNNS	Shanklin
AHIKLNRS	rinkhals
AHIKLRSY	rakishly
AHIKNPRS	prankish
AHIKRSSW	Sikh Wars
AHILLMOU	halloumi
AHILLMPS	phallism
AHILLMSS	smallish
AHILLMTU	thallium
AHILLNRT	in thrall
AHILLNSW	Swan Hill
	Whillans
AHILLPST	tall ship
AHILLSVY	lavishly
AHILMNOT	Hamilton
AHILMOST	mailshot
AHILMQSU	qualmish
AHILOORT	Lothario
AHILOPST	hospital
AHILORSS	hair loss
AHILPTWY	play with
AHILRSTY	trashily
AHILRTWY	wrathily
AHIMMNSU	humanism
AHIMMORZ	mahzorim
AHIMMOSV	moshavim
AHIMNOSW	womanish
AHIMNSTU	humanist
AHIMNTUY	humanity
AHIMOPRS	aphorism
AHIMPPSS	sapphism □
AHIMRSST	smartish
AHIMSTVZ	mitzvahs
AHINNNOR	Rhiannon
AHINNNSY	nannyish
AHINNOPT	antiphon
AHINOPTY	Hay Point
AHINORRS	Harrison
AHINOSST	astonish
AHINPPSS	snappish
AHINPRST	tranship
AHINQSUV	vanquish
AHINRRUY	in a hurry
AHIOPRST	aphorist
AHIORSTV	tovarish
AHIOTTTU	hit out at
AHIPPSST	sapphist
AHIPRSSW	warships
AHIPRTTW	part with
AHIQRSSU	squarish
AHISTTWY	stay with
AHJLNOPU	John Paul
AHJNNOOS	Johanson
AHJNNOOT	Jonathon
AHKLOPRT	Klaproth
AHKLOPST	talk shop
AHKLOSTW	talk show
AHKMNOST	Tom Hanks
AHKMORTU	Khartoum
AHKNNOST	no thanks
AHKNOSTT	thanks to
AHKNOTUY	thank you
	thankyou
AHLLMOTU	all mouth
AHLLNOTW	town hall
AHLLOSSW	shallows
AHLLOSTY	tally-hos
AHLMMOPY	lymphoma
AHLMNOOR	hormonal
AHLMOOPS	omphalos
AHLMOPTY	polymath
AHLOPRSU	Sholapur
AHLORRTY	harlotry
AHLRTTWY	thwartly
AHMNNNOU	non-human
AHMNNSTU	huntsman □
AHMNORSU	man-hours
AHMNSSUY	Huysmans
AHMOOPSS	shampoos
AHMOORSW	washroom
AHMORSST	R S Thomas
AHMORSSU	sour mash
AHMORTTW	Tamworth
AHMPSTYY	sympathy
AHMQSSUU	musquash
AHNOOPTU	upon oath
AHNOORRY	honorary
AHNOPPSW	pawnshop
AHNOPRST	not sharp
AHNOPSST	snapshot
AHNOPSTT	hot pants
AHNORSTV	Torshavn
	Tórshavn
AHNOSTUX	xanthous
AHOOSSTY	soothsay
AHOPSTUW	southpaw
AHORTTUW	watt-hour
AIIILNST	initials
AIIJKNNS	Nijinska
AIIKKSUY	sukiyaki
AIIKLLMN	Millikan
AIIKLNRR	larrikin
AIIKMNNN	mannikin
AIIKNNNP	pannikin
AIIKORTY	yakitori
AIIKTTZZ	tzatziki
AIILLMNO	a million
AIILLMSW	Williams
AIILLNNV	vanillin
AIILLNOP	pollinia
AIILLNOT	illation
AIILLNVY	villainy
AIILLPRS	spirilla
AIILLWWW	williwaw
AIILMNST	Latinism
AIILMNTT	militant
AIILMPUV	impluvia
AIILMRTY	limitary
	military
AIILNOPS	Pasolini
AIILNOPT	oil paint
AIILNOPV	pavilion
AIILNOST	sail into
AIILNOSV	visional
AIILNPST	tailspin
AIILNQRU	Quirinal
AIILNRSU	Silurian
AIILNSTT	Latinist
AIILNSTY	salinity
AIILOPPS	papilios
AIILRSTT	trialist
AIILSTTW	wait-list
AIILTTVY	vitality

AIIMMNNY	minyanim
AIIMNNOS	insomnia
AIIMNOPT	point aim
AIIMNRSU	Arminius
AIIMNSTV	nativism
AIIMNTTU	titanium
AIIMORTT	imitator
AIIMOSST	amitosis
AIIMRUVV	vivarium
AIIMSSTT	mastitis
AIINNOPS	pianinos
AIINNOSV	invasion
AIINNSTY	insanity
AIINPRST	Pristina
AIINRRTT	irritant
AIINSSST	assist in
AIINSTTV	nativist
	visitant
AIINTTVY	nativity
AIINTYZZ	in a tizzy
AIIORSTV	ovaritis
AIIORTTV	vitiator
	Vittoria
AIIPRRST	airstrip
AIIRSSTT	satirist
AIJKKNOU	kinkajou
AIJKLMNU	junk mail
AIJLLOOR	jillaroo
AIJLLOVY	jovially
AIJLNTUY	jauntily
AIJMNOOR	Joan Miró
AIJMNOSS	Joan Sims
AIJMORTY	majority
AIJNOPPY	popinjay
AIKKLLRW	Kirkwall
AIKKLOSW	Kowalski
AIKKLOSY	silky oak
AIKKNOTY	kantikoy
AIKLLRSS	all-risks
AIKLNOPS	Polanski
AIKLNOTT	talk into
AIKLNOTW	walk into
AIKLOSUV	souvlaki
AIKLOTTW	kilowatt
AIKNNOOS	nainsook
AIKNNOST	Atkinson
AIKNOSTT	stotinka
AIKNPSST	ski pants
AIKNRRSU	run a risk
AIKNRSST	Sanskrit
AILLMOOV	Malvolio
AILLMOSS	Limassol
AILLMOST	misallot
AILLMPRY	primally
AILLMRUY	arum lily
AILLMUUV	alluvium
AILLNOPP	papillon
AILLNOST	stallion
AILLNOSU	allusion
AILLNOTW	Low Latin
AILLNOWW	wallow in

AILLNPTY	pliantly
AILLNSUV	Sullivan
AILLOPPY	apply oil
AILLORTT	littoral
	tortilla
AILLOSTY	loyalist
AILLPRSY	spirally
AILLPRTY	paltrily
AILLRSTY	rallyist
AILLRTUY	ritually
AILLSUVY	visually
AILMMNOO	monomial
AILMMORS	moralism
AILMMORT	immortal
AILMMRSY	smarmily
AILMNNPP	Lippmann
AILMNOOP	palomino□
AILMNOOR	monorail
AILMNOPY	Olympian
	palimony
AILMNPTU	platinum
AILMNRUY	luminary
AILMOPRX	proximal
AILMORST	moralist
AILMORSU	solarium
AILMORSY	royalism
AILMORTY	molarity
	morality
AILMOSTU	solatium
AILMPPSY	misapply
AILMPSST	psalmist
AILMRSTU	altruism
	muralist
	ultraism
AILNNOOT	notional
AILNNOSU	unisonal
AILNNOSW	son-in-law
AILNOOPT	optional
AILNOPRU	unipolar
AILNOPTY	ponytail
AILNOSTU	Lusitano
AILNOTTY	tonality
AILNPPSY	snappily
AILNPRUV	pulvinar
AILNPSTU	nuptials
AILNPSUU	nauplius
AILNQRTU	tranquil
AILNQTUY	quaintly
AILNRRTU	trial run
AILNRTTU	turn tail
AILNRUWY	unwarily
AILNSSUV	Silvanus
AILNSTTU	lutanist
AILNSTUU	nautilus
AILNSTVY	Navy List
AILOOPZZ	Paolozzi
AILOORRS	sororial
AILOORTV	violator
AILOPRRV	proviral
AILOPRTV	Port-Vila
AILOPRTY	polarity

AILORSTU	sutorial
AILORSTY	royalist□
	solitary
AILORTTU	tutorial
AILORTUV	outrival
AILOTTTY	totality
AILPRSTU	stipular
AILRRSTY	starrily
AILRRTUY	rurality
AILRSTTU	altruist
	ultraist
AILRSUVV	survival
AIMMMNOU	ammonium
AIMMNNOS	Mosimann
AIMMOSSU	miasmous
AIMMRRSY	mismarry
AIMNNOOU	uno animo
AIMNNORU	our man in
AIMNNOTU	mountain
AIMNNOTY	antimony
	antinomy
AIMNNRTU	ruminant
AIMNOORV	Monrovia
AIMNORTU	Minotaur
AIMNORTY	minatory
AIMNOSTU	manitous
AIMNOTTU	Mount Tai
	mutation
AIMNPRSU	up in arms
AIMNRSTT	Tantrism
	transmit
AIMNRSTU	naturism
AIMOPRTT	impart to
AIMOPSST	impastos
AIMOPSSY	symposia
AIMORRSU	rosarium
AIMORRTY	Moriarty
AIMORRUV	variorum
AIMORTVY	vomitary
AIMOSTTW	Tom Waits
AIMPRSTY	partyism
AIMRRSTT	Tristram
AIMRTTUY	maturity
AINNNOST	santonin
AINNOOTT	notation
AINNOSTU	Antonius
AINNOTTU	nutation
AINNPPSS	snip-snap
AINNSSTT	Instants
AINNSTTY	nystatin
AINOOPTT	potation
AINOORTT	rotation
AINOOSTT	ostinato
AINOPRTV	proviant
AINOPSSS	passions
AINOPSST	pass into
AINOPSTT	at points
	Pattison
AINOPTUW	wait upon
AINORSST	arsonist
AINORSTU	sutorian

AINORUWY	in our way
AINOSSUU	Ausonius
AINPPRUW	wrap up in
AINPRSSU	Prussian
AINPRSTU	Rasputin
AINPSSSY	synapsis
AINPSSTU	puissant
AINPSTTU	pant suit
AINQTTUY	quantity
AINRSTTU	naturist
AINRTUXY	X-ray unit
AIOOORRT	oratorio
AIOPRRSS	Pissarro
AIOPRRTT	portrait
AIOPRSST	protasis
AIORRSTV	varistor
AIORSTTV	votarist
AIORSTUV	virtuosa
AIOSSSTY	isostasy
AIPPRSTT	Trappist
AIPPRSTY	papistry
AIPPTTTY	pitty-pat
AIPRRTTY	tray-trip
AIPRSSTU	upstairs
AIPRSSTY	sparsity
AIRRSTTY	artistry
AJLLNOOS	Al Jolson
AJLNORSU	journals
AJMNSSTU	Jan Smuts
AJPSSSTU	just pass
AKLLNOTW	wall knot
AKLLNPRU	pull rank
AKLMNOOW	moonwalk
AKLNNOPT	plankton
AKLOORWY	look awry
AKLOSTVY	Saltykov
AKLPRRSU	larkspur
AKMMNOOR	monomark
AKMMNRSU	Murmansk
AKMOPRST	postmark
AKNNOSTZ	Konstanz
AKOPRRTW	partwork
AKOPRSTU	spark out
AKORSWWX	waxworks
ALLLOOPU	Ullapool
ALLLOSSU	All Souls
ALLLPRUY	plurally
ALLMNORY	normally
ALLMOPSX	smallpox
ALLMORTY	mortally
ALLMTUUY	mutually
ALLNOOPY	Apollyon
ALLNOOTW	not allow
ALLNORSS	lasslorn
ALLOPSTY	postally
ALLOPTUU	pull out a
ALLRUUVY	uvularly
ALMMMOOW	Mo Mowlam
ALMMORTW	maltworm
ALMNNOOR	non-moral
ALMNORTY	matronly
ALMOPPST	lamppost
ALMOSTTU	sum total
ALNNOPTW	town plan
ALNNOTWY	wantonly
ALNOOSTU	not a soul
ALNOPPTT	pot plant
ALNOPPUY	play upon
ALNOPRST	plastron
ALNOPTTU	plant out
ALNORRWY	narrowly
ALNORSVY	sovranly
ALNOTWWY	tawny owl
ALNPPSTU	supplant
ALNRRTUU	nurtural
ALOOPPRS	proposal
ALOORSUV	valorous
ALOPPSUU	papulous
ALOPPTUY	play up to
ALOPRRSU	sporular
ALOPRSTU	postural
ALOPSSSU	spousals
ALORSTTW	saltwort
ALORTUWY	outlawry
ALPPSTUY	platypus
AMMNPTUY	tympanum
AMNNORSY	mansonry
AMNNOSTW	townsman
AMNNSTTU	stuntman
AMNOOPPS	pompanos
AMNOOTTU	amount to
AMNOOTUY	autonomy
AMNOOTXY	taxonomy
AMNOTTUU	To Autumn
AMNRSTTU	tantrums
AMOOORSS	amorosos
AMOORRRT	rotor arm
AMOORTWY	motorway
AMOOTTUY	autotomy
AMOPRSXY	paroxysm
AMOPSTTU	stamp out
AMOQSSUU	squamous
AMORRTUY	mortuary
AMORSTTU	outsmart
ANNOORST	sonorant
ANNOPRTY	non-party
ANNOSSTU	stannous
ANOOPRRT	pronator
ANOOPRSS	sopranos
ANOOPRTT	pro tanto
ANOOSTTY	not to say
	say not to
ANOPPSSU	pass upon
ANORSTTT	not start
ANPRSTUU	pursuant
ANRRSTTU	star turn
AOOOPRTZ	protozoa
AOOPRSSU	saporous
AOOPRSTT	pot roast
	pot-roast
AOOPRSTW	soapwort
AOOPRSUV	vaporous
AOORRTTY	rotatory
AOPPRSST	passport
AORRSSYY	say sorry
AORRSTTW	starwort
AORSTTTU	start out

B

BBBCEOWY	cobwebby
BBBEOOTU	boob tube
BBBGILNU	bubbling
BBBIITTY	bit by bit
BBBINOPY	bobby-pin
BBCDERSU	scrubbed
BBCEILRS	scribble
BBCELORS	cobblers
BBCELORY	cobblery
BBCEMNOU	buncombe
BBCERRSU	scrubber
BBCGIINR	cribbing
BBCGIKSU	big bucks
BBCGILNO	cobbling
BBCGILNU	clubbing
BBCHKSUU	bushbuck
BBCILRSY	scribbly
BBCKLOOU	book club
BBDEEMNU	benumbed
BBDEFOOR	robbed of
BBDEILMY	Dimbleby
BBDEILRU	bluebird
BBDEIMOV	dive-bomb
BBDEINOR	dobber-in
BBDELOOS	be so bold
BBDELSTU	stubbled
BBDGINRU	drubbing
BBDILORT	bird-bolt
BBDLOOWY	body blow
BBDOSUYY	busybody
BBEEGLOS	Goebbels
BBEEHMOR	Beerbohm
BBEEHTYY	by the bye
BBEEIIRR	beriberi
BBEELLLU	bluebell
BBEFIMOR	fire-bomb
BBEGLOPU	gobble up
BBEILQRU	quibbler
BBEILRRY	bilberry
BBEIMMOT	time bomb
	time-bomb
BBEIMOST	bombsite
BBEKNOOT	bontebok
BBELLOUY	bell buoy
BBELLRUY	lubberly
BBELNRUU	burn blue
BBELORSY	slobbery
BBENOORT	born to be
BBENORSY	snobbery
BBERRRUY	Burberry
BBGHILNO	hobbling
BBGIILNN	nibbling
BBGILMNU	bumbling
BBGILNNO	nobbling

BBGILNOW	wobbling
BBGILNOY	lobbying
BBGILNSU	slubbing
BBGINNSU	snubbing
BBHILOSS	slobbish
BBHINOSS	snobbish
BBHIRSUY	rubbishy
BBIKLNOO	bobolink
BBILLOYY	billy boy
BBILOSTY	lobbyist
BBILOSUU	bibulous
BBIMNOSS	snobbism
BBLLOUYY	bully boy
	bully-boy
BBNORSTU	stubborn
BCCEHIOY	by choice
BCCEHIRU	cherubic
BCCEIIIS	cicisbei
BCCEIILO	libeccio
BCCEILRU	crucible
BCCEMRUU	cucumber
BCCIIMOR	microbic
BCCILOOR	broccoli
BCCKLMOU	bum-clock
BCCLOOOO	cocobolo
BCCSSUUU	succubus
BCDEEEMR	December
BCDEEHNR	bedrench
BCDEEIKN	Benedick
BCDEEILR	credible
BCDEEILU	educible
BCDEEINT	Benedict
BCDEEIRS	describe
BCDEEIST	bisected
BCDEEKRU	reedbuck
BCDEEORV	bedcover
BCDEERUY	reduce by
BCDEFKOR	Beckford
BCDEHINS	disbench
BCDEHLOT	blotched
BCDEIKRR	brick-red
	redbrick
BCDEILRY	credibly
BCDEIMNO	combined
BCDEINOU	icebound
BCDEKLRU	Delbrück
BCDEKOSS	bedsocks
BCDEMNOU	uncombed
BCDENRUU	uncurbed
BCDEORSU	obscured
BCDIIMOR	bromidic
BCDIIPSU	bicuspid
BCDIKMOY	Moby Dick
BCDINRUU	rubicund
BCEEEFIN	benefice
BCEEEHRS	breeches
BCEEEINR	Berenice
BCEEEQRU	Quebecer
BCEEERSU	berceuse
BCEEFILN	fencible
BCEEHKSU	buckshee
BCEEHNRU	unbreech
BCEEHNTU	beech nut
BCEEIILM	imbecile
BCEEIORR	Corbiere
BCEELRTU	tubercle
BCEEMNRU	encumber
BCEEMOOT	come to be
BCEEMRRU	cerebrum
BCEERRSU	Cerberus
BCEFILOR	forcible
BCEFLSUU	Blefuscu
BCEGHILN	belching
BCEGIMNO	becoming
BCEGLNOO	conglobe
BCEHHIRT	the birch
BCEHILPU	blue-chip
BCEHIMRS	besmirch
BCEHIMRU	cherubim
BCEHINRU	cherubin
BCEHINSY	by inches
BCEHIRST	britches
BCEHLOSW	Welsh Cob
BCEHNRSU	Burschen
BCEHORRU	brochure
BCEHRSTU	butcher's
	Schubert
BCEHRTTU	Cuthbert
BCEHRTUY	butchery
BCEIIKLN	iceblink
BCEIILMS	miscible
BCEIILNV	vincible
BCEIIMRS	imbrices
BCEIINRS	inscribe
BCEIKLNY	Nickleby
BCEIKLOO	booklice
BCEIKNNT	Bentinck
BCEILPRU	republic
BCEIMORS	microbes
BCEIMOSW	combwise
BCEINOVX	biconvex
BCEIOOPS	bioscope
BCEIOOVX	voice-box
BCEIORRS	cribrose
BCEIORST	bisector
BCEJNOOT	no object
BCEJOORT	objector
BCEJOOTT	object to
BCEJSSTU	subjects
BCEKLNUU	unbuckle
BCEKLOTU	buckle to
BCEKNRRU	Bruckner
BCELORUV	over-club
BCEOORTU	cube root
BCEORRWY	cowberry
BCFFILMO	climb off
BCFFKLOO	block off
BCFGLLOU	golf club
BCFILORY	forcibly
BCFLRTUU	Turf Club
BCGHIINR	birching
BCGHIMOR	Gombrich
BCGHINNU	bunching
BCGHINOT	botching
BCGIIKST	big stick
BCGIILMN	climbing
BCGIKKRU	grub kick
BCGIKLNO	blocking
BCGILOPU	go public
BCGINNOU	bouncing
BCHIILTY	bitchily
BCHIISSU	hibiscus
BCHIKLOS	blockish
BCHILLRU	Burchill
BCHILSTU	Lubitsch
BCHIOORY	choirboy
BCHJOSUY	cushy job
BCHKNORU	buckhorn
BCHKOSTU	buckshot
BCHNOORS	bronchos
BCHNORSU	bronchus
BCIILNPU	in public
BCIIMNOO	bionomic
BCIISSTU	biscuits
BCIISTUY	biscuity
BCIKKNSU	buckskin
BCIKLOOT	bootlick
BCILLPUY	publicly
BCILMOSY	symbolic
BCILNOUY	bouncily
BCIMOSUX	music box
BCINOSSU	subsonic
BCINOSTU	subtonic
BCIOORST	robotics
BCKKOOOO	cookbook
BCKLLOOS	bollocks
BCKLNOSU	sunblock
BCKLOOTU	block out
BCKOOOPY	copybook
BCKOSTTU	buttocks
BCLMOSUU	Columbus
BCLOORTU	clubroot
BCMORSUU	cumbrous
BCOORSSW	crossbow
BCORSTTU	obstruct
BDDDEEEM	embedded
BDDDEIRY	red biddy
BDDEEFLU	befuddle
BDDEEIMO	embodied
BDDEEINT	indebted
BDDEEINW	bindweed
BDDEEIRS	birdseed
BDDEENRU	burdened
BDDEEORR	bordered
BDDEGINR	Bridgend
BDDEILNR	brindled
BDDEILOO	bloodied
BDDEINNU	unbidden
BDDEINRU	underbid
BDDEIORS	disorbed
	disrobed
BDDELOOR	blood-red
BDDEOTYY	Teddy boy

BDDGOOSY	dogsbody
BDDGUUYY	Buddy Guy
BDDHIMSU	Buddhism
BDDHISTU	Buddhist
BDDMNOUW	dumb down
BDEEEGIS	besieged
BDEEEHTU	hebetude
BDEEEILV	believed
BDEEEIRV	Bedivere
BDEEELLV	bevelled
BDEEELPU	Deep Blue
BDEEEMMR	membered
BDEEENOS	Bodensee
BDEEFFRU	buffered
BDEEFINR	befriend
BDEEFOOR	forebode
BDEEGGRU	begrudge
BDEEGILN	bleeding
BDEEGILU	beguiled
BDEEGIMR	begrimed
BDEEGINR	breeding
BDEEGRSV	Svedberg
BDEEHIRS	Hebrides
BDEEHLNO	beholden
BDEEHLOR	beholder
BDEEHMOR	home-bred
BDEEHNST	the bends
BDEEHORT	bothered
BDEEIILN	inedible
BDEEIKRS	kerbside
BDEEILLU	eludible
BDEEILNN	bed linen
	bed-linen
BDEEILNO	bone idle
	bone-idle
BDEEILNV	vendible
BDEEILOR	erodible
BDEEILRW	bewilder
BDEEIMRT	timbered
BDEEINOT	obedient
BDEEINSW	bendwise
BDEEIRST	bestride
BDEEIRSY	Birdseye
BDEELLRW	well-bred
BDEELMNO	embolden
BDEELORU	redouble
BDEEMNRU	numbered
BDEEMORR	emborder
BDEEMOSS	embossed
BDEEORRR	borderer
BDEEORSV	observed
BDEEORTU	outbreed
BDEEOSSS	obsessed
BDEEOSTT	besotted
BDEEPRRU	pure-bred
BDEFINRR	fernbird
BDEFLOOY	fooled by
BDEGGLOR	Goldberg
BDEGHHIR	high-bred
BDEGHILT	blighted
BDEGHINO	go behind
BDEGILNN	blending
BDEGINSY	by design
BDEGIORX	Oxbridge
BDEGLNOU	bludgeon
BDEGLOOR	Belgorod
BDEGNOOY	go beyond
BDEGORRY	Dogberry
BDEHIRST	The Birds
BDEHLSUV	bushveld
BDEIILMR	bird-lime
BDEIILTY	debility
BDEIIRTU	Itúrbide
BDEILNOY	bodyline
BDEILNPW	Blind Pew
BDEILNRU	unbridle
BDEILNVY	vendibly
BDEILORV	lovebird
BDEILOSS	bodiless
BDEILOSW	disbowel
BDEILRRY	lyrebird
	lyre-bird
BDEILRST	bristled
BDEIMNOR	Benidorm
BDEINORV	bind over
	ovenbird
BDEINOSU	Bedouins
BDEINOTT	in debt to
BDEINRSU	Burnside
BDEIRSSU	disburse
BDEKLMOO	blokedom
BDEKOOPU	booked-up
BDELLOOR	bordello
	doorbell
BDELLOOT	let blood
BDELLOUZ	bulldoze
BDELMRUU	delubrum
BDELNOOW	new blood
BDELNOSS	boldness
BDELNOTU	unbolted
BDELNOUU	undouble
BDELNOUW	unblowed
BDELNPUU	bundle up
BDELOPUU	double up
BDELORTU	troubled
BDEMNSSU	dumbness
BDEMOOSY	somebody
BDENNRUU	unburden
BDENOORR	border on
BDENOORU	Eurobond
BDENOOTW	bentwood
BDENRSUU	unbrused
BDENRUUY	underbuy
BDEOORRW	borrowed
BDEOPTTU	put to bed
BDEORRTU	obtruder
BDERSTUU	subtrude
BDFFIPRU	puffbird
BDFGNOOU	fogbound
BDFILLLO	bill-fold
BDFINORU	foribund
BDFINOTY	by dint of
BDFINRUU	furibund
BDFLOTUU	doubtful
BDGIILNN	blinding
BDGIILNU	building
BDGILNOU	doubling
BDGINOOR	brooding
BDGINORS	bird song
	songbird
BDGINOTU	doubting
BDGIRSUU	Duisburg
BDGKOOOO	good book
BDGNRUUY	burgundy□
BDHIIPRW	whipbird
BDHIMOOR	rhomboid
BDHIMORT	birthdom
BDHIORST	birdshot
BDHLMOTU	Humboldt
BDHMOSUW	dumb show
BDHNRSUU	unshrubd
BDHOOPSY	body shop
BDIIINRS	Brindisi
BDIIJOTU	Djibouti
BDIILLRT	drill bit
BDIIMRUU	rubidium
BDIIOOTX	idiot box
BDILLLOO	ill blood
BDILLOOY	bloodily
BDILMORY	morbidly
BDILNNSU	sunblind
BDILNOOW	boil down
BDILNPRU	purblind
BDILRTUY	turbidly
BDIMNORU	moribund
BDIMOOSS	disbosom
BDIMOSTU	misdoubt
BDINNRUW	windburn
BDIOSTUY	bodysuit
BDKOOORW	wordbook
	word-book
BDKOORWY	bodywork
BDLNOOOU	doubloon
BDLNOOTW	bolt down
BDLOSTUW	dust bowl
BDNNORUW	burn down
BDNOOTUU	outbound
BDORUWZZ	buzz word
BEEEEFLN	enfeeble
BEEEENQU	queen bee
BEEEGRTT	begetter
BEEEHLRT	herbelet
BEEEHNOY	honey bee
BEEEILLL	libellee
BEEEILRV	believer
BEEEKLRY	Berkeley
BEEELMNS	ensemble
BEEELMRS	resemble
BEEELMZZ	embezzle
BEEELRVY	Beverley
BEEEMMRR	remember
BEEEMNSU	unbeseem
BEEEMRSS	Bessemer

Words marked □ can also be spelled with an initial capital letter

BEEEPRUZ	breeze up
BEEFFORT	bereft of
BEEFGINR	befringe
BEEFGIST	bigfeets
BEEFGOOR	go before
BEEFILLT	lifebelt
BEEFILLX	flexible
BEEFILNU	unbelief
BEEFIOTW	wife-to-be
BEEFLORW	beflower
BEEFNORR	Born Free
	freeborn
BEEFOORT	freeboot
BEEGHILW	big wheel
BEEGHLRU	Breughel
	Brueghel
BEEGIILL	eligible
BEEGILNT	beetling
BEEGINNR	beginner
BEEGINRW	Weinberg
BEEGLNOR	Grenoble
BEEGLRUY	blue-grey
BEEGMRSU	submerge
BEEGORTT	go better
BEEHHMOT	behemoth
BEEHILMN	Blenheim
BEEHLLNT	hell-bent
BEEHLOOR	borehole
BEEHLOTW	the elbow
BEEHLPST	the plebs
BEEHLSTU	the blues
BEEHMORT	be mother
BEEHMORW	home brew
	home-brew
BEEHNOOP	neophobe
BEEHNORS	nose-herb
BEEHNRRT	brethren
BEEHNRVZ	Brezhnev
BEEIILST	Tebilise
BEEIINOS	ebionise
BEEIINOZ	ebionize
BEEIISTZ	bitesize
BEEIJSTU	bejesuit
BEEIKLTU	tubelike
BEEIKLWY	bi-weekly
BEEILLNU	Blue Nile
	Nile blue
BEEILLTT	belittle
BEEILNSS	sensible
BEEILNST	stilbene
	tensible
BEEILNSU	nebulise
BEEILNUZ	nebulize
BEEILRRT	terrible
BEEILRSZ	Berzelis
BEEILRYZ	breezily
BEEIMRTT	embitter
BEEINNSV	Ben Nevis
BEEIORSS	soberise
BEEIORSZ	soberize
BEEIOSTW	be wise to
BEEIRSSU	suberise
BEEIRSUZ	suberize
BEEIRTVY	every bit
BEEISSUU	Eusebius
BEEJLOWX	jewel-box
BEEKNOST	steenbok
BEEKPSUY	keep busy
BEELLNTT	bell tent
BEELLSUY	bull's eye
	Bullseye
	bull's-eye
BEELMNNO	noblemen
BEELMRRT	trembler
BEELNNOT	Ben Elton
BEELNOSS	boneless
BEELNOTU	blue note
BEELNSSU	blueness
BEELOOST	obsolete
BEELRTUU	true-blue
BEELSSTU	tubeless
BEEMNORV	November
BEEMOPRT	obtemper
BEEMRSSU	submerse
BEEMRSTU	bum steer
BEENNOOY	one by one
BEENORTV	verboten
BEENRTTU	brunette
BEENSTTX	next best
BEEOORRT	root beer
BEEOORTT	beetroot
BEEORRSV	observer
BEEORSSU	suberose
BEEORSTU	to be sure
	tuberose
BEERRTTU	rebutter
BEERSSUV	subserve
BEESTTTU	test tube
BEFGIINR	briefing
BEFHINOS	fishbone
BEFHIRSU	bushfire
BEFILLMU	blue film
BEFILLXY	flexibly
BEFILOUY	lifebuoy
BEFILSTY	by itself
BEFKLNUU	blue funk
BEFLLLUY	bellyful
BEFLORUW	furbelow
BEFLSTUU	tubefuls
BEFNOOST	be soft on
BEFOOTTU	tube foot
BEGGIINN	bingeing
BEGGINRS	Ginsberg
BEGHIILP	philibeg
BEGHIIRT	Ghiberti
BEGHILRT	blighter
BEGHINRT	brighten
BEGHITWY	by weight
BEGHLNOU	bunghole
BEGIIISS	sigisbei
BEGIILLY	eligibly
BEGIIMRT	big timer
BEGIINOS	big noise
BEGIKMOS	big smoke
BEGILLLU	gullible
BEGILNNY	benignly
BEGILNOV	beloving
BEGILNSS	blessing
	glibness
BEGIMNSU	bemusing
BEGINNOR	ringbone
BEGINNTU	Tübingen
BEGINORS	sobering
BEGKNORR	Kornberg
BEGLLORY	gor-belly
BEGLLOTU	globulet
BEGLMRRU	grumbler
BEGLNOOT	belong to
BEGLNOOU	Boulogne
BEGLOOVX	glove box
BEGLOTUU	bulge out
BEGNNRRU	Nürnberg
BEGNSSUU	subgenus
BEHHOOSU	Hobhouse
BEHHOTUW	who but he
BEHIKLOS	blokeish
BEHIKPSU	push-bike
BEHILLOS	shoebill
BEHILLTY	blithely
BEHILMRW	whimbrel
BEHILORR	horrible
BEHIMNOO	bonhomie
BEHINNOS	shinbone
BEHINOSW	wishbone
BEHINOTT	on the bit
BEHINRTW	new birth
BEHINRTY	the briny
BEHIOSTU	Boethius
BEHJNOOT	on the job
BEHLLOOT	bolthole
BEHNORTX	The Bronx
BEHOOOST	boothose
BEHOORST	theorbos
BEHOOSUY	houseboy
BEHORRST	brothers
BEIILMMO	immobile
BEIILMOS	mobilise
BEIILMOZ	mobilize
BEIILNNR	bin-liner
BEIILOPR	periboli
BEIILRST	trilbies
BEIILRSU	Liberius
BEIILRTT	libretti
BEIILSSU	Sibelius
BEIINSTT	stibnite
BEIIRSTU	Tiberius
BEIISSTU	subitise
BEIISTUZ	subitize
BEIJMOSU	jumboise
BEIJMOUZ	jumboize
BEIKLMRY	Kimberly
BEIKLOTY	kilobyte
BEIKNNOR	broken in

BEILLMSS limbless
BEILLNRU Lilburne
BEILLNTU bulletin
BEILMMOS embolism
BEILMNOU nobelium
BEILMNRU unlimber
BEILMNTU tumble in
BEILMPRU limber up
BEILMRSS brimless
BEILNNTU buntline
BEILNOOV Benvolio
BEILNOVY bovinely
BEILNSSY sensibly
BEILOORV boil over
BEILOPPW blowpipe
BEILOPSS possible
BEILORST strobile
BEILORTT libretto
BEILRRTY terribly
BEILRSTY blistery
BEILRTTY bitterly
BEILSTTU subtitle
BEIMMOOT boom time
BEIMNSSU nimbuses
BEIMOORS ribosome
BEIMORRV brim over
BEIMORTY biometry
BEINNOSS boniness
BEINRSTU turbines
BEINSSSU business
BEIOORST robotise
BEIOQTUU boutique
BEIORSTY sobriety
BEIOTTZZ bozzetti
BEJJMOTU jumbo jet
BEJLMPUU jumble up
BEJORTTU turbojet
BEKLLLPU bull kelp
BEKLNORY brokenly
BEKLNTTU Blunkett
BEKLOOOT look to be
BEKLORUV overbulk
BEKLSSUY Sky blues
BEKNNORU unbroken
BEKNOOOP open book
BEKNOOOT notebook
BEKNOORR Brookner
BEKOOORV overbook
BEKOOTTX textbook
BELLMNOU Léon Blum
BELLNORW well-born
BELLOPTY pot belly
pot-belly
BELLOSWX swell box
BELMNOSU nelumbos
BELMOORS bloomers
BELMOPRS problems
BELMORST temblors
BELMORSY sombrely
BELMOTTU tumble to
BELMPTUU tumble up
BELMRRUY mulberry
BELNNOWW new-blown
BELNOORT noble rot
BELNOSUU nebulous
BELNSTUU unsubtle
BELOOOSX loose box
BELOORVW blow over
bowl over
overblow
BELOOSST bootless
BELOPTTU bottle up
BELORSTU troubles
BELOSSUY bless you
BELOSTUY obtusely
BELPRSUY superbly
BELRSSSU Brussels
BELRSTTU rust belt
BELRSTUY blustery
BELSTTUY subtlety
BEMNNSSU numbness
BEMNOORT trombone
BEMNOORW new broom
BEMNOOXY moneybox
money-box
BEMNORSY embryons
BEMOORRS sombrero
BEMORTUW tube worm
BENNNOTU unbonnet
BENNNOTY Tony Benn
BENNOOPU bone up on
BENNOSSU snub nose
BENNOSTU be nuts on
BENORRSU suborner
BENORRUV overburn
BENRRTUY by return
BENSSSUY busyness
BEOORRRW borrower
BEOPRRSV Proverbs
BEOPRSSX press box
BEOQSTUU bouquets
BEORSSSU sorbuses
BEORSTUU tuberous
BEORSUVY overbusy
BEPRTTUU butter up
BERRSTUU surrebut
BERSSTTU buttress
BERSSTUV subverst
BFFGINOR bring off
BFFHORSU brush off
brush-off
BFFNOORU rub off on
BFFNOSUX snuffbox
BFFOSSTU sob-stuff
BFGILMNU fumbling
BFGIORRU Fribourg
BFGLLORU bullfrog
BFGOOOTY go by foot
BFIIORSS fibrosis
BFILLSSU blissful
BFILOOST soft-boil
BFIMNORU nubiform
BFIMORTU tubiform
BFIOPRTY profit by
BFLNOOOR fool-born
BFLOORSU subfloor
BGGIILNO obliging
BGGIILNY gibingly
BGGILNNU bungling
BGHHINOR highborn
high-born
BGHHIORW highbrow
BGHHIRUY Highbury
BGHILMNU humbling
BGHILNSU blushing
BGHILRTY brightly
BGHIMOTU big mouth
bigmouth
big-mouth
BGHINORT Brighton
BGHINRSU brushing
BGHIOSST big shots
BGHIRSTY by rights
BGHJNNOY John Byng
BGHNNUUY bunny-hug
BGIIKLNN blinking
BGIILNOR broiling
BGIILNRS brisling
BGIIMMNR brimming
BGIINRSU bruising
BGILLNOU globulin
BGILLNUY bullying
BGILMMNU mumbling
BGILMNOO blooming
BGILMNPU plumbing
BGILMNRU rumbling
BGILMNTU tumbling
BGILMORY gorblimy
BGILNORW bring low
BGILNORY boringly
BGILNOTT blotting
BGILNSTU bustling
BGINNORW browning❑
BGINNORZ bronzing
BGINOOST boosting
BGINORSW browsing
BGINORTU bring out
BGINRSTU bursting
BGIOOSTT go to bits
BGKNOOOS songbook
BGLOORXY glory box
BGRRUUWZ Würzburg
BHHOOTUU tohu bohu
BHIILMPS blimpish
BHIIOPRT prohibit
BHIJNORT John Birt
BHIKLLOO billhook
BHILLNOR hornbill
BHILLORT Billroth
BHILLPUW bullwhip
BHILLSTU bullshit
BHILORRY horribly
BHILOSYY boyishly

BHIMNORT	thrombin
BHINOPSU	unbishop
BHINORSW	brownish
BHISTUWY	busy with
BHKMNOOY	hymn-book
BHKNOOOR	hornbook
BHKOOOPS	bookshop
BHLOOOTT	tolbooth
BHMMOTTU	Tom Thumb
BHMORSTU	thrombus
BHMPSTUU	thumbs up
	thumbs-up
BHMPTTUU	tub-thump
BIIKMRSS	Simbirsk
BIILLNOS	billions
BIILMOTY	mobility
BIILNOOV	oblivion
BIILNOTY	nobility
BIILNTUY	nubility
BIILORST	strobili
BIIMMNSY	nimbyism
BIIORSTT	botritis
BIIQTUUY	ubiquity
BIIRSSTU	bursitis
BIKLOOST	book list
BIKMNOOY	in my book
BIKMTTUU	Timbuktu
BIKOOUUZ	bouzouki
BILLMWYY	by my will
BILLNOOU	bouillon
BILLNOTU	bull into
BILLSTUU	Tibullus
BILMMPSU	plumbism
BILMOSTU	botulism
BILNNOOY	loony bin
BILOORST	sorbitol
BILOPSSY	possibly
BILOPSUY	Polybius
BILORSST	bristols
BIMNOPTU	bump into
BIMNOSTY	symbiont
BIMNRUUV	viburnum
BIMOSTTU	submit to
BINNOORS	Robinson
BINNOTTU	butt in on
BIOPRSTW	bowsprit
BIORRSTU	burritos
BIOSTTUY	obtusity
BJOPPTUU	put-up job
BKKOOORW	workbook
BKLNOORY	Brooklyn
BKMOOORW	bookworm
BLMOOOST	tombolos
BLMOOOTY	lobotomy
BLMOOSSY	blossomy
BLNOORWW	brown owl
BLNOOTUW	blown-out
BLOOSSTY	slyboots
BLORSTUY	robustly
BLORTTUU	blurt out
BLOSTUUU	tubulous
BMOORSTU	motor-bus
BNNORTUW	nut-brown
BNNOTTUU	unbutton
BNNRSTUU	sunburnt
BNOOOSUY	sonobuoy
BNOPTTUU	button up
BNORRUUW	unburrow
BNORTTUU	burnt out
BNRSSTUU	sunburst
BOOORRTW	to borrow
BOPRRTUY	ruby port
BORSTTUU	burst out
	outburst

C

CCCEEILT	eclectic
CCCEGOSY	coccyges
CCCIINSU	succinic
CCCILNOY	cyclonic
CCCINSTU	succinct
CCCIOORS	scirocco
CCCKOORW	cockcrow
	cock-crow
CCDEEENR	credence
CCDEEHIL	clichéed
CCDEEHLN	clenched
CCDEEKOY	cock-eyed
CCDEENOR	conceder
CCDEHLTU	declutch
CCDEHORS	scorched
CCDEIINO	coincide
CCDEINOT	Occident
CCDEIOPU	occupied
CCDELNOU	conclude
CCDELORU	occluder
CCDENOOR	Concorde
CCDHIIOR	dichroic
CCDINOTU	conducti
CCDKOOOW	woodcock
CCDLOSTU	cold cuts
CCEEHKRS	checkers
CCEEHMOO	Ecce Homo
CCEEHRSY	screechy
CCEEILNR	encircle
CCEEILNT	elenctic
CCEEILPY	epicycle
CCEEILRT	electric
CCEEINOR	cicerone
CCEEINOV	conceive
CCEEIORV	coercive
CCEEIRSV	cervices
CCEEKLOR	cockerel
CCEEKNRW	crew neck
CCEELMNY	clemency
CCEELOSS	scoleces
CCEEMMNO	commence
CCEEMMOR	commerce
CCEENNOS	ensconce
CCEENORT	concrete
CCEENRST	crescent□
CCEEOORT	coco-tree
CCEFFHKO	check off
CCEFIIPS	specific
CCEFLOOS	floccose
CCEGHIKN	checking
CCEGILOO	ecologic
CCEGNOOS	cognosce
CCEHIIMR	chimeric
CCEHIINZ	zecchini
CCEHILNR	clincher
CCEHILOR	choleric
CCEHILOY	choicely
CCEHINOR	enchoric
CCEHINOZ	zecchino
CCEHINST	technics
CCEHIORT	ricochet
CCEHIOST	choicest
CCEHKOTU	check out
	checkout
CCEHLMOR	cromlech
CCEHLSTU	clutches
CCEHORRS	scorcher
CCEHORTT	crotchet
CCEIILNT	enclitic
CCEIILPT	ecliptic
CCEIILST	scilicet
CCEIINOR	ciceroni
CCEIIRRT	circiter
CCEIIRTZ	critcize
CCEILNUY	unicycle
CCEILOSS	scolices
CCEILRTY	tricycle
CCEILRUU	curlicue
CCEIMNOO	economic
CCEIMOST	cosmetic
CCEIMRRU	mercuric
CCEINNOS	insconce
CCEINNOV	convince
CCEINOOR	coercion
CCEINOOZ	Cenozoic
CCEINOPT	concepti
CCEINORT	concerti
	necrotic
CCEINOTT	concetti
	tectonic
CCEINOTU	cut no ice
CCEINPRT	precinct
CCEINRTU	cincture
CCEIOOTX	ecotoxic
CCEIOPRU	occupier
CCEIORST	cortices
CCEIOSTT	Scottice
CCEIPRTU	cut price
	cut-price
CCEIPSUV	Vespucci
CCEKORRY	crockery
CCEKORSU	cocksure
CCELOPSY	Cyclopes
CCELOSSY	cycloses
CCENNORS	concerns
CCENOORT	concerto
CCENRRUY	currency

Words marked □ can also be spelled with an initial capital letter

CCEOOORR	corocore
CCEOPRUY	re-occupy
CCEORSSU	crocuses
CCFFKLOO	clock off
CCFIIRUX	crucifix
CCFIKNOY	cocknify
CCFILLOU	flocculi
CCFILNOT	conflict
CCFKLLOU	full-cock
CCFNOOOU	con fuoco
CCGHHIOU	hiccough
CCGHINOU	couching
CCGIILNR	circling
CCHHIINN	chin-chin
CCHHIITY	ichthyic
CCHHINOT	chthonic
CCHHLRUY	churchly
CCHHNRUU	unchurch
CCHHOOPP	chop-chop
CCHHOOWW	chow-chow
CCHIINUZ	zucchini
CCHKLOSY	schlocky
CCHKOTUU	chuck out
CCHLNTUU	unclutch
CCHNRSUY	scrunchy
CCIIKKPW	Pickwick
CCIILLRY	Cyrillic
CCIILNOP	clip coin
CCIIMNSY	cynicism
CCIKKLOP	picklock
CCIKKOTT	tick-tock
CCIKNORT	con trick
CCILLMNU	McCullin
CCILLOPP	clip-clop
CCILOOPS	piccolos
CCINORSY	cryonics
CCIOORSS	siroccos
CCIOOTXY	oxytocic
CCIRSSUY	circussy
CCKLOOTU	clock out
CCKMOOOR	moorcock
CCKOOPST	stopcock
CCLLOOPP	clop-clop
CCLLOTUY	occultly
CCLOOOSZ	zoccolos
CCMOOORS	moroccos
CCOOSSUU	couscous
CCORSSTU	crosscut
CCOSSTTU	cut costs
CDDDIIOY	diddicoy
CDDEEEIV	deceived
CDDEEEJT	dejected
CDDEEHNR	drenched
CDDEEINO	decide on
CDDEEIRT	directed
CDDEEKUW	duckweed
CDDEELMO	comeddle
CDDEELSU	secluded
CDDEELUX	excluded
CDDEELUY	deucedly
CDDEEORR	recorded
CDDEFIIO	codified
CDDEGIIN	deciding
CDDEGINO	decoding
CDDEHIRT	Redditch
CDDEILNU	included
CDDEIORV	divorced
CDDELLOW	cold-weld
CDDELPUU	cuddle up
CDDEOORR	corroded
CDDEOPRU	produced
CDDGHILO	godchild
CDDGHIOT	ditch-dog
CDDGILOS	gold disc
CDDHILOS	cloddish
CDDOOORW	cordwood
CDEEEFNS	defences
CDEEEHRT	the Creed
CDEEEHST	tedesche
CDEEEINV	evidence
CDEEEIPS	epicedes
CDEEEIRV	deceiver
	received
CDEEEJRT	rejected
CDEEELST	deselect
	selected
CDEEEMNT	cemented
CDEEEMRS	Mercedes
CDEEENRS	screened
CDEEEPTX	excepted
	expected
CDEEERRS	screeder
CDEEERSS	recessed
CDEEETUX	executed
CDEEFIIL	field ice
CDEEFINN	fenced in
CDEEFINT	infected
CDEEFIRR	Frederic
CDEEFKLR	freckled
CDEEFNNU	unfenced
CDEEFNOR	enforced
CDEEFORS	frescoed
CDEEFORT	defector
CDEEGIIR	regicide
CDEEGINO	genocide
CDEEGINR	receding
CDEEGINS	seceding
CDEEGIOS	geodesic
CDEEGIOT	geodetic
CDEEHIKL	helideck
CDEEHIPR	decipher
CDEEHIST	tedeschi
CDEEHLSU	schedule
CDEEHNNU	Duchenne
CDEEHNQU	quenched
CDEEHRTW	wretched
CDEEHSSU	duchesse
CDEEIILR	Eric Idle
CDEEIIMN	medicine
CDEEIIMP	epidemic
CDEEIINT	indictee
CDEEIISV	decisive
CDEEIITT	dietetic
CDEEIKNS	sickened
CDEEILNS	licensed
CDEEILNT	denticle
CDEEILRT	derelict
CDEEIMNR	endermic
CDEEIMOR	mediocre
CDEEIMOT	time code
CDEEINNS	incensed
CDEEINNT	indecent
CDEEIORV	divorcee
CDEEIPRT	decrepit
	depicter
CDEEIPRU	pedicure
CDEEIRRT	redirect
CDEEIRST	discreet
	discrete
CDEEIRSY	Criseyde
CDEEIRUY	Eurydice
CDEEKLOP	keep cold
CDEEKLPS	speckled
CDEEKNOR	reckoned
CDEEKORV	deck over
CDEEKORW	rockweed
CDEEKOST	socketed
CDEEKPRU	puckered
CDEELNOS	enclosed
CDEELNOV	Clevedon
CDEELNPU	peduncle
CDEELNTY	decently
CDEELOOW	locoweed
CDEELOPU	decouple
CDEELPRU	preclude
CDEEMORT	ectoderm
CDEENNOS	condense
CDEENNOU	denounce
CDEENNTY	tendency
CDEENORR	cornered
CDEENORS	seconder
CDEENOTX	coextend
CDEENPRU	prudence □
CDEENSTY	encysted
CDEEOOTV	dovecote
CDEEOPRS	proceeds
CDEEORRR	recorder
CDEEORTT	detector
CDEEOSST	cosseted
CDEEPRST	sceptred
CDEFHILL	elf-child
CDEFIIIL	filicide
CDEFIIOR	codifier
CDEFILOS	Scofield
CDEFILSW	W C Fields
CDEFINNO	confined
CDEFINNU	infecund
CDEFLORY	forcedly
CDEFNORU	unforced
CDEFNOSU	confused
CDEGHIOR	Goderich
CDEGIILO	Goidelic
CDEGILOO	Coolidge

CDEGINRY	decrying
CDEGORSW	scrowdge
CDEHHOTU	Dutch hoe
CDEHIIMO	homicide
CDEHIINO	echinoid
CDEHIIRT	Dietrich
CDEHIKNR	Dick Hern
CDEHIKRW	herdwick
CDEHILNR	children
CDEHILOR	chloride
CDEHILRS	Childers
CDEHILRT	eldritch
CDEHIMOT	methodic
CDEHINOS	hedonics
CDEHISTT	stitched
CDEHKLSU	shelduck
CDEHLMTU	Dutch elm
CDEHLOOS	deschool
	schooled
CDEHMNTU	Dutchmen
CDEHOORR	rheocord
CDEHORRS	Schröder
CDEHORTY	Docherty
CDEIIKKS	sidekick
CDEIILMO	domicile
CDEIILNN	inclined
CDEIILNO	indocile
CDEIILOT	idiolect
CDEIILPS	disciple
CDEIILPU	pediculi
CDEIILRU	ridicule
CDEIILRW	wild rice
CDEIINNT	incident
CDEIINOS	decision
CDEIINRT	in credit
	indirect
CDEIIOPR	periodic
CDEIIOPS	episodic
CDEIIPRR	cirriped
CDEIIRTU	diuretic
CDEIKLNR	crinkled
CDEIKLWY	wickedly
CDEIKNTU	tunicked
CDEIKORR	Roderick
CDEIKSTY	city desk
CDEILLOY	docilely
CDEILLPU	pellucid
CDEILMRU	dulcimer
CDEILNOS	closed in
CDEILNRY	cylinder
CDEILORU	crude oil
CDEILOSS	disclose
CDEILPPR	crippled
CDEILRTY	directly
CDEILSXY	dyslexic
CDEIMOST	domestic
CDEIMPRS	scrimped
CDEINNOW	wind cone
CDEINORS	consider
CDEINORT	doctrine
	on credit
CDEINOTU	eduction
CDEINOUV	unvoiced
CDEINPRS	prescind
CDEINRUV	curved in
	incurved
CDEIOPRT	depictor
CDEIOPST	despotic
CDEIOPTY	copy-edit
CDEIORRT	creditor
	director
CDEIORSV	discover
CDEIPRSY	cyprides
CDEKLNOU	unlocked
CDEKLOPU	locked up
	uplocked
CDEKNOOU	uncooked
CDEKOOPP	poop deck
CDEKOOPU	cooked-up
CDEKOORV	rock dove
CDELLNOU	Culloden
CDELLORS	scrolled
CDELLORU	colluder
CDELMNOO	monocled
CDELMNOU	columned
CDELMPRU	crumpled
CDELNOOR	condoler
CDELNOSS	coldness
CDELNOSU	unclosed
CDELNOSY	secondly
CDELOORS	cold sore
CDELOORU	coloured
	decolour
CDELORSS	cordless
CDELRSUY	cursedly
CDELRTUU	cultured
CDEMNOOW	come down
	comedown
CDEMNOSU	consumed
CDEMNOTU	document
CDEMOOPS	composed
CDENNOUY	uncoyned
CDENOORR	on record
CDENRTUU	undercut
CDEOOPPU	cooped up
CDEOOPST	postcode
CDEOORSU	decorous
CDEOPRRU	producer
CDEORRSS	Red Cross
CDEOSSTU	custodes
CDERSTTU	destruct
CDFFILOR	Clifford
CDFIILSU	fluidics
CDFIKOPR	Pickford
CDFIKORS	disfrock
CDFKOORR	Rockford
CDFKRSUU	surf duck
CDFNNOOU	confound
CDGHIILN	childing
CDGHIINT	ditching
CDGIIKSW	Sidgwick
CDGIINNU	inducing
CDGIKLNU	duckling
CDGIKLOR	gridlock
CDGILNOS	scolding
CDGILOOU	I could go
CDGKLOOU	good luck
CDGLNOOO	go cold on
CDHHIILS	childish
CDHIIORT	trichoid
CDHIIOSZ	schizoid
CDHIISST	distichs
CDHIMNOR	Richmond
CDHIOOPW	woodchip
CDHIOORT	trochoid
CDHIOPRW	whipcord
CDHIOSUV	disvouch
CDHNOOPW	chop down
CDIIKPST	dipstick
CDIILOTY	docility
CDIILTUY	lucidity
CDIINSTT	distinct
CDIIPTUY	cupidity
CDIIRSTT	district
CDIJNSTU	disjunct
CDIKKNOW	kickdown
CDIKKOPR	drop-kick
CDIKLPUY	lucky dip
CDIKNOSW	windsock
CDIKORST	do tricks
CDILLOUY	cloudily
CDILOORT	lordotic
CDIMMOSU	modicums
CDIMOORT	microdot
CDINNQUU	quidnunc
CDINORSW	discrown
	in crowds
CDINORTU	inductor
CDINOSTU	discount
CDIOOPRS	prosodic
CDIOORRR	corridor
CDJLNOUY	jocundly
CDKLMORU	Lord Muck
CDKLOORW	cold-work
CDKOPSUU	Duck Soup
CDLNOOOW	cool down
CDLNORTU	turn cold
CDLOORSU	sour-cold
CDLOOSTW	Cotswold
CDLOPRUW	World Cup
CDMMOOSU	Commodus
CDMNOOPU	compound
CDMNORUU	corundum
CDOORRUY	corduroy
CDOPRSTU	products
CEEEFINR	enfierce
CEEEGITX	exegetic
CEEEHIST	ice sheet
CEEEHKOR	Cherokee
CEEEHNNY	Cheyenne
CEEEIJTV	ejective
CEEEILNN	lenience
CEEEILNS	licensee

CEEEILRT	erectile
CEEEILTV	elective
CEEEIMNN	eminence
CEEEIMRR	rere-mice
CEEEINNT	enceinte
CEEEINOP	one-piece
CEEEIPRV	perceive
CEEEIPST	set piece
CEEEIRRV	receiver
CEEEIRSX	exercise
CEEEIRTT	et ceteri
CEEEJRRT	rejecter
CEEELLNR	crenelle
CEEELMNT	Clemente
CEEELPRT	pre-elect
CEEELRTT	electret
CEEEMNRT	cerement
CEEEMRTY	cemetery
CEEEMSUX	excuse me
	excuse-me
CEEENNPT	ten pence
CEEENNST	sentence
CEEENNSV	Cévennes
CEEENPRS	presence
CEEENPRT	pretence
CEEENQSU	sequence
CEEENRRS	screener
CEEENRTW	New Crete
CEEENSST	centeses
CEEERSST	sesterce
CEEERSWY	screw eye
CEEERTUX	executer
CEEFFFNO	fence off
CEEFFINT	in effect
CEEFFORT	effector
CEEFHIKR	kerchief
CEEFHLRT	fletcher□
CEEFHLRU	cheerful
CEEFHORT	the Force
CEEFIKKR	free kick
CEEFILRY	fiercely
CEEFINRT	frenetic
CEEFKLSS	feckless
CEEFLNOR	Florence
CEEFLNTU	feculent
CEEFLRUU	flue-cure
CEEFNORR	confrère
CEEFNRVY	fervency
CEEFOPRR	perforce
CEEFORRS	frescoer
CEEFORSS	frescoes
CEEFORST	cost-free
	of secret
	scot free
	scot-free
CEEFORSU	use force
CEEGGILS	egg-slice
CEEGHINR	cheering
CEEGHLLS	Schlegel
CEEGHLOW	cogwheel
CEEGIMNS	miscegen
CEEGINOR	erogenic
CEEGINPR	creeping
CEEGINST	genetics
CEEGINSU	eugenics
CEEGINXY	exigency
CEEGKNOR	Greenock
CEEGMMOR	commerge
CEEGNNOO	oncogene
CEEGNNOR	congener
CEEGNORV	Congreve
	converge
CEEHHIRS	Cheshire
CEEHHLRS	Herschel
CEEHHMNN	hench-men
CEEHIIST	ethicise
CEEHIITZ	ethicize
CEEHIKLY	cheekily
CEEHILLM	Michelle
CEEHILLN	chenille
	Hellenic
CEEHILMT	Michelet
CEEHILRW	clerihew
CEEHILRY	cheerily
CEEHILSV	vehicles
CEEHILTV	Helvetic
CEEHIMNR	Michener
CEEHIMRT	hermetic
CEEHINOR	coinhere
CEEHINPR	encipher
CEEHINPT	phenetic
CEEHINST	sithence
CEEHIORS	cheerios
CEEHIOSV	cohesive
CEEHIPRT	herpetic
CEEHKLRT	The Clerk
CEEHKNOR	Honecker
CEEHKOTY	cheeky to
CEEHKRST	sketcher
CEEHLNOO	Holocene
CEEHLNOS	echelons
CEEHLNOT	enclothe
CEEHLNSU	elenchus
CEEHLOSS	echoless
CEEHLRSU	Hercules
CEEHLRUV	Chevreul
CEEHMMOO	come home
CEEHNNRT	entrench
CEEHNORT	coherent
CEEHNQRU	quencher
CEEHNRRT	retrench
	trencher
CEEHOPRY	coryphee
	coryphée
CEEHOPTT	pochette
CEEHORVW	chew over
CEEHRSTU	the curse
CEEHTTTU	cut teeth
CEEIIMNP	mince pie
CEEIIMRT	eremitic
CEEIINPS	in pieces
	in specie
CEEIINST	niceties
CEEIJLLO	Jellicoe
CEEIJLNO	Joceline
CEEIJNOT	ejection
CEEIJORR	rejoicer
CEEIJRUV	verjuice
CEEIKLNN	neckline
CEEIKLPR	pickerel
CEEIKNRW	Wernicke
CEEIKPRT	picketer
CEEILLLP	pellicle
CEEILLNT	lenticle
CEEILLNW	clew-line
CEEILMPS	semplice
CEEILNNY	leniency
CEEILNOP	Pliocene
CEEILNOT	election
CEEILNOV	violence
CEEILNRR	recliner
CEEILNRS	silencer
CEEILNRV	vernicle
CEEILORR	recoiler
CEEILOSS	solecise
CEEILOSZ	solecize
CEEILPRS	Pericles
CEEILQSU	liquesce
CEEILRSV	versicle
CEEILRTU	reticule
CEEILRTY	celerity
CEEILSTT	testicle
CEEIMMRS	mesmeric
CEEIMNPS	specimen
CEEIMORT	meteoric
CEEINNOP	pine cone
CEEINNPZ	pince-nez
CEEINNSS	niceness
CEEINNST	nescient
CEEINORT	erection
	neoteric
CEEINORV	overnice
	over-nice
CEEINORX	exocrine
CEEINOSS	senecios
CEEINPST	pectines
CEEINPSX	sixpence
CEEINRST	in secret
	scienter
	secretin
CEEINRSU	insecure
	sinecure
CEEINRTT	reticent
CEEINRTU	ceinture
	enuretic
CEEINSSX	in excess
CEEINSTY	cysteine
CEEIOPPR	pericope
CEEIOPST	to pieces
CEEIOPTU	piece out
CEEIOPTW	two-piece
CEEIORST	esoteric
CEEIORSX	exorcise

CEEIORTT	erotetic
CEEIORXZ	exorcize
CEEIPPRT	precepit
CEEIPPTU	eupeptic
CEEIPRST	receipts
CEEIRRTU	ureteric
CEEIRSSV	services
CEEIRSTV	vertices
CEEIRSVX	cervixes
CEEJORRT	rejector
CEEKKNPS	kenspeck
CEEKLRSS	clerkess
	reckless
CEEKNORR	reckoner
CEEKOPRX	ox-pecker
CEELLMOU	molecule
CEELLMST	stem cell
CEELLRVY	cleverly
CEELLSSU	clueless
CEELMOPT	complete
CEELNOPT	Poncelet
CEELNOPU	opulence
CEELNORT	electron
CEELNOSS	Les Noces
CEELNPTU	centuple
CEELNRTY	recently
CEELNSTU	esculent
CEELORSS	sclerose
CEELORST	corselet
	electors
	electros
	selector
CEELORTV	coverlet
CEELOSST	close-set
CEELOSSU	coleuses
CEELPRST	plectres
CEELRRTU	lecturer
CEELRSTU	lectures
CEELRSTY	secretly
CEELRSUY	securely
CEELSSUU	Seleucus
CEEMMNTU	cementum
CEEMNNOW	Newcomen
CEEMNOOR	once more
CEEMNORW	newcomer
CEEMNORY	ceremony
CEEMNOSW	Newcomes
CEEMNOTX	come next
CEEMOORV	come over
	overcome
CEEMORTU	come true
CEENNORT	centre on
	cretonne
CEENNORU	renounce
CEENNORV	convener
CEENNOST	centones
CEENOORV	once-over
CEENOPRU	en cuerpo
CEENOPTW	two pence
	twopence
CEENORSV	conserve
	converse
CEENORTT	trecento
CEENORTU	en croûte
CEENORVY	reconvey
CEENRRSU	censurer
CEENRSTU	unsecret
CEENSSTU	cuteness
CEEOORRW	orecrowe
CEEOORST	creosote
CEEOPRRT	receptor
CEEOQTTU	coquette
CEEORRRS	sorcerer
CEEORRSU	recourse
	resource
CEEORRVY	recovery
CEEORSSS	Scorsese
CEEORSSY	cross-eye
CEEORSTX	cortexes
CEEORTTV	corvette
	Corvette®
CEEORTUX	executor
CEEOSSTX	to excess
CEEPPRST	precepts
CEEPPSTY	type spec
CEEPRRSU	precurse
CEEPRSST	respects
CEERSSTW	setscrew
CEERSTTU	cruet set
CEFFFHOT	fetch off
CEFFHKOO	choke off
CEFFILWY	Wycliffe
CEFFIORS	officers
CEFFIORU	coiffeur
	coiffure
CEFFIRSU	sufficer
CEFFLOOS	close off
CEFFLORU	forceful
CEFFOORS	score off
CEFGHINT	fetching
CEFGLNUY	fulgency
CEFHIIMS	mischief
CEFHILNR	flincher
CEFHILRT	flichter
	rich-left
CEFHINSU	fuchsine
CEFHOSSU	sous-chef
CEFHOTTU	fetch out
CEFIILTY	felicity❑
CEFIIRRT	terrific
CEFIKLOR	firelock
CEFILLLO	follicle
CEFILMRU	merciful
CEFILOPY	file copy
CEFINNOS	confines
CEFINORS	forensic
CEFINOTT	confetti
CEFIORTY	ferocity
CEFIRSTU	frutices
CEFKLLOS	elflocks
CEFKLOOR	forelock
CEFLNRUU	furuncle
CEFLNUWY	Cynewulf
CEFMMOOR	come from
CEFOORRV	cover for
CEFOORST	soft-core
CEFOORSU	of course
CEFOORTU	force out
CEFORSTU	fructose
CEGGILRS	scriggle
CEGGIORS	Georgics
CEGGLNOY	glycogen
CEGGMORR	McGregor
CEGHHHIT	high tech
CEGHHIMO	come high
CEGHIINY	hygienic
CEGHIMNS	scheming
CEGHINRT	retching
CEGHINVY	Givenchy
CEGHNORS	groschen❑
CEGIILOS	logicise
CEGIILOZ	logicize
CEGIINNT	enticing
CEGIINPR	piercing
CEGIINTX	exciting
CEGIIOST	egoistic
CEGIKNRW	wrecking
CEGILNRY	glycerin
CEGILRSY	lysergic
CEGINOOP	geoponic
CEGINOOR	orogenic
CEGINORV	covering
CEGINOTV	coveting
CEGINRSU	securing
CEGINSUX	excusing
CEGKSTTU	get stuck
CEGLLOOU	collogue
CEGLLORY	glycerol
CEGLNOTY	cogently
CEGMNNOO	cognomen
CEGMNORV	McGovern
CEGNNPUY	pungency
CEGNORSS	congress❑
CEGNORSU	scrounge
CEGORRSU	scourger
CEHHLOTT	the cloth
CEHHOPTY	hypothec
CEHIILLS	chillies
CEHIILMN	Michelin
CEHIILNT	lecithin
CEHIILOT	eolithic❑
CEHIIMPT	mephitic
CEHIIMRT	hermitic
CEHIIOPT	Ethiopic
CEHIIRSS	Chrissie
CEHIIRST	Christie
CEHIISTT	theistic
CEHIKLRS	clerkish
CEHIKLSU	such like
CEHIKMOS	homesick
CEHIKOST	thickoes
CEHIKSTT	thickset
CEHILLMT	Mitchell

Words marked ❑ can also be spelled with an initial capital letter

CEHILLRS	Schiller
CEHILNOP	pinochle
CEHILNOR	chlorine
CEHILNSS	chinless
CEHILORT	clothier
CEHILPTY	phyletic
CEHILTTY	tetchily
CEHIMNOP	phonemic
CEHIMNOR	Nichrome®
CEHIMNOW	chow mein
CEHIMNTZ	Chemnitz
CEHIMORT	chromite
	trichome
CEHIMOTW	come with
CEHINNRT	intrench
CEHINOOS	cohesion
CEHINOPT	phonetic
	Pinochet
CEHINOPU	euphonic
CEHINORU	unheroic
CEHINOSY	hyoscine
CEHINPRU	uncipher
CEHINRSS	richness
CEHINRST	christen
	snitcher
CEHINRSW	Schwerin
CEHIOPRU	euphoric
CEHIOPST	postiche
CEHIOPTW	cope with
CEHIORRT	rhetoric
CEHIRSTT	stitcher
CEHIRSTY	hysteric
CEHIRTTW	twitcher□
CEHIRTWY	witchery
CEHISSTW	switches
CEHISSUW	suchwise
CEHKLLOS	skelloch
CEHKLOSY	Shockley
CEHKNPUY	keypunch
CEHKRSTU	huckster
CEHLLOUY	louchely
CEHLMSSU	much less
CEHLNNOU	luncheon
CEHLNOOT	clothe on
CEHLNOSS	Loch Ness
CEHLNOTU	unclothe
CEHLORSU	sloucher
CEHLPPSY	schleppy
CEHLQSUY	squelchy
CEHLRRSY	Chrysler®
CEHLSSSU	Schüssel
CEHMNRTU	truch-men
CEHMOOSZ	schmooze
CEHMORUV	overmuch
CEHMRUVY	very much
CEHNNOSU	nonesuch
CEHNOORS	schooner
CEHNSTTU	chestnut
CEHOORSU	ochreous
CEHOOSUW	cowhouse
CEHOPPRY	prophecy
CEHOPSTW	Chepstow
CEHOPSUY	chop suey
CEHORSSZ	scherzos
CEHORSTU	scouther
CEHORSTW	scowther
CEHRSTTY	stretchy
CEIIILSV	civilise
CEIIILVZ	civilize
CEIIINOS	Ionicise
CEIIINOZ	Ionicize
CEIIINSS	sinicise
CEIIINSV	incisive
CEIIINSZ	sinicize
CEIIKLMR	limerick□
CEIIKMMR	mimicker
CEIIKNSS	kinesics
CEIIKNST	kinetics
CEIILLPT	elliptic
CEIILNNP	pencil in
CEIILNOS	silicone
CEIILOPS	policies
CEIILOTZ	zeolitic
CEIILPRT	perlitic
CEIILPRU	pirlicue
CEIILPTX	explicit
CEIILPTY	pyelitic
CEIILRTV	verticil
CEIIMORS	isomeric
CEIIMOST	semiotic
CEIIMRRT	trimeric
CEIINNOT	nicotine
CEIINNRT	intrince
CEIINORS	recision
CEIINOSX	excision
CEIINOTV	eviction
CEIINRSU	sciurine
CEIINSTU	cutinise
CEIINSTZ	citizens
CEIINTUZ	cutinize
CEIIQRTU	critique
CEIIRSTV	veristic
CEIISTVV	vivisect
CEIJLNOS	Joscelin
CEIKKNRS	knickers
CEIKKRRS	skerrick
CEIKLMNY	McKinley
CEIKLMPR	Mr Pickle
CEIKLNSZ	Selznick
CEIKLOSV	lovesick
CEIKLRST	stickler
	strickle
CEIKLRSY	sickerly
CEIKMNOR	monicker
CEIKMPPU	pick-me-up
CEIKNOPT	in pocket
CEIKNORT	Cronkite
CEIKNOTY	cytokine
CEIKNRST	stricken
CEIKNSSS	sickness
CEIKORTV	tick over
CEIKQSTU	quickset
CEIKRRTY	trickery
CEILLLOY	ice lolly
CEILLNOU	nucleoli
CEILLOPS	pollices
CEILLORY	colliery
CEILLRTU	telluric
CEILMMUY	mycelium
CEILMNOP	compline
CEILMNOT	monticle
CEILMNSU	muscle in
CEILMOPR	compiler
CEILMOPS	polemics
CEILMOSS	solecism
CEILMOSU	coliseum□
CEILMTUU	lutecium
CEILNNSY	syncline
CEILNOOS	colonise
	eclosion
CEILNOOZ	colonize
CEILNOPT	leptonic
CEILNPRY	princely
CEILNSUU	unsluice
CEILOOVW	low voice
CEILOPRW	low-price
CEILOPTU	poultice
CEILORST	cloister
CEILORTY	cryolite
CEILOSST	solstice
CEILOSSU	coulisse
CEILOTVY	velocity
CEILPPRS	clippers
CEILPRSU	surplice
CEIMMNNO	mnemonic
CEIMMNOU	encomium
	meconium
CEIMNNOO	come in on
	encomion
CEIMNNOU	enconium
CEIMNNOY	neomycin
CEIMNOOT	come in to
	come into
	emoticon
CEIMNORT	intercom
CEIMNRST	centrism
CEIMNSSU	meniscus
CEIMOOSZ	Mesozoic
CEIMOPRS	comprise
CEIMORSX	exorcism
CEIMORTU	Mercutio
CEIMRRTU	turmeric
CEIMSSTY	systemic
CEINNNOT	innocent□
CEINNORV	conniver
CEINNOTU	continue
CEINOOTZ	enzootic
CEINOPRS	conspire
CEINOPRT	entropic
CEINOPRU	Couperin
	in cuerpo
CEINOPRV	province
CEINOPTU	put on ice

CEINORRS	resorcin
CEINORRT	tricorne
CEINORSS	Ericsson
	necrosis
CEINORSU	in course
CEINORTT	contrite
	cornetti
CEINORTU	neurotic
CEINORTV	contrive
CEINOSSS	cosiness
CEINOSTT	stenotic
CEINOSTU	counties
CEINOSTY	cytosine
CEINOTTU	Teutonic
CEINPRSS	princess
CEINRSTT	centrist
CEINRSVV	crivvens
CEINRTTU	intercut
	tincture
CEIOOPTV	co-optive
CEIOOTUV	outvoice
CEIOPRRU	croupier
CEIOPRSU	precious
CEIOPRTU	outprice
CEIOPSSU	specious
CEIORRTU	courtier
CEIORSTV	vortices
CEIORSTX	exorcist
CEIPRRST	rescript
CEIPRSTU	crepitus
	pictures
CEIPRSUU	Epicurus
CEIRRSTT	restrict
CEIRSSSU	scissure
CEIRSTUY	security
CEISSSTU	cistuses
CEJLOOSY	jocosely
CEJNORRU	conjurer
CEJNRTUU	juncture
CEKKNORS	knockers
CEKKNTUY	Kentucky
CEKLLSSU	luckless
CEKLNOOP	polo neck
	polo-neck
CEKLOORV	overlock
CEKLRRTU	truckler
CEKNNOOR	reckon on
CEKNOPRU	reckon up
CEKNOPST	penstock
CEKNOSTU	unsocket
CEKOOORV	overcook
CEKOORRS	rock rose
CEKOORRW	coworker
	co-worker
CEKOPRST	sprocket
CEKORRTY	rocketry
CEKPPRUU	pucker up
CELLMORW	Cromwell
CELLNORW	Cornwell
CELLNSUU	nucellus
CELLOOQU	colloque
CELLOOST	Costello
CELLOSSY	cloyless
CELLRSUY	scullery
CELMNOTU	Uncle Tom
CELMNOTY	cloyment
CELMNOUY	uncomely
CELMOOOT	locomote
CELMPRTU	plectrum
CELMPSUU	speculum
CELNNOTY	nocently
CELNOORS	consoler
CELNOORU	encolour
CELNOOSS	coolness
CELNOOST	not close
CELNOOVV	convolve
CELNOPUU	uncouple
CELNORSU	run close
CELNORWY	clownery
CELNOSUV	convulse
CELNOSVY	solvency
CELNOVXY	convexly
CELOOPSS	cesspool
CELOORVY	overcloy
CELOOSTU	cut loose
CELOPTTU	octuplet
CELORSST	crosslet
CELORSSU	sclerous
CELORSUU	Coelurus
	ulcerous
CELORSUY	crousely
CELORTVY	covertly
CELOSTTU	culottes
CELPRSSU	scruples
CELPRSUY	sprucely
CELRSTUY	clustery
CEMMNOOR	commoner
CEMMNOOS	consommé
CEMMORTU	commuter
CEMNOOPU	come upon
CEMNOOTY	monocyte
CEMNOPTT	contempt
CEMNORSU	consumer
	mucrones
CEMNRSTU	centrums
CEMOOPRS	composer
CEMOOPTU	come up to
CEMOPRSS	compress
CEMOPRTU	computer
CEMORSTU	costumer
	customer
CEMPRSTU	spectrum
CENNOOPR	corn pone
CENNOOPU	pounce on
CENNOORV	convenor
CENNORTU	nocturne
CENNOSTT	contents
CENOOPRT	Eton crop
CENOORSU	corneous
CENOORVY	conveyor
CENOPRSY	necropsy
CENOQSTU	conquest
CENORSTU	construe
CENORSUY	cynosure
CENORTUY	Courtney
CENORTVY	Coventry
CENOSSTU	countess
CENPRTUU	puncture
CENRSSTU	curtness
CEOOOPST	otoscope
CEOOPRRV	overcrop
CEOORSTU	score out
CEOOSTUV	covetous
CEOPPRST	prospect
CEOPRRRU	procurer
CEOPRSTT	Prescott
CEOPRTUW	power cut
CEOQRTUY	coquetry
CEORRSTY	corsetry
CEORSTUY	courtesy
CEORSUWY	screw you
CEPPRSUU	spruce up
CEPPRTUU	uppercut
CERSSUUX	excursus
CFFGINOS	scoffing
CFFHINOY	chiffony
CFFHMOOO	mooch off
CFFHOOTU	touch off
CFFIKLNU	cufflink
CFFIRTUY	fructify
CFFKKNOO	knock off
CFFKLOPU	pluck off
CFGHIILN	filching
CFGINORT	crofting
CFGINOSU	focusing
CFHIIORR	horrific
CFHIKORS	rockfish
CFHILPTY	flypitch
CFHIMOSS	scomfish
CFHOORUV	vouch for
CFIIILSY	silicify
CFIIKNYZ	zinckify
CFIIKQUX	quick fix
CFIILOPR	prolific
CFIIMNOS	somnific
CFIINORT	friction
CFIKKORS	for kicks
CFIKLNOS	in flocks
CFIMNORU	unciform
CFINNOTU	function
CFIOSTTY	Scottify
CFKKLOOR	folk rock
CFKORSTU	stuck for
CFLMRSUU	fulcrums
CFLNORSU	scornful
CFLOOPSU	scoopful
CFLOPRSU	cropfuls
CFNNOORT	confront
CFNOOOTU	con out of
CFOOORTW	crowfoot
CFRSTUUU	usufruct
CGGGILNO	clogging
CGGIILNN	clinging

CGGIINNR	cringing
CGHHIIKK	high kick
CGHHINNU	hunching
CGHHIOST	high-cost
CGHIILLN	chilling
CGHIINNP	pinching
CGHIINPR	chirping
CGHIINPT	pitching
CGHIKNOS	shocking
CGHILNNY	lynching
CGHILNOT	clothing
CGHILNRU	lurching
CGHINNPU	punching
CGHINOOS	choosing
CGHINOTU	touching
CGHINRSU	crushing
CGHIORRW	grow rich
CGHNOOSU	souchong
CGIIINNT	inciting
CGIIKLNT	tickling
CGIIKMMY	gimmicky
CGIIKNPR	pricking
CGIIKNPS	pickings
CGIIKNRT	tricking
CGIIKNST	sticking
CGIILNOP	policing
CGIILNPP	clipping
CGIILOST	logistic
CGIIMNNO	incoming
CGIINNOT	noticing
CGIINORT	trigonic
CGIINRSU	cruising
CGIKKNNO	knocking
CGIKLNOR	rockling
CGIKLNSU	suckling ❑
CGIKMNOS	smocking
CGIKNOST	stocking
CGIKNRTU	trucking
CGILLNSU	sculling
CGILMNUU	cingulum
CGILNNOW	clowning
CGILNOOY	cooingly
CGILNOPU	coupling
CGILNOSW	scowling
CGILNOTT	clotting
CGILOORU	urologic
CGIMMNSU	cummings
CGIMNNOO	oncoming
CGIMNOPU	coming up
	upcoming
CGINNORW	crowning
CGINNOTU	counting
CGINORSS	crossing
CGINORSU	coursing
	scouring
	sourcing
CGINORTU	courting
CGINOSTU	scouting
CGINOUVY	Young Vic
CGINSTTU	cuttings
CGLMOOYY	mycology
CGLNOOOY	oncology
CGLOOTYY	cytology
CGLRSUUY	Lycurgus
CGNOORTU	Goncourt
CHHIILTY	hitchily
CHHIINPT	pinch-hit
CHHILRSU	churlish
CHHIMRTY	rhythmic
CHHIOPST	chip shot
CHHNORSU	rhonchus
CHIIKLST	ticklish
CHIILLLY	chillily
CHIILNNP	linchpin
CHIILOST	holistic
CHIILPRY	chirpily
CHIILQSU	cliquish
CHIIMPRU	pichurim
CHIIORST	historic
CHIKLLOY	hillocky
CHIKLORS	Horlicks®
CHIKLTUW	with luck
CHIKMNPU	chipmunk
CHIKNOOR	Korchnoi
CHIKNOTT	not thick
CHIKOPTY	kyphotic
CHIKORST	trochisk
CHILLOOT	oilcloth
CHILLOTU	chill out
CHILNOOS	scholion
CHILNOSW	clownish
CHILNPSY	lip-synch
CHILOSSU	Huis Clos
CHILOSYY	coyishly
CHILOTUY	touchily
CHILOTYY	Holy City
CHIMMORU	chromium
CHIMNOSU	insomuch
CHINOPTY	hypnotic
	pythonic
	typhonic
CHINORTU	cothurni
CHINOSTW	switch on
CHINOSUY	cushiony
CHINSTTU	unstitch
CHIOORSZ	chorizos
CHIOORTT	orthotic
CHIOPRST	strophic
CHIOSSTT	Scottish
CHIPRRUY	chirrupy
CHIPRTTY	triptych
CHIPSTTU	stitch up
CHIRRSSU	scirrhus
CHIRSSTU	Christus
CHKMMOUY	hummocky
CHKOORRS	Horrocks
CHLNOOOP	colophon
CHLOPSTY	splotchy
CHMNORRU	crumhorn
CHMOOSSU	so much so
CHNOOPTT	top notch
	top-notch
CHNORSTU	cothurns
CHNORTUU	churn out
CHOOPSTU	octopush
CHORSTTU	cut short
	short cut
	short-cut
CIIILMPT	implicit
CIIILTVY	civility
CIIINNOS	incision
CIIINTVY	vicinity
CIIJRSTU	juristic
CIIKLLOS	oil slick
CIIKLLSY	sicklily
CIIKLOPT	politick
CIIKLPST	lipstick
CIIKLRTY	trickily
CIIKLSST	sick list
CIIKLSTY	stickily
CIIKMNPX	pick-'n'-mix
CIILLSUU	Lucilius
CIILMNOT	Miltonic
CIILMOSS	sciolism
CIILMRSY	lyricism
CIILOPST	politics
CIILORST	clitoris
CIILOSST	sciolist
CIILOSTY	solicity
CIILRSTY	lyricist
CIILRTUU	utriculi
CIIMNOST	monistic
CIIMORST	trisomic
CIIMOSST	misticos
	stoicism
CIIMRTTU	triticum
CIINNSTT	instinct
CIINOOST	isotonic
CIINOSSS	scission
CIINOSTV	Visconti
CIINPSTU	sinciput
CIIOOPST	isotopic
CIIOQTUX	quixotic
CIIOTTXY	toxicity
CIIPRRTU	pruritic
CIIPRSTU	puristic
CIIRSTTU	truistic
CIISSTTY	cystitis
CIJKLMUY	Lucky Jim
CIJKOSTY	joystick
CIJNNOOT	conjoint
CIJNNOTU	junction
CIJOOSTY	jocosity
CIKKNRTU	kick turn
CIKLLPUY	pluckily
CIKLOSTY	stockily
CIKNNOST	non-stick
CIKNOTTU	tuck into
CIKORTTU	trick out
CIKOSSTT	stockist
CIKOSTTU	stick out
CIKOSTTW	two ticks
CIKPSSTU	up sticks

CILLMSUY	clumsily
CILLNORS	inscroll
CILLOORS	criollos
CILMNUUV	vinculum
CILMOORS	miscolor
CILMPRSY	scrimply
CILNNOOS	Nicolson
CILNOORU	colour in
	unicolor
CILNOOST	colonist
CILNOOTU	locution
CILNOPTU	plutonic
CILNORTU	Trinculo
CILOORYZ	Zircoloy®
CILOOSSU	sciolous
CILOSSTY	systolic
CILOSSUU	luscious
CILRSTTY	strictly
CILRSTUY	crustily
CILRSUVY	scurvily
CIMMNNOO	in common
CIMNOPRT	comprint
CIMNOSTU	miscount
CIMOORSS	Moriscos
CIMOSTUY	mucosity
CINNOOTU	continuo
CINNOOTX	non-toxic
CINNOOVY	in convoy
CINNQUUX	quincunx
CINOOOPT	co-option
CINOOPRS	scorpion ❑
CINOOTXY	oxytocin
CINOPSTY	synoptic
CINOSTTU	unit cost
CINOSTUV	viscount
CINRSTTU	instruct
CINRSTUY	scrutiny
CIOOPRSS	Scorpios
CIOOPRST	porticos
CIOOQSTU	coquitos
CIOOSSTU	stocious
CIOPRSSU	Scorpius
CIORSSSS	scissors
CIOTTTUU	cut it out
CIQRSTUY	cry quits
CJNOORRU	conjuror
CKKNOOTU	knock out
	knockout
	knock-out
CKKNOPRU	punk rock
CKLMMOSU	slummock
CKLNOOOT	lock on to
CKLOOORW	rock wool
CKNOOSTT	Stockton
CKNORSTU	struck on
CKOOPSTT	stockpot
CKOPSTUU	suck up to
CKOSSTUY	tussocky
CLLLOOPT	clotpoll
CLLLSUUU	Lucullus
CLLNNOOY	Connolly

CLLOOQUY	colloquy
CLMMNOOY	commonly
CLNOORST	controls
CLOOOPRT	protocol
CLOOPRUU	colour up
CLOOSSSU	colossus
CLOPRSTU	sculptor ❑
CMMNNOOU	uncommon
CMNOOPRT	Crompton
CNNOOOTT	cotton on
CNOOOORT	octoroon
CNOORSTU	contours
	cornutos
	outscorn
CNOOTTUU	count out
CNOSTUUU	unctuous
COOOPRRT	root crop
COOOPSTU	scoop out
COORSSTU	cross out
	outcross

D

DDDEEEFN	defended
DDDEEENR	reddened
DDDEEENU	undeeded
DDDEEEPY	deep-dyed
DDDEEGOO	good deed
DDDEEIKN	Dedekind
DDDEIINV	dividend
DDDEINOR	dendroid
DDEEEFNR	defender
DDEEEFRR	deferred
DDEEEHNU	unheeded
DDEEEIWY	wide-eyed
DDEEELPT	depleted
DDEEELSS	deedless
DDEEEMNT	demented
DDEEENNU	unneeded
DDEEENPX	expended
DDEEENSU	unseeded
DDEEENTX	extended
DDEEENUW	unweeded
DDEEERST	deserted
DDEEERSV	deserved
DDEEESTT	detested
DDEEEWYY	dewy-eyed
DDEEFFNO	offended
DDEEFILW	field-dew
DDEEFIPR	drip-feed
DDEEFMOR	deformed
DDEEFNRU	underfed
DDEEGINR	enridged
DDEEGINS	designed
DDEEGOPS	Godspeed
DDEEGOTW	two-edged
DDEEGPRU	dredge up
DDEEHILS	shielded
DDEEHRRS	shredder
DDEEIKNW	Wedekind
DDEEILMN	meddle in
DDEEILMW	mildewed

DDEEIMOS	Diomedes
DDEEINNT	indented
	intended
DDEEINOS	one-sided
DDEEINRT	dendrite
DDEEINST	destined
DDEEINTU	unedited
DDEEIPRV	deprived
DDEEISTV	divested
DDEELLOP	deed poll
DDEELOPX	exploded
DDEELOVV	devolved
DDEEMNOR	endoderm
DDEENNOP	depend on
DDEENNTU	untended
DDEENOPR	perdendo
DDEENOPW	deep down
DDEENORS	endorsed
DDEENRSU	sundered
DDEEOPRT	deported
DDEEOPRW	powdered
DDEFFISU	diffused
DDEFIILM	midfield
DDEFIIMO	modified
DDEFILLO	Oldfield
DDEFIOOV	devoid of
DDEFLNOU	unfolded
DDEGGIOU	guide dog
DDEGGLOY	doggedly
DDEGHINS	shedding
DDEGILMN	meddling
DDEGILNP	peddling
DDEGILNS	sledding
DDEGILNU	deluding
	indulged
DDEGILOS	dislodge
DDEGILUV	divulged
DDEGINUU	unguided
DDEGIORT	dog-tired
DDEGNOOR	Dordogne
DDEGNORU	grounded
	underdog
DDEGOOOR	do-gooder
DDEGOOWW	Wedgwood
DDEGRRUY	drudgery
DDEHIISS	side dish
DDEHILNY	hiddenly
DDEHINNU	unhidden
DDEHNRSU	hundreds
DDEHOOSW	woodshed
DDEHOOWY	how-d'ye-do
DDEHORSU	shrouded
DDEHRSUY	shuddery
DDEIIKLS	disliked
DDEIILNR	dieldrin
DDEIILOZ	idolized
DDEIIOXZ	oxidized
DDEIIPUV	divide up
DDEIIRSV	dividers
DDEIKMOT	Mike Todd
DDEILNPS	splendid

DDEILNRU	unriddle
DDEILOPS	lopsided
	lop-sided
DDEILRST	striddle
DDEILRTW	twiddler
DDEIMMNU	undimmed
DDEIMNNU	unminded
DDEIMNOS	so-minded
DDEIMNUV	videndum
DDEIMOQU	idem quod
DDEIMOSU	medusoid
DDEIMRSU	side drum
	side-drum
DDEINORW	ride down
DDEINOSW	disendow
	disowned
	downside
DDEIOPRS	dropsied
DDEIOPRV	provided
DDEIOPSS	disposed
DDEIORRS	disorder
DDEIOSTW	two-sided
DDEIPSTU	disputed
DDELMPUU	muddle up
DDELNSUY	suddenly
DDEMNOST	oddments
DDEMNOUU	duodenum
DDEMNPUU	pudendum
DDEMOOTU	outmoded
DDENNOSW	send down
DDENOOPR	Don Pedro
DDENOOUW	unwooded
DDENORSW	send word
DDFGIILN	fiddling
DDFIIOSU	fiddious
DDFMNOUU	dumfound
DDGGINNO	ding-dong
DDGHINTU	thudding
DDGHLOOO	hold good
DDGIIINV	dividing
DDGIILMN	middling
DDGIILNP	piddling
DDGILMNU	muddling
DDGILNOP	plodding
DDGILNPU	puddling
DDGINNOU	ding doun
DDGINOPR	prodding
DDGINSTU	studding
DDGIORTY	dirty dog
DDGLNOOS	long odds
DDGLOSTU	gold dust
DDGOOOOT	do good to
DDGOOORW	good word
DDHILOSY	shoddily
DDHLNOOW	hold down
DDIIMRSU	druidism □
	siddurim
DDIINOPU	dupondii
DDIIQTUY	quiddity
DDILOOWW	wildwood
DDILORSY	sordidly
DDIMOSUY	didymous
DDINNOWW	downwind
	wind down
DDINOOOT	odontoid
DDINOOWW	woodwind
DDLLOORW	Old World
	old-world
DDLMORSU	doldrums
DDMNORTU	Dortmund
DDNOOPRW	drop down
DDNOOSSW	doss down
DDNOOUWY	Dunwoody
DEEEEFRZ	defreeze
DEEEEGKR	kedgeree
DEEEEKNP	knee-deep
DEEEEMRR	redeemer □
DEEEEMST	esteemed
DEEEFIIX	idée fixe
DEEEFIRW	fireweed
DEEEFIRY	fire-eyed
DEEEFLOS	felo de se
DEEEFMNR	freedmen
DEEEFORV	overfeed
DEEEFRRR	deferrer
DEEEFRST	festered
DEEEFRTT	fettered
DEEEGIPR	pedigree
DEEEGISW	edgewise
DEEEGLSS	edgeless
DEEEGLSV	selvedge
DEEEGNNR	engender
DEEEHLMT	helmeted
DEEEHLRT	Ethelred
DEEEHLRW	wheedler
DEEEHLSS	heedless
DEEEHRTT	tethered
DEEEILRV	relieved
DEEEINRR	reindeer
DEEEINRS	nereides
DEEEINTV	eventide
DEEEIPTX	expedite
DEEEIRRR	derrière
DEEEIRSS	diereses
DEEEISST	Teesside
DEEEKOPW	pokeweed
DEEELLLV	levelled
DEEELLNT	dentelle
DEEELLNW	newelled
DEEELLPR	repelled
DEEELLPX	expelled
DEEELNPU	unpeeled
DEEELNSS	needless
DEEELPST	steepled
DEEELRTT	lettered
DEEELSSS	seedless
DEEELSSW	weedless
DEEENOPY	open-eyed
DEEENORS	endorsee
DEEENPRT	repetend
DEEENPSS	deepness
DEEENRRR	renderer
DEEENRRV	reverend
DEEEOPRT	deportee
DEEEOSTV	devotees
DEEEPPPR	peppered
DEEEPRST	pestered
DEEEQSUZ	squeezed
DEEERRST	deserter
DEEERRSV	reserved
	reversed
DEEFFNOR	offender
DEEFGINR	fingered
DEEFGLNU	engulfed
DEEFGLOO	feelgood
DEEFGLUW	gulfweed
DEEFHLOR	freehold
DEEFHORR	Hereford
DEEFIILN	fedelini
DEEFIINT	definite
DEEFIIRS	fireside
DEEFIIRV	verified
DEEFILNS	Seinfeld
DEEFILPR	pilfered
DEEFILRT	filtered
DEEFIMTU	tumefied
DEEFINRR	inferred
DEEFINRZ	frenzied
DEEFINST	infested
DEEFIOSS	seised of
DEEFLORW	deflower
DEEFMPRU	perfumed
DEEFNOST	softened
DEEFNRRU	refunder
DEEFNSST	deftness
DEEFORST	De Forest
	deforest
	forested
DEEFRSTW	Fred West
DEEFRTUY	duty-free
DEEGGHHO	hedgehog
DEEGGIJR	jiggered
DEEGGLOR	doggerel
DEEGGNOR	engorged
DEEGHHOP	hedge-hop
DEEGHITW	weighted
DEEGHOPS	sheepdog
DEEGHORW	hedgerow
DEEGIISS	diegesis
DEEGILMP	impledge
DEEGILNR	engirdle
DEEGILNS	seedling
DEEGILRY	greedily
DEEGINPS	speeding
DEEGINRS	designer
	redesign
	resigned
DEEGINSS	edginess
DEEGIRST	digester
DEEGJPRU	prejudge
DEEGLOOT	edge tool
DEEGLOPR	pledgeor
DEEGNOOV	good-even

Words marked □ can also be spelled with an initial capital letter

DEEGOOST	go to seed
DEEGRRTU	Gertrude
DEEHHPRS	shepherd
DEEHILNS	enshield
DEEHILNW	New Delhi
DEEHILSV	dishevel
DEEHILTV	the Devil
DEEHIMMN	hemmed in
DEEHIMRT	Meredith
DEEHINNT	in the end
DEEHINRR	hinderer
DEEHINRS	drisheen
DEEHINRT	in the red
DEEHIPPS	sheep-dip
DEEHIPRS	perished
DEEHIRRT	ditherer
DEEHIRTW	withered
DEEHIRTY	heredity
DEEHKNSU	skene-dhu
DEEHLORV	verdelho
DEEHMNOS	send home
DEEHNORR	dehorner
DEEHNORT	dethrone
	threnode
DEEHNOTT	to the end
DEEHNOWY	honeydew
DEEHNSTU	enthused
DEEHOORT	Theodore
DEEHORSU	house red
	rose-hued
DEEIILMT	idle time
DEEIILNS	sideline
DEEIILRV	liveried
DEEIIMRS	dimerise
DEEIIMRZ	dimerize
DEEIIMTZ	itemized
DEEIINRS	reside in
DEEIIPRU	prie-dieu
DEEIIRST	siderite
DEEIIRSV	derisive
DEEIISSS	disseise
DEEIISSW	sidewise
DEEIISSZ	disseize
DEEIISVW	side view
DEEIKLLR	killdeer
DEEIKLNN	enkindle
DEEIKLNR	rekindle
DEEIKLOV	dovelike
DEEIKNPS	skin-deep
DEEIKNRS	deerskin
DEEIKPSS	deep kiss
DEEIKSTT	diskette
DEEILLMN	Medellín
DEEILLRV	rivelled
DEEILLST	let slide
DEEILMOS	melodise
DEEILMOZ	melodize
DEEILNOT	deletion
DEEILNRU	underlie
DEEILNSS	idleness
DEEILNTT	entitled
DEEILOPT	lepidote
DEEILORV	evildoer
	evil-doer
DEEILPSY	speedily
DEEILRSU	leisured
DEEILRSV	desilver
DEEILRTT	littered
DEEILRTV	let drive
DEEILRVY	delivery
DEEILSUV	delusive
DEEILTUY	Yuletide
DEEIMMRS	immersed
DEEIMNOO	Idomeneo
DEEIMNOR	domineer
DEEIMNOS	demonise
DEEIMNOZ	demonize
DEEIMNPT	pediment
DEEIMNRR	reminder
DEEIMNRV	vermined
DEEIMNST	sediment
DEEIMNSY	mind's eye
DEEIMPRS	premised
DEEIMRST	demister
DEEINNRT	interned
DEEINNTV	invented
DEEINOPS	open side
DEEINOPW	wide open
	wide-open
DEEINORT	oriented
DEEINORV	Don Revie
DEEINOSV	nosedive
	nose-dive
DEEINPSS	dispense
DEEINQSU	sequined
DEEINRST	Dniester
	inserted
	resident
DEEINRSU	uredines
DEEINRSV	versed in
DEEINRTV	inverted
DEEINRTX	dextrine
DEEINSSW	dewiness
	wideness
DEEIOPRX	peroxide
DEEIORRV	override
DEEIORSV	overside
DEEIORTV	tide over
DEEIPPQU	equipped
DEEIPRSS	disperse
DEEIPSST	sidestep
	side-step
DEEIPSTU	deputise
DEEIPTUZ	deputize
DEEIQRRU	required
DEEIQRTU	requited
DEEIQTUU	quietude
DEEIRRRV	Red River
DEEIRRTV	verditer
DEEIRSSV	disserve
	dissever
DEEIRSVX	sex drive
DEEJPRRU	perjured
DEEKKOOY	okey-doke
DEEKLLNY	Ned Kelly
DEEKLOWY	Koldewey
DEEKMRSU	musk deer
DEEKNOPW	keep down
DEELLMOR	modeller
DEELLNOW	well done
	well-done
DEELLORY	yodeller
DEELLSUW	well-used
DEELMNOO	melodeon
DEELMNOW	new-model
DEELMOPR	empolder
DEELMOPY	employed
DEELMRUY	demurely
DEELNOOS	loose end
DEELNOOV	loved one
DEELNORT	redolent
DEELNORV	overlend
DEELNPRS	resplend
DEELNRTU	underlet
DEELNRTY	tenderly
DEELNSSW	lewdness
DEELNWWY	newly-wed
DEELNXYY	lynx-eyed
DEELOPRY	redeploy
DEELORRS	solderer
DEELORSV	resolved
DEELORTT	dotterel
DEELORTV	revolted
DEELPRSU	repulsed
DEELPTTY	pettedly
DEEMMORS	mesoderm
DEEMNOQU	queendom
DEEMNORY	no remedy
DEEMNOTT	dome tent
DEEMNOUY	money due
DEEMORTU	udometer
DEEMPRSU	presumed
DEEMPSSU	messed up
DEEMRRRU	murderer
DEEMRTTU	muttered
DEENNOPT	deponent
DEENNORW	renowned
DEENNRUV	unnerved
DEENNSSU	nudeness
DEENOORV	overdone
DEENOOST	Oostende
DEENOPRS	rope's end
DEENORRS	endorser
DEENORRW	wonderer
DEENORTU	deuteron
DEENRRTU	returned
DEENRSSU	rudeness
DEENRSTU	dentures
	underset
DEENRSUV	unversed
DEENSTTU	untested
DEEOORSV	overdose
DEEOPRRT	reported

DEEOPRSY	eye drops
DEEOPSSU	espoused
DEEORRST	restored
DEEORRUV	devourer
DEEORRVW	Verwoerd
DEEORSTX	dextrose
DEEORSUV	overused
DEEOSTUX	tuxedoes
DEEPRSTU	pertused
DEEPRSUY	pseudery
DEERRTTU	turreted
DEERRTUX	extruder
DEERSSST	stressed
DEERTTUX	textured
DEFFHLSU	shuffled
DEFFILOV	fivefold
DEFFIORV	off-drive
DEFFIRSU	diffuser
DEFFMOOR	formed of
DEFFPPUU	puffed up
DEFFSSUU	suffused
DEFGIILN	defiling
	Fielding
DEFGIINY	edifying
DEFGILNU	field gun
DEFGILTY	giftedly
DEFGIORT	get rid of
DEFGJORU	forjudge
DEFGLOOY	old fogey
DEFHIINS	fiendish
	finished
DEFHIISV	fish dive
DEFHIOOW	wifehood
DEFHLOOS	selfhood
DEFHLOOT	the Flood
DEFHOOPR	hoped-for
DEFHOORS	serfhood
DEFHORRT	Hertford
DEFHORTT	Thetford
DEFHOSTU	soft-hued
DEFIIKNR	Friedkin
DEFIILLO	oilfield
DEFIILLW	wildlife
DEFIILMS	misfield
DEFIILOR	oil-fired
DEFIILPS	flip side
DEFIILRW	wildfire
DEFIILSU	fluidise
DEFIILTY	fidelity
DEFIILUZ	fluidize
DEFIIMNN	fine mind
DEFIIMOR	modifier
DEFIINRW	Winifred
DEFIINTU	finitude
DEFIINTY	identify
DEFIIOSS	ossified
DEFIIOTV	videofit
DEFIIPRU	purified
DEFIIPTY	typified
DEFILLNU	unfilled
DEFILMOW	demi-wolf
DEFILNNO	ninefold
DEFILNRS	Flinders
DEFILNRU	urnfield
DEFILNRY	friendly
	-friendly
DEFILORU	fluoride
DEFILOTU	outfield
DEFILPRU	prideful
DEFILPTU	lifted up
	uplifted
DEFILRRU	flurried
DEFILRVY	fervidly
DEFIMNOR	informed
DEFIMRSU	Dumfries
DEFINNRU	reinfund
DEFINRTT	drift-net
DEFINSYY	Disneyfy
DEFINTTU	unfitted
DEFIOORR	fire door
DEFIOORT	to die for
DEFIOORW	firewood
DEFIOTXY	detoxify
DEFIRSSU	fissured
DEFKLORY	forkedly
DEFLLOOR	folderol
DEFLNORU	flounder
	unfolder
DEFLNOUW	wondeful
DEFLNRUU	unfurled
DEFLOORV	overfold
DEFMNORU	unformed
DEFMOOOR	foredoom
DEFNNOSS	fondness
DEFNNOUW	new-found
DEFNOORS	frondose
DEFNOPRS	forspend
DEFNRRUU	underfur
DEFOORRW	foreword
DEFOPRST	Stepford
DEFORRUW	furrowed
DEFRSSUY	Dreyfuss
DEGGILNS	sledging
DEGGILOO	lie doggo
DEGGIORS	disgorge
DEGGIPRS	sprigged
DEGGLRUY	ruggedly
DEGHHIIT	high tide
DEGHILPT	plighted
DEGHILRT	red light
DEGHINNU	unhinged
DEGHINOT	Deighton
DEGHLOOP	good help
DEGHNOOU	Donoghue
DEGHNORT	thronged
DEGHNORY	hydrogen
DEGHOOST	the goods
DEGHOOSU	house-dog
DEGIIIRS	rigidise
DEGIIIRZ	rigidize
DEGIIIST	digitise
DEGIIITZ	digitize
DEGIILNS	sideling
DEGIILNT	diligent
DEGIILNY	yielding
DEGIIMNP	impeding
DEGIIMSU	misguide
DEGIINNT	indigent
DEGIINNW	widening
DEGIINNX	indexing
DEGIINOS	indigoes
DEGIINRS	desiring
	ringside
DEGIINRV	deriving
DEGIINST	indigest
DEGIINSV	devising
DEGIISSU	disguise
DEGIJMSU	misjudge
DEGIKLOV	kid-glove
DEGILLNW	dwelling
DEGILMNO	gold mine
DEGILNOS	sidelong
DEGILNWY	wingedly
DEGILOOY	ideology
DEGILOWY	go widely
DEGILPSU	pulsidge
DEGILRZZ	grizzled
DEGIMNOS	smidgeon
DEGIMORR	Gordimer
DEGINNNU	unending
DEGINNOT	denoting
DEGINNPS	spending
DEGINNRU	enduring
DEGINNSU	unsigned
DEGINOPS	disponge
DEGINORR	ordering
DEGINORV	ring-dove
DEGINPSU	dispunge
DEGINRSS	dressing
DEGINRST	stringed
DEGIOPRR	porridge
DEGJMNTU	judgment
DEGKNRTU	get drunk
DEGLLNOY	goldenly
DEGLLOPS	Godspell
DEGLOOUU	duologue
DEGNOORS	drongoes
DEGNOOSS	goodness
DEGNOOSW	good news
DEGNOPSU	pug-nosed
DEGNORTU	get round
DEGOORVY	very good
DEGRRSUU	drug user
DEHIILLS	hillside
DEHIILSV	devilish
DEHIINSU	Hinduise
DEHIINUZ	Hinduize
DEHIIOTT	The Idiot
DEHIISTW	side with
DEHIJMNO	demijohn
DEHIKNOW	Windhoek
DEHIKNRT	the drink
DEHILLRT	thrilled

DEHILMNW	helm wind
DEHILMOS	demolish
DEHILNPY	diphenyl
DEHILOPS	polished
DEHILPSU	sulphide
DEHILRTW	writhled
DEHIMNOS	hedonism
	Sondheim
DEHINOST	hedonist
DEHINOTW	done with
DEHINPSU	pushed in
DEHINRSS	in shreds
DEHINSTW	send with
DEHINSUW	unwished
DEHIOPRS	spheroid
DEHIORSS	dishorse
DEHIOSSU	dishouse
DEHIOSSW	sideshow
DEHIRRST	red shirt
DEHKNOOO	hooked on
DEHLLOOW	hollowed
DEHLLOPY	phyllode
DEHLMORY	hydromel
DEHLOOPT	potholed
	pot-holed
DEHLOORV	hold over
	overhold
DEHLOOSW	woolshed
DEHLOPRU	upholder
DEHLORSU	shoulder
DEHLORTW	the world
DEHLRSWY	shrewdly
DEHMOORW	whoredom
DEHNNOOT	on the nod
DEHNOORU	honoured
DEHNOOTT	on the dot
DEHNORSU	enshroud
DEHNORTY	threnody
DEHNOSTU	Southend
DEHNOTWY	the downy
DEHNRTUY	thundery
DEHOOPRT	Theropod
DEHOORTU	out-Herod
DEHOPRST	potsherd
DEIIINSV	divinise
DEIIINVZ	divinize
DEIIISVV	divisive
DEIIKKLS	disklike
DEIIKLNS	disliken
DEIILLMT	ill-timed
DEIILMRU	delirium
DEIILNPV	vilipend
DEIILNVY	divinely
DEIILORS	idoliser
DEIILORZ	idolizer
DEIILPSS	sideslip
DEIIMMST	mistimed
DEIIMSVW	midwives
DEIINORS	derision
	Ironside
DEIINOST	sedition
DEIINPPW	windpipe
DEIINPRS	inspired
DEIINPRT	intrepid
DEIINPRY	pyridine
DEIINQSU	quinsied
DEIINRST	disinter
DEIINSST	tidiness
DEIINSSU	in disuse
DEIINSTU	disunite
	nudities
DEIINTTY	identity
DEIIORTX	trioxide
DEIIORXZ	oxidizer
DEIIPRST	spirited
DEIIPTTY	tepidity
DEIIQSTU	disquiet
DEIJORRY	joyrider
DEIKKLNO	Klondike
DEIKLNRW	wrinkled
DEIKLNSS	kindless
DEIKLORS	Roskilde
DEIKNNSS	kindness
DEIKRSSU	Rusedski
DEILLNTU	untilled
DEILLNUW	unwilled
DEILLSTU	duellist
DEILMNOO	melodion
DEILMNSS	mildness
	mindless
DEILMOOT	dolomite
DEILMOPR	impolder
DEILMORT	old-timer
DEILMOST	melodist
DEILMPSU	displume
DEILNNOT	indolent
DEILNOOS	solenoid
DEILNORS	disenrol
DEILNOSU	delusion
	unsoiled
DEILNOVV	involved
DEILNOVW	live down
DEILNPST	split end
DEILNRSS	rindless
DEILNRSW	swindler
DEILNRTY	trendily
DEILNSSW	wildness
	windless
DEILNSTU	insulted
	unlisted
DEILNTTU	untitled
DEILNTUY	unitedly
DEILNUWY	unwieldy
DEILOOPW	woodpile
DEILORSS	soldiers
DEILOSSV	dissolve
DEILOSTU	solitude
DEILPPST	stippled
DEILPSTU	stipuled
DEILPTWY	wild type
DEILRSVY	diversly
DEILSTUY	sedulity
DEILSTWW	Wild West
DEIMMNOS	demonism
DEIMMOST	immodest
DEIMNNOP	open mind
DEIMNNOY	endymion ❑
DEIMNOOS	dominoes
DEIMNOOT	demotion
DEIMNOOX	monoxide
DEIMNPRU	unprimed
DEIMNPSS	misspend
DEIMNPTU	impudent
DEIMNRTU	rudiment
DEIMOPRS	promised
DEIMOPRT	imported
DEIMOPRV	improved
DEIMORRS	misorder
DEIMORUX	exordium
DEIMRSSU	surmised
DEIMRSUU	residuum
DEINNNOU	innuendo
DEINNOOT	noontide
DEINNOSW	snowed in
DEINNOTT	intend to
DEINNOWW	winnowed
DEINNPRU	underpin
DEINNRSU	in sunder
DEINNRTV	TV dinner
DEINOOPS	poisoned
	Poseidon
DEINOOPW	pinewood
DEINOOTV	devotion
DEINOPPW	pipe down
DEINOPSS	dopiness
DEINORSV	in droves
DEINORTU	diner-out
	inured to
DEINORTW	tire down
DEINORVW	overwind
DEINOSSV	voidness
DEINOSSZ	doziness
DEINOSWZ	downsize
DEINPRUZ	unprized
DEINRRTU	intruder
DEINRSTT	strident
DEINRSTU	sit under
DEINSTUU	unsuited
DEIOORTV	overdo it
DEIOPRRV	provider
DEIOPRSV	disprove
DEIOPRSW	dropwise
DEIOPTUW	wiped out
DEIORRSY	derisory
DEIORRTU	outrider
DEIORSSU	desirous
DEIORSTU	outsider
DEIORTTU	tired out
	tired-out
DEIORTUV	drive out
DEIPPRST	stripped
DEIPRSSU	dispurse
DEIPRSTU	disputer

DEIRRRSY	dry riser
DEIRSSST	distress
DEIRSTTU	detritus
DEISTTTU	duettist
DEJMPPUU	jumped up
	jumped-up
DEJNOPRU	June drop
DEJOOOTY	Ode to Joy
	ode to joy
DEKKLNOY	Klondyke
DEKLMOOY	yokeldom
DEKMORSY	smoke-dry
DEKNORUW	unworked
DEKOOPRV	provoked
DEKOPRUW	worked up
	worked-up
DELLMOOS	modellos
DELLNOPU	unpolled
DELLNSSU	dullness
DELLOOTW	well-to-do
DELLOPTU	polluted
DELLORRY	drollery
DELLORSS	lordless
DELLOSTY	Old Style
	old style
DELLOTUW	outdwell
DELMNORY	modernly
DELMNOTW	meltdown
DELMNPUU	pendulum
DELMORSU	smoulder
DELMOSTY	modestly
DELNOORS	Old Norse
DELNOOSU	nodulose
DELNOOTW	low-toned
DELNOOWY	woodenly
DELNOPTW	pelt down
DELNORSU	unsolder
DELNORSY	Reynolds
DELNORWW	New World
DELNOSSU	loudness
DELNOSUV	unsolved
DELOOOOT	toodle-oo
DELOORRV	overlord
DELOORRW	word-lore
DELOORTY	rootedly
DELOOSSW	woodless
DELOPSTW	spot-weld
DELORSSW	wordless
DELORSUY	delusory
DELORTUU	ruled out
DELORUVY	very loud
DELOSSUU	sedulous
DELOTUVY	devoutly
DELSTUUV	Deus vult
DEMMNSUU	unsummed
DEMMRRUU	murmured
DEMNNOOT	Edmonton
DEMNOOVW	move down
DEMNORSY	syndrome
DEMNOSTU	mudstone
DEMOOPRR	prodrome
DEMOOPRT	promoted
DEMOORST	doomster
DEMOORSU	dormouse
DEMOORTY	odometry
DEMORRUU	rumoured
DENNOOOZ	endozoon
DENNOORW	no wonder
DENNOOTW	note down
	tone down
DENNORTU	turned on
	turned-on
DENNOSTW	sent down
DENNOTUW	unwonted
DENNRRUU	underrun
DENOOOPR	open door
DENOOPRS	prodnose
DENOORTX	next door
	next-door
DENOOTVW	vote down
DENOPRUV	unproved
DENOPSTU	outspend
DENOPSTW	step down
	step-down
DENOPSUW	snowed up
DENOQTUU	unquoted
DENORRSU	rounders
DENORSSU	dourness
DENORSTU	tonsured
	unsorted
DENORSTY	dry-stone
DENORTUW	undertow
DENOTUUV	undevout
DENPRTUU	upturned
DENRRSUY	dry-nurse
DENSSTTU	students
DEOOORSW	rosewood
DEOOPPRS	proposed
DEOOPRST	doorstep
	torpedos
DEOOPRTU	uprooted
DEOORRSW	sorrowed
DEOOSTWW	Westwood
DEOPPRSU	purposed
DEOPPSSU	supposed
DEOPRRTU	protrude
DEOPRSST	top-dress
DEORRTTU	tortured
DEORSTUX	dextrous
DEOSSSUY	Odysseus
DEOSSTTU	testudos
DEPPSSYY	dyspepsy
DEPRRTUU	ruptured
DFFFIORT	drift off
DFFHIOOS	food-fish
DFFIILUY	fluidify
DFFIKNOR	drink off
DFFLOORU	fourfold
DFFNOORU	round off
DFFNOOSU	sound off
DFFOOOST	soft food
DFFOORUW	woodruff
DFGGHIOT	dogfight
DFGHILOS	goldfish
DFGIIIRY	rigidify
DFGIILRY	frigidly
DFGIINNS	findings
DFGIINRT	drifting
DFGILLOO	gold foil
DFGILNNO	fondling
DFGILNOO	flooding
DFGINNOU	founding
DFGINORY	dying for
DFGLNOOR	Longford
DFGMOOOR	good form
DFGNOOOS	Son of God
DFHIIMUY	humidify
DFHJNOOR	John Ford
DFHLOOOT	foothold
DFHNOOUX	foxhound
DFIIINVY	divinify
DFIILOSY	solidify
DFIILTUY	fluidity
DFILLORY	floridly
DFILLOWW	wild fowl
	wildfowl
DFIMNORW	firm down
DFINRSUW	windsurf
DFIOOPRS	disproof
DFLNOOWW	wolf down
DFLOOOSU	soul food
DFNOOPRU	profound
DFOOOSTW	softwood
DGGGIINS	diggings
DGGGINRU	grudging
DGGHINOT	night-dog
DGGIINNR	grinding
DGGIINNW	wingding
DGGILNOS	lodgings
DGGIRSTU	druggist
DGHHHILO	hold high
DGHIILNS	hidlings
DGHIIMNT	midnight
DGHIINNW	hindwing
DGHILNOS	holdings
DGHILNRU	hurdling
DGHILOOR	girlhood
DGHINNOU	hounding
DGHLORSU	gold rush
DGHNOTUU	doughnut
DGHOOOST	hot goods
DGHOOOTT	dog-tooth
DGHORRUY	rough-dry
DGIIINNV	divining
DGIIIRTY	rigidity
DGIIKLNN	kindling
DGIIKNNR	drinking
DGIILLNR	drilling
DGIILLRR	drill rig
DGIINNRW	windring
DGIINORR	gridiron
DGIINPPR	dripping
DGIKLOOY	kidology

DGIKNOOW	kingwood
DGILLOOW	good will
	goodwill
DGILLOSW	God's will
DGILMNOU	moulding
DGILMNPU	dumpling
DGILMSUY	smudgily
DGILNOTY	dotingly
DGILOSTY	stodgily
DGILRTUY	turgidly
DGIMMNRU	drumming
DGINNOOT	doting on
DGINNOPU	pounding
DGINNOSU	sounding
DGINNOUW	wounding
DGINOOPR	drooping
DGINOPPR	dropping
DGINOTUY	dying out
	dying-out
DGINSTUY	studying
DGKNOOSW	God knows
DGLLOORY	Old Glory
DGLNOPUW	gulp down
DGLOOOXY	doxology
DGNNOOOW	go down on
DGNOOORV	Novgorod
DGNOOOTW	go down to
DGNOORTU	good turn
DHHILOTW	hold with
	withhold
DHIIIMNS	diminish
DHIIKWZZ	whizz kid
DHIIMNOO	hominoid
DHIIMNSU	Hinduism
DHIIMPSS	midships
DHIIMTUY	humidity
DHIINSTW	whinid'st
DHIIORSS	hidrosis
DHIKNOOW	hoodwink
DHIKNORT	hot drink
DHILLNOW	downhill
DHILMOPY	lymphoid
DHILMOSY	modishly
DHILOPRS	lordship☐
DHILOPSS	slipshod
DHILORRY	horridly
DHIMNOST	hindmost
DHINOTWW	down with
DHIOOPRZ	rhizopod
DHJNOORY	John Dory
DHJOPRSU	jodhpurs
DHKMNOOO	monkhood
DHLLNOUW	hull-down
DHLNOOOT	hold on to
DHLNOOWW	howl down
DHLNOSTU	shouldn't
DHLORXYY	hydroxyl
DHNNOTUW	hunt down
DHNOOPRU	Proudhon
DHNOOSWW	showdown
DHNOPSUW	push down
DHNORSUU	unshroud
DHNOSTUW	shut down
	shutdown
DHOOORTX	orthodox
DHOOPRST	drop-shot
DIIIKMNS	minidisk
DIIILRSW	wild iris
DIIILTVY	lividity
DIIIMTTY	timidity
DIIINOSV	division
DIIINTVY	divinity
DIIIPRST	dispirit
DIIIRTVY	viridity
DIIJNOST	disjoint
DIILLMNW	windmill
DIILLMPY	limpidly
DIILLMTY	dimly lit
DIILLQUY	liquidly
DIILLSTY	idyllist
DIILNOTU	dilution
DIILNTUY	untidily
DIILOPRT	triploid
DIILOSTY	solidity
DIIMNNOO	dominion
DIIMNOPT	midpoint
	mid-point
DIIMRUUV	duumviri
DIIMTTUY	tumidity
DIINNOSU	disunion
DIINOORT	Triodion
DIINOSSU	sinusoid
DIINSTUY	disunity
DIKLNNUY	unkindly
DIKLRUUU	durukuli
DIKMOORW	Mirkwood
DIKNOOPW	pinkwood
DILLMNOP	millpond
DILLOSTY	stolidly
DILMNOSW	slim down
DILNOUWY	woundily
DILOOPRY	droopily
DILOORSS	lordosis
DILOORSU	louis d'or
	louis-d'or
DILOOSTT	to-do list
DILOOSUY	odiously
DILOPRTY	torpidly
DILORRTY	torridly
DILORSTW	word-list
DILORSWY	drowsily
DILPRTUY	putridly
DILPSTUY	stupidly
DILRSTUY	sturdily
DIMMNORY	myrmidon
DIMMNOTY	to my mind
DIMNOOST	monodist
DIMNORTU	drum into
DIMNORUY	your mind
DIMNOSTU	dismount
DIMNOSUW	unwisdom
DIMOOPPU	Pompidou
DIMORSWY	rowdyism
DIMRSUUV	duumvirs
DINNOOPR	drop in on
DINNOORS	rondinos
DINNOOST	tondinos
DINNORUW	win round
DINOORSU	nidorous
DINOOSTY	nodosity
DINOPRTY	dry-point
DINOPSSW	piss down
DINOSSUY	Dionysus
DINRSTUY	industry
DIOORSTT	ridottos
DIOSSTUU	studious
DIRSSTTU	distrust
DJRTUUYY	jury duty
DKLNOOOW	look down
DKNNOOTW	don't know
DKOOORWW	woodwork
DLLNOPUW	pull down
DLNOOSUU	nodulous
DLNOOSWW	slow down
	slowdown
DLNORTUY	rotundly
DLOOOORS	doloroso
DLOOORSU	dolorous
DLOOPPUW	pulpwood
	wood pulp
DLOORSTY	old story
DMMNRUUY	dummy run
DMNOORWY	on my word
DMNOOSTW	downmost
DMOOORWW	woodworm
	wormwood
DMPPPUUY	mudpuppy
DNNOOTWW	downtown
	down-town
DNNORTUW	downturn
	turn down
	turn-down
DNOOPPRU	propound
DNOOPRSW	snowdrop
DNOOPRUW	downpour
	pour down
DNOOPSTW	stop down
DNOOPTUW	two pound
DNOORSUW	wondrous
DNOOSTUU	sound out
DNORRSUU	surround
DOOOPRST	doorpost
	doorstop
DOOORSTU	outdoors
DOOORTTW	Trotwood
DOOPPRTU	top-proud
DOORRSUU	ordurous

E

EEEEFNRZ	enfreeze
EEEEGGRR	greegree
EEEEGNSV	Genevese
EEEEGQSU	squeegee

Words marked ☐ can also be spelled with an initial capital letter

EEEEHRSW	see where
EEEEHRTV	The Reeve
EEEEHTTY	eye teeth
EEEELLPX	expellee
EEEELMST	let me see
EEEENRRV	veneerer
EEEEOTYY	eye to eye
EEEEPRRV	repreeve
EEEFFGIR	fee-grief
EEEFFLOR	forefeel
EEEFFLTY	effetely
EEEFFNRT	efferent
EEEFFORT	forefeet
EEEFFRVW	feverfew
EEEFGMRR	germ-free
EEEFIKLL	feel like
EEEFILPR	life peer
EEEFIMRT	free time
EEEFINRR	free rein
EEEFINRT	Tenerife
EEEFLORV	free love
EEEFNORS	foreseen
EEEFNRRT	rent-free
	tree fern
EEEFNRSS	freeness
EEEFNRTT	enfetter
EEEFNRUZ	unfreeze
EEEFORTV	free vote
EEEFPRUZ	freeze-up
EEEGGILN	negligee
EEEGGLPY	Peggy Lee
EEEGHINT	eighteen
EEEGHORS	here goes!
EEEGHRTT	get there
EEEGINNR	engineer
EEEGINRS	energise
	greenies
EEEGINRZ	energize
EEEGISSX	exegesis
EEEGITVV	vegetive
EEEGKKRY	Greek key
EEEGMNRT	emergent
EEEGMORT	geometer
EEEGNNOR	renege on
EEEGNOSV	Genovese
EEEGNRRU	reneguer
EEEGNRRV	revenger
EEEGNRRY	greenery
EEEGOPRT	protégée
EEEGQQUU	Queequeg
EEEHIRST	etherise
EEEHIRTZ	etherize
EEEHITWY	white-eye
EEEHKLNO	kneehole
EEEHLMPT	helpmeet
EEEHLNTV	eleventh
EEEHLOPP	peephole
EEEHLORV	heel over
EEEHMNTV	vehement
EEEHMNTY	the Enemy
EEEHMRYY	eye rhyme
EEEHNNPT	nepenthe
EEEHNNTV	even then
EEEHNPRS	ensphere
EEEHNRTT	Ethernet
EEEHNRVW	whenever
EEEHORRS	Hereroes
EEEHRRVW	wherever
EEEIKLMS	seem like
EEEIKLPS	Spike Lee
EEEIKMPT	keep time
EEEIKNPS	Pekinese
EEEILLRV	reveille
EEEILMMN	Emmeline
EEEILNPR	pelerine
EEEILNRT	tree line
EEEILNST	enlistee
	selenite
EEEILRRV	reliever
EEEILSSW	elsewise
EEEILSTV	televise
EEEILTVW	teleview
EEEIMNRU	meunière
EEEIMPRR	premiere
	première
EEEIMPRS	emperise
EEEIMPRZ	emperize
EEEIMRTT	remittee
EEEINNNT	nineteen
EEEINNRT	internee
EEEINNST	seine net
EEEINNSV	Viennese
EEEINRSS	eeriness
EEEINRST	eternise
EEEINRTZ	eternize
EEEIPRRV	reprieve
EEEIPRST	Pieterse
EEEIQSUX	exequies
EEEIRRTV	retrieve
EEEIRRVW	reviewer
EEEJKKNR	knee-jerk
EEEJLLRW	jeweller
EEEKKNSY	Ken Kesey
EEEKLNNR	enkernel
EEEKLORV	keel over
EEEKLPSW	ekpweles
EEEKMNSS	meekness
EEEKMRSS	kermesse
EEEKNNSS	keenness
EEEKNORS	kerosene
EEEKNSWW	Newsweek
EEEKPPST	keep step
EEELLLRV	leveller
EEELLNQU	quenelle
EEELLPRR	repeller
EEELLRRV	reveller
EEELMNST	elements
EEELMOPY	employee
EEELMOTT	omelette
EEELMPRS	REM sleep
EEELMRTU	muleteer
EEELNOPP	Penelope
EEELNOPV	envelope
EEELNOSV	novelese
EEELNRSW	newsreel
EEELNRSY	serenely
EEELNRTY	Terylene®
EEELPRSS	peerless
EEELRSST	treeless
EEELRSTT	resettle
EEELRSVY	severely
EEELTTTX	teletext
EEEMNNTT	tenement
EEEMORRV	ever more
	evermore
EEEMORTV	overteem
EEEMRSST	semester
EEENNOPR	neoprene
EEENNSSV	evenness
EEENORSV	Veronese
EEENORVY	everyone
EEENPPRS	prepense
EEENPRRT	repenter
EEENPRSS	ens per se
EEENPRSY	Pyrenees
EEENPSSX	expenses
EEENRRTV	reverent
EEENRSTY	yestreen
EEENRSUV	revenues
EEENSSTW	tweeness
EEEOPRRV	overpeer
EEEORRSV	overseer
EEEPRRST	pesterer
EEEPRRSV	perverse
	preserve
EEEPRRTW	pewterer
EEEPSTTT	septette
EEEQRSUZ	squeezer
EEERRRSV	reverser
EEERRSSV	reserves
EEERRSTT	resetter
EEERSTVX	vertexes
EEERSTWZ	tweezers
EEFFFKLU	kefuffle
EEFFGIRT	free gift
EEFFGORY	Geoffrey
EEFFHIKY	keffiyeh
EEFFISUV	effusive
EEFFJRSY	Jeffreys
EEFFLLOV	level off
EEFFLMOR	flee from
EEFFLNTU	effluent
EEFFLOPS	sleep off
EEFFMORR	free-form
EEFFRRSU	sufferer
EEFGIILR	filigree
EEFGILNS	feelings
EEFGILNT	fleeting
EEFGINRZ	freezing
EEFGIRRU	refigure
EEFGLNRY	greenfly
EEFGLNUV	vengeful
EEFGNOOR	foregone

EEFGORRT	tree frog
EEFHILLR	hellfire
EEFHILST	The Flies
EEFHILTW	feel with
EEFHIORS	fire hose
EEFHIRSV	feverish
EEFHIRTY	etherify
EEFHLLPS	Self-Help
EEFHLLWY	flywheel
EEFHLMST	themself
EEFHLNOS	one flesh
EEFHMORR	herefrom
EEFHMORY	Meyerhof
EEFHNORT	forehent
EEFHNRSW	fresh-new
EEFHORRT	therefor
EEFHORRW	wherefor
EEFHORSW	foreshew
EEFIIKLL	lifelike
EEFIILLN	lifeline
EEFIILMT	lifetime
EEFIILSZ	life-size
EEFIIMNN	feminine
EEFIIMNS	feminise
EEFIIMNZ	feminize
EEFIIRRV	verifier
EEFIJNNR	Jennifer
EEFIKNNP	penknife
EEFILLMR	Mill Reef
EEFILLOV	love life
EEFILLRW	free will
EEFILLSS	lifeless
EEFILNOT	Leontief
EEFILNSS	fineless
EEFILPPU	flue pipe
EEFILPRR	pilferer
EEFILRSS	fireless
EEFINNSS	fineness
EEFINNTU	fine-tune
EEFINOPR	open fire
EEFINRRY	refinery
EEFINRSS	rifeness
EEFIRRSU	sure-fire
EEFIRSTY	esterify
EEFISSSW	fess-wise
EEFKMOPR	keep from
EEFKNORT	reef knot
EEFKOPRS	for keeps
EEFLLLNU	Fluellen
EEFLLORT	foretell
	toll-free
EEFLLOSV	self-love
EEFLLRSU	self-rule
EEFLLRXY	reflexly
EEFLLSSS	selfless
EEFLNORW	enflower
EEFLNOSS	one's self
EEFLNTUV	eventful
EEFLOPTU	feel up to
EEFLORRW	flowerer
EEFLORTV	left over
	leftover
	left-over
EEFLORTW	floweret
EEFLORWW	werewolf
EEFLOSUX	flexuose
EEFMNORT	fomenter
EEFMORRR	reformer
EEFMPRRU	perfumer
EEFNORST	enforest
	softener
EEFNORTU	fourteen
EEFNORTW	Freetown
EEFNQRTU	frequent
EEFNRTTU	unfetter
EEFOPRRT	Freeport
EEFOPRST	post-free
EEFOPRTU	of repute
EEFORRST	forester□
	fosterer
	reforest
	steer for
EEFORRSU	ferreous
EEFORRTY	feretory
EEFORSUV	feverous
EEGGHLLS	eggshell
EEGGHNOR	Honegger
EEGGIJRR	rejigger
EEGGIMNR	emerging
EEGGIMRT	egg-timer
EEGGINNR	greening
EEGGINRT	greeting
EEGGMORS	Rees-Mogg
EEGGORTT	go-getter
EEGGPRRS	preggers
EEGGPSUY	Peggy Sue
EEGHHIKN	knee-high
EEGHHINT	heighten
EEGHIIST	eighties
EEGHILLV	give hell
EEGHILNW	wheeling
EEGHILTW	white-leg
EEGHINRS	greenish
EEGHINST	seething
	sheeting
EEGHINTT	teething
EEGHINWZ	wheezing
EEGHIRST	Thesiger
EEGHISST	sightsee
EEGHISTY	eyesight
EEGHLNNT	lengthen
EEGHMNOY	hegemony
EEGHNNRU	enhunger
EEGHNOPS	phosgene
EEGHNOPY	hypogene
EEGHNSSU	hugeness
EEGHNSTT	the gents
EEGHORTT	together
EEGHOSTT	ghettoes
EEGHPTTU	get het up
EEGHRSTY	the Greys
EEGHRTTY	The Tyger
EEGIILNR	lingerie
EEGIILNV	give line
	inveigle
EEGIINRV	give rein
EEGIINTV	genitive
EEGIKLNN	kneeling
EEGILLRV	Greville
EEGILNPS	sleeping
EEGILNRR	lingerer
EEGILNRU	reguline
EEGILNSV	sleeving
EEGILOPU	epilogue
EEGILOSU	eulogies
	eulogise
EEGILOUZ	eulogize
EEGILRSU	regulise
EEGILRTV	verligte
EEGILRUZ	regulize
EEGIMNNS	meninges
EEGIMNRT	regiment
EEGIMNRU	meringue
EEGINNPR	preening
EEGINNRS	sneering
EEGINNRT	entering
EEGINNRW	renewing
EEGINNSU	unseeing
EEGINNSV	evenings
EEGINNSZ	sneezing
EEGINNTV	eventing
EEGINPST	steeping
EEGINPSW	sweeping
EEGINRRS	resigner
EEGINRST	steering
EEGINRSU	seigneur
EEGINRSV	severing
EEGINRUZ	Zigeuner
EEGINSSU	geniuses
EEGINSUU	Eugenius
EEGINTTV	vignette
EEGINTTW	tweeting
EEGIORST	ergotise
EEGIORTZ	ergotize
EEGIORVV	give over
EEGIPRST	prestige
EEGIRRST	register
EEGIRSTT	grisette
EEGISSTV	vestiges
EEGKNSSS	Skegness
EEGLMRSS	germless
EEGLNOPY	polygene
EEGLNPRS	Spengler
EEGLORTW	get lower
EEGMNOST	gemstone
EEGMNTTU	tegument
EEGMORSU	gruesome
EEGMORTY	geometry
EEGNNORT	roentgen□
EEGNNOSV	evensong
EEGNOORV	engroove
EEGNOPTY	genotype
EEGNORST	estrogen

EEGNORSU	generous
EEGNORSY	eryngoes
EEGNPRRS	Sprenger
EEGNPRTY	Peer Gynt
EEGNPRUX	expunger
EEGNRSSY	greyness
EEGNRSUY	guernsey□
EEGNRTUV	Turgenev
EEGOPRSU	superego
	super-ego
EEGORSTW	get worse
EEHHILTW	the while
EEHHIPSS	sheepish
EEHHIRST	The Shire
	this here
EEHHIRTW	herewith
EEHHLMOP	home help
EEHHORTT	the other
EEHHRRST	thresher
EEHIILTW	white lie
EEHIITTW	white tie
EEHIKLLT	hell-kite
EEHIKLMO	homelike
EEHIKRRS	shrieker
EEHILLNP	helpline
EEHILNNO	nine-hole
EEHILNPW	pinwheel
EEHILORT	hotelier
EEHILRSS	heirless
EEHILRST	St Helier
EEHILWYZ	wheezily
EEHIMNOR	Hermione
EEHIMPST	epithems
EEHIMRST	The Miser
EEHIMSTT	The Times
EEHIMTTW	meet with
	teem with
EEHINNQU	henequin
EEHINNRS	enshrine
EEHINNRT	inherent
EEHINPRS	insphere
EEHINPRT	nephrite
	trephine
EEHINRTT	thirteen
EEHIORST	isothere
	theorise
EEHIORTZ	theorize
EEHIPPTY	epiphyte
EEHIPRRS	perisher
EEHIPSST	steepish
EEHIPSUU	euphuise
EEHIPUUZ	euphuize
EEHIQRSU	queerish
EEHIRRSW	wherries
EEHIRSTT	tee shirt
	tee-shirt
EEHIRTVY	thievery
EEHJLOWY	joy-wheel
EEHKLOOR	look here!
EEHKLOWY	Holy Week
EEHKMOST	the Smoke
EEHLLPSS	helpless
EEHLLSTW	the wells
EEHLMOPS	so help me
EEHLMORU	home rule
EEHLMOSS	homeless
EEHLNOTT	telethon
EEHLNSST	St Helens
EEHLOOPS	lose hope
EEHLOPSS	hopeless
EEHLORSV	shoveler
EEHLOSSS	shoeless
EEHLPRSU	spherule
EEHLPRTY	three-ply
EEHMMOPR	morpheme
EEHMMORT	ohmmeter
EEHMNORS	horsemen
EEHMOOPS	some hope
EEHMORVW	whomever
EEHNNORT	enthrone
EEHNNSTU	unnethes
EEHNOORS	one-horse
EEHNOPRU	hereupon
EEHNOPTY	neophyte
EEHNORTT	not there
EEHNORTU	hereunto
EEHNOSTV	Hot Seven
EEHNPRSU	unsphere
EEHNPRYY	Henry Pye
EEHNRTTU	untether
EEHOORSV	overshoe
	over-shoe
EEHOOTTY	eye tooth
EEHPRSSU	Hesperus
EEIIKLPP	pipelike
EEIIKLSW	likewise
EEIILLMM	millième
EEIILMNT	ilmenite
EEIILNNT	Leninite
EEIILNPP	pipeline
EEIILNTV	lenitive
EEIILRVW	live wire
EEIILSTW	lewisite
EEIIMRSS	miseries
EEIIMSST	Semitise
EEIIMSSV	emissive
EEIIMSTZ	Semitize
EEIINNST	Einstein
	nineties
EEIINPPR	piperine
EEIINRRV	riverine
EEIINRSS	in series
	resinise
	sirenise
EEIINRSZ	resinize
	sirenize
EEIIQSTU	equities
EEIIRSTV	verities
EEIJLNNU	julienne
EEIJLNUV	juvenile
EEIKLNSS	likeness
EEIKLORS	roselike
EEIKLORT	lorikeet
EEIKLPST	spikelet
EEIKLRST	triskele
EEIKNORS	kerosine
EEIKNPRT	Peterkin
EEIKNRRT	tinkerer
EEILLLMV	Melville
EEILLLVW	live well
EEILLMPR	impeller
EEILLNST	stelline
EEILLNSY	ley lines
	senilely
EEILLPSS	ellipses
EEILLPSY	sleepily
EEILLTTV	Villette
EEILMNOS	Seminole
EEILMNSU	selenium
EEILMOPS	polemise
EEILMOPZ	polemize
EEILMOST	lose time
EEILMRRS	Mirrlees
EEILMSST	timeless
EEILMSVV	Mevlevis
EEILNNOR	one-liner
EEILNNST	sentinel
EEILNOPR	leporine
EEILNORS	Elsinore
EEILNOSV	novelise
EEILNOVZ	novelize
EEILNPPZ	zeppelin□
EEILNPRS	Pilsener
EEILNPRU	perilune
EEILNPRV	replevin
EEILNRST	Leinster
	listener
EEILNRTY	entirely
EEILNSSV	evilness
	vileness
EEILNSTT	settle in
EEILORRT	loiterer
EEILORST	literose
EEILORSV	relievos
EEILORVV	overlive
	overveil
EEILPPSS	pipeless
EEILPPSY	epilepsy
EEILPSST	epistles
EEILPSSV	pelvises
EEILPSTY	epistyle
EEILRSST	riteless
	tireless
EEILRSSW	wireless
EEIMMORS	memories
	memorise
EEIMMORT	more time
EEIMMORZ	memorize
EEIMMOST	sometime
EEIMMRST	meristem
	mismetre
EEIMNORS	emersion
EEIMNOST	monetise

Words marked □ can also be spelled with an initial capital letter

	semitone	EEIPSSTW	stepwise	EELORSTU	resolute
EEIMNOTZ	monetize	EEIQRRRU	requirer	EELORSTY	Tyrolese
	time zone	EEIQRRTU	requiter	EELORTTU	roulette
EEIMNPRU	perineum	EEIQSSSU	esquisse	EELORTUV	revolute
EEIMNRTU	mutineer	EEIRRSST	resister		truelove
EEIMNRTV	virement	EEIRSTVY	severity	EELPPSTU	septuple
EEIMNSTW	news item	EEIRTTTZ	terzetti	EELPRTXY	expertly
EEIMNSUV	Museveni	EEJJLNUY	jejunely	EELPSSUX	plexuses
EEIMOPRS	promisee	EEJPRRRU	perjurer	EELPSTTU	settle up
	re-impose	EEKKNRSY	Kerensky	EELPSTUX	sextuple
EEIMORST	tiresome	EEKLLPTW	well-kept	EELRRSTW	wrestler
EEIMORTV	overtime	EEKLNNNU	unkennel	EELRSSST	restless
EEIMOSSW	somewise	EEKLNOST	skeleton	EELRSTWY	westerly
EEIMPRSS	premises	EEKLORST	Koestler	EEMMNOST	mementos
EEIMRRTT	remitter	EEKMNOYY	key money	EEMMNOTV	movement
	trimeter	EEKNOSTY	keystone	EEMNNRSU	Mensuren
EEIMRSTU	emeritus	EEKNSSSW	skewness	EEMNOOPT	tone poem
EEIMRTTY	temerity	EELLLLMP	pell-mell	EEMNPRSS	pressmen
EEINNNPS	Pennines	EELLLNWY	Llewelyn	EEMNPRTU	untemper
EEINNPTT	penitent	EELLLOVW	low-level	EEMNSSTU	muteness
EEINNRTT	renitent	EELLNOOS	Ole Olsen		tenesmus
EEINNRTV	in ventre	EELLNSTU	entellus	EEMNSTTV	vestment
	re-invent	EELLOOST	let loose	EEMOORRV	moreover
EEINNSTT	sentient	EELLORSV	oversell	EEMOORVV	move over
EEINOPPR	peperoni	EELLORTX	extoller	EEMOQTTU	moquette
EEINOPRS	in repose	EELLORVW	well over	EEMORSST	Somerset
	isoprene	EELLORVY	volleyer	EEMORSTT	remotest
EEINORRT	reorient	EELLOSSV	loveless	EEMORSUV	muse over
EEINORSV	eversion	EELLOSWY	Wolseley	EEMOTTTU	teetotum
EEINORTT	tenorite	EELLRSSU	ruleless	EEMRRTTU	mutterer
EEINORTX	exertion	EELLRVWY	very well	EENNNOSS	nonsense
EEINOSTT	noisette	EELMNOOS	lonesome	EENNNOTV	non-event
EEINPPTZ	Zentippe	EELMNSUY	unseemly	EENNNPWY	new penny
EEINPRSS	ripeness	EELMNTUY	unmeetly	EENNOOOT	one-to-one
EEINPRTX	inexpert	EELMOPRY	employer	EENNOORT	rotenone
EEINQRRU	enquirer	EELMORST	molester	EENNOPSS	openness
EEINRRST	inserter	EELMORTY	remotely	EENNOPTX	exponent
EEINRRSU	reinsure	EELMPPRU	empurple	EENNOPUV	even up on
EEINRSSU	enuresis	EELMSSST	stemless	EENOOPRS	open sore
EEINRSTT	interest	EELNNUVY	unevenly	EENOORTV	overtone
EEINRSTU	esurient	EELNOORS	loosener	EENOPRSS	response
EEINRSTV	reinvest	EELNOPPU	unpeople	EENOPRST	Peterson
EEINRSTX	intersex	EELNOQTU	eloquent	EENOPRTT	entrepot
EEINRSTY	serenity	EELNOSSS	noseless		entrepôt
EEINRSUV	universe	EELNOSST	noteless	EENOPRXY	pyroxene
EEINRTTY	entirety		toneless	EENORRTW	Rowntree
	eternity	EELNOSTT	settle on	EENORSSS	soreness
EEINSSSX	sexiness	EELNOTVV	on velvet	EENORSSU	neuroses
EEINSTTW	tentwise	EELNSSTU	tuneless	EENORSTX	extensor
	twenties	EELNSTTU	unsettle	EENORSUV	venerous
EEINSTTX	existent	EELNSTWY	New Style	EENOSSST	stenoses
EEIOPRRT	portière	EELOOSST	set loose	EENPRSST	pertness
EEIOPRRV	overripe	EELOPRRX	explorer	EENPRSSU	pureness
EEIOPRRW	wire rope	EELOPRTT	teleport	EENPSSSU	suspense
EEIORRTX	exterior	EELOPSTU	outsleep	EENRRTUV	venturer
EEIORSVZ	oversize		sleep out	EENRSSSU	sureness
EEIORVVW	overview	EELOQRUY	requoyle	EENRSSTU	trueness
EEIPPRRS	perspire	EELORRSV	resolver	EENRSTUW	wet nurse
EEIPRSTT	pretties	EELORRTV	revolter		wet-nurse
EEIPRSTX	pre-exist	EELORRUV	overrule	EEOOOTTT	toe to toe
EEIPRTUV	eruptive	EELORRVV	revolver	EEOOPRRV	pore over

EEOORRZZ	zero-zero
EEOPRRRT	reporter
EEOPRRRV	reprover
EEOPRRTT	potterer
EEOPRRTX	exporter
EEOPRSSS	espresso
EEOPRSSU	repoussé
EEOPRSSX	expresso
EEOPRSTV	overstep
EEOPRSTY	serotype
EEOPRSUX	exposure
EEOPRTTU	peter out
EEOPRTVY	overtype
EEOPSSTW	sweetsop
EEORRRST	resorter
	restorer
	retrorse
EEORRSSV	reversos
EEORRTTT	totterer
EEORRTUV	overture
	trouvère
EEORSTUV	serve out
EEORSTVX	vortexes
EEPRRSSU	pressure
EEPRSTTU	upsetter
EERSSTTU	trustees
EFFGHIOW	weigh off
EFFGHTUY	get huffy
EFFGINOR	offering
EFFGIOTT	get it off
EFFGNOOT	get off on
EFFHIISW	fishwife
EFFHIITT	fiftieth
EFFHIOTW	off-white
EFFHLRSU	shuffler
EFFHOORS	offshore
EFFHOOSV	shove off
EFFHRSTU	stuff her
EFFIKOSV	skive off
EFFILNRS	sniffler
EFFIMOST	smite off
EFFINOSU	effusion
EFFIOPRS	pifferos
EFFIOPST	off-piste
EFFIORST	forfeits
EFFIORTW	write off
	write-off
EFFLMNUU	unmuffle
EFFLNRSU	snuffler
EFFLNRUU	unruffle
EFFLOOPS	slope off
EFFOOORT	forefoot
EFFOORSW	worse off
EFFORRUV	overruff
EFGGIINN	feigning
EFGGILOS	solfeggi
EFGGIOST	foggiest
EFGHHIIL	high life
EFGHHIIV	high-five
EFGHIILR	Hilfiger
EFGHINRT	frighten
EFGHINSU	feng shui
EFGHIOSY	fogeyish
EFGHORST	The Frogs
EFGIINNR	infringe
	refining
EFGIINRU	figurine
EFGIITUV	fugitive
EFGILLNO	lifelong
EFGILLUU	guileful
EFGILMOR	filmgoer
EFGILNOR	florigen
EFGILNTW	left-wing
EFGIMRUU	refugium
EFGINOOR	go on fire
EFGINORU	figure on
EFGINORV	forgiven
EFGINORW	forewing
EFGINPUY	pinguefy
EFGINRSU	refusing
EFGINRTY	gentrify
EFGIOPTT	pettifog
EFGIORTT	forget it
EFGLOOVX	foxglove
EFGLORWY	grey wolf
EFGNORSU	Ferguson
EFGNSSUU	funguses
EFGOOTTU	get out of
EFHIIKLS	fish-like
EFHIILMN	Niflheim
EFHIINRS	finisher
EFHIIPPS	pipefish
EFHIIPRS	fireship
EFHILTWY	whitefly
EFHIORTT	fortieth
EFHKLNOU	funkhole
EFHKLOOR	folk hero
EFHLNORS	hornfels
EFHLNOTY	on the fly
EFHLNSUY	unfleshy
EFHLOOST	elf-shoot
EFHLORSY	horsefly
EFHLOSTU	flesh out
EFHLOSUY	housefly
EFHOORSW	foreshow
EFHORSTT	set forth
EFHRSTTU	furthest
EFIIILRV	vilifier
EFIIINNT	infinite
EFIILLNT	tefillin
EFIILLRS	frillies
EFIILNOU	in lieu of
EFIILNST	in itself
EFIILNTY	finitely
EFIILRSU	fusilier
EFIIMMNS	feminism
EFIIMNOS	fisnomie
EFIIMNST	feminist
EFIIMRSS	miss fire
EFIINORR	inferior
EFIINOVW	in view of
EFIINPSV	fivepins
EFIINRSY	resinify
EFIINSUV	infusive
EFIIPRRU	purifier
EFIIPRST	spitfire □
EFIIPRTY	typifier
EFIIRVVY	revivify
EFIJLORS	frijoles
EFIKLOOR	rooflike
EFIKLORW	life-work
EFIKLRUY	like fury
EFIKNNOS	finnesko
EFIKNORS	foreskin
EFIKNRSU	refusnik
EFIKORRW	firework
EFILLLSW	self-will
EFILLMOR	Fillmore
EFILLMTU	full time
	full-time
EFILLORV	overfill
EFILLORZ	Florizel
EFILLOSU	fusel-oil
EFILLRUY	irefully
EFILLSTY	stellify
EFILLTUY	futilely
EFILMORV	film over
EFILMSUY	emulsify
EFILNORU	fluorine
EFILNORW	in flower
EFILNOST	soft line
EFILOORT	roof tile
EFILOPRR	pro-lifer
EFILORTU	fluorite
EFILOSTT	loftiest
EFILPPSU	pipefuls
EFILPSTU	spiteful
EFILPSTY	self-pity
EFILRSST	riftless
EFILSTTW	swiftlet
EFIMNORR	informer
	reinform
	reniform
EFIMNRSS	firmness
EFIMNSTT	fitments
EFIMORRT	retiform
EFIMOSTT	ofttimes
EFINNORS	infernos
EFINORRT	frontier
EFIORRTT	retrofit
EFIOSTTU	fit to use
EFIPPRRY	frippery
EFIPRRUY	repurify
EFIPRTTY	prettify
EFIRSTUX	fixtures
EFKLLOOR	folklore
EFKNOORW	foreknow
EFKOORRV	fork over
EFKOOTUY	out of key
EFKORRTW	fretwork
EFLLLOWY	fellowly
EFLLLPTU	full-pelt
EFLLNOOW	lone wolf

Words marked □ can also be spelled with an initial capital letter

EFLLNSSU	fullness
EFLLNTUY	fluently
EFLLOORW	follower
EFLLORUV	overfull
EFLLOSST	soft sell
EFLLOUWY	woefully
EFLLRUUY	ruefully
EFLLSUUY	usefully
EFLMMRUY	flummery
EFLMOOTW	Tom Wolfe
EFLMORRY	formerly
EFLMORSS	formless
EFLNOOTW	wolf note
EFLNOPTY	plenty of
EFLNORTT	frontlet
EFLNOSST	soft lens
EFLNOSSU	foulness
EFLNOSSW	self-sown
EFLNOSTY	stonefly
EFLOORSS	roofless
EFLOORSW	foreslow
EFLOORVW	flow over
	overflow
EFLOOSST	footless
EFLOPRUW	powerful
EFLORSUY	yourself
EFLOSUUX	flexuous
EFLRSTUY	flustery
EFLRTTUY	fluttery
EFMOORST	foremost
EFMOORSU	foursome
EFNNOOOR	forenoon
EFNNOOTT	not often
EFNNOOTY	Fontenoy
EFNNORST	fornenst
EFNOOOTT	footnote
EFNOPSTU	soften up
EFNOSSST	softness
EFOOORST	footsore
EFOOPSTT	footstep
EFOORSTT	footrest
EFOPRRSS	press for
EFORRSST	fortress
EFORRSTY	forestry
EFORSSUV	fuss over
EGGGILNS	leggings
EGGGINOT	get going
EGGGNNOR	ronggeng
EGGGOOOS	goosegog
EGGHIINW	weighing
EGGHIRWY	Whiggery
EGGHRTUY	thuggery
EGGIINNR	reigning
EGGIINRV	grieving
EGGIKNOS	gingkoes
	ginkgoes
EGGILNRY	gingerly
EGGILQSU	squiggle
EGGILRRW	wriggler
EGGINOST	set going
EGGINPRU	ginger up
EGGINSSU	guessing
EGGIPRRY	priggery
EGGLMRSU	smuggler
EGGLNNOO	long-gone
EGGLRSTU	struggle
EGGMNTUY	nutmeggy
EGGNOOPS	egg-spoon
EGGNORTW	get wrong
EGGNRSUY	snuggery
EGGOORSU	gorgeous
EGGOOTUU	gouge out
EGGOPTTY	Peggotty
EGHHIIMT	high time
EGHHIIRS	high-rise
EGHHIIRW	high wire
EGHHILNO	high-lone
EGHHILTY	eighthly
EGHHINSS	highness
EGHHINTT	The Thing
	the thing
EGHHIPRU	higher-up
EGHHIPTY	type-high
EGHHORUW	rough-hew
EGHIILNR	hireling
EGHIINTV	thieving
EGHIINTW	in weight
EGHIIPRS	Respighi
EGHIIRST	tigerish
EGHILLNS	shelling
EGHILLNW	well-nigh
EGHILLOR	Holliger
EGHILNPT	light pen
EGHILNSS	shingles
EGHILNSV	shelving
EGHILNUW	glühwein□
EGHILRST	slighter
EGHINORV	hovering
EGHINPRS	Pershing
EGHINPSS	sphinges
EGHINRSW	Gershwin
EGHINSTT	The Sting
EGHIOPSU	pishogue
EGHIORSV	sigh over
EGHIOSTV	eightvos
EGHIOTUW	outweigh
	weigh out
EGHIQRTU	requight
EGHIRSTT	set right
EGHJNNOW	Gwen John
EGHLLNOR	Gellhorn
EGHLMNOO	long home
EGHLNRUY	hungerly
EGHLOORY	rheology
EGHLOOTY	ethology
	theology
EGHLORST	short leg
EGHMNOOY	homogeny
EGHMOPUY	hypogeum
EGHNOOST	The Goons
EGHNOPTU	gone phut
EGHNORUV	hung over
EGHNOTUU	Huguenot
EGHNOTUY	the young
EGHNRSTT	strength
EGIIKKLN	kinglike
EGIIKNSZ	king-size
EGIILNOR	religion□
EGIILNRS	Riesling
EGIILNRV	reviling
EGIILNSW	wiseling
EGIIMNRT	ring-time
EGIIMOPT	impetigo
EGIINNPR	ripening
EGIINNPW	Winnipeg
EGIINOPR	peignoir
EGIINORS	seignior
EGIINOTV	give in to
	give into
EGIINPRX	expiring
EGIINRRT	retiring
EGIINRSU	signieur
EGIINRSW	ringwise
EGIINRTU	intrigue
EGIINRTV	riveting
EGIINRVV	reviving
EGIINSTX	existing
EGIIOTTV	give it to
EGIITUXY	exiguity
EGIJNNNS	Jennings
EGIKKNRT	trekking
EGIKLNSS	kingless
EGIKLNSY	Kingsley
EGIKNORV	revoking
EGILLMNS	smelling
EGILLNOR	Negrillo
EGILLNOV	livelong
EGILLNOW	Lilongwe
EGILLNQU	quelling
EGILLNSW	swelling
EGILLOOR	gloriole
EGILLOTT	little go
EGILLRUV	Gulliver
EGILMNOT	long time
EGILMNPU	implunge
EGILMNST	smelting
EGILMOUU	eulogium
EGILNNST	nestling
EGILNNTT	nettling
EGILNORW	lowering
EGILNOSU	ligneous
EGILNOSW	longwise
EGILNOVV	evolving
EGILNRRY	erringly
EGILNRST	ringlets
	sterling
EGILNSSU	ugliness
EGILNSSW	wingless
EGILNSTT	settling
EGILNSUW	Lewis gun
EGILNTUX	exulting
EGILNTUY	Tinguely
EGILNVXY	vexingly

EGILRTTY	glittery
EGIMNOOR	Geronimo
EGIMNORS	Negroism
EGIMNPTT	tempting
EGIMNPTY	emptying
EGIMNRSS	grimness
EGIMNSTU	Mengistu
EGIMORST	ergotism
EGINNORS	nose-ring
EGINNORT	nitrogen
EGINNRRU	unerring
EGINNSSU	Guinness
EGINOORR	Rio Negro
EGINOORV	ingroove
EGINOOTV	give on to
	give onto
EGINOPRS	reposing
EGINOPRU	Perugino
EGINOPRY	pigeonry
EGINOPUV	give up on
EGINORRY	iron-grey
EGINORSS	goriness
EGINORST	Negritos
EGINORSV	sign over
EGINORTU	outreign
EGINORTW	towering
EGINORVW	overwing
EGINPRSS	pressing
EGINQRUY	querying
EGINQSTU	questing
EGINRRST	stringer
EGINRRTU	ring true
EGINRSSY	syringes
EGINRSTT	strigent
EGINRSVW	swerving
EGINRTTU	uttering
EGIORSST	strigose
EGIORSSU	griseous
EGIORSUV	grievous
EGIOSUUX	exiguous
EGIRRSTY	registry
EGISSYYZ	syzygies
EGJLNORU	jongleur
EGLLNNWY	Nell Gwyn
EGLMNOOP	long poem
EGLMNORT	long-term
EGLMNSSU	glumness
EGLMORSS	gormless
EGLNNTUY	ungently
EGLNOOOY	oenology
EGLNOOPY	penology
EGLNOORV	overlong
EGLNOOSV	love-song
EGLNORUU	longueur
EGLNRTUY	urgently
EGLOOPRU	prologue
EGLOOPTY	logotype
EGLOORSY	serology
EGLOOSXY	sexology
EGLORSSW	grow less
EGLORSUY	rugosely
EGMNOOOS	mongoose
EGMNSSSU	smugness
EGNNOOTY	ontogeny
EGNNOOUY	young one
EGNNOSTU	gunstone
EGNNOTUV	Vonnegut
EGNNRSUY	Grey nuns
EGNNSSSU	snugness
EGNNSTTU	tungsten
EGNOORRV	governor
EGNOORTT	go rotten
EGNOOSSS	Goossens
EGNOOTUX	ox-tongue
EGNOPPRU	oppugner
EGNORRST	stronger
EGNORSST	songster
EGNORSTU	sturgeon
EGNORSUW	wrong use
EGNSSTUU	Tunguses
EGOOORTV	go over to
EGOOPRRU	prorogue
EGOORRVW	overgrow
EGOORSTT	grottoes
EGOPRRSS	progress
EGOPRRSU	groupers
EGORTTTY	try to get
EHHIISTV	thievish
EHHILMNT	helminth
EHHILPTW	help with
EHHIOPTW	with hope
EHHIORTT	hitherto
EHHIOTTW	white-hot
EHHIRSSW	shrewish
EHHISSTT	the shits
EHHJMNOU	John Hume
EHHMNOTT	The Month
EHHMPRUY	Humphrey
EHHNOOPT	on the hop
EHHNOORS	shoehorn
EHHNOOSS	Shoshone
EHHNPSTY	Nephthys
EHHOOSTU	hothouse
EHHOPRTW	Hepworth
EHIIKLNS	Helsinki
EHIIKLRS	Irish elk
EHIIKLST	like this
EHIIKMNO	Khomeini
EHIIKNSV	Kishinev
EHIILMOS	homilies
EHIILMST	Eli Smith
EHIILMTT	the limit
EHIILRSV	liverish
EHIILTVW	live with
EHIIMPST	mephitis
EHIINNQU	heniquin
EHIINSVX	vixenish
EHIIPRST	ship-tire
EHIIPRSV	viperish
EHIIRRTX	heritrix
EHIIRSTT	thirties
EHIIRTTW	Whittier
EHIISTTX	sixtieth
EHIJLSWY	Jewishly
EHIKLOOP	hooplike
EHIKRSSW	whiskers
EHIKRSWY	whiskery
EHILLLMO	molehill
EHILLMOY	homelily
EHILLNSW	Shinwell
EHILLPTY	phyllite
EHILLRRT	thriller
EHILLRTY	litherly
EHILLSWW	wish well
EHILMNOP	Philemon
EHILMOOR	heirloom
EHILMQUU	umquhile
EHILNOSS	holiness
EHILNOST	Holstein
EHILNOSV	novelish
EHILNOTX	xenolith
EHILNSWY	newishly
EHILOOPZ	zoophile
EHILOPRS	pilhorse
EHILOPRT	heliport
EHILORTY	rhyolite
EHILPSST	pithless
EHILPSTU	sulphite
EHILRSTW	whistler❑
EHILRSTY	slithery
EHILRTTW	whittler
EHIMMRSY	shimmery
EHIMNNOO	home in on
EHIMNOPR	morphine
EHIMNORT	thermion
EHIMNOST	mine host
EHIMNOTU	home unit
EHIMNPST	shipment
EHIMOOST	smoothie
EHIMORST	isotherm
EHIMPPSS	psephism
EHIMPRSU	murphies
EHIMPSUU	euphuism
EHIMSSTY	methysis
EHINNOTU	the Union
EHINNOTW	non-white
EHINNRST	thinners
EHINNSST	thinness
EHINNSSU	sunshine
EHINOOPT	in the poo
EHINOPPR	hornpipe
EHINOPRY	Hyperion
EHINOPTT	the point
EHINORTY	in theory
EHINOSTU	outshine
EHINOTTW	tone with
EHINPSSX	sphinxes
EHIOOSST	stooshie
EHIORRTW	worthier
EHIORSTT	theorist
EHIORSTW	worthies
EHIORTVW	over with
EHIORTWZ	howitzer

EHIOSSTU	house-sit
EHIOTTUW	white out
	white-out
EHIPQSUY	physique
EHIPRSST	hipsters
	thripses
EHIPRSTW	whipster
EHIRSTTW	rest with
EHISSTUW	thuswise
EHJKMNOP	John Kemp
EHJNNNOV	John Venn
EHJOPSSU	Josephus
EHKLOSTY	lekythos
EHKLSSTU	the sulks
EHKMOORW	homework
EHKMORSW	meshwork
	mesh-work
EHKNNRSU	shrunken
EHKORSTW	the works
EHLLLOWY	Holywell
EHLLNSTU	nutshell
EHLLOOOP	loophole
EHLLOSTU	shell out
EHLMOORW	wormhole
EHLMORTY	motherly
EHLMOSUU	Mulhouse
EHLNOPSU	sulphone
EHLNOSTY	honestly
	on the sly
EHLNSSSU	lushness
EHLOOPRT	porthole
EHLOPPRT	thropple
EHLORSTT	throstle
EHLORSTY	hostelry
EHLORTTT	throttle
EHLOSSTY	thyloses
EHLRSSTU	ruthless
EHMMOOPR	romp home
EHMNOOST	smoothen
EHMNOOTW	home town
EHMNOOTY	hot money
EHMNOPSU	homespun
EHMOPRSU	Morpheus
EHMORSTY	smothery
EHMORTUV	vermouth□
EHMOSTTU	Thutmose
EHMOTUWY	Weymouth
EHMOTUZZ	mezuzoth
EHMRTUYY	eurythmy
EHNNOOPX	Xenophon
EHNNORRT	northern
EHNNORTU	on the run
	unthrone
EHNOOPPS	open shop
EHNOORVZ	Voronezh
EHNOOSSW	snowshoe
	snow-shoe
EHNOPPSU	push open
EHNORSTU	southern□
EHNOSTUU	nuthouse
	nut-house
EHNRSSTU	huntress
EHOOPRTY	orthoepy
EHOOPSTU	housetop
EHOOPTYZ	zoophyte
EHOORRUZ	zero hour
EHOORSST	orthoses
EHOORSTV	overshot
EHOOSTUU	outhouse
EHOPPRSS	shoppers
EHOPPRST	prophets
EHOPPRSY	prophesy
EHOPRSST	hot-press
EHOPRSUV	pushover
	push-over
EHORSTTT	the trots
EHORSTTW	the worst
EIIILMSS	similise
EIIILMSZ	similize
EIIIMMNS	minimise
EIIIMMNZ	minimize
EIIKLLMN	limekiln
EIIKLLMT	kill time
EIIKNNSS	inkiness
EIIKNNSW	wineskin
EIIKNRST	strike in
EIILLLVY	livelily
EIILLMNN	Minnelli
EIILLMNR	milliner
EIILLMNU	illumine
EIILLNTT	in little
EIILLOST	Sillitoe
EIILLPSS	ellipsis
EIILLSUV	illusive
EIILMNNS	Leninism
EIILMNNT	liniment
EIILMNOT	limonite
EIILMNSS	liminess
EIILMNST	Milstein
EIILMOPT	impolite
EIILMSSS	missiles
EIILMSTT	mistitle
EIILMSTY	myelitis
EIILNNST	Leninist
	listen in
EIILNOPT	pile it on
EIILNOSS	oiliness
EIILNSSW	wiliness
EIILNSTW	wine list
EIILNSTY	senility
EIILNTTU	intitule
EIILOTTV	Olivetti
EIILOTVV	volitive
EIILPRSU	plurisie
EIILPRTT	let it rip
EIILPSST	pitiless
EIILPSTY	pyelitis
EIILPTUV	live it up
EIILRTUZ	utilizer
EIILSSTU	Tiselius
EIIMMNNT	imminent
EIIMMNSU	immunise
EIIMMNUZ	immunize
EIIMMPRU	imperium
EIIMNNOT	in no time
EIIMNOPT	pimiento
EIIMNORT	Minorite
EIIMNOSS	emission
EIIMNOST	Timonise
EIIMNOTV	monitive
EIIMNOTZ	Timonize
EIIMNRST	minister
EIIMNRTT	intermit
EIIMNRTX	intermix
EIIMOPST	optimise
EIIMOPTZ	optimize
EIIMOSSV	omissive
EIIMOTVV	vomitive
EIIMPRSS	misprise
EIIMPRSZ	misprize
EIIMRSTW	miswrite
EIINNNPS	ninepins
EIINNOSU	unionise
EIINNOSV	envision
EIINNOUZ	unionize
EIINNPSS	spinnies
EIINNSST	tininess
EIINNSTV	invest in
EIINOPRS	ripienos
EIINOPTT	petition
EIINORRT	interior
EIINORSV	revision
EIINORTW	wire into
EIINOTVW	into view
EIINOVVZ	Zinoviev
EIINPRRS	inspirer
EIINPRST	pristine
EIINPSTZ	pint-size
EIINPTUV	punitive
EIINQRRU	inquirer
EIINQTUY	inequity
EIINRSST	sinister
EIINRSSW	wiriness
EIINRSTU	neuritis
EIINSTTZ	Steinitz
EIIOPRST	Poitiers
EIIOPSTV	positive
EIIORSTT	rise to it
EIIOSSTT	osteitis
EIIPPRTV	pit viper
EIIPRSTT	rispetti
EIIPRSTY	pyritise
EIIPRTYZ	pyritize
EIJJNTUY	jejunity
EIJLOOSU	Joe Louis
EIJNORTU	jointure
EIJNOSTT	jettison
EIKKLLOO	look like
EIKKLNNY	Kilkenny
EIKLLMNU	Mulliken
EIKLLNTW	well-knit
EIKLLNUY	unlikely
EIKLLORV	overkill

EIKLLOTY	likely to
EIKLMNOO	moonlike
EIKLMNOS	moleskin
EIKLNOOR	oerlikon □
EIKLNPRS	sprinkle
EIKLNRST	strinkle
EIKLNRTW	twinkler
EIKLOORT	rootlike
EIKLSSTT	skittles
EIKMNOPT	Potemkin
EIKMNOST	tokenism
EIKNNPSS	pinkness
EIKNOPRS	rose-pink
EIKNOPTY	key point
EIKNORST	on strike
EIKNPRTU	turnpike
EIKNRSTT	trinkets
EIKNSSTT	skin test
EIKOPPRW	pipework
EIKOPRSV	overskip
EIKORRWW	wirework
EIKPRRSU	spruiker
EIKPRSTU	strike up
EILLLNTY	lent-lily
EILLLPUV	pulville
EILLMNOS	Sémillon
EILLMNOU	linoleum
EILLMOPS	plimsole
EILLMOTT	Little Mo
EILLMPSS	misspell
EILLMPTU	multiple
EILLMUVX	vexillum
EILLNSTY	silently
	tinselly
EILLNSVY	snivelly
EILLOOSW	woollies
EILLOPRW	lower lip
EILLOPTX	exit poll
EILLOPTY	politely
EILLORST	trilloes
	trollies
EILLOTUY	I tell you
EILLRSTT	testrill
EILLRSVY	silverly
EILLRTUV	Tulliver
EILLSSST	listless
EILLSTTT	littlest
EILMMNOU	Moulmein
EILMNOOR	Leo Minor
EILMNOSU	emulsion
EILMNOTT	melt into
EILMNOTY	mylonite
EILMNPSS	limpness
EILMNRST	minstrel
EILMNSSS	slimness
EILMNTUY	minutely
	untimely
EILMOOPS	liposome
EILMOOST	toilsome
EILMOPRS	sperm oil
EILMOPST	milepost
	polemist
EILMOSTT	time slot
EILMOSUV	volumise
EILMOUVZ	volumize
EILMPRUY	impurely
EILMRSSY	remissly
EILMTTUU	lutetium
EILMTTUY	multeity
EILNNOST	insolent
EILNNOSW	snowline
EILNNPTY	in plenty
EILNNTTY	intently
EILNOOPS	polonise
EILNOOPZ	polonize
EILNOOST	oilstone
EILNOOTT	Ottoline
EILNOPRT	Interpol
EILNOPTY	Linotype®
EILNOSTT	listen to
EILNOSTU	outlines
EILNOSTV	novelist
EILNOTUV	involute
EILNPRST	splinter
EILNPSSU	splenius
EILNPSTU	listen up
EILNPSUY	supinely
EILNQUUY	uniquely
EILNRSTU	result in
EILNRSUU	Ursuline
EILNRTUV	virulent
EILNRTWY	winterly
EILNSSTU	utensils
EILNSSTW	westlins
EILNSTTU	lutenist
EILNSUWY	unwisely
EILOORWW	wire wool
EILOPRSU	perilous
EILOPRSV	overslip
EILOPSTX	exploits
EILOPTUV	live up to
EILORRTU	ulterior
EILORSTU	Ortelius
EILORTTY	toiletry
EILOSTTT	stiletto
EILPPPRU	upper lip
EILPPPRY	preppily
EILPPRST	stippler
EILPPRSU	supplier
EILPPRSY	slippery
EILPPRTU	pulpiter
EILPPSSU	supplies
EILPRSTT	splitter
EILPRSTY	priestly
EILPRSUU	purlieus
EILPRSUY	pleurisy
EILPRTTY	prettily
EILPRTUZ	Pulitzer
EILQRRSU	squirrel
EILQRSUY	squirely
EILRSSST	stirless
EILRSSTY	sisterly
EILRSTTU	surtitle
EILRSTTW	wristlet
EIMMMNOT	immoment
EIMMMORZ	momzerim
EIMMNORS	misnomer
EIMMNOTU	immune to
EIMMOPRU	emporium
EIMMORRT	Mortimer
EIMMOSTT	totemism
EIMMPRSU	premiums
EIMMRRST	Strimmer®
EIMNNOOV	move in on
EIMNNOTT	ointment
EIMNOOPS	impose on
EIMNOORT	remotion
EIMNOORV	omnivore
EIMNOOST	emotions
EIMNOPRT	orpiment
EIMNOPST	nepotism
	pimentos
EIMNOPTT	impotent
EIMNORSU	Monsieur
EIMNORTW	timeworn
	time-worn
EIMNORTY	enormity
EIMNPRSS	primness
EIMNPSST	misspent
EIMNRSST	trimness
EIMNRSTU	muster in
	terminus
EIMNRSTY	entryism
EIMOORST	motorise
EIMOORTZ	motorize
EIMOPPRR	improper
EIMOPRRS	primrose □
	promiser
EIMOPRRT	importer
EIMOPRRV	improver
EIMOPRST	imposter
EIMOPRUU	europium
EIMOPTTU	up to time
EIMOQSTU	misquote
EIMORRST	mortiser
EIMORRTT	remittor
EIMORRWW	wireworm
EIMORSTU	misroute
	moisture
EIMORSTV	mist over
EIMORSVW	overswim
EIMORTTW	two-timer
EIMOSSTZ	mestizos
EIMOSTTT	totemist
EIMOSTTU	titmouse
EIMQSTUY	mystique
EIMRRSSU	surmiser
EIMRSSST	mistress
EINNNOTT	intent on
EINNOORZ	zero in on
EINNOPRS	in person
EINNORSV	environs
EINNORTU	neutrino

Words marked □ can also be spelled with an initial capital letter

EINNORTV	inventor
EINNORWW	winnower
EINNOSSS	nosiness
EINNOSTU	not in use
EINNPSSU	puniness
EINNPSSY	spinneys
EINNPSXY	sixpenny
EINNRRTU	in return
EINNRTTU	nutrient
EINOOPRS	poisoner
EINOORST	senior to
EINOORZZ	ozonizer
EINOOSSZ	ooziness
EINOPQRU	in querpo
EINOPRRS	prisoner
EINOPRSS	ropiness
EINOPRST	pointers
EINOPRTU	eruption
EINOPSTT	nepotist
	set point
	step into
	step on it
EINOQSTU	question
EINOQTTU	not quite
	quotient
EINOQTUU	unique to
EINORRTU	Tournier
EINORSSS	rosiness
EINORSSU	neurosis
	resinous
EINORSTV	investor
EINORSTY	tyrosine
EINORSUV	souvenir
EINORTTU	ritenuto
EINORTTW	witter on
EINOSSSS	Sessions
EINOSSST	stenosis
EINOSTVY	venosity
EINPPSST	snippets
EINPPSTY	snippety
EINPRRST	sprinter
EINPRRTU	prurient
EINPRSST	spinster
EINPRSTU	unpriest
EINPRTTU	inputter
EINQRSTU	squinter
EINRSSST	instress
EINRSSXY	syrinxes
EINRSTTY	entryist
EINSSSSU	Senussis
EIOOPPRS	porpoise
EIOOPPST	opposite
EIOORRSS	sororise
EIOORRSZ	sororize
EIOORSTT	tortoise
EIOPRRSS	prioress
EIOPRRSU	superior □
EIOPRSTV	sportive
EIOPRSUV	pervious
	previous
	viperous
EIOPRTUZ	outprize
EIORRSST	resistor
EIORRSVY	revisory
EIORSSTT	Rossetti
EIORSTTU	tutorise
EIORSTUV	virtuose
	vitreous
EIORTTUW	write out
EIORTTUZ	tutorize
EIPPRRST	stripper
EIPQRSTU	quipster
EIPRRSSU	surprise
EIPRRSTZ	spritzer
EIQRRSTU	squirter
EIRTTTWY	twittery
EISSUUVV	Vesuvius
EJMNOOST	Tom Jones
EJMOPRUV	jump over
	overjump
EJNOOORT	Joe Orton
EJNORSUY	journeys
EJNSSSTU	justness
EKKMORSY	kromesky
EKLMNOSS	Smolensk
EKLNOOOR	looker-on
	onlooker
EKLOOORV	look over
	look-over
	overlook
EKLORSST	Klosters
EKLORSSW	workless
EKMOOSTU	smoke out
EKMORSSU	musk rose
EKMRSTUY	musketry
EKNNOPSU	unspoken
EKNOOPRW	open work
	openwork
EKOOPRRV	provoker
EKOORRVW	overwork
	work over
EKOPRSTU	upstroke
ELLLMOWY	mellowly
ELLLNSUY	sullenly
ELLMNOSY	solemnly
ELLMNOTY	moltenly
ELLMOORS	morellos
ELLMORUV	mull over
ELLMOSTT	Smollett
ELLMOSTU	smell out
ELLNNSSU	nullness
ELLNOORV	lovelorn
ELLNOPUW	well up on
ELLNORWW	well-worn
ELLNOSVY	slovenly
ELLNOUVY	unlovely
ELLOOPRT	Trollope
ELLOORRV	roll over
	roll-over
ELLOPRST	pollster
ELLOPRUV	pull over
	pullover
ELLOPSST	plotless
ELLOPSTU	spell out
ELLORRST	stroller
ELLORSTY	trolleys
ELLOSSSU	soulless
ELLOSTUW	outswell
ELLPPSUY	supplely
ELMMNOTY	momently
ELMNOOSS	moonless
ELMNOOSZ	zoom lens
ELMNOPSU	pulmones
ELMNORUY	Mulroney
ELMNUUZZ	unmuzzle
ELMOOPSY	polysome
ELMOORST	tremolos
ELMOORSY	morosely
ELMOOSSY	lysosome
ELMOPSYY	polysemy
ELMOSYYZ	lysozyme
ELNNOOSU	unloosen
ELNOOPSU	loosen up
ELNOPTTY	potently
ELNORSTU	turnsole
ELNORSVY	slovenry
ELNORTTY	rottenly
ELNOSSSW	slowness
ELNPPSUU	unsupple
ELNPRTUU	purulent
ELOOPRUW	owerloup
ELOORSST	rootless
ELOOSTUU	Toulouse
ELOPPRRY	properly
ELOPRRTY	porterly
ELOPRSTT	plotters
ELOPRSTY	prostyle
ELOPRSYY	pyrolyse
ELOPRYYZ	pyrolyze
ELOPSSST	spotless
	stopless
ELPRSSSU	spurless
ELPRSTTU	splutter
ELPRSTUU	rustle up
ELSSSTUY	styluses
EMMMNOTU	momentum
EMMNNOTU	monument □
EMMNORSU	summoner
EMMNOTTU	tomentum
EMMNOTYY	metonymy
EMMOORRS	Mrs Moore
EMMRRRUU	murmurer
	remurmur
EMMRSTYY	symmetry
EMNNOOOT	monotone
EMNOOPTY	monotype
	Monotype®
EMNOORST	monteros
	Montrose
EMNOORSU	enormous
EMNOORSW	newsroom
EMNOOSUV	venomous
EMNOOTUV	outvenom

EMNORSUU	numerous
EMNORTUX	Montreux
EMOOPRRT	promoter
EMOORRST	rest room
EMOPPRRT	prompter
EMOPRSSU	supremos
EMOPTTUY	empty out
EMORSSTU	strumose
EMOSSTVZ	zemstvos
EMPRRTUY	trumpery
EMPRSTTU	strumpet
ENNNOSTY	Tennyson
ENNOOOPT	open on to
	open onto
ENNOOORS	no sooner
ENNOOOTZ	entozoon
ENNOOPPT	opponent
ENNOORST	norteños
ENNOOSTT	nonettos
ENNOPRSU	unperson
ENNOPRUV	unproven
ENNOPTWY	twopenny
ENNPPTUY	tuppenny
ENNPRRUU	runner-up
ENOOORTW	one or two
ENOOOSSZ	zoonoses
ENOOPPST	postpone
ENOOPRSS	poorness
ENOORSVY	very soon
ENOPRTTU	putter-on
ENOPRTUW	uptowner
ENOPSSSY	synopses
ENORRTTU	return to
ENORRTUU	Tourneur
ENORRTUV	overturn
	turn over
	turnover
ENORSSSU	sourness
ENOSSSUU	sensuous
ENPRSSSY	spryness
ENRRRTUU	nurturer
EOOOPRSS	soporose
EOOPPRRS	proposer
	Prospero
EOOPPSST	postpose
EOOPRRST	troopers
EOOPRRTU	Europort
EOOPRRUV	pour over
EOOPRSTV	stop over
	stopover
EOOPRTUW	outpower
EOORRRSW	sorrower
EOORRSTT	resort to
EOORSSTU	oestrous
EOOSTTTW	set to two
EOPPRRTY	property
EOPPRSSU	supposer
EOPRRSTU	posturer
EOPRRUVY	purveyor
EOPRSSTU	press out
EOPRSTTZ	St-Tropez
EOPSTTUU	put to use
EOQQTUUU	tu quoque
EORRRTTU	torturer
EORRSSST	stressor
EORRSSTU	trousers
EORRSTTT	trotters
EORRSUVY	surveyor
EORRTUUV	trouveur
EORSSTTU	tutoress
EORSSTWY	Oswestry
EPPPRTUY	puppetry
EPPRSSSU	suppress
EPRSTTUY	sputtery

F

FFFGHIOT	fight off
FFGGINOO	going off
FFGHIIRT	Griffith
FFGHIORT	fight for
	right off
FFGHORSU	shrug off
FFGIILNP	piffling
FFGIINNS	sniffing
FFGIINPS	spiffing
FFGILMNU	muffling
FFGILNRU	ruffling
FFGINORW	wring off
FFGINSTU	stuffing
FFGLLOOU	full of go
FFHIIOTT	hit it off
FFHIISST	stiffish
FFHIISTY	fiftyish
FFHIMSTU	stuff him
FFHLORTY	froth-fly
FFHMOOTU	mouth off
FFHOOOST	offshoot
	shoot off
FFHOORTW	throw off
FFHOSTTU	hot stuff
FFIILNSY	sniffily
FFIILNTY	flintify
FFILLOPP	flip-flop
FFILLTUY	fitfully
FFILOPST	split off
FFILRTUU	fruitful
FFILSTUY	stuffily
FFIMORSU	fusiform
FFINOPRT	offprint
FFINOSTU	sniff out
FFIOPRST	strip off
FFKLORSU	forkfuls
FFLMNOOU	moufflon
FFNOSTUU	snuff out
FFOOORTU	four-foot
FFOOPSTU	spout off
FFOORRUU	frou-frou
FFOSTUUY	stuff you
FGGGIINR	frigging
FGGGILNO	flogging
FGGHIINT	fighting
FGGHINTU	gunfight
FGGIINRU	figuring
FGHIIKNS	kingfish
FGHIILNT	in-flight
FGHIINST	shifting
FGHIITTW	Whitgift
FGHILNSU	Flushing
FGHILRTU	rightful
FGHINORT	frothing
FGHINOST	of nights
FGHLORUU	furlough
FGIILNPP	flipping
FGIILNRT	trifling
FGIILNST	stifling
FGIILNTT	flitting
FGIINNSU	infusing
FGIINNUY	unifying
FGIINSTT	fittings
FGILNOOR	flooring
FGILNOOT	footling
FGILNOPP	flopping
FGILNOTU	fling out
FGILNTYY	fly-tying
FGILOTUY	guilty of
FGINNORT	fronting
FGINORRT	ring fort
FGINORST	frosting
FGKLNOOS	folk-song
FGLNORUW	wrongful
FGLOOOST	footslog
FGNOOOST	go soft on
FHHOORST	shofroth
FHIIKNTT	think fit
FHIILLTY	filthily
FHIILSTY	shiftily
FHIINPSU	finish up
FHIKMNOS	monkfish
FHILLOOT	foothill
FHILLORT	hill fort
	hill-fort
FHILMPSU	lumpfish
FHILMRTU	mirthful
FHILOOTW	fool with
FHILOPST	shoplift
FHILORSU	flourish
FHILORTY	frothily
FHIMPRSU	frumpish
FHIOOPTT	Photofit®
FHIORSTY	fortyish
FHLLOSTU	slothful
FHLMOTUU	mouthful
FHLORTUY	fourthly
FHLOTUUY	youthful
FHLRTTUU	truthful
FHOOORST	forsooth
	shoot for
FHOORRST	for short
	short for
FHOORTWY	worthy of
FHOPRTTU	put forth
FIIINNTY	infinity
FIIJMORU	Fujimori

FIIKLRSY	friskily
FIILLMSY	flimsily
FIILLNTY	flintily
FIILMNOR	film noir
FIILMNRY	infirmly
FIILMOPR	piliform
FIILMPSY	simplify
FIILTTUY	futility
FIIMOPRS	pisiform
FIIMOSTY	moistify
FIINNOSU	infusion
FIINORTU	fruition
FIIQUYZZ	quizzify
FIKKLNOS	kinsfolk
FILLLTTU	full tilt
	full-tilt
FILLLUWY	wilfully
FILLNORS	no frills
	no-frills
FILLNSUY	sinfully
FILLOPPY	floppily
FILNOOOT	fool into
FILNOOTY	if only to
FILOOPRS	spoil for
FILORSTY	frostily
FILRSTTU	tristful
FILSTTUY	stultify
FIMNNOOR	inform on
FIMORTUY	fumitory
FIMRSTUU	futurism□
FINOPRTU	put in for
FINORRTU	run for it
FIOORSSU	furiosos
FIORTTUY	fortuity
FIPRSSUY	Prussify
FIRSTTUU	futurist
FIRTTUUY	futurity
FJLLOUYY	joyfully
FKOOORTW	footwork
FLLMNOOU	full moon
FLLNOOOW	follow on
	follow-on
FLLNOTUY	not fully
FLLOOPUW	follow up
	follow-up
	upfollow
FLLOPSTU	full stop
FLLOSSTU	full toss
FLMNORUU	mournful
FLMOOORW	moorfowl
FLMOORSU	roomfuls
FLMOPPRU	plump for
FLNOOPSU	spoonful
FLOOSSTW	soft-slow
FLRSTTUU	trustful
FMNOORTT	Montfort
FMOORSSU	Formosus
FMRSSTUU	frustums
FNOORTUU	run out of
FNOORTUW	outfrown
FOOOPTTU	opt out of
FOOPSSTT	soft spot
FOORRRSY	sorry for

G

GGGGIILN	giggling
GGGIILNN	niggling
GGGIJLNU	juggling
GGGILNPU	plugging
GGGILNRU	gurgling
GGHHIISW	Whiggish
GGHHISTU	thuggish
GGHIILNT	lighting
GGHIIMSW	Whiggism
GGHIINST	sighting
GGHIIPRS	priggish
GGHILSSU	sluggish
GGHKNNOO	Hong Kong
GGHNORUY	go hungry
GGIIINNT	igniting
GGIIINNV	giving in
	giving-in
GGIILLNR	grilling
GGIILMNN	mingling
GGIILMNY	ginglymi
GGIILNNS	gin sling
GGIILNNT	glinting
	tingling
GGIINNOR	groining
	ignoring
GGIINNRW	wringing
GGIINNST	stinging
GGIINNSW	swinging
GGIINNUV	ungiving
GGIINPPR	gripping
GGIINPUV	giving up
	giving-up
GGIIRRSS	grisgris
GGIKKNNO	King Kong
GGILNNOU	lounging
GGILNNPU	plunging
GGILNORW	growling
GGILNORY	glorying
GGILNUZZ	guzzling
GGILQSUY	squiggly
GGINNOOS	goings-on
GGINNOPP	ping pong
	ping-pong
GGINNOPS	sponging
GGINNOSS	singsong
GGINNOTU	tonguing
GGINNRTU	grunting
GGINOOTU	going out
	going-out
	outgoing
GGINOPRU	grouping
GGINORTU	grouting
GGLLOOWY	gollywog
GGLLOPUW	glow plug
GGLLPUUY	plug-ugly
GGOOOORR	groo-groo
GHHIIKRS	high-risk
GHHIILST	lightish
GHHIJMPU	high jump
GHHILOSU	ghoulish
GHHINNOO	High Noon
	high noon
GHHIOPST	high spot
GHHIORSU	roughish
GHHIOSTU	toughish
GHHOORTU	thorough
GHHOSTTU	thoughts
GHIIKNNT	thinking
GHIIKNPS	kingship
GHIIKNRS	shirking
GHIILLNS	shilling
GHIILMST	mislight
GHIILMTY	mightily
GHIILNRW	whirling
GHIILTTW	twilight
GHIINNNT	thinning
GHIINOTW	go in with
GHIINPPS	shipping
GHIINPPW	whipping
GHIINRRW	whirring
GHIINRTV	thriving
GHIINWZZ	whizzing
GHIIORSU	Ishiguro
GHIIORSV	vigorish
GHIIOSTV	Visigoth
GHIIRSTT	rightist
GHIISTTT	sit tight
GHIJKNNO	King John
GHIKLNTY	knightly□
GHIKLSTY	skylight
GHIKMRUU	Gurmukhi
GHIKNNTU	unknight
GHILLSTY	slightly
GHILNOPS	longship
GHILNOPU	plough in
GHILNRUY	hungrily
GHILNSTU	sunlight
GHILOPRS	shop-girl
GHILORSW	showgirl
GHILPRTY	triglyph
GHIMNOPR	morphing
GHIMNPTU	thumping
GHIMNSTU	gunsmith
GHINNNSU	shunning
GHINNORT	northing
GHINOOST	shooting
	soothing
GHINOPPS	shopping
GHINOPPW	whopping
GHINORTT	not right
GHINORTW	right now
	Worthing
GHINOSSU	housings
GHINOSTU	shouting
GHINOSUY	youngish
GHINOTTU	outnight
GHINSSTU	hustings
GHINSTTU	shutting

GHIORTTU	outright
	right out
GHIPRTTU	put right
GHJNRUUY	hung jury
GHLMOOOY	homology
GHLNNOOR	Longhorn
GHLNOORU	hourlong
GHLOOORY	horology
GHMNNOTU	Thom Gunn
GHNNOPUU	hung up on
GHNOSTUU	unsought
GHOORTUU	rough out
GHOORTUY	yoghourt
GHOOTTUU	tough out
GIIILMNT	limiting
GIIILNNU	linguini
GIIILNNV	living-in
GIIILOTV	vitiligo
GIIILSUV	Vigilius
GIIINNOR	in origin
GIIINNOT	ignition
GIIINNTV	inviting
GIIINSTV	visiting
GIIJMNOS	jingoism
GIIJNNOT	jointing
GIIJNOST	jingoist
GIIKMMNS	skimming
GIIKMNPS	skimping
GIIKNNST	stinking
GIIKNNTT	knitting
GIIKNPPS	skipping
GIIKNRST	skirting
	striking
GIILLNRT	Trilling
GIILLPSW	pigswill
GIILLTUY	guiltily
GIILLTYZ	glitzily
GIILMMNS	slimming
GIILMPSU	pugilism
GIILNNPU	lining up
GIILNNSY	lyings-in
GIILNOPS	spoiling
GIILNOPT	piloting
GIILNPPR	rippling
GIILNPPS	slipping
GIILNQSU	quisling ❑
GIILNQTU	quilting
GIILNRST	Stirling
GIILNRSW	swirling
GIILNRTW	twirling
GIILNRVY	virginly
GIILNSTT	stilting
GIILNSTU	linguist
GIILNSTY	stingily
GIILNSZZ	sizzling
GIILPSTU	pugilist
GIIMMNRT	trimming
GIIMMNSW	swimming
GIIMNNOY	ignominy
GIIMNOPS	imposing
GIIMNOTT	omitting
GIIMNOTV	vomiting
GIINNNPS	spinning
GIINNNSW	winnings
GIINNNTW	twinning
GIINNOPT	pointing
GIINNPPS	snipping
GIINNPRT	printing
GIINNRTU	untiring
GIINNSTT	stinting
GIINOPTV	pivoting
GIINORST	roisting
GIINPRSU	uprising
GIINPSTT	spitting
GIINQTTU	quitting
GIINQUZZ	quizzing
GIINRRST	stirring
GIINRSTV	striving
GIINRSTW	writings
GIINSTTW	twisting
GIIORRST	rigorist
GIIPRSTZ	spritzig
GIJKLNOY	jokingly
GIJNOSTT	jottings
GIKKLNSU	skulking
GIKLNNRU	knurling
GIKNNOST	Kingston
	stonking
GIKNOPRW	grow pink
GIKNORSW	workings
GILLMOOY	gloomily
GILLNOPS	long slip
GILLNOSY	losingly
GILLNOVY	lovingly
GILLNPUY	pulingly
GILLNSUY	sullying
GILLOSSY	glossily
GILMMNSU	slumming
GILMMTUY	multigym
GILMNOPY	mopingly
GILMNOTT	mottling
GILMNOVY	movingly
GILMNSUY	musingly
GILMPRUY	grumpily
GILNNORU	iron lung
GILNNOSU	Longinus
GILNNOUV	unloving
GILNNRSU	nursling
GILNOOSY	Sinology
GILNOOWY	wooingly
GILNOPPT	toppling
GILNOPSY	posingly
	spongily
GILNOPTT	plotting
GILNOTUY	outlying
GILNPRYY	pryingly
GILNPUZZ	puzzling
GILNRSTU	rustling
GILNRTYY	tryingly
GILOOORS	rosoglio
GILOOOST	oologist
GILOORSU	glorious
GILOORVY	virology
GILOOSSS	isogloss
GIMMNRUY	gin rummy
GIMNNORS	mornings
GIMNNORU	mourning
GIMNNOTU	mounting
GIMNNOUV	unmoving
GIMNOPTU	gumption
GIMNORRW	ringworm
GIMNORST	storming
GIMNOSYY	misogyny
GINNNSTU	stunning
GINNOOPS	snooping
GINNOOSZ	snoozing
GINNOOTU	go in unto
GINNOPRS	spring on
GINNOPTU	gunpoint
GINNOPUW	owning-up
GINNORST	snorting
GINNPRSU	spurning
GINNRSTU	unstring
GINOOPPS	opposing
GINOOPST	stooping
GINOORTW	grow into
GINOPPST	stopping
GINOPRST	sporting
GINOPSST	signpost
GINOPSTT	spotting
GINORRWY	worrying
GINORSTT	Storting
GINORTTU	tutoring
GINORTUW	wring out
GINOSTTW	swotting
GINPPRSU	spring up
	upspring
GINPRSTU	spurting
	string up
GINPRSUU	pursuing
	usurping
GINRSSTU	trussing
GINRSTTU	trusting
GIOOORSV	vigoroso
GIOOPRRS	porrigos
GIOORRSU	rigorous
GIOORSUV	vigorous
GIOPRRSU	prurigos
GIORSTUY	rugosity
GJLMNOPU	long jump
GLLOOPTY	polyglot ❑
GLLOOSWY	go slowly
GLMNOOOT	glom on to
	monoglot
GLMNRTUU	ngultrum
GLMOORWW	glowworm
	glow-worm
GLNOOOSY	nosology
GLNOOOTY	ontology
GLNOOPST	long stop
GLNOPYYY	polygyny
GLNORSTY	strongly
GLNORTUW	lungwort

GLNOTTUY gluttony
GLOOOPSY posology
GLOOOPTY topology
GLOORSUU orgulous
GMMNOTUY tommy-gun
GMNNOOYY monogyny
GNNRSTUU unstrung
GNOOOTTW go to town
GNPRSTUU strung up
GOOOPTTT got to pot
GOOPPPRU pop group
GOORSSTU gross out

H

HHHHSSUU hush-hush
HHIIOORT Hirohito
HHIIPSST phthisis
HHIISTTW with this
HHJNNOTU John Hunt
HHJNORTU John Hurt
HHJNOSSU John Huss
HHMPRSUY Humphrys
HHOOOOPP pooh-pooh
HHOOPPRS phosphor
HHORRSUU rush hour
HIIILMNS nihilism
HIIILNST nihilist
HIIILNTY nihility
HIIILPPP Philippi
HIIINRST rhinitis
HIIJNOTW join with
HIIKLNTW link with
HIIKMNST misthink
HIIKMRSS skirmish
HIIKOPRS piroshki
HIIKOPRZ pirozhki
HIIKQRSU quirkish
HIIKSSTT skittish
HIILLPPS Phillips
HIILMOST homilist
HIILMPSY impishly
HIILMSWY whimsily
HIILMTUY humility
HIILPSSY syphilis
HIILRSTY shirtily
HIIMNSTT tinsmith
HIIMOPSS phimosis
HIINORST histrion
HIIORSST histrios
HIIPPQSU quippish
HIJMPPSU jump ship
HIKNNOTT not think
HIKNOOST in shtook
HIKNOTTU outthink
out-think
think out
HIKOOPSS spookish
HIKOPSSY kyphosis
HIKORTWW work with
HILLLOSU Solihull
HILLMSUY mulishly
HILLNOUY unholily
HILMNOOT monolith
HILMOPSY mopishly
HILNOSTY tonishly
HILOORST short-oil
HILOOTTY toothily
HILOPPSU polish up
HILOPPSY popishly
HILORTWY Holy Writ
holy writ
worthily
HILOSTYY toyishly
HILPPRSU purplish
HILPPSUY uppishly
HILSSTTU sluttish
HIMMOPRU Phormium
HIMOOPRS isomorph
HIMOPRSW shipworm
HIMORSTU humorist
HIMOTTVZ mitzvoth
HINNORTW worn thin
HINNSSUY sunshiny
HINOORST hornitos
HINOORSU Honorius
HINOPSSY hypnosis
HINOPSTU push into
HINOPSTW township
HINORTXY thyroxin
HINOSTTU Tithonus
HINRSTTU thrust in
HIOORSST orthosis
HIOOSSTT shootist
HIOPSTWY show pity
HIORRSSY sorryish
HIOSSTTU stoutish
HIPSSSUY Sisyphus
HJKNNOOX John Knox
HJNOOOPR poor-John
HJNOOOTT Otto John
HJNOORSS John Ross
HKMOOORW hookworm
HKOOPRSW workshop
HLLLOOWY hollowly
HLLMNOOU monohull
HLLNOOUU Honolulu
HLMOOSTY smoothly
HLMOPTUY Plymouth
HLNOOSUW Hounslow
HLOOPRRY lorry-hop
HLPRSUUY sulphury
HMMNOOTU Monmouth
HMMOORSU mushroom
HMNOOOST moonshot
HMNOOPST Thompson
HMNOOSTU unsmooth
HMNOPSYY symphony
HMNOPYYY hyponymy
HMOOORSW showroom
HMOORSUU humorous
HNOOPRRT Northrop
HNORRSTU run short
HNORTUWY unworthy
HOOOSTTU shoot-out
HOOOSTTW two hoots
HOORTTUW outworth
throw out
HOOSTTUU shout out
HOPPRRYY porphyry❑
HOPRRSTU Portrush
HPRSTTUU upthrust

I

IIIIPPRR piri-piri
IIIKLNPS spilikin
IIILLMNP minipill
IIILLNOS Illinois
IIILMRSV virilism
IIILNOPP Pilipino
IIILRTVY virility
IIIMMNST intimism
IIIMMPRS imprimis
IIINPRST inspirit
IIINQTUY iniquity
IIJJSTUU jiu-jitsu
IIJKNNSY Nijinsky
IIJNNSTU ninjitsu
IIJRSSUU sui juris
IIKKORSS Sikorski
IIKLMPSY skimpily
IIKLQRUY quirkily
IIKNNSTU sink unit
IIKNOPST Tok Pisin
IIKNOSTT stotinki
IILLLPUV pulvilli
IILLMNOS millions
IILLMRTU trillium
IILLNOSU illusion
IILLNOSZ zillions
IILLOPUV pulvilio
IILMNOSU Limousin
IILMOTTY motility
IILNNOOT nolition
IILNOOTV volition
IILNOPST slip into
IILNPPST split pin
IILOPSSS psilosis
IILOPSTY pilosity
IIMMNTUY immunity
IIMMOPST optimism
IIMNNOOT in motion
monition
IIMNNOSU unionism❑
IIMNNOTU munition
IIMNOOSS omission
IIMNOPRS imprison
IIMNOPST mispoint
IIMNORTT intromit
IIMNORTY minority
IIMNPRST misprint
IIMNPTUY impunity
IIMNRSTY ministry
IIMOPSTT optimist

IIMORSSU	Missouri
IIMOTTVY	motivity
IIMPRTUY	impurity
IIMRRTTU	trimurti❑
IIMRRTUV	triumvir
IIMSSTUW	swimsuit
IINNNOSU	in unison
IINNOOPS	opinions
IINNOPPT	pinpoint
	pin-point
IINNOSST	insist on
IINNOSTU	unionist
IINNRTTU	turn it in
IINNSTTU	tinnitus
IINOOPST	position
IINOSTVY	vinosity
IINPRSTW	wrist pin
IINRTTUY	triunity
IIOOPSTV	oviposit
IIOOQRSU	Iroquois
IIOOSTTY	otiosity
IIOPRRTY	priority
IIORSSTV	visitors
IIORSTUV	virtuosi
IIPRRSTU	pruritis
IJLLORTU	Trujillo
IJMOPTTU	jump to it!
IJMPSTUU	jumpsuit
IJNNSTUU	ninjutsu
IJNOORTU	junior to
IKKLNOOP	look pink
IKKLNOSY	kolinsky
IKKORSSY	Sikorsky
IKLLOOTV	kilovolt
IKLMORSW	silkworm
IKLNNOOO	look in on
IKLNOOOT	look into
IKLNOPST	slipknot
IKLNPSSU	spun silk
IKLOOPSY	spookily
IKLOPSTY	sky pilot
IKNOOPPS	Spion Kop
IKNOORTW	work into
IKNOSTTU	stink out
IKOPSSTU	kiss up to
IKORSSTU	kurtosis
ILLLMOPS	plimsoll
ILLLOOPP	lollipop
ILLMOSSY	lissomly
ILLMPTUY	multiply
ILLOOPRT	Portillo
ILLOORSZ	zorillos
ILLOPPSY	sloppily
ILLOPRXY	prolixly
ILLORSUY	illusory
ILLOSTUW	swill out
ILLOTTWY	wittolly
ILLRSTUY	sultrily
ILMNOOPU	polonium
ILMNOSUU	luminous
ILMOPPSU	populism

ILMORSTY	stormily
ILMOSTUY	timously
ILMPSTUY	stumpily
ILMSSTUU	stimulus
ILMSTTUY	smuttily
ILNNOTUW	until now
ILNOOPSU	Polonius
ILNOOPSV	volpinos
ILNOOPSY	spoonily
ILNOOPTW	low point
ILNOOSTU	solution
ILNOOSTY	snootily
ILNOOTUV	volution
ILNOPSTU	Plotinus
	unspoilt
ILNOSSTW	stowlins
ILNOSTTY	snottily
ILNPSUUV	pulvinus
ILOORSTU	risoluto
ILOPPSTU	populist
ILOPRSTY	sportily
ILOPSTTY	spottily
ILRSTTUY	trustily
IMMRTTUU	rum-ti-tum
IMNNOOOZ	zoom in on
IMNNOOTT	monotint
IMNNOSUU	numinous
IMNOORRS	Morrison
IMNOORST	trominos
IMNOORTY	monitory
	tiny room
IMNOORVY	omnivory
IMNOPPRU	pump iron
IMNOSTUU	mutinous
IMOOPRRS	promisor
IMOOPRST	impostor
IMOOQSTU	mosquito
IMOORSTT	motorist
IMOORSTU	sumotori
	timorous
IMOORTVY	vomitory
IMORSTTZ	St Moritz
IMRSSTTU	mistrust
IMRSSTTY	mistryst
INNNNOOU	non-union
INNOOPSS	sponsion
INNOOPSU	unpoison
INNORTTU	turn into
INNPRRTU	print run
INOOPPTT	top point
INOOPRST	positron
INOOPSTT	spittoon
INOOPTTU	outpoint
	point out
INOORSTY	sonority
INOPRTTU	printout
INOPSSSY	synopsis
INORSSUV	sun visor
INORTTWY	try to win
INPRTTUU	turn it up
IOOPRRSV	provisor

IOOPRSSV	provisos
IOOPRSTY	isotropy
	porosity
IOORRSTY	sorority
IOORSSTT	risottos
IOORSSUV	voussoir
IOORSTUV	virtuoso
IOORSUUX	uxorious
IOOSSTTU	stotious
IOOSTTUZ	zoot suit
IOPRRSUV	provirus
IOPRSSUU	spurious
IOPRSTTU	outstrip
	strip out
IOPRSTUU	poursuit
IOQRTUXY	quixotry
IORRSUVV	survivor
IORSSUUU	usurious
IORSTTUY	touristy
IORSTUUV	virtuous
IPRRSTUU	pruritus

J

JLNOSTUY	only just
JLNSTUUY	unjustly
JLOOSUYY	joyously
JMNOOPTU	jump onto

K

KKLMUYYZ	Kyzyl-Kum
KKOOOSUY	Yokosuko
KLLMNSUU	numskull
KLNOOOOT	look onto
KLNOOOPU	look upon
KLNORSTY	klystron
KLOOOPTU	look up to
KLOOORVY	Korolyov
KMOOORRW	workroom
KNOOOOOR	Oroonoko
KNOOPRUW	work upon
KNOORTWY	Yorktown
KNRRTTUU	turn Turk
KOOPRSTW	stop work

L

LLNOORST	stroll on!
LLOOPRTY	trollopy
LLOOPRYY	roly-poly
LMNOOOPY	monopoly
	Monopoly®
LMOORSWW	slowworm
LMOPPRTY	promptly
LMRSSTUU	lustrums
LNOOOPRT	poltroon
LNOOPPRY	propylon
LNOOSWWY	snowy owl
LOOOORSS	olorosos
LOOPPSUU	populous
LOOPPSUY	polypous
LOOPRSTT	STOLport
LORSSTUU	lustrous

M

MMNOPSUU summon up
MMOORTTY tommyrot
tommy-rot
MNNOOOTY monotony
MNNOSYYY synonymy
MNOOORST Nostromo
MNOOORXY oxymoron
MNOOPTYY toponymy
MNORSTUU surmount
MNOSTUUU Mount Usu
MOOORRTW tomorrow
MOORSTUU tumorous
MORSSTUU strumous

N

NNOORTUU run out on
NNOPRTUU turn upon
NOOORSSU sonorous
NOOPSTUW swot up on
NORRSTUU turn sour
NRSTTUUY untrusty

O

OOOTTTUU out to out
OOPRSTTU outsport
OORRTUWY worry out
OORSTTUU tortuous
OORSTTYY Toy Story
OPPRSTUU sprout up
OPRSSSUU sourpuss
RRSSSUUU susurrus

9 letters

A

AAAABCLLV balaclava❑
AAAABDDHM Ahmadabad
AAAABDHLL Allahabad
AAAABIKLL balalaika
AAAABIRRT Barataria
AAAABJLMY jambalaya
AAAACCHMT tacamahac
AAAACCLLR Caracalla
AAAACDDNY Canada Day
AAAACDIMM macadamia
AAAACDJNR jacaranda
AAAACMNRT catamaran
AAAADILLM Dalai Lama
dalai lama
AAAAGNPRU Paranagua
AAAAHHJMR maharajah
AAAAHLPTU Atahualpa
AAAAHMNPT panama hat
AAAAILLPR paralalia
AAAAINSST Anastasia
AAAAKKNRT Karnataka
AAAAMPRTT paramatta
AAAANNSTY Santayana
AAABBDEIS Adis Abeba
AAABBDINR Barbadian
AAABBENNS be bananas
AAABBINRR barbarian
AAABCCHLN bacchanal❑
AAABCCHNR charabanc
AAABCDRRU barracuda
AAABCEIRS scarabaei
AAABCEKKM make a back
AAABCEKKT take aback
AAABCELTU acetabula
AAABCESSY easy as ABC
AAABCIKTT katabatic
AAABCIMOR Maracaibo
AAABCINPR pan-Arabic
AAABCKNNT cantabank
AAABCLMOR carambola
AAABCLMRU ambulacra
AAABCLNOT canal-boat
AAABDEHNR bear a hand
AAABDELNR Aldebaran
AAABDELPT adaptable
AAABDENRS sarabande
AAABDGIMR Digambara
AAABDHHKS Ashkhabad
AAABDILLS sabadilla
AAABDILMS Islamabad
AAABDINWY in a bad way
AAABDLNNO à l'abandon
AAABEHHSV have a bash
AAABEHHTV have a bath
AAABEHKTT take a bath
AAABEHLLV have a ball
AAABEHSTV have a stab
AAABEILLV available
AAABEKPRR parabrake
AAABEKRWY break away
breakaway
AAABELLNN Annabella
AAABELLPT palatable
AAABELNST Alan Bates
AAABELRST alabaster
AAABELWYZ blaze away
AAABGLNOR Anglo-Arab
AAABGLWYY Galway Bay
AAABGNNOS go bananas
AAABHIMSY Shibayama
AAABHLRTZ balthazar
AAABHNOST Naas Botha
AAABILLTV ablatival
AAABILLVY availably
AAABILNRR Brian Lara
AAABLLPTY palatably
AAABLOPRS parabolas
AAABMNSTY Tasman Bay
AAABNNOPT top banana
AAACCCHHH cha-cha-cha
AAACCCKNR crack a can
AAACCDELV cavalcade
AAACCHTWY catch away
AAACCINSU Caucasian
AAACCIRTT ataractic
AAACDDNRY Canada Dry®

AAACDEKMR	make a card
AAACDHNRS	sandarach
AAACDNRSS	Cassandra
AAACEEFKM	make a face
AAACEEHRV	have a care
AAACEGLNT	at a glance
AAACEGNRT	Cartagena
AAACEHLNV	avalanche
AAACEHSWY	chase away
AAACEIMNR	Americana
AAACEIMNT	catamenia
AAACEIMPR	paramecia
AAACEKLLM	make a call
AAACELLPP	a cappella
AAACELRWY	clear away
AAACEMMNR	cameraman
AAACFILNT	fanatical
AAACGHLLN	Callaghan
AAACGINRU	Nicaragua
AAACGLLSW	scallawag
AAACGLNRS	Carl Sagan
AAACHIMNT	matachina
AAACHIRSZ	Zacharias
AAACHKKMT	Kamchatka
AAACHLLLT	call a halt
AAACHLNRT	charlatan
AAACHLPRR	chaparral
AAACHLRRT	catarrhal
AAACILLMR	camarilla
AAACILNOR	Aaronical
AAACILNRT	lactarian
AAACILNRU	lacunaria
AAACILNST	satanical
AAACILRTU	actuarial
AAACINOPR	paranoiac
AAACINOTT	catatonia
AAACKLLNR	Alan Clark
AAACKLSSV	Caslavska
AAACKLSWY	slack away
AAACLMMPW	macaw-palm
AAACLMNPU	campanula
AAACMORST	sarcomata
AAACRRWYY	carry away
AAADDHMRY	hamadryad
AAADDLSSY	salad days
AAADEEKLM	make a deal
AAADEFFNR	fanfarade
AAADEGKLR	Lake Garda
AAADEGLMN	Magdalena
AAADEGNTV	advantage
AAADELMMR	marmalade
AAADELNRX	Alexandra
AAADEMNOT	adenomata
AAADEMNSU	ad nauseam
AAADEPRST	tapaderas
AAADFNRSY	András Fay
AAADGILRU	La Guardia
AAADGLRVX	gravadlax
AAADGNNRT	D'Artagnan
AAADGNPPR	grandpapa
AAADHHPRZ	haphazard

AAADHIOPR	adiaphora
AAADHNNTY	at any hand
AAADILMNT	Dalmatian
AAADILPRS	paradisal
AAADINRYY	a rainy day
AAADIOPPR	parapodia
AAADKMNRS	Samarkand
AAADLMNTY	adamantly
AAADLNNSY	analysand
AAADNRSSS	Sassandra
AAADPRRRT	radar trap
AAAEEEGNS	Aegean Sea
AAAEEHMNR	maharanee
AAAEEKKLT	take a leak
AAAEEKLMM	make a meal
AAAEEKMRW	make aware
AAAEEKSTT	take a seat
AAAEFHKLW	half-awake
AAAEGGRTV	aggravate
AAAEGHOTV	have a go at
AAAEGILNS	analgesia
AAAEGIQRU	aqua regia
AAAEGLMTU	Guatemala
AAAEGLNNT	at an angle
AAAEGLSSV	vassalage
AAAEHHSVW	have a wash
AAAEHLNOV	have a loan
AAAEHLPVW	alpha wave
AAAEHMMOT	haematoma
AAAEHMNST	anathemas
AAAEIKLNZ	Elia Kazan
AAAEIMNRS	Amerasian
AAAEIQTUV	aqua vitae
AAAEKKLTW	take a walk
AAAEKLNSY	Lake Nyasa
AAAEKNTWY	taken away
AAAEKPRTT	take apart
AAAELLMRS	small area
AAAELLNPT	panatella
AAAELMMRT	alma mater
AAAELNNTT	antenatal
AAAELNPQU	aquaplane
AAAELRRRU	rural area
AAAELSTWY	steal away
AAAELSVWY	slave away
AAAEMNSST	Tasman Sea
AAAEMPRST	aspartame
AAAENRTTY	at any rate
AAAEPRRTT	tear apart
AAAEPRSSS	apsarases
AAAESTWWY	waste away
AAAFGIPST	fat as a pig
AAAFGLRRT	Trafalgar
AAAFGMSTU	Famagusta
AAAFGORSS	go as far as
AAAFIKNRS	Afrikaans
AAAFILMNT	animal fat
AAAFINRSS	in as far as
AAAFLLPRT	fall apart
AAAFLMRSY	Alf Ramsay
AAAFLORST	solfatara

AAAFRSSSS	sassafras
AAAGGLOPS	galapagos
	Galápagos
AAAGHMPRS	Sarah Gamp
AAAGHPPRR	paragraph
AAAGILNST	Galatians
AAAGIMNOT	angio-mata
AAAGIMNRV	gravamina
AAAGIMRRT	margarita
AAAGINSST	as against
AAAGJNNRU	Nagarjuna
AAAGLNRSU	Alan Sugar
AAAGMMRSY	gamma rays
AAAGNORRT	Tarragona
AAAGORSSS	Saragossa
AAAGPRSSU	asparagus
AAAHHLLMS	mashallah
AAAHIKNRT	Katharina
AAAHILMSY	Himalayas
AAAHIMNRU	marihuana
AAAHJNRST	Rajasthan
AAAHKMOTV	Akhmatova
AAAHKNNOR	Hank Aaron
AAAHKNRST	astrakhan □
AAAHLLOTY	ayatollah □
AAAHLLSTT	as all that
AAAHLOPSS	lhasa apso
AAAHMNNTT	Manhattan
AAAHMNRTT	harmattan
AAAHMOPRS	Ramaphosa
AAAHNOPTT	apathaton
AAAHSSTWY	stash away
AAAIIJNRY	Irian Jaya
AAAIINQTU	Aquitania
AAAIINRST	sanitaria
AAAIJMNRU	marijuana
AAAIJPPRT	Prajapati
AAAILMMMN	mammalian
AAAILMNSY	Malaysian
AAAILMORT	amatorial
AAAILNNOT	Anatolian
AAAILNNPR	planarian
AAAILNSST	assailant
AAAILPPRS	appraisal
AAAILRSTU	Australia
AAAILRTWY	trail away
AAAIMNNOZ	Amazonian
AAAIMNNST	Tasmanian
AAAIMNORT	inamorata
AAAIMNOST	Toamasina
AAAIMNRST	Samaritan
	Sarmatian
AAAINORST	sanatoria
AAAINORTT	natatoria
AAAINPSSU	Pausanias
AAAIPPRZZ	paparazzi
AAAIRSSTV	Sarasvati
AAAIRSSTW	Saraswati
AAAKMRSTU	Kama Sutra
	Kamasutra
AAALLMPSS	Las Palmas
AAALNRTTU	tarantula
AAALOOPPS	Appaloosa
AAALPPRTY	play a part
AAAMMNRST	man-at-arms
AAANNNPRU	Annapurna
AAAOPPRZZ	paparazzo
AAAPPRSTU	apparatus
AABBCCIRR	bric-à-brac
AABBCDKOR	backboard
AABBCEHLL	beach-ball
AABBCEINR	Caribbean
AABBCEKLN	black bean
AABBCEKLR	black bear
AABBCENOR	carob bean
AABBCILMS	cabbalism □
AABBCILST	cabbalist
AABBCKLLL	blackball
AABBCKLRT	Black Bart
AABBCKMRR	barmbrack
AABBCORSS	barbascos
AABBDDNOR	broadband
AABBDEELT	debatable
AABBDENOR	broad bean
AABBDNRSS	brass band
AABBEEKLR	breakable
AABBEEKRT	breakbeat
AABBEELLM	blameable
AABBEGLNR	Alban Berg
AABBEHHST	Bathsheba
AABBEHILT	habitable
AABBEINRT	rabbinate
AABBEIRRS	barbarise
AABBEIRRZ	barbarize
AABBEISST	sabbatise
AABBEISTZ	sabbatize
AABBEKMMO	make a bomb
AABBELLMY	blameably
AABBELOTW	at a low ebb
AABBERSTW	rabbet saw
AABBFFINY	Baffin Bay
AABBGORTU	brag about
AABBHILTY	habitably
AABBHKKOR	Bar Kokhba
AABBIILLL	ballabili
AABBIMRRS	barbarism
AABBIRRTY	barbarity
AABBNOTYY	Botany Bay
AABBNRTYY	Bantry Bay
AABBORRSU	barbarous
AABCCEEMS	Maccabees
AABCCEFKL	blackface
AABCCEHLT	catchable
AABCCEKPS	backspace
AABCCHHKT	hatchback
AABCCHKKU	huckaback
AABCCHNST	bacchants
AABCCIKKP	pickaback
AABCCIKLM	claim back
AABCCIORT	acrobatic
AABCCJKKL	blackjack
AABCCKKRT	backtrack

AABCCKLLO	coal-black
AABCCKRRY	carry back
AABCDDEFL	bald-faced
AABCDDORR	cardboard
AABCDEEFR	barefaced
AABCDEEHH	beachhead
AABCDEELN	danceable
AABCDEETY	beta decay
AABCDEHKL	blackhead
AABCDEILN	Alice band
AABCDEINT	can't abide
AABCDEIRR	barricade
AABCDEKLP	back-pedal
AABCDELRT	card table
AABCDEMSU	ambuscade
AABCDENNR	barn dance
AABCDENNU	abundance
AABCDHILN	baldachin
AABCDHILR	Archibald
AABCDIMNO	Cambodian
AABCDKRSW	backwards
AABCDNOOR	carbonado
AABCDORST	broadcast
AABCEEELP	peaceable
AABCEEHLR	reachable
AABCEEHLT	teachable
AABCEEKLS	leaseback
AABCEELLV	cleavable
AABCEELPS	escapable
AABCEELPY	peaceably
AABCEELRS	calabrese ❑
AABCEELRT	traceable
AABCEELTT	cabalette
AABCEENRR	aberrance
AABCEFILN	fanciable
AABCEFIRT	fabricate
AABCEFLOP	capable of
AABCEFORY	Bay of Acre
AABCEFOSU	fabaceous
AABCEFOTU	about-face
AABCEFRST	bare facts
AABCEGIKV	give a back
AABCEGILR	algebraic
AABCEGKST	backstage
AABCEGKTT	get back at
AABCEHINR	branchiae
AABCEHIRT	brachiate
AABCEHKTT	at the back
AABCEHLMP	Palm Beach
AABCEHLTW	watchable
AABCEILLM	claimable
AABCEILMN	imbalance
AABCEILMR	bicameral
AABCEILNP	incapable
AABCEILNT	cantabile
AABCEILRT	bacterial
	calibrate
AABCEILST	Baltic Sea
AABCEIMNR	mainbrace
AABCEINOR	anaerobic
AABCEISSS	abscissae
AABCEJKMR	amberjack
AABCEKKLS	slack-bake
AABCEKMPR	break camp
AABCEKPPR	paperback
AABCEKRTW	back water
	backwater
AABCELLLO	allocable
AABCELMNU	ambulance
AABCELNNO	on balance
AABCELNNU	unbalance
AABCELNOR	Barcelona
AABCELNPU	uncapable
AABCELNTU	unactable
AABCELOOS	calaboose
AABCELORR	barcarole
AABCELPPR	crab apple
AABCELRST	Castlebar
AABCELRTT	tractable
AABCELRTU	trabecula
AABCELRTY	traceably
AABCENORT	carbonate
AABCENRRY	aberrancy
AABCEORTU	care about
AABCEOSTU	sauce boat
AABCEOTUV	a cut above
AABCERRTU	carburate
AABCFGKLL	black flag
AABCFHKLS	flashback
AABCFHLOT	batch loaf
AABCFKSTU	a fast buck
AABCFNORU	Afro-Cuban
AABCGILNN	balancing
AABCHHIRT	bath chair ❑
AABCHIKTT	hit back at
AABCHMNOS	hansom-cab
AABCIKLLM	blackmail
AABCIKLNR	lack-brain
AABCILLSY	basically
AABCILNOT	botanical
AABCILNPY	incapably
AABCILOPR	parabolic
AABCILRUV	vibracula
AABCIMNOR	macrobian
AABCISSSS	abscissas
AABCKKLMR	black mark
AABCKLLMP	lamp-black
AABCKLLRT	trackball
AABCKLLST	backstall
AABCKLMSS	black mass
AABCKLNSW	black swan
AABCKLRST	black arts
AABCKRSTT	start back
AABCLLNUV	Naval Club
AABCLLOTU	Cat Ballou
AABCLMNOR	Marc Bolan
AABCLRTTU	Clara Butt
AABCLRTTY	tractably
AABCMNOTT	combatant
AABCOSTTU	cast about
AABDDDEGP	padded bag
AABDDEGLS	saddlebag

AABDDEHOR	headboard
AABDDEHRY	Hyderabad
AABDDEINR	brain-dead
AABDDENNO	abandoned
AABDDHORR	hardboard
AABDDHORS	dashboard
AABDDNNST	bandstand
AABDEEGLL	bald eagle
AABDEEKLN	Baekeland
AABDEELLP	pleadable
AABDEELLR	balladeer
AABDEELMN	amendable
AABDEENNO	abandonee
AABDEFHKL	half-baked
AABDEGINR	gabardine
AABDEGMOS	gambadoes
AABDEGORT	abrogated
AABDEHHLT	bad health
AABDEHITV	have it bad
AABDEHKNR	handbrake
AABDEHKRU	Ehud Barak
AABDEHLSY	abashedly
AABDEHNSU	unabashed
AABDEIILN	inaidable
AABDEIKNU	aduki bean
AABDEILMR	admirable
AABDEILOV	avoidable
AABDEILRV	adverbial
AABDEILSV	advisable
AABDEINST	bastinade
AABDEKRSY	Drake's Bay
AABDELLNT	tableland
AABDELLST	stable lad
AABDEMNNR	brand name
	brand-name
	name brand
AABDEMORT	dreamboat
AABDEMRTU	adumbrate
AABDEORSV	bravadoes
AABDGIILR	garibaldi□
AABDGJLLR	J G Ballard
AABDGNNOW	bandwagon
AABDGNOSV	vagabonds
AABDHLOTY	hold at bay
AABDHLRSU	Hasdrubal
AABDHORSW	washboard
AABDILMNO	abdominal
AABDILMRY	admirably
AABDILNQU	baldaquin
AABDILNRS	Rab Island
AABDILNST	stand bail
AABDILORS	bad sailor
	sailboard
AABDILORT	tailboard
AABDILSVY	advisably
AABDINNRT	trainband
AABDINOST	bastinado
AABDINPRT	in bad part
AABDINSTW	waistband
AABDKLNRW	draw blank
AABDLNORX	Arnold Bax
AABDLNSST	sandblast
AABDLORUY	day-labour
AABDNORTU	bat around
AABDORRST	starboard
AABDORSWY	broadways
AABEEEGLR	agreeable
AABEEFNST	beanfeast
AABEEGGLU	gaugeable
AABEEGLLL	glabellae
AABEEGLLT	bagatelle
AABEEGLRY	agreeably
AABEEGLTT	get-at-able
AABEEGRRT	Great Bear
AABEEHKLS	shakeable
AABEEHLPS	shapeable
AABEEHLRT	herbal tea
AABEEHRTT	heartbeat
AABEEILLN	alienable
AABEEILNT	be in a tale
AABEEILRS	raiseable
AABEEINRS	Béarnaise
AABEEKLPS	speakable
AABEEKMRV	make brave
AABEEKOTW	be awake to
AABEEKPTY	keep at bay
AABEELLLM	malleable
AABEELLNN	Annabelle
AABEELLRT	alterable
AABEELLRV	alla breve
AABEELMMT	emblemata
AABEELNTU	uneatable
AABEELORT	elaborate
AABEELPRR	reparable
AABEELPRS	separable
AABEELPRY	repayable
AABEELRTT	treatable
AABEELRTW	tableware
AABEELSTZ	set ablaze
AABEELTTX	battleaxe
	battle-axe
AABEEMNST	abasement
AABEEMNTT	abatement
AABEEQRSU	arabesque
AABEERRTW	water bear
AABEFGILT	fatigable
AABEFILRU	Albufeira
AABEFKRST	breakfast
AABEFLLMM	flammable
AABEFLLOT	floatable
AABEFLLPP	flappable
AABEFLMSU	flambeaus
AABEFLMUX	flambeaux
AABEFORST	abreast of
AABEGHIMT	The Gambia
AABEGHLLU	laughable
AABEGILNV	navigable
AABEGINRR	bargainer
AABEGIRRT	arbitrage
AABEGLMNP	Palembang
AABEGLNOR	Bangalore
AABEGLNRT	grantable

AABEGLPRS	graspable
AABEGLRTV	travel bag
AABEGNRUZ	Aurangzeb
AABEHHNPR	Aphra Behn
AABEHITTU	habituate
AABEHLLRT	earth ball
AABEHLOTW	whaleboat
AABEHMNST	abashment
AABEHMSTT	steam bath
AABEIILLS	labialise
AABEIILLZ	labialize
AABEIIMNR	bain-marie
AABEIIRTU	aubrietia
AABEIIRTV	bivariate
AABEIJKLR	break jail
	jailbreak
AABEIKLNS	Balkanise
AABEIKLNZ	Balkanize
AABEIKNRR	karabiner
AABEILLLR	albarelli
AABEILLNR	ballerina
AABEILLRT	bilateral
AABEILNPT	paintable
AABEILNRT	Albertina
	trainable
AABEILTTW	wait table
AABEIMNOT	abominate
AABEINPST	be at pains
AABEINRST	abstainer
AABEINRVW	brainwave
AABEINSST	Sebastian
AABEIRRTT	arbitrate
AABEJMNSU	Jan Mabuse
AABEKKNRR	break rank
AABEKLLTT	Table Talk
AABEKLNST	beanstalk
AABEKLRTY	Art Blakey
AABEKPRRT	Pat Barker
AABELLLMR	alarm-bell
AABELLLOW	allowable
AABELLMST	meatballs
AABELLNPT	plantable
AABELLSTT	table salt
AABELLSUV	valuables
AABELMNOR	malar bone
AABELMNST	stableman
AABELMSSU	assumable
AABELNNOS	nasal bone
AABELNSUV	unsavable
AABELNSUY	unsayable
AABELOPRR	polar bear
AABELORRZ	razorable
AABELORST	astrolabe
AABELORTT	rotatable
AABELPRRY	reparably
AABELPRSY	separably
AABELPRYY	play by ear
AABELRSSU	assurable
AABELRSTU	saturable
AABELRTTU	tablature
AABEMOSTT	steamboat
	steam-boat
AABEMRRSS	embarrass
AABENNSTV	Van Basten
AABENOPRT	Bonaparte
AABEOPPRT	approbate
AABEORTUV	rave about
AABEOSTTU	about east
AABERSTUX	beaux arts
AABFFFOTU	faff about
AABFIIMNS	Fabianism
AABFIINST	Fabianist
AABFIKNRS	Fairbanks
AABFILLOR	ball of air
AABFIMORT	fibromata
AABFLLOTU	fall about
AABGGRRYY	argy-bargy
AABGHILRT	Galbraith
AABGHLLUY	laughably
AABGHNOTU	hang about
AABGHOPRR	barograph
AABGIINWY	in a big way
AABGILNVY	navigably
AABGILRRT	Gibraltar
AABGINNOR	born again
	born-again
AABGINTVY	vanity bag
AABGJSTYY	Jay Gatsby
AABGLNOYY	by analogy
AABGNORSZ	garbanzos
AABGORTVY	gravy boat
AABHHIKSU	hibakusha
AABHIILRZ	bilharzia
AABHIIMNP	amphibian
AABHIIOPP	apiphobia
AABHIMMRU	Hammurabi
AABHIMNOT	Ian Botham
AABHINOPP	panphobia
AABHINRSW	brainwash
AABHINSSW	washbasin
AABHKKLNU	Kubla Khan
AABHKLRRT	Karl Barth
AABHLLOWX	boxwallah
AABHMRRTU	barathrum
AABIIKNNS	Iain Banks
AABIILNRR	librarian
AABIILNRZ	Brazilian
AABIINNRT	Britannia
AABIINRTT	Brittania
AABILLLOW	allow bail
AABILLNPT	paintball
AABILLNST	in ballast
AABILMNOS	anabolism
AABILMOPY	amblyopia
AABILMORS	ambrosial
AABILMPST	baptismal
AABILNOTT	battalion
AABILSVWY	Walvis Bay
AABIMNNOU	buonamani
AABIMNORS	ambrosian
AABINOSTW	boatswain
AABIRRRTY	arbitrary

AABJJLLNU	Ljubljana
AABKLORTU	lark about
AABKLOTTU	talk about
AABKLOTUW	walkabout
AABKLSTVY	Blavatsky
AABLLLOWY	allowably
AABLLMSYY	abysmally
AABLLNTTY	blatantly
AABLLRSYY	syllabary
AABLLRTUY	tabularly
AABLMNTUY	untamably
AABLMSSUY	assumably
AABLNORTU	Ulan Bator
AABLOPTUY	play about
AABLORSST	albatross
AABLORTTU	tabulator
AABMNOSTW	batswoman
AABNNSTTU	Bantustan
AABNOOSSV	bossa nova
	bossanova
AABNOSTUW	swan about
AABRSSTTU	substrata
AACCCHIOP	capocchia
AACCDDINY	candidacy
AACCDEILM	acclaimed
AACCDEIMS	academics
AACCDEJNY	adjacency
AACCDELPR	place card
AACCDGINS	cascading
AACCDIINR	circadian
AACCDIMNO	mandiocca
AACCDIOSU	Caucasoid
AACCDNORT	accordant
AACCDORSS	as accords
AACCEEIRR	cercariae
AACCEELNR	clearance
AACCEENRT	cancerate
AACCEGHPR	charge-cap
AACCEHJKP	cheapjack
	cheap-jack
AACCEHRRT	character
AACCEHSTW	watchcase
AACCEIILN	caecilian
AACCEILMT	acclimate
AACCEINTV	vaccinate
AACCEJKSU	Jack-sauce
AACCEKNRS	crankcase
AACCEKRRT	race track
	racetrack
AACCELLTU	calculate
AACCELMNU	calcaneum
AACCELMTY	cyclamate
AACCELNSU	calcaneus
AACCEORTT	coarctate
AACCFGOOS	cacafogos
AACCHIKSW	Chickasaw
AACCHILNY	china clay
AACCHINRS	saccharin
AACCHIRTT	cathartic
AACCHIRTU	autarchic
AACCHKUWY	chuck away

AACCIINTT	tactician
AACCILLSS	classical
AACCILNNO	canonical
AACCILPRT	practical
AACCILTTY	catalytic
AACCIMNOR	carcinoma
	macaronic
AACCINOTT	catatonic
AACCINPTY	captaincy
AACCINRTT	Antarctic
AACCIOPRT	capacitor
AACCIOPSU	capacious
AACCIRSST	sarcastic
AACCLLLLO	local call
AACCLMORY	cyclorama
AACCLMSTY	cataclysm
AACCMNOPY	accompany
AACCOPRRS	sarcocarp
AACCORTUY	autocracy
AACCOSSTT	staccatos
	stoccatas
AACDDEETU	decaudate
AACDDEHMR	dead-march
AACDDEINT	candidate
AACDDELNO	do a candle
AACDDENSU	Sadducean
AACDDHIMV	David Mach
AACDDIIST	Dadaistic
AACDDLMNO	MacDonald
	Macdonald
AACDDMORU	docudrama
AACDEEFLT	defalcate
AACDEEHHR	headreach
AACDEEIMT	emaciated
AACDEEIRT	eradicate
AACDEEKPP	peaked cap
AACDEELRT	lacerated
AACDEELST	escalated
AACDEELTU	aculeated
AACDEEMNS	damascene
AACDEEMRT	demarcate
AACDEETVX	excavated
AACDEFFHL	half-faced
AACDEFFIN	affianced
AACDEFHRS	headscarf
AACDEFLRS	false-card
AACDEGLNO	decagonal
AACDEGNOS	gasconade
AACDEHILN	enchilada
AACDEHLRT	cathedral
AACDEHORT	octahedra
AACDEHPST	pas de chat
AACDEIKSV	ask advice
AACDEILLN	dalliance
AACDEILLT	dialectal
AACDEILNO	Laodicean
AACDEILNT	cadential
AACDEILTU	acidulate
AACDEIMNO	Macedonia
AACDEIMPR	paramedic
AACDEIMSS	camisades

AACDEINNV	in advance
AACDEINOT	diaconate
AACDEINOV	avoidance
AACDEIRSS	ascarides
AACDEISST	cast aside
AACDEJKMP	jam-packed
AACDEKLRY	lardy cake
AACDEKNRS	ransacked
AACDELLNU	calendula
AACDELMNO	Damoclean
AACDELMNS	Candlemas
AACDELNOT	anecdotal
AACDELNPS	landscape
AACDELNRR	Carl Andre
AACDEMNTU	manducate
AACDEMORS	cream soda
AACDENNNO	cannonade
AACDENNST	ascendant
AACDENOTU	coadunate
AACDENPRT	tap-dancer
AACDERSTT	castrated
AACDERSWY	Sacred Way
AACDERTTT	attracted
AACDFHLRS	flash card
AACDFHNRT	handcraft
AACDFIILT	fatidical
AACDFLNOO	food canal
AACDGINNV	advancing
AACDHIIRR	Richardia
AACDHILMY	chlamydia
AACDHINNP	cap in hand
AACDHINOR	arachnoid
AACDHIRSY	chairdays
AACDHLLLO	hold a call
AACDHLNPS	clap hands
AACDHLNPU	launch pad
AACDHLNRS	crashland
AACDHPRRS	card-sharp
AACDIILTV	vaticidal
AACDIIMNO	amino acid
AACDIISST	diastasic
AACDIISTT	diastatic
AACDILLRY	radically
AACDILOPR	parodical
AACDILPRU	Paul Dirac
AACDIMOSS	camisados
AACDIMRST	dramatics
AACDINNOR	draconian ❑
AACDIOSUU	audacious
AACDIQRTU	quadratic
AACDIRSTY	caryatids
AACDJNTUY	adjutancy
AACDMRRST	smart card
AACDNNSTT	can't stand
AACDORSTW	coastward
AACDPRRSY	scrapyard
AACEEEKMP	make peace
	make-peace
AACEEFINN	fainéance
AACEEFIRT	cafeteria
AACEEFLPS	safe place
AACEEFLPT	face plate
AACEEFLUV	face value
AACEEFRRT	aftercare
AACEEFRSV	face-saver
AACEEGHNS	sea change
AACEEGILL	elegiacal
AACEEGKLN	angel cake
AACEEGKNO	Genoa cake
AACEEGLLR	cellarage
AACEEGLLS	legal case
AACEEGNRR	carrageen
AACEEHHRT	heartache
AACEEHLPV	have place
AACEEHNOR	Chaeronea
AACEEHPRT	cheap-rate
AACEEHRTT	tracheate
AACEEHSUV	have cause
AACEEJLTU	ejaculate
AACEEKLMR	make clear
AACEEKLPT	take place
AACEEKMPR	pacemaker
AACEEKNPT	keep an act
AACEEKRRT	caretaker
AACEELNPT	placentae
AACEELPRT	Paraclete
AACEELRTT	altercate
AACEEMNNY	Mycenaean
AACEEMRRW	creamware
AACEENNRT	nectarean
AACEENORY	once a year
AACEENRTX	excarnate
AACEENSTY	cast an eye
AACEEOPRS	aerospace
AACEERSTT	estate car
AACEFFIRT	affricate
AACEFGNRR	fragrance
AACEFGOPR	forage-cap
AACEFHLST	half-caste
AACEFINST	fascinate
AACEFLLPU	pull a face
AACEGHLNR	archangel ❑
AACEGHLTT	Gaeltacht
AACEGHMNP	champagne
AACEGHNOR	anchorage ❑
AACEGHRST	gatecrash
AACEGILNS	analgesic
AACEGILRS	Algeciras
AACEGILRT	cartilage
AACEGIMNO	come again
	come again?
	egomaniac
AACEGINNO	once again
AACEGISTT	castigate
AACEGLMOU	guacamole
AACEGLOST	galactose
AACEGLOTU	catalogue
	coagulate
AACEGNORR	arrogance
AACEGNORT	Goa trance
AACEGNRSU	cane-sugar
	sugar cane

AACEGOPST	scapegoat
AACEGORTT	greatcoat
AACEHHIRZ	Zechariah
AACEHHMRR	March hare
AACEHIIMS	ischaemia
AACEHILLO	echolalia
AACEHILMT	malachite
AACEHILNS	selachian
AACEHILPT	caliphate
AACEHIMNR	Charmaine
AACEHIMNT	machinate
AACEHIMTT	athematic
AACEHINRS	anarchise
AACEHINRT	Catharine
	Catherina
AACEHINRZ	anarchize
AACEHIOPT	apothecia
AACEHIOST	Taoiseach
AACEHIPTT	apathetic
AACEHIRST	catharise
AACEHIRSY	easy chair
AACEHIRTZ	catharize
AACEHKLNO	kalanchoe
AACEHKMOR	hackamore
AACEHKMPU	Kampuchea
AACEHKRSV	haversack
AACEHKRTY	Thackeray
AACEHLLLR	Clare Hall
AACEHLMUU	chalumeau
AACEHLNSW	wash clean
AACEHMNRU	human race
AACEHMRSU	cause harm
AACEHMRSY	camera-shy
AACEHNORS	sea anchor
AACEHNRRT	Hart Crane
AACEHNSSS	Sassenach
AACEHPRTU	parachute
AACEHRSST	catharses
AACEIILNT	laciniate
AACEIINRR	cineraria
AACEIINRS	raise Cain
AACEIIRTV	vicariate
AACEILLPT	capitella
AACEILLRV	varicella
AACEILLTV	vacillate
AACEILMNN	Alemannic
AACEILMNP	campanile
AACEILMPS	eclampsia
AACEILMTV	calmative
AACEILNNR	carnelian
AACEILNNT	cantilena
	lancinate
AACEILNPP	appliance
AACEILNPT	analeptic
	Placentia
AACEILNRS	carnalise
AACEILNRZ	carnalize
AACEILORT	aleatoric
AACEILPTV	placative
AACEILRSS	sacralise
AACEILRSZ	sacralize
AACEILSSU	casualise
AACEILSTU	actualise
AACEILSTX	catalexis
AACEILSUZ	casualize
AACEILTUZ	actualize
AACEIMNNW	Ian McEwan
AACEIMNPT	mancipate
AACEIMNTU	acuminate
AACEIMRST	marcasite
AACEIMSTT	masticate
AACEINNRT	incarnate
AACEINNSY	in any case
AACEINPRS	in a scrape
AACEINPRT	Patna rice
AACEINPSU	cause pain
AACEINRST	ascertain
	Cartesian
	sectarian
AACEIORRT	acroteria
AACEIOSST	associate
AACEIPPRT	per capita
AACEIPSTU	auspicate
AACEIPTTV	captivate
AACEIRSST	staircase
AACEISTUV	causative
AACEJKLNT	Jack-a-Lent
AACEJKLSV	Jack-slave
AACEJOSSU	soja sauce
AACEKLPRT	plate rack
AACEKLPSW	space walk
	space-walk
AACEKNRRS	ransacker
AACELLMNS	call names
AACELLNOT	all at once
AACELLNOW	allowance
AACELLNPT	placental
AACELLNST	castellan
AACELLSUU	clausulae
AACELMNTT	cattleman
AACELMRST	smart alec
AACELNOTT	Canaletto
AACELNPST	placentas
AACELNRST	ancestral
	Lancaster
AACELNSTU	Anacletus
AACELOPRT	Cleopatra
AACELORST	escalator
AACELOSTT	cattaloes
AACELOTUV	autoclave
AACELPSTU	aspectual
AACELPSTY	catalepsy
AACELPTXY	cataplexy
AACELRRTY	carrytale
AACELRTUW	caterwaul
AACEMNNOR	Connemara
AACEMNRST	sacrament ❑
AACEMOPRT	come apart
AACEMORRT	macerator
AACENNNOY	annoyance
AACENNOSS	assonance
AACENRSSU	anacruses

	assurance
AACENRSSV	canvasser
AACENSSTT	castanets
AACEOOPPT	apocopate
AACEORTVX	excavator
AACEORWWY	cower away
AACEOSSUY	soya sauce
AACEOSTTV	cast a vote
AACERRSST	Carstares
AACFFIRRT	craft fair
AACFGILRY	fly agaric
AACFGLNRY	flagrancy
AACFGNRRY	fragrancy
AACFHKLRT	half-track
AACFIILNN	financial
AACFILNOT	factional
AACFILORT	factorial
AACFINSTT	fantastic
AACFJNOOR	Joan of Arc
AACFKRSTT	fast-track
AACFLLTUY	factually
AACFMNRRZ	Franz Marc
AACFMNRST	craftsman
AACGGHINN	chain gang
AACGGIKNP	packaging
AACGHIIMN	Chiang Mai
AACGHILPR	graphical
AACGHIMOR	Archimago
AACGHINTT	attaching
AACGHNORS	charangos
AACGHOPSZ	gazpachos
AACGHORSU	guacharos
AACGILLMY	magically
AACGIMOTU	autogamic
AACGIMPRT	pragmatic
AACGIOSSU	sagacious
AACGLLSWY	scallywag
AACGLNOOT	octagonal
AACGLNOTU	coagulant
AACGLRSSU	Carl Gauss
AACGNNSTY	stagnancy
AACGNRRTY	Cary Grant
AACHHHIUU	chihuahua □
AACHHKKNU	Chanukkah
AACHHNSSS	Hans Sachs
AACHIILMN	chain mail
AACHIILNP	Chaliapin
AACHIILPT	aliphatic
AACHIIMNT	matachini
AACHIIMRS	mariachis
AACHIIPRS	pharisaic □
AACHILOPR	parochial
AACHILOPT	chipolata
AACHILORS	Charolais
AACHILPST	asphaltic
AACHILSST	thalassic
AACHIMNOR	harmonica
AACHIMNRS	anarchism
AACHIMRRT	matriarch
AACHIMSTT	asthmatic
AACHINOPR	anaphoric
	Pharaonic
AACHINRST	anarchist
AACHIPRRT	patriarch
AACHIRSST	catharsis
AACHKSSTY	Haystacks
AACHLLMRY	lachrymal
AACHLMOST	stomachal
AACHMMNSY	Sammy Cahn
AACHMNNOR	anchorman
AACHMNORW	charwoman
AACHMNSTY	yachtsman
AACHMPRST	march past
	march-past
AACHMRRTU	MacArthur
AACHNNOTY	anthocyan
AACHNOSTU	acanthous
AACHOPPRY	Apocrypha
AACHQSSTU	sasquatch
AACIILLRT	altricial
AACIILMNP	campanili
AACIILMRS	racialism
AACIILMST	Lamaistic
AACIILPRT	piratical
AACIILRST	racialist
	satirical
AACIIMMST	miasmatic
AACIIMOTX	axiomatic
AACIINNOP	poinciana
AACIINNOT	nicotiana
AACIINPRT	patrician
AACIIPRST	parasitic
AACIIRRTU	urticaria
AACIISTTV	atavistic
AACIJNOTT	jactation
AACILLMMN	Macmillan
AACILLMNY	manically
AACILLNOT	allantoic
AACILLNRY	ancillary
AACILLNTY	actinally
AACILLOXY	coaxially
AACILLPRY	capillary
AACILLPTY	capitally
AACILMPST	plasmatic
AACILMRSU	simulacra
AACILNOPT	placation
AACILNOTT	lactation
AACILNPPT	applicant
AACILNPSV	pan-Slavic
AACILNQTU	quantical
AACILNRTY	carnality
AACILNRUV	navicular
AACILORTU	auctorial
AACILOSSU	salacious
AACILPRSU	spiracula
AACILPRTY	paralytic
AACILQTTU	acquittal
AACILRRTU	articular
AACILRRUU	auricular
AACILRSTT	Scarlatti
AACILRSTY	rascality
	satyrical

AACILSSTY	catalysis
AACILSTUY	causality
AACILTTUY	actuality
AACIMNNNU	Mancunian
AACIMNOPR	panoramic
AACIMNORS	macaronis
AACIMNOTT	mactation
AACIMORTU	amaurotic
AACIMOTTU	automatic
AACIMRRSU	sacrarium
AACIMRTTU	traumatic
AACINNORT	carnation
AACINNOST	santonica
AACINNPRT	captain RN
AACINOOTV	avocation
AACINOPRS	caparison
AACINOPST	capitanos
AACINOSTU	causation
AACINOTTU	actuation
AACINRRVY	arrivancy
AACINRSST	sacristan
AACINRSSU	anacrusis
AACIOPRSU	rapacious
AACIORTTV	activator
AACIOSTTW	waistcoat
AACIRSSUU	Carausius
AACJKRSTW	Jack Straw
AACKLMNPX	Max Planck
AACKORSTT	toast rack
AACLLMNTY	clamantly
AACLLTTUY	tactually
AACLNOORT	root canal
AACLNOPTU	cantaloup
AACLNPRTU	crapulant
AACLNRUUV	avuncular
AACLOOPST	tapacolos
AACLOPRRT	patrol car
AACLOPRTY	placatory
	play actor
	play-actor
AACLOPSTU	tapaculos
AACLPRSUY	scapulary
AACMOOSTT	scotomata
AACNNOSTT	Constanta
AACNOPRST	not a scrap
AACNORTUU	au courant
AACNOSTTY	at any cost
AACNRSTUY	sanctuary
AACNRSTUZ	Santa Cruz
AACORRSTU	Tuscarora
AACORSSWY	cassowary
AACPRSSTU	Spartacus
AADDDGNRY	grandaddy
AADDEEFHT	fat-headed
AADDEEMRY	ready-made
AADDEENRU	Audenarde
AADDEGLOO	a good deal
AADDEGMNU	undamaged
AADDEHHMN	ham-handed
AADDEHIOR	Radiohead
AADDEHIRV	David Hare
AADDEHLNN	lend a hand
AADDEHRTW	deathward
AADDEILNO	adenoidal
AADDEILNV	David Lean
AADDEILTV	validated
AADDEILWY	idled away
AADDEINRW	Edwardian
AADDEKLNY	naked lady
AADDELLNS	sandalled
AADDELMNN	landdamne
AADDELORU	read aloud
AADDELRST	astraddle
AADDEMNOR	Andromeda
AADDEORST	roadstead
AADDEORTW	awarded to
AADDHLLOR	Roald Dahl
AADDHNNST	handstand
AADDIIMRY	dairymaid
AADDIINRV	Dravidian
AADDILMSY	lady's maid
AADDINORS	Diana Dors
AADDINPRT	dandiprat
AADDIRRWY	Irrawaddy
AADDKNORY	Dan Aykrod
AADDLNRSW	landwards
AADDLRSTY	dastardly
AADDNRSST	standards
AADEEFILS	false idea
AADEEFLPR	flap-eared
AADEEGHMT	megadeath
AADEEGHST	Gateshead
AADEEGILV	give a lead
AADEEGLMN	Magdalene
AADEEGLRT	great deal
AADEEGNOR	orangeade
AADEEGNPP	appendage
AADEEGNRT	Great Dane
	Teagarden
AADEEHHRX	hexahedra
AADEEHHTT	at the head
	heat death
AADEEHISV	have ideas
AADEEHLSW	alewashed
AADEEHPRS	spearhead
AADEEHRRT	heart-dear
AADEEHRTT	death rate
AADEEIKST	take aside
AADEEIKWW	wide awake
	wide-awake
AADEEILMV	mediaeval
AADEEILNT	alienated
AADEEILPV	Deepavali
AADEEIRRT	reradiate
AADEEISVW	wave aside
AADEEJMNS	James Dean
AADEEJMSS	James Eads
AADEEKMNS	damaskeen
AADEEKMRR	earmarked
AADEEKMRY	make ready
	makeready
AADEELLMN	allemande

AADEELNNR	lend an ear
AADEELNPS	esplanade
AADEELNRX	Alexander
AADEELTUV	devaluate
AADEEMNRT	tradename
AADEEMNST	Seated Man
AADEEMRSU	admeasure
AADEENSST	sense data
AADEENSTU	nauseated
AADEEORTT	toad-eater
AADEEPRST	paederast
	separated
AADEERSTY	Easter Day
AADEESTTV	devastate
AADEFGHOO	go ahead of
AADEFGLNN	fandangle
AADEFGRSU	safeguard
AADEFHNOR	aforehand
AADEFHNPS	fan-shaped
AADEFIORS	aforesaid
AADEFIRRT	trade fair
AADEFJNNO	Jane Fonda
AADEFLNOR	farandole
AADEFLNSW	false dawn
AADEFMRST	farmstead
AADEFNNRU	Anna Freud
AADEFOSTU	autos-da-fé
AADEFSSTT	steadfast
AADEGHINV	give a hand
AADEGHNRY	hydrangea
AADEGIMNT	diamagnet
AADEGIMNV	give a damn
AADEGINRT	tragedian
AADEGIPRS	disparage
AADEGIQRU	quadrigae
AADEGKNOT	go and take
AADEGLLOP	gallopade
AADEGLNNR	engarland
AADEGLOTV	dataglove
AADEGRRRU	rearguard
AADEGRRSS	as regards
AADEGRRVY	graveyard
AADEHHITV	have had it
AADEHHKNS	handshake
AADEHHMNW	hem and haw
AADEHHRRT	had rather
AADEHHRTW	hard wheat
AADEHIMNV	have a mind
AADEHINRS	Adar Sheni
AADEHIORR	diarrhoea
AADEHIPRT	apartheid
	hit parade
AADEHLLPU	pull ahead
AADEHLLST	headstall
AADEHLMNN	manhandle
AADEHLMPS	lampshade
AADEHLMSY	ashamedly
AADEHLNRT	heartland
AADEHMNSU	unashamed
AADEHPRTT	deathtrap
AADEHRSTT	death star
	head start
AADEIILRS	radialise
AADEIILRZ	radialize
AADEIIRRT	irradiate
AADEILMNS	ladies' man
AADEILMNT	laminated
AADEILNNR	adrenalin
AADEILNSV	vandalise
AADEILNVZ	vandalize
AADEILPPR	laid paper
AADEILPRU	praeludia
AADEILRTY	radiately
AADEILTUV	laudative
AADEILTVW	tidal wave
AADEIMMSS	mass media
AADEIMRRR	ram-raider
AADEIMRST	dramatise
AADEIMRTZ	dramatize
AADEINPTT	patinated
AADEINRST	steradian
AADEINRTT	attainder
AADEIOPTU	audiotape
AADEIORVW	radio wave
AADEIPPRS	disappear
AADEIPRST	disparate
AADEIRVWY	drive away
AADEKMRRT	trademark
AADEKNNYY	Danny Kaye
AADELLMRY	alarmedly
AADELLNNO	one and all
AADELLQRU	quadrella
AADELLSSY	saleslady
AADELMMOR	melodrama
AADELMNRU	unalarmed
AADELMPSU	Lampedusa
AADELNQUY	Dan Quayle
AADELNRRU	Laura Dern
	rural dean
AADELNSTW	wasteland
AADELPRSY	paralysed
AADELRSWY	seawardly
AADELRSYY	early days
AADELRTTY	latter-day
AADEMMNOR	memoranda
AADEMMRST	Amsterdam
AADEMNPRS	ampersand
AADEMNRST	tradesman
AADEMOTTU	automated
AADEMPSTT	date-stamp
AADEMRRTU	dura mater
AADEMSTTU	State Duma
AADENNRST	Santander
AADENNTTT	attendant
AADENPPRS	sandpaper
AADENRRTT	retardant
AADENRRTW	warranted
AADENSSTY	stand easy
AADEOPRRS	paradores
AADEOPRST	tapaderos
AADEOPSSS	passadoes
AADEORSTW	soda water

AADERRRSW	rearwards
AADERRSVY	adversary❑
AADERSSTW	eastwards
AADERSTTU	saturated
AADERSTWW	war-wasted
AADFFIITV	affidavit
AADFGNNOS	fandangos
AADFGNORR	Fragonard
AADFHHLRY	half-hardy
AADFHILNT	lift a hand
AADFIILNN	Finlandia
AADFILNRY	fairyland❑
AADFIMNRY	man Friday❑
AADFINNSS	ifs and ans
AADFNSSTT	stand fast
AADGGHLRY	haggardly
AADGGIINR	Diana Rigg
AADGHIMPR	diaphragm
AADGHINRT	Adi Granth
AADGHNNOR	hand organ
AADGILNOR	girandola
AADGILORT	gladiator
AADGILRRU	guardrail
AADGIMMNO	gammadion
AADGIMNRU	marauding
AADGIMORR	radiogram
AADGIMORU	audiogram
AADGIMRRS	Mardi Gras
AADGINORT	gradation
AADGINRUZ	Dzungaria
AADGLLNRU	glandular
AADGLLNSY	Sandy Gall
AADGLLRUY	gradually
AADGLMNRS	grand slam
AADGLNOOW	wagonload
AADGLNRSS	grassland
AADGMNOOY	a good many
AADGMNORS	dragomans
AADGMNRSU	guardsman
AADGNNRTU	grand-aunt
AADHHMNUW	hum and haw
AADHIMMST	Adam Smith
AADHINNNY	in any hand
AADHINPSU	Upanishad
AADHIPSSY	dysphasia
AADHJMNOS	John Adams
AADHKMNTU	Kathmandu
AADHKNRTU	Hardaknut
AADHLLNST	hallstand
AADHLMNRS	marshland
AADHLNRYY	hardly any
AADHNSSTW	washstand
AADHORRSU	Hadrosaur
AADHORSUZ	hazardous
AADIIKLNU	Niki Lauda
AADIILLMY	Daily Mail
AADIILSUV	visual aid
AADIIMMOT	ommatidia
AADIINNRS	Sardinian
AADIINNRW	Darwinian
AADIINORT	radiation
AADIINPRY	pray in aid
AADIINRRT	irradiant
AADIIORTU	auditoria
AADILLMOR	armadillo
AADILLMPS	Aldis lamp
AADILLMPU	palladium
AADILLNNS	land snail
AADILLNPU	paludinal
AADILLOPS	sapodilla
AADILLSSU	Ladislaus
AADILMNSV	vandalism
AADILMNTU	Tamil Nadu
AADILMOPS	plasmodia
AADILMORT	maladroit
AADILMPRY	pyramidal
AADILMRTY	Admiralty
AADILNOPT	antipodal
AADILNOTU	adulation
	laudation
AADILNRTY	radiantly
AADILNSWZ	Swaziland
AADILOSVW	disavowal
AADILPSSY	dysplasia
AADILRSTY	Daily Star
AADILSYYZ	lazy-daisy
AADIMNNOR	Dan Marino
AADIMNNOT	damnation
AADIMNQSU	damasquin
AADIMNUVZ	avizandum
AADIMQRSU	maquisard
AADIMRSTT	dramatist
AADINNNOT	andantino
AADINNORV	Andrianov
AADINOORT	adoration
AADINORSS	Diana Ross
AADINSSTY	saint's day
AADIPSSUY	ups-a-daisy
AADIRSWXY	Six-Day War
AADKLPSUU	Paul Dukas
AADKLRWWY	awkwardly
AADKNOPRS	ask pardon
AADKPRRSW	parkwards
AADLLNORU	all around
AADLMNPSW	swampland
AADLMOORV	Almodovar
AADLNOPRU	pal around
AADLORTUY	adulatory
	laudatory
AADLRWWYY	waywardly
AADMNORTY	damnatory
	mandatory
AADMNOSTY	Tony Adams
AADNOORRS	Aaron's rod
AADOPPRST	strappado
AAEEEKLTV	take leave
AAEEFGRST	fare stage
	fare-stage
AAEEFHNSV	safe haven
AAEEFINNS	feiseanna
AAEEFKMRT	make after
AAEEFKRTT	take after

AAEEFLLMP	maple leaf
AAEEFLMNS	false name
AAEEFLRTW	water flea
AAEEFLTTY	Lafayette
AAEEFMNRT	name after
AAEEFPRRY	fare-payer
AAEEGGGRT	aggregate
AAEEGHKLS	shake a leg
AAEEGILNR	generalia
AAEEGINTV	evaginate
AAEEGIRTV	variegate
AAEEGKLLM	make legal
AAEEGKLNO	Lake Onega
AAEEGKMUV	make vague
AAEEGLLMR	large meal
AAEEGLLRY	legal year
AAEEGLNST	sea tangle
AAEEGLRST	Great Seal
AAEEGLSVW	wage slave
AAEEGMNNS	manganese
AAEEGMNST	stage name
	stage-name
AAEEGMRRV	Mr Average
AAEEGNORV	on average
AAEEGNPRT	parentage
AAEEGNRRR	rearrange
AAEEGNRTT	gnateater
AAEEGNRTU	guarantee
AAEEGNRWY	Greenaway
AAEEGRTTW	water gate
	Watergate
AAEEHIMTT	haematite
AAEEHIRTT	eat the air
AAEEHKLMO	make a hole
AAEEHKMST	make haste
AAEEHKNNT	Akhenaten
AAEEHKPST	take shape
AAEEHKRTT	take heart
AAEEHLMTW	wheatmeal
AAEEHLRRS	rehearsal
AAEEHMNTU	Athenaeum
AAEEHMNTX	exanthema
AAEEHMPST	metaphase
AAEEHMSST	the same as
AAEEHPSVW	waveshape
AAEEHRRRT	rare earth
AAEEHRRSW	shareware
AAEEHRRTT	at the rear
AAEEHRSTV	have a rest
AAEEHRTWY	thereaway
AAEEHRWWY	where away?
AAEEIKLMU	leukaemia
AAEEILLMN	El Alamein
AAEEILLST	ill at ease
AAEEILLTV	alleviate
AAEEILMNS	Melanesia
AAEEILRTT	retaliate
AAEEIMNRT	reanimate
AAEEIMNTX	exanimate
AAEEINPSY	naye paise
AAEEIPTTX	expatiate
AAEEISTTV	aestivate
AAEEJLMSX	Alex James
AAEEJNPSS	Japaneses
AAEEKLMQU	make equal
AAEEKLNNP	palankeen
AAEEKMMOV	make a move
AAEEKMMSS	make a mess
AAEEKMRTW	make water
AAEEKMSVW	make waves
AAEEKPPRT	keep apart
AAEEKPRRT	parrakeet
AAEEKRSTT	take a rest
AAEELLLTT	tell a tale
AAEELLMNS	sallee-man
AAEELLPPT	appellate
AAEELLQRU	aquarelle
AAEELLRRT	Alter-Réal
AAEELMSTT	stalemate
AAEELNOPR	aeroplane
AAEELNRTT	alternate
AAEELPPSX	sex appeal
AAEELPRST	lapse rate
AAEEMMNNS	name names
AAEEMMNTZ	amazement
AAEEMMPTZ	temazepam
AAEEMNNSS	anamneses
AAEEMPRRT	parameter
AAEENRRTW	warrantee
AAEENRSSW	awareness
AAEENTTTU	attenuate
AAEEOPRTV	evaporate
AAEEPRRTY	ratepayer
AAEEPRSST	separates
AAEEPSSYY	easy-peasy
AAEEPSTTU	put at ease
AAEERRTTW	water rate
AAEERTVWW	water-wave
AAEFFGLNO	Fongafale
AAEFFIILT	affiliate
AAEFGHLNT	hang a left
AAEFGIKMT	make a gift
AAEFGILTT	flagitate
AAEFGINRS	seafaring
AAEFGIRSX	saxifrage
AAEFGLRVW	flag-waver
AAEFGORRS	farragoes
AAEFHHITV	have faith
AAEFHLLPT	half-plate
AAEFHLLRT	earthfall
AAEFHLOST	false oath
AAEFHMRTT	aftermath
	hamfatter
AAEFHRTTT	after that
AAEFIINST	Fantaisie
AAEFIKNRR	Afrikaner
AAEFILMRR	fire alarm
AAEFILRTY	fairy tale
	fairytale
	fairy-tale
AAEFIMMNR	mainframe
AAEFINNRS	safranine

AAEFINSST	fantasise
AAEFINSTZ	fantasize
AAEFINTTU	infatuate
AAEFKMSSU	make a fuss
AAEFKNNNR	Anne Frank
AAEFKOPRT	partake of
AAEFLLLRY	fallalery
AAEFLLPSY	play false
AAEFLLRTW	waterfall
AAEFLLSTU	at full sea
AAEFLNRRT	fraternal
AAEFLORTZ	Fortaleza
AAEFLOSTT	set afloat
AAEFLRRST	flare star
AAEGGILRV	gilravage
AAEGGINOR	Georgiana
AAEGGINRU	rain gauge
	rain-gauge
AAEGGIRRS	gargarise
AAEGGIRRZ	gargarize
AAEGGLLNO	gallonage
AAEGGMMSU	a mug's game
AAEGGNPSU	snap gauge
AAEGHKLMU	make laugh
AAEGHLLPY	hypallage
AAEGHLNOX	hexagonal
AAEGHLNPR	phalanger
AAEGHLNPS	phalanges
AAEGHNOPR	orphanage
AAEGHNRRU	haranguer
AAEGHORRT	Harrogate
AAEGHRTWY	gather way
AAEGIILNT	genitalia
AAEGIILQU	aquilegia
AAEGIKLTV	give a talk
AAEGIKMNS	make a sign
AAEGIKNNW	awakening
AAEGILLNT	allegiant
	tell again
AAEGILNNN	annealing
AAEGILNNT	galantine
AAEGILNOS	analogise
AAEGILNOZ	analogize
AAEGILNPP	appealing
	lagniappe
AAEGILNRU	neuralgia
AAEGILNSV	galvanise
AAEGILNVZ	galvanize
AAEGIMMNS	mismanage
AAEGIMNNS	magnesian
AAEGIMNNT	man-eating
	manganite
AAEGIMNRR	margarine
AAEGIMNRT	marginate
AAEGIMRSY	Magyarise
AAEGIMRYZ	Magyarize
AAEGINNRT	Argentina
AAEGINORT	aragonite
AAEGINORV	over again
AAEGINPPR	appearing
AAEGINPPS	appeasing
AAEGINPTZ	Gaziantep
AAEGINRRR	arraigner
AAEGINRSU	guaranies
AAEGINRSY	asynergia
	gainsayer
AAEGINRTT	gratinate
AAEGIORRT	gear ratio
AAEGIRTTV	gravitate
AAEGISTTT	sagittate
AAEGJLNSS	Jena glass
AAEGKMNRY	make angry
AAEGKNOSS	Agnes Oaks
AAEGKRRSS	grass-rake
AAEGLLNRY	laryngeal
AAEGLMNST	gas mantle
AAEGLMPSY	play games
AAEGLMTTU	glutamate
AAEGLNOPU	a plague on
AAEGLNRTU	granulate
AAEGLPRRY	pearl-gray
AAEGLRSSW	glassware
AAEGLRSTT	Great Salt
AAEGMMNNO	Agamemnon
AAEGMNNOR	Orangeman
AAEGMNNPR	pan-German
AAEGMNPRT	pentagram
AAEGMNRTT	termagant
AAEGMOSST	moss agate
AAEGMRSTT	stratagem
AAEGNOPRS	parsonage
AAEGNOPRT	patronage
AAEGNPRTY	pageantry
AAEGNRRST	a stranger
AAEGNRSTV	Stavanger
AAEGNRTTU	great-aunt
AAEGOPPRT	propagate
AAEGPRSTU	pasturage
AAEGRRSTZ	stargazer
	star-gazer
AAEHHIMNN	Minnehaha
AAEHHIMTV	have-at-him
AAEHHINPZ	Zephaniah
AAEHHISTV	have a shit
AAEHHMNNN	Hahnemann
AAEHHOPTW	what a hope
AAEHHOSTV	have a shot
AAEHIKNRT	Katharine
AAEHILLNN	Annie Hall
AAEHILNNT	Nathaniel
AAEHILNRT	in a lather
AAEHILNTV	leviathan ◻
AAEHILORT	hariolate
AAEHILWWY	while away
AAEHIMNOT	theomania
AAEHIRSTW	Artie Shaw
AAEHKLNRS	ranshakle
AAEHKMPPY	make happy
AAEHKMRRS	Marrakesh
AAEHKNNOT	Akhenaton
AAEHKNSYZ	Ashkenazy
AAEHLLPUY	Up-Helly-Aa

Words marked ◻ can also be spelled with an initial capital letter

AAEHLLSTU	haustella
AAEHLLTWY	all the way
AAEHLMSTU	steam-haul
AAEHLNPSX	phalanxes
AAEHLNRTT	later than
AAEHLNSTT	Athelstan
AAEHLOPPR	phalarope
AAEHLPSTT	alpha test
	alphatest
AAEHLTTWX	wealth tax
AAEHMNOSU	A E Housman
AAEHMNRSW	washerman
AAEHMOSTT	haemostat
AAEHMRSTU	shamateur
AAEHNNTUY	Netanyahu
AAEHNPSST	pheasants
AAEHPRSVY	heavy spar
AAEIILMNS	animalise
AAEIILMNZ	animalize
AAEIILNRT	inter alia
AAEIILPTX	epitaxial
AAEIILRST	aerialist
AAEIIMNNT	inanimate
AAEIIMRST	artemisia
AAEIINNOS	Ionian Sea
AAEIKKRST	take a risk
AAEIKLLRZ	lazar-like
AAEIKLMNP	make plain
AAEIKLMPS	make a slip
AAEIKLMST	make a list
AAEIKLTTV	talkative
AAEIKMPRT	make a trip
AAEIKMRST	make a stir
AAEIKMSST	take amiss
AAEIKNPST	take pains
AAEIKPRRY	perikarya
AAEILLMMM	mammillae
AAEILLNPS	sailplane
AAEILLNPT	tailplane
AAEILLNTV	élan vital
AAEILLPPT	papillate
AAEILLPRT	plate rail
AAEILLPSS	paillasse
	palliasse
AAEILMMST	melismata
AAEILMNRT	Lamartine
AAEILMNSS	Messalina
AAEILMPRV	primaeval
AAEILMRST	materials
AAEILMSWY	miles away
AAEILNNSU	annualise
AAEILNNUZ	annualize
AAEILNORT	rationale
AAEILNPRT	perinatal
AAEILNSTT	tantalise
AAEILNTTT	tantalite
AAEILNTTZ	tantalize
AAEILORTV	variolate
AAEILPPTT	palpitate
AAEILPRST	psalteria
AAEILPRTZ	trapezial
AAEILRRTV	air travel
AAEILRRTW	water rail
AAEILRSSW	wassailer
AAEILRSTU	estuarial
AAEILRSTW	altarwise
AAEIMMNTY	many a time
AAEIMMRRS	marmarise
AAEIMMRRZ	marmarize
AAEIMNNNR	in a manner
AAEIMNNOT	emanation
AAEIMNNSS	anamnesis
AAEIMNNTX	examinant
AAEIMNOST	anatomise
AAEIMNOTZ	anatomize
AAEIMNPRR	repairman
AAEIMNRTW	water main
AAEIMNTTY	at any time
AAEIMORST	aromatise
AAEIMORTZ	aromatize
AAEIMPRRS	spermaria
AAEIMPRRV	Primavera
AAEIMPRST	spermatia
AAEINPPRT	appertain
AAEINPSSV	Vespasian
AAEINQTTU	antiquate
AAEINRRRS	in arrears
AAEINRRTV	narrative
AAEINRSST	star-anise
AAEINRSTZ	St-Nazaire
AAEIPPRRS	appraiser
AAEIPRSST	parasites
AAEIPSSTV	passivate
AAEIRRSTT	tartarise
AAEIRRTTZ	tartarize
AAEIRTWWY	write away
AAEISSSUV	assuasive
AAEJKLRWY	jaywalker
AAEJMSTTW	James Watt
AAEKKTYYY	yakety-yak
AAEKLLSST	sales talk
AAEKMMORR	make or mar
AAEKMRRTW	watermark
AAEKNNRTU	nunataker
AAEKNORRW	Korean War
AAEKNPRST	Pasternak
AAEKNRTTU	take a turn
AAELLLNRY	nearly all
AAELLLPTW	wall plate
AAELLLRTY	laterally
AAELLMORT	moral tale
AAELLMPTY	palmately
AAELLMRST	smell a rat
AAELLMSWY	may as well
AAELLNPPT	appellant
AAELLOPRW	wall a rope
AAELLOPRY	play a role
AAELLPPRW	wallpaper
AAELLPRTT	tell apart
AAELLQRSU	all square
AAELLSUXY	asexually
AAELMMNOS	melanomas

AAELMMORR	marmoreal
AAELNORTZ	Lanzarote
AAELNPRTY	planetary
AAELNRSTT	translate
AAELNRTUU	au naturel
AAELNSTTU	sultanate
AAELOPPRY	Propylaea
AAELOPRST	pastorale
AAELOPSSU	asepalous
AAELORRSY	solar year
AAELORTTZ	lazaretto
AAELORTUV	evaluator
AAELPPRRS	pearl spar
AAELPQRTU	equal part
AAELPRRSY	paralyser
AAELPSTTU	spatulate
AAELRRSTV	traversal
AAELRSSTU	as a result
	assaulter
	australes
AAELRSTTW	saltwater
AAELSSTWY	leastways
AAEMMNRST	armaments
AAEMMNSST	amassment
AAEMNORTU	neuromata
AAEMNORTZ	Mozartean
AAEMNPRTT	apartment
AAEMNSSTT	statesman
AAEMORSTT	amarettos
AAEMPRRTY	prayer mat
AAEMPRSTY	paymaster
AAEMRRSST	smart arse
AAENNPSST	en passant
AAENOPRRT	pro re nata
AAENORRTV	Terranova
AAENPRSTY	peasantry
AAENRRRST	Stranraer
AAENRRRTW	warranter
AAENSTTTT	attestant
AAEOOPPRS	soap opera
AAEOPRRST	separator
AAEOPRSTT	pastorate
AAEPPRRST	spare part
AAEPRSSTW	pass water
AAFFGNRSU	suffragan
AAFFINPRY	paraffiny
AAFFOPSSS	pass off as
AAFGHLORU	for a laugh
AAFGILNRS	franglais
AAFGINRWY	wayfaring
AAFGLLMNO	fall among
AAFGOORSS	go so far as
AAFGORTTU	autograft
AAFHHNNUY	funny ha-ha
AAFHLMOTU	Fomalhaut
AAFHLNRSS	Frans Hals
AAFHLSTTT	that's flat
AAFHLSUWY	flush away
AAFIIRRYY	airy-fairy
AAFILMMNY	family man
AAFILMNOR	foraminal

AAFILMWYY	family way
AAFILNOOV	of no avail
AAFILNOTX	aflatoxin
AAFILORUW	rauwolfia
AAFIMORRW	Mia Farrow
AAFIMORTU	fumatoria
AAFINORSS	in so far as
	insofar as
AAFINSSTT	fantasist
AAFKLNOUU	Nuku'alofa
AAFMOPRRT	apart from
AAFMORRTW	marrowfat
AAFORRSTT	for a start
AAGGIINTT	agitating
AAGGIMNOR	angiogram
AAGGIMNPR	rampaging
AAGGINNRR	arranging
AAGGINOST	go against
AAGGINOWY	going away
AAGGINSSU	assuaging
AAGGKLNNP	gangplank
AAGHHILRT	high altar
AAGHIKMNY	haymaking
AAGHIKMOS	Kagoshima
AAGHILLMN	Allingham
AAGHILMOS	Lismahago
AAGHILNRS	Shangri-La
	Shangri-la
AAGHINNRU	Hungarian
AAGHINRSS	harassing
AAGHIRTWY	right away
AAGHLNPRY	pharyngal
AAGHLNSTU	galanthus
AAGHNOTTU	hang out at
AAGHNPRST	strap-hang
AAGHOPRTU	autograph
AAGIIKNNS	Kisangani
AAGIIMNNT	animating
AAGIIMNRY	imaginary
AAGIINNTT	attaining
AAGIINOTT	agitation
AAGIINRTT	antitragi
AAGIKLMNW	law-making
AAGIKLNNO	Algonkian
AAGIKMRSS	kissagram
AAGIKNPRT	partaking
AAGILLNPP	appalling
AAGILLNTV	gallivant
AAGILLNVY	vaginally
AAGILLORT	alligator
AAGILMMNU	magnalium
AAGILMNNS	signalman
AAGILMNNT	malignant
AAGILMNSV	galvanism
AAGILMNYZ	amazingly
AAGILMRST	magistral
AAGILNOST	nostalgia
AAGILNRUU	inaugural
AAGILNRUV	vulgarian
AAGILNWYY	waylaying
AAGILQUUY	Guayaquil

AAGIMNPRS	Grampians	AAHMNOUVX	vox humana
AAGIMNPRT	ptarmigan	AAHMNPSST	phantasms
AAGINNRTU	turn again	AAHMOPRRX	Harpo Marx
AAGINOPRS	sporangia	AAHNOTTWY	at a why-not
AAGINORTV	navigator	AAHNPPRSY	nappy rash
AAGINPRSU	Singapura	AAHORTWWY	throw away
AAGINPSTU	up against		throwaway
AAGINRSTT	giant star		throw-away
AAGIPSSTY	paysagist	AAIIILMRT	militaria
AAGKNNRUU	Guru Nanak	AAIIILMSY	Ismailiya
AAGLLLNTY	gallantly	AAIIKNNRU	Ukrainian
AAGLLNOPY	play along	AAIIKNPST	Pakistani
AAGLLNRTY	gallantry	AAIIKPRTT	Tripitaka
AAGLLOPUW	go up a wall	AAIILLMNS	snail mail
AAGLMNORU	granuloma	AAIILMMNS	animalism
AAGLMPRSU	sugar palm	AAIILMNST	animalist
AAGLNOOSU	analogous	AAIILMNTY	animality
AAGMOOPSU	apogamous	AAIILMPRT	impartial
AAGMRSSSU	sargassum	AAIILNOSU	Louisiana
AAGNNORTU	orang utan	AAIILNSTU	Lusitania
	orang-utan	AAIILRRRS	arris rail
AAGNNOTUY	agony aunt	AAIILRUXY	auxiliary
AAGNORRTU	guarantor	AAIIMNNOT	animation
AAGNORSTU	Argonauts	AAIIMORST	Timisoara
AAGOPRSSU	sugar soap	AAIIMPPRR	primipara
AAGORSSSS	sargassos	AAIINNRTU	Unitarian
AAGPRSTTY	stag party	AAIINNRTV	invariant
AAHHIIMRS	maharishi	AAIINORTV	variation
AAHHIJPRS	rajahship	AAIINOSTT	satiation
AAHHILLNS	inshallah	AAIINRRTU	Ruritania
AAHHKMRSW	marsh hawk	AAIIPSTVY	pay a visit
AAHHSTTTT	that's that	AAIIQRTZZ	Tariq Aziz
AAHHSTTWW	what's what	AAIJMMNNT	Jan Timman
AAHIILNTU	Lithuania	AAIJNNOST	Saint Joan
AAHIKMNNR	Imran Khan	AAIJNRSSY	janissary
AAHILMTUZ	azimuthal	AAIKKTYYY	yakity-yak
AAHILORST	sailor-hat	AAIKLLMRY	Rik Mayall
AAHILORTU	authorial	AAIKLLPRV	Villa Park
AAHIMMNSS	shamanism	AAIKLNORW	walk on air
AAHIMNOST	Thomasina	AAIKLOSUV	souvlakia
AAHIMNPST	phantasim	AAIKMNRTW	Mark Twain
AAHIMNSST	shamanist	AAIKRRRST	ra-ra skirt
AAHIMNSTU	amianthus	AAIKRSTTU	autarkist
AAHINOORR	honoraria	AAILLMMRY	mamillary
AAHINPTTY	antipathy	AAILLMMXY	maximally
AAHINRRTU	Arthurian	AAILLMOPP	papilloma
AAHIORSTU	haustoria	AAILLMORT	tamarillo
AAHIPRRSY	hairspray	AAILLMRRY	armillary
AAHKLLMRS	hallmarks	AAILLMRSY	amaryllis
AAHKLNORS	loan shark	AAILLMRTY	maritally
	loan-shark		martially
AAHKLNOTW	walkathon	AAILLMRXY	maxillary
AAHLLSTTT	Hallstatt	AAILLNOST	allantois
AAHLMNNTU	lanthanum	AAILLNSST	All Saints
AAHLMRSST	salt marsh	AAILLNTVY	valiantly
AAHLOPRST	alphasort	AAILLPPRY	papillary
AAHLOSTTU	lash out at	AAILLPRTY	partially
AAHLPPPSY	slaphappy	AAILLPSTY	spatially
	slap-happy	AAILMNOST	atonalism
AAHLPRSSU	Pharsalus	AAILMNSST	talismans
AAHMNOSTX	xanthomas	AAILMNTTU	matutinal

AAILMORSU	malarious
AAILMORTY	amorality
AAILMPRSU	marsupial
AAILMPRTU	multipara
AAILNNOPS	Annapolis
AAILNNPQU	palanquin
AAILNOOTV	to no avail
AAILNOPSS	passional
AAILNOPVV	Pavlovian
AAILNORZZ	lazzaroni
AAILNOSTT	saltation
AAILNOSTV	salvation
AAILNOTTY	atonality
AAILNOTUV	valuation
AAILNPRTU	tarpaulin
AAILNSSTW	Stanislaw
AAILOORRT	oratorial
AAILOPRRT	raptorial
AAILOPRRY	pair-royal
AAILOPRST	pastorali
AAILOPRTT	partial to
AAILORRST	sartorial
AAILPRSSY	paralysis
AAILRRRTY	tirra-lyra
AAIMMNNOO	monomania
AAIMMNRST	Martinmas
AAIMNNORS	San Marino
AAIMNNORU	Roumanian
AAIMNOORT	inamorato
AAIMNOPRY	pyromania
AAIMNORTZ	Mozartian
AAIMNOSTT	anatomist
AAIMOORRT	moratoria
AAIMORRSW	Maori Wars
AAIMORSSU	amaurosis
AAIMQRSUU	aquariums
AAINNORRT	narration
AAINNORTT	Tarantino
AAINNPRSY	spin a yarn
AAINNRSTU	Saturnian
AAINOPSTT	antipasto
AAINORSSY	Yossarian
AAINQRTUY	antiquary
AAINQTTUY	a quantity
AAINSSSTT	assistant
AAIOPPRRT	pro patria
AAIOPRRST	aspirator
AAIOPRTTV	Pavarotti
AAIOPSTTU	autopista
AAIORRTTT	trattoria
AAIPPRSSU	pari passu
AAIPSSTWW	wasp waist
AAIPSTWYY	pay its way
AAJLOPRTY	A J P Taylor
AAJMORRSU	Ursa Major
AAJNORRTW	Trojan War
AAKKMMOOS	mako-makos
AAKLLLMST	small talk
AAKLNNOTT	Alan Knott
AAKNOOSST	Saskatoon
AALLLMOST	almost all
AALLMOPRY	royal palm
AALLMRSSY	mass rally
AALLNNOPY	Pollyanna
AALLNRTUY	naturally
AALLNSTUY	Aunt Sally
AALLORRUY	aurorally
AALLORSVY	Yaroslavl
AALLPPRTU	pull apart
AALLPRTWY	party wall
AALMNNNOU	non-manual
AALMNNPST	plantsman
AALMNOOSU	anomalous
AALMNOPRT	patrolman
AALMNPRTY	rampantly
AALMOOSTU	autosomal
AALMORSTY	royal mast
AALMORTYY	mayoralty
AALNNNORY	Nolan Ryan
AALNNOOPT	pantaloon
AALNNRTUU	unnatural
AALNOPRTT	Port Natal
AALNOPSTT	postnatal
AALNSSTWY	slantways
AALNSSUYZ	lazy Susan
AALOPRRTY	portrayal
AALORSTTY	saltatory
AAMMNNOWX	Manxwoman
AAMNNOSTY	not as many
AAMNNOTUY	any amount
AAMNOORSW	oarswoman
AAMNOOTTU	automaton
AAMNOPRTU	paramount
AAMNORRST	Monsarrat
AAMNQRTUY	Mary Quant
AANNOORTT	annotator
AANORRRTW	warrantor
AANORRRTY	narratory
AANORRTWY	Norway rat
AANORSTTU	astronaut
AANPRSSSU	Parnassus
ABBBCELLU	clubbable
ABBBDOTTU	Bud Abbott
ABBBEMNOO	Bob Beamon
ABBCDELRY	crabbedly
ABBCDIKLR	blackbird
ABBCDKLOY	black body
ABBCEELNU	Benbecula
ABBCEHOSY	Beach Boys
ABBCEIKLL	black bile
ABBCEIKRT	backbiter
ABBCEILLM	climbable
ABBCEKLLT	black belt
ABBCEKLLU	blue-black
ABBCGIKNR	bring back
ABBCHJKOS	Jack Hobbs
ABBCIKRST	brickbats
ABBCILPRU	public bar
ABBCIMOST	bombastic
ABBCKLLUY	buckyball
ABBCKLNRU	Blackburn
ABBCMOOST	cost a bomb

ABBDEEERT	breed-bate
ABBDEILOT	bobtailed
ABBDELSUU	subduable
ABBDGIILN	ad-libbing
ABBDHLOOT	bloodbath
	blood-bath
ABBDIINRR	birdbrain
ABBDILLOR	billboard
	broadbill
ABBDILNUY	Dublin Bay
ABBDILTUY	dubitably
ABBDKLNOO	blood bank
ABBDRRSUY	Bradburys
	Bradbury's
ABBEEEHRS	Beersheba
ABBEEHLRT	the rabble
ABBEEHTTY	baby teeth
ABBEEKLRU	rebukable
ABBEELMOT	be to blame
ABBEENORS	bare bones
ABBEENRST	Ernst Abbe
ABBEEORRS	sea robber
	sea-robber
ABBEFOWYY	be by way of
ABBEGIJNR	jabbering
ABBEGINRY	yabbering
ABBEHLOTU	tabbouleh
ABBEILMOT	bombilate
ABBEILMSU	Abu Simbel
ABBEIMNOR	Barenboim
ABBEIMNOS	bombasine
ABBEIMNOT	bombinate
ABBEJLLYY	jelly baby
ABBEKKLRU	break bulk
ABBEKOOSY	absey book
ABBELLMSY	semblably
ABBELMOOZ	bamboozle
ABBELMORY	Bob Marley
ABBELOSTY	stableboy
ABBELQRSU	squabbler
ABBENORRW	brown bear
ABBENORST	absorbent
ABBENORSU	Enobarbus
ABBEORSWY	Bob Sawyer
ABBFHLLSU	flashbulb
ABBGILLNO	billabong
ABBGILMNR	brambling
ABBGILOOT	obbligato
ABBGINORS	absorbing
ABBHOOTTY	baby tooth
ABBJMRUUU	Bujumbura
ABBLLOOTX	ballot-box
ABBMSTTUY	Matt Busby
ABBOOORTW	a bob or two
ABBOOPRTY	booby-trap
ABBOORRWY	barrow-boy
ABCCCKKLO	blackcock
ABCCDIIOR	boric acid
ABCCDIRUY	cubic yard
ABCCEEFRY	cybercafé
ABCCEENRU	buccaneer
ABCCEFKOR	force back
ABCCEHKKO	choke back
ABCCEINOV	biconcave
ABCCEINRW	cabin crew
ABCCELNRU	carbuncle
ABCCEMNRU	cumbrance
ABCCEMORY	come by car
ABCCEOOST	tobaccoes
ABCCFIINO	Fibonacci
ABCCGHLTU	clutch bag
ABCCHHKNU	hunchback
ABCCHKLOT	backcloth
ABCCHNOOR	Conchobar
ABCCIKLLO	acock-bill
ABCCILLUY	cubically
ABCCILNOO	obconical
ABCCKKKNO	knock back
	knock-back
ABCCKKOOR	crookback
ABCCKNOTU	cut back on
ABCCKORSS	back-cross
ABCCKORTU	backcourt
ABCCLLSSU	club class
ABCCMOORY	mobocracy
ABCDDEEHU	debauched
ABCDDEILU	adducible
ABCDDEIRT	debit card
ABCDDEKLO	blockaded
ABCDEEEHU	debauchee
ABCDEEILM	medicable
ABCDEEJKT	bed-jacket
ABCDEEKRT	bracketed
ABCDEGIMR	Cambridge
ABCDEHKLO	blockhead
ABCDEIKLS	backslide
ABCDEIKRS	disc brake
ABCDEIKRU	rudbeckia
ABCDEIKRV	drive back
ABCDEILRS	crab-sidle
ABCDEKORR	order back
ABCDELLNO	blond-lace
ABCDELMRS	scrambled
ABCDELOSU	cloud base
ABCDELOTU	double act
ABCDENORR	corn bread
ABCDENORS	absconder
ABCDENOSU	subdeacon
ABCDEOORT	obcordate
ABCDEOSST	bad cess to
ABCDHINRS	disbranch
ABCDHIOPR	chipboard
ABCDHIRSY	Charybdis
ABCDHNRTU	Dutch barn
ABCDIKRRY	brickyard
ABCDILSUY	subacidly
ABCDINOOT	bandicoot
ABCDINOTU	abduction
ABCDKLOOR	roadblock
ABCDKLOOW	blackwood
ABCDKOOSW	backwoods
ABCDLNRSU	scrubland

ABCDNOOXX	Box and Cox
ABCEEELLR	cerebella
ABCEEELLT	electable
ABCEEELRT	celebrate
ABCEEELRX	execrable
ABCEEERRT	cerebrate
ABCEEFFOR	coffee bar
ABCEEFHRU	Feuerbach
ABCEEFIRS	briefcase
ABCEEFKLT	Blackfeet
ABCEEFOSU	because of
ABCEEGKNR	greenback
ABCEEHIOT	cohabitee
ABCEEHIRT	Rechabite
ABCEEHKTT	back teeth
ABCEEHLLP	Pachelbel
ABCEEHLLY	bellyache
	belly-ache
ABCEEILSX	excisable
ABCEEILTX	excitable
ABCEEINOS	obeisance
ABCEEIRST	bacterise
ABCEEIRTZ	bacterize
ABCEEKKNR	breakneck
ABCEEKPRS	backspeer
ABCEEKPSW	sweepback
ABCEELMNS	semblance
ABCEELNRT	celebrant
ABCEELNUU	nubeculae
ABCEELOPS	placeboes
ABCEELORV	revocable
ABCEELOTV	covetable
ABCEELRST	bracelets
ABCEELRSU	securable
ABCEELRXY	execrably
ABCEELSUX	excusable
ABCEEMMOR	Morecambe
ABCEEMMRT	Camembert
ABCEEMORT	embrocate
ABCEENRTY	cybernate
ABCEEORST	obsecrate
ABCEEOSSU	sebaceous
ABCEEOSTU	cause to be
ABCEEPRRU	cup-bearer
ABCEFFHNO	Offenbach
ABCEFHILT	batch file
ABCEFIRTU	bifurcate
ABCEFOSTU	obfuscate
ABCEFRTTU	brute fact
ABCEGHILN	bleaching
ABCEGHLNO	Long Beach
ABCEGHORV	Gorbachev
ABCEGILOT	cogitable
ABCEGIMNR	embracing
ABCEGKMSU	megabucks
ABCEGKOTT	get back to
ABCEGRSUU	sugar-cube
ABCEHHMRT	Beth March
ABCEHINNO	bone china
ABCEHINOT	aitchbone
ABCEHKLLL	hell-black
ABCEHKLLO	black hole
ABCEHKMNR	benchmark
ABCEHKORS	horseback
ABCEHKOTT	to the back
ABCEHKTUW	buckwheat
ABCEHLOTU	touchable
ABCEHLRSU	crushable
ABCEHOQRU	quebracho
ABCEHRSTU	Bucharest
ABCEIILLN	cabilline
ABCEIILNS	sibilance
ABCEIILRS	irascible
ABCEIIMRT	imbricate
ABCEIJNOT	abjection
ABCEIKPRS	backspeir
ABCEIKRTW	write back
ABCEILMOT	metabolic
ABCEILNRU	incurable
ABCEILNVY	bivalency
ABCEILORT	cabriolet
ABCEILRTU	lubricate
ABCEILRUX	Excalibur
ABCEIMOTV	combative
ABCEIMRTU	bacterium
ABCEIMSTU	beat music
ABCEINORS	carbonise
ABCEINORZ	carbonize
ABCEIORRS	barricoes
ABCEIRRSU	carburise
ABCEIRRTU	rubricate
ABCEIRRUZ	carburize
ABCEISSSS	abscisses
ABCEJNSTU	subjacent
ABCEKKLNR	bank clerk
ABCEKLLLW	Blackwell
ABCEKLNSS	blackness
ABCEKLPRU	parbuckle
	Pearl Buck
ABCEKNRSS	brass neck
ABCEKPSTW	sweptback
ABCEKRTUW	waterbuck
ABCELLRSW	screwball
ABCELMOOR	rocambole
ABCELMOSY	cymbaloes
ABCELMPRU	clamber up
ABCELMRRS	scrambler
ABCELNOST	constable ❑
ABCELNOTU	countable
ABCELNRUU	uncurable
ABCELORSS	crossable
ABCELORVY	revocably
ABCELOSTT	ectoblast
ABCELRTTY	battle cry
	battle-cry
ABCELRTUU	lucubrate
ABCELSUXY	excusably
ABCEMOOTU	come about
ABCEMORSS	crossbeam
ABCENORTY	baronetcy
ABCENRRRY	cranberry
ABCENSSTU	substance

ABCEOPRRY	reprobacy
ABCEORSST	caber toss
ABCFFHNOR	branch off
ABCFFIRRU	fur fabric
ABCFGHIKT	fight back
ABCFIIRSU	Fabricius
ABCFKLOOT	Blackfoot
ABCFKOOTU	back out of
ABCGGIKPY	piggyback
ABCGHINNR	branching
ABCGIKLNS	slingback
ABCGIKNOR	king cobra
ABCGIKNSW	backswing
ABCGINNOS	sonic bang
ABCHHKSUW	bushwhack
ABCHIIKTT	a bit thick
ABCHIILLN	chilblain
ABCHIKKNT	think back
ABCHILMOS	shambolic
ABCHILNOR	bronchial
ABCHIOORS	borachios
ABCHJNOOT	John Cabot
ABCHKMTTU	thumbtack
ABCHKORTW	throw back
	throwback
ABCHLLOTT	latch bolt
ABCHNORTU	branch out
ABCIIIKLW	bailiwick
ABCIIKLRS	Black Iris
ABCIILLMU	umbilical
ABCIILLST	ballistic
ABCIILMOR	microbial
ABCIILNSY	sibilancy
ABCIILORU	Roubiliac
ABCIILRSY	irascibly
ABCIINRRU	rubrician
ABCIINRTT	Brittanic
ABCIIRSTY	sybaritic❑
ABCIKKOTU	kick about
ABCIKLLST	blacklist
ABCILMSTY	cymbalist
ABCILNNOU	connubial
ABCILNORU	binocular
ABCILNRTU	lubricant
ABCILNRUY	incurably
ABCILOPSY	polybasic
ABCILORRU	orbicular
ABCIMOSTU	subatomic
ABCINORTU	incubator
ABCINOSTY	obstinacy
ABCKKLLOO	black look
ABCKLLOOP	Blackpool
ABCKLOPST	black spot
ABCKMOTUU	muck about
ABCKNORSU	Osnabrück
ABCKNORUY	Ayckbourn
ABCKOOPRS	scrapbook
ABCKORSUY	buckayros
ABCLMNNOT	Mont Blanc
ABCLMNOUW	clubwoman
ABCLMORSU	Lambrusco
ABCLNOWYY	Colwyn Bay
ABCLOORRU	colour bar
ABCMOSSUU	submucosa
ABCNORSTU	obscurant
ABCNORSTY	corybants
ABCOORTUW	crow about
ABCRSSTTU	substract
ABDDEEGHI	big headed
	bigheaded
	big-headed
ABDDEELLU	deludable
ABDDEELMO	beadledom
ABDDEEPRS	bedspread
ABDDEILNT	blind date
ABDDEIORS	broadside
	sideboard
ABDDEIRRU	ribaudred
ABDDEISSU	disabused
ABDDELOSW	saddlebow
ABDDENNRU	unbranded
ABDDFILOR	forbiddal
ABDDGORUY	bodyguard
ABDDHINTW	bandwidth
ABDDILNNS	sand-blind
ABDDJMNOO	odd-jobman
ABDEEEFLR	deferable
ABDEEEGLL	delegable
ABDEEFHLR	half-breed
ABDEEFILN	definable
ABDEEFORY	day before
ABDEEGGLR	bedraggle
ABDEEGHIN	beheading
ABDEEGINR	gaberdine
ABDEEGMOR	embargoed
ABDEEGNRR	bergander
ABDEEGORR	garderobe
ABDEEGRRY	greybeard
ABDEEHINR	Hebridean
ABDEEHRSW	shewbread
ABDEEHRTT	had better
ABDEEIILR	diablerie
ABDEEILMS	Ambleside
ABDEEILNR	breadline
ABDEEILNS	disenable
ABDEEILRS	desirable
ABDEEILRT	liberated
ABDEEILRV	derivable
	driveable
ABDEEILST	side-table
ABDEEILTT	tide table
ABDEEINSW	Wiesbaden
ABDEEINTU	butadiene
ABDEEITTU	beatitude
ABDEEKLLW	well-baked
ABDEEKLNT	blanketed
ABDEEKORV	overbaked
ABDEELLLY	Leadbelly
ABDEELLPS	speedball
ABDEELLTY	belatedly
ABDEELMSS	assembled
ABDEELMTT	embattled

ABDEELNOR	banderole
	bandoleer
ABDEELNPR	prebendal
ABDEELNPS	spendable
ABDEELNRU	endurable
ABDEELNST	steel band
ABDEELOPS	deposable
ABDEELRSS	beardless
ABDEELRSY	Beardsley
ABDEEMNOU	beau monde
ABDEEMNRT	debarment
ABDEEMPRT	bad temper
ABDEENRRT	bartender
ABDEENRRU	underbear
ABDEENTTU	débutante
ABDEEOPST	speedboat
ABDEERRST	redbreast
ABDEFFGLU	duffel bag
ABDEFILNY	definably
ABDEFINRR	firebrand
ABDEFLTUY	by default
ABDEFORSS	brassed of
ABDEGGINR	badgering
ABDEGGLSU	sluggabed
ABDEGGMRU	Magdeburg
ABDEGGOSW	Wade Boggs
ABDEGHILN	lag behind
ABDEGIIRR	brigadier
ABDEGILNO	no big deal
ABDEGILOT	obligated
ABDEGIMRS	game birds
ABDEGINNO	in bondage
ABDEGINRR	debarring
ABDEGNOST	Edgbaston
ABDEGNSTU	Bundestag
ABDEGRTUY	budgetary
ABDEHIINT	inhabited
ABDEHILNO	hobnailed
ABDEHILOS	abolished
ABDEHIRTW	Whitbread
ABDEHLOTW	death blow
	death-blow
ABDEHNRRT	Bernhardt
ABDEHOPSW	bow-shaped
ABDEHORST	the boards
ABDEHRRTY	Bert Hardy
ABDEHRTYY	by the yard
ABDEIIKLR	like a bird
ABDEIILNU	inaudible
ABDEIILOS	diabolise
ABDEIILOZ	diabolize
ABDEIILTV	devil a bit
ABDEIKLMN	make blind
ABDEIKLNR	Birkeland
	drinkable
ABDEIKMRS	disembark
ABDEIKNRS	snakebird
ABDEIKNRW	break wind
	windbreak
ABDEILLOY	Old Bailey
ABDEILLTU	dilutable
ABDEILMNS	mandibles
ABDEILMOR	bromeliad
ABDEILNNO	bandoline
ABDEILNOR	bandolier
	bird-alone
ABDEILORV	olive drab
ABDEILOST	idle boast
ABDEILRRY	early bird
ABDEILRSY	desirably
ABDEILRVY	derivably
ABDEILRWY	bridleway
ABDEINNPW	pin and web
	web and pin
ABDEINRSS	rabidness
ABDEINSSU	unbiassed
ABDEINSSW	bawdiness
ABDEIORSW	broadwise
ABDEIRRTW	water bird
ABDEJMNOS	James Bond
ABDEJORTT	objet d'art
ABDEKLRSU	Dark blues
ABDEKMRRU	brake drum
	drum brake
ABDEKNORW	break down
	breakdown
ABDELLMOU	mouldable
ABDELLNOO	ballooned
ABDELNNSS	blandness
ABDELNOSV	bond-slave
ABDELNRUY	endurably
ABDELNSTU	Dunstable
ABDELOOPS	paso doble
ABDELORUV	boulevard
ABDEMNNOR	Dobermann
ABDEMNRRT	Rembrandt
ABDEMNSTY	Stand By Me
ABDEMOOSY	a somebody
ABDENNOYY	annoyed by
ABDENNTTU	Butenandt
ABDENOPPR	bond paper
ABDENOPRS	bad person
ABDENORRY	errand-boy
ABDENORSS	broadness
ABDENORST	adsorbent
ABDENOSTU	eastbound
ABDENRRST	St Bernard
ABDENRSTU	Bundesrat
ABDENRSTY	bystander
	stander-by
ABDEOORRV	overboard
ABDEOORWZ	zebrawood
ABDEOSTWY	body waste
ABDFGLMOO	Lamb of God
ABDFHILLN	half-blind
ABDFHLLOO	half-blood
ABDFIIRRR	friarbird
ABDFLLNUY	full and by
ABDFORRSU	surfboard
ABDGHORTU	go hard but
ABDGIILNS	disabling
ABDGIILNY	abidingly

ABDGIIMNT	bad timing
ABDGINNOU	abounding
ABDGINOOR	Brigadoon
ABDGINRRY	brigandry
ABDGIRRSU	sugar bird
ABDHIINNR	hindbrain
ABDHIMNRY	mynah bird
ABDHIMORY	hybridoma
ABDHIMRTY	dithyramb
ABDHIOPRS	board ship
	shipboard
ABDHLNSUY	husbandly
ABDHNOSUY	Hudson Bay
ABDHNRSUY	husbandry
ABDIIILLN	libidinal
ABDIILLRS	billiards
ABDIILMOS	diabolism
ABDIILNUY	inaudibly
ABDIILOST	diabolist
ABDIIMRST	tribadism
ABDIINPTU	put in a bid
ABDILLMOR	millboard
ABDILLPRU	pull a bird
ABDILNOOR	Bardolino
ABDILOTUW	wild about
ABDILRRRY	Larry Bird
ABDILRSSU	disbursal
ABDIMNNOT	badminton
ABDIMNOTT	Tom and Tib
ABDIMPQSU	damp squib
ABDINOWWY	bay window
ABDINRSTW	wristband
ABDIRSTUY	absurdity
ABDKLNORW	World Bank
ABDKNOOST	bookstand
ABDLMOOOR	broadloom
ABDMMNOSU	ombudsman
ABDMNNOOW	bondwoman
ABDMNORTU	Dumbarton
ABDMNORUU	bum around
ABDMOOORR	boardroom
ABDNNOSTY	on standby
	on stand-by
ABDNOORSW	snowboard
ABEEEEFRT	beefeater❑
ABEEEERSZ	sea breeze
ABEEEFKRR	break free
ABEEEFKST	beefsteak
ABEEEFLOS	beefaloes
ABEEEFLRR	referable
ABEEEFLRZ	freezable
ABEEEGLLR	relegable
ABEEEGLNS	Bengalese
ABEEEGLRU	beleaguer
ABEEEGLTV	vegetable
ABEEEGNNR	green bean
ABEEEGSTU	Beau Geste
ABEEEHLSW	wheelbase
ABEEEHRTW	wheat beer
ABEEEKNRV	break even
ABEEEKPRR	barkeeper
	bar-keeper
ABEEELMPR	permeable
ABEEELMTY	may beetle
ABEEELNRT	enterable
ABEEELNRV	venerable
ABEEELNRW	renewable
ABEEELRST	steerable
ABEEELRSV	severable
ABEEENNTV	an even bet
ABEEERRTT	terebrate
ABEEERRTV	vertebrae
ABEEERTUX	exuberate
ABEEFFILN	ineffable
ABEEFGLOR	forgeable
ABEEFILNR	inferable
ABEEFILRS	bas relief
	bas-relief
ABEEFLORY	lay before
ABEEFLRSU	refusable
ABEEFLRTU	refutable
ABEEFLSSU	self-abuse
ABEEFORRS	forebears
ABEEFORTX	before tax
ABEEGGINU	béguinage
ABEEGHILW	weighable
ABEEGHINV	have being
ABEEGILLR	Gabrielle
ABEEGILLV	give a bell
ABEEGIMTU	image tube
ABEEGINRS	Bering Sea
ABEEGINRU	aubergine
ABEEGKORR	brokerage
ABEEGLLMO	Malebolge
ABEEGLNPR	pregnable
ABEEGLNPS	bespangle
ABEEGLNVY	vengeably
ABEEGLOPR	bargepole
	porbeagle
ABEEGLSSU	guessable
ABEEGLTVY	vegetably
ABEEGMORS	embargoes
ABEEGNORZ	Bronze Age
ABEEGNRSU	subgenera
ABEEGRSTU	sugar beet
ABEEHHKSS	baksheesh
ABEEHHNST	Hans Bethe
ABEEHILRT	heritable
ABEEHILST	Elisabeth
ABEEHILTZ	Elizabeth
ABEEHIMSV	misbehave
ABEEHIMTW	whitebeam
ABEEHINRT	breathe in
	hibernate
	inbreathe
ABEEHKORS	brake shoe
ABEEHKOSU	bakehouse
ABEEHLLUW	blue whale
ABEEHLMPS	blaspheme
ABEEHLNOW	whalebone
ABEEHLTTT	The Tablet
ABEEHMNOT	on the beam

ABEEHNORT	breathe on
ABEEHNOTT	on the beat
ABEEHNRTY	Abernethy
ABEEHORTU	hereabout
ABEEIINRT	inebriate
ABEEIKLST	beastlike
ABEEIKMRT	breaktime
ABEEIKNST	snakebite
ABEEILMRS	miserable
ABEEILMST	estimable
ABEEILMTT	timetable
ABEEILNTW	table wine
ABEEILQTU	equitable
ABEEILRSV	revisable
	verbalise
ABEEILRTV	avertible
	veritable
ABEEILRVV	revivable
ABEEILRVZ	verbalize
ABEEILSTW	tablewise
ABEEIORSV	rise above
ABEEIOTTT	bite to eat
ABEEIRRSS	brasserie
	brassiere
	brassière
ABEEJLLNO	banjolele
ABEEJLLNY	jelly bean
ABEEJLNOY	enjoyable
ABEEKLMOR	Blakemore
ABEEKLNSS	bleakness
ABEEKLORV	revokable
ABEEKNOPR	break open
ABEEKNPSU	unbespeak
ABEEKOTUW	week about
ABEEKPRST	break step
ABEEKRRSU	Sue Barker
ABEELLMRS	small beer
ABEELLMSS	blameless
ABEELLMTU	umbellate
ABEELLORT	tolerable
ABEELLORV	be all over
ABEELMMOR	memorable
ABEELMNRU	numerable
ABEELMORV	removable
ABEELMPRT	Temple Bar
ABEELMPRY	permeably
ABEELMRSS	assembler
ABEELMRSU	resumable
ABEELNNTU	untenable
ABEELNRVY	venerably
ABEELOPRV	proveable
ABEELPRSU	superable
ABEELPRTU	reputable
ABEELRRTV	vertebral
ABEELRTTU	utterable
ABEEMNTTT	battement
ABEEMORRT	barometer
ABEEMRRSU	embrasure
ABEENRSST	steenbras
ABEENRTUX	exuberant
ABEEOPRRT	reprobate
ABEEOSTUU	beauteous
ABEEPRSTT	bespatter
ABEFFILNY	ineffably
ABEFFLOSU	buffaloes
ABEFGILNR	frangible
ABEFIILLR	fibrillae
ABEFIILNU	unifiable
ABEFIIMRT	fimbriate
ABEFILLOR	liable for
ABEFILLRT	filtrable
ABEFILNRU	funebrial
ABEFILTUU	beautiful
ABEFINORR	forebrain
ABEFIRRTU	bear fruit
ABEFIRSST	first base
ABEFKLORT	flat broke
ABEFKLSTU	basketful
ABEFKNORT	to be frank
ABEFKOORT	foot brake
ABEFLLLUY	balefully
ABEFLLNUY	banefully
ABEFLLRRU	barrefull
	barrelful
ABEFLNOSW	wolfsbane
ABEFLOSUW	blow a fuse
ABEFLRTUY	refutably
ABEFMNORU	a number of
ABEFMNOSY	by means of
ABEFOPRRU	bear up for
ABEFORRTY	ferry-boat
ABEGGINSS	bagginess
ABEGGLLRU	bugger all
ABEGHHILT	high table
ABEGHILRT	rightable
ABEGHINRR	harbinger
ABEGHINRT	breathing
ABEGHMRRU	hamburger
ABEGHRSSU	sagebrush
ABEGIILNS	abseiling
ABEGIILNT	ignitable
ABEGIILRR	irrigable
ABEGIINOR	aborigine□
ABEGIINOS	a big noise
ABEGILLLN	labelling
ABEGILLMN	emballing
ABEGILLOS	globalise
ABEGILLOZ	globalize
ABEGILLST	Bill Gates
ABEGILMNY	beamingly
ABEGILRSU	Bulgarise
ABEGILRUZ	Bulgarize
ABEGIMRRS	ambergris
ABEGINNNT	benignant
ABEGINNRT	bantering
ABEGINNRU	unbearing
ABEGINOST	obsignate
ABEGINRRT	bartering
ABEGINRTT	battering
ABEGIORRY	Yogi Berra
ABEGIUVZZ	give a buzz
ABEGJLNOU	jugal bone

ABEGJLRRS	Jarlsberg
ABEGJORTU	objurgate
ABEGJSTUU	subjugate
ABEGLLORS	bargellos
ABEGLMORU	beglamour
ABEGLMRTU	grumble at
ABEGLNORU	Boulanger
	lounge bar
ABEGLRSSU	bluegrass
ABEGMMMRU	brummagem
ABEGMNOOR	boomerang
ABEGMNOSY	moneybags
ABEGNOOVY	bon voyage
ABEGNORUY	bear young
ABEGOORST	botargoes
ABEGORSTU	subrogate
ABEGRRSST	Strasberg
ABEHHNOST	on the bash
ABEHIINNR	Hibernian
ABEHIITTW	whitebait
ABEHIKLNT	thinkable
ABEHIKNTT	bethankit
ABEHIKRTW	break with
ABEHILLLY	Bill Haley
ABEHILMOP	amphibole
ABEHILMRS	herbalism
ABEHILMSU	Basil Hume
ABEHILRST	herbalist
ABEHILRSY	bearishly
ABEHILRTY	breathily
	heritably
ABEHILSST	establish
ABEHIMRRU	herbarium
ABEHINOOP	neophobia
ABEHINOST	on the bias
ABEHINRST	the brains
ABEHIORUV	behaviour
ABEHIPRRS	herb-Paris
ABEHKNRSS	Hans Krebs
ABEHLLNOT	on the ball
ABEHLMPSY	blasphemy
ABEHLOPRY	hyperbola
ABEHLORTT	betrothal
ABEHLORTW	bowler hat
ABEHNORRT	abhorrent
ABEHNOTTU	thenabout
ABEHNRRTU	heartburn
ABEHNRSSS	brashness
ABEHNRSTU	sunbather
ABEHOOSTU	boathouse
	boat-house
	houseboat
ABEHQRSUU	harquebus
ABEIIKMNR	minibreak
ABEIILLLR	illiberal
ABEIILLMT	limitable
ABEIILNRT	nail-biter
ABEIILRRT	irritable
ABEIILRTV	vibratile
ABEIILSST	stabilise
ABEIILSTV	visitable
ABEIILSTZ	stabilize
ABEIINNRT	inebriant
ABEIIPRTT	bipartite
ABEIIRSSV	vibrissae
ABEIIRTVV	vibrative
ABEIJLLNY	Billy Jean
ABEIKMSTY	by mistake
ABEIKNNOR	break in on
ABEIKNNTY	taken in by
ABEIKNORT	break into
ABEILLLNT	libellant
ABEILLLRY	liberally
ABEILLNOT	not liable
	note a bill
ABEILLNPU	unpliable
ABEILLPSU	plausible
ABEILLSSU	subsellia
ABEILLSSY	syllabise
ABEILLSYZ	syllabize
ABEILMMOV	immovable
ABEILMMSW	swimmable
ABEILMMTU	immutable
ABEILMNSS	balminess
ABEILMORT	Baltimore
ABEILMPTU	imputable
ABEILMRSV	verbalism
ABEILMRSY	miserably
ABEILMRTU	umbratile
ABEILMSTU	sublimate
ABEILMSTY	estimably
ABEILNPRT	printable
ABEILNPSU	subalpine
ABEILNRRY	inerrably
ABEILNRSS	brainless
ABEILNRSU	insurable
ABEILNRWY	barely win
ABEILORRT	liberator
ABEILORST	strobilae
ABEILPRTY	bit player
ABEILQTUY	equitably
ABEILRRYZ	bizarrely
ABEILRSTU	brutalise
ABEILRSTV	verbalist
ABEILRTTY	at liberty
ABEILRTUZ	brutalize
ABEILRTVY	veritably
ABEILRVVY	revivably
ABEILSTTW	twistable
ABEILSUVY	abusively
ABEIMNOST	absit omen
ABEIMNRST	brainstem
	tribesman
ABEIMNRSU	submarine
ABEIMNRTU	inumbrate
ABEIMNRUV	brevi manu
ABEIMOTTU	time about
ABEIMSSST	Miss Bates
ABEINNOPT	pinto bean
ABEINNRST	bannister❏
ABEINNSTT	abstinent
ABEINNTYZ	Byzantine

ABEINOSTT	obstinate
ABEINPRST	breastpin
ABEINRSST	banisters
ABEINRTTU	tribunate
	turbinate
ABEIRRRST	barrister
ABEIRRSST	arbitress
ABEIRTTTU	attribute
ABEJLNOYY	enjoyably
ABEKKMOOR	bookmaker
ABEKLLMOS	smoke-ball
ABEKLLPRU	pull baker
ABEKLNNSS	blankness
ABEKLNOST	Léon Bakst
ABEKLOOPT	bookplate
ABEKLOOUV	book value
ABEKLORTW	worktable
ABEKMNPRS	sperm bank
ABEKMOORT	bootmaker
ABEKNNOST	banknotes
ABELLMNTY	lambently
ABELLORTY	tolerably
ABELLORUY	royal blue
ABELLOSWY	Boyle's law
ABELLRSST	Tsar's Bell
ABELMMORY	memorably
ABELMNOUV	unmovable
ABELMNPRU	penumbral
ABELMNRUY	numerably
ABELMNSTT	blastment
ABELMORVY	removably
ABELNOSUX	Saxon blue
ABELNOSYZ	lazybones
	lazy-bones
ABELNPTUY	untypable
ABELNRSTU	subaltern
ABELNRTTU	turntable
ABELOOPPS	opposable
ABELOOTVY	obovately
ABELOPRTY	pot barley
ABELOPRVY	proveably
ABELORRSU	labourers
ABELOSTTY	stylobate
ABELPRSUY	superably
ABELPRTUY	reputably
ABELRSUYY	Aylesbury
ABEMNNOSY	by no means
ABEMNORSW	Sam Browne
ABEMOOPRR	broomrape
ABEMOOPTU	mope about
ABEMOOTUV	move about
ABEMORRRY	Barrymore
ABEMORRTU	arboretum
ABEMOSSTU	mess about
ABENNNNOY	Anne Bonny
ABENOQSTU	Bosanquet
ABENORSTV	observant
ABENORTUZ	brazen out
ABENOSSST	stone bass
ABEOORRSU	arboreous
ABEORTTTY	try to beat
ABEOSTTUW	west-about
ABEPRRRSY	raspberry
ABEPRSSSY	passers-by
ABERSSTTU	substrate
ABERTTTUW	water butt
	water-butt
ABFGGHILT	flight bag
ABFGIOPSY	Bay of Pigs
ABFHLLSUY	bashfully
ABFHLNRSU	flash burn
ABFHLRSTU	flat brush
ABFHSTTTU	butt-shaft
ABFIILLRR	fibrillar
ABFIIORSU	bifarious
ABFILLSYY	syllabify
ABFILMSUY	subfamily
ABFILNSSU	basinfuls
ABFILOTTU	flit about
ABFJOOOTU	out of a job
ABFLLLSTU	full blast
	full-blast
ABFLOOOTU	fool about
ABFNOPPRZ	Franz Bopp
ABGGIINNR	barging-in
ABGGIKNPY	piggy-bank
ABGGLOORY	garbology
ABGHILMNS	shambling
ABGHINWZZ	whizz-bang
ABGHIOPRY	biography
ABGIILLNU	bilingual
ABGIIMTUY	ambiguity
ABGIINNOT	obtaining
ABGIINRTV	vibrating
ABGIKLLNY	balkingly
ABGILNORU	labouring
ABGILOOST	obligatos
ABGIMOSSU	subimagos
ABGIMOSUU	ambiguous
ABGINOSTW	swingboat
ABGLLNOOW	bowl along
ABGLMOPSU	plumbagos
ABHHILOTT	batholith
ABHHIRRSU	hairbrush
ABHIILLMS	bismillah
ABHIKLLSW	hawksbill
ABHIKMRRT	birthmark
ABHILMNTU	thumbnail
ABHILMOPY	amphiboly
ABHILNORT	Bartholin
ABHILNRTY	labyrinth
ABHILTTTY	Blyth Tait
ABHIMPTUW	with a bump
ABHIOOOPZ	zoophobia
ABHIOPSTU	about-ship
ABHJNORRY	Barry John
ABHLLMSTU	all thumbs
ABHLOPSTY	hypoblast
ABHMNRTUY	urban myth
ABHNORRUU	unharbour
ABIIILLTY	liability
ABIIILNTY	inability

ABIIILTVY	viability	ACCCDHLOT	catch cold
ABIILLLRY	Billy Liar	ACCCEIIRT	cicatrice
ABIILLNRT	brilliant	ACCCEILLO	calcicole
ABIILMRST	tribalism	ACCCEIOPT	copacetic
ABIILNOOT	abolition	ACCCHKOOR	cockroach
ABIILNOOV	boliviano	ACCCHNOTY	cony-catch
ABIILNORY	nobiliary	ACCCIILLY	alicyclic
ABIILRRTY	irritably	ACCCIILMT	climactic
ABIILSTTY	stability	ACCCIIOPR	capriccio ❑
ABIILSTUY	usability	ACCCILORU	Carluccio
ABIIMOSTU	ambitious	ACCCNOPUY	occupancy
ABIINNNUV	Ivan Bunin	ACCDDEEEN	decadence
ABIINOOTV	obviation	ACCDDEILS	discalced
ABIINORTV	vibration	ACCDDIIST	didactics
ABIINSTVW	bavin wits	ACCDDIORS	disaccord
ABILLNOPT	ballpoint	ACCDEEEHN	déchéance
ABILLORRZ	razorbill	ACCDEEHIK	chickadee
ABILLPSUY	plausibly	ACCDEEIST	desiccate
ABILMMOVY	immovably	ACCDEELLN	cancelled
ABILMMTUY	immutably	ACCDEELNO	concealed
ABILMOORS	ribosomal	ACCDEELOS	coalesced
ABILMPTUY	imputably	ACCDEFILY	decalcify
ABILMRSTU	brutalism	ACCDEGLNO	clog dance
ABILNORTY	Tony Blair	ACCDEHKOT	cocked hat
ABILNRTUZ	brazil nut	ACCDEHRST	scratched
ABILNRTVY	vibrantly	ACCDEIILN	Icelandic
ABILOORSU	laborious	ACCDEIILT	dialectic
ABILRSSUY	Salisbury	ACCDEINST	desiccant
ABILRSTUY	salubrity	ACCDEIORW	cowardice
ABILRTTUY	brutality	ACCDELLOO	local code
ABIMMNRUU	manubrium	ACCDELMOR	cold cream
ABIMNTUYZ	Byzantium	ACCDEMNOO	cacodemon
ABIMORRTT	Britomart	ACCDEMOPT	compacted
ABINNOTVV	bon vivant	ACCDEMORR	camcorder
ABINOOPRT	probation	ACCDEMORY	democracy
ABINOPSTU	subtopian	ACCDEORRS	scorecard
ABINRSSUY	Sainsbury	ACCDEORSW	sacred cow
ABIORRTVY	vibratory	ACCDFIILO	folic acid
ABIPRSTTY	baptistry	ACCDFILLY	flaccidly
ABIRRTTUY	tributary	ACCDGINOR	according
ABJLLOOTY	jollyboat	ACCDHHRUY	archduchy
ABJOSTTUU	just about	ACCDHIIOR	radicchio
ABKLLOOST	bookstall	ACCDHOORT	octachord
ABKNPRSTU	Knabstrup	ACCDHORTW	catchword
ABLLLOOST	stoolball	ACCDIIIRT	diacritic
ABLLLOOTU	loll about	ACCDIIOPT	apodictic
ABLMNNOTZ	Boltzmann	ACCDILLOY	cycloidal
ABLMNORSU	subnormal	ACCDINOOR	accordion
ABLMNOUVY	unmovably		Concordia
ABLNNTUUY	untunably	ACCDKNORW	crack down
ABLNRSUUY	sublunary		crackdown
ABLOOPTYY	play booty	ACCDLOPTU	cloud-capt
ABMOOORTT	motor boat	ACCDNOORT	concordat
ABMPRSTTU	bump start	ACCDOOSST	stoccados
ABNORTTUU	about-turn	ACCEEELNR	canceleer
	turn about	ACCEEELRS	recalesce
	turnabout	ACCEEENRR	recreance
ABNOSTTUU	nuts about	ACCEEGHMN	McGeechan
ABOOPRSTT	bootstrap	ACCEEHIST	catechise
ABRRSTTUW	bratwurst	ACCEEHITY	haecceity
ACCCDEEIN	accidence	ACCEEHITZ	catechize

ACCEEHKMT	checkmate
ACCEEHLOT	cochleate
ACCEEHNPR	perchance
ACCEEILNR	cancelier
ACCEEIQSU	acquiesce
ACCEEIRTV	accretive
ACCEEISTX	exsiccate
ACCEEKLOT	cockateel
ACCEELMNO	come clean
ACCEELNOR	concealer
ACCEELNPR	pre-cancel
ACCEELPST	spectacle
ACCEENNST	canescent
ACCEENRRY	recreancy
ACCEENRSU	recusance
ACCEEORSU	ceraceous
ACCEESSUU	Ceausescu
ACCEFFFIL	cliff face
	cliff-face
ACCEFGILU	calcifuge
ACCEFHIRT	catch fire
ACCEFHLNU	chanceful
ACCEFHLOT	face-cloth
ACCEFIIRS	sacrifice
ACCEFILSU	fascicule
ACCEGIKNO	Cockaigne
ACCEGINPT	accepting
ACCEGIORT	categoric
ACCEHHNOW	how chance?
ACCEHILLN	ill-chance
ACCEHILNO	cochineal
ACCEHILNT	technical
ACCEHILOR	choleraic
ACCEHIMNS	mechanics
	mischance
ACCEHIMST	catechism
	schematic
ACCEHINRY	chicanery
ACCEHIRTT	architect
ACCEHISTT	catechist
ACCEHLOOT	chocolate
ACCEHMNTT	catchment
ACCEHNORS	charnecos
ACCEHORTU	cartouche
ACCEHORTY	theocracy
ACCEHRRST	scratcher
ACCEIIMNT	cinematic
ACCEIINOS	cocainise
ACCEIINOZ	cocainize
ACCEIIRST	cicatrise
ACCEIIRTZ	cicatrize
ACCEIISTV	siccative
ACCEIKKLP	place kick
ACCEIKLOT	cockatiel
ACCEIKPRS	spice rack
ACCEIKRSW	wisecrack
ACCEILNTU	inculcate
ACCEILOPR	precocial
ACCEILPST	sceptical
ACCEILRTU	circulate
ACCEINOOZ	Caenozoic
ACCEINORT	accretion
ACCEINOSS	accession
ACCEINSTU	encaustic
	succinate
ACCEINTXY	excitancy
ACCEIPSTY	cityscape
ACCEJORYY	Joyce Cary
ACCEKNORR	corncrake
ACCELLLOS	close call
ACCELLOOT	collocate
ACCELMORY	real McCoy
ACCELNOOR	con calore
ACCELNOPY	cyclopean
ACCELNOTU	cancel out
ACCELNOVY	concavely
ACCELNPTY	peccantly
ACCEMNRTU	accrument
ACCEMNRTY	McCartney
ACCENNOST	Constance
ACCENNRST	CT scanner
ACCENORSU	cancerous
ACCENRSUY	recusancy
ACCEORRSW	scarecrow
ACCEORSSY	accessory
ACCEORSTU	coruscate
	court case
ACCFFHHIN	chaffinch
ACCFIILOR	calorific
ACCFIILSU	fasciculi
ACCFIISST	fascistic
ACCFIKNSY	fancy-sick
ACCFINNOU	Confucian
ACCFIORTX	Arctic fox
ACCFKOORT	frock-coat
ACCGHHNNU	Changchun
ACCGHIIKN	chiacking
ACCGIKLNR	crackling
ACCHHIINP	Pichincha
ACCHHMNRU	churchman
ACCHHORRS	Rorschach
ACCHILLOO	alcoholic
ACCHILLOT	laccolith
ACCHIMOPR	camphoric
ACCHIMORT	chromatic
ACCHIMORX	Chico Marx
ACCHIMOST	stomachic
ACCHINPTU	catch up in
ACCHIRTTY	trachytic
ACCHKLOST	sackcloth
ACCHKOOOP	cock-a-hoop
ACCHKOORW	coachwork
ACCHKORST	crack shot
ACCHLOOPS	school cap
ACCHLOORT	ochlocrat
ACCHLOOSW	slowcoach
ACCHLOOTY	chocolaty
ACCHNOOPY	cacophony
ACCHNORSU	chancrous
ACCHOORTU	coach tour
ACCHOSSTU	succotash
ACCHPRSUU	crush a cup

ACCIIILNN	clinician
ACCIILLSY	salicylic
ACCIILLVY	civically
ACCIILNOR	conciliar
ACCIILOPT	occipital
ACCIILTVY	acclivity
ACCIINOOZ	Cainozoic
ACCIINRTY	intricacy
ACCIIORST	isocratic
ACCIISSTU	casuistic
ACCIJKKXY	Jacky Ickx
ACCIKNOSW	cockswain
ACCILLMOY	comically
ACCILLNOY	conically
ACCILLNYY	cynically
ACCILLRUY	crucially
ACCILNORV	clavicorn
ACCILOSUV	acclivous
ACCILRRSU	circulars
ACCILRRUU	curricula
ACCILRTUU	cuticular
ACCIMNORY	acronymic
ACCIMOORS	crocosmia
ACCIMORTY	timocracy
ACCINOPRR	Capricorn
ACCINOSTY	oscitancy
ACCINOTVY	concavity
ACCINSTTY	syntactic
ACCIOPRTY	procacity
ACCIOPSST	spiccatos
ACCIOSSTU	acoustics
ACCLMNOTY	Tom Clancy
ACCLMOPTY	compactly
ACCLORTUY	clay court
ACCMMOORS	macrocosm
ACCMNOORY	monocracy
ACCMNOTUY	contumacy
ACCNNOOTU	no-account
	on account
ACCNNOSTY	constancy
ACCNOOTTU	to account
ACCNOPSTU	occupants
ACCNORSTU	coruscant
ACCOPRRUY	procuracy
ACCORSSTU	cut across
ACDDDEEIT	dedicated
ACDDDEIRS	discarded
ACDDEEEIT	dedicatee
ACDDEEIMT	medicated
ACDDEEORT	decorated
ACDDEFGOO	goodfaced
ACDDEGIRS	disgraced
ACDDEGNOO	dodecagon
ACDDEIINS	discandie
ACDDEIINT	indicated
ACDDEIITV	addictive
ACDDEIJNU	jaundiced
ACDDEILPS	displaced
ACDDEINRX	card-index
ACDDEIORT	dedicator
ACDDELNRU	underclad
ACDDENRRU	undercard
ACDDHHNSU	dachshund
ACDDHIILM	maid-child
ACDDIILOS	discoidal
ACDDIILRU	druidical
ACDDIINOT	addiction
ACDDIMSSU	Sadducism
ACDDNOORR	donor card
ACDDNRTUY	cut and dry
ACDEEEHNP	cheapened
ACDEEEHNR	adherence
ACDEEEMRT	decametre
ACDEEEPPS	deep space
ACDEEEPRT	deprecate
ACDEEEPRV	Cape Verde
ACDEEERST	desecrate
ACDEEERTU	re-educate
ACDEEFGKU	fudge cake
ACDEEFHMR	chamfered
ACDEEFHWY	whey-faced
ACDEEFIRR	Frederica
ACDEEFKRT	after deck
ACDEEFNTU	fecundate
ACDEEFRRT	refracted
ACDEEGHNX	exchanged
ACDEEGLNO	congealed
ACDEEGLOU	Decalogue
ACDEEGNRR	green card
ACDEEGOPU	decoupage
	découpage
ACDEEHINN	enchained
ACDEEHIOV	head voice
ACDEEHIPP	epedaphic
ACDEEHKNY	hackneyed
ACDEEHLLN	chandelle
ACDEEHNNT	enchanted
ACDEEHNST	chastened
ACDEEHPSY	speech day
ACDEEHRRT	chartered
ACDEEHRRY	cherryade
ACDEEIILP	epicedial
ACDEEIINP	epicedian
ACDEEIJTV	adjective
ACDEEILMR	declaimer
ACDEEILNN	celandine
	decennial
ACDEEILNR	Icelander
ACDEEILNU	Euclidean
ACDEEILRT	decalitre
ACDEEILTU	elucidate
ACDEEIMNP	impedance
ACDEEINOS	oceanides
ACDEEINRS	increased
ACDEEIPRT	predicate
ACDEEIRRT	traceried
ACDEEITUV	educative
ACDEEKKNR	knackered
ACDEELLNV	Cleveland
ACDEELLOT	decollate
	ocellated
ACDEELNOP	penal code

ACDEELNTT	tentacled		acid house
ACDEELORR	Carol Reed		acid-house
ACDEELORW	coral weed	ACDEHIPRT	dirt cheap
ACDEELTTU	Claudette		dirt-cheap
ACDEEMMUV	vade-mecum	ACDEHIRSV	crash dive
ACDEEMNOR	Decameron	ACDEHKOST	headstock
ACDEENNRT	entranced	ACDEHLMSY	chlamydes
ACDEENNRU	endurance	ACDEHLNOT	decathlon
ACDEENOPR	rope-dance	ACDEHLNRY	chandlery
ACDEENOSS	deaconess	ACDEHLNTU	unlatched
ACDEENRTY	day centre	ACDEHLPRY	parchedly
ACDEEORRR	care order	ACDEHMNTU	unmatched
ACDEEPRRT	red carpet	ACDEHMPRY	pachyderm
ACDEERSST	Descartes	ACDEHNOPR	cardphone
ACDEERSTT	scattered	ACDEHNOTU	head count
ACDEERSTU	reductase	ACDEHNRTU	uncharted
ACDEESSTU	decussate	ACDEHNRUY	hue and cry
ACDEFFHKO	hacked off	ACDEHNSTU	unscathed
ACDEFFILR	Radcliffe	ACDEHNTUW	unwatched
ACDEFFILT	afflicted	ACDEIIINT	dietician
ACDEFFIST	disaffect	ACDEIILMN	medicinal
ACDEFFLLO	called off	ACDEIILNT	identical
ACDEFFLLU	full-faced	ACDEIILRV	veridical
ACDEFFMOR	cofferdam	ACDEIILST	deistical
ACDEFGLNO	long-faced	ACDEIIMMY	immediacy
ACDEFHINR	arch-fiend	ACDEIIMRT	diametric
ACDEFHINT	thin-faced		matricide
ACDEFHITW	faced with	ACDEIINTV	vindicate
ACDEFHLTU	Dutch leaf	ACDEIIPRR	parricide
ACDEFILLO	coalfield	ACDEIIPRT	patricide
ACDEFILLU	Caulfield	ACDEIKRST	sidetrack
ACDEFILNY	idle fancy	ACDEIKTTY	ticket day
ACDEFILOR	coal-fired	ACDEILLMY	decimally
ACDEFLLOR	called for		medically
	called-for	ACDEILLOU	lodiculae
ACDEFLMOR	cold frame	ACDEILLOZ	localized
ACDEFLNOR	force-land	ACDEILLTY	edictally
ACDEFMNOO	moon-faced	ACDEILMNU	unclaimed
ACDEFORSS	cross-fade	ACDEILMPS	misplaced
ACDEFRRTU	fractured	ACDEILNOU	Deucalion
ACDEGGIMO	demagogic	ACDEILOOR	air-cooled
ACDEGGIOP	pedagogic	ACDEILORX	Delacroix
ACDEGHINR	chagrined	ACDEILOST	dislocate
ACDEGHINT	detaching	ACDEILOTV	dolce vita
ACDEGHIRS	discharge	ACDEILPTU	duplicate
ACDEGHNNU	unchanged	ACDEILRTU	curtailed
ACDEGIILR	regicidal	ACDEIMNNO	dominance
ACDEGILNO	genocidal	ACDEIMNNT	mendicant
ACDEGIMNP	decamping	ACDEIMNOP	compendia
ACDEGINNS	ascending	ACDEIMNTY	mendacity
ACDEGIRRT	cartridge	ACDEIMORT	decimator
ACDEGLLRU	guard cell	ACDEIMORU	ami de cour
ACDEGMNOO	come and go	ACDEIMOSY	Samoyedic
ACDEHHIKT	thickhead	ACDEINNOR	ordinance
ACDEHHIRS	rhachides	ACDEINNOT	contadine
ACDEHHORX	hexachord		contained
ACDEHIINS	side chain	ACDEINNST	instanced
ACDEHIITT	diathetic	ACDEINORR	coriander
ACDEHINNR	hindrance	ACDEINORT	redaction
ACDEHINSV	Cavendish	ACDEINOTU	education
ACDEHIOSU	Acid House	ACDEINSTY	asyndetic

syndicate
ACDEIPRST practised
ACDEIPRSW swipe card
ACDEIPSTU cuspidate
ACDEIQTTU acquitted
ACDEIRTTX direct tax
ACDEISSTY ecdysiast
ACDEKMOOS mockadoes
ACDEKNOPU pound cake
ACDEKOPTU packed out
ACDEKRSSU duck's arse
ACDELLOPS collapsed
scalloped
ACDELMOOR moral code
ACDELMOPR placoderm
ACDELMORY comradely
ACDELNNOO colonnade
ACDELNOSW scale down
ACDELNRTY trancedly
ACDELOSTW cold sweat
ACDEMMNOR commander
ACDEMOORT motorcade
ACDEMORSU Scudamore
ACDENNRST transcend
ACDENORST Doncaster
ACDENORSY secondary
ACDENORTU undercoat
ACDENRRSU run scared
ACDENRRTU undercart
ACDENRTTU truncated
ACDEOORRT decorator
ACDEOORTT doctorate
ACDEOPSTU spaced out
ACDEOPTTU coup d'état
ACDEORRST store card
ACDEORRTT detractor
ACDEORSUZ cruzadoes
ACDEORTUY educatory
ACDFFHNSU handcuffs
ACDFHINOO food chain
ACDFIIRUY fiduciary
ACDFIKLNO Nick Faldo
ACDFINNOT confidant
ACDFINTUY facundity
ACDFNTTUY candytuft
ACDFOORTW woodcraft
ACDGILNSS scaldings
ACDGIMORW magic word
ACDGINRSU crusading
ACDGINRTU traducing
ACDGLLOOR dog-collar
ACDGLOOST Gold Coast
ACDHIIIRR Richard II
ACDHIIIST stichidia
ACDHIILMO homicidal
ACDHIIMOR chromidia
ACDHIKPRT pitch-dark
ACDHILRSY chrysalid
ACDHILRUY hydraulic
ACDHILSTT last-ditch
ACDHIMORT chromatid
ACDHINORS disanchor
ACDHIOPRS rhapsodic
ACDHLORTU Coulthard
ACDHMOOTW doomwatch
matchwood
ACDHNORRU round arch
ACDHORRTU hard court
Tudor arch
ACDHORTWW watchword
ACDHRSTUW Dutch Wars
ACDIIIMOT idiomatic
ACDIIJLRU juridical
ACDIIJRUY judiciary
ACDIILLTY callidity
ACDIILNOR crinoidal
ACDIILOST diastolic
ACDIILPTY placidity
ACDIILSTU dualistic
ACDIIMNNO Dominican
ACDIIMPRY pyramidic
ACDIINNOT contadini
ACDIINORT indicator
ACDIINOTT dictation
ACDIINRTY rancidity
ACDIJLORY Cyril Joad
ACDIKKLRY Kirkcaldy
ACDIKKNST kickstand
ACDIKNQSU quicksand
ACDIKRSTY yardstick
ACDILLLOO colloidal
ACDILLLUY ludically
ACDILLORY cordially
ACDILLOSU caudillos
ACDILMOPY diplomacy
ACDILNORT doctrinal
ACDILNORU rain-cloud
ACDILOPRS dropsical
ACDILORSW crowd sail
ACDILOSTU custodial
ACDILOSUU acidulous
ACDILOTUV oviductal
ACDIMMNNO in command
ACDIMOPSS spasmodic
ACDINOSTU custodian
ACDIORTTY dictatory
ACDJLNTUY adjunctly
ACDJOORTU coadjutor
ACDKNORTW track down
ACDKORSTY stockyard
ACDLLNORU call round
Lord Lucan
ACDLMNOPW clamp down
clampdown
ACDMMNOOS commandos
ACDMOOSUV muscovado
ACDMORSUU Scudamour
ACDNNOOPR pro and con
ACDNNRTUU cut and run
ACDOORRSS crossroad
ACDORRSUY your cards
ACDORRTUY courtyard

ACEEEFHLP	feel cheap
ACEEEFIRS	ceasefire
	cease-fire
ACEEEFIRT	cafetière
ACEEEFLNR	freelance
ACEEEGHKU	Aguecheek
ACEEEGHPR	repechage
ACEEEGNNV	vengeance
ACEEEHIPT	petechiae
ACEEEILMP	piecemeal
ACEEEIMPT	peacetime
ACEEEIPPP	peace-pipe
ACEEEKNOW	once a week
ACEEEKRRT	racketeer
ACEEELNPS	Pleasence
ACEEELNRT	crenelate
ACEEELNRV	relevance
ACEEELNTU	enucleate
ACEEELNTY	acetylene
ACEEELSSS	ceaseless
ACEEEMNNR	remanence
ACEEEMNPR	permeance
ACEEENPPT	appetence
ACEEENPRS	esperance
ACEEENRSV	severance
ACEEENRTW	new-create
ACEEFFHRU	réchauffé
ACEEFFITV	affective
ACEEFFLNU	affluence
ACEEFFLTU	effectual
ACEEFFNRY	fancy-free
ACEEFGMOO	come of age
ACEEFHHKL	half-cheek
ACEEFHLNP	halfpence
ACEEFHORR	forereach
ACEEFHSTT	fact sheet
ACEEFILPR	fireplace
ACEEFINRT	interface
ACEEFIRSS	fricassee
ACEEFLLLS	leaf cells
ACEEFLOTV	volte-face
ACEEFLRRX	reflex arc
ACEEFMORT	come after
	forcemeat
ACEEFNORV	confervae
ACEEFRRSU	resurface
ACEEGHIOR	heroic age
ACEEGHIRU	gaucherie
ACEEGHISV	give chase
ACEEGHLLN	challenge
ACEEGHNRX	exchanger
ACEEGHOPT	go the pace
ACEEGIILS	gaelicise
ACEEGIILZ	gaelicize
ACEEGILNT	genetical
ACEEGILPV	give place
ACEEGILRS	sacrilege
ACEEGIMNR	Germanice
ACEEGINRV	grievance
ACEEGIRTT	cigarette
ACEEGLLOU	colleague
ACEEGLNRT	rectangle
ACEEGLRSS	graceless
ACEEGNORT	grace note
ACEEGNORU	encourage
ACEEGNRSV	scavenger
ACEEGNRSY	sergeancy
ACEEGRTTU	curettage
ACEEHHLRW	wheel arch
ACEEHHORT	each other
ACEEHHRRT	the Archer
ACEEHHRST	the Arches
ACEEHHTUX	Hexateuch
ACEEHIIPR	hairpiece
	hair-piece
ACEEHILMS	alchemise
ACEEHILMZ	alchemize
ACEEHILPT	petechial
ACEEHILRT	heretical
ACEEHILRV	chevalier □
ACEEHIMNS	achimenes
	mechanise
ACEEHIMNZ	mechanize
ACEEHINRT	Catherine
	heritance
ACEEHINST	hesitance
ACEEHIRSS	Erica Hess
ACEEHISTT	aesthetic
ACEEHKPTW	keep watch
ACEEHLMNO	chameleon □
ACEEHLMPV	champlevé
ACEEHLNRU	herculean □
ACEEHLNSS	seneschal
ACEEHLNTU	Neuchâtel
ACEEHLRTW	cartwheel
ACEEHMOTY	haemocyte
ACEEHMRST	The Scream
ACEEHMTTU	humectate
ACEEHNNRT	enchanter
ACEEHNOPR	chaperone
ACEEHNPSS	cheapness
ACEEHNRTT	entrechat
ACEEHNSTU	chanteuse
ACEEHORRS	racehorse
ACEEHORRV	overreach
ACEEHPRTY	archetype
ACEEHRRRT	charterer
ACEEHRRTT	chatterer
ACEEHRRTY	treachery
ACEEHRSUV	ever such a
ACEEHSTTX	the sex act
ACEEIILPT	tailpiece
ACEEIKLSV	sick leave
ACEEIKMNZ	Mackenzie
ACEEIKRST	ice-skater
ACEEILLMS	limescale
ACEEILLRT	reticella
ACEEILLST	celestial
ACEEILLTV	vellicate
ACEEILMOV	come alive
ACEEILMRR	reclaimer
ACEEILMRT	Carmelite

ACEEILMST	time scale
	timescale
ACEEILNRT	interlace
	reclinate
ACEEILOPV	piacevole
ACEEILPRS	periclase
	sale price
ACEEILPRT	replicate
ACEEILPTX	explicate
ACEEILRST	cartelise
ACEEILRTZ	cartelize
ACEEILSUV	vesiculae
ACEEIMMNN	immanence
ACEEIMMNT	mincemeat
ACEEIMNPR	mepacrine
ACEEIMNSX	exciseman
ACEEIMPRT	imprecate
ACEEIMPST	empaestic
	space-time
ACEEIMRRS	careerism
ACEEIMRTT	metricate
ACEEINNRT	nectarine
ACEEINNTU	enunciate
ACEEINPRU	epicurean
ACEEINPTT	pectinate
ACEEINRSS	scenarise
ACEEINRST	cisternae
ACEEINRSZ	scenarize
ACEEIORTX	excoriate
ACEEIOSSS	écossaise
ACEEIOTVV	evocative
ACEEIPPRR	rice paper
ACEEIPRST	set a price
ACEEIPRTT	crepitate
ACEEIPRTV	precative
ACEEIPSTX	expiscate
ACEEIRRST	careerist
ACEEIRSTU	cauterise
ACEEIRSTV	viscerate
ACEEIRSVV	vice versa
ACEEIRTTX	extricate
ACEEIRTUZ	cauterize
ACEEISSST	ecstasise
ACEEISSTZ	ecstasize
ACEEKORTV	take cover
ACEELLORT	electoral
ACEELMNPT	placement
ACEELNNSS	cleanness
ACEELNORT	tolerance
ACEELNOST	Slate Cone
ACEELNPTU	petulance
ACEELNRSS	clearness
ACEELNRTU	calenture
ACEELNRTW	law centre
ACEELNRVY	relevancy
ACEELNSSW	Wenceslas
ACEELNSTW	Newcastle
ACEELOOSU	oleaceous
ACEELOPRT	percolate
ACEELOPRV	place over
ACEELORRT	correlate
ACEELORSS	casserole
ACEELORSW	lower-case
ACEELORTU	urceolate
ACEELOSST	lose caste
ACEELPSSS	spaceless
ACEELPSTU	speculate
ACEELPSTY	type scale
ACEELPTUX	exculpate
ACEELRSST	traceless
ACEELRTTU	reluctate
ACEELRTUY	electuary
ACEEMNNRY	remanency
ACEEMNNTT	enactment
ACEEMNRRY	mercenary
ACEEMORTT	octameter
ACEEMOVZZ	mezza voce
ACEEMRRTU	mercurate
ACEEMRSTV	Steve Cram
ACEENNOPR	can-opener
ACEENNORS	resonance
ACEENNOST	Cantonese
ACEENNRST	renascent
ACEENNRTY	centenary
ACEENOPPS	open space
ACEENORTZ	Zenocrate
ACEENPPTY	appetency
ACEENPRRT	carpenter
ACEENPTTX	expectant
ACEENRSSY	necessary
ACEENRSTV	Cervantes
ACEENRTTU	utterance
ACEENSSTU	acuteness
ACEENSSTX	exactness
ACEENTTUX	executant
ACEEOOPRT	cooperate
	co-operate
ACEEOPRRT	procreate
ACEEORRTT	rectorate
ACEEORRTV	overreact
ACEEORTUY	eucaryote
ACEEORTVX	over-exact
ACEEOSSTU	setaceous
ACEEPPRSU	upper-case
ACEEPRRTU	recapture
ACEEPRSSV	cap verses
ACEERRSTT	scatterer
ACEERRSTY	secretary
ACEERRTUW	water cure
ACEERSSTU	secateurs
ACEFFFLRU	carfuffle
ACEFFGINT	affecting
ACEFFGLNO	glance off
ACEFFHRUU	chauffeur
ACEFFIIOT	officiate
ACEFFINOT	affection
ACEFFIORT	forficate
ACEFFOSTU	suffocate
ACEFGHINT	Night Café
ACEFGHIRT	right face!
ACEFGHLNU	changeful
ACEFGLNOR	gerfalcon

ACEFHIINT	chieftain
ACEFHILPR	half-price
ACEFHINRS	franchise
ACEFHIPRY	preachify
ACEFHIRTW	watch fire
ACEFHMNNR	Frenchman
ACEFHMORT	homecraft
ACEFHORRS	search for
ACEFHOSUV	vouchsafe
ACEFIILMS	facsimile
ACEFIILRR	clarifier
ACEFIINNR	financier
ACEFIIPRX	fix a price
ACEFIIRRS	scarifier
ACEFIIRRT	artificer
ACEFIIRTV	fricative
ACEFIISST	satisfice
ACEFIITTV	factitive
ACEFIJKKN	jackknife
ACEFIKRTU	fruitcake
ACEFILNOP	in place of
ACEFILSTU	faculties
ACEFIMNOR	main force
ACEFINNSS	fanciness
ACEFINORT	certain of
ACEFIORST	factorise
ACEFIORSU	feracious
ACEFIORTZ	factorize
ACEFIOSTU	facetious
ACEFIRSSW	scarfwise
ACEFKORST	task force
	task-force
ACEFLLLSU	full-scale
ACEFLLRUY	carefully
ACEFLMNOS	flamencos
ACEFLNORR	conferral
ACEFLOOPU	a couple of
ACEFLPTUU	teacupful
ACEFLRSUU	saucerful
ACEFLTTUU	fluctuate
ACEFMOPRS	from space
ACEFNORSV	confervas
ACEFNRSTT	transfect
ACEFORRRT	refractor
ACEFOSTUU	tufaceous
ACEFRTTUU	fructuate
ACEGGHTTU	get caught
ACEGGINOS	Gascoigne
ACEGHHINT	each thing
ACEGHILRT	lethargic
ACEGHILTT	tight-lace
ACEGHIMPR	graphemic
ACEGHIMPS	game chips
ACEGHIMRS	mischarge
ACEGHINNN	enhancing
ACEGHINPR	preaching
ACEGHINRS	searching
ACEGHIRST	Reichstag
ACEGHMORT	hectogram
ACEGHOPTU	Hugo Capet
ACEGHOPTY	phagocyte
ACEGHRRSU	surcharge
ACEGIIKKV	give a kick
ACEGIILLS	Gallicise
ACEGIILLZ	Gallicize
ACEGIILNS	anglicise
ACEGIILNV	vigilance
ACEGIILNZ	anglicize
ACEGIIMNT	enigmatic
ACEGIIRRT	geriatric
ACEGIKRST	gear-stick
ACEGILLOT	colligate
ACEGILNNO	congenial
ACEGILNNS	cleansing
ACEGILNRU	neuralgic
ACEGILRTU	Géricault
	graticule
ACEGILRTY	large city
ACEGIMMRS	scrimmage
ACEGIMNRS	screaming
ACEGIMNTU	mutagenic
ACEGIMNUY	gynaecium
ACEGINNOR	ignorance
ACEGINNSU	unceasing
ACEGINPPR	recapping
ACEGINPRT	carpeting
ACEGINPRY	panegyric
ACEGINRST	recasting
ACEGIOPRR	paregoric
ACEGIRSTT	strategic
ACEGJNOTU	conjugate
ACEGLMNOO	come along
ACEGLMNRY	clergyman
ACEGLNNOU	uncongeal
ACEGLNNPY	plangency
ACEGLORST	L'Escargot
ACEGMMRSU	scrummage
ACEGNNOTT	cotangent
ACEGNNPRY	pregnancy
ACEGORRTU	corrugate
ACEGORSST	get across
ACEHHIRRY	hierarchy
ACEHHIRSS	rhachises
ACEHHLSTT	shtetlach
ACEHHMNTT	hatchment
ACEHHOOTT	toothache
ACEHHPRTY	heptarchy
ACEHIILTU	halieutic
ACEHIINRT	trichinae
ACEHIISTT	atheistic
ACEHIKNPP	Peckinpah
ACEHIKORT	artichoke
ACEHIKRST	heartsick
ACEHILLLY	helically
ACEHILLTY	ethically
ACEHILMMO	chamomile
ACEHILMST	alchemist
ACEHILNOR	enchorial
ACEHILNPR	Prince Hal
ACEHILNTU	unethical
ACEHILORR	Charleroi
ACEHILPRS	spherical

ACEHILPRY	preachily
ACEHILRUV	vehicular
ACEHILSTT	athletics
ACEHIMMNS	mechanism
ACEHIMNRY	machinery
ACEHIMRTU	rheumatic
ACEHINORT	anchorite
ACEHINRRU	hurricane □
ACEHINRSS	chariness
ACEHINRSU	sea urchin
ACEHINRTT	in the cart
ACEHINRTY	tyre chain
ACEHINSTY	hesitancy
ACEHINTTU	authentic
ACEHIOOTZ	zoothecia
ACEHIOPRY	coryphaei
ACEHIORST	rhotacise
ACEHIORTZ	rhotacize
ACEHIPPSS	spaceship
ACEHIRRST	Charteris
ACEHIRSTT	theatrics
ACEHIRSTU	Eucharist
ACEHJLNOR	John Clare
ACEHKLNSU	unshackle
ACEHKORST	shortcake
	track shoe
ACEHKOSVW	shock wave
ACEHLLLOR	chlorella
ACEHLLNOP	phone call
ACEHLLOOR	Local Hero
ACEHLLOPY	holy place
ACEHLMOST	moschatel
ACEHLMRSS	charmless
ACEHLMSST	matchless
ACEHLMSSY	chlamyses
ACEHLNNOY	Lon Chaney
ACEHLNNPU	up-Channel
ACEHLNNRU	uncharnel
ACEHLNOSY	anchylose
ACEHLNPTY	phlyctena
ACEHLOPSW	showplace
ACEHLORRT	trochlear
ACEHLORTT	Charlotte
ACEHLOTUV	have clout
ACEHLRSVY	cry halves
ACEHLSSUY	Aeschylus
ACEHMNPRT	parchment
ACEHMNRST	Ernst Mach
ACEHMNTTU	humectant
ACEHMORST	stomacher
ACEHMORTV	overmatch
ACEHMOSTU	moustache
ACEHMPRTY	champerty
ACEHMSTTT	test match
ACEHNNRTT	trenchant
ACEHNORRS	rancheros
ACEHNORSS	anchoress
ACEHNORTU	near touch
ACEHNOSTT	stonechat
	The Cantos
ACEHNRSUZ	Schnauzer

ACEHOOSTU	housecoat
ACEHOPRRS	sharecrop
ACEHORRST	orchestra
ACEHORSTU	search out
ACEHORTVW	overwatch
	watch over
ACEHOSSUW	show cause
ACEHOSTUY	easy touch
ACEHPRRSU	purchaser
ACEHPRTTT	Pratchett
ACEHPSTTT	patch test
ACEHPSTTY	petty cash
ACEHRRTTU	the cratur
ACEHRSSTT	crash-test
ACEIIILNS	siciliane
ACEIIILST	italicise
ACEIIILTZ	italicize
ACEIIKMNT	kinematic
ACEIILMPR	empirical
ACEIILMPT	implicate
ACEIILMST	climatise
ACEIILMSV	vicesimal
ACEIILMTZ	climatize
ACEIILNNT	anticline
ACEIILNNV	vicennial
ACEIILNST	inelastic
	sciential
ACEIILOSS	socialise
ACEIILOST	socialite
ACEIILOSV	viliacoes
ACEIILOSZ	socialize
ACEIILPRT	pearlitic
ACEIILRST	eristical
	realistic
ACEIILRTT	triticale
ACEIILSTV	calvities
ACEIIMMNR	Cimmerian
ACEIIMMRU	americium
ACEIIMNRT	criminate
ACEIIMNSS	Messianic
ACEIIMRST	armistice
ACEIINOTV	noviciate
ACEIINPRS	precisian
ACEIINRTT	intricate
ACEIINTTT	nictitate
ACEIIPRST	peirastic
ACEIISTTT	steatitic
ACEIJKNPS	jack-snipe
ACEIJLPTU	juliet cap
ACEIKKLPT	kick pleat
ACEIKLLNN	lack-linen
ACEIKLPRS	spraickle
ACEIKLRYZ	like crazy
ACEIKNOQU	a quick one
ACEIKNSST	tackiness
ACEIKNSSW	wackiness
ACEIKOPST	kopasetic
ACEIKPSTY	tipsy cake
ACEILLLXY	lexically
ACEILLMOP	polemical
ACEILLMOT	collimate

	local time
ACEILLNOR	collinear
	coralline
ACEILLNPS	spellican
ACEILLNPT	plant-lice
ACEILLOST	oscillate
	tesla coil
ACEILLPRS	callipers
ACEILLPSY	specially
ACEILLPTY	plicately
ACEILLRSW	Carl Lewis
ACEILLSSU	sulcalise
ACEILLSUZ	sulcalize
ACEILMNNU	luminance
ACEILMNOP	policeman
ACEILMNOR	coalminer
ACEILMNRU	numerical
ACEILMNSU	masculine
ACEILMNTU	culminate
ACEILMRRU	mercurial
ACEILMRTU	climature
ACEILNNOR	cornelian
ACEILNNOT	octennial
ACEILNNTY	anciently
ACEILNOPR	porcelain
ACEILNOPT	point-lace
ACEILNORS	censorial
ACEILNOST	coastline
	sectional
ACEILNOSV	volcanise
ACEILNOTU	inoculate
ACEILNOVZ	volcanize
ACEILNPTU	inculpate
ACEILNRST	larcenist
ACEILNRTY	certainly
ACEILNSSS	scaliness
ACEILNSTU	unelastic
ACEILNSUV	vulcanise
ACEILNTUV	vulcanite
ACEILNTXY	inexactly
ACEILNUVZ	vulcanize
ACEILOORR	air cooler
ACEILOPPS	episcopal
ACEILOQUV	equivocal
ACEILORRT	rectorial
ACEILORST	sclerotia
	sectorial
ACEILORTT	tectorial
ACEILPPPR	paperclip
ACEILPRST	particles
ACEILPSSU	Asclepius
	capsulise
ACEILPSTU	spiculate
ACEILPSTY	specialty
ACEILPSUZ	capsulize
ACEILPTUY	eucalypti
ACEILRRTU	recruital
	reticular
ACEILRSSZ	Carl Zeiss
ACEILRTUV	lucrative
ACEILTTUV	cultivate
ACEIMMNNY	immanency
ACEIMMNOT	comminate
ACEIMMOSS	come amiss
ACEIMNORT	cremation
ACEIMNOST	encomiast
ACEIMNOTT	omittance
ACEIMNOTX	income tax
ACEIMNPTU	pneumatic
ACEIMNRST	miscreant
ACEIMNSST	semantics
ACEIMNSTU	mint sauce
ACEIMNTYZ	enzymatic
ACEIMORVW	microwave
ACEIMOSST	as it comes
ACEIMPRST	spermatic
ACEIMRTTU	micturate
ACEINNNSS	canniness
ACEINNORR	in a corner
ACEINNORT	container
ACEINNOSS	ascension □
ACEINNOST	cantonise
ACEINNOTZ	cantonize
ACEINNRRY	inerrancy
ACEINNRSU	insurance
ACEINNRTU	encurtain
	runcinate
	uncertain
ACEINNRTY	ancientry
ACEINNSST	incessant
ACEINOOTV	evocation
ACEINORRV	carnivore
ACEINORSS	scenarios
ACEINORST	narcotise
ACEINORTU	Cointreau®
ACEINORTZ	narcotize
ACEINOSST	cessation
ACEINOSTU	tenacious
ACEINOTTY	to a nicety
ACEINPRTT	crepitant
ACEINPRUY	pecuniary
ACEINPSSU	puissance
ACEINQTTU	quittance
ACEINRSSZ	craziness
ACEINRTTY	certainty
ACEINRTUV	incurvate
ACEINSSSU	sauciness
ACEINSSTT	cattiness
	tacitness
ACEINSTTY	intestacy
ACEIOPRST	patricoes
ACEIOPRSU	auriscope
ACEIOPRTV	proactive
ACEIOPTTT	petticoat
ACEIORSST	ostracise
	Socratise
ACEIORSTZ	ostracize
	Socratize
ACEIORSUV	veracious
ACEIOSSTW	coastwise
ACEIPRSTT	scarpetti
ACEIRSTTU	rusticate

ACEISSSTU	suitcases
ACEISSTTU	suscitate
ACEJJKNOS	Jack Jones
ACEJKKRSY	skyjacker
ACEJKMOOS	James Cook
ACEJLMSUU	majuscule
ACEKKMRRU	muck-raker
ACEKKOSTT	stocktake
	take stock
ACEKLNPSU	slacken up
ACEKLNSSS	slackness
ACEKLOPRW	workplace
ACEKLRSST	trackless
ACEKMOORS	smackeroo
ACEKMORRR	rocker arm
ACEKNNTTU	Nantucket
ACEKNORSU	cankerous
ACEKOPPRW	power pack
ACEKPRSSU	sapsucker
ACEKRSTUW	awestruck
ACELLLORS	solar cell
ACELLMORS	all comers
ACELLMORU	molecular
ACELLMRSU	Marcellus
ACELLNNUY	uncleanly
ACELLNOTU	Launcelot
ACELLNRTY	centrally
ACELLOQUY	coequally
ACELLPSSS	scalpless
ACELLRSUY	secularly
ACELLSSSS	classless
ACELMMNOS	commensal
ACELMMNSU	muscleman
ACELMMOSU	mamelucos
ACELMNOOR	clean room
ACELMNTUU	tenaculum
ACELMOPST	ectoplasm
ACELNNOTU	Launceton
ACELNOOST	consolate
ACELNOOSV	volcanoes
ACELNOPRV	Provençal
ACELNORSU	larcenous
ACELNORTT	central to
ACELNORTU	recountal
ACELNOSTU	consulate
ACELNPRTU	crapulent
ACELNPTUY	petulancy
ACELNRTTU	reluctant
ACELOOPRR	corporeal
ACELOORTW	water-cool
ACELOOSST	cast loose
ACELOPRRU	opercular
ACELOPRTU	parcel out
	peculator
ACELORRST	stercoral
ACELORSSU	caroluses
ACELORTTV	travel-cot
ACELOSSTU	cassoulet
	lost cause
ACELOSTUU	cautelous
ACEMMNOOR	Common Era
ACEMMOTTU	commutate
ACEMNOOPS	moonscape
ACEMNOPSS	encompass
ACEMNORTU	mucronate
ACEMORRSU	sour cream
ACEMOSTVY	vasectomy
ACEMPPSTU	set up camp
ACEMPRSUY	supremacy
ACENNNORU	announcer
ACENNOOTT	connotate
ACENNOSTU	Antonescu
ACENNPTUU	nuncupate
ACENNSSST	scantness
ACENOORST	corantoes
ACENOPRRT	procreant
ACENOPSTW	townscape
ACENOPSTY	syncopate
ACENORRTU	raconteur
ACENORSST	ancestors
ACENORSTU	courtesan
	nectarous
ACENORSUV	cavernous
ACENORUVV	Vancouver
ACENOSSST	contessas
ACENOSSTZ	scazontes
ACENOSTUU	cutaneous
ACENPRRTY	carpentry
ACENPRSUU	pursuance
ACENPTTUU	punctuate
ACENRRSTU	Cresta Run
ACENRRSUY	cursenary
ACENRSSSS	crassness
ACENRSTUU	Centaurus
ACEOOPRRT	corporate
ACEOOPRSS	ascospore
ACEOORSSU	rosaceous
ACEOPRRTY	precatory
ACEOPRSSY	caryopses
ACEOPRSTT	spectator
ACEORRRTT	retractor
ACEORRRVY	carry over
ACEORRSTU	craterous
ACEORRTTX	extractor
ACEOSSTTW	West Coast
ACERRTUUV	curvature
ACFFGHILN	cliffhang
ACFFIILNO	officinal
ACFFIINOT	officiant
ACFFIINRT	traffic in
ACFFILMOR	falciform
ACFFIMNPU	muffin-cap
ACFFLOSTW	cowl-staff
ACFGHMORR	frogmarch
ACFGIINNN	financing
ACFGIINPY	pacifying
ACFGINORT	acting for
ACFGINRSU	surfacing
ACFGIOSUU	fugacious
ACFGLNORY	gyrfalcon
ACFHHHILT	half hitch
	half-hitch

ACFHIILRT	chairlift
ACFHILNTU	cut in half
ACFHLLORT	call forth
ACFHLMRSU	scrum half
ACFHLNORW	half-crown
ACFHLORSS	half-cross
ACFHLORTW	flow chart
ACFHMORSU	forasmuch
ACFHOOSTU	out of cash
ACFIIILOR	orificial
ACFIILLNY	finically
ACFIILNOT	fictional
ACFIKRRTU	Friar Tuck
ACFILMORT	film actor
ACFILMORU	formulaic
ACFILNNOR	francolin
ACFILNPPY	flippancy
ACFILNRTY	franticly
ACFILNRUU	funicular
ACFILOPTY	typical of
ACFIMOOST	motoscafi
ACFIMORRY	formicary
ACFINORRT	infractor
ACFINORTU	furcation
ACFIOOPST	ipso facto
ACFIORSTU	fractious
ACFIORSUU	furacious
ACFJKORST	Jack Frost
ACFKNORWY	fancywork
ACFKORRTW	craftwork
ACFLLTTUY	tactfully
ACFLNTTUU	fluctuant
ACFLOORTY	olfactory
ACFMORSUX	Marcus Fox
ACFMOSTTU	factotums
ACFORTTUY	outcrafty
ACGGHNNPU	gang-punch
ACGGILRSY	scraggily
ACGGIMNOP	go camping
ACGGINOTT	cottaging
ACGGIOORS	coraggios
ACGHHHIIR	high-chair
ACGHHILSS	high-class
ACGHIIJKN	hijacking
ACGHIILNR	China Girl
ACGHIINRW	wing chair
ACGHIIPRT	graphitic
ACGHILNNU	launching
ACGHILORY	oligarchy
ACGHILPRY	graphicly
ACGHIMOSW	magic-show
ACGHINNOT	gnathonic
ACGHINNST	snatching
ACGHLMNOR	long march
ACGHLMOOY	logomachy
ACGHNNOTU	Connaught
ACGHOOOST	go cahoots
ACGHORSTU	roughcast
ACGIILLLO	illogical
ACGIILLNV	cavilling
ACGIILLOR	cigarillo
ACGIILMNS	Anglicism
ACGIIMSTT	stigmatic
ACGIINNOR	inorganic
ACGIINQRU	acquiring
ACGIIORST	orgiastic
ACGIKNPPU	packing-up
ACGILLLOY	logically
ACGILLNOR	collaring
ACGILLOST	collagist
ACGILNNST	scantling
ACGILNOST	nostalgic
ACGILNOXY	coaxingly
ACGILNPRY	carpingly
ACGILRRYZ	Girl Crazy
ACGIMMNOO	monogamic
ACGIMNNOO	cognomina
ACGIMNNOR	romancing
ACGIMNOOR	agronomic
ACGIMNORR	cairngorm
ACGIMNOSS	gasconism
ACGIMNSTY	gymnastic
	nystagmic
ACGIMOPRT	pictogram
ACGIMOTYZ	zygomatic
ACGINNOOT	cognation
	contagion
ACGINNOPY	poignancy
ACGINNOST	cognisant
ACGINNOTZ	cognizant
ACGINOPSW	coping-saw
ACGINORSU	carousing
ACGINORTU	Agincourt
ACGINORTV	cavorting
ACGINPPRS	scrapping
ACGINPRSS	scrapings
ACGINPTUY	pugnacity
ACGIOORSS	graciosos
ACGJNORRU	currajong
ACGKOOORT	go crook at
ACGLMOORY	macrology
ACGLNOOSY	cosy along
ACGMNNOOR	Cro-Magnon
ACGMOPRTY	cryptogam
ACGNNOOST	contangos
ACGNORRUW	currawong
ACGORRSUY	surrogacy
ACHHILNOR	rhonchial
ACHHILORT	haircloth
ACHHILSTW	clash with
ACHHIMRTW	march with
ACHHIMTTW	match with
ACHHINNOT	chthonian
ACHIILMSW	whimsical
ACHIIMNST	machinist
ACHIINPSY	physician
ACHIINRST	Christian
	Christina
	trichinas
ACHIIOPST	pistachio
ACHIIPRSV	vicarship
ACHIIRRTT	arthritic

ACHIIRSTV	archivist
ACHIKLMST	mahlstick
ACHIKNNOT	Ninotchka
ACHILLLOY	allicholy
ACHILLMSU	music hall
ACHILLNTY	Chantilly
ACHILLOST	sailcloth
ACHILMPTY	lymphatic
ACHILNORV	Lochinvar
ACHILNRUY	raunchily
ACHILNSTY	snatchily
ACHILOPTU	patchouli
ACHILORTV	archivolt
ACHILOSST	scholiast
ACHILRSSY	chrysalis
ACHILRSTY	starchily
ACHILSTTY	cattishly
ACHIMMNOS	monachism
ACHIMMNTX	mix 'n' match
ACHIMMORZ	machzorim
ACHIMNORS	harmonics
ACHIMNORT	chromatin
	march into
ACHIMNOST	macintosh
ACHIMOSTU	mustachio
ACHIMRSST	Christmas
ACHIMRSSW	scrimshaw
ACHINNOST	stanchion
ACHINNOTW	Chinatown
ACHINOOST	in cahoots
ACHINOPPS	pansophic
ACHINORST	crash into
ACHINOSTU	Antiochus
ACHINPRST	chinstrap
ACHIOOPST	sociopath
ACHIOPRRZ	rhizocarp
ACHIORSTV	tovarisch
ACHIPRSUY	haruspicy
ACHISTUWZ	Auschwitz
ACHKKKOOS	Kokoschka
ACHKLOPTU	chalk up to
ACHKOPRTW	patchwork
ACHLLORSY	scholarly
ACHLMOORR	Loch Morar
ACHLMORSW	slow-march
ACHLMOSTW	slow match
ACHLMSTYZ	schmaltzy
ACHLNOOTT	latch on to
	latch onto
ACHLNOTUU	outlaunch
ACHLNSTUY	staunchly
ACHLOOSTU	holocaust
ACHLOPRYY	polyarchy
ACHMMSSUY	Symmachus
ACHMNOSTU	not as much
ACHMNRSTU	truchmans
ACHMOPTTU	match up to
ACHNOPSTY	sycophant
ACHOORSTT	short-coat
ACHOPSTTW	stopwatch
ACHOPSTUY	hypocaust
ACHORTTTU	cut-throat
ACIIIMNST	animistic
ACIIINPPR	principia
ACIIINPST	sincipita
ACIIKSTTT	stick at it
ACIILLNOS	isoclinal
ACIILLNST	scintilla
ACIILLOPT	political
ACIILLPRS	Priscilla
ACIILMNPU	municipal
ACIILMNSV	Calvinism
ACIILMNTY	militancy
ACIILMOSS	socialism
ACIILMOSU	malicious
ACIILMQTU	quitclaim
ACIILNOOT	coalition
ACIILNOVV	convivial
ACIILNOVY	inviolacy
ACIILNPPR	principal
ACIILNSTV	Calvinist
ACIILOPRT	pictorial
ACIILOSST	socialist
ACIILOSTY	sociality
ACIILQUZZ	quizzical
ACIILTTTY	tactility
ACIIMMPST	psammitic
ACIIMNNOS	aniconism
	insomniac
ACIIMNOPT	impaction
ACIIMNORT	mortician
ACIIMNOSU	minacious
ACIIMNOTT	manicotti
ACIIMOPST	simpatico
ACIIMORTT	triatomic
ACIIMOSST	mosaicist
ACIIMOTTY	atomicity
ACIIMPRST	prismatic
ACIIMSTUV	viaticums
ACIINNOST	aniconist
	onanistic
	Toscanini
ACIINNOTT	nictation
ACIINNOTU	incaution
ACIINOORT	octonarii
ACIINORTV	Victorian
ACIINOTTY	atonicity
ACIINPRTU	Paricutín
ACIINPRVY	in privacy
ACIIOPRTT	patriotic
ACIIOPTZZ	pizzicato
ACIIORSUV	vicarious
ACIIOSUVV	vivacious
ACIIPRSTT	patristic
ACIIPTTVY	captivity
ACIISSTTT	statistic
ACIJKNNOU	Union Jack
ACIKKNNOT	antiknock
ACIKKRSTT	kick-start
ACIKLLSST	Catskills
ACIKLMSTU	maulstick
ACIKLOPRS	spark coil

ACIKLOSTT	tailstock
ACIKLPSST	slapstick
ACIKNORST	Kit Carson
ACIKRSTTU	tracksuit
ACILLLRYY	lyrically
ACILLMSUY	musically
ACILLNOOT	collation
ACILLOOQU	colloquia
ACILLOPTY	optically
	topically
ACILLORST	cloistral
ACILLOSTY	callosity
	stoically
ACILLOTXY	toxically
ACILLPTYY	typically
ACILLSSTU	Callistus
ACILMMOTT	committal
ACILMNNOU	in a column
ACILMNOPT	complaint
	compliant
ACILMNSUU	unmusical
ACILMOORS	lacrimoso
ACILMPTUU	capitulum
ACILMSSTU	simulcast
ACILNNNUY	uncannily
ACILNNOTU	continual
ACILNNRUU	ranunculi
ACILNOPRT	prolactin
ACILNORTT	contralti
ACILNPTUY	untypical
ACILOOPRS	acropolis ❑
ACILOOPST	apostolic
ACILOPPPU	Lucia Popp
ACILOQTUY	loquacity
ACILORSTU	ocularist
	suctorial
ACILOSSTV	vocalists
ACILPPRSY	scrappily
ACILRRTUU	utricular
ACILSSTTY	systaltic
ACIMMORSS	commissar
ACIMNNOOP	companion
ACIMNNOPY	in company
ACIMNOOTU	autonomic
ACIMNOOTX	taxonomic
ACIMNORST	narcotism
ACIMNOUVX	nux vomica
ACIMORSST	ostracism
ACIMORSTT	stromatic
ACIMRSTTU	strumatic
ACINNORST	constrain
ACINNOSST	sanctions
ACINNRTUU	uncurtain
ACINOORST	consortia
ACINORSST	croissant
ACINOSSSU	Sans Souci
	saucisson
ACINPRSUW	Punic Wars
ACINRSSSU	narcissus ❑
ACIOOPRSZ	saprozoic
ACIOORSTU	atrocious
ACIOORSUV	voracious
ACIOPRSTY	piscatory
ACIRSSTUY	casuistry
ACJLLORUY	jocularly
ACJLOORTU	joculator
ACKLLNRTU	trunk call
ACKLMOOOR	cloakroom
ACKLNOPRT	rock plant
ACKLORSSW	crosswalk
ACKRSTTUY	Cutty Sark
ACLLLOSUY	callously
ACLLOORRY	corollary
ACLLOOTTU	call out to
ACLLORSSW	scroll-saw
ACLMMNOOW	common law
ACLMNOORU	monocular
ACLMOOOPR	Marco Polo
ACLMOORSS	classroom
ACLMOORSU	clamorous
ACLMOPSTY	cytoplasm
ACLMSSUUV	vasculums
ACLNNORTU	nocturnal
ACLNOORTT	contralto
ACLNOORTU	colourant
ACLOORUWY	colourway
ACLOPRSTU	Patroclus
ACLOPRSTY	pyroclast
ACLOPRSUU	crapulous
ACLOPRTTU	plutocrat
ACLOPSTTU	Paul Scott
ACLORSUUY	raucously
ACLOSTUUY	Autolycus
ACLOSUUVY	vacuously
ACMNOORRT	cormorant
ACMNOOSTU	cosmonaut
ACMORSTUY	customary
ACNNNOOST	consonant
ACNOORRSU	rancorous
ACNORRSSU	run across
ACOORSSTU	autocross
ACOPRRSST	sports car
ACOPRSSTU	put across
ACORRSTTU	scrutator
ACORSSSWY	crossways
ADDDEEHNR	redhanded
	red-handed
ADDDEEIRT	dead tired
ADDDEEKLS	skedaddle
ADDDEFIIN	dandified
ADDDEGLOP	dog-paddle
ADDDEIINS	disdained
ADDDEIMNO	diamonded
ADDEEEGLT	delegated
ADDEEEPRT	depredate
ADDEEERSS	addressee
ADDEEFIIX	fixed idea
ADDEEFILL	Delafield
ADDEEFNNT	defendant
ADDEEFRRU	defrauder
ADDEEGHIP	pigheaded
	pig-headed

ADDEEGHRU	rug-headed
ADDEEGINN	deadening
ADDEEGINR	André Gide
ADDEEGNSW	sand wedge
ADDEEHHOT	hotheaded
	hot-headed
ADDEEHMNT	the damned
ADDEEHOSU	deadhouse
ADDEEHRSS	headdress
ADDEEHRTY	dehydrate
ADDEEIILZ	idealized
ADDEEILMR	middle ear
ADDEEILPT	depilated
ADDEEILRV	daredevil
	dare-devil
ADDEEIOTX	deoxidate
ADDEEIPRU	Depardieu
ADDEELNRU	laundered
ADDEELRSS	dreadless
ADDEEMNOS	Desdemona
ADDEEMNRU	undreamed
ADDEEMNST	damnedest
ADDEENNPT	dependant
ADDEENOST	stone-dead
ADDEENSWY	Wednesday
ADDEEOPRS	desperado
ADDEEPRSU	persuaded
ADDEEPRTY	Pat Eddery
ADDEEPSUX	pas de deux
ADDEERSSS	addresses
ADDEFFHNO	offhanded
ADDEFFLOS	offsaddle
ADDEFFPRU	puff adder
ADDEFHILN	field hand
ADDEFILRW	fieldward
ADDEFINNR	Ferdinand
ADDEFINSS	faddiness
ADDEFIRSV	Fred Davis
ADDEGGINR	degrading
ADDEGGOOT	dog-eat-dog
ADDEGHINR	hag-ridden
ADDEGIITT	digitated
ADDEGIMNN	demanding
	maddening
ADDEGINNS	saddening
ADDEGIRRS	disregard
ADDEGKNRU	grand duke
ADDEGLLMO	gold medal
ADDEGLRUY	guardedly
ADDEGNOOR	gadrooned
ADDEGNORW	downgrade
ADDEGNRUU	unguarded
ADDEHIMUV	David Hume
ADDEHINRY	anhydride
ADDEHINSY	hendiadys
ADDEHIOPV	David Hope
ADDEHIRRW	hard-wired
ADDEHLRRU	hard-ruled
ADDEHNNRU	underhand
ADDEHNORS	hard-nosed
ADDEHNOTW	two-handed
ADDEHOOTT	do to death
ADDEHRSTU	shudder at
ADDEHTTUY	death duty
ADDEIIIMT	dimidiate
ADDEIILNX	Dixieland
ADDEIINNR	Indian red
	Red Indian
ADDEIKNPP	Kidnapped
ADDEILLNS	landslide
ADDEILMMN	middleman
ADDEILMWY	middle way
ADDEILNNO	dandelion
ADDEILNNW	Edwin Land
ADDEILOSV	David Sole
ADDEILPSY	displayed
ADDEILSVY	advisedly
ADDEIMNOT	dominated
ADDEIMNSY	many-sided
ADDEIMORT	dermatoid
ADDEINNTU	inundated
ADDEINOPT	dead point
ADDEINOVW	David Owen
ADDEINRTW	trade wind
ADDEINSUV	unadvised
ADDEIRSSW	sidewards
ADDEJNORU	adjourned
ADDELNOSY	olden days
ADDELNOTU	nodulated
ADDELNSUW	unswaddle
ADDELNTUU	undulated
ADDELOSSU	Dead Souls
ADDEMORRY	dromedary
ADDENNORU	unadorned
ADDENNRTU	redundant
ADDENNTUU	undaunted
ADDENOORT	deodorant
ADDENOPTU	unadopted
ADDENORTW	trade down
ADDENORVW	dove-drawn
ADDENOSTU	astounded
ADDENRRUW	underdraw
ADDEPQRUU	quadruped
ADDFGHNOO	hand of God
ADDFIIQRU	quadrifid
ADDFLNNOO	land of Nod
ADDFLOOSY	days of old
ADDGGIJNU	adjudging
ADDGGINRR	Gradgrind
ADDGILNTW	twaddling
ADDGNOOST	stand good
ADDHHIOOR	hardihood
ADDHHLNOS	hold hands
ADDHIILLV	David Hill
ADDHLOOTU	adulthood
ADDHNNORU	hand round
ADDHNNOSW	hands down
ADDHRSTUY	study hard
ADDINRSWW	windwards
ADDLLNORY	dandy-roll
ADDLMOPTY	toddy-palm
ADDMNOOTU	odd man out

ADDNNOPUW	up and down
	up-and-down
ADDNNOSTW	stand down
ADDNORSWW	downwards
ADDRSSTUY	dry as dust
	Dryasdust
ADEEEEGLY	eagle-eyed
ADEEEFHRT	feathered
ADEEEFIRR	federarie
ADEEEFNRR	referenda
ADEEEFRRT	free trade
	free-trade
ADEEEFRTU	defeature
ADEEEGLRV	everglade
ADEEEGLST	delegates
ADEEEGORT	to a degree
ADEEEHINT	The Aeneid
ADEEEHPRT	Peterhead
ADEEEHRTW	weathered
ADEEEHVYY	heavy-eyed
ADEEEILMN	madeleine□
ADEEEILNT	delineate
ADEEEIRSS	diaereses
ADEEEKKNW	weak-kneed
ADEEEKNSW	snakeweed
ADEEELLMN	enamelled
ADEEELLNS	lease-lend
	lend-lease
ADEEELPRS	seed-pearl
ADEEEMPRT	permeated
ADEEEMRSV	Mesa Verde
ADEEENRRS	serenader
ADEEENRTV	enervated
	venerated
ADEEEPRST	desperate
ADEEEPRTW	deep water
ADEEERTTU	deuterate
ADEEFFILR	fieldfare
ADEEFGINN	deafening
ADEEFGLLR	Lagerfeld
ADEEFGLMO	female dog
ADEEFHILR	had liefer
ADEEFHLMS	made flesh
ADEEFIKLW	Wakefield
ADEEFIKMX	make fixed
ADEEFILMS	Masefield
ADEEFILOT	defoliate
ADEEFIMST	defeatism
ADEEFINOR	Freedonia
ADEEFIORT	foederati
ADEEFISTT	defeatist
ADEEFLLMW	well-famed
ADEEFLLST	stall-feed
ADEEFLMST	Flamsteed
ADEEFLNNR	Fernandel
ADEEFLORT	deflorate
	floreated
ADEEFLRTU	defaulter
ADEEFMNOR	forenamed
ADEEFNOST	stone-deaf
ADEEGGHPS	egg-shaped
ADEEGGINN	engaged in
ADEEGGINS	disengage
ADEEGGIRV	aggrieved
ADEEGGITU	tide gauge
ADEEGGJLT	jet-lagged
ADEEGGLNO	golden age
ADEEGGMOU	demagogue
ADEEGGNNU	unengaged
ADEEGGNRR	Red Grange
ADEEGGOPU	pedagogue
ADEEGGRST	staggered
ADEEGHIRR	Gerhardie
ADEEGHSTW	get washed
ADEEGIIRV	give a ride
ADEEGILLR	galleried
ADEEGILLT	get laldie
ADEEGILLZ	legalized
ADEEGILNR	Geraldine
ADEEGILNW	wide-angle
ADEEGIMNN	demeaning
ADEEGIMOV	video game
ADEEGINNR	endearing
	grenadine
ADEEGINRR	grenadier
	rereading
ADEEGINRT	denigrate
ADEEGINST	designate
ADEEGISTV	stage-dive
ADEEGKPRU	keep guard
ADEEGLLLY	allegedly
ADEEGLNNR	Greenland
ADEEGLNNT	entangled
ADEEGLNOT	elongated
ADEEGLNRY	legendary
ADEEGLRTU	regulated
ADEEGMNRS	gendarmes
ADEEGMNTU	augmented
ADEEGNORS	renegados
ADEEGNRST	estranged
ADEEGNRSU	dungarees
ADEEGNRSV	Gravesend
ADEEGSTTU	degustate
ADEEHHITW	whitehead□
ADEEHHLLT	hell-hated
ADEEHHLRT	The Herald
ADEEHHLRY	Heyerdahl
ADEEHHNPY	hedyphane
ADEEHHOPT	The Phaedo
ADEEHIISV	Heaviside
ADEEHIKLT	deathlike
	death-like
ADEEHIKTV	khedivate
ADEEHILMO	Ideal Home
ADEEHILNR	headliner
ADEEHILNT	in the lead
ADEEHILRV	had liever
ADEEHILST	the ladies
ADEEHILTW	white lead
ADEEHINRT	herniated
ADEEHINSS	headiness
ADEEHIRTW	Whiteread

Words marked □ can also be spelled with an initial capital letter

ADEEHKLRS	sheldrake
ADEEHLLOS	leasehold
ADEEHLSSS	shadeless
ADEEHLSST	deathless
ADEEHMNOT	methadone
ADEEHMOST	do the same
	homestead
ADEEHNOST	headstone
ADEEHNPPR	apprehend
ADEEHNRST	adherents
ADEEHNRTU	unearthed
ADEEHOPTY	pay heed to
ADEEHORSV	overheads
	overshade
ADEEHPRSY	sharp-eyed
ADEEHRRTY	rehydrate
ADEEHRSST	shed tears
ADEEHRSTT	shattered
ADEEHRSTW	draw-sheet
	watershed
ADEEHSSTY	these days
ADEEHSTUX	exhausted
ADEEIILRZ	idealizer
ADEEIIMMT	immediate
ADEEIIMST	mediatise
ADEEIIMTV	mediative
ADEEIIMTZ	mediatize
ADEEIIRSS	diaeresis
ADEEIKLMR	dreamlike
ADEEIKLPS	spadelike
ADEEIKMRT	make tired
ADEEIKMRW	make wider
ADEEIKSST	take sides
ADEEILLMW	well-aimed
ADEEILLSY	easily led
ADEEILMNN	Mendelian
ADEEILMNS	Mélisande
ADEEILMPR	epidermal
ADEEILMTY	mediately
ADEEILNOV	devil a one
ADEEILNRT	tail-ender
ADEEILOTT	etiolated
	etoliated
ADEEILPRR	lip-reader
ADEEILPRS	pearlised
ADEEILPRZ	pearlized
ADEEILPSS	displease
ADEEIMMNS	misdemean
ADEEIMNNO	menadione
ADEEIMNRR	remainder
ADEEIMNSW	news media
ADEEIMPPR	pipe dream
	pipe-dream
ADEEIMSST	demitasse
ADEEIMSTT	estimated
ADEEINPRR	Periander
ADEEINPST	pedantise
ADEEINPTZ	pedantize
ADEEINRSS	readiness
ADEEINRSW	send a wire
ADEEINRTT	denitrate
ADEEINRUW	unwearied
ADEEIOPTV	videotape
ADEEIPRRS	draperies
ADEEIPRTU	repudiate
ADEEIPRTV	predative
ADEEIRSTV	advertise
ADEEIRSTW	waterside
ADEEIRTTX	extradite
ADEEISSTT	stateside ❑
ADEEJLNRY	Leyden jar
ADEEJMRSU	mudéjares
ADEEKLMRT	market-led
ADEEKMRSS	dressmake
ADEEKNNSS	nakedness
ADEEKNRTU	undertake
ADEEKORRT	take order
ADEELLMRW	well-armed
ADEELLNNP	pannelled
ADEELLNRY	learnedly
ADEELLRTV	travelled
ADEELLRVW	draw level
ADEELLSST	tasselled
ADEELLSTT	stellated
ADEELLTXY	exaltedly
ADEELMNOP	pademelon
ADEELMORU	remoulade
	rémoulade
ADEELMRSS	dreamless
ADEELNNRU	unlearned
ADEELNORV	Eve Arnold
ADEELNPTU	pendulate
ADEELNRRS	slanderer
ADEELNRSU	underseal
ADEELNRTU	unaltered
	unrelated
ADEELNRUX	unrelaxed
ADEELNSTY	Steely Dan
ADEELNTUX	unexalted
ADEELORST	desolater
ADEELORTT	related to
	tolerated
ADEELPRST	plastered
ADEELPSSU	pas de seul
ADEELRRTU	adulterer
ADEELRSTY	steelyard
ADEELRSVY	adversely
ADEELRTVY	avertedly
ADEEMMNNT	amendment
ADEEMMOXY	myxoedema
ADEEMNOPR	promenade
ADEEMNORU	demeanour
	enamoured
ADEEMOORR	aerodrome
ADEEMOPRR	madrepore
ADEEMORTT	trematode
ADEEMPSTU	despumate
	steamed up
ADEENOPRT	ponderate
ADEENORUV	endeavour ❑
ADEENORVY	oven-ready
ADEENPRSS	panderess

ADEENPRTT	patterned		Mansfield
ADEENPSST	adeptness	ADEFILNNZ	Zinfandel
ADEENQSTU	Dantesque	ADEFILNOT	deflation
ADEENRRTU	underrate		defoliant
	under-rate	ADEFILNTY	defiantly
ADEENRRUW	underwear	ADEFILORT	floriated
ADEENRSTY	sedentary	ADEFIMNNR	man friend
ADEENRTTU	untreated	ADEFIMORS	aside from
ADEENRTTV	advertent	ADEFIMOTY	time of day
ADEENRTUV	adventure	ADEFINOST	DiStefano
ADEENRTUW	unwatered		instead of
ADEENSSST	satedness	ADEFINRST	stand fire
ADEENSSVY	Seven Days	ADEFKLOTU	flaked out
ADEEOPRSV	eavesdrop	ADEFLLLSU	ladlefuls
ADEEORRTV	over-trade	ADEFLLMSY	damselfly
ADEEORRTZ	zero-rated	ADEFLMMOR	malformed
ADEEORTVX	overtaxed	ADEFLNOTU	default on
ADEEPPRST	speed trap	ADEFLNOWY	Fay Weldon
ADEEPRRSU	persuader	ADEFLOPST	soft pedal
ADEEPRRTU	departure		soft-pedal
ADEEPRSTU	depasture	ADEFLORUV	flavoured
ADEERRSSU	reassured	ADEFLPSSU	spadefuls
ADEERRSTU	treasured	ADEFLRSTW	leftwards
ADEERRSTV	traversed	ADEFMNNTU	fundament
ADEERSTYY	yesterday	ADEFNNOSU	nefandous
ADEFFGOOR	fear of God	ADEFNNOTU	fanned out
ADEFFHNOR	harden off	ADEFOOPRR	proofread
ADEFFIILS	falsified	ADEFOOTTU	out of date
ADEFFNORS	saffroned		out-of-date
ADEFFNORT	affronted	ADEFORRTV	overdraft
ADEFFNORW	wander off	ADEFORRTW	afterword
ADEFGGOTU	fagged out		Waterford
ADEFGHORT	godfather	ADEFRRSTU	fraudster
ADEFGIIRT	gratified	ADEGGHHIR	high-grade
ADEFGILLO	field goal	ADEGGHILN	hang-glide
ADEFGILNT	deflating	ADEGGINNR	gardening
ADEFGILRU	lifeguard	ADEGGINRR	regarding
ADEFGIRRU	fireguard	ADEGGINUW	wind gauge
ADEFGLOOT	floodgate	ADEGHHILT	headlight
ADEFGLRRU	regardful	ADEGHIILV	Diaghilev
ADEFHIIPT	Edith Piaf	ADEGHILPT	glide path
ADEFHIMST	ham-fisted	ADEGHINNR	hardening
ADEFHINOS	fashioned	ADEGHINPU	heading up
ADEFHIRST	head first	ADEGHINSU	anguished
ADEFHLNOZ	half-dozen	ADEGHIOPR	ideograph
ADEFHLOOS	falsehood	ADEGHIORU	rough idea
ADEFHNORU	unheard of	ADEGHIRST	sight-read
	unheard-of	ADEGHMORU	home guard
ADEFIILMP	amplified	ADEGHNNOS	Ogden Nash
ADEFIILNZ	finalized	ADEGHNOPY	endophagy
ADEFIILQU	qualified	ADEGHOOPS	good shape
ADEFIILRT	Eid al-Fitr	ADEGIILNT	detailing
ADEFIINRV	vide infra	ADEGIILOS	dialogise
ADEFIIPRR	rapid fire	ADEGIILOZ	dialogize
ADEFIIRSZ	fair-sized	ADEGIIMNT	mediating
ADEFIISST	dies fasti	ADEGIINNR	ingrained
	satisfied	ADEGIINTV	deviating
ADEFIKKLR	frikkadel	ADEGIIORS	go airside
ADEFIKNRT	after kind	ADEGIKNNR	darkening
ADEFILLSU	fusillade	ADEGILLOS	gladioles
ADEFILMNS	fieldsman	ADEGILMOR	Golda Meir

ADEGILNOR	girandole
	negroidal
ADEGILNOS	alongside
ADEGILNRU	gerundial
ADEGILNTW	delta-wing
ADEGILORV	Gore Vidal
ADEGILSUY	easily dug
ADEGIMNNN	demanning
ADEGIMNNP	dampening
ADEGIMNTU	magnitude
ADEGIMOST	dogmatise
ADEGIMOTZ	dogmatize
ADEGINNPW	Wig and Pen
ADEGINNPX	expanding
ADEGINNRT	integrand
ADEGINNRW	wandering
ADEGINNTT	attending
ADEGINOOT	go on a diet
ADEGINORR	Rio Grande
ADEGINORS	dragonise
	grandiose
ADEGINORW	wrong idea
ADEGINORZ	dragonize
	organized
ADEGINOSS	diagnoses
ADEGINPRS	spreading
ADEGINPRT	departing
ADEGINPRV	depraving
ADEGINRRW	rewarding
ADEGINRTU	giant rude
ADEGINSSU	gaudiness
ADEGIPRRT	partridge ❑
ADEGIRTTU	gratitude
ADEGKRRTU	drug taker
ADEGLLOPT	gold plate
	gold-plate
ADEGLNNSU	Langesund
ADEGLNOST	Gladstone
ADEGLNRUW	Grünewald
ADEGLNSTU	angel dust
ADEGLOOPY	paedology
ADEGLOOUV	good value
ADEGLORST	old stager
ADEGLORTW	Goldwater
ADEGMNOOZ	Mao Zedong
ADEGMNRTU	Nemrut Dag
ADEGMOPRR	deprogram
ADEGNNRSS	grandness
ADEGNOORS	goosander
ADEGNOPRT	godparent
ADEGNORSU	dangerous
ADEGNORTU	get around
ADEGNOSTW	downstage
ADEGOORST	stage door
ADEGOORSY	goodyears
ADEGOOSTT	good taste
ADEHHIPRS	rhaphides
ADEHHISTW	death wish
ADEHHORST	short-head
ADEHIIKLV	khedivial
ADEHIILNP	delphinia

ADEHIIMNS	maidenish
ADEHIINRT	in a dither
ADEHIIRRR	hairdrier
ADEHIISST	diathesis
ADEHIJMNU	mujahedin
ADEHIKLOR	Lake Ohrid
ADEHIKMOT	The Mikado
ADEHIKNPS	handspike
ADEHIKNRT	in the dark
ADEHILLPY	daily help
ADEHILMNS	mishandle
ADEHILMOT	ethmoidal
ADEHILNOR	lie hard on
ADEHILNPR	philander
ADEHILNRR	hardliner
ADEHILNRS	hard lines
ADEHILPTW	plead with
ADEHILTTW	dealt with
ADEHILTWY	white lady
ADEHIMMNO	ad hominem
ADEHIMNOR	rhodamine
ADEHIMNRS	Sanhedrim
ADEHIMOSU	housemaid
ADEHIMRST	Hard Times
	hard times
ADEHIMRTY	diathermy
ADEHINNRS	Sanhedrin
ADEHINNSS	handiness
ADEHINNST	set in hand
ADEHINORS	rhodanise
ADEHINORT	in the road
ADEHINORZ	rhodanize
ADEHINRRT	Reinhardt
ADEHINRSS	hardiness
ADEHINRST	interdash
	tarnished
ADEHINSSS	shadiness
ADEHINTWY	win the day
ADEHIOPRS	do a perish
ADEHIOPRT	Aphrodite
	atrophied
ADEHIRRRY	hairdryer
ADEHIRRTT	third-rate
ADEHIRSTW	dishwater
ADEHIRSVW	hivewards
ADEHJLOSU	Judas-hole
ADEHJNNOR	John Arden
ADEHKNOSW	shake down
ADEHKORRS	dark horse
ADEHKRSTU	Turk's head
ADEHLLOTT	death toll
ADEHLLRSW	hellwards
ADEHLOOWZ	Hazelwood
ADEHLOPRY	polyhedra
ADEHLORST	Aldershot
ADEHLORTW	hold water
ADEHMMOTU	mouth-made
ADEHMNORY	hard money
ADEHMNSTU	them and us
ADEHMOORT	Motorhead
ADEHMOORV	Hoover Dam

ADEHMOPRY	hypoderma
ADEHMORSW	homewards
ADEHNOORT	On the Road
	on the road
ADEHNORST	stone-hard
ADEHNORTU	under oath
ADEHNORUV	have round
ADEHNOSTT	set hand to
ADEHNPPRU	upper hand
ADEHOORSU	roadhouse
ADEHOORTW	heartwood
ADEHOOSTT	statehood
ADEHORRSW	shoreward
ADEHORSVW	have words
ADEHOSTUW	washed out
	washed-out
ADEHRSTUY	Dusty Hare
ADEHTUVYY	heavy-duty
ADEIIINNS	Indianise
ADEIIINNZ	Indianize
ADEIIINPR	peridinia
ADEIIINTT	dietitian
ADEIILLMS	misallied
ADEIILMST	Miltiades
ADEIILNST	disentail
ADEIILORT	editorial
ADEIILORV	D'Oliveira
ADEIILPRS	presidial
ADEIILPTX	pixilated
ADEIILQTU	liquidate
ADEIIMNOT	mediation
ADEIIMSSV	misadvise
ADEIINNOS	Indonesia
ADEIINOTV	deviation
ADEIINPPR	drainpipe
ADEIINPRS	Pindarise
ADEIINPRZ	Pindarize
ADEIINSTZ	sanitized
ADEIIPRRS	disrepair
ADEIIPRSS	dispraise
ADEIIPSST	dissipate
ADEIIPSSY	diapyesis
ADEIIRRTT	irritated
ADEIIRSTT	distraite
ADEIJLMNS	James Lind
ADEIJLOSU	jalousied
ADEIKMORS	kaiserdom
ADEIKMRTY	make dirty
ADEIKMYZZ	make dizzy
ADEIKNPPR	kidnapper
ADEIKNPRS	spikenard
ADEIKNPRT	predikant
ADEIKNRRR	rank-rider
ADEILLMNO	medallion
ADEILLMOT	metalloid
ADEILLMRT	treadmill
ADEILLMST	medallist
ADEILLNNV	Ivan Lendl
ADEILLPRS	spiralled
ADEILLPRU	preludial
ADEILLQRU	quadrille
ADEILLRSY	Sally Ride
ADEILMNNO	mandoline
ADEILMNPT	implanted
ADEILMNST	dismantle
ADEILMOPT	diplomate
ADEILMOPY	polyamide
ADEILMPTU	amplitude
ADEILMSTU	simulated
ADEILMTTU	mutilated
ADEILNNSW	Dennis Law
ADEILNOPT	planetoid
ADEILNORU	lie around
ADEILNRRT	interlard
ADEILNRSW	draw lines
ADEILNRTT	tridental
ADEILNRTU	uitlander
ADEILNRUY	unreadily
ADEILNSTU	insulated
ADEILOQSU	odalisque
ADEILPRSS	dispersal
ADEILPTTU	platitude
ADEILSSTU	lassitude
ADEIMMRST	midstream
ADEIMNNOT	nominated
ADEIMNNTU	indumenta
ADEIMNORS	randomise
ADEIMNORZ	randomize
ADEIMNOST	Maidstone
ADEIMNPRR	reprimand
ADEIMNPRS	spiderman
ADEIMNPST	pedantism
ADEIMNRRU	unmarried
ADEIMNRSU	nursemaid
ADEIMNRSY	year's mind
ADEIMNSTV	Vedantism
ADEIMOORV	road movie
ADEIMOPST	impastoed
ADEIMORTT	trematoid
ADEIMORTY	mediatory
ADEIMPRST	spermatid
ADEIMRRUU	Du Maurier
ADEIMRTUX	admixture
ADEIMRTXY	taxidermy
ADEINNNSU	Dunsinane
ADEINNRSS	randiness
ADEINNRTU	untrained
ADEINNSSS	sandiness
ADEINNSTU	unstained
ADEINNTTU	untainted
ADEINOOPS	poinadoes
ADEINOPPT	appointed
ADEINOPRR	preordain
ADEINOPST	antipodes
ADEINORTT	Andreotti
ADEINORTY	arytenoid
ADEINOTUX	exudation
ADEINPPRS	sandpiper
ADEINPPST	standpipe
ADEINPRSS	rapidness
ADEINPRSU	unpraised
ADEINPSSV	vapidness

ADEINPSVY	vin de pays
ADEINRRTY	Tyrian red
ADEINRSST	Streisand
	tardiness
ADEINRSTU	turn aside
ADEINSSST	staidness
ADEINSSTU	sustained
ADEINSTTU	disattune
ADEINSTTV	Adventist
ADEIOPRSV	privadoes
ADEIOPRTZ	trapezoid
ADEIPPRSU	dispauper
ADEIPPSSY	dyspepsia
ADEIPRSTV	drive past
ADEIPRSUU	Epidaurus
ADEIPRSUV	vide supra
ADEIPRTVY	depravity
ADEIRRSUY	residuary
ADEIRSTVY	adversity
ADEISTTTU	attitudes
ADEKKMNRU	make drunk
ADEKMNNOW	made known
ADEKMOPRU	make proud
ADEKNOOTW	tae kwon do
ADEKNORSW	dear knows
ADEKNSTUU	Eduskunta
ADEKOPRSW	spadework
ADELLLOWY	allowedly
ADELLMRUY	medullary
ADELLNOOT	Donatello
ADELLNOUY	unalloyed
ADELLNPSU	all ends up
ADELLNSTW	stand well
ADELLNSYY	Sandy Lyle
ADELLORRT	tall order
ADELLORRW	real world
ADELLRTXY	dextrally
ADELMNNOS	Mandelson
ADELMNNUY	mundanely
ADELMNOPS	endoplasm
ADELMORST	old master
ADELMSSUY	assumedly
ADELNNNPU	unplanned
ADELNNORW	landowner
ADELNNPTU	unplanted
ADELNOOST	loadstone
ADELNORRV	Land Rover®
ADELNORTU	outlander
ADELNORUY	roundelay
ADELNOSSW	Les Dawson
ADELNPRUY	underplay
ADELNRSSU	laundress
ADELNRTVY	verdantly
ADELNSSTU	dauntless
ADELOPPTU	populated
ADELOPTUY	played out
	played-out
ADELPQRUU	quadruple
ADELRSSUY	assuredly
ADEMNNORT	adornment
ADEMNNORU	maunder on
ADEMNOPRS	mad person
ADEMNORSU	meandrous
ADEMNRRSU	snare-drum
ADEMNRTUU	unmatured
ADEMOORRT	moderator
ADEMOORST	astrodome
ADEMOPPRU	pauperdom
ADEMOPRST	arms depot
ADEMORRSW	Romewards
ADEMORRTT	Rotterdam
ADENNNSTU	sun-tanned
ADENNORRU	do a runner
ADENNORSS	Sanderson
ADENNOSST	sandstone
ADENNOSTY	asyndeton
ADENNSSTW	news-stand
ADENNTTWY	and twenty
ADENOORST	tornadoes
ADENOORTT	detonator
ADENOPRTV	davenport□
ADENOPRUV	up-and-over
ADENOPRUZ	Ezra Pound
ADENORRUY	year-round
ADENORRVW	overdrawn
ADENORSTV	stand over
ADENORSTW	stare down
ADENORTTU	rotundate
ADENORTWW	water down
ADENOSUVW	sound wave
ADENOTTWY	wyandotte□
ADENPRSSU	underpass
ADENRRSTW	sternward
ADENRSSTW	St Andrews
ADEOPRRTW	top drawer
	top-drawer
ADEOPRRTY	predatory
ADEOPRSTU	outspread
	spread out
ADEORRSWW	swear-word
ADEPPPRUW	wrapped up
ADERSSTWW	westwards
ADFFHRSTU	hard stuff
ADFFIIMRS	disaffirm
ADFFILNTU	find fault
	find-fault
ADFGHIRSU	Fishguard
ADFGINORS	sangfroid
	sang-froid
ADFGLNORY	dragonfly
ADFGOORRW	go forward
ADFGOORTU	drag out of
ADFHINRST	firsthand
	first-hand
ADFHKLNRU	half-drunk
ADFHLLOOY	lay hold of
ADFHLOORY	foolhardy
ADFHNOOTU	out of hand
ADFIILOOP	filopodia
ADFILRSTY	first lady
ADFIMNRST	stand firm
ADFINORSZ	sforzandi

ADFIORSUV	disfavour
ADFLLLOOW	floodwall
ADFLLOOOS	Adolf Loos
ADFLLOOST	faldstool
ADFLNOOPT	plant food
ADFLORRWY	forwardly
	frowardly
ADFLORUUY	Raoul Dufy
ADFMNORST	stand from
ADFMOOPPR	damp-proof
ADFNOORSZ	sforzando
ADFNORRTW	frontward
ADFOPRSUW	upwards of
ADGGILNRY	niggardly
ADGGINPRU	upgrading
ADGGINRRU	guard ring
ADGGLOORV	Volgograd
ADGHHINRT	right-hand
ADGHHOOPR	hodograph
ADGHILLLU	guildhall
ADGHILNRV	grindhval
ADGHILNSY	dashingly
ADGHIMOSU	Mogadishu
ADGHINNST	and things
ADGHINOSW	shadowing
ADGHINRTU	indraught
ADGHIRRTW	rightward
ADGHORRUW	rough-draw
ADGIIILNT	digitalin
ADGIIILST	digitalis
ADGIIJNNO	adjoining
ADGIILNSS	glissandi
ADGIIMNRS	disarming
ADGIIMNSY	dismaying
ADGIIMNTT	admitting
ADGIINNNT	indignant
ADGIINNRW	drawing-in
	in drawing
ADGIINOSS	diagnosis
ADGIINRTY	dignitary
ADGIIRTVY	gravidity
ADGIKLNRS	darklings
ADGILLNUY	languidly
ADGILLOSU	gladiolus
ADGILNNOT	Aldington
ADGILNNOU	unloading
ADGILNORY	adoringly
ADGILNOSS	glissando
ADGILNRTY	dartingly
ADGILOORY	radiology
ADGIMMOST	dogmatism
ADGIMNNOS	Mandingos
ADGIMOSTT	dogmatist
ADGINNOOU	iguanodon ❑
ADGINNORS	Grandison
ADGINNORW	Winogrand
ADGINNRST	stranding
ADGINOPRY	parodying
ADGINPRRX	Grand Prix
ADGLLNOOP	plod along
ADGLNNORW	long-drawn
ADGLNOORY	andrology
ADGLNOOTY	odontalgy
ADGLNOUYY	young lady
ADGMOORRU	guardroom
ADGMRRSTU	smart drug
ADGNNNNOU	Dungannon
ADGNNNOOO	go on and on
ADGNOORTU	a good turn
ADGNORRTU	grand tour
ADGOOORST	a good sort
ADGOOPRST	gastropod
ADGOORSTW	go towards
ADHHNORST	shorthand
ADHIIKLNR	drink-hail
ADHIILORZ	rhizoidal
ADHIIMMRS	Midrashim
ADHIIMPSS	amidships
ADHIKMNNU	humankind
ADHIKNORW	handiwork
ADHIKNSSS	kiss hands
ADHILLMNO	Damon Hill
ADHILLOSW	dishallow
ADHILLTWY	dally with
ADHILMSTY	Ladysmith
ADHILNNUY	unhandily
ADHILNOOY	on holiday
ADHILNOPY	hypnoidal
ADHILOPTY	typhoidal
ADHINNRTU	hit-and-run
ADHINOOST	sainthood
ADHINORTY	hydration
ADHINRTWW	withdrawn
ADHINSTTW	stand with
	withstand
ADHISTWWY	widthways
ADHKMOSTY	Thomas Kyd
ADHKNORTW	Dankworth
ADHLNOOWY	any old how
ADHLNORUU	haul round
ADHLOTTUW	would that
ADHMNOOOW	womanhood
ADHMORTTU	Dartmouth
ADHNNRSTU	hand's turn
ADHNOORYZ	hydrozoan
ADHNORRTW	northward
ADHNORSUY	anhydrous
ADHNOSSTU	thousands
ADHOOPRRT	arthropod
ADHOOSTTW	what's to do?
ADHORSTTY	hydrostat
ADHORSTUW	southward
ADIIIKNNN	Indian ink
ADIILLNVY	invalidly
ADIILMPVY	impavidly
ADIILMSSS	dismissal
ADIIMNOSS	admission
ADIIMNRSW	Darwinism
ADIINNOST	disanoint
ADIINOOTX	oxidation
ADIINOQTU	quotidian
ADIINORTT	tradition

Words marked ❑ can also be spelled with an initial capital letter

ADIINORTV	divinator
ADIINOSST	soi-disant
ADIINRSTT	distraint
ADIINRSTW	Darwinist
ADIIPRSTY	disparity
ADIISSTUY	assiduity
ADIKKNNSY	Kandinsky
ADIKLMNRS	alms-drink
ADIKMNNOW	womankind
ADIKMRRTY	dirty mark
ADILLNRUY	diurnally
ADILLQSUY	squalidly
ADILMNOST	daltonism❑
ADILMNOWW	wild woman
ADILMNRUU	Duralumin®
ADILMSTTU	Talmudist
ADILNOPSY	on display
ADILNORSW	solar wind
ADILNPSWY	wild pansy
ADILNSTTY	distantly
ADILORRWW	World War I
ADILPRTWY	wild party
ADIMNNTUY	mundanity
ADIMORRTY	Amy Dorrit
ADINNNOUZ	D'Annunzio
ADINNOOST	donations
ADINNOSST	dissonant
ADINNPRTU	tip and run
ADINOOSTW	satinwood
ADINOPRRS	raindrops
ADINORSTU	sit around
ADINPSTTU	disputant
ADIOOPSTU	adoptious
ADIOPPTTU	put paid to
ADIORRSTT	traditors
ADIOSSSUU	assiduous
ADIPSSUYY	upsy-daisy
ADJMMOOOR	major-domo
ADKLNORTU	talk round
ADKNORRWW	drawn work
ADKOORRSW	roadworks
ADLLNSSUV	Sundsvall
ADLMNORTY	mordantly
ADLMOOPRR	prodromal
ADLMOORRY	Lord Mayor
ADLMOORTU	modulator
ADLNOPRYY	polyandry
ADLNRSSTU	Stralsund
ADLOOOSTT	toadstool
ADLOPRSWY	swordplay
ADLORSUUY	arduously
ADLORTUWY	outwardly
ADLPQRUUY	quadruply
ADMMORRTY	martyrdom
ADMNOOOST	odontomas
ADMNOORSZ	smorzando
ADMNORSST	sand storm
	sandstorm
ADMNORSSW	swordsman
ADMOOPPRU	pompadour
ADMPSTTUY	stamp duty
ADNNOORTU	not around
ADNNOPSTU	stand upon
ADNNORRUU	run around
	runaround
ADNOOTTUU	out and out
	out-and-out
ADNOPRRUW	wrapround
ADNOPRSSU	pass round
ADNOPRSTU	Port Sudan
ADNOPSTTU	stand up to
ADNOQSTUW	squat down
ADOOORRWW	arrowwood
ADOOPSSSS	Dos Passos
AEEEEHMPR	ephemerae
AEEEEHRRW	here we are
AEEEELMRS	Release Me
AEEEETTTT	tête-à-tête
AEEEFFLRT	feel after
AEEEFGNRR	free-range
AEEEFHLLN	fellaheen
AEEEFHRRT	hereafter
AEEEFIRRT	fire-eater
AEEEFKRST	seek after
AEEEFLMRZ	ramfeezle
AEEEFOSSU	ease of use
AEEEFRRTV	ever after
AEEEFSTTT	estafette
AEEEGGGNR	greengage
AEEEGGNNR	engrenage
AEEEGGRST	Easter egg
	segregate
AEEEGHLRW	gearwheel
AEEEGHTTX	get the axe
AEEEGIJNN	Jean Genie
AEEEGIKNV	give a knee
AEEEGILVV	give leave
AEEEGIMNR	menagerie
AEEEGJNNT	Jean Genet
AEEEGLRRV	gear-lever
AEEEGMNNP	empennage
AEEEGMNRT	agreement
AEEEGNRSS	eagerness
AEEEGNSTV	Stevenage
AEEEGRTTZ	gazetteer
AEEEHHNST	ensheathe
AEEEHLMPR	ephemeral
AEEEHLMRS	Haslemere
AEEEHLMRT	the real me
AEEEHLPRR	Harper Lee
AEEEHMPRS	ephemeras
AEEEHMRTX	hexameter
AEEEHNNRT	enhearten
AEEEHNRTW	enwreathe
AEEEHRRRS	rehearser
AEEEIKLPV	keep alive
AEEEILLRU	Laurie Lee
AEEEILNPY	pineal eye
AEEEIMNRX	re-examine
AEEEIMRRT	Téméraire
AEEEIRRTT	reiterate
AEEEJNNTT	Jeannette

AEEEKLLMV	make level
AEEEKMNSS	make sense
AEEEKMNST	make tense
AEEEKMPRT	keep a term
AEEEKMRRT	marketeer
AEEEKNRST	tree snake
AEEELLMNT	elemental
AEEELLNRS	all serene
AEEELLSST	tessellae
AEEELMSTW	sweetmeal
AEEELNUVZ	Venezuela
AEEELPTTU	epaulette
AEEEMNRST	erasement
AEEEMNRTU	enumerate
AEEEMPRTT	temperate
AEEEMRRSU	remeasure
AEEEMSTTW	sweetmeat
AEEENNNQU	Queen Anne
	Queen-Anne
AEEENNPRT	perennate
AEEENORTX	exonerate
AEEENPRTT	penetrate
AEEENRTTV	eventrate
AEEENSSSV	seven seas
AEEENTTUV	eventuate
AEEENTTUX	extenuate
AEEERRVYY	every year
AEEERSTTW	Teeswater
AEEFFFMUW	fee-faw-fum
AEEFFILRT	afterlife
	after-life
AEEFGGLUU	fuel gauge
AEEFGGNOR	engage for
AEEFGILMS	self-image
AEEFGILPR	pilferage
AEEFGINRS	far-seeing
AEEFGLLOT	flageolet
AEEFGORST	forestage
AEEFHIKPT	keep faith
AEEFHLRTT	heartfelt
	heart-felt
AEEFHORTT	at the fore
AEEFHOSSU	safe house
AEEFILLMN	en famille
AEEFILMPR	relief map
AEEFILNRT	interleaf
AEEFILOTX	exfoliate
AEEFILRST	reistafel
AEEFILRSV	life-saver
AEEFILRWY	life-weary
AEEFIMORT	aforetime
AEEFINSTT	festinate
AEEFINSTX	antefixes
AEEFIQTUW	quite a few
AEEFIRRTW	firewater
	fire-water
AEEFKLOVW	folk-weave
AEEFKMOSU	make use of
AEEFKOPRS	forespeak
AEEFLLLMS	feel small
AEEFLLOOS	loose-leaf
AEEFLMNRT	Fremantle
AEEFLNRST	fenestral
AEEFLNSSS	falseness
AEEFLPSST	false step
AEEFLRRTT	flatterer
AEEFMNORS	Freemason
AEEFMNORW	freewoman
AEEFMNRTT	frame tent
AEEFNNORT	foreanent
AEEFNSTTY	safety net
AEEFOPRRT	perforate
AEEFORSTT	foretaste
AEEGGILNR	ginger ale
AEEGGIRUW	wire gauge
AEEGGLNOY	genealogy
AEEGGNPRY	energy gap
AEEGGNRSU	grease gun
AEEGGRRSW	swaggerer
AEEGGRTUY	tyre gauge
AEEGHILST	Eastleigh
AEEGHIMRT	hermitage ❑
AEEGHINNU	guinea hen
AEEGHINRS	garnishee
AEEGHIRTW	agree with
AEEGHLPRT	telegraph
AEEGHLRWY	grey whale
AEEGHMNOP	megaphone
AEEGHMNOT	on the game
AEEGHMRTW	wheat germ
AEEGHMRTZ	megahertz
AEEGHNRSW	greenwash
AEEGHOSTU	gatehouse
AEEGIILNS	genialise
AEEGIILNZ	genialize
AEEGIKNNW	weakening
AEEGILLNS	all-seeing
AEEGILLRS	galleries
AEEGILLRV	villagree
AEEGILLST	legislate
AEEGILMNN	meningeal
AEEGILMNR	greenmail
AEEGILNNR	in general
AEEGILNNT	eglantine
	inelegant
AEEGILNPR	repealing
AEEGILNRV	revealing
AEEGILNSW	anglewise
AEEGILNTV	elevating
AEEGILPTT	title page
AEEGILRTU	gauleiter
AEEGILUVY	Ivy League
AEEGIMNNV	given name
AEEGIMNRS	Germanise
AEEGIMNRT	germinate
AEEGIMNRZ	Germanize
AEEGIMNST	magnetise
AEEGIMNTT	magnetite
AEEGIMNTZ	magnetize
AEEGIMPTT	pegmatite
AEEGIMRRT	remigrate
AEEGINNRT	Argentine

	tangerine
AEEGINNSU	Gneisenau
AEEGINNUW	New Guinea
AEEGINOPS	espionage
AEEGINOTT	negotiate
AEEGINPRT	interpage
	repeating
AEEGINPRV	grapevine
AEEGINRST	stingaree
AEEGINRTT	integrate
AEEGINSSW	seesawing
AEEGIPSUV	give pause
AEEGIRUWZ	wire gauze
AEEGJNORR	jargoneer
AEEGLLNOR	organelle
AEEGLLNRY	generally
AEEGLLNTY	elegantly
AEEGLMNNT	gentleman
AEEGLMNRY	germanely
AEEGLMNST	segmental
AEEGLMORT	glomerate
AEEGLMORU	Rogue Male
AEEGLNNOR	enlarge on
AEEGLNNOS	Angelenos
AEEGLNNPT	pentangle
AEEGLNOPS	espagnole
AEEGLNORS	sloganeer
AEEGLNRSS	largeness
AEEGLORST	alter egos
AEEGLORVZ	overglaze
AEEGLPRRY	pearl-grey
AEEGLQRSU	square leg
AEEGLRSSV	graveless
AEEGMNOTY	gate money
	gate-money
AEEGMNRRS	merganser
AEEGMOPRW	power game
AEEGMORST	gasometer
	megastore
AEEGNNSTW	newsagent
AEEGNOPRS	personage
AEEGNORRT	generator
AEEGNORTT	teratogen
AEEGNORTU	entourage
AEEGNOTTW	wagonette
AEEGNOTXY	oxygenate
AEEGNPRSS	passenger
AEEGNRSST	greatness
AEEGNRSSV	graveness
AEEGNSSUV	vagueness
AEEGOPRRT	reportage
AEEGORTTW	gate-tower
AEEGPRTUX	expurgate
AEEGRRTVY	very great
AEEGRSTTU	gesture at
	Trésaguet
AEEHHILRT	healthier
AEEHHINST	insheathe
AEEHHIPRU	Uriah Heep
AEEHHITTW	white heat
AEEHHKNRS	Shere Khan
AEEHHKSST	the shakes
AEEHHLMTT	at the helm
AEEHHLOSW	hawsehole
AEEHHNPTY	hyphenate
AEEHHNSTU	unsheathe
AEEHHOOVY	yo-heave-ho
AEEHHRRTT	the rather
AEEHIKMTW	make white
AEEHIKNRT	Katherine
AEEHILLRS	raise hell
AEEHILMNW	meanwhile
AEEHILMRZ	Alzheimer
AEEHILNRS	Earl Hines
AEEHILNSS	Sinhalese
AEEHILNTV	Helvetian
AEEHILPST	ephialtes
AEEHILSTW	white sale
AEEHIMNST	mainsheet
AEEHIMPSS	emphasise
AEEHIMPST	empathise
AEEHIMPSZ	emphasize
AEEHIMPTZ	empathize
AEEHIMRST	timeshare
AEEHIMSTW	white-seam
AEEHIMTTT	at the time
AEEHIMTTW	white meat
AEEHINPRS	Hesperian
AEEHINPSS	Ephesians
AEEHINPST	Stephanie
AEEHINRRT	in the rear
AEEHINRSV	haversine
AEEHINRTT	Henrietta
AEEHINRTW	inwreathe
AEEHINSSV	heaviness
AEEHIPPSW	hawsepipe
AEEHIPRSS	apheresis
AEEHIPRST	therapies
AEEHKLMOW	make whole
AEEHKLMRW	wheelmark
AEEHKLPSW	sheepwalk
AEEHKMNOT	on the make
AEEHKMORS	shoemaker ❑
AEEHKMPRT	theme park
AEEHKNOTT	on the take
AEEHKORST	take horse
AEEHLLMOW	wholemeal
AEEHLLNOW	Hallowe'en
AEEHLLOSW	wholesale
AEEHLLPRT	Peter Hall
AEEHLMMNT	Emmenthal
AEEHLMNOO	Home Alone
AEEHLMOPT	home plate
AEEHLMSSS	shameless
AEEHLMTTY	methylate
AEEHLNOPS	anopheles
AEEHLOPST	telophase
AEEHLORST	lose heart
AEEHLORTW	waterhole
AEEHLOTTU	out at heel
AEEHLPSSS	shapeless
AEEHLPTTY	telepathy

AEEHLRSST	heartless
AEEHLRTTT	The Tatler
AEEHLSTTT	the latest
AEEHLSTXY	hexastyle
AEEHMMORT	hammer-toe
AEEHMMPSY	emphysema
AEEHMNNOP	phenomena
AEEHMNOPT	Amenhotep
AEEHMNOTT	moth-eaten
AEEHMNSTX	exanthems
AEEHMOPRS	semaphore
AEEHMPRST	petersham
AEEHMRRTU	Arthur Mee
AEEHMRTTT	the matter
AEEHMSSST	the masses
AEEHMSTTW	Westmeath
AEEHNNOTW	on the wane
AEEHNORTW	weather on
AEEHNPRRS	sharpener
AEEHNPRSW	new phrase
AEEHNPTTU	up the ante
AEEHNRTTY	Henry Tate
AEEHNRTUW	unwreathe
AEEHORRST	heart-sore
AEEHORRTT	to the rear
AEEHORSTW	whatsoeer
AEEHORSUW	warehouse
AEEHPRSST	set phrase
AEEHPRSTU	Euphrates
	superheat
AEEHRRSTV	harvester
AEEHSSTTT	the States
AEEIIKRST	Erik Satie
AEEIILMNT	eliminate
AEEIILQRU	reliquiae
AEEIILRSS	serialise
AEEIILRST	Israelite
	realities
AEEIILRSZ	serialize
AEEIIMNRR	marinière
AEEIIMNST	amenities
AEEIINNTV	Vientiane
AEEIINRSY	yersiniae
AEEIINRTT	itinerate
AEEIIPPRT	peripetia
AEEIIRSTV	varieties
AEEIIRTTV	iterative
AEEIIRTVZ	vizierate
AEEIJLNQU	Jaqueline
AEEIJMNSS	jessamine
AEEIJPRSS	jasperise
AEEIJPRSZ	jasperize
AEEIKKLNS	snakelike
AEEIKLMUW	Milwaukee
AEEIKLNNP	Lenin Peak
AEEIKLNSS	leakiness
AEEIKLRTW	like water
AEEIKNNSY	Keynesian
AEEIKNSSW	snakewise
AEEIKRSTW	awestrike
AEEIKSSTU	take issue
AEEILLMOT	emolliate
AEEILLMOZ	Emile Zola
AEEILLMST	metallise
AEEILLMTZ	metallize
AEEILLPST	palletise
AEEILLPTZ	palletize
AEEILLSTT	satellite
AEEILLTTV	Little Eva
AEEILMMRS	marmelise
AEEILMMRZ	marmelize
AEEILMMST	lemmatise
AEEILMMTZ	lemmatize
AEEILMNNT	lineament
AEEILMORT	meliorate
AEEILMRST	misrelate
AEEILMRTT	altimeter
AEEILMRTW	limewater
AEEILNNPP	peneplain
AEEILNNPR	perennial
AEEILNNTV	Levantine
	valentine ❑
AEEILNORR	earlier on
AEEILNOTV	elevation
	élevation
AEEILNPPP	pineapple
AEEILNRSS	earliness
AEEILNRSU	unrealise
AEEILNRSV	in several
	vernalise
AEEILNRTU	retinulae
AEEILNRTW	waterline
AEEILNRUZ	unrealize
AEEILNRVZ	vernalize
AEEILNSST	essential
AEEILNSSV	aliveness
AEEILNSTT	state line
AEEILNTTV	ventilate
AEEILORRT	arteriole
AEEILPRST	prelatise
AEEILPRTZ	prelatize
AEEILRRTV	retrieval
AEEILRSSW	weariless
AEEILRSTU	at leisure
AEEILRSTV	relatives
	versatile
AEEILRSTY	seriately
AEEILRTTU	elutriate
AEEILSSUX	sexualise
AEEILSUXZ	sexualize
AEEILSVVY	evasively
AEEIMNNZZ	mezzanine
AEEIMNOTT	at one time
AEEIMNPRT	in a temper
AEEIMNRTT	terminate
AEEIMNRTV	verminate
AEEIMNSSS	seaminess
AEEIMNSST	meatiness
AEEIMNTVV	vivamente
AEEIMOPPR	peperomia
AEEIMORST	osmeteria
AEEIMORSW	wearisome

AEEIMPRRT	prime rate
AEEIMPRSS	Parseeism
AEEIMPRST	spare time
AEEIMPRTT	impetrate
AEEIMRTTX	extra time
	taximeter
AEEIMSTTW	waste time
AEEINNNPS	Apennines
AEEINNNSS	inaneness
AEEINNPST	septennia
AEEINNRST	in earnest
AEEINNRTT	entertain
AEEINNRTV	innervate
AEEINNSST	insensate
AEEINNSSV	naïveness
AEEINOPPT	appointee
AEEINORTT	orientate
AEEINPPST	pepsinate
AEEINPRSS	passerine
AEEINPSVX	expansive
AEEINQSTU	sequentia
AEEINRRST	retainers
AEEINRRTV	veratrine
AEEINRSSW	weariness
AEEINRSTT	reinstate
AEEINRSTU	estuarine
AEEINRSTV	invertase
AEEINSTTT	intestate
	satinette
AEEINTTTV	attentive
	tentative
AEEIOPRTV	evaporite
	operative
AEEIPPRST	appetiser
AEEIPPRSU	pauperise
AEEIPPRTW	water pipe
AEEIPPRTZ	appetizer
AEEIPPRUZ	pauperize
AEEIPPSTW	waste pipe
AEEIPRRTV	privateer
AEEIPRSSV	aspersive
AEEIPRSTW	taperwise
AEEIPRSVV	pervasive
AEEIPRTTX	extirpate
AEEIPSSST	epistases
AEEIRRSTV	East River
AEEIRRSTZ	rasterize
AEEIRSSTT	sestertia
AEEIRSSTV	assertive
AEEJLMRSU	Jerusalem
AEEJMORTT	majorette
AEEJNNORT	Janet Reno
AEEKLLNSY	Sean Kelly
AEEKLORVW	leave work
AEEKLSTTW	sweet talk
	sweet-talk
AEEKMMNOY	make money
AEEKMMPTY	make empty
AEEKMMRRY	make merry
AEEKMMRST	make terms
AEEKMNRTW	newmarket❑
AEEKMORSW	make worse
AEEKORSST	keratoses
AEEKORSTV	skate over
AEEKORTUY	eukaryote
AEEKPSSTT	take steps
AEELLLSTT	tell tales
AEELLLSUV	vulsellae
AEELLMRSS	realmless
AEELLMRSW	Sam Weller
AEELLNPRT	repellant
AEELLNRTY	eternally
AEELLOPST	Sellotape®
AEELLOSWY	Yellow Sea
AEELLRRTV	traveller
AEELLRSVY	severally
AEELLSSUV	valueless
AEELMMNRT	entrammel
AEELMNOST	telamones
AEELMNPSS	ampleness
AEELMNRTV	ravelment
AEELMORST	elastomer
AEELMOSWY	awesomely
AEELMPRXY	exemplary
AEELMPTTY	type metal
AEELMRTTU	tremulate
AEELNNNPY	Penny Lane
AEELNNOSS	aloneness
AEELNNRWY	nearly new
	nearly-new
AEELNOSYY	lay eyes on
AEELNPRTV	prevalent
AEELNRSST	alertness
AEELNRSTX	externals
AEELNRSTY	earnestly
AEELNRTTY	ternately
AEELNRTVY	Trevelyan
AEELNRTWY	Trelawney
AEELNSSST	staleness
AEELOPRTV	leave port
AEELOPSUY	please you
AEELORSTW	lose water
AEELORTVW	water vole
AEELORTVY	elevatory
AEELORUVV	overvalue
AEELOSTTW	tea towels
AEELPPRRU	puerperal
AEELPPRSS	paperless
AEELPPRTU	perpetual
AEELPQTTU	plaquette
AEELPRRST	plasterer
AEELPRRSU	pleasurer
AEELPRSTT	saltpetre
AEELPSSSU	pauseless
AEELQSTUZ	quetzales
AEELQUVZZ	Velázquez
AEELRRSTU	serrulate
AEELRSSTW	waterless
AEELRSTUY	austerely
AEELRSTVY	every last
AEELSSSTT	stateless
	tasteless

AEEMMNORT	manometer
AEEMMNSTU	amusement
AEEMMORTT	atmometer
AEEMMRRST	stammerer
AEEMNNOPR	praenomen
AEEMNNOTT	atonement
AEEMNNPRT	permanent
AEEMNOPST	steam open
AEEMNOPSU	menopause
AEEMNORTW	worm-eaten
AEEMNORUV	manoeuvre
AEEMNOSYY	easy money
AEEMNPRTY	repayment
AEEMNPSST	passement
AEEMNQRUY	Queen Mary
AEEMNRSST	steersman
AEEMNRTTT	treatment
AEEMNSSTY	mateyness
AEEMNSTTT	statement
	testament
AEEMOPRTW	pome-water
AEEMPRRTU	premature
AEEMPRSUU	measure up
AEEMPRTTT	trampette
AEEMPRTTU	permutate
AEEMRSSTT	smear test
AEEMRSSTY	easy terms
AEEMRTTTW	wattmeter
AEENNNPTY	ten a penny
AEENNOPTT	panettone
AEENNPRRT	trepanner
AEENNPRTT	penetrant
	repentant
AEENOPPRT	notepaper
AEENOPRST	Esperanto
	personate
AEENOPTTT	potentate
AEENOQRSU	square one
AEENORRST	nor'-easter
AEENORSTW	stoneware
AEENPPRRT	entrapper
AEENPPRRU	unprepare
AEENPPRSW	newspaper
AEENPRRTU	enrapture
AEENPRSSS	spareness
AEENPRSTT	at present
AEENRRSTU	saunterer
AEENRRTUV	Eva Turner
AEENRSSTU	Sauternes
AEENSSSUV	suaveness
AEEOOPRTZ	azeotrope
AEEOPPRRV	paper over
AEEOPPRSU	pea-souper
AEEOPPRVW	wove paper
AEEOPRRST	patereros
AEEOPRSTT	poetaster
AEEOPRSTX	extrapose
AEEOPRVWW	wave power
AEEORRSTV	overstare
AEEORRTUW	outerwear
AEEORRVWY	overweary
AEEORSTTV	overstate
AEEORSUWY	as you were
AEEPPRSTT	test paper
AEEPRRSTU	repasture
AEEPRRSTY	spare tyre
AEEPRSTTU	pertusate
AEEPRSTXY	apteryxes
AEEQRSSTU	sequestra
	set square
	set-square
AEEQRTTTU	quartette
AEERRRSSU	reassurer
AEERRRSTU	treasurer
AEERRRSTV	traverser
AEERRTTVX	extravert
AEESTTTTU	statuette
AEFFFOORR	for fear of
AEFFGOORR	forage for
AEFFGORTT	off target
	off-target
AEFFHIORT	off the air
AEFFHMOPT	off the map
AEFFIILRS	falsifier
AEFFIIPRR	pifferari
AEFFIKPST	pikestaff
AEFFILOWY	way of life
AEFFIRSTW	stiffware
AEFFKMNOU	make fun of
AEFFLLRUY	fearfully
AEFFLLTUY	fatefully
AEFFLNOPT	pantoffle
AEFFLORSW	safflower
AEFFLORTT	rattle off
AEFFMORST	off-stream
AEFFNOOSS	offseason
AEFFOQRSU	square off
AEFFORSTV	overstaff
AEFGHILNS	angel-fish
AEFGHILST	safe light
AEFGHILTW	white flag
AEFGHINST	night safe
AEFGHLRTU	flaughter
AEFGHORRT	forgather
AEFGIILTV	give a lift
AEFGIIMNR	magnifier
AEFGILLNN	Llangefni
AEFGILLRY	fragilely
AEFGILNRT	faltering
AEFGILOTT	fail to get
AEFGILRUY	lay-figure
AEFGINNST	fastening
AEFGINNTT	fattening
AEFGINRRT	raftering
AEFGIORSS	ossifrage
AEFGIRRRY	Grey Friar
AEFGKLNRU	Garfunkel
AEFGKSUWY	Guy Fawkes
AEFGLLLMU	flagellum
AEFGLNOST	flagstone
AEFGLORTW	afterglow
AEFGLRTUU	fulgurate

AEFGMNRST	fragments
AEFGNNOOR	far gone on
AEFGNOPRT	front-page
AEFGNORRT	frontager
AEFHHLLTU	healthful
AEFHHLORT	other half
AEFHIKMST	makeshift
AEFHILLTT	half-title
AEFHILMNU	human life
AEFHILSST	faithless
AEFHIMNRS	fisherman
AEFHINORS	fashioner
	refashion
AEFHINRTW	wafer-thin
AEFHIPRSS	spearfish
AEFHKNORR	hanker for
AEFHLLTTU	at the full
AEFHLLTUY	hatefully
AEFHLNNPY	halfpenny
AEFHLNSSW	newsflash
AEFHLORSV	flash-over
AEFHLOSSW	false show
AEFHMORSU	farmhouse
AEFHNRTTU	hunt after
AEFHORRTU	Our Father
AEFIIKLRY	fairylike
AEFIILMPR	amplifier
AEFIILNNT	infantile
AEFIILQRU	qualifier
AEFIILRRT	air filter
	trial-fire
AEFIIMNNS	Fenianism
AEFIINNRT	train fine
AEFIINRTU	infuriate
AEFIJLRST	rijstafel
AEFIKLNSS	flakiness
AEFIKMNTU	make unfit
AEFILLNPT	plant life
AEFILLOST	fellatios
AEFILMMOR	oriflamme
AEFILMNOS	Isle of Man
AEFILMNTU	fulminate
AEFILMORS	formalise
AEFILMORZ	formalize
AEFILMRSW	welfarism
AEFILNNUZ	influenza
AEFILNORT	reflation
AEFILNRSS	frailness
AEFILORTU	foliature
AEFILPRSU	praiseful
AEFILRSTW	welfarist
AEFIMMNRT	firmament
AEFIMNOSS	foaminess
AEFIMNOST	manifesto
AEFIMNOTX	tamoxifen
AEFIMNRST	first name
AEFIMORSS	misfeasor
AEFIMORTV	formative
AEFINNRYZ	in a frenzy
AEFINNSST	faintness
AEFINOPRR	poriferan
AEFINORSS	Sanforise
AEFINORSU	nefarious
AEFINORSZ	Sanforize
AEFINPSTY	safety pin
AEFINRRTY	fairy tern
AEFINRSSS	sans serif
AEFINRTZZ	frizzante□
AEFINSSTT	fattiness
AEFIORTUV	favourite
AEFIRRSTT	first rate
	first-rate
AEFIRRSTY	first-year
AEFJLOOSU	jealous of
AEFKKRRTW	Kraftwerk
AEFKLLOST	folk tales
	folktales
AEFKLLUWY	wakefully
AEFKLNOSW	snowflake
AEFKLOOPR	leakproof
AEFKLOORT	look after
AEFKMOPRU	make up for
AEFKMORRW	framework
AEFKNNRSS	frankness
AEFKNOPTU	poke fun at
AEFKOOPST	to speak of
AEFLLNOSW	Owen Falls
AEFLLNTTU	flatulent
AEFLLORST	forestall
AEFLLRTUY	tearfully
AEFLLSSTU	faultless
AEFLMORST	steal from
AEFLMORTU	formulate
AEFLMORWY	mayflower□
AEFLMRSTU	masterful
AEFLNOOSS	aloofness
AEFLNOOTW	now of late
AEFLNOPRY	profanely
AEFLNOPTU	pantoufle
AEFLNORRY	royal fern
AEFLNSSUW	awfulness
AEFLOOPTT	footplate
AEFLOORRY	foreroyal
AEFLOPRSU	up for sale
AEFLORTWW	waterfowl
AEFLORWWX	wax flower
AEFLOSSTT	falsettos
AEFLPRRUY	prayerful
AEFLRSTTU	lust after
AEFMNOORW	forewoman
AEFMORRRT	terraform
AEFMORRTT	formatter
AEFNNOORT	afternoon
AEFNORRSW	answer for
AEFNORSTU	Nosferatu
AEFNORTTU	fortunate
AEFNRSSTU	transfuse
AEFOOPPRV	approve of
AEFOPRRTY	prefatory
AEFRRSTTU	frustrate
AEGGGINRU	ring gauge
AEGGHINRT	gathering

AEGGHJMOS	James Hogg
AEGGHOPRY	geography
AEGGIINNR	regaining
AEGGIINPU	guinea pig
AEGGIIOTV	give it a go
AEGGILNNR	enlarging
AEGGIMOPT	maggot-pie
AEGGINNRV	engraving
AEGGINOOR	gorgoneia
AEGGINOSY	easygoing
	easy-going
AEGGINPRS	presaging
AEGGIOPRS	arpeggios
AEGGLNRRY	glengarry
AEGGLRRST	straggler
AEGGNOSUY	synagogue
AEGGNPRSS	pressgang
	press-gang
AEGGORRSS	aggressor
AEGGORUVY	gyrovague
AEGHHINST	sheathing
AEGHHIRTW	high water
AEGHHNNOY	Honeyghan
AEGHIILNS	Ghislaine
AEGHIKMRT	make right
AEGHIKNNR	hankering
AEGHIKNRS	shrinkage
AEGHILLMS	megillahs
AEGHILLMT	light meal
AEGHILLNY	healingly
AEGHILNRS	shearling
AEGHILNRT	earthling
	heartling
AEGHILRRT	rear light
AEGHILRSS	Alger Hiss
AEGHILRTY	light-year
AEGHILSTT	set alight
AEGHIMMNR	hammering
AEGHIMNPR	hampering
AEGHIMNRT	nightmare
AEGHIMNWY	Hemingway
AEGHIMOTT	Gothamite
AEGHINNPP	happening
AEGHINNRT	near thing
AEGHINNST	hastening
AEGHINPRS	reshaping
AEGHINRTW	wreathing
AEGHIOOPS	oesophagi
AEGHIOPST	go ape-shit
AEGHIORWY	go haywire
AEGHIPPRY	epigraphy
AEGHIPRRS	serigraph
AEGHIPSTT	spaghetti
AEGHIRSTT	tight arse
AEGHIRTUW	argue with
AEGHLNOOS	hang loose
AEGHLOOPR	oleograph
AEGHLORTT	larghetto
AEGHLRSTU	slaughter
AEGHNNORS	hangers-on
AEGHNOPTY	pathogeny

AEGHNOSTU	shogunate
AEGHNPRSY	pharynges
AEGHOORTT	go to earth
AEGHOOTTV	have got to
AEGHORRTU	ore-raught
AEGHRTTUX	extraught
AEGIILLNN	lilangeni
AEGIILLRS	grisaille
AEGIILLSS	gallisise
AEGIILLSZ	gallisize
AEGIILMSV	vigesimal
AEGIILNSS	signalise
AEGIILNSZ	signalize
AEGIILNTV	genitival
	vigilante
AEGIILNTY	geniality
AEGIILSTV	vestigial
AEGIIMMRT	immigrate
AEGIIMNNR	remaining
AEGIIMSSV	give a miss
AEGIINORT	originate
AEGIINRRU	Guarnieri
AEGIINRST	granitise
AEGIINRTZ	granitize
AEGIINSTT	instigate
AEGIISSTV	visagiste
AEGIJNORS	jargonise
AEGIJNORZ	jargonize
AEGIKKMNR	kingmaker
AEGIKLLSS	glasslike
AEGIKLLST	Gaitskell
AEGIKMNRT	marketing
AEGIKNQSU	squeaking
AEGIKNRST	streaking
AEGIKNSSW	gawkiness
AEGILLLLY	illegally
AEGILLMRU	malgré lui
AEGILLNNP	panelling
AEGILLNPR	pellagrin
AEGILLNRV	ravelling
AEGILLPPR	Grappelli
AEGILLPSX	Plexiglas®
AEGILLRRU	guerrilla
AEGILLRSS	salesgirl
AEGILMMOR	malgré moi
AEGILMNNT	alignment
	lamenting
AEGILMNNY	meaningly
AEGILMNRY	Mayerling
AEGILMNSU	San Miguel
AEGILMNTU	emulating
	glutamine
AEGILMORR	rigmarole
AEGILMORS	glamorise
AEGILMORZ	glamorize
AEGILMRSV	alms-giver
AEGILNNOR	angle iron
AEGILNOOT	go it alone
AEGILNORY	legionary
AEGILNOSS	sloganise
AEGILNOSZ	sloganize

AEGILNPRS	relapsing
AEGILNPRY	parleying
AEGILNQSU	equal sign
	squealing
AEGILNRSV	slavering
AEGILNRTY	ingrately
AEGILNRWY	wearingly
AEGILNSST	eastlings
AEGILNSSW	wine glass
AEGILNSTY	teasingly
AEGILOOPS	apologies
	apologise
AEGILOOPZ	apologize
AEGILOOTY	aetiology
AEGILORSS	seraglios
AEGILRRRU	irregular
AEGILRSUV	vulgarise
AEGILRUVZ	vulgarize
AEGIMMNOT	gemmation
AEGIMMNRU	germanium
AEGIMMNST	magnetism
AEGIMMNSU	magnesium
AEGIMNNNU	unmeaning
AEGIMNNOT	Montaigne
AEGIMNNSS	manginess
AEGIMNNSY	gymnasien
AEGIMNOPT	game point
AEGIMNPPR	pampering
AEGIMNPRT	tampering
AEGIMNRST	streaming
AEGIMNRSU	measuring
AEGIMNRTT	mattering
AEGINNORS	reasoning
AEGINNORW	Norwegian
AEGINNORZ	organzine
AEGINNOSS	seasoning
AEGINNPPR	Perpignan
AEGINNPRT	parenting
AEGINNRST	gannister
AEGINNSST	assenting
	tanginess
AEGINNSTU	unseating
AEGINOOPT	pogoniate
AEGINOPPT	Giant Pope
AEGINOPRS	Singapore
AEGINOPRT	operating
	orange-tip
AEGINORRV	overgrain
AEGINORRZ	organizer
AEGINOSTT	gestation
AEGINPPRR	preparing
AEGINPRTT	pattering
AEGINQRUV	quavering
AEGINRRST	arresting
AEGINRRTU	garniture
AEGINRSTU	signature
AEGINRTTU	Ungaretti
AEGINSSSS	gassiness
AEGINSSST	staginess
AEGINSSUZ	gauziness
AEGINSTUU	Augustine
AEGIOTVWY	give way to
AEGIPRTUV	purgative
AEGIRRRST	registrar
AEGIRRSSW	wire grass
AEGISTTUV	gustative
AEGLLNOST	gallstone
AEGLLORTU	lager lout
AEGLLOSSW	gallowses
AEGLLRRUY	regularly
AEGLLRTUY	tegularly
AEGLMNORW	Low German
AEGLNOSTU	langouste
AEGLNOSTV	Galveston
AEGLNRRST	strangler
AEGLNRSST	strangles
AEGLNRSTY	strangely
AEGLORRTU	regulator
AEGLORTTY	tetralogy
AEGLRSSSS	grassless
AEGLRSSSU	sugarless
AEGMMOPRR	programme
AEGMNNORT	magnetron
AEGMNORRW	warmonger
AEGMNORTU	augmentor
AEGMNOTTU	mange tout
	mangetout
AEGMNRTTU	gutter-man
AEGMOOSUX	exogamous
AEGMORSSY	gossamery
AEGNNNOTU	agent noun
AEGNNOORT	not go near
AEGNNPRTU	repugnant
AEGNNSSTU	gauntness
AEGNOOSWY	go one's way
AEGNORRWY	garryowen
AEGNORSUV	vargueños
AEGNRSSTU	assurgent
AEGOOPRRT	prorogate
AEGOOSTTW	go to waste
AEGOOSWYZ	wayzgoose
AEGOPRRTY	party-goer
AEGOPRRUW	groupware
AEGORRRTT	garrotter
AEGORRSSV	overgrass
AEGORRSTU	surrogate
AEGPRRRUY	prayer rug
AEHHHITTY	hit the hay
AEHHILLLT	ill health
	ill-health
AEHHILLOP	halophile
AEHHILLTY	healthily
AEHHIMPRS	Hampshire
AEHHIORRS	horsehair
AEHHIPPSS	shipshape
AEHHIRRST	ratherish
AEHHISTWW	whitewash
AEHHLNTUY	unhealthy
AEHHLPRSW	Welsh harp
AEHHMOOPT	homeopath
AEHHMORRT	Rotherham
AEHHNORTT	other than

AEHHNORTW	Hawthorne
AEHHNRSSS	harshness
AEHHOPPST	phosphate
AEHHOSSUW	washhouse
AEHIILMTU	humiliate
AEHIILNSY	hyalinise
AEHIILNYZ	hyalinize
AEHIILTVW	alive with
AEHIIMNNT	in the main
AEHIIMNST	histamine
AEHIIMNTT	a thin time
AEHIINOPT	Ethiopian
AEHIINRSS	hairiness
AEHIIPSTT	hepatitis
AEHIJLOSU	jailhouse
AEHIKKLMS	milk shake
AEHIKLNOR	Heraklion
AEHIKLOST	like a shot
AEHIKNOST	shake on it
AEHIKNPSW	whip snake
AEHIKNSSS	shakiness
AEHIKNTTW	taken with
AEHIKQRSU	Quakerish
AEHILLNSV	Nashville
AEHILLPTY	philately
AEHILLTTY	lethality
AEHILLTWY	wealthily
AEHILMNPS	nephalism
AEHILNNOT	anthelion
	on the nail
AEHILNOPR	parhelion
AEHILNORT	lion-heart
AEHILNPRS	planisher
AEHILNPST	nephalist
AEHILNQRU	harlequin
AEHILORST	horsetail
AEHILOSSW	shoalwise
AEHILOSTT	heliostat
	lie at host
AEHILPRRV	River Alph
AEHILRSTV	The Rivals
AEHILRSTY	hairstyle
AEHIMMNNT	Tim Henman
AEHIMNORS	harmonies
	harmonise
AEHIMNORZ	harmonize
AEHIMNPSS	misshapen
AEHIMNPST	pantheism
AEHIMNSST	in the mass
AEHIMORST	Aerosmith
AEHIMPRSS	seraphims
AEHIMPSST	steamship
AEHIMQSSU	squeamish
AEHINNOST	Esthonian
AEHINNRSS	in harness
AEHINOPST	pantihose
AEHINORSS	hoariness
AEHINOTVW	have in tow
AEHINPPRT	paper-thin
AEHINPPSS	happiness
AEHINPPTX	Xanthippe
AEHINPRSS	seraphins
AEHINPSTT	in the past
	pantheist
AEHINRRSU	Arrhenius
AEHINRRSV	varnisher
AEHINRSSW	sherwanis
AEHINSSST	hastiness
AEHINSTTT	hestitant
AEHIORSTU	authorise
AEHIORTTV	hortative
AEHIORTUZ	authorize
AEHIOTTUV	have it out
AEHIPRSTT	therapist
AEHIPRSTW	ship water
AEHIRTTTW	treat with
AEHJKNOST	John Keats
AEHJLNOPP	apple-John
AEHJLNOWY	John Elway
AEHJMNSTU	James Hunt
AEHJNNOOS	John Soane
AEHJNNOWY	John Wayne
AEHKLNOPV	Plekhanov
AEHKLNORU	Lake Huron
AEHKLNSST	thankless
AEHKLRRSU	Karlsruhe
AEHKMNORR	horn-maker
AEHKORRTW	earthwork
AEHKORSTT	take short
AEHKPRSTU	Petrushka
AEHLLMRTY	thermally
AEHLLPRTY	L P Hartley
AEHLLPSSY	haplessly
AEHLLPTUW	up the wall
AEHLLRSST	star shell
AEHLLSSTU	thalluses
AEHLMOOST	loathsome
AEHLMOSSU	alms-house
AEHLMPPST	pamphlets
AEHLNNOPR	alpenhorn
AEHLNNOPT	panthenol
AEHLNORTW	lower than
AEHLNOSST	loathness
AEHLNRTUY	unearthly
AEHLOPRSY	horseplay
AEHLOPSUY	playhouse ❑
AEHLORTWY	holy water
AEHLPRRSU	spherular
AEHLRSSTU	Althusser
AEHLRSTUW	The Walrus
AEHMMORTU	hammer out
AEHMNNSSU	humanness
AEHMNOOTT	not at home
AEHMNRSTU	transhume
AEHMOPRST	Tom Sharpe
AEHMORRTW	earthworm
AEHMORSTW	what's more
AEHMOSTTT	at the most
AEHMOSTTW	Thomas Tew
AEHNNOPRT	Parthenon
AEHNNRSSU	unharness
AEHNOOPRR	harpooner

AEHNOOPSX	saxophone
AEHNORSTT	north-east
AEHNPPRSU	sharpen up
AEHNPRSSS	sharpness
AEHNPRSXY	pharynxes
AEHOOPRRY	pyorrhoea
AEHOOPSTT	osteopath
AEHOOPTTT	the potato
AEHOORSTX	orthoaxes
AEHOORUWY	how are you?
AEHOPPSSY	apophyses
AEHOPRSTU	put ashore
AEHOPRSUV	a pushover
AEHOPSSTT	posthaste
	post-haste
AEHORSSTU	authoress
AEHORSTVW	short wave
AEHORSTVY	overhasty
AEHORSTWY	seaworthy
AEHOSSSTU	South Seas
AEHOSSTTU	South-East
	south-east
AEHRSSTUU	thesaurus
AEIIILNTW	lie in wait
AEIIILRVZ	vizierial
AEIIILTVX	lixiviate
AEIIIMTTV	imitative
AEIIJLNUV	juvenilia
AEIIKKTTW	kittiwake
AEIIKLLNS	snail-like
AEIIKLLTT	take it ill
AEIIKLNOS	kaolinise
AEIIKLNOT	kaolinite
AEIIKLNOZ	kaolinize
AEIIKLNST	saintlike
AEIIKLNSV	skin alive
AEIIKLRST	triskelia
AEIIKRSTT	keratitis
AEIILLMNN	millennia
AEIILLMRS	Ramillies
AEIILLTTT	titillate
AEIILMNNR	mainliner
AEIILMNSU	aluminise
AEIILMNUZ	aluminize
AEIILMRSS	serialism
AEIILMRTT	literatim
	time trial
AEIILNNRT	triennial
AEIILNNSV	venial sin
AEIILNOPT	epilation
AEIILNORV	live on air
AEIILNOTV	inviolate
AEIILNPRT	reptilian
AEIILNPST	platinise
AEIILNPTV	plaintive
AEIILNPTZ	platinize
AEIILNRRT	interrail
AEIILNRTY	in reality
AEIILNSTW	waistline
AEIILNSWY	win easily
AEIILORST	solitaire
AEIILORSV	Lavoisier
AEIILQSTU	qualities
AEIILRRST	arris tile
AEIILRSTU	ritualise
	uralitise
AEIILRTUZ	ritualize
	uralitize
AEIILSSUV	visualise
AEIILSUVZ	visualize
AEIIMMRSS	Semiramis
AEIIMNNTU	in a minute
AEIIMNPST	impatiens
AEIIMNPTT	impatient
AEIIMNRTT	Marinetti
AEIIMNRTU	miniature
AEIIMPRRS	impresari
AEIIMPRSS	mispraise
AEIIMPRSV	vampirise
AEIIMPRVZ	vampirize
AEIIMPSSV	impassive
AEIINNNTV	antivenin
AEIINNQTU	inquinate
AEIINNRSS	raininess
AEIINNRTT	itinerant
AEIINNRTU	uraninite
AEIINNSTU	insinuate
AEIINOPTX	expiation
AEIINORTT	iteration
AEIINOTTV	novitiate
AEIINPRTV	in private
AEIINRRTY	itinerary
AEIINRSSY	yersinias
AEIINRSTZ	sanitizer
AEIINSTTY	insatiety
AEIIPRSTV	privatise
AEIIPRTTV	partitive
AEIIPRTVV	privative
AEIIPRTVZ	privatize
AEIIPSTTT	stipitate
AEIIRRSTV	arriviste
AEIIRSSTW	stairwise
AEIITTTTV	tittivate
AEIJKKRVY	Reykjavík
AEIJMORST	Jose Marti
AEIKKLLOO	lookalike
	look-alike
AEIKKRRST	risk-taker
AEIKLLNRT	Linklater
AEIKLLNRY	Killarney
AEIKLLOOV	look alive
AEIKLMNOW	womanlike
AEIKLNNSS	lankiness
AEIKLNNVW	Van Winkle
AEIKLNORT	oil-tanker
AEIKLNOST	like as not
AEIKLNRUW	unwarlike
AEIKLPRSS	sparklies
AEIKLQSUY	squeakily
AEIKLRSTW	strawlike
AEIKLRSTY	streakily
AEIKLRSVY	Valkyries

AEIKMNOTT	not make it
AEIKMQRSU	Quakerism
AEIKNNPRS	spinnaker
AEIKNNSSS	snakiness
AEIKNOPTW	weak point
AEIKNORTU	ketonuria
AEIKNOTTW	take in tow
AEIKNQSSU	quakiness
AEIKORSST	keratosis
AEIKPPQSU	pipsqueak
AEIKPRSTY	strike pay
AEILLLMSS	all smiles
AEILLLRTY	literally
AEILLMMST	small-time
AEILLMNRY	millenary
AEILLMNSY	seminally
AEILLMSSY	aimlessly
AEILLNNRW	inner wall
AEILLNOPS	Pisanello
AEILLNOPT	pollinate
AEILLNORW	Orwellian
AEILLNPRY	plenarily
AEILLNPSS	palliness
AEILLNPST	panellist
AEILLNRST	reinstall
	re-install
AEILLNRTU	ill nature
	tellurian
AEILLNSTY	saliently
AEILLOPPT	papillote
	popliteal
AEILLPRSU	pluralise
AEILLPRUZ	pluralize
AEILLPSTU	pulsatile
AEILLRRTY	artillery
AEILLRSSV	rivalless
AEILLRSTW	stairwell
AEILLRTVY	vitellary
AEILLRTWY	water lily
AEILLRVXY	vexillary
AEILLSTTY	statelily
AEILMMNPS	Pelmanism
AEILMMORS	memorials
AEILMNNOT	melatonin
AEILMNNPS	plainsmen
AEILMNNSS	manliness
AEILMNOOT	emotional
AEILMNOPR	prolamine
AEILMNORS	normalise
AEILMNORZ	normalize
AEILMNOSS	loaminess
AEILMNOTU	emulation
AEILMNPRT	reimplant
AEILMNPTU	penultima
AEILMNRVY	liveryman
AEILMNTTY	mentality
AEILMORRZ	moralizer
AEILMORST	mortalise
	solar time
AEILMORTZ	mortalize
AEILMSSVY	massively
AEILMSTTU	stimulate
AEILMSTUU	mutualise
AEILMTUUZ	mutualize
AEILNNOPR	nonpareil
AEILNNORT	reliant on
AEILNNOSV	Slovenian
AEILNNOSY	Lyonnaise
AEILNNOTV	anti-novel
	Valentino
AEILNNPSS	plainness
AEILNNPSU	peninsula
AEILNNPTY	pinnately
AEILNNTUV	univalent
AEILNOOPS	polonaise
AEILNOPST	Platonise
AEILNOPTT	potential
AEILNOPTZ	Platonize
AEILNORST	relations
AEILNORSV	versional
AEILNOSSS	sessional
AEILNOSSV	Slavonise
AEILNOSVZ	Slavonize
AEILNPRTY	interplay
	party line
AEILNPSTY	sapiently
AEILNPTTY	patiently
AEILNPTUV	pulvinate
AEILNQTUY	antiquely
AEILNRSUV	universal
AEILNRTTV	trivalent
AEILNRTUY	unreality
AEILNSSST	saltiness
	stainless
AEILNSSTW	slantwise
AEILNSTUY	sinuately
AEILNSUUX	unisexual
AEILNTUVW	wine vault
AEILOPRST	saprolite
AEILORSST	tailoress
AEILORSTT	Aristotle
	totaliser
AEILORTTZ	totalizer
AEILPQRSU	pasquiler
AEILPQSTU	plastique
AEILPRSVY	privy seal
AEILPRTVY	privately
AEILPSSVY	passively
AEILPSTTU	stipulate
AEILPSTUV	pulsative
AEILQRRUY	reliquary
AEILRSSTV	Silvestra
AEILRTUUX	luxuriate
AEILSSUVY	suasively
AEILSTUXY	sexuality
AEIMMMNOT	mammonite
AEIMMNNOT	in a moment
AEIMMNNRS	mannerism
AEIMMNOPT	pantomime
AEIMMNSTY	many times
AEIMMRSSU	summarise
AEIMMRSUZ	summarize

AEIMMSTUV	summative
AEIMNNNQU	mannequin
AEIMNNOPU	pneumonia
AEIMNNORS	Normanise
AEIMNNORZ	Normanize
AEIMNNOST	Minnesota
AEIMNNOSY	anonymise
AEIMNNOSZ	Neo-Nazism
AEIMNNOYZ	anonymize
AEIMNNRST	mannerist
AEIMNNTUY	any minute
AEIMNOPRT	protamine
AEIMNOPTU	upon a time
AEIMNORST	main store
	matronise
	steam iron
AEIMNORTV	normative
AEIMNORTZ	matronize
AEIMNORWZ	womanizer
AEIMNOSWW	wise woman
AEIMNOSWY	in some way
AEIMNOTUY	you name it
AEIMNPRST	spearmint
AEIMNRSTU	antiserum
AEIMNRSTX	Axminster
AEIMNRTTY	maternity
AEIMNSTUX	Maxentius
AEIMOPRRT	imperator
AEIMOPRTX	proximate
AEIMOPSTT	optimates
AEIMORSTT	estimator
AEIMORSTV	movie star
AEIMORTTU	autotimer
AEIMPPRSU	pauperism
AEIMPRRTT	part-timer
AEIMPRSSY	pyramises
AEIMPRTUZ	trapezium
AEIMRRRTU	terrarium
AEIMRRSTY	martyrise
AEIMRRTYZ	martyrize
AEINNNOTV	non-native
AEINNOPSX	expansion
AEINNOPTT	panettoni
AEINNORST	Rosinante
AEINNORTV	vernation
AEINNOSST	sensation
AEINNOSTW	wantonise
AEINNOTTT	attention
AEINNOTWZ	wantonize
AEINNPSST	inaptness
AEINNRSTT	transient
AEINNRSTU	saturnine
AEINNRSTY	tyrannise
AEINNRTYZ	tyrannize
AEINNSSST	nastiness
AEINNSSTT	nattiness
AEINOOPRT	operation
AEINOPPRT	reappoint
AEINOPRSS	aspersion
AEINOPRST	patronise
	Petrosian
AEINOPRSV	pervasion
AEINOPRSY	aepyornis
AEINOPRTT	pertain to
AEINOPRTU	epuration
AEINOPRTV	overpaint
AEINOPRTZ	patronize
AEINOPSSS	soapiness
AEINOQRTU	inquorate
	ortanique
AEINORRST	serration
AEINORRTV	overtrain
AEINORSST	assertion
AEINORSTT	stationer
AEINOSSST	assientos
AEINPPPSS	Pan's pipes
AEINPPSSS	sappiness
AEINPRRST	transpire
AEINPRTTY	paternity
AEINPSSST	pastiness
AEINRRSST	tarriness
AEINRRSTT	restraint
AEINRRSVW	Swan River
AEINRSSTT	resistant
AEINRSSTU	sustainer
AEINRSTTT	in tatters
AEINSSSTT	tastiness
AEINSSTTT	tattiness
AEIOPRRVZ	vaporizer
AEIOPRTTV	portative
	vaporetti
AEIOPRTXY	expiatory
AEIORRRWZ	razor wire
AEIORRTTT	trattorie
AEIORTUVV	uvarovite
AEIOSTUVX	vexatious
AEIPPRRTY	Tipperary
AEIPRRSTU	rapturise
AEIPRRTUZ	rapturize
AEIPRSTUZ	trapezius
AEIPRSTYZ	party-size
AEIPSSTTV	tipstaves
AEIQRRTTU	triquetra
AEIQRTTUZ	quartzite
AEIRRSSTT	traitress
AEIRRTTTU	triturate
AEIRSSTTU	tessitura
AEIRSTTUY	austerity
AEISSTTUW	sweatsuit
AEJLLOSUY	jealously
AEJLNOPSU	Paul Jones
AEJMNOSTW	Jamestown
AEJMORSSS	James Ross
AEJMPRTUW	water jump
AEJNNOPRU	Juan Perón
AEJOPSTUX	juxtapose
AEKKMNNOW	make known
AEKKMNOOS	kakemonos
AEKLLSSST	stalkless
AEKLMOORT	toolmaker
AEKLMORTW	metalwork
AEKLMPTTY	empty talk

AEKLNOPRW	panel-work
AEKLOOOPP	Lake Poopó
AEKMNOORR	moonraker
AEKMNOPRS	pranksome
AEKMNOPSS	spokesman
AEKMNOPTW	kept woman
AEKMOOWYZ	make woozy
AEKNNORTT	Tarkenton
AEKNPRRST	prankster
AEKNRSSST	starkness
AEKNRSTTU	take turns
AEKOOPSST	so to speak
	soopstake
AEKOPPRRW	paperwork
AEKOPRTYY	karyotype
AELLLMOWY	Amy Lowell
AELLLPTUU	pullulate
AELLLRSTU	stellular
AELLLSSWY	lawlessly
AELLMNOSZ	manzellos
AELLMNOTT	allotment
AELLMNSSS	smallness
AELLMOPRY	permalloy
AELLMORST	martellos
AELLMORTU	Tullamore
AELLMRSVY	very small
AELLNORTY	not really
AELLNOSTW	stonewall
AELLNQUUY	unequally
AELLNRTUY	neutrally
AELLNRTVY	ventrally
AELLNSSUY	sensually
AELLOOPRT	allotrope
AELLOPRRT	patroller
AELLOPRTY	prolately
AELLOPTUV	pole vault
AELLORTTY	allottery
AELLOSUYZ	zealously
AELLRSSTY	artlessly
AELLRSTUW	Ullswater
AELLRSUUU	usual rule
AELMMORST	maelstrom
AELMMOSUU	mausoleum
AELMNNNTU	annulment
AELMNNOOP	monoplane
AELMNOOPR	lampooner
AELMNOPPY	empanoply
AELMNORTT	lemon tart
AELMNORWW	lawnmower
AELMNRSTU	menstrual
	Ulsterman
AELMOPRSS	slope arms
AELMOPSTT	palmettos
AELMRTWXY	wax myrtle
AELNNORTY	not nearly
AELNNOSUX	non-sexual
AELNOOPTY	lay open to
AELNOPRSY	lay person
	layperson
AELNORTVW	navelwort
AELNOTUVV	vol-au-vent

AELNRRUVY	vulnerary
AELNRSTTU	resultant
AELNSSSUU	usualness
AELOOPRTW	water polo
AELOOPRVY	parleyvoo
AELOOSSTY	stay loose
AELOPRRTW	pearlwort
AELOPRSTU	sporulate
AELOPSSSU	espousals
AELOPSTTU	postulate
AELORSTTY	lay to rest
AELPPRTUW	Wuppertal
AELPRSSST	strapless
AELPRSSTU	pertussal
AELPSTTUU	pustulate
AELQRRTUY	quarterly
AELRSSTVY	Sylvestra
AEMMNNOTY	momentany
AEMMNORTY	manometry
	momentary
AEMMNOTUZ	Montezuma
AEMMNRSTU	sarmentum
AEMMOORST	steam room
AEMMRSTYY	asymmetry
AEMNNORST	ornaments
AEMNNORTT	remontant
AEMNNOTTU	Mount Etna
AEMNORRTU	numerator
AEMNORSTY	monastery
AEMNORTTT	not matter
AEMNPRSTU	smarten up
AEMNRSSST	smartness
AEMNRSSSU	Rasmussen
AEMNRSTTU	transmute
AEMOOPRRS	spare room
AEMOORSTT	stateroom
AEMOPRRTY	temporary
AEMOPRSTU	mouse-trap
AEMOPSTTY	asymptote
AEMORRSVW	swarm over
AEMORSTWY	Tom Sawyer
AEMPPRTUW	water pump
AEMPRTUXZ	Max Perutz
AEMQRRTUY	marquetry
AENNOOSWY	on one's way
AENNOPTWY	two a penny
AENNPSSTU	unaptness
AENNSSTUY	Sun Yat-Sen
AENOOPSST	soapstone
AENOORRST	resonator
AENOORRTV	renovator
AENOORSTV	oven-roast
AENOPPRRT	en rapport
AENOPRRTW	part-owner
AENOPRSST	patroness
	transpose
AENOPRSUV	supernova
AENORSTTY	attorneys
AENPSSSTW	wasp's nest
	wasps' nest
AENQSSSTU	squatness

AENRRTTUX	tax return
AENRSSTTV	transvest
AEOOPRTTV	vaporetto
AEOORRSTZ	Zoroaster
AEOORTTUU	autoroute
AEOPRRRTY	portrayer
AEOPRRSSY	aspersory
AEOPRRSTT	prostrate
AEOPRRSTU	pterosaur
AEOPRSTTT	protest at
AEOQRRSSU	squarrose
AEORRSTTV	start over
AEORRSTZZ	terrazzos
AEORSSTUU	trousseau
AEORSTTVW	straw vote
AEPPRSTUU	suppurate
AEPQRRTUY	parquetry
AEPRRSSTU	superstar
AEQRSSTTU	squatters
AERRSSTUU	susurrate
AERRSSVYY	arsy-versy
AFFFNOORT	not far off
AFFGGINUW	guffawing
AFFGIIRST	sgraffiti
AFFGIKNOT	taking off
AFFGILNOY	laying-off
AFFGIORST	sgraffito
AFFHILRSY	raffishly
AFFHOOSTT	hats off to
AFFIILNPT	plaintiff
AFFILNRUY	ruffianly
AFFIMORRT	far from it
AFFIPSSTT	tipstaffs
AFFKNORRT	Frankfort
AFFKNRRTU	Frankfurt
AFFLOOTTU	footfault
AFFMNNRUY	funny farm
AFGGIINTU	fatiguing
AFGHHILLT	half-light
AFGHIIMNS	famishing
AFGHILLNS	halflings
AFGHILLNT	nightfall
AFGHIPRTW	whip-graft
AFGHNRTUU	unfraught
AFGIILLNN	falling-in
AFGIILMNN	inflaming
AFGIILNNU	unfailing
AFGIILRTY	fragility
AFGIIMSTU	fastigium
AFGIINRRY	fairy ring
AFGIKLNOT	talking of
AFGIKNORS	forsaking
AFGILLMNY	flamingly
AFGILLNRY	flaringly
AFGILLNST	flatlings
AFGILLNTY	lying flat
AFGILLNUY	gainfully
AFGILLOPT	pilot flag
AFGILMNOS	flamingos
AFGILMNOY	foamingly
AFGILNNTU	flaunting
AFGILNNWY	fawningly
AFGILNRTZ	Fritz Lang
AFGILRTUY	frugality
AFGIMORTU	fumigator
AFGINNPRY	frying-pan
AFGINORUV	favouring
AFGLLSSSU	glassfuls
AFGNNOOSU	son of a gun
AFHHLRTTU	half-truth
AFHIIKNOP	kniphofia
AFHIILOTT	fail to hit
AFHIINNOS	in fashion
AFHIKLOTT	of that ilk
AFHIORSTY	forsythia
AFHIORTTW	throw a fit
AFHLLMRUY	harmfully
AFHLLORST	fall short
	shortfall
AFHLMORTU	harmful to
AFHMMNORU	human form
AFHMOOTTU	fathom out
AFHOORRST	hoar-frost
AFHOPPRST	prop shaft
AFIIILNOT	filiation
AFIILNNOR	Arnolfini
AFIILNNOT	inflation
AFIILNOOT	foliation
AFIIMNRRY	infirmary
AFIIOORRT	a fortiori
AFIIORRTU	fioritura
AFIIORTTW	wait for it!
AFILLNPUY	painfully
	pay in full
AFILLNRUV	Furnivall
AFILLOOPR	April fool
AFILLOPSU	Fallopius
AFILLORST	for all it's
AFILMMORS	formalism
AFILMNNTU	fulminant
AFILMNOOW	Naomi Wolf
AFILMORST	formalist
AFILMORTY	formality
AFILNOOTT	flotation
AFILNORST	frost-nail
AFILOORSS	fossorial
AFIMNNORT	informant
AFIMNOORT	formation
AFINOOPRR	rainproof
AFINOPRTY	profanity
AFIORRSST	Froissart
AFIORTTTT	tit for tat
AFIOSTTUU	fatuitous
AFIPRRSTT	first part
AFIRRSTTU	star fruit
AFIRRTTTU	fruit tart
AFKLLMRSU	full marks
AFKLOOSTT	footstalk
AFKLOOTTU	talk out of
AFKMNORRS	form ranks
AFKMOORST	footmarks
AFKOORRTW	work of art

AFLLLPUYY	playfully
AFLLMNOUY	moanfully
AFLLMOOST	most of all
AFLLNOOPR	floor plan
AFLLOOSSW	as follows
AFLMORRUY	formulary
AFLOOPSTY	splay foot
AFLOOPTUY	out of play
AFLOORSUV	flavorous
AFLOPRRSU	fluorspar
AFLOSTUUY	fatuously
AFMNORRST	transform
AFMNORRTW	warm front
AFMOPRRTY	for my part
AFMORRSTY	stray from
AFNORSTWY	frontways
AFOOOPPRS	apropos of
AFOORSSTZ	sforzatos
AGGGILLNY	laggingly
AGGGINRSY	Ryan Giggs
AGGGLNOOO	Goolagong
AGGHHILSY	haggishly
AGGHHNOTU	hang tough
AGGHHNRTU	Hugh Grant
AGGHILOOY	hagiology
AGGHILSWY	waggishly
AGGHINSTT	stag night
AGGHLOOPR	logograph
AGGIIIMNN	imagining
AGGIILLNP	pillaging
AGGIILMNN	maligning
AGGIILNNT	ting-a-ling
AGGIILNVW	law-giving
AGGIIMNRT	migrating
AGGIIMNST	gigantism
AGGIINNOZ	agonizing
AGGIINVWY	giving way
AGGILLLNY	gallingly
AGGILLNOP	galloping
AGGILLNRY	glaringly
AGGILNNOS	ganglions
	singalong
AGGILNNPS	spangling
AGGILNNRW	wrangling
AGGILNOOW	going AWOL
AGGILNPSY	gaspingly
AGGILNRTY	gratingly
AGGIMMNRU	rummaging
AGGINORRS	grosgrain
AGGMOORRT	mortgagor
AGGNNOPYY	Pyongyang
AGGNORRWY	grow angry
AGGOORSST	go to grass
AGHHILTUY	haughtily
AGHHINRST	thrashing
AGHHLOOPR	holograph
AGHHMOOPR	homograph
AGHIILNRT	light rain
AGHIIMMMN	Immingham
AGHIIMNNT	main thing
AGHIINNSU	in anguish
AGHIINNSV	vanishing
AGHIINRSV	ravishing
AGHIINRTW	Ian Wright
AGHIIORSV	viragoish
AGHIKRRTW	Arkwright
AGHILLLOP	Gallophil
AGHILLMPT	lamplight
AGHILLNOW	hallowing
AGHILLNST	all things
AGHILLNTY	haltingly
AGHILMORT	algorithm
	logarithm
AGHILNOTW	along with
AGHILNPSS	splashing
AGHILNPTY	plaything
AGHILNTUY	naughtily
AGHILOOPT	Lotophagi
AGHILRSTT	starlight
AGHIMNRST	hamstring
AGHIMORST	histogram
AGHINNOTT	not a thing
AGHINORRW	harrowing
AGHINPSUW	washing-up
AGHINRRSY	garnishry
AGHINRTTW	thwarting
AGHKMOPRY	kymograph
AGHLLOOPY	haplology
AGHLMNOPU	ploughman
AGHLMOOPR	lagomorph
AGHLMOOTU	goalmouth
AGHLNOOTY	anthology
AGHLNOPSU	push along
AGHLNOSTU	onslaught
AGHLOOPTY	pathology
AGHLOPPRY	polygraph
AGHLORSSU	hourglass
AGHMNOOPR	monograph
	nomograph
AGHMNRSTU	hamstrung
AGHNOOPRS	sonograph
AGHOOPRRT	rotograph
AGHOOPRRY	orography
AGHOPRRUY	urography
AGHORSTTY	hygrostat
AGIIIMNPR	impairing
AGIIIMNTT	imitating
AGIIKLMNR	grimalkin
AGIILLNRY	railingly
AGIILLNWY	wailingly
AGIILMNSY	mislaying
AGIILMNTY	malignity
AGIILNNPT	pantiling
AGIILNNWZ	Zwinglian
AGIILNOST	intaglios
	isolating
AGIILNSSS	isinglass
AGIILORTT	litigator
AGIIMMNRT	immigrant
AGIIMNORT	migration
AGIIMNPRT	imparting
AGIIMNSSS	misassign

AGIIMORTT	mitigator
AGIINNORS	Signorina
AGIINNORT	rationing
AGIINNPSS	in passing
AGIINNRST	straining
AGIINNRTT	intrigant
AGIINSSST	assisting
AGIIRSSTT	gastritis
AGIIRSTTU	guitarist
AGIJLNRRY	jarringly
AGIJNORST	jargonist
AGIKLNOSY	soakingly
AGIKLNOTT	talking-to
AGIKLNPRS	sparkling
AGIKLNQUY	quakingly
AGIKMNNSU	unmasking
AGIKMORSS	kissogram
AGIKNNPRW	king prawn
AGIKNOPSU	soaking-up
AGIKNOTTU	taking out
AGILLLNUY	lingually
AGILLNNNU	annulling
AGILLNOPW	walloping
AGILLNOTT	totalling
AGILLNOWW	wallowing
AGILLNSTY	lastingly
AGILMNNOO	Mongolian
AGILMNOPY	Pygmalion
AGILMNSUY	amusingly
AGILMOORS	lagrimoso
AGILMRSUV	vulgarism
AGILNNOPS	plainsong
AGILNNOQU	Algonquin
AGILNNOTY	atoningly
AGILNNPTY	pantingly
AGILNNRTY	rantingly
AGILNNWYY	yawningly
AGILNOOTT	agnolotti
AGILNORRY	roaringly
AGILNORSY	soaringly
AGILNORVY	vainglory
AGILNOSTW	wagon-lits
	wagons-lit
AGILNPRSW	sprawling
AGILNPRSY	raspingly
	sparingly
AGILNPRTT	prattling
AGILNPRTY	pratingly
AGILNPRYY	prayingly
AGILNPSTU	pulsating
AGILNPSUY	pausingly
AGILNRSTT	startling
AGILNRSTY	staringly
AGILNSSUY	ugly as sin
AGILOOPST	apologist
AGILRRTUY	garrulity
AGILRTUVY	vulgarity
AGIMMNSUY	gymnasium
AGIMNNOOR	marooning
AGIMNNORS	ransoming
AGIMNORSU	ignoramus
AGIMORRTY	migratory
AGINNOPSS	passing on
AGINNORRW	narrowing
AGINNORST	on a string
AGINNOSTU	Antigonus
AGINNPRSU	unsparing
AGINNRUVY	unvarying
AGINOORRT	Tongariro
AGINOPPRV	approving
AGINOPRTU	purgation
AGINOPTUY	paying-out
AGINORSTY	signatory
AGINOSTTU	gustation
AGINOTTTU	guttation
AGINPPRST	strapping
	trappings
AGINPPRSW	wrappings
AGIOORSTU	autogiros
AGIOPRRSY	spirogyra
AGJKNORRU	kurrajong
AGKLNOORY	look angry
AGKLOORYY	karyology
AGKLPPRSU	spark plug
AGKMNOPRU	Mungo Park
AGKNORSST	knot grass
	knotgrass
AGLLLNOOR	roll along
AGLLNOOPY	polygonal
AGLLOOSSW	glass wool
AGLMOORSU	glamorous
AGLMPRSUU	sugar-lump
AGLOOOSSW	go so low as
AGLOORSST	glossator
AGLOORSTY	astrology
AGLOOTTUY	tautology
AGLOPPRUY	playgroup
AGLORRSUU	garrulous
AGLORSSTW	glasswort
AGMMNOORS	groomsman
AGMNNOSSU	Magnusson
AGMNORRST	Armstrong
	strongarm
AGMNSSTUY	nystagmus
AGNNOPPTU	oppugnant
AGNOOOSTY	go on to say
AGNPRSSUU	spun sugar
AGNRRSTUY	strangury
AGOORSTUY	autogyros
AGOPRRTUY	purgatory ❑
AGORSTTUY	gustatory
AGRSTTTTU	Stuttgart
AHHIIMORS	Hiroshima
AHHIIRRST	hair shirt
AHHIKLSWY	hawkishly
AHHIKOSTU	Sukhothai
AHHILLWWY	whillywha
AHHIMSSST	Smash Hits
AHHISTTWW	what's with
AHHMOSTUW	mouthwash
AHHNORRST	hartshorn
AHHOOPRSS	Oh So Sharp

Words marked ❑ can also be spelled with an initial capital letter

AHHOPPRUY	happy hour
AHHORSTTU	thrash out
AHIILMNTU	humiliant
AHIILNOPS	Ian Hislop
AHIILORSU	hilarious
AHIILOSST	halitosis
AHIIMMRST	Mithraism
AHIINORST	historian
AHIINSTWY	in this way
AHIIPRSSZ	sizarship
AHIIRRSTT	arthritis
AHIJMNNNO	John Inman
AHIKKNRSS	sharkskin
AHIKLMSWY	mawkishly
AHIKLNSVY	knavishly
AHIKLRSTU	hula skirt
AHIKNOTWW	I know what
AHILLOORS	hors la loi
AHILLOPRT	prothalli
AHILLOSSW	sallowish
AHILLPSSY	splashily
AHILLPSTW	whipstall
AHILLPTUW	all up with
AHILLSSTY	saltishly
AHILLSSVY	slavishly
AHILLTTWY	tally with
AHILMNNUY	inhumanly
AHILMORST	hailstorm
AHILMPRTU	triumphal
AHILNOPTY	notaphily
AHILNORTT	triathlon
AHILNPPUY	unhappily
AHILNSVWY	vinyl wash
AHILOORST	Lotharios
AHILOPPTY	Hippolyta
AHILORTTY	throatily
AHILPPTUW	pal up with
AHILPSSWY	waspishly
AHILQSSUY	squashily
AHIMMMNOS	mammonish
AHIMMMOSS	shammosim
AHIMMNORU	harmonium
AHIMNNORY	in harmony
AHIMNORST	harmonist
AHIMNOSST	smash into
AHIMNRTUU	anthurium
AHIMRSTWW	swarm with
AHINOOPTY	hypotonia
AHINOORTT	hortation
AHINPRSST	transship
AHIOPPSSY	apophysis
AHIOPRSUV	vapourish
AHIORRTWY	airworthy
AHIORTTUY	authority
AHJJMNOOR	John Major
AHJLMNOOO	Jonah Lomo
AHJMNOOWY	John Mayow
AHJNOORST	John Astor
AHKLOOPRS	look sharp
AHKLOOPYY	play hooky
AHKMOORSW	Hawksmoor
AHKNPRSTU	Pankhurst
AHKORSTUW	Southwark
AHLLLOSWY	shallowly
AHLLMORUY	humorally
AHLLOPSUY	aphyllous
AHLMMNOTU	Multnomah
AHLMOPSUX	Max Ophuls
AHLMOPTYY	polymathy
AHLOPSSTU	splash out
AHMNOOPTY	taphonomy
AHMOOPRSU	amorphous
AHMOPRTTU	mouthpart
AHNNNOOTY	hootnanny
AHNNORSTT	Northants
AHNOPSTYY	hyponasty
AHNORRSTT	North Star
AHOOOPTTT	hot potato
AHOOPSTTT	photostat
	Photostat®
AHOORRTTY	hortatory
AHPRSSTTU	push-start
AIIILLNTY	initially
AIIIMNOTT	imitation
AIIINNNOT	inanition
AIIINNSTY	asininity
AIIINORTT	initiator
AIIINOTTV	vitiation
AIIJLNPTU	put in jail
AIIJLOTVY	joviality
AIIJNNSTU	Justinian
AIILLMRSY	similarly
AIILLNPRT	in ill part
AIILLPRST	pillarist
AIILLPSTU	it is all up
AIILLRSTT	triallist
AIILLRTVY	trivially
AIILMMNUU	aluminium
AIILMNORT	trinomial
AIILMNSST	Stalinism
AIILMORST	similar to
AIILMPRRY	primarily
AIILMRSTU	ritualism
AIILNOOST	isolation
AIILNOOTV	violation
AIILNOPST	pianolist
AIILNOTTU	tuitional
AIILNRSST	sinistral
AIILNSSTT	Stalinist
AIILPRSST	spritsail
AIILPRSTU	spiritual
AIILRSTTU	ritualist
AIIMMPRSV	vampirism
AIIMNNOPT	main point
AIIMNNTUY	unanimity
AIIMNOPRS	prosimian
AIIMNOPSS	impassion
AIIMNORTY	a minority
AIIMNOSTY	animosity
AIIMNPSTT	timpanist
AIIMRSTUU	Mauritius
AIIMRSUVV	vivariums

AIINNNOOT	Antonioni	AILMNOSUU	aluminous
AIINNOPRS	sopranini	AILMNSTTU	stimulant
AIINNORST	Santorini	AILMORSTU	simulator
AIINNORTT	nitration	AILMORTTU	mutilator
AIINNORTU	ruination	AILMORTTY	mortality
	urination	AILMOSSTY	atmolysis
AIINNOSTU	sinuation	AILMPRSTY	palmistry
AIINNOTTX	antitoxin	AILMTTUUY	mutuality
AIINNRSTT	in transit	AILNNOPTU	Plutonian
AIINOOQRU	Iroquoian	AILNNOSSW	sons-in-law
AIINOPRST	spiration	AILNNSTTY	instantly
AIINOPRTT	partition	AILNOOPRT	portolani
AIINOPRTV	privation	AILNOORST	tonsorial
AIINORSTT	striation		torsional
AIINORSVY	visionary	AILNOOSTV	solvation
AIINORTTT	attrition	AILNOOTUV	ovulation
	titration	AILNOPSTT	Platonist
AIINOSTTU	situation	AILNOPSTU	platinous
AIINQTTUY	antiquity		pulsation
AIIOPRSSS	psoriasis		put on sail
AIIOPRSTT	topiarist	AILNORSTU	insulator
AIIOPRTVY	oviparity	AILNOSUXY	anxiously
AIIPRTTUY	pituitary	AILNOTTWZ	waltz into
AIIPSSTVY	passivity	AILNPPSTU	suppliant
AIKLLNOTW	know-it-all	AILNPQTUY	piquantly
AIKLMNNNS	Klinsmann	AILNRSTUY	rusty nail
AIKLNOSSY	ankylosis	AILNRTUUX	luxuriant
AIKLRRUVY	Valkyriur	AILOOPRST	spoliator
AIKMMNOOS	makimonos	AILOOPTTU	autopilot
AIKMMRRST	trim marks	AILOOTTUV	voilà tout
AIKMNNOSW	kinswoman	AILORRTTY	traitorly
AIKMNOTWZ	Mankowitz	AILORSUVY	savourily
AIKMPRSTZ	Mark Spitz		variously
AIKNNOPRS	Parkinson	AILOSSTUY	autolysis
AIKPRSTTU	put at risk	AIMMMMNOS	mammonism
AILLLPRUV	pulvillar	AIMMMNOST	mammonist
AILLMMORY	immorally	AIMMNORTY	matrimony
AILLMMPST	stamp mill	AIMMNOSTU	summation
AILLMNNOY	nominally	AIMMPRSUU	marsupium
AILLMOPTY	optimally	AIMMRSSTU	summarist
AILLMPRSU	pluralism	AIMNNOORT	nominator
AILLNNSTU	uninstall	AIMNNOSUU	unanimous
AILLNORST	tonsillar	AIMNNOTYY	anonymity
AILLNOTUU	ululation	AIMNOPRSY	parsimony
AILLNRSUY	insularly	AIMNOPRTT	important
AILLOPRST	Tirol Alps	AIMNOPRTY	patrimony
AILLOPTVY	pivotally	AIMNORRST	rainstorm
AILLORUXY	uxorially	AIMNORRSU	Ursa Minor
AILLPRSTU	pluralist	AIMNORRTU	ruminator
AILLPRTUY	plurality	AIMNORRTY	marry into
AILLRTTUY	titularly	AIMNOSSSY	Simon says
AILLRTUVY	virtually	AIMNPSTTY	tympanist
AILMMOORT	immolator	AIMNRSSTU	saturnism
AILMMRSUY	summarily	AIMOOPRUZ	Mario Puzo
AILMMSTUU	mutualism	AIMOORTTV	motivator
AILMMTTUU	ultimatum	AIMOPRSUW	Opium Wars
AILMNOOPS	palominos	AIMOPSSTU	potassium
AILMNOPRT	trampolin	AIMSSSSTY	miss stays
AILMNOPST	Platonism	AINNNOSTU	Antoninus
AILMNOPSU	Paul Simon		unisonant
AILMNORTY	normality	AINNOOPRS	sopranino

AINNOORTV	innovator
AINNORSTT	start in on
AINOOPPRT	apportion
AINOOQTTU	quotation
AINOORTTU	ration out
AINOOSSTT	ostinatos
AINOOSTTV	ottavinos
AINOPPRRT	in rapport
AINOPRSTT	into parts
AINOPRSTU	put on airs
	supinator
AINOPRSUU	uniparous
AINORSTTU	outstrain
AINPSSTTU	pants suit
AIOOORRST	oratorios
AIOOPRSUV	oviparous
AIOPRSSTT	spit-roast
AIORRSSTU	sartorius
AJMNORUWY	jurywoman
AJMPRSTTU	jump start
AKLLLMOOS	look small
AKLLMMOWY	mollymawk
AKLMNORWY	workmanly
AKLMOORST	look smart
AKLNOOTUW	walk out on
AKLORSSTW	saltworks
AKMNOORWW	workwoman
AKMNORSTU	Turkomans
AKMORRSWY	marrowsky
AKNOORTTW	not at work
ALLLNNSUY	Sally Lunn
ALLMNOSTW	small-town
ALLNOPTTU	pollutant
ALLNSUUUY	unusually
ALLOOPRTY	allotropy
ALLOPPRUY	popularly
ALLOPRSTW	straw poll
ALLOPSUWW	swallow up
ALLORSTTY	tall story
ALLRSTUUY	suturally
ALMMNRUUY	nummulary
ALMNNOOOS	monsoonal
ALMNNOUWY	unwomanly
ALMNOOSTT	almost not
ALMNOPRUY	pulmonary
ALMOORSUY	amorously
ALMOSSTUU	most usual
ALNOPPRUU	unpopular
ALNOPSTTU	postulant
ALNORTUVY	voluntary
ALOOOPRTZ	protozoal
ALOOPRSTV	Stavropol
ALOPPRSSU	prolapsus
ALOPRSTTU	Port Salut
ALOPRSTUW	sprawl out
ALOPRSTUY	pulsatory
ALOPRTUVY	voluptary
AMNNOOSTY	not so many
AMNNOOSUY	anonymous
AMNNOOSWW	Woman's Own
AMNOOPSTW	postwoman
	woman post
AMNOORSTY	astronomy
AMNOOSSTU	Mount Ossa
AMNOPRSST	sportsman
AMPRSTUUY	sumptuary
ANNORSTUY	tyrannous
ANOOOPRTZ	protozoan
ANOOPSSWY	spoonways
ANOORSTWY	Stornoway
ANOPRRSTT	transport
ANOPRTTWY	tawny port
ANORSUUVY	unsavoury
AOOORRRTW	arrowroot
AOOORRTTV	Rotovator®
AOPRRSTUU	rapturous
AOQSSTTUU	Status Quo
	status quo
AORSTTTUY	statutory

B

BBBEEELMU	bumblebee
	bumble-bee
BBBEEELUZ	Beelzebub
BBBEELORS	beslobber
BBBEELRSU	beslubber
BBCCHKLOU	Chubb® lock
BBCDIRRSU	scrub-bird
BBCEHLOTY	Toby Belch
BBCEHLOUY	cubbyhole
	cubby-hole
BBCEILRRS	scribbler
BBCEIRSSU	subscribe
BBCGILMOO	logic bomb
BBCGINRSU	scrubbing
BBCILLOSY	Bill Cosby
BBCKKLOOO	book block
BBDDEESYY	beddy-byes
BBDDEJOOR	odd-jobber
BBDDILLUY	Billy Budd
BBDEEIORT	bride-to-be
BBDEIORRW	bowerbird
BBDELLOOU	blue blood
BBDENORUY	Bounderby
BBDIMORTY	dirty bomb
BBDOORRUU	Borobudur
BBEEEHLMU	humble-bee
BBEEELLRY	beer belly
	beer-belly
BBEEFIORT	to be brief
BBEEINOSV	bene vobis
BBEEIRRSU	rubberise
BBEEIRRUZ	rubberize
BBEELRRUY	blueberry
BBEELTTUY	Betty Blue
BBEGGNOOW	wobbegong
BBEGHIIRS	gibberish
BBEGHILOS	bobsleigh
BBEGINSSU	gubbinses
BBEGLMTUU	tumble-bug
BBEHHIOTT	The Hobbit
BBEHILLOY	Holy Bible

BBEHKOOTY	by the book
BBEHLLMOS	bombshell
BBEHRRSUY	shrubbery
BBEINSSTU	tubbiness
BBEKMMOOS	smoke-bomb
BBELNOTTU	to be blunt
BBEMNRSUY	by numbers
BBEOORVVY	bovver boy
BBFMOOOPR	bombproof
	bomb-proof
BBGHILLTU	light bulb
BBGHILNOO	hobgoblin
BBGHINORT	throbbing
BBGIILNQU	quibbling
BBGIIOSTY	gibbosity
BBGILNOSY	sobbingly
BBGILOSUY	gibbously
BBGJNOORR	Bjorn Borg
BBGOORTUY	rugby boot
BBHILOSYY	yobbishly
BBIIILNRU	bilirubin
BBIIKMTUZ	kibbutzim
BBIINNORS	in ribbons
BBIKMNOST	stink bomb
BBILLMMOS	Mills bomb
BBILOSSTY	lobbyists
BBLLOSUUY	bulbously
BCCCHIINU	cubic inch
BCCCIMOOX	coxcombic
BCCCKMOOS	cockscomb
BCCDEHKOY	body-check
BCCDKLOOY	body clock
BCCEEIKTU	ice bucket
BCCEEILOR	coercible
BCCEHIKNP	pinchbeck
BCCEIIILM	imbecilic
BCCEIILOS	libeccios
BCCEILORY	coercibly
BCCEINNOU	concubine
BCCEINORS	conscribe
BCCEKOSTU	stock cube
BCCFIOOTU	cubic foot
BCCIILSTY	bicyclist
BCCIORSTU	scorbutic
BCCMOSTUU	succumb to
BCDDDEEIY	decided by
BCDDEEILU	deducible
BCDDEEIRS	described
BCDDIIKRY	Dicky Bird
	dicky-bird
BCDEEEFIN	beneficed
BCDEEEINO	obedience
BCDEEESUX	be excused
BCDEEHIIR	herbicide
BCDEEHITW	bewitched
BCDEEILRU	reducible
BCDEEIRRS	describer
BCDEEJSTU	subjected
BCDEELLOR	corbelled
BCDEELRTU	tubercled
BCDEEMNTU	decumbent
BCDEIILNU	inducible
BCDEIJSUU	sub judice
BCDEJNOOS	second job
BCDEKLNOU	unblocked
BCDELLLOO	blood cell
BCDELNRUU	underclub
BCDEORRSS	crossbred
BCDEORRUY	body-curer
BCDGIKLOR	gold brick
BCDHHIIOT	dhobi itch
BCDIIMMUY	cymbidium
BCDIINNOO	ionic bond
BCDILMNOW	climb down
BCDIOPSUW	Cupid's bow
BCDKLOOOW	wood block
	woodblock
BCDKNOOOS	boondocks
BCDKNOORU	rock-bound
BCDOOOOSY	Scooby Doo
BCDOPRTUY	by-product
BCEEEEHTT	tête-bêche
BCEEEGHIS	big cheese
BCEEEHKNO	cheekbone
BCEEEHLRY	Cheeryble
BCEEEKLPS	bespeckle
BCEEEKQRU	Quebecker
BCEEELQRU	becquerel ❑
BCEEFILNS	fencibles
BCEEGHINR	breeching
BCEEGINRS	big screen
BCEEHHLNO	bench-hole
BCEEHORTT	brochette
BCEEHRTTU	trebuchet
BCEEIILNV	evincible
BCEEIJOTV	objective
BCEEIKNST	Steinbeck
BCEEILLMO	become ill
BCEEILLOS	bellicose
BCEEILMNY	Cymbeline
BCEEILPUY	public eye
BCEEILRTY	celebrity
BCEEIMNOR	recombine
BCEEINOOT	coenobite
BCEEINRWY	Eric Newby
BCEEIOQSU	Québecois
BCEEIORSX	boxercise
BCEEIPRRS	prescribe
BCEEIPSSU	sub specie
BCEELNOSY	obscenely
BCEELOOSS	obsolesce
BCEEMMOOR	Morecombe
BCEEMNRTU	recumbent
BCEEMRRSU	cerebrums
BCEENPSTU	pubescent
BCEFFLOOR	corbel off
BCEFFNOOU	bounce off
BCEFIIKRR	firebrick
BCEFIJOTY	objectify
BCEFKLTUU	bucketful
BCEGHORRU	Cherbourg
BCEGIIKNR	bickering

BCEGRRSUW	grub screw	BCHIIRSTU	hubristic
BCEHILNTU	in the club	BCHIKLSUY	buckishly
BCEHIMRSU	cherubims	BCHILOOPY	lyophobic
BCEHINOOP	neophobic	BCHKNORTU	buckthorn
BCEHIPSSU	spicebush	BCHKOOTTU	bucktooth
BCEHKNORW	workbench	BCHLNOPUW	punch bowl
BCEHLNORY	Chernobyl	BCHLOOOSY	schoolboy
BCEHLNOTU	on the club	BCHLOTUUY	youth club
BCEHLOSUU	clubhouse	BCIIIMRST	Briticism
BCEHLRTUY	butcherly	BCIILMSUU	umbilicus
BCEHMNOOY	honeycomb	BCIILPSTU	publicist
BCEHMSTUY	set much by	BCIILPTUY	publicity
BCEHNSSTU	butchness	BCIILRTUY	lubricity
BCEHORRSU	brochures	BCIIMNOOS	bionomics
BCEIIIRST	Briticise	BCIIMOSTY	symbiotic
BCEIIIRTZ	Briticize	BCIKKORRW	brickwork
BCEIILNVY	evincibly	BCIKNNRSU	Innsbruck
BCEIILPSU	publicise	BCIKNOOOR	Robin Cook
BCEIILPUZ	publicize	BCIKNRSUW	Brunswick
BCEIIMORT	biometric	BCILLORSS	crossbill
BCEIINOST	bisection	BCILMMOUU	columbium
BCEIINRRS	inscriber	BCILMNOOT	climb on to
BCEIINSSU	subincise	BCILPRSTU	strip club
BCEIISSTU	Ctesibius	BCIMNOOOS	sonic boom
BCEIJNOOT	objection	BCIOOPRSS	proboscis
BCEIKNOST	steinbock	BCIOPRSTU	subtropic
BCEIKOOPR	book price	BCIORSTUY	obscurity
BCEILMNOU	columbine	BCIPRSSTU	subscript
BCEILMORY	cor blimey	BCMOSSUUU	submucous
BCEIMNNOU	uncombine	BCRSSTTUU	substruct
BCEIMNNTU	incumbent	BDDDEEFLU	befuddled
BCEIMNOOU	coenobium	BDDDEEINR	bedridden
BCEIMNORY	embryonic		bed-ridden
BCEINORRW	brown rice	BDDDEILOY	Bo Diddley
BCEINOSTY	obscenity	BDDEEGIRR	Redbridge
BCEIOPRRS	proscribe	BDDEEIOSY	disobeyed
BCEIORSST	crossbite	BDDEENRRU	underbred
BCEIORSTT	obstetric	BDDEFINOR	forbidden
BCEJOSTTU	subject to	BDDEFLOOU	blood-feud
BCEKLOOTV	block vote	BDDEFNOOW	bed of down
BCEKNPRUY	cyberpunk	BDDEGLOOU	doodlebug
BCELLOSUU	Cleobulus	BDDEHINOU	hidebound
BCELMOOTY	lobectomy		hide-bound
BCELNOSSU	Luc Besson	BDDEHLOOS	bloodshed
BCELOORTU	corbel out		shed blood
BCELOOSSU	colobuses	BDDEIILLO	Bill Oddie
	lobscouse	BDDEIILNS	blind side
BCELORSUY	obscurely	BDDEIISUV	subdivide
BCEMOTTUY	tubectomy	BDDEILNRU	unbridled
BCEPRTTUU	buttercup	BDDEIMOSY	disembody
BCFHILLNU	bullfinch	BDDEINRSU	disburden
BCFIKSUZZ	buck's fizz ❑	BDDEIRSTU	disturbed
BCGHILNTU	nightclub	BDDEKNOSU	desk-bound
	night-club	BDDELSUUY	subduedly
BCGIIMNNO	combining	BDDEMNORU	odd number
BCGIKRSUV	Vicksburg	BDDENNOUU	unbounded
BCGILMNRU	crumbling	BDDENOTUU	undoubted
BCGILMNSU	scumbling	BDDENSUUU	unsubdued
BCGKNOPRU	prongbuck	BDDFILLNO	blindfold
BCHHIIISU	shibuichi	BDDFMNOUU	dumbfound
BCHIIOPRS	bishopric	BDDGIINOR	doing bird

BDDIIORWW	widow bird
BDDILNORW	word-blind
BDDINNOUW	windbound
BDDNOTUUY	duty-bound
BDEEEEFLN	enfeebled
BDEEEELRV	belvedere ❑
BDEEEGIRV	Beveridge
BDEEEGLRR	Lederberg
BDEEEGRSY	by degrees
BDEEEHNST	sheet bend
BDEEEHTTW	wet the bed
BDEEEIOTW	woe betide
BDEEEISST	set beside
BDEEELNOS	nosebleed
BDEEELORT	dor beetle
BDEEENRTU	debenture
BDEEFIILS	disbelief
BDEEFIORR	fire-robed
BDEEFLLOW	bedfellow
BDEEFLORW	flower-bed
BDEEGGLOW	bow-legged
BDEEGHINT	benighted
	get behind
BDEEGMRSU	submerged
BDEEHIILN	lie behind
BDEEHIITX	exhibited
BDEEHILMS	blemished
BDEEHNOTY	the Beyond
BDEEHORTT	betrothed
BDEEHTUUX	Buxtehude
BDEEIILLN	indelible
BDEEIKLNR	blinkered
BDEEILMOR	embroiled
BDEEILMSS	dissemble
BDEEILNSV	vendibles
BDEEILRST	blistered
BDEEILRTV	drive belt
BDEEIMMRS	dismember
BDEEIMORR	embroider
BDEEINRRT	interbred
BDEEINRTU	underbite
BDEEIRSTT	bedsitter
	bed-sitter
BDEEIRTVY	riveted by
BDEEKNRUU	unrebuked
BDEELLSSY	blessedly
BDEELNOUV	unbeloved
BDEELNRRU	blunderer
BDEELOSTV	best-loved
BDEEMPPSU	speed bump
BDEEMRSSU	submersed
BDEENNOOY	beyond one
BDEEORVYY	everybody
BDEEPRRTU	perturbed
BDEFFLNOU	bundle off
BDEFGORTU	budget for
BDEFIKLOO	field book
BDEFILLOO	lifeblood
BDEFINORY	boyfriend
BDEFIOORW	wood fibre
BDEFLORUW	flower-bud
BDEFLOSTU	self-doubt
BDEFOOTTU	out of debt
BDEGHILNR	Lindbergh
BDEGHINRU	Edinburgh
BDEGIIILR	dirigible
BDEGIILOS	disoblige
BDEGIIPPR	big dipper
BDEGIKOOU	guidebook
BDEGILNNY	bendingly
BDEGILOOT	obliged to
BDEGIMRUY	Muybridge
BDEGINNNU	unbending
BDEGINORR	bordering
BDEGLNORU	Oldenburg
BDEGLOTUW	low-budget
BDEGMMTUU	mum-budget
BDEHIIINT	inhibited
BDEHIIRSY	hybridise
BDEHIIRYZ	hybridize
BDEHILNRU	Brunhilde
BDEHILPSU	published
BDEHINOOY	hyoid bone
BDEHINRSU	burnished
BDEHIORSU	bird-house
BDEHJLOOR	job-holder
BDEHNOSTU	South Bend
BDEHNRSUU	underbush
BDEIIILSV	divisible
BDEIIILTY	edibility
BDEIILLNY	indelibly
BDEIISSSU	subsidise
BDEIISSUZ	subsidize
BDEIKLLRR	kerb drill
BDEILLNPS	spellbind
BDEILMNOW	Wimbledon
BDEILNNSS	blindness
BDEILNRSU	Dubliners
BDEILOQTU	quodlibet
BDEILORUV	overbuild
BDEIMNOST	disentomb
BDEIMORSU	mousebird
BDEIMSTTU	submitted
BDEINNORW	windborne
	wind-borne
BDEINOOST	do one's bit
BDEINORTX	tinderbox
BDEINORTZ	Trebizond
BDEINRSSU	sideburns
BDEIORSTU	subeditor
BDEIRSTTY	bide tryst
BDEKOOOTU	booked-out
BDELLOOOS	lose blood
BDELLOORS	bordellos
BDELLOOSS	bloodless
BDELLOPUW	Bud Powell
BDELLORUZ	bulldozer
BDELMNPUU	unplumbed
BDELMRTUY	tumble-dry
BDELNNRUU	unbundler
BDELNOSSU	boundless
BDELOOPRU	pure-blood

BDELOOPTY	blood type
BDELOOSTT	blood test
BDELOPTTU	bottled-up
BDELORSTU	Bulstrode
BDELOSSTU	doubtless
BDEMMNOSU	Ombudsmen
BDENNOSSU	snub-nosed
BDENNRSUU	sunburned
BDENOOUYY	beyond you
BDENOSTUW	westbound
BDFLLOOOW	blood-flow
BDGIILNSU	buildings
BDGIINNNU	unbinding
BDGIINSSU	subsiding
BDGINNORW	bring down
BDHIIMRSY	hybridism
BDHIIRTYY	hybridity
BDHINOOOR	Robin Hood
BDHKOORSU	Dukhobors
BDHLOOOST	bloodshot
BDHOOORTY	Boothroyd
BDHOORSUW	brushwood
BDIIILSVY	divisibly
BDIIKNOST	sitbodkin
BDIIMORTY	morbidity
BDIIRTTUY	turbidity
BDIKNORUV	Dubrovnik
BDILNNOSW	snow-blind
BDILNOPST	blind spot
BDILNOPUU	build upon
BDILOSUUY	dubiously
BDINOOWWW	bow window
BDINOOWWX	window box
BDLLOOOWY	Bollywood
BDLLOOSTU	bloodlust
BDNNOOSUW	snowbound
BDORSUWZZ	buzz words
BEEEEEKPR	beekeeper
BEEEEMRRY	Meyerbeer
BEEEFGLOR	leg before
BEEEFINSS	beefiness
BEEEFORST	set before
BEEEGGRUZ	Zeebrugge
BEEEGLNRT	green belt
BEEEGNOOW	woebegone
BEEEGNOTW	go between
	go-between
BEEEGRTTT	get better
BEEEHHLMT	Bethlehem
BEEEHKTWY	by the week
BEEEHLLOR	hellebore
BEEEHLRTT	Ethelbert
BEEEHNOTV	Beethoven
BEEEIILNV	believe in
BEEEIKLLR	rebel-like
BEEEILLOT	oil beetle
BEEEILMMS	emblemise
BEEEILMMZ	emblemize
BEEEILNUV	unbelieve
BEEEILRSV	believers
	eversible
BEEEIMRSV	semibreve
BEEEINNTW	in-between
BEEEINORT	bête noire
BEEEINRRS	Bernières
BEEEISTUV	sieve tube
BEEEKORRT	Robert Kee
BEEELLSTU	steel-blue
BEEELLSTV	level best
BEEELMRZZ	embezzler
BEEELPRTU	Blue Peter
	blue peter
BEEELSSSU	sublessee
BEEEMMNRW	new member
BEEEMPRST	September
BEEENORST	tenebrose
BEEENOSSS	obeseness
BEEFFGIRU	febrifuge
BEEFFORTT	better off
BEEFFOSTW	web offset
BEEFIILMS	misbelief
BEEFILNNO	non-belief
BEEFILRSS	briefless
	fibreless
BEEFINRSS	briefness
BEEFLNNUW	funnel-web
BEEFLNOSY	by oneself
BEEFNOORW	before now
BEEFNORTU	befortune
BEEGGGIRT	get bigger
BEEGGIINS	besieging
BEEGGNRTU	Gutenberg
BEEGIILLL	illegible
BEEGIILNV	believing
BEEGIKLLO	globelike
BEEGILLNR	rebelling
BEEGILLNW	wellbeing
	well-being
BEEGILNNN	Nigel Benn
BEEGILNRS	inselberg
BEEGILNUU	unbeguile
BEEGILPRS	Spielberg
BEEGINNRT	Tinbergen
BEEGINSTT	besetting
BEEGKORRS	go berserk
BEEGLNOOS	Bolognese
BEEGMNRRU	Nuremberg
BEEGNORRS	Rosenberg
BEEHIINRS	hibernise
BEEHIINRZ	hibernize
BEEHIKRRS	Berkshire
BEEHILLMS	embellish
BEEHILMPU	humble pie
BEEHILTUZ	Buthelezi
BEEHIOPRS	biosphere
BEEHIORRS	herborise
BEEHIORRV	herbivore
BEEHIORRZ	herborize
BEEHLOPRY	hyperbole
BEEHLOTTT	the bottle
BEEHMORUY	homebuyer
BEEHNOOPX	xenophobe

BEEHNOOTT	to the bone
BEEIILNRT	libertine
BEEIILRST	liberties
BEEIINRTY	inebriety
BEEIKLMRU	berkelium
BEEIKLMRY	Kimberley
BEEIKLSSU	blue-skies
BEEIKOSTV	Steve Biko
BEEILLNOR	rebellion
BEEILLNTU	ebullient
BEEILLRTT	belittler
BEEILLRTU	rubellite
BEEILMOUV	blue movie
BEEILNOPX	exponible
BEEILNRSU	blue rinse
BEEILNRUZ	nebulizer
BEEILOTTU	oubliette
BEEILRRSV	vers libre
BEEILSTUV	vestibule
BEEIMNRST	tenebrism
BEEIMRRSU	reimburse
BEEINNOTT	bentonite
BEEINNRST	Bernstein
BEEINNRTU	inner tube
BEEINORST	tenebrios
BEEINRSTU	Trubenise
BEEINRTTY	tenebrity
BEEIOQSSU	obsequies
BEEIOSSSV	obsessive
BEEIQRTTU	briquette
BEEIRRTTU	retribute
BEEJNRRUY	Juneberry
BEEJOOSST	Jesse Boot
BEEKLRRSY	berserkly
BEEKNORST	kerbstone
BEELLORSU	resoluble
BEELLORTW	bell tower
BEELMNORU	Melbourne
BEELMNOTY	money belt
BEELMORST	temblores
BEELMRRSU	slumberer
BEELNNOSS	nobleness
BEELORSVY	obversely
	verbosely
BEELOSSTU	boletuses
BEELQRSUU	burlesque
BEELRRSTU	blusterer
BEELRSTTU	subletter
BEEMMNNOR	non-member
BEEMNNORU	number one
BEEMNNRTU	Number Ten
BEEMNORST	Mrs Beeton
BEEMOPRRY	pre-embryo
BEENNOOPU	be one up on
BEENNOTUV	ben venuto
BEENOQSTU	obsequent
BEENORRST	resorbent
BEENORSSS	soberness
BEENORSTU	tenebrous
BEEORSSUU	subereous
BEEORSTTU	soubrette
BEEPRRSTY	presbyter
BEERRSTUV	subverter
BEFFGINTU	buffeting
BEFFHINTU	in the buff
BEFFHIOTT	off the bit
BEFFINOTT	bitten off
BEFFLNSSU	bluffness
BEFFMNORU	number off
BEFGIINTT	befitting
BEFGILNSU	fungibles
BEFGLNRSU	Flensburg
BEFHIORRS	Frobisher
BEFHIRRSU	furbisher
	refurbish
BEFHKLOOS	bookshelf
BEFIILNSU	infusible
BEFIINORT	be in for it
BEFIKLOOR	brief look
BEFILLMSU	blue films
BEFILRWYY	fly-by-wire
BEFINOPRU	ibuprofen
BEFIORSTT	frostbite
BEFLLLOPY	belly-flop
BEFLLLSUU	full blues
BEFLRTTUY	butterfly
BEFNNNOUY	funny bone
BEGGGILNY	beggingly
BEGGGLOOX	goggle-box
BEGGIILNU	beguiling
BEGGIINNN	beginning
BEGGILNNO	belonging
BEGGINOSS	bogginess
BEGGIOORV	go over big
BEGGJLOOS	Joe Bloggs
BEGHHORTU	be through
BEGHIIRTV	give birth
BEGHILLNT	night-bell
BEGHIMNOR	bring home
BEGHINORT	bothering
BEGHINORU	neighbour
BEGIIILNT	ignitible
BEGIILLLY	illegibly
BEGIIMNRT	timbering
BEGIINNTY	benignity
BEGIJRTTU	jitterbug
BEGILMNOS	Mel Gibson
BEGILMNRT	trembling
BEGILMNRU	lumbering
BEGILMORY	gorblimey
BEGILMRRU	Limburger
BEGILRSTW	W S Gilbert
BEGIMNNRU	numbering
BEGIMNOSS	embossing
BEGINNORU	Ben Gurion
	Ben-Gurion
BEGINOOSS	besognios
BEGINOOSU	biogenous
BEGINORRV	bring over
BEGIOORSU	bourgeois❑
BEGLLOPUY	go belly up
	go belly-up

Words marked ❑ can also be spelled with an initial capital letter

BEGLMRUUX	Luxemburg
BEGLOORTT	globe-trot
BEGMORRST	Bergström
BEGPRRSSU	Pressburg
BEHHLLORT	hell-broth
BEHHMOOOP	homophobe
BEHHOSTUW	who but she
BEHIIINRT	inhibiter
BEHIILPST	phlebitis
BEHIIORTX	exhibitor
BEHIKLOSV	Bolshevik
BEHILLNNY	Benny Hill
BEHILLNTY	thin-belly
BEHILNOOT	on the boil
BEHILNORS	Niels Bohr
BEHILNSUW	blush wine
BEHINSSSU	bushiness
BEHIORRVY	herbivory
BEHIORSTY	be history
BEHIRRSUW	wire brush
BEHKSUVYY	Kuybyshev
BEHLORRTY	brotherly
BEHMOORST	thrombose
BEHMORSSU	rhombuses
BEHNOOORT	on the broo
BEHNOOPXY	xenophoby
BEHOPRTYY	bryophyte
BEIIILNSV	invisible
BEIIKLLSS	Bill Sikes
BEIILLNSY	sibylline
BEIILLTTT	little bit
BEIILMORZ	mobilizer
BEIILMOSS	omissible
BEIILMSSU	sublimise
BEIILMSUZ	sublimize
BEIILNRTT	litter bin
BEIILOOPR	periboloi
BEIILORTT	trilobite
BEIILOTVZ	Leibovitz
BEIILSSTU	subtilise
BEIILSTUZ	subtilize
BEIINRTTU	Tribunite
BEIIORSST	sorbitise
BEIIORSTZ	sorbitize
BEIJLLLOY	Billy Joel
BEIKLNSSU	bulkiness
BEIKMOORT	motorbike
	motor-bike
BEIKNRSSS	briskness
BEIKORTWZ	Berkowitz
BEILLLOSU	libellous
BEILLLTUW	well-built
BEILLMNPU	plumb line
	plumb-line
BEILLMRUY	beryllium
BEILLMSUY	sublimely
BEILLNORU	Bernoulli
BEILLNOSU	insoluble
BEILLOQUY	obliquely
BEILLOTTY	little boy
BEILLRTTY	brittlely
BEILMNOSW	women's lib
BEILMOSSY	symbolise
BEILMOSYZ	symbolize
BEILMPPRU	upper limb
BEILNNUVY	Blue Vinny
BEILNORTU	in trouble
BEILNPRTU	blueprint
BEILOOPRT	pot-boiler
BEILOPSSS	possibles
BEILORSTT	librettos
BEIMNNRSU	in numbers
BEIMNORST	brimstone
BEIMNOSSU	omnibuses
BEIMNPSSU	bumpiness
BEIMOSSTW	misbestow
BEIMRSTTU	submitter
BEIMRTTUY	ytterbium
BEINNRSUW	Swinburne
BEINOORSV	obversion
BEINOOSSS	obsession
BEINORUVV	bon viveur
BEIOOPRRU	pourboire
BEIOPRSTU	bite or sup
BEIOQRSTU	sobriquet
BEIORSTTW	Two Tribes
BEIORSTUV	obtrusive
BEIORSTVY	verbosity
BEIRRSTUW	bierwurst
BEJNNNOOS	Ben Jonson
BEKLMOORS	Mel Brooks
BEKNNNOUW	unbeknown
BELLOPTUY	belly up to
BELMMOOSS	emblossom
BELMNOSTU	stumble on
BELMOOORW	elbow-room
BELMOOTTY	Bottomley
BELNNSSTU	bluntness
BELNOORRS	born loser
BELNOORVW	overblown
BELNRTTUU	turbulent
BELOPRSTU	bolster up
BELORSSSU	sublessor
BELQRSUUY	brusquely
BEMNOOSTT	tombstone
BEMNORTUU	outnumber
BEMNORTUW	number two
BEMOORRSS	sombreros
BENNORSSW	brownness
BENOORRST	Robertson
BENOOSTUU	bounteous
BENOPRSTU	burst open
BENORRSWY	snowberry
BERRSTTUY	burst tyre
BFGHILLTU	bullfight
BFGIIJLNY	flying jib
BFGLORSUW	Wolfsburg
BFIIILLNR	fibrillin
BFIILMORY	myofibril
BFILNOTUU	bountiful
BFINORRST	first-born
BFLLLNOUW	full-blown

BFOORTUWY	two-by-four
BGGILLNUY	bulgingly
BGGILMNRU	grumbling
BGGINOSUY	Guy Gibson
BGHHHIIRT	high birth
BGHHIORSW	highbrows
BGHILLOTW	light blow
BGHILMNTU	thumbling
BGHINSTUY	buy things
BGHIOORTT	too bright
BGHOPRTUU	upbrought
BGHORRSUU	Burroughs
BGIIIKPRR	kirbigrip❑
BGIILLNOW	billowing
BGIILMOOR	imbroglio
BGIILMPRS	limb sprig
BGIILNRST	bristling
BGIILOOST	biologist
BGIINNTTU	butting-in
BGIKNOPRS	springbok
BGILMNNUY	numbingly
BGILMNOOY	myoglobin
BGILMNSTU	stumbling
BGILNNRUY	burningly
BGILNORTU	troubling
BGILNUYZZ	buzzingly
BGILOORTY	tribology
BGIMNSSUU	subsuming
BGINNNOOT	Bonington
BGINNORTU	binturong
BGINOORRW	borrowing
BGLMOOSYY	symbology
BGNOORSTX	strongbox
BHHIMORTY	biorhythm
BHHIRSSTU	bush shirt
BHIIINORT	inhibitor
BHIIKLMPY	Kim Philby
BHIILLLLY	hillbilly
BHIILLNOT	billionth
BHILLLSUY	bullishly
BHILLNORT	thornbill
BHILMNOTY	bimonthly
BHILOORSY	boorishly
BHILRSTUY	brutishly
BHIMOOSTY	tomboyish
BHIMOOTTT	hit bottom
BHIORRTTW	birth-wort
BHJOORSTW	jobsworth
BHKMNOTTU	thumb knot
BHKORRSUW	brushwork
BHLLOOOTT	tollbooth
BHNOPRSUU	brush up on
BIIILNSVY	invisibly
BIIKNNOTV	Botvinnik
BIILLOSUY	biliously
BIILMSTUY	sublimity
BIILOOSUV	oblivious
BIILOQTUY	obliquity
BIIMNOORR	Borromini
BIIMOPRTY	improbity
BIIMOSSSY	symbiosis
BIISSTTYY	itsy-bitsy
BIKNOORSW	Bronowski
BILLNOPTU	bull point
BILLNORST	stillborn
BILLNOSUY	insolubly
BILMMOSSY	symbolism❑
BILMOORST	Stromboli
BILMOQSTU	Blomquist
BILMOSSTY	symbolist
BILOOPRTU	politburo❑
BILOOSUVY	obviously
BILORSSTU	strobilus
BIMNORTTU	Tim Burton
BIMOPSTUU	bumptious
BINNORSTU	burst in on
BINOOOSUX	obnoxious
BINOORSTU	obtrusion
BKLLMNSUU	numbskull
BKOOORSTY	storybook
	story-book
BLMORSSUU	slumbrous
BMMMOSUYY	mummy's boy
BMOOOTTTU	bottom out
BMOOPSTTU	bottoms up
BNNORRTUW	turn brown
BOOPPRRTU	turboprop

C

CCCDENOOT	concocted
CCCEEINRT	eccentric
CCCEIILPY	epicyclic
CCCENOORT	concocter
CCCGINOOO	gonococci
CCCHHIKOT	Hitchcock
CCCHILMOU	colchicum
CCCIILOSY	isocyclic
CCCIOORSS	sci-roccos
CCCNOOORT	concoctor
CCDDELNOU	concluded
CCDEEERSU	succeeder
CCDEEHIKW	chickweed
CCDEEHKNU	unchecked
CCDEEIINN	incidence
CCDEEILNR	encircled
CCDEEINNY	indecency
CCDEEINOT	conceited
CCDEEINSU	succeed in
CCDEELLOT	collected
CCDEENNOR	concerned
CCDEENNOS	ensconced
CCDEENNOT	connected
CCDEENORS	crescendo
CCDEENORT	concerted
CCDEEORTU	decocture
CCDEEOSTU	succeed to
CCDEILOOR	crocodile
CCDEIMOOR	microcode
CCDEINNOV	convinced
CCDEINOOT	decoction
CCDEINOTV	convicted
CCDEINOUV	conducive

Words marked ❑ can also be spelled with an initial capital letter

CCDELNOTU	occludent
CCDENOSSU	concussed
CCDHKOOUW	woodchuck
CCDIILNRY	cylindric
CCDIIOORT	corticoid
CCDKKLNOO	knock cold
CCDKLLOUY	cuckoldly
CCDKLORUY	cuckoldry
CCDNOORTU	conductor
CCEEEFLNU	feculence
CCEEEHHRR	recherché
CCEEEHNOR	coherence
CCEEEHRRS	screecher
CCEEEINNS	nescience
CCEEEINRT	reticence
CCEEEMMOR	e-commerce
CCEEFILLY	life-cycle
CCEEGINOR	concierge
CCEEHIKOY	ice hockey
	ice-hockey
CCEEHKORV	check over
	overcheck
CCEEHLORT	cerecloth
CCEEHOTTU	couchette
CCEEIIPPR	precipice
CCEEIKRRT	cricketer
CCEEILNNO	on-licence
CCEEILNOR	reconcile
CCEEIMNOU	oecumenic
CCEEIMNSU	ecumenics
CCEEINNNO	innocence
CCEEINORS	cicerones
CCEEIRRST	rectrices
CCEEIRSTT	tectrices
CCEEKLLOR	Cockerell
CCEELLORT	recollect
CCEENNORT	concenter
	concentre
	connecter
CCEFHIOOR	for choice
CCEFIIPSS	specifics
CCEFKNOYY	cockneyfy
CCEGGHOST	Scotch egg
CCEGIIKLN	Cecil King
CCEGILNRY	recycling
CCEGINNOO	oncogenic
CCEGLNOSY	song cycle
CCEHHHRTU	the church
CCEHHMNRU	churchmen
CCEHIKLST	checklist
CCEHIKNNO	no chicken
CCEHILNOR	chronicle
CCEHINOSZ	zecchinos
CCEHIORST	orchestic
CCEHKLNOT	neckcloth
CCEHKOPST	spot check
	spot-check
CCEHLOTTU	the occult
CCEHORTTY	crotchety
CCEHOTTUZ	zucchetto
CCEIIIRST	criticise
CCEIIIRTZ	criticize
CCEIIKNPR	picnicker
CCEIILNOT	niccolite
CCEIINORS	crescioni
CCEIKLLOY	kilocycle
CCEIKLMOT	time clock
CCEIKLOSW	clockwise
CCEIKNOSS	cockiness
CCEILNOSY	concisely
CCEILORST	sclerotic
CCEILOSUV	occlusive
CCEIMNOOS	economics
CCEIMOSST	cosmetics
CCEINNORT	in concert
CCEINORRT	incorrect
CCEINOSTT	tectonics
CCEINPRST	precincts
CCEIOPRST	cost price
CCEIOPRTY	precocity
CCEKORRSW	corkscrew
CCELLMRSU	McCullers
CCELLNOOY	colonelcy
CCELLOORT	collector
CCELNSTUU	succulent
CCELOPRSU	corpuscle
CCELOPSSY	Cyclopses
CCELORRTY	correctly
CCELORTUU	coculture
CCENNNORU	unconcern
CCENNOORT	connector
CCENOORST	concertos
CCENOORSU	concourse
CCENOORTV	convector
CCENORRTU	occurrent
CCEOORRRT	corrector
CCEOPPRUY	preoccupy
CCEORRSUU	succourer
CCEORSSSU	successor
CCFGHIKOT	cockfight
CCFHIINOO	finocchio
CCFHKLLOU	chock-full
CCFIMORRU	cruciform
CCFINOSUU	Confucius
CCFKOOOST	cocksfoot
CCFLLOSUU	flocculus
CCFLOOOOS	locofocos
CCGHIILNN	clinching
CCGHIKLNU	chuckling
CCGHINORS	scorching
CCGILMOOY	mycologic
CCGINNOOO	cocooning
CCGINORRU	occurring
CCHHILLRU	Churchill
CCHHOOPST	hopscotch
CCHIIKNTU	chuck it in
CCHIINOOP	Pinocchio
CCHIINSUZ	zucchinis
CCHIIORRT	trichroic
CCHIKLLOO	cook-chill
CCHINRSTY	strychnic
CCHIOPSTY	psychotic

CCIIILNRT	triclinic
CCIIIMRST	criticism
CCIILNNOU	in council
CCIILOOST	scoliotic
CCIILOPRT	proclitic
CCIINNOOS	concision
CCIIRRTUY	circuitry
CCIKNORST	con tricks
CCILMOSTU	occultism
CCILNOOSU	occlusion
CCILORSUU	curculios
CCILOSTTU	occultist
CCIMMOORS	microcosm
CCIMOOPRY	microcopy
CCINOOSSU	conscious
CCINOPRST	conscript
CCINORSTT	constrict
CCIOOTTXY	cytotoxic
CCKKLOORW	clockwork
CCKKNOOPY	knock copy
CCKOOPPPY	poppycock
CCLNOORTY	cyclotron
CCNORSTTU	construct
CCOOSTTUU	tucotucos
CCOSTTUUU	tucutucos
CDDDEEILY	decidedly
CDDDEEINU	undecided
CDDDEILNO	condiddle
CDDEEENRS	descender
CDDEEHLSU	scheduled
CDDEEIKRU	eider duck
CDDEEINRS	rescinded
CDDEEIPRT	predicted
CDDEEISST	dissected
CDDEEITUV	deductive
CDDEEKOTU	decked out
CDDEELPRU	precluded
CDDEEMNNO	condemned
CDDEENNOS	condensed
	descend on
CDDEGLOOR	old codger
CDDEHIJNU	Judi Dench
CDDEHKLSU	sheldduck
CDDEHORRT	Dordrecht
CDDEIILMO	domiciled
CDDEIINRT	dendritic
CDDEIIRST	discredit
CDDEILOSS	disclosed
CDDEILTUU	dulcitude
CDDEINOTU	deduction
CDDEIOSUU	deciduous
CDDELNOUU	unclouded
CDDENORUW	uncrowded
CDDGHLOTU	Dutch gold
CDDHHILOO	childhood
CDDHIILMN	childmind
CDDIKLNOR	cold drink
CDDILORSW	Discworld
CDEEEEFNR	deference
CDEEEFFOR	force-feed
CDEEEFHOS	cheesed of
CDEEEFITV	defective
CDEEEFKLR	fleckered
CDEEEFPRT	perfected
CDEEEGINX	exceeding
CDEEEGLNT	neglected
CDEEEHKNP	henpecked
CDEEEHQRU	chequered
CDEEEIMRT	decimetre
CDEEEINPT	centipede
CDEEEINRS	residence
CDEEEINRT	intercede
CDEEEINUV	undeceive
CDEEEIPTV	deceptive
CDEEEITTV	detective
CDEEELLOT	décolleté
CDEEELNOR	redolence
CDEEELORT	electrode
CDEEEMNRT	decrement
CDEEENPRT	precedent
CDEEEORRT	retrocede
CDEEEORRV	recovered
CDEEEPRST	respected
CDEEFIINT	deficient
CDEEFIIPS	specified
CDEEFIIRT	certified
CDEEFIKRR	Frederick
CDEEFILTU	deceitful
CDEEFINOT	defection
CDEEFIORT	fore-cited
CDEEFKNSU	fen-sucked
CDEEFKOST	feedstock
CDEEFLORT	deflector
CDEEFLRUU	flue-cured
CDEEFNOSS	confessed
CDEEGHOOR	good cheer
CDEEGIILN	diligence
CDEEGIIMR	germicide
CDEEGIINN	indigence
CDEEGIINV	deceiving
CDEEGIJNT	dejecting
CDEEGILOR	Coleridge
CDEEGILRY	glyceride
CDEEGINPR	preceding
CDEEGLORT	get colder
CDEEGNOST	congested
	decongest
CDEEHHIRS	cherished
CDEEHIKNT	thickened
CDEEHILNS	Schleiden
CDEEHILSW	disc wheel
CDEEHINOT	ethnocide
CDEEHINRS	Schneider
CDEEHINST	dehiscent
CDEEHIORT	ditrochee
CDEEHLORY	hydrocele
CDEEHRSTT	stretched
CDEEIILRT	decilitre
CDEEIIMNT	menticide
CDEEIIMRV	decemviri
	vermicide
CDEEIIPRR	cirripede

CDEEIIPST	pesticide
CDEEIIPTV	depictive
CDEEIIRTV	directive
CDEEIISTT	dietetics
CDEEIJNOT	dejection
CDEEIJPRU	prejudice
CDEEIKMRY	Dick Emery
CDEEILNNO	indolence
CDEEILPRT	predilect
CDEEILRST	derelicts
CDEEILTXY	excitedly
CDEEIMNPU	impudence
CDEEIMRSV	decemvirs
CDEEINNOR	endocrine
CDEEINOPT	deception
CDEEINORT	recondite
CDEEINOTT	detection
CDEEINQUY	De Quincey
CDEEINRST	stridence
CDEEINRSY	residency
CDEEINTTX	extincted
CDEEINTUX	unexcited
CDEEIRTTU	certitude
	rectitude
CDEEIRTUV	reductive
CDEEISTUV	seductive
CDEEJOPRT	projected
CDEEKLORW	lower deck
CDEELLMOP	compelled
CDEELMNTU	demulcent
CDEELMOPT	completed
CDEELNORY	redolency
CDEELRSTU	clustered
CDEELRTTU	cluttered
CDEEMMNOR	recommend
CDEEMNORU	come under
CDEEMOOPS	decompose
CDEEMOORS	Morse code
CDEENNORS	condenser
CDEENNORT	contender
CDEENNORU	denouncer
CDEENNOTT	contented
CDEENOOPS	endoscope
CDEENOPRS	drop-scene
CDEENOQRU	conquered
CDEENORTV	converted
CDEENORUV	uncovered
CDEENOSTT	contested
CDEENRSSU	crudeness
CDEENRSUU	unsecured
CDEEOPRRU	procedure
	reproduce
CDEEOPRSS	processed
CDEEOPRTT	protected
CDEEORSSY	cross-eyed
CDEEPPRSU	scuppered
CDEEPRSUW	screwed up
	screwed-up
CDEEPSSTU	suspected
CDEFGIINU	fungicide
CDEFHIILL	Lichfield
CDEFHIIRR	Friedrich
CDEFIINST	disinfect
CDEFIMNOR	confirmed
CDEFINNOT	confident
CDEFINTUY	fecundity
CDEFNOSUU	unfocused
CDEGHHIIV	high-viced
CDEGHINNR	drenching
CDEGIILNN	declining
CDEGIINRT	directing
CDEGILNUX	excluding
CDEGILOOP	police dog
CDEGILOSU	glucoside
CDEGILOSY	glycoside
CDEGINNOS	consigned
	seconding
CDEGINORR	recording
CDEGLORST	goldcrest
CDEHHINTU	unhitched
CDEHIIKLL	childlike
CDEHIKLSU	shielduck
CDEHILLOV	love child
	love-child
CDEHILLSS	childless
CDEHILNOT	clothed in
CDEHILNSS	childness
CDEHILPST	stepchild
CDEHINORT	threnodic
CDEHINOSU	cushioned
CDEHIOORT	Theodoric
CDEHKNOOR	Rodchenko
CDEHKNOOW	choke down
CDEHLLOOS	hold close
CDEHLMOUV	much loved
CDEHLNOTU	unclothed
CDEHLOSTU	The Clouds
CDEHNOTUU	untouched
CDEHNOTUV	Dutch oven
CDEHORTTU	Dutrochet
CDEHPPSUY	psyched up
CDEIIILSV	civilised
CDEIIILVZ	civilized
CDEIIKMTW	mid-wicket
CDEIILLNO	decillion
CDEIILNNU	include in
CDEIILOSU	delicious
CDEIILRRU	ridiculer
CDEIILTVY	declivity
CDEIIMNOS	meniscoid
CDEIIMNTY	mendicity
CDEIIMRST	misdirect
CDEIINOPT	depiction
CDEIINORT	direction
CDEIINOXZ	zinc oxide
CDEIINRTT	interdict
CDEIINTUV	inductive
CDEIIOOSU	dioecious
CDEIIOPRT	peridotic
CDEIIORUX	uxoricide
CDEIIRRTX	directrix
CDEIJNNOO	conjoined

CDEILLLOU	celluloid®
CDEILMNOU	unmelodic
CDEILNNOU	cloud nine
CDEILNOOZ	colonized
CDEILNSSU	lucidness
CDEILOPRW	low-priced
CDEILOSUU	I could use
CDEILOSUV	declivous
CDEILRTUY	credulity
CDEIMMNOO	incommode
CDEIMMOTT	committed
CDEIMMSUY	music-demy
CDEIMNNOT	condiment
CDEIMNOPR	princedom
CDEIMNORU	indecorum
CDEIMNOSU	Nicodemus
CDEINNOTU	continued
	unnoticed
CDEINORST	doctrines
CDEINORTU	introduce
	reduction
CDEINORTV	contrived
CDEINOSTU	seduction
CDEINPPRR	Dr Crippen
CDEINRSTY	stridency
CDEIORRST	directors
CDEIORRTY	directory ❑
CDEIORSSU	discourse
CDEIORSVY	discovery ❑
CDEIOSSTT	Docetists
CDEIPPSTY	dyspeptic
CDEKLOORY	crookedly
CDEKNOORU	undercook
CDEKNOOTU	conked out
CDELLOSSU	cloudless
CDELMNORU	lemon curd
CDELNOOOR	con dolore
CDELNOORT	decontrol
CDELNOORU	undercool
CDELNOOST	stone-cold
CDELNOOSW	close down
CDELNOOTY	cotyledon
CDELNOPUU	uncoupled
CDELNORSU	scoundrel
CDELOORUV	cloud over
	overcloud
CDELORSUU	credulous
CDEMMOOOR	commodore
CDEMNOORU	come round
CDEMNOSTU	documents
CDENNORUW	uncrowned
CDENNOTUU	uncounted
CDENOOPRS	drop-scone
CDENOOPSY	endoscopy
CDENOORTT	contorted
CDENORSSU	uncrossed
CDENPRTUU	punctured
CDEOORRVW	overcrowd
CDEOORSWW	woodscrew
CDEOPRRTU	corrupted
CDEORSTUV	dust cover
CDEORTUUV	curved out
CDFFIILTU	difficult
CDFFNOOOR	cordon off
CDFGHILNO	goldfinch
CDFGIINNO	confiding
CDFGIOOTY	city of God
CDFHINORY	chondrify
CDFIIMOST	discomfit
CDFIIORSU	sudorific
CDFIMMOOY	commodify
CDFKOOTUU	duck out of
CDFLNOORT	cold front
CDFOOORTU	food court
CDGHNOOUW	cough down
CDGHOOPRU	cough drop
	cough-drop
CDGIILNNU	including
CDGIIOTYZ	dizygotic
CDGILLNOU	colluding
CDGILNNOY	condignly
CDGINNNOO	condoning
CDGINOORR	corroding
CDGINOPRU	producing
CDGLNOORW	gold crown
CDGOOSTTU	Doug Scott
CDHHIILTW	with child
CDHHIIOTY	ichthyoid
CDHHILOST	dish-cloth
CDHIIMOPR	dimorphic
CDHIIMORS	dichroism
CDHIIORRS	scirrhoid
CDHIMOOTY	dichotomy
CDHIOOPRY	chiropody
CDHLLOOOS	old school
CDHLOORTU	hold court
CDHMOOOTU	do too much
CDHNOOORT	notochord
CDHNOOTUW	touch down
CDHOOOTUW	touch wood
	touchwood
CDIIINNOT	indiction
CDIIISTVY	viscidity
CDIIJOSUU	judicious
CDIIKNNOS	Dickinson
CDIILPTUY	duplicity
CDIILTTUY	ductility
CDIINNOOT	condition
CDIINNOTU	induction
CDIIOPRST	dioptrics
CDIIPRSTU	tricuspid
CDIJNOTUY	jocundity
CDIKMRSTU	drumstick
CDILOORSU	discolour
CDILORSUU	ludicrous
CDIMMNOOS	discommon
CDIMMOOTY	commodity
CDIMNORSY	syndromic
CDINNOOPU	pound coin
CDINORSSW	crosswind
CDINOSTUY	in custody
CDIOORSSU	Dioscorus

CDKKNNOOW	knock down
	knock-down
CDKKNOOOR	doorknock
CDKKNOOOW	knock wood
CDMNNORUU	conundrum
CDOORRSSW	crossword
CEEEEEHSW	ewe-cheese
CEEEEFNRR	reference
CEEEEGMNR	emergence
CEEEEHMNV	vehemence
CEEEENRRV	reverence
CEEEFFHOS	cheese off
CEEEFFITV	effective
CEEEFFLNU	effluence
CEEEFHLTT	fléchette
CEEEFINNR	inference
CEEEFINPV	five pence
CEEEFLNSS	fenceless
CEEEFNORR	re-enforce
CEEEGIMNS	miscegene
CEEEGINRT	energetic
CEEEGLNOR	conger eel
CEEEGMNRY	emergency
CEEEHIKLL	leechlike
CEEEHILPS	sheep-lice
CEEEHILST	scheelite
CEEEHKNPR	henpecker
CEEEHLRSS	cheerless
CEEEHNRVW	whencever
CEEEHOPRS	ecosphere
	pre-echoes
CEEEHOPST	sheepcote
CEEEHPRST	the creeps
CEEEHQRUX	exchequer
CEEEIIMPT	timepiece
CEEEILLNT	clientele
	clientèle
CEEEILNOP	Pleiocene
CEEEILNST	Celestine
CEEEILPSS	epicleses
CEEEILRST	electrise
	Leicester
CEEEILRTZ	electrize
CEEEILSTV	selective
CEEEIMRRS	mercerise
CEEEIMRRZ	mercerize
CEEEINNPT	penitence
CEEEINNSS	in essence
CEEEINNST	sentience
CEEEINPRT	epicentre
CEEEINRSU	esurience
CEEEINSTX	existence
CEEEIPRTV	receptive
CEEEIRRSX	exerciser
CEEEIRSSV	recessive
CEEEIRSSX	exercises
CEEEIRSTV	secretive
CEEEIRSVV	Vic Reeves
CEEEIRTVX	excretive
CEEEISSVX	excessive
CEEEITUVX	executive
CEEEKORRT	rocketeer
CEEELLNTX	excellent
CEEELNOQU	eloquence
CEEELNOSY	Ceylonese
CEEELOPST	telescope ❑
CEEELORVX	excel over
CEEELPRST	preselect
CEEEMNRTX	excrement
CEEENNORV	reconvene
CEEENNSST	senescent
CEEENNSSU	unessence
CEEENORTT	entrecôte
CEEENRSST	erectness
CEEEORRRV	recoverer
CEEEPRRST	respecter
CEEEPRSTU	persecute
CEEFFFORT	for effect
CEEFFGINT	effecting
CEEFFIINT	efficient
CEEFFILOR	life-force
CEEFFIOOR	o're-office
CEEFFIORS	Escoffier
CEEFFIOSU	coiffeuse
CEEFFNORS	screen off
CEEFFNORT	off-centre
CEEFFOOPT	coffee pot
CEEFGINNR	ring-fence
CEEFGLNTU	genuflect
CEEFHIIST	fetichise
CEEFHIITZ	fetichize
CEEFHIPSY	speechify
CEEFHLNRU	free lunch
CEEFHMNNR	Frenchmen
CEEFIILRT	feliciter
CEEFIINTV	infective
CEEFIIRRT	certifier
	rectifier
CEEFILNNU	influence
CEEFILRTY	electrify
CEEFIMORT	focimeter
CEEFIMPRT	imperfect
CEEFINORR	reinforce
CEEFINORT	refection
CEEFINTTU	fettucine
CEEFIORSV	of service
CEEFLNORT	reflect on
	tenor clef
CEEFLOORS	foreclose
CEEFLORRT	reflector
CEEFLORSS	forceless
CEEFLORSU	fluoresce
CEEFLPRTY	perfectly
CEEFNOOPR	force open
CEEFNQRUY	frequency
CEEFNRSTU	rufescent
CEEFOPRST	perfectos
CEEFOPRTX	except for
CEEFORRTY	refectory
CEEFORSTW	crow's feet
CEEFORSUX	excuse for
CEEGGILRS	egg slicer

CEEGHINOR	re-echoing	CEEHRSSTW	the screws
CEEGHINRW	Greenwich	CEEIIJNOR	rejoice in
CEEGHORRT	The Grocer	CEEIIKLNS	nickelise
CEEGIILPS	spicilege	CEEIIKLNZ	nickelize
CEEGIIMNS	miscegine	CEEIILPPT	epileptic
CEEGIINRV	receiving	CEEIILPSS	epiclesis
CEEGILLNX	excelling	CEEIIMMNN	imminence
CEEGILNOO	Oligocene	CEEIIMNRS	reminisce
CEEGILNRY	glycerine	CEEIIMPRS	imprecise
CEEGIMNNT	cementing	CEEIIMRST	metricise
CEEGIMNOS	see coming	CEEIIMRTZ	metricize
CEEGIMORT	geometric	CEEIINNRS	insincere
CEEGINNOS	consignee	CEEIINNTV	incentive
CEEGINNRS	screening	CEEIINPRT	recipient
CEEGINORS	congeries	CEEIINPTV	inceptive
	recognise	CEEIINRST	cretinise
CEEGINORZ	recognize	CEEIINRSV	in service
CEEGINPTX	excepting		in-service
	expecting	CEEIINRTZ	cretinize
CEEGIORRS	groceries	CEEIINSST	scientise
CEEGLMNRY	clergymen	CEEIINSTZ	scientize
CEEGORTTU	courgette	CEEIINTVV	invective
CEEHHIRVW	whichever	CEEIIOPST	poeticise
CEEHIILNP	Chile pine	CEEIIOPTZ	poeticize
CEEHIILRU	Richelieu	CEEIIORRT	écritoire
CEEHIIPTT	epithetic	CEEIIORST	eroticise
CEEHIKNRT	Kitchener	CEEIIORTZ	eroticize
CEEHIKRST	shit creek	CEEIIPRSS	Persicise
CEEHILMNY	Michel Ney	CEEIIPRSU	epicurise
CEEHIMRST	hermetics	CEEIIPRSZ	Persicize
CEEHIMRSW	shrewmice	CEEIIPRUZ	epicurize
CEEHINPST	phenetics	CEEIJLSSU	juiceless
CEEHINPSU	euphenics	CEEIJNORT	rejection
CEEHINQTU	technique	CEEIJNRTT	interject
CEEHINRTT	threnetic	CEEIJRRRY	Jerry Rice
CEEHINRVY	every inch	CEEIKNQRU	quickener
CEEHINSTZ	Nietzsche		requicken
CEEHINSUU	eunuchise	CEEIKOPRW	workpiece
CEEHINUUZ	eunuchize	CEEILLLTU	cellulite
CEEHIOPSW	showpiece	CEEILLNOR	Corneille
CEEHIORSS	co-heiress	CEEILLNPR	penciller
CEEHIORTT	theoretic	CEEILLNTT	intellect
CEEHIRRST	Streicher	CEEILMNNT	inclement
CEEHJLNOO	Joel Cohen	CEEILMNPR	Crimplene®
CEEHKNNOR	Chernenko	CEEILMNSU	luminesce
CEEHKNORV	Cherenkov	CEEILMRSS	merciless
CEEHLLNOP	cellphone	CEEILNNOS	insolence
CEEHLLNOV	Loch Leven	CEEILNORT	centriole
CEEHLORSU	lecherous	CEEILNOST	selection
CEEHLORTV	Chevrolet	CEEILNOTT	Nicolette
CEEHLPRSU	sepulchre	CEEILNPST	splenetic
CEEHLQRSU	squelcher	CEEILNRSY	sincerely
CEEHLRWYY	Wycherley	CEEILNRTV	ventricle
CEEHMNORZ	chernozem	CEEILNRUV	virulence
CEEHMRSTW	screw them	CEEILOPTU	poeticule
CEEHNOPRR	Percheron	CEEILORSX	excelsior
CEEHOORTT	to the core	CEEILOSSS	isosceles
CEEHOPRRV	overperch	CEEILOSSV	voiceless
CEEHORRST	Rochester	CEEILPRSS	priceless
CEEHORRTU	retoucher	CEEILPRSY	precisely
CEEHRRSTT	stretcher	CEEILRSUV	reclusive

CEEILSSTT	testicles
CEEILSUVX	exclusive
CEEIMMNSU	ecumenism
CEEIMMOTT	committee
CEEIMNNRT	increment
CEEIMNOOS	economise
CEEIMNOOZ	economize
CEEIMNOPT	impotence
CEEIMNOST	centesimo
CEEIMNOWX	New Mexico
CEEIMNSTU	intumesce
CEEIMRRSU	mercurise
CEEIMRRUZ	mercurize
CEEINNORS	recension
CEEINOPRS	pericones
	preconise
CEEINOPRT	creep into
	reception
CEEINOPRZ	preconize
CEEINOPTX	exception
CEEINORRS	encierros
CEEINORSS	recession
CEEINORST	necrotise
	resection
	secretion
CEEINORTX	excretion
CEEINORTZ	necrotize
CEEINOSSS	secession
CEEINOSSY	synoecise
CEEINOSYZ	synoecize
CEEINOTUX	execution
CEEINPRRU	prurience
CEEINPRST	prescient
CEEINPRTT	intercept
CEEINQRTU	quercetin
CEEINQSTU	quiescent
CEEINRRSV	scrivener
CEEINRSTT	intersect
CEEINRSTV	virescent
CEEINRSUY	esuriency
CEEINSSTY	necessity
CEEIOORVV	voice-over
CEEIOPPRS	periscope
CEEIOPRRV	overprice
CEEIORRST	corsetier
CEEIORSST	sectorise
CEEIORSSU	sericeous
CEEIORSTV	vectorise
CEEIORSTZ	sectorize
CEEIORTVW	twice over
CEEIORTVZ	vectorize
CEEIRRRTU	recruiter
CEEIRRSUV	recursive
CEEIRSUVX	excursive
CEEIRTUXX	executrix
CEEJORRTT	retroject
CEEKLPSSS	speckless
CEEKOOPRT	Peter Cook
CEELLLOSU	cellulose
CEELLMNTY	clemently
CEELLRSUY	reclusely

CEELMNOUW	unwelcome
CEELNOORT	contrôlée
CEELNORSU	enclosure
CEELNOSSS	closeness
CEELNPRUU	purulence
CEELORSSS	scleroses
CEELORSSV	coverless
CEELOSTTU	select out
CEEMMNORT	commenter
CEEMNOPRT	contemper
CEEMNOPTT	competent
CEEMNSTTU	tumescent
CEEMOORSS	Morescoes
CEEMOSSTY	ecosystem
CEENNORRU	renouncer
CEENNORTU	encounter ❑
CEENNRSSU	sunscreen
CEENOORSV	e converso
CEENOORTV	cover note
CEENOPRRT	precentor
CEENOPSTT	Pentecost
CEENOPTTX	not expect
CEENORRTU	recounter
CEENORRTV	converter
	reconvert
CEENORSTT	contester
CEENORSTW	sweetcorn
CEENRRRTU	recurrent
CEEOORRSV	overscore
CEEOPPRRT	preceptor
CEEOPRRSS	reprocess
CEEOPRRTX	excerptor
CEEOPRSTT	top secret
	top-secret
CEEOPRSTU	prosecute
CEEOQRTTU	croquette
CEEORRSSS	sorceress
CEEORRSSU	recourses
	resources
CEEORRSTW	Worcester
CEEORRSTY	secretory
CEEORRSUV	verrucose
CEEORRTXY	excretory
CEEORTUXY	executory
CEEPRRRRU	precurrer
CEEPRRSSU	repercuss
CEERRRSTU	resurrect
CEFFHINRY	Frenchify
CEFFHNRRY	French fry
CEFFIINOT	coffinite
CEFFIIOOX	ex officio
CEFFIKNPS	Pecksniff
CEFFILSTU	Sutcliffe
CEFFIMOOT	come off it!
CEFFOORSU	off course
	off-course
CEFGINORU	configure
CEFHIILSS	fish slice
CEFHIIOTT	fiochetti
CEFHMOORT	come forth
	forthcome

CEFHOORSU	corfhouse	CEGILOOST	ecologist
CEFIIKNTY	finickety	CEGILORRV	cover girl
CEFIIKQRU	quick-fire	CEGIMNOOR	ergonomic
CEFIILNPV	pelvic fin	CEGIMNOPT	competing
CEFIILNRT	inflicter	CEGIMNOUY	gynoecium
CEFIINNOT	infection	CEGINNOOT	ontogenic
CEFIINTTU	cut it fine	CEGINNORS	consigner
	fettucini	CEGINOOPS	geoponics
CEFIKNORS	sicken for	CEGINOPRU	recouping
CEFIMNOOR	come in for	CEGINOPRY	pyrogenic
CEFIMNORU	cuneiform	CEGINOPTY	genotypic
CEFIMORST	come first	CEGINORSV	coverings
CEFIMORTT	tectiform	CEGINOSST	cosseting
CEFINNNOU	unconfine	CEGINRRRU	recurring
CEFINORTU	confiture	CEGIOOPRT	geotropic
CEFIOORSU	ferocious	CEGMNNOOS	cognomens
CEFIOOSTV	soft voice	CEGNNORTU	congruent
CEFIORRSS	crossfire	CEGNORRSU	scrounger
CEFIORSST	frescoist	CEGOOPRSY	gyroscope
CEFKLOPTU	pocketful	CEHHHIIKT	hitch-hike
CEFKOORRW	workforce	CEHHIMOST	shochetim
CEFLNNOTU	confluent	CEHHIMSTT	hem-stitch
CEFLNOSTY	confestly	CEHHLOOTU	touch-hole
CEFMNOORR	conformer	CEHIIKLRS	lickerish
CEFMOOOTU	come out of	CEHIIKLTW	witchlike
CEFNOORSS	confessor	CEHIIKTTW	hit wicket
CEFNOOSST	confess to	CEHIILMOT	homiletic
CEFOOPSTY	fetoscopy	CEHIILNOT	neolithic ❑
CEFOORRTU	forecourt	CEHIIMSTY	mythicise
CEFOORSTV	soft-cover	CEHIIMTYZ	mythicize
CEGGIOORR	Correggio	CEHIINNOT	on thin ice
CEGHIINNR	enriching	CEHIINPPT	pitchpine
CEGHIINSY	hygienics	CEHIINPRT	nephritic
CEGHIIOST	gothicise	CEHIINRST	Christine
CEGHIIOTZ	gothicize	CEHIINSST	itchiness
CEGHIKNST	sketching	CEHIINTTY	ethnicity
CEGHILLNS	Schelling	CEHIINTWZ	zinc white
CEGHILLOU	guilloche	CEHIIRSTU	heuristic
CEGHILMTU	gemütlich	CEHIKLPRS	clerkship
CEGHILNTV	vetchling	CEHIKLSTY	sketchily
CEGHINNQU	quenching	CEHIKNSST	thickness
CEGHINNRW	wrenching	CEHIKORTW	work ethic
CEGHINOOT	Neo-Gothic	CEHIKPRSW	shipwreck
	neo-gothic	CEHIKSSTT	the sticks
CEGHKNORU	roughneck	CEHILLNOS	ill-chosen
CEGHLOOUY	euchology	CEHILMNOS	Michelson
CEGIIILNT	eliciting	CEHILMNTU	lunchtime
CEGIIJNOR	rejoicing	CEHILMOOS	molochise
CEGIIKNNS	sickening	CEHILMOOZ	molochize
CEGIILNNR	reclining	CEHILNNPU	punchline
CEGIILNNS	silencing	CEHILNOTU	touchline
CEGIINOTV	cognitive	CEHILNSTZ	schnitzel
CEGIINRSV	servicing	CEHILOPPT	pitch-pole
CEGIIOSTT	egotistic	CEHILORTW	wire cloth
CEGIKNNOR	reckoning	CEHILOSTW	close with
CEGIKNOPT	pocketing	CEHIMMOPR	morphemic
CEGIKNORT	rocketing	CEHIMMORS	micromesh
CEGILMMNO	commingle	CEHIMNNOU	ichneumon
CEGILMNOW	welcoming	CEHIMNOPS	phonemics
CEGILNNOS	enclosing	CEHIMRSTY	chemistry
CEGILNRSU	surcingle	CEHINOPST	phonetics

CEHINPRST	sphincter
CEHINSTTY	synthetic
CEHIOPPRT	prophetic
CEHIOPRTT	prothetic
CEHIOPRTU	eutrophic
	Petruchio
CEHIOPRTV	overpitch
CEHIOPRTY	hypocrite
CEHIORRST	chorister
CEHIORSUV	ECHO virus
	echo virus
CEHIORTVW	cover with
CEHIOSSST	schistose
CEHIRSSTY	hysterics
CEHIRSTTY	stitchery
CEHITTTWY	witchetty
CEHJKLNOO	John Locke
CEHKLNORS	schnorkel
CEHKOSTTU	sketch out
CEHLLORUY	holy-cruel
CEHLMNOUU	homuncule
CEHLNOSZZ	schnozzle
CEHLOOPRS	preschool
CEHLOOPSS	Sophocles
CEHMMNOOT	the common
CEHMNOPRS	McPherson
CEHMOOPRT	ectomorph
CEHMOORST	come short
CEHMORSWY	show mercy
CEHNNORTU	truncheon
CEHNORRRS	schnorrer
CEHOOOPRS	horoscope
CEHOORSTU	court shoe
	court-shoe
CEHOPSSSY	psychoses
CEHOPTTUY	touch-type
CEIIILMNS	Miliciens
CEIIIMSTV	victimise
CEIIIMTVZ	victimize
CEIIINNPT	incipient
CEIIIPSTT	pietistic
CEIIJNNOT	injection
CEIIJNSSU	juiciness
CEIIJNSTU	injustice
CEIIKLRTY	ricketily
CEIIKMQTU	quick time
CEIIKNPRT	nit-picker
CEIIKNRST	Rick Stein
CEIIKRSTU	Turkicise
CEIIKRTUZ	Turkicize
CEIILLMNT	Millicent
CEIILMOSV	Milosevic
CEIILMPSS	simplices
CEIILNNOR	crinoline
CEIILNPPR	principle
CEIILNSUV	inclusive
CEIILOQRU	liquorice
CEIILOSSU	siliceous
CEIILPRST	price list
CEIILPRTU	pleuritic
CEIILSTUV	Leviticus

CEIIMNOST	semitonic
CEIIMNOVY	in my voice
CEIIMNRST	cretinism
CEIIMNSST	scientism
CEIIMOPST	impeticos
CEIIMORST	eroticism
	isometric
CEIIMOSST	semiotics
CEIIMOSTX	exoticism
CEIIMPRSU	epicurism
CEIINNOPT	inception
CEIINNOTV	Vincentio
CEIINNOTW	tonic wine
CEIINNRTY	inner city
	inner-city
CEIINOPRS	precision
CEIINORRT	criterion
CEIINPRTU	unit price
CEIINPSSS	spiciness
CEIINRSTX	extrinsic
CEIINRSTY	sincerity
CEIINRSUV	incursive
CEIINRTTY	intercity
CEIINRTYZ	citizenry
CEIINSSTT	scientist
CEIIOOPTZ	epizootic
CEIIORSTU	triecious
CEIIPSTTY	septicity
CEIIRSSTU	rusticise
CEIIRSTUZ	rusticize
CEIJKMOSY	jockeyism
CEIJKNOST	Jock Stein
CEIJNORTT	introject
CEIKLNORT	interlock
CEIKLNOST	close-knit
CEIKLNSSS	slickness
CEIKLOPST	stockpile
CEIKLOSTV	livestock
CEIKMNORS	misreckon
CEIKMNSSU	muckiness
CEIKMORST	tricksome
CEIKMPSTU	stick 'em up!
CEIKNORSS	corkiness
	rockiness
CEIKNQSSU	quickness
CEIKOPRRT	rock tripe
CEIKPPRSU	pick-purse
CEIKPQSTU	quickstep
CEIKPRSTW	Prestwick
CEIKRRSTT	trickster
CEILLOPPT	pole-clipt
CEILLOSUV	collusive
CEILLPSTY	sylleptic
CEILMNNOO	monocline
CEILMNOOS	semicolon
CEILMNSUU	minuscule
CEILMOPRY	micropyle
CEILMRTUU	reticulum
CEILNNOOP	encolpion
CEILNNOOS	cloisonné
	close in on

CEILNOORZ	colonizer
CEILNOOTU	elocution
CEILNORST	sclerotin
CEILNORSU	Cornelius
	inclosure
	reclusion
CEILNORUV	involucre
	volucrine
CEILNOSSU	seclusion
CEILNOSUX	exclusion
CEILNRSSU	curliness
CEILNSSTU	linctuses
CEILOOPRT	coprolite
CEILOORSU	colourise
CEILOORUZ	colourize
CEILOPPRT	proleptic
CEILORSSS	sclerosis
CEILORSST	cloisters
CEILOSTVY	costively
CEILRSTUU	Lucretius
CEILRSUVY	cursively
CEIMMNOOR	monomeric
CEIMMNOSU	communise
	encomiums
CEIMMNOTU	comminute
CEIMMNOTY	metonymic
CEIMMNOUZ	communize
CEIMMOORT	microtome
CEIMNNOOY	coin money
CEIMNNORS	encrimson
CEIMNOOST	economist
CEIMNOOTU	come out in
CEIMOOPST	composite
CEIMOORSS	Moriscoes
CEIMOPRST	prime cost
CEIMORSTU	costumier
	Tom Cruise
CEIMOSSTU	customise
CEIMOSTUV	muscovite❑
CEIMOSTUZ	customize
CEINNNOOX	connexion
CEINNNOTT	continent
CEINNOOTT	not notice
CEINNOPRT	Princeton
CEINNORSS	corniness
CEINNORTU	centurion
CEINNPRUW	cup-winner
CEINOORST	cortisone
CEINOORTV	cover into
CEINOPPRU	porcupine
CEINOPRRS	conspirer
CEINOPRRT	intercrop
CEINOPRST	inspector
CEINOPRSV	provinces
CEINOPSST	Scots pine
CEINORRSU	recursion
CEINORRTV	contriver
CEINORRTW	town crier
CEINORSTT	cornetist
CEINORSTU	countries
	cretinous
CEINORSUX	excursion
CEINOTVXY	convexity
CEINPRSSS	crispness
CEIOOPRST	porticoes
CEIOORRSV	corrosive
CEIORRSTT	tortrices
	trisector
CEIORRSTU	scrutoire
CEIORRSUZ	cruzeiros
CEIORRTUU	couturier
CEIORSSSW	crosswise
CEIPPRRST	prescript
CEIPRRSTU	scripture❑
CEIRRSTTU	stricture
CEJKOOTUY	outjockey
CEJNOPRUU	conjure up
CEJOOPRRT	projector
CEKKNOORV	knock over
CEKKNOPRU	knocker-up
CEKKORSTY	skyrocket
	sky-rocket
CEKLNORTW	town clerk
CEKLORSUW	worse luck
CELLMOORY	Collymore
CELLMOPXY	complexly
CELLMSTUU	scutellum
CELLNOSUU	nucleolus
CELLOOPTY	collotype
CELMNOSUU	lucumones
CELMNOTUY	contumely
CELMOOSSU	colosseum
CELMOOTUY	leucotomy
CELMOPRUU	operculum
CELMPRSTU	plectrums
CELNOOTUV	convolute
CELNOPRST	plectrons
CELNOPRTU	corpulent
CELNOSSTU	countless
CELNRRTUY	currently
CELNRTTUU	truculent
CELNTTTUU	nut cutlet
CELOOPRSU	supercool
CELOOPSTU	close up to
CELORRSUU	soul-curer
CELPRSTUU	sculpture
CELPRTTUU	clutter up
CEMMNNOOT	comment on
	no comment
CEMMNOORS	commoners
CEMNNOOPT	component
CEMNOOOQU	monocoque
CEMNOOORS	Monoceros
CEMNORSSU	consumers
CEMNORSUY	mercy on us
CEMOOOTUY	come to you
CEMOOPRSU	composure
CEMORRSUU	mercurous
CEMORSSTU	customers
CENNNORSU	Cernunnos
CENNOOPPY	opponency
CENNOOPRU	pronounce

CENNOOSTT	consent to
CENNORSTU	Nocturnes
CENNOSSSU	consensus
CENOOPRST	stonecrop
CENOOPRTU	open court
CENOOQRRU	conqueror
CENOORRTV	convertor
CENOORTUV	overcount
CENORSSSS	crossness
CENORSSTW	crow's nest
CEOOOSTTV	sotto voce
CEOOPRRSS	processor
CEOOPRRTT	protector
CEOOPSSTU	octopuses
CEOORRSSU	sorcerous
CEOORSTUU	courteous
	outsource
CEOPPRSST	prospects
CEOPRRRSU	precursor
CEOPRRRTU	corrupter
CEOPRRSSU	procuress
CEORRSUUV	verrucous
CERRSTTUU	structure
CERSSTTUU	suetcrust
CFFHIOSTW	switch off
CFFIIOOSU	officious
CFFKORSTU	struck off
CFFLOOORU	off colour
	off-colour
CFFMORSTU	storm cuff
CFFOOSSTU	soft focus
CFGIILLMN	clingfilm
CFGIINNNO	confining
CFGINNOSU	confusing
CFHIINOOR	honorific
CFHIKOPRT	pitchfork
CFHIKOSST	stockfish
CFHLOPSUU	pouchfuls
CFHMOORSU	so much for
CFHOOSTTU	soft touch
CFIIIMNOU	Fiumicino
CFIILMMOR	microfilm
CFIILNORT	inflictor
CFIILORST	floristic
CFIIOOPRS	soporific
CFIKLLNOT	flintlock
CFIKLLOOR	folkloric
CFIKLMOSU	folk music
CFILLNRUY	in full cry
CFIMORRUV	curviform
CFINNOOSU	confusion
CFINOOSST	consist of
CFIOOPRRY	corporify
CFKLOOTUU	out of luck
CFLLOORUU	colourful
CFLNOORRU	cornflour
CFLOOOSTT	coltsfoot
CFLOOPSSU	scoopfuls
CFLOORTUU	out of curl
CFMNOOORT	conform to
CFNOOSTUY	out of sync
CFOOORSTW	crow's foot
CFOORRTUY	cry out for
CFOORTTUU	cut out for
CFORSTUUU	fructuous
CGGHIKNNU	Chungking
CGGHINNOQ	Chongqing
CGGINORSU	scourging
CGHHIORTU	High Court
	high court
CGHIILLNS	schilling
CGHIILNST	chitlings
CGHIILORR	choirgirl
CGHIINSTT	stitching
CGHIINSTW	switching
CGHIINTTW	twitching
CGHILNOOS	schooling
CGHILNORT	chortling
CGHILNOSU	slouching
CGHILOOOR	horologic
CGHILORUY	grouchily
CGHINORTW	night-crow
CGHIOPRTY	copyright
CGHKLOTUU	tough luck
CGHLOOPYY	phycology
CGIIIKMMN	mimicking
CGIIILNNN	inclining
CGIIKLNNR	crinkling
CGIIKLNPR	prickling
CGIIKMMRY	gimmickry
CGIIKNNTU	tucking-in
CGIILNPPR	crippling
CGIILOSST	logistics
CGIIMNPRS	scrimping
CGIINNNOV	conniving
CGIINNOOT	cognition
	incognito
CGIINNTTU	cutting-in
CGIJNNORU	conjuring
CGIKLMNOY	mockingly
CGIKLNRTU	truckling
CGIKLOQUY	go quickly
CGIKNOPRS	prick-song
CGIKNOSST	stockings
CGIKOOPST	pogo stick
CGILLNORS	scrolling
CGILMNOOY	cynomolgi
CGILMNOPY	complying
CGILNNNUY	cunningly
CGILNNOOS	consoling
CGILNOOOT	ontologic
CGILNOOOY	iconology
CGILNOORU	colouring
CGILNOPUV	loving-cup
CGILOOOSY	sociology
CGIMMNNOU	communing
CGIMNNOSU	consuming
CGIMNOOTU	coming out
	coming-out
CGINNOORS	consignor
CGINNORTU	trouncing
CGINNRUUV	uncurving

CGINORSSU	scourings
CGINORTUY	congruity
CGINPTTUU	cutting up
CGKNOOOOR	go crook on
CGLMOOOSY	cosmology
CGMNOOOSY	cosmogony
CGNOORSUU	congruous
CGOOORTTU	go to court
CHHHIIMNO	Ho Chi Minh
CHHIIKTTW	thick with
CHHINTTUW	witch hunt
CHHKLLOOY	hollyhock
CHIIILPPP	philippic
CHIIKLPST	thick-lips
CHIIKLSSY	sickishly
CHIIKLSTY	kitschily
CHIIKSTTW	stick with
CHIILLOPY	lyophilic
CHIILMORT	microlith
CHIILORTY	rhyolitic
CHIILPTTY	typhlitic
CHIIMNOST	Mitchison
CHIIMPSSY	physicism
CHIIMSTTY	mythicist
CHIINOPTT	pitch into
CHIINOSTU	chitinous
CHIIOPSST	sophistic
CHIIORRSS	cirrhosis
CHIIORSST	trichosis
CHIIPSSTY	physicist
CHIIRSSTT	strictish
	tristichs
CHIKLMOST	locksmith
CHIKOOPTT	toothpick
CHIKOPSTW	whipstock
CHILLNOOT	loincloth
CHILLOPPT	pitch-poll
CHILMNOUU	homunculi
CHILNNOOS	Nicholson
CHILNOPSU	sulphonic
CHILPRSUU	sulphuric
CHILRRSUY	currishly
CHIMNOORY	chironomy
CHIMNOPSY	symphonic
CHINOOPTY	hypotonic
CHIOOPRTT	orthoptic
CHIOORSTT	orthotics
CHIOPRSTU	courtship
CHIOPRSYY	hypocrisy
CHIOPSSSY	psychosis
CHIORRSSU	scirrhous
CHJNORRUY	John Curry
CHKLMOOST	Stockholm
CHKLNOORS	lock horns
CHLNOTUUY	uncouthly
CHLOPPTYY	polyptych
CHMNOOSTU	not so much
CHNNORSYY	synchrony
CHNOOPTUU	touch upon
CHOOOPPTY	photocopy
CHOOOPRSY	horoscopy
CIIILLLTY	illicitly
CIIILLSTV	civil list
CIIILMOPT	impolitic
CIIILORTV	vitriolic
CIIILOSSS	silicosis
CIIILOSSU	silicious
CIIIMSTTW	witticism
CIIINNRST	intrinsic
CIIKNNOTY	cytokinin
CIIKNOSTT	stick into
CIIKOSTTT	stick it to
CIILLNOOS	collision
CIILLNOOT	octillion
CIILLNUVY	uncivilly
CIILLOPTY	politicly
CIILMPRSY	scrimpily
CIILNNOSU	inclusion
CIILNOPTU	punctilio
CIILOOPST	politicos
CIILOORST	solicitor
CIILOOSSS	scoliosis
CIILOSUVY	viciously
CIILSSTTY	stylistic
CIIMMSSTY	mysticism
CIIMNORUZ	zirconium
CIIMORSTV	vorticism □
CIIMRSSTU	rusticism
CIINNNOTU	inunction
CIINNORSU	incursion
CIINNOSST	consist in
CIINNOSSW	Wisconsin
CIINOPSSU	suspicion
CIINORSUU	incurious
CIINPSSTU	sinciputs
CIIOOPRST	isotropic
CIIORSTTU	touristic
CIIORSTTV	vorticist
CIIORSTUY	curiosity
CIIOSSTVY	viscosity
CIIOSTUXY	Sioux City
CIIRSTTUY	rusticity
CIJKOSSST	joss-stick
CIJNNOTTU	T-junction
CIKKLOOQU	quick look
CIKLLNUUY	unluckily
CILLNOOSU	collusion
CILLOOOST	ocotillos
CILMNOSTU	columnist
CILMOORSU	miscolour
CILMOSSUU	soul music
CILNNOORT	in control
CILNOORUU	unicolour
CILOOPSUY	copiously
CILOORRTU	tricolour □
CILOORSTU	colourist
CILORRSUY	cursorily
CILORSUUY	curiously
CILOSSSTT	list costs
CIMMMNOSU	communism
CIMMNNOOU	communion □
CIMMNOOOT	commotion

Words marked □ can also be spelled with an initial capital letter

CIMMNOSTU	communist
CIMMNOTUY	community
CIMNNOTUU	continuum
CIMNOOPTY	toponymic
CIMNOOTXY	mycotoxin
CIMORSUXY	Roxy Music
CINNOORST	in consort
CINNOOSTU	continuos
	contusion
CINNOOSUU	innocuous
CINOOORRS	corrosion
CINOOTTXY	cytotoxin
CINOPRRTU	incorrupt
CINOSTUVY	viscounty
CIOOPPRSU	Procopius
CIOOPSSTU	posticous
CKLLNOORR	rock 'n' roll
CKMNOOOTU	Mount Cook
CKMOOORST	stockroom
CKNOOPSTU	stock up on
CKOOORSTT	rootstock
CKOOPRSTT	Stockport
CLMOOOORT	locomotor
CLMOOOSTY	colostomy
CLMOORSTU	colostrum
CLNOOPRSU	proconsul
CLNOOSUUY	nocuously
CLOPRRTUY	corruptly
CMMNOOORS	Roscommon
CMOOORRTU	courtroom
CMOOORSST	motocross
CNNOOORST	contornos
CNNOOPTUU	count upon
CNOOOPRSS	cosponsor
CNOPRRTUU	uncorrupt
CNOPRTUUY	up-country

D

DDDEEINST	distended
DDDEEISTU	Deusdedit
DDDEENORS	reddendos
DDDEGINOR	doddering
DDDEIILVY	dividedly
DDDEIINUV	undivided
DDEEEFILP	deep field
DDEEEFNRU	underfeed
DDEEEGIPR	pedigreed
DDEEEILTT	title deed
DDEEELOPV	developed
DDEEENNOP	open-ended
DDEEENNPT	dependent
DDEEENOPT	deep-toned
DDEEENPRT	pretended
DDEEEPRSS	depressed
DDEEERTTX	Ted Dexter
DDEEESTUU	desuetude
DDEEFGINN	defending
DDEEFGLNU	unfledged
DDEEFGNOR	Fredegond
DDEEFIIMY	demi-deify
DDEEFILNU	undefiled
DDEEFINNU	undefined
DDEEFINOP	dope-fiend
DDEEFNNOR	end for end
DDEEFNORU	foundered
DDEEGGILT	gilt-edged
DDEEGHILT	delighted
DDEEGINNR	reddening
DDEEGLOOT	edged tool
DDEEHINNR	hinder end
DDEEIILMT	delimited
DDEEIINRV	I never did!
DDEEIIOSX	deoxidise
DDEEIIOXZ	deoxidize
DDEEIIPPT	dipeptide
DDEEILLRS	seed drill
DDEEILRSV	Red devils
DDEEIMMNO	demi-monde
DDEEIMNPU	unimpeded
DDEEINOPS	dispondee
DDEEINORW	eiderdown
DDEEINRSS	dressed in
DDEEINRSU	underside
	undesired
DDEEIOORS	deodorise
DDEEIOORZ	deodorize
DDEEIPRRS	red spider
DDEEIPRSS	dispersed
DDEEIRSSS	side-dress
DDEELOTVY	devotedly
DDEENNORU	underdone
DDEENORTU	outredden
DDEENPSSU	suspended
DDEENRSSU	undressed
DDEEOOTTV	devoted to
DDEEORSTY	destroyed
DDEFFIINT	diffident
DDEFFIIOV	divide off
DDEFGIIIN	dignified
DDEFGILLO	goldfield
DDEFILOOT	floodtide
DDEFLNORU	fold under
DDEFNNOUU	unfounded
DDEFNNRUU	underfund
DDEGIIMSU	misguided
DDEGIINSS	giddiness
DDEGIISSU	disguised
DDEGIJLLU	ill-judged
DDEGIJMSU	misjudged
DDEGIJNRU	juddering
DDEGIKMNO	kingdomed
DDEGINNOT	Eddington
DDEGINRRU	undergird
DDEGIORRU	Ruddigore
DDEGISSTU	disgusted
DDEGLNOOR	goldenrod
DDEGNOVWY	down-gyved
DDEHHNRTU	hundredth
DDEHIIRSY	yiddisher ❑
DDEHIORXY	hydroxide
DDEHLOOST	the old sod
DDEIIJNOS	disjoined

DDEIIKRSV	disk drive
DDEIILLST	distilled
DDEIILLSU	disillude
DDEIIMSSS	dismissed
DDEIIMTTW	dimwitted
	dim-witted
DDEIINSST	dissident
DDEIINSTU	disunited
DDEIIOTUV	divide out
DDEILMNOT	Middleton
DDEILMNOW	low-minded
DDEILNRRU	unriddler
DDEILNTUU	undiluted
DDEILORWW	worldwide
DDEILSTUV	dust-devil
DDEILSTUY	studiedly
DDEIMNOPU	impounded
DDEIMNSSU	muddiness
DDEINOSSW	dowdiness
DDEINRSSU	dissunder
	ruddiness
DDEINSTUU	unstudied
DDEIOPPRU	proud-pied
DDEIORSTT	distorted
DDEIPRSTU	disrupted
DDELOORTT	odd-lotter
DDEMNNOOS	Edmondson
DDENNOOTW	toned down
DDENNORTU	untrodden
DDENNORUU	unrounded
DDENNOSUU	unsounded
DDENOOOTU	odd one out
DDENOORSW	do wonders
DDENOORUW	underwood❑
DDENOPRUU	rounded up
DDENORSSW	dress down
DDEOORRRW	word order
DDFGILORU	Guildford
DDFIOORTW	driftwood
DDFOORTUY	do duty for
DDGIILNNW	dwindling
DDGIILNTW	twiddling
DDGILNNOY	noddingly
DDGINNORW	grind down
DDGINNOWY	dying-down
DDHIOOOWW	widowhood
DDHOOOUWY	how-d'you-do
DDIIKKNWY	kiddywink
DDIMNOOUY	do you mind?
DDIORRTWY	dirty word
DEEEEFHST	sheet-feed
DEEEEGNRY	green-eyed
DEEEEHPRT	three deep
DEEEEKNRW	weekender
DEEEENSTW	sweetened
DEEEFGIKN	knife-edge
DEEEFHRRS	refreshed
DEEEFINSV	defensive
DEEEFMNOR	enfreedom
DEEEFMNRT	deferment
	fermented
DEEEFPRRR	preferred
DEEEFRRYZ	freeze-dry
DEEEGGHIR	Heidegger
DEEEGHNOT	on the edge
DEEEGIMNR	redeeming
DEEEGINNP	deepening
DEEEGINRS	seeing red
DEEEGISWW	wedgewise
DEEEGLNOY	GoldenEye
	golden-eye
DEEEGNOST	set on edge
DEEEGNRTT	detergent
DEEEHILLW	idle wheel
DEEEHILPS	ephelides
DEEEHINPR	ephedrine
DEEEHISTT	diet sheet
DEEEHLRST	sheltered
DEEEHNPRR	reprehend
DEEEHNRRU	hereunder
DEEEIILSS	dieselise
DEEEIILSZ	dieselize
DEEEILLMP	millepede
DEEEILNRT	tree-lined
DEEEILRRV	deliverer
	redeliver
DEEEILSSW	edelweiss
DEEEIMNRT	determine
DEEEIMSST	disesteem
DEEEINNNZ	endenizen
DEEEINNSS	neediness
DEEEINPTX	expedient
DEEEINQTU	quietened
DEEEINRRS	reindeers
DEEEINRST	teredines
DEEEINSSS	seediness
DEEEINSSW	weediness
DEEEKNPRU	keep under
DEEELLPSW	speedwell
DEEELNOPV	enveloped
DEEELOPRV	developer
DEEELPPRX	perplexed
DEEELRRTT	red-letter
DEEEMNNOV	envenomed
DEEEMNOSY	seed money
DEEEMNRTT	determent
DEEEMOPRT	pedometer
DEEEMORSU	mouse-deer
DEEEMPRST	destemper
DEEENNRUW	unrenewed
DEEENNSSS	denseness
DEEENPPRU	underpeep
DEEENPRRT	pretender
DEEENPRST	presented
DEEENRRTT	deterrent
DEEENRSUV	undeserve
DEEEOPRRS	pedereros
DEEEORRST	ore-rested
DEEEORSTV	stevedore
DEEEPPPRR	Red Pepper
	red pepper
DEEEPRRSS	repressed

DEEEPRRSV preserved
DEEEPRRTV perverted
DEEEPRSSU supersede
DEEEPRSSX expressed
DEEEQRSTU requested
DEEFFHILS Sheffield
DEEFFHLOU heedful of
DEEFFINRT different
DEEFGIIRS Siegfried
DEEFGILNY feignedly
DEEFGILRS Selfridge
DEEFGINNU unfeigned
DEEFGJORU forejudge
DEEFHINRT The Friend
DEEFHLLUY heedfully
DEEFHLORT threefold
DEEFHLORY Fred Hoyle
DEEFIILNR infielder
DEEFIILQU liquefied
DEEFIILSZ life-sized
DEEFIIPRT petrified
DEEFIIRRT terrified
DEEFIISST dies festi
DEEFILNRY refinedly
DEEFILPRS self-pride
DEEFILPXY fix deeply
DEEFILRSV self-drive
DEEFINNPR pen-friend
DEEFINNRU unrefined
DEEFINRRU underfire
DEEFINSST fetidness
DEEFINSSX fixedness
DEEFIOPRV deprive of
DEEFIORRT torrefied
DEEFIPRRV perfervid
DEEFIPRTU putrefied
DEEFIPSTU stupefied
DEEFIRSTU surfeited
DEEFJKNNY J F Kennedy
DEEFKKLRW F W De Klerk
F W de Klerk
DEEFLLNNU funnelled
DEEFLLNUY needfully
DEEFLLPSU full-speed
DEEFLNOSV sevenfold
DEEFLNRTU underfelt
DEEFLOOTW Fleetwood
DEEFLRSTU flustered
DEEFMOPRR performed
DEEFNOOPS spoon-feed
DEEFNOPRS forespend
DEEFNOSTU fondue set
DEEFOPRSS professed
DEEFORRST defroster
DEEFPRRRY Fred Perry
DEEGGIRSU ruggedise
DEEGGIRUZ ruggedize
DEEGGSSTU suggested
DEEGHHIPS high-speed
DEEGHHSTU Ted Hughes
DEEGHILNW wheedling
DEEGHINNU unheeding
DEEGHINTT tightened
DEEGHINUW unweighed
DEEGHIPUW weighed-up
DEEGHNOTU toughened
DEEGHORTW Edgeworth
DEEGIILNU guideline
DEEGIILNV inveigled
DEEGIILRT ridge-tile
DEEGIISTV digestive
DEEGILLOR liege lord
DEEGILNRT ringleted
DEEGILOOU ideologue
DEEGIMNPT pigmented
DEEGIMNRY remedying
DEEGINNPX expending
DEEGINNRR rendering
DEEGINNRS Red Ensign
DEEGINNRT tendering
DEEGINORT redingote
DEEGINRRR derringer
DEEGINRRT deterring
DEEGINRSV deserving
DEEGINRTT ridge tent
DEEGINRTV divergent
DEEGINRUV gerundive
DEEGIOSST geodesist
DEEGIPRST predigest
DEEGIPSST get pissed
DEEGIRRUU de rigueur
DEEGJMNTU judgement
DEEGKLNOW knowledge
DEEGKOPRW powder keg
DEEGLNNOW Gwendolen
DEEGMOORS Sedgemoor
DEEGNNNOU endungeon
DEEGNNORU gone under
DEEGNOORW green wood
greenwood□
DEEGNOOSS good sense
DEEGNOPTU put on edge
DEEGNORRU reguerdon
DEEGNORSS engrossed
DEEGNOUYY young-eyed
DEEGOSTTU get used to
DEEHHMOTT the method
DEEHHPSTT the depths
DEEHIINPT pethidine
DEEHIINRT inherited
DEEHIKRSW whiskered
DEEHILNUY unheedily
DEEHILSTV The Devils
DEEHIMOOV home video
DEEHIMORV drive home
DEEHIMOST methodise
DEEHIMOTZ methodize
DEEHINNOV Eindhoven
DEEHINNTU in the nude
DEEHINOST on the side
DEEHIOPRT the period
DEEHIORST other side

DEEHIOTTW	to the wide
DEEHIPRSW	whispered
DEEHISSTW	sweet dish
DEEHLNOOT	on the dole
DEEHMNNOT	on the mend
DEEHMNOTW	new method
DEEHMOORT	hodometer
DEEHMORST	smothered
DEEHNNORS	Henderson
DEEHNOPTY	endophyte
DEEHNORST	shortened
DEEHNORTW	down there
DEEHOORTX	heterodox
DEEHOOSUW	Wodehouse
DEEIILLMP	millipede
DEEIILLOS	diesel oil
DEEIIMNTT	midinette
DEEIIMNTU	in due time
DEEIIMPRS	epidermis
DEEIIPRSU	Euripides
DEEIIPSSW	side-swipe
DEEIIRRSV	riverside❑
DEEIIRTVV	divertive
DEEIJNNOR	enjoinder
DEEIJNORR	rejoinder
DEEIKLLLW	well-liked
DEEIKLLRS	killdeers
DEEIKLOVY	yoke-devil
DEEIKNSTW	stinkweed
DEEILLLOW	well-oiled
DEEILLMNO	ill-omened
DEEILLMST	mild steel
DEEILLMTW	well-timed
DEEILLNRV	Rivendell
DEEILLNTT	little end
DEEILLRSU	slide-rule
DEEILMNTV	devilment
DEEILNNRU	underline
DEEILNOPS	slide open
DEEILNOPT	depletion
DEEILNOTV	delve into
DEEILNPTU	plenitude
DEEILNRTU	interlude
DEEILNTVY	evidently
DEEILOPPS	dispeople
DEEILOPRS	despoiler
DEEILOPTX	exploited
DEEILPPRS	slippered
DEEILPRSS	prideless
DEEILRRSS	riderless
DEEILRRTY	retiredly
DEEILRSVY	diversely
DEEILRTUY	eruditely
DEEIMMOOR	Demi Moore
DEEIMNNOT	mentioned
DEEIMNNRU	undermine
DEEIMNNRV	never mind
DEEIMNORS	modernise
DEEIMNORZ	modernize
DEEIMNOSS	Des Moines
DEEIMNPST	spend time
DEEIMNRTT	detriment
DEEIMNRTU	unmerited
DEEIMOORT	meteoroid
DEEIMORST	dosimeter
DEEIMPRSS	impressed
DEEIMPRST	distemper
DEEIMPRTT	permitted
DEEIMRSTU	Demetrius
DEEIMRTUU	deuterium
DEEINNNPS	Pendennis
DEEINNOOS	on one side
DEEINNOOY	onion-eyed
DEEINNORT	internode
DEEINNOTT	detention
DEEINNPRU	unripened
DEEINNRST	dinner set
DEEINNRTU	indenture
DEEINNSSS	snideness
DEEINOOST	to one side
DEEINOPTX	pentoxide
DEEINORST	desertion
DEEINPRSS	dispenser
DEEINPRST	president
DEEINRSST	dissenter
	residents
	tiredness
DEEINRSSW	weirdness
DEEIOPRVW	power dive
DEEIORRRV	overrider
DEEIORRTV	overtired
DEEIORRVV	overdrive
DEEIOTTVX	videotext
DEEIPRSTU	disrepute
DEEIRSTTV	test drive
DEEIRSTUV	servitude
DEEIRTTXY	dexterity
DEEISTTTU	destitute
DEEJOORVY	overjoyed
DEEKKOOYY	okey-dokey
DEEKRRTUY	Turkey red
DEELLMOOR	role model
DEELLMRTU	red mullet
DEELLNOVW	level down
DEELLNRSU	undersell
DEELLNRSY	slenderly
DEELLNSSY	endlessly
DEELLOOPP	old people
DEELMOORV	velodrome
DEELNNPTY	pendently
DEELNOOST	lodestone
DEELNOPPU	unpeopled
DEELNPRRU	plunderer
DEELNRSTU	end result
DEELNSTTU	unsettled
DEELNSWWY	newlyweds
DEELOORSV	Dover sole
DEELOPRSY	reposedly
DEELORRSS	orderless
DEELPRTUY	reputedly
DEEMNNOTW	endowment
DEEMNOPRS	endosperm

DEEMNORTT	tormented
DEEMNSSTU	must needs
	mutedness
DEEMORRSW	mere words
DEEMPRTTU	trumpeted
DEEMRRSSU	murderess
DEENNORTU	undernote
	undertone
DEENNRSTU	nurse-tend
DEENOPRRV	provender
DEENOPRSV	overspend
DEENOPRUX	expounder
DEENORSTU	run to seed
DEENPRSSU	suspender
DEENRRRSU	surrender
DEENRRTTU	Ted Turner
DEENRSTTU	Ernst Udet
DEENRSTUV	undervest
DEENRSTYY	dysentery
DEENRTTUU	unuttered
DEEOOPRST	torpedoes
DEEOOPSTX	exposed to
DEEOPPRSS	oppressed
DEEOPPSTU	up to speed
DEEOPRRSS	depressor
DEEOPSSSS	possessed
DEEORRSSV	overdress
DEEORRSTX	dextrorse
DEEORRSTY	destroyer
DEEORSTUX	dexterous
DEEPRRSSU	pressured
DEFFGIINR	differing
DEFFGINNO	offending
DEFFHPTUU	up the duff
DEFFIIORT	fortified
DEFFIISUV	diffusive
DEFFILLLU	fulfilled
DEFFILSUY	diffusely
DEFFIOPSS	pissed off
DEFFLNRUU	unruffled
DEFFNORTU	turned off
DEFFOPTUU	puffed out
	puffed-out
DEFGGIINT	fidgeting
DEFGGILLN	fledgling
DEFGGIOOR	good grief
DEFGHILOT	eightfold
DEFGHLOOT	get hold of
DEFGHMOOO	home of God
DEFGIINNR	friending
DEFGIIRSU	disfigure
DEFGILLNO	long field
DEFGINOTW	get wind of
DEFGOOPRR	drop-forge
DEFHIILTW	Whitfield
DEFHIIORR	horrified
DEFHILLOY	Holyfield
DEFHINRSU	furnished
DEFHIORRS	rodfisher
DEFHIORSW	wished-for
DEFHLOOOW	wholefood
DEFHNORRY	Henry Ford
DEFHNORST	send forth
DEFHOPRSU	pushed for
DEFIIJSTU	justified
DEFIILLNU	nullified
DEFIILLRR	fire drill
DEFIILLTT	ill-fitted
DEFIILMRU	Muirfield
DEFIILPRT	field trip
DEFIIMMMU	mummified
DEFIIMNNY	indemnify
DEFIIMORT	mortified
DEFIIMRWY	midwifery
DEFIIMSTY	mystified
DEFIINRTY	denitrify
DEFIINSST	disinfest
DEFIIPRTY	perfidity
DEFIIRSVY	diversify
DEFIIRTVY	devitrify
	fervidity
DEFIKLOOX	fixed look
DEFIKLORW	fieldwork
DEFILLRUY	direfully
DEFILMNRU	remindful
DEFILMSUY	demulsify
DEFILNORT	interfold
DEFILNOSW	snowfield
DEFILNSSU	fluidness
DEFIMNNOO	of one mind
DEFIMNORU	uniformed
DEFIMORRT	triformed
DEFIMORTY	deformity
DEFIMSTYY	demystify
DEFINNORT	intend for
DEFIOOPSS	dispose of
DEFIOOSTU	outside of
DEFIORSST	disforest
DEFIORTTU	fortitude
DEFIOTTTU	fitted out
DEFKLOOOR	looked-for
DEFLLLOUY	dolefully
DEFLLRSSU	full dress
DEFLMMOUX	flummoxed
DEFLNOORW	new for old
DEFLNORUW	underflow
	wonderful
DEFNOORTU	underfoot
DEFNOOSTT	soft-toned
DEGGIILRU	Girl Guide
DEGGIINNS	designing
DEGGIINRV	diverging
DEGGIORTU	rigged out
DEGHHINOT	high-toned
DEGHIILNS	shielding
DEGHIILNT	delight in
DEGHIILST	sidelight
DEGHIINNR	hindering
DEGHIINRT	dithering
DEGHIIRST	right side
DEGHIJPSU	judgeship
DEGHILMSU	gumshield

DEGHILOTW	white gold
DEGHIMNRU	humdinger
DEGHINOWW	weigh down
DEGHINSTU	unsighted
DEGHMOORT	godmother
DEGHNNRUU	underhung
DEGHNORUY	greyhound❑
DEGHOOOTT	to the good
DEGHOORTW	the word go
DEGIIIMRS	dirigisme
	semi-rigid
DEGIIIRST	dirigiste
DEGIIIRTZ	digitizer
DEGIIKNSZ	king-sized
DEGIILLNR	Dillinger
DEGIILNNR	red-lining
DEGIILNNU	indulge in
DEGIILNOV	evil-doing
DEGIIMNNP	impending
DEGIIMNNR	reminding
DEGIIMNOT	doing time
DEGIINNSS	dinginess
DEGIINOST	digestion
DEGIINRSS	rigidness
DEGIINRTU	intrigued
DEGIINRTV	diverting
DEGIIRRSV	verdigris
DEGIKMOOS	Eskimo dog
DEGIKNNOO	De Kooning
DEGIKNNUU	Kunigunde
DEGILLMNO	modelling
DEGILLNOV	long-lived
DEGILLNSW	dwellings
DEGILLOTT	Little Dog
DEGILNNRU	underling
DEGILNNTU	indulgent
DEGILNNYY	denyingly
DEGILNOOR	gondolier
DEGILNORS	soldering
DEGILNOSS	godliness
DEGILNOTU	longitude
DEGILOSTT	glottides
DEGILSSUW	wild guess
DEGIMNRRU	demurring
DEGINNNOY	no denying
DEGINNOPR	pondering
DEGINNORS	endorsing
DEGINNORW	wondering
DEGINNOTT	tending to
DEGINNRRU	under-ring
DEGINNRSU	undersign
DEGINNRUW	underwing
DEGINOORV	overdoing
DEGINOOSS	goodiness
DEGINOPSS	podginess
DEGINORRW	rewording
DEGINORSW	wrong side
DEGINORUV	devouring
DEGINPSSU	pudginess
DEGIOOQTU	quite good
DEGIOORTW	tigerwood
DEGIOPSTU	guidepost
DEGIORRTW	grow tired
DEGIORTUU	tour guide
DEGKLORTU	Kurt Gödel
DEGLLOSSY	godlessly
DEGLMORUY	grey mould
DEGLNOOPR	prolonged
DEGLNORSU	groundsel
DEGMNOORU	ungroomed
DEGMOORST	good terms
DEGNOORRW	wrongdoer
DEGNOOTTW	get down to
DEGNOPRUW	gunpowder
DEGOOPRSS	good press
DEGOORUVW	vogue word
DEHHIIMNT	Hindemith
DEHHIIOSY	Hideyoshi
DEHHIKMOS	sheikhdom
DEHHILNOS	Holinshed
DEHHINOSY	hoydenish
DEHHLLNOU	hellhound
DEHHLOOSU	household
DEHHLORST	threshold
DEHIIINST	histidine
DEHIILRSS	disrelish
DEHIIMNNT	in the mind
DEHIIMNSU	disinhume
DEHIINNTW	in the wind
DEHIIOOPX	pixie hood
DEHIIOPST	it is hoped
DEHIIPRST	Petri dish
DEHIISTWW	widthwise
DEHIKNORT	Thorndike
DEHILLNOR	Hölderlin
DEHILNNOR	innholder
DEHILNPSU	Delphinus
DEHILOORT	rhodolite
DEHILOSTW	dishtowel
DEHILOSUY	hideously
DEHILRRUY	hurriedly
DEHIMMOST	Methodism
DEHIMNORT	Trondheim
DEHIMNOSY	hoydenism
DEHIMNSSU	humidness
DEHIMOSTT	Methodist
DEHIMOSTU	Methodius
DEHINNOPR	endorphin
DEHINOORT	rhodonite
DEHINORST	disthrone
DEHINORVW	wind-hover
DEHINOSST	dishonest
DEHINRRUU	unhurried
DEHIOORSW	Isherwood
DEHIOOTWW	whitewood
DEHJNNNOO	John Donne
DEHKLOOST	stokehold
DEHLMNOPY	lymph node
DEHLMOORW	wormholed
DEHLNOSSW	seldshown
DEHLORSYY	hydrolyse
DEHLORTYY	hydrolyte

DEHLORYYZ	hydrolyze
DEHLPRSUU	desulphur
DEHMNOOPR	endomorph
DEHNNOSUW	newshound
DEHNOORWY	Henry Wood
DEHNORSTU	undershot
DEHNPRTUU	upthunder
DEHOOOSUW	Woodhouse
DEHOORSTU	Herodotus
DEHOOSSSU	dosshouse
DEHRRRSYY	dry sherry
DEIIIKNTT	identikit□
DEIIILLMT	illimited
DEIIILMSS	dissimile
DEIIILQSU	liquidise
DEIIILQUZ	liquidize
DEIIINNQU	quinidine
DEIIIPSTX	ipse dixit
DEIIKKLNR	kilderkin
DEIIKLLNS	skilled in
DEIIKLNNX	index-link
DEIIKNRSV	skin-diver
DEIILLMPY	impliedly
DEIILLMTY	limitedly
DEIILLOPS	ellipsoid
DEIILLRST	distiller
DEIILLSTU	ill-suited
DEIILMNTU	unlimited
DEIILMRSU	deliriums
DEIILNNUV	unlived-in
DEIILNSSV	lividness
DEIILORSU	delirious
DEIIMMRSU	disimmure
DEIIMNNOS	dimension
DEIIMNNTY	indemnity
DEIIMNRUW	Edwin Muir
DEIIMNSST	timidness
DEIIMPRSU	presidium
DEIINNNOT	indention
DEIINNORT	rendition
DEIINNOTT	dentition
DEIINNOTV	vendition
DEIINNOUZ	unionized
DEIINNRTW	interwind
DEIINNSSW	windiness
DEIINNTUV	uninvited
DEIINOPRT	perdition
DEIINOPSS	indispose
DEIINORST	disorient
DEIINORSV	diversion
DEIINORTT	detrition
DEIINORTU	erudition
DEIINORTV	drive into
DEIINOSST	on its side
DEIINOSTU	inside out
	outside in
DEIINOTTZ	Donizetti
DEIINPSTU	in dispute
DEIINPSTZ	pint-sized
DEIINRSST	dirtiness
DEIINSSTV	disinvest
DEIINSSVV	vividness
DEIINSSZZ	dizziness
DEIINSTUV	unvisited
DEIIOPRSS	presidios
DEIIORSSS	siderosis
DEIIOSSTU	seditious
DEIIRSTVY	diversity
DEIIRSUVV	redivivus
DEIJLNNNY	Jenny Lind
DEIJNNOTU	unjointed
DEIJNNRUU	uninjured
DEIKKLNOR	klondiker
DEIKKNOOP	pondokkie
DEIKLLNSU	unskilled
DEIKLMOST	most-liked
DEIKLNPRS	sprinkled
DEIKMNNOW	womenkind
DEIKNSSSU	duskiness
	sun-kissed
DEILLMNOU	mullioned
DEILLNSUU	unsullied
DEILLOOTT	Doolittle
DEILLORSY	soldierly
DEILLSTTY	stiltedly
DEILMOOST	Dolomites
DEILMOOSU	melodious
DEILMPRSY	Simply Red
DEILMTTUU	multitude
DEILNNOOS	Londonise
DEILNNOOZ	Londonize
DEILNOORS	soldier on
DEILNOOSU	loud noise
DEILNOPRU	purloined
DEILNOPSU	unspoiled
DEILNOPTY	pointedly
DEILNORSS	lordiness
DEILNOSSS	solidness
DEILNOSSU	delusions
DEILNRSSU	luridness
DEILNSTTY	stintedly
DEILOOPPT	toodle-pip
DEILORRWY	worriedly
DEILORVWW	world-view
DEILOSSTU	dissolute
DEILOSTUY	tediously
DEILOSUVY	deviously
DEIMMMRSU	midsummer
DEIMMNORS	modernism□
DEIMMNOUY	neodymium
DEIMMOSTY	immodesty
DEIMNNOOO	onion dome
DEIMNOOPS	imposed on
DEIMNOOSS	moodiness
DEIMNOPRU	impounder
DEIMNORST	modernist
DEIMNORTY	modernity
DEIMNPRTU	imprudent
DEIMNPSSU	dumpiness
DEIMNRSTU	rudiments
DEIMNSSTU	tumidness
DEIMOPPUY	yuppiedom

Words marked □ can also be spelled with an initial capital letter

DEIMOPSST	despotism
DEIMORSUX	exordiums
DEINNNOSU	innuendos
DEINNOOTU	dine out on
DEINNOPTU	unpointed
DEINNOSSW	downiness
DEINNSSUY	sunny side
DEINNSTTU	unstinted
DEINOORRT	in order to
DEINOOSSW	woodiness
DEINOOSTV	devotions
DEINOPRTV	provident
DEINOPRUV	unprovide
DEINOPSTU	put on side
DEINORRUW	unworried
DEINORSSW	rowdiness
	wordiness
DEINORTWW	write down
	write-down
DEINOSSTT	dottiness
DEINOSTTU	duettinos
DEINPSTWW	windswept
DEINRRSTU	unstirred
DEINRSTTY	dentistry
DEINRSTUV	drive nuts
DEINSSSTU	dustiness
DEIOOPRST	depositor
DEIOPRSTU	dipterous
DEIOPRTTU	torpitude
DEIPRRSSU	surprised
DEIPRRSTU	disrupter
DEIPRTTUU	turpitude
DEIRSSSTU	dress suit
DEKKLNORY	klondyker
DEKLNNRUY	drunkenly
DEKNOOTUZ	zonked out
DEKNORRUW	underwork
DEKOPRSTU	stud poker
DELLMOSWY	Lymeswold
DELMNOOPR	lemon drop
DELMNOUVY	unmovedly
DELMNPSUU	pendulums
DELMNUUZZ	unmuzzled
DELNOORWW	lower down
DELNOPRSU	splendour
DELNOPSUU	pendulous
DELNORTWX	next world
DELNOSSSU	soundless
DELNPRTUY	prudently
DELOOORRV	drool over
DELOOOSUW	woodlouse
DELOORSSU	odourless
DELORSTUY	desultory
DELOSTUUY	duteously
DELPRSUUY	usurpedly
DEMNNOOWY	money down
DEMNOORUV	move round
DEMNOPSUY	pseudonym
DEMNORRTU	tenor-drum
DEMNORSTU	undermost
DEMORRSUU	murderous
DEMPPRTUU	trumped-up
DENNOOOST	on one's tod
DENNOOSTU	do one's nut
DENNOOTTU	tend out on
DENNORSSU	roundness
DENNORSUW	snow under
	sundowner
DENNOSSSU	soundness
DENNRRTUU	turn under
DENOOPPST	postponed
DENOOPPSU	unopposed
DENOOPRST	respond to
DENOOPRSU	ponderous
DENOORSTU	tournedos
DENOPPSTU	unstopped
DENOPRSSW	press down
DENOPSTTU	unspotted
DENORTTUU	turned out
	untutored
DEOOOPPST	opposed to
DEOORRSTU	Tudor rose
DEOPPPRTU	rod puppet
DEOPPRRTU	purported
DEOPPRSTU	supported
DEORRSUUV	verdurous
DEPRSSSTU	press stud
DFFFOOSTU	foodstuff
DFFIINOSU	diffusion
DFFIKSSTU	kids' stuff
DFFILMNOU	mindful of
DFGIIIRTY	frigidity
DFGIIMNOY	modifying
DFGIINNUY	undignify
DFGILNNOU	foundling
	unfolding
DFGILNNOW	fling down
DFGLOOOPT	pot of gold
DFHHLOORT	hold forth
DFHILOORY	hydrofoil
DFHIORSSW	swordfish ❑
DFHLNOOUW	wolfhound
	wolf-hound
DFHLNSSUU	slush fund
DFIILORTY	floridity
DFIINPRST	spindrift
DFIKLNOPY	Pink Floyd
DFIKNORST	soft drink
DFILLMNUY	mindfully
DFILLTUUY	dutifully
DFILMNNUU	unmindful
DFILNTUUU	undutiful
DFIMNOOTU	out of mind
DFINOOPRW	windproof
DFINORSTW	snowdrift
DFINORTTY	try to find
DFNOOOPTU	foot-pound
DFNRSTTUU	trust fund
DFOOOPRTU	drop out of
DGGHILOSY	doggishly
DGGHINOOT	good thing
	goodnight

DGGHNOORU	groundhog
DGGIILLNY	glidingly
DGGIILNOW	go wilding
DGGINNOOW	going down
	going-down
DGGINNORU	grounding
DGHHIINST	hindsight
DGHHILOTT	hold tight
DGHHINOPT	diphthong
DGHHIORSW	high words
DGHHOORSU	roughshod
DGHILMOST	goldsmith❑
DGHILNOPU	upholding
DGHILOTUY	doughtily
DGHINNOOT	do nothing
	do-nothing
DGHINORTW	downright
	right down
	right-down
DGHIOOSTW	wish to God
DGHJNNOOO	John Ogdon
DGHLOORYY	hydrology
DGHOORSTW	ghost word
DGHOORSUU	sourdough
DGHORSTTU	God's truth
DGHRRTTUU	truth drug
DGIIILNOZ	idolizing
DGIIINNTY	indignity
DGIIJNORY	joy-riding
DGIIKNSVY	sky-diving
DGIILLNSY	slidingly
DGIILNNSW	swindling
DGIILNNWY	windingly
DGIILNRST	stridling
DGIILNRZZ	drizzling
DGIIMNSSU	Sigismund
DGIINNNUW	unwinding
DGIINNOSW	disowning
DGIINNPUW	winding-up
DGIINNRTU	intruding
DGIINOPRV	providing
DGIINSSTU	in disgust
DGIIRTTUY	turgidity
DGIJMNOOR	Jo Grimond
DGILLNORW	worldling
DGILLNOUY	ungodlily
DGILLOPSY	splodgily
DGILMNOOO	Mongoloid
DGILNNORY	droningly
DGILNNOWY	lying down
DGILNNUYY	undyingly
DGILNOOPT	gold point
DGILNORRW	Ringworld
DGIMNRSUY	Grundyism
DGINNOPSU	pound sign
DGINNOSWW	downswing
DGINOOOPT	good point
DGINOOPRY	Podgorniy
DGINOOPST	stop doing
DGINOPPRS	droppings
DGINORTUY	drying out
DGINORUVY	ground ivy
DGKLOOOOS	good looks
DGMNRRSUY	Mrs Grundy
DGNNORTUU	groundnut
DGNOOOOUY	good on you
DGNOOORTU	go round to
DGNOORRWW	wrong word
DHHIKNSUU	Hindu Kush
DHIIIPSTY	hispidity
DHIILNRWW	whirlwind
DHIILOSTW	solid with
DHIINOORT	ornithoid
DHIKLSSUY	duskishly
DHILLOSTY	doltishly
DHILMPSUY	dumpishly
DHILNORSY	dronishly
DHILPRSUY	prudishly
DHIMNOSTY	hymnodist
DHIMORSTW	wordsmith
DHIMORSUU	dishumour
DHINNORTW	north wind
DHINNOTUW	whodunnit
DHINOOPRS	rhodopsin
DHINOORSU	dishonour
DHINOPRUW	whip-round
DHIOOTTUW	do without
DHIORRTTW	throw dirt
DHKMNOOOS	monkshood
DHKNORUYY	hunky-dory
DHLLOOOWY	Hollywood
DHLMOOTUU	loudmouth
	loud-mouth
DHLNOOOTU	hold out on
DHLNOOPTU	put on hold
DHMNOOPWY	wood nymph
DHMOOPTUY	Humpty Doo
DHNOOOSTW	shoot down
DHNOORTWW	throw down
DHNOOSTUW	shout down
	Southdown
DHOOORTXY	orthodoxy
DHOPRSTYY	dystrophy
DIIILMPTY	limpidity
DIIILNPSY	insipidly
DIIILQTUY	liquidity
DIIINOSSU	insidious
DIIINOSUV	invidious
DIIKKNNRY	rinky-dink
DIIKLPSSU	Pilsudski
DIIKNNPSY	skinny-dip
DIILLNORT	drill into
DIILOSTTY	stolidity
DIIMNNPTU	put in mind
DIINOPRSS	disprison
DIINOSSUY	Dionysius
DIIOPRTTY	torpidity
DIIPRTTUY	putridity
DIIPSTTUY	stupidity
DIKLMNORU	milk round
DIKLOORTY	dirty look
DIKNNOOTW	I don't know

Words marked ❑ can also be spelled with an initial capital letter

DIKNOOSTW	stinkwood
DIKORRTWY	dirty work
DILLOOPPY	polyploid
DILOOPTUW	tulipwood
DIMMNORSY	Myrmidons
DIMNORSTW	windstorm
DIMOORRTY	dormitory
DINNOPRSU	spin round
DINOOPRST	piston rod
DINOPRSTW	strip down
DINORTTUY	rotundity
DIOOPRSST	prosodist
DKLNOORSW	Lord knows
DKORSTUWY	work study
DLLNOPRUU	pull round
DLLNORUWY	unworldly
DLNNOSUUY	unsoundly
DLNOOOSTW	down tools
DLOOORSUY	odorously
DMNOORRUW	roundworm
DMOOORRST	storm door
DMOOPRRSU	prodromus
DMORSSTTU	dust-storm
DNNORRTUU	turn round
DNOOORRTU	ororotund
DNOOPTTUW	put down to
DNOORRTWY	don't worry
DNOORRWWY	worry down
DNORRSSUU	surrounds
DOOSTTTUU	out to stud

E

EEEEFHLRW	freewheel
EEEEFHRST	freesheet
EEEEFRRSV	free verse
EEEEGGRRS	greegrees
EEEEGINVV	Genevieve
EEEEGJNOR	Joe Greene
EEEEGNRRV	evergreen
EEEEHLRSW	elsewhere
EEEEIJLNN	Jennie Lee
EEEEKRVWY	every week
EEEELLRSZ	Zeller See
EEEELMPTY	Eye Temple
EEEELMRTT	telemeter
EEEELNSSV	elevenses
EEEELNTVV	velveteen
EEEENNSST	Tennessee
EEEENNSTV	seventeen
EEEENOPRY	eye-opener
EEEENRRVV	Never Ever
EEEENRSTW	sweetener
EEEEPRRSV	persevere
EEEFFMNOT	Toffeemen
EEEFGKNRU	fenugreek
EEEFHNOPR	freephone
EEEFHNRRS	refreshen
EEEFHORRT	therefore
EEEFHORRW	wherefore
EEEFHORSU	free house
EEEFHORTT	foreteeth
EEEFHRRRS	refresher
EEEFILLTU	feuilleté
EEEFILMPS	fee simple
EEEFILRVX	reflexive
EEEFINRRT	interfere
EEEFISSSW	fesse-wise
EEEFLNSST	fleetness
EEEFLRSTY	freestyle
EEEFMNORW	freewomen
EEEFNORST	freestone
EEEFORTUZ	freeze out
EEEGGORTT	georgette □
EEEGHOPRS	geosphere
EEEGIKNPS	Pekingese
EEEGILLNR	leger-line
EEEGILNNR	Nile green
EEEGINNOT	eigentone
EEEGINNRV	veneering
EEEGINPRR	peregrine □
EEEGINRRZ	energizer
EEEGINRST	Serengeti
EEEGINRTT	teetering
EEEGINRUV	Guinevere
EEEGINRVV	revengive
EEEGIRSTY	tiger's eye
EEEGISTTX	exegetist
EEEGKLLNY	Gene Kelly
EEEGLLNTY	genteelly
EEEGMNRSS	messenger
EEEGNNRSS	greenness
EEEGNORRV	overgreen
EEEHHIRST	Shere Hite
EEEHILLNS	Hellenise
EEEHILLNZ	Hellenize
EEEHILNST	Heseltine
EEEHILRWW	wire wheel
EEEHIMPRS	ephemeris
EEEHIMPSU	euphemise
EEEHIMPUZ	euphemize
EEEHIMSTT	time sheet
EEEHKOPSU	keep house
EEEHLNOPT	telephone
EEEHLNRST	enshelter
EEEHLOPPT	The People
EEEHLRRST	shelterer
EEEHLTTVW	the Twelve
EEEHMNOPR	ephemeron
EEEHMORST	threesome
EEEHMORSW	somewhere
EEEHNORSW	whensoeer
EEEHNRSSS	sheerness □
EEEHNSSTW	news sheet
	news-sheet
EEEHOPRSX	exosphere
EEEHRRSTW	tree shrew
EEEHRSTTU	usherette
EEEIINRSW	Ernie Wise
EEEIKLNQU	queenlike
EEEIKNNPR	innkeeper
EEEIKPQTU	keep quiet
EEEILLLMR	Lee Miller

EEEILLMRV	vermeille
EEEILLPST	pelletise
EEEILLPTZ	pelletize
EEEILNNRV	enlivener
EEEILNSTX	extensile
EEEILPTVX	expletive
EEEILRSTX	exsertile
EEEIMMNNO	Menominee
EEEIMMRSS	mesmerise
EEEIMMRSZ	mesmerize
EEEIMMSST	misesteem
EEEIMNRTX	extermine
EEEIMORTT	meteorite
EEEIMPRRT	perimeter
EEEIMRRTZ	terze rime
EEEIMRSTV	serve time
EEEIMRTVY	every time
EEEINNPRS	persienne
EEEINNRTV	intervene
EEEINNSTT	St-Étienne
EEEINORRT	orienteer
EEEINORST	neoterise
EEEINORTZ	neoterize
EEEINPRRS	reserpine
EEEINPSVX	expensive
EEEINQSUZ	queen-size
EEEINRRSV	in reserve
EEEINRTTV	retentive
EEEINSSTV	seventies
EEEINSTVX	extensive
EEEIPRRTT	preterite
EEEIPRSTX	expertise
EEEIPRTXZ	expertize
EEEIQTTTU	etiquette
EEEIRRRTV	retriever
EEEIRSTTV	serviette
EEEIRSTVX	exsertive
EEEJKNRTU	junketeer
EEEJLLRWY	jewellery
EEEJNPRSS	Jespersen
EEEJNRSWY	New Jersey
EEEKLMPRR	Klemperer
EEEKLNSSS	sleekness
EEEKMRSTU	musketeer
EEEKOSSTV	seek votes
EEELLMNOP	lemon peel
EEELLNPRT	repellent
EEELLNSSV	levelness
EEELLPSSS	sleepless
EEELMMNOP	Melpomene
EEELMNOPT	elopement
EEELMOPSY	employees
EEELMRTTY	telemetry
EEELMRTXY	extremely
EEELNORVW	wolverene
EEELNOTTV	novelette
EEELNRRTY	terrenely
EEELNRSSV	nerveless
EEELNSSSS	senseless
EEELOPRSV	oversleep
	sleep over
EEELOPRTW	peel-tower
EEELRRSVY	reversely
EEELRSTTT	letterset
EEEMNNOVY	even money
EEEMNORRV	nevermore
EEEMNRSTT	entremets
EEEMNRSTY	mesentery
EEEMNRTTV	revetment
EEEMOPRTX	extempore
EEENNORST	sonneteer
EEENNSSST	tenseness
EEENOSSTY	set eyes on
EEENPRRST	presenter
	represent
	re-present
EEENPRSUV	supervene
EEENPSSST	steepness
EEENQRSSU	queerness
EEENQSSTU	sequentes
EEENRRSTW	westerner
EEENRRSUV	unreserve
EEENRSSST	terseness
EEENSSSTW	sweetness
EEEORRSTV	oversteer
EEEORRTVX	overexert
EEEORSTVW	oversweet
EEEPPPRTU	puppeteer
EEEPRRRSV	preserver
EEEQRRSTU	requester
EEEQRSSTU	sequester
EEERRTTUX	retexture
EEFFFKLRU	kerfuffle
EEFFFMNOT	feoffment
EEFFFOORT	for toffee
EEFFGHOPT	off the peg
	off-the-peg
EEFFGLNTU	effulgent
EEFFHILLS	shelf-life
EEFFHINTT	fifteenth
EEFFHLRSU	reshuffle
EEFFINOSV	offensive
EEFFINRST	stiffener
EEFFIORRT	forfeiter
EEFFJNORS	Jefferson
EEFFLOOTT	fleet-foot
EEFFORSTT	off-street
EEFGGIKRT	Greek gift
EEFGGOORX	George Fox
EEFGHIRRT	freighter
EEFGILLNY	feelingly
EEFGILNNU	unfeeling
EEFGINORR	foreigner
EEFGINRST	festering
EEFGIORRV	grieve for
EEFGIORTV	forgetive
EEFGIPRRU	prefigure
EEFGLLLUY	gleefully
EEFGLNRTU	refulgent
EEFGLRRTU	regretful
EEFHIIKLT	thief-like
EEFHIISST	fetishise

EEFHIISTZ	fetishize	EEFMORRST	E M Forster
EEFHILLRS	shellfire	EEFMPRRUY	perfumery
EEFHILOTT	to the life	EEFNNOSST	oftenness
EEFHINSST	heftiness	EEFNORSTW	New Forest
EEFHIORST	the rise of	EEFORRRST	Forrester
EEFHIOSUW	housewife	EEFORRTTU	ferret out
EEFHIQRSU	queer fish	EEFPRSSUU	superfuse
EEFHLLSSS	fleshless	EEGGHHIRT	get higher
EEFHLLTUW	Ethelwulf	EEGGIILNT	gelignite
EEFHLMNST	fleshment	EEGGIKNOP	keep going
EEFHLOSTW	flow sheet	EEGGILNNT	negligent
EEFHMORRT	therefrom	EEGGILOOS	geologise
EEFHMORRW	from where	EEGGILOOZ	geologize
EEFHNPRSU	freshen up	EEGGINNRV	revenging
EEFHNRSSS	freshness	EEGGINRRS	sniggerer
EEFHOORRS	foreshore	EEGGINRST	greetings
EEFHOORTT	to the fore	EEGGIORSU	egregious
EEFIIKLLS	like flies	EEGGNOOOS	gone goose
EEFIILMTX	flexitime	EEGGORSST	St George's
EEFIILNRT	infertile	EEGHHIITT	eightieth
EEFIILQRU	liquefier	EEGHHILLV	high-level
EEFIILRST	fertilise	EEGHHISTT	the eights
EEFIILRTZ	fertilize	EEGHIIKLM	Mike Leigh
EEFIINRSS	fieriness	EEGHIKNTW	weeknight
EEFIINRTT	Nefertiti	EEGHIKOTV	give the OK
EEFIIRRSV	versifier	EEGHILNNT	enlighten
EEFIIRSTT	testifier	EEGHIMOST	egotheism
EEFIJLNOY	enjoy life		eightsome
EEFIKNRSU	refusenik	EEGHINSST	see things
EEFILLPTY	pelletify	EEGHIORVW	overweigh
EEFILLRTY	fertilely	EEGHIOSTT	ghettoise
EEFILLSTY	lifestyle	EEGHIOTTZ	ghettoize
EEFILMPXY	exemplify	EEGHIRSST	sightseer
EEFILNNRS	inner self	EEGHLORTY	leg theory
EEFILNORX	reflexion	EEGHMNOST	theme song
EEFILSTVY	festively	EEGHNNORR	greenhorn
EEFIMNRTT	refitment	EEGHNORTU	toughener
EEFINORST	Firestone	EEGIIKNNP	in keeping
	forestine	EEGIILLPS	Gillespie
	set on fire	EEGIILNRV	inveigler
EEFINPRSU	superfine		relieving
EEFINRSTU	interfuse	EEGIILNST	gentilise
EEFIOPRRT	profiteer	EEGIILNTZ	gentilize
EEFIOPRRW	fire-power	EEGIILOPS	epilogise
EEFIORSTT	set fire to	EEGIILOPZ	epilogize
EEFIOSTTV	set to five	EEGIILORS	religiose
EEFIPRSTU	stupefier	EEGIILPRV	privilege
EEFIRRRTU	fruiterer	EEGIILRUX	religieux
EEFKLLTTU	kettleful	EEGIINNNO	ion engine
EEFKNOORT	foretoken	EEGIINRSU	signeurie
EEFLNOOST	to oneself	EEGIISTTZ	Zeitgeist
EEFLNRSTU	resentful	EEGIJLNRY	jeeringly
EEFLNRTVY	fervently	EEGIKNNRT	Kentigern
EEFLOPRSU	reposeful	EEGILLLNV	levelling
EEFLORRSY	feel sorry	EEGILLNPR	repelling
EEFLORRTX	retroflex	EEGILLNRV	Grenville
EEFLORSTT	settle for		revelling
EEFLORSTV	leftovers	EEGILLNRY	leeringly
EEFLSSTTY	tsetse-fly		reelingly
EEFMNOORW	forewomen	EEGILLSSU	guileless
EEFMOPRRR	performer	EEGILMNSY	seemingly

EEGILNNRT relenting
EEGILNNSS lessening
EEGILNNST single ten
EEGILNNUY genuinely
EEGILNOOS neologise
EEGILNOOZ neologize
EEGILNORV line-grove
EEGILNPWY weepingly
EEGILNRTT lettering
EEGILNRVY veeringly
EEGILNTXY exigently
EEGILOPSS gospelise
EEGILOPSZ gospelize
EEGILORST sortilege
EEGILORUZ eulogizer
EEGILRTVY Trygve Lie
EEGIMNNSU unseeming
EEGIMNOVY give money
EEGIMNPRR Preminger
EEGIMNPRT tempering
EEGINNNUU ungenuine
EEGINNOPR reopening
EEGINOOSS oogenesis
EEGINORSS egression
EEGINORSV sovereign
EEGINOSSS gneissose
Sosigenes
EEGINOSXY oxygenise
EEGINOTTU tongue-tie
EEGINOXYZ oxygenize
EEGINPRST pestering
EEGINPSSW sweepings
EEGINQSUZ squeezing
EEGINRRST restringe
EEGINRRSV reversing
EEGINRSSY synergise
EEGINRSTW westering
EEGINRSYZ synergize
EEGIOPRSS serpigoes
EEGIOSTTW get wise to
EEGIRRSST registers
EEGIRRSSU régisseur
EEGKNNORZ Egon Krenz
EEGLLLPRU leg-puller
EEGLLNOTW get on well
EEGLLOOTY teleology
EEGLLORRV groveller
EEGLNOOVV oven glove
EEGLNORTT lorgnette
EEGLNSSUY glueyness
EEGLOOPST go to sleep
EEGLOORVZ gloze over
EEGLPRSUU superglue
Superglue®
EEGMNOORR Green Room
green room
greenroom
EEGMNORSS moss green
EEGMORSTZ Esztergom
EEGNOORST oestrogen
EEGNOORSU erogenous
EEGNOOSSY gooeyness
EEGNOOSUX exogenous
EEGNORSSV governess
EEGNRRSTU resurgent
EEGOOPSST goose-step
EEGOPPRRU peer group
EEGOPRTUU Portuguee
EEGOQRSTU grotesque
EEGORRSUV surge over
EEGORRTTU tregetour
EEHHINOSS shoeshine
EEHHINPSY hyphenise
EEHHINPYZ hyphenize
EEHHIOPTW white hope
EEHHIRSST the Shires
EEHHIRTTW therewith
EEHHIRTWW wherewith
EEHHOORSS horseshoe
EEHHOOSSU houseshoe
EEHIILNTW white line
White Nile
EEHIILRTT Hitlerite
EEHIILSTW white lies
EEHIINNRW Rhine wine
EEHIINNTT ninetieth
EEHIINTWW white wine
EEHIIRSTT there it is
EEHIIRSTW where it is
EEHIJNOPS Josephine
Joséphine
EEHIKLMTT milk teeth
EEHIKMNSV Menshevik
EEHIKNPSS sheepskin
EEHILLLMW mill wheel
EEHILLMNS Hellenism
EEHILLMRT The Miller
EEHILLNST Hellenist
EEHILLTVW level with
EEHILMOST lithesome
EEHILNNOO hole in one
EEHILNOOP oenophile
EEHILNORS shoreline
EEHILNPRS replenish
EEHILNPSW wheel spin
EEHILNRST inshelter
EEHILNSST litheness
EEHILOPTW elope with
EEHILOPTY heliotype
EEHILPRTU Prue Leith
EEHILPSTW sleep with
EEHILPSVY peevishly
EEHILRSTW erstwhile
EEHIMMOOV home movie
EEHIMMPSU euphemism
EEHIMNTTU the minute
EEHIMPRRW whimperer
EEHINNOPT in the open
EEHINNORT threonine
EEHINNOTV Einthoven
EEHINOPST phonetise
EEHINOPSU euphonise

EEHINOPTZ	phonetize
EEHINOPUZ	euphonize
EEHINORST	on the rise
EEHINORSV	overshine
EEHINORTT	thereinto
EEHINOSUW	house wine
EEHINPQSU	queenship
EEHINPRRT	trephiner
EEHINSSTW	whiteness
EEHINSTTX	sixteenth
EEHINTTTW	twentieth
EEHIOQRTU	theorique
EEHIORRST	rhetorise
EEHIORRTZ	rhetorize
	theorizer
EEHIORSTW	otherwise
EEHIPPRRY	periphery
EEHIPPSSY	epiphyses
EEHIPRRSW	whisperer
EEHIQRSTU	The Squire
EEHIRRSST	heritress
EEHIRTVWY	every whit
EEHJKNOPS	John Speke
EEHKLOORW	look where
EEHKOPRSU	keep hours
EEHKORSTW	worksheet
EEHLLLNVY	Helvellyn
EEHLLORST	hosteller
EEHLLORSV	shoveller
EEHLMOOSW	wholesome
EEHLMORVW	overwhelm
EEHLMORWW	worm wheel
EEHLMPSSY	emphlyses
EEHLMRSSY	rhymeless
EEHLNOPTY	polythene
	telephony
EEHLNOSSW	wholeness
EEHLNSTVY	seventhly
EEHLOOPTT	telephoto
EEHLOPRST	the proles
EEHLPRSUW	spur wheel
EEHMMNOTT	the moment
EEHMNOOPR	pheromone
EEHMNOORW	home-owner
EEHMNOOTV	on the move
EEHMNORTY	heteronym
EEHMNPTTU	umpteenth
EEHMOORST	some other
EEHMOOSUV	move house
EEHMOPRSS	press home
EEHMORRST	smotherer
EEHMRRSTY	rhymester
EEHMSSTTY	the system
EEHNNOORT	none other
EEHNNOOST	on the nose
EEHNOOPSU	open house
EEHNOPPTY	phenotype
EEHNOPRTU	thereupon
EEHNOPRUW	whereupon
EEHNOPSTU	penthouse □
EEHNORSST	otherness
EEHNORTUW	whereunto
EEHNOSTTW	whetstone
EEHNPPRSU	penpusher
	pen-pusher
EEHNSSSTY	syntheses
EEHOORSSV	over-shoes
EEHOORSVW	howsoever
	whosoever
EEHOPRRSU	superhero
EEHOPRSTY	hey-presto
EEHOPRTXY	xerophyte
EEHORRRTT	the Terror
EEHPRTTXY	hypertext
EEIIKLLMN	Nellie Kim
EEIILLNTV	vitelline
EEIILNNRT	interline
EEIILNQSU	Esquiline
EEIILNRST	resilient
EEIILNSTU	luteinise
EEIILNTUZ	luteinize
EEIILRSST	Listerise
	sterilise
EEIILRSSV	silverise
EEIILRSTZ	Listerize
	sterilize
EEIILRSVZ	silverize
EEIIMMPRT	prime time
EEIIMMRST	eremitism
EEIIMNOPT	in epitome
EEIIMOPST	epitomise
EEIIMOPTZ	epitomize
EEIIMORSS	isomerise
EEIIMORSZ	isomerize
EEIIMRSSV	remissive
EEIINNRTV	intervein
EEIINNSTT	intestine
EEIINNSTV	intensive
EEIINNTVV	inventive
EEIINQRSU	enquiries
EEIINRSTT	enteritis
EEIINRSTW	winterise
EEIINRTVW	interview
EEIINSSST	sensitise
EEIINSSTV	sensitive
EEIINSSTZ	sensitize
EEIIOPQSU	equipoise
EEIIOSSTV	sovietise
EEIIOSTVZ	sovietize
EEIIPRSSW	spirewise
EEIIQRSTU	requisite
EEIIQSTUX	exquisite
EEIJKLLLY	jelly-like
EEIJKNRSS	jerkiness
EEIKKLMOS	like smoke
EEIKLLMPW	Will Kempe
EEIKLMORT	kilometre
EEIKLRTWY	tri-weekly
EEIKNNOST	Tonkinese
EEIKNPRSS	perkiness
EEIKNSTTX	sex kitten
EEIKOPSSW	spokewise

Words marked □ can also be spelled with an initial capital letter

EEILLMNOR	Niemöller
EEILLMNOT	emollient
EEILLMNPT	impellent
EEILLMPRT	ill temper
	ill-temper
EEILLNNTY	leniently
EEILLNOTT	little one
EEILLNRSV	sniveller
EEILLOPSW	powellise
EEILLOPWZ	powellize
EEILLORTT	title role
EEILLRSTT	rillettes
EEILLRSTU	tellurise
EEILLRSUV	surveille
EEILLRSUY	leisurely
EEILLRSVY	servilely
EEILLRTUZ	tellurize
EEILLSUVY	elusively
EEILMMNPT	implement
EEILMMNSY	immensely
EEILMMORT	milometer
EEILMNNTY	eminently
EEILMNOSS	solemnise
EEILMNOST	limestone
	milestone
EEILMNOSZ	solemnize
EEILMNPPR	pimpernel
EEILMORUX	Emile Roux
	Émile Roux
EEILMOSTT	mistletoe
EEILMOSVW	semivowel
EEILNNPSS	penniless
EEILNNSTY	intensely
EEILNOPRT	interlope
	repletion
EEILNOPRW	power line
EEILNOPST	sleep on it
EEILNOPSX	Polixenes
EEILNORVW	wolverine
EEILNOSSS	noiseless
EEILNOSTV	novelties
EEILNOTTX	lie next to
EEILNPSSS	spineless
EEILNPSTT	pestilent
EEILNPSVY	pensively
EEILNRSST	listeners
EEILNRSVY	inversely
EEILOPRTX	exploiter
EEILOPSSW	slopewise
EEILOPSVX	explosive
EEILORRTT	Tortelier
EEILPPRTU	pulpiteer
EEILPRSTY	peristyle
	Priestley
EEILPRSUV	prelusive
	pulverise
	repulsive
EEILPRUVZ	pulverize
EEILPSUVX	expulsive
EEILRRSSV	riverless
EEILRSTVY	restively
EEILRSUVV	revulsive
EEIMMMRSS	mesmerism
EEIMMNNTU	minutemen
EEIMMNRRT	merriment
EEIMMNRTT	remitment
EEIMMORRT	memoriter
EEIMMOSST	sometimes
EEIMMRSST	mesmerist
EEIMMRSTW	swimmeret
EEIMMRSTX	extremism
EEIMNNOST	minestone
EEIMNNRTT	interment
EEIMNNRTU	inurement
EEIMNNSSU	Nine Muses
EEIMNNSTT	sentiment
EEIMNOPTX	exemption
EEIMNORSS	sermonise
EEIMNORSZ	sermonize
EEIMNPQTU	equipment
EEIMNPRRU	en primeur
EEIMNPSST	emptiness
EEIMNRRSS	merriness
EEIMNRTTT	remittent
EEIMNSSSS	messiness
EEIMOPRST	temporise
EEIMOPRTZ	temporize
EEIMOSSST	so it seems
EEIMPPRRS	perisperm
EEIMPSSTU	impetuses
EEIMRSSTY	mysteries
EEIMRSTTX	extremist
EEIMRTTXY	extremity
EEIMSSSTY	systemise
EEIMSSTYZ	systemize
EEINNNOPS	en pension
EEINNNRSU	nunneries
EEINNOPPS	Nipponese
EEINNOPRS	pensioner
EEINNOPRT	interpone
	tin-opener
EEINNORTT	enter into
	retention
EEINNOSST	sonnetise
EEINNOSTX	extension
EEINNOSTZ	sonnetize
EEINNPRST	spinneret
EEINNPRTT	pertinent
EEINNPSST	ineptness
EEINNPSWY	penny-wise
EEINNRSST	inertness
EEINNRSSV	Inverness
EEINNSSSW	newsiness
EEINOPPPR	pepperoni
EEINOPPRS	prise open
EEINOPPST	peptonise
	pipestone
EEINOPPTZ	peptonize
EEINOPRSS	personise
EEINOPRST	interpose
EEINOPRSZ	personize
EEINOPSTT	potentise

EEINOPTTZ	potentize
EEINOQRUV	Véronique
EEINORRSV	reversion
EEINOSSTV	ostensive
EEINOSTTU	Teutonise
EEINOTTUZ	Teutonize
EEINPRRTT	interpret
EEINPRSSW	winepress
EEINPRTTY	Intertype®
EEINPSSTT	pettiness
EEINQSSTU	quietness
EEINQTTTU	quintette
EEINRSSTT	triteness
EEINRSSTW	witnesser
EEINRSSUV	Severinus
EEINSSSTT	testiness
EEIOOPRSV	overpoise
EEIOPPSTV	stovepipe
EEIOPRRVZ	overprize
EEIOPRTTU	pirouette
EEIORRRST	roisterer
	terrorise
EEIORRRSV	reservoir
EEIORRRTZ	terrorize
EEIORRTVW	overwrite
EEIORSSUV	overissue
EEIPRSSST	priestess
EEIPRSSUV	supervise
EEIPRTTWY	typewrite
EEIRRSSTV	reservist
EEIRRTTTW	twitterer
EEIRSSSTT	tristesse
EEIRSTTUX	texturise
EEIRSTUVX	extrusive
EEIRTTUXZ	texturize
EEJKLLOST	tell jokes
EEJLNOPRU	pleno jure
EEJMNNOTY	enjoyment
EEJMPQUUU	queue-jump
EEJNORRUY	journeyer
EEJPSSTUW	Jesus wept
EEKKORSTY	keystroke
EEKLLMOSS	sell smoke
EEKLMOSSS	smokeless
EEKLNPRSU	spelunker
EEKLORSTW	steelwork
EEKMNOPSS	spokesmen
EEKNOPPTU	not keep up
EEKNORRTW	networker
EELLMNOOS	lemon sole
EELLNNRTU	tunneller
EELLNPSTW	well-spent
EELLOOSTW	steel wool
EELLOPPRR	propeller
EELLORSVW	overswell
EELLPSSSY	syllepses
EELLSSSUY	uselessly
EELMMNOTU	emolument
EELMMRSUW	Welsummer
EELMNNORT	enrolment
EELMNOTTX	extolment
EELMNPSTU	Sun Temple
EELMOOPST	leptosome
EELMOOPTT	totem pole
EELMOPRSY	employers
EELMOPRTU	petroleum
EELMORTTV	voltmeter
EELMOSTVW	twelvemos
EELMPRSUY	supremely
EELNNOPRS	personnel
EELNOOSSS	looseness
EELNOPSTU	plenteous
EELNORSTV	resolvent
EELNORTUV	volunteer
EELNOSSST	stoneless
EELNPRSTY	presently
EELOOPRSW	lose power
EELOOPRSY	operosely
EELOORSTV	Roosevelt
EELOPPRSS	prolepses
EELOPRRTU	pétroleur
	poulterer
EELOPRSSW	powerless
EELOPRSTY	polyester
	proselyte
EELORSSUV	ourselves
EELPPSTTU	septuplet
EELPRSSXY	expressly
EELPRSTUU	sepulture
EELPSTTUX	sextuplet
EELRSSTVY	Sylvester
EEMMNOORT	metronome
	monometer
	monotreme
EEMNNOPST	penstemon
EEMNOPRSU	presume on
EEMNORRTY	Monterrey
EEMNRSTTW	strewment
EEMNSSTTV	vestments
EEMOOPPRS	prose poem
EEMOOPRTT	optometer
EEMOPRRTY	pyrometer
EEMOSTTTU	teetotums
EEMPRRTTU	trumpeter
EEMPRSSTT	temptress
EENNOPRSS	proneness
EENNOPRSW	new person
EENNOPRTU	enter upon
EENNORSTU	entre nous
EENNOSSTV	Stevenson
EENNOTTWY	twenty-one
EENNPRTUY	truepenny
EENNRSSST	sternness
EENOORRSU	erroneous
EENOPPRRS	per person
EENOPPRTT	prepotent
EENOPRSTW	Peter Snow
EENORRSTW	nor'wester
EENPRRTUV	unpervert
EENRSSTTU	utterness
EEOOPRRVW	overpower
EEOORRTVW	overtower

	tower over
EEOOSSSTX	exostoses
EEOOSSTTV	ovotestes
EEOPPRSSU	superpose
EEOPRRRSS	repressor
EEOPRRRST	reporters
EEOPRRRTY	repertory
EEOPRRSSV	overpress
EEOPRRSTT	protester
EEOPRSSSS	espressos
	repossess
EEOPRSSTU	proteuses
EEOPRSTTU	route-step
EEOPRSTUX	exposture
EEOPSSTTU	poussette
EEOPSSTTW	sweet spot
EEORRRTTV	retrovert
EEORRSSTU	retroussé
EEORRSTTU	teruteros
EEORRSTUV	overtures
EEORRSTVW	overwrest
EEORRTTVX	extrovert
EEORSSTUW	sou'wester
EEORSTTTU	tetterous
EEORSTTTZ	terzettos
EEOSSSTTT	sestettos
EEPRRSTTU	sputterer
EERRSTTTU	stutterer
EFFGINRSU	suffering
EFFGLORTU	forgetful
EFFGNRSSU	gruffness
EFFHIKSWW	skew-whiff
EFFHINSSU	huffiness
EFFHLLSSU	shelf-fuls
EFFHMSTTU	stuff them
EFFIIORRT	fortifier
EFFIKLORT	off kilter
EFFIKORST	strike off
EFFILMUUV	effluvium
EFFILNOUX	effluxion
EFFINOOSS	noises off
EFFINPSSU	puffiness
EFFINSSST	stiffness
EFFIOOPRR	fireproof
	fire-proof
EFFIORTVY	forty-five
EFFISSUUV	suffusive
EFFLLRTUY	fretfully
EFFNOORRT	forefront
EFFOORRTY	offertory
EFGGIINNR	fingering
EFGGIIWZZ	Fezziwigg
EFGGILOOS	solfeggio
EFGGINOOR	foregoing
EFGGINOSS	fogginess
EFGHHIILR	high-flier
EFGHHILRY	high flyer
	high-flyer
EFGHIILNT	nightlife
EFGHILNSS	fleshings
EFGHILTWY	flyweight
EFGHIOOTT	eightfoot
	eight-foot
EFGHIORST	foresight
	grief-shot
EFGHIORTV	give forth
EFGHNORRU	hunger for
EFGHOOSTT	get shot of
EFGIILNPR	pilfering
EFGIINNRR	infringer
EFGIINRTT	refitting
EFGIINRVY	verifying
EFGIKNOTT	gift token
EFGILNORW	flowering
EFGIMNNOT	fomenting
EFGIMNORR	reforming
EFGINNOST	softening
EFGINORST	fostering
EFGIORTUU	figure out
EFGLLNTUY	fulgently
EFGLNORSW	self-wrong
EFGLOOTUV	tug-of-love
EFGNOORTT	forgotten
	not forget
EFGOOOOST	goosefoot
EFHHIISTW	white fish
EFHHILLSS	shellfish
EFHHNOOOT	on the hoof
EFHIIMSST	fetishism
EFHIINSSS	fishiness
EFHIISSTT	fetishist
EFHIJLLSY	jellyfish
EFHIKNORT	forethink
EFHILLORS	fill-horse
EFHILLSSY	selfishly
EFHILNSSU	unselfish
EFHILSSST	shiftless
EFHINORRT	firethorn
EFHINOSST	stonefish
EFHIOPSTT	stop thief
EFHLLLPUY	helpfully
EFHLLNPUU	unhelpful
EFHLLOPUY	hopefully
EFHLLOSUU	full house
EFHLLOSUV	shovelful
EFHLLOTTU	to the full
EFHLLTTWY	twelfthly
EFHLORSST	frothless
EFHLORSTW	self-worth
EFHLOSSUU	housefuls
EFHNORRTU	further on
EFHOOORTT	the root of
EFHORSSTU	short fuse
EFIIJRSTU	justifier
EFIIKLOUY	if you like
EFIILLLST	still life
EFIILLMOR	mollifier
EFIILLNRU	nullifier
EFIILLORT	oil filter
EFIILMNSS	filminess
EFIILMOTT	leitmotif
EFIILNNOX	inflexion

EFIILOSSS	fossilise
EFIILOSSZ	fossilize
EFIILPRTT	filter-tip
EFIILRTTY	fertility
EFIIMNSST	feminists
EFIIMRSTT	first time
EFIIMRSTY	mystifier
EFIINNOPT	fine point
EFIINNRTU	run it fine
EFIINNSST	niftiness
EFIINNSTY	intensify
EFIINOPST	in spite of
EFIIORRTU	fioriture
EFIISTTVY	festivity
EFIKLORST	frostlike
EFIKNNOTX	next of kin
EFIKOOPRV	Prokofiev
EFIKORRST	foreskirt
EFIKORRSW	fireworks
EFILLNPTU	plentiful
EFILLOORT	floor tile
EFILMNOSY	solemnify
EFILMORSU	formulise
EFILMORUZ	formulize
EFILNNOOS	no flies on
EFILNNORT	front line
EFILNOORS	Solferino
EFILNOOSU	felonious
EFILNOOTU	out of line
EFILNORTW	interflow
EFILNOSST	loftiness
EFILNRSTU	run itself
EFILOOTUV	live out of
EFILORSTY	life story
EFILORSVX	silver fox
EFILOTUZZ	fizzle out
EFILPPUUY	yuppie flu
EFILQRUUV	quiverful
EFILRSSTU	fruitless
EFILRTUVY	furtively
EFIMMORRS	reformism
EFIMMORRV	vermiform
EFIMNNOPR	penniform
EFIMNNOTY	Tom Finney
EFIMNORST	in terms of
EFIMOOTTU	out of time
EFIMORRST	fire-storm
	reformist
EFIMORSTV	first move
EFIMORSTX	exist from
EFINNNSSU	funniness
EFINNSSTU	unfitness
EFINOOPRT	forepoint
EFINOOSTT	set foot in
EFINOPRSU	perfusion
EFINOPRSY	personify
EFINORSTW	frontwise
EFINRRSSU	furriness
EFINRRTUU	furniture
EFINRSSTU	turfiness
EFINSSSSU	fussiness
EFINSSSTU	fustiness
EFINSSSTW	swiftness
EFINSSUZZ	fuzziness
EFIOPRTTU	petit four
EFIORRSTV	strive for
EFIORTTTU	outfitter
EFIOSTTTY	testify to
EFIPRSSTT	first step
EFJNOOORT	not for Joe
EFKLMNOOW	womenfolk
EFKNOOPRS	spoken for
EFLLLMOSU	foul smell
EFLLMOSUY	fulsomely
EFLLMSUUY	musefully
EFLLNTUUY	tunefully
EFLLOORSW	followers
EFLLOOVWW	vow-fellow
EFLLORRUY	Roy Fuller
EFLLRSTUY	restfully
EFLLSTUYZ	zestfully
EFLNNTUUU	untuneful
EFLNORSST	frontless
EFLNORSUW	sunflower
EFLOOOOST	footloose
EFLOOPRTW	flowerpot
EFLOOSTTW	Lowestoft
EFLOPRSUY	profusely
EFLORSSST	frostless
EFLPRSUUX	superflux
EFLRSSSTU	stressful
EFMOOOTUV	move out of
EFNOOOSTT	footnotes
	set on foot
EFNOOTTUU	out of tune
EFOOPPRSU	of purpose
EFOOPRRSS	professor
EFOOPSTTU	out of step
EFOOQRRTU	Roquefort
EFOORTTUU	out of true
EGGGIIJNR	rejigging
EGGGILMSU	misguggle
EGGGINOTT	go-getting
EGGHIILNS	sleighing
EGGHIINNW	whingeing
EGGHIINTW	weighting
EGGHIJNOR	John Greig
EGGHILORU	Lou Gehrig
EGGHINNRU	hungering
EGGIILNNR	lingering
EGGIINNSW	swingeing
EGGIINOOR	Giorgione
EGGIINOPR	Prigogine
EGGILLNRU	gruelling
EGGILNORW	glowering
EGGILOOST	geologist
EGGIMNSSU	mugginess
EGGINNNOR	Groningen
EGGINNORV	governing
EGGINNOTT	getting on
EGGINNRTU	ginger nut
EGGINOORS	gorgonise

EGGINOORV	going-over
EGGINOORZ	gorgonize
EGGINORSU	gingerous
EGGINORTY	Tony Greig
EGGINOSSS	sogginess
EGGINRTTU	guttering
EGGIORRTU	outrigger
EGGLNPSUU	snuggle up
EGGLRRSTU	struggler
EGGNNOORW	gone wrong
EGHHIITWW	weigh with
EGHHIKNTT	The Knight
EGHHILNTU	Leigh Hunt
EGHHNORUW	rough-hewn
EGHHNOTTU	thoughten
EGHHNOUZZ	Zhengzhou
EGHIIKNRS	shrieking
EGHIILLMT	limelight
EGHIILNTV	the living
EGHIILTWY	weightily
EGHIIMNTT	night-time
EGHIINNTW	whitening
EGHIINOTW	weigh into
EGHIINPRS	perishing
EGHIINRSV	shivering
EGHIINRTV	the Virgin
EGHIINRTW	withering
EGHIINSTY	hygienist
EGHIINTTW	get in with
EGHIIRSTZ	rightsize
EGHIITTTW	get with it
EGHIKLOST	ghostlike
EGHILLMOT	megilloth
EGHILLNTY	lengthily
EGHILNNOR	Lohengrin
EGHILNNOT	neon light
EGHILNPTU	lighten up
EGHILNRTU	night-rule
EGHILNSST	lightness
EGHILORST	sole right
EGHILOSTW	go whistle
EGHILPRTU	uplighter
EGHILRTVY	Very light
EGHILSSST	sightless
EGHILSSTT	slightest
EGHIMNOST	something
EGHIMORTT	tiger moth
EGHINNOTW	on the wing
EGHINOPUW	weigh upon
EGHINORSU	rehousing
EGHINORSW	reshowing
EGHINORTV	overnight
EGHINOSTY	histogeny
EGHINOTTW	get on with
EGHINRSST	rightness
EGHINRSTU	sure thing
EGHINRTUW	wuthering
EGHINSSTT	tightness
EGHIOPRTT	tightrope
EGHIORSTU	righteous
EGHIORSTV	oversight
EGHIORTWW	grow white
EGHJLNNNO	John Glenn
EGHLLOORY	glory hole
EGHLMNOPU	ploughmen
EGHLMOOOU	homologue
EGHLNOOPY	nephology
	phenology
EGHLNOORS	longshore
EGHLNOOTY	ethnology
EGHLNOPYY	phylogeny
EGHLOOORR	horologer
EGHLOOTUV	tough love
EGHMNOORW	home-grown
EGHMOOPSS	gomphoses
EGHNNOOTU	not enough
EGHNOPTYY	phytogeny
EGHNORSSU	roughness
EGHNOSSTU	toughness
EGIIKNRSS	Kissinger
EGIILLRTY	Tiger Lily
	tiger lily
EGIILNNST	enlisting
	listening
EGIILNNTT	letting in
EGIILNNUV	unveiling
EGIILNORT	loitering
EGIILNTTY	gentility
EGIILOORS	religioso
EGIILORSU	religious
EGIILSTTZ	Stieglitz
EGIIMNNSS	mingginess
EGIIMNPRS	simpering
EGIIMNRSS	griminess
EGIIMOPST	impetigos
EGIINNORS	nigrosine
	signorine
EGIINNOST	ingestion
EGIINNOSU	ingenious
EGIINNQRU	enquiring
EGIINNRSW	inswinger
EGIINNSTV	investing
EGIINNTUY	ingenuity
EGIINPPQU	equipping
EGIINQRRU	requiring
EGIINQRUV	quivering
EGIINRRTU	intriguer
EGIINRRTW	rewriting
EGIINRSST	resisting
	sistering
EGIINRSTT	string tie
EGIINRTTT	tittering
EGIINRTTY	integrity
EGIJKNNTU	junketing
EGIJLNSTY	jestingly
EGIKLNNOO	inglenook
EGIKNORRW	reworking
EGILLLNTY	tellingly
EGILLMNTY	meltingly
EGILLMORU	glomeruli
EGILLMOTU	guillemot
EGILLNNOT	Ellington

EGILLNORS	Negrillos
EGILLNOTT	ill-gotten
EGILLNOTW	towelling
EGILLNOTX	extolling
EGILLNPTY	peltingly
EGILLOSSY	syllogise
EGILLOSYZ	syllogize
EGILLSSTU	guiltless
EGILMNOOS	Mongolise
	neologism
EGILMNOOZ	Mongolize
EGILMOOSY	semiology
EGILMOSUU	eulogiums
EGILNNOOS	loosening
EGILNNOST	singleton
EGILNNOTX	Lexington
EGILNNOUY	Neil Young
EGILNNRSU	nurseling
EGILNOOST	neologist
EGILNORTV	revolting
EGILNORVV	revolving
EGILNOSTU	single out
EGILNOTVY	longevity
EGILNRSTU	resulting
EGILNRSTW	wrestling
EGILNSSST	stingless
EGILNSSTT	settlings
EGILOOPRS	prologise
EGILOOPRZ	prologize
EGILOORTT	Rigoletto
EGILORSTY	sortilegy
EGILOSSTT	glottises
EGIMMNSSU	gumminess
EGIMNNORT	mentoring
EGIMNNOSS	messing on
EGIMNORSV	misgovern
EGIMNPRSU	presuming
EGIMNRSSY	synergism
EGIMNRTTU	muttering
EGINNNNPU	unpenning
EGINNNRUV	unnerving
EGINNOPPU	opening-up
EGINNORSW	worsening
EGINNOSUU	ingenuous
EGINNRRTU	returning
EGINNRSTT	stringent
EGINNRSTU	insurgent
	unresting
EGINNTTUV	vingt-et-un
EGINOPPRS	pop singer
EGINOPRRR	porringer
EGINOPRRT	reporting
EGINOPRRV	reproving
EGINOPRST	progestin
EGINOPRTT	pottering
EGINOPTUV	not give up
EGINORRST	restoring
	rostering
EGINORRTV	Vortigern
EGINORRTW	intergrow
EGINORSUY	Sigourney
EGINORTTT	tottering
EGINOSSTU	goutiness
EGINPPSUW	spewing up
EGINPSTTU	setting up
	setting-up
	upsetting
EGINPSTWW	sweptwing
EGINRSUVY	surveying
EGINSSSTU	gustiness
	gutsiness
EGIOPPRSS	gossipper
EGIPPRTTU	gruppetti
EGIPSTUZZ	Zugspitze
EGKNOOTTW	get to know
EGKORSSUW	guesswork
EGLLMNORY	mongrelly
EGLMNOOOU	monologue
EGLMOOORV	overgloom
EGLMOOTYY	etymology
EGLNNOSUU	sun lounge
EGLNNPTUY	pungently
EGLNOOOPY	poenology
EGLNOORUY	neurology
EGLNOOSUV	longevous
EGLNOSTUU	glutenous
EGLOOOSTY	osteology
EGLOOPRTY	petrology
EGLOOPSTY	pestology
EGLOORSSV	gloss over
EGMNOOOSS	mongooses
EGMNOORRS	Gros Morne
EGNNNRRUU	gunrunner
EGNNOOSUY	young ones
EGNNORSSW	wrongness
EGNOOOSSW	snow goose
EGNOOPRSS	prognoses
EGNOORRSV	governors
EGNOORRVW	overgrown
EGNOOSUXY	oxygenous
EGNOOTTUU	outtongue
EGNOPRSUW	newsgroup
EGNORSSSS	grossness
EGNORSTUY	youngster
EGNPRSSUU	sun spurge
EGNRRTTUU	turret-gun
EGOOPRSST	go to press
EHHIINSTT	in the shit
EHHIIRTTT	thirtieth
EHHIJNORT	John Reith
EHHILLLSY	hellishly
EHHILLORT	Hollerith
EHHILOPRS	philhorse
EHHILOTTT	to the hilt
EHHINORTW	no whither
EHHIOPRSW	horsewhip
EHHIOSTVY	yeshivoth
EHHJNNORY	John Henry
EHHLLMOTZ	Helmholtz
EHHLOOPTY	holophyte
EHHLPSSTY	The Sylphs
EHHMNNOPP	Phnom Penh

EHHMNOOOP	homophone
EHHMNOSUY	hush money
EHHMORTTU	home truth
EHHMRTUYY	eurhythmy
EHHNOORTU	on the hour
EHHNOSTUU	house-hunt
EHHOOPSTY	theosophy
EHIIINRVY	Henry VIII
EHIIINTTW	tie in with
EHIIKLMTW	milk-white
EHIIKNNPT	in the pink
EHIIKNSTT	kittenish
EHIILLNPT	tephillin
EHIILLNSS	hilliness
EHIILLRSW	ill-wisher
EHIILLTWY	lily-white
EHIILMRST	Hitlerism
EHIILPSSY	syphilise
EHIILPSYZ	syphilize
EHIILRSTT	Hitlerist
EHIILRSTW	Wiltshire
EHIIMNSTW	in the swim
EHIIMRSTT	tritheism
EHIINNSSS	shininess
EHIINORRT	inheritor
EHIINPPRW	whipper-in
EHIINPRST	nephritis
EHIINPSST	pithiness
EHIIPPSSY	epiphysis
EHIIPRSTT	the Spirit
EHIIPTTUW	tie up with
EHIIRSSTW	Irish stew
EHIIRSTTT	tritheist
EHIJNOPPR	John Piper
EHIKLLPSY	sylphlike
	sylph-like
EHIKLNPRY	hyperlink
EHIKLORTZ	kilohertz
EHIKNNOTW	in the know
EHIKNORTV	think over
EHIKNPRRS	pre-shrink
EHIKNSSSU	huskiness
EHIKORRSY	Yorkshire
EHILLNOPT	on the pill
EHILLOSTY	hostilely
EHILLOSWY	yellowish
EHILLRSTU	Ruth Ellis
EHILLSSTU	shell suit
EHILMNOST	monthlies
EHILMNPTU	in the lump
EHILMRSST	mirthless
EHILNOOPT	lithopone
	phonolite
EHILNOSUY	heinously
EHILOOSTT	hostile to
EHILOPSSU	Sophus Lie
EHILOPTYY	heliotypy
EHILPSTTY	pettishly
EHIMNNOOS	moonshine
EHIMNOPUU	euphonium
EHIMNRTUU	ruthenium
EHIMNSTTU	tunesmith
EHIMORRRT	The Mirror
EHIMORSTT	short time
EHIMPRRTU	triumpher
EHINNOPSS	phoniness
EHINNORSS	horniness
EHINNOSTW	whinstone
EHINNSSTU	Nissen hut
EHINOOPST	point shoe
EHINOORST	Hortensio
EHINOPRSW	ownership
EHINOPSTT	phonetist
EHINOPSTU	in the soup
EHINOPSTY	hypnotise
EHINOPTYZ	hypnotize
EHINORRSU	nourisher
EHINORSSS	horsiness
EHINORTXY	thyroxine
EHINOSSSW	showiness
EHINOSTWW	snow-white
EHINPSSSU	pushiness
EHINRTTUW	turn white
EHINSSSTY	synthesis
EHINSTTWY	twentyish
EHIOPRSST	prothesis
EHIOPRTTW	white port
EHIORSTTW	worthiest
EHJLNNOOT	Elton John
EHJLNORTY	John Tyler
EHJNNOOST	Johnstone
EHKOORRSW	workhorse
EHKOORSUW	housework
EHLLMOPSY	mesophyll
EHLLORSST	sell short
EHLLOSTUW	Southwell
EHLNNOTTU	Len Hutton
EHLNOOPPY	polyphone
EHLNOOPRT	North Pole
	north pole
EHLNOOPXY	xylophone
EHLNOOSTY	holystone
EHLNOPSWY	Welsh Pony
EHLNORRTY	northerly
EHLOOPSTU	South Pole
	south pole
EHLOOPSTY	photolyse
EHLOOSSTT	toothless
EHLOPRSTU	upholster
EHLOPSTYY	hypostyle
EHLORSSTW	worthless
EHLORSTUY	southerly
EHMMNOORY	monorhyme
EHMMOOPRS	mesomorph
EHMNNOOOY	honeymoon
EHMNORRST	Ernst Röhm
EHMNOSTUU	mouse-hunt
EHMOOORSU	houseroom
EHMOOOSTT	toothsome
EHMOOPSTU	shoot-'em-up
EHMORRSTT	short-term
EHMPRRTUY	pyrethrum

EHNNOOTTW	On the Town	EIILMOTTV	leitmotiv
EHNNORTTU	on the turn	EIILMPSUV	impulsive
EHNOOOPPT	optophone	EIILNNOQU	quinoline
EHNOOPPTY	phonotype	EIILNPSST	splenitis
EHNOOPRTW	throw open	EIILNPSTY	pensility
EHNOOPSTT	on the spot	EIILNQTUY	inquietly
	on-the-spot	EIILNSTTY	tensility
EHNOORTTT	on the trot	EIILNTUVY	unitively
EHNOOSTUW	town house	EIILPRTUY	puerility
	town-house	EIILRSSUV	Silverius
EHNOOTTTT	Hottentot	EIILRSTTY	sterility
EHNOPRTTU	pot-hunter	EIILRSTTZ	strelitzi
EHNOPSSTY	pythoness	EIILRSTVY	servility
EHNORSSST	shortness	EIIMMNORS	immersion
EHNORSTTW	north-west	EIIMMNSTY	immensity
EHNRSTTUU	unshutter	EIIMMORST	memoirist
EHOOOPRSU	poorhouse	EIIMMPSSS	pessimism
EHOOORSTV	overshoot	EIIMNOPST	pimientos
EHOOPRRTV	hoverport	EIIMNORSS	missioner
EHOOPRSST	posthorse		remission
EHOOPSSTU	posthouse	EIIMNRSST	ministers
EHOORRTVW	overthrow	EIIMNSSST	mistiness
	throw over	EIIMOPRSU	imperious
EHOPPSSTU	set up shop	EIIMOPRSV	improvise
EHOSSTTUW	South-West	EIIMOPSTT	epitomist
	south-west	EIIMOSSTV	sovietism
EIIILMMTT	time limit	EIIMPSSST	pessimist
EIIILNNSV	live in sin	EIINNNOST	intension
EIIILSTTU	utilities	EIINNNOTT	intention
EIIIMPRTV	primitive	EIINNNOTV	invention
EIIINQRSU	inquiries	EIINNORST	insertion
EIIINRSTT	retinitis	EIINNORSV	inversion
EIIINTTUV	intuitive	EIINNOSSS	in session
EIIJLMSSU	Miss Julie		noisiness
EIIJNNORT	interjoin	EIINNPPSS	nippiness
EIIJNOSSU	join issue	EIINNPSSS	spininess
EIIKKLNST	like stink	EIINNSSTT	insistent
EIIKKNNSS	kinkiness	EIINNSTTY	intensity
EIIKLMNSS	milkiness	EIINOPRSV	prevision
EIIKLNNRT	interlink	EIINOPTVW	viewpoint
EIIKLNRSW	wrinklies	EIINORSTU	routinise
EIIKLNSSS	silkiness	EIINORSTY	seniority
EIIKLORST	strike oil	EIINORTUZ	routinize
EIIKNNRTT	interknit	EIINPRSST	persist in
EIIKNRSSS	riskiness	EIINPSSST	tipsiness
EIILLMNRY	millinery	EIINQTTTU	quintetti
EIILLMSST	limitless	EIINRSTUV	intrusive
EIILLNNOP	penillion	EIINRTTUV	nutritive
EIILLNOOR	neroli oil		vetturini
EIILLNSSS	silliness	EIINSSSSS	sissiness
EIILLOPRS	pillorise	EIINSSTTW	wittiness
EIILLOPRZ	pillorize	EIINSTTTU	institute
EIILLSTUV	Vitellius	EIIPRRTUV	irruptive
EIILMNORV	vermilion	EIJKLLOOU	kilojoule
EIILMNOST	St-Émilion	EIJLLLMOV	Jim Lovell
EIILMNOSU	limousine	EIJLLNOSS	jolliness
EIILMNPPS	mislippen	EIJLMNPTU	mint-julep
EIILMNPRU	primuline	EIJMNPSSU	jumpiness
EIILMNSSS	sliminess	EIJNNOSST	jointness
EIILMOPRV	Primo Levi	EIJNORRSU	surrejoin
EIILMOPSV	implosive	EIJPRTTUY	petit jury

EIKLLRTUW	Kurt Weill
EIKLMMORZ	klezmorim
EIKLMORSY	irksomely
EIKLNNRUW	unwrinkle
EIKLNPRRS	sprinkler
EIKLNSSSU	sulkiness
EIKMNOORS	mono-skier
EIKMNOSSS	smokiness
EIKMNOSTY	Mike Tyson
EIKMNOTTT	Tom Kitten
EIKMNRSSU	murkiness
EIKMNSSSU	muskiness
EIKNNOPRT	pinkerton
EIKNOPSTY	key points
EIKNORRTW	interwork
EIKNORSTV	overstink
EIKNRRTTY	trinketry
EIKORSTTU	outstrike
	strike out
EILLLOTTW	little owl
EILLMNOST	millstone
EILLMORST	still more
EILLMOSSY	lissomely
EILLMPTUX	multiplex
EILLMRTUU	tellurium
EILLNOPRU	nullipore
EILLNORST	stornelli
EILLNOSSW	lowliness
EILLNOTVY	violently
EILLNSSST	stillness
EILLNSSSY	sinlessly
EILLOOPRV	Liverpool
EILLOOTTT	too little
EILLOPRSV	overspill
	spill over
	spillover
EILLOPRTY	pellitory
EILLOPRWW	willpower
EILLOPSST	pilotless
EILLPRSUW	pull wires
EILLPSSSY	syllepsis
EILLSSTWY	witlessly
EILMMOPSY	misemploy
EILMNOORR	minor role
EILMNOOSY	noisomely
EILMNOPST	simpleton
EILMNOPSU	on impulse
EILMNORTT	tormentil
EILMNOSTY	solemnity
EILMNOSWY	winsomely
EILMNPSSU	lumpiness
EILMOOSTY	ileostomy
EILMOSTUY	timeously
EILNNOSTV	insolvent
EILNOOPSX	explosion
EILNOOTUV	evolution
EILNOPRSU	repulsion
EILNOPSST	pointless
EILNOPSSU	spinulose
EILNOPSUX	expulsion
EILNORSSY	sensorily
EILNORSTY	storyline
EILNORSUV	revulsion
EILNORTUY	routinely
EILNOSSSU	lousiness
EILNOSUVY	enviously
EILNPQTUU	quintuple
EILNPRSTY	splintery
EILNQTUUY	unquietly
EILNRSSSU	surliness
EILNRSTTU	turnstile
EILNRTUUV	vulturine
EILNSSSTU	lustiness
EILOPPRSS	prolepsis
EILOPRSTV	liver spot
EILOPSTTT	test pilot
EILOPSTUY	piteously
EILORRTVW	liverwort
EILORSSUY	seriously
EILOSSTTT	stilettos
EILRRTUWZ	Wurlitzer®
EILRSSTTW	wristlets
EIMMNOPRS	persimmon
EIMMOOPRU	prooemium
EIMMOPRSU	emporiums
EIMMOPSTU	impostume
EIMNNOPRT	prominent
EIMNNORST	innermost
EIMNNPTUU	neptunium
EIMNNRTTU	nutriment
EIMNOOOPR	prooemion
EIMNOOPRV	improve on
EIMNOORSS	roominess
EIMNOORST	trominoes
EIMNOPRTU	importune
EIMNORRTW	worriment
EIMNORSSU	sensorium
EIMNORSUV	verminous
EIMNOSSSS	mossiness
EIMNOSSST	moistness
EIMNOSSSU	mousiness
EIMNOSTTY	testimony
EIMNOTTZZ	mezzotint
EIMNSSSTU	mustiness
EIMNSSUZZ	muzziness
EIMOORRSW	worrisome
EIMOPRRST	misreport
EIMOPRSTU	imposture
EIMOPSTUU	impetuous
EIMORRRST	terrorism
EIMORRSTU	trimerous
EIMORSUVY	voyeurism
EINNNOTTY	nonentity
EINNNSSSU	sunniness
EINNOORST	ironstone
	serotonin
EINNOPSTT	not in step
EINNORSTU	neutrinos
EINNORTVY	inventory
EINNOSSST	stoniness
EINNOSSSW	snowiness
EINNOSSTY	syntonise

EINNOSTYZ	syntonize
EINNPRSTW	newsprint
EINNQSTTU	St-Quentin
EINNRTTUW	unwritten
EINNSSTTU	nuttiness
EINOOPRST	sore point
EINOOPSSW	spoonwise
EINOORRTT	retortion
EINOORTTX	extortion
EINOORTTY	notoriety
EINOOSSST	sootiness
EINOOSSWZ	wooziness
EINOPPSSS	soppiness
EINOPRRTU	erruption
EINOPRRTV	overprint
EINOPRSSS	prosiness
EINOPRSTU	Petronius
EINOPRSUU	penurious
EINOPRTVY	in poverty
EINOPSSSU	piousness
EINOPSSSY	synopsise
EINOPSSTT	pottiness
EINOPSSYZ	synopsize
EINOQSSTU	questions
EINORRSSS	sorriness
EINORRTTV	introvert
EINORSTTU	ritenutos
EINORSTUX	extrusion
EINORSVYY	very noisy
EINOSSTUU	Suetonius
EINOSTTVY	ventosity
EINPRRTTU	interrupt
EINRSSSTU	rustiness
EIOOPRRST	posterior
EIOOPRSSV	provisoes
EIOOPRSTX	expositor
EIOPPRRTY	propriety
EIOPPRSUV	purposive
EIOPRSTTU	proustite
EIOPRSTTY	posterity
EIOQRSTUU	turquoise
EIORRRSTT	terrorist
EIORRRTTY	territory
EIPQRTTUY	triptyque
EIPRRRSSU	surpriser
EIPRSSSTU	pertussis
EIQRSSTTU	questrist
EIRRSTVXY	River Styx
EJLLOSSYY	joylessly
EJMNORUWY	jurywomen
EJNOORRSU	sojourner
EKLLNNOWW	well known
	well-known
EKLMMNOSU	musk melon
EKLNOOORS	lookers-on
	onlookers
EKMNNOORS	non-smoker
EKMNNOTUY	monkey nut
EKNOOPRUV	unprovoke
EKNOOPSTU	outspoken
EKNOORSTW	stonework
EKNORSSTU	sunstroke
EKOORRTUW	outworker
EKOORSTTW	set to work
ELLMOOTUW	mellow out
ELLMOSUUY	emulously
ELLMRSTUU	surmullet
ELLNOPRSU	prunellos
ELLNOPTUY	opulently
ELLNOTTTY	Lyttelton
ELMMNSSUU	Mussulmen
ELMNNOOST	somnolent
ELMNOORTV	Lermontov
ELMNPPSSU	plumpness
ELMORSSST	stormless
ELMORSTUU	tremulous
ELNOORSTU	turn loose
ELNOORSUY	onerously
ELNORSUVY	nervously
ELNOSTUUY	tenuously
ELOOPPTTT	pottle-pot
ELOORSTVY	love story
ELOPPPUVY	puppy love
ELOPPRSUY	purposely
ELOPRRSUW	rowel-spur
ELOPRRSUY	prelusory
ELOPTUUZZ	puzzle out
ELOQRSUUU	querulous
ELORSTTUU	outlustre
ELPRSTTUY	spluttery
EMMNOOOSS	meno mosso
EMMNOOSTU	momentous
EMMNOSSSU	summonses
EMNNOOOST	moonstone
EMNNOORUU	numero uno
EMNOOPSUY	eponymous
EMNOORRTT	tormentor
EMNOORTUV	overmount
EMOOORRST	storeroom
EMOOPRTTY	optometry
EMOOPSSSU	espumosos
EMOORSTTU	outermost
EMOPPRRTU	prompture
EMOPPRSTU	uppermost
EMOPRRTUV	overtrump
EMOPRRTYY	pyrometry
EMORSTTTU	uttermost
EMORSTTUU	muster out
ENNNOOOSW	on one's own
ENNNOOPRS	non-person
ENNOOOPTT	not open to
ENNOOPPRT	proponent
ENNOOPPST	opponents
ENNOOPRTV	not proven
ENNORSTTU	turnstone
ENNPRRSUU	runners-up
ENOOPPRSU	on purpose
ENOOPPRTU	opportune
ENOOPRRSS	responsor
ENOOPRRTU	root-prune
ENOORSTTT	Otto Stern
ENOORSTTW	stonewort

ENOOSSTTU	sostenuto
ENOPPRSTU	unstopper
ENOPTTTWY	top twenty
ENORSSTUU	strenuous
ENOSSSTTU	stoutness
EOOOPRRTU	Europoort
EOOORTUVY	over to you!
EOOPPRRSS	oppressor
EOOPPRTTY	prototype
EOOPRRSTT	protestor
EOOPRSSSS	possessor
EOPPRRSTU	supporter
EOPPRSSST	stop press
EORRSSSST	strossers
EORRSTUXY	extrusory
EORSSSTTU	stress out

F

FFFHIINOS	finish off
FFFOOPTUU	out of puff
FFGGIINOV	giving-off
FFGHIILNW	whiffling
FFGHILNSU	shuffling
FFGHILRTU	frightful
FFGHIOOTW	go off with
FFGHOPRUU	rough-puff
FFGIILNNS	sniffling
FFGILNNSU	snuffling
FFGILNOXY	flying fox
FFGILNPUY	puffingly
FFGINOPRS	offspring
FFHHILSUY	huffishly
FFHILOOPS	polish off
FFHLORSUU	four-flush
FFIILLNOR	fill in for
FFIILMOST	off limits
	off-limits
FFIILMRXY	fix firmly
FFILLOPTU	pull it off
FFILMOORR	floriform
FFINNOORT	in front of
FFINOSSUU	suffusion
FFIOORSTT	first-foot
FFIOOSSTT	toss it off
FFIORSTTU	soft fruit
FFLMNOOSU	moufflons
FFLOOOOPR	foolproof
FFNOPSTUU	up to snuff
FFORRSUUU	furfurous
FGGHIINOS	go fishing
FGGIINORV	forgiving
FGHHILNOW	high-flown
FGHHOOTTU	thought of
FGHIIINNS	finishing
FGHIILLTY	flightily
FGHIINORT	in right of
FGHILOPTT	top-flight
FGHINORTT	fortnight
FGHMOORTU	frogmouth
FGIIILLNN	filling-in
FGIIILNVY	vilifying
FGIIINVVY	vivifying
FGIILLLRT	flirt-gill
	gillflirt
FGIILLNRU	in full rig
FGIILNNOW	inflowing
FGIILNPTU	uplifting
FGIILNSTY	siftingly
FGIILNTTY	fittingly
FGIILRTUU	ugli® fruit
FGIIMNNOR	informing
FGIINNTTU	unfitting
FGIINPRUY	purifying
FGIKLLNOS	golf links
FGILLNOOW	following
FGILLNOWY	flowingly
FGILNNOUV	fun-loving
FGILNNOUW	unflowing
FGILNNRUU	unfurling
FGILNNRUY	Funny Girl
FGILOOSTU	ufologist
FGINNOORT	go in front
FGLLNORUW	full-grown
FGLLNOSUY	songfully
FGNOOORTW	wrong-foot
FGOOORTUW	grow out of
FHHIORTTW	forthwith
FHIIIKLLS	killifish
FHIILRTTW	flirt with
FHIILRTTY	thriftily
FHIIORSTX	hit for six
FHIIORSTY	historify
FHIKMORRS	shirk from
FHILLOOSY	foolishly
FHILLOSWY	wolfishly
FHILLSUWY	wishfully
FHILOPPSY	foppishly
FHIMORSTX	sixth form
FHINNRSUU	unfurnish
FHINRTTUY	unthrifty
FHIOOOTTT	hotfoot it
FHIORRSTT	thirst for
FHLLPSUUY	pushfully
FHLLRTUUY	hurtfully
	ruthfully
FHLMOSTUU	mouthfuls
FHLOOOPRS	shop floor
FHLOOORSW	floor show
FHMOOOPRT	mothproof
FHMOORRST	short form
FHNORRTTU	turn forth
FHOOPRRTU	pour forth
FHOORRTTW	Fort Worth
FIIIKRTUW	kiwi fruit
FIIILNOPS	Filipinos
FIIIMNRTY	infirmity
FIIKLNNST	skinflint
FIILLMORV	villiform
FIILLPTUY	pitifully
FIILORTVY	frivolity
FIIMMNORS	misinform
FIIMNOPRS	spiniform

FIIMORRTU	triforium
FIIMORRTV	vitriform
FIINNOOPT	in point of
FIJMNOTUU	Mount Fuji
FIKLLLSUY	skilfully
FIKLLNSUU	unskilful
FILLLPSTU	full-split
FILLNOPTU	full point
FILLSTUWY	wistfully
FILMMORTU	multiform
FILMNORUY	uniformly
FILMORUVV	vulviform
FILOOOPRT	portfolio
FILOORSUV	frivolous
FILORRSTY	floristry
FILORSUUY	furiously
FILOSSTUU	fistulous
FINNOOPRT	non-profit
FINOOPRSU	profusion
FINOOPRTT	footprint
FKLNOOSTW	townsfolk
FKLNRSTUU	trunkfuls
FKOOORTUW	out of work
FKOORRSTW	frostwork
FLLLOSUUY	soulfully
FLLLSTUUY	lustfully
FLLNOORRY	forlornly
FLLOOOTUW	follow out
FLLOOPTUU	pull out of
FLNOOPSSU	spoonfuls
FLOOOOSTT	footstool
FLOORRSUW	sorrowful
FLOPRSSUU	plus-fours
FMNNOOORW	from now on
FMNOOORRT	front room
FNNOOORTT	front onto
FNNOOPRUW	frown upon
FOOORRRSW	sorrow for
FOOPSSTUY	pussyfoot
	pussy-foot

G

GGGIILNRW	wriggling
GGGILMNSU	smuggling
GGGILNTUY	tuggingly
GGHHHIILT	highlight
GGHHILOSY	hoggishly
GGHHINORW	high-grown
GGHHOORTU	go through
GGHIIILRW	whirligig
GGHIILNNT	lightning
GGHIILNST	slighting
GGHIILNSY	sighingly
GGHIILPSY	piggishly
GGHIINRTW	right wing
	right-wing
GGHIINSST	sight-sing
GGHILNNOT	nightlong
GGHILNSUY	gushingly
GGHILORTW	grow light
GGHINNOTW	nightgown
GGHLOORYY	hygrology
GGIIIMNNP	impinging
GGIIIMNSV	misgiving
GGIILNNRY	ringingly
GGIILNNSY	singingly
GGIILNPRY	gripingly
GGIILNRZZ	grizzling
GGIIMNOSS	go missing
GGIINNNOS	signing on
GGIINNORW	ingrowing
GGIINNPRS	springing
GGIINNPSU	signing up
	signing-up
GGIINNSWW	swing-wing
GGIINOPSS	gossiping
GGIINOTUV	giving-out
GGILLNNOY	longingly
GGILLNOWY	glowingly
GGILMNSUY	ginglymus
GGILMOOSY	gismology
GGILMOOYZ	gizmology
GGILNOPRY	gropingly
GGILNORUY	young girl
GGINOOSTU	outgoings
GGINOPRUW	growing up
GHHHIIMST	Highsmith
GHHIIJKNS	high jinks
GHHIILPST	lightship
GHHIINOPT	high point
GHHMNORUU	Hugh Munro
GHIIKNNRS	shrinking
GHIIKNSTT	skintight
	skin-tight
GHIIKNTTT	tight-knit
GHIILLNRT	thrilling
GHIILLOTW	go ill with
GHIILLRSY	girlishly
GHIILNNSY	shiningly
GHIILNNTY	hintingly
GHIILNNWY	whiningly
GHIILNOPS	polishing
GHIILNOST	night-soil
GHIILNSSY	hissingly
GHIILRSTY	tigrishly
GHIIMNPRS	shrimping
GHIINNPSU	punishing
GHIINNRSU	inrushing
GHIINOPPT	piping hot
GHIINRSTT	thirsting
GHILLOOPY	philology
GHILLOOTY	lithology
GHILLPTTU	pull tight
GHILMNOOT	moonlight
GHILNOOPT	pot-holing
GHILNOORY	rhinology
GHILNOPTU	light upon
GHILNPSUY	pushingly
GHILNSTUY	unsightly
GHILOOSTY	histology
GHILOPSTT	spotlight
	stoplight

GHILORSUY	roguishly
GHILOSTTU	lights out
GHILPRSTY	sprightly
GHILPRTUY	uprightly
GHIMMNTUY	thingummy
GHIMNORUU	humouring
GHIMNOSST	songsmith
GHIMORSST	Grossmith
GHINNOORU	honouring
GHINNORSU	onrushing
GHINOOTTW	not go with
GHINOPRST	hot spring
GHINOPSTT	nightspot
GHINOPSUW	showing up
GHINORSST	strongish
GHINOTUWY	with young
GHINRSTTU	thrusting
GHIOOTTUW	go out with
	go without
GHIOPSTTT	tight spot
GHLMNOOYY	hymnology
GHLMOOTYY	mythology
GHLNOOOPY	phonology
GHLNOOPYY	hypnology
GHMNOOSUU	humongous
GHMNOSUUU	humungous
GHNNOOPRR	pronghorn
GHNOOSTTW	ghost town
GHOOORSTT	Ostrogoth
GHOORTTUW	outgrowth
GHOPRTUUW	upwrought
	wrought-up
GIIILNNOZ	lionizing
GIIILOSTU	litigious
GIIINNORS	signorini
GIIINNPRS	inspiring
GIIINNQRU	inquiring
GIIINNRTW	in writing
GIIINOSSS	Issigonis
GIIINRTVY	virginity
GIIJKLMNO	Kim Jong Il
	Kim Jong-Il
GIIJKNORS	ski-joring
GIIJNNOPU	joining up
GIIKLLMNS	Kingsmill
GIIKLMNSU	Kim Il-sung
GIIKLNNTW	twinkling
GIIKLNNWY	winkingly
GIIKNSVVY	skivvying
GIILLLNWY	willingly
GIILLMNPY	limpingly
GIILLMNSY	smilingly
GIILLNNUW	unwilling
GIILLNOTU	Guillotin
GIILLNOTW	willing to
GIILLNPSY	lispingly
GIILMNNSU	unsmiling
GIILMNOPR	imploring
GIILMNSSY	missingly
GIILNNNWY	winningly
GIILNNOST	Islington

GIILNNPPY	nippingly
GIILNNSTU	insulting
GIILNNTWY	twiningly
GIILNOSUU	uliginous
GIILNPRST	stripling
GIILNPRSY	springily
GIILNPSTT	splitting
GIILNPTYY	pityingly
GIILNRSTY	stringily
GIILNTTWY	wittingly
GIIMMNRST	trimmings
GIIMNOPRS	promising
GIIMNOPRV	improving
GIIMNOTTW	two-timing
GIIMNRSSU	surmising
GIIMPRSTU	spirit gum
GIINNPRST	sprinting
GIINNPTUY	unpitying
GIINNQSTU	squinting
GIINNRSSU	Rising Sun
GIINNSSTU	unsisting
GIINNTTUW	unwitting
GIINPPRST	stripping
GIINQRSTU	squirting
GIINRSUVV	surviving
GIJKLNORW	J K Rowling
GIJKNNOOT	not joking
GIJLLNOTY	joltingly
GIJLNTTUY	juttingly
GIKLNNNSY	King's Lynn
GIKLNNOOO	onlooking
GIKLNNOWY	knowingly
GIKNNNOUW	unknowing
GIKNNOSTW	Kingstown
GIKNOOPRV	provoking
GIKNOOPTU	poking out
GIKNOOTWW	kowtowing
GIKOORSTW	Grotowski
GILLLLNOY	lollingly
GILLMNOOY	limnology
GILLMOSSY	syllogism
GILLNNORU	unrolling
GILLNOPSY	slopingly
GILLNOPTU	polluting
GILLNORST	strolling
GILLNORUY	louringly
GILLOOOPY	oligopoly
GILLOORSU	orgillous
GILMMNOOS	mongolism
GILMNNOTY	Lymington
GILMNOPRY	rompingly
GILNNNPUY	punningly
GILNNNRUY	runningly
GILNOPPTY	toppingly
GILNOPSUW	slowing-up
GILNOPTUY	poutingly
GILNORSUY	rousingly
GILNORTUU	ruling out
GILNOSTUU	glutinous
GILNPPSUY	supplying
GILNPRRUY	purringly

GILOOORST	orologist
GILOOOSTT	otologist
GILOOOSTZ	zoologist
GILOORSTU	urologist
GIMMNPSUU	summing-up
GIMMNRRUU	murmuring
GIMNNOORS	Monsignor
GIMNOOPRT	promoting
GIMNOORSU	ginormous
GIMNOPPRT	prompting
GIMOPRUUY	uropygium
GINNNOOTV	non-voting
GINNOOPRT	Orpington
GINNOOTTV	not voting
GINNORSST	no strings
GINNORTTU	turning to
GINNRRTUU	nurturing
GINOOPRSS	prognosis
GINOOPRST	gros point
GINOOPRTU	uprooting
GINOORRSW	sorrowing
GINOORSTU	trigonous
GINOPPSSU	supposing
GINOPRSTU	outspring
	posturing
	sprouting
GINOPSSTU	stop using
GINOPTTTU	totting-up
GINORSTTU	string out
GINRSTTTU	strutting
GKNORTUUY	Young Turk
GLNOORSTY	long story
GNOORRSTY	Roy Strong
GNORSTTUU	strung out
GORRSTUWY	worryguts

H

HHIIKNTTW	think with
HHIJMNOST	John Smith
HHIORTTWW	Whitworth
HHKLOOOSV	Sholokhov
HHMMOOOPR	homomorph
HHMNOOOPY	homophony
HHNOORRST	shorthorn ❑
HIIISTTVW	visit with
HIILLMNOT	millionth
HIILLOOOP	hoi polloi
HIILLOSWW	willowish
HIILMPSSU	silphiums
HIILMPSWY	wimpishly
HIILNSSWY	swinishly
HIILNTYZZ	Thin Lizzy
HIILOSTTY	hostility
HIILPSTTY	typhlitis
HIILRSTTY	thirstily
HIIMNOSST	Shintoism
HIIMORSSS	Irish moss
HIIMORSST	hit or miss
	hit-or-miss
HIINOSSTT	Shintoist
HIINOTTTW	not with it
HIIOTTTUW	out with it!
HIJLLMNOS	John Mills
HIKLMOOTT	milk tooth
HIKNNORST	stinkhorn
HIKNSSVYY	Vyshinsky
HILLMORUU	ill-humour
HILLMPSUY	lumpishly
HILLNSTTU	still-hunt
HILLOOPRW	whirlpool
HILLOSTUY	loutishly
HILLOSVWY	wolvishly
HILLSSTYY	stylishly
HILMMPSUY	mumpishly
HILMOOTTY	lithotomy
HILMOPRSY	rompishly
HILNNOSTY	tonnishly
HILOOPRST	polo shirt
HILOPRSST	short slip
HILORSSTT	shortlist
	short-list
HILORSSUY	sourishly
HILOSSTTY	sottishly
HILRSTUUV	vulturish
HIMNNOOSY	moonshiny
HIMNOPSTY	hypnotism
HINNOOPTT	thin on top
HINOPSTTY	hypnotist
HINORSTTU	North Uist
HIOOPPRST	troop-ship
HIOOPPTUW	whoop it up
HIOORSTTT	orthotist
HIOPRSSTY	sophistry
HIOPRSTTU	tutorship
HIOSSTTUU	South Uist
HIPPTTUUW	put up with
HJJNNOORU	John Junor
HKKNNOOTY	honky-tonk
HKMMNORRU	krummhorn
HLLOOOTUW	hollow out
HLMOOPPXY	pompholyx
HLNOOPPYY	polyphony
HLOOORTWW	Woolworth
HLOOPPRSY	sporophyl
HMOOOPRTU	poor-mouth
HMOOOSTTU	smooth out
HNOOPSTUW	put on show
HOOPRSSTT	stop short
HOOPRSTTU	Southport
HORSTTTUU	thrust out

I

IIIKMNRST	mini skirt
	miniskirt
IIILNOSTV	violinist
IIILNTTUY	inutility
IIIMPRSST	spiritism
IIIMRRTUV	triumviri
IIINNNRTT	Rin Tin Tin
IIINNOTTU	intuition
IIINSSSTU	sinusitis
IIIPRSSTT	spiritist

IIJNORSUU	injurious
IIKKMNOSW	Minkowski
IIKNTTTUU	Inuktitut
IILLLOPUV	pulvillio
IILLNNNOO	nonillion
IILMNOOPS	implosion
IILMNOPSU	impulsion
IILMNORTU	in turmoil
IILMNOSSU	Mussolini
IILMOPSSS	solipsism
IILMOPSUY	impiously
IILNOOPST	postilion
IILNTTUWY	unwittily
IILOPRTXY	prolixity
IILOPSSST	solipsist
IILOSTVVZ	slivovitz
IIMNNOSTU	munitions
IIMOPRTXY	proximity
IIMOQSTUX	quixotism
IIMRRSTUV	triumvirs
IINNOOPRT	Pinot Noir
IINNORSTU	intrusion
IINNORTTU	nutrition
IINOOPRSV	provision
IINOOPSVY	poison ivy
IINOPRRTU	irruption
IINOSSTUY	sinuosity
IINOSSTVY	synovitis
IIOOPRSST	spiritoso
IIRSTUUVV	Vitruvius
IJMNOOPSS	O J Simpson
IKKNOOPRT	Kropotkin
IKLMOSTTU	milk stout
IKMOPPRUY	Yom Kippur
IKNSSWYYZ	Wyszynski
IKORSSTTU	outskirts
ILLNOOPSU	pollusion
ILLNOOPTU	pollution
ILLNOPTUW	up till now
ILLOOPRTY	poorly lit
ILLOOQSUY	soliloquy
ILLORSSSW	Swiss roll
ILMNOOPRT	Port Limon
ILMNOOSUY	ominously
ILMNOPTUU	plutonium
ILNNOSSTW	stownlins
ILNOOSUXY	noxiously
ILNOPPSTU	plus point
ILNOPSSUU	spinulous
ILNORSUUY	ruinously
ILNOSSUUY	sinuously
ILOOPPUVX	vox populi
ILOOPRSTU	Port Louis
ILOORSTUY	riotously
ILOPRSSYY	pyrolysis
ILORSSUVW	slow virus
ILORSUUUX	luxurious
IMMMNOORS	Mormonism
IMMOPPRTU	impromptu
IMMOPSSUY	symposium
IMNOOOPRT	promotion
IMNOOSSTU	miss out on
IMNORRRSS	Mrs Norris
IMNORSTTU	strontium
IMOOPPSTY	pomposity
IMOORSSTU	sumotoris
IMORSUVXY	myxovirus
INNOOQRTU	quintroon
INNOOSSUU	unisonous
INOOOPSSU	poisonous
INOOORSTU	notorious ❑
INOOSTTWW	in two twos
INRSTTTUU	unit trust
IOOPPRRTU	potpourri
	pot-pourri
IOOPRRSVY	provisory
IOORSSTUV	virtuosos
IOPRSTTUU	poursuitt

J

JKOORSSTU	Kurt Jooss

K

KKNORRTUW	trunk-work
KLNOOOOTU	look out on

L

LMOOPPSUY	pompously
LORSTUUUV	vulturous

M

MMORRSUUU	murmurous
MNNOOOPSY	monopsony
MNOORSSTU	monstrous
MNOORSSTW	snow storm
	snowstorm
MOPSSTUUU	sumptuous

N

NNOOOPRSU	non-porous
NOOOOPRTV	Porto Novo

O

OOPRSSTUU	stuporous
OORRSTTUU	torturous

10 letters

A

AAAABBDDIS	Addis Ababa
AAAABCCLNP	Capablanca
AAAABCCLNS	Casablanca
AAAABDFILS	Faisalabad
AAAABEINRS	Arabian Sea
AAAABEMPRT	parabemata
AAAABLRSTU	tabula rasa
AAAACDGMRS	Madagascar
AAAACDMMRT	tarmacadam □
AAAACGMNRT	Magna Carta
AAAACLMNRT	almacantar
AAAADELLLN	Allan-a-Dale
AAAADELMMT	Alma-Tadema
AAAADEMNNS	Andaman Sea
AAAADFNRWY	far and away
AAAAEGLMMT	amalgamate
AAAAEIKLMS	Lake Saimaa
AAAAGGGGWW	Wagga Wagga
AAAAGGLMNR	Mangalarga
AAAAGHJNNT	Jagannatha
AAAAGHRSTY	satyagraha
AAAAGNORSX	Anaxagoras
AAAAHIMMRS	Amarasimha
AAAAILRTTV	La Traviata
AAAAIMNNNP	Panamanian
AAAAIMNRST	Santa Maria
AAAAKKLMNT	Takla Makan
AAAALLORTV	Alvar Aalto
AAAALMNRSZ	salmanazar
AAAAMPRRTT	parramatta
AAABBCILST	sabbatical
AAABBEPRRY	Barbary ape
AAABBMPRRY	Barbara Pym
AAABBORRSS	Barbarossa
AAABCCCHRT	catch a crab
AAABCCEHLN	Bacchanale
AAABCCKNSV	canvasback
AAABCDDEFG	Bagdad Café
AAABCDEIRS	scarabaeid
AAABCDELNR	candelabra
AAABCEGGNR	garbage can
AAABCEHNST	Athabescan
AAABCEKKNT	taken aback
AAABCEKLTT	attackable
AAABCELSTT	cabalettas
AAABCIKLMR	Black Maria
AAABDDEINT	aid and abet
AAABDDHIRY	bad hair day
AAABDEEGLM	damageable
AAABDEGGNR	garage band
AAABDEKRTY	at daybreak
AAABDKLNRW	draw a blank
AAABDLMSSU	Abdus Salam
AAABDMNRSY	Bryan Adams
AAABDMORSS	ambassador
AAABDORRST	astarboard
AAABEEGLMN	manageable
AAABEEKKRT	take a break
AAABEELMNS	able seaman
AAABEERVWY	beaver away
AAABEGLLSU	Elagabalus
AAABEGLMNY	manageably
AAABEHHMST	The Bahamas
AAABEIJNRZ	Azerbaijan
AAABEIKKLL	Lake Baikal
AAABEILLSS	assailable
AAABEILNTT	attainable
AAABEINPST	anabaptise
AAABEINPTZ	anabaptize
AAABEKKORR	karaoke bar
AAABEKPRRT	break apart
AAABELMNST	Abel Tasman
AAABELNRRT	narratable
AAABEMRSTV	Svetambara
AAABFHILXY	Halifax Bay
AAABIKNNNS	banana skin
AAABILRSTV	Bratislava
AAABIMNPRS	pan-Arabism
AAABIMNPST	Anabaptism
AAABIMOPRR	Paramaribo
AAABINPSTT	Anabaptist
AAABKLNRSW	Balkan Wars
AAACCEHKRV	have a crack
AAACCEIPTT	capacitate
AAACCHILNR	anarchical
AAACCINRTT	Antarctica
AAACCLMNOS	calamancos
AAACDDENSU	Sadducaean
AAACDEEGMR	arcade game
AAACDEHLPY	alpha decay
AAACDEIMMS	macadamise
AAACDEIMMZ	macadamize
AAACDELMRS	salad cream
AAACDGIILR	cardialgia
AAACDIIPRS	paradisaic
	paradisiac
AAACDILLTY	call it a day
AAACDILNOP	pina colada
	piña colada
AAACEEENVV	venae cavae
AAACEENPPR	appearance
AAACEFILTU	café au lait
AAACEFLQTU	catafalque
AAACEHKNSV	have a snack
AAACEINPRS	parascenia
AAACEINPSS	Caspian Sea
AAACEINPST	anapaestic
AAACEINRTV	at variance
AAACEJKNPS	jackanapes
AAACEKLSST	take a class

Words marked □ can also be spelled with an initial capital letter

AAACELMPRT	metacarpal
AAACESSTUY	satay sauce
AAACFHIILR	facial hair
AAACFINNPR	pan-African
AAACFKNPRR	Frank Capra
AAACGGIORV	Caravaggio
AAACGHNRTT	tragacanth
AAACGILLNO	analogical
AAACGINSTT	act against
AAACHIINPT	Cap Haitian
AAACHIMNSU	naumachias
AAACHIPTWY	chip away at
AAACHJOPRS	chaparajos
AAACHLNOTU	anacolutha
AAACHNPRTY	pyracantha
AAACHOSSUY	ayahuas-cos
AAACIKLRTU	autarkical
AAACILLMNU	animalcula
AAACILLMNY	maniacally
AAACILLNTY	analytical
AAACILLRTU	Ural-Altaic
AAACILMNOT	anatomical
AAACILNRSS	carnassial
AAACILNRST	scarlatina
AAACIMNNOR	narcomania
AAACIMNPTY	Panama City
AAACLMNRTU	almucantar
AAACLMNRVY	cavalryman
AAACLNSSTU	Santa Claus
AAACMNNRTT	marcantant
AAACMRSSTY	Mary Cassat
AAACPRSTWW	Warsaw Pact
AAADDEEMNV	Adam and Eve
AAADDEGNTV	advantaged
AAADDELMPT	maladapted
AAADDHMRSY	Hamadryads
AAADEEGLRT	a great deal
AAADEEKRST	take as read
AAADEFIKMR	make afraid
AAADEFIOST	asafoetida
AAADEFNNRR	far and near
	near and far
AAADEGGRTV	aggravated
AAADEGINRV	devanagari □
AAADEGKLLO	Lake Ladoga
AAADEGNRRV	Ava Gardner
AAADEGNRTV	avant-garde
AAADEGNSTV	advantages
AAADEHINTW	what an idea!
AAADEHLPRT	hard palate
AAADEHNNRT	near at hand
AAADEIINST	Anita Desai
AAADEILNRX	Alexandria
AAADEIMNNT	adamantine
AAADEIMSTT	diastemata
AAADEKMNST	make a stand
AAADELMNRS	salamander
AAADELMPPS	Adam's apple
AAADELRSTY	lead astray
AAADEOPSTZ	zapateados
AAADEPSSWY	passed away
AAADGINNPT	giant panda
AAADGLLNOR	allargando
AAADGMMMNR	grandmamma
AAADGMNORR	mandragora
AAADGNOPPR	propaganda
AAADHLLNTT	and all that
AAADHLLNTW	and what all
AAADIILNPR	lapidarian
AAADIIMMNR	Maid Marian
AAADIIOSTU	Said Aouita
AAADIKLPST	Das Kapital
AAADILNNSU	Andalusian
AAADILRSUV	Laura Davis
AAADINOPTT	adaptation
AAADKNNNOR	Donna Karan
AAADLNQRTU	quadrantal
AAADNOTUWY	out and away
AAADORSTTU	autostrada
AAAEEHHRTV	have a heart
AAAEEHIRRS	raise a hare
AAAEEKMPPR	make appear
AAAEFJNOPS	Sea of Japan
AAAEFLLMRS	false alarm
AAAEFLMNST	malfeasant
AAAEGGIMNT	gametangia
AAAEGILMNR	managerial
AAAEGILPPR	paraplegia
AAAEGINPRS	asparagine
AAAEGNNTTT	at a tangent
AAAEGPSSWY	passageway
AAAEHHLNNT	Nathan Hale
AAAEHIMRTU	haematuria
AAAEHINSTU	euthanasia
AAAEHITVWY	have it away
AAAEHKNOTT	take an oath
AAAEHPPRRS	paraphrase
AAAEHPRTVY	have a party
AAAEHRRSTT	start a hare
AAAEIILNTT	Italianate
AAAEIKLLMW	Lake Malawi
AAAEILLPST	palatalise
AAAEILLPTZ	palatalize
AAAEILMRTU	tularaemia
AAAEILNPRT	planetaria
AAAEIMNPRS	paramnesia
AAAEIMNQRU	aquamarine
AAAEIMNRSW	Samian ware
AAAEIMNRTU	Mauretania
AAAEINNRTV	Tananarive
AAAEKLMPSU	Musala Peak
AAAEKLNPRR	Alan Parker
AAAEKLPRRW	parawalker
AAAEKMRSTT	make a start
AAAELLNRTT	tarantella
AAAELMMNOT	melanomata
AAAELMPPSS	mass appeal
AAAELMRSTT	metatarsal
AAAELPRSTY	pray a tales
AAAELSSTWY	leastaways
AAAEMORTTT	teratomata
AAAEPRRSYY	say a prayer

AAAEQRSUWY	square away
AAAFFKKNRZ	Franz Kafka
AAAFGHNRSW	Afghan Wars
AAAFHKNORR	Frank O'Hara
AAAFIJNNRS	Rafsanjani
AAAFIKPRRS	safari park
AAAFILMMNR	Animal Farm
AAAFIMNRST	Marat Safin
AAAFKNPPRZ	Frank Zappa
AAAFLORSST	solfataras
AAAFLOSTTY	stay afloat
AAAFNORTWY	not far away
AAAGGNNRTU	gargantuan□
AAAGHIMRRT	margharita
AAAGHINSVY	having a say
AAAGHNPSTU	agapanthus
AAAGIILMNR	marginalia
AAAGIKNNTY	Tanganyika
AAAGIKNTWY	taking away
	taking-away
AAAGILLMNO	Gallomania
AAAGIMMNRR	grammarian
AAAGINNOPT	Patagonian
AAAGINRSTT	start again
AAAGKORTYY	Yogyakarta
AAAGLNRSTU	natural gas
AAAGLPTUWY	plug away at
AAAGMNSTTY	syntagmata
AAAHIIJMRY	jamahiriya
AAAHILMRRS	air-marshal
AAAHILNSST	thalassian
AAAHINSSTU	Athanasius
AAAHKKNSTZ	Kazakhstan
AAAHLMNPST	phantasmal
AAAHLOPSSS	lhasa apsos
AAAHMNOTTX	xanthomata
AAAHPPRRST	paraphrast
AAAIILLNTT	natalitial
AAAIIMNRTU	Mauritania
AAAIINNRST	sanitarian
AAAIKLMNPR	animal park
AAAIKMMRSW	Wasim Akram
AAAILLLPTY	palatially
AAAILLMNNZ	manzanilla□
AAAILLMNPR	rampallian
AAAILLMRTW	martial law
AAAILLORTV	lavatorial
AAAILMNORZ	Mario Lanza
AAAILMRRTT	martial art
AAAILNORTT	natatorial
AAAILNRSTU	Australian
	saturnalia□
AAAILOPRSV	Valparaiso
	Valparaíso
AAAIMNORST	inamoratas
AAAINNOTTT	Anatotitan
AAAINSSSTU	Anastasius
AAALMNOPRR	paranormal
AAALNOORSV	Savonarola
AAALNPRSSY	nasal spray
AAAMNNORTT	tramontana

AAAMNPSSTU	Maupassant
AAAMRTZZZZ	razzmatazz
AABBBELORS	absorbable
AABBCCKKOT	back to back
AABBCDEEGR	red cabbage
AABBCDEKLR	black bread
	Blackbeard
AABBCDKLOR	blackboard
AABBCDNRSU	unscabbard
AABBCEILRS	ascribable
AABBCELNRU	Crab nebula
AABBCIILNR	rabbinical
AABBCIJKRT	jack rabbit
AABBCNNOOR	Brabanõcon
AABBDDEORR	breadboard
AABBDDEORS	broad-based
AABBDEEELT	debateable
AABBDEEKNS	baked beans
AABBDEEKRR	break bread
AABBDEGORR	barge-board
AABBDEOORV	above board
	above-board
AABBDRSTUY	Bustard Bay
AABBEEGILT	aglet babie
AABBEEHLRT	breathable
AABBEEIRTV	abbreviate
AABBEELLRT	barbellate
AABBEELNRU	unbearable
AABBEELNTU	unbeatable
AABBEEMUXY	Meaux Abbey
AABBEESSUY	busy as a bee
AABBEHRTTY	The Tar Baby
AABBEILLLS	ballabiles
AABBEILMNO	abominable
AABBEILNOT	obtainable
AABBEIMNRS	babe in arms
AABBEIMNWZ	Zimbabwean
AABBEKLLST	basketball
AABBEKLORT	Béla Bartók
AABBEKLRWY	baby-walker
AABBELLMNU	unblamable
AABBELNRUY	unbearably
AABBIKORUY	Aboukir Bay
AABBILMNOY	abominably
AABBMMNPYY	namby-pamby
AABBOOSTTU	boast about
AABCCCIKRR	crack a crib
AABCCEEHHT	The Bacchae
AABCCEELPT	acceptable
AABCCEHKNY	hackney cab
AABCCEHNST	bacchantes
AABCCEILPT	accept bail
AABCCEKKPR	backpacker
AABCCELLLU	calculable
AABCCELPTY	acceptably
AABCCGIKLM	black magic
AABCCIKLLL	Cilla Black
AABCCIORST	acrobatics
AABCCLLLUY	calculably
AABCDDEHKN	backhanded
	back-handed

AABCDDEKLS	saddleback
AABCDEEHLT	detachable
AABCDEEILR	eradicable
AABCDEEKNR	breakdance
AABCDEELLR	declarable
AABCDEERSU	bread sauce
AABCDEFIRT	fabricated
AABCDEFRSS	brass-faced
AABCDEHKLT	Black Death
AABCDEHKNR	back-hander
AABCDEIILS	Alcibiades
AABCDELNNU	unbalanced
AABCDELPRW	parcel-bawd
AABCDENORT	carbonated
AABCDERSTT	abstracted
AABCDGKLRU	blackguard
AABCDHOPRT	patchboard
AABCDIILLO	diabolical
AABCDIINOT	abdication
AABCDIORRS	barricados
AABCDKLRWY	backwardly
AABCDMNOPY	bad company
AABCDMOSSU	ambuscados
AABCDNNORT	contraband
AABCDNOORS	carbonados
AABCEEEFFL	effaceable
AABCEEERTX	exacerbate
AABCEEGHLN	changeable
AABCEEGHLR	chargeable
AABCEEHILV	achievable
AABCEEHLMP	peach melba
AABCEEIMRT	bacteremia
AABCEEINNY	in abeyance
AABCEEIRTU	eubacteria
AABCEEIRTV	abreactive
AABCEEKRTT	battercake
AABCEEKSST	basket case
	basket-case
AABCEELLLR	recallable
AABCEELNRT	tabernacle
AABCEELRTU	trabeculae
AABCEFFLNO	off balance
	off-balance
AABCEGHLNY	changeably
AABCEGHLRY	chargeably
AABCEGHMRS	gas chamber
AABCEGIRRR	carrier bag
AABCEGKLLR	Clark Gable
AABCEGLMNN	blancmange
AABCEGLSUV	Savage Club
AABCEHIIMM	Miami Beach
AABCEHILNN	Balanchine
AABCEHILPT	alphabetic
AABCEHILRT	charitable
AABCEHKLLW	black whale
AABCEHLMRR	Marble Arch
AABCEIINTU	beautician
AABCEILLMP	implacable
AABCEILLPP	applicable
AABCEILLPS	slip a cable
AABCEILNOT	actionable
AABCEILPSZ	capsizable
AABCEINORT	abreaction
AABCEIORST	aerobatics
AABCEKKMRR	backmarker
AABCEKNRSW	answer back
AABCEKOPTT	packet boat
	packet-boat
AABCELLORR	barcarolle
AABCELLORS	caballeros
AABCELMOPR	comparable
AABCELMTUU	acetabulum
AABCELNOTU	balance out
	outbalance
AABCELOPRR	arable crop
AABCELRRTU	trabecular
AABCEOPRRT	Robert Capa
AABCERRTUU	bureaucrat
AABCFIKLOS	lack of bias
AABCFIORRT	fabricator
AABCFKLLNO	fall back on
AABCGIILLM	galliambic
AABCGIKKNT	taking back
AABCGIKNRR	barracking
AABCGKMMNO	backgammon
	back-gammon
AABCGLRRTU	cat burglar
	cat-burglar
AABCHHIMPR	amphibrach
AABCHILRTY	charitably
AABCHIOOPR	acrophobia
AABCHLNOOR	halocarbon
AABCIILLMY	iambically
AABCIILPTY	capability
AABCIILTTY	actability
AABCIKRSST	backstairs
AABCILLMPY	implacably
AABCILLNNY	cannibally
AABCILLPPY	applicably
AABCILMORU	columbaria
AABCILMOST	catabolism
AABCILNOTY	actionably
AABCILNSUV	subclavian
AABCIQSTUU	subaquatic
AABCKRSSST	brass tacks
AABCLLNNNO	cannonball
AABCLMOPRU	labour camp
AABCLMOPRY	comparably
AABCLNOOVY	Volcano Bay
AABCLORUVY	vocabulary
AABCLRSTTY	abstractly
AABCNORSST	contrabass
AABCORTUYZ	crazy about
AABDDDEEHL	bald-headed
AABDDEEEHR	bareheaded
AABDDEEGLR	degradable
AABDDEEHNR	barehanded
AABDDEELMN	demandable
AABDDEHLMO	hebdomadal
AABDDEHLRS	balderdash
AABDDEILRY	daily bread
AABDDEIMNR	madbrained

AABDDELOPT	paddle-boat
AABDDIMNOO	in a bad mood
AABDDKLNUY	Dundalk Bay
AABDDMNNOR	Don Bradman
AABDEEELMS	sealed-beam
AABDEEFLRY	defrayable
AABDEEHRRT	threadbare
AABDEEILNT	detainable
AABDEEILRU	Baudelaire
AABDEELNPX	expandable
AABDEELNRU	unreadable
AABDEELPRS	spreadable
AABDEELRRW	rewardable
AABDEFFLOR	affordable
AABDEFINRT	fatbrained
AABDEFKORY	break of day
AABDEGGINR	brigandage
AABDEGGNRS	sandbagger
AABDEGHLNS	Bangladesh
AABDEGIMRS	bragadisme
AABDEGLNOY	Donegal Bay
AABDEGLNRY	by and large
AABDEGORST	goatsbeard
AABDEHINNR	bear in hand
AABDEHINPS	in bad shape
AABDEHINRT	brain death
AABDEHINWY	win by a head
AABDEHITTU	habituated
AABDEHLLPS	ball-shaped
AABDEHLNST	stable hand
AABDEHRRTW	draw breath
AABDEIJMRS	James Braid
AABDEIKKOR	kodiak bear ❑
AABDEIKNUZ	adzuki bean
AABDEILLNR	banderilla
AABDEILLSY	dialysable
AABDEINNOR	Aberdonian
AABDEINRSU	Diane Arbus
AABDEINSST	bastinades
AABDEINSTT	in bad taste
AABDEIRSST	bastardise
AABDEIRSTZ	bastardize
AABDEJLSTU	adjustable
AABDEKLLMS	masked ball
AABDEKMNOW	Meadowbank
AABDEKORST	skateboard
AABDELLNNO	belladonna
AABDELLORS	sell abroad
AABDELNOPR	pardonable
AABDELRSTU	balustrade
AABDELRTTY	treat badly
AABDEMNNNO	one-man band
AABDEMNNRS	bad manners
AABDEMNRST	bandmaster
AABDEMOORV	move abroad
AABDEMORRT	Robert Adam
AABDENORSY	dry as a bone
AABDEOPPRR	paperboard
AABDEOPRST	pasteboard
AABDESSTTY	as stated by
AABDFHLNOT	not half bad
AABDGIILNW	law-abiding
AABDGILNOY	loading bay
AABDGINNNO	abandoning
AABDHLORRU	hard labour
AABDHMNNSU	husbandman
AABDHNORRW	hand-barrow
AABDIINNRR	brain drain
AABDILLLUY	illaudably
AABDILMNRU	mandibular
AABDILQTUY	bad quality
AABDIORRST	stir abroad
AABDJLSTUY	adjustably
AABDLNNTUY	abundantly
AABDLNOPRY	pardonably
AABDNNPRSY	brandy snap
AABDNOSTTU	stand about
AABEEELLPR	repealable
AABEEELLRV	revealable
AABEEELPRT	repeatable
AABEEELRRT	talebearer
AABEEFIKRT	take a brief
AABEEGIKNW	being awake
AABEEGKRST	break gates
AABEEGLLST	Bagatelles
AABEEGLMSS	assemblage
AABEEGLTTZ	Bazalgette
AABEEHHRTV	have breath
AABEEHIRTT	beat the air
AABEEHKRRT	heartbreak
AABEEHKRTT	take breath
AABEEHLLNU	unhealable
AABEEHLQTU	bequeathal
AABEEHMMMR	hammer beam
AABEEHPRTT	beat the rap
AABEEHRRTV	Braveheart
AABEEIKLLM	make liable
AABEEILLRZ	realizable
AABEEILMNX	examinable
AABEEILNRT	retainable
AABEEINRTV	native bear
AABEEJKMRS	James Baker
AABEEJKNRT	Janet Baker
AABEEJKRST	break a jest
AABEEKLLRT	Lake Albert
AABEEKLMRR	remarkable
AABEEKLMRT	marketable
AABEEKLMST	make stable
AABEEKLRRW	lawbreaker
	law-breaker
AABEEKPRRS	Breakspear
AABEEKRRTW	breakwater
AABEELLMNT	lamentable
AABEELLPRR	pall-bearer
AABEELMNNU	unamenable
AABEELMNTU	untameable
AABEELMRSU	measurable
AABEELNORS	reasonable
AABEELNOSS	seasonable
AABEELNPTT	patentable
AABEELNRSW	answerable
AABEELOPRV	evaporable

AABEELPPRY prepayable
AABEELRRST arrestable
AABEELRTTW water table
AABEELSSSS assessable
AABEELSTTT attestable
AABEENRSST Barents Sea
AABEEOPPRT appear to be
AABEEORTVW above water
AABEEQRSSU Arabesques
AABEERRSTT street Arab
street arab
AABEFFMOWY way off beam
AABEFFOPRU opera buffa
AABEFGILTU fatiguable
AABEFHIKRT break faith
AABEFHLMOT fathomable
AABEFILLNT inflatable
AABEFILPPR papal brief
AABEFIMORS framboesia
AABEFINRRT Barnet fair
AABEFLORUV favourable
AABEGGIINN begin again
AABEGGORRT Greta Garbo
AABEGHORRU harbourage
AABEGIILMN imaginable
AABEGIJOTV give a jab to
AABEGIKLOR Gabriel Oak
AABEGILNOZ zabaglione
AABEGILNRY laying bare
AABEGILNSS assignable
AABEGILRST algebraist
AABEGINNOT abnegation
AABEGINRST Great Basin
AABEGLNRUU unarguable
AABEHIILTT habilitate
AABEHKLNSU unshakable
AABEHLQSSU squashable
AABEHLRSZZ Belshazzar
AABEHRRSTW water-brash
AABEIILNRV invariable
AABEIILNST insatiable
AABEIILSST assibilate
AABEIINNST in absentia
AABEIJLOSU Beaujolais
AABEIKLMST mistakable
AABEILLMPP impalpable
AABEILLNUV invaluable
AABEILMMRU barium meal
AABEILMNTV ambivalent
AABEILMPSS impassable
AABEILMSUX ambisexual
AABEILNRSY inerasably
AABEILNRUV unvariable
AABEILOPRS parabolise
AABEILOPRZ parabolize
AABEILRSTU tabularise
AABEILRTUZ tabularize
AABEIMNORU Maria Bueno
AABEIMPRTV vampire bat
AABEINORRT aberration
AABEKLMRRY remarkably
AABEKLNOOR Alanbrooke
AABEKOPSTU speak about
AABELLLORS albarellos
AABELLMNSY by all means
AABELLMNTY lamentably
AABELLNNTY Ballantyne
AABELLSSST stable lass
AABELMNNOT Monte Albán
AABELMNORS ransomable
AABELMNTUY untameably
AABELMOSTT Melba toast
AABELMRSUY measurably
AABELNORSY reasonably
AABELNORTU learn about
AABELNOSSY seasonably
AABELNPRST Barnstaple
AABELNPSSU unpassable
AABELNRSWY answerably
AABELNSUWY unswayable
AABELOORRT elaborator
AABELPRSTU pasturable
AABEMMORVY Emma Bovary
AABEMNNSYY by any means
AABEMRSTTU masturbate
AABFFIILTY affability
AABFGINORR bargain for
AABFIILOTT a bit of tail
AABFILLOTU flail about
AABFLMNOTY flamboyant
AABFLORUVY favourably
AABGGIINNR bargaining
AABGIILMNY imaginably
AABGIILNOR aboriginal
AABGIINNST abstaining
AABGINOORT abrogation
AABGINORTU outbargain
AABGIRSSTU bass guitar
AABGLNRUUY unarguably
AABGNRTTTY Grant Batty
AABHIINNTT inhabitant
AABHIINOTT habitation
AABHIJLLMU Majuba Hill
AABHIJLLNU Najibullah
AABHIKKLNU Kublai Khan
AABHILLTUY habitually
AABHILORTY habilatory
AABHIMMNRS Brahmanism
AABHIMRTVZ bar mitzvah
AABHIMTTVZ bat mitzvah
AABHIOOPTU autophobia
AABHKLNSUY unshakably
AABHLLLOOU hullabaloo
AABIIILMTY amiability
AABIIKMNNS Iain M Banks
AABIILNRVY invariably
AABIILNSTY insatiably
AABIILRTTY ratability
AABIINNSSY Abyssinian
AABIINPRST bipartisan
AABIJNORTU abjuration
AABILLMNUY bimanually

AABILLMPPY	impalpably
AABILLNNUY	biannually
AABILLNOOT	oblational
AABILLNRUY	binaurally
AABILLNUVY	invaluably
AABILMNOTU	ambulation
AABILMPSSY	impassably
AABILMRSST	strabismal
AABILNOTTU	tabulation
AABILPRTUY	patibulary
AABINRRSTY	binary star
AABIORRRTT	arbitrator
AABISTTTTU	Battistuta
AABKKOORRU	kookaburra
AABLLMNORY	abnormally
AABLMMPSTU	stamp album
AABLMORTUY	ambulatory
AABLOORRTY	laboratory
AABLRSSTTU	substratal
AABLSTTTUY	statutably
AABNOORRTW	narrow boat
	narrow-boat
AABORRSSUU	Barosaurus
AACCCDEIIT	acetic acid
AACCCDENOR	accordance
AACCCDIILT	lactic acid
AACCCEEILO	Lee Iacocca
AACCCEENPT	acceptance
AACCCEILTT	catalectic
AACCCIJKLO	Calico Jack
AACCCINRUY	inaccuracy
AACCDDEHKN	cack-handed
AACCDEENSU	succedanea
AACCDEEPST	space cadet
AACCDEERRZ	care-crazed
AACCDEHIRS	saccharide
AACCDEHNOR	archdeacon
AACCDEIILM	maleic acid
AACCDEILNT	accidental
AACCDEIMRS	disc camera
AACCDELLTU	calculated
AACCDENNSY	ascendancy
AACCDENRRW	Cancer Ward
AACCDEORSS	access road
AACCDERSTY	scaredy-cat
AACCDGIILL	gallic acid
AACCDHPRST	scratch pad
AACCDIILOX	oxalic acid
AACCDIINNT	tannic acid
AACCEEELRT	accelerate
AACCEEFFOT	face to face
	face-to-face
AACCEEFGHN	change face
AACCEEGPRS	scapegrace
AACCEEIKNP	pancake ice
AACCEEKLTT	cattle cake
AACCEELLNT	cancellate
AACCEENTTU	accentuate
AACCEEORTV	coacervate
AACCEEPRSU	caper sauce
AACCEFIIPT	pacificate
AACCEFPRST	spacecraft
AACCEGHKNT	change tack
AACCEGHOST	stagecoach
AACCEHILMN	mechanical
AACCEHINNT	cachinnate
AACCEHINRS	saccharine
AACCEHIRSS	saccharise
AACCEHIRSZ	saccharize
AACCEHLNOT	coelacanth
AACCEHLNRT	lancet arch
AACCEHLNST	last-chance
AACCEHLPRT	chapel cart
AACCEHNNOT	not a chance
AACCEHORSS	saccharose
AACCEHRRST	characters
AACCEHRRTT	rat-catcher
AACCEILPTT	cataleptic
AACCEINORV	covariance
AACCEINPRT	pancreatic
AACCEINRTU	inaccurate
AACCEIRRTU	caricature
AACCEISTUV	accusative
AACCEJKKOR	crack a joke
AACCEKORRT	carrot cake
AACCELMTUU	accumulate
AACCELORSU	calcareous
AACCELRTUY	accurately
AACCENNRST	CAT scanner
AACCENRSTU	crustacean
AACCFHIRSY	saccharify
AACCFILLRY	farcically
AACCFINNRS	Franciscan
AACCGHOPRY	cacography
AACCGIIILP	I Pagliacci
AACCGIJKNR	carjacking
AACCGIKLNO	caking coal
AACCHHINTW	watch chain
AACCHILNPY	chaplaincy
AACCHIMORT	achromatic
AACCHKNPPU	pack a punch
AACCHNORST	cast anchor
AACCHOPRTY	coach party
AACCIILLNU	canaliculi
AACCIINPTY	incapacity
AACCILLTTY	tactically
AACCILMMUY	immaculacy
AACCILNOOS	occasional
AACCILOSTU	acoustical
AACCILRTUY	articulacy
AACCIMNORS	carcinomas
AACCINORTV	vaccinator
AACCINOSTU	accusation
AACCIOPTTY	to capacity
AACCIORTTU	autocratic
AACCLLORTU	calculator
AACCNNOTTU	accountant
AACCNORSST	sacrosanct
AACCORSTUY	accusatory
AACDDEEHLR	decahedral
AACDDEEIMP	aide-de-camp
AACDDEEMNS	damascened

AACDDEEMRT	demarcated
AACDDEIJTU	adjudicate
AACDDEINST	candidates
AACDDEOSTU	add sauce to
AACDDIIMMR	MacDiarmid
AACDDIOTTU	autodidact
AACDEEELST	de-escalate
AACDEEEMNS	damasceene
AACDEEFFLS	false-faced
AACDEEFHMS	shamefaced
AACDEEFHNR	face-harden
AACDEEFPPR	paper-faced
AACDEEGNOT	anecdotage
AACDEEHLRT	thread-lace
AACDEEHNRS	case-harden
AACDEEHRRT	race hatred
AACDEEHRTT	tracheated
AACDEEHRTX	ex cathedra
AACDEEILRT	dilacerate
AACDEEINRT	deracinate
AACDEEIPTT	decapitate
AACDEEITTV	deactivate
AACDEEKMRS	make sacred
AACDEELOSS	escaladoes
AACDEELRRW	declare war
AACDEENNTT	attendance
AACDEEOPRS	escape road
AACDEEOPSS	escapadoes
AACDEFGLSS	glass-faced
AACDEFINRR	Africander
AACDEFINRU	fricandeau
AACDEFINST	fascinated
AACDEFJNSU	Janus-faced
AACDEFLORT	defalcator
AACDEFPSTY	pasty-faced
AACDEGHHNR	charge hand
AACDEGLOTU	coagulated
AACDEHHTTW	deathwatch
	death-watch
AACDEHILNS	enchiladas
AACDEHINRS	sedan-chair
AACDEHIORS	icosahedra
AACDEHJKLT	Jack the Lad
AACDEHLLPY	Lady Chapel
AACDEHLNNR	Archenland
AACDEHLORT	octahedral
AACDEHMNOR	Andromache
AACDEHNTTU	unattached
AACDEHOTTT	attached to
AACDEIILRS	radicalise
AACDEIILRZ	radicalize
AACDEIIPRT	paediatric
AACDEIIRRT	irradicate
AACDEIIRTV	divaricate
AACDEIJLTV	adjectival
AACDEIKLLP	Lake Placid
AACDEILMNO	demoniacal
AACDEILNNO	Caledonian
AACDEILNSS	scandalise
AACDEILNSZ	scandalize
AACDEIMNTT	admittance
AACDEINQTU	acquainted
AACDEINQUY	inadequacy
AACDEINRST	discarnate
AACDEIORRT	eradicator
AACDEIOSST	associated
AACDEIPTTV	captivated
AACDEIRSTY	caryatides
AACDEJLNTY	adjacently
AACDEJNOTT	adjacent to
AACDEKLOWY	locked away
AACDEKNTTU	unattacked
AACDEKTUWY	tucked away
AACDELLLOS	also called
AACDELMRSU	clear as mud
AACDELNSST	sandcastle
AACDELOPRT	leopard-cat
AACDELORST	sacerdotal
AACDEOPRRS	radarscope
AACDEORRVW	draw a cover
AACDEORSUV	cadaverous
AACDFGILRS	fiscal drag
AACDFHINRT	handicraft
AACDFIINOO	aficionado
AACDGGINRR	drag-racing
AACDGHHINR	Chandigarh
AACDGIKOSS	sick as a dog
AACDGIMORR	cardiogram
AACDGINNPT	tap-dancing
AACDGNRSUY	sugar candy
AACDGORSTU	coastguard
AACDHIINSY	daisy-chain
AACDHILLMY	chlamydial
AACDHJMMNO	John McAdam
AACDHKORRS	hard as rock
AACDHLMNRS	marchlands
AACDHLORSY	day-scholar
AACDHNNORY	Chardonnay
AACDHOSSTW	shadowcast
AACDIILMRS	radicalism
AACDIILMRT	matricidal
AACDIILPRR	parricidal
AACDIILPRT	patricidal
AACDIJLLUY	Judaically
AACDILLMTU	Talmudical
AACDILLNRY	cardinally
AACDILLOOR	local radio
AACDILMORY	myocardial
AACDIMMRSU	music drama
AACDIMNRTU	undramatic
AACDINNOST	contadinas
AACDLNOSSU	scandalous
AACDMMNNOT	commandant
AACDOOPRRT	paradoctor
AACDORSSTW	coastwards
AACEEEHKPS	Chesapeake
AACEEEKMPR	peacemaker
AACEEEKNSY	eye askance
AACEEELNOP	Palaeocene
AACEEFKORT	take care of
AACEEGGHNR	change gear
AACEEGHKRT	take charge

AACEEGHNRR	carragheen	AACEGHOTTT	act the goat
AACEEGHRUV	Che Guevara	AACEGIIMNT	emaciating
AACEEGILLN	allegiance	AACEGIINRR	Craig Raine
AACEEGKPTW	wage packet	AACEGILLLT	illegal act
	wage-packet	AACEGILNRT	lacerating
AACEEGLLRS	large-scale	AACEGILNST	escalating
AACEEGLNTU	acute angle	AACEGILORT	categorial
AACEEGNOST	act one's age	AACEGILPPR	paraplegic
AACEEHILNT	châtelaine	AACEGIMNPR	campaigner
AACEEHJMSS	James Chase	AACEGINRTV	vintage car
AACEEHKPST	cheapskate	AACEGLMORY	acromegaly
AACEEHLLSW	Lech Walesa	AACEGLORTU	cataloguer
AACEEHLMNO	Chamaeleon	AACEHHHNUV	have a hunch
AACEEHLPST	sphacelate	AACEHHKLMS	hamshackle
AACEEHMPPR	paper-mâché	AACEHHLMPT	health camp
AACEEIJNNR	Jean Racine	AACEHHMNTT	hatchet man
AACEEILMRS	caramelise	AACEHIIMNR	hemicrania
AACEEILMRZ	caramelize	AACEHIKLMR	like a charm
AACEEILPRT	altarpiece	AACEHILLLY	heliacally
AACEEILSTT	elasticate	AACEHILMMS	Michaelmas
AACEEIMNPT	emancipate	AACEHILNOP	Cephalonia
AACEEIMSST	Siamese cat	AACEHILNPT	china plate
AACEEIPPRT	appreciate	AACEHILNRS	Lancashire
AACEEIRTTV	reactivate	AACEHILPRS	seraphical
AACEEKLRRT	Crater Lake	AACEHILPST	chaptalise
AACEELLLUV	valleculae	AACEHILPTZ	chaptalize
AACEELLNOT	lanceolate	AACEHILRTT	theatrical
AACEELLPUV	place value	AACEHIMMPR	amphimacer
AACEELMSTU	emasculate	AACEHIMNRT	carthamine
AACEELOPSU	paleaceous		Rachmanite
AACEELRTVY	acervately	AACEHIMNSU	Manichaeus
AACEENNRSS	arcaneness	AACEHINPTY	pay the cain
AACEENORSU	arenaceous	AACEHINRTT	anthracite
AACEENOSSY	Sean O'Casey	AACEHIORST	Oireachtas
AACEENRRTV	veteran car	AACEHIRRTV	architrave
AACEFFGLOS	scaffolage	AACEHJKMMR	jackhammer
AACEFFIMNR	affirmance	AACEHJOPRS	chaparejos
AACEFFKLMO	lack of fame	AACEHKLMRS	ramshackle
AACEFGINSV	face-saving	AACEHKLNRS	ranshackle
AACEFGLMOU	camouflage	AACEHKMMRT	matchmaker
AACEFGRSTT	stagecraft	AACEHKMRTW	watchmaker
AACEFHLLNR	fallen arch	AACEHKOPRT	karate chop
AACEFHRTTW	watch after	AACEHKORVW	wreak havoc
AACEFIILTT	facilitate	AACEHLMMRW	claw hammer
AACEFIIMPR	prima facie	AACEHLMUUX	chalumeaux
AACEFIINRS	Africanise	AACEHLNPTY	phlyctaena
AACEFIINRZ	Africanize	AACEHLPRTY	archetypal
AACEFIINST	fanaticise	AACEHLRRSY	Ray Charles
AACEFIINTZ	fanaticize	AACEHMNPRY	parenchyma
AACEFILNSU	final cause	AACEHMNRRT	Carmarthen
AACEFILRSY	fiscal year	AACEHMNTTT	attachment
AACEFJKKLT	flak jacket	AACEHMOPRS	Chamaerops
AACEFKLRST	flare stack	AACEHMOPRT	camphorate
AACEFLLLOR	flea collar	AACEHMORST	Samothrace
AACEFLLOTW	tallow-face	AACEHNPPRT	panther cap
AACEFLMORT	malefactor	AACEHOPPRS	approaches
AACEFLNORV	naval force	AACEHOPRTY	apothecary
AACEFRRTTW	watercraft	AACEHRSTTT	at a stretch
AACEFRSTTT	statecraft	AACEIILLNN	in alliance
AACEGHILNR	alcheringa	AACEIILPST	capitalise
AACEGHINOR	archegonia	AACEIILPTZ	capitalize

AACEIIMNOT	emaciation
AACEIIMPRT	parmacitie
AACEIINPTT	anticipate
AACEIINTTV	inactivate
	vaticinate
AACEIIOPSS	Cassiopeia
AACEIIPRTT	patriciate
AACEIKLLRS	rascal-like
AACEIKLRTT	racket-tail
AACEIKNOTT	take action
AACEILLMNU	animalcule
AACEILLNOS	escallonia
AACEILLNTT	cantillate
AACEILLOSU	alliaceous
AACEILLPRT	prelatical
AACEILLPRU	Lupercalia
AACEILLRVY	cavalierly
AACEILLSTY	salicylate
AACEILMMTU	immaculate
AACEILMNPS	campaniles
AACEILMNRT	reclaimant
AACEILMNRU	unicameral
AACEILMNSU	main clause
AACEILMNTU	calumniate
AACEILMRRT	tricameral
AACEILMRTU	tularaemic
AACEILNORT	laceration
AACEILNOST	escalation
AACEILNPPS	appliances
AACEILNRTU	retinacula
AACEILOOPZ	Palaeozoic
AACEILPTTU	capitulate
AACEILRTTU	articulate
AACEILSSTU	casualties
AACEIMMPRU	Paramecium
AACEIMNNOR	necromania
AACEIMNNRU	un-American
AACEIMNNST	anamnestic
AACEIMNORS	macaronies
AACEIMNORT	maceration
	racemation
AACEIMNORU	oceanarium
AACEIMNRRW	Crimean War
AACEIMNRWX	Mexican War
AACEIMOPST	aposematic
AACEIMPRRT	parametric
AACEIMRRSU	Camerarius
AACEINNNTU	annunciate
AACEINNOWY	once in a way
AACEINNPRT	pancreatin
AACEINORTU	aeronautic
AACEINOTUV	evacuation
AACEINOTVX	excavation
AACEINPRST	Persian cat
AACEINPRTY	at any price
AACEINRSST	incrassate
	Isaac Stern
AACEINSSST	assistance
AACEINSTVY	vanity case
	vanity-case
AACEIOSSST	associates
AACEIRTTTV	attractive
AACEJKNNVY	Jan Van Eyck
	Jan van Eyck
AACEJKNRRW	Jack Warner
AACEJKNRTT	natterjack
AACEKKMRST	make tracks
AACEKKTYYY	yackety-yak
AACEKLMRST	smart aleck
AACEKLNORS	coral snake
AACELLLMSS	small-scale
AACELLLORT	collateral
AACELLLRST	saltcellar
AACELLPRRY	carpellary
AACELLPRST	past recall
AACELLPSST	cast a spell
AACELMNRVY	cavalrymen
AACELMORST	scleromata
AACELMPRST	campestral
AACELMPRTW	Walter Camp
AACELMRRSU	secular arm
AACELNNUVY	Uncle Vanya
AACELNOPTU	cantaloupe
AACELNRRUV	vernacular
AACELNRRUW	nuclear war
AACELNRTTU	tentacular
AACELNSSSU	casualness
AACELOPPSY	apocalypse □
AACELORSTY	escalatory
AACELPRSSU	Paracelsus
AACELSTTUU	auscultate
AACEMNOPRS	campaneros
	mascarpone
AACEMNOPSW	spacewoman
AACEMNORST	Sacramento
AACEMPRSTU	metacarpus
AACENNORRV	Caernarvon
AACENNSSTV	vacantness
AACENRSTTY	Stan Tracey
AACEORRTTT	terracotta
AACEPSTTTU	statute cap
AACFFIJMRT	traffic jam
AACFGIIMNT	magnificat □
AACFGILNRT	flat racing
AACFHKNRST	crankshaft
AACFHLNORW	half-a-crown
AACFHMOSTT	fat stomach
AACFIIILRT	artificial
AACFIILNOR	California
AACFIILSTT	fatalistic
AACFIIMNST	fanaticism
AACFIIMORR	formicaria
AACFILLMOU	claim a foul
AACFILLOSU	fallacious
AACFILMOOT	coat of mail
AACFILNORT	fractional
AACFILORSV	varifocals
AACFILTTUY	factuality
AACFINOSTT	fantastico
AACFMNNOWY	fancy woman
AACFMOORST	coat of arms
	coat-of-arms

AACFNRSTTU	surfactant
AACFOPSSUY	cup of assay
AACFRRTTYY	arty-crafty
AACGGLLMNO	McGonagall
AACGHHIKMR	Graham Hick
AACGHHOPRT	tachograph
AACGHIOPRS	sarcophagi
AACGHKLMOR	Graham Lock
AACGHLSSTW	watchglass
AACGIILNOT	glaciation
AACGIIMSTT	astigmatic
AACGIINNOS	San Ignacio
AACGIKNNRS	ransacking
AACGILLLNS	call signal
AACGILLRSW	Gallic Wars
AACGILLRTY	tragically
AACGILMNNY	malignancy
AACGILNORS	cor anglais
AACGILNPTY	play-acting
AACGIMNORT	morganatic
AACGIMPRST	pragmatics
AACGIMRSTY	magistracy
AACGINOUUV	Nova Iguacu
AACGINRSTY	cry against
AACGLNORTU	octangular
AACGLOORTU	coagulator
AACHHHINUU	Chihuahuan
AACHHILNPT	naphthalic
AACHHLNPUY	play a hunch
AACHHLOPTT	hatch a plot
AACHIIRSSU	Saurischia
AACHIKMORT	Marita Koch
AACHILNNPT	plainchant
AACHILPRSU	haruspical
AACHIMMNRS	Rachmanism
AACHIMNOOS	monochasia
AACHIMNORS	maraschino
AACHIMNORT	machinator
AACHIMNORW	chairwoman
AACHIMNPST	phantasmic
AACHIMNSSU	in as much as
	inasmuch as
AACHIMPRST	pharmacist
AACHIMRRTY	matriarchy
AACHIMRSTT	Maastricht
AACHINRSTU	Carthusian
AACHIPRRTY	patriarchy
AACHIRSTTU	autarchist
AACHLMMOOS	school-ma'am
AACHLNNNOT	nonchalant
AACHLOPPRY	apocryphal
AACHMNNORR	Norman arch
AACHMOOPRT	apochromat
AACHNOOPST	Pocahontas
AACHPRSTTW	watchstrap
AACIILLNNT	anticlinal
AACIILLOPT	apolitical
AACIILMNOS	simoniacal
AACIILMNPS	Panislamic
AACIILMNST	talismanic
AACIILMNTX	anticlimax
AACIILMPST	capitalism
AACIILNNST	annalistic
AACIILNOST	antisocial
AACIILPSTT	capitalist
AACIILRRTU	urticarial
AACIIMNSTT	Instamatic®
AACIIMNSTV	Vaticanism
AACIINOPTT	capitation
AACIINORTV	victoriana □
AACIINOTTV	activation
	cavitation
AACIINPRST	patricians
AACIINSTTT	antistatic
AACIINSTTV	Vaticanist
AACIIORSUV	avaricious
AACIJMNORS	Canis Major
AACIKLMMRS	Lamarckism
AACIKNSSTY	Kansas City
AACILLMOSY	mosaically
AACILLMOTY	lay claim to
AACILLNOOT	allocation
AACILLNTUY	nautically
AACILLOOPR	coprolalia
AACILLOPTT	to cap it all
AACILLRWXY	wax lyrical
AACILLSTTY	statically
AACILLTVWY	cavity wall
AACILMNOTU	maculation
AACILMNOTY	claymation
AACILMOSTU	calamitous
AACILMPPRY	Paralympic
AACILMPSTU	capital sum
AACILNNRTY	tyrannical
AACILNOOTV	vocational
AACILNOPPT	panoptical
AACILNOPTY	nyctalopia
AACILNORTT	tractional
AACILNPPST	applicants
AACILOORRT	oratorical
AACILOPPRT	applicator
AACILPRRTU	particular
AACIMMNNOO	monomaniac
AACIMNOPRY	pyromaniac
AACIMORSTT	masticator
AACINNOSTT	Constantia
AACINOOSTV	Nova Scotia
AACINORSTT	castration
AACINORTTT	attraction
AACINORTUY	auctionary
	cautionary
AACIOOPTVZ	Octavio Paz
AACIORRSTT	aristocrat
AACIPPRSST	Paris Pacts
AACJLNORSU	Juan Carlos
AACKLNOTUY	you can talk
AACLLORRUY	oracularly
AACLLOSSTT	at all costs
AACLLRSUVY	vascularly
AACLMNNOSW	clanswoman
AACLMOPRSS	sarcoplasm
AACLMPSTUY	Paul McStay

AACLOORRTU	coloratura
AACLOPPRSS	papal cross
AACMNOPRUY	paramouncy
AACMOPSSSW	compass saw
AACNNNOSTT	constantan
AACNNOPTTU	put on an act
AACNNORSTY	Nancy Astor
AACNORRSTT	transactor
AACNORRSTW	narrowcast
AACOOPPRSU	apocarpous
AADDDDGNRY	granddaddy
AADDDEEHHR	hard-headed
AADDDEELPT	addle-pated
AADDDEELUV	value added
AADDDEILST	add details
AADDDGRSUY	sugar daddy
AADDDHNNYY	handy-dandy
AADDEEFHIR	fair-headed
AADDEEGGRS	Edgar Degas
AADDEEGMNR	grande dame
AADDEEGRRS	regarded as
AADDEEHHOT	head to head
AADDEEHHST	death's-head
AADDEEHIMN	Maidenhead
AADDEEHNNT	neat-handed
AADDEEHNRR	hard-earned
AADDEEIRST	desiderata
AADDEEIRWY	day-wearied
AADDEELRRW	Edward Lear
AADDEEMRRY	daydreamer
AADDEENORU	Oudenaarde
AADDEESTTV	devastated
AADDEFINRW	far and wide
AADDEGHLNR	glad-hander
AADDEGIILT	digladiate
AADDEGIRRT	tardigrade
AADDEGMNOR	Armageddon
AADDEHIKRR	dark-haired
AADDEHIMNN	handmaiden
AADDEHNORS	Esarhaddon
AADDEHORRT	hard to read
AADDEHQSTU	death squad
AADDEHRSTW	deathwards
AADDEIILPT	dilapidate
AADDEILMMY	midday meal
AADDEILMRR	red admiral
AADDEIMMTV	David Mamet
AADDEIRRSY	disarrayed
AADDELMUWY	muddle away
AADDELOPSS	saddle soap
AADDGILMOY	amygdaloid
AADDGNRSTU	stand guard
AADDGORSTU	add sugar to
AADDHHINNN	hand in hand
AADDHHNNOT	hand to hand
	hand-to-hand
AADDHIKSSY	say Kaddish
AADDIILNOT	additional
AADDIJNOSV	David Jason
AADDILLLOV	Valladolid
AADDILNRSZ	sand lizard
AADDINORRT	ritardando
AADDLLNORS	sand dollar
AADDLNOOSW	sandalwood
AADDNNRRUU	Duran Duran
AADEEEFLLM	female lead
AADEEEJMMS	James Meade
AADEEEKNRW	reawakened
AADEEFGHOR	forge ahead
AADEEFGHOT	get ahead of
AADEEFGLRT	deflagrate
AADEEFHORY	head of year
AADEEFLNRT	trade-falne
AADEEFLRRY	Alfred Ayer
AADEEGGINR	reading age
AADEEGIRTV	variegated
AADEEGLRVW	Waldegrave
AADEEGMNRW	game warden
AADEEGNRST	degreasant
AADEEGNRTU	guaranteed
AADEEHHLRX	hexahedral
AADEEHHMMR	hammerhead
AADEEHIMTV	have it made
AADEEHINOV	have no idea
AADEEHKKOV	have a dekko
AADEEHLTWY	lead the way
AADEEHMNTY	name the day
AADEEHMRST	headmaster
AADEEHMRVY	heavy-armed
AADEEHNPRT	pentahedra
AADEEHNRVW	heavenward
AADEEHPPRS	pear-shaped
AADEEHPRSS	press ahead
AADEEHQRSU	headsquare
AADEEHRRTT	tetrahedra
AADEEHRTTY	at the ready
AADEEILMNT	delaminate
AADEEILNNR	adrenaline
AADEEILNST	desalinate
AADEEIMMNN	maiden name
AADEEIMNRT	reanimated
AADEEINQTU	inadequate
AADEEIPRST	deaspirate
AADEEJMRSW	James Dewar
AADEEKKKOT	take a dekko
AADEEKKMRR	make darker
AADEEKMMNS	make amends
AADEEKOTWY	a week today
AADEELLOTW	a lead towel
AADEELMPRR	palm reader
AADEELMRTT	maltreated
AADEELNNWZ	New Zealand
AADEELNRSX	alexanders
AADEELQRSU	square deal
AADEELQTUY	adequately
AADEELRSSW	easselward
AADEELRTTU	adulterate
AADEEMQRSU	masquerade
AADEEMQSTU	desquamate
AADEENPPSU	suppedanea
AADEENSTVZ	Zend-Avesta
AADEENTTTU	attenuated

AADEEOPRTV	evaporated
AADEEORSTY	easy to read
AADEERRTTW	tread water
AADEFFIILT	affiliated
AADEFFNORT	fore-and-aft
AADEFGLNNS	fandangles
AADEFGLOOT	get a load of
AADEFGNNOS	fandangoes
AADEFGRSSU	safeguards
AADEFHHIOR	head of hair
AADEFHIIRR	fair-haired
AADEFHLNRT	fatherland
AADEFHRSTY	Father's Day
AADEFILLRT	falderal it
AADEFIMNOT	defamation
AADEFINSTZ	fantasized
AADEFINTTU	infatuated
AADEFKLNOR	do a flanker
AADEFMORTY	defamatory
AADEFNRRSW	Dawn Fraser
AADEFRRSTW	afterwards
AADEGGINRS	aggrandise
AADEGGINRZ	aggrandize
AADEGGOSSU	sausage dog
	sausage-dog
AADEGILMNN	leading man
AADEGILPRR	paraglider
AADEGILRST	saltigrade
AADEGILTTY	agitatedly
AADEGIMMNS	mismanaged
AADEGIMNPR	map-reading
AADEGINOTT	toad-eating
AADEGINRRS	disarrange
AADEGIORST	Deo gratias
AADEGIPRRS	disparager
AADEGLNQRU	quadrangle
AADEGLNRTU	granulated
AADEGLNSTW	sweat gland
AADEGMRRSY	Gerry Adams
AADEGMRRTU	dramaturge
AADEGNNRRU	unarranged
AADEGNOPRR	grand opera
AADEGNORSS	Sangradoes
AADEGNRSTY	Great Sandy
AADEHHKNSS	shake hands
AADEHHNNOS	Shenandoah
AADEHHRTWY	the hard way
AADEHIILRS	dish aerial
AADEHIIMNR	maidenhair
AADEHIINRT	antheridia
AADEHIIPRS	sphaeridia
AADEHIKNNT	take in hand
AADEHILORR	diarrhoeal
AADEHINRSS	hansardise
AADEHINRSZ	hansardize
AADEHKMRRT	thread mark
AADEHLNNPR	panhandler
AADEHLNPRR	Ralph Nader
AADEHLRSSY	harassedly
AADEHMNOSY	Moshe Dayan
AADEHMPRSS	Sam Shepard
AADEHNSSTV	handstaves
AADEIILMNN	Indian meal
AADEIILNOT	ideational
AADEIILNTV	invalidate
AADEIIMNNR	Amerindian
AADEIIMNNT	maintained
AADEIIMNST	disanimate
	mediastina
AADEIIMPRS	imparadise
AADEIINPPR	India paper
AADEIKLNSW	Wake Island
AADEILLPPT	papillated
AADEILMNNR	mainlander
AADEILMNPT	Dame Pliant
AADEILMNTY	animatedly
AADEILMORT	tailor-made
AADEILMRTX	taxidermal
AADEILNNTV	native land
AADEILNOPR	Adrianople
AADEILNPRT	land-pirate
AADEILNRSU	unsalaried
AADEILNSTU	andalusite
AADEILOPSS	palisadoes
AADEILPPRS	disapparel
AADEILPTVY	adaptively
AADEIMMNNO	domain name
AADEIMMNRR	married man
AADEIMNRTV	animadvert
AADEIMNSUX	à deux mains
AADEINNQRU	quadrennia
AADEINNRWW	win and wear
AADEINNSTW	stand in awe
AADEINORTY	arytaenoid
AADEINPQSU	pasquinade
AADEINPRSU	unparadise
AADEINQTTU	antiquated
AADEIORSTV	advisorate
AADEIPRRTV	drive apart
AADEIRSSTU	raise a dust
AADEJNORST	Oranjestad
AADEJPRRSU	Raj Persaud
AADEKKNRST	stark naked
	stark-naked
AADEKLLMNS	Dan Maskell
AADEKMNOSU	make a sound
AADEKMORSS	damask rose
AADEKMRRST	trademarks
AADEKMRRTT	dark matter
AADELLLMTY	Tam Dalyell
AADELLMORT	mortadella
AADELLNPTT	platteland
AADELLNRTY	Talleyrand
AADELLORRT	a tall order
AADELLORSV	El Salvador
AADELLPRUU	Paul Eluard
AADELMORST	loadmaster
AADELMOSTT	made to last
AADELNNOST	stand-alone
AADELNRTTU	adulterant
AADEMMNSSU	mandamuses
AADEMNOORS	enamorados

AADEMNOQRU	Andromaque
AADEMOQRTU	Torquemada
AADENNRTTU	denaturant
AADENNSTTT	attendants
AADENORRRY	Ray Reardon
AADENORRSU	arse around
AADENORRTW	draw near to
AADENQRSTU	quadrantes
AADENRSTTT	stand treat
AADENRSTTU	transudate
AADEOPRRUX	paradoxure
AADEORSTTV	devastator
AADEQRRSUY	square yard
AADEQRRTUU	quadrature
AADFFFNORU	faff around
AADFFGINST	fading fast
AADFFHNSST	handstaffs
AADFHIKLOR	Frida Kahlo
AADFILMRYY	My Fair Lady
AADFILRSTU	fruit salad
AADFNORRTU	fart around
AADGGILMNY	damagingly
AADGHIPRSY	dysgraphia
AADGHNNORU	hang around
AADGIIIRSS	giardiasis
AADGIILNTV	validating
AADGIIMNRR	ram-raiding
AADGIINNRT	grant-in-aid
AADGIINOTV	divagation
AADGILLNOY	diagonally
AADGILMNSU	salmagundi
AADGILMRSU	gradualism
AADGILNOOT	odontalgia
AADGILNRST	Stalingrad
AADGILRSTU	gradualist
AADGILRTUY	graduality
AADGINNOPR	grand piano
AADGINORRY	Dorian Gray
AADGINORTU	graduation
AADGLMNSUY	salmagundy
AADGLNORTT	grand total
AADGMRRTUY	dramaturgy
AADGMRSSTU	mustard gas
AADGNNOPRS	snapdragon
AADHILLMOO	homaloidal
AADHILRTWW	withdrawal
AADHINOPSU	diaphanous
AADHINORRS	hard as iron
AADHINPSSU	Upanishads
AADHIOTWWY	do away with
AADHIRRSTY	dysarthria
AADHLLNNOS	on all hands
AADHLNNOSY	lay hands on
	lay on hands
AADHLNORWY	Andy Warhol
AADIILNOTT	dilatation
AADIILNOTV	validation
AADIILNPRW	Rawalpindi
AADIIMNOPS	dipsomania
AADIIMNORT	admiration
AADIINNRSW	Indian Wars
AADIINRRSY	in disarray
AADIIPRSST	aspidistra
AADIIRRSTV	Stradivari
AADIJNORTU	adjuration
AADILLMORS	armadillos
AADILNOPTT	top and tail
AADILNRSTT	stand trial
AADIMNNOPR	prima donna
AADIMNNRST	sand martin
AADINNNOST	andantinos
AADJMNNPRU	panjandrum
AADJMNOOSY	Joy Adamson
AADKLMMPSU	damask plum
AADKLNOOSY	look and say
AADKLNORRU	lark around
AADLMNNNOS	No Man's Land
AADLMNORTU	Laundromat®
AADLMNPSUY	Palm Sunday
AADLNOPRUY	play around
AADMNOOOTT	odontomata
AADNNORSUW	swan around
AADNOPRRUW	wraparound
AADNOPRSSU	pass around
AADOPPRSST	strappados
AAEEEGGLLL	legal eagle
AAEEEGGRTX	exaggerate
AAEEEGKLNV	Lake Geneva
AAEEEGLSST	easselgate
AAEEEGMNRU	Eugene Aram
AAEEEGNRRW	wage-earner
AAEEEHRSST	heartsease
	heart's-ease
AAEEEIKMRS	make easier
AAEEEILLMM	mealie meal
AAEEEKKMRW	make weaker
AAEEEKMSTY	make eyes at
AAEEELLNOV	leave alone
AAEEELNPRS	paraselene
AAEEELRSTT	real estate
AAEEELRTUV	re-evaluate
AAEEEMNNOS	sea anemone
AAEEENRSTU	ease nature
AAEEEPRSTX	exasperate
AAEEERSSTV	asseverate
AAEEFGIMRT	after-image
AAEEFGKMMO	make game of
AAEEFGLLLT	flagellate
AAEEFHLLPS	half-asleep
AAEEFHRSTV	aftershave
AAEEFKKQSU	Kafkaesque
AAEEFLLLPS	fall asleep
AAEEFLPSST	fast asleep
AAEEFLRSSV	Lassa fever
AAEEFRSTTT	aftertaste
AAEEGGIPRT	arpeggiate
AAEEGGKORR	Karageorge
AAEEGGMSTU	steam gauge
AAEEGGPPRU	paper gauge
AAEEGGPRTU	taper gauge
AAEEGGRTUW	water gauge
AAEEGHLLRT	all the rage

AAEEGHLNOT	halogenate
AAEEGHLPRY	harpy eagle
AAEEGHRRTT	Great-heart
AAEEGIJNPT	Jean Piaget
AAEEGILMNN	emalangeni
AAEEGILNTT	gelatinate
AAEEGIMNRT	emarginate
AAEEGIMNTT	meat-eating
AAEEGIMSSX	Sexagesima
AAEEGINRTV	vegetarian
AAEEGJMPST	James Paget
AAEEGKLMRR	make larger
AAEEGKLRST	Great Lakes
AAEEGKMRRV	grave-maker
AAEEGKMSSU	make a guess
AAEEGLRRTX	extra large
	extra-large
AAEEGLRSSY	Gale Sayers
AAEEGLRSTV	Great Slave
AAEEGMMNNT	management
AAEEGMMORR	aerogramme
AAEEGMNRSS	manageress
AAEEGMNRTV	ravagement
AAEEGMRRSV	Mrs Average
AAEEGNPRRR	prearrange
AAEEGNSSSV	savageness
AAEEGQRRTU	quarterage
AAEEHIKRTT	take the air
AAEEHILRTX	exhilarate
AAEEHIMPRY	hyperaemia
AAEEHIMPTT	epithemata
AAEEHIPRSS	aphaeresis
AAEEHKMNPP	make happen
AAEEHKPRTT	take the rap
AAEEHKQRTU	earthquake
AAEEHLLMST	all the same
AAEEHLLNNT	Ethan Allen
AAEEHLMTVY	heavy metal
AAEEHLNNST	The Annales
AAEEHLNTTT	latent heat
AAEEHLQRSU	equal share
AAEEHLSTTT	at the least
AAEEHMNORR	amenorrhea
AAEEHMNRTW	weatherman
AAEEHMPRST	metaphrase
AAEEHMPRTW	weather map
AAEEHNNRSW	Shane Warne
AAEEHNOSTT	eat one's hat
AAEEHNPRSV	Enver Pasha
AAEEHPTVWY	pave the way
AAEEHRRSTW	shearwater
AAEEHRTVWY	heavy water
AAEEIJLNSS	Jean Alessi
AAEEIKLMNS	seamanlike
AAEEIKMNOS	make a noise
AAEEIKSTTY	take it easy
AAEEILLLRV	lavallière
AAEEILLNST	lateen sail
AAEEILLQTU	illaqueate
AAEEILLRTT	alliterate
AAEEILMNNS	Melanesian
AAEEILMORT	ameliorate
AAEEILNPRT	penetralia
AAEEILPRTU	eutrapelia
AAEEILTUVV	evaluative
AAEEIMNNSX	Anaximenes
AAEEIMNOTT	one at a time
AAEEIMNRSU	in a measure
AAEEINPPRV	papaverine
AAEEINPRSS	paraenesis
AAEEIOPRRS	opera seria
AAEEIPRRTT	repatriate
AAEEIPRRTV	reparative
AAEEIPRTTX	expatriate
AAEEJJMNSS	James Jeans
AAEEJLMNPR	Jane Marple
AAEEJNNSTU	Jane Austen
AAEEJNQTTU	Jaquenetta
AAEEKLLPTY	keep a tally
AAEEKLMRYY	Mary Leakey
AAEEKLNNRV	Lake Vänern
AAEEKLNRSS	Lake Nasser
AAEEKMNOTT	take to mean
AAEEKMNSUY	make uneasy
AAEEKNRSTW	water snake
AAEEKPRTTU	take-up rate
AAEEKRSTTU	take as true
AAEELLNNRR	Alan Lerner
AAEELLNNSW	Anna Sewell
AAEELMPRRT	marprelate
AAEELMQRSU	square meal
AAEELNNPTU	pennatulae
AAEELNPRRT	parenteral
AAEELNRRRW	Earl Warren
AAEELPRSTU	at pleasure
AAEELPRSTY	separately
AAEEMNNSSU	amanuenses
AAEEMPRRST	parameters
AAEEMSSSTT	metastases
AAEENORRYY	year-on-year
AAEENRTTUV	at a venture
AAEEPPRSTW	waste paper
AAEERRSTXX	Artaxerxes
AAEFFHLLMO	hall of fame
AAEFFHOPTV	have off pat
AAEFFILLNR	farfalline
AAEFFILORV	love affair
AAEFGGHRTU	fraughtage
AAEFGHILNU	half guinea
AAEFGIISTT	fastigiate
AAEFGLLLNS	Angel Falls
AAEFGLLLNT	flagellant
AAEFGLMNRT	fragmental
AAEFGNORRR	arrange for
AAEFHHLMRT	health farm
AAEFHIKLLS	like a flash
AAEFHINRTT	faint-heart
AAEFHLLRYY	half-yearly
AAEFIILLMN	animal life
AAEFIILSTT	fatalities
AAEFIKRRTT	traik after
AAEFILMMNY	family name

AAEFILNNOT	La Fontaine
AAEFILNNOV	vienna loaf
AAEFIMRRRT	terra firma
AAEFINOOPR	one of a pair
AAEFINRSTZ	fantasizer
AAEFKKNORT	take rank of
AAEFKLLUWY	fully awake
AAEFKPPRRT	kraft paper
AAEFLLMNOS	all means of
AAEFLLNPTU	fault plane
AAEFLLNSTU	fustanella
AAEFLLORRS	solar flare
AAEFLLRSTW	Fats Waller
AAEFLOPSTT	soft palate
AAEFLORTZZ	to a frazzle
AAEFLRSSTT	false start
AAEFLSSTTY	Safety Last
AAEFMRSSTT	fast stream
AAEFORRSTT	after a sort
AAEGGILNSW	Glaswegian
AAEGHHIRTV	have a right
AAEGHIKNTW	wake a night
AAEGHILLSS	Galashiels
AAEGHILPSY	hypalgesia
AAEGHINNRT	a near thing
AAEGHIRSTT	Ishtar Gate
AAEGHLNOPT	heptagonal
AAEGHLNPRY	pharyngeal
AAEGHLNRRT	larger than
AAEGHLOSTU	hasta luego
AAEGHPPPRR	graph paper
AAEGIILNNT	alienating
AAEGIILPRS	plagiarise
AAEGIILPRZ	plagiarize
AAEGIINNTV	invaginate
AAEGIINRTT	ingratiate
AAEGIKLLNR	Karl Nägeli
AAEGILLMQU	maquillage
AAEGILLNOT	allegation
AAEGILLPRS	aspergilla
AAEGILMNRT	martingale
AAEGILNNTT	tangential
AAEGILNSWX	sealing-wax
AAEGILOPRS	paralogise
AAEGILOPRZ	paralogize
AAEGIMNRRS	misarrange
AAEGIMNRVY	Marvin Gaye
AAEGIMPRST	pragmatise
AAEGIMPRTZ	pragmatize
AAEGIMRSTT	magistrate
	sterigmata
AAEGINNOST	antagonise
AAEGINNOTZ	antagonize
AAEGINNSTU	nauseating
AAEGINPRST	separating
AAEGINRTUU	inaugurate
AAEGINSSTT	set against
AAEGIRRSTV	stravaiger
AAEGIRSTTV	give a start
AAEGKLOOTT	get a look at
AAEGKNRSSS	grass snake

AAEGLLPSST	plate glass
AAEGLLRRTY	art gallery
AAEGLMORSU	megalosaur
AAEGLNNOPT	pentagonal
AAEGLNORTT	tetragonal
AAEGLOPRSS	opera-glass
AAEGLPRRRT	larger part
AAEGLPRRYY	Gary Player
AAEGLRSSTW	waterglass
AAEGMMNOOT	a moment ago
AAEGMOPRSU	rampageous
AAEGNORSTY	gone astray
AAEHHINTWY	The Hay Wain
AAEHHJLLLU	hallelujah
AAEHHKLRSW	whale shark
AAEHHLPRTY	hypaethral
AAEHHNRRTT	rather than
AAEHHRRSTU	Arthur Ashe
AAEHIILMNS	leishmania
AAEHIILNNT	annihilate
AAEHIILRSV	Rhea Silvia
AAEHIKPPSS	speak a ship
AAEHIKRRST	hairstreak
AAEHILMMNP	Manila hemp
AAEHILNOTX	exhalation
AAEHILPSTW	Westphalia
AAEHILRSVY	Rhea Sylvia
AAEHIMNPSS	seamanship
AAEHIMNPST	phantasime
AAEHIMNSTY	myasthenia
AAEHIMRSTU	amateurish
AAEHIMTTTT	at that time
AAEHINNORV	Hanoverian
AAEHIPSTXY	asphyxiate
AAEHLLMRRS	marshaller
AAEHLNNOOV	have on loan
AAEHLNNOSS	Hans Sloane
AAEHLORTTY	lay to heart
AAEHMNORST	Thomas Arne
AAEHMNORTW	Earthwoman
	woman-hater
AAEHMNRSST	harassment
AAEHMNRSTV	harvestman
AAEHMOSTTY	stay-at-home
AAEHMPRSTT	metaphrast
AAEHNNRSTU	Tannhäuser
AAEHNOPRST	anastrophe
AAEHNPRSST	trans-shape
AAEHPPRSSY	paraphyses
AAEHRSTTTT	at the start
AAEIIILNST	Italianise
AAEIIILNTZ	Italianize
AAEIIKLLNS	alkalinise
AAEIIKLLNZ	alkalinize
AAEIIKNNTV	take in vain
AAEIILLPTV	palliative
AAEIILMMRT	immaterial
AAEIILMNRS	laminarise
AAEIILMNRZ	laminarize
AAEIILMSST	assimilate
AAEIILNNOT	alienation

AAEIILNNST	salientian
AAEIILNPSY	Ian Paisley
AAEIILNSTV	insalivate
AAEIILPRST	partialise
	patrialise
AAEIILPRTZ	partialize
	patrialize
AAEIIMNNRS	seminarian
AAEIIMNNRT	maintainer
AAEIIMPPRR	primiparae
AAEIIPRSST	parasitise
AAEIIPRSTZ	parasitize
AAEIKLMNOZ	Amazon-like
AAEIKLMORT	tailormake
AAEIKLNSTY	like a tansy
AAEIKNPRTT	take part in
AAEILLLMUX	maxillulae
AAEILLLNPR	in parallel
AAEILLLRST	saltarelli
AAEILLMNPT	palliament
AAEILLMRTY	materially
AAEILLMSTT	at all times
AAEILLNORT	relational
AAEILLNRTU	unilateral
AAEILLRRTT	trilateral
AAEILLRTTY	laterality
AAEILLRTVY	varietally
AAEILMNNSS	Las Meninas
AAEILMNPRT	parliament
AAEILMNPTU	manipulate
AAEILMNRTT	alternatim
AAEILMNRTY	alimentary
AAEILMPRRT	premarital
AAEILNNOPT	Neapolitan
AAEILNNOTV	venational
AAEILNOPST	spaniolate
AAEILNORST	senatorial
AAEILNORTT	alteration
AAEILNORTX	relaxation
AAEILNOTTX	exaltation
AAEILNOTUV	evaluation
AAEILNRRVW	new arrival
AAEILNRSTU	naturalise
AAEILNRTUZ	naturalize
AAEILOQRTU	equatorial
AAEILORRTT	retaliator
AAEILPPRSS	paralipses
AAEILPPRST	epiplastra
AAEILPSSSY	pass easily
AAEILQRSSU	square sail
AAEILSTUXY	asexuality
AAEIMMNRST	mainstream
AAEIMMNRTT	main matter
AAEIMMPRTU	at a premium
AAEIMMRSTU	amateurism
AAEIMNNOPR	Pomeranian
	praenomina
AAEIMNNOSY	mayonnaise
AAEIMNNSSU	amanuensis
AAEIMNNTTT	attainment
AAEIMNOPPT	Papiamento
AAEIMNPRTZ	nitrazepam
AAEIMNQRTU	Quatermain
AAEIMNRTTT	antimatter
AAEIMNRTVW	Vietnam War
AAEIMPRSST	separatism
AAEIMRSTTU	traumatise
AAEIMRTTUV	maturative
AAEIMRTTUZ	traumatize
AAEIMSSSTT	metastasis
AAEINNNOTX	annexation
AAEINNQRTU	quarantine
AAEINNSSST	Saint-Saëns
AAEINOPRRT	praetorian
	reparation
AAEINOPRST	separation
AAEINOPSST	passionate
AAEINPRRSW	Persian War
AAEINRRTTZ	tartrazine
AAEINRSSTU	Russian tea
AAEINRTTTT	tarte tatin
AAEIOPSSTT	apostatise
AAEIOPSSTZ	apostasize
AAEIOPSTTZ	apostatize
AAEIPRRTVW	private war
AAEIPRSSTT	separatist
AAEJMMNOSS	James Mason
AAEJMNNOOT	Joe Montana
AAEJRSTTYY	Jay's Treaty
AAEKKMMRRS	maker's mark
AAEKKOSTTT	take to task
AAEKLLLMWY	walk lamely
AAEKLMMORS	smoke alarm
AAEKLNNOOT	take on loan
AAEKMMRSST	mass market
	mass-market
AAEKMNORRW	make narrow
AAEKMPRSTU	take up arms
AAEKMRSSTT	taskmaster
AAEKRRSTUU	sauerkraut
AAELLLLPRY	parallelly
AAELLLMNOS	salmonella
AAELLMNRTY	maternally
AAELLMORTT	martellato
AAELLMORZZ	mozzarella
AAELLMPPSU	slap-up meal
AAELLMPQTU	Malplaquet
AAELLMPRTY	malapertly
AAELLNOSSY	seasonally
AAELLNPRTY	parentally
	paternally
AAELLNPSTY	pleasantly
AAELLNRSTU	Stan Laurel
AAELLOSSWW	sea swallow
AAELLPRUVY	Paul Valéry
AAELMNNORT	ornamental
AAELMNNPUW	Paul Newman
AAELMNOPSU	menopausal
AAELMNORVV	removal van
AAELMNOSSW	saleswoman
AAELMNOUVX	Max von Laue
AAELMNRSUY	aneurysmal

AAELMRRTUX	extramural
AAELNNNPRU	penannular
AAELNNPSTU	pennatulas
	unpleasant
AAELNOPRUV	no par value
AAELNORRTT	alternator
AAELNPPRTY	apparently
AAELNPRRSU	suprarenal
AAELNPRSTT	transeptal
AAELNPRSTY	pleasantry
AAELNPRTTW	water-plant
AAELNRSTUV	transvalue
AAELOPPRST	poles apart
AAELOPRSST	pastorales
AAELORRTTV	travelator
AAELORSTTZ	lazarettos
AAELPRSSUU	as per usual
AAEMNNORTT	tramontane
AAEMNNRSTV	manservant
AAEMNOOSST	anastomose
AAEMPRSSTT	past master
AAEMRSSTTU	metatarsus
AAENNPPRTU	unapparent
AAENOPSWYY	pay one's way
AAENORTUUV	Art Nouveau
AAENQRRTUY	quaternary ☐
AAENRRSTTU	restaurant
AAEOOPRRTV	evaporator
AAEQRRSTUW	quarter-saw
AAEQRSTUUY	quaestuary
AAFFGIMNRU	ragamuffin
AAFFILLRTW	tariff wall
AAFGGILLNS	signal flag
AAFGGILNVW	flag-waving
AAFGIINNPR	frangipani
AAFGKLOORW	go for a walk
AAFGLLNRTY	flagrantly
AAFGLLOSST	float glass
AAFGLNNRTY	granny flat
AAFGLNRRTY	fragrantly
AAFGMOORWY	go away from
AAFHHLRRSY	flash Harry
AAFHIINNOS	in a fashion
AAFHIITTUW	au fait with
AAFHIMORRS	Omar Sharif
AAFHLLORTT	for all that
AAFIIILRSS	filariasis
AAFIILLMRY	familiarly
AAFIILMNRU	unfamiliar
AAFIINRTVY	Vanity Fair
AAFIIRSSTU	safari suit
AAFILNOOTT	floatation
AAFIMOORRS	afrormosia
AAFIOQRSTU	aqua fortis
AAFLNPRSTY	flan pastry
AAFMNOORST	sonata form
AAFMNORSTW	man of straw
AAGGHHINRT	hang a right
AAGGHLNNSW	slang-whang
AAGGIINNSY	gainsaying
AAGGINNSTT	stagnating
AAGGINRSTZ	stargazing
AAGGLLLOSS	galloglass
AAGGLLNNYY	ylang-ylang
AAGHHILLMR	Graham hill
AAGHHIMNWY	highwayman
AAGHIIKNNT	think again
AAGHIKNQSU	quaking ash
AAGHILMNSW	Walsingham
AAGHILNPST	phalangist
AAGHILOPPY	polyphagia
AAGHILORTY	hagiolatry
AAGHIMNORS	Ngaio Marsh
AAGHMOORTT	Otto Graham
AAGHMORSTY	Thomas Gray
AAGHNOPPRT	pantograph
AAGHNRTUUU	Tungurahua
AAGHOPRSTY	Pythagoras
AAGHOPRTUY	autography
AAGIIILNRT	tagliarini
AAGIIINNRV	viraginian
AAGIILLNVY	availingly
AAGIILMPRS	plagiarism
AAGIILNNUV	unavailing
AAGIILPRST	plagiarist
AAGIINNOTV	navigation
AAGIINPSTT	pit against
AAGIJKLNWY	jaywalking
AAGIKMNNWY	yawn-making
AAGIKNPRTT	taking part
AAGILLMNRY	alarmingly
	marginally
AAGILLNOSZ	gallinazos
AAGILLSTTY	sagittally
AAGILMNORS	organismal
AAGILMOPRS	paralogism
AAGILNNOQU	Algonquian
AAGILNNRTU	Alan Turing
AAGILNPRSY	paralysing
AAGILNRRTU	triangular
AAGILNRTUY	angularity
AAGILOSUVY	Yugoslavia
AAGIMMNRWY	Mary Wigman
AAGIMMPRST	pragmatism
AAGIMNNNRY	Mary Anning
AAGIMNNOST	antagonism
AAGIMNNPRW	warming-pan
AAGIMPRSTT	pragmatist
AAGINNORTW	wagon train
AAGINNOSTT	antagonist
	stagnation
AAGINNRSUY	sanguinary
AAGINOORRT	arrogation
AAGINRRTVY	gravy train
AAGLLNOPTT	topgallant
AAGLLNRRUY	granularly
AAGLMNORSU	granulomas
AAGLNNOOSX	Anglo-Saxon
AAGLNNSTTY	stagnantly
AAGLNORRTY	arrogantly
AAGLRSSTUU	astragulus
AAGMOOSTUU	autogamous

AAGOOPPRRT	propagator
AAGOOPRRST	Protagoras
AAHHILMOPT	ophthalmia
AAHHIMMMSS	shammashim
AAHHIMRRTY	arrhythmia
AAHHMMNNUU	Nahum Nahum
AAHIIKLLMT	Mikhail Tal
AAHIILNNOT	inhalation
AAHIILNNTU	Lithuanian
AAHIILNOPS	Hispaniola
AAHIIMMMRX	Hiram Maxim
AAHIIMNOPP	hippomania
AAHIIMPRSS	pharisaism
AAHIKNOOST	Takashi Ono
AAHILLOPRT	prothallia
AAHILMNSTU	Malthusian
AAHILNNOPT	antiphonal
AAHINOPRTW	on a par with
AAHISSTTTY	it says that
AAHKKNNPYY	hanky-panky
AAHKLLLOOR	Lalla Rookh
AAHKLNOSTT	thanks a lot
AAHKLORRSW	ashlar-work
AAHKMNNSTY	many thanks
AAHLLORSTU	at all hours
AAHLOPRSTY	hyoplastra
AAHLPRTTWY	Twyla Tharp
AAHMMNNOST	Thomas Mann
AAHMNNORSW	Norman Shaw
AAHMOORRST	Ramos-Horta
AAHNOPRTTU	naturopath
AAHNORTWWY	thrown away
AAHOPRRRSZ	razor-sharp
AAHOPRRTTU	Utahraptor
AAHRSTTWWY	thwartways
AAIIILMMNT	militiaman
AAIIILMMNX	Maximilian
AAIIJKNSTT	Tajikistan
AAIIJLNORT	janitorial
AAIIJMOQRU	Jamiroquai
AAIIKLLNTY	alkalinity
AAIIKMNNST	Kantianism
AAIILLNOPT	palliation
AAIILLNUXY	uniaxially
AAIILMMNRT	Minimal Art
AAIILMMRST	martialism
AAIILMMSTX	maximalist
AAIILMNNOT	lamination
AAIILNORRT	irrational
AAIILNORST	solitarian
AAIILNOSTV	salivation
AAIILNRSTY	sanitarily
AAIILPPRSS	paralipsis
AAIILPRTTY	partiality
	patriality
AAIILPSTTY	spatiality
AAIILRRRRT	tirra-lirra
AAIIMMNRST	Martin Amis
AAIIMNNNOT	antinomian
AAIIMNRTTV	intra vitam
AAIIMPPRRS	primiparas
AAIIMPRSST	parasitism
AAIINNOPTT	patination
AAIINNOSTT	sanitation
AAIINNRRTU	Ruritanian
AAIINNRSTY	insanitary
AAIINOPPRT	apparition
AAIINOPRST	aspiration
AAIIPRSTWY	spirit away
AAIJNNOQSU	San Joaquin
AAIKLPRSTV	vital spark
AAILLMNNOZ	Manzanillo
AAILLNNOTY	nationally
AAILLNOPST	spallation
AAILLNORTY	notarially
	rationally
AAILLNPRST	in all parts
AAILLRSTUY	salutarily
AAILMNNOPR	nominal par
AAILMNOTTU	mutational
AAILMNPSSV	pan-Slavism
AAILMNRRTU	intramural
AAILMNRSTU	naturalism ❑
AAILNNOOTT	notational
AAILNNOPTT	plantation
AAILNNOTTU	nutational
AAILNNRTUY	annularity
AAILNOPRST	Alain Prost
AAILNOPTUV	vapulation
AAILNOPVVV	Ivan Pavlov
AAILNOSTTU	salutation
AAILNPQSTU	pasquilant
AAILNPSSTV	pan-Slavist
AAILNRSTTU	naturalist
AAILNRSTUY	insalutary
AAILNSSSTU	Stanislaus
AAILORSTTT	altostrati
AAILRSSTTY	Lysistrata
AAILRSSTUV	visual arts
AAIMMOSSTU	miasmatous
AAIMMOSTTU	automatism
AAIMMRSTTU	traumatism
AAIMNNOOSW	Ian Woosnam
AAIMNOORST	inamoratos
AAIMNOOTTU	automation
AAIMNOPRUV	Paavo Nurmi
AAIMNOPTTU	amputation
AAIMNORSTU	sanatorium
AAIMNORTTU	maturation
AAIMNPRSST	Spartanism
AAIMOSTTTU	automatist
AAINNNOOST	San Antonio
AAINNNOOTT	annotation
AAINNRSTUY	unsanitary
AAINORSTTU	saturation
AAINORSTTV	starvation
AAINORSTTY	stationary
AAINPPRSTY	spray-paint
AAIORRSTTT	trattorias
AAJKKLNRSY	Karl Jansky
AAKKLLTWYY	walky-talky
AAKKMOSVYY	Mayakovsky

Words marked ❑ can also be spelled with an initial capital letter

AAKLNOPRTW	walk-on part	ABBDEEELNR	Ben Bradlee
AAKLNORSUY	ankylosaur	ABBDEEGILR	bridgeable
AAKMMNORSW	markswoman	ABBDEEHLPS	pebbledash
AAKMNNORTY	Mark Antony	ABBDEEKNOR	doner kebab
AAKMORRSTY	ask to marry	ABBDEELNNU	unbendable
AALLLLOTWW	wall-to-wall	ABBDEFIORR	fibreboard
AALLMNTUUY	autumnally	ABBDEFLNOW	ebb and flow
AALLNOTUWY	all you want	ABBDEGIINR	Bainbridge
AALLOPRSTY	pastorally	ABBDEHIINS	Bishan Bedi
AALLORSSUU	Allosaurus	ABBDEHINRS	behind bars
AALLPSSWYY	palsy-walsy	ABBDEHIORY	ride a hobby
AALLRSTTWY	stalwartly	ABBDEILNRU	blue riband
AALMOOPPRS	malapropos	ABBDEIMORR	bombardier
AALMOOPRTY	laparotomy	ABBDEINORS	absorbed in
AALMOPRSXY	paroxysmal	ABBDEKLNOU	double-bank
AALNNNORTU	non-natural	ABBDELMOOZ	bamboozled
AALNNPRSTT	transplant	ABBDELORSY	absorbedly
AALNNRRSTU	translunar	ABBDELOSSU	double bass
AALNOOPPRV	on approval	ABBDENORRW	brown bread
AALNOPRSST	transposal	ABBDGILLNY	dabblingly
AALNORRSTT	translator	ABBEEEILLV	believable
AALNPRTTUY	play truant	ABBEEEKLRT	bark beetle
AALOORRTTV	travolator	ABBEEERTTT	a better bet
AALOPRRSTU	Australorp	ABBEELORSV	observable
AALOPSTTUY	autoplasty	ABBEELRTTU	rebuttable
AALORSTTUY	salutatory	ABBEENORST	breastbone
AAMNNOTTTU	tantamount	ABBEENORTW	browbeaten
AAMNOOSTTU	automatons	ABBEENRTTU	butter bean
AAOOPPRRST	paratroops	ABBEEORRTW	browbeater
ABBBBEHLTU	bubble bath	ABBEFGNOOS	bag of bones
ABBBBINORY	baby-ribbon	ABBEFILNSS	flabbiness
ABBBCEKLPU	bubble pack	ABBEGNRTTU	Battenburg
ABBBCEORRR	robber-crab	ABBEHIKMOT	Thabo Mbeki
ABBBCLMOOT	cobalt bomb	ABBEHINSSS	shabbiness
ABBBDENRRU	rubber band	ABBEHLRSSU	sable brush
ABBBDNOSSY	Bobby Sands	ABBEHOPRRS	barbershop
ABBBEILNRU	unbribable	ABBEILMOPR	improbable
ABBBEIRRRT	Brer Rabbit	ABBEILNOTU	obnubilate
ABBBEMOORY	baby boomer	ABBEILOPSY	Bob Paisley
ABBCCEKNOU	bounce back	ABBEIRSTTY	baby-sitter
ABBCCKKLOS	back-blocks	ABBELMOORZ	bamboozler
ABBCDEKLOU	double back	ABBELMSSUU	subsumable
ABBCDEMRRU	breadcrumb	ABBELNNRUU	unburnable
ABBCDKLOOR	blockboard	ABBELORSVY	observably
ABBCDKMOUY	Bombay duck	ABBGHINRRU	rhubarbing
ABBCEINRSS	crabbiness	ABBGILNQSU	squabbling
ABBCEINSSS	scabbiness	ABBGILNSTY	stabbingly
ABBCEKLRRY	blackberry	ABBGINORTU	bring about
ABBCEKMNRU	back number	ABBHILMSUU	Lubumbashi
ABBCEKNRRU	back burner	ABBHJNORTY	John Bratby
ABBCELMOPR	parcel bomb	ABBIILLORR	Barbirolli
ABBCELNUYY	Cluny Abbey	ABBILMOPRY	improbably
ABBCEMORRY	Abercromby	ABBILORSTU	suborbital
ABBCENORSY	absorbency	ABBMMOORRT	mortar-bomb
ABBCGIIKNT	backbiting	ABCCCEFIOS	beccaficos
	back-biting	ABCCDEINTY	by accident
ABBCHIOTTU	bitch about	ABCCDIIORS	sorbic acid
ABBCIILLLY	biblically	ABCCEEILMP	impeccable
ABBCIIRRTU	barbituric	ABCCEEILSS	accessible
ABBCIMMOOT	atomic bomb	ABCCEEKNRT	centre-back
ABBDDEEILO	able-bodied	ABCCEELLRY	recyclable

ABCCEEPRSY	cyberspace
ABCCEFILPU	public face
ABCCEIIRTY	acerbicity
ABCCEILMPY	impeccably
ABCCEILNOU	bon accueil
ABCCEILORU	corbiculae
ABCCEILSSY	accessibly
ABCCEKMOOT	come back to
ABCCHIIRRT	tribrachic
ABCCHIKLPT	pitch-black
ABCCHIKSTT	backstitch
ABCCHIKSTW	switchback
ABCCIKLTTU	Kitcat Club
ABCCILLOSU	social club
ABCCILORXY	carboxylic
ABCCNOOPRY	carbon copy
	carbon-copy
ABCDDEIRUV	David Bruce
ABCDEEELLT	delectable
ABCDEEELRT	celebrated
ABCDEEELTT	detectable
ABCDEEERSY	decrease by
ABCDEEFFTY	affected by
ABCDEEHMOR	become hard
ABCDEEHRUY	debauchery
ABCDEEILLN	declinable
ABCDEEILNU	ineducable
ABCDEEILPR	predicable
ABCDEEILPS	despicable
ABCDEEILRT	creditable
ABCDEEIRSS	describe as
ABCDEELLNY	belly-dance
ABCDEELLTY	delectably
ABCDEELLUX	excludable
ABCDEELMRS	descramble
ABCDEFOSTU	obfuscated
ABCDEGKMOS	gobsmacked
ABCDEHIILR	herbicidal
ABCDEHILSU	child abuse
ABCDEHKMPU	hump-backed
ABCDEHNORU	unbroached
ABCDEHORSS	chessboard
ABCDEHORSY	body-search
ABCDEIILNT	indictable
ABCDEIILNV	vindicable
ABCDEIKLRS	backslider
ABCDEILLNU	includable
ABCDEILPSY	despicably
ABCDEILRTY	creditably
ABCDEINORY	binary code
ABCDEIPRRS	crispbread
	spider crab
ABCDEKLOTU	blacked out
ABCDELMNRU	Cumberland
ABCDELNNOO	condonable
ABCDEOORRS	scoreboard
ABCDGINNOS	absconding
ABCDGKNORU	background
ABCDHIILNR	brainchild
ABCDHINNRU	nudibranch
ABCDHIOOPR	brachiopod
ABCDHKRRTU	Burckhardt
ABCDHLOORR	Cold Harbor
ABCDIILLSY	disyllabic
ABCDIILNNP	blind panic
ABCDIILNNU	Indian club
ABCDIKLOWW	black widow
ABCDIKOPRR	drop a brick
ABCDILLNOO	bill and coo
ABCEEEELSS	Celebes Sea
ABCEEEFFNO	coffee bean
ABCEEEFLTT	beef cattle
ABCEEEIKRR	icebreaker
ABCEEEILNT	enticeable
ABCEEEILRV	receivable
ABCEEEJLRT	rejectable
ABCEEEKMOW	become weak
ABCEEELLRR	cerebellar
ABCEEELMOP	become pale
ABCEEELPTX	expectable
ABCEEELTUX	executable
ABCEEENRUX	exuberance
ABCEEFHNNR	French bean
ABCEEFIILN	beneficial
ABCEEFINRV	cabin fever
ABCEEFNORT	benefactor
ABCEEHKLPS	black sheep
ABCEEHKLST	sketchable
ABCEEHLLRY	belly-acher
ABCEEHLLTT	bell the cat
ABCEEHLNQU	quenchable
ABCEEHLNSU	Chelsea bun
ABCEEHMOYZ	become hazy
ABCEEHNORR	abhorrence
ABCEEHORSU	herbaceous
ABCEEIJLNT	injectable
ABCEEILLNR	reclinable
ABCEEILLPX	explicable
ABCEEILMMT	emblematic
ABCEEILNNU	enunciable
ABCEEILNOT	noticeable
ABCEEILRTX	extricable
ABCEEINNOZ	benzocaine
ABCEEINNST	abstinence
ABCEEIOPRV	above price
ABCEEJKLTU	bluejacket
ABCEEJNSST	abjectness
ABCEEKORRV	break cover
ABCEEKRSTT	back street
ABCEEKSTTU	bucket seat
ABCEELNNOV	convenable
ABCEELNOVY	conveyable
ABCEELNRSU	censurable
ABCEELOPRW	pace-bowler
ABCEELORRT	celebrator
ABCEELPTXY	expectably
ABCEEMRSTU	Burmese cat
ABCEENOPRR	reprobance
ABCEENORSV	observance
ABCEEOPPRS	space probe
ABCEGHISTT	the big cats
ABCEGIKLNN	blackening

ABCEGINNNY	benignancy
ABCEGKLOSW	swage block
ABCEGLNOOT	conglobate
ABCEGNOORR	Roger Bacon
ABCEHHJOTT	hatchet job
ABCEHHNNOU	haunch bone
ABCEHHORTY	Tycho Brahe
ABCEHIKLNT	in the black
ABCEHILPRT	birthplace
ABCEHILRST	Christabel
ABCEHIMNRT	Chambertin
ABCEHIMRRT	hermit crab
ABCEHIPPRR	paper birch
ABCEHJKSTU	bush jacket
ABCEHKPRSY	Becky Sharp
ABCEHLLOTT	tablecloth
ABCEHLNRSS	branchless
ABCEHLPUYY	buy cheaply
ABCEHMMNRU	Mach number
ABCEHMOPRT	chamberpot
ABCEHOQRSU	quebrachos
ABCEHORTTX	chatterbox
ABCEHRSTTU	bruschetta
ABCEIIJNOS	Jacobinise
ABCEIIJNOZ	Jacobinize
ABCEIILLMT	bimetallic
ABCEIILLNR	brilliance
ABCEIILMTU	umbilicate
ABCEIILPST	epiblastic
ABCEIINTUV	incubative
ABCEIISSTU	sea biscuit
ABCEIKKRST	strike back
ABCEIKLMPU	make public
ABCEIKLRRY	bricklayer
ABCEILLNPU	inculpable
ABCEILLNRS	crane's bill
	cranesbill
ABCEILLSSU	casus belli
ABCEILLSUV	Savile Club
ABCEILLTUV	cultivable
ABCEILMOPT	compatible
ABCEILNOSU	unsociable
ABCEILNOTY	noticeably
ABCEILNPRU	republican
ABCEILNRRU	incurrable
ABCEIMORRT	barometric
ABCEINORSS	escribanos
ABCEINOSTU	Count Basie
ABCEINRRST	transcribe
ABCEINRSTU	be curtains
ABCEKKLRUY	lucky break
ABCEKKORST	backstroke
ABCEKLLNOU	unlockable
ABCEKLOPRW	Black Power
	black power
ABCELLLORU	blue-collar
ABCELLMOOR	Clare Bloom
ABCELLNOOR	collarbone
ABCELLNOOS	consolable
ABCELLOORS	Carlos Belo
ABCELMMOTU	commutable
ABCELMNOSU	consumable
ABCELMNRRU	Brunel Marc
ABCELMNRSU	unscramble
ABCELMOPTU	computable
ABCELNOSTU	locust bean
ABCELNRSUU	subnuclear
ABCELNRSUY	censurably
ABCELOPRRU	procurable
ABCELRRTUU	tubercular
ABCELSTUUY	subacutely
ABCEMNOOTZ	combat zone
ABCEMOSSUU	submucosae
ABCENOOPTU	ponce about
ABCENORSTY	corybantes
ABCENORSUW	brown sauce
ABCENORTTU	obtruncate
ABCENRRTUY	Canterbury
ABCEOORRST	Serbo-Croat
ABCEORRRTY	Robert Cray
ABCERRSTTU	subtracter
ABCFGIIKNR	backfiring
ABCGGIIKNV	giving back
	giving-back
ABCGHIIOPR	biographic
ABCGHKLOPU	plough back
ABCGIILLOO	biological
ABCGIKNOPX	packing-box
ABCGIKNPRS	spring back
ABCGILMNRS	scrambling
ABCGILNOSY	cognisably
ABCGILNOYZ	cognizably
ABCHHIOPRS	archbishop
ABCHHJNNOU	John Buchan
ABCHIILMOP	amphibolic
ABCHIKKNRS	shrink back
ABCHIKLLLS	Black Hills
ABCHIKLMST	blacksmith
ABCHIKLRST	Blackshirt
ABCHIMOORZ	Chimborazo
ABCHINOOPY	cynophobia
ABCHJKNOSU	John Backus
ABCHKKOOTU	chukka boot
ABCHKLNORT	blackthorn
ABCIIINOTT	antibiotic
ABCIILLNRY	brilliancy
ABCIILLOTY	biotically
ABCIILLSST	ballistics
ABCIILRTUY	curability
ABCIIMRSST	strabismic
ABCIINNOTU	incubation
ABCILLMOSY	symbolical
ABCILLNPUY	inculpably
ABCILLRRUY	rubrically
ABCILMOPTY	compatibly
ABCILMOSUX	musical box
ABCILNNOPT	Pinot Blanc
ABCILNORSU	binoculars
ABCILNOSUY	unsociably
ABCILORRTU	lubricator
ABCIMNOORS	coram nobis
ABCIORRRTU	rubricator

ABCKKNOOTU	knock about
	knockabout
ABCKLMPSTU	black stump
ABCKMMNOSU	summon back
ABCKNPRTUY	bankruptcy
ABCLLOORUY	colourably
ABCLMOSSUU	submucosal
ABCLORRTUY	Rotary Club
ABCLORSSUY	scabrously
ABCNORSTTY	by contrast
ABCORRSTTU	subtractor
ABDDDENORW	Edward Bond
ABDDEEEFLN	defendable
ABDDEEEHNO	bone-headed
ABDDEEELNP	dependable
ABDDEEGGLR	bedraggled
ABDDEEGHIR	bridgehead
ABDDEEHLLU	bull-headed
ABDDEELNPY	dependably
ABDDEELRST	bestraddle
ABDDEFGOOO	abode of God
ABDDEGINRU	unabridged
ABDDEGIRRW	drawbridge
ABDDEGNNOO	dog and bone
ABDDEHHINN	behindhand
ABDDEHILOR	hard-boiled
ABDDEHILUV	David Hubel
ABDDEHNORY	hard done by
ABDDEHORST	add herbs to
ABDDEIIMRS	bridesmaid
ABDDEIIOVW	David Bowie
ABDDEIORSS	sideboards
ABDDELMORU	Boulder Dam
ABDDELNORR	borderland
ABDDHNRSUY	dandy-brush
ABDDIIOORT	idiot board
ABDDINOORU	in bad odour
ABDDOORRSW	broadsword
ABDEEEELMR	redeemable
ABDEEEFHRT	feather bed
	featherbed
ABDEEEFLRR	deferrable
ABDEEEFORV	bereaved of
ABDEEEFRST	breastfeed
	breast-feed
ABDEEEGGLR	barelegged
ABDEEEGLLP	pledgeable
ABDEEEHNRV	heaven-bred
ABDEEEHQTU	bequeathed
ABDEEEILLN	delineable
ABDEEEILMR	remediable
ABDEEEILRT	deliberate
ABDEEEINRV	aberdevine
ABDEEEKLNN	needle bank
ABDEEELMRY	redeemably
ABDEEELNPX	expendable
ABDEEELNRR	renderable
ABDEEELNTX	extendable
ABDEEELRYY	bleary-eyed
ABDEEELSTT	detestable
ABDEEEMNST	debasement
ABDEEEMNTT	debatement
ABDEEENRTT	Bernadette
ABDEEEPPRR	be prepared
ABDEEEPRST	breast-deep
ABDEEERSTW	sweetbread
ABDEEFFHLU	bufflehead
ABDEEFGILN	bad feeling
ABDEEFHIMS	be famished
ABDEEFHNOR	beforehand
ABDEEFIKNR	bread knife
ABDEEFLNRU	refundable
ABDEEFOORT	barefooted
ABDEEFRSST	Fred Basset
ABDEEGHIRT	big-hearted
ABDEEGILNS	designable
ABDEEGILRT	ledger-bait
ABDEEGLNPS	bespangled
ABDEEGLNUW	unwedgable
ABDEEHIKNR	Birkenhead
ABDEEHILLS	déshabillé
ABDEEHILLV	ill-behaved
ABDEEHILRR	halberdier
ABDEEHIRTW	white-beard
ABDEEHITTW	debate with
ABDEEHORST	broadsheet
ABDEEIILTT	debilitate
ABDEEIINRT	inebriated
ABDEEIKNNY	kidney bean
ABDEEILMRY	remediably
ABDEEILNNU	undeniable
ABDEEILPRU	repudiable
ABDEEINNOR	Edna O'Brien
ABDEEINNRR	Bernardine
ABDEEIORUV	De Beauvoir
ABDEEISTTV	Bette Davis
ABDEEJLORT	job-related
ABDEEKOPPY	Pobedy Peak
ABDEEKORRY	keyboarder
ABDEEKRRRT	kerb-trader
ABDEELLLNU	unlabelled
ABDEELLOPR	deplorable
ABDEELLSTY	sell-by date
ABDEELPRRU	perdurable
ABDEELSTTY	detestably
ABDEEMOOOR	oboe d'amore
ABDEENOSSY	beyond seas
ABDEENPRRY	prebendary
ABDEERRSTT	Bradstreet
ABDEFFORSS	brassed off
ABDEFHILLN	fall behind
ABDEFHILOR	hold a brief
ABDEFIILMO	modifiable
ABDEFIIMRT	fimbriated
ABDEFILMOR	formidable
ABDEFILNOS	bed of nails
ABDEFINRSS	Fassbinder
ABDEFIRRTU	breadfruit
ABDEFLLOTU	double flat
ABDEFLOORT	after blood
ABDEGGIRRU	budgerigar
ABDEGHIIRT	bright idea

ABDEGHOOTT	go to the bad
ABDEGILNSY	debasingly
ABDEGILNTY	debatingly
ABDEGIMNRT	abridgment
ABDEGIMRRU	Bermuda rig
ABDEGINNOR	broadening
ABDEGIRRTW	Bridgwater
ABDEGJSTUU	subjugated
ABDEGNOSYY	bygone days
	days gone by
ABDEGOOSYY	say goodbye
ABDEHIILLS	dishabille
ABDEHIKLNW	walk behind
ABDEHILNSU	Danish blue
ABDEHIMRTU	thumb a ride
ABDEHINRTT	hard-bitten
ABDEHINSTY	stay behind
ABDEHIRSSU	brush aside
ABDEHLLMOT	mothballed
ABDEHNORRS	shard-borne
ABDEHNORTU	earthbound
ABDEHNRSTU	subtrahend
ABDEHNRTUY	Thunder Bay
ABDEHORRST	shortbread
ABDEHORTTU	outbreath'd
ABDEHOSUWY	bawdy-house
ABDEIIKLLS	dislikable
ABDEIILMSS	admissible
ABDEIIMNNR	bear in mind
ABDEIKNNRR	André Brink
ABDEILLLNY	blind alley
ABDEILLLSY	disyllable
ABDEILNNUY	undeniably
ABDEILNOPY	pineal body
ABDEILNORY	debonairly
ABDEILNRTV	Vanderbilt
ABDEILNSUY	unbiasedly
ABDEILOPRV	providable
ABDEILOPSS	disposable
ABDEILPSTU	disputable
ABDEILRTTW	wattlebird
ABDEIMNRST	disbarment
ABDEIMNSTU	submediant
ABDEIMRTUW	dumb-waiter
ABDEINORSU	boundaries
ABDEINPSTU	bite and sup
ABDEINRTTU	turbinated
ABDEKLLOTU	Double Talk
	double talk
	double-talk
ABDEKLMOOS	make so bold
ABDEKLOPRU	double-park
ABDELLNSUY	buy and sell
ABDELLOPRY	deplorably
ABDELLORST	Lord's Table
ABDELMMOOT	Tom o' Bedlam
ABDELMOPUY	Paul Dombey
ABDELNOORS	bandoleros
ABDELNOSUV	unabsolved
ABDELOOSTW	sweat blood
ABDELORSTU	double star
ABDELORTUY	obdurately
ABDELPRRUY	perdurably
ABDENNOTTW	batten down
ABDENOORTU	broaden out
ABDENORRSW	Rob Andrews
ABDENORTTW	batter down
ABDENRSSSU	absurdness
ABDENRSSTY	standers-by
ABDENSSTUY	Sunday best
ABDEOORRTU	order about
ABDEORRSWY	worry beads
ABDERRTTYY	dry battery
ABDFFNOUYY	Bay of Fundy
ABDFGHLOOR	grab hold of
ABDFGIINOR	fair-boding
ABDFGOORSX	Oxford bags
ABDFHIORTY	day of birth
ABDFILMORY	formidably
ABDFILNORU	floribunda
ABDFINSSTU	ifs and buts
ABDFLOOORR	floorboard
ABDFNORRWW	brown dwarf
ABDGGINNOR	go and bring
ABDGIINPRU	upbraiding
ABDGINNRST	string band
ABDGINNSTY	standing by
ABDGLLNOTU	bulldog ant
ABDHNOSSUY	Hudson's Bay
ABDIIILSTY	disability
ABDIIILTUY	audibility
ABDIILNOOS	obsidional
ABDIILPTUY	dupability
ABDIILRTUY	durability
ABDIIRSSUY	subsidiary
ABDILNOOST	bloodstain
ABDILNRUZZ	Buzz Aldrin
ABDILOORWZ	brazilwood
ABDILPSTUY	disputably
ABDINRSTTU	disturbant
ABDKLNOORS	Brooklands
ABDLMOORYY	bloody Mary
ABDMNNOOSW	bondswoman
ABDNOORSSU	boss around
ABDNOORTUU	round about
	roundabout
ABDOORRSTY	storyboard
ABDOORRTUU	troubadour
ABDOOTTTUY	dotty about
ABEEEFLORS	forseeable
ABEEEFLPRR	preferable
ABEEEFLRRR	referrable
ABEEEFNRTW	far between
ABEEEGLSTT	stag beetle
ABEEEGLSTV	vegetables
ABEEEHKRRS	break sheer
ABEEEHRSTT	hartebeest
ABEEEIKRRT	tie-breaker
ABEEEILLRV	relievable
ABEEEILRVW	reviewable
ABEEEKLPRT	Peter Blake
ABEEEKMRTT	make better

ABEEELMRSS	reassemble
ABEEELNPRT	penetrable
ABEEELQSUZ	squeezable
ABEEERRSST	Basseterre
	Basse-Terre
ABEEERRTTV	vertebrate
ABEEFFHMOT	off the beam
ABEEFFLMNT	bafflement
ABEEFFLRSU	sufferable
ABEEFGNRTU	be great fun
ABEEFHLMTY	fly the beam
ABEEFHLRST	self-breath
ABEEFHLRTT	better half
ABEEFIILRV	verifiable
ABEEFIIRTU	beautifier
ABEEFILLRT	filterable
ABEEFILNRR	inferrable
ABEEFILNSU	unfeasible
ABEEFILNTT	flea-bitten
ABEEFILPST	past belief
ABEEFKNORT	be taken for
ABEEFLLNSU	self-unable
ABEEFLMORR	reformable
ABEEFLPRRY	preferably
ABEEFLRSSU	self-abuser
ABEEFLSTTY	safety belt
ABEEFMOOTT	beef tomato
ABEEGGIKMR	make bigger
ABEEGHISTW	be ages with
ABEEGHNTTU	beat the gun
ABEEGILNOT	negotiable
ABEEGLNOPS	spongeable
ABEEGLNORV	governable
ABEEGLNSTW	West Bengal
ABEEGMMNNO	gombeen-man
ABEEGNNNRT	Tannenberg
ABEEGNRSTT	abstergent
ABEEHILLRS	relishable
ABEEHILPRS	perishable
ABEEHKLOSU	Bleak House
ABEEHKNORS	boneshaker
ABEEHLLOST	ballet shoe
ABEEHLLRST	three balls
ABEEHLLSTT	all the best
ABEEHLMPRS	blasphemer
ABEEHLRSST	breathless
ABEEHMORTT	bathometer
ABEEHNRSTY	Henry Bates
ABEEHNRTTT	better than
ABEEHOORRS	seborrhoea
ABEEHORSTU	hereabouts
ABEEHORTTU	breathe out
	thereabout
ABEEHORTUW	whereabout
ABEEHRRTTT	Brett Harte
ABEEIILLMN	eliminable
ABEEIILLRS	liberalise
ABEEIILLRZ	liberalize
ABEEIILNTV	inevitable
ABEEIILSST	bestialise
ABEEIILSTZ	bestialize
ABEEIJMOSW	James Bowie
ABEEIKLLLS	Klebsiella
ABEEIKLNRT	ankle-biter
ABEEIKMNST	be mistaken
ABEEILLMNR	Bellarmine
ABEEILLNNT	table linen
ABEEILLNRT	Albert Nile
ABEEILLNRU	unreliable
ABEEILLNSS	liableness
ABEEILLNTV	ventilable
ABEEILLRTT	Little Bear
ABEEILMNRT	terminable
ABEEILMNUZ	albumenize
ABEEILMOST	metabolise
ABEEILMOTT	metabolite
ABEEILMOTZ	metabolize
ABEEILMRRY	irremeably
ABEEILMSSS	assemblies
ABEEILNNUV	unenviable
ABEEILNOPR	inoperable
ABEEILNORX	inexorable
ABEEILNPSX	expansible
ABEEILNRSS	bleariness
ABEEILNRTU	untireable
ABEEILORTT	obliterate
ABEEILQRTU	requitable
ABEEINRTUX	exurbanite
ABEEIRSSTV	abstersive
ABEEJLLMSU	jumble sale
ABEEJMMNNT	enjambment
ABEEKLLMRT	market-bell
ABEEKLNRSV	blank verse
ABEEKLNTTW	wet blanket
ABEEKLOORS	break loose
ABEEKMMNNT	embankment
ABEEKNOPST	keep tabs on
ABEEKOPRRW	power brake
ABEELLLNTU	untellable
ABEELLMNOT	noble metal
ABEELLMOPY	employable
ABEELLNRUV	vulnerable
ABEELLNTTY	Betty Allen
ABEELLORSV	resolvable
ABEELMMMNT	embalmment
ABEELMNRRU	real number
ABEELMNRSU	Lebensraum
	mensurable
ABEELMNTTT	battlement
ABEELMORSW	seam bowler
ABEELMPRTU	permutable
ABEELNNNOY	Anne Boleyn
ABEELNOPRS	personable
ABEELNOTTZ	battle zone
ABEELNPRTY	penetrably
ABEELNQTTU	blanquette
ABEELNRRTU	returnable
ABEELNSSST	stableness
ABEELNSSSU	usableness
ABEELOOPPT	boat people
ABEELOPRRT	reportable
ABEELOPRTX	exportable

ABEELORRST	restorable
ABEENNNORT	Anne Brontë
ABEENNNRRU	runner bean
ABEENNRRSS	barrenness
ABEENNRSSU	urbaneness
ABEENNRSSZ	brazenness
ABEENORRTW	waterborne
ABEENORSTU	Eastbourne
ABEENRRSSV	brass nerve
ABEEOORTVW	tower above
ABEEPRRTTU	perturbate
ABEFFGILRU	febrifugal
ABEFFHLNOO	on behalf of
ABEFFILLOR	ball of fire
	bill of fare
ABEFFILORS	offers bail
ABEFFLRSUY	sufferably
ABEFGILORV	forgivable
ABEFGILRSS	fibreglass
	glass fibre
ABEFGINORR	forbearing
ABEFHIRRTT	afterbirth
ABEFHIRRTZ	Fritz Haber
ABEFHKORRT	break forth
ABEFIILLLN	infallible
ABEFIILLRT	fibrillate
ABEFIILNOT	notifiable
ABEFIILNTU	infibulate
ABEFILLLNU	unfallible
ABEFILMORR	moral fibre
ABEFILOPRT	profitable
ABEFKLSSTU	basketfuls
ABEFLLLMUY	blamefully
ABEFLLOORT	footballer
ABEFLLRRSU	barrelfuls
ABEFLMOORT	to blame for
ABEFLORSTW	fast bowler
ABEFMNORST	absent from
ABEFNOORSY	by reason of
ABEFNORSTY	Fray Bentos
ABEFNORTUY	Fortune Bay
ABEFNRRRYY	Bryan Ferry
ABEGGHILNU	be laughing
ABEGGINNOO	go on a binge
ABEGGNOORT	tobogganer
ABEGHHIRST	breast-high
ABEGHIKLRT	brake light
ABEGHIKMRT	make bright
ABEGHILNRT	blathering
ABEGHIMNNU	human being
ABEGHIOPRR	biographer
ABEGHLLOOP	Gallophobe
ABEGHLLOPU	ploughable
ABEGHLNOOP	anglophobe □
ABEGHNOPST	sponge bath
ABEGHNRRSU	bushranger
ABEGHQSUUU	usquebaugh
ABEGIILNNT	intangible
ABEGIILNRT	liberating
ABEGIINNRT	brigantine
ABEGIKNPRU	breaking-up
ABEGILLNOY	all-obeying
ABEGILLOSU	Bela Lugosi
ABEGILMNPU	impugnable
ABEGILNRSS	singles bar
ABEGILRRSU	burglarise
ABEGILRRUZ	burglarize
ABEGIMNNOT	bang on time
ABEGINNQTU	banqueting
ABEGINNRST	string bean
ABEGINRSSU	ear-bussing
ABEGINRSTU	gas turbine
ABEGLNORRY	loganberry
ABEGMNOOTY	Montego Bay
ABEGMORSUU	umbrageous
ABEGNOORTU	Baton Rouge
ABEGORRSSY	Gary Sobers
ABEHHILLST	sheathbill
ABEHHORRTT	heart-throb
ABEHIILMNT	habiliment
ABEHIJNNOR	John Braine
ABEHIKLNRS	shrinkable
ABEHIKRSWY	by a whisker
ABEHILLPTY	pay the bill
ABEHILMNST	habilments
ABEHILNPSU	punishable
ABEHILOPST	hospitable
ABEHILORTV	Bath Oliver
ABEHILPRSY	perishably
ABEHILPSTT	battleship
ABEHILPSTU	bisulphate
ABEHILTTTW	battle with
ABEHIMNNST	banishment
ABEHIMRRSU	herbariums
ABEHIMTTTY	by that time
ABEHINNORT	on the brain
ABEHINOOPX	xenophobia
ABEHINOPRV	vibraphone
ABEHINORTW	The Rainbow
ABEHIRRTWY	Barry White
ABEHIRSSTW	white brass
ABEHJNNORS	John Barnes
ABEHKLRSUW	bushwalker
ABEHKOOPRS	phrase book
ABEHLLMOTU	be all mouth
ABEHLNOORU	honourable
ABEHMORSTU	a sore thumb
ABEHMRTTYY	bathymetry
ABEHNOPRTY	hyperbaton
ABEHNORSST	basset horn
ABEHNOSTTU	thenabouts
ABEHORRSSS	horse brass
ABEIIILLMN	bimillenia
ABEIIILMNT	inimitable
ABEIILLMRS	liberalism
ABEIILLNNY	biennially
ABEIILLNOV	inviolable
ABEIILLRST	liberalist
ABEIILLRTY	liberality
ABEIILLTUZ	utilizable
ABEIILMNSS	lesbianism
ABEIILMNSU	albuminise

ABEIILMNUZ	albuminize
ABEIILMPRT	impartible
ABEIILNORT	liberation
ABEIILNOTT	nobilitate
ABEIILNPXY	inexpiably
ABEIILNRSY	inerasibly
ABEIILNTTY	tenability
ABEIILNTVY	inevitably
ABEIILQTUY	equability
ABEIILRSST	stabiliser
ABEIILRSSU	Belisarius
ABEIILRSTU	burial site
ABEIILRSTZ	stabilizer
ABEIILSTTY	bestiality
ABEIIMNTTU	bituminate
ABEIINNRSS	braininess
ABEIINNRTW	New Britain
ABEIINRRSV	river basin
ABEIJLNOTT	join battle
ABEIJMNOST	James Tobin
ABEIKLNNSU	unsinkable
ABEIKNOPRT	break point
ABEIKNSTUZ	Uzbekistan
ABEILLLNRW	Berlin Wall
ABEILLMNRT	Martin Bell
ABEILLMSTU	stimulable
ABEILLNORT	Lionel Bart
ABEILLNRUY	unreliably
ABEILLRSUY	leisurably
ABEILLSUXY	bisexually
ABEILMMOST	metabolism
ABEILMNRTY	terminably
ABEILMNSSU	unmissable
ABEILMOOTU	automobile
ABEILMOPRV	improvable
ABEILMRSSU	surmisable
ABEILNNRUY	inurbanely
ABEILNNUVY	unenviably
ABEILNOPRY	inoperably
ABEILNORXY	inexorably
ABEILNPRUZ	unprizable
ABEILNPSXY	expansibly
ABEILNSTUU	unsuitable
ABEILOPRRV	proverbial
ABEILORSTT	strobilate
ABEILORTVY	abortively
ABEILRSTUV	vestibular
ABEILRSUVV	survivable
ABEIMMOQUZ	Mozambique
ABEIMNNOTT	obtainment
ABEIMNOORR	Brian Moore
ABEIMNORTT	montbretia
ABEIMNORTU	tambourine
ABEIMNRRSU	submariner
ABEIMOSSTU	abstemious
ABEINNOPRU	bear in upon
ABEINNORTV	native-born
ABEINNOSST	sanbenitos
ABEINNOSTT	abstention
ABEINNRRTU	interurban
ABEINNRSSW	brawniness
ABEINOPPTT	bon appetit
ABEINOPRRW	brainpower
ABEINORSST	abstersion
ABEINORTTX	exorbitant
ABEINRSSSS	brassiness
ABEIOPPRSY	presbyopia
ABEIOPRSTV	absorptive
ABEIOSSSST	asbestosis
ABEIPRSTTY	baptistery
ABEIRRRSST	barristers
ABEIRSTTTU	attributes
ABEJMNORSW	James Brown
ABEKKMOORR	bookmarker
ABEKKORSTW	basketwork
	basket-work
	workbasket
ABEKLNNOUW	unknowable
ABEKLNORUW	unworkable
ABEKMNNOTU	mountebank
ABEKMNOPRU	embark upon
ABEKMORRST	Bram Stoker
ABEKMORRUY	marker buoy
ABEKNNOOOP	an open book
ABEKNOPRRW	pawnbroker
ABEKOOPRRY	prayer book
	prayerbook
	prayer-book
ABEKORRSTW	breastwork
ABELLLLOVY	volleyball
ABELLLORRR	barrel roll
ABELLLOSUW	Saul Bellow
ABELLNOSUV	unsolvable
ABELLOORWY	woolly bear
ABELLOSTUY	absolutely
ABELLSSSUY	syllabuses
ABELMMNOSU	summonable
ABELMNNOOW	noblewoman
ABELMNOUVY	unmoveably
ABELMOORSU	laboursome
ABELMPRSUY	presumably
ABELNNORUV	verbal noun
ABELNOOPST	tablespoon
ABELNOPRUV	unprovable
ABELNOPTXY	penalty box
ABELNORRTT	latter-born
ABELNORTTT	battle-torn
ABELNOSUXY	Saxony blue
ABELOOPSST	Sebastopol
ABELOORTUV	vote Labour
ABELOOSSTT	osteoblast
ABELOOTTUW	out at elbow
ABELOPPSSU	supposable
ABELOPRSTT	table-sport
ABELORRTUX	Albert Roux
ABELORSTYY	lay store by
ABELRSSTUY	abstrusely
ABELRSTTTU	salt-butter
ABEMMNRSSU	mass number
ABEMNNORSS	sans nombre
ABENOPPRRW	brown paper
ABENOPRSTU	beansprout

ABENORRSTZ	Bronze Star
ABENPRSSTU	abruptness
ABEOORSTUU	rouseabout
ABEOPSTTUY	beauty spot
ABEOQSSUUU	subaqueous
ABERRRSTWY	strawberry
ABFFGILLNY	bafflingly
ABFGILNOTY	flying boat
ABFGOPRRSU	up for grabs
ABFHILMTTU	thumb a lift
ABFHIOSTTU	shift about
ABFIIILRTY	friability
ABFIILLLNY	infallibly
ABFIILLRRY	fibrillary
ABFIILNORV	riboflavin
ABFILLOSTT	fall to bits
ABFILOPRTY	profitably
ABFINORRST	Fortinbras
ABFJLORSUY	frabjously
ABFKNNORRU	Frank Bruno
ABFLLOSTUY	boastfully
ABFLLOSUUY	fabulously
ABGGGILNRY	braggingly
ABGGILLNRU	Raging Bull
ABGGINOOTU	going about
ABGHIIINNT	inhabiting
ABGHIIMMNR	Birmingham
ABGHINNSTU	sunbathing
ABGHINPRST	birth-pangs
ABGHIORTTU	right about
ABGHIRRRSU	Harrisburg
ABGHLORRUY	royal burgh
ABGIIILNNT	nail-biting
ABGIILNNTY	intangibly
ABGIILNOOT	obligation
ABGIKKMNOO	bookmaking
ABGIKMNOOT	bootmaking
ABGILLMNRY	ramblingly
ABGILLNNOO	ballooning
ABGILLNRWY	warblingly
ABGILLNSUU	sublingual
ABGILMOSUY	bigamously
ABGILNOTUW	bawling-out
ABGILOORTY	obligatory
ABGINNORRT	Barrington
ABGINOORTW	rowing boat
ABGINRSSST	string bass
ABGJORSTUU	subjugator
ABGKLOORTU	Olga Korbut
ABGKNOPRTU	go bankrupt
ABGLLLORUY	globularly
ABGLMOORUY	glamour boy
ABGNORRSUW	brown sugar
ABGORRSSTU	Strasbourg
ABHHIMOOOP	homophobia
ABHHNORSSW	hash browns
ABHIIMOPSU	amphibious
ABHIIOOPTX	toxiphobia
ABHIKNOTTU	think about
ABHILLTTUY	I'll buy that
ABHILOOSTU	Louis Botha
ABHILOPSTY	hospitably
ABHILORTUW	labour with
ABHIMNOPTU	thumb piano
ABHIOOPPRY	pyrophobia
ABHIPRRSSU	bursarship
ABHJNNNOUY	John Bunyan
ABHKORRSUY	Sky Harbour
ABHLNOORUY	honourably
ABHOORTTUW	throw about
ABIIILLPTY	pliability
ABIIILMNTY	inimitably
ABIIILNOST	sibilation
ABIIINOSST	antibiosis
ABIIIORSTT	tibiotarsi
ABIIJLNOTU	jubilation
ABIILLMNSU	subliminal
ABIILLNOVY	inviolably
ABIILLNSTY	sibilantly
ABIILMOTVY	movability
ABIILMPRTY	impartibly
ABIILMPSSY	impassibly
ABIILMTTUY	mutability
ABIILNOOSV	bolivianos
ABIILNOTTY	bitonality
	notability
ABIILOPRTY	bipolarity
ABIIMRSSTY	sybaritism
ABIINNRTUY	inurbanity
ABIINORSTV	vibrations
ABIINOTTTU	titubation
ABIINRTTYY	Trinity Bay
ABIIORSTTU	obituarist
ABIIQRTUUY	ubiquitary
ABIJLLNTUY	jubilantly
ABIKLNNOPT	point-blank
ABIKNOPRTU	prink about
ABILLLOOSV	Villa-Lobos
ABILLNOOST	balloonist
ABILLNOSVY	insolvably
ABILLOORSZ	Laszlo Biro
ABILMNOOTU	out on a limb
ABILMOPRVY	improvably
ABILMOSSTU	absolutism
ABILNOOSTU	absolution
ABILNSTUUY	unsuitably
ABILORSSUU	salubrious
ABILOSSTTU	absolutist
ABIMNORRST	brainstorm
ABIMRSSSTU	strabismus
ABINOOPRST	absorption
ABINOOSSST	bassoonist
ABINOSSTTU	substation
ABKMORSSYZ	Szymborska
ABLOOPRTTT	Port Talbot
ABLOPPSSUY	supposably
ABMRSSTTUU	substratum
ABNOORRSTU	brontosaur
ABOORRTUWY	worry about
ACCCDEIIPT	pectic acid
ACCCDIIIRT	citric acid
ACCCEEEKLS	Eccles cake

ACCCEEHITT	catechetic
ACCCEFHKOR	cockchafer
ACCCEHIKOR	Chick Corea
ACCCEHLNOO	Coco Chanel
ACCCEIIRST	cicatrices
ACCCEIKORT	cockatrice ❑
ACCCEILLNY	encyclical
ACCCEILMOP	accomplice
ACCCGLNOOO	gonococcal
ACCCHHILOO	chocaholic
ACCCHKOPST	spatchcock
ACCCHLOORY	ochlocracy
ACCCIIOPRS	capriccios
ACCCIKMORR	microcrack
ACCCILLLYY	cyclically
ACCCINOPPU	cappuccino
ACCDDEEIRT	accredited
ACCDDEEIST	desiccated
ACCDDEIRRT	credit card
ACCDEEHLOT	cochleated
ACCDEEHQRU	cheque card
ACCDEEINNS	incandesce
ACCDEEISTX	exsiccated
ACCDEELPST	spectacled
ACCDEELPTY	acceptedly
ACCDEELRTY	trade cycle
ACCDEGIINN	ice dancing
ACCDEHLNOY	chalcedony
ACCDEIILNY	indelicacy
ACCDEIILST	dialectics
ACCDEIIOPT	apodeictic
ACCDEIKLNW	candlewick
ACCDEILLOP	peccadillo
ACCDEILNOT	occidental ❑
ACCDEILOPY	cyclopedia
ACCDEIMNNY	mendicancy
ACCDEIMORT	democratic
ACCDEINNTU	inductance
ACCDEIORST	desiccator
ACCDELRSUY	accursedly
ACCDEMOSTU	accustomed
ACCDENORTT	contracted
ACCDEOPRST	cadet corps
ACCDFIILTY	flaccidity
ACCDFIIMOR	formic acid
ACCDHHRRUW	churchward
ACCDHHRRUY	churchyard
ACCDHIINOR	diachronic
ACCDHILNOO	conchoidal
ACCDHILORV	clavichord
ACCDIIINRT	nitric acid
ACCDIILSST	cladistics
ACCDINORTT	contradict
ACCDLOORSV	vocal cords
ACCDNNOORT	concordant
ACCEEEEHKS	cheesecake
ACCEEEHILR	chelicerae
ACCEEEHIST	seecatchie
ACCEEEHNNV	even chance
ACCEEEHRTY	eye-catcher
ACCEEELMNU	Clemenceau
ACCEEELPRT	receptacle
ACCEEENNRS	renascence
ACCEEGISSV	give access
ACCEEGLLOP	college cap
ACCEEHHKOS	cheechakos
ACCEEHILNP	encephalic
ACCEEHIRTZ	catechizer
ACCEEHISST	catechesis
ACCEEHMNTU	catechumen
ACCEEHNORR	encroacher
ACCEEILMNU	ecumenical
ACCEEIMSST	access time
ACCEEIORST	Eric Coates
ACCEEIORSU	ericaceous
ACCEEIRTUX	excruciate
ACCEEKOOPR	peacock-ore
ACCEEKOPRY	peacockery
ACCEELNOST	coalescent
ACCEELNOSV	convalesce
ACCEELNPRU	crapulence
ACCEELNRTU	reluctance
ACCEELOPRR	cereal crop
ACCEELPSST	spectacles
ACCEELRTWY	water cycle
ACCEEMOSTY	ascomycete
ACCEENNOVY	conveyance
ACCEENOPSS	open access
ACCEENORST	consecrate
ACCEENPTXY	expectancy
ACCEENRSSS	scarceness
ACCEEORRSU	racecourse
	Sacre Coeur
ACCEEORSTU	cretaceous ❑
ACCEFFIINY	inefficacy
ACCEFFIITY	efficacity
ACCEFHLRTY	flycatcher
ACCEFIILPS	specifical
ACCEFIIRRS	sacrificer
ACCEFILLOR	calciferol
ACCEFILRSU	flea circus
ACCEFINOST	confiscate
ACCEFLLOTU	flocculate
ACCEGILLOO	ecological
ACCEGILNNO	concealing
ACCEGINNOR	carcinogen
ACCEGINNOS	cognisance
ACCEGINNOZ	cognizance
ACCEHHIIRR	hierarchic
ACCEHHIMRS	Carchemish
ACCEHHIPRT	heptarchic
ACCEHHMRSU	Schumacher
ACCEHIILMR	chimerical
ACCEHIINNT	technician
ACCEHIINPT	epicanthic
ACCEHIKLNU	Auchinleck
ACCEHIKOPS	peacockish
ACCEHILLMY	chemically
ACCEHILLTY	hectically
ACCEHILPRS	Cecil Sharp
ACCEHILPRV	pelvic arch
ACCEHINNRY	in chancery

ACCEHIOPRT choice part
ACCEHIOPRV pro hac vice
ACCEHIORTT theocratic
ACCEHIRTVZ czarevitch
ACCEHKOORS a-cockhorse
ACCEHLLNOR chancellor
ACCEHLOOST chocolates
ACCEHLOOTY chocolatey
ACCEHNNOPU chance upon
ACCEHNNPTY catchpenny
ACCEHNNRTY trenchancy
ACCEHNORTT technocrat
trench coat
ACCEHNORVX convex arch
ACCEHOORSU ochraceous
ACCEIILNOT conciliate
ACCEIILRRT rectricial
ACCEIILSSS classicise
ACCEIILSSZ classicize
ACCEIIMSST asceticism
ACCEIINNOR Ciceronian
ACCEIINPRT in practice
ACCEIINRST Cistercian
ACCEIIRSTX cicatrixes
ACCEIKLPRT Celtic Park
ACCEIKMNNO Connie Mack
ACCEIKRSSW wisecracks
ACCEILLNSY scenically
ACCEILMMOR commercial
ACCEILMNOO economical
ACCEILMNOP compliance
ACCEILMOPT complicate
ACCEILNOTU noctilucae
ACCEILOPPT apoplectic
ACCEILOPRR reciprocal
ACCEIMOOPR comic opera
ACCEINNNOV connivance
ACCEINNORT concertina
ACCEINNSSY incessancy
ACCEINOOST consociate
ACCEIOORSU coriaceous
ACCEIOPPSY episcopacy
ACCEIOSSTT sticcatoes
ACCEIRRSTT tractrices
ACCEKLORTW water clock
ACCEKNRRTU nutcracker
ACCELLSSUU calculuses
ACCELMNOPT complacent
ACCELNOPTU conceptual
ACCEMNNORY necromancy
ACCEMOORSS come across
ACCENNNOOS consonance
ACCENNORSS as concerns
ACCENORTTU counteract
ACCENRSUVY Cyrus Vance
ACCEORSUUV curvaceous
ACCFFFFHHI chiffchaff
chiff-chaff
ACCFHIRTTW witchcraft
ACCFIIIMPS pacificism
ACCFIIIPST pacificist
ACCFIMOPTY compactify
ACCFNOORTU account for
ACCGHHILTT catch light
ACCGHHIORT Gothic arch
ACCGHHISTT catch sight
ACCGHIILOR oligarchic
ACCGHINRST scratching
ACCGHIOPTY phagocytic
ACCGHORSSU couch grass
ACCGIIMORT tragicomic
ACCGIKNPRU cracking-up
ACCGILNSUY accusingly
ACCGINNOTU accounting
ACCHHIILLN chinchilla
ACCHIIMSST schismatic
ACCHIINORT anchoritic
ACCHIINRST stracchini
ACCHIKMQRU quick march
ACCHIKMSTT matchstick
ACCHILMOPS accomplish
ACCHILNNPS splanchnic
ACCHILNNUU Cú Chulainn
ACCHILNOOT catholicon
ACCHILOSST scholastic
ACCHILRSTY scratchily
ACCHIMNORY chiromancy
ACCHINORST stracchino
ACCHIOPRSZ schizocarp
ACCHIOSSTT stochastic
ACCHJKLNOO John Alcock
ACCHKLMRUY lucky charm
ACCHMOOORT motor-coach
ACCHMORSST cross-match
ACCHNOPSST Scotch snap
ACCHNOPSYY sycophancy
ACCHOPRSST crosspatch
ACCIIILLLP piccalilli
ACCIIINNNT Cincinnati
ACCIILLLNY clinically
ACCIILLNOY iconically
ACCIILLRTY critically
ACCIILMOTY comicality
ACCIILMSSS classicism
ACCIILNRTU uncritical
ACCIILSSST classicist
ACCIIOPRSU capricious
ACCIISTTUY causticity
ACCIKKKKNN knick-knack
ACCILLMOSY cosmically
ACCILLRRUY circularly
ACCILMNOOS iconoclasm ❑
ACCILNOOST iconoclast
ACCILNOPTY nyctalopic
ACCILNORTU inculcator
ACCILNOTUX council tax
ACCILOPPRY polycarpic
ACCILRRRUU curricular
ACCIMNOOPR monocarpic
ACCIMNOOPT compaction
ACCIMNOORT monocratic
ACCINNOOOS on occasion

ACCINNORTT	contract in
ACCINNOTTU	cunctation
ACCINOOPRU	cornucopia
ACCINOOPTU	occupation
ACCINOPRSY	conspiracy
ACCINORSTY	Carson City
ACCLOPRTUY	plutocracy
ACCNNNOOSY	consonancy
ACCNOORRTT	contractor
ACDDDEGIPY	giddy-paced
ACDDDEIOTT	addicted to
ACDDDGIRTU	drug addict
ACDDEEEINP	dependacie
ACDDEEEKNU	Dundee cake
ACDDEEENOS	Dodecanese
ACDDEEENRT	dead centre
ACDDEEHLOO	cool-headed
ACDDEEHLTY	detachedly
ACDDEEHNOR	decahedron
ACDDEEKORW	Edward Coke
ACDDEELLRY	declaredly
ACDDEELLSY	Clydesdale
ACDDEELNRU	undeclared
ACDDEELNTY	decadently
ACDDEENNST	descendant
ACDDEENTUU	uneducated
ACDDEEOPRW	Edward Cope
ACDDEGHIRS	discharged
ACDDEHIKNP	hand-picked
ACDDEHINTU	The Dunciad
ACDDEHIPSS	disc-shaped
ACDDEHNNOS	second hand
	second-hand
ACDDEHOORT	head doctor
ACDDEIIJTU	dijudicate
ACDDEIINOT	dedication
ACDDEIINTV	vindicated
ACDDEIIRRS	Cader Idris
ACDDEILMOU	duodecimal
ACDDEILOST	dislocated
ACDDEINNSS	candidness
ACDDEIORTY	dedicatory
ACDDEIPSTU	cuspidated
ACDDEIRSTT	distracted
ACDDEKLLNO	landlocked
ACDDEKLORS	dreadlocks
ACDDELMNOW	calmed down
ACDDELNNOO	colonnaded
ACDDELNOSW	scaled-down
ACDDENNRUY	redundancy
ACDDFHIORU	chaudfroid
ACDDGHILNR	grandchild
ACDDGHNRUY	grand duchy
ACDDGIINRS	discarding
ACDDHILNVY	David Lynch
ACDDINORST	discordant
ACDEEEELRT	decelerate
ACDEEEEPRS	predecease
ACDEEEFLNR	fer-de-lance
ACDEEEFMNN	defenceman
ACDEEEFMNT	defacement
ACDEEEGNRY	degeneracy
ACDEEEHHRS	hard cheese
ACDEEEHLTT	decathlete
ACDEEEIKSV	seek advice
ACDEEEIPRT	depreciate
ACDEEENNTT	antecedent
ACDEEENRTV	advertence
ACDEEEORRT	redecorate
ACDEEERRST	desecrater
ACDEEFFHIO	head office
ACDEEFFHRT	far-fetched
ACDEEFFLOR	declare off
ACDEEFFLTY	affectedly
ACDEEFFNTU	unaffected
ACDEEFGOOP	peace of God
ACDEEFIIRR	Fredericia
ACDEEFINOT	defecation
ACDEEFKOPR	poker-faced
ACDEEFMORR	armed force
ACDEEFPRTY	Perfect Day
ACDEEGHLLN	challenged
ACDEEGHNNO	hendecagon
ACDEEGIIMN	mediagenic
ACDEEGIKLR	girdle cake
ACDEEGINNR	grand-niece
ACDEEGINRS	decreasing
ACDEEGINRT	centigrade
ACDEEGLLRW	well-graced
ACDEEGLNRT	rectangled
ACDEEGNORU	encouraged
ACDEEHILNR	chandelier
ACDEEHIMNZ	mechanized
ACDEEHIMRS	Archimedes
ACDEEHLLNN	channelled
ACDEEHLLST	satchelled
ACDEEHLNRW	D H Lawrence
ACDEEHLORT	cloth-eared
ACDEEHMNTT	detachment
ACDEEHNOPS	cone-shaped
ACDEEHNRTT	tented arch
ACDEEHOPPR	copperhead
ACDEEIILMS	decimalise
	medicalise
ACDEEIILMZ	decimalize
	medicalize
ACDEEIILNT	indelicate
ACDEEIIRRV	a rivederci
ACDEEILLNR	Cinderella
ACDEEILLTY	delicately
ACDEEILMPR	premedical
ACDEEILNRS	calendries
ACDEEILNRT	credential
ACDEEILOSV	devocalise
ACDEEILOVZ	devocalize
ACDEEILRTT	red lattice
	red-lattice
ACDEEIMMNT	medicament
ACDEEINNTU	denunciate
ACDEEINPPS	appendices
ACDEEINPTT	pectinated
ACDEEINSST	desistance

ACDEEIORTV	decorative
ACDEEIORTX	excoriated
ACDEEIOTTX	detoxicate
ACDEEIPRRT	trade price
ACDEEITTUX	exactitude
ACDEEKLMOR	make colder
ACDEEKLNRY	cankeredly
ACDEEKMRUV	make curved
ACDEELLLPW	well-placed
ACDEELLNRU	unrecalled
ACDEELLOTT	Dolcelatte
ACDEELMORT	ectodermal
ACDEELNOST	adolescent
ACDEELNOTU	cleaned out
ACDEELOORT	decolorate
ACDEELORRT	correlated
ACDEELORTU	edulcorate
ACDEELPRTU	curled-pate
ACDEEMMNOR	commandeer
ACDEEMMNPT	decampment
ACDEEMORSU	saucer dome
ACDEENNOST	condensate
ACDEENNRTY	dry canteen
ACDEENOPRR	rope-dancer
ACDEENOPRT	Pete Conrad
ACDEENORST	second-rate
ACDEENRSSS	sacredness
ACDEENRSTT	stand erect
ACDEENRTTU	detruncate
ACDEENRTVY	advertency
ACDEEOPRRT	deprecator
	tape-record
ACDEEORRST	desecrator
ACDEEORVWY	covered way
ACDEFFLORS	scaffolder
ACDEFFLOTU	duffel coat
ACDEFGILNY	defacingly
ACDEFGLLNO	golden calf
ACDEFHNNRW	Dawn French
ACDEFIIINT	nidificate
ACDEFIILSS	classified
ACDEFIINST	sanctified
ACDEFIIRRT	fratricide
ACDEFILSSY	declassify
ACDEFINNOT	confidante
ACDEFLNORS	land forces
ACDEFLOOSY	close of day
ACDEFNOORS	for a second
ACDEFNORRU	uncared-for
ACDEFNRSSY	fancy dress
ACDEGGIOPS	pedagogics
ACDEGGNOOR	go-go dancer
ACDEGHIRRS	discharger
ACDEGHNNOW	change down
ACDEGHNORW	charge down
ACDEGHRRSU	surcharged
ACDEGIILMR	germicidal
ACDEGIINRS	in disgrace
ACDEGILRTT	cattle grid
ACDEGINNUY	undecaying
ACDEGINORR	corrigenda
ACDEGINORT	decorating
ACDEGINRTY	garden city
ACDEGIORSU	discourage
ACDEGIRRST	cartridges
ACDEGKNORR	rock garden
ACDEGKORRT	tracker dog
ACDEGLNNRU	grand-uncle
ACDEGLNORS	cradle song
ACDEGORRTU	corrugated
ACDEHHOPRT	heptachord
ACDEHIINNS	disenchain
ACDEHIIORR	diarrhoeic
ACDEHILLMT	ill-matched
ACDEHILMOT	methodical
ACDEHILORT	chloridate
ACDEHIMMST	mismatched
ACDEHINNRS	hindrances
ACDEHINNST	disenchant
ACDEHINOPT	dictaphone
ACDEHINRSZ	scherzandi
ACDEHKLNSU	unshackled
ACDEHLOOPP	cephalopod
ACDEHLRSTY	starchedly
ACDEHMNOOT	come to hand
ACDEHMOSTU	moustached
ACDEHNOORT	octahedron
ACDEHNOPRT	pentachord
ACDEHNORST	on the cards
ACDEHNORSZ	scherzando
ACDEHRTTTU	Dutch treat
ACDEIIILST	idealistic
ACDEIIINTV	indicative
ACDEIIKNNS	Dickensian
ACDEIILLOT	idiolectal
ACDEIILMPT	implicated
ACDEIILMRS	disclaimer
ACDEIILMRT	direct mail
ACDEIILNNT	incidental
ACDEIILNOT	Diocletian
ACDEIILOPR	periodical
ACDEIILORS	cordialise
ACDEIILORZ	cordialize
ACDEIIMNOT	decimation
	medication
ACDEIIMRTX	taxidermic
ACDEIINNRY	incendiary
ACDEIIOSST	dissociate
ACDEIIPPRY	cypripedia
ACDEIJRTUU	judicature
ACDEILMNOS	Colin Meads
ACDEILMOPR	proclaimed
ACDEILNNOR	endocrinal
ACDEILNPSS	placidness
ACDEILNPTU	inculpated
ACDEILORSW	Oscar Wilde
ACDEILORTU	elucidator
ACDEILOSUY	edaciously
ACDEILPSTU	disculpate
ACDEILTTUV	cultivated
ACDEIMMORY	immoderacy
ACDEIMNNNO	demi-cannon

ACDEIMNNOP	pandemonic
ACDEIMNORU	androecium
ACDEIMNOSU	mendacious
ACDEIMOPRR	madreporic
ACDEINNOSS	dissonance
ACDEINNOST	sanctioned
ACDEINNRSS	rancidness
ACDEINOORT	carotenoid
	coordinate
	co-ordinate
	decoration
ACDEINORTT	detraction
ACDEINOSTT	anecdotist
ACDEINPRST	discrepant
ACDEINSTTU	sanctitude
ACDEIOPRSU	predacious
ACDEIOPSSU	spadiceous
ACDEIORSTZ	ostracized
ACDEIPQRSU	quadriceps
ACDEIQRSTU	quadrisect
ACDEIRRVYZ	drive crazy
ACDEIRSSTU	crassitude
ACDEIRSTTU	rusticated
ACDEJKSTTU	dust jacket
ACDEKKMOPR	pockmarked
ACDEKMPRSU	muckspread
ACDELLORWY	yellow card
ACDELMNOTU	documental
ACDELNNOOY	Conan Doyle
ACDELNOORW	Noël Coward
ACDELNPRUU	peduncular
ACDELNRSSU	underclass
ACDELOOPST	postal code
ACDELOPPTU	clapped-out
ACDELOPRRU	procedural
ACDELORSTY	cost dearly
ACDEMMOSTU	custom-made
ACDEMNORST	Doc Martens®
ACDEMNORTU	mucronated
ACDEMOPRSU	damp-course
ACDENORSTT	contrasted
ACDENPTTUU	punctuated
ACDENRRRTU	redcurrant
ACDENRRSTU	transducer
ACDEOORRVW	woodcarver
ACDEOPPRSU	pseudocarp
ACDEOPRRTT	protracted
ACDEOPRSUU	drupaceous
ACDFGIILNU	fungicidal
ACDFGNOOSY	fancy goods
ACDFHLLOOP	clap hold of
ACDFIILLUY	fiducially
ACDGGIINRS	disgracing
ACDGHNOOTU	touch and go
	touch-and-go
ACDGIINNST	distancing
ACDGIINOST	diagnostic
ACDGIKNNNU	King Duncan
ACDGILNOOT	odontalgic
ACDGILOORY	cardiology
ACDGIMMNNO	commanding

ACDHIIIIRR	Richard III
ACDHIILOSZ	schizoidal
ACDHILLPSY	child's play
ACDHILLRYY	hydrically
ACDHILRSST	third class
	third-class
ACDHILRSSY	chrysalids
ACDHILRSUY	hydraulics
ACDHINOOOP	Ophiacodon
ACDHINOOOX	chionodoxa
ACDHINORRS	Richardson
ACDHIOPRSW	cowardship
ACDHIORRSW	disc harrow
ACDHLOORSW	schoolward
ACDHLOOSSY	schooldays
ACDHMNOTUW	Dutchwoman
ACDHNOOPRR	drop anchor
ACDHNORSUW	dawn chorus
ACDIIINNOT	indication
ACDIIJLLUY	judicially
ACDIILLSUY	suicidally
ACDIILMOPT	diplomatic
ACDIILNOSV	Colin Davis
ACDIILORST	clostridia
ACDIILORTY	cordiality
ACDIILORUX	uxoricidal
ACDIIMNOSY	isodynamic
ACDIIMNOTU	coatimundi
ACDIINOORT	carotinoid
ACDIINOORV	Ordovician
ACDIINORSU	dinosauric
ACDIINORTV	vindicator
ACDIINORTY	dictionary
	indicatory
ACDIIOSSSU	Dio Cassius
ACDIKKNORU	kick around
ACDIKNQSSU	quicksands
ACDILLMNOT	call to mind
ACDILMPRUY	Plaid Cymru
ACDILNOPRS	spinal cord
ACDILNRSTU	translucid
ACDILOPRTU	duplicator
ACDIMMORUY	myocardium
ACDINNORSU	Andronicus
ACDINOORRT	rain-doctor
ACDINORSTY	syndicator
ACDJKLNNOO	Jack London
ACDKLMOSSY	lady's smock
ACDKMNORUU	muck around
ACDLLOOPSW	codswallop
ACDLLOPTYY	polydactyl
ACDLLORSSW	world-class
ACDLLORSTU	collar stud
ACDLMNOOSY	condylomas
ACDLNOOSTT	scot and lot
ACDMMNNOOO	on commando
ACDMOOSSUV	muscovados
ACDOORRSSS	crossroads
ACEEEEGNPR	Greenpeace
ACEEEFFKTT	take effect
ACEEEFFMNT	effacement

ACEEEFFTTU	effectuate
ACEEEFIPRS	fire escape
ACEEEGILNN	inelegance
ACEEEGILTX	exegetical
ACEEEGINRT	great-niece
ACEEEGNPRT	percentage
ACEEEGNRRY	regeneracy
ACEEEHIRTT	hereticate
ACEEEHKLPP	keep chapel
ACEEEHPSTT	set the pace
ACEEEHRRRS	researcher
ACEEEIPPRV	apperceive
ACEEEIPRRV	Peace River
ACEEEIRRST	secretaire
ACEEEIRSTV	eviscerate
ACEEEIRTVX	execrative
ACEEEKMRSU	make secure
ACEEELLNRT	crenellate
ACEEELNPRV	prevalence
ACEEELNRTW	T E Lawrence
ACEEELOPRV	peace-lover
ACEEELORTT	electorate
ACEEELPRVY	every place
ACEEELRSTT	telecaster
ACEEELRTUX	exulcerate
ACEEELSTTU	sea lettuce
ACEEEMMNRT	amercement
ACEEEMNNPR	permanence
ACEEEMNNST	encasement
ACEEEMNORR	come nearer
ACEEEMNPRT	temperance
ACEEEMNPST	escapement
ACEEENNPRT	repentance
ACEEENNSTV	evanescent
ACEEENNTTW	wet canteen
ACEEEPPPRR	crêpe paper
ACEEEPRRTU	recuperate
ACEEFFFHOT	off the face
ACEEFFHLOT	halo effect
ACEEFFHSUU	chauffeuse
ACEEFFILRT	café filtre
ACEEFFIMNY	effeminacy
ACEEFFLOTY	feet of clay
ACEEFFNRSU	sufferance
ACEEFHHTTW	chew the fat
ACEEFHINRS	franchisee
ACEEFHLNRT	centre-half
ACEEFHLNTU	Neufchâtel
ACEEFHORRS	rose-chafer
ACEEFHOSTU	the cause of
ACEEFIILTT	felicitate
ACEEFILMNT	maleficent
ACEEFILNSS	facileness
ACEEFIORTV	vociferate
ACEEFIRRTV	refractive
ACEEFLLNTU	flatulence
ACEEFLLORV	cloverleaf
ACEEFLLPUY	peacefully
ACEEFLNSTV	flavescent
ACEEFLORST	forecastle
ACEEFMOPRS	escape from
ACEEFNOOST	to one's face
ACEEFORRST	forecaster
ACEEGGHOPR	egg poacher
ACEEGGNORT	congregate
ACEEGGRSTU	curate's egg
ACEEGHHRTW	chew the rag
ACEEGHILNT	genethliac
ACEEGHINNP	cheapening
ACEEGHINNX	in exchange
ACEEGHLLNR	challenger
ACEEGHLNSS	changeless
ACEEGHLRTV	Cleve-Garth
ACEEGHNNOP	Copenhagen
ACEEGHNORV	changeover
	change-over
ACEEGHNSSU	gaucheness
ACEEGHORRV	overcharge
ACEEGIKTTW	get a wicket
ACEEGILLOT	collegiate
ACEEGILNTU	geniculate
ACEEGIMNOR	cinema-goer
ACEEGIOPTT	cottage pie
ACEEGIORST	categorise
ACEEGIORTZ	categorize
ACEEGIOTTX	excogitate
ACEEGJNORS	Grace Jones
ACEEGKNOPS	sponge cake
ACEEGLNORV	glance over
ACEEGLNRTU	great-uncle
ACEEGNNORV	governance
ACEEGNNPRU	repugnance
ACEEGNNSWY	news agency
ACEEGNRSVY	scavengery
ACEEHHILRW	wheelchair
ACEEHHLMNT	Cheltenham
ACEEHHLNNT	the Channel
ACEEHHNNOT	Ethan Cohen
ACEEHHNOPT	on the cheap
ACEEHHPTTU	Heptateuch
ACEEHIIPRT	perithecia
ACEEHIKMRR	make richer
ACEEHIKNTT	kitchen tea
ACEEHILMRT	hermetical
ACEEHILNNS	channelise
ACEEHILNNZ	channelize
ACEEHILNRT	in the clear
ACEEHILNST	anthelices
ACEEHILPTT	telepathic
ACEEHIMNPZ	chimpanzee
ACEEHIMNSX	Sex Machine
ACEEHIMPRY	hyperaemic
ACEEHIMPTT	empathetic
ACEEHIMSST	schematise
ACEEHIMSTZ	schematize
ACEEHIORRT	charioteer ❑
ACEEHISSTT	aesthetics
ACEEHISTUW	white sauce
ACEEHLLMPW	wheel clamp
ACEEHLLNOP	Cellophane®
ACEEHLLRTV	latch lever
ACEEHLMSTU	Telemachus

ACEEHLNNOP	encephalon
ACEEHLNPRU	leprechaun
ACEEHLNPTY	phlyctenae
ACEEHLOSSV	close shave
ACEEHLRSST	thale cress
ACEEHMMRSU	meerschaum
ACEEHMNNST	encashment
ACEEHMNRST	Manchester
ACEEHMOOTV	come to have
ACEEHMORTT	tachometer
ACEEHMRTTY	tachymeter
ACEEHNOPRS	each person
ACEEHNPTTU	Pentateuch
ACEEHNSSST	chasteness
ACEEHOPRRR	reproacher
ACEEHOPRSU	proseuchae
ACEEHORRTT	the Creator
ACEEHPRRSU	repurchase
ACEEHRRSTU	chartreuse
ACEEIILNTT	licentiate
ACEEIILPSS	specialise
ACEEIILPSZ	specialize
ACEEIILSST	elasticise
ACEEIILSTZ	elasticize
ACEEIIMNPT	impatience
ACEEIIMRRU	Marie Curie
ACEEIINNRT	incinerate
ACEEIIPSST	asepticise
ACEEIIPSTZ	asepticize
ACEEIIRRST	sericteria
ACEEIIRTTV	recitative
ACEEIITTVX	excitative
ACEEIJLMSV	Clive James
ACEEIJLNQU	Jacqueline
ACEEIKKMTY	mickey-take
ACEEIKLLTT	cattlelike
ACEEIKLMNS	simnel cake
ACEEIKLNRT	trance-like
ACEEIKLRRS	arse-licker
ACEEIKNOTT	take notice
ACEEIKPRTT	ticker tape
ACEEILLMPS	small piece
ACEEILLMTY	emetically
ACEEILLNNS	clean lines
ACEEILLNRW	wine cellar
	wine-cellar
ACEEILLORS	El Escorial
ACEEILLPSY	especially
ACEEILMNNT	Clementina
ACEEILMNOR	ceremonial
ACEEILMNOT	melaconite
ACEEILMNRT	mercantile
ACEEILNNUV	univalence
ACEEILNPRT	epicentral
ACEEILNRST	centralise
ACEEILNRSU	nuclearise
ACEEILNRTV	cantilever
	trivalence
ACEEILNRTZ	centralize
ACEEILNRUZ	nuclearize
ACEEILPPRT	tea clipper
ACEEILPRSW	parcelwise
	parcel-wise
ACEEILRRSU	curselarie
ACEEILRRTT	retractile
ACEEILRSSU	secularise
ACEEILRSUZ	secularize
ACEEILRTTU	reticulate
ACEEILRTUV	ulcerative
ACEEILRTVY	creatively
	reactively
ACEEILSTUV	vesiculate
ACEEIMNRSS	creaminess
ACEEIMNRSV	serviceman
ACEEIMNRTT	remittance
ACEEIMPRST	spermaceti
ACEEINNRST	transience
ACEEINORRT	recreation
	re-creation
ACEEINORTU	auctioneer
ACEEINORTX	execration
ACEEINPPRT	apprentice
ACEEINPRST	interspace
ACEEINRSST	resistance
ACEEINRTUV	uncreative
ACEEINSSTV	activeness
ACEEIOPPST	episcopate
ACEEIOQTUV	equivocate
ACEEIPPRTY	party piece
ACEEIPQRSU	picaresque
ACEEIQRSTU	requiescat
ACEEIRRTTV	retractive
ACEEJJMOSY	James Joyce
ACEEJLMNOT	cajolement
ACEEKLLRSS	sales clerk
	salesclerk
ACEEKLRRTW	water clerk
ACEEKNRRRT	rack-renter
ACEEKNRTTV	track event
ACEELLLMOU	columellae
ACEELLRSSY	carelessly
ACEELMNOTY	melanocyte
ACEELNOPST	opalescent
ACEELNOPSY	clap eyes on
ACEELNPRSY	screenplay
ACEELNRRTY	recreantly
ACEELNSSUW	Wenceslaus
ACEELOORSU	oleraceous
ACEELOPRTU	operculate
ACEELPRSTT	select part
ACEELQRRUU	craquelure
ACEEMMNNPT	encampment
ACEEMMNOTT	commentate
ACEEMMORSU	commeasure
ACEEMNNPRY	permanency
ACEEMNOORT	come near to
ACEEMNOPST	compensate
ACEEMNPRST	escarpment
ACEEMOSTUZ	eczematous
ACEEMPPSTY	empty space
ACEENNOPRV	provenance
ACEENNOPSU	pennaceous

ACEENNORTV	contravene
	covenanter
ACEENNOTTZ	canzonette
ACEENNRSSV	cravenness
ACEENNSSTU	sustenance
ACEENOOSTU	coetaneous
ACEENOPRTT	pernoctate
ACEENORSSS	coarseness
ACEENORSTU	nectareous
	raconteuse
ACEENORSTX	Xenocrates
ACEENPRRST	Carpenters
ACEENPRUVY	purveyance
ACEENRSSTW	newscaster
ACEENSSTTV	Cat Stevens
ACEEOPRSTU	outer space
ACEEOPSSTU	pesto sauce
ACEEORRSTT	stercorate
ACEEORRTVX	extra cover
ACEEORRTXY	execratory
ACEEOSSTTU	testaceous
ACEERRSSTW	watercress
ACEFFGINSU	suffigance
ACEFFGNSUU	face fungus
ACEFFHHILT	Heathcliff
ACEFFHLNOR	French loaf
ACEFFIIMNO	main office
ACEFFIKNRT	craft knife
ACEFFIKRRT	trafficker
ACEFFINOST	affections
ACEFFIRSST	scare stiff
ACEFFKLNOS	slacken off
ACEFFLOOSS	loss of face
ACEFFOSTUU	tuffaceous
ACEFGHINOR	in charge of
ACEFGILNST	self-acting
ACEFGIRTUU	cut a figure
ACEFGLLRUY	gracefully
ACEFGLNRUU	ungraceful
ACEFHIINTT	fianchetti
ACEFHILPST	felspathic
ACEFHILRTU	ultrafiche
ACEFHINOTT	fianchetto
ACEFHINRRS	franchiser
ACEFHIORSS	coarse fish
ACEFHIPSTT	the cap fits
ACEFHKMMOU	make much of
ACEFHKORST	aftershock
ACEFHLOOTT	act the fool
ACEFHLRRSY	Charles Fry
ACEFHMPPTU	fetch a pump
ACEFHOORTU	out of reach
ACEFHOOTTU	cheat out of
ACEFHORRTV	hovercraft
ACEFHORSTU	housecraft
ACEFIIILST	facilities
ACEFIILMSS	facsimiles
ACEFIILPST	spiflicate
ACEFIINRST	sanctifier
ACEFIKLNPS	clasp knife
ACEFILOOSU	foliaceous
ACEFILORTV	vital force
ACEFILPRST	first place
ACEFIMNOSS	Neofascism
ACEFINNPRY	Fanny Price
ACEFINORRT	for certain
	refraction
ACEFINORUY	in-your-face
ACEFINOSST	Neofascist
ACEFINRSST	craftiness
ACEFIRRTTU	trifurcate
ACEFIRSSTU	first cause
ACEFJKLNOT	Jack of Lent
ACEFKLNORS	cornflakes
ACEFKMORTY	Mary of Teck
ACEFLLNOOR	once for all
ACEFLLNTUY	flatulency
ACEFLNOOTU	clean out of
ACEFLOOPTU	out of place
ACEFLPSTUU	teacupfuls
ACEFLRSSUU	saucerfuls
ACEFNOPRTT	Pontefract
ACEFORRRTY	refractory
ACEGGHILNN	changeling
ACEGGILLOO	geological
ACEGGINNOO	ocean-going
ACEGGINRSS	cragginess
ACEGHHILPS	high places
ACEGHHINOT	high-octane
ACEGHHOPRT	hectograph
ACEGHIILMT	megalithic
ACEGHIIMTW	white magic
ACEGHIINRS	cashiering
ACEGHIIPPR	epigraphic
ACEGHILMPT	phlegmatic
ACEGHILPSY	hypalgesic
ACEGHIMNNU	machinegun
	machine-gun
ACEGHINNNT	enchanting
ACEGHINNOT	change into
ACEGHINNST	chastening
ACEGHINOPT	pathogenic
ACEGHINOTT	Tao-te-ching
ACEGHINRTT	chattering
ACEGHLORUY	Guy Laroche
ACEGHRRRSU	surcharger
ACEGIIKNST	ice-skating
ACEGIILLST	legalistic
ACEGIILMTY	legitimacy
ACEGIILNNO	lignocaine
ACEGIILOST	egoistical
ACEGIIMOTT	Giacometti
ACEGIIMPTT	pegmatitic
ACEGIINNRS	increasing
ACEGIINORT	iatrogenic
ACEGIIOTTV	cogitative
ACEGIIRRST	geriatrics
ACEGIKLNNS	slackening
ACEGILMNNY	menacingly
ACEGILNNOT	congenital
ACEGILNOPY	clay pigeon
ACEGILNOTU	glauconite

ACEGILNTXY	exactingly
ACEGILOOPT	apologetic
ACEGIMNNOR	coming near
ACEGIMNPRS	scampering
ACEGIMNRSU	Germanicus
ACEGIMORSU	gracious me
ACEGINNNRT	entrancing
ACEGINNRST	transgenic
ACEGINNTUX	unexacting
ACEGINOPRS	saprogenic
ACEGINORTV	overacting
ACEGINRSTT	scattering
ACEGKORSTU	goatsucker
ACEGLMOSUU	glumaceous
ACEGLNNOUY	agony uncle
ACEGLNOOOY	oceanology
ACEGLOOPSY	escapology
ACEGNRSSUY	assurgency
ACEGOOPRRY	Gary Cooper
ACEGOORSUU	courageous
ACEGOPRRSU	supercargo
ACEHHIINRT	in the chair
ACEHHIKSTT	hit the sack
ACEHHILTWZ	witch hazel
ACEHHIPTTW	whip the cat
ACEHHMRRTU	much rather
ACEHHNORSU	ranchhouse
ACEHHNOTTW	on the watch
ACEHIILLPT	philatelic
ACEHIILMRT	hermitical
ACEHIILTTY	ethicality
ACEHIIMRTT	arithmetic
ACEHIINNOP	Phoenician
ACEHIINNRT	interchain
ACEHIINOTV	inchoative
ACEHIINTTT	antithetic
ACEHIIPRRT	peritricha
ACEHIIRSTT	tracheitis
ACEHIKLNSS	chalkiness
ACEHIKMNOS	chain-smoke
ACEHIKMNTW	Twickenham
ACEHIKPPST	packet-ship
ACEHILLNTY	ethnically
ACEHILLOOS	alcoholise
ACEHILLOOZ	alcoholize
ACEHILLORY	heroically
ACEHILLPRY	Caerphilly
ACEHILLTTY	thetically
ACEHILMMST	mischmetal
ACEHILMNNS	Schliemann
ACEHILMOTY	haemolytic
ACEHILNORT	chlorinate
ACEHILNOTY	inchoately
ACEHILOPRT	arctophile
ACEHILORRT	rhetorical
ACEHILPSST	sales pitch
ACEHILRSTU	Heraclitus
ACEHILRSTY	hysterical
ACEHIMMSST	schematism
ACEHIMNNOR	enharmonic
ACEHIMNORS	monarchise
ACEHIMNORZ	monarchize
ACEHIMNPTU	unemphatic
ACEHIMNRSV	revanchism
ACEHIMOPRT	amphoteric
ACEHIMORTW	Marco White
ACEHIMOSTX	chemotaxis
ACEHINNRST	Ernst Chain
ACEHINORST	chain store
	search into
ACEHINORTV	chevrotain
ACEHINPSST	patchiness
ACEHINPSTU	epicanthus
ACEHINQRSU	square inch
ACEHINRSTV	revanchist
ACEHINSSTT	chattiness
ACEHIOPSST	post chaise
	post-chaise
ACEHIPRSSU	haruspices
ACEHIRSTTT	tetrastich
ACEHIRSTTV	tsarevitch
ACEHIRTVWY	Vichy water
ACEHKLMMOR	hammerlock
ACEHKLNOST	Shackleton
ACEHLLMNOY	melancholy
ACEHLLNSSY	Nelly Sachs
ACEHLLPRSU	sepulchral
ACEHLMORSY	lachrymose
ACEHLNNOPT	cannot help
ACEHLNORSS	anchorless
ACEHLNORST	Charleston
ACEHLNORUV	overlaunch
ACEHLOORST	orthoclase
ACEHLORRST	Clare Short
	orchestral
ACEHLPRTYY	phylactery
ACEHMNOTUV	avouchment
ACEHMOOTTU	eat too much
ACEHMORRTU	route-march
ACEHNORRTT	trochanter
ACEHNORTTT	Chatterton
ACEHNPRSTT	stench trap
ACEHORTTWW	watchtower
	watch-tower
ACEHOSSUUY	shoyu sauce
ACEHPRRSSU	purchasers
ACEIIILMSS	Islamicise
ACEIIILMSZ	Islamicize
ACEIIINTTV	incitative
ACEIIIRTTV	recitativi
ACEIIISTTV	activities
ACEIIJLSTU	jesuitical
ACEIIKMNST	kinematics
ACEIIKNRTT	kinetic art
ACEIIKRSTT	rickettsia
ACEIILLLPT	elliptical
ACEIILLNPR	periclinal
ACEIILLNRY	irenically
ACEIILLOSU	liliaceous
ACEIILLRTY	illiteracy
ACEIILLSTT	satellitic
ACEIILMMST	melismatic

ACEIILMNST	melanistic
ACEIILMOPT	atomic pile
ACEIILMPSS	specialism
ACEIILNOPT	Capitoline
ACEIILNOSX	saxicoline
ACEIILNTVY	inactively
ACEIILORSZ	socializer
ACEIILPPRT	participle
ACEIILPRTT	triplicate
ACEIILPSST	plasticise
	specialist
ACEIILPSTY	speciality
ACEIILPSTZ	plasticize
ACEIILSTTV	active list
ACEIILSTTY	elasticity
ACEIIMNORS	Micronesia
ACEIIMNRRU	cinerarium
ACEIINNQRU	quinacrine
ACEIINNRTY	itinerancy
ACEIINOPST	speciation
ACEIINORTT	recitation
ACEIINOSTV	vesication
ACEIINOTTX	excitation
	intoxicate
ACEIINPPRT	principate
ACEIINPSTT	antiseptic
	psittacine
ACEIINRTVY	inveracity
ACEIIRTTVY	creativity
ACEIJKMNTU	minute-jack
ACEIKLRSTV	travel sick
	travel-sick
ACEIKNORTV	native rock
ACEIKNPSTT	septic tank
ACEIKORTUY	eukaryotic
ACEIKPSTTY	sticky tape
ACEILLLNPU	Pulcinella
ACEILLLOPW	pillow-lace
ACEILLLPRU	pellicular
ACEILLMNSY	miscellany
ACEILLMRTY	metrically
ACEILLNNNO	cannelloni
ACEILLNOOT	ocellation
ACEILLNRTU	lenticular
ACEILLOPSW	pillowcase
ACEILLOPTY	poetically
ACEILLOSTY	societally
ACEILLOTXY	exotically
ACEILLPRUY	peculiarly
ACEILLPSTY	septically
ACEILLRTUV	victualler
ACEILLRTVY	vertically
ACEILMMNSS	clamminess
ACEILMNOPR	complainer
ACEILMNRST	centralism
ACEILMNRUW	lawrencium
ACEILMOPRR	proclaimer
ACEILMRRUV	vermicular
ACEILMRSSU	secularism
ACEILMRSUY	early music
ACEILMSSTU	salicetums
ACEILMTUUV	cumulative
ACEILNNOOP	Napoleonic
ACEILNNOTU	nucleation
ACEILNNUVY	univalency
ACEILNOORT	iconolater
	relocation
ACEILNOPRT	pratincole
ACEILNOPST	pleonastic
ACEILNOPTU	peculation
ACEILNORTU	ulceration
ACEILNOSSS	socialness
ACEILNOSTU	inosculate
ACEILNOTTV	violent act
ACEILNPPSU	suppliance
ACEILNPPTU	put in place
ACEILNRSTT	centralist
ACEILNRSTU	lacustrine
ACEILNRTTY	centrality
ACEILNRTVY	trivalency
ACEILNRUUX	luxuriance
ACEILOOSUV	olivaceous
ACEILOPRTU	peculiar to
ACEILPPSTU	supplicate
ACEILPRTUU	apiculture
ACEILRRSUV	versicular
ACEILRSSTU	secularist
ACEILRSTTU	testicular
ACEILRSTUY	secularity
ACEILRTUUV	aviculture
ACEILSTUWZ	Clausewitz
ACEIMMNORT	manometric
ACEIMMRSTY	asymmetric
ACEIMNNRUY	innumeracy
ACEIMNOPRT	importance
ACEIMNOPSS	campesinos
ACEIMNORSU	main course
ACEIMNRRTU	current aim
ACEIMORRTT	meritocrat
ACEIMORSVW	microwaves
ACEIMRSTUW	Water Music
ACEIMSSTTY	systematic
ACEINNOPTT	pentatonic
ACEINNORTU	enunciator
ACEINNOTTU	continuate
ACEINNRSTY	transiency
ACEINNRTTU	net curtain
ACEINNRTUU	nunciature
ACEINNSSST	scantiness
ACEINOORTV	revocation
ACEINOPRTU	precaution
ACEINOPSTT	constipate
ACEINORRTT	retraction
ACEINORSTU	Carnoustie
ACEINORTTU	eructation
ACEINORTTW	tonic water
ACEINORTTX	extraction
ACEINRRRTU	air-current
ACEIOOPRTZ	azeotropic
ACEIOOPTTV	co-optative
ACEIOORTTU	autoerotic
ACEIOPRRSU	precarious

ACEIORSTVY	vesicatory
ACEIORTTXY	excitatory
ACEIRRRTUW	raw recruit
ACEJKLLOWY	Yellow Jack
ACEJKLMMNO	Jack Lemmon
ACEJORRTTY	trajectory
ACEKKMOSST	smokestack
ACEKLLLRTY	tally clerk
ACEKLLRSTU	lacklustre
ACEKLNOPST	alpenstock
ACEKLNORSS	close ranks
ACEKLORSTY	York Castle
ACEKPRRSSY	skyscraper
ACELLMOSTU	Samuel Colt
ACELLNOSSW	callowness
ACELLOPRTY	pectorally
ACELLORSSW	lower-class
ACELLPRSTY	spectrally
ACELLSSTTY	tactlessly
ACELMMNOOS	common seal
ACELMNNOTT	malcontent
ACELMNOORT	Monte Carlo
ACELNNOSSU	consensual
ACELNNOSTU	Launceston
ACELNNOTUV	conventual □
ACELNOPRSY	narcolepsy
ACELNOPSTY	nyctalopes
ACELNOTTUX	contextual
ACELNOTTXY	not exactly
ACELNRTTUY	truncately
ACELOOPRRS	Poor Clares
ACELOOPRRT	percolator
ACELOOSSTT	osteoclast
ACELOPRSTU	speculator
ACELORRSTY	clearstory
ACELPPRSSU	upper class
	upper-class
ACELPSTUUY	eucalyptus
ACEMMNORTY	commentary
ACEMMNOSTU	consummate
ACEMMOSTTY	mastectomy
ACEMNNNOTT	cantonment
ACEMNNORST	monstrance
ACEMOOPSST	come to pass
ACEMOOSTTY	come to stay
ACENNOORTV	covenantor
ACENNORRWY	Cannery Row
ACENNORSTV	conversant
ACENNOSTTT	contestant
ACENOOPRVY	overcanopy
ACENORRSWY	cornerways
ACEOOOPRRT	co-operator
ACEOOPRRRT	procreator
ACEOOPSSTT	statoscope
ACEOORRTVY	revocatory
ACEOPRSSTT	spectators
ACFFGHILNY	chaffingly
ACFFGIILNT	afflicting
ACFFGILLNO	calling-off
ACFFGINOST	casting-off
ACFFIILLOY	officially
ACFFIILNNO	coffin-nail
ACFFIILNOT	affliction
ACFFIILNOU	unofficial
ACFFIIOORT	officiator
ACFFILLNUY	fancifully
ACFFOPRSST	staff corps
ACFGHMORRS	frog's-march
ACFGILNNOO	cooling fan
ACFGILOPRY	profligacy
ACFGILRSTU	gastric flu
ACFGINOPTU	facing up to
ACFHKLSSUU	Klaus Fuchs
ACFHKOOTUW	out of whack
ACFHLLTUWY	watchfully
ACFHLMOOST	smooth calf
ACFHLMOSTU	stomachful
ACFHLNTUUW	unwatchful
ACFHMNOOTU	not much of a
ACFHOOSTTU	a soft touch
ACFIIILNTY	finicality
ACFIIIORTV	factor VIII
ACFIILNOPT	pontifical
ACFIILNORT	frictional
ACFIINNORS	infrasonic
ACFIINNORT	infarction
	infraction
ACFIIOSTTU	factitious
ACFILLLORU	follicular
ACFILNNOOT	conflation
ACFILNNOTU	functional
ACFILNOOPT	focal point
ACFILNOOST	tonic sol-fa
ACFILOSTUY	factiously
ACFILRSSST	first-class
ACFINNSTUY	unsanctify
ACFINOORRT	fornicator
ACFINOORSU	facinorous
ACFINRSSSW	Swiss franc
ACFLLOORSS	collar of SS
ACFLNOORTW	contraflow
ACFLNRRUUU	furuncular
ACFMNOORSW	can of worms
ACGGHIILOO	hagiologic
ACGGHINNNU	unchanging
ACGGHINOTT	chittagong □
ACGGIILLOT	Glagolitic
ACGGIINOTT	cogitating
ACGGIINRSU	icing sugar
ACGGILLNNY	glancingly
ACGHHNOSSU	Hugh Casson
ACGHIINNNU	unchaining
ACGHIINSST	chastising
ACGHIKMNOR	Rockingham
ACGHILLMNU	McLaughlin
ACGHILMNRY	charmingly
ACGHILNSST	nightclass
ACGHILNSTY	scathingly
ACGHIMNNNU	Cunningham
ACGHIMNNOP	champignon
ACGHIMNNTU	unmatching
ACGHINNPTU	hunting-cap

ACGHINPPTU	patching up
ACGHINPRSU	purchasing
ACGHINPTTU	chatting up
ACGHIOPPRT	pictograph
ACGHIOPRRU	urographic
ACGHLLOOPR	collograph
ACGIILLORS	cigarillos
ACGIILLOST	logistical
ACGIILLOTY	logicality
ACGIILLRTU	liturgical
ACGIILNORY	royal icing
ACGIILNOSU	caliginous
ACGIILNOVZ	vocalizing
ACGIIMNORS	organismic
ACGIINOOTT	cogitation
ACGIINPRST	practising
ACGIJKKNSY	skyjacking
ACGIKKMNRU	muck-raking
ACGILLNOPS	collapsing
ACGILLNORW	wing collar
ACGILLOOOR	orological
ACGILLOOOZ	zoological
ACGILLOORU	urological
ACGILLRSUY	surgically
ACGILNNPRY	prancingly
ACGILNOPSS	Panglossic
ACGILNOPTU	copulating
ACGILORSUY	graciously
ACGIMNOORS	agronomics
ACGIMNORRS	Cairngorms
ACGIMNSSTY	gymnastics
ACGINNORRT	Carrington
ACGINNORRY	carrying-on
ACGINOOSTU	contagious
ACGINOPRST	Racing Post
ACGINOPSUU	pugnacious
ACGINORSUU	ungracious
ACGINOSTTU	casting out
ACGJLLNOUY	conjugally
ACGMOPRRTY	cryptogram
ACGNNOPPUY	oppugnancy
ACGORRSSTU	grass court
ACHHILMOPT	ophthalmic
ACHHILMRTY	rhythmical
ACHHIMRRTY	arrhythmic
ACHHINOSTU	South China
ACHHIOPPRS	Hipparchos
ACHHJNNOSY	Johnny Cash
ACHHNOOTTU	autochthon
ACHHOPPSTY	psychopath
ACHIIIRSST	trichiasis
ACHIILLMPS	phallicism
ACHIILLNTW	within call
ACHIILNOPT	notaphilic
ACHIILORST	historical
ACHIIMNSTU	humanistic
ACHIIMNSUV	chauvinism
ACHIIMOPPP	hippocampi
ACHIINNOOT	inchoation
ACHIINNORT	Corinthian
ACHIINORTT	chittaroni
ACHIINRSTT	Antichrist
ACHIINSTUV	chauvinist
ACHIIOPRST	aphoristic
ACHIIOPSST	pistachios
ACHIISSSTU	such as it is
ACHIJLNNOV	John Calvin
ACHIKLOORW	workaholic
ACHIKMNOST	mackintosh ▫
ACHIKMNRSS	scrimshank
ACHILLMOOS	alcoholism
ACHILLMTYY	mythically
ACHILLNNSY	clannishly
ACHILLNOPY	phonically
ACHILLPSYY	physically
ACHILMOPTY	polymathic
ACHILMPSSY	scampishly
ACHILNNOTU	launch into
ACHILNOORS	isochronal
ACHILORSUV	chivalrous
ACHIMMNORS	monarchism
ACHIMNORST	monarchist
ACHIMORRTT	trichromat
ACHIMOSSTU	mustachios
ACHINORSTU	Sun Chariot
ACHINSTTUY	unchastity
ACHIOOPSTY	sociopathy
ACHIOPSTTY	hypostatic
ACHIPRSTYY	psychiatry
ACHIRSTTWW	wristwatch
ACHJKNNOOR	John Cranko
ACHKMOOOST	Thomas Cook
ACHKNOOTTU	Nouakchott
ACHLLLLOYY	allycholly
ACHLLOOPSY	playschool
ACHLMMOORS	schoolmarm
	school-marm
ACHLMNORUU	homuncular
ACHLNNORSY	synchronal
ACHLOORSUW	colourwash
ACHNNORSYY	asynchrony
ACIIIKLNOT	kaolinitic
ACIIILLMNY	inimically
ACIIILMSST	Islamicist
ACIIILNOPT	politician
ACIIILNOSS	sicilianos
ACIIINNOTT	incitation
ACIIINRSTT	inartistic
ACIIINSTTV	nativistic
ACIIINTTVY	inactivity
ACIIJLRSTU	juristical
ACIIJRSTUY	justiciary
ACIIKTTUWY	Kuwait City
ACIILLMNRY	criminally
ACIILLNNOS	Scillonian
ACIILLNORY	ironically
ACIILLRTTY	tritically
ACIILMNSUY	musicianly
ACIILMORST	moralistic
ACIILMSTUY	musicality
ACIILNOPRV	provincial
ACIILOPTTY	topicality

ACIILOSSUV	lascivious
ACIILPSTTY	plasticity
ACIILPTTYY	typicality
ACIILRSTTU	altruistic
ACIIMMNOPT	pantomimic
ACIIMMNOST	commit a sin
ACIIMMNSTU	numismatic
ACIIMNNORS	Canis Minor
ACIIMNPTTY	tympanitic
ACIIMNRSSS	narcissism
ACIIMOPRSS	prosaicism
ACIINNOOTV	invocation
ACIINNOSTU	insouciant
ACIINNOTTX	intoxicant
ACIINOOSTT	oscitation
ACIINORTTU	urtication
ACIINOSTUU	incautious
ACIINRSSST	narcissist
ACIIOPRRST	scriptoria
ACIIOPSSUU	auspicious
ACIIOPSTZZ	pizzicatos
ACIIORSTVY	varicosity
ACIIPSSTTY	spasticity
ACIIQRTTUZ	quartzitic
ACIISSSTTT	statistics
ACIJLORTUY	jocularity
ACIKKLMNOR	Kilmarnock
ACIKKOPRUW	kick up a row
ACIKLMRTTU	multi-track
ACIKLNNOPT	planktonic
ACIKLOORSW	social work
ACIKLPRSTY	play tricks
ACIKNRRTTU	turn a trick
ACIKOPRTYY	karyotypic
ACILLLNOOY	colonially
ACILLLOOQU	colloquial
ACILLMNNOO	monoclinal
ACILLMOORT	collimator
ACILLMOTUU	altocumuli
ACILLMOTUV	multivocal
ACILLMSTYY	mystically
ACILLNORSW	Cornwallis
ACILLNORUV	involucral
ACILLNOSUY	unsocially
ACILLNOUVY	univocally
ACILLOOPRT	allotropic
ACILLOORST	oscillator
ACILLOPRTY	tropically
ACILLORTVY	vortically
ACILLRSTUY	rustically
ACILMNOOOS	nosocomial
ACILMNOPST	complaints
ACILMNOSUU	calumnious
ACILMNOTUU	cumulation
ACILMNRSUU	minuscular
ACILMOOPTY	polyatomic
ACILMORSUU	miraculous
ACILMPRSUU	spiraculum
ACILNNOOOT	on location
ACILNOOORT	coloration
ACILNOOPTU	copulation
ACILNOORSU	Coriolanus
ACILNOORTU	inoculator
ACILNOORTY	iconolatry
ACILNOOSSS	Colossians
ACILNOOSTU	osculation
ACILNOOTTT	cottontail
ACILNORRTY	contrarily
ACILNORSST	Latin cross
ACILNORSTU	ultrasonic
ACILNOSTTY	oscitantly
ACILNPPSTU	supplicant
ACILNRTTUY	taciturnly
ACILOOPRRT	proctorial
ACILOOQSUU	loquacious
ACILOOSSUX	saxicolous
ACILOPSSUY	spaciously
ACILOPSTUY	captiously
ACILORTTUV	cultivator
ACILOSTUUY	cautiously
ACILPRRSTU	scriptural
ACIMNNOOPS	companions
ACIMNNORTU	unromantic
ACIMNNOSTY	sanctimony
ACIMNOOPRS	comparison
ACIMNOOPSS	compassion
ACIMNOORST	astronomic
ACIMNOOSST	onomastics
ACIMNOPPRS	prison camp
ACIMNOPRTY	importancy
	patronymic
ACIMNOPSST	tonic spasm
ACIMNPRSTU	manuscript
ACIMOOPRTT	compatriot
ACIMOORTVY	varicotomy
ACIMOPSTTY	asymptotic
ACINNNOSTT	inconstant
ACINNOOORT	coronation
ACINNORSTT	constraint
	in contrast
ACINNORTTU	truncation
ACINNOTUWY	you can't win
ACINOOOPTT	co-optation
ACINOORSTT	cartoonist
ACINOORTVY	invocatory
ACINOPRSTU	Count Paris
ACINORSSTU	Sanctorius
ACINPRRSTT	transcript
ACIOORSTVY	Ivory Coast
ACKKNRSTUW	knackwurst
ACKLMMNOOT	common talk
ACKLMNOORS	rock salmon
ACLLLLOORR	rollcollar
ACLLLRTUUY	culturally
ACLLMMNOUY	communally
ACLLMNNOOO	monoclonal
ACLLMRSUUY	muscularly
ACLLNPTUUY	punctually
ACLLOOPRRY	corporally
ACLLPRSTUU	sculptural
ACLMMNOOTY	commonalty
ACLNNOSTTU	consultant

ACLNNOSTTY	constantly
ACLNNPTUUU	unpunctual
ACLNNRSUUU	ranunculus
ACLNOORSTT	contraltos
ACLNOORSUY	canorously
ACLNOPSTUY	postulancy
ACLOORSSST	across lots
ACLOORSTUY	osculatory
ACLRRSTTUU	structural
ACMMOORTTU	commutator
ACMNNORTUY	countryman
ACMNOOSSTW	Scotswoman
ACNNNOSTTU	unconstant
ACNOOPRSTY	syncopator
ACNOORRTTY	contrary to
ACOOPRRRTT	protractor
ACOOPRRRTU	procurator
ACOOPRTTUY	pay court to
ADDDEEHNRU	dunderhead
ADDDEEHRTY	dehydrated
ADDDEEILSS	sidesaddle
ADDDEELLPW	well-padded
ADDDEGILOV	David Lodge
ADDDEGINWY	wedding day
ADDDEHNNOW	handed down
ADDDGORSTU	add drugs to
ADDEEEEPST	deep-seated
ADDEEEFHNR	free-handed
ADDEEEFNTU	undefeated
ADDEEEGHRY	grey-headed
ADDEEEHNNV	even-handed
ADDEEEIRST	desiderate
ADDEEELLSW	Weddell Sea
ADDEEELNTT	deadnettle
	dead-nettle
ADDEEERRWY	Edward Eyre
ADDEEFHLNT	left-handed
ADDEEFHNOR	forehanded
ADDEEFHOST	soft-headed
ADDEEFIINN	definienda
ADDEEFILOT	defoliated
ADDEEGGHLU	head-lugged
ADDEEGGINS	disengaged
ADDEEGHITW	dead-weight
ADDEEGINRR	dead ringer
ADDEEGINST	designated
ADDEEGLLNR	Gelderland
ADDEEGNRRU	unregarded
ADDEEGORRZ	razor-edged
ADDEEHLNRU	unheralded
ADDEEHNNOP	open-handed
ADDEEHNORV	overhanded
ADDEEHPTUY	deputy head
ADDEEHRRTY	dehydrater
ADDEEIINRT	ride and tie
	ride-and-tie
ADDEEIKMNW	weak-minded
ADDEEILMMN	middle name
ADDEEILMST	Middle East
ADDEEILNSS	deadliness
ADDEEILPSS	displeased
ADDEEILRWY	widely read
	widely-read
ADDEEILSTV	David Steel
ADDEEIMNOT	dead on time
ADDEEIMNRR	mind-reader
ADDEEIMRXY	ready mixed
ADDEEIPPRV	dive-dapper
ADDEEIPRSW	widespread
ADDEEKMNNU	Edmund Kean
ADDEELLSSS	saddleless
ADDEELMNOY	almond-eyed
ADDEELMOTU	demodulate
ADDEELOORV	overloaded
ADDEELORSS	saddle sore
	saddle-sore
ADDEELPRST	stepladder
ADDEELPRVY	depravedly
ADDEENNTTU	unattended
ADDEENOPRS	dead person
ADDEENOTTT	attended to
ADDEENQRSU	squandered
ADDEENRRUW	unrewarded
ADDEEOPRSS	desperados
ADDEFGINRU	defrauding
ADDEFGLORR	Gerald Ford
ADDEFHILRS	fish-ladder
ADDEFHIRST	hard-fisted
ADDEFHNORU	four-handed
ADDEFIIMNR	fair-minded
ADDEFIKNTY	fat-kidney'd
ADDEFILRSW	fieldwards
ADDEFJLLOR	Alfred Jodl
ADDEFLLRUY	dreadfully
ADDEFLOORS	saddle roof
ADDEGGILNN	gladdening
ADDEGHHHIN	high-handed
ADDEGHLNOR	dog-handler
ADDEGIORVW	David Gower
ADDEGLLOPT	gold-plated
ADDEGPTUWY	Deputy Dawg
ADDEHHPRSU	hard-pushed
ADDEHIJMNU	mujaheddin
ADDEHILNNR	hinderland
ADDEHILSTW	saddle with
ADDEHIMNOO	maidenhood
ADDEHINNOR	iron-handed
ADDEHLLNOR	landholder
ADDEHLNOOR	door-handle
ADDEHLOSTY	the old days
ADDEHMNNOW	hand-me-down
ADDEHMNORY	home and dry
ADDEHNOORT	horned toad
ADDEHNORSW	Howards End
ADDEHNORSY	dandy-horse
ADDEHORRTY	dehydrator
ADDEHORSTT	short-dated
ADDEIILLSV	ill-advised
ADDEIILQTU	liquidated
ADDEIINNVV	David Niven
ADDEIIPSST	dissipated
ADDEILLOSW	disallowed

ADDEILMTTY admittedly
ADDEILNNRY dinner lady
ADDEILNOYZ daily dozen
ADDEIMNSUY undismayed
ADDEINNOTU denudation
ADDEINNRRU underdrain
ADDEINOORS radiosonde
ADDEJOSTTU adjusted to
ADDEKMNOOS make no odds
ADDEKMNORW marked-down
ADDELNNORW wonderland ❑
ADDELNNRSU Sunderland
ADDELNOORW woodlander
ADDELNOPWY played-down
ADDEMNNOPW dampen down
ADDENNRSTU understand
ADDENOQRSU squadroned
ADDFGIOORY Good Friday
ADDFIILNSU disdainful
ADDFILMORY myriadfold
ADDFIORSTV David Frost
ADDGGLOOOS good as gold
ADDGHHINRY high and dry
ADDGHINNOT Haddington
ADDGIILNRY daily grind
ADDGILLNWY dawdlingly
ADDGINNOPU up and doing
ADDGNOPRTU Pont du Gard
ADDGORRSUW sword-guard
ADDHIILMOS old-maidish
ADDHIOSTTW at odds with
ADDIIILNUV individual
ADDIIINNOT in addition
ADDIILMRTW draw it mild
ADDILLLLYY dilly-dally
ADDILNNRST Lindstrand
ADDLNORWWY downwardly
ADDNNOOTUW down and out
down-and-out
ADEEEEGNRT degenerate
ADEEEFHKOT take heed of
ADEEEFHNOV have need of
ADEEEFIIRS dies feriae
ADEEEFILRS federalise
ADEEEFIRTV federative
ADEEEFLORR freeloader
ADEEEFMNNS defenseman
ADEEEFNOST East of Eden
ADEEEFNOTV Deo favente
ADEEEGGLNR near-legged
ADEEEGGRST segregated
ADEEEGHITT get the idea
ADEEEGJNRT grande jeté
ADEEEGLNRS Greenslade
ADEEEGLOPV Lope de Vega
ADEEEGLRSV Everglades
ADEEEGLRTU deregulate
ADEEEGRSTW water's edge
ADEEEHLNOT heel and toe
ADEEEHLNRT the Red Lane
ADEEEHLNSV sleevehand
ADEEEHLRTT letterhead
ADEEEHMNOT meet head on
meet head-on
ADEEEHORTV overheated
ADEEEIKLRU Auld Reekie
ADEEEIOPSU peau de soie
ADEEEIPRRT pied-à-terre
ADEEEIPTTX expeditate
ADEEEIRSTT Eastertide
ADEEEKMNRT make tender
ADEEELLNRW well-earned
ADEEELNNUV unleavened
ADEEELNRSU underlease
ADEEELNRUV unrevealed
ADEEELNRUW Leeuwarden
ADEEELPRTY repeatedly
ADEEELRRTW Walter Reed
ADEEEMNNRT endearment
man-entered
ADEEEMOOST oedematose
ADEEENORTX exonerated
ADEEENRRSW newsreader
ADEEENSSST sedateness
ADEEFGGLRT ragged left
ADEEFGHIRU figurehead
ADEEFGLNNW newfangled
new-fangled
ADEEFGLNRS self-danger
ADEEFGLRRS self-regard
ADEEFGMNRT defragment
fragmented
ADEEFHLORW flower-head
ADEEFHNRTU unfathered
ADEEFIILMN a minefield
ADEEFILLNS self-denial
ADEEFILMRS federalism
ADEEFILNRR real friend
ADEEFILOUX folie à deux
ADEEFILRST federalist
ADEEFINORT federation
ADEEFINORZ fazendeiro
ADEEFIOPRS safe period
ADEEFIORSV fore-advise
ADEEFIRSTU disfeature
ADEEFKORTU freaked out
ADEEFLLORW fallow deer
ADEEFLLSSY fadelessly
ADEEFMNORW freedwoman
ADEEFMNRTY defrayment
ADEEFMORRV far-removed
ADEEFNNSTU unfastened
ADEEFNOPRT Peter Fonda
ADEEFOPRRT perforated
ADEEFORSTU foederatus
ADEEGGHJRU jugged hare
ADEEGGHLOR loggerhead
ADEEGGHPTU depth gauge
ADEEGGJNSS jaggedness
ADEEGGNORS George Sand
ADEEGGNRSS raggedness
ADEEGHILNY Headingley

ADEEGHIRRY grey-haired
ADEEGIINSS diagenesis
ADEEGIJLNR Darjeeling
ADEEGILNOT delegation
ADEEGILNRR ringleader
ADEEGIMNNR meandering
ADEEGIMRRT get married
ADEEGINNRS Grenadines
ADEEGINRRT intergrade
ADEEGINRTT integrated
ADEEGINRTU green audit
ADEEGIORTV derogative
ADEEGIRSTT get astride
ADEEGLLNRY enlargedly
ADEEGLMNNO golden mean
ADEEGLNRUZ underglaze
ADEEGLORTY derogately
ADEEGLPPRY dapple-grey
ADEEGLRRSS regardless
ADEEGMNRSS gensdarmes
ADEEGNNOTY get annoyed
ADEEGORRRT retrograde
ADEEHHILST heat shield
ADEEHHINST in the shade
ADEEHHNORX hexahedron
ADEEHHNPTY hyphenated
ADEEHHNRTU headhunter
ADEEHHOTTT to the death
ADEEHIIKRR Keir Hardie
ADEEHIIKTV khediviate
ADEEHIINSV have inside
ADEEHIIRRW wire-haired
ADEEHIKLNT and the like
ADEEHILNOT endothelia
ADEEHILOPP paedophile
ADEEHILPRS dealership
leadership
ADEEHILSVY adhesively
ADEEHILSWY daisy-wheel
ADEEHIMNSU dehumanise
ADEEHIMNUZ dehumanize
ADEEHIMPRY hypermedia
ADEEHINNRV have dinner
ADEEHINRST dishearten
ADEEHINRSX share index
ADEEHINSTV Edith Evans
ADEEHIPRRS readership
ADEEHIRRSS sherardise
ADEEHIRRSZ sherardize
ADEEHIRRTY hereditary
ADEEHKLLNT death-knell
ADEEHKLLRS shelldrake
ADEEHKNOOY hook-and-eye
ADEEHKNOTT death-token
ADEEHLLNRT enthralled
ADEEHLNOTW down at heel
down-at-heel
ADEEHLRRVY hardly ever
ADEEHMMNOR remand home
ADEEHMNOTU haute monde
ADEEHMNPRU unhampered
ADEEHNNRTU underneath
ADEEHNRSTT and the rest
ADEEHOPRTT deep throat
ADEEHORTTY the year dot
ADEEHRRSTT Thar Desert
ADEEIIJNRR jardinière
ADEEIIKLMN maidenlike
ADEEIILMNT eliminated
ADEEIILMTT delimitate
ADEEIILNSS desalinise
ADEEIILNSZ desalinize
ADEEIILNTV evidential
ADEEIILSTV devitalise
ADEEIILTVZ devitalize
ADEEIIMTTV meditative
ADEEIIRTVV derivative
ADEEIJOPRS jeopardise
ADEEIJOPRZ jeopardize
ADEEIKKPRT keep it dark
ADEEIKLLWW weak-willed
ADEEIKNRRT dreikanter
ADEEIKPRSW Paderewski
ADEEILLMNV Mandeville
ADEEILLMRY remedially
ADEEILLMVY medievally
ADEEILLPRS espadrille
ADEEILLRTT ill-treated
ADEEILLUVV vaudeville
ADEEILMNRT derailment
ADEEILMORS demoralise
ADEEILMORZ demoralize
ADEEILNNRW Andrew Neil
New Ireland
ADEEILNORT delineator
ADEEILNPRT interplead
ADEEILNRTU adulterine
ADEEILNRUZ unrealized
ADEEILNSSV disenslave
ADEEILNTTT dilettante
ADEEILOPRS depolarise
ADEEILOPRZ depolarize
ADEEILORSV devalorise
ADEEILORVZ devalorize
ADEEILPRST pilastered
ADEEIMMORT immoderate
ADEEIMNNOT denominate
emendation
ADEEIMNNTT detainment
ADEEIMNORV maiden over
ADEEIMNOTT meditate on
ADEEIMNPRS Parmenides
ADEEIMNRSS dreaminess
ADEEIMNRTT terminated
ADEEIMNSTW tandemwise
ADEEIMORTU audiometer
ADEEIMOTTV demotivate
ADEEIMQRRU quadrireme
ADEEINOTTV denotative
ADEEINPPSX appendixes
ADEEINPRST pedestrian
ADEEINRRSS dreariness

ADEEINRRST restrained
ADEEINRSTT straitened
ADEEINRSTU denaturise
ADEEINRTTT tridentate
ADEEINRTUZ denaturize
ADEEINSSST steadiness
ADEEINSSTU use instead
ADEEIOSSTY easy does it
ADEEIOSXYY oxeye daisy
ADEEIPRSTT tapestried
ADEEIPRTUV depurative
ADEEIRRRWW wiredrawer
ADEEIRRSTV advertiser
ADEEISSTVV Steve Davis
ADEEKLMORU make louder
ADEEKMMNOR make modern
ADEEKMNRRU unremarked
ADEEKMOSTU make used to
ADEEKMRRSS dressmaker
ADEEKNRRTU undertaker
ADEEKORRST take orders
ADEELLNQUU unequalled
ADEELLNRUV unravelled
ADEELLOSTY desolately
ADEELMNPUX unexampled
ADEELMOPSY employed as
ADEELMORTY moderately
ADEELMRSUY measuredly
ADEELNNPPR preplanned
ADEELNNQSU Queensland
ADEELNNTTU untalented
ADEELNRTTU laundrette
ADEELNRUUV undervalue
ADEELOPPTU depopulate
ADEELOPRSS leopardess
ADEELOPRVY overplayed
ADEELPPRRY preparedly
ADEELRRSSW rewardless
ADEELRRSTU serrulated
ADEELRSSTU adulteress
ADEEMNNNRU unmannered
ADEEMNNORT ornamented
ADEEMNOPRR promenader
ADEEMNORST sordamente
ADEEMNORTY emendatory
ADEEMNORYY ready money
ADEEMNPRTT department
ADEEMNRRTT retardment
ADEEMNRSTU unstreamed
ADEEMOOSTU oedematous
ADEEMORSST dermatoses
ADEEMRRSUY dry measure
ADEENNORSU unreasoned
ADEENNOSSU unseasoned
ADEENNPRTT pretendant
ADEENNRSUW unanswered
ADEENPPRRU unprepared
ADEENPPRSS dapperness
ADEENPRRTU enraptured
ADEENPRSST depressant
ADEENPRSTY present-day
ADEENQRRSU squanderer
ADEENRRTUV adventurer
ADEENRRTUW underwater
ADEENRSTTU understate
ADEENRSTUV adventures
ADEENSTTTU unattested
ADEEOOPSTT seed-potato
ADEEOPPRRR order paper
ADEEOPPSTT at top speed
ADEEOPRRSV overspread
spread over
ADEEOPRSSV passed over
ADEEORRTTU trade route
ADEEORSTTV overstated
ADEERRSTTW streetward
ADEERRSTYY starry-eyed
ADEERSSSTW stewardess
ADEESTTTUY estate duty
ADEFFGHINO heading off
ADEFFHLMOR half-formed
ADEFFIKLNR Frank Field
ADEFFLOOTT flat-footed
ADEFGGINOR God-fearing
ADEFGHIRST far-sighted
ADEFGIINOR foreign aid
ADEFGILNTU defaulting
ADEFGILRSU Life Guards
ADEFGILRTZ FitzGerald
Fitzgerald
ADEFGINNOR in danger of
ADEFGINORR in regard of
ADEFGLLOOS GoodFellas
ADEFGNOORR roof garden
ADEFHHLOOT health food
ADEFHHOOPT pad the hoof
ADEFHHOORT fatherhood
ADEFHILMSS damsel fish
damselfish
ADEFHILTTW halfwitted
half-witted
ADEFHINPRT pathfinder
ADEFHIRSTV drive shaft
ADEFHIRTWW white dwarf
ADEFHKLOOT take hold of
ADEFHMNOTU unfathomed
ADEFHNNORY Henry Fonda
ADEFHOORSW foreshadow
ADEFIIILNN Indian file
ADEFIILLRT field trial
ADEFIINQTU quantified
ADEFIINRTU infuriated
unratified
ADEFIINRTW draw it fine
ADEFIIRSTT stratified
ADEFIKNNOO one of a kind
ADEFILLLRY all-firedly
ADEFILLLSU full-sailed
ADEFILMORS Fidel Ramos
ADEFILOORT defoliator
ADEFILORTU fluoridate
ADEFIMRRRT dirt farmer

ADEFINOORR	foreordain
ADEFINRSTX	transfixed
ADEFIOPPRS	apprised of
ADEFKLORST	tradesfolk
ADEFKNORSU	unasked-for
ADEFLLMNNU	full-manned
ADEFLLRTWY	leftwardly
ADEFLNRTUU	fraudulent
ADEFMNOORT	not dream of
ADEFMNORRW	wander from
ADEFMOORRS	reformados
ADEFMOPRRT	depart from
	parted from
ADEFNNOPRU	unprofaned
ADEFNOORRW	for a wonder
ADEFOORSYY	days of yore
ADEFORSSTW	soft sawder
ADEFRRSTTU	frustrated
ADEGGGINNR	darning egg
ADEGGHHIRR	high regard
ADEGGHILNR	hang-glider
ADEGGILLRU	drill gauge
ADEGGIMOPS	pedagogism
ADEGGIPRSW	digger-wasp
ADEGGNOPTU	get-up-and-go
ADEGGOORSV	grave goods
ADEGHHILNR	highlander
ADEGHHINST	nightshade
ADEGHHLOOT	good health
ADEGHIKKLN	King Khaled
ADEGHILLNO	Heligoland
ADEGHILNOR	long-haired
ADEGHILNOW	Goldie Hawn
ADEGHINPRS	ring-shaped
ADEGHIOPRY	ideography
ADEGHLNORT	Grand Hotel
ADEGHLOOPY	edaphology
ADEGHLRTUY	daughterly
ADEGHMOPRY	demography
ADEGHNOPTU	upon the gad
ADEGHNORST	headstrong
ADEGHOOPTT	gap-toothed
ADEGHORRSY	Gary Rhodes
ADEGHORRTU	rough trade
ADEGHORSUU	guardhouse
ADEGIIILST	digitalise
ADEGIIILTZ	digitalize
ADEGIIIMNS	disimagine
ADEGIILLRR	Girardelli
ADEGIILLSU	seguidilla
ADEGIILMNS	misaligned
	misleading
ADEGIILNPR	lip-reading
ADEGIILTTY	digitately
ADEGIIMNNU	unimagined
ADEGIIMNRS	misreading
ADEGIINPRS	despairing
ADEGIIOPRR	prairie dog
ADEGILLNNY	Glyn Daniel
ADEGILLNPY	pleadingly
ADEGILLNYY	delayingly
ADEGILMNRY	dreamingly
ADEGILMRTU	multigrade
ADEGILNNNO	non-aligned
ADEGILNNNT	landing-net
ADEGILNNRS	sanderling
ADEGILNNRU	laundering
ADEGILNORV	drive along
ADEGILNOSY	agonisedly
ADEGILNOYZ	agonizedly
ADEGILNPPR	dapperling
ADEGILNRRR	errand-girl
ADEGILOSTW	slow-gaited
ADEGIMNNRU	maundering
ADEGIMNOPU	impoundage
ADEGIMNORS	gormandise
ADEGIMNORT	moderating
ADEGIMNORZ	gormandize
ADEGIMORRV	Roger Vadim
ADEGINNRSW	wanderings
ADEGINOOPS	poignadoes
ADEGINOORT	derogation
ADEGINORRT	denigrator
	in regard to
ADEGINORTX	axe to grind
ADEGINOSST	assigned to
ADEGINPRSW	wingspread
ADEGIPRRST	partridges
ADEGIRRTTY	dirty great
ADEGKNRRRU	krugerrand□
ADEGKORRRW	grow darker
ADEGLLMNOP	Golden Palm
ADEGMMOPRR	programmed
ADEGMNORSS	Dream Songs
ADEGNOORTU	good nature
ADEGNORSSU	sandgrouse
ADEGOOPRST	gasteropod
ADEGOORRTY	derogatory
ADEHHHNPRY	hard hyphen
ADEHHIIPRT	diphtheria
ADEHHIORTT	hit the road
ADEHHIRSSW	dishwasher
ADEHHLLOOR	holohedral
ADEHHOOPPS	hoop-shaped
ADEHIILMST	Delia Smith
ADEHIILMTU	humiliated
ADEHIILOPU	audiophile
ADEHIIMNNV	have in mind
ADEHIIMRTT	mithridate
ADEHIKMOTW	make do with
ADEHILLORU	loudhailer
	loud-hailer
ADEHILNNRT	hinterland
ADEHILNORT	threnodial
ADEHILNRST	disenthral
ADEHILOPRS	spheroidal
ADEHIMNORZ	harmonized
ADEHIMORTU	rheumatoid
ADEHINOSST	astonished
ADEHINPRSW	wardenship
ADEHINQSUV	vanquished
ADEHIOPRSS	rhapsodise

Words marked □ can also be spelled with an initial capital letter

ADEHIOPRST	Portishead
ADEHIOPRSZ	rhapsodize
ADEHIORTUZ	authorized
ADEHKNORRW	work-harden
ADEHLLNOUW	unhallowed
ADEHLLOPRY	polyhedral
ADEHLMNORT	motherland
ADEHLMNOSY	handsomely
ADEHLMOOSU	Samuel Hood
ADEHLNRSTU	Sutherland
ADEHLORRUY	Harold Urey
ADEHLRTTWY	thwartedly
ADEHMNNOSU	unhandsome
ADEHMNOOPS	moon-shaped
ADEHMNOTTU	muttonhead
ADEHMORRTW	threadworm
ADEHMORSTU	Thomas Edur
ADEHMORSTY	Mother's Day
ADEHMRTUUW	durum wheat
ADEHNNNOTW	now and then
ADEHNNOOST	to one's hand
ADEHNOOPRT	parenthood
ADEHNOPPRS	sand hopper
ADEHOORSVW	overshadow
ADEHOOSTTW	saw-toothed
ADEHOPTTTU	put to death
ADEHORRSSW	shorewards
ADEHORSTWW	westward ho!
ADEIIILMST	Militiades
ADEIIIMNTT	intimidate
ADEIILLPTX	pixillated
ADEIILLSTT	distillate
ADEIILMMTU	multimedia
ADEIILMNOR	meridional
ADEIILMNSU	unidealism
ADEIILMPPS	misapplied
ADEIILMSSV	Miles Davis
ADEIILNOPT	depilation
ADEIILNTTT	dilettanti
ADEIILORST	idolatrise
ADEIILORTZ	idolatrize
ADEIIMMNOS	Maimonides
ADEIIMNNOR	Iron Maiden
	iron maiden
ADEIIMNNOT	antimonide
ADEIIMNOTT	meditation
ADEIIMNOTV	dominative
ADEIIMNPRU	unimpaired
ADEIIMNRST	administer
ADEIIMORST	Radio Times
ADEIIMPRSU	praesidium
ADEIIMRSTT	dermatitis
ADEIINNNOS	Indonesian
ADEIINNORT	inordinate
ADEIINNOTW	nationwide
ADEIINNOTX	indexation
ADEIINNPPT	pinnatiped
ADEIINNRST	disentrain
ADEIINNRVY	Andy Irvine
ADEIINNSST	daintiness
ADEIINNSTU	insinuated
ADEIINNSTW	West Indian
ADEIINORTV	derivation
ADEIINPPRS	drainpipes
ADEIINPRST	inside part
ADEIINPTTU	inaptitude
ADEIIPRRSY	presidiary
ADEIIPRTTU	tripudiate
ADEIIPRTTW	pittie-ward
ADEIIPRTVZ	privatized
ADEIIRRTVX	Taxi Driver
ADEIIRSSTT	sit astride
ADEIISSSUV	dissuasive
ADEIJMMNRW	windjammer
ADEIJNOPRY	in jeopardy
ADEIKLLLRY	lady-killer
ADEIKLLMMT	malted milk
ADEIKLLNUY	unladylike
ADEIKMNTUY	make untidy
ADEIKOPSWW	widow's peak
ADEILLMPUX	all mixed up
ADEILLMSTW	Willemstad
ADEILLNOOS	solenoidal
ADEILLNOPR	Pirandello
ADEILLNOSS	on all sides
ADEILLNPSS	pallidness
ADEILLNRTU	ill-natured
ADEILLNRUV	unrivalled
ADEILLORSZ	Leo Szilard
ADEILLRRST	ill-starred
ADEILMNNUY	unmaidenly
ADEILMNOPR	palindrome
ADEILMNRTU	rudimental
ADEILMNSSS	dismalness
ADEILMNSTU	dentaliums
ADEILMOORS	ladies' room
ADEILMOPSS	psalmodise
ADEILMOPSZ	psalmodize
ADEILMSTTU	stimulated
ADEILMTTUU	a multitude
ADEILNOOST	desolation
ADEILNOOTV	devotional
ADEILNORTY	ordinately
ADEILNPRTU	prudential
ADEILNPTUV	pulvinated
ADEILNQTUU	unqualited
ADEILNRSTY	strainedly
ADEILNSTUY	unsteadily
ADEILNSTWY	Walt Disney
ADEILOORST	oestradiol
ADEILOPRTW	tidal power
ADEILOPRTY	depilatory
ADEILORSST	idolatress
ADEILOSSTT	solid-state
ADEILPSTTU	stipulated
ADEILRRRSU	Rural Rides
ADEILRSTTU	stridulate
ADEILRTTXY	dextrality
ADEIMMNRST	mastermind
ADEIMMRSUZ	summarized
ADEIMNNORT	ordainment
ADEIMNNOSS	idem sonans

ADEIMNOORT	moderation
ADEIMNORRZ	randomizer
ADEIMNORSW	randomwise
ADEIMNRRTT	Mitterrand
ADEIMORSTT	Mister Toad
ADEINNOORS	in ones road
ADEINNOOTT	denotation
	detonation
ADEINNOPWW	windowpane
ADEINNORTU	trade union
ADEINNRTYZ	tyrannized
ADEINOPRTU	depuration
ADEINOPTTU	deputation
ADEINORRWW	Rear Window
ADEINORSST	adroitness
	intradoses
ADEINOSTVY	video nasty
ADEINOSTWW	window seat
ADEINPRSSY	dispensary
ADEINRSSTW	tawdriness
ADEINSSSTU	unassisted
ADEINSSTTV	Adventists
ADEIOPPRSV	disapprove
ADEIOPRRTU	repudiator
ADEIOPRSTY	depositary
ADEIORRSTT	traditores
ADEIORSSTT	siderostat
ADEIPPRRTY	day-tripper
ADEIRRSSTW	ward sister
ADEIRSSTWY	strideways
ADEJKNORRU	jerk around
ADEJLNOPVY	J P Donleavy
ADEJMNORZZ	modern jazz
ADEJMNSTTU	adjustment
ADEJOPSTUX	juxtaposed
ADEKMNORTW	down-market
ADEKNOOPRU	poke around
ADEKNORSUZ	Konrad Zuse
ADELLNOOTW	not allowed
ADELLNOOWY	Woody Allen
ADELLNORRU	all-rounder
ADELLNORWW	Wonderwall
ADELLNTUUY	undulately
ADELLOOTTT	allotted to
ADELMMOPSS	plasmodesm
ADELMNOPRT	trampled on
ADELNNNOOY	one and only
ADELNNOOOR	Lorna Doone
ADELNNPRTU	underplant
ADELNORSSU	slanderous
ADELNRSTUW	wanderlust
ADELOPSTTU	postulated
ADELORSTUU	adulterous
ADELPQRTUU	quadruplet
ADELPQRUUX	quadruplex
ADELRSTWWY	westwardly
ADEMMMNORU	memorandum
ADEMMRRSSU	mass murder
ADEMNNORSS	randomness
ADEMNNORST	adornments
ADEMNOORUV	move around
ADEMNOOTUW	amount owed
ADEMNORSSU	mess around
ADEMNORSTW	downstream
ADEMNRRSSV	Mrs Danvers
ADENNOORSU	nose around
ADENNOPTTU	put an end to
ADENNORRRU	roadrunner
ADENNPRSTU	underpants
ADENOORTUV	over and out
ADENOPPRUV	unapproved
ADENOPRSST	transposed
ADENOPRSTV	Van der Post
ADENORRSWY	Roy Andrews
ADENORRTUY	ready to run
ADENPRRSUW	under wraps
ADENPRSSUW	upwardness
ADENRRSSTW	sternwards
ADEOOPPRSW	soap powder
ADEOPRRSTT	prostrated
ADEORRSTTW	Rod Stewart
ADFFGINORW	warding off
ADFFHLLOOS	flash flood
ADFFILNSTU	find faults
ADFGHHORTU	hard-fought
ADFGHORRTU	rough-draft
ADFGIILRRY	girl Friday ❑
ADFGIIOPRT	dig a pit for
ADFGILMNTU	fling mud at
ADFGILMOOY	good family
ADFGILOORY	fairly good
ADFGIMNRTU	grand Mufti
ADFGINORRW	forwarding
ADFGMNOOOW	woman of God
ADFGNOOORT	go to and fro
ADFHILRSWY	dwarfishly
ADFHINNORU	four-in-hand
ADFHLOOSTT	hold fast to
ADFHNOORST	and so forth
ADFIIILPTT	Fittipaldi
ADFIIKMNRU	fair dinkum
ADFIILLTUV	vital fluid
ADFIILQSUY	disqualify
ADFIIOSSTU	fastidious
ADFIISSSTY	dissatisfy
ADFIKNOOTW	two of a kind
ADFILLMNOY	manifoldly
ADFILOSTTU	studio flat
ADFIMNNOOT	not of a mind
ADFIMNOOST	Fats Domino
ADFINNOOTU	foundation
ADFINNORST	stand in for
ADFINNORSU	infrasound
ADFINRRTTU	turn adrift
ADFLLNNOOW	fall down on
ADFLLNOOPT	plot of land
ADFLNOOORU	fool around
ADFNOORSSZ	sforzandos
ADFNOPRSTU	stand up for
ADFNORRSTW	frontwards
ADFOORRSWW	war of words
ADFOPRRTUW	put forward

ADGGGINNOR	dragging on
ADGGHINOOT	a good thing
ADGGHIRRTU	right guard
ADGGINNOOR	gadrooning
ADGGINNORU	gain ground
ADGHHILNOW	high and low
ADGHHIORTW	go hard with
ADGHIINRSS	disgarnish
ADGHIMNOPP	hopping mad
ADGHINNOTU	handing out
	handing-out
ADGHINNOTY	do anything
ADGHINNPRS	handspring
ADGHINRRTW	right-drawn
ADGHIRRSTW	rightwards
ADGHIRSTTU	distraught
ADGHLLMNPY	lymph gland
ADGHLMOOST	Thomas Gold
ADGIIILMNO	Modigliani
ADGIIKNNPP	kidnapping
ADGIILMNOU	gadolinium
ADGIILMNRY	admiringly
ADGIIMNNOT	dominating
ADGIINNPRW	drawing-pin
ADGIINOOOZ	zoogonidia
ADGIINPRTW	writing-pad
ADGIKNORWY	working day
ADGILLNNOS	Long Island
ADGILLNRWY	drawlingly
ADGILLNYZZ	dazzlingly
ADGILLOPRW	grow pallid
ADGILLOPRY	prodigally
ADGILMNSTU	sling mud at
ADGILNNORT	Darlington
ADGILNNTUU	undulating
ADGILNOSSS	glissandos
ADGILOOORS	good sailor
ADGIMMNORS	gormandism
ADGIMNOSTY	nystagmoid
ADGINNOOTU	go in and out
ADGINNOSTU	astounding
ADGINNPSTU	upstanding
ADGINOOPRT	in good part
ADGINORTUW	drawing out
ADGINPRRSX	grands prix
ADGINRRSTW	drawstring
ADGIORSSWW	grass widow
ADGJNORRRU	grand juror
ADGLNNOPRU	groundplan
ADGLNOPRUY	playground
ADGLNOTUUY	young adult
ADGNOPSTUW	wasp-tongu'd
ADHHJNOORW	John Howard
ADHHMOOOST	Thomas Hood
ADHHNOSTTU	thousandth
ADHHOPRTYY	hydropathy
ADHIIKKNNT	kith and kin
ADHIILMNOT	Midlothian
ADHIIMMNPS	midshipman
ADHIIMNSST	hit and miss
	hit-and-miss
ADHIIMSTTU	humidistat
ADHIINNSTU	Hindustani
ADHIKLNOTU	think aloud
ADHILLNOPY	hold in play
ADHILLNOSY	Holy Island
ADHILLPRUW	uphillward
ADHILNOSTU	outlandish
ADHILOOPRS	drosophila
ADHIMNORSY	disharmony
ADHINNOOOT	nationhood
ADHINOOPRT	anthropoid
ADHINOOPSU	diaphonous
ADHINOPSTU	Diophantus
ADHINOSSWW	sash window
	window sash
ADHINSTUWY	Whit Sunday
	Whitsunday
ADHIOPRSST	rhapsodist
ADHIPRRTTY	third party
ADHIRRRTYY	Dirty Harry
ADHJLNNOOT	John Dalton
ADHLMOORST	Thomas Lord
ADHLNOPSSW	splash down
	splashdown
ADHMORTTUW	throw mud at
ADHNOOPRSU	shop around
ADHNOPRSUU	push around
ADHNORRSTW	northwards
ADHNORSTWW	Wandsworth
ADHOORRTWY	roadworthy
ADHORSSTUW	southwards
ADIIILMRSS	dissimilar
ADIIILNOSV	divisional
ADIIILNTVY	invalidity
ADIIINNOTV	divination
ADIILLORTY	dilatorily
ADIILMOPRR	primordial
ADIILNOOTZ	idolizaton
ADIILNORRY	ordinarily
ADIILNOSSU	sinusoidal
ADIILNRSTU	industrial
ADIILOQRTU	liquidator
ADIILORRWW	World War II
ADIILORSTY	solidarity
ADIILQSTUY	squalidity
ADIIMMMOTU	ommatidium
ADIIMNNNOO	anno Domini ❑
ADIIMNNOOT	admonition
	domination
ADIIMORTUU	auditorium
ADIIMQRUUV	quadrivium
ADIINNNOTU	inundation
ADIINNOORT	ordination
ADIINNORRY	in ordinary
ADIINOPPST	disappoint
ADIINOPSSS	dispassion
ADIINORSTT	traditions
ADIINORTVY	divinatory
ADIINOSSSU	dissuasion
ADIKLLLTWY	talk wildly
ADIKLNORTZ	Karl Dönitz

ADIKMORSTT	ditto marks	AEEEFFKNOR	offer a knee
ADILLLOSYY	disloyally	AEEEFGILNR	Generalife
ADILLMNORU	mill around	AEEEFHLSTT	false teeth
ADILLMNOTT	Matt Dillon	AEEEFHPRSU	refuse-heap
ADILLNNOST	still and on	AEEEFHRRTT	thereafter
ADILLNSSTT	stand still	AEEEFHRRTW	whereafter
	standstill	AEEEFINRTZ	antifreeze
ADILLOSTYY	disloyalty	AEEEFKMRRT	free-market
ADILMMNNOO	Moominland	AEEEFLLNST	fenestella
ADILMMOPSU	plasmodium	AEEEFLMNSS	femaleness
	sodium lamp	AEEEFLMPRS	free sample
ADILMNNOTY	dominantly	AEEEFLNOOZ	Zeno of Elea
ADILMNOOTU	modulation	AEEEFNRRST	transferee
ADILMORTUY	modularity	AEEEFNRSTT	fenestrate
ADILNNNOOT	Anton Dolin	AEEEGGHLOR	George Hale
ADILNNOOTU	nodulation	AEEEGGMNNT	engagement
ADILNNOTUU	undulation	AEEEGHINNT	heat engine
ADILNOPSUU	paludinous	AEEEGHNRRT	green earth
ADILNRSTTU	stridulant	AEEEGILNRS	generalise
ADILOORSTU	idolatrous	AEEEGILNRZ	generalize
ADILOPRSTY	Daily Sport	AEEEGILNSV	evangelise
ADILOPRTUY	plauditory	AEEEGILNUV	eigenvalue
ADIMNOORTY	admonitory	AEEEGILNVZ	evangelize
ADIMNRRTUV	Trivandrum	AEEEGINNRT	ingenerate
ADIMORSTUU	sudatorium	AEEEGINRTV	generative
ADINNOPSTT	standpoint	AEEEGITTVV	vegetative
ADINNOSSTU	ins and outs	AEEEGKLOPR	goalkeeper
	outs and ins	AEEEGLMNRT	regalement
ADINNOSTTW	stand to win	AEEEGLSSSY	eyeglasses
ADINOOPRST	adsorption	AEEEGMNNTV	avengement
ADINOPRSSU	piss around	AEEEGMNNTY	enemy agent
ADINORSSTW	downstairs	AEEEGMNRSS	meagreness
ADIORSSSTU	disastrous	AEEEGMRRST	agree terms
ADIORSSSUY	dissuasory	AEEEGNNRTV	nerve agent
ADJLOPRTUU	plat du jour	AEEEGNPPRR	green paper
ADKLLLOTUY	talk loudly	AEEEGNRVWY	wave energy
ADKLNOOTTW	talk down to	AEEEHHINST	heathenise
ADLLLNNOOW	London Wall	AEEEHHINTZ	heathenize
ADLLNORRUY	rally round	AEEEHHISTV	the heavies
ADLMOOORSU	malodorous	AEEEHHLTTW	at the wheel
ADLNOORRSS	Ronald Ross	AEEEHIRSTW	weatherise
ADLNORSTUU	ultrasound	AEEEHIRTWZ	weatherize
ADLNORTUUY	undulatory	AEEEHLLRTY	ethereally
ADLNORTUWY	untowardly	AEEEHLRTWW	water-wheel
ADMNNOORSU	monandrous	AEEEHMPRTT	heptameter
ADMNORRSUW	swarm round	AEEEHMSSTT	metatheses
ADMPRSSTUW	draw stumps	AEEEHNNNPT	nepenthean
ADNNOORRWW	narrow down	AEEEHNNRTT	thereanent
ADNNORRTUU	turn around	AEEEHNNSTV	heaven-sent
	turnaround	AEEEHNORTY	honeyeater
ADNOOORRTU	root around		honey-eater
ADNOOSTUYY	you don't say!	AEEEHORRUY	here you are
ADNOPSSTUY	Sunday Post	AEEEHRSTTW	sweetheart
AEEEEGKMPR	gamekeeper	AEEEIILRRS	earlierise
AEEEEGKPRT	gatekeeper	AEEEIILRRZ	earlierize
AEEEEGNRRT	regenerate	AEEEIIPPRT	peripeteia
AEEEEHKLTT	eat the leek	AEEEILLMRV	à merveille
AEEEEHRTWY	weather eye	AEEEILLMSS	Leslie Ames
AEEEENRTTX	exenterate	AEEEILNRST	eternalise
AEEEFFGLRU	effleurage	AEEEILNRTV	interleave
AEEEFFIMNT	effeminate	AEEEILNRTZ	eternalize

AEEEILNSSY	easily seen
AEEEIMNRTT	intemerate
AEEEIMNSTV	Vietnamese
AEEEIMPRTV	permeative
AEEEINNNTV	antivenene
AEEEINRSTT	entreaties
AEEEINRTTV	inveterate
AEEEINRTVV	enervative
AEEEINRTVW	interweave
AEEEIPRTVY	Private Eye
	private eye
AEEEIRRVVW	rave review
AEEEJJMSSS	Jesse James
AEEEJKRRRT	tear-jerker
AEEEJMNRRV	Jan Vermeer
AEEEJNRTUV	rejuvenate
AEEEKLNUWY	Lee Kuan Yew
AEEEKMRRSV	verse-maker
AEEEKPSSTW	sweepstake
AEEELLLRTT	tale-teller
AEEELLRTVW	water level
AEEELLSSTT	tessellate
AEEELMMNRT	Emmentaler
AEEELMNNTT	lentamente
	tenemental
AEEELMNRTT	terne metal
AEEELMNRTY	elementary
AEEELNNOSY	anyone else
AEEELPRRUV	Paul Revere
AEEEMMNORT	anemometer
AEEEMNOPSS	open sesame
AEEEMNPRTT	pentameter
AEEEMNRRTU	remunerate
AEEEMRRTTT	tetrameter
AEEEMRSTTW	watersmeet
AEEENPRSST	Sea Serpent
	sea serpent
AEEENRSSSV	averseness
AEEEOPRRST	patereroes
AEEEPPRRST	Peter Pears
AEEEPPRRTT	perpetrate
AEEEPPRTTU	perpetuate
AEEERRSTYY	yesteryear
AEEERSSTTY	Easy Street
	easy street
AEEFFHORRT	forefather
AEEFFLLORR	free-for-all
AEEFFLSTUX	exsufflate
AEEFFMORSU	measure off
AEEFFORRST	reafforest
AEEFGGHIRT	freightage
AEEFGHINRT	feathering
AEEFGHORRT	foregather
AEEFGILPRS	persiflage
AEEFGILRRS	Serge Lifar
AEEFGINORW	orange-wife
AEEFGLPRSU	presageful
AEEFHHINRT	Fahrenheit
AEEFHIKLRT	fatherlike
AEEFHIRSTX	the fair sex
AEEFHIRTTW	water thief
AEEFHLLORT	hear tell of
AEEFHLOPPR	leaf-hopper
AEEFHLRSST	fatherless
AEEFHMORTT	fathometer
AEEFHORRTW	whore after
AEEFHPRSTT	stepfather
AEEFHRRSTW	freshwater
AEEFIILLNR	in real life
AEEFIIRRRS	fire-raiser
AEEFIJORRZ	Joe Frazier
AEEFIKKNST	steak knife
AEEFIKLNPT	knife pleat
AEEFIKNPPR	paper-knife
AEEFIKNRSS	freakiness
AEEFILMRTY	family tree
AEEFILNORR	free on rail
AEEFILNRST	fenestrial
AEEFILOPRT	perfoliate
AEEFILPRSS	self-praise
AEEFINRRST	fraternise
AEEFINRRTZ	fraternize
AEEFINRSTU	tea infuser
AEEFKLNOSS	ask oneself
AEEFKMORSU	make sure of
AEEFKNOOTT	take note of
AEEFLLMORS	false morel
AEEFLLNNOT	fontanelle
AEEFLLNNSS	fallenness
AEEFLLNRUY	funereally
AEEFLLRSSY	fearlessly
AEEFLMOPRX	for example
AEEFLMORSY	fearsomely
AEEFLOPRSV	prove false
AEEFNNSSSU	unsafeness
AEEFOPPRRR	prepare for
AEEGGHHNTT	get the hang
AEEGGHINRS	Hans Geiger
AEEGGHOPRR	geographer
AEEGGIKRRY	Reggie Kray
AEEGGINRRS	grangerise
AEEGGINRRZ	grangerize
AEEGGINTTV	vegetating
AEEGGIRSSV	aggressive
AEEGGJORRY	Joe Gargery
AEEGGNNOVW	Geneva gown
AEEGHIIINP	Iphigeneia
AEEGHIILMP	hemiplegia
AEEGHIIRTV	give the air
AEEGHIJLNT	Janet Leigh
AEEGHILLTV	The Village
AEEGHILNRT	leathering
AEEGHILNSS	Singhalese
AEEGHILRST	lethargise
AEEGHILRTW	Large White
AEEGHILRTZ	lethargize
AEEGHINNRT	heartening
AEEGHINRRS	rehearsing
AEEGHINRTW	weathering
AEEGHINSTT	seeing that
AEEGHIRTTW	great white
AEEGHKNNRS	greenshank

AEEGHLLLNS	hell's angel
AEEGHLLSTU	The Seagull
AEEGHLMORT	geothermal
AEEGHLNOWW	wagon wheel
AEEGHLNSTU	The Angelus
AEEGHLNTVW	wavelength
AEEGHLORTT	altogether
AEEGHLPRTY	telegraphy
AEEGHMNORT	thereamong
AEEGHMORTY	game theory
	heterogamy
AEEGHNOSTU	house agent
AEEGHSSTUV	have guests
AEEGIILLLS	illegalise
AEEGIILLLZ	illegalize
AEEGIILLNV	villeinage
AEEGIILMTT	legitimate
AEEGIILNST	gelatinise
AEEGIILNTZ	gelatinize
AEEGIIMNNT	ingeminate
AEEGIIMNST	enigmatise
AEEGIIMNTZ	enigmatize
AEEGIJLMNN	Jan Leeming
AEEGIJNNRS	Jean Ingres
AEEGIKNRST	tiger snake
AEEGIKORTV	give or take
AEEGILLMNN	enamelling
AEEGILLORS	allegorise
AEEGILLORZ	allegorize
AEEGILMNRR	malingerer
AEEGILMNRT	regimental
AEEGILMNSV	evangelism □
AEEGILNORT	regelation
	relegation
AEEGILNRST	generalist
AEEGILNRTY	generality
AEEGILNSTV	evangelist □
AEEGILNTVY	negatively
AEEGILOSTY	lay siege to
AEEGILRRSU	regularise
AEEGILRRUZ	regularize
AEEGILRTUV	regulative
AEEGIMNOTV	give name to
AEEGIMNPRT	impregnate
AEEGIMNRTZ	magnetizer
AEEGIMNSTU	mutagenise
AEEGIMNTUZ	mutagenize
AEEGIMRRTU	marguerite
AEEGIMRRTV	gravimeter
AEEGINNNSU	ensanguine
AEEGINNORT	generation
	renegation
AEEGINNRRT	interregna
AEEGINNRST	Tangerines
AEEGINNRTT	entreating
AEEGINNRTV	enervating
AEEGINORRZ	reorganize
AEEGINORTV	overeating
AEEGINOTTV	vegetation
AEEGINPRRS	Paris green
	Paris-green
AEEGINPRSY	panegyrise
AEEGINPRYZ	panegyrize
AEEGINRRSY	ear syringe
AEEGINRSSS	greasiness
AEEGIPPRRT	paper tiger
AEEGIPRRTW	gripe-water
AEEGKLMNOR	make longer
AEEGKORRWW	grow weaker
AEEGLLNOSS	Los Angeles
AEEGLLORTT	allegretto
AEEGLLSTWY	galley-west
AEEGLMOPSU	plaguesome
AEEGLMRRSW	leg-warmers
AEEGLNORST	estrangelo
AEEGLNORTU	outgeneral
AEEGLNORTV	graveolent
AEEGLORTUV	travelogue
AEEGLRSUUX	sexual urge
AEEGMNNOOS	on one's game
AEEGMNNOST	mangosteen
AEEGMNOOTV	get a move on
AEEGMNRSTY	segmentary
AEEGMORRST	stereogram
AEEGMPRTUU	up a gumtree
AEEGMPSTTU	get up steam
AEEGMRRTTY	grey matter
AEEGNNORSS	sense organ
	sense-organ
AEEGNOOPRS	go on a spree
AEEGNOPRSW	spongeware
AEEGNOPSST	set a sponge
AEEGNORRRV	Range Rover®
AEEGNORSSU	sea surgeon
AEEGNORSTV	gravestone
AEEGNOSTWY	get one's way
AEEGNPRRTY	Green Party
	green party
AEEGNPRSSS	passengers
AEEGNPRSST	press agent
AEEGOORSSV	go overseas
AEEGOPRSSU	repoussage
AEEGPRRTUX	expurgater
AEEHHHINST	heathenish
AEEHHILTWW	white whale
AEEHHIMNST	heathenism
AEEHHIMSST	The Messiah
AEEHHJNNNO	John Heenan
AEEHHKNPSS	sheepshank
AEEHHLMSTU	methuselah □
AEEHHLOTWW	wholewheat
AEEHHNOOPV	have no hope
AEEHHNORVX	Enver Hoxha
AEEHHPSSTU	Hephaestus
AEEHIILLPT	epithelial
AEEHIINVVW	have in view
AEEHIKLMNW	minke whale
AEEHIKLNNP	enkephalin
AEEHILLMTT	all the time
AEEHILMRST	thermalise
AEEHILMRSZ	Alzheimer's
AEEHILMRTZ	thermalize

AEEHILMTTW	white metal
AEEHILNOVY	lie heavy on
AEEHILPPRR	peripheral
AEEHILPRST	sphalerite
AEEHILPRTW	pearl white
AEEHILRTTT	triathlete
AEEHILSTVW	white slave
AEEHIMSSTT	metathesis
AEEHIMSTTU	The Timaeus
AEEHINNPRT	pantherine
AEEHINPRST	interphase
AEEHINPSTT	stephanite
AEEHINQTTU	the antique
AEEHINRSST	earthiness
	heartiness
AEEHINSSTT	antitheses
AEEHIOPRST	rosehip tea
AEEHIPPRRS	periphrase
AEEHIPPRTW	white paper
AEEHIQTTUW	equate with
AEEHIRSTTW	where it's at
AEEHIRTTWW	white water
AEEHISTUVX	exhaustive
AEEHJMNRSY	Henry James
AEEHKLLOTW	walk to heel
AEEHKLOSWY	keyhole saw
AEEHKMMORT	home market
AEEHKNSTTU	take the sun
AEEHKORSTT	heatstroke
AEEHKORSTV	Tereshkova
AEEHKOSSTU	steakhouse
AEEHLLLPRS	pearl-shell
AEEHLLLSWY	Wesley Hall
AEEHLLMORT	all the more
AEEHLLORSW	wholesaler
AEEHLMNNOP	phenomenal
AEEHLMPRSW	sperm whale
AEEHLNORTT	on the alert
AEEHLNOSTT	on the slate
AEEHLNPSTT	The Planets
AEEHLNRSST	lesser than
AEEHLNRSTT	nettlerash
AEEHLOPSTT	at the slope
AEEHLOSTWY	lose the way
AEEHLPPRUZ	Purple Haze
AEEHLPPSSS	she's apples
AEEHLRSSTW	Walter Hess
AEEHLRSTTX	tax shelter
AEEHLRSTTY	Hattersley
AEEHMNNSSU	humaneness
AEEHMNOORR	menorrhoea
AEEHMNOPRT	Promethean
AEEHMNOSTT	not the same
AEEHMNPTTY	Pat Metheny
AEEHMOPRST	atmosphere
AEEHMORRTV	earthmover
AEEHMORSUX	hexamerous
AEEHNNOORT	one another
AEEHNNOPSX	Xenophanes
AEEHNNPRSY	penny share
AEEHNOOPRR	harpooneer
AEEHNOPTWY	open the way
AEEHNORSSS	hoarseness
AEEHNOSSST	The Seasons
AEEHNPPTVY	happy event
AEEHNRSTTV	The Servant
AEEHOOPRSU	opera house
AEEHOOPSST	apotheoses
AEEHORRTVW	or whatever
AEEHORSTUW	Waterhouse
AEEHORSTVW	whatsoever
AEEHORTTUW	weather out
AEEHORTTXY	heterotaxy
AEEHORTVWY	over the way
AEEHPRRSTT	three-parts
AEEHPRSTXY	sex therapy
AEEIIKNRST	keratinise
AEEIIKNRTZ	keratinize
AEEIILLRST	literalise
AEEIILLRTT	illiterate
AEEIILLRTZ	literalize
AEEIILMNRS	mineralise
AEEIILMNRZ	mineralize
AEEIILNNPR	en plein air
AEEIILNSTT	lie in state
AEEIILRSTV	relativise
AEEIILRTVZ	relativize
	revitalize
AEEIIMNNST	inseminate
AEEIIMNSTT	anti-semite
AEEIIMPRTV	imperative
AEEIINNPRS	Parisienne
AEEIINPRSS	Persianise
AEEIINPRSZ	Persianize
AEEIIPRSST	patisserie
AEEIJKNNRS	Jenkin's Ear
AEEIJLLMNT	Jean Millet
AEEIJNNORR	Jean Renoir
AEEIJOPRTV	pejorative
AEEIKKMSST	Kiss Me Kate
AEEIKKRSTT	take strike
AEEIKLLMVY	make lively
AEEIKLNSSW	weakliness
AEEIKMMPRU	make impure
AEEIKMNNRR	reim-kennar
AEEIKNNSSS	sneakiness
AEEIKNRRSV	Snake River
AEEIKRRSTW	water-skier
AEEILLLLNV	villanelle
AEEILLMRSS	Marseilles
AEEILLNTVV	inlet valve
AEEILLPSTT	stipellate
AEEILLRSSV	Versailles
AEEILLRTVY	relatively
AEEILLSSTT	satellites
AEEILLSTUV	televisual
AEEILMMNPT	impalement
AEEILMNNOS	Liam Neeson
AEEILMNNST	lineaments
AEEILMNNTT	entailment
AEEILMNORS	neorealism
AEEILMNPRT	planimeter

AEEILMNRST	streamline
AEEILMNSSS	measliness
AEEILMORRS	remoralise
AEEILMORRZ	remoralize
AEEILMPSST	metalepsis
AEEILMQRSU	square mile
AEEILNNNPY	penny-a-line
AEEILNNPST	septennial
AEEILNNRST	real tennis
AEEILNNSTT	sentential
AEEILNNTTU	lieutenant
AEEILNOPRT	peritoneal
AEEILNORST	neorealist
AEEILNORTV	revelation ◻
AEEILNPRSS	pearliness
AEEILNQSTU	sequential
AEEILNQTUV	equivalent
AEEILNRRTV	irrelevant
AEEILNRSTU	neutralise
AEEILNRTUZ	neutralize
AEEILNSSST	essentials
AEEILNSSSU	sensualise
AEEILNSSSZ	sleaziness
AEEILNSSUZ	sensualize
AEEILOPRST	periosteal
AEEILORRSV	revalorise
AEEILORRVZ	revalorize
AEEILPRRRV	Pearl River
AEEILPRRTV	River Plate
AEEILPRSSY	erysipelas
AEEILPRSTX	Praxiteles
AEEILRRTTU	literature
AEEIMMRSSU	mismeasure
AEEIMNNPRT	pine marten
AEEIMNNRTT	retainment
AEEIMNNRTU	innumerate
AEEIMNOPRT	permeation
AEEIMNORSY	raise money
AEEIMNORTT	marionette
AEEIMNOSTT	maisonette
AEEIMNRRTU	remain true
AEEIMNRSSS	smeariness
AEEIMNSSST	steaminess
AEEIMORRTV	variometer
AEEIMQRSUV	semiquaver
AEEINNNSST	innateness
AEEINNNTVY	in any event
AEEINNORTV	enervation
	veneration
AEEINNOTTT	Antoinette
AEEINNRTUV	aventurine
AEEINNSSSU	uneasiness
AEEINNSSTV	nativeness
AEEINOPTTT	potentiate
AEEINPRSTU	resupinate
AEEINQRSTU	equestrian
AEEINQSSSU	queasiness
AEEINRRRST	restrainer
AEEINRRTTV	travertine
AEEINRRTVY	veterinary
AEEINRSSTW	wateriness
AEEINRSTTT	interstate
AEEINRVWYY	in every way
AEEIOPRRSV	overpraise
AEEIPPRVWY	pay-per-view
AEEIPRSSTT	striptease
AEEIPRSSTU	pasteurise
AEEIPRSSUV	persuasive
AEEIPRSTUZ	pasteurize
AEEIPRTTUV	reputative
	vituperate
AEEIQRSSUW	squarewise
AEEIRRTTWY	Terry Waite
AEEJJLMOSU	James Joule
AEEJLNORSU	journalese
AEEKLLMNOY	Molly Keane
AEEKLLMNUW	make unwell
AEEKLMOOTV	make love to
AEEKLNNUVW	uneven walk
AEEKLOPRRW	rope-walker
AEEKMMNORY	money-maker
AEEKMMNOTW	weak moment
AEEKMMNPRY	kempery-man
AEEKMMRRRY	merrymaker
AEEKMNOPRT	open market
AEEKMPRRTV	verkrampte
AEEKMRSTTT	test-market
AEELLLSTTU	stellulate
AEELLLSTTY	stellately
AEELLMMRRT	trammeller
AEELLMNOTV	malevolent
AEELLMNQRU	man-queller
AEELLMNRTU	allurement
AEELLMNSSY	namelessly
AEELLNOTTY	Lotte Lenya
AEELLNPRST	all-present
AEELLNRTVY	relevantly
AEELLNRTXY	externally
AEELLNTUVY	eventually
AEELLORTTY	tea trolley
AEELLOTTTY	teetotally
AEELLQRRRU	quarreller
AEELLRRSTV	travellers
AEELLRSTTW	Wall Street
AEELMNORSS	moral sense
AEELMNORTW	watermelon
AEELMOPPSS	ampelopses
AEELMOPSTT	palmettoes
AEELMORTTV	voltameter
AEELMPRSTT	streetlamp
AEELMRSSST	masterless
AEELMRSWYY	Mary Wesley
AEELNNORSW	New Orleans
AEELNNQSTU	lansquenet
AEELNOORYZ	ozone layer
AEELNOPSSW	weaponless
AEELNORTTV	relevant to
AEELNPRSST	parentless
AEELNPRSTT	street plan
AEELNPRTTW	wentletrap
AEELOPSSTT	salopettes
AEELORRTVV	travel over

AEELORRTVY	revelatory
AEELORSTTU	lotus-eater
AEELRRRVYY	very rarely
AEELRRSTUW	lustreware
AEEMMNOSSW	Mason Weems
AEEMNNOOST	to one's name
AEEMNNOPRS	praenomens
AEEMNNORRT	ornamenter
AEEMNNORUV	mavourneen
AEEMNNPRTT	entrapment
AEEMNNRSST	Stresemann
AEEMNNTTTU	attunement
AEEMNOPPRR	proper name
AEEMNOPPRY	paper money
AEEMNOQRSU	Romanesque
AEEMNORRTU	enumerator
AEEMNORRUV	manoeuvrer
AEEMNORSST	sarmentose
	sea monster
AEEMNORSUV	manoeuvres
AEEMNPPRST	sapperment
AEEMNPPRTY	prepayment
AEEMNRSTTU	menstruate
AEEMNSSSST	assessment
AEEMOORTTT	tree tomato
AEEMORRSTV	overmaster
AEEMORSSTU	Mateus Rosé
AEEMORSTUU	measure out
	outmeasure
AEEMPRRSTY	Mary Peters
AEEMRSSSST	seamstress
AEENNNRTTW	new entrant
AEENNOOPSS	open season
AEENNOPRSW	a new person
AEENNORSST	ornateness
AEENNPSSTT	patentness
AEENOPQSSU	opaqueness
AEENOPRRTT	penetrator
AEENOPRRTU	neuroptera
AEENOPRSUV	supernovae
AEENORSTUX	extraneous
AEENPPRSSW	newspapers
AEENPPRSTT	step-parent
AEENPRSSSS	sparseness
AEENQRSSSU	squareness
AEENRRSSTV	transverse
AEENRRSTUU	untreasure
AEENSSSTTU	astuteness
AEENSSTTTU	sustentate
AEEOPPRRST	praeposter
AEEOPRRTWW	water power
AEEORRTTWW	water tower
AEEPRRSSST	trespasser
AEEQSSTTUU	statuesque
AEESSSSTUX	East Sussex
AEFFFGIRST	Steffi Graf
AEFFFIRSTU	suffer a fit
AEFFGHINRT	affrighten
AEFFGINORT	fit of anger
AEFFHKMORT	off the mark
AEFFHLLOTW	off the wall
	off-the-wall
AEFFIKLLOW	walk of life
AEFFILNSTU	insufflate
AEFFLLNTUY	affluently
AEFFLMOOPR	flameproof
AEFFLNORST	false front
AEFFNRSSTU	staff nurse
AEFFOOSTTU	affettuoso
AEFGHIILNV	having life
AEFGHIIRRT	air freight
AEFGHIKLTT	take flight
AEFGHIKRTT	take fright
AEFGHILLPT	fill the gap
AEFGHILNRS	angler fish
AEFGHINRRW	wharfinger
AEFGHNOORT	gate of horn
AEFGIILLOR	florilegia
AEFGIILMNN	Ian Fleming
AEFGIILNNR	fingernail
AEFGIILNSV	life-saving
AEFGIINNRR	refraining
AEFGIINSTU	ignes fatui
AEFGIIOPVW	View of a Pig
AEFGIIRTUV	figurative
AEFGIKMNRR	fingermark
AEFGILLNPY	flying leap
AEFGILMNNU	meaningful
AEFGILMNOS	flamingoes
AEFGILNNTT	flattening
AEFGILNOUW	guinea fowl
AEFGILNRTT	flattering
AEFGILOPRT	profligate
AEFGIPRRTU	grapefruit
AEFGIRRRSY	Grey friars
	Greyfriars
AEFGLLRTUY	gratefully
AEFGLMRSTU	Gulf Stream
AEFGLNRTUU	ungrateful
AEFGLSSTTU	Gulf States
AEFGORRTTW	grow fatter
AEFHHLNRTU	half-hunter
AEFHHLORTY	Holy Father
AEFHIIRRTW	White Friar
	white friar
AEFHIKLRSY	freakishly
AEFHILLORT	fall heir to
AEFHILNRTT	flint-heart
AEFHILNSSS	flashiness
AEFHILNSSY	Hessian fly
AEFHILRSST	half-sister
AEFHIMMNST	famishment
AEFHINOPTY	in the pay of
AEFHINOTWY	in the way of
AEFHLLMSUY	shamefully
AEFHLLNNOS	half nelson
AEFHLMNTTW	twelfth man
AEFHLMOPRT	Ampleforth
AEFHLMOSST	fathomless
AEFHOOPSTU	out of phase
	out of shape
AEFHORRTTU	fourth-rate

AEFHRRSSTT	fresh start
AEFIIINNTT	infinitate
AEFIILNOTU	unifoliate
AEFIILNRTT	infiltrate
AEFIILORTT	trifoliate
AEFIIMNNOS	infamonise
AEFIIMNNOZ	infamonize
AEFIINQRTU	quantifier
AEFIINSSTU	fustianise
AEFIINSTUZ	fustianize
AEFIKLNNRZ	Franz Kline
AEFIKMOSUY	if you ask me
AEFIKNOPRS	fair-spoken
AEFILLLNOV	fall in love
AEFILLMORT	for all time
AEFILLNNRY	infernally
AEFILLNNUZ	influenzal
AEFILLRTVY	rift valley
AEFILLRUWY	wearifully
AEFILMNSTY	manifestly
AEFILMORRT	formaliter
AEFILMRTTU	left atrium
AEFILNNRTV	ventral fin
AEFILNORTU	fluorinate
AEFILNPRTU	turnip flea
AEFILNSSTU	faultiness
AEFILOQRTU	quatrefoil
AEFILPQRUY	pre-qualify
AEFIMNOSST	manifestos
AEFINNRSSU	unfairness
AEFINOOPRT	fortepiano
	pianoforte
AEFINOPRTT	point after
AEFINORRST	rainforest
AEFINORTTU	refutation
AEFINRRTTY	fraternity
AEFIORRSUU	auriferous
AEFKLLOOTT	take toll of
AEFKLNORSY	forsakenly
AEFKLNOSSW	snowflakes
AEFKLOORSW	sale of work
AEFKOPPRSU	speak up for
AEFLLLOOSV	of all loves
AEFLLLOPWY	playfellow
AEFLLLORWW	wallflower
AEFLLLPTTU	at full pelt
AEFLLLSSWY	flawlessly
AEFLLNSSUW	lawfulness
AEFLLOORRY	ferro-alloy
AEFLLPSUUY	pausefully
AEFLLSTTUY	tastefully
AEFLLSTUWY	wastefully
AEFLMNNSSU	manfulness
AEFLNOOSTT	float-stone
AEFLNORTUY	Fauntleroy
AEFLNOTTTU	flatten out
AEFLNRSSTU	artfulness
AEFMMNOORT	for a moment
AEFMNORRTU	from nature
AEFMNOSSSU	famousness
AEFMOPRRST	permafrost
AEFNORRRST	transferor
AEFNORRTTW	waterfront
AEFNRRSSTU	transfuser
AEFOOPRRTW	waterproof
AEFOOQRSTU	square foot
AEFOQRRSUU	four-square
AEGGGILNNY	engagingly
AEGGGINRST	staggering
AEGGGINRSW	swaggering
AEGGHHIINT	gain height
AEGGHHIMNR	High German
AEGGHHLNOU	Lough Neagh
AEGGHIINTW	gain weight
AEGGHILNRT	right angle
	right-angle
AEGGHINSSS	shagginess
AEGGHIORST	The Gorgias
AEGGIILMPR	pilgrimage
AEGGIILNVW	living wage
AEGGILNRTU	regulating
AEGGINNPRS	gingersnap
AEGGINNRST	estranging
AEGGINORSS	aggression
AEGGINQSSU	quagginess
AEGGIORRSU	gregarious
AEGGJNRTUU	juggernaut
AEGGLORRRW	grow larger
AEGGMNNORR	Greg Norman
AEGGNNORSU	gangrenous
AEGHHHINRT	higher than
AEGHHHLLSU	Hughes Hall
AEGHHILLLS	shillelagh
AEGHHILOPR	heliograph
AEGHHILRTW	right whale
AEGHHILRUU	Hugh Laurie
AEGHHINOSS	high season
AEGHHINRST	hear things
AEGHHMOPPT	apophthegm
AEGHIILOST	goliathise
AEGHIILOTZ	goliathize
AEGHIINRSV	vinegarish
AEGHIINSTT	hesitating
AEGHIIPRST	graphitise
AEGHIIPRTZ	graphitize
AEGHIKMMNO	homemaking
AEGHIKMNOS	shoemaking
AEGHIKRRST	tiger shark
AEGHILLLOP	Gallophile
AEGHILMNNS	Englishman
AEGHILMPWY	pigmy whale
AEGHILNOOT	theologian
AEGHILNORW	wholegrain
AEGHILOPRT	light opera
AEGHILPRXY	lexigraphy
AEGHIMMOPR	mimeograph
AEGHINNPPS	happenings
AEGHINNRTU	unearthing
AEGHINNRTV	night-raven
AEGHINPRRS	rephrasing
AEGHINRSSS	garishness
AEGHINRSTT	shattering

	straighten
AEGHINRSTV	harvesting
AEGHINSTUX	exhausting
AEGHIOSTWY	go easy with
AEGHIPRRSY	serigraphy
AEGHIRSTUW	white sugar
AEGHIRTTTW	watertight
AEGHJLLPRY	jellygraph
AEGHLMOOOT	homologate
AEGHLNNOOP	anglophone ❑
AEGHLNOOSU	halogenous
AEGHLNOSTU	tongue-lash
AEGHLNSTWY	lengthways
AEGHLOOORR	logorrhoea
AEGHLOOPRY	oleography
AEGHLOOPTY	hepatology
AEGHLORSTT	larghettos
AEGHLORSUV	overslaugh
AEGHLOSSSU	glasshouse
AEGHMNOOPR	gramophone
AEGHNNOOTW	on the wagon
AEGHNOOORR	gonorrhoea
AEGHNOPRST	stenograph
AEGHNORRST	short-range
AEGHOOPSSU	oesophagus
AEGHOPPSTT	stop the gap
AEGHOPRRXY	xerography
AEGIIILNTV	invigilate
AEGIIIMTTV	mitigative
AEGIIJMNNZ	Jiang Zemin
AEGIILLLTY	illegality
AEGIILMNRT	trigeminal
AEGIILMNST	time signal
AEGIILNNPX	explaining
AEGIILNPRV	prevailing
AEGIILRTTT	glitterati
AEGIIMNNOT	gemination
	not imagine
AEGIIMNORT	emigration
AEGIIMNSTV	negativism
	time-saving
AEGIIMSSTT	stigmatise
AEGIIMSTTZ	stigmatize
AEGIINNRTT	intrigante
AEGIINORTV	invigorate
AEGIINPPST	appetising
AEGIINPPTZ	appetizing
AEGIINSTTV	negativist
AEGIINTTVY	negativity
AEGIIRTTVY	give it a try
AEGIKLMMOR	kilogramme
AEGIKLMNOV	lovemaking
	love-making
	making love
AEGIKLNNSY	sneakingly
AEGIKLNPRY	pearly king
AEGIKLNPSY	speakingly
AEGIKLRSTV	Lagerkvist
AEGIKMNOTT	Tom Keating
AEGIKNOSTW	soaking wet
AEGILLNORY	regionally
AEGILLNPSY	pleasingly
AEGILLNRTV	travelling
AEGILLNRTY	integrally
AEGILLNSTY	stealingly
AEGILLORST	legislator
AEGILMNOOP	monoplegia
AEGILMNORY	mineralogy
AEGILMSTTU	multi-stage
AEGILNNOOT	elongation
AEGILNNOSU	lanuginose
AEGILNNRYY	yearningly
AEGILNNSSS	slanginess
AEGILNNSUY	sanguinely
AEGILNOOSU	oleaginous
AEGILNORTT	relating to
AEGILNORTU	regulation
	urogenital
AEGILNOSTU	gelatinous
AEGILNOTUV	leaving out
	leaving-out
AEGILNPRRT	large print
AEGILNPRST	plastering
AEGILNPRTY	taperingly
AEGILNQSSU	equals sign
AEGILNRSTV	starveling ❑
AEGILNRVWY	waveringly
AEGILNRWYY	wearyingly
AEGILNSSSS	glassiness
AEGILOPRTT	graptolite
AEGILRRTUY	regularity
AEGILRSWWY	lawyer's wig
AEGIMMNRST	stammering
AEGIMMORSS	seismogram
AEGIMNNSST	assignment
AEGIMNOPRS	angiosperm
AEGIMNORSU	gramineous
AEGIMNPRTY	pigmentary
AEGIMNRRST	ringmaster
	ring-master
AEGIMNRSTT	smattering
AEGIMRRTVY	gravimetry
AEGINNNPRT	trepanning
AEGINNORRS	engarrison
AEGINNORST	resonating
AEGINNRSTT	astringent
AEGINNRSTU	sauntering
AEGINNRUVW	unwavering
AEGINNRUWY	unwearying
AEGINOORTT	negotiator
AEGINORTUW	wearing out
AEGINPRSTU	supergiant
AEGINPRSTY	panegyrist
AEGINQRRTU	quartering
AEGINRRSSU	reassuring
AEGINRRSTV	traversing
AEGINRSSSS	grassiness
AEGINRSSSU	sugariness
AEGIRSSTTT	strategist
AEGJLOSUUY	Jealous Guy
AEGKLMMOOY	make gloomy
AEGKLNOSVW	Volkswagen®

AEGKLPRRUU	Paul Kruger
AEGKMNORST	make strong
AEGKMNOSXY	oxygen mask
AEGKMOORTT	go to market
AEGLLLLNNO	Llangollen
AEGLLMRTUY	metallurgy
AEGLLNNPTY	plangently
AEGLLNORSW	swell organ
AEGLLOPRSU	pellagrous
AEGLMNOOOV	avgolemono
AEGLMNOOSY	mosey along
AEGLMOPRTU	promulgate
AEGLMORTTU	malgré tout
AEGLNNPRTY	pregnantly
AEGLNOOPRT	prolongate
AEGLNRRSST	Stranglers
AEGLNSSSSU	sunglasses
AEGLOOOPTW	a peg too low
AEGLOORRST	astrologer
AEGLORRTUY	regulatory
AEGMMOPRRR	programmer
AEGMNOORST	gastronome
AEGMNORTTU	Tantum ergo
AEGNNNPRTU	unpregnant
AEGNOORTXY	oxygenator
AEGNOOSTUU	autogenous
AEGNRRSSST	transgress
AEGNSSSTUU	augustness
AEGNSTUVYY	Yves Tanguy
AEGOORSTUU	outrageous
AEGOPRRSSU	sour grapes
AEGOPRRTUX	expurgator
AEGPRRSSSU	supergrass
AEHHIKMNST	think shame
AEHHILNSTU	helianthus
AEHHIMOTTW	at home with
AEHHINOPRT	hierophant
AEHHINPRST	pantherish
AEHHINRTWY	anywhither
AEHHLNOPTT	heptathlon
AEHHLOOPRS	holophrase
AEHHLOOPRT	poor health
AEHHMOOOPT	homoeopath
AEHHMOOPTY	homeopathy
AEHHNOOPRT	anthophore
AEHHOSTWWY	show the way
AEHHPSSTTU	Hatshepsut
AEHIIKLRTW	wraith-like
AEHIIKMTTW	make it with
AEHIILLLNT	Lilienthal
AEHIILLMNW	Wilhelmina
AEHIILOPRS	Hierapolis
AEHIIMNORS	mashie iron
AEHIIMNSTU	humanities
AEHIIMSTTT	at this time
AEHIINOSTT	hesitation
AEHIINPRTU	up in the air
AEHIINRTWY	in their way
AEHIINSSTT	antithesis
AEHIJNNOPR	John Napier
AEHIKKNOPT	Pinakothek

AEHIKLLLRW	hillwalker
AEHIKLNSSY	sneakishly
AEHIKMRSTV	Vikram Seth
AEHIKNRSSS	rakishness
AEHIKOPPRT	pork-pie hat
AEHIKPTTUW	take up with
AEHILLOPTW	pilot whale
AEHILLSTTY	stealthily
AEHILMNNUY	inhumanely
AEHILMOSSY	haemolysis
AEHILNNOTV	on the anvil
AEHILNOOST	shoot a line
AEHILNORSS	lion's share
AEHILNSSSV	lavishness
AEHILNSTTY	hesitantly
AEHILRSTVY	shrievalty
AEHIMMNORT	hammer into
AEHIMMPRRT	trip hammer
AEHIMMRSTU	rheumatism
AEHIMNNPPS	penmanship
AEHIMNORUU	iure humano
AEHIMNOTUX	exhumation
AEHIMNRSTV	ravishment
AEHIMNSSTU	enthusiasm
AEHIMORSTT	a short time
AEHIMORSTW	what is more
AEHIMPRTTW	tamper with
AEHIMPSSTY	sympathise
AEHIMPSTYZ	sympathize
AEHIMPTTUW	team up with
AEHINNOPPT	happen into
AEHINNRRTY	Tyrrhenian
AEHINNSTTT	the instant
AEHINOPSTT	on the tapis
AEHINORSTU	house-train
AEHINORSTW	reason with
	with reason
AEHINORTTW	in hot water
AEHINOSTUX	exhaustion
AEHINQRSUV	vanquisher
AEHINRSSST	trashiness
AEHINSSTTU	enthusiast
AEHIOOPSST	apotheosis
AEHIORSSST	air hostess
AEHIQRSTUW	square with
AEHIRSSTTW	sweatshirt
	sweat-shirt
AEHIRSTTWW	thwartwise
AEHJMNORUU	jure humano
AEHJNOPSSW	Joseph Swan
AEHKLNOSTT	honest talk
AEHKLNOSTY	honey-stalk
AEHKMMOOST	make smooth
AEHKNOORRT	North Korea
AEHKNORRST	other ranks
AEHKNORSTT	taken short
AEHKOORSTU	South Korea
AEHLLMRSSY	harmlessly
AEHLLOOPRT	Hartlepool
AEHLLOOSTY	say hello to
AEHLLOPRXY	phylloxera

AEHLMNOSWW	Welshwoman
AEHLMOOSUX	homosexual
AEHLMORRYY	rhyme royal
	rhyme-royal
AEHLNNOPTT	pentathlon
AEHLNNOSTT	on the slant
AEHLNOPPRT	thorn apple
AEHLNOPSTU	house plant
	sulphonate
AEHLORSTUV	horse vault
AEHLPRSTUU	sulphurate
AEHMMOORST	Thomas More
AEHMNNOORT	no more than
AEHMNOORSU	manor-house
AEHMNOORSW	horsewoman
AEHMNOORTW	other woman
AEHMNOOSUY	shame on you
AEHMNORRTT	Matterhorn
AEHMNPRSUU	superhuman
AEHMNPRTWY	water nymph
AEHMOPSTTU	put to shame
AEHMORSTTT	thermostat
AEHNNOORST	sooner than
AEHNNOORTT	not another
AEHNNOPPPU	happen upon
AEHNOOPSSU	sousaphone
AEHNOOTTWY	on the way to
AEHNOPPRST	Shepparton
AEHNORRTTU	run to earth
AEHOOPPRST	apostrophe
AEHOOPRRTT	orthoptera
AEHOOPSSTZ	zoothap-ses
AEHOOPSTTT	toothpaste
AEHOOPSTTY	osteopathy
AEHOORSSTY	soothsayer
AEHOPPRSTY	saprophyte
AEHOPSSSTY	hypostases
AEHORSTTTU	utter oaths
AEHORSTTTW	at the worst
AEHPRSSTTY	strathspey
AEIIIILNST	initialise
AEIIIILNTZ	initialize
AEIIIINTTV	initiative
AEIIILMRST	militarise
AEIIILMRTZ	militarize
AEIIILNNTW	wait in line
AEIIILRSTV	trivialise
AEIIILRTVZ	trivialize
AEIIILSTTV	vitalities
AEIIIMNRST	ministeria
AEIIIMNSTV	vitaminise
AEIIIMNTVZ	vitaminize
AEIIIMRRTU	iure mariti
AEIIIRRTTV	irritative
AEIIKLLNNW	walk in line
AEIIKLLNPR	painkiller
AEIIKLRSST	strike sail
AEIILLLMMS	millesimal
AEIILLLMNN	millennial
AEIILLLTVY	illatively
AEIILLMNOR	mineral oil
AEIILLMNTU	illuminate
AEIILLMPRY	imperially
AEIILLMRST	literalism
AEIILLOSTV	volatilise
AEIILLOTVZ	volatilize
AEIILLRRTY	literarily
AEIILLRSTT	literalist
AEIILMMMOR	immemorial
AEIILMNNOS	nominalise
AEIILMNNOZ	nominalize
AEIILMNORT	eliminator
AEIILMNTTY	intimately
AEIILMOPST	optimalise
AEIILMOPTZ	optimalize
AEIILMOSSS	isoseismal
AEIILMRSTV	relativism
AEIILMRSVV	revivalism
AEIILNNORS	rosaniline
AEIILNNSTT	intestinal
AEIILNOOTT	etiolation
AEIILNOPRT	oil painter
AEIILNOPSS	spaniolise
AEIILNOPSZ	spaniolize
AEIILNORST	Toni Sailer
AEIILNORSV	revisional
AEIILNOTTV	levitation
AEIILNPRZZ	Lipizzaner
AEIILNQTUY	inequality
AEIILORTTV	vitriolate
AEIILRSTTV	relativist
AEIILRSTTZ	strelitzia
AEIILRSTVV	revivalist
AEIILRTTVY	relativity
AEIIMMMNOR	In Memoriam
	in memoriam
AEIIMMNPRT	impairment
AEIIMMNSSS	Messianism
AEIIMMRSTT	mime artist
AEIIMNNNOS	Nina Simone
AEIIMNNNOT	innominate
AEIIMNNOTV	nominative
AEIIMNOSTT	estimation
AEIIMNOTTT	intimate to
AEIIMNQRTU	Martinique
AEIIMNQTUY	equanimity
AEIIMNRSST	seminarist
AEIIMNRTUV	ruminative
AEIIMOPRRS	impresario
AEIIMPRSTT	team spirit
AEIINNOTVV	innovative
AEIINOPPST	inapposite
AEIINOPRTX	expiration
AEIINOPSTT	poinsettia
AEIINOPSTU	utopianise
AEIINOPTUZ	utopianize
AEIINOQTTU	equitation
AEIINPRSTU	puritanise
AEIINPRTUZ	puritanize
AEIINPSSST	antisepsis
	inspissate
AEIINQSTTU	quantities

AEIINRRSTV	intra vires
AEIINRSSSU	Russianise
AEIINRSSUZ	Russianize
AEIINRSTTV	transitive
AEIIOPPRTT	propitiate
AEIIPRRTTT	tripartite
AEIJKLRSUZ	Jaruzelski
AEIJLNORSU	journalise
AEIJLNORUZ	journalize
AEIJMNOSSS	jam session
AEIJMORSVY	James Ivory
AEIJNNSSTU	jauntiness
AEIJNOOPRT	pejoration
AEIKLLLNRY	nearly kill
AEIKLMNORW	menial work
AEIKLMNSTY	mistakenly
AEIKLMPPRR	ripple-mark
AEIKLOPRRT	parrot-like
AEIKMNOSTT	not mistake
AEIKNNORRY	Ronnie Kray
AEIKNOPRRY	perikaryon
AEIKNOPTTY	take pity on
AEIKNORSTU	keratinous
AEILLLMOSU	Louis Malle
AEILLLMOTW	all-time low
AEILLLSUVY	allusively
AEILLMNRTY	terminally
AEILLMPRVY	primevally
AEILLMTTUY	ultimately
AEILLNNRTY	internally
AEILLNOPTT	potentilla
AEILLNORTY	orientally
AEILLNPSSY	painlessly
AEILLNRTTU	Tertullian
AEILLNRTUY	tenurially
AEILLOPSTT	postillate
AEILLRSSTV	liver salts
AEILLRSTTU	illustrate
AEILMMRTUY	immaturely
AEILMNNNOY	in name only
AEILMNNOTY	nominately
AEILMNNSTT	instalment
AEILMNOPRS	impersonal
AEILMNOPRT	trampoline
AEILMNORTU	tourmaline
AEILMNRSTU	neutralism
AEILMNSSSU	sensualism
AEILMNSSVY	levy in mass
AEILMNSTTU	last-minute
AEILMPPSST	palimpsest
AEILMPRSST	slipstream
AEILMPRTUU	pari-mutuel
AEILMRRSSU	surrealism □
AEILNNOPSY	Polynesian
AEILNNORST	non-realist
AEILNNORTT	intolerant
AEILNNPRSU	peninsular
AEILNNPRTT	interplant
AEILNOORTT	toleration
AEILNOOSTT	nose to tail
AEILNOPRTV	portal vein
AEILNORRTT	torrential
AEILNORRTY	anteriorly
AEILNORTTV	ventilator
AEILNOSTTU	Titus Alone
AEILNOTTUX	exultation
AEILNPPRRU	Purple Rain
AEILNPRSST	paltriness
AEILNRSTTU	neutralist
AEILNRSTUU	Laurentius
AEILNRTTUY	neutrality
AEILNRTTWW	written law
AEILNSSSTU	sensualist
AEILNSSTUU	nautiluses
AEILNSSTUY	sensuality
AEILOOPSST	apostolise
AEILOOPSTZ	apostolize
AEILOPPRSU	popularise
AEILOPPRUZ	popularize
AEILOPPSTY	appositely
AEILOPRSSU	plesiosaur
AEILOPRSTY	epistolary
AEILOPTTVY	optatively
AEILORRTTU	elutriator
AEILPRRTWY	play-writer
AEILPRSSTU	sur le tapis
AEILQSTUYY	say quietly
AEILRRSSTU	surrealist
AEILRRSSTV	Silver Star
AEILRRSTUV	ultra vires
AEILRSTTUZ	Austerlitz
AEIMMNORST	monetarism
AEIMMNPRTT	impartment
AEIMMNRSSS	smarminess
AEIMMNRTTU	manumitter
AEIMMOOPRR	pro memoria
AEIMNNNORW	inner woman
AEIMNNNOTT	anointment
AEIMNNOPRS	in personam
AEIMNNORTU	numeration
	ruminate on
AEIMNOOPZZ	mezzo-piano
AEIMNOPRTT	portamenti
AEIMNOPRWZ	prizewoman
AEIMNOPTTT	temptation
AEIMNORRST	ironmaster
AEIMNORSTT	monetarist
AEIMNORTTU	mature into
AEIMNPPRST	pentaprism
AEIMNPSTTY	tympanites
AEIMNRRRTY	intermarry
AEIMNRRSTT	retransmit
AEIMNRSSTU	antiserums
AEIMOOTTUV	automotive
AEIMPRSTUZ	trapeziums
AEIMPSSTUV	assumptive
AEIMQRSTUZ	quizmaster
AEIMRRRSTU	terrariums
AEINNNOQSU	sine qua non
AEINNOOPRZ	Renzo Piano
AEINNOOPTT	at one point
AEINNOORTV	renovation

AEINNOPRSY	pensionary
AEINNOQRTU	quaternion
AEINNORRSU	raisonneur
AEINNORSTT	stentorian
AEINNOSTTT	attentions
AEINNOTTVW	native town
AEINNPPSSS	snappiness
AEINNQSSTU	quaintness
AEINNRRTTU	Tina Turner
AEINNRSSUW	unwariness
AEINOOPRRT	peroration
AEINOOPRST	operations
AEINOPPRRS	Prosperina
AEINOPRRST	periastron
AEINOPRSSS	aspersions
AEINOPRSSU	persuasion ❑
AEINOPRTTU	reputation
AEINORRSTU	souterrain
AEINORRSTV	overstrain
AEINORSSTY	tyrosinase
AEINORSTTY	stationery
AEINPPRSTW	wit-snapper
AEINPRRSTU	in raptures
AEINPRRTTU	parturient
AEINRRSSST	starriness
AEINRRSSTT	restraints
AEINRSTUYZ	suzerainty
AEIOPRRRST	respirator
AEIOPRRSTU	Praetorius
AEIOPRRTTX	extirpator
AEIOSTTTUW	sweat it out
AEJLLLORYY	royal jelly
AEJMNNORUY	journeyman
AEKKLRTTUY	talk turkey
AEKLLMRUWY	lukewarmly
AEKLMNOSTY	money talks
AEKLNOPRTT	petrol tank
AEKLOPPPRR	Karl Popper
AEKLOPRSTY	stroke play
AEKLORTTWW	wattle-work
AEKMNNOORS	on one's mark
AEKMNNOTUY	Mount Kenya
AEKMNORTTW	market town
AEKMORRSTW	masterwork
AEKNNNOSTT	Stan Kenton
AEKNOOTTTW	take to town
AEKNOPRRSY	nosy parker
AEKNOQRSTU	square knot
AEKOOPRRTY	prokaryote
AEKORRSTWW	waterworks
AELLMNNOUY	noumenally
AELLMOPRTY	temporally
AELLMOPSSY	plasmolyse
AELLMOPSYZ	plasmolyze
AELLMORSUV	marvellous
AELLNOPPRT	propellant
AELLNOPRSY	personally
AELLNORTTY	tolerantly
AELLNOSSSW	sallowness
AELLNPRSUY	supernally
AELLNPTTUY	petulantly
AELLNRSTTY	slatternly
AELLNTTUXY	exultantly
AELLOOSTUW	allow to use
AELLOPPRSU	all-purpose
AELLPRSTUU	sepultural
AELLRTTUXY	texturally
AELMMNNOTU	monumental
AELMMOOPSS	plasmosome
AELMNNNRUY	unmannerly
AELMNNOOTV	monovalent
AELMNOOOSW	loose woman
AELMNOOPRY	lampoonery
AELMNOPRST	Palmerston
AELMNOPRTU	Paul Merton
AELMNORSSS	ransomless
AELMNPRRUW	Plum Warner
AELMOOPRTU	tropaeolum
AELMOPPRUY	propylaeum
AELMOPRTTU	petrolatum
AELMOPSSST	Epsom salts
AELMOQSSUU	squamulose
AELMORSSTU	somersault
AELMPPRSUY	maple syrup
AELMRSSTTU	mulattress
AELMTTTUUU	tumult-uate
AELNNOORSZ	San Lorenzo
AELNNOPRYY	pennyroyal
AELNNORSTY	resonantly
AELNOOOTTT	not too late
AELNOPPRTW	power plant
AELNOPRSYZ	lazy person
AELNOPSTTT	talent-spot
AELNORRTVW	travel-worn
AELNORSUVY	ravenously
AELNOSSUUY	nauseously
AELNPPRSTU	supplanter
AELOOPRTTW	total power
AELOOPSSTV	Sevastopol
AELOPRRSUY	super-royal
AELORSSSUV	savourless
AELPPSSTUY	platypuses
AEMNNNNOUV	Von Neumann
AEMNNNOPTY	non-payment
AEMNNOOSST	stonemason
AEMNNORTTU	tournament
AEMNNRRSUY	nurseryman
AEMNOOPRTT	portamento
AEMNOORRST	astronomer
AEMNOPRRSY	Perry Mason
AEMNOPRSSW	presswoman
AEMNOPRSUW	superwoman
AEMNORRSTT	Montserrat
AEMNORSSTT	assortment
AEMNORSSTU	sarmentous
AEMNRRSTTU	transmuter
AEMOPRSSTT	postmaster
AEMORRSTTY	astrometry
AEMPRSSSTU	pass muster
AEMRSSSTTY	star system
AENNNOSSTW	wantonness
AENNORRSSW	narrowness

Words marked ❑ can also be spelled with an initial capital letter

AENNORRSTT	non-starter
AENOOPRRST	personator
AENOOQRRTU	quarteroon
AENOORSSTU	treasonous
AENOPPPRTU	put on paper
AENOPRRSST	transposer
AENOPRSSUV	supernovas
AENOPRSTTT	protestant □
AENOQRSTUW	town square
AENORSTTUW	run to waste
AENPRRSTTU	transputer
AENRSTTTUV	Sturtevant
AEOOPRSTTV	vaporettos
AEOOQRRSTU	square root
AEOPQRSTUU	square up to
AEOPRRSSTW	sportswear
AEOPRSTTUW	waterspout
AEORSSSTUU	trousseaus
AEORSSTUUX	trousseaux
AEORSTTTUY	stay true to
AEOSTTUWWY	Way Out West
AEPPRSSTTY	pretty pass
AFFFGILLNO	falling-off
AFFFLLLOOU	fall foul of
AFFGIKMNOR	marking off
AFFGILNOST	sling off at
AFFGIMRSSU	suffragism
AFFGINNORT	affronting
AFFGINOSTV	staving off
AFFGIRSSTU	suffragist
AFFGNOORST	stroganoff
AFFHILLNOR	half florin
AFFHILLTUY	faithfully
AFFHILNTUU	unfaithful
AFFHILOTTU	faithful to
AFFIIMNRSU	ruffianism
AFFILLORST	first of all
AFFINOORUV	in favour of
AFFMNOORRT	not far from
AFFPPRSTUY	puff pastry
AFGGGILNNU	unflagging
AFGGIIMNNY	magnifying
AFGGIINRTY	gratifying
AFGHHILLST	flashlight
AFGHHILPTT	flight path
AFGHIINNOS	fashioning
AFGHILLNPT	flight plan
AFGHIORTWY	right of way
AFGHNOORTU	hang out for
AFGIILNQUY	qualifying
AFGIILOSTU	flagitious
AFGIIMNOTU	fumigation
AFGIINORTU	figuration
AFGIINSSTY	satisfying
AFGIKLNOTU	flaking-out
AFGILLNOTU	falling-out
AFGILLNOTY	floatingly
AFGILLNSST	flint glass
AFGILNORUV	flavouring
AFGIMNOSTV	fast-moving
AFHHLLORUY	half-hourly
AFHIILLNTW	fall in with
AFHILNOPST	flash point
AFHILNPSSY	Spanish fly
AFHIOORTTY	tooth fairy
AFHIORTUVW	with favour
AFHKLLNTUY	thankfully
AFHKLNNTUU	unthankful
AFHLLORSTY	sally forth
AFHLLORSUY	royal flush
AFHLLORTUW	fourth wall
AFHLLRTUWY	wrathfully
AFHOOPRSTU	push too far
AFIILLRRTY	fritillary
AFIILNORTT	filtration
	flirtation
AFIKLLMNOS	man of skill
AFIKNORRSU	run a risk of
AFILLLLTYY	tilly-fally
AFILLLTTTU	at full tilt
AFILLMNORY	informally
AFILLNPPTY	flippantly
AFILLOSSUX	Sioux Falls
AFILMNOSUY	infamously
AFILNRSTZZ	Franz Liszt
AFIMNOORSU	foraminous
AFIMOOPRRV	vaporiform
AFIMORRSTT	stratiform
AFIORRSTYY	fairy story
AFLLLNUUWY	unlawfully
AFLLMNNUUY	unmanfully
AFLLMNOTUU	full amount
AFLLMNOUWY	womanfully
AFLLNOORSU	on all fours
AFLLNRTUUY	unartfully
AFMNNNOUWY	funny woman
AGGGIIINNV	gaingiving
AGGGILNNTU	gatling gun
	gatling-gun
AGGGILNRST	straggling
AGGHHIINPY	high-paying
AGGHHOPRRY	hygrograph
AGGHIILLMN	Gillingham
AGGHILLNUY	laughingly
AGGHILNNSY	gnashingly
AGGHILNNUU	unlaughing
AGGHINPTUW	gang up with
AGGHIORSTT	go straight
AGGHLOOPRY	graphology
AGGIIIMNTT	mitigating
AGGIILMNSV	almsgiving
	alms-giving
AGGIIMNNNS	singing-man
AGGIINNORZ	organizing
AGGILLNNTY	tanglingly
AGGILLNORR	rag-rolling
AGGILLNOTY	gloatingly
AGGILNNTWY	twangingly
AGGILNPRSY	graspingly
AGGINOORRT	raring to go
AGGINORRTT	garrotting
AGGLNNOOOT	not long ago

Words marked □ can also be spelled with an initial capital letter

AGGLNOOORZ	Gorgonzola
AGGNORSSTU	sugar tongs
AGHHHOTTUW	what though
AGHHIIILTT	hightail it
AGHHILOPRT	lithograph
AGHHLLORTU	all through
AGHHLOOPRY	holography
AGHHOOPPRT	photograph
AGHIIILLNS	Lilian Gish
AGHIILNORS	Anglo-Irish
AGHIIMNNUZ	humanizing
AGHIINNRST	tarnishing
AGHIINNRSV	varnishing
AGHIINPRRS	hairspring
AGHIKNRRTU	King Arthur
AGHILLNOTY	loathingly
AGHILNNTUY	hauntingly
AGHILOPPRY	lipography
AGHILOPPSY	gypsophila
AGHILPRTWY	playwright
AGHILRSTTY	straightly
AGHIMNNOTT	Nottingham
AGHINNOSTW	Washington
AGHINOPSTV	stop having
AGHINORSTT	straight-on
AGHINORSTU	sharing out
AGHIOPSTTT	a tight spot
AGHIPRSTTU	straight up
	straight-up
AGHJMNNOOR	John Morgan
AGHKMOPRYY	kymography
AGHLNOOORT	orthogonal
AGHLORSTWY	Galsworthy
AGHMMOOOSU	homogamous
AGHMNOOPRY	nomography
AGHMNOORTU	mouth-organ
AGHMOOPRTY	tomography
AGHNOOPRSY	nosography
AGHOOOPSUZ	zoophagous
AGHOOPPRTY	topography
AGHOPPRTYY	typography
AGIIIINNTT	initiating
AGIIILMNNN	mainlining
AGIIILNOTT	litigation
AGIIIMNOTT	mitigation
AGIIINNNRT	in training
AGIIINORRT	irrigation
AGIIINRRTT	irritating
AGIIKNPSST	piss-taking
AGIILLNNST	installing
AGIILLNNUU	unilingual
AGIILLNORY	originally
AGIILLNPRS	spiralling
AGIILLNRTU	trilingual
AGIILLNRTY	trailingly
AGIILLNRVY	virginally
AGIILLNTVY	vigilantly
AGIILLRTTY	gratillity
AGIILMNORZ	moralizing
AGIILNNORU	unoriginal
AGIILNNSTU	insulating
AGIILNPRST	springtail
AGIILNPRSY	aspiringly
	praisingly
AGIILNRSTY	laryngitis
AGIIMMOSST	misogamist
AGIIMMSSTT	stigmatism
AGIIMNNOWZ	womanizing
AGIIMNNPRS	mainspring
AGIIMNNRTU	ruminating
AGIIMNORSU	migrainous
AGIIMNOSSS	Miss Saigon
AGIIMNOTTV	motivating
AGIIMORTTY	mitigatory
AGIIMSSTTT	stigmatist
AGIINNOSTT	stationing
AGIINNRTTU	intriguant
AGIINNSSTU	sustaining
AGIINOORRT	originator
AGIINOPRRR	rip-roaring
AGIINORSTT	instigator
AGIINORSUV	viraginous
AGIKKLNRSY	skylarking
AGIKLLNNOW	all-knowing
AGIKLMNOOT	toolmaking
AGIKLMNOSS	loss-making
AGIKLNNORW	low-ranking
AGIKLNNPRY	prankingly
AGIKLNNPSY	spankingly
AGIKMMORXY	Maxim Gorky
AGIKMNNORW	working man
AGIKMNORTU	marking out
AGILLLNRUY	alluringly
AGILLLNRYY	rallyingly
AGILLNNRSY	snarlingly
AGILLNNSTY	slantingly
AGILLNOPRT	patrolling
AGILLNOSWW	swallowing
AGILLNRSUY	singularly
AGILLNTTTY	tattlingly
AGILMNOPTU	go platinum
AGILMNRTUU	Triangulum
AGILMNSSUY	assumingly
AGILMOOSTU	gliomatous
AGILMOPSTY	polygamist
AGILNNNOYY	annoyingly
AGILNNOPTY	poignantly
AGILNNORTY	ignorantly
AGILNNPPSY	snappingly
AGILNNRSTU	turn signal
AGILNNTTUY	tauntingly
AGILNNTUVY	vauntingly
AGILNRSTTY	startingly
AGILORSSST	glossarist
AGIMMNOOST	monogamist
AGIMMNOSSU	Simon Magus
AGIMMNSSUY	gymnasiums
AGIMNNNNRU	Running Man
AGIMNNSSUU	unassuming
AGIMNOOPRU	amino group
AGIMNOORST	agronomist
AGIMNOPRSU	sporangium

AGINNOPTTU	at gunpoint
AGINNORRTW	Warrington
AGINNPPSUW	swan-upping
AGINNPRSUW	pruning-saw
AGINOOOPRS	sporogonia
AGINOPSSTU	passing-out
AGINORRRST	Ringo Starr
AGINORSTTU	Titus Groan
AGINPRSSSU	surpassing
AGINRSSTTU	start using
AGIORSTTUU	gratuitous
AGKNNNORTY	granny knot
AGKNRSTYYZ	Kyrgyzstan
AGLLLLOPPU	Gallup poll
AGLLLOOPRY	pyrogallol
AGLLMOPRSU	small group
AGLLNOOPYY	palynology
AGLLRTTUUY	gutturally
AGLMNNOOTU	Mount Logan
AGLMOOPSUY	polygamous
AGLNOORSUU	languorous
AGLOOPPRYY	papyrology
AGLORTTUUZ	Turgut Ozal
AGMMNOOOSU	monogamous
AGMMNOPSUU	magnum opus
AGMNNOOUWY	young woman
AGMNOORSTY	gastronomy
AGNOPRUWWY	wrong way up
AHHHIRSTTW	thrash with
AHHILLWWWY	whillywhaw
AHHIMNOSTY	Mishnayoth
AHHIOPRSTU	authorship
AHHIPRSTTW	thwartship
AHHISSWWYY	wishy-washy
AHHLMNNOTU	Holman Hunt
AHIIIMMPSX	amphimixis
AHIIJKMNSW	Jim Hawkins
AHIIKMNRSS	Krishnaism
AHIILLNOPS	nail polish
AHIILPRSST	split hairs
AHIIMNNOTU	inhumation
AHIIMNNTUY	inhumanity
AHIIMNORSW	Irishwoman
AHIJKNNORW	John Kirwan
AHIKKMNRSS	skrimshank
AHIKLMSTWY	malt whisky
AHIKLPRSSY	sparkishly
AHIKNPRRSW	shrink-wrap
AHIKNRSTUV	Turkish Van
AHILLMQSUY	qualmishly
AHILMNOPYY	Polyhymnia
AHILMNOSWY	womanishly
AHILNOORTZ	horizontal
AHILNOPSTU	sulphation
AHILNPPSSY	snappishly
AHILNPSSTU	sultanship
AHIMNOORRU	honorarium
AHIMNOORSU	harmonious
AHIMNOPRTY	Amphitryon
AHIMNPRTTU	triumphant
AHIMNPSTYY	in sympathy
AHIMPPPRSU	parish pump
	parish-pump
AHINOPPSST	pansophist
AHINOPRSTY	notaryship
AHIOOPSTTX	phototaxis
AHIOPSSSTY	hypostasis
AHJMNNOOSY	Amy Johnson
AHKKMOORRT	Mark Rothko
AHKLLOOPSU	All Shook Up
AHKMNNSTUU	Knut Hamsun
AHKNNOOSTT	no thanks to
AHKNNOPSSY	shank's pony
AHLLMORSSU	small hours
AHLLOPRSST	sports hall
AHLLOPRSTU	prothallus
AHLLOPTXYY	phyllotaxy
AHLMNNORTU	lunar month
AHLMNOORST	solar month
AHLMPRSUWY	Murphy's law
AHLNOPSTUY	polyanthus
AHLOOPSTTY	play host to
AHMOOSSTTY	stay shtoom
AHMOPRSTTU	mouthparts
AHNOOPRRXY	oropharynx
AHNOPPRTTY	tryptophan
AIIIILMNST	initialism
AIIIINNOTT	initiation
AIIILLMNTU	illuminati
AIIILLMRTY	militarily
AIIILMMMNS	minimalism
AIIILMMNST	minimalist
AIIILMMRST	militarism
AIIILMNOTT	limitation
AIIILMRSTT	militarist
AIIILMRSTY	similarity
AIIILNOPTX	pixilation
AIIILORSTV	visitorial
AIIILRTTVY	triviality
AIIIMNNOTT	intimation
AIIIMNOPSS	pianissimo
AIIINNOOST	ionisation
AIIINNOOTZ	ionization
AIIINNOTTV	invitation
AIIINORRTT	irritation
AIIINORTTT	tritiation
AIIINORTTY	initiatory
AIIINOSTTV	visitation
AIIINOTTTV	titivation
AIIIPRSSTY	pityriasis
AIIIPRTVVY	viviparity
AIIJJLLMSW	JJ Williams
AIIKLMNOSW	Malinowski
AIILLMNNTU	illuminant
AIILLMNTTY	militantly
AIILLNOOTV	volitional
AIILLNOSUV	villainous
AIILLNOSVY	visionally
AIILLNOTUV	outvillain
AIILLORSTY	solitarily
AIILLOSSTT	solstitial
AIILLOTTVY	volatility

AIILMMNNOS	nominalism
AIILMMNOOT	immolation
AIILMMORTY	immorality
AIILMNNOST	nominalist
AIILMNOORT	monitorial
AIILMNOSTU	simulation
AIILMNOTTU	mutilation
AIILMRRTUV	triumviral
AIILNNOOST	insolation
AIILNNOSTU	insulation
AIILNOOPST	positional
	spoliation
AIILNRSSUY	urinalysis
AIILNRSTUY	insularity
AIILRTTUVY	virtuality
AIIMMNNOTU	ammunition
AIIMMPRRTU	imprimatur
AIIMMRTTUY	immaturity
AIIMNNNOOT	nomination
AIIMNNOPST	main points
AIIMNNORTU	rumination
AIIMNNRSTT	ministrant
AIIMNOOTTV	motivation
AIIMNOPSTU	utopianism □
AIIMNOPTTU	imputation
AIIMNORSSY	missionary
AIIMNPRSTU	puritanism □
AIIMNPSSTU	impuissant
AIIMOPRSTT	patriotism
AIIMOSSTTT	stomatitis
AIINNNOOTT	intonation
AIINNNOOTV	innovation
AIINNOPSTT	snap into it
AIINNORSTT	transition
AIINNORSTU	insinuator
AIINNTTUVY	vanity unit
AIINOOPPST	apposition
AIINORTTUY	tuitionary
AIINQRSTUU	Tarquinius
AIIOPRSUVV	viviparous
AIIPPRSSTU	Aristippus
AIIPRSSSTT	piss artist
AIJLMNORSU	journalism
AIJLNORSTU	journalist
AIJNNOPTUX	put a jinx on
AIKKRRSTWY	Kirsty Wark
AIKLLLMOST	almost kill
AIKLLLOPTW	pillow talk
AIKLNORVVY	Ivan Krylov
AIKMMNORSS	Simon Marks
AIKMMORRRS	Mark Morris
AIKNNOPRSS	Parkinson's
AIKNRSSTVY	Stravinsky
AILLLLTVYY	tilly-vally
AILLLMNNUV	Liv Ullmann
AILLLMNOWY	Willy Loman
AILLLOOOPR	Paolo Rolli
AILLMMORTY	immortally
AILLMNOOPY	polynomial
AILLMNPRST	small print
AILLMOOSTT	tomatillos
AILLMOPRXY	proximally
AILLNNOOTY	notionally
AILLNNOSUY	unisonally
AILLNOOPTY	optionally
AILLNQRTUY	tranquilly
AILLOORRSY	sororially
AILLOQTUWY	low quality
	low-quality
AILLORTTUY	tutorially
AILMNNOOPR	pronominal
AILMNNRTUY	ruminantly
AILMNOOPST	lampoonist
AILMNORTUY	unmorality
AILMOOPRRT	implorator
AILMOOSSUZ	Luis Somoza
AILMORSTTU	stimulator
AILNOOPPTU	population
AILNOOPRSS	sponsorial
AILNOPRTTU	put on trial
AILNORSTTU	lustration
AILNPSSTUY	puissantly
AILOOPRSTY	spoliatory
AILOPPRTUY	popularity
AILOPRSTTU	stipulator
AIMMNORSTU	stramonium
AIMMOORRTU	moratorium
AIMNNOWWYY	in my own way
AIMNOOSTTX	taxonomist
AIMNOPSSTU	assumption □
AIMNORRSTU	intra muros
AIMNRSTTUU	nasturtium
AIMOQSSTUY	squamosity
AINNOOPRSS	sopraninos
AINNOOPRTT	anti-proton
AINNOORTVY	innovatory
AINNOPRSTT	strapontin
AINOOPPTTU	up to a point
AINOOPSSTU	out-passion
AINOOSTTTU	outstation
AINOPRSTUU	usurpation
AINORRSSTT	transistor
AINORRSTTY	transitory
AINPRSTUUV	pursuivant
AIOOPRRSUU	uproarious
AIOOPRSTVY	vaporosity
AIOORRSTTU	traitorous
AIOPRRSUVV	parvovirus
AIORRRTTTU	triturator
AIORSSTTTW	at its worst
AKLNOOPPSY	look snappy
ALLOOPPRRT	poll-parrot
ALLOORSUVY	valorously
ALMMNSSSUU	Mussulmans
ALMOOPPRST	protoplasm
ALMOPPSSUY	play possum
ALNOOOPRST	portolanos
ALNPRSTUUY	pursuantly
ALOOPPRSTT	protoplast
ALOOPPRTTY	prototypal
ALOOPRSUVY	vaporously
ALOPRTUUVY	voluptuary

ALORSSTTUU	Lotus Sutra
AMNNOOSTUY	antonymous
AMNNOOSTWW	townswoman
AMNNOSTTUW	stuntwoman
AMNOOOSTUU	autonomous
AMOORSSTTU	stromatous
AMOPPRSTTU	postpartum
ANNOOOSTTY	not say no to
ANOOOPRSTZ	protozoans
ANOOPPRTTU	not up to par
AOOPPSTTTU	put a stop to
AOORRSSTUU	Torosaurus

B

BBBDEEINOR	beribboned
BBBEELORUV	bubble over
BBBEGILNRU	blubbering
BBBEILNORU	blue ribbon
BBBEJNOOSY	Bobby Jones
BBBEMOOORY	Bobby Moore
BBBLLOOWWY	blow-by-blow
BBCEEKNRRU	rubberneck
BBCEGILNOR	clobbering
BBCEHINSSU	chubbiness
BBCEIRRSSU	subscriber
BBCGINORSY	Bing Crosby
BBDDEILNOU	double bind
BBDDELNOOU	double bond
BBDEEEISYZ	be seized by
BBDEEHORTY	bothered by
BBDEEIMORV	dive-bomber
BBDEEINSWY	Sidney Webb
BBDEEIRRUZ	rubberized
BBDEELNOTU	bent double
BBDEIKNOOR	bookbinder
BBDEILLLOU	double bill
BBDEILLNOU	I'll be bound
BBDEKLOOOU	double-book
BBEEEFGRRU	beefburger
BBEEELLSUV	bull-beeves
BBEEELORTT	beer bottle
BBEEELOVYY	Bye Bye Love
BBEEERRRTU	rubber tree
BBEEILLNRU	Berlin blue
BBEELLOTTU	bluebottle
BBEELMORTT	letter bomb
BBEGHIORRT	Big Brother
BBEGINRSSU	grubbiness
BBEHHILOST	shibboleth
BBEHHOORSY	hobby-horse
BBEHJNNOOW	John Benbow
BBEILLNOSY	Billy Bones
BBEILNOSSW	wobbliness
BBEILNOSUY	boys in blue
BBEINOORWX	box Brownie®
BBEINOPRRT	Ribbentrop
BBEINSSSTU	stubbiness
BBELMOOPRT	petrol bomb
BBELOORRTT	Robert Bolt
BBEMNRRTUU	burnt umber
BBFGILMNOY	flying bomb
BBFHIINORS	ribbonfish
BBFIMNOOSU	fusion bomb
BBGHILLNOY	hobblingly
BBGIILLNNY	nibblingly
BBGILNNSUY	snubbingly
BBHHINOOTW	hobnob with
BBHIIPRSTU	rubbish tip
BBHILNOSSY	snobbishly
BBHJLNOOWY	John Bowlby
BBIIKKNTUZ	kibbutznik
BBILLNORSY	Bill Bryson
BBILLOSUUY	bibulously
BBILMOOOTT	bombolotti
BBIMNOORRW	ribbonworm
BBJMMMOOUU	mumbo-jumbo
BBLNORSTUY	stubbornly
BBNNOORRUU	Bruno Bruno
BCCDEEEMNU	decumbence
BCCDEELMOO	become cold
BCCDEEMNUY	decumbency
BCCEEEMNRU	recumbence
BCCEEENPSU	pubescence
BCCEEIMRTU	cubic metre
BCCEEINRTY	cybernetic
BCCEEKLRSY	Krebs cycle
BCCEEMNRUY	recumbency
BCCEHIILOS	libecchios
BCCEHIIMRU	cherubimic
BCCEHKRRUY	Chuck Berry
BCCEIINOOT	coenobitic
BCCEILORTU	Bertolucci
BCCEIMNNUY	incumbency
BCCEJLOTTU	cult object
BCCGIMNSUU	succumbing
BCCHHIINNY	inch by inch
BCCHIINORT	bronchitic
BCCLNOOTTU	Cotton Club
BCDDEEEIVY	deceived by
BCDDEEIMOW	Widdecombe
BCDEEEFIMN	minced beef
BCDEEEFNOR	corned beef
BCDEEEIINT	benedicite
BCDEEEILTT	detectible
BCDEEEKLPS	bespeckled
BCDEEEMNRU	encumbered
BCDEEFINNO	be confined
BCDEEHIMRS	besmirched
BCDEEHLOST	bedclothes
BCDEEIILNR	incredible
BCDEEIIPRR	bride-price
BCDEEIMOOV	become void
BCDEEINSSU	subsidence
BCDEEINSTU	Benedictus
BCDEEIPRRS	prescribed
BCDEEKLLNU	bull-necked
BCDEENOSST	second-best
BCDEEORRSS	crossbreed
BCDEFHILRU	Burchfield
BCDEGHINOU	debouching
BCDEHILNOU	double chin
BCDEIILLNU	includible

BCDEIILNRY	incredibly
BCDEILOPRU	producible
BCDEIOPRRS	proscribed
BCDEKLNOUW	buckle down
BCDEKNOTUW	bucket down
BCDELNOORU	cordon bleu
BCDELNORSU	Drones Club
BCDEMMNNOO	common bend
BCDEMMNRUU	cummerbund
BCDEORSTTU	obstructed
BCDGKLOOUY	by good luck
BCDHHIILRT	childbirth
BCDIIMMSUY	cymbidiums
BCDIIOPRRT	tropicbird
BCDIKKSTUU	Dick Butkus
BCDILORSTU	locust bird
BCDKLOOOST	bloodstock
BCDKMRSTUU	dumbstruck
BCDLNOOOTU	blood count
BCDLORSTUU	cloudburst
BCEEEEHKOO	Okeechobee
BCEEEFIMNO	become fine
BCEEEFINNT	beneficent
BCEEEFLLRT	treble clef
BCEEEFMOOR	come before
BCEEEGHINS	beseeching
BCEEEIJLRT	rejectible
BCEEEILLNU	ebullience
BCEEEIMOPR	become ripe
BCEEELLMRU	cerebellum
BCEEELLNRS	bell screen
BCEEELMOSS	become less
BCEEENORRS	resorbence
BCEEFIMMOR	become firm
BCEEFIOPRS	fibrescope
BCEEFLLRUW	curfew-bell
BCEEFORRTU	brute force
BCEEGHMOOU	gobemouche
BCEEGHNORS	Schoenberg
BCEEGIINOT	biogenetic
BCEEGINRSU	subgeneric
BCEEGNNORR	Cronenberg
BCEEHHNNOT	on the bench
BCEEHIMNOT	become thin
BCEEHMNRSU	Übermensch
BCEEHMORUU	embouchure
BCEEHNORRX	Bronx cheer
BCEEHRSTTU	bruschette
BCEEIILPST	plebiscite
BCEEIILTYZ	Belize City
BCEEIJOSTV	objectives
BCEEIJSTUV	subjective
BCEEILLNPU	blue pencil
	blue-pencil
BCEEILLNUY	ebulliency
BCEEILMOST	comestible
BCEEILNORT	Colbertine
BCEEILNOTY	by-election
BCEEIPRRRS	prescriber
BCEEJLOSST	objectless
BCEEKLLNNU	Kennel Club
BCEEKLNOTT	bottleneck
BCEELNNRUY	Lenny Bruce
BCEELNQSUU	Queen's Club
BCEELNRTUU	turbulence
BCEEMMORSU	cumbersome
BCEEMOORTU	Umberto Eco
BCEEMOORVY	overcome by
BCEEOOORRR	corroboree
BCEFFIKOOO	office-book
BCEFHILLOX	Felix Bloch
BCEFIIMORR	microfibre
BCEFIJSTUY	subjectify
BCEFIKKLNO	knife block
BCEFKLSTUU	bucketfuls
BCEFLMORRU	Reform Club
BCEGHIINTW	bewitching
BCEGHIKNNS	King's Bench
BCEGIILORR	corrigible
BCEGILLNOR	corbelling
BCEGILMNOY	becomingly
BCEGIMNNOU	unbecoming
BCEHIIMOST	biochemist
BCEHIINSST	bitchiness
BCEHILNOOR	bronchiole
BCEHILOPRY	hyperbolic
BCEHINNSSU	bunchiness
BCEHINOOPX	xenophobic
BCEHKLNOOT	on the block
BCEHKLOORS	horse block
BCEHKLOOSU	blockhouse
BCEHKOORRT	Robert Koch
BCEHKOPSTU	bucket shop
BCEHLNOOSU	be no slouch
BCEHMRSTUW	thumbscrew
BCEIIILMMS	immiscible
BCEIIILMTY	imbecility
BCEIIILNNV	invincible
BCEIIKLLLS	sicklebill
BCEIIKLRRT	rib-tickler
BCEIILLOTT	Botticelli
BCEIIMORST	biometrics
BCEIJNOSTU	subjection
BCEIKLOORT	bootlicker
BCEIKNOOPT	bone to pick
BCEIKOOTTY	tickety-boo
BCEILNORSU	Berlusconi
BCEILNRTUU	tuberculin
BCEINNOSSU	bounciness
BCEINORTTU	contribute
BCEINOSSTU	subsection
BCEIOPPRSY	presbyopic
BCEIOPRRRS	proscriber
BCEIORSSTT	obstetrics
BCEJNOSTTU	not subject
BCEKLOOPRW	power block
BCEKLOORTW	tower block
BCEKOOORSU	coursebook
BCEKRSTTUU	rust-bucket
BCELLNOTTU	button cell
BCELMMNOOU	common blue
BCELOORSSU	lob's course

BCELRSTUUU	subculture
BCEMNOPRTU	procumbent
BCEMNOSSUV	Venus's comb
BCENOORSSS	crossbones
BCGIIKKNOX	kick boxing
BCGIKNPRSU	springbuck
BCHHIMOOOP	homophobic
BCHIINORST	bronchitis
BCHIIOPSSY	biophysics
BCHIKNNORY	Nick Hornby
BCHIMOORTT	thrombotic
BCIIILNNVY	invincibly
BCIIILORTT	trilobitic
BCIILNOPSY	psilocybin
BCIILORSUU	lubricious
BCIJKOPSTU	stick-up job
BCIKKORRSW	brickworks
BCIKMNOOTT	Nick Bottom
BCIKMOORST	broomstick
BCIKNOPTTU	pin-buttock
BCIMNOOSTU	combustion
BCINOSSSTU	consubsist
BCKMOOORTT	rock bottom
	rock-bottom
BCLMORSUUY	cumbrously
BCOORRSTTU	obstructor
BDDDEELOOR	red-blooded
BDDEEEILLS	Bill Deedes
BDDEEEILLV	bedevilled
BDDEEEILRW	bewildered
BDDEEEIMRX	mixed breed
BDDEEFFNOY	offended by
BDDEEIISSY	side by side
BDDEEILMSS	dissembled
BDDEEIMNNR	mind-bender
BDDEEINNTU	unindebted
BDDEEINOTT	indebted to
BDDEFILLOU	full-bodied
BDDEGGNOOW	bogged down
BDDEGILLOU	double-gild
BDDEHINOOR	behind-door
BDDEHLOOOT	hot-blooded
BDDEIIKNOR	ride bodkin
BDDEIIPRRS	bird-spider
BDDEIIRSUV	subdivider
BDDEILMORW	middlebrow
BDDEILNRUU	underbuild
BDDEIMOUVY	buddy movie
BDDELOOORU	double door
BDDFGIINOR	forbidding
BDDHLLOUYY	Buddy Holly
BDDHLNOOOU	bloodhound
BDDIKLNNRU	blind drunk
BDDLNOOOOR	blood donor
BDEEEEGNSU	Eugene Debs
BDEEEEJLLW	bejewelled
BDEEEEMMRR	remembered
BDEEEEPRTY	Peter Debye
BDEEEFHNOT	be the end of
BDEEEFILNS	defensible
BDEEEGHILR	Heidelberg
BDEEEGLNTU	dung beetle
	dung-beetle
BDEEEHILTW	bleed white
BDEEEHLLNR	hellbender
BDEEEIILSV	disbelieve
BDEEEILLOS	Léo Delibes
BDEEEILNTX	extendible
BDEEEILSTW	wildebeest
BDEEEIMRTT	embittered
BDEEEINRRT	interbreed
BDEEELMTUW	tumbleweed
BDEEELORRT	dorr beetle
BDEEELRRRY	elderberry
BDEEEPRRSS	bedpresser
BDEEERRSVW	bed-swerver
BDEEFGGLOO	foolbegged
BDEEFGIINR	debriefing
BDEEFHILNT	left behind
BDEEFIINST	disbenefit
BDEEFILNSY	defensibly
BDEEFINRST	best friend
BDEEFOORSS	bed of roses
BDEEGHIRTT	get the bird
BDEEGIILST	digestible
BDEEGIINNR	inbreeding
BDEEGILLOR	gor-bellied
BDEEGIMOSU	disembogue
BDEEGINOTT	get into bed
BDEEGINPRS	big spender
BDEEGINTTW	bed-wetting
BDEEGIOPRR	rope bridge
BDEEGIORST	Gobi Desert
BDEEGNNORY	bond energy
BDEEGNORSW	Swedenborg
BDEEGNOTXY	oxygen debt
BDEEGOORSU	bodegueros
BDEEHIIMNT	behind time
BDEEHILLLY	Delhi belly
BDEEHIMRSU	Humberside
BDEEHINOTW	be done with
BDEEHIRRSY	Derbyshire
BDEEHLNNOR	hornblende
BDEEHNOOPY	beyond hope
BDEEIILMOS	demobilise
BDEEIILMOZ	demobilize
BDEEILLOPT	potbellied
	pot-bellied
BDEEILMOSW	disembowel
BDEEILMOTU	double time
BDEEILMRSS	dissembler
BDEEILNNOS	disennoble
BDEEILNORR	borderline
BDEEILNOTY	obediently
BDEEILORSW	bowdlerise
BDEEILORWZ	bowdlerize
BDEEIMMNOT	embodiment
BDEEIMNRTU	untimbered
BDEEIMOOSS	somebodies
BDEEIMORRY	embroidery
BDEEINOOTT	obedient to
BDEEINOSSY	by one's side

BDEEIORSSS	sobersides
BDEEIORVWY	review body
BDEEKNORRV	kerb-vendor
BDEELLNRUY	underbelly
BDEELMOPYY	employed by
BDEELMRRUU	blue murder
BDEELOORVW	bowled over
BDEELOPRUW	powder blue
BDEELOSTTY	besottedly
BDEELQRSUU	burlesqued
BDEEMNNRUU	unnumbered
BDEEMNORSU	burdensome
BDEENNNOTU	unbonneted
BDEENOORTV	Denver boot
BDEENOOSST	do one's best
BDEENORRUV	overburden
BDEENORSUV	unobserved
BDEFFIILSU	diffusible
BDEFFIORST	bored stiff
BDEFFNOORW	browned off
BDEFGINOOR	foreboding
BDEFGIOORT	footbridge
BDEFHJOOOT	do the job of
BDEFILOOST	soft-boiled
BDEFIOPRRY	bird of prey
BDEFKLLOOU	blood fluke
BDEFLOORUX	Oxford blue
BDEGGGINRU	begrudging
BDEGHIMOTU	big-mouthed
BDEGHINNRU	Hindenburg
BDEGIILNRU	rebuilding
BDEGIINNRR	ring binder
BDEGIINORR	Ironbridge
BDEGILLORT	toll bridge
	tollbridge
BDEGILNNOT	Bedlington
BDEGILNNRU	blundering
BDEGILNSSU	blind guess
BDEGIMOORR	bridegroom
BDEGINNRRU	bring under
BDEGINORTW	Bridgetown
BDEGINRRST	Strindberg
BDEGIOPRRT	Bridgeport
BDEGIORRTW	Trowbridge
BDEGIRRRSU	Rusbridger
BDEHIIOPRT	prohibited
BDEHILLLOT	the old Bill
BDEHILNOOT	in the blood
BDEHIMNTUX	thumb index
	thumb-index
BDEHINRSTU	disburthen
BDEHIRSTTU	butter dish
BDEHNOOSUU	housebound
BDEHNRRSUU	underbrush
BDEIIILNRV	biliverdin
BDEIIKRRST	bird strike
BDEIILMORS	disembroil
BDEIIRSSUZ	subsidizer
BDEIIRSTTU	distribute
BDEIJLRRUY	jerry-build
BDEIKMRSTU	strike dumb
BDEILLOSSU	dissoluble
BDEILLOTUX	billet-doux
BDEILNNOST	stone-blind
BDEILNNOTY	Enid Blyton
BDEILNOOSS	bloodiness
BDEIMMNOUY	immune body
BDEIMMOOSS	disembosom
BDEIMNORSS	morbidness
BDEINOORSS	broodiness
BDEINOSSSU	do business
BDEINRSSTU	turbidness
BDEIOOPSTX	deposit box
BDEIOORTTW	bitterwood
BDEKNNOORW	broken down
	broken-down
BDELLNOPSU	spellbound
BDELLORTUY	troubledly
BDELMMNOUY	molybdenum
BDELMNOTUW	tumbledown
	tumble-down
BDELMOOSUY	Moody Blues
BDELNOOOST	bloodstone
BDELNORTUU	untroubled
BDELOOTTTU	blotted out
BDENNOTTUU	unbuttoned
BDENOPTTUU	buttoned up
BDENPRSTUU	run up debts
BDFLLOTUUY	doubtfully
BDFNOORSTU	frostbound
BDGGINOORT	bring to God
BDGHIILNNT	night-blind
BDGIIKNNRY	by-drinking
BDGIILNPUU	building-up
	upbuilding
BDGIINOORT	riding-boot
BDGIINRSTU	disturbing
BDGILNOORY	broodingly
BDGILNOTUY	doubtingly
BDGINNORRU	bring round
BDGLNOOOUY	young blood
BDGMNOORSU	bongo drums
	bongo-drums
BDGNOOORSW	brown goods
BDHIIIINST	disinhibit
BDHIILRRWY	whirlybird
BDHILNOOOT	in hot blood
BDHIMNOORY	monohybrid
BDHINOOORS	Robin Hood's
BDHKOOORSU	Doukhobors
BDHLNOOTTU	buttonhold
BDHMNOSTUW	thumbs down
	thumbs-down
BDHNNOORTU	northbound
BDHNOOSTUU	southbound
BDIIIILNST	libidinist
BDIIILNOSU	libidinous
BDIKOORSTY	dirty books
BDILLNPRUY	purblindly
BDILNOOOTW	boil down to
BDILNRSTTU	blind trust
BDINNOORRU	round robin

BDKNNOOORY	Donnybrook
BDMNOORSTU	stormbound
BDNORSTUWY	brown study
BEEEEFLNSS	feebleness
BEEEEFLRTT	feel better
BEEEEGIKNP	beekeeping
BEEEEGLSTU	Betelgeuse
BEEEEGNRRT	Green Beret
BEEEEILNPT	pine beetle
BEEEELORRT	Robert E Lee
BEEEELORTV	rove beetle
BEEEERRSTT	Beer Street
BEEEFGILNN	enfeebling
BEEEFILLRX	reflexible
BEEEFIMORT	beforetime
	time before
BEEEFINRRV	nerve fibre
BEEEFOORRT	freebooter
BEEEGGINRR	ginger beer
BEEEGGORST	George Best
BEEEGGRRUV	vegeburger
BEEEGHINRS	Heisenberg
BEEEGHLOSU	glebe-house
BEEEGILNRS	inselberge
BEEEGINRRW	Weinberger
BEEEHHRSTT	the three B's
BEEEHIILNW	wheelie bin
BEEEHINTVW	be even with
BEEEHKNOTW	bow the knee
BEEEHLLRTW	bell-wether
BEEEIILMSV	misbelieve
BEEEIILOSV	I believe so
BEEEIIRSSW	Weisse Bier
BEEEIKLLRT	Tel-El-Kebir
BEEEIKLRTT	like better
BEEEILNRUV	unbeliever
BEEEILNSTX	extensible
BEEEILRRSV	reversible
BEEEILRRTV	revertible
BEEEINRSSZ	breeziness
BEEEIRRSTW	sweet brier
BEEEKKOOPR	bookkeeper
BEEEKLMSTU	musk beetle
BEEELLRSST	bestseller
BEEELLTUVV	Blue Velvet
BEEELNNOTV	benevolent
BEEELOPRRT	Robert Peel
BEEEMNNRUV	even number
BEEEMNRTTT	betterment
BEEENPTTUW	put between
BEEEOQSUXZ	squeeze-box
BEEFFHNOOR	Bonhoeffer
BEEFFNORUZ	buffer zone
BEEFGLNOOR	before long
BEEFGRSTUU	subterfuge
BEEFIIKNOW	bowie knife
BEEFIILLNX	inflexible
BEEFILLMRU	umbellifer
BEEFILNOSS	sensible of
BEEFIORTVY	every bit of
BEEFLLLORW	bell-flower
BEEFLMORRT	tremble for
BEEFNNOOOR	before noon
BEEGGGNORY	George Byng
BEEGGHORSU	George Bush
BEEGGIILLN	negligible
BEEGGLOORT	bootlegger
BEEGGNRRSU	Regensburg
BEEGHIIMTT	the big time
BEEGHIKRTW	kerb weight
BEEGHILLLS	sleigh bell
BEEGHILNRT	blethering
BEEGHIORTV	give bother
BEEGHIRSTY	Bright Eyes
BEEGHMNRUU	huge number
BEEGHOOTTT	get the boot
BEEGIIILLN	ineligible
BEEGIILNST	ingestible
BEEGIINNNR	inner being
BEEGIINOSS	biogenesis
BEEGILMNRS	resembling
BEEGILNNNU	Nibelungen
BEEGILNNSU	Blue Ensign
BEEGINNNSS	benignness
BEEGINRTTW	Wittenberg
BEEGNSSSUU	subgenuses
BEEGOORRSY	gooseberry
BEEGPRRSTU	Petersburg
BEEGRRSTTU	Grub Street
BEEHIIITVX	exhibitive
BEEHILMMOO	mobile home
BEEHILMOST	blithesome
BEEHILNSST	blitheness
BEEHILOSSV	bolshevise
BEEHILOSVZ	bolshevize
BEEHIMMPRS	membership
BEEHISSSTW	best wishes
BEEHKMNOOR	broken home
BEEHLLLLSS	hell's bells
BEEHLMNSSU	humbleness
BEEHLMORRT	Herbert Lom
BEEHLORSSU	Blue Horses
BEEHLRSSTU	bus shelter
BEEHMOORST	bothersome
BEEHMOORTT	mother-to-be
BEEHNOOSTT	to be honest
BEEIIJORTU	bijouterie
BEEIIKLMRT	kimberlite
BEEIILLLRV	Libreville
BEEIILMRSS	remissible
BEEIILNNSS	insensible
BEEIILRSST	resistible
BEEIIMMTTY	item by item
BEEIKKNORR	knobkerrie
BEEIKLLNRT	Tinkerbell
BEEIKLNPRS	besprinkle
BEEILLLOVW	boll-weevil
BEEILLLOWY	yellow bile
BEEILLORSU	rebellious
BEEILLOSSW	Boswellise
BEEILLOSWZ	Boswellize
BEEILLRSTT	belletrist

BEEILMNNSS	nimbleness
BEEILNOPRZ	Nobel Prize
	Nobel prize
BEEILNOSST	ostensible
BEEILNOTTW	wine bottle
BEEILSSTTU	subtleties
BEEIMORRTT	tribometer
BEEIMORSSV	misobserve
BEEINNORRT	Norbertine
BEEINORSTU	tenebrious
BEEINRSSTT	bitterness
BEEINRSTTU	burnettise
BEEINRTTUZ	burnettize
BEEIRSSUVV	subversive
BEEJNNORSU	Burne-Jones
BEEJNOSSTV	Steven Jobs
BEEKLLOORS	bookseller
BEEKLOORRV	love-broker
BEEKNNOOPT	poke-bonnet
BEEKNNORSS	brokenness
BEEKNORTTW	know better
BEEKOOPRRT	Peter Brook
BEEKORRTTT	Robert Kett
BEELLOOSTY	obsoletely
BEELMMNSUW	mumble-news
BEELMNNOOW	noblewomen
BEELMNRSSU	numberless
BEELMOQSUU	Blue Mosque
BEELNSSSTU	subtleness
BEELORSTUV	oversubtle
BEEMMNNOTT	entombment
BEEMNORSSS	sombreness
BEEMOPRRSY	pre-embryos
BEENOSSSTU	obtuseness
BEENPRSSSU	superbness
BEENQSSTUU	subsequent
BEEORSSTTY	set store by
BEEPPSSTTY	step by step
	step-by-step
BEEPRRSTYY	presbytery
BEFFNOORUY	buffoonery
BEFGIIKNRS	king's brief
BEFGIINNOR	fibrinogen
BEFGILNORW	fingerbowl
BEFGINNOOR	fibronogen
BEFGKOOORR	go for broke
BEFHIILLTT	fit the bill
BEFHILLMTU	thimbleful
BEFIILLNXY	inflexibly
BEFIILLORS	fibrillose
BEFIILRSTU	filibuster
BEFILMORTW	timber wolf
BEFIMORRTU	tuberiform
BEFIORTUVY	by virtue of
BEFLLMRTUU	tumblerful
BEFLLOSTTU	bottlefuls
BEFNOORRST	forest-born
BEGGGIORRW	grow bigger
BEGGHMRUUY	humbuggery
BEGGHNORTU	Gothenburg
BEGGIILLNY	negligibly
BEGGIINNNS	beginnings
BEGGIINNSU	begin using
BEGGILNNOS	belongings
BEGGINNORU	burgeoning
BEGGINRRUZ	Zurbriggen
BEGGRSSUUY	Guy Burgess
BEGGRSTTUY	Gettysburg
BEGHIILMRT	thimblerig
BEGHIILNRT	blithering
BEGHIINRRT	rebirthing
BEGHILLSTU	Light blues
BEGHINPRTU	brighten up
BEGHINRSST	brightness
BEGHOORSTT	borghettos
BEGIIILLNY	ineligibly
BEGIIILLTY	legibility
BEGIIKLRTZ	blitzkrieg
BEGIIKMNOS	Mike Gibson
BEGIILLNTT	belittling
BEGIILMNTT	timing belt
BEGIILNRST	blistering
BEGIKLNRUY	rebukingly
BEGILLNOTY	boil gently
BEGILMNRSU	slumbering
BEGILMOORS	embroglios
BEGILNORSY	soberingly
BEGILNRSTU	blustering
BEGILNSTTU	subletting
BEGILOOOXY	exobiology
BEGINNORSS	boringness
BEGINNOSTX	nesting-box
BEGINNRSTU	set burning
BEGINPRRTU	perturbing
BEGJKLNOOU	Jungle Book
BEGLMOORYY	embryology
BEGLMORUUX	Luxembourg
BEGMOOPSSU	goose bumps
BEGOOPPRST	gobstopper
BEHIIIINTV	inhibitive
BEHIIINOTX	exhibition
BEHIIMSTTY	by this time
BEHIKLLNOR	Broken Hill
BEHIKLLNRU	Bunker Hill
BEHIKLNNOT	on the blink
BEHILLOPTT	top the bill
BEHILMOSSV	Bolshevism
BEHILOSSTV	Bolshevist
BEHIMSSSTU	miss the bus
BEHINOSSSY	boyishness
BEHJJOSTTU	just the job
BEHJNNNOOS	Ben Johnson
BEHLMOOPTY	phlebotomy
BEHLNOORRW	Hornblower
BEHLNOOTTU	buttonhole
BEHMOORSST	thromboses
BEHMPRTTUU	tub-thumper
BEHNOOORTU	on the buroo
BEHRRSSUWY	Shrewsbury
BEIIILMMOS	immobilise
BEIIILMMOZ	immobilize
BEIIIMNSTU	bituminise

BEIIIMNTUZ	bituminize
BEIILLOSSU	solubilise
BEIILLOSUZ	solubilize
BEIILLPRTT	bitter pill
BEIILMMOOZ	immobolize
BEIILMOPSS	impossible
BEIILMRTUY	muliebrity
BEIILNNSSY	insensibly
BEIILORSTU	boiler suit
BEIILRSSTY	resistibly
BEIILRSTTT	librettist
BEIILRSTTW	Birtwistle
BEIILSUYZZ	busy Lizzie
	busy lizzie
BEIIMSSSUV	submissive
BEIINNOQUU	ubiquinone
BEIINNRSTU	Rubinstein
BEIINORSTY	insobriety
BEIJLRRTUY	jerry-built
BEIKLLMOTT	milk bottle
BEIKNOORUY	on your bike
BEILLNSUUU	Luis Buñuel
BEILMMNSUU	nelumbiums
BEILMNOOTT	bottom line
BEILMOOORR	boiler room
BEILMOOOST	lobotomise
BEILMOOOTZ	lobotomize
BEILMORSYZ	symbolizer
BEILNNSSUY	unsensibly
BEILNOPRSW	spin-bowler
BEILNOPSSU	unpossible
BEILNOSSTY	ostensibly
BEILRRSUVY	ruby silver
BEIMNORSSU	submersion
BEINNOSTUV	subvention
BEINNRSTTU	sunbittern
BEINOPRSTU	subreption
BEINORSSUV	subversion
BEINORSTUU	subroutine
BEINOSSSUU	bonus issue
BEINOSSTWX	witness box
BEINSSSTTU	subsistent
BEIOOQSSUU	obsequious
BEIOORSSTU	boisterous
BEIOQRSTUU	soubriquet
BEIORSTTUY	tuberosity
BEIPRRSSUY	by surprise
BEISSTTTUU	substitute
BEJLLMRSYY	Mrs Jellyby
BEKLNNORUY	unbrokenly
BEKMOORSTU	muster-book
BEKNOORSTY	stony broke
	stony-broke
BELLNOSUUY	nebulously
BELLOOSSTY	bootlessly
BELLORSTUY	trolleybus
BELMOOSSTT	bottomless
BELMORSSUU	slumberous
BELNNRRUYY	Yul Brynner
BELNOORSWW	snowblower
BELORSTTUU	outbluster
BEMNOPRSUU	penumbrous
BEMOOPRRSY	proembryos
BENNOORSTW	brownstone
BENORSSSTU	robustness
BEORRTTTUW	butterwort
BFFFIOSTTU	bit of stuff
BFFNOOORTU	rub off on to
BFFOORRUUY	four-by-four
BFGHILNTYY	fly-by-night
BFGHINORRT	bring forth
BFGILLMNUY	fumblingly
BFHORRSTTU	burst forth
BFIIILSTUY	fusibility
BFIIIORSST	fibrositis
BFIILLORSU	fibrillous
BFILLLSSUY	blissfully
BGGIILLNOY	obligingly
BGGIINNPRU	bringing up
	bringing-up
	upbringing
BGGILLNNUY	bunglingly
BGGILNOTUU	bulging out
BGHHIIRRTT	birthright
BGHHIJNORT	John Bright
BGHIIIINNT	inhibiting
BGHIILNPSU	publishing
BGHIINNRSU	burnishing
BGHIJNOOSS	Josh Gibson
BGHILLMNUY	humblingly
BGHILLNSUY	blushingly
BGHILNNSUU	unblushing
BGHILNORTW	light brown
BGHINNOTTU	nothing but
BGHINNOTUX	hunting-box
BGHIPRSTTU	Pittsburgh
BGIIILNOTY	ignobility
BGIIKLNNNU	unblinking
BGIILLNOPT	top billing
BGIILMNOWX	mixing bowl
BGIILMOORS	imbroglios
BGIINORSUU	rubiginous
BGIINSSSTU	subsisting
BGIJLLMNUY	jumblingly
BGILLMMNUY	mumblingly
BGILLMNRUY	rumblingly
BGILMNOOSS	blossoming
BGILORSUUU	lugubrious
BGIMNNOOSU	unbosoming
BGIMNOOORR	robing-room
BGINOORRSW	borrowings
BHHOORSTTU	toothbrush
BHIIIINNOT	inhibition
BHIIIMRSST	Britishism
BHIIINORTY	inhibitory
BHIILLRSTT	stillbirth
BHIMOORSST	thrombosis
BHINORRSTW	Brownshirt
BHJNNOORTU	John Bruton
BHLLOOSSUU	holus-bolus
BHLLRRUUYY	hurly-burly
BHNOPSTTUU	push-button

BIIIILRSTY	risibility
BIIIILSTVY	visibility
BIIILMMOTY	immobility
BIILLLLSYY	silly-billy
BIILLOSTUY	solubility
BIILLOTUVY	volubility
BIIMNOSSSU	submission
BIIMNOSTUU	bituminous
BIIOQSTUUU	ubiquitous
BIKLLORSST	stork's bill
BIMNOORSTT	trombonist
BIMOOPPRRU	opprobrium
BINOOORRSY	Roy Orbison
BLLLMMOOOY	Molly Bloom
BMMOOOSTTT	bottommost

C

CCCCIIMOOR	micrococci
CCCDEIMRUU	circumduce
CCCDIMRTUU	circumduct
CCCEEINNOS	conscience
CCCEEINRST	crescentic
CCCEELNSUU	succulence
CCCEENORRU	occurrence
CCCEHKORSS	crosscheck
	cross-check
CCCEIIMRSU	circumcise
CCCEIIRSTY	cysticerci
CCCEILOPRR	crop circle
CCCEINNOOP	Concepción
CCCEINNORT	concentric
CCCEIOOPRT	eccoprotic
CCCELNSUUY	succulency
CCCGNOOOSU	gonococcus
CCCHHILOOO	chocoholic
CCCHIKOPST	spitchcock
CCCHILMOOY	homocyclic
CCCHILMOSU	colchicums
CCCIKLMNOT	McClintock
CCCILNSTUY	succinctly
CCCINNOOOT	concoction
CCCLOORSSY	cyclo-cross
CCDDEENNOS	condescend
CCDDEKLORU	curled dock
CCDEEEENPR	precedence
CCDEEEHINS	dehiscence
CCDEEEHRSU	curd cheese
CCDEEEIORV	ice-covered
CCDEEERRSU	recrudesce
CCDEEFIINY	deficiency
CCDEEFINNO	confidence
CCDEEGINSU	succeeding
CCDEEHHTUW	chew the cud
CCDEEHNOSY	synecdoche
CCDEEIIIPT	epideictic
CCDEEIILRT	dielectric
CCDEEIKLRV	clever dick
CCDEEILNOR	reconciled
CCDEEIMORT	ectodermic
CCDEEIORRU	cri de coeur
CCDEELNNOO	condolence
CCDEENORSS	crescendos
CCDEHILLOS	cold chisel
CCDEHILNOR	chronicled
CCDEHLNTUU	Dutch uncle
CCDEIIIRTZ	criticized
CCDEIINNOR	endocrinic
CCDEIINNOT	coincident
CCDEIINOPU	occupied in
CCDEIJKOSY	disc jockey
CCDEIKLOSU	cuckoldise
CCDEIKLOUZ	cuckoldize
CCDEINNOST	disconnect
CCDEINOOPS	endoscopic
CCDEINOPUU	unoccupied
CCDEINORST	disconcert
CCDELNOOTU	to conclude
CCDELOOORU	colour code
	colour-code
CCDFKOORRS	Crockford's
CCDGIIINNO	coinciding
CCDGIILOSY	glycosidic
CCDGILNNOU	concluding
CCDGILOOOY	codicology
CCDGINNOTU	conducting
CCDHIIIORT	dichroitic
CCDIMNOSTU	misconduct
CCDINNOOTU	conduction
CCDLMMNOOO	common cold
CCEEEELLNX	excellence
CCEEEENNSS	senescence
CCEEEFNNOR	conference ❏
CCEEEIINPR	recipience
CCEEEINPRS	prescience
CCEEEINQSU	quiescence
CCEEEINRSV	virescence
CCEEELLNXY	Excellency
CCEEEMMNOR	recommence
CCEEEMNOPT	competence
CCEEEMNSTU	tumescence
CCEEENRRRU	recurrence
CCEEENRSTX	excrescent
CCEEFFIINY	efficiency
CCEEFFILNO	off-licence
CCEEFHHRRU	Free Church
CCEEFINOOV	conceive of
CCEEFINTTU	fettuccine
CCEEFLNNOU	confluence
CCEEGHINRS	screeching
CCEEGIMNSU	ecce signum
CCEEGINNOR	congeneric
CCEEGINORT	egocentric
	geocentric
CCEEGNNORU	congruence
CCEEHHIRST	Chichester
CCEEHIINST	technicise
CCEEHIINTZ	technicize
CCEEHILNRY	Henry Cecil
CCEEHINOSS	choiceness
CCEEHLORST	Colchester
CCEEHNOSTU	escutcheon
CCEEIIINNP	incipience

CCEEIILMRS	semicircle
CCEEIINPRY	recipiency
CCEEILLOTV	collective
CCEEILMNNY	inclemency
CCEEILNOPT	pleonectic
CCEEILNORR	reconciler
CCEEILNORT	electronic
CCEEILOPST	telescopic
CCEEILORVY	coercively
CCEEIMOSTU	cut some ice
CCEEINNNOT	continence
CCEEINNOTV	connective
CCEEINNRTU	encincture
CCEEINORST	concretise
CCEEINORTZ	concretize
CCEEINOSSV	concessive
CCEEINOTVV	convective
CCEEINQSUY	quiescency
CCEEINRRSU	currencies
CCEEINRTTY	city centre
CCEEIOPRSS	crosspiece
CCEEIORRTV	corrective
CCEEISSSUV	successive
CCEEJNORTU	conjecture
CCEEKKLOYY	cocky-leeky
CCEELMOORS	come closer
CCEELNOPRU	corpulence
CCEELNORTY	concretely
CCEELNRTUU	truculence
CCEELOSTTU	cos lettuce
CCEELPRSUU	crepuscule
CCEEMNOPTY	competency
CCEENOOSSX	ex concesso
CCEENOPRRT	preconcert
CCEFHIIMOR	microfiche
CCEFHIMOOR	from choice
CCEFHKLOOT	of the clock
CCEFIIINST	scientific
CCEFIINPSU	unspecific
CCEFIKLSTT	cleft stick
CCEFILLLRU	full-circle
CCEFILMRUX	circumflex
CCEFIMRSUU	circumfuse
CCEFINNOOT	confection
CCEFLLNOTU	flocculent
CCEFLSSSUU	successful
CCEGGILNOY	glycogenic
CCEGHHORRU	churchgoer
CCEGHIILNO	conchiglie
CCEGHINORT	crocheting
CCEGIILNNR	encircling
CCEGIMMNNO	commencing
CCEGINNNOR	concerning
CCEGINNNOT	connecting
CCEGINORSY	cryogenics
CCEGNNORUY	congruency
CCEHHILOTV	clove hitch
CCEHIINNOS	cinchonise
CCEHIINNOZ	cinchonize
CCEHIKMOOR	mock-heroic
CCEHIKNNRU	chicken run
CCEHIKNOPT	checkpoint
CCEHIKNOPX	chickenpox
CCEHIKNOTU	chicken out
CCEHIKPRRY	cherry-pick
CCEHIKSSTT	Schick test
CCEHILNORR	chronicler
CCEHILNORS	chronicles □
CCEHILORRU	hour-circle
CCEHIMOSSY	ecchymosis
CCEHIOORRV	Verrocchio
CCEHMOORTY	cytochrome
CCEHNOPRUW	cowpuncher
CCEHOSTTUZ	zucchettos
CCEIIINNPY	incipiency
CCEIILOSST	solecistic
CCEIIMOORS	seriocomic
CCEIIMOTXY	Mexico City
CCEIIMPSST	scepticism
CCEIIOPPRS	periscopic
CCEIIOSSTT	Scotticise
CCEIIOSTTZ	Scotticize
CCEIKKOPPT	pickpocket
	pick-pocket
CCEILLNOOT	collection
CCEILNNOSU	nucleonics
CCEILNOSUV	conclusive
CCEIMMRRUU	circummure
CCEIMNNOOU	uneconomic
CCEIMNRTUV	circumvent
CCEIMOOPRS	microscope □
CCEIMOPRSU	circumpose
CCEIMORRST	miscorrect
CCEINNNOOT	connection
CCEINNOOPT	conception □
CCEINNOORT	concertino
	concretion
CCEINNOOSS	concession
CCEINNOOTV	convection
CCEINOORRT	correction
CCEINOPRSU	Copernicus
CCEINOSSSU	succession
CCEIOOPRSU	precocious
CCEKLOORTW	clock tower
CCELLOSTYY	cyclostyle
CCELMOORTY	motorcycle
	motor-cycle
CCELNOPRUY	corpulency
CCELNOSSTU	occultness
CCENNORRTU	concurrent
CCENOOPRSY	necroscopy
CCENOPSSTU	conspectus
CCENORRSTU	cut corners
CCEORSSSSU	successors
CCFIILNNOT	in conflict
CCGHHHHIRU	High Church
CCGHLNOOOY	conchology
CCGIINNNOV	convincing
CCGINNORRU	concurring
CCGIOOPRSY	gyroscopic
CCHHHOOPTT	hotchpotch
	hotch-potch

CCHHIIOTTY	ichthyotic
CCHIILNNOO	conchiolin
CCHIINORTY	chronicity
CCHILMNNOU	column inch
CCHIMNOOOR	monochroic
CCHIMOSSTT	Scotch mist
CCHINNORSY	synchronic
CCHINORTUW	concur with
CCHIOOOPRS	horoscopic
CCHIORSSTU	trochiscus
CCHKLNOSUU	no such luck
CCHMNOOPTU	not much cop
CCHOOPSSUU	hocus-pocus
CCIIILOSST	sciolistic
CCIIKKQRTU	quick trick
CCIIKKQSTU	quick-stick
CCIILLNOPY	polyclinic
CCIILMNNOY	lincomycin
CCIILMOPTY	complicity
CCIILORTUV	civil court
CCIILRSTTY	tricyclist
CCIIMOPRST	comic strip
CCIINNNOTY	concinnity
CCIINNOOTV	conviction
CCIIORSTUU	circuitous
CCIKNOOPTU	cuckoo pint
CCILLNOORU	councillor
CCILMRRUUU	curriculum
CCILNNOOSU	conclusion
CCIMOOPRSY	microscopy
CCINNOOSSU	concussion
CCINOSTUVY	viscountcy
CCIORRSSSS	crisscross
	criss-cross
CCJLNNOTUY	conjunctly
CCNOORRTUW	crown court
CDDEEEENNP	dependence
CDDEEEINUV	undeceived
CDDEEEJLTY	dejectedly
CDDEEELNOR	needlecord
CDDEEENNPY	dependency
CDDEEENTTU	undetected
CDDEEFFIIN	diffidence
CDDEEGGLOR	egg coddler
CDDEEGINNS	descending
CDDEEIINSS	dissidence
CDDEEIJPRU	prejudiced
CDDEEINORS	considered
CDDEEINRTU	undirected
CDDEEINTUY	Dundee City
CDDEEIORSV	discovered
CDDEEKMRXY	Eddy Merckx
CDDEELLSUY	secludedly
CDDEELMOSU	cuddlesome
CDDEEMNOTU	documented
CDDEEMOOPS	decomposed
CDDEENORRU	unrecorded
CDDEEOPRRU	reproduced
CDDEFFHISU	dischuffed
CDDEFNNOOU	confounded
CDDEGIKLOR	gridlocked
CDDEHISTUY	Thucydides
CDDEIILNNU	included in
CDDEIMMNOS	discommend
CDDEIMMOOS	discommode
CDDEIMOOSU	duodecimos
CDDEINNOSW	second wind
CDDEINORTU	introduced
CDDEINOSTU	discounted
CDDEMNOOPU	decompound
CDDENOPRTU	end-product
CDDHIILORW	wild orchid
CDDILOOPSU	diplodocus ❑
CDDNOORRUW	crowd round
CDEEEEGILP	Ledge Piece
CDEEEEINPX	expedience
CDEEEENRRT	deterrence
CDEEEFFHOS	cheesed off
CDEEEFFINR	difference
CDEEEFFIST	side effect
CDEEEFILST	self-deceit
CDEEEFILTV	deflective
CDEEEFINOV	evidence of
CDEEEGINRV	divergence
CDEEEGITTX	get excited
CDEEEHINRS	Chinese red
CDEEEHIPRR	decipherer
CDEEEHLNSU	enschedule
CDEEEHLRSU	reschedule
CDEEEHNNRT	entrenched
CDEEEIINNV	in evidence
CDEEEIINPS	desipience
CDEEEIINRS	decree nisi
CDEEEILOPV	velocipede
CDEEEILQSU	deliquesce
CDEEEIMNNO	comedienne
CDEEEINPXY	expediency
CDEEEINRRT	interceder
CDEEELLNUX	unexcelled
CDEEELMNOT	dolcemente
CDEEELMOPS	Empedocles
CDEEELOPST	telescoped
CDEEELORRT	telerecord
CDEEELPTXY	expectedly
CDEEENPTUX	unexpected
CDEEENTUUX	unexecuted
CDEEEOPTTX	expected to
	to expected
CDEEEPRSTU	persecuted
CDEEERRSTT	street cred
CDEEFGILNT	deflecting
CDEEFIINRT	dentifrice
CDEEFIIORS	crise de foi
CDEEFILNNU	influenced
CDEEFILNOT	deflection
CDEEFINNTU	uninfected
CDEEFINORR	reinforced
CDEEFLNORT	centrefold
CDEEFLNORY	enforcedly
CDEEFLNOSS	second self
CDEEFNNORU	unenforced
CDEEFNORSS	forcedness

CDEEGHHITT	get hitched
CDEEGIINOR	Ceredigion
CDEEGIKNNR	ring-necked
CDEEGILNNU	indulgence
CDEEGILNOV	Venice gold
CDEEGILNUV	divulgence
CDEEGILPST	get spliced
CDEEGINOPR	proceeding
CDEEGINORZ	recognized
CDEEGINRRS	screen grid
CDEEHHIKTT	hit the deck
CDEEHIMNOR	echinoderm
CDEEHINRST	christened
CDEEHLNOSU	on schedule
CDEEHLOORS	deschooler
CDEEHLRTWY	wretchedly
CDEEHMNOOS	second home
CDEEHMNOPR	comprehend
CDEEHORRST	Dorchester
CDEEIIILSV	decivilise
CDEEIIILVZ	decivilize
CDEEIIINSV	indecisive
CDEEIILNNO	Celine Dion
CDEEIILSVY	decisively
CDEEIIMPRS	spermicide
CDEEIINRRR	dernier cri
CDEEIINRST	indiscreet
	indiscrete
	iridescent
CDEEIIPRTV	predictive
CDEEIIRSSV	disservice
CDEEIKNSSW	wickedness
CDEEILNNOS	declension
CDEEILNNSU	unlicensed
CDEEILNNTY	indecently
CDEEILNOOS	decolonise
CDEEILNOOZ	decolonize
CDEEILNOSS	disenclose
CDEEILNOSU	nucleoside
CDEEILNOTU	nucleotide
CDEEILNRTU	interclude
CDEEILNRUV	curved line
CDEEILNRVY	Inverclyde
CDEEILOORZ	decolorize
CDEEILORST	cloistered
CDEEILRSTY	discreetly
	discretely
CDEEIMNNTU	inducement
CDEEIMNPRU	imprudence
CDEEINNRSW	windscreen
CDEEINOPRV	providence □
CDEEINORRS	reconsider
CDEEINORTT	credit note
CDEEINPRRU	underprice
CDEEINPRSY	presidency
CDEEINRSST	directness
CDEEIOPRRV	overpriced
CDEEIOPSTU	deceptious
CDEEIORRSV	discoverer
CDEEIORRVV	cover drive
CDEEIPRSST	disrespect

CDEEIRRSTT	derestrict
	restricted
CDEEKKKNNO	knock-kneed
CDEEKNNORU	unreckoned
CDEEKOOORV	overcooked
CDEEKOOPRW	woodpecker
CDEELNNOSU	unenclosed
CDEELNOORS	second role
CDEELNOVXY	convexedly
CDEEMNNOOU	come undone
CDEEMOOPRS	decomposer
CDEEMOPRSS	compressed
	decompress
CDEENNORST	contenders
CDEENOORRS	rood screen
CDEENORRSU	underscore
CDEENORRUV	under cover
	undercover
CDEENORSTU	unescorted
CDEENOSTUU	consuetude
CDEENRRSTU	undercrest
CDEENSSSSU	cussedness
CDEEOPRRRU	reproducer
CDEEOPRRSU	procedures
CDEERSSSTU	seductress
CDEFFHILOO	hold office
CDEFFILNRU	undercliff
CDEFGHIKLT	flight deck
CDEFHINORU	four-inched
CDEFHLMORS	Chelmsford
CDEFILLOUV	full-voiced
CDEFILNOUU	fluid ounce
CDEFINNNOU	unconfined
CDEFINNOTU	defunction
CDEFIOSSTX	fixed costs
CDEFLNORUY	unforcedly
CDEFLNOSUY	confusedly
CDEFMOOOPS	composed of
CDEFNOOPRU	pound force
CDEFNORRTU	undercroft
CDEGHHIIPR	high-priced
CDEGHHIMOY	high comedy
CDEGHINNRU	chundering
CDEGIILNNY	incedingly
CDEGIINNRS	discerning
	rescinding
CDEGIINSST	dissecting
CDEGIKNOST	stockinged
CDEGILNSUY	seducingly
CDEGIMNNNO	condemning
CDEGINNNOT	contending
CDEGKLNOOR	Golden Rock
CDEGMNORUU	curmudgeon
CDEGNOOORR	go on record
CDEHHIJNOR	John Edrich
CDEHIILOPS	discophile
CDEHIILORS	chloridise
CDEHIILORZ	chloridize
CDEHIINOST	hedonistic
CDEHIKORTT	do the trick
CDEHILOPTW	low-pitched

CDEHIMOPRY hypodermic
CDEHINOPTY endophytic
CDEHLNOOSU unschooled
CDEHLOOPPR clodhopper
CDEHMMNOOR common herd
CDEHMNOTUW Dutchwomen
CDEHNOOORT octohedron
CDEHOOPRSY hydroscope
CDEIIIILNS in deliciis
CDEIIILNNS disincline
CDEIIILNPS discipline
CDEIIIMRSV recidivism
CDEIIIMTVZ victimized
CDEIIINNOS indecision
CDEIIINTVV vindictive
CDEIIIRSTV recidivist
CDEIIKLSST sick-listed
CDEIILNNOT inclined to
CDEIILNOSS disinclose
CDEIILNPPR principled
CDEIILNRTY indirectly
CDEIILOSTU solicitude
CDEIIMNNTT indictment
CDEIIMORRS misericord
CDEIIMORTY mediocrity
CDEIIMPPSU piped music
CDEIINOPRT prediction
CDEIINORST directions
discretion
CDEIINOSST dissection
CDEIIOORRS sororicide
CDEIIORTTY city editor
CDEIIRSSUV discursive
CDEILLLOVY Clive Lloyd
CDEILLLPUY pellucidly
CDEILNOSSU cloudiness
CDEILNOTUU include out
CDEILORSSU disclosure
CDEIMMNOOT come to mind
CDEIMMNOPU compendium
CDEIMNOOSY diseconomy
CDEIMNOSUU mucedinous
CDEIMOOPSS discompose
CDEIMORSTU Democritus
CDEIMOSTUZ customized
CDEINNOSTT discontent
CDEINOORSU indecorous
CDEINOPRTY decryption
CDEINORSTU discounter
CDEINPRSTU unscripted
CDEINRSTTU instructed
CDEIOPRRST descriptor
CDEIOPRTUV productive
CDEIORRSSU discourser
CDEIRRSTTU strictured
CDEKKNOOTU knocked out
CDEKLORTUY cold turkey
CDELLNOORT controlled
CDELMOOPSY composedly
CDELNOORUU uncoloured
CDELNOOTUV convoluted
CDELNORRTU turn colder
CDELNRTUUU uncultured
CDELOORSUY decorously
CDELPRSTUU sculptured
CDEMNNOOOW come down on
CDEMNNOSUU unconsumed
CDEMNOOOTW come down to
CDENNOOPRU pronounced
CDENOOPRRS correspond
CDENOPRTUW new product
CDENORRUUV curve round
CDEOORRRTU court order
CDERRSTTUU structured
CDFFIILTUY difficulty
CDFHILOOPR childproof
CDFIMOORST discomfort
CDFINNOOTU confound it
CDGHILOORY hydrologic
CDGHILOPSU disc plough
CDGIIILNRU ridiculing
CDGIIKNNOO in good nick
CDGIINOPRR riding-crop
CDGIKLLOOS goldilocks
CDGILLNOSY scoldingly
CDHHIILLSY childishly
CDHHILORST Rothschild
CDHILLORSY Chris Lloyd
CDHILORTYY hydrolytic
CDHINOOPRY hydroponic
CDHKNNPRUU punch-drunk
CDHKNOORSU Rock Hudson
CDHLLMNOOO Loch Lomond
CDIIINNSTT indistinct
CDIIKNPRTU Dick Turpin
CDIIKRRTTY dirty trick
CDIILNOOSU nidicolous
CDIILNSTTY distinctly
CDIILORSUU ridiculous
CDIINNOOST conditions
CDIINOPSUU cupidinous
CDIINOSSSU discussion
CDILMORSUW world music
CDIMMOOOSU commodious
CDINNOOORS con sordino
CDINOOPRST spin doctor
CDINOOPRTU production
CDLMOORSTU storm cloud
CDLNOORTUY old country
CDLOOOPRST Doctor Slop
CDNOOOOTTW cottonwood
CDNOOPSSTU pound Scots
CDNOSSSTUU Duns Scotus
CEEEEFFRSV effervesce
CEEEEFHPRS free speech
CEEEEFLLSS fleeceless
CEEEEFLRST free-select
CEEEEFNPRR preference
CEEEEHNPRT threepence
CEEEEINPRX experience
CEEEEKPRST keep secret
CEEEELLNPR repellence

CEEEFFGLNU	effulgence
CEEEFFLORS	effloresce
CEEEFGLNRU	refulgence
CEEEFHNNOT	on the fence
CEEEFILRTV	reflective
CEEEFINRRS	firescreen
CEEEFINRSS	fierceness
CEEEFIPRTV	perfective
CEEEFPRRTU	prefecture
CEEEGGILNN	negligence
CEEEGINRTV	vice-regent
CEEEGLLNOW	New College
CEEEGNRRSU	resurgence
CEEEHHMRTU	Erechtheum
CEEEHHRSTU	Erechtheus
CEEEHIKNSS	cheekiness
CEEEHINRSS	cheeriness
CEEEHJLNOS	John Cleese
CEEEHKPRTU	up the creek
CEEEHKRSSS	Cherkesses
CEEEHLLSSY	Seychelles
CEEEHLMOOT	come to heel
CEEEHLPSSS	speechless
CEEEHMORTT	hectometre
CEEEHNOPQU	open cheque
CEEEHNOPSS	ecphoneses
CEEEHNORSS	chersonese
CEEEHOQRUU	Eurocheque
CEEEHORRST	threescore
CEEEIILNRS	resilience
CEEEIINNOP	in one piece
CEEEIKKPTW	keep wicket
CEEEILLTVY	electively
CEEEILMNNT	clementine ❑
CEEEILMRTT	telemetric
CEEEILNNRT	centre-line
CEEEILNPRT	percentile
CEEEILNPST	pestilence
CEEEIMNNTT	enticement
CEEEIMNNTV	evincement
CEEEIMNRSV	servicemen
CEEEIMNRTT	centimetre
CEEEIMNTTX	excitement
CEEEINNPPY	penny-piece
CEEEINNPRT	pertinence
CEEEINNQSU	in sequence
CEEEINTTWY	winceyette
CEEEIPPRTV	perceptive
	preceptive
CEEEIPRSTV	respective
CEEEISTUVX	executives
CEEEKKLNPS	kenspeckle
CEEEKOPRRW	crow-keeper
CEEEKRRSSU	seersucker
CEEELLNPRY	repellency
CEEELNRSSV	cleverness
CEEELNSSST	selectness
CEEELORSTT	corselette
CEEELORSTV	Secret Love
CEEELPSSTX	exceptless
CEEEMNOPRS	recompense
CEEEMNORRT	centromere
CEEENNRSST	recentness
CEEENOPPRT	prepotence
CEEENOPRST	open secret
CEEENRSSSU	secureness
CEEENRSSTT	screen test
CEEFFFLNOU	offenceful
CEEFFHILNS	Schlieffen
CEEFFHOOPS	coffee shop
CEEFFILLMO	coffee mill
CEEFFINPTY	fifty pence
CEEFFIOORV	overoffice
CEEFGHINNR	greenfinch
CEEFGINOSU	Cienfuegos
CEEFGINPRT	perfecting
CEEFGINRTU	centrifuge
CEEFGLLNTU	neglectful
CEEFGLNRUY	refulgency
CEEFHHNORT	henceforth
CEEFHIPRTV	fever pitch
CEEFHLLRUY	cheerfully
CEEFIILNTV	inflective
CEEFIJLNST	self-inject
CEEFIKLNSS	fickleness
CEEFILMOOT	come to life
	life to come
CEEFILNNRU	influencer
CEEFILNNSU	influences
CEEFILNORT	reflection
CEEFINOPRT	perfection
CEEFINOSSX	in excess of
CEEFKLLSSY	fecklessly
CEEFLNORST	florescent
CEEFLPPRTU	pluperfect
CEEFLPRSTU	respectful
CEEFMNNORT	conferment
CEEFORRRSS	cross-refer
CEEFORRSST	C S Forester
CEEGHHOPTT	get the chop
CEEGHIILMP	hemiplegic
CEEGHIKNNP	henpecking
CEEGHIMOST	geochemist
CEEGHOSTUW	cough sweet
CEEGIILNTV	Gil Vicente
CEEGIINOTV	give notice
CEEGIINSTT	geneticist
CEEGILNNOT	neglection
CEEGILNPRY	creepingly
CEEGIMMNSU	e e cummings
CEEGINNQSU	sequencing
CEEGINNRSS	screenings
CEEGINNRST	nigrescent
CEEGINNRSU	insurgence
CEEGINOORT	orogenetic
CEEGINOOST	osteogenic
CEEGINOPRS	precognise
CEEGINOPRZ	precognize
CEEGINORRV	recovering
CEEGINORRZ	recognizer
CEEGINOSTV	congestive
CEEGINPRST	respecting

Words marked ❑ can also be spelled with an initial capital letter

CEEGINRSTY	synergetic
CEEGIOOPST	go to pieces
CEEGKORRSS	Greek cross
CEEGLLNNOS	Glenn Close
CEEGLOOSTT	get close to
CEEGLORSTU	Gloucester
CEEGNNOORV	converge on
CEEGNNORTV	convergent
CEEGNPRSUU	upsurgence
CEEGNRSTTU	turgescent
CEEHHIMORT	come-hither
CEEHHMNNOW	henchwomen
CEEHIIRRST	heritrices
CEEHIKORST	the Rockies
CEEHILNOPR	necrophile
CEEHILNOPT	telephonic
CEEHILOPRT	helicopter
CEEHILORTT	hectolitre
CEEHILOSVY	cohesively
CEEHILPSST	ecthlipses
CEEHIMMPSY	emphysemic
CEEHIMNNRT	enrichment
CEEHIMNRTT	Metternich
CEEHIMNTTU	technetium
CEEHIMOPTU	mouthpiece
CEEHIMSSTU	sheet music
CEEHINNORT	incoherent
CEEHINRSTW	Winchester
	Winchester®
CEEHINSSTT	tetchiness
CEEHIOPRSX	exospheric
CEEHIOPSTT	The Poetics
CEEHIPRRRY	Cherry Ripe
CEEHIRRSTV	Chris Evert
CEEHIRSTTY	hysteretic
CEEHIRSTWZ	Schweitzer
CEEHJKNORT	John Eckert
CEEHKKOOYY	hokey cokey
	hokey-cokey
CEEHLLNOSW	well-chosen
CEEHLNORTY	coherently
CEEHLNQSSU	quenchless
CEEHMOOPRT	hoc tempore
CEEHNOOPRT	ctenophore
CEEHNORRYY	Henry Royce
CEEHNORSTT	Chesterton
CEEHOOPSST	post-echoes
CEEIIINSTZ	citisenize
CEEIIINTZZ	citizenize
CEEIILLMRV	vermicelli
CEEIILNOSU	isoleucine
CEEIILNRSY	resiliency
CEEIILNRTT	centilitre
CEEIILPRSV	lip service
	lip-service
CEEIILTTVY	electivity
CEEIIMNNTT	incitement
CEEIIMORTT	meteoritic
CEEIIMPRRT	perimetric
CEEIIMPSSS	speciesism
CEEIIMPSST	epistemics
CEEIINNPPR	en principe
CEEIINNSST	insistence
CEEIINOSST	sectionise
CEEIINOSTZ	sectionize
CEEIINPPRT	percipient
CEEIINRSTT	interstice
CEEIIOPPSS	episcopise
CEEIIOPPSZ	episcopize
CEEIIOQTUV	quiet voice
CEEIIORRST	escritoire
CEEIIPSSST	speciesist
CEEIIRSSTU	securities
	securitise
CEEIIRSTUZ	securitize
CEEIJLOPRT	projectile
CEEIKLOPRS	corpse-like
CEEIKNPRTY	pernickety
CEEILLNRST	stenciller
CEEILLORSS	recoilless
CEEILMNOPT	incomplete
CEEILMNORT	clinometer
CEEILMNOSS	comeliness
CEEILNOORW	wine cooler
CEEILNORVY	overnicely
CEEILNRSUY	insecurely
CEEILORRST	cloisterer
CEEILORSST	sclerotise
CEEILORSTZ	sclerotize
CEEILPRSUV	preclusive
CEEIMMOOTT	time to come
CEEIMMORRT	micrometer
	micrometre
CEEIMNNOPR	prominence
CEEIMNOORZ	economizer
CEEIMNSSSU	meniscuses
CEEINNNOTV	convenient
CEEINNPRTY	pertinency
CEEINOPPRT	perception
CEEINOPRSS	precession
CEEINOPRTV	optic nerve
CEEINOPRTX	excerption
CEEINORRSW	cornerwise
CEEINORSTV	ventricose
CEEINOSSTX	exoticness
CEEINOSTTX	coexistent
	co-existent
CEEINRRSTU	scrutineer
CEEINRSSTY	syncretise
CEEINRSTTT	trecentist
CEEINRSTTV	vitrescent
CEEINRSTYZ	syncretize
CEEINRTTUX	extincture
CEEIOPRTTV	protective
CEEIOPRVWY	review copy
CEEIORRTUU	couturière
CEEIPRRSUV	precursive
CEEIPRSSUV	percussive
CEEIPSSTUV	susceptive
CEEJNOOSSS	jocoseness
CEEKLLRSSY	recklessly
CEEKLNRTTU	turtle-neck

CEEKLORRWW	crewelwork
CEEKNOORRV	overreckon
CEELLMOPTY	completely
CEELMMNOPT	complement
CEELMNNOOS	somnolence
CEELMNRSUU	Uncle Remus
CEELNORSVY	conversely
CEELOOPRRT	Cole Porter
CEELORRSTY	clerestory
CEEMMOTXYY	myxomycete
CEEMNOOPSS	meconopses
CEEMNOPRTU	recoupment
CEEMNORSTT	most recent
CEEMNPSSTU	spumescent
CEEMOORSTT	come to rest
CEENNOQSTU	consequent
CEENNORRTU	rencounter
CEENOPPPRR	peppercorn
CEENOPPRTY	prepotency
CEENORRTUV	rev counter
CEENORSSTV	covertness
CEENORSTUU	countersue
CEENPRSSSU	spruceness
CEENPRSTTU	putrescent
CEEOPRRSTT	retrospect
CEEOPRRSTU	persecutor
CEERSSSUUX	excursuses
CEFFFFHOTU	off the cuff
	off-the-cuff
CEFFHIINOR	chiffonier
CEFFHNOORR	French roof
CEFFIIKKLN	flick knife
	flick-knife
CEFFIINSTU	sufficient
CEFFIOOPST	Post Office
CEFFLLORUY	forcefully
CEFFMNOOOT	not come off
CEFGHILRTW	flight crew
CEFGIIKLNR	flickering
CEFGIINRTY	rectifying
CEFGINNORR	conferring
CEFGINORSU	using force
CEFGLOORSU	golf course
CEFHHINORT	Richthofen
CEFHHNNORR	French horn
CEFHHOOPRT	for the chop
CEFHILPRTU	pitcherful
CEFHILPRTY	flypitcher
CEFHILSTTU	cuttlefish
CEFHKNNORT	French knot
CEFHLNOOOV	cloven hoof
CEFIIILNTY	infelicity
CEFIIJRTUU	fruit juice
CEFIIKMNNY	Mickey Finn
CEFIILNNOT	inflection
CEFIILNOQU	cinquefoil
CEFIILOSTU	felicitous
CEFIIMNNTU	munificent
CEFIINOPRT	proficient
CEFIINOPST	pontifices
CEFIINOSTU	infectious
CEFIJNOORS	join forces
CEFILLMRUY	mercifully
CEFILMNRUU	unmerciful
CEFILMOORR	recoil from
CEFILMOORS	frolicsome
CEFILMOPXY	complexify
CEFILOPRRS	rifle-corps
CEFILORSUU	luciferous
CEFINNNOOT	innocent of
CEFINNOOSS	confession
CEFINOORSU	coniferous
CEFINORSUU	nuciferous
CEFINRSSSU	scurfiness
CEFIOORSUV	vociferous
CEFKLOPSTU	pocket-fuls
CEFLLSTTUU	scuttleful
CEFLNOORRW	cornflower
CEFOOOPSTY	foetoscopy
CEGGHIMNUW	chewing-gum
CEGHHIINRS	cherishing
CEGHIIKNNT	thickening
CEGHIILLNS	chiselling
CEGHIINNUY	unhygienic
CEGHIINOST	histogenic
CEGHILNOOP	nephologic
CEGHILNOST	close thing
CEGHIMMNOO	home-coming
CEGHINOOPT	photogenic
CEGHINOTTU	get in touch
CEGHINRSTT	stretching
CEGHIOPSSY	geophysics
CEGHLNOOTY	technology
CEGHOOPRSY	hygroscope
CEGIIJNORS	rejoicings
CEGIIKNNQU	quickening
CEGIILLNNP	pencilling
CEGIILNNSS	clinginess
CEGIILNNTY	enticingly
CEGIILNPRY	piercingly
CEGIILNTXY	excitingly
CEGIILOSTU	eulogistic
CEGIILPRSS	Spice Girls
CEGIINNPST	inspecting
CEGIINNRSV	scrivening
CEGIINNTUX	unexciting
CEGIINOSST	Gnosticise
CEGIINOSTX	coexisting
CEGIINOSTZ	Gnosticize
CEGIINRRTU	recruiting
CEGIJNOPRT	projecting
CEGIKNOOPR	rock pigeon
CEGIKNSTTU	get stuck in
CEGILLMNOP	compelling
CEGILLMOSU	collegiums
CEGILLOOXY	lexicology
CEGILMNOOP	monoplegic
CEGILMNOPT	completing
CEGILNNOST	clingstone
CEGILNORWY	coweringly
CEGILNOTVY	covetingly
CEGILOORUV	give colour

CEGILOSSTT	Giles Scott
CEGIMNNSSU	McGuinness
CEGIMNOORS	ergonomics
CEGIMNOORV	overcoming
CEGINNNOST	consenting
CEGINNNOTT	contingent
CEGINNOOST	congestion
CEGINNOQRU	conquering
CEGINNORST	constringe
CEGINNORSV	conserving
CEGINNORUV	uncovering
CEGINNRRUU	unrecuring
CEGINNRSTY	stringency
CEGINNRSUY	insurgency
CEGINOORRV	Congo River
CEGINOPRSS	processing
CEGINOPRTT	protecting
CEGINPSSTU	suspecting
CEGKLNOOTY	cook gently
CEHHHIIKRT	hitchhiker
CEHHHKRSUV	Khrushchev
CEHHILNRTU	in the lurch
CEHHIMRTUY	eurhythmic
CEHHIOOPST	theosophic
CEHHIOPTTY	hypothetic
CEHHLLOOTW	whole cloth
CEHHLORTTW	Letchworth
CEHIIINRST	trichinise
CEHIIINRTZ	trichinize
CEHIIKNTTW	think twice
CEHIIKRTTV	Trevithick
CEHIILLNSS	chilliness
CEHIILLOOP	oleophilic
CEHIILMORT	Roche limit
CEHIILMOST	homiletics
	mesolithic ❑
CEHIILNORS	chlorinise
CEHIILNORZ	chlorinize
CEHIILOPTY	heliotypic
CEHIIMNORT	thermionic
CEHIIMRTYZ	mythicizer
CEHIINORST	trichinose
CEHIINPRSS	chirpiness
CEHIINPSST	pitchiness
CEHIINSSTT	in stitches
CEHIIPRSTY	sphericity
CEHIIPSTUU	euphuistic
CEHIIRRTTU	urethritic
CEHIJKOPSY	jockeyship
CEHIKNORTW	reckon with
CEHIKOQTTU	to the quick
CEHILMORUX	Michel Roux
CEHILORSTY	chrysolite
CEHILTUWZZ	Chuzzlewit
CEHIMMNSSU	chumminess
CEHIMNOOPR	microphone
CEHIMOPTUW	come up with
CEHIMOSSUU	house music
CEHIMRSTUY	Eurythmics
CEHIMSSTTT	stem stitch
CEHIMSSTTU	miss the cut
CEHINNNPPY	penny-pinch
CEHINNRSTU	unchristen
CEHINNRSTY	strychnine
CEHINOORRS	rhinoceros
CEHINOOSSS	choosiness
CEHINOPPTY	phenotypic
CEHINOPRSS	censorship
CEHINOPRSY	hypersonic
CEHINOPRTY	hypertonic
CEHINOSSTU	touchiness
CEHINPSTTT	pitch tents
CEHIOORRRT	retrochoir
CEHIOPRRST	rectorship
CEHIOPRSTT	prosthetic
CEHIOQSTTU	coquettish
CEHIORRSST	choristers
CEHIORSSTV	Victor Hess
CEHIORSTTU	Theocritus
CEHIRSSTTW	Schwitters
CEHKLMNOOT	klootchmen
CEHKNOORST	on the rocks
CEHKOOPPRR	rock-hopper
CEHLMOOPRY	polychrome
CEHLMOPTYY	lymphocyte
CEHLNOOPTU	clothe upon
CEHLNOPRUW	power lunch
CEHLOOOPRT	tocopherol
CEHMMNOOOR	monochrome
CEHMMOOORS	chromosome
CEHMNOORSU	much sooner
CEHMNOOTTU	touch-me-not
CEHMOOPRTY	ectomorphy
CEHMPRTTUY	pretty much
CEHNOOPRRS	corner shop
CEHNOORSST	on the cross
CEHNOOSTTU	touchstone ❑
CEHNOPRSTU	Scunthorpe
CEHNOPRSTY	phenocryst
CEHNORTTUY	the country
CEHOOPRSTU	octopusher
CEHORSTTTU	outstretch
	stretch out
CEIIIILSTV	civilities
CEIIILLNNP	penicillin
CEIIILNOSU	Ion Iliescu
CEIIILNPTX	inexplicit
CEIIILNSVY	incisively
CEIIILOPST	politicise
CEIIILOPTZ	politicize
CEIIIMMPRS	empiricism
CEIIIMOSSS	isoseismic
CEIIIMPRST	empiricist
CEIIIMRTVZ	victimizer
CEIIJNNTUV	injunctive
CEIIKKLNPT	tickle pink
CEIIKLNSSS	sickliness
CEIIKNRSST	trickiness
CEIIKNSSST	stickiness
CEIILLORRT	Torricelli
CEIILLPTXY	explicitly
CEIILMOPST	polemicist

CEIILMSSTV	victimless
CEIILNOSTU	licentious
CEIILNOSTV	novelistic
CEIILNPPRS	principles
CEIILNQSSU	cliquiness
CEIILOOPRT	riot police
CEIILOOPST	politicoes
CEIIMNNOST	omniscient
CEIIMNRTUV	centumviri
CEIIMORSST	isometrics
CEIINNNOTU	continue in
CEIINNOPST	inspection
CEIINNOTTX	extinction
CEIINNSSTY	insistency
CEIINOPRSU	pernicious
CEIINOPRTV	voiceprint
CEIINOPSTT	nepotistic
CEIINORSSS	rescission
CEIINORSTT	trisection
CEIINPRSTU	in pictures
CEIINRSSTU	scrutinise
CEIINRSTUY	insecurity
CEIINRSTUZ	scrutinize
CEIIOOPSTZ	epizootics
CEIIOORSTU	trioecious
CEIIOPRSTY	preciosity
CEIIOPSSTY	speciosity
CEIIORSTVV	vivisector
CEIJNOOPRT	projection
CEIKKORRWW	wickerwork
CEIKLLORTT	Little Rock
CEIKLNPSSU	pluckiness
CEIKNOSSST	stockiness
CEILLMNOOT	Monticello
CEILLOOQSU	colloquise
CEILLOOQUZ	colloquize
CEILLORSSW	scrollwise
CEILMMNOPT	compliment
CEILMNNOSU	muscle in on
CEILMNOOPT	completion
CEILMNOOPX	complexion
CEILMNOSSU	miscounsel
CEILMNPSSU	clumpiness
CEILMNSSSU	clumsiness
CEILMOOOTV	locomotive
CEILMOOPST	leptosomic
CEILMOPSUV	compulsive
CEILMOPTXY	complexity
CEILMOSTUU	meticulous
CEILNNNOTY	innocently
CEILNNOSVY	insolvency
CEILNOOPRS	necropolis
CEILNOORRS	resorcinol
CEILNOPRSU	preclusion
CEILNORSTU	uncloister
CEILNORTTY	contritely
CEILNOSSST	costliness
CEILNOSUVV	convulsive
CEILNPRSSY	princessly
CEILOPRSUY	preciously
CEILOPSSUY	speciously
CEILORRTUY	courtierly
CEILORSSST	cloistress
CEIMMMNOOT	common time
CEIMMMNOTT	commitment
CEIMMNOORT	metronomic
CEIMMNOQUU	communiqué
CEIMMNORTY	metronymic
CEIMMOOPRS	compromise
CEIMMOPSTU	miscompute
CEIMMORRTY	micrometry
CEIMMORTUX	commixture
CEIMNOOOSU	monoecious
CEIMNOPRSU	proscenium
CEIMNORSUU	ceruminous
CEIMNRSSTY	syncretism
CEIMOOPRTT	competitor
CEIMOORSTY	sociometry
CEIMOPRRTY	pyrometric
CEINNNOOTT	contention
CEINNNOOTV	convention ❑
CEINNOORSV	conversion
CEINNOPSSU	in one's cups
CEINNOPTUX	expunction
CEINNORTTU	uncontrite
CEINNOSSTT	consistent
CEINOOPRSS	procession
CEINOOPRTT	protection
CEINOOPRTV	cover point
CEINOORSSU	censorious
CEINOORTTV	contortive
CEINOPRSSU	percussion
	supersonic
CEINOPRSTT	introspect
CEINOPRSTU	supertonic
CEINOQTUYZ	Quezon City
CEINORRSST	intercross
CEINORSTTT	cornettist
CEINOSTTTU	constitute
CEINRSSSTT	strictness
CEINRSSSTU	crustiness
CEINRSSSUV	scurviness
CEINRSSTTY	syncretist
CEIOOPRRST	proctorise
CEIOOPRRTU	Puerto Rico
CEIOOPRRTY	corporeity
CEIOOPRRTZ	proctorize
CEIOPPRRTT	protreptic
CEIOPRRTTX	protectrix
CEIOPRRTUV	corruptive
CEIOPRRTWY	copywriter
CEIOQRSSTU	quit scores
CEIPPRSTTY	typescript
CEIPRRSSTU	Scriptures
CEJJKMOPUY	jump-jockey
CEKLLLSSUY	lucklessly
CEKLMOOORR	locker room
CEKLMPRSUU	lumpsucker
CEKMNOOOTW	come to know
CEKNNOPSTY	penny stock
CELLLNTUUY	luculently
CELLNOORRT	controller

CELLNOORSU	counsellor
CELLOOORSU	lose colour
CELLOORRSY	Rolls-Royce®
CELLOORSSU	colourless
CELLORSUUY	ulcerously
CELMMOPTUY	lumpectomy
CELMNNOOSY	somnolency
CELMNOOSSY	Ceylon moss
CELOOPRRTU	colporteur
CELOOSSSSU	colossuses
CELOOSTUVY	covetously
CELPRSSSTU	sculptress
CEMMNNOOSS	commonness
CEMNNOOPST	components
CEMNOPRSTU	sperm count
CEMOOPRRSS	compressor
CENNNNOOTT	non-content
CENOORRTTV	controvert
CEOOPPRRST	prospector
CEOOPRRSTU	prosecutor
CEOPPRSSTU	prospectus
CEOPRRRSUY	precursory
CEOPRRSSTU	Procrustes
CEPPRRSTUU	upper crust
	upper-crust
CFFFIISSTU	fisticuffs
CFFFMOORRY	cry off from
CFFFMOORTU	cut off from
CFFGIIKNOT	ticking-off
CFFGILNOSY	scoffingly
CFFGINOTTU	cutting-off
CFFHILMNOR	flinch from
CFFOOOSTUU	out of focus
CFGIIMNNOR	confirming
CFGIINNORU	Finno-Ugric
CFGIINNOSY	consignify
CFGIKNNORU	unfrocking
CFGILOUYZZ	fuzzy logic
CFGIMNNOOR	conforming
CFGIMNOORT	comforting
CFHHIILRTY	filthy rich
CFHIIKSSTT	stick shift
CFHIMORSTW	switch from
CFHIOORSTT	Otto Frisch
CFHLLOOORT	floorcloth
CFHLMOOORR	chloroform
CFHMOOORTU	too much for
CFHNOOSTUY	out of synch
CFHOOOTTUU	out of touch
CFIIILNNOT	infliction
CFIIIOSTTU	fictitious
CFIILNOPRU	unprolific
CFIINNNOOT	non-fiction
CFIIOORRST	Cristofori
CFIIRSTTUU	futuristic
CFIKLLQUYY	fly quickly
CFIKOORTTU	trick out of
CFIKOPRSTU	stick up for
CFILMOOPRU	poculiform
CFIMMNOORS	conformism
CFIMNOORST	conformist
CFIMNOORTY	conformity
CFKOOOSTTU	out of stock
CFLLNORSUY	scornfully
CFLOORRSSY	flory cross
CFLOORSSUU	scrofulous
CFOOORTTUU	out of court
CGGIILNNRY	cringingly
CGGINNORSU	scrounging
CGHHILOOS	high school
CGHHILLNTU	light lunch
CGHHILOORU	high colour
CGHHILORTT	torchlight
CGHIILMORT	microlight
CGHIILNNPY	pinchingly
CGHIILNTWY	witchingly
CGHIILOOST	histologic
CGHIILPRTY	triglyphic
CGHIINNOSU	cushioning
CGHIINPRRU	chirruping
CGHIKLNOSY	shockingly
CGHIKNORTW	thick-grown
CGHILLOORS	schoolgirl
CGHILNOSTT	longstitch
CGHILNOTUY	touchingly
CGHILNRSUY	crushingly
CGHILOORTY	trichology
CGHIMNOORY	chirognomy
CGHIOORTUV	Victor Hugo
CGHLNOOORY	chronology
CGHLOOPSYY	psychology
CGHOPRTUUU	cut up rough
CGIIIILNVZ	civilizing
CGIIIJNOST	jingoistic
CGIIIKNNPT	nit-picking
CGIIILNNTY	incitingly
CGIIILNOST	soliciting
CGIIILNSTU	linguistic
CGIIILPSTU	pugilistic
CGIIJNNNOO	conjoining
CGIIKLLNOR	rollicking
CGIIMNOSST	Gnosticism
CGIINNNOTU	continuing
CGIINNOOST	incognitos
CGIINNOPRS	conspiring
CGIINNORTV	contriving
CGIINOTTUY	contiguity
CGIKLLNOOR	rollocking
CGIKLNOPRS	spring lock
CGIKNNOOTU	conking-out
CGIKNOSSTU	King's Scout
CGILLNOSWY	scowlingly
CGILLOSSYY	glycolysis
CGILMOOSTY	mycologist
CGILMOOSUY	musicology
CGILNNOPUU	uncoupling
CGILNNOSTU	consulting
CGILNOOOST	oncologist
CGILOOOTXY	toxicology
CGILOOSTTY	cytologist
CGIMNNOOOS	coming soon
CGIMOPRSUU	music group

CGINNPRTUU	puncturing
CGINOOPRST	prognostic
CGINOOSTUU	contiguous
CGINOPRRTU	corrupting
CGINOTTTUU	cutting-out
CGLOOOPRTY	proctology
CGNOOOSTUY	octogynous
CHHIIMRSST	Chris Smith
CHHIIOSSTY	ichthyosis
CHHIIPSTTW	whip-stitch
CHHILLRSUY	churlishly
CHHILOOPTY	holophytic
CHHIMNOOOP	homophonic
CHHIMPTUUW	chum up with
CHHIOOPPRS	phosphoric
CHHLLOOPRY	chlorophyl
CHIIIILNST	nihilistic
CHIIILPSTY	syphilitic
CHIIINORST	histrionic
CHIIKLLSTY	ticklishly
CHIIKLRSTY	trickishly
CHIIKMNTUW	muck in with
CHIILMNOOT	monolithic
CHIILOSTTY	histolytic
CHIIMOOPRS	isomorphic
CHIIMOPRRT	trimorphic
CHIIMORRST	trichroism
CHIINORSTU	trichinous
	unhistoric
CHIKNOQRTU	quickthorn
CHIKORSSTW	how's tricks?
CHILLNOSWY	clownishly
CHILLOPSTY	splotchily
CHILMOPTWY	comply with
CHILNOOPPY	polyphonic
CHILNOPSSU	consulship
CHILOOPTTY	photolytic
CHIMNNOOOP	monophonic
CHIMNRSSTY	strychnism
CHIMOOPRSY	hypocorism
CHIMOORTTY	trichotomy
CHIMOSSSTT	moss stitch
CHINOOPRSY	rhinoscopy
CHINRSSSYY	synchrysis
CHIOOPRSTT	orthoptics
CHIORSTTTW	stitchwort
CHKLOOORSW	schoolwork
CHLMNOSUUU	homunculus
CHLMOOPRYY	polychromy
CHLNOOTTUU	out to lunch
CHORRSSTTU	shortcrust
CIIIIKLOPT	poikilitic
CIIIILNTVY	incivility
CIIILLMPTY	implicitly
CIIILMPSST	simplistic
CIIILMPSSU	Simplicius
CIIILMPSTY	simplicity
CIIILNTUVY	uncivility
CIIILPRTTY	triplicity
CIIIMOPSTT	optimistic
CIIIMSSTTW	witticisms
CIIJNNNOTU	injunction
CIIKNOSTTW	in two ticks
CIIKOSTTTU	stick it out
CIILLNOOPS	cipollinos
CIILLNOOTU	illocution
CIILNOPSTU	punctilios
CIILOOSSTU	solicitous
CIILOPRTVY	proclivity
CIILRRSTUY	scurrility
CIILSSSTTY	stylistics
CIIMMNOOSS	commission
CIIMNOPRRT	microprint
CIINNNOOPT	conniption
CIINNOORTT	contrition
CIINNOTTUY	continuity
CIINOOPRST	con spirito
CIIOORSTUV	victorious
CIIOPRSTTU	prosciutti
CIIOPSSSUU	suspicious
CIJLNNOOTY	conjointly
CIKLLOSSTT	stock-still
CILLMNOOST	Tom Collins
CILLMOOQUU	colloquium
CILLMORSUY	collyriums
CILLOPRSTU	portcullis
CILLOPSTUY	Polyclitus
CILLOSSUUY	lusciously
CILMNOOOOT	locomotion
CILMNOOPSU	compulsion
CILMNOSTUU	monticulus
CILMOOSSTU	music stool
CILNNOOSUV	convulsion
CILORRSSUU	scurrilous
CIMNNOOOPP	nincompoop
CIMNNOSTUU	continuums
CIMNOOORXY	oxymoronic
CIMNOORSTU	consortium
CIMOOOPRST	compositor
CIMOORSSTU	roots music
CINNOOORTT	contortion
CINNOOPRSU	pronuncios
CINNOOSTUU	continuous
CINOOPRRTU	corruption
CINOORSSTY	consistory
CINOORSUUV	nucivorous
CINORRSTTU	instructor
CINORSTTUY	Tony Curtis
CINOSTTUUY	unctuosity
CIOOPRSTTU	prosciutto
CIOPPRSSTT	postscript
CIPPRRSTUU	stirrup cup
CKKNORSTUW	knockwurst
CKLLOORRSW	scrollwork
CKMNOORSTU	moonstruck
CKOOSSTUUY	sucks to you!
CLLMNNOOOY	Mo Connolly
CLMMNNOOUY	uncommonly
CLMOOOORTU	oculomotor
CLMOOOORTY	locomotory
CLMOOPRSUY	compulsory
CLNOOOOTTW	cotton wool

	cottonwool
CLNOORRTUU	turn colour
CLNOSTUUUY	unctuously
CLOOOPRRTU	prolocutor
CLOPRSSUUU	scrupulous
CMMMNOOOOR	common room
CMMMNOOOST	most common
CMMNNNOOOU	common noun
CNNOOOOTTT	cotton on to
	cotton onto
CNNOOTTUWY	county town

D

DDDDDFUUYY	fuddy-duddy
DDDEEEFNNU	undefended
DDDEEEHLOR	deed holder
DDDEEFIOST	eisteddfod
DDDEEIORRS	disordered
DDDEGIIOOR	didgeridoo
DDDEHLNORU	Old Hundred
DDDEINOORW	Edwin Drood
DDDELOORYY	Roddy Doyle
DDEEEEELTW	Tweedledee
DDEEEEMNRU	unredeemed
DDEEEFGIKN	knife-edged
DDEEEGINRS	redesigned
DDEEEGRSST	get dressed
DDEEEHIKNP	keep hidden
DDEEEHIRST	three-sided
DDEEEIMNPT	pedimented
DDEEEIMNRT	determined
DDEEEINRVY	in very deed
DDEEELLMOR	remodelled
DDEEELMMOS	meddlesome
DDEEELMNTY	dementedly
DDEEELMTUW	Tweedledum
DDEEELNTXY	extendedly
DDEEELRSVY	deservedly
DDEEENRRTU	undeterred
DDEEENRSUV	undeserved
DDEEENRSUX	undersexed
DDEEEOOPRT	deep-rooted
DDEEEPRSSU	superseded
DDEEFFLNOY	offendedly
DDEEFIIINT	identified
DDEEFIILLN	ill-defined
DDEEFIILMR	midfielder
DDEEFINNRU	unfriended
DDEEFIOPRV	deprived of
DDEEFIOSTV	divested of
DDEEFLMORY	deformedly
DDEEFMOOOR	foredoomed
DDEEGGHOOP	hodgepodge
	hodge-podge
DDEEGGNOSS	doggedness
DDEEGHLLNO	Glen Hoddle
DDEEGIINST	indigested
DDEEGILNSY	designedly
DDEEGILSTY	digestedly
DDEEGINNSU	undesigned
DDEEGJLLUW	well-judged
DDEEHILMOS	demolished
DDEEHILMTW	meddle with
DDEEHILNSU	unshielded
DDEEHINNRU	unhindered
DDEEHINORR	ride herd on
DDEEHINTUW	endued with
DDEEHNORSU	enshrouded
DDEEIIKLLR	riddle-like
DDEEIIKLMN	like-minded
DDEEIILMNV	evil-minded
DDEEIILNVW	wild endive
DDEEIINRSW	sidewinder
DDEEIIORXZ	deoxidizer
DDEEIIQSTU	disquieted
DDEEIKMORS	smoke-dried
DDEEILLMNW	well-minded
DDEEILLNRT	tendrilled
DDEEILLRSS	ill-dressed
DDEEILNNTY	intendedly
DDEEILNOSY	one-sidedly
DDEEILNOTT	dotted line
DDEEILSTTU	lust-dieted
DDEEIMNNOP	open-minded
DDEEIMNNRU	undermined
DDEEIMNORZ	modernized
DDEEINNNTU	unintended
DDEEINNOTT	intended to
DDEEINRRUV	underdrive
DDEEINRRUW	underwired
DDEEINRSUZ	undersized
DDEEIOORRZ	deodorizer
DDEEIRSSST	distressed
DDEELLOORW	olde-worlde
DDEELNOPUX	unexploded
DDEELRRSSU	rudderless
DDEENNOPST	despondent
DDEENNOSSS	soddenness
DDEENNPRSU	underspend
DDEENNSSSU	suddenness
DDEENOOTTT	dotted note
DDEENRRSSU	underdress
DDEEOORTTV	dotted over
DDEEORSTTT	dotted rest
DDEFFILSUY	diffusedly
DDEFGIIRSU	disfigured
DDEFGINOOR	good friend
DDEFHIILTW	fiddle with
DDEFHIIMUY	dehumidify
DDEFHLNORU	fundholder
DDEFIIILOS	solidified
DDEFIIMNOU	unmodified
DDEFILLNOU	ill-founded
DDEFKNNRUU	dunderfunk
DDEFLLOOSW	Oddfellows
DDEFLORSSU	Düsseldorf
DDEFMNORUU	dumfounder
DDEGGGILOR	gold-digger
DDEGHHIIMN	high-minded
DDEGHILNNO	Golden Hind
DDEGHINRSU	shuddering
DDEGIILNRY	deridingly

DDEGILNNOW	longwinded
	long-winded
DDEGILNUUV	undivulged
DDEGINNORS	dog's dinner
DDEGLLLOOR	rolled gold
DDEGLNOORY	dendrology
DDEGLNORUY	groundedly
DDEGNNORUU	ungrounded
DDEHIIIMNS	diminished
DDEHIIKNSY	kidney dish
DDEHIILNSW	windshield
DDEHIIMOST	Dodie Smith
DDEHINOSSS	shoddiness
DDEHJNNORY	John Dryden
DDEHLNOSTU	Huddleston
DDEHLOOSTU	the ould sod
DDEIIIKKNW	kiddiewink
DDEIIIMPSY	epididymis
DDEIIIPRST	dispirited
DDEIIJNOST	disjointed
DDEIIKNRRV	drink-drive
DDEIIMNNOU	diminuendo
DDEIINOPSS	indisposed
DDEIINORRS	in disorder
DDEIKNNOOS	do one's kind
DDEIKNNRUW	wunderkind
DDEILLNPSY	splendidly
DDEILLTTUW	dull-witted
DDEILOPSSY	disposedly
DDEILORRSY	disorderly
DDEIMMOSSU	desmodiums
DDEINOPSUW	upside down
	upside-down
DDEINORRSW	Red Windsor
DDEINORSSS	sordidness
DDEINPSTUU	undisputed
DDEIOOPSST	disposed to
DDELNORRUW	underworld
DDENNOORUZ	round dozen
DDENOORSTU	understood
DDENORRSUU	surrounded
DDENRSTUUY	understudy
DDGGIILNOS	dislodging
DDGGILNRUY	drudgingly
DDGGOOOOYY	goody-goody
DDGHIIRRYY	hirdy-girdy
DDGHILNTUY	thuddingly
DDGHRRUUYY	hurdy-gurdy
DDGIILLNRY	riddlingly
DDGILLNOPY	ploddingly
DDGILMNOUW	Ludwig Mond
DDGLOOOTUW	would to God
DDHILORRTW	Third World
DDHOOOOUWY	how do you do?
DDNNOOOPRW	drop down on
DDOOOOORRT	door-to-door
DEEEEEFPRZ	deep-freeze
DEEEEFNRTT	tenderfeet
DEEEEHLLLW	well-heeled
DEEEEIJLLL	jellied eel
DEEEEIKLLN	needle-like

DEEEEILMNT	needle time
DEEEEILNNP	pine needle
DEEEELMNVY	Mendeleyev
DEEEEOPRRS	pedereroes
DEEEFFOORT	free-footed
DEEEFHILWX	fixed-wheel
DEEEFHLORR	freeholder
DEEEFIJOUX	feux de joie
DEEEFILMNT	defilement
DEEEFILNTV	field event
DEEEFIMNNT	definement
DEEEFLORRW	deflowerer
DEEEFMNORW	freedwomen
DEEEFMNRRU	referendum
DEEEFNORWZ	freeze down
DEEEFNRTTU	unfettered
DEEEFORRRT	referred to
DEEEGGGLOY	goggle-eyed
DEEEGHHINT	heightened
DEEEGHLNNT	lengthened
DEEEGILLNR	ledger-line
DEEEGILMTY	gimlet-eyed
DEEEGILNRW	Gene Wilder
DEEEGIMNRT	regimented
DEEEGINRSS	greediness
DEEEGINRSU	under siege
DEEEGIRRST	deregister
	registered
DEEEHIKRRT	Erik the Red
DEEEHILRVW	drive-wheel
DEEEHIPRSS	Hesperides
DEEEHLLSSY	heedlessly
DEEEHLNORS	lederhosen
DEEEHLPRTU	The Prelude
DEEEHNORTY	heterodyne
DEEEHNRRTU	thereunder
DEEEHNRRUW	whereunder
DEEEHNRTTU	untethered
DEEEIIMNPR	meperidine
DEEEIKLLRW	weedkiller
DEEEILMRSS	remediless
DEEEILNRSS	slenderise
DEEEILNRUV	unrelieved
DEEEILORRV	Oliver Reed
DEEEILPRTT	deep litter
DEEEILPTXY	expeditely
DEEEIMMRSZ	mesmerized
DEEEIMNOST	demonetise
DEEEIMNOTZ	demonetize
DEEEIMNRRT	determiner
DEEEIMNRRW	Windermere
DEEEIMNRST	densimeter
DEEEIMORTU	eudiometer
DEEEIMPRTV	redemptive
DEEEIMRSSY	Merseyside
DEEEIMRSTV	time-served
DEEEINNPTV	pendentive
DEEEINORST	désorienté
DEEEINPRST	predestine
DEEEINPSSS	speediness
DEEEINRSTT	interested

DEEEINSSTW	tweediness
DEEEIPRSSV	depressive
DEEEIRSTWX	dexterwise
DEEEKLNORW	needlework
DEEEKOOPRR	doorkeeper
	door-keeper
DEEEKOPPST	keep posted
DEEELLNORW	ne'er-do-well
DEEELLNSSY	needlessly
DEEELLRSVW	well-versed
DEEELNOOTV	Deo volente
DEEELNRTTU	unlettered
DEEELPPPRU	Deep Purple
DEEELRRSVY	reservedly
	reversedly
DEEEMNNOTT	denotement
DEEEMNNOTU	denouement
	dénouement
DEEEMNOTTV	devotement
DEEEMNPRTU	untempered
DEEEMNRSSU	demureness
DEEENNRSST	tenderness ❑
DEEENOORVW	wood veneer
DEEENORTVX	extend over
DEEENOSTTW	sweet-toned
DEEENPRRST	Pretenders
DEEENRRSTU	understeer
DEEENRRSUV	undeserver
	unreserved
DEEENRSSSS	dress sense
DEEEPRRSSU	superseder
DEEFFGSTTU	get stuffed!
DEEFFNORSS	offendress
DEEFGGILLN	fledgeling
DEEFGHINRT	frightened
DEEFGIINRT	gentrified
DEEFGINSST	giftedness
DEEFHKLOOP	keep hold of
DEEFHNOOTT	to the end of
DEEFIIINNT	indefinite
DEEFIIINTV	definitive
DEEFIILNRS	friendlies
DEEFIILNTY	definitely
DEEFIINRUV	unverified
DEEFIINRVW	viewfinder
DEEFILLLSW	self-willed
DEEFILLRSU	fleur-de-lis
DEEFILLSTT	self-titled
DEEFILMOSU	field mouse
	fieldmouse
DEEFILNRSS	friendless
DEEFILNRSV	self-driven
DEEFILNRYZ	frenziedly
DEEFILORTU	outfielder
DEEFINNRTX	next friend
DEEFINRSSV	fervidness
DEEFLLMORW	well-formed
DEEFLLOTVW	twelvefold
DEEFLLPSUY	speedfully
DEEFLLRSUY	fleur-de-lys
DEEFLLSSTY	self-styled
DEEFLMRRSU	self-murder
DEEFMNORRU	unreformed
DEEFNOORTT	tenderfoot
DEEFNORSTU	unforested
DEEFOOQRTU	fore-quoted
DEEFOORSTU	sure-footed
DEEFORRUWW	furrow-weed
DEEGGGIMRU	Muggeridge
DEEGGGLLNO	long-legged
DEEGGNRSSU	ruggedness
DEEGGRSTUY	greedy guts
DEEGHIKNRT	The Red King
DEEGHINOTV	give the nod
DEEGHINOUY	honeyguide
DEEGHINRRR	red herring
DEEGHINSTU	Gesundheit
DEEGIIINNS	indigenise
DEEGIIINNZ	indigenize
DEEGIILNSU	guidelines
DEEGIILPRV	privileged
DEEGIINNRT	ingredient
DEEGIIRSSV	digressive
DEEGILNOPV	developing
DEEGILNRSY	resignedly
DEEGILRSST	stridelegs
DEEGINOOPT	pigeon-toed
DEEGINORST	resigned to
DEEGINOTTU	tongue-tied
DEEGINPPSU	speeding-up
DEEGINPRSS	depressing
DEEGIORRST	Rod Steiger
DEEGIORRSV	give orders
DEEGJJMORU	Medjugorje
DEEGKNOTTT	get knotted
	get knotted!
DEEGLLMRRU	Gerd Muller
DEEGLLNORU	golden rule
DEEGLNOORS	Golden Rose
DEEGNNOOSU	endogenous
DEEGNNOPRU	green pound
DEEGNNORUV	ungoverned
DEEHHIILMS	Hildesheim
DEEHIIRSTT	hereditist
DEEHILLRSV	shrivelled
DEEHILLSWW	well-wished
DEEHILMORS	demolisher
DEEHILNOTW	The Wild One
DEEHILOOTT	theodolite
DEEHIMRSTY	Mister Hyde
DEEHINOOPV	videophone
DEEHINORSV	Devonshire
DEEHINORVV	vinho verde
DEEHIORRRS	horserider
DEEHIORSTV	Shrovetide
DEEHJNNORS	John Enders
DEEHJNNORV	John Denver
DEEHLLOOWY	hollow-eyed
DEEHLMNOSW	seldom when
DEEHLMNRUW	underwhelm
DEEHLNOSUU	unhouseled
DEEHMORRTY	hydrometer

DEEHNRSSSW	shrewdness
DEEHOORTXY	heterodoxy
DEEHOPPRSU	dope pusher
DEEHOSSTYY	The Odyssey
DEEIIINPPR	piperidine
DEEIIKLNRT	tinder-like
DEEIIKLOSW	do likewise
DEEIIKMNNP	keep in mind
DEEIILMPST	speed limit
DEEIILNSTT	disentitle
DEEIILRSSV	silverside
DEEIILRSTZ	sterilized
DEEIILRSVY	derisively
DEEIIMMNPT	impediment
DEEIIMMNRS	immersed in
DEEIIMPRST	spider mite
DEEIINNRTT	Tridentine
DEEIINNSSV	divineness
DEEIINNSTW	disentwine
DEEIINOPTX	expedition
DEEIINPTTU	ineptitude
DEEIINQSTU	disquieten
DEEIINQTUU	inquietude
DEEIINSSTW	West Indies
DEEIINSSTZ	sensitized
DEEIIOPRSX	peroxidise
DEEIIOPRTT	peridotite
DEEIIOPRXZ	peroxidize
DEEIJNOSTT	jettisoned
DEEIJPRSTU	jeu d'esprit
DEEIKKNPRU	dukkeripen
DEEIKNNRSU	Iskenderun
DEEIKORSST	sidestroke
DEEILLMNUW	mulled wine
DEEILLSTUW	well-suited
DEEILLSUVY	delusively
DEEILMNOST	olden times
DEEILNNNRU	underlinen
DEEILNNQTU	delinquent
DEEILNOPSV	disenvelop
DEEILNORRS	orderlines
DEEILNOTTT	entitled to
DEEILNRSSW	wilderness
DEEILNRTVY	invertedly
DEEILPRUVZ	pulverized
DEEIMNNOPR	prime donne
DEEIMNNRRU	underminer
DEEIMNNRUV	menu-driven
DEEIMNOOTV	Montevideo
DEEIMNOPRT	redemption
DEEIMNORRZ	modernizer
DEEIMNORTV	Monteverdi
DEEIMNRSTW	Midwestern
DEEIMNRSWW	Wim Wenders
DEEIMNSTTV	divestment
DEEIMOPRSW	disempower
DEEINNNOSU	innuendoes
DEEINNOPRS	prednisone
DEEINNRSST	trendiness
DEEINNRSUV	unversed in
DEEINNSSTU	unitedness
DEEINOPRSS	depression
DEEINOPRST	interposed
DEEINORRUY	reioyndure
DEEINPPQUU	unequipped
DEEINPRRST	rinderpest
DEEINPRSTY	predestiny
DEEINQRRUU	unrequired
DEEINQRTUU	unrequited
DEEINQSTUY	squint-eyed
DEEINRRTUW	underwrite
DEEINRSSSS	dressiness
DEEINSSTTU	testudines
DEEIOPPRRT	propertied
DEEIOPPRSS	predispose
DEEIOPRSTT	test period
DEEIOPRSUX	Oedipus Rex
	superoxide
DEEIOQRRTU	required to
DEEIORRRTZ	terrorized
DEEIORRSTV	overstride
DEEJMOSTUX	jeux de mots
DEEKLMRTTU	kettledrum
	kettle-drum
DEEKLOOORV	overlooked
DEEKNOOTVY	donkey vote
DEEKOORRVW	overworked
DEELLMNOUW	unmellowed
DEELLMOOSY	dolesomely
DEELLNORTY	redolently
DEELLNRTUW	well-turned
DEELLORSVY	resolvedly
DEELMMNOPU	nom de plume
	nom-de-plume
DEELMNOPTY	deployment
DEELMNOPUY	unemployed
DEELMOPRSU	supermodel
DEELNNOSSU	unlessoned
DEELNOPRUX	unexplored
DEELNORSUV	unresolved
DEELNOSTTW	settle down
DEELOORSTV	resolved to
DEELOOVVYY	lovey-dovey
DEELOPRRTY	reportedly
DEELOPRSTW	spot-welder
DEELORTTUV	turtledove
DEEMNNOPRT	ponderment
DEEMNNORTW	wonderment
DEEMNNOSTW	endowments
DEEMNOORRY	money order
DEEMNOPRTT	deportment
DEEMNORSTU	tremendous
DEEMOORSTV	overmodest
DEEMOPRRTY	redemptory
DEENNOPRST	respondent
DEENOORSST	rootedness
DEENOORSTU	endorse out
DEENOQRTUU	underquote
DEENORRTUV	overturned
DEENORSUVZ	rendezvous
DEENOSSTUV	devoutness
DEENPRSSSU	suspenders

DEENRSUUVY	unsurveyed
DEEOQRSTUU	Tudoresque
DEEPPRSSSU	suppressed
DEFFFGINNO	fending off
DEFFHIMORS	sheriffdom
DEFFIMNOOR	informed of
DEFFOOORTU	four-footed
DEFFOORSWW	of few words
DEFFOPPRUW	powder puff
DEFGGILLRU	full-rigged
DEFGGILNOR	Goldfinger
DEFGHIITTW	fidget with
	gifted with
DEFGHILLTU	delightful
DEFGHOOOSU	house of God
DEFGIILNRR	girlfriend
DEFGIILNYY	edifyingly
DEFGIINNUY	unedifying
DEFGILLNUW	full-winged
DEFGILNNSY	send flying
DEFGINNORU	foundering
DEFGIOOOTV	give food to
DEFGNOORRU	foreground
DEFHIIIMRU	humidifier
DEFHIILNSY	fiendishly
DEFHIINNSU	unfinished
DEFHIINPRS	friendship
DEFHIIOSST	this side of
DEFHIKLOTY	Keith Floyd
DEFHILORSU	flourished
DEFHIOOPPR	hipped roof
DEFHLNOSUW	flesh wound
DEFHLORSSU	Rudolf Hess
DEFHNOOOTT	on the dot of
DEFHNOOPRU	unhoped-for
DEFHORRRTU	rutherford□
DEFIIILMPS	simplified
DEFIIILNTY	infidelity
DEFIIINNOT	definition
DEFIIINNTU	infinitude
DEFIILLNRY	friendlily
DEFIILORSU	fluoridise
DEFIILORUZ	fluoridize
DEFIILOSSZ	fossilized
DEFIINORST	iron-fisted
DEFIINPRUU	unpurified
DEFIIOPRSU	perfidious
DEFILLORWW	wild flower
	wildfowler
DEFILLPRUY	pridefully
DEFILNNRUY	unfriendly
DEFILNORSS	floridness
DEFILNORWW	windflower
DEFILOPRSW	wolf spider
DEFIMNNORU	uninformed
DEFIMORSST	desist from
DEFIMRSTTU	Fred Titmus
DEFINRRSUW	windsurfer
DEFIOOPRRV	provide for
DEFIOPPRST	stripped of
DEFIOPRSSS	disprofess

DEFLNOTTWY	twentyfold
DEFNOOORSW	of one's word
DEFNOORSTY	end of story
DEFOOORRTU	out of order
DEFOORSSTW	soft sowder
DEGGHNOOOU	good enough
DEGGIIKNSU	King's Guide
DEGGIINRSS	digressing
DEGGINNORU	going under
DEGGINORUV	give ground
DEGHIILTTW	twilighted
DEGHINNRTU	thundering
DEGHINOSSU	doughiness
DEGHINRSST	nightdress
DEGHIOOSSW	good wishes
DEGHIOOSTW	white goods
DEGHLNOPUU	unploughed
DEGIIINSSU	in disguise
DEGIILLMRX	mixed grill
DEGIILLNTY	diligently
DEGIILLNYY	yieldingly
DEGIILNNTY	indigently
DEGIILNNUY	unyielding
DEGIILNOPS	despoiling
DEGIILOOST	ideologist
DEGIILOPSS	idle gossip
DEGIIMNOOT	in good time
DEGIINNOSU	indigenous
DEGIINNSST	dissenting
DEGIINORRV	overriding
DEGIINORSS	digression
DEGIINPRST	spring tide
	springtide
DEGIKLMOOR	grimlooked
DEGIKLORST	strike gold
DEGILLOOTY	deltiology
DEGILMNORU	mouldering
	remoulding
DEGILMNRSU	mud-slinger
DEGILNNNUY	unendingly
DEGILNNPRU	plundering
DEGILNNRUY	enduringly
	underlying
DEGILNOOSS	goodliness
DEGILNOSTU	singled out
DEGILNRSTU	disgruntle
DEGILOOPST	pedologist
DEGIMNORTW	wrong-timed
DEGIMNSSSU	smudginess
DEGINNOPUX	expounding
DEGINNORST	grindstone
	stringendo
DEGINNORSU	resounding
DEGINORSTY	destroying
DEGINOSSST	stodginess
DEGIOORSTW	Tiger Woods
DEGKLOOOOR	good-looker
DEGLMNOOOY	demonology
DEGLNNRSUU	underslung
DEGLNOOOTY	deontology
DEGLNORSSU	groundless

DEGLOORTTY	troglodyte
DEGNNOOOTY	odontogeny
DEGNNOOPSW	sponge down
DEGNOORRUV	overground
DEGNOORTTU	get round to
DEGOOORSUW	wood grouse
	woodgrouse
DEHHILORTW	withholder
DEHHLNOOOR	holohedron
DEHHMOOORT	motherhood
DEHHNOOPRY	hydrophone
DEHHOPRTYY	hydrophyte
DEHIIINRST	disinherit
DEHIIJKOOT	Hideki Tojo
DEHIIKLLOO	likelihood
DEHIIKLNTW	linked with
DEHIILLOOV	livelihood
DEHIILLSVY	devilishly
DEHIILMNPU	delphinium
DEHIILNPSS	displenish
DEHIIMNSTT	in the midst
DEHIINOPSY	hypnoidise
DEHIINOPYZ	hypnoidize
DEHIIOPRST	editorship
DEHIIPTTUW	tied up with
DEHIIRSTVW	whist drive
DEHIJKNOPU	John Updike
DEHIKNOORW	hoodwinker
DEHIKORSST	kiss the rod
DEHILNOPSU	unpolished
DEHILNORTU	unitholder
DEHILNORTW	in the world
DEHILORSTV	short-lived
DEHIMMPSSY	dysphemism
DEHIMNOSSS	modishness
DEHIMNRTTU	The Tin Drum
DEHIMOOPPR	hippodrome
DEHIMOPRSY	hypodermis
DEHINNPSUU	unpunished
DEHINOORRS	her indoors
DEHINOPTYZ	hypnotized
DEHINORRSS	horridness
DEHINORSTT	threnodist
DEHINOSSTY	dishonesty
DEHINOTTUW	without end
DEHIOOPRST	priesthood
DEHIOORSST	sisterhood
DEHIOOSSTU	Theodosius
DEHIOPPRSW	worshipped
DEHIORSTWZ	Dershowitz
DEHIRRSSST	dress-shirt
DEHJNNOPPY	Johnny Depp
DEHLLLLOOY	Hello Dolly
DEHLNOOPRY	polyhedron
DEHLNOUUZZ	unhouzzled
DEHLOORRSY	holy orders
DEHLOORSSU	Lord's house
DEHMOORSSY	hydrosomes
DEHMORRTYY	hydrometry
DEHNNOORUU	unhonoured
DEHNOOOPRS	personhood
DEHNOORRSU	horrendous
DEHNOORSTU	undershoot
DEHNORSTUU	thunderous
DEHOOPRRWY	hydropower
DEHOOPRSUU	house-proud
DEIIILMSTU	similitude
DEIIILQRSU	liquidiser
DEIIILQRUZ	liquidizer
DEIIILSVVY	divisively
DEIIIMNPRY	pyrimidine
DEIIIMNTUV	diminutive
DEIIIMSSSV	dismissive
DEIIINNSTT	tendinitis
DEIIINORUV	iure divino
DEIIJNORUV	jure divino
DEIIKLNNSS	kindliness
DEIIKLNNTU	unit-linked
DEIILLNORW	iron-willed
DEIILLNUWY	unwieldily
DEIILLRSTY	distillery
DEIILMNOOT	demolition
DEIILMNPSS	limpidness
DEIILMNSTT	distilment
DEIILMOOST	dolomitise
DEIILMOOTZ	dolomitize
DEIILNNOVV	involved in
DEIILNNRTY	dirty linen
DEIILNOPTY	yield point
DEIILNOSVV	disinvolve
DEIILNPRTY	intrepidly
DEIILPRSTY	spiritedly
DEIILQSTUY	disquietly
DEIIMNNOSS	dimensions
DEIIMNOPRS	imprisoned
DEIIMOPRSV	disimprove
	improvised
DEIIMORRRS	side mirror
DEIIMPRSSU	presidiums
DEIINNORSV	disenviron
DEIINNOSSS	dissension
DEIINNOSST	distension
DEIINNOSTT	tendonitis
DEIINNPRSU	uninspired
DEIINNSSTU	untidiness
DEIINOOPST	deposition
DEIINOPRSS	dispersion
	pieds noirs
DEIINOPRXY	pyridoxine
DEIINRSSST	in distress
DEIIPRSTUV	disruptive
DEIKNNNORR	non-drinker
DEIKNNNSSU	unkindness
DEIKNNRSUW	swine-drunk
DEIKNORSTW	strike down
DEIKNRRSTU	underskirt
DEILLMMOSU	slime mould
DEILLMNSSY	mindlessly
DEILLNNOTY	indolently
DEILLNORSS	lordliness
DEILMMOSTY	immodestly
DEILMNORSW	world's mine

DEILMNOSSU	mouldiness
DEILMNPTUY	impudently
DEILMSTTUU	multitudes
DEILNNNTUW	wind tunnel
DEILNNOUVV	uninvolved
DEILNOOTUV	devolution
DEILNOPPTW	tipple down
DEILNOPRSW	wild person
DEILNOSSST	stolidness
DEILNRSTTY	stridently
DEILOORRTV	lord it over
DEILOPRSUU	preludious
DEILORSSUY	desirously
DEILOSTTWW	slow-witted
DEIMMNORSW	simmer down
DEIMNNNOOS	on one's mind
DEIMNNOSTW	disownment
DEIMNOPRUV	unimproved
DEIMNORTYY	dirty money
DEIMOPPRST	prompt side
DEINNNOSUW	unsinnowed
DEINNRSTUV	driven nuts
DEINOOPRSS	droopiness
DEINOOPRST	desorption
DEINOOQTUX	Don Quixote
DEINOORRTZ	torrid zone
DEINOORSWW	rose window
DEINOOSSSU	odiousness
DEINOPRRTU	put in order
DEINOPRSST	torpidness
DEINORRSST	torridness
DEINORRTTT	dirt-rotten
DEINORSSSW	drowsiness
DEINPSSSTU	stupidness
DEINRSSSTU	sturdiness
DEIOOPRSTY	depository
DEIOPSSSSS	dispossess
DEJLLLMOUY	jelly mould
DEJLNOOPUY	Joey Dunlop
DEJNOORSSU	de nos jours
DEKKNOORWY	donkeywork
	donkey-work
DEKLOOOPTU	looked up to
DEKLORSSVV	Sverdlovsk
DEKNOOPRUV	unprovoked
DEKOOORRWW	woodworker
DEKOOSSTVY	Dostoevsky
DELLLOPTUY	pollutedly
DELLNOPTUU	unpolluted
DELLORSSWY	wordlessly
DELLOSSUUY	sedulously
DELNNOPSSU	nonplussed
DELNNOTUWY	unwontedly
DELNOPRSSU	splendours
	splendrous
DELOOORRSW	wood sorrel
DELOOPRRWW	world power
DELOPPSSUY	supposedly
DELORRTTUY	torturedly
DELORSTUXY	dextrously
DEMMNOORST	most modern
DEMNOOPRST	post-modern
DEMNOPPRTU	unprompted
DEMNORSTUU	surmounted
DEMOOOPRRW	powder room
DEMOORRSST	Söderström
DENNOOPRSU	pundonores
DENNORSSTU	rotundness
DENOOORTTX	next door to
DENOOPPRRU	propounder
DENOOPRSWW	powder snow
DENOPRRTTU	protrudent
DENOPSSTUU	stupendous
DEOOPPSSTU	supposed to
DFFFOOSSTU	foodstuffs
DFGHIINORS	fishing-rod
DFGHILLOOT	floodlight
DFGIILNTUY	find guilty
DFGIMNOOOR	in good form
DFGOOOORUY	good for you
DFHIINRSSU	disfurnish
DFHILORTTY	thirtyfold
DFHLOOORTU	hold out for
DFIIKNORTT	fit to drink
DFIIKNRYZZ	fizzy drink
DFIIOOOPRT	idiot-proof
DFIKLOPPSY	floppy disk
DFILORRSTW	First World
DFIMNOOSTW	of two minds
DFINOPRTUY	profundity
DFLNOOPRUY	profoundly
DFLOOORTTU	Rudolf Otto
DFNOOOPRSU	soundproof
	sound-proof
DFOOOORSTU	out of doors
	out-of-doors
DGGGILNRUY	grudgingly
DGGGINNRUU	ungrudging
DGGHINORRU	rough-grind
DGGIILLNOW	God willing
DGGIILNNRY	grindingly
DGGIINSSTU	disgusting
DGGINNOORW	wrongdoing
DGGNOOORTU	go to ground
DGHHIKNOOT	knighthood
DGHHNOORTU	nod through
DGHIILLNNO	Hillingdon
DGHIILMNTY	midnightly
DGHILLNOOW	go down hill
	go downhill
DGHINNNOTU	Huntingdon
DGHINOOSTT	do things to
DGHINOOTWW	go down with
DGHLNOORST	stronghold
DGHMOOORUU	good humour
DGIIIKNNSV	skin-diving
DGIIKLOOST	kidologist
DGIILNOSSV	dissolving
DGIILNYYZZ	dizzyingly
DGIIMNNOOR	dining-room
DGIIMNNOPU	impounding
DGIIMNOORT	in good trim

DGIINNOSWZ	downsizing
DGIIOOPRSU	prodigious
DGILLRTUUU	Ruud Gullit
DGILNNOSUY	soundingly
DGILNNOUWY	woundingly
DGILNOOPRY	droopingly
DGIMNNOOVW	moving down
DGINNOOPRW	roping-down
DGINOPRRTU	protruding
DGKLNOOOOO	look good on
DGKNOORRUW	groundwork
DGLNOOOOTY	odontology
DGOPRSTUUY	study group
DHIIKNNOTT	I don't think
DHIIMMOPRS	dimorphism
DHILLRSUWY	rush wildly
DHILORSSYY	hydrolysis
DHIMMNNOST	month's mind
DHIMOOPRSU	dimorphous
DHINOOPSWW	shop window
	window-shop
DHINOPRSTY	dystrophin
DHJLNNOOPU	John Dunlop
DHNOOORTUX	unorthodox
DHOORRSTWW	Wordsworth
DIIIINPSTY	insipidity
DIIIMMORSU	osmiridium
DIIIMNNOTU	diminution
DIILLMNOSY	silly mid-on
DIILLNOSWW	windowsill
DIILLRSTTW	twist drill
DIIMMOPRRU	primordium
DIIMNNOSTW	in two minds
DIIMORSSSY	dismissory
DIINOOPSSU	Posidonius
DIINOORSTT	distortion
DIINOPRSTU	disruption
DIIOOPRSTW	wood spirit
DILLOOPPYY	polyploidy
DILOPSTTUY	pilot study
DILORSSTUU	stridulous
DILOSSTUUY	studiously
DIMOPRSSUY	dysprosium
DINOORTTUY	orotundity
DIOOPQQRUU	quid pro quo
DKLNNOOOOW	look down on
DLLOOORSUY	dolorously
DLNOORSUWY	wondrously
DNORSTTTUU	turn to dust

E

EEEEEGPRST	Pete Seeger
EEEEEGPSSX	epexegeses
EEEEFFNSST	effeteness
EEEEFKLRSS	self-seeker
EEEEFLMSST	self-esteem
EEEEFORRVZ	freeze over
EEEEGILNST	genteelise
EEEEGILNTZ	genteelize
EEEEGMNRRT	re-emergent
EEEEHIMRSU	euhemerise
EEEEHIMRUZ	euhemerize
EEEEHNPSST	epentheses
EEEEHORRSW	wheresoeer
EEEEHRRVWY	everywhere
EEEEIILLSW	Elie Wiesel
EEEEIKMPRT	timekeeper
EEEEILLLOR	Lorelei Lee
EEEELLSSSV	sleeveless
EEEELMOPPT	meet people
EEEENNRRVV	never-never
EEEENNRSSS	sereneness
EEEENNTWYY	teeny-weeny
EEEENRSSSV	severeness
EEEERRRTTV	terre verte
EEEFFHINTT	the Fifteen
EEEFFHLORT	off the reel
EEEFFIIMNS	effeminise
EEEFFIIMNZ	effeminize
EEEFFILORT	tree of life
EEEFFIRRST	strife-free
EEEFGIINNR	fire engine
EEEFGLNRUV	revengeful
EEEFHHRSTT	the three F's
EEEFHNOOTV	on the eve of
EEEFHOORRT	heretofore
EEEFILNRRT	life-renter
EEEFILRRSV	file server
EEEFIMNNRT	refinement
EEEFINORRV	over-refine
EEEFINRRRT	interferer
EEEFINRSVW	swine fever
EEEFKNOPRS	free-spoken
EEEFLLMSTT	self-mettle
EEEFLLORRT	foreteller
EEEFLNOSST	set oneself
EEEFLRRSTY	freestyler
EEEFMNPRRT	preferment
EEEFNNOOST	on one's feet
EEEFNNORSU	unforeseen
EEEFNOORVY	every one of
EEEFNQRRTU	frequenter
EEEGGGHLOR	Georg Hegel
EEEGGHHNRU	Hugh Greene
EEEGGNOORS	Goose Green
EEEGHHIMST	high esteem
EEEGHHINTT	eighteenth
EEEGHKLNNT	knee-length
EEEGHNNOST	Stonehenge
EEEGHNORSU	greenhouse
EEEGHNORTW	get nowhere
EEEGIILRSU	religieuse
EEEGIINRSS	greisenise
EEEGIINRSZ	greisenize
EEEGILMNST	genteelism
EEEGIMNNRT	enregiment
EEEGIMORST	geometrise
EEEGIMORTZ	geometrize
EEEGINNPTY	Gene Pitney
EEEGINNSTW	sweetening
EEEGINOPRY	epeirogeny
EEEGINORSV	overseeing

EEEGINRRST	enregister
	interreges
EEEGIORRVV	grieve over
EEEGIRRSSV	regressive
EEEGLMNRTY	emergently
EEEGLNNSST	gentleness
EEEGLOPSTT	get to sleep
EEEHHIMPRS	hemisphere
EEEHHISTTW	seethe with
EEEHHLLSTT	hell's teeth
EEEHHLOSUW	wheelhouse
EEEHHRRSTT	the three R's
EEEHIKLPRS	spherelike
EEEHILMORT	heliometer
EEEHILNOTT	toe the line
EEEHILNOTV	the Evil One
EEEHILNPRS	prehensile
EEEHILRRTV	River Lethe
EEEHIMNRST	smithereen
EEEHIMRSTT	three times
EEEHINNNTT	nineteenth
EEEHINNTTV	in the event
EEEHINORSW	Eisenhower
EEEHINSSWZ	wheeziness
EEEHINSTTV	seventieth
EEEHKLLOTT	kettle hole
EEEHKOPPRS	shopkeeper
EEEHLLMRUV	Leverhulme
EEEHLLNOTV	on the level
EEEHLLNTVY	eleventhly
EEEHLMNTVY	vehemently
EEEHLORTWW	two-wheeler
EEEHLPRSSS	sphereless
EEEHMOPRSS	mesosphere
EEEHMORRRT	Rothermere
EEEHMORSTT	meet others
EEEHMPRTTT	the Tempter
EEEHMPSTTT	The Tempest
EEEHNNPRTY	threepenny
EEEHNOPPRS	Persephone
EEEHNORRVW	or whenever
EEEHNORSSS	horse sense
EEEHNORSVW	whensoever
EEEHNOSTUY	See You Then
EEEHNRRVYY	Henry Every
EEEHOPPRRT	tree hopper
EEEHOPRSTU	Peterhouse
EEEHORRRVW	or wherever
EEEHORRTVY	every other
EEEHORSTTT	set to three
EEEHPRSSTX	The Express
EEEIINNSST	Eisenstein
EEEIIPRTTV	repetitive
EEEIJNRSUV	rejuvenise
EEEIJNRUVZ	rejuvenize
EEEIKLMSWY	semi-weekly
EEEIKLNNPR	pine kernel
EEEILLNRVW	well I never!
EEEILLNUVV	Villeneuve
EEEILMMORT	mileometer
EEEILMNRTV	revilement
EEEILMNSSS	seemliness
EEEILMNSTY	mesitylene
EEEILNOPPS	penelopise
EEEILNOPPZ	penelopize
EEEILNPSSS	sleepiness
EEEILNSSST	sleetiness
	steeliness
EEEILPSTVX	expletives
EEEIMMNNOS	Menominees
EEEIMNNPRT	pre-eminent
EEEIMNORST	remonetise
EEEIMNORTZ	remonetize
EEEIMNPRTX	experiment
EEEIMNRRTT	retirement
EEEIMPPRTV	pre-emptive
EEEINNPRST	serpentine
EEEINNPRTV	prevenient
EEEINNRRTV	intervener
EEEINNRSST	entireness
EEEINPRRST	enterprise
EEEINPRSST	serpentise
EEEINPRSSU	purse-seine
EEEINPRSTZ	serpentize
EEEINPRTVV	preventive
EEEINQTTTU	netiquette
EEEINRRRTV	irreverent
EEEINRSSTW	westernise
EEEINRSTWZ	westernize
EEEINSSTWY	eyewitness
	eye-witness
EEEIOPRRRT	repertoire
EEEIPRRSSV	repressive
EEEIPRRTTU	répétiteur
EEEIPRSSVX	expressive
EEEIRSSTTW	streetwise
EEEJJNNSSU	jejuneness
EEEJKMNORR	Jerome Kern
EEEJLNRSUV	Jules Verne
EEEJNOSSSW	Jesse Owens
EEEJNOSSTV	Steve Jones
EEEKLLLTTW	Kettlewell
EEEKLORRTW	teleworker
EEEKMNORTV	revokement
EEELLLORVW	lower-level
EEELLMSSTW	sweet smell
EEELLNPSUV	eleven-plus
EEELLNRRTY	Ellen Terry
EEELLNRSST	relentless
EEELLPRSSY	peerlessly
EEELMMOSTT	mettlesome
EEELMNOPTU	Mount Pelée
EEELMNSTTT	settlement
EEELNOPRTT	open letter
EEELNOTTVW	twelve-tone
EEELNPPRSY	prepensely
EEELNRRTVY	reverently
EEELNRSTTW	newsletter
EEELOPRRRT	Peter Lorre
EEELOPRSTU	pétroleuse
EEELORSVWW	werewolves
EEELPRRSVY	perversely

EEEMNNRSTT	resentment	EEFIINRRST	Finisterre
EEEMNOPRST	treponemes	EEFIIPPRRS	fripperies
EEEMNORSST	remoteness	EEFIIPRRST	free spirit
EEEMORSTTX	to extremes	EEFIKLLRUV	liver fluke
EEENNNOOTV	not even one	EEFILLLSSY	lifelessly
EEENNNSSUV	unevenness	EEFILMRSTU	muster-file
EEENORSTWZ	sneezewort	EEFILNNORT	florentine ❑
EEENOSTTUW	outsweeten	EEFILNOPST	pit oneself
EEENPRSSTX	expertness	EEFILNPPTT	felt-tip pen
EEEOOPRSVX	overexpose	EEFILOORSU	oleiferous
EEEOPRSTTY	stereotype	EEFILORTTU	true-to-life
EEEOQSTUUZ	squeeze out	EEFILOSTWX	Felixstowe
EEEOSTTTVV	Steve Ovett	EEFIMNOSTT	oftentimes
EEEPRSTTTY	typesetter	EEFIMNSTUW	few minutes
EEFFGHILRT	free flight	EEFIMORRRT	retire from
EEFFGINORR	forefinger	EEFINNORRT	interferon
EEFFHHILTW	fifth wheel	EEFINNQRTU	infrequent
EEFFIILLNO	line of life	EEFIORRRTX	fox-terrier
EEFFIILLRZ	Zeffirelli	EEFKLLOOWY	yoke-fellow
EEFFILSUVY	effusively	EEFKLNOOST	Folkestone
EEFFIORRTU	forfeiture	EEFLLNNRRU	fell-runner
EEFFIRTUUW	future wife	EEFLLORSSW	flowerless
EEFFLORSST	effortless	EEFLMORRSU	remorseful
EEFFNORRTY	effrontery	EEFLMORRTT	form letter
EEFGGILNTU	gut feeling	EEFLNNTUUV	uneventful
EEFGHHIILR	high relief	EEFLNOSSUW	woefulness
EEFGHINNRS	freshening	EEFLNQRTUY	frequently
EEFGHINRRS	refreshing	EEFLNRSSUU	ruefulness
EEFGHLNOSU	hug oneself	EEFLNSSSUU	usefulness
EEFGHLOOSS	gooseflesh	EEFLOPTTUU	feel put out
EEFGIILLLN	ill feeling	EEFLRSSTTU	streetfuls
	ill-feeling	EEFLRSSTUU	futureless
EEFGIILLNS	single file	EEFMMNOSTW	few moments
EEFGIILOTV	give life to	EEFMMOORRT	remote from
EEFGILLNRY	fleeringly	EEFMMOPRTX	exempt from
EEFGILLNTY	fleetingly	EEFMOORTZZ	mezzo forte
EEFGILNRSS	fingerless		mezzo-forte
EEFGILNRTW	left-winger	EEFMOPRRRS	performers
EEFGIMNNRT	fermenting	EEFNNORRRU	forerunner
EEFGKLLNOT	gentlefolk	EEFNOORRTU	en route for
EEFGLLNUVY	vengefully	EEGGGHIMNU	Guggenheim
EEFGLMNNTU	engulfment	EEGGHILNRT	green light
EEFHHILNST	in the flesh	EEGGHOORTT	go together
EEFHHLNOST	on the shelf	EEGGIINNRW	ginger wine
EEFHHLOOTW	the whole of	EEGGIINNRZ	energizing
EEFHHLORSS	horseflesh	EEGGIMNRST	stem ginger
EEFHIKLOST	the likes of	EEGGISSTUV	suggestive
EEFHILNSSS	fleshiness	EEGGNOORTW	George Town
EEFHILRSVY	feverishly		Georgetown
EEFHINNORT	the Inferno	EEGHHIRSTT	high street
EEFHLNOORS	Holofernes	EEGHHNOTUV	even though
EEFHLPRSSS	press flesh	EEGHHORSTU	see through
EEFHNORTTU	fourteenth		see-through
EEFHNPRSTY	Stephen Fry	EEGHHPSTTU	get the push
EEFIIKLLNX	Felix Klein	EEGHIKLRSU	kieselguhr
EEFIILMNNY	femininely	EEGHILLPST	light sleep
EEFIILMRSU	emulsifier	EEGHILMRTT	light meter
EEFIILRRST	fertiliser	EEGHILNOOP	pigeonhole
EEFIILRRTZ	fertilizer		pigeon-hole
EEFIIMNNNU	unfeminine	EEGHILNSTW	lengthwise
EEFIINNSST	finiteness	EEGHILOOST	theologise

EEGHILOOTZ	theologize
EEGHILOSTW	lose weight
EEGHILRTVY	Verey light
EEGHILSSTW	weightless
EEGHIMNOOS	homogenise
EEGHIMNOOZ	homogenize
EEGHINPRST	regentship
EEGHINRTVY	everything
EEGHIORTVW	overweight
EEGHKMORRU	Khmer Rouge
EEGHLLNOUW	well enough
EEGHLNOOSW	go on wheels
EEGHLNORST	Glenrothes
EEGHLOORTY	heterology
EEGHLOPRSU	sleep rough
EEGHMORRTY	hygrometer
EEGHNNRSTT	strengthen
EEGHNOORTY	heterogony
EEGHNORSUU	sure enough
EEGHNORTTU	untogether
EEGHOORTUY	there you go
EEGHOSSTUU	guest house
	guesthouse
	house guest
EEGIIILMST	legitimise
EEGIIILMTZ	legitimize
EEGIILNNNV	enlivening
EEGIILNNST	lentigines
EEGIILNORR	religioner
EEGIILNRVV	ever-living
EEGIILOPSU	epiloguise
EEGIILOPUZ	epiloguize
EEGIINNOPR	pioneering
EEGIINPRSS	serpigines
EEGIINRRRV	Niger River
EEGIINRSSU	sui generis
EEGIINRSTV	vertigines
EEGIIORSTV	give rise to
EEGIJNSTTT	jet-setting
EEGIKLNOPS	spongelike
EEGIKMNOPV	keep moving
EEGIKNPRTY	keep trying
EEGILLOPSS	gospellise
EEGILLOPSZ	gospellize
EEGILMMNNT	minglement
EEGILMNORS	mongrelise
EEGILMNORZ	mongrelize
EEGILNNPRS	leg spinner
EEGILNNPSU	unsleeping
EEGILNNRSY	sneeringly
EEGILNNSSS	singleness
EEGILNNSUY	unseeingly
EEGILNORRV	linger over
EEGILNPPRX	perplexing
EEGILNPSST	single-step
EEGILNPSWY	sweepingly
EEGILNRSTW	sweltering
EEGILORRST	sortileger
EEGIMNNOOR	engine room
EEGIMNNOTT	mignonette
EEGIMNNTTU	integument
EEGIMNOORT	goniometer
EEGIMNOPRW	empowering
EEGINNORST	röntgenise
EEGINNORTZ	röntgenize
EEGINNPRST	presenting
EEGINNPRUY	penguinery
EEGINNPRUZ	Prinz Eugen
EEGINOORSS	orogenesis
EEGINORRSS	regression
EEGINORRTU	rerouteing
EEGINORSTY	generosity
EEGINOTTVV	give vent to
EEGINPRRTV	perverting
EEGIOORTVV	give over to
EEGLLMRTUY	grey mullet
EEGLLNOOSY	selenology
EEGLLOOPSY	speleology
EEGLMORSUY	gruesomely
EEGLNNOOSS	on one's legs
EEGLNORSUY	generously
EEGLRSSTTU	get results
EEGMNNORSW	newsmonger
EEGMNNORTV	government
EEGMOOORRR	Roger Moore
EEGNNORSUU	ungenerous
EEGNNOTTXY	oxygen tent
EEGNOOOSTT	not go to see
EEGNOSTUVY	Steve Young
EEGOPRSTUU	Portuguese
EEGORRRSST	retrogress
EEHHIKNRTT	The Thinker
EEHHILMPTT	pith helmet
EEHHILORTW	otherwhile
EEHHILPSSY	sheepishly
EEHHIMNOST	henotheism
EEHHINOSTT	henotheist
EEHHINRTTT	thirteenth
EEHHIORRSS	shire horse
EEHHIORSTW	white horse
	Whitehorse
EEHHIOSTUW	house white
EEHHIRSSTV	the shivers
EEHHLNOOTW	on the whole
EEHHLOOTTW	tooth-wheel
EEHHLRSTTU	The Hustler
EEHHNOOSTU	on the house
EEHHOORSUW	whorehouse
EEHHOPSSTY	hypotheses
EEHIIKNPTW	keep in with
EEHIILLSTW	the willies
EEHIILMPTU	epithelium
EEHIILNOPR	perihelion
EEHIIMNNOT	methionine
EEHIINOSTW	white noise
EEHIIRRSTX	heritrixes
EEHIJNNNOR	John Rennie
EEHIKLLNNO	Hellenikon
EEHIKLMORT	motherlike
EEHIKMORST	strike home
EEHIKNOPTW	keep on with
EEHIKNOTTT	tie the knot

EEHIKOSSTT	to the skies
EEHIKPPTUW	keep up with
EEHILLLNSW	Helen Wills
EEHILLRSWW	well-wisher
EEHILMNOSS	homeliness
EEHILMOPRT	thermopile
EEHILNNRTY	inherently
EEHILNOSTT	on the tiles
EEHILNRTUW	whereuntil
EEHILNSTUV	Nevil Shute
EEHILOOPRT	heliotrope
EEHILOSTTU	silhouette
EEHILSTTTW	settle with
EEHIMNNOTY	in the money
EEHIMRSSTV	verse-smith
EEHINNOPRS	prehension
EEHINNORST	enthronise
	rhinestone
EEHINNORTZ	enthronize
EEHINNOSST	tennis shoe
EEHINNOSTT	to the nines
EEHINNSSSW	newishness
EEHINOOPRS	ionosphere
EEHINOQTTU	on the quiet
EEHINORSTW	no the wiser
EEHINPRSST	in the press
EEHINSSSTX	sixth sense
EEHINSSSTY	synthesise
EEHINSSTTY	synthetise
EEHINSSTYZ	synthesize
EEHINSTTYZ	synthetize
EEHIOPPRST	epistrophe
EEHIRSSSTY	hysteresis
EEHJLNNOVY	John Evelyn
EEHJLNOSWY	John Wesley
EEHKLNORRV	Herrenvolk
EEHKMOOPST	keep shtoom
EEHKMOOSSU	smokehouse
EEHKNOORTT	tenterhook
EEHLLLPSSY	helplessly
EEHLLMORTW	Motherwell
EEHLLOPSSY	hopelessly
EEHLMORSST	motherless
EEHLNNNRYY	Lenny Henry
EEHLNOOOST	on the loose
EEHLOORSUW	lower house
EEHMNNNOOP	phenomenon
EEHMNNOOTY	on the money
EEHMNOORRY	Henry Moore
EEHMNOORTY	heteronomy
EEHMNORSTT	nethermost
EEHMOOPRTT	photometer
EEHMOOSSUU	house mouse
EEHMOPRSTT	stepmother
EEHMOPRSTU	Prometheus
EEHMOPRSTY	hypsometer
EEHMOQRSUU	humoresque
EEHMORSSUW	shrewmouse
EEHMOSSTTT	the mostest
EEHNNOPSST	Stephenson
EEHNNOPSSY	phoneyness
EEHNNORRRT	northerner ◻
EEHNOOPRST	on the ropes
EEHNOORTTU	on the outer
EEHNOPRSUY	Euphrosyne
EEHNOPSSTU	penthouses
EEHNOPSTUY	hypotenuse
EEHOOPRRSW	horsepower
EEHOOPRSUW	powerhouse
	power-house
EEHOOPRTTV	over the top
	over-the-top
EEHOORRSVW	overshower
EEHOORRTTW	two or three
EEHOORSSTU	storehouse
EEHOORSTUY	here's to you
EEHOPPRSST	prophetess
EEHOPPRSUU	upper house
EEHOPRRSTV	Shreveport
EEHOPRSSST	prostheses
EEHOPSSTUU	set up house
EEIIIMMRSS	immiserise
EEIIIMMRSZ	immiserize
EEIIKLLNSS	likeliness
EEIIKLNPRW	periwinkle
EEIIKLPRST	priestlike
EEIIKLQRSU	squirelike
EEIILLMMRT	millimetre
EEIILLNSSV	liveliness
EEIILMMNPT	limpet mine
EEIILMMPST	simple time
EEIILMNOSW	Simone Weil
EEIILMNSST	timeliness
EEIILMPRTT	triple time
EEIILNNNTX	next in line
EEIILNOSTV	television
EEIILOPSST	epistolise
EEIILOPSTZ	epistolize
EEIILOPTVX	exploitive
EEIILORSTT	toiletries
EEIILRRSTZ	sterilizer
EEIIMNNOST	in one's time
EEIIMNNPTT	impenitent
	pentimenti
EEIIMNRSTX	in extremis
EEIIMNRTTW	wintertime
EEIIMNRTZZ	intermezzi
EEIIMOPRTZ	epitomizer
EEIIMPRSSV	impressive
	permissive
EEIIMPRSTV	septemviri
EEIINNNSTT	insentient
EEIINNRTTW	intertwine
EEIINNSSTT	intestines
EEIINOPRTT	petitioner
	repetition
EEIINORTVV	invite over
EEIINOSSSV	see visions
EEIIORRSST	rotisserie
EEIIPQRSTU	perquisite
EEIIPRSSTV	persistive
EEIJLLNUVY	juvenilely

EEIJLRRSWY	Jerry Lewis
EEIKLLRVYY	very likely
EEIKLMMRSU	summerlike
EEIKLNNSSU	unlikeness
EEIKLNPSTT	kettle-pins
EEIKORRSTV	overstrike
EEILLLLNTT	Little Nell
EEILLLLRWW	well-willer
EEILLLNOWY	yellow line
EEILLLOTVW	well-to-live
EEILLLPSTV	split-level
EEILLMNSSS	smelliness
EEILLMPPPR	pepper mill
	peppermill
EEILLNNOSS	loneliness
EEILLNOSSV	loveliness
EEILLNOSTT	little ones
EEILLOORSV	loose-liver
EEILLPRRUW	wire-puller
EEILLRSSTY	tirelessly
EEILLSSVWY	viewlessly
EEILMMNPST	implements
EEILMNNSTT	enlistment
EEILMNOPRT	Montpelier
EEILMNOSSU	mousseline
EEILMNPSSS	simpleness
EEILMOPRSY	polymerise
EEILMOPRTT	polite term
EEILMOPRYZ	polymerize
EEILMORSTY	tiresomely
EEILMOSSTV	motiveless
EEILNNPTTY	penitently
EEILNNSSST	silentness
EEILNOOTVV	evolve into
EEILNOPRRT	interloper
EEILNOPSST	politeness
EEILNORTVV	intervolve
EEILNPRTXY	inexpertly
EEILNRSTUY	esuriently
EEILOPPRSS	Persepolis
EEILORRSTU	irresolute
EEILORRTTW	Rottweiler
EEILORRTXY	exteriorly
EEILORSVWY	overwisely
EEILPPRTXY	perplexity
EEILPRSTTU	supertitle
EEILRSSTTZ	strelitzes
EEIMMMRSTU	summer time
	summertime
EEIMMOPRRV	prime mover
EEIMMRSSTY	symmetrise
EEIMMRSTYZ	symmetrize
EEIMNNNRTT	internment
EEIMNNOPTT	pentimento
EEIMNNORST	minestrone
EEIMNNSSTT	sentiments
EEIMNNSSTU	minuteness
EEIMNNSTTV	investment
EEIMNOPPRT	pre-emption
EEIMNOPRTU	peritoneum
EEIMNORRSZ	sermonizer
EEIMNORTZZ	intermezzo
EEIMNOSSTX	sixteenmos
EEIMNPPPRT	peppermint
EEIMNPRSSU	impureness
EEIMNRSSSS	remissness
EEIMNRSSTU	terminuses
EEIMOPRRTZ	temporizer
EEIMOPRSTU	periosteum
EEIMPPRRUU	puerperium
EEIMPRRSSU	presurmise
EEIMPRSSTV	septemvirs
EEIMPRSTUV	resumptive
EEINNNSSTT	intentness
EEINNOPPRT	porpentine
EEINNOPRSS	pensioners
EEINNOPRST	pretension
	pre-tension
EEINNOPRTV	prevention
EEINNOSSTT	set in stone
EEINNPRSSU	unripeness
EEINNPRTTU	turpentine
EEINNPSSSU	in suspense
	supineness
EEINNQSSUU	uniqueness
EEINNSSSUW	unwiseness
EEINOOSSST	otioseness
EEINOPRRSS	repression
EEINOPRRSV	perversion
EEINOPRSSV	responsive
EEINOPRSSW	wise person
EEINOPRSSX	expression
EEINOPRSXY	epoxy resin
EEINOQRSTU	questioner
EEINORRSUV	overinsure
EEINORRTVW	overwinter
EEINPRSSTT	persistent
	prettiness
EEINPSSSUV	suspensive
EEINRRSTWW	news-writer
EEIOPPRSSV	oppressive
EEIOPRRSTV	resorptive
EEIOPRSTTT	operettist
EEIOPSSSSV	possessive
EEIPPRTTUY	perpetuity
EEIPRRSSSU	pressurise
EEIPRRSSUZ	pressurize
EEIPRRSTVY	perversity
EEIPRRTTWY	typewriter
EEIRRSSSTV	reservists
EEIRSSSTTU	sestertius
EEJNORRSTY	Terry Jones
EEKKNNOOTW	keen to know
EEKLLNOPSW	well-spoken
EEKLLNRSSU	Ken Russell
EEKLOOPPRW	workpeople
	work-people
EELLMMORSS	mess or mell
EELLMNOOSY	lonesomely
EELLMNOSSW	mellowness
EELLMNTTUY	temulently
EELLMOSSVY	movelessly

EELLNNSSSU	sullenness
EELLNOPPRT	propellent
EELLNOQTUY	eloquently
EELLNOSSTY	tonelessly
EELLNOSSWY	yellowness
EELLORSTUY	resolutely
EELLPRTTWY	pretty well
EELLRSSSTU	lustreless
EELLRSSSTY	restlessly
EELMMNOPTY	employment
EELMMNOSTU	emoluments
EELMNNOSSS	solemnness
EELMNPPSTU	supplement
EELMNPTUZZ	puzzlement
EELMOORRSS	more or less
EELMORSTUY	temerously
EELNNOOTVW	twelve noon
EELNNORTUU	Eurotunnel
EELNOPPRSY	propensely
EELNPPSSSU	suppleness
EELOOPPRTV	topple over
EELOOPPSSS	opposeless
EELOOPRSTY	proteolyse
EELOPPSTTU	put to sleep
EELOPRUVZZ	puzzle over
EELORRRSTY	retrorsely
EELORSSUVY	yourselves
EELPPRSSSU	supperless
EELPRRSTTU	splutterer
EELRSSSSST	stressless
EEMMOORSTT	most remote
EEMNNOPSTT	pentstemon
EEMNOORSSS	moroseness
EEMNOPRSSW	presswomen
EEMOOPPRRT	pro tempore
EEMOPPRRTY	peremptory
EENNNNOOSS	no-nonsense
EENNOOOSST	on one's toes
EENNOPRSTT	not present
EENNOQRSTU	quernstone
EENNORSSTT	rottenness
EENNOSSSTY	syntenoses
EENNRSSSUU	unsureness
EENOPPRRSS	properness
EENORRSSST	Stroessner
EENORSTTTU	neutrettos
EEOPPPRSSU	presuppose
EEOPPRRSUW	superpower
EEOPPRSSSS	prepossess
EEOPRRSSTU	superstore
EEOPRSTTYY	stereotypy
EEORRSSSTV	overstress
EESSSSTUWX	West Sussex
EFFFFHLOSU	shuffle off
EFFFHIPRSU	puffer fish
EFFFILLLOU	full of life
EFFFILNSSU	fluffiness
EFFFINOOOT	foot of fine
EFFFMORRSU	suffer from
EFFGGIORRT	trigger off
EFFGHIINRS	fish-finger
EFFGHORSTU	Geoff Hurst
EFFGIINNST	stiffening
EFFGILLNOT	telling-off
EFFGINOSTT	setting-off
EFFHHKOOOT	off the hook
EFFHILOSTW	whistle off
EFFHOORSTU	fresh out of
EFFIIKLOSS	kiss of life
EFFIINNSSS	sniffiness
EFFILLMNTU	fulfilment
EFFILLOOSS	loss of life
EFFILLOSSU	fossil fuel
EFFILNSSTU	fitfulness
EFFINNOOPS	pension off
EFFINORTTW	written off
EFFINSSSTU	stuffiness
EFFNNOOSTU	off one's nut
EFGGHINRTU	gunfighter
EFGGIIILNV	life-giving
EFGGIILNNR	fingerling
EFGGINORTT	forgetting
EFGHIIKNRS	kingfisher
EFGHILLSST	flightless
EFGHILLTUW	full weight
EFGHIMNORS	fishmonger
EFGHLLLNTU	full-length
EFGHLLNORU	flugelhorn
	flügelhorn
EFGHLLOOUY	Lough Foyle
EFGHOOPPRR	frog-hopper
EFGIIILNNR	firing line
	firing-line
EFGIILNQUY	liquefying
EFGIILTUVY	fugitively
EFGIINPRSY	presignify
EFGIINPRTY	petrifying
EFGIINRRTY	terrifying
EFGIKLNORS	folk-singer
EFGIKORRUW	figurework
EFGILLLUUY	guilefully
EFGILLNOSV	self-loving
EFGILLNRSU	self-ruling
EFGILMNORS	Single Form
EFGILNRTTU	fluttering
EFGIMNOPRR	performing
EFGIMNORRS	resign from
EFGIMOORTV	give form to
EFGINNORUV	unforgiven ❑
EFGINOPRST	finger-post
EFGINPRTUY	putrefying
EFGINPSTUY	stupefying
EFGJLLNOUW	jungle fowl
EFGLLLNOOW	Longfellow
EFGNOOPRTU	Group of Ten
EFGOOOOSST	goosefoots
EFGOOOSTUU	go out of use
EFHHIJNORS	John Fisher
EFHHIOORTT	hit the roof
EFHHNOPSTY	soft hyphen
EFHIILNRST	Flintshire
EFHIILNSST	filthiness

EFHIILRSSV	silverfish
EFHIILRTTW	trifle with
EFHIINSSST	shiftiness
EFHILLOPSW	fellowship
EFHILOPRST	shoplifter
EFHILORSTW	whistle for
EFHILRSSTT	thriftless
EFHINORSST	frothiness
EFHINORTTZ	on the fritz
EFHJLNOOSW	John Fowles
EFHLLMOOOW	follow home
EFHLLOOPRS	shellproof
EFHLLOSSUV	shovelfuls
EFHLOOORTT	to the floor
EFIIIINNTV	infinitive
EFIIILMPRS	simplifier
EFIIILNNTY	infinitely
EFIIIMNNTY	femininity
EFIIKNRSSS	friskiness
EFIILLLSST	still lifes
EFIILLNRSS	frilliness
EFIILLNUVW	in full view
EFIILMNSSS	flimsiness
EFIILNNSST	flintiness
EFIILNORRY	inferiorly
EFIILOPRSU	piliferous
EFIILRSTTU	stultifier
EFIINOORRT	inferior to
EFIINORTUV	in virtue of
EFIIPRRSTZ	first prize
EFIKLNOORW	line of work
EFIKLNOSSS	folksiness
EFILLMORST	stelliform
EFILLNORTU	ill fortune
	ill-fortune
EFILLNSSUW	wilfulness
EFILLPSTUY	spitefully
EFILNNSSSU	sinfulness
EFILNOORSS	solferinos
EFILNOPPSS	floppiness
EFILOPRSST	profitless
EFIMMNOORY	in memory of
EFIMNOORRV	overinform
EFIMNORSTU	misfortune
EFINOOPRSS	profession
EFINOORRST	in store for
EFINORSSST	frostiness
EFJLNOSSUY	joyfulness
EFKLLOORWW	work-fellow
EFKLMMOORY	folk-memory
EFKLMNOOSW	womenfolks
EFKLNOOPSU	foul-spoken
EFKNOOPSST	soft-spoken
EFLLLNNOSU	full nelson
EFLLMORSSY	formlessly
EFLLNNORRY	Errol Flynn
EFLLNSUUUY	unusefully
EFLLOPRUWY	powerfully
EFLMOOORTY	tomfoolery
EFLMORRSTU	result from
EFLNORSSUW	Sunflowers
EFLOPPRSUU	purposeful
EFMMNOORYY	for my money
EFMNNNOUYY	funny money
EFMOOORSST	set of rooms
EFMOOPRRTU	outperform
EFNNOORRSU	non-ferrous
EFOOPPRRSS	press proof
EFOOPRRSTU	four-poster
EGGGHILMSU	mishguggle
EGGGIINNRS	sniggering
EGGGINORSS	grogginess
EGGGINSSTU	suggesting
EGGHHORTTU	get through
EGGHIIKLLT	klieg light ❑
EGGHIILNNT	lightening
EGGHIINNTT	tightening
EGGHIINNUW	unweighing
EGGHIINPUW	weighing up
	weighing-up
EGGHIJLTUW	juggle with
EGGHINNOTU	toughening
EGGHORSSUU	rough guess
EGGIIILNNV	inveigling
EGGIILMMNR	glimmering
EGGIILNNST	glistening
EGGIILNRTT	glittering
EGGIILNRVY	grievingly
EGGIINNRST	signet-ring
EGGIINORVV	giving-over
EGGILLLNPU	leg-pulling
EGGILLNORV	grovelling
EGGILNNRSU	gunslinger
EGGILNSSUY	guessingly
EGGILOORST	Georg Solti
EGGINNORSS	engrossing
EGGINOPRRU	regrouping
EGGINOSSTU	suggestion
EGGLNOOPSS	gospel song
EGGLNOORRW	grow longer
EGGLNORSTU	struggle on
EGGLOOPTYY	Egyptology
EGGLOORSUY	gorgeously
EGHHHLUUXY	Hugh Huxley
EGHHIILNTT	in the light
EGHHIILTTW	white light
EGHHIINNST	The Shining
EGHHIINNTT	the in thing
EGHHIINRTT	in the right
EGHHIIPRST	high priest
EGHHIITTWW	with weight
EGHHILOPRY	hieroglyph
EGHHILOSTU	lighthouse
EGHHIOPTTW	hop the twig
EGHHMOPTTU	got the hump
EGHHOORSUU	rough-house
EGHHOPRTYY	hygrophyte
EGHHORTTUW	wet through
EGHIIJPSTU	the jig is up
EGHIILLLNV	living hell
EGHIILRSTY	tigerishly
EGHIIMMNRS	shimmering

EGHIIMNPRS	Pringsheim
EGHIIMNPRW	whimpering
EGHIINNSTW	in the wings
EGHIINPRSW	whispering
EGHIINSTUX	extinguish
EGHIJLNOPR	John Pilger
EGHILLNOST	hostelling
EGHILLOTWW	go well with
EGHILMNOOV	home-loving
EGHILMOOOS	homologise
EGHILMOOOZ	homologize
EGHILNORST	Nigel Short
EGHILNORVY	hoveringly
EGHILNSSST	slightness
EGHILOORST	rheologist
EGHILOPSUW	ploughwise
EGHILORSST	sole rights
EGHILOSTTT	set light to
EGHIMNOPRS	phorminges
EGHIMNORST	smothering
EGHINNORST	shortening
EGHINNORTW	in the wrong
EGHINNPPSU	pen-pushing
EGHINNRSSU	hungriness
EGHINNRSTT	in strength
EGHINNRSTU	Night Nurse
EGHIORSTTW	ghost-write
EGHJMMNORU	John Gummer
EGHJMNPTUU	jump the gun
EGHLNOOPRY	nephrology
EGHLOOPPSY	psephology
EGHLOPPRTY	petroglyph
EGHMNOOOSU	homogenous
EGHMOOOTYZ	homozygote
EGHMORRTYY	hygrometry
EGHMPRSWYY	pygmy shrew
EGHNRRUVYY	very hungry
EGHOORRTVW	overgrowth
EGIIILMPRS	pilgrimise
EGIIILMPRZ	pilgrimize
EGIIILNNPP	pipelining
EGIIILNORR	irreligion
EGIIIMNNST	meningitis
EGIIJNNOOS	Inigo Jones
EGIIKLLTUY	guilty-like
EGIIKLNNSS	kingliness
EGIIKLNORV	King Oliver
EGIIKLNPRS	springlike
EGIILLLRTT	little girl
EGIILLNNSV	snivelling
EGIILLNOTU	guillotine
EGIILLNRVY	revilingly
EGIILLNSVW	swivelling
EGIILLRSTV	silver-gilt
EGIILNNPRY	repiningly
EGIILNNSTT	settling-in
EGIILNRRTY	retiringly
EGIILNRSSS	grisliness
EGIILNRVVY	rev ivingly
EGIILNSSTU	guiltiness
EGIILOPSTT	epiglottis
EGIIMMNORZ	memorizing
EGIIMNOPRT	primogenit
EGIIMNPRST	springtime
EGIINNORSS	ingression
EGIINNPPST	stepping-in
EGIINNSSST	stinginess
EGIINORRST	roistering
EGIINORRTT	intertrigo
EGIINPPRRS	perspiring
EGIINPRSST	persisting
EGIINRTTTW	twittering
EGIINSTTTV	vignettist
EGIJNNORUY	journeying
EGIKLNNPSU	spelunking
EGIKLOORTW	grow to like
EGIKNOORST	go on strike
EGIKOPRUVW	give up work
EGILLLNPSY	spellingly
EGILLLNSWY	swellingly
EGILLMMNPU	pummelling
EGILLNNNTU	tunnelling
EGILLNNOTW	wellington ❑
EGILLNORWY	loweringly
EGILLNPRSW	wellspring
	well-spring
EGILLNTUXY	exultingly
EGILMMNPTU	plummeting
EGILMNOOOS	mo-nologise
EGILMNOOOZ	mo-nologize
EGILMNOOSS	gloominess
EGILMNOPTT	melting-pot
EGILMNOSUU	leguminous
EGILMNPTTY	temptingly
EGILMOOSSY	seismology
EGILNNRRUY	unerringly
EGILNNSTTU	unsettling
EGILNOOOST	oenologist
EGILNOOPST	penologist
EGILNORRUV	overruling
EGILNORTWY	toweringly
EGILNOSSSS	glossiness
EGILNOSTTU	gluttonise
EGILNOSTUU	lounge suit
EGILNOTTUZ	gluttonize
EGILNPRSSS	springless
EGILNPRSSY	pressingly
EGILNQRUYY	queryingly
EGILNQSTUY	questingly
EGILOOPRSU	prologuise
EGILOOPRUZ	prologuize
EGILOORSST	serologist
EGILOOSSTX	sexologist
EGILORSUVY	grievously
EGILOSUUXY	exiguously
EGIMMNNPTU	impugnment
EGIMNNOORR	ironmonger
EGIMNNOOWY	money owing
	owing money
EGIMNNORTT	tormenting
EGIMNOORST	ergonomist
EGIMNPRSSU	grumpiness

EGIMNPRTTU	trumpeting
EGIMOOPRST	geotropism
EGIMOORRSU	morigerous
EGINNOOPTU	opening-out
EGINNOPSSS	sponginess
EGINNRSUVW	unswerving
EGINOOPPST	pigeon-post
EGINOOPRRT	progenitor
EGINOPPSTW	sopping wet
EGINOPRRSS	in progress
EGINOPRSTT	protesting
EGINOPRTUW	pouring wet
EGINORRSTW	songwriter
EGINORRUVY	Ivor Gurney
EGINORSTUW	outswinger
EGINOSTTTU	setting-out
EGINPPPSTU	stepping-up
EGINPRRSSU	pressuring
EGINRSSTTV	string vest
EGINRSTTTU	stuttering
EGJLLOORRY	Jolly Roger
EGLMNOOOTY	entomology
EGLMNOORUY	numerology
EGLMNOOYYZ	enzymology
EGMMNOORTY	Montgomery
EGMMNOPRSY	gymnosperm
EGMOOORRSU	grouse moor
EGNNORSSSU	Guns 'n' Roses
EGNOOPRSUY	pyrogenous
EGNORRSTUV	overstrung
EGNORSSSST	songstress
EGOPPRRSUU	supergroup
EHHIILLMSW	Wilhelm His
EHHIILOPPP	hippophile
EHHIILSTVY	thievishly
EHHILNOPTW	help on with
EHHILOPRSU	Herophilus
EHHILOPTTY	lithophyte
EHHILORTWW	worthwhile
EHHILRSSWY	shrewishly
EHHIMORSTT	hithermost
EHHINOPSST	in the shops
EHHINORTTW	whitethorn
EHHIOPPPTY	hippety-hop
EHHIOPRRSS	Shropshire
EHHIOPSSTY	hypothesis
EHHJNNORTU	John Hunter
EHHKLLMOTU	Helmut Kohl
EHHLOOOSTW	whole shoot
EHHNORSTUW	run the show
EHHOORRRST	the horrors
EHHOPPSSYY	hypophyses
EHIIILNNTW	in line with
EHIIILNPST	philistine
EHIIILPPPS	Philippise
EHIIILPPPZ	Philippize
EHIIINRRTX	inheritrix
EHIIJMMTWY	Jimmy White
EHIIKLNPSX	sphinxlike
EHIIKMRRSS	skirmisher
EHIILLLOWY	holy Willie ❑
EHIILLMNOT	the million
EHIILLOOPS	Heliopolis
EHIILLOPSY	lyophilise
EHIILLOPYZ	lyophilize
EHIILNOTVW	in love with
EHIILNQRSU	relinquish
EHIILNSTTW	tin whistle
EHIIMMMSTT	Emmit Smith
EHIIMNOPSX	phoenixism
EHIIMNOSST	The Mission
EHIIMNPSSS	impishness
EHIIMNSSSW	whimsiness
EHIIMNSTTU	this minute
EHIIMOPRSV	impoverish
EHIINNTTTW	with intent
EHIINNTTUW	in tune with
EHIINPPSSW	whippiness
EHIIRRSTTU	urethritis
EHIJKLNOSW	John Wilkes
EHIJLLNOTT	Little John
EHIKLNORTW	Kenilworth
EHIKLNPSXY	Sphynx-like
EHIKLOPRSY	pokerishly
EHILLNPTTU	up till then
EHILLNRSSS	shrillness
EHILLNSTUV	Huntsville
EHILMNSSSU	mulishness
EHILMOPSTY	polytheism
EHILNNOSSU	unholiness
EHILNOSSSW	owlishness
EHILOOPRTY	heliotropy
EHILOOPSTU	pilot house
EHILOPSTTY	polytheist
EHILOSSTTW	sow thistle
EHILPRSSUU	sulphurise
EHILPRSUUZ	sulphurize
EHIMMNOOST	monotheism
EHIMMOPRTU	promethium
EHIMNNOORS	moonshiner
EHIMNNPSTU	punishment
EHIMNOOSTT	monotheist
EHIMNOPRST	mentorship
EHIMORRSTT	thermistor
EHIMPRRTUY	triumphery
EHINNOORTW	on their own
EHINOOPSUU	euphonious
EHINOOPTTT	to the point
EHINOOSSTT	toothiness
EHINORSSTW	worthiness
EHINPPSSSU	uppishness
EHINPRSUYZ	Zephyrinus
EHINRRTTUW	Winterthur
EHIOORSSTX	six-shooter
EHIOPPRRSW	worshipper
EHIOPRRSTY	prehistory
EHIOPRSSST	prosthesis
EHJLLORTTU	Jethro Tull
EHJLNNNNOO	John Lennon
EHJMOPRSUW	showjumper
EHLLNOOSSW	hollowness
EHLLRSSTUY	hurtlessly

	ruthlessly
EHLMOPPSUY	Polyphemus
EHLMORSSUU	humourless
EHLNOOPRTW	on the prowl
EHLNORSTUY	southernly
EHLOOPPRRY	plerophory
EHLOPRSTUY	upholstery
EHMNOOOTTV	venom-tooth
EHMNOOSSST	smoothness
EHMNOPSTTU	on the stump
EHMOOORSTV	smooth over
EHMOOPRTTY	photometry
EHMOPRSTYY	hypsometry
EHMRRSTTUU	truth serum
EHNNOPRTWY	pennyworth
EHNOORRSTW	Worsthorne
EHNOORTTWY	noteworthy
EHNORSTWWY	newsworthy
EHOOPPRSTY	sporophyte
EHOPPPSTUW	puppet show
EHOPPSTTUU	up the spout
EIIILLLMRT	millilitre
EIIILORSTV	vitriolise
EIIILORTVZ	vitriolize
EIIILPRSTV	evil spirit
EIIIMNOSSS	missionise
EIIIMNOSSZ	missionize
EIIIMPRSTU	impurities
EIIIOPRRST	prioritise
EIIIOPRRTZ	prioritize
EIIJLNTUVY	juvenility
EIIJMNRTUY	injury time
EIIJMNSTTU	just-in-time
EIIKKLOSSW	Kieslowski
EIIKLLNRTW	winterkill
EIIKLMORRR	mirrorlike
EIIKLNORST	triskelion
EIIKMNPSSS	skimpiness
EIIKMOPRRS	morris-pike
EIIKNNOSTT	tie in knots
EIIKNORSTT	strike into
EIIKNQRSSU	quirkiness
EIILLLNOTT	Little Lion
EIILLLOSUV	Louisville
EIILLLOTVW	will to live
EIILLLSUVY	illusively
EIILLMMNNU	millennium
EIILLMNORV	vermillion
EIILLMOPTY	impolitely
EIILLMPRTU	multiplier
EIILLNOPST	septillion
EIILLNORRT	ritornelli
EIILLNORSS	Rossellini
EIILLNORTT	tortellini
EIILLNOSTX	sextillion
EIILLPPRSY	slipperily
EIILLPSSTY	pitilessly
EIILMMNNTY	imminently
EIILMNNSTT	instilment
EIILMNOSST	lentissimo
EIILMNOSTY	mylonitise
EIILMNOTYZ	mylonitize
EIILMORTTU	outer limit
EIILMOSUXY	eximiously
EIILMPPRTU	upper limit
EIILNNNOST	listen in on
EIILNNOSTT	listen in to
EIILNORRTY	interiorly
EIILNOSSSV	visionless
EIILNPPSSS	slippiness
EIILNRSSTY	sinisterly
EIILOPSTVY	positively
EIILPRSSST	spiritless
EIIMMNRRSV	Mrs Miniver
EIIMMOPRSV	misimprove
EIIMMPRSUY	perimysium
EIIMNNOSTU	Ismet Inönü
EIIMNOPRSS	impression
	permission
EIIMNORSTT	minister to
EIIMOOPSTY	episiotomy
EIIMOPRRSV	improviser
EIIMOPRSUV	impervious
EIIMORRRSW	mirrorwise
EIIMORSSTU	moisturise
EIIMORSTUZ	moisturize
EIINNNOSTT	intentions
EIINNOQSTU	in question
EIINOOPRST	reposition
	re-position
EIINOOPSTX	exposition
EIINOPPTTT	petit point
EIINORSTVV	inter vivos
EIINORTTWZ	zwitterion
EIINPRSSSS	prissiness
EIINPRSSST	stripiness
EIINRSTTTU	instituter
EIINRSTTTW	intertwist
EIINRSTUVY	university
EIIOPPSSTT	petits pois
EIJKLNORRT	J R R Tolkien
EIJKNNORSY	Roy Jenkins
EIJLMPPRTU	triple jump
EIKLLLOOVY	look lively
	look lively!
EIKLLMOSTY	most likely
EIKLNNOPRS	link person
EIKLNNOPSS	Leon Spinks
EIKLOSTTTU	skittle out
EIKNNOSSTT	knottiness
EIKNOOPSSS	spookiness
EIKOORRSTT	strike root
EIKORSTTTY	Trotskyite
EILLLLSSWY	willlessly
EILLLOORTT	toilet roll
EILLLSSSTY	listlessly
EILLMNOTTV	Nevill Mott
EILLMOOSTY	toilsomely
EILLNNOSTY	insolently
EILLNOORRT	ritornello
EILLNOORTT	little or no
EILLNOOSSW	woolliness

EILLNOPTUY	unpolitely
EILLNOSSTT	stone-still
EILLNOSTVW	Townsville
EILLNRTUVY	virulently
EILLOPRSUY	perilously
EILLORRTUY	ulteriorly
EILLORTTTU	litter-lout
EILMMSSSTU	summitless
EILMNNSTTU	insultment
EILMNOOOPS	monopolise
EILMNOOOPZ	monopolize
EILMNOOSST	motionless
EILMNOPTTY	impotently
EILMNRSSTY	minstrelsy
EILMOOPRST	metropolis
EILMOPPRRY	improperly
EILMSSTTTU	litmus test
EILNNNOOTV	non-violent
EILNNRSSUU	unruliness
EILNOOOPTV	love potion
EILNOOPSSX	explosions
EILNOOPTVW	vowel point
EILNOORSTU	resolution
EILNOORTUV	revolution
EILNOPPRTW	nipplewort
EILNOPPSSS	sloppiness
EILNOPPSTU	suppletion
EILNOPRSST	portliness
EILNORRSTY	introrsely
EILNORSSUY	resinously
EILNPQTTUU	quintuplet
EILNPRRTUY	pruriently
EILNPRSSTY	spinsterly
EILNRSSSTU	sultriness
EILOOPPSTY	oppositely
EILOPPRSUV	propulsive
EILOPRRSUY	superiorly
EILOPRSTUY	pyrolusite
EILOPRSTVY	sportively
EILOPRSUVY	perviously
	previously
	viperously
EILOPSSSTX	Sex Pistols
EILORSSSTU	soul sister
EILRRSTUVW	liverwurst
EIMNNOOPTT	omnipotent
EIMNNOPRST	prisonment
EIMNNOSSYY	synonymise
EIMNNOSYYZ	synonymize
EIMNNRSTTU	instrument
EIMNOOPPSU	impose upon
EIMNOOPRSS	spoonerism
EIMNOORSST	in some sort
EIMNOPRRTU	importuner
EIMNOPRSTU	resumption
EIMNORSSST	storminess
EIMNORSSSU	sensoriums
EIMNPSSSTU	stumpiness
EIMNSSSTTU	smuttiness
EIMOOQSSTU	mosquitoes
EIMOOTTTWW	two-two time
EIMORSSTUY	mysterious
EINNNORSTU	in one's turn
EINNOOPPRS	open prison
	propension
EINNOOPSTU	out-pension
EINNOOSSST	snootiness
EINNOPSSSU	suspension
EINNOSSSTT	snottiness
EINOOOPRTZ	zero option
EINOOPPRSS	oppression
EINOOPPRTW	power point
EINOOPRRST	resorption
EINOOPSSSS	possession
EINOORSSST	rootsiness
EINOORTTTT	Tintoretto
EINOPPRSTY	propensity
EINOPRRRST	ripsnorter
EINOPRSSST	sportiness
EINOPSSSTT	spottiness
EINOQRTTUU	tourniquet
EINPRSSSUY	syrupiness
EINRSSSTTU	trustiness
EIOOOPPSTT	opposite to
EIOOPPRRRT	proprietor
EIOOPPRRST	prepositor
EIOOPRRSTU	superior to
EIOOPRRSTY	repository
EIOOPRSSTT	strepitoso
EIOOPRSTUV	previous to
EIOOPRSTXY	expository
EIOORRSSTU	roisterous
EIOORRTVWY	ivory tower
	ivory-tower
EIOPPRRSTU	Propertius
EIOPPRRSTY	prosperity
EIOPPRSTUV	supportive
EIOPRRSSUV	supervisor
EIOPRRSTUV	protrusive
EIOPRRTTVY	protervity
EIOPRSTTTU	prostitute
EIORRRSTUV	retrovirus
EIORRSTTTU	restitutor
EIPPRRSUVY	Privy Purse
EJNNSSSTUU	unjustness
EJNOOSSSUY	joyousness
EKLOORRTUW	work to rule
	work-to-rule
EKORRTTTUY	turkey-trot
ELLLOSSSUY	soullessly
ELLMOOPRRS	Moser-Proll
ELLMOOSVWY	move slowly
ELLNPRTUUY	purulently
ELLOOOSTTY	Leo Tolstoy
ELLOPSSSTY	spotlessly
ELMNOORSUY	enormously
ELMNOOSUVY	venomously
ELMNORSUUY	numerously
ELMNPPSTUY	supplyment
ELMOOPSSUY	polysemous
ELMOPPPRTU	petrol pump
ELMORSTTYY	stylometry

ELNOOOPRTU	poultroone
ELNOPPRRUY	unproperly
ELNOSSSUUY	sensuously
ELNRRTTTUU	turn turtle
ELOORSTTVY	try to solve
ELOPPRSUVY	oversupply
EMMNRSSTUU	menstruums
EMMOOPRSTT	post-mortem
EMNNOOPTUY	put money on
EMNOPPRSST	promptness
EMNORRSTUU	surmounter
ENNNORRTUV	Trevor Nunn
ENNOOPPRRU	proper noun
ENOOPRRSSY	responsory
ENOOPRSSSU	porousness
ENOOPRSTTU	portentous
ENOOPRSTUY	Peyton Rous
ENOOSSSSTY	synostoses
ENOPRSSSUY	suspensory
ENOPRSTTUU	put to nurse
EOOORRRSVW	sorrow over
EOOOSSTTTV	voetstoots
EOOPPRRSSU	prosperous
EOORRSSTTU	stertorous
EOPPRRSSSU	suppressor
EOPPRRSSTU	supporters
EOPRRSTTUW	power trust
EOPRSSSTTU	set spurs to

F

FFFFIITTYY	fifty-fifty
FFGHHIOSTY	fight shy of
FFGHIILNSY	fly-fishing
	Flying Fish
	flying fish
FFGHIIOPPR	hippogriff
FFGHINOOSW	showing off
	showing-off
FFGHORSTUU	rough-stuff
FFGIILLLNU	fulfilling
FFGIILNNSY	sniffingly
FFGIINOPPR	ripping off
FFGIINORTY	fortifying
FFGILLNOPU	pulling-off
FFGINNNORU	running off
FFGINOPTTU	off-putting
	putting-off
FFHINORTUW	run off with
FFILLRTUUY	fruitfully
FFILNRTUUU	unfruitful
FFILOORRST	first floor
FFIMOOPRRT	profit from
FFIOOPRRST	first proof
FGGHHIILNY	high-flying
FGGHIIINNT	infighting
	in-fighting
FGGIILNORY	glorifying
FGHHIINSTT	night shift
FGHHIMNOOR	from on high
FGHHIORRTT	forthright
FGHHLOTTUU	thoughtful
FGHIILNSTU	insightful
FGHIILRSTT	first light
FGHIINNRSU	furnishing
FGHIINORRY	horrifying
FGHIINRSTT	first night
	first thing
FGHIIOTTTU	fight it out
FGHILLRTUY	rightfully
FGHILOOSTT	footlights
FGHINNOORT	for nothing
FGHIOOSTTU	out of sight
FGHLLORTUW	full growth
FGIIILLNTT	ill-fitting
FGIIJNSTUY	justifying
FGIIKLNRSY	friskingly
FGIILLMNOY	mollifying
FGIILLNNUY	nullifying
FGIILLNRTY	flirtingly
	triflingly
FGIILLNSTY	stiflingly
FGIILNOSUU	fuliginous
FGIILNPPTY	fly-tipping
FGIILNSTUY	flying suit
FGIIMNORTY	mortifying
FGIIMNSTYY	mystifying
FGIINOTTTU	outfitting
FGILLNOTUY	floutingly
FGILNNORWY	frowningly
FGILNOOTUW	outflowing
FGILNOPSTY	flyposting
FGLLNORUWY	fully-grown
	wrongfully
FGLOORTUUY	futurology
FHHIIINSTW	finish with
FHHIOPRSTT	thrift shop
FHIIKNORSW	finish work
FHIILLPTUW	fill up with
FHIILPSSTT	split shift
FHIKMNORRS	shrink from
FHILLMRTUY	mirthfully
FHILOPRSUW	worshipful
FHINNOOORU	in honour of
FHLLLOSTUY	slothfully
FHLLOTUUYY	youthfully
FHLLRTTUUY	truthfully
FHLNRTTUUU	untruthful
FHNOORTUWY	unworthy of
FHOOPRSTTU	spout forth
FIILLMNOOS	millions of
FIIMNORTUY	uniformity
FIIMOORSST	fortissimo
FIINORTTUU	futurition
FIJNOOOTTU	out of joint
FIKLLOORST	folklorist
FIKNORSTWY	forty winks
FILLOOPTTY	toploftily
FILLOOSTUW	follow suit
FILNOORSUU	uniflorous
FILOOOPRST	portfolios
FINOOOPSTT	soft option
FINOOPRSTT	footprints

FINOOPRTTU	out of print
FIOORSTTUU	fortuitous
FJJMOOPRUY	jump for joy
FLLLOOSWWY	flow slowly
FLLMNORUUY	mournfully
FLLMORSTUY	stormfully
FLLNOOOPUW	follow up on
FLLOPRSTUY	sportfully
FLLRSTTUUY	trustfully
FLNRSTTUUU	untrustful
FNNOORSTTU	not for nuts
FNNORSTUYY	funny story
FOOORSSTTU	out of sorts

G

GGGIILLNNY	nigglingly
GGGIJLLNUY	jugglingly
GGGILNRSTU	struggling
GGHHIIILNV	high living
GGHHIILSWY	Whiggishly
GGHHIILTTT	light-tight
GGHIILPRSY	priggishly
GGHILLSSUY	sluggishly
GGHILNOSTU	oughtlings
GGHINOOPPS	go shopping
GGIIIINSTV	gingivitis
GGIIIMNSSV	misgivings
GGIIINNRTU	intriguing
GGIILLMNNY	minglingly
GGIILNNSTY	stingingly
GGIILNNSWY	swingingly
GGILLNNOUY	loungingly
GGILLNORWY	growlingly
GGILNNRTUY	gruntingly
GGIMORSSSU	Gus Grissom
GGINNNNRUU	gunrunning
GGLLNNOOOW	Wollongong
GHHIILSTTY	tightishly
GHHIINRSTT	nightshirt
GHHIIPRSTW	shipwright
GHHILLOPTY	lithoglyph
GHHILLOSUY	ghoulishly
GHHINOPRTT	triphthong
GHHINORTUW	win through
GHHLOORTUY	thoroughly
GHHNORRTUU	run through
	run-through
GHHNORSSTU	song thrush
GHHOORTTUU	throughout
GHHOPRTTUU	put through
	throughput
GHIIKLNNTY	thinkingly
GHIIKNNNTU	unthinking
GHIILLNOTW	Linlithgow
GHIILLOPTT	pilot light
GHIILNRTWY	wr ithingly
GHIILNWYZZ	whizzingly
GHIIMNPRTU	triumphing
GHIINNNOST	not shining
GHIINNORSU	nourishing
GHIKLNNTUY	unknightly
GHIKNNORTW	think wrong
GHILMNPTUY	thumpingly
GHILMOOORU	Horologium
GHILNOOPST	phlogiston
GHILNOOPTU	plough into
GHILNOOSTY	soothingly
GHILNOSTTU	gluttonish
GHILNOSTUY	shoutingly
GHILNRRUYY	hurryingly
GHILOOORST	horologist
GHILOOPSYY	physiology
GHILOOSTWW	go slow with
GHIMMNOPTU	humming-top
GHINOPRTUW	throwing up
GHIOOTTTUU	tough it out
GHLMOOOOSU	homologous
GHLMOOOPRY	morphology
GHLMOOOSTY	go smoothly
GHLNOOPSUW	snowplough
GHMOOOSUYZ	homozygous
GIIIIMMNNZ	minimizing
GIIILLNNST	instilling
GIIILNNTVY	invitingly
GIIIMNNPRT	imprinting
GIIINNNTUV	uninviting
GIIKLLNNTY	tinklingly
GIIKLMMNSY	skimmingly
GIIKLMNPSY	skimpingly
GIIKLMNRSY	smirkingly
GIIKLNNOPT	Pilkington
GIIKLNNPRS	sprinkling
GIIKLNPPSY	skippingly
GIIKLNRSTY	strikingly
GIILLNNOPR	rolling-pin
GIILLNNOTW	not willing
GIILLNPPRY	ripplingly
GIILLNSYZZ	sizzlingly
GIILMMNRTY	trimmingly
GIILMMNSWY	swimmingly
GIILMNNOTW	Wilmington
GIILMNOORV	living-room
GIILMNOPSY	imposingly
GIILNNNOTY	intoningly
GIILNNOPRU	purloining
GIILNNOSTV	Livingston
GIILNNSTTY	stintingly
GIILNOORSU	inglorious
GIILNOOSST	Sinologist
GIILNPPRTY	trippingly
GIILNRRSTY	stirringly
GIILNRSTVY	strivingly
GIILNTTTWY	twittingly
GIILOORSTV	virologist
GIILOPPRST	pistol grip
GIIMNNNORU	in mourning
GIIMNNOORS	Monsignori
GIIMNNOORT	monitoring
GIIMNORRRW	wing mirror
GIIMNOSSTY	misogynist
GIINNNSTTU	unstinting
GIINNOPRST	piston ring

GIINNRRSTU	unstirring
GIINOTTTUW	outwitting
GIINPRRSSU	surprising
GIJNOTTTUU	jutting out
GIKKLLNSUY	skulkingly
GIKMNNNOOS	non-smoking
GIKNNOORTW	not working
	Workington
GIKNOORTUW	working out
	working-out
GILLNNOUVY	unlovingly
GILLNOOPRT	trolloping
GILLNOPRRS	spring roll
GILLNOPRWY	prowlingly
GILLNOPTTY	plottingly
GILLNPUYZZ	puzzlingly
GILLNRSTUY	rustlingly
GILLOORSUY	gloriously
GILMMNOOUY	immunology
GILMNNORUY	mourningly
GILMNOOSVW	slow-moving
GILNNNOPSU	nonplusing
GILNNNSTUY	stunningly
GILNNOOSWY	swooningly
GILNNORSTY	snortingly
GILNOOOSST	nosologist
GILNOOPSTY	stoopingly
GILNOPRSTY	sportingly
GILNORRWYY	worryingly
GILNPRSUUY	pursuingly
	usurpingly
GILNRSTTUY	trustingly
GILOORRSUY	rigorously
GILOORSUVY	vigorously
GIMMPPTUYY	gippy tummy
GIMNNOOPUV	Moving On Up
GIMNNOORSS	Monsignors
GIMNOOSSUY	misogynous
GINNOOPPST	postponing
GINNRSTTUU	untrusting
GINOOORTTU	rooting-out
GINOOPRTUU	outpouring
GINOORSTTU	sorting out
GINOPPPSTU	stopping-up
GINOPPRRTU	purporting
GINOPPRSTU	supporting
GKMMNOOOPS	Kompong Som
GKMORSSSUY	Mussorgsky
GLNOORSUWY	wrongously
GLNOOSTTUU	gluttonous
GMMPPTUYYY	gyppy tummy
GMNNOOOSUY	monogynous
GMNOOORRST	strongroom
GNNOOOOTTW	go to town on

H

HHHMNNOSUY	Houyhnhnms
HHIILOPPRT	Philip Roth
HHILOOPPSY	philosophy
HHIOPPSSYY	hypophysis
HHJNNOOSTU	John Huston
HHOOPPRSSU	phosphorus
HHOPPSSTUU	shut up shop
HIIJNOPTUW	join up with
HIIKLNPTUW	link up with
HIIKLSSTTY	skittishly
HIILLNORTT	trillionth
HIILOPPSTW	pistol-whip
HIILORTTTY	lithotrity
HIILOSSSTY	histolysis
HIIMOPRSSW	misworship
HIINOORSST	ornithosis
HIINORRSUV	rhinovirus
HIIOOOPRST	oophoritis
HIIOOTTTYY	hoity-toity
HIJKNNORSU	John Ruskin
HIJLMNNOOT	John Milton
HIJLMNOOTW	John Wilmot
HIKORSSUWY	whisky sour
HILLNOTTUW	Will Hutton
HILLSSTTUY	sluttishly
HILMNORTTY	trimonthly
HILNOOPPSU	polish up on
HILNORTUWY	unworthily
HILOOPRSTY	polyhistor
HILOOPSSTY	photolysis
HILOPPSTUY	Hippolytus
HIOOOSTTTU	shoot it out
HIOOPPRRSY	porphyrios
HIOOPRSTTT	orthoptist
HIOOPRTTXY	thixotropy
HIORSSTTUU	struthious
HJMNNOOORT	John Morton
HLLOOPPRSY	sporophyll
HLMOORSUUY	humorously
HLOPRSSUUU	sulphurous
HMMOOORTTU	motormouth
HMOOPRSTTU	Portsmouth
HMOOPSSTUU	posthumous
HNORSSTTUY	Stonyhurst
HOORRSSTTY	short story
	short-story

I

IIIMNOOPST	imposition
IIIMNOPRSS	misprision
IIIMOPSSTV	positivism
IIINOQRSTU	inquisitor
IIINOQSTUU	iniquitous
IIIOPSSTTV	positivist
IIJNOPRSTT	strip joint
IIKLLLMSTU	multiskill
IIKLOOPSTT	Ostpolitik
IILLLLNWYY	willy-nilly
IILLLLWWYY	willy-willy
IILLLOPPSW	pillowslip
IILLNOOPPS	poison pill
IILLNOOPST	postillion
IILMNOSTUY	luminosity
IILNNOOOPW	low opinion
IILNNOOTUV	involution
IILNOPSTTW	split in two

IILOOPRSUX	prolixious
IILOPRSSTW	low spirits
IINOOOPPST	opposition
IINOOPRSSV	provisions
IINORSTTTU	institutor
IINORSTTUU	nutritious
IIOOOPRSTV	ovipositor
IIOOPPRSTU	propitious
IIOPRSSTUU	spirituous
IIORSTTUVY	virtuosity
IJLNOOOSTT	joint-stool
IKLLOOPPSY	look slippy
IKMORSSTTY	Trotskyism
IKORSSTTTY	Trotskyist
ILLMNOSUUY	luminously
ILLMOQTUUY	multiloquy
ILMNOOOPST	monopolist
ILMNOOOPSY	polyominos
ILMNOOOSTW	slow-motion
ILMNOOSUUV	voluminous
ILMNOSTUUY	mutinously
ILMOORSTUY	timorously
ILNOOPPRSU	propulsion
ILOOPPRSST	spoilsport
ILOORSTTUY	tortiously
ILOORSUUXY	uxoriously
ILOPRSSUUY	spuriously
ILORSSUUUY	usuriously
ILORSTUUVY	virtuously
IMNOOORSUV	omnivorous
IMOOPRRSSY	promissory
INOOOPPRRT	proportion
INOOPRRSTU	protrusion

L

LLOOPPSUUY	populously
LLORSSTUUY	lustrously
LMNOOPSUUY	upon my soul!
LMOSTTUUUU	tumultuous
LNOOORSSUY	sonorously
LOOPSTUUUV	voluptuous
LOORSTTUUY	tortuously
LORRSTUUYY	yours truly

M

MMOOPRRSUU	rumpus room
MMPPPRUUYY	rumpy-pumpy
MNNOOOOSTU	monotonous
MNNOOSSUYY	synonymous
MNOOOPRRTY	promontory
NOOORRTTWY	not to worry
OPRSTTUVYY	topsy-turvy

11 letters

A

AAAAABBCDRR	abracadabra
AAAAABHHMRT	Mahabharata
AAAAACLMNNP	Panama Canal
AAAAADGJLRU	Guadalajara
AAAAAGLMMRS	garam masala
AAAAAHMNNST	hasta mañana
AAAAANRRTTT	taratantara
AAAABBBDNRS	Bandar Abbas
AAAABBCHILN	Bahia Blanca
AAAABBDRRRW	Barbara Ward
AAAABBINRST	Sabbatarian
AAAABCCHILN	bacchanalia
AAAABCCILNN	baccanalian
AAAABCHINNS	Sanni Abacha
AAAABCHINPT	Captain Ahab
AAAABDEKKLS	baked Alaska
AAAABDGHMNR	Grand Bahama
AAAABDIIRSU	Saudi Arabia
AAAABEHSTTV	have a stab at
AAAABHLRSTT	Shatt al-Arab
AAAABIJLMOR	labia majora
AAAACDGLLNU	Guadalcanal
AAAACDGMOSV	Vasco da Gama
AAAACEGLMNP	à la campagne
AAAACEGMMMR	gamma camera
AAAACEHKLLP	Lake Chapala
AAAACEJNSTV	Ajanta caves
AAAACGILPSS	passacaglia
AAAACGINNRR	Gran Canaria
AAAACILLMRS	Maria Callas
AAAADEGLMMT	amalgamated
AAAADELMRSS	Dar es Salaam
AAAAEHIMNSV	have as an aim
AAAAEKMPSST	make a pass at
AAAAFGNOSTT	Antofagasta
AAAAFINRRST	Rastafarian
AAAAGHIPPRR	paragraphia
AAAAHHMRRST	Maharashtra
AAAAHMNPSTT	phantasmata
AAAAIMORRST	Ars Amatoria
AAAALLMNRSY	Allan Ramsay
AAAALNNOPVV	Anna Pavlova
AAABBCELLPS	baseball cap
AAABBCHJKMR	Jack Brabham
AAABBCLOOSV	Vasco Balboa
AAABBDEJKMO	make a bad job
AAABBDILNST	blind as a bat
AAABCCEHLTZ	catch ablaze
AAABCCKLLOS	black as coal
AAABCCLLOWY	Cab Calloway
AAABCDDIRRY	bradycardia
AAABCDEEINR	abecedarian
AAABCDELNRS	candelabras
AAABCDENORR	radar beacon
AAABCDGINRY	Cardigan Bay
AAABCDLOOST	bald as a coot

AAABCEEIMRT	bacteraemia
AAABCEGKPSS	back passage
AAABCEHINRT	abranchiate
AAABCILLNTY	abactinally
AAABCILLOPR	parabolical
AAABCLLOPSS	Pablo Casals
AAABDDENORW	draw a bead on
AAABDEELRTW	Walter Baade
AAABDEELRWY	Delaware Bay
AAABDEGGLNU	bad language
AAABDEGIMNR	brain damage
AAABDELORRS	Labrador Sea
AAABEEGLLSV	salvageable
AAABEFLOTTU	A Tale of a Tub
AAABEGILNPR	plea bargain
	plea-bargain
AAABEGNOPRZ	garbanzo pea
AAABEHIMNPS	amphisbaena
AAABEIIJNRZ	Azerbaijani
AAABEIILNRS	Rabelaisian
AAABEILLNUV	unavailable
AAABEILLRTZ	blaze a trail
AAABEILPPRS	appraisable
AAABEKLLNOT	Lake Balaton
AAABELLNPTU	unpalatable
AAABELNRRTW	warrantable
AAABEMRSTTT	Stabat Mater
AAABGHIOOPR	agoraphobia
AAABGORSSZZ	Zsa Zsa Gabor
AAABHIOPRST	astraphobia
AAABIILMNOR	labia minora
AAABILLNUVY	unavailably
AAABILMNOTU	ablutomania
AAABILNNPST	banana split
AAABINNORVY	Navarino Bay
AAABINPSSTT	Anabaptists
AAABLLNPTUY	unpalatably
AAABLNRRTWY	warrantably
AAACCCEILTT	acatalectic
AAACCCEINPT	capacitance
AAACCCILLTT	catallactic
AAACCDEIIMN	academician
AAACCDHIRTY	tachycardia
AAACCEEHKNT	take a chance
AAACCEEHSTT	attaché case
	attaché-case
AAACCEFLOST	catafalcoes
AAACCEGLNST	cast a glance
AAACCEHINPU	ipecacuanha
AAACCEILLOR	calceolaria
AAACCELMNOS	calamancoes
AAACCEORTTV	caveat actor
AAACCGHLLMR	Marc Chagall
AAACCGILNPT	pan-galactic
AAACCHILLRY	archaically
AAACCHILRTT	cathartical
AAACCHILRTU	autarchical
AAACCIKNPTT	panic attack
AAACCILLNRU	canalicular
AAACCILLPRT	parallactic
AAACCILMNOT	acclamation
AAACCILRRTU	caricatural
AAACCILSTUV	accusatival
AAACCIMNORT	carcinomata
AAACCLMORTY	acclamatory
AAACDEEGKLP	package deal
AAACDEEIKMR	Madeira cake
AAACDEEIMRR	camaraderie
AAACDEEKLNS	Cakes and Ale
AAACDEELLOV	Ada Lovelace
AAACDEENPRW	War and Peace
AAACDEGNOOS	Canada goose
AAACDEHINRT	acidanthera
AAACDEIIRST	Adriatic Sea
AAACDEILMPR	paramedical
AAACDEILNRT	cardinalate
AAACDEINSTT	at a distance
AAACDEIRRWY	carried away
AAACDEPRTTU	data capture
AAACDGMNNRY	Grand Cayman
AAACDILOPRX	paradoxical
AAACEEFKMST	make faces at
AAACEEFLMNS	malfeasance
AAACEELLNST	a clean slate
AAACEENRTTV	caravanette
AAACEGHILLP	cephalalgia
AAACEGILMNO	egomaniacal
AAACEGIRRWY	carriageway
AAACEHILLPR	parheliacal
AAACEHIMRRY	Mariah Carey
AAACEHKRTTT	heart attack
AAACEHLLVVV	Vaclav Havel
AAACEIKLMST	stake a claim
AAACEILLMNR	all-American
AAACEILMRSS	Las Americas
AAACEIMNNPR	pan-American
AAACEINRSTV	caravan site
AAACEJKLMNR	Jean Lamarck
AAACEJKMMSY	James Mackay
AAACELLMTUU	macula lutea
AAACELMNRST	sacramental
AAACELMOPRT	paracetamol
AAACERRSTTU	tartar sauce
AAACFILLNTY	fanatically
AAACFILNSTT	fantastical
AAACFIMNRRT	aircraftman
AAACGHIPPRR	paragraphic
AAACGHNOOTT	Chattanooga
AAACGILLNTY	agnatically
AAACGILMMRT	grammatical
AAACHIILPRS	pharisaical
AAACHIKPPRT	apparatchik
AAACHILMRRT	matriarchal
AAACHILNOTU	anacoluthia
AAACHILPRRT	patriarchal
AAACHINPRST	Carpathians
AAACHLLLOTT	call a halt to
AAACIILMOTX	axiomatical
AAACIILPRST	parasitical
AAACIIMNPST	Isaac Pitman
AAACIIMOSSV	Isaac Asimov
AAACILLNNPS	spinal canal

AAACILLNORV	Convallaria
AAACILLNSTY	satanically
AAACILLRTUY	actuarially
AAACILMMNOS	sal ammoniac
AAACILNNRST	Lancastrian
AAACIRRTWYY	carry it away
AAACJLMNORY	Ramón y Cajal
AAADDDDEOOS	dead as a dodo
AAADDEFRTYY	day after day
AAADDEHMRSY	hamadry-ades
AAADDEHORTW	draw to a head
AAADDEIMNSV	David Seaman
AAADDEIMRRR	Madara Rider
AAADDEINORR	Andrea Doria
AAADDELNOST	adelantados
AAADDFHNRST	hard and fast
	hard-and-fast
AAADDIMNUVZ	ad avizandum
AAADEEFHHVW	have had a few
AAADEEGGNSS	ages and ages
AAADEEGHNRV	have a gander
AAADEEHKMMS	make ashamed
AAADEEHKMWY	make headway
AAADEEHLSVY	heavy as lead
AAADEENRRTW	tear and wear
	wear and tear
AAADEENSSTT	stand at ease
AAADEFFGNRV	Van de Graaff
AAADEFFNNOR	fanfaronade
AAADEFGNOTV	of advantage
AAADEFOPSST	deaf as a post
AAADEGHHMNS	Meghnad Saha
AAADEGINRSS	Andre Agassi
AAADEGNOTTV	to advantage
AAADEHHHTTV	have had that
AAADEHINRTT	radiant heat
AAADEHINSTT	that's an idea
AAADEHLNOOV	have a load on
AAADEHLNPRS	Alan Shepard
AAADEILMPTV	maladaptive
AAADEILMRRR	rear admiral
AAADEILNNRX	Alexandrian
AAADEILPRSS	Sal Paradise
AAADEILRRSV	adversarial
AAADEIMNNRX	Anaximander
AAADEKKMRWW	make awkward
AAADEKKNOTZ	Takada Kenzo
AAADELLMPRT	Mar del Plata
AAADELMRSTW	Walter Adams
AAADENNRRTV	rant and rave
AAADFFHHLLN	half-and-half
AAADGILNORT	gradational
AAADGILORXY	radio galaxy
AAADGIMNRRT	Armatrading
AAADGINNNOW	now and again
AAADHHLPRYZ	haphazardly
AAADHILMMMU	Muhammad Ali
AAADHILNRSS	hard as nails
AAADHIMMMUZ	Muhammad Zia
AAADHLNNRUY	hardy annual
AAADILNNRSS	Aran Islands
AAADLLNRSTW	warts and all
AAADLNORSSV	San Salvador
AAAEEELNPRS	paraselenae
AAAEEFKLMMO	make a meal of
AAAEEFKMORW	make aware of
AAAEEGGMNST	stage-manage
AAAEEGINPRS	paragenesia
AAAEEGMSSTU	sausage meat
AAAEEHHRTTV	have at heart
AAAEEHINSST	anaesthesia
AAAEEHLLSST	Tallahassee
AAAEEHLNRRS	Alan Shearer
AAAEEHMNTTX	exanthemata
AAAEELMNPSX	as an example
AAAEELNPRTY	penalty area
AAAEERSTTVX	extravasate
AAAEFFIJNRX	Jane Fairfax
AAAEFHHKMOS	make a hash of
AAAEGHINNPP	happen again
AAAEGHLPTUW	what a plague
AAAEGIILNRT	egalitarian
AAAEGIKMNST	make against
AAAEGIKNPTU	take up again
AAAEGIKNSTT	take against
AAAEGILMMNO	megalomania
AAAEGILNPRY	playing area
AAAEGILNRWY	in a large way
AAAEGINRWWY	wearing away
AAAEGJLMSWY	James Galway
AAAEGLMNOUY	Maya Angelou
AAAEGLOPRSS	paraglossae
AAAEGNOSSTU	not a sausage
AAAEGNRTTVX	extravagant
AAAEGORSSSS	Sargasso Sea
AAAEHHLNNPT	naphthalane
AAAEHIILMPT	epithalamia
AAAEHIKNRST	thin as a rake
AAAEHILNOPR	aeolian harp
AAAEHILNPRT	paranthelia
AAAEHLLRSUY	Laura Ashley
AAAEHLMNRSS	Las Hermanas
AAAEHPPRRRS	paraphraser
AAAEILMNSTW	animal waste
AAAEILMRRTW	raw material
AAAEILNPWXY	explain away
AAAEINSSSST	assassinate
AAAEKKLNRTU	Lake Turkana
AAAEKMOORTT	take a room at
AAAENNPRSTU	Punta Arenas
AAAENPRSSTW	Peasants' War
AAAEPPRSSTU	apparatuses
AAAFFFILNST	Falstaffian
AAAFGHINNST	Afghanistan
AAAFILLMRTY	family altar
AAAFILMMNRS	farm animals
AAAFLOPRRTY	lay a trap for
AAAGGGINRTV	aggravating
AAAGGHHIOPR	Hagiographa
AAAGGINORTV	aggravation
AAAGHHIIOPS	Hagia Sophia
AAAGIILNPRS	parasailing

AAAGIINRSTT	Sagittarian
AAAGILNNPQU	aquaplaning
AAAGINPRSTY	pray against
AAAGINPSSWY	passing away
	passing-away
AAAGINSTWWY	wasting away
AAAGKNOORRT	kangaroo rat
	rat kangaroo
AAAGLLORSSV	Vargas Llosa
AAAGLMNORTU	granulomata
AAAGMMRRRSS	marram grass
AAAGMPPRSSS	pampas grass
AAAHHHNORSS	Rosh Hashana
AAAHIKMNRRS	Ramakrishna
AAAHIKNRRSV	Ravi Shankar
AAAHILMOPRT	prothalamia
AAAHILNPSXY	anaphylaxis
AAAHIMNRRUZ	Ziaur Rahman
AAAHKMMORYY	Omar Khayyám
AAAIILLNNPR	Rila Planina
AAAIILMRSST	Alastair Sim
AAAIILNORTV	variational
AAAIILNPSTU	saintpaulia
AAAIINNQRTU	antiquarian
AAAIINQRRRW	Iran-Iraq War
AAAIJRSTTYY	Satyajit Ray
AAAILLMNSWY	in a small way
AAAILLMORTY	amatorially
AAAILLNNPSZ	Spallanzani
AAAILLNOTUV	valuational
AAAILLORSTT	saltatorial
AAAILNNRSTU	Saturnalian
AAAILNORTVV	Navratilova
AAAILNPPRTY	play a part in
AAAILOPRRTT	raptatorial
AAAIMNNOOST	antonomasia
AAAIMNOOPRS	paronomasia
AAAJNNNOOTV	Jana Novotna
AAAMNORRTTU	Mount Ararat
AAAOPRSSTUU	apatosaurus ❏
AABBBCDEINR	bib and brace
AABBBCEKRST	back-stabber
AABBCCIILST	cabbalistic
AABBCCKLNOR	carbon black
AABBCDEINRT	brace and bit
AABBCEEKKRR	backbreaker
AABBCEINORT	bicarbonate
AABBCEKLTUY	Black Beauty
AABBCFIOSYY	Bay of Biscay
AABBDDDENOR	bed and board
AABBDEEHLVY	behave badly
AABBDEEHRTT	bated breath
AABBDEEIRTV	abbreviated
AABBDEEKRST	bread basket
AABBDEILSSY	Baily's beads
AABBDEINOTT	Diane Abbott
AABBDLORSSS	bold as brass
AABBDRRRUYY	Ray Bradbury
AABBEEIRRTV	rebarbative
AABBEEKLNRU	unbreakable
AABBEFGLNOY	Bay of Bengal

AABBEFGLRST	flabbergast
AABBEGILLNR	ball-bearing
AABBEHIILNT	inhabitable
AABBEIMNRSS	Babes in Arms
AABBEIRRTTU	barbiturate
AABBEKMOOOO	make a booboo
AABBHIKOSUZ	Bashi-Bazouk
AABBIIILMNO	bibliomania
AABBLORRSUY	barbarously
AABCCCDIIOR	boracic acid
AABCCCHKRST	backscratch
AABCCDKLNOR	Conrad Black
AABCCEELMPT	accept blame
AABCCEHNNYY	by any chance
AABCCEILPRT	practicable
AABCCEKRSTT	backscatter
AABCCELNOTT	contactable
AABCCELNOTU	accountable
AABCCERRUUY	bureaucracy
AABCCGIKKNP	backpacking
AABCCILMOST	saltimbocca
AABCCILPRTY	practicably
AABCCKNNOTU	bank account
AABCCLNOTUY	accountably
AABCDDIKMNO	diamond-back
AABCDEEERTX	exacerbated
AABCDEEFLRY	barefacedly
AABCDEEHIRS	raised beach
AABCDEEKNRR	breakdancer
AABCDEEORRT	beat a record
AABCDEHIMMR	chambermaid
AABCDEHLMTY	Lady Macbeth
AABCDEILMSY	as claimed by
AABCDEILNRY	clay-brained
AABCDEILNST	elastic band
AABCDEINNNU	in abundance
AABCDEINOOR	radio beacon
AABCDEIORRS	barricadoes
AABCDELLNPS	cap and bells
AABCDELMNRU	candelabrum
AABCDEMORTY	Tremadoc Bay
AABCDEMOSSU	ambuscadoes
AABCDENOORS	carbonadoes
AABCDEORRST	broadcaster
	rebroadcast
AABCDFIKLLN	back and fill
AABCDGGIOOR	braggadocio
AABCDGHIKNN	handing back
AABCDGIKNRW	drawing back
AABCDGKORSW	go backwards
AABCDHHNRST	Brands Hatch
AABCDHIRRSY	Richards Bay
AABCDHMNORY	rhabdomancy
AABCDINOORR	radiocarbon
AABCEEELLPR	replaceable
AABCEEFNORR	forbearance
AABCEEGLLNO	congealable
AABCEEHKLRT	leather-back
AABCEEHLNRU	unreachable
AABCEEHLNTU	unteachable
AABCEEHMNRT	antechamber

Words marked ❏ can also be spelled with an initial capital letter

AABCEEILLMR	reclaimable	AABCENOPPRR	carbon paper
AABCEEILMNV	ambivalence	AABCFFJOSST	Jacob's staff
AABCEEILNPS	inescapable	AABCFGIIMSY	as if by magic
AABCEEILNQU	equibalance	AABCFGIKLLN	falling back
AABCEEILNRS	increasable	AABCFIINORT	fabrication
AABCEEILPPR	appreciable	AABCFIKLRRS	Black friars
AABCEELNORV	overbalance		Blackfriars
AABCEELNPSS	capableness	AABCFLMNOYY	flamboyancy
AABCEELNRTU	untraceable	AABCGGHIKNN	hanging-back
AABCEELRRTT	retractable	AABCGHIOOPR	agoraphobic
AABCEELRTTU	trabeculate	AABCHHIOOPT	tachophobia
AABCEELRTTX	extractable	AABCHIINNTY	inhabitancy
AABCEFHKOTT	at the back of	AABCHILLRTY	charity ball
AABCEFINOTT	tabefaction	AABCHJLNORY	John Barclay
AABCEFLMNOY	flamboyance	AABCIIILMTY	amicability
AABCEFLNOTU	confabulate	AABCIILLPTY	placability
AABCEGHNORT	baton charge	AABCIILMNNS	cannibalism
	baton-charge	AABCIILNORT	calibration
AABCEGILNNT	enabling act	AABCILLNOTY	botanically
AABCEGMNNSU	Angus McBean	AABCILLORSS	Carlo Blasis
AABCEHIIMRT	Marie Bichat	AABCILNRTTY	intractably
AABCEHIINNT	inhabitance	AABCINNOORT	carbonation
AABCEHILLRY	Hebraically	AABCINORSTT	abstraction
AABCEHILMNR	chamberlain ❑	AABCKLLLNOU	Alan Bullock
AABCEHILNRU	hibernacula	AABCKLLORWY	rock wallaby
AABCEHINORT	haricot bean	AABCKMOORRR	barrack-room
AABCEHKLRTT	the black art	AABDDEEELRW	Edward Albee
AABCEHKORTT	back to earth	AABDDEEGHLR	Hedda Gabler
AABCEHLLMRS	Charles Lamb	AABDDEELNRR	brand leader
AABCEHMRRST	Star Chamber	AABDDEEMNNR	bad-mannered
AABCEIIINRR	carabinieri	AABDDEGGORR	daggerboard
AABCEIILNNS	cannibalise	AABDDEGLLLR	gall bladder
AABCEIILNNZ	cannibalize	AABDDEHMORY	hebdomadary
AABCEIIMRST	basmati rice	AABDDEIILVY	David Bailey
AABCEIKLLMR	blackmailer	AABDDEINOTV	David Beaton
AABCEIKMRSS	Bismarck Sea	AABDDEITTVY	David Beatty
AABCEILLMRY	reclaimably	AABDDELNNOY	abandonedly
AABCEILLORY	aerobically	AABDDERRRUW	Edward Burra
AABCEILLPRU	burial place	AABDDHHIMOR	Bodhidharma
	burial-place	AABDDNRSSTU	substandard
AABCEILLRTU	articulable	AABDEEEHKLW	beaked whale
AABCEILLSTY	syllabicate	AABDEEFIRRS	free as a bird
AABCEILMNVY	ambivalency	AABDEEGIMRR	marriage-bed
AABCEILNNOT	containable	AABDEEGNNSV	Geneva bands
AABCEILNPSY	inescapably	AABDEEHHRRS	haberdasher
AABCEILNRTT	intractable	AABDEEHINRR	harebrained
AABCEILPPRY	appreciably		hare-brained
AABCEIMNPRR	Precambrian	AABDEELPRSU	persuadable
AABCEJLMORY	Jacob Marley	AABDEELRSTW	wastel bread
AABCEKKLMRT	black market	AABDEEMRRSS	embarrassed
	black-market	AABDEEOSTTV	above-stated
AABCEKLLRRT	trackerball	AABDEFFLOOR	loaf of bread
AABCEKLNNRT	central bank	AABDEFIKMOR	make a bid for
AABCEKMRUUV	vacuum brake	AABDEGIJOSS	Jagadis Bose
AABCEKQRRTU	quarterback	AABDEGILNOR	load-bearing
AABCELLLOPS	collapsable	AABDEGILNOS	diagnosable
AABCELLOORT	collaborate	AABDEGINOSV	vagabondise
AABCELMRSTU	Albert Camus	AABDEGINOVZ	vagabondize
AABCELNORTY	carbonylate	AABDEHIILTT	habilitated
AABCELOORST	car boot sale	AABDEHIINRR	hair-brained
AABCELRRTVY	travel by car	AABDEHOSTTT	stab to death

AABDEHRSTWY	breadthways
AABDEIILNSV	inadvisable
AABDEIILRTY	readability
AABDEILLNOT	labiodental
AABDEILLRVY	adverbially
AABDEILLSTY	Bastille Day
AABDEILNOUV	unavoidable
AABDEILNSUV	unadvisable
AABDEINOORS	noise abroad
AABDEINOSST	bastinadoes
AABDEKLOTTU	talked about
AABDEKNOORT	take on board
AABDEKNRRTZ	Bernard Katz
AABDELLLNOO	lead balloon
AABDELLNORR	Allan Border
AABDELNOPRU	Pablo Neruda
AABDELORRUY	day-labourer
AABDEMNNNOT	abandonment
AABDFIIINPS	spina bifida
AABDFILNORS	Island of Rab
AABDGHIILNT	in a bad light
AABDGIINRSW	bias-drawing
AABDGKLNOUW	dak bungalow
AABDHIKLNOY	bank holiday
AABDHINNOPS	abandon ship
AABDHIOSTTV	Bodhisattva
AABDIILLTUY	laudability
AABDIILMNTY	damnability
AABDIILMOTT	admit to bail
AABDIILNRSS	Brian Aldiss
AABDILLMNOY	abdominally
AABDILLNOOS	bold as a lion
AABDILNORTU	Adrian Boult
AABDILNOUVY	unavoidably
AABDILNSUVY	unadvisably
AABDIMNORTU	adumbration
AABDIMPSSUY	bumpsadaisy
AABDIORRSST	Broadstairs
AABDLLNOOST	boots and all
AABDLNOPRTY	Portland Bay
AABDMOORRRT	mortarboard
	mortar-board
AABDNOOPRSX	Pandora's box
AABDNOORRWW	bow and arrow
AABDNOOTTUU	out and about
AABDOPRRSTY	pastry board
AABEEEEGRRV	eager beaver
AABEEEFKRRS	safe-breaker
AABEEEHLLNW	baleen whale
AABEEEHMRTW	weather beam
AABEEEKSTVW	basketweave
AABEEERRRTW	Water Bearer
	Water-bearer
AABEEFORSTU	Beaufort Sea
AABEEGGIIRR	argie-bargie
AABEEGGLLRR	argle-bargle
AABEEGKMRTU	take umbrage
AABEEGLMNTU	augmentable
AABEEGLNOSV	noble savage
AABEEGLNTTU	ungetatable
	unget-at-able

AABEEHILNTZ	Elizabethan
AABEEHILPST	alphabetise
AABEEHILPTZ	alphabetize
AABEEHIRRRT	heat barrier
AABEEHKLNSU	unshakeable
AABEEHKLRTW	break the law
AABEEIILLNN	inalienable
AABEEIJKLRR	jailbreaker
AABEEIJMRRS	James Barrie
AABEEILLNNU	unalienable
AABEEILLNPX	explainable
AABEEILLNRT	inalterable
AABEEILMNSS	amiableness
AABEEILNPRS	inseparable
AABEEILNRUW	unweariable
AABEEILORTV	elaborative
AABEEILPRRR	irreparable
AABEEINNNST	Annie Besant
AABEEINRRRT	train-bearer
AABEEINRRST	brainteaser
	brain-teaser
AABEEKKMORR	make or break
	make-or-break
AABEEKLNPSU	unspeakable
AABEEKOPTUW	be a wake-up to
AABEELLNRTU	unalterable
AABEELLNSSV	Vanessa Bell
AABEELLORTY	elaborately
AABEELLOTUV	All About Eve
AABEELLPRRY	pearl barley
AABEELLPRSU	pleasurable
AABEELMPRTU	perambulate
	preambulate
AABEELNOORT	elaborate on
AABEELNORST	treasonable
AABEELNORTU	unelaborate
AABEELNRTTU	entablature
	untreatable
AABEELNRTUV	unavertable
AABEELPRSTT	breastplate
AABEELRRSTT	sabre-rattle
AABEELRRSTV	traversable
AABEELRRTWY	barley water
AABEELSSUUX	sexual abuse
AABEFFIILLS	falsifiable
AABEFGIILMN	magnifiable
AABEFHILNOS	fashionable
AABEFHILPST	half-baptise
AABEFHILPTZ	half-baptize
AABEFIILLQU	qualifiable
AABEFIILSST	satisfiable
AABEFILLMMN	inflammable
AABEFILLNTT	final battle
AABEFKRSTTV	breakfast TV
AABEFLLNPPU	unflappable
AABEFLMNTUU	funambulate
AABEFLNOPSY	Bay of Naples
AABEGIIMRRV	Gambia River
AABEGIKLNRW	law-breaking
AABEGILNNUV	unnavigable
AABEGIRRRTU	arbitrageur

AABEGJSSTUU	assubjugate	AABGHILNOOP	anglophobia
AABEGKLOSTW	blow a gasket	AABGHINNOTU	hang about in
AABEGLLRSTU	Glauber salt	AABGIILNNVY	innavigably
AABEGLNOPTU	Paul Boateng	AABGIILNOST	sailing boat
AABEGLNORRR	barrel organ	AABGIKNNSSV	savings bank
AABEGLRRSUY	barley sugar	AABGILMNRSU	submarginal
AABEHILNRST	tarnishable	AABGINNOSTW	angwantibos
AABEHILORUV	behavioural	AABHIINNSTT	inhabitants
AABEHKLLMTW	Lambeth Walk	AABHIINOTTU	habituation
AABEHLPRRSV	phrasal verb	AABHJMNORRT	John Bartram
AABEHLRSTUU	hurl abuse at	AABHLLLLOOU	hullaballoo
AABEIILLNNY	inalienably	AABHMOOSSTU	Matsuo Basho
AABEIILLSTY	saleability	AABHNOOPRTU	harp on about
AABEIILMMOR	memorabilia	AABIIILRTVY	variability
AABEIILMNTY	amenability	AABIIILSTTY	satiability
AABEIILNRRT	libertarian	AABIILMOOTU	automobilia
AABEIILRTTY	rateability	AABIILNORTV	vibrational
AABEIILRTWY	wearability	AABIILORSTU	atrabilious
AABEIJLMNRU	Julian Bream	AABIILPSSTY	passability
AABEIKMNORT	embarkation	AABIILRRRTY	arbitrarily
AABEILLLRTY	bilaterally	AABIIMNNOOT	abomination
AABEILLMNPU	manipulable	AABIINORRTT	arbitration
AABEILLNNUY	unalienably	AABILLMNNRU	Alan Milburn
AABEILLNRTY	inalterably	AABILLMORSY	ambrosially
AABEILLRRTZ	trailblazer	AABILLMPSTY	baptismally
	trail-blazer	AABILLNORRT	anti-roll bar
AABEILLRSUY	subaerially	AABILLRTUUV	burial-vault
AABEILLRVZZ	Brazzaville	AABILMNORTY	abnormality
AABEILMNPRS	Persian lamb	AABILNOPRSU	labour pains
AABEILNOORT	elaboration	AABILNSSTTU	substantial
AABEILNPRSY	inseparably	AABINOOPPRT	approbation
AABEILNSSTU	sustainable	AABLNNORRTU	natural-born
AABEILOPRVZ	vaporizable	AABLNPRRSUW	urban sprawl
AABEILPRRRY	irreparably	AABLOPRRTUY	Labour Party
AABEILPRTYY	play it by ear	AABOOPPRRTY	approbatory
AABEIMNRRTT	arbitrament	AACCCDHLOTT	catch cold at
AABEINNPRTT	Brian Patten	AACCCDHRRST	scratchcard
AABEINOPSTT	be at pains to	AACCCDIILRY	acrylic acid
AABEKKOOPRT	poke borak at	AACCCEILPTT	cataplectic
AABEKLNPSUY	unspeakably	AACCCEINORT	Arctic Ocean
AABEKNOPRTU	put a brake on	AACCCGHIOPR	cacographic
AABEKNORSTV	karbovanets	AACCCHHILLT	catch a chill
AABELLNRTUY	unalterably	AACCCIILLMT	climactical
AABELLORTTY	battle royal	AACCCILMSTY	cataclysmic
AABELLPRSUY	pleasurably	AACCCNNOTUY	accountancy
AABELLRRTUV	barrel vault	AACCDEEELRT	accelerated
AABELNORSTY	treasonably	AACCDEELLNT	cancellated
AABELNOSTUY	beauty salon	AACCDEELNOR	accelerando
AABELPRSSSU	surpassable	AACCDEELPRS	sacred place
AABENOSTUUY	uneasy about	AACCDEIILLT	dialectical
AABFHILNOSY	fashionably	AACCDEIILRV	valeric acid
AABFIKNORSU	Burkina Faso	AACCDEIIMMS	academicism
AABFILLMMNY	inflammably	AACCDEIIPRR	pericardiac
AABFIMNORST	abstain from	AACCDEILMNU	unacclaimed
AABFLLLSTTU	at full blast	AACCDEILOPY	cyclopaedia
AABFLLNPPUY	unflappably	AACCDEIMNOP	accompanied
AABFLLOORTW	Football War	AACCDEIRRTU	caricatured
AABGGHINOTW	go with a bang	AACCDEMMOOT	accommodate
AABGHHINRST	Granth Sahib	AACCDFKNORW	crack of dawn
AABGHIJKLRT	J K Galbraith	AACCDGINORS	according as
AABGHILLMRY	Billy Graham	AACCDHHORTT	hard to catch

AACCDIIILRT	diacritical
AACCDLNORTY	accordantly
AACCEEFKRRS	safecracker
	safe-cracker
AACCEEHILNP	in each place
AACCEEHLOPT	to each place
AACCEEILPSS	special case
AACCEEILRSV	Alcaic verse
AACCEEILTTT	atelectatic
AACCEEINPRS	parascience
AACCEEINRRT	incarcerate
AACCEEJNOTU	Jean Cocteau
AACCEEKLRRW	crackleware
AACCEELLNOT	collectanea
AACCEELMNRR	Marcel Carné
AACCEELORRT	accelerator
AACCEELPRTU	receptacula
AACCEENNOTT	concatenate
AACCEFILNOT	calefaction
AACCEFKNRRS	César Franck
AACCEGHOPRR	cacographer
AACCEGIKNPS	packing-case
AACCEGILORT	categorical
AACCEGIMPRT	magic carpet
AACCEHHILNR	Charlie Chan
AACCEHHIMNS	cash machine
AACCEHHPRST	catch phrase
AACCEHIIMNN	mechanician
AACCEHILMOT	machicolate
AACCEHILMST	catechismal
AACCEHINRRT	in character
AACCEHIRSST	catachresis
AACCEHLNNNO	nonchalance
AACCEHNRRTY	carry the can
AACCEHOPRSU	couch a spear
AACCEHORRSS	reach across
AACCEIILMST	acclimatise
AACCEIILMTZ	acclimatize
AACCEIKLNSV	Salk vaccine
AACCEILLNST	Callanetics
AACCEILLSTY	ascetically
AACCEILMPRT	malpractice
AACCEILPSTY	typical case
AACCEIMPRSU	America's Cup
AACCEINNORT	Eric Cantona
AACCEINQTTU	acquittance
AACCEJKKORU	Jack Kerouac
AACCEKKTYYY	yackety-yack
AACCEKMNOTT	make contact
AACCELLMNOW	Ewan MacColl
AACCELLNOTU	calculate on
AACCELLNTUY	accentually
AACCELMNUUV	vacuum-clean
AACCELNRSYY	scarcely any
AACCELPRSTU	spectacular
AACCELRTTUU	acculturate
AACCENNORSS	Carcassonne
AACCFHILOTT	fail to catch
AACCFIIILRS	sacrificial
AACCFIILLPY	pacifically
AACCGILLNTU	calculating
AACCHHIINTU	t'ai chi ch'uan
AACCHIIMRST	charismatic
AACCHIINRST	anarchistic
AACCHILLOTY	chaotically
AACCHILMNOR	monarchical
AACCHILMOST	stomachical
AACCHLLOTTW	tallow-catch
AACCHORRRTY	carry a torch
AACCIILLNTY	actinically
AACCIILMPRT	impractical
AACCIILSSTU	casuistical
AACCIILSTTT	stalactitic
AACCIINNOTV	vaccination
AACCIINOSTU	acoustician
AACCIINTTVY	Vatican City
AACCILLLNOY	laconically
AACCILLLSSY	classically
AACCILLNNOY	canonically
AACCILLNOTU	calculation
AACCILLNRTU	curtain call
AACCILLNSUU	canaliculus
AACCILLOSSS	social class
AACCILLPRTY	practically
AACCILLSTUY	caustically
AACCILNPRTU	unpractical
AACCILNSTTY	syntactical
AACCILOPPTY	apocalyptic
AACCILOPSUY	capaciously
AACCILRRSUW	circular saw
AACCILSSSUY	Cassius Clay
AACCIMNOPST	accompanist
AACCIORRSTY	aristocracy
AACCKNORTTU	a nut to crack
AACCLMORTUU	accumulator
AACCLNOOPRT	Locarno Pact
AACCLNORTTU	contractual
AACCMNNORTT	contract man
AACDDEEEHLR	clear-headed
AACDDEEHRTW	Edward Teach
AACDDEEIMPS	aides-de-camp
AACDDEEIORR	Eddie Arcaro
AACDDEGILNR	leading card
AACDDEHINPP	handicapped
AACDDEIIRTV	divaricated
AACDDEINRTU	candidature
AACDDIJORTU	adjudicator
AACDDIKNORS	Adirondacks
AACDDNORRTY	dot and carry
AACDEEEHHRT	head teacher
	headteacher
AACDEEEIMRR	cameraderie
AACDEEEMPRS	speed camera
AACDEEFFINT	caffeinated
AACDEEFILRR	free radical
AACDEEGHNRR	Grande Arche
AACDEEGLNTU	acute-angled
AACDEEHILMX	hexadecimal
AACDEEHMOOT	come to a head
AACDEEHNNOS	Dean Acheson
AACDEEHRSSV	headscarves
AACDEEIILRS	deracialise

AACDEEIILRZ	deracialize
AACDEEIIRTV	eradicative
AACDEEILNRS	calendarise
AACDEEILNRZ	calendarize
AACDEEILRSS	desacralise
AACDEEILRSZ	desacralize
AACDEEILRTV	declarative
AACDEEILSTT	elasticated
AACDEEIMNPT	emancipated
AACDEEIMORV	video camera
AACDEEINNNT	dance in a net
AACDEEIPPRT	appreciated
AACDEEKLNPP	pack and peel
AACDEELLNOT	lanceolated
AACDEELLSTT	castellated
AACDEEMNNTV	advancement
AACDEENQRSU	square dance
	square-dance
AACDEFGLMOU	camouflaged
AACDEFGORSY	days of grace
AACDEFILNOT	defalcation
AACDEFINNOV	in advance of
AACDEFINRUX	fricandeaux
AACDEGGILOP	pedagogical
AACDEGHHNNS	change hands
AACDEGHIPRS	cigar-shaped
AACDEGIIMNT	diamagnetic
AACDEGLNRSU	Angus Calder
AACDEHINOTT	anticathode
AACDEHINPPR	handicapper
AACDEHINRST	cantharides
AACDEHINRTU	Hardicanute
AACDEHJLMOT	Maja Clothed
AACDEHLNOST	close at hand
AACDEHORSTY	cathode rays
AACDEHPRRRS	card-sharper
AACDEHRRTYY	carry the day
AACDEIILMNO	Iain Macleod
AACDEIILMRT	diametrical
AACDEIILMRV	vice-admiral
AACDEIILPRR	pericardial
AACDEIINNNO	Indian Ocean
AACDEIINNNR	incarnadine
AACDEIINNRT	incardinate
AACDEIINORT	eradication
AACDEIINPTT	anticipated
AACDEIIORTV	radioactive
AACDEIIPRST	paediatrics
AACDEIIPRSU	parasuicide
AACDEILLLTY	dialectally
AACDEILLMOT	Camaldolite
AACDEILLOTV	La Dolce Vita
AACDEILMNOT	declamation
AACDEILNORT	declaration
AACDEILNOTU	educational
AACDEILNPRS	Iceland spar
AACDEILNRSS	radicalness
AACDEILORRT	redactorial
AACDEILRSTT	strait-laced
AACDEILRTTU	articulated
AACDEILRTTY	dairy cattle
AACDEIMNORT	demarcation
AACDEIMNORY	aerodynamic
AACDELLLMOY	Ally Macleod
AACDELLNOTY	anecdotally
AACDELMNNOR	Roman candle
AACDELMORTY	declamatory
AACDELNPTTY	pentadactyl
AACDELORRTY	declaratory
AACDEMORRRU	armoured car
AACDENNRSUV	under canvas
AACDENPSTTU	cut and paste
AACDEORRTVW	draw a covert
AACDEORTTTT	attracted to
AACDFHNORTY	factory hand
AACDFIILLTY	fatidically
AACDFIILRRT	fratricidal
AACDFIINOOS	aficionados
AACDFINNRYY	Nancy Friday
AACDFINOOTY	day of action
AACDGGHIKNU	Dick Gaughan
AACDGHIOPRR	cardiograph
AACDGIILNRS	radical sign
AACDGILNPRY	playing-card
AACDGIMRRTU	dramaturgic
AACDHIIOPRS	aphrodisiac
AACDHIJMNSW	jam sandwich
AACDHILMOPY	holiday camp
AACDHILOPRS	rhapsodical
AACDHIMMNTU	I'm a Dutchman
AACDHINPPTY	pitch and pay
AACDHMOPRSY	psychodrama
AACDIILMNRU	adminicular
AACDIILMPRY	pyramidical
AACDIILORTT	dictatorial
AACDIIMNOPS	dipsomaniac
AACDIJKKNSW	Jack Dawkins
AACDIKNNRRU	rack and ruin
AACDILLMNOY	nomadically
AACDILLMNYY	dynamically
AACDILLNORS	coral island
AACDILLRSTY	drastically
AACDILMOPSS	spasmodical
AACDILMPRSU	Admiral's Cup
AACDILOSUUY	audaciously
AACDIMMOOTY	mycodomatia
AACDINOSTTU	at a discount
AACDLMNOOTY	condylomata
AACDRRSTTTU	custard tart
AACEEEHKKTT	take the cake
AACEEEHKMPS	make a speech
AACEEEHKMPT	make the pace
AACEEEHLNST	a clean sheet
AACEEEHMRTT	tame cheater
AACEEEIRRSV	service area
AACEEELNPSW	a clean sweep
AACEEEPRTTY	peace treaty
AACEEFFMNRT	Raman effect
AACEEFGORRY	year of grace
AACEEFILLOP	all of a piece
AACEEFIMNSS	misfeasance
AACEEFIRRTV	rarefactive

AACEEFLLPTT	cleft palate
AACEEFNNNOS	non-feasance
AACEEGHLMNR	Charlemagne
AACEEGHLRST	Castlereagh
AACEEGHRRST	gatecrasher
	gate-crasher
AACEEGHRRTX	extra charge
AACEEGIKMNP	peacemaking
	peace-making
AACEEGILLLY	elegiacally
AACEEGILLNV	evangelical
AACEEGJMNSY	James Cagney
AACEEGKORTT	Cottage Rake
AACEEHHLTUX	hexateuchal
AACEEHILRRT	clear the air
AACEEHIMPPR	papier-mâché
AACEEHINSTT	anaesthetic
AACEEHLNNPY	anencephaly
AACEEHLNNSV	clean-shaven
AACEEHLNPTY	phlyctaenae
AACEEHLNSTT	The Analects
AACEEHLORTT	leather-coat
AACEEHLRTWY	clear the way
AACEEHPSTTY	stay the pace
AACEEIIMNPR	American Pie
AACEEIIMNRS	Americanise
AACEEIIMNRZ	Americanize
AACEEIIMPST	septicaemia
AACEEIJLTUV	ejaculative
AACEEIKKTTW	take a wicket
AACEEIKLLRW	Alice Walker
AACEEIKLMRT	make it clear
AACEEIKMNRT	make certain
AACEEIKNSVW	view askance
AACEEIKPTTV	take captive
AACEEILLMNS	mésalliance
AACEEILMMOT	camomile tea
AACEEILNNRS	encarnalise
AACEEILNNRZ	encarnalize
AACEEILNRTT	intercalate
AACEEILRRST	secretarial
AACEEILSSTT	atelectasis
AACEEIMNNNT	maintenance
AACEEIMNOTT	matinée coat
AACEEIMNVWX	Mexican wave
AACEEINNNRT	centenarian
AACEEINNRRT	reincarnate
AACEEINNRSS	necessarian
	renaissance
AACEEIPRRTV	prevaricate
AACEEIRRRVW	carrier wave
AACEEIRRSTT	secretariat
AACEEJKLNOS	Leos Janácek
AACEEJKMSTT	steam jacket
AACEEJKRTTW	water jacket
AACEEKLMNNU	make unclean
AACEEKLMNRU	make unclear
AACEEKLMPRT	marketplace
	market-place
AACEEKMPSTT	steam-packet
AACEELLNRRW	crawler lane
AACEELLORSV	Ellora caves
AACEELMORSY	Mary Seacole
AACEELNNPUZ	Paul Cézanne
AACEELNOPSY	play one's ace
AACEELNPSTU	encapsulate
AACEELRRTTT	treacle tart
AACEELRSTTW	Alec Stewart
AACEENNRTWY	entranceway
AACEENPRRTT	pattern race
AACEENRRSSU	reassurance
AACEFFHINRS	affranchise
AACEFFINOTT	affectation
AACEFFLRSTU	flat surface
AACEFGHINRR	far-reaching
AACEFGILNOR	Fra Angelico
AACEFGLNORT	conflagrate
AACEFGLOOTT	cottage loaf
AACEFHISSTW	wash its face
AACEFHMSTTY	safety match
AACEFIILLNS	fiançailles
AACEFIILNRT	interfacial
AACEFILLLMY	malefically
AACEFILLORR	for all I care
AACEFILMNOT	malefaction
AACEFILMRSU	surface mail
AACEFILTTUV	facultative
AACEFINORRT	rarefaction
AACEFINORSU	farinaceous
AACEFINORTT	fractionate
AACEFKKMMOU	make a muck of
AACEFKRRSTT	fast-tracker
AACEFLLOSTU	cause to fall
AACEFLLPSTU	pull faces at
AACEFLMORSU	formal cause
AACEFLMORTY	malefactory
AACEFLNSSTU	factualness
AACEFMNRTUU	manufacture
AACEGGILPTU	Tegucigalpa
AACEGGINRRU	gun carriage
AACEGGINRSV	saving grace
AACEGGMUUUV	vacuum gauge
AACEGHILOPR	archipelago
AACEGHLLMNS	small change
AACEGHLOORY	archaeology
AACEGHNORTU	autochanger
AACEGIILLPR	periglacial
AACEGIIMRRS	miscarriage
AACEGILLLNY	angelically
AACEGILLLOR	allegorical
AACEGILLNOT	legal action
AACEGILLOPS	plagioclase
AACEGILLRTV	village cart
AACEGILNPRY	panegyrical
AACEGILOSTU	cataloguise
AACEGILOTUZ	cataloguize
AACEGILRSTT	strategical
AACEGIMNNPR	permanganic
AACEGIMNOPT	compaginate
AACEGIMQRSU	magic square
AACEGINPPRT	rate-capping
AACEGKOPRTU	package tour

AACEGLNRRTU	rectangular
AACEGRRSSTU	caster sugar
AACEHHINTTT	Cat in the Hat
AACEHHIPRRS	Archie Sharp
AACEHIILLMV	Machiavelli
AACEHIILMPT	epithalamic
AACEHIILSTT	atheistical
AACEHIIMMNS	Manichaeism
AACEHILLMNO	melancholia
AACEHILLNPP	Ian Chappell
AACEHILLNTU	hallucinate
AACEHILLRTW	Willa Cather
AACEHILPSTT	at this place
AACEHILRSTT	theatricals
AACEHIMMSTT	mathematics
AACEHIMNNOY	haemocyanin
AACEHIMNRRS	in arm's reach
AACEHIMORST	achromatise
AACEHIMORTT	haematocrit
AACEHIMORTZ	achromatize
AACEHIMOSTT	haemostatic
AACEHINOPRS	coin a phrase
AACEHINOTTU	Teotihuacán
AACEHIPRSTU	haruspicate
AACEHLLRSSW	Charles's law
AACEHLMOOTT	come to a halt
AACEHLMORSY	Charles Mayo
AACEHLSSTTT	the last cast
AACEHMMNNRT	merchant man
	merchantman
AACEHMMOTWY	come what may
AACEHNOSTUY	an easy touch
AACEHOPRSTT	catastrophe
AACEHOPSSTU	spathaceous
AACEHPRRSTY	search party
AACEHPRSTUX	purchase tax
AACEIIKLMNT	kinematical
AACEIILLMNS	misalliance
AACEIILMRRR	mail-carrier
AACEIILNRRT	interracial
AACEIILPPRR	pericarpial
AACEIILPPTT	Pitti Palace
AACEIIMMNRS	Americanism
AACEIINORTT	ratiocinate
AACEIIOSSTV	associative
AACEIIPPRTT	participate
AACEIJLNOTU	ejaculation
AACEIJQSTTU	Jacques Tati
AACEIKLRSTU	Lake Scutari
AACEILLLNPS	in all places
AACEILLLSTY	elastically
AACEILLMNRY	clay mineral
AACEILLMNSU	animalcules
AACEILLMPRY	miracle play
AACEILLNTTY	tetanically
AACEILLNTVY	venatically
AACEILLPRRT	caterpillar
AACEILLRRTY	erratically
AACEILLRSST	rascalliest
AACEILMNORT	reclamation
AACEILMNOTX	exclamation

AACEILMPRST	spermatical
AACEILMRTTU	matriculate
AACEILNORTT	altercation
AACEILNPSTU	incapsulate
AACEILNRRTY	intercalary
AACEILORTVV	aortic valve
AACEILPRTTU	particulate
AACEILRSSUV	vascularise
AACEILRSUVZ	vascularize
AACEILSTUVY	causatively
AACEIMNNOTT	contaminate
AACEIMNOPRT	emancipator
AACEIMOPRTV	comparative
AACEINNORTT	recantation
AACEINNOSTW	Isaac Newton
AACEINORRTY	reactionary
AACEINORSTU	aeronautics
AACEINOSTVX	excavations
AACEINRSSTU	sanctuarise
AACEINRSTUZ	sanctuarize
AACEIOPRSTT	aspect ratio
AACEJLORTUY	ejaculatory
AACEKKLNOOS	look askance
AACEKLQRSUV	quacksalver
AACELLLNOOV	Leoncavallo
AACELLLOPST	to all places
AACELLLORTT	total recall
AACELLNRSTY	ancestrally
AACELLOPRTY	acropetally
AACELMORSST	scleromatas
AACELMORTXY	exclamatory
AACELNORSTT	translocate
AACELNPRRTT	central part
AACELPRSSTT	plaster cast
AACELQRTUUU	aquaculture
AACEMNORRST	Sam Torrance
AACEMNORSUY	mornay sauce
AACEMOOSTTU	tomato sauce
AACENNNORTW	water cannon
AACENOOPSSU	saponaceous
AACENORSSST	ansate cross
AACEOPPRSUY	papyraceous
AACFFIOORTU	Out of Africa
AACFFMORRTY	factory farm
AACFGIINNST	fascinating
AACFGIMNOPR	campaign for
AACFGINOTWY	way of acting
AACFHIORSTU	South Africa
AACFIILLNNY	financially
AACFIILORTT	facilitator
AACFIINNOST	fascination
AACFILLNRTY	frantically
AACFKLMSUUV	vacuum flask
AACFLLNTUUW	unlawful act
AACFMNOORSW	a can of worms
AACFMNORSTW	craftswoman
AACFMNORTUY	manufactory
AACFNORSTUU	anfractuous
AACFOORRRTY	carry too far
AACGGHHMOOR	Graham Gooch
AACGGIIMNNP	campaigning

AACGGIINSTT	castigating
AACGGILNOTU	cataloguing
AACGHHIOSTT	at a high cost
AACGHHPRTYY	tachygraphy
AACGHIKMNTW	watchmaking
AACGHILLPRY	calligraphy
	graphically
AACGHINOPPR	approaching
AACGHINPPRY	Phrygian cap
AACGHIOPRTU	autographic
AACGHLNOORY	arachnology
AACGHNOOPRR	coronagraph
AACGHOPRRTY	cartography
AACGHOPRSSU	sarcophagus
AACGIIKKNST	kick against
AACGIILLNTV	vacillating
AACGIILLNTW	call waiting
AACGIILLOOX	axiological
AACGIILMNNS	Anglicanism
AACGIILMSTT	stalagmitic
AACGIILNNOR	Carolingian
AACGIINNQTU	acquainting
AACGIINOSTT	castigation
AACGIINPTTV	captivating
AACGILLNORY	organically
AACGILNOOTU	coagulation
AACGILNORSS	cors anglais
AACGILOPRRU	racial group
AACGILOSSUY	sagaciously
AACGIMMMNOU	gum ammoniac
AACGIMNOPRT	coming apart
AACGINPRVYZ	crazy paving
AACGIORSTTY	castigatory
AACGLLNOOTY	octagonally
AACGLMNOOPY	campanology
AACHIIMNNOT	machination
AACHIIMNSST	shamanistic
AACHIINPPST	captainship
AACHIKNOOPT	Captain Hook
AACHILLMNOP	Campion Hall
AACHILLNOPV	Pancho Villa
AACHILLOPRY	parochially
AACHIMMORST	achromatism
AACHIMNNORS	anachronism
AACHIMNNORV	Rachmaninov
AACHIMNORSS	maraschinos
AACHINNNOTY	anthocyanin
AACHINORSST	anthracosis
AACHIPRSTTU	parachutist
AACHLNNOOTU	anacoluthon
AACHLNOPSTU	Polacanthus
AACHMMRRSUU	harum-scarum
AACHMNNOORW	anchorwoman
AACHMNOSTWY	yachtswoman
AACHMOPTTTU	put a match to
AACHMOSTTWY	cost what may
AACHNNOOPTT	not a patch on
AACHNNOORTY	Anthony Caro
AACIIILNNOT	laciniation
AACIIILNPST	initial caps
AACIIILPPRT	participial
AACIIJNOTTT	jactitation
AACIILLMNRW	criminal law
AACIILLMRTU	multiracial
AACIILLNOOT	coalitional
AACIILLNOTV	vacillation
AACIILLNTTY	titanically
AACIILLPRTY	capillarity
	piratically
AACIILLRSTY	satirically
AACIILMNOST	anomalistic
AACIILMNRRW	war criminal
AACIILNOPPT	application
AACIILNPRTU	puritanical
AACIILOPRST	piscatorial
AACIILPTTYY	atypicality
AACIIMNOSTT	mastication
AACIINNNORT	incarnation
AACIINNNOTT	incantation
AACIINOOSST	association
AACIINOPRST	piscatorian
AACIINOPRTT	anticipator
AACIINOPSTU	auspication
AACIINOPTTV	captivation
AACIINOSTTV	vacationist
AACIINPPRTT	participant
AACILLMOSTY	somatically
AACILLNOPRS	rapscallion
AACILLNRTUW	curtain wall
AACILLOOPST	apostolical
AACILLOPRSY	prosaically
AACILLOSSUY	salaciously
AACILLPRTUY	capitularly
AACILLPSSTY	spastically
AACILLRRUUY	auricularly
AACILMNNOPT	complainant
AACILMNOPST	complaisant
AACILMNORTU	calumniator
AACILNOOTUV	vacuolation
AACILNORTVY	clairvoyant
AACILOPRSUY	rapaciously
AACILOPSTTU	autoplastic
AACILORRTTU	articulator
AACILPRRSTU	particulars
AACIMNNNOTT	contaminant
AACIMNPRSTT	transit camp
AACIMORSTTY	masticatory
AACINNORSTT	transaction
AACINNORTTY	incantatory
AACINNRRSTU	transuranic
AACKLMOSSTU	mock-assault
AACKLNOTTUY	you can't talk
AACLMMOPSSY	mycoplasmas
AACLNNNOOST	consonantal
AACLNORSSTU	cast a slur on
AACLOOPPRSY	laparoscopy
AACLORSTTUU	auscultator
AACMNOPPRTY	part company
AACMNOPRTUY	paramountcy
AACMOORSSTU	sarcomatous
AADDDDEEEHL	addle-headed
AADDDEIILPT	dilapidated

AADDDEILRRT	tarradiddle
AADDDELNORW	Donald Dewar
AADDEEFIMTT	admit defeat
AADDEEFLLRR	Alfred Adler
AADDEEGHNNR	hand grenade
AADDEEGLRRW	Edward Elgar
AADDEEHHNVY	heavy-handed
AADDEEHHRRT	hard-hearted
AADDEEHHRTW	Edward Heath
AADDEEHLPRY	paraldehyde
AADDEEIKLNS	naked ladies
AADDEEILRSY	sidereal day
AADDEEIMNOZ	a dime a dozen
AADDEEIMRST	dedramatise
AADDEEIMRTZ	dedramatize
AADDEEINNRR	André Derain
AADDEEIPPRS	disappeared
AADDEELRTTU	adulterated
AADDEENRRTW	Dawn Treader
AADDEFGMNNU	managed fund
AADDEFILMNN	final demand
AADDEGILLNY	leading lady
AADDEGIMNRY	daydreaming
	day-dreaming
AADDEGINORT	degradation
AADDEGINRRS	disarranged
AADDEHILLNV	De Havilland
AADDEHLNNOT	lend a hand to
AADDEIILNTV	invalidated
AADDEIKNPRR	park-and-ride
AADDEILNPTY	painted lady
AADDEIMOPRR	period drama
AADDEINRSST	standardise
AADDEINRSTZ	standardize
AADDEIPRRSW	Edward Sapir
AADDEJLMSTU	maladjusted
AADDELNORRW	law and order
AADDELPQRUU	quadrupedal
AADDENNORTW	draw to an end
AADDFHNNOOT	hand and foot
AADDFIORSTV	Star of David
AADDGHILNNR	hard landing
AADDGHINRRY	daring-hardy
AADDGIILNOV	David Ginola
AADDGJLNRUY	Judy Garland
AADDGLMNNOR	grand old man
AADDIIINNRT	Trinidadian
AADDIINNNRW	wind and rain
AADDILLOOPR	olla-podrida
AADDIMNOWWW	Widow Wadman
AADDINORRST	ritardandos
AADDINOTUYY	day in day out
AADDNNNORST	non-standard
AADEEEFHLLN	halfendeale
AADEEEFNRSY	free and easy
	free-and-easy
AADEEEGGRTX	exaggerated
AADEEEGLPRS	spread-eagle
AADEEEHLNRS	hand release
AADEEEHLPRT	pale-hearted
AADEEELLPSW	deep as a well
AADEEEMNPRR	André Ampère
AADEEEPPRTU	depauperate
AADEEEPRSTX	exasperated
AADEEFHHLRT	half-hearted
AADEEFHHOTT	at the head of
AADEEFHIMOT	ahead of time
AADEEFHOSTT	head of state
AADEEFIRRST	Fred Astaire
AADEEFOQRTU	adequate for
AADEEGHNNOT	on the agenda
AADEEGHRTTU	The Graduate
AADEEGIKKRR	Kierkegaard
AADEEGIKNTV	give and take
	give-and-take
AADEEGILPSV	pale-visaged
AADEEGNPRRR	prearranged
AADEEHILRTX	exhilarated
AADEEHJNRRW	Wanderjahre
AADEEHKORTT	take the road
AADEEHLLPTY	deathly pale
AADEEHLNNPV	have planned
AADEEHLNNRT	Neanderthal
AADEEHLNPRT	pentahedral
AADEEHLRRTT	tetrahedral
AADEEHLRTWY	weatherlady
AADEEHMRRTW	warm-hearted
AADEEHNORTT	near to death
AADEEHNRSVW	heavenwards
AADEEHNRTVW	and whatever
AADEEIKMNNR	make a dinner
AADEEIKNNOT	Diane Keaton
AADEEILLMVY	mediaevally
AADEEILNNRX	alexandrine
AADEEILNRTX	alexandrite
AADEEINRSTT	tear-stained
AADEEIRRTTV	retardative
AADEEJKMNRR	Derek Jarman
AADEEKMORTU	make a detour
AADEELNOOST	at a loose end
AADEELORSTT	sad to relate
AADEEMMNSSU	assumed name
AADEEMORTWW	water meadow
AADEEMQRRSU	masquerader
AADEENNRTWY	Tyne and Wear
AADEENPRSTU	unseparated
AADEENRSWYY	New Year's Day
AADEERSTTUV	Deus avertat
AADEFGHNRRT	grandfather
AADEFGIISTT	fastigiated
AADEFGLORSU	sugar of lead
AADEFGMNNSU	fun and games
AADEFHHNOTT	at the hand of
AADEFHJOSTW	jaws of death
AADEFHLLOPU	pull ahead of
AADEFHLLOTW	wall of death
AADEFHLRSTV	half-starved
AADEFIKLNNR	rank and file
AADEFILLNRS	rise and fall
AADEFIMNORT	foraminated
AADEFLMNNTU	fundamental
AADEFLOPRRW	leap forward

AADEFLSSTTY	steadfastly
AADEFNORSWY	send away for
AADEFORSTUY	area of study
AADEGGGHLNU	hand-luggage
AADEGGHNRSS	haggardness
AADEGGILNNR	landing gear
	landing-gear
AADEGGIORRY	Yegor Gaidar
AADEGHINOTV	give a hand to
AADEGHINRRW	hard-wearing
AADEGHINRTU	The Guardian
AADEGHINSTY	an eight days
AADEGHNRTTT	granted that
AADEGIILPRZ	plagiarized
AADEGILLNNP	pineal gland
AADEGILMNPR	palm reading
	reading-lamp
AADEGILNOTW	long-awaited
AADEGILNPRT	plantigrade
AADEGIMNNRV	Venn diagram
AADEGINNOTZ	antagonized
AADEGINSTTV	devastating
AADEGLMMMNO	Emma Goldman
AADEGMNRRST	Grand Master
	grand master
	grandmaster
AADEGMORSSW	meadow grass
AADEGMRRRSW	warm regards
AADEGNNPRRT	grandparent
AADEGNPRRTY	garden party
AADEHHJLNNO	John Haldane
AADEHHLNOOV	have a hold on
AADEHIILOPP	paedophilia
AADEHIINNRR	Adrian Henri
AADEHILLMNR	mail handler
AADEHILLNOS	hollandaise
AADEHILMMMO	Mohammed Ali
AADEHILMNNO	nominal head
AADEHILRTTU	titular head
AADEHIMNNOO	hedonomania
AADEHINOPPY	hypnopaedia
AADEHJMNORS	John-a-dreams
AADEHKMNPPR	Hampden Park
AADEHLMNSUY	unashamedly
AADEHLNORSV	Harold Evans
AADEHLORTTY	Ready-to-Halt
AADEHLRRRUY	Harry Lauder
AADEHNORSST	hard as stone
AADEHPRSSTT	spatterdash
AADEIILMNRV	remain valid
AADEIILMORT	mediatorial
AADEIILMSST	assimilated
AADEIIPRSSS	pass airside
AADEIKMNORS	make inroads
AADEILLMRTY	diametrally
AADEILMMORY	Memorial Day
AADEILMNRRT	intradermal
AADEILNNQRU	quadrennial
AADEILNOTUV	devaluation
AADEILNRTUZ	naturalized
AADEILORRTV	advertorial
AADEILPRSTY	disparately
AADEIMMNRST	disarmament
AADEIMNNOSW	madonnawise
AADEIMNRSTV	maidservant
AADEINOPRTV	depravation
AADEINORRTT	retardation
AADEINOSTTV	devastation
AADEINPQRSU	pasquinader
AADEINRTTUV	durante vita
AADEIPSSTWW	wasp-waisted
AADEKNORSTU	skate around
AADEKNRSSWW	awkwardness
AADELLMNOSX	Alex Salmond
AADELLNNORT	rallentando
AADELLPUUVX	Paul Delvaux
AADELNOPQSU	Don Pasquale
AADELNPRSTU	pastureland
AADELORSVWY	Oswald Avery
AADEMNNNRWY	Randy Newman
AADEMNORSTW	tradeswoman
AADEMOORRSU	Dromaeosaur
AADENNRRTUW	unwarranted
AADENRRSTTU	understrata
AADENRSSWWY	waywardness
AADENRSTTUU	unsaturated
AADEORRRTTY	retardatory
AADFFORRSTW	fast-forward
AADFGHHNNOU	Afghan hound
AADFGHILLNN	half-landing
AADFGHIMORR	rhagadiform
AADFGILLNNP	landing flap
AADFHILNRST	hard as flint
AADFHINRSTT	at first hand
AADFILLLPRY	fall rapidly
AADFILNSSUU	Susan Faludi
AADFKNOSUXY	Sandy Koufax
AADFLLLOOSY	All Fools' Day
AADFMNOORRS	mansard roof
AADGGGGMNOO	Gog and Magog
AADGGHILOSU	Douglas Haig
AADGGIILNPR	paragliding
AADGGIINPRS	disparaging
AADGGILNNRZ	grazing land
AADGGOOOUUU	Ouagadougou
AADGHHOPRSW	shadowgraph
AADGHIIJNRV	Rajiv Gandhi
AADGHIKLNNO	Alan Hodgkin
AADGHILMNNN	manhandling
AADGHILNOST	hold against
AADGHIOPRRY	radiography
AADGHMNRSTU	draughtsman
AADGIIKLNNR	Kaliningrad
AADGIILNNNO	Anglo-Indian
AADGIILNRRU	Laura Riding
AADGILLNNST	all standing
AADGILMNNSU	salmangundi
AADGIMNRSUV	vanguardism
AADGINNOSTT	stand to gain
AADGLLLNRUY	glandularly
AADGLLNPPUY	plug-and-play
AADHHINSTTT	this and that

AADHHKORSWW	Howard Hawks
AADHHMORSTY	Thomas Hardy
AADHIILNOPR	dolphinaria
AADHIOPPRTY	paratyphoid
AADHIOPRRTY	parathyroid
AADHJMMNNOO	Joan Hammond
AADHKNOORTT	North Dakota
AADHKOOSTTU	South Dakota
AADHLMNOSTY	Dylan Thomas
AADHLORSUYZ	hazardously
AADHMOORSTY	hydrosomata
AADHNOPQRUY	quadraphony
AADHNORRRVY	Harry Vardon
AADIIINNNOR	Indo-Iranian
AADIIINORRT	irradiation
AADIILLLMUW	William Laud
AADIILLMNSW	wild animals
AADIILLNTTU	latitudinal
AADIILNORTT	traditional
AADIILOSUUV	audiovisual
AADIINNOTTX	antioxidant
AADIINOSTTV	idiot savant
AADILLLLNST	still and all
AADILLMNNOY	Madonna-lily
AADILLMNOOT	amontillado
AADILLMORTY	maladroitly
AADILLMPRYY	pyramidally
AADILOORSTV	vasodilator
AADILOPPRSV	disapproval
AADIMNNOPRS	prima donnas
AADIMNORSTU	Surinam toad
AADINPSSTTT	distant past
AADKNNOPRSW	Sandown Park
AADLLLOSSUY	All Souls Day
	All Souls' Day
AADLLMORSWY	Mrs Dalloway
AADLMNORSWY	lay down arms
AADLOPRRSTW	worlds apart
AAEEEERRRSV	reserve area
AAEEEFFLMMT	femme fatale
AAEEEFKLOTV	take leave of
AAEEEGHNSTV	Heaven's Gate
AAEEEGIIRSS	raise a siege
AAEEEGKMRRT	make greater
AAEEEGMMRRT	Margaret Mee
AAEEEGMNOST	manage to see
AAEEEGNNRSZ	Gene Sarazen
AAEEEGNRSSV	averageness
AAEEEGNSTTT	estate agent
AAEEEHKPRSS	Shakespeare
AAEEEHNRRTW	earthenware
AAEEEIKLMRR	make earlier
AAEEEILLSXY	Alexei Sayle
AAEEELNPPSS	epanalepses
AAEEEMNPPST	appeasement
AAEEEMORRST	remote areas
AAEEEMPRSTU	tape measure
AAEEFFOPRST	separate off
AAEEFGIKMRU	make a figure
AAEEFGLLLNN	fallen angel
AAEEFGMRRRW	germ warfare
AAEEFHIOVVW	have a view of
AAEEFHIRRTW	fair-weather
AAEEFHKNRRT	hanker after
AAEEFHLMTWY	meet halfway
AAEEFHLORSV	have for sale
AAEEFHMRRRS	sharefarmer
AAEEFHORRTT	at the rear of
AAEEFIJLNTT	Jean Lafitte
AAEEFJMRRSZ	James Frazer
AAEEFKMMOSS	make a mess of
AAEEFKMNOOT	make a note of
AAEEFLORSVY	vale of years
AAEEFLSTVVY	safety valve
	safety-valve
AAEEGGGLRTY	aggregately
AAEEGGGNNRS	gas gangrene
AAEEGGHLORS	George Halas
AAEEGGIMNRV	graven image
AAEEGGINNRW	wage-earning
AAEEGGLMORT	agglomerate
AAEEGGNNORT	Agent Orange
AAEEGGORRTX	exaggerator
AAEEGHHMORR	haemorrhage
AAEEGHLMNUU	Human League
AAEEGHLMPTY	play the game
AAEEGHLNRTW	Walter Hagen
AAEEGHLOOPS	oesophageal
AAEEGHNRRTT	greater than
AAEEGIKLNTV	leave-taking
AAEEGIKNNRW	reawakening
AAEEGILLLTT	tagliatelle
AAEEGILMMNT	mental image
AAEEGILMMNY	Amin Gemayel
AAEEGILMNTT	latent image
AAEEGILMSSX	sexagesimal
AAEEGIMNOTV	give a name to
AAEEGINNOPS	neopaganise
AAEEGINNOPZ	neopaganize
AAEEGINPRSS	paragenesis
AAEEGINPRST	greasepaint
AAEEGLLLSVY	galley slave
	galley-slave
AAEEGLLRTTY	Tate Gallery
AAEEGLMMRSU	rummage sale
AAEEGLNRTTV	travel agent
AAEEGLPRSTY	pearly gates
AAEEGLRSSTY	early stages
AAEEGMNNRRT	arrangement
AAEEGMNOPRT	pomegranate
AAEEGMNSSTU	assuagement
AAEEGNNPTTT	patent agent
AAEEGNNSUVZ	Suzanne Vega
AAEEGPRRRTT	greater part
AAEEHHKLMTY	make healthy
AAEEHHKOTTT	take the oath
AAEEHHLNNPT	naphthalene
AAEEHHORSVW	have a shower
AAEEHIILMNS	leishmaniae
AAEEHIKLMNO	make a hole in
AAEEHILMOPR	hemeralopia
AAEEHILNNST	Saint Helena

AAEEHILNRRT	earlier than
AAEEHIMMNPT	amphetamine
AAEEHIMMSTT	mathematise
AAEEHIMMTTZ	mathematize
AAEEHINSSST	anaesthesis
AAEEHKLLTTW	take the wall
AAEEHKMOPTY	take home pay
	take-home pay
AAEEHKMRSTV	save the mark
AAEEHKORTTT	take to heart
AAEEHLMNRSS	Shalmaneser
AAEEHLSTTTT	at the latest
AAEEHMMRRTW	water hammer
AAEEHMNOORR	amenorrhoea
AAEEHNOOSVZ	have a snooze
AAEEHNOSSVY	have one's say
AAEEHNOSVWY	have one's way
AAEEHNPSSTT	the peasants
AAEEIILLTVV	alleviative
AAEEIILMRST	materialise
AAEEIILMRTZ	materialize
AAEEIILNSST	Ilie Nastase
AAEEIILRRST	arterialise
AAEEIILRRTZ	arterialize
AAEEIILRTTV	retaliative
AAEEIKKLRST	like a streak
AAEEIKMNSST	skaines mate
AAEEILLLNRT	lateral line
AAEEILLLPRS	parallelise
AAEEILLLPRZ	parallelize
AAEEILLMPRX	premaxillae
AAEEILLPPTV	appellative
AAEEILLQRTU	equilateral
AAEEILMNRRT	remain alert
AAEEILNRTTV	alternative
AAEEILPPRSS	paraleipses
AAEEIMSSSTT	metastasise
AAEEIMSSTTZ	metastasize
AAEEINOPTTX	expatiate on
AAEEINRRSTT	tea strainer
AAEEIOPRTVV	evaporative
AAEEJKLMMNS	James Kelman
AAEEKKMMRRT	market maker
AAEEKLLMMRS	make smaller
AAEEKLNRSTT	rattlesnake
AAEEKLRSTTW	Walter Skeat
AAEEKMMNOOV	make a move on
AAEEKMNOSWY	make one's way
AAEEKNOSTWY	take one's way
AAEELLLMNOS	salmonellae
AAEELLNRTTY	alternately
AAEELLNSTTV	at all events
AAEELLOOSST	a slate loose
AAEELNNPTTV	pentavalent
AAEELNRRSTT	retranslate
AAEELNRTTTV	tetravalent
AAEELOPRTTX	extrapolate
AAEELPRRTTW	Walter Pater
AAEELPRSSTT	sales patter
AAEELRRSTTU	serratulate
AAEELRRTVWY	travel-weary
AAEEMMNNNTT	Emma Tennant
AAEEMMPRTUY	empyreumata
AAEEMPPRSST	Pete Sampras
AAEEMRSTTTW	waste matter
AAEENNOPPRR	non-appearer
AAEENNOPPRU	pan-European
AAEENNRSSUW	unawareness
AAEEOPRSTTU	separate out
AAEFFIIMRTV	affirmative
AAEFFKLMOOO	make a fool of
AAEFFKMOSSU	make a fuss of
AAEFGILLNRT	tear-falling
AAEFGILLRRY	fairly large
AAEFGLLLORT	flagellator
AAEFGLMNORY	Morgan le Fay
AAEFGLSSSTY	safety glass
AAEFGMNRRTY	fragmentary
AAEFGMORTWY	get away from
AAEFHHIINTV	have faith in
AAEFHILNRTW	father-in-law
AAEFHKMOOSW	make a show of
AAEFHLMNOTW	The Man of Law
AAEFHLNOPST	half past one
AAEFIIILMRS	familiarise
AAEFIIILMRZ	familiarize
AAEFIIORRSV	savoir-faire
AAEFIKMOPRT	make a profit
AAEFILMNRTY	filamentary
AAEFILOPRRT	prefatorial
AAEFIRRTTWY	fritter away
AAEFKLLOOTT	take a toll of
AAEFLLMNNOR	all manner of
AAEFLLMNNOW	fallen woman
AAEFLLNRRTY	fraternally
AAEFLNORTUW	law of nature
AAEFLNRRRST	transferral
AAEFLOPSTTY	state of play
AAEFLORSSTU	as a result of
AAEFNNRRRST	transfer RNA
AAEFOPRRSTT	set a trap for
AAEFORRSTYZ	safety razor
AAEGGGINORT	aggregation
AAEGGILNNVZ	navel-gazing
AAEGGILNTTU	agglutinate
AAEGGINNRRR	rearranging
AAEGGINRSTU	strain gauge
AAEGGNORRUW	narrow-gauge
AAEGHHIIKST	high as a kite
AAEGHHIPPRY	hyperphagia
AAEGHIMNORR	menorrhagia
AAEGHIMNPRS	managership
AAEGHINNNSS	shenanigans
AAEGHINOPRV	have a grip on
AAEGHIRTWWW	wage war with
AAEGHISSTTT	at this stage
AAEGHITTWWY	get away with
AAEGHLLNOXY	hexagonally
AAEGHLLOTWY	go all the way
AAEGHLMOOTY	haematology
AAEGHLPSSTT	the last gasp
AAEGHMOOPTY	pay homage to

AAEGHMOPRRS	phraseogram
AAEGHMRTTUU	thaumaturge
AAEGHNOPRTY	Pythagorean
AAEGHNORSST	North Sea gas
AAEGHNPRRST	strap-hanger
AAEGIIIMNTV	imaginative
AAEGIIKNOPP	a pig in a poke
AAEGIILLNTV	alleviating
AAEGIILMNRS	marginalise
AAEGIILMNRZ	marginalize
AAEGIILMRST	magisterial
AAEGIILNRRY	air layering
AAEGIILNRSU	Ligurian Sea
AAEGIILPRRZ	plagiarizer
AAEGIIMNNRT	reanimating
AAEGIIMNSTT	against time
AAEGIINNNRT	Argentinian
AAEGIINNOTV	evagination
AAEGIINORTV	variegation
AAEGIKLNPTU	Paul Keating
AAEGIKLOTTV	give a talk to
AAEGIKMNPST	masking tape
AAEGILLNPPY	appealingly
AAEGILLNRTV	gallivanter
AAEGILLNSTT	tell against
AAEGILMNPST	Leptis Magna
AAEGILMNTWY	melting away
AAEGILNNPPU	unappealing
AAEGILNNRTT	alternating
AAEGILNPPSY	appeasingly
AAEGILNQRUU	equiangular
AAEGILNRTTU	triangulate
AAEGILNSTWY	laying waste
AAEGIMNNRRT	arraignment
AAEGIMNPTUY	Egyptian Mau
AAEGIMNRSTY	gain mastery
AAEGINNPPRT	parapenting
AAEGINOPRTV	evaporating
AAEGINORSTV	over against
AAEGINOSTTV	vote against
AAEGINPRRTT	in great part
AAEGIOPPRTV	propagative
AAEGIOPSTTY	steatopygia
AAEGLLNNTTY	tangentally
AAEGLLNOPTY	penalty goal
AAEGLLNORTV	travel along
AAEGLLORSSU	sausage roll
AAEGLMNORTU	large amount
AAEGLMNRTTY	termagantly
AAEGLMOPRRU	parlour game
AAEGLNNPRTU	pentangular
AAEGLNRSTTU	strangulate
AAEGLPRRSTT	largest part
AAEGNNORTWY	orange-tawny
AAEGNORRSTT	a stranger to
AAEGRRSTTUY	treasury tag
AAEHHIILMOP	haemophilia
AAEHHIKNRRS	Hare Krishna
AAEHHILNPST	naphthalise
AAEHHILNPTZ	naphthalize
AAEHHLMPSTT	health stamp

AAEHHMNOSST	Thomas Nashe
AAEHHOTUVWY	what have you
AAEHIILLMRW	William Hare
AAEHIILMNSS	leishmanias
AAEHIJLNNOU	Jean Anouilh
AAEHIKLLVWY	walk heavily
AAEHIKSTTTW	what it takes
AAEHILNOSTT	East Lothian
AAEHILNSSTU	ailanthuses
AAEHILSTWWY	whistle away
AAEHILTTWWY	whittle away
AAEHIMOSSST	haemostasis
AAEHIMPRSST	metaphrasis
AAEHINPPSST	as it happens
AAEHINPRSTT	Thespian art
AAEHJNNORSU	Johannes Rau
AAEHKMNNTTU	Tutankhamen
AAEHKMPRSST	pass the mark
AAEHLLNPRRU	Ralph Lauren
AAEHLLOOTVW	allow to have
AAEHLNNORTT	no later than
AAEHMNNRTUU	human nature
AAEHMNORSTT	Tam O'Shanter
	tam-o'-shanter
AAEHMNORSWW	washerwoman
AAEHNRRSTUV	Arthur Evans
AAEIIILRSUX	auxiliaries
AAEIIKNRSST	raise a stink
AAEIILLMNNR	millenarian
AAEIILLMNRT	matrilineal
AAEIILLNOPR	Apollinaire
AAEIILLNOTV	alleviation
AAEIILLNPRT	patrilineal
AAEIILLPTXY	epitaxially
AAEIILMMRST	materialism
AAEIILMNNTY	inanimately
AAEIILMNRRT	air terminal
AAEIILMRSTT	materialist
AAEIILMRTTY	materiality
AAEIILNNNTV	Valentinian
AAEIILNNOST	nationalise
AAEIILNNOTZ	nationalize
AAEIILNNPST	Palestinian
AAEIILNORST	rationalise
AAEIILNORTT	retaliation
AAEIILNORTZ	rationalize
	realization
AAEIILNPRRT	patrilinear
AAEIILNRTTV	tire-valiant
AAEIILNSTTY	insatiately
AAEIILPPRSS	paraleipsis
AAEIILQTTUV	qualitative
AAEIIMNNORT	reanimation
AAEIIMNNOTX	examination
AAEIINNPPRT	paripinnate
AAEIINNSTTT	instantiate
AAEIINOPTTX	expatiation
AAEIINOSTTV	aestivation
AAEIKLLNOST	Nikola Tesla
AAEIKLLTTVY	talkatively
AAEIKLMNOPT	kleptomania

AAEIKLNOORT Lake Ontario
AAEIKLNOSST as like as not
AAEIKMNOSUX make anxious
AAEIKNOPSTT take pains to
AAEILLLMPRS parallelism
AAEILLLOSTV sal volatile
AAEILLMNOTT no time at all
AAEILLMPRVY primaevally
AAEILLMRTVV mitral valve
AAEILLNOPPT appellation
AAEILLNOPRY play a role in
AAEILLORTTU ratatouille
AAEILLRSUVZ Luis Alvarez
AAEILMMORRW war memorial
AAEILMNNOTT lamentation
AAEILMNORST monasterial
AAEILMNPRST paternalism
AAEILMNPRTU planetarium
AAEILMNRRSS Silas Marner
AAEILMNRRTU ultramarine
AAEILNNOPTX explanation
AAEILNNORTT alternation
AAEILNNOSST sensational
AAEILNNPRST transalpine
AAEILNOOPRT operational
AAEILNOPPRY player piano
player-piano
AAEILNOPRRT proletarian
AAEILNOSSTY seasonality
AAEILNRRTTU nature trail
AAEILNRRTVY narratively
AAEILNRSTTV at intervals
AAEILOPRRTT proletariat
AAEILORRTTY retaliatory
AAEIMMNORUU Naomi Uemura
AAEIMOPPRTX approximate
AAEINNOPRSZ Arno Penzias
AAEINNOPRTT trepanation
AAEINNOTTTU attenuation
AAEINNRRSVY anniversary
AAEINOOPRTV evaporation
AAEINOPPRRT preparation
AAEINOPPRTT appertain to
AAEINORRRST in arrears to
AAEINOSTTTT attestation
AAEINPRRSSW Persian Wars
AAEIOPPPRRT appropriate
AAEIOPPRRSS appressoria
AAEIOPPRSST so it appears
AAEIORRTTVW Ottawa River
AAEJKLNOOPY play a joke on
AAEJKLPRRSS Karl Jaspers
AAEJLNNRSTW lantern jaws
AAEJMMRRSUY James Murray
AAEJMNOSSTW James Watson
AAEKLLLORVW walk all over
AAELLLMNOSS salmonellas
AAELLLORSST saltarellos
AAELLMORSUV moral values
AAELLOPSSTT Elastoplast®
AAELLORRSTT stellarator
AAELMNPQTUU quantum leap
AAELMNRRTUY Mary Renault
AAELMOPRRTU armour-plate
AAELNNRSSTU naturalness
AAELNOPRTXY explanatory
AAELNORSSTY royal assent
AAELNRRSSTV transversal
AAEMNNORTUV verumontana
AAEMNOOPRTT protonemata
AAEMNOOSSST anastomoses
AAEMNOPRTTU portmanteau
AAEMNOSSTTW stateswoman
AAEMNPPRTTY part payment
AAEMNRSTTTU transmutate
AAEMOOPRSTZ spermatozoa
AAEMOPSSSZZ passamezzos
AAEMORSSTTT toastmaster
AAENNNORSTY Ayrton Senna
AAENNPPRTTU appurtenant
AAENNPRRSTT transparent
AAENNPRSTTU supernatant
AAEOOPPRRRT paratrooper
AAEOPPRRRTY preparatory
AAEOPRRTUVW water vapour
AAFFGILOPST gaff-topsail
AAFFIIILNOT affiliation
AAFFIIMNORT affirmation
AAFFNNNORTZ Frantz Fanon
AAFGHIILNTT failing that
AAFGHIMRSTW Graham Swift
AAFGIINNSTZ fantasizing
AAFGILLMRUY gallimaufry
AAFGILLNRST falling star
falling-star
AAFGILNOSTT stagflation
AAFGILOPRST fail to grasp
AAFHILLLLSY fallalishly
AAFHLOPSTTW half past two
AAFHMORSWYY shy away from
AAFIIILLRRT fritillaria
AAFIIILMRTY familiarity
AAFIILLMTTW William Taft
AAFIILNNPST in a flat spin
AAFIILNRSTU fustilarian
AAFIINNOTTU infatuation
AAFILLMNORW laminar flow
AAFILMNOORT formational
AAFIMNNNRTY infantryman
AAFINNOOPRT profanation
AAFLNNOORST nasofrontal
AAFMNORRUWY run away from
AAFNOOPRRTY profanatory
AAGGGHILNSU laughing gas
AAGGGILNSSZ glass-gazing
AAGGHHIOPRY hagiography
AAGGHINOPRY angiography
AAGGIINRRUY Yuri Gagarin
AAGGILNPUUU Paul Gauguin
AAGGNNOORTU orang-outang
AAGHHLOPPRY haplography
AAGHIIINRRS hair-raising

AAGHIILLNOP	anglophilia	AAHIIMORSST	a hit or a miss
AAGHIILNRTV	rival-hating	AAHIINPRSST	antiphrasis
AAGHIINRRST	right as rain		artisanship
AAGHILLMNRS	marshalling	AAHIKKLNOSV	kalashnikov
AAGHILNRSSY	harassingly	AAHIKLNPSSW	walk Spanish
AAGHIMNRSTT	straight man	AAHIKNOOPRS	Anish Kapoor
AAGHKNOOOPR	kangaroo-hop	AAHILLMNOPY	phyllomania
AAGHLNOOTTY	thanatology	AAHILLPSTVY	Sylvia Plath
AAGHMMMOPRY	mammography	AAHILMNTTWW	Walt Whitman
AAGHMRTTUUY	thaumaturgy	AAHIMMNNOPY	nymphomania
AAGHNOPRRUY	uranography	AAHIMNNOSTU	mountain ash
AAGIIIMNNOT	imagination	AAHIMNOPRSS	oarsmanship
AAGIIKNNPST	painstaking	AAHIMRSSTTU	Mathias Rust
AAGIILLLNWW	Wailing Wall	AAHINOPTTTT	at that point
AAGIILMNNTY	animatingly	AAHINRTUWWY	run away with
AAGIILMNRTY	marginality	AAHIOSSTTTY	that is to say
AAGIILNNTTZ	tantalizing	AAHKNOSTUYY	say thank you
AAGIILNPPTT	palpitating	AAHKOPRRSWW	sparrowhawk
AAGIIMMNNTY	magnanimity	AAHLLMMORSW	marshmallow
AAGIIMMSSTT	astigmatism	AAHLLMORTYY	Royal Lytham
AAGIIMRSSUU	Gaius Marius	AAHMMNOORRY	Ram Mohan Roy
AAGIINNORSS	anagnorisis	AAHMNNRSTTU	transhumant
AAGIINNOSST	assignation	AAHNNOPRSXY	nasopharynx
AAGIINNSTUU	Augustinian	AAHNOPRTTUY	naturopathy
AAGIINORTTV	gravitation	AAHOPRRTTWY	throw a party
AAGIINPSTTU	up against it	AAHPRRSSSTU	Arthur's Pass
AAGIIRSSTTU	Sagittarius	AAIIILNRTTU	utilitarian
AAGIJKNOPRT	joking apart	AAIIIMNNNOT	inanimation
AAGIKNORSTW	work against	AAIIINNRRTT	Trinitarian
AAGILLLNPPY	appallingly	AAIIJKLMNOR	Kilimanjaro
AAGILLLOOSS	glossolalia	AAIILLLPSUZ	lapis lazuli
AAGILLMNNTY	malignantly	AAIILLMPRTY	impartially
AAGILLNRTUV	Vulgar Latin	AAIILLNPRST	pillar-saint
AAGILNNOPSS	Panglossian	AAIILMMNORT	matrimonial
AAGILNNORTU	granulation	AAIILMMNPSS	Panislamism
AAGILNOOPRS	sporangiola	AAIILMNNOST	nationalism
AAGILNOORSU	Louis Aragon	AAIILMNNOTV	nominatival
AAGILNORSTV	vital organs	AAIILMNOPRT	patrimonial
AAGILNOSUVY	Yugoslavian	AAIILMNOPST	maintopsail
AAGILNRRTUY	granularity	AAIILMNORST	rationalism
AAGILOPRRTU	purgatorial	AAIILNNOSTT	nationalist
AAGIMMNNOSU	magnanimous	AAIILNNOTTY	nationality
AAGINNNRUWY	running away	AAIILNOPPTT	palpitation
	running-away	AAIILNORSTT	rationalist
AAGINNOPRST	roasting pan	AAIILNORTTT	attritional
AAGINNRSTTU	turn against	AAIILNORTTY	rationality
AAGINNRTUWY	turning away	AAIILNOSTTU	situational
AAGINOOPPRT	propagation	AAIIMMNORSV	Moravianism
AAGINORRTUU	inaugurator	AAIIMNNORST	Mastroianni
AAGLLNOOSUY	analogously	AAIIMNOPRTT	impartation
AAGLMNNNOOR	Anglo-Norman	AAIIMNORRST	Rotarianism
AAGLMOOPSUY	apogamously	AAIIMNRSSTU	sanitariums
AAGNNOSSSTU	Susan Sontag	AAIINNNNSTT	in an instant
AAGOPRSTTUU	Port Augusta	AAIINRSSTTV	transit visa
AAHHHLMPRTY	alpha rhythm	AAIIOPSTTVY	pay a visit to
AAHHMMNOPPT	Hamp Hampton	AAIJMNNOTTW	want jam on it
AAHIIKLMRWZ	al-Khwarizmi	AAILLLOSTWW	swallow tail
AAHIILNNORT	annihilator		swallowtail
AAHIILNNRSV	nail varnish	AAILLNOPSTT	at all points
AAHIILNOORT	hariolation	AAILLORRSTY	sartorially
AAHIIMNNPSS	Spanish Main	AAILMMNOSTU	summational

AAILMMOPPRS	malapropism
AAILMNOPRTU	manipulator
AAILMNPSSTU	nuptial Mass
AAILMNRSTTT	transmittal
AAILMOPRSST	pastoralism
AAILNNORSTT	translation
AAILNOPPSSY	passion play
AAILNOSSTTU	salutations
AAILOORSTTT	Totalisator
AAILOORTTTZ	Totalizator
AAILOPRRTUV	vapour trail
AAIMMNOSSUY	immunoassay
AAIMNOOPSST	pass a motion
AAIMNORSSTU	sanatoriums
AAIMNORSTTU	natatoriums
AAINNNOPRST	non-partisan
AAINNOPRSTT	patron saint
AAINOORRSTZ	Zoroastrian
AAKLLMPRUUU	Kuala Lumpur
AAKLNNOOSSW	also known as
AALLMMNOSTU	small amount
AALLNNRTUUY	unnaturally
AALLOOPSSTW	allow to pass
AALMMOPPRRS	Mrs Malaprop
AALMNNOPSTW	plantswoman
AALMNOOPRTW	patrolwoman
AALMNOOTTTU	total amount
AALMNOPRTUY	paramountly
AALNNRRSTUY	translunary
AALORSSTTTU	altostratus
AAMNPRSSTTY	smartypants
AAMOOPRRTUU	out-paramour
AANNORRSTUY	tyrannosaur
ABBBDELOORW	wobble board
ABBBDINOSST	bits and bobs
ABBBEHITWYY	Whitby Abbey
ABBBENNORWY	newborn baby
ABBBINNRTUY	bunny rabbit
ABBCCDEHKNU	bunch-backed
ABBCCEEHKNR	backbencher
ABBCCEEHMOR	beachcomber
ABBCCHIORTT	Bob Cratchit
ABBCDEEFIKO	biofeedback
ABBCDEEILRS	describable
ABBCDEEKRUV	Dave Brubeck
ABBCDEENRSS	crabbedness
ABBCEEEKNRU	Beckenbauer
ABBCEEKLORT	beta-blocker
ABBCEHIRRRS	Chris Barber
ABBCEJKORWY	Jabberwocky
ABBCELMNORU	nuclear bomb
ABBCGIIIMNN	minicabbing
ABBCHIMNOOP	Bob Champion
ABBCHINPRTU	rabbit punch
ABBCILMOPST	plastic bomb
ABBCKLMOOTT	black bottom
ABBCKLNORYY	black bryony
ABBCKMOOORY	backroom-boy
ABBCKNNNORU	Bannockburn
ABBDDEIINRR	bird-brained
ABBDDOOORWW	Bob Woodward
ABBDEEGLNUU	unbudgeable
ABBDEELORTU	redoubtable
ABBDEEMMORR	board member
ABBDEEMORRR	armed robber
ABBDEGILNOT	bold-beating
ABBDEGIORSY	Boys' Brigade
ABBDEGNNRRU	Brandenburg
ABBDEHLLORU	Deborah Bull
ABBDEHNOSTU	husband-to-be
ABBDEIILNTU	indubitable
ABBDEIILNTY	bendability
ABBDEIINRRU	India rubber
ABBDELNOTUU	undoubtable
ABBDELNSUUU	unsubduable
ABBDEMMNORT	bombardment
ABBDGGINNOR	Brobdingnag
ABBDGIIINNS	bias binding
ABBDGINNRUY	bring-and-buy
ABBDHLNORRU	L Ron Hubbard
ABBDIILNTUY	indubitably
ABBEEEGILNV	Geneva Bible
ABBEEFFNOOR	baron of beef
ABBEEGIKRSU	Sergei Bubka
ABBEEHLOSTY	lose the baby
ABBEEHMMORX	Max Beerbohm
ABBEEKOORRV	Beaverbrook
ABBEELMSSSU	subassemble
ABBEELORRSU	rabble-rouse
ABBEFIILLMY	family Bible
ABBEFNORRSY	Bryan Forbes
ABBEGIJLNRY	jabberingly
ABBEGIKLMOO	go like a bomb
ABBEGINORRT	bring to bear
ABBEGINORTW	browbeating
ABBEHHIPRSU	rubbish heap
	rubbish-heap
ABBEHILRSTW	Welsh rabbit
ABBEHINSSSY	babyishness
ABBEHLLMSTU	be all thumbs
ABBEHNOORTT	Berthon-boat
ABBEILRSTVY	silver tabby
ABBEIMNRRTU	Martin Buber
ABBEINRSSUU	suburbanise
ABBEINRSTUU	suburbanite
ABBEINRSUUZ	suburbanize
ABBELNPRRTU	rubber plant
ABBEMPRRSTU	rubber stamp
	rubber-stamp
ABBENOSTTUU	be nuts about
ABBGGIRRRSY	Barry Briggs
ABBGIINSTTY	baby-sitting
ABBGILNORSY	absorbingly
ABBIILMNOOT	bombilation
ABBIILOPRTY	probability
ABBIIMNNOOT	bombination
ABBINNOORRS	Brian Robson
ABCCCELNORY	carbon cycle
ABCCCHIJKOS	Jacob Schick
ABCCCHKKLOO	chock-a-block
ABCCCILMOOX	coxcombical
ABCCDEEIIRT	bactericide

ABCCDEHHKNU	hunchbacked
ABCCDEIINOZ	benzoic acid
ABCCDEIKNRR	carrick bend
ABCCDEKKOOR	crookbacked
ABCCDEKLMOY	black comedy
ABCCDHHORRU	Broad Church
ABCCDOPRRUY	cry cupboard
ABCCEEELMOR	become clear
ABCCEEERSTW	Rebecca West
ABCCEEFFKLO	black coffee
ABCCEEHHINR	Reichenbach
ABCCEEHHMOR	echo chamber
ABCCEEILNOT	Cecil Beaton
ABCCEEILNOV	conceivable
ABCCEEKLOPU	peacock-blue
ABCCEELLLOT	collectable
ABCCEELNNOT	connectable
ABCCEEMNNRU	encumbrance
ABCCEEMRSUU	sea cucumber
ABCCEGINNOU	concubinage
ABCCEGKLLRY	black clergy
ABCCEHIILMO	biochemical
ABCCEHILNNN	Chenin Blanc
ABCCEHKLRRY	black cherry
ABCCEIILPTY	peccability
ABCCEIKKLST	stickleback
ABCCEIKLNPR	Black Prince
ABCCEILNOTV	convictable
ABCCEILNOVY	conceivably
ABCCEILOSTT	ectoblastic
ABCCGIKLRRU	Garrick Club
ABCCGIKNTTU	cutting back
ABCCIILLNSU	subclinical
ABCCIIMOORT	macrobiotic
ABCCIKORTTY	Toby Crackit
ABCCILLLOUY	bucolically
ABCCINOOSTT	tobacconist
ABCCKNOOOTU	account-book
ABCCKNORTUY	back-country
ABCCLLNORTU	Carlton Club
ABCCNORSTTU	subcontract
ABCDDEEFLOU	double-faced
ABCDDEEHKLO	blockheaded
ABCDDEEHLUY	debauchedly
ABCDDEFILRR	fiddler crab
ABCDDEFINOR	forbiddance
ABCDDHIIRRR	Richard Bird
ABCDDHIRRRY	Richard Byrd
ABCDEEEERRT	decerebrate
ABCDEEEHORS	cheese board
ABCDEEGILRR	Bracegirdle
ABCDEEHNORY	beyond reach
ABCDEEIJKOR	Derek Jacobi
ABCDEEILLMN	clean-limbed
ABCDEEILMOV	become valid
ABCDEEILMOW	bid a welcome
ABCDEEILPRT	predictable
ABCDEEINORS	decarbonise
ABCDEEINORZ	decarbonize
ABCDEEKLNNU	unblackened
ABCDEELLNOW	clean bowled
ABCDEELLNRU	Leander Club
ABCDEELLNRY	belly-dancer
ABCDEELMMNO	commendable
ABCDEELMNNO	condemnable
ABCDEELMORU	double cream
ABCDEELMOTU	become adult
ABCDEELOPSU	double-space
ABCDEENORRT	centreboard
ABCDEFFILTY	afflicted by
ABCDEFIINRR	bird-fancier
ABCDEGIKNNS	sending back
ABCDEHILSTW	switchblade
ABCDEHIRRTW	birdwatcher
ABCDEIILTUY	educability
ABCDEIIORTT	obiter dicta
ABCDEILPRTY	predictably
ABCDEILRRST	blister card
ABCDEILSSSU	discussable
ABCDEINRRST	transcribed
ABCDEINRSTU	disturbance
ABCDEKLMRUX	Max Delbrück
ABCDEKLOOOS	a closed book
ABCDELMMNOY	commendably
ABCDELMNRUU	Cumbernauld
ABCDELORRWY	Clyde Barrow
ABCDENNORSY	body scanner
ABCDGHIKLNO	holding-back
ABCDGHINOOV	Bogdanovich
ABCDGIIKLNS	backsliding
ABCDGIKNNOW	backing-down
ABCDHIIRSTU	hudibrastic
ABCDHIOPSTX	dispatch box
ABCDHIORSTW	switchboard
ABCDHNOORRY	hydrocarbon
ABCDIILORYY	ciliary body
ABCDIILOSSY	dissociably
ABCEEEFFKOR	coffee break
ABCEEEFFLOT	coffee table
	coffee-table
ABCEEEFIINT	beneficiate
ABCEEEFLNOR	enforceable
ABCEEEHIKRT	break the ice
ABCEEEILNRX	inexecrable
ABCEEEILPRV	perceivable
ABCEEEILRSV	serviceable
ABCEEEILRSX	exercisable
ABCEEELMNRS	resemblance
ABCEEELMOPR	become paler
ABCEEELORRV	recoverable
ABCEEELPRRU	recuperable
ABCEEELPRST	respectable
ABCEEEMMNRR	remembrance □
ABCEEEMMNRT	embracement
ABCEEEMORRR	become rarer
ABCEEFHIKRR	chief barker
ABCEEFIILPS	specifiable
ABCEEFIILRT	certifiable
	rectifiable
ABCEEFIINRY	beneficiary
ABCEEFIMNOT	become faint
ABCEEFINNOT	benefaction

Words marked □ can also be spelled with an initial capital letter

ABCEEFINRTU	rubefacient
ABCEEFKORTY	take by force
ABCEEFNORTY	benefactory
ABCEEGIINOT	abiogenetic
ABCEEGIJMRR	Jim Bergerac
ABCEEGILNRT	celebrating
ABCEEGLNORS	Serge Blanco
ABCEEGMNORY	become angry
ABCEEHIMNVY	Maeve Binchy
ABCEEHINNRS	Sennacherib
ABCEEHKLNQU	blank cheque
ABCEEHLLLRS	Charles Bell
ABCEEHLRSST	Charles Best
ABCEEHLRSTT	stretchable
ABCEEHORRRT	torchbearer
ABCEEIJOTTV	objectivate
ABCEEILLNTU	ineluctable
ABCEEILNOPT	beneplacito
ABCEEILNORT	celebration
ABCEEILNSUX	inexcusable
ABCEEILNTUX	unexcitable
ABCEEILOOTT	bootlace tie
ABCEEILORRV	irrevocable
ABCEEILPRVY	perceivably
ABCEEILRRSU	irrecusable
ABCEEILRSVY	serviceably
ABCEEINNRTY	bicentenary
ABCEEINORRT	cerebration
ABCEEINORTX	exorbitance
ABCEEKKLNRU	bare-knuckle
ABCEEKLLTVV	black velvet
ABCEEKLRRRW	kerb-crawler
ABCEELNOQRU	conquerable
ABCEELNORST	carbon steel
ABCEELNORSV	conservable
ABCEELNOSTT	contestable
ABCEELNRSSU	curableness
ABCEELORRTY	celebratory
ABCEELPRSTY	respectably
ABCEELRTTUU	tuberculate
ABCEEMRRTTU	butter cream
ABCEENORRST	arborescent
ABCEFHKNOOT	on the back of
ABCEFIILRTY	certifiably
ABCEFIKORTZ	Rifat Ozbeck
ABCEFILMNOR	confirmable
ABCEFINORTU	rubefaction
ABCEFKLORST	Black Forest
ABCEFLMNOOR	conformable
ABCEFLMOORT	comfortable
ABCEFLMRRSU	Farmers Club
ABCEFLOORRU	labour force
ABCEGHILLNY	belly-aching
ABCEGILLMTU	magic bullet
ABCEGILMNRY	embracingly
ABCEGILNNOS	consignable
ABCEGILNOPW	pace-bowling
ABCEGKLORSU	black grouse
ABCEGLLORSU	bogus caller
ABCEHHKRSUW	bushwhacker
ABCEHHNNRSU	Hans Buchner
ABCEHIIMRSW	Micawberish
ABCEHIKNRSU	Chris Eubank
ABCEHILNORV	olive branch
ABCEHINOOPR	necrophobia
ABCEHINPSTY	spy in the cab
ABCEHKLNOSU	unshockable
ABCEHLLOSTT	tablecloths
ABCEHLNOTUU	untouchable
ABCEHNOORRT	Robert Cohan
ABCEHRSSTTU	bruschettas
ABCEIIKLNRT	tickle-brain
ABCEIILMRTY	imbricately
ABCEIILNOSV	cablevision
ABCEIIMNOTV	combinative
ABCEIKLPRST	blister pack
ABCEIKNOOPT	a bone to pick
ABCEIKNSSWW	Bewick's swan
ABCEILLLLLU	Lucille Ball
ABCEILLLOPS	collapsible
ABCEILLNTUY	ineluctably
ABCEILLRTUV	carvel-built
ABCEILMOPRT	problematic
ABCEILNRSTU	inscrutable
ABCEILNSUXY	inexcusably
ABCEILORRSU	orbiculares
ABCEILORRVY	irrevocably
ABCEILORSTT	obstetrical
ABCEILRRSUY	irrecusably
ABCEILRTUVY	Variety Club
ABCEIMNOORT	embrocation
ABCEINNSSTU	in substance
ABCEINRRRST	transcriber
ABCEIRSTTUV	subtractive
ABCEJMNORSU	James Coburn
ABCEKLLMNOT	mental block
ABCELLMOSTU	costume ball
ABCELLNSSTU	sanctus bell
ABCELNNORTU	contubernal
ABCELNNOTUU	uncountable
ABCELNORSVY	conversably
ABCELORSSUU	scaberulous
ABCENNNOOST	be consonant
ABCENRRSTUY	canterburys
ABCEOOORRRT	corroborate
ABCEOORRSST	cross to bear
ABCEORRRTTU	carburettor
ABCFGIKLNOW	flowing-back
ABCFGIKORST	bag of tricks
ABCFHINOOST	son of a bitch
	sonofabitch
ABCFIINORTU	bifurcation
ABCFINOOSTU	obfuscation
ABCFKNOORTT	back to front
ABCFLMNOORY	conformably
ABCFLMOORTY	comfortably
ABCFOORSTUY	obfuscatory
ABCGHILNORU	Brian Clough
ABCGHOORRSU	Scarborough
ABCGIIKLNRY	bricklaying
ABCGIILLOST	go ballistic
ABCGIKKLNOO	looking back

ABCGIKLLNPU	pulling back
ABCHHILOOOP	ochlophobia
ABCHHIOPRSS	archbishops
ABCHIILOPSY	biophysical
ABCHIKKNOTT	think back to
ABCHILOPSTY	hypoblastic
ABCHIMOTTUU	much about it
ABCHINOOPTY	nyctophobia
ABCHOSTTUWY	cut both ways
ABCIIILOSTY	sociability
ABCIIKLNRSY	brainsickly
ABCIIKLNSUW	Kiwanis Club
ABCIILLPTUY	culpability
ABCIILLRSTY	trisyllabic
ABCIILNOPTU	publication
ABCIILNORTU	lubrication
ABCIIMNNOOT	combination
ABCIINORRTU	rubrication
ABCILLNNOUY	connubially
ABCILLNORUY	binocularly
ABCILLNORYY	Byronically
ABCILLORRUY	orbicularly
ABCILLPSUYY	say publicly
ABCILMNNUUU	incunabulum
ABCILNRSTUY	inscrutably
ABCILOPRSTU	subtropical
ABCIMNOORTY	combinatory
ABCINNOORTU	conurbation
ABCINNOPTTU	panic button
ABCINOORSTU	obscuration
ABCINORSTTU	subtraction
ABCLLRSTUUU	subcultural
ABCNORRSTUY	subcontrary
ABCORRSSTTU	substractor
ABDDDEGLNOU	Donald Budge
ABDDDEIMNOR	broad-minded
ABDDDIIMNOR	diamond bird
ABDDEEEMPRT	bad-tempered
ABDDEEHINRT	tread behind
ABDDEEIILTT	debilitated
ABDDEEPRSUY	persuaded by
ABDDEFFILNN	eff and blind
ABDDEFHLLOO	half-blooded
ABDDEFILOTU	fiddle about
ABDDEGIKORR	Dirk Bogarde
ABDDEGNNOOS	banned goods
ABDDEHLLNOO	lo and behold
ABDDEHNNSUU	unhusbanded
ABDDEIILNUV	undividable
ABDDEILLNRU	dull-brained
ABDDEILLOUY	daily double
ABDDEIMNNST	disbandment
ABDDEKLOOOS	blood-soaked
ABDDEKOORSS	address book
ABDDELMOORW	warm-blooded
ABDDHLOOORT	Bardo Thodol
ABDDLNOOSUY	body and soul
ABDEEEEGLRU	beleaguered
ABDEEEGLLOU	double eagle
ABDEEEHILNV	leave behind
ABDEEEHILRT	hereditable
ABDEEEHIMRT	ride the beam
ABDEEEHLLVW	well behaved
	well-behaved
ABDEEEHRRRT	Herbert Read
ABDEEEILLRV	deliverable
ABDEEEILPPP	apple-pie bed
ABDEEEKLNTW	blanketweed
ABDEEELLOPV	developable
ABDEEELNSST	belatedness
ABDEEELORSV	sleeve board
ABDEEELRRRW	reed-warbler
ABDEEEPRSTT	bespattered
ABDEEFGIIRR	fire brigade
ABDEEFGILNS	bad feelings
ABDEEFIILNN	indefinable
ABDEEFIINRT	defibrinate
ABDEEFILLTT	battlefield
ABDEEFILNNU	undefinable
ABDEEFILNRT	Alfred Binet
ABDEEFLLNOR	Alfred Nobel
ABDEEFNOORR	free on board
ABDEEFOORSS	a bed of roses
ABDEEGGINRR	gingerbread
ABDEEGHHOTY	go by the head
ABDEEGHLOPS	globe-shaped
ABDEEGHNORY	honey badger
ABDEEGIMNRT	abridgement
ABDEEGLNOTU	double agent
ABDEEGLNRSS	garbledness
ABDEEHILSST	established
ABDEEHIRSTW	breadthwise
ABDEEHLOSTT	tables-d'hôte
ABDEEHLOTTU	at the double
ABDEEHMRTTU	beat the drum
ABDEEIIKLLS	dislikeable
ABDEEIILRST	detribalise
ABDEEIILRTZ	detribalize
ABDEEIILSST	destabilise
ABDEEIILSTZ	destabilize
ABDEEILMNST	disablement
ABDEEILMSSS	disassemble
ABDEEILNNOO	Daniel Boone
ABDEEILNPSS	dispensable
ABDEEILNRSU	undesirable
ABDEEILORRT	deliberator
ABDEEILORTT	obliterated
ABDEEINNRRW	breadwinner
ABDEEIRTTTU	deattribute
ABDEEKLOPSU	doublespeak
ABDEEKNORSZ	baker's dozen
ABDEELLLORR	rollerblade
ABDEELLNOPW	Baden-Powell
ABDEELMNORZ	bronze medal
ABDEELMNRUY	denumerably
ABDEELNNRRU	Blade Runner
ABDEELNNRUU	unendurable
ABDEELNOSST	bloatedness
ABDEELNRSSU	durableness
ABDEELORRTW	world-beater
ABDEELRSSTT	battledress
ABDEEMRSSUY	Burmese Days

ABDEEORRRSW sword-bearer
ABDEFGIIRRT frigate bird
frigatebird
ABDEFGINORR fingerboard
ABDEFGIRSSU figured bass
ABDEFIILNNY indefinably
ABDEFLLOTUU double fault
double-fault
ABDEGGHINOR be hard going
ABDEGGINORR ragged robin
ABDEGHLORSU shoulder bag
shoulder-bag
ABDEGHMNRTU bang the drum
ABDEGIILNNT dining-table
ABDEGIKNOOR reading-book
ABDEGIKNORY keyboarding
ABDEGINNPSW spawning-bed
ABDEGKNORRU break ground
ABDEGLNNOOU go a bundle on
ABDEGLNOOOR blood orange
ABDEGOOORRV go overboard
ABDEHHMOORR rhombohedra
ABDEHIINNPR hairpin bend
ABDEHIINNTU uninhabited
ABDEHLOORSV shovelboard
ABDEHLOPRSU double sharp
ABDEHMOORRT motherboard
ABDEHNOSSTU basset-hound
ABDEIIILNTY deniability
ABDEIILLTWY weldability
ABDEIILMNOT indomitable
ABDEIINRSST Saint Bride's
ABDEIINRTTU inturbidate
ABDEIKNNNOS skin-and-bone
ABDEIKNORTW break it down
ABDEILLLSSY dissyllable
ABDEILMNOPU impoundable
ABDEILMSSSY disassembly
ABDEILNPSSY dispensably
ABDEILNRSUY undesirably
ABDEILNSSUY unbiassedly
ABDEILOPRSS bolas spider
ABDEINORSTU subordinate
ABDEKLLOPSY speak boldly
ABDEKMNOOTU make no doubt
ABDELMOORST bloodstream
ABDELOORRWW wood warbler
ABDEMNOORWW meadow brown
ABDENNORSTV bondservant
ABDENOORRSW snowboarder
ABDENOPRSUU superabound
ABDENORSTVY body servant
ABDEOOOPRTT torpedo boat
ABDEOPRRSST ports de bras
ABDFFIJNOOR find a job for
ABDFGHIILNN half-binding
ABDFIILLSYY disyllabify
ABDFIILNNUU infundibula
ABDFKNNOORS Frank Dobson
ABDGHHJNOOO John Habgood
ABDGHIILNNS blandishing
ABDGHINPSSU spud-bashing
ABDGIILLLNU all-building
ABDGIINNNOU abounding in
ABDGINOPRRS springboard
ABDGKNNOORS Gordon Banks
ABDGMOORRSS smorgasbord
ABDGNNNORSY granny bonds
ABDHHIOOPRY hydrophobia
ABDHINOOPRS on shipboard
ABDHJNNOOUU John Audubon
ABDHLMOOOST Thomas Blood
ABDIIILRTVY drivability
ABDIILLMRWY William Byrd
ABDIILMNOTY indomitably
ABDILLNRTWY Willy Brandt
ABDILMNORUU burial mound
ABDIMNNOSTU subdominant
ABDLNOOOSTT odontoblast
ABEEEEFLORS foreseeable
ABEEEEGLNRR regenerable
ABEEEEIKLMV make believe
make-believe
ABEEEELRTTW water beetle
ABEEEEMNRTV bereavement
ABEEEERRRTV reverberate
ABEEEFFILLS false belief
ABEEEFIRRRR barrier reef
ABEEEFLMNRT fermentable
ABEEEGGKLOR George Blake
ABEEEGILRRS bersagliere
ABEEEGIRRTV verbigerate
ABEEEGLORSW elbow grease
elbow-grease
ABEEEGLRRTT regrettable
ABEEEHINRRT Bertie Ahern
ABEEEHMNRRV Bremerhaven
ABEEEHNNORT near the bone
ABEEEHNRRSY Barry Sheene
ABEEEHORRTV over-breathe
ABEEEIILNPS plebeianise
ABEEEIILNPZ plebeianize
ABEEEILLLMN Nellie Melba
ABEEEILMMPR impermeable
ABEEEILMMST emblematise
ABEEEILMMTZ emblematize
ABEEEILNNOT be in one tale
ABEEEILPRRY Pierre Bayle
ABEEEILRRTV retrievable
ABEEEIMNSST absenteeism
ABEEEKNRRSV reserve bank
ABEEELMNRRU remunerable
ABEEELNPRST presentable
ABEEELNPRTV preventable
ABEEELPRRST Albert Speer
ABEEELPRRSV preservable
ABEEELPSTUY beauty sleep
ABEEEMOPRTT obtemperate
ABEEENQTUUY beauty queen
ABEEENRRRTV reverberant
ABEEFFILORT forfeitable
ABEEFFMMRST staff member

ABEEFFRSTTU	buffer state
ABEEFGILNRR	refrangible
ABEEFHMNOTY	by the name of
ABEEFIILLQU	liquefiable
ABEEFILNRSS	friableness
ABEEFILRRTU	irrefutable
ABEEFKLMNNY	Fanny Kemble
ABEEFLLNSSU	balefulness
ABEEFLMOPRR	performable
ABEEGGIILLV	give leg bail
ABEEGGLNORS	Glen Seaborg
ABEEGHIKNST	baking sheet
ABEEGHILPPT	the Big Apple
ABEEGIINNRR	bearing rein
ABEEGIINOSS	abiogenesis
ABEEGIKLNNT	telebanking
ABEEGILMNPR	impregnable
ABEEGILRRST	registrable
ABEEGINORRV	overbearing
ABEEGIRRTTT	Great Bitter
ABEEGLMNRRU	large number
ABEEGLMOPPR	problem page
ABEEGLNOSTU	obtuse angle
ABEEGLRRTTY	regrettably
ABEEGMMNRSU	numbers game
ABEEGMNRRTU	great number
ABEEHHILORS	Hore-Belisha
ABEEHHPRSTY	bathysphere
ABEEHIILNRT	inheritable
ABEEHILMNST	habilements
ABEEHILRSST	establisher
	re-establish
ABEEHILSTUX	exhaustible
ABEEHINORTT	breathe into
ABEEHINRSST	breathiness
ABEEHKNORRT	heartbroken
	heart-broken
ABEEHKORRTW	Robert Hawke
ABEEHLNORTT	the noble art
ABEEHLOORST	Athole brose
ABEEHLORRWW	wheelbarrow
ABEEHNOPRRY	hyperborean
ABEEHNOPRTU	breathe upon
ABEEHNORSTW	Noah Webster
ABEEHNORTTT	on the batter
ABEEHORSTTU	thereabouts
ABEEHORSTUW	whereabouts
ABEEIIKLMSV	make visible
ABEEIILMNST	inestimable
ABEEIILNQTU	inequitable
ABEEIILQRTU	equilibrate
ABEEIKLNNRX	Karen Blixen
ABEEILLNORT	intolerable
ABEEILLNPSS	pliableness
ABEEILLOPTX	exploitable
ABEEILMMOSV	immoveables
ABEEILMMPRY	impermeably
ABEEILMNNOT	mentionable
ABEEILMNNRU	innumerable
ABEEILMNRTU	unmeritable
ABEEILMORRV	irremovable
ABEEILMORST	steam boiler
ABEEILNNOPS	pensionable
ABEEILNNSTT	table tennis
	table-tennis
ABEEILNPRSU	insuperable
ABEEILNSSST	beastliness
ABEEILPRSSU	persuasible
ABEEILRRTVY	retrievably
ABEEINORRTV	verberation
ABEEINORSSU	Buenos Aires
ABEEINRRSSZ	bizarreness
ABEEINRSSTW	bear witness
ABEEINSSSUV	abusiveness
ABEEIOPRRTV	reprobative
ABEEIRRTTTU	reattribute
ABEEKLNORTW	T-Bone Walker
ABEEKMNOOSW	make one's bow
ABEEKMOSSST	Moses basket
ABEEKNOOPTU	keep on about
ABEEKNOORUZ	Kenzaburo Oë
ABEELLLMSSY	blamelessly
ABEELLLMTUY	umbellately
ABEELLLNQUU	unquellable
ABEELLORSST	Ballesteros
ABEELLRRTVY	vertebrally
ABEELMMNORU	unmemorable
ABEELMNORUV	unremovable
ABEELMNOSSV	movableness
ABEELMNPRTU	number plate
ABEELMNSTTT	battlements
ABEELNNOSST	notableness
ABEELNOOSTW	at one's elbow
ABEELNORRTY	learn by rote
ABEELNPRSTY	presentably
ABEELNRTTUU	unutterable
ABEELNRTUXY	exuberantly
ABEELORTTTW	water bottle
ABEELOSTUUY	beauteously
ABEELQQRUUU	Albuquerque
ABEEMMNOSSY	by some means
ABEENNORTUV	Bonaventure
ABEEOPRRRTY	Robert Peary
ABEEOPRRTTU	protuberate
ABEFFGHLOTW	blow the gaff
ABEFFGIKNOR	breaking-off
ABEFFIILORT	fortifiable
ABEFFLLNOSU	full of beans
ABEFGHIIMNS	be famishing
ABEFGHRRRSU	Fraserburgh
ABEFGIILNNR	infrangible
ABEFGIINTUY	beautifying
ABEFGIMNORT	bring fame to
ABEFGLMOORR	gambrel roof
ABEFHHLORRT	half-brother
ABEFHILNOTW	the final bow
ABEFHLNSSSU	bashfulness
ABEFHNORRTW	Father Brown
ABEFHOORTTU	out of breath
ABEFIIILSTY	feasibility
ABEFIIJLSTU	justifiable
ABEFIILNOSS	fissionable

ABEFIKLNNUU	in a blue funk
ABEFILLTUUY	beautifully
ABEFILNNNOR	Flann O'Brien
ABEFILORSTU	suitable for
ABEFILRRTUY	irrefutably
ABEFLLNOORT	frontal lobe
ABEFLMOOSTT	false bottom
ABEFLNOPTYY	Bay of Plenty
ABEFMNNORUY	any number of
ABEFNNNRUYY	Fanny Burney
ABEFNOOPRTT	not be part of
ABEFNOORSTV	observant of
ABEGGHIMNRT	German Bight
ABEGGIILNOR	globigerina
ABEGGLMNRVY	Melvyn Bragg
ABEGHIIMNSV	misbehaving
ABEGHIIMSTT	as it might be
ABEGHIINNRT	hibernating
ABEGHIKMNNO	home banking
ABEGHILMNOO	haemoglobin
ABEGHIMNNSU	human beings
ABEGIIINNRT	inebriating
ABEGIIKMNRS	Kim Basinger
ABEGIILNRVZ	verbalizing
ABEGIIMNSSU	subimagines
ABEGIIRRSTU	subirrigate
ABEGIJMNNPU	jumping-bean
ABEGIKLNOOT	be looking at
ABEGIKNOSST	Basingstoke
ABEGILMNOSW	seam bowling
ABEGILMNPRY	impregnably
ABEGILNNNTY	benignantly
ABEGILNNRTY	banteringly
ABEGILRRYZZ	grizzly bear
ABEGIOTUVZZ	give a buzz to
ABEGLLORSSW	glass-blower
ABEGMORRSTU	burgomaster
ABEHHILNNOS	Hans Holbein
ABEHHJNORSY	John Ashbery
ABEHHORSTTU	thresh about
ABEHIILMOPT	amphibolite
ABEHIILPRST	blepharitis
ABEHIIMMNOS	bohemianism □
ABEHIINNORT	hibernation
ABEHIKLNNTU	unthinkable
ABEHILLLRTY	liberty hall
ABEHILPPRST	slipper bath
ABEHILPSSTT	battleships
ABEHIMOSSTT	miss the boat
ABEHINOORTT	botheration
ABEHINPRRTT	birth parent
ABEHJKNOPSS	Joseph Banks
ABEHJLMNORT	John Lambert
ABEHLMOORTW	Bartholomew
ABEHLMOPSSU	blasphemous
ABEHLMORTWY	blameworthy
ABEHLNORRTY	abhorrently
ABEHNORSTTY	east-by-north
	north by east
ABEHOSSTTUY	east-by-south
	south by east
ABEHPRRRTUY	Hubert Parry
ABEHRSTTWYY	Aberystwyth
ABEIIIILLST	liabilities
ABEIIILLLMT	illimitable
ABEIIILLNOR	billionaire
ABEIIILLRTY	reliability
ABEIIILMTTU	Mutabilitie
ABEIIINNORT	inebriation
ABEIIKLNORW	rainbow-like
ABEIILLLLRY	illiberally
ABEIILLMMST	bimetallism
ABEIILLMPSU	implausible
ABEIILMNSTY	inestimably
ABEIILMOTVY	moveability
ABEIILNNOOP	piano nobile
ABEIILNQTUY	inequitably
ABEIILOPPRT	propitiable
ABEIILOPRTY	operability
ABEIIMOPRTV	improbative
ABEIIRTTTUV	attributive
ABEIKLLNOOT	kite-balloon
ABEIKNORTTU	tinker about
ABEILLLOPSS	all possible
ABEILLLRSTY	trisyllable
ABEILLNOOTT	not liable to
ABEILLNORTY	intolerably
ABEILLNRSSY	brainlessly
ABEILMNNRUY	innumerably
ABEILMOORTV	Oliver Tambo
ABEILMORRVY	irremovably
ABEILMORSUY	Louis B Mayer
ABEILNNORTT	Leon Brittan
ABEILNNPRTU	unprintable
ABEILNNSTTY	abstinently
ABEILNOOSSS	obsessional
ABEILNORSSU	Belorussian
ABEILNOSTTY	obstinately
ABEILNPRSUY	insuperably
ABEILNRSSUU	Russian Blue
ABEILORSSTW	belowstairs
ABEIMNNSSSU	businessman
ABEIMNORSTW	tribeswoman
ABEINOOPRRT	probationer
	reprobation
ABEINOORSTV	observation
ABEINSSTTUV	substantive
ABEIPSSSTTT	past its best
ABEIRSSTTUV	substrative
ABEKLMNOPRT	Belmont Park
ABEKMNOOTUY	monkey about
ABEKMORSTTY	take by storm
ABEKOOSTTTU	statute book
ABELLMMNRSU	small number
ABELLMNOORW	below normal
ABELLNNOTTY	tantony bell
ABELMOOPSSS	Peasblossom
ABELNOOPRSU	Paul Robeson
ABELNOPPSTU	unstoppable
ABELNORSTVY	observantly
ABELNRTTUUY	unutterably
ABELOPPRSTU	supportable

ABEMNNOTTTU	Mountbatten
ABEMNOSSSTU	bums on seats
ABENNOORSTU	no reason but
ABENNORSTUV	unobservant
ABENOPRRTTU	protuberant
ABEOOPRRRTY	reprobatory
ABEOOPRTTTU	potter about
ABEOORRSTVY	observatory
ABFFFFILOTU	a bit of fluff
ABFFILLMSTU	bull-mastiff
ABFGHNOORRU	Farnborough
ABFGIILNNRY	infrangibly
ABFGIILNORT	floating rib
ABFGILNOSTW	fast bowling
ABFIIILLLTY	fallibility
ABFIIIMNORT	fimbriation
ABFIIJLSTUY	justifiably
ABFIILORSUY	bifariously
ABFIINOOTTT	not a bit of it
ABFILLLNSTU	in full blast
ABFILMNSTUU	funambulist
ABFLNOOORRS	Flora Robson
ABGGGINNOOT	tobogganing
ABGGILOORST	garbologist
ABGGINOOSTT	tobogganist
ABGHIINSTTU	bathing suit
ABGHIKLNSUW	bushwalking
ABGHILMOOPY	amphibology
ABGHINNTTUY	anything but
ABGHLMOORRU	Marlborough
ABGIIILMMTY	immitigably
ABGIIILNTTY	tangibility
ABGIILLLNUY	bilingually
ABGIILLNRST	star billing
ABGIILMNTUY	unmitigably
ABGIILNOOST	obligations
ABGIJNOORTU	objurgation
ABGIJNOSTUU	subjugation
ABGIKLNOOTW	walking-boot
ABGIKNNOPRW	pawnbroking
ABGILLNNOSW	snowballing
ABGILMOSUUY	ambiguously
ABGIMNOSUUU	unambiguous
ABGINOORSTU	subrogation
ABGINOPRSST	bring to pass
ABGLNORSTUY	Glastonbury
ABGMOORSSTT	bottom-grass
ABGOORRTTUW	Otto Warburg
ABHHIIOOPPP	hippophobia
ABHHIKRSTTU	Turkish bath
ABHHIOOOPPT	photophobia
ABHIIMRRSTW	British warm
ABHIKLLLNSY	Bill Shankly
ABHIKNORSVY	Baryshnikov
ABHILMMNOPT	phantom limb
ABHILRRSSTU	Arthur Bliss
ABHIOPRSSSW	Bishops' Wars
ABHJMNNOOOR	John Boorman
ABHMNOORSTW	Thomas Brown
ABHMORRSTTU	Arthur's Tomb
ABHNORRRTUW	Arthur Brown
ABHPRRSSTUY	pastry brush
ABIIIILMTTY	imitability
ABIIILLLMTY	illimitably
ABIIILNSTTY	instability
ABIIILNTUVY	unviability
ABIIILSTTUY	suitability
ABIIKLORTWY	workability
ABIILLLNRTY	brilliantly
ABIILLMPSUY	implausibly
ABIILMNOSTU	sublimation
ABIILMOSTUY	ambitiously
ABIILNORTTU	tribulation
ABIILNRSTUY	insalubrity
ABIILOPRTTY	portability
ABIILOQTTUY	quotability
ABIILRRTTUY	tributarily
ABIIMNORSTT	nimbostrati
ABIIMNOSTUU	unambitious
ABIINOORSTT	abortionist
ABIINORTTTU	attribution
ABIJLRRTUYY	Trial by Jury
ABILLNPSUUY	unplausibly
ABILLOORSUY	laboriously
ABILLOPRRSW	sparrow-bill
ABILLOSTTTU	built to last
ABILMORSTUU	umbratilous
ABIMOOPRRTY	improbatory
ABINNOORSTU	subornation
ABJOOSTTTUU	just about to
ABLNOPPSTUY	unstoppably
ABLOPPRSTUY	supportably
ABMNOPPTTUY	Natty Bumppo
ABMOORSSTTY	smartyboots
ACCCDEHILNO	chalcedonic
ACCCDEIILNU	nucleic acid
ACCCDEIKRRT	crack credit
ACCCDENNOOR	concordance
ACCCDENNOTU	conductance
ACCCDHIILOR	chloric acid
ACCCDIIIILS	silicic acid
ACCCDIMOPST	compact disc
ACCCEEELNOS	coalescence
ACCCEEHISTT	catechetics
ACCCEEILRRT	electric arc
ACCCEELMNOP	complacence
ACCCEHIISTT	catechistic
ACCCEHNORTY	technocracy
ACCCEIILMRT	climacteric
ACCCEIKNRST	cancer-stick
ACCCELMNOPY	complacency
ACCCHHIMPUU	Machu Picchu
ACCCHIILLOT	laccolithic
ACCCHILOORT	ochlocratic
ACCCIIOOPRS	capriccioso
ACCCIKLMOOT	atomic clock
ACCCIMMOORS	macrocosmic
ACCCIMOOPRS	macroscopic
ACCCINOPPSU	cappuccinos
ACCCNOOSTTU	cost-account
ACCDDEINORS	discordance
ACCDDIIIMST	didacticism

ACCDEEEENNT	antecedence
ACCDEEELNOS	adolescence
ACCDEEFHHKL	half-checked
ACCDEEFNORY	confederacy
ACCDEEGOPRU	coup de grâce
ACCDEEHIMNO	machine code
ACCDEEHINRS	hard science
ACCDEEHIORS	archdiocese
ACCDEEIORTT	decorticate
ACCDEEKKNNN	neck and neck
ACCDEEKLOPS	close-packed
ACCDEELNNOU	unconcealed
ACCDEEMNSUU	succedaneum
ACCDEENORST	consecrated
ACCDEFKLORU	Fleur Adcock
ACCDEFNOSTU	safe conduct
	safe-conduct
ACCDEHHRSSU	archduchess
ACCDEHINORW	choice-drawn
ACCDEHKLNPU	packed lunch
ACCDEIILLTY	deictically
ACCDEIINOST	desiccation
ACCDEIKLNST	candlestick
ACCDEILLOPS	peccadillos
ACCDEILMOPT	complicated
ACCDEINOOTU	coeducation
ACCDEINPRSY	discrepancy
ACCDEKNNOPR	neck and crop
ACCDEKORRRT	track record
ACCDELMOPTY	compactedly
ACCDELNOSSS	second class
	second-class
ACCDENORTUV	cut and cover
ACCDFHHLOOT	catch hold of
ACCDFIIKNRS	Dick Francis
ACCDGGILNNO	clog-dancing
ACCDGILNOOR	cooling card
ACCDGILNORY	accordingly
ACCDGINOORT	according to
ACCDHHNSSUU	such-and-such
ACCDHHRRSUW	churchwards
ACCDHIIMORT	dichromatic
ACCDHIINOOP	Capodichino
ACCDHINORYY	hydrocyanic
ACCDIILLNRY	cylindrical
ACCDIIPRSSU	prussic acid
ACCDIIPRUVY	pyruvic acid
ACCDIKMOPST	compact disk
ACCDIMOSSTU	disaccustom
ACCDKNNOORW	crack down on
ACCEEEEHMRS	cream cheese
ACCEEEENNSV	evanescence
ACCEEEFIKOP	piece of cake
ACCEEEFILMN	maleficence
ACCEEEFLNRT	reflectance
ACCEEEHHKOS	cheechakoes
ACCEEEHHTTY	catch the eye
ACCEEEHLLRS	Carl Scheele
ACCEEEHNNTV	chance event
ACCEEEIKKLO	cockaleekie
	cock-a-leekie
ACCEEELNOPS	opalescence
ACCEEELNPST	en spectacle
ACCEEELNRST	recalescent
ACCEEFIIPST	specificate
ACCEEFIIRTT	certificate
ACCEEFIKLOS	slice of cake
ACCEEFIKRRR	firecracker
ACCEEFIOSTY	café society
ACCEEFLORST	Corfe Castle
ACCEEGHILMO	geochemical
ACCEEGHINTY	eye-catching
ACCEEGHKRUY	Chuck Yeager
ACCEEGHORRV	cover charge
ACCEEGILRRT	great circle
ACCEEGINORS	agroscience
ACCEEHHIRST	Cheshire Cat
ACCEEHILMNO	chameleonic
ACCEEHILNRT	chanticleer
ACCEEHKORTW	weather-cock
ACCEEHLLNRY	chancellery
ACCEEHLLOPS	local speech
ACCEEHMMORY	cache memory
ACCEEIILNRT	electrician
ACCEEIINQSU	acquiesce in
ACCEEIKKLOP	peacock-like
ACCEEIKNPRS	science park
ACCEEIKRRSW	wisecracker
ACCEEILLLRT	all-electric
ACCEEILMNOU	oecumenical
ACCEEILOOPR	Alice Cooper
ACCEEILRRTY	electric ray
ACCEEINQSTU	acquiescent
ACCEEIOPRRT	reciprocate
ACCEEIORSSS	accessories
	accessorise
ACCEEIORSSZ	accessorize
ACCEEIORTTX	excorticate
ACCEELMNNOT	concealment
ACCEEMNNORR	necromancer
ACCEEMNOPPU	come-uppance
ACCEENNNOTU	countenance
ACCEENNORSV	conversance
ACCEENNORTT	concentrate
ACCEENNORVY	conveyancer
ACCEENORRRT	catercorner
ACCEFFHNNRR	French franc
ACCEFFIIOSU	efficacious
ACCEFFILLOO	local office
ACCEFHHKLNR	French chalk
ACCEFHIINTY	chieftaincy
ACCEFILOPST	sceptical of
ACCEFILORSU	calciferous
ACCEGGIKNRT	get cracking
ACCEGHLLRTU	gull-catcher
ACCEHHNSTTU	catch the sun
ACCEHIILOST	catholicise
ACCEHIILOTZ	catholicize
ACCEHIIMNST	mechanistic
ACCEHIIRSTU	eucharistic ❑
ACCEHIKPRTY	parity check
ACCEHILLMNO	melancholic

ACCEHILLNTY	technically
ACCEHILMNNO	non-chemical
ACCEHIMNNOR	chrominance
ACCEHIMRTTY	McCarthyite
ACCEHLLNORT	concert-hall
ACCEHLLNORY	chancellory
ACCEHMNOORS	comancheros
ACCEHNOPRTU	coup the cran
ACCEIIINPRT	accipitrine
ACCEIIINRST	intricacies
ACCEIILLMRS	clericalism
ACCEIILLNPR	preclinical
ACCEIILRRSU	circularise
ACCEIILRRUZ	circularize
ACCEIIMNOST	cosmetician
	encomiastic
ACCEIIMORTT	Matteo Ricci
ACCEIINNOSU	insouciance
ACCEIINOSTX	exsiccation
ACCEIIRRSTT	criticaster
ACCEIKNRSSS	carsickness
	car-sickness
ACCEILLLMRS	small circle
ACCEILLNRTY	centrically
ACCEILLPSTY	sceptically
ACCEILMOPST	ectoplasmic
ACCEILNNOTY	anticyclone
ACCEILNOPRT	Eric Clapton
ACCEILORSSY	accessorily
ACCEIMMNOTU	communicate
ACCEIMNNORT	necromantic
ACCEIMNRSTU	trance music
ACCEIMORRTY	meritocracy
ACCEINNNOTU	continuance
ACCEINNOORS	cancioneros
ACCEINNORTV	contrivance
ACCEINORSTU	cater-cousin
ACCEINORTTV	contractive
ACCEINSSSTU	causticness
ACCEIORSTUU	urticaceous
ACCEJLNORTU	conjectural
ACCELLOSTTU	coal scuttle
ACCELMMNOOP	commonplace
ACCELNNOSTT	contact lens
ACCELPRRSUU	crepuscular
ACCEMNOOPRT	comportance
ACCEMNOPSST	compactness
ACCENNORSVY	conservancy
ACCENOOPRTU	pococurante
ACCENOPRRTT	precontract
ACCENPRTUUU	acupuncture
ACCFHILLORT	chill factor
ACCFIILOPRY	prolificacy
ACCFILMNNOO	Finn mac Cool
ACCFINOORST	confiscator
ACCFNNOOOTU	of no account
	on account of
ACCGHIIIOPS	pichiciagos
ACCGIILNRTU	circulating
ACCGILLMOOY	mycological
ACCGILLOOTY	cytological
ACCGINORSTU	coruscating
ACCHHIPTTUW	catch up with
ACCHHJKNNOO	John Hancock
ACCHHLNNOOR	Loch Rannoch
ACCHHMNORUW	churchwoman
ACCHHORRTUU	Arthur Couch
ACCHIILMOST	Catholicism
ACCHIILOSST	scholiastic
ACCHIILOTTY	catholicity
ACCHIIOOPST	sociopathic
ACCHIIOPRRZ	rhizocarpic
ACCHIIPRSTY	psychiatric
ACCHILLNORY	chronically
ACCHILLPSYY	psychically
ACCHIMMRSTY	McCarthyism
ACCHINOPSTY	sycophantic
ACCHIOOPTTT	phototactic
ACCHIOORRSU	chiaroscuro
ACCHKNNOOTY	Tony Hancock
ACCHNOOOPSU	cacophonous
ACCHOOOPTTU	couch potato
ACCHOPRSTTU	up to scratch
ACCIIILNSTV	Calvinistic
ACCIIILRTTY	criticality
ACCIILLOPTY	occipitally
ACCIILNNOTU	inculcation
ACCIILNOORT	conciliator
ACCIILNORTU	circulation
ACCIILOSTUV	acclivitous
ACCIILRRTUY	circularity
ACCIINNNSTU	Cincinnatus
ACCIINORRSU	Rosicrucian
ACCIJNNOTUV	conjunctiva
ACCIKKKKNNS	knickknacks
	knick-knacks
ACCILLMOSTY	Ally McCoist
ACCILLNOOOT	collocation
ACCILLNOSSU	call cousins
ACCILLPRTYY	cryptically
ACCILMOPSTY	cytoplasmic
ACCILNOOTTU	occultation
ACCILOPRSTY	pyroclastic
ACCILOPRTTU	plutocratic
ACCILORRTUY	circulatory
ACCIMMNNOTU	communicant
ACCIMNNOOTT	concomitant
ACCIMNOTTUY	contumacity
ACCINNNOSTY	inconstancy
ACCINNOOOSS	on occasions
ACCINNOOOTV	convocation
ACCINNOOPRU	cornucopian
ACCINNOORTT	contraction
ACCINOORSTU	coruscation
ACCINOPRRSU	Capricornus
ACCKLLNOOTY	Tony Allcock
ACCKLORRSTY	rock crystal
ACCLLLOOORU	local colour
ACCLMNOOPTU	coconut palm
	coconut-palm
ACCLNNOSTUY	consultancy
ACCLOPRRSUU	corpuscular

ACCNNNOOOTU	on no account
ACCNOORTTTU	contract out
ACCORSSSTUW	crosscut saw
ACDDDEINRTU	cut and dried
	cut-and-dried
ACDDEEERRTU	reduced rate
ACDDEEFFIST	disaffected
ACDDEEGIKLR	griddle-cake
ACDDEEGIKNW	wedding cake
ACDDEEHHIKT	thick-headed
ACDDEEHILOT	load the dice
ACDDEEHIPPW	widechapped
ACDDEEHLNOS	close-handed
ACDDEEHLORT	cold-hearted
ACDDEEHNORW	crowned head
ACDDEEIKRST	sidetracked
ACDDEEIMRRV	David Mercer
ACDDEEIMSSU	Sadduceeism
ACDDEEINNNR	dinner-dance
ACDDEEMNNOR	modern dance
ACDDEENNOPT	co-dependant
ACDDEENNSST	descendants
ACDDEENORTU	undecorated
ACDDEFIILOW	codified law
ACDDEGIORSU	discouraged
ACDDEHILMMR	Middlemarch
ACDDEHLLOST	saddlecloth
ACDDEHMNRUV	Edvard Munch
ACDDEHOPPRR	dropped arch
ACDDEIIOSST	dissociated
ACDDEILLMSS	middle class
	middle-class
ACDDEILORRY	Daily Record
ACDDEINOORT	co-ordinated
ACDDEIOPSTY	Space Oddity
ACDDELNORUU	under a cloud
ACDDNOORRUW	crowd around
ACDEEEFLNRT	needlecraft
ACDEEEFNORT	confederate
ACDEEEGLLOT	décolletage
ACDEEEIKMTX	make excited
ACDEEEILNRV	deliverance□
ACDEEEIMPRT	premedicate
ACDEEEINRTV	revendicate
ACDEEEIPRTT	decrepitate
ACDEEEIPRTV	deprecative
ACDEEELLNRT	crenellated
ACDEEELLSST	Leeds Castle
ACDEEELORRT	decelerator
ACDEEERRSTT	trade secret
ACDEEFILNOP	piece of land
ACDEEFIMNOP	peace of mind
ACDEEFLNRUU	fraudulence
ACDEEFMORRS	armed forces
ACDEEFORRTT	tractor feed
ACDEEGHHPRT	depth charge
	depth-charge
ACDEEGHINSS	change sides
ACDEEGHIRRR	Richard Gere
ACDEEGHNRRU	undercharge
ACDEEGHORRV	overcharged
ACDEEGINPRT	deprecating
ACDEEGINRST	desecrating
ACDEEGIORTZ	categorized
ACDEEGKLNOW	acknowledge
ACDEEHIIMNT	Medicine Hat
ACDEEHILLTV	Edith Cavell
ACDEEHILNPP	Chippendale
ACDEEHILPSY	psychedelia
ACDEEHIMNRS	merchandise
ACDEEHIMNRZ	merchandize
ACDEEHINRTW	windcheater
ACDEEHLLMTW	well-matched
ACDEEHLLOSU	close-hauled
ACDEEHMNORW	reach-me-down
ACDEEHMNOSW	Chad Newsome
ACDEEHNPRSS	parchedness
ACDEEHNRRTU	unchartered
ACDEEIILLTV	divellicate
ACDEEIILLTY	eidetically
ACDEEIILPSZ	specialized
ACDEEIILTUV	elucidative
ACDEEIIMMNN	medicine man
ACDEEIIMRST	mediatrices
ACDEEIINPST	pedanticise
ACDEEIINPTZ	pedanticize
ACDEEIINRTV	revindicate
ACDEEIIPRTV	predicative
ACDEEIIRRRV	arrivederci
ACDEEIJLTVY	adjectively
ACDEEIJPRTU	prejudicate
ACDEEIKMRTT	dream ticket
ACDEEILLMNY	endemically
ACDEEILNNST	clandestine
ACDEEILNOTT	delectation
ACDEEILNRST	credentials
ACDEEILNTTU	denticulate
ACDEEILPRTU	reduplicate
ACDEEIMNPRT	predicament
ACDEEIMORST	democratise
ACDEEIMORTZ	democratize
ACDEEIMOSTT	domesticate
ACDEEINNRST	disentrance
ACDEEINOPRT	deprecation
ACDEEINORST	considerate
	desecration
ACDEEINORTU	re-education
ACDEEIORRTT	directorate
ACDEEJMNRTU	muntjac deer
ACDEEKLLSTW	well-stacked
ACDEEKLORVW	covered walk
ACDEEKQRRTU	quarter deck
	quarterdeck
ACDEELMNOTU	Claude Monet
ACDEELMORRS	scleroderma
ACDEELNOSTU	Doune Castle
ACDEELNPTUU	pedunculate
ACDEELNRRSY	dry cleaner's
ACDEELOORTW	water-cooled
ACDEELRSTTY	scatteredly
ACDEELSSTUY	decussately
ACDEEMNNOOT	come to an end

ACDEEMNOPSS	encompassed
ACDEEMNRTTU	traducement
ACDEEOPRRTY	deprecatory
ACDEFFIIRTV	diffractive
ACDEFFIRSST	scared stiff
ACDEFGILRSU	disgraceful
ACDEFHILPST	feldspathic
ACDEFIIINNT	infanticide
ACDEFIIINOT	deification
	edification
ACDEFILORST	Fidel Castro
ACDEFINNOTU	fecundation
ACDEFLLMMRU	crammed full
ACDEFLLMOTT	mottled calf
ACDEFLLNORU	full-acorned
	uncalled-for
ACDEFLMMNOS	self-command
ACDEFLNRUUY	fraudulency
ACDEFLOPTUY	place of duty
ACDEFMOORRW	come forward
ACDEFMORRTT	detract from
ACDEGHHIOWY	Highway Code
ACDEGHHIRTW	charged with
ACDEGHIILNP	hiding-place
ACDEGHIIOPR	ideographic
ACDEGHILLNT	candlelight
ACDEGHIMOPR	demographic
ACDEGHINNOT	changed into
ACDEGHNNORU	change round
ACDEGIILLOO	ideological
ACDEGIKNNPS	send packing
ACDEGIMORTY	tragicomedy
ACDEGLOORST	cold storage
ACDEHIIKMNT	kitchenmaid
ACDEHIIMNNW	wind machine
ACDEHIIOPRT	diaphoretic
ACDEHIKLNSU	and suchlike
ACDEHILLLPY	delphically
ACDEHILOPTV	hold captive
ACDEHILRSSY	chrysalides
ACDEHILRSTT	stilted arch
ACDEHIMMNRU	drum machine
ACDEHIMOPRS	comradeship
ACDEHIMOSTU	mustachioed
ACDEHINOORS	icosahedron
ACDEHIOOPRT	orthopaedic
ACDEHIPSTTY	dyspathetic
ACDEHJLLNNO	John Cleland
ACDEHKLNNST	landsknecht
ACDEHKMRSTU	Deutschmark
ACDEHLLLOPY	phylloclade
ACDEHLNPRTU	thunderclap
ACDEHLRSTTY	Strathclyde
ACDEHMOORTW	doomwatcher
ACDEHNOORST	octahedrons
ACDEHNORSSZ	scherzandos
ACDEHORRTWW	draw the crow
ACDEIIILMOT	domiciliate
ACDEIIINTVV	vindicative
ACDEIIJLPRU	prejudicial
ACDEIIKNRST	inside track
ACDEIILLMNY	medicinally
ACDEIILLNTY	identically
ACDEIILLRVY	veridically
ACDEIILLSTY	deistically
ACDEIILMNOT	malediction
ACDEIILMPRS	spermicidal
ACDEIILNNOS	Nico Ladenis
ACDEIILNNOT	declination
ACDEIILNNST	incidentals
ACDEIILNORT	directional
ACDEIILNOTU	elucidation
ACDEIILNOTV	valediction
ACDEIILNPTU	in duplicate
ACDEIILOPRW	periodic law
ACDEIILORRT	directorial
ACDEIILRTUV	diverticula
ACDEIIMORTU	audiometric
ACDEIIMPRRU	pericardium
ACDEIINOPRT	predication
ACDEIINORRT	doctrinaire
ACDEIINOTTX	intoxicated
ACDEIINPRSS	Princess Ida
ACDEIINPRST	practised in
ACDEIINRTTX	indirect tax
ACDEIKLQRUY	read quickly
ACDEILMNOSU	Claude Simon
ACDEILMORTY	maledictory
ACDEILNNOSY	Coney Island
ACDEILNOOST	consolidate
ACDEILNORSY	secondarily
ACDEILOORRS	social order
ACDEILORTUY	elucidatory
ACDEILORTVY	valedictory
ACDEIMNOOPT	Capodimonte
ACDEIMNORRS	morris dance
	morris-dance
ACDEINNORST	constrained
ACDEINNORTU	denunciator
ACDEINOORST	coordinates
	co-ordinates
	decorations
ACDEINOPSTT	constipated
ACDEINOSTTU	outdistance
ACDEINPRSTU	unpractised
ACDEINPRSTY	candy stripe
ACDEINRRVYZ	driven crazy
ACDEIOPRSSY	caryopsides
ACDEIRSTTUY	daisy-cutter
ACDEJORRTUU	carte du jour
ACDEKLNNOST	Ken Scotland
ACDELLOORRT	call to order
ACDELMNOTTU	laced mutton
ACDELOPRTTY	pterodactyl
ACDEMMMNNOT	commandment
ACDEMMNOSTU	consummated
ACDEMNNORTU	countermand
ACDEMNORTUY	documentary
ACDEMOORSTW	come towards
ACDEMOPRSSU	mass-produce
ACDENNNNOUU	unannounced
ACDENNOOPRU	ponce around

ACDENOORSTY	secondary to
ACDENORRTUW	counterdraw
ACDEOOPRSTU	cause to drop
ACDEORRSSST	star-crossed
ACDFFGIINNT	fact-finding
ACDFFGILNOS	scaffolding
ACDFFIILMOO	officialdom
ACDFFIINORT	diffraction
ACDFIMMNNOO	in command of
ACDFOORRTUW	ward of court
ACDGGHIINRS	discharging
ACDGHIIINNR	dining-chair
ACDGHILNORR	Richard Long
ACDGHIOPRSY	discography
ACDGIIILMNS	disclaiming
ACDGIIINNTV	vindicating
ACDGIIKNPRS	disc parking
ACDGIILNPTU	duplicating
ACDGIINOPRR	road pricing
ACDGIINRSTT	distracting
ACDGIIORSSU	disgracious
ACDGIKNNORW	knowing card
ACDGILNRTUY	traducingly
ACDGIMNNOPU	up and coming
	up-and-coming
ACDGINOORVW	woodcarving
ACDHHIKNRRU	Richard Kuhn
ACDHHIOPRRS	harpsichord
ACDHHIOPRTY	hydropathic
ACDHIINOOPR	radiophonic
ACDHIIRRSVV	Viv Richards
ACDHIMNOORT	trichomonad
ACDHIOPRSTT	drop a stitch
ACDHIORSTTY	hydrostatic
ACDHLLOOOOW	wood alcohol
ACDHLNNSUUY	Sunday lunch
ACDHLNOOORT	notochordal
ACDHLOORSSW	schoolwards
ACDIIILLOTY	idiotically
ACDIIILMORY	domiciliary
ACDIIINNOST	indications
ACDIIINNOTV	vindication
ACDIIJLLRUY	juridically
ACDIIKLOPST	optical disk
ACDIILLLLYY	idyllically
ACDIILMNOPR	palindromic
ACDIILMNSSY	syndicalism
ACDIILNNOOT	conditional
ACDIILNNOTU	inductional
ACDIILNOOST	dislocation
ACDIILNOPTU	duplication
ACDIILNSSTY	syndicalist
ACDIIMORSTY	myocarditis
ACDIINNOSTY	syndication
ACDIINORSTT	distraction
ACDIINORSTU	nitrous acid
ACDIINORTVY	vindicatory
ACDIKKPSTUU	kick up a dust
ACDIKLNOOSS	Cook Islands
ACDIKNOPRTW	Downpatrick
ACDIKNORSTU	stick around
ACDILLNORTY	doctrinally
ACDILLNOSYY	synodically
ACDILLORSTY	crystalloid
ACDILNOSSTU	locus standi
ACDINNNOOOT	condonation
ACDINOOORRT	co-ordinator
ACDKKNNOORU	knock around
ACDKLLNOORR	rock and roll
ACDLMNNOOPW	clamp down on
ACDLNNOORUW	clown around
ACDMMNOOPST	command post
ACDMNOOOPUZ	azo-compound
ACDMORRSSUU	Sursum Corda
ACDOPRRSTUY	drop a curtsy
ACEEEEFLLNV	Lee Van Cleef
ACEEEEFNNRT	entrance fee
ACEEEEHLPSW	escape wheel
ACEEEEHPRRS	cheeseparer
ACEEEEKPRST	keep a secret
ACEEEFFFRTT	after effect
	after-effect
ACEEEFFKNOT	take offence
ACEEEFHLNRV	French leave
ACEEEFIOPPP	pipe of peace
ACEEEFKLOPR	keep clear of
ACEEEFLMRSW	female screw
ACEEEGGORRY	George Carey
ACEEEGHRRST	Three Graces
ACEEEGIMNNR	generic name
ACEEEGIMNST	miscegenate
ACEEEGLOTTT	telecottage
ACEEEGMNOPR	peace-monger
ACEEEGNRSTT	centre stage
	secret agent
ACEEEHIIMPR	epicheirema
ACEEEHIMNTV	achievement
ACEEEHIORVV	overachieve
ACEEEHKLNRT	leather-neck
ACEEEHKMPRS	speech-maker
ACEEEHLLNRT	chanterelle
ACEEEHMNNNT	enhancement
ACEEEHPRSTT	teacher's pet
ACEEEHRSSTW	cheese straw
ACEEEILMNPS	mise en place
ACEEEILMNPT	mantelpiece
ACEEEILNPPR	pipe-cleaner
ACEEEILNQUV	equivalence
ACEEEILNRRV	irrelevance
ACEEEIMPRST	masterpiece
ACEEEINPRST	rest in peace
ACEEEINRSSS	necessaries
ACEEEINSSTT	necessitate
ACEEEJKLPST	steeplejack
ACEEEKLLNRU	Lake Lucerne
ACEEELLMNOV	malevolence
ACEEELLRSTT	tell a secret
ACEEELLSSSY	ceaselessly
ACEEELMMNPT	emplacement
ACEEELMNPRT	replacement
ACEEELMNRTX	excremental
ACEEELNORST	Rene LaCoste

ACEEENRRSSV	screen saver
ACEEEOPRTTX	expectorate
ACEEFFFNOOS	off one's face
ACEEFFHINOT	in the face of
ACEEFFIILOS	officialese
ACEEFFILNTU	ineffectual
ACEEFFILTVY	affectively
ACEEFFLLTUY	effectually
ACEEFHINNRS	enfranchise
ACEEFHINORT	in the care of
ACEEFHLLOOR	alcohol-free
ACEEFHMORRT	form teacher
ACEEFHNRRTU	furtherance
ACEEFIKOPSS	kiss of peace
ACEEFILLNVY	venefically
ACEEFILNRSU	increaseful
ACEEFILRSTV	service flat
ACEEFIMNORS	Freemasonic
ACEEFIMNTTU	tumefacient
ACEEFINRSSY	if necessary
ACEEFKKOPRT	keep track of
ACEEFKMOPRT	pomfret cake
ACEEFLLNRST	crestfallen
ACEEFLLNRUU	nuclear fuel
ACEEFLNRSSU	carefulness
ACEEFLRRSTY	Carl Seyfert
ACEEFMNOPRR	performance
ACEEGGHNOOR	George Cohan
ACEEGGIMNOT	geomagnetic
ACEEGGLORSU	George Lucas
ACEEGHHORSU	charge-house
ACEEGHHPRRY	hypercharge
ACEEGHILPRT	telegraphic
ACEEGHINNRT	interchange
ACEEGHINRRS	researching
ACEEGHJORVZ	Jorge Chavez
ACEEGHLLNRS	challengers
ACEEGHLNOOS	loose change
ACEEGHLOPST	close the gap
ACEEGHMMORT	hectogramme
ACEEGHNRRSU	charge nurse
ACEEGHNRRTY	entry charge
ACEEGHORTTT	act together
ACEEGHPRRSU	supercharge
ACEEGIINPRR	ear-piercing
ACEEGIKNNPP	kneecapping
ACEEGILLNRS	selling race
ACEEGILLNRY	generically
ACEEGILLNTY	genetically
ACEEGILLNUY	eugenically
ACEEGILMNRS	single cream
ACEEGILMORT	geometrical
ACEEGILNOPV	peace-loving
ACEEGILNPRS	sleeping car
ACEEGILOPTV	give place to
ACEEGILSTTU	gesticulate
ACEEGIMMNRT	centigramme
ACEEGINNORS	Grecian nose
ACEEGINORTT	teratogenic
ACEEGKNORRT	rocket range
ACEEGLLRSSY	gracelessly
ACEEGLMNNOT	congealment
ACEEGLMNORS	camerlengos
ACEEGMNORRS	scaremonger
ACEEGMORSTU	come a gutser
ACEEGNNOSST	cognateness
ACEEGNORSSV	Geneva cross
ACEEHHIRTTT	Thatcherite
ACEEHHMMSTU	much the same
ACEEHHMNRTT	The Merchant
ACEEHHNORST	sheet-anchor
ACEEHHOPTTY	hypothecate
ACEEHIIKLMN	machine-like
ACEEHIILNST	antihelices
ACEEHIINNRT	inheritance
ACEEHIIPPRT	perihepatic
ACEEHIIRSTT	theatricise
ACEEHIIRTTZ	theatricize
ACEEHIKNRTW	kitchenware
ACEEHILLNNP	panhellenic
ACEEHILLRTY	heretically
ACEEHILMNOW	Michael Owen
ACEEHILMOPR	hemeralopic
ACEEHILNRTT	chain letter
	threnetical
ACEEHILNSST	ethicalness
ACEEHILORTT	theoretical
ACEEHILRSSV	Charles Ives
ACEEHIMMNPT	impeachment
ACEEHIMNNNT	enchainment
ACEEHIMNNSU	unmechanise
ACEEHIMNNUZ	unmechanize
ACEEHINNSTZ	Nietzschean
ACEEHINORTT	The Creation
ACEEHINPRSS	preachiness
ACEEHINPRTT	parenthetic
ACEEHIOPRST	spirochaete
ACEEHIPRRST	Petrarchise
ACEEHIPRRTZ	Petrarchize
ACEEHIPRTTU	therapeutic
ACEEHIPRTVY	hyperactive
ACEEHJLNORR	John Le Carré
ACEEHKNNSSY	Hans Eysenck
ACEEHKNOPTW	keep watch on
ACEEHLLNTTU	call the tune
ACEEHLLQRUW	Raquel Welch
ACEEHLOPPTU	the populace
ACEEHMMNNRT	merchantmen
ACEEHMNNNTT	enchantment
ACEEHMNNRRT	trencherman
ACEEHMNORVY	have mercy on
ACEEHNNRSST	enchantress
ACEEHNOPRTT	on the carpet
ACEEHORRSTT	orchestrate
ACEEHORRSTU	treacherous
ACEEIIKNNTZ	Citizen Kane
ACEEIIKRSTT	rickettsiae
ACEEIILLNPT	penicillate
ACEEIILLNRT	rectilineal
ACEEIILNRRT	rectilinear
ACEEIILPRSU	peculiarise
ACEEIILPRSZ	specializer

ACEEIILPRUZ	peculiarize
ACEEIILPTVX	explicative
ACEEIIMNRRT	recriminate
ACEEIINRSST	canisterise
ACEEIINRSTZ	canisterize
ACEEIINRTTV	interactive
ACEEIIPPRTT	peripatetic
	precipitate
ACEEIIRSSTT	cassiterite
ACEEIJNNRTT	interjacent
ACEEIKLMNRT	Maeterlinck
ACEEIKNSSSS	seasickness
ACEEILLLSTY	celestially
ACEEILLNNRS	Carl Nielsen
ACEEILLNNSS	cleanliness
ACEEILLNPST	splenetical
ACEEILLOPST	all to pieces
ACEEILMNNRT	incremental
ACEEILMNORT	Trincomalee
ACEEILMNOSS	Monica Seles
ACEEILMNRRY	mercenarily
ACEEILMORRT	calorimeter
ACEEILMORST	elastomeric
ACEEILMPSST	esemplastic
ACEEILMPSTU	time capsule
ACEEILMRTUV	vermiculate
ACEEILNNORT	intolerance
ACEEILNNTUY	lieutenancy
ACEEILNOPTX	exceptional
ACEEILNORSS	recessional
ACEEILNPRTT	centripetal
ACEEILNPSSS	specialness
ACEEILNPTTY	pectinately
ACEEILNRRVY	irrelevancy
ACEEILNRSSY	necessarily
ACEEILNRTTY	Eternal City
ACEEILOPSTT	police state
ACEEILORRTV	correlative
ACEEILORTUX	executorial
ACEEILOTVVY	evocatively
ACEEILPSTUV	speculative
ACEEIMMORST	commiserate
ACEEIMNNOTT	cementation
ACEEIMNQRTU	acquirement
ACEEINNSSTX	inexactness
ACEEINOORRU	iure coronae
ACEEINOPTTX	expectation
ACEEINORSST	estancieros
ACEEINPRRST	transpierce
ACEEINRRSTV	transceiver
ACEEIOOPRTV	co-operative
ACEEIOPRRTV	procreative
ACEEIORRTTV	retroactive
	retro-active
ACEEIORSSTU	cause to rise
ACEEIPRRSTW	space writer
ACEEIRSSTTU	resuscitate
ACEEJMNNORS	Carmen Jones
ACEEKKLMRSY	mackerel sky
ACEEKKPRRRY	Kerry Packer
ACEEKMNNSTT	Mack Sennett
ACEEKMNOPPY	keep company
ACEEKNRSTTV	track events
ACEEKPRRSST	racket-press
ACEELLMNRSS	small screen
ACEELLNORTY	coeternally
ACEELLNOSTT	constellate
ACEELLRSSTY	tracelessly
ACEELLSSSUY	causelessly
ACEELMMNORS	Carlos Menem
ACEELMNNOOV	monovalence
ACEELMNOPTT	contemplate
ACEELMORTXY	more exactly
ACEELNNNSSU	uncleanness
ACEELNNRSSU	unclearness
ACEELNOOPRT	coleopteran
ACEELNOOSSS	close season
ACEELNOPSTT	Pentecostal
ACEELNORSTU	counterseal
ACEELNOSTWY	wet one's clay
ACEELNPTTXY	expectantly
ACEELOPPPRT	copperplate
ACEELORSTTW	water closet
ACEEMMMOORT	commemorate
ACEEMNNORTU	connumerate
ACEEMNORTTU	meat counter
ACEEMOPRTTU	computerate
ACEENNNORSY	Sean Connery
ACEENNOPRTU	counterpane
ACEENNORSTT	consternate
ACEENNRSSUY	unnecessary
ACEENOORSTT	cotoneaster
ACEENOPRTTX	expectorant
ACEEORRSTUW	watercourse
ACEEPRRSSUU	acupressure
ACEFFFILOST	facts of life
ACEFFGHILNR	cliffhanger
	cliff-hanger
ACEFFGILNTY	affectingly
ACEFFHKORTT	off the track
ACEFFIILPST	spifflicate
ACEFFIITTVY	affectivity
ACEFFILOSST	last offices
ACEFFIOSTUV	suffocative
ACEFFORSSTU	soft surface
ACEFGGIMNOO	coming of age
ACEFGHLLNOT	focal length
ACEFGHLLNUY	changefully
ACEFGHNNORT	change front
ACEFGHNOOTU	change out of
ACEFGIIMNNT	magnificent
ACEFGIIMNOS	magnificoes
ACEFGIINNRT	interfacing
ACEFGILNRTU	centrifugal
ACEFGILNTTU	leaf-cutting
ACEFGINORST	forecasting
ACEFGINORTU	configurate
ACEFGMNNORY	fancy monger
ACEFHHINRSS	Hans Fischer
ACEFHIILNOR	Nicole Farhi
ACEFHIJLMOX	Michael J Fox
ACEFHILMOOT	Michael Foot

ACEFHILORRT trefoil arch
ACEFHILRSTY self-charity
ACEFHIRSTTY city fathers
ACEFHLOPRRU reproachful
ACEFHMNNORW Frenchwoman
ACEFHNNOOPR francophone
ACEFHNORSTT French toast
ACEFHOORSUU hour of cause
ACEFIIIMNRT rifacimenti
ACEFIIINORT reification
ACEFIILNNSS finicalness
ACEFIILNRTV vertical fin
ACEFIILPRSU superficial
ACEFIINOPTT pontificate
ACEFIINORST fractionise
ACEFIINORSU facinerious
ACEFIINORTZ fractionize
ACEFILLORUW cauliflower
ACEFILMMOTU comme il faut
ACEFILORSST trace fossil
ACEFILOSTUY facetiously
ACEFIMNOTTU tumefaction
ACEFINNORST for instance
ACEFINPRSTY presanctify
ACEFINRRRTU franc-tireur
ACEFKKOOSTT take stock of
ACEFKLOOPRW place of work
ACEFKLOORST lose track of
ACEFKORRSUW work surface
ACEFLNSSTTU tactfulness
ACEFOOPSTTX ex post facto
ACEGGHILLNN challenging
ACEGGINNORU encouraging
ACEGGINRSSS scragginess
ACEGGKLORSU Georg Lukács
ACEGGLNOOYY gynaecology
ACEGHHILRST searchlight
ACEGHHIMORZ Chaim Herzog
ACEGHHINORW weigh anchor
ACEGHHITTWW weight-watch
ACEGHHMNRRU hunger march
ACEGHHNORST short-change
ACEGHHOOPRR choreograph
ACEGHIILPRX lexigraphic
ACEGHIKMNOP epoch-making
ACEGHILLOOR rheological
ACEGHILLOOT theological
ACEGHILNOST a close thing
ACEGHILNRSY searchingly
ACEGHILOPSY geophysical
ACEGHIMNORU archegonium
ACEGHIMNRSY crying shame
ACEGHINORRS horse-racing
ACEGHINORRV overarching
ACEGHINPRSS graphicness
ACEGHINPRTU put in charge
ACEGHIOPRRX xerographic
ACEGHIRRTWY carry weight
ACEGHLOOSTY eschatology
ACEGHOOPRSU creophagous
ACEGHOOPSTY phagocytose
ACEGIIKKOTV give a kick to
ACEGIIKLNRS arse-licking
ACEGIIKNPRS asking price
ACEGIILLNNV clean-living
ACEGIILNNRT interlacing
ACEGIILOSTT egotistical
ACEGIILRSST sacrilegist
ACEGIIMNPST camping-site
ACEGIIMRRTV gravimetric
ACEGIINRRRR ring-carrier
ACEGIKLNNOT Nat King Cole
ACEGILLMRTU metallurgic
ACEGILLNNOY congenially
ACEGILLNOOO oenological
ACEGILLNOOP penological
ACEGILLOORS serological
ACEGILMNORS camerlingos
ACEGILMNRSY screamingly
ACEGILNNNOU uncongenial
ACEGILNNOOT congelation
ACEGILNNPRS spring-clean
ACEGILNNSUY unceasingly
ACEGILNOORS Nicolas Roeg
ACEGILNORRS carol-singer
ACEGILNRSSY caressingly
ACEGILNTUUU unguiculate
ACEGILPRRSS garlic press
ACEGILRRTUU agriculture
ACEGIMNNOOT cognominate
ACEGINNNOSU consanguine
ACEGINNRSTY astringency
ACEGINNSSTW newscasting
ACEGINOOPRT co-operating
ACEGINORTTU gut reaction
ACEGIORSSTT get it across
ACEGKRSSTTU stage-struck
ACEGLLOSTYY glycosylate
ACEGLMNORWY clergywoman
ACEGLNORTUY granulocyte
ACEGMNNORSS congressman
ACEGMNOORRR Roger Corman
ACEGMOPRRST spectrogram
ACEGNOORRTT gerontocrat
ACEGOOPRSST gastroscope
ACEGRRSSTTU grass-cutter
ACEHHIIMRRS hierarchism
ACEHHIINNTY hyacinthine
ACEHHIINRTW within reach
ACEHHILLPRU Paul Ehrlich
ACEHHIMOOPT homeopathic
ACEHHIMRSTT Thatcherism
ACEHHINRRST Hans Richter
ACEHHLNOORT anthochlore
ACEHHMNNSUU Münchhausen
ACEHHMOOTUV have too much
ACEHHOORSTY chaos theory
ACEHIIINPSS hispanicise
ACEHIIINPSZ hispanicize
ACEHIILLMOT homiletical
ACEHIILMSTT athleticism
ACEHIILNOPR necrophilia

ACEHIILNPST	in this place
ACEHIILRSVW	swivel-chair
ACEHIIMRSTT	arithmetics
	theatricism
ACEHIIMSSST	schismatise
ACEHIIMSSTZ	schismatize
ACEHIINNOPT	phonetician
ACEHIINNTTU	inauthentic
ACEHIINORRT	rhetorician
ACEHIINPSTT	pantheistic
ACEHIKLPRRS	parish clerk
ACEHIKLPRTY	prickly heat
ACEHIKMNORS	chain-smoker
ACEHIKMRTUY	rheumaticky
ACEHILLMRTY	thermically
ACEHILLORTW	white-collar
ACEHILLPRSY	spherically
ACEHILMNOOT	machine tool
ACEHILMPSTW	Limp Watches
ACEHILNORSU	A Chorus Line
ACEHILNPRST	sphincteral
ACEHILOPSTT	to this place
ACEHILRSSSY	chrysalises
ACEHIMMNSTU	The Music Man
ACEHIMMOPRT	metamorphic
ACEHIMNORSS	marchioness
ACEHIMNOSYY	hyoscyamine
ACEHIMOPRST	atmospheric
ACEHIMOPRTW	compare with
ACEHIMORRST	choirmaster
ACEHIMPSSTY	metaphysics
ACEHIMPSTTY	sympathetic
ACEHINNNRTT	intrenchant
ACEHINNOOTT	canine tooth
ACEHINNPSSU	paunchiness
ACEHINNRSSU	raunchiness
ACEHINOOPRZ	Phanerozoic
ACEHINOPRRS	chairperson
ACEHINORRSU	hurricanoes
ACEHINPSSTT	pentastichs
ACEHINRSSST	starchiness
ACEHINSSSTT	cattishness
ACEHIOOPSTT	osteopathic
ACEHIOPPRST	Hippocrates
ACEHIPRRSST	strip search
ACEHKNOSSTU	Stockhausen
ACEHKOPRSST	stock phrase
ACEHLLMRSSY	charmlessly
ACEHLLMSSTY	matchlessly
ACEHLNNRTTY	trenchantly
ACEHLNORSTW	Charlestown
ACEHLOOSSTT	state school
ACEHLPPPRTU	purple patch
ACEHMNRRTTU	return match
ACEHMOORTTY	tracheotomy
ACEHNNSSSTU	staunchness
ACEHNOORSTT	on that score
ACEHOOPRRST	prothoraces
ACEHOPRRSSY	chrysoprase
ACEHORSSTTV	torch-staves
ACEIIIILNSV	civilianise
ACEIIIILNVZ	civilianize
ACEIIILMNRS	criminalise
ACEIIILMNRZ	criminalize
ACEIIILMPTV	implicative
ACEIIILNOTT	elicitation
ACEIIIMNNRT	incriminate
ACEIIIMNSTT	anti-Semitic
ACEIIIQSTUV	acquisitive
ACEIIKLLNNV	Calvin Klein
ACEIIKLLOOR	kilocalorie
ACEIIKLRSTT	rickettsial
ACEIIKNRSSS	airsickness
ACEIIKRSSTT	rickettsias
ACEIILLLTVY	levitically
ACEIILLMMTY	mimetically
ACEIILLMNNU	illuminance
ACEIILLMPRY	empirically
ACEIILLNSTT	scintillate
ACEIILMNSSU	masculinise
ACEIILMNSUZ	masculinize
ACEIILNNNNO	on an incline
ACEIILNOPRT	replication
ACEIILNOPTX	explication
ACEIILNOQTU	equinoctial
ACEIILNOSSV	Slavonicise
ACEIILNOSVZ	Slavonicize
ACEIILNOTUV	inoculative
ACEIILNPRUY	pecuniarily
ACEIILNRRUV	curvilinear
ACEIILNRSTU	unrealistic
ACEIILNRTTY	intricately
ACEIILPPRST	psi particle
ACEIILPRSST	plasticiser
ACEIILPRSTT	peristaltic
ACEIILPRSTZ	plasticizer
ACEIILPRTUY	peculiarity
ACEIILRTTVY	verticality
ACEIIMNNORS	Micronesian
ACEIIMNOPRT	imprecation
ACEIIMNORST	Creationism
	miscreation
	romanticise
ACEIIMNORTZ	romanticize
ACEIIMNPRRU	pericranium
ACEIIMNPSSU	impuissance
ACEIIMNSSTT	semanticist
ACEIINNNOTU	enunciation
ACEIINNOPST	case in point
ACEIINNOPTT	pectination
ACEIINNORRT	incinerator
ACEIINNORTT	interaction
ACEIINOORTX	excoriation
ACEIINOPRTT	crepitation
ACEIINORSTT	creationist
ACEIINORTTX	extrication
ACEIINPRTTY	antipyretic
	pertinacity
ACEIIORSTTV	recitativos
ACEIJMMRRTY	Jimmy Carter
ACEIJNRSUUY	cause injury
ACEIKKLMQUY	make quickly

ACEIKKLNPTY	penalty kick
ACEIKKMOSUY	make you sick
ACEIKKNOSTT	take stock in
ACEIKLORTTW	latticework
	lattice-work
ACEIKLPPRRY	prickly pear
ACEIKMNOOST	ask to come in
ACEIKNOPSWY	pick one's way
ACEIKPRSSTU	Sitka spruce
ACEIKQSSSTU	quick assets
ACEILLLMNOR	lamellicorn
ACEILLLMOPY	polemically
ACEILLLNRUU	unicellular
ACEILLLRSTW	Will Scarlet
ACEILLMNNOT	non-metallic
ACEILLMNOOV	Monaco-Ville
ACEILLMNRUY	numerically
ACEILLMNSUY	masculinely
ACEILLMPRRY	primary cell
ACEILLMRRUY	mercurially
ACEILLNNOTY	octennially
ACEILLNORST	Sir Lancelot
ACEILLNOSTY	sectionally
ACEILLNOTTY	tonetically
ACEILLNRSTY	crystalline
ACEILLOPPSY	episcopally
ACEILLOPSSW	pillowcases
ACEILLOPTTY	act politely
ACEILLOQUVY	equivocally
ACEILLORTVY	vectorially
ACEILLRRTUY	reticularly
ACEILLRSSTY	crystallise
ACEILLRSTYZ	crystallize
ACEILLRTUVY	lucratively
ACEILMMNOSU	communalise
ACEILMMNOTY	metonymical
ACEILMMNOUZ	communalize
ACEILMMRSTY	symmetrical
ACEILMNNSUU	unmasculine
ACEILMNOOPS	scopolamine
ACEILMNOOPW	policewoman
ACEILMNRTTU	curtailment
ACEILMNSSSU	musicalness
ACEILNNNOSS	nonsensical
ACEILNNNOTT	continental
ACEILNNOOPT	Neoplatonic
ACEILNNRTUY	uncertainly
ACEILNNSSTY	incessantly
ACEILNOOPRR	incorporeal
ACEILNOOPRT	neotropical
	percolation
ACEILNOORRT	correlation
ACEILNOORTU	unicolorate
ACEILNOPSST	lost in space
ACEILNOPSTU	speculation
ACEILNOPTUX	exculpation
ACEILNOQUUV	unequivocal
ACEILNORSTT	intercostal
ACEILNORTUV	countervail
	involucrate
ACEILNOSTUY	tenaciously
ACEILNRRTUV	ventricular
ACEILOOPPRU	colour a pipe
ACEILOPRRTT	protractile
ACEILOPRTXY	explicatory
ACEILORSUVY	veraciously
ACEILPRSTTY	spectrality
ACEILQRTUUU	aquiculture
ACEIMMORRTU	crematorium
ACEIMMOTTUV	commutative
ACEIMMPRSSU	supremacism
ACEIMNNNOTT	containment
ACEIMNOSSST	in most cases
ACEIMOPRRTY	imprecatory
ACEIMPRSSTU	supremacist
ACEIMSSSTTY	systematics
ACEINNNNSSU	uncanniness
ACEINNNOSTT	Constantine
ACEINNOOTTV	connotative
ACEINNOSSTT	cast in stone
ACEINNRSSSW	scrawniness
ACEINNRTTUY	uncertainty
ACEINOOOPRT	co-operation
ACEINOOPRRT	incorporate
	procreation
ACEINOOPRTU	aponeurotic
ACEINOPPRTU	put a price on
ACEINOPRSTU	precautions
ACEINORRTTY	contrariety
ACEINORSTTV	contrastive
ACEINORSUUV	unveracious
ACEINPPRSSS	scrappiness
ACEINRSSSSU	narcissuses
ACEIOOPRTVV	provocative
ACEIOOQRTUV	equivocator
ACEIOPRRRTT	Port Cartier
ACEIOPRRSTT	triceratops □
ACEJKLLRSSU	Jack Russell
ACEKKLOPTTU	take pot luck
ACEKKMORSTT	stock market
ACEKLLRSSTY	tracklessly
ACEKLOPSSTU	pale tussock
ACEKOORTTTU	take to court
ACELLLMORUY	molecularly
ACELLMMNOSY	commensally
ACELLMPRTTU	trumpet call
ACELLNORSUY	larcenously
ACELLNOSSSU	callousness
ACELLNRTTUY	reluctantly
ACELLOOPRRY	corporeally
ACELLSSSUUU	Aulus Celsus
ACELMNNOORU	mononuclear
ACELMNNOOVY	monovalency
ACELMRSTUUU	musculature
ACELNNOOPVX	plano-convex
ACELNNRSTTU	translucent
ACELNORSUVY	cavernously
ACELNOSSSUV	calvousness
ACELNOSSTTU	sansculotte
ACELNOSTTTU	talent scout
ACELNPRTTTU	plantcutter
ACELOOPRRTY	corporately

Words marked □ can also be spelled with an initial capital letter

ACELOORRTUW	watercolour
ACELOOSSTTY	stay close to
ACELOPPRRTY	act properly
ACELOPRTUXY	exculpatory
ACELORSTTTW	Walter Scott
ACEMMNOORTT	commentator
ACEMMNOPRTT	compartment
ACEMOOOPSTT	come to a stop
ACEMORRSUYY	Seymour Cray
ACENNORRSTZ	Rosencrantz
ACENNOSSTTT	contestants
ACENOORRSTV	conservator
ACENOPPRSTU	supportance
ACENOPRRSTU	Procrustean
ACENOPRRSUU	run up a score
ACENOPRRTTU	counterpart
ACENORSSSUU	raucousness
ACENORSTTUY	country seat
ACENOSSSUUV	vacuousness
ACENPRRSSTU	pass current
ACEORSSSSSY	syssarcoses
ACEOSTTTUUW	cut out waste
ACFFFIKKOOR	for a kick-off
ACFFGGILNNO	glancing-off
ACFFGIIKNRT	trafficking
ACFFGINOSTU	suffocating
ACFFIIILMOS	officialism
ACFFINOOSTU	suffocation
ACFGIIINNST	significant
ACFGILLMOPY	Olympic Flag
ACFGILNTTUU	fluctuating
ACFGINNOOTZ	cognizant of
ACFGINRSSTU	surfcasting
ACFHIINSUVV	Vivian Fuchs
ACFHKOPRSWZ	Schwarzkopf
ACFHLMOSSTU	stomachfuls
ACFHOOPRSTY	factory shop
ACFIIILLMRY	mirifically
ACFIIINNOTU	unification
ACFIILMNORU	californium
ACFIILMORST	formalistic
ACFIILMSSSY	misclassify
ACFIILNOPST	pontificals
ACFIIMNOORT	formication
ACFIIMNORST	informatics
ACFIINNOORT	fornication
ACFIKKPSSUU	kick up a fuss
ACFILMNNOTU	malfunction
ACFILMORTUY	family court
ACFILNOTTUU	fluctuation
ACFILORSTUY	fractiously
ACFINNOOTTU	confutation
ACFINNORSTW	Francistown
ACFINNORTUY	functionary
ACFINOOOTTU	out of action
ACFIOOTTTTU	cut it too fat
ACFORRRUUVY	curry favour
ACGGHILOOPR	graphologic
ACGGILOSTWY	Glasgow City
ACGHHIILLMN	Chillingham
ACGHHILOOPR	holographic
ACGHHIOPRRY	chirography
ACGHHNOOPRR	chronograph
ACGHIILMNPT	itching palm
ACGHIILMORT	algorithmic
	logarithmic
ACGHIIMNNOP	championing
ACGHIIPRSST	sphragistic
ACGHIKLNNSU	unshackling
ACGHIKMOPRY	kymographic
ACGHILLOOOR	horological
ACGHILMOOST	logomachist
ACGHILNNSTY	snatchingly
ACGHILNOSTT	cast light on
ACGHIMNOOPR	gramophonic
	monographic
	nomographic
ACGHINOOPRS	nosographic
ACGHINOOPRY	iconography
ACGHINPRSTW	watchspring
ACGHIOOPPRT	topographic
ACGHIOPPRTY	pictography
	typographic
ACGHIOPRSTY	hypogastric
ACGHIRSSTTW	twitch grass
ACGHLOOPRRU	choral group
ACGHMOORRUX	Groucho Marx
ACGHNOOOPRR	coronograph
ACGHOPPRRTY	cryptograph
ACGIIILMNPT	implicating
ACGIIILNOSZ	socializing
ACGIIKLMNPS	lip-smacking
ACGIILLLLOY	illogically
ACGIILLLNRW	Will Carling
ACGIILLNOST	oscillating
ACGIILLOORV	virological
ACGIILMNNOP	complaining
ACGIILMNNTU	culminating
ACGIIMNOSST	agnosticism
ACGIINNNOST	incognisant
ACGIINNNOTZ	incognizant
ACGIINNOSTW	wainscoting
ACGIINORRTY	tragic irony
ACGIJJKMNPU	jumping-jack
ACGIJLNOTUY	conjugality
ACGIJNNOOTU	conjugation
ACGIKKNOSTT	stocktaking
ACGILLMOORS	oscillogram
ACGILLMOOTY	climatology
ACGILLNOOOS	nosological
ACGILLNOOOT	ontological
ACGILLNOSTY	gnostically
ACGILLNRRYY	rallying cry
	rallying-cry
ACGILLNRSSU	ruling class
ACGILLNRSWY	scrawlingly
ACGILLOOOPT	topological
ACGILNOOSTT	costing a lot
ACGILNORSUY	carousingly
ACGIMNNOORT	morning coat
ACGIMNOORRT	motor racing
ACGIMNOORST	gastronomic

ACGINNORRSY	carryings-on
ACGINNORSTT	contrasting
ACGINOOPRTU	action group
ACGINOORRTU	corrugation
ACGINORRTUY	carrying out
	carrying-out
ACGLLNOOOVY	volcanology
ACGLLNOOUVY	vulcanology
ACGLMNNOOUY	agony column
ACGMOOPRSSY	gyrocompass
ACHHILOPRSS	scholarship
ACHHIORSTUY	ichthyosaur
ACHHJKNOOST	John Toshack
ACHHJLMNOUY	John Mauchly
ACHHNOOSTTU	autochthons
ACHHNORRSST	Scharnhorst
ACHHOPPSTYY	psychopathy
ACHIIIMNPSS	hispanicism
ACHIILLLPTU	Paul Tillich
ACHIILLMSWY	whimsically
ACHIILMPSSY	physicalism
ACHIILNRSTY	Christianly
ACHIILOPSST	sophistical
ACHIILPSTYY	physicality
ACHIINNORST	Corinthians
ACHIINNPSTU	put in chains
ACHIINNRSTU	unchristian
ACHIINOTTUW	with caution
ACHIKKOSTVY	Tchaikovsky
ACHILLMNOOP	Champollion
ACHILNNOPSY	non-physical
ACHIMOOPRSY	hypocorisma
ACHIMOPPPSU	hippocampus
ACHIMRSSSTY	Christmassy
ACHIOOPPRST	apostrophic
ACHIOOPRTTU	autotrophic
ACHIOPPRSTY	saprophytic
ACHIOPRRSTU	curatorship
ACHKLMNOOST	klootchmans
ACHKMMNOOSY	Noam Chomsky
ACHKMNOOPRT	Rockhampton
ACHLLNORSUY	unscholarly
ACHLLOOPRST	chloroplast
ACHLMMOOORS	chromosomal
ACHLMNOORTU	motor launch
ACHLNOPRTYY	lycanthropy
ACHLOOOSTTT	a colt's tooth
ACHMMOPPSTU	stomach pump
ACHNOOORSTW	cartoon show
ACHOPRSTUXY	choux pastry
ACIIILLNORS	nicrosilial
ACIIILMNOPT	implication
ACIIILMNRTY	criminality
ACIIILNNNOT	inclination
ACIIILRSTTU	ritualistic
ACIIIMNNORT	crimination
ACIIINNOTTT	nictitation
ACIIINOQSTU	acquisition
ACIIINPTTVY	in captivity
ACIIJNNOOTT	joint action
ACIILLLOPTY	politically
ACIILLMNOOS	colonialism
ACIILLMNOOT	collimation
ACIILLMNPUY	municipally
ACIILLMOSUY	maliciously
ACIILLMOTTY	mitotically
ACIILLNOOST	colonialist
	oscillation
ACIILLNOVVY	convivially
ACIILLNPPRY	principally
ACIILLOPRTY	pictorially
ACIILLPRSTU	pluralistic
ACIILLQSTTU	call it quits
ACIILLQUYZZ	quizzically
ACIILMNNOTU	culmination
ACIILMNOOPT	compilation
ACIILMNSTUY	masculinity
ACIILNNOOTU	inoculation
ACIILNNOPTU	inculpation
ACIILNNORSY	synclinoria
ACIILNOTTUV	cultivation
ACIILORSUVY	vicariously
ACIILOSUVVY	vivaciously
ACIIMMMNOST	mammonistic
ACIIMMNNOOT	commination
ACIIMMNORST	romanticism ❑
ACIIMMNOSST	monasticism
ACIIMNOORSU	acrimonious
ACIIMNORSTT	romanticist
ACIINNORRTU	Iron Curtain
ACIINNORTUV	incurvation
ACIINOOSSST	iconostasis
ACIINOPRTTU	unpatriotic
ACIINORSTTU	rustication
ACIINRTTTUY	taciturnity
ACIIOPSSSTT	psittacosis
ACIJKLMNOST	Milt Jackson
ACIJKLNNOTY	Tony Jacklin
ACIJNNOORTU	conjuration
ACIKLPQSSUY	pass quickly
ACILLMNOPTY	compliantly
ACILLMOOSTY	osmotically
ACILLMOTYYZ	zymotically
ACILLNNOTUY	continually
ACILLOORSTY	oscillatory
ACILMMRSSUU	simulacrums
ACILMORSTUY	customarily
ACILMRSTUUY	muscularity
ACILNNOOOST	consolation
ACILNOOORTU	colouration
ACILNOPRTUY	inculpatory
ACILNORSSTU	ultrasonics
ACILNPTTUUY	punctuality
ACILOORSTUY	atrociously
ACILOORSUVY	voraciously
ACILOSSTUUY	astuciously
ACIMMNOOTTU	commutation
ACIMMOPSTTY	symptomatic
ACIMNNNOORT	non-romantic
ACIMNNOOOST	onomasticon
ACIMNOOPTTU	computation
ACIMNOPRTUY	importunacy

Words marked ❑ can also be spelled with an initial capital letter

ACIMOOPRRST	corporatism
ACINNNNOOST	inconsonant
ACINNNOOOTT	connotation
ACINNOOPRTT	contraption
ACINNOOPSTY	syncopation
ACINNOPTTUU	punctuation
ACINNORSSTT	constraints
ACINOOOPRRT	corporation
ACINOOOPRTV	provocation
ACINOOPRRST	conspirator
ACINOOPRRTT	protraction
ACINOORRSUV	carnivorous
ACIOPRSSTTU	put it across
ACJKNOOPRST	Port Jackson
ACKLOPPRSTU	lack support
ACLLMOORSUY	clamorously
ACLLMOSTUUU	altocumulus
ACLLNNORTUY	nocturnally
ACLLOORSUUY	oraculously
ACLMNOORRST	arms control
ACLNNNOOSTY	consonantly
ACLNOOORSTY	consolatory
ACLNOOPRRSU	proconsular
ACLNOORRSUY	rancorously
ACLOOPPRSUY	polycarpous
ACMNOOOPRSU	monocarpous
ACMNORSTUUY	uncustomary
ACMOOOSSTTU	scotomatous
ADDDDENNOSS	odds and ends
ADDDDNOOSSS	odds and sods
ADDDEEGIRRS	disregarded
ADDDEEHNSTU	sudden death
ADDDEEIMMTU	medium-dated
ADDDEFGORRT	draft-dodger
ADDDEGGLOPY	doggy-paddle
ADDDEIMNOOV	diamond dove
ADDDEIORSWY	Edward Doisy
ADDDERSSTTU	star-studded
ADDDGLOOOSY	good old days
ADDDNNOOSST	dos and don'ts
	do's and don'ts
ADDEEEEFHTT	the defeated
ADDEEEEGNRT	degenerated
ADDEEEEHLLV	level headed
	level-headed
ADDEEEFILLM	E M Delafield
ADDEEEFILNO	Daniel Defoe
ADDEEEFILSU	defeudalise
ADDEEEFILUZ	defeudalize
ADDEEEGGILN	leading edge
ADDEEEHHITT	die the death
ADDEEEHIKNS	hide-and-seek
ADDEEEHLLPW	paddle wheel
ADDEEEHLLSW	swelled head
ADDEEEHMPTY	empty-headed
ADDEEEHPRTT	the departed
ADDEEEOPRSS	desperadoes
ADDEEEORRRS	A Red, Red Rose
ADDEEFMNORU	undreamed-of
ADDEEGGIRRV	Edvard Grieg
ADDEEGHHILT	light-headed
ADDEEGHILPY	pigheadedly
ADDEEGHNORW	wrong-headed
ADDEEGHOORT	good-hearted
ADDEEGHORTT	add together
ADDEEGIKNRS	reading-desk
ADDEEGINORW	edge in a word
ADDEEGLLORY	gold-layered
ADDEEGNRSSU	guardedness
ADDEEHHNRTU	thunderhead
ADDEEHIKNRT	kind-hearted
ADDEEHILMRT	Middle-Earth
ADDEEHILNST	in the saddle
ADDEEHLNORV	overhandled
ADDEEHMNPTY	empty-handed
ADDEEHNORTW	downhearted
	down-hearted
ADDEEHPPPUY	puppy-headed
ADDEEHPRRSS	hard-pressed
ADDEEIILTVZ	devitalized
ADDEEIINNNW	wine and dine
ADDEEILLSVW	well-advised
ADDEEILMNRW	Edward Milne
ADDEEILMORZ	demoralized
ADDEEILNOTT	not detailed
ADDEEIMNNOT	denominated
ADDEEIMRSTU	desideratum
ADDEEINOPRR	preordained
ADDEEINOPRT	depredation
ADDEEIRTTWY	ready-witted
ADDEELLRSSY	dreadlessly
ADDEELNPRUY	underplayed
ADDEELNRUUV	undervalued
ADDEEMNNNRU	undermanned
ADDEEMOORRT	made to order
ADDEEMRSSTU	Mustard-seed
ADDEENORTWW	watered-down
ADDEENPRSUU	unpersuaded
ADDEENRSTTU	understated
ADDEEOPPPRT	add pepper to
ADDEEPRSUWY	Edward Pusey
ADDEFFHLNOY	offhandedly
ADDEFGHINOT	dead of night
ADDEFHILNTY	find the lady
ADDEFHINSSS	faddishness
ADDEFIIMOTW	midwife toad
ADDEFNORRSW	send forward
ADDEGGHORTU	goddaughter
ADDEGGIIIRT	digitigrade
ADDEGHHINRT	right-handed
ADDEGHNORTU	dreadnought □
ADDEGIIMNNR	mind-reading
ADDEGIKNRRS	kind regards
ADDEGILMNNY	maddeningly
ADDEGIMNNNU	undemanding
ADDEGLNRUUY	unguardedly
ADDEGNOORTU	good-natured
ADDEHHLOORT	hold the road
ADDEHHNORST	shorthanded
	short-handed
ADDEHIILMOT	thalidomide
ADDEHIKNRRR	hard drinker

ADDEHILNORS	Rhode Island
ADDEHILNSSS	laddishness
ADDEHILORST	add relish to
ADDEHINORTY	dehydration
ADDEHINOSWW	window shade
ADDEHMNNOSW	hand-me-downs
ADDEHNRRTTU	thunderdart
ADDEIIIKLVW	David Wilkie
ADDEIIIMNTT	intimidated
ADDEIIINTUV	individuate
ADDEIILMNNO	Neil Diamond
ADDEIILNNRW	Edwin Aldrin
ADDEIINOOTX	deoxidation
ADDEIJNOPRY	pride and joy
ADDEIKKNNRS	dark-skinned
ADDEILLMMNS	small-minded
ADDEILLMORV	David Mellor
ADDEILLNNST	still and end
ADDEILNSUVY	unadvisedly
ADDEINNOTVY	Danny Devito
ADDEIOOPPSU	pseudopodia
ADDELLNORVY	Dolly Varden
ADDELLORSTU	older adults
ADDELMOORTU	demodulator
ADDELNNRTUY	redundantly
ADDELNNTUUY	undauntedly
ADDELNOOPRS	Donald Soper
ADDEMNOOORT	rodomontade
ADDEMRSTUWY	Muddy Waters
ADDENOORRRU	order around
ADDENOPRSSU	passed round
ADDENORSTTW	tend towards
ADDENRSSTTU	sudden start
ADDEOOPRRTY	ready to drop
ADDFFLOORRT	Old Trafford
ADDGGINNORW	downgrading
ADDGGINOPSU	sago pudding
ADDGHILLNNO	landholding
ADDGHILNOOR	roadholding
ADDGHINNOOS	in good hands
ADDGHLORSUU	Douglas Hurd
ADDGIMNOOOO	in a good mood
ADDGLNNOSUU	Douglas Dunn
ADDGNNOOPUW	go up and down
ADDHJLNNOOW	John Dowland
ADDHLLLOORY	Harold Lloyd
ADDIIIKLLMW	William Kidd
ADDIIILNSUV	individuals
ADDIIIORVZZ	David Rizzio
ADDIINORSTU	suraddition
ADDIJNOSUWW	Judas-window
ADDILLNNOUV	null and void
ADDILMNORTY	dirty old man
ADDILOPPRRY	drop rapidly
ADDINOOOPST	add poison to
ADDMNOOOTUW	odd woman out
ADDNNOOSTUW	down-and-outs
ADDNNOPSSUW	ups and downs
ADEEEEFIRSS	disease-free
ADEEEEGGRST	desegregate
ADEEEEGHHTV	have the edge
ADEEEENNRTU	nuée ardente
ADEEEFHNRTW	weather-fend
ADEEEFIKVWY	five-day week
ADEEEFILNRT	deferential
ADEEEFNRSSV	vas deferens
ADEEEFNRSTT	fenestrated
ADEEEGGLLNO	golden eagle
ADEEEGGLMOR	George Medal
ADEEEGHLMPT	dephlegmate
ADEEEGHPRST	gather speed
ADEEEGILMNR	legerdemain
ADEEEGILNRZ	generalized
ADEEEGIMNRR	gendarmerie
ADEEEGIMNST	demagnetise
ADEEEGIMNTZ	demagnetize
ADEEEGINNRT	in great need
	tragedienne
ADEEEGLLNRT	legal tender
ADEEEGMNNRT	derangement
ADEEEGNOTXY	deoxygenate
ADEEEHILNSY	Denis Healey
ADEEEHIMPSS	de-emphasise
ADEEEHIMPSZ	de-emphasize
ADEEEHIRSTW	weather side
ADEEEHIRTVY	the very idea
ADEEEHLLORS	leaseholder
ADEEEHNOPRT	open-hearted
ADEEEHNRRSU	unrehearsed
ADEEEHPRSST	spreadsheet
ADEEEHRRTTU	truehearted
ADEEEIILNTV	delineative
ADEEEIIMMOR	aide-mémoire
ADEEEILMNTY	demyelinate
ADEEEILMSSY	Lyme disease
ADEEEILSSUX	desexualise
ADEEEILSUXZ	desexualize
ADEEEIMNRTT	determinate
ADEEEIMPPRR	pipe-dreamer
ADEEEIMPRTT	premeditate
ADEEEINNRTV	Venetian red
ADEEEINPRTW	in deep water
ADEEEINRSVY	never say die
ADEEEIORRTT	deteriorate
ADEEEIPPRSU	depauperise
ADEEEIPPRUZ	depauperize
ADEEEIPRRST	pieds-à-terre
ADEEEKKLNWY	weak-kneedly
ADEEEKLRRST	deerstalker
ADEEELLNSWY	Wensleydale
ADEEELLPSTT	steel-plated
ADEEELLSSTT	tessellated
ADEEELMNNOW	needlewoman
ADEEELNNOUV	leave undone
ADEEELNNRSS	learnedness
ADEEELNRSST	relatedness
ADEEELNRTTU	launderette
ADEEELNSSTX	exaltedness
ADEEELPRSTY	desperately
ADEEEMNPRTT	département
ADEEEMNRRTU	remunerated
ADEEEMOSTWW	meadowsweet

ADEEENRSTTX next dearest
ADEEFFHNOOS off one's head
ADEEFFIINRT differentia
ADEEFGIINNR fine-grained
ADEEFGILNNY deafeningly
ADEEFGILNOR freeloading
ADEEFGINNRR rangefinder
ADEEFGIRTVY gravity-feed
ADEEFGORRTY get ready for
ADEEFHNRSTT farthest end
ADEEFHOOTVY heavy-footed
ADEEFHORSTT soft-hearted
ADEEFIILNST fine details
ADEEFIINSST dies nefasti
ADEEFIKMNRS make friends
ADEEFILMRRS self-admirer
ADEEFILNSUU unfeudalise
ADEEFILNUUZ unfeudalize
ADEEFINORSZ fazendeiros
ADEEFINRRTW water-finder
ADEEFIOPSST safe-deposit
ADEEFIRRSTV drive faster
ADEEFISSSTX fixed assets
ADEEFLLORSV severalfold
ADEEFLLPSTU at full speed
ADEEFLRSSSU self-assured
ADEEFMMNOOY made of money
ADEEFMNOORU enamoured of
ADEEFMNRRTU Fred Trueman
ADEEFMOORRS reformadoes
ADEEFNRRRST transferred
ADEEFPRSTTU superfatted
ADEEGGGIRRV grave-digger
ADEEGGHLORS loggerheads
ADEEGGIINRS disagreeing
ADEEGGINRRT garden tiger
ADEEGGLORTW waterlogged
ADEEGGMORUY demagoguery
ADEEGHIKLTT take delight
ADEEGHILSTY see daylight
ADEEGHINRST near-sighted
ADEEGHLNORS golden share
ADEEGHLRSTU slaughtered
ADEEGHMOPRR demographer
ADEEGHNNPRW grand-nephew
ADEEGHNOOSV good heavens
ADEEGHNORTY hydrogenate
ADEEGIILSTV give details
ADEEGIIORRV Diego Rivera
ADEEGIKKNPR keeping dark
ADEEGILLNOR leading role
ADEEGILNNOT leading note
ADEEGILNNRY endearingly
ADEEGILNNST disentangle
ADEEGILNORS Gorée Island
ADEEGILNRSW lead-swinger
ADEEGILNTTU deglutinate
ADEEGILRTUV travel guide
ADEEGIMNPRT impregnated
ADEEGJLMNTU judgemental
ADEEGKNOPRU keep guard on
ADEEGLNOSTU Tsung-Dao Lee
ADEEGMNNORY danger money
ADEEGMNRRRY gerrymander
ADEEGNNRSTU stun grenade
ADEEGNRTUWY get under way
ADEEGORSTUV Gustave Doré
ADEEHHIIRTW white-haired
ADEEHHIMSST missheathed
ADEEHHLORRS shareholder
ADEEHHNORSX hexahedrons
ADEEHHORTTY the other day
ADEEHHPRSTU The Phaedrus
ADEEHIKSTWY this day week
ADEEHILMSTV The Maldives
ADEEHILNOPT elephantoid
ADEEHILNORT lion-hearted
ADEEHILNPRR philanderer
ADEEHILNRTW draw the line
ADEEHILNSST deathliness
ADEEHILPSTW pleased with
ADEEHINNOTT the anointed
ADEEHIPSTTT despite that
ADEEHIRRRSS hairdresser
ADEEHIRRRSW washer-drier
ADEEHIRRSTW Harris tweed®
ADEEHKORSTT death-stroke
ADEEHKORTTW take the word
ADEEHLMNOTT mentholated
ADEEHMNNOST and then some
ADEEHNNNOTY Anthony Eden
ADEEHNNOPRT pentahedron
ADEEHNNORVY on every hand
ADEEHNNPRSU unsharpened
ADEEHNOOUVY have you done?
ADEEHNOPRRT The Pardoner
ADEEHNORRTT tetrahedron
ADEEHNOSSTW stonewashed
ADEEIIKNPRT take pride in
ADEEIILMMSV medievalism
ADEEIILMMTY immediately
ADEEIILMSSV Miles Davies
ADEEIILMSTV medievalist
ADEEIILNNOT delineation
ADEEIILNRST residential
ADEEIILNSST de-Stalinise
ADEEIILNSTZ de-Stalinize
ADEEIIMMNPT impedimenta
ADEEIIMNNPT pentamidine
ADEEIIMNRSS in medias res
ADEEIIMNSST disseminate
ADEEIIMRSTX taxidermise
ADEEIIMRTXZ taxidermize
ADEEIINNRSS in readiness
ADEEIINNSTW etesian wind
ADEEIINPSTT stipendiate
ADEEIINRTVY evidentiary
ADEEIIPRTUV repudiative
ADEEIKMORRW make worried
ADEEIKMRSST make strides
ADEEIKNRRST dreikanters
ADEEILLMNNR ill-mannered

ADEEILLMRSV	silver medal
ADEEILLNRTW	well-trained
ADEEILMNNST	enlisted man
ADEEILMNRST	streamlined
ADEEILMNRTT	detrimental
ADEEILMOSVY	easily moved
ADEEILMPPUU	ami du peuple
ADEEILMSTUU	demutualise
ADEEILMTUUZ	demutualize
ADEEILNNPUX	unexplained
ADEEILNRSTY	sedentarily
ADEEILOPPRT	Lepidoptera
ADEEILPRSSU	displeasure
ADEEILRRSVV	slave-driver
ADEEILRRTTU	literatured
ADEEILRSUVX	sexual drive
ADEEIMNNRTT	determinant
	detrainment
ADEEIMNNTTU	edutainment
ADEEIMNOPRT	predominate
ADEEIMNRSTY	sedimentary
ADEEIMPRSSU	mispersuade
ADEEINNPRRV	André Previn
ADEEINNRSSU	unreadiness
ADEEINNRTTV	inadvertent
ADEEINOPRST	desperation
ADEEINORRST	raison d'être
ADEEINOSTTT	detestation
ADEEINPPRRT	Peter Pindar
ADEEINPRRSU	underpraise
ADEEIPRRSTW	water spider
ADEEKLMMORY	Melody Maker
ADEEKLOPRSU	loudspeaker
ADEELLLNNPW	well-planned
ADEELLMRSSY	dreamlessly
ADEELLNNRUY	unlearnedly
ADEELNOOSST	at loose ends
ADEELNOPRSU	sleep around
ADEELNOPSSU	sound asleep
ADEELNOSSST	stoss and lee
ADEELNRRUUV	undervaluer
ADEELNRTTVY	advertently
ADEELORSSWW	weasel words
ADEEMMNOORR	more and more
ADEEMMNORTY	dynamometer
ADEEMNNOOOW	wood anemone
ADEEMNOPPRR	name-dropper
ADEEMNORSTT	demonstrate
ADEEMNRRRWY	merry-andrew
ADEEMORSSUY	Musée d'Orsay
ADEENNNPPSY	spend a penny
ADEENNOSWWY	wend one's way
ADEENNPRTTU	unpatterned
ADEENOOPRSV	eavesdrop on
ADEENOORRVV	over and over
ADEENRRRSTU	under arrest
ADEENRSSSSU	assuredness
ADEENRSSTUV	adventuress
ADEERRSSTTW	streetwards
ADEFFILLOSU	full of ideas
ADEFFILNOTU	in default of
ADEFFILNRTU	fault-finder
ADEFFIMMNOR	frame of mind
ADEFFIORSST	disafforest
ADEFGHLOOTT	flog to death
ADEFGILNRSY	lady's finger
ADEFGITTUUY	fatigue-duty
ADEFGKNOORS	God-forsaken
ADEFGKOORSS	for God's sake
ADEFGLLRRUY	regardfully
ADEFGNOORTU	out of danger
ADEFHIKOSST	kiss of death
ADEFHILLORT	Adolf Hitler
ADEFHINNOSU	unfashioned
ADEFHORRTWW	whet forward
ADEFIILLQUY	qualifiedly
ADEFIILNOOT	defoliation
ADEFIILNQUU	unqualified
ADEFIILNRTT	infiltrated
ADEFIINSSTU	unsatisfied
ADEFILLORUV	ill-favoured
ADEFILLRSTY	lady-trifles
ADEFILMNOSW	fieldswoman
ADEFILMRRUY	Murrayfield
ADEFILSSTTU	distasteful
ADEFIMNNORW	woman friend
ADEFIMNOORT	deformation
ADEFIMNOOTY	not my idea of
ADEFIMNOSTT	state of mind
ADEFINNOPRU	under pain of
ADEFINORSWW	in a few words
ADEFIOOPRTT	fried potato
ADEFISSSTUU	dies faustus
ADEFLLLOPRY	Alfred Polly
ADEFLLNOSST	dental floss
ADEFLNOORRS	fool's errand
ADEFLOOPSTY	splay-footed
ADEFMNORRST	transformed
ADEFMOORRVW	move forward
ADEFNOOPRSS	ropes of sand
ADEFNORRSSW	forwardness
	frowardness
ADEFOPRRSTW	step forward
ADEGGGHIRRT	ragged right
ADEGGHILNRT	right-angled
ADEGGHLRSTU	The Sluggard
ADEGGHNORRU	Darren Gough
ADEGGIIJMOO	Joe DiMaggio
ADEGGIINNRT	denigrating
ADEGGIINNRW	wide-ranging
ADEGGILNRUU	unguligrade
ADEGGILRSSU	sluggardise
ADEGGILRSUZ	sluggardize
ADEGGINOSTY	going steady
ADEGGKLOORS	look daggers
ADEGGNNOOPS	egg-and-spoon
ADEGGNORRYY	Andy Gregory
ADEGHHIILRT	light-haired
ADEGHHILNNP	helping hand
ADEGHHINNTU	headhunting
ADEGHHINRRT	right-hander
ADEGHHLNORU	rough-handle

ADEGHHORRTU	read through
ADEGHHORTUW	wade through
ADEGHIIKNNT	The King and I
ADEGHIILNTV	devil a thing
	living death
ADEGHIILNTW	dealing with
ADEGHILNNOV	hand in glove
ADEGHINNNRU	running head
ADEGHINOOPS	in good shape
ADEGHINOORT	in good heart
ADEGHINOTTW	two and eight
ADEGHLMOOSU	Douglas-Home
ADEGHMNORRT	grandmother
ADEGHNOORWW	Gwen Harwood
ADEGHNORRTU	gather round
ADEGHNRRTUU	run the guard
ADEGIILLNNT	ending it all
ADEGIILNPSS	displeasing
ADEGIILOPRS	prodigalise
ADEGIILOPRZ	prodigalize
ADEGIIMNOSS	misdiagnose
ADEGIIMNPST	die-stamping
ADEGIIMNRST	mistreading
ADEGIIMNRSV	serving-maid
ADEGIIMNTTU	unmitigated
ADEGIIMSTTZ	stigmatized
ADEGIINNORT	denigration
ADEGIINNOST	designation
ADEGIINNTUV	undeviating
ADEGIINORSS	disorganise
ADEGIINORSZ	disorganize
ADEGIINORTV	invigorated
ADEGIINRRWW	wiredrawing
ADEGIINRSTV	advertising
	driving seat
ADEGIINRTTU	ingratitude
ADEGIIPRSTV	tripe-visag'd
ADEGIKMNRSS	dressmaking
ADEGIKNNRTU	undertaking
ADEGILLOSSU	gladioluses
ADEGILLPTUY	plead guilty
ADEGILMMNRY	Me and My Girl
ADEGILNNRRR	Ring Lardner
ADEGILNNRWY	wanderingly
ADEGILNNSSU	languidness
ADEGILNORSY	grandiosely
ADEGILNPRSY	spreadingly
ADEGILNPRTY	panty girdle
ADEGILNPRVY	depravingly
ADEGILNSTTY	settling day
ADEGILOOPST	paedologist
ADEGIMNOORR	reading-room
ADEGIMNORRZ	gormandizer
ADEGIMNORSU	gourmandise
ADEGIMNORUZ	gourmandize
ADEGINNORTW	tearing-down
ADEGINNORUZ	unorganized
ADEGINNORWW	wearing down
	wearing-down
ADEGINNPRTU	put in danger
ADEGINNQRSU	squandering
ADEGINNRRUW	unrewarding
ADEGINORRTY	denigratory
ADEGLMOORTY	dermatology
ADEGLNORSUY	dangerously
ADEGMNNOORS	good manners
ADEGNNOORSU	on one's guard
ADEGNOOPRRU	grope around
ADEGNOORTTU	get around to
ADEGNORSTUW	waste ground
ADEHHILMNSU	human shield
ADEHHILPRSY	her ladyship
ADEHHIMNRTT	The Third Man
ADEHHIORRSS	horseradish
ADEHHIRRTTW	thitherward
ADEHHIRRTWW	whitherward
ADEHHJNOPSY	Joseph Haydn
ADEHHMMRTTU	thrummed hat
ADEHIIMNOPR	diamorphine
ADEHIIMNRST	Damien Hirst
ADEHIIMNRTU	antheridium
ADEHIIMRSTT	Mithridates
ADEHIIOPRSS	diaphoresis
ADEHIKNRSST	strike hands
ADEHIKOORST	Theodorakis
ADEHILLMMRR	hammer drill
ADEHILLNRST	disenthrall
ADEHILMNRYY	Myra Hindley
ADEHILORRVY	Oliver Hardy
ADEHIMMPPUY	happy medium
ADEHIMNOPRS	preadmonish
ADEHIMNPSSS	dampishness
ADEHIMOPRST	Thomas Pride
ADEHINNNSSU	unhandiness
ADEHINNRSTU	untarnished
ADEHINNRSUV	unvarnished
ADEHINNRTTW	handwritten
ADEHINOORTZ	antherozoid
ADEHINORRTY	rehydration
ADEHINOSSSW	shadowiness
ADEHINOSSTY	in those days
ADEHINOSTTT	that's done it
ADEHINRSTTW	withstander
ADEHIOPPSSY	diapophyses
ADEHIOPRRTY	pyritohedra
ADEHIPRSSTW	stewardship
ADEHIPRSTTW	sharp-witted
ADEHIRSTVYY	this very day
ADEHJLNOOSW	hold one's jaw
ADEHJLOOOSU	jealoushood
ADEHJMNOOOR	Mohenjo-daro
ADEHKLNORTW	work the land
ADEHKLOORTW	The Woodlark
ADEHLLLMORS	smallholder
ADEHLLLORTW	all the world
ADEHLLNOSTW	show and tell
ADEHLLOOSSU	A Doll's House
ADEHLMOOPRT	leopard-moth
ADEHLORRTUW	would rather
ADEHLORSTTW	the last word
ADEHMNOORWY	Woody Herman
ADEHNNNOOSS	on one's hands

ADEHNNOPSTU	open-and-shut
ADEHNNORSTY	try one's hand
ADEHNOORRSU	horse around
ADEHNOORTTW	down to earth
	down-to-earth
ADEHOORRTTW	tooth-drawer
ADEHOORRTTY	dehortatory
ADEHOPRSSTW	shop steward
ADEHRRRTVYY	try very hard
ADEIIILMSST	dissimilate
ADEIIINNTTU	uninitiated
ADEIIINPRRS	in disrepair
ADEIIIOPSTV	diapositive
ADEIIIPSSTV	dissipative
ADEIILLLNSS	Ellis Island
ADEIILLLOPS	ellipsoidal
ADEIILLMNTU	illuminated
ADEIILLMRSY	Daisy Miller
ADEIILLMSTW	Ted Williams
ADEIILLNNSS	Line Islands
ADEIILLNPQU	Daniel Quilp
ADEIILLORTY	editorially
ADEIILMNNOS	dimensional
ADEIILMOPST	diplomatise
ADEIILMOPTZ	diplomatize
ADEIILMSSTU	dissimulate
ADEIILNNNST	stand in line
ADEIILOPRRT	trial period
ADEIIMMNSTU	mediastinum
ADEIIMNNSSS	Dennis Amiss
ADEIIMNOPSS	impassioned
ADEIIMOPPTW	meadow pipit
ADEIIMRSTTX	taxidermist
ADEIINNNOTT	indentation
ADEIINNOOPT	opinionated
ADEIINNOSTT	destination
ADEIINNRSVY	Sandy Irvine
ADEIINNSTUZ	unsanitized
ADEIINOPRTT	trepidation
ADEIINOPRTU	repudiation
ADEIINOPRTV	deprivation
ADEIINOPSST	Passiontide
ADEIINORSTY	seditionary
ADEIINORTTX	extradition
ADEIINPRSTY	stipendiary
ADEIINQSTTU	equidistant
ADEIIRRSSTT	Dire Straits
	dire straits
ADEIJNORRRV	River Jordan
ADEIJPRSSTU	Judas Priest
ADEIKLLNSST	Kiss and Tell
	kiss-and-tell
ADEILLORSST	ill-assorted
ADEILLOSVWW	swallow-dive
ADEILLRSTTU	illustrated
ADEILMNNORW	annelid worm
ADEILNNTTUY	untaintedly
ADEILNOOPRT	deploration
	periodontal
ADEILNPPRST	spider plant
ADEILNQSSSU	squalidness
ADEILNRSTWZ	Switzerland
ADEILNSSTUY	sustainedly
ADEILOPRRTY	predatorily
ADEIMMNNOPU	pandemonium
ADEIMNNOORT	denominator
ADEIMNNOPRT	predominant
ADEIMNNORRY	ordinary men
ADEIMNNOTUW	mountain dew
ADEIMNORSTT	more distant
ADEIMNOTTUV	unmotivated
ADEIMNRRSUY	nurserymaid
ADEIMNRRTUY	rudimentary
ADEIMNRSTUV	adventurism
ADEINNORRWY	Winona Ryder
ADEINNORSTU	trades union
ADEINNPRRTY	dinner party
ADEINOOPRTT	deportation
ADEINPPPRUW	wrapped up in
ADEIOPRRTTY	trepidatory
ADEIPPSSTTU	past dispute
ADEJMNNORTU	adjournment
ADEJMOORRRS	major orders
ADEKOORRTWY	ready to work
ADELLMMORTY	troll-my-dame
ADELLMNORSW	small wonder
ADELLNOPRTU	unpatrolled
ADELLNSSTUY	dauntlessly
ADELMNORRTU	ultra-modern
ADELMOOORTU	outdoor meal
ADELNOOPRSW	snow leopard
ADELNOPPTUU	unpopulated
ADELNOPRSTW	plaster down
ADELNORRTUV	travel round
ADELNORSWWY	Wayne's World
ADELOOPRRST	postal order
ADELOPPRSUU	dual-purpose
ADEMMMNORSU	memorandums
ADEMMNNORSU	Donna Summer
ADEMMNNOUYY	Maundy money
ADEMNNOPTWY	down payment
ADEMNOOTTUU	Ode to Autumn
ADEMOORSTVW	move towards
ADEMOPRSTUY	made-up story
ADEMOPRSUVW	move upwards
ADENNOORTTU	done to a turn
ADENNOPRRST	transponder
ADENOPRRSSU	press around
ADENOPRRSTT	transported
ADENORSSSUU	arduousness
ADENORSSTUW	outwardness
ADENORSTUUV	adventurous
ADENPRSSSUU	unsurpassed
ADENRSTTUUY	nature study
ADEOOOPPSST	as opposed to
ADFFFFHNPUU	huff and puff
ADFFHINOSST	standoffish
	stand-offish
ADFGHIINOOT	in good faith
ADFGHLNOORY	hand of glory
ADFGIINQRSU	firing squad
ADFGILLNNOW	falling-down

ADFGILNNOST	soft landing
ADFGILNQSUY	flying squad
ADFGOOOORSS	so far so good
ADFHHNOOSSW	show of hands
ADFHINORSTU	shift around
ADFHOPRRSUW	push forward
ADFHORRRSUW	rush forward
ADFIIIKRSTT	first aid kit
ADFIIILLNNU	nullifidian
ADFIIIMNNTU	ad infinitum
ADFINNOOSTU	foundations
ADFLMOORSUW	world-famous
ADFMNOORSWY	of many words
ADFMOORRTUW	outward form
ADFOOPPRRRW	prop forward
ADGGGHIILNN	hang-gliding
ADGGGHLOOSU	Douglas Hogg
ADGGHILMOTY	God-almighty
ADGGIINNNWW	wing-and-wing
ADGGIINRSTU	guiding star
ADGGINNOORU	going around
ADGHHIINRTT	hard-hitting
ADGHHILNOPT	diphthongal
ADGHHOPRRYY	hydrography
ADGHIILMNNS	mishandling
ADGHIINNRTW	handwriting
ADGHIKNORRW	hard working
	hardworking
	hard-working
ADGHINNNNRU	hand-running
ADGHINOOORU	in a good hour
ADGHINORRUW	draw in rough
ADGHIOPRTTY	dittography
ADGHLLLOUUY	laugh loudly
ADGHNNOORSW	hang on words
ADGIIINNNOT	indignation
ADGIILLMOSY	sigmoidally
ADGIILLNNPU	pain-dulling
ADGIILMNNST	dismantling
ADGIILNNNTY	indignantly
ADGIILOORST	radiologist
ADGIILOPRTY	prodigality
ADGIINNNOOV	Don Giovanni
ADGIINORRSS	disgarrison
ADGIINORSTY	grandiosity
ADGIJLOPRTU	Judit Polgar
ADGIKKLORSU	Kirk Douglas
ADGILOPRRWY	grow rapidly
ADGIMMNORSU	gourmandism
ADGIMNOORRW	drawing-room
ADGINNOOTTW	wanting to do
ADGINNOSTTU	outstanding
	standing out
ADGINOPRSTT	trading post
ADGNNNOOTWW	town and gown
ADGNNOORSUY	androgynous
ADHHJMNNOWY	John Wyndham
ADHHMNOOTTU	hand to mouth
	hand-to-mouth
ADHHMPRUVYY	Humphry Davy
ADHIINNSTTW	stand in with
ADHILLNNOSW	Don Whillans
ADHILMNOOSW	old-womanish
ADHILNNORST	North Island
ADHILNOSSTU	South Island
ADHIMNOOPSW	woodmanship
ADHINPPRSUW	whip and spur
ADHIOPRTTTU	hard put to it
ADHKOOORRTW	work too hard
ADHLNORRTWY	northwardly
ADHLORSTUWY	southwardly
ADHNOORRTUW	throw around
ADIIILNOOTZ	idolization
ADIIILNOQTU	liquidation
ADIIIMNORTT	intimidator
ADIIIMOSSTT	mastoiditis
ADIIINOPSST	dissipation
ADIIJLMMMSY	dismal Jimmy
ADIILMOPSTT	diplomatist
ADIIMORSTUU	auditoriums
ADIINOPPPTU	point d'appui
ADIINOPSTTU	disputation
ADIIOOPRSUV	avoirdupois
ADIKLOOSTVV	Vladivostok
ADIKNOPRRSW	Windsor Park
ADILLMOPSYY	sympodially
ADILNNORTWY	Tiny Rowland
ADILNNOSSTY	dissonantly
ADILORRSTTU	stridulator
ADILOSSSUUY	assiduously
ADIMNOOOPRR	Romano Prodi
ADIMNOSSTTT	most distant
ADKOORRSTWW	work towards
ADLLOOOSWWW	wood-swallow
ADLNOOPRSUY	polyandrous
ADLNOOPRSWY	play on words
ADMOOPPRSTT	Tom Stoppard
ADNNORSSTTU	toss and turn
ADNOORSUUYY	you and yours
ADNOPRSSTUY	Sunday Sport
ADOOOPPRRSU	Prosauropod
AEEEEFFMRRZ	freeze-frame
AEEEEFGGLRU	feeler gauge
AEEEEFGILPR	life peerage
AEEEEFLNOSS	ease oneself
AEEEEFNORYY	eye for an eye
AEEEEGHHTTV	get the heave
AEEEEGKNRTV	take revenge
AEEEEGLMSST	Telemessage®
AEEEEGMRRSV	game reserve
AEEEEHILRST	etherealise
AEEEEHILRTZ	etherealize
AEEEEKNNOPY	keep an eye on
AEEEEKNRSUV	Keanu Reeves
AEEEELOPPRT	people-eater
AEEEENRSVWY	New Year's Eve
AEEEEPRRSTV	perseverate
AEEEFFHOTTT	at the feet of
AEEEFFKNOST	take offense
AEEEFFLOPPT	toffee apple
AEEEFFNRRST	transfer fee
AEEEFGIKNPS	safekeeping

	safe-keeping
AEEEFGIRRRT	refrigerate
AEEEFHIKLRT	featherlike
AEEEFHINRRT	hereinafter
AEEEFHORSVY	have eyes for
AEEEFILLNRT	eternal life
AEEEFILNRRT	referential
AEEEFKMNOSS	make sense of
AEEEFLLNNTT	flannelette
AEEEFLNOSWY	feel one's way
AEEEFLRSSTU	featureless
AEEEFPRSTTU	superfetate
AEEEGGILNOS	genealogise
AEEEGGILNOZ	genealogize
AEEEGHHLOTV	heave the log
AEEEGHILLNS	Alleghenies
AEEEGHLNRST	The Gleaners
AEEEGHNPRTW	great-nephew
AEEEGHNPRTY	gene therapy
AEEEGHRSTTT	the greatest
AEEEGIKKNNV	Kevin Keegan
AEEEGILMMRR	lammergeier
AEEEGILMNNV	evening meal
AEEEGIMNNRT	in agreement
AEEEGIMNNST	steam engine
AEEEGINPRRT	peregrinate
AEEEGINRRTT	reintegrate
AEEEGLMMRRY	lammergeyer
AEEEGLMNNRT	enlargement
AEEEGMNNRSS	germaneness
AEEEGNORRRT	regenerator
AEEEGNORRTT	get nearer to
AEEEGNSSSTV	St Agnes's Eve
AEEEHHLORST	shoe leather
AEEEHIKLTTV	take the veil
AEEEHILNNPT	elephantine
AEEEHILPSTT	telepathise
AEEEHILPTTZ	telepathize
AEEEHIMRSTX	hexametrise
AEEEHIMRTXZ	hexametrize
AEEEHIMSSTT	metathesise
AEEEHIMSTTZ	metathesize
AEEEHIPRSST	aspheterise
AEEEHIPRSTZ	aspheterize
AEEEHIRSTWW	weather-wise
AEEEHISSTTX	The Exstasie
AEEEHKMOOPW	make whoopee
AEEEHLMPPRT	pamphleteer
AEEEHLNTUVY	lay the venue
AEEEHLORRTV	overleather
AEEEHLPRRWY	prayer wheel
AEEEHMRSTVY	the very same
AEEEHNNORRW	nowhere near
AEEEHNOPRTU	The European
AEEEHNPRSST	parentheses
AEEEHOPRRTT	Heteroptera
AEEEHORRTUY	there you are
AEEEHORRTVW	overweather
AEEEHORRUWY	where you are
AEEEIIRRTTV	reiterative
AEEEIKMQRTU	make quieter
AEEEILLLPWY	peelie-wally
AEEEILMPRST	time-pleaser
AEEEILNORRS	Sierra Leone
AEEEILNRRTT	interrelate
AEEEILNRRTV	reverential
AEEEILNRSTV	interleaves
AEEEILNRSTX	externalise
AEEEILNRTXZ	externalize
AEEEILNSTUV	eventualise
AEEEILNTUVZ	eventualize
AEEEIMNPRTT	impenetrate
	intemperate
AEEEIMNRSTT	Eastern Time
AEEEIMNRTTX	exterminate
AEEEIMNRWZZ	Ezer Weizman
AEEEINNRRTT	entertainer
AEEEINOPRSU	Europeanise
AEEEINOPRUZ	Europeanize
AEEEINORRTT	reorientate
AEEEINORTVX	exonerative
AEEEINPRTTV	penetrative
AEEEINSSSVV	evasiveness
AEEEINTTUVX	extenuative
AEEEJLMSSTY	lese-majesty
AEEEKLLOSTX	exoskeletal
AEEEKLLPRSW	sleepwalker
AEEEKMNPRVY	Mervyn Peake
AEEEKPSSSTW	sweepstakes
AEEELLLMNTY	elementally
AEEELLORTTT	teetotaller
AEEELMMNNPT	empanelment
AEEELMNNSTV	enslavement
AEEELMPRTTY	temperately
AEEELMRSSSU	measureless
AEEELMSSSTV	steam vessel
AEEELNPQRUY	pearly queen
AEEELORSTUY	see you later
AEEELRSTTUV	street value
AEEEMMNPRTT	temperament
AEEEMMNRSTU	measurement
AEEEMNNNRST	ensnarement
AEEEMNOSSSW	awesomeness
AEEEMNRSTTT	restatement
AEEEMORRSUV	overmeasure
AEEEMPRRTTU	temperature
AEEEMQRRSTU	square metre
AEEENNNRRST	Ernest Renan
AEEENNRSSST	earnestness
AEEEORRSTUV	auto-reverse
AEEEQRSSTTU	sequestrate
AEEFFFFIMUW	fee-fi-faw-fum
AEEFFGMNOOS	off one's game
AEEFFGRSTTU	suffragette
AEEFFHORRST	forefathers
AEEFFIKMOTT	take time off
AEEFFILMRTU	feature film
AEEFFLMOSTT	let off steam
AEEFFLNRSSU	fearfulness
AEEFFLNSSTU	fatefulness
AEEFGHORRTT	heterograft
AEEFGIKLNRS	Finger Lakes

AEEFGIKNRST free skating
AEEFGILLNSS self-sealing
AEEFGILNPRU plane figure
AEEFGINRRRT refrigerant
AEEFGIPRRTU prefigurate
AEEFGMNNRTT engraftment
AEEFGOOPRRS greaseproof
AEEFHHILMTT half the time
AEEFHILMRTT film theatre
AEEFHILNNRW finner whale
AEEFHILNRST Riefenstahl
AEEFHIMNNOT in the name of
AEEFHIMOTTT at the time of
AEEFHLLMNST mantelshelf
AEEFHLNOSSW wash oneself
AEEFHLNRSTT fresh talent
AEEFHLNSSTU hatefulness
AEEFHNNORTW no fewer than
AEEFIILNNRT inferential
AEEFIILOSTZ fail to seize
AEEFIILOTVX exfoliative
AEEFIKLLNWX Felix Wankel
AEEFIKLOPSV speak evil of
AEEFILLNOST eat one's fill
AEEFILLNRST self-reliant
AEEFILNSTTY festinately
AEEFILOPRRT proliferate
AEEFILOPSUY if you please
AEEFIMNOSST manifestoes
AEEFIMORRTV reformative
AEEFIMSSTTT fastest time
AEEFINORRRZ Enzo Ferrari
AEEFINRRRTZ fraternizer
AEEFKLLOPSW speak well of
AEEFKLNSSUW wakefulness
AEEFLLOORST for all to see
AEEFLLORRST forestaller
AEEFLMNOPRU funeral poem
AEEFLMNORUV roman fleuve
AEEFLMRSSTY self-mastery
AEEFLNRSSTU tearfulness
AEEFLOPPRRS proper-false
AEEFLOPRRST false report
AEEFLRRSSTT self-starter
AEEFMMNRRSZ Franz Mesmer
AEEFMNOPRTY forepayment
AEEFMNORRSY Freemasonry
AEEFNNOPRSS profaneness
AEEFNORRSVW war of nerves
AEEFNORRTWZ frozen water
AEEFNRRRRST transferrer
AEEFOQRRRTU forequarter
AEEFPPRRSTU aftersupper
AEEGGGINRST segregating
AEEGGGMOORW George Gamow
AEEGGGNNRRZ Grenzgänger
AEEGGILNOST genealogist
AEEGGINORST segregation
AEEGGINQSTU gigantesque
AEEGGIRRTTU regurgitate
AEEGGNOOSTT get one's goat
AEEGHHINNRT hang in there
AEEGHHITVWY heavy weight
heavyweight
AEEGHIILMNS Hegelianism
AEEGHIKLMRT make lighter
AEEGHILLTVW give the wall
AEEGHILNPRS generalship
AEEGHILRRTW weathergirl
AEEGHIMNRSS Germain Hess
AEEGHIMPSTU the game is up
AEEGHINNRTT threatening
AEEGHIPRRRS serigrapher
AEEGHLLORTT all together
AEEGHLNNPTU elephant gun
AEEGHLNORUY early enough
AEEGHLNOTTW get the law on
AEEGHLNUVWY Evelyn Waugh
AEEGHLRRSTU slaughterer
AEEGHMNNRSY Syngman Rhee
AEEGHMOPTTY gametophyte
AEEGHOPRRST stereograph
AEEGIIKLNTV give a tinkle
AEEGIILLSTV legislative
AEEGIILMNPT leaping-time
AEEGIILNNOR legionnaire
AEEGIILNORS regionalise
AEEGIILNORZ regionalize
AEEGIILNRSU seigneurial
AEEGIINNRVW wine vinegar
AEEGIINNTVW vintage wine
AEEGIINRTTV vinaigrette
AEEGIINSTTV investigate
AEEGIIRSTTV give it a rest
AEEGIJKNRRT tear-jerking
AEEGIKKLNPW keep walking
AEEGIKLNRRY Gary Lineker
AEEGILLNNTY inelegantly
AEEGILLNOSV give one's all
AEEGILLRSTU legislature
AEEGILMNNRT realignment
AEEGILMNNSS meaningless
AEEGILMNRST regimentals
AEEGILNNORV leaning over
AEEGILNNRTT intertangle
AEEGILNNRUV unrevealing
AEEGILNRSTV everlasting ▫
AEEGIMMNSST mass meeting
AEEGIMNORSV give a sermon
AEEGIMNOSTV give means to
AEEGIMSSTTU guesstimate
AEEGINNORTX Generation X
AEEGINNPRTT penetrating
AEEGINNTTUX extenuating
AEEGINOPRRS opera singer
AEEGINORRRV Orange River
AEEGINORRTT interrogate
AEEGIOPRRTV prerogative
AEEGLLMNNTY gentlemanly
AEEGLLMNSTY segmentally
AEEGLLOOPSY spelaeology
AEEGLMNNOTW gentlewoman

Words marked ▫ can also be spelled with an initial capital letter

AEEGLMNOOPR	prolegomena
AEEGLMNORSU	long-measure
AEEGLNNPRST	green plants
AEEGLNOORSS	lose one's rag
AEEGLNORRRR	Errol Garner
AEEGLNORRSY	solar energy
AEEGNNORTUV	gouvernante
AEEGNNRSSST	strangeness
AEEGNOOSSTT	get one's oats
AEEGNOSSSSU	gaseousness
AEEGOPRRSTT	report stage
AEEHHHLLTTW	what the hell
AEEHHILLLTW	all the while
AEEHHILNSST	healthiness
AEEHHILRTWW	wherewithal
AEEHHISTVWX	have sex with
AEEHHLMNPRY	Henry Pelham
AEEHHMMNOST	shame on them
AEEHHMORRTT	mother earth
AEEHIINNOTV	have it in one
AEEHIKLLLRW	killer whale
AEEHIKLMNOS	make holes in
AEEHIKLMOST	make hostile
AEEHIKMNNRT	make thinner
AEEHIKNSTTV	have kittens
AEEHIKPSSTT	take the piss
AEEHILNPPRS	planisphere
AEEHILNPSSS	shapeliness
AEEHILNRSST	earthliness
AEEHILNSSTW	wealthiness
AEEHILPSTTT	telepathist
AEEHIMMNRST	Hammerstein
AEEHIMNNNRT	in the manner
AEEHIMNNRST	Martin Sheen
AEEHIMNORTT	another time
AEEHIMRSTTV	harvest-time
AEEHIMRTTTW	white matter
AEEHINORSST	the reason is
AEEHINPRSST	parenthesis
AEEHIOOPRTT	heterotopia
AEEHIOOPSST	apotheosise
AEEHIOOPSTZ	apotheosize
AEEHIORSTTX	heterotaxis
AEEHIORTTVX	exhortative
AEEHIPPPRTY	pay the piper
AEEHIPPRRSS	periphrases
AEEHIPPSTUX	exhaust pipe
AEEHJLLMOSW	James Howell
AEEHJMRSSSU	James Ussher
AEEHJMSSTTU	just the same
AEEHJNNORTV	John Tavener
AEEHJNORSVY	Harvey-Jones
AEEHKLNSTVV	velvet shank
AEEHKMNORTT	on the market
AEEHKMORRST	make shorter
AEEHKMPRRTY	hypermarket
AEEHKNNOSVW	heaven knows
AEEHLLMRSYY	Mary Shelley
AEEHLLMSSSY	shamelessly
AEEHLLNORTT	not all there
AEEHLLNORTY	lonely heart
	lonely-heart
AEEHLLORTWY	Yellow Earth
AEEHLLPSSST	sell the pass
AEEHLLRSSTY	heartlessly
AEEHLMNNRTT	enthralment
AEEHLMOSTTY	stately home
AEEHLNORTZZ	on the razzle
AEEHLNPSSSS	haplessness
AEEHLOPPRTY	pelotherapy
AEEHLOPSTUY	pleaseth you
AEEHLPPRRTU	Purple Heart
	purple heart
	purpleheart
AEEHLRRTTTU	turret lathe
AEEHMMNOTTT	at the moment
AEEHMORRRTT	earth-tremor
AEEHMORSSTU	housemaster
AEEHMORSTVW	whatsomever
AEEHMRSSTTT	the smart set
AEEHNNOPRSW	answerphone
AEEHNOQRSTU	on the square
AEEHNORRSTT	north-easter
AEEHNORRTWW	weather-worn
AEEHOOSTTTW	a sweet tooth
AEEHORRSSTU	house arrest
AEEHOSTTTTU	at the outset
AEEHPSSSTTT	pass the test
AEEHRSSSTUU	thesauruses
AEEIIILMPRS	imperialise
AEEIIILMPRZ	imperialize
AEEIIINNNST	Einsteinian
AEEIIJLMORV	Jamie Oliver
AEEIIKLLNPS	spaniel-like
AEEIIKMSSYY	Issey Miyake
AEEIILLRSTW	Water Lilies
AEEIILLRWWY	Weary Willie
AEEIILLSSTT	satellitise
AEEIILLSTTZ	satellitize
AEEIILMMORS	memorialise
AEEIILMMORZ	memorialize
AEEIILMNRRZ	mineralizer
AEEIILMORTV	meliorative
AEEIILNNPTT	penitential
AEEIILNNRRT	interlinear
AEEIILNNRST	internalise
AEEIILNNRTZ	internalize
AEEIILNNSST	inessential
AEEIILNORST	orientalise
AEEIILNORTZ	orientalize
AEEIILNSTTX	existential
AEEIILNTTVV	ventilative
AEEIILRTTVY	iteratively
AEEIIMMSSTT	misestimate
AEEIINNTTTV	inattentive
AEEIINOPRTV	inoperative
AEEIINORRTT	reiteration
AEEIIPRRSTV	reprivatise
AEEIIPRRTVZ	reprivatize
AEEIKLLLSTY	least likely
AEEIKLLOSUY	Louis Leakey
AEEIKLPRSTT	strike plate

AEEIKNOPSSW	Passion week
AEEIKNQSSSU	squeakiness
AEEIKNRSSST	streakiness
AEEIKOPRRST	perestroika
AEEIKOPRSST	strike a pose
AEEILLMMNPT	implemental
AEEILLMPRXY	exemplarily
AEEILLNNPRY	perennially
AEEILLNNPSY	plainly seen
AEEILLNNSXY	sexennially
AEEILLNOPPT	en papillote
AEEILLNRTVY	eviternally
AEEILLNSSTY	essentially
AEEILLPRSTV	silver plate
AEEILLRSSWY	wearilessly
AEEILLRSTVY	versatilely
AEEILMNNSTT	sentimental
AEEILMNORRS	renormalise
AEEILMNORRZ	renormalize
AEEILMNORST	salinometer
AEEILMNPRST	sempiternal
AEEILMNPTTU	penultimate
AEEILMNSSSS	aimlessness
AEEILMNSSWY	Wesleyanism
AEEILMORSWY	wearisomely
AEEILMOSTTT	teetotalism
AEEILMSTTTU	statute mile
AEEILNNOPTX	exponential
AEEILNNPSTU	peninsulate
AEEILNNSSTU	unessential
AEEILNNSSTY	insensately
AEEILNOPRSS	personalise
AEEILNOPRSZ	personalize
AEEILNOPRTT	interpolate
AEEILNORRSV	reversional
AEEILNPSVXY	expansively
AEEILNRRTUZ	neutralizer
AEEILNRSTUX	intersexual
AEEILNSSSTT	stateliness
AEEILNTTTVY	attentively
	tentatively
AEEILNTTUVY	eventuality
AEEILOPPRTT	toilet paper
AEEILOPRRVV	prevail over
AEEILOPRTVX	explorative
AEEILOPRTVY	operatively
AEEILOPSTUY	please it you
AEEILORSSXY	Alexis Soyer
AEEILORTTTW	toilet water
AEEILPPQRSU	apple-squire
AEEILPPRRSV	silver paper
AEEILPRSTUV	superlative
AEEILPRSVVY	pervasively
AEEILPSSTUY	easily upset
AEEILRRRSTT	terrestrial
AEEILRSSTVY	assertively
AEEIMMNNPRT	impermanent
AEEIMMNOPRR	Roman Empire
AEEIMMNPRST	pentamerism
AEEIMMQRSSU	Requiem Mass
AEEIMNNNOQU	menaquinone
AEEIMNNOPRT	prenominate
AEEIMNNORTU	enumeration
	mountaineer
AEEIMNNOSTT	maisonnette
AEEIMNNSTTT	instatement
AEEIMNOPRST	impersonate
AEEIMNOPRSU	Europeanism
AEEIMNORRST	Rose Tremain
AEEIMNRSSST	streaminess
AEEIMNRSTTV	Steve Martin
AEEIMNSSSSV	massiveness
AEEIMOPRRST	temporaries
AEEIMOPRSST	Marie Stopes
AEEIMORRSTU	temerarious
AEEIMSSSTTY	systematise
AEEIMSSTTYZ	systematize
AEEINNOORTX	exoneration
AEEINNOPRTT	penetration
AEEINNORSTV	anteversion
AEEINNOTTUX	extenuation
AEEINOPRSTU	Europeanist
AEEINOPRSTV	pet aversion
AEEINORRSTV	reservation
AEEINPRRSTT	inter partes
AEEINPRRTVY	in every part
AEEINPRSSTT	Esperantist
AEEINPRSSTV	privateness
AEEINPSSSSV	passiveness
AEEINQRSSTU	equestrians
AEEINQRSSUV	quaveriness
AEEINRSSTUV	unassertive
AEEIOPPRRTX	expropriate
AEEIORRSTTV	restorative
AEEIPRRSTUZ	pasteurizer
AEEJLLLMOSV	James Lovell
AEEJLLNRSSU	Jane Russell
AEEJLLOSSTW	Tessa Jowell
AEEJMMNOORS	James Monroe
AEEJMNORSUY	Jane Seymour
AEEJNORRTUV	rejuvenator
AEEKLLORRST	roller-skate
AEEKLLPRSSW	Kepler's laws
AEEKLMORRTW	metalworker
AEEKLNOPPSY	speak openly
AEEKLNORRST	Lake Torrens
AEEKMNORSUV	make nervous
AEEKMPRRSTU	supermarket
AEEKNOPRRSY	nosey parker
AEEKNORSTVW	weaver's knot
AEEKNPRRSTU	supertanker
AEELLLNPRTY	repellantly
AEELLLORTWY	yellow alert
AEELLMMNOTU	emolumental
AEELLMORRST	steamroller
	steam-roller
AEELLNORSTW	stonewaller
AEELLNPRTVY	prevalently
AEELLNRSTWW	Western Wall
AEELLNSSSSW	lawlessness
AEELLPPRRUY	puerperally
AEELLPPRTUY	perpetually

AEELLPSSSUY	pauselessly
AEELLSSSTTY	tastelessly
AEELMMORSSU	Samuel Morse
AEELMNNPRTY	permanently
AEELMOPRRTV	trample over
AEELMOQRRSU	quarrelsome
AEELMPPSSUY	Samuel Pepys
AEELMPRRTUY	prematurely
AEELNNOOPST	on one's plate
AEELNNPRTTY	repentantly
AEELNNQSSUU	unequalness
AEELNOOSSWY	lose one's way
AEELNOPPRTT	rotten apple
AEELNOPRSSS	salesperson
AEELNOSSSUZ	zealousness
AEELNRSSSST	artlessness
AEELOOPSSUY	so please you
AEELOORSUVZ	overzealous
	over-zealous
AEELOPSTTUX	expostulate
AEELORSSTTU	Lotus-eaters
AEELPRSSSTU	pastureless
AEEMNNRSSTV	men-servants
AEEMNOPRSTU	pentamerous
AEEMNORRRTU	remunerator
AEEMNORRSTT	remonstrate
AEEMNORSSTT	easternmost
AEEMNPRRSST	present arms
AEEMOPRRTXY	extemporary
AEEMOPRSTUU	measure up to
AEENNNPRTTU	unrepentant
AEENOOPRSSU	aponeuroses
AEENOOSSTTT	to one's taste
AEENOPRRSTT	paternoster❑
AEENOQRRTTU	quarter tone
AEENORTTUXY	extenuatory
AEENPRSSTUW	pastures new
AEENRRTTUVY	at every turn
AEEOOPSTTTW	sweet potato
	sweet-potato
AEEOPPRRRTT	perpetrator
AEEOPPRRTTU	perpetuator
AEEORRRSTVY	reservatory
AEFFFFILOST	staff of life
AEFFFGHIOTW	get a whiff of
AEFFGHNOOTW	off the wagon
AEFFGIMSTUU	suffumigate
AEFFGINOPRT	tapering off
AEFFGLORRTU	grateful for
AEFFHHILTTU	the Faithful
AEFFHIKMOTW	make off with
AEFFHILORST	off the rails
AEFFHINRSSS	raffishness
AEFFIMNORRR	refrain from
AEFFKNRRRTU	frankfurter
AEFFLLNRUUY	unfearfully
AEFFLLORSUY	full of years
AEFFLOSTTUX	state of flux
AEFFNOOOSST	off one's oats
AEFGGHIINNR	hanging fire
AEFGGHILNNT	left hanging

AEFGGHILOPS	Phileas Fogg
AEFGGHIRSTT	stage fright
AEFGHHLORTU	leaf through
AEFGHHORRTU	throughfare
AEFGHIKLMOT	make light of
AEFGHILMNRS	self-harming
AEFGHORSTTU	sought after
	sought-after
AEFGIIINRRS	fire-raising
AEFGIILNRSS	self-raising
AEFGIILOTTV	give a lift to
AEFGIINNPRT	finger-paint
AEFGIKLLLNW	fell-walking
AEFGILLNRST	fingerstall
AEFGILLNRTY	falteringly
AEFGILNNOOR	gonfalonier
AEFGILNNRTU	unfaltering
AEFGILNORSU	soul-fearing
AEFGINNNSTU	unfastening
AEFGINNORRW	forewarning
AEFGINORRSW	forswearing
AEFGINRRSTU	transfigure
AEFGIRRSSTU	sugar sifter
AEFGLLOOPRY	galley proof
AEFGLMNRRSU	farmer's lung
AEFGLNNORSU	funeral song
AEFGLNRRTUW	Furtwängler
AEFHHIIRSTT	hatti-sherif
AEFHHIMOTTW	at the whim of
AEFHHLLLTUY	healthfully
AEFHHLLNTUU	unhealthful
AEFHHNRRTTU	further than
AEFHIILMNTY	in the family
AEFHIINORTV	have it in for
AEFHIIRRSTW	White friars
AEFHIKLNNRT	The Franklin
AEFHILLSSTY	faithlessly
AEFHIMNOPRS	HMS Pinafore
AEFHKOORTTU	out of the ark
AEFHLLOOPTY	play the fool
AEFHLMNRSSU	harmfulness
AEFHMOOORRV	have room for
AEFHNOOPRTT	on the part of
AEFHOOORTTT	at the root of
AEFHOOTTUWY	out of the way
	out-of-the-way
AEFIILLNNTU	influential
AEFIILMORST	formalities
AEFIILMORTT	militate for
AEFIILNOOTX	exfoliation
AEFIIMNORTV	informative
AEFIINNOSTT	infestation
	sinfonietta
AEFIINNRSTT	transfinite
AEFIINORSTT	fire station
AEFIKMMNORU	make uniform
AEFIKMNORST	mistaken for
AEFIKMOORTW	a work of time
AEFIKOOTTTU	take it out of
AEFILLRRTTU	ultrafilter
AEFILMNOSTU	filamentous

AEFILMOPRTY	play for time
AEFILMORRSU	formularise
AEFILMORRUZ	formularize
AEFILMRSTTY	state firmly
AEFILNNPSSU	painfulness
AEFILNOOPST	point of sale
AEFILNORSUY	nefariously
AEFILOOPRST	fore-topsail
AEFILOOPSTY	play footsie
AEFILOPRRTY	prefatorily
AEFILOPRSSS	press of sail
AEFILORSSTW	fossil water
AEFIMNNNRTY	infantrymen
AEFIMNNOOTT	fomentation
AEFIMNOORRT	reformation
AEFIMOPRRTZ	trapeziform
AEFINNNOPTU	fountain pen
AEFINNRRRST	transferrin
AEFINOOPRRT	perforation
AEFINOOPRST	pianofortes
AEFINOORSTT	forestation
AEFINOOTTTT	not fit to eat
AEFINORSSWW	sinews of war
AEFJMMNOORY	money for jam
AEFKLLORSTW	flower-stalk
AEFKLOPSSTY	speak softly
AEFKMMOOORR	make room for
AEFKMNOORSY	ask for money
AEFKOORSSTV	ask for votes
AEFLLLNORTU	on full alert
AEFLLLNTTUY	flatulently
AEFLLLOPRUW	all powerful
	all-powerful
AEFLLLSSTUY	faultlessly
AEFLLMRSTUY	masterfully
AEFLLNPSSUY	playfulness
AEFLLOOPRVY	play for love
AEFLLORSSUV	flavourless
AEFLLPRRUYY	prayerfully
AEFLMOORSUV	flavoursome
AEFLNNOOPTY	on penalty of
AEFLNOOPSTU	teaspoonful
AEFLNORTTUY	fortunately
AEFMNORRRST	transformer
AEFMNORRTTT	front matter
	frontmatter
AEFMOOPPRRT	tamperproof
	tamper-proof
AEFMOORRRTY	reformatory
AEFNNORSTTU	fast neutron
AEFNNORTTUU	unfortunate
AEFNOOOSSTU	out of season
AEFNOSSSTUU	fatuousness
AEFORRRSSTT	for starters
AEGGGNORSTU	go great guns
AEGGHHIKNNS	Genghis Khan
AEGGHHILOTV	high-voltage
AEGGHIILNNT	nightingale ▫
AEGGHIILNSX	Alex Higgins
AEGGHIIMMST	Maggie Smith
AEGGHIINNRT	ingathering
AEGGHIIRRRT	hair trigger
AEGGHINNORV	overhanging
AEGGHINSSSW	waggishness
AEGGHMNORST	Gormenghast
AEGGHMNORTU	Grangemouth
AEGGIIILMNV	living image
AEGGIIKMNTT	Mike Gatting
AEGGIIKNSST	kissing gate
AEGGIILLNST	legislating
AEGGIILMNNR	malingering
AEGGIILNRUV	give a ruling
AEGGIINRTTU	ingurgitate
AEGGIJNNORS	Jane Grigson
AEGGILMORTU	Miguel Torga
AEGGIMNRSST	gangsterism
AEGGINPRRSU	spur gearing
AEGGINPSTUY	paying guest
AEGGINRRTTU	regurgitant
AEGGNRRSSTU	Günter Grass
AEGHHIILLMT	all-time high
AEGHHILLUVY	value highly
AEGHHILMRTU	Hugh Latimer
AEGHHILMTTY	the Almighty
AEGHHILOPRY	heliography
AEGHHINORST	high treason
AEGHHINORTV	have no right
AEGHHINSSTU	haughtiness
AEGHHKORRTU	rake through
AEGHHLLOPUW	Hugh Walpole
AEGHHLOPRSU	ploughshare
AEGHHNOPRTY	ethnography
AEGHHORRTUW	wear through
AEGHIIKMNNT	in the making
AEGHIIMNRST	time-sharing
AEGHIINNRTW	wearing thin
	within range
AEGHIINRTTW	weight-train
AEGHIKNOOPR	reaping hook
	reaping-hook
AEGHILLMPRT	lamplighter
AEGHILLMSTW	might as well
AEGHILLNNRT	enthralling
AEGHILNOOST	anthologise
AEGHILNOOTZ	anthologize
AEGHILNSSST	ghastliness
AEGHILNSTTT	latest thing
AEGHILPPRTW	grapple with
AEGHILQRSTU	equal rights
AEGHIMNNRST	garnishment
AEGHIMOPRSS	seismograph
AEGHINNSSTU	naughtiness
AEGHINNSTTU	hunting-seat
AEGHINORSUW	warehousing
AEGHINPRSTX	Great Sphinx
AEGHIOOSTTV	give a shot to
AEGHIRSTTWW	straw-weight
AEGHJNNORST	John Sargent
AEGHKLMORUY	make roughly
AEGHLLNOOSY	hang loosely
AEGHLLOOTTW	go to the wall
AEGHLLOPTUW	go up the wall

AEGHLNOOORR	gonorrhoeal
AEGHLOOPRSY	phraseology
AEGHMNNORRY	Henry Morgan
AEGHMNOOPRR	monographer
AEGHNOOPRRS	nosographer
AEGHNOPRSTY	stenography
AEGHNOSTTTU	set at nought
AEGHOOPPRRT	topographer
AEGHOPPRRRY	reprography
AEGHOPPRRSS	grasshopper
AEGHOPPRRTY	typographer
AEGHRSSTTTU	thrust stage
AEGIIILMNPR	primigenial
AEGIIINORTV	originative
AEGIIINSTTV	instigative
AEGIIKNRSTW	water-skiing
AEGIILLNOST	legislation
AEGIILLNTVY	genitivally
AEGIILMNORS	regionalism
AEGIILMNTUV	lignum vitae
AEGIILNORRY	religionary
AEGIILNRSSU	singularise
AEGIILNRSUZ	singularize
AEGIIMMMNUW	minimum wage
AEGIIMMORRR	mirror image
AEGIIMNNORT	germination
AEGIIMNNORV	Merovingian
AEGIIMNNPRS	spring a mine
AEGIIMNNRTT	terminating
AEGIIMNOPRT	impignorate
AEGIIMNSTTW	time-wasting
AEGIINNNORT	Ignorantine
AEGIINNOOTT	negotiation
AEGIINNORST	resignation
AEGIINNORTT	integration
AEGIINNOSTT	negationist
AEGIINNRRST	restraining
AEGIINNRTTU	intriguante
AEGIINPPRTW	wiretapping
AEGIINRRTVX	extra virgin
AEGIJMNORTT	majoretting
AEGIJNNNPST	Pat Jennings
AEGIKLNQSUY	squeakingly
AEGIKMMNNOY	moneymaking
	money-making
AEGIKMMNRRY	merrymaking
AEGIKNNNPSW	spanking new
AEGILLMNNTY	lamentingly
AEGILLMOOPS	megalopolis
AEGILLNNOSW	Nigel Lawson
AEGILLNNRUV	unravelling
AEGILLNOPRY	role-playing
AEGILLNQRRU	quarrelling
AEGILLNRSVY	slaveringly
AEGILLRRRUY	irregularly
AEGILMNNNUY	unmeaningly
AEGILMNNOPS	plasminogen
AEGILMNOPRU	pelargonium
AEGILMNORST	gila monster
AEGILMNRSTY	streamingly
AEGILMOOPST	plagiostome
AEGILNNNRTU	running late
AEGILNNOSTU	langoustine
AEGILNNSSST	lastingness
AEGILNNSSTY	assentingly
AEGILNOOSSX	xenoglossia
AEGILNORSTU	regulations
AEGILNQRUVY	quaveringly
AEGILNRSUUV	unvulgarise
AEGILNRTTYY	yatteringly
AEGILNRUUVZ	unvulgarize
AEGILOOSTTU	tautologise
AEGILOOTTUZ	tautologize
AEGILPRTUVY	purgatively
AEGILRSTTUU	gutturalise
AEGILRTTUUZ	gutturalize
AEGIMMOPRSU	gemmiparous
AEGIMNNNRTU	running mate
AEGIMNNORUV	manoeuvring
AEGIMNNOSWW	sewing woman
AEGIMNOOPRS	spermogonia
AEGIMNOPRRS	Piers Morgan
AEGIMNORSSU	ignoramuses
AEGIMNPRSTU	get up in arms
AEGIMOOORTV	give a room to
AEGINNNOPRS	none-sparing
AEGINNNORSU	unreasoning
AEGINNOOTXY	oxygenation
AEGINNOPPRT	opening part
AEGINNOPSTV	paving stone
	paving-stone
AEGINNORRTT	interrogant
AEGINNOSSUU	sanguineous
AEGINNPRSSS	sparingness
AEGINOPPRRT	preparing to
AEGINOPRSSV	passing over
AEGINOPRSTW	Spiro T Agnew
AEGINOPRTTV	vintage port
AEGINOPRTUX	expurgation
AEGINPRSSST	trespassing
AEGINRRSTUV	invert sugar
AEGIPRRRTYY	pyrargyrite
AEGKLNOOOTT	take too long
AEGLLMORRSW	grow smaller
AEGLLNOOPTY	planetology
AEGLMNNOOTU	Léon Gaumont
AEGLPPRSTUY	great supply
AEGMOOORRST	storage room
AEGNNOPRTTU	repugnant to
AEGNOOPRSSU	saprogenous
AEGNOOPRSSY	greasy spoon
AEGOORRRTUV	rotogravure
AEGORSSSTUU	stegosaurus ❑
AEHHIILRTTT	hit the trail
AEHHILLNTUY	unhealthily
AEHHILOPSTY	lithophysae
AEHHIMOPRTY	hypothermia
AEHHIMRSTVY	Harvey Smith
AEHHINNOPTY	hyphenation
AEHHINOPRST	on the parish
AEHHIOPPSST	phosphatise
AEHHIOPPSTZ	phosphatize

Words marked ❑ can also be spelled with an initial capital letter

AEHHIOPRSST	ship the oars
AEHHIORTTTW	whitethroat
AEHHLOPPSYY	hypophyseal
AEHHMOOOPTY	homoeopathy
AEHHNOORRYY	Hooray Henry
AEHHOOPPRST	phosphorate
AEHHRRSTTUW	water thrush
AEHIIILMTUV	humiliative
AEHIIKLLNTT	in at the kill
AEHIILLPSTT	philatelist
AEHIILMMPTU	epithalmium
AEHIILNPSTW	White Plains
AEHIILOPRRT	horripilate
AEHIILOPSST	hospitalise
AEHIILOPSTZ	hospitalize
AEHIILPRSTT	peristalith
AEHIINOPRRS	parishioner
AEHIINPTTTW	patient with
AEHIIORSTTU	authorities
AEHIIOTTVWW	with a view to
AEHIIPPRRSS	periphrasis
AEHIKLMTWYY	the Milky Way
AEHIKLNNRSW	Hans Winkler
AEHIKMNNORT	ink-horn-mate
AEHIKMNSSSW	mawkishness
AEHIKMORSTY	make history
AEHIKNNPPRT	Pink Panther
AEHIKNNSSSV	knavishness
AEHIKNPTTUW	taken up with
AEHILLMTTUU	Ultima Thule
AEHILLNNSTU	in a nutshell
AEHILLOPRST	hospitaller
AEHILLORTVW	all over with
AEHILMNORTW	mother-in-law
AEHILMNRSTU	Lutheranism
AEHILMQSSUY	squeamishly
AEHILNOOPRS	Sophia Loren
AEHILNORSST	shorten sail
AEHILNOSTTW	West Lothian
AEHILNPRRTY	platyrrhine
AEHILNSSSST	saltishness
AEHILNSSSSV	slavishness
AEHILNTTUWW	white walnut
AEHILOOPPRR	plerophoria
AEHILORTTVY	hortatively
AEHILQRRTUW	quarrel with
AEHIMNNNSSS	mannishness
AEHIMNNNSSU	inhumanness
AEHIMNOOPSS	homo sapiens □
AEHIMNOPRST	misanthrope
AEHIMNORSTU	house martin
AEHIMNSSTUU	enthusiuasm
AEHIMOOSSST	homeostasis
AEHIMOPSSTY	haemoptysis
AEHIMPRSTYZ	sympathizer
AEHINNORWWY	in her own way
AEHINNPPSSU	unhappiness
AEHINOOPRST	share option
AEHINOORTTX	exhortation
AEHINOPRSTT	antistrophe
AEHINOPSSTT	stephanotis
AEHINOPTTWY	point the way
AEHINORRRSX	Rex Harrison
AEHINORSSTT	throatiness
AEHINPPRRST	partnership
	transhipper
AEHINPSSSSW	waspishness
AEHINRSSSTW	swarthiness
AEHIOPSSSTY	hypostasise
AEHIOPSSTTY	hypostatise
AEHIOPSSTYZ	hypostasize
AEHIOPSTTYZ	hypostatize
AEHIORSTVWY	variety show
AEHJJNOPRSS	Jasper Johns
AEHJNOORRST	Trojan Horse
AEHKLLNSSTY	thanklessly
AEHKLOOPRTT	look the part
AEHKMNOOSST	smooth snake
AEHKMOPRTTU	up to the mark
AEHKOPRSTTU	take up short
AEHLLMOOSTY	loathsomely
AEHLLMORRSY	Larry Holmes
AEHLLNOSSSW	shallowness
AEHLMNOOTUW	whole amount
AEHLMNOQSSU	lemon squash
AEHLOPRTUUX	Paul Theroux
AEHMMRRRTUU	heart murmur
AEHMNNOORTT	not more than
AEHMNOORSTV	harvest moon
AEHMNOPPTTU	put on the map
AEHMORRSTTY	Terry-Thomas
AEHNNOORSST	Sharon Stone
AEHNOOPRRTT	orthopteran
AEHNOOPRSWW	whooper swan
AEHNOORSSUY	honours easy
AEHNOOTTUWY	on the way out
AEHNOPPRTTY	tryptophane
AEHNOPSSUWY	push one's way
AEHOOPRRSTX	prothoraxes
AEHOORRTTXY	exhortatory
AEHOPRRRTTY	Harry Potter
AEIIILLMNOR	millionaire
AEIIILMMPRS	imperialism
AEIIILMNNOT	elimination
AEIIILMNRST	ministerial
AEIIILMPRST	imperialist
AEIIILMRRSV	verisimilar
AEIIILMTTVY	imitatively
AEIIIMNNRTU	in miniature
AEIIIMNOTTZ	itemization
AEIIIMNRSTU	miniaturise
AEIIIMNRTUZ	miniaturize
AEIIINNSTUV	insinuative
AEIIKLLOPRT	realpolitik
AEIIKLMNPRS	marlinspike
AEIIKLMORRR	like a mirror
AEIIKLOSTUY	As You Like It
AEIILLLLMTW	William Tell
AEIILLMNNPW	William Penn
AEIILLNNRTY	triennially
AEIILLNOSTX	lex talionis
AEIILLNOTVY	inviolately

AEIILLNPRTY	reptilianly
AEIILLNPTVY	plaintively
AEIILLNRSUY	uniserially
AEIILMMORST	immortalise
AEIILMMORTZ	immortalize
AEIILMNNOPS	Minneapolis
AEIILMNOORT	melioration
AEIILMNOSTT	testimonial
AEIILMNOSTV	love-in-a-mist
AEIILMNPRRY	preliminary
AEIILMNPTTY	impatiently
AEIILMPSSVY	impassively
AEIILMQTTUY	quality time
AEIILMSTTUV	stimulative
AEIILNNNOTT	intentional
AEIILNNORST	insertional
AEIILNNOTTV	ventilation
AEIILNNRTTY	itinerantly
AEIILNNSSST	saintliness
AEIILNOPRSV	previsional
AEIILNORSTT	Orientalist
AEIILNORTTU	elutriation
AEIILNRSSTV	trivialness
AEIILNRSSTW	sister-in-law
AEIILNRTUUX	luxuriate in
AEIILORRRTT	territorial□
AEIILPRSSST	peristalsis
AEIILPRTTVY	partitively
AEIILPRTVVY	privatively
AEIILRSTTVY	versatility
AEIILTTTUVY	attuitively
AEIIMMNNSSW	Weismannism
AEIIMMRRTTU	termitarium
AEIIMNNORST	inseminator
AEIIMNNORTT	termination
AEIIMNPSSTT	in times past
AEIIMOPPRRT	impropriate
AEIIMOPRRSS	impresarios
AEIIMRRTTUV	triumvirate
AEIINNNOSVV	non-invasive
AEIINNNOTTT	inattention
AEIINNNQQUU	quinquennia
AEIINNOOPRT	in operation
AEIINNOORTT	orientation
AEIINOPPRTT	Point-a-Pitre
AEIINOPRRST	Airstrip One
	respiration
AEIINOPRRTT	repartition
AEIINOPRTTX	extirpation
AEIINOPRTTY	petitionary
AEIINORRSVY	revisionary
AEIINPRSSSU	Prussianise
AEIINPRSSUZ	Prussianize
AEIIOOPRRST	a posteriori
AEIIORRSVVV	savoir-vivre
AEIJLNNPSSU	Juan-les-Pins
AEIJMNNNPTY	Jenny Pitman
AEIJMNNOORS	Marion Jones
AEIKKLMNORW	workmanlike
AEIKLMPRRSU	Muriel Spark
AEIKLNNOPPS	plainspoken
	plain-spoken
AEIKLNNORRW	lower in rank
AEIKLNOOSWY	Wole Soyinka
AEIKNNRSTTU	take in turns
AEIKNOOTTTU	take it out on
AEIKORSSTUY	strike you as
AEILLLLMNTY	mentally ill
AEILLMNOOTY	emotionally
AEILLMNTTUV	multivalent
AEILLMOOSTT	tomatilloes
AEILLNNOSTY	tensionally
AEILLNOPTTY	potentially
AEILLNOSSSY	sessionally
AEILLNRSTUV	surveillant
AEILLNRSUVY	universally
AEILLNSSSTY	stainlessly
AEILLNSSTTY	taintlessly
AEILLNSUUXY	unisexually
AEILLORTTUV	ultraviolet
AEILMMNORTY	momentarily
AEILMNNNSSU	unmanliness
AEILMNNOOTU	unemotional
AEILMNNOSSW	womanliness
AEILMNNRTTU	nutrimental
AEILMNOOSTT	molestation
AEILMNORSTT	Simon Rattle
AEILMNORTVY	normatively
AEILMNTTUWZ	Minute Waltz
AEILMOPRRTY	polarimetry
	temporarily
AEILMOPRTXY	proximately
AEILMPPRSTU	litmus paper
AEILMPSSTTY	state simply
AEILMRTTTWY	Walter Mitty
AEILNNOSUUX	sexual union
AEILNNRSTTY	transiently
AEILNOOPRTX	exploration
AEILNOPPRUV	prevail upon
AEILNOPRSTY	personality
AEILNOPSSSS	passionless
AEILOORRTTV	Il Trovatore
AEILOPRSTTW	water pistol
AEILOSTUVXY	vexatiously
AEILRSSSTUV	Lévi-Strauss
AEIMMNPPRSS	panspermism
AEIMMNRSSSU	summariness
AEIMMOPSTTU	impostumate
AEIMMORSTTU	tautomerism
AEIMMPRSSTU	Suprematism
AEIMNNOPPTT	appointment
AEIMNNORSTT	ornamentist
AEIMNNORSTU	mensuration
AEIMNNSSTTU	sustainment
AEIMNOORSST	astronomise
AEIMNOORSTZ	astronomize
AEIMNOPRTTU	importunate
	permutation
AEIMNOPSTTT	Temptations
AEIMNPPRSST	panspermist
AEIMNRRSTTT	transmitter
AEIMOORSTTU	autoerotism

Words marked □ can also be spelled with an initial capital letter

AEINNNORTTU	antineutron
	anti-neutron
AEINNOOPRST	personation
AEINNOOSTTT	ostentation
AEINNOPSTTY	spontaneity
AEINNORSTUV	intravenous
AEINNOSSSUX	anxiousness
AEINNRRSTTU	unrestraint
AEINOOPRSSU	aponeurosis
AEINOOPRTTX	exportation
AEINOORRSTT	restoration
AEINOPRSSSV	vasopressin
AEINORSSSUV	savouriness
	variousness
AEINPRRSTTU	nature strip
AEIOPPRRRTY	proprietary
AEIOPRRRSTY	respiratory
AEIOPRRRTTU	portraiture
AEIOPRRTTXY	extirpatory
AEIPPRSTUUV	suppurative
AEJKMMOPUUY	make you jump
AEJMNNOORTW	Trojan Women
AEKLLOPSSWY	speak slowly
AEKLLPRSSSY	sparklessly
AEKLOPRRSTW	plasterwork
AEKMNNOORSS	on one's marks
AEKMNOOPSSW	spokeswoman
AEKMNOPPTUU	put make-up on
AEKMNOPRSTU	put one's mark
AEKNOPRSTTU	turn to speak
AELLMPPPSUY	ample supply
AELLNPRSTUU	ne plus ultra
AELLOPRSSUX	solar plexus
AELLOQRRSUU	quarrellous
AELMMRSSTUU	summersault
AELMNORSTUW	Ulsterwoman
AELMORSSSTY	solar system
AELMPRSTYYY	mystery play
AELNNSSSUUU	unusualness
AELNOPPSTTY	penalty spot
AELOOPRRTXY	exploratory
AELOOPSSTTY	osteoplasty
AELPPRSTUWY	water supply
AEMMNNOSTTY	nasty moment
AEMNNNOORST	Norman Stone
AEMNNORRSTT	remonstrant
AEMNOOPRSTY	trypanosome
AEMNOORSSSU	amorousness
AEMNOPPRRTY	property man
AEMNOPRTTWY	Pretty Woman
AEMOOPPRRRU	amour-propre
AENNOOOSTWY	on one's way to
AENNOOPRSSS	parson's nose
AENNOOPSSTU	spontaneous
AENNOPPRSST	Prestonpans
AENNORRSTTU	neutron star
AENOOPPRSTT	top one's part
AENOPRRRSTT	transporter
AENORRSTTTU	sternutator
AENPPRSSSTU	suppressant
AEOOPPPRRTY	party-pooper
AEOPPRRTTVY	poverty trap
AEOPRRRSSTY	rotary press
AEOPRRSSTTW	water sports
AFFGGGILNOS	slagging off
	slagging-off
AFFGHIORSTT	straight off
AFFGHLLRTUU	full-fraught
AFFGIILMNRY	affirmingly
AFFHIKLOTWW	walk off with
AFFHKLNORTU	thankful for
AFFIINOSTUX	suffixation
AFFLLLNORTU	full-frontal
AFFOOORTUUV	out of favour
AFGGHIIMNNT	fighting man
AFGGIILNTUY	fatiguingly
AFGHHHIINOS	high fashion
AFGHHIILNTU	highfalutin
AFGHHLLORTU	fall through
AFGHILMOPRY	filmography
AFGHIORSTWY	right-of-ways
	rights-of-way
AFGHIPPTTUU	put up a fight
AFGHJNNOOTU	John of Gaunt
AFGIIINNRTU	infuriating
AFGIIKLNOOS	looking as if
AFGIILLNNTY	inflatingly
AFGIILLNNUY	unfailingly
AFGIILMNNTU	fulminating
AFGIILNOVWY	way of living
AFGIINNNORU	Finno-Ugrian
AFGIINSSTUU	ignis fatuus
AFGILLNNTUY	flauntingly
AFGILLORRUU	augur ill for
AFGILNPRTYY	flying party
AFGILNRSTTY	flying start
AFGINOOPPTT	foot-tapping
AFGINRRSTTU	frustrating
AFHIILLLLTW	fall ill with
AFHIILOTTUW	without fail
AFHILNOPSSW	Spanish fowl
AFHIMMNNORU	in human form
AFHINORRSTU	sharon fruit
AFHLOOSSTTY	soothfastly
AFIIIILNNTV	infinitival
AFIIILMNNST	infantilism
AFIIILNRSTU	fustilirian
AFIILLMORTW	Fort William
AFIILMNNOTU	fulmination
AFIILMNORTY	informality
AFIILNNRUWY	win unfairly
AFIILNORRTT	infiltrator
AFIILORSTTU	flirtatious
AFIIMNNOORT	information
AFIIMNOORSU	omnifarious
AFIIMORSTUV	favouritism
AFIINNORSTX	transfixion
AFIIOPRSSSU	fissiparous
AFIKLLLNPSU	skilful plan
AFILLMOOPRT	oil platform
AFILMMNOORS	Milos Forman
AFILMNOORTU	formulation

AFILMNORTUY	fulminatory
AFIMMORSTUU	fumatoriums
AFINNORSSTU	transfusion
AFINOOPPRST	Port of Spain
AFINOOPSTTU	snap out of it
AFINORRSTTU	frustration
AFLLOPRUUXY	lap of luxury
AGGHHIIKNNR	high-ranking
AGGHIIJMNTU	thingumajig
AGGHIILNNSU	languishing
AGGHIILOOST	hagiologist
AGGHILNOOTW	go along with
AGGHMMOPRSY	sphygmogram
AGGIIINNORT	originating
AGGIIINNSTT	instigating
AGGIILNNOSY	agonisingly
AGGIILNNOYZ	agonizingly
AGGILLMORRU	glamour girl
AGGILLNNOST	long-lasting
AGGILLNNTWY	twanglingly
AGGILNNORST	string along
AGGINOPSSTT	staging post
AGHHIILQTUY	high quality
	high-quality
AGHHIIMNRST	nightmarish
AGHHIIRSSTT	straightish
AGHHIJMNORS	John Grisham
AGHHILOPRTY	lithography
AGHHILORSTU	sail through
AGHHIMNRSTU	human rights
AGHHINOTTUW	hang out with
AGHHKOORSTU	soak through
AGHHNOOPPRY	phonography
AGHHOOPPRTY	photography
AGHHOOPRRTY	orthography
AGHHOPPRSYY	hypsography
AGHHOPRSSTU	pass through
AGHIIILMNTU	humiliating
AGHIIKLLLNW	hillwalking
AGHIILLPPSS	Philip Glass
AGHIILMNOOS	hooliganism
AGHIILMPRRS	A Shrimp Girl
AGHIILNNSVY	vanishingly
AGHIILNRSVY	ravishingly
AGHIIMNNORZ	harmonizing
AGHIIMRRTTU	right atrium
AGHIINNOSST	astonishing
AGHIINNQSUV	vanquishing
AGHIINPRSTY	pharyngitis
AGHIKNORSUW	waking hours
AGHILNOOSTT	anthologist
AGHILNORRWY	harrowingly
AGHILNRTTWY	thwartingly
AGHILOOPSTT	pathologist
AGHILOOTTWW	go to law with
AGHIMNNRSTY	Granny Smith
AGHIMNOORRU	hog in armour
AGHINOORSTW	shooting war
AGHINOOSSTY	soothsaying
AGHINOPSSST	passing shot
AGHINRRSTTY	Starry Night
AGHIORSTTTU	straight out
AGHIPRSTTTU	put straight
AGHLOSSTTUV	Gustav Holst
AGHMNOOSTUY	Thomas Young
AGHNOOPPRRY	pornography
AGHNORRTUUY	Arthur Young
AGIIIKLLNNP	painkilling
AGIIILLNTTT	titillating
AGIIILMNSTV	vigilantism
AGIIILNNOPT	oil painting
	oil-painting
AGIIILNNORS	original sin
AGIIILNORTV	invigilator
AGIIILNORTY	originality
AGIIILNPSST	salpingitis
AGIIILNSTTW	waiting-list
AGIIIMMNORT	immigration
AGIIINNNSTU	insinuating
AGIIINNOORT	origination
AGIIINNOSTT	instigation
AGIIKLNNOTT	talking into
AGIIKNPRSSY	sky-aspiring
AGIILMNSTTU	stimulating
AGIILMOOSST	gliomatosis
AGIILNRSTUY	singularity
AGIIMMNRSUZ	summarizing
AGIIMNOORTW	waiting-room
AGIIMNRSTTW	arm-twisting
AGIINNOPRST	stop raining
AGIINNOPRTZ	patronizing
AGIINORSTTT	tritagonist
AGIKKMNNNOW	making known
AGIKLLNPRSY	sparklingly
AGIKLMSTTUV	Gustav Klimt
AGIKLNOPSTT	stop talking
AGIKMNNORSS	king's ransom
AGILLLNPTUU	pullulating
AGILLMNNOOU	monolingual
AGILLNRSTTY	startlingly
AGILMNPPRSS	Palm Springs
AGILNNOSSUW	Angus Wilson
AGILNNPRSUY	unsparingly
AGILNOPPRVY	approvingly
AGILNOPRUVY	vapouringly
AGILOORSSYY	Assyriology
AGILPRTTUYY	guilty party
AGIMNNORRST	Morning Star
	morning star
AGIMNORSTTU	outsmarting
AGINNOPRSST	transposing
AGINOOOPRRT	prorogation
AGINOOPRSTT	protagonist
AGINORRSSYY	saying sorry
AGINPPRSTUU	suppurating
AGLLLNOOPYY	polygonally
AGLLLOOPTTY	polyglottal
AGLLMOORSUY	glamorously
AGLLOOPSTTT	glottal stop
AGLLORRSUUY	garrulously
AGLMOOOSTTY	stomatology
AGLMOOPRRTU	promulgator

AGLMOPRSSUU	glamourpuss
AGLOOOSTTUU	tautologous
AHHIJKNNOSW	John Hawkins
AHHILNOORTU	holothurian
AHHILOPPSYY	hypophysial
AHHIMNOPSSW	showmanship
AHHIPRSSTTW	thwartships
AHHJKNNOSWY	John Hawkyns
AHIIILMNOTU	humiliation
AHIIILNPPPS	Philippians
AHIIINNORTT	into thin air
AHIIJLLMNOS	John Millais
AHIIKLRRSTU	Turkish lira
AHIILLNOSTT	hill station
AHIILLNRTTY	Trinity Hall
AHIILLORSUY	hilariously
AHIILMNOPST	notaphilism
AHIILMORTUY	humiliatory
AHIILNOPRRT	horripilant
AHIILNOPSTT	notaphilist
AHIILOPSTTY	hospitality
AHIILRSSTTY	hairstylist
AHIIMNNRRTU	antirrhinum
AHIIMOOPPPT	hippopotami
AHIINNOSWWY	in his own way
AHIINNSSTTT	this instant
AHIINOPSTTT	at this point
AHIKKOORRSW	kwashiorkor
AHIKLOTTUWW	walk out with
AHIKMNOPRSW	workmanship
AHIKPPRRSTU	Arthur Kipps
AHILLNNOPSY	pollyannish
AHILLOPSTXY	phyllotaxis
AHILMNPPRST	shrimp plant
AHILNOPRSTY	rhinoplasty
AHILOORRSTY	oral history
AHILOORRTTY	hortatorily
AHILOPPRSXY	prophylaxis
AHIMNOOPSTT	taphonomist
AHIMNOORRSU	honorariums
AHIMNOPRSTY	misanthropy
AHIMNOPSSSS	Spanish moss
AHIMOORSTUZ	rhizomatous
AHINNOORRST	horrisonant
AHINNOPSSTW	Spanish Town
AHINOOPSSTX	saxophonist
AHINOPRTTTW	not part with
AHINORSTTTT	that's torn it!
AHIORSTTTTW	to start with
AHJKMNOOOSU	Joshua Nkomo
AHJMNNOORST	John Marston
AHLMOOPRSUY	amorphously
AHLNOOPSSTU	splash out on
AHLOPRRSTUU	sulphurator
AHMNNOOPRTT	Northampton
AHMNOOPSTTU	Southampton
AIIILLLNPTU	Lilliputian
AIIILLMPTTW	William Pitt
AIIILLNOPTX	pixillation
AIIILLNOTTT	titillation
AIIILMNOSST	in altissimo
AIIILMNOSTT	limitations
AIIILNNOOST	in isolation
AIIILNNOOTZ	lionization
AIIILNNOTTU	intuitional
AIIILNOTTUZ	utilization
AIIIMNRSTTU	miniaturist
AIIIMPSSTVY	impassivity
AIIINNNOSTU	insinuation
AIIINNOPRST	inspiration
AIIINNOTTUZ	unitization
AIIJJLNNOPS	Janis Joplin
AIIJLLMNSUV	Jim Sullivan
AIIJLLMPRSW	JPR Williams
AIIKNRSSSTT	Sanskritist
AIILLMNORTU	illuminator
AIILLNNOOPT	pollination
AIILLNORSUY	illusionary
AIILLNRSSTY	sinistrally
AIILLPRSTUY	spiritually
AIILMMORTTY	immortality
AIILMNOOPRT	imploration
AIILMNOOSST	solmisation
AIILMNOOSTZ	solmization
AIILMNOSTTU	stimulation
AIILNNOOSTT	notionalist
AIILNNORTTU	nutritional
AIILNOOPRSV	provisional □
AIILNOPRTUY	unipolarity
AIILNOPSTTU	stipulation
AIILNOSTTYZ	stylization
AIILNPRSTUU	unspiritual
AIILNQRTTUY	tranquility
AIIMMNNOSSU	manumission
AIIMMNOPSTT	pantomimist
AIIMMNSSTTU	numismatist
AIIMNOOPRTT	importation
AIIMNOPRTTZ	Martin Opitz
AIINNNOOQUY	Ninoy Aquino
AIINNOOOTZZ	ozonization
AIINNORSTUY	insinuatory
AIINOPRRSTY	inspiratory
AIINOPRRTTU	parturition
AIINORRTTTU	trituration
AIIOOPPRRTT	propitiator
AIIPPRRSTTY	party spirit
AIJLNORSSTU	journalists
AIKMMNOSTTY	Tommy Atkins
AIKNOORSTTW	work station
	workstation
AILLLMNOOPP	lollipop man
AILLLNOPTUU	pullulation
AILLLNOSUVY	villanously
AILLNORTUVY	voluntarily
AILLNPPSTUY	suppliantly
AILLNRTUUXY	luxuriantly
AILLOPPPRTU	tulip poplar
AILLORRSTTU	illustrator
AILMNNOSUUY	unanimously
AILMNOOOPRT	promotional
AILMNOPRTTY	importantly
AILMNORSTUV	voluntarism

AILMOOPRRTY	imploratory
AILMOPRSTUU	multiparous
AILNNORTUVY	involuntary
AILNOOPSTTU	postulation
AILNORSUUVY	unsavourily
AILOOPQRTUY	poor quality
	poor-quality
AILOOPRSUVY	oviparously
AILOPRSTTUY	stipulatory
AILORSTTTUY	statutorily
AIMMNORRTUU	murmuration
AIMMOORRSTU	moratoriums
AIMMOOSSTXY	myxomatosis
AIMNNOOPTTU	mountain top
AIMNNOORRSV	Van Morrison
AIMNNOOSTUU	mountainous
AIMNNOPRTTU	unimportant
AIMNOPPPRSY	Mary Poppins
AINNOORUWWY	in our own way
AINOOPRRSTT	prostration
AINOPPRSTUU	suppuration
AINORRRTTTU	turn traitor
AINORRSSTUU	susurration
AJLLMOOPRYY	jam roly-poly
AJMMNPQTUUU	quantum jump
AJMMOOORRTW	jam tomorrow
AKLNNOOOPTZ	zooplankton
ALLNOOOPPRR	propranolol
ALMNNOOSUYY	anonymously
ALMNOORSTTU	salmon trout
ALNNORSTUYY	tyrannously
ALOPRRSTUUY	rapturously
AMMNOOORRST	Marston Moor
AMNNOOOPPRT	ma non troppo
AMNOOPRSSTW	sportswoman
AMNOOPRSTTU	put to ransom
ANOPPRSTTUU	put on a spurt

B

BBBBNOOORSY	Bobby Robson
BBBDEELNRUU	bubble under
BBCDEEEEIKR	Beiderbecke
BBCDEEEMOOR	become bored
BBCDEHIIKRT	thick-ribbed
BBCDEHIRRTU	butcherbird
BBCEEEKLORZ	breeze block
BBCEEHHIRRT	breech birth
BBCEEHNNOOU	bonne-bouche
BBCEEIKORRS	Boris Becker
BBCEEORRRTU	Robert Bruce
BBCEILMOSTU	combustible
BBCEIORSSTU	subscribe to
BBCEIRRSSSU	subscribers
BBCEJKOORST	stockjobber
BBCEKLORSTU	blockbuster
BBCELMORSTU	cluster bomb
	cluster-bomb
BBDDEELLOOU	blue-blooded
BBDDEILLNOU	double-blind
BBDDEIRSTUY	disturbed by
BBDDENOOTUY	beyond doubt
BBDEEELOUYY	blue-eyed boy
BBDEEHHLOOY	hobbledehoy
BBDEEHILNUW	Edwin Hubble
BBDEELLORWY	Lloyd Webber
BBDEFFLLOUU	double bluff
BBDEGIIMNOV	dive-bombing
BBDEINNOPUU	be bound up in
BBDELNRSSUU	blunderbuss
BBDELRRSUUU	Ruud Lubbers
BBDGHLOOOTU	blood-bought
BBDGIIKNNOO	bookbinding
BBEEENOSSTT	one's best bet
BBEEGIILLNR	gibberellin
BBEEGILMRSU	submergible
BBEEILMRSSU	submersible
BBEEINNNOOR	be borne in on
BBEELOORRSV	slobber over
BBEELOORRTY	Robert Boyle
BBEENORRSYY	boysenberry
BBEGHKOOOTY	go by the book
BBEGIINSSSU	big business
BBEGIKLNOOR	Bolingbroke
BBEHIIILLOP	bibliophile
BBEHIKLORST	hobble skirt
BBEHINRSSSU	shrubbiness
BBEIILMSSSU	submissible
BBEILLNRTUY	Billy Bunter
BBEIMMOORRT	Bob Mortimer
BBELLMOOSTT	bell-bottoms
BBELLNOTTUY	belly-button
BBEMNNOORTU	neutron bomb
BBENORRRSTU	Robert Burns
BBFLLOOORWW	blow for blow
BBGHILNORTY	throbbingly
BBGIILLNQUY	quibblingly
BBGIKNOOORT	bring to book
BBGMOORRSUY	borborygmus
BBIILLLNTUY	Billy Butlin
BBJMMMOOSUU	mumbo-jumbos
BCCCEHHHNRU	church-bench
BCCCEIILLPY	bicycle clip
BCCDEEHKLOU	double-check
BCCDEIKLLOU	double-click
BCCDEINNOVY	convinced by
BCCEEEEFINN	beneficence
BCCEEEENRSU	erubescence
BCCEEEIKLLT	click beetle
BCCEEHILRTU	The Crucible
BCCEEILNNOT	connectible
BCCEEILORRT	Robert Cecil
BCCEEINRSTY	cybernetics
BCCEFFIKLOO	office block
BCCEIILNORU	ribonucleic
BCCEIINOORT	necrobiotic
BCCEILMPPUY	bicycle pump
BCCEINOOPPR	corn cob pipe
BCCELLRTUUU	Culture Club
BCCGHLOORUU	Groucho Club
BCCHHILOOOP	ochlophobic
BCCHHOORSTT	Scotch broth
BCCLNORTUUY	Country Club

	country club
BCDDDEEEIOT	to be decided
BCDDDELLOOO	cold-blooded
BCDDEEIIRTT	direct debit
BCDDEHLOTUU	double Dutch
BCDDILLNOOO	in cold blood
BCDEEEEIRRS	decerebrise
BCDEEEEIRRZ	decerebrize
BCDEEEFIMOX	become fixed
BCDEEEIINNT	Benedictine
BCDEEEIMORT	become tired
BCDEEEIMORW	become wider
BCDEEHILNPT	pitchblende
BCDEEHMNOOY	honeycombed
BCDEEHMNOTU	debouchment
BCDEEIILNRS	discernible
BCDEEIILRRU	irreducible
BCDEEIIMRSS	misdescribe
BCDEEIINNOT	benediction
BCDEEIMNRSU	disencumber
BCDEEINORTY	benedictory
BCDEEJOSTTU	subjected to
BCDEEKLNRUU	buckle under
BCDEELMNTUY	decumbently
BCDEFJNOOTU	found object
BCDEGHILMOU	much obliged
BCDEGHNRRSU	bergschrund
BCDEHILNNOR	hornblendic
BCDEHKLLOOT	the old block
BCDEIIILRTY	credibility
BCDEIILNRSY	discernibly
BCDEIILRRUY	irreducibly
BCDEIILSSSU	discussible
BCDEIKLOQUU	double-quick
BCDEIOOPRSS	proboscides
BCDEKLNOOOS	do one's block
BCDEKLOORSU	bloodsucker
BCDELMNOSUU	muscle-bound
BCDELOORSSU	double-cross
BCDEOORRRSS	cross-border
BCDFIKORSUY	Dick Fosbury
BCDGIIKMNOR	mockingbird
BCDGILLLOPU	bulldog clip
BCDHHIOOPRY	hydrophobic
BCDHILNNORU	unborn child
BCDIILOOPTY	body politic
BCDILLNOORU	colour-blind
BCEEEELMRRU	crème brulée
BCEEEELNNOV	benevolence
BCEEEEMNOTW	come between
BCEEEFILPRT	perfectible
BCEEEGINPTX	be expecting
BCEEEGMNRSU	submergence
BCEEEHIMOTW	become white
BCEEEHNNQSU	Queen's Bench
BCEEEILPPRT	perceptible
BCEEELLMRSU	cerebellums
BCEEENQSSUU	subsequence
BCEEFIIKNST	sick benefit
BCEEFILORRW	Wilberforce
BCEEFNNOOST	be of consent
BCEEGHILMOT	become light
BCEEGIMNNOO	come on begin
BCEEHHNOOPT	technophobe
BCEEHIIINRS	hibernicise
BCEEHIIINRZ	hibernicize
BCEEHILPRTU	The Republic
BCEEHIMNTTW	bewitchment
BCEEHIOORRS	seborrhoeic
BCEEHJKLOWY	cheek by jowl
BCEEHLOSSTT	best clothes
BCEEIIJOSTV	objectivise
BCEEIIJOTVZ	objectivize
BCEEIJLOTVY	objectively
BCEEIKOORSV	servicebook
	service-book
BCEEILLLOSY	bellicosely
BCEEILMNPUY	Public Enemy
	public enemy
BCEEILMOSST	comestibles
BCEEILNORTV	convertible
BCEEILORRSU	Le Corbusier
BCEEILORRTV	Robert Clive
BCEEILPPRTY	perceptibly
BCEEILPSSTU	susceptible
BCEEILRSTUU	tuberculise
BCEEILRTUUZ	tuberculize
BCEEINOOOSS	biocoenoses
BCEEINSSSTU	subsistence
BCEEIPRRSSU	superscribe
BCEEJLSSSTU	subjectless
BCEEKLLORTT	block letter
BCEEKMNNOOW	become known
BCEELMNRTUY	recumbently
BCEELNOOSST	obsolescent
BCEELNOSTTT	scent bottle
BCEEMNNOSUY	become sunny
BCEEMNOSTTU	obmutescent
BCEENOORRTU	counterbore
BCEFFKORSTU	be struck off
	buffer stock
BCEFFNORTUU	counterbuff
BCEFIIOPRST	fibre optics
BCEGHHIMOWY	High Wycombe
BCEGHILNNNU	unblenching
BCEGHILOPRU	police burgh
BCEGIINPRRS	prescribing
BCEGILLNSSU	singles club
BCEHHIIMRTT	timber hitch
BCEHIIIMNRS	Hibernicism
BCEHIILRRSV	silver birch
BCEHIIMNOTW	combine with
BCEHIJLNOTU	join the club
BCEHIJPSSTU	subjectship
BCEHILLORWY	yellow birch
BCEHILNOSST	blotchiness
BCEHILOPSUU	public house
BCEHKLMOOPU	Pumblechook
BCEHLORRSYY	chrysoberyl
BCEIIJMOSTV	objectivism
BCEIIJOSTTV	objectivist
BCEIIJOTTVY	objectivity

BCEIILLOSTY bellicosity
BCEIILLRSUW Bruce Willis
BCEIIMNOOST coenobitism
BCEIINOORSS necrobiosis
BCEIIORRSTW Eric Bristow
BCEIJNSTUUV subjunctive
BCEIKMNORSU broken music
BCEILLORSSU brucellosis
BCEILMNNTUY incumbently
BCEILMNRSSU crumbliness
BCEILMORTUU microtubule
BCEILNORTVY convertibly
BCEILOPRRTU corruptible
BCEILPPRSUU public purse
BCEILPSSTUY susceptibly
BCEINNOOORR Conor O'Brien
BCEIOOPRSSS proboscises
BCEIORSTTUV obstructive
BCEKKOORRST stockbroker
BCELMOOOSTW come to blows
BCELNOORTUW counterblow
BCENOOORSST botoné cross
BCEOOOPRSST stroboscope
BCEOORRSTTT Robert Scott
BCFIIILORTY forcibility
BCGHINOORSU Conisbrough
BCGIIIKLNRT rib-tickling
BCGIIILNPUZ publicizing
BCGIIKLNOOT bootlicking
BCGILOOORYY cryobiology
BCHIIIPSSTU ship biscuit
BCHMOOOTTTU touch bottom
BCHNOORSSTU hot cross bun
BCIIIILMSTY miscibility
BCIIIILNTVY vincibility
BCIILLLNNOT Bill Clinton
BCIJNNOOTUX junction box
BCIJNNOSTUU subjunction
BCIKLOPRSUW public works
BCILMOSTTUU custom-built
BCILOPRRTUY corruptibly
BCINOORRTTU contributor
BCINOORSTTU obstruction
BDDDEEEGLOU double-edged
BDDDEEIIMOS disembodied
BDDDEFMNOUU dumbfounded
BDDEEFILRUY Durbeyfield
BDDEEFLSSUU self-subdued
BDDEEIINOST disobedient
BDDEEILMNNO noble-minded
BDDEEIMNRSU disemburden
BDDEEKMNRUU Edmund Burke
BDDEELOOPRU pure-blooded
BDDEENSSSUU subduedness
BDDEFILNORY forbiddenly
BDDEFLLLOOU full-blooded
BDDEFMNORUU dumbfounder
BDDEGIIMNNN mind-bending
BDDEGINRUWY ruby wedding
BDDEHIMNSUZ Zen Buddhism
BDDEHINRRTU thunderbird
BDDEINRSTUU undisturbed
BDDELNNOUUY unboundedly
BDDELNOTUUY undoubtedly
BDDENOORSWY beyond words
BDDFILLNNOU unblindfold
BDDGILNOOOP blood doping
BDEEEEHIRST therebeside
BDEEEEIIMRR Biedermeier
BDEEEEKNOPS keep one's bed
BDEEEFILLRW well-briefed
BDEEEFILOOU oeil-de-boeuf
BDEEEHIKRSW bewhiskered
BDEEEHILLMS embellished
BDEEEIILRSV disbeliever
BDEEEIIRRSV Sir Bedivere
BDEEEILMNTV bedevilment
BDEEEILMRTT Bette Midler
BDEEEILOSTW boiled sweet
BDEEEIMNNTZ bedizenment
BDEEEIMORRR embroiderer
BDEEELNSSSS blessedness
BDEEEMNSSSU bemusedness
BDEEENOPRTT pretend to be
BDEEFFGIJRS Jeff Bridges
BDEEFFGIORT beg to differ
BDEEFGOOTTU get out of bed
BDEEFHIIRRT The Firebird
BDEEFIIINRS defibrinise
BDEEFIIINRZ defibrinize
BDEEFIIOTTT fit to be tied
BDEEFIIRRTY terrified by
BDEEGGHIIRW weighbridge
BDEEGGLLNOO Golden Globe
BDEEGIIINNV Divine Being
divine being
BDEEGIILLNR ill-breeding
BDEEGIILNRW bewildering
BDEEGINORTU outbreeding
BDEEGINOTTT get into debt
BDEEGINRRTT Trent Bridge
BDEEHHLLOTT hold the belt
BDEEHHOPRSY shepherd boy
BDEEHILLOUX double helix
BDEEHILMNSU unblemished
BDEEHILSSTW blessed with
BDEEHISTTTU bite the dust
BDEEHLNRTUU Blut und Ehre
BDEEIILNSST distensible
BDEEIIMRSTT disembitter
BDEEILLMOOS loose-limbed
BDEEILLNPRS spellbinder
BDEEILLRRUV D'Urberville
BDEEILMRRTU tumble-drier
BDEEILORRWZ bowdlerizer
BDEEIMMNRUX mixed number
BDEEIMNNRUX index number
BDEEINNSSSU business end
BDEEJLORSTU Jules Bordet
BDEELLOOSSV blood vessel
BDEELNORTUY double-entry
BDEELPRRTUY perturbedly

BDEENPRRTUU	unperturbed
BDEFFLNNOUU	bundle of fun
BDEFGINOORY	foreign body
BDEFHILMNOS	Flemish bond
BDEFHIORRST	for the birds
BDEFHNOOORU	bed of honour
BDEFILORSTU	double first
BDEFIMNOORS	bosom friend
BDEGGIINRSW	swing bridge
BDEGHIOOTTW	go to bed with
BDEGHKOOOOT	the Good Book
BDEGIILMNSS	dissembling
BDEGIIOPRTV	pivot bridge
BDEGILNNNUY	unbendingly
BDEGINNNRUU	unburdening
BDEGINNOORR	bordering on
BDEGIORRSTU	Stourbridge
BDEGLNNOORW	golden brown
BDEGLNOORUW	below ground
BDEGLOOSSUY	God bless you
BDEHHOOORRT	brotherhood
BDEHIIINNTU	uninhibited
BDEHIIKLLTY	Billy the Kid
BDEHIILPRSU	shipbuilder
BDEHIINNPTU	nip in the bud
BDEHIKLNOTU	doublethink
BDEHILNPSUU	unpublished
BDEHIOOPVVY	hooped bivvy
BDEHIOTTTUW	without debt
BDEHLNORTTU	thunderbolt
BDEIIIILNSV	indivisible
BDEIIIILNTY	inedibility
BDEIIILMMOZ	immobilized
BDEIIILNTVY	vendibility
BDEIIISSUVV	subdivisive
BDEIILLLRWY	Billy Wilder
BDEIKNORSTU	strikebound
BDEILLLNORR	roller blind
BDEILLOSTUX	billets-doux
BDEILNNOOOS	in one's blood
BDEILNTTTUW	blunt-witted
BDEILOORSST	blood-sister
BDEIMMNOPRU	Premium Bond
BDEINNORTTU	run into debt
BDEINOSSSUU	dubiousness
BDEISSTTTUU	substituted
BDELLOSSTUY	doubtlessly
BDEMNOORTUW	do number two
BDFGIIKNORS	king of birds
BDFKOOOORSW	book of words
BDFLNOOOOSY	nobody's fool
BDFLOOOORTU	out for blood
BDFNOOOSTUU	out of bounds
BDGGIIILNOS	disobliging
BDGHIIMMNRU	hummingbird
	Humming-Bird
BDGIILMNNOW	mind-blowing
BDGIILNNOOW	boiling-down
BDGIILNNORT	Bridlington
BDGIILNOTUU	outbuilding
BDGIIMMNNNU	mind-numbing
BDGIIMNNORT	bring to mind
BDGIINNPRUW	bring up wind
BDGNNOOORRW	Gordon Brown
BDHINOPTUUW	bound up with
BDHKOORSTUY	Dukhobortsy
BDHNNOOORUU	honour-bound
BDIIIILNSVY	indivisibly
BDIIINOSSUV	subdivision
BDIIORRSTTU	distributor
BDLOOOPRSST	blood sports
BEEEEGIMNST	besiegement
BEEEEIMNTTW	betweentime
BEEEFHINRSS	fines herbes
BEEEFILNOST	bet one's life
BEEEFLMOPRR	problem-free
BEEEFLORRTU	trouble-free
BEEEGGLOOOR	George Boole
BEEEGGOORRY	George Robey
BEEEGHILPST	The Big Sleep
BEEEGIINNOR	bioengineer
BEEEGILLNRT	belligerent
BEEEGILMNSY	beseemingly
BEEEGILMNTU	beguilement
BEEEGIMMNRR	remembering
BEEEGINOSUY	be seeing you
BEEEGNOORTT	go one better
BEEEHORRSTV	The Observer
BEEEILNNORV	nonbeliever
	non-believer
BEEEILNPRTV	preventible
BEEEILPRRSS	repressible
BEEEILPRSSX	expressible
BEEEIMMMRRS	misremember
BEEEINNRSTV	Ernest Bevin
BEEEIOPRRRS	Robespierre
BEEEIRSTTTW	bittersweet
BEEELMNNNOT	ennoblement
BEEENORSSSV	verboseness
BEEFFINOOTT	of benefit to
BEEFGILNORW	wrong belief
BEEFGINOORT	freebooting
BEEFGLLOORW	globeflower
BEEFILRSTTU	butterflies
BEEFKLLRUUY	rebukefully
BEEGGHORSUW	George W Bush
BEEGGILSSTU	suggestible
BEEGGINSTTX	next biggest
BEEGGNOORRW	George Brown
	George-Brown
BEEGGNOORRY	George Byron
BEEGGNORRSU	George Burns
BEEGHIISSTU	The Big Issue
BEEGHIKMOST	the Big Smoke
BEEGHILNORT	bring to heel
BEEGHILNRTT	gentle birth
BEEGHINNORR	herringbone
	herring-bone
BEEGHLNOORT	the long robe
BEEGIILLNVY	believingly
BEEGIILNNUV	unbelieving
BEEGIIMNRTT	embittering

BEEGIKKNOOP	bookkeeping
BEEGIKLNNSY	Ben Kingsley
BEEGILLNSST	bestselling
BEEGILLRRTY	Gilbert Ryle
BEEGILNNOSS	ignobleness
BEEGILNSSSU	leg-business
BEEGILORTUV	give trouble
BEEGIMNOSTT	misbegotten
BEEGIMNOSTY	bygone times
BEEGPRRRSSU	Pressburger
BEEHIIKNNRS	Henrik Ibsen
BEEHIILNRRU	Henri Breuil
BEEHIIMSSST	Bessie Smith
BEEHILMNOOP	mobile phone
BEEHILNNPTT	Phil Bennett
BEEHILNOTTU	into the blue
BEEHILOPRSY	hyperbolise
BEEHILOPRYZ	hyperbolize
BEEHIMNOORT	theobromine
BEEHINSSSTU	the business
BEEHJNOOTTW	new to the job
BEEHJNORSTW	John Webster
BEEHJOPSSUY	Joseph Beuys
BEEHKMNORRY	broken rhyme
BEEHKNOORSU	house-broken
BEEHKOOORRT	Robert Hooke
BEEHLLNOOPR	Bellerophon
BEEHLMNORUW	whole number
BEEHLOORSTW	The Rose Bowl
BEEHLRRTTTU	Rhett Butler
BEEHOPRRSTT	stepbrother
BEEIILMPRSS	impressible
	permissible
BEEIILNOPST	bite one's lip
BEEIILNSSSV	visibleness
BEEIIRRTTUV	retributive
BEEIJLPRSTY	J B Priestley
BEEIKLLNOTT	Klein bottle
BEEILLLNTUY	ebulliently
BEEILLRRRTU	bull-terrier
BEEILLSTTTY	set little by
BEEILMMNORT	embroilment
BEEILMNORTT	bitter lemon
BEEILMNORTY	Emily Brontë
BEEILMNSSSU	sublimeness
BEEILNNOSTW	tennis elbow
BEEILNOPRSS	responsible
BEEILNOQSSU	obliqueness
BEEILNRSSTT	brittleness
BEEILORSSSV	brisés volés
BEEILPRRSSY	repressibly
BEEIMMNPRRU	prime number
BEEINNOORTU	boutonnière
BEEINORSTTY	tenebrosity
BEEINRSSTUV	subservient
BEEINRTTUUV	Venturi tube
BEEJOORTTUV	objet trouvé
BEEKMNOORTY	more by token
BEELLLLOWYY	yellow-belly
BEELMNORTTU	Mount Elbert
BEELMOORSTU	troublesome
BEEMNORRRRY	Rory Bremner
BEENNNOTTTY	Tony Bennett
BEENOORRRST	Robert Ensor
BEENQRSSSUU	brusqueness
BEFGHILLRTU	bullfighter
BEFGIILNORT	bring to life
BEFGIILNTTY	befittingly
BEFGIINNTTU	unbefitting
BEFHIILLLLT	fill the bill
BEFHILLMSTU	thimblefuls
BEFHILLOOTT	foot the bill
BEFHLMORTUU	rule of thumb
BEFIIILLTXY	flexibility
BEFIMORRSUU	umbriferous
BEFINORSTTT	frostbitten
BEFLLMRSTUU	tumblerfuls
BEFLLOOPRTU	bulletproof
	bullet-proof
BEFOORRRSTT	Robert Frost
BEGGGILNOOT	bootlegging
BEGGHILNORS	Helsingborg
BEGGIILLNUY	beguilingly
BEGGIINNORS	Ronnie Biggs
BEGGINOORRS	Bognor Regis
BEGHIINOTTW	to begin with
BEGHIIORTTV	give birth to
BEGHILNORUY	neighbourly
BEGHIMNOORT	bring home to
BEGHINNOOTT	be nothing to
BEGIIIILLTY	eligibility
BEGIILLNNOR	be rolling in
BEGIINRSTUV	Vitus Bering
BEGILLMNRTY	tremblingly
BEGILNORSVY	observingly
BEGINRSSTTU	buttressing
BEGMNNORRUW	wrong number
BEHHMRSSTUU	the bum's rush
BEHIIIOPRTV	prohibitive
BEHIINPRSTU	tribuneship
BEHIINRSSST	Britishness
BEHIKKOOSST	kiss the book
BEHIKNOOSSS	bookishness
BEHILLNSSSU	bullishness
BEHILMOPRSY	hyperbolism
BEHINOORSSS	boorishness
BEHINRSSSTU	brutishness
BEHIOORRSUV	herbivorous
BEHJNNOOORS	John Osborne
BEHLLLSSSUY	blushlessly
BEHLOORRSTU	soul brother
BEHMNOORTUU	Bournemouth
BEHMOOOTTTT	to the bottom
BEHNNOOTTTU	on the button
BEHNORSTTWY	north by west
BEHOORRSSTX	boxer shorts
	boxer-shorts
BEHOSSTTUWY	south by west
BEIIILMMORZ	immobilizer
BEIIILMNRST	libertinism
BEIIILMQRUU	equilibrium
BEIIILNSSTY	sensibility

BEIIILQRSTU	equilibrist
BEIILLORSTV	Orbitsville
BEIILMPRSSY	permissibly
BEIILNOSSSU	biliousness
BEIILNRSSST	bristliness
BEIILRRSSTV	verslibrist
BEIINNPSTXY	sixpenny bit
BEIINORRTTU	retribution
BEIKLNNOOTW	bowline knot
BEILLLLOSUY	libellously
BEILLMPSTUU	submultiple
BEILLNORSVW	Brownsville
BEILLORRSUY	irresolubly
BEILMNOOOTT	Milton Obote
BEILMOORSTT	mortise bolt
BEILMPRRSTU	rumble strip
BEILNOPRSSY	responsibly
BEILORSTUVY	obtrusively
BEIMNOPSSTU	montes pubis
BEIMPSSTUUV	subsumptive
BEINNOPTTWY	twopenny bit
BEINOOSSSUV	obviousness
BEINOPRRSTU	stirrup bone
BEINORSTUUV	unobtrusive
BEINSSTTTUU	substituent
BELLMOSSSUY	bless my soul!
BELLNRTTUUY	turbulently
BELMNOOPRSU	numbers pool
BELMNORSTUU	Mount Elbrus
BELNNNOORSY	Byron Nelson
BELNOOOPSTW	blow one's top
BELNOOSTUUY	bounteously
BELOOORRSTW	Robert Solow
BELOOPRSTTU	trouble spot
BEMOOPRRSTY	Port Moresby
BENOORTTTUU	turn out to be
BFFLOOPRSUY	Fosbury flop
BFIKLOOOSST	list of books
BFILLLMNOOU	in full bloom
BFILLNOTUUY	bountifully
BFLLOORUUYY	bully for you
BGGHIILLNTY	blightingly
BGGILLMNRUY	grumblingly
BGGINNOORUU	bourguignon
BGHHKOOORTU	book through
BGHIIINOPRT	prohibiting
BGHIIINRRTV	Virgin Birth
BGHIINOPPWY	whipping-boy
BGHIKNOSTWY	know by sight
BGHIMNPTTUU	tub-thumping
BGIIILLLTUY	gullibility
BGIILMNOSYZ	symbolizing
BGIILNNOPSW	spin-bowling
BGIILOORSTT	tribologist
BGILLMNSTUY	stumblingly
BGILNOOTTTU	blotting out
	blotting-out
BGINNNOSTUW	snow bunting
BHIIIINNOST	inhibitions
BHIIINOOPRT	prohibition
BHIILLLRSUY	Silbury Hill
BHIILMRSTUW	Wilbur Smith
BHIIOOPRRTY	prohibitory
BHIKNNOOSTW	with knobs on
BHIKOOOTTUW	without book
BHILMOOSTYY	tomboyishly
BHIMNOOPRRT	prothrombin
BIIILOPSSTY	possibility
BIIKNOORSSV	Novosibirsk
BIILLNOORTU	tourbillion
BIILLOOSUVY	obliviously
BIILOOOSTUV	oblivious to
BIIMNOOSTUX	moxibustion
BIIMOPRSSTU	Möbius strip
BILMOPSTUUY	bumptiously
BILNOOOSUXY	obnoxiously
BIMNNOORRSS	Mrs Robinson
BIMNOPSSTUU	subsumption
BIMOOOSSTUV	most obvious
BIMORSSTUUU	rumbustious
BINOOPSSSTU	Puss in Boots
BIOOOPPRRSU	opprobrious
BLLMORSSUUY	slumbrously
BLLOORSTUUY	troublously
BMMMMNOSUUU	summum bonum
BMMNOTTTUUY	tummy-button
BMORSSTUUUU	rumbustuous

C

CCCCKKLOOOU	cuckoo clock
CCCDEEIINNO	coincidence
CCCEEEENRSX	excrescence
CCCEEFLLNOU	flocculence
CCCEEIILMST	eclecticism
CCCEEIINRTV	civic centre
CCCEENNORRU	concurrence
CCCEENORRSU	occurrences
CCCEFILMRTU	circumflect
CCCEILORSST	Celtic cross
CCCEIMPRSTU	circumspect
CCCEINNOTTU	Connecticut
CCCEINOOPRS	necroscopic
CCCGIKNOORW	cock-crowing
CCCIIMMOORS	microcosmic
CCCIIMOOPRS	microscopic
CCDDEEENORS	decrescendo
CCDEEEEINNR	Nicene Creed
CCDEEEFHIKN	chickenfeed
CCDEEEGINOT	genetic code
CCDEEEIINRS	iridescence
CCDEEELLORT	recollected
CCDEEENRRST	Red Crescent
CCDEEFINOOS	food science
CCDEEHILPSY	psychedelic
CCDEEIIINST	insecticide
CCDEEIIRRST	directrices
CCDEEILNOPY	encylopedic
CCDEEILNOTY	conceitedly
CCDEEILRRSS	dress circle
CCDEEIOPPRU	preoccupied
CCDEELLLOTY	collectedly
CCDEELLNOTU	uncollected

CCDEELNNOOS	condolences
CCDEELNNORY	concernedly
CCDEELNNOTY	connectedly
CCDEENNNORU	unconcerned
CCDEENNNOTU	unconnected
CCDEFINNOOV	convinced of
CCDEHHIKLNO	hold in check
CCDEIMOOOST	octodecimos
CCDEINNNOUV	unconvinced
CCDEINNOUUV	unconducive
CCDEINOOTUV	conducive to
CCDEINORSTT	constricted
CCDENORSSTU	conductress
CCDENORSTTU	deconstruct
CCDFLMOOORT	cold comfort
CCDGILNNOUY	conducingly
CCDHHILLOOS	schoolchild
CCDHIILORWY	wild chicory
CCDHILOOPYY	hypocycloid
CCDHIOORTTW	witch doctor
CCDHIOOSTUU	studio couch
CCDILLMNNOU	Don McCullin
CCEEEEILLRT	electric eel
CCEEEEILRTY	electric eye
CCEEEEINPRT	centrepiece
CCEEEFHIKNR	neckerchief
CCEEEFIILNS	life science
CCEEEFLNORS	florescence
CCEEEGINNRS	nigrescence
CCEEEGNNORV	convergence
CCEEEGNRSTU	turgescence
CCEEEHHLOST	cheesecloth
CCEEEHIKKNP	keep in check
CCEEEHINNOR	incoherence
CCEEEIINPPR	percipience
CCEEEILSTWY	sweet cicely
CCEEEINNNOV	convenience
CCEEEINOPRV	preconceive
CCEEEINOSTX	coexistence
CCEEEINRRST	Cirencester
CCEEEINRSTV	vitrescence
CCEEEIRSTUX	executrices
CCEEELORTTU	electrocute
CCEEENNOQSU	consequence
CCEEENPRSTU	putrescence
CCEEFFIINOT	coefficient
CCEEFFIINSU	sufficience
CCEEFHNRRUV	French curve
CCEEFIIMNNU	munificence
CCEEFILNOST	self-conceit
CCEEFILOOPR	police force
CCEEFINOSST	soft science
CCEEGLLORSV	clever clogs
	cleverclogs
CCEEGNNOOST	cognoscente
CCEEGNOOPRS	precognosce
CCEEHIIKNRW	chicken wire
CCEEHMOPTYY	phycomycete
CCEEIILNOSS	soil science
CCEEIILRTTY	electricity
CCEEIIMMNSU	ecumenicism
CCEEIIMNNOS	omniscience
CCEEIIMNOSV	misconceive
CCEEIIMNTUY	ecumenicity
CCEEIIMOSST	cosmeticise
CCEEIIMOSTZ	cosmeticize
CCEEIINOPTV	nociceptive
CCEEILNNOTV	conventicle
CCEEILNORST	electronics
	stone circle
CCEEILPPRRU	upper circle
CCEEILPPRTU	peptic ulcer
CCEEIMNOORT	econometric
CCEEIMNRSTU	music centre
CCEEINNOOTV	not conceive
CCEEINNOQTU	cinquecento
CCEEINNOSSS	conciseness
CCEEINNOSST	consistence
CCEEINOORTW	once or twice
CCEEINORRTU	Eurocentric
CCEEINORSTU	scenic route
CCEEINOSSSX	ex concessis
CCEEINOSTUV	consecutive
CCEEIOPSTTU	cut to pieces
CCEEJNOOOSS	Jose Conseco
CCEELMOOOST	come close to
CCEELSSSSSU	successless
CCEEMNNNORT	concernment
CCEENNNOORT	non-concrete
CCEENOPSSTU	conceptuses
CCEENORRSST	correctness
CCEEOORRRTV	overcorrect
CCEFFIINSUY	sufficiency
CCEFHIIMORS	microfiches
CCEFHIIORST	first choice
CCEFHIKNRST	French stick
CCEFIIIPSTY	specificity
CCEFIINNOPS	non-specific
CCEFIINOPRY	proficiency
CCEFINORSST	cross-infect
CCEGHHORRSU	churchgoers
CCEGHINOPSY	psychogenic
CCEGIILNNOR	reconciling
CCEGILMNOOS	coming close
CCEGILNOORY	eccrinology
CCEGINNNOTY	contingency
CCEGINNOOST	cognoscenti
CCEHHIMRSTU	Church Times
CCEHHIOSSTT	schottische
CCEHHKOOORT	crochet hook
CCEHHMORSUU	church-mouse
CCEHHORRTUW	church tower
CCEHIILNOPR	necrophilic
CCEHIINPRST	sphincteric
CCEHIIPRRTY	hyper-critic
CCEHIKKOSTY	hockey stick
CCEHIKSSSTT	Schick's test
CCEHILNOPTY	polytechnic
CCEHIMOOPRT	ectomorphic
CCEHINNOTTW	connect with
CCEHINNRSSU	crunchiness
CCEHKLOSTTU	shuttlecock

CCEHKMOORTU	Cockermouth
CCEHKNPRSUU	sucker-punch
CCEHNNOORSW	show concern
CCEIIILMOPU	Emilio Pucci
CCEIIJMNORT	microinject
CCEIIKLRSTY	city slicker
CCEIIKNSSTT	stick insect
CCEIIMMORRT	micrometric
CCEIIMOORST	sociometric
CCEIINOPRTU	open circuit
CCEIIOPRRTY	reciprocity
CCEIJNNOTUV	conjunctive
CCEIKLNOPRU	cupro-nickel
CCEILMORUVV	circumvolve
CCEILNNOTTU	noctilucent
CCEILNORRTY	incorrectly
CCEILOOPRTU	police court
CCEINNNOOST	connections
CCEINNOORST	concertinos
CCEINNOOSTU	consecution
CCEINNOPRRW	crown prince
CCEINNOSSTY	consistency
CCEINOOPSTU	conceptious
CCEJNNORTUU	conjuncture
CCEKMNOSTUU	come unstuck
CCELLNSTUUY	succulently
CCELORSSSUU	succourless
CCENORRSTTU	constructer
	reconstruct
CCFGIILNNOT	conflicting
CCFIIINORUX	crucifixion ❑
CCFINOOOSSU	conscious of
CCGGHHINORU	church-going
CCGHIIKMNOT	thick-coming
CCGHILNORSY	scorchingly
CCGHIOOPRSY	hygroscopic
CCGIIINRRTU	ring circuit
CCGINOSTTTU	cost-cutting
CCHHMNOOPTU	not much chop
CCHIIILNOPS	silicon chip
CCHIIMNOOPR	microphonic
CCHIINOOPRS	rhinoscopic
CCHILMOOPRY	polychromic
CCHILMOOSSU	music school
CCHIMMNOOOR	monochromic
CCHIOOOPRST	orthoscopic
CCHIORSSSTT	cross-stitch
CCIIKKQSSTU	quick-sticks
CCIIMMNOORS	in microcosm
CCIIMMNOSTU	communistic
CCIINNOOSTV	convictions
CCIINOPRTTY	nyctitropic
CCIJNNNOOTU	conjunction
CCILMRRSUUU	curriculums
CCILNNOOSSU	conclusions
CCILNNOOTUW	town council
CCILNOOSSUY	consciously
CCILNOOSTUU	noctilucous
CCIMNNOOPTU	compunction
CCINNOOSSUU	unconscious
CCINOOPSSUU	conspicuous
CCINOORRSTT	constrictor
CCINOORSSSU	cross cousin
CCLNNOOORWY	crown colony
CCNOORRSTTU	constructor
CCNOORTTUUY	county court
CDDDEEEINSS	decidedness
CDDDEEENNSU	undescended
CDDDEEIIRST	discredited
CDDDEEILNUY	undecidedly
CDDEEEEPRSU	reduce speed
CDDEEEHIPPT	deep-pitched
CDDEEEILPRT	predilected
CDDEEEIPRTU	decrepitude
CDDEEEMMNOR	recommended
CDDEEFIINST	disinfected
CDDEEFILNSU	self-induced
CDDEEGIORTV	get divorced
CDDEEIILLLR	Eric Liddell
CDDEEIIMRST	misdirected
CDDEEIINORT	rodenticide
CDDEEIINRTT	interdicted
CDDEEILMNOS	close-minded
CDDEEILTUVY	deductively
CDDEEINPRRU	underpriced
CDDEEINPRTU	unpredicted
CDDEEIOORRV	video-record
CDDEELOORUV	clouded over
CDDEENNNOSU	uncondensed
CDDEENNOPSY	despondency
CDDEENOORRT	not recorded
CDDEENRRTUY	eddy current
CDDEEOORRVW	overcrowded
CDDEEORSTUV	dust-covered
CDDEFGHIILT	gifted child
CDDEFIIKLST	fiddlestick
CDDEFIIMOST	discomfited
CDDEGIINPRU	rice pudding
CDDEHIILMNR	childminder
CDDEHIKLTUW	The Wild Duck
CDDEHILNORW	wonder child
CDDEHIORTWW	crowded with
CDDEIIILNNS	disinclined
CDDEIIILNPS	disciplined
CDDEIILNNOT	inclinded to
CDDEIILPPSS	slipped disc
CDDEIINNOOT	conditioned
CDDEIKOPSTT	spotted dick
CDDEILNOSSU	undisclosed
CDDEILOORSU	discoloured
CDDEIMOOPSS	discomposed
CDDEIOPSTUU	cut up didoes
CDDELLLMOOY	mollycoddle
CDDELMOORUU	mud-coloured
CDDELOORRRW	world record
CDDHILOOOOV	Voodoo Child
CDEEEEFFLNS	self-defence
CDEEEEFLNSS	defenceless
CDEEEEHKRRT	three-decker
CDEEEEINPRX	experienced
CDEEEEORRTV	tree-covered
CDEEEFFINRS	differences

Words marked ❑ can also be spelled with an initial capital letter

CDEEEFGLOTT	get cold feet
CDEEEFHIMNR	chemin de fer
CDEEEFHORUV	chef d'oeuvre
	chef-d'oeuvre
CDEEEFIILNS	fin de siècle
CDEEEFILTVY	defectively
CDEEEFIORRT	fore-recited
CDEEEFLNRST	self-centred
CDEEEFLORSV	self-covered
CDEEEGHRTTU	hedgecutter
CDEEEGILNXY	exceedingly
CDEEEGINORS	derecognise
CDEEEGINORZ	derecognize
CDEEEIINSST	necessitied
CDEEEIIOPPR	period piece
CDEEEILNOST	deselection
CDEEEILORTT	lie detector
CDEEEILPTVY	deceptively
CDEEEINSSTX	excitedness
CDEEEIORSSX	do exercises
CDEEEIORTVX	overexcited
CDEEELNPRTY	precedently
CDEEEMMNORR	recommender
CDEEENNOPRS	respondence
CDEEENORRTT	retrocedent
CDEEENORSST	rose-scented
CDEEENORSVY	every second
CDEEEOOPRRW	woodcreeper
CDEEEOPRRSS	predecessor
CDEEERRRSTU	resurrected
CDEEFFIKNST	stiff-necked
CDEEFHOORUV	forevouched
CDEEFIIINNT	deficient in
CDEEFIILNTY	deficiently
CDEEFIINPSU	unspecified
CDEEFIIORRX	ferric oxide
CDEEFILLTUY	deceitfully
CDEEFILNORS	close friend
CDEEFILNORY	eco-friendly
CDEEFILNRUU	Lucien Freud
CDEEFILOPPR	Copperfield
CDEEFILOSST	close-fisted
CDEEFINORRT	Fredericton
CDEEFLNOSSY	confessedly
CDEEFNNORST	frondescent
CDEEFNORSTT	soft-centred
CDEEFOORRTU	tour de force
CDEEFOPRRTW	word-perfect
	WordPerfect®
CDEEGGINTTU	cutting edge
CDEEGGLORSS	cross-legged
CDEEGHIINPR	deciphering
CDEEGINOPRS	proceedings
CDEEGNOSSSU	second-guess
CDEEHHINRSU	uncherished
CDEEHIINNOS	Indo-Chinese
CDEEHIINNST	indehiscent
CDEEHIKPRSW	shipwrecked
CDEEHILMNNR	men-children
CDEEHIMNOST	Demosthenic
CDEEHIOOSSS	choose sides
CDEEHIOQSTU	discotheque
	discothèque
CDEEHNOORRT	on the record
CDEEHNOORSU	echo-sounder
CDEEIIKLNSS	slickenside
CDEEIILNORT	dereliction
CDEEIIMOSST	domesticise
CDEEIIMOSTZ	domesticize
CDEEIINORRT	redirection
CDEEIINPTUV	input device
CDEEIINRSTV	viridescent
CDEEIINRTTU	incertitude
CDEEIIOORTV	Côte d'Ivoire
CDEEIIPRSTV	descriptive
CDEEIKLNNOO	nickelodeon
CDEEIKLNORT	interlocked
CDEEIKOPSTZ	pocket-sized
CDEEIKPPPSU	pick up speed
CDEEILLOPPS	close-lipped
CDEEILLRTWY	city-dweller
CDEEILNNQUY	delinquency
CDEEILNOPRT	predilecton
CDEEILOORSU	decolourise
CDEEILOORUZ	decolourize
CDEEILRSUVY	decursively
CDEEILRTUVY	reductively
CDEEILSTUVY	seductively
CDEEIMNNRST	discernment
	rescindment
CDEEIMNNSTU	inducements
CDEEIMNOPRS	endospermic
CDEEINOORTT	condottiere
CDEEINOPRTV	open verdict
CDEEINORRTU	reintroduce
CDEEINORSUU	in due course
CDEEINPRSUU	superinduce
CDEEIORRTXY	ex-directory
CDEEIRRRSVW	screwdriver
CDEEIRSTTUV	destructive
CDEEKLLOSTW	well-stocked
CDEEKNOORSS	crookedness
CDEELLMNOPU	uncompelled
CDEELLMOOPT	compelled to
CDEELMNOPTU	uncompleted
CDEELNNOTTY	contentedly
CDEELNRRTUY	decurrently
CDEELNRTTUU	uncluttered
CDEELPSSTUY	suspectedly
CDEEMNNNOTU	uncontemned
CDEEMNOOPUY	compound eye
CDEEMOORSTY	Comedy Store
CDEENNOPRSY	respondency
CDEENNOQRUU	unconquered
CDEENNORTUV	unconverted
CDEENNOSTTU	uncontested
CDEENOORTTV	converted to
CDEENOPRSSU	unprocessed
CDEENOPRTTU	unprotected
CDEENPSSTUU	unsuspected
CDEEOOPRRUV	overproduce
CDEEORRSTUV	rust-covered

CDEFFGIOOOS	good offices	CDEIIMOSTTY	domesticity
CDEFFIORTUY	duty officer	CDEIINNOORT	conditioner
CDEFHILLORW	flower child		recondition
CDEFHIOOPRT	pitched roof	CDEIINNOSTU	discontinue
CDEFHNNOORU	confound her	CDEIINOORTT	condottieri
CDEFIINNTUY	infecundity	CDEIINOPRST	description
CDEFIINORTU	countrified	CDEIJOOSTTU	do justice to
CDEFILNNOTY	confidently	CDEILNNNOOU	on cloud nine
CDEFIMNNORU	unconfirmed	CDEILNNOTUY	continuedly
CDEFIMOORRV	divorce from	CDEILNOORUU	unicoloured
CDEFINNNOOT	not confined	CDEILNOPSST	split second
CDEFINNTUUY	unfecundity	CDEILNORSUU	incredulous
CDEFINORTUY	countryfied	CDEILOORRTU	tricoloured
CDEGHHHIIPT	high-pitched	CDEILORSTTY	Ridley Scott
CDEGHIILNSU	child genius	CDEIMMNOPSU	compendiums
CDEGHILNOOS	deschooling	CDEIMMNOTTU	uncommitted
CDEGHINORRS	Schrödinger	CDEIMMOOPRS	compromised
CDEGHINOSST	second sight	CDEIMNOOPSU	compendious
CDEGIINNORS	considering	CDEINNOORST	not consider
CDEGIINOOOV	in good voice	CDEINNOPRST	nondescript
CDEGIKMMNOO	kingdom come	CDEINOORTTU	introduce to
CDEGIMNOOPS	decomposing	CDEINORSTTU	destruction
CDEGIMNORRU	corrigendum	CDEINORSTUY	countryside
CDEGNOORRUV	ground cover	CDEINORTUWY	countrywide
CDEHIIKLPPT	thick-lipped		country-wide
CDEHIILLNOT	decillionth	CDEIORSSTUY	discourtesy
CDEHIILLOTW	collide with	CDEKKLNNOUW	knuckle down
CDEHIIMOOST	dichotomise	CDEKMPRRTUU	dumper truck
CDEHIIMOOTZ	dichotomize	CDELLLOSSUY	cloudlessly
CDEHIKLSTTU	lick the dust	CDELLNORSUY	scoundrelly
CDEHIKMNPRU	Humperdinck	CDELLORSUUY	credulously
CDEHILPRTUU	pulchritude	CDELMOOORTW	world to come
CDEHIMNOOPR	endomorphic	CDELOOORTUW	tow-coloured
CDEHIMNOOUX	xenodochium	CDENOOPRRTU	put on record
CDEHIMNORST	Christendom	CDENOPRRTUU	uncorrupted
CDEHIMORRTY	hydrometric	CDEOPRRRUWY	curry powder
CDEHINNOSUY	Deinonychus	CDFFIILLTUY	difficultly
CDEHINNOTTW	contend with	CDFGHLLOOOT	cloth of gold
CDEHINOPRRY	Pondicherry	CDFGIILNNOY	confidingly
CDEHLNOSTTU	old chestnut	CDFGIMNOOSY	Song of my Cid
CDEIIILNSUV	uncivilised	CDFGINNNOOU	confounding
CDEIIILNUVZ	uncivilized	CDFHIMNNOOU	confound him
CDEIIINNORT	indirection	CDFILLOSUUU	dulcifluous
CDEIIINORTX	nitric oxide	CDFINNOSTUY	dysfunction
CDEIIINSTTV	distinctive	CDFNNOOOUUY	confound you
CDEIIIOPRTY	periodicity	CDGHILNOOPP	clodhopping
CDEIIIRTTVY	directivity	CDGIIKNSTTU	sitting duck
CDEIIISSTUV	vicissitude	CDGIINNOSTU	discounting
CDEIIJNSTUV	disjunctive	CDGILNNOOSW	closing-down
CDEIIKKLNPT	tickled pink	CDGILOORTTY	troglodytic
CDEIIKQTTUW	quick-witted	CDGINOOTTUW	woodcutting
CDEIILLMNOS	millisecond	CDHHIILOPRY	hydrophilic
CDEIILLOORV	cod-liver oil	CDHHIOPRTYY	hydrophytic
CDEIILLOSUY	deliciously	CDHIIMORRSU	Iris Murdoch
CDEIILLPTUY	pellucidity	CDHIIOOPRST	chiropodist
CDEIILNOSTU	unsolicited	CDHIISSSTUW	discuss with
CDEIILNRTUY	incredulity	CDHIMOOOSTU	dichotomous
CDEIILNTUVY	inductively	CDHINOOPRSY	hydroponics
CDEIILOSTUV	declivitous	CDIIIJNOSUU	injudicious
CDEIIMMOOST	commodities	CDIIINNNOOT	in condition
CDEIIMNORST	modernistic	CDIIINNOSTT	distinction

CDIIJLOSUUY	judiciously
CDIIKRRSTTY	dirty tricks
CDIILMORSTU	clostridium
CDIILOPSTUU	duplicitous
CDIIMMNNOOU	condominium
CDIINNNOOOT	on condition
CDIKLNOPSSU	spondulicks
CDILLORSUUY	ludicrously
CDKKNNOOOOW	knock on wood
CDOORRSSSSW	cross swords
CEEEEEGHNRS	green cheese
CEEEEEGMNRR	re-emergence
CEEEEEPRRRT	tree-creeper
CEEEEHLMNOS	lemon cheese
CEEEEHNSSTT	set the scene
CEEEEILNORT	electioneer
CEEEEIMNNPR	pre-eminence
CEEEEIMNNSS	mise en scène
	mise-en-scène
CEEEEINPRSX	experiences
CEEEEINRRRV	irreverence
CEEEEJNRSUV	rejuvenesce
CEEEEKOPRRS	score-keeper
CEEEENNRRTV	nerve centre
CEEEENPPRST	Peter's pence
CEEEFFGINOV	give offence
CEEEFFHIOTW	white coffee
CEEEFFHOOSU	coffee house
CEEEFFIINTV	ineffective
CEEEFFILTVY	effectively
CEEEFHIIPRS	speechifier
CEEEFHNRRTV	trench fever
CEEEFIKQRUZ	quick-freeze
CEEEFILRSSV	self-service
CEEEFKLLORR	Rockefeller
CEEEFLLOOST	feel close to
CEEEFLPRSST	self-respect
CEEEFLRRTUY	cruelty-free
CEEEFMNNORT	enforcement
CEEEFNPRSST	perfectness
CEEEGGNORRR	greengrocer
CEEEGHILNOS	Egon Schiele
CEEEGHLOSTU	The Eclogues
CEEEGIINOPR	epeirogenic
CEEEGINNNTV	Gene Vincent
CEEEHHINORT	Erechtheion
CEEEHHKLNOP	heckelphone
CEEEHHMMRSY	rhyme-scheme
CEEEHHNRSTT	the Trenches
CEEEHIKNTTT	kitchenette
CEEEHIMNRTU	hermeneutic
CEEEHINNRTT	in the centre
CEEEHINRSTT	in the secret
CEEEHIORRSV	heroic verse
CEEEHIQRSUW	chequerwise
CEEEHJNOOTZ	John Coetzee
CEEEHLMORST	chrome steel
CEEEHLNPRSU	ensepulchre
CEEEHLOPRST	Cleethorpes
CEEEIIKLNTT	telekinetic
CEEEIIMNNPT	impenitence
CEEEIIMPRSV	misperceive
CEEEIINNNRT	internecine
CEEEIINNSTX	in existence
CEEEIINSSST	necessities
CEEEIIPRRRU	Pierre Curie
CEEEIKNNRSS	snickersnee
CEEEILLSTVY	selectively
CEEEILNNOTV	non-elective
CEEEILNOPST	Pleistocene
CEEEILNSTUV	unselective
CEEEILOSTVX	voix céleste
CEEEILRSSVY	recessively
CEEEILRSTVY	secretively
CEEEILSSVXY	excessively
CEEEILTUVXY	executively
CEEEIMMPSUU	museum piece
CEEEIMNNSTT	enticements
CEEEINNOPRV	provenience
CEEEINNOSTV	venesection
CEEEINORTUX	executioner
CEEEINOSTVX	coextensive
CEEEINPRSSS	preciseness
CEEEINPRSST	persistence
CEEEINPRTUV	unreceptive
CEEEINRSTVV	revivescent
CEEEIOPRRSV	overprecise
	over-precise
CEEEIPPRSTV	perspective
CEEEIRSTUXX	executrixes
CEEEJNNSTUV	juvenescent
CEEEKLNOPSU	keep counsel
CEEEKMNORSS	smokescreen
CEEELLLNTXY	excellently
CEEELLNOPPR	prepollence
CEEELLORSTY	electrolyse
CEEELLORTTY	electrolyte
CEEELMMOTTU	telecommute
CEEELNOQSTU	closet queen
CEEELNRSSSU	recluseness
CEEELOPRTTY	electrotype
CEEEMOPRSTU	computerese
CEEENNPTTWY	twenty pence
CEEEOOPRSST	stereoscope
CEEEORSSTUW	sweet course
CEEEPPRRSST	preceptress
CEEFFHIIORS	Irish coffee
CEEFFHINRRS	French fries
CEEFFIIINNT	inefficient
CEEFFIILNTY	efficiently
CEEFFINQRUU	queer cuffin
CEEFGIMOORT	come to grief
CEEFHHNORTT	thenceforth
CEEFHHNORTW	whenceforth
CEEFHIILMRS	Emil Fischer
CEEFHILNOTU	feel in touch
CEEFHMNNORW	Frenchwomen
CEEFIIMNORR	Enrico Fermi
CEEFIIPRSSU	superficies
CEEFIKKLNOS	kick oneself
CEEFIKKNOPT	pocket knife
	pocket-knife

CEEFIKOOPRW	piece of work
CEEFILMPRTY	imperfectly
CEEFILNNOSS	confineless
CEEFILOSUVX	exclusive of
CEEFIMNNNOT	confinement
CEEFIMOORTV	motive force
CEEFINNQRUY	infrequency
CEEFINOPRST	in respect of
CEEFINORTTU	counterfeit
CEEFINOSSTY	of necessity
CEEFINPRSTU	superinfect
CEEFLNOPRTU	reflect upon
CEEFLNORSTU	fluorescent
CEEFLOORRSU	foreclosure
CEEFLORRSUU	resourceful
CEEFMOORRRV	recover from
CEEGGKMNOOR	George Monck
CEEGGKOORRU	George Cukor
CEEGGKOPRRY	Gregory Peck
CEEGGOORRSS	George Cross
CEEGGOORSTT	George Scott
CEEGHIKNPSS	King's Speech
CEEGHILNRSS	Schlesinger
CEEGHINRSST	sight screen
CEEGIIMNOST	see it coming
CEEGIINPRST	string piece
CEEGIIOOTVV	give voice to
CEEGIJJLNUU	jungle juice
CEEGILNNOSY	geosyncline
CEEGILNPTXY	expectingly
CEEGINNOOSS	oncogenesis
CEEGINNOOTT	ontogenetic
CEEGINOORST	oestrogenic
CEEGLNNORTU	electron gun
CEEGLOORSTT	get closer to
CEEHHIIMPRS	hemispheric
CEEHHILNOPT	technophile
CEEHHIMNSTU	the munchies
CEEHIIINORS	chinoiserie
CEEHIIKNSTT	kinesthetic
CEEHIILLNST	Hellenistic
CEEHIILLRSS	schillerise
CEEHIILLRSZ	schillerize
CEEHIIMNOPS	phonemicise
CEEHIIMNOPZ	phonemicize
CEEHIIMPSTU	euphemistic
CEEHIIMRTTY	hermeticity
CEEHIINOOTW	within cooee
CEEHIINOPST	phoneticise
CEEHIINOPTZ	phoneticize
CEEHIINPPRR	perinephric
CEEHIKNOPTU	keep in touch
CEEHIKNSSST	sketchiness
CEEHIKORSST	The Sick Rose
CEEHIKPRSTU	up shit creek
CEEHILNOOST	the Colonies
CEEHILORTVW	white clover
CEEHILPRSTU	lectureship
CEEHIMOPTTW	compete with
CEEHIOPPRTW	white copper
CEEHIOPRRST	Terpsichore
CEEHIORSTTX	The Exorcist
CEEHIPRSTTW	with respect
CEEHJMNNOOR	John McEnroe
CEEHKLNOSUY	honeysuckle
CEEHKLORRST	rock shelter
CEEHLLNOOPW	Enoch Powell
CEEHLLOORST	cholesterol
CEEHLLORSUY	lecherously
CEEHLMRSTWZ	Weltschmerz
CEEHMNOORRT	chronometer
CEEHMNOPRTY	nephrectomy
CEEHNNORRTU	truncheoner
CEEHNOOPRRY	Henry Cooper
CEEHNOORRTT	orthocentre
CEEHNOQSTTU	the Conquest
CEEHOOPSSTT	stethoscope
CEEHOORRRST	The Sorceror
CEEHORRSTTV	overstretch
CEEHORRTTYY	erythrocyte
CEEIIINNSTV	incentivise
CEEIIINNTVZ	incentivize
CEEIIKNRSST	ricketiness
CEEIILMPRSY	imprecisely
CEEIILMRTUV	vermiculite
CEEIILNNRSY	insincerely
CEEIILNRSTV	virilescent
CEEIILSTTVY	selectivity
CEEIIMMNOTT	in committee
CEEIIMNNPTY	impenitency
CEEIIMNNRST	reminiscent
CEEIIMOPTTV	competitive
CEEIIMORSST	esotericism
CEEIINORSTV	insectivore
CEEIINRSTVV	reviviscent
CEEIIPRTTVY	receptivity
CEEIIRRSTTV	restrictive
CEEIJLOPRST	projectiles
CEEIJRRSUVY	jury service
CEEIKLNORSU	Louis Necker
CEEIKLSSTWY	sickly sweet sickly-sweet
CEEIKNNORSS	snick or snee
CEEIKNORSST	stick or snee
CEEILLMNNTY	inclemently
CEEILLMRSSY	mercilessly
CEEILLPRSSY	pricelessly
CEEILLSUVXY	exclusively
CEEILMNNSTU	luminescent
CEEILMOORRT	colorimeter
CEEILMOPSTU	Telescopium
CEEILNNNOOV	non-violence
CEEILNOOPRS	necropoleis
CEEILNPRSST	split screen
CEEILNPRSTY	presciently
CEEILNQSTUY	quiescently
CEEILRRRUVW	Curlew River
CEEILRRSTUU	sericulture
CEEILRSUVXY	excursively
CEEIMNNOOOZ	economize on
CEEIMNNOOPT	omnipotence
CEEIMNNOPTT	incompetent

CEEIMNNORTU	countermine
CEEIMNNSTTU	intumescent
CEEIMNOORSU	ceremonious
CEEIMNOPSTU	pumice stone
CEEIMNRRTTU	recruitment
CEEIMOORRSV	room service
CEEIMOPRSSV	compressive
CEEIMOPRSTU	computerise
CEEIMOPRTUZ	computerize
CEEINNOORRT	reconnoitre
CEEINOOPRST	retinoscope
CEEINOPRRTT	interceptor
CEEINOPRSTU	persecution
CEEINORRSST	intercessor
CEEINORRSTU	intercourse
CEEINOSSSTU	necessitous
CEEINPRSSTY	persistency
CEEIOPPRSTV	prospective
CEEIOPRRTUV	overpicture
CEEIOPRSTTY	stereotypic
CEEIPPRSTUY	perspecuity
CEEIPQRSTUU	picturesque
CEEIRSTTVVY	civvy street
CEEJLNORSWW	crown jewels
CEEKMNOOPTY	pocket money
CEEKOORRRTT	retro-rocket
CEELLNOPPRY	prepollency
CEELLORSVYY	very closely
CEELMNNOSTU	locum tenens
CEELMNOOPTT	not complete
CEELMNOPSSX	complexness
CEELMNOPSTY	splenectomy
CEELMNOPTTY	competently
CEELMOPRSUW	muscle power
CEELNORSTUW	stone curlew
	stone-curlew
CEELNRRRTUY	recurrently
CEELPRSTTUY	put secretly
CEEMMNNOOSS	common sense
	commonsense
	common-sense
CEEMMOORSTT	come to terms
CEEMNNNOTTT	contentment
CEEMNNORTTU	recountment
CEEMNOPRRTU	procurement
CEEMNOPRSTT	contretemps
CEEMNORRSTT	storm centre
CEEMNORRTUU	countermure
CEENNOORRST	cornerstone
	corner-stone
CEENOORRSTV	seroconvert
CEENOORTTUV	counter-vote
CEENOQSSTUU	Queen's Scout
CEEOOPRRTTV	overprotect
CEEOOPRSSTY	stereoscopy
CEEOPRRSSTT	protectress
CEEORRRRSTU	resurrector
CEERRRSTTUU	restructure
CEFFHIINNOR	chiffonnier
CEFFHILNORT	Northcliffe
CEFFHIOORSU	office hours
CEFFHIRSSTT	festschrift
CEFFIORRSUU	furciferous
CEFGHILMRTY	mercy flight
CEFGHIORTUV	gift voucher
CEFGIIINPRX	price-fixing
CEFGNOORRST	strong force
CEFHIIISSTT	fetishistic
CEFHILLRTUY	filthy lucre
CEFHMOOORST	come short of
CEFIIIKNNSS	finickiness
CEFIILNOSUV	inclusive of
CEFIIMNORST	come in first
CEFIKNNOTUY	function key
CEFILLLOOSU	folliculose
CEFILNOORTU	counterfoil
CEFILNORTUY	Country Life
CEFILOORSUY	ferociously
CEFINNOOSSS	confessions
CEFINOOPRSS	in process of
CEFKOOOPTTU	out of pocket
CEFLLNNOTUY	confluently
CEFLLNOORST	self-control
CEFLMOORSST	comfortless
CEFLOOOPRSU	fluoroscope
CEFLORRSSUY	fleury cross
CEFNOOORSTU	of course not
CEFNOPRRTUY	perfunctory
CEGGGIIKLSW	Giggleswick
CEGHHIIOSTY	high society
CEGHHKORSTU	rough sketch
CEGHHMOORTU	come through
CEGHIINNRST	christening
CEGHILMOOTT	come to light
CEGHILNOOOU	euchologion
CEGHILNOOPR	phrenologic
CEGHILNOOTV	Gothic novel
CEGHILORSTU	light source
CEGHIMORRTY	hygrometric
CEGHINOPRTU	ethnic group
CEGHINORRTT	tight corner
CEGHINORSSU	grouchiness
CEGHIOOPRST	geostrophic
CEGHLNOOORR	chronologer
CEGHLNOTTUY	touch gently
CEGIIJLNORY	rejoicingly
CEGIIKLNNSY	sickeningly
CEGIILLNNST	stencilling
CEGIILMOOSS	seismologic
CEGIILNOOST	neologistic
CEGIILNOTVY	cognitively
CEGIILOOPST	geopolitics
CEGIIMMNOST	coming times
CEGIINNOORT	recognition
CEGIINNOTTX	not exciting
CEGIINORRSU	crinigerous
CEGIKKLNPSU	pig's knuckle
CEGILLMNOWY	welcomingly
CEGILLNNOSU	counselling
CEGILMNNOUW	unwelcoming
CEGILNOOSTY	Scientology
CEGIMNNNOST	consignment

CEGIMOOPRST	come to grips
CEGINNNNSSU	cunningness
CEGINNOOPST	coping stone
	coping-stone
CEGINNOPRTY	corn in Egypt
CEGINNORSTU	countersign
CEGORRRSUYY	cryosurgery
CEHHIMOOPRT	theomorphic
CEHHIMRSTUY	eurhythmics
CEHHIOPRRST	Christopher
CEHHLMOOSTT	clothes moth
CEHHLOOOSSU	schoolhouse
CEHHMNORSSY	synchromesh
CEHHMOOOPRR	chromophore
CEHIIINOTVW	voice within
CEHIIINPSTZ	citizenship
CEHIIIORSST	historicise
CEHIIIORSTZ	historicize
CEHIIIRSTTT	tritheistic
CEHIIJPSSTU	justiceship
CEHIIKKNNST	kitchen sink
	kitchen-sink
CEHIIKLLRSY	lickerishly
CEHIIKLNOPS	pick holes in
CEHIIKLORST	ostrich-like
CEHIIKNNTTU	kitchen unit
CEHIILOOPRT	heliotropic
CEHIIMNOPST	phonemicist
CEHIIMNORST	thermionics
CEHIIMOSSUV	mischievous
CEHIIMPRSST	Mister Chips
CEHIINOORSS	isochronise
CEHIINOORSZ	isochronize
CEHIINOPRST	Eric Shipton
CEHIIOPRRST	prehistoric
CEHIIOSSSVY	vichyssoise
CEHIJRSSSTU	Jesus Christ
CEHIKNOPSTU	soup kitchen
CEHIKOOPRTT	tooth-picker
CEHILOOPSSY	Coelophysis
CEHIMMNOTUW	commune with
CEHIMMOOPRS	mesomorphic
CEHIMOOPRTT	photometric
CEHIMOOTTUW	come out with
CEHIMOPRSTY	hypsometric
CEHINNORSSY	synchronise
CEHINNORSYZ	synchronize
CEHINOPRSSY	hypersonics
CEHIOPRSSTT	prosthetics
CEHKNOOSSTT	on the stocks
CEHLOPRSSUU	sepulchrous
CEHMMNOOORS	common-shore
CEHMMOOORSX	X-chromosome
CEHMMOOORSY	Y-chromosome
CEHMNOORRTU	Hector Munro
CEHMOORSTWY	show mercy to
CEHMOOSSTUU	custom house
CEHNNORTTUU	hunt counter
CEHNNOSSTUU	uncouthness
CEHOORRSSTV	cover shorts
CEIIILLMNPU	penicillium
CEIIILLNSST	illicitness
CEIIILMPRST	simpliciter
CEIIILNNPPR	in principle
CEIIILNNPTY	incipiently
CEIIIMNOPRS	imprecision
CEIIIMPSSST	pessimistic
CEIIINNRSTY	insincerity
CEIIINNSTTV	instinctive
CEIIINOSTVV	vivisection
CEIIINPRSTV	inscriptive
CEIIIOPRSTT	periostitic
CEIIIORSSTU	curiosities
CEIIJLOORTU	Joliot-Curie
CEIIKKLNNNO	Neil Kinnock
CEIIKLLPSTT	lickspittle
CEIIKLNPRSS	prickliness
CEIIKLNPRST	pencil-skirt
CEIIKLPSTTY	lickety-spit
CEIIKLQRSUV	quicksilver
CEIILLLSSSY	Scilly Isles
CEIILLNSUVY	inclusively
CEIILNNOPPR	on principle
CEIILNRTUUV	viniculture
CEIILRTTUUV	viticulture
CEIILSTUVXY	exclusivity
CEIIMNOOPTT	competition
CEIIMNOPSUU	impecunious
CEIIMNPRSSS	scrimpiness
CEIINNNNOTT	incontinent
CEIINORRSTT	restriction
CEIINOSSSUV	viciousness
CEIINRRSTUZ	scrutinizer
CEIINRSTTUV	instructive
CEIIOPPRSTU	precipitous
CEIIORSSSSW	scissorwise
CEIIORSTUVY	voyeuristic
CEIIPPRSTUY	perspicuity
CEIJLLOOPRY	Jilly Cooper
CEIJNNOQSUY	Quincy Jones
CEIKLMOORST	mortise lock
CEIKLMOQUVY	move quickly
CEIKLNNSSUU	unluckiness
CEIKLQRUVYY	very quickly
CEIKNNORSTU	countersink
CEIKNORTWYY	New York City
CEIKNRSSSTU	tinker's cuss
CEILLLNOOOV	violoncello
CEILLLOSUVY	collusively
CEILLNOOPST	ponticellos
CEILMMNOPST	compliments
CEILMNOORSS	moline cross
CEILMOORRTY	colorimetry
CEILNNNOTTY	continently
CEILNOOPRTU	perlocution
CEILNOPRRTW	triple crown
CEILNORSSTU	courtliness
CEILNPRSTUU	insculpture
CEILOOOPRST	protocolise
CEILOOOPRTZ	protocolize
CEILOORRSVY	corrosively
CEIMMNORSSU	consumerism

CEIMMOOSTUV	move to music
CEIMNOOPRSS	compression
CEIMNOORSTU	coterminous
CEIMNOPSTUV	consumptive
CEIMNORSSTU	misconstrue
CEIMOOPRSTT	competitors
CEINNNOOSTV	conventions
CEINNOORSSU	connoisseur
CEINNOOSTTU	contentious
CEINNOSTTTU	constituent
CEINOOPRSTU	prosecution
CEINOOPRSTY	retinoscopy
CEINOOPSSSU	copiousness
CEINORSSSUU	curiousness
CEINOSSSSUV	viscousness
CEINOSSSTUV	viscountess
CEIOOOPRRTZ	Proterozoic
CEIOPPRSSUU	perspicuous
CEIPPRRSSTU	superscript
CEKLLMPPTUU	plume-pluckt
CEKLNORSTUY	try one's luck
CEKMOOORRTT	rocket motor
CEKNOORRTUW	counterwork
CELLLOOOSTU	Lou Costello
CELLMOOPRRT	comptroller
CELLNNOOPTU	pollen count
CELLNOOORST	lose control
CELLNOPRTUY	corpulently
CELLNRTTUUY	truculently
CELLOORTUVY	courtly love
CELMMMNOOOR	common morel
CELMNOORTUU	monoculture
CELNOOPRTTU	counter-plot
CELOORSTUUY	courteously
CEMMNOOPRTT	comportment
CEMMOOOPRTY	Tommy Cooper
CENOOPRSSTT	potent cross
CENOORRSTVY	controversy
CENOPRRSSTU	corruptness
CEPRRSSTTUU	superstruct
CFFGIINRTUY	fructifying
CFFGIKKNNOO	knocking off
CFFGINOORSU	offscouring
CFFHILMNOTU	fifth column
CFFIILOOSUY	officiously
CFFINOOPTTU	cut-off point
CFGHIIKLQTU	quick flight
CFGHIILLNNY	flinchingly
CFGHIILNNNU	unflinching
CFGHIMNOORT	forthcoming
CFGIINNNOTU	functioning
CFGINNNOORT	confronting
CFHHIKMNOTU	think much of
CFHIINORTWY	within cry of
CFHILOORSST	first school
CFIILNOPPTU	Pulp Fiction
CFIINNNOOSU	in confusion
CFIINORSSTU	first cousin
CFIKKNOORSX	knock for six
CFIKOORSTTU	stick out for
CFILMOOPPRY	microfloppy
CFILNNOOORT	in control of
CFINORSTUUU	infructuous
CFLLLOORUUY	colourfully
CFLNORSUUUU	furunculous
CFLOOOPRSUY	fluoroscopy
CFNORSTUUUU	unfructuous
CGGIILMMNNO	commingling
CGHHIKOSTTU	thought-sick
CGHHILNOOST	night school
CGHHILOOTYY	ichthyology
CGHHINNOSTU	no such thing
CGHHIOPRTYY	hygrophytic
CGHIILOOPSY	physiologic
CGHILOORSTY	Christology
CGHIMNOORST	shortcoming
CGIIILNSSTU	linguistics
CGIIKMNOQUV	quick-moving
CGIIKNOSTTU	sticking out
CGIILLOSSTY	syllogistic
CGIILMNOORY	criminology
CGIILOOOSST	sociologist
CGIINNORTUY	incongruity
CGIINOPRTWY	copy-writing
CGIKLOQRUWY	grow quickly
CGILLNNOORT	controlling
CGILLNNOOSY	consolingly
CGILLOOPTTY	polyglottic
CGILMOOOSST	cosmologist
CGINNNOOTTU	not counting
CGINNOORSUU	incongruous
CGINOORSTUU	outsourcing
CGLNOORSUUY	congruously
CHHIILOOPPS	philosophic
CHHIILOPTTY	lithophytic
CHHIINOTTUW	in touch with
CHHIMMOOOPR	homomorphic
CHHKOOORRRS	shock horror
	shock-horror
CHHLLLOOPRY	chlorophyll
CHIIIMORSST	historicism
CHIIINORSST	histrionics
	trichinosis
CHIIIORSSTT	historicist
CHIIIORSTTY	historicity
CHIILLLNOPS	Phil Collins
CHIILLNOOTT	octillionth
CHIINOOPRSW	icon worship
CHIIOOPRTTX	thixotropic
CHIIOPPRRTY	porphyritic
CHIJLLNNOOS	John Collins
CHIKOPSTTUW	stock up with
CHILMOOPPRY	polymorphic
CHILOORSTUU	ulotrichous
CHIMMNOOOPR	monomorphic
CHIMNOOPPPY	hypnopompic
CHIMNOOPRRS	prochronism
CHINOOORSSU	isochronous
CHIOOPPRRST	proctorship
CHIOOPPRSTY	sporophytic
CHIOOSTTTUW	without cost
CHIOPSTTTUY	touch-typist

CHMNOOPSTTU	mutton chops
CHMNOOPTTUU	not up to much
CHNNOORRSTY	synchrotron
CHNNOORSSUY	synchronous
CHRRRRSUUYY	hurry-scurry
CIIILLMOPTY	impoliticly
CIIILOPSSST	solipsistic
CIIIMNORTTU	micturition
CIIINNOPRST	inscription
CIIINORSTUY	incuriosity
CIIKLLQSTUY	list quickly
CIILLNNOOSU	in collusion
CIILLOORSTT	torticollis
CIILNOOPSTU	liposuction
CIILNOPSTUU	punctilious
CIILNORSUUY	incuriously
CIIMMNNOOTU	comminution
CIIMNOOOPST	composition
CIIMNRSSTTU	misinstruct
CIIMOPRSTUY	promiscuity
CIINNORSTTU	instruction
CIIOOPRSSUV	piscivorous
CIJKLNOOSWY	Jocky Wilson
CIJLNOOPSTT	Scott Joplin
CIKNOOPRUWY	pick-your-own
CILLMOOQSUU	colloquiums
CILMNNOOOSU	monoclinous
CILNNOOOTUV	convolution
CILNNOOSSUV	convulsions
CILNNOOSUUY	innocuously
CILNOOORSUU	unicolorous
CILNOPRRTUY	incorruptly
CILOOOPRSTT	protocolist
CIMNNOOPSTU	consumption
CIMNOORSSTU	consortiums
CIMNOPPSTUU	suction pump
CIMOOPRSSUU	promiscuous
CIMOPRSSTUU	scrumptious
CIOOPRSSTTU	prosciuttos
CLLNOOSUUVV	convolvulus
CNNOOOPRRSU	pour scorn on

D

DDDEEFIOSST	eisteddfods
DDDEEGIMOSS	demigoddess
DDDEEIILMSZ	middle-sized
DDDEEINORSS	dodderiness
DDDEFHLNORU	hundredfold
DDDEFILOOTU	diddle out of
DDDEIILNUVY	undividedly
DDDENNOORTW	downtrodden
	down-trodden
DDDENNOORUW	rounded down
DDEEEFILLNW	well-defined
DDEEEFILORV	delivered of
DDEEEGHIRRT	third degree
DDEEEHILLSV	dishevelled
DDEEEIIINRV	Eddie Irvine
DDEEEILLRSW	well-desired
DDEEEILLRVW	well-derived
DDEEEILMNRT	intermeddle
DDEEEIMORRS	more desired
DDEEEINNNPT	independent
DDEEEINNPRT	interdepend
DDEEEINPRST	predestined
DDEEEKNNOUW	Wounded Knee
DDEEELLNOWW	well-endowed
DDEEELLORRW	well-ordered
DDEEELLRSSW	well-dressed
DDEEELNOPUV	undeveloped
DDEEELNPRTY	pretendedly
DDEEENNNOPT	dependent on
DDEEENOSSTV	devotedness
DDEEENOSTWY	Sweeney Todd
DDEEEORRSSV	overdressed
DDEEEORTTUV	true-devoted
DDEEFIIIRSV	diversified
DDEEFLLNOUW	well-founded
DDEEGHILLTY	delightedly
DDEEGHINOWW	weighed down
	weighed-down
DDEEGILLNOO	golden oldie
DDEEGILNNPY	dependingly
DDEEGILNOWW	window ledge
DDEEGINNNOP	depending on
DDEEGINNRSU	undersigned
DDEEGINNRTY	tender-dying
DDEEGLNORRU	ground elder
DDEEGMNORRU	Rumer Godden
DDEEHIILMNT	in the middle
DDEEHIILMTW	Middle White
DDEEHILMOTT	to the middle
DDEEHIMPRUY	Eddie Murphy
DDEEHINOTWW	endowed with
DDEEHIORRST	ride the rods
DDEEHOORSTV	over the odds
DDEEIILNSTT	disentitled
DDEEIINORST	disoriented
DDEEIIQSTUU	disquietude
DDEEIKNNRSS	kindredness
DDEEILNNOTU	tunnel diode
DDEEILPRSSY	dispersedly
DDEEIMNPTTY	petty-minded
DDEEIOPPRSS	predisposed
DDEEIOSSWWW	widow's weeds
DDEELLNORTW	well-trodden
DDEELLNORUW	well-rounded
DDEELMOORUY	Dudley Moore
DDEENNORSUW	snowed under
DDEENRRSSUU	under duress
DDEFFIILNTY	diffidently
DDEFGIIINNU	undignified
DDEFLNNOUUY	unfoundedly
DDEGGHHINOU	high dudgeon
DDEGGIINNRW	wedding ring
DDEGHIIMNRT	right-minded
DDEGHLNNORU	long hundred
DDEGHLNOPRY	dendroglyph
DDEGIILMSUY	misguidedly
DDEGIILNRTU	guilt-ridden
DDEGIILSSUY	disguisedly
DDEGIINORST	Otis Redding

DDEGIINSSUU	undisguised
DDEGILMNOST	dislodgment
DDEGILNRSTU	disgruntled
DDEGILSSTUY	disgustedly
DDEGINOOORR	in good order
DDEGINORSWW	winged words
DDEGINPSTUU	suet pudding
DDEGNNORRUU	underground
DDEHHIIRSTT	dish the dirt
DDEHIIKNPRS	kindredship
DDEHIINRSSW	widdershins
DDEHILNOTTY	on the tiddly
DDEHILOOTWW	The Wild Wood
DDEHINNOTWW	down the wind
DDEHINOORSU	dishonoured
DDEHINORSSU	disenshroud
DDEHINORSTW	short-winded
DDEHJNOOORW	John Redwood
DDEHLMOOTUU	loud-mouthed
DDEHLMORSTU	the doldrums
DDEHNOORSTU	do the rounds
DDEIIKNRRRV	drink-driver
DDEIILLOPSS	ill-disposed
DDEIIMNNOSU	diminuendos
DDEIIMOORRV	room-divider
DDEILNNOOPR	London pride
DDEINORSTTU	undistorted
DDELNNOORRY	Londonderry
DDEMNOSTTUU	Desmond Tutu
DDFGHILNNOU	fundholding
DDFIMNNOOSU	of sound mind
DDFOOORRRWW	word for word
	word-for-word
DDGGGGIILNO	gold-digging
DDGHIMOOTWY	Dwight Moody
DDGIIINNORV	divining rod
DDGILMNPPUU	plum pudding
DDGINOOOORU	in good odour
DDIIIMRTTUY	rumti-iddity
DDIIKLNSTWY	tiddlywinks
DDLLNOOSUUY	sound loudly
DEEEEFGNRUV	dengue fever
DEEEEFLORST	Lee De Forest
DEEEEHIMPRS	ephemerides
DEEEEHLNRTU	under the lee
DEEEEHNQRTU	The Red Queen
DEEEEIRRSSV	reverse side
DEEEELLNRTW	well-entered
DEEEEMOPRST	speedometer
DEEEENNSTUW	unsweetened
DEEEEQRSSTU	sequestered
DEEEFFFNOOS	off one's feed
DEEEFFNOOST	toffee-nosed
DEEEFHLNSSU	heedfulness
DEEEFIIJLLO	fille de joie
DEEEFILNSTV	field events
	self-evident
DEEEFILNSVY	defensively
DEEEFINNRSS	refinedness
DEEEFINORRV	overrefined
	over-refined
DEEEFLNNOSY	deny oneself
DEEEFLNNSSU	needfulness
DEEEFLNPRSY	spend freely
DEEEFMNRRSU	referendums
DEEEGGINNNR	engendering
DEEEGHIKNST	keen-sighted
DEEEGHILNNT	enlightened
DEEEGINNNRV	never ending
	never-ending
DEEEGINOSXY	deoxygenise
DEEEGINOXYZ	deoxygenize
DEEEGINQSUU	Queen's Guide
DEEEGIRSTTU	street guide
DEEEGLORRSU	guelder rose
DEEEGLORRSV	gold reserve
DEEEGMNORRU	nom de guerre
DEEEHHPRSSS	shepherdess
DEEEHIRSTTU	three-suited
DEEEHKNOORT	three-nooked
DEEEHLMNOTY	the old enemy
DEEEHLMORVW	overwhelmed
DEEEHLNRSTU	unsheltered
DEEEHLORSTW	see the world
DEEEHMNOSST	Demosthenes
DEEEHMOPRTT	hot-tempered
DEEEIIJORVV	joie de vivre
DEEEIILRSSV	desilverise
DEEEIILRSVZ	desilverize
DEEEIINNPTX	inexpedient
DEEEIINSSST	desensitise
DEEEIINSSTZ	desensitize
DEEEIKLNRSV	linked verse
DEEEILLMPRT	ill-tempered
DEEEILLNPPZ	Led Zeppelin
DEEEILLNRSS	elderliness
DEEEILLORWY	lower eyelid
DEEEILMMNPT	implemented
DEEEILMMNUV	mendelevium
DEEEILNNOPT	needlepoint
DEEEILNPTXY	expediently
DEEEILORSTU	deleterious
DEEEILPPRUY	upper eyelid
DEEEIMNOPTT	mont-de-piété
DEEEINPRTUX	expenditure
DEEEINQSSUY	Disneyesque
DEEEINRRSSV	vine-dresser
DEEEINRRTUV	unretrieved
DEEEINRSSSV	diverseness
DEEEIOPRRSV	preside over
DEEELLNRRSU	underseller
DEEELLPPRXY	perplexedly
DEEELMNNORY	moneylender
	money-lender
DEEELMNOPTV	development
DEEELNNPRST	resplendent
DEEELNNRSSS	slenderness
DEEELNNSSSS	endlessness
DEEELNOPSST	send to sleep
DEEELOOPPRV	overpeopled
DEEELOOPRVV	overdevelop
DEEELRRSSUV	verdureless

DEEEMNNORST	endorsement
DEEENOPRSSS	reposedness
DEEENOPRSUX	underexpose
DEEENPRRSSU	unrepressed
DEEENPRRSUV	unpreserved
DEEENPRSSUX	unexpressed
DEEENQRSTUU	unrequested
DEEENRRRRSU	surrenderer
DEEENRRSTTT	trendsetter
DEEEOOPRRVW	overpowered
DEEEOPRSTTY	stereotyped
DEEEORRTTVX	extroverted
DEEEPRRSSST	pre-stressed
DEEFFIILOVW	field of view
DEEFFIINNRT	indifferent
DEEFFILNNOS	find oneself
DEEFFILNRTY	differently
DEEFFINSSSU	diffuseness
DEEFGGILNOO	good feeling
DEEFGHILOOT	the good life
DEEFGHIORST	foresighted
DEEFGIINSST	fidgetiness
DEEFGILNNSY	self-denying
DEEFGILNNUY	unfeignedly
DEEFGILNORS	gird oneself
DEEFGIOORTT	tiger-footed
DEEFHILPPRW	Fred Whipple
DEEFHINOOST	on the side of
DEEFHNRSTTU	furthest end
DEEFIIIMNNR	indemnifier
DEEFIIINNST	intensified
DEEFIINOPRS	personified
DEEFIJOORST	Jodie Foster
DEEFIKLNRRY	drink freely
DEEFIKLORRW	field worker
	fieldworker
DEEFILLRSSU	fleurs-de-lis
DEEFILMNNRU	Dunfermline
DEEFILMOPSS	self-imposed
DEEFILNORWW	Wilfred Owen
DEEFILOSTTU	outside left
DEEFIOPRTUZ	deputize for
DEEFIOSTTTU	destitute of
DEEFKLMOPRU	Rudolf Kempe
DEEFLLNOSSU	dolefulness
DEEFLLRSSUY	fleurs-de-lys
DEEFLNRSTUU	unflustered
DEEFLOPRSSY	professedly
DEEFNOORSTT	tenderfoots
DEEFNOPRSTU	turn of speed
DEEGGILNORR	dégringoler
DEEGGINNOOV	good-evening
DEEGGINSTTU	getting used
DEEGGLLOORY	Lloyd-George
DEEGGLNOOOS	golden goose
DEEGHHINRST	ring the shed
DEEGHHIOPRW	high-powered
DEEGHHOPTTU	deep thought
DEEGHILNNOT	Len Deighton
DEEGHILNOOP	pigeonholed
DEEGHINORSW	Winged Horse
DEEGHINORSY	hydrogenise
DEEGHINORYZ	hydrogenize
DEEGHINRTUW	underweight
DEEGHIORSUV	Hugo De Vries
DEEGHLLLNOO	golden hello
DEEGHLMOOPS	so help me God
DEEGHOOPSUW	P G Wodehouse
DEEGIIKNPSS	deep kissing
DEEGIILSTVY	digestively
DEEGIIMNNOR	domineering
DEEGIIMNNRT	determining
DEEGIINNRST	ingredients
DEEGIINRSSV	dissevering
DEEGILLMNOR	remodelling
DEEGILNORUV	overindulge
	over-indulge
DEEGILNRSVY	deservingly
DEEGILNRTVY	divergently
DEEGINNORSS	engrossed in
DEEGINNOSTW	get one's wind
DEEGINNRSUV	undeserving
DEEGINNRTUU	ungenitured
DEEGLLMOORW	well-groomed
DEEGLLNORUV	ground-level
DEEGLNOSSSS	godlessness
DEEHHILLNOT	hold the line
DEEHHILNNNO	Hohenlinden
DEEHHLOORSU	householder
DEEHHOPRRSY	hydrosphere
DEEHIIKLNTW	like the wind
DEEHIILNNRT	thin red line
DEEHIIMPRSU	hesperidium
DEEHIIOPRSS	spheroidise
DEEHIIOPRSZ	spheroidize
DEEHIKLNPTY	think deeply
DEEHIKLNRTU	thunder-like
DEEHILLNOPS	spindle hole
DEEHILLORTT	title-holder
DEEHILMNOTU	endothelium
DEEHILNOWWW	wheel window
DEEHIMNNOTW	Down the Mine
DEEHIMOSTTW	wisdom teeth
DEEHINOPSTY	dehypnotise
DEEHINOPTYZ	dehypnotize
DEEHINOSSSU	hideousness
DEEHINRRSSU	hurriedness
DEEHINSSTYZ	synthesized
DEEHIORSTTU	The Outsider
DEEHKOOPRRT	red-hot poker
DEEHLLNRRTU	Ruth Rendell
DEEHLMNNOSS	Mendelssohn
DEEHLNORRTW	nether world
DEEHMNOOPTU	open-mouthed
DEEHMOORSTU	The Dormouse
DEEHNNORSTU	underhonest
	unshortened
DEEHNNRSTUU	under the sun
DEEHOORRSUV	hors d'oeuvre
DEEIIIKKNNX	Nikkei index
DEEIIKLLMRV	milk-livered
DEEIIKLLMSS	semi-skilled

DEEIIKLLORS	soldierlike
DEEIILLLRVY	lily-livered
DEEIILLPPQU	ill-equipped
DEEIILMNSST	limitedness
DEEIIMMNRST	determinism
DEEIIMNNNOT	mentioned in
DEEIIMNNOPS	demi-pension
DEEIIMNRRST	irredentism
DEEIIMNRSTT	determinist
DEEIINNSSTT	dissentient
DEEIINPRSTY	serendipity
DEEIINRRSTT	irredentist
DEEIINRSSTT	disinterest
DEEIIOPSTUX	expeditious
DEEIJPRSTUX	jeux d'esprit
DEEIKLLORSV	Volkslieder
DEEILMMOSST	seldom-times
DEEILMNRTUY	unmeritedly
DEEILMOSTUW	it would seem
DEEILNOOPTV	develop into
DEEILNOPTUX	unexploited
DEEILNORRSS	orderliness
DEEILNSSSTT	stiltedness
DEEILOPPPTY	polypeptide
DEEILQRRRSU	red squirrel
DEEIMMNORST	Modern Times
DEEIMMNORTU	endometrium
DEEIMNNNOTU	unmentioned
DEEIMNOPRSY	money spider
DEEIMNORUYY	mind your eye
DEEIMNPRSSU	unimpressed
DEEINNNORST	non-resident
DEEINNOPSST	pointedness
DEEINNOQTUW	quieten down
DEEINNOSTTU	tendentious
DEEINNPRSTU	superintend
DEEINNSSSTT	stintedness
DEEINOPRRVW	power-driven
DEEINORRSSW	worriedness
DEEINORRTTV	introverted
DEEINOSSSTU	tediousness
DEEINOSSSUV	deviousness
DEEINPRRTTU	interrupted
DEEINRRRTUW	underwriter
DEEIPRRSSUZ	pressurized
DEEJNNORSUY	journey's end
DEEJRSSSTTU	just deserts
DEEKLRSSTTU	Studs Terkel
DEEKNNNRSSU	drunkenness
DEELLNORTWW	town-dweller
DEELLNSTTUY	unsettledly
DEELMNORTTY	tormentedly
DEELORSTUXY	dexterously
DEEMNOORTUY	Deuteronomy
DEEMNOSSSSY	syndesmoses
DEEMOORSTVY	overmodesty
DEENNOOOORV	do one over on
DEENNSSSTTU	stuntedness
DEENRRSSSTU	under stress
DEEOOPPRRST	doorstepper
DEEOPPPRSSU	presupposed
DEEORSSSTTU	stressed out
	stressed-out
DEFFGILLRUU	full-figured
DEFFIILORSS	fossil-fired
DEFFIILSUVY	diffusively
DEFFIINORTU	unfortified
DEFFILLLNUU	unfulfilled
DEFFNOOSSTU	do one's stuff
DEFGHIISTTT	tight-fisted
DEFGHILOOSY	old-fogeyish
DEFGHILOOTT	light-footed
DEFGIILNNSW	self-winding
DEFGIILNPRS	Springfield
DEFGIINORSZ	frigid zones
DEFGILLNSUY	sdeignfully
DEFGILNRSSY	fly-dressing
DEFGNOOORTU	good fortune
DEFHHLOORTT	hold the fort
DEFHIINNOST	not finished
DEFHIINRSTW	friends with
DEFHIMNORTU	mouth-friend
DEFHINNRSUU	unfurnished
DEFHINOPRSU	punished for
DEFHINORSUW	unwished-for
DEFHINPRSTT	spendthrift
DEFHIOORRSX	Oxfordshire
DEFHKOOORTW	do the work of
DEFHLLMOTUU	full-mouthed
DEFHLMOOTUU	foul-mouthed
DEFIIIMNSTY	misidentify
DEFIIJNSTUU	unjustified
DEFIILLMNOR	ill-informed
DEFIILLNOPS	flip one's lid
DEFIIMMNORS	misinformed
DEFILMNNSSU	mindfulness
DEFILNSSTUU	dutifulness
DEFILOPRSST	field sports
	sports field
DEFILRSSSTU	distressful
DEFIMNOORUY	remind you of
DEFINNNOPSU	pension fund
DEFIOOORRSU	odoriferous
DEFKLNOOORU	unlooked-for
DEFLLNORUWY	wonderfully
DEGGHHHIIST	high-sighted
DEGGHIJLNOU	John Gielgud
DEGGHILNOST	long-sighted
DEGGHOOOSTT	go to the dogs
DEGGIILNNSY	designingly
DEGGIILNRVY	divergingly
DEGGKLRSUUY	skulduggery
DEGHHIILMOT	high old time
DEGHHIINSTY	high-density
DEGHHILNORT	hold the ring
DEGHHILNOST	shed light on
DEGHIIINRTV	divine right
DEGHIILLLPT	gild the pill
DEGHIILLLTY	gild the lily
DEGHIILNNRY	hinderingly
DEGHIILPPTT	tight-lipped
DEGHIINORRS	horse-riding

DEGHILNOORV	holding-over
DEGHIMNOOST	do something
DEGHINNOORY	hydrogen ion
DEGHINNOOST	do one's thing
DEGHINOSSTU	doughtiness
DEGHLMOOOTY	methodology
DEGHNOOOSTT	honest-to-God
DEGHNOOPTTU	put on the dog
DEGHNOORSTU	go the rounds
DEGHNOORSUY	hydrogenous
DEGHNOORTTU	to the ground
DEGHNORRTUW	undergrowth
DEGIIINNOST	indigestion
DEGIIINQSTU	disquieting
DEGIIKNRSTW	writing-desk
DEGIILNNNRU	underlining
DEGIILNRTVY	divertingly
DEGIIMNNNRU	undermining
DEGIIMNNORZ	modernizing
DEGIINNNOTT	intending to
DEGIINRSSST	distressing
DEGIINRSTTV	driving test
DEGIJMMNSTU	misjudgment
DEGILLNNTUY	indulgently
DEGILLNOPRY	deploringly
DEGILMNORSU	smouldering
DEGILNNOPRY	ponderingly
DEGILNNORWY	wonderingly
DEGILNNOSSU	ungodliness
DEGILNNOSTW	lend wings to
DEGILNOPSSS	splodginess
DEGILNORUVY	devouringly
DEGINOPRSST	top-dressing
DEGINOPRSUW	wrong side up
DEGLLNORSUW	ground swell
DEGLNOOOSST	stolen goods
DEGLNOPRSUY	golden syrup
DEGMNOOORST	on good terms
DEGNNOORSTU	stoneground
DEHHILMOORS	holohedrism
DEHHLNOSTUU	sleuth-hound
DEHHNNORSUY	Henry Hudson
DEHIIIJMNRX	Jimi Hendrix
DEHIIKNNNST	thin-skinned
DEHIILLMNPS	Mendip Hills
DEHIILMNPSU	delphiniums
DEHIIMNORSW	in her wisdom
DEHIINSTTUW	Whitsuntide
DEHILLMORUU	ill-humoured
DEHILNOPTTU	put the lid on
DEHILNOSSTY	dishonestly
DEHILNOSTTW	thistledown
DEHILNRRUUY	unhurriedly
DEHILORSSTT	shortlisted
DEHIMNSSTYY	Sydney Smith
DEHINORSSTU	drouthiness
DEHINPRSSSU	prudishness
DEHLNNOOOSW	hold one's own
DEHLNOOPRSY	polyhedrons
DEHMMORSTUW	mum's the word
DEHMOOPPRSU	pseudomorph

DEHNRRSTTUU	underthrust
DEIIIMNPRSU	peridiniums
DEIIINNPSSS	insipidness
DEIIINOSSTT	seditionist
DEIIINPRTTY	intrepidity
DEIIKKLMMMS	skimmed milk
DEIILLORSUY	deliriously
DEIILMMNPSS	Simple Minds
DEIILMPRSTW	limp-wristed
DEIILNOORWW	oriel window
DEIILNOPRRY	pyrrolidine
DEIILOPRSTW	low-spirited
DEIILOSSTUY	seditiously
DEIIMNOPRTV	improvident
DEIINNOQRSU	inquirendos
DEIINNORTUV	invite round
DEIINORSSTY	inside story
DEIINOSSSTU	dissentious
DEIINOSTTTU	destitution
DEIKLNNOWWY	widely known
	widely-known
DEILLMOOSUY	melodiously
DEILLNORSSW	worldliness
DEILLORSTUY	desultorily
DEILLORSWWY	worldly wise
	worldly-wise
DEILLOSSTUY	dissolutely
DEILMNOOSUU	unmelodious
DEILMNPRTUY	imprudently
DEILNOPRTVY	providently
DEILPPRSSUY	supply-sider
DEILPRRSSUY	surprisedly
DEIMMNNSTUU	indumentums
DEIMMRSSTYY	dissymmetry
DEIMNNNOOVW	Devon minnow
DEIMNNOPSTU	put one's mind
DEIMNOOPRSU	imponderous
DEIMNOORRRS	minor orders
DEIMOPPRTTU	promptitude
DEINNOPRTUV	unprovident
DEINNORTTWW	written down
DEINNPSSUUY	sunny side up
DEIOPPRRSTY	disproperty
DEKNOORRSWW	work wonders
DELLNOPSUUY	pendulously
DELLNOSSSUY	soundlessly
DELMORRSUUY	murderously
DELNOOORSTT	rondolettos
DELNOOORSUW	would sooner
DELNOOPRSSU	splendorous
DELNOOPRSUY	ponderously
DELOOPRSTUU	trous-de-loup
DELOPPRRSSU	Lord's Supper
DELOPPRRTUY	purportedly
DEMMOORSTYY	Tommy Dorsey
DENNNOSSSUU	unsoundness
DENNOOOOPSW	wooden spoon
DENOOORSSSU	odorousness
DENOOORSSTW	do one's worst
DENOPPRSTUU	unsupported
DFFGHIJOORS	Josh Gifford

DFFIIISTUVY	diffusivity
DFFIILLMOSY	silly mid-off
DFFLOOORSWW	flow of words
DFGGINOOPRR	drop-forging
DFGHIIOPRRT	right of drip
DFGIIKNNNSU	sinking fund
DFGIILLNOWW	wildfowling
DFGIINNRSUW	windsurfing
DFHMOOORTUW	word of mouth
	word-of-mouth
DFIILLLMNOO	millionfold
DFIIMNNOPTU	put in mind of
DFILLMNNUUY	unmindfully
DFILLNTUUUY	undutifully
DFILRSSTTUU	distrustful
DGGHIIILNRT	riding-light
DGGHINNOOTU	good hunting!
DGGIIILLNRR	drilling rig
DGGIILMNNSU	mudslinging
	mud-slinging
DGGIKLNOOOO	good-looking
DGGIMNNOOOR	good-morning
DGHHHIOOPTU	up to high doh
DGHHIILNOTW	withholding
DGHHIINOSWW	High Windows
DGHHLOOPRTU	plod through
DGHIIIIMNNS	diminishing
DGHIIINSSTU	distinguish
DGHIIKNNOOW	hoodwinking
DGHIIMNNSTU	midnight sun
DGHILNOOPST	stop holding
DGHILOORSTY	hydrologist
DGHLOORSTWY	Goldsworthy
DGIIIINPRST	dispiriting
DGIIINNORRV	driving iron
DGIILLNSWWY	swing wildly
DGIILNOPSSY	disposingly
DGIINNOOOOP	good opinion
DGIINOORRSW	word origins
DGIINRSSTTU	distrusting
DGIIOOPRSST	good spirits
DGIKNNORRST	strong drink
DGILLNNOPUW	pulling-down
DGINNNNORUW	running-down
DGINNNORTUW	turning-down
DGINNORRSUU	surrounding
DGNNOOORSTU	Gordonstoun
DGNNOORRTUU	run to ground
DHHIILOPRSS	his lordship
DHHILNOOTTW	not hold with
DHHIOOPRTYY	hypothyroid
DHHNOOOSTTU	hound's-tooth
DHIIIMNOSSW	in his wisdom
DHIMOOOSTTW	wisdom tooth
DHIOOORTTUW	without-door
DHIOORRSTWY	word history
DHNOOORTUXY	unorthodoxy
DIIIKNOPSST	od's-pitikins
DIIILLNOSSU	disillusion
DIIILNOSSUY	insidiously
DIIILNOSUVY	invidiously
DIIIMNOPRSS	disimprison
DIIINOOPRSV	pro indiviso
DIIINOOPSST	disposition
DIILLMPTTUY	put it mildly
DIILNOOSSTU	dissolution
DIILNOPSSTY	spondylitis
DIINORSSTUU	industrious
DIKLLNORSWY	drink slowly
DIKNNOORSTW	Windsor knot
DILNOOORSUY	inodorously
DIMNOORSTWW	storm window
DLOOOPRRSTV	Lord Provost
DNNOOOORSTV	Rostov-on-Don

E

EEEEEEOSTYY	see eye to eye
EEEEFFLLNOS	feel oneself
EEEEFFLNORS	free oneself
EEEEFHMRSTT	Set Them Free
EEEEFILPRSS	life peeress
EEEEFLMORRS	feel remorse
EEEEFLRSTTT	Fleet Street
EEEEGILLNRW	green-wellie
EEEEGLNNSST	genteelness
EEEEGNPPPRR	green pepper
EEEEHKLNOUW	Leeuwenhoek
EEEEHKLOPRT	hotel-keeper
EEEEHKOPRSU	housekeeper
EEEEHNNSTTV	seventeenth
EEEEHORRSVW	wheresoever
EEEEIINRTVW	interviewee
EEEEIMNPRSW	minesweeper
EEEEINOPPSY	pipe one's eye
EEEEINPRRSV	persevere in
EEEEKOPRRST	storekeeper
EEEELLNQRUY	Ellery Queen
EEEELLRSTTV	street-level
EEEELMNOOSS	someone else
EEEELNPRSST	repleteness
EEEEMMORRTX	more extreme
EEEEMORRSTT	stereometer
EEEEMPRSTTW	sweet temper
EEEENPRRSTV	ever-present
EEEEPPPRSTW	sweet pepper
EEEEQRRSTTU	Queer Street
EEEFFILORTW	Eiffel Tower
EEEFGIIKLLN	feeling like
EEEFGIKLNSS	self-seeking
EEEFGILLNSS	feelingless
EEEFGILNOSV	give oneself
EEEFGINRSTT	setting free
EEEFGJLNRUV	Jungle Fever
	jungle fever
EEEFHIKNRRT	freethinker
	free-thinker
EEEFHIKSSTT	kiss the feet
EEEFHILRRSW	Ferris wheel
EEEFHLLNOPS	help oneself
EEEFHLORRTU	rule of three
EEEFHMNRRST	refreshment
EEEFHOORRTT	theretofore

EEEFIINNRRT	interfere in
EEEFILLRVXY	reflexively
EEEFLLNOOSS	lose oneself
EEEFLLORVWY	yellow fever
EEEFLMPRSSU	perfumeless
EEEFLPRSSSX	self-express
EEEFMOORRRV	for evermore
	forevermore
EEEGGGOORRV	George Grove
EEEGGHORTTT	get together
	get-together
EEEGGIINNNR	engineering
EEEGGILLORS	George Ellis
EEEGGILOORT	George Eliot
EEEGGJLNNRU	jungle-green
EEEGGMNNORT	engorgement
EEEGGMOOORR	George Moore
EEEGHHILSTT	see the light
EEEGHIKNPRT	keep the ring
EEEGHIMNOST	eighteenmos
EEEGHINTTVW	get even with
EEEGIILMORS	Emilio Segrè
EEEGIINPPRW	weeping-ripe
EEEGIKLNORV	keeling-over
EEEGILMNORS	Simon Legree
EEEGILNRSTW	swingletree
EEEGILNRSVY	every single
EEEGIMPRRST	Peter Grimes
EEEGINNNSSU	genuineness
EEEGINNORVW	overweening
EEEGINNRRTW	wintergreen
EEEGINPRRSV	persevering
EEEGKMNNORY	green monkey
EEEGLLNSSSS	leglessness
EEEGLNOOPST	gone to sleep
EEEGLNRRTTU	green turtle
EEEGMNORRSV	verse-monger
EEEGNORRSTU	tree surgeon
EEEGRRRSTUY	tree surgery
EEEHHILOPRS	heliosphere
EEEHHILPPTW	Hepplewhite
EEEHHILRSTW	elsewhither
EEEHIINNPPR	epinephrine
EEEHILLMTTT	tell the time
EEEHILMNNRR	Helen Mirren
EEEHILNPRRS	replenisher
EEEHILPPRTW	whippletree
EEEHIMNNOPS	phenomenise
EEEHIMNNOPZ	phenomenize
EEEHIMNOPPR	Oppenheimer
EEEHIMNRSST	smithereens
EEEHIMOOSTT	so mote I thee
EEEHINNRTTT	the Internet
EEEHINPSSSV	peevishness
EEEHINRSTUV	The Universe
EEEHINRTTTY	the entirety
EEEHIPPPRTW	white pepper
EEEHIRRRSTV	Three Rivers
EEEHLNNOSST	none the less
	nonetheless
EEEHLORTTTT	to the letter
EEEHMMORRTT	thermometer
EEEHMNOQRTU	queen mother
EEEHNORSTTT	on the street
EEEHRRSSTWY	sweet sherry
EEEIIKLNSST	telekinesis
EEEIILMNRST	Lise Meitner
EEEIIMRSTTX	extremities
EEEIINNPSVX	inexpensive
EEEIINNRRST	Niersteiner
EEEIINRRSTW	Winterreise
EEEIINRRTVW	interviewer
EEEIIORRSTX	exteriorise
EEEIIORRTXZ	exteriorize
EEEIKLNOSST	skeletonise
EEEIKLNOSTZ	skeletonize
EEEIKLNPRST	serpentlike
EEEILLLPRTY	Peter Lilley
EEEILMNNNTV	enlivenment
EEEILMNNTTT	entitlement
EEEILNNOPSS	in one's sleep
EEEILNNPSSS	pensileness
EEEILNNQSSU	queenliness
EEEILNPRRTT	teleprinter
EEEILNPSVXY	expensively
EEEILNRTTVY	retentively
EEEILNSSTVV	velvetiness
EEEILNSTVXY	extensively
EEEIMMNNSSS	immenseness
EEEIMMNOORT	one more time
EEEIMNORSTT	tensiometer
EEEIMNPRSTT	present-time
EEEIMNQQRUU	quinquereme
EEEIMNQRRTU	requirement
EEEIMOPRSTX	extemporise
EEEIMOPRTXZ	extemporize
EEEIMORRTTV	terremotive
EEEIMPRSTWY	Peter Wimsey
EEEINNNSSST	intenseness
EEEINNPRTUX	unexperient
EEEINNPSSSV	pensiveness
EEEINOQRTUV	queen it over
EEEINPPPRSS	pepperiness
EEEINPRRRTT	interpreter
EEEINPRRSST	enterprises
	intersperse
EEEINRSSSTV	restiveness
EEEKKLNOSTY	skeleton key
EEEKLNOOSTX	exoskeleton
EEEKLNRSTUV	trunksleeve
EEEKLORRSTW	steelworker
EEELLLNPRTY	repellently
EEELLLOSTVW	lowest level
EEELLLPSSSY	sleeplessly
EEELLNRSSVY	nervelessly
EEELLNSSSSY	senselessly
EEELMNNOPTV	envelopment
EEELMORRSSS	remorseless
EEELMPRRSTY	Meryl Streep
EEELNSSSSSU	uselessness
EEELNSSSSSX	sexlessness
EEELOOOPRTT	Peter O'Toole

EEELORRSTVW	overwrestle
EEELPRRSSTT	letterpress
EEEMMMRSTUU	Terme Museum
EEEMMNOPRTW	empowerment
EEEMMORSTTX	most extreme
EEEMNNOSTUX	exeunt omnes
EEEMNNPRSTT	presentment
EEEMNORSTUV	venturesome
EEEMNPRSSSU	supremeness
EEEMNPRSTTY	empty-nester
EEEMORRSTTY	stereometry
EEENOPRRSVY	every person
EEEOPPRRRTT	Peter Porter
EEEOPRRSTTY	stereotyper
EEFFFHHLOST	off the shelf
EEFFGHIILST	gefilte fish
EEFFGILNRSU	glue-sniffer
EEFFGLLNTUY	effulgently
EEFFHILNTTY	fifteenthly
EEFFIILLORY	life of Riley
EEFFIILRRVY	River Liffey
EEFFIINNOSV	inoffensive
EEFFILNOSVY	offensively
EEFFIMOPRTT	fit of temper
EEFFLNRSSTU	fretfulness
EEFGGIOPRTT	pettifogger
EEFGHHORTTU	freethought
EEFGHIILRRT	firelighter
EEFGHIKOPST	keep sight of
EEFGHINRRST	frighteners
EEFGHIORRTV	overfreight
EEFGHIORTTT	fit together
EEFGHLMNORS	fleshmonger
EEFGIINNRRT	interfering
EEFGILLNNUY	unfeelingly
EEFGILLNORT	foretelling
EEFGILNNOUX	genuflexion
EEFGILNORRU	foreign rule
EEFGILNRSSV	self-serving
EEFGINNORSS	foreignness
EEFGINNRTTU	unfettering
EEFGINORRRT	referring to
EEFGINORSSV	forgiveness
EEFGIOORSTY	Siege of Troy
EEFGLLOORXY	reflexology
EEFGLLRRTUY	regretfully
EEFGLNRRTUU	unregretful
EEFGMNOORTT	forget-me-not
EEFGNOOORRV	go on for ever
EEFHHILNOTY	Heyhoe Flint
EEFHIILNRSU	Henri Fuseli
EEFHIIMNOTT	in the time of
EEFHIIOSTTZ	the size of it
EEFHILNSSSS	selfishness
EEFHILOSUWY	housewifely
EEFHINRTTUU	in the future
EEFHIORRSTW	the wiser for
EEFHIORSUWY	housewifery
EEFHKOOSSUY	House of Keys
EEFHLLNPSSU	helpfulness
EEFHLNOOSSW	show oneself
EEFHLNOPSSU	hopefulness
	push oneself
EEFHLNORRWY	Henry Fowler
EEFHMNOORRW	from nowhere
EEFHMORRRTU	furthermore
EEFHMORRSTU	furthersome
EEFHNOORRST	foreshorten
EEFHNOOTTTU	to the tune of
EEFHOORRSTW	for the worse
	the worse for
EEFIIINNRST	intensifier
EEFIIISSTTV	festivities
EEFIIKKLLOR	like for like
EEFIILRTVXY	reflexivity
EEFIINOPRRS	personifier
EEFIKLLLNOS	kill oneself
EEFIKLLNOWY	Yellowknife
EEFILLLMNTU	mellifluent
EEFILLOPRTU	of ill repute
EEFILMNOSSS	miss oneself
EEFILMORSST	St Elmo's fire
EEFILNORSSW	floweriness
EEFILNOSSTU	suit oneself
EEFILOOPRRT	profiterole
EEFIMMORRST	former times
EEFINRSSTUV	furtiveness
EEFIOPRSSTU	pestiferous
EEFLLNORTTU	fortune-tell
EEFLLNORUUV	Ulf von Euler
EEFLLNRSTUY	resentfully
EEFLLOPRSUY	reposefully
EEFLMNOSSSU	fulsomeness
EEFLNNSSTUU	tunefulness
EEFLNOPPSTW	Steppenwolf
EEFLNPSSSUU	suspenseful
EEFLNRSSSTU	restfulness
EEFLNSSSTUZ	zestfulness
EEFLOOPRRWW	flower power
EEFMOOPRTTU	out of temper
EEFNOPRSSSU	profuseness
EEFOPRRRRSU	fore-spurrer
EEGGGOORRSZ	George Grosz
EEGGHHIINNT	heightening
EEGGHIINSST	sightseeing
EEGGHILNNNT	lengthening
EEGGILLNNTY	negligently
EEGGILNNRVY	revengingly
EEGGILORSUY	egregiously
EEGGNORRSTT	get stronger
EEGHHILRTWW	wheelwright
EEGHHIPSTUV	give the push
EEGHHOPRSTU	seep through
EEGHIIILNVV	Vivien Leigh
EEGHIIKNPST	keep in sight
EEGHIILPSTV	give the slip
EEGHIIMNTTW	teeming with
EEGHIINNSTV	this evening
EEGHIINNSTW	White Ensign
EEGHIINPRST	ship it green
EEGHIINSSTW	weightiness
EEGHIKNNPST	Stephen King

EEGHIKNOPPS shopkeeping
EEGHILNNSST lengthiness
EEGHILRSTTT streetlight
EEGHIMNOOTY homogeneity
EEGHIMORTTX mix together
EEGHINNPTWY pennyweight
EEGHINOORTV in the groove
EEGHINOPTTT get the point
EEGHIORTTVW get over with
EEGHLOOPRTY herpetology
EEGHMNOOOSU homogeneous
EEGHMNOORRW whoremonger
EEGHNOORTTT not together
EEGHNORRTTU run together
EEGHOOPTTTT get to the top
EEGHOPRTTTU put together
EEGIIILNORS religionise
EEGIIILNORZ religionize
EEGIIIMNPST impetigines
EEGIILLNNTT intelligent
EEGIILLTVWY give it welly
EEGIILMNNRT intermingle
EEGIIMMNNPT impingement
EEGIIMMNRSZ mesmerizing
EEGIIMNNNRS Minnesinger
EEGIIMNNOPT opening time
EEGIIMNRSTV time-serving
EEGIINNNRTV intervening
EEGIINNORST nitrogenise
EEGIINNORTZ nitrogenize
EEGIINNRSTT interesting
EEGIINNRTTW wire netting
EEGIINOPRTV progenitive
EEGIKKNORWW working week
EEGIKLNORTW teleworking
EEGIKORRSVY Sergey Kirov
EEGILLLMNNR Glenn Miller
EEGILLLNPRY repellingly
EEGILLLSSUY guilelessly
EEGILLOOSTT teleologist
EEGILLORRRU guerrillero
EEGILMOOSTY etymologise
EEGILMOOTYZ etymologize
EEGILNNNRTU unrelenting
EEGILNNPRTY repentingly
EEGILNNRSTY resentingly
EEGILNORSVY sovereignly
EEGILNOSSSV give lessons
EEGILNPRSTY pesteringly
EEGILOPRSTT poltergeist
EEGIMMNOORT Montgomerie
EEGIMNNOOPV opening move
EEGIMNNORSU Monseigneur
EEGIMNNPRTU untempering
EEGIMNNRRTU interregnum
EEGIMNORSTW swingometer
EEGINNOOSST ontogenesis
EEGINNPRSST Springsteen
EEGINOORRTU rouge-et-noir
EEGINOORTVV given over to
EEGINOPRTTU petering out
EEGINORSTVY sovereignty
EEGINPRSTTU guttersnipe
EEGINPSTTTY typesetting
EEGIOOPRTVW give power to
EEGIOPRRSSV progressive
EEGKORRSTUW guest worker
EEGLMOOORTY meteorology
EEGLNOOPPUY young people
EEGLNSSSSTU gutlessness
EEGLOPPPTUV glove puppet
EEGLOQRSTUY grotesquely
EEGMNNORSST engrossment
EEGNOOORSTU erotogenous
EEGOQRRSTUY grotesquery
EEGPRRSSTTU gutter press
EEHHIJKOPST Keith Joseph
EEHHIKLOTTW the whole kit
EEHHILLNSSS hellishness
EEHHILLORTV over the hill
EEHHILOPRST lithosphere
EEHHINORSTT in the throes
EEHHIOOPSST theosophise
EEHHIOOPSTZ theosophize
EEHHIOPSSTY hypothesise
EEHHIOPSTTY hypothetise
EEHHIOPSTYZ hypothesize
EEHHIOPTTYZ hypothetize
EEHHIORSSTW white horses
EEHHLLOOTTW the whole lot
EEHHLMOPRTT port the helm
EEHHMOPRTUV over the hump
EEHHNNOORTT on the throne
EEHHNOORRTW whether or no
EEHHNORSTUU house-hunter
EEHHOOPPRST photosphere
EEHHOOPRRTT heterotroph
EEHHOPPRSTT the prophets
EEHIIIMPTTT it pitieth me
EEHIIKNPSTY pie in the sky
EEHIILLMNWW Wilhelm Wien
EEHIILMNTUW minute-while
EEHIIMPPRRS premiership
EEHIIMSSTTV Stevie Smith
EEHIINRRSST inheritress
EEHIJLNNNOT John Tenniel
EEHIKLLLNRU run like hell
EEHILLMNRRY Henry Miller
EEHILNOPSTT telephonist
EEHILNOSTTV novelettish
EEHILNSTTXY sixteenthly
EEHILOPRSST priest's hole
EEHILRSTTWW wrestle with
EEHILSSTTUW shuttlewise
EEHIMNOPRSS Shimon Peres
EEHIMNOTTTU to the minute
EEHIMOPRSTU hemipterous
EEHINNOOPTT into the open
EEHINNORRST northernise
EEHINNORRTZ northernize
EEHINNOSSSU heinousness
EEHINOPSTVY hypotensive

EEHINORSSTU	southernise	EEIKMNORSSS	irksomeness
EEHINORSTUZ	southernize	EEILLMNOPRT	Montpellier
EEHINPSSSTT	pettishness	EEILLMNOTTW	Little Women
EEHINRSSSTU	hirsuteness	EEILLMOOPRT	trompe l'oeil
EEHINRSSSTY	synthesiser		trompe-l'oeil
EEHINRSSTYZ	synthesizer	EEILLMPRTUX	multiplexer
EEHIOORRSTW	or otherwise	EEILLMRSSUW	Weissmuller
EEHIOPRRSST	The Prioress	EEILLNNOSWX	Lennox Lewis
EEHIPRSSTTU	trusteeship	EEILLNOSSSY	noiselessly
EEHJNOPRRST	Prester John	EEILLNPSSSY	spinelessly
EEHJNORSSTU	John Surtees	EEILLNPSTTY	pestilently
EEHKNOORSTT	on the stroke	EEILLOOPRSU	leisure pool
	tenterhooks	EEILLOPSVXY	explosively
EEHKNOSTUVY	Yevtushenko	EEILLORRVWY	Yellow River
EEHLLMOOSWY	wholesomely	EEILLPRSUVY	prelusively
EEHLMMOOPRS	pommel horse		repulsively
EEHLMNOOSUW	unwholesome	EEILMMNORRW	Erwin Rommel
EEHLMNOTTVW	twelvemonth	EEILMNNOOVW	Women in Love
EEHLOOSSUVY	She Loves You	EEILMNNOTVV	involvement
EEHLOPRRSTU	upholsterer	EEILMNOOSST	emotionless
EEHMMNORSTU	The Summoner	EEILMNRTTTY	remittently
EEHMMOOPRRT	emperor moth	EEILNNOPPTT	plenipotent
EEHMMORSSUU	summerhouse	EEILNNPRTTY	pertinently
EEHMNNOOORY	honeymooner	EEILNNSSSSS	sinlessness
EEHMNOOORTV	over the moon	EEILNOORSTV	Oliver Stone
EEHMOPPRSTY	spermophyte	EEILNOPRTVY	poverty line
EEHMOPRRSTT	short temper	EEILNORSSTV	Silverstone
EEHNOOOPRSZ	ozonosphere	EEILNOSSTVY	ostensively
EEHNOOPRSTY	stereophony	EEILNOSTTTV	novelettist
EEHNOPQSTUY	Pythonesque	EEILNSSUUWY	use unwisely
EEHNORRSTTW	north-wester	EEILOPRSSTY	proselytise
EEHOOPPRRST	troposphere	EEILOPRSTYZ	proselytize
EEIIIMNNSTU	einsteinium	EEILORSTVXY	extorsively
EEIIINNSSTV	insensitive	EEIMMMNOORT	memento mori
EEIIKLLNNNS	Enniskillen	EEIMMNOPRTV	improvement
EEIIKLNNRTU	interleukin	EEIMNNNORTV	environment
EEIILLNORVV	live-in lover	EEIMNNOOSSS	noisomeness
EEIILLNRSTY	resiliently	EEIMNNOPRST	omnipresent
EEIILLPPRST	pipistrelle	EEIMNNOSSSW	winsomeness
EEIILLPRSTV	spirit level	EEIMNNSSTTV	investments
EEIILMMNPRT	imperilment	EEIMNOQSTUU	Montesquieu
EEIILMNOSSU	emulsionise	EEIMNORSTZZ	intermezzos
EEIILMNOSUZ	emulsionize	EEIMNPPRTUU	in perpetuum
EEIILMNRSSS	miserliness	EEIMNRSSTTW	Westminster
EEIILNNPRRT	line printer	EEIMOOPRTVW	motive power
EEIILNNSTVY	intensively	EEIMOPPRSSU	superimpose
EEIILNNTVVY	inventively	EEIMPPRSTUV	presumptive
EEIILNSSTVY	sensitively	EEINNNOSTTX	non-existent
EEIILQSTUXY	exquisitely	EEINNOPRSST	pretensions
EEIILRSSTVY	resistively	EEINNORSSTU	routineness
EEIIMNNPRTT	impertinent	EEINNORTTUV	venture into
EEIINNOOPRT	Pointe Noire	EEINNOSSSUV	enviousness
	Pointe-Noire	EEINNOSSTTU	sententious
EEIINNPRRWZ	prizewinner	EEINNQSSTUU	unquietness
	prize-winner	EEINOORRTTX	extortioner
EEIINOSSTTV	sensitive to	EEINOPRSSSX	expressions
EEIINRSTTUV	investiture	EEINOPRSTTU	pretentious
EEIIOPRSTTU	repetitious	EEINOPSSSTU	piteousness
EEIIORRRSTT	territories	EEINORSSSSU	seriousness
EEIIRSTTTUV	restitutive	EEINPRRRTTU	interrupter
EEIJMNORRSY	Jeremy Irons	EEINPRTTTWY	typewritten

EEINRRSTUWW Wienerwurst
EEIPPRSSSUV suppressive
EEJLNOSSSSY joylessness
EEKKOORRRTV Voortrekker
EEKLLMOSSSY smokelessly
EEKLLOPRRSW spellworker
EEKLORRSTTW trestlework
EEKMNOOPSSW spokeswomen
EELLNOOPRUV pull one over
EELLNOORSSW Orson Welles
EELLNOPSTUY plenteously
EELLNORRSTW western roll
EELLNORTVWY not very well
EELLNPRTUUV pulverulent
EELLOPRSSWY powerlessly
EELLORRSTTY storyteller
EELMMNOPTTU Temple Mount
EELMNNOOSTY stolen money
EELMNOSSSUU emulousness
EELMOPRRSTT storm petrel
EELNNSSSSSU sunlessness
EELNOOPPSTW townspeople
EELNOORRSUY erroneously
EELNOPRSTYY polystyrene
EELOPPRSSSU purposeless
EEMMORWZZZZ Mezz Mezzrow
EEMNORSSTTW westernmost
EEMOPSSTTTT tempest-tost
EEMOPSSTTUU tempestuous
EENNOORSSSU onerousness
EENNOORSTTT rottenstone
EENNORSSSUV nervousness
EENNOSSSTUU tenuousness
EENNPPRTTYY pretty penny
EEOOPRRRRTV Trevor-Roper
EEOOPRRSSSS repossessor
EEOPPRRSTUY upper storey
EEOPQRSSTTU request stop
EFFFGINORUU figure of fun
EFFFINORSTZ frozen-stiff
EFFFIOORRTW write off for
EFFGHIINNOT in the offing
EFFGIOOPRUV Group of Five
EFFGLLORTUY forgetfully
EFFHHILOPTW help off with
EFFHHKOOOST off the hooks
EFFHINOOPTT off the point
EFFIJNOORTT joint effort
EFFILOORRSU floriferous
EFFIOORRRTT fit of terror
EFGGHIINNRT frightening
EFGGHIIRRST triggerfish
EFGHHIILOPR high profile
EFGHHOORTTU forethought
EFGHIIILNNS fishing-line
EFGHIILMRTY Light My Fire
EFGHIILNSST flightiness
EFGHIILOSTW Isle of Wight
EFGHIINOPRT in the grip of
EFGHIJLMNNO John Fleming
EFGHILNPSWY when pigs fly
EFGHILOOSST lose sight of
EFGHINNOORT for one thing
EFGHNNOSUUY honey fungus
EFGIIILNRTZ fertilizing
EFGIIINRVVY revivifying
EFGIILLMORU florilegium
EFGIILLNPRY pilferingly
EFGIILLNTTW well-fitting
EFGIILMNNOT filet mignon
EFGIILMNSTT filmsetting
EFGIIMNORTT more fitting
EFGIINNPRRT fingerprint
EFGIINNSSTT fittingness
EFGIKLLLNRU fell-lurking
EFGIKNNOORW foreknowing
EFGILLLORWY gillyflower
EFGILLNNNRU fell-running
EFGILMNOORT Montgolfier
EFGILNOORVW overflowing
EFGINOOORST fons et origo
EFGINORRSUU ferruginous
EFGLMNOOTTU leg-of-mutton
EFGMOPRRSTU Forrest Gump
EFHHOOPPRRT froth-hopper
EFHIINRSSTT thriftiness
EFHIKLLNOTW think well of
EFHILLNSSUY unselfishly
EFHILLOSTWW wolf whistle
EFHILLSSSTY shiftlessly
EFHILNOOSSS foolishness
EFHILNOSSSW wolfishness
EFHILNSSSUW wishfulness
EFHINOPPSSS foppishness
EFHLLNOPUUY unhopefully
EFHLNOOOPRR forlorn hope
EFHLNRSSTUU hurtfulness
EFHLOSTTUUY theftuously
EFHMORRSTTU furthermost
EFHOOOPRRSW showerproof
EFIIILNOTTV fit to live in
EFIIILNRTTY infertility
EFIIINORRTY inferiority
EFIIKRRSSTT first strike
EFIILNNOOPS self-opinion
EFIILNOPTTU put life into
EFIILNPSSTU pitifulness
EFIINNOPRST finer points
EFIINNORSTU interfusion
EFIINOOPTVW point of view
EFIINOPRSSU spiniferous
EFIKLLNSSSU skilfulness
EFIKLOORTTU out of kilter
EFILLLMOSUU mellifluous
EFILLLNPTUY plentifully
EFILLNOOSUY feloniously
EFILLRSSTUY fruitlessly
EFILNSSSTUW wistfulness
EFILPRSTUUY superfluity
EFIMNNORSSU uniformness
EFIMNOORSSU somniferous
EFINORSSSTW frowstiness

EFINORSSSUU	furiousness
EFLLNNTUUUY	untunefully
EFLLNORSSTY	frontlessly
EFLLNOSSSUU	soulfulness
EFLLNSSSTUU	lustfulness
EFLNNOORRSS	forlornness
EFLOPPRSSTU	self-support
EFLOPRSSUUU	superfluous
EFMMOOORTUY	From Me To You
EFMNOOOPSTY	pots of money
EFMNOOORRUY	for our money
EFNNNORRRTU	front-runner
EFNOOPRRTTY	port of entry
EGGGILNNOOS	gone gosling
EGGGINOPRRU	ginger group
EGGHHHIILRT	highlighter
EGGHHIILTTW	lightweight
EGGHHINOSSS	hoggishness
EGGHIINPSSS	piggishness
EGGHIINRRTW	right-winger
EGGHLNOORSW	hornswoggle
EGGHLNOOSTT	go to lengths
EGGIIKNNNPU	king penguin
EGGIILLNNRY	lingeringly
EGGIILNNSWY	swingeingly
EGGILNNORSV	long-serving
EGGINOPRRSS	progressing
EGGINOSSSTU	suggestions
EGGLMMNOOOR	gloom-monger
EGGLNOOORTY	gerontology
EGHHHLOPRTU	help through
EGHHHOORSTU	hog-shouther
EGHHIIINTWW	weigh in with
EGHHIIKNTTW	white knight
EGHHIINNOST	high-tension
EGHHILNNORS	English horn
EGHHILOPRSY	hieroglyphs
EGHHILORTUV	live through
EGHHILOSSTU	house lights
EGHHIMNOSSU	Simon Hughes
EGHHKNOTTUW	hunt-the-gowk
EGHHLOSSTTU	thoughtless
EGHIIIMNTTW	whiting-time
EGHIIKLNNOT	The Lion King
EGHIIKLNRSY	shriekingly
EGHIILLNRSV	shrivelling
EGHIILNNOST	in one's light
EGHIILNNPSS	plenishings
EGHIILNPRSY	perishingly
EGHIILNRSSS	girlishness
EGHIILNRSVY	shiveringly
EGHIILNRTWY	witheringly
EGHIILNSSST	sightliness
EGHIINNRRVY	Henry Irving
EGHIINOTTTW	get it on with
EGHIINRSSTT	night sister
EGHIKMNOORW	homeworking
EGHILLMOTVY	move lightly
EGHILLSSSTY	sightlessly
EGHILMNOORT	moonlighter
EGHILMOOSTY	Mythologies
	mythologise
EGHILMOOTYZ	mythologize
EGHILNOOPST	nephologist
	phenologist
EGHILNOOSTT	ethnologist
EGHILNOSSST	ghostliness
EGHILORSSTV	Silver Ghost
EGHILORSTUY	righteously
EGHIMNNORSU	nursing home
EGHINNNOSST	nothingness
EGHINNOPTUW	upon the wing
EGHINNORRST	Sherrington
EGHINOPTTUW	put on weight
EGHINORSSSU	roguishness
EGHINORSTUU	unrighteous
EGHINPRSSTU	uprightness
EGHIOORTTTV	right to vote
EGHIORRSTTW	ghost writer
EGHIORSSTTT	set to rights
EGHLMOPRTUY	methyl group
EGHNOPRRUWY	power-hungry
EGHOOPRRTUY	group theory
EGHOORRTUVW	overwrought
EGIIIKKLNNW	like winking
EGIIIKNNOTY	ignition key
EGIIILNNNRT	interlining
EGIIILORRSU	irreligious
EGIIILORSTY	religiosity
EGIIINNOPRT	pre-ignition
EGIIINNOPTT	petitioning
EGIIJNNOSTT	jettisoning
EGIIKKLLNOO	looking like
EGIIKLNOOSY	kinesiology
EGIILLLLMNS	ill-smelling
EGIILLMNPSS	misspelling
EGIILLNNSSW	willingness
EGIILLNORTY	loiteringly
EGIILLNPRUW	wire-pulling
EGIILLNRSTW	ill-wresting
EGIILLORSUY	religiously
EGIILMNPRSY	simperingly
EGIILNNOSTU	lentiginous
EGIILNNOSTV	Livingstone
EGIILNNOSUY	ingeniously
EGIILNORSUU	unreligious
EGIILNQRUVY	quiveringly
EGIILNRSSST	gristliness
EGIILNRSSTY	resistingly
EGIIMNNOPPU	impinge upon
EGIIMNNORSZ	sermonizing
EGIIMNNRTTU	unremitting
EGIIMNOPRTZ	temporizing
EGIIMNSTTTU	Mistinguett
EGIINNNORVW	winning over
EGIINNOPRST	interposing
EGIINNOQSTU	questioning
EGIINNPRSSS	springiness
EGIINNRSSST	stringiness
EGIINNRSSTU	unresisting
EGIINOPRSSU	spinigerous
EGIINOPRTTU	pirouetting

EGIINORRRTZ	terrorizing
EGIINORRSTT	intertrigos
EGIINORSTUV	vertiginous
EGIINPRSSUV	supervising
EGIINPRTTWY	typewriting
EGIIOPRSSTU	prestigious
EGIKLLNNORS	snorkelling
EGIKLLNOSWY	King's-yellow
EGIKLNOOORV	overlooking
EGIKMNOOPSU	go up in smoke
EGIKNNNOSSW	knowingness
EGIKNNORRTW	ring network
EGILLLSSTUY	guiltlessly
EGILLMNORUV	mulling over
	mulling-over
EGILLMNOSTU	smelling-out
EGILLNORTVY	revoltingly
EGILMNNOSTW	melting snow
EGILMNOOOSU	monologuise
EGILMNOOOUZ	monologuize
EGILMNOORTY	terminology
EGILMNPRSUY	presumingly
EGILMNRTTUY	mutteringly
EGILMOOSTTY	etymologist
EGILNNOOPSU	loosening up
EGILNNOSUUY	ingenuously
EGILNNRSTTY	stringently
EGILNNRSTUY	unrestingly
EGILNNRTUVY	venturingly
EGILNOOOPST	stool pigeon
EGILNOORSTU	neurologist
EGILNOPRRTY	reportingly
EGILNOPRRVY	reprovingly
EGILNOPRTTY	potteringly
EGILNORTTTY	totteringly
EGILNPRSTTU	spluttering
EGILOOORSTY	soteriology
EGILOOOSSTT	osteologist
EGILOOPRSSY	perissology
EGILOOPSSTT	pestologist
EGIMNNOORRY	ironmongery
EGINNNORRUV	overrunning
EGINNNRTTUX	running text
EGINNOORSTU	nitrogenous
EGINOOPRRSS	progression
EGINOOPRRST	progenitors
EGMMNNOOTTU	Mount Egmont
EGNNOOPRSUY	young person
EHHIILNOSSS	His Holiness
EHHIINRRSTU	Irish Hunter
EHHIINRSSTW	withershins
EHHIJMOPSST	Joseph Smith
EHHILOOPPRS	philosopher
EHHILOPTTTU	up to the hilt
EHHILOPTTUW	without help
EHHIMRSTTUY	eurhythmist
EHHIOOPPRSS	phosphorise
EHHIOOPPRSZ	phosphorize
EHHIOOPRRSW	hero worship
	hero-worship
EHHIOOPSSTT	theosophist

EHHLOOSTTUY	youth hostel
EHHNNOPSTUU	upon the shun
EHHNOOSSTTU	shoot the sun
EHHOOPPRSTY	hypostrophe
EHHOOPSSTTW	stop the show
EHHOPPRRTYY	hypertrophy
EHIIILNPPPS	Philippines
EHIIILOSSTT	hostilities
EHIIIPRSTTW	white spirit
EHIIKKLLNTY	think likely
EHIILMRSSTV	silversmith
EHIIMNPSSSW	wimpishness
EHIINNORSST	in one's shirt
EHIINNSSSSW	swinishness
EHIINPRSSST	spinsterish
EHIINRSSSTT	thirstiness
EHIJNNNOSTU	honest Injun
EHILLMRSSTY	mirthlessly
EHILMNPSSSU	lumpishness
EHILMOOSSTU	Lossiemouth
EHILNOPTTUW	with no let-up
EHILNOSSSTU	loutishness
EHILNSSSSTY	stylishness
EHILOPSSTTW	whistle-stop
EHIMNNORSTU	nourishment
EHIMOPRRTUV	triumph over
EHINNOOPSTY	hypotension
EHINORRSTTU	North Utsire
EHINORRTUVW	overrun with
EHIOOOPRRSU	eriophorous
EHIORSSTTUU	South Utsire
EHJKLNNOOST	John Skelton
EHJLNOOPSSY	Joseph Lyons
EHJNOORRSTV	John Vorster
EHKNOOPRSST	short-spoken
EHLLOOOOPPT	loop the loop
EHLLORSSTWY	worthlessly
EHLMNOPTUWY	New Plymouth
EHLMOOOSTTY	toothsomely
EHLNNOOSSTY	Holy Sonnets
EHLOPRSSUUU	sulphureous
EHMOOOPRSTU	homopterous
EHMOOSTTTTU	to the utmost
EHOOPPRSSTW	show-stopper
EIIIINQSTUV	inquisitive
EIIILMPRTVY	primitively
EIIILNNPSTY	insipiently
EIIILNTTUVY	intuitively
EIIIMNNOPTT	point in time
EIIIMNNOTTT	Tito Menniti
EIIIMNORSSV	revisionism
EIIIMNORSVX	vision mixer
EIIINNOQRTU	inquire into
EIIINOPRSTT	peritonitis
EIIINOQRSTU	requisition
EIIINORSSTV	revisionist
EIIINSSTTVY	sensitivity
EIIIRSSTTVY	resistivity
EIIKKLLOOST	it looks like
EIIKKNORSSS	kirk session
EIIKLNPSSTT	skittle-pins

EIILLLMSSTY limitlessly
EIILLMMNNSU millenniums
EIILLMPSUVY impulsively
EIILLOOQSSU soliloquise
EIILLOOQSUZ soliloquize
EIILMOPRSUY imperiously
EIILMORSTTU outer limits
EIILNNSSTTY insistently
EIILNOOPPRT lipoprotein
EIILNOPPRTT triple point
EIILNOQSUUZ Louis-Quinze
EIILNRSTUVY intrusively
EIILNRTTUVY nutritively
EIILOPPRSTY propylitise
EIILOPPRTYZ propylitize
EIILORSTTVW Oliver Twist
EIILPRRTUVY irruptively
EIIMNNOOPRT premonition
EIIMNNOOSTT set in motion
EIIMNOPRSSS impressions
EIIMNOPSSST miss one's tip
EIIMNOPSSSU impiousness
EIIMNRRTTTY Trinity term
EIIMOORRSTU meritorious
EIIMOPPRRTY impropriety
EIIMOPRSSST prestissimo
EIIMOPSTTUY impetuosity
EIIMORRSTUZ moisturizer
EIINNNOSSTT insistent on
EIINOOPPRST preposition
EIINOPRSSUV supervision
EIINORRSSST sinistrorse
EIINORSTTTU restitution
EIIOPRRSTUY superiority
EIJJLLNNOOO Jonjo O'Neill
EIJKMMRSSUU Rijksmuseum
EIJLOOSTUUV Louis Jouvet
EIKLLNNOTTW little known
little-known
EIKMNORRSTY York Minster
EILLNOOORVV Ivor Novello
EILLNOORRST ritornellos
EILLNOORTYY Tony O'Reilly
EILLNOPSSTY pointlessly
EILLOPRRSUY prelusorily
EILMNNOPRTY prominently
EILMNOOOPRZ monopolizer
EILMNOPRTUY importunely
EILMNOSTUUY untimeously
EILMOPRSSTY proselytism
EILMOPSTUUY impetuously
EILMORSTTUY multistorey
EILNNOOSTTT not listen to
EILNOOPSTTW lowest point
EILNOPRSUUY penuriously
EILOOPRRSTY posteriorly
EILOPPRRSTW slipperwort
EIMNNOOSSSU ominousness
EIMNNRSSTTU instruments
EIMNOOPRRTY premonitory
EIMNOOQSTTU mosquito net
EIMNOOSTTZZ mezzotintos
EIMNOPPRSTU presumption
EIMOOPRSTTT optometrist
EINNOOPPRTU inopportune
EINNOOPSSTT post-tension
EINNOOSSSUX noxiousness
EINNOQRSTUU non sequitur
EINNORSSSUU ruinousness
EINNOSSSSUU sinuousness
EINOOPSSSSS possessions
EINOORSSSTU riotousness
EINOPPRSSSU suppression
EINOPRRRTTU interruptor
EINORSSTTUY strenuosity
EIOOPPRRRST proprietors
EIOPRRSSSUV supervisors
EIOPRRSSUVY supervisory
EIORRSSTTUU trouser suit
EIORRSTTTUY restitutory
EKLLRRSSTUU Kurt Russell
EKLNOOPSTUY outspokenly
EKLNOORSTTY Leon Trotsky
EKNNNNOSSUW unknownness
ELLMNNOOSTY somnolently
ELLMORSTUUY tremulously
ELLNORTTUUW turn out well
ELLOPPRTTYY Pretty Polly
ELLOQRSUUUY querulously
ELMMNOOSTUY momentously
ELMNNORSUYY Lynn Seymour
ELMNOPPSUYY money supply
ELNNOORSTUW slow neutron
ELNOOOPRRTY poltroonery
ELNOOPPRTUY opportunely
ELNORSSTUUY strenuously
ELNORSTUUVY venturously
ELOPPRSSSTU supportless
EMNOOPPSSSU pompousness
EMORRSTTUYY mystery tour
ENNOORSTTTU turn to stone
ENOPRSSSTTU put stress on

F

FFGGHIIINTT fighting fit
FFGHILLNSUY shufflingly
FFGHILLRTUY frightfully
FFGIINNOSTU sniffing-out
FFHIIINRSST finish first
FGGHIINNOTT nothing-gift
FGGIIKKNNOS king of kings
FGGIINNORUV unforgiving
FGHHILOPRTU flip through
FGHHNOOTTUU unthought-of
FGHIILNOPST shoplifting
FGHIILNORSU flourishing
FGHIINNRSSU furnishings
FGHILLNOOWW Howling Wolf
FGHILNORTTY fortnightly
FGHILOPTTTU put to flight
FGHIMNOSSTU sum of things
FGHINOOSSSW show signs of

FGHINORRTTU ring of truth
FGIILLNNSUW in full swing
FGIILLNPTUY upliftingly
FGIILNNTTUY unfittingly
FGIILNSTTUY stultifying
FHHIORRSSTT short shrift
FHIIKNOOTTT to think of it
FHIILNRTTUY unthriftily
FHIIOPRSTTW with profits
FHIMOORTTUW from without
FHJMNOOOPRU John Profumo
FHLLMNOOTWY monthly flow
FHLPRSTTUUU sulphur tuft
FHMOOORTUUU out of humour
FHOOOPRSSTT stop short of
FIIMMNOSSTZ Fitzsimmons
FIIMOORSTTT fritto misto
FIINNOOPRSU in profusion
FIIOOPPRRST proof spirit
FIIRTTTTTUU Tutti Frutti
tutti-frutti
FILLOORSUVY frivolously
FILMOPPRSTU split up from
FILMRSSTTUU mistrustful
FILNOORSSTY frontolysis
FLLOORRSUWY sorrowfully

G

GGGINNOORST going strong
GGHIIILNNTV living thing
GGHIILLNSTY slightingly
GGHIINNOQTU Quintin Hogg
GGHIOORSTUU Hugo Grotius
GGIINNPPRSU springing-up
GGILNNNNORU long-running
GHHHIORTTUW through with
GHHHNORTTUU hunt through
GHHHOPRSTUU push through
GHHIIINNOOP high opinion
GHHIIIPRSST high spirits
GHHILNNOOTT nothing loth
GHHILOPRTTT troth-plight
GHHINNNORTU hunting-horn
GHHKLOOORTU look through
GHHKOORRTUW work through
GHHLLOPRTUU pull through
GHHLOPRSUUY push roughly
GHHMNNOOOPT monophthong
GHHMOOPRRTU romp through
GHIIINNNOTT nothing in it
GHIIKLNNRSY shrinkingly
GHIIKLNTTTY tightly-knit
GHIIKNNNRSU unshrinking
GHIILLLNRTY thrillingly
GHIILLNNOTT Notting Hill
GHIILLNORTW Illingworth
GHIILLNOSWW show willing
GHIILLNSTWY whistlingly
GHIILLOOPST philologist
GHIILLOOSTT lithologist
GHIILNNPSUY punishingly
GHIILNOORST rhinologist
GHIILOOSSTT histologist
GHIIMNNORST this morning
GHIIMNNOSST miss nothing
GHIINNOOTTT nothing to it
GHIINNOPTYZ hypnotizing
GHIINOPPRSW worshipping
GHIJMNOPSUW showjumping
show-jumping
GHIKNNNOOTW know-nothing
GHILMMNRTUY thrummingly
GHILMNOOSTY hymnologist
GHILMOOSTTY mythologist
GHILNOOOPST phonologist
GHILNOOORTY ornithology
GHIMMNOORSU mushrooming
GHIMNOOPSYY physiognomy
GHINNNOSTTU Huntington's
GHINOORRTUW wrought iron
GHINOORTTUW throwing out
GHIOPRSTTTU put to rights
GIIIINNPRST inspiriting
GIIIKLMNNSS missing link
GIIILLNNORT rolling in it
GIIILLOSTUY litigiously
GIIILNNPRSY inspiringly
GIIILNNQRUY inquiringly
GIIIMNNOOSU ignominious
GIIINNNPRSU uninspiring
GIIINNOOPST positioning
GIIKLLLNOSU soul-killing
GIIKLNPRSSU prusik sling
GIILLLNNUWY unwillingly
GIILLMNOOST limnologist
GIILLMNOPRY imploringly
GIILLMNPTUY multiplying
GIILLNNSTUY insultingly
GIILMNOPRSY promisingly
GIILMNOPRVY improvingly
GIILNNQSTUY squintingly
GIILNNTTUWY unwittingly
GIILNPPSTTU splitting-up
GIIMNNOPRSU unpromising
GIIMNOORSTT sitting-room
GIIMOORRRST rigor mortis
GIINNNOOPRS spring onion
GIINNNOPSTW winning-post
GIINNOOPTTU pointing-out
GIINNOPRRST ripsnorting
GIINRTTTTYY nitty-gritty
GIKLNNNOUWY unknowingly
GIKLNOOPRVY provokingly
GIKNNNNORTU running knot
GIKNOOPRSTW stop working
GILLNOSTUUY glutinously
GILLNPRSSTU pull strings
GILMMNRRUUY murmuringly
GILNORRTTUY torturingly
GILNRSTTTUY struttingly
GIMMNNOPSUU summoning-up
GIMNNORSTUU surmounting

GINNOOPPSTT not stopping
GINNOOPRSTT strong point
GINOOPPSTTU stopping-out

H

HHILMOOPSTY holophytism
HHKNOOOSWWW know who's who
HHOOOPPRSSU phosphorous
HIILLNNNOOT nonillionth
HIILOPRSTTY lithotripsy
HIIMMOOPRSS isomorphism
HIIMMOPRRST trimorphism
HIIMNOOPRST monitorship
HIKOORTTUWW without work
HILNOOPSTXY xylophonist
HILNOORSSTU honours list
HIMNOOPSSUY symphonious
HIMOOOPRSSU isomorphous
HIMOOPRRSTU trimorphous
HINOOPPRSSS sponsorship
HJNOORSSTTW St John's wort
HLOPPRSSTUY short supply
HMNNOOPTTYY Monty Python
HORRSTTTUWY trustworthy

I

IIIIMMPRSTV primitivism
IIIIMPPSSSS Mississippi
IIIINNOQSTU inquisition
IIILLMNOPST pointillism
IIILLMNOSSU illusionism
IIILLNOPSTT pointillist
IIILLNOSSTT tonsillitis
IIILLNOSSTU illusionist
IIINNOSTTTU institution
IIJLNORSUUY injuriously
IILLNNOOOPP opinion poll
IILLOOQSSTU soliloquist
IILLORSSTUU illustrious
IILMOORTTUY utility room
IILNNOOSUXY innoxiously
IILOOPRRSVY provisorily
IIMNNOOPTTU put in motion
IIMNOPRTTUY importunity
IIMOOPRSSTT soroptimist❑
IINNOPPRSTU put in prison
IINOOOPPRST proposition
IINOOPPSSTU supposition
IINOPPQRTUY propinquity
IIOOPPRRTTY top-priority
IJKLNOORTWY work jointly
IJLNNOSTUWY only just win
IKKLOOSSTVY Tsiolkovsky
ILLOPSSUWWY pussy willow
ILLORSUUUXY luxuriously
ILMNOPRSSUU plus or minus
ILNNNOOSSTY Sonny Liston
ILNOOOPSSUY poisonously
ILNOOORSTUY notoriously
IMNOOPPRSTU opportunism
IMNOORSSTTY monstrosity
IMOOPPRSTTU pittosporum
IMOPSSTTUUY sumptuosity
IMPPPRRSTUU stirrup pump
INOOOPPRRST proportions
INOOPPRSTTU opportunist
INOOPPRTTUY opportunity
IOOPPRSSTUY suppository

L

LLNOOORRUWY roll-your-own
LMMORRSUUUY murmurously
LMNOORSSTUY monstrously
LMOPSSTUUUY sumptuously

12 letters

A

AAAAAABCNNNN Canaan Banana
AAAAAALMRSTT taramasalata
AAAAABBNRRST Santa Barbara
AAAAABCDLMNS Canada balsam
AAAAADLNRSTW Anwar al-Sadat
AAAAAEGNPSST apage Satanas
AAAABBDHMRRY Abraham Darby
AAAABBJMORRR Major Barbara
AAAABCCHILNN bacchanalian
AAAABDGGHITV Bhagavad Gita
AAAABDGILMOV viola da gamba
AAAABEERTVWY beaver away at
AAAABEHISSSV have as a basis
AAAABILNPRSV Bavarian Alps
AAAACCCCIRTU acciaccatura
AAAACDIILPRS paradisaical
AAAACDIIMORT acaridomatia
AAAACDIMOORT acarodomatia
AAAACEINRRSV caravanserai
AAAACELLLLPP alla cappella
AAAACHILNPPS Appalachians
AAAACIMNRSST antimacassar
AAAADEELRTTT at a later date
AAAADEFHLSSZ Hafez al-Assad
AAAADEGLMNNR an arm and a leg
AAAADEHMRSTT mad as a hatter
AAAADELNRSTW Anwar el-Sadat
AAAADILRSTUY Australia Day
AAAAEEGKMTWY make a getaway
AAAAEFFHINRV have an affair
AAAAEFMMORRS Sea of Marmara
AAAAEFRRSSTY Yasser Arafat
AAAAEGGLNPRU paralanguage
AAAAEGHLNOSV have as an goal
AAAAEGNRTVXZ extravaganza
AAAAEHILMSST thalassaemia

AAAAEIKNNNNR Anna Karenina
AAAAEIMMNRRT armamentaria
AAAAFGILLNRS Niagara Falls
AAAAGHHMMRRT Martha Graham
AAAAGHHNRSUV Sarah Vaughan
AAAAGILMMNOT amalgamation
AAAAHILSSTTV hasta la vista
AAAAHIMNNOTT thanatomania
AAAAILLPRRSS sarsaparilla
AAAAILNRSSTU Australasian
AAAAINNNORTV Antananarivo
AAABBBCHKLST Black Sabbath
AAABBCEEINRS Caribbean Sea
AAABBCEGOSVY savoy cabbage
AAABBDLNOORZ blazon abroad
AAABBEEFHMTT abaft the beam
AAABBEHHOSVY have as a hobby
AAABBELNSTTT Blatant Beast
AAABBILLMRRS Barbara Mills
AAABCDEELLNW weal-balanced
AAABCDEEMNRS Danse Macabre
AAABCDHHIPTT hit a bad patch
AAABCEELLLRS clear as a bell
AAABCEERSSSU scarabaeuses
AAABCEGIORRS Casare Borgia
AAABCEHILLPT alphabetical
AAABCEHILNPT analphabetic
AAABCEHIMRSU Beaumarchais
AAABCEHLOPPR approachable
AAABCEIILNSZ Isaac Albéniz
AAABCEILLNRT trial balance
AAABCEILLPSS Blaise Pascal
AAABCEILNPTY Placentia Bay
AAABCELLLNRU Lauren Bacall
AAABCHKKLRWW Black Hawk War
AAABCIILRRUV vibracularia
AAABDDJNNORY Darby and Joan
AAABDEEFHLPT deaf alphabet
AAABDEILMNPR Brian De Palma
AAABDEINNRSV drive bananas
AAABDEMMORVY Madame Bovary
AAABDEMRSSSS ambassadress
AAABDGHMNRSS smash-and-grab
AAABDIILPTTY adaptability
AAABDILMRTYY Admiralty Bay
AAABDLLMNOOR abnormal load
AAABDNRRRSST Barnard's star
AAABEEERRTTT beat a retreat
AAABEEGHINRT breathe again
AAABEEGIKNTT take a beating
AAABEEGILMRR marriageable
AAABEEGLMNNU unmanageable
AAABEELNPPSU unappeasable
AAABEFHIKMOT make a habit of
AAABEFKLLMOS make a balls of
AAABEFLMOTTZ Battle of Zama
AAABEHHKKLLS Lake Balkhash
AAABEHIKPPPT Phi Beta Kappa
AAABEHMSSTTY that's as may be
AAABEIIJNRSZ Azerbaijanis
AAABEIILMNNT maintainable
AAABEILLNSSU unassailable
AAABEILNNTTU unattainable
AAABEILRRSTV variable star
AAABEINNSSST San Sebastian
AAABELLLPRRS parallel bars
AAABELLNNSUY unanalysable
AAABELLNRSTT translatable
AAABELNOOPTY palaeobotany
AAABELQSTTUU absquatulate
AAABEMNORTTW water boatman
AAABFILMRRSS friar's balsam
AAABGGLNNPRU Luang Prabang
AAABGLLMRRRU burglar alarm
AAABHIKLLMOR Kimball O'Hara
AAABIIILLTVY availability
AAABIILLPTTY palatability
AAABIKKLNOTU Kota Kinabalu
AAABIKLNNNOT national bank
AAABILLNQRRU Barranquilla
AAABILNPRSSU Assurbanipal
AAACCCDILLSY saccadically
AAACCCHLNRSU Lucas Cranach
AAACCDEEGNRS Cascade Range
AAACCDEILLMY academically
AAACCDEILMNO decalcomania
AAACCDEILMRU camera lucida
AAACCDHNRRSY cash and carry
cash-and-carry
AAACCDIIPRST aspartic acid
AAACCDIIRRTT tartaric acid
AAACCEHNOSTU acanthaceous
AAACCEIIKLTT Lake Titicaca
AAACCEIINPTT incapacitate
AAACCEILLNTU canaliculate
AAACCEINNQTU acquaintance
AAACCFILNTTU in actual fact
AAACCHILLNRY anarchically
AAACCHILNPTY anaphylactic
AAACCILORSTU accusatorial
AAACDDEGNRUV advance guard
AAACDDHIMRRS Richard Adams
AAACDDHNRTWW watch and ward
AAACDEEHINVY have a nice day
AAACDEEKMNSV make advances
AAACDEENNPST Peasant Dance
AAACDEGIIPRR carriage-paid
AAACDEGINNNO once and again
AAACDEINNPVY pay in advance
AAACDEINRSTT tradescantia
AAACDELMRSSU as clear as mud
AAACDFIIILNN financial aid
AAACDGHNPRTU Chandragupta
AAACDGIIMMRT diagrammatic
AAACDGIIMPRT paradigmatic
AAACDHKKLLNT chalk and talk
AAACDIINNNSV Scandinavian
AAACDILLMRTY dramatically
AAACDLNNOOPR Aaron Copland
AAACDLRSTUWY casualty ward
AAACEEENPPRR reappearance
re-appearance

AAACEEFILMNS	animal faeces
AAACEEFKMORS	make a case for
AAACEEFKMRWY	make a wry face
AAACEEGLNRRT	Angela Carter
AAACEEGNRTVX	extravagance
AAACEERRSTTU	tartare sauce
AAACEFIMNORR	Afro-American
AAACEFINSTTT	fantasticate
AAACEGILMMNO	megalomaniac
AAACEGORSTTT	at a great cost
AAACEHILMMTT	mathematical
AAACEHIPRRTT	patriarchate
AAACEHJMMMNS	James Mancham
AAACEHKNSSTW	Saskatchewan
AAACEHNORSTU	near as a touch
AAACEILMOOST	osteomalacia
AAACEILMPRRT	parametrical
AAACEILNORTU	aeronautical
AAACEINNNSST	as an instance
AAACEKLMRRSU	casual remark
AAACELMORSUY	Rose Macaulay
AAACELNNRRTU	carnal nature
AAACELOSTTUY	autocatalyse
AAACELOTTUYZ	autocatalyze
AAACFGILNNRU	lingua franca
AAACFIINRRTT	anti-aircraft
AAACFIMNRRST	aircraftsman
AAACGGILLNOY	anagogically
AAACGGILLOPY	apagogically
AAACGIILNPST	capital gains
AAACGIKNSSTT	stack against
AAACGILLLNOY	analogically
AAACGILLLNVY	galvanically
AAACHIIKPPRT	apparatchiki
AAACHIKPPRST	apparatchiks
AAACHILMNRST	charlatanism
AAACHMNNOPPR	panpharmacon
AAACIILNNOTZ	canalization
AAACILLLNNOT	national call
AAACILLLNTYY	analytically
AAACILLMNOTY	anatomically
AAACILMMNNOO	monomaniacal
AAACLLMNORSY	nasolacrymal
AAACLMMOPSTY	mycoplasmata
AAADDDEEILNV	dead-and-alive
AAADDEEELPPS	Dead Sea apple
AAADDEGINSTV	disadvantage
AAADDEGLLNNR	adrenal gland
AAADDEGLLNSS	leads and lags
AAADDEGLNOPT	Ponta Delgada
AAADDEHHNNRT	heart and hand
AAADDFHLLOOO	all of a doodah
AAADDFLLORSW	Waldorf salad
AAADDGLMOSSU	Douglas Adams
AAADDGLNNNOW	Gondwanaland
AAADDILLORSV	Salvador Dali
AAADDLMNPRST	standard lamp
AAADEEFGGLNU	deaf language
AAADEEFNRRTU	turn a deaf ear
AAADEEGHNRRV	have arranged
AAADEEGMMRRT	Margaret Mead
AAADEEHMMNSS	Nasseem Hamad
AAADEEHNRTTT	near that date
AAADEEIILLNP	India Pale Ale
AAADEEILORST	isolated area
AAADEEINRRSV	Sierra Nevada
AAADEEIRRSST	disaster area
AAADEEKKKOTT	take a dekko at
AAADEEKLMOST	take as a model
AAADEEKMNNRR	make an errand
AAADEELLNRTY	early and late
AAADEELPPRST	spread a plate
AAADEEMQRSSU	masquerade as
AAADEFHILMNT	time and a half
AAADEFIKMOTY	make a day of it
AAADEFLMORWY	lead away from
AAADEGIIMNNT	time and again
AAADEGIMQRSU	Quadragesima
AAADEGLNNORR	Ronald Reagan
AAADEGNOSTUV	advantageous
AAADEHINORST	raise a hand to
AAADEHLLRSWY	Layard's whale
AAADEHLOPRST	pastoral head
AAADEHMMMNRR	Armand Hammer
AAADEIILNPTT	Adelina Patti
AAADEILLOPRT	Rio de la Plata
AAADEIMMNRST	near as dammit
AAADELMNRRUX	André Malraux
AAADELNRSTUY	Austen Layard
AAADEMNNSSWY	ways and means
AAADFINRSTWY	waif and stray
AAADFKLLNRSW	Falklands War
AAADGGINRSTU	guard against
AAADGHHIMNSW	Aswan High Dam
AAADGIILLORT	gladiatorial
AAADGIMNRSTV	avant-gardism
AAADGINNSSTT	stand against
AAADGINRSTTV	avant-gardist
AAADGLMMMNRY	mammary gland
AAADGLNQRRUU	quadrangular
AAADGLOORSVW	Avogadro's law
AAADHHNSTTTT	and that's that
AAADHILLNRSW	Hadrian's Wall
AAADILLNSSTY	All Saints' Day
AAADILMOQRSU	maquiladoras
AAADILNRSSSU	Russian salad
AAADINNORTTU	Antoni Artaud
AAAEEELQTUVV	ave atque vale
AAAEEGGLMNTU	metalanguage
AAAEEGGPRSSV	passage grave
AAAEEGHMNORT	manage to hear
AAAEEGINNRSX	sexagenarian
AAAEEGMNNPRT	permanganate
AAAEEHHINRSV	have a share in
AAAEEHIMNSTT	anathematise
AAAEEHIMNTTZ	anathematize
AAAEEHIPRSST	paraesthesia
AAAEEHORRSTT	treat as a hero
AAAEEIKKMMST	make a mistake
AAAEEILMRTTT	at a later time
AAAEEJLMRRSY	James Earl Ray
AAAEEKLLLMPR	make parallel

AAAEEKNRSTUW	take unawares
AAAEEKRRSTTT	steak tartare
AAAEFFIJLTVV	Tel Aviv-Jaffa
AAAEFIIKLMMR	make familiar
AAAEFIILMMNR	familiar name
AAAEFKLMOPRY	make a play for
AAAEFKMORTWY	take away from
AAAEFMOPRRTW	marrowfat pea
AAAEGGINRSTU	argue against
AAAEGHLOPPRY	palaeography
AAAEGILLNORV	all over again
AAAEGINNNNOR	nonagenarian
AAAEGJMOORSS	José Saramago
AAAEGLMNORTU	a large amount
AAAEGNRSSSUU	as sure as a gun
AAAEHHITVWWY	have a way with
AAAEHIILLMPT	epithalamial
AAAEHIKMTWWY	make away with
AAAEHLNPRTTY	natal therapy
AAAEHMOPRRTY	aromatherapy
AAAEHNPRSTTY	parasyntheta
AAAEIIKKNRTW	Kiri Te Kanawa
AAAEIILNNRSS	Alain Resnais
AAAEILMNOPPR	paralipomena
AAAEILMRRTTX	extramarital
AAAEIMNNRRRW	Marina Warner
AAAEKLNOOTTU	take out a loan
AAAELLLSSTVY	Telly Savalas
AAAELPRSTTWY	play at waster
AAAELQQRSUUV	quaquaversal
AAAEMMRRSSTT	master-at-arms
AAAENOPRSUYY	pay-as-you-earn
AAAFGILLNPRT	falling apart
AAAFHHLMNORT	half marathon
	half-marathon
AAAFIILMNWYY	in a family way
AAAFIINORTWY	in a fair way to
AAAFIKNNRRST	Frank Sinatra
AAAFKLMORWWY	walk away from
AAAFMORSTWYY	stay away from
AAAGGIOPPRTU	appoggiatura
AAAGHHIJKNNR	Jahangir Khan
AAAGHIIMPRST	amphigastria
AAAGHIRSTTWY	straight away
	straightaway
AAAGIILNNOTV	navigational
AAAGKOPRRSVY	Gary Kasparov
AAAHHHHNORSS	Rosh Hashanah
AAAHIIMNNRTU	humanitarian
AAAHIKLTWWWY	walk away with
AAAHLLMNPSTY	phantasmally
AAAHLPPRRSYY	happy as Larry
AAAIILLMMMRS	mammillarias
AAAIILMPRRTY	paramilitary
AAAIILNNOSTZ	nasalization
AAAIILNORTTT	totalitarian
AAAIKLNNOPRT	national park
AAAILLNOSTTU	salutational
AAALMMOOPSST	plasmosomata
AAALNORRRTWY	royal warrant
AABBBCCEKMOY	Baby Come Back
AABBBCGIKNST	back-stabbing
AABBCCIKOSST	back to basics
AABBCDEKLLNU	black-and-blue
AABBCDEMNOPY	be bad company
AABBCEEEKLNY	black-eye bean
AABBCEEGHITW	cabbage white
AABBCEGIKKNR	backbreaking
	back-breaking
AABBCGIKLLLN	blackballing
AABBCIILLNRY	rabbinically
AABBDDEEHLVY	badly behaved
	badly-behaved
AABBDEEFLOTU	feel bad about
AABBDEEHNNNR	Brendan Behan
AABBDEGNRRUY	Barnaby Rudge
AABBDEHIORUV	bad behaviour
AABBEEEHRTTY	Abbey Theatre
AABBEIINORTV	abbreviation
AABBEILNNOTU	unobtainable
AABBEILOSTUY	A Suitable Boy
AABBEILRTTTU	attributable
AABBEIMMNPSY	namby-pambies
AABBEIORRTVY	abbreviatory
AABBELMOORTT	Alberto Tomba
AABBFHOOORTY	a broth of a boy
AABBHIIILTTY	habitability
AABCCCDIILOR	carbolic acid
AABCCCDIINOR	carbonic acid
AABCCCDIIORS	ascorbic acid
AABCCDEIKNRR	crackbrained
	crack-brained
AABCCEEHHINU	Chinua Achebe
AABCCEEHLNRT	carte blanche
AABCCEELNPTU	unacceptable
AABCCEELORST	obstacle race
AABCCEHIINNT	china cabinet
AABCCEILLLNU	incalculable
AABCCEIRRTUU	bureaucratic
AABCCEKLORTT	crack a bottle
AABCCELNORTT	contractable
AABCCELNPTUY	unacceptably
AABCCENOORSU	carbonaceous
AABCCFINNORS	Francis Bacon
AABCCHHIIMPR	amphibrachic
AABCCIKLLOPT	block capital
AABCCILLLNUY	incalculably
AABCCKLNRRTU	blackcurrant
AABCDDDEEKLS	saddlebacked
AABCDDEHIKMV	David Beckham
AABCDDEJLORS	Jacob's ladder
AABCDDEKLRRW	bladder wrack
	bladderwrack
AABCDDEKLRST	straddleback
AABCDDGINORR	boarding card
AABCDEEEKLPY	black-eyed pea
AABCDEEHKLRT	black-hearted
AABCDEEIILNR	ineradicable
AABCDEEKORRR	break a record
AABCDEELLLNW	well balanced
	well-balanced
AABCDEELLNRT	ballet dancer

	ballet-dancer
AABCDEELRTTU	trabeculated
AABCDEFINSTY	fascinated by
AABCDEGHIRTW	with bad grace
AABCDEGIKNNR	breakdancing
	break-dancing
AABCDEGINNRV	Dancing Brave
AABCDEHIKRTY	birthday cake
AABCDEHORRTY	carbohydrate
AABCDEIILNRY	ineradicably
AABCDEIPTTVY	captivated by
AABCDEKNRSSW	backwardness
AABCDELOPPRR	clapperboard
AABCDELRSTTY	abstractedly
AABCDENOPRSW	bow and scrape
AABCDEOPRRRS	scraperboard
AABCDFHKNORT	back and forth
AABCDFKNORST	stand back for
AABCDGGIOORS	braggadocios
AABCDGINNORT	carbon dating
AABCDGINORST	broadcasting
AABCDGKLLRUY	blackguardly
AABCDGLNRRSU	Carl Sandburg
AABCDIILLLOY	diabolically
AABCDKMNOOSW	backwoodsman
AABCDLMNNORY	Raymond Blanc
AABCEEEFFILN	ineffaceable
AABCEEEGHLNX	exchangeable
AABCEEEGHLRR	rechargeable
AABCEEEHLNST	balance sheet
AABCEEFFILNY	ineffaceably
AABCEEFIPRRT	prefabricate
AABCEEGHLNNU	unchangeable
AABCEEGHLNXY	exchangeably
AABCEEHILNNT	in the balance
AABCEEHILNUV	unachievable
AABCEEHLMNRT	merchantable
AABCEEHLNRSU	unsearchable
AABCEEHLOPRR	reproachable
AABCEEIKMNRT	cabinet-maker
AABCEEIKMNYZ	Mackenzie Bay
AABCEEILLMMT	emblematical
AABCEEILMNSS	amicableness
AABCEEIMRRRR	barrier cream
AABCEEINORTX	exacerbation
AABCEEINOSST	Sebastian Coe
AABCEEJNNORS	Arne Jacobsen
AABCEELLLNRU	unrecallable
AABCEELLNPSS	placableness
AABCEFGILNNR	Belgian franc
AABCEFHIKLNW	finback whale
AABCEFIILLSS	classifiable
AABCEFIILLTY	beatifically
AABCEFKLORRT	Roberta Flack
AABCEFNNNORT	Anne Bancroft
AABCEGGHINRR	bring a charge
AABCEGHILMTW	Abel Magwitch
AABCEGHLNNUY	unchangeably
AABCEGIKLNNR	clearing bank
AABCEGILLMNR	all-embracing
AABCEHHNOOPR	arachnophobe
AABCEHILNRTU	uncharitable
AABCEHIRRRRS	crash barrier
AABCEHKMNNRT	merchant bank
AABCEHKNOPTT	pat on the back
AABCEHLMNORS	elasmobranch
AABCEHLNRSUY	unsearchably
AABCEHLRRRSY	Charles Barry
AABCEHMNORRT	Bonham-Carter
AABCEHOPRSSU	habeas corpus
AABCEIIILPST	capabilities
AABCEIILLNPP	inapplicable
AABCEIILMMRS	bicameralism
AABCEIILRTTY	traceability
AABCEILLLLTY	balletically
AABCEILMNNOT	contaminable
AABCEILMNOPR	incomparable
AABCEILMORVW	microwavable
AABCEILNNOST	sanctionable
AABCEINRRSTT	scatterbrain
AABCEKNORTTU	back to nature
	back-to-nature
AABCELMOOPRT	comparable to
AABCENORRSTY	carry one's bat
AABCENRSSSTT	abstractness
AABCFIILNRSY	Francis Baily
AABCFKLLNOPU	fall back upon
AABCGHIILOPR	biographical
AABCGHKLLNOY	by a long chalk
AABCGHNOPPRW	Cappagh-brown
AABCGILLLSUY	subglacially
AABCHIIMORTT	microhabitat
AABCHIINOOTT	cohabitation
AABCIIILNPTY	incapability
AABCIIKLNPTT	Paint It Black
AABCIILLNPPY	inapplicably
AABCIILMRSST	strabismical
AABCIILRTTTY	tractability
AABCIKLNRSSU	black Russian
AABCILLLLSYY	syllabically
AABCILLNNOTU	National Club
AABCILMNOPRY	incomparably
AABCILMNOSST	saltimbancos
AABCILOOPPSS	Pablo Picasso
AABCIMOPRRSU	coram paribus
AABCLLOOORRT	collaborator
AABCLNORSTUY	constabulary
AABCMNNNOOTT	non-combatant
AABDDDEEILNR	addle-brained
AABDDDEEIMTY	it may be added
AABDDEEILLLN	dead-ball line
AABDDEFOORRT	Board of Trade
AABDDEGLORSU	Douglas Bader
AABDDEHHNRST	hand's breadth
AABDDEHLLMOY	hebdomadally
AABDDEHORRTW	draw the board
AABDDEILLMVY	David Bellamy
AABDDELMNORS	old man's beard
AABDDGHORRTU	draughtboard
AABDDIJNRTTU	adjutant bird
AABDEEEFLNTU	undefeatable
AABDEEEGILRS	disagreeable

AABDEEEKLLNO	Leo Baekeland
AABDEEELNRSS	readableness
AABDEEELPRRT	Peter Abelard
AABDEEGILRSY	disagreeably
AABDEEHHLOWW	bowhead whale
AABDEEHLRTTW	draw the table
AABDEEHORRTW	weatherboard
AABDEEIILRSV	adverbialise
AABDEEIILRVZ	adverbialize
AABDEEILRTTX	extraditable
AABDEELMNNSS	damnableness
AABDEELNORSS	adorableness
AABDEENOORVV	over and above
AABDEFGILLMO	balm of Gilead
AABDEGGLNOST	Gladstone bag
AABDEGGLNOUY	body language
AABDEGHINORT	bring to a head
AABDEGIIMSTU	disambiguate
AABDEGJKMOOO	make a good job
AABDEHHIRRST	hair's-breadth
AABDEHHORSTY	by a short head
AABDEHIOTTTU	habituated to
AABDEHNOPRRU	bear hard upon
AABDEIJLMNSW	James Baldwin
AABDEILLNOSS	ballon d'essai
AABDEILNNOTT	national debt
AABDEIMRRSSS	disembarrass
AABDEINOPPRT	pipe and tabor
AABDELLNOSSU	sound as a bell
AABDELNNOPRU	unpardonable
AABDELOPRRST	plasterboard
AABDENNORTUV	overabundant
AABDFFIILNNS	Baffin Island
AABDGIMNOORV	moving abroad
AABDGINOPRSS	boarding pass
AABDIIIINSTV	absit invidia
AABDIIILSTVY	advisability
AABDIILRUUXY	auxiliary bud
AABDIMOOPSSY	boomps-a-daisy
AABDLMNNOORR	Marlon Brando
AABEEEFGLTTV	vegetable fat
AABEEEFMORSU	be a measure of
AABEEEGGLLTT	gateleg table
AABEEEGIKMRR	image-breaker
AABEEEGLMPRS	gas-permeable
AABEEEGLORVW	below average
AABEEEGLTVWX	vegetable wax
AABEEEHKRRRT	heart-breaker
AABEEEHNOSVV	heavens above
AABEEELLNSSS	saleableness
AABEEELMNNSS	amenableness
AABEEELMNRWY	Wembley Arena
AABEEELNPRTU	unrepeatable
AABEEELRRTTU	terebratulae
AABEEFGILRRR	irrefragable
AABEEFGILRRU	Gabriel Fauré
AABEEFILMNST	manifestable
AABEEFJLNOTT	Battle of Jena
AABEEFLNRRST	transferable
AABEEGHHRRTT	gather breath
AABEEGHIMRTY	Hermitage Bay
AABEEGIILRTY	agreeability
AABEEGILMNTZ	magnetizable
AABEEGILNRST	rebel against
AABEEGIRRSTT	gastarbeiter❑
AABEEGLNNTUW	Blaenau Gwent
AABEEHIILRTT	rehabilitate
AABEEHLNRRTY	learn by heart
AABEEHLOSTTV	above the salt
AABEEHLRRSTY	Breathalyser®
AABEEIIKLRST	Lake Tiberias
AABEEIKKRRST	break a strike
AABEEIKLMSTU	make suitable
AABEEILLLNPP	inappellable
AABEEILLOPRT	parietal lobe
AABEEILLPRRY	irrepealably
AABEEILMMRSU	immeasurable
AABEEILNOPRT	parietal bone
AABEEILNPRRU	unrepairable
AABEEILNRSSV	variableness
AABEEILPTTTU	Tibet Plateau
AABEEIMMRRRT	Marie Rambert
AABEEINNNRUV	Aneurin Bevan
AABEEINRSSSV	abrasiveness
AABEEKLLRTTW	Bakewell tart
AABEEKLMNRRU	unremarkable
AABEELLMORUV	more valuable
AABEELLNSSUV	valuableness
AABEELMNORUV	manoeuvrable
AABEELNNORSU	unreasonable
AABEELNNOSSU	unseasonable
AABEELNNRRUW	urban renewal
AABEELNNRSUW	unanswerable
AABEELNPSSSS	passableness
AABEELRRSTTU	terebratulas
AABEELRSSUUX	sexual abuser
AABEENNRRSTU	subterranean
AABEENNRTUUV	Buenaventura
AABEENRRTTWY	Warren Beatty
AABEFFIILRTW	water bailiff
AABEFFLORTUW	water buffalo
AABEFGILRRRY	irrefragably
AABEFHLMNOTU	unfathomable
AABEFIILNQTU	quantifiable
AABEFLLMMNNO	non-flammable
AABEFLLMMNOT	not flammable
AABEFLNORUUV	unfavourable
AABEGGGILMMN	gambling game
AABEGHIKNORT	oath-breaking
AABEGHIKNRTT	breathtaking
	breath-taking
AABEGHILLOSU	Heliogabalus
AABEGHILNOST	Althea Gibson
AABEGHIMNTTW	bantamweight
AABEGHNORUUW	Auberon Waugh
AABEGIILMNNU	unimaginable
AABEGIINRRTT	Great Britain
AABEGIINSSUU	Guinea-Bissau
AABEGIJLNOTU	Jubilate Agno
AABEGIMNRRSS	embarrassing
AABEGIMNRRTT	battering-ram
AABEGLLRSSTU	Glauber's salt

AABEGLMMOPRR programmable
AABEGLNOSTVY Galveston Bay
AABEHIIILNRS Isaiah Berlin
AABEHILNQSUV vanquishable
AABEHILNSSTU habitualness
AABEHLLNOTWY on the wallaby
AABEHLOPRRRU Pearl Harbour
AABEIIKLLLMW William Blake
AABEIILLLMTY malleability
AABEIILLMRST bilateralism
AABEIILLRTTY alterability
AABEIILPRSTY separability
AABEIINOORSS anaerobiosis
AABEIINRRTTV Vera Brittain
AABEIJNOPSTT patient as Job
AABEIKLMNSTU unmistakable
AABEILLMNNTU in all but name
AABEILLNRRTU turbellarian
AABEILLNRSSW Barnes Wallis
AABEILLPRRTY Liberal Party
AABEILMMRSUY immeasurably
AABEILMNPRTU unimpartable
AABEILNPRRST transpirable
AABEINNOPRWY binary weapon
AABEINSSTTTU substantiate
AABEIORSTTTU as a tribute to
AABEKKMNPRTU make bankrupt
AABELLMNNRTY R M Ballantyne
AABELMMNOSTU somnambulate
AABELMNOOSSS beso las manos
AABELMNORRTT Robert Altman
AABELMNRSTTU transmutable
AABELMNRSUUY unmeasurably
AABELMOPRRTU perambulator
AABELNNORSUY unreasonably
AABELNNOSSUY unseasonably
AABELNNRSUWY unanswerably
AABELNOPRSST transposable
AABELORRSTTY solar battery
AABFHLMNOTUY unfathomably
AABFIILLMMTY flammability
AABFLLMNOTYY flamboyantly
AABFLNORUUVY unfavourably
AABGGGINRRYY argy-bargying
AABGGIILLMRW William Bragg
AABGHIINNRSW brainwashing
AABGHIKKNRSS basking shark
AABGHILNORTT bring to a halt
AABGIIILNTVY navigability
AABGIILLNORY aboriginally
AABGIILMNNUY unimaginably
AABGIKLNORTU larking about
AABGILNORSUV labour-saving
AABHIIINNOTT inhabitation
AABHIIKNRTYZ Yitzhak Rabin
AABHIILOOPRU ailurophobia
AABHIKMNORSU Hosni Mubarak
AABIIJMNOSSV Jonas Savimbi
AABIILNNNTTU tintinnabula
AABIINNORTUZ urbanization
AABIKLMNSTUY unmistakably
AABILLLNOORT trial balloon
AABILLMRSUXY submaxillary
AABILNSSTTUV substantival
AABILOPRRSTU supraorbital
AABIMNORSTTU masturbation
AABINOOPRRTY probationary
AABLMMNNOSTU somnambulant
AABLMNRSTTUY transmutably
AABLNSTTTUUY unstatutably
AABLORRRSTUY barratrously
AABMNNOOTTUW man about town
man-about-town
AACCCDEINNOR in accordance
AACCCEEHILTT catechetical
AACCCEEKMRRR cream cracker
AACCCEHHKNOY hackney coach
AACCDDEHIIRS disaccharide
AACCDDIILLTY didactically
AACCDDIIOTTU autodidactic
AACCDEEFHHTT hatchet-faced
AACCDEEHHIKS sick headache
AACCDEEIMNSS academicness
AACCDEEINRRT incarcerated
AACCDEHIINOT ethanoic acid
AACCDEHIPSST dispatch case
AACCDEIIILNT dialectician
AACCDEIILMTZ acclimatized
AACCDEIKNOPT action-packed
AACCDEILLNTY accidentally
AACCDEKMPUUV vacuum-packed
AACCDELLLTUY calculatedly
AACCDELLNTUU uncalculated
AACCDELORSTW Cawdor Castle
AACCDEMNORSS random access
AACCDFKNNORY Fanny Cradock
AACCDGINRRRY card-carrying
AACCDIILNOTU claudication
AACCDILLLTYY dactylically
AACCDILLMRTU lacrimal duct
AACCDLNORTUU Count Dracula
AACCEEEFIKOP a piece of cake
AACCEEELMMRR crème caramel
AACCEEELPSSU escape clause
AACCEEGHIMNN Ian McGeechan
AACCEEGILNRT accelerating
AACCEEHIILMN Michael Caine
AACCEEHILNNP anencephalic
AACCEEHIRRST characterise
AACCEEHIRRTZ characterize
AACCEEIILLPR capercaillie
AACCEEIILPRZ capercailzie
AACCEEILNORT acceleration
AACCEEILRRTT recalcitrate
AACCEEKLNSUX lack an excuse
AACCEENRSSTU accurateness
AACCEFGHKLNO lack of change
AACCEGHILNOS Nicholas Cage
AACCEGILORSS social graces
AACCEHHIILRR hierarchical
AACCEHILLMNO melancholiac
AACCEHILLMNY mechanically

AACCEHILPRTY archetypical
AACCEHIMPRTU pharmaceutic
AACCEHLMOPRY macrocephaly
AACCEHLNORRS Rachel Carson
AACCEIILLNRT anticlerical
AACCEIIMRSUU amicus curiae
AACCEIKLOPST peacock's tail
AACCEIKNOOST take occasion
AACCEILLLMNR Carmen Callil
AACCEILLMSTU miscalculate
AACCEILLNNOT cancellation
AACCEILLNOSS neoclassical
AACCEILLOPPT apoplectical
AACCEILLOPSU capillaceous
AACCEILLSTTY ecstatically
AACCEILMNOPS complaisance
AACCEILMTUUV accumulative
AACCEILNORVY clairvoyance
AACCEILNRRTT recalcitrant
AACCEILNRTUY inaccurately
AACCEILSTUVY accusatively
AACCEIMRSSTT smear tactics
AACCEINNORST transoceanic
AACCEINNOTTU accentuation
AACCEKNPRRRW prawn cracker
AACCELLRRSTY crystal clear
crystal-clear
AACCELNNOOPV plano-concave
AACCEMOORSSS come across as
AACCFIIINOPT pacification
AACCFIILMOPT fait accompli
AACCFIINPRST transpacific
AACCFIIOPRTY pacificatory
AACCFINNORSS San Francisco
AACCGHHIPRTY tachygraphic
AACCGHIILLOR oligarchical
AACCGHILOPTY phagocytical
AACCGHIOPRRT cartographic
AACCGIILMORT tragicomical
AACCGILLOOST scatological
AACCGIMNNOPY accompanying
AACCHIILMSST schismatical
AACCHIMNOPRT panchromatic
AACCHIMOOPRT apochromatic
AACCHIOPRSTT catastrophic
AACCHLLNORYY acronychally
AACCIIILPSTT capitalistic
AACCIILMPRST practicalism
AACCIILMRSST critical mass
AACCIILNRTUY inarticulacy
AACCIILNTTTY Atlantic City
AACCIILOPPRT paroccipital
AACCIILPRSTT practicalist
AACCIILPRTTY practicality
AACCIIORRSTT aristocratic
AACCIIRRSTTU caricaturist
AACCIJKKLNSU Jack Nicklaus
AACCILLLNOVY volcanically
AACCILLNOOSY occasionally
AACCILLNORTY narcotically
AACCILLNOSTU calculations
AACCILLORSTY acrostically
Socratically
AACCILLOSTUY acoustically
AACCILMNOTUU accumulation
AACCILMOPRSS sarcoplasmic
AACCILNOOPTU occupational
AACCILNORVYY clairvoyancy
AACCILNRSTUU lunar caustic
AACCILOPRSST capital cross
AACCLORRSSVY Calvary cross
AACCNNNOOTUY on any account
AACCOOOSSTTT coast-to-coast
AACDDDIIORRV David Ricardo
AACDDEEEHLTY acetaldehyde
AACDDEEEHNRS case-hardened
AACDDEEHIMRR Richard Meade
AACDDEEIMPSV David Campese
AACDDEELLNVW well-advanced
AACDDEELNSSV less advanced
AACDDEGNNNOS song and dance
AACDDEHNNOST at second hand
AACDDEIILNOT dedicational
AACDDEIJQSUV Jacques David
AACDDGGLNNOO Donald Coggan
AACDDGIIKRRV David Garrick
AACDDGLMNOSU Gus Macdonald
AACDDIIJNOTU adjudication
AACDDIIKNORT Anita Roddick
AACDDIKMNNRU mandarin duck
AACDEEEFFINT decaffeinate
AACDEEEHNRVY each and every
AACDEEEIILMR Mircea Eliade
AACDEEFFNORR force and fear
AACDEEFGLRRS Gerald Scarfe
AACDEEFHLMSY shamefacedly
AACDEEGHILMR Michael Grade
AACDEEGHLNNO hendecagonal
AACDEEGHLNTU langue de chat
AACDEEGINOPR proceed again
AACDEEGLLMOR drama college
AACDEEHLLRTY Ely Cathedral
AACDEEHNPSTT stand the pace
AACDEEHORSTT scare to death
AACDEEIILPST decapitalise
AACDEEIILPTZ decapitalize
AACDEEIKLRTT racket-tailed
AACDEEILMRVY devil-may-care
AACDEEILNNOW New Caledonia
AACDEEILNOST de-escalation
AACDEEILRTTU dearticulate
AACDEELLMOPS same old place
AACDEENSSSSU cause sadness
AACDEFFILNNR Ann Radcliffe
AACDEFHISSTU fidus Achates
AACDEFIILPTX fixed capital
AACDEFIKNRRS Francis Drake
AACDEFIMNRSU Francis Maude
AACDEFINOSTT act instead of
AACDEFMNRTUU manufactured
AACDEGILLNNY cleaning lady
AACDEGILNORR carried along

AACDEGILNORT	leading actor
AACDEGILNRSW	scale drawing
AACDEGINNPRS	parascending
AACDEGLNOPRR	drop a clanger
AACDEHILLLRY	heraldically
AACDEHJKPPRS	Jack Sheppard
AACDEHLOPRRT	procathedral
AACDEHORRRTW	Howard Carter
AACDEIILMNTU	adminiculate
AACDEIILNNRX	cranial index
AACDEIIMRSTY	Armistice Day
AACDEIINNORT	deracination
AACDEIINNOSS	Isaac Dineson
AACDEIINOPTT	decapitation
AACDEIINOTTV	deactivation
AACDEIIOSSST	disassociate
AACDEIJLLTVY	adjectivally
AACDEIKMNNNR	mandarin neck
AACDEILLMNOY	demoniacally
AACDEILLNOSW	disallowance
AACDEILLNPTY	pedantically
AACDEILMMORT	melodramatic
AACDEILNNOOT	national code
AACDEILNOSTT	anecdotalist
AACDEILNOSTW	in a cold sweat
AACDEIMNNOTT	contaminated
AACDEIMNORST	demarcations
AACDEIMNORSY	aerodynamics
AACDEIMOOSTU	diatomaceous
AACDEIMORRTV	overdramatic
AACDEINNOSSY	Ascension Day
AACDEINNQTUU	unacquainted
AACDEINOSSTU	unassociated
AACDELLLNOTW	tallow-candle
AACDELLORSTY	sacerdotally
AACDELMNRSUU	Samuel Cunard
AACDELOORSTW	draw to a close
AACDELPPRSTU	custard apple
AACDEMMNOPPR	command paper
AACDFFIINOOS	afficionados
AACDFFIINRTY	affinity card
AACDFGILNNRT	landing craft
	landing-craft
AACDFIIILNNT	infanticidal
AACDFILNPSTU	capital funds
AACDFJNOORRW	Joan Crawford
AACDFLNOPRRU	Rudolf Carnap
AACDFORRRRWY	carry forward
AACDGHIIOPRR	radiographic
AACDGHILNNPP	handclapping
AACDGHILNNPU	launching-pad
AACDGHILNNRS	crash-landing
AACDGHINNSTY	sand-yachting
AACDGHIOPRRY	cardiography
AACDGIILLOOR	radiological
AACDGILLMOTY	dogmatically
AACDHIILNPRS	cardinalship
AACDHILLNRTU	natural child
AACDHILMRRUY	hydraulic ram
AACDHIMRSSTY	Christmas Day
AACDHINOPQRU	quadraphonic
AACDIIINORTV	divarication
AACDIILLNOTY	diatonically
AACDIILNOOPU	Paulo DiCanio
AACDIKNNPPSS	spick and span
	spick-and-span
AACDILLNORSY	sardonically
AACDILLNSTYY	dynastically
AACDILLOPRSY	sporadically
AACDIMOOPRSS	radio compass
AACDKLNRRUYZ	Darryl Zanuck
AACDLLNOSSUY	scandalously
AACEEEFFHNTV	have an effect
AACEEEFGIRRR	carriage-free
AACEEEFHLOPS	chapel of ease
AACEEEFLMRRX	reflex camera
AACEEEFNOSSV	save one's face
AACEEEGHNRTX	exchange rate
AACEEEHKRRTT	The Caretaker
AACEEEIRRSSU	air-sea rescue
AACEEELMMRSY	Mary McAleese
AACEEENPRSVY	severance pay
AACEEFFINOTT	affectionate
AACEEFGHHORV	have charge of
AACEEFGHKORT	take charge of
AACEEFHILLMO	Michael Foale
AACEEFHOPRSV	have space for
AACEEFHOSTVW	have two faces
AACEEFIILOPT	a piece of tail
AACEEFKMOPRS	make space for
AACEEFOPSSTW	waste of space
AACEEFRRSTUW	surface water
AACEEGGILLNO	genealogical
AACEEGHILPST	Satchel Paige
AACEEGHNPRTX	part-exchange
AACEEGHOPSTT	The Scapegoat
AACEEGIJLNSS	Jessica Lange
AACEEGILNRRV	vicar-general
AACEEGIMNPTT	magnetic tape
AACEEGLNORST	at close range
AACEEGLNRTVY	travel agency
AACEEHHHMRRT	The March Hare
AACEEHHIKRTT	take the chair
AACEEHHLLLRS	Charles Hallé
AACEEHHMNRTU	the human race
AACEEHHRRTTW	weather chart
AACEEHINTTTU	authenticate
AACEEHIOPRST	apothecaries
AACEEHKMNRRS	snake-charmer
AACEEHLLNNRT	entrance hall
	entrance-hall
AACEEHLNNRTW	water-channel
AACEEHLNOTUV	not have a clue
AACEEHLNPTTU	Pentateuchal
AACEEHMORRTY	archaeometry
AACEEHNNPPST	happenstance
AACEEIILNSTT	Elias Canetti
AACEEIILPRST	recapitalise
AACEEIILPRTZ	recapitalize
AACEEIINRSST	sectarianise
AACEEIINRSTZ	sectarianize
AACEEIIPPRTV	appreciative

AACEEIJMRSSY	Jeremy Isaacs
AACEEILLRRSX	Alexis Carrel
AACEEILMPPRS	pre-eclampsia
AACEEILMRRUV	Maurice Ravel
AACEEILNORRT	recreational
AACEEILPRTTU	recapitulate
AACEEIMMNORS	Mesoamerican
AACEEINPRSST	paracentesis
AACEEIPRRRRS	spear-carrier
AACEEIPRRSST	separatrices
AACEEIRRRRTW	Water-carrier
AACEEJKMNRVY	every man Jack
AACEEJLLLMSV	James Clavell
AACEEJMMNORS	James Cameron
AACEEJORRRSS	José Carreras
AACEEKLNQSUY	squeaky clean
	squeaky-clean
AACEELLLNOTY	lanceolately
AACEELNRSTUW	nuclear waste
AACEEMOPRTTV	caveat emptor
AACEENNPPRTU	appurtenance
AACEENOPRRSW	narrow escape
AACEENOPSSTT	set one's cap at
AACEFFILNORV	naval officer
AACEFFMORTTT	matter-of-fact
AACEFFORSTTY	safety factor
AACEFGHINNRU	French Guiana
AACEFGIKNORT	taking care of
AACEFGMNOORU	man of courage
AACEFHOPRTTT	act the part of
AACEFIILLNTU	in actual life
AACEFIILSSTU	facial tissue
AACEFIKLNOTT	line of attack
AACEFINOSSST	of assistance
AACEFINOSSTT	fantasticoes
AACEFIORRSTU	surface-to-air
AACEFLLNORTU	call of nature
AACEFLLPRUWY	pull a wry face
AACEFMNRRTUU	manufacturer
AACEFNORRTTX	extractor fan
AACEGGHILOPR	geographical
AACEGGHINRST	gatecrashing
AACEGGIIORRS	Sergio Garcia
AACEGHHIIPRT	at a high price
AACEGHHPRRTY	tachygrapher
AACEGHIIKLMN	Lake Michigan
AACEGHILLMPT	phlegmatical
AACEGHILLPRR	calligrapher
AACEGHILOPRS	archipelagos
AACEGHNOOPRY	oceanography
AACEGHOPRRRT	cartographer
AACEGIIINRRT	geriatrician
AACEGIILLOOT	aetiological
AACEGIIMMPRT	epigrammatic
AACEGIIMMRST	grammaticise
AACEGIIMMRTZ	grammaticize
AACEGIINNRST	ascertaining
AACEGILLMNRY	Germanically
AACEGILLMNTY	magnetically
AACEGILLMSST	Glamis Castle
AACEGILLNOSU	gallinaceous
AACEGILLOOPT	apologetical
AACEGILLORSU	argillaceous
AACEGILLORTY	categorially
AACEGILMNNRT	magic lantern
AACEGILNOOST	A Song to Celia
AACEGILNRTUW	caterwauling
AACEGIMNORSU	graminaceous
AACEGINNOORT	octogenarian
AACEGINNORTT	octane rating
AACEGLNORTTU	congratulate
AACEGLRRSTYZ	crystal-gazer
AACEGMRRSUVY	Marcus Garvey
AACEHHIILMOP	haemophiliac
AACEHHKKLLTW	walk the chalk
AACEHHNORSUV	have a crush on
AACEHIILLMNP	Michael Palin
AACEHIILLOPT	palaeolithic ◻
AACEHIILLPRS	Schiaparelli
AACEHIILNTTT	antithetical
AACEHIILOPRS	parochialise
AACEHIILOPRZ	parochialize
AACEHIINPTTT	antipathetic
AACEHIINRRST	Christian era
AACEHIKMNPPS	Sam Peckinpah
AACEHIKMRSTT	strike a match
AACEHILLLTTY	athletically
AACEHILLMPTY	emphatically
AACEHILLMTTY	thematically
AACEHILLPRSY	seraphically
AACEHILLPTTY	pathetically
AACEHILLRTTY	theatrically
AACEHILMNPRU	alphanumeric
AACEHILMOPRT	metaphorical
AACEHILMPSTY	metaphysical
AACEHIMMNNOR	harmonic mean
AACEHIMNORRT	North America
AACEHIMORSTU	South America
AACEHIMPRSTU	Ramapithecus
AACEHLLOOPRR	rhopaloceral
AACEHMNNRSTU	transhumance
AACEHMNNRTVY	merchant navy
AACEHORSSTWY	across the way
AACEIIKLLNTU	like a lunatic
AACEIIKLORTV	Lake Victoria
AACEIIKOPRTV	Victoria Peak
AACEIILLMNTU	nautical mile
AACEIILLMRWY	William Carey
AACEIILNOPTZ	capitalize on
AACEIILNPRTT	antiparticle
AACEIILNRTTU	inarticulate
AACEIIMNNOPT	emancipation
AACEIIMNORTZ	racemization
AACEIIMNRSST	sectarianism
AACEIINNNRTW	win in a canter
AACEIINOPPRT	appreciation
AACEIINORTTV	reactivation
AACEIJKRSTTT	straitjacket
AACEIJLLMSTY	majestically
AACEIJLMNORU	Julia Cameron
AACEIJLRSSUU	Julius Caesar
AACEIKLLSTTY	Salt Lake City

AACEIKLMNOPT	kleptomaniac
AACEILLLLMTY	metallically
AACEILLLLOPV	Valpolicella
AACEILLLPRTY	prelatically
AACEILLMMTUY	immaculately
AACEILLMNOTY	noematically
AACEILLMNSTY	semantically
AACEILLNNRSU	Carl Linnaeus
AACEILLNOPST	pleonastical
AACEILLNPTUY	paniculately
AACEILLOPRTY	operatically
AACEILLRTTUY	articulately
AACEILMMRSTY	asymmetrical
AACEILMNOSTU	emasculation
AACEILNOORSY	Casino Royale
AACEILNOPRTY	action replay
AACEILOPRSTT	spectatorial
AACEILRTTTVY	attractively
AACEIMNNNORT	ancient Roman
AACEINOPSSTT	space station
AACEINORRTTT	retractation
AACEINORRTUV	avant-courier
AACEINRTTTUV	unattractive
AACEIOPRRRTV	prevaricator
AACEJJKNNOST	Janet Jackson
AACEJNNOPRRS	Jasper Conran
AACEKNNORSTU	cantankerous
AACEKNOOPTTT	open to attack
AACELLLLORTY	collaterally
AACELLMNRTUY	Tracey Ullman
AACELLNOPSST	cast a spell on
AACELLNRRUVY	vernacularly
AACELMNNOSTU	Manon Lescaut
AACELMNORSTW	scarlet woman
AACELNNNORTW	Walter Cannon
AACELOOPRRTU	corpora lutea
AACELORRSSTV	travel across
AACEMNOPRTTU	Truman Capote
AACENNPRRSTY	transparency
AACENPRTTTVY	Pretty Vacant
AACFFIIKLMOR	official mark
AACFGHINRRRS	Ragnar Frisch
AACFGHOPRRTY	fractography
AACFGIIINOST	gasification
AACFGIILLMNY	magnifically
AACFGILMMORU	magic formula
AACFIIILLRTY	artificially
AACFIIILNNST	financialist
AACFIIILNOTT	facilitation
AACFIIIMNORT	ramification
AACFIIINNOTZ	Nazification
AACFIIINORTT	ratification
AACFIILLLSVY	salvifically
AACFIILMNOST	factionalism
AACFIILNNPTT	Captain Flint
AACFIILNOOTZ	focalization
AACFIINOSSTT	satisfaction
AACFILLLOSUY	fallaciously
AACFILLNORTY	fractionally
AACFILNNOOPT	plan of action
AACFINOORRTT	fractionator
AACFIORSSTTY	satisfactory
AACGGHHIIOPR	hagiographic
AACGGHIILLOO	hagiological
AACGGIILLNTY	gigantically
AACGHILLNOOR	grain alcohol
AACGHILLOOPT	pathological
AACGHIMNOPRR	marconigraph
AACGHINOPRRU	uranographic
AACGHLMOOPRY	pharmacology
AACGIIINNPTT	anticipating
AACGIIKNNOTT	action-taking
AACGIILMNNTU	calumniating
AACGIINNOSTT	antagonistic
AACGIKLMRSSU	surgical mask
AACGILLLLNRY	rallying call
AACGILLOORST	astrological
AACGILLOOTTU	tautological
AACGILLRRTUU	agricultural
AACGILMNORST	marginal cost
AACGILNRTTTY	attractingly
AACGIMMNOOUZ	Giacomo Manzú
AACGINNOSTTU	count against
AACGINOPPRTU	group captain
AACGLMOOSTUU	glaucomatous
AACHHILMOPTY	hypothalamic
AACHHLNOOTTU	autochthonal
AACHIILLNPSY	Hispanically
AACHIILMOPRS	parochialism
AACHIILOPRTY	parochiality
AACHIIMNNOST	machinations
AACHIINQTTUW	acquaint with
AACHIJMMORTU	Joachim Murat
AACHIKLMOOTY	Oklahoma City
AACHIKORSTUW	autorickshaw
AACHILLMNORY	harmonically
AACHILOPSTTY	hypostatical
AACHIMNOPRRS	parachronism
AACHINOPRTTU	naturopathic
AACHINOSTTTY	yacht station
AACHLLNNNOTY	nonchalantly
AACIIINNOPTT	anticipation
AACIIINSSTTT	statistician
AACIIKLLLMRW	William Clark
AACIILLLOPTY	apolitically
AACIILLMNOSY	simoniacally
AACIILLMOTTY	amitotically
AACIILLNOOTV	Italo Calvino
AACIILLNOOTZ	localization
AACIILLNOSTY	antisocially
AACIILLPPSTY	papistically
AACIILLRSTTY	artistically
AACIILLSTTUY	autistically
AACIILMMNOPT	pantomimical
AACIILMMORSS	commissarial
AACIILMNNOTU	calumniation
AACIILNNOOPS	Nicola Pisano
AACIILNOOTVZ	vocalization
AACIILNOPTTU	capitulation
AACIILNORTTU	articulation
AACIILNPRRTU	in particular
AACIILNRSTTU	naturalistic

AACIILOOPRRV	corpora vilia
AACIILORSUVY	avariciously
AACIIMMORSST	commissariat
AACIIMNNORST	animatronics
AACIINNNNOTU	Annunciation
AACIINNNOOTZ	canonization
AACIINOOSSST	associations
AACIINOPRTTY	anticipatory
AACIINPPRSTT	participants
AACIIOPPRRTT	participator
AACIJKPRRSSU	Jurassic Park
AACIKLNSSSTY	slack in stays
AACILLLNOPTY	call into play
	platonically
AACILLLRTVWY	cavalry twill
AACILLMNORTY	romantically
AACILLMNOSTY	monastically
AACILLMOSTUY	calamitously
AACILLNNRTYY	tyrannically
AACILLNOOTVY	vocationally
AACILLOORRTY	oratorically
AACILLOPTTUY	autoptically
AACILLPRRTUY	particularly
AACILMNOOPRT	proclamation
AACILMNOORST	astronomical
AACILMNORTUY	calumniatory
AACILMOPSTTY	asymptotical
AACILMORRTTU	court martial
	court-martial
AACILNOSTTUU	auscultation
AACILOSSSTTU	social status
AACIMNOOPRST	paronomastic
AACIMOORSSST	sarcomatosis
AACINNNPRTTU	turn cat in pan
AACINNORSSTT	transactions
AACINORSSTTU	astronautics
AACLLNNORTUY	connaturally
AACLMOOPRRTY	proclamatory
AACLNNOPRTTU	contrapuntal
AACLORSTTUUY	auscultatory
AACMOORSSTTY	astrocytomas
AACMOPRSSTUU	Camptosaurus
AADDDEIJMNOR	Jared Diamond
AADDDEINRSTZ	standardized
AADDDGLNORST	gold standard
AADDDHNOPSWY	Paddy Ashdown
AADDEEEFLORV	leave for dead
AADDEEEGLPRS	spread-eagled
AADDEEEGRRSV	Edgard Varèse
AADDEEEHLLNW	wheel and deal
AADDEEEHLRTT	rattle-headed
AADDEEFGLRTU	Grateful Dead
AADDEEFHILNT	life-and-death
AADDEEFHRRTU	hard-featured
AADDEEGHILNT	death-dealing
AADDEEHHNORV	hand over head
AADDEEHNOPRT	hand-operated
AADDEEHNSSWY	Ash Wednesday
AADDEEILOPRT	Port Adelaide
AADDEELLNRWY	Edward Alleyn
AADDEEMNORTU	Edouard Manet
AADDEFFIILST	fit as a fiddle
AADDEFHORRUV	hard-favoured
AADDEFILNOTV	feal and divot
AADDEFLLNOSU	all of a sudden
AADDEFNNOSSU	safe and sound
AADDEGHLNNOV	hand and glove
AADDEGLLNORS	Donald Glaser
AADDEGLLOOSU	logodaedalus
AADDEHHNNORV	hand over hand
AADDEHMORSTW	Edward Thomas
AADDEHNORRSZ	Zandra Rhodes
AADDEHNRSSUW	Shaun Edwards
AADDEHOORSTT	at death's door
AADDEIKMNNOS	diamond snake
AADDEIKMNNRT	meat and drink
AADDEIMNRSTT	standard time
AADDEINRRSTZ	standardizer
AADDEINRSSTT	stand astride
AADDELLMNORS	salmon ladder
AADDEMNOSTTU	dead as mutton
AADDENOPRRSU	spread around
AADDFMOORTYY	from day to day
AADDGGLOOOSS	as good as gold
AADDGHHINNNO	go hand in hand
AADDGHIIINNR	Indira Gandhi
AADDGHINNRST	hard-standing
AADDGILNOPRT	parotid gland
AADDHINORSSS	Sarah Siddons
AADDIIILNOPT	dilapidation
AADDIILLNOTY	additionally
AADDKLNORRSU	drunk as a lord
AADDLLNNRSUY	all and sundry
AADDNNNNNOOO	on and on and on
AADEEEEHHLTV	heave the lead
AADEEEFHLRST	false-hearted
AADEEEFILSTY	defeat easily
AADEEEGGMNRR	Graeme Garden
AADEEEGHKMRT	make the grade
AADEEEGHLRRT	large-hearted
AADEEEGHNNOV	have an edge on
AADEEEGLNNRS	Greenland Sea
AADEEEGLNRSV	lasagne verde
AADEEEHHRTVY	heavy-hearted
AADEEEHIPSTV	adhesive tape
AADEEEHIRSST	heart disease
AADEEEHLLNWX	wheel and axle
AADEEEILRRSY	sidereal year
AADEEEKLMRRT	market leader
AADEEEMPRRTW	Peter Medawar
AADEEENQSSTU	adequateness
AADEEFFNORRT	fore-and-after
AADEEFGHOSTT	gates of death
AADEEFHINRTT	faint-hearted
AADEEFHIORST	the aforesaid
AADEEFIKORRT	take for a ride
AADEEFILLMRT	fleet admiral
AADEEFKMORRY	make ready for
AADEEGGGIRST	disaggregate
AADEEGHHNNOS	hang one's head
AADEEGIILNNR	radial engine
AADEEGIKLMOR	go like a dream

AADEEGILLRSV	legal adviser
AADEEGILMOTV	give a medal to
AADEEGILNORT	Daniel Ortega
AADEEGINRTUV	unvariegated
AADEEGKMNRRT	market garden
AADEEGKNOPTW	take down a peg
AADEEGLLNRRW	well-arranged
AADEEGLNRRRT	Gerald Ratner
AADEEHHINTTT	in at the death
AADEEHHMRTTT	The Mad Hatter
AADEEHILNQRU	harlequinade
AADEEHILNTTY	late in the day
AADEEHLLLNOT	Land o' the Leal
AADEEHLNPTTY	death penalty
AADEEHLNSTTW	The Waste Land
AADEEHLOPRST	hard to please
	hard-to-please
AADEEHMRRSSU	hard measures
AADEEHOPRRTZ	trapezohedra
AADEEHQRRSTU	headquarters
AADEEHRRSTVY	the Adversary
AADEEIIKNPRT	take a pride in
AADEEIILMNRV	live in a dream
AADEEIIMNNRT	antemeridian
AADEEILLNNRV	live and learn
AADEEILLNTUV	unalleviated
AADEEILNNOWW	in weal and woe
AADEEILNPRRY	lead in prayer
AADEEILNQTUY	inadequately
AADEEILNRSST	Easter Island
AADEEILNRSTU	denaturalise
AADEEILNRTUZ	denaturalize
AADEEIMQSTUV	desquamative
AADEEIMRRSTT	married state
AADEEJLNNRTW	lantern-jawed
AADEELLLNPRU	unparalleled
AADEELLNORRS	Ronald Searle
AADEELLRZZZZ	razzle-dazzle
AADEELMNPRTT	departmental
AADEEMMNRSTW	New Amsterdam
AADEENRSSTUY	Easter Sunday
AADEFFIIILST	disaffiliate
AADEFFIILNTU	unaffiliated
AADEFFIILOTT	affiliated to
AADEFFILLORR	ride for a fall
AADEFGGHLORT	dagger of lath
AADEFGGINRSU	safeguarding
AADEFGHLLLNO	fall headlong
AADEFGILNORT	deflagration
AADEFHHNOSTT	at the hands of
AADEFHILLMRS	field marshal
AADEFHILLORT	all of a dither
AADEFHINNOTU	fountainhead
	fountain-head
AADEFHLLNOTW	law of the land
AADEFIIILMRZ	familiarized
AADEFIILMMNT	animated film
AADEFILLPSSY	false display
AADEFILMORTY	defamatorily
AADEFILNNPST	find pleasant
AADEFILNORSS	Faroe Islands
AADEFILNORTY	deflationary
AADEFILNRSTU	Alfred Austin
AADEFILOSTTW	Two Fat Ladies
AADEFINNOSTW	stand in awe of
AADEFLMMNRTY	Marty Feldman
AADEFLMNNSTU	fundamentals
AADEFLNOORRS	a fool's errand
AADEGGGILNOU	loading gauge
AADEGGILNNRR	Darling Range
AADEGGILNNRS	danger signal
AADEGGILNNST	landing-stage
AADEGHHILNNP	a helping hand
AADEGHIKLNST	Talking Heads
AADEGHILLLOY	legal holiday
AADEGHIOPPRR	Herod Agrippa
AADEGHIOPRRR	radiographer
AADEGIIINRVW	Virginia Wade
AADEGIILLNNP	plain-dealing
AADEGIILPQRU	quadriplegia
AADEGIIMMNST	diamagnetism
AADEGIINPPRS	disappearing
AADEGIINPRST	Giant Despair
AADEGILNSSST	stained glass
AADEGIMNNOTV	not give a damn
AADEGIMPRRTY	Great Pyramid
AADEGINNSTVW	standing wave
AADEGINOPPRS	propagandise
AADEGINOPPRZ	propagandize
AADEGLLNNSUY	Auld Lang Syne
	auld lang syne
AADEGLNPRSST	star-spangled
AADEGOPRSTTU	postgraduate
AADEHHIILLPP	Philadelphia
AADEHIILMRTW	white admiral
AADEHIKLMORY	holidaymaker
AADEHIKMRTTW	marked with a T
AADEHILMNPRS	aldermanship
AADEHILORSST	heads or tails
AADEHIMNOORZ	mazarine hood
AADEHINOPRST	Herod Antipas
AADEHIOPRRTY	radiotherapy
AADEHKMNORSU	Ahmed Sukarno
AADEHLNORSTU	heart and soul
AADEHMOOPSTT	mashed potato
AADEHNNSSSTT	thés dansants
AADEHPRRSTTU	Uttar Pradesh
AADEIIILNOTZ	idealization
AADEIILLNOTY	ideationally
AADEIILLNUVV	vaudevillian
AADEIILNNOST	desalination
AADEIILNNOTZ	nationalized
AADEIILNNTUV	antediluvian
AADEIILNORTV	derivational
AADEIILNORTZ	rationalized
AADEIIMNNNTU	unmaintained
AADEIINNNORW	neo-Darwinian
AADEIJMMNOSS	James Madison
AADEIKLMNNRU	Milan Kundera
AADEIKMNNOST	and no mistake
AADEILNNNORR	noradrenalin
AADEILNNPRSS	salad spinner

AADEILNNSSTT	Staten Island
AADEILNORTTU	adulteration
AADEILNQRTUV	quadrivalent
AADEILOPRSST	Paradise Lost
AADEILRSSTYY	it's early days
AADEIMNOQSTU	desquamation
AADEJLNORRTU	trade journal
AADEKNNRSTUW	drunk as a newt
AADELLMNOPRR	Arnold Palmer
AADELLNNORST	rallentandos
AADELMMNOPRS	random sample
AADELMNNRTUU	ultramundane
AADELMOPRRTU	armour-plated
AADELNNNPSTU	sun-and-planet
AADEMNNPRSUU	supramundane
AADEMNOPPRTU	put a damper on
AADEMOQRSTUY	desquamatory
AADFFHLORRSW	flash forward
	flashforward
AADFIINNNOVW	Favonian wind
AADFILNNOOTU	foundational
AADGGILMMNOR	Mid Glamorgan
AADGHHIMNNRT	right-hand man
AADGHIIMMNNT	might and main
AADGHIINPRSU	guardianship
AADGHINNNORU	hang around in
AADGIIILNNTV	invalidating
AADGIIIMPRRV	primigravida
AADGIILMRTUV	multigravida
AADGIILNNNOZ	Anzio Landing
AADGIILNNORT	national grid
AADGIILQRUUV	Guadalquivir
AADGIINNNRWW	award-winning
AADGIINNOOTU	Antonio Gaudí
AADGILLNPPUY	applaudingly
AADGIMNPRSTT	trading stamp
AADGIMRRSTTU	dramaturgist
AADGINOPPRST	propagandist
AADGLMNNRRUY	Gunnar Myrdal
AADHIIILNNTW	Withnail and I
AADHILLMNORT	Harold Tilman
AADHILNNOOTT	tooth and nail
AADHILNOOPRT	anthropoidal
AADHILNOPSUY	diaphanously
AADHINORRSSV	Sharron Davis
AADHINORRTUY	Arundhati Roy
AADHINPRSSTY	Danish pastry
AADHJKLMMORS	Hammarskjöld
AADHLORSTUYY	Holy Saturday
AADIIILNNOPS	Indianapolis
AADIIILNNOTV	invalidation
AADIIINNNORR	Irina Rodnina
AADIIKNNRSST	Kristiansand
AADIILLLLSWW	Will Ladislaw
AADIILMNOQRU	quadrinomial
AADIIMNNOOTZ	nomadization
AADIIRRSSTUV	Stradivarius
AADILLMNOOST	amontillados
AADILLNNNOST	still and anon
AADILMNNOSUY	Mail on Sunday
AADILNOPPRST	postprandial
AADINNORSTTU	transudation
AADMNOQRSUUU	quadrumanous
AAEEEEGNRSTY	teenage years
AAEEEEKNOSST	take one's ease
AAEEEFGILLOS	Sea of Galilee
AAEEEFLRSTTW	welfare state
AAEEEGGGHRTT	the aggregate
AAEEEGGHMNRR	Graham Greene
AAEEEGGLNNRT	agent-general
AAEEEGNRRSTT	Great Eastern
AAEEEHHHRTTV	have the heart
AAEEEHILSSTT	telaesthesia
AAEEEHINRSTT	raise the ante
AAEEEHINSSTT	anaesthetise
AAEEEHINSTTZ	anaesthetize
AAEEEHKLOOSV	have a look-see
AAEEEHLLNPST	elephant seal
AAEEEHLPPRSY	happy release
AAEEEHMNSSUY	Seamus Heaney
AAEEEILMRRTT	meat retailer
AAEEEILPRSTT	tapsalteerie
AAEEEJMNNORU	Jeanne Moreau
AAEEEKLMPUWY	make up leeway
AAEEEKLPRSTU	take pleasure
AAEEEKMRSSTU	take measures
AAEEEKNOSSTT	take one's seat
AAEEELLPRSTU	Pasteurellae
AAEEELOPRTTU	poet laureate
AAEEEMORRSTT	remotest area
AAEEENPRSSST	separateness
AAEEFFGLNRST	general staff
AAEEFFHLMNST	fan the flames
AAEEFFKMNORT	make an effort
AAEEFGILNRUV	give an earful
AAEEFHILMOTW	whale of a time
AAEEFHLORSSV	half-seas-over
AAEEFHLRTTUV	have a flutter
AAEEFHOSSSSU	safe as houses
AAEEFIILRRSS	laisser-faire
AAEEFIILRSSZ	laissez-faire
AAEEFIINRSST	East Friesian
AAEEFIMOSTTW	a waste of time
AAEEFKMOPRWY	keep away from
AAEEFLLLRSTW	last farewell
AAEEFMNNRRTT	tenant farmer
AAEEFMOPRRST	separate from
AAEEFNNOORTT	afternoon tea
AAEEFNNPRSST	snap-fastener
AAEEGGGHMORR	George Graham
AAEEGGIKLMOR	Lake Maggiore
AAEEGGIMNRTV	Gram-negative
AAEEGGINORTT	get into a rage
AAEEGGINORTX	exaggeration
AAEEGGLLNSSU	languageless
AAEEGGLNNOTU	tone language
AAEEGHILNNPT	panel heating
AAEEGHINRSTT	thereagainst
AAEEGHLNOOSV	have one's goal
AAEEGHLNORTW	weather along
AAEEGHLRSSTW	weather glass
AAEEGHMNOPRT	on the rampage

AAEEGIIMMNTZ	Time Magazine
AAEEGIKLLNTT	take a telling
AAEEGILNNORT	generational
AAEEGILRSSUV	liver sausage
AAEEGIMNOPRR	open marriage
AAEEGIMNORST	ménage à trois
AAEEGIMNTTUV	augmentative
AAEEGIMPSSTU	Septuagesima
AAEEGINNORSW	Norwegian Sea
AAEEGINNRSTV	Geraint Evans
AAEEGINNSTUX	exsanguinate
AAEEGINPRSTX	exasperating
AAEEGJLMNORR	major general
	major-general
AAEEGKMNNPRT	make pregnant
AAEEGKNOORRT	tree kangaroo
AAEEGLLRTUVY	value greatly
AAEEGLMNNORW	New Mangalore
AAEEGLMNORTV	galvanometer
AAEEGLMNRRTV	Great Malvern
AAEEGLOPRSSS	opera-glasses
AAEEGMNNRRST	arrangements
AAEEGMNOPTTU	mangetout pea
AAEEGPRRSTTT	greatest part
AAEEHHIMPRTT	amphitheatre
AAEEHHLMNNRS	Helen Sharman
AAEEHHLNOTVW	have the law on
AAEEHHMNRSTW	what's-her-name
AAEEHHORRTTT	heart-to-heart
AAEEHHOSSSST	Ashes To Ashes
AAEEHIIKNSST	kinaesthesia
AAEEHIILRTVX	exhilarative
AAEEHIKNOSTT	take a shine to
AAEEHILOPRST	heteroplasia
AAEEHIMNSTWY	in the same way
AAEEHINORRST	tear one's hair
AAEEHINORSST	raise one's hat
AAEEHINSSTTT	anaesthetist
AAEEHIRRSSTY	East Ayrshire
AAEEHKMORRTT	katharometer
AAEEHLMNPRRW	Pelham Warner
AAEEHLORRTTY	Theatre Royal
AAEEHLSTUVVX	exhaust valve
AAEEHMNORSUW	warehouseman
AAEEHMNPRTTT	The Apartment
AAEEHOORRSTT	steatorrhoea
AAEEHORSTTVY	Savoy Theatre
AAEEIIKKLLTW	walkie-talkie
AAEEIILLRTTV	alliterative
AAEEIILMNTTV	alimentative
AAEEIILMORTV	ameliorative
AAEEILLLPRSW	parallelwise
AAEEILLNPRUV	Paul Verlaine
AAEEILLPRSVV	all-pervasive
AAEEILMNRRTW	mineral water
AAEEILMNRSST	materialness
AAEEILMORRST	alstroemeria
AAEEILNORTUV	re-evaluation
AAEEILNPRSST	pleasantries
AAEEILPRSSTU	it's a pleasure
AAEEIMNPPRST	appraisement
AAEEIMNPPRTT	apparent time
AAEEIMNPRSTV	private means
AAEEINOPRSTX	exasperation
AAEEINORSSTV	asseveration
AAEEJKMMNRTZ	katzenjammer
AAEEJLLMMSWX	James Maxwell
AAEEJMMNPRXY	Jeremy Paxman
AAEEJMRSSTTW	James Stewart
AAEEKKMMNORS	make one's mark
AAEEKLNNOOTW	an oaken towel
AAEEKMQRRSTU	market square
AAEELLMMPRSU	Samuel Palmer
AAEELLNPRRTY	parenterally
AAEELLPRSSTU	Pasteurellas
AAEELMMNRTTT	maltreatment
AAEELMNPRSST	malapertness
AAEELNNOPPRU	European plan
AAEELNNPSSST	pleasantness
AAEEMNNPPRSW	newspaperman
AAEEMNNPRTWY	permanent way
AAEEMNNSSTTW	New Statesman
AAEEMNORSSTW	Western Samoa
AAEEMNRSTTTY	testamentary
AAEENNPPRSST	apparentness
AAEENNPRSTUU	superannuate
AAEENPRSTTWY	Payne Stewart
AAEERRRSTTUU	restaurateur
AAEFFGIMORRS	fromage frais
AAEFFHLMNORS	an arm of flesh
AAEFGGLLNOUU	foul language
AAEFGHHIILNT	Faith Healing
	faith healing
AAEFGHIKMNOT	make a thing of
AAEFGHIKRTTT	take fright at
AAEFGIKLMNRW	walking-frame
AAEFGILLLNOT	flagellation
AAEFGILLNOPT	foliage plant
AAEFGILNNORY	lay a finger on
AAEFGILNORTY	fly into a rage
AAEFGINNORTT	engraftation
AAEFGKLNRRTU	Art Garfunkel
AAEFHHLMNORT	more than half
AAEFHHLOSUWY	halfway house
AAEFHILNOPST	fashion plate
AAEFHILNRSTW	fathers-in-law
AAEFHIMRTTTW	what matter if
AAEFHINPRSST	fresh as paint
AAEFIILMORRV	overfamiliar
	over-familiar
AAEFIKMNOOPT	make a point of
AAEFILLNSSSY	self-analysis
AAEFILNORRTY	reflationary
AAEFILORSSTY	forestaysail
AAEFIORRTWWY	write away for
AAEFKKLNORRW	work a flanker
AAEFKLLLNPRU	pull a flanker
AAEFKLMMNRRZ	Franz Klammer
AAEFKLMNOPRS	make plans for
AAEFLLNOPSTU	pull a fast one
AAEFLLOPPRSV	self-approval
AAEFNNOOSSTT	as often as not

AAEGGGIKMNRU	marking gauge
AAEGGGILNNSU	sign language
AAEGGHIINSTW	weigh against
AAEGGHOPRSSU	rough passage
AAEGGILMNPRS	palm-greasing
AAEGGIMRRRSY	merry as a grig
AAEGGINRSTTT	starting gate
AAEGHHIKNRST	earth-shaking
AAEGHHIORTTV	have a right to
AAEGHHKMOSTU	make as though
AAEGHHNNRUVY	Henry Vaughan
AAEGHIIKMRTT	make airtight
AAEGHIILLMUW	William Hague
AAEGHIILNRTX	exhilarating
AAEGHIMMNPSS	gamesmanship
AAEGHIMNRRTW	heartwarming
	heart-warming
AAEGHIOORSTT	Horatio Gates
AAEGHLLNNOTT	ten-gallon hat
AAEGHLMNRSTT	at arm's length
AAEGHLMNRSTU	manslaughter
AAEGHLMRSTUV	Gustav Mahler
AAEGHNOPRRRU	uranographer
AAEGHNOPRRTW	narrow the gap
AAEGHNOQRSSU	orange squash
AAEGIIKKLLMN	make a killing
AAEGIILLNOST	legalisation
AAEGIILLNOTZ	legalization
AAEGIKLNPRTV	valet parking
AAEGILLLQSSU	Lalique glass
AAEGILLNNPUV	Paul Langevin
AAEGILLNNTTY	tangentially
AAEGILMNNORT	marginal note
AAEGILNNOPPR	Angela Rippon
AAEGILNNSTUY	nauseatingly
AAEGILNPRRTT	integral part
AAEGIMMNNPRS	pan-Germanism
AAEGIMNNOTTU	augmentation
AAEGIMNRRSTT	transmigrate
AAEGINNOPTTV	vantage point
AAEGINPRSTTT	setting apart
AAEGINSSSTTW	wasting asset
AAEGLLNNOPTY	pentagonally
AAEGLLNORTTY	tetragonally
AAEGLMOOPSTU	gamopetalous
AAEGLMORSSUU	megalosaurus □
AAEGLNORSSUX	sexual organs
AAEGMOPPSSTT	postage stamp
AAEHHIIKMTTW	make a hit with
AAEHHIINRSTU	hiatus hernia
AAEHHILMOPTX	exophthalmia
AAEHHIMNSSTW	what's-his-name
AAEHHKLPRSSY	speak harshly
AAEHHNOPRTTW	on the warpath
AAEHIILNORTX	exhilaration
AAEHIINNPSST	pain in the ass
AAEHIINOPRTZ	azathioprine
AAEHIKPRTTTW	take part with
AAEHILLMORSV	Villahermosa
AAEHILLNNNPY	phenylalanin
AAEHILMNPSSS	salesmanship
AAEHILMOSSTY	haematolysis
AAEHILMRSTUY	amateurishly
AAEHIMNNSSSU	haussmannise
AAEHIMNNSSUZ	haussmannize
AAEHIMNSSTTW	what's-its-name
AAEHIMPRSTTW	Matthew Paris
AAEHINOPRSST	Aristophanes
AAEHIPPRRSST	star sapphire
AAEHJMMNSSTY	James Nasmyth
AAEHKKLLNPTW	walk the plank
AAEHKKMMNRUW	Kwame Nkrumah
AAEHLLMORSTW	Thomas Waller
AAEHLMNOPTWY	play the woman
AAEHLNNORTTT	not later than
AAEHLRSSTTTW	the last straw
AAEHMMNOTTTT	at that moment
AAEHMNOOPRSS	anamorphoses
AAEHMNOPSSYY	A Sea Symphony
AAEHMNORTTTW	no matter what
AAEHMOOPRSTT	potato masher
AAEHMORSSTVY	Thomas Savery
AAEHOPPPRSSY	parapophyses
AAEIIILMSSTV	assimilative
AAEIIJLLMMSW	William James
AAEIIKLLOTVW	A View to a Kill
AAEIIKNRTTTW	Katerina Witt
AAEIILLLMPWY	William Paley
AAEIILLLNOST	Alan Sillitoe
AAEIILLMMRTY	immaterially
AAEIILLNORTT	alliteration
AAEIILLNPSTY	sapientially
AAEIILMNNOTT	alimentation
AAEIILMNOORT	amelioration
AAEIILMNPTUV	manipulative
AAEIILNNOPTZ	penalization
AAEIILNOQTUZ	equalization
AAEIILNORSTT	Aristotelian
AAEIILNORTVZ	velarization
AAEIILPPRSVY	appraisively
AAEIIMPPRSTU	Marius Petipa
AAEIINNRSSST	sanitariness
AAEIINOPRRTT	repatriation
AAEIINOPRTTX	expatriation
AAEIINQTTTUV	quantitative
AAEIJLMNRSUZ	Jules Mazarin
AAEIKLLNPPSY	speak plainly
AAEIKLMMNNTU	Immanuel Kant
AAEIKMNNNTTY	Matti Nykanen
AAEIKMNPPSTY	make it snappy
AAEILLLMRTTU	multilateral
AAEILLLNORTY	relationally
AAEILLLNRTUY	unilaterally
AAEILLLRRTTY	trilaterally
AAEILLMNNOUV	nominal value
AAEILLMNNSUY	semi-annually
AAEILLNNNOTW	Antonine Wall
AAEILLNORSTY	senatorially
AAEILLOQRTUY	equatorially
AAEILLPPSUVY	applausively
AAEILMMNNORR	Norman Mailer
AAEILMMOPRTV	primeval atom

AAEILMNNOSTT	Lamentations
AAEILMNORSTV	malversation
AAEILMNRSSTT	mistranslate
AAEILNNNPSVY	Pennsylvania
AAEILNNOPTTX	explantation
AAEILNNRSTUU	unnaturalise
AAEILNNRTUUZ	unnaturalize
AAEILNOPSSTY	passionately
AAEILNPRSSTT	plaster saint
AAEILNRSSSTU	salutariness
AAEIMNOOOOPT	onomatopoeia
AAEINNOPRSXY	expansionary
AAEINNOPTTTY	pay attention
AAEINNORSSTU	Austronesian
AAEINOPPRRST	preparations
AAEIPPRRSTTV	private parts
AAEIRRSSSTTU	Erasistratus
AAEJKMNOOTTY	Jomo Kenyatta
AAEJLLMNNOUY	Joanna Lumley
AAEKLMNORRUW	manual worker
AAEKLMORRTWW	low-watermark
AAEKLMRRRUWY	Murray Walker
AAEKMOPRSTUY	make up a story
AAELLMMNOSSU	Seamus Mallon
AAELLMNNORTY	ornamentally
AAELLNNPSTUY	unpleasantly
AAELMMNNNORY	Norman Manley
AAELMNNORTTU	ultramontane
AAELMOOPRSTZ	spermatozoal
AAELNNPRRSTT	transplanter
AAELNOPRTTWY	Walter Payton
AAELNPRRSTUU	supernatural
AAELNRSSSTTW	stalwartness
AAELOOPRRTTX	extrapolator
AAELOPRSSTUU	Plateosaurus
AAEMNNNORSTT	transmontane
AAEMNOOPRSTZ	spermatozoan
AAEMNOPRSTTU	portmanteaus
AAEMNOPRTTUX	portmanteaux
AAEOPPRSSTTU	passe-partout
AAFFFHJLNOST	John Falstaff
AAFFHJNNOOST	John Atansoff
AAFHIIILMRTW	familiar with
AAFHILNOPTWY	halfway point
AAFIIILNNOTZ	finalization
AAFIILMMNNOT	inflammation
AAFIILNNORTY	inflationary
AAFIINRRSSTU	Austin friars
AAFILMMNOORT	malformation
AAFILMMNORTY	inflammatory
AAFINNNORSTT	for an instant
AAFKLLMNOORW	man-of-all-work
AAGGHHIINNTV	having a thing
AAGGIIILLNUV	Luigi Galvani
AAGGIIINNRTT	ingratiating
AAGHIILMNRST	animal rights
AAGHIINNOSTW	Washingtonia
AAGHIJLLNNOO	John Galliano
AAGHILLNRTTU	natural light
AAGHILNNOOTV	having a lot on
AAGHIMNSSTTU	assuming that
AAGHINORTWWY	throwing-away
AAGHIPRRSTTY	stratigraphy
AAGHIRSSTTWY	straightways
AAGHKNNNOSSS	on Shanks's nag
AAGIIILLNNPS	plain sailing
AAGIIINNNOTV	invagination
AAGIIINNORTT	ingratiation
AAGIIKLNNORW	walking on air
AAGIILNNRSUY	sanguinarily
AAGIILOSSSUZ	Louis Agassiz
AAGIINNOORST	organisation
AAGIINNOORTZ	organization
AAGIINNORTUU	inauguration
AAGIKMNNORSS	a king's ransom
AAGILLLORSSY	glossarially
AAGILLMNTUWY	mulligatawny
AAGILLNRRTUY	triangularly
AAGILMNNNNOT	non-malignant
AAGILNNSSTWY	slantingways
AAGILOOPRSTY	parasitology
AAGIMNNOOTTU	mountain goat
AAGINNOOSTTW	station wagon
AAGINPRRRSTT	starring part
AAGLOPRSSUZZ	Zsuzsa Polgar
AAGOPRRRSSSW	sparrow-grass
AAHHIIMMSSSV	Miss Havisham
AAHHIINNRRSS	Sirhan Sirhan
AAHHIORRTTWY	Rita Hayworth
AAHHIRRRRSTU	Arthur Harris
AAHHLMOPSTUY	hypothalamus
AAHIIILNNNOT	annihilation
AAHIIMNNOTUZ	humanization
AAHIINOPSTXY	asphyxiation
AAHIINPPRSST	partisanship
AAHIJKMMMRSU	Jammu-Kashmir
AAHIKMMNPRSS	marksmanship
AAHILLNNOPSY	pollyannaish
AAHILLNNOPTY	antiphonally
AAHILMNOOPRT	prothalamion
AAHIMNOOPRSS	anamorphosis
AAHINNORRTTU	not turn a hair
AAHJLNOORTTV	John Travolta
AAHLNORRSTUY	anarthrously
AAHMNOORSTTW	Thomas Warton
AAHMNRRRSTUY	Harry S Truman
AAHNNNOSSTUY	Susan Anthony
AAIIILMNOSST	assimilation
AAIIILMNOSTZ	Islamization
AAIIILMPRTTY	impartiality
AAIIILNOTTVZ	vitalization
AAIIILORSTTV	visitatorial
AAIIIMMNNORR	Marino Marini
AAIIIMNNRSTU	Unitarianism
AAIIINNOSTTZ	sanitization
AAIIKLNRSSSY	risk analysis
AAIILLMORSTW	William Astor
AAIILLNNOSTT	installation
AAIILLNORRTY	irrationally
AAIILMNNOPTT	implantation
AAIILMNNOPTU	manipulation
AAIILMNOORTZ	moralization

AAIILMNOOTTV	motivational
AAIILMNOSSTT	saltationism
AAIILNNORSTT	transitional
AAIILNOOPRST	polarisation
AAIILNOOPRTZ	polarization
AAIILNOORTVZ	valorization
AAIILNORRTUZ	ruralization
AAIILNOSSTTT	saltationist
AAIILNOSSTTV	Salvationist
AAIIMNNOORTZ	Romanization
AAIIMNOORSTT	amortisation
AAIIMNOORTTZ	amortization
AAIINNOPRSTT	strain a point
AAIINNOQTTUZ	quantization
AAIINOOPRTVZ	vaporization
AAIJORRRSWZZ	Jazz Warriors
AAIKLNSSSTVY	Stanislavsky
AAILLMNOPRTT	all-important
AAILLMNOTTUY	mutationally
AAILLMOPRTYY	morality play
AAILLNOOPTWW	wallop in a tow
AAILLORSTTUY	salutatorily
AAILMNOPRTUY	manipulatory
AAILOORSSTTU	saltatorious
AAIMMNOORRTU	Mount Roraima
AAINOPRRRSTT	air transport
AAIOOPPPRRRT	appropriator
AAKLNORSSUUY	Ankylosaurus
AALLMOOPPRST	protoplasmal
AALLNOORSWYY	Rosalyn Yalow
AALMMNNNOORT	Norman Lamont
AAMMNNOOOTWW	woman-to-woman
AAMNNOOTTTTU	tantamount to
ABBBBBBEEILL	bibble-babble
ABBBCEEHLNOT	technobabble
ABBBCEHLOPSY	psychobabble
ABBBCEILRSSU	subscribable
ABBBDELORYZZ	bobby-dazzler
ABBBEESTTTUY	test-tube baby
ABBBEGHIILNS	Bible-bashing
ABBBEHLMORTU	blabbermouth
ABBBGGIILNOS	Bilbo Baggins
ABBCCEGHIMNO	beachcombing
ABBCDEFKNOOY	back of beyond
ABBCEEEEHLRS	Charles Beebe
ABBCEEEGGORR	George Crabbe
ABBCEEJKMORT	bomber jacket
ABBCEEMMOORY	Morecombe Bay
ABBCEIKRRSTU	rabbit-sucker
ABBCELOOORRR	corroborable
ABBCGIMNOOST	costing a bomb
ABBDDEEEGINT	being debated
ABBDDEEILNSS	biddableness
ABBDDEGINORW	Edward Gibbon
ABBDDEMNRRUU	Edmund Rubbra
ABBDEEEGINRT	bate-breeding
ABBDEEFLORSS	self-absorbed
ABBDEEGIILRY	Bailey bridge
ABBDEGHOORTY	go by the board
ABBDEGNRRSUU	garden suburb
ABBDEHIILRYZ	hybridizable
ABBDELOOOSST	be so bold as to
ABBDENRRTTUY	brandy butter
ABBDIILLLRWY	Willard Libby
ABBEEEILLNUV	unbelievable
ABBEEELMMRRY	rememberably
ABBEEFLOORTW	Tower of Babel
ABBEEGMNORRR	barber-monger
ABBEEGMORRTU	Robert Mugabe
ABBEEILLNUVY	unbelievably
ABBEEILMRRSU	reimbursable
ABBEEILRRTTU	irrebuttable
ABBEEINNRTTY	Tintern Abbey
ABBEELOPRSTV	l'Abbé Prévost
ABBEELORRRSU	rabble-rouser
ABBEFHIIJSUU	Jusuf Habibie
ABBEFHIORRSY	Frobisher Bay
ABBEGIILLLNN	enabling bill
ABBEGIINNOTT	babingtonite
ABBEHHMOOSST	Thomas Hobbes
ABBEHIMORRRS	Bomber Harris
ABBEHLNORRTY	Albert Hornby
ABBEILLMNOTU	Bill Beaumont
ABBEILNOORTT	borlotti bean
ABBEIMNNORTT	Norman Tebbit
ABBELLLRSTUU	tubular bells
ABBFIILLLPSU	spill a bibful
ABBFLLOOOOTT	football boot
ABBGHIILOPRY	bibliography
ABBHLOORTWWY	throw a wobbly
ABCCCEHIILNY	bicycle chain
ABCCDEEELPST	bespectacled
ABCCDEEHILNN	blanc-de-chine
ABCCDEEIMNOR	become rancid
ABCCDEFHINNY	find by chance
ABCCDEHILMNO	chemical bond
ABCCDEHILORU	coachbuilder
ABCCDEHLMORU	cloud chamber
ABCCDEIKNOPY	by cock and pie
ABCCDEILNOSU	build a sconce
ABCCDEINOOSY	occasioned by
ABCCDHILRSTU	scratchbuild
ABCCEEEELRSU	cause célèbre
ABCCEEEHLNRT	treble chance
ABCCEEEHMNTY	meet by chance
ABCCEEEILLNT	table licence
ABCCEEEIMOTV	become active
ABCCEEEKPRRT	bracket-creep
ABCCEEELNORT	concelebrate
ABCCEEENORRS	arborescence
ABCCEEGINNRU	buccaneering
ABCCEEHKLOTT	beat the clock
ABCCEEIILNSS	inaccessible
ABCCEEIKKNRR	Rickenbacker
ABCCEEILLNOR	reconcilable
ABCCEELMNRRU	Bruce McLaren
ABCCEENORRTU	counterbrace
ABCCEHIIMNOS	biomechanics
ABCCEHILLRUY	cherubically
ABCCEHIMMRSU	chamber music
ABCCEHINRTUW	Bruce Chatwin
ABCCEHLOOOTX	chocolate-box

ABCCEIILNSSY	inaccessibly
ABCCEIINRRSU	cabin cruiser
ABCCEILLNORY	reconcilably
ABCCEILMMNOU	communicable
ABCCEILNORTT	contractible
ABCCEILORSTU	scrobiculate
ABCCEIOPRSSS	basic process
ABCCEKLMNOOY	black economy
ABCCELNOSTUY	bouncy castle
ABCCHHILOOOP	ochlophobiac
ABCCIILLSTUY	cubistically
ABCCIIMOORST	macrobiotics
ABCCILLOOSTY	octosyllabic
ABCCILMMNOUY	communicably
ABCDDGIKLNPU	black pudding
ABCDEEEGGMOR	become ragged
ABCDEEEHILPR	decipherable
ABCDEEEILNUV	undeceivable
ABCDEEEINRTY	Aberdeen City
ABCDEEEKMORR	become darker
ABCDEEELNRTU	uncelebrated
ABCDEEELNTTU	undetectable
ABCDEEFFNTUY	unaffected by
ABCDEEFILNNU	bad influence
ABCDEEGHLORU	double-charge
ABCDEEHIINRU	Richie Benaud
ABCDEEHIPPRR	bread-chipper
ABCDEEIILLMN	medicine ball
ABCDEEILLMOP	become pallid
ABCDEEILMNSS	dissemblance
ABCDEEILNORS	considerable
ABCDEEILORSV	discoverable
ABCDEEKKLNRU	bare-knuckled
ABCDEEKKLORW	break wedlock
ABCDEELMOOPS	decomposable
ABCDEELRTTUU	tuberculated
ABCDEFHKOOTY	Dock of the Bay
ABCDEGHIILNR	childbearing
	child-bearing
ABCDEGHORRTU	turbocharged
ABCDEHHLOOOR	bachelorhood
ABCDEHINOOPS	scaphoid bone
ABCDEHMOORST	hors de combat
ABCDEHMOORTY	hard to come by
ABCDEHNRRRYY	cherry brandy
ABCDEIILLNNY	indeclinably
ABCDEIINNSTZ	Citizens' Band
ABCDEILLMNOT	metallic bond
ABCDEILNNORS	Blanc de Noirs
ABCDEILNORSY	considerably
ABCDEILNOSTU	discountable
ABCDEILORRTU	direct labour
ABCDEINRSSSU	business card
ABCDEIORSVYY	Discovery Bay
ABCDELLNOOST	second ballot
ABCDELNNOOTV	covalent bond
ABCDEOOORRRT	corroborated
ABCDFHKLMOOR	hold back from
ABCDGHIINRTW	bird-watching
ABCDGIILMNNO	limbo-dancing
ABCDGIKLNOOP	blood packing
ABCDGIKNNOUW	back-wounding
ABCDLLNOPRTU	Portland Club
ABCEEEEKMORW	become weaker
ABCEEEELNPTW	place between
ABCEEEFFIORR	office-bearer
ABCEEEFHKOST	see the back of
ABCEEEFLNORS	brace oneself
ABCEEEFMORTT	become fatter
ABCEEEGLMORR	become larger
ABCEEEIKRRSV	break service
ABCEEEKLLORS	block release
ABCEEEKLSTVY	Steve Backley
ABCEEELLMORT	become taller
ABCEEEMMNRRR	remembrancer
ABCEEEMMNRRS	remembrances
ABCEEEMNNRTU	cetane number
ABCEEFIILLNY	beneficially
ABCEEFIILNOT	beneficial to
ABCEEFINORST	sorbefacient
ABCEEFKORRSU	be a sucker for
ABCEEFNOORUY	before you can
ABCEEGILLLNO	eco-labelling
ABCEEGILNORZ	recognizable
ABCEEHIKLMRU	Michael Buerk
ABCEEHILLPST	slip the cable
ABCEEHKMNRRT	kerb-merchant
ABCEEHKMOSTT	Thomas Becket
ABCEEHLNNPTY	penalty bench
ABCEEHLNNQUU	unquenchable
ABCEEHMORRSY	Harry Secombe
ABCEEIILLNPX	inexplicable
ABCEEIILLTTY	electability
ABCEEIILNRTX	inextricable
ABCEEIJNOPST	Jacob Epstein
ABCEEILNNOTU	unnoticeable
ABCEEILNORSU	ribonuclease
ABCEEILNOSSS	sociableness
ABCEEILNPRRT	Prince Albert
ABCEEILRSSTU	resuscitable
ABCEEINRRSTU	canterburies
ABCEEKSSTTUW	sweat buckets
ABCEELLRSSSU	Brussels lace
ABCEELOPRSTU	prosecutable
ABCEELORSTUU	cause trouble
ABCEEMNNORTU	octane number
ABCEEMNOORRW	become narrow
ABCEENNORTUY	Encounter Bay
ABCEENOPRRTU	protuberance
ABCEFHILOPRT	place of birth
ABCEFHKRSTTU	furthest back
ABCEFHLLNORW	Blanchflower
ABCEFIILOPRT	optical fibre
ABCEFILOPRTY	cap of liberty
ABCEGGHINRRS	bring charges
ABCEGHORRRTU	turbocharger
ABCEGIILNNOZ	incognizable
ABCEGIINNORS	in banco regis
ABCEGIKNORST	backing store
ABCEGILMNOST	single combat
ABCEGILNORSY	recognisably
ABCEGILNORYZ	recognizably

ABCEGILOORTY	bacteriology
ABCEGLLNOOTU	conglobulate
ABCEHHIIKKTT	kick the habit
ABCEHHINOOPT	technophobia
ABCEHIILLNRY	Hibernically
ABCEHIJKNOTX	jack-in-the-box
ABCEHIKNRSSS	brackishness
ABCEHIKPPTTU	pick up the tab
ABCEHILSTTTY	chastity belt
ABCEHIRRRRSU	crush barrier
ABCEHKLRSSUW	swashbuckler
ABCEHLLOOSTW	blow the coals
ABCEHLMOOPSS	peach blossom
ABCEIIILLRST	liberalistic
ABCEIIILTTXY	excitability
ABCEIILLNPXY	inexplicably
ABCEIILMNOPT	incompatible
ABCEIILNRTUV	vibratiuncle
ABCEIILNRTXY	inextricably
ABCEIILORTVY	revocability
ABCEIILPRSTY	plebiscitary
ABCEIINORRRS	sonic barrier
ABCEIINORSTT	obstetrician
ABCEIIRSTTUW	water biscuit
ABCEILLNNOOS	inconsolable
ABCEILLNTUUV	uncultivable
ABCEILMNOPTU	incomputable
ABCEILNNOTUY	unnoticeably
ABCEIMMNORTU	atomic number
ABCEINRRSTUY	bear scrutiny
ABCEKNNORSTU	turn one's back
ABCELLLNOORT	controllable
ABCELLLOOSTY	octosyllable
ABCELMNNOSUU	unconsumable
ABCELNORSTTU	counterblast
ABCENORSSSSU	scabrousness
ABCENOSSTUUU	subcutaneous
ABCFFKLLOOST	block of flats
ABCFLNOOORRU	fluorocarbon
ABCFMORRSTTU	subtract from
ABCGGIKNOPRU	backing group
ABCGHHIKNSUW	bushwhacking
ABCGHIIKKNNT	thinking back
ABCGHINNORTU	branching out
	branching-out
ABCGIIILLOST	go ballisitic
ABCGIIKLMNPU	making public
ABCGIILLLOOY	biologically
ABCGIKMNOTUU	mucking about
ABCGILLMNRSY	scramblingly
ABCHIMORSSTX	Christmas box
ABCIIIILRSTY	irascibility
ABCIIIKLSTTY	stickability
ABCIIILMNOTU	umbilication
ABCIIILNRTUY	incurability
ABCIILMNOPTY	incompatibly
ABCIILNOPPRY	principal boy
ABCIJKMMRTUY	Jimmy Tarbuck
ABCILLLMOSYY	symbolically
ABCILLLOPSYY	polysyllabic
ABCILLMNOOSY	monosyllabic
ABCILLNNOOSY	inconsolably
ABCILMMNOSTU	noctambulism
ABCILMMNOTUY	incommutably
ABCILMNNOSUY	inconsumably
ABCILMNOSTTU	noctambulist
ABCILNOPRTUY	notary public
ABCIMNOOPRSY	by comparison
ABCIMNORSSTU	obscurantism
ABCINORSSTTU	obscurantist
ABCKMNOOTTUU	not muck about
ABCKMOOORTTT	at rock bottom
ABCOOOORRRRT	corroborator
ABDDDEELRSSY	badly-dressed
ABDDDEENOORW	Edward De Bono
ABDDEEEGRRRU	Gerard Debreu
ABDDEEELLORU	double-dealer
ABDDEEELNNPU	undependable
ABDDEEFORRSW	Edward Forbes
ABDDEEGGLORU	double dagger
ABDDEEGLLOUZ	double-glazed
ABDDEEIMNNST	absent-minded
ABDDEGILNNPT	bedding plant
ABDDEHIILRTV	David Hilbert
ABDDEIILMRTV	David Trimble
ABDDEILNOOST	bloodstained
ABDDEMNNOOSY	Dombey and Son
ABDDGIINNPSU	pudding basin
ABDDGIMNNPRU	bump and grind
ABDDHILMNNOO	hoodman-blind
ABDDILNNOOOR	blood and iron
ABDDIOORSVYY	advisory body
ABDEEEEGGLOR	George Beadle
ABDEEEEILMRR	irredeemable
ABDEEEFGNRST	Stefan Edberg
ABDEEEFIILNS	indefeasible
ABDEEEGILLRT	great-bellied
ABDEEEGLRRSW	sedge warbler
ABDEEEIILMRR	irremediable
ABDEEEIILRTV	deliberative
ABDEEEILLRTY	deliberately
ABDEEEILMNRT	determinable
ABDEEEILMRRY	irredeemably
ABDEEEIMSTTW	time-bewasted
ABDEEEKLORRR	broker-dealer
ABDEEELMNTZZ	bedazzlement
ABDEEENOOPTT	open to debate
ABDEEEOPRRSU	pas de bourrée
ABDEEFFJNTUU	Jean Dubuffet
ABDEEFHILMRT	half-timbered
ABDEEFHINORV	heaven forbid
ABDEEFIIILNT	identifiable
ABDEEFIILNSY	indefeasibly
ABDEEFIIRRTY	dietary fibre
ABDEEFINRTTY	Betty Friedan
ABDEEFINSTUU	subinfeudate
ABDEEFLPRSST	flat-bed press
ABDEEFNORTTU	debt of nature
ABDEEGGHIPRT	bridge the gap
ABDEEGHNORTT	band together
ABDEEGKLLNOW	knowledgable
ABDEEGLNOSTU	obtuse-angled

ABDEEHILLOTY	the Old Bailey
ABDEEHLLNRTY	enthralled by
ABDEEHLNOVYY	heavenly body
ABDEEHLRSTTU	lust-breathed
ABDEEHNORTUW	weather-bound
ABDEEIIKLRST	East Kilbride
ABDEEIILMRRY	irremediably
ABDEEIILNORT	deliberation
ABDEEILMNOPR	imponderable
ABDEEILMNRTY	determinably
ABDEEILNNRRV	Bernard Levin
ABDEEILNRSSU	undesirables
ABDEEILPRSTU	disreputable
ABDEEIMNOOSS	sesamoid bone
ABDEEIMOPPRR	bromide paper
ABDEEINNSSSU	unbiasedness
ABDEEINOPRRY	beyond repair
ABDEEJNORTUY	journey-bated
ABDEEKLMNOOS	make old bones
ABDEEKLNNRTU	underblanket
ABDEELMNORST	demonstrable
ABDEELMOPRRT	Peter Lombard
ABDEEOORRSTT	bored to tears
ABDEFIIILNTY	definability
ABDEGGNOORUU	Bourdon gauge
ABDEGGNORRUU	bugger around
ABDEGIIILNTT	debilitating
ABDEGIKNNORW	breaking-down
ABDEGILNORTW	world-beating
ABDEGINNNORT	bring to an end
ABDEGKLLNOWY	knowledgably
ABDEGLNORTTU	battleground
ABDEGMNNNOOY	Benny Goodman
ABDEGNOPRSSY	Porgy and Bess
ABDEHHLMOORR	rhombohedral
ABDEHIIILMNS	diminishable
ABDEHIILSSST	disestablish
ABDEHILMNNST	blandishment
ABDEHILOTTTW	do battle with
ABDEHIMNNNOR	Hermann Bondi
ABDEHNNORSSU	rub one's hands
ABDEIIILMNSS	inadmissible
ABDEIIILMTXY	mixed-ability
ABDEIIILNOTT	debilitation
ABDEIIILRSTY	desirability
ABDEIIILRTVY	driveability
ABDEIILMNORT	Lamberto Dini
ABDEIILNPSTU	indisputable
ABDEIILORSTU	subeditorial
ABDEIILTTUVY	dubitatively
ABDEIINORTVY	by derivation
ABDEIIRSTTUV	disturbative
ABDEIKNNNOSS	skin and bones
ABDEILLOPRRX	pillar-box red
ABDEILPRSTUY	disreputably
ABDEIMORSTUX	ambidextrous
ABDEIOORRTUW	worried about
ABDELMNORSTY	demonstrably
ABDELOOQRRTU	quarter-blood
ABDEMOORRTTW	bottom drawer
ABDENOQRRTUU	quarter bound
ABDFGGINOORS	Frodo Baggins
ABDFGINORRRW	bring forward
ABDFHIKLNOTY	think badly of
ABDFIILNNRUU	infundibular
ABDFIILNOOOV	bioflavonoid
ABDFINNOSSTU	no ifs and buts
ABDFINOOTTUU	find out about
ABDGGIILNNOR	bridging loan
ABDGHILNRTUY	burn daylight
ABDGHINOOSWX	shadow-boxing
ABDGHNNOSUUY	Younghusband
ABDGIILLLOOR	Lollobrigida
ABDGIILOOORY	radiobiology
ABDGILNORRUU	burial ground
ABDGINNNORRU	running-board
ABDGINNOORSW	snowboarding
ABDIIIILNTUY	inaudibility
ABDIIILMNSSY	inadmissibly
ABDIIILRSSUY	subsidiarily
ABDIIIRSSTUY	subsidiarity
ABDIILNPSTUY	indisputably
ABDLNNOSSTTU	nuts and bolts
ABDLNOORTUUY	roundaboutly
ABEEEELPRSUZ	breeze up sale
ABEEEFHNOQSU	Queen of Sheba
ABEEEFLNOOSV	above oneself
ABEEEGHLORTT	Globe Theatre
ABEEEGIIKLLM	make eligible
ABEEEGILLOTV	vegetable oil
ABEEEGILPRRT	Peter Gabriel
ABEEEGLRRSST	Lee Strasberg
ABEEEHILMPTU	eat humble pie
	eat humble-pie
ABEEEHILNOTV	above-the-line
ABEEEHKKNNRT	Kenneth Baker
ABEEEHKNRSTW	break the news
ABEEEHKORRSU	housebreaker
	house-breaker
ABEEEHORSTTY	be here to stay
ABEEEIKLLNSS	likeableness
ABEEEILMNPRT	impenetrable
ABEEEINQRTUX	Queen Beatrix
ABEEEINRRTTV	invertebrate
ABEEELMMNTTT	embattlement
ABEEELMNOSSV	moveableness
ABEEEMMNQRTU	embarquement
ABEEEOPRRSTT	obstreperate
ABEEEORRRRTV	reverberator
ABEEERRSSTWY	brewer's yeast
ABEEFFILNRSU	insufferable
ABEEFHHJOOTV	have the job of
ABEEFHILRTYZ	Elizabeth Fry
ABEEFIILNRUV	unverifiable
ABEEFIINOPRS	Bias of Priene
ABEEFILMORRR	irreformable
ABEEFILNNRTY	Albert Finney
ABEEFKLNOORW	foreknowable
ABEEGGHINOVY	be heavy going
ABEEGGIILNOR	globigerinae
ABEEGHIINSTV	have its being
ABEEGHIKMRRT	make brighter

ABEEGIJNNNRT Jan Tinbergen
ABEEGILLLLNW all being well
ABEEGILLMNRS Elgin marbles
ABEEGILNNSST tangibleness
ABEEGILNORRY Eleanor Rigby
ABEEGLNNORUV ungovernable
ABEEGMNRRSTU great numbers
ABEEGMORRTUW Robert Mugawe
ABEEGORRRSTV Robert Graves
ABEEHIILLTVW liveable with
ABEEHIILMPRS imperishable
ABEEHILPRSST pre-establish
ABEEHILRRSTW welsh rarebit ❑
ABEEHJJMNNOT John Betjeman
ABEEHJMRRSTU James Thurber
ABEEHKLMRSST bless the mark
ABEEHKLNNOTT on the blanket
ABEEHLLMRSTU The Umbrellas
ABEEHLLNSSTT St Benet's Hall
ABEEHLLOSTTW below the salt
ABEEHLLRSSTY breathlessly
ABEEHNNRRRUY Henry Raeburn
ABEEHNOPRRSY Hyperboreans
ABEEHOPRSTTW powers that be
ABEEIIILLLRS illiberalise
ABEEIIILLLRZ illiberalize
ABEEIIJLNSSU Jean Sibelius
ABEEIILMNNRT interminable
ABEEIILMPRTY permeability
ABEEIILNPSST pitiableness
ABEEIILORTTV obliterative
ABEEIILOSSUV Silva Eusebio
ABEEIJNORTUZ Benito Juarez
Benito Juárez
ABEEIKLMOPSS make possible
ABEEIKLNORSY easily broken
ABEEIKLRSTTT litter basket
ABEEIKMOPRRS break-promise
ABEEIKNNOPRR Bonnie Parker
ABEEIKNNORRR Ronnie Barker
ABEEILLMNSSY assembly line
ABEEILLNNRUV invulnerable
ABEEILLPRUVZ pulverizable
ABEEILLRSTVY livery stable
ABEEILMNPRTY impenetrably
ABEEILMNRRSU serial number
ABEEILNOQSTU questionable
ABEEILNSSSTU suitableness
ABEEILORRTVY Trevor Bailey
ABEEILRRSTTW water blister
ABEEIMNNSSSU mean business
ABEEIMNRSTTU steam turbine
ABEEINNORSSU use one's brain
ABEEINOPRRRT Robert Napier
ABEEINORRTTV vertebration
ABEEINPRRSTY presbyterian
ABEEIPRSSTUX beaux esprits
ABEEJLLMOSSW James Boswell
ABEEKLMORRTU troublemaker
ABEEKLNORSSW workableness
ABEEKMRRSTUY buyer's market
ABEEKNORSTTU Buster Keaton
ABEEKORRSSTT breaststroke
ABEELLMNOPUY unemployable
ABEELLMOOPRT temporal lobe
ABEELLMRSTUU Samuel Butler
ABEELLNORSTW snowball tree
ABEELLNORSUV unresolvable
ABEELLNORTUV vulnerable to
ABEELLORSTUU absolute rule
ABEELLORSTUW water-soluble
ABEELMMNNOTZ emblazonment
ABEELMNOOPRT temporal bone
ABEELNOPRSST personal best
ABEELNOSSSTU absoluteness
ABEELNOSSTUV solvent abuse
ABEELOORSTUZ absolute zero
ABEEMNNNOOSW be one's own man
ABEEMNQRRSUU square number
ABEENOPSSSTT past one's best
ABEENORRRRTW Robert Warren
ABEENPRTTTUU peanut butter
ABEENRSSSSTU abstruseness
ABEFFGGHIOTT gift of the gab
ABEFFGNRSTUU Stauffenburg
ABEFFHIKORTW break off with
ABEFFIIILNTY ineffability
ABEFFILNRSUY insufferably
ABEFGIINRRTU fruit-bearing
ABEFGIKNOSST king of beasts
ABEFGILNORRY forbearingly
ABEFGILNORUV unforgivable
ABEFGINNRRTU afterburning
ABEFHHIINOTT in the habit of
ABEFHILLNOTW the final blow
ABEFHINOOSST on the basis of
ABEFILMORRRY irreformably
ABEFILNOPRTU unprofitable
ABEFLLOOORUV labour of love
ABEFLLOOOSTT Battle of Loos
ABEFLNOSSSTU boastfulness
ABEFLNOSSSUU fabulousness
ABEGGHINORTV overnight bag
overnight-bag
ABEGGHIOOPRY biogeography
ABEGHHIOTTUV have bought it
ABEGHHKORRTU break through
breakthrough
ABEGHIMNNORS bring shame on
ABEGHIMNORST bring shame to
ABEGHJNNORSU Johannesburg
ABEGHNOORTTU Attenborough
ABEGIILNRTTW writing-table
ABEGIINRSSSU agribusiness
ABEGIKLMNORT Goblin Market
ABEGIKLNNOOR book-learning
ABEGILNNPUXY inexpugnably
ABEGIMNOSSTU messing about
ABEGINOQRTUU bouquet garni
ABEGINORSSSU agrobusiness
ABEGIOOOSTTV give a boost to
ABEGLLRRUUYY buy regularly

Words marked ❑ can also be spelled with an initial capital letter

ABEGLMORSUUY	umbrageously
ABEGLNNORUVY	ungovernably
ABEGLNORSSSU	glabrousness
ABEHIIILRTTY	heritability
ABEHIILLTUVY	heavily built
ABEHIILMPRSY	imperishably
ABEHIILNNRTY	labyrinthine
ABEHIILNOPST	inhospitable
ABEHIIMORSUV	behaviourism
	misbehaviour
ABEHIIORSTUV	behaviourist
ABEHILNOPTYZ	hypnotizable
ABEHILNORRTW	brother-in-law
ABEHIMNOOOPT	entomophobia
ABEHINNORSTU	Born in the USA
ABEHJMNNORRY	John Berryman
ABEHMNOORSTW	Thomas Browne
ABEHNORSTTUU	hunt saboteur
ABEIIILLLRTY	illiberality
ABEIIILLNNRT	brilliantine
ABEIIKLLMRUW	William Burke
ABEIIKMNNOTU	mountain bike
ABEIILLLMPTU	multipliable
ABEIILLORTTY	tolerability
ABEIILMMORTY	memorability
ABEIILMNNRTY	interminably
ABEIILMNPRTU	unimpartible
ABEIILMNRTUY	numerability
ABEIILMORTVY	removability
ABEIILNNTTUY	untenability
ABEIILNOORTT	obliteration
ABEIILOQRRTU	equilibrator
ABEIINOQRTUU	inquire about
ABEIINORSTUZ	suberization
ABEIJLMNOPSU	jump one's bail
ABEIJLORRSTU	Julia Roberts
ABEIKNNOORZZ	Zinzan Brooke
ABEIKNPRSSSU	business park
ABEILLNNOPPT	ballpoint pen
ABEILLNNRUVY	invulnerably
ABEILLOPRRVY	proverbially
ABEILLORRSVY	irresolvably
ABEILMOSSTUY	abstemiously
ABEILNOQSTUY	questionably
ABEILNORSSUY	Byelorussian
ABEILNORTTXY	exorbitantly
ABEILNPRSSUU	Prussian blue
ABEILOPRRRVY	irreprovably
ABEIMNRSSTYY	binary system
ABEINOPRRTTU	perturbation
ABEIOPRTTTUY	pay tribute to
ABEKLOOORRTY	Brooke-Taylor
ABELLLLOPSYY	polysyllable
ABELLLMNOOSY	monosyllable
ABELMMOORSSY	assembly room
ABELMNORSTUU	surmountable
ABELNOORSWYY	so early by now
ABEMNOOSSTTU	not mess about
ABENOOPRRSTT	Pat Robertson
ABFFIKLOORRS	Boris Karloff
ABFGHIIMNORT	habit-forming
ABFGIIILNRTY	frangibility
ABFHILRSSTTU	at first blush
ABFIIILLNORT	fibrillation
ABFIIILNNOTU	infibulation
ABGGHIMNORUY	Brigham Young
ABGGHINOORSU	Gainsborough
ABGGHINORSTT	bang to rights
ABGGIILNRSTT	grit blasting
ABGGILLNOSSW	glass-blowing
ABGHHIKORTUW	rough hawkbit
ABGHHJNNORUV	John Vanbrugh
ABGHIIILLLMW	William Bligh
ABGHIIMMNSTW	swimming-bath
ABGHILOOPTTT	potato blight
ABGHILOORSTU	Boutros-Ghali
ABGIIILLMNSU	bilingualism
ABGIILLMRSUW	Williamsburg
ABGIILLOORTY	obligatorily
ABGIILNORRTT	bring to trial
ABGILNOSSTUU	Boussingault
ABGIMOSSTUUU	August Möbius
ABGINOOPRSTT	bring to a stop
ABGMMMNNOSUU	magnum bonums
ABHIIKMNNPRS	brinkmanship
ABHIILLMOOTW	William Booth
ABHIILNOPSTY	inhospitably
ABHIINOPRSTV	vibraphonist
ABHIMNNORRTU	Northumbrian
ABHLNNNOTTUY	Anthony Blunt
ABHLNNOOSUVW	Hans von Bülow
ABIIIILRRTTY	irritability
ABIIILLPSTUY	plausibility
ABIIILMMOTVY	immovability
ABIIILMMTTUY	immutability
ABIIILMNOOST	abolitionism
ABIIILMNOOTZ	mobilization
ABIIILNOOSTT	abolitionist
ABIIILLLMNSUY	subliminally
ABIIILLNOOPRT	abortion pill
ABIILMNOORSV	Simon Bolivar
	Simón Bolívar
ABIILNORSSUU	insalubrious
ABIILNORSTTU	tribulations
ABIILOOPPSTY	opposability
ABIKOPRSSSSY	Boris Spassky
ABILLORSSUUY	salubriously
ABILMMMNOSSU	somnambulism
ABILMMNOSSTU	somnambulist
ABILMNORSTUY	subnormality
ABIMNNOORRSY	Mary Robinson
ABIMNORSSTTU	nimbostratus
ABINOORRTTUW	rainbow trout
ABKLLNOOSSTT	lots to blanks
ABLMOSSSTTUY	status symbol
ABNOORRSSTUU	brontosaurus□
ACCCCDIIINSU	succinic acid
ACCCCEIILRRT	Arctic Circle
ACCCDEEIRSST	direct access
ACCCDHIORTTU	thoracic duct
ACCCEEEELNRS	recalescence
ACCCEEEINQSU	acquiescence

Words marked □ can also be spelled with an initial capital letter

ACCCEEHKLTTU cut the cackle
ACCCEEHMNOTU accouchement
ACCCEEIILSST ecclesiastic
ACCCEEILLLTY eclectically
ACCCEELNOSTY nectocalyces
ACCCEEMOOPTT come to accept
ACCCEGIINNOR carcinogenic
ACCCEHINORTT technocratic
ACCCEHKLORTW clock-watcher
ACCCEIJMNRTU circumjacent
ACCCEIMNRSTU circumstance
ACCCFIIKNRRS Francis Crick
ACCCHHIILLOT Chalcolithic
ACCCHIIOPRRT chiropractic
ACCCHIIOPRSZ schizocarpic
ACCCHIKOSSTT shock tactics
ACCCIILNNOTY anticyclonic
ACCCIILNOOST iconoclastic
ACCDDEEHINOR Eddie Cochran
ACCDEEEELMNN Clemence Dane
ACCDEEENORST deconsecrate
ACCDEEFIIRTT certificated
ACCDEEFILLMS Macclesfield
ACCDEEGILNNR eccrine gland
ACCDEEIIILPT epideictical
ACCDEEILLLNO ill-concealed
ACCDEEILLOPS peccadilloes
ACCDEEILNOPY encyclopedia
ACCDEEINNNST incandescent
ACCDEEINORTX exotic dancer
ACCDEELLRSUY succeed rally
ACCDEELMORTT clotted cream
ACCDEENNORTT concentrated
ACCDEENOSSUU succedaneous
ACCDEFHIKLNO Hancock Field
ACCDEGHORTUU Dutch courage
ACCDEGIILRSY lysergic acid
ACCDEHHNRRUW churchwarden
ACCDEHILMOPS accomplished
ACCDEHNRRRUY hard currency
ACCDEIILMOUX calcium oxide
ACCDEIILNNOT coincidental
ACCDEIINORTT direct action
ACCDEILLNOTY occidentally
ACCDEILNOORU Cain-coloured
ACCDEIMNORTU undemocratic
ACCDELNORTTY contractedly
ACCDEMNOSTUU unaccustomed
ACCDEMOOSTTU accustomed to
ACCDENNORTUY country dance
ACCDFFHIILRR Cliff Richard
ACCDFIIINOOT codification
ACCDHHIIKKNT hitch and kick
ACCDHIINORTW in accord with
ACCDHIKLNNWY Lynn Chadwick
ACCDHILLOOST Old Catholics
ACCDHILOOOSU I should cocoa
ACCDHINOTTUU Dutch auction
ACCDHIORRSTT Richard Scott
ACCDIINOORST accordionist
ACCDILNOOSSS Cocos Islands
ACCDIMNOPSTU stand-up comic
ACCDLNNOORTY concordantly
ACCEEEFHILMR chemical-free
ACCEEEFHIMRR crème fraîche
ACCEEEFHOPRT force the pace
ACCEEEGLLLOR Clare College
ACCEEEHINRST earth science
ACCEEEILSSST Ecclesiastes
ACCEEELRRSVY scarcely ever
ACCEEFGIIMNN magnificence
ACCEEFHIKMOO make choice of
ACCEEFHIMSTU face the music
ACCEEGHNORSU change course
ACCEEGINNORS recognisance
ACCEEGINNORZ recognizance
ACCEEHIKPSTT stick the pace
ACCEEHILNRTU Chaunticleer
ACCEEHILRRST Richter scale
ACCEEHIORTTT heterotactic
ACCEEHIRRTTU architecture
ACCEEHLMNRSY sclerenchyma
ACCEEHLMORTY the real McCoy
ACCEEHMNNORT encroachment
ACCEEHOPRSSX express coach
ACCEEHORRSTW The Scarecrow
ACCEEIINPPRT precipitance
ACCEEIKLNRRW Carl Wernicke
ACCEEILLLRTY electrically
ACCEEILLMNUY ecumenically
ACCEEILNPTTU centuplicate
ACCEEILNRTTY tetracycline
ACCEELNNOSTV convalescent
ACCEELNNRSTU translucence
ACCEELPRRWYY creepy-crawly
ACCEEMNORTTU accoutrement
ACCEEMOOPPRR come a cropper
ACCEENNORSTU unconsecrate
ACCEFFIIJKNO jack-in-office
ACCEFGIIINNS significance
ACCEFIILLMRY family circle
ACCEFIILLPSY specifically
ACCEFILOOTTU cut a lot of ice
ACCEGHHIOPRT hectographic
ACCEGHLLOOOT chocolate log
ACCEGHLNOORU change colour
ACCEGIIJRSTU gastric juice
ACCEGIINNNOZ incognizance
ACCEGIINRTUX excruciating
ACCEGILLLOOY ecologically
ACCEGILNNORT Anglocentric
ACCEGILNNOSV convalescing
ACCEGIMRRTUY circumgyrate
ACCEGINNNORS as concerning
ACCEGINNNOVY conveyancing
ACCEGNOORRTY gerontocracy
ACCEHHIIKNRT kitchen chair
ACCEHHIKPRTW crack the whip
ACCEHHILOSSZ eschscholzia
ACCEHHLOOOTT hot chocolate
ACCEHIILLMRY chimerically
ACCEHIILLNST callisthenic

ACCEHIILNOPR	necrophiliac
ACCEHIILNTTY	technicality
ACCEHIKMNSTY	chimney stack
ACCEHILLLORY	cholerically
ACCEHILMOPRS	accomplisher
ACCEHILNNNOT	non-technical
ACCEHILOPRTY	chalcopyrite
ACCEHINNNOPT	pantechnicon
ACCEHINORRTT	trochanteric
ACCEHINRSSST	scratchiness
ACCEHIOPSTVY	psychoactive
ACCEHLLOSTWY	watch closely
ACCEHMNORRTU	countercharm
	countermarch
ACCEIIILPSST	specialistic
ACCEIIKKMNRS	camiknickers
ACCEIILLLNTY	enclitically
ACCEIILLOSST	solecistical
ACCEIILMMORT	microclimate
ACCEIILMRRSU	semicircular
ACCEIILNRSST	criticalness
ACCEIILORRTV	overcritical
ACCEIIMORRTT	meritocratic
ACCEIINORTUX	excruciation
ACCEIINPPRTY	precipitancy
ACCEIIPPRSTY	perspicacity
ACCEILLMMORY	commercially
ACCEILLMNOOY	economically
ACCEILLMOORT	Camille Corot
ACCEILLMOSTY	cosmetically
ACCEILLNOTTY	tectonically
ACCEILLNSTYY	synectically
ACCEILLOPRRY	reciprocally
ACCEILMMNORU	uncommercial
ACCEILMNNOOU	uneconomical
ACCEILMNORTU	counter-claim
ACCEILNNOOTV	convectional
ACCEILNOORRT	correctional
ACCEILNOSSSU	successional
ACCEIMNRTTUU	circumnutate
ACCEINNOORST	consecration
ACCEINNORSTV	contrivances
ACCEINOORRSU	Enrico Caruso
ACCEINQRTTUY	cry quittance
ACCEIOOPRRRT	reciprocator
ACCELLLOOOPU	Paolo Uccello
ACCELLMNOPTY	complacently
ACCELLMORSUU	ocular muscle
ACCELMNOOPSY	close company
ACCELNNRSTUY	translucency
ACCELNOOPPRY	cyclopropane
ACCELNSSSTUY	successantly
ACCENOPRRTTY	concert party
ACCFFNOOORTU	for account of
ACCFGHHIOSTT	catch sight of
ACCFGIIINNSY	significancy
ACCFHIIOPSTU	South Pacific
ACCFIIMNNOSU	Confucianism
ACCFIINNOOST	confiscation
ACCFIINNOSTU	Confucianist
ACCFILLNOOTU	flocculation
ACCFILNOORST	olfactronics
ACCFILNOORUW	council of war
ACCFINOORSTY	confiscatory
ACCGHIIKLNOT	Catholic King
ACCGHIIKNORR	rocking-chair
ACCGHIIOPPRT	pictographic
ACCGHILNRSTY	scratchingly
ACCGIILLOOOS	sociological
ACCGILLMOOOS	cosmological
ACCHHHIPRRSU	parish church
ACCHHIIIRSSS	rachischisis
ACCHHINOORTX	xanthochroic
ACCHHIOPPSTY	psychopathic
ACCHHJMNORTY	John McCarthy
ACCHIIINSTUV	chauvinistic
ACCHIILOPRTY	hypocritical
ACCHIIMMORST	chromaticism
ACCHIIMORRTT	trichromatic
ACCHIIMORTTY	chromaticity
ACCHILLNNOOO	non-alcoholic
ACCHILLOPTTY	phyllotactic
ACCHILOOPSSY	psychosocial
ACCHILOPPRTY	prophylactic
ACCHIMNOOPPT	phonocamptic
ACCHIOOPRRRT	chiropractor
ACCHIOORRSSU	chiaroscuros
ACCIIILNNOOT	conciliation
ACCIIINRSSST	narcissistic
ACCIILLNRTUY	uncritically
ACCIILMNOOPT	complication
ACCIILNOORTY	conciliatory
ACCIILOPRSUY	capriciously
ACCIJKLNNOOS	Colin Jackson
ACCIJLNNOTUV	conjunctival
ACCIJNNOOTTU	joint account
ACCIKLLNOUUY	Lucky Luciano
ACCIKMMNNOOP	common ink cap
ACCIMMNNOSTU	communicants
ACCIMMNOORTU	communicator
ACCIMNOOSTUU	contumacious
ACCINNOORSTT	contractions
ACCKMMMNOOSU	common as muck
ACCMNORSTUUU	autumn crocus
ACDDDEEHNOOR	dodecahedron
ACDDEEEFNORT	confederated
ACDDEEEGMOSS	coded message
ACDDEEEHIMST	semi-detached
ACDDEEELLTUW	well-educated
ACDDEEGKLNOW	acknowledged
ACDDEEHILNRY	cylinder head
ACDDEEHINNST	disenchanted
ACDDEEHORRST	hard-sectored
ACDDEEILMORR	recorded mail
ACDDEEIMOSTT	domesticated
ACDDEELNPTUU	pedunculated
ACDDEGHIMNRW	wedding march
ACDDEGHNRSSU	grand duchess
ACDDEGIILLNO	dialling code
ACDDEGIINNRS	discandering
ACDDEHIILMNO	Donald Michie
ACDDEHIKNOVY	David Hockney

ACDDEHILSSTT	saddle stitch
ACDDEIIKNRST	sick and tired
ACDDEIILNORU	radionuclide
ACDDEIINORST	endocarditis
ACDDEIINRTTY	identity card
ACDDEILLOSTY	dislocatedly
ACDDEILNOOST	consolidated
ACDDEILRSTTY	distractedly
ACDDEKLOORRU	dark-coloured
ACDDELNOORSU	sand-coloured
ACDDEMOPRSSU	mass-produced
ACDDGHHRTTUU	Dutch Draught
ACDDGIILNNOR	iron-cladding
ACDDHIMNORYY	hydrodynamic
ACDDHJNNPUUY	Punch and Judy
ACDDILNORSTY	discordantly
ACDEEEEFFNOS	feed one's face
ACDEEEEHHRSZ	Schéhérézade
ACDEEEFFFLST	self-affected
ACDEEEFFLPTY	affect deeply
ACDEEEFFNSST	affectedness
ACDEEEGINRTT	cigarette end
ACDEEEGLNOOU	eau de Cologne
	eau-de-cologne
ACDEEEGLNPTU	get cleaned up
ACDEEEGNNRRT	garden centre
ACDEEEHINRUV	underachieve
ACDEEEHLRRTT	cattleherder
ACDEEEHMNOSS	damson cheese
ACDEEEIIPRTV	depreciative
ACDEEEIKNPST	keep distance
ACDEEEILLLRW	well I declare!
ACDEEEILNORT	deceleration
ACDEEEILNRST	decentralise
ACDEEEILNRSU	denuclearise
ACDEEEILNRTZ	decentralize
ACDEEEILNRUZ	denuclearize
ACDEEEILNSST	delicateness
	delicatessen □
ACDEEEILORTV	overdelicate
ACDEEEINNRTV	inadvertence
ACDEEELLNOOV	leave one cold
ACDEEELNNTTY	antecedently
ACDEEEMNNRRT	remand centre
ACDEEENPRRST	centre spread
ACDEEEOPRRRT	tape recorder
ACDEEFFIINNO	in defiance of
ACDEEFFLNTUY	unaffectedly
ACDEEFFNORRT	Fort de France
	Fort-de-France
ACDEEFHHIKNR	handkerchief
ACDEEFHILLRW	child welfare
ACDEEFHNORRW	henceforward
ACDEEFILMTTU	multifaceted
ACDEEFILNRTU	declare unfit
ACDEEFILOPPR	pride of place
ACDEEFIMMNNO	Of Mice and Men
ACDEEFLMMNOO	female condom
ACDEEFLMOOTW	Fleetwood Mac
ACDEEFLORRTU	federal court
ACDEEFNNOOPR	do penance for

ACDEEFNORRTU	Tour de France
ACDEEFNOSSTW	two-facedness
ACDEEGGIINUV	give guidance
ACDEEGHILRST	clear-sighted
ACDEEGHINNRT	interchanged
ACDEEGHLLNNU	unchallenged
ACDEEGILLOTY	geodetically
ACDEEGILMNOY	Ealing comedy
ACDEEGILNNRU	Lucinda Green
ACDEEGILNORS	close-grained
ACDEEGILNRSY	decreasingly
ACDEEGINNNQU	Dancing Queen
ACDEEGMNOORR	Grande Comore
ACDEEGNNORTV	Covent Garden
ACDEEGNNOSTT	decongestant
ACDEEGNORSST	get one's cards
ACDEEHIINNRR	Adrienne Rich
ACDEEHIKLPSS	sickle-shaped
ACDEEHIKNTTY	The Naked City
ACDEEHILLOOS	de-alcoholise
ACDEEHILLOOZ	de-alcoholize
ACDEEHILMNOR	echinodermal
ACDEEHILNNRT	Netherlandic
ACDEEHIMNRRS	merchandiser
ACDEEHKMRSTU	Deutsche Mark
	Deutsche mark
ACDEEHLNNOOR	Leonard Cohen
ACDEEHLNOPRT	elephant cord
ACDEEHLOOSTT	close to death
ACDEEHNOPRRU	unreproached
ACDEEIILLMPY	epidemically
ACDEEIILLNTY	indelicately
ACDEEIILLTTY	dietetically
ACDEEIINOPRT	depreciation
ACDEEIINPRRR	Pierre Cardin
ACDEEIINQSTU	equidistance
ACDEEIINTTUX	inexactitude
ACDEEIKLOOPS	kaleidoscope
ACDEEIKNNNSS	snick and snee
ACDEEIKNNRRU	reduce in rank
ACDEEILMNPST	displacement
ACDEEILMORRS	sclerodermia
ACDEEILMRTUV	vermiculated
ACDEEILORTVY	decoratively
ACDEEILRTTVY	detractively
ACDEEIMNNOPR	predominance
ACDEEIMNOSST	some distance
ACDEEINNORRT	André Citroën
ACDEEINNRTVY	inadvertency
ACDEEINOOPRT	coin-operated
ACDEEINOORRT	redecoration
ACDEEINOSUUV	Dieu avec nous
ACDEEIOPPRTU	propaedeutic
ACDEEIOPRRTY	depreciatory
ACDEEIRSSTTU	resuscitated
ACDEEJKKNOTY	donkey jacket
ACDEEKLLMMOR	Derek Malcolm
ACDEEKLORTTW	Derek Walcott
ACDEEKMPRRSU	muckspreader
ACDEEKOPRRTY	Peter Ackroyd
ACDEELMNNOTT	malcontented

Words marked □ can also be spelled with an initial capital letter

ACDEELNOPRTU counterplead
ACDEELOPRRRY record-player
ACDEEMNOPPTY appendectomy
ACDEENNNRSTT transcendent
ACDEENNORSTU second nature
ACDEFFIINOST disaffection
ACDEFGHIMNNO change of mind
ACDEFGHINNOW wind of change
ACDEFHHOORTT thatched roof
ACDEFHIINRSS disfranchise
ACDEFHOORSSU house of cards
ACDEFIILMRTY family credit
ACDEFIILNNOT confidential
ACDEFIILNSSU unclassified
ACDEFIILNSTY sanctifiedly
ACDEFIINNSTT disinfectant
ACDEFIINNSTU unsanctified
ACDEFILLOPSU Paul Scofield
ACDEFINORRSU François Rude
ACDEFLLNOORT not called for
ACDEGGHLOORS ragged school
ACDEGHIMNOTT method acting
ACDEGHIOPRRS discographer
ACDEGIIKMNST magnetic disk
ACDEGIIKNRST sidetracking
ACDEGIILLNSS sliding scale
ACDEGIILPQRU quadriplegic
ACDEGIINRRTT credit rating
ACDEGILLOOTY dialectology
ACDEGILNRTTY detractingly
ACDEGIMMNRTU magnetic drum
ACDEGINORRSS cross-grained
ACDEHHHNOTTW down the hatch
ACDEHHILOPTW hold pace with
ACDEHIIPRTYY hyperacidity
ACDEHILLMOTY methodically
ACDEHILMNOTU unmethodical
ACDEHIMOOPPR paedomorphic
ACDEHINNOPSW open sandwich
ACDEHINOPTTU put the acid on
ACDEHIOOPRST orthopaedics
ACDEHJJNNORY John Jarndyce
ACDEHJNOOPRS Joseph Conrad
ACDEHMMNOORT doom merchant
ACDEHMNNOORS enchondromas
ACDEIIILNTVY indicatively
ACDEIIILOSSS dissocialise
ACDEIIILOSSZ dissocialize
ACDEIIILRTVY veridicality
ACDEIIIMNNRS incendiarism
ACDEIIIMNNRT incriminated
ACDEIIIMNRST discriminate
ACDEIIIMORST isodiametric
ACDEIIINPPST appendicitis
ACDEIIINRSTT disintricate
ACDEIIIPRRST pericarditis
ACDEIIKLMNNO Nicole Kidman
ACDEIIKLNOPR a rod in pickle
ACDEIILLNNTY incidentally
ACDEIILLOPRY periodically
ACDEIILLOPSY episodically
ACDEIILMNOPT decimal point
ACDEIILMNOST maledictions
ACDEIILNORST discretional
ACDEIILRRTUV diverticular
ACDEIINNNOTU denunciation
ACDEIINNORTT indoctrinate
ACDEIINOORTV co-ordinative
ACDEIINORSTT at discretion
ACDEIINOSTTU educationist
ACDEIJLNTUVY adjunctively
ACDEIKLNOTTU induce to talk
ACDEIKMNNORT one-track mind
ACDEIKNORSTT stock-in-trade
ACDEILLMOSTY domestically
ACDEILLNSTYY syndetically
ACDEILLOPSTY despotically
ACDEILMNNOOT come in to land
ACDEILMNOPRU unproclaimed
ACDEILMNOSUY mendaciously
ACDEILNNOTWW lancet window
ACDEILNOORTY co-ordinately
ACDEILNOOSST disconsolate
ACDEILNORSSW cowardliness
ACDEILNTTUUV uncultivated
ACDEILOORRUV varicoloured
ACDEIMMNNOOT commendation
ACDEIMMOOORR air-commodore
ACDEIMNNNOOT condemnation
ACDEINNNOOST condensation
ACDEINNNOSTU unsanctioned
ACDEINNORTTU detruncation
ACDEINNORTUY denunciatory
ACDEINOOPRRT incorporated
ACDEINORSTTU discount rate
ACDEIORRSTUV radius vector
ACDEJMNOOQSU Jacques Monod
ACDELLLOSTUW Ludlow Castle
ACDELMNOORUY many-coloured
ACDELMOPRTUW talcum powder
ACDELNOORTYY cotyledonary
ACDELOPRRTTY protractedly
ACDEMMNOORTY commendatory
ACDEMNNOORTY condemnatory
ACDEMOOORRTU Doctor Moreau
ACDEOPRSTTUW waste product
ACDEORSTTTUU autodestruct
ACDFGIKLNOOT floating dock
ACDFHHIINPSS fish and chips
ACDFHIOPRRTW pitch forward
ACDFIIIINNOT nidification
ACDFIIILNTVY divinity calf
ACDFIIIMNOOT modification
ACDFIKMOPRRY Mary Pickford
ACDFILMOORTY family doctor
ACDFIMNNORTY Nancy Mitford
ACDGGIINORSU discouraging
ACDGGIOOORSU good gracious
ACDGHHIOPRRY hydrographic
ACDGHILLOORY hydrological
ACDGHINNOSTW Washington DC
ACDGIILOORST cardiologist

ACDGIINNOORT	co-ordinating
ACDGIKNNORTW	tracking-down
ACDGILMMNNOY	commandingly
ACDHHIILNTWY	wild hyacinth
ACDHHINOOPRY	hypochondria
ACDHIIMMORST	dichromatism
ACDHIIMNOORT	mitochondria
ACDHIINNORRX	Richard Nixon
ACDHIINOOPRS	radiophonics
ACDHIIOPRSTT	dictatorship
ACDHIIORRRSV	Ivor Richards
ACDHILNNOORT	Conrad Hilton
ACDHILNNOUWW	launch window
ACDHINOOPQRU	quadrophonic
ACDHINPPTTTU	pitch and putt
ACDHIOPRRRRY	Richard Pryor
ACDHIORSSTTY	hydrostatics
ACDHLNOOSSUY	Sunday school
ACDHNRSTTTUU	cut and thrust
ACDIIIJLLNUY	injudicially
ACDIIILNPRSY	disciplinary
ACDIIINNOORT	air-condition
ACDIIINOOSST	dissociation
ACDIIIOSSTTU	adscititious
ACDIILLMNPTU	multiplicand
ACDIILMNOPTU	undiplomatic
ACDIILMNPSTU	platinum disc
ACDIINNOOORT	co-ordination
ACDIINORSSYY	idiosyncrasy
ACDIIOOORTVW	Victoria Wood
ACDILLOOPRSY	prosodically
ACDILMOORSUY	mordaciously
ACDILNNOOSTU	non-custodial
ACDILNOOORST	consolidator
ACDILNORSUUU	iracundulous
ACDIMORRSSUU	Sir Scudamour
ACDINOOQRSTU	conquistador
ACDLLMNOOOPY	Collop Monday
ACDNOOORSTTW	Doctor Watson
ACEEEEEHKPPT	keep the peace
ACEEEEFNRRSS	carefreeness
ACEEEEHHORST	see each other
ACEEEEHLPSST	steeplechase
ACEEEEILMRST	Marie Celeste
ACEEEELMNRTT	trace element
ACEEEELNORTT	coelenterate
ACEEEENPRRSV	perseverance
ACEEEFFFRSTT	after effects
	after-effects
ACEEEFFGHORR	free of charge
	Roger Chaffee
ACEEEFHKLMRU	make cheerful
ACEEEFILLNRS	self-reliance
ACEEEFJMORRU	force majeure
ACEEEFLLRSUV	level surface
ACEEEFLNNOSV	Anne of Cleves
ACEEEFLNPSSU	peacefulness
ACEEEFLOORTV	force to leave
ACEEEFLORRST	steer clear of
ACEEEFLRRSTV	scarlet fever
ACEEEFNNRRST	transference

ACEEEGGHHLNT	change the leg
ACEEEGGORRRV	George Carver
ACEEEGHINNRS	search engine
ACEEEGHINPRS	cheeseparing
	cheese-paring
ACEEEGIKNNRT	ancient Greek
ACEEEGIKNRRT	racketeering
ACEEEGILLTXY	exegetically
ACEEEGILMNPT	meeting-place
ACEEEGIMNPPS	specimen page
ACEEEGINRRST	generatrices
ACEEEGLNSSTY	Casey Stengel
ACEEEGNNRRUY	unregeneracy
ACEEEGNORSVW	news coverage
ACEEEHHILLLS	Achilles' heel
ACEEEHHLNRTT	health centre
ACEEEHHLRTTW	ratchet-wheel
ACEEEHIISSTT	aestheticise
ACEEEHIISTTZ	aestheticize
ACEEEHIKPPTW	keep pace with
ACEEEHIMNSTV	achievements
ACEEEHKLNRST	Ernst Haeckel
ACEEEHLLOPST	lose the place
ACEEEHNNPRST	Stephen Crane
ACEEEHNOORRS	one-horse race
ACEEEHNPRRTT	The Carpenter
ACEEEHNRSSTY	the necessary
ACEEEHORRSTU	terrace house
ACEEEHORRSUV	have recourse
ACEEEIIMNRTV	cinéma vérité
	cinéma-vérité
ACEEEIKOPSTT	take to pieces
ACEEEILLNPST	license plate
ACEEEILRTVXY	execratively
ACEEEIMMNNPR	impermanence
ACEEEIMNNPRT	intemperance
ACEEEIMNRSVX	ex-serviceman
ACEEEINRSSTV	creativeness
	reactiveness
ACEEEIOPRSTT	tear to pieces
ACEEEIPRRTUV	recuperative
ACEEEIRRRRTV	river-terrace
ACEEEJLNNOPT	Jean Poncelet
ACEEEKLMMOPT	make complete
ACEEEKNNNRTT	Tennant Creek
ACEEEKNNOSSV	save one's neck
ACEEELLOPRTT	electroplate
ACEEELMMNPST	emplacements
ACEEELNNSTVY	evanescently
ACEEELNRSSSS	carelessness
ACEEELORSSTT	settle a score
ACEEEMPRSSUU	supreme sauce
ACEEENNPSSST	pass sentence
ACEEENNRRTTY	tercentenary
ACEEFFFGILNS	self-effacing
ACEEFFGHILNO	change of life
ACEEFFGLLOST	staff college
ACEEFFHOTTTT	to that effect
ACEEFFIKLRTT	raffle-ticket
ACEEFFILOPRS	special offer
ACEEFFINOPTT	Patent Office

ACEEFFINOTTU	effectuation
ACEEFFLNNOSY	fancy oneself
ACEEFFNNORSU	on sufferance
ACEEFGHNNOOT	change of tone
ACEEFGILNRST	self-catering
ACEEFGKLNORY	lack of energy
ACEEFGLNRSSU	gracefulness
ACEEFGNNOOST	age of consent
ACEEFHIKKMNT	Mack The Knife
ACEEFHINNOSU	finance house
ACEEFHLOPRRS	self-reproach
ACEEFHLORRST	Charles Forte
ACEEFHMORTTY	at the mercy of
ACEEFHNOOSSW	show one's face
ACEEFHNORSTU	on the surface
ACEEFHOPPRST	part of speech
ACEEFIIOPPSS	a piece of piss
ACEEFIKNNNRS	frankincense
ACEEFIKNOOTT	take notice of
ACEEFILLNRTY	frenetically
ACEEFILLOPST	fall to pieces
ACEEFILMMOTU	mute of malice
ACEEFILOPRRT	prefectorial
ACEEFILPRSTU	false picture
ACEEFINORSSU	surface noise
ACEEFINPSTTU	stupefacient
ACEEFIPRTTUV	putrefactive
ACEEFIPSTTUV	stupefactive
ACEEFKLLSTUW	sweet fuck all
ACEEFKMORRST	market forces
ACEEFLLRSUUY	use carefully
ACEEFMNORSST	centre of mass
ACEEFNOOPSTU	one's cup of tea
ACEEFNOORSWY	force one's way
ACEEFNOPPRST	copper-fasten
ACEEFORRSTUU	outer surface
ACEEGGHIINRV	give in charge
ACEEGGHINNRV	ever-changing
ACEEGGHLLPPR	Greg Chappell
ACEEGGMNORRW	Ewan McGregor
ACEEGHHILPST	highest place
ACEEGHIKMNPS	speech-making
ACEEGHILLMNO	Michelangelo
ACEEGHILNOSU	chaise-longue
ACEEGHLLORTT	call together
ACEEGHLORSTV	graveclothes
ACEEGHPRRRSU	supercharger
ACEEGHPRRSSS	press charges
ACEEGIILNSTV	evangelistic
ACEEGIIMMNNT	magnetic mine
ACEEGIIMNORT	geometrician
ACEEGIKNNRRV	nerve-racking
ACEEGILLLOOT	teleological
ACEEGILLLRTY	telergically
ACEEGILLNTUY	geniculately
ACEEGILNNSSU	Alec Guinness
ACEEGILNPSTT	place setting
ACEEGINPRRTU	recuperating
ACEEGLMNOORT	conglomerate
ACEEGMMOPRTU	computer game
ACEEGMNOPRRT	carpetmonger
ACEEGMOSTTUU	Auguste Comte
ACEEGNNORTTU	counter-agent
ACEEGOPRRSSU	supercargoes
ACEEHHILMSTT	The Alchemist
ACEEHHIPRRSU	hire purchase
	hire-purchase
ACEEHHLNORSU	charnel house
ACEEHHMOPRTY	chemotherapy
ACEEHHNOPRSU	Schopenhauer
ACEEHHORRSTU	charterhouse □
ACEEHHORSSTT	share the cost
ACEEHHORSTTT	cost the earth
ACEEHIIKNSTT	kinaesthetic
ACEEHIILLNRT	trichinellae
ACEEHIILNNOW	once in a while
ACEEHIILNPST	encephalitis
ACEEHIIMSSTT	Aestheticism
ACEEHIINORTT	theoretician
ACEEHIINSTUU	haute cuisine
ACEEHIKLMNRT	merchantlike
ACEEHILLMRTY	hermetically
ACEEHILLOPPT	leptocephali
ACEEHILNTVYY	heavenly city
ACEEHILOPRSX	exospherical
ACEEHILRRTTY	Lyric Theatre
ACEEHIMNPRST	parchmentise
ACEEHIMNPRTZ	parchmentize
ACEEHIMNSSTT	chastisement
ACEEHIMRSSTV	Christmas Eve
ACEEHIMRSTTU	music theatre
ACEEHINORUUV	nouveau riche
ACEEHIPRSTTU	therapeutics
ACEEHKKLNNRT	Kenneth Clark
ACEEHLLMOSTY	Halley's comet
ACEEHLLOORSV	school-leaver
ACEEHLNRSTTU	turn the scale
ACEEHLPSSTTU	space shuttle
ACEEHNNORRST	Hernán Cortés
ACEEHNNSSSTU	unchasteness
ACEEHOPPRRRS	sharecropper
ACEEHOPRSTTT	The Spectator
ACEEHORTTUUU	haute couture
ACEEIILLRTTV	verticillate
ACEEIILMPRRT	perimetrical
ACEEIILMRRSU	mercurialise
ACEEIILMRRUZ	mercurialize
ACEEIILNOPRS	porcelainise
ACEEIILNOPRZ	porcelainize
ACEEIILNORST	neorealistic
ACEEIILNOSST	sectionalise
ACEEIILNOSTZ	sectionalize
ACEEIIMNNPRT	impertinance
ACEEIIMNNSTT	ancient times
ACEEIIMNPRSU	Epicureanism
ACEEIINNORST	containerise
ACEEIINNORTZ	containerize
ACEEIINNRTUV	renunciative
ACEEIINORSTV	evisceration
ACEEIINRRRT	cairn terrier
ACEEIKLLQUVY	leave quickly
ACEEIKLMMNTY	Mickey Mantle

ACEEIKMRRSTT	make stricter
ACEEIKNOSSTT	season ticket
ACEEILLLNTTU	intellectual
ACEEILLLPTTT	Citlaltépetl
ACEEILLLTTUW	Lucie Attwell
ACEEILLMNORY	ceremonially
ACEEILLMNSTY	centesimally
ACEEILLMNTUV	multivalence
ACEEILLMORTY	meteorically
ACEEILLMOSTY	meet socially
ACEEILLNNORT	crenellation
ACEEILLNOPRS	porcellanise
ACEEILLNOPRZ	porcellanize
ACEEILLNORTY	neoterically
ACEEILLNRSUV	surveillance
ACEEILLNSSSU	cause illness
ACEEILLOPRRS	Pierre Laclos
ACEEILLOPSTT	total eclipse
ACEEILLORSTY	esoterically
ACEEILLORTXY	exoterically
ACEEILLPRSUV	all-up service
ACEEILLRTTUY	reticulately
ACEEILMMNPST	misplacement
ACEEILNOPPRT	perceptional
ACEEILNOPRSS	precessional
ACEEILNRSSTV	verticalness
ACEEILOOPRRS	corporealise
ACEEILOOPRRZ	corporealize
ACEEILOPPRRT	preceptorial
ACEEILRRTTVY	retractively
ACEEIMMNNPRY	impermanency
ACEEIMNNORTT	conterminate
ACEEIMNORSSX	cross-examine
ACEEIMNORSVW	servicewoman
ACEEIMOOPQRU	opéra comique
ACEEINNRRTTY	tricentenary
ACEEINOOPRTV	pine overcoat
ACEEINOORRTV	overreaction
ACEEINOPPPRT	apperception
ACEEINOPRRTU	recuperation
ACEEINOPRSTT	inspectorate
ACEEINOPSTTX	expectations
ACEEINORSTVV	conservative
ACEEJJKNOSSS	Jesse Jackson
ACEEKMNORSTV	make converts
ACEEKPRRTTUY	Turkey carpet
ACEELLORSSSW	lower classes
ACEELMNNORTU	nomenclature
ACEELMNRSTTY	Clytemnestra
ACEELMORSSST	Maltese cross
ACEELMPRRTUU	permaculture
ACEELNNOVWYY	Yvonne Cawley
ACEELNOORRSS	Eleanor Cross
ACEELNOPRRUW	nuclear power
ACEELNSSSSTT	tactlessness
ACEELOOPPPTT	Popocatepetl
ACEELOOPRSTY	Astley Cooper
ACEELPPRSSSU	upper classes
ACEELPSSTUUY	eucalyptuses
ACEEMMNOORST	come on stream
ACEEMMNORSTU	commensurate
ACEEMNNNNOTU	announcement
ACEEMNNORRST	remonstrance
ACEEMNOOPRST	compare notes
ACEEMOPRSTTY	spermatocyte
ACEENOPRSTUU	percutaneous
ACEEOOPRRTTT	protectorate
ACEEOPSTTTWZ	Aztec two-step
ACEFFFFHIOST	chief of staff
ACEFFGINNOTT	not affecting
ACEFFGOOORST	go off at score
ACEFFHILLLWY	Wycliffe Hall
ACEFFHOOORTU	out of reach of
ACEFFIIKNNPS	Pecksniffian
ACEFFILNNSSU	fancifulness
ACEFFORRSUUU	furfuraceous
ACEFGIIKNNRV	carving-knife
ACEFGILMNTUX	magnetic flux
ACEFGILNRSUY	flying saucer
ACEFGIMMOPRR	perform magic
ACEFHHIJNNOT	Johann Fichte
ACEFHKOOSSTT	state of shock
ACEFHLNSSTUW	watchfulness
ACEFHORRSSTU	rhesus factor
ACEFIIILNOST	fictionalise
ACEFIIILNOTT	felicitation
ACEFIIILNOTZ	fictionalize
ACEFIIINORTV	verification
ACEFIILLNNOT	inflectional
ACEFIILLRRTY	terrifically
ACEFIILNNOOT	line of action
ACEFIILNOOTT	fail to notice
ACEFIILNOQTU	liquefaction
ACEFIIMNORTV	confirmative
ACEFIINOORTV	vociferation
ACEFIINOPRTT	petrifaction
	pontificater
ACEFIIORRSTV	versificator
ACEFIIORRTVY	verificatory
ACEFIIRRTTVY	refractivity
ACEFILLNORSY	forensically
ACEFILNNOOSS	confessional
ACEFILORRRTY	refractorily
ACEFIMNOOPRT	of importance
ACEFINNOTUVW	wave function
ACEFINOPRTTU	putrefaction
ACEFINOPSTTU	stupefaction
ACEFINOSTTTU	Così Fan Tutte
ACEFLLMOOPRW	camp-follower
ACEFLLOORSSU	false colours
ACEFNOORRTWY	factory-owner
ACEGGGINTTUU	cutting gauge
ACEGGHINORRV	overcharging
ACEGGIILLNSS	glass ceiling
ACEGGIINNSST	giganticness
ACEGGIKRSSTW	swagger-stick
ACEGGILLLOOY	geologically
ACEGGIMNORTY	gyromagnetic
ACEGGINNOORT	congregation
ACEGHHIILOPR	heliographic
ACEGHHINOPRT	ethnographic
ACEGHHNORRST	short-changer

ACEGHHOOPRRY	choreography
ACEGHIILLNYY	hygienically
ACEGHIILLOOR	hierological
ACEGHIILPRST	special right
ACEGHIIMNOTV	have it coming
ACEGHIIMOTTW	atomic weight
ACEGHILLNNOU	hallucinogen
ACEGHILLNOOP	nephological
	phenological
ACEGHILLNOOT	ethnological
ACEGHILMOOOT	Homage to Clio
ACEGHILMOPYY	hypoglycemia
ACEGHILNNNTY	enchantingly
ACEGHILNOPRV	graphic novel
ACEGHILOPRXY	lexicography
ACEGHINOPRST	stenographic
ACEGHINORRTT	a tight corner
ACEGHINORTVW	watching-over
ACEGHIOPPRRR	reprographic
ACEGHLMNOOST	magnet school
ACEGHNOOPRSU	necrophagous
ACEGHOPPRRST	spectrograph
ACEGIIILLMTY	illegitimacy
ACEGIIINSTTV	negativistic
ACEGIIKKMNTY	mickey-taking
ACEGIILLOOPT	geopolitical
ACEGIILLOSTY	egoistically
ACEGIILNNOTY	congeniality
ACEGIILNNRSY	increasingly
ACEGIILNPRSS	Alice Springs
ACEGIILORSSU	sacrilegious
ACEGIIMNORST	gastrocnemii
ACEGIINOOTTX	excogitation
ACEGIINOQTUV	equivocating
ACEGILLLNOOY	neologically
ACEGILLMOOTY	etymological
ACEGILLNNOTY	congenitally
ACEGILLNOORU	neurological
ACEGILLNORSY	early closing
ACEGILLNRTTY	clatteringly
ACEGILLOOOST	osteological
ACEGILMMOPSY	Olympic Games
ACEGILNNOTTU	conglutinate
ACEGILNOOOST	oceanologist
ACEGILNOOPTU	unapologetic
ACEGILNOORTY	oryctolagine
ACEGILNRSTTY	scatteringly
ACEGILOOPSST	escapologist
ACEGIMMMNOST	Magic Moments
ACEGIMNNOPSS	encompassing
ACEGINNORRTU	raconteuring
ACEGINORSSSU	graciousness
ACEGLNOORSUY	acrogenously
ACEGLOORSUUY	courageously
ACEGLORRSSTU	regular costs
ACEHHILMOPTX	exophthalmic
ACEHHILOPTTY	hypothetical
ACEHHINOPRTT	theanthropic
ACEHHJLNNORY	John Charnley
ACEHHKNNOOTV	Anton Chekhov
ACEHHKOPRSTY	shock therapy
ACEHHLLOSSTT	call the shots
ACEHHMORSTTY	chrestomathy
ACEHHNOOSTTU	autochthones
ACEHIIINRSST	christianise
ACEHIIINRSTZ	christianize
ACEHIIKPRTTW	Patrick White
ACEHIIKRRSWW	Warwickshire
ACEHIILLNRST	trichinellas
ACEHIILNPRST	sphincterial
ACEHIILPRSTY	sphericality
ACEHIIMNNNRY	Henry Mancini
ACEHIIMNOPTW	white campion
ACEHIINSSTTU	enthusiastic
ACEHIINTTTUY	authenticity
ACEHIIOPPRST	Hippocratise
ACEHIIOPPRTZ	Hippocratize
ACEHIIOPSSTT	sophisticate
ACEHIIPPRRST	periphrastic
ACEHIJLNNOOS	Celia Johnson
ACEHIKLLLRRS	Karl Schiller
ACEHIKRRSSSW	kirschwasser
ACEHILLMNOPY	phonemically
ACEHILLNOPTY	phonetically
ACEHILLORRTY	rhetorically
ACEHILLRSTYY	hysterically
ACEHILMOPSTW	Sopwith Camel
ACEHILNNNSSS	clannishness
ACEHILNOORSW	Nicholas Rowe
ACEHILNOPPTY	phenotypical
ACEHIMMNNRSY	Mercian Hymns
ACEHIMNOSTUY	human society
ACEHIMNPSSSS	scampishness
ACEHIMOORTTY	atomic theory
ACEHIMOPRSST	atmospherics
ACEHIMOPSSTY	scyphistomae
ACEHIMORSTTT	thermostatic
ACEHIMPRSTUY	music therapy
ACEHINNOORRS	horrisonance
ACEHINOPSSTY	sycophantise
ACEHINOPSTYZ	sycophantize
ACEHIOPRRSTT	orchestra pit
ACEHJLNNOORT	John Coltrane
ACEHKMRRSSTT	stretch marks
ACEHKNOPRTTU	put on the rack
ACEHLLLORRSS	Charles Rolls
ACEHLLMNOPSY	shell company
ACEHLLMORSYY	lachrymosely
ACEHLMMNOOTW	commonwealth ▫
ACEHLMNOORSY	close harmony
ACEHLMOORSST	schoolmaster
ACEHLOPSSUXY	psychosexual
ACEHMNOORTTT	Cotton Mather
ACEHMNORRRTT	trench mortar
ACEHMNRTUVWY	want very much
ACEHMOORSTTY	tracheostomy
ACEHOORRRSTT	orchestrator
ACEHOORSSTTY	athrocytoses
ACEIIILMNPSU	municipalise
ACEIIILMNPUZ	municipalize
ACEIIILNSTTY	inelasticity
ACEIIILRSTTV	relativistic

ACEIIILRSTVV	revivalistic	ACEILOPRRSUY	precariously
ACEIIINNNORT	incineration	ACEIMNNNORTT	conterminant
ACEIIINNRSTT	intrinsicate	ACEIMNNOOPST	companion set
ACEIIINPRSST	precisianist		compensation
ACEIIJLLSTUY	jesuitically	ACEIMNNOOSST	Monte Cassino
ACEIILLLLPTY	elliptically	ACEIMNNOPRTU	unimportance
ACEIILLLNSUV	all-inclusive	ACEIMNOOOOPT	onomatopoeic
ACEIILLMNSST	miscellanist	ACEIMNORSSTV	conservatism
ACEIILLMOPST	compile a list	ACEIMNPSTTUU	mispunctuate
ACEIILLNORSW	Willie Carson	ACEIMNSSTTUY	unsystematic
ACEIILLNORTY	collinearity	ACEIMOOPRSTZ	spermatozoic
ACEIILMMNRST	mercantilism	ACEIMPRRRSTW	writer's cramp
ACEIILMNOSST	sectionalism	ACEINNNOOSTU	Ion Antonescu
ACEIILMNRSTT	mercantilist	ACEINNOOPRTT	pernoctation
ACEIILMOPRST	semi-tropical	ACEINNOORSTV	conservation
ACEIILNNORST	non-realistic		conversation
ACEIILNOPRST	inspectorial	ACEINNOOSTTT	contestation
ACEIILNORTTU	reticulation	ACEINNORRSST	contrariness
ACEIILNRSTTT	clarinettist	ACEINNORRTUY	renunciatory
ACEIILNRSTVV	civil servant	ACEINNORSTTU	encrustation
ACEIILOQTUVY	equivocality	ACEINOPPRRTU	Port-au-Prince
	voice quality	ACEINOPSSSSU	spaciousness
ACEIILPRRSUY	superciliary	ACEINOPSSSTU	captiousness
ACEIILRRSSTU	surrealistic	ACEINOSSSTUU	cautiousness
ACEIILRRTTTY	retractility	ACEIORRSSTTU	resuscitator
ACEIIMNOPRST	imprecations	ACEJKOPRSSTT	sports jacket
ACEIIMNORRRT	recriminator	ACELLNNOOPRT	control panel
ACEIINNNORTU	renunciation	ACELLNNOSSUY	consensually
ACEIINOOQTUV	equivocation	ACELLNOTTUXY	contextually
ACEIINOPRRTT	practitioner	ACELMMNOSTUY	consummately
ACEIINOPRSTU	pertinacious	ACELMNOOPRTT	contemplator
ACEIINORRSTW	contrariwise	ACELMNPRSUUU	supernaculum
ACEIJKLLNOSV	Jacksonville	ACELMOPRRSTU	Marcel Proust
ACEIKKLNNSTY	Kilkenny cats	ACELNNRSSUUU	ranunculuses
ACEIKLOORRSW	social worker	ACEMNOOPRRTY	contemporary
ACEIKMOOPRRT	Patrick Moore	ACEMNOOPRSTY	compensatory
ACEIKNNORSST	in one's tracks	ACENNNORSTUV	unconversant
ACEIKORRRTTT	trick or treat	ACENNOORSTTU	turn one's coat
ACEILLLNRTUY	lenticularly	ACENOOQRTTTU	quattrocento
ACEILLLORRSW	Lewis Carroll	ACENOORRSTVY	conservatory
ACEILLMORTUY	molecularity	ACENOPRRRTUY	counter-parry
ACEILLMTUUVY	cumulatively	ACENOPRRSUWY	Norway spruce
ACEILLNORTUY	neurotically	ACEOPRRSSSTT	sportscaster
ACEILLNOTTUY	Teutonically	ACEPRRSTTTUY	pastry cutter
ACEILMNNOOPT	componential	ACFFGGHIILNN	cliffhanging
ACEILMNOOPTY	come into play		cliff-hanging
ACEILMOOPSTT	leptosomatic	ACFFHJNNORUY	Johann Cruyff
ACEILMORTTTU	Lucretia Mott	ACFFIILLNOUY	unofficially
ACEILNNNOOTV	conventional	ACFGIIILNOTU	uglification
ACEILNNOPRTT	central point	ACFHIIIMNOTU	humification
ACEILNNORTTY	certainly not	ACFHIILLORRY	horrifically
ACEILNOOPRSS	processional	ACFHILLOOSTY	act foolishly
ACEILNOORTUY	elocutionary	ACFHILNNOOST	infant school
ACEILNOPQTUU	pauciloquent	ACFIIIILNOTV	vilification
ACEILNOPRSSU	percussional	ACFIIIINOTVV	vivification
ACEILNORSUXY	exclusionary	ACFIIILNOPST	spiflication
ACEILNOSTTUV	consultative	ACFIIINNOOTT	notification
ACEILOOPRRST	prosectorial	ACFIIINOOSST	ossification
ACEILOOPRRTV	Velociraptor	ACFIIINOPRTU	purification
ACEILOOPRRTY	corporeality	ACFIIINOPTTY	typification
ACEILOOPSSTT	osteoplastic	ACFIIJORSTTU	justificator

ACFIILLLOPRY	prolifically
ACFIILLNOPTY	pontifically
ACFIILNNNOOT	non-fictional
ACFIILOSTTUY	factitiously
ACFIIMNNOORT	confirmation
ACFIINORRTTU	trifurcation
ACFIIOPRRTUY	purificatory
ACFIKLLNOOTU	out of all nick
ACFILLNNOTUY	functionally
ACFIMNNOOORT	conformation
ACFIMNOORRTY	confirmatory
ACGGIILLLMOO	Camillo Golgi
ACGHHIILOPRT	lithographic
ACGHHIOOPPRT	photographic
ACGHHIOOPRRT	orthographic
ACGHHORRRTUY	carry through
ACGHIIKNNOTT	not hacking it
ACGHIILLLOOP	philological
ACGHIILLLOOT	lithological
ACGHIILLNOOR	rhinological
ACGHIILLOOST	histological
ACGHIILNRTWW	crawling with
ACGHIINPRSTY	scintigraphy
ACGHIIPRSSST	sphragistics
ACGHIJMNNOOS	Magic Johnson
ACGHIKNOOSTW	what's cooking?
ACGHILLMOOTY	mythological
ACGHILLNOOOP	phonological
ACGHILLOOPRS	oscillograph
ACGHINOOPPRR	pornographic
ACGHIOOPSSTY	phagocytosis
ACGHKLOPPUYY	happy-go-lucky
ACGHLNOORSTU	laugh to scorn
ACGHOPPRRTYY	cryptography
ACGIIILLLOTY	illogicality
ACGIIINNOTTX	intoxicating
ACGIIKKLNSTW	walking stick
	walking-stick
ACGIILLLMNOO	limnological
ACGIILLLRTUY	liturgically
ACGIILMNOSUU	mucilaginous
ACGIILNPPSTU	supplicating
ACGIIMORRTVY	microgravity
ACGIINNOSTTW	wainscotting
ACGIKKMNOSST	stocking mask
ACGIKLNORSSW	working class
	working-class
ACGIKNNNRRTU	running-track
ACGILLLOOOYZ	zoologically
ACGILLMNNOOY	gnomonically
ACGILMOPRSUU	musical group
ACGILNOOSTUY	contagiously
ACGILNOPSUUY	pugnaciously
ACGILNORSUUY	ungraciously
ACGIMNOOPRTU	compurgation
ACGLLNOORSUY	clangorously
ACHHIIINORST	Ornithischia
ACHHIILMNOPR	philharmonic
ACHHIIMNOPPS	championship
ACHHIIMOSTTY	stichomythia
ACHHIIMOSTYZ	schizothymia
ACHHIKOOSSTV	Shostakovich
ACHHILLMRTYY	rhythmically
ACHHINNOPTXY	phycoxanthin
ACHIIILMSTWY	whimsicality
ACHIIIMNPSSU	musicianship
ACHIIINNNNOX	Nixon in China
ACHIIINRSTTY	Christianity
ACHIIKLNNOTY	lay in on thick
ACHIIKLNOTTY	lay it on thick
ACHIILLLOSTY	holistically
ACHIILLORSTY	historically
ACHIILNNOORT	chlorination
ACHIILNOPRST	rhinoplastic
ACHIILOPRSTT	cartophilist
ACHIIMNOPRST	misanthropic
ACHIIPRSSTTY	psychiatrist
ACHIKMORTUUV	kurchatovium
ACHILLNOORSY	isochronally
ACHILLNOPTYY	hypnotically
ACHILLORSUVY	chivalrously
ACHIMNNORSSY	asynchronism
ACHIMOPSSSTY	scyphistomas
ACHINNOOSTTT	not a stitch on
ACHINNORSTTU	turn into cash
ACHINOPRSSTY	Cornish pasty
ACHIOOPRRSUZ	rhizocarpous
ACHIOPRSSSTY	astrophysics
ACHLLMNOOORS	normal school
ACHNNOORSSUY	asynchronous
ACHOOPRRRTTU	Port Harcourt
ACIIIILMRSTT	militaristic
ACIIIILNOSTV	civilisation
ACIIIILNOTVZ	civilization
ACIIILMNOPST	implications
ACIIILMNPTUY	municipality
ACIIILNOOSTT	coalitionist
	solicitation
ACIIILNOPRTT	triplication
ACIIILNOTVVY	conviviality
ACIIILNPPRTY	principality
ACIIILQTUYZZ	quizzicality
ACIIIMNORSTV	Victorianism
ACIIINNOOTTX	intoxication
ACIIINOPSSUU	inauspicious
ACIIINOQSSTU	acquisitions
ACIIJLLRSTUY	juristically
ACIIJLNORSTU	journalistic
ACIIKKPRSSTU	kick upstairs
ACIIKNOPSTTU	put a sock in it
ACIILLNOPRVY	provincially
ACIILLNRTUUV	vinicultural
ACIILLOQTUXY	quixotically
ACIILLOSSUVY	lasciviously
ACIILLPRSTUY	puristically
ACIILLRTTUUV	viticultural
ACIILMNNOOTU	columniation
ACIILNNOOOST	colonisation
ACIILNNOOOTZ	colonization
ACIILNNOSTUY	insouciantly
ACIILNOPPSTU	supplication
ACIILNOSTUUY	incautiously

ACIILOPSSUUY	auspiciously
ACIILPRSTTUU	apiculturist
ACIIMMOOPRRS	comprimarios
ACIIMNNOOPRS	in comparison
ACIIMNOPRTTU	protactinium
ACIINNNOOORT	incoronation
ACIINNNOOTTU	continuation
ACIINNOOPSTT	constipation
ACIINNORSTTU	incrustation
ACIINOPRRSUV	picornavirus
ACIINOPSSUUU	unauspicious
ACIIOOPRRTTV	Port Victoria
ACIKLNOOPRST	split on a rock
ACILLLLOOQUY	colloquially
ACILLMNNOPSU	spinal column
ACILLMNOSUUY	calumniously
ACILLMOOOTYZ	zootomically
ACILLMORSUUY	miraculously
ACILLNOPSTYY	synoptically
ACILLOOPRRTY	proctorially
ACILLOOQSUUY	loquaciously
ACILLPRRSTUY	scripturally
ACILMMNNOOTT	non-committal
ACILMNOOOPST	cosmopolitan ❑
ACILMOOPPRST	protoplasmic
ACILMOOPRRRT	Corporal Trim
ACILNNNOSTTY	inconstantly
ACILNNOOSTTU	consultation
ACILOOPPRTTY	prototypical
ACILOPPRSTUY	supplicatory
ACILORSSSTTU	tourist class
ACIMMNNOOSTU	consummation
ACINNNORSTTU	unconstraint
ACINNOORSTTT	in contrast to
ACINOOPRRSTT	strip cartoon
ACINORRSSSSU	Russian cross
ACIORRRSSTTU	cirrostratus
ACLLLMMOORWY	Malcolm Lowry
ACLLLPRSTUUY	sculpturally
ACLLMMMNOOOW	common mallow
ACLLMNOORTUU	monocultural
ACLLNNPTUUUY	unpunctually
ACLNOORSTTUY	consultatory
ACMNNNOOORWY	No Woman, No Cry
ACMNNOORTUWY	countrywoman
ADDDDEEEHNRU	dunderheaded
ADDDDEEEIRSW	Eddie Edwards
ADDDDEEFFILL	fiddle-faddle
ADDDEEFIOSTU	eisteddfodau
ADDDEEIIMPRS	diadem spider
ADDDEELPRRSU	rudder pedals
ADDDEFILNORU	fiddle around
ADDDEILNNNOS	Donald Sinden
ADDEEEEFLNRS	self-endeared
ADDEEEEGGRST	desegregated
ADDEEEEGLLRY	Alderley Edge
ADDEEEFGNNOR	Garden of Eden
ADDEEEFIIRTV	additive-free
ADDEEEFIKLRR	Freddie Laker
ADDEEEHHINOS	hide one's head
ADDEEEHINRST	disheartened
ADDEEEHLNNVY	even-handedly
ADDEEEIIRSTV	desiderative
ADDEEEIMPRTT	premeditated
ADDEEEIORRTT	deteriorated
ADDEEEJLLMSW	James Weddell
ADDEEEJNNRRW	Edward Jenner
ADDEEEKLPSST	pedestal desk
ADDEEELLRRTW	Edward Teller
ADDEEENPPTXY	expanded type
ADDEEFFNRSTU	understaffed
ADDEEFHLLNTY	left-handedly
ADDEEFHLMORY	formaldehyde
ADDEEFIKRRST	Frederikstad
ADDEEFINOORR	foreordained
ADDEEFIRRRST	Freddie Starr
ADDEEFLLOPST	soft-pedalled
ADDEEFLNRSSU	dreadfulness
ADDEEGGILLNN	dingle-dangle
ADDEEGGILNOR	dégringolade
ADDEEGHILNNS	single-handed
ADDEEGHILNOR	golden-haired
ADDEEGHKNRTU	The Grand Duke
ADDEEGILNNST	disentangled
ADDEEGILNPRU	plague-ridden
ADDEEGINNSTU	undesignated
ADDEEGINPPSU	pease pudding
ADDEEHLLMNOY	Edmond Halley
ADDEEHLNSTUW	sudden wealth
ADDEEHMNOTTU	mutton-headed
ADDEEHMORSUY	Hydromedusae
ADDEEHOPRRTU	proud-hearted
ADDEEIILNSVZ	Denzil Davies
ADDEEIIMMNNO	demi-mondaine
ADDEEIKLMNWY	weak-mindedly
ADDEEILLPSSY	displeasedly
ADDEEINRSTUV	unadvertised
ADDEEJLLSTUW	well-adjusted
ADDEELLMNRUW	Edmund Waller
ADDEENNORRVW	Edward Vernon
ADDEENOOOSSW	seasoned wood
ADDEFGIILLNN	landing-field
ADDEFGILRRSU	disregardful
ADDEFHILNOOS	old fashioned
	old-fashioned
ADDEFIIILQSU	disqualified
ADDEFIIISSST	dissatisfied
ADDEFINORRSW	fire and sword
ADDEFLNNNOUW	Newfoundland
ADDEGGIINRRS	disregarding
ADDEGHIINRRT	third reading
ADDEGHILNORS	Das Rheingold
ADDEGHILRRUW	Ludwig Erhard
ADDEGIINORSS	disorganised
ADDEGIINORSZ	disorganized
ADDEGILNNRWY	Wendy Darling
ADDEGINNRRUW	underdrawing
ADDEGLOOSSST	add glosses to
ADDEHHLORRSU	hard shoulder
ADDEHHOSSTTW	what's the odds?
ADDEHILNOSTY	in the old days
ADDEHINNORTW	down the drain

ADDEHLLMNSTU	St Edmund Hall
ADDEIILLLSVY	ill-advisedly
ADDEIILLNSSV	Devil's Island
ADDEIILMSSVY	misadvisedly
ADDEIILPSSTY	dissipatedly
ADDEIINOPPST	disappointed
ADDEILMNOOTU	demodulation
ADDEILMNOPRS	promised land
ADDEILMNSSTW	West Midlands
ADDEILNORSWW	Edward Wilson
ADDEIMMMRSUY	Midsummer Day
ADDEIMNNORRW	narrow-minded
ADDEINOOPRTT	traded option
ADDEINRRSUVY	Sunday driver
ADDELMNOORSU	same old round
ADDEMNOOORRT	rodomontader
ADDEMNOOPSSU	pseudomonads
ADDFIILLNSUY	disdainfully
ADDFILLNOOTW	Donald Wolfit
ADDGGINNOOST	good standing
ADDGHHILNNOS	holding hands
ADDGHIIKNNRR	hard drinking
ADDGHILNORTY	thyroid gland
ADDGHIMNOORU	rough diamond
ADDGIIILLNVW	dividing wall
ADDGIILNSSTU	studdingsail
ADDGILLNOOPP	paddling-pool
ADDGINNNOSTW	standing-down
ADDGKMNOOOOR	Komodo dragon
ADDGLLNOSSUY	Guys and Dolls
ADDHINNNOSWW	win hands down
ADDIIILLNUVY	individually
ADDIIINNOOTT	in addition to
ADDILLMOOSTY	till doomsday
ADDILNRRTUYY	dirty laundry
ADEEEEGINRTV	degenerative
ADEEEEGLNRTY	degenerately
ADEEEEHHNRRT	here and there
ADEEEEHKNOPS	keep one's head
ADEEEEKMMNST	make ends meet
ADEEEEMNPRTW	deepwatermen
ADEEEFFFRSTU	suffer defeat
ADEEEFFIINRT	differentiae
ADEEEFFILSTT	defeat itself
ADEEEFFPRRTY	deep-fat fryer
ADEEEFGIKNNO	on a knife edge
ADEEEFGLNNRR	Fernand Léger
ADEEEFGNORST	drag one's feet
ADEEEFHIKLTT	take the field
ADEEEFHILSSV	self-adhesive
ADEEEFIIKMNT	make definite
ADEEEFILLRST	alder-liefest
ADEEEFINPRRR	referred pain
ADEEEFNNOSST	tone-deafness
ADEEEFOPRRST	desperate for
ADEEEFRSVWYY	every few days
ADEEEGGHLNOR	George Handel
ADEEEGGINNRT	degenerating
ADEEEGHIRRST	head register
ADEEEGHLMMRS	sledgehammer
ADEEEGIMNRST	disagreement
ADEEEGIMNRTZ	demagnetizer
ADEEEGINNORT	degeneration
ADEEEGINPRST	predesignate
ADEEEGINRRTT	redintegrate
ADEEEGLNNNRW	New Englander
ADEEEGMNNNRT	endangerment
ADEEEGMPSTTU	get steamed up
ADEEEHHLORTW	wholehearted
	whole-hearted
ADEEEHHNNRTT	then and there
	there and then
ADEEEHIMNRTT	hereditament
ADEEEHINSSSV	adhesiveness
ADEEEHIRRTTT	tetrahedrite
ADEEEHLNNRRT	Netherlander
ADEEEHLNOOSS	lose one's head
ADEEEHNOORSV	over one's head
ADEEEIILMNRS	demineralise
ADEEEIILMNRZ	demineralize
ADEEEIILMRST	sidereal time
ADEEEIILNPTX	expediential
ADEEEIIMMNRT	ante meridiem
ADEEEIIMNRTT	intermediate
ADEEEIKLRRTW	Kielder Water
ADEEEILLMMOS	mademoiselle ❑
ADEEEILMNORT	radioelement
ADEEEILNRRTT	interrelated
ADEEEILRRRTW	leader-writer
ADEEEILRRTTY	reiteratedly
ADEEEILRSSUX	sexual desire
ADEEEIMMORTT	Edmé Mariotte
ADEEEIMNRTTX	exterminated
ADEEEIMPRSTT	distemperate
ADEEEINPRSTT	predestinate
ADEEEINPRSTW	in deep waters
ADEEEJNOORRS	rejoneadores
ADEEEKLLMRSS	Skelmersdale
ADEEEKLLNOST	endoskeletal
ADEEEKOPPTTU	keep up to date
ADEEELLMNNRW	well-mannered
ADEEELLMNOSV	dolman sleeve
ADEEELLNORSW	well-reasoned
ADEEELLNOSSW	well-seasoned
ADEEELNNQRSU	Queenslander
ADEEELNOORSU	Eleonora Duse
ADEEELNOSSST	desolateness
ADEEELNPRSVY	evenly spread
ADEEELOPPRST	tradespeople
ADEEEMNORSST	moderateness
ADEEENOPPRRT	preponderate
ADEEENPPRRSS	preparedness
ADEEENPRRTUV	peradventure
ADEEENRRTTWW	Derwent Water
ADEEEOPPRRSV	eavesdropper
ADEEEOPRRSUV	overpersuade
ADEEERRRSTTT	street-trader
ADEEFFHILORT	thread of life
ADEEFFHOORST	Feast of Herod
ADEEFFIILNRT	differential
ADEEFGHHORTT	The Godfather
ADEEFGHILNRS	hard feelings

Words marked ❑ can also be spelled with an initial capital letter

ADEEFGILLSSS	field glasses
	field-glasses
ADEEFGINNRST	free-standing
ADEEFGINORRT	foreign trade
ADEEFGIRSSTU	fatigue-dress
ADEEFGLLNNWY	newfangledly
ADEEFGLNORSU	guard oneself
ADEEFGLORRSS	regardless of
ADEEFGNORSVY	Godfrey Evans
ADEEFHILLNOT	lie of the land
ADEEFHILLPTY	play the field
ADEEFHILNRRY	Harry Enfield
ADEEFHILNRTT	flint-hearted
ADEEFHIMOTTY	the time of day
ADEEFHINNOSW	new-fashioned
ADEEFHLNNPSU	funnel-shaped
ADEEFHOORRTT	at the order of
ADEEFIIMNOSS	admission fee
ADEEFIKLNRSY	Alfred Kinsey
ADEEFILLRSSY	Alfred Sisley
ADEEFILMOSSV	devil of a mess
ADEEFILRSTXY	stare fixedly
ADEEFKKMNORR	Frank Kermode
ADEEFLLPRSTU	apfel strudel
ADEEFMOORRRY	ready for more
ADEEGGHIRSTT	straightedge
ADEEGGIQRRSU	square-rigged
ADEEGGLNOPPR	doppelgänger
ADEEGHHILRTT	light-hearted
ADEEGHIIRSTW	disagree with
ADEEGHIKLMOY	like hey-go-mad
ADEEGHILNSTW	swing the lead
ADEEGHINNRRT	heart-rending
ADEEGHINRSTT	straightened
ADEEGHLNOSST	The Golden Ass
ADEEGHNOOOST	go to one's head
ADEEGHORRTTW	draw together
ADEEGIILLRSS	Gilles de Rais
ADEEGIINRSTT	disintegrate
ADEEGIJNNRWW	wandering Jew
ADEEGIKMMOOT	make good time
ADEEGIKNNRRT	kindergarten
ADEEGIKPRRRU	Gerard Kuiper
ADEEGILNORTU	deregulation
ADEEGILORTVY	derogatively
ADEEGINNORUV	endeavouring
ADEEGINNRRTW	winter garden
ADEEGIOPRRTV	prerogatived
ADEEGIOSSTTY	easy to digest
ADEEGLLNOTTW	golden wattle
ADEEGLLRRSSY	regardlessly
ADEEGLRSTUVV	velvet-guards
ADEEGMNNRRTU	undergarment
ADEEGNORRTUW	go under water
ADEEGNORSTTT	get started on
ADEEGNPRTUUX	unexpurgated
ADEEHHIKNRRS	headshrinker
ADEEHHILTTVW	what the devil
ADEEHHINOTVW	have done with
ADEEHHLOOTTW	toothed whale
ADEEHHMORTTY	rhyme to death
ADEEHHNNNOOT	on the one hand
ADEEHHNOOSSW	show one's head
ADEEHIILRRTY	hereditarily
ADEEHIINNRSS	rise and shine
ADEEHIINRSTW	raise the wind
ADEEHIJMNOPS	Joseph Damien
ADEEHIKNRRVY	heavy drinker
ADEEHILLPSTW	with all speed
ADEEHILLPTVY	play the devil
ADEEHILMORTT	maître d'hôtel
ADEEHIMMNRSU	her name is mud
ADEEHIMNPPRS	misapprehend
ADEEHIMRSSST	headmistress
ADEEHINORSTU	house-trained
ADEEHIOSTTTU	at the outside
ADEEHKKMORST	Thomas Dekker
ADEEHLMMOTUY	mealy-mouthed
ADEEHLPRSTUU	desulphurate
ADEEHMNNOSSS	handsomeness
ADEEHNNOPRST	pentahedrons
ADEEHNNORSTU	turn one's head
	under one's hat
ADEEHNORRSTT	tetrahedrons
ADEEHNORSTTY	stony-hearted
ADEEHORRSSTT	tear to shreds
ADEEHORSTTTU	stout-hearted
ADEEIIILMRST	demilitarise
ADEEIIILMRTZ	demilitarize
ADEEIIILMTTV	delimitative
ADEEIIILORST	editorialise
ADEEIIILORTZ	editorialize
ADEEIIJLLOSS	jolies laides
ADEEIIJNOORR	Rio de Janeiro
ADEEIILLNTVY	evidentially
ADEEIILMMNPT	impedimental
ADEEIILMTTVY	meditatively
ADEEIILNPRST	presidential
ADEEIILRTVVY	derivatively
ADEEIIMNNRSU	unseminaried
ADEEIIMNOPTT	monte di pietà
ADEEIIMNPRST	mean-spirited
ADEEIIMNRRTY	intermediary
ADEEIINNRRVW	Andrew Irvine
ADEEIINORSTT	disorientate
ADEEIINRRSTY	residentiary
ADEEIINRRTVW	water-diviner
ADEEIIPPRSSU	dispauperise
ADEEIIPPRSUZ	dispauperize
ADEEIJLNRSUW	Julie Andrews
ADEEIKLLNSSY	ladylikeness
ADEEIKLMNOVV	make involved
ADEEIKLMPPRR	ripple-marked
ADEEIKMNRSSS	semi-darkness
ADEEIKNRRRTW	water-drinker
ADEEILLNOTTU	andouillette
ADEEILLOSSVY	easily solved
ADEEILLOSTVW	old wives' tale
ADEEILLPRSTV	silver-plated
ADEEILLRTVWY	travel widely
ADEEILMMORTY	immoderately
ADEEILMOSTVY	move steadily

ADEEILMPRTTY timely-parted
ADEEILNNTTUV unventilated
ADEEILNOPRSZ personalized
ADEEILNOPRTT latent period
ADEEILNOTTVY denotatively
ADEEILNRRSTY restrainedly
ADEEIMMNORSU misdemeanour
ADEEIMNRSTUV misadventure
ADEEIMSSTTYZ systematized
ADEEINNOOPRU Indo-European
ADEEINNRRSTU unrestrained
ADEEINNSSSTU unsteadiness
ADEEINORRSTV overstrained
ADEEINSSTTTU United States
ADEEIOPSSSTT Pott's disease
ADEEKLNORRSW Arnold Wesker
ADEEKNORSSYY donkey's years
ADEELLLRSSSW Sadler's Wells
ADEELLMMNRTU untrammelled
ADEELLMNNORW Andrew Mellon
ADEELLMORUZZ muzzle-loader
ADEELMNOSTTT Old Testament
ADEELNPPRRUY unpreparedly
ADEEMMRRRSSU mass murderer
ADEEMNNNORTU unornamented
ADEEMNNOSSWY mend one's ways
ADEEMNNPRSUU supermundane
ADEEMNNPRTUY underpayment
ADEENNOPPRRT preponderant
ADEENOORSSTW eat one's words
ADEENOORSUUY see you around
ADEENOPRRSST tradesperson
ADEENORSSTUW sweet-and-sour
ADEFFGHILRTY affrightedly
ADEFFGNOORSU off one's guard
ADEFFHHRSTTU the hard stuff
ADEFFHNNOOSS off one's hands
ADEFFHORSSTT short-staffed
ADEFGHHILNOT height of land
ADEFGHIKORSY skreigh of day
ADEFGHILNRTT right-and-left
ADEFGHILRSTY far-sightedly
ADEFGHLNOSTY length of days
ADEFGIILLNPY playing-field
ADEFGIILMNRS self-admiring
ADEFGIIMMNRX mixed farming
ADEFGIINRRST first reading
ADEFGORRRSUW surge forward
ADEFHHIIOTTW with the aid of
ADEFHHLNRSTU thunderflash
ADEFHILMNOOS fashion model
ADEFHILNORRS Ronald Fisher
ADEFHIMNOORS fore-admonish
ADEFHINORSTV hand over fist
ADEFHIORTUVW favoured with
ADEFHLLORTTU full-throated
ADEFHOOORTTU out of the road
ADEFIIKLLPRW wildlife park
ADEFIIKNRSTT after its kind
ADEFIILNOSTT deflationist
ADEFIILNPRSU Freudian slip
ADEFIIMNNORS fide non armis
ADEFIKLLNRTY friendly talk
ADEFILLNOOSS on all sides of
ADEFILMNNOSS manifoldness
ADEFINOPRRSY person Friday
ADEFIOOPPRSV disapprove of
ADEFLLLMNORS Moll Flanders
ADEFLLNRTUUY fraudulently
ADEFLMOOOPPS apple of Sodom
ADEFMNOOORTV move to and fro
ADEFOPRRSSTW steps forward
ADEGGHHILRRY regard highly
ADEGGHIILLNT leading light
ADEGGHIINRST sight-reading
ADEGGHNORRTU gather ground
ADEGGINNORRR organ-grinder
ADEGHHHORSUW Howard Hughes
ADEGHHILLUVY highly valued
ADEGHHILNOOT in good health
ADEGHHILNORS shareholding
ADEGHHOPRRRY hydrographer
ADEGHIILNNPR philandering
ADEGHIINRRSS hairdressing
ADEGHIINRRST in this regard
ADEGHINORRST horsetrading
horse-trading
ADEGHINORRTW worth reading
ADEGHIORRTTW with regard to
ADEGHIOSTTWY go steady with
ADEGHLLNORST stranglehold
ADEGHNOPRSTU sharp-tongued
ADEGIILLMNSY misleadingly
ADEGIILLNNOT dialling tone
ADEGIILMNORZ demoralizing
ADEGIILNOOTT go into detail
ADEGIILNORSS digressional
ADEGIILNPRSY despairingly
ADEGIINNRSTU turning aside
turning-aside
ADEGIJKNNOST standing joke
ADEGIKLNRRRU regular drink
ADEGILLNORUV all-devouring
ADEGILLNORUZ lounge-lizard
ADEGILNNPRUY underplaying
ADEGILOORRTY derogatorily
ADEGIMNNOPPR name-dropping
ADEGINOPRRWW drawing power
ADEGINORSTUU Auguste Rodin
ADEGIOPPRSSS spread gossip
ADEGLNNOORUU lounge around
ADEGNOOORSTU stooge around
ADEHHIIRSTVW ravished with
ADEHHILLPPSU philadelphus
ADEHHINNORTY hither and yon
ADEHHINORTTW Edith Wharton
ADEHHIOOTTVW have to do with
ADEHHIRRSTTW thitherwards
ADEHHIRRSTWW whitherwards
ADEHHNNOOSSW show one's hand
ADEHHOPRRTYY hydrotherapy
ADEHIIIMRSTT mithridatise

ADEHIIIMRTTZ	mithridatize
ADEHIILNSTTT	dilettantish
ADEHIIMMNSSU	his name is mud
ADEHIIMNORSS	disharmonise
ADEHIIMNORSZ	disharmonize
ADEHIIORSSTU	disauthorise
ADEHIIORSTUZ	disauthorize
ADEHIJLOPSUU	Philo Judaeus
ADEHIKLMNNOY	milk and honey
ADEHIKLMRTUW	Kurt Waldheim
ADEHIKNORSSW	whiskerandos
ADEHILLOORWY	woolly-haired
ADEHILMNOPSU	sulphonamide
ADEHILMNORSU	malnourished
ADEHILMNSWWY	Wyndham Lewis
ADEHILNOPRRT	Harold Pinter
ADEHILOTTUWY	without delay
ADEHIMMNNNOS	Hammond Innes
ADEHIMMNNOST	admonishment
ADEHIMNOOSST	Thomas Edison
ADEHINNQSUUV	unvanquished
ADEHINOORSSS	hors de saison
ADEHINORTUUZ	unauthorized
ADEHINQRRSTU	hindquarters
ADEHIOOPRSTT	orthopaedist
ADEHKNNOORTV	overhand knot
ADEHLLNOOSTW	Shetland wool
ADEHLLOSUUXY	Aldous Huxley
ADEHLMMNOTYY	Tommy Handley
ADEHLMNNOSUY	unhandsomely
ADEHLNNOPSTY	Shetland pony
ADEHLOORSVWY	hold sway over
ADEHMORRRTTU	Morte d'Arthur
ADEHNNOPPTUU	on the up and up
ADEHOORRRTVW	Trevor Howard
ADEIIILMNOTT	delimitation
ADEIIIMNOPTT	monti di pietà
ADEIIIMNOSTV	deviationism
ADEIIINNORRV	vin ordinaire
ADEIIINOSTTV	deviationist
ADEIIINSTTTU	attitudinise
ADEIIINTTTUZ	attitudinize
ADEIIKKLNTTY	take it kindly
ADEIILLMNORY	meridionally
ADEIILLNPRUV	Liverpudlian
ADEIILMNOSVY	Emily Davison
ADEIILMNSTTT	dilettantism
ADEIILNNORTY	inordinately
ADEIILNOOPST	depositional
	despoliation
ADEIILNOPRTV	providential
ADEIILNORSST	dilatoriness
ADEIILQSSSTU	liquid assets
ADEIILSSSUVY	dissuasively
ADEIIMMNNRSU	Indian summer
ADEIIMMNOORT	immoderation
ADEIIMNNNOOT	denomination
ADEIIMNNOORT	in moderation
ADEIIMNNOPRT	Piet Mondrian
ADEIIMNNORSW	neo-Darwinism
ADEIIMNNOSTU	mountainside

ADEIIMNNRSTT	distrainment
ADEIIMNOPRST	postmeridian
ADEIIMNORSST	disseminator
ADEIINNNNRRU	Indian runner
ADEIINNOPSST	dispensation
ADEIINNORRSS	ordinariness
ADEIINNORSTW	neo-Darwinist
ADEIINORRSVY	diversionary
ADEIINORSSTT	dissertation
ADEIINOSTTUV	adventitious
ADEIIOOOPRST	radioisotope
ADEIKKLNOTTY	take kindly to
ADEIKNNORRTU	tinker around
ADEILLLNOOSY	solenoidally
ADEILLLNRTUY	ill-naturedly
ADEILLLORRSV	silver dollar
ADEILLNOOTVY	devotionally
ADEILLNPRTUY	prudentially
ADEILLPPRSSY	lady's slipper
	lady's-slipper
ADEILMNNOORY	Leonard Nimoy
ADEILMORSSTT	artist's model
ADEILNNORSWW	Andrew Wilson
ADEILNOOPPTU	depopulation
ADEIMMOPRSUY	praseodymium
ADEIMNNOORTW	Andrew Motion
ADEIMOOPRSTZ	spermatozoid
ADEINNOORSSZ	senza sordino
ADEINNSSSTTW	witness stand
ADEJLORSSSTU	loss adjuster
ADEKLNNOORRZ	Konrad Lorenz
ADEKMNNOORUY	monkey around
ADELLMMORSTY	troll-my-dames
ADELLMOOSSWY	Oswald Mosley
ADELLNORSSUY	slanderously
ADELLORSTUUY	adulterously
ADELOPPRSSUW	slope upwards
ADEMNOORRSTT	demonstrator
ADEMOPRRSSTU	superstardom
ADENNORSSTUW	untowardness
ADENOOPRSSSW	pass one's word
ADFFGIILNNTU	fault-finding
ADFGGINOORRW	going forward
ADFGHINPSTTU	stand-up fight
ADFGHOOPRRTU	draught-proof
ADFGIILLNRYZ	flying lizard
ADFGINOORTUW	out of drawing
ADFHIMNOOORU	maid of honour
ADFHIMORRTWW	withdraw from
ADFHINOORRRS	Harrison Ford
ADFHMNOOOTTU	foot-and-mouth
ADFHNOORRSTU	rush to and fro
ADFIIILNOTUZ	fluidization
ADFIIIOOPRRZ	Porfirio Díaz
ADFIILOSSTUY	fastidiously
ADFIMNNOOOTT	not of a mind to
ADGGGILNNORU	Grand Guignol
ADGGHIILNOOT	in a good light
ADGGHIKLNSTY	Gladys Knight
ADGGIIMNNORZ	gormandizing
ADGGIINNNOOS	a good innings

ADGGILNNNOST	long-standing
ADGHHIIRRSTU	Irish Draught
ADGHIIMMNSST	Midnight Mass
ADGHIINNSTTW	withstanding
ADGHIINRSTWY	dirty washing
ADGHIKLNORSW	world-shaking
ADGHILLLMNOS	smallholding
ADGHINORSTTW	straight down
ADGHINPRSTTU	stand upright
ADGHLMNOOPUY	Plough Monday
ADGHLNNOORST	long-and-short
ADGIIIIMNNTT	intimidating
ADGIIIINOTTZ	digitization
ADGIIIMNOSSS	misdiagnosis
ADGIILLNNOTU	longitudinal
ADGIILNNPRST	landing-strip
ADGIINOPPRSV	disapproving
ADGIKNNORRRU	roaring drunk
ADGIKNOOOPRS	Goodison Park
ADGILLNNTUUY	undulatingly
ADGILNNOSTUY	astoundingly
ADGIMNNOOOST	Santo Domingo
ADGINNNNPRUU	up and running
ADGLLLNOSUUY	glandulously
ADGLNNOORTUW	long-drawn-out
ADGMNOOORSTW	go down a storm
ADHHIOPRSTTY	hydropathist
ADHIILMNOPRU	dolphinarium
ADHIIMOPRSST	diastrophism
ADHIINOOPRST	radiophonist
ADHILLNOORSW	Harold Wilson
ADHILLNOSTUY	outlandishly
ADHILMMOTUYY	holiday tummy
ADHILOPRSUYY	your ladyship
ADHLLOPSSUYY	dasyphyllous
ADHLMNOOORST	hold to ransom
ADIIIIMNNOTT	intimidation
ADIIIINNOTVZ	divinization
ADIIILLMRSSY	dissimilarly
ADIIILLNOSTT	distillation
ADIIILMORSST	dissimilar to
ADIIIMNORTTY	intimidatory
ADIIINORSTTT	traditionist
ADIIKLLNRSSU	Kuril Islands
ADIILLMOPRRY	primordially
ADIILLNOSSUY	sinusoidally
ADIILLNRSTUY	industrially
ADIILMNOPRST	palindromist
ADIILMORSSTU	dissimulator
ADIILNORSTTU	stridulation
ADIILNOSTTUU	latitudinous
ADIIOPSSTTUU	disputatious
ADILLLLOOPPY	lollipop lady
ADILLMNOOOPY	monopodially
ADILLNRSTTUY	stridulantly
ADILLOORSTUY	idolatrously
ADILNOPPSTUY	put on display
ADILORRSTTUY	stridulatory
ADILORSSSTUY	disastrously
ADIMMNNOORSW	Norman Wisdom
ADINNRSTTTUW	twist and turn
ADINOOPRRUVY	Yuri Andropov
ADLLNOOORTUY	Royal Doulton
AEEEEELMNSSV	levée en masse
AEEEEGHHITVV	give the heave
AEEEEGHLPRST	telegraphese
AEEEEGINRRTV	regenerative
AEEEEGMPRRSV	game preserve
AEEEEGNNRRSW	Arsene Wenger
AEEEEGNNRRTU	unregenerate
AEEEEHHKLTTW	take the wheel
AEEEEHNOSTYY	easy on the eye
AEEEEHNSSSTV	the Seven Seas
AEEEEIIPRSTT	tapsieteerie
AEEEEKLNNNOV	on an even keel
AEEEEKNOPTUY	keep an eye out
AEEEELPRRSSS	press release
AEEEFFHPRRST	Peter Shaffer
AEEEFFILMNTY	effeminately
AEEEFFKMMORR	make free from
AEEEFGIINNRT	retaining fee
AEEEFGIOSSTT	state of siege
AEEEFGLNNORS	range oneself
AEEEFHHIRTTW	white feather
AEEEFHHLOSTT	at the heels of
AEEEFHHOSTUV	have the use of
AEEEFHIKMRTW	make free with
AEEEFHILOTTY	tail of the eye
AEEEFHINRRRS	air-freshener
AEEEFHINRRTT	thereinafter
AEEEFHINRSST	featheriness
AEEEFHLMOPRT	Temple of Hera
AEEEFHLNNOTV	have none left
AEEEFHPRRTVY	fever therapy
AEEEFIKLNPTT	palette knife
AEEEFILNPRRT	preferential
AEEEFILPRSTT	repeat itself
AEEEFIMNRTTV	fermentative
AEEEFKOPRSST	for pete's sake
AEEEFLMNOSSU	amuse oneself
AEEEFLMNSSSS	selfsameness
AEEEFLNOOSST	feel one's oats
AEEEFLNRSSSS	fearlessness
AEEEFNOSSSTT	sense of taste
AEEEGGHLNSTT	snaggleteeth
AEEEGGINNRRT	regenerating
AEEEGGINRRST	steering gear
AEEEGGNRSTUY	get a guernsey
AEEEGHHKSSTT	get the shakes
AEEEGHINNNRT	enheartening
AEEEGHNPRSST	The Passenger
AEEEGHNRRSVY	Henry Segrave
AEEEGIKLNNNW	Wankel engine
AEEEGILNNPSS	palingeneses
AEEEGILNOPPT	people-eating
AEEEGILNOPTV	negative pole
AEEEGILNPRRU	Paule Régnier
AEEEGILTTVVY	vegetatively
AEEEGIMNRRTT	René Magritte
AEEEGINNORRT	regeneration
AEEEGINNSSTV	negativeness
AEEEGIRRSTTV	tergiversate

AEEEGKMNORSY	grease monkey
AEEEGLLNSSTT	tassel-gentle
AEEEGLMNNNTT	entanglement
AEEEGMMNORTT	magnetometer
AEEEGMNNRRSS	messenger RNA
AEEEGMNNRSTT	estrangement
AEEEGMNOPRSU	pergameneous
AEEEGMORRRSS	error message
AEEEGNORRRTY	regeneratory
AEEEGNRRSTTW	Great Western
AEEEHHIRSTVW	share the view
AEEEHHMNNRSS	Hermann Hesse
AEEEHHMNOOSV	have one's home
AEEEHHORSTVW	have the worse
AEEEHIKNRSTT	take the reins
AEEEHILMPRTY	ephemerality
AEEEHILNNSSV	heavenliness
AEEEHIMNNOPP	epiphenomena
AEEEHIMORTTV	movie theatre
AEEEHINPPRSV	apprehensive
AEEEHINPRSST	parenthesise
AEEEHINPRSTZ	parenthesize
AEEEHINRRTTW	interwreathe
AEEEHKMMNOOS	make one's home
AEEEHLMNSTTY	the last enemy
AEEEHLMOORTV	leave the room
AEEEHLORSTUX	heterosexual
AEEEHMNRTTTT	the treatment
AEEEHNORSSTT	Eratosthenes
AEEEHQRRRTTU	three-quarter
AEEEHRSTTTTW	test the water
AEEEIIKLLMNN	Melanie Klein
AEEEIILMNRRS	remineralise
AEEEIILMNRRZ	remineralize
AEEEIILMPRTT	temperalitie
AEEEIILNPRTX	experiential
AEEEIILRSTVZ	relative size
AEEEIKLMNOPS	make one's pile
AEEEIKMNOSTT	take one's time
AEEEILLNPRTT	interpellate
AEEEILLQTUVY	leave quietly
AEEEILMNPRTX	experimental
AEEEILMNRTTY	intemerately
AEEEILNRSSTV	relativeness
AEEEILNRTTVY	inveterately
AEEEILOPRSTZ	Zola Pieterse
AEEEIMNRRTUV	remunerative
AEEEIMORSTTV	overestimate
AEEEINNRRSTT	entertainers
AEEEINOQRTTU	requite atone
AEEEINPRTTVV	preventative
AEEEIPRRSTVV	preservative
AEEEKLRRSTTW	streetwalker
	street-walker
AEEELLLLNOTW	let well alone
AEEELLLMRSUW	Samuel Weller
AEEELLORSSSV	sell overseas
AEEELMNNSSSS	namelessness
AEEELMNORSYY	eleemosynary
AEEELNOOSSST	lose one's seat
AEEEMMNRSSTU	measurements
AEEEMNNPPRSW	newspapermen
AEEEMNNSTTTW	New Testament
AEEEMNORSSTT	eat one's terms
AEEEMNRSSSST	reassessment
AEEFFFIKLNRU	in a kerfuffle
AEEFFFLOORRS	offer for sale
AEEFFGHIRRTU	father-figure
AEEFFHHIKTTT	take the Fifth
AEEFFHKOORST	for the sake of
AEEFFHORSSTT	soft feathers
AEEFGGHHNOTT	get the hang of
AEEFGGINNORT	foreign agent
AEEFGHHNOOUV	have enough of
AEEFGIILNNRV	never-failing
AEEFGIKRRSTU	figure skater
AEEFGILLNPSS	self-pleasing
AEEFGIORRRRT	refrigerator
AEEFGLNORSUX	Alex Ferguson
AEEFGLNRSSTU	gratefulness
AEEFHHINOPST	in the shape of
AEEFHHMORRTT	from the heart
AEEFHIIKPRTW	keep fair with
AEEFHIILNRTT	left in the air
AEEFHIKNRSSS	freakishness
AEEFHILNNPRS	Ralph Fiennes
AEEFHIOORRST	raise the roof
AEEFHKLOORTT	take the floor
AEEFHKMMOPRR	keep from harm
AEEFHLLMOPRT	platform heel
AEEFHLLOOSTW	follow the sea
AEEFHLMNSSSU	shamefulness
AEEFHLMORRTW	flame-thrower
AEEFHLOOSTTT	athlete's foot
AEEFHOOPRRTW	weatherproof
AEEFHORSTTTU	fourth estate
AEEFIIILMPPRR	preamplifier
AEEFIIILNORTT	interfoliate
AEEFIINQRRTU	inquire after
AEEFIKLLMOTT	make little of
AEEFIKLNNSTY	Stanley knife®
AEEFIKMMORTT	take it from me
AEEFIKNNNRST	Frankenstein
AEEFILNSSSTW	false witness
AEEFILOPRRUW	power failure
AEEFIMNNORTT	fermentation
AEEFINNORSTT	fenestration
AEEFIORSTUVY	of easy virtue
AEEFJLLLRRWY	Jerry Falwell
AEEFJORRRSTY	Jay Forrester
AEEFKLNORRSS	Frank Loesser
AEEFKMOORRTV	take over from
AEEFKNNORSSS	forsakenness
AEEFLLNOPPSY	apply oneself
AEEFLLNSSSSW	flawlessness
AEEFLMNORSTT	man of letters
AEEFLNOORSSY	Alfonso Reyes
AEEFLNSSSTTU	tastefulness
AEEFLNSSSTUW	wastefulness
AEEFMNNORSTY	means of entry
AEEFMOORRTTY	Treaty of Rome
AEEFNNORTTUV	enfant trouvé

AEEFNOPRRSTT	foster parent
AEEFOSSTTUUZ	Statue of Zeus
AEEGGGGHHILL	higgle-haggle
AEEGGGILNOTW	get a wiggle on
AEEGGGLLOPRU	George Gallup
AEEGGHHNORTT	hang together
AEEGGHIINRTW	agreeing with
AEEGGHNOOSTT	go on the stage
AEEGGIINNOSS	angiogenesis
AEEGGIINNSTV	negative sign
AEEGGIJJLLNN	jingle-jangle
AEEGGILLMMNN	mingle-mangle
AEEGGILOPTUV	give a leg up to
AEEGGILRSSVY	aggressively
AEEGGIMMNOST	geomagnetism
AEEGGIMORSTU	mortise gauge
AEEGGINNTTTW	wetting agent
AEEGGINORSST	Saint George's
AEEGGINRSSUV	unaggressive
AEEGGIQRRRSU	square-rigger
AEEGGMNRRTTU	nutmeg grater
AEEGGNOOPRTT	George Patton
AEEGHHIINSTV	heave in sight
AEEGHHIKNTTW	wake the night
AEEGHHILNRTT	the real thing
AEEGHHIMNRTT	The Nightmare
AEEGHHJNNOOT	Johann Goethe
AEEGHHNOPRRT	ethnographer
AEEGHILLNRSY	Early English
AEEGHILNOPSU	leaping-house
AEEGHILNORTW	watering-hole
AEEGHILORRUV	heliogravure
AEEGHILPRSTT	telegraphist
AEEGHINOPSST	pathogenesis
AEEGHINOPSTT	get into shape
AEEGHIPRSSTW	stage whisper
AEEGHLMNNORV	Hermann Vogel
AEEGHLNNOORV	no longer have
AEEGHLNOPRSY	selenography
AEEGHMNOPRRS	phrasemonger
AEEGHMOORSTU	heterogamous
AEEGHNOPRRST	stenographer
AEEGHNOPSSTT	step on the gas
AEEGHOPPRRRR	reprographer
AEEGHOPRRSTY	stereography
AEEGHORSSTTU	argue the toss
AEEGIIILLMTT	illegitimate
AEEGIIILNRRV	Virginia reel
AEEGIIKLNNPW	Lake Winnipeg
AEEGIILLMTTY	legitimately
AEEGIILMNORS	mineralogise
AEEGIILMNORZ	mineralogize
AEEGIINNNRTT	entertaining
AEEGIINORRTV	reinvigorate
AEEGIJLMRSTU	Jules Maigret
AEEGIJLNNTUY	Jean Tinguely
AEEGIJMMRSVY	Jimmy Greaves
AEEGIJNNRTUV	rejuvenating
AEEGIKLLNPSW	sleepwalking
AEEGIKLNSTTW	sweet-talking
AEEGIKMNPRRT	parking meter
AEEGIKMORSST	Great Smokies
AEEGIKNRSTUY	key signature
AEEGILLLMNNS	Nigel Mansell
AEEGILLLNPST	selling plate
AEEGILNNNOPR	open learning
AEEGILNNPRST	single parent
AEEGILNNRTTY	entreatingly
AEEGILOOOSTV	give a loose to
AEEGIMNNOSTT	segmentation
AEEGIMOPPSTT	stoppage time
AEEGIMPRSSST	Mistress Page
AEEGINNNSSSU	sanguineness
AEEGINNRTUVV	Ivan Turgenev
AEEGINOPRRRT	peregrinator
AEEGJLNORTYY	enjoy greatly
AEEGKMNORRST	make stronger
AEEGKMOPRRSS	make progress
AEEGKNOORSTU	keratogenous
AEEGKNRTWYYZ	Wayne Gretzky
AEEGLLMNOOPR	prolegomenal
AEEGLLMNRUWZ	mangel-wurzel
AEEGLLPRRSSY	press gallery
AEEGLMNNORTV	governmental
AEEGMMNORTTY	magnetometry
AEEGNORRSTTY	Sergeant Troy
AEEHHHILNSTY	heathenishly
AEEHHHINOPTV	have on the hip
AEEHHILOPRTY	heliotherapy
AEEHHIMNPRSW	New Hampshire
AEEHHIMPRRTY	hyperthermia
AEEHHLMPRRTY	hyperthermal
AEEHHLORRSTT	health resort
AEEHHLOSSTTW	steal the show
AEEHHNNOPSVY	shove ha'penny
AEEHHNORRTUY	Henry Thoreau
AEEHIIKNSSST	kinaesthesis
AEEHIILMOPST	epitheliomas
AEEHIIMNRSST	Henri Matisse
AEEHIINNOPRT	in the open air
AEEHIJKRRTTT	Keith Jarrett
AEEHIKLMOTVW	make love with
AEEHIKLRSTVY	The Valkyries
AEEHIKMNORTT	Mike Atherton
AEEHIKNPPPRT	The Pink Paper
AEEHILLMNNPS	Panhellenism
AEEHILLNNOTY	lay on the line
AEEHILLNNPST	Panhellenist
AEEHILMMNRST	Simmenthaler
AEEHILMSSTTW	steam whistle
AEEHILNOORSS	lose one's hair
AEEHILNRSSSS	hairlessness
AEEHILNSSSTT	stealthiness
AEEHILOPRTTV	private hotel
AEEHILPRSTUW	with pleasure
AEEHILSTUVXY	exhaustively
AEEHIMNOPRTZ	promethazine
AEEHIMOPRSSV	overemphasis
AEEHINNOPPRS	apprehension
AEEHINPRSTVY	Pythian verse
AEEHIOPPSTTV	stovepipe hat
AEEHIORRRRST	hair restorer

AEEHIPRRSTTW	weather strip
AEEHIPRSSTTX	sex therapist
AEEHKKNOOOST	take one's hook
AEEHKMNOPTTU	put the make on
AEEHLLMMORWY	yellowhammer
AEEHLLMNNOPY	phenomenally
AEEHLLMNNOTT	Lotte Lehmann
AEEHLLMORTXY	exothermally
AEEHLLMPPSSU	Samuel Phelps
AEEHLMNRSSSS	harmlessness
AEEHLMORSTTW	Tower Hamlets
AEEHLNNRSTYY	Henry Stanley
AEEHLNOPRTTU	upon the alert
AEEHLNOPRTUY	polyurethane
AEEHLNRRSTTW	Walther Nerst
AEEHLOPRSTTY	heteroplasty
AEEHLORRSTTU	rule the roast
AEEHMMOOPRST	metamorphose
AEEHMNNOPRTY	hymenopteran
AEEHMNORRTTU	mother nature
AEEHMOPRSTTU	The Mousetrap
AEEHMORSSTUV	harvest mouse
AEEHNNORRSTT	north-eastern
AEEHNOOPRSST	epanorthoses
AEEHNORRSTWY	Wayne Shorter
AEEHNORSSTTU	south-eastern
AEEHNRRSTTUU	treasure hunt
AEEHOPRRSSTT	stratosphere
AEEIIKLLLRRS	serial killer
AEEIIKLMNNNR	in like manner
AEEIILLLRTTY	illiterately
AEEIILLMSTWW	sweet william
AEEIILLNPPSU	uillean pipes
AEEIILLNPSTT	pestilential
AEEIILLRRTVY	irrelatively
AEEIILMPRTVY	imperatively
AEEIILNNPRTY	perenniality
AEEIILNNRSUV	leave in ruins
AEEIILNRSSTU	Arne Tiselius
AEEIILNRSSUV	universalise
AEEIILNRSTUY	uniseriately
AEEIILNRSUVZ	universalize
AEEIILOPTTVX	exploitative
AEEIILPRSTVV	Private Lives
AEEIIMNSSSTW	Siamese twins
AEEIINNPRTTY	penitentiary
AEEIINNRRTTU	intrauterine
AEEIIPRTTUVV	vituperative
AEEIJKMNNRSS	James Skinner
AEEIJLOPRTVY	pejoratively
AEEIJMMOPRRS	major premise
AEEIJNNORTUV	rejuvenation
AEEIKLOPRRSU	Lake Superior
AEEIKLPQSTUY	speak quietly
AEEIKMNNSSST	mistakenness
AEEIKMNOQSTU	make question
AEEIKNNOSSSV	save one's skin
AEEILLLLTVYY	tilley-valley
AEEILLLSTUVY	televisually
AEEILLMNRTTT	ill-treatment
AEEILLNNPSTY	septennially
AEEILLNNSTTY	sententially
AEEILLNOSSTT	tessellation
AEEILLNOSSTV	volatileness
AEEILLNPRSTY	presentially
AEEILLNQSTUY	sequentially
AEEILLNQTUVY	equivalently
AEEILLNRRSTT	interstellar
AEEILLNRRTVY	irrelevantly
AEEILLORTTTU	retail outlet
AEEILLTTTTTT	tittle-tattle
AEEILMNNNRSS	mannerliness
AEEILMNRSSST	masterliness
AEEILMQRRRTU	quarter-miler
AEEILNNNOSST	non-essential
AEEILNNOPRUX	E Annie Proulx
AEEILNNPSSSS	painlessness
AEEILNNRTTUY	lieutenantry
AEEILNNSSSUU	unsensualise
AEEILNNSSUUZ	unsensualize
AEEILNOQTTUV	equivalent to
AEEILNPRRRST	laser printer
AEEILNRTTTUX	intertextual
AEEILPPRRSTU	pleasure trip
AEEILPRSSUVY	persuasively
AEEILPRTTUVY	reputatively
AEEIMMNRSSTU	immatureness
AEEIMMNRSTTT	mistreatment
AEEIMMRRTTXX	mixter-maxter
AEEIMNNOORSY	raise money on
AEEIMNNORRTU	remuneration
AEEIMNORRTTX	exterminator
AEEIMNORRTUV	ruminate over
AEEINNNOPRSS	insane person
AEEINNOPRSTT	presentation
AEEINNOPSSTT	state pension
AEEINNPRRRTU	intrapreneur
AEEINOOPRTTV	not operative
AEEINOORTTTX	extortionate
AEEINOPPRRTT	perpetration
AEEINOPPRTTU	perpetuation
AEEINOPPSSST	appositeness
AEEINOPRRSTV	preservation
AEEINORRRSVY	reversionary
AEEINORRSSTV	reservations
AEEINORRSTVX	extraversion
AEEINPRRSSTX	express train
AEEINPRSTUXY	Saint-Exupéry
AEEINRSSTTTV	transvestite
AEEINRSTTTUV	sternutative
AEEIPPRRTTTT	pitter-patter
AEEKKLOOOPTU	keep a lookout
AEEKLLNNUVWY	walk unevenly
AEEKLLORRRST	roller-skater
AEEKLLORSTWY	yellow streak
AEEKLMOPSSUV	speak volumes
AEEKLNNNOSST	talk nonsense
AEEKMORRSSTT	masterstroke
AEEKNNORSTTU	take one's turn
AEELLLMNOTVY	malevolently
AEELLLNOPSWY	Naples-yellow
AEELLMNPPSTU	supplemental

AEELLNOORTTW	allow to enter
AEELLPRRSSYY	prayerlessly
AEELMMNORTUY	emolumentary
AEELMNPRRSTU	premenstrual
AEELMORRSSTU	somersaulter
AEELMSSSTUWY	sweet alyssum
AEELNORRRSTU	sale or return
AEELNORSTUXY	extraneously
AEELNRRSSTVY	transversely
AEELOPRSTUUV	superovulate
AEELORRSTTVY	travesty role
AEELQSSTTUUY	statuesquely
AEEMNOORTUUV	outmanoeuvre
AEEMNORRRTUY	remuneratory
AEEMOPRRSTUY	temporary use
AEEMORRSSTWY	Rosemary West
AEENNOOOPRST	open to reason
AEENNOPRRSTU	neuropterans
AEENNORSSSUV	ravenousness
AEENNOSSSSUU	nauseousness
AEENNPPRTTYY	a pretty penny
AEENOPRSSSTT	statesperson
AEENORRSSTXY	extrasensory
	extra-sensory
AEENORRSTTUY	treasury note
AEEOQRRSSTTU	sequestrator
AEEORRRTTTUW	water torture
AEFFFGILNORY	Fear of Flying
AEFFGGHIINNY	hang in effigy
AEFFGNOOORTU	out of range of
AEFFHILNSSTU	faithfulness
AEFFHNOORTTT	at the front of
AEFFIILMNRST	fireman's lift
AEFFIKLMRTUU	make fruitful
AEFFILNOSTUX	exsufflation
AEFFILRRSSTU	first refusal
AEFFINNORSTY	fry in one's fat
AEFFLLOORTTU	all-out effort
AEFFMMOORRTT	matter of form
AEFGGGILNOPR	leap-frogging
AEFGGHINORRT	forgathering
AEFGHHOORRTU	thoroughfare
AEFGHHOORTTU	aforethought
AEFGHHORTTTU	afterthought
AEFGHIINNORS	refashioning
AEFGHIINRRTT	freight-train
AEFGHIKNORST	for the asking
AEFGIILRTUVY	figuratively
AEFGIINNRRTZ	fraternizing
AEFGIINPPSWW	wife-swapping
AEFGIKLMNOST	king of metals
AEFGIKLNOORT	looking after
	looking-after
AEFGILLMNNUY	meaningfully
AEFGILLNORST	forestalling
AEFGILLNRTTY	flatteringly
AEFGILLNSSUW	wineglassful
AEFGILLOPRTY	profligately
AEFGILMNOORT	for a long time
AEFGILMNOPSU	go up in flames
AEFGILNNRTTU	unflattering
AEFGILNOOQTU	equal footing
AEFGILNRSSTT	self-starting
AEFGILOOOPRZ	apologize for
AEFGIMNNORRT	morning after
AEFGINNNRRTU	running after
AEFGINNOPRTU	put a finger on
AEFGINOOPRSS	song of praise
AEFGINOOPRTT	potato finger
AEFGLLNRTUUY	ungratefully
AEFGLLORRUUW	augur well for
AEFHHIINNOST	in the fashion
AEFHHINOOSSU	fashion house
AEFHIILPRTWY	play with fire
AEFHIKLNRTTW	Frank Whittle
AEFHIKMOORTT	make it hot for
AEFHIMMORTTT	from that time
AEFHINOOPTTT	at the point of
AEFHKKOOOSST	Sea of Okhotsk
AEFHKLMORSST	Thermos® flask
AEFHKLNNSSTU	thankfulness
AEFHLLNOSSTU	loathfulness
AEFHLNRSSTUW	wrathfulness
AEFHNOPRRSTU	turn of phrase
AEFHOOPRRSTT	shatterproof
AEFIIILMNSST	semifinalist
AEFIIILNORTW	lie in wait for
AEFIIIMNNSTT	anti-feminist
AEFIIKNNOPTT	at knife-point
AEFIILLMORTW	water milfoil
AEFIILNOOPRT	perfoliation
AEFIIMNNNOTT	infotainment
AEFIKLLNNOOR	Keiron Fallon
AEFILLMPRSTT	splatter film
AEFILMMNNOOT	monofilament
AEFILMNRSTUY	it's my funeral
AEFILNNRSTUU	sinful nature
AEFILNOOPRSS	professional
AEFILNRRSSTT	transfer list
AEFILOOPRRSS	professorial
AEFILOPRRSTT	self-portrait
AEFIMNNORRST	frontiersman
AEFINNOOPRSS	for one's pains
AEFINNRRTUUV	furniture van
AEFINOORTUVV	vote in favour
AEFIOPPPRRST	paper profits
AEFLLMNORSTU	small fortune
AEFLLNNSSUUW	unlawfulness
AEFLMNNOORRW	Norman Fowler
AEFLMNOOPRYY	play for money
AEFLNOOPSSTU	teaspoonfuls
AEFLOPPRSTUU	put up for sale
AEFMNNOORRST	Norman Foster
AEFMNOOPRSSU	famous person
AEFOOPPRRSTU	a supporter of
AEFOQRRSTTUU	Four Quartets
AEGGGILNRSTY	staggeringly
AEGGGILNRSWY	swaggeringly
AEGGGIMNOTTU	Montague Tigg
AEGGHHIILNTV	health-giving
AEGGHIINNOTW	weighing a ton
AEGGHILNNOOS	hanging loose

AEGGHILNOTTW	get along with
AEGGHINNOSTY	Anything Goes
AEGGHINNRSTT	gain strength
AEGGHIOORSTU	South Georgia
AEGGHIPPRRTY	trigger-happy
AEGGHLNOOSTT	snaggletooth
AEGGHOOOPRYZ	zoogeography
AEGGIIILNNRV	Virginia Leng
AEGGIJMNRSUU	measuring jug
AEGGILORRSUY	gregariously
AEGGIMNNORRW	warmongering
	war-mongering
AEGGINNPRSSS	graspingness
AEGHHHMOSSTU	Thomas Hughes
AEGHHIIKNNRR	higher in rank
AEGHHILOPRRT	lithographer
AEGHHIPRSUWY	superhighway
AEGHHMOPRRTY	thermography
AEGHHOOPPRRT	photographer
AEGHHOOPRRRT	orthographer
AEGHIIILRTVW	give it a whirl
AEGHIIKLNNTY	like anything
AEGHIIKLRSTT	strike a light!
AEGHIILLNTTV	having little
AEGHIILMNSST	almightiness
AEGHIILNSTTY	hesitatingly
AEGHIINNSTTU	unhesitating
AEGHIINOPRTU	go up in the air
AEGHIKLORRSY	Arshile Gorky
AEGHIKLORSWY	Whisky Galore
AEGHIKNNRRTT	knight-errant
AEGHILLPRSTU	sugar the pill
AEGHILLQTUUY	laugh quietly
AEGHILMNNOSW	Englishwoman
AEGHILOOPSTT	hepatologist
AEGHILQRRTTU	quarterlight
AEGHIMMNORTU	hammering-out
AEGHIMNNNORU	running a home
AEGHIMNORSUW	housewarming
	house-warming
AEGHIMNORTTV	Gherman Titov
AEGHIMOPRSSY	seismography
AEGHINOPRRSW	power-sharing
AEGHINPRSTTU	straighten up
AEGHINRSSSTT	straightness
AEGHIORSTTTV	vote straight
AEGHKMORRTTW	growth market
AEGHLLOOSTTW	go to the walls
AEGHLMOORTUY	rheumatology
AEGHLORSSTUU	slaughterous
AEGHNOOPPRRR	pornographer
AEGHOPPRRTUY	group therapy
AEGHOPPSSYYZ	zygapophyses
AEGIIIILTTTV	vitilitigate
AEGIIIKLNNPS	Alpine skiing
AEGIIILNRTVZ	revitalizing
AEGIIINNPRSW	awe-inspiring
AEGIIINRSTVW	West Virginia
AEGIIKLMNSSY	Kingsley Amis
AEGIILLMRRTY	Terry Gilliam
AEGIILLNNOTW	Wellingtonia
AEGIILLNPRVY	prevailingly
AEGIILMNOPRT	primogenital
AEGIILMNORST	mineralogist
AEGIILNNNSSU	ungainliness
AEGIILNNORTU	urinogenital
AEGIILNNRTUZ	neutralizing
AEGIILNPPSTY	appetisingly
AEGIILNPPTYZ	appetizingly
AEGIILNPRSTT	ear-splitting
AEGIILNRSTVV	vestal virgin
AEGIILRRRTUY	irregularity
AEGIIMNNOPRT	impregnation
AEGIIMNNOPTT	pigmentation
AEGIIMOPRSTV	Gram-positive
AEGIINNNRSTT	intransigent
AEGIINNOOSTT	negotiations
AEGIINNPPTUZ	unappetizing
AEGIINORRSTT	registration
AEGIINORSTTV	investigator
AEGIIOPRRSTT	prestigiator
AEGIKLNNORRW	lower-ranking
AEGILLMPRSSU	aspergillums
AEGILLMRSTTU	metallurgist
AEGILLNNPSUY	unpleasingly
AEGILMMNRSTY	stammeringly
AEGILMNNNNOT	non-alignment
AEGILMNNOQTU	magniloquent
AEGILMNRSTTY	smatteringly
AEGILNNNOSTU	sanguinolent
AEGILNNRSTTY	astringently
AEGILNNRSTUY	saunteringly
AEGILNNRUVWY	unwaveringly
AEGILNPRSSUY	use sparingly
AEGILNRRSSUY	reassuringly
AEGIMMMNNOTU	gain momentum
AEGIMNNOSTWY	money-wasting
AEGIMPPRRRST	strippergram
AEGINNORSSTU	nugatoriness
AEGINOORRRTT	interrogator
AEGINOPRSTWY	staying power
AEGLLLLNNSUY	Sally Gunnell
AEGLLMOSSSTY	all systems go
AEGLMNNPSTTU	tungsten lamp
AEGLOORSTUUY	outrageously
AEGNNOOOSWWY	go one's own way
AEGNNOORRSTT	no stranger to
AEGNORRRSSST	transgressor
AEGOOPSSTTUY	steatopygous
AEHHIILNTTWW	within the law
AEHHILLLPTWY	play hell with
AEHHILLNORTY	roll in the hay
AEHHILMMNPSS	helmsmanship
AEHHILMNORST	Othniel Marsh
AEHHILNOOPRT	in poor health
AEHHILNOPPRT	philanthrope
AEHHILOPSTTU	thiosulphate
AEHHIMNOPRSS	horsemanship
AEHHIMNORSTT	shot in the arm
AEHHINNOSTWY	Antony Hewish
AEHHIPPRTTUU	put up the hair
AEHHLMOOPSTX	exophthalmos

AEHHLMOPSTUX	exophthalmus
AEHHLMOSTUXY	Thomas Huxley
AEHHMOOSTTWY	smooth the way
AEHHNOPPRTYY	hypnotherapy
AEHHOOPRRSST	sharpshooter
AEHHOPRSSTTU	Theophrastus
AEHIIILNOPSS	hispaniolise
AEHIIILNOPSZ	hispaniolize
AEHIIKLNOSST	Thessaloníki
AEHIILLNPTTY	paint the lily
AEHIILMNPTTU	put in the mail
AEHIILNNORUV	in an evil hour
AEHIILNOPRST	relationship
AEHIILPRRSTT	hair-splitter
AEHIIMNORSTT	in a short time
AEHIIMNOTWWZ	womanize with
AEHIINNORSTW	within reason
AEHIINOPRRSS	parishioners
AEHIINRSSTUW	White Russian
AEHIINSSTTWW	with a witness
AEHIIRRSSTTW	shirtwaister
AEHIJKLSTTTU	just like that
AEHIJLLNUUXY	Julian Huxley
AEHIJLNOPSST	Joseph Stalin
AEHILLMORSTY	isothermally
AEHILLMRRRTU	Arthur Miller
AEHILMNORSTW	mothers-in-law
AEHILMNRRTTU	Martin Luther
AEHILNNOPTUV	upon the anvil
AEHILOQTTUUW	without equal
AEHIMMMOPRST	metamorphism
AEHIMMNNNOOT	man in the moon
AEHIMMNOSTTT	at this moment
AEHIMMOPSTTU	imposthumate
AEHIMNNOPPSU	one-upmanship
AEHIMNNOSSSW	womanishness
AEHIMNNOSSTT	astonishment
AEHIMNNPRSTT	transhipment
AEHIMNNQSTUV	vanquishment
AEHIMNOPRSTW	with open arms
AEHIMNOSTTUW	without means
AEHIMOOOSSST	homoeostasis
AEHIMOPPRRST	primrose path
AEHINNNOSTTT	on the instant
AEHINNOPRTTX	xanthopterin
AEHINNPPSSSS	snappishness
AEHINNQSSSTU	squash tennis
AEHINOORSTTX	exhortations
AEHINOOSSTTU	station house
AEHINPPSSSST	Spanish Steps
AEHIOOPPRSST	apostrophise
AEHIOOPPRSTZ	apostrophize
AEHIOPRRSTWY	praiseworthy
AEHJNOOPPSTX	Joseph Paxton
AEHLMNPRSUUY	superhumanly
AEHLMOOSSTWY	Thomas Wolsey
AEHLNOPRSSTU	Southern Alps
AEHLNOPSSTUY	polyanthuses
AEHMMMNOOPST	Emma Thompson
AEHMMNORRSTU	Thomas Murner
AEHMOOOPRTTT	Room at the Top
AEHNNNOOORST	no sooner than
AEHNOOPRRSSU	sarrusophone
AEHNOORSSTTW	a stone's throw
AEHNORRSSSTY	synarthroses
AEHOOPRSSSTT	pass to others
AEIIIILRSTTV	trivialities
AEIIILLLMNNZ	Liza Minnelli
AEIIILLMNTUV	illuminative
AEIIILNOPPRS	Pier Pasolini
AEIIILPRSSTU	spiritualise
AEIIILPRSTUZ	spiritualize
AEIIILRSTTTV	relativitist
AEIIIMMNSSTT	anti-Semitism
AEIIIMNNNOST	insemination
AEIIIMNORSSS	missionaries
	missionarise
AEIIIMNORSSZ	missionarize
AEIIIMNRSTTV	ministrative
AEIIINNRSTTV	intransitive
AEIIIOPPRTTV	propitiative
AEIIJMORTVWY	majority view
AEIIKKNORSSY	karyokinesis
AEIIKLNNPRVW	Rip Van Winkle
AEIILLLLMMSY	millesimally
AEIILLLMRWWY	William Wyler
AEIILLMMMORY	immemorially
AEIILLNQRSTU	tranquillise
AEIILLNQRTUZ	tranquillize
AEIILLRSTTUV	illustrative
AEIILMMNOOST	emotionalism
AEIILMNNOTVY	nominatively
AEIILMNRSSUV	universalism ❑
AEIILMNRTUVY	ruminatively
AEIILMNSTTUY	simultaneity
AEIILMPRTTTU	multipartite
AEIILMPTTUVY	imputatively
AEIILNNNQQUU	quinquennial
AEIILNNOORTT	in relation to
AEIILNNOPSTT	salient point
AEIILNOOPSTX	expositional
AEIILNOOPTTX	exploitation
AEIILNOPPSTY	inappositely
AEIILNOPTTTY	potentiality
AEIILNORSSST	solitariness
AEIILNQTTUVY	quantitively
AEIILNRSSSTW	sisters-in-law
AEIILNRSSTUV	Universalist
AEIILNRSTTVY	transitively
AEIILNRSTUVY	universality
AEIILNSTUUXY	unisexuality
AEIIMMNOORTZ	memorization
AEIIMNNOPSSX	expansionism
AEIIMNNORRTU	Mount Rainier
AEIIMNNRRSTV	Vernis Martin
AEIIMNRSSSTV	transmissive
AEIIMPPRSSTT	past its prime
AEIIMPRRSSUY	primary issue
AEIINNNORTTU	antineutrino
	anti-neutrino
AEIINNOPRSTU	resupination
AEIINNOPSSTX	expansionist

Words marked ❑ can also be spelled with an initial capital letter

AEIINOPPRRST	perspiration
AEIINOPRTTUV	vituperation
AEIINOPSSTTU	point at issue
AEIJLLNORTVY	Jayne Torvill
AEIJLMORRTUY	majority rule
AEIKMNNRSTTU	Turkmenistan
AEIKMNOQRSTU	question mark
AEIKMRSSSSTT	taskmistress
AEILLMNOPRSY	impersonally
AEILLMNPRSUU	superluminal
AEILLNNORTTY	intolerantly
AEILLNNOSTTT	to all intents
AEILLNORRTTY	torrentially
AEILLORSTTTU	to illustrate
AEILMNNOOPST	Neoplatonism
AEILMNNOSSTW	Winston-Salem
AEILMNNRSTTU	instrumental
AEILMNOOPRTT	metropolitan
AEILMNOPPRSW	Piers Plowman
AEILMNOQSUUY	equanimously
AEILMNOSSTUU	simultaneous
AEILNNOOPSTT	Neoplatonist
AEILNNQRSSTU	tranquilness
AEILNNRTTUWW	unwritten law
AEILNOOPRRSS	responsorial
AEILNOORTUVY	evolutionary
AEILNOPRRTUU	Paul Tournier
AEILNOPSSSWY	slip one's ways
AEILNPPRRTUY	Tyrian purple
AEILNPRSTTTY	strepitantly
AEILOPRSSTUU	Louis Pasteur
AEIMMOPSSTTY	symptomatise
AEIMMOPSTTYZ	symptomatize
AEIMNNNOTUWY	any minute now
AEIMNNOPPSTT	appointments
AEIMNNORSTTU	menstruation
AEIMNNORTTUY	monetary unit
AEIMNOOPRRST	impersonator
AEIMNRSSSTTV	transvestism
AEINNNORSSTT	non-resistant
AEINNOOPRSTU	put one's oar in
AEINNORSTTTU	sternutation
AEINOOPRSTTT	protestation
AEINOOPRSTTW	power station
AEINOOSSTTTU	ostentatious
AEINOPRRSTTT	train-spotter
AEIOOPPRRRTX	expropriator
AEIOPRRTTTUV	private tutor
AEKLLPPSSTUU	pull up stakes
AEKLNRRRSTUY	slurry tanker
AEKLOOPRRSTW	postal worker
AEKLOORRTTVW	travel to work
AEKNOOOPRSST	sport one's oak
AELLLMORSUVY	marvellously
AELLMMNNOTUY	monumentally
AELLMNOOOSSS	solomon's seal ❑
AELMNNOSTTUY	Mount Stanley
AELMOPSSSTTY	postal system
AELOOPRSTTUX	expostulator
AEMNNOORSSTY	stonemasonry
AEMNOOOPRSTZ	spermatozoon
AEMNOOOPRSZZ	mezzo-soprano
AEMNOORRRSTT	remonstrator
AEMOORRRSTTT	starter motor
AENOOPRSSSUV	vaporousness
AENORRSTTTUY	sternutatory
AEOOOPRRRTTU	tour operator
AFFGILNNORTY	affrontingly
AFFHILLNTUUY	unfaithfully
AFFHINOOOSTU	out of fashion
AFFIINOOPRTT	partition off
AFFIKLMORRSY	ask for firmly
AFGGHHIILNTU	highfaluting
AFGGIILNRTYY	gratifyingly
AFGHIIRSSTTT	at first sight
AFGIIKMNOPRT	profit-making
AFGIILLOSTUY	flagitiously
AFGIILNSSTYY	satisfyingly
AFGIIMNOPRRT	profit margin
AFGIINNSSTUY	unsatisfying
AFGIKNOORSTT	toasting-fork
AFGIMNNORRST	transforming
AFGIMNORRSTY	transmogrify
AFGLLNOOORSU	go on all fours
AFHIINOORTTU	out of thin air
AFHILOTTTUUW	without fault
AFHNOOORRSUW	honours of war
AFHOOOORSTTW	sawtooth roof
AFHOOOPRRSTU	author's proof
AFIIILMNNOST	inflationism
AFIIILNNORTT	infiltration
AFIIILNNOSTT	inflationist
AFIILMORSTUU	multifarious
AFIILOPRSSTT	spirit of salt
AFIINOPRSSTU	passion fruit
AFILMNOOOSTW	laws of motion
AFLNOOPPRRTU	popular front
AGGGILLNRSTY	stragglingly
AGGHHIIKNSWY	King's highway
AGGHHILMOTUW	Gough Whitlam
AGGHHMOPPRSY	sphygmograph
AGGHIIKLNPRT	parking-light
AGGHIIKNNSTV	thanksgiving
AGGHIILNNRTW	warning light
AGGHILMNNRSY	rhyming slang
AGGHILOOPRST	graphologist
AGGHINNOOSTW	what's going on
AGGHLNOOPRYY	pharyngology
AGGHLOPPRTYY	glyptography
AGGIIINNORTV	invigorating
AGGIIKLLNOOO	Nikolai Gogol
AGGIKLLNOOSS	looking-glass
AGGIKMNOORST	Magnitogorsk
AGGILMNOPRTU	promulgating
AGHHIIMNNOTU	mountain-high
AGHHILNNOOTT	nothing loath
AGHHILNOPRTT	triphthongal
AGHHINORSTTU	thrashing-out
AGHHIOPPRSYY	physiography
AGHHLORRTTUW	trawl through
AGHIIMNRSTWW	swarming with
AGHIINNOSTTW	it was nothing

AGHIINNPPRST	transhipping
AGHIINOPSTTT	in a tight spot
AGHIKLNOOPRS	sharp-looking
AGHIKNOORSTW	Hawk Roosting
AGHILLMNOPPS	shopping mall
AGHILLMRSTWY	slightly warm
AGHILLNNOORT	all-or-nothing
AGHILMNOOOOT	homologation
AGHIMNOOPRST	monographist
AGHINOORSSTT	shooting star
	shooting-star
AGHJNOSSTUUU	Augustus John
AGHLLNOOORTY	orthogonally
AGHLNOOOPRTY	anthropology
AGIIIILNNOTV	invigilation
AGIIIKLNNNTW	in a twinkling
AGIIILLMNNTU	illuminating
AGIIINNOORTV	invigoration
AGIIINNOPRTT	partitioning
AGIIKLMNSTTU	multitasking
AGIIKLNNOPTT	talking point
	talking-point
AGIILLLMNTUU	multilingual
AGIILLNNPSUU	Linus Pauling
AGIILLOPSSSS	salpiglossis
AGIILMNNOPRT	trampolining
AGIILMNNRTUY	ruminatingly
AGIILMNOOPRS	slip a mooring
AGIILNOORSUV	vainglorious
AGIKMNNOORWW	working woman
AGIKNOPRRSTW	working parts
AGIKNOPRRTWY	working party
AGIKNORRSTTW	start working
AGILMNNSSUUY	unassumingly
AGILMNOOPRTU	promulgation
AGILNNOOOPRT	prolongation
AGILNOOPSSTT	signal to stop
AGILNPRSSSUY	surpassingly
AGILOOPPRSTY	papyrologist
AGILORSTTUUY	gratuitously
AGIMNNORRSTW	storm warning
AGIMNOORSSTT	gastronomist
AGINNOOPPRTU	propugnation
AGINNOPRRSTT	transporting
AGLLMOOPSUYY	polygamously
AGLLNOORSUUY	languorously
AGMMNNOORUUV	Novum Organum
AHHILLLLSSYY	shilly-shally
AHHILNOPPRTY	philanthropy
AHIIIKLLNPPR	Philip Larkin
AHIIIKMMOSUY	Yukio Mishima
AHIIJLLMNOSW	John Williams
	William Johns
AHIIKLLMPPRS	Mark Phillips
AHIIKMNRRSTU	Krishnamurti
AHIIKNOSTTWW	know what it is
AHIILMMPRSTU	triumphalism
AHIILMPRSTTU	triumphalist
AHIIMNNOORSU	inharmonious
AHIJNNNOSTUY	Johnny Unitas
AHIKLOORTTUW	kilowatt hour

AHILLNOORTYZ	horizontally
AHILMNOORSUY	harmoniously
AHILMNPRTTUY	triumphantly
AHILNOPRSTUU	sulphuration
AHIMMNPSSTUY	Spanish tummy
AHIMMOOPSSTU	amphistomous
AHIMNNOORSUU	unharmonious
AHIMNOOPRSST	misanthropos
AHIMOOPPPSTU	hippopotamus
AHINOOOSSSST	so soon as this
AIIIIMMNNOTZ	minimization
AIIILLLNPSTU	Lilliputians
AIIILLMNNOTU	illumination
AIIILLNNOSTT	instillation
AIIILMMNORST	trinomialism
AIIILMNOOSST	isolationism
AIIILMNORSTT	trinomialist
AIIILMPRSSTU	spiritualism
AIIILNOOSSTT	isolationist
AIIILPRSSTTU	spiritualist
AIIILPRSTTUY	spirituality
AIIIMMNNOTUZ	immunization
AIIIMNNORSTT	ministration
AIIIMNOOPTTZ	optimization
AIIIMNOSSTTU	situationism
AIIINOOPPRTT	propitiation
AIIINOPRRTTT	tripartition
AIIKMNNOPRSS	parkinsonism
AIILLLNOOTVY	volitionally
AIILLLNOSUVY	villainously
AIILLLOSSTTY	solstitially
AIILLMNOORTY	monitorially
AIILLMOPRTUW	William Prout
AIILLNOOPRTU	air pollution
AIILLNORSTTU	illustration
AIILLNQRTTUY	tranquillity
AIILMNNNOOTU	mountain lion
AIILMNNORTTU	malnutrition
AIILMNOPRSTT	trampolinist
AIILNNOPRSTU	non-spiritual
AIILNOOOPPST	oppositional
AIILNOPSSTTU	stipulations
AIILNORRSSST	sinistrorsal
AIILNORRSTTY	transitorily
AIILOPRSUVVY	viviparously
AIIMNNORSSST	transmission
AIIMNOOORTTZ	motorization
AIIMNOOPRSSU	parsimonious
AIIMNOOQSTTU	misquotation
AIIOOPPRRTTY	propitiatory
AIJMNRRSTTUY	Justin Martyr
AIKLLLMMOPRS	Plimsoll mark
AIKMOPPRRUWY	Yom Kippur War
AILLMNNOOPRY	pronominally
AILLORRSTTUY	illustratory
AILMNORSTUVY	voluntaryism
AILNOOOPPRRT	proportional
AILNOPPRTUUY	unpopularity
AILOOPRRSUUY	uproariously
AILOORRSTTUY	traitorously
AIMNOOPRRSTT	port in a storm

AKMOOORSSUUY	Yamoussoukro
ALMNOOOSTUUY	autonomously
ALMOOPPRRSTU	moral support

B

BBBBBEEHLLUU	hubble-bubble
BBBCEFHIORSY	Bobby Fischer
BBBEELMMORUY	bubble memory
BBCCEEILLORY	Colley Cibber
BBCCEEILMOPU	become public
BBCCIIMRSTUU	biscuit-crumb
BBCEEEGGIMOR	become bigger
BBCEEEHQRRUU	rubber cheque
BBCEEEMNRRTU	rubber cement
BBCEEGIMNOOR	become boring
BBCEGHILNRTU	nightclubber
BBCELLLOOSWY	collywobbles
BBCENOORRSTU	bronco-buster
BBCGIILLNRSY	scribblingly
BBCGIILMNOOT	climbing-boot
BBDDELNNOTUU	Blut und Boden
BBDDGIILNOUY	body-building
BBDEEEELORTW	beetle-browed
BBDEEEFILNOY	beyond belief
BBDEEEHLNOTW	bend the elbow
BBDEEGGKLOOO	gobbledegook
BBDEEILLOORU	double boiler
BBDEELLMOOTT	bell-bottomed
BBDEGGKLOOOY	gobbledygook
	gobblydegook
BBDEGHMNOORY	hydrogen bomb
BBDEHLOOORRT	blood-brother
BBDEIIILSSUV	subdivisible
BBDEILNOORTW	Born to be Wild
BBDGIINOORTY	orbiting body
BBEEEHLLOTTW	below the belt
BBEEGGORSSTU	George Stubbs
BBEEGILLORRT	Robbe-Grillet
BBEEGMNORRUY	money-grubber
BBEEHKNOOOST	be on the books
BBEEILLMNRRY	Billy Bremner
BBEEILMMRSTU	Mister Bumble
BBEEILNORSTT	brittle bones
BBEENNNRRSUU	Bunsen burner
BBEENNORRSTU	Robert Bunsen
BBEENOOOSSTT	bet one's boots
BBEENOORRRTW	Robert Browne
BBEFIIIIKNRS	bikini briefs
BBEGILLNRSUY	slubberingly
BBEGINOORRST	Robert Gibson
BBEHINNOSSSS	snobbishness
BBEILLNOORWY	yellow ribbon
BBEILNOSSSUU	bibulousness
BBENNORSSSTU	stubbornness
BBGHIMMNOTUY	thingummybob
BCCCEIIMRRSU	circumscribe
BCCDEEELMOOR	become colder
BCCDEEIJORTT	direct object
BCCDEELMOOUY	become cloudy
BCCEEEEFIINN	beneficience
BCCEEEILLRTU	electric blue
BCCEEELNOOSS	obsolescence
BCCEEFIIOPST	to be specific
BCCEEIILNOSV	obliviscence
BCCEHHINOOPT	technophobic
BCCEHNNOOORT	corn on the cob
BCCEHNOOOPRS	bronchoscope
BCCEHORSTTTU	butterscotch
BCCEILMOORTY	motor-bicycle
BCCEILOPRSTU	public sector
BCCGIIKLMNOR	rock-climbing
BCCHILLOOPSU	public school
BCCINOOSSSUU	subconscious
BCCIOOOPRSST	stroboscopic
BCCKOORSSTTU	cross-buttock
BCDDEEEIINOS	disobedience
BCDDEEEKLORU	double-decker
BCDDEIIILTUY	deducibility
BCDEEEEKNSTW	between-decks
BCDEEEEMNORT	become tender
BCDEEEEMNRSZ	Mercedes-Benz®
BCDEEEEOPTTX	to be expected
BCDEEEFFILOO	code of belief
BCDEEEGGINST	eggs Benedict
BCDEEEHINSTY	Sidney Bechet
BCDEEFHIILNT	child benefit
BCDEEFIIKLRR	brickfielder
BCDEEFIJOSTU	bed of justice
BCDEEIIOPPRR	bodice-ripper
BCDEEILLOORR	Border collie
BCDEEILOPRRU	reproducible
BCDEEILRSTTU	destructible
BCDEEINORRSS	incrossbreed
BCDEEKLLOSTY	blocked style
BCDEELOORSUW	could be worse
BCDEGIINOPRY	body piercing
BCDEHIIMNOTW	combined with
BCDEHKNOOOST	the boondocks
BCDEIIILRTUY	reducibility
BCDEIIILNORTU	introducible
BCDEIIILNPUUZ	unpublicized
BCDEIIMORTTU	obiter dictum
BCDEILLORTTY	bitterly cold
BCDEIMOSSUUV	Deus vobiscum
BCDEINORSTUU	subintroduce
BCDELLLNOOOO	Colonel Blood
BCDENORSTTUU	unobstructed
BCDGIKLNOOSU	bloodsucking
BCDGIKNOOSTY	body stocking
BCDIIKLLQUUY	build quickly
BCEEEEEHKNRS	knee-breeches
BCEEEEFNPRRY	by preference
BCEEEEGHRRSU	cheeseburger
BCEEEEGILLNR	belligerence
BCEEEEGKLLLO	Keble College
BCEEEEIIKRSX	exercise bike
BCEEEEKMNNOO	become keen on
BCEEEFILNNTY	beneficently
BCEEEFNORRTY	enter by force
BCEEEGHILNSY	beseechingly
BCEEEGILLNRY	belligerency
BCEEEGLMNOOR	become longer

BCEEEILLMOVY	become lively
BCEEEINRSSUV	subservience
BCEEELLMMOOW	become mellow
BCEEELMOORSW	become slower
BCEEELNORTTU	electron tube
BCEEEMNOORTT	become rotten
BCEEFHILLLRU	Hell-fire Club
BCEEFILNORSS	forcibleness
BCEEGGHNORRU	Georg Büchner
BCEEGHLORTTU	club together
BCEEGIMNNOSS	becomingness
BCEEHIIKLRST	lick the birse
BCEEHILLNRSU	Brunelleschi
BCEEHLLNOSST	Stellenbosch
BCEEIIJSSTUV	subjectivise
BCEEIIJSTUVZ	subjectivize
BCEEIJLSTUVY	subjectively
BCEEIJNNOOTV	non-objective
BCEEILMNOOST	become lost in
BCEEILMNOPTT	contemptible
BCEEILMOPRSS	compressible
BCEEILOOPSTW	blow to pieces
BCEEINORRRTU	Robert Runcie
BCEEINRSSUVY	subserviency
BCEELMMORTTU	commuter belt
BCEELMNOPRUU	Melbourne Cup
BCEELRRRTTUU	butter curler
BCEFFHIIOOTX	box-office hit
BCEFFHINOSUV	bunch of fives
BCEFGIILPRUU	public figure
BCEGHIILNTWY	bewitchingly
BCEGHLOOORSU	close borough
BCEGIIILNORR	incorrigible
BCEGIKLNOSTU	bluestocking
BCEGILMNNOUY	unbecomingly
BCEHHIILLNOR	Heinrich Böll
BCEHHKOORSTU	butcher's hook
BCEHIIKLLNSY	kill by inches
BCEHIIMORSTY	biochemistry
BCEHIINOSTTY	biosynthetic
BCEHILNNNOOS	Ben Nicholson
BCEHIMOORSTW	witches' broom
BCEHIMORSTWW	West Bromwich
BCEHKKOOOOST	cook the books
BCEIIILLRTVY	civil liberty
BCEIIJMSSTUV	subjectivism
BCEIIJSSTTUV	subjectivist
BCEIILLLLMNY	Billy McNeill
BCEIILNRSTTU	instructible
BCEIINORTTUV	contributive
BCEIKNNRSUWW	New Brunswick
BCEILMNOPTTY	contemptibly
BCEILORSSTUU	tuberculosis
BCEINNNOSTTU	subcontinent
BCEINOORTTTU	contribute to
BCEIOOORSTTY	Rosie Boycott
BCELLNOOOOSW	blow one's cool
BCEMOOOPPRTT	copper-bottom
BCERRSSTTUUU	substructure
BCGHIKNOORRT	Brighton Rock
BCGIIILMNNOR	climbing iron
BCGIIILNORRY	incorrigibly
BCGIIKLLNNOO	lino blocking
BCGIILMOOORY	microbiology
BCGIILOOOOSY	sociobiology
BCGIINNORTTU	contributing
BCHHIMOOORRT	orthorhombic
BCHIIIOPSSTY	biophysicist
BCHIIIPSSSTU	ship's biscuit
BCIIKLLQTUUY	quickly built
BCIILLMOOOTY	locomobility
BCIINNOORSSU	Robin Cousins
BCIINNOORTTU	contribution
BCIINOPRSSTU	subscription
BCIKNOOOOPRS	book-scorpion
BCILMMNOSUUU	cumulonimbus
BCINOORRTTUY	contributory
BCINOORSSTTU	obstructions
BCNOOORSSTTY	bottony cross
BDDDEGILNOOW	Blood Wedding
BDDDEILMNOOY	bloody-minded
BDDEEEEFILMN	feeble-minded
BDDEEEFIMORX	of mixed breed
BDDEEEFINNRU	unbefriended
BDDEEEIMNRTY	determined by
BDDEEEINNSST	indebtedness
BDDEEEMNORYY	beyond remedy
BDDEEENORRUV	overburdened
BDDEEENRRTUY	undeterred by
BDDEEFHIORRS	Bedfordshire
BDDEEFKLLOUU	double fluked
BDDEEGGINOOR	good breeding
BDDEEHNNORTU	round the bend
BDDEEILMOSUX	mixed doubles
BDDEEILORWWW	World Wide Web
BDDEFINOORRW	bird of wonder
BDDEGHNNOORY	hydrogen bond
BDDEGILLORSY	Lloyd Bridges
BDDEHINORRSW	reddish-brown
BDDENORRSUUY	surrounded by
BDDFGIILNORY	forbiddingly
BDEEEEMMNRRU	unremembered
BDEEEFIILNNS	indefensible
BDEEEFIOOPRR	period before
BDEEEFMNOORT	forebodement
BDEEEGILLRUY	blue-eyed girl
BDEEEGLNORTU	ground beetle
BDEEEHIISTWZ	be seized with
BDEEEHINRTTT	the bitter end
BDEEEIIMNOST	bide one's time
BDEEEIIRSVWY	bird's eye view
BDEEEILMNRTW	bewilderment
BDEEEJORTTUV	objet de vertu
BDEEELMNORTU	redoublement
BDEEENOSSSTT	besottedness
BDEEFGHINRTY	frightened by
BDEEFHINORTY	The Boy Friend
BDEEFIILNNSY	indefensibly
BDEEFILMNOOT	nimble-footed
BDEEFLOOOPPY	body of people
BDEEGHHIINRS	Denbighshire
BDEEGIIILNST	indigestible

BDEEGIIILNSV	disbelieving
BDEEGIILRRTY	Bridget Riley
BDEEGIIMMNRS	dismembering
BDEEGIIMNORR	embroidering
BDEEGIINORUW	Brownie Guide
BDEEGIMMRRUU	Murrumbidgee
BDEEGJLMPTUU	get jumbled up
BDEEGLNOOTUU	double-tongue
BDEEHIILLMSS	disembellish
BDEEHIINOSTT	bit on the side
BDEEHIOSSSTW	obsessed with
BDEEIILMNTTW	nimble-witted
BDEEIILNNOTY	inobediently
BDEEIILNORZZ	Lizzie Borden
BDEEIILOORSV	Oliver de Bois
BDEEIIRRSTTU	redistribute
BDEEILNNSTUU	Blut und Eisen
	Eisen und Blut
BDEEIMNRSSTU	disbursement
BDEEINNORSTV	inverted snob
BDEEINOORRRT	Robert De Niro
BDEELNORSUVY	unobservedly
BDEFGGIILNRY	flying bridge
BDEFGILNOORY	forebodingly
BDEFHNOOORTU	debt of honour
BDEFIIINNOTY	by definition
BDEFILNNOOST	festoon blind
BDEFLNOSSTUU	doubtfulness
BDEGHHOORRTU	thoroughbred ❏
BDEGHJNNOOOY	Johnny B Goode
BDEGIIILNSTY	indigestibly
BDEGIILLNNPS	spellbinding
BDEGILLNNRUY	blunderingly
BDEGILLNOOTT	bloodletting
	blood-letting
BDEGINOSTTUY	begin to study
BDEHHMNOOORR	rhombohedron
BDEHINOPTUUY	put behind you
BDEHLORRSSUU	rub shoulders
BDEHNOOORSSY	Rhodes Boyson
BDEIIIORSTVY	biodiversity
BDEIIIRSTTUV	distributive
BDEIIKNRSTTU	Denis Burkitt
BDEIILLNOSSU	indissoluble
BDEIILNOOSUV	double vision
BDEIINNOSSSU	do business in
BDEIKLLOOOST	like old boots
BDEILMNNOOSW	blow one's mind
BDELLLMOOOOP	Leopold Bloom
BDELLNORTUUY	untroubledly
BDELNORRSTUY	Burt Reynolds
BDFGHILLOOSW	goldfish bowl
BDGGGIILMNNO	mind-boggling
BDGGLRRSSTUU	Struldbruggs
BDGHIIILNPSU	shipbuilding
BDGHIIORRUVY	hybrid vigour
BDGILNNOTUUY	undoubtingly
BDGINOOORSUV	Boris Godunov
BDHIINNOSTUW	within bounds
BDHILOORSTTY	bloodthirsty
BDHIOOTTTUUW	without doubt
BDHJOOOPRSTU	jodhpur boots
BDIIILLNOSUY	libidinously
BDIIINORSTTU	distribution
BDIILLNOSSUY	indissolubly
BEEEEEFLMNNT	enfeeblement
BEEEEEHKNSST	the bee's knees
BEEEEGHNOTTW	The Go-Between
BEEEEGILLNRT	Berline-Tegel
BEEEEGNORRRT	Robert Greene
BEEEEHNNPSTT	Stephen Benét
BEEEEHNPRRST	Peter Behrens
BEEEEIMNSTTW	between times
	betweentimes
BEEEELMMNTZZ	embezzlement
BEEEFHLMPTUU	be up the flume
BEEEFHORRTTT	for the better
BEEEGGIORSTZ	Georges Bizet
BEEEGHILOTVW	give the elbow
BEEEGIILLMNS	ill-beseeming
BEEEGILRSSTU	Geissler tube
BEEEGIMNPRSU	Supreme Being
	supreme being
BEEEGIMOORSU	embourgeoise
BEEEHILLNOTW	below-the-line
BEEEHLNOOPTX	telephone box
BEEEIILRRRSV	irreversible
BEEEILLMNTTT	belittlement
BEEEILNNSSSS	sensibleness
BEEEILOPPRST	tribespeople
BEEEILOPRRUZ	Pierre Boulez
BEEEIMMNRTTT	embitterment
BEEELLNNOTVY	benevolently
BEEELNOOPRTT	bottle opener
BEEELNOOSSST	obsoleteness
BEEENOSTTUWW	between us two
BEEFFFGINRTU	finger buffet
BEEFFHLOOTTT	off the bottle
BEEFGGLOORTT	Gottlob Frege
BEEFHILLOTTW	lift the elbow
BEEFHIOSSTTX	six of the best
BEEFHLOOTTUU	out of the blue
BEEFIILRRSTU	filibusterer
BEEFILMNNOOT	Bloemfontein
BEEFIORRSTUU	tuberiferous
BEEGGIIOOOOW	boogie-woogie
BEEGHHILLRST	she'll be right
BEEGHIILLMNS	embellishing
BEEGHIILRTTW	Gilbert White
BEEGHOOPRRTU	Peterborough
BEEGHOORSTWY	go by the worse
BEEGIIILLLNT	intelligible
BEEGIINNSSTT	besetting sin
BEEGKNOOOSST	get one's books
BEEGLOORRTTT	globetrotter
BEEGPRRSSTTU	St Petersburg
BEEHHILOTTTT	hit the bottle
BEEHHLMPTUUY	hump the bluey
BEEHIIILTVXY	exhibitively
BEEHIIINORTX	exhibitioner
BEEHIILLNNTU	thin blue line
BEEHIINNOOST	in the boonies

BEEHILLLRSVY	Beverly Hills
BEEHILLMOSTY	blithesomely
BEEHILMOOPST	phlebotomise
BEEHILMOOPTZ	phlebotomize
BEEHILNORRSS	horribleness
BEEHINOPTTTU	put the bite on
BEEHJMMOPSTU	jump the besom
BEEHKNOORRST	honest broker
BEEHLORRRTWY	whortleberry
BEEHMNORRTUY	number theory
BEEHNOOPRRTU	porte-bonheur
BEEHNOOSSSTT	one's best shot
BEEIIILMRRSS	irremissible
BEEIIILRRSST	irresistible
BEEIIKLNSSSU	businesslike
	business-like
BEEIILRRRSVY	irreversibly
BEEIKLNNOTTW	let it be known
BEEILLLORSUY	rebelliously
BEEILMPRSUUY	impulse buyer
BEEILPPRSSSU	suppressible
BEEKNNNORSSU	unbrokenness
BEEKOOPRRRTU	Rupert Brooke
BEELLLOORRTW	Robert Lowell
BEELLMNRSSUY	numberlessly
BEELMNORSTUW	lowest number
BEELNNOSSSUU	nebulousness
BEELNQSSTUUY	subsequently
BEENOQSSTTUU	subsequent to
BEEOOPRRSSTU	obstreperous
BEFFGIINNRUY	burn in effigy
BEFFHIOOTUWY	be off with you
BEFGHIINRRSU	refurbishing
BEFHIKNNOORT	on the brink of
BEFHIMOOOPRS	Bishop of Rome
BEFHINNOOORS	one for his nob
BEFIIMNOOPRS	pisiform bone
BEFILLNSSSSU	blissfulness
BEGGGHINOOTU	be tough going
BEGGHIINNORU	neighbouring
BEGGHIINNOTY	in the by-going
BEGGIILNNOSS	obligingness
BEGHIKLNNOOT	go on the blink
BEGHINORRSWY	greyish-brown
BEGHORSSSTTU	Ghostbusters
BEGIIIILLLTY	illegibility
BEGIIILLLNTY	intelligibly
BEGIIILNNRRV	Irving Berlin
BEGIILOOOSTX	exobiologist
BEGILLMNRSUY	slumberingly
BEGILLNRSTUY	blusteringly
BEGILMOORSTY	embryologist
BEGIMNORRSTT	bring to terms
BEGINOPRRTUU	Tribune group
BEHHJNOORSTY	John Sotherby
BEHIIILPRSTT	Blithe Spirit
BEHIINOSSSTY	biosynthesis
BEHIJLLNNORU	John Lilburne
BEHINOOPTTTU	put in the boot
	put the boot in
BEHINOSSSSUW	show business
BEHKORRSSSTU	brush strokes
BEHLOOORSTTU	troubleshoot
BEHNNORTTUUY	bounty hunter
BEHOORSSTTUY	your best shot
BEIIIIKLNNSV	invisible ink
BEIIILLMMNSU	bimilleniums
BEIIILLNOSSU	insolubilise
BEIIILLNOSUZ	insolubilize
BEIIILRRSSTY	irresistibly
BEIILLOORSTU	Louis Blériot
BEIILMMMOPRU	primum mobile
BEIILMSSSUVY	submissively
BEIILNORSSTY	Boris Yeltsin
BEIIMNSSSUUV	unsubmissive
BEIINNOOPRTW	brownie point ❑
BEIINOOSSSST	obsessionist
BEIISSTTTUUV	substitutive
BEIKLORSSTTV	Brest-Litovsk
BEIKNOOOSSTU	suit one's book
BEILLOORSSTT	stilboestrol
BEILMNRSTTUU	butter-muslin
BEILOOQSSUUY	obsequiously
BEILOORSSTUY	boisterously
BEILOPPRSTUU	purpose-built
BELLMORSSUUY	slumberously
BENNOOOSTTUZ	snooze button
BEOOORRSTTUU	tuberous root
BFGGHIILLNTU	bullfighting
BFGHIILLORST	Bill of Rights
	bill of rights
BFIIILNNORSY	fibrinolysin
BGGHHLOOORUU	Loughborough
BGGHIILNORTT	bring to light
BGHHHMORTTUU	thumb through
BGHHINOORRTU	honour bright
BGHHORRSTTUU	burst through
BGHIILRRTUWW	Wilbur Wright
BGHILLNNSUUY	unblushingly
BGHILLNOOOPT	polling-booth
BGIIILNNOOPT	boiling point
BGIIKLLNNNUY	unblinkingly
BGIILMMNNOOU	immunoglobin
BGILLORSUUUY	lugubriously
BHIINNOSSTTU	in his buttons
BIIIIILNSTVY	invisibility
BIIILLNOSTUY	insolubility
BIIKLLNOOPSY	kill by poison
BIIKOOORSSTV	visitors' book
BIILOQSTUUUY	ubiquitously
BIINNOOPPTTY	point by point
BIINOSSTTTUU	substitution
BILLORSSTUUY	subsultorily
BILOORSSTUUY	robustiously

C

CCCCEENOORRU	co-occurrence
CCCDEEILNOPY	encyclopedic
CCCEEHILORTY	heterocyclic
CCCEEHKNORTU	countercheck
CCCEEIINRTTY	eccentricity
CCCEEILNNOTU	noctilucence

Words marked ❑ can also be spelled with an initial capital letter

CCCEHINOPRTT concert pitch
CCCEIINNOOST conic section
CCCEILMORTUU circumlocute
CCCEINNOPSTU concupiscent
CCCEINNSSSTU succinctness
CCCEIOOPRSTT streptococci
CCCGIIILORTU logic circuit
CCCHHHIRRSTU Christ Church
Christchurch
CCCIIIMNORSU circumcision
CCCIIIMORRTU microcircuit
CCCIIKLRSTTY trick cyclist
CCCIIORRTTUU circuit court
CCDDEEENNOPY co-dependency
CCDDEEENORSS decrescendos
CCDDEEHIILNR cliché-ridden
CCDDEEINNOST disconnected
CCDDEEINORST disconcerted
CCDEEEEFHPST speech defect
CCDEEEEHINPR crêpe de chine
CCDEEEEMNSTU detumescence
CCDEEEFIILNV civil defence
CCDEEEFNNORS frondescence
CCDEEEHIINNS indehiscence
CCDEEEHIPRST direct speech
CCDEEEIINRSV viridescence
CCDEEEINOPRV preconceived
CCDEEENRRSTU recrudescent
CCDEEFIINNNO in confidence
CCDEEIILLNOV ill-conceived
CCDEEIIMNOSV misconceived
CCDEEILMORRS sclerodermic
CCDEELOPRRSU red corpuscle
CCDEGIMNNOOS Second Coming
CCDEHIIINOTW coincide with
CCDEHIIOPTUW occupied with
CCDEIILNNOTY coincidently
CCDEILNOORWY Colin Cowdrey
CCDEINNOOSSU second cousin
CCDEIOORRTUV divorce court
CCDENOPRSTUU superconduct
CCDHHILOORRY hydrochloric
CCDIINOTTUVY conductivity
CCDNNNOOORTU non-conductor
CCEEEEHILRSS cheese slicer
CCEEEEIIKKLO cockieleekie
CCEEEEJNNSUV juvenescence
CCEEEELLRRVV clever-clever
CCEEEFIILNSS life sciences
CCEEEFINNNOR in conference
CCEEEFLNORSU fluorescence
CCEEEHINNOST ethnoscience
CCEEEHKLLPRS spellchecker
CCEEEIILNRSV virilescence
CCEEEIIMNNRS reminiscence
CCEEEILLORTV recollective
CCEEEILMNNRT encirclement
CCEEEILMNNSU luminescence
CCEEEILOPRST secret police
CCEEEIMNNOPT incompetence
CCEEEIMNNSTU intumescence
CCEEEIMOOPST come to pieces
CCEEEINNNOST consentience
CCEEELOOPRST electroscope
CCEEEMMMNNOT commencement
CCEEENNOQSSU consequences
CCEEENNORSST concreteness
CCEEFFIIINNY inefficiency
CCEEFGINNNOR conferencing
CCEEFHIPPRTT perfect pitch
CCEEFINNOORT confectioner
CCEEGGOORSTT George C Scott
CCEEGILLOOSY ecclesiology
CCEEGINOSTTY cytogenetics
CCEEHHIKNNTW kitchen-wench
CCEEHIILNORT heliocentric
CCEEHIKPRRRY cherry picker
CCEEHIMOSTYZ schizomycete
CCEEHINNORTT ethnocentric
CCEEHKLOORST electroshock
CCEEHKNORSTW socket-wrench
CCEEHLMOORSU colour scheme
CCEEIIIIKKKW kickie-wickie
CCEEIIILRSVV civil service
CCEEIIKOPPST pick to pieces
CCEEIILLOSTV collectivise
CCEEIILLOTVZ collectivize
CCEEIINNNNOT incontinence
CCEEIINNOSST conscientise
CCEEIINNOSTZ conscientize
CCEEIINNPRTV Vincent Price
CCEEILLLOTVY collectively
CCEEILLNOORT recollection
CCEEILLORTTY electrolytic
CCEEILNNOTVY connectively
CCEEILOOPRTT electro-optic
CCEEILSSSUVY successively
CCEEIMNNOPTY incompetency
CCEEIMNOORST econometrics
CCEEINNNORTT interconnect
CCEEINOORRRT correctioner
CCEEIOOPRSST stereoscopic
CCEEKLLOOTVW twelve o'clock
CCEEKNORSSSU cocksureness
CCEENORRRUUY Eurocurrency
CCEEOOPPRSST spectroscope
CCEFHIKNOOTU chicken out of
CCEFIIINNSTU unscientific
CCEFINNORRST first concern
CCEFKLOOORUW cuckoo flower
CCEFLLSSSUUY successfully
CCEFLNSSSUUU unsuccessful
CCEFOOOPRRRT proof-correct
CCEGHIIKQRTU get-rich-quick
CCEGIINNOTTU cutting no ice
CCEGINOPPRUY preoccupying
CCEHIINOORRT rhinocerotic
CCEHIKLORTVY cover thickly
CCEHILLOQRUU Quiller-Couch
CCEHILNOOSUU council house
CCEHIMNOORRT chronometric
CCEHINOPRSTY pyrotechnics

CCEHIOOPSSTT	stethoscopic
CCEHKLORSTUU	culture shock
CCEHNOOSTTTU	count the cost
CCEIIKKSTTWY	sticky wicket
CCEIILLMOSTV	collectivism
CCEIILNNOSUV	inconclusive
CCEIILPRSTUU	pisciculture
CCEIINNNNOTY	incontinency
CCEIINNOSSSU	in succession
CCEIINORSTTV	constrictive
CCEIINRSSTTY	syncretistic
CCEIKNOSSTTU	cut one's stick
CCEILLNOSUVY	conclusively
CCEILLOOOPSS	oscilloscope
CCEILNOOPRRT	price control
CCEILOOPRSUY	precociously
CCEINNOSTTUY	constituency
CCEINOORSSST	cross section
	cross-section
CCEINOPSTTUY	conspectuity
CCEINORSTTUV	constructive
CCEKLLOOORRU	cuckoo-roller
CCELNNORRTUY	concurrently
CCENORRRSSTU	cross-current
CCEOOPPRSSTY	spectroscopy
CCEORSSSSTUY	success story
CCFGGHIIKNOT	cockfighting
	fighting cock
CCFIIMNORSUU	circumfusion
CCFILOOOPRSU	fluoroscopic
CCGHILNOOOST	conchologist
CCGIILNNNOVY	convincingly
CCGIINNNNOUV	unconvincing
CCGIKKNNOOPY	knocking copy
CCHHHHIIISWW	which is which?
CCHHIIIIQQUU	chiquichiqui
CCHHIIMOSTYZ	schizothymic
CCHIIOOPRSTY	hypocoristic
CCHIIORRSTTU	short circuit
	short-circuit
CCHINOORRSSS	Cornish cross
CCHIOOPPRSTY	psychotropic
CCIIKKORSSSS	scissors kick
CCIILNNNOOSU	in conclusion
CCIILNNNSTUU	cunnilinctus
CCIILNOPRUVY	Privy Council
CCIILORSTUUY	circuitously
CCIIMMOOPRSU	Microscopium
CCIINNOOPRST	conscription
CCIINNOORSTT	constriction
CCIKLNOORSTT	control stick
CCIKLNOORSUW	works council
CCILMOORSTTY	motorcyclist
CCILMORRSUUU	cirrocumulus
CCIMNOOPSTUU	compunctious
CCIMNORSSTTU	misconstruct
CCIMNORSTUUY	country music
CCINNOORSTTU	construction
CCNOORRSSTUY	cross-country
CDDDEEFIIOST	eisteddfodic
CDDDEEFILNOS	second fiddle

CDDDELLLMOOY	mollycoddled
CDDEEEEINNNP	independence □
CDDEEEEJNSST	dejectedness
CDDEEEGIMOOS	geodesic dome
CDDEEEILLRTW	well-directed
CDDEEEINNNPY	independency
CDDEEHIORRST	Desert Orchid
CDDEEHLNNOSU	non-scheduled
CDDEEHLNORTU	underclothed
CDDEEIJNPRUU	unprejudiced
CDDEEILMORSU	middle course
CDDEEINNORSU	unconsidered
CDDEEINNOSTT	discontented
CDDEEINORSUV	undiscovered
CDDEENOPRRUU	under-produce
CDDEFIIKLSST	fiddlesticks
CDDEFLNNOOUY	confoundedly
CDDEGIIINRST	discrediting
CDDEGLLOOORU	gold-coloured
CDDEHILLMOOS	middle school
CDDEHILNOSSS	cloddishness
CDDEHLLOORSU	cold shoulder
	cold-shoulder
CDDEHLNORTUU	thundercloud
CDDEIINNOSTU	discontinued
CDDLNNOORTUW	turn down cold
CDEEEEFGLLNO	golden fleece
CDEEEEFILNSV	self-evidence
CDEEEEFILRSV	self-deceiver
CDEEEEGIINVV	give evidence
CDEEEEIINNPX	inexpedience
CDEEEEIIRRVW	wide receiver
CDEEEEILRRST	Red Leicester
CDEEEEKOPRRR	record-keeper
CDEEEELNNPRS	resplendence
CDEEEENPRSSU	supersedence
CDEEEENSSTTW	sweet-scented
CDEEEFFIINNR	indifference
CDEEEFHILRST	chesterfield □
CDEEEFHORSUV	chefs d'oeuvre
CDEEEFIILLNN	feel inclined
CDEEEFINRRSS	crise de nerfs
CDEEEFLMNRTU	Clement Freud
CDEEEGIILNOS	geodesic line
CDEEEGIKLNRS	single-decker
CDEEEGINOSTV	decongestive
CDEEEHIKNOTW	the wicked one
CDEEEHILNNOT	on the decline
CDEEEHIMNPRT	decipherment
CDEEEHNOSSTX	The Second Sex
CDEEEHNRSSTW	wretchedness
CDEEEIIINSTZ	decitisenize
CDEEEIIINTZZ	decitizenize
CDEEEIINNPXY	inexpediency
CDEEEIINSSSV	decisiveness
CDEEEIIORRST	erotic desire
CDEEEILNQSTU	deliquescent
CDEEEINNNORS	non-residence
CDEEEINRSSST	discreetness
	discreteness
CDEEEKNOOPRR	keep on record

Words marked □ can also be spelled with an initial capital letter

CDEEELNNPRSY	resplendency
CDEEELNPTUXY	unexpectedly
CDEEEMNNNOTU	denouncement
CDEEEMNNOORS	encomenderos
CDEEFFFIILOR	field officer
CDEEFFHILOOR	office-holder
CDEEFFHOORRT	off the record
	off-the-record
CDEEFGILNORZ	freezing cold
CDEEFGIOOOPS	piece of goods
CDEEFHIINTTW	infected with
CDEEFHLNOOOV	cloven-hoofed
CDEEFHOORRRT	for the record
CDEEFILNNNUU	uninfluenced
CDEEFLLOORSU	self-coloured
CDEEFLNOOOTV	cloven-footed
CDEEFLRSSTTU	self-destruct
CDEEGIILLPRV	pelvic girdle
CDEEGIILRRTY	triglyceride
CDEEGIIORTTV	give credit to
CDEEGIKNOPRR	pecking order
CDEEGIMMNNOR	recommending
CDEEGINNORUZ	unrecognized
CDEEGMMNNOOR	common gender
CDEEGPPRSTUU	get spruced up
CDEEHILMOPST	domestic help
CDEEHINORSST	Édith Cresson
CDEEHLMOOSTU	close-mouthed
CDEEHLNORSTU	underclothes
CDEEHNOORSTU	Côtes du Rhône
CDEEHORSTTTU	outstretched
	stretched out
CDEEIIILNSVY	indecisively
CDEEIIILOPST	depoliticise
CDEEIIILOPTZ	depoliticize
CDEEIIINNSTV	disincentive
CDEEIILNOPRT	predilection
CDEEIILNRSTY	indiscreetly
	indiscretely
	iridescently
CDEEIILPRTVY	predictively
CDEEIILRSTVY	discretively
CDEEIIMNOPRV	improvidence
CDEEIINNRSST	indirectness
CDEEIKNORSST	second strike
CDEEILLNPSSU	pellucidness
CDEEILRRSTTY	restrictedly
CDEEIMMNOOXY	mixed economy
CDEEIMOOSSTX	sextodecimos
CDEEIMOPRTUZ	computerized
CDEEINRRSTTU	unrestricted
CDEEIOPRRTUV	reproductive
CDEEIOPSSSUY	pseudocyesis
CDEEIORRSSSW	crossed wires
CDEEKKLNNRUU	knuckle under
CDEELMNOOPTT	not completed
CDEELOOORRSU	rose-coloured
CDEEMOOPRRSS	decompressor
CDEENNNOOOST	second to none
	second-to-none
CDEENNRRRTUU	undercurrent
CDEFFHOOPSTU	depth of focus
CDEFFIIILSTU	difficulties
CDEFGHIOOTTY	The City of God
CDEFGIINORRV	driving force
CDEFHINNORWW	French window
CDEFHMNNOOTU	confound them
CDEFIIINNOST	disinfection
CDEFIIMORSTU	discomfiture
CDEFILLOORSU	field colours
CDEFILMNOORR	record on film
CDEFILNNNOUY	unconfinedly
CDEGHHIIKSTT	thick-sighted
CDEGHHILOORU	high-coloured
CDEGHINNOOSU	echo-sounding
CDEGHNOORSTW	second growth
CDEGIINNNRSU	undiscerning
CDEGINNORRSU	underscoring
CDEGINNORSST	second string
CDEGINOORRVW	overcrowding
CDEGLMNORUUY	curmudgeonly
CDEHHIILNSSS	childishness
CDEHHIMNOOPT	phonic method
CDEHIIILPPSS	discipleship
CDEHIIKKNNST	thick-skinned
CDEHIIKNORTY	hydrokinetic
CDEHIINNRSTT	herd instinct
CDEHIIOPRRST	directorship
CDEHILLOOOST	old school tie
	old-school tie
CDEHILORSTTY	dirty clothes
CDEHIMNOOTWW	come down with
CDEHIMORTTYY	rhytidectomy
CDEHIORRTTWY	creditworthy
CDEIIIILNNPS	indiscipline
CDEIIIJRSTUV	jurisdictive
CDEIIILNTVVY	vindictively
CDEIIIMNORST	misdirection
CDEIIINNORST	indiscretion
CDEIIINNORTT	interdiction
CDEIIKNOTTWW	ticket window
CDEIILMRTUUV	diverticulum
CDEIILNNPPRU	unprincipled
CDEIILRSSUVY	discursively
CDEIIMMNOOSS	commissioned
	decommission
CDEIIMMRSSTY	dissymmetric
CDEIIMNOPRRT	microprinted
CDEIIMNORSTU	reductionism
CDEIINNOOPRT	precondition
CDEIINNSSSTT	distinctness
CDEIINOOPRST	periodontics
CDEIINORRTTY	interdictory
CDEIINORSTTU	reductionist
CDEIJOORTUVY	Victor de Jouy
CDEIKMOORSTW	domestic work
CDEILLNOQTUU	dulciloquent
CDEILNOORSUY	indecorously
CDEILOPRTUVY	productively
CDEIMMNOOPTU	compound time
CDEIMNORSSTU	misconstrued
CDEIMOOPRSSU	discomposure

CDEINOOPRRTU	reproduction
CDEINOPRTUUV	unproductive
CDEIOORSSTUU	discourteous
CDEJKLLOORTY	Doctor Jekyll
CDEKNORRSTUW	wonder-struck
CDELLNNOORTU	uncontrolled
CDELNNOOPRUY	pronouncedly
CDELNNOORRTU	under control
CDELNOOOSTUY	cotyledonous
CDELOORRSTUU	rust-coloured
CDEMNNOOOPUW	come down upon
CDENNNOOPRUU	unpronounced
CDENOOOPRRST	correspond to
CDENRRSTTUUU	unstructured
CDFGIIIMNOST	discomfiting
CDFGILNOORTY	flying doctor
CDFHILOORRUY	hydrofluoric
CDFHILOOSSTT	Scottish Fold
CDFINNOORTUW	function word
CDGGGIIIKNST	digging stick
CDGGIKLLNUUY	ugly duckling
CDGIIINNNOOT	conditioning
CDGIIKLNOSSU	cloud-kissing
CDGIILNNNOTU	not including
CDGIIMMNNOOR	common-riding
CDGIKKNNNOOW	knocking-down
CDGMMNNOOORU	common ground
CDHIIIMOOPRS	isodimorphic
CDHIKMNOORTU	drink too much
CDHINOOORSTT	orthodontics
CDIIIJNORSTU	jurisdiction
CDIIILNNSTTY	indistinctly
CDIIIMNNSTTU	Nunc Dimittis
	nunc dimittis
CDIILLORSUUY	ridiculously
CDIIMMNOOOSU	incommodious
CDIINNOORTTU	introduction
CDIIOPRTTUVY	productivity
CDILMMOOOSUY	commodiously
CDINNOOOPTUW	two pound coin
CDINOORRTTUY	introductory
CEEEEFFNRSTV	effervescent
CEEEEFHNOSST	of the essence
CEEEEFHORTTV	cover the feet
CEEEEFILNNST	life sentence
CEEEEFINNPRR	in preference
CEEEEFINNRRT	interference
CEEEEGGLLNOR	Green College
CEEEEHNOPRRY	honeycreeper
CEEEEHNORSVW	whencesoever
CEEEEHNPQSSU	Queen's Speech
CEEEEIINNPRX	inexperience
CEEEEIKKPRTW	wicket-keeper
CEEEEILLLSTV	Celesteville
CEEEEILMNNOO	Come on Eileen
CEEEEIPRRRSV	reserve price
CEEEELMORRTT	electrometer
CEEEEMNQSTUV	Steve McQueen
CEEEEPRSTTUZ	crêpe suzette
CEEEFFGIOTTV	give effect to
CEEEFFILPPRT	ripple effect
CEEEFFINNOTV	non-effective
CEEEFFLNOORS	force oneself
CEEEFFLNORST	efflorescent
CEEEFGHHIMRT	Fehmgerichte
CEEEFGHIIOPT	piece of eight
CEEEFHHILNPT	feel the pinch
CEEEFHLNRRTT	French letter
CEEEFHLNRSSU	cheerfulness
CEEEFILLRTVY	reflectively
CEEEFILPRTVY	perfectively
CEEEFKLNSSSS	fecklessness
CEEEGGNORRRY	greengrocery
CEEEGHMOORTT	come together
CEEEGIILLNNT	intelligence
CEEEGIINRSTV	receiving-set
CEEEGIKNNORT	rocket engine
CEEEGILLLOOR	Oriel College
CEEEGINOOSTT	osteogenetic
CEEEGJLLOSSU	Jesus College
CEEEHHIINSTW	Chinese white
CEEEHHIRSTTW	Three Witches
CEEEHIIPRRSV	receivership
CEEEHIJNOPPS	Joseph Niepce
CEEEHILLOPRT	electrophile
CEEEHIMNPSWY	chimney-sweep
CEEEHIMNRSTU	hermeneutics
CEEEHKMNNNRY	Henry Mencken
CEEEHKORSTTY	street hockey
CEEEHLLPSSSY	speechlessly
CEEEHLNORTUW	counter-wheel
CEEEHMNNNRTT	entrenchment
CEEEHMNNRRTT	retrenchment
CEEEHNOSTTTU	cut one's teeth
CEEEIIMNNPRT	impertinence
CEEEIIMPPRTV	imperceptive
CEEEIINPRTTV	interceptive
CEEEIIPRRSTV	irrespective
CEEEILNNOPPT	plenipotence
CEEEILNRRSSV	silver screen
CEEEILPPRTVY	perceptively
CEEEILPRSTVY	respectively
CEEEIMNNOPRS	omnipresence
CEEEIMNORSVW	servicewomen
CEEEIMNPPSTY	type specimen
CEEEIMORRSTT	stereometric
CEEEINNNOSTX	non-existence
CEEEINNQSSTU	quintessence
CEEEINRRRSTW	screen writer
	screenwriter
CEEEIORRSSTV	retrocessive
CEEEIPRRSSUV	repercussive
CEEEJOPRRTTX	export reject
CEEEKLNOOOPS	keep one's cool
CEEEKLNRSSSS	recklessness
CEEELMMORTTU	telecommuter
CEEELMNOPSST	completeness
CEEELMOORUWY	you're welcome
CEEELMORRTTY	electrometry
CEEELORRSSSU	resourceless
CEEELORSTTVV	velvet-scoter
CEEEMNNNORTU	renouncement

CEEEMOPRRSTT	spectrometer
CEEEMRSSSTTY	secret system
CEEENNPRTUUV	venepuncture
CEEEOOPRRTTX	exteroceptor
CEEFFFHIPRTT	perfect fifth
CEEFFFIMOORT	term of office
CEEFFGIORTUY	city of refuge
CEEFFIKOORRW	office worker
CEEFFIMNNOOR	minor offence
CEEFFINPRTTY	fifty per cent
CEEFFIOPRRSS	press officer
CEEFFIOPRTTY	petty officer
CEEFFLNORSSU	forcefulness
CEEFGHIINPSY	speechifying
CEEFGIILNRTY	electrifying
CEEFGILLNRTY	reflectingly
CEEFGILNNOTU	genuflection
CEEFGLLLNTUY	neglectfully
CEEFHHJLNORT	John Fletcher
CEEFHIIKLMNO	Michel Fokine
CEEFHKMOORSW	scheme of work
CEEFHLOOSSTT	set of clothes
CEEFIILRTTVY	reflectivity
CEEFIIMNOPRT	imperfection
CEEFIINOPRST	frontispiece
CEEFIJLNORTU	fuel injector
CEEFILMNRSSU	mercifulness
CEEFILNNOORT	on reflection
CEEFILNOSUVY	veneficously
CEEFIMNOOPRY	price of money
CEEFINOOPRTT	to perfection
	to prefection
CEEFIOORSTUV	out of service
CEEFLLPRSTUY	respectfully
CEEFLNOQRUWY	low frequency
CEEFMOORRRTU	recomforture
CEEGGIKLLNOS	King's College
CEEGGILLNNTY	neglectingly
CEEGGILNORSV	leg-coverings
CEEGGNOORRUZ	George Curzon
CEEGHIINOSTT	histogenetic
CEEGHILNOPTY	phylogenetic
CEEGHIMORSTY	geochemistry
CEEGHINOORTT	orthogenetic
CEEGHINORTUW	counterweigh
	counter-weigh
CEEGHINPRSTU	Peter Cushing
CEEGHKLOORTT	lock together
CEEGHKNORSTT	G K Chesterton
CEEGHMNNOOSU	hoc genus omne
CEEGIILLNPRS	selling price
CEEGIINNPRTT	intercepting
CEEGIINNRSTT	intersecting
CEEGIINOPRTV	precognitive
CEEGIKKNNOOR	knee-crooking
CEEGIKLLNOPS	glockenspiel
CEEGILLNNNOR	Lincoln green
CEEGILNNOORS	corno inglese
CEEGINOPRRSS	reprocessing
CEEGMNOORRST	costermonger
CEEHHHJLNORS	John Herschel

CEEHHIILNNRZ	Heinrich Lenz
CEEHHIINOSTT	henotheistic
CEEHHMOOPRRS	chromosphere
CEEHHOOPPRSS	phosphoresce
CEEHIIILLNOR	Lionel Richie
CEEHIILLNPRS	spine-chiller
CEEHIILNNSTT	Lichtenstein
CEEHIINOOTVW	with one voice
CEEHIINPRTTU	in the picture
CEEHIKKLNTUW	white-knuckle
CEEHIKLMRUVY	like very much
CEEHIKMNOSSS	homesickness
CEEHILMOORTV	motor vehicle
CEEHILMOSSTT	Themistocles
CEEHILNNORTY	incoherently
CEEHIMNOOSTT	The Economist
CEEHIMNOOSTU	home counties
CEEHIMOORTVW	overcome with
CEEHINNNPPRY	penny-pincher
CEEHINOOPRST	stereophonic
CEEHINOORRSS	rhinoceroses
CEEHINOORRST	rhinocerotes
CEEHINRRRTWY	winter cherry
CEEHINRSSSTT	stretchiness
CEEHIOPRSTUU	picture-house
CEEHIOPRSTUX	executorship
CEEHKKNNOORT	on the knocker
CEEHKNOORSTW	know the score
CEEHLLMOORWY	chrome yellow
CEEHLLNPRRUY	Henry Purcell
CEEHLLNQSSUY	quenchlessly
CEEHLMOOPRTU	thermocouple
CEEHLMOPSTUY	The Lucy Poems
CEEHMORSTTYY	hysterectomy
CEEHNOOQRRTU	the Conqueror
CEEHNRRSTTUW	turn the screw
CEEHOOPRRSTU	urethroscope
CEEIIIMNPPRT	impercipient
CEEIIINNSSSV	incisiveness
CEEIIJNNORTT	interjection
CEEIIKKLLRST	stickler-like
CEEIIKLORRTU	courtierlike
CEEIILLMNPSX	mill-sixpence
CEEIILLNORVV	live in clover
CEEIILMOPSTX	complexities
CEEIILNPSSTX	explicitness
CEEIIMNOOTVW	come into view
CEEIIMOPRSSU	semi-precious
CEEIIMORRSTU	meretricious
CEEIINNNNOTV	inconvenient
CEEIINNOPRTT	interception
CEEIINNORSST	intercession
CEEIINNORSTT	intersection
CEEIINNSSTTW	New Scientist
CEEIINOPRSTT	receptionist
CEEIINORSSUX	excursionise
CEEIINORSUXZ	excursionize
CEEIINOSSSST	secessionist
CEEIIPPRRSTV	prescriptive
CEEIIPPRTTVY	perceptivity
CEEIKLMNPPRU	pumpernickel

CEEIKMNOORYY Mickey Rooney
CEEIKNNOOPST in one's pocket
CEEIKNNORSTV Kevin Costner
CEEIKNRRTTTU return ticket
CEEILLMNOPTY incompletely
CEEILLOPPSTU pull to pieces
CEEILLORSSTY electrolysis
CEEILLPRSUVY preclusively
CEEILMNNNOOS insomnolence
CEEILMOOPRSY co-polymerise
CEEILMOOPRYZ co-polymerize
CEEILMRRTUUV vermiculture
CEEILNNNOTVY conveniently
CEEILNOOPRSS necropolises
CEEILOOPRSTT coleopterist
CEEILOPRTTVY protectively
CEEILPRSSUVY percussively
CEEIMMNNORTU intercommune
CEEIMNOOPRST contemporise
CEEIMNOOPRTZ contemporize
CEEINNNOQSTU inconsequent
CEEINNOORRRT reconnoitrer
CEEINNOPRTUY Courtney Pine
CEEINNORRTTV interconvert
CEEINNPRTUUV venipuncture
CEEINNRRRTTU intercurrent
CEEINOOPRSTU counterpoise
CEEINOORRSST retrocession
CEEINOORRSVV cover version
CEEINOPRRSSU repercussion
CEEINOPRRSTT in retrospect
CEEINOPRSSSU preciousness
CEEINOPSSSSU speciousness
CEEINORRRSTU resurrection
CEEINORRSSTY intercessory
CEEINORSTTTU reconstitute
CEEINPPRRRTU Prince Rupert
CEEIOPRRTTTW write protect
write-protect
CEEKLLOORTWY yellow rocket
CEEKLNOOSTTY cytoskeleton
CEEKNNOOPSTU up to one's neck
CEEKOOPRRSSU pressure-cook
CEELLNOOOOSS lose one's cool
CEELMMNOOOPP Common People
common people
CEELMNORSTTY most recently
CEELNNOQSTUY consequently
CEELOOOPRSTU coleopterous
CEEMMORRRSUU Correr Museum
CEEMOPRRSTTY spectrometry
CEEMOPRRSTUU Supreme Court
supreme court
CEENNOORRTTU counter-tenor
CEENOOOPPRSS snooperscope
CEENOOSSSTUV covetousness
CEENORSTTUUV Venture Scout
CEEOOPRRSTTU Puerto Cortes
CEEOPPRSSSTU prospectuses
CEFFFIIORRST first officer
CEFFHIILORST life of Christ
CEFFHIJLNOWY John Wycliffe
CEFFHIORRSTU sheriff court
CEFFHMNOOPSU off one's chump
CEFFIIINNSTU insufficient
CEFFIILNSTUY sufficiently
CEFFIILOOPRT pilot officer
CEFFIORRSTUU fructiferous
CEFFMOOORSTW come off worst
CEFGHINOORSU forcing-house
CEFGIIIKLNNR fingerlickin'
CEFGIIKLLNRY flickeringly
CEFGIILNOSTT close-fitting
CEFHHIIKNOTT in the thick of
CEFHHILNOPRS French polish
French-polish
CEFIIILNOSTU infelicitous
CEFIIINNOPRT proficient in
CEFIILLOSTUY felicitously
CEFIILMNNTUY munificently
CEFIILNOPRSS prolificness
CEFIILNOPRTY proficiently
CEFIILNORSST frictionless
CEFIILNOSTUY infectiously
CEFIIMNOOTUZ Zeno of Citium
CEFIINNOPRTU unproficient
CEFILLMNRUUY unmercifully
CEFILLMOORSY frolicsomely
CEFILLOORRTU colour filter
CEFILLORRTUU floriculture
CEFILNNOSSTU functionless
CEFILOORSUVY vociferously
CEFKKLOORRSW clerk of works
CEFKKLOORSTU stroke of luck
CEFLNNORSSSU scornfulness
CEGGGHMOORRU Roger McGough
CEGGHILOSTTW toggle switch
CEGHHIILOPRY hieroglyphic
CEGHHILNOSTT nightclothes
CEGHHLNOPRTU trench-plough
CEGHHLOOSTTU close thought
CEGHIIOPSSTY geophysicist
CEGHIJORSTUU rough justice
CEGHILLOSTTY close tightly
CEGHILNOOORS chronologise
CEGHILNOOORZ chronologize
CEGHILOOPSSY psychologise
CEGHILOOPSYZ psychologize
CEGHIMORTUUX cough mixture
CEGHINNOSSTU touchingness
CEGIIILNNORS corni inglesi
CEGIIKLLMNRY mercy killing
CEGIIKLNNORT interlocking
CEGIILNNPSTY inspectingly
CEGIINNOOPRT precognition
CEGIKLNNOSSU King's Counsel
CEGIKNOSTTTU get stuck into
CEGILNNNOSTY consentingly
CEGILNNNOTTY contingently
CEGILNNOQRUY conqueringly
CEGILNNOSTTY contestingly
CEGILNOOORTW cooling tower

CEGILNOPRTTY	protectingly	CEIILOOSSTTV	solicit votes
CEGIMNOORRSU	microsurgeon	CEIILOPRSSUU	supercilious
CEGIMNOORSTT	come it strong	CEIIMMNOORSS	commissioner
CEGIMORRRSUY	microsurgery	CEIIMMNOPRTU	minicomputer
CEGINNNNOOTT	contingent on	CEIIMNNNOTTZ	zinc ointment
CEGINNPSSTUU	unsuspecting	CEIINNNORSTU	internuncios
CEGINOORRSSV	crossing over	CEIINNNOSSTT	inconsistent
CEGINORRSSTU	string course	CEIINNORRSTU	insurrection
CEGINPRSSTTU	press cutting	CEIINOOPRRTY	incorporeity
CEGLNOOOPPSS	pop one's clogs	CEIINOPPRRST	prescription
CEGMNNOOORST	come on strong	CEIINORRSSTT	restrictions
CEHHIIJNORST	John Christie	CEIINORSSTUX	excursionist
CEHHIILLOSTV	Cheviot Hills	CEIIOPPRRSTV	proscriptive
CEHHIILOPRST	lithospheric	CEIIPRRRSTTW	scriptwriter
CEHHILNRSSSU	churlishness	CEIKKMNORSTY	monkey tricks
CEHHILOOPRTY	hypochlorite		monkey-tricks
CEHHIMOOPSTT	photochemist	CEIKLLORSTUY	kill-courtesy
CEHHIOPPRRTY	hypertrophic	CEILLLNOOOSV	violoncellos
CEHHOOORSTTW	shoot the crow	CEILLMOPSUVY	compulsively
CEHIIIKRRSTT	strike it rich	CEILLMOSTUUY	meticulously
CEHIIJLLMNOT	Joni Mitchell	CEILLNOSUVVY	convulsively
CEHIIKLNSSST	ticklishness	CEILMNOOSTUU	contumelious
CEHIILLNNORS	Lincolnshire	CEILNNOSSTTY	consistently
CEHIILNQSSSU	cliquishness	CEILNOORRTTU	interlocutor
CEHIILOPSTTY	polytheistic	CEILNOORSSUY	censoriously
CEHIIMNOOSTT	monotheistic	CEILNOSSSSUU	lusciousness
CEHIIMOORSTT	trichotomise	CEILOOSSSSUW	colossus-wise
CEHIIMOORTTZ	trichotomize	CEIMMNOOPSST	compos mentis
CEHIIOPRTTUW	without price	CEIMNNOOPRSU	mispronounce
CEHIJNNOORSS	John Ericsson	CEIMNNOORSTU	conterminous
CEHILLNNOPSU	Punchinellos	CEIMNOPRSTTY	streptomycin
CEHILNNOSSSW	clownishness	CEINNOOPRTTU	counterpoint
CEHILOQSTTUY	coquettishly	CEINNOSSTTTU	constituents
CEHILORRTTUU	horticulture	CEINORRSSTUU	run its course
CEHIMNORRTYY	erythromycin	CEINPSSSTTUU	intussuscept
CEHINNORRSYZ	synchronizer	CEINRRSSSTTU	instructress
CEHIOOPPRRST	tropospheric	CEKLNOORTUYY	country yokel
CEHJNOOPRSTT	John Prescott	CELMOPRSTUUU	corpus luteum
CEHKLNOPSSUU	push one's luck	CELNOOORRTTW	control tower
CEHLMMOORSSU	summer school	CEMMNNNOOSSU	uncommonness
CEHLOOOOPPST	scoop the pool	CEMMNNOOOPRS	common person
CEHMOOOOPRTY	oophorectomy	CEMNOOOOPTTU	come out on top
CEHMOOPRSTTU	host computer	CEMNOOPSTTUU	contemptuous
CEHNOORSTUUY	country house	CENNOORRTTUU	run counter to
CEHOOPRRSTUY	urethroscopy	CENNOSSSTUUU	unctuousness
CEIIIIILNSTV	incivilities	CFFGIIIOORRS	frigorificos
CEIIIKOSTTTV	stick-to-it-ive	CFFGINOORSSU	offscourings
CEIIILMNPSST	implicitness	CFFHKLNOPSUU	Suffolk Punch
CEIIINOPRSST	precisionist		Suffolk punch
CEIIJLNNTUVY	injunctively	CFGHHIKLORTU	flick through
CEIIKLLNOPSS	lick one's lips	CFGHIIKLORTT	trick of light
CEIIKLLPSTTY	lickety-split	CFGIILNOOSTV	cost of living
CEIIKLQRSUVY	quicksilvery	CFGILLMNNOUY	flying column
CEIIKLQRTUWY	write quickly	CFGILMNOORTY	comfortingly
CEIIKLSSTWZZ	swizzle-stick	CFGINOORRTUY	crying out for
CEIIKRRSSTUY	security risk	CFHIINOOPRSS	scorpion fish
CEIILLNOSTUY	licentiously	CFIIILOSTTUY	fictitiously
CEIILLRSTUUV	silviculture	CFIIOOPSSSUU	suspicious of
CEIILMNNOSTY	omnisciently	CFIMNNOORTUY	unconformity
CEIILNOOSTTU	elocutionist	CFIOORRSTUUV	fructivorous
CEIILNOPRSUY	perniciously	CFLNOOOORTTU	out of control

CFNOOORTTTUU	not cut out for
CGGILNNORSTU	curling tongs
CGHHIILLNORT	rolling hitch
CGHHIINOPSTT	hitching post
CGHHILLOTTUY	touch lightly
CGHIIIKNNRST	stinking rich
CGHIILOOOPRT	oligotrophic
CGHIILOORSTT	trichologist
CGHIIMNOOPSY	physiognomic
CGHIJKLNNOSU	John Suckling
CGHIKKNNOOPS	knocking shop
	knocking-shop
CGHIKLNNORUW	working lunch
CGHILNOOORST	chronologist
CGHILOOPSSTY	psychologist
CGHINOOOPPTY	photocopying
CGIIIILNNOOT	ignition coil
CGIIINNRSTUZ	scrutinizing
CGIILMOOSSTU	musicologist
CGIILNNOPRSY	conspiringly
CGIILOOOSTTX	toxicologist
CGIIMMNOOPRS	compromising
CGILMNOOPSSU	gossip column
CGILNOOSTUUY	contiguously
CGILOOOPRSTT	proctologist
CGINNNORSSTU	running costs
CGINOOOSTTUU	contiguous to
CHIILNOOPRTY	Trichinopoly
CHIIMNNRSSTY	strychninism
CHIINOOPPRSW	whip scorpion
CHIINOPSSTUV	viscountship
CHIKNOPSSTTU	stockpunisht
CHIMOOORSTTU	trichotomous
CHIOOOPRRSTV	Rostropovich
CHKLMOOPRTUY	Plymouth Rock
CHKOORRRRSTU	horror-struck
CHMMNOOORSST	short commons
CIIILLMPTTUY	multiplicity
CIIIMMNNOOSS	in commission
CIILLOOSSTUY	solicitously
CIILMNOOOPST	monopolistic
CIILMOOOTTVY	locomotivity
CIILOORSTUVY	victoriously
CIILOPSSSUUY	suspiciously
CIIMNOPRSTTY	nyctitropism
CIINNOOSTTTU	constitution
CIINNORSSTTU	instructions
CIINOOPPRRST	proscription
CIINOPSSSUUU	unsuspicious
CIJLNORSSTUU	jurisconsult
CIJMMNNOORSY	Jimmy Connors
CILLMOOPRSUY	compulsorily
CILLORRSSUUY	scurrilously
CILNNOOOSTUV	convolutions
CILNNOOSTUUY	continuously
CILNORSSTUUY	scrutinously
CILOPRSSTUUY	scrupulosity
CIMNNOOSSTUU	customs union
CLLOPRSSUUUY	scrupulously
CLNOPRSSUUUU	unscrupulous

D

DDDDEEILLNNO	niddle-noddle
DDDEEEEFNNOS	se defendendo
DDDEEENRRSSU	underdressed
DDDEEFHILRSU	Huddersfield
DDDEEGINORWW	wedding-dower
DDDEEGINRSSW	wedding dress
DDDEEIIIMPSY	epididymides
DDDEEIINORST	Denis Diderot
DDDEEINOSTTW	sodden-witted
DDDEELMMTTUY	muddy-mettled
DDDEGILMNORU	middle ground
DDDEHNNOOORR	rhododendron
DDDEIIINOTVW	divided in two
DDEEEEFHNRTT	tender-hefted
DDEEEELLRSVW	well-deserved
DDEEEEMNNSST	dementedness
DDEEEENORTVX	overextended
DDEEEFGINNRU	underfeeding
DDEEEFIINNNR	friend in need
DDEEEGGILRST	stridelegged
DDEEEGGNORSS	Green Goddess
DDEEEGILLNSW	well-designed
DDEEEGINRSST	get dressed in
DDEEEGMOOPRT	good-tempered
DDEEEGNRSSTU	get undressed
DDEEEILMNRTY	determinedly
DDEEEILOPVWX	exploded view
DDEEEIMNNRTU	undetermined
DDEEEIMNORTT	determined to
DDEEEINNOSSS	one-sidedness
DDEEELNOPPRU	underpeopled
DDEEELNOPRUV	under-develop
DDEEELNRSUVY	undeservedly
DDEEFFGLLLUY	fully fledged
	fully-fledged
DDEEFFHILOPT	depth of field
DDEEFFIIILNU	unified field
DDEEFGLORRRU	flour dredger
DDEEFHIIIMRU	dehumidifier
DDEEFIIINNTU	unidentified
DDEEFIIKLLMO	Mike Oldfield
DDEEFILLORSU	Rudolf Diesel
DDEEGGHHOOOW	wood hedgehog
DDEEGGINRRSU	designer drug
DDEEGHIILMTW	middleweight
DDEEGIILMNNS	single-minded
DDEEGILMNOST	dislodgement
DDEEGILNNSUY	undesignedly
DDEEGINNRRUW	red underwing
DDEEGLLNORUW	well-grounded
DDEEGNOORRTX	Dexter Gordon
DDEEHIILORRS	hired soldier
DDEEHLNORSTW	the world's end
DDEEIIIIKKNW	kiddiewinkie
DDEEIILLMNVY	evil-mindedly
DDEEIILMMNPS	simple-minded
DDEEIIMNNOSU	diminuendoes
DDEEIKNNRRUW	wunderkinder
DDEEILLOPRVW	well-provided

DDEEILLOPSSW	well-disposed
DDEEILMMNOTY	motley-minded
DDEEILNNPSSS	splendidness
DDEEILNOPSSS	lopsidedness
DDEEILNSTUVY	undivestedly
DDEEIOPSSSSS	dispossessed
DDEELNNOPSTY	despondently
DDEFFILOSTUY	field of study
DDEFGIMNRSUU	Sigmund Freud
DDEFGINNNRUU	underfunding
DDEGGHINOOTW	Dwight Gooden
DDEGHIINPTUW	white pudding
DDEGHILNRSUY	shudderingly
DDEGHMOOORUU	good-humoured
DDEGIIIILNNV	dividing-line
DDEGIKLLOSTU	like gold dust
DDEGILNNOPSY	despondingly
DDEGILNOORST	dendrologist
DDEGIMNNORST	strong-minded
DDEGINNORSSW	dressing-down
DDEGLNNORUUY	ungroundedly
DDEHHOOSSTTU	shout the odds
DDEHIIIMNNSU	undiminished
DDEHINOORSTU	ride to hounds
DDEHINOORTTY	do the dirty on
DDEHMMNOOTUV	venom'd-mouth'd
DDEIIILPRSTY	dispiritedly
DDEIIJLNOSTY	disjointedly
DDEIIMNOSUVV	modus vivendi
DDEILMNNOSUW	Edmund Wilson
DDEILNOPRUVY	unprovidedly
DDEILNPSTUUY	undisputedly
DDEIMNOORRWW	dormer window
DDEIMOOPPSUU	pseudopodium
DDFGGGIINPUY	figgy pudding
DDFIMOOORSWW	word of wisdom
DDGIIIKNNRRV	drink-driving
DDIIIMPRTTUY	rumpti-iddity
DDILMNOOUUWY	would you mind?
DEEEEEGHLNTT	get the needle
DEEEEEMNPRTV	even-tempered
DEEEEFHIKLPT	keep the field
DEEEEGIILNNS	diesel engine
DEEEEGMOORST	to some degree
DEEEEGRRRSUU	ruse de guerre
DEEEEHHLNRTU	under the heel
DEEEEHLNNORT	Heldentenöre
DEEEEHLNSSSS	heedlessness
DEEEEILMMNUV	mendeleevium
DEEEEILMPRTV	evil-tempered
DEEEEILNNPTT	lite pendente
	pendente lite
DEEEEIMNPRRT	predetermine
DEEEELNNSSSS	needlessness
DEEEENRRSSSV	reservedness
DEEEFFINNOST	find one's feet
DEEEFGIILMNX	mixed feeling
DEEEFGLRSTTU	get flustered
DEEEFHILNNOT	end of the line
DEEEFHOOSSTW	sow the seed of
DEEEFIINNSST	definiteness
DEEEFILLRSSU	fille des rues
DEEEFILNOPRS	pride oneself
DEEEFLLMOPSY	self-employed
DEEEFNNQRTUU	unfrequented
DEEEGGLMNORR	Gregor Mendel
DEEEGHIMMRRT	hedgetrimmer
DEEEGIINNRRV	engine driver
	engine-driver
DEEEGIKLNNNY	Nigel Kennedy
DEEEGIKMOOPT	keep good time
DEEEGINNOOTV	Ode to Evening
DEEEGINNRSSS	resignedness
DEEEGINNRSSV	evening dress
	evening-dress
DEEEGJMNPRTU	prejudgement
DEEEGLLMNOPT	Golden Temple
DEEEHHIORSTT	the other side
DEEEHHIPPRSS	shepherd's pie
DEEEHHLOOTTW	toothed wheel
DEEEHIIPPPRT	The Pied Piper
DEEEHILMNSTV	dishevelment
DEEEHILPRTTT	Pitt the elder
DEEEHISSTUWY	Eyes Wide Shut
DEEEHLNNORST	Helden-tenors
DEEEHLRRSSSW	Welsh dresser
DEEEHMNNORTT	dethronement
DEEEHOOSTTTW	sweet-toothed
DEEEIINNRSTT	interested in
DEEEIINRSSSV	derisiveness
DEEEIINRSSTZ	desensitizer
DEEEIKMNNOPS	keep one's mind
DEEEILLMRSSY	remedilessly
DEEEILLNRSVW	well-versed in
DEEEILMOPRSY	depolymerise
DEEEILMOPRYZ	depolymerize
DEEEILNRSTTY	interestedly
DEEEILNSSSUV	delusiveness
DEEEILRRSSTV	reserved list
DEEEIMNNOSUY	mud in one's eye
DEEEIMNOPSTT	monts-de-piété
DEEEIMNORRSS	reindeer moss
DEEEIMNRSSTV	disseverment
DEEEIMOPRTXZ	extemporized
DEEEINNRSTTU	uninterested
DEEEINORSTVW	Stevie Wonder
DEEEINRSSTTU	entertissued
DEEEIPRRSSSU	depressurise
DEEEIPRRSSUZ	depressurize
DEEEKLNNOOST	endoskeleton
DEEEKNOOPRSW	keep one's word
DEEELMNOPSTV	developments
DEEELNORSSSV	resolvedness
DEEELNRRSUVY	unreservedly
DEEFFHOOORRT	of the order of
DEEFFIILNRRY	friendly fire
DEEFFILNOORS	rid oneself of
DEEFFINNOOPS	pensioned off
DEEFGHINOTTW	get the wind of
DEEFGIILNNOS	dig oneself in
DEEFGIKORTTY	Kitty Godfree
DEEFGILNNOSS	find one's legs

DEEFGIOOSTTU	get outside of
DEEFGOOOPRTU	of good repute
DEEFHIINNSSS	fiendishness
DEEFHINOORRT	in the order of
DEEFHJKNNNOY	John F Kennedy
DEEFHJLNNOOY	John of Leyden
DEEFIIILNNTY	indefinitely
DEEFIIILNTVY	definitively
DEEFIILNNRSS	friendliness
DEEFIIOPRSST	dies profesti
DEEFILLMNORW	well-informed
DEEFILLNOSTT	lend itself to
DEEFILLNOSVV	self-involved
DEEFILNORRVY	over-friendly
DEEFILNRRSUY	user-friendly
DEEFINORRSTW	Edwin Forrest
DEEFLOORSTUY	surefootedly
DEEFLORSSSTY	style of dress
DEEFMNOPRRRU	underperform
DEEGGIILLNNV	living legend
DEEGGIKRRSSU	Greg Rusedski
DEEGHHIKNRTT	The Red Knight
DEEGHHILNPRS	shepherdling
DEEGHHINNOTT	the done thing
DEEGHHLOORTT	hold together
DEEGHIINNSTW	winding-sheet
DEEGHIINSTUX	extinguished
DEEGHILOOTTV	go to the devil
DEEGHINOORTT	go into the red
DEEGHINOOTTV	give the nod to
DEEGHINPTTUW	get the wind up
DEEGHNNOOTUY	honey-tongued
DEEGIIILPRSV	disprivilege
DEEGIILMOOPY	epidemiology
DEEGIILNNSSY	yieldingness
DEEGIILNPRTV	diving petrel
DEEGIILRSSVY	digressively
DEEGIJMMNSTU	misjudgement
DEEGILMNNNOY	moneylending
	money-lending
DEEGILNNPRTY	pretendingly
DEEGILNNRSTU	Guildenstern
DEEGILNPRSSY	depressingly
DEEGINNOPRSV	overspending
DEEGINNRSTTT	trendsetting
DEEGINOORSVW	give one's word
DEEGIOORRSTV	give orders to
DEEGLLNOOPRV	golden plover
DEEGNNOOORRW	Ron Greenwood
DEEGNOORRSTT	Gordon setter
DEEHHHLOOSTU	the Household
DEEHHINORTVW	The Windhover
DEEHIIKRSSSW	side whiskers
DEEHIILLSTTW	Edith Sitwell
DEEHIILNSSSV	devilishness
DEEHIIMOPRSV	impoverished
DEEHIINPSSTW	dispense with
DEEHILLPRSUV	shrivelled up
DEEHILLPSSSY	Les Sylphides
DEEHILNOOTWY	dye in the wool
DEEHILOORRSS	horse soldier
DEEHILPRSSUU	desulphurise
DEEHILPRSUUZ	desulphurize
DEEHIMMRRSUY	medium sherry
DEEHIMNOORTU	time-honoured
DEEHINNOPPRS	Dennis Hopper
DEEHINOOSTTU	on the outside
DEEHIOPPRTTY	pteridophyte
DEEHLLMMSTUY	sell the dummy
DEEHLOORRTVW	the world over
DEEHNNORSTTU	thunder-stone
DEEHOORRSSUV	hors d'oeuvres
DEEIIILLLNNS	Dennis Lillie
DEEIIIMNRTTV	divertimenti
DEEIIINSSSVV	divisiveness
DEEIILNNNNSS	Dennis Nilsen
DEEIILNNSSUW	unwieldiness
DEEIIMMOPRST	post meridiem
DEEIIMNNRSTT	disinterment
DEEIIMNORSTT	endometritis
DEEIIMNORTTV	divertimento
DEEIINNPRSST	intrepidness
DEEIINPRSSST	spiritedness
DEEIJLNOOOST	loose-jointed
DEEIKKNNRRSU	underskinker
DEEIKMNNOPSU	end up in smoke
DEEIKMNOPRSY	spider monkey
DEEILLLPPSUW	well-supplied
DEEILLNNQTUY	delinquently
DEEILMNNSSSS	mindlessness
DEEILMNRTTUY	unremittedly
DEEILNNSTUWY	Edwin Lutyens
DEEILNPRRTTU	triple-turned
DEEILNQRTUUY	unrequitedly
DEEIMOPPRSSU	superimposed
DEEINNOOPSTU	put on one side
DEEINNOQSTUU	unquestioned
DEEINOOPSTTU	put to one side
DEEINOPPRRTU	Pierre Du Pont
DEEINPRSSUUV	unsupervised
DEEKMNOOPRWY	powder monkey
DEEKNOORRRWW	wonder-worker
DEELMNORSTUY	tremendously
DEELNORSSSSW	wordlessness
DEELNOSSSSUU	sedulousness
DEELPPRSSSUY	suppressedly
DEENNNOSSTUW	unwontedness
DEENOOPRRRTY	Rodney Porter
DEENOOPRSSST	dessertspoon
DEENOPRRSTTU	under protest
DEENORSSSTUX	dextrousness
DEFFGHOOOORT	for the good of
DEFFHIRSSTTU	stuffed shirt
DEFFHLNOOPSU	pound of flesh
DEFGGINOOORS	foreign goods
DEFGHHIIILTY	high fidelity
DEFGHILLLTUY	delightfully
DEFGIIINRSVY	diversifying
DEFGIILMNOOV	mode of living
DEFGILMNNOOY	folding money
DEFHHIIINSTW	finished with
DEFHHLLOOORT	hold the floor

DEFHIIINTTWY	identify with
DEFHIILNRTWY	friendly with
DEFHIIMNOSTT	in the midst of
DEFHILOPPRST	Doppler shift
DEFHIMNOOORT	in the mood for
DEFHIMNOORST	hindforemost
DEFHLOOORSSU	House of Lords
DEFHOOOOTTUW	out of the wood
DEFIILLNNRUY	unfriendlily
DEFIILOPRSUY	perfidiously
DEFIKMMNOOUU	Duke of Omnium
DEFILNOOSTUW	swindle out of
DEFILOORSTUY	do-it-yourself
DEFILRSSSTTU	self-distrust
DEFIMORRSSST	Mistress Ford
DEFINOOOPRRT	point of order
DEFMNOORRTUU	out from under
DEFNNOOPRSSU	profoundness
DEGGGINNRSSU	grudgingness
DEGGGLMRRSUU	drug-smuggler
DEGGHHIIILNY	high-yielding
DEGGHILLORRS	shrill-gorged
DEGGHILNNOTU	hunting-lodge
DEGGHILNOOSU	lodging house
DEGGINNORSSW	dressing-gown
DEGHHHILORSU	shoulder-high
DEGHHIIIPRST	high-spirited
DEGHHIINOPST	diphthongise
DEGHHIINOPTZ	diphthongize
DEGHHINORTTW	thronged with
DEGHHIORRTUV	drive through
DEGHHIORSSTT	shortsighted
	short-sighted
DEGHIIINNSST	things inside
DEGHIIKLNNST	light-skinned
DEGHIIORSTTU	outside right
DEGHIOORTUWY	Woody Guthrie
DEGHLOOORTTW	go to the world
DEGHNNOOSTUU	hound's-tongue
DEGHNORRTUUW	underwrought
DEGIIIKLNNNX	index-linking
DEGIILLNNUYY	unyieldingly
DEGIILLOOSTT	deltiologist
DEGIILNNOSUY	indigenously
DEGIILNNSSTY	dissentingly
DEGIILNORSSS	Doris Lessing
DEGIINNNNPRU	underpinning
DEGIINNOSSUU	disingenuous
DEGIINNRRTUW	underwriting
DEGIINOOPPSS	opposing side
DEGIINOPRRVW	driving-power
DEGIKLMNOORW	working model
DEGIKNOORRRW	working order
DEGILLNORSTW	strong-willed
DEGILNNORSUY	resoundingly
DEGILOOPRSTT	proglottides
DEGIMNNORRSS	morning dress
DEGINNOPPSTW	stepping-down
DEGINNORRTUW	winter-ground
DEGINOORSTUW	wrong side out
DEGLLNORSSUY	groundlessly
DEGLNNORSTYY	deny strongly
DEGMNOORRRUY	merry-go-round
DEGOOOPSTTUU	put to good use
DEHHILOSSSTU	South Shields
DEHHNOOORSTU	do the honours
DEHIIILNPPSY	Philip Sidney
DEHIIIMMNNST	diminishment
DEHIIKLLNOOU	unlikelihood
DEHIILNOPRRV	river dolphin
DEHIIMMOOSVV	moshvei ovdim
DEHILLOOOSWY	Hollywoodise
DEHILLOOOWYZ	Hollywoodize
DEHILMORSTWY	the world is my
DEHILNOOPRRS	hold prisoner
DEHILOOPRRSV	overlordship
DEHIMNOOORTY	domino theory
DEHINNOOQRUY	hydroquinone
DEHINOOPRSST	spinsterhood
DEHINOORRRST	in short order
DEHINOORRSTW	in other words
DEHINOOTTUWW	out the window
DEHINPPTTUUW	put the wind up
DEHLLOORRTWY	otherworldly
	other-worldly
DEHLLOORSTTW	The Lost World
DEHLNOORRSUY	horrendously
DEHLNORSTUUY	thunderously
DEHLOOOSTTTW	two-toed sloth
DEHMNORRSTTU	thunderstorm
DEHNOOORSTUW	southernwood
DEIIILMNTUVY	diminutively
DEIIILMSSSVY	dismissively
DEIIKNNPPRSY	skinny-dipper
DEIILLORRTTT	Little Dorrit
DEIILMNNOPSS	slip one's mind
DEIILOPSSTUY	dispiteously
DEIILPRSTUVY	disruptively
DEIINOOPRSTT	periodontist
DEIINOORSTUX	nitrous oxide
DEIJNPRRSTUU	jurisprudent
DEIKNOPRRSTW	printed works
DEILLMORTUXY	dolly mixture
DEILNOORUVWW	louvre window
DEINNNOORRTZ	Norton Zinder
DEINNOOPRSST	send to prison
DEINOSSSSTUU	studiousness
DEIOPRSTTUVY	topside-turvy
DEKLNOOPRUVY	unprovokedly
DELNOPSSTUUY	stupendously
DEMNOOOSSTTU	do one's utmost
DEMNOOPSSUUY	pseudonymous
DENNOOPRRSSU	roundsperson
DENNOORSSSUW	wondrousness
DFGILLSSTUUY	disgustfully
DFGOOOPRRSUW	group of words
DFHNOOOORRUW	word of honour
DFIIILLLNTUY	fill untidily
DFLOOORRSSTW	lost for words
DGGGHIIILNTU	guiding light
DGGHHIINNOSU	high-sounding
DGGHIIINNOOT	go into hiding

DGGHIILNNORT	lightning-rod
DGGHIINNNOOT	nothing doing
DGGHINNOTTUU	doughnutting
DGGIILNSSTUY	disgustingly
DGGIINNORRSU	rising ground
DGHIIMNNOOST	do-nothingism
DGHIINNOORSU	dishonouring
DGHIMNOOOUWY	mind how you go
DGIILOOPRSUY	prodigiously
DGIIMMNNOPSW	swimming-pond
DGIIMNNOPRST	spring to mind
DGILMOORSTTY	troglodytism
DGILNOOOOSTT	odontologist
DGINNORRSSUU	surroundings
DGNOOPRRSSTU	sports ground
DHIKOOORTVVZ	Todor Zhivkov
DHILOORRSUWY	I should worry!
DHIMOOPRRSTY	hydrotropism
DHINOOORSTTT	orthodontist
DHMMPPTTUUYY	Humpty-Dumpty
	humpty-dumpty
DIIIINOQSSTU	disquisition
DIKLNNOOTUWW	I wouldn't know
DINOOPRSTTUW	put into words
DNOOOPRSTTUW	put down roots

E

EEEEEFFLNOST	feel one's feet
EEEEFGLLNOSS	feel one's legs
EEEEFLLNOSST	steel oneself
EEEEFLNNOPRS	preen oneself
EEEEFLNORSTX	exert oneself
EEEEGGINNNOU	Eugene Onegin
EEEEGHMORSTW	get somewhere
EEEEGIILNPSS	spiegeleisen
EEEEGILLNNOU	Eugene O'Neill
EEEEGLMOPSST	get some sleep
EEEEHHKOPSTU	keep the house
EEEEHIMNRTTX	in the extreme
EEEEHKLPRSTU	keep the rules
EEEEHLMNOPRT	nephelometer
EEEEHLNRSSTV	nevertheless
EEEEHNOSSTTT	set one's teeth
EEEEIMNPRRTX	experimenter
EEEEINNQRSTU	equestrienne
EEEEKNNRTTVY	Kenny Everett
EEEELLPRRSST	Peter Sellers
EEEELMNOOSSS	someone else's
EEEELNOPSSUV	up one's sleeve
EEEELNPRSSSS	peerlessness
EEEEMMNPRSST	empressement
EEEENNPRRRTU	entrepreneur
EEEENNSSTWYY	teensy-weensy
EEEENPRRSSSV	perverseness
EEEEPPRRRSSU	peer pressure
EEEFFFLNOORS	offer oneself
EEEFFGHOORWY	Geoffrey Howe
EEEFFIILNNTT	in fine fettle
EEEFFINOSTTV	Tet Offensive
EEEFFINSSSUV	effusiveness
EEEFGGHINRTT	get the finger
EEEFGGINNRRS	green fingers
EEEFGHINNRRS	refreshening
EEEFGHNOORTV	on the verge of
EEEFGIILNOSV	give one's life
EEEFGILNNSST	fleetingness
EEEFGILNORSY	foreseeingly
EEEFGLLNOOST	let oneself go
EEEFGLLNRUVY	revengefully
EEEFGLNNSSUV	vengefulness
EEEFHHINOTTT	in the teeth of
EEEFHHLNOOST	on the heels of
EEEFHINNOTTV	in the event of
EEEFHINRRRSW	Renfrewshire
EEEFHINRSSSV	feverishness
EEEFHLLMORTW	helmet flower
EEEFHMNRRSST	refreshments
EEEFHOOPRTTT	top of the tree
EEEFIIKLLNSS	lifelikeness
EEEFIILLLLMU	millefeuille
EEEFIIMNNNSS	feminineness
EEEFILLNOOSS	lose one's life
EEEFILLNSSSS	lifelessness
EEEFILNRSSTT	self-interest
EEEFJLNNOOSY	enjoy oneself
EEEFLLNOORSW	lower oneself
EEEFLLNSSSSS	selflessness
EEEFLLOOPPRW	flower people
EEEFLLORRSST	forset-seller
EEEFLLORSSST	fosset-seller
EEEFNNQRSSTU	frequentness
EEEFNOORSTVY	every so often
EEEFOORSTTUV	refuse to vote
EEEFOSSSTTTV	Steve Fossett
EEEGGGILLNPV	level pegging
EEEGGHINRTTT	getting there
EEEGGKOORSST	George Stokes
EEEGGLLOORRW	George Orwell
EEEGGOOPRRRT	George Porter
EEEGHHILMSTY	esteem highly
EEEGHHILNTTY	eighteenthly
EEEGHIILOTTV	give the lie to
EEEGHIILTTTV	give the title
EEEGHIKNOPSU	housekeeping
EEEGHILORTTV	live together
EEEGHILRTTWW	welterweight
EEEGHIMNOSTU	meeting-house
EEEGHIMNTTTT	get the mitten
EEEGHINSTTVY	seventy-eight
EEEGHNNRRSTT	strengthener
EEEGHNORRRWZ	Werner Herzog
EEEGHNORSSTT	togetherness
EEEGHOORTTYZ	heterozygote
EEEGIIILLTVW	give it wellie
EEEGIILMNNTV	inveiglement
EEEGIINNORRT	orienteering
EEEGILRRSSVY	regressively
EEEGIMNRSSSU	Messeigneurs
EEEGINNPRRST	representing
EEEGINOOSSST	osteogenesis
EEEGIOQRRSTU	grotesquerie
EEEGLNNNSSTU	ungentleness

EEEGMNORSSSU gruesomeness
EEEGMOORSTTX go to extremes
EEEGNNOOORTV get one over on
EEEGNNORSSSU generousness
EEEGNOOPRRRS Roger Penrose
EEEGNOOPRRST progesterone
EEEHHILLOSTW oil the wheels
EEEHHINPSSSS sheepishness
EEEHHJLLOPRS Joseph Heller
EEEHHLNORTUV eleventh-hour
EEEHHLNOSSTV on the shelves
EEEHHMOPRRST thermosphere
EEEHILLOSTTT stiletto heel
EEEHILMNNORY Leonine rhyme
EEEHILNNNTTY nineteenthly
EEEHIMNRSTTU hermeneutist
EEEHIMORSSTX heterosexism
EEEHINNOPRRS reprehension
EEEHINNORSTW none the wiser
EEEHINPRSTVY hypertensive
EEEHIORSSTTX heterosexist
EEEHJMOPRRTY Jeremy Thorpe
EEEHJMPQTUUU jump the queue
EEEHKLNNNOST Kenneth Olsen
EEEHLLNOPTYY polyethylene
EEEHLLNPSSSS helplessness
EEEHLMNOPRTY nephelometry
EEEHLMNOSSSS homelessness
EEEHLNOPSSSS hopelessness
EEEHLOPRRSSS sheep's sorrel
EEEHLOPRSTTW potter's wheel
EEEHMNNNORTT enthronement
EEEHMOORRSTU heteromerous
EEEHMOORRSTW meteor shower
EEEHNOPRRRSY reprehensory
EEEHNORSSTTT on the streets
EEEHNRRSTTUV serve the turn
EEEIIKLNORSY Kyrie eleison
EEEIILPRTTVY repetitively
EEEIIMNPSTTV intempestive
EEEIINNNRTTV intervenient
EEEIINNPRSST serpentinise
EEEIINNPRSTZ serpentinize
EEEIINPRRTTV interpretive
EEEIINPRSSVX inexpressive
EEEIIPQRRSTU prerequisite
EEEIJLNNSSUV juvenileness
EEEILLLOPPTT little people
EEEILLPRSSVY Elvis Presley
EEEILMNNPRTY pre-eminently
EEEILMNNSSSU unseemliness
EEEILMNORSTU son et lumière
EEEILMNSSSST timelessness
EEEILNNPRSTY serpentinely
EEEILNPRTVVY preventively
EEEILNRRRTVY irreverently
EEEILNRSSSST tirelessness
EEEILNRSSSTW Western Isles
EEEILPRRSSVY repressively
EEEILPRSSVXY expressively
EEEIMNNPRSTT presentiment
EEEIMNORSSST tiresomeness
EEEIMNORSSTT sensitometer
EEEIMNPRRSST misrepresent
EEEIMNQRRSTU requirements
EEEIMOORRSST stereoisomer
EEEIMOPRRRST respirometer
EEEIMOPRSTUX time exposure
EEEINNNOSSSS in one's senses
EEEINNPRSSTX inexpertness
EEEINNPRSTUV supervenient
EEEINPRSSUVX unexpressive
EEEIOOPSTVWX expose to view
EEEJLLORSWYY yellow jersey
EEEKLOOPPPSS spokespeople
EEEKMNORTVVY vervet monkey
EEELLLNRSSTY relentlessly
EEELMNNOOSSS lonesomeness
EEELMOPPRRTT Teleprompter
EEELNOPRSSSS responseless
EEELNORSSSTU resoluteness
EEELNRSSSSST restlessness
EEEMNOOSTTTX to some extent
EEEMNORSTTUV Mount Everest
EEEMPRSSTTXY expert system
EEENOOPSSTUY up to one's eyes
EEENOORSSTTT testosterone
EEENOPRSSTTU up one's street
EEEOOPRRSUVX overexposure
EEEOPRRRSTTT Street-Porter
EEFFFLNOSSTU stuff oneself
EEFFGHHINOST off the hinges
EEFFGHILLORY Geoffrey Hill
EEFFGHILLSTU gefüllte fish
EEFFGILNNNUY funny feeling
EEFFGLLNORUY full of energy
EEFFHIKLOSTT kettle of fish
EEFFHIMOORTT for the time of
EEFFHLLRRSUY refreshfully
EEFFLLORSSTY effortlessly
EEFFLOORRRSY feel sorry for
EEFGGIILNRSU single-figure
EEFGGINNOPRS sponge finger
EEFGGIOPRTTY pettifoggery
EEFGHHIOPRTU of high repute
EEFGHIIKNNRT freethinking
free-thinking
EEFGHIILNRRT freightliner
EEFGHIIPRRTZ prizefighter
prize-fighter
EEFGHILMNOTT length of time
EEFGHILNRRSY refreshingly
EEFGHINORSST sense of right
EEFGHINOSSST sense of sight
EEFGIILLNRTT little finger
EEFGIILMNPXY exemplifying
EEFGIIMNNNRT infringement
EEFGIINOPRRT profiteering
EEFGIINSSTUV fugitiveness
EEFGIKNOOPTU out of keeping
EEFGILLNSSUU guilefulness
EEFGINPPPRTU finger puppet

EEFGNOOPRSUV	Group of Seven
EEFHHILNOOTW	in the whole of
EEFHHMMMOOOR	home from home
EEFHILNNOOST	on the lines of
EEFHILNOPPST	slip of the pen
EEFHINOOPRTW	in the power of
EEFHLNORTTUY	fourteenthly
EEFHMMNOORTT	for the moment
EEFHMOOORTTY	Otto Meyerhof
EEFHNOOORTUW	out of nowhere
EEFIIINNNSST	infiniteness
EEFIIKLNORSS	Leif Eriksson
EEFIIMNORSSU	seminiferous
EEFILNNQRTUY	infrequently
EEFILNOORRTX	retroflexion
EEFILNPSSSTU	spitefulness
EEFIMNOPRRST	serpentiform
EEFJMNNOORTY	for enjoyment
EEFKLLOORRWW	fellow worker
	fellow-worker
EEFLLMORRSUY	remorsefully
EEFLLNORSSUV	overfullness
	over-fullness
EEFLMNORRSUU	unremorseful
EEFLMNORSSSS	formlessness
EEFLNOOPPRST	people's front
EEFLNOPRSSUW	powerfulness
EEFNNNOOPRUY	fourpenny one
EEFNNORSTTUV	turn of events
EEFOOPPRSSTU	of set purpose
EEGGGGHMRRUU	hugger-mugger
EEGGGINORRRS	Ginger Rogers
EEGGHIILNNNT	enlightening
EEGGHIINNRTT	teething ring
EEGGHIIOTTVW	give weight to
EEGGHOORRTTW	grow together
EEGGILSSTUVY	suggestively
EEGGJMMOORRY	memory-jogger
EEGGNOORSSSU	gorgeousness
EEGHHHILMRTT	right the helm
EEGHHINRTTVY	the very thing
EEGHHIORSTTU	see it through
EEGHHIORTTTW	together with
EEGHHIPRRSSU	high-pressure
EEGHIIIMSTTX	six-eight time
EEGHIINOSSST	histogenesis
EEGHIINPRRTZ	the prize-ring
EEGHIINRSTUX	extinguisher
EEGHIJNOORTT	join together
EEGHIKLNORTT	link together
EEGHIKNRRSTU	hunger strike
	hunger-strike
EEGHIKORSTVW	give the works
EEGHILLLPSTY	sleep lightly
EEGHILMNORVW	overwhelming
EEGHILNOOPRS	phrenologise
EEGHILNOOPRZ	phrenologize
EEGHILNOPPST	teleshopping
EEGHILNOPSSY	phylogenesis
EEGHINNOSTTW	sweet nothing
EEGHINOORSST	orthogenesis
EEGHINOPSSTY	phytogenesis
EEGHINOSSTUW	Westinghouse
EEGHIOORSTTV	give to others
EEGHKOORRTTW	work together
EEGHLLOOPRST	hot gospeller
EEGHLLOPRTTU	pull together
EEGHLOOOPRTT	pool together
EEGHLOOORSTU	heterologous
EEGHMMOPRSTY	sphygmometer
EEGHMNOORTTU	mother tongue
EEGHNNOOSTUY	The Young Ones
EEGHNOOORSTU	heterogonous
EEGHNOORSSUU	house-surgeon
EEGHOOOPRTTV	go over the top
EEGHOORSSTTY	the story goes
EEGHOORSTUYZ	heterozygous
EEGIIKLMNOUY	Kylie Minogue
EEGIILLLMNSV	evil-smelling
EEGIILLLNPPS	sleeping pill
	sleeping-pill
EEGIILLNPRST	still-peering
EEGIILNNSTTY	single entity
EEGIIMNNOPTT	meeting-point
EEGIINNPRRST	enterprising
EEGIINNRRTTY	eternity ring
EEGIINNRRTUV	give in return
EEGIINNSTTTW	Wittgenstein
EEGIIRRSSTVY	regressivity
EEGIJMNPQUUU	queue-jumping
EEGILLNNPSUX	sun-expelling
EEGILLNOOSST	selenologist
EEGILLNPPRXY	perplexingly
EEGILLOOPSST	speleologist
EEGILLORRRSU	guerrilleros
EEGILMNOOOST	entomologise
EEGILMNOOOTZ	entomologize
EEGILMOOPPSS	goose-pimples
EEGILMOOPSTY	epistemology
EEGILNOORRSW	lower regions
EEGILNOPRTTU	triple-tongue
EEGILQRRRSUY	grey squirrel
EEGIMNNNORTV	in government
EEGIMNNRRSTU	interregnums
EEGINNNRRSSU	unerringness
EEGINNPRSTUV	prevent using
EEGINOOPRRVW	overpowering
EEGINOORRSTU	outer regions
EEGINOPPRSTV	overstepping
EEGINOPRRSST	progenitress
EEGINOPRSTTY	stereotyping
EEGINORSSSUV	grievousness
EEGINOSSSUUX	exiguousness
EEGLMNNOOOPR	prolegomenon
EEGLNNOOPSSU	upon one's legs
EEHHIINSSSTV	thievishness
EEHHIKLLMNUW	Wilhelm Kühne
EEHHILNRTTTY	thirteenthly
EEHHJKOOOPRS	Joseph Hooker
EEHHLLOPRTYY	heterophylly
EEHHLLRTTTTU	tell the truth
EEHHLNOOPTUW	upon the whole

EEHHMOOPRRTY heteromorphy
EEHHNOORRTTW whether or not
EEHHOOPRRTTY heterotrophy
EEHHOOSSUUYY housey-housey
EEHIIIMNNRTT in the interim
EEHIILLLRTTT little Hitler
EEHIILNPRSTY prehensility
EEHIIMNPPRRU perinephrium
EEHIINOPRRVX River Phoenix
EEHIINOQTUVV on the qui vive
EEHIJLOPRSST Joseph Lister
EEHIKLLNRRTU hunter-killer
EEHILLPRSTUW pull the wires
EEHILMNORSST motherliness
EEHILNNOPTTU put on the line
EEHILNOPRSTT Peter Shilton
EEHILOPSTTTV split the vote
EEHILPSTTTUW settle up with
EEHIMNOOPRTV on the improve
EEHINNOORTVZ event horizon
EEHINNOPRSTY hypertension
EEHINORSSTTW show interest
EEHJNOPRRSTU Joseph Turner
EEHKMNORSSUY rhesus monkey
EEHKNOOPRSTW know the ropes
EEHLLLOOPSWY Sleepy Hollow
EEHLNRSSSSTU ruthlessness
EEHLOORRSTTU rule the roost
EEHMNOOORSTU heteronomous
EEHMNRRRSUYY nursery rhyme
EEHNNOOORSTW one-horse town
EEHNNORRSTTW north-western
EEHNORSSTTUW south-western
EEHOOPPRSTTU to the purpose
EEIIINRSSSTW sinisterwise
EEIIINRSSTUV universities
EEIIKLLNNSSU unlikeliness
EEIILLNSSSUV illusiveness
EEIILMNNPTTY impenitently
EEIILMNNSSTU untimeliness
EEIILMNOPSST impoliteness
EEIILMPRSSVY impressively
permissively
EEIILNPPRSSS slipperiness
EEIILNPSSSST pitilessness
EEIILNRSSSST sisterliness
EEIILOPSTVXY expositively
EEIILOSSTTTU toilet tissue
EEIIMNNRTTTT intermittent
EEIIMNOQSTTU question time
EEIIMNPRRSTT misinterpret
EEIIMNPRSSUV unimpressive
EEIIMNRRTTUX intermixture
EEIINNNORTTV intervention
EEIINNORSTTT retentionist
EEIINNPPSSST snippetiness
EEIINOPSSSTV positiveness
EEIINPPRTTUY in perpetuity
EEIINPRRTTUV interruptive
EEIIOOPRSSTV seropositive
EEIJNNORTTUV joint venture
EEIKLMNNOSTY Milton Keynes
EEIKOOPRSSTX expose to risk
EEIKOPRRRSTW worker priest
EEILLNNOQTUY ineloquently
EEILLNNOSSSV slovenliness
EEILLNNOSSUV unloveliness
EEILLNSSSSST listlessness
EEILLORRSTUY irresolutely
EEILLRSSSSTY resistlessly
EEILMMNNOPTY in employment
EEILMOOPRSST metropolises
EEILMOPPRRTY peremptorily
EEILMOPRSSTW Mister Wopsle
EEILMORSSSTU moistureless
EEILMPRSTUVY resumptively
EEILNNOPQSTU Nelson Piquet
EEILNOORRSTU resolutioner
EEILNOPRSSSU perilousness
EEILNOPRSSVY responsively
EEILNOQSSSTU questionless
EEILNPRSSTTY persistently
EEILNPSSSUVY suspensively
EEILOPPRSSVY oppressively
EEILOPRRSTYZ proselytizer
EEILOPSSSSVY possessively
EEIMMMNSSTUY immune system
EEIMNNNOPRSY moneyspinner
money-spinner
EEIMNNORSTTX nonextremist
EEINNOOPQSTU open question
EEINNOPRSSUV unresponsive
EEINNOPRSTUV supervention
EEINNORRSSTV Steven Norris
EEINOOPPSSST oppositeness
EEINOOPRSSSS repossession
EEINOORRRSTV retroversion
EEINOORRSTVX extroversion
EEINOPRSSSSU supersession
EEINOPRSSSTV sportiveness
EEINOPRSTTUV Peter Ustinov
EEINORSSSTUV vitreousness
EEINRRSSTTUV serve its turn
EEIOPPRRRSST proprietress
EEKLMNOPUYZZ monkey puzzle
EEKNNOORSTTT Stoke-on-Trent
EEKNNOORUVWY you never know
EEKNOOPPRSSS spokesperson
EELLNNNNOOSS Nelson Nelson
EELLNNNOOSSV nolens volens
EELLNOOOSVWY loosely woven
EELLNOSSSSSU soullessness
EELMMNNOPTUY unemployment
EELMMNPSSTUY plenum system
EELMOOPRSTTY Ptolemy Soter
EELMOPRRSTTY stormy petrel
EELNNPPSSSUU unsuppleness
EELNOORSSSST rootlessness
EELNOPSSSSST spotlessness
EELOPRRSSTUY streperously
EEMNNOOORRTU motor neurone
EEMNNOOPPSTT postponement

EEMNNOORSSSU	enormousness
EEMNNOOSSSUV	venomousness
EEMNNORSSSUU	numerousness
EENNNOOOPRSS	on one's person
EENNOOOPRTUV	put one over on
EENNOOPPRSSU	on one's uppers
EENNOSSSSSUU	sensuousness
EENNRRRSSUUY	nursery nurse
EENNTTTTWWYY	twenty-twenty
EEOOPPRRSSTU	preposterous
EEPPRRTTTTYY	pretty-pretty
EFFGGIILNNSU	glue-sniffing
EFFGHIIOTTTW	get it off with
EFFILNRSSTUU	fruitfulness
EFFIMOORRTUU	four-four time
EFFINNNOOOOS	off one's onion
EFGGGIINOPTT	pettifogging
EFGGILNORTTY	forgettingly
EFGGILOORTUW	wriggle out of
EFGHHIILNOTT	in the light of
EFGHHIINOSTT	in the sight of
EFGHHILNTTTW	Twelfth Night
EFGHIKOORRSY	Yorkshire fog
EFGHILNRSSTU	rightfulness
EFGHINOOPRTW	Night of Power
EFGHINORRTTY	right of entry
EFGIIINNNSTY	intensifying
EFGIIKNNNPRU	pruning-knife
EFGIILNOOSTT	loose-fitting
EFGIILNORSUV	griseofulvin
EFGIILNRRTYY	terrifyingly
EFGIINNPRRST	fingerprints
EFGILLLMNOSU	foul-smelling
EFGILLOORSSU	self-glorious
EFGLNNORSSUW	wrongfulness
EFHHILLOOOSY	holy of holies
EFHIKNORRSTU	run the risk of
EFHILLMNORTU	run of the mill
	run-of-the-mill
EFHILLRSSTTY	thriftlessly
EFHILMNRSSTU	mirthfulness
EFHILNOOPTTU	put on the foil
EFHILOORRSUV	overflourish
EFHILOORTVWW	overflow with
EFHINNOOOPTT	on the point of
EFHJNOOOPRST	not for Joseph
EFHLLNOSSSTU	slothfulness
EFHLNNOOPRTY	horn of plenty
EFHLNOSSTUUY	youthfulness
EFHLNRSSTTUU	truthfulness
EFIIIILNNTVY	infinitively
EFIIIMNNNTUY	unfemininity
EFIIINOPRSTW	spirit of wine
EFILLOPRSSTY	profitlessly
EFILNORRSSUW	snow flurries
EFLLOPPRSUUY	purposefully
EFLMNNORSSUU	mournfulness
EFLNRSSSTTUU	trustfulness
EFNOOPRRSTTU	return of post
EGGGIILNNRSY	sniggeringly
EGGGIILORTYY	György Ligeti
EGGHHIINNRSY	Henry Higgins
EGGHHOORTTTU	get through to
EGGHIIKLNNSS	King's English
EGGHIINNNOPT	opening night
EGGHIINPRSSS	priggishness
EGGHILNSSSSU	sluggishness
EGGHILRSTTUW	struggle with
EGGIIINORSTV	giving rise to
EGGIILLMMNRY	glimmeringly
EGGIILLNRSTY	glisteringly
EGGIILLNRTTY	glitteringly
EGGILOOPSTTY	Egyptologist
EGGIMNOOPRSS	gossip-monger
EGHHHOORRTTU	through-other
EGHHIINOPSTT	highest point
EGHHIJNNOPRS	John Pershing
EGHHIJOPRSTW	Joseph Wright
EGHHILNOSSSU	ghoulishness
EGHHINNOSTUU	house-hunting
EGHHNOOOSTTU	go on the shout
EGHHNOOPRSTW	the wrong shop
EGHHNOORSSTU	thoroughness
EGHIIIMNRSTV	shriving-time
EGHIILMNPRWY	whimperingly
EGHIILNOTTWZ	twilight zone
EGHIILNPRSWY	whisperingly
EGHIIMNNNORT	in the morning
EGHIINNNNRTU	in the running
EGHIINOSSTTU	house-sitting
EGHILMNORSTY	smotheringly
EGHILNNNORTU	in the long run
EGHILNOOPRST	phrenologist
EGHILOOPPSST	psephologist
EGHIMNOOORSU	rooming-house
EGHIMNORSSTW	women's rights
EGHINOOPRRSV	governorship
EGHLLOOOPSTT	go to the polls
EGIIIKLNNNRT	interlinking
EGIIILLNNRSV	silver lining
EGIIIMNOPSTU	impetiginous
EGIIINNNPRWZ	prize-winning
EGIIKLLNNORR	inking roller
EGIIKLNPPRRS	klipspringer
EGIIKNOPPPRS	skipping-rope
EGIILLMNOTUY	I'm telling you
EGIILMOOSSST	seismologist
EGIILNNNOSTT	not listening
EGIILNNNRTTU	running title
EGIILNNOORSU	non-religious
EGIILNNPRSST	Silent Spring
EGIILNPRSSTY	persistingly
EGIILNRSSTTW	West Stirling
EGIILNRTTTWY	twitteringly
EGIIMNOOPRRT	primogenitor
EGIIMNOORRST	risorgimento
EGIINNPRRTTU	interrupting
EGIINOOPSTTV	give points to
EGIINPRRSSUZ	pressurizing
EGILLNNOORST	rolling stone
EGILLNORSTTY	story-telling
EGILMNNORTTY	tormentingly

EGILMNOOOSTT	entomologist
EGILMNOORSTU	numerologist
EGILMNOOSTYZ	enzymologist
EGILNNRSUVWY	unswervingly
EGILNOORSSSU	gloriousness
EGILNOPRSTTY	protestingly
EGILNPRSTTUY	sputteringly
EGILNRSTTTUY	stutteringly
EGIMNOORRTTY	trigonometry
EGINNOPRSTTU	unprotesting
EGINNOPSSSSU	unpossessing
EGINOORRSSSU	rigorousness
EGINOORSSSUV	vigorousness
EGINORRSTTUV	overtrusting
EGKNNOORSSTU	surgeon's knot
EGKNNORTTUUV	Kurt Vonnegut
EGMMNOORRRUU	rumour-monger
EHHIIJNORTTW	John Whittier
EHHIILOOPPSS	philosophise
EHHIILOOPPSZ	philosophize
EHHILOPPSTUY	hyposulphite
EHHINNOOORTZ	on the horizon
EHHNOOPRTTTU	put to the horn
EHIIIILNPSST	Philistinise
EHIIIILNPSTZ	Philistinize
EHIIILORSTTT	lithotritise
EHIIILORTTTZ	lithotritize
EHIIIOPTTTUY	it pitieth you
EHIIKNSSSSTT	skittishness
EHIILLOPSTWW	will-o'-the-wisp
EHIILLSTTTTW	Wilt the Stilt
EHIILMOOPRST	heliotropism
EHIILOPRRTTT	lithotripter
EHIIMNOPSSTT	miss the point
EHIIMOPSTTTU	up to this time
EHIINORSTTUY	Trinity House
EHIJMMNOORRT	John Mortimer
EHIJNNOOSSSS	John Sessions
EHILLMOPPSTU	multiple shop
EHILMMOOPPRS	pleomorphism
EHILNNOSSTYZ	Solzhenitsyn
EHILNOOPSUUY	euphoniously
EHILNOORTTWY	noteworthily
EHILNORSTTUW	with no result
EHILNSSSSTTU	sluttishness
EHILOPRSSUWY	whisperously
EHIMMOPSSTUY	The Symposium
EHIMMORRSSTT	short-termism
EHIMOOPPRRTY	pyromorphite
EHINNORSSTUW	unworthiness
EHINOORRSSTV	short version
EHINOPPSTTTU	put in the post
EHINOPRTTTUZ	put on the Ritz
EHIOORRRTTUW	without error
EHKLNOOOOTTU	on the lookout
EHKMNOOOPSST	smooth-spoken
EHLMMOOOSTVY	move smoothly
EHMMNNOORRST	the morn's morn
EHMMOOOPRSSU	mesomorphous
EHMNNOORRSTT	northernmost
EHMNOORSSSUU	humorousness
EHMNOORSSTTU	southernmost
EHNOOPPSTTTU	put on the spot
EHOOOPRRSTTU	orthopterous
EIIIMNNORSST	intermission
EIIIMPRTTTVY	permittivity
EIIJLLNNOOPS	Lionel Jospin
EIILLLLMNOPS	Plimsoll line
EIILLOOQRSUZ	soliloquizer
EIILLPRSSSTY	spiritlessly
EIILMNOOQSSU	somniloquise
EIILMNOOQSUZ	somniloquize
EIILMNOOSTUV	evolutionism
EIILMOPRSUVY	imperviously
EIILNNNOSTUV	tunnel vision
EIILNOOOPPST	pole position
EIILNOORRSTU	irresolution
EIILNOOSTTUV	evolutionist
EIILNOPRSTUY	polyneuritis
EIIMMNNOPRST	imprisonment
EIIMNNNQQUUU	quinquennium
EIIMOPRSSSST	prestissimos
EIINNNOPSSSU	in suspension
EIINNOORRSTV	introversion
EIINNOPRRTTU	interruption
EIINOORSTTTX	extortionist
EIINOPRSSTTU	superstition
EIIOOPPSSTTV	postpositive
EIKLLMNOSTUY	most unlikely
EIKMNNOSSTUZ	Simon Kuznets
EILLLLRSSUWY	Willy Russell
EILLMNOQTTUU	multiloquent
EILLMOPRTUVY	overmultiply
EILMNNOOPTTY	omnipotently
EILMOPPRSTUU	multipurpose
EILMORSSTUYY	mysteriously
EILOPPRSTUVY	supportively
EILOPRRSTUVY	protrusively
EIMNNNOOOTTT	not to mention
EIMNNNOSSSUU	numinousness
EIMNNOOPTTUY	put money into
EIMNNOSSSTUU	mutinousness
EIMNOOOPPRRT	proper motion
EIMNOORSSSTU	timorousness
EINNOPRSSSUW	win one's spurs
EINOORSSSUUX	uxoriousness
EINOPRRSSTTW	winter sports
EINOPRSSSSUU	spuriousness
EINOQRTTTTUU	Trout Quintet
EINORSSSTUUV	virtuousness
EIOOOOPRSSST	osteoporosis
EIOOPPRSTTUV	supportive to
EIOORRSTTTUU	tourist route
EKLOOOORTTUW	lookout tower
ELLNOORSTUUY	ultroneously
ELNOOPRSTTUY	portentously
ELOOPPRRSSUY	prosperously
ELOORRSSTTUY	stertorously
EMOPPRSSTUUU	presumptuous
ENNOOORSSSSU	sonorousness
ENOOPPRRSSST	sportsperson
ENOORSSSTTUU	tortuousness

F

FFFFGIIOTTYY go fifty-fifty
FFGGHHIIINST fighting fish
FFHHIIIOTTTW hit it off with
FFLLOOSSTTYY softly-softly
FGGHIIINTTTT tight-fitting
FGGHIILMPSTY pigs might fly
FGGHIINOPSTT stop fighting
FGGHINNOOORT go for nothing
FGGHIOOOSTTU go out of sight
FGHHIIJNOTTW John Whitgift
FGHHILORRTTY forthrightly
FGHHLLOTTUUY thoughtfully
FGHIILNORRYY horrifyingly
FGHIINNNOOTT nothing if not
FGHIINORSSTW first showing
FGHILLNRTUUY unrightfully
FGHILLPRSTUY sprightfully
FGIILLNOSUUY fuliginously
FGIILMNSTYYY mystifyingly
FGINOOPSSTUY pussyfooting
FHIILOOSTTWY foolish-witty
FHILLOPRSUWY worshipfully
FHLLNRTTUUUY untruthfully
FIILMMORTTUY multiformity
FIIOOPRSSTTU out of spirits
FILLMNOSUUUX luminous flux
FILOORSTTUUY fortuitously
FMNNOORSSTUU from sun to sun

G

GGGHHHIIILNT highlighting
GGGHHINOORTU going-through
GGGILLNRSTUY strugglingly
GGHHILNRSTUY highly-strung
GGHIIILNNSTV living things
GGHIIJMMNTUY thingummyjig
GGHIILMNNOOT moonlighting
GGHIINOOTTUW going-without
GGHIINORSTTV voting rights
GGIIILLNNOTU guillotining
GGIIILNNRTUY intriguingly
GHHHIKNORTTU think through
GHHHORRRTUUY hurry through
GHHIIIOPRRTY high-priority
GHHIIOSTTTUW without sight
GHHILNOORTTW throw light on
GHHMNPRRSTUY sprung rhythm
GHIIKLNNNTUY unthinkingly
GHIILNNORSUY nourishingly
GHIILNOPPSST shopping list
GHIILOOPSSTY physiologist
GHIINNOOORST shooting iron
GHIKNOORRSUW working hours
GHILMOOOPRST morphologist
GIIIMNOPRSTV moving spirit
GIIINNPRTTUW put in writing
GIIKKOORRSSY Igor Sikorsky
GIILLNNNOTUW not unwilling
GIILLNOORSUY ingloriously
GIILMMNOOPSW swimming-pool
GIILMMNOOSTU immunologist
GIILMNNOOOPZ monopolizing
GIILMNNOOSTU monolinguist
GIILMNORSSST Stirling Moss
GIILNNNSTTUY unstintingly
GIILNORRSSTU soul-stirring
GIILNPRRSSUY surprisingly
GIINNNOPRTTU turning-point
GIINNPRRSSUU unsurprising
GILNOOQRRSTU strong liquor
GINNNNOORTUU running out on
GLLNOOSTTUUY gluttonously
GOOPPPRRSTUU support group

H

HHHJMNOPRSUY John Humphrys
HHIKLMOORSTY Miklós Horthy
HHIMMMOOOPRS homomorphism
HHINOOPRRTTY thyrotrophin
HHIOOTTTUUWW tu-whit tu-whoo
HHJNNOOOPRRT John Northrop
HHMMOOOOPRSU homomorphous
HHMMOOOTTTUU mouth-to-mouth
HIIIILMNPSST philistinism
HIIIILMNSTTW within limits
HIIILMOTTTUW without limit
HIILOOPRRTTT lithotriptor
HIIMMNOORSTU Ornithomimus
HIIMNNOSSTTW Winston Smith
HIINOPRSTTUU in hot pursuit
HILMMOOPPRSY polymorphism
HIMOOOPPRSTT phototropism
HIMOORSTTTWY thirty-twomos
HLMMNOOOSUYY homonymously
HLMOOOPPRSUY polymorphous
HLMOOPSSTUUY posthumously
HMMNOOOOPRSU monomorphous
HMNNOOOPRUUY upon my honour

I

IIIIMMNNNPYY niminy-piminy
IIILNOPRSSTW in low spirits
low in spirits
IIILNOQSTUUY iniquitously
IIIMNNOORSST intromission
IIIMNOORTTUV vomiturition
IIINNOOOPPST in opposition
IIINNORSTTTU nutritionist
IIINNORSTTUU innutritious
IIIOPRSSTTUY spirituosity
IILMOOPRRSSY promissorily
IILNORSSSTUY sinistrously
IILNORSTTUUY nutritiously
IILOOPPRSTUY propitiously
IIMNNOOORRST Toni Morrison
IINNOOOPPTTT point-to-point
IINOOOPPSSTT postposition
IINOOPPRSTUU unpropitious
IINOOPRSTTTU prostitution
ILLMNOOSUUVY voluminously

ILLMOOQSTUUU multiloquous
ILLNNNOORSSY Sonny Rollins
ILNORSTUUUVY unvirtuously
ILOPRSTTUVYY topsy-turvily
INNNOOOOPSSU non-poisonous

L

LLMOSTTUUUUY tumultuously
LLOOPSTUUUVY voluptuously
LMMNOOPSTUUY Mount Olympus
LMNNOOOOSTUY monotonously
LMNNOOSSUYYY synonymously

M

MNPPRRSTTUUU turn up trumps

13 letters

A

AAAAADEGNNTTV at an advantage
AAAAADGGIINNN again and again
AAAAAHKMNNOTV Anna Akhmatova
AAAABBCELRRST Barbara Castle
AAAABBDEGGGGN bag and baggage
AAAABCDIILLTY adiabatically
AAAABCEEKKSTT take a back seat
AAAABCEIKLMOR Lake Maracaibo
AAAABCIMNNRRU Carmina Burana
AAAABDDEENRRS Andreas Baader
AAAABDILMORSS ambassadorial
AAAABEEIKLLMV make available
AAAABHHINNNRR Brian Hanrahan
AAAACCDIIKLLS lackadaisical
AAAACCEELPRSS Caesar's Palace
AAAACCHIMNRST act as chairman
AAAACCHRSTTTW catch at a straw
AAAACCILLLPRT parallactical
AAAACEELLPRTT at a later place
AAAACEGIKLNRU Lake Nicaragua
AAAACEILNPSST at a snail's pace
AAAACEIMMNORS American Samoa
AAAACEKLRSSVV Vera Caslavska
AAAACFHLMMNNO Man of La Mancha
AAAACGHHMMNPR Graham Chapman
AAAACIIKLMORV Alicia Markova
AAAADEEGKNRTT take a gander at
AAAADEGHLMNOP alpha and omega
AAAADFFLNNORU fauna and flora
flora and fauna
AAAADILMNOPTT maladaptation
AAAAEEGHJMMPT The Pajama Game
AAAAEEHILMRRT Amelia Earhart
AAAAEGIMMNRST anagrammatise
AAAAEGIMMNRTZ anagrammatize
AAAAEGKMNORRT make arroganat
AAAAEHILNPPRR paraphernalia
AAAAEIKLLMMSU salaam aleikum
AAAAEJLMNPRTU Jean Paul Marat
AAAAGILLNNOUV Galina Ulanova
AAAAGPRRSSTTW grasp at a straw
AAAAIKKORRSUW Akira Kurosawa
AAAALMRSSSTTU assault at arms
AAABBCCIILLST cabbalistical
AAABBCDDILOOU Claudio Abbado
AAABBCEFINORR Afro-Caribbean
AAABBDEFJKMOO make a bad job of
AAABBELNPRSTY Barnstaple Bay
AAABBHMMOORSS Abraham's bosom
AAABCCCEKLLTU back-calculate
AAABCCEMORRSU camera obscura
AAABCCENNRSSU bancassurance
AAABCCHILOPRR parabolic arch
AAABCCILLORTY acrobatically
AAABCDEGHIRTW with a bad grace
AAABCDEHINRTU Chateaubriand
AAABCEEEHKPSY Chesapeake Bay
AAABCEEILNRST ascertainable
AAABCEFHKNRRU Frank Auerbach
AAABCEFKKMSTU make a fast buck
AAABCEGILLLRY algebraically
AAABCEHJMNNSU James Buchanan
AAABCEHMNRRTY Carmarthen Bay
AAABCEILLNORY anaerobically
AAABCEILLNTTU nautical table
AAABCHHINOOPR arachnophobia
AAABCILLLOPRY parabolically
AAABCKLNNORUY Alan Ayckbourn
AAABDDDENRRRW Edward Barnard
AAABDDELNTTUW wattle and daub
AAABDEGHHNRTY hang by a thread
AAABDEGIILMTY damageability
AAABDELLNPSTU Spandau Ballet
AAABDGHINNSST Hastings Banda
AAABDHHINNSSW washhand basin
AAABEEEGKLRRT Great Bear Lake
AAABEEEHKRRTT take a breather
AAABEEELLRTUV rateable value
AAABEEGHKRRTT Akbar the Great
AAABEEGKMRTTU take umbrage at
AAABEEGLLNSUV unsalvageable
AAABEFILOPTTV Battle of Pavia
AAABEFLNORTTV Battle of Varna
AAABEGIILMNTY manageability
AAABEHIMSTTTY be that as it may
AAABEILLMNPTU manipulatable
AAABEILMMNPST baptismal name
AAABEILNTTUVV tableau vivant
AAABELNNRRTUW unwarrantable
AAABGHIINNRST Arabian Nights
AAABGPRRRSSST part brass rags
AAABIIILNTTTY attainability
AAABIIKLNNOTZ Balkanization
AAABILNNRSSUY Alan Sainsbury
AAABLNNRRTUWY unwarrantably
AAACCDEIIMNNO Nadia Comaneci

AAACCDEIINPTT	incapacitated
AAACCDEIIPSTT	discapacitate
AAACCDEILLNTU	canaliculated
AAACCDEIRRRST	cardiac arrest
AAACCDHIILNOR	archidiaconal
AAACCEEFHLOTT	at the coalface
AAACCEEHMNRTT	catchment area
AAACCEELMMRRU	Marcel Marceau
AAACCEGILLNPT	galactic plane
AAACCEGILLPTY	legal capacity
AAACCEHIMNRRT	main character
AAACCEHKLMRSY	Charles Mackay
AAACCEHNRSTUW	catch unawares
AAACCEHPRRRTT	character part
AAACCEIPPRSTY	spare capacity
AAACCELLLNOPR	local parlance
AAACCELLPRSTY	Crystal Palace
AAACCGIMMNNOR	Norman MacCaig
AAACCHRSSTTTW	catch at straws
AAACCIILMSSTT	salami tactics
AAACCILLLTTYY	catalytically
AAACCILLMNORY	macaronically
AAACCILLRSSTY	sarcastically
AAACDDEGNNNOS	a song and dance
AAACDDELLMNNO	Donald Maclean
AAACDDINNORSU	Isadora Duncan
AAACDEEFLLLRW	Alfred Wallace
AAACDEEGJKNRT	Jack Teagarden
AAACDEEINPPRS	disappearance
AAACDEELLMORT	moderate a call
AAACDEGINRRSS	airs and graces
AAACDEGLMOSUY	amygdalaceous
AAACDEHHKNRRS	Chandrasekhar
AAACDEHNNPSTY	cheap and nasty
AAACDEIIINPRT	paediatrician
AAACDEIINNRRV	Canadian River
AAACDEIMORSTT	act as mediator
AAACDELNPPRRT	part and parcel
AAACDFNRRSSTT	Arts and Crafts
AAACDGHIIMPRT	diaphragmatic
AAACDGILMRRTU	dramaturgical
AAACDHHINNRRY	Richard Hannay
AAACDHILMRRTY	Admiralty Arch
AAACDILLOPRXY	paradoxically
AAACDILMNNSSY	Cayman Islands
AAACDILNNRSSY	Canary Islands
AAACDILNORTUY	auditory canal
AAACEEEGILMNR	American eagle
AAACEEFHILTTU	Château Lafite
AAACEEFLNNORT	Anatole France
AAACEEHKLMRTY	the real Mackay
AAACEEILMRSTU	material cause
AAACEEINRSTTV	set at variance
AAACEEKKMNPPU	pancake make-up
AAACEENNNOPPR	non-appearance
AAACEFIILNNRY	financial year
AAACEFIKLMOPT	make capital of
AAACEFMORRRTT	cream of tartar
AAACEGILMTTUY	Guatemala City
AAACEGIMMNPRS	smear campaign
AAACEGIMQRRUZ	García Márquez
AAACEHIILLMNV	Machiavellian
AAACEHIIMMNTT	mathematician
AAACEHILLMTTY	athematically
AAACEHILLPPRT	alpha particle
AAACEHILLPTTY	apathetically
AAACEHILMMRSY	Michael Ramsay
AAACEHILNPRTU	Alpha Centauri
AAACEHIMOOPPR	pharmacopoeia
AAACEHLMNORST	steal a march on
AAACEHLORRSTT	Scarlett O'Hara
AAACEHNRRRSTW	search warrant
AAACEIILMNNRT	Latin-American
AAACEILPSSSTT	capital assets
AAACEKLLNOTUY	all you can take
AAACELLMNRSTY	sacramentally
AAACELLOPRSTV	cast a pall over
AAACELNRSSTUU	natural causes
AAACFHLNORSTY	Choral Fantasy
AAACFIIMNNPRS	pan-Africanism
AAACFILLNSTTY	fantastically
AAACFIMNORRTW	aircraftwoman
AAACGILLMMRTY	grammatically
AAACGILLMPRTY	pragmatically
AAACGILMMNRTU	ungrammatical
AAACGILNNOTTU	anticoagulant
AAACHHIKNRTTU	Khatchaturian
AAACHHKMRRRTU	Arthur Rackham
AAACHIILLPRSY	pharisaically
AAACHIKKLNPST	thick as a plank
AAACHILLMSTTY	asthmatically
AAACHILLNOPRY	anaphorically
AAACHILNRSSSU	Halicarnassus
AAACHLORRTYYZ	Zachary Taylor
AAACIILLMOTXY	axiomatically
AAACIILLPRSTY	parasitically
AAACIILNOTTUZ	actualization
AAACIINSTTTVY	cast a nativity
AAACIKOPRRSST	sick as a parrot
AAACILLLMPSST	small capitals
AAACILLMOTTUY	automatically
AAACILLMRTTUY	traumatically
AAACILNNRSTTT	transatlantic
AAACILOSSTTUY	autocatalysis
AAACINNNOOOTV	Antonio Canova
AAACMOORSTTTY	astrocytomata
AAADDDEEINNOS	Dido and Aeneas
AAADDDEELMNPS	dead man's pedal
AAADDDEELTUVX	value-added tax
AAADDDEGINSTV	disadvantaged
AAADDDEGNRRST	Standard grade
AAADDEEELMMST	Madame de Staël
AAADDEEGILMSY	easily damaged
AAADDEEILNPSS	palais de danse
AAADDEGGNRSTU	standard gauge
AAADDEGIMNOOR	Diego Maradona
AAADDEHHISTVY	have had its day
AAADDEHHMPRSY	Madhya Pradesh
AAADDEHHNPRRS	Andhra Pradesh
AAADDGLLRSWYY	Gladys Aylward
AAADDLNORRSTY	royal standard
AAADEEELMNORV	Éamon de Valera

AAADEEEMRRSTU	tread a measure
AAADEEFHNRRTT	tar and feather
AAADEEFLLLMNU	Manuel de Falla
AAADEEFLLRRVZ	Alfred Alvarez
AAADEEFRTTTUU	at a future date
AAADEEGGGRTTV	get aggravated
AAADEEGHHORTT	gather to a head
AAADEEGHILNRX	Alexander Haig
AAADEEGHKRTWW	The Awkward Age
AAADEEGILNNSS	Aegean Islands
AAADEEGKLMMOO	make a good meal
AAADEEGLLNOPR	Edgar Allan Poe
AAADEEGLMMNRY	Mary Magdalene
AAADEEHHLNRTY	hale and hearty
AAADEEHIMNTTZ	anathematized
AAADEEHLLORUV	have a dual role
AAADEEILQRTUU	audita querela
AAADEELMNPRSW	Pamela Andrews
AAADEFGKLMNRU	Gerald Kaufman
AAADEFHHILMNV	have half a mind
AAADEFHIRSSSY	fresh as a daisy
AAADEFINQRRSU	fair and square
	fair-and-square
AAADEGGILNNRU	guardian angel
AAADEGGINRSST	gas and gaiters
AAADEGIINSSTV	advise against
AAADEGILMQRSU	quadragesimal
AAADEGINORTVW	give an award to
AAADEGINRSTTV	avant-gardiste
AAADEHHNPRSSZ	haphazardness
AAADEHILLNOSW	Lewis Alan Hoad
AAADEHMMNNRST	Arms and the Man
AAADEIILMNOPR	Daniel arap Moi
AAADEIKMNNOOT	make a donation
AAADEILLQRRTU	quadrilateral
AAADELMMOPSST	plasmodesmata
AAADEMOORSSTU	use as a doormat
AAADFLLORRSUW	Dwarf Allosaur
AAADFNNOOPTUY	Antony of Padua
AAADGILLNORTY	gradationally
AAADGILLNRSVY	salivary gland
AAADGILNNNORT	Grand National
AAADGILNNORTU	National Guard
AAADGIMNOORST	good Samaritan
AAADHLLLLOSWY	All Hallows' Day
AAADIIMNORTTZ	dramatization
AAADILLNSSTTT	at a standstill
AAADKKLLRWWWY	walk awkwardly
AAAEEEGKNRTWY	Kate Greenaway
AAAEEEHKNPRSS	Shakespearean
AAAEEFGILLRSS	as large as life
AAAEEFGLORSVW	law of averages
AAAEEFILORSTV	Teresa of Avila
AAAEEGHHIMTVW	have a game with
AAAEEGHKOSSTT	take as hostage
AAAEEGHLOPPRR	palaeographer
AAAEEGKLLRSTT	Great Salt Lake
AAAEEGMMMNNNT	man-management
AAAEEHIKNPRSS	Shakespearian
AAAEEHILTTTTV	leave it at that
AAAEEHLLRSSVW	walls have ears
AAAEEILMNOPPR	paraleipomena
AAAEEJLLMNNSV	James Van Allen
AAAEEJLLNNRRY	Alan Jay Lerner
AAAEENORSSUVY	save as you earn
AAAEFFHINORST	after a fashion
AAAEFGMOPRSSS	passage of arms
AAAEFHIKSTTTU	take a shufti at
AAAEFIILMMRST	materfamilias
AAAEFIILMPRST	paterfamilias
AAAEFKMMORRTY	make a martyr of
AAAEGGIMNOPRS	megasporangia
AAAEGHILNSTTW	against the law
AAAEGIILNNRSV	earn a living as
AAAEGILOPRSTU	à la Portugaise
AAAEGLLLMOPRR	parallelogram
AAAEGLNRTTVXY	extravagantly
AAAEHHIMNRRRT	Harriet Harman
AAAEHILTTTWWY	whittle away at
AAAEHJMNRSTTY	James Hanratty
AAAEHLMRTTTUW	Walter Matthau
AAAEIILLMRRSW	Maria Walliser
AAAEIKNQSTTTU	take a squint at
AAAEILMNPRRTY	parliamentary
AAAEILNNPRTTW	water plantain
AAAEILNNRSTUW	New Australian
AAAEINORSTTVX	extravasation
AAAEKLMMNNSSW	Selman Waksman
AAAELLMNOPRRS	personal alarm
AAAELLSSSTUUX	sexual assault
AAAELPRSSTTWY	play at wasters
AAAFILLMORTWY	away from it all
AAAFILMNNOSTW	Tasmanian wolf
AAAFLMORSSSTU	assault of arms
AAAGGGILNRTVY	aggravatingly
AAAGGHLOPRSSY	shaggy parasol
AAAGGIINNRSTT	starting again
AAAGGKNOORRSS	kangaroo grass
AAAGIILNNOTVZ	galvanization
AAAGIILNORTTV	gravitational
AAAGIKLNRSSUV	Sunil Gavaskar
AAAGIMMNPRSTT	pangrammatist
AAAGPRRSSSTTW	grasp at straws
AAAHHIILMSTTW	what ails him at?
AAAHHINOPRSTT	a Parthian shot
AAAHIINORRTTU	authoritarian
AAAHIMNOQSSTU	Thomas Aquinas
AAAIILNNOTTTZ	tantalization
AAAIIMNNOOTTZ	anatomization
AAAIINNOSSSST	assassination
AAAILLNNORSTT	translational
AAAILMNORSTVY	Salvation Army
AAAILNNNORSTT	transnational
AAAKLNOOPRTVY	Anatoly Karpov
AABBBIILORSTY	absorbability
AABBCCDELLNNS	Blanc de Blancs
AABBCCDHKLOOR	Harold Babcock
AABBCDEEEKLNY	black-eyed bean
AABBCDEELNRST	belt-and-braces
AABBCEEHILNOS	Belisha beacon
AABBCEHIKNSTT	stab in the back
AABBCEHILMRRU	burial chamber

AABBCELORRRTY	Robert Barclay
AABBCILLMOSTY	bombastically
AABBCIMNOORTU	bamboo curtain
AABBDDDINRRSS	dribs and drabs
AABBDDEEGILOR	biodegradable
AABBDEEFGLRST	flabbergasted
AABBDEEINRTUV	unabbreviated
AABBDEGIRRTWY	Bridgwater Bay
AABBDIKNOPRRT	rabbit and pork
AABBEEEFSSTTT	Babette's Feast
AABBEEEKLNRSS	breakableness
AABBEEFNNOTYY	Fontenay Abbey
AABBEEGIMRTWZ	Great Zimbabwe
AABBEEHILLSST	establishable
AABBEEHILNSST	habitableness
AABBEEHKLLRST	break the balls
AABBEEILRUVXY	Rievaulx Abbey
AABBEFLLLOOTT	table football
AABBEHIILNNTU	uninhabitable
AABBEIILLOSSU	bouillabaisse
AABBEKKLLNNTY	blankety-blank
AABBENORRSSSU	barbarousness
AABCCCEHKRRST	backscratcher
	back-scratcher
AABCCDDEENOTU	dead-cat bounce
AABCCDDIORRTY	cardboard city
AABCCDEHLLORU	Claude Chabrol
AABCCEEEHLMSU	béchamel sauce
AABCCEEHLMRRT	charm bracelet
AABCCEELLNNOU	unconcealable
AABCCEFKKKNOW	knock back a few
AABCCEHILNPRS	Special Branch
AABCCEHKNOSTW	watch one's back
AABCCEIILMPRT	impracticable
AABCCEIILPTTY	acceptability
AABCCEILLMOSV	clavicembalos
AABCCEILMNRSV	canvas-climber
AABCCELMOPRTY	campylobacter
AABCCELNNOTUU	unaccountable
AABCCIIILLNOT	actinobacilli
AABCCIIILNNST	cannibalistic
AABCCIIJLLNOY	Jacobinically
AABCCIILMPRTY	impracticably
AABCCILLRSUUV	subclavicular
AABCCLLNOSTUY	by all accounts
AABCCLNNOTUUY	unaccountably
AABCDEEHNNOTT	that can be done
AABCDEELRRSTT	battle-scarred
AABCDEENNORUV	overabundance
AABCDEFILMNNO	balance of mind
AABCDEGILLNNT	ballet-dancing
AABCDEHIKLNTW	black and white
	black-and-white
AABCDEHINOSTW	shadow cabinet
AABCDEIILNSTU	East India Club
AABCDEIILTTUY	educatability
AABCDEIIMPRST	side-impact bar
AABCDEKLLLNRY	Lady Bracknell
AABCDEKLLNOST	ball and socket
AABCDEKMORSVW	move backwards
AABCDGIILMOPT	diplomatic bag

AABCDHIINSTTW	bait and switch
AABCDHIMNORRS	Chris Boardman
AABCDHNNOORRT	root and branch
	root-and-branch
AABCDINNORSTT	contrabandist
AABCDNOORSTUY	bad scran to you
AABCEEEELNPSS	peaceableness
AABCEEEFMOORW	become aware of
AABCEEEGGGSSX	excess baggage
AABCEEEIKMNOS	make obeisance
AABCEEEILLPRR	irreplaceable
AABCEEELLNSSV	cleavableness
AABCEEFLORSTU	Beaufort scale
AABCEEGGLNRRW	Lawrence Bragg
AABCEEGHIOPRT	bacteriophage
AABCEEGLNOORS	barnacle goose
AABCEEHHMMOST	Thomas Beecham
AABCEEHILMNPU	unimpeachable
AABCEEHKMOSTT	Thomas à Becket
AABCEEHOOPRRV	above reproach
AABCEEIILLMRR	irreclaimable
AABCEEIILNPPR	inappreciable
AABCEEIJMRRTU	Maurice Béjart
AABCEEILLPRRY	irreplaceably
AABCEEILMORVW	microwaveable
AABCEEILPRSTT	beta particles
AABCEEINNPTUY	put in abeyance
AABCEEIRRSTUU	bureaucratise
AABCEEIRRTUUZ	bureaucratize
AABCEEKQRRSTU	square bracket
AABCEELLPRRSY	cerebral palsy
AABCEELNRSSTT	tractableness
AABCEENNOOSSV	save one's bacon
AABCEERRSSTTV	abstract verse
AABCEFFHLNOOT	act on behalf of
AABCEFGIMOTTU	combat fatigue
AABCEFIIINOTT	beatification
AABCEFIINORTT	abortifacient
AABCEGHIIINRV	Virginia Beach
AABCEGHIILNTY	changeability
AABCEGHNOOTUU	Château Bougon
AABCEGILNNPRS	spring balance
AABCEHHIMPTTT	champ at the bit
AABCEHHKLMPUW	humpback whale
AABCEHIIILTVY	achievability
AABCEHILLLMNR	lamellibranch
AABCEHILLPSTY	heptasyllabic
AABCEHINORRSW	rainbow-chaser
AABCEHINORSSW	chase rainbows
AABCEHINRSTTT	in the abstract
AABCEHKLNOPST	slap on the back
AABCEIILLMRRY	irreclaimably
AABCEIILNPPRY	inappreciably
AABCEIINNNRSS	cannabis resin
AABCEILLMOPRT	problematical
AABCEILLOORTV	collaborative
AABCEILMNNOOP	companionable
AABCEILNNNOTU	uncontainable
AABCEILNNORUV	navicular bone
AABCEILORSSTV	variable costs
AABCEILRSTTVY	abstractively

AABCEINOORRST	Serbo-Croatian
AABCELNOOPRTY	polycarbonate
AABCELNRRSTTU	Burt Lancaster
AABCFFIILPRSU	public affairs
AABCFIKMNOORT	back-formation
AABCFILNNOOTU	confabulation
AABCGGIMNRRUY	Barry McGuigan
AABCGILLNOORT	collaborating
AABCHINOPRSUZ	Baruch Spinoza
AABCHIORRSSUU	brachiosaurus ❑
AABCIIILLMPTY	implacability
AABCIIILLPPTY	applicability
AABCIILLNOSTY	syllabication
AABCIILMOPRTY	comparability
AABCIINNOORST	carbonisation
AABCIINNOORTZ	carbonization
AABCIKLLMNPTU	platinum black
AABCILLNOOORT	collaboration
AABCILMNNOOPY	companionably
AABCNNOOORSST	contrabassoon
AABDDDELNOOST	boot and saddle
AABDDEEILLLOR	radiolabelled
AABDDELNORSTW	below standard
AABDDIILNSSUY	indissuadably
AABDEEEGNNRSU	Aberdeen Angus
AABDEEEHMNOTV	the above-named
AABDEEEHNOOSV	above one's head
AABDEEELNOOST	be at a loose end
AABDEEFGIILNT	indefatigable
AABDEEFHNOPRY	pay beforehand
AABDEEFLNOSTT	Battle of Sedan
AABDEEGIRSSTU	sugar diabetes
AABDEEGJORSSU	sober as a judge
AABDEEHORSTVW	behave towards
AABDEEIKKLOOR	read like a book
AABDEEILNRRTT	rattle-brained
AABDEEIPPRTVY	private pay bed
AABDEEKLLNORX	Alexander Blok
AABDEEKMRSTTY	masked battery
AABDEELLRRTUV	barrel-vaulted
AABDEELNPRSUU	unpersuadable
AABDEELORSTUW	sweated labour
AABDEEMNRRSSU	unembarrassed
AABDEENORSSTY	Satyendra Bose
AABDEERRSTTTU	statute-barred
AABDEFGIILNTY	indefatigably
AABDEFGIOPRSS	bird of passage
AABDEFGKORSST	dog's breakfast
AABDEGIILRRWY	railway bridge
AABDEGIINNRRT	grin and bear it
AABDEGLLNRTUY	Argyll and Bute
AABDEHIIILSTT	dishabilitate
AABDEHIINOSSV	Siobhan Davies
AABDEHILNSTTW	withstandable
AABDEHLNORRST	Roland Barthes
AABDEHMNORSTY	Arms and the Boy
AABDEIKLLORRY	Royal Birkdale
AABDEILMRTUVY	adumbratively
AABDELLMNRSTU	umbrella-stand
AABDENNPRSTUU	superabundant
AABDFFIILORTY	affordability
AABDGIKNNOORT	taking on board
AABDHIMNORSTT	rhabdomantist
AABDHIMRRRTUU	Arthur Rimbaud
AABDHMMMMOSTU	Muhammad's Tomb
AABDIIJLSTTUY	adjustability
AABDIILLMNRUW	William Dunbar
AABDIILNNRSTU	Austrian blind
AABEEEEGLNRSS	agreeableness
AABEEEEHNRTTW	weather-beaten
AABEEEFGLLNOT	flageolet bean
AABEEEFLMNSST	self-abasement
AABEEEHILRSTY	breathe easily
AABEEEHPRSTTT	breast the tape
AABEEEIKLMMRS	make miserable
AABEEELLLMNSS	malleableness
AABEEELLNORTU	Nobel laureate
AABEEELNORSST	elaborateness
AABEEELNPRSSS	separableness
AABEEELOORRTV	overelaborate
	over-elaborate
AABEEFGILTTTU	battle fatigue
AABEEFHHLLTTT	half the battle
AABEEFIKMRSST	make first base
AABEEFILNNOTU	Fontainebleau
AABEEFLNRRRST	transferrable
AABEEGHIKNRRT	heartbreaking
	heart-breaking
AABEEGHILMRSY	Bashir Gemayel
AABEEGHILRSTT	Basil the Great
AABEEGHLORTTW	Walter Bagehot
AABEEGILMORST	metagrabolise
AABEEGILMORTZ	metagrabolize
AABEEHHLLLRTT	The Albert Hall
AABEEHILNRTYZ	Elizabeth Ryan
AABEEHIMNOSTT	in the same boat
AABEEHINOPSTT	beat into shape
AABEEHLLNOTTY	lay on the table
AABEEILLNNPUX	unexplainable
AABEEILLNORTY	inelaborately
AABEEILLSSTTU	least suitable
AABEEINPPRSTW	wastepaper bin
AABEELNNORSTW	not answerable
AABEEMMNRRSST	embarrassment
AABEEMNNNRTTW	Barnett Newman
AABEFGHIIKNRT	breaking faith
AABEFGHINOVWY	way of behaving
AABEFGIKPRSST	pig's breakfast
AABEFHILNNOSU	unfashionable
AABEFIILNSSTU	unsatisfiable
AABEFILLMMNNU	uninflammable
AABEFILNRSTUU	Laurent Fabius
AABEFLMNORRST	transformable
AABEGGHILPRSS	A Bigger Splash
AABEGGILLLLOV	global village
AABEGGILLNRTV	travelling bag
AABEGGIMMNNRR	Ingmar Bergman
AABEGHHIMOTUV	have a big mouth
AABEGHHLLNTWY	hang by the wall
AABEGHINQRSSU	square-bashing
AABEGIILLNOUV	bougainvillea
AABEGIJKLNRWY	jawbreakingly

AABEGILLOOOPY	palaeobiology
AABEGILNORRTU	gubernatorial
AABEGILNRRSTT	sabre-rattling
AABEGLLOPPRSS	palpable-gross
AABEHIILORRTT	rehabilitator
AABEHIKORTTUW	without a break
AABEHILLORUVY	behaviourally
AABEHIMNRRTTU	Harriet Tubman
AABEHLMOPPRSS	blepharospasm
AABEHNOOPPTTU	about to happen
AABEIIILMNTXY	examinability
AABEIIKLMRTTY	marketability
AABEIILLLOTVZ	volatilizable
AABEIILLMNRSW	William Barnes
AABEIILMNNTUY	unamenability
AABEIILNORTVZ	verbalization
AABEIILNRSTWY	answerability
AABEIILRRUVXY	auxiliary verb
AABEIINRRRSST	arbitrariness
AABEIKKKLLOOT	talk like a book
AABEIKNNOORRT	Anita Brookner
AABEILLNNPUXY	unexplainably
AABEILMNNOTTU	Table Mountain
AABEILMNOPRTU	perambulation
AABEILMNRSTTT	transmittable
AABEILNNSSTUU	unsustainable
AABEILNOORSTV	observational
AABELLNPRSUUY	unpleasurably
AABELMNNRRTUU	natural number
AABELMOPRRTUY	perambulatory
	preambulatory
AABELNOPRRSTT	transportable
AABELNPRSSSUU	unsurpassable
AABELOPRRTUUY	beauty parlour
AABFFIIILLMNW	William Baffin
AABFGHIMNOUUZ	Naguib Mahfouz
AABFGHINRRSST	brass farthing
AABFHILNNOSUY	unfashionably
AABFHLORRRTUU	Arthur Balfour
AABFIIMMSSUUX	Fabius Maximus
AABGGILLMMNOU	gamma globulin
AABGGILLMNORW	global warming
AABGHHINOTTUW	hang about with
AABGHIOOPRTUY	autobiography
AABGHKOOOPRTU	autograph book
AABHIIILNPRRS	librarianship
AABHILLNOOORT	hot-air balloon
AABHILNOORRTZ	horizontal bar
AABHILOPTTUWY	play about with
AABIIIILNRTVY	invariability
AABIIIILNSTTY	insatiability
AABIIILLMPPTY	impalpability
AABIIILMPSSTY	impassability
AABIIILNOSTTZ	stabilization
AABIILLLMOTTW	William Talbot
AABIILNNSSTTU	insubstantial
AABIILNORTTUZ	brutalization
AABILLNSSTTUY	substantially
AABILNNSSTTUU	unsubstantial
AABIMMNNNORRT	Martin Bormann
AABINNOOOPPRT	on approbation

AACCCDIIILLSY	salicylic acid
AACCCEEILNRRT	recalcitrance
AACCCEGIKLORR	carriage clock
AACCCEHHINTTT	catch in the act
AACCCEHIILSTT	catechistical
AACCCEHIJQRSU	Jacques Chirac
AACCCEHILMOPR	macrocephalic
AACCCEIILLMRT	climacterical
AACCCFIIILNOT	calcification
AACCCHILLOORT	ochlocratical
AACCCIIILMNTT	anticlimactic
AACCCIILLLMTY	climactically
AACCCILMOOPST	social compact
AACCCILNOOSTT	social contact
AACCCLLNOOTTU	call to account
AACCDDEHINORR	Richard Deacon
AACCDEEENRRTY	day care centre
AACCDEEILNOPY	encyclopaedia
AACCDEEINNOTV	advance notice
AACCDEFHIOPRT	edaphic factor
AACCDEFHNRRTY	fetch and carry
AACCDEGHHNNOP	chop and change
AACCDEHIJKMSW	James Chadwick
AACCDEHLMMPRU	Marcel Duchamp
AACCDEHLNORRS	Charles Conrad
AACCDEIILLLTY	dialectically
AACCDEIINORTT	accreditation
AACCDEILNOOTU	coeducational
AACCDEIMNNOPU	unaccompanied
AACCDENNNOSTU	send an account
AACCDENORTTUV	to cut and carve
AACCDFFGHORTU	catch off guard
AACCDFIIIINOT	acidification
AACCDGIMMNOOT	accommodating
AACCDHIILNOOT	diacatholicon
AACCDHIKPRSTW	pack cards with
AACCDHILORSTY	cold as charity
AACCDHIMRRSST	Christmas card
AACCDIILLOPTY	apodictically
AACCDIILNOSSS	Caicos Islands
AACCDIINOOPPR	propanoic acid
AACCDILNORRSS	cardinal cross
AACCDIMMNOOOT	accommodation
AACCEEEGLPRTY	accept eagerly
AACCEEEHHNRST	the chances are
AACCEEFILORST	calefactories
AACCEEFIRSTUV	surface-active
AACCEEFLLSSUY	accuse falsely
AACCEEFMNOSSS	means of access
AACCEEHHIMNNT	the main chance
AACCEEHHLLRST	Harlech Castle
AACCEEHIMNSVW	wave mechanics
AACCEEHIMORRT	archaeometric
AACCEEHIMRRST	saccharimeter
AACCEEHKNOPST	chance to speak
AACCEEHLRRSST	characterless
AACCEEHMNNORS	chance one's arm
AACCEEILMRRSV	cervical smear
AACCEEILPPRTU	picture-palace
AACCEEILRSSTT	Caister Castle
AACCEEKLNNOST	Lake Constance

AACCEELMNRUUV	vacuum cleaner
AACCEFHMOPSST	fetch a compass
AACCEFKMNOOTU	make account of
AACCEFKNOOTTU	take account of
AACCEGGHILNNP	changing place
AACCEGHINOOPR	oceanographic
AACCEGHKOOPRU	cook up a charge
AACCEGIILNRTT	intergalactic
AACCEGILLNOOO	oceanological
AACCEGILLORTY	categorically
AACCEGILLOTTY	geotactically
AACCEHIINNORT	chain reaction
AACCEHIKMRSST	Christmas cake
AACCEHILLMRSV	clishmaclaver
AACCEHILLMSTY	schematically
AACCEHILOPRST	Social Chapter
AACCEHILRRTTU	architectural
AACCEHIMPRSTU	pharmaceutics
AACCEHIMRRSTY	saccharimetry
AACCEHIPPRRST	sharp practice
AACCEHKLRRRTU	Arthur C Clarke
AACCEIILMNOST	encomiastical
AACCEIILNRSWY	scenic railway
AACCEIINNORRT	incarceration
AACCEIJKLOPRT	practical joke
AACCEIKLLNSTW	Alnwick Castle
AACCEIKLRSTWW	Warwick Castle
AACCEILLMRTUV	circumvallate
AACCEILMMOOTX	come to a climax
AACCEILNPRSST	practicalness
AACCEIMMNNOPT	accompaniment
AACCEIMNRRSTU	American crust
AACCEINNNOOTT	concatenation
AACCEINOPSSSU	capaciousness
AACCEKNORTTTU	counter-attack
AACCELLNOOPRR	lance-corporal
AACCELLPRSTUY	spectacularly
AACCELMNPRTUY	Paul McCartney
AACCELNOPRTTU	Conceptual Art
AACCELNPRSTUU	unspectacular
AACCFIIILLRSY	sacrificially
AACCFIIILNORT	clarification
AACCFIIINORST	scarification
AACCFIILORRTY	clarificatory
AACCGHILLNOOT	Anglo-Catholic
AACCGILLLNTUY	calculatingly
AACCHIILMRSSU	musical chairs
AACCHIIMORTTY	achromaticity
AACCHIINNORST	anachronistic
AACCHILLMORTY	chromatically
AACCHILMNOORT	Roman Catholic
AACCIIILLNSTV	Calvinistical
AACCIIINORTTZ	cicatrization
AACCIILLMOPTY	apomictically
AACCIILLMPRTY	impractically
AACCIILLSSTUY	casuistically
AACCIILMNOOSS	occasionalism
AACCIILNOOSST	occasionalist
AACCIIMMNNOTU	in contumaciam
AACCIIMOSSSTT	staccatissimo
AACCIKLNOPRTW	prawn cocktail
AACCIKMNOORRY	Rocky Marciano
AACCILLNSTTYY	syntactically
AACCILNORTTUU	acculturation
AACCILOOSSTTU	social outcast
AACCINNNOOOSY	on any occasion
AACCINORSSTTY	sacrosanctity
AACDDDEGINOOR	a good riddance
AACDDEEELLNVV	Advanced level
AACDDEEGIINST	decide against
AACDDEEHHILRR	Richard Hadlee
AACDDEEHORSTT	scared to death
AACDDEEIILMMR	Middle America
AACDDEEILNOTY	delayed action
AACDDEEIMOSSW	mad cow disease
AACDDEGHIIMNN	adding machine
AACDDEGIKLNOT	like cat and dog
AACDDEGJLNORU	Jean-Luc Godard
AACDDEHLLNOOT	hold a candle to
AACDDEIIOSSST	disassociated
AACDDEMNNORTU	ordnance datum
AACDDFHIKNNNO	finnan haddock
AACDEEEFLNRSU	declare unsafe
AACDEEEHLNPSS	Passchendaele
AACDEEEIILLPR	pedicellariae
AACDEEGHKMNNR	heck and manger
AACDEEGHLLMOW	Wadham College
AACDEEGINRRRU	undercarriage
AACDEEGINRSTT	great distance
AACDEEGNNNORR	non-regardance
AACDEEHIKLRRY	Richard Leakey
AACDEEHIMNSUX	deus ex machina
AACDEEHINOSTW	see what I can do
AACDEEHINTTTU	authenticated
AACDEEHIOSTUZ	autoschediaze
AACDEEIIKMNOS	make a decision
AACDEEIILNOSS	salade niçoise
AACDEEILLRTVY	declaratively
AACDEEILORSST	sacerdotalise
AACDEEILORSTZ	sacerdotalize
AACDEEIMNNOTT	decontaminate
AACDEEINPPRTU	unappreciated
AACDEEIQRSTTU	acquired taste
AACDEELLNRSTU	Arundel Castle
AACDEELMSSSTU	Damascus steel
AACDEELNORRTX	adrenal cortex
AACDEENNNNOTT	non-attendance
AACDEFFIIMNRS	disaffirmance
AACDEFFINRRTW	traffic warden
AACDEFGHIRSTT	straight-faced
AACDEFHILMNNO	Adolf Eichmann
AACDEFHMMNOOV	have command of
AACDEFLLNNOOR	once and for all
AACDEGGILLOPY	pedagogically
AACDEGHINRRRW	Richard Wagner
AACDEGHIOPRRR	cardiographer
AACDEGIILLOPR	glacial period
AACDEGIINRTTU	Educating Rita
AACDEGINNQRSU	square-dancing
AACDEGJKLNNOS	Glenda Jackson
AACDEGLMNNORS	scandalmonger
AACDEHHILMORW	Michael Howard

AACDEHIIMNRRT	archimandrite
AACDEHIJLMNOR	Michael Jordan
AACDEHILNRRSW	Charles Darwin
AACDEHIMOSSTU	autoschediasm
AACDEHINRRTWY	Richard Tawney
AACDEHIORRSTT	trisoctahedra
AACDEHLNNNOSU	Claude Shannon
AACDEHMNNOORT	enchondromata
AACDEHNOPRSST	stop-and-search
AACDEIILLMRTY	diametrically
AACDEIILNORTV	valedictorian
AACDEIILRSTTU	disarticulate
AACDEIINNPTTU	unanticipated
AACDEIINNRSTT	transactinide
AACDEIKLLNPST	slap and tickle
AACDEILLLORRU	cellular radio
AACDEILLMORTY	declamatorily
AACDEILLNORRU	Claude Lorrain
AACDEILLNOTUY	educationally
AACDEILLORRTY	declaratorily
AACDEILMORSST	sacerdotalism
AACDEILORSSTT	sacerdotalist
AACDEILPQRTUU	quadruplicate
AACDEIMNNNOTT	decontaminant
AACDEIMNPRSSV	scrimp and save
AACDEINNOPRSX	expansion card
AACDEINNORSUU	arundinaceous
AACDEINOSSSUU	audaciousness
AACDEIORRRTTY	carotid artery
AACDEJKNNORSW	Andrew Jackson
AACDELLNOSVWY	advance slowly
AACDELMMMSUUU	summa cum laude
AACDELMNNRSSU	underclassman
AACDEMMNNOOST	at one's command
AACDEMNORRRVY	Raymond Carver
AACDEOQRRSSTU	quadrate cross
AACDFFILNOPUW	a capful of wind
AACDFFLNNORUY	Carol Ann Duffy
AACDFIIIMNNOT	damnification
AACDGHILNOSSS	Chagos Islands
AACDGIIINNOST	diagnostician
AACDHIIMNRRRT	Richard Martin
AACDHILLLRUYY	hydraulically
AACDHILLOPRSY	rhapsodically
AACDHILORSTTY	hydrostatical
AACDHIMMOOSSS	sado-masochism
AACDHINOPQRSU	quadraphonics
AACDIIILLMOTY	idiomatically
AACDIIIORTTVY	radioactivity
AACDIIJLLSTUY	Judaistically
AACDIIJORSSTU	Judas Iscariot
AACDIIKNNNOPR	rack and pinion
AACDIILLLSTUY	dualistically
AACDIILLMPRYY	pyramidically
AACDIILLORTTY	dictatorially
AACDIILNNOPRT	cardinal point
AACDIILNOOORT	radiolocation
AACDIIMNORRTY	dramatic irony
AACDILLMOPSSY	spasmodically
AACDNNNOOORRS	Sandra O'Connor
AACEEEEHPRSTW	swear the peace

AACEEEEKMNOPS	make one's peace
AACEEEFFKNOTT	take offence at
AACEEEGHHNRTX	heat exchanger
AACEEEGHLRTTT	rattle the cage
AACEEEGILMNRS	crème anglaise
AACEEEHIKMPTW	make peace with
AACEEEHJKLRTT	leatherjacket
	leather-jacket
AACEEEHKLLNTU	Lake Neuchâtel
AACEEEIJKMNTT	matinée jacket
AACEEEKLNOPST	take one's place
AACEEEKMNRSSY	make necessary
AACEEELNORSTW	Lawrence Oates
AACEEENNPSSST	pass a sentence
AACEEENORSTVY	cast an eye over
AACEEFFGIILTV	give a facelift
AACEEFFLOPSTY	place of safety
AACEEFGHHNORT	change of heart
AACEEFGHNOSTT	change of state
AACEEFHHIJSTZ	Jascha Heifetz
AACEEFHHLRSTT	Charles the Fat
AACEEFHILNPST	slap in the face
AACEEFHNRRRTW	trench warfare
AACEEFIKMNORT	make certain of
AACEEFILNRRRU	Friar Laurence
AACEEFILNRSSU	life assurance
AACEEFLNRSSSU	self-assurance
AACEEGGHMNOPR	George Chapman
AACEEGHILOPRS	archipelagoes
AACEEGHLMNRST	segmental arch
AACEEGIINNRSV	Gianni Versace
AACEEGILLLNVY	evangelically
AACEEGLLOOOPY	palaeoecology
AACEEHHLLMTTT	that'll teach me
AACEEHIILRSTT	theatricalise
AACEEHIILRTTZ	theatricalize
AACEEHIIMMSTT	mathematicise
AACEEHIIMMTTZ	mathematicize
AACEEHIIMNPRT	ramapithecine
AACEEHIJQSTTU	Hattie Jacques
AACEEHIKLPRRR	Charlie Parker
AACEEHILLMMNY	Michael Manley
AACEEHILLSTTY	aesthetically
AACEEHILLSTUV	ethical values
AACEEHILMNOPR	pinhole camera
AACEEHILNPRTT	parenthetical
AACEEHILPRTVY	heavy particle
AACEEHINPRRRT	Catherine Parr
AACEEHKKLMRRS	mackerel shark
AACEEHLNNOPPR	parencephalon
AACEEHLPPRSST	pass the parcel
AACEEHNOPPSTU	cause to happen
AACEEHOPRRTXY	archaeopteryx
AACEEIILNNOPT	Neapolitan ice
AACEEIIMNNRSU	un-Americanise
AACEEIIMNNRUZ	un-Americanize
AACEEIIMPPRST	misappreciate
AACEEIINNRSST	necessitarian
AACEEIJKRSTTW	Jackie Stewart
AACEEIJLNRTTU	interjaculate
AACEEILLMNRSS	Leslie Scarman

AACEEILLPRTTT	capital letter
AACEEILNORRST	race relations
AACEEILNRRSUV	vernacularise
AACEEILNRRUVZ	vernacularize
AACEEIMNNRSTT	ascertainment
AACEEINPPRRST	Persian carpet
AACEELLLRRTUX	extracellular
AACEELLMNORSY	Sorley MacLean
AACEELNNOPRUW	nuclear weapon
AACEENNPPRSTU	appurtenances
AACEFFGHINRRW	Erwin Chargaff
AACEFFGLLMORR	fall from grace
AACEFGLLLNOPU	pull a long face
AACEFHHMMNOTT	man of the match
AACEFHIILLNNP	financial help
AACEFHIINNOTW	within an ace of
AACEFIIIILRST	artificialise
AACEFIIIILRTZ	artificialize
AACEFIILNORST	fractionalise
AACEFIILNORTV	African violet
AACEFIILNORTZ	fractionalize
AACEFIINRRSVX	Francis Xavier
AACEFILLLNOPT	fall into place
AACEFILLMNRUY	nuclear family
AACEFILLTTUVY	facultatively
AACEFINRSTTUY	safety curtain
AACEFKKMORRST	make tracks for
AACEFKNOPRSTW	Sack of Antwerp
AACEFLLLMOPRS	from all places
AACEFLLNRSSUU	full assurance
AACEFLLOORRUY	for all you care
AACEFLOOPPRTU	Court of Appeal
AACEFMNNOOSTW	Scent of a Woman
AACEFNOPRRSTT	transport café
AACEFNOPRSSSV	press of canvas
AACEGGHJKNNNU	Kangchenjunga
AACEGGILNOPSU	Paul Gascoigne
AACEGGLOPRTTY	Clara Peggotty
AACEGHHIIKKNS	Chiang Kai Shek
	Chiang Kai-Shek
AACEGHHINPRTY	grape hyacinth
AACEGHIILLPRX	lexigraphical
AACEGHILLLRTY	lethargically
AACEGHILMOPYY	hypoglycaemia
AACEGHILOORST	archaeologist
AACEGHIMNOPRT	cinematograph
AACEGHOPRSSSU	sarcophaguses
AACEGIIILMRRV	civil marriage
AACEGIIKNPTTV	taking captive
AACEGIILLMNOR	mineralogical
AACEGIILLMNTY	enigmatically
AACEGIILLNNTY	antigenically
AACEGIILNPRSV	scrape a living
AACEGIINPRRTV	prevaricating
AACEGIIORRTTV	Great Victoria
AACEGIKNNNRRY	Nancy Kerrigan
AACEGILLLLORY	allegorically
AACEGILLLMRTU	metallurgical
AACEGILLNPRYY	panegyrically
AACEGILLRSTTY	strategically
AACEGILMNNNOW	cleaning woman
AACEGILMOPRSW	magical powers
AACEGIMNOPSTU	come up against
AACEGINOSSSSU	sagaciousness
AACEGLLNRRTUY	rectangularly
AACEGLMNORRSS	marrons glacés
AACEGMORRRTTU	Margaret Court
AACEHHINOSSTU	South China Sea
AACEHHLLSTTTU	that'll teach us
AACEHHLMNOPSU	Alphonse Mucha
AACEHHMMOPSTU	Thomas Peachum
AACEHIIIMNRTT	arithmetician
AACEHIILLSTTY	atheistically
AACEHIILNPSTT	pantheistical
AACEHIILRTTTY	theatricality
AACEHIIMMNNWZ	Chaim Weizmann
AACEHIIMNNOTZ	mechanization
AACEHIIMNNRST	christian name ❑
AACEHIIOSSTTW	associate with
AACEHILLMRTUY	rheumatically
AACEHILLNTTUY	authentically
AACEHILMOPRST	atmospherical
AACEHILNOPRSS	parochialness
AACEHINORTTTU	authenticator
AACEHLLMORSTY	Thomas Carlyle
AACEHLNOPSSYY	psychoanalyse
AACEHLOOPSTUU	autocephalous
AACEHMMNORRST	Thomas Cranmer
AACEHMSSSSTTU	Massachusetts
AACEHNOPPTTUU	put a cheat upon
AACEIIILMRSTT	materialistic
AACEIIINORTTV	ratiocinative
AACEIIINPPRTT	participate in
AACEIIKLOORST	Alistair Cooke
AACEIILLLRSTY	realistically
AACEIILLNPSTY	epinastically
AACEIILLPRSTY	peirastically
AACEIILMMNRSU	unicameralism
AACEIILMNRSTU	unicameralist
AACEIILMNTTUV	licentia vatum
AACEIILNNORTT	intercalation
AACEIILNNOSTT	cat-o'-nine-tails
AACEIILNNPSST	castle in Spain
AACEIILNPRSTT	paternalistic
AACEIILPRRSTU	particularise
AACEIILPRRTUZ	particularize
AACEIIMMOSTTU	semi-automatic
AACEIINNNORRT	reincarnation
AACEIINOPRRTV	prevarication
AACEIINORTTUZ	cauterization
AACEIINRRRSTU	curtain-raiser
AACEIKPRSTWYZ	Patrick Swayze
AACEILLLNRRTU	intracellular
AACEILLMNPTUY	pneumatically
AACEILMOPRTVY	comparatively
AACEILMRRSTUY	security alarm
AACEILNNOPSTU	encapsulation
AACEILNNORSTU	connaturalise
AACEILNNORTUZ	connaturalize
AACEILNOORSTT	trail one's coat
AACEILNOSSSSU	salaciousness
AACEILNPRRSTU	interscapular

Words marked ❑ can also be spelled with an initial capital letter

AACEIMNOOPSST	compassionate
AACEINOPRRSTT	procrastinate
AACEINOPRRTUY	precautionary
AACEINOPRSSSU	rapaciousness
AACEINORSTTTX	sex attraction
AACEJOPRRRSTT	Jasper Carrott
AACELNOOPPSWY	Apocalypse Now
AACELORSSSTUU	assault course
AACEMNNOPPRTY	parent company
AACENNOPRRSTT	transportance
AACENOORSTTTX	at no extra cost
AACFFIIILNOST	falsification
AACFFIILMOPST	official stamp
AACFGIIIMNNOT	magnification
AACFGIIINORTT	gratification
AACFGILNNOORT	conflagration
AACFGILNNORST	Francis Galton
AACFGIMNNRTUU	manufacturing
AACFGINNNOSUX	cunning as a fox
AACFHIMNPRSST	craftsmanship
AACFIIIILRTTY	artificiality
AACFIIILMNOPT	amplification
AACFIIILNNNRU	financial ruin
AACFIIILNOQTU	qualification
AACFIIILNORTT	not artificial
AACFIILLORSTV	Victoria Falls
AACFIILNORSTT	fractionalist
AACFIILOQRTUY	qualificatory
AACFIINNOORTT	fractionation
AACFIINOORTTZ	factorization
AACFORRSSTTTU	fractostratus
AACGGHIKLMPSY	shaggy milk cap
AACGGHILLOOPR	graphological
AACGGHILMNNST	slanging match
	slanging-match
AACGGILLLLOOY	algologically
AACGGILNRSTYZ	crystal-gazing
AACGHHIMNNTTW	night-watchman
AACGHIILLNNTU	hallucinating
AACGHIILLPRST	calligraphist
AACGHIIPRRSTT	stratigraphic
AACGHILLNNOTY	gnathonically
AACGHILMNOOPR	monographical
AACGHILNOORST	arachnologist
AACGHILOOPPRT	topographical
AACGHILOPPRTY	typographical
AACGHIMRSTTUU	thaumaturgics
AACGHKLLMOOPR	Graham Pollock
AACGIIILNNOTZ	anglicization
AACGIIINPPRTT	participating
AACGIILLLNTVY	vacillatingly
AACGIILLMSTTY	stigmatically
AACGIILLNNORY	inorganically
AACGIILLNOSTY	agonistically
AACGIILNORSTU	cartilaginous
AACGIILNORTTU	graticulation
AACGIIMNNNOTT	contaminating
AACGILLLNNOOO	Anglo-Colonial
AACGILLLNOSTY	nostalgically
AACGILLMNSTYY	gymnastically
AACGILMNOOPST	campanologist
AACGIMMMNOORT	monogrammatic
AACGINNORRSTW	narrowcasting
AACGKNOOORRTU	kangaroo court
AACHHILMPRRTU	triumphal arch
AACHHILOPTVWY	play havoc with
AACHIILLNNOTU	hallucination
AACHIINOPRSTU	haruspication
AACHILLLMPTYY	lymphatically
AACHILLNORSTY	thrasonically
AACHILLNORTUY	hallucinatory
AACHILMOPSTTU	optic thalamus
AACHILNNOORRT	North Carolina
AACHILNOORSTU	South Carolina
AACHILOPRSSTY	astrophysical
AACHIMMNOOPST	Thomas Campion
AACHJKMNOOSST	Thomas Jackson
AACHLNNOORSUY	anachronously
AACHLNOPSSTYY	psychoanalyst
AACIIIILNOTTZ	italicization
AACIIILLNPSTY	pianistically
AACIIILLPPRTY	participially
AACIIILNNOSTT	nationalistic
AACIIILNOOSST	socialisation
AACIIILNOOSTZ	socialization
AACIIILNORSTT	rationalistic
AACIIILNOSTTY	antisociality
AACIIINNOORTT	ratiocination
AACIIINOPPRTT	participation
AACIILLMORTTY	triatomically
AACIILLMOSTTY	atomistically
AACIILLMPRSTY	prismatically
AACIILLNPRTUY	puritanically
AACIILLOPRTTY	patriotically
AACIILLOSSTTY	isostatically
AACIILLSSTTTY	statistically
AACIILMNORTTU	matriculation
AACIILMPRRSTU	particularism
AACIILNNOTUVZ	vulcanization
AACIILNPPPRRT	principal part
AACIILNPPRTTY	participantly
AACIILPRRTTUY	particularity
AACIIMMNNORTU	communitarian
AACIIMNNNOOTT	contamination
AACIINNOORTTZ	narcotization
AACIIOPPRRTTY	participatory
AACIKMNNOPRST	Patrick Manson
AACILLLOOPSTY	apostolically
AACILLMNOOSTY	onomastically
AACILLMNOOTXY	taxonomically
AACILLMNOPSTY	complaisantly
AACILLMNSTUUY	lunatic asylum
AACILMNNOPSTU	uncomplaisant
AACILMNOOPTTU	computational
AACILMNRRSTUU	intramuscular
AACILMORRSTTU	court martials
	courts martial
AACILNNOORSTT	translocation
AACILNPRSSTYY	cryptanalysis
AACINNOOOQRUZ	Corazon Aquino
AACJLMNNORSTU	Trajan's Column
AACLQRRSTTUYZ	quartz crystal

AACORRSSSTUUY	Styracosaurus
AADDDEEILNNOR	Daniel Deronda
AADDDEHIPPRSV	David Sheppard
AADDDGLLNOOSU	Donald Douglas
AADDEEEGLLMNR	Gerald Edelman
AADDEEELMNPTX	expanded metal
AADDEEELMPRST	paddle steamer
	paddle-steamer
AADDEEGHRRSTW	Gareth Edwards
AADDEEGIMNNRT	in great demand
AADDEEGNRRTUU	undergraduate
AADDEEGORSTYY	ready, steady, go
AADDEEHHIPSSW	waspish-headed
AADDEEHHLRRTY	hard-heartedly
AADDEEIMQRSSU	Marquis de Sade
AADDEEKMMNNOS	make demands on
AADDEEKMNNRTU	make redundant
AADDEELNRTTUU	unadulterated
AADDEELORRTTU	Edouard Lartet
AADDEFHHOOSTW	shadow of death
AADDEGGHNRRTU	granddaughter
AADDEGHIMNOOV	have a good mind
AADDEGHNORRUY	rough and ready
	rough-and-ready
AADDEGILNRSSS	salad dressing
AADDEGINORRRY	Ordinary grade
AADDEHILPPSUY	head-up display
AADDEHIMNSSSU	Saddam Hussein
AADDEHIMPPRSY	pyramid-shaped
AADDEHNNNOSST	stand one's hand
AADDELMNNORSU	Roald Amundsen
AADDENNOORTTT	door attendant
AADDENORRRRST	standard error
AADDFFNNNOOST	stand off and on
AADDFGILNORUV	add flavouring
AADDFGLLNOOOR	for good and all
AADDFINNORUWY	find a way round
AADDGHHINRSTY	Hard Day's Night
AADDHIMNOOSST	Thomas Addison
AADDHLLOOORRW	Harold Larwood
AADDIILMNSSWY	Midway Islands
AADDKLNNOPUWW	walk up and down
AADEEEFNORRVY	for ever and aye
AADEEEGGLRTXY	exaggeratedly
AADEEEGGNRTUX	unexaggerated
AADEEEGLLNORS	alleged reason
AADEEEGLMNRST	send a telegram
AADEEEHHKNOSS	shake one's head
AADEEEHINSTTZ	anaesthetized
AADEEEHMNNOST	one and the same
AADEEEIILMRST	dematerialise
AADEEEIILMRTZ	dematerialize
AADEEEIMNNRRT	Mediterranean
AADEEELNOPPRX	Alexander Pope
AADEEEMMORSTU	made to measure
	made-to-measure
AADEEENPRRTUW	a new departure
AADEEFFIKMNOR	make a friend of
AADEEFGHKORST	of the Dark Ages
AADEEFHHLLRTY	half-heartedly
AADEEFIRRTTWY	frittered away
AADEEFKMMNORS	make amends for
AADEEFNSSSSTT	steadfastness
AADEEGGHLORST	at loggerheads
AADEEGHHHNOUV	have had enough
AADEEGHIMOOTV	have a good time
AADEEGHNRSTUW	great unwashed
AADEEGIILNRTT	in great detail
AADEEGIIMMRRX	mixed marriage
AADEEGIKNNRUW	rude awakening
AADEEGILNNSTV	leave standing
AADEEGIMNPRST	disparagement
AADEEGIMNRRTT	reading matter
AADEEGINNRRTY	radiant energy
AADEEGINORSSV	Andrés Segovia
AADEEGINRSTTT	trading estate
AADEEHHNPRSTT	at the sharp end
AADEEHIKLNPRT	leap in the dark
AADEEHIKMRRTT	raid the market
AADEEHILNRTTW	draw the line at
AADEEHIMMMNOS	Mohammedanise
AADEEHIMMMNOZ	Mohammedanize
AADEEHINRRSTT	head restraint
AADEEHKKNNNTU	Kenneth Kaunda
AADEEHKOORTTT	take to the road
AADEEHLLRRTTY	tetrahedrally
AADEEHLMRRTWY	warm-heartedly
AADEEIILNNOST	denationalise
AADEEIILNNOTZ	denationalize
AADEEILLMSVWX	Maxwell Davies
AADEEILLNNRVY	lay in lavender
AADEEILMMORST	melodramatise
AADEEILMMORTZ	melodramatize
AADEEILNNNORR	noradrenaline
AADEEILNOPPSS	epanadiploses
AADEEILNRTTTV	travel-tainted
AADEEILORRVVW	draw a veil over
AADEEIMNOPRST	mains-operated
AADEEIMORRTVZ	overdramatize
AADEEINPRSSST	disparateness
AADEEKMNRSSTU	keen as mustard
AADEELLMNNNOS	Nelson Mandela
AADEELLMNORTW	Walter Mondale
AADEELLMNRRVW	Andrew Marvell
AADEELMNOORRS	Roman de la Rose
AADEELNNRRSTU	sale and return
AADEELNPPPRST	pepper-and-salt
AADEEMPRRSSTU	mass departure
AADEENNPRSTUU	superannuated
AADEFFGINORRT	fore-and-aft rig
AADEFFHJMRRUY	Madhur Jaffrey
AADEFFMNOORSW	meadow saffron
AADEFGHHINORR	hard of hearing
AADEFGHHIOORT	a hair of the dog
AADEFGHLNRRTY	grandfatherly
AADEFIKLMNPRS	Mansfield Park
AADEFILOOPRSS	fool's paradise
AADEFKLNOORRT	foot-land-raker
AADEFLLMNNTUY	fundamentally
AADEFLLMNORTU	dental formula
AADEGGKLOORST	look daggers at
AADEGGLLNORUW	world language

AADEGHHLOOSST	hold as hostage
AADEGHILNRTUW	daughter-in-law
AADEGHINNRRRW	Warren Harding
AADEGHLOPRTTY	play hard to get
AADEGIIIMPRRV	primigravidae
AADEGIIILMRTUV	multigravidae
AADEGIINNOOTV	give a donation
AADEGILNSTTVY	devastatingly
AADEGINNRSTTW	water-standing
AADEGLOORRSUV	Avogadro's rule
AADEGMMNORRUU	rummage around
AADEGMORRRTTU	Margaret Tudor
AADEHHILMOORR	haemorrhoidal
AADEHHIORTVWW	have a word with
AADEHHNNOSSSW	wash one's hands
AADEHHOOORRTW	a hard row to hoe
AADEHIILMOSSY	haemodialysis
AADEHIILNPSUZ	sulphadiazine
AADEHILMNRSSU	Salman Rushdie
AADEHLLNOTWWY	lay down the law
AADEHLMNORSTU	sound the alarm
	Thomas Arundel
AADEHLMNORTTW	Matthew Arnold
AADEHNNORSTTY	try one's hand at
AADEHNORRSTTW	north-eastward
AADEHNORSSSUZ	hazardousness
AADEHORSSTTUW	south-eastward
AADEIIIILMNSST	assimilated in
AADEIIILMSSST	disassimilate
AADEIILLMMRTY	Military Medal
AADEIILLMORTY	mediatorially
AADEIILLNRRTY	interradially
AADEIILMMNRST	maladminister
AADEIILNRSSTU	disnaturalise
AADEIILNRSTUZ	disnaturalize
AADEIIMNNOORT	enantiodromia
AADEIIMNNORSV	animadversion
AADEIIMNORRTT	Mario Andretti
AADEIINOPSSST	dispassionate
AADEIIPQRRTTU	quadripartite
AADEIKKMNPSSU	kiss and make up
AADEIKNPPRRSU	drunk as a piper
AADEILLNNQRUY	quadrennially
AADEILLPRRTYY	radial-ply tyre
AADEILMNORSST	maladroitness
AADEILNORRRRT	trial and error
	trial-and-error
AADEILNRSSTTW	Stewart Island
AADEINORRRTXY	extraordinary
AADEIOPRRSSTW	aspire towards
AADEJLMMNSTTU	maladjustment
AADELLOQRRRTU	quarter dollar
AADELNNRRTUWY	unwarrantedly
AADELNRRSSSUU	Ursula Andress
AADELORRSTTVW	travel towards
AADEMOPRRRSUU	spread a rumour
AADENNOORSSTT	stand to reason
AADFHHIMNNOSS	man of his hands
AADFHIINRSTTW	stand fair with
AADFHLLOOSTTY	Lady of Shalott
AADFIKLLMOORW	maid of all work
	maid-of-all-work
AADFJJMNNORTU	Franjo Tudjman
AADGGIILNPRSY	disparagingly
AADGHIINOTWWY	doing away with
AADGHILMMORRS	marsh marigold
AADGHILNNPPSY	happy landings
AADGHMNORSTUW	draughtswoman
AADGIIILNNTWY	lady-in-waiting
AADGIIIMPRRSV	primigravidas
AADGIILMRSTUV	multigravidas
AADGILLNOPSTW	pit and gallows
AADGILNNOPRST	prostaglandin
AADGILNNOPRUY	playing around
AADHHILMNOPRS	Harold Shipman
AADHIILLNNRST	Rathlin Island
AADHMNNOORTTW	not worth a damn
AADIIILNNNOSS	Ionian Islands
AADIILLNOORTZ	dollarization
AADIILLNORTTY	traditionally
AADIILLOSUUVY	audiovisually
AADIILNNORTTU	untraditional
AADIIMNNOORTZ	randomization
AADIIMNORRSTT	administrator
AADIJMMNRSSVY	Sammy Davis Jnr
AADIKNNNOORTV	Antonín Dvorák
AADIMNNOPSTUU	unpaid amounts
AADINNOPSSSUY	Passion Sunday
AAEEEEKLNOSTV	take one's leave
AAEEEFFKNOSTT	take offense at
AAEEEFGLNSSTT	Fêtes Galantes
AAEEEGGHINORW	here we go again
AAEEEGGHMORST	George Eastham
AAEEEGGLNNRST	agents-general
AAEEEGGMNORST	George Eastman
AAEEEGHORRSTT	storage heater
AAEEEGILMNPVX	give an example
AAEEEGLMMNRSS	German measles
AAEEEGMNNRRRT	rearrangement
AAEEEGNOPRRSV	average person
AAEEEGNPRRTUV	average punter
AAEEEHHNNORTV	heaven on earth
AAEEEHIILLSSS	Haile Selassie
AAEEEHILPPRRT	Pre-Raphaelite
AAEEEHIMMSTTT	at the same time
AAEEEHLNPRTTT	patent leather
AAEEEIKNPRSTV	native speaker
AAEEELLPPPPUU	appel au peuple
AAEEELMMNOPSU	male menopause
AAEEELMMNPRTT	temperamental
AAEEEMNNPRTVW	permanent wave
AAEEENRRSSVWY	Seven Years' War
AAEEFFGNRSSTT	staff sergeant
AAEEFFKNORRTU	freak of nature
AAEEFGIKNNNSW	Finnegans Wake
AAEEFGILNRSSW	false swearing
AAEEFGINRRTWY	wayfaring-tree
AAEEFGIOPRSST	rite of passage
AAEEFGJLNRRUW	jungle warfare
AAEEFGLORSSSV	Leaves of Grass
AAEEFHHLOSTTT	state of health
AAEEFHHORRSTT	heart of hearts

AAEEFHIIMOTTV	have a time of it
AAEEFHIMRTTTT	after that time
AAEEFHJLMOTTW	The Jew of Malta
AAEEFHKOPRTTT	take the part of
AAEEFHLNOTUVV	vault of heaven
AAEEFHOPRTVWY	pave the way for
AAEEFHORSTTTT	state of the art
	state-of-the-art
AAEEFIMRTTTUU	at a future time
AAEEFINNOPPRT	appear often in
AAEEFIOPRRSTT	state of repair
AAEEFKKMMNOOY	make a monkey of
AAEEFKLMORTUW	make foul water
AAEEGGINNOPRT	generation gap
AAEEGHHLPTTUW	what the plague
AAEEGHIJMNSTU	James Naughtie
AAEEGHILLRRTW	Walter Raleigh
AAEEGHIMOPSTT	apothegmatise
AAEEGHIMOPTTZ	apothegmatize
AAEEGHKNORSST	no great shakes
AAEEGIIKLPSTW	sweat like a pig
AAEEGIIMMPRST	epigrammatise
AAEEGIIMMPRTZ	epigrammatize
AAEEGIIMNRRRT	intermarriage
AAEEGIKMNPRUW	wearing make-up
AAEEGIKMNRSTT	make it strange
AAEEGILLMSSXY	sexagesimally
AAEEGILMNOORR	oleomargarine
AAEEGILNRRTTY	literary agent
AAEEGIMMMNNST	mismanagement
AAEEGIMNRTTUV	argumentative
AAEEGJLNPTTUY	Jean Paul Getty
AAEEGJMNORRST	sergeant-major
AAEEGKLLRRTUY	take regularly
AAEEGKLMNNOOS	make a long nose
AAEEGLLLMNSUY	Samuel Langley
AAEEGLNNORRSS	Sloane Rangers
AAEEHHILNRTTW	White Hart lane
AAEEHHIMOSSTV	have as its home
AAEEHIILMNSSS	leishmaniases
AAEEHIILMOPTT	epitheliomata
AAEEHIILNPSST	elephantiasis
AAEEHIINNPRST	pain in the arse
AAEEHILLNNNPY	phenylalanine
AAEEHILRRSSTU	russia leather ❑
AAEEHINNRRSTY	Tyrrhenian Sea
AAEEHINOPRTTW	weather a point
AAEEHINOSTVWY	have it one's way
AAEEHKMPRRTTW	Matthew Parker
AAEEHKORRTTTT	Tarka the Otter
AAEEHLLOOPRTT	Apollo Theatre
AAEEHLOSSTTTY	to say the least
AAEEHMNNOPPTT	meant to happen
AAEEHNORSSTTT	east-north-east
AAEEHOSSSTTTU	east-south-east
AAEEHRRRRSSUU	Herrerasaurus
AAEEIIILMMRST	immaterialise
AAEEIIILMMRTZ	immaterialize
AAEEIILMNNRTT	interlaminate
AAEEIIMNNORTX	re-examination
AAEEIKLMNSSTT	statesmanlike
AAEEIKLNSSTTV	talkativeness
AAEEILLLPPTVY	appellatively
AAEEILLNRTTVY	alternatively
AAEEILMMNORST	mean solar time
AAEEILNPRSSTT	essential part
AAEEILNRRSTTT	transliterate
AAEEILOPRTTVX	extrapolative
AAEEILPPRRTVY	preparatively
AAEEILPRSSSSZ	laissez-passer
AAEEIMNNPPRTT	appertainment
AAEEIMPRRTTTV	private matter
AAEEINNPRSTTY	spiny anteater
AAEEINORRTUYY	year in year out
AAEEIPRRSTTTZ	trapeze artist
	trapeze-artist
AAEEKMMNPRSTU	amusement park
AAEEKNNOOSSTW	take as one's own
AAEELLLLPRRRU	parallel ruler
AAEELLNOPPRTY	Appleton layer
AAEELNPRRRTTU	preternatural
AAEEMQRRRSTTU	quartermaster
AAEENOSTTTTVX	to a vast extent
AAEEPRRSSTTUU	supersaturate
AAEFFHIIILTTW	affiliate with
AAEFFIILMRTVY	affirmatively
AAEFFIIMNORRT	reaffirmation
AAEFFINOORSTT	afforestation
AAEFFIOPRRSTT	tear a strip off
	tear off a strip
AAEFFLOPRSTYY	play for safety
AAEFGHHINORTV	have a thing for
AAEFGIKNOPSWY	way of speaking
AAEFGILLNNSSY	self-analysing
AAEFGILMNRRTY	fragmentarily
AAEFGILNORSUY	yourself again
AAEFGIMNNORTT	fragmentation
AAEFHHIINNOTV	have no faith in
AAEFHHILNNPST	flash in the pan
AAEFHHOOORRRV	have a horror of
AAEFHIILMPPSY	happy families
AAEFHLLLNOTWY	a fly on the wall
AAEFHLMORSTTW	Waltham Forest
AAEFHLOPPRTTY	play the part of
AAEFHMORRTTTT	for that matter
AAEFHNOORRSTT	for that reason
AAEFIILLNNRSS	in all fairness
AAEFIILNNORRU	Alain-Fournier
AAEFIIMNNOSTT	manifestation
AAEFIJNORRSST	Jean Froissart
AAEFIKMNORRTU	make a run for it
AAEFILLNORRRW	Fallen Warrior
AAEFILLOPRRTY	prefatorially
AAEFILNOOPSTT	at point of sale
AAEFJMORRRRSY	Marjory Fraser
AAEFKKLMPRSSY	make sparks fly
AAEFLLMNORSTU	a small fortune
AAEGGHILLNNVY	hanging valley
AAEGGHILNRSTT	at right angles
	straight angle
AAEGGIILNTTUV	agglutinative
AAEGGIINORSTV	give a roasting

AAEGGILMNOORT	agglomeration
AAEGGLMNORSTW	West Glamorgan
AAEGGLNNRSSSY	granny glasses
AAEGHHIKMRRTW	high-water mark
AAEGHHNNOPSTU	hang up one's hat
AAEGHIKMNOPRT	kinematograph
AAEGHILMOOSTT	haematologist
AAEGHIMNOTTUW	manage without
AAEGHIMOORSTT	a short time ago
AAEGHINNOTTVW	wanting to have
AAEGHIPRRRSTT	stratigrapher
AAEGHMORRTTUY	Great Yarmouth
AAEGIIILMNTVY	imaginatively
AAEGIIIMNNTUV	unimaginative
AAEGIIKKLNOTT	take a liking to
AAEGIIKLNNPPS	plain speaking
	plain-speaking
AAEGIIKNNSSWY	easy as winking
AAEGIILLLORST	legislatorial
AAEGIILLMRSTY	magisterially
AAEGIILLNNRTW	retaining wall
AAEGIILNNTTTY	tangentiality
AAEGIIMNNOTTZ	magnetization
AAEGIIMNQQSUU	Quinquagesima
AAEGIKLPRRSTV	Pär Lagerkvist
AAEGIKMMNRSST	mass-marketing
AAEGILLNPSSUU	lapsus linguae
AAEGILLNRTTUY	triangulately
AAEGILMNNOPST	Leamington Spa
AAEGILNQRTTUY	large quantity
AAEGIMNNNORTU	mountain range
AAEGIMNNORTTU	argumentation
AAEGINOORSTTY	geostationary
AAEGLLNOOOPTY	palaeontology
AAEGLNNOOSSSU	analogousness
AAEHHILMOPRTX	xerophthalmia
AAEHHIMNORSTT	a shot in the arm
AAEHHLLOPRSWY	Harlow Shapley
AAEHIIILMNSSS	leishmaniasis
AAEHIIIMNNSTT	antihistamine
AAEHIIKKKMNN	Mikka Hakkinen
AAEHIILLMRVWY	William Harvey
AAEHIIORTTTUV	authoritative
AAEHIIRRSSTWY	with a siserary
AAEHIKLMNPRTZ	Itzhak Perlman
AAEHIKMMOPSST	Thomas à Kempis
AAEHILNNOSSST	Thessalonians
AAEHIMNPSSSTT	statesmanship
AAEHINNRSSSSU	Nasser Hussain
AAEHKMMORTUWY	make a wry mouth
AAEHKMNNORSSS	on Shanks's mare
AAEHKMNNRRSSS	shark's manners
AAEHLMNNSSTTY	Lytham St Anne's
AAEHLNNOPTTWY	play the wanton
AAEHLNNOQTUYY	Anthony Quayle
AAEHMNORRRSTU	Arthur Ransome
AAEIIIKNNNSSX	Iannis Xenakis
AAEIIILMMRTTY	immateriality
AAEIIILNORRST	irrationalise
AAEIIILNORRTZ	irrationalize
AAEIIILNORSTZ	serialization
AAEIIKLMNPSST	Semipalatinsk
AAEIILLLMNRTY	matrilineally
AAEIILLLNPRTY	patrilineally
AAEIILLMNNOTT	in no time at all
AAEIILLMNOTTZ	metallization
AAEIILLMNRSTU	unilateralism
AAEIILLMRRSTT	trilateralism
AAEIILLNRSTTU	unilateralist
AAEIILLNRTTUY	unilaterality
AAEIILLQTTUVY	qualitatively
AAEIILLRRSTTT	trilateralist
AAEIILMNPRSST	impartialness
AAEIILNNNORTT	international
AAEIILNNORSTV	vernalisation
AAEIILNNORTVZ	vernalization
AAEIINNNSTTTY	instantaneity
AAEIINNOPPRRT	in preparation
AAEIINOPPPRRT	inappropriate
AAEIINOPPRTUZ	pauperization
AAEIIRRSTTTVY	variety artist
AAEIJLMNORRTV	major interval
AAEIJMMORRSTY	James Moriarty
AAEIKLLNOSSTY	as likely as not
AAEIKNNOPRTTT	not take part in
AAEILLNNOSSTY	sensationally
AAEILLNOPRTXY	explanatorily
AAEILMNORRSTY	Rila Monastery
AAEILMOPPRTXY	approximately
AAEILNNPRRSUW	Peninsular War
AAEILNOOORTTV	laevorotation
AAEILNOOPRTTX	extrapolation
AAEILNPPRSTUU	paper nautilus
AAEILOPPPRRTY	appropriately
AAEILOPPRRRTY	preparatorily
AAEIMMNPPRSST	panspermatism
AAEIMNNNOORTT	ornamentation
AAEIMNNOSTTUY	ayuntamientos
AAEIMNPPRSSTT	panspermatist
AAEIMOOPPRTTX	approximate to
AAEINNNOSSTTU	instantaneous
AAEIOOPPPRRTT	appropriate to
AAELLMMNORSTU	smaller amount
AAELLNRRSSTVY	transversally
AAELMNNOOSSSU	anomalousness
AAELNNNRSSTUU	unnaturalness
AAELNNOPRRSST	transpersonal
AAELNNPRRSTTY	transparently
AAELNOPPRSTTU	put a plaster on
AAELOOPRRTTXY	extrapolatory
AAEOOPPRRRTTY	preparatory to
AAFGGILLNOPUW	Wolfgang Pauli
AAFGIILNNOORT	floating on air
AAFGIIMNNORST	inform against
AAFGIMNNOPRST	Naming of Parts
AAFHIJNNOSTTW	Jonathan Swift
AAFHINOOPRRST	parrot-fashion
AAFHMOORSTUWY	out of harm's way
AAFIIILMNRTUY	unfamiliarity
AAFIIKLLMNRSW	Frank Williams
AAFIILMNNOORT	informational
AAFIILMNOORTZ	formalization

AAFILNNNOORTT	National Front
AAGGHHIIOPRST	hagiographist
AAGGHIINNSSTV	Gavin Hastings
AAGGIIIMNOORR	Giorgio Armani
AAGGIILNNNRSW	warning signal
AAGGIILNNOTTU	agglutination
AAGHHNOOPPRTY	anthropophagy
AAGHIIIKKLLMN	Mikhail Glinka
AAGHIIIMNNRST	Martina Hingis
AAGHIILMNORTT	antilogarithm
AAGHIKNORRSTU	Turkish Angora
AAGHIMNNORSTW	Winston Graham
AAGHIMRSTTTUU	thaumaturgist
AAGHINOPPRRTV	having rapport
AAGHINPSTTUWY	put things away
AAGIIJNNOORST	jargonisation
AAGIIJNNOORTZ	jargonization
AAGIIKLNNPSTY	painstakingly
AAGIILLNNPRTT	trailing plant
AAGIILLNNSTTY	tantalisingly
AAGIILLNNTTYZ	tantalizingly
AAGIILMNOORTZ	glamorization
AAGIILNNORTTU	triangulation
AAGIILNORTUVZ	vulgarization
AAGIILNRRTTUY	triangularity
AAGIIMNNPRSTY	praying mantis
AAGIIMNOPPRTX	approximating
AAGIINNPPRSTY	spray-painting
AAGIKLMNOVWWY	moving walkway
AAGIKNNSSUUUY	Aung San Suu Kyi
AAGILMMNNOSUY	magnanimously
AAGILMNORRSTT	mortal-staring
AAGILNNNPRSTT	transplanting
AAGILNNORSTTU	strangulation
AAGILNPRSSTTU	pulsating star
AAGIMNORRRSTT	transmigrator
AAHHIIKMRSTYZ	Yitzhak Shamir
AAHHKNOSTTWWW	know what's what
AAHHLMMOSSTTU	Thomas Malthus
AAHIIILNNOTYZ	hyalinization
AAHIIKLLMPTWW	walk with a limp
AAHIIMNNOORTZ	harmonization
AAHIINOORTTUZ	authorization
AAHIJMMOOOTYY	Yohji Yamamoto
AAHINOPSSSSTT	shop assistant
	shop-assistant
AAHJNNORSSSTU	Johann Strauss
AAHMNORRTTTUW	throw a tantrum
AAIIILNNOPRST	inspirational
AAIIILNORRTTY	irrationality
AAIIILNORTTUZ	ritualization
AAIIILNOSTUVZ	visualization
AAIIIMMNNNOST	antinomianism
AAIIINNOSSTTT	sanitationist
AAIIINOPRTTVZ	privatization
AAIILLLMNOTWW	William Walton
AAIILLMMNORTY	matrimonially
AAIILLMNNOTTU	multinational
AAIILLMNNOTVY	nominatively
AAIILLMNOPRTY	patrimonially
AAIILLNNOSSTT	installations
AAIILLNOPRTUZ	pluralization
AAIILMNNOORTZ	normalization
AAIIMMNORSTUZ	summarization
AAIIMNOOPPRTX	approximation
AAIINNNORTTYZ	tyrannization
AAIINNOPRRSTT	transpiration
AAIINNORRSTTY	transitionary
AAIINOOPPPRRT	appropriation
AAIJMNNORSTUU	Jura Mountains
AAIKLMNNOOPRS	Roman Polanski
AAIKLNNOPRSSW	Parkinson's law
AAIKNNNOORSTW	Rowan Atkinson
AAILLMOOPPSTU	papillomatous
AAILMNNORSTUU	Ural Mountains
AAILNNOPPSTTU	supplantation
AAILNNORSTTTU	National Trust
AAIMMNNNNOOST	Anton Mosimann
AAIMNNORSTTTU	transmutation
AAKLNNNNNOOPT	nannoplankton
AAMNOORRSTXYY	X-ray astronomy
AANNORRSSTUUY	tyrannosaurus □
AAOOOQRSSTTTU	Torquato Tasso
ABBBBCEEHLMRU	bubble-chamber
ABBBCHLNOORTY	Bobby Charlton
ABBBDEEGHJRUY	Jedburgh Abbey
ABBCDEEIILNRS	indescribable
ABBCDEEILNRSU	undescribable
ABBCDEHILNOSU	Blanche Du Bois
ABBCDEIILNRSY	indescribably
ABBCDEIMOSTTY	domestic tabby
ABBCEEEFKLSTU	Beefsteak Club
ABBCEEEIMORRS	Ambrose Bierce
ABBCEEHJKORTW	The Jabberwock
ABBCEEHKNOOTT	to the backbone
ABBCEEIJLNOOT	objectionable
ABBCEEORRSTTY	Robert Catesby
ABBCEGILNOPUU	bubonic plague
ABBCEHKOORRSS	shock absorber
	shock-absorber
ABBCEIJLNOOTY	objectionably
ABBCEILNORTTU	contributable
ABBDDDEIILMVY	David Dimbleby
ABBDEEEEELNRV	Venerable Bede
ABBDEEFNORSTU	beast of burden
ABBDEEHNOSTTU	beat the bounds
ABBDEFGIOORST	bridge of boats
ABBDEHINPRSTU	put behind bars
ABBDEILLNORTU	bulletin board
ABBDFFILMNNSU	blind man's buff
ABBDHILNOORRS	Harold Robbins
ABBDHINOOORSY	Robin Hood's Bay
ABBEEEEFHMORT	before the beam
ABBEEHINRRSSU	Henri Barbusse
ABBEEILMPRRTU	imperturbable
ABBEELMMNOOTZ	bamboozlement
ABBEELNPRRTUU	unperturbable
ABBEGGHINORTY	Big Bang theory
ABBEGGIMNNORY	money-grabbing
ABBEGGIOOORRT	Roberto Baggio
ABBEGILLNOSST	Stella Gibbons
ABBEGILNORRSU	rabble-rousing

Words marked □ can also be spelled with an initial capital letter

ABBEHINORTTUZ	Benazir Bhutto
ABBEHKLNRRTUU	Luther Burbank
ABBEIIILOPRST	probabilities
ABBEILMPRRTUY	imperturbably
ABBEILSSTTTUU	substitutable
ABBFGHNOORRUY	burgh of barony
ABBFGLLOORTUY	rugby football
ABBIIILMOPRTY	improbability
ABCCCDEEINNOS	bad conscience
ABCCCILLMOOXY	coxcombically
ABCCDDEHINORR	Richard Cobden
ABCCDEEHLLORR	corbelled arch
ABCCDEGNOTTUU	budget account
ABCCDIILLMORU	umbilical cord
ABCCEEFLORTTY	Battle of Crécy
ABCCEEHHIKNOR	Herbie Hancock
ABCCEEHHKRTTY	Becky Thatcher
ABCCEEIILMMRS	immarcescible
ABCCEEIILNNOV	inconceivable
ABCCEHIILLMOY	biochemically
ABCCEIIILMPTY	impeccability
ABCCEIIILSSTY	accessibility
ABCCEIILLMORS	social climber
ABCCEIILLOOPT	occipital lobe
ABCCEIILNNOVY	inconceivably
ABCCEIILNOOPT	occipital bone
ABCCEIIMMNRTU	circumambient
ABCCEILLLMNOP	Colin Campbell
ABCCEILNNOUVY	unconceivably
ABCCEINNOOPTY	Conception Bay
ABCCELNORSTTU	constructable
ABCCHHIIOPRRS	archbishopric
ABCCHKOQTTTUU	quatch-buttock
ABCCIIINNSSTT	Basic Instinct
ABCCIINORSTTU	antiscorbutic
ABCCILMNOPPUY	public company
ABCCNOORRSTTU	subcontractor
ABCDDEEEHNSSU	debauchedness
ABCDDEEFIINOT	bid defiance to
ABCDDEEHNRRUU	Eduard Buchner
ABCDDEEIILRST	discreditable
ABCDDEEILTTUX	tax-deductible
ABCDDEEIMNNOW	Ann Widdecombe
ABCDDEELSSUUY	Claude Debussy
ABCDDEIILRSTY	discreditably
ABCDDEIINOORX	carbon dioxide
ABCDEEEEINPRX	bad experience
ABCDEEEHLRRST	barrel-chested
ABCDEEEHORRTT	beat the record
ABCDEEELMMNOR	recommendable
ABCDEEFIMNNOS	absence of mind
ABCDEEGGORRUY	George Cadbury
ABCDEEGHILNOR	breech-loading
ABCDEEGHIRSTU	discharge tube
ABCDEEHLLOOOW	whole caboodle
ABCDEEHLRRRTU	Albrecht Dürer
ABCDEEIILLTTY	delectability
ABCDEEIILMNNU	unmedicinable
ABCDEEIILMNOV	become invalid
ABCDEEIILNOST	decision table
ABCDEEIILOPRT	periodic table
ABCDEEIINPSST	bits and pieces
ABCDEEILLOSTY	celestial body
ABCDEEILNPRTU	unpredictable
ABCDEEILOORTW	eat boiled crow
ABCDEEIRRRSTY	secretary bird
ABCDEELLOPRST	corps de ballet
ABCDEELLRSSUY	Darcey Bussell
ABCDEELMMNORY	recommendably
ABCDEEMNOOPRY	beyond compare
ABCDEGHLMOTUY	Clyde Tombaugh
ABCDEGIINORTU	auction bridge
ABCDEGMNOOOPY	be good company
ABCDEHIILNNRR	brainchildren
ABCDEHILORRRT	Robert Aldrich
ABCDEHILRRRTU	Richard Butler
ABCDEIIILLNPS	disciplinable
ABCDEIIILNTUY	ineducability
ABCDEIILMNORV	Vince Lombardi
ABCDEIILPSUVV	bicuspid valve
ABCDEILNPRTUY	unpredictably
ABCDEILORRRTY	trial by record
ABCDELLNNOSUW	Lansdowne Club
ABCDGHHIIRRRT	Richard Bright
ABCDGHINOOPPR	chopping-board
ABCDHIILLOPUY	public holiday
ABCDHINORRRTU	Richard Burton
ABCDIINRRSTTU	urban district
ABCEEEEGMORRT	become greater
ABCEEEFLNNORU	unenforceable
ABCEEEGGHMORT	George Macbeth
ABCEEEGHIMMNN	Menachem Begin
ABCEEEIILMPRV	imperceivable
ABCEEEILNOPTX	exceptionable
ABCEEEILNRSUV	unserviceable
ABCEEEILNSSTX	excitableness
ABCEEEILORRRV	irrecoverable
ABCEEEKLMSTTU	Samuel Beckett
ABCEEELLMMORS	become smaller
ABCEEELNORRUV	unrecoverable
ABCEEELNPRSTU	unrespectable
ABCEEFGHNOTYY	by the agency of
ABCEEFIILNRTU	unrectifiable
ABCEEGHHKNNTY	hang by the neck
ABCEEGILLNPRU	general public
ABCEEGIRTTTTU	cigarette butt
ABCEEGJNOPRRS	Jacob Sprenger
ABCEEGKNOPSTU	get one's back up
ABCEEHHOORRSS	horseshoe crab
ABCEEHIILLLOR	Hilaire Belloc
ABCEEHILLPTUW	the public weal
ABCEEHIMOPRRS	promise-breach
ABCEEHNRRSTUY	Treasury bench
ABCEEIIILRTVY	receivability
ABCEEIILNPRSU	republicanise
ABCEEIILNPRUZ	republicanize
ABCEEIKLPPRSU	public speaker
ABCEEILNNOSTT	incontestable
ABCEEILNNRRST	Carl Bernstein
ABCEEILNOPRRS	cerebrospinal
ABCEEILNOPTXY	exceptionably
ABCEEILORRRVY	irrecoverably

ABCEEILRRSTTU	battle-cruiser
ABCEEIMNOSSTV	combativeness
ABCEEJMRSTTTU	subject matter
ABCEEKMNRRSTU	numbers racket
ABCEEKNOPSSTU	set one's back up
ABCEELMMNORSU	commensurable
ABCEELMNOTUVY	Can't Buy Me Love
ABCEELMOOPPRU	become popular
ABCEELNNOOPRU	pronounceable
ABCEELNNOQRUU	unconquerable
ABCEENNNOORSV	non-observance
ABCEENOSTTTUY	beauty contest
ABCEEOPRRSUVX	procès-verbaux
ABCEFGHIINRTW	watching brief
ABCEFGIIILNNT	filing cabinet
ABCEFGIILMMNR	climbing-frame
ABCEFHIILLMRU	Liebfraumilch
ABCEFHNRRSTUZ	Franz Schubert
ABCEFHORRSTTU	breach of trust
ABCEFINOORRSU	carboniferous ◻
ABCEFINORRSTU	be curtains for
ABCEFLMNNOORU	unconformable
ABCEFLMNOORTU	uncomfortable
ABCEGHHILNOST	High Constable
ABCEGHIKLNOSS	slingback shoe
ABCEGHILOPRTY	copyrightable
ABCEGHIMNNSUU	submachine-gun
ABCEGIILLOOOX	exobiological
ABCEGILLMOORY	embryological
ABCEGILNNNOOZ	non-cognizable
ABCEGILNOORST	bring solace to
	bring to a close
ABCEGIMNOOTYZ	zygomatic bone
ABCEGINORRSSZ	zebra crossing
ABCEHHHIINRRT	Heinrich Barth
ABCEHIIIKLMNS	mashie niblick
ABCEHIKLNSTTT	blanket stitch
ABCEHILOPSTTU	absolute pitch
ABCEHJLNNOOST	John Constable
ABCEHKLNOPTTU	put the black on
ABCEHMOOORTTU	too much to bear
ABCEHMOOPSSTX	box the compass
ABCEIILLLMPTU	multiplicable
ABCEIILMNPRSU	republicanism
ABCEIILMORRUV	Columbia River
ABCEIIMNNOORT	recombination
ABCEILLLPSTTU	plastic bullet
ABCEILLORSTTY	obstetrically
ABCEILNNOSTTY	incontestably
ABCEILNORTTUU	tuberculation
ABCEILNPRSTUV	public servant
ABCEILORRRTUU	arboriculture
ABCEIOOORRRTV	corroborative
ABCEKNNNORRTU	Anton Bruckner
ABCELMMNORSUY	commensurably
ABCELMORSSSTU	stumble across
ABCFFGIILOOSU	bogus official
ABCFLMNNOORUY	unconformably
ABCFLMNOORTUY	uncomfortably
ABCGHIKLNSSUW	swashbuckling
ABCGIILLMNNPT	climbing plant
ABCHIILLRSTUY	hubristically
ABCHIKNOORRRS	Brian Horrocks
ABCIIILLNPTUY	inculpability
ABCIIILMOPTTY	compatibility
ABCIIILNOSTUY	unsociability
ABCIILLMOSTYY	symbiotically
ABCIILLMRSTUU	biculturalism
ABCILLOPRSTUY	subtropically
ABCINOOOORRRT	corroboration
ABCLRRSSTTUUU	substructural
ABDDDEGOORRRT	Robert Goddard
ABDDDEILMNORY	broadmindedly
ABDDEEEGHINSS	bigheadedness
	big-headedness
ABDDEEEHPRRSS	be hard pressed
ABDDEEEIKNNRY	red kidney bean
ABDDEEEIMNNRS	bedside manner
ABDDEEELORTTX	dead-letter box
ABDDEEGILLNOU	double dealing
	double-dealing
ABDDEEHLLORSU	shoulder blade
ABDDEEHMOOSST	Thomas Beddoes
ABDDEEIILNPTY	dependability
ABDDEEIIORVWW	wide-broad view
ABDDEELNOTTUY	doubly dentate
ABDDEFHLLNOOS	flesh and blood
ABDDEHLNOORRS	no holds barred
	no-holds-barred
ABDDEIKLNTTUV	David Blunkett
ABDDEIMNOSSXY	body mass index
ABDDGIIOOORRR	Rodrido Borgia
ABDEEEEHINRRS	Aberdeenshire
ABDEEEGGHRRRR	Gerhard Berger
ABDEEEGHILNRT	bleeding heart
ABDEEEGIIKLLP	bleed like a pig
ABDEEEGILLNRS	designer label
ABDEEEGKLLNOW	knowledgeable
ABDEEEGKLNOSW	knowledge base
ABDEEEHIKMRST	beside the mark
ABDEEEHILORTV	hard to believe
ABDEEEHKNORRT	brokenhearted
	broken-hearted
ABDEEEHLNOPTY	beyond the pale
ABDEEEHLNOSTY	lead by the nose
ABDEEEHLNRTTU	under the table
ABDEEEHMNNORS	on her beam-ends
ABDEEEHNRRRTU	thunder-bearer
ABDEEEHOPRSTW	sweep the board
ABDEEEILNRSSU	undesireables
ABDEEEIORRSWY	raised eyebrow
ABDEEEKNOOSTT	take to one's bed
ABDEEELLNOSST	tell one's beads
ABDEEEMNORSUY	beyond measure
ABDEEFFILLOTT	field of battle
ABDEEFIJLNNOY	find enjoyable
ABDEEFLOORRTT	order of battle
ABDEEGGNRSTTU	butter-and-eggs
ABDEEGHIILNNV	leaving behind
ABDEEGILMNNOU	double meaning
	double-meaning
ABDEEGILNRSST	dressing-table

Words marked ◻ can also be spelled with an initial capital letter

ABDEEGKLLNOWY	knowledgeably
ABDEEGKNORRRU	groundbreaker
	ground-breaker
ABDEEHIINOSTT	a bit on the side
ABDEEHILNSSTU	unestablished
ABDEEHMRSSTTU	The Dam Busters
ABDEEHNPRRUUY	Audrey Hepburn
ABDEEIILNNNTV	Venetian blind
ABDEEIILNNPSS	indispensable
ABDEEIILNPTXY	expendability
ABDEEIILNTTXY	extendability
ABDEEIILSTTTY	detestability
ABDEEILLNORRS	banderilleros
ABDEEILMRRSTU	master builder
ABDEEILNNRTUY	turn a blind eye
ABDEEINNOPRRR	Pierre Bonnard
ABDEEKNOORRSW	break one's word
ABDEELLLNORRV	Bernard Lovell
ABDEELMNORSTT	Mandelbrot set
ABDEELNNNORTT	Arnold Bennett
ABDEELNNOORTY	Arnold Toynbee
ABDEELNORRVWW	Brave New World
ABDEEMORRRRWY	Drew Barrymore
ABDEENORRSTYY	born yesterday
ABDEFHNRSTUUU	future husband
ABDEFIILLORRT	defibrillator
ABDEFIILNNTUU	infundibulate
ABDEFIMNOORTU	informed about
ABDEGGIILLNRU	large building
ABDEGGIIMNNRR	Ingrid Bergman
ABDEGGILLNOUZ	double-glazing
ABDEGHINOORSU	boarding-house
ABDEGIIIMNNNR	bearing in mind
ABDEGILMOOSVY	viol-de-gamboys
ABDEGINOPRTTU	bring up to date
	bring up-to-date
ABDEGNOSSSUYY	anybody's guess
ABDEHHILMOSTT	Theobald Smith
ABDEHIIILLLOY	Billie Holiday
ABDEHILMNNSST	blandishments
ABDEHILNOORSU	dishonourable
ABDEHINSSSSUY	shady business
ABDEHMORRSSTU	Bermuda shorts
ABDEHNNOOPPTU	bound to happen
ABDEIIIILQRSU	disequilibria
ABDEIILLOPRTY	deplorability
ABDEIILNNPSSY	indispensably
ABDEIINNORSTU	insubordinate
ABDEIINORSTUV	subordinative
ABDEIKLNOOSUZ	Zuleika Dobson
ABDEILMNNORRU	ordinal number
ABDEILMNNRRTU	Martin Brundle
ABDEILNORSTUY	subordinately
ABDEINOORSTTU	subordinate to
ABDEKRRTUUYZZ	turkey buzzard
ABDELNNOPTUUW	unputdownable
ABDFIIILMORTY	formidability
ABDFNOOOOPRSS	basso profondo
ABDFNOOOPRSSU	basso profundo
ABDGGIIOOORRR	Rodrigo Borgia
ABDGIIKNORRST	skirting-board
ABDGIILNNNORT	bring in to land
ABDGILMNNORSU	Bildungsroman
ABDGINNOOORRU	Giordano Bruno
ABDHIIINORTYZ	hybridization
ABDHILNOORSUY	dishonourably
ABDHIOOTTTUUW	without a doubt
ABDIIIILMSSTY	admissibility
ABDIIILNOSSUV	subdivisional
ABDIINNOORSTU	subordination
ABDIIOPRTTUYY	pituitary body
ABDILLMNNOPTU	platinum-blond
ABDINNORSTUWY	in a brown study
ABDMMNOOOPRSS	mops and brooms
ABEEEEEHLLLLN	La Belle Hélène
ABEEEEFHLRRTY	breathe freely
ABEEEEFILLMRS	feel miserable
ABEEEEFLNORSU	unforeseeable
ABEEEEGLMNRTU	beleaguerment
ABEEEEILMMPRS	semi-permeable
ABEEEEIRRRTVV	reverberative
ABEEEELNNRSSV	venerableness
ABEEEELNPRRST	representable
ABEEEEMNPSTTT	tempest-beaten
ABEEEFFILNNSS	ineffableness
ABEEEFFKMORRR	break free from
ABEEEFHHOSTTT	at the behest of
ABEEEFHKMOSTT	make the best of
ABEEEFHMORSTT	before the mast
ABEEEFIILLMPX	exemplifiable
ABEEEFLNNOSST	absent oneself
ABEEEGGHMNORT	George Bentham
ABEEEGGOQRRSU	Georges Braque
ABEEEGHHIMNTV	might-have-been
ABEEEGHILLOTT	goliath beetle
ABEEEGHILNNVY	heavenly being
ABEEEGHKORRTZ	Zorba the Greek
ABEEEGIMRSTUV	give a bum steer
ABEEEGINRRRTV	reverberating
ABEEEGLOORTTV	root vegetable
ABEEEGMNRRRTU	greater number
ABEEEHHLLSTYY	lay by the heels
ABEEEHIKMRSTT	strike the beam
ABEEEHJMMNRTY	Jeremy Bentham
ABEEEIIKLRSTT	take liberties
ABEEEIILRRRTV	irretrievable
ABEEEILLMRSSS	Les Miserables
	Les Misérables
ABEEEILNPRRTT	interpretable
ABEEEILNQSSTU	equitableness
ABEEEINORRRTV	reverberation
ABEEELLMNSSSS	blamelessness
ABEEELLNORSST	tolerableness
ABEEELNNNSSTU	untenableness
ABEEELNNPRTUV	unpreventable
ABEEEMMNNOOSS	be someone's man
ABEEENOSSSTUU	beauteousness
ABEEEORRRRTVY	reverberatory
ABEEFFFMMORST	member of staff
ABEEFFHHIOTTW	The Wife of Bath
ABEEFGLNORTTU	unforgettable
ABEEFKMNNOOOS	make no bones of

ABEEFLOPRSTTY	Battle of Ypres
ABEEGGILLNNRS	Allen Ginsberg
ABEEGHHLPRSTU	bush telegraph
ABEEGHIKNORSU	housebreaking
	house-breaking
ABEEGHILNRRRT	Albert Herring
ABEEGHLORSTTT	ghetto-blaster
ABEEGIKNRRTUY	Yekaterinburg
ABEEGILMOORST	metagrobolise
ABEEGILMOORTZ	metagrobolize
ABEEGILNNNOOT	non-negotiable
ABEEGILNORRVY	overbearingly
ABEEGIORTTTTU	Ettore Bugatti
ABEEHHIOOPPRT	herpetophobia
ABEEHIILNOTVY	be heavily into
ABEEHIILNSTUX	inexhaustible
ABEEHIIORSTTT	rise to the bait
ABEEHILLNPSST	spill the beans
ABEEHILMNSSTT	establishment □
ABEEHILOPRTTZ	Port Elizabeth
ABEEHILRSSSYY	Shirley Bassey
ABEEHKNOPRTTU	put the brake on
ABEEHLMNOPTTU	put the blame on
ABEEHLNRSTTTU	turn the tables
ABEEHMNOOPRTT	on the port beam
ABEEHOORRSTTU	or thereabouts
ABEEIILNPRTTY	penetrability
ABEEIILNRRSST	irritableness
ABEEIILOPRRSV	proverbialise
ABEEIILOPRRVZ	proverbialize
ABEEIILQSTUYZ	squeezability
ABEEIILRRRTVY	irretrievably
ABEEILLNPSSSU	plausibleness
ABEEILMMNSSTU	immutableness
ABEEILMNNNOTU	unmentionable
ABEEILNNRSSSS	brainlessness
ABEEILNNSTTUU	sublieutenant
ABEEINORSSTTW	bear witness to
ABEEKMNNORTUY	mountebankery
ABEELLMORRTWX	Robert Maxwell
ABEELLOOPRRTW	Robert Walpole
ABEELLORRSTUU	absolute ruler
ABEELNNNORRTU	non-returnable
ABEELOOPRSTUW	absolute power
ABEFFIIMOPRST	baptism of fire
ABEFFNNOOOSTW	off one's own bat
ABEFGIILNRRRY	irrefrangibly
ABEFHMOOOTTTT	at the bottom of
ABEFIIIILNSTY	infeasibility
ABEFIIIILRTVY	verifiability
ABEFIIJLNSTUU	unjustifiable
ABEFIILMORRTY	reformability
ABEFIKLLOORTY	look briefly at
ABEFILOSSSTTU	Battle of Issus
ABEFIMNNOSSSU	man of business
ABEFIMNOORRSU	neurofibromas
ABEFKLOORRSTU	ask for trouble
ABEFLLNOOPSTU	tablespoonful
ABEGGIIMNNOPT	opening gambit
ABEGGLNORSTUW	blow great guns
ABEGHIIIMMNRS	Birminghamise
ABEGHIIIMMNRZ	Birminghamize
ABEGHIIMNNOOT	The Mabinogion
ABEGIIILLMNOW	William Boeing
ABEGIIILNOTTY	negotiability
ABEGIKLMNORTU	troublemaking
ABEGILNNNRTTU	running battle
ABEGIMNOSSSUU	ambiguousness
ABEGLLMOPRRUU	umbrella group
ABEGLMORRSUUX	Rosa Luxemburg
ABEHHINNOORST	Heath-Robinson
ABEHIIILPRSTY	perishability
ABEHIIJMMNNST	Benjamin Smith
ABEHIILNSTUXY	inexhaustibly
ABEHIINNPTTTU	pain in the butt
ABEHILNORRSTW	brothers-in-law
ABEHIMOSSTTUW	mess about with
ABEHINNOOSSTT	The Bostonians
ABEHJLOOPRSTT	Joseph Rotblat
ABEHLLMOPSSUY	blasphemously
ABEHLMNORTUWY	unblameworthy
ABEIIIILNTTVY	inevitability
ABEIIILLNRTUY	unreliability
ABEIIILMNORST	liberationism
ABEIIILMNRTTY	terminability
ABEIIILNOPRTY	inoperability
ABEIIILNORSTT	liberationist
ABEIIILNORTXY	inexorability
ABEIIILNPSTXY	expansibility
ABEIIILLNRTUVY	vulnerability
ABEIILLORSTVY	resolvability
ABEIILMNRSSST	transmissible
ABEIILMNRSTUY	mensurability
ABEIILMPRTTUY	permutability
ABEIILNORSSTV	vibrationless
ABEIILOPRTTXY	exportability
ABEIILRTTTUVY	attributively
ABEIIMNOSSSTU	ambitiousness
ABEIIMOORSTUV	overambitious
ABEIINSSSTTUV	substantivise
ABEIINSSTTUVZ	substantivize
ABEIKMMNNOSTU	mountebankism
ABEIKNNNOOOSY	in anyone's book
ABEILLNOOSSSY	obsessionally
ABEILMNNORRUY	Brian Mulroney
ABEILMNNOSTUU	Blue Mountains
ABEILMNNSSTTY	by instalments
ABEILNNOOPSTX	expansion bolt
ABEILNOORSSSU	laboriousness
ABEILNOPPRSTU	insupportable
ABEILNSSTTUVY	substantively
ABEILNSSTUUUY	use unsuitably
ABEIMNNOSSSUW	businesswoman
ABEINNORSTUVY	subventionary
ABEKMNNOOORRS	Norman Brookes
ABELLNOOSTTUY	absolutely not
ABELNOPRRTTUY	protuberantly
ABFGHHIIMOSTT	that's big of him
ABFGIILLNOSTT	falling to bits
ABFHILOOOTTUW	fool about with
ABFIIIILLLNTY	infallibility
ABFIIILOPRTTY	profitability

Words marked □ can also be spelled with an initial capital letter

ABFIIJLNSTUUY	unjustifiably
ABGGGIILLNORT	ballot-rigging
ABGGHIILLLNNT	ball lightning
ABGHIIMMNSSTW	swimming-baths
ABGIIIILNNTTY	intangibility
ABGIILNNOPRTY	bring into play
ABGIIMNNORRST	brainstorming
ABGILLORRSUUY	burglariously
ABGILMNOSUUUY	unambiguously
ABHIIKMNNPRSS	brinksmanship
ABHIILNOORTUY	honourability
ABIIIIILMNTTY	inimitability
ABIIIILLNOTVY	inviolability
ABIIILLMNORSW	Robin Williams
ABIIILNOSTTUZ	subtilization
ABIIILNSTTUUY	unsuitability
ABIIILRSTUVVY	survivability
ABIIKLNORTUWY	unworkability
ABIILMNOOSTYZ	symbolization
ABILNOPPRSTUY	insupportably
ACCCCILLLNOYY	concyclically
ACCCDEEEINNNS	incandescence
ACCCDIIIINNOT	nicotinic acid
ACCCEEELNNOSV	convalescence
ACCCEEILLNRTY	eccentrically
ACCCEFHIIRTTU	fetch a circuit
ACCCEFKLNNOOR	lack of concern
ACCCEFKLOSSSU	lack of success
ACCCEGILMNNOO	meningococcal
ACCCEHHKLOTTW	watch the clock
ACCCEHIINORTT	architectonic
ACCCEILNNOORS	social concern
ACCCEIMMNOOOR	macroeconomic
ACCCEIMNRSSTU	circumstances
ACCCELOOPRSTT	streptococcal
ACCCHILOOPSTY	staphylococci
ACCCIIKKLOSTT	cocktail stick
ACCCIMMNOOSTU	common caustic
ACCDDEEEEFNOT	concede defeat
ACCDEEEFIIOPV	piece of advice
ACCDEEEHKLRST	clear the decks
ACCDEEEIKMNOT	make conceited
ACCDEEEILMNRT	medical centre
ACCDEEENNNRST	transcendence
ACCDEEENNORTT	deconcentrate
ACCDEEENORRRT	catercornered
ACCDEEGMOSTTU	get accustomed
ACCDEEGNOORTT	grande cocotte
ACCDEEHHIKLPT	thick-pleached
ACCDEEHIILNPX	cephalic index
ACCDEEIILLSWY	Cecil Day-Lewis
ACCDEEIILNOST	occidentalise
ACCDEEIILNOTZ	occidentalize
ACCDEEINNOPRT	accident-prone
ACCDEELLNORSY	secondary cell
ACCDEELMOORRU	cream-coloured
ACCDEENNNRSTY	transcendency
ACCDEENNORSTU	unconsecrated
ACCDEFHHIRTTT	catch the drift
ACCDEFILMNORT	armed conflict
ACCDEHHILOPRY	hydrocephalic
ACCDEHIKNOOPS	pick and choose
ACCDEHILNSUVY	Lucy Cavendish
ACCDEHINOORTW	with one accord
ACCDEIIKLOOPS	kaleidoscopic
ACCDEIKLORSST	cocktail dress
ACCDEILMMOSUY	musical comedy
ACCDEILMNOPTU	uncomplicated
ACCDGIINNORTT	contradicting
ACCDHHINOOPRY	hypochondriac
ACCDHIILNOPSU	sulphonic acid
ACCDHIILPRSUU	sulphuric acid
ACCDHILLNOOTU	Dutch Colonial
ACCDHILLOOPYY	hypocycloidal
ACCDHIMNOPSYY	psychodynamic
ACCDHLNOOOTTU	hold to account
ACCDIIINOOPPR	propionic acid
ACCDIIINORSTY	idiosyncratic
ACCDIILLLNRYY	cylindrically
ACCDIIMMNNOOU	incommunicado
ACCDIINNOORTT	contradiction
ACCDINOORRTTY	contradictory
ACCEEEEGHOSTT	cottage cheese
ACCEEEELLNPRX	par excellence
ACCEEEFINOPPR	Prince of Peace
ACCEEEGHIRRSV	service charge
ACCEEEIIRSTVV	active service
ACCEEEJKNQRSU	Jacques Necker
ACCEEEKNOPRTU	account-keeper
ACCEEENNNORRT	Terence Conran
ACCEEENPRRSTY	Spencer Tracey
ACCEEFFIILRSS	self-sacrifice
ACCEEGGHIINNP	changing-piece
ACCEEGHIKLRRT	trickle-charge
ACCEEGHILLMOY	geochemically
ACCEEGHILNOPS	sleeping coach
ACCEEGHKNOSTX	stock exchange
ACCEEGHNORRTU	countercharge
ACCEEGILNORRT	electric organ
ACCEEHHILLNUV	launch vehicle
ACCEEHHLOORST	schoolteacher
ACCEEHIKLNSST	kitchen scales
ACCEEHILMOPRT	petrochemical
ACCEEHILNNSST	technicalness
ACCEEHKNRRTTU	The Nutcracker
ACCEEHORRSTTY	oystercatcher
ACCEEIILMMNSU	ecumenicalism
ACCEEIILMMORS	commercialise
ACCEEIILMMORZ	commercialize
ACCEEIILMNOSU	Louis MacNeice
ACCEEIIMNPRRU	Prince Maurice
ACCEEIIOPRRTV	reciprocative
ACCEEIKLNOPRS	cocker spaniel
ACCEEILMNOORT	econometrical
ACCEEILNOPSTU	conceptualise
ACCEEILNOPTUZ	conceptualize
ACCEEILNQSTUY	acquiescently
ACCEEILORSTTT	electrostatic
ACCEEIMMNOTUX	excommunicate
ACCEEIMORSSTT	microcassette
ACCEEINNNNOTU	in countenance
ACCEEINNPSTTV	Cape St Vincent

ACCEEINOPRTTV	contraceptive
ACCEEINORTTUV	counteractive
ACCEELLMMOORU	macromolecule
ACCEELNNOSSTT	contact lenses
ACCEEMNORSTTU	accoutrements
ACCEENNNOORTT	concentrate on
ACCEENNOORTTY	octocentenary
ACCEENORRSTTU	counter-caster
ACCEEOORRSSTU	stercoraceous
ACCEEORRSSTXY	carry to excess
ACCEFFIIINOSU	inefficacious
ACCEFFIILOSUY	efficaciously
ACCEFGHIORSST	right of access
ACCEFHKKLOOTW	cock of the walk
ACCEFHNOORTTU	for the account
ACCEFHOORRSTU	Court of Arches
ACCEFIIINOPST	specification
ACCEFIIINORTT	certification
	rectification
ACCEFIIKLNSTT	in a cleft stick
ACCEFIOOPRTTU	out of practice
ACCEGHHIOOPRR	choreographic
ACCEGHIILOPRX	lexicographic
ACCEGHILLNOOT	technological
ACCEGHILMOPYY	hypoglycaemic
ACCEGHILNNORY	encroachingly
ACCEGIILNQSUY	acquiescingly
ACCEGIKKLNOPS	speaking clock
ACCEGINNNORTT	concentrating
ACCEGINOORRTT	gerontocratic
ACCEGIOPPRRTU	group practice
ACCEHHHINOPTT	catch on the hip
ACCEHHILMOOPT	photochemical
ACCEHHILMOPTY	phytochemical
ACCEHHILNRSUW	Church in Wales
ACCEHHILOSSTZ	eschscholtzia
ACCEHHORRRTTY	carry the torch
ACCEHHORRSSTT	Rorschach test
ACCEHIILLNSST	callisthenics
ACCEHIILMOSTT	Catholic Times
ACCEHIILPRRTY	hypercritical
ACCEHIKLLMOOT	milk chocolate
ACCEHILLNOPRT	phallocentric
ACCEHILLNOPRY	chronicle play
ACCEHILLOOPSS	special school
ACCEHNOORSTTV	convert to cash
ACCEIIILLNRSV	Clive Sinclair
ACCEIIKLNOSTW	anticlockwise
ACCEIIKNNPRST	panic-stricken
ACCEIILMMMORS	commercialism
ACCEIILMMORTY	commerciality
ACCEIILMNOSSS	neoclassicism □
ACCEIILOPRRTY	reciprocality
ACCEIIMMNOTUV	communicative
ACCEIINOOPRRT	reciprocation
ACCEIIOPPRSSU	perspicacious
ACCEILMNNNOOP	non-compliance
ACCEILMNOPSTU	conceptualism
ACCEINNNOOOOS	on one occasion
ACCEINNNOORTT	concentration
ACCEINNOOPRTT	contraception
ACCEINNOORSSY	concessionary
ACCEINNOORTTU	counteraction
ACCEINOOPPRTU	preoccupation
ACCEJLLNORTUY	conjecturally
ACCELOOPRRSST	pectoral cross
ACCENNOPRSSTY	Constance Spry
ACCFGINNOORTU	accounting for
ACCFHIIORRSTV	Vicar of Christ
ACCFIIKLORTTU	fruit cocktail
ACCFILMOORSTU	court of claims
ACCFINNOOTTUU	unit of account
ACCFLMORSTUUU	fractocumulus
ACCGHIILLOORT	trichological
ACCGHILLNOOOR	chronological
ACCGHILLOOPSY	psychological
ACCGHILOOPRSY	hygroscopical
ACCGHIOPPRRTY	cryptographic
ACCGIILLMOOSU	musicological
ACCGIILLOOOTX	toxicological
ACCGIILMORRSU	microsurgical
ACCHIILMOSSST	scholasticism
ACCHIILNOPRSU	parish council
ACCHIINNOTTTW	in contact with
ACCHIINNOTTUW	in account with
ACCHIJKLNNOOS	Jack Nicholson
ACCHILMOOPRTY	polychromatic
ACCHILNOOSSTT	Nicholas Scott
ACCHIMMNOOORT	monochromatic
ACCHIMOOPSSTY	psychosomatic
ACCHIOOPRSSUZ	schizocarpous
ACCIIILNNORTU	in circulation
ACCIIILNOPRTT	critical point
ACCIILLNNQUUY	quincuncially
ACCIILLPRSTUU	piscicultural
ACCIILMNORRTU	criminal court
ACCIIMMNNOOTU	communication
ACCIINOORRSTY	Socratic irony
ACCIIOORRSSTV	Victoria Cross
ACCILMNNOOTTY	concomitantly
ACCIMNOOPRSTU	pococurantism
ACCINPRSTTUUU	acupuncturist
ACCLLORRSSTUU	cross-cultural
ACCNNOORTTTUU	turn to account
ACDDDEEEIILSY	easily decided
ACDDDEEEIINPV	peace dividend
ACDDEEEFHNRSU	schadenfreude
ACDDEEEGINNRX	Grande Dixence
ACDDEEEIIIMMR	Marie de Médici
ACDDEEEILNRTZ	decentralized
ACDDEEEKMNOPR	promenade deck
ACDDEEENOPRTT	top dead-centre
ACDDEEEOORRTV	overdecorated
ACDDEEFFIIITU	fide et fiducia
ACDDEEFFILSTY	disaffectedly
ACDDEEGINNORS	second reading
ACDDEEHLLORTY	cold-heartedly
ACDDEEILNORRU	Claude Dornier
ACDDEENNOOPRT	ordnance depot
ACDDEFFHINNOR	Ferdinand Foch
ACDDEFHINNNOR	Ferdinand Cohn
ACDDEGILLNOOR	dendrological

ACDDEGINORSUU undiscouraged
ACDDEGLLNSSTU ductless gland
ACDDEHIIPRRST dispatch rider
ACDDEINNOORTU uncoordinated
unco-ordinated
ACDDEINORSTTU trade discount
ACDDEIORRSTTW direct towards
ACDDELMMMNOOU command module
ACDDHIMNORSYY hydrodynamics
ACDDIOPRRSTUY dairy products
ACDEEEEFILNSV false evidence
ACDEEEEHNNSTT death sentence
ACDEEEENRRSST René Descartes
ACDEEEFGHLQRU chequered flag
ACDEEEFGIKPRR Frederick Page
ACDEEEFIJKNRR Frederick Jane
ACDEEEFKOOPRR keep a record of
ACDEEEGIORSTV storage device
ACDEEEHHKNNRT harden the neck
ACDEEEHIINNTV Death in Venice
ACDEEEHILRRST Richard Steele
ACDEEEHINRRUV underachiever
ACDEEEHLMNTVY evenly matched
ACDEEEHLNOOPS hold one's peace
ACDEEEHMNPRST speed merchant
ACDEEEHORRSTU terraced house
ACDEEEHORSSTU reduce to ashes
ACDEEEIOSSTTV videocassette
ACDEEEKNORRRY ready reckoner
ACDEEELLNOPRY declare openly
ACDEEELMORTTT metal detector
ACDEEELNPRRSU supercalender
ACDEEELOPRSST Apostles' Creed
ACDEEENNOPPRR preponderance
ACDEEFFIIRTUX feux d'artifice
ACDEEFGIILMNT magnetic field
ACDEEFHHIKNRS handkerchiefs
ACDEEFHNORRTW thenceforward
ACDEEFIILNPRS special friend
ACDEEFILNNOST self-contained
ACDEEFINNOORT confederation
ACDEEFINOOSUY see if you can do
ACDEEFNORRRTW centre-forward
ACDEEGGINNRTU reducing agent
ACDEEGHINOSTT go the distance
ACDEEGHNNOPRS changed person
ACDEEGIIPRRRT Eric Partridge
ACDEEGILLLNPW dwelling-place
ACDEEGILLNORW Darwin College
ACDEEGILNNORX exocrine gland
ACDEEGILNPRTY deprecatingly
ACDEEGIMMNNOR commandeering
ACDEEGINOPRRT tape-recording
ACDEEGORRRSST cross-gartered
ACDEEHHKLNNTU The Naked Lunch
ACDEEHIIKMNNY kidney machine
ACDEEHIILMNNR André Michelin
ACDEEHIKLOTTT tickle to death
ACDEEHILNORTY holiday centre
ACDEEHIMOPRRT Arc de Triomphe
ACDEEHINPRSSS cash dispenser
ACDEEHLNNOORR hole-and-corner
ACDEEHNNOSTWY show a tendency
ACDEEIIILMNRS decriminalise
ACDEEIIILMNRZ decriminalize
ACDEEIILLNNNP inclined plane
ACDEEIILNNSST identicalness
ACDEEIILNOSTY easily noticed
ACDEEIILPRTUV reduplicative
ACDEEIILPRTVY predicatively
ACDEEIIMMNNOW medicine woman
ACDEEIIMNNRTY indeterminacy
ACDEEIIMNOPRT premedication
ACDEEIINNNOSV send an invoice
ACDEEIINNORST inconsiderate
ACDEEIINOPRTT decrepitation
ACDEEIKMNPRUY numeric keypad
ACDEEIKNOPSTU induce to speak
ACDEEIKNQRSUW quick-answered
ACDEEILLMORRT all-time record
ACDEEILLNNSTY clandestinely
ACDEEILMMSSTY decimal system
ACDEEILNNPTUV Vincent de Paul
ACDEEILNORSTY considerately
ACDEEILNPPRRU perpendicular
ACDEEILNRSSSU Anders Celsius
ACDEEILOPRRTY deprecatorily
ACDEEIMNNRTUY maiden century
ACDEEIMNORSTU documentarise
ACDEEIMNORTUZ documentarize
ACDEEIMNOSTTU undomesticate
ACDEEIMOPRRSS compressed air
ACDEEINNORSSS secondariness
ACDEELNRSSTTU Dunster Castle
ACDEFFIIKLMTU make difficult
ACDEFGHINNOSW winds of change
ACDEFGILLRSUY disgracefully
ACDEFHILLLOTW Call of the Wild
ACDEFHLNOPRTU clap of thunder
ACDEFHOOSTUVY have custody of
ACDEFIIILNNOS final decision
ACDEFIIILNOTZ fictionalized
ACDEFIIIMNTUV mundificative
ACDEFIILNNOSS non-classified
ACDEFILMORRTV formal verdict
ACDEFIORRSTVY first-day cover
ACDEFMNORRTTU truncated form
ACDEGGHILORSW glow discharge
ACDEGGHIOORTW with good grace
ACDEGGINORRSS grade crossing
ACDEGHHHIMOST high-stomached
ACDEGHIIMNNRS merchandising
ACDEGHIKLPTTY tightly packed
ACDEGHIORRRRS Richard Rogers
ACDEGHLNOORRS Charles Gordon
ACDEGHLNOORSU Charles Gounod
ACDEGIILLMRUY demiurgically
ACDEGILLNOOOT deontological
ACDEGIMMNNORW wing commander
ACDEGINPSTUUU C Auguste Dupin
ACDEGIRRSTUUY security guard
ACDEHHIKOORRR Richard Hooker

ACDEHHLOPRSUY	hydrocephalus
ACDEHIILLRRTT	Little Richard
ACDEHIINRSTUV	Christian Duve
ACDEHIIOPSSTT	sophisticated
ACDEHIKLNRRSS	Schindler's Ark
ACDEHILLNOOSV	shield volcano
ACDEHILMORRTY	hydrometrical
ACDEHIMMNORTY	thermodynamic
ACDEHMRSTTTUU	cut the mustard
ACDEHNOORSSSW	show one's cards
ACDEIIJLLPRUY	prejudicially
ACDEIIKNNORWW	Dionne Warwick
ACDEIILNNOTTU	denticulation
ACDEIILNOOSTV	consolidative
ACDEIILNOPRTU	reduplication
ACDEIILNRSTYY	say indirectly
ACDEIILRSTTVY	distractively
ACDEIIMNOOSTT	domestication
ACDEIINNOORST	consideration
ACDEIINORRSTY	discretionary
ACDEIKKNOSSWY	knock sideways
ACDEIKLPQRSUY	spread quickly
ACDEILLMMOUWY	cadmium yellow
ACDEILLPPSTYY	dyspeptically
ACDEILMNORTUY	documentarily
ACDEILNNORSTY	constrainedly
ACDEILNOOSTTW	Clint Eastwood
ACDEILNORSSTW	Windsor Castle
ACDEILNORSSUU	consider usual
ACDEILOOORRRV	Colorado River
ACDEILOOPRRTU	particoloured
	parti-coloured
ACDEILOPRSSTY	perissodactyl
ACDEIMNNOOTTU	documentation
ACDEIMNORRSTU	arms reduction
ACDEINNNORSTU	unconstrained
ACDEKLLNOPSYY	Sydney Pollack
ACDFIIILMNOTU	amniotic fluid
ACDFILNNOSTUY	dysfunctional
ACDFOORSSTTUU	Doctor Faustus
ACDGGIMNNOPRU	camping-ground
ACDGHINOOOPRT	gonadotrophic
ACDGHIOOORTVZ	Doctor Zhivago
ACDGIILNRSTTY	distractingly
ACDGIIMNNORRS	morris dancing
ACDGILLNOOOOT	odontological
ACDGILLOORTTY	troglodytical
ACDGIMNOPRSUY	group dynamics
ACDHHIINOOORS	Soichiro Honda
ACDHIIINORRST	Christian Dior
ACDHIIKKNPSUY	kick up a shindy
ACDHIILMNOORT	mitochondrial
ACDHIINOPSSTU	custodianship
ACDHINOOPQRSU	quadrophonics
ACDIIIILMNOOT	domiciliation
ACDIIILLORSTY	dioristically
ACDIIILNORTVY	vindicatorily
ACDIIIMNORRST	discriminator
ACDIILLMNORRW	criminal world
ACDIILLMOOSTY	sodomitically
ACDIILLNNOOTY	conditionally

ACDIILLNOOPST	Platonic solid
ACDIILLQRSTUY	liquid crystal
ACDIILNNNOOOT	conditional on
ACDIILNNNOOTU	unconditional
ACDIILNNOOOST	consolidation
ACDIILNOOORST	discoloration
ACDIILNRSTTUY	translucidity
ACDIINNOORRTT	indoctrinator
ACDIMNOOPSSWW	compass window
ACDINOOQRSSTU	conquistadors
ACEEEEFFFLNOS	efface oneself
ACEEEEFHMPRTT	fête champêtre
ACEEEEFLOPRTT	letter of peace
ACEEEEGINNSTV	give a sentence
ACEEEEGMRSSST	secret message
ACEEEEHILNSSV	Chinese leaves
ACEEEEHINSTVX	have existence
ACEEEEHLPRSST	steeplechaser
ACEEEELLMNTTT	Clement Attlee
ACEEEENNPPPRY	cayenne pepper
ACEEEEPPRRSTW	carpet-sweeper
ACEEEFFHJRRRY	Jeffrey Archer
ACEEEFGHLNNOS	change oneself
ACEEEFGHNNOUV	change of venue
ACEEEFGHPRRRS	prefer charges
ACEEEFHILNNUV	have influence
ACEEEFIKLOTTV	ticket of leave
ACEEEFINOPRTT	perfectionate
ACEEEFINRRSTU	user interface
ACEEEFMORRRTT	refractometer
ACEEEGGGLSSUX	excess luggage
ACEEEGGHILMOR	George Michael
ACEEEGHINSVWX	exchange views
ACEEEGHIOPSTV	give a speech to
ACEEEGHLOPRTT	place together
ACEEEGILLNRTY	energetically
ACEEEGIMNNNRY	in an emergency
ACEEEGINOORVV	give a once-over
ACEEEGLMNORTT	electromagnet
ACEEEGLNNRRUY	nuclear energy
ACEEEGLNRSSSS	gracelessness
ACEEEGMNNORTU	encouragement
ACEEEHHPPRSTY	speech therapy
ACEEEHIJMMNRS	James Michener
ACEEEHIKKMTTY	take the mickey
ACEEEHIKLLMNO	chameleon-like
ACEEEHILMNRTU	hermeneutical
ACEEEHIMQRRRU	Erich Remarque
ACEEEHINNORST	on the increase
ACEEEHIPRSTTT	set the price at
ACEEEHKKLNNRT	Kenneth Clarke
ACEEEHKLMORRS	horse mackerel
ACEEEHKOPRTVW	keep watch over
ACEEEHLMNNOPS	mesencephalon
ACEEEHLMRTTUY	Lyceum Theatre
ACEEEIILLNNOP	all in one piece
ACEEEIILNRRSV	irrelevancies
ACEEEIINNRSTV	intensive care
ACEEEIKLNSSTX	exact likeness
ACEEEIKNOPTTX	take exception
ACEEEILLPRSTV	Peveril Castle

ACEEEILMNNRTT	interlacement
ACEEEILMRRVWY	receive warmly
ACEEEILNNNRTT	tercentennial
ACEEEILRRRRTT	letter-carrier
ACEEEIMNNPRSS	Prince Nasseem
ACEEEINNOPRVX	Aix-en-Provence
ACEEEINORSSTV	at one's service
ACEEEINOSSTVV	evocativeness
ACEEELLNOOPSS	lose one's place
ACEEELLNORTTV	electrovalent
ACEEELLRRSTTT	scarlet letter
ACEEFFGIKLLNO	lack of feeling
ACEEFFHINOOTT	on the face of it
ACEEFFILLNTUY	ineffectually
ACEEFGHHINORT	in the charge of
ACEEFGHILMTTU	The Magic Flute
ACEEFGHILNNRU	lingue franche
ACEEFGHINNORX	in exchange for
ACEEFGHKKNOTT	get the knack of
ACEEFGIJOSTTU	gate of justice
ACEEFGIMNNRST	fencing-master
ACEEFGIMNORRT	ferromagnetic
ACEEFGLLMOORS	College of Arms
ACEEFHIIKMMRS	mischief-maker
ACEEFHIIPRTTX	fix the price at
ACEEFHIKLMNOT	Michael of Kent
ACEEFHIKLNOOT	look in the face
ACEEFHJOPRSSU	Joseph Surface
ACEEFIILNNRSU	life insurance
ACEEFIINNRRSU	fire insurance
ACEEFILNOPRSW	Prince of Wales
ACEEFILNOQSTU	acquit oneself
ACEEFIMNNOOPR	free companion
ACEEFINOSSSTU	facetiousness
ACEEFKMORRSSY	for mercy's sake
ACEEFLOOPSSTV	Aspects of Love
ACEEFMNOOPRST	compensate for
ACEEFNNOOPSTU	put on one's face
	put one's face on
ACEEFOOPRSSVY	a copy of verses
ACEEGGGINNNOR	George Canning
ACEEGGHIILMPS	Gilgamesh Epic
ACEEGGHIKMORW	George Wickham
ACEEGGIJKNORS	Reggie Jackson
ACEEGGILNOTTT	telecottaging
ACEEGGINPRRRY	Percy Grainger
ACEEGGIOORTUV	give courage to
ACEEGHHMNRRRU	hunger-marcher
ACEEGHHOOPRRR	choreographer
ACEEGHIIMNNSW	sewing-machine
ACEEGHIKOSTTV	give the sack to
ACEEGHILNOPRS	selenographic
ACEEGHILOPRRX	lexicographer
ACEEGHIMNNNRU	machine-gunner
ACEEGHINNOTTT	get in on the act
ACEEGHINOTTTT	get into the act
ACEEGHLOPRSTT	clasp together
ACEEGHMNRRSTU	surchargement
ACEEGIIMNNOST	miscegenation
ACEEGIINNNRST	intransigence
ACEEGIKNNRRVW	nerve-wracking
ACEEGIKOORTTV	give a rocket to
ACEEGILLLNOOS	selenological
ACEEGILLLOOPS	speleological
ACEEGILLMORTY	geometrically
ACEEGILMNNOQU	magniloquence
ACEEGILNNNOSS	congenialness
ACEEGILNNORRT	Central Region
ACEEGILNNRRUV	learning curve
ACEEGINOPPPRS	popping crease
	popping-crease
ACEEHHHOORRSS	horseshoe arch
ACEEHHIILMPRS	hemispherical
ACEEHHIRVWWYY	every which way
ACEEHHORTTTWW	The Watchtower
ACEEHHRRRSTTU	Chester Arthur
ACEEHIIJMRSST	James Christie
ACEEHIIKNNNPT	pain in the neck
ACEEHIILLLNST	Hellenistical
ACEEHIJKPPRRT	Jack the Ripper
ACEEHIKNRSSST	heart-sickness
ACEEHILLLMOPW	Michael Powell
ACEEHILLNPRTY	phrenetically
ACEEHILLORTTY	theoretically
ACEEHILMPRRTY	hypermetrical
ACEEHILNPRSSS	sphericalness
ACEEHILOPRSTT	heteroplastic
ACEEHIMOPSSST	smash to pieces
ACEEHIMRRSSTT	Christmas tree
ACEEHIMRRSSTU	Maurits Escher
ACEEHINOPRRST	terpsichorean
ACEEHINPRTTTU	cut the painter
ACEEHIOOPRTTW	co-operate with
ACEEHKLOORRTW	work the oracle
ACEEHLMMNOOTW	the common weal
ACEEHLMNORRTU	thermonuclear
ACEEHLMNSSSST	matchlessness
ACEEHLNRSSTTU	turn the scales
ACEEHLORRSTUY	treacherously
ACEEHLPPRSTUY	supply teacher
ACEEHMNOPPRRT	rapprochement
ACEEHNNOORSTU	Southern Ocean
ACEEHNOOPSSSW	show one's paces
ACEEHNOPSSTTW	watch one's step
ACEEHNRSTTTUW	water chestnut
ACEEHORSSTTUY	stay the course
ACEEIIIKKLLNR	Killiecrankie
ACEEIIIMNRRTV	recriminative
ACEEIIINPSSTT	antisepticise
ACEEIIINPSTTZ	antisepticize
ACEEIIKLLNRRT	Eric Linklater
ACEEIIKLMRSUW	Maurice Wilkes
ACEEIILLMNSTY	miscellaneity
ACEEIILLNRRTY	rectilinearly
ACEEIILMNRSST	Cesar Milstein
ACEEIILPPRTTY	precipitately
ACEEIILSSSTTU	elastic tissue
ACEEIIMNNOSST	amniocentesis
ACEEIIMNOPRTV	private income
ACEEIINNORTTW	winter aconite
ACEEIINNRSSTT	intricateness
ACEEIIRSSTTUV	resuscitative

ACEEIJLNOPRSU	Jules Poincaré
ACEEIKLLSSTVW	Sackville-West
ACEEIKLMORRRW	miracle-worker
ACEEIKLRRSTTW	Walter Sickert
ACEEIKORSSTTU	take its course
ACEEILLLNPSTY	splenetically
ACEEILLLNRRTU	intercellular
ACEEILLLNSTTU	intellectuals
ACEEILLMNOSSU	miscellaneous
ACEEILLNNNSSU	uncleanliness
ACEEILLNOPTXY	exceptionally
ACEEILLNPRSST	in all respects
ACEEILLORRTVY	correlatively
ACEEILLPSTUVY	speculatively
ACEEILLRRSSTY	recrystallise
ACEEILLRRSTYZ	recrystallize
ACEEILMNOPTTV	contemplative
ACEEILMNOTTXY	exactly on time
ACEEILMNPRTTU	mental picture
ACEEILMOPRSTU	precious metal
ACEEILNNOPTUX	unexceptional
ACEEILNNOQSTU	consequential
ACEEILNNRRTUW	nuclear winter
ACEEILNNRSSUY	unnecessarily
ACEEILNORSTTU	interosculate
ACEEILNOSTTUX	contextualise
ACEEILNOTTUXZ	contextualize
ACEEILNRRSUUV	universal cure
ACEEILOOPRTVY	co-operatively
ACEEILOPRSSTV	postal service
ACEEILOPRSTTY	stereotypical
ACEEILORRTTVY	retroactively
ACEEIMMMOORTV	commemorative
ACEEIMNNOOPTU	once upon a time
ACEEIMNOORVVW	microwave oven
ACEEIMNPRTTUY	pneumatic tyre
ACEEIMPPRRRTU	turmeric paper
ACEEINNNORSST	non-resistance
ACEEINNNQRTUY	quincentenary
ACEEINNNSSSST	incessantness
ACEEINNOSSSTU	tenaciousness
ACEEINOOPRTTX	expectoration
ACEEINOOPRTUV	unco-operative
ACEEINOORRSTV	conservatoire
ACEEIOPRRSTTV	private sector
ACEEKLNNOOPSW	know one's place
ACEEKMMNOORTY	market economy
ACEEKMOPPRSTU	computerspeak
ACEELLLLOORRT	electoral roll
ACEELLOORRRST	rollercoaster
ACEELLOPRSSTU	supercollate
ACEELMMNOPRTY	complementary
ACEELNNOPRRTY	penalty corner
ACEELNNRRRSTU	scarlet runner
ACEEMMNNOPSST	encompassment
ACEENOOPRRSST	Oscar Peterson
ACEFFFIMOORRS	officer of arms
ACEFFGIILNNNS	self-financing
ACEFFHIINOTTW	with affection
ACEFGGHOPRSTY	Peggy Ashcroft
ACEFGHIIIILMN	Michela Figini
ACEFGHIILMNNY	flying machine
ACEFGHIINORSS	coarse fishing
ACEFGHILORSST	list of charges
ACEFGHINNOSTT	Night of Ascent
ACEFGIIIINSTV	significative
ACEFGIILMNNTY	magnificently
ACEFGIILNNRTU	lunatic fringe
ACEFGIILNOOPR	place of origin
ACEFGILLNRTUY	centrifugally
ACEFHHIIINPST	chieftainship
ACEFHHIINORTW	within reach of
ACEFHHLMNOOTT	man of the cloth
ACEFHIJNOPRSS	Francis Joseph
ACEFHILLNOTWY	thylacine wolf
ACEFHKMMOOOTU	make too much of
ACEFHLLOPRRUY	reproachfully
ACEFHLNOOORTV	have control of
ACEFHOORSSTWY	Way of the Cross
ACEFIIIJSTTUV	justificative
ACEFIIILNOSTT	felicitations
ACEFIIINOPRTT	petrification
ACEFIIINORSTV	versification
ACEFIILLPRSUY	superficially
ACEFIKLMNOOOT	lack of emotion
ACEFILMNOPRTU	capture on film
ACEFILNNORSUU	nuclear fusion
ACEFILNNPRUUY	funny peculiar
	funny-peculiar
ACEFINNORRTTY	confraternity
ACEFINOORRSTU	fusion reactor
ACEFINORSSSTU	fractiousness
ACEFJKKLNOORT	Norfolk jacket
ACEFLNOOORRSU	fear no colours
ACEFLOOPPTTUU	put out of place
ACEFMOOORSTUV	favours to come
ACEFOPRRSTTTU	Pott's fracture
ACEGGGHIINNNR	change-ringing
ACEGGHHLNORTU	glance through
ACEGGHIINNNRT	interchanging
ACEGGHILLLNNY	challengingly
ACEGGHIOOOPRZ	zoogeographic
ACEGGILNNORUY	encouragingly
ACEGGILNOOSTY	gynaecologist
ACEGHHHINTTTW	The Night Watch
ACEGHHINRSUVY	Harvey Cushing
ACEGHHIORTTUW	without charge
ACEGHHNOOPRRR	chronographer
ACEGHHOPRRSTU	scrape through
ACEGHIIKLNNRT	clear-thinking
ACEGHIILOPSTT	phlogisticate
ACEGHIINOPTTY	pathogenicity
ACEGHILLLOOTY	ethologically
	theologically
ACEGHILLNOOPR	phrenological
ACEGHILLOOPPS	psephological
ACEGHILMNOOTW	come along with
ACEGHILMNRSSU	Charles Mingus
ACEGHILMORRTY	hygrometrical
ACEGHILNORSSU	soul-searching
ACEGHILOOSSTT	eschatologist
ACEGHIMNNORTT	magnetic north

ACEGHOPPRRRTY	cryptographer
ACEGHOPPRRSTY	spectrography
ACEGIIILNOSSS	Alec Issigonis
ACEGIIKLLNNPT	nickel-plating
ACEGIILLMOOSS	seismological
ACEGIILLNOOST	neologistical
ACEGIILLOSTTY	egotistically
ACEGIILNOSTTU	gesticulation
ACEGIIMMNORST	commiserating
ACEGIINPRRSTT	starting price
ACEGILLLOORSY	serologically
ACEGILLMNOOOT	entomological
ACEGILLMNOORU	numerological
ACEGILLMNOORY	ergonomically
ACEGILLNNOOTY	ontogenically
ACEGILLNOPTYY	genotypically
ACEGILLOOPRTY	geotropically
ACEGILMNOPSTY	salpingectomy
ACEGILNNOORSS	congressional
ACEGILNOPPPST	stopping-place
ACEGILNPRSTTY	trysting-place
ACEGIMMNORSTT	magnetic storm
ACEGIMNORSSTU	gastrocnemius
ACEGINOOPRSTT	prognosticate
ACEGMNNOORSSW	congresswoman
ACEHHIILMNNTT	anthelminthic
ACEHHIINOPRSZ	schizophrenia
ACEHHIIORSTTW	score a hit with
ACEHHIJKOPTTT	hit the jackpot
ACEHHILPPRSYY	hyperphysical
ACEHHLNNOPSUY	play one's hunch
ACEHHMMNRSTUY	chrysanthemum
ACEHHMOOOPRRT	chromatophore
ACEHHOPPRSTYY	psychotherapy
ACEHIIILOSTWZ	socialize with
ACEHIIILRSTTT	tritheistical
ACEHIIIMNSTTT	a stitch in time
ACEHIIINNORST	corinthianise
ACEHIIINNORTZ	corinthianize
ACEHIIINNPRTT	antinephritic
ACEHIIKLNOPST	lick into shape
ACEHIILLLMOTY	homiletically
ACEHIILLOOPRT	heliotropical
ACEHIILLRSTUY	heuristically
ACEHIILOPRRST	prehistorical
ACEHIIMPSSTTY	metaphysicist
ACEHIINNOPRST	container ship
ACEHIIPRTTVYY	hyperactivity
ACEHIJKLOORSU	Jailhouse Rock
ACEHIJKLPRSSY	physical jerks
ACEHIJLLMMORT	Major Mitchell
ACEHILLLOPRTY	plethorically
ACEHILLNORSSS	scholarliness
ACEHILLNSTTYY	synthetically
ACEHILLOPPRTY	prophetically
ACEHILMOPRSTT	thermoplastic
ACEHILNNOORSS	Charles Onions
ACEHILOOPRSTV	private school
ACEHILORRSSTT	orchestralist
ACEHILPPRSSUY	superphysical
ACEHIMNPSTTUY	unsympathetic
ACEHIMORRSSST	Christmas rose
ACEHINOORRSTT	orchestration
ACEHINOORSTTT	at short notice
ACEHINOPPRRST	copartnership
ACEHINOPRSTTT	stretch a point
ACEHIOPPRSSTT	spectatorship
ACEHIOPRRSSTT	stratospheric
ACEHLNOORSTTT	at the controls
ACEHLNOORTTTW	Charlottetown
ACEHLNOOSTTTY	The Last Tycoon
ACEHLOOOPRRSU	rhopalocerous
ACEHLOOPRRTUY	colour therapy
ACEHNNOORRTTY	on the contrary
ACEHNOORRTTTY	to the contrary
ACEHNOORSTTTU	cut one's throat
ACEHORRSTTTUW	hot-water crust
ACEIIIILMPRST	imperialistic
ACEIIIIPPRRSU	piri-piri sauce
ACEIIILLMPTVY	implicatively
ACEIIILLNRSSW	Sinclair Lewis
ACEIIILNOPRSV	provincialise
ACEIIILNOPRVZ	provincialize
ACEIIILNOSTVV	vivisectional
ACEIIILQSTUVY	acquisitively
ACEIIIMNNORRT	recrimination
ACEIIINOPPRTT	precipitation
ACEIIKLMOSTTU	stick out a mile
ACEIILLMOPRWW	William Cowper
ACEIILLMORSTY	isometrically
ACEIILLNOQTUY	equinoctially
ACEIILLNRSTXY	extrinsically
ACEIILMNOPRRW	crown imperial
ACEIILMNOSSSU	maliciousness
ACEIILNNOPSST	non-specialist
ACEIILNOOPSTT	police station
ACEIILNPPRTTY	precipitantly
ACEIILNPQTTUU	quintuplicate
ACEIIMMNOORST	commiseration
ACEIIMNNOOOTZ	economization
ACEIIMNORRRTY	recriminatory
ACEIIMOORSTTU	autoeroticism
ACEIINNOOOPRT	in co-operation
ACEIINNOORSVZ	conversazioni
ACEIINORSSTTU	resuscitation
ACEIINOSSSUVV	vivaciousness
ACEIINPRRSTTV	transcriptive
ACEIIORRTTTVY	retroactivity
ACEIKLMNOPSSS	smack one's lips
ACEIKMMMNOPSU	Communism Peak
ACEIKMMNNOOTU	take communion
ACEILLLLMRTUU	multicellular
ACEILLLLPSTYY	sylleptically
ACEILLLOPPRTY	proleptically
ACEILLMMNOTYY	metonymically
ACEILLMMRSTYY	symmetrically
ACEILLMOSSWZZ	Czeslaw Milosz
ACEILLNNNOSSY	nonsensically
ACEILLNNOOSTT	constellation
ACEILLNOOPRRY	incorporeally
ACEILLNOQUUVY	unequivocally
ACEILLOPRSTUY	plural society

ACEILMMNOPRTY complimentary
ACEILMMNRSTUY unsymmetrical
ACEILMMOTTUVY commutatively
ACEILMNNOOPSS companionless
ACEILMNNOOPTT contemplation
ACEILMNOPRVYY livery company
ACEILNNOOSSTU Nicolaus Steno
ACEILNOORRRSS Lorraine cross
ACEILNOORRSTV controversial
ACEILNOPRRSSY Princess Royal
ACEILOOPRTVVY provocatively
ACEIMMMNOOORT commemoration
ACEIMOOPRRRSS air-compressor
ACEINNNOORSTT consternation
ACEINNNOORTTV contravention
ACEINNOOPRSTT cornet-à-piston
ACEINNOORSTTW Coniston Water
ACEINNORTTUVY native country
ACEINOORSSSTU atrociousness
ACEINOORSSSUV voraciousness
ACEKKLLMOOPTU poke mullock at
ACEKLLLOOOSTY look at closely
ACEKLMNNOORRY Norman Lockyer
ACEKLNORSTTUY try one's luck at
ACELLMNOORSTY Stan Collymore
ACELLNNRSTTUY translucently
ACELMNOORSSSU clamorousness
ACEMMNNOOORTU Mount Cameroon
ACEMNNOOPPRTT component part
ACENNOORRSSSU rancorousness
ACEORRSSTTTUY carry out tests
ACFFFGHILNOTY flight of fancy
ACFFGILNOSTUY suffocatingly
ACFFIIINOORTT fortification
ACFFIINNOOPTT in point of fact
ACFGIIIINNNST insignificant
ACFGIIIINNOST signification
ACFGIIILNNSTY significantly
ACFGIIILNOORT glorification
ACFGIIINNOPTT pontificating
ACFGIILNNSTYY sanctifyingly
ACFGIINNOORTU configuration
ACFGILNNOOORT gain control of
ACFHIIIMNOSTV fashion victim
ACFHIILLNOORY honorifically
ACFHIKLNORRSV Karl von Frisch
ACFIIIINNORTT nitrification
ACFIIIINORTTV vitrification
ACFIIIJLLNOOT jollification
ACFIIIJNOSTTU justification
ACFIIILLMNOOT mollification
ACFIIILLNNOTU nullification
ACFIIIMMMNOTU mummification
ACFIIIMNOORTT mortification
ACFIIIMNOSTTY mystification
ACFIIINOPPTUY yuppification
ACFIIINORSSTU Russification
ACFIIJORSTTUY justificatory
ACFIILLLORSTY floristically
ACFIILMNNOSTU functionalism
ACFIILNNOSTTU functionalist
ACFILNNNNOOTU non-functional
ACFILOOOPRRSU pair of colours
ACFIMMOOPSTTY symptomatic of
ACFINNNOOORTT confrontation
ACFLLMOPRRSTU call for trumps
ACGGHIKLNOSTU laughing-stock
ACGHHIIOPPRSY physiographic
ACGHHIIOPRRST chirographist
ACGHHIMNOSTTU shouting match
shouting-match
ACGHIILLOOPSY physiological
ACGHIINSSTTTY stay stitching
ACGHILLLMOOOY homologically
ACGHILLMOOOPR morphological
ACGHIMMMOORSU magic mushroom
ACGHIMNORSSST Christmas song
ACGHMNOOPSSTU Compsognathus
ACGIIIILNNSTU linguistician
ACGIIIIMNNNRT incriminating
ACGIIIILLNNSTT scintillating
ACGIIIILLSSUUU Gaius Lucilius
ACGIIIMNNORTZ romanticizing
ACGIILLMMNOOU immunological
ACGIILLMNNOPY complainingly
ACGIILLMOOSTT climatologist
ACGIILMNNNOPU uncomplaining
ACGIILRRSTTUU agriculturist
ACGIIMMNOORRS micro-organism
ACGIINNNOSTUY consanguinity
ACGILLLNOOOTY ontologically
ACGILLLOOOPTY topologically
ACGILLNOOSTUV vulcanologist
ACHHIIINNORST ornithischian
ACHHIILLOOPPS philosophical
ACHHIILNOPPRT philanthropic
ACHHILMMOORSS school-marmish
ACHHMNNOOPSTY Thomas Pynchon
ACHHNOOOSTTUU autochthonous
ACHIILLOPSSTY sophistically
ACHIILNNRSTUY unchristianly
ACHIIMMORRSTT trichromatism
ACHIIMNNOOPPS companionship
ACHIIMNNOPTWY in company with
ACHILLORRTTUU horticultural
ACHILMOOPRRSY primary school
ACHMNOOPRRTTU Arthur Compton
ACHOORRSSTUUY Corythosaurus
ACIIIIMNNNORT incrimination
ACIIIIMNOTTVZ victimization
ACIIIILLNNOSTT scintillation
ACIIILLNNRSTY intrinsically
ACIIILMNOPRSV provincialism
ACIIILNNOPRST inscriptional
ACIIILNOPRSTV provincialist
ACIIILNOPRTVY provinciality
ACIIIMNNORRTY incriminatory
ACIILLLMOOQSU colloquialism
ACIILLNNSTTUY instinctually
ACIILMNOORSUY acrimoniously
ACIILMORRSSTY Military Cross
ACIILNNOPRSTU Upton Sinclair

ACIILNNORSTTU	instructional
ACIILNOOORTUZ	colourization
ACIILOPPRSTTY	party politics
ACIIMNNNOTTUY	continuity man
ACIIMNNOOSSTU	sanctimonious
ACIIMNOOSTTUZ	customization
ACIINNNOOPRTU	pronunciation
ACIINNOOOPRRT	incorporation
ACIINNOOPTTTU	put into action
ACIINNOPRRSTT	transcription
ACIKKLLOOQTUY	look quickly at
ACIKLLLMOOPWY	woolly milk cap
ACILLLMRTTUUU	multicultural
ACILMNOSSSTTU	sansculottism
ACILMOOPRRSTT	tropical storm
ACILMRRSSTTUU	structuralism
ACILNNNNOOSTY	inconsonantly
ACILNNPTTUUUY	unpunctuality
ACILNOORRSUVY	carnivorously
ACILNOSSSTTTU	sansculottist
ACILRRSSTTTUU	structuralist
ACINNOPRSTTTU	contrapuntist
ACKKMNNOOPSST	postman's knock
ACLMORSSTTUUU	stratocumulus
ACNOOOPPRSSTT	contrappostos
ADDDEEEFGIMNN	demand feeding
ADDDEEEFLRSSS	self-addressed
ADDDEEEIINRSS	disease-ridden
ADDDEEEKNNRWY	Edward Kennedy
ADDDEEGILLMNN	Middle England
ADDDEEHLNNRUY	underhandedly
ADDDEEIIMNOWW	maiden-widowed
ADDDEEIMNNOOV	video-on-demand
ADDDEGGLLNOSY	daddy longlegs
	daddy-long-legs
ADDDEIIMNNNOT	Dandie Dinmont
ADDDEMNNOORST	Edmond Rostand
ADDDFFMOOORRX	Ford Madox Ford
ADDEEEEEGHILT	Eddie The Eagle
ADDEEEEHNRRTT	tender-hearted
ADDEEEEKMPRSS	make depressed
ADDEEEFILMRSU	Die Fledermaus
ADDEEEGHINPSS	pig-headedness
ADDEEEGILNNNR	darning-needle
ADDEEEGINRRTT	redintegrated
ADDEEEGIRRSST	Reader's Digest
ADDEEEHHNOSST	hot-headedness
ADDEEEHLLNOSW	swollen-headed
ADDEEEHMNOSSS	dead men's shoes
ADDEEEHNNORRY	here and yonder
ADDEEEHNNPPRU	unapprehended
ADDEEEIILLNTV	Live and Let Die
ADDEEEILNNRSW	Edwin Landseer
ADDEEENPPRRRU	underprepared
ADDEEFFHNNOSS	offhandedness
ADDEEFFLRRSUY	Alfred Dreyfus
ADDEEFGILNNNR	Alfred Denning
ADDEEFHOORRTY	order of the day
ADDEEFIKKNNRW	Frank Wedekind
ADDEEFLNNPRUY	penny dreadful
ADDEEFLNOSTUY	defeat soundly
ADDEEGHIIMNNN	hidden meaning
ADDEEGHLNORWY	wrong-headedly
ADDEEGIINRSTT	disintegrated
ADDEEGIMNNOTU	maiden-tongued
ADDEEGIORSUUV	Dieu vous garde
ADDEEGLLLRRRU	Gerald Durrell
ADDEEGNNRSSUU	unguardedness
ADDEEHIKLNRTY	kind-heartedly
ADDEEHJKLLNYY	Jekyll and Hyde
ADDEEHJOPPRRW	her jaw dropped
ADDEEHMPRRWWY	Edward Whymper
ADDEEHNNNORSU	under one's hand
ADDEEHNRRRTTU	thunder-darter
ADDEEHOPRRSTW	spread the word
ADDEEIILLQUVY	divide equally
ADDEEIINORSTT	disorientated
ADDEEIMNNPRRU	unreprimanded
ADDEEINNSSSUV	unadvisedness
ADDEENNNSSTUU	undauntedness
ADDEFFMOORRSS	form of address
ADDEFIILLLRRZ	frilled lizard
ADDEFNOORRSTY	Dornford Yates
ADDEGHHILNRSS	Highland dress
ADDEGIILNRSTY	dirty dealings
ADDEGINNNRSTU	understanding
ADDEGINNORRST	standing order
ADDEGLNOORTUY	good-naturedly
ADDEHHHILNSTW	with hands held
ADDEHHINNORTY	hither and yond
ADDEHHNNOORSU	Horse and Hound
ADDEHIJNOOPSS	Joseph Addison
ADDEHIJOPPRSW	his jaw dropped
ADDEHILLMNRUY	Edmund Hillary
ADDEIIIILNSUV	individualise
ADDEIIIILNUVZ	individualize
ADDEIIINOOTXZ	deoxidization
ADDEIILNORSTY	disordinately
ADDEIINOOORTZ	deodorization
ADDEIINOPRSTU	superaddition
ADDEILNNPRRST	Per Lindstrand
ADDEIMNNRSSTU	misunderstand
ADDEIMNOOPRSU	modus operandi
ADDEMNNOOPUVW	move up and down
ADDEMNOORSVWW	move downwards
ADDGHHIKNOORW	Howard Hodgkin
ADDGIILLLLNYY	dilly-dallying
ADDGNOOOORTTU	do a good turn to
ADDIIIILMNSUV	individualism
ADDIIIILNSTUV	individualist
ADDIIIILNTUVY	individuality
ADDIIIINNOTUV	individuation
ADDILLLNOOWWY	wild and woolly
ADDKLNNOOOPUW	look up and down
ADEEEEEHLLRRW	wheeler-dealer
ADEEEEFLMNNOS	demean oneself
ADEEEEGGLLNRR	general ledger
ADEEEEGHHNOTV	have the edge on
ADEEEEGHKLPTT	take the pledge
ADEEEEGNNRRTU	unregenerated
ADEEEEGRRSTVV	Steve Redgrave
ADEEEEHHLORSV	head over heels

ADEEEEHKLNNNY	Helena Kennedy
ADEEEEHNNORST	enter one's head
ADEEEEHNRTTVY	three-day event
ADEEEEILNPPPW	pineapple weed
ADEEEEILOTTTU	eau-de-toilette
ADEEEEMNRRRUU	René de Réaumur
ADEEEENPRSSST	desperateness
ADEEEFFGILNST	self-defeating
ADEEEFFGIORRT	agree to differ
ADEEEFFIINRTT	differentiate
ADEEEFFIKMNRT	make different
ADEEEFHHKNOST	seek the hand of
ADEEEFHHLRRSY	Alfred Hershey
ADEEEFHHNORTT	end of the earth
ADEEEFHIKOSTT	take the side of
ADEEEFHILOSST	The Odessa File
ADEEEFILLNRTY	deferentially
ADEEEFILNNORS	read oneself in
ADEEEGGIMNNST	disengagement
ADEEEGGINORST	desegregation
ADEEEGHHORRTT	Herod the Great
ADEEEGHILNRST	single-hearted
ADEEEGHINOPRT	pigeon-hearted
ADEEEGHLNORSS	drag one's heels
ADEEEGLLLRTUW	well-regulated
ADEEEGLNORRSY	Roy Greenslade
ADEEEGOPRRTUY	daguerreotype
ADEEEHHNNORTW	the here and now
ADEEEHIILRSTV	raise the devil
ADEEEHIKKNPRT	keep in the dark
ADEEEHLLNORRU	Leonhard Euler
ADEEEHLNSSSST	deathlessness
ADEEEHNPRSTTY	the present day
ADEEEIILNRTVY	in every detail
ADEEEIIMMNSST	immediateness
ADEEEIIMNNRTT	indeterminate
ADEEEIIMNRTTV	determinative
ADEEEIIMPRTTV	premeditative
ADEEEIINOPRRT	trainee period
ADEEEIINPRSST	pedestrianise
ADEEEIINPRSTZ	pedestrianize
ADEEEIKLNNORR	Kornelia Ender
ADEEEILMNRTTY	determinately
ADEEEILNNNRUV	Inland Revenue
ADEEEILNOPRSS	depersonalise
ADEEEILNOPRSZ	depersonalize
ADEEEIMNPRTTV	tamper-evident
ADEEEIMNRSTTU	underestimate
ADEEEIMNRSTTV	advertisement
ADEEEIMORSTTV	overestimated
ADEEEINOPQRTU	equiponderate
ADEEEIPRRRTUU	Pierre Trudeau
ADEEELLLLRTVW	well-travelled
ADEEELLMNOPSW	Epsom and Ewell
ADEEELLMNOPTV	developmental
ADEEELLNORSTT	State Enrolled
ADEEELNNNRSSU	unlearnedness
ADEEELNNRSSTU	unrelatedness
ADEEELNOSSSTY	needless to say
ADEEFFHIKLOTT	take the lid off
ADEEFFIILSSST	self-satisfied
ADEEFGHILOSTT	lag of the tides
ADEEFGIILOSTV	give details of
ADEEFHHINOSTT	soft in the head
ADEEFHHINOTVW	have the wind of
ADEEFHIJLMNOS	John Masefield
ADEEFHIKMNOST	of the same kind
ADEEFHIKMORTW	wide of the mark
ADEEFHIKNORRW	Frankie Howerd
ADEEFHIKNRRSV	Frederikshavn
ADEEFHIMMNOST	of the same mind
ADEEFHJLMNOST	John Flamsteed
ADEEFHLNORSVY	Evelyn Ashford
ADEEFHLOORRTU	rule of the road
ADEEFHNOOORRT	one for the road
ADEEFHNOOOSTU	out of one's head
ADEEFIILLLQUW	well-qualified
ADEEFIILLNSSY	elysian fields
ADEEFIILOQRUV	overqualified
ADEEFILMNOYZZ	fizzy lemonade
ADEEFILNOPPST	self-appointed
ADEEFINOORSTT	deforestation
ADEEFIOPSSTTY	safety-deposit
ADEEFLNNRTUUV	undulant fever
ADEEFLNOPRSUW	draw oneself up
ADEEFOORRTTVY	Treaty of Dover
ADEEGGNNOORST	Georges Danton
ADEEGGNOPRSTU	tread upon eggs
ADEEGHHNORVYY	heavy hydrogen
ADEEGHIIKLMRT	like grim death
ADEEGHIINNRST	disheartening
ADEEGHIINRRTT	ride at the ring
ADEEGHILNRSTY	near-sightedly
ADEEGHINNNOST	get one's hand in
ADEEGHINNOSSV	have designs on
ADEEGHLNOSTTY	The Longest Day
ADEEGHNORSTTT	stand together
ADEEGIIINRTTT	interdigitate
ADEEGIINORRTT	deteriorating
ADEEGIINORRTV	reinvigorated
ADEEGILLMNNOT	Gideon Mantell
ADEEGILLNORWZ	well-organized
ADEEGILNNNNOO	Lonnie Donegan
ADEEGILNNOOPS	old-age pension
ADEEGILORRSUU	Louis Daguerre
ADEEGINOPPRSV	eavesdropping
ADEEGJMNPSSTU	pass judgement
ADEEGLNNOORRT	Greater London
ADEEGMNNRRSTU	undergarments
ADEEGNNORSSSU	dangerousness
ADEEHHHLORRTY	Thor Heyerdahl
ADEEHHILMRTTY	hardly the time
ADEEHHILNNRST	Netherlandish
ADEEHHILNOOTT	toad in the hole
	toad-in-the-hole
ADEEHHILNTTUY	unhealthy diet
ADEEHHIMOPRRT	hermaphrodite
ADEEHHINPSTTU	put in the shade
ADEEHHLMNOOSU	household name
ADEEHIILLSSTT	satellite dish
ADEEHIIOSSTUV	avoid the issue
ADEEHIKLMOOWZ	Mike Hazelwood

ADEEHILLRTVWW	draw level with
ADEEHILMNORST	sidereal month
ADEEHILMSSTUY	Heysel Stadium
ADEEHILOPTTVY	the devil to pay
ADEEHIMMOPRTX	mixed metaphor
ADEEHIMNOORRU	Honoré Daumier
ADEEHINORTWWW	weather window
ADEEHIPRRSSTV	harvest spider
ADEEHJNOPRSSW	Joseph Andrews
ADEEHKMNORSTU	make the rounds
ADEEHKOPRTTUW	take up the word
ADEEHLNOOTUVW	would to heaven
ADEEHLORSTTTW	the latest word
ADEEHMMOOOSUW	Emma Woodhouse
ADEEHMNOORRSY	dysmenorrhoea
ADEEHMNRRSTTU	thunder-master
ADEEHNNOOSSTT	set one's hand to
ADEEHNORSSTTW	short and sweet
ADEEHORSSTUVY	Shrove Tuesday
ADEEIIIMMNPRR	prime meridian
ADEEIIKLLLORV	live like a lord
ADEEIIKLRRTTT	treat like dirt
ADEEIILLSSSST	Still's disease
ADEEIIMMNNNOT	eminent domain
ADEEIIMNNORTT	determination
ADEEIIMNNOSTT	sedimentation
ADEEIIMNOPRTT	premeditation
ADEEIINOORRTT	deterioration
ADEEIINOPRTXY	expeditionary
ADEEIINRRRSUV	River Eridanus
ADEEIIOPSSSTU	adipose tissue
ADEEIKLMMOORS	make more solid
ADEEIKMNNOPSS	speak one's mind
ADEEILLMNRTTY	detrimentally
ADEEILLNNRTTY	interdentally
ADEEILLNOPPTW	well-appointed
ADEEILMNNOSTT	last-mentioned
ADEEILMNORTTT	detrimental to
ADEEILMNPPRSU	pure and simple
ADEEILMOSSTUW	as it would seem
ADEEILMPQRTUU	quadruple time
ADEEILNNRTTVY	inadvertently
ADEEILNOPRTUV	Andrei Tupolev
ADEEIMNORSTTV	demonstrative
ADEEIMNPRRTTT	printed matter
ADEEINNNSSTTU	untaintedness
ADEEINNOSSTTW	at one's wits' end
ADEEINOPRRSST	predatoriness
ADEEINOPRRSTU	superordinate
ADEEINORRTUVY	auditory nerve
ADEEKLLNOSTWY	Daltons Weekly
ADEEKOOSTTWWY	two weeks today
ADEELLNOOSTWY	say well done to
ADEELMNOORSST	star-nosed mole
ADEELNNNQSTUU	Queensland nut
ADEELNNSSSSTU	dauntlessness
ADEELNOORRUVV	revolve around
ADEELOOPPRTUV	overpopulated
ADEEMORRSSSUW	measure swords
ADEENOOPRSTTU	persuade not to
ADEENPRRTTUUW	put under water
ADEFFHIORRSST	Staffordshire
ADEFFLLLORUUV	full-flavoured
ADEFGHHILNOST	sleight of hand
	sleight-of-hand
ADEFGHIIINRRT	riding the fair
ADEFGHINOORSW	foreshadowing
ADEFGHOORRRSW	show regard for
ADEFGNNOOOORT	good afternoon
ADEFHIIISSTTW	satisfied with
ADEFHIILLOPST	field hospital
ADEFHILNOORSS	foolhardiness
ADEFHLMNOORTW	man of the world
ADEFHLMOORSTT	Thomas Telford
ADEFIINSSSTUU	dies infaustus
ADEFIJMMORRSU	Reform Judaism
ADEFILLLORUVY	ill-favouredly
ADEFILLSSTTUY	distastefully
ADEFILMOOPRSW	pearl of wisdom
ADEFMNOOORRST	Stanford Moore
ADEFNOOOORSTU	out of one's road
ADEGGHIIINOTV	give a hiding to
ADEGGIILNNNST	disentangling
ADEGGIILNNRSS	niggardliness
ADEGGINNOORVW	wood engraving
ADEGHHHORTTUY	through the day
ADEGHHIINNNTW	hang in the wind
ADEGHHLLNORUY	handle roughly
ADEGHHOPRRSTU	spread through
ADEGHIKLLNNSY	Kenny Dalglish
ADEGHINNOORTY	hydrogenation
ADEGHINOORSVW	overshadowing
ADEGHINOPRSWW	washing powder
ADEGHLMNORRTY	grandmotherly
ADEGIIIMNNRST	administering
ADEGIIIMNOSSV	give admission
ADEGIILLMNOOT	all in good time
ADEGIILLNPSSY	displeasingly
ADEGIILMNTTUY	unmitigatedly
ADEGIILNOOSTT	go into details
ADEGIIMMNNRST	masterminding
ADEGIINNNPRTU	underpainting
ADEGIKLNNOTWY	take lying down
ADEGIKMNOORRY	Andrei Gromyko
ADEGILLMNOUZZ	muzzle-loading
ADEGILLMNPPPU	apple dumpling
ADEGILMOORSTT	dermatologist
ADEGILNNOOUVW	go down in value
ADEGILNNOQRTU	grandiloquent
ADEGILNNQRSUY	squanderingly
ADEGILNOPRSTX	exploding star
ADEGIMNNORSTT	demonstrating
ADEGINNNOSSTT	standing stone
ADEGINNOSSTTU	standing to sue
ADEGJLMNNNOTU	non-judgmental
ADEGLLMNOSUWY	Samuel Goldwyn
ADEHHIILMNPTU	Paul Hindemith
ADEHHIILNPRTW	philander with
ADEHHIKNORSTT	shot in the dark
ADEHHILLLOSST	old as the hills
ADEHHINNOSSTW	with one's hands
ADEHHLMOOPSTU	hold up to shame

ADEHHOPRRSSTW	sharp's the word
ADEHIIMNOPTTT	at the midpoint
ADEHIIPPSSSUU	push up daisies
ADEHILLLLORSW	heads will roll
ADEHILMNSSSTY	Myles Standish
ADEHIMMOOPPRS	paedomorphism
ADEHIMNNOOTTW	The Tin Woodman
ADEHIMOOPRRST	moderatorship
ADEHINRSTUVYY	heavy industry
ADEHJNNNOORSW	Andrew Johnson
ADEHLLLORTWWY	worldly wealth
ADEHLLNNOOTWY	Anthony Dowell
ADEHLMNOOPSTY	Daley Thompson
ADEHLOPRRSSTU	shoulder strap
ADEHNNOOPSTTU	put one's hand to
ADEHNOORRTUWY	other way round
ADEHNORRSTTWW	north-westward
ADEIIILLMNSTU	disilluminate
ADEIIILNPSTTU	platitudinise
ADEIIILNPTTUZ	platitudinize
ADEIIILNRSSTU	industrialise
ADEIIILNRSTUZ	industrialize
ADEIIIMNNOSST	dissemination
ADEIIINRRSSTT	in dire straits
ADEIIINRTTTUZ	attitudinizer
ADEIILLMMMOOR	immemorial old
ADEIILLMNNTUU	unilluminated
ADEIILMNRRTUY	rudimentarily
ADEIILNQSTTUY	equidistantly
ADEIILPSTTUVY	disputatively
ADEIIMNNOORTZ	modernization
ADEIIMNNOPSSU	unimpassioned
ADEIIMNNORSTU	trade unionism
ADEIIMNORSTTU	sodium nitrate
ADEIINNNOSTTU	United Nations
ADEIINNOOPRRT	preordination
ADEIINNORSTTU	trade unionist
ADEIINOPRSTTU	disreputation
ADEIJLLORSUUX	Julius Axelrod
ADEIJNOPPRTUY	put in jeopardy
ADEIKLNNORSSY	Orkney Islands
ADEILLNOPSUWW	swallowed up in
ADEILLOPRRSVY	Lord Privy Seal
ADEILMNNOPRTY	predominantly
ADEILNOORTUVY	devolutionary
ADEIMNNOORSTT	demonstration
ADEINNOPPRSST	point-and-press
ADEINOPRSTUVY	vapour density
ADEINOSSSSSUU	assiduousness
ADEKMNNRSSSUU	Knud Rasmussen
ADELLMOOPRRST	Lords Temporal
ADELNNOORSSSV	Sons and Lovers
ADELNOPRRSTTY	transportedly
ADELNORSTUUVY	adventurously
ADELNPRSSSUUY	unsurpassedly
ADEMNOORSSTUU	Edmontosaurus
ADEMOPRRRSSUU	spread rumours
ADENNORSTUUUV	unadventurous
ADFFGHILLNOOS	flash flooding
ADFFHIILNTTUW	find fault with
ADFFHIMNNOSTU	Dustin Hoffman
ADFGGHHIILLNN	Highland fling
ADFGHNOOORRUU	guard of honour
ADFGIIINORSTU	disfiguration
ADFGIIINSSSTY	dissatisfying
ADFGIIKLNNOOV	A Kind of Loving
ADFGIINNNORST	standing in for
ADFGILNNOOORU	fooling around
ADFGIMNOORRVW	moving forward
ADFGLLNOOSUUW	unlawful goods
ADFHHKLLNOOOO	Hook of Holland
ADFIKLLNNOORS	Norfolk Island
ADFILORRRSTWW	First World War
ADFKLOOOORRTW	look forward to
ADGGHHHIIMNTY	high and mighty
	high-and-mighty
ADGGHIINNNOWW	window hanging
ADGGIIKLNNRSS	drinking-glass
ADGGIIMNNORUZ	gourmandizing
ADGHHILLNOPTY	diphthongally
ADGHHNOOORRTU	no through road
ADGHIILNNOPPS	island-hopping
ADGHINNOOOPRT	gonadotrophin
ADGIIILLMNOWW	William Godwin
ADGIIILMNSSTU	dissimulating
ADGIIILNNRSSV	Virgin Islands
ADGIIILNPRSSY	dispraisingly
ADGIIINNOPPST	disappointing
ADGIIKLNNOORW	inward-looking
ADGIJLNOPPRWY	jawdroppingly
ADGILNNOSTTUY	outstandingly
ADGILNOOQRSUU	grandiloquous
ADGIOOPRRSUVY	advisory group
ADGNNOORRUWWY	wrong way round
ADHHJKNNOORTW	John Dankworth
ADHHNNOORSTTU	North and South
ADHIILLNOQRTU	quadrillionth
ADHIILMNOPRSU	dolphinariums
ADHIIMNOORSSU	disharmonious
ADHIINSSSTTWY	St Swithin's Day
ADHIMNOPRSSSW	swordsmanship
ADHINOOSTTUUW	without a sound
ADHJNOOOPSSSS	John Dos Passos
ADHKNOOOTUWWY	what do you know?
ADIIIILMRSSTY	dissimilarity
ADIIIILNNOQTU	in liquidation
ADIIILLMORRTW	William Dorrit
ADIIILMNOSSTU	dissimulation
ADIIILMNPRTUV	Vladimir Putin
ADIIILMNRSSTU	industrialism
ADIIILMOPRRTY	primordiality
ADIIILNRSSTTU	industrialist
ADIILMNOORRTZ	monitor lizard
ADIILNOPSTTUU	platitudinous
ADIINNRSTTUYY	Trinity Sunday
ADIMNNOORSSWY	in so many words
ADLNOOPPRSUWY	play upon words
AEEEEFGGIKOOR	Georgia O'Keefe
AEEEEFGIINRRV	give a free rein
AEEEEFHLOPPTY	apple of the eye
AEEEEFLLNOPSS	please oneself
AEEEEFLLNORSV	reveal oneself

AEEEEGGHHORTV heave the gorge
AEEEEGGHMSSTT get the message
AEEEEGGIMNRRR Germaine Greer
AEEEEGHHHOTTV get the heave-ho
AEEEEHHNNSTVV seventh heaven
AEEEEHLMNOOSV leave one's home
AEEEEHRRSTTTT street theatre
AEEEEIILNQSUV Queenie Leavis
AEEEEIMNPRSST passementerie
AEEEEKMMNORST meet one's maker
AEEEEMNPRSSTT temperateness
AEEEENRRRSTUV nature reserve
AEEEFFGILSTUV Gustave Eiffel
AEEEFFGLNOTUY get an eyeful of
AEEEFFHKMORTT make the effort
AEEEFGGMNOORR George Foreman
AEEEFGHHIRTTW featherweight
AEEEFGHINRRTT fringe theatre
AEEEFGHLNRTTU feature-length
AEEEFGIIRRRTV refrigerative
AEEEFGNOOSUVY Eugene of Savoy
AEEEFHHORRSST horsefeathers
AEEEFHINQRTUY The Fairy Queen
AEEEFHLNOOSTV have to oneself
AEEEFHMNOQTUY Queen of the May
AEEEFHNPRRSST Stephen Frears
AEEEFIIKLMNRT make infertile
AEEEFIIMMRTTT time after time
AEEEFILLNRRTY referentially
AEEEFILRSSSTV self-assertive
AEEEFINQRTTUV frequentative
AEEEFIRRRTTUW feature-writer
AEEEFLNORSSST assert oneself
AEEEGGHNORSSU greenhouse gas
AEEEGGLMNNORT Georg Telemann
AEEEGGORRSSTU Georges Seurat
AEEEGGPRRSSUU pressure gauge
AEEEGHHLORTTT the altogether
AEEEGHIMPRRRT the grim reaper
AEEEGHKLNPTTU take the plunge
AEEEGHLNOPRRS selenographer
AEEEGHMNOPRST magnetosphere
AEEEGHNOTTTUX to a huge extent
AEEEGIKLLLOPS sleep like a log
AEEEGIKLLMNNT gentlemanlike
AEEEGIKLMNRTT telemarketing
AEEEGILLNSTTV televangelist
AEEEGILNORRTX exterior angle
AEEEGINOPPPSU Giuseppe Peano
AEEEGINORSSTT teratogenesis
AEEEGMNORSSSU Graeme Souness
AEEEHHILNPTTW white elephant
AEEEHHINOSTTV the noes have it
AEEEHHLNPRSTW elephant shrew
AEEEHHMORRSTT Mother Theresa
AEEEHHNOPRSST asthenosphere
AEEEHHOPPRSTU paper the house
AEEEHIIMMNNTT in the meantime
AEEEHILMNNOPS phenomenalise
AEEEHILMNNOPZ phenomenalize
AEEEHIMOPRSVZ overemphasize
AEEEHLLMNORTT tell me another
AEEEHLMNSSSSS shamelessness
AEEEHLNPSSSSS shapelessness
AEEEHLNRSSSST heartlessness
AEEEHMMNORTTV earth-movement
AEEEHMNNOOOSV have someone on
AEEEHMNNOPTTV on the pavement
AEEEHPPPRTTTU puppet theatre
AEEEHRSSTTTTW test the waters
AEEEIILNRRRTV irreverential
AEEEIJLMMRRSS James Mirrlees
AEEEIKLLMPRST kapellmeister
AEEEIKNORRSVW weaker version
AEEEILLNRRTVY reverentially
AEEEILMNPRSSX exemplariness
AEEEILMNPRTTY intemperately
AEEEILNORSSTU at one's leisure
AEEEILNPRTTVY penetratively
AEEEILNRSSSTV versatileness
AEEEIMMNORSSU in some measure
AEEEIMMPRSTUY empyreumatise
AEEEIMMPRTUYZ empyreumatize
AEEEIMNNNRTTT entertainment
AEEEIMNNORSTW write one's name
AEEEIMNNRSTTT reinstatement
AEEEIMNORSSSW wearisomeness
AEEEIMNPPPRTT peppermint tea
AEEEINNNSSSST insensateness
AEEEINNPSSSVX expansiveness
AEEEINNSSTTTV attentiveness
tentativeness
AEEEINOPRSSTV operativeness
AEEEINPRSSSVV pervasiveness
AEEEINRSSSSTV assertiveness
AEEEIORRSSTVV over-assertive
AEEEIRRSSTUUX très au sérieux
AEEEJLMNSSSTU Jules Massenet
AEEEKLLMRRSST seller's market
sellers' market
AEEEKLMOPRSSW make powerless
AEEEKMORRSTUV make overtures
AEEELLLOORTVW to a lower level
AEEELNNOOSSST set one's seal on
AEEELNOOOPRSV Paolo Veronese
AEEELNOOSSSTT set one's seal to
AEEELNSSSSSTT tastelessness
AEEEMMPRRSTTU supreme matter
AEEEMNORSTTTV overstatement
AEEENOPRRSTTT enter a protest
AEEENOPRSSTTT poste restante
AEEEORRRSSTTU treasure-store
AEEEORRRSTTUV treasure-trove
AEEFFGHHILRTT flight-feather
AEEFFGHORTTUU The Art of Fugue
AEEFFGRRRRTYY Gerry Rafferty
AEEFFHIKLOSTT a kettle of fish
AEEFFHILLNRTU in full feather
AEEFFHNOORTTU of the nature of
AEEFGGHILNNRY hanging freely
AEEFGHHHIINRT in high feather
AEEFGHHNOORUV have enough for

AEEFGHILNORSV	half sovereign
AEEFGHINOTTWY	get in the way of
AEEFGHLLRSSTU	self-slaughter
AEEFGHNORTTTY	Treaty of Ghent
AEEFGIIKLLOTV	fit like a glove
AEEFGIILMNNSX	self-examining
AEEFGIINORRRT	refrigeration
AEEFGILLLLOSW	if all goes well
AEEFGILNRSSST	self-asserting
AEEFGIMNNORST	Magersfontein
AEEFGINORRSTU	argentiferous
AEEFGIORRRRTY	refrigeratory
AEEFGJLLORSUU	Jules Laforgue
AEEFGMOOPSSTT	mess of pottage
AEEFHHIIKPTTW	keep faith with
AEEFHHKLOOOTV	have the look of
AEEFHHLNOORST	one's other half
AEEFHIKNORTTW	war to the knife
AEEFHILNSSSST	faithlessness
AEEFHIMNNNORT	in the manner of
AEEFHIMNOORTV	have no time for
AEEFHIMNORTTT	in the matter of
AEEFHINNORTTU	in the nature of
AEEFHKMMOOSTT	make the most of
AEEFHLLOOPRTY	play the role of
AEEFHLMOOPRRT	mother-of-pearl
AEEFHMNNOOSST	son of the manse
AEEFHNORRTTUY	turn of the year
AEEFHOOPRRSUY	house of prayer
AEEFHOOSSSTTU	House of States
AEEFIILLNNRTY	inferentially
AEEFIINRRSSTT	fire-resistant
AEEFIKMMNNOOT	make mention of
AEEFILMORRRTT	air letter form
AEEFILNNORSST	strain oneself
AEEFILNORSSST	self-assertion
AEEFILNRRSSTT	self-restraint
AEEFINNORSSSU	nefariousness
AEEFINOPRRTVY	in every part of
AEEFINOPRSTTU	superfetation
AEEFKLLNOOSTT	talk to oneself
AEEFLLNSSSSTU	faultlessness
AEEFLLOORRTTV	foot-traveller
AEEFLMNOORUVY	value for money
AEEFLMNRSSSTU	masterfulness
AEEFLNPRRSSUY	prayerfulness
AEEFLOORSTTUV	refusal to vote
AEEFMNNOOPRSS	person of means
AEEGGIINNNPRT	genre painting
AEEGGIINNPRRT	peregrinating
AEEGGIJMRRSST	Mister Jaggers
AEEGGINNORSSV	non-aggressive
AEEGGLLMOORRY	George Mallory
AEEGGLLORRSUY	rogues' gallery
AEEGHHIOPPRTT	height to paper
AEEGHIIKNNSSV	heaven-kissing
AEEGHIILMNSTU	Haile Mengistu
AEEGHIIMNSSST	Missing the Sea
AEEGHIJNRSTZZ	The Jazz Singer
AEEGHILMNPTTV	pavement light
AEEGHILNNRRTU	Henri Regnault
AEEGHILNNRTTY	threateningly
AEEGHIMMNNOST	mean something
AEEGHIMOPRRSS	seismographer
AEEGHINNPRSTZ	Sherpa Tenzing
AEEGHINOSSTTU	housing estate
AEEGHLLNOOTTW	gone to the wall
AEEGHLMNOOOTU	theologoumena
AEEGHLNOORTZZ	go on the razzle
AEEGIIINSTTVV	investigative
AEEGIIKLNOSXY	Alexei Kosygin
AEEGIIKLNOTUV	eke out a living
AEEGIILLLSTVY	legislatively
AEEGIILMNORSS	generalissimo
AEEGIILMNORST	Gloria Steinem
AEEGIILNNORRT	interior angle
AEEGIILNNOTTV	gentian violet
AEEGIILNNSSTY	easy listening
AEEGIILNPRSTY	Israel in Egypt
AEEGIIMNNORTT	regimentation
AEEGIIMNNRTTX	exterminating
AEEGIIMNRSTTU	time signature
AEEGIINNOPRRT	peregrination
AEEGIINORRTTV	interrogative
AEEGIKLNRSTTW	street-walking
AEEGILLNRSTVY	everlastingly
AEEGILNNNOOST	not a single one
AEEGILNNPRTTY	penetratingly
AEEGILNNTTUXY	extenuatingly
AEEGILOPRRTVY	prerogatively
AEEGIMMNOOTTV	magnetomotive
AEEGIMNNNNSSU	unmeaningness
AEEGIMNNRTTUY	integumentary
AEEGINNPPRSTT	step-parenting
AEEGINNRSTTUU	signature tune
AEEGINRRSSSTV	transgressive
AEEGIORRRSTTV	tergiversator
AEEGLLMNNNTUY	ungentlemanly
AEEGLMNOOPRRY	prolegomenary
AEEGMNOOOSSWY	go someone's way
AEEGMNORRRTTT	German Trotter
AEEGNNOOSTWWY	get one's own way
AEEGNOPPRRTTY	property agent
AEEHHIIMPTTWZ	empathize with
AEEHHIINNOPTZ	phenothiazine
AEEHHIIPPRSTW	white sapphire
AEEHHILLLNOTW	hole in the wall
AEEHHILNNSSTU	unhealthiness
AEEHHIMNNRTTW	with the manner
AEEHHIMRTTTTW	the matter with
AEEHHLMORRTTY	earth-motherly
AEEHHLOPRSSTY	play the horses
AEEHHNNORTTTU	turn on the heat
	turn the heat on
AEEHIIIPPRSTT	perihepatitis
AEEHIIKLRSTTT	treat like shit
AEEHIIKSSTTUW	take issue with
AEEHIILLLPPPS	Philippe Sella
AEEHIILLNRSWW	Willie Renshaw
AEEHIILMNOSSS	leishmanioses
AEEHIILNNRTTV	in the interval
AEEHIIMNRSTUW	within measure

AEEHIINNPRSST	in parenthesis
AEEHIJLMRSSTW	James Whistler
AEEHIKLMOOSTT	make hostile to
AEEHIKMNORSST	Thomas Erskine
AEEHIKMOTTUWY	take me with you
AEEHILLMNSSTT	in the smallest
AEEHILMMNNOPS	phenomenalism
AEEHILMNNOPST	phenomenalist
AEEHILMNOPRST	Le Misanthrope
AEEHILNNRSSTU	unearthliness
AEEHIMNNPSSSS	misshapenness
AEEHIMNNRSTTU	human interest
AEEHIMNPRSSUU	superhumanise
AEEHIMNPRSUUZ	superhumanize
AEEHIMNQSSSSU	squeamishness
AEEHIMOPPRRTY	hypermetropia
AEEHIMOQRSSUV	over-squeamish
AEEHINOPSSTTY	enhypostatise
AEEHINOPSTTYZ	enhypostatize
AEEHINORSSSTW	seaworthiness
AEEHIPRRRSSTU	treasurership
AEEHKLNNSSSST	thanklessness
AEEHLMNOOSSST	loathsomeness
AEEHLNORRSTTY	north-easterly
AEEHLNOSSTUWW	New South Wales
AEEHLORRSTTYY	Roy Hattlersey
AEEHLORSSTTUY	south-easterly
AEEHLPPRSSTTU	The Last Supper
AEEHMMOOPRSST	Metamorphoses
AEEHMMOPSSTUY	emphysematous
AEEHMOOPPRRST	spermatophore
AEEHMOPPRSTTY	spermatophyte
AEEHOPRRSTTVY	the party's over
AEEIIILMNPRRS	preliminaries
AEEIIIMNSSTTV	imitativeness
AEEIILLLMMPTW	William Temple
AEEIILLNNPTTY	penitentially
AEEIILLNSTTXY	existentially
AEEIILMNOPRSS	impersonalise
AEEIILMNOPRSZ	impersonalize
AEEIILMNRTTVY	terminatively
AEEIILNNORRTT	interrelation
AEEIILNNPRRTV	live-in partner
AEEIILNNPSSTV	plaintiveness
AEEIILNNTTTVY	inattentively
AEEIILNORSTTV	revelationist
AEEIILNQSTTUY	sequentiality
AEEIILNRRSTTV	silver nitrate
AEEIIMNNORTTX	extermination
AEEIIMNPSSSSV	impassiveness
AEEIIMNQRSSTU	equestrianism
AEEIINNOQRSTU	questionnaire
AEEIINOOPRRTT	Pietro Aretino
AEEIJLMNNOTUW	Jewel Mountain
AEEIKLMNNOSTV	make insolvent
AEEILLLMNNSST	mental illness
AEEILLLMNRSTY	Stanley Miller
AEEILLLNOPPPP	Pineapple Poll
AEEILLMNNSTTY	sentimentally
AEEILLMNPRSTY	sempiternally
AEEILLNNOPTXY	exponentially
AEEILLNNOSTXY	extensionally
AEEILLNORRSVY	reversionally
AEEILLNOSTTTW	satellite town
AEEILLOPRRTTU	Paul Tortelier
AEEILLPRSTUVY	superlatively
AEEILLRRRSTTY	terrestrially
AEEILLRTTTTTT	tittle-tattler
AEEILMMNNPRTY	impermanently
AEEILMNNNORTV	environmental
AEEILMNNNSTTU	unsentimental
AEEILMNOOORTV	overemotional
	over-emotional
AEEILMOPRRTXY	extemporarily
AEEILMOPRSTTV	splatter movie
AEEILMORRSTUY	temerariously
AEEILNNNOPRST	anti-personnel
AEEILNNOOORSS	lie on one's oars
AEEILNNOPRRST	interpersonal
AEEILNNOPRSTT	septentrional
AEEILNNOQRUVX	vernal equinox
AEEILNNQQTUUV	quinquevalent
AEEILNNRSSSUV	universalness
AEEILNNRSTTTY	stare intently
AEEILNNSSSSST	stainlessness
AEEILOPSTTUVX	expostulative
AEEILORRSTTVY	restoratively
AEEIMNOPPRSST	past one's prime
AEEIMNOPRRSST	temporariness
AEEIMNORRSTTV	remonstrative
AEEINNOSSSTWY	set in one's ways
AEEINOPRSSTTT	Protestantise
AEEINOPRSTTTZ	Protestantize
AEEINOQRSSTTU	sequestration
AEEINOSSSTUVX	vexatiousness
AEEIOOPPRSTTV	post-operative
AEEIPPRRSSSTT	asset-stripper
AEEJLLORRSTVY	traveller's joy
AEEKLLMMSSUUY	Samuel Slumkey
AEEKLMNOPSSTU	take one's lumps
AEEKLNNORRTUW	neural network
AEELLMOORRTTW	martello tower
AEELLMOQRRSUY	quarrelsomely
AEELMNPPRSTUY	supplementary
AEELNNOPRRSTU	neutral person
AEELNOOORRRST	sooner or later
AEELNOPPRRSWY	plenary powers
AEELNOPRSTTTT	talent spotter
AEELNRSSTTUVY	Yves St Laurent
AEEMNPRRRSUUY	supernumerary
AEEMNPRRSTTUW	trumpeter swan
AEEOOPRRRTUVW	pour water over
AEEOORSSSSTTT	Ettore Sotsass
AEFFGHILOORST	go off the rails
AEFFGIMRSSTTU	suffragettism
AEFFHHIIOTTVW	have it off with
AEFFHHSSTTTTU	that's the stuff!
AEFFHMNNNORST	Ernst Hoffmann
AEFFHMOPRSTYY	offer sympathy
AEFFIIKNNSTTU	take it in snuff
AEFFIILLOQTUY	quality of life
AEFGGIIKNRSTU	figure skating

AEFGGMMORSTUU	Fogg Art Museum
AEFGHHIKLOPSY	speak highly of
AEFGHIKMNNOOT	make nothing of
AEFGHILNORTTU	light of nature
AEFGHINNNPRTY	penny farthing
	penny-farthing
AEFGHNORSTTUU	unsought-after
AEFGHOOOTTUWY	go out of the way
AEFGIINNOORSV	range of vision
AEFGIINOPRRTU	prefiguration
AEFGILLNNRTUY	unfalteringly
AEFGILNNOOSSU	using one's loaf
AEFGILNOPPRSV	self-approving
AEFGMNNOORTTY	Margot Fonteyn
AEFHHLLLNTUUY	unhealthfully
AEFHIINOPSTTT	in spite of that
AEFHILLNOORTW	will not hear of
AEFHILOPRTTXY	trial of the pyx
AEFHIMNNOOSTT	Timon of Athens
AEFHIMOORRSTT	for a short time
AEFHINNOORSTT	this afternoon
AEFHINOORRSST	for this reason
AEFHKKNNOORTY	Anthony Fokker
AEFHLNNOOOSST	Solon of Athens
AEFHNOORRTTUW	worth a fortune
AEFHOORRSTTTY	The Story of Art
AEFIIIILMNNST	infinitesimal
AEFIIILNORSTT	fertilisation
AEFIIILNORTTZ	fertilization
AEFIILLLNNTUY	influentially
AEFIILLMORTWY	William of Tyre
AEFIILLOPPRSU	papilliferous
AEFIILLPRSTTU	fruit pastille
AEFIILMNNOOTT	fail to mention
AEFIILNOOPRRT	proliferation
AEFIIMNNORTUV	uninformative
AEFIIMNORSSTU	staminiferous
AEFIINNORTTUV	Trevi Fountain
AEFIINRRSTTTY	interstratify
AEFIKLLOOSTTT	take its toll of
AEFIKNNOPRSWY	Erwin Panofsky
AEFIKOPRRRTWY	firework party
AEFILMNOPRSTT	self-important
AEFILNRSSTUVY	transfusively
AEFIMNORRSTUU	frumentarious
AEFINOOPRRRSW	prisoner of war
AEFIOOPRSTTUV	favourite spot
AEFIOQRRSTUUZ	quartziferous
AEFLLMNORSTUW	menstrual flow
AEFLNNORTTUUY	unfortunately
AEFMMNNOOORTT	not for a moment
AEFMNOORSTTUU	run out of steam
AEGGGGINNOTUW	tongue-wagging
AEGGHHIKLLSTU	Hugh Gaitskell
AEGGHIIIMNNST	imagine things
AEGGHIINNRSTT	straightening
AEGGHILNNOSTU	tongue-lashing
AEGGHILNOORTW	woolgathering
	wool-gathering
AEGGHINNOORST	shooting range
AEGGHLNNOOTTY	go to any length
AEGGIIIMNPSTT	spitting image
AEGGIIINNSTTV	investigating
AEGGIILNNRRST	Stirling Range
AEGGIINORRTTU	regurgitation
AEGGIINRSTTTT	sitting target
AEGGILLMNRRUY	Gerry Mulligan
AEGGIMMNORSTY	gyromagnetism
AEGGINNNOORSS	non-aggression
AEGGINNNORTYZ	Tenzing Norgay
AEGGLLOORRTUY	go to regularly
AEGHHIKMMNSTU	make things hum
AEGHHILMNOSTU	lighthouseman
AEGHHINNNOOTV	have nothing on
AEGHHIOPPRRSY	physiographer
AEGHHKLOSSTTW	the ghost walks
AEGHHLORRTTUV	travel through
AEGHHOOPPRRST	photographers
AEGHIIINNRSTV	The Virginians
AEGHIIKLLOTTU	out like a light
AEGHIIKNNPRSS	pinking shears
	pinking-shears
AEGHIIKNNSTTV	having kittens
AEGHIILNRTTTT	tilt at the ring
AEGHIINRRRSTT	heart-stirring
AEGHIIPRRRSST	registrarship
AEGHIKNNRRSTT	knights-errant
AEGHILLLLNTUY	hunt illegally
AEGHILORSSTTW	with great loss
AEGHIMNORTTUW	mouthwatering
	mouth-watering
AEGHINNNOOPPS	happening soon
AEGHINNNOPTTT	nothing patent
AEGHINNOORSST	on a shoestring
AEGHINNPRRSSU	pruning-shears
AEGHINOOORTUV	give a honour to
AEGHINORSTTTU	straighten out
AEGHINORSTTVY	overnight stay
AEGHIOPRRSSTU	surrogateship
AEGHLLMOOORTY	moral theology
AEGHLMMOORTTY	thremmatology
AEGIIIKLLMNPS	Spike Milligan
AEGIIIMMNNNNO	moaning minnie
AEGIIINNNOOPV	give an opinion
AEGIIINNOSTTV	investigation
AEGIIINNRSSUU	iure sanguinis
AEGIILLLLNRTY	Lillie Langtry
AEGIILNNPRRST	laser printing
AEGIIMNOPRRTY	primogenitary
AEGIINNNSTTTT	sitting tenant
AEGIINNOORRTT	interrogation
AEGIINNORRTUY	genito-urinary
AEGIINOORSTTT	giant tortoise
AEGIINORSTTVY	investigatory
AEGIJLNRRRSWY	Jerry Rawlings
AEGIKLLNORRST	roller-skating
AEGILLNOOPSTT	planetologist
AEGILLNOSSSTT	on its last legs
AEGILMNNORRST	Neil Armstrong
AEGILNNNORSUY	unreasoningly
AEGILNNORSTTU	transit lounge
AEGILOPRRSTUW	Walter Gropius

AEGINNNPRSSSU	unsparingness
AEGINNOPRSSSU	gain one's spurs
AEGINNORRSSST	transgression
AEGINOORRRTTY	interrogatory
AEGINQRRSTTTU	string quartet
AEGLMNNOORTYY	Antony Gormley
AEGLNORRSSSUU	garrulousness
AEGLNRSSSSTUY	Ulysses S Grant
AEHHIIILMNSST	helminthiasis
AEHHIILNORSTW	in a short while
AEHHIILORSTTV	health visitor
AEHHIIMNORTWZ	harmonize with
AEHHIINOPPSTW	whip into shape
AEHHIIOTTTUVW	have it out with
AEHHIKLLNORTT	I'll thank her to
AEHHILMMOOORT	homoiothermal
AEHHINORRRSTY	North Ayrshire
AEHHIOPPRSTYY	physiotherapy
AEHHIORRSSTUY	South Ayrshire
AEHHLLOPSTTUW	push to the wall
AEHHLOOPPRSTY	phosphorylate
AEHIIIMNTTTUW	titanium white
AEHIIKLLNOSUV	Sihanoukville
AEHIILLMOORVW	William Hoover
AEHIILLMOPPRW	Philip Marlowe
AEHIIMNRSSTTU	Austin hermits
AEHIINNORTWWY	in their own way
AEHIINNPPRRST	in partnership
AEHIINORRSSTW	airworthiness
AEHIJNNNOORSV	Earvin Johnson
AEHIJOPSTTUWX	juxtapose with
AEHIKKNOOSSTT	soak to the skin
AEHILLMNNNSWY	Manny Shinwell
AEHILLMNNOOPT	Lionel Hampton
AEHILLMNPRSTT	the small print
AEHILMOOSTUXY	homosexuality
AEHILNNOOORST	Horatio Nelson
AEHIMMNOPRTUY	immunotherapy
AEHIMMOOPRSST	metamorphosis □
AEHIMNOPPSSTU	put emphasis on
AEHINOORSTTUW	without reason
AEHJLMNNOOSSU	Samuel Johnson
AEHLLNNOOPTWY	Anthony Powell
AEHLMNOOPRTVW	Wolverhampton
AEHLNOORSSTTW	worth one's salt
AEHLOQRRRTUUY	quarter-hourly
AEHMNOOPRRTTY	anthropometry
AEHMNOOPRSSSU	amorphousness
AEHMNOOPRTTWY	Oh, Pretty Woman
AEHMNOQRTTUUY	quantum theory
AEHMOOQRSUUUU	aqueous humour
AEHNNOOTTUWWY	when you want to
AEIIIKLLLMNVW	William Kelvin
AEIIILLMNNNOO	one in a million
AEIIILLMNPRRY	preliminarily
AEIIILLMNRSTY	ministerially
AEIIILLMRRSVY	verisimilarly
AEIIILNORSSTT	sterilisation
AEIIILNORSTTZ	sterilization
AEIIILPRRSTUZ	spiritualizer
AEIIINNORSSSV	visionariness

AEIIINNORTTWZ	winterization
AEIIINNOSSTTZ	sensitization
AEIIKMNOOPRSV	make provision
AEIIKNNRSTTTU	take it in turns
AEIILLLMMNSWY	Emlyn Williams
AEIILLMMNOPSW	William Empson
AEIILLMNSSUVW	Venus Williams
AEIILLNNNOTTY	intentionally
AEIILLNNORTVY	inventorially
AEIILLNQRRSTU	tranquilliser
AEIILLNQRRTUZ	tranquillizer
AEIILLORRRTTY	territorially
AEIILMMNOSSSS	Missa Solemnis
AEIILMNNOOSTZ	solemnization
AEIILMNNOPSTU	emulsion paint
AEIILMNNORRTV	minor interval
AEIILMNOPRRTX	interproximal
AEIILMNOPRSTY	impersonality
AEIILMNORSSST	trim one's sails
AEIILNNNNOTTU	unintentional
AEIILNNOOPRTT	interpolation
AEIILNOOPPRST	prepositional
AEIILNOOPSTTX	sexploitation
AEIILNOORSTTT	tolerationist
AEIILNOPPSTTU	Pontius Pilate
AEIILNOPRTUVZ	pulverization
AEIILNPRSSSTU	spiritualness
AEIILOOPPRRRT	proprietorial
AEIIMNNOOPRST	impersonation
AEIIMNOOPRTTZ	temporization
AEIINOOPPRRTX	expropriation
AEIINOORRRTTZ	terrorization
AEIINORRSSSTT	transistorise
AEIINORRSSTTZ	transistorize
AEIKKLMNNORUW	unworkmanlike
AEIKLLNOOSTTT	take its toll on
AEIKLMNOPRSST	sportsmanlike
AEIKOPPPRRSTY	pork-pie pastry
AEILLMNNOOTUY	unemotionally
AEILLNOPRTTWW	willow pattern □
AEILMMNNOORRY	Marilyn Monroe
AEILMNNNOSSUW	unwomanliness
AEILMNOPRSSTT	less important
AEILMNOPRTTUY	importunately
AEILNOOPRSTTT	petrol station
AEILNOOPSTTUX	expostulation
AEILNOORRTUVY	revolutionary
AEILOOQRSTUUZ	Louis-Quatorze
AEIMMNOPPRTUU	put a premium on
AEIMNNOOPPRTT	apportionment
AEIMNNOORRSTT	remonstration
AEIMNNOORSWWY	worm one's way in
AEIMNNQSSSTUY	Quentin Massys
AEIMNOPRSSTTT	Protestantism
AEIMORSSSSTTT	toastmistress
AEIMPRRRSSSTY	primary stress
AEINNORSSSUUV	unsavouriness
AEINOOOPPRRTT	proportionate
AEJKKLMNOOPSX	James Knox Polk
AELLMNOPRRSUY	supernormally
AELMNNORRSTTY	remonstrantly

Words marked □ can also be spelled with an initial capital letter

AELMNOORRTTUY	Mary Lou Retton
AELNNOOPSSTUY	spontaneously
AELOOPRSTTUXY	expostulatory
AEMMNNORSTUUV	verumontanums
AEMNOOOPRSSZZ	mezzo-sopranos
AENNNOOPSSTUU	unspontaneous
AFFMOOOOPRRRU	armour of proof
AFGGGINNOOORS	going for a song
AFGGHHIIRSTTT	straight fight
AFGHHIORRSTTT	straightforth
AFGHIIKNNOTWY	way of thinking
AFGHIINOPRRST	profit-sharing
AFGHIMOPRSSST	pass from sight
AFGIIILNNRTUY	infuriatingly
AFGIIILNOORVW	Virginia Woolf
AFGILNRRSTTUY	frustratingly
AFGNOOOPRTTUW	put a foot wrong
AFHIILMORSTYY	family history
AFHMNOPSSTUYY	Faust Symphony
AFIIILNOOSSTZ	fossilization
AFIIKLNOORSSY	ask for noisily
AFIILLORSTTUY	flirtatiously
AFIILOPRSSSTT	spirits of salt
AFIILOPRSSSUY	fissiparously
AFIIMNNNOOOPR	form an opinion
AFIKLMNOOTWWZ	Wolf Mankowitz
AFKLLNOOORUWY	for all you know
AGGHHIIPRSTTT	straight-pight
AGGHHMOPPRSYY	sphygmography
AGGHIILLNNSUY	languishingly
AGGHIKLNOOPPR	grappling-hook
AGGIIILNNSTTY	instigatingly
AGGIILLNOPRVY	payroll giving
AGGIILNNOPPRR	grappling-iron
AGGINPSSTUUUU	Augustus Pugin
AGHHIILMNRSTY	nightmarishly
AGHHIIMNNOSTU	mountains-high
AGHHIINPRSTTU	run a tight ship
AGHHINOOPPRST	in photographs
AGHHINOOPRSST	sharpshooting
AGHHIOOPRRSTT	orthographist
AGHHLLMOOOPTY	ophthalmology
AGHIIILNPRSTT	hair-splitting
AGHIIKOORSUUZ	Kazuo Ishiguro
AGHIILNNOSSTY	astonishingly
AGHIKLMNOOSTT	smooth-talking
AGHINNOOPSTTT	stop at nothing
AGHINOPPSSTTU	supposing that
AGHLLMOORSUUW	gallows humour
AGHOOOPPPRRSY	prosopography
AGIIILLLNTTTY	titillatingly
AGIIILLMNRSTU	trilingualism
AGIIILNNNOOPT	no oil painting
AGIIILNNNSTUY	insinuatingly
AGIIILNNORTUY	unoriginality
AGIILLNNOPRTY	rallying-point
AGIILNNOPRSSU	ruling passion
AGIILNNOPRSTY	patronisingly
AGIILNNOPRTYZ	patronizingly
AGIILOORSSSTY	Assyriologist
AGIIMNOORRSUV	graminivorous
AGIINNOPRSTTT	starting point
	starting-point
	Trainspotting
	train-spotting
AGILNNOPPRUVY	unapprovingly
AGLLOOOSTTUUY	tautologously
AGOOPRSSTTTUU	put out to grass
AHHIIKLLMNOTT	I'll thank him to
AHHIIMNNORTWY	in harmony with
AHHIMOOPSSTTW	Thomas Sopwith
AHHNOOOPPRSTY	anthroposophy
AHIIILLPSTTUW	it is all up with
AHIIILNOOPRRT	horripilation
AHIILNOORTTYZ	horizontality
AHIIMNOPRSSTT	misanthropist
AHIKLLNOOTTUY	I'll thank you to
AHILMMNOORTYY	Holy Matrimony
	holy matrimony
AHIMNOPPRSSST	sportsmanship
AHKLNNOOPPTTY	phytoplankton
AHKNNNOOPSSSY	on Shanks's pony
AHLLMOPRTUUWY	pull a wry mouth
AHOOOPPPRSSTT	passport photo
AIIIILNNOQSTU	inquisitional
AIIIILNOQRSTU	inquisitorial
AIIIIMNOPSSSS	pianississimo
AIIILLMMORRSW	William Morris
AIIILLMNNOSTU	illuminations
AIIILLMNPSTUY	pusillanimity
AIIILNNOSTTTU	institutional
AIIIMNNORSSTT	ministrations
AIIIMNOOOPRTT	poor imitation
AIIIMNOOPRSTV	improvisation
AIIINNNOOSTTV	innovationist
AIIJNOOPSTTUX	juxtaposition
AIILLMNOPSSUU	pusillanimous
AIILLNNORTUVY	involuntarily
AIILLNOOPRSVY	provisionally
AIILLNPRSTUUY	unspiritually
AIILNOOPPSSTU	suppositional
AIINNNOPSSTUU	Antoninus Pius
AIINNOOPRSSTT	transposition
AIIOOOPRSUVVV	ovoviviparous
AILMOOOPSSSTX	toxoplasmosis
AILORRSTTUUUV	ultra-virtuous
AIMMNOOPRSTTT	most important
ALMNOOOPSTUUY	almost upon you

B

BBBEEEKLRSUYY	Busby Berkeley
BBCDEEELMORRU	become blurred
BBCDEEELORTTU	could be better
BBCDEEIILORTY	liberty bodice
BBCDGIIKLLNOU	building block
BBCEEEIILMOSV	become visible
BBCEEHKOSSTYZ	Sketches By Boz
BBCEEHLORRTTT	Bertolt Brecht
BBCEEIMOOOSUV	become obvious
BBCEEIORRSSUV	oversubscribe
BBCEGHIILNNPU	Bible-punching
BBCEHMOORRSTU	butcher's broom

BBCEIILMNOSTU	incombustible
BBCGGHIILNNTU	nightclubbing
BBCIILMNOSTUY	incombustibly
BBDDEEGIILRRU	bridge-builder
BBDEEEHILSSTW	be blessed with
BBDEEGHHRRTUU	Hubert de Burgh
BBDEEGIORRRST	Robert Bridges
BBDEEHKNOOOTY	done by the book
BBDEHINOPTUUW	be bound up with
BBDEHLOOORRST	Blood Brothers
BBEEEEEEHIIJS	heebie-jeebies
BBEEEGILNRTUY	burying beetle
BBEEEHILLTTTU	bite the bullet
BBEEHILLLRRUY	Blueberry Hill
BBEEHILNOSTUY	the boys in blue
BBEEHIMNOSTTU	bite one's thumb
BBEGGIMNNORUY	money-grubbing
BBEGHIILMNPTU	Bible-thumping
BBEGHKOOOORRU	Brookeborough
BCCCDEIIMRRSU	circumscribed
BCCCEEHILPRUZ	Czech Republic
BCCDEEEIILLLM	Cecil B De Mille
BCCDEIKLLNORY	cylinder block
BCCDELNOOOTUU	double coconut
BCCDKMMNOOORU	common burdock
BCCEEEIMMOORR	Eric Morecombe
BCCEEEIMNOTTX	become extinct
BCCEEFIMNOORS	combine forces
BCCEEHIKKKTTU	kick the bucket
BCCEEKMNOSTUU	become unstuck
BCCEHHINOOOSS	Hobson's choice
BCCEIIIJOSTTV	objectivistic
BCCEILNORSTTU	constructible
BCCGIILLMOOSY	symbolic logic
BCDDDELLLOOOY	cold-bloodedly
BCDDEEEILNSSU	deducibleness
BCDDEEFILLORU	Bruce Oldfield
BCDDEEFINNOOT	confined to bed
BCDDGILLNOORU	bloodcurdling
BCDEEEFIMNORS	become friends
BCDEEEIMOOSTU	become tedious
BCDEEGINORRSS	cross-breeding
BCDEEHHLPRSSU	shepherd's club
BCDEEIIILLMRW	Willie McBride
BCDEEIIILNNRS	indiscernible
BCDEEIILNNRSU	undiscernible
BCDEEKKNRTUYY	Kentucky Derby
BCDEELMRRRUUY	cry blue murder
BCDEELOORRSSU	double-crosser
BCDEIIIILNRTY	incredibility
BCDEIIILNNRSY	indiscernibly
BCDEIILNNRSUY	undiscernibly
BCDGHIIKKRRTU	Kirkcudbright
BCEEEEEKNOORZ	Ebenezer Cooke
BCEEEEFKNOORR	reference book
BCEEEFMNPRRTU	perfect number
BCEEEGHIKTTUV	give the bucket
BCEEEGIINORST	bioenergetics
BCEEEGILLNORT	cobelligerent
BCEEEHILNOSTT	be in the closet
BCEEEHIMNNORT	become thinner
BCEEEHMOORRST	become shorter
BCEEEIILMPPRT	imperceptible
BCEEEIJNOSSTV	objectiveness
BCEEEIJOSTTTV	objective test
BCEEELMMOPPRU	become plumper
BCEEELNOOPRRT	electron probe
BCEEGIIMNNOOT	come into being
BCEEHIILLMOTW	become ill with
BCEEHIJKNNOST	John Steinbeck
BCEEHIKORRRRT	Robert Herrick
BCEEHILMOOOTT	come to the boil
BCEEHILOORRTZ	Hector Berlioz
BCEEHKLOOORTW	crook the elbow
BCEEIILMPPRTY	imperceptibly
BCEEIINNNORTV	Vincent O'Brien
BCEEILNPSSTUU	unsusceptible
BCEEINNOORRTT	Ronnie Corbett
BCEELMMNOPRUX	complex number
BCEFHIMNOOOTT	fine-tooth comb
BCEFHINOOSSST	sons of bitches
BCEFIJOORTTUV	object of virtu
BCEFJMOOORRST	Job's comforter
BCEGHILNOOOTY	biotechnology
BCEGHIMNORRST	Ernst Gombrich
BCEGHKOOOPRTU	pocket borough
BCEHIIJLLLRUU	Julie Burchill
BCEHILNRSSTTU	Ernst Lubitsch
BCEHIMMORRTTU	Robert Mitchum
BCEHINORRRTTU	Burton Richter
BCEIILNNORTVY	inconvertibly
BCEIILNOPRRTU	incorruptible
BCEIILNPSSTUY	insusceptibly
BCEIJLNSTUUVY	subjunctively
BCEILORSTTUVY	obstructively
BCEIMNOOORSSU	cessio bonorum
BCEKLMNOOOSUY	colobus monkey
BCFGIIMMNNOOR	combining form
BCGHNOOORTUUY	county borough
BCGIILOOORSTY	cryobiologist
BCHIKMOOORTTT	hit rock bottom
BCIIIIILNNTVY	invincibility
BCIIILLPTTUUY	public utility
BCIIILNPQRUUY	public inquiry
BCIILNOPRRTUY	incorruptibly
BCIINNOORSTTU	contributions
BCIKLLNNOPUWY	publicly known
BCILLLLNNOOYY	Billy Connolly
BDDDEEGILNOUW	double wedding
BDDDEELMNNNUU	Edmund Blunden
BDDEEEGGILLOR	George Biddell
BDDEEEGGINNNR	gender-bending
BDDEEFOORRRRT	Robert Redford
BDDEEGGGNOOTW	get bogged down
BDDEEGILNNSUY	begin suddenly
BDDEEIILNOSTY	disobediently
BDDEEIJLNOOTU	double-jointed
BDDEEINOPSTUY	beyond dispute
BDDEENNNOSSUU	unboundedness
BDDEGHILMORSU	Middlesbrough
BDDEILNNORSSW	word-blindness
BDEEEEEGHORTV	be over the edge

BDEEEEFILNOSS	beside oneself
BDEEEEGHNOSST	hedge one's bets
BDEEEFGILNOTT	feeding bottle
BDEEEFHINORTW	before the wind
BDEEEGIINNRRT	interbreeding
BDEEEGIJLLNOU	golden jubilee
BDEEEHIINNRRS	Inner Hebrides
BDEEEHILLMNSU	unembellished
BDEEEHIORRSTU	Outer Hebrides
BDEEEIILMPRRU	empire-builder
BDEEEILLLLOWY	yellow-bellied
BDEEEIMMMNRST	dismemberment
BDEEEIORRRRRT	Border terrier
BDEEEJORSTTUV	objets de vertu
BDEEEKNNNOOSY	beyond one's ken
BDEEEKNNORRTY	Robert Kennedy
BDEEELNNORSTU	under one's belt
BDEEELNPRSSTU	suspender belt
	suspender-belt
BDEEFGILORSUU	double figures
BDEEFHIINRSTW	be friends with
BDEEFIIILNSTY	defensibility
BDEEGHLLNOOTW	The Golden Bowl
BDEEGHNOOTTUW	go down the tube
BDEEGIILLNRWY	bewilderingly
BDEEGIILMNSSX	mixed blessing
BDEEGIINORRUW	Brownie Guider
BDEEGINNNNSSU	unbendingness
BDEEGNNNOORTT	Gordon Bennett
BDEEHIOOORRTV	Theodor Boveri
BDEEIIILNTTXY	extendibility
BDEEILMNOORST	slide trombone
BDEELLMNOOSTW	bellows to mend
BDEELLNOOSSSS	bloodlessness
BDEELNNOSSSSU	boundlessness
BDEELOOPRRSSU	blood pressure
BDEEOPRSSSTUX	express doubts
BDEFFHILLOOTW	blow the lid off
BDEFFNOOOPRRU	burden of proof
BDEFHILOORSTW	Bosworth Field
BDEGGINNOORVY	governing body
BDEGHHINOOORU	neighbourhood
BDEGIIIILSTTY	digestibility
BDEGIILLMNSSY	dissemblingly
BDEGIILMNNSSU	undissembling
BDEGIILOORSUY	religious body
BDEGINNOOOPRT	pontoon bridge
BDEHHMNOOORRS	rhombohedrons
BDEHHMNOSTTUW	the thumbs-down
BDEHILNNOORTU	run in the blood
BDEHJKOOPRSSY	Joseph Brodsky
BDEHNOOOPRSTU	boustrophedon
BDEILNNNOSSSW	snow blindness
BDEILOOQRSTUU	double or quits
BDEKLNOOORTWY	old-boy network
BDELMNOOORRTU	Robert Muldoon
BDFFIIIILSTUY	diffusibility
BDFHMOOORTUWY	by word of mouth
BDFOOOPPRSTUY	body of support
BDGGIIILLNOSY	disobligingly
BDHINNNOOORUU	in honour bound
BDHNOOORSTTUW	throw doubts on
BEEEEFHIMMPRS	membership fee
BEEEEFHINORRT	thereinbefore
BEEEEGGHORRRT	George Herbert
BEEEEHHLSSTTY	set by the heels
BEEEEHILNPRRS	reprehensible
BEEEEHILNSTWW	betweenwhiles
BEEEEHKLOPRRT	brothel-keeper
BEEEEHMNRRSSY	Henry Bessemer
BEEEELLLRSSTT	belles-lettres
BEEEFFGIINNRT	fringe benefit
BEEEFGHNORRTU	rub of the green
BEEEFHLLMNOSU	humble oneself
BEEEFIMNOORTT	not before time
BEEEGGINRTTTT	getting better
BEEEGHHORRTUZ	breeze through
BEEEGHNNORRTU	rub on the green
BEEEGIIMNRTTT	time-bettering
BEEEGILLLNRTY	belligerently
BEEEGILMNNSUY	unbeseemingly
BEEEGMNOPRSST	September Song
BEEEHHOORRRTV	Herbert Hoover
BEEEHIKMOPRRS	Pembrokeshire
BEEEHILLMMNST	embellishment
BEEEHILNPRRSY	reprehensibly
BEEEHINNPRTTY	threepenny bit
BEEEHKLLOORST	The Bookseller
BEEEHKLNOOOPT	telephone book
BEEEIIJLLRSUV	silver jubilee
BEEEIILNPRSSX	inexpressible
BEEEIILPRRRSS	irrepressible
BEEEIMMNRRSTU	reimbursement
BEEEINNORRRTW	Norbert Wiener
BEEEINOSSSSSV	obsessiveness
BEEEIOORRSTTW	Bertie Wooster
BEEELMMNOOTVW	bowel movement
BEEFGILNORSSV	self-observing
BEEFGINRRSTTU	butterfingers
BEEFHHKLOOOTT	The Book of Thel
BEEFHIKNORTTT	think better of
BEEFHIMNRRSTU	refurbishment
BEEFIIILLRTXY	reflexibility
BEEFILLMORSUU	umbelliferous
BEEGGHINORRTT	bring together
BEEGGIINNNNSW	new beginnings
BEEGGIIORSTTZ	George Stibitz
BEEGGIJMNNPUU	bungee jumping
BEEGHHIIIMTTT	hit the big time
BEEGHIOOOTTTV	give the boot to
BEEGHJKLNOOTU	The Jungle Book
BEEGHLNORSTTW	below strength
BEEGIILLNNUVY	unbelievingly
BEEGIIMNNOSTY	in times gone by
BEEGMNORRSSTU	Sune Bergström
BEEHHLOPSTTTU	push the bottle
BEEHILLORSTWW	whistle-blower
BEEHILMNOOTTT	the bottom line
BEEHILNOPSTTT	spin the bottle
BEEHILNORRSST	brotherliness
BEEHIMNPRRSUU	her number is up
BEEHIMOORRSTT	Berthe Morisot

BEEHLLOORRTVY	brotherly love
BEEHLOOPSTTUW	up to the elbows
BEEHMNNOOSSTU	thumb one's nose
BEEHOORRSTTUY	Robert Southey
BEEIIILMMPRSS	impermissible
BEEIIILRRSTVY	reversibility
BEEIILMMMRRUV	membrum virile
BEEIILNOPRRSS	irresponsible
BEEIILNPRSSXY	inexpressibly
BEEIILPRRRSSY	irrepressibly
BEEIILRRTTUVY	retributively
BEEILLORSSTTW	Osbert Sitwell
BEEILNPRSSSUY	supersensibly
BEEILNRSSTUVY	subserviently
BEEINOOQRSTUU	bone turquoise
BEEINORSSSTUV	obtrusiveness
BEEINORSSTTUV	subservient to
BEEJOORSSTTUV	objets trouvés
BEELLMOORSTUY	troublesomely
BEENNOOSSSTUU	bounteousness
BEFFHILRSTTUY	butterfly fish
BEFGHMMORSUUU	Hofburg Museum
BEFHILLMORTTU	full to the brim
BEFIIIILLNTXY	inflexibility
BEFIKLRSSTTUY	butterfly kiss
BEFILNNOSSTUU	bountifulness
BEFINNNSSSUUY	funny business
BEFIORSSTTTUU	substitute for
BEGGHIIOORTVW	go over big with
BEGGIIIILLNTY	negligibility
BEGGILNOORTTT	globetrotting
	globe-trotting
BEGHHIOORSTTW	show to be right
BEGHHOORRSTUW	browse through
BEGHIILLNORTT	Little Bighorn
BEGHILNNORUUY	unneighbourly
BEGHLLOPRTUUW	well-brought-up
BEGHMOOOTTTT	go to the bottom
BEGHNOOORRTTU	rotten borough
BEGIIIIILLNTY	ineligibility
BEGIILMNPSUUY	impulse buying
BEGIILNNNOPTW	tenpin bowling
	ten-pin bowling
BEGILOPRSSSUV	viper's bugloss
BEHHNOPSTTTUU	push the button
BEHIIIIMNOSTX	exhibitionism
BEHIIIINOSTTX	exhibitionist
BEHIIILOPRTVY	prohibitively
BEHIIMMRSSTUU	British Museum
BEHIIMNPRSSUU	his number is up
BEHILNOOSTWWY	The Winslow Boy
BEHIMNOOSSSTY	tomboyishness
BEHIMNORTTUUW	without number
BEHINNNOORRSY	Henry Robinson
BEIIIILMRSSTY	remissibility
BEIIIILNNSSTY	insensibility
BEIIIILOPSSST	possibilities
BEIIIILRSSTTY	resistibility
BEIIILMMPRSSY	impermissibly
BEIIILNOSSTTY	ostensibility
BEIILNOOSSSUV	obliviousness
BEIILNOPRRSSY	irresponsibly
BEIILNORSTUVY	inobtrusively
BEIILOPQSSTUY	quite possibly
BEIIOPRSSTTUU	subreptitious
BEIKNNOORSSTW	knit one's brows
BEILMOOPSSTTT	bottomless pit
BEILNNOOPSTTU	button one's lip
BEILNORSTUUVY	unobtrusively
BEIMNOPSSSTUU	bumptiousness
BEINNOOOSSSUX	obnoxiousness
BEINNOORRSTTW	Robert Winston
BGHIIILNRSTTW	bristling with
BGHINNOOORRTU	bring honour to
BGIIILNNORSST	Birgit Nilsson
BGIILMOQSSTTU	Stig Blomquist
BGINNOORSSTTU	burst into song
BHLMOOPRSTTUU	sulphur-bottom
BIIIILMOPSSTY	impossibility
BIIJOOOPRSTTZ	Josip Broz Tito
BILLMOPTTUWYY	multiply by two
BILOOOPPRRSUY	opprobriously

C

CCCCEEINNOPSU	concupiscence
CCCCEGIIMNNOO	meningococcic
CCCCEIIKKLLTY	clickety-click
CCCCEIOOPRSTT	streptococcic
CCCDDEFNOOOTU	code of conduct
CCCDEEEENRRSU	recrudescence
CCCDEIIMNRSUU	uncircumcised
CCCEEEEFILNRT	electric fence
CCCEEEFIMNRRU	circumference
CCCEEEIILNOPT	poetic licence
CCCEEFHIKNRRT	French cricket
CCCEEILOOPRST	electroscopic
CCCEHIIMOSTYZ	schizomycetic
CCCEIIILORSUV	vicious circle
CCCEIIMMNOOOR	microeconomic
CCCEIINNORTTY	concentricity
CCCEILMPRSTUY	circumspectly
CCCEIMNPRSTUU	uncircumspect
CCCEOOPRSSTTU	streptococcus
CCDDEEGINNNOS	condescending
CCDDEELLNOTUW	well-conducted
CCDDEFLNOORTU	occluded front
CCDEEEEEFNRSV	defervescence
CCDEEEEFNRSVY	defervescency
CCDEEEEILNQSU	deliquescence
CCDEEEFIILLRT	electric field
CCDEEEFILNOST	self-conceited
CCDEEEFLLLOST	self-collected
CCDEEEHOQRSSU	crossed cheque
CCDEEEINNOSST	conceitedness
CCDEEELLLORTY	recollectedly
CCDEEELLNOSST	collectedness
CCDEEENNNORSS	concernedness
CCDEEHIILNNPY	phencyclidine
CCDEEHILORRTY	hydroelectric
CCDEEHINNORTW	concerned with
CCDEEHINNOTTW	connected with
CCDEEIJNSSTUU	just succeed in

CCDEEILNOPSTY	encyclopedist
CCDEEINNNOOSS	condescension
CCDEEINOOPRUW	owner-occupied
CCDEEINRRRTTU	direct current
CCDEELNNNORUY	unconcernedly
CCDEFHIOOORSW	choice of words
CCDEFOOORRRTU	court of record
CCDEGIINNORST	disconcerting
CCDEGINNNOORT	connecting rod
CCDEHKLNOORTU	round the clock
	round-the-clock
CCDEIIIMMOSTU	commit suicide
CCDEIINNNOOST	disconnection
CCDEIINNOORST	disconcertion
CCDEILLMNOOPS	minced collops
CCDEIMNOORSTU	semiconductor
CCDGINNNNOOTU	non-conducting
CCDIIILNNOOTU	induction coil
CCDIIORRSTTTU	district court
CCEEEEEFFNRSV	effervescence
CCEEEEEINNPPT	ten pence piece
CCEEEEFFLNORS	efflorescence
CCEEEEINOPPTW	two pence piece
CCEEEEIRRSSTV	secret service
CCEEEFFIOSTTV	cost-effective
CCEEEFILNNORS	inflorescence
CCEEEFINPRSTT	perfect insect
CCEEEFNNOOQSU	of consequence
CCEEEFNOORRRT	ferroconcrete
CCEEEHHIKNORR	Erich Honecker
CCEEEHMOOPRRT	chemoreceptor
CCEEEIILOPRTZ	piezoelectric
CCEEEIIMNNRSS	reminiscences
CCEEEIINNNNOV	inconvenience
CCEEEILMNNORT	reconcilement
CCEEEILMORRTT	electrometric
CCEEEIMMNSSUU	Science Museum
CCEEEINNNOQSU	in consequence
	inconsequence
CCEEEINNRRRTU	intercurrence
CCEEEIORSSTTY	secret society
CCEEENOPRRSSS	screen process
CCEEFFIILOOPR	police officer
CCEEFFKKNNOOT	knock-on effect
CCEEFIMNOOORT	come into force
CCEEFINNOORTY	confectionery
CCEEFLNOOPSUY	occupy oneself
CCEEGHINOPSTY	psychogenetic
CCEEGIIMNORST	geocentricism
CCEEGIINORTTY	egocentricity
CCEEGILNNORTY	nitrogen cycle
CCEEHHIIOOPSS	Sophie's Choice
CCEEHHNRRSTUW	Western Church
CCEEHIILLOPRT	electrophilic
CCEEHILOOPRTT	photoelectric
CCEEHILOOPRTU	heroic couplet
CCEEHIMMNOOOS	home economics
CCEEIIJOPSTTU	poetic justice
CCEEIINOPSTTU	cut into pieces
CCEEIJMNORSTU	misconjecture
CCEEILLNOORST	recollections
CCEEILMOORRTT	electric motor
CCEEILMORRSTT	electric storm
CCEEILNOORTTU	electrocution
CCEEILNOSTUVY	consecutively
CCEEILOOPRSTT	electro-optics
CCEEIMMOPRRTU	computer crime
CCEEIMOPRRSTT	spectrometric
CCEEINNOOPPRT	preconception
CCEEINNORRSST	incorrectness
CCEEINOOPRRUW	owner-occupier
CCEEIOPRRSSTU	prosecutrices
CCEELLSSSSSUY	successlessly
CCEELOORSSTUY	oestrous cycle
CCEFFHKLOOOTT	cock of the loft
CCEFFIIINNSUY	insufficiency
CCEFGHIILLORT	circle of light
CCEFILNOOSSSU	self-conscious
CCEGHIIKNNPRS	spring chicken
CCEGHIIKNPRRY	cherry-picking
CCEGILLNNOOSU	co-counselling
CCEGILOOOOTXY	ecotoxicology
CCEGINNNORSTY	constringency
CCEHHIINOPRSZ	schizophrenic
CCEHIINNORTTW	in concert with
CCEHIKOQTTTUU	cut to the quick
CCEHIMOPRSSTY	psychometrics
CCEHIOOPRRSTU	urethroscopic
CCEHIOPPRSSWY	psychic powers
CCEIILMNOOPSY	incomes policy
CCEIILNNNOSTY	inconsciently
CCEIIMNNOOPST	misconception
CCEIIMNNORTUV	circumvention
CCEIIMNOOSSSU	semiconscious
CCEIINNNOSSTY	inconsistency
CCEIINNOOSSTU	conscientious
CCEIJLNNOTUVY	conjunctively
CCEIKKKLLOORW	like clockwork
CCEILNOORRSTU	cruise control
CCEIMMOOPRRTU	microcomputer
CCEINNOOPRRST	prince consort
CCEINNOOSSSSU	consciousness
CCEINNOPRRSSW	crown princess
CCENOOORRRSTU	coroner's court
CCENOORRRSTTU	reconstructor
CCGGHIILNOOPP	logic-chopping
CCGIIKNNOOPTT	cotton-picking
CCHHHIIIMNOTY	Ho Chi Minh City
CCHIINNORSTYY	synchronicity
CCHIIOPRRSSTU	Corpus Christi
CCHIJLMOOORSW	Jim Crow school
CCIIJNNNNOOTU	in conjunction
CCIINNOOPSSUU	inconspicuous
CCILNNOOSSUUY	unconsciously
CCILNOOPSSUUY	conspicuously
CCINNOORSTUUY	country cousin
CCLLMNNOOORTU	control column
CDDDEEINOOOTT	decide not to do
CDDEEEENNPRTU	unprecedented
CDDEEEFIKKRRU	Duke Frederick
CDDEEEHIRSTTW	wide-stretched
CDDEEEIOORRRV	video recorder

CDDEEELNOORRS	enclosed order
CDDEEIILLNORS	ill-considered
CDDEEIKLMNNOS	condensed milk
CDDEEILLMOSTU	deltoid muscle
CDDEEILNNRSUY	undiscernedly
CDDEEINOSSSUU	deciduousness
CDDEFFILOORST	Clifford Odets
CDDEHILNOSTUY	held in custody
CDDEIIILNNPSU	undisciplined
CDDEIINNNOOTU	unconditioned
CDDEIOOOPRRTU	Doctor Proudie
CDDGIINNOOOOT	good condition
CDDGILLLMNOOY	mollycoddling
CDDHILNOOSTUY	hold in custody
CDEEEEEHMMNRT	crème de menthe
CDEEEEFIIPRST	pesticide-free
CDEEEEFINSSTV	defectiveness
CDEEEEFLLNSSY	defencelessly
CDEEEEHNORRRT	three-cornered
CDEEEEIINNPRX	experienced in
	inexperienced
CDEEEEIMNORVY	money received
CDEEEEINPSSTV	deceptiveness
CDEEEEIQRSTUZ	credit squeeze
CDEEEELLPRSTW	well-respected
CDEEEFFLNOSSS	self-confessed
CDEEEFFLOPPRT	Doppler effect
CDEEEFILNNOST	line of descent
CDEEEFILNOPST	self-deception
CDEEEFILNSSTU	deceitfulness
CDEEEGHINOPST	pigeon-chested
CDEEEGIIKNNSV	King's evidence
CDEEEGKLNNOOW	On Wenlock Edge
CDEEEHHKLLOOW	hollow-cheeked
CDEEEHORRSTTV	overstretched
CDEEEIINNRRSV	dinner service
CDEEEIINPRSTV	vice-president
CDEEEIKMPQRTU	quick-tempered
CDEEEIMNORTVX	void excrement
CDEEEIMOPRSSV	decompressive
CDEEEINNORSST	reconditeness
CDEEEINRSSTUV	reductiveness
CDEEEINSSSTUV	seductiveness
CDEEEKMOORSTT	smoke detector
CDEEELLOORSTU	steel-coloured
CDEEELLOPRTTW	well-protected
CDEEELMNOPSSX	complexedness
CDEEENNNOSSTT	contentedness
CDEEEPRRSTTUU	deep structure
CDEEFFIILLNST	self-inflicted
CDEEFFILNNOST	self-confident
CDEEFFINOORRT	rodent officer
CDEEFGIIORRTV	give credit for
CDEEFGINOOPRU	piece of ground
CDEEFHKMOOORT	Dome of the Rock
CDEEFIIIKLMRT	certified milk
CDEEFIILNORST	self-direction
CDEEFILPRSSTU	disrespectful
CDEEFINNOORTV	overconfident
	over-confident
CDEEGIILNNPSU	sleep-inducing
CDEEGIINNOORT	derecognition
CDEEGILNNNNOU	non-indulgence
CDEEGILNNOOST	golden section
CDEEHHILMNORS	children's home
CDEEHIIKLLNSS	childlikeness
CDEEHIIKLNSTV	Kitchen Devils®
CDEEHILMNNORW	women-children
CDEEHIMMNOPRS	miscomprehend
CDEEHIMMRSSST	Messerschmidt
CDEEHLNOOPSTU	the clouds open
CDEEIIIMNRSTT	deterministic
CDEEIIKNNOTUV	Duke Vincentio
CDEEIILNORSST	directionless
CDEEIILPRSTVY	descriptively
CDEEIINOORRTV	eviction order
CDEEIINORRSTT	derestriction
CDEEIINORRTTU	indirect route
CDEEIJNPRRSUU	jurisprudence
CDEEIKNOPSTUY	keep in custody
CDEEIKNORRTTY	kitty-cornered
CDEEILLORSVWY	discovery well
CDEEILMMRTUUU	culture medium
CDEEILNPRRSSY	cylinder press
CDEEILOORRSUV	versicoloured
CDEEILRSTTUVY	destructively
CDEEIMNNOOTUV	move unnoticed
CDEEIMNOOPRSS	decompression
CDEEINOPQSTTU	cinque-spotted
CDEEIOPPRRSST	esprit de corps
CDEEKKLNRSTUU	knuckleduster
CDEEKNOOPSSTW	keep costs down
	keep down costs
CDEELMOOORSUU	mouse-coloured
CDEELNORSSSUU	credulousness
CDEELNPSSTUUY	unsuspectedly
CDEENNOOPRRST	correspondent
CDEFFGLMOOTUY	Get Off My Cloud
CDEFIILNNOSTU	self-induction
CDEFIKKNOORSX	knocked for six
CDEFOOOOPRRSS	food processor
CDEFOORSSTUUY	course of study
CDEGHHIKOSTTU	sick-thoughted
CDEGHIIKNRSWY	Henry Sidgwick
CDEGHILLOORTU	light-coloured
CDEGHILNNORTU	underclothing
CDEGHMMNOOOOT	the common good
CDEGIIIKLNSVW	Nevil Sidgwick
CDEGIILNNORSY	consideringly
CDEGILNNOOORY	endocrinology
CDEGINNOOPRRS	corresponding
CDEGINORRSSSS	cross-dressing
CDEGMNOOORSSU	consumer goods
CDEHHILMMSTTU	Helmut Schmidt
CDEHHIOOORRST	rhodochrosite
CDEHIIIOPRSTY	spheroidicity
CDEHIIKLTTTWY	thick-wittedly
CDEHIIKMNSTTU	stick-in-the-mud
CDEHIIKNORSTY	hydrokinetics
CDEHIIMNOPRRU	perichondrium
CDEHILNOORSTW	clothe in words
CDEHIMOOPPRSU	pseudomorphic

CDEHINOOSSTUU	discount house
CDEHKNRRSTTUU	thunderstruck
CDEHMMOORTTYY	Tommy Docherty
CDEHMOPRRRTUU	Rupert Murdoch
CDEHNNOORSSSY	synchondroses
CDEIIILNSTTVY	distinctively
CDEIIIMPRSSTV	descriptivism
CDEIIINNSTTUV	undistinctive
CDEIIJLNSTUVY	disjunctively
CDEIIJNOSSSUU	judiciousness
CDEIIKLQTTUWY	quick-wittedly
CDEIIMNOOOPST	decomposition
CDEIINORSTTUU	rectitudinous
CDEIINRRSSTTU	district nurse
CDEILLMOORTUU	multicoloured
	multi-coloured
CDEILLNORSUUY	incredulously
CDEILMNOOPSUY	compendiously
CDEILNNOPRSTY	nondescriptly
CDEILNORSSSUU	ludicrousness
CDEILOORTUUUX	tic douloureux
CDEIMNNNOOPST	Dennis Compton
CDEIMNNOORSSS	cross one's mind
CDEINNOOPRTUV	non-productive
CDEINOOSTTUWZ	cut down to size
CDEKKLNNOOTUW	knuckle down to
CDELMNNOOOOTY	monocotyledon
CDEOOOPRRRSSW	word processor
CDFGILNNNOOUY	confoundingly
CDFIIMNOORSTY	disconformity
CDGHIIKNORSTW	Dickson Wright
CDGIIINNNOSTU	discontinuing
CDHHIMNOOPRUY	hypochondrium
CDHIIMNNOOORT	mitochondrion
CDHILMOOOSTUY	dichotomously
CDHLMMOOORSUU	mushroom cloud
CDIIIJLNOSUUY	injudiciously
CDIIINNOSTTUY	discontinuity
CDIINNOOSSTUU	discontinuous
CDILMOORRTUUV	victor ludorum
CDKKNOOOPRSTU	knockout drops
CEEEEEGHLNRSS	Scheele's green
CEEEEEGLLORTX	Exeter College
CEEEEFFINSSTV	effectiveness
CEEEEFFNOPRRR	for preference
CEEEEFLNOSSUX	excuse oneself
CEEEEFLPRRTTT	letter-perfect
CEEEEGHINORTT	heterogenetic
CEEEEGHIOPRTT	piece together
CEEEEGIIMNNRS	éminence grise
CEEEEGIMNRSTT	secret meeting
CEEEEGIMNRTXY	emergency exit
CEEEEGINNOOSU	Eugène Ionesco
CEEEEGLLNOQSU	Queens' College
CEEEEHLNRSSSS	cheerlessness
CEEEEILNRRSTU	leisure centre
CEEEEINNNPPTY	tenpenny piece
CEEEEINPRSSTV	receptiveness
CEEEEINRSSSSV	recessiveness
CEEEEINRSSSTV	secretiveness
CEEEEINSSSSVX	excessiveness
CEEEEJNNRSTUV	rejuvenescent
CEEEENRRTTUUV	revenue cutter
CEEEFFIILNTVY	ineffectively
CEEEFHINNOSTT	sit on the fence
CEEEFHIORSSTU	force the issue
CEEEFHMOOSTTT	meet the cost of
CEEEFIINNSSTV	infectiveness
CEEEFILLNRTTV	left ventricle
CEEEFIMNNORRT	reinforcement
CEEEFINORRTTU	counterfeiter
CEEEFLMNOOOST	come to oneself
CEEEFNOOQSTUU	out of sequence
CEEEGGINORRTU	Geiger counter
CEEEGGIORRSUV	Georges Cuvier
CEEEGHIKNNOTU	tongue in cheek
	tongue-in-cheek
CEEEGHIMNOOTV	give the come-on
CEEEGHIPRTTTU	get the picture
CEEEGIIILNNRV	civil engineer
	receiving-line
CEEEGIIKNNRTY	kinetic energy
CEEEGLLLNOSWY	Selwyn College
CEEEGLLMNOORT	Merton College
CEEEHHHIIINNR	Heinrich Heine
CEEEHHIPQRTTU	queer the pitch
CEEEHIILNNSTT	Liechtenstein
CEEEHIJLLMSTU	Jules Michelet
CEEEHIKKLNOSS	kick one's heels
CEEEHIKORTTVW	over the wicket
CEEEHILLLMOSU	hemicellulose
CEEEHILMNOPRT	nephelometric
CEEEHILNPSUZZ	Chinese puzzle
CEEEHIMNOPRSV	comprehensive
CEEEHINNORSTT	in on the secret
CEEEHKLOPRSTW	sprocket wheel
CEEEHLLNOOOSS	cool one's heels
CEEEHLNORSSSU	lecherousness
CEEEHNSSTTTUW	sweet chestnut
CEEEIILRRSSVV	silver service
CEEEIIMNNRTTT	intermittence
CEEEIIMNPRSSS	impreciseness
CEEEIINNOSTTX	into existence
CEEEIINNPPSXY	sixpenny piece
CEEEIINORRSSV	senior service
CEEEIINPPRSTV	in perspective
CEEEILLNSTUVY	unselectively
CEEEILMNRSSSS	mercilessness
CEEEILMOORTTV	electromotive
CEEEILMOPRRSY	more precisely
CEEEILNOSSSSV	voicelessness
CEEEILNPRSSSS	pricelessness
CEEEILNRSSSUV	reclusiveness
CEEEILNSSSUVX	exclusiveness
CEEEILPPRSTVY	perspectively
CEEEINNOPPTWY	twopenny piece
CEEEINRSSSUVX	excursiveness
CEEEIOPRRSTTV	retrospective
CEEELMNNOSTTU	locum tenentes
CEEELNNOQSSUU	Queen's Counsel
CEEFFFGIINOOR	foreign office
CEEFFHIKLRRSS	sheriff clerks

CEEFFHIKNPSST	Seth Pecksniff
CEEFFHIKORSTU	Turkish coffee
CEEFFHOPRRTTU	perfect fourth
CEEFFIIILNNTY	inefficiently
CEEFFIJNORSTY	Jefferson City
CEEFFINOPTTTU	put into effect
CEEFFKNOOORRS	off one's rocker
CEEFGHHINQRUY	high frequency
CEEFGIIKNRRST	grief-stricken
CEEFHHLNOOOTV	the cloven hoof
CEEFHIIIMNRST	chief minister
CEEFHINOORSTU	in the course of
CEEFHNORRRTTT	French Trotter
CEEFIIILNSSTT	life scientist
CEEFIIJLNNOTU	fuel-injection
CEEFIILLNOTWZ	fellow citizen
CEEFIILNOSUVY	veneficiously
CEEFIIMNOPRST	perfectionism
CEEFIINOPRSTT	perfectionist
CEEFIKNOOORTU	fortune cookie
CEEFILMMNOOST	commit oneself
CEEFILNOORRTT	retroflection
CEEFILNORTTUY	counterfeitly
CEEFINNNOORTV	convenient for
CEEFINOORSSSU	ferociousness
CEEGGIINOOPST	going to pieces
CEEGGILLNOORT	Girton College
CEEGHHIIILNTT	hit the ceiling
CEEGHHIMNOSSU	housing scheme
CEEGHIIKLMTTU	Gemütlichkeit
CEEGHIIRRSTUW	cruiserweight
CEEGHIKORSTTT	stick together
CEEGHIMNOOPRT	morphogenetic
CEEGHINOPSSSY	psychogenesis
CEEGHINORTTUW	counter-weight
CEEGHKKNOORTT	knock together
CEEGIINRRSTTW	secret writing
CEEGIKKKNNNOS	knocking knees
CEEGIKNNOOSTW	get on one's wick
CEEGILMMNNOPT	complementing
CEEGILMMNOTTU	telecommuting
CEEGJMORSTTUY	Jeremy Guscott
CEEHHHIINRRTZ	Heinrich Hertz
CEEHHIMMOOORT	homoeothermic
CEEHHIMOOPRRT	heteromorphic
CEEHHIOOPRRTT	heterotrophic
CEEHHIOPSTTUW	without speech
CEEHHJMNNORRY	Johnny H Mercer
CEEHHNORSSTTU	horse chestnut
CEEHIIMNRSTTZ	Chester Nimitz
CEEHIJMMRTTWY	Jemmy Twitcher
CEEHILLNNOPSU	Punchinelloes
CEEHILOOPRRTU	Hercule Poirot
CEEHIMMNOOOST	home economist
CEEHIMMRSSSTT	Messerschmitt
CEEHIMNNOOPRS	comprehension
CEEHIMNNORSTT	ethnocentrism
CEEHINNORSTTT	ethnocentrist
CEEHINOPPRSST	propheticness
CEEHIOPRSTTTW	with respect to
CEEHKKMNOSTUY	suck the monkey
CEEHKLLOOORSU	lecherous look
CEEHKLMORTTTU	The Mock Turtle
CEEHLOOPRRSTU	electrophorus
CEEHMMOOORSSX	sex chromosome
CEEHNNORRRTTU	turn the corner
CEEHNOORSSTTW	stone the crows
	stone the crows!
CEEHNOPRSTTUW	put on the screw
CEEHOOOPPRRTT	photoreceptor
CEEHPPRRSTTUU	the upper crust
CEEIIILMRSSSU	cruise missile ❑
CEEIIINNORSTZ	senior citizen
CEEIIKMMMRSTW	Mister Wemmick
CEEIILMNNRSTY	reminiscently
CEEIILRRSTTVY	restrictively
CEEIIMPPRSSTV	perspectivism
CEEIINOOPRRSV	over-precision
CEEIINOPRSTTV	introspective
CEEIJLNORTUUV	juvenile court
CEEIKOORRRRSV	reservoir rock
CEEILLLOOSSTV	Elvis Costello
CEEILLMNOQTUU	multiloquence
CEEILMMNOOPTT	polite comment
CEEILMNNOPTTY	incompetently
CEEILMNOORSUY	ceremoniously
CEEILNOOPRRST	scleroprotein
CEEILNOSSSTUY	necessitously
CEEILOPPRSTVY	prospectively
CEEILORSTTTUY	courtesy title
CEEILPQRSTUUY	picturesquely
CEEILRSSTTUUU	tissue culture
CEEIMNNOORSUU	unceremonious
CEEIMNOOOPRRT	reception room
CEEIMNOOPSSST	compositeness
CEEINNORSTTTU	reconstituent
CEEINOOPRRSTT	retrospection
CEEINOOPRSSTU	precious stone
CEEINOORRSSSV	corrosiveness
CEEINOPRRSSSU	repercussions
CEEIOPPPRRSTY	copper pyrites
CEEIOPRRSSTUX	prosecutrixes
CEELMNOOORRTT	remote control
CEELNNOSSSSTU	countlessness
CEELNOOSSSSTU	cut one's losses
CEELPQRSSTUUU	sculpturesque
CEEMNNNOOPRTU	pronouncement
CEEMOPPPRRTTU	copper trumpet
CEEMOPPRRSTUU	supercomputer
CEENOORSSSTUU	courteousness
CEEOOPRRRRTTU	court reporter
CEEOPRRSSSSTT	St Peter's cross
CEFFFGIILNORY	flying officer
CEFFFGIILNSSU	self-sufficing
CEFFFIINORSTU	sufficient for
CEFFHILLORTUW	with full force
CEFFIINOOPRRS	prison officer
CEFFIINOOSSSU	officiousness
CEFGILNOOORRV	floor-covering
CEFHLOOORRSST	cross the floor
CEFHMNOOORRTY	cry for the moon
CEFIIINORRTTW	fiction writer

CEFIILLLOSSSY	Isles of Scilly	CEIINNORSSSUU	incuriousness
CEFIJLMOOPRRT	film projector	CEIINNRSTTUUV	uninstructive
CEFIKMOPRRRST	perform tricks	CEIINOOPRSSTT	retinoscopist
CEFILNOPRRTUY	perfunctorily	CEIINOOPRSTTT	protectionist
CEFIOOPRRSTUU	furor poeticus	CEIINOORSSTUV	insectivorous
CEFLLLLOOOSWY	follow closely	CEIINOPRSSSTU	percussionist
CEFLLNOORSSUU	colourfulness	CEIJMMOPRRTUY	commit perjury
CEGGHLNOOOORY	geochronology	CEIKLMMNNOTUY	Mount McKinley
CEGGINOPRRSUY	Gregory Pincus	CEILLMNOOSTTY	tonsillectomy
CEGHHIILOPRSY	hieroglyphics	CEILMNNOOOSSU	mononucleosis
CEGHHIINNSUUW	Chien-Shiung Wu	CEILMNOPSTUVY	consumptively
CEGHIIILLNNPS	spine-chilling	CEILNNOOSTTUY	contentiously
CEGHIIMNOOSTT	come into sight	CEILNOORRTTUY	interlocutory
CEGHIINNNNPPY	penny-pinching	CEILNORRRTUUY	Cyril Tourneur
CEGHIKNNNOORT	neck or nothing	CEILOPPRSSUUY	perspicuously
CEGHILORSTTUY	courtesy light	CEIMMNOOOPRST	not compromise
CEGHIMNNOOOTT	come to nothing	CEIMNOOPPRSTU	income support
CEGHOPRRSSUYY	psychosurgery	CEINNNOOSSSUU	innocuousness
CEGIIMMNNOSTU	time-consuming	CEINOOQRSSSTU	cross-question
CEGIINNNOORRT	reconnoitring	CEIOOOPPPRRRT	proprioceptor
CEGINRRRSTTUU	restructuring	CELLMNNNOOSSU	Nelson's Column
CEHHIILLLNRST	Chiltern Hills	CENNOOPRRSTUY	country person
CEHHIMNNORSTT	the morn's nicht	CFFIIILNOOSUY	inofficiously
CEHHOOPRTTTTU	put to the torch	CFFIKKLORRTTU	fork-lift truck
CEHIIIINNTTVY	in the vicinity	CFFKKNOOOPSST	knock spots off
CEHIIIKLNNOPT	pile in on thick	CFGHIILLNNNUY	unflinchingly
CEHIIIKLNOPTT	pile it on thick	CFGHIMNNOORTU	unforthcoming
CEHIIKLNOSSTT	on the sick list	CFGIKLNOOSTTU	floutingstock
CEHIILMOSSUVY	mischievously	CFGILLNOORSUY	flying colours
CEHIIMNRRSSTT	Christminster	CFIINNOOOPSSU	on suspicion of
CEHIIMOORSTTY	stoichiometry	CFILNORSTUUUY	infructuously
CEHIIMOOTTTUW	come out with it	CFIMNNNOOORST	nonconformist
CEHIJNOORTTUW	to conjure with		non-conformist
CEHILNNNOOSTY	Holy Innocents	CFIMNNNOOORTY	nonconformity
CEHIMMMNOOTUY	community home		non-conformity
CEHIOOPRRSTTU	trichopterous	CFLLNOOOORSST	loss of control
CEHLNOORRSSUY	nursery school	CGGHHINOOOPUW	whooping cough
CEHMNOORRTTUY	mother country	CGGILNNOORRWY	crowning glory
	mother-country	CGHHIILLOORSS	schoolgirlish
CEHNNNOORRRTW	Northern Crown	CGHHIILOOSTTY	ichthyologist
CEHNNOORRSTUW	Southern Crown	CGHIIIKKNNQTU	quick-thinking
CEHNOORRSSSTU	Southern Cross	CGHIIKNOOSSTT	shooting stick
CEIIIKLLLNOSW	Wilkie Collins	CGHIILNORRSTY	Christ in Glory
CEIIILNNSTTVY	instinctively	CGIIIKNNOPSTT	sticking-point
CEIIILNPRSTVY	inscriptively	CGIIILLOOOPST	oligopolistic
CEIIIMNNOOPTT	in competition	CGIIILMNOORST	criminologist
CEIIIMNOPSTUY	impecuniosity	CGIIIMMNNOOSS	commissioning
CEIIJNOOPRSTT	projectionist	CGIINNNOOPRTW	crowning point
CEIIKLNOPSTTW	Wilson Pickett	CGILNNOORSUUY	incongruously
CEIILLLNOOSTV	violoncellist	CGIMMNOOOOPRS	composing room
CEIILMNOPSUUY	impecuniously	CHIIIKKLLNORT	Kirkintilloch
CEIILNNNNOTTY	incontinently	CHILMMNNOOOUY	Holy Communion
CEIILNNOORTTU	interlocution	CHILNOOORSSUY	isochronously
CEIILNOPSSSSU	suspicionless	CHLNNOORSSUYY	synchronously
CEIILNRSTTUVY	instructively	CIIILNRSTTUUV	viniculturist
CEIILOOPPRSTW	power politics	CIIILRSTTTUUV	viticulturist
CEIILOPPRSTUY	precipitously	CIILLNOPSTUUY	punctiliously
CEIILRRSSTTUU	sericulturist	CIIMNOPSTTUVY	consumptivity
CEIIMNNORRTTU	micronutrient	CIINNOOORSTTT	contortionist
CEIIMNOOPRTTU	motion picture	CIINOOPPRSTTU	opportunistic
CEIINNOOPRSTT	introspection	CIKMMNOORTUWY	community work

CILMOOPRSSUUY promiscuously
CILMOPRSSTUUY scrumptiously

D

DDDEEEGNNPRTU drug-dependent
DDDEGIKNNNOOY nodding donkey
DDDEILLMNORWY worldly-minded
DDEEEEFFLNNOS defend oneself
DDEEEEIMNPRRT predetermined
DDEEEEINORRSW dree one's weird
DDEEEELLLOPVW well-developed
DDEEEFGILNRRS fiddler's green
DDEEEGHILNSST delightedness
DDEEEIIMPRRST red spider mite
DDEEEIINOPSUY deep inside you
DDEEEIINRSSTT disinterested
DDEEEILNNNPTY independently
DDEEEINNOQTUW quietened down
DDEEEMNNPRSSU Edmund Spenser
DDEEFHIILMNOT in the middle of
DDEEFHILORRSW Wilfred Rhodes
DDEEGHHINRTUW hundredweight
DDEEGHNOOSSTT send to the dogs
DDEEGIIILMSSU guided missile
DDEEGILLNOPTU get dolled up in
DDEEGOOOPRSTX exported goods
DDEEHILLORSWY reddish-yellow
DDEEHILNOOTWY dyed in the wool
dyed-in-the-wool
DDEEHINORTTYZ The Dirty Dozen
DDEEHLMNRSSUU Edmund Husserl
DDEEHLNORRTUW The Underworld
DDEEIIKMNRRST Kidderminster
DDEEIIMNORSSU serious-minded
DDEEIKLLORSST dressed to kill
DDEEILNOPRRST Lord President
DDEFHILOORSUW field wood rush
DDEGGHHIINNOU in high dudgeon
DDEGGIINOOPRR doing porridge
DDEGGINNOPPSU sponge pudding
DDEGHHLMORTUU muddle through
DDEGHIIINSSTU distinguished
DDEGIIKMNNOTU United Kingdom
DDEGIILNSSUUY undisguisedly
DDEGIMMNPRSUU summer pudding
DDEGIMOOOPRST imported goods
DDEGINOPRSTUW dusting powder
DDEHHLOOORSUW household word
DDEHILMNORSTU in the doldrums
DDEIIIILMSSTU dissimilitude
DDEIIILLNOSSU disillusioned
DDEIIINOOTTVW divide into two
DDEIKLMNOORUW Under Milk Wood
DDEIMMNOORRSS Desmond Morris
DDEIMNOORSSTU misunderstood
DDEMNNOORSSWY Down's syndrome
DDENOOORRRUWY Rory Underwood
DDFIIMNNOOTUY if you don't mind
DDFIMNNNOOSUU of unsound mind
DDNNOORRSSUUU surround sound
DEEEEFFGIRRRZ fridge-freezer
DEEEEFFILNSSV self-defensive
DEEEEFGLLNOPS pledge oneself
DEEEEFHHOTTTT fed to the teeth
DEEEEFLNOOSTV devote oneself
DEEEEGGHOORTV go over the edge
DEEEEHHNRRTTU The Deer Hunter
DEEEEILOPPRRT retired people
DEEEEKNNOPPSU keep one's end up
DEEEELLPRRSVW well preserved
well-preserved
DEEEELLPRSSWX well-expressed
DEEEFGIILNNRR life-rendering
DEEEFGILLNRRW fringe-dweller
DEEEFGKLNOORW foreknowledge
DEEEFHHIORRRS Herefordshire
DEEEFHIKNNRTU under the knife
DEEEFHOOSSSTW sow the seeds of
DEEEFIJLNRRSY Jerry Seinfeld
DEEEFILLNNOSV find one's level
DEEEFILNOPPRS People's Friend
DEEEFILNORSTV divert oneself
DEEEFIMNNOORT forementioned
DEEEFINOORSVY on every side of
DEEEFLLLOPPRS self-propelled
DEEEFLOPSSSSS self-possessed
DEEEFNOORRSTV order of events
DEEEGGHILNPST sign the pledge
DEEEGGINNRSST send greetings
DEEEGHILNNNTU unenlightened
DEEEGHINRRRTV Right Reverend
DEEEGHLMOORST Gödel's theorem
DEEEGHLOORSWY heels o'er gowdy
DEEEGHNOOSTUV Steve Donoghue
DEEEGIIILNORS dereligionise
DEEEGIIILNORZ dereligionize
DEEEGIIPPRSUV Giuseppe Verdi
DEEEGILLORSTU Rouget de Lisle
DEEEGINNNORSU sound engineer
DEEEGINNORRST non-registered
DEEEHHIILTTVW The White Devil
DEEEHHNNPRSTY Stephen Hendry
DEEEHIINNSTWY in the wind's eye
DEEEHILNOORTW lied ohne worte
DEEEHJKNNOPSY Joseph Kennedy
DEEEHLMNNOOWY honeydew melon
DEEEHLNOPRSTT the old serpent
DEEEHMOPRRSTT short-tempered
DEEEIILNNPTXY inexpediently
DEEEILLORSTUY deleteriously
DEEEINOPRRRST retired person
DEEEINOQSTUVX vexed question
DEEELLNNPRSTY resplendently
DEEELNNSSSTTU unsettledness
DEEEMNORRSSYY Reye's syndrome
DEEEMOPSSSTTT tempest-tossed
DEEENNNOORSSU under one's nose
DEEENOPRRSUUX underexposure
DEEENORSSSTUX dexterousness
DEEENPRRRSSUU under pressure
DEEFFFIMNORRT different from
DEEFFFINORRST first offender

DEEFFGNNOORUY	young offender
DEEFFIIINORTW	fortified wine
DEEFFIILLORTW	well-fortified
DEEFFIILNNRTY	indifferently
DEEFFIINSSSUV	diffusiveness
DEEFGGHIILNRT	light-fingered
DEEFGGHINORTU	feeding trough
DEEFGHIILNNRY	Henry Fielding
DEEFGIIMNRSTU	disfigurement
DEEFGILLNNSTU	self-indulgent
DEEFGILLNNSYY	self-denyingly
DEEFHHIORRRST	Hertfordshire
DEEFHIIJLNTUW	June Whitfield
DEEFHILLMNRUW	Wilhelm Freund
DEEFHILNNOTTU	until the end of
DEEFHMNOORRST	shortened form
DEEFIILLMSSUY	elysium fields
DEEFIILNNOTTY	definitely not
DEEFILLOPRRSU	Rudolf Peierls
DEEFILNNOORYZ	ozone-friendly
DEEFILNOPRSSU	splendiferous
DEEFILNOPSTUY	tidy oneself up
DEEFILNORRSTU	Rudolf Steiner
DEEFLNORRUUVY	Rudolf Nureyev
DEEGGHIOOSTTV	give to the dogs
DEEGGINOSTTTU	getting used to
DEEGHHINOOSTU	in the doghouse
DEEGHHINOPTTU	deep in thought
DEEGHILLNOSUW	dwelling-house
DEEGHILMNNRUW	underwhelming
DEEGHILMOOSTY	demythologise
DEEGHILMOOTYZ	demythologize
DEEGHILNNOOST	on the long side
DEEGHILNOORST	The Gondoliers
DEEGHKOOOPRSU	keep good hours
DEEGIIIKMNNNP	keeping in mind
DEEGIKLLNNOTU	Duke Ellington
DEEGILNNORTUV	overindulgent
DEEGILNNRSUVY	undeservingly
DEEGILNORSTUV	silver-tongued
DEEGIMNNNOPSY	spending money
DEEGINNORSTTW	Downing Street
DEEGINNOSSTUW	sweet-sounding
DEEGINOPRRSSW	power dressing
DEEGIOORRRSSV	Reservoir Dogs
DEEHHIIMNNUUY	Yehudi Menuhin
DEEHHIOOPRSTT	the priesthood
DEEHHIOPPRRTY	hypertrophied
DEEHHLLOORTWW	the whole world
DEEHHLOORRTTW	the other world
DEEHIIMNPSTTW	spend time with
DEEHIINORSSTT	hit one's stride
DEEHIKNRRSTTU	thunderstrike
DEEHILOORRSSS	horse soldiers
DEEHINNRRSSUU	unhurriedness
DEEHINOORTTWW	down to the wire
DEEHKNORRSTTU	thunder-stroke
DEEHLMNOOOOST	hold someone to
DEEHNNOPPRSTY	the penny drops
DEEHNOOOOPRTT	open the door to
DEEIIINOPRSTY	Sidney Poitier
DEEIIINOQRSTU	derequisition
DEEIIKNNNNRSS	Dennis Skinner
DEEIILNORSSSU	deliriousness
DEEIILOPPRSTT	lepidopterist
DEEIILOPSTUXY	expeditiously
DEEIIMNOORSST	endometriosis
DEEIINOPRSSTU	serendipitous
DEEIINOSSSSTU	seditiousness
DEEIJNNOPRRSU	injured person
DEEIKKLLORRSW	skilled worker
DEEIKLLNOPRSS	skilled person
DEEILLNNOOORT	rolled into one
DEEILMNOOSSSU	melodiousness
DEEILNNOSTTUY	tendentiously
DEEILNORSSSTU	desultoriness
DEEILNOSSSSTU	dissoluteness
DEEILNPRRTTUY	interruptedly
DEEILOOPPRSTU	lepidopterous
DEEIMNNNOOSST	set one's mind on
DEEIMNNOOSSTT	set one's mind to
DEEINNPRRTTUU	uninterrupted
DEEIOPRSTTUVY	topside-turvey
DEEIORSSSTTWY	West Side Story
DEELLNORTTUUW	well-turned-out
DEELNNOPSSSUU	pendulousness
DEELNNOSSSSSU	soundlessness
DEELOOOPRSSTU	sleep outdoors
DEEMMRRRSTUYY	murder mystery
DEEMNORRSSSUU	murderousness
DEENNOOPRSSSU	ponderousness
DEENOORRRRTTU	order to return
DEFFFHIILLOTT	lift the lid off
DEFFGIIKNNORR	drink offering
DEFFGILNNNOUY	unoffendingly
DEFFIIILNOOSV	field of vision
DEFGHMOOORRTW	from the word go
DEFGIILRRTTUY	fertility drug
DEFHIILLOPSSW	disfellowship
DEFHILMRRTTYY	Merthyr Tydfil
DEFHIMORRRTUU	rutherfordium
DEFHLOOOPRTTW	top of the world
DEFHMOOOOPPRT	prophet of doom
DEFHOOOOSTTUW	out of the woods
DEFIILPRSTUUY	superfluidity
DEFIIMMNOOTTU	time out of mind
DEFILLRSSSTUY	distressfully
DEFILMNNNSSUU	unmindfulness
DEFILOOORRSUY	odoriferously
DEFIMNNOOOSTU	out of one's mind
DEFLNNOOOORTW	Tower of London
DEGGHHORRTTUU	trudge through
DEGGHIIILNNPS	pidgin English
DEGGHNNOOOOTU	not good enough
DEGHHINOOPPST	do the shopping
DEGHIIIINNRST	disinheriting
DEGHIIILPRSTT	light-spirited
DEGHIIJLLNNOR	John Dillinger
DEGHIIKLOSTVW	with kid gloves
DEGHIMNOOOSTT	something to do
DEGHMNOOOSTTU	smooth-tongued
DEGIIILNPSSTT	side-splitting

DEGIIILNQSTUY disquietingly
DEGIILNNOORRS soldering-iron
DEGIILNRSSSTY distressingly
DEGIINNNNPRSU underpinnings
DEGIINOPRSSTU true-disposing
DEGIKNNOORRWW wonder-working
DEGILNNOPRSTU pound sterling
DEGILNOOORRVV revolving door
DEGOOOOPPRSTU to good purpose
DEHHIMOPRRSUY Doris Humphrey
DEHHOOOORSTTW show the door to
DEHIILNOPTTTU put the lid on it
DEHIINOOPPSST deipnosophist
DEHIKNOPSSTTU put the skids on
DEHINORSTTTUW round the twist
DEHOOPRSTTTUW put to the sword
DEIIILOPSSTVY dispositively
DEIIINNOSSSSU insidiousness
DEIIINNOSSSUV invidiousness
DEIIINOOPRSTT periodontitis
DEIIKNNOOSTUW know inside out
DEIILMNOPRTVY improvidently
DEIILNOOSTTUV devolutionist
DEIIMNNNOOTTT don't mention it
DEIINNORSTTUU turn inside out
turn inside-out
DEIINOOPSSSSS dispossession
DEILLMORRTUUW murder will out
DEILLNNORSSUW unworldliness
DEIMMNOOPRSST Post-Modernism
Post-modernism
DEIMNNOOPSTTU put one's mind to
DELLOOPRSTTUY protest loudly
DELNOPPRSTUUY unsupportedly
DFGGHIILLNOOT floodlighting
DFGHILMNORTUW fling throw mud
DFGIINNOOOOPS food poisoning
DFILLRSSTTUUY distrustfully
DGGGGILMNRSUU drug-smuggling
DGHHHIIINSTTW with hindsight
DGHIIIILMNNSY diminishingly
DGHIKLLNRSTUY slightly drunk
DGHILMNORSTUW sling throw mud
DGIIIILNPRSTY dispiritingly
DGIIIKNNNPPSY skinny-dipping
DGIIINOOPRSST in good spirits
DGINNNORRRSUU run rings round
DHIIIMMOOPRSS isodimorphism
DHIIMOOOPRSSU isodimorphous
DIIIINNOOPSST indisposition
DIILMNOSTTUUU multitudinous
DIILNORSSTUUY industriously
DIINOOOPPRRST disproportion
DILLMOPRSTUWY multiply words
DILNOOOORSWWW Woodrow Wilson
DIMNOOORRTTWY dormitory town
DMOPPPRRSTUUU drum up support

E

EEEEEHLMORSSW somewhere else
EEEEEIKNPRRSV keep in reserve
EEEEENNPRRSTU entrepreneuse
EEEEFGNNOOSTT get on one's feet
EEEEFGNOOSTTT get to one's feet
EEEEFILNRSSVX reflexiveness
EEEEFKLNOOPST keep to oneself
EEEEGHILMORST eightsome reel
EEEEGHILNRSTW steering-wheel
EEEEGHINORSST heterogenesis
EEEEGHINORTTY heterogeneity
EEEEGHLOPRSTT sleep together
EEEEGHMNRRTUX extreme hunger
EEEEGHNOORSTU heterogeneous
EEEEGIINOPRSS epeirogenesis
EEEEGILLNNNVY Evelyn Glennie
EEEEGILMNOPPT meeting people
EEEEHHOQRSTUV shove the queer
EEEEHINRRSTVW never the wiser
EEEEHKLLRRSTT helter-skelter
EEEEHKNOOPPSU keep open house
EEEEHLLORTTUW roulette wheel
EEEEHLNNSTTVY seventeenthly
EEEEIINPRRRRV Pierre Vernier
EEEEIJLLRRSWY Jerry Lee Lewis
EEEEIKKNOTUWW week in week out
EEEEILMNNNOST in one's element
EEEEILNNPRTTT Triple Entente
EEEEIMNORSSTV serve one's time
EEEEINNPSSSVX expensiveness
EEEEINNRSSTTV retentiveness
EEEEINNSSSTVX extensiveness
EEEEINQRRSTTU in queer street
EEEEJJKMMOORR Jerome K Jerome
EEEEJNNSSTTUV Just Seventeen
EEEELLMOPRRST Ellesmere Port
EEEELLNPSSSSS sleeplessness
EEEELMNOOSSTU let someone use
EEEELMNOQRSUZ lemon squeezer
EEEELNNOORSSV lose one's nerve
EEEELNNRSSSSV nervelessness
EEEELNNSSSSSS senselessness
EEEEMOPRRSTUX exposure meter
EEEENNNORSSSV nonsense verse
EEEFFGILLLNOW fellow feeling
fellow-feeling
EEEFFGILLNORY forefeelingly
EEEFFGLNOORST forget oneself
EEEFFHLLOOSST feel the loss of
EEEFFINNOSSSV offensiveness
EEEFFLNOORSSU sure of oneself
EEEFGILNNNSSU unfeelingness
EEEFGILNNORSS resign oneself
EEEFGINOOPRSW power of seeing
EEEFGLNRRSSTU regretfulness
EEEFHHLOORRSS horseflesh ore
EEEFHHLPRSSST press the flesh
EEEFHIIMMNNRY feminine rhyme
EEEFHIINRRTTW interfere with
EEEFHIMORRTTU three-four time
EEEFHLLNOOPST help oneself to
EEEFHNOPRRSTT for the present
EEEFHNOPRSSTT Stephen Foster

EEEFHORRSUVWY	every few hours
EEEFIILNNOSTX	file extension
EEEFILNPRSSTT	present itself
EEEFILOORRSTT	restore to life
EEEFLLNORRTTU	fortune-teller
EEEFLNNRSSSTU	resentfulness
EEEFNNOOOSTTU	out on one's feet
EEEFNOOORSTTU	out of one's tree
EEEFNOPPSTTUU	put one's feet up
EEEGGHIORTTTT	get it together
EEEGGINORSSSU	egregiousness
EEEGHIILLSTTW	get the willies
EEEGHIJRSTTTT	get the jitters
EEEGHILMNNNTT	enlightenment
EEEGHILNNQSSU	Queen's English
EEEGHINNRTVWY	green with envy
EEEGHIOOTTTVV	give the vote to
EEEGHOPRRSSTT	press together
EEEGIIMNRRSST	Meistersinger
EEEGILLMNSSTW	sweet-smelling
EEEGILLNNRVWY	Greville Wynne
EEEGILLNSSSSU	guilelessness
EEEGILNPRRSVY	perseveringly
EEEGIMMMNRSSU	summer-seeming
EEEGIMNNORSST	remote sensing
EEEGINOPRRSTW	power steering
EEEGIORRRSSTV	retrogressive
EEEGNNOOPSSTU	get up one's nose
EEEGNOQRSSSTU	grotesqueness
EEEHHHLNOOSTT	hot on the heels
EEEHHIILNPRTW	three-line whip
EEEHHIORRSTVW	whithersoever
EEEHHJKLNOOOR	John Lee Hooker
EEEHHLNOOSSSW	show one's heels
EEEHHLNRTTTTU	hunt the letter
EEEHHNOOSSTTW	show one's teeth
EEEHIIILNNPPT	in the pipeline
EEEHIIMNNRSST	in smithereens
EEEHILLMPRSTY	Shirley Temple
EEEHILMNNPRST	replenishment
EEEHILNRSSTTT	enter the lists
EEEHIMMOORSTT	some other time
EEEHIMNNNOOPP	epiphenomenon
EEEHLLNOOPSTT	telephoto lens
EEEHLMNOOSSSW	wholesomeness
EEEHOOPRRSTTU	heteropterous
EEEIILNNPSVXY	inexpensively
EEEIINNNSSSTV	intensiveness
EEEIINNNSSTVV	inventiveness
EEEIINNSSSSTV	sensitiveness
EEEIINORSSTVV	oversensitive
	over-sensitive
EEEIINQRSSSTU	requisiteness
EEEIINQSSSTUX	exquisiteness
EEEIIPQRRSSTU	prerequisites
EEEIJLNRRSUUY	Julius Nyerere
EEEILLMOPPSSY	Smiley's People
EEEILNNNPSSSS	pennilessness
EEEILNNOSSSSS	noiselessness
EEEILNNPSSSSS	spinelessness
EEEILNOPSSSVX	explosiveness
EEEILNORSSUVY	sue one's livery
EEEILNPRSSSUV	repulsiveness
EEEIMNNORSSTV	montes veneris
EEEIMNOOPRTTT	potentiometer
EEEIMOPPRSTUY	Upper Yosemite
EEEIMOPRSSTUV	Supreme Soviet
EEEINNOPPSSTU	tune one's pipes
EEEINNOPRSSWX	new expression
EEEINOPRSSSTX	set expression
EEEJNOOPRSSTT	Otto Jespersen
EEEKLMNOOSSSZ	smokeless zone
EEEKLMOOPRRTT	Otto Klemperer
EEELLMORRSSSY	remorselessly
EEELMNORSTUVY	venturesomely
EEELMOPPPRRRU	purple emperor
EEELNNOPSSSTU	plenteousness
EEELNOPRSSSSW	powerlessness
EEENNOORRSSSU	erroneousness
EEENNORRSSTUV	serve one's turn
EEFFFLLLNOOSU	full of oneself
EEFFGGHIIORTU	figure of eight
EEFFGLNORSSTU	forgetfulness
EEFFHHKLOOOTT	let off the hook
EEFFHIIKLOSST	the kiss of life
EEFFIILNNOSVY	inoffensively
EEFFKNOOORSST	off one's stroke
EEFFNNOORSTTU	off one's nutter
EEFGGGIINRRRT	trigger finger
EEFGGHHLNOOTT	go the length of
EEFGGIILNRSSU	single figures
EEFGGILNNORST	strong feeling
EEFGGILNNORSV	self-governing
EEFGGILSSSTTU	suggest itself
EEFGHIINNOORT	in the region of
EEFGHILORSSTU	self-righteous
EEFGIILMNOORT	Legion of Merit
EEFGIILNNRRTY	interferingly
EEFGIINNOPRTZ	freezing point
EEFGILLOORSTX	reflexologist
EEFGINNOORSST	frontogenesis
EEFGINOORRRRT	Reign of Terror
	reign of terror
EEFHHHILOPTTW	with the help of
EEFHHINOOSSTW	on the wishes of
EEFHIILLLNOTY	lily of the nile
EEFHILNNSSSSU	unselfishness
EEFHILNSSSSST	shiftlessness
EEFHIMOOPTTTU	up to the time of
EEFHKNOOORSTT	on the stroke of
EEFHLNORSSTTU	thrust oneself
EEFHNNORRTTUU	fortune-hunter
EEFHNOOOPRRTT	on the report of
EEFHOOPPRRTTY	the property of
EEFIILLMNNOOS	fill someone in
EEFIILOPRRSTU	reptiliferous
EEFILLLLMNTUY	mellifluently
EEFILLNNPSSTU	plentifulness
EEFILNNNOOOST	not on one's life
EEFILNNOOSSSU	feloniousness
EEFILNOOPSTTU	step out of line
EEFILNRSSSSTU	fruitlessness

EEFILOPRSSTUY	pestiferously
EEFMNOORRSSTT	stern-foremost
EEGGGGIINORSS	George Gissing
EEGGHHHLOOOTW	go the whole hog
EEGGHINNNRSTT	strengthening
EEGGHMNOOORST	George Thomson
EEGGHNOOORTTT	not go together
EEGGHOOPRRTTU	group together
EEGGIIILMNORS	in gremio legis
EEGGIINOSSSTU	suggestionise
EEGGIINOSSTUZ	suggestionize
EEGGIJKOPRRYY	jiggery-pokery
EEGGIJLNOPPRS	jogger's nipple
EEGGIJNNOORSW	jow one's ginger
EEGGILNPPSSYY	Sleeping Gypsy
EEGGILOPRSTTT	Lester Piggott
EEGGLOPRRSTUW	power struggle
EEGHHIILLNORZ	Heinz Holliger
EEGHHIILOPSVX	high explosive
EEGHHIIPRSSST	high priestess
EEGHHIOPSTTUV	give the push to
EEGHHNNORSTTT	on the strength
EEGHHOORRTTTW	throw together
EEGHIIIKNNPTW	in keeping with
EEGHIIKLMNOST	something like
EEGHIILNNNPSW	spinning-wheel
EEGHIKNRRRSTU	hunger-striker
EEGHILLNOTTWW	get on well with
EEGHILMMNOSST	gentilshommes
EEGHILNSSSSST	sightlessness
EEGHILOOPRSTT	herpetologist
EEGHIMNOOPRSS	morphogenesis
EEGHIMNORSTTT	thermosetting
EEGHINNOSSTTW	sweet nothings
EEGHINORSSSTU	righteousness
EEGHIOPRTTTTU	put it together
EEGHLMNNOOOPY	phenomenology
EEGIIIMNOPRTV	primogenitive
EEGIILLLMSUVY	Sylvie Guillem
EEGIILLLNNTTY	intelligently
EEGIILLNNNTTU	unintelligent
EEGIILLNOPWWW	weeping willow
EEGIILNNOSSSV	give lessons in
EEGIILNNRSTTY	interestingly
EEGIILNORSSSU	religiousness
EEGIIMNOPRRTU	primogeniture
EEGIIMNOPRTXZ	extemporizing
EEGIINNNOSSSU	ingeniousness
EEGIINNNRSTTU	uninteresting
EEGIKLNPPPSUY	keep supplying
EEGILLNNNRTUY	unrelentingly
EEGILLNSSSSTU	guiltlessness
EEGILMOOORSTT	meteorologist
EEGILNNNOORSU	no longer in use
EEGILOPRRSSVY	progressively
EEGIMMNNORSTV	misgovernment
EEGIMNOOPRRTT	Otto Preminger
EEGINNNOSSSUU	ingenuousness
EEGINNNRSSSTT	stringentness
EEGINNOPPSSTT	stepping-stone
EEGINNOPPSSUV	even supposing
EEGINOORRRSST	retrogression
EEGINOPPRSSSS	prepossessing
EEGINOPRRSSUV	unprogressive
EEGINORSTTTUW	tongue-twister
EEGJMMNOOORSY	jog one's memory
EEGLMNOOOPRSU	prolegomenous
EEGOPPRRRSSUU	pressure group
EEHHHLOOOSTTW	the whole shoot
EEHHIIIMPTTTT	it pitieth them
EEHHIINNOOPTW	Winnie-the-Pooh
EEHHILRSTTTUW	with the result
EEHHINOPPRSTT	Pepin the Short
EEHHMMNOOOPPR	morphophoneme
EEHIIINPPRRST	perinephritis
EEHIIKLMOOSTT	Some Like It Hot
EEHIKORRSSTWY	West Yorkshire
EEHILLOORSSTT	tortoiseshell❑
EEHILMNRSSSST	mirthlessness
EEHILNNORRSST	northerliness
EEHILNOORSSST	lose one's shirt
EEHILNOORSSTT	Ornitholestes
EEHIMNOPTTTUU	up to the minute
	up-to-the-minute
EEHIMORRSTTVY	very short time
EEHIMORSSSSTU	housemistress
EEHKNNOOORSTT	on tenterhooks
EEHLLLNNOOTYY	Only the Lonely
EEHLLMNOOSUWY	unwholesomely
EEHLMNNOSSTTU	Mount St Helens
EEHLNORRSTTWY	north-westerly
EEHLNORSSSSTW	worthlessness
EEHLORSSTTUWY	south-westerly
EEHMMNOOPTTTU	up to the moment
	up-to-the-moment
EEHMNOOPRSTUY	hymenopterous
EEHMNOOPSTTUV	put the moves on
EEHNNOORRTTUW	nowhere to turn
EEHNORSSTTTWW	west-north-west
EEHOOPRSTTTUW	put to the worse
EEHOSSSTTTUWW	west-south-west
EEIIIINSSSTTV	sensitivities
EEIIILNNSSTVY	insensitively
EEIIIMMNPRRST	prime minister
EEIIIMNPRSSTV	primitiveness
EEIIINNRSTTTY	in its entirety
EEIIINNSSTTUV	intuitiveness
EEIIJKNNPRRTT	ink-jet printer
EEIILLMNSSSST	limitlessness
EEIILMNNPRTTY	impertinently
EEIILMNPSSSUV	impulsiveness
EEIILMOOSSTTY	osteomyelitis
EEIILNOORSTUV	revolutionise
EEIILNOORTUVZ	revolutionize
EEIILNOQRSTUV	ventriloquise
EEIILNOQRTUVZ	ventriloquize
EEIILOPPRSTVY	prepositively
EEIILOPRSTTUY	repetitiously
EEIIMNNNOOSTW	in one's own time
EEIIMNOPRSSSU	imperiousness
EEIIMNOPRSSSX	expressionism❑
EEIINNOPRRSST	interspersion

EEIINNRSSSTUV	intrusiveness
EEIINOPRSSSTX	Expressionist
EEILLMOPRSTTU	multiple store
EEILLNOOPQRSU	nolle prosequi
EEILMMMNOPSTY	misemployment
EEILMNNRTTTUY	unremittently
EEILMPPRSTUVY	presumptively
EEILNNOPSSSST	pointlessness
EEILNNOSSTTUY	sententiously
EEILNOOPSSTTV	split one's vote
EEILNOPRSSSTU	sur les pointes
EEILNOPRSTTUY	pretentiously
EEIMNOPSSSTUU	impetuousness
EEINNNOPRSSTT	non-persistent
EEINNOPRSSSUU	penuriousness
EEINNOPRSTTUU	unpretentious
EEINOPPRRSSTU	pressure point
EEINOPPRSSSUV	purposiveness
EEKLRRTTUUUVY	turkey vulture
EEKNNOOPSSSTU	outspokenness
EEKNOOPPRSSSS	spokespersons
EELLNOOPPPRYY	polypropylene
EELLOPPRSSSUY	purposelessly
EELMNORSSSTUU	tremulousness
EELMOPSSTTUUY	tempestuously
EELNOPRRSSSUY	nursery slopes
EELNOQRSSSUUU	querulousness
EEMMNNOOSSSTU	momentousness
EEMMPRRSSTUYY	supersymmetry
EEMNORSSSTUVY	nervous system
EEMOOOPPRSSTU	to some purpose
EENNOOPPRSSTU	opportuneness
EENNORSSSSTUU	strenuousness
EENOPPRRSSTUU	put pressure on
EFFGGILNNORSU	long-suffering
EFFGHHIRSTTTU	The Right Stuff
EFFGHILNRSSTU	frightfulness
EFFHIOOOPRTTT	to the profit of
EFFIILOORSSSU	fossiliferous
EFFILLMNNNOTU	non-fulfilment
EFFKNNOOSSTUW	know one's stuff
EFGGGGHIINRUU	figure-hugging
EFGGHIIILNTTW	weightlifting
EFGGHIIINPRTZ	prizefighting
	prize-fighting
EFGGHIILNNRTY	frighteningly
EFGGINNOORTTT	not forgetting
EFGGLNNOOORTT	long-forgotten
EFGHHILOOSTTT	the footlights
EFGHHILOOTTWW	go with the flow
EFGHHILORRTTU	filter through
EFGHHLLOOTTUW	well-thought-of
EFGHIIILMNTWY	mini-flyweight
EFGHIILMMORTY	Tommy Hilfiger
EFGIKLNNOORWY	foreknowingly
EFGIKNOORRRST	king of terrors
EFGILLNOORVWY	overflowingly
EFGOOPPRRSTTU	get support for
EFHIIINOPSSTT	in spite of this
EFHIIKLLNOTTT	think little of
EFHIINNRSSTTU	unthriftiness
EFHIKMNNOOORT	think no more of
EFHMMNOORTTTU	moment of truth
EFIIIMNRRSSTT	first minister
EFIIINOOPSSTV	five positions
EFIIINOPRSSTW	spirits of wine
EFIKLLMNORTUY	Mull of Kintyre
EFIKLLNNSSSUU	unskilfulness
EFIKLMNOORSTY	Trofim Lysenko
EFILLLLMOSUUY	mellifluously
EFILLOOPRRSUY	proliferously
EFILNOOPPRRST	splinter-proof
EFINOOOQSTTUU	out of question
EFLLOPRSSUUUY	superfluously
EFLNOORRSSSUW	sorrowfulness
EGGHHIOOTTTUV	give thought to
EGGHIIIKLLNNT	like lightning
EGGHIINOOPRSS	Sophie Grigson
EGGHIJMNNPTUU	jumping the gun
EGGHILLNOOPST	hot gospelling
EGGHIMMNOOORS	Georg Simon Ohm
EGGHLMOOOOPRY	geomorphology
EGGIIILMNNNRT	intermingling
EGGILNOOORSTT	gerontologist
EGHHIINOPPRSW	horsewhipping
EGHHIKORRSTTU	strike through
EGHHLLOSSTTUY	thoughtlessly
EGHHMNOOORRTW	growth hormone
EGHIIIMMMNTUW	minimum weight
EGHIIINRTTTWY	with integrity
EGHIILLORRTVW	Orville Wright
EGHIILNNOSTTU	ethnolinguist
EGHIILNNSSSTU	unsightliness
EGHIILNPRSSST	sprightliness
EGHIIMNOPSSTU	something is up
EGHIKLMNNOOWY	howling monkey
EGHIKLNNOOOSS	sling one's hook
EGHILNORSTUUY	unrighteously
EGHILOPRSTUUY	uprighteously
EGHINNNOOTTTX	next to nothing
EGHINNOPRTTUW	put in the wrong
EGHLLLNOPPTUU	pull the plug on
EGIIIILNORRST	irreligionist
EGIIIKLNOOSST	kinesiologist
EGIIILLORRSUY	irreligiously
EGIIILNOSSSTU	litigiousness
EGIIINNOOPRST	repositioning
EGIIJNNNNNPSY	spinning-jenny
EGIIKNNNORRSW	inner workings
EGIILLNNNSSUW	unwillingness
EGIILMNNRTTUY	unremittingly
EGIILMNOPRSTY	temporisingly
EGIILMNOPRTYZ	temporizingly
EGIILNNOQSTUY	questioningly
EGIILNNORSTUU	neurolinguist
EGIILNNRSSTUY	unresistingly
EGIILNOPRSTYZ	proselytizing
EGIILNORSTUVY	vertiginously
EGIILOOOSSTTV	sovietologist
EGIIMNOORRSST	risorgimentos
EGIIMOPRRSSSV	progressivism
EGIINNNOOOPTV	given no option

EGIINNNOQSTUU	unquestioning
EGIINNNSSTTUW	unwittingness
EGIINNOPQRSUX	spring equinox
EGIINNOPRRRRT	printing error
EGIINNPPRRSST	printing press
EGIIOPRRSSSTV	progressivist
EGIKLOOPRSTWY	grow like Topsy
EGIKNNOOPRRSW	working person
EGILLNNOORSST	Rolling Stones
EGILLNPRSTTUY	splutteringly
EGILNNOSSSTUU	glutinousness
EGILNOPPRRSTU	splinter group
EHHHIOOPPPSTY	hypophosphite
EHHIIKLNOSTWW	with whole skin
EHHIILLOSTWWY	whitish-yellow
EHHIILOOPPRSZ	philosophizer
EHHIMMNOORSTU	Monmouthshire
EHHIMNOOPRSTT	Mother Shipton
EHHINNORRSTTU	in the short run
EHHKOOORSSTTW	shoot the works
EHHMMOOORRSSU	horse mushroom
EHIIILLOPPPSU	Louis Philippe
	Louis-Philippe
EHIIKLOSSSTTW	kist o' whistles
EHIILLOPSSTWW	will-o'-the-wisps
	wills-o'-the-wisp
EHIINOOOPPSTT	the opposition
EHIKLMNNOOSTU	Thelonius Monk
EHILLNNOOPQUY	phylloquinone
EHILLNORSTUVY	rush violently
EHIMOPRSSSTTU	stir the possum
EHKNNNOOOOOSW	on one's own hook
EHLLOPRSSUUUY	sulphureously
EHMMNOORRSTUU	Mount Rushmore
EIIIILNQSTUVY	inquisitively
EIIIINNSSTTVY	insensitivity
EIIILLMOOPSTY	poliomyelitis
EIIILNSTTTUVY	institutively
EIIIMMNOPRSSS	Impressionism
EIIIMNOPRSSST	impressionist
EIIINNOOPRSTT	interposition
EIIJNNORSSSUU	injuriousness
EIILMNOOPRRTY	premonitorily
EIILMNOORSTUV	revolutionism
EIILMNOQRSTUV	ventriloquism
EIILMOORRSTUY	meritoriously
EIILNOORSTTUV	revolutionist
EIILNOQRSTTUV	ventriloquist
EIILNORRSSSTY	sinistrorsely
EIIMNNOOOPSSS	Siméon Poisson
EIIMNPPPRRSTU	Sturmer Pippin
EIINNNQSSTUUU	Quintus Ennius
EIINNOOSSTTVY	tenosynovitis
EIINOPRSSSTTU	superstitions
EIIOPRRSSTTUU	surreptitious
EIIOPRSSSTTUU	superstitious
EIJOORSSSSTTU	Just So Stories
EILMMNOPRSSTY	Myrtle Simpson
EILNNOOPPRTUY	inopportunely
EILNORSSSUUUX	luxuriousness
EILOQRRSTTUUY	triquetrously
EINNOOOPSSSSU	poisonousness
EINNOOORSSSTU	notoriousness
ELMMNNOOOOPYY	Monopoly money
EMNNOORSSSSTU	monstrousness
EMNOPSSSSTUUU	sumptuousness

F

FGHHHIIKLNOTY	think highly of
FGHHLLOOORTUW	follow through
	follow-through
FGHIIINNOPSST	finishing post
FGHIILLNORSUY	flourishingly
FGHIOOPSTTTUU	put out of sight
FGIJJMNOOPRUY	jumping for joy
FGLMNNOOOOOSS	Song of Solomon
FHIIJKNOSTTTU	just think of it
FHIILLORSTTUW	without frills
FHINNOOOOPRTU	point of honour
FIJNOOOPTTTUU	put out of joint
FILLMRSSTTUUY	mistrustfully

G

GGGHHINOOORTU	thoroughgoing
GGHHHIOORTTUW	go through with
GGHHHLOOPRTUU	plough through
GGHHIIKLLMNSU	Hugh Kingsmill
GGHIIILNPRSTT	strip lighting
GGHIIINNPPRTT	night-tripping
GGHIIKOORUVYZ	Giorgiy Zhukov
GGHIILNNNRSTU	running lights
GHHIIIINPRSST	in high spirits
GHHIINNNOOTTW	with nothing on
GHHILNOOSTTTU	lost in thought
GHIIILLNSSTXY	sixty shilling
GHIILNOOORSTT	ornithologist
GHIIMNOOPSSTY	physiognomist
GHIINPPTTTUUW	putting up with
GHIMNNNOORSTU	smooth-running
GHMMOOPRSSUYY	gypsy mushroom
GIIIILNNPRSTY	inspiritingly
GIIIKLLLMNSTU	multiskilling
GIIILLMNSTTUU	multilinguist
GIIILMNNOOSUY	ignominiously
GIILMNRSSTTUY	mistrustingly

H

HHIMMOOOOPRSS	homomorphosis
HIIILLNNOQTTU	quintillionth
HIINOOPPSTTTU	up to this point
HILNOPPRSSTUY	in short supply
HILORRSTTTUWY	trustworthily
HNORRSTTTUUWY	untrustworthy

I

IIINNOOPPSTTU	put in position
IILLLORSSTUUY	illustriously
IILNOOOPSSTTU	lotus position
IIMNOOOPPRRST	misproportion
INNOOPPPSTTUU	put upon points

14 letters

A

AAAAACEFKLNPST	flat as a pancake
AAAAADFGIILMRS	Sagrada Familia
AAAAAEFRRRSSTY	Yasser Ar Arafat
AAAAAHMNRSSTUY	Mahayana Sutras
AAAABBCJKNORRS	Barbara Jackson
AAAABBIIMNRSST	Sabbatarianism
AAAABCCEJLNOPS	José Capablanca
AAAABCEHLLOTTT	attach a label to
AAAABDDILLNRSS	Aldabra Islands
AAAABDEFGGLOOR	a load of garbage
AAAABEEHINRVVW	have a brainwave
AAAACCDEGIMRSS	cardiac massage
AAAACCILLPRTTY	paratactically
AAAACDDILLNNOR	Canadian dollar
AAAACDEFHILMRY	Michael Faraday
AAAACDEHKLNRTZ	Kazan Cathedral
AAAACDGIILMMRT	diagrammatical
AAAACDGIILMPRT	paradigmatical
AAAACEGHJLLMNS	James Callaghan
AAAACEHLLOPRTV	Hoare-Laval Pact
AAAACHLMMOSTUY	Thomas Macaulay
AAAADDEEEKMSTT	make a dead set at
AAAADDEILLNOPR	Andrea Palladio
AAAADDEJNPRRRS	Rajendra Prasad
AAAADDFGIMMMRU	Muammar Gaddafi
AAAADEEGMNNNRT	Andrea Mantegna
AAAADEGINNQRRU	quadragenarian
AAAADELLLNORRV	Andorra-la-Vella
AAAADHHNNORSWW	Anna Howard Shaw
AAAADHJLLNTTZZ	and all that jazz
AAAAEEGILMRRST	steal a marriage
AAAAEELLLNRSUY	Leaellynasaura
AAAAEGIKKLNNTY	Lake Tanganyika
AAAAEGLNRSTTUW	natural wastage
AAAAEIMNRRSSTT	Martin Sarasate
AAAAFIIMNRRSST	Rastafarianism
AAAAGHIMNOPRST	phantasmagoria
AAAAILLNPRSSTU	Australian Alps
AAAAILMOPPRRTU	Pamulaparti Rao
AAABBBCEEGHLRS	Charles Babbage
AAABBCEEEGHRTT	cabbage-tree hat
AAABBCEILNNPRU	banana republic
AAABBCEINOSSTT	Sebastian Cabot
AAABBEEGLLNOOR	Boolean algebra
AAABCCFIIINPRS	Francis Picabia
AAABCCILMNNOOY	cyanocobalamin
AAABCDDENORSUW	Edward Casaubon
AAABCDEEFLNORT	balance of trade
AAABCDEEGLMNRR	Le Grand Macabre
AAABCDEGINOSTU	Santiago de Cuba
AAABCDILLLLRSY	Lyrical Ballads
AAABCEEEINRSSU	Béarnaise sauce
AAABCEEFLNNOTT	Battle of Cannae
AAABCEEGGGILMR	baggage reclaim

AAABCEEGGGIRRR	baggage-carrier
AAABCEEIKLNRST	strike a balance
AAABCEEIMNRTUY	American Beauty
AAABCEHILLLPTY	alphabetically
AAABCEHKLORRWZ	razorback whale
AAABCEHLNOPPRU	unapproachable
AAABCEILMNRRTU	interambulacra
AAABCELLLMORST	Balmoral Castle
AAABCEMMNORRRT	Robert McNamara
AAABCEMNNORSTV	Marco Van Basten
AAABCHILLMNNOR	Abraham Lincoln
AAABCHILNOPPRY	inapproachably
AAABCHLNOPPRUY	unapproachably
AAABDDEENRRRST	standard-bearer
AAABDDELMMNRRU	Bernard Malamud
AAABDEEGGGHLNR	baggage-handler
AAABDEEGGLNSUU	use bad language
AAABDEEGIMNOTV	give a bad name to
AAABDEEIIJLLNS	Isabelle Adjani
AAABDEFGILLMOS	balsam of Gilead
AAABDEGILNNORU	Nadia Boulanger
AAABDEHHNRRRST	Sarah Bernhardt
AAABDEHMORSSST	The Ambassadors
AAABDEILMNORRV	random variable
AAABDELNNORRWW	Andrew Bonar Law
AAABDEMNNOORTT	Donato Bramante
AAABDHIMOPRSSS	ambassadorship
AAABDIINORSTTZ	bastardization
AAABEEEGLMNNSS	manageableness
AAABEEGHINNORV	have a bearing on
AAABEEGIMRRRUU	marriage bureau
AAABEEILNNSSTT	attainableness
AAABEFGLMORTTW	Battle of Wagram
AAABEFINORRSTV	Bavarian Forest
AAABEFKLLMOPSU	make a balls-up of
AAABEGIIKNRRST	strike a bargain
AAABEGIILLNOUV	bougainvillaea
AAABEGKMNOOSTU	make a song about
AAABEIIILMNRSS	Rabelaisianism
AAABEIILLMNPRR	prima ballerina
AAABEIILMNNNTU	unmaintainable
AAABEIILMNNRTT	Britannia metal
AAABEIILMNRTTT	Brittania metal
AAABEILMOORRTV	Alberto Moravia
AAABEILNRRSTTU	Alastair Burnet
AAABEILOORRRSU	aurora borealis
AAABELLNNPRSTT	transplantable
AAABGHLMOPRTUU	autograph album
AAABIIILLNTUVY	unavailability
AAABIILLNRTTUY	natural ability
AAACCCEHORRRTT	character actor
AAACCCEINNORTT	Antarctic Ocean
AAACCDEEIKLLRT	care killed a cat
AAACCDEFNORTVY	advance factory
AAACCDEGINNNSY	gain ascendancy
AAACCDILORRSUV	cardiovascular

AAACCEEFHHKLTT at the chalkface
AAACCEEHIKKNRT take a raincheck
AAACCEGHILLOOR archaeological
AAACCEHILMPRTU pharmaceutical
AAACCEHLLMRSSV clash-ma-clavers
AAACCEIKLMNRRS Animal Crackers
AAACCGHHILPRTY tachygraphical
AAACCGHILLNOOR arachnological
AAACCGIIINNPTT incapacitating
AAACCHILLMORTY achromatically
AAACCHILLNNORY anachronically
AAACCHLRSTTTUW clutch at a straw
AAACCIIINNOPTT incapacitation
AAACCIKLLMNUUY Macaulay Culkin
AAACCILLORTTUY autocratically
AAACCLLOOOPRRS corpora callosa
AAACDDEGGKLNOR cloak-and-dagger
AAACDDENORSTVW advance towards
AAACDEEGINRSTT a great distance
AAACDEEIKMNQTU make acquainted
AAACDEEINNTTTW wait attendance
AAACDEGHIKLOPY package holiday
AAACDEGIILMNST declaim against
AAACDEGIMRRSTT scatter diagram
AAACDEGINNORST ascending aorta
AAACDEGINNRSVY advancing years
AAACDEHILMNNPT mental handicap
AAACDEIIIMNNNR American Indian
AAACDEIIMNOPRS Cinema Paradiso
AAACDEIJLLNNRU Julian calendar
AAACDEILLMOPRS Camelopardalis
AAACDEILMNNNRW Cardinal Newman
AAACDELLMNORRU all-round camera
AAACDFHIMNNRST handicraftsman
AAACDGHLLLMNRY lachrymal gland
AAACDHHILMNSST Chatham Islands
AAACDHILNOOPRS achondroplasia
AAACDHINNRSTTU Tristan da Cunha
AAACDIIILNORST radicalisation
AAACDIIILNORTZ radicalization
AAACDIILNNOSTZ scandalization
AAACDIIMRRSTTT dramatic artist
AAACDILLMNNORR mandarin collar
AAACEEEGHNNTVW what a vengeance
AAACEEEHLNPSTV Elephanta caves
AAACEEFLLNSSTY lay a false scent
AAACEEHILPSSTV have as its place
AAACEEHKLMMNOR Karma Chameleon
AAACEEIILLMPPR Imperial Palace
AAACEEIILPRSST specialist area
AAACEEIIMNNRTV Native American
AAACEEILNNNPSW clean as a new pin
AAACEEKLLMNOSW make allowances
AAACEFGINNORSS Françoise Sagan
AAACEFGIORSSUX saxifragaceous
AAACEFIILNNSTT financial state
AAACEFIIORTTVY area of activity
AAACEGHHIIRSTT Agatha Christie
AAACEGIMNRSTUU argumenti causa
AAACEGINSSTUWY Giant's Causeway
AAACEHHIKKLTWW watch like a hawk
AAACEHIILMRRSV air-vice-marshal
AAACEHIILNPTTT antipathetical
AAACEHILLLMPRY alphamerically
AAACEHILLMMTTY mathematically
AAACEHILLMNPRU alphanumerical
AAACEHILLPPRST alpha particles
AAACEHILNOPPRT palaeanthropic
AAACEHIMNNOPTV have an impact on
AAACEHJMPSSTTY the cat's pyjamas
AAACEIILLLLMWW William Wallace
AAACEIILMNORTZ caramelization
AAACEIILNNNORR Carolina Nairne
AAACEIIMMNNPRS pan-Americanism
AAACEILLMNNSTY anamnestically
AAACEILLNORTUY aeronautically
AAACEILMMNRSST sacramentalism
AAACEILMNRSSTT sacramentalist
AAACEIMNOSSTUV mass evacuation
AAACFIMNORRSTW aircraftswoman
AAACGGHHIILOPR hagiographical
AAACGHILNOPRRU uranographical
AAACGHIMNOPRST phantasmagoric
AAACGIIINNOTTW awaiting action
AAACGIILLMSTTY astigmatically
AAACGILLMNORTY morganatically
AAACGIMNOPPRTT pantopragmatic
AAACHILLLLOPTY allopathically
AAACHILMOPRRSY Cyril Ramaphosa
AAACIIILNOPTTZ capitalization
AAACIKMOOPRSSS Kaposi's sarcoma
AAACNNOPPTTWYY Can't Pay, Won't Pay
AAADDDEEHLMNNS dead man's handle
AAADDDHILLOYYY Lady Day Holiday
AAADDEEFNORRVY for ever and a day
AAADDEEGHINRRS dead as a herring
AAADDEEGINSSTT dead set against
AAADDEEGMOOORV Amedeo Avogadro
AAADDEEHHNOSVY have had one's day
AAADDEEHLNNSTW Leda and the Swan
AAADDEEKLNORRX Alexander Korda
AAADDEEKNNORRU Konrad Adenauer
AAADDEELMNRSUX Alexandre Dumas
AAADDEELNORRST Andrea del Sarto
AAADDEELRRSTTY already started
AAADDEFFIILSST as fit as a fiddle
AAADDEGGNRRSTW at daggers drawn
AAADDEHHNRSSTW heads and thraws
AAADDEHLLNRRUY Laurel and Hardy
AAADDFINNORUWY find a way around
AAADDGHHIMNNOS Mohandas Gandhi
AAADDLMNORRSST moral standards
AAADEEEFINRSTV vasa deferentia
AAADEEEHILMRTT Almeida Theatre
AAADEEELLMRRTW Walter De La Mare
Walter de la Mare
AAADEEFGIJLMRS James A Garfield
AAADEEFHLLMSTU full steam ahead
AAADEEFLMNRRTT flame-retardant
AAADEEFLNNRRXZ Franz Alexander
AAADEEFNORRTTU turn a deaf ear to
AAADEEGHHINSTT against the head

AAADEEGHHMSTTW	what's the damage?
AAADEEGHIMNRTV	have a great mind
AAADEEGJNOPRSW	Japanese War God
AAADEEGLMMNNNT	land management
AAADEEGNNNVYYY	Gennady Yanayev
AAADEEHLLORTTT	lead to the altar
AAADEEIKLLMNRS	salamander-like
AAADEELNPPPRSS	apples and pears
AAADEEMNQSSUUU	usque ad nauseam
AAADEERRSSTTUY	Easter Saturday
AAADEFGHHLTUUV	have had a gutful
AAADEGHIIRSSTT	straight as a die
AAADEGIMNNRSTU	unarmed against
AAADEGLNOSTUVY	advantageously
AAADEGMOORRTTW	Margaret Atwood
AAADEHHNOTUVWY	and what have you
AAADEHIIMMNSTU	Anaheim Stadium
AAADEHIKNORRSV	Andrei Sakharov
AAADEHKMRRSSTT	hard taskmaster
AAADEHMNPSTTYY	tea and sympathy
AAADEIILMNNSTV	Tasmanian devil
AAADEIILNNRTUV	valetudinarian
AAADEILNNOPRRX	Alexandr Oparin
AAADEIMNNORRSY	ordinary seaman
AAADEINNNOORSX	Ariadne on Naxos
AAADEMMNNNPRSU	Man and Superman
AAADFHHIMMMRSU	Muhammad Sharif
AAADFHNNOOPTUY	Anthony of Padua
AAADFINRSSSTWY	waifs and strays
AAADGINNPSSTTU	stand up against
AAADGLLNQRRUUY	quadrangularly
AAADIIILNNRTTU	latitudinarian
AAADIKLLNORSWY	all in a day's work
AAAEEEFILNNORS	a flea in one's ear
AAAEEEGKLLRSTV	Great Slave Lake
AAAEEEKMMNSTTT	make a statement
AAAEEFGIKMOPRS	make a pig's ear of
AAAEEFGMMMNNRT	farm management
AAAEEGGGLNRTTU	target language
AAAEEGGILNNTUV	native language
AAAEEGGMNRRRST	Margaret Sanger
AAAEEGHIKMMNRT	take a hammering
AAAEEGINNPPUUW	Papua New Guinea
AAAEEGINNPRSTU	septuagenarian
AAAEEGOPRSSTWY	go separate ways
AAAEEHHNORRTTW	wear another hat
AAAEEHIIMNRRTT	Henrietta Maria
AAAEEHIMNSSTWY	in the same way as
AAAEEIKMNOPRRT	make reparation
AAAEEINNOTTTUW	Antoine Watteau
AAAEEJLNPRRSTU	Jean-Paul Sartre
AAAEEKLPQRRTUU	take up a quarrel
AAAEELNPPRSSTY	present as a play
AAAEFFFIORSSTT	affairs of state
	state of affairs
AAAEFGIMNNOORT	Fontana Magiore
AAAEFHIKLNNRRT	Aretha Franklin
AAAEFIILMMRSST	matresfamilias
AAAEFIILMPRSST	patresfamilias
AAAEFIILNORRRT	irrational fear
AAAEFKNOORSTTT	at a rate of knots

AAAEFLLOOPPRSV	seal of approval
AAAEFLNOPPRTYY	pay a penalty for
AAAEGGILLNNOSU	analogue signal
AAAEGIIILMNRST	egalitarianism
AAAEGIIMNNRSTT	Tasmanian tiger
AAAEGIINNPRRRS	arrange in pairs
AAAEGIKOSTUUWY	Ieyasu Tokugawa
AAAEGMMNORRTTT	Tetragrammaton
AAAEHHIITTVWWY	have it away with
AAAEHILMNNNOTT	national anthem
AAAEHIMOPRRSTT	aromatherapist
AAAEHINPPRRSST	as a partnership
AAAEHLLRSSSUXY	harass sexually
AAAEIILLNORTTZ	lateralization
AAAEIILMNOOPTZ	Emiliano Zapato
AAAEIIMNNOSSTX	Ioannis Metaxas
AAAEILMOPPPRRT	malappropriate
AAAEILNSSSSSTT	sales assistant
AAAEIMMMNRRSTU	armamentariums
AAAEKLPPPRSSTT	Krapp's Last Tape
AAAELLLLLMOPRS	parallel slalom
AAAELLQQRSUUVY	quaquaversally
AAAFFGILNOPSTY	play off against
AAAFGHHINOOSTW	Song of Hiawatha
AAAGIILNNOORTZ	organizational
AAAGIINNNOOTTZ	antagonization
AAAHHLMORSTTTU	Lothar Matthaus
AAAHILORSSTTUU	South Australia
AAAIILMNNOSTTU	Altai Mountains
AAAIILNNORTTUZ	naturalization
AAAIIMNORTTTUZ	traumatization
AAAILMNNOSSTTU	Atlas Mountains
AAAIMMNNORSTTU	Matra Mountains
AAAIMNNORSTTTU	Tatra Mountains
AABBCCDIIIRRTU	barbituric acid
AABBCCEEEGHINS	Chinese cabbage
AABBCCEEINNRRT	Barbican Centre
AABBCDEGHIRRRU	Richard Burbage
AABBCEEFHKKORT	break the back of
AABBCEEKLLOTTX	battle-axe block
AABBCEFGLOORTY	cabbage-root fly
AABBCEGHLMRSTU	Bamburgh Castle
AABBDDEENNOOVY	above and beyond
AABBDEEHIMNORT	broad in the beam
AABBDEIINRSSTY	Saint Bride's Bay
AABBDFHILOORSU	a load of rubbish
AABBDGGIINNNOR	Brobdingnagian
AABBEEEHIRSTTW	The Water-Babies
AABBEEENORSSTT	beat one's breast
AABBEEFLNOSTTY	Battle of Naseby
AABBEEGHIMNRTY	Nightmare Abbey
AABBEEHLMMRTTW	Matthew Bramble
AABBEEINNORSST	beat one's brains
AABBEEKMOORRVX	Max Beaverbrook
AABBEFGGILNRST	flabbergasting
AABBEFINNOSTUY	Fountains Abbey
AABBFKKMNNOORT	from bank to bank
AABBHIKKMNOORS	Simon Bar Kokhba
AABCCCDEIILMRU	calcium carbide
AABCCCDIILORXY	carboxylic acid
AABCCCGHIKNRST	backscratching

AABCCDEEKNORSW	answer back code
AABCCDEILLNNOU	Caledonian Club
AABCCDEKKLLNOT	block and tackle
AABCCEEEIKLMSS	make accessible
AABCCEEELMOPRT	more acceptable
AABCCEEELNPSST	acceptableness
AABCCEEFHIKLNT	black in the face
AABCCEELNNORTU	counterbalance
AABCCEENRRRSUY	cranberry sauce
AABCCEHILLMOPS	accomplishable
AABCCEILMMRTUU	circumambulate
AABCCGIILMNORT	bring acclaim to
AABCCIIILPRTTY	practicability
AABCCIILNOTTUY	accountability
AABCCIKLNRSSSU	Black Narcissus
AABCDDEEKNPSTU	bucket and spade
AABCDDEIKRRSVW	drive backwards
AABCDDEILMNOPR	bladder campion
AABCDDELLLMNOP	Donald Campbell
AABCDEEEGHNRUU	bureau de change
AABCDEEEHLMRTV	valet de chambre
AABCDEEFHLORRT	Brother Cadfael
AABCDEEFILLMNU	field ambulance
AABCDEEGLNOSSU	sebaceous gland
AABCDEEHHLLRST	Charles the Bald
AABCDEEHILNNOY	hold in abeyance
AABCDEEHIMNRST	Bedrich Smetana
AABCDEEHKPRSTY	speak by the card
AABCDEEHLLORTT	called to the bar
AABCDEEHLNOORZ	Honoré de Balzac
AABCDEEHNNRUZZ	nebuchadnezzar ❑
AABCDEEHORTTUY	cathode-ray tube
AABCDEEIKRRSTV	back-seat driver
AABCDEEINRRSTT	scatterbrained
	scatter-brained
AABCDEEKLNSSUY	black-eyed Susan
	black-eyed susan
AABCDEELNOPSUU	double saucepan
AABCDEENNPRSUU	superabundance
AABCDEENRSSSTT	abstractedness
AABCDEFIIMORRS	Birds of America
AABCDEFLLNRSSY	fancy dress ball
AABCDEGIKLNRRT	blank cartridge
AABCDEHIKLRRUY	hydraulic brake
AABCDEHOORRSST	across-the-board
AABCDEILMNNRRU	cardinal number
AABCDEIMNNNORT	recombinant DNA
AABCDEKLNORRST	stock and barrel
AABCDELLNRSUUV	vascular bundle
AABCDHINNORRRS	Richard Branson
AABCDIILNNORSS	Nicobar Islands
AABCEEEEFLNOSV	leave of absence
AABCEEEGHLNNSS	changeableness
AABCEEEHILLMNP	Blenheim Palace
AABCEEEKKLMRRT	black-marketeer
AABCEEEMNOPPRT	become apparent
AABCEEFHHLORTW	breach of the law
AABCEEFLLMOTTY	Battle of Mycale
AABCEEFLNOOPRW	balance of power
AABCEEGGJLNOTU	object language
AABCEEGHINPRST	breathing space
	breathing-space
AABCEEGHLNORUX	labour exchange
AABCEEGINORRSS	Isaac Rosenberg
AABCEEGMNNOSTT	become stagnant
AABCEEHILNRSST	charitableness
AABCEEHILOPRRR	irreproachable
AABCEEHINSTTUU	eustachian tube ❑
AABCEEHLNNRTTU	turn the balance
AABCEEILLLMMTY	emblematically
AABCEEILLMNPSS	implacableness
AABCEEKMNOOPSY	pay someone back
AABCEFGHIORTTU	right about face!
AABCEFGILLLOOT	Gaelic football
AABCEFGILNNOOT	floating beacon
AABCEFIIINOTTU	beautification
AABCEFIILLNSSU	unclassifiable
AABCEFIINOPRRT	prefabrication
AABCEFILMOTTTU	Battle of Actium
AABCEFKLNNOOST	flat on one's back
AABCEGHILPRSTT	graphics tablet
AABCEHIILLRSTY	Hebraistically
AABCEHILLPRTYY	hyperbatically
AABCEHILOPRRRY	irreproachably
AABCEHKMNNOORS	man on horseback
AABCEIIILNPSTY	inescapability
AABCEIILLOORTY	aerobiotically
AABCEIILRTTTXY	extractability
AABCEIKNNORRSS	rack one's brains
AABCEILLMORRTY	barometrically
AABCEILNNOORST	torsion-balance
AABCEILNOOORRS	Corona Borealis
AABCEIMMRRSSTY	asymmetric bars
AABCEIMNOOPRRS	bear comparison
AABCEINOORRSTV	observation car
AABCGHIILLMOOP	amphibological
AABCGHIILLOPRY	biographically
AABCGILNNNOSUV	Sauvignon Blanc
AABCHILOOPRSTU	claustrophobia
AABCIIILNRTTTY	intractability
AABCIILLLOPSTY	collapsability
AABCILLORRRTUU	arboricultural
AABCILMNNOOTTU	noctambulation
AABCJKNOOPRSTY	Port Jackson Bay
AABCNOOPRRSSYY	coronary bypass
AABDDDEEEHLNSS	bald-headedness
AABDDDELNORSTU	double standard
AABDDEEHIILTVZ	Elizabeth David
AABDDEEIMNNORT	one-armed bandit
AABDDEELNNRSTU	understandable
AABDDEFHINNSUW	husband and wife
AABDDEFIIOPRRS	Bird of Paradise
	bird of paradise
AABDDEFLNNOTTU	Adolf Butenandt
AABDDEGIINOORT	biodegradation
AABDDEGILNORYZ	badly organized
AABDDEGNNRRRST	Grand St Bernard
AABDDGHIINNRTW	bad handwriting
AABDEEEFHINRRT	feather-brained
AABDEEEHILNNNR	banner headline
AABDEEEHILNRTV	live and breathe
AABDEEEHNNORUV	have been around

AABDEEELNNRSSU	unreadableness
AABDEEENNRRSTT	Anne Bradstreet
AABDEEFLNOORVY	Adolf von Baeyer
AABDEEGIMRRSSU	Marburg disease
AABDEEHHLLTTTY	That'll Be The Day
AABDEEHINPRTTU	habit and repute
AABDEEILMNOTTY	motte and bailey
AABDEEILNNOTTY	not bat an eyelid
AABDEELNORRTUY	Robert Delaunay
AABDEEMORRRSTW	wardrobe master
AABDEFGJKMOOOO	make a good job of
AABDEFHKLNORSS	Hans Adolf Krebs
AABDEFILMOTTWY	Battle of Midway
AABDEGGHIINOTV	give a big hand to
AABDEGHILNRRTY	bright and early
AABDEGIILOOPRT	Pietro Badaglio
AABDEGILNRRRSU	Alan Rusbridger
AABDEGIMNNNNRR	Bernard Manning
AABDEGLORRRTWY	Barry Goldwater
AABDEHIIKNNRRT	Bernard Haitink
AABDEHILNNRRTU	Bernard Hinault
AABDEIIILLORSV	Basil D'Oliveira
AABDEIIKMNORST	disembarkation
AABDEIIOPPRSTV	disapprobative
AABDEIKLLNNNOS	all skin and bone
AABDEILLNNSTWY	Stanley Baldwin
AABDEILMOORTUZ	Bartolomeu Diaz
AABDEINNOOPRSX	expansion board
AABDFLLNNOORUV	Rudolf von Laban
AABDGHIILNPTTU	put in a bad light
AABDGIIIMNOSTU	disambiguation
AABDGNNNOOOOTU	go on and on about
AABDHILMNOSSUY	busman's holiday
AABDIIIILNSTVY	inadvisability
AABDIIILNOTUVY	unavoidability
AABDIINOOPPRST	disapprobation
AABDIOOPPRRSTY	disapprobatory
AABEEEEHRRTTTT	beat the retreat
AABEEEFHIJNNRR	Jean Henri Fabre
AABEEEHHLLNOWW	whalebone whale
AABEEEHKLMRSST	make breathless
AABEEEHKNORRST	break one's heart
AABEEEHKNORSTT	take one's breath
AABEEEHNORSSTV	save one's breath
AABEEEINORRSWY	raise an eyebrow
AABEEEKLLMNRUV	make vulnerable
AABEEEKLMMORST	make more stable
AABEEEKLMNRRSS	remarkableness
AABEEELNNORSSS	reasonableness
AABEEELNNOSSSS	seasonableness
AABEEFGGILNNST	self-abnegating
AABEEFGILNNOST	self-abnegation
AABEEFGLMNORRU	a large number of
AABEEFGMNORRTU	a great number of
AABEEFHKMORSTT	mark of the Beast
AABEEFHLMNORTT	Battle of Arnhem
AABEEFKOPRRSTW	power breakfast
AABEEFLNNRRSTU	untransferable
AABEEFLNORSSUV	favourableness
AABEEGGHRSTTTY	The Great Gatsby
AABEEGGIIKMNNN	make a beginning
AABEEGHHINRTVY	heavy breathing
AABEEGHHKNNNRT	Kenneth Branagh
AABEEGILNOPRTT	operating table
AABEEGORRSTTTY	storage battery
AABEEHIIILRTTV	rehabilitative
AABEEHIIINORTX	exhibition area
AABEEHKNRSTTTU	burn at the stake
AABEEHKOOSTTTT	take to the boats
AABEEHMNNRRTTU	near that number
AABEEIIKLLNRRT	all-terrain bike
AABEEIILNNSSST	insatiableness
AABEEIILNOPRST	Isabelita Perón
AABEEIILNRRRST	irrestrainable
AABEEILLMMORRT	Albert Memorial
AABEEILMNPSSSS	impassableness
AABEEILNNRRSTU	unrestrainable
AABEEIMNNORTUV	mountain beaver
AABEEJKKMOOSTU	make jokes about
AABEEKNOOSTTTU	take out one's bat
AABEEKNOQRRSSU	break no squares
AABEFGIKLLPRRU	ballpark figure
AABEFHHIIKRTTW	break faith with
AABEFIKLMOORTT	make a bolt for it
AABEFILLMMNNNO	non-inflammable
AABEFILLNOPSTU	Fallopian tubes
AABEFIMNOORRTU	neurofibromata
AABEFLLMMNORSU	a small number of
AABEFLMOORSTUV	most favourable
AABEGHIINNORTT	into the bargain
AABEGHINNNOTVY	not be having any
AABEGHIOOPRRTU	autobiographer
AABEGILLNRRRUU	urban guerrilla
AABEHHIOSTTVWY	have it both ways
AABEHHJMNNORSS	Johannes Brahms
AABEHIIILNORTT	rehabilitation
AABEHLLOPPRSTY	blepharoplasty
AABEIIIILLNNTY	inalienability
AABEIIILLNORTZ	liberalization
AABEIIILLNRTTY	inalterability
AABEIIILMNRRST	libertarianism
AABEIIILNPRSTY	inseparability
AABEIIILPRRRTY	irreparability
AABEIILLMNNNRW	William Brennan
AABEIILLMNOSTW	William Bateson
AABEIILLMNRTWZ	William Barentz
AABEIILMNORSUV	bulimia nervosa
AABEIILNNNTTTU	tintinnabulate
AABEIILNSSSTTU	substantialise
AABEIILNSSTTUZ	substantialize
AABEIIMPPRSTTV	private baptism
AABEIINOPPSSTW	boatswain's pipe
AABEIKNOPRRSST	Boris Pasternak
AABEILMNNORRTU	rational number
AABEILMNNRSTTU	intransmutable
AABEIMNNNRRTUV	Martin Van Buren
AABEIMPRRRTTYY	primary battery
AABEKMRRRRSTWY	strawberry mark
AABELMNOORSSTU	neuroblastomas
AABFFIIIILLSTY	falsifiability
AABFGHIILLORTT	a bit of all right
AABFIIILLMMNTY	inflammability

AABFIILLNPPTUY unflappability
AABGGIIIOORRSV Giorgio Vasarib
AABGIINNSSTTTU substantiating
AABHIIIKKLMNNU Mikhail Bakunin
AABIIILMNNRSSU annus mirabilis
AABIIILNSSTTUY sustainability
AABIILLNOOPTTX blaxploitation
AABIILMNSSSTTU substantialism
AABIILNSSSTTTU substantialist
AABIILNSSTTTUY substantiality
AABIINNOSSTTTU substantiation
AABILLNSSTTUVY substantivally
AABILMMNNOOSTU somnambulation
AACCCEEFHHIRRT chief character
AACCCEEHILLTTY catechetically
AACCCEEIILLSST ecclesiastical
AACCCEHIIRRSTT characteristic
AACCCEHILMORST chromatic scale
AACCCEILLLLORR clerical collar
AACCCGIKNORRST stock-car racing
AACCCHLLOOPSTY staphylococcal
AACCCILNOORSTT social contract
AACCCNNOOSTTTU cost-accountant
AACCDDDEEHHNRT catch red-handed
AACCDDEEHKNNSS cack-handedness
AACCDDEIMMOOST disaccommodate
AACCDEEEIILOSS coeliac disease
AACCDEEHHNOSTT catch one's death
AACCDEEHIINORS reach a decision
AACCDEEHLNRRST cradle-snatcher
AACCDEEIINRRST disincarcerate
AACCDEELNORRRW Clarence Darrow
AACCDEGHIMOORR echocardiogram
AACCDEGIPRSTUU Auguste Piccard
AACCDEHHILLORT Catholic Herald
AACCDEHILOPRSY polysaccharide
AACCDEHIMNOORS monosaccharide
AACCDEIILLOPTY apodeictically
AACCDEIILMOTTZ acclimatized to
AACCDEIINNORTT contraindicate
AACCDEIKLLRSTU calculated risk
AACCDEILLMORTY democratically
AACCDEILMOORST social democrat
AACCDEILNNOSSV Slavonic Dances
AACCDELLLNOTUU Launcelot du Lac
AACCDENPRSSSUU cups and saucers
AACCDFHIMMNNOO chain of command
AACCDHHJMNOOSU John Couch Adams
AACCDHIILLNORY diachronically
AACCDHNNNOORRW crown and anchor
AACCDIINNNORTT contraindicant
AACCDIKNORRSTT carrot and stick
AACCEEEHHILMMR Michael Meacher
AACCEEEHIMNORS macaroni cheese
AACCEEEHKNNOST take one's chance
AACCEEFHLRRSSU Charles Surface
AACCEEFKNOPRTT Pontefract cake
AACCEEGHKMMRRR grammar checker
AACCEEHLLRSSUY Charles Causley
AACCEEILNNRSTU natural science
AACCEEIMRRSTUY security camera
AACCEEINNNORSS reconnaissance
AACCEELNNOPSTU clean up one's act
AACCEELNORRRTU nuclear reactor
AACCEFFILNOORT area of conflict
AACCEFHLLRTUWY watch carefully
AACCEFHOORRTTU out of character
AACCEFIILLORUV calorific value
AACCEFILNOSSTU self-accusation
AACCEFIMNNNOPY finance company
AACCEGGHILNNPS changing places
AACCEGGILLNOOY gynaecological
AACCEGHILLLLTY catch illegally
AACCEGHILLOOST eschatological
AACCEGIIMNRTUV circumnavigate
AACCEHHIILLNPR Charlie Chaplin
AACCEHHIILLRRY hierarchically
AACCEHIILOPPRS archiepiscopal
AACCEHIJKLMNOS Michael Jackson
AACCEHIJKLNORT Jackie Charlton
AACCEHILLNORSU Charles Luciano
AACCEHILLORTTY theocratically
AACCEHIPPRRSST sharp practices
AACCEHLMOOPRSU macrocephalous
AACCEHOOOPRSST cast a horoscope
AACCEIIILPRSTT practicalities
AACCEIJKLOPRRT practical joker
AACCEIJKLOPRST practical jokes
AACCEILLLOPPTY apoplectically
AACCEILLMTUUVY accumulatively
AACCEILNNOOSSS occasionalness
AACCEILPRSTTUY spectacularity
AACCEIMMNNOPST accompaniments
AACCENNORSSSST sacrosanctness
AACCFHIILMMNNU Finn mac Cumhail
AACCFHOORRRRTY carry a torch for
AACCFIIILNOSST classification
AACCFIIINNOSTT sanctification
AACCFIILORSSTY classificatory
AACCFNNORTTTUU turf accountant
AACCGHIJKMNNNU Jack Cunningham
AACCGHNNOOSTUU à chacun son goût
chacun à son goût
AACCGIILLLMOOT climatological
AACCGIILLMORTY tragicomically
AACCGIILNOTTTV tactical voting
AACCGIIORSTTUU acoustic guitar
AACCGILLLNOOUV vulcanological
AACCHIIILMRRST Lacrima Christi
AACCHIILLMSSTY schismatically
AACCHILLLOPTTY phyllotactical
AACCHILLLOSSTY scholastically
AACCHILNNOORSU canonical hours
AACCHILNOPSTYY psychoanalytic
AACCHLRSSTTTUW clutch at straws
AACCIIILMPRTTY impracticality
AACCIILLMNOSTU miscalculation
AACCIILLNNOOTT call into action
AACCIILMNRSTTU circumstantial
AACCIILOOPRSTV vicar-apostolic
AACCIILPRSSTTU rustic capitals
AACDDDHILORTUV David Coulthard

AACDDEEFILLLNN	Decline and Fall
AACDDEEHIPRSTT	death-practised
AACDDEEIJQRRSU	Jacques Derrida
AACDDEEILOSTVV	devil's advocate
AACDDEEIMNNOTT	decontaminated
AACDDEELLORSSS	Dead Sea Scrolls
AACDDEFGILLNOO	Colonel Gaddafi
AACDDEIIIMMNOV	Divina Commedia
AACDDEIILRSTTU	disarticulated
AACDDEKLMORRTT	cold dark matter
AACDDGHHIIMMRU	Hugh MacDiarmid
AACDDHIIKNRRSW	Richard Dawkins
AACDDHILMNORYY	hydrodynamical
AACDEEEEGHHNTX	heated exchange
AACDEEEEHJLNNU	Jean-Luc Dehaene
AACDEEEFHMNSSS	shamefacedness
AACDEEEGINNRRW	Andrew Carnegie
AACDEEEIRRRSTT	restricted area
AACDEEFFKLLTWY	walk affectedly
AACDEEFGKOOORT	take good care of
AACDEEGHHNORST	chase the dragon
AACDEEGHIIMNNR	reading-machine
AACDEEGILNRSST	leading actress
AACDEEHHLLPRTY	hardly the place
AACDEEHHLRTTWY	Aldwych Theatre
AACDEEHIINNTUW	with an audience
AACDEEHIJLNRSW	Jewish calendar
AACDEEHILMRRST	Reims Cathedral
AACDEEHIORRTTT	read the riot act
AACDEEHLLLRSTW	Wells Cathedral
AACDEEHLMOPPRX	Phaedra complex
AACDEEHLNPPSSU	pleased as Punch
AACDEEHLOORSTU	could eat a horse
AACDEEHLPRRSTY	The Card Players
AACDEEIIMPPRST	misappreciated
AACDEEILLMMNTY	medicamentally
AACDEEILPRRTTU	ultracrepidate
AACDEELLNNSUVY	Lucas van Leyden
AACDEELNNNRSTT	transcendental
AACDEENORSSSUV	cadaverousness
AACDEFGNOOOPTU	put a good face on
AACDEFHILNORSW	Earl of Sandwich
AACDEFHIMNNRRY	Richard Feynman
AACDEFHMMNOOTT	at the command of
AACDEFIIINNOTZ	denazification
AACDEFIINRTTTV	find attractive
AACDEFIMMNOOVW	command a view of
AACDEGGHIOORTW	with a good grace
AACDEGHHILLNTT	Highland cattle
AACDEGHILLMOSU	Michael Douglas
AACDEGIILLMRRR	Marc Girardelli
AACDEGINOPRSST	data processing
AACDEHIINQTTUW	acquainted with
AACDEHIINRSSTT	Christian Stead
AACDEHIIOSSTTW	associated with
AACDEHILLMNNRR	Richard Ellmann
AACDEHILLNNNSS	Channel Islands
AACDEHILLNORST	The Coral Island
AACDEHILNOPRRT	Ripon Cathedral
AACDEHINRRTTUW	draw the curtain
AACDEHIOPRSTUY	acid-house party
AACDEIIILLLSTY	idealistically
AACDEIIILMNOTZ	decimalization
AACDEIIILMORST	isodiametrical
AACDEIILLORTVY	radial velocity
AACDEIILNOSTTU	educationalist
AACDEIILNRRTUV	cardinal virtue
AACDEIMNNNOTTU	uncontaminated
AACDEIMNNOORTT	decontaminator
AACDEINOOPRTTT	data protection
AACDFLMMNOOOTX	common toadflax
AACDGGHHIORRRT	Richard Hoggart
AACDGHIIMNRRRS	Richard Ingrams
AACDGHIMORRTTW	dramatic growth
AACDGIILNNOSST	social standing
AACDHHIKLRRTUY	Richard Hakluyt
AACDHIIILLOPTY	idiopathically
AACDHIKLLOORSY	kailyard school
AACDHILLOTTUWY	what-d'you-call-it
AACDHIRRRSSSTU	Richard Strauss
AACDHLLLNOOPTU	put a call on hold
AACDIIIILNNPRS	disciplinarian
AACDIIIILNNRVW	Indian Civil War
AACDIIILNORSTV	Victoria Island
AACDIIINOOSSST	disassociation
AACDIILLLMOPTY	diplomatically
AACEEEEGHIMNTV	achievement age
AACEEEEKMNOPSS	make one's escape
AACEEEFFHNNOTV	have an effect on
AACEEEFGHNORTX	rate of exchange
AACEEEFGHORRTY	the Year of Grace
AACEEEFHINRSTT	stare in the face
AACEEEFHKLOPTT	take the place of
AACEEEFINORRST	rate of increase
AACEEEGGLNRSTU	secret language
AACEEEGHINNTVW	with a vengeance
AACEEEGIKMNNRZ	Mackenzie Range
AACEEEGINOPRST	cease operating
AACEEEHHILNNOT	an ace in the hole
AACEEEHIMNNOST	in the same canoe
AACEEEHIMNRRST	Increase Mather
AACEEEHKMRRRST	market research
AACEEELLNSSTVW	Wallace Stevens
AACEEELLPRRSTV	space traveller
AACEEELPRSSTTY	cassette player
	cassette-player
AACEEFFILNOTTY	affectionately
AACEEFGILORRTT	of great article
AACEEFGLNNPRSY	false pregnancy
AACEEFHIMNNOTT	act in the name of
AACEEFHLORRTWY	clear the way for
AACEEFIKOPRTTU	take a picture of
AACEEFILLORRUW	cauliflower ear
AACEEFKLLORSTU	Oak-leaf Cluster
AACEEFMNOPRRRT	performance art
AACEEGGILLLNOY	genealogically
AACEEGHHHLRSUY	Charles Haughey
AACEEGHHINRRST	heart-searching
AACEEGHIKRRRTT	Garrick Theatre
AACEEGHILLLNTY	genethliacally
AACEEGHILMPRYY	hyperglycaemia
AACEEGHILNNRTT	central heating

AACEEGHKLMOPSU keep a calm sough
AACEEGHNNOSSWY change one's ways
AACEEGIIKLLLMP Gamaliel Pickle
AACEEGIILLMNSV evangelicalism
AACEEGILLNRSTV vertical angles
AACEEGILLNSTTT Tintagel Castle
AACEEGIMNOPSTT compete against
AACEEHHHLLRTTT that'll teach her
AACEEHHNOPPRST on the scrap heap
AACEEHIILNRSTT castle in the air
AACEEHIINNRTTX inheritance tax
AACEEHILLLPTTY telepathically
AACEEHILMMMRST Michaelmas term
AACEEHILNNOPRT in another place
AACEEHILNNPSTU a place in the sun
AACEEHILRRTUVX extravehicular
AACEEHLLLNPRRS Charles Parnell
AACEEHLLOPPRTT apple charlotte
AACEEHLMORRRTT thermal reactor
AACEEHLNOOPRTT to another place
AACEEHLNOOPTTT the clean potato
AACEEHMNPPPRRT parchment paper
AACEEHMOOSTTVY have come to stay
AACEEIIKLLNOTW A Town Like Alice
AACEEIILOPRSTV overcapitalise
AACEEIILOPRTVZ overcapitalize
AACEEIILPPRTVY appreciatively
AACEEIILPRTTUV recapitulative
AACEEIINPPRTUV unappreciative
AACEEILLLMSTTY telesmatically
AACEEILLNNPRSU annular eclipse
AACEEILMMNSSTU immaculateness
AACEEILNPRTTUV venture capital
AACEEILNRSSTTU articulateness
AACEEIMNOPRRTW a warm reception
AACEEINNOPRRST a certain person
AACEEINOPRSSTT stare into space
AACEEINRSSTTTV attractiveness
AACEEKLLNPRSUY speak unclearly
AACEEKLOSSSTTY Stokesay Castle
AACEEKMNNORSTV make conversant
AACEEKNNORSTTU take a scunner to
AACEELLNOPPRRT Peter Pan collar
AACEELOOPRRRTX extracorporeal
AACEEOOPRRSTTT corporate state
AACEFFGIILLLRT illegal traffic
AACEFFHIILORTT article of faith
AACEFFHILNRSTY Charles Tiffany
AACEFFINORRRTW warrant officer
AACEFFLMORTTTY matter-of-factly
AACEFGGINNOOTV coign of vantage
AACEFGIILNSTTV self-activating
AACEFGMNOOORUW woman of courage
AACEFHMNNOOSST canon of the mass
AACEFIIILMNNST Financial Times
AACEFIILLMNOPT file a complaint
AACEFILLNOSSSU fallaciousness
AACEFLOOPPRSTU court of appeals
AACEGGHILLOPRY geographically
AACEGGILNNOORT congregational
AACEGHHIILLOPR heliographical
AACEGHHILNOPRT ethnographical
AACEGHHIMOPPTT apophthegmatic
AACEGHIILLNRTW with an ill grace
AACEGHIIMNNRSV vanishing cream
AACEGHILLLMPTY phlegmatically
AACEGHILLOOPRS phraseological
AACEGHIMNOPRTY cinematography
AACEGHLNNOOPSZ Pancho Gonzales
AACEGHLNNSTUUW Weltanschauung
AACEGIIIILLMRW William Craigie
AACEGIILLLLSTY legalistically
AACEGIINOORSTT categorisation
AACEGIINOORTTZ categorization
AACEGILLLOOPTY apologetically
AACEGILNNOOTUU union catalogue
AACEGILNORTTUV congratulative
AACEGILNRRTTUY rectangularity
AACEGLLMMNORST Malcolm Sargent
AACEGLNNOOORSW score an own goal
AACEHHHILLMTTT that'll teach him
AACEHHIIMMNNSS Hamish MacInnes
AACEHHIKORTVWW wreak havoc with
AACEHHLLOTTTUY that'll teach you
AACEHIILLMRTTY arithmetically
AACEHIILLNTTTY antithetically
AACEHIILMMNRST Ismail Merchant
AACEHIILMMNSUV male chauvinism
AACEHIILMNSTUV male chauvinist
AACEHIIMNOSTTZ schematization
AACEHIINNOTTTU authentication
AACEHIKLMNNOSW Coleman Hawkins
AACEHILLMNNORY enharmonically
AACEHILLMNOPTY phonematically
AACEHILLMOPRSY semaphorically
AACEHILLMOPRTY metaphorically
AACEHILLMPSTYY metaphysically
AACEHILNPRSTUY physical nature
AACEHKKLLNOSSW walk one's chalks
AACEHLNOPRRSSS Charles Parsons
AACEHLNOPRSSYY psychoanalyser
AACEIIILNOPSTZ specialization
AACEIIILNPTTVY anticipatively
AACEIILLLMRTTY altimetrically
AACEIILLNPSTTY antiseptically
AACEIILLNRTTUY inarticulately
AACEIILNNORTTZ centralization
AACEIILNNORTUZ nuclearization
AACEIILNNPSSST castles in Spain
AACEIILNOOPPSU papilionaceous
AACEIILNOPRTTU recapitulation
AACEIILNORSTUZ secularization
AACEIINNNRTTUY certain annuity
AACEIINORSSSUV avariciousness
AACEIKPRRSSTTU surprise attack
AACEILLLNOPSTY pleonastically
AACEILLMMRSTYY asymmetrically
AACEILLMSSTTYY systematically
AACEILMNORRTTY moral certainty
AACEILMRRSSUUU Marcus Aurelius
AACEILNNOOPRSW Napoleonic Wars
AACEILNNOORSTV conservational

conversational
AACEILNPRRSSTU particularness
AACEILOPRRRTUV overparticular
over-particular
AACEILOPRRTTUY recapitulatory
AACEILRSSSTUUV vascular tissue
AACEIMMNSSTUUV Vatican Museums
AACEIMNOPPRTVY private company
AACEIMNOPRSTTU storm in a teacup
AACEINNRTTTUUY curtate annuity
AACEINOPRSSSST cast aspersions
AACEKLNNORSTUY cantankerously
AACELLNOPPSSTU cast a spell upon
AACENOORRRRTYY coronary artery
AACFGHILMOPRRU graphic formula
AACFGILNORRTUV vulgar fraction
AACFGNOOORSTTT contrafagottos
AACFHILNOOPRST Chilon of Sparta
AACFIIIILLNRTY inartificially
AACFIIILNOQSTU qualifications
AACFIIINNOOPST saponification
AACFIIINNOQTTU quantification
AACFIIINORSTTT stratification
AACFIIKLLOTTVY lack of vitality
AACFIILORSSTTY satisfactorily
AACFINORSSTTUY unsatisfactory
AACGGIILLMOSST Glagolitic Mass
AACGHHILOOPRRT orthographical
AACGHHMOOPRRTY chromatography
AACGHIIJKLLMRT I'm all right, Jack
AACGHIIMNOPRST panoramic sight
AACGHILLLOOPTY pathologically
AACGHILMOOPRST pharmacologist
AACGHLOOPPRSYY parapsychology
AACGHMNOORSSTT a strong stomach
AACGIIILNPRSTU paralinguistic
AACGIIINNNOPTT action painting
AACGIIKLNOPRTW working capital
AACGIIMNOOPRRS microsporangia
AACGIINNOOSTTT antagonistic to
AACGILLLOORSTY astrologically
AACGILLLOOTTUY tautologically
AACGILLLRRTUUY agriculturally
AACGILNNOORTTU congratulation
AACGKLNORSTTTY attack strongly
AACGLNOORRTTUY congratulatory
AACHIILLNNOPTY antiphonically
AACHIILLOPRSTY aphoristically
AACHIKMORRSSTW mark with a cross
AACHILLOORTTUY local authority
AACHILLOPSTTYY hypostatically
AACHILNOPSSSYY psychoanalysis
AACHKKKKOOORSS Oskar Kokoschka
AACIIIINNNOPTT in anticipation
AACIIILLLSTTVY vitalistically
AACIIILLMMRSTU multiracialism
AACIIILLNRSTTY inartistically
AACIIILMNOPPST misapplication
AACIIILNOPRTTY anticipatorily
AACIILLLRSTTUY altruistically
AACIILLMMNOPTY pantomimically
AACIILLMMNSTUY numismatically
AACIILLOPPRTTY party political
AACIILLPQTTUYY typical quality
AACIILMOOPTTTU automatic pilot
AACIILNOOPRRST conspiratorial
AACIILNPPPRRST principal parts
AACIIMMNOSSTTU atomic mass unit
AACIINNOOSSTTT action stations
AACILLLNORSTUY ultrasonically
AACILLMNOORSTY astronomically
AACILLMOPSTTYY asymptotically
AACILLNOOPRSTT castor oil plant
AACILMOOPPRSTT protoplasmatic
AACILNNNOSTTUV anticonvulsant
AACIMNNORSSTUU Marcus Antonius
AACINOOOPRRTTX corporation tax
AACINOOPRRRSTT procrastinator
AADDDEEEHHNRSS hard-headedness
AADDDEEEHIMMMO Mohammed Aideed
AADDDEEHIISSTY hydatid disease
AADDDEFHLLMOTY daddy of them all
AADDDEILLNORSS lords and ladies
lords-and-ladies
AADDEEEHLNNORR Hero and Leander
AADDEEFGHLOORS flog a dead horse
AADDEEGGILNRRR Gerald Gardiner
AADDEEGIJKLNSU Daniel Gajdusek
AADDEEGINNPSTW Peasant Wedding
AADDEEHHHMOSTT death's-head moth
AADDEEHILLLNTV the devil and all
AADDEEIILLNSWY Daniel Day-Lewis
AADDEEIILNNOTZ denationalized
AADDEEILLNRSSW Leeward Islands
AADDEEKMNNORRT non-trademarked
AADDEELNOPPRTW Edward Appleton
AADDEELNOQRRSU squadron leader
AADDEELNPPRSUY appear suddenly
AADDEGIIJLNRSV J David Salinger
AADDEGIJLNORSU Douglas Jardine
AADDEGNORRSTUV stand guard over
AADDEHHMNRRTTU thread and thrum
AADDEIIILMNOTT additional time
AADDEIILLNNORW in an ideal world
AADDELMOOOPRRV Pedro Almodovar
AADDELOOORSTUY do as you are told
AADDEOPRRSSTUW spread outwards
AADDFFHLNOSTUU A Handful of Dust
AADDFFKNOORSUX Sandford Koufax
AADDHHHIINNNTW hand in hand with
AADDHJLNNNOOOS Donald Johanson
AADEEEEGGORRTT to a great degree
AADEEEFFHILRTT life after death
AADEEEFFHNOOST eat one's head off
AADEEEFGIOPRST pâté de foie gras
AADEEEFHORSSTT streets ahead of
AADEEEGGHHIOTV give the go-ahead
AADEEEGHLLNNRW Greenland whale
AADEEEGNNOSTWY get one's end away
AADEEEHHILPRTT Adelphi Theatre
AADEEEHIILRSVY Heaviside layer
AADEEEHILLLNPS lead apes in hell

AADEEEHIMMRRTT	Mermaid Theatre
AADEEEILPPRRSY	easily prepared
AADEEELMNRSSTT	elder statesman
AADEEELNOPSSTT	set on a pedestal
AADEEEMNNSSTTT	send a statement
AADEEFFHIMMORS	homme d'affaires
AADEEFGGHLNRTY	Gandalf the Grey
AADEEFGIKLLLRR	Karl Lagerfield
AADEEFGILLLRTZ	Ella Fitzgerald
AADEEFGKNORRTT	take for granted
AADEEFGLLNRRUV	glandular fever
AADEEFHIKLNNRT	the rank and file
AADEEFHILNRTTY	faint-heartedly
AADEEFHJMNOOPU	one jump ahead of
AADEEFHLMNOOST	old man of the sea
AADEEFIIKMOTVW	take a dim view of
AADEEFIILNORTZ	federalization
AADEEFIJLMNNSY	Jayne Mansfield
AADEEFKNOSSUWY	a week of Sundays
AADEEFMNNOOTTY	Day of Atonement
AADEEGGIMNNRTZ	aggrandizement
AADEEGHIIILNRT	Dante Alighieri
AADEEGHILNPRST	triangle-shaped
AADEEGHILOPRRT	radiotelegraph
AADEEGHIMORRTW	Maria Edgeworth
AADEEGHINNSTTT	stand in the gate
AADEEGHKMORSTV	God save the mark
AADEEGHLNNOPST	golden pheasant
AADEEGILLLNRTT	Little and Large
AADEEGIMNNRRST	disarrangement
AADEEGINRRSUUX	au grand sérieux
AADEEHHINNNOSV	have in one's hand
AADEEHIILNNNPT	Indian elephant
AADEEHKMNORRSV	mover and shaker
AADEEIILNPQSSU	sesquipedalian
AADEEIKLMOPRTV	evaporated milk
AADEEILMNORTTT	tatterdemalion
AADEEILMNTTTTU	mental attitude
AADEEILNNOSSTV	Adlai Stevenson
AADEEILNRRSSTU	Treasure Island
AADEEIMNRRSTTU	unmarried state
AADEEINNPRSSTT	antidepressant
AADEELLMNPRTTY	departmentally
AADEELMNNOORRX	Alexander Monro
AADEELNOPPSTTU	put on a pedestal
AADEENNORSSSST	Tessa Sanderson
AADEENNPPRSSTT	Past and Present
AADEFFGHIORRTY	ready for a fight
AADEFHHLOOORRT	Harold Harefoot
AADEFHIINTTTUW	infatuated with
AADEFHNNOOOSTU	one of a thousand
AADEFHNNORSSST	Fathers and Sons
AADEFIIJKLSSTU	Afsluitdijk Sea
AADEFIILMNORST	self-admiration
AADEFILMMNNSTU	fundamentalism □
AADEFILMNNSTTU	fundamentalist
AADEFILMNNTTUY	fundamentality
AADEFIORRSSSTW	Disasters of War
AADEGGIINNOORV	avoid going near
AADEGGINORSSWY	going-away dress
AADEGHILNRSTUW	daughters-in-law
AADEGHMMNNORST	hammer and tongs
AADEGILNOORTVW	vowel gradation
AADEGINOORRRTT	retrogradation
AADEGMNNORRSST	Anders Ångström
AADEHHHIKNSSTW	shake hands with
AADEHHILOPRRSS	A Shropshire Lad
AADEHHINOPRUVW	have a whip-round
AADEHHLLMOSSTW	Thomas Shadwell
AADEHIIJKLNNPV	Nihanj Kapil Dev
AADEHIILLMNPSU	sulphanilamide
AADEHILNORSTWZ	Alan Dershowitz
AADEHINNNOOSTU	one in a thousand
AADEHINNOPSSSU	diaphanousness
AADEHJLNNORSTU	Joan Sutherland
AADEHLLLNORSSX	Halldór Laxness
AADEHLNNNOOSSY	lay one's hands on
AADEHNORRSSTTW	north-eastwards
AADEIIILLMMPRW	William Dampier
AADEIIILNNOSST	desalinisation
AADEIIILNNOSTZ	desalinization
AADEIIILNOTTVZ	devitalization
AADEIIIMNRSTTV	administrative
AADEIILLLMNTWY	William Tyndale
AADEIILLLNTUVY	antediluvially
AADEIILMNNNOOT	denominational
AADEIILMNOORTZ	demoralization
AADEIILNOOPRTZ	depolarization
AADEIIMNNNOSST	Sistine Madonna
AADEIIMNNORSSV	animadversions
AADEIIOPPPRRST	disappropriate
AADEIKLLNSTUWY	walk unsteadily
AADEILMMRRSTYY	radial symmetry
AADEILMNOORTYY	early day motion
AADEILNNORTUUV	undervaluation
AADEILNOOPSSST	at one's disposal
AADEINOPPPRRTU	unappropriated
AADELNNOOPSWWY	lay down weapons
AADFFIIIILNOST	disaffiliation
AADFFIIILNPQRU	liquid paraffin
AADFFIIIMNORST	disaffirmation
AADFFINORSSTUU	fast and furious
AADFGIILLNNOST	floating island
AADFHILLNOORYY	hooly and fairly
AADFIIILNNNOST	Finlandisation
AADFIIILNNNOTZ	Finlandization
AADFIIILNNRSSS	Frisian Islands
AADGGIINNOPPRZ	propagandizing
AADGGINNORRRWY	Garry Winogrand
AADGHHIMNNORTW	right-hand woman
AADGHHINNORTUW	hang around with
AADGHILNOOOTTV	having a lot to do
AADGHILNOOSTTU	hold out against
AADGIILNPRTTUY	pituitary gland
AADGINNOORSTUY	Rogation Sunday
AADGINNOOSSTUU	Augusto Sandino
AADHHLOOSSSUWY	as who should say
AADHILMNSSTWYY	Wayland's Smithy
AADHILNOPRTUWY	play around with
AADHIMNRRSSTTY	Tristram Shandy
AADHLMNNNOOORT	London Marathon
AADHOOOSTTUWYY	what do you say to?

Words marked □ can also be spelled with an initial capital letter

AADIIILMNORSTT traditionalism
AADIIILNNOOTVV Antonio Vivaldi
AADIIILNNORSTU solitudinarian
AADIIILNORSTTT traditionalist
AADIIILNORTTTY traditionality
AADIIIMNNORSTT administration
AADIILNNNOORTT nontraditional
AADIMNOOORRSTY radio astronomy
AAEEEEFLMNORSS means of release
AAEEEEGGHMNRTU Hague Agreement
AAEEEEGHLLNRTW the general weal
AAEEEEGLNRSSTT Estates General
AAEEEEGNPRRTWY Peter Greenaway
AAEEEEHKKNSTTW weak at the knees
AAEEEFGHNOORST The Age of Reason
AAEEEFHKNORSSV for heaven's sake
AAEEEFHLMNOPTT Temple of Athena
AAEEEFINORRSTT area of interest
AAEEEFKMOORSST make so free as to
AAEEEFLMNSSTTT false statement
AAEEEGHHKMNNRT Kenneth Grahame
AAEEEGHIMRSTTT State Hermitage
AAEEEGHINORVVY have a roving eye
AAEEEGHLMNRRSY Hamersley Range
AAEEEGLNORTTTX to a large extent
AAEEEGMNNPRRRT prearrangement
AAEEEGNORTTTTX to a great extent
AAEEEHHHKRRSTT the Earthshaker
AAEEEHHIPRSSTY hyperaesthesia
AAEEEHHLMNNPTT The Elephant Man
AAEEEHHMNOOSSV have as one's home
AAEEEHIKMRRSTT raise the market
AAEEEHILLOOSTV have a tile loose
AAEEEHKKKNRSTW The Kraken Wakes
AAEEEIKLNPRSTU take pleasure in
AAEEEILLSSTTTT satellite state
AAEEEILMNRTTVY maternity leave
AAEEEILNPRTTVY paternity leave
AAEEEILPPSTTUX sexual appetite
AAEEEJLNOPPPPR jalapeño pepper
AAEEEKLLMMNRSU Emmanuel Lasker
AAEEEKMMNOOPSY make someone pay
AAEEEKMMORRTWY make more watery
AAEEENRRSSTVVW transverse wave
AAEEFFFOORSTTW a waste of effort
AAEEFFILLNOOSV avail oneself of
AAEEFGGLRRSTTU after a struggle
AAEEFGHHHLOTUV have the laugh of
AAEEFGHILLNRRT larger than life
AAEEFGHORSSTTY The Forsyte Saga
AAEEFGINOORRSV give a reason for
AAEEFGIOPRSSST rites of passage
AAEEFGLLMRRRTU Margaret Fuller
AAEEFHHLORSTTT salt of the earth
AAEEFIKKMOOTTU take a mike out of
AAEEFIKOORSTTU take a rise out of
AAEEFILLNOSTTX self-exaltation
AAEEFILMNNSTTT final statement
AAEEFILMNPRSST present as a film
AAEEFILMNRSSTT flame-resistant
AAEEFIMNORSTTY Treaty of Amiens
AAEEFLMMNOOPRT Temple of Amon-Ra
AAEEGGHIIMMNRV give a hammering
AAEEGGHIMNORRT the roaring game
AAEEGGHLLMORRS George Marshall
AAEEGGHMNOOPRT go on the rampage
AAEEGGIIILLLLO Galileo Galilei
AAEEGGMNRRSSUV Musgrave Ranges
AAEEGHHLORSTTU tough as leather
AAEEGHIKMRTTTW make watertight
AAEEGHIKNSSTTY take things easy
AAEEGHIRRSTWYY Eighty Years' War
AAEEGIILNNORTZ generalization
AAEEGIILNNOTVZ evangelization
AAEEGIILORSSTV Évariste Galois
AAEEGILNORSSSS raise one's glass
AAEEGILNRSSTVY asseveratingly
AAEEGKOPRRRSSS A Rake's Progress
AAEEGLMNPRRTUY regular payment
AAEEGMNOPRSSSU rampageousness
AAEEGMNORSTTTU greatest amount
AAEEGNOPRSSTTY one-stage pastry
AAEEHIIKMNSTWW What Maisie Knew
AAEEHIILLMORSZ Alois Alzheimer
AAEEHILMPPRSSS plasmapheresis
AAEEHILOPRRTTT the proletariat
AAEEHIMNRSSSTU amateurishness
AAEEHINORSTTTW weather station
AAEEHKLLMNOSTY Thomas Keneally
AAEEHMNNOOOTVY have one too many
AAEEHOPRRSTUWY warehouse party
AAEEIILLMNRSSW Serena Williams
AAEEIILNNORTTZ eternalization
AAEEIILNOPRRST proletarianise
AAEEIILNOPRRTZ proletarianize
AAEEIJLMMNPRSS Miss Jane Marple
AAEEIKMMNNOSST mistake one's man
AAEEILMNRSTTTY testamentarily
AAEEILMOPSTUYY may it please you
AAEEILNNPRRTTY interplanetary
AAEEILNPPRSTTY paisley pattern
AAEEIMNPRSTTTV pavement artist
AAEEINNOPSSSST passionateness
AAEEINRRSSTTTW water-resistant
AAEEKLLNOPRSTY take personally
AAEELNNNPSSSTU unpleasantness
AAEELNNOOTTTVW not want to leave
AAEEMNNOPPRSWW newspaperwoman
AAEENOPRRSSSYY say one's prayers
AAEFFIIILMORST forisfamiliate
AAEFFILNOSTTUX in a state of flux
AAEFGHIIKLNORV have a liking for
AAEFGHIIKMNOTT make a night of it
AAEFGIMMORSUVY give a summary of
AAEFGLLNOOPRTT fore-topgallant
AAEFGLOOPPRRTV get approval for
AAEFHHMMOOTTTU foam at the mouth
AAEFHIILMNTWYY in the family way
AAEFHIMNOOORSS Heraion of Samos
AAEFIINNORRSTT fraternisation
AAEFIINNORRTTZ fraternization
AAEFILLLNNOOTW fellow national

AAEFILNNOORRTU funeral oration
AAEFILOPPRRSST plaster of Paris
AAEFIMNORRSTTV transformative
AAEFKKNNNORRTT Frank Tarkenton
AAEFLLNNOOPSTU pull a fast one on
AAEFLLNOPRRRUU funeral parlour
AAEFLNOORRTWZZ worn to a frazzle
AAEGGGLNNORSTU strong language
AAEGGHIIINNSTV inveigh against
AAEGGHIILMMNRT thermal imaging
AAEGGHIINNNTTY eating anything
AAEGGIIILLNNRW Gillian Wearing
AAEGGIIKLNOTTV give a talking-to
AAEGHHLLMNORRT Martha Gellhorn
AAEGHIILLNRTXY exhilaratingly
AAEGHIIRRSTTTV right as a trivet
AAEGHIKLOPRTTW walk a tightrope
AAEGHILNOOSTTW against the wool
AAEGHIMNOPRSTY Pythagoreanism
AAEGHINOSTTUWY what's eating you?
AAEGIIILNNOTTZ gelatinization
AAEGIILMRSSTUU Miguel Asturias
AAEGIILNNPSTTU insulating tape
AAEGIILNQRTUUY equiangularity
AAEGIINNNRSSSU sanguinariness
AAEGIINNOORRTZ reorganization
AAEGILLMNNOPRT Long Parliament
AAEGILNNNORRST internal organs
AAEGILNNNORTTW wanting to learn
AAEGILRSSTTTUU sagittal suture
AAEGIMNNSSTUUW August Weismann
AAEGLLMMNNRRUY Murray Gell-Mann
AAEHIILLMMNRSW William Sherman
AAEHIILLMNRSTW William Shatner
AAEHIIMOORTVWW A Room with a View
AAEHILLMNOPSTT mental hospital
AAEHIRRRSTTWYY Thirty Years' War
AAEHJMOOORRSST José Ramos-Horta
AAEHKLOPPRSSTY speak sharply to
AAEHKMMOOOPRTU make a poor mouth
AAEHLMNNOOSTUX xanthomelanous
AAEIIIILNRSTTU utilitarianise
AAEIIIILNRTTUZ utilitarianize
AAEIIIKLLMNNRW William Rankine
AAEIIIKNNORTTZ keratinization
AAEIIILLMMNNRS millenarianism
AAEIIILMNNORTZ mineralization
AAEIIILNNOORST Antonio Salieri
AAEIIILNORTTVZ revitalization
AAEIIINNNRSSST insanitariness
AAEIIINNRRSTUV universitarian
AAEIILLNNORSTT reinstallation
AAEIILLNPRSTTY interspatially
AAEIILLRRTTUVY virtual reality
AAEIILMNNOSSST sensationalism
AAEIILNNORTTUZ neutralization
AAEIILNNOSSSTT sensationalist
AAEIILNQTTTUVY quantitatively
AAEIIMOPPPRRST misappropriate
AAEIINNPPRRSTT antiperspirant
anti-perspirant
AAEIINOPRSSTTU pasteurisation
AAEIINOPRSTTUZ pasteurization
AAEIJKMNNOPRSS James Parkinson
AAEILLLMNOOPRT parallel motion
AAEILLMNNNPSTT instalment plan
AAEILLMNNPPRTW Walter Lippmann
AAEILMMNPPRRTU Rump Parliament
AAEILNORRRSTTT transliterator
AAEINNNOPRSTUU superannuation
AAEINNOOPTTTTY pay attention to
AAEJLLNNOOOPRT Joanna Trollope
AAEKNOPRRRSSTW work as partners
AAELLMNOPRUVVY pulmonary valve
AAELLNPRRSTUUY supernaturally
AAEOORRRSSUYYY say you are sorry
AAEORRRRSSSTTU Sartor Resartus
AAFFFHINOOORRU affair of honour
AAFGHIINNOPSSS passing fashion
AAFGIILLMNNNPY family planning
AAFGINOPPRRSTY past praying for
AAFHIIILMNRTUW unfamiliar with
AAFIIIMNNORRTU uniformitarian
AAFIIKMNNOORST ask information
AAFIINOORRTTTW war of attrition
AAFIMNNOORRSTT transformation
AAGGHLMNOORSTU South Glamorgan
AAGGIIILNNRTTY ingratiatingly
AAGHHIILLMORTW William Hogarth
AAGHIIPRRSSTTT stratigraphist
AAGHILMNNOQSUV having no qualms
AAGIIIMNNSSTUU Augustinianism
AAGIIIMNOSTTTZ stigmatization
AAGIIINNNOOPSV Giovanni Pisano
AAGIILOOPRSSTT parasitologist
AAGIIMNNORRSTT transmigration
AAGILLNRSSSTTT starting stalls
AAGIMNORRRSTTY transmigratory
AAHIIILLLMTTWZ William Hazlitt
AAHIKLMNOPRRTT Martin Klaproth
AAHILLNRRSTUUV Arthur Sullivan
AAHILNORRSTTUY natural history
AAHMMNOORSSSTU satan's mushroom
AAIIIILMNORTTZ militarization
AAIIIILMNRSTTU utilitarianism
AAIIIILNORTTVZ trivialization
AAIIIIMNNRRSTT Trinitarianism
AAIIIKLLNOOVVV Nikolai Vavilov
AAIIILLNOOTTVZ volatilization
AAIIILMMNORSTT arms limitation
AAIIILMNOOPTTZ optimalization
AAIIINNORSSTUZ Russianization
AAIIJKLNNSSVVY Vaslav Nijinsky
AAIILLLNORSTTU illustrational
AAIILLMNOOTTVY motivationally
AAIILLNNORSTTY transitionally
AAIILMNNORSSST transmissional
AAIILMNNORSSTT mistranslation
AAIILNOOPPRTUZ popularization
AAIIMNOORRSSTZ Zoroastrianism
AAIKMNNOORSTUZ Ozark Mountains
AAILMNNORSSTWY Wynton Marsalis

AAILMNNORSTTTU	ultramontanist
AAINNOOPRRSTTT	transportation
ABBCDEEEHMORRS	robes-de-chambre
ABBCDEEHIKNNOS	behind one's back
ABBCDEEIMOORST	discomboberate
ABBCDEGHIKMPRU	humpback bridge
ABBCDEIIMNNORY	incendiary bomb
ABBCDEILMOOSTU	discombobulate
ABBCEEEIMNOORR	become airborne
ABBCEEFFIIKNST	Babinski effect
ABBCEGLLNOOOTU	Launcelot Gobbo
ABBCEHLNNOSTTU	Hubble constant
ABBCEHLNOORRSU	Charles Bourbon
ABBCEIILLMOTTW	William Cobbett
ABBCIJKNOOORSW	Jacob Bronowski
ABBDDEEELORSTU	double-breasted
ABBDEEEEFORSTT	best-before date
ABBDEEEHLNRSST	Bran the Blessed
ABBDEEEIJMNSWW	James Edwin Webb
ABBDEFHINNORST	forbid the banns
ABBDEGIIORRTTT	Brigitte Bardot
ABBDFIILNNOOTT	not a blind bit of
ABBDGIIILNNRRY	library binding
ABBDIIIILNTTUY	indubitability
ABBEEEFFHLLORT	bear off the bell
ABBEEEKLLORRTW	Robert Bakewell
ABBEEFHHIINOTT	be in the habit of
ABBEEHHIIRTTTW	The White Rabbit
ABBEEHINNOOPRT	phenobarbitone
ABBEEIJLMNNRTU	Benjamin Butler
ABBEEIKNNNOTTY	not be taken in by
ABBEEINNOOPRTT	pentobarbitone
ABBEGILLMNRRTU	tumbling-barrel
ABBEHNOOORTTTU	not bother about
ABBEIIIILLMORSW	Robbie Williams
ABCCCEEEEENRSX	exacerbescence
ABCCCEEHKLNSUY	Buckley's chance
ABCCCEHILMNORU	chamber council
ABCCDEFIILOORS	blood-sacrifice
ABCCDEGINORRTT	contract bridge
ABCCEEEELRSSSU	causes célèbres
ABCCEEELORRRTX	cerebral cortex
ABCCEEFHILNOST	chief constable
ABCCEEHIIKNNTT	kitchen cabinet
ABCCEEIIKRRRTU	circuit-breaker
ABCCEEIILLNORR	irreconcilable
ABCCEEILLNNORU	unreconcilable
ABCCEHHLMRSSUY	Church Assembly
ABCCEHLOORSTTY	Charles Boycott
ABCCEIIILNOTVY	conceivability
ABCCEIILLNORRY	irreconcilably
ABCCEIILMMNNOU	incommunicable
ABCCEIILNNPSUU	public nuisance
ABCCEILMNNOSTU	Uncle Tom's Cabin
ABCCEILNNNOOSU	unconscionable
ABCCGINNOORTTU	bring to account
ABCCHILOOPRSTU	claustrophobic
ABCCIILMMNNOUY	incommunicably
ABCCILNNNOOSUY	unconscionably
ABCCINOOORRSTT	boa constrictor
ABCDDEEILNNORT	Benedict Arnold
ABCDDEELMNOOPU	decompoundable
ABCDDIIINNNOOT	in bad condition
ABCDEEEELLNSST	delectableness
ABCDEEEELORSTU	decree absolute
ABCDEEEEORRRRT	breeder reactor
ABCDEEEHIILNPR	indecipherable
ABCDEEEHKORRRT	break the record
ABCDEEEHLNNOPT	cannot be helped
ABCDEEELLOOORT	Colorado beetle
ABCDEEFLLNORTY	reflect badly on
ABCDEEGHIIMRRS	Cambridgeshire
ABCDEEGHIJNSTU	subject heading
ABCDEEGIKNORRR	record-breaking
ABCDEEHINPRSSS	herbs and spices
ABCDEEHNOOPRRY	beyond reproach
ABCDEEIILNNORS	inconsiderable
ABCDEFIIMOORRT	imbricated roof
ABCDEGIIILPRTY	credibility gap
ABCDEGIILLMPTU	Public Image Ltd
ABCDEGILNOSTTU	Doubting-Castle
ABCDEHILLNNORS	Charles Blondin
ABCDEIIILPRTTY	predictability
ABCDEIILNNORSY	inconsiderably
ABCDEIMNNOOORX	carbon monoxide
ABCDEINNORRTTU	burnt to a cinder
ABCDENOOORRRTU	uncorroborated
ABCDIIIILOSSTY	dissociability
ABCEEEEEHKKLOO	Lake Okeechobee
ABCEEEEFHLNSTT	fence the tables
ABCEEEEILNRSSV	receivableness
ABCEEEFHINNOST	in the absence of
ABCEEEFLORRTTY	refectory table
ABCEEEGMNNOPRT	become pregnant
ABCEEEHHLLPSTY	clap by the heels
ABCEEEHIILMNNT	Michael Bentine
ABCEEEHMRRRSTU	Herbert Marcuse
ABCEEEIILPRSST	respectabilise
ABCEEEIILPRSTZ	respectabilize
ABCEEEMNOSSSTT	asbestos cement
ABCEEFGHILLNOX	bill of exchange
ABCEEGHIKLOORT	globe artichoke
ABCEEGILLLLLOO	Balliol College
ABCEEGILLNRSUY	subgenerically
ABCEEGILNNORUZ	unrecognizable
ABCEEGKNNOOSTW	get one's own back
ABCEEGORSTTUUV	Gustave Courbet
ABCEEHHHRTTTUY	bury the hatchet
ABCEEHIIKSTTTU	take the biscuit
ABCEEIIIILRSTVY	serviceability
ABCEEIILORRTVY	recoverability
ABCEEIILPRSTTY	respectability
ABCEEIKLLMNOOR	Colin Blakemore
ABCEEILMNOOSTT	most noticeable
ABCEEILNNNORUY	Laurence Binyon
ABCEEILNNOSSSU	unsociableness
ABCEEILNOOPRSS	sociable person
ABCEEINORRRSST	Cartier-Bresson
ABCEEIORRSSSTT	cross batteries
ABCEELLLRRSTUV	Travellers Club
ABCEELMORRSTUY	Curtley Ambrose
ABCEELNOPSTTTY	petty constable

ABCEEMMMNORSUU	mucous membrane
ABCEEOOPRRSSTU	a sop to Cerberus
ABCEFFFHKOOOTT	off the back foot
ABCEFIIIINOSTV	beatific vision
ABCEGHHIKLNORT	knight bachelor
	knight-bachelor
ABCEGHIKNPSSTU	passing the buck
ABCEGHIMNOSTTU	bathing costume
	bathing-costume
ABCEGIIKLNPPSU	public speaking
ABCEGIILOORSTT	bacteriologist
ABCEHHIILORRST	British cholera
ABCEHIILMOPTTW	compatible with
ABCEHILLLOPRYY	hyperbolically
ABCEHLMNOOPRTU	Roehampton Club
ABCEHLNNOORRSS	Charles Bronson
ABCEHMNNORRSTU	Robert Schumann
ABCEIIIILNTTXY	inexcitability
ABCEIIILNTTUXY	unexcitability
ABCEIIILORRTVY	irrevocability
ABCEIIKLLLMUWY	William Buckley
ABCEIILRRSSTUY	irresuscitably
ABCEIINOOPSSUV	above suspicion
ABCEIINOPRRRTT	Robert Pitcairn
ABCEIKKLNRSTUY	Stanley Kubrick
ABCEKNNNOORSTU	turn one's back on
ABCELLLNNOORTU	uncontrollable
ABCELMMNOOORRU	common labourer
ABCELMNPRRTUUU	lumbar puncture
ABCELNOSSTUUUY	subcutaneously
ABCFIILMNOORTY	conformability
ABCFKNOOPRTTTU	put back to front
ABCGHHILLMNRUU	Hurlingham Club
ABCHIIKLNOSTUY	unshockability
ABCIIILLLOPSTY	collapsibility
ABCIIILLOORSUU	Louis Roubiliac
ABCIIILNRSTTUY	inscrutability
ABCIILMNOOSTUU	bituminous coal
ABCILLLNNOORTY	incontrollably
ABCILMNORSTUUY	rambunctiously
ABCLLLNNOORTUY	uncontrollably
ABDDDEEMOORVYY	over my dead body
ABDDEEEHLLNSSU	bull-headedness
ABDDEEEHNNOOST	on one's deathbed
ABDDEEFFINOOOX	of no fixed abode
ABDDEEHHNOORTT	hot and bothered
ABDDEEIIJLMNOU	diamond jubilee
ABDDEEILMNNSTY	absent-mindedly
ABDDEFGHIINOTT	at the bidding of
ABDDEFGIMORRST	Stamford Bridge
ABDDEGIINNNRSW	bending inwards
ABDDEGIINNORUV	David Ben-Gurion
ABDDEIIKORTVWZ	David Berkowitz
ABDDELNOORTUUY	roundaboutedly
ABDDFMNOOORRWX	Ford Madox Brown
ABDEEEEILNRSST	deliberateness
ABDEEEELNSSSTT	detestableness
ABDEEEGHINRSST	big-heartedness
ABDEEEGHNORTTY	the Great Beyond
ABDEEEGILNOTUV	double negative
ABDEEEGILNRSST	single-breasted
ABDEEEGINOPRST	pigeon-breasted
ABDEEEHILNNORT	on the breadline
ABDEEEHILNOSVY	heavenly bodies
ABDEEEHINNOOST	on one's head be it
ABDEEEIILLRTVY	deliberatively
ABDEEEIILMNNRT	indeterminable
ABDEEEIINNOPZZ	benzodiazepine
ABDEEEILNNNSSU	undeniableness
ABDEEEILNOPRTU	deliberate upon
ABDEEEIMNNOOTV	above-mentioned
ABDEEELLNOPRSS	deplorableness
ABDEEEMNNNOOSS	on one's beam ends
	on one's beam-ends
ABDEEFHHINRSTT	farthest behind
ABDEEFHHOORRTT	Order of the Bath
ABDEEFHIMNNRSS	fisherman's bend
ABDEEFHNOOPSTU	bend out of shape
ABDEEFIIILNNTU	unidentifiable
ABDEEFILLLNORS	bells of Ireland
ABDEEFILMNORSS	formidableness
ABDEEFLNORTTUV	Battle of Verdun
ABDEEGHIILNTTW	being dealt with
ABDEEGHIIRSSST	Bright's disease
ABDEEGIKMNNPRS	Dennis Bergkamp
ABDEEGKNNORRUW	break new ground
ABDEEHIIILRTTY	hereditability
ABDEEHKOOOORRT	Dorothea Brooke
ABDEEIIILQRSTU	disequilibrate
ABDEEIIJMNORSS	Miss Jean Brodie
ABDEEIILMNNRTY	indeterminably
ABDEEIILMNSSSS	admissibleness
ABDEEILMMSTUWY	Wembley Stadium
ABDEEILMNNORST	indemonstrable
ABDEEINNORSSSS	in sober sadness
ABDEELLNORRSTY	Albert Reynolds
ABDEELMNNORSTU	undemonstrable
ABDEELNNORSSSU	danseurs nobles
ABDEFGHLLNOSUU	bundle of laughs
ABDEFHILLNNSSS	flash blindness
ABDEFHLLLNORSS	Blashford-Snell
ABDEFIIILLNORT	defibrillation
ABDEFIILMNOPRT	find it a problem
ABDEFMOOORRSTW	from bad to worse
ABDEGGIKNNORRU	ground-breaking
ABDEGHIIJLNOOR	John Logie Baird
ABDEGHLMNORTUU	rough-and-tumble
ABDEGHLNOORTWW	draw the long bow
ABDEGIILLNNRRY	lending library
ABDEGIILLNRSST	Gilbert Islands
ABDEGIIOSSTUVY	give a subsidy to
ABDEGINOOPRRUY	I beg your pardon?
ABDEHHLMNRSTUY	rhythm and blues
ABDEHILNOPRSUY	Rhapsody in Blue
ABDEHLMNNORRTU	Northumberland
ABDEIIIILMNOOTZ	demobilization
ABDEIIILNORRTY	library edition
ABDEIILMMNOOPS	Bolson de Mapimi
ABDEIILNOORTWZ	bowdlerization
ABDEILMNNORSTY	indemonstrably
ABDEILMORSTUXY	ambidextrously
ABDEINNNOORSSY	in one's born days

ABDENNOORSSTUU	roundaboutness
ABDFGHOORRRTUW	brought forward
ABDFLLMNNORTUU	Rudolf Bultmann
ABDFNOOOPRSSSU	basso profundos
ABDGHIMNOOSTTU	doubting Thomas
ABDGIINOOORSTV	Good Vibrations
ABDIIIILMNOTTY	indomitability
ABDIIINORSTTTU	disattribution
ABDIILMOPRTUWY	upward mobility
ABEEEEFHMORSTU	be the measure of
ABEEEEHILNQTUZ	Queen Elizabeth
ABEEEFGHNOORTZ	The Age of Bronze
ABEEEFHLNORSTT	one's better half
ABEEEFIIKLMNST	mistaken belief
ABEEEFILMMORRT	fail to remember
ABEEEFILNNRRTT	enfant terrible
ABEEEGGKMNNOOT	engagement book
ABEEEGHHIMOTTW	weigh to the beam
ABEEEGHIIKMMTT	make the big time
ABEEEGILLNPSTT	sleeping tablet
ABEEEGIMNNRTUV	negative number
ABEEEHIILLLSTV	Elisabethville
ABEEEHIJKNOPRS	Josephine Baker
ABEEEHIKLNNTYZ	Elizabeth Kenny
ABEEEHIKLRTTTY	take the liberty
ABEEEHKMNOSTTY	by the same token
ABEEEHLNRSSSST	breathlessness
ABEEEIILNNRSTT	Albert Einstein
ABEEEIILNNSSTV	inevitableness
ABEEEIKMOPRRRS	promise-breaker
ABEEEILMNNRSST	terminableness
ABEEEILNNOPRSS	inoperableness
ABEEEINORRRSTV	reverberations
ABEEELLNNRSSUV	vulnerableness
ABEEELMMNORSTY	Belém Monastery
ABEEELNNOPRSSS	personableness
ABEEERRRRSTTWY	strawberry tree
ABEEFGGNOPRRST	Gräfenberg spot
ABEEFGIORSSTTT	get to first base
ABEEFHIIKLNRTZ	Elizabeth Frink
ABEEFHIMNOORST	Bohemian Forest
ABEEFIIKLNOPTT	Battle of Pinkie
ABEEFIILMNRTTY	fermentability
ABEEFILNOPRSST	profitableness
ABEEFKLMOOORRS	break loose from
ABEEFMNORRRSTY	embryo transfer
ABEEFORSSTTTTY	battery of tests
ABEEGGHIINNNTT	at the beginning
ABEEGGLNORRSUY	George Lansbury
ABEEGHHIKNRSTT	high-street bank
ABEEGHIILNSTUX	extinguishable
ABEEGHINPRRRTU	bring up the rear
ABEEGIIIJKLLNN	Billie Jean King
ABEEGILMNNRRSU	in large numbers
ABEEGIMNNRRSTU	in great numbers
ABEEGINNORRRST	Roger Bannister
ABEEHHIQRRSTTU	Herbert Asquith
ABEEHILNOPSSST	hospitableness
ABEEHILNRRTTUU	turn the air blue
ABEEHKNOPRSTTU	put the brakes on
ABEEHLMNNOPRRT	Robert Helpmann
ABEEHLNNOORSSU	honourableness
ABEEHLOORTTTTW	hot-water bottle
ABEEIIILMMPRTY	impermeability
ABEEIIILMNNSST	inimitableness
ABEEIIILNNOTVZ	Annie Leibovitz
ABEEIILLNNOSSV	inviolableness
ABEEIILMNOPRSS	impressionable
ABEEIIMNNNNOOT	innominate bone
ABEEIKPRRSSTUY	take by surprise
ABEEILLPRRSTYY	presbyterially
ABEEILMNNNOSTU	unmentionables
ABEEILNNOOSWWY	elbow one's way in
ABEEILNNOQSTUU	unquestionable
ABEEILNNSSSTUU	unsuitableness
ABEEIMNOSSSSTU	abstemiousness
ABEEKLNNORSSUW	unworkableness
ABEENNNNOORTVW	Anton von Webern
ABEFFGHHIORTTT	right off the bat
ABEFFHIIKORTTW	break it off with
ABEFGGNNOORSTU	burn one's faggot
ABEFGIIILNRRTY	refrangibility
ABEFGNNOOORRTU	gone for a Burton
ABEFHHILLOOSTT	Battle of Shiloh
ABEFIIILRRTTUY	irrefutability
ABEFILNOOPRSST	self-absorption
ABEFKLOOOOSTTV	Battle of Kosovo
ABEFLLNOOPSSTU	tablespoonfuls
ABEGGHHINORRTU	rough breathing
ABEGGIIIILMNNO	Beniamino Gigli
ABEGHHLNOOOSTW	whole bang shoot
ABEGHHMOPRRTUY	Humphrey Bogart
ABEGHILMNOPRSV	having problems
ABEGHKNORRRRTU	Arthur Kornberg
ABEGHNNORSSTUY	Anthony Burgess
ABEGHNORRTUWWY	rub the wrong way
ABEGIIILLLMRTW	William Gilbert
ABEGIIILMNPRTY	impregnability
ABEGIILNOORSST	obligatoriness
ABEGIINNRRRRSU	barrier nursing
ABEGIINORRTTVY	bring variety to
ABEGILMNRSTTUU	Sturmabteilung
ABEHHIJNOPSTTT	John the Baptist
ABEHHKOOORTTTW	throw the book at
ABEHHOOPSTTTUU	push the boat out
ABEHIILLMNNOWY	William H Bonney
ABEHIKNNOOTTUW	in the know about
ABEHINNNORSTUY	Hanbury-Tenison
ABEIIILLNORTTY	intolerability
ABEIIILMNNRTUY	innumerability
ABEIIILMORRTVY	irremovability
ABEIIILNPRSTUY	insuperability
ABEIIILPRSSTUY	persuasibility
ABEIIKLLMNORRT	Robert Millikan
ABEILLMOOSSTTT	Tobias Smollett
ABEILMNNORSTUU	insurmountable
ABEILMNOSSTTUU	most unsuitable
ABEILNNOQSTUUY	unquestionably
ABEILNORSSSSUU	salubriousness
ABEINORRSSTTTU	burst into tears
ABELMNNORSTUUU	unsurmountable
ABFIIIIJLSTTUY	justifiability

ABFLMMOOOSSTUU	Tomb of Mausolus
ABGHIINOSTTUWY	what's biting you?
ABGIIIKMNNNOTU	mountain biking
ABGLNOORRSTTUY	Glastonbury Tor
ABHIIINOOPRRTY	prohibitionary
ABIIIILLMPSTUY	implausibility
ABIIIILMMNOOTZ	immobilization
ABIILLNORSSUUY	insalubriously
ABILMNNORSTUUY	insurmountably
ABILNOOOPPRRTY	proportionably
ACCCDEEEEFNPRT	perfect cadence
ACCCDEEEIILMNS	medical science
ACCCDEEFIOOPRT	code of practice
ACCCEEEHISSSUV	achieve success
ACCCEEEIILLNPS	special licence
ACCCEEFFHINORY	Chancery Office
ACCCEEHIILLPRR	parhelic circle
ACCCEEHKLNNOSU	chance one's luck
ACCCEEIILLRRTV	vertical circle
ACCCEEIILSSSTU	Ecclesiasticus
ACCCEFINOOPRRT	Tropic of Cancer
ACCCEHHHIILNTT	technical hitch
ACCCEHIILLNNOR	chilli con carne
ACCCEHIINOORSS	onchocerciasis
ACCCEHIINORSTT	architectonics
ACCCEILLNNORTY	concentrically
ACCCEIMMNOOORS	macroeconomics
ACCCENNOOPRUWY	owner-occupancy
ACCCENNORRTTUU	current account
ACCCGIIIMNOOPU	Giacomo Puccini
ACCCGINNOOSTTU	cost-accounting
ACCCHLOOPSSTUY	staphylococcus
ACCCILLOSSSSUU	locus classicus
ACCCILNOOSSSSU	class-conscious
ACCDDDEKLOOOOO	cock-a-doodle-doo
ACCDDEEEHIILRV	heraldic device
ACCDEEEEEKNPRT	take precedence
ACCDEEEEELMMRR	crème de la crème
ACCDEEEFHINNOV	have confidence
ACCDEEEHHIKNRT	chicken-hearted
ACCDEEEHNPRSST	crescent-shaped
ACCDEEEINNPRSS	ens per accidens
ACCDEEFFIILMOR	Medical Officer
	medical officer
ACCDEEHIKLNRSS	Charles Dickens
ACCDEEHIKRRRTT	three-card trick
ACCDEEILOORRST	crocodile tears
ACCDEEIMNOPPTY	appendicectomy
ACCDEEINNNOSTU	discountenance
ACCDEEINNOORST	deconsecration
ACCDEELLOOSTUW	allow to succeed
ACCDEEMNOSSSTU	accustomedness
ACCDEENNNORTTU	unconcentrated
ACCDEFNNOORTUU	unaccounted-for
ACCDEGIILLNOOV	Calvin Coolidge
ACCDEGMOORSTUW	grow accustomed
ACCDEHIIORRRST	director's chair
ACCDEHILMNOPSU	unaccomplished
ACCDEHINORSSUW	sandwich course
ACCDEHLLLNOORR	Lord Chancellor
ACCDEIILLNNOTY	coincidentally

ACCDEIINNNOSTU	discontinuance
ACCDEIMMNOORTY	romantic comedy
ACCDEINOOPSTTU	deposit account
ACCDEMMMNNOOOY	command economy
ACCDEMNOOSTTUU	unaccustomed to
ACCDHHIIOOPPRS	phosphoric acid
ACCDHIMNOPSSYY	psychodynamics
ACCEEEFFIINSTU	efficient cause
ACCEEEFHIKLOST	slice of the cake
ACCEEEFHLLNNOR	conference hall
ACCEEEFHOPRTTU	Peace of Utrecht
ACCEEEFILNPTXY	life expectancy
ACCEEEFLLNNOOS	conceal oneself
ACCEEEGILLLNOR	Linacre College
ACCEEEHHILMRRS	Schleiermacher
ACCEEEHIKNOOST	take one's choice
ACCEEEHKLPPRTU	perpetual check
ACCEEEILOPSTVY	escape velocity
ACCEEELLMOPRTX	Electra complex
ACCEEELLNORTVY	electrovalency
ACCEEENNOPSTUX	expense account
ACCEEEORRSSTUW	Worcester sauce
ACCEEFILLMORTV	collective farm
ACCEEFLLORRSTU	Colles' fracture
ACCEEGHIIKNNOT	icing on the cake
ACCEEGIILRRTTU	electric guitar
ACCEEGIINNORSS	carcinogenesis
ACCEEGILLNNORU	general council
ACCEEGILLNORTY	geocentrically
ACCEEHIILLMOTT	chemical toilet
ACCEEIILLMNORT	electronic mail
ACCEEIINNOORSS	concessionaire
ACCEEIJORRTTUX	juice extractor
ACCEEILLLNORTY	electronically
ACCEEILLLOPSTY	telescopically
ACCEEILLOOPRTT	electro-optical
ACCEEILMOPRSTU	proceleusmatic
ACCEEILNOPRSST	reception class
ACCEEILNOPSTTT	plate tectonics
ACCEEILORSSTTT	electrostatics
ACCEELLMNRSTUY	menstrual cycle
ACCEELLNRRTTUU	cultural centre
ACCEENORSSSUUV	curvaceousness
ACCEFFGIIINNOS	of significance
ACCEFGGHHIINNT	fighting chance
ACCEFGIIIINNNS	insignificance
ACCEFHHIJKORSS	Joschka Fischer
ACCEFHILLMOTUU	Michel Foucault
ACCEFIIILLNSTY	scientifically
ACCEFIIINOPSST	specifications
ACCEFILNNOPRSU	Francis Poulenc
ACCEFILNOOSTTU	Council of State
ACCEFINOOORSTU	course of action
ACCEGGHINNORSU	changing course
ACCEGHHILNOOST	schoolteaching
ACCEGHIILLNNOU	hallucinogenic
ACCEGHIIMNNPRR	Prince Charming
ACCEGHINNOPRST	sporting chance
ACCEGHIOPPRRST	spectrographic
ACCEGIILNRTUXY	excruciatingly
ACCEGIKLLNNORT	central locking

ACCEGKLOPPRUUU	pluck up courage
ACCEHHILLNOPRS	chancellorship
ACCEHHJMOPRSTY	Joseph McCarthy
ACCEHIILLLMNOS	Michael Collins
ACCEHIKLLMOORY	mock-heroically
ACCEHIKMNNOPUY	capuchin monkey
ACCEHILMMNOPST	accomplishment
ACCEHILMNOORRT	chronometrical
ACCEHILNPRSSUY	nuclear physics
ACCEHIMNOPRRSU	proscenium arch
ACCEIIILNNOORT	reconciliation
ACCEIIKKLMPSUW	Samuel Pickwick
ACCEIIKLNNOPRS	Cecil Parkinson
ACCEIILLLOSSTY	solecistically
ACCEIILLMRRSUY	semicircularly
ACCEIILMMNORTT	critical moment
ACCEIILNNRSSTU	uncriticalness
ACCEIILNOORRTY	reconciliatory
ACCEIILORSSTUY	social security
ACCEIINOPRSSSU	capriciousness
ACCEILLNOSSSUY	successionally
ACCEILMMNNOOSS	commonsensical
ACCEILNOORSSST	cross-sectional
ACCEIMMNOORTUX	excommunicator
ACCEIMNOOPRSTU	pococuranteism
ACCELLMOOPRSTT	stamp collector
ACCFFIIINORTTU	fructification
ACCFGILNOORTTT	clotting factor
ACCFHHIKLLNRRU	Frank Churchill
ACCFHHILLLLRSU	Churchill Falls
ACCFIIIIILNOST	silicification
ACCFINNOOOPTTT	point of contact
ACCGHHIILLOOTY	ichthyological
ACCGIILLLMOORY	micrologically
ACCGIIMNORRTUY	circumgyration
ACCGINNOORSSTU	Toucan crossing
ACCHHIMOOORRTT	orthochromatic
ACCHIILLOPRTYY	hypocritically
ACCHIILOOPRSTY	hypocoristical
ACCHILLNNORSYY	synchronically
ACCHNOOPRSTTTU	not up to scratch
ACCIILMNOPRTUU	municipal court
ACCIIMMNNOOSTU	communications
ACCILLOPPRRTYY	procryptically
ACCILMNOOSTUUY	contumaciously
ACCILNNOORSTTU	constructional
ACCIMMNNNNOOTU	non-communicant
ACCJKKLLNOOOPS	Jackson Pollock
ACCLLMOOPRSSUU	corpus callosum
ACDDDEEIILMNST	middle distance
ACDDEEEEIILSVY	easily deceived
ACDDEEEFNNOOTV	deed of covenant
ACDDEEEHLNOOSS	cool-headedness
ACDDEEEINNRSSU	sudden increase
ACDDEEELORSTTY	Decorated style
ACDDEEEMNORRTU	document reader
ACDDEEENORSVYY	every second day
ACDDEEFNNOSSST	stand confessed
ACDDEEGIKLNOSW	disacknowledge
ACDDEEGILNNNOR	endocrine gland
ACDDEEGKLNNOUW	unacknowledged

ACDDEEHHLORRSU	shouldered arch
ACDDEEIKNOPSUW	upside-down cake
ACDDEEIMNOSTTU	undomesticated
ACDDEFIIKNORST	sick and tired of
ACDDEFILOOPPRS	apple of discord
ACDDEGHIORRRRS	Richard Rodgers
ACDDEGHLNOORSS	Charles Dodgson
ACDDEHMNNOOORW	come down hard on
ACDDEIIINNOORT	air-conditioned
ACDDEIIKLNOSVZ	David O Selznick
ACDDEIKMNOORRR	Roderick Random
ACDDELMNOORRTV	Trevor McDonald
ACDDELNOORRSWW	Second World War
ACDDGHINOORRRS	Gordon Richards
ACDDGIILMNOOOP	Plácido Domingo
ACDEEEEGILMNNT	magnetic needle
ACDEEEEHILPRSV	deliver a speech
ACDEEEEHLLRRSW	well-researched
ACDEEEELNNRSUU	Laurence Eusden
ACDEEEFFGILNOR	goal difference
ACDEEEFFHNRSST	far-fetchedness
ACDEEEFFNNSSTU	unaffectedness
ACDEEEFHIRSUVX	chevaux-de-frise
ACDEEEFILNNORT	dolce far niente
ACDEEEFMNNOSTU	come unfastened
ACDEEEGHLLLORS	Herald's College
ACDEEEGHNNOSST	chanson de geste
ACDEEEHHIKNRSV	handkerchieves
ACDEEEHIIMNSTU	Eudemian Ethics
ACDEEEHIMNOPRW	machine-powered
ACDEEEHKLNNRSY	Charles Kennedy
ACDEEEHLLOPRRU	chorale prelude
ACDEEEHNRSTTTU	student teacher
ACDEEEIIMNNPTT	patent medicine
ACDEEEILNORRSY	royal residence
ACDEEEILOOPRST	radio telescope
ACDEEEINNOPQRU	equiponderance
ACDEEEINORSSTV	decorativeness
ACDEEELLLORSTY	closely related
ACDEEELNOPRRUW	nuclear-powered
ACDEEEMOPRRSTU	Peter Scudamore
ACDEEENRRRSTUY	under-secretary
ACDEEFHIINNRSS	disenfranchise
ACDEEFHORRSSTW	chest of drawers
	chest-of-drawers
ACDEEFILLMOPRS	self-proclaimed
ACDEEFINOQRRUY	radio frequency
ACDEEFINRRRSTT	credit transfer
ACDEEGHIIMNNNV	vending machine
ACDEEGHILOOSSW	wild-goose chase
ACDEEGHIMNNNOS	change one's mind
ACDEEGHINNRRTT	right and centre
ACDEEGHLNORRTU	clear the ground
ACDEEGIILNNRSY	declining years
ACDEEGIILNPRTY	depreciatingly
ACDEEGIIMNORRZ	organized crime
ACDEEGIIRSTTTV	digestive tract
ACDEEGILNNOQRU	grandiloquence
ACDEEGIMNORSTU	discouragement
ACDEEGKLMNNOTW	acknowledgment
ACDEEGNOORSTUU	cause to undergo

ACDEEHHIKNSTTW	what the dickens
ACDEEHHILMNORR	Michael Hordern
ACDEEHHILNOPST	Daphnis et Chloé
ACDEEHHINNRSVY	Henry Cavendish
ACDEEHHKKNNOOT	knock on the head
ACDEEHIIINNRST	disinheritance
ACDEEHIIINRSST	dechristianise
ACDEEHIIINRSTZ	dechristianize
ACDEEHIILLNRRV	Richard Neville
ACDEEHIINRSTTW	Christian de Wet
ACDEEHILLNNOST	Achilles' tendon
ACDEEHILMNOSST	methodicalness
ACDEEHIMNNNSTT	disenchantment
ACDEEHINNOOPRT	drop in the ocean
ACDEEHINOOPPRT	apprenticehood
ACDEEHMNNOOOST	come to one's hand
ACDEEILMRSSTTU	striated muscle
ACDEEIMMMOPRRS	promise-crammed
ACDEEIMMNNOORT	recommendation
ACDEEIMMNOOPRS	remain composed
ACDEEIMMNORSTV	inverted commas
ACDEEIMNNOSTWW	casement window
ACDEELLMNNOTTY	malcontentedly
ACDEELNNNRSTTY	transcendently
ACDEEMMNOORRTY	recommendatory
ACDEENNORRSUVY	Ordnance Survey
ACDEENOOOORTVW	wooden overcoat
ACDEFHMNNOPRRY	pardon my French
ACDEFIIIINNOTT	identification
ACDEFIIINNOSTY	Disneyfication
ACDEFIIINOOTTX	detoxification
ACDEFIILLNNOTY	confidentially
ACDEFIIMOORSST	dissociate from
ACDEGHHIIKOSSU	his cake is dough
ACDEGHHIILLMNO	Michael Holding
ACDEGHILLMOOOT	methodological
ACDEGHIMNORRRS	marching orders
	marching-orders
ACDEGIIIKMNNOS	decision-making
ACDEGIILLOOSTT	dialectologist
ACDEGIMNNNORTU	countermanding
ACDEGIMNOPRTTU	computer dating
ACDEGINOORRRTU	corrugated iron
ACDEGMMNNOOORR	common or garden
	common-or-garden
ACDEHHIIMOPRRT	hermaphroditic
ACDEHHILLMOORY	Michael Holroyd
ACDEHHLOOPRSUY	hydrocephalous
ACDEHHNNOORSTW	Theodor Schwann
ACDEHIILLMMOTY	immethodically
ACDEHIILLNORSY	Nicholas Ridley
ACDEHIILNRSSTT	child-resistant
ACDEHIILPPPSSY	applied physics
ACDEHIIMORRSTY	radiochemistry
ACDEHIKKLNORUV	Leonid Kravchuk
ACDEHIKNOQRTUW	quick on the draw
ACDEHILLMNOTUY	unmethodically
ACDEHILLMOPRYY	hypodermically
ACDEHILPRRSSUY	hydraulic press
ACDEHIMMNORSTY	thermodynamics
ACDEHINOSSTTTW	cast to the winds
ACDEIIIIMNNRST	indiscriminate
ACDEIIIIMNRSTV	discriminative
ACDEIIIKMNNSTT	make indistinct
ACDEIIILMNRSTY	discriminately
ACDEIIILNNORTU	indication rule
	unidirectional
ACDEIIINNOORRT	air-conditioner
ACDEIIIOORSTTV	Vittorio De Sica
ACDEIILLNORSTY	discretionally
ACDEIILMMNOPTY	limited company
ACDEIILMMRSSTY	dissymmetrical
ACDEIILNNOOOTZ	decolonization
ACDEIILNNOPSST	in a split second
ACDEIILNOSSSTY	Society Islands
ACDEIILPRSTUVV	tricuspid valve
ACDEIINOOPRRST	disincorporate
ACDEILLMNOOSTY	endosmotically
ACDEILLNOOSSTY	disconsolately
ACDEILMNNOORRS	consider normal
ACDEINNORSTUUY	consuetudinary
ACDEINOOQRSSTU	conquistadores
ACDEKMNOOORSTU	ask to come round
ACDENORRSSSSTW	St Andrew's cross
ACDFFHILNOOPSY	hands-off policy
ACDFFIOPPRRSST	Stafford Cripps
ACDFGHILMNNTUY	Flying Dutchman
ACDFHIIIIMNOTU	humidification
ACDFIIIIINNOTV	divinification
ACDFIIIILNOOST	solidification
ACDFIIKLLMMNOR	Malcolm Rifkind
ACDGGIILNORSUY	discouragingly
ACDGHILLLOORYY	hydrologically
ACDGHILMNNOOPY	holding company
ACDGIIIIMNNRST	discriminating
ACDHHINOOPRSTY	hypochondriast
ACDHILLNOOPRYY	hydroponically
ACDHILOOOPRSTT	hospital doctor
ACDHILOPRSSUUU	sulphurous acid
ACDIIIILNNNOST	disinclination
ACDIIIILNOOSSV	social division
ACDIIIIMNNORST	discrimination
ACDIIIJLNORSTU	jurisdictional
ACDIIIILNNOOTTY	conditionality
ACDIIIILOSSTTUY	adscititiously
ACDIIIMNORRSTY	discriminatory
ACDIIINNNOORTT	indoctrination
ACDIILNNOOOSST	disconsolation
ACDIILNOOORSTU	discolouration
ACDILMNORTTUUU	mutual inductor
ACDIMNOOPRSSTU	mass production
	mass-production
ACDMMNOOORSTUY	yours to command
ACEEEEEGILRRVY	receive eagerly
ACEEEEEHNPQSTU	the queen's peace
ACEEEEFFFLMNST	self-effacement
ACEEEEFFLNOSTV	leave no effects
ACEEEEFLMPPRTX	perfect example
ACEEEEGHNRSTTT	The Secret Agent
ACEEEEGILLPTXY	epexegetically
ACEEEEHHILNRTW	Catherine wheel
ACEEEEHINNRSWY	Chinese New Year

ACEEEEILSSTUVX sales executive
ACEEEEKLMRSSSU make less secure
ACEEEEKMMORRSU make more secure
ACEEEELNNRRSTU Laurence Sterne
ACEEEFGHLNRTTT the gentle craft
ACEEEFHIIIMNNX examine-in-chief
ACEEEFHIMRRTUV rheumatic fever
ACEEEFLLNNOPSU clean oneself up
ACEEEFLNNSSSTU self-sustenance
ACEEEFMOPRRRTU recuperate from
ACEEEGGHIINNVX give in exchange
ACEEEGGHNRRSWZ Schwarzenegger
ACEEEGHHINNTWX win the exchange
ACEEEGHLLMNNOW Newnham College
ACEEEGHLNNSSSS changelessness
ACEEEGHNNNOSTU change one's tune
ACEEEGHOPRRSTT scrape together
ACEEEGIILNNORS social engineer
ACEEEGILNSSSTT cassette single
ACEEEGIMMOSTTT committee stage
ACEEEGIMNORRTV image converter
ACEEEGINNPRSTT genetic parents
ACEEEGKLMNNRSY clergyman's knee
ACEEEGLLNNOSST St Anne's College
ACEEEGLMNORSTT Egremont Castle
ACEEEHHIIMMNTT The Time Machine
ACEEEHHILNOPTV live on the cheap
ACEEEHIKOPPRTW a prophetic week
ACEEEHILNNNRST Chinese lantern
ACEEEHKKLNNRTU near the knuckle
ACEEEHKLNOPRVV Pavel Cherenkov
ACEEEHLNORRRTV trochlear nerve
ACEEEHLOPRRTTY electrotherapy
ACEEEHOORRSTUV have recourse to
ACEEEIIINNRSSZ increase in size
ACEEEIIKMNRRVZ Mackenzie River
ACEEEIINOORSSV raise one's voice
ACEEEIKLNNPRRT percentile rank
ACEEEILLMNOSXY examine closely
ACEEEILMORRSTT stereometrical
ACEEEIMNORSVWX ex-servicewoman
ACEEELMNNOORTT Ornette Coleman
ACEEELNNPRSSTY Stanley Spencer
ACEEEMNOOPRSTV overcompensate
ACEEEMNORRSTUU countermeasure
ACEEFFFHILNOTY fly in the face of
ACEEFFGIILNOOR regional office
ACEEFFHIMNORSV charm offensive
ACEEFFHKMNOOOS hack someone off
ACEEFFIILNTTUY ineffectuality
ACEEFFILNOOPRS on special offer
ACEEFFMMNORSUY summary offence
ACEEFGIILNRSTU centrifugalise
ACEEFGIILNRTUZ centrifugalize
ACEEFHILORSSTW as the crow flies
ACEEFHIOPPRRTY pay the price for
ACEEFHLOOSSSTU cause the loss of
ACEEFIIILPRSSU superficialise
ACEEFIIILPRSUZ superficialize
ACEEFIIINORSTT esterification
ACEEFIIKLNNPRR Franklin Pierce
ACEEFIKLNORSTT lack of interest
ACEEFIKNNOOOTT take no notice of
ACEEFILMNOPRST self-importance
ACEEFILMPRRSTU simple fracture
ACEEFINNOORSWY force one's way in
ACEEFINNORSSTU surface tension
ACEEFINORRRSST refractoriness
ACEEFLLOOPRRSW powers of recall
ACEEFMOORRSTTU matter of course
ACEEGGHHINNRST ring the changes
ACEEGGHLLSSTUU August Schlegel
ACEEGGIILLMOOT geological time
ACEEGGIMNNORRS scaremongering
ACEEGHIKKLOOST go like hot cakes
ACEEGHLNOORTTY Charlotte Yonge
ACEEGHMNRRTTTU gutter-merchant
ACEEGIIMNPRSTT magnetic stripe
ACEEGIINNNORTT traction engine
ACEEGILLLLOOTY teleologically
ACEEGILLMOOORT meteorological
ACEEGILLNOPRTT electroplating
ACEEGLLNNORSSU consuls general
ACEEGNOORSSSUU courageousness
ACEEHHIKSTTTTT that's the ticket
ACEEHHINOPRRSU on hire purchase
ACEEHHMOOPRRST chromatosphere
ACEEHIIKNNOSTT skate on thin ice
ACEEHIILMNRSTV Michael Ventris
ACEEHIILMPPTTT Michael Tippett
ACEEHIIMNNSSTZ Nietzscheanism
ACEEHIINPPPRST apprenticeship
ACEEHIKNNRSSTY think necessary
ACEEHILLLNOPTY telephonically
ACEEHILLMORTXY exothermically
ACEEHINORSUUVX nouveaux riches
ACEEHKMNORSTTT shock treatment
ACEEHKMOPSSSTU mocks the pauses
ACEEHLOPPPRSTU copper sulphate
ACEEHLORRSSTTU charlotte russe
ACEEHMMNNOOSTW Thomas Newcomen
ACEEHMNORRSSUU human resources
ACEEHNOORRSSST cross one's heart
ACEEHPRRRTTTTY Terry Pratchett
ACEEIIILNRRTTY rectilinearity
ACEEIIIPRRSTTV creative spirit
ACEEIIJLNNORTT interjectional
ACEEIIKLLMNPSY Mickey Spillane
ACEEIILMNNOPST special mention
ACEEIILNNNNQTU quincentennial
ACEEIILNNORSST intercessional
ACEEIILNNORSTT intersectional
ACEEIILNORRSST intercessorial
ACEEIIMNRSSTTU street-musician
ACEEIINORSSTTV service station
ACEEIINRRSSTTZ citizen's arrest
ACEEIKLNORRTTW Walter Cronkite
ACEEIKLNRSSSTV travel sickness
ACEEILLLLNTTUY intellectually
ACEEILLLNNTTUU unintellectual
ACEEILMMNORTUV Victor Emmanuel
ACEEILMMOOPSTT metal composite

ACEEILMNOPSSTT	Pentecostalism
ACEEILNOPSSTTT	Pentecostalist
ACEEILNORSTVVY	conservatively
ACEEIMMNNORSTU	incommensurate
ACEEIMNORRSSST	Martin Scorsese
ACEEINNOORSSVZ	conversaziones
ACEEINNPRTTTUU	interpunctuate
ACEEINOPRRSSSU	precariousness
ACEEJLMORRSSSU	Jerusalem cross
ACEELMMNORSTUY	commensurately
ACEELNOPRSTUUY	percutaneously
ACEELOORRRSTWY	Royal Worcester
ACEENOPRRSSSTU	Paterson's curse
ACEFFGLNORSTTY	affect strongly
ACEFFHIIOORRST	Chariots of Fire
ACEFFIIILLMOSY	semi-officially
ACEFFIIILNOORS	liaison officer
ACEFFIILLNOOPY	open officially
ACEFFIIOSSTTUY	suffice it to say
ACEFFIMOOPRRTU	form a picture of
ACEFFINOOQSTTU	question of fact
ACEFGHILNNNRSU	channel surfing
ACEFGIIINNORTT	gentrification
ACEFHHNOOSTTUU	a touch of the sun
ACEFHIIIOTTVVY	hive of activity
ACEFHILOOPPRSW	place of worship
ACEFIIIINNORST	resinification
ACEFIIIINORTVV	revivification
ACEFIIILMNOSTU	emulsification
ACEFIIILPRSTUY	superficiality
ACEFIIINOPRTTT	prettification
ACEFIILMNOPRST	simple fraction
ACEFIILNNORSSU	nuclear fission
ACEFIINOSSSTTU	factitiousness
ACEFIIOOPRRSST	pro aris et focis
ACEFILLLLORRSU	cure for all ills
ACEFILMNOOPRSS	self-comparison
ACEFILOOPRRSTT	tropical forest
ACEFINOOPPRRRT	proper fraction
ACEFINRRRSTTUU	infrastructure
ACEFLLNOORSTTW	Wollstonecraft
ACEGGHINNNOTVV	Vincent Van Gogh
ACEGGIILNNNPRS	spring-cleaning
ACEGGILLNOOORT	gerontological
ACEGGILLNOOSTY	geognostically
ACEGHHIILLOPRY	hieroglyphical
ACEGHHIKNORTTT	on the right tack
ACEGHHILNNNOPP	channel hopping
ACEGHIIIKLMMNN	milking machine
ACEGHIIKLLNRSV	Granville Hicks
ACEGHIILLNOSTY	histogenically
ACEGHIILNNOPST	nothing special
ACEGHIILOPRSTX	lexicographist
ACEGHIINNORSST	right ascension
ACEGHILLLNOOTY	ethnologically
ACEGHIOPPRRSSU	supercargoship
ACEGHKNNOORTTW	on the wrong tack
ACEGHLMOOPSTYY	metapsychology
ACEGIIILLLOOPTY	geopolitically
ACEGIILLLOSTUY	eulogistically
ACEGIILLMNOORT	terminological
ACEGIIILLNRSSTT	Stirling Castle
ACEGIIILLOOORST	soteriological
ACEGIIILLORSSUY	sacrilegiously
ACEGIIILNNNOTUY	uncongeniality
ACEGIIINOOPRSTV	Victoria sponge
ACEGIKLMNORRSS	closing remarks
ACEGIKLNORSSSW	working classes
ACEGILLLMOOTYY	etymologically
ACEGILLLNOORUY	neurologically
ACEGILLLOOPRTY	petrologically
ACEGILMNNOOORT	conglomeration
ACEGILNOPRSSTU	plastic surgeon
ACEGILPRRSSTUY	plastic surgery
ACEGIMMMOPRRSU	programme music
ACEGINNNOOSSUU	consanguineous
ACEGINNORSSSUU	ungraciousness
ACEGINOOPRSSTT	operating costs
ACEHHIINOPSSUY	house-physician
ACEHHIJLMNNOOS	Michael Johnson
ACEHHILLOOPSTY	theosophically
ACEHHILLOPTTYY	hypothetically
ACEHHLMOOOPPST	ophthalmoscope
ACEHHLNNOORSTT	Charlton Heston
ACEHHMNORSTTTU	turn the stomach
ACEHIIINNRSSTU	unchristianise
ACEHIIINNRSTUZ	unchristianize
ACEHIIKKNNPSTT	kick in the pants
ACEHIILLPSTUUY	euphuistically
ACEHIINNORSTTY	ancient history
ACEHIINNSSTTUU	unenthusiastic
ACEHIINOOPRTTU	eutrophication
ACEHILNORSSSUV	chivalrousness
ACEHIMNOOPRRTT	anthropometric
ACEHIMNOOPRSYY	Eroica Symphony
ACEHIMOPPRSTTY	spermatophytic
ACEHINNORSSSTY	narcosynthesis
ACEHINNORSTTVW	conversant with
ACEHLLMMOORSTW	Thomas Cromwell
ACEHLNORSTTTYY	Lytton Strachey
ACEHNOOPPRSTUW	throw up one's cap
ACEIIIKLLNQRSU	acquire skill in
ACEIIIILLMOPRTY	Military Police
	military police
ACEIIILLOPSTVW	political views
ACEIIIMMNOORSS	commissionaire
ACEIIIMMNTTUVY	active immunity
ACEIIKNNOORSST	stick one's oar in
ACEIILLMNNOOOS	neocolonialism
ACEIILLMORRTUU	Maurice Utrillo
ACEIILLNNOOOST	neocolonialist
ACEIILLNNOQSTU	call in question
ACEIILLPSSUUUU	Lucius Apuleius
ACEIILNNNOSSTY	nonsensicality
ACEIILNNOOPRST	in loco parentis
ACEIILNNPSSTTT	plant scientist
ACEIILNOOPRRTY	incorporeality
ACEIILNOPRSTUY	pertinaciously
ACEIILNOSSSSUV	lasciviousness
ACEIINNOSSSTUU	incautiousness
ACEIINOPSSSSUU	auspiciousness
ACEIKLNNOPSTTU	pocket an insult

ACEILLLMORTUVY	volumetrically
ACEILLNNNOOTVY	conventionally
ACEILLNOOPRSST	cross-pollinate
ACEILLNOPRSSUY	supersonically
ACEILMNORSSSUU	miraculousness
ACEILNNNNOOTUV	unconventional
ACEILNOOPRRTUY	perlocutionary
ACEILNOOQSSSUU	loquaciousness
ACEILOORRSTTUW	watercolourist
ACEIMMOORTTTUY	come to maturity
ACEIMNNNOOPPSY	company pension
ACEIMNNNOOPRTU	pronunciamento
ACEIMNOORRRRST	narcoterrorism
ACEIMNOQRSTTTU	quattrocentism
ACEINNOOPRRSTY	carry one's point
ACEINNOOPRSSTT	cornet-à-pistons
ACEINOQRSTTTTU	quattrocentist
ACEINORRSSTTUY	strain courtesy
ACELLMNNOOPRSU	personal column
ACELRRRSTTTUUU	ultrastructure
ACEMNNOOPPRSTT	component parts
ACEOOPPRRSSTTT	spectator sport
ACFFGHILOSTTUY	faculty of sight
ACFGIIILMNORTT	limiting factor
ACFGIILMNNNOTU	malfunctioning
ACFHHIIINNNOTW	within an inch of
ACFIIIILMNOPST	simplification
ACFIIILNOSTTTU	stultification
ACFIILLNNOORSV	François Villon
ACFIMNOOORSTTT	comfort station
ACFINOOOPTTTUU	put out of action
ACGHHIJLLMNNOU	John McLaughlin
ACGHIIKNNOSTTT	stick at nothing
ACGHIILLLLOOPY	philologically
ACGHIILLLOOSTY	histologically
ACGHIILLNOOORT	ornithological
ACGHIILMNOOPSY	physiognomical
ACGHILLLMOOTYY	mythologically
ACGHIMNNORSTTU	stomach-turning
ACGIIIJLLNOSTY	jingoistically
ACGIIILLLNSTUY	linguistically
ACGIIILLLPSTUY	pugilistically
ACGIIILNOPPRRV	Gavrilo Princip
ACGIIILPRRSSTU	surgical spirit
ACGIILLNPPSTUY	supplicatingly
ACGIIMMNOORRSS	micro-organisms
ACGILLLOOOPRTY	tropologically
ACGINOOOPRRSTT	prognosticator
ACHHILNOPSSTYY	sycophantishly
ACHHLMNOOPRSYY	Choral Symphony
ACHIIILLNORSTY	histrionically
ACHIIIMMNNOOST	Naomi Mitchison
ACHIIIMNOORSST	trichomoniasis
ACHIIINOOPSSTT	sophistication
ACHIILLLOSTTYY	histolytically
ACHIIMMNNOOORT	harmonic motion
ACHIIOPRSSSTTY	astrophysicist
ACHIJLNOSSSUUV	Julius von Sachs
ACHIOOPPRRRSTU	procuratorship
ACHLNNOORSSUYY	asynchronously
ACIIIIILNOOPTTZ	politicization
ACIIIILPRSSTTU	spiritualistic
ACIIILLLMPSSTY	simplistically
ACIIILLMNOPTTU	multiplication
ACIIILLMOPSTTY	optimistically
ACIIILNOPSSUUY	inauspiciously
ACIIINNORSTTUZ	scrutinization
ACIILNNOOPSSSU	Nicolas Poussin
ACIILNNOOSTTTU	constitutional
ACIINNOOOPRSTT	contraposition
ACIKMNNOORSTUY	Rocky Mountains
ACILLMMNNOOTTY	non-committally
ACILLNOOQRTTUY	quality control
ACILLNPRRSTUUY	unscripturally
ACILMOOPRRRSUY	primary colours
ACILNOPRSSTUUY	transpicuously
ADDDDEEEHLLMUY	muddleheadedly
ADDDDEGIIMNNOW	diamond wedding
ADDDEEEEHLRRTW	Edward the Elder
ADDDEEEELNOPPV	padded envelope
ADDDEEEINRSTTT	tried and tested
ADDDEEHHNRSTUY	the Hundred Days
ADDDEEHILNORRS	Rhode Island Red
ADDDEEHLOORTTW	dead to the world
ADDDEGHLOOOSTY	the good old days
ADDEEEEFHNNRSS	free-handedness
ADDEEEEFNNOOST	dead on one's feet
ADDEEEEHNNNSSV	even-handedness
ADDEEEFILMNTXY	extended family
ADDEEEGNNOPRRS	deranged person
ADDEEEHINRRSTU	hidden treasure
ADDEEEHLNPSSTU	Stephen Dedalus
ADDEEEHNNNOPSS	open-handedness
ADDEEEIKMNNSSW	weak-mindedness
ADDEEEILMPRTTY	premeditatedly
ADDEEEILNNNPSS	pins and needles
ADDEEEILNNRSTT	landed interest
ADDEEEIMNPRTTU	unpremeditated
ADDEEEIMNRSTTU	underestimated
ADDEEEKMNNOPST	make despondent
ADDEEELLNRSUVY	reveal suddenly
ADDEEFIIMNNRSS	fair-mindedness
ADDEEFNNOOORST	Fernando de Soto
ADDEEGGHHILRRY	highly regarded
	highly-regarded
ADDEEGHHHINNSS	high-handedness
ADDEEGHILLNNSY	single-handedly
ADDEEGIIILNNRS	insider dealing
ADDEEGIIMNNORR	Nadine Gordimer
ADDEEHHLNOOPSU	hold up one's head
ADDEEHIKLNNPSS	spindle-shanked
ADDEEHLNOORSTW	The Woodlanders
ADDEEHNNOOORST	Hernando de Soto
ADDEEIIOPRRSTV	drive to despair
ADDEEILMNORRST	mental disorder
ADDEEILNOOQSTU	loaded question
ADDEEILNRRSUVY	arrive suddenly
ADDEEINNNORSWY	nine days' wonder
ADDEEKMNOORSTU	make understood
ADDEELMRRSSSTY	smartly dressed
ADDEELNOPPRTUU	underpopulated
ADDEFGILLRRSUY	disregardfully

ADDEFIILNNSSSU	disdainfulness
ADDEGHHINOOSTW	wood nightshade
ADDEGHINNOORTW	go down the drain
ADDEGIKLNNOUWW	walking wounded
ADDEGLLNNOOORS	Gordon Lonsdale
ADDEGNOOOORSSW	good as one's word
ADDEHIIIMNOTYZ	azidothymidine
ADDEHIILMNOSSS	old-maidishness
ADDEILMNNORRWY	narrow-mindedly
ADDEIOOPPRRRST	trapdoor spider
ADDFGIIILMNORT	fair to middling
ADDGHLNOOOTUUY	young adulthood
ADDGHLNOORTWYY	Andy Goldworthy
ADDGIIKLNPRRUY	Rudyard Kipling
ADEEEEEGNNRSST	degenerateness
ADEEEEEILLLNST	Danielle Steele
ADEEEEFFGHKOTT	take the edge off
ADEEEEFHINRSUW	auf Wiedersehen
ADEEEEFIMPRRRT	Pierre de Fermat
ADEEEEFNORRRVV	for ever and ever
ADEEEEGHILLNRW	wheeler-dealing
ADEEEEHHLMMPST	Hemel Hempstead
ADEEEEIILMNNST	senile dementia
ADEEEEIKLMNRRW	Lake Windermere
ADEEEEIMNPRRTT	predeterminate
ADEEEELNNNRRVV	Never-Never Land
	never-never land
ADEEEFGHHLRTTU	feel the draught
ADEEEFGHIKMNRT	make frightened
ADEEEFGILORRTU	Tierra del Fuego
ADEEEFGLNNNSSW	newfangledness
ADEEEFHHORTTTW	draw the teeth of
ADEEEFHMNNORTU	under the name of
ADEEEFHNOOSSTY	one of these days
ADEEEFIILLSTTX	fixed satellite
ADEEEFILNRRSST	self-restrained
ADEEEFILRRSSTV	self-advertiser
ADEEEFIMNNOORT	aforementioned
ADEEEFINNORSTT	defenestration
ADEEEFLNNNOOST	land on one's feet
ADEEEGGHILRTTU	Gielgud Theatre
ADEEEGGIJMNTUV	give a judgement
ADEEEGHHMNPRRS	German Shepherd
ADEEEGHINORRRS	garnishee order
ADEEEGHJMMORTT	jammed together
ADEEEGHKOOOPSU	keep a good house
ADEEEGHNNORRTT	Enter the Dragon
ADEEEGIILMRRST	registered mail
ADEEEGIIMNNRST	in disagreement
ADEEEGILOQUVZZ	Diego Velázquez
ADEEEGJLMNTUUV	value judgement
ADEEEGLNRRSSSS	regardlessness
ADEEEGNOOPRSTX	expose to danger
ADEEEHHILNNOTT	Death on the Nile
ADEEEHHIRSTTTT	the third estate
ADEEEHHLLORTWY	wholeheartedly
	whole-heartedly
ADEEEHHLNNRSTT	The Netherlands
ADEEEHHMMNRRTU	under the hammer
ADEEEHIINRRSST	hereditariness
ADEEEHIKMNOSSU	housemaid's knee
ADEEEHIKNNNOPS	keep one's hand in
ADEEEHIKNOSSSS	shake one's sides
ADEEEHJLNORRTT	Dear John letter
ADEEEHMNOORTTY	enemy at the door
ADEEEHORSTUVWY	what you deserve
ADEEEIILLLNTVV	live and let live
ADEEEIILLNPTXY	expedientially
ADEEEIILMNNOSS	Léonide Massine
ADEEEIILMNRTTY	intermediately
ADEEEIIMMQRSUV	demisemiquaver
ADEEEIKLNPRSTW	spend like water
ADEEEILLLNTTVW	well-ventilated
ADEEEILNPRSTUV	penal servitude
ADEEEIMMNORSST	immoderateness
ADEEEKNPPRRSUW	keep under wraps
ADEEELMNNOPRST	Peter Mandelson
ADEEELNRRRSUUV	surrender value
ADEEEMNNRSTTTU	understatement
ADEEENNPPRRSSU	unpreparedness
ADEEFFFGHILRST	self-affrighted
ADEEFFHINOORST	on the far side of
ADEEFFIILLNRTY	differentially
ADEEFFIINORRTT	differentiator
ADEEFFIKLNRSTY	ask differently
ADEEFFILNRSTYY	say differently
ADEEFFLNOOSSTT	flat-footedness
ADEEFGHILNNORS	no hard feelings
ADEEFGHILRRRSY	Harry Selfridge
ADEEFGHINRSSST	farsightedness
	far-sightedness
ADEEFGILNNRRSS	Flinders Ranges
ADEEFGMOOORRSU	for good measure
ADEEFHIILPRSTT	depart this life
ADEEFHIKLLOTTV	talk of the devil
ADEEFHILLNOSTU	the life and soul
ADEEFIIKNORRTT	Frankie Dettori
ADEEFIILLLRRTY	field artillery
ADEEFIKLMNRRRY	friendly remark
ADEEFKMOORRRST	take orders from
ADEEFLLLMRSSUU	Les Fleurs du Mal
ADEEFLNNNORSTY	Alfred Tennyson
ADEEFLNNOPRTUY	under penalty of
ADEEFNORSSSTTU	state of undress
ADEEGGHIMNNORT	dog in the manger
ADEEGHHILLRTTY	light-heartedly
ADEEGHHILNOSSY	highly seasoned
	highly-seasoned
ADEEGHHIMNOSTT	do the same thing
ADEEGHHINNORTW	wrong in the head
ADEEGHILNRSSTU	daughterliness
ADEEGHNNNOOSST	get one's hands on
ADEEGHNNOPRRTU	Uther Pendragon
ADEEGIIIMNNNRT	main ingredient
ADEEGIINORRSTT	deregistration
ADEEGINOORRSST	derogatoriness
ADEEGJLMNNNOTU	non-judgemental
ADEEGLLNOPRSSW	Oswald Spengler
ADEEGLNOPRRSUU	pleasure ground
ADEEGORRSSTTUW	gesture towards
ADEEHHHNNOORTT	on the other hand
ADEEHHILLNOSTW	how the land lies

ADEEHHLNORRTTU	Leonhard Hutter
ADEEHHOORTTWWY	woe worth the day
ADEEHIKLLLRSTY	The Ladykillers
ADEEHILLORTTVW	drive to the wall
ADEEHILLPRTUVW	drive up the wall
ADEEHILORSSTTU	horse latitudes
ADEEHLOPRRRSTY	the Lord's Prayer
ADEEHLORSTTTUY	stout-heartedly
ADEEHNOOPRRSTZ	trapezohedrons
ADEEIIIMNNORTT	intermediation
ADEEIIINORSSST	radiosensitise
ADEEIIINORSSTV	radiosensitive
ADEEIIINORSSTZ	radiosensitize
ADEEIILLLOOTTZ	Eliza Doolittle
ADEEIILMNNOTVY	denominatively
ADEEIILNPSSTVY	dispensatively
ADEEIILOPRRSTV	private soldier
ADEEIILPQSSTUY	sesquipedality
ADEEIINNNORSST	inordinateness
ADEEIINNOPRSTT	predestination
ADEEIJLMNOORTU	Romeo and Juliet
ADEEIKLLNNSSUY	unladylikeness
ADEEIKMMNNOPSU	make up one's mind
ADEEILLNNORTTU	Lord Lieutenant
ADEEILMNOSTUVY	move unsteadily
ADEEILNNRRSTUY	unrestrainedly
ADEEILNORRSSWW	world-weariness
ADEEIMNNOPRRST	Modern Painters
ADEEIMNSSTTUYZ	unsystematized
ADEEKMNNOORSSU	make one's rounds
ADEELLLNOOORWY	Leonard Woolley
ADEELMMNOORRYY	read only memory
ADEELNNOPPRRTY	preponderantly
ADEEMMNNOORTVW	onward movement
ADEFFGHINNORTU	founding father
ADEFFGHOOOORST	shortage of food
ADEFFHILLNOSUY	fully-fashioned
ADEFFIJNNNORST	Fridtjof Nansen
ADEFGHHILNOTTY	lady of the night
ADEFGHHILORUVY	highy-flavoured
ADEFGHIMOORRTY	fairy godmother
ADEFHIIIKKLNRS	drink like a fish
ADEFHINOOOORTT	a foot in the door
ADEFHINOORRTTU	for the duration
ADEFHLLLOORRTW	for all the world
ADEFHLNOOORTUW	would not hear of
ADEFHNNNOOORSW	for one's own hand
ADEFHNOOORRSVW	have no words for
ADEFIIKNORRTUV	favourite drink
ADEFIILMMNNORT	Milton Friedman
ADEFIINNOOORRT	foreordination
ADEFIINOSSSSTU	fastidiousness
ADEFIIOORSSTUV	overfastidious
	over-fastidious
ADEFNORRSSTTUY	stand surety for
ADEGGGHHORTTUU	grudge a thought
ADEGGHIINNRSTT	riding the stang
ADEGGIIINNRSTT	disintegrating
ADEGHHLLNNOOYY	Lloyd Honeyghan
ADEGHHLLNOOSSW	Sheldon Glashow
ADEGHHLNOPSSTU	plough the sands
ADEGHHLOOORTUY	your good health
ADEGHIIJLMOPRS	Joseph Grimaldi
ADEGHIINOOSTTW	a wise thing to do
ADEGHILNNOPRTT	holding pattern
ADEGHILNOOPRST	The Prodigal Son
ADEGHINNNOSSSU	using one's hands
ADEGHINOPTTTTU	putting to death
ADEGIIILMNNRUU	Miguel Indurain
ADEGIIILNNPRVW	prevailing wind
ADEGIIINNORSTT	disintegration
ADEGIIKLOORTVY	give a dirty look
ADEGIILLMNPRSY	pyramid selling
ADEGIILLNNOOPV	Golden Pavilion
ADEGIILNRSSSST	distress signal
ADEGIKMNNORRSU	make rings round
ADEGILLNOPTTUY	plead not guilty
ADEGNNOOPRSTUU	put on one's guard
ADEHHIIILNPPRS	Philip Sheridan
ADEHIILNNOPSSX	Phoenix Islands
ADEHIIMNNNOPTW	with an open mind
ADEHIINNRSTTWW	straw in the wind
ADEHIJKNNOORRT	Jan Hendrik Oort
ADEHILNNOSSSTU	outlandishness
ADEHIMNORSSTUW	mess around with
ADEHINNNOOSSST	sit on one's hands
ADEHINOORRSSTW	roadworthiness
ADEHJLNOORSSUY	Joshua Reynolds
ADEHJMNOPPPSTU	hop, step and jump
ADEHLNORRSSTUV	Luther Vandross
ADEHLOORRSSTYY	Dorothy L Sayers
ADEHNNNOORSTTU	turn one's hand to
ADEHNNOOORRTTW	not another word
ADEHNORRSSTTWW	north-westwards
ADEHORSSSTTUWW	south-westwards
ADEIIINNOORSTT	disorientation
ADEIILLNOPRTVY	providentially
ADEIILMNNNOOSX	Mason-Dixon Line
ADEIILMNNOOSTW	two-dimensional
ADEIILNOPRSSTY	dispensatorily
ADEIILNOSTTUVY	adventitiously
ADEIIMNNOPPSTT	disappointment
ADEILLMNORSWWY	Worldly Wiseman
ADEINNOOPRRRSY	ordinary person
ADEKLLLMOORTUY	talk more loudly
ADEMNNOPRSSTTU	stand upon terms
ADEOOORRRTTTXY	dextrorotatory
ADFGGIINNNOORT	toing and froing
ADFGIKLNOOORRW	forward-looking
	looking forward
ADFHILNOOORTUW	fool around with
ADFIIIMNNOORST	disinformation
ADFILNOOOORRSU	Orlando Furioso
ADGGIIILLLMNOW	William Golding
ADGGIIKNNORRWW	working drawing
ADGGIINNNORRTU	training ground
ADGGIMNNOPRSTU	stamping-ground
ADGGINNNOPRSUW	spawning-ground
ADGIIIINNNPRSU	Indian Uprising
ADGIIIINNTTTUZ	attitudinizing
ADGIILLLNNOTUY	longitudinally
ADGIILNOPPRSVY	disapprovingly

ADGIKLNOOORTUW outward-looking
ADGINNNORRRSUU run rings around
ADHHNOORSTTTUU stouth and routh
ADHIJKMNOPPPSU hop, skip and jump
ADIIIILNOQSSTU disquisitional
ADIILLOPRRSSTU Lords Spiritual
ADIILOPSSTTUUY disputatiously
ADIIMMMNNOPTUU ammunition dump
ADIKLNNOOOOORS Oroonoko Island
ADILLMNNOOOSSS Solomon Islands
AEEEEEKLPRRSSU pleasure-seeker
AEEEEEMNNRRSTV en ventre sa mère
AEEEEFFIMNNSST effeminateness
AEEEEFGKNORRTV take revenge for
AEEEEFHNOPSTTX at the expense of
AEEEEFLNOOPPSY apple of one's eye
AEEEEFLNOPPRRS prepare oneself
AEEEEFLPPRRRUV puerperal fever
AEEEEGHHHIOTVV give the heave-ho
AEEEEGILNRRTVY regeneratively
AEEEEGINNRSSTV generativeness
AEEEEGINSSTTVV vegetativeness
AEEEEGLLMRRTXY extremely large
AEEEEGNRSTTTTX greatest extent
AEEEEHKNNORTTW water on the knee
AEEEEHLMNOOSTV let someone have
AEEEEHNNOOSSVY have one's eyes on
AEEEEILMNNRSST elementariness
AEEEEINNPRRTTT interpenetrate
AEEEEINPRRSTTV representative
AEEEELLNPRRTTW water-repellent
AEEEEMNOPRSTTZ temperate zones
AEEEFFGORRSTTT greatest effort
AEEEFFIRRSSUUZ suffer a seizure
AEEEFFLLNNOOST fall on one's feet
AEEEFFLLNORSTT flatter oneself
AEEEFGHHLLOSTT The Gates of Hell
AEEEFGHIKOSTTU take the guise of
AEEEFGILLNOPZZ Felipe González
AEEEFGILLNOSSY Isle of Anglesey
AEEEFGILNOORSS Siege of Orléans
AEEEFGILNPRRSV relapsing fever
AEEEFGMOPRRRST stage performer
AEEEFHHLLLORRT hell for leather
AEEEFHLLORTTTW letter of the law
AEEEFHOQRSTTTU at the request of
AEEEFILLNPRRTY preferentially
AEEEFLNOORSTUW wear oneself out
AEEEFLNOORSTVX overtax oneself
AEEEFLNOPRRSST present for sale
AEEEGGHHORRTTT gather together
AEEEGGIMNNRSTT Strange Meeting
AEEEGGINRSSSSV aggressiveness
AEEEGGLNNORRSU surgeon general
AEEEGHHINRTVVY have everything
AEEEGHHIOPRTTW great white hope
AEEEGHHNOPPRTT happen together
AEEEGHHNRRRTTU hunter-gatherer
AEEEGHIIKNPRTT keep a tight rein
AEEEGHLNPRSTTT grasp the nettle
AEEEGIILMNSSTT legitimateness
AEEEGIINQTTUVY negative equity
AEEEGIKLLNPRTV keep travelling
AEEEGILLLLNRTY enter illegally
AEEEGILMRSTUUU Auguste Lumière
AEEEGILOPRSTUV give pleasure to
AEEEGILRRRTTUY grey literature
AEEEGIMNOOSTTT get someone at it
AEEEGINORSSTTV sovereign state
AEEEGLLNNNNSUZ Suzanne Lenglen
AEEEGLNOPPRRSU general-purpose
AEEEHHHILNORTT hole in the heart
AEEEHHIILMNNTW in the meanwhile
AEEEHHIMNNOOSV have one's home in
AEEEHHINOPRTTX Phoenix Theatre
AEEEHHKNOPRSST Hesketh Pearson
AEEEHHLMNNOSTY Henley-on-Thames
AEEEHHOPPRRTTW weather prophet
AEEEHIILORRTTV Olivier Theatre
AEEEHIKMMNNOOS make one's home in
AEEEHIKNNOOPRS keep one's hair on
AEEEHILLLMMNRV Herman Melville
AEEEHILNPPRSVY apprehensively
AEEEHILNPRTTVY hyperventilate
AEEEHILNRSTTTW The Winter's Tale
AEEEHIMNNRSTTT man in the street
AEEEHINNPPRSUV unapprehensive
AEEEHJKLNNOPRS Johannes Kepler
AEEEHKLOPRRSUY keep early hours
AEEEHKLRSSTTTW walk the streets
AEEEHLMOPRRSTT The Last Emperor
AEEEHLORSSTTTU The Lotus-Eaters
AEEEHNNOORSSTT set one's heart on
AEEEIILLNPRTXY experientially
AEEEIILMNNSSTT sentimentalise
AEEEIILMNNSTTZ sentimentalize
AEEEIILRRRTVWY Literary Review
AEEEIIMNPRSSTV imperativeness
AEEEIINPRRTTTV interpretative
AEEEILLMNPRTXY experimentally
AEEEILLNPRSTTU Pauline Letters
AEEEILLNSSSSTT stainless steel
AEEEILNOPRSTUV superelevation
AEEEILOPRRRSSU Pierre Larousse
AEEEIMNNRRTUUV unremunerative
AEEEINNOPRRSTT representation
AEEEINPRSSSSUV persuasiveness
AEEEIOOPRRRTTV retro-operative
AEEEKNOOOSSTTT take to one's toes
AEEELLLMMRSTXY extremely small
AEEELLOPRSSSTU Pasteurelloses
AEEELNOOPRRSST personal stereo
AEEEMNNOPPRSWW newspaperwomen
AEEEMNOOPRSTUX extemporaneous
AEEENNORSSSTUX extraneousness
AEEENQSSSSTTUU statuesqueness
AEEFFFLNOOPSSS pass oneself off
AEEFFGGIORSTUV give suffrage to
AEEFFGILLNRSTT self-flattering
AEEFFGLOORRTYY Geoffrey Taylor
AEEFFHILLMOOSU house of ill fame
AEEFFHILLNOOSV have one's fill of

AEEFFIILMNSSTT	manifest itself
AEEFGGHJNNORSU	Johannes Fugger
AEEFGGILLNRSTU	self-regulating
AEEFGHINNNOPPT	happening often
AEEFGHJLLNOTUW	law of the jungle
AEEFGHKNOORRTY	Gareth of Orkney
AEEFGIILLNNPSX	self-explaining
AEEFGIINRRTTUW	feature-writing
AEEFGIINRSSTUV	figurativeness
AEEFGIKNORSSSV	ask forgiveness
AEEFGILMNNNSSU	meaningfulness
AEEFGIMMNORRST	ferromagnetism
AEEFGINOORRSSV	give reasons for
AEEFGLNNRSSTUU	ungratefulness
AEEFGLRRSSTTUY	Fergus Slattery
AEEFGOOPRRRSST	rate of progress
AEEFHHHOORSTTV	have the hots for
AEEFHHLNNOPSVY	shove-halfpenny
AEEFHIINRRTTWZ	fraternize with
AEEFHIKMNORRTT	in the market for
AEEFHILMORSTTT	for the last time
AEEFHILNNNPRSU	Ranulph Fiennes
AEEFHLLLMMOPST	smell of the lamp
AEEFHLLOPPRRST	propeller shaft
AEEFHLLOSTTTTU	taste to the full
AEEFHLMOSSTTWY	system of wealth
AEEFHLNOORSTTW	throw oneself at
AEEFHMMMNNOOTT	man of the moment
AEEFHNOORSSSTU	The Four Seasons
AEEFHOORRSSSTW	Wars of the Roses
AEEFILMNOSSTTY	false testimony
AEEFLLLMOOOPPT	Temple of Apollo
AEEFLLNOOOPSTW	at one fell swoop
AEEFLLNOOPPSTY	apply oneself to
AEEFLMNOORSTTW	woman of letters
AEEGGGIINOORVV	give a going-over
AEEGGHHIINNNRT	hanging in there
AEEGGHHNORRRTU	Arthur Honegger
AEEGGHIMNNNORR	Hermann Goering
AEEGGHINOORRRS	George Harrison
AEEGGIILLMRTUV	Maggie Tulliver
AEEGGIINORSSTT	segregationist
AEEGGILNNOOSSV	Love Songs in Age
AEEGGILNORSTVV	revolving stage
AEEGGINORRSSSU	gregariousness
AEEGHHIIMRTTTT	at the right time
AEEGHHIKNNPSTW	Stephen Hawking
AEEGHHILORSSTV	have sole rights
AEEGHHKMORTTUW	make wet through
AEEGHHLORSSTUU	slaughterhouse
AEEGHHMNNOORTU	more than enough
AEEGHIIKLMNOST	something like a
AEEGHIIPRRRSST	parish register
AEEGHIKMNNNRTU	make the running
AEEGHILNNOOPTY	pile on the agony
AEEGHILNOPPTUY	pile up the agony
AEEGHILPPRRTUW	purple with rage
AEEGHLNNNOPSTT	Stephen Langton
AEEGIIILLLMTTY	illegitimately
AEEGIIILLNNRST	inertia selling
AEEGIIILLNNSTT	intelligentsia
AEEGIILMNORSSS	generalissimos
AEEGIILNNNORSV	earn one's living
AEEGIILNNNRTTY	entertainingly
AEEGIIMNNNORTU	mountaineering
AEEGIINORRSTTV	tergiversation
AEEGIKNNOPSSTU	speak in tongues
AEEGILLNOPRSUV	pleasure-loving
AEEGILMPRRSSTY	impress greatly
AEEGILNNOOSSSU	oleaginousness
AEEGINOOPRRSTU	supererogation
AEEGLLNNOOSSST	on one's last legs
AEEGMNOOPRSSSU	grass someone up
AEEGNOORSSSTUU	outrageousness
AEEGOOPRRRSTUY	supererogatory
AEEHHHIIMPTTWZ	emphathize with
AEEHHIIITTTTWW	whittie-whattie
AEEHHIIORSTTTU	the authorities
AEEHHINNOORTTW	one with another
AEEHHLLOOPRSTV	all over the shop
AEEHHOPPPRSSTU	superphosphate
AEEHIIILLLNTTW	in a little while
AEEHIIILLLTWWW	Willie Whitelaw
AEEHIIILNPPPPT	Philippe Pétain
AEEHIIMPRSSTTU	serum hepatitis
AEEHIJNNOPRSST	Saint-John Perse
AEEHIKLLNOSTVY	shake violently
AEEHILLMNOTTTW	the little woman
AEEHILLMOSTTVY	move stealthily
AEEHILMNNOSSTT	less than no time
AEEHILMNOOSTTZ	Simon the Zealot
AEEHILMNPRRRTT	thermal printer
AEEHIMORSTTUUW	without measure
AEEHINPPPPRRSW	whippersnapper
AEEHJLLMNNORSU	Johannes Müller
AEEHKLORRRSTTU	Arthur Koestler
AEEHKMNOPRTTTU	put on the market
AEEHLMORRSTTUY	your heart melts
AEEHLOPPPRSSUY	pleurapophyses
AEEIIIKKLNSTTV	at it like knives
AEEIIILLMMNSSW	William Siemens
AEEIIILMMMMORT	time immemorial
AEEIIILMNOSSTT	testimonialise
AEEIIILMNOSTTZ	testimonialize
AEEIIILMNSSTTX	existentialism
AEEIIILNNNORTT	interlineation
AEEIIILNSSTTTX	existentialist
AEEIIILORRRSTT	territorialise
AEEIIILORRRTTZ	territorialize
AEEIILLLNPSTTY	pestilentially
AEEIILLMNNSSTT	small intestine
AEEIILLNNOPRTT	interpellation
AEEIILMMNNOPTT	implementation
AEEIILMMNNSSTT	sentimentalism
AEEIILMNNSSTTT	sentimentalist
AEEIILMNNSTTTY	sentimentality
AEEIILNNPSSTTV	sensitive plant
AEEIILNNQSSTTU	quintessential
AEEIILNQRSSTUU	tequila sunrise
AEEIILPRTTUVVY	vituperatively
AEEIIMNOORSTTV	overestimation
AEEIIMORRRRRVW	rear-view mirror

AEEIINNNOSSTVV innovativeness
AEEIINNOPPSSST inappositeness
AEEIINNOPRRTTT interpretation
AEEIINNORSTTWZ westernization
AEEIKKLOOPSSTW swoopstake-like
swoop-stake-like
AEEIKMNOPRRSSX expression mark
AEEILLLNOSTTTW tell its own tale
AEEILLNNRSSSTT slatternliness
AEEILMNNNNRSSU unmannerliness
AEEILMNNOOOSST on someone's tail
AEEILMOPRRSTUY use temporarily
AEEILNNOORSSTT listen to reason
AEEILNOORTTTXY extortionately
AEELLMNORSSSUV marvellousness
AEELNNNORRTUVV non-return valve
AEENNOOORRSSST rest on one's oars
AEFFGIILNNORTT not lift a finger
AEFFHILNNSSTUU unfaithfulness
AEFFHIOORSTTUW fish out of water
AEFFIILPPPRSTU a stiff upper lip
AEFGGNOORRSSYY Gregory of Nyssa
AEFGHHILLNORRY harrying of hell
AEFGHHIMNORSTT The Rights of Man
AEFGHLOPSTTTUU put the flags out
AEFGIILMNNNORV manner of living
AEFGIILNNSSSTU self-sustaining
AEFGIILNOORRSW Wars of Religion
AEFGIILNOSSSTU flagitiousness
AEFGIINNOPRRST in foreign parts
AEFGIKLLLNORTV travelling folk
AEFGIMNOPRRRST performing arts
AEFGINOOPRRSTT to foreign parts
AEFGNOOOOSTUWY go out of one's way
AEFHHLNNOPRTWY halfpennyworth
AEFHIILLLNOTVW fall in love with
AEFHIILMNNRTUY run in the family
AEFHIILNNOPRTY hyperinflation
AEFHIINNNOOPST pin one's faith on
AEFHIKKMNOOTUY make you think of
AEFHIKMNNORSST fisherman's knot
AEFHIKNORSTVWY have forty winks
AEFHKLNNNSSTUU unthankfulness
AEFHLLLORTTTTU at full throttle
AEFHMNNOOOTTWW woman of the town
AEFHMOOPRRSTTT for the most part
AEFIIKMNRSSSWY Swiss army knife
AEFIILLMMNOOST self-immolation
AEFIIMNOORRSTT reformationist
AEFILLNOOPRSSY professionally
AEFILLOOPRRSSY professorially
AEFILNNOOPRSSU unprofessional
AEFILNORRSTUUY it's your funeral
AEFIMMORSSTXYY axis of symmetry
AEFIMNNOORRSTW frontierswoman
AEFKLLLOOOORRV look all over for
AEFMNNOOOOORSW A Room of One's Own
AEFMNOOPPRSSTU means of support
AEGGHHMMORRTUU rummage through
AEGGHIIIMNSSVV have misgivings
AEGGHIIINNRTTW weight-training
AEGGHILLNOOTTW going to the wall
AEGGHINNOOPRTV photoengraving
AEGGHLLLNOOSTT go to all lengths
AEGGHLNNOOSTTY go to any lengths
AEGGIIINNORRTV reinvigorating
AEGGIILLNNOSTT ill-gotten gains
AEGGIILNNOPRSS singapore sling
AEGGINOOSSTTUU auto-suggestion
AEGHHIKLLNOOTY healthy-looking
AEGHHILLORSSTW laser-light show
AEGHIIILLNNNPS in plain English
AEGHIIILNNSTTT sting in the tail
AEGHIILNNOORSS losing one's hair
AEGHIILNNSTTUY unhesitatingly
AEGHIIMNNOOOTZ homogenization
AEGHIKLMNPRSTT Knights Templar
AEGHIKMNOOPSST smooth-speaking
AEGHILMOORSTTU rheumatologist
AEGHIMMMNORTUU omnium-gatherum
AEGHIMNOPSTTTU put something at
AEGHLLORSSTUUY slaughterously
AEGHMNOPPRSUYY Prague Symphony
AEGIIIILMNOSTT legitimisation
AEGIIIILMNOTTZ legitimization
AEGIIINNOORRTV reinvigoration
AEGIIKMNOPSSSV passive smoking
AEGIIKNNOPRRST taking prisoner
AEGIILLLNNRTUY interlingually
AEGIILLRRSTUVY visit regularly
AEGIILNNNRSTTY intransigently
AEGIILNOPRRSTU Negro spiritual
AEGIILNQRRSTUV living quarters
AEGIILORRRSTUV regular visitor
AEGIINNNPRRRSU running repairs
AEGIINPPRSSSTT asset-stripping
AEGILLMNNOQTUY magniloquently
AEGILMNOOORSTU osmoregulation
AEGILNNPPRSTTU snapping turtle
snapping-turtle
AEGIMMNOOPRSTU spermatogonium
AEGIMNNNSSSSUU unassumingness
AEGIMNNOPRRRSY morning prayers
AEGIMNPRRSSSTT spring mattress
AEHHHILNOORTTU holier-than-thou
AEHHIILLLLRSSY shilly-shallier
AEHHIIMPSTTWYZ sympathize with
AEHHIKLLMNOTTT I'll thank them to
AEHHINNOPTTTTU put the tin hat on
AEHHMMNOPTTUWY put the whammy on
AEHHNNOORRSTTT north-north-east
AEHHOOSSSTTTUU south-south-east
AEHIILLLNOOTTT Otto Lilienthal
AEHIILNOORTTTW with relation to
AEHIILOPRRSTWY praiseworthily
AEHIINOORSSTTV have its roots in
AEHIIOORRSSTTT osteoarthritis
AEHIKNNNOPRSTY Anthony Perkins
AEHILLNNPSTTUU put in a nutshell
AEHILLORSSSTUU Louis Althusser
AEHILNOPRSSTTW slap on the wrist
AEHIMNNOORSSSU harmoniousness

AEHIOOORRSSSTT	osteoarthrosis
AEHJMNNNNNOOUV	John Von Neumann
AEHMMNORRTTUWY	the worm may turn
AEIIILNNOOPTVY	opinionatively
AEIIILNNRSTTVY	intransitively
AEIIILNPRSSTUU	unspiritualise
AEIIILNPRSTUUZ	unspiritualize
AEIIILORRRTTTY	territoriality
AEIIINOQRRSTUY	requisitionary
AEIIJLMNORSTTY	silent majority
AEIIJLNNORSTUV	universal joint
AEIIJNNNOOPSTX	expansion joint
AEIIKNOOPPSTTU	take up position
AEIILLLRSTTUVY	illustratively
AEIILLMNOOPRSW	William Spooner
AEIILLNNNQQUUY	quinquennially
AEIILMNOOPRSTY	polymerisation
AEIILMNOOPRTYZ	polymerization
AEIILMNRSSSTVY	transmissively
AEIIMNNOORTTUW	in a minute or two
AEIIMNOORRSSTT	restorationism
AEIIMNRSSSTTTV	transvestitism
AEIINNNOOOPRTT	not in operation
AEIINNORRSSSTT	transitoriness
AEIINOPRSSSUVV	viviparousness
AEIJMOOOPPRRRS	Marjorie Proops
AEILLMNNRSTTUY	instrumentally
AEILLMNOSSTUUY	simultaneously
AEILNOOSSTTTUY	ostentatiously
AEIMMNNOOORTTW	in a moment or two
AEINNOOPPRRRTY	non-proprietary
AEINNOOSSTTTUU	unostentatious
AEINOOPQSTTTUU	put a question to
AEINOOPRRSSSUU	uproariousness
AEINOORRSSSTTU	traitorousness
AEKMNOOOORTVWW	know a move or two
AFFFIILLMNOORR	fill in a form for
AFFGHHIIRRRTTU	Arthur Griffith
AFGGHHILLNORTU	falling-through
AFGGHIIMNNNOOS	fashionmonging
AFGHHINOORTTTU	train of thought
AFGHINNOOOSTTY	to say nothing of
AFHMNNOOOORRTU	matron of honour
AFIIIMMNNOORST	misinformation
AFIILLMORSTUUY	multifariously
AGGGHIILNNOOTW	going along with
AGGHIIILNNOSTT	Sailing Tonight
AGGHIINORTTUUW	without arguing
AGGHILNOOOTUWY	go along with you
AGGIIILMNNRRUV	Irving Langmuir
AGGLLNOOOORTYY	otolaryngology
AGHHIIOOPRRSTY	historiography
AGHHJLNOORSTWY	John Galsworthy
AGHHLOOOPPTTYY	phytopathology
AGHIIINNNOPSTV	vanishing point
AGHIILLNORRTWY	Ray Illingworth
AGHIILPPSSTUUU	Philip Augustus
AGHIINNORTTUWW	without warning
AGHILNOOOPRSTT	anthropologist
AGHINNOOOSTTTY	nothing to say to
AGIIIIILNOTTTV	vitilitigation
AGIIILLNNQRTUZ	tranquillizing
AGIIKNORRSSTVY	Igor Stravinsky
AGIIILLMMNNOOSU	monolingualism
AGIIILLNOORSUVY	vaingloriously
AGILMNOORRSSTU	Louis Armstrong
AGILNNOPRRSTTY	transportingly
AGLMMOOOPSTTYY	symptomatology
AHHHIKORTTTWWY	Kathy Whitworth
AHHIILNOPPRSTT	philanthropist
AHHIIMNPSTTWYY	in sympathy with
AHHIKNNNOOPSTY	Anthony Hopkins
AHHIOPSTTUUWWY	what's up with you?
AHIILMNNOORSUY	inharmoniously
AHIJLLMNORSTTU	John Stuart Mill
AIIIIIKKKKRTTV	Rikki-Tikki-Tavi
AIIILOOPPRRTTY	propitiatorily
AIIILPRRSTTUUV	Trivial Pursuit®
AIIIMNRSSSTTVY	transmissivity
AIIINNNOOSTTUW	no-win situation
AIILLNORRSSSTY	sinistrorsally
AIILMNOOPRSSUY	parsimoniously
AIKKKMOORRSSVY	Rimsky-Korsakov
AILLNOOOPPRRTY	proportionally

B

BBBCCEEEHIMORU	become chubbier
BBBCDEEEEIIKRX	Bix Beiderbecke
BBBCIINOORSTUU	Bourbon biscuit
BBBDEEGHOORTTU	be brought to bed
BBBEEEGIIILLNV	Bible-believing
BBBEILLOOSSWYY	boys will be boys
BBCEEEEFFILLOR	forcible feeble
BBCEEEEILMNOSS	become sensible
BBCEEEELMOOOST	become obsolete
BBCEEEGHLOORTT	cobble together
BBCEEEHORRRTTU	Robert the Bruce
BBCGIKLLMNOSTU	stumbling-block
BBCIIILMOSTTUY	combustibility
BBCILNOOOOPPRU	pro bono publico
BBDDEEFILLORSY	Sybille Bedford
BBDDEGGIIILNRU	bridge-building
BBDEEGIMOOORRT	bridegroom-to-be
BBDEEHHHILOOSY	hobbledehoyish
BBDEHOOORTTTYY	Betty Boothroyd
BBEEEEEENRRRWZ	Ebenezer Brewer
BBEEEEFHORRTTT	be the better for
BBEEEGHJLOOPSS	Joseph Goebbels
BBEEEGILLNOOSS	noblesse oblige
BBEEEILLNOORRX	Boxer Rebellion
BBEEHHMMRRTTUU	Humbert Humbert
BBEFHJOOORSSTY	jobs for the boys
BBEGGHIKNOOOTY	going by the book
BBEGGIIINNNORT	bring into being
BBEGGIILLORSSU	big girl's blouse
BBEGHIILNOORTT	bring to the boil
BBEGIIILMRSTUY	submergibility
BBEGINNOORRRTW	Robert Browning
BBEIIILMRSSTUY	submersibility
BBEIIKLLNOOSSY	Sibylline Books
BBFIIMMNOOSSTZ	Bob Fitzsimmons
BBIKNNOOOORRSS	Brooks Robinson

BCCDDEEHLLOTUU double-declutch
BCCDEEEENOORTT Benedetto Croce
BCCDEEIIJNORTT indirect object
BCCDEELNOOORTU double concerto
BCCEEEEGILRTTU iceberg lettuce
BCCEEEGIIMNOTX become exciting
BCCEEEHKLORTUV cover the buckle
BCCEEHMNNRRRUU number-cruncher
BCCEEIKKKNORRS knickerbockers
BCCEFHHIKNOPTU pick of the bunch
BCCEIIIJSSTTUV subjectivistic
BCCEIILLRTUVYY City Livery Club
BCCFIIIORSSSTY cystic fibrosis
BCCILNOOSSSUUY subconsciously
BCDDEEEHHILNSU behind schedule
BCDDEEGIINSSSU being discussed
BCDEEEEFIIMNOT become definite
BCDEEEEHILRRVY breech delivery
BCDEEEEMOOPSSU become espoused
BCDEEEHJORSTUU Jude the Obscure
BCDEEEIILNNRSS incredibleness
BCDEEFFIMNOORT combined effort
BCDEEFGIKRRRSU Fredericksburg
BCDEEFHIMMNOOR come from behind
BCDEEHILLLOOTW white blood cell
BCDEEIIILNPRST indiscerptible
BCDEEIILNRSTTU indestructible
BCDEELNOOORSST stone-cold sober
BCDEEMOOOPPRTT copper-bottomed
BCDEENOOORTTUY cry out to be done
BCDEEOORSTTUUY cry out to be used
BCDEFIINORRRSU furor scribendi
BCDEGIILNNPPSU public spending
BCDEGILNOORSSU double-crossing
BCDEHIKNNOOOST in the boondocks
BCDEHIMOPRRTUY hybrid computer
BCDEIIILPPRSTU public-spirited
BCDEIILNRSTTUY indestructibly
BCDENNOOOOPRUZ zero-coupon bond
BCDFIILNNOOTUY bodily function
BCDGHIIMNOOTWY Midnight Cowboy
BCDGILMNNOOOSU blood-consuming
BCDHHIIOOPRTYY hydrophobicity
BCEEEEEHLLRSTU Hercules beetle
BCEEEEHNPRRRST Herbert Spencer
BCEEEELLNOORTV lector benevole
BCEEEFIINOSTTY benefit society
BCEEEFINNORRTU Brief Encounter
BCEEEHHJLNNNOY Johnny Lee Bench
BCEEEHILMNOPRS comprehensible
BCEEEHKNPRRTUY Peter Henry Buck
BCEEEHLNOOOSTT close to the bone
BCEEEIJNSSSTUV subjectiveness
BCEEEIKLNORTUV Lee Buck Trevino
BCEEELLOORSSVY observe closely
BCEEFHJNOOSTTU on the subject of
BCEEFIIILPRTTY perfectibility
BCEEGILLOOORTY electrobiology
BCEEGIMNNNOSSU unbecomingness
BCEEHHIILNORRS Heinrich Olbers
BCEEHILMNOPRSY comprehensibly
BCEEIIILPPRTTY perceptibility
BCEEILNOORRTTV controvertible
BCEGIIJNORSTTU bring to justice
BCEIIILNORTTVY convertibility
BCEIIILPSSTTUY susceptibility
BCEILNOORRTTVY controvertibly
BCEINNOOORRSSU Robinson Crusoe
BCEMNNOOPRTTTU Compton-Burnett
BCFGHIKLLMOORT block light from
BCFGIINNOORSTU bring into focus
BCGHIINNNOORST Chris Bonington
BCGIIILMOOORST microbiologist
BCIIILOPRRTTUY corruptibility
BCIIMNOORSSTTU obstructionism
BCIINOORSSTTTU obstructionist
BCIINOPRSSTTUV subscription TV
BCIKMNNOPRTUUY country bumpkin
BDDEEEEFILLMNY feeble-mindedly
BDDEEEELNNORTU double entendre
BDDEEEILMOORSU edible dormouse
BDDEEGGINNORRU breeding-ground
BDDEEGHNORRUYY Greyhound Derby
BDDEELNNOOPRSU drop one's bundle
BDDEFFIINORRTU forbidden fruit
BDDEFGIINNORSS forbiddingness
BDDEHLLLNOOPSU hold spellbound
BDDHJLNNOOOPUY John Boyd Dunlop
BDEEEEHHHILNTW behind the wheel
BDEEEFFHLOOORT before the flood
BDEEEFGIILMNNR nimble-fingered
BDEEEFGINRRTTU butter-fingered
BDEEEFLNNORSUV bundle of nerves
BDEEEGIMMNOSTU disemboguement
BDEEEHHIIMNSTT behind the times
BDEEEHIINOPSTT beside the point
BDEEEHILNNORVZ Leonid Brezhnev
BDEEEHINSSSSTW send best wishes
BDEEEIILNOOSTV I don't believe so
BDEEEILMMNOSTW disembowelment
BDEEEIMNNOOSST in someone's debt
BDEEEINNOPRRSS inbred response
BDEEEKLOORRTWY Robert Koldewey
BDEEELOOPRSUUX double exposure
BDEEEMNNORSSSU burdensomeness
BDEEGGHHLNOOTU The Golden Bough
BDEEGGHLNOOOTY The Long Goodbye
BDEEGHILLNORST Gilbert Sheldon
BDEEGHNOOSTTUW go down the tubes
BDEEGIIILMNPRU empire-building
BDEEGILLNRSTUW Tunbridge Wells
BDEEGLNOOOPSTU get one's blood up
BDEEHMNNORSTUU under one's thumb
BDEEHNOOORTTXY the boy next door
BDEEIINNOOOSST die in one's boots
BDEEILLNOSUWWY bull's eye window
BDEEINNOOQSTUY beyond question
BDEEINNOOSSSSU do one's business
BDEELMNNORRSUY Reynolds number
BDEEOOORSTTTWY Betsey Trotwood
BDEFFGIIILMNNOU being mindful of
BDEFFHILNOOORR hold no brief for

BDEFHIILNORTWY	Winifred Holtby
BDEGGHILOOOPRW	Whoopi Goldberg
BDEGGIMMNORRSU	Sigmund Romberg
BDEGHIILLMNOST	Billings method
BDEGHIILNNNSST	night-blindness
BDEGIILMNSSTUY	system building
BDEHIIKLNORSTY	Sybil Thorndike
BDEHIILLORSTTT	thrilled to bits
BDEHIKLOPRSSUW	published works
BDEIIILNNOSSSU	libidinousness
BDEIIILRSTTUVY	distributively
BDEIIIMNNOOSTU	omnibus edition
BDEIIINORRSTTU	redistribution
BDEIMNNNORRSUU	in round numbers
BDHIILLOORSTTY	bloodthirstily
BDHJLNNNNOOOSY	Lyndon B Johnson
BDIIIIIILNSTVY	indivisibility
BEEEEEGGKLORRY	George Berkeley
BEEEEEGHPRTTUZ	get the breeze up
BEEEEFGHORTTTT	get the better of
BEEEEFIMNOORST	before one's time
BEEEEGHILPRRTU	Pieter Breughel
	Pieter Brueghel
BEEEEGHLNORRST	Ethel Rosenberg
BEEEEGINNRSTVW	Steven Weinberg
BEEEEHHOORSTTZ	shoot the breeze
BEEEEKLLNNORXY	Lennox Berkeley
BEEEFFGIINNRST	fringe benefits
BEEEFFGIKNOOST	get off one's bike
BEEEFIILLNNSSX	inflexibleness
BEEEGGIIINNNOR	bioengineering
BEEEGHILOOTTVW	give the elbow to
BEEEGHLLNNOORT	longhorn beetle
BEEEGILLNNNORT	nonbelligerent
BEEEHHLNOOOPTT	telephone booth
BEEEHKNORSTUVY	The Rokeby Venus
BEEEHLORRRSTVY	Everly Brothers
BEEEIILNPRSSSX	inexpressibles
BEEEILLNORSSSU	rebelliousness
BEEEILNOPPSSSU	businesspeople
BEEEJMNOORRTTY	remote job entry
BEEEKMOOSSTUUZ	Mobutu Seze Seko
BEEELLNOOOSSTT	lose one's bottle
BEEFGHINOORRTT	bring to the fore
BEEFGILNNOORST	bring oneself to
BEEFIILNNOSSSU	line of business
BEEFILNOOPRRSS	responsible for
BEEFLNNOORSTUU	burn oneself out
BEEGGHIIINNNNT	in the beginning
BEEGHIILLLMNSY	embellishingly
BEEGHIILMNNORV	Emil von Behring
BEEGIIILLLNNTU	unintelligible
BEEGIIOOPRSTTU	petit bourgeois
BEEHHHMPRRTUUY	Hubert Humphrey
BEEHHILLOSTTWW	blow the whistle
BEEHIIOOPPSTTW	be opposite with
BEEHJNOOPRSSTU	Bustopher Jones
BEEHLOOORRSTTU	troubleshooter
BEEHNOPRSSTTTU	press the button
BEEIIILNOOPRST	obiit sine prole
BEEIILLLLTTTTY	little by little
BEEIILLPRRRTTU	pit bull terrier
BEEIILNPPRSSSU	insuppressible
BEEIILOPRSSTVX	visible exports
BEEIIMNOPRSTUV	positive number
BEEIIMNSSSSSUV	submissiveness
BEEIKLLMNORRTU	Robert Mulliken
BEEIKMNNOSSSUY	monkey business
BEEILNNOOPRSST	not responsible
BEEILNPPRSSSUU	unsuppressible
BEEIMNNNNPRSUY	in penny numbers
BEEIMNOOPPRSTU	opposite number
BEEINOOQSSSSUU	obsequiousness
BEEINOORSSSSTU	boisterousness
BEELOOPRRSSTUY	obstreperously
BEFGILNRSSTTUY	flying buttress
BEFIILOPRTTTUY	to put it briefly
BEFKLLOOOORRTU	look for trouble
BEGGHIILNORSTT	strobe lighting
BEGGIIILSSTTUY	suggestibility
BEGHLLLNOOPTUW	pull the long bow
BEGILLNNOOOTTW	wellington boot
BEGILNORSSSUUU	lugubriousness
BEHHIILMOSTTUW	without blemish
BEHHIKNOOPSTTU	put the kibosh on
BEHIKNNRRRSSUU	Burrhus Skinner
BEHILLNOORSWWY	yellowish brown
	yellowish-brown
BEIIIILMPRSSTY	permissibility
BEIIILMOPRSSTV	visible imports
BEIIILNOPRSSTY	responsibility
BEIILNPPRSSSUY	insuppressibly
BEIILSSTTTUUVY	substitutively
BELOPRRSSSSTUU	brussels sprout ❑
BFGGHIINNORRST	bringings forth
BFGILLNORSTTUU	full to bursting
BHIIIINOOPRSTT	prohibitionist
BHMMNOOORSTTUU	button mushroom

C

CCCDEEELNOPRSY	cycle per second
CCCDEEGINNOOOS	good conscience
CCCDEFINNOOSST	soft-conscienc'd
CCCEEEHHHIINNR	chincherinchee
CCCEEFIIINNOST	science fiction
	science-fiction
CCCEEFILLLMORU	come full circle
CCCEIIMMNOOORS	microeconomics
CCCEIIMNOPRSTU	circumspection
CCCEILMORRRUUU	core curriculum
CCCIIIMNNORSUU	uncircumcision
CCCIILMNOORTUU	circumlocution
CCCILMOORRTUUY	circumlocutory
CCDDEEIIIMMOOS	Cosimo de' Medici
CCDDEEILNNOSTY	disconnectedly
CCDDEENNNOOPSU	condescend upon
CCDEEEEGINORTV	give credence to
CCDEEEFFILNNOS	self-confidence
CCDEEEFGIINPRS	gender-specific
CCDEEEFINNOORV	overconfidence
	over-confidence
CCDEEEGNOORRSS	Green Cross Code

CCDEEEHIIKLNRV	chicken-livered
CCDEEEHIINPRST	indirect speech
CCDEEEHLOORRST	close the record
CCDEEEIINNNNOV	inconvenienced
CCDEEEINNNORTT	interconnected
CCDEEELNOPRRTY	preconcertedly
CCDEEENNOOPRRS	correspondence
CCDEEFHIINOPRR	Frédéric Chopin
CCDEEFLNNOOSTU	conduct oneself
CCDEEGIIILNNRV	driving licence
CCDEEGIMNNNOOO	non-comedogenic
CCDEEIILNORTWW	electric window
CCDEEKLLOORSTW	collected works
CCDEELOOOPPRRU	copper-coloured
CCDEGIIMNNOSTU	semiconducting
CCDEHILNORRSTU	children's court
CCDEIIINPRRTTU	printed circuit
CCDEIILMOORTTY	clitoridectomy
CCDEIIOOORRSTT	corticosteroid
CCDEIKLOPQRUUY	produce quickly
CCDEINNOORSTTU	deconstruction
CCDENOOPRRSTUU	superconductor
CCDHHHOOORRTUX	Orthodox Church
CCEEEEEFIINPPV	five pence piece
CCEEEEEJNNRSUV	rejuvenescence
CCEEEEFHIITUVX	chief executive
CCEEEEFNNNORSW	news conference
CCEEEEFNORRRSS	cross-reference
CCEEEEHHHOORTT	cheer to the echo
CCEEEEHMNNOOST	come on the scene
CCEEEEMMMNNORT	recommencement
CCEEEFFIMNOOTT	come into effect
CCEEEFHMNRSUXY	excuse my French
CCEEEFLLLNOOST	collect oneself
CCEEEFLNNNOORS	concern oneself
CCEEEGJLNNORTU	concrete jungle
CCEEEHHILLMRUV	Michel Chevreul
CCEEEHILMORRTT	thermoelectric
CCEEEHILMORSTT	electrochemist
CCEEEILLLORTVY	recollectively
CCEEEINSSSSSUV	successiveness
CCEEELNNOORSTU	close encounter
CCEEENOOPRRTTY	concrete poetry
CCEEFFIILOORST	Coriolis effect
CCEEFHIKKNNRRS	French knickers
CCEEFIMNOOORSU	source of income
CCEEFLNSSSSSUU	successfulness
CCEEGHILLORSST	Christ's College
CCEEGIILLOOSST	ecclesiologist
CCEEGILLLLNNOO	Lincoln College
CCEEGINORRTUVY	give currency to
CCEEGLLOORSSST	St Cross College
CCEEHIIIPRRSTY	hypercriticise
CCEEHIIIPRRTYZ	hypercriticize
CCEEHIILLMOPTU	multiple-choice
CCEEHILOPRSTUW	white corpuscle
CCEEHKNOOPRSTU	checkout person
CCEEILLMOORSTT	collector's item
CCEEILLNNOOTUV	collective noun
CCEEILNNOSSSUV	conclusiveness
CCEEILNOSSSSSU	successionless
CCEEINOOPRSSSU	precociousness
CCEEINORRSTTUV	reconstructive
CCEELNORRTTUUU	counter-culture
CCEFHNOOOSTTTU	count the cost of
CCEFIJOORSTTUU	court of justice
CCEFLLNSSSUUUY	unsuccessfully
CCEGNOOOORRSST	concerto grosso
CCEHIIIMOORSTT	stoichiometric
CCEHIIIMPRRSTY	hypercriticism
CCEHIMOOSSTUYZ	schizomycetous
CCEIILLNNOSUVY	inconclusively
CCEIILORRSTUUV	virtuous circle
CCEIINORSSSTUU	circuitousness
CCEILNORSTTUVY	constructively
CCEIMOOOPRRRSS	microprocessor
CCEINNOORRSTTU	reconstruction
CCGHHIKLOPRSTU	Christoph Gluck
CCGHIIOOPRSTYY	hygroscopicity
CCHIIOPRRRTVYY	Pyrrhic victory
CCIIIJNNOSTTUV	conjunctivitis
CCIIILPRSSTTUU	pisciculturist
CCIIMNORSSTTUV	Constructivism
CCILLNNOOORTUW	town councillor
CCILMNOOPSTUUY	compunctiously
CCILNNOORSSTUY	try conclusions
CDDDEEFIKORRSY	Frederick Soddy
CDDDEEHLLOORSU	cold shouldered
CDDEEEFIMRRRUY	Freddie Mercury
CDDEEEIIMORSVW	received wisdom
CDDEEENOOPRRRT	not prerecorded
CDDEEGHLMNOOTU	dodge the column
CDDEEGIIINNRSV	dividing screen
CDDEEGIINOORRV	video recording
CDDEEIKLNNOUVY	Ludovic Kennedy
CDDEEILNNOSTTY	discontentedly
CDDEGIIILLNRRT	direct drilling
CDDEHIILMOORSU	sodium chloride
CDEEEEEIINPRWX	wide experience
CDEEEEEINNQSUV	Queen's evidence
CDEEEEFIKLORRW	Frederick Loewe
CDEEEEFMNNNOSS	mend one's fences
CDEEEEHOPPRRST	reported speech
CDEEEENNPSSTUX	unexpectedness
CDEEEFGILLNNSU	self-indulgence
CDEEEFILORRTTT	letter of credit
CDEEEFIMNNOPRS	presence of mind
CDEEEFLLORRUVY	fully recovered
CDEEEGILNNORUV	overindulgence
CDEEEHIINNRRSV	Vreni Schneider
CDEEEIIINNSSSV	indecisiveness
CDEEEIIMMNOSTV	decisive moment
CDEEEINOOPRRRT	reception order
CDEEEINPRTTUUX	cut expenditure
CDEEEINRRSSSTT	restrictedness
CDEEEIORSTTTVY	detective story
CDEEELNNNOOORT	nolo contendere
CDEEFGHINNRRSS	French dressing
CDEEFGIIKNRSTY	sticky-fingered
CDEEFGIOORSSTY	dregs of society
CDEEFHKNOOOSTW	neck of the woods
CDEEFHLLRSTTUY	fully stretched

CDEEFIIILLNPSS	self-discipline
CDEEFLLLNOORST	self-controlled
CDEEGGILLNNOOW	Downing College
CDEEGHIIKLNPRR	pickled herring
CDEEGILNNORXYY	oxygen cylinder
CDEEHHINORRTTU	Henri Dutrochet
CDEEHIIIORRSTW	Cider with Rosie
CDEEHIKNORTTUW	round the wicket
CDEEHLMOOORTTW	the world to come
CDEEHLOOOORSTT	close the door to
CDEEHNNOORRRTU	round the corner
CDEEIIINNSSTVV	vindictiveness
CDEEIIMMNOORSS	decommissioner
CDEEIINRSSSSUV	discursiveness
CDEEIJLOOPRRST	slide projector
CDEEIKNNORRSTW	wonder-stricken
CDEEILLNNNNOOS	Ninon de Lenclos
CDEEILLNOOPTUY	polynucleotide
CDEEILMOOPPSUX	Oedipus complex
CDEEILNOORRSUX	exclusion order
CDEEILOPRRTUVY	reproductively
CDEEIMNNNOSTTT	discontentment
CDEEINNOORSSSU	indecorousness
CDEEINOPRSSTUV	productiveness
CDEEKNOORRRUVW	undercover work
CDEELLRRSTTUUW	well-structured
CDEELOPRRSSTUU	produce results
CDEENNOOPRRSST	correspondents
CDEENNOORSTTVY	send to Coventry
CDEENRRRSTTUUU	understructure
CDEFFIIIILNSTU	in difficulties
CDEFFNOOOOPRTU	foot-pound force
CDEFGHOOOORRTT	go for the doctor
CDEFGIINORRRST	first recording
CDEFGINOOPRRTU	foreign product
CDEFHIIKPPRRRU	Friedrich Krupp
CDEFHLLOOORTWW	follow the crowd
CDEGHHIIILNPPR	high-principled
CDEGHHIILNORSY	consider highly
CDEGHHNOOSSTTU	second thoughts
CDEGHLOOPRRUUY	produce roughly
CDEGIIINNNOORT	reconditioning
CDEGINOOPRRSSW	word-processing
CDEGINOOPRRSUW	scouring powder
CDEHIILLNRSSST	Schindler's List
CDEHILMNNOOPTT	hold in contempt
CDEHINNNORSUYZ	unsynchronized
CDEHINOOPRRSTW	correspond with
CDEIIIILRSTTUV	diverticulitis
CDEIIIINRSSTTY	identity crisis
CDEIIIKLMNNOSY	Emily Dickinson
CDEIIINNNSSSTT	indistinctness
CDEIILNNOOPRTU	production line
CDEIILNORSSSUU	ridiculousness
CDEIINNOORRTTU	reintroduction
CDEIINNOPSSSUU	cupidinousness
CDEIIOPRRTTUVY	reproductivity
CDEIKLNNOOSSUW	lick one's wounds
CDEILOORSSTUUY	discourteously
CDEIMMNOOOSSSU	commodiousness
CDEKLNNNOOOSUW	down on one's luck
CDELLLNNOORTUY	uncontrolledly
CDFFHIIILTTUWY	with difficulty
CDFIINNOOOOTTU	out of condition
CDGNNOOORSTUWY	God's own country
CDHJNNOOSSSTUU	John Duns Scotus
CDHMOOOORTTTUY	try to do too much
CDIILMMNOOOSUY	incommodiously
CDIILNOORRTTUY	introductorily
CDIIMNNOOORTTU	induction motor
CDINOOOPPRSTTU	post-production
CEEEEFFKNOSTTY	keystone effect
CEEEEFGINNQRUY	eigen-frequency
CEEEEFHNORSSTT	set the scene for
CEEEEFILNRSSTV	reflectiveness
CEEEEFINNOPRRT	in preference to
	reference-point
CEEEEGIILNNORT	electioneering
CEEEEGIINNRSVV	evening service
CEEEEHIILRRSST	Leicestershire
CEEEEHLNPSSSSS	speechlessness
CEEEEHLORSSTTT	settle the score
CEEEEIKNOPRRWX	work experience
CEEEEILMNNPSST	simple sentence
CEEEEINPPRSSTV	perceptiveness
CEEEEINPRRSTVY	in every respect
CEEEEPRSSSTTUZ	crêpes suzettes
CEEEFFGHIOPRSU	figure of speech
CEEEFFGIIORRST	register office
CEEEFFGILNRSVY	effervescingly
CEEEFFILPRSTTU	Peter Sutcliffe
CEEEFGILNPRSST	self-respecting
CEEEFGLLNNSSTU	neglectfulness
CEEEFHNNORSSSU	rush one's fences
CEEEFIILMPRTVY	imperfectively
CEEEFIIOPRRSTV	irrespective of
CEEEFILOORRSSX	floor exercises
CEEEFLNNOQSSTU	self-consequent
CEEEFLNPRSSSTU	respectfulness
CEEEGGGKLLLLOO	Kellogg College
CEEEGGGMNOORRV	George McGovern
CEEEGHIIKNNTTT	get it in the neck
CEEEGHIINORSUV	receiving-house
CEEEGHLLLNOTYY	ethylene glycol
CEEEGIILLNNNTU	unintelligence
CEEEGILNORRTTV	covering letter
CEEEGLMNOSTUUW	unwelcome guest
CEEEHHIIKKNTTT	kick in the teeth
CEEEHHIIMNNOST	mose in the chine
CEEEHHIINRSVWW	In Which We Serve
CEEEHHILOPRRST	Christopher Lee
CEEEHIJNOPSTTU	step on the juice
CEEEHIKNNOPPSU	keep one's chin up
CEEEHIMORSSTTY	hysterectomise
CEEEHIMORSTTYZ	hysterectomize
CEEEHIORRRSSTW	Worcestershire
CEEEHMMOPSSSTY	metempsychoses
CEEEHMNNOOORTU	roche moutonnée
CEEEHNNOOSTTTU	cut one's teeth on
CEEEIIKNNPRSST	pernicketiness
CEEEIILPRRSTVY	irrespectively
CEEEIIMOORRSST	stereoisomeric

CEEEIKLNNOOPST line one's pocket
CEEEILMNNOPSST incompleteness
CEEEILNORRRSTU senior lecturer
CEEEIMNNORTTUX extreme unction
CEEEINNOOPRSSS con espressione
CEEEINOPRSSTTV protectiveness
CEEEIOOPRRTTVV overprotective
over-protective
CEEEKOOPRRRSSU pressure cooker
CEEELLOPPRRRSW screw propeller
CEEENOORSSTUYY cry one's eyes out
CEEENORRRSSTUU ruse contre ruse
CEEFFFFHIIORRS sheriff officer
CEEFFFIILNSSTU self-sufficient
CEEFGIINNORTTU counterfeiting
CEEFGLLLNOOOSW Wolfson College
CEEFHHILLNRTTU left in the lurch
CEEFHINOOPRSST in the process of
CEEFHINORTTUWY The Country Wife
CEEFHMNOOORTTT come to the front
CEEFIILORRSSTZ cross-fertilize
CEEFIINNOSSSTU infectiousness
CEEFIJOOSSSTUY Society of Jesus
CEEFILMNNRSSUU unmercifulness
CEEFINOORSSSUV vociferousness
CEEFLLNNOOORST control oneself
CEEFLMNOOOPRST comport oneself
CEEGGHHLLOSSTU St Hugh's College
CEEGGOORRSSSST St George's cross
CEEGHIILNRRTTV right ventricle
CEEGHIILRSTUVX exclusive right
CEEGHINNOPPRST shopping centre
CEEGHJLLNOOSST St John's College
CEEGIILLNORTTY Trinity College
CEEGIILNNORRTY nitroglycerine
CEEGIIMNNORRSV morning service
CEEGIINNNPRRST screen printing
CEEGILMNNORSTU steering column
steering-column
CEEGNNOOPRRTUU encounter group
CEEHHHIINORRRR Heinrich Rohrer
CEEHHINOOOPSUW whoopee cushion
CEEHHINQRRSTTU thirst-quencher
CEEHHKLLMOORSS Sherlock Holmes
CEEHHMOOORRSTU heterochromous
CEEHHNOOPPRSST phosphorescent
CEEHIILNNOPRSS phenolic resins
CEEHIILNOPSSTT sit on the splice
CEEHIIMNOOPTTT the competition
CEEHIIMOORSTTY stoicheiometry
CEEHIINOSSTTUX the Six Counties
CEEHILLOORSTUV Louis Chevrolet
CEEHILMNOOPSTU photoluminesce
CEEHILMORSSTUV The Music Lovers
CEEHIMMMNOSTTT The Commitments
CEEHIMMOPSSSTY metempsychosis
CEEHIMOOOPRST oophorectomise
CEEHIMOOOPRTZ oophorectomize
CEEHIMOPRRSTTY petrochemistry
CEEHINNNOOSTTW with one consent
CEEHINOQSSSTTU coquettishness
CEEHINORRRSTUU run their course
CEEHKLNOOORSTV Love on the Rocks
CEEHNOOPRSSSUY psychoneuroses
CEEHNOPRSSTTUW put the screws on
CEEIIINNORSSTZ senior citizens
CEEIILMORRSTUY meretriciously
CEEIILNNNNOTVY inconveniently
CEEIILNNOSSSTU licentiousness
CEEIILNORSSTTW winter solstice
CEEIILNPSSTUVY insusceptively
CEEIILPPRRSTVY prescriptively
CEEIINNOPRSSSU perniciousness
CEEIINNORRSTTV non-restrictive
CEEIKMMOORSTTW works committee
CEEIKNORRRRSTT terror-stricken
CEEILLLMOORRVW Oliver Cromwell
CEEILMMORSSSTU summer solstice
CEEILMNOSSSTUU meticulousness
CEEILMOOORSSST electro-osmosis
CEEILMOORSTUUV over-meticulous
CEEILNNNOQSTUY inconsequently
CEEILNNOOPRSSU Cornelius Nepos
CEEILNORRSSUYY yours sincerely
CEEIMNOOPRRSST Inspector Morse
CEEINNNOPRSTTU supercontinent
CEEINNOORSSSSU censoriousness
CEEINOOPRRSTTU counter-riposte
CEEKNNOOOSSTTT Stockton-on-Tees
CEELLRRTTUUUUV culture vulture
CEEPRRRSSTTUUU superstructure
CEFFGIINNORRSU nursing officer
CEFFIIILNNSTUY insufficiently
CEFFINOOOPRSST score points off
CEFGHINOORSSST sign of the cross
CEFGIIKLLNORST stocking filler
CEFHHIOPRRRSTY Christopher Fry
CEFHHJNOOORSST John of the Cross
CEFHILNNOOORTT in the control of
CEFHMMNOOOOSSU House of Commons
CEFHNOOORTTTUU out for the count
CEFILNNOOSSTTT list of contents
CEFINOOORSSSTU Court of Session
CEGHHIINOTTTUW get in touch with
CEGHHIKLORRTTU trickle through
CEGHNOOORTTTUY go to the country
CEGIIIKLNQRSUV quicksilvering
CEGIIIMNNOOTVW coming into view
CEGILNNPSSTUUY unsuspectingly
CEHHHIORSTTTWW throw the switch
CEHHIKLMNPRRUY Humphry Clinker
CEHHILOPRRSSTY Christopher Sly
CEHHIMOOPRSTTY photochemistry
CEHHINOOPSTTTY photosynthetic
CEHIIIKLMOOPRT poikilothermic
CEHIINNOSSTTTW consistent with
CEHIJLNOOORSTU join the colours
CEHIKLLNOORSST kill on the cross
CEHIKNOORRRRST horror-stricken
CEHIKRRSSTTTUW Kurt Schwitters
CEHILMOORSSSST schoolmistress
CEHILOPRRSSTUY holy Scriptures

CEIIIINOSSTTVV vivisectionist
CEIIIMOOPRSTTV over-optimistic
CEIIIMPPRRSSTV prescriptivism
CEIIKMNNOOSSST motion sickness
CEIILLOPRSSUUY superciliously
CEIILNNNOSSTTY inconsistently
CEIILNOOSSSSTU solicitousness
CEIILOPPRRSTVY proscriptively
CEIIMNNOOOPSSU pneumoconiosis
CEIINNOORSTTTU reconstitution
CEIINOORSSSTUV victoriousness
CEIINOPPRRSSTU superscription
CEIINOPSSSSSUU suspiciousness
CEIKNOOPRSSTTU up to one's tricks
CEILLMNOOSTUUY contumeliously
CEILNORRSSSSUU scurrilousness
CEIMMMMOOORTTY commit to memory
CEINNNOOSSSTUU continuousness
CEKLMOOPRSTTUU mock turtle soup
CELMNOOPSTTUUY contemptuously
CELNOPRSSSSUUU scrupulousness
CELOOPRRSSUUUV overscrupulous
CFFHIILMNOSTTU fifth columnist
CFGIILMNNOORSU soul-confirming
CFGIINNNNNOOTU non-functioning
CFGIINNNNOOTTU not functioning
CGHHIIIMMNOOSS High Commission
CGIIILNNORTTUY continuity girl
CGIIILNNRSSTUY scrutinisingly
CGIIILNNRSTUYZ scrutinizingly
CGIIILNOOOPSST oligopsonistic
CGIILNNOOSTUUY incontiguously
CGIIMMNNOOPRSU uncompromising
CGILMNNOOORSTU consulting room
CHHJMNOOORSSTY John Chrysostom
CHHKNOORSSTTUW not worth shucks
CHIIKKNOOORRTV Viktor Korchnoi
CHIILORRSTTTUU horticulturist
CHILMOOORSTTUY trichotomously
CIILNOPSSSUUUY unsuspiciously
CLLNOPRSSUUUUY unscrupulously

D

DDDEEEEELNOPRUV underdeveloped
DDDEEIIJKLNSUU Julius Dedekind
DDDEEIIMNNORSU Edmund Ironside
DDEEEEFHILNOPT dip of the needle
DDEEEEGHHIRRTT the third degree
DDEEEEGHNOOTWW the wooden wedge
DDEEEEHINNNPTT The Independent
DDEEEEINNNPRTT interdependent
DDEEEELMMNOSSS meddlesomeness
DDEEEFLLLOPUVY fully-developed
DDEEEGHHLORTTU huddle together
DDEEEHILNOSTTW let the side down
DDEEEIIKLMNNSS like-mindedness
DDEEEIIMORTUUX deuterium oxide
DDEEEIMNNNOPSS open-mindedness
DDEEEIMNNNORTU undermentioned
DDEEELOORSTTVY Teddy Roosevelt
DDEEFIIMOORSST from side to side
DDEEGHHIIMNNSS high-mindedness
DDEEGHINOOSSSW send good wishes
DDEEGIILLMNNSY single-mindedly
DDEEGILNNNOSSW long-windedness
DDEEHIINNOSTWY on the windy side
DDEEHINNORRSUU undernourished
DDEEIIIILMNOTT limited edition
DDEEIIINPRSSST dispiritedness
DDEEIIJNNOSSST disjointedness
DDEEIILNORRSSS disorderliness
DDEEIIMNOORTTU Dieu et mon droit
DDEELMNOOORTUY Old Deuteronomy
DDEEMNOOOOPRSU do someone proud
DDEFHIMNOSTTUY study of the mind
DDEFIIILMOOQSU semi-liquid food
DDEFLLNOORRUWW Wonderful World
DDEGGINOOOOSSY goody-goodiness
DDEGHHLOOOOSSU household goods
DDEGHLMOOORUUY good-humouredly
DDEGHLNNOOORSU hold one's ground
DDEGIINNORSSWW window dressing
window-dressing
DDEHIIIMNNORST third dimension
DDEHIILOPRSUUX sulphur dioxide
DDEHIMNNOPSTUW down in the dumps
DDEINNOPRSTUUW turn upside down
turn upside-down
DDGHHIKNOOORTY Dorothy Hodgkin
DEEEEFILNRSSTT self-interested
DEEEEGGHIMORRT George Meredith
DEEEEGGIINNNRS design engineer
DEEEEGHHILMSTY highly esteemed
DEEEEGNORSSSTT get one's deserts
DEEEEHNNPPRSST Stephen Spender
DEEEEILLMMOSSS Mesdemoiselles
DEEEEIMNPRRSST misrepresented
DEEEEINRSSTTTV vested interest
DEEEENNRRSSSUV unreservedness
DEEEFFGHIMORRT freedom fighter
freedomfighter
DEEEFFHIPRSSTU sheriff deputes
DEEEFFIMNOOORS ride someone off
DEEEFGHIORTTTT fitted together
DEEEFHILORRUVW four-wheel drive
DEEEFHIMNOOTTT to the end of time
DEEEFIIINNNSST indefiniteness
DEEEFIIINNSSTV definitiveness
DEEEFIILNPRRST Flinders Petrie
DEEEFILNNOOPRS pride oneself on
DEEEFILNNRSSSS friendlessness
DEEEFLLMNNOOOS model oneself on
DEEEGHIILNNOSS dig in one's heels
dig one's heels in
DEEEGIIKLNNNTT knitting needle
DEEEGINNOSSTTU tongue-tiedness
DEEEGIOPRRSSTT registered post
DEEEGMNNOOOSTW get someone down
DEEEHHLOORSTTT three-toed sloth
DEEEHHPPRRSSSU shepherd's purse
DEEEHIINNOOSSS die in one's shoes
DEEEHLLMOOOPPS old people's home

DEEEHLLNOPRRST	Stephen Dorrell
DEEEIIMNNNOSSY	in one's mind's eye
DEEEIIMNPRRSTT	misinterpreted
DEEEIIMNRSSTTV	divertissement
DEEEIINORRSSVV	Revised Version
DEEEIKMNNNOOPS	keep one's mind on
DEEEILNOPRRSVY	delivery-person
DEEEINNNPRSTTU	superintendent
DEEEINORRRRSST	dernier ressort
DEEEMNNORSSSTU	tremendousness
DEEFFHHLOORSTU	off the shoulder
DEEFFHILLOORST	Lord of the Flies
DEEFGHIIOPRSTV	deprive of sight
DEEFGHILLNSSTU	delightfulness
DEEFHLNOORRSUZ	frozen shoulder
DEEFHLNOORSTWW	News of the World
DEEFHNOOOPSTTU	out of one's depth
DEEFIIILMOPRSV	oversimplified
DEEFIILNNNRSSU	unfriendliness
DEEFIIMNNORSTT	first-mentioned
DEEFIINOPRSSSU	perfidiousness
DEEFINNOOSSTTY	Stone of Destiny
DEEFLOORRRTTUW	four-letter word
DEEFMMNOOORTVX	Oxford Movement
DEEGGMNNOORTTW	don't get me wrong
DEEGHHHILORSTU	shoulder-height
DEEGHHIINOSTTT	on the tight side
DEEGHIIMNOPRSW	whispering dome
DEEGHILNOOTVWW	give the low-down
DEEGHIMNOOORST	do someone right
DEEGHLNNOOOSTU	hold one's tongue
DEEGIIILLPSYZZ	Dizzy Gillespie
DEEGIIILMOOPST	epidemiologist
DEEGIIINNORRST	interior design
DEEGIIJMNNSTTU	sit in judgement
DEEGIINNSTTUUV	uninvited guest
DEEGILMNNRSTTU	disgruntlement
DEEGILNNNPRTUY	unpretendingly
DEEGLNNORSSSSU	groundlessness
DEEGMNNOOOORSW	do someone wrong
DEEGMNOPRTTTUU	trumpet-tongued
DEEHHIILNOSTWW	how the wind lies
DEEHHINOORSSTT	on the short side
DEEHHLNOOORSSS	hold one's horses
DEEHIKLNNORRTZ	Hendrik Lorentz
DEEHINOOPPRRRU	Pierre Proudhon
DEEHKLNOORSSTT	the Lord's tokens
DEEHKMNOOOORSW	do one's homework
DEEHLLMMOSTTUY	sell the dummy to
DEEHMMMNOOORST	Theodor Mommsen
DEEHNNOORRSSSU	horrendousness
DEEIIIILMRSTUV	verisimilitude
DEEIIIMNNSSTUV	diminutiveness
DEEIIKNORRRSSU	serious drinker
DEEIILNOPSSSST	split one's sides
DEEILNNSSTTUYY	study intensely
DEEIMNNNOOOPSW	pin someone down
DEEIMNNNOOPRSY	prey on one's mind
DEENNOOOOPRSST	on one's doorstep
DEENNOPSSSSTUU	stupendousness
DEFFHHLOOORRTT	hold the fort for
DEFGHILLOOOPSW	good fellowship
DEFGHIMNNORSTT	strength of mind
DEFGHIMNOOORST	do something for
DEFGNOOOORSSUW	goods for own use
DEFHHJNOORRRTU	John Rutherford
DEFHILLNOQTTUU	not the full quid
DEFHINOOOTTUWW	out of the window
DEFHLNOOORRTTW	not for the world
DEFIIJKLOPSSUZ	Józef Pilsudski
DEFIIKNOOORRRW	indoor firework
DEFLMMNNOOOSUU	Museum of London
DEGHHIIKLRSTTU	Turkish delight
DEGHHILORSSTTY	short-sightedly
DEGHHOOORSTTTW	throw to the dogs
DEGHILNOOPRTUW	go up in the world
DEGHIMNNOOOSTT	not do something
DEGHINNNOOOSTW	do one's own thing
DEGIIIKMNNPRTU	drinking-up time
DEGIIKLNNNOSSV	loving-kindness
DEGIIKNNOORRRW	in working order
DEGIILNNOSSUUY	disingenuously
DEGILNOORSSTUY	soul-destroying
DEHHHILNOOSSTW	hold one's whisht
DEHHIMNNOOTTUW	down in the mouth
DEHIILNNOPTTTU	put the tin lid on
DEHIILOOPPRRSW	idol-worshipper
DEHIIMOOOPPRST	photoperiodism
DEHIIOPSTTTUUW	without dispute
DEHILNNOORRTTW	Thornton Wilder
DEHIMMOOPPRSSU	pseudomorphism
DEIIIILLNOSSSU	disillusionise
DEIIIILLNOSSUZ	disillusionize
DEIIINOOPPRSST	predisposition
DEIIMNNNRSTTUW	wind instrument
DELMNOOPSSUUYY	pseudonymously
DFGGHINNOOOORT	good-for-nothing
DFGHIIILLMNSTW	fight windmills
DFHHIIILNOORSUW	Irish wolfhound
DFHILOOORSTTUW	out of this world
DGGHIIIINNSSTU	distinguishing
DGHIINNOOPPSWW	window-shopping
DGHINORRSTTUWY	growth industry
DGIIIKLNNQSUUV	Vidkun Quisling
DHHIIMOOPRSTYY	hypothyroidism

E

EEEEEENOOSTTYY	not see eye to eye
EEEEEFGLNNORSV	revenge oneself
EEEEEFILLNORSV	relieve oneself
EEEEEFINPRRRST	free enterprise
	free-enterprise
EEEEEGGHORRTTY	Georgette Heyer
EEEEFFGGJORRSY	George Jeffreys
EEEEFFHLNORRSS	refresh oneself
EEEEFFLMOORRRS	feel remorse for
EEEEFGHHILNSST	The Selfish Gene
EEEEFGIINORRTV	give free rein to
EEEEFGLNNRSSUV	revengefulness
EEEEFIMNNORRTV	over-refinement
EEEEFIMNORRRTT	interferometer
EEEEFINOORSSTT	rise to one's feet

EEEEFJLNOPRRSU perjure oneself
EEEEFKNNOPRSSS free-spokenness
EEEEFLNNOPRSST present oneself
EEEEFLNNOPRSTV prevent oneself
EEEEFLNOPRSSSX express oneself
EEEEGGLNOORSTV get one's leg over
EEEEGGNNOOSSSU Eugene Goossens
EEEEGHLLOTTVVV the velvet glove
EEEEGHMOSSTTUY get some shut-eye
EEEEGILLMNNRTT little green men
EEEEGINRRSSSSV regressiveness
EEEEGJLLORRSUW jeweller's rouge
EEEEHILNPRRSVY reprehensively
EEEEHIMMNORRTT retirement home
EEEEHIMNPRSTTT the present time
EEEEHJRRSSTTUV just the reverse
EEEEIINPRSSTTV repetitiveness
EEEEILLLNOPPVY Penelope Lively
EEEEINNOPRRSTZ enterprise zone
EEEEINNPRRTTTU turpentine tree
EEEEINPRSSSSVX expressiveness
EEEELLNNRSSSST relentlessness
EEEELMNOOPRSST lose one's temper
EEEENNOORRSUVY run one's eye over
EEEFFFGHIORRSY Geoffrey Fisher
EEEFFFHILMOORT for the life of me
EEEFFFNNOORSTU run off one's feet
EEEFFHIILLORTY the life of Riley
EEEFFHIJLOSSTU The Life of Jesus
EEEFFHLNOORTUW wheel of Fortune
wheel of fortune
EEEFFILMMORSST Mr Mistoffelees
EEEFFLNORSSSST effortlessness
EEEFGGHIILNNRT flight engineer
EEEFGIILNOPSUV give up one's life
EEEFGLMNNORSTV self-government
EEEFHHLNOOPSTU upon the heels of
EEEFHKOOPRSTWY power of the keys
EEEFHLOOOPRTVW The Power of Love
EEEFILLNNRSTWX twin-lens reflex
EEEFILNOPRSSSX self-expression
EEEFLLMMNOPSTY self-employment
EEEFLLMNNOOPSU plume oneself on
EEEFLMNNRTUXYY extremely funny
EEEFLMNORRSSSU remorsefulness
EEEFLNNNSSTUUV uneventfulness
EEEFNOOPPRSSSU sense of purpose
EEEGGGHINORRSW George Gershwin
EEEGGHINNORSTW wigs on the green
EEEGGHLLOORTTW go well together
EEEGGIMNNOORSS Georges Simenon
EEEGGINOORRSSS one's gorge rises
EEEGGINSSSSTUV suggestiveness
EEEGHIINORSTTV give the reins to
EEEGHILNSSSSTW weightlessness
EEEGHKLORRSUYY keyhole surgery
EEEGIIKMNOPPRS promise-keeping
EEEGIIMNRRSSST Meistersingers
EEEGILLLLMRUUV Lemuel Gulliver
EEEGILLMNORTUY you're telling me
EEEGIMNNOPPRRU emperor penguin
EEEGLNNOOOSSTU lose one's tongue
EEEGNNNORSSSUU ungenerousness
EEEHHILMOPPSST Mephistopheles
EEEHIINPRSSSTY hypersensitise
EEEHIINPRSSTVY hypersensitive
EEEHIINPRSSTYZ hypersensitize
EEEHILNOSSTTWW wet one's whistle
EEEHIORRSTTUVW without reserve
EEEHJNOOPRRSTW Joseph Rowntree
EEEHLNNNOORSTU turn on one's heel
EEEHMNOOOORRST someone or other
EEEHNOOSSSTTUY shut one's eyes to
EEEHNOPPRSTTTU up to the present
EEEIILMNPRSSTT simple interest
EEEIILMNPSTTVY intempestively
EEEIILNPRRTTVY interpretively
EEEIIMNORSUVWY Yoweri Museveni
EEEIIMNPRSSSSV impressiveness
permissiveness
EEEIKNNNOOOPSS poke one's nose in
EEEILMNNPRSTUY supereminently
EEEILNOPRSSSSX expressionless
EEEILNORRSSSTU irresoluteness
EEEIMMNNOPRSSU immune response
EEEIMNOOPSSTUW put someone wise
EEEIMNOPPRRSST peremptoriness
EEEINNOPRSSSSV responsiveness
EEEINOPPRSSSSV oppressiveness
EEEINOPSSSSSSV possessiveness
EEEIPPRRSTTTTY pretty-pretties
EEEJLLLMOPRTUY petroleum jelly
EEEKLMNNOOOSTW let someone know
EEEKLNNOOOOPSW keep one's wool on
EEELMOPRSSSUVX express volumes
EEEMMMNNOOSTVW women's movement
EEFFFILLLMNSTU self-fulfilment
EEFFFILLNNOSSU fluff one's lines
EEFFFILNOORSTY fortify oneself
EEFFGGILNORSTT self-forgetting
EEFFHHILLOORTT for the hell of it
EEFFHHOOPRSSTT hot off the press
EEFFHILOOORTTV for the love of it
EEFFHINNOORRTT in the forefront
EEFFILNNOORRSU run for one's life
EEFFIMNOOOPSSS piss someone off
EEFFLLNOOORSTY off one's trolley
EEFGHIILNOTTUW without feeling
EEFGHIKOOPSTTU keep out of sight
EEFGHILPRSTUWY super-flyweight
EEFGHINNOORRST foreshortening
EEFGIIILNNPRRT relief printing
EEFGIIKLLLNNOS killing oneself
EEFGIINNNNORRT non-interfering
EEFGIKNOORSSTU stroke of genius
EEFGILLLNOPPRS self-propelling
EEFGILLNNORTTU fortune-telling
EEFGILNNOOPPST topping oneself
EEFGLNOOQRTTUY go to frequently
EEFHHILOORSSTW two for his heels
EEFHILMNNPSSTU self-punishment
EEFHILNRSSSSTT thriftlessness

EEFHJLLNOOTTUY	enjoy to the full
EEFHLLLOORSTUW	follow the rules
EEFHLLOOOSTTWW	lowest of the low
EEFHLNNOOORSTW	throw oneself on
EEFIIMMMOORTTT	from time to time
EEFILLNNOOOPSW	in one fell swoop
EEFILNOOPSSSSS	self-possession
EEFLLMNORRSUUY	unremorsefully
EEFLLNNOOOOSSW	follow one's nose
EEFLMNOOOORRVY	for love or money
EEFLNOOPPRSSTU	support oneself
EEFLNOPPRSSSUU	purposefulness
EEGGGHIKLNORTY	George Knightly
EEGGHHIILNNSTT	sheet lightning
EEGGHHIOPSTTUV	give up the ghost
EEGGHIILNRRSTV	reversing light
EEGGHINORSTTTV	give strength to
EEGGIIIPPSSTUU	Giuseppe Giusti
EEGGIILNNNSTTT	stinging nettle
EEGGNOOOPRRTTW	Port Georgetown
EEGHHHINOOPRST	on the high ropes
EEGHHHNOORSTTU	through the nose
EEGHHIILNPSSTW	sheep-whistling
EEGHHIOORSTTWW	go with the worse
EEGHHLOPRSTTTU	the gospel truth
EEGHHNOORRTTTW	thrown together
	thrown-together
EEGHIIKNNRRSSY	Henry Kissinger
EEGHIILOORSSUU	religious house
EEGHIIMNOQSTTU	quite something
EEGHILLMNNORTW	Wilhelm Röntgen
EEGHILLMNORVWY	overwhelmingly
EEGHILLNOPSTUW	pull one's weight
EEGHILNNOOPSTT	single hoop tent
EEGHINOPRTTTUY	Pitt the younger
EEGIIIILNPRRUV	Pier Luigi Nervi
EEGIIIMNOPRSSV	give permission
EEGIIKLNNNOSTV	Ken Livingstone
EEGIILMNORTTUU	ultimogeniture
EEGIILMOOPSSTT	epistemologist
EEGIILNNNPRSTY	serpentiningly
EEGIILNNPRRSTY	enterprisingly
EEGIIMNNRSSTUY	men in grey suits
EEGIINNNORSTTT	not interesting
EEGIINNNPRRSTU	unenterprising
EEGIKLOOORRSVY	Sergei Korolyov
EEGILLNORRTTWY	terry towelling
EEGILNOOPRRSVW	resolving power
EEGILNOOPRRVWY	overpoweringly
EEGINOOPPSSTUV	give up one's post
EEGKLNNNOOOPRS	no longer spoken
EEHHHIJNNNORYZ	Henry John Heinz
EEHHIILLOSTWWY	yellowish-white
EEHHILNOORSTWW	worth one's while
EEHHINNOORSTTT	sit on the throne
EEHHIOPPPPTTYY	hippety-hoppety
EEHHIOPPRSTTUW	with the purpose
EEHHLLOOPRSTUY	heterophyllous
EEHHLLOORSTTUY	youth hosteller
EEHHMOOOORRSTW	somehow or other
EEHIILMNNQRSTU	relinquishment
EEHIIMMNOPRSTV	impoverishment
EEHIINOOPSSSTT	photosensitise
EEHIINOOPSSTTZ	photosensitize
EEHIIOPRSTTTUW	without respite
EEHIJLOPPRSTUZ	Joseph Pulitzer
EEHIMOOPRRRSTU	mother superior
EEHINNNOOOPPSS	pin one's hopes on
EEHINNOORSSTTW	noteworthiness
EEHINNOPRRTTTU	three-point turn
EEHINOOPPQSTTU	pop the question
EEHKNOOPRSTTWY	The New York Post
EEHLMNORSSSSUU	humourlessness
EEIIIIKLLLSTTT	tell it like it is
EEIILMNNRTTTTY	intermittently
EEIILNOPRRSSVY	irresponsively
EEIILNPRRTTUVY	interruptively
EEIILNPRSSSSST	spiritlessness
EEIILOPRSSTTUV	positive result
EEIILPRRSSTUUU	leisure pursuit
EEIIMMNNNORRSS	nine men's morris
EEIIMNNNOOOPST	pin it on someone
EEIIMNOPRSSSUV	imperviousness
EEIINOPRRSSSTT	Pointer Sisters
EEIKLMNOQRRSUY	squirrel monkey
EEILMNNNNOOTVV	non-involvement
EEILMNNOOSSSST	motionlessness
EEILNOOPSSSTTV	split one's votes
EEIMNORSSSSTUY	mysteriousness
EEINNNOORSSTUV	nervous tension
EEINNOOOPQSTTU	open to question
EEINOOOOPRRTZZ	zero-zero option
EELOOPPRRSSTUY	preposterously
EENNOOOPPRRSST	person-to-person
EENNOOPRSSSTTU	portentousness
EENNOOPRSSTTUU	turn up one's toes
EENOORRSSSSTTU	stertorousness
EFFFGIILLLLNSU	self-fulfilling
EFFGHIIJNORRTY	Griffith-Joyner
EFFGIIJLNSSTUY	self-justifying
EFFGIINNOPRSTT	offset printing
EFFILNNRSSTUUU	unfruitfulness
EFFNORSSSTTTUU	strut one's stuff
EFGGHHIILLTTWY	light-flyweight
EFGGHIIKKNNOST	The King of Kings
EFGGIIINNNOPRT	finger-pointing
EFGGOOORRRSTUY	Gregory of Tours
EFGHHHIJMOPRTU	for the high jump
EFGHHIILNOPTTT	in the top flight
EFGHHINORRSSTT	forthrightness
EFGHHLNOSSTTUU	thoughtfulness
EFGHILLNORSTTW	strength of will
EFGHINNNORTTUU	fortune-hunting
EFGHLNOOORSTWY	glory of the snow
EFGIILLNQRRSUY	flying squirrel
EFGILNOPPRSSTU	self-supporting
EFHHHMOOSTTTUU	shut the mouth of
EFHHIIKLNRSTUW	wishful thinker
EFHHIOOOPRSSUW	house of worship
EFHHLNOOOOPRST	on the shop floor
EFHHMOOOPSTTTU	stop the mouth of
EFHIIMMNOORSTT	from this time on

EFHILNOPRSSSUW	worshipfulness
EFHKLOOORRTTUU	further outlook
EFHLNNRSSTTUUU	untruthfulness
EFILOOOPRRSSUY	soporiferously
EFINOORSSSTTUU	fortuitousness
EGGGHHINORTTTU	getting-through
EGGHHIIILLNSTY	eighty shilling
EGGHIIILMNPTTU	lighting-up time
EGGHIINNORTTWW	get in wrong with
EGGHIIOPRSTTTW	get to grips with
EGGIIKLMNRSTWY	Mrs Tiggy-Winkle
EGGIILOOPRRSUU	religious group
EGGILLMNNORSST	strong-smelling
EGGINNOOOPRSTU	outgoing person
EGHHILNNOOOTTT	long in the tooth
EGHHIMNNOOOPST	monophthongise
EGHHIMNNOOOPTZ	monophthongize
EGHHINOPSTTTTU	putting the shot
EGHHJNOORRTUUY	journey through
EGHHLLOOTTTUUW	well-thought-out
EGHIIKNNNNSSTU	unthinkingness
EGHIILLMORSTTT	grist to the mill
EGHIINNNOORSTW	in one's own right
EGHIJLLNNOORSV	Long John Silver
EGHILLNPRSSTTU	pull the strings
EGHNNOOOOTTTUW	go out on the town
EGIIIJKNNNPRTT	ink-jet printing
EGIIILLLLNNORT	Lionel Trilling
EGIIILMMNNORVY	in living memory
EGIILNNOORSSSU	ingloriousness
EGIINNPRRSSSSU	surprisingness
EGIJKOORRSTWYZ	Jerzy Grotowski
EHHIILMOPSTTTU	push to the limit
EHHIIOOPRSTTVW	with the proviso
EHHIKNOORRRSTY	North Yorkshire
EHHIKOORRSSTUY	South Yorkshire
EHHINNOOSTTUWY	Whitney Houston
EHHINOOPSSSTTY	photosynthesis
EHHNNOORRSTTTW	north-north-west
EHHOOSSSTTTUUW	south-south-west
EHIIIKLLMOTTTW	with time to kill
EHIIOOPPPRRRST	proprietorship
EHIJMNNPSSTTUU	just punishment
EHILNNOOORSTTW	throw in one's lot
EHIMOORRSTUUUV	vitreous humour
EHINNOOPRSSTTU	put one's shirt on
EHMMOOORRSSTUY	oyster mushroom
EIIIINOQRSSTTU	requisitionist
EIIIKLLMOPRTTU	like it or lump it
EIILLNNOOOPSTU	noise pollution
EIILMNOOQRSUUY	querimoniously
EIILOOPPSSTTVY	postpositively
EIINNORSSSTTUU	nutritiousness
EIINOOPPPRSSTU	presupposition
EIINOOPPRSSSTU	propitiousness
EIINOPRSSSSTUU	spirituousness
EIJLLNOORTUUVY	July Revolution
EIKNNNNOOOOSSW	know one's onions
EIKNOORRRTTUYY	Yukon Territory
EILMNNOOSSSUUV	voluminousness
EIMMMORRRRSTYY	mirror symmetry
EIMMNOPPRSSSUU	immunosuppress
EIMNOOOPRRSSTY	promissory note
EIMNOPRSSSSTTU	stir one's stumps
EIMOOOPPPPRSTT	opposite prompt
EINOPRSSSTTUVY	topsy-turviness
ELMNOSSSTTUUUU	tumultuousness
ELMOPPRSSTUUUY	presumptuously
ELNOOPSSSTUUUV	voluptuousness

F

FGHHIIKNNNOOTT	think nothing of
FGHHINNOOORSTT	nothing short of
FGHHLLNOTTUUUY	unthoughtfully
FIIIIILLNOPPPP	Filippino Lippi

G

GHIILLLNOOPTTU	light pollution
GIIKMMNNRSSTUW	swimming trunks

I

IIINNOOOOPPSTT	in opposition to
IIIOOPPSSSTTUU	supposititious
IINNOOOOPPRRTT	in proportion to

15 letters

A

AAAAABBCDLNRRRT	Barbara Cartland
AAAAACEEHKLLRRT	Haleakala Crater
AAAAACEIILMNPST	aplastic anaemia
AAAAADEEGKNTTTV	take at advantage
AAAABCCDEJMSSUU	Judas Maccabaeus
AAAABCEEEKKLMNR	make a clean break
AAAABDHNOPPSSYY	happy as a sandboy
AAAACCDEEHHLNRT	Aachen Cathedral
AAAACCDIIKLLLSY	lackadaisically
AAAACCEEEKMPRST	act as peacemaker
AAAACCEFHIOPTVY	have a capacity of
AAAACCEHHIMNPTT	Captain MacHeath
AAAACCEIMMNOPRR	panoramic camera
AAAACCHIMNORSTW	act as chairwoman
AAAACDDIKNORRVZ	Radovan Karadzic
AAAACDDIMMNNOSS	Cosmas and Damian
AAAACDDLMMNORSY	Ramsay MacDonald
AAAACDEGIINPRRR	carriage and pair
AAAACDEGILRRUWY	dual carriageway
AAAACDELLLMMOPR	Palma de Mallorca
AAAACDHNOORSSSU	as sound as a roach
AAAACDIILNPQRSU	Aquila and Prisca
AAAACEEIKNPRRTT	take part in a race
AAAACEFFMORSTTT	as a matter of fact
AAAACEGILNOPSST	go at a snail's pace
AAAACEIILLMNRST	Alistair Maclean
AAAACEILLMNNRTY	alimentary canal
AAAACGGIIMNNPST	campaign against
AAAACGIILNPSTTX	capital gains tax
AAAACHIKKLNPSST	as thick as a plank
AAAADDDEILNOORS	dead as a doornail
	dead as a door-nail
AAAADEEFGKNOTTV	take advantage of
AAAADEEGILMMORR	Marriage à la Mode
AAAADEGGIKNNTTV	taking advantage
AAAADEGIINOPSST	A Passage to India
AAAADGIJMNNORRT	Joan Armatrading
AAAADHIIILNNSSW	Hawaiian Islands
AAAAEEGGNNORSTY	George Santayana
AAAAEEHMNNPRTTZ	Tarzan the Ape Man
AAAAEEIIKMNNNTV	take a name in vain
AAAAEEILNNRSTTV	as an alternative
AAAAEFHIOPRRRYZ	Prayer of Azariah
AAAAEGGLLNNRTUU	natural language
AAAAEHHJLLNRRUW	Jawaharlal Nehru
AAAAEIILMNNPRRT	parliamentarian
AAAAEILLMNNQRTU	Allan Quatermain
AAAAGHIIKLMNRST	Marghanita Laski
AAAAHKMPRSTTTUU	Mustapha Atatürk
AAAAIILLNNRSSTY	Larissa Latynina
AAAAILORRRSSTUU	aurora australis
AAAAIMNOOOSSSTZ	Anastasio Somoza
AAABBCEEEILLMOV	become available
AAABBCEFILMORTT	Battle of Cambrai
AAABBDDEEFKNRST	bed and breakfast
AAABBDEEGLMRRRT	Margaret Drabble
AAABBDEHHIRRSTY	by a hair's breadth
AAABBDEINRRRSST	Barbra Streisand
AAABBDHHIILLMRU	Abdullah Ibrahim
AAABBEEEHLLRTWY	bear away the bell
AAABBEEIJLNOPST	Japanese Bobtail
AAABBEHHOPRRRTW	Barbara Hepworth
AAABBIIIILLOTVY	bioavailability
AAABCCEILLNOOST	occasional table
AAABCCFINNORSSY	San Francisco Bay
AAABCDDGHILORRR	Archibald Garrod
AAABCDEHIKPRSTT	strike a bad patch
AAABCDEIILLNRSS	Balearic Islands
AAABCDFNNOORRTW	contraband of war
AAABCDIIIIORRSS	Isidor Isaac Rabi
AAABCDLMNNRUVYY	Army and Navy Club
AAABCEEEEILNNVY	leave in abeyance
AAABCEEFKORTWYY	take away by force
AAABCEEFLNNORTU	balance of nature
AAABCEEFNOPRTUV	put a brave face on
	put on a brave face
AAABCEEHIKLNRTW	break a lance with
AAABCEEHKRSTTTU	take a butcher's at
AAABCEEILMRSSTU	Beaumaris Castle
AAABCEEILNNRSTU	unascertainable
AAABCEILNOPSTTU	Captain Absolute
AAABCHIILOPPRTY	approachability
AAABCHILNOPRRST	Caspar Bartholin
AAABDDEELMNNORU	Andromeda nebula
AAABDDEELNNRRXY	brandy Alexander
AAABDEEHILORRRV	verbal diarrhoea
AAABDEFHIIMRTTW	Fatima Whitbread
AAABDLLLLMMNSSY	by small and small
AAABEEEHLORRRVV	have over a barrel
AAABEEELLMORSUV	above all measure
AAABEEFIKKMORRT	make a break for it
AAABEEHKLLNSTVY	Helena Blavatsky
AAABEEIIMNNORTX	bear examination
AAABEFIKLNSSSTU	Sebastian Faulks
AAABEFILLMOSSTT	Battle of Salamis
AAABEHLMOQSTUUV	have qualms about
AAABFFLLNOOSTTY	fantasy football
AAABIIILLNSSTUY	unassailability
AAACCDDEEENNNTT	dance attendance
AAACCDDEGNNNOST	song-and-dance act
AAACCDEEMOPRRYY	camera-ready copy
AAACCDEGIIMNNPR	permanganic acid
AAACCDEGIMNNOTU	cut and come again
AAACCDHKNORRTTU	a hard nut to crack
AAACCEEFHILMRRW	chemical warfare
AAACCEEGHIKNRRY	hackney carriage
	hackney-carriage
AAACCEELLORSSTU	escalator clause
AAACCEFHILLPTTY	pathetic fallacy
AAACCEFHIOPRTTY	capacity for heat

AAACCEFIIRRRRT	aircraft carrier
AAACCEGHILNOOPR	oceanographical
AAACCEGIOPRSTTY	storage capacity
AAACCEIKMNOSSTU	make accusations
AAACCFIIMNORRSU	François Mauriac
AAACCHILMORRSST	A Christmas Carol
AAACCIIILMNOTTZ	acclimatization
AAACCIILLNOPRTY	capillary action
AAACCILLLOPPTYY	apocalyptically
AAACDDDHILMNNNO	Madonna and Child
AAACDDEEELLNRRX	Alexander Calder
AAACDDEEELMNRRY	lead a merry dance
AAACDDEEINNRSVY	advanced in years
AAACDDEELLNNOPS	Donald Pleasance
AAACDDEHHLMRRTU	Durham Cathedral
AAACDDEILOPPRUV	Papa Doc Duvalier
AAACDDGINNORSST	rain cats and dogs
AAACDEEEIILPRSZ	specialized area
AAACDEEEMMNRSTU	amusement arcade
AAACDEEFFGHIRRS	chargé d'affaires
AAACDEEGHMNNRTX	Exchange and Mart
AAACDEEHHITTUVY	have the audacity
AAACDEEHIJLMNOT	Michael Ondaatje
AAACDEEILLMNORT	moderate in a call
AAACDEEILRSSSUV	vascular disease
AAACDEFJKLLORST	jack-of-all-trades ❑
AAACDEHOORSSTVW	cast a shadow over
AAACDEILLMNORYY	aerodynamically
AAACDEILLNORSSS	Coral Sea Islands
AAACDEIMNNOORTT	animated cartoon
AAACDEJKMNNOSSS	Sam Jackson Snead
AAACDFFIKMPRRRS	Cardiff Arms Park
AAACDFJLNOORSTU	Acts of Adjournal
AAACDGILMNOOORR	Girolamo Cardano
AAACDHILLLMMNOR	Harold Macmillan
AAACEEEEKLMNPSW	make a clean sweep
AAACEEEGHILNSTU	Hanseatic League
AAACEEFGLLLOSUX	La Cage aux Folles
AAACEEFHILNNPRT	African elephant
AAACEEFINPPRRST	first appearance
AAACEEGGHILMNNU	machine language
AAACEEGILNORTTV	lactovegetarian
AAACEEGINNRSSUV	give an assurance
AAACEEHILLMORTT	Charlotte Amalie
AAACEEHILLNSSTW	clean as a whistle
AAACEEHILLNSTTY	anaesthetically
AAACEEILNORSSSW	social awareness
AAACEEKOPRSTTTU	cause to take part
AAACEFGHINORRVV	have a craving for
AAACEFGILNPRRSV	Francis Palgrave
AAACEFGINOSTTVY	Fantastic Voyage
AAACEFHHIILMRRS	air-chief-marshal
AAACEFHKKLLNOOP	knock all of a heap
AAACEFHMNOOPPRS	means of approach
AAACEFILLLMNOWY	family allowance
AAACEFILMNOPRTT	Act of Parliament
AAACEGILLNPRSST	Pascal's triangle
AAACEHHMNOOPRST	Athena Promachos
AAACEHIILNPRSSS	pharisaicalness
AAACEHILLORRSSW	Clarissa Harlowe
AAACEHLLORSSTWY	all the way across

AAACEIKLMMNORTX	exclamation mark
AAACEILNORSTTUY	Cautionary Tales
AAACEIMNOPRSTTU	a storm in a teacup
AAACEINNNOQSSUU	causa sine qua non
AAACFGHINOPPRST	fast approaching
AAACFGIILLNOPTT	floating capital
AAACFIILNOPRRTT	partial fraction
AAACFILMNOOSSTW	law of mass action
AAACGIIKNPSTTTU	put a tick against
AAACIILLLMNOSTY	anomalistically
AAACILLMOOSTTUY	Louisa May Alcott
AAACILMOOOORTTX	locomotor ataxia
AAACILNOORRSSTU	Corona Australis
AAADDDDEEILORRU	Edouard Daladier
	Édouard Daladier
AAADDDEEIMNPRRV	Père Armand David
AAADDEEEHNORRSV	over head and ears
AAADDEEINRSSSUY	Raynaud's disease
AAADDEELLLNORSV	Salvador Allende
AAADDEELNOPPRTT	Tadpole and Taper
AAADDEGHIINNSTY	in this day and age
AAADDEGINOSSTUV	disadvantageous
AAADDEHJNNORSTW	Jonathan Edwards
AAADDEHNNNOOSTU	a thousand and one
AAADDELMNNOOPRT	Madonna del Prato
AAADDFIKLLLNNSS	Falkland Islands
AAADDGHJKLMMORS	Dag Hammarskjöld
AAADDGHLLNNOUWY	laugh and lay down
AAADDIINNORSTTZ	standardization
AAADEEEFLMNNRSU	under a false name
AAADEEEGHMRRSST	regard as the same
AAADEEEGNRRSSVV	Vanessa Redgrave
AAADEEEHNNOSVWY	have one's end away
AAADEEEIILNRRST	residential area
AAADEEFGILMPRRS	Admiral Graf Spee
AAADEEFHHMORTTT	The Death of Marat
AAADEEFMNNSSTWY	sweet Fanny Adams
AAADEEGIILMMRTT	legitimate drama
AAADEEGILLMNPRT	leading male part
AAADEEILNRSSSUV	Andreas Vesalius
AAADEEMNOOPSTTT	meat and potatoes
AAADEFHHILMNOTV	have half a mind to
AAADEFHHOOPRTTT	at the drop of a hat
AAADEGGLNRRSTUU	granulated sugar
AAADEGHIIKLLNRU	laugh like a drain
AAADEGHNOOSTTVW	show to advantage
AAADEGINOPRRRTU	praetorian guard
AAADEGLNORRRSUY	Sugar Ray Leonard
AAADEGMNPSSTUUY	Guy de Maupassant
AAADEGNNORTTTUV	turn to advantage
AAADEHIMNRRSTVY	Martha's Vineyard
AAADEIILLMNNTVW	William Davenant
AAADEIILLNNSSTU	Aleutian Islands
AAADEILOPPRSTUW	as it would appear
AAADELLNOORSSTV	Alessandro Volta
AAADFILLNNSTUUW	Wallis and Futuna
AAADGGHHIILNNSU	Guiana Highlands
AAADGHIOOPRRTUY	autoradiography
AAADGIIILLNRRST	Alistair Darling
AAADGIILLLLMNNW	William Langland
AAADHILLLMNRSSS	Marshall Islands

Words marked ❑ can also be spelled with an initial capital letter

AAAEEEEGHLNNNRT Nathanael Greene
AAAEEEEGLNRSTTT real-estate agent
AAAEEEFHIKMRRTW make fair weather
AAAEEEFKLMMNOPX make an example of
AAAEEEGGHIMTVWY give the game away
AAAEEEGKMNOSTWY make one's getaway
AAAEEEHIMMSSTTT at the same time as
AAAEEEHLRRSSTVW wear several hats
AAAEEEHNOPRSSSV have as a response
AAAEEEIILMNRRTT at an earlier time
AAAEEEKLMMNNOTT make a mental note
AAAEEFGKLMOPRTY make great play of
AAAEEFHNOPRSTTZ Tarzan of the Apes
AAAEEFLLMORRSTW A Farewell to Arms
AAAEEGHILRSTTTT at the trial stage
AAAEEGIKLLMNOST make allegations
AAAEEGIMNPRRRRT marriage partner
AAAEEHHIKSTTTVW have what it takes
AAAEEHHINOTVWWY have a way with one
AAAEEHHLMMNNNSU Samuel Hahnemann
AAAEEHHLNRRTTUW Walther Rathenau
AAAEEHILNNORTTT National Theatre
AAAEEILMRRSTTXX extramarital sex
AAAEEINNOORRSVX anorexia nervosa
AAAEFFGGNNOOTTT go off at a tangent
AAAEFGGLLMNOORV Vale of Glamorgan
AAAEFGJMNOORRTU Margaret of Anjou
AAAEFHKNOOPSSTT take a snapshot of
AAAEFHLMNORSUZZ Lazarus Zamenhof
AAAEGGHIINNRSTT against the grain
AAAEGIIILMNSTTT militate against
AAAEGIIKLMNSTTT talk against time
AAAEGIILMMMNNST animal magnetism
AAAEGIKNOPSSTTU speak out against
AAAEGILLLNNORTY National Gallery
AAAEGNNNOOPRRST persona non grata
AAAEHHLOPRSSTTY thalassotherapy
AAAEIIILMNORTTZ materialization
AAAEIILLMNPRRTY parliamentarily
AAAEIILMMNPRRST parliamentarism
AAAEIILMNNOORTX oral examination
AAAEILLNRRSSTUU Australian Rules
AAAEILMNNPRRTUY unparliamentary
AAAELLLSSSTUUXY assault sexually
sexually assault
AAAFFIKMMNNRRTU Frankfurt am Main
AAAFIIIILMNORTZ familiarization
AAAFLMOOPPPRSTV stamp of approval
AAAGHIILLMNSUVW Vaughan Williams
AAAGIILLNORTTVY gravitationally
AAAGIINNOORSTTV astro-navigation
AAAHIIIMMNNRSTU humanitarianism
AAAHLOOPPRRSSUU Parasaurolophus
AAAIIILMNORSTTT totalitarianism
AAAIIILNNNOOTTZ nationalization
AAAIIILNNOORTTZ rationalization
AAAILLNNNOORSTT loan-translation
AAAILMNNORSTTTU transmutational
AAAILNNNOPRSTTT transplantation
AABBBDEEKLNQSUU bubble and squeak
bubble-and-squeak
AABBCCDHJKORRTU Jacob Burckhardt
AABBCDDEILORUVY Baby Doc Duvalier
AABBCDLLMMORRUY Malcolm Bradbury
AABBCEHLMOPRRRY Ralph Abercromby
AABBDDDIINNRRSS in dribs and drabs
AABBDEEEHHSTTWY wet the baby's head
AABBDEEELRRSUYY Aubrey Beardsley
AABBDEEGGNNRRTU Brandenburg Gate
AABBDEEHHIRTTTW with bated breath
AABBDEEIILMNNOR Daniel Barenboim
AABBDEGILNNRSUY bring and buy sale
AABBDEHOOSTTUUV have doubts about
AABBDGGIINNNORS Brobdingnagians
AABBEEGHNNORRTY Northanger Abbey
AABBEFIILNORTTT Battle of Britain
AABBELMNORSSTUU stubborn as a mule
AABBGHINORSTTTU bright as a button
AABBIINNORSTUUZ suburbanization
AABCCCELMOORSUU cool as a cucumber
AABCCDEEEEIMMOT become emaciated
AABCCDEEHILLNSY hendecasyllabic
AABCCDEELMNRSUU Cumberland sauce
AABCCEEHHHINNRS Hans Reichenbach
AABCCEEHHNORSTT catch one's breath
AABCCEEHLLRSSTU Chelsea Arts Club
AABCCEEIKLMMORR commercial break
AABCCEEILNPRSST practicableness
AABCCEELNNOSSTU accountableness
AABCCEGIILLOORT bacteriological
AABCCEIILNPTTUY unacceptability
AABCCELLLLMMMOP Malcolm Campbell
AABCCIIILLLNTUY incalculability
AABCCIIILLMNPST clinical baptism
AABCDDDEEKLOORV broad-leaved dock
AABCDDEEEKLNRUX Alexander Dubcek
AABCDDEEFIKLNRR Frederick Blanda
AABCDDEGHLNOTUW caught and bowled
AABCDDFIIIRRSUV David Frabricius
AABCDDIINNNOOWY cowboy and Indian
AABCDEEEEILMNOT become alienated
AABCDEEEGILNNRR Anne Bracegirdle
AABCDEEEHIILPRV Cepheid variable
AABCDEEEHLLLNSY hendecasyllable
AABCDEEHHKLMPUW humpbacked whale
AABCDEEHIMORRSX embarras de choix
AABCDEEHLNORSTT cards on the table
AABCDEEILLMORRT Liberal Democrat
AABCDEGHHIKLNST black nightshade
AABCDEHHJNOOOTT do a hatchet job on
AABCDEHIIKLNNTW in black and white
AABCDEHILLMNORR Lord Chamberlain
AABCDEHIMORRSUX embarras du choix
AABCDEIINNOORTZ decarbonization
AABCDEIINORRTUZ decarburization
AABCDEIMNOORSTU sodium carbonate
AABCDEMNNSSSTUU sum and substance
AABCDGIKKLNOORW backward-looking
AABCEEEFKLRRTVW blackwater fever
AABCEEEGHILNNRT interchangeable
AABCEEEGHLLLNNU unchallengeable
AABCEEEGKMRRTTT Margaret Beckett

AABCEEELLNNOOSS lose one's balance
AABCEEELMMNNRRU nuclear membrane
AABCEEFKLMMOORT make comfortable
AABCEEFLLORTTTU Battle of Leuctra
AABCEEGHIILNTXY exchangeability
AABCEEGHILNNRTY interchangeably
AABCEEHHIMMPRRS Ephraim Chambers
AABCEEHHJLLNNOP Johann Pachelbel
AABCEEHIKNOOPTV have a bone to pick
AABCEEHILMNNORW Owen Chamberlain
AABCEEHIMNORRRT anterior chamber
AABCEEHLRRSTTTU Arts Theatre Club
AABCEEIKKMNNORT Aaron Temkin Beck
AABCEEIKNNOPRSS pin back one's ears
AABCEEIKPPRRRTW Paperback Writer
AABCEEILOPPRRRU Paul Pierre Broca
AABCEEKNOOQRSTU back to square one
AABCEELNORRSSTT Osbert Lancaster
AABCEELNRRSTTUY Canterbury Tales
AABCEFFHLNOORTW throw off balance
AABCEFFINORRSTU Francis Beaufort
AABCEFIMNNORSTU Francis Beaumont
AABCEFLNNOORTTU Battle of Corunna
AABCEGHIILNNTUY unchangeability
AABCEGIIIMNNOUV Giovanni Cimabué
AABCEGIKKLNNOOR Look Back in Anger
AABCEGKLMNOORTT get back to normal
AABCEHIILLMNRTW Wilt Chamberlain
AABCEILLLMOPRTY problematically
AABCEINNOSSTTTU consubstantiate
AABCELMNNORSTTT Constant Lambert
AABCENOORRSTTUY carry out one's bat
AABCFIIILLNOSTY syllabification
AABCIIIILLNPPTY inapplicability
AABCIIILMNOPRTY incomparability
AABCIILLNNOOORT in collaboration
AABDDDELNOOSSST boots and saddles
AABDDEEGHLNNORT Bel and the Dragon
AABDDEEILLNTTVY badly ventilated
AABDDEHMNOORRRS Dr Barnardo's home
AABDEEEOPRRTTTY battery-operated
AABDEEFFHIORRST birds of a feather
AABDEEFLMMRTTUY Madame Butterfly
AABDEEGHINORRTW weatherboarding
AABDEEGIIILRSTY disagreeability
AABDEEGILMNRRTU Bermuda Triangle
AABDEEHILMMNORY hyaloid membrane
AABDEEHIMNNNRRR Bernhard Riemann
AABDEEHLLOORRRV hold over a barrel
AABDEEILMNOORVW bowl a maiden over
AABDEEILNNOSSUV unavoidableness
AABDEEKLMNNORTW mental breakdown
AABDEFJLLNOTTTU Battle of Jutland
AABDEHHINORSTWY win by a short head
AABDEIIILNORTTZ detribalization
AABDEIKLLNNNOSS all skin and bones
AABDEILNORRRRTY by trial and error
AABDEINNSSTTTUU unsubstantiated
AABDELNNPRSTUUY superabundantly
AABDFINRSSSTTTY by fits and starts
AABDIIKLMNOORVV Vladimir Nabokov
AABDILNNORSTUUW rub salt in a wound
AABEEEEFIKLMNOR make a beeline for
AABEEEEHHORTTVW above the weather
AABEEEFHLNOTTTV Battle of the Neva
AABEEEGGHOPRRST The Beggar's Opera
AABEEEGGLLNNORR General Belgrano
AABEEEGIKLRRTTT Great Bitter Lake
AABEEEGIKMNOSTT take some beating
AABEEEGLLMNRSSY General Assembly
AABEEEHHIMNRSTT in the same breath
AABEEEHIMNNORTT Three Men in a Boat
AABEEEHLMNORSSV have one's marbles
AABEEEHLNORSSTT breathe one's last
AABEEEHNORSSTTW waste one's breath
AABEEEILLNNRSST inalterableness
AABEEEJMNOOPRRT Jérôme Bonaparte
AABEEELLNNRSSTU unalterableness
AABEEELNNORSSST treasonableness
AABEEFFHKLNOOPS speak on behalf of
AABEEFGLMNOORTT Battle of Marengo
AABEEFGLRSTTUUV Gustave Flaubert
AABEEFHILNNOSSS fashionableness
AABEEFLLNOOPTTT Battle of Lepanto
AABEEFLLNOORSTT Battle of Salerno
AABEEFLLOPSSTTY Battle of Plassey
AABEEFLNNNORRST non-transferable
AABEEGLORRSTTYY lay great store by
AABEEHHHORTTTVY have by the throat
AABEEHILLORTTYZ Elizabeth Taylor
AABEEHILNOPRUVY bear heavily upon
AABEEHINNORRTTW water on the brain
AABEEIIILLMNSTT mental abilities
AABEEILMMNRSTUU Albertina Museum
AABEELNNNOOPSST on one's pantables
AABEFGGHIIKMNOT make a big thing of
AABEFGIIILRRRTY irrefragability
AABEFHIINORRUUV unfair behaviour
AABEFHILMOORRTW Bartholomew Fair
AABEFHLOPSSTTTU Battle of Thapsus
AABEFIIJLMOOTTW Battle of Iwo Jima
AABEFIILNRRSTTY transferability
AABEFILLNSSSTTU self-substantial
AABEFILNOOPPRST self-approbation
AABEFLNORRTTUZZ burnt to a frazzle
AABEGGHIINNNORV having no bearing
AABEGIIMMNNRRUY imaginary number
AABEHIIKNORTTUW without a break in
AABEHLNOOPRTTTT Neath Port Talbot
AABEIILLMMNOTUW William Beaumont
AABEIILMNORTUVY manoeuvrability
AABEILLNOORSTVY observationally
AABEIMMMNNORRTU Mr Tambourine Man
AABFHIILMNOTTUY unfathomability
AABFIKNOORSTTWY a nasty bit of work
AABGHIIKKLLMOUV Mikhail Bulgakov
AABGHIJNNNOORRT Jonah Barrington
AABGIIIKLLNNNOU Nikolai Bulganin
AABHIIKKLNNORUY Nikolay Bukharin
AABIILLNNSSTTUY insubstantially
AABIILMNRSTTTUY transmutability

AACCCDDHIINORYY	hydrocyanic acid
AACCCDEFIIILNOT	decalcification
AACCCDEILMOORSY	social democracy
AACCCEEHHKRRSTT	character sketch
AACCCEEHILLOORT	chocolate éclair
AACCCEEIIJNPRTU	pancreatic juice
AACCCEHIIRRSSTT	characteristics
AACCCFFINNOORRS	Francisco Franco
AACCCHIMRSSSTTU	Christmas cactus
AACCCILLMMOORSY	macrocosmically
AACCCILLMOOPRSY	macroscopically
AACCDEEEHILNNRS	Chinese calendar
AACCDEEGHILPRRT	charged particle
AACCDEEHILLORRV	Richard Lovelace
AACCDEEHINNNSTY	in the ascendancy
AACCDEEIIJLPRRU	racial prejudice
AACCDEENORSSSUY	secondary causes
AACCDEFGINOORSY	Francisco de Goya
AACCDEFHIIPRRRS	Caspar Friedrich
AACCDEFIILMNORT	decimal fraction
AACCDEGIILNSTTY	delaying tactics
AACCDEHLOORRTTY	Charlotte Corday
AACCDEILNOOPRST	accordion pleats
AACCDGILMMNOOTY	accommodatingly
AACCDGIMMNNOOTU	unaccommodating
AACCDHHILNOOPRY	hypochondriacal
AACCDHILNOOPRST	achondroplastic
AACCEEEEGHHNRTX	exchange teacher
AACCEEEFLOOSSTU	cause to lose face
AACCEEEGILNPRRT	general practice
AACCEEEGLMNORSS	Glencoe Massacre
AACCEEFGNNOORTV	covenant of grace
AACCEEFILNOOPRT	force into a place
AACCEEHHILPRTTW	Whitechapel cart
AACCEEHIJLMPRSS	Cecil James Sharp
AACCEEHILLNOOTV	have a collection
AACCEEHILORSSTT	the coast is clear
AACCEEIKMNNNOOT	make a connection
AACCEEILNNORRTU	nuclear reaction
AACCEEILORRSSTY	social secretary
AACCEEJOQSSTUUU	Jacques Cousteau
AACCEEKMMMNOOSU	make common cause
AACCEELLMNRSTTY	Stella McCartney
AACCEFFHIIOPRTW	War of the Pacific
AACCEFGHILMOPST	catch a glimpse of
AACCEFHINOOORSV	have occasion for
AACCEFKNNOOOTTU	take no account of
AACCEGHIILLOPRX	lexicographical
AACCEGHIIMNOPRT	cinematographic
AACCEGHIKLNOSTT	against the clock
AACCEGHILMNORST	German Catholics
AACCEGIILLNNOSS	social cleansing
AACCEGIMMNOPSST	magnetic compass
AACCEHHHLMPRRSU	Ralph Schumacher
AACCEHIILLMNSTY	mechanistically
AACCEHIKMNOTTTW	make contact with
AACCEHILLRRTTUY	architecturally
AACCEHKORRSSSTT	across the tracks
AACCEIIILLMNRST	anticlericalism
AACCEIILLMNOSTY	encomiastically
AACCEIILNNORSSU	social insurance
AACCEIIMNRSTTTU	circumstantiate
AACCEIKNNOOTTTU	take into account
AACCEILLMNNORTY	necromantically
AACCFFFGHKLOOOT	go off at half cock
AACCFIIINOPRSSU	Scipio Africanus
AACCGIIILNNNOOP	Niccolò Paganini
AACCGIIMNORRTUV	circumnavigator
AACCHHIIOOPPRTT	Hippocratic oath
AACCHHIORSTTTUW	without a scratch
AACCHILLNOPSTYY	sycophantically
AACCIIILLLOSSTY	socialistically
AACCIMNNNOOOSSY	on many occasions
AACCKLNNNOPSSTT	Planck's constant
AACDDDEEFHINSTT	catted and fished
AACDDEEEFHHLOSU	ahead of schedule
AACDDEEEFHHNOTT	The Dance of Death
AACDDEEFGHNORSS	change of address
AACDDEFIMNNORRS	Ferdinand Marcos
AACDDEGGHIOTTTY	act the giddy goat
AACDDEGGIINRSST	Giscard d'Estaing
AACDDEHHILNNOPS	Daphnis and Chloe
AACDDEHLMNNORRY	Raymond Chandler
AACDDEIILNNOORV	Leonardo da Vinci
AACDDEMNRRSSSTU	mustard and cress
AACDDHIILNNSSSW	Sandwich Islands
AACDDILLLMOOPRY	dollar diplomacy
AACDEEEEFFIKMNR	make a difference
AACDEEEEHLRRTTX	Exeter Cathedral
AACDEEEEHNNORVY	each and every one
AACDEEEFHILPRRR	Frederic Raphael
AACDEEEGGLLLMNO	Magdalen College
AACDEEEGHILMRRV	Michael Redgrave
AACDEEEGHLLLRSU	Charles de Gaulle
AACDEEEHHILRRTW	Rachel Whiteread
AACDEEEHHKNPRSY	hackneyed phrase
AACDEEEHLPRRSTY	Speyer Cathedral
AACDEEEHNPRRSTV	chapter and verse
AACDEEFHILSSTTY	child-safety seat
AACDEEFLNOOPRRR	place an order for
AACDEEGGNNOOPRS	egg-and-spoon race
AACDEEGHIINNRST	hearing distance
AACDEEGHLLMOOSU	Alec Douglas-Home
AACDEEGHLNOPRTU	golden parachute
AACDEEGHLOORRSY	Charles Goodyear
AACDEEGIILLNPPS	special pleading
AACDEEGKLLNNORW	carnal knowledge
AACDEEHHINORRTW	Catherine Howard
AACDEEHHMNORSSY	Sydenham's chorea
AACDEEHIKLMMNRS	Hammer and Sickle
	hammer and sickle
AACDEEHINNOOPRT	a drop in the ocean
AACDEEHINNTTTUU	unauthenticated
AACDEEIILMNNORT	demarcation line
AACDEEIIMNNOTTV	decontaminative
AACDEEIJKLLLNUY	Jean Claude Killy
AACDEEILNNSSTTU	indecent assault
AACDEEIOOPRRRRT	corporate raider
AACDEFFGINRSSTU	facts and figures
AACDEFHOPPRRSST	strapped for cash
AACDEFNPRRSSTYY	fancy-dress party
AACDEGHIILLOPRY	ideographically

AACDEGHIMORSTWY say the magic word
AACDEGIIIKKLNNV alive and kicking
AACDEGIILMOOOPR Giacomo Leopardi
AACDEGILLMNOOPT lodge a complaint
AACDEHHIILNPRST Christadelphian
AACDEHHKNOORSTT horse and hattock
AACDEHIINOSSSUV have a discussion
AACDEHLMMNOOTWY Commonwealth Day
AACDEIIKLMNNOOT make conditional
AACDEIILNORSSTT dictatorialness
AACDEIIMNNNOOTT decontamination
AACDEIIMNOORTTZ democratization
AACDEIINNOOPSTV advance position
AACDEIKNNNPPSSW spick and span new
AACDEILNOPRSTTU custodial parent
AACDEIMNNOOPRRY Raymond Poincaré
AACDFGHIMNORRRW marching forward
AACDFHIILNOOPRY Fyodor Chaliapin
AACDFHLLOOORTTW hard act to follow
AACDFIIINOSSSTT dissatisfaction
AACDGIKNNOORRTU go to rack and ruin
AACDHHIILMNORRT Richard Hamilton
AACDHHILLOPRTYY hydropathically
AACDHHILNOPRRRS Ralph Richardson
AACDHIIILOTTVYY activity holiday
AACDHIILMNRSSST Christmas Island
AACDHIJMNNOQSUY John Quincy Adams
AACDIIILNNPRSST Pitcairn Islands
AACDIILNOPQRTUU quadruplication
AACDILMNOOPRRUY cardiopulmonary
AACEEEEFHKLNRTV take French leave
AACEEEEGKNNNOTV take vengeance on
AACEEEEINNNNPRS near as ninepence
AACEEEFHINNQRTU The African Queen
AACEEEFHORRSTTW weather forecast
AACEEEFIKMMMNOT make mincemeat of
AACEEEFLNRRSTUX external surface
AACEEEGHLLRRRSY Charles Earl Grey
AACEEEGIIMRRRSV marriage service
AACEEEGILLNNRST scalene triangle
AACEEEGINNRRTTT Terence Rattigan
AACEEEHHORSSTUV have as the source
AACEEEHILLLMNUW wheel animalcule
AACEEEHLLLOPRTV all over the place
AACEEEHLOORSSVW have a screw loose
AACEEEIKMNNOPTX make an exception
AACEEEILMMNNRTX animal excrement
AACEEEILNRSSSST sales resistance
AACEEEINOOPRSST cease operations
AACEEFFGIILOTTV give a facelift to
AACEEFHINNOSTTT at the instance of
AACEEFHJLMORSSX Charles James Fox
AACEEFHNOOPRTTU another cup of tea
AACEEFIINOORSST free association
AACEEFILNORSSTT essential factor
AACEEFJKLLLMTTU Full Metal Jacket
AACEEFMNOPPRRST past performance
AACEEGHHLLOSTTW cheat the gallows
AACEEGHILLLPRTY telegraphically
AACEEGHIMNOPRRT cinematographer
AACEEGILLNNOPRS nearing collapse
AACEEGIMNOQRTTU magnetic equator
AACEEGKLNOORTTU encourage to talk
AACEEHHHLLMTTTT that'll teach them
AACEEHHIINPRRTY reichian therapy ❑
AACEEHHIMNRRRST Carmarthenshire
AACEEHHJKNNORST Johannes Eckhart
AACEEHIILLMNRSY Shirley MacLaine
AACEEHIILNRSSTT castles in the air
AACEEHILLNPRTTY parenthetically
AACEEHILLPRTTUY therapeutically
AACEEHILNNOOOST a hole in one's coat
AACEEHIORSSSTUV have as its source
AACEEHLNOORRSTT clear one's throat
AACEEHMNOPRRTWW come the raw prawn
AACEEIILNNORSTV national service
AACEEIKNOPRSTTU take precautions
AACEEILMMPRSSTU male supremacist
AACEEIMNORRRSTV Sacramento River
AACEEIMNORRRTTT American Trotter
AACEELOQRRSSTTU at close quarters
AACEFFKNNOOPRTT pocket an affront
AACEFGGINOORSST act of aggression
AACEFHHIMRRSSTT Father Christmas
AACEFHIIIOTTVVY a hive of activity
AACEFHKLNORSSYY Charles Yanofsky
AACEFIILMNNSSTY financial system
AACEGHHLLNORSTU Charles Laughton
AACEGHILLMOORTU rheumatological
AACEGIILLMORSVW William Cosgrave
AACEGIIMNORSSTV moving staircase
AACEGILLMNNOPSS all-encompassing
AACEGKLNOOORRSU kangaroo closure
AACEHHIIMNRRSTW within arm's reach
AACEHHILLMOOPTY homeopathically
AACEHIILMNNOSSW Nicholas Wiseman
AACEHIINNNNOTTU The Annunciation
AACEHIJLLMNNOOP Jean Champollion
AACEHILLMOPRSTY atmospherically
AACEHILLMPSTTYY sympathetically
AACEHILMOOORRTV Violeta Chamorro
AACEHLMORSSTUUW walrus moustache
AACEIIIILMNOPPSS episcopalianism
AACEIILLMNNRSTY manneristically
AACEIILLMOPRRSS Camille Pissarro
AACEIILMNOPRRTT malpractitioner
AACEIILNNOOPTTT action potential
AACEIIMNOPRRTUX Proxima Centauri
AACEIJLMOOPRRST pectoralis major
AACEILLNNOOTTTT call attention to
AACEILLNNORSSUU Carolus Linnaeus
AACEILMNOOPSSTY compassionately
AACEIMMNOPRRSSS Mariner's Compass
AACEIMNNOOPSSTU uncompassionate
AACEIMOOPPRSTTX approximate cost
AACELLLMNOORRTY Monte Carlo Rally
AACFFIIINORSSSS Francis of Assisi
AACFFIKNOORSTUV stack in favour of
AACFFILLLNOOPRT final port of call
AACFGIILNNOORTU configurational
AACFHIIKLLMMOOW William of Ockham
AACFHIJJKLMNPSU Jumpin' Jack Flash

AACGGHLNNOOPSSU lapsang souchong
AACGGIIIMNOOOST Giacomo Agostini
AACGHHIILOPPRSY physiographical
AACGHIILLLMORTY logarithmically
AACGHILLMNOOPRY gramophonically
AACGHILLNOOOPRT anthropological
AACGHILLOOPPRTY topographically
AACGHILLOPPRTYY typographically
AACGHLLOPRRSTYY crystallography
AACGIIIINNNOSSV Giovanni Cassini
AACGIIILNPRSSTU paralinguistics
AACGIIKNNORSTTT tracking station
AACGIILLRRSTTUU agriculturalist
AACGIINNOPRRSTT procrastinating
AACGILNNOORSTTU congratulations
AACGIMNOOORSTTW room to swing a cat
AACHHIILLNOPPRT philanthropical
AACHIIILNPRSSVW Spanish Civil War
AACHIIKLLMOSTVY Michail Saltykov
AACHIMNOPPRTTWY part company with
AACIIIILMNNORST criminalisation
AACIIIILMNNORTZ criminalization
AACIIILLLRSTTUY ritualistically
AACIIILNRRSSUVW Russian Civil War
AACIIILSSSTTTTV vital statistics
AACIIIMNNOORTTZ romanticization
AACIILLLMOPSTUY political asylum
AACIILLNORSSTTY crystallisation
AACIILLNORSTTYZ crystallization
AACIILNNOPRRSTT transcriptional
AACIINNOOPRRSTT procrastination
AACIINNOORRSTTU Arturo Toscanini
AACILLMMOPSTTYY symptomatically
AADDDEEEGIPRRRU Gérard Depardieu
AADDDEIMNNNOORS Adrian Edmondson
AADDDENOPRRSSWW spread downwards
AADDDIILNNRSSWW Windward Islands
AADDEEEFHHILRTW Alfred Whitehead
AADDEEEHHNRRSST hard-heartedness
AADDEEGHHILNRVY leave high and dry
AADDEEGHHKLNNOS golden handshake
AADDEEGIKMNNOOR make a good dinner
AADDEEGINNNRSTV Evening Standard
AADDEEHIMNPRRUU Daphne Du Maurier
AADDEEHMRRRTTWY Edward the Martyr
AADDEEHNRRRSUWY Hundred Years' War
AADDEEIMMNNNPTY demand in payment
AADDEGHIJNNORRT Django Reinhardt
AADDEGHILLNNOUW laugh and lie down
AADDEGHILNNRSST Standard English
AADDEGHIMNOOOTV have a good mind to
AADDEHILLNNSSST Shetland Islands
AADDEILOOOPRUZZ Eduardo Paolozzi
AADDGGHIMNORRST Thomas Gradgrind
AADDGHHIILLMORR Lord High Admiral
AADDILLLMNNOOPU London Palladium
AADEEEEEGHLRRSW Where Eagles Dare
AADEEEEFGGILRTV feel aggrieved at
AADEEEEHHKRRTWW Hereward the Wake
AADEEEEIILRRRRT Airedale terrier
AADEEEELMNOPRTV development area
AADEEEFHHIMOSTT ahead of the times
AADEEEFHIMNOOST ahead of one's time
AADEEEGHLLNNRST Hansel and Gretel
AADEEEGILLLMNOR leading male role
AADEEEGLLMPSTTU get all steamed up
AADEEEHLLORSVWY Lee Harvey Oswald
AADEEEHMNRRSSTW warm-heartedness
AADEEEHNNPQRRSU Harpers and Queen
AADEEEHNOORRSTT dear to one's heart
AADEEEIILNNRRVX Alexander Irvine
AADEEEIKLNNRSVX Alexander Nevski
AADEEEILMNPRSTT departmentalise
AADEEEILMNPRTTZ departmentalize
AADEEEKLNNRSVXY Alexander Nevsky
AADEEEKMMNOOSSY make someone's day
AADEEFFHMORSTTU The Raft of Medusa
AADEEFFIINNRTWY in a different way
AADEEFHILNOSSSV loaves and fishes
AADEEGHIIMORTTV give a hard time to
AADEEGHKLMMNOTU don't make me laugh
AADEEGHLMMNNORY Gene Myron Amdahl
AADEEGIILNPRSTT Patient Griselda
AADEEGIIMNNOTTZ demagnetization
AADEEHHILLMMSTT Dashiell Hammett
AADEEHHILNSSTVY The Lady Vanishes
AADEEHHINNNOSSV have in one's hands
AADEEHIILNNRSTW sail near the wind
AADEEHILLMNOSTU Thelma and Louise
AADEEHINNOORSST raise one's hand to
AADEEHMNOORRSUW Donmar Warehouse
AADEEILMMNPRSTT departmentalism
AADEEILNNSSTTVY St Valentine's Day
AADEEJKMMNSSTTU make adjustments
AADEFFGIKMOOOST make a good fist of
AADEFGHILNNTTTT flight attendant
AADEFHHNNOOSSSW wash one's hands of
AADEFHILMMNOORS horns of a dilemma
AADEFILLLNNOUVW fall down in value
AADEFILMNNNTTUU fundamental unit
AADEFLMNOORRTTV travel to and from
AADEGIIIILNNSTW ladies-in-waiting
AADEGIILNNPSSTU sustaining pedal
AADEGIINNOOOTTV give a donation to
AADEGINNORRRSUU surrounding area
AADEHHILLLOSSST as old as the hills
AADEHHNOPRSSTTU pass round the hat
AADEIIILNOORTTV Adriano Olivetti
AADEIIKMNNOORST make inroads into
AADEIILNOPSSSTY dispassionately
AADEIILNORRRTXY extraordinarily
AADEILLLNOORSUV Love is All Around
AADEINNOORTTTTW draw attention to
AADEINPRRSSSSTT Stars and Stripes
AADELMNNOORSSWY lay down one's arms
AADELNOPRSTTUUY polyunsaturated
AADEMMNOORSSTWY motorway madness
AADFGHILNNNOOSY laying-on of hands
AADFGHIORRRSTTW straightforward
AADFGILNNNOPRRW forward planning
AADFHMNNOOSSTUY a month of Sundays
AADFIINNRSSSTTT in fits and starts

AADFLOOORRSSSTW	at a loss for words
AADGHHIMNPRSSTU	draughtsmanship
AADGIIINNOORSTZ	disorganization
AADGIINNNOOSTTV	standing ovation
AADGLNOOOOPPRSV	goods on approval
AADHKOORRRSTTTW	start to work hard
AADIIKKLNNSSWYY	Wasily Kandinsky
AADIILLMMNORSWY	Raymond Williams
AADIIMMNSSTTTUU	mutatis mutandis
AAEEEEFHHNNOSVV	heaven of heavens
AAEEEEFKLNOOSTV	take one's leave of
AAEEEEGLLNRRTVW	New Age traveller
AAEEEFGHINOTTXY	The Age of Anxiety
AAEEEFGILNOSVWY	give oneself away
AAEEEFGLMMNNRRT	gentleman farmer
AAEEEFHILOSSSTY	The Essays of Elia
AAEEEFHOOPPRRTU	The Rape of Europa
AAEEEGILLNNRRTT	eternal triangle
AAEEEGIMRSTTTUU	Auguste Mariette
AAEEEGMMMNNNOTY	money management
AAEEEGMMNNNPRTT	permanent magnet
AAEEEHHIMMMNPTT	methamphetamine
AAEEEHHINNOSTTV	one's native heath
AAEEEHHKOPRSTTT	speak to the heart
AAEEEHIKRSTTTVW	whatever it takes
AAEEEHKNOORSTTT	take to one's heart
AAEEEHMMMNOSTTT	at the same moment
AAEEEHNNOORRSTT	near to one's heart
AAEEEHNOORSTTTU	eat one's heart out
AAEEEHOOPRSTTTT	The Potato Eaters
AAEEEIIKLORTTTV	take it or leave it
	take-it-or-leave-it
AAEEEIIMNNORTTT	Marie Antoinette
AAEEEIJKNNNNRTT	Jeannette Rankin
AAEEEILMNNPTTTU	antepenultimate
AAEEEILNORTTTVV	Alternative Vote
AAEEEIMNSSSTTTU	issue a statement
AAEEELLMMNPRTTY	temperamentally
AAEEEMNPRRRTTUU	run a temperature
AAEEFFHKOPRSTTW	take the wraps off
AAEEFFINOORRSTT	reafforestation
AAEEFGHILLLNOTT	The Flagellation
AAEEFGIMNNRRSST	fragmentariness
AAEEFGMORRRRSTT	Margaret Forster
AAEEFHILLNOOSTV	The Isle of Avalon
AAEEFHILRSSSTTT	the fatal sisters
AAEEFHILRSSTTVV	harvest festival
AAEEFIILMNNOSTX	self-examination
AAEEFIIOPRRSSTT	Treaties of Paris
AAEEFIJLORRSSTV	Jaroslav Seifert
AAEEFILLNNRSTTV	Lantern Festival
AAEEFILMNNOPRTY	one-parent family
AAEEFLLNOPRSTXY	self-explanatory
AAEEFNOOPRSTTUV	put a fast one over
AAEEGGIIIILLLLO	Galilieo Galilei
AAEEGGIIILMNRSZ	girlie magazines
AAEEGGJMNOSTTTU	just manage to get
AAEEGHHIMOPPTTZ	apophthegmatize
AAEEGHHINOOPPST	hope against hope
AAEEGHHINRRSTTT	earth-shattering
AAEEGHHIOSTVWWY	give the show away
AAEEGHIKNNRSSST	snake in the grass
AAEEGHKNORTTWWY	take the wrong way
AAEEGHMMMORSSTU	Somerset Maugham
AAEEGIIIMNNSSTV	imaginativeness
AAEEGILMNRTTUVY	argumentatively
AAEEGIMNORRSTVY	gain mastery over
AAEEGINQRRTTTUY	greater quantity
AAEEGKNOOPRSSSW	work one's passage
AAEEHHMORTTTTUW	water at the mouth
AAEEHIIJLLMNOTW	Joe Willie Namath
AAEEHILLNOPRTTW	wallop in a tether
AAEEHILMNSTTTTU	at the last minute
AAEEHINNRRSSTUV	Svante Arrhenius
AAEEHINOORRSTTU	tear one's hair out
AAEEHINOPRRSTVY	aversion therapy
AAEEHLLMOOSTTUY	all the same to you
AAEEHLMMMNOSSUU	Ashmolean Museum
AAEEHLMNSSTTTWY	Stanley Matthews
AAEEHLNPRRSTTUU	the supernatural
AAEEHNNOOORRTWY	one way or another
AAEEIILNNORTTXZ	externalization
AAEEIINNOOPRTUZ	Europeanization
AAEEIKMNNNORTVY	make an inventory
AAEEILLNORSSTUX	sexual relations
AAEEILLRRSTTTUX	extra-illustrate
AAEEILNPRRSSTUU	supernaturalise
AAEEILNPRRSTUUZ	supernaturalize
AAEEIMNOPPRRRTY	proprietary name
AAEEIMNOPPRSSTX	approximateness
AAEEINOPPPRRSST	appropriateness
AAEEKMNOOOPSSTY	ask someone to pay
AAEELLNPRRRTTUY	preternaturally
AAEELLOPRRSSTTT	Pastoral Letters
AAEELMNRRRSTTWY	Ernst Walter Mayr
AAEELNNOPRRSSTU	natural response
AAEENNNPRRSSSTT	transparentness
AAEFFHIOORSTTUW	a fish out of water
AAEFGGHILLNNPRY	flying phalanger
AAEFGGHILNNOORV	have a longing for
AAEFGHIIILMRTTW	get familiar with
AAEFGIILLMNOORW	William of Orange
AAEFGLLOPRRRUYY	pay for regularly
AAEFHHIILLRRTTY	heath fritillary
AAEFHHLNOORRSTT	horns of the altar
AAEFHIIIILMRTWZ	familiarize with
AAEFIIILMORRTVY	overfamiliarity
	over-familiarity
AAEFIIKLLLMNRUW	William Faulkner
AAEGHHINOOPPRTT	anthropophagite
AAEGHHNOOOSTTTV	not to have a ghost
AAEGHIIILNNRSTT	in a straight line
AAEGHIIINORSSTV	have as its origin
AAEGHIIKLLNNRTT	lateral thinking
AAEGHILLLNOTTTU	let it all hang out
AAEGHJKKLNRSTUY	Karl Guthe Jansky
AAEGHLLNOORTTUY	natural theology
AAEGIIILNNOORST	regionalisation
AAEGIIILNNOORTZ	regionalization
AAEGIIKNNNPSSST	painstakingness
AAEGIIMNOOPRRRT	marriage portion
AAEGIINNOOOTTVV	give an ovation to

AAEGIINNOPRRSTT	Tigran Petrosian
AAEGIKNNNOOSSTW	taking as one's own
AAEGILLNOOOPSTT	palaeontologist
AAEGILNNORRSSST	transgressional
AAEGIMMNNNOSSSU	magnanimousness
AAEGINNPPRRRRST	sparring partner
AAEHIIILLLMTWWW	William Whitelaw
AAEHIIILNNOPRST	in a relationship
AAEHIILORTTTUVY	authoritatively
AAEHIKLNNNORRTW	lower in rank than
AAEHILLLOPRTTUW	without parallel
AAEHILNOPRSSTTW	a slap on the wrist
AAEHINOPRRTTTUW	without a partner
AAEHLLLMMNORSUW	al-hallown summer
AAEHLLNORSSTUUW	slower than usual
AAEIIIKNNOOPSTW	in a weak position
AAEIIILNNNORTTZ	internalization
AAEIIINOPRRTTVZ	reprivatization
AAEIILLLMMRSTTU	multilateralism
AAEIILLLMRSTTTU	multilateralist
AAEIILLMNNRSTTU	transilluminate
AAEIILLNNNORTTY	internationally
AAEIILMNNOORRST	renormalisation
AAEIILMNNOORRTZ	renormalization
AAEIILMORRRRTTY	Territorial Army
AAEIILNNOOPRSTZ	personalization
AAEIILNNORRSTTT	transliteration
AAEIILNOPPPRRTY	inappropriately
AAEIIMNOSSTTTYZ	systematization
AAEIJKKLNOORRTW	work like a Trojan
AAEIKKLLNOSSTWY	Stanley Kowalski
AAEILLNNOORTTTY	National Lottery
AAEILMNNOQTUUUX	autumnal equinox
AAEILMNPRRSSTUU	supernaturalism
AAEILMNSSSSSTYY	systems analysis
AAEILNNNOSSTTUY	instantaneously
AAEILNPRRSSTTUU	supernaturalist
AAEINNNOOPTTTTY	not pay attention
AAEOOOOPPRSSTTT	propose a toast to
AAFGGGIILMNNSSY	magnifying glass
AAFGIINNORRSTTU	transfiguration ❑
AAFGILMOPRRTTVY	gravity platform
AAFHILNORRTTTUV	Valiant-for-Truth
AAFIIIMMNOOPRST	spirit of ammonia
AAGGHILMNNORTTW	malignant growth
AAGGMMNNNOSSSUU	Magnus Magnusson
AAGIIILNNORSTUZ	singularization
AAGIIKLNNOPRSST	stinking parasol
AAGIMNNOORSSTUZ	Zagros Mountains
AAHIIILLMNORRSW	William Harrison
AAHIIILNOOPSTTZ	hospitalization
AAHIINNNOPPRSST	non-partisanship
AAHILMOORRSTTWY	story with a moral
AAHLMMOOOPRRSSU	parasol mushroom
AAIIIIMNNORTTUZ	miniaturization
AAIIILLNNOPRSTY	inspirationally
AAIIILMMNOORTTZ	immortalization
AAIIILMNNNOOPTT	ion implantation
AAIIJLNOOPSTTUX	juxtapositional
AAIILMMNNRTTUUY	natural immunity
AAIILNNOOPRSSTT	transpositional
AAIIMNOOPRSSSTY	trypanosomiasis
AAIINNOOPRSTTTU	saturation point
AAIMNNORSSTTUUU	Taurus Mountains
ABBBDEEGIILNRRY	Beryl Bainbridge
ABBBEFGIORRRSYY	Greyfriars Bobby
ABBCDDEHIILMRRY	Richard Dimbleby
ABBCDEEFHKNOOTY	the back of beyond
ABBCEEEEFMMMOOR	become a member of
ABBCEEEFFKLOOOT	coffee-table book
ABBCEEHKNNORRTU	on the back burner
ABBCEEIJLNNOOTU	unobjectionable
ABBCEFGIIKLNORT	bring back to life
ABBCEHLNNOSSTTU	Hubble's constant
ABBCEIJLNNOOTUY	unobjectionably
ABBCHIIILMORSTU	British Columbia
ABBDDELNOORTTUY	total body burden
ABBDEEEHIMMNORT	Meindert Hobbema
ABBDEEGHINRRTYZ	bright and breezy
ABBDEEHKLOOPTYY	played by the book
ABBDEEIILNNSSTU	indubitableness
ABBDEEIMNORRSSU	Ambrose Burnside
ABBDEGHILORRTYY	daylight robbery
ABBDEHIJNOORSUY	Josiah Bounderby
ABBEEEEHILNNTTZ	Elizabeth Bennet
ABBEEEFHLOORTTW	The Tower of Babel
ABBEEEFILORTTTU	feel bitter about
ABBEEEHLNOORSTW	below one's breath
ABBEEHHIILOPSTZ	Elizabeth Bishop
ABBEEIIJMNNNRTT	Benjamin Britten
ABBEEILOPRRRSSW	blow raspberries
ABBEFILNOORRSVY	Rivers of Babylon
ABBEFKLOORSTTTU	Battles of Tobruk
ABCCCDEIIILNORU	ribonucleic acid
ABCCCEHKKLOPTTU	put back the clock
	put the clock back
ABCCCGIIKLLLOOO	biological clock
ABCCEEEIKLLNRTT	electric blanket
ABCCEEEILRRTTTY	electric battery
ABCCEEHLNNOOSSW	blow one's chances
ABCCEEIILLNNORU	unreconciliable
ABCCEFHINOORRSU	François Boucher
ABCCEFIIIJNOOTT	objectification
ABCCEGHINOPRSST	batch processing
ABCCEHIKLNOORRS	black rhinoceros
ABCCEHKMOOORRTT	reach rock bottom
ABCCEIIIILNSSTY	inaccessibility
ABCCEIIILLNORTY	reconcilability
ABCCEIIILNPPRSS	basic principles
ABCCIIKLMNNOOOT	combination lock
ABCDDEEEIILPSSY	place side by side
ABCDDEEENNNORUY	beyond endurance
ABCDDEEGINNORRV	David Cronenberg
ABCDDEEHIIOTWWW	a widow bewitched
ABCDEEEEGMNORST	become estranged
ABCDEEEEHHIORST	beside each other
ABCDEEEHLLLNSTY	sell by the candle
ABCDEEFGHILRUUW	Ludwig Feuerbach
ABCDEEFHIOOORUV	code of behaviour
ABCDEEGHILNOPRW	bleaching powder
ABCDEEGHILNRSTU	Edinburgh Castle

ABCDEEGIIMNNNOT become indignant
ABCDEEHIIILPRTY decipherability
ABCDEEHILLLORVW Clive Howard Bell
ABCDEEIILNOSSSS dissociableness
ABCDEFIIKLLMORW William Beckford
ABCDEFKKLOORSTU stroke of bad luck
ABCDEGHIINNOTTW can't be doing with
ABCDEGHIKNNORTU in the background
ABCDEIKLLOORRWY yellow brick road
ABCDEILNOOORRUW rainbow-coloured
ABCEEEEEHHRRSTW wear the breeches
ABCEEEEILNRSSSV serviceableness
ABCEEEEIMOOPRTV become operative
ABCEEEELNORRSSV recoverableness
ABCEEEFHLORSTUW below the surface
ABCEEEFIMMNNORR in remembrance of
ABCEEEFMNOPRRST best performance
ABCEEEGHKORRTTT bracket together
ABCEEEGINSSSTUW subsistence wage
ABCEEEHHINORSTT raise to the bench
ABCEEEHKLNNOOSS back on one's heels
ABCEEEIIKNOPRST break into pieces
ABCEEEIILLNOSTV cable television
ABCEEEILNNOPTUX unexceptionable
ABCEEEINRSSSTTU cause bitterness
ABCEEELMNNNORST Clemens Brentano
ABCEEELNNORSSSV conversableness
ABCEEFFHLLORRTY carry off the bell
ABCEEFHIMOOPRRS breach of promise
ABCEEFHKORTTTUU Back to the Future
ABCEEFILNOPSSSU place of business
ABCEEFLLNOOOSTT Battle of Colenso
ABCEEGGIIKNNOSV give one's backing
ABCEEGHIKKNNOPT keep nothing back
ABCEEGHINORSSTT tossing the caber
ABCEEGHKOPRTTTU put back together
ABCEEHHILNOPTTU built on the cheap
ABCEEHILLMNORST Albert Michelson
ABCEEHKNNORSTTU South Bank Centre
ABCEEHLNOORRTTT Charlotte Brontë
ABCEEIIIMNNRSTT cabinet minister
ABCEEIKLNRSTTUY security blanket
ABCEEILMMNNORSU incommensurable
ABCEEILMNNNOOOU once in a blue moon
ABCEEILNNOPTUXY unexceptionably
ABCEELLMNORRTUV vertebral column
ABCEFLNOOOPRRRU perfluorocarbon
ABCEGHHIIKMNRSU Buckinghamshire
ABCEGLLLORRSTUU globular cluster
ABCEHHIKLMNSTTU thumbnail sketch
ABCEIIIILLNPTXY inexplicability
ABCEIIIKLLMNNTW William Bentinck
ABCEIIIKLMNRSWW Wilkins Micawber
ABCEIIILLMPRSTT bimetallic strip
ABCEIILLNOPRSTU public relations
ABCEIILMMNOPTVX vitamin B complex
ABCEIILNNOPTTTU public attention
ABCEIKNNOOPSTTU put one's back into
ABCFKNNOORRTTTU turn back to front
ABCIIIILMNOPTTY incompatibility
ABCIIILLNNOOSTY inconsolability
ABCIILLLNOORTTY controllability
ABCIILORRRSTTUU arboriculturist
ABDDDEEIMNNORSS broad-mindedness
ABDDEEEFHILOOTV abode of the devil
ABDDEEEFLNORSTT Battle of Dresden
ABDDEEEHNOORSUW bonded warehouse
ABDDEEFFLLNOOTT Battle of Flodden
ABDDEEFILNNOPRT Forbidden Planet
ABDDEGINNOORRSW Edward G Robinson
ABDDEGINNORSTUW bending outwards
ABDDGGIIIINORTZ digitizing board
ABDEEEEFHINOSST be on the safe side
ABDEEEEILMNPRRT predeterminable
ABDEEEEMNNOTUWY between you and me
ABDEEEGHJLORRSU Joshua Lederberg
ABDEEEGHLNPRSTY send by telegraph
ABDEEEHILLLSSTW well-established
ABDEEEHNNOPRSST spend one's breath
ABDEEEHNNORRSTU under one's breath
ABDEEEIKLNRSSTT beer and skittles
ABDEEEILNNRSSSU undesirableness
ABDEEFGIINORRST bearer of tidings
ABDEEFHNNOORTTU under the baton of
ABDEEFIIIILNSTY indefeasibility
ABDEEFINNORSSTT to absent friends
ABDEEGGGINORTUV don't give a bugger
ABDEEGHILLNOSST long-established
ABDEEGHKLMORSST God bless the mark
ABDEEGIILLMORTT Gottlieb Daimler
ABDEEHHLNOOORSU Leonard Hobhouse
ABDEEHIKLORSSTW established work
ABDEEHIMNNRSTUW white man's burden
ABDEEHLLNSSTTUU hustle and bustle
ABDEEIILLLNNORU Daniel Bernoulli
ABDEEIILMNNOSST indomitableness
ABDEEILMNNOOPUU double pneumonia
ABDEEILNNORTTUY turn a blind eye to
ABDEELLNRRRSSTU Bertrand Russell
ABDEELNORSSTUUV Sunset Boulevard
ABDEFHILNNOORST land of one's birth
ABDEGGHHIILLNOT Heligoland Bight
ABDEGGHHIILLNRV high-gravel-blind
ABDEGHHNNORSTTY by the strong hand
ABDEGHIIILNSSTU distinguishable
ABDEGIILNNOORTU under obligation
ABDEIILNNORSTUY insubordinately
ABDENOOORRTTUUU roundabout route
ABDGHLOOOOSSTTU tough as old boots
ABDGILLMNNOTUWZ Ludwig Boltzmann
ABDHHINOORRSTUY birthday honours
ABDIIIIILMNSSTY inadmissibility
ABDIIINNNOORSTU insubordination
ABEEEEEGLNNRRWY renewable energy
ABEEEEILLNORRST Easter Rebellion
ABEEEELLORSSSTV Seve Ballesteros
ABEEEFFGKNSSTUU beefsteak fungus
ABEEEFHILLNOTTT Battle of the Nile
ABEEEFHOPRRTTTT the better part of
ABEEEGGHLLORRSY Borghese Gallery
ABEEEGGILNNPRRT ginger beer plant
ABEEEGGINNORSST get one's bearings

ABEEEGHHHLNOSTW	the whole shebang
ABEEEGHNNOORTTT	go one better than
ABEEEGORRSSTTTY	set great store by
ABEEEHHOPRSTTTW	the powers that be
ABEEEHIILNNPPRS	inapprehensible
ABEEEHIILNRRTTV	Ivan the Terrible
ABEEEHILLPPRSTU	Isabelle Huppert
ABEEEHILMNRSSTT	re-establishment
ABEEEHJLNNNOSTW	John Bennet Lawes
ABEEEHLLNOOSTTW	bottlenose whale
ABEEEIILNNQSSTU	inequitableness
ABEEEIINPRRSSTY	Presbyterianise
ABEEEIINPRRSTYZ	Presbyterianize
ABEEEILLNNORSST	intolerableness
ABEEEILMNNNRSSU	innumerableness
ABEEEILNRRSTUVV	vestibular nerve
ABEEEIMNOOOSTTT	beat someone to it
ABEEELLMNOORSSS	lose one's marbles
ABEEELLMOPPSSSY	People's Assembly
ABEEELNPPRRSTUU	Peter Paul Rubens
ABEEFFGGHHIOTTT	the gift of the gab
ABEEFFGHOORRRUU	harbour of refuge
ABEEFFHNOOPRSTT	bore the pants off
ABEEFFMNOOORSSS	brass someone off
ABEEFGHIKMNOSTT	making the best of
ABEEFGNOORRRSTU	Berengar of Tours
ABEEFHHILLOOSVY	behave foolishly
ABEEFHLMOOSSSUY	House of Assembly
ABEEFIIJLNSSSTU	justifiableness
ABEEFILNOORSSTV	self-observation
ABEEFILORSTTTUY	Statue of Liberty
ABEEFNOOORSSTWW	sweat of one's brow
ABEEGGIKLNRSSTU	like gangbusters
ABEEHHMORRRSTTX	The Marx Brothers
ABEEHIIILMNNSTV	The Invisible Man
ABEEHIILMMNOORT	binomial theorem
ABEEHILMNORSSTW	blameworthiness
ABEEHMNNNOORRTT	to the manner born
ABEEHNNNORRRUVW	Wernher von Braun
ABEEIIILLLMNSST	illimitableness
ABEEIIILMNPRTTY	impenetrability
ABEEIIMNPRRSSTY	Presbyterianism
ABEEILLMNOORRRY	Lionel Barrymore
ABEEILLMNORSUWY	Yellow Submarine
ABEEINNSSSSTTUV	substantiveness
ABEENNOOOPRSSTU	about one's person
ABEFGGHILORRTUY	burgh of regality
ABEFHHILRSSTTTU	at the first blush
ABEFHIIMNORRRST	Martin Frobisher
ABEFHIINNOSSSSU	fashion business
ABEFIIJLMOORRTU	Alberto Fujimori
ABEFILMNORSSTTU	burst into flames
ABEFINNORRRSSUW	Barrow-in-Furness
ABEGHHILNOORRTU	Right Honourable
ABEGHHIOORTTTTU	to the right about
ABEGIIIILLNNNOV	Giovanni Bellini
ABEGIILNNORTUVY	ungovernability
ABEGILLMNOPPRRT	trembling poplar
ABEGIMNNOSSSUUU	unambiguousness
ABEGOOPRSSTTTUU	be put out to grass
ABEHHHIORRSSTTY	by the short hairs
ABEHHINORRRTTTU	burr in the throat
ABEHIIIILMPRSTY	imperishability
ABEHIOOOPPRRRSU	harbour porpoise
ABEIIILLNNRTUVY	invulnerability
ABEIINNNNORSTTU	Anton Rubinstein
ABEIINNRRRSTTUU	Artur Rubinstein
ABEIKMNNOOOPPTT	appointment book
ABEINOOOPRSSTTV	observation post
ABGHHIIILNORRST	British longhair
ABGHKNNOOPSSSYY	go by shanks's pony
ABGIIMNORRTTTUY	bring to maturity
ABHHIJJNOORSTTU	Thojib N J Suharto
ABHIIILNNORRSSU	annus horribilis
ABHIIILNOPTTYYZ	hypnotizability
ABHIINNOPRSSTUW	burn with passion
ABIINORSSTTTUUY	substitutionary
ACCCCCDEIIILRTY	citric acid cycle
ACCCCEEIIJMNRSU	circumjacencies
ACCCDDKLLNOOOUU	Cloudcuckooland
	cloud-cuckoo-land
ACCCDEEILMNRRUY	decimal currency
ACCCDEEINNOORTT	concerted action
ACCCDEFHHIKLORT	Alfred Hitchcock
ACCCEEEHILLMORT	electrochemical
ACCCEEFHILLLOOR	cholecalciferol
ACCCEEGIILLLOOS	ecclesiological
ACCCEEHHIIILORS	Escherichia coli
ACCCEEIIILMSSST	ecclesiasticism
ACCCEEIILLNNNOS	in all conscience
ACCCEEILOORSTTU	electroacoustic
ACCCEHMOOPRSTTU	come up to scratch
ACCCEILOOPRSTUU	acoustic coupler
ACCCEIMNNOOOTTT	come into contact
ACCCELLMNORRSSU	Carson McCullers
ACCCIILLMOOPRSY	microscopically
ACCCIINNOORRTVY	carry conviction
ACCDDEEEFINOOSS	deed of accession
ACCDDEEEHLSSSTU	scheduled castes
ACCDDEEFILNNORU	road fund licence
ACCDDEEINNNOSTU	discountenanced
ACCDDEIIKNNOOST	cask-conditioned
ACCDDEIMMNNNOOS	second-in-command
ACCDEEEIILMNNRU	nuclear medicine
ACCDEEEIILNSSUY	succeed in easily
ACCDEEEIKLQRSUY	decrease quickly
ACCDEEEILNNNORT	declare innocent
ACCDEEHIILMORRR	Mordecai Richler
ACCDEEIIMNOOOST	come to a decision
ACCDEEILMNORSTY	electrodynamics
ACCDEELLNORSSTU	couldn't care less
ACCDEFGHHLNNORU	Church of England
ACCDEFINNNOOSTU	find one's account
ACCDEFLNOORSSTU	curse of Scotland
ACCDEFNNOOOORSW	of one's own accord
ACCDEHIKKLNNSUW	knuckle sandwich
ACCDEHLNOOORSSY	secondary school
ACCDEIIILMNNSTU	incidental music
ACCDEIILMORRSTU	musical director
ACCDEIOPPRRSTTU	picture postcard
ACCDELNOOORRSUY	secondary colour
ACCDFFLMMOOORRT	Cold Comfort Farm

ACCDIILMOOPPRST diplomatic corps
ACCDIILNOORRTTY contradictorily
ACCEEEEFFILRSSV self-service café
ACCEEEEHILLMMNT chemical element
ACCEEEELNPPRRSV Spencer Perceval
ACCEEEFFGHORRUY Geoffrey Chaucer
ACCEEEGILMNORTT electromagnetic
ACCEEEHHIMMNOTT The Iceman Cometh
ACCEEEHIMNRRSTV merchant service
ACCEEEILLMORRTT electrometrical
ACCEEFFIINOSSSU efficaciousness
ACCEEFHILLNORST electronic flash
ACCEEFIIILNORTT electrification
ACCEEGHIILNNNST ethnic cleansing
ACCEEGHIMMNNNRU Merce Cunningham
ACCEEGHLNNOORTX exchange control
ACCEEGHLNOOPSTY space technology
ACCEEGIIMOPRSUV Amerigo Vespucci
ACCEEHHIMOORRTT heterochromatic
ACCEEHIINOPRRSV vice-chairperson
ACCEEIIKLNQRSUY increase quickly
ACCEEIIMMNOOTTT action committee
ACCEEIIOPPRRTTY cryoprecipitate
ACCEEIKMNNOOSSS make concessions
ACCEEILLMORRSTT electrical storm
ACCEEILNNOOPRUU European Council
ACCEEILNORSSTUU Seleucus Nicator
ACCEEKNOORRSSTV cover one's tracks
ACCEENNOPSSSTUU suspense account
ACCEFFGIIILNRSS self-sacrificing
ACCEFFIIILNOSUY inefficaciously
ACCEFGIIIPRSTVY specific gravity
ACCEFHHMMNOSSUU much of a muchness
ACCEFHHOOPRSSST Pasch of the Cross
ACCEFIKMNOOOSSU make conscious of
ACCEFILNOOSSTTU Council of States
ACCEGHILLLNOOTY technologically
ACCEGHIMMNORTUY community charge
ACCEGIILNNOPRSS pelican crossing
ACCEGNNOOOOSTTU go to one's account
ACCEHHIINNOPSSS cash in one's chips
ACCEHIILLPRRTYY hypercritically
ACCEHIILNORSSTT interscholastic
ACCEHIILPPRSSTY particle physics
ACCEHIIMMNOTTUW communicate with
ACCEHINNNOOOSTW show a connection
ACCEHINNOOPRRTT anthropocentric
ACCEIIKNNORSSTW stick in one's craw
ACCEIILMMNOTUVY communicatively
ACCEIILMRRTUUUV curriculum vitae
ACCEIILOPPRSSUY perspicaciously
ACCEIIMMNNOOTUX excommunication
ACCEIIMMNNOTUUV uncommunicative
ACCEIINOPPRTTTU put into practice
ACCEIKMNNOOSSUU make unconscious
ACCEILMOOPRRSTU ultramicroscope
ACCEIMORRSTTTUU atomic structure
ACCFIIIMNNOORTT romantic fiction
ACCGHILLLNOOORY chronologically
ACCGHILLLOOPSYY psychologically
ACCGIIIINNRRTTU circuit training
ACCGIILLLOOOTXY toxicologically
ACCHHILMOOOPPST ophthalmoscopic
ACCHILMMNOOPRRT Richmal Crompton
ACCIKLLMOOOOTTV Molotov cocktail
ACCILMOOPRRSTUY ultramicroscopy
ACCINOOORRSSTTV vasoconstrictor
ACDDDEEEEINNNPY Independence Day
ACDDDEEINOORTWW decorated window
ACDDDFGIINOORTU drug of addiction
ACDDDHINOORRUWY Richard Dunwoody
ACDDEEEELNNPSTU dependent clause
ACDDEEEFFINSSST disaffectedness
ACDDEEEHILMSSTU Dutch elm disease
ACDDEEEHLNNOSSS close-handedness
ACDDEEEHLNORSST cold-heartedness
ACDDEEEHORRRSTW Edward Rochester
ACDDEEEIILRRTVV deliver a verdict
ACDDEEFHILLLNOU Holden Caulfield
ACDDEEFINORSTTU after deductions
ACDDEEGGHINNOOR nodding ogee arch
ACDDEEGHHORRRRS Gerhard Schröder
ACDDEEHIILNNNTW Candle in the Wind
ACDDEEHIINRSTUV Christian de Duve
ACDDEEHILMNNOUY Unchained Melody
ACDDEEILNOPPRSS displaced person
ACDDEEKKLNNORUY under lock and key
ACDDEFFGHLNNOSU golden handcuffs
ACDDEFGILNORSUU Figure and Clouds
ACDDEFHIRRRSSUY Richard Dreyfuss
ACDDEFLMOOORSSW sword of Damocles
ACDDEIILNORRSUU Claudius Dornier
ACDDHIIMNORSTYY hydrodynamicist
ACDDIIIIILNSTUV individualistic
ACDEEEEGHKLNRST the Greek calends
ACDEEEEGHNRRSTT The Secret Garden
ACDEEEEGILNORUX Eugène Delacroix
ACDEEEEIKNPRSTU take up residence
ACDEEEEILLNNRSS lesser celandine
ACDEEEEILNNORTT entente cordiale
ACDEEEFFHIINRTW with a difference
ACDEEEFGIKNRRRS Frederick Sanger
ACDEEEFGILNPRST self-deprecating
ACDEEEFIINRRTVX refractive index
ACDEEEFILNOPRST self-deprecation
ACDEEEGHIKPPRST pick gather speed
ACDEEEGHNNSTTUX exchange student
ACDEEEGKLMNNOTW acknowledgement
ACDEEEGLLNORRVV Grover Cleveland
ACDEEEGNNORRTUV undercover agent
ACDEEEHHNNORSTT ascend the throne
ACDEEEHIILMNRRT Marlene Dietrich
ACDEEEHILMORRUV armoured vehicle
ACDEEEHIMNORRSV Devonshire cream
ACDEEEIILLPRSVY special delivery
ACDEEEIIMNPRSSV manic-depressive
ACDEEEIJLNPQRUU Jacqueline du Pré
ACDEEEINNORSSST considerateness
ACDEEELLLNRRRUW Lawrence Durrell
ACDEEFFFHIOORTY officer of the day
ACDEEFGIINOORST age of discretion
ACDEEFHIKNORRST Frederick Ashton

ACDEEFIKLORRRTY	Frederick Taylor
ACDEEFILNOPRRTW	in a perfect world
ACDEEFILNORRRTU	funeral director
ACDEEFKOQRRSSUW	Wackford Squeers
ACDEEFLMNNORRRT	Clermont-Ferrand
ACDEEFMMNNOORSY	comedy of manners
ACDEEGGHIINPRRS	graphic designer
ACDEEGHHIINORTU	higher education
ACDEEGHIILOPSTT	dephlogisticate
ACDEEGHMPPRRTUU	trumped-up charge
ACDEEGIIILLMOOP	epidemiological
ACDEEGIIKMNRRTT	direct marketing
ACDEEGIILLPRSSV	privileged class
ACDEEGIMMNOOORR	coram domino rege
ACDEEHHINOPRRST	Christopher Dean
ACDEEHIMNOORSTU	echinodermatous
ACDEEHIMNOQSTUY	Thomas De Quincey
ACDEEHINOOPRSST	drop one's aitches
ACDEEHLLMNNOOOY	Ode on Melancholy
ACDEEHLLOPPRRSU	shoulder-clapper
ACDEEHLNNOORTUV	Under the Volcano
ACDEEHMNNOOOVWY	come down heavy on
ACDEEIIKLNPRSTY	speak indirectly
ACDEEIILNNORSTY	inconsiderately
ACDEEIINNOORRST	reconsideration
ACDEEIKLPPQRRUY	quickly prepared
ACDEEILLNPPRRUY	perpendicularly
ACDEEIMMNNOORST	recommendations
ACDEEIMMORSSTTT	domestic matters
ACDEELMNORSTTUV	travel documents
ACDEEMMMNNNOSTT	Ten Commandments
ACDEEMNNNOORSTY	stand on ceremony
ACDEENNNOORRSST	stand one's corner
ACDEFFLOOOPRSSY	pay off old scores
ACDEFHIILMOORTU	A Child of our Time
ACDEFHIMOOPPRSY	Pyramid of Cheops
ACDEFIIIIMNNNOT	indemnification
ACDEFIIIINORSTV	diversification
ACDEFIIILNNOTTY	confidentiality
ACDEFIIIMNOSTTY	demystification
ACDEGGHINNORRUY	greyhound-racing
ACDEGHHIKLNOORT	chalking the door
ACDEGHIINNORSTT	considering that
ACDEGIIILLLMOOW	William Coolidge
ACDEGILNNNOSTTU	consenting adult
ACDEGINORSTTTUY	cottage industry
ACDEHHINORRSTTW	throw in the cards
ACDEHHOPRRSTTUW	throw up the cards
ACDEHIIKLLQTUWY	deal with quickly
ACDEHIIMNOOOPRR	radio microphone
ACDEHIINOPSSTTU	unsophisticated
ACDEHILLNOORTWY	The Cowardly Lion
ACDEIIILLNNORST	in all directions
ACDEIIILMNNOORT	omnidirectional
ACDEIIILNORRSTY	discretionarily
ACDEIIINNNOORST	inconsideration
ACDEIIINNORRTYZ	ordinary citizen
ACDEIIMNOOSTTUY	situation comedy
ACDEIKMNPQRTTUY	pretty damn quick
ACDEIKNOOSTTTUY	take into custody
ACDEIMNORSSSTTU	mass destruction
ACDEKNNOOSSSSTT	stocks and stones
ACDELNOOOPRRTUW	pour cold water on
ACDGHIMNNOOPRRY	gynandromorphic
ACDGIIIINNNOORT	air-conditioning
ACDGIILLNNORRTY	Cyril Darlington
ACDGILNOOOPRRSS	Colorado Springs
ACDHHIINOOPRSSY	hypochondriasis
ACDHHILLNNOOORS	Harold Nicholson
ACDHIINNNOOOTTT	on condition that
ACDIIINNNOOSTTU	discontinuation
ACDIILLNNNOOTUY	unconditionally
ACDIILOOOORSTUV	Ludovico Ariosto
ACDIINNORSSTTUU	Titus Andronicus
ACEEEEEFKMNORRT	make reference to
ACEEEEEHINRSSVV	have seen service
ACEEEEEHLLPSSSV	leave speechless
ACEEEEFHHLMNTUU	The Female Eunuch
ACEEEEFILLMRRSU	merciful release
ACEEEEFILNPRUWX	awful experience
ACEEEEGHHLNOSTX	lose the exchange
ACEEEEGHLNRSTTX	exchange letters
ACEEEEGILLNNORT	general election
ACEEEEGILNORTTV	electronegative
ACEEEEGLLLMMNOU	Emmanuel College
ACEEEEHILLPRSST	celestial sphere
ACEEEELPPRRSTTU	upper-case letter
ACEEEEMNNRSSTTU	cause resentment
ACEEEENOORSSTVY	cast one's eye over
ACEEEFFILNNSSTU	ineffectualness
ACEEEFFLNOPRSST	personal effects
ACEEEFGGHINNORX	foreign exchange
ACEEEFGILNNOPRR	peregrine falcon
ACEEEFGILNORRST	steering clear of
ACEEEFHHILNPRTT	in perfect health
ACEEEFHIMNNNRST	enfranchisement
ACEEEFIINNORRTT	centre of inertia
ACEEEFILNPRRTTV	perfect interval
ACEEEGGNOORRUVV	George Vancouver
ACEEEGHILLLRRSV	Charles Greville
ACEEEGHIMMNNRTU	Munich Agreement
ACEEEGHIMNNNRTT	interchangement
ACEEEGHINNOPRTT	parthenogenetic
ACEEEGHINNOSVWX	exchange views on
ACEEEGHINNPRRTV	prevent reaching
ACEEEGIIINPRRRV	Virginia creeper
ACEEEGIMNOPRSTT	spermatogenetic
ACEEEHHHLNOOPRX	hexachlorophene
ACEEEHHILLNRTUV	leave in the lurch
ACEEEHHIPPRSSTT	speech therapist
ACEEEHHNOORTTTX	next to each other
ACEEEHHORSTTTVW	whatever the cost
ACEEEHIILLRRSST	Leslie Charteris
ACEEEHIINRSTTTZ	Citizen's Theatre
ACEEEHIKLLPPRST	like the clappers
ACEEEHIKORRSTTU	take their course
ACEEEHILLMNRTUY	hermeneutically
ACEEEHKMMNOORTT	come on the market
ACEEEHNOOPRSSSU	shape one's course
ACEEEHNORRSSSTU	treacherousness
ACEEEIILLLNSTTU	intellectualise
ACEEEIILLLNTTUZ	intellectualize

ACEEEIILLNORRUV	Laurence Olivier
ACEEEIILMMORRSV	memorial service
ACEEEIINPPRSSTT	precipitateness
ACEEEIKNOOPTTTX	take exception to
ACEEEILLORRSTWY	Aleister Crowley
ACEEEILMNOSSSUU	mousseline sauce
ACEEEILNOPQRSUV	picaresque novel
ACEEEILNPSSSTUV	speculativeness
ACEEEIMMNPPPRRT	peppermint cream
ACEEEINNNRSSSSU	unnecessariness
ACEEEINNQRSSTUY	sesquicentenary
ACEEELLLMOPRTXY	relax completely
ACEEELLMNOPRSSU	peroneal muscles
ACEEEMMNOOOSSWY	come someone's way
ACEEFFFFHKOPSTU	speak off the cuff
ACEEFFHHIKLLOTT	take the chill off
ACEEFFHLLOPRRSU	self-reproachful
ACEEFFILNNNOORS	François Fénelon
ACEEFFILNOSTTUY	affluent society
ACEEFGHIKLNOSTT	king of the castle
ACEEFGHIMORSSST	message of Christ
ACEEFGIILLNOPST	falling to pieces
ACEEFGILNRRTTUU	ultracentrifuge
ACEEFGINORRTTVY	centre of gravity
ACEEFGNOOOPRRSU	person of courage
ACEEFHIILNPRSTT	in the first place
ACEEFHILNNOPRSY	French Polynesia
ACEEFHLNOPRRSSU	reproachfulness
ACEEFHOOPRRRSTU	par for the course
ACEEFIIILMNOPTX	exemplification
ACEEFIIINNOSTTX	extensification
ACEEFIILNPRSSSU	superficialness
ACEEFIINNOOPTTX	in expectation of
ACEEFILLLNRSTUY	listen carefully
ACEEFINORRSTTUY	it's a free country
ACEEGGIILLNNORT	training-college
ACEEGHHHIOORTTW	go with each other
ACEEGHHINORSTTT	costing the earth
ACEEGHIKLLNRSSY	Charles Kingsley
ACEEGIIKLNNOOPT	go on a picket line
ACEEGIILLMNORVW	William Congreve
ACEEGIILLMOOPST	epistemological
ACEEGILLNNOOTTY	ontogenetically
ACEEGILMNNOPPUU	pneumonic plague
ACEEGLLLLLOOSSU	All Souls College
ACEEGLLMNNOORTV	local government
ACEEGLMORRRSTUU	regular customer
ACEEGMNNORRTTUU	counter-argument
ACEEHHIIKNNOTTT	take it on the chin
ACEEHHIILLLMRSW	William Herschel
ACEEHHIKRSSSTTW	the cat's whiskers
ACEEHIIJLLNNOTT	lethal injection
ACEEHIILLLLNSTY	Hellenistically
ACEEHIILLMPSTUY	euphemistically
ACEEHIILMNORTVV	thermionic valve
ACEEHIIMMORSTTW	commiserate with
ACEEHIIMNNOORRS	come rain or shine
ACEEHIKMNOPPTWY	keep company with
ACEEHILLLORSTTV	Charlottesville
ACEEHILMMNRSTTY	mental chemistry
ACEEHILOORRSSST	atherosclerosis
ACEEHILOORSSTWW	with a screw loose
ACEEHIMMNOPRSTU	the Paris Commune
ACEEHNOORRSTTUY	cry one's heart out
ACEEIIILRSTTUVY	leisure activity
ACEEIIINQSSSTUV	acquisitiveness
ACEEIILLLMNSTTU	intellectualism
ACEEIILLLNTTTUY	intellectuality
ACEEIILNNNOOSTV	conventionalise
ACEEIILNNNOOTVZ	conventionalize
ACEEIILNNNOQSTU	inconsequential
ACEEIJLNNNORSSU	Cornelius Jansen
ACEEIKNOPPRRSSU	prick up one's ears
ACEEILLLMNOSSUY	miscellaneously
ACEEILLMMNOPRTY	complementarily
ACEEILLMNOPTTVY	contemplatively
ACEEILLNNOQSTUY	consequentially
ACEEILMNNOPTTUY	complete annuity
ACEEILMPRSSTUUZ	trapezius muscle
ACEEILNNNNOSSSS	nonsensicalness
ACEEILNNOQSSUUV	unequivocalness
ACEEILNPRRSSSVY	scrivener's palsy
ACEEIMMNNNNOTTU	ancient monument
ACEEIMNNOOPRTTY	contemporaneity
ACEEIMNOORSSSTU	music to one's ears
ACEEINORRRRSTUY	resurrectionary
ACEELLMNNNOORUY	Maureen Connolly
ACEELLOORSTTUUU	Toulouse-Lautrec
ACEEMNNOOOPRSTU	contemporaneous
ACEFFHOOOPPRRSU	proof of purchase
ACEFHHLMNOOOTTW	woman of the cloth
ACEFIIIINNNOSTT	intensification
ACEFIIINNOOPRST	personification
ACEFKNNOOORSTVW	covenant of works
ACEFLMNOOOPSVWY	Company of Wolves
ACEFMMNOOOPRSTU	common of pasture
ACEGHHIKNORRTTT	on the right track
ACEGHHILNOSSTTW	swathing-clothes
ACEGHIIIMNNNPRT	printing-machine
ACEGHIMNNRTUVWY	wanting very much
ACEGHINOOPSTTUU	Augusto Pinochet
ACEGIIKLNPRSSTT	sticking-plaster
ACEGILLLMNOOOTY	entomologically
ACEGILNNOPPRSST	processing plant
ACEHHIKNORTTUVW	have no truck with
ACEHHINOPPRSTTU	Pithecanthropus
ACEHHIOPPRSSTTY	psychotherapist
ACEHIIINOSSTTTU	situation ethics
ACEHIIJMNRSSTTY	Christ in Majesty
ACEHIIKLLLMOSWY	William Shockley
ACEHIILLLMOOPRT	Michael Portillo
ACEHIILLLOOPRTY	heliotropically
ACEHIILLNOORSTV	historical novel
ACEHIILLOPRRSTY	prehistorically
ACEHIILMMNNOSTT	Mont-Saint-Michel
ACEHILMMPSSTTYY	lymphatic system
ACEHINOOPRRSSTW	ancestor-worship
ACEHLMMOOSSTUUU	Holocaust Museum
ACEHMNNOORSSTTU	turn one's stomach
ACEIIIKLLLMMNWY	William McKinley
ACEIIILLMPSSSTY	pessimistically
ACEIILLLLMOSSTV	still small voice

ACEIILLLMMNNOOR Lincoln Memorial
ACEIILLMNOPPRRS moral principles
ACEIILMNNNOOSTV conventionalism
ACEIILMNOOPRRST pectoralis minor
ACEIILNNNOOSTTV conventionalist
ACEIILNNNOOTTVY conventionality
ACEIILNNSSSTTUX sexual instincts
ACEIIMNOOPRTTUZ computerization
ACEIINNOORSSTTV conservationist
ACEIINNORRRSTUY insurrectionary
ACEIKLNNOOOORST a crook in one's lot
ACEILLNOORRSTVY controversially
ACEILLNOPRSTTUY personality cult
ACEILMMNNOPRTUY uncomplimentary
ACEINNOPRSTTTTU constituent part
ACELLMNORSTUUVY voluntary muscle
ACELMMNOOOPSSUW common-law spouse
ACELPRRRSSTTUUU superstructural
ACFGIIIILNNNSTY insignificantly
ACFGIIIMNNOSSTT most significant
ACFGILNNOOPRTUU functional group
ACFHIIJLNNOORUW Julian of Norwich
ACFHIORRRTUUVWY curry favour with
ACFIIMNNOOOSTTY comity of nations
ACFIINNNNOOORTT in confrontation
ACGGKLNOORSUVYY György von Lukacs
ACGHHIIIOOPRRST historiographic
ACGHHLLMNNOPSUU ploughman's lunch
ACGHHLOOOPPSTYY psychopathology
ACGHIILLLOOPSYY physiologically
ACGIILLLLOSSTYY syllogistically
ACGIILLLMMNOOUY immunologically
ACGIINNOOOPRSTT prognostication
ACHHHKOOPRRSSST short sharp shock
ACHHIILLLOOPPSY philosophically
ACHHIMNOOOPPRRT anthropomorphic
ACHIIIMOOSSSSST schistosomiasis
ACHIINNNOORSTYZ synchronization
ACHKLMNOOOOTTTU not much to look at
ACHLOOOPRRSSUUY Cryolophosaurus
ACIIILLLNOOPSTU optical illusion
ACIIILNNOPQTTUU quintuplication
ACIILMMNOOORSSY Royal Commission
royal commission
ACIILMNNOOSSTUY sanctimoniously
ADDDEEEHNNNRSSU underhandedness
ADDDEEEMNNOOSST do one's damnedest
ADDDEEFHILMOORT middle-of-the-road
ADDDEELNNOORSST Old Red Sandstone
ADDDGNNNOOORRUU go round and round
ADDEEEEEHLLNSSV level-headedness
ADDEEEEFGHNNORT The Garden of Eden
ADDEEEEFMNPRRTY deferred payment
ADDEEEFFIIOSSTX fixed set of ideas
ADDEEEFGHILMOST of the Middle Ages
ADDEEEFGILNORRU folie de grandeur
ADDEEEFGIMNNRSS dead men's fingers
ADDEEEFHHNOORTT the end of the road
ADDEEEFINNRRTUY deferred annuity
ADDEEEGGINNORSS engrossing a deed
ADDEEEGHHILNSST light-headedness
ADDEEEGHNNORSSW wrong-headedness
ADDEEEGNNOPRSTU get one's dander up
ADDEEEGNNORRSSS send one's regards
ADDEEEHIKNNRSST kind-heartedness
ADDEEEHLMOPRTUV move up the ladder
ADDEEEHLPPRSTTU step up the ladder
ADDEEEHNNORSSTW downheartedness
ADDEEEINOPRRRRS Pierre de Ronsard
ADDEEFGHLORRTTU The Artful Dodger
ADDEEGHIIKNOSSS Hodgkin's disease
ADDEEGIIKLNNORS like a dog's dinner
ADDEEHHINNORRTY hither and yonder
ADDEEHHNNORSTTU send round the hat
ADDEEHINNOORTVW over and done with
ADDEEIIIILNRSSTU deindustrialise
ADDEEIIIILNRSTUZ deindustrialize
ADDEEIIIILNRUVVY every individual
ADDEEILLMMNNSSS small-mindedness
ADDEELMNNOPRSUY many-splendoured
ADDEFFIILLPRSTY play first fiddle
ADDEFGINOORTTWW get to windward of
ADDEGGIINNNORWW window gardening
ADDEGHHINOOSTWY woody nightshade
ADDEGHINNORRTTU Arthur Eddington
ADDEGILNNNRSTUY understandingly
ADDEGNNNOORSSTU stand one's ground
ADDEHHIIJNNOSTW with hands joined
ADDEHILMMNOOSTT Thomas Middleton
ADDEIMNNNOPQSSS mind one's p's and q's
ADDHINNOPSSTUWW with ups and downs
ADEEEEEGLORRSST to a lesser degree
ADEEEEGIRRSSTTT State Registered
ADEEEEHHMORTTTT armed to the teeth
ADEEEEHHNRRTTUW under the weather
ADEEEEHIMMSTTTU meditate the muse
ADEEEEIIMNOSSTZ time-zone disease
ADEEEEILLLMNRSS Ellesmere Island
ADEEEFGHINORSTU under the aegis of
ADEEEFHHILLNOTT the lie of the land
ADEEEFHLNOPRTTW Peter and the Wolf
ADEEEFHNORSSSTT soft-heartedness
ADEEEGGHIIILRSV Sergei Diaghilev
ADEEEGGHIIMNRRT Martin Heidegger
ADEEEGGHINORTTW get the wrong idea
ADEEEGGIMORRRUU George Du Maurier
ADEEEGHLOPPRSST spread the gospel
ADEEEGILLLNNRTT little Englander
ADEEEGILMNNNSTT disentanglement
ADEEEGILNNOOPRS old-age pensioner
ADEEEGILNNOORRT older generation
ADEEEHHHIILNSTT hit the headlines
ADEEEHHHNOSSTUW haud one's wheesht
ADEEEHHHORSSTTW sheathe the sword
ADEEEHIIILORSVV Oliver Heaviside
ADEEEHIILMNORST residential home
ADEEEHILNNORSST lion-heartedness
ADEEEHNNNORTVWY every now and then
ADEEEIILMNNRTTY indeterminately
ADEEEIILNNOSTTV Ninette De Valois
Ninette de Valois
ADEEEIILNOPPPRR in apple-pie order

ADEEEIILNRSTTVY relative density
ADEEEILLMMNRSUY Süleyman Demirel
ADEEEILMNRRSUVY universal remedy
ADEEEIMNNOORTTY money-orientated
ADEEEINNOOTTTTV devote attention
ADEEELLLMNOPTVY developmentally
ADEEEMNOPRRSTTT department store
ADEEFFFHHLLNOTY fly off the handle
ADEEFFGIIINNRTT differentiating
ADEEFFIIINNORTT differentiation
ADEEFFIMMNOOPRR freedom from pain
ADEEFFIMNORSSTT disafforestment
ADEEFGGIKLNNOOW gain knowledge of
ADEEFGHIILLNPTY playing the field
ADEEFGIILLRSTTZ Alfred Stieglitz
ADEEFGKNOOORSSS for goodness sake
ADEEFHHORRRSTUY Rutherford Hayes
ADEEFHIIKMNRSTW make friends with
ADEEFHILLNSTTUW whistle and flute
ADEEFHILMNRSTTW Matthew Flinders
ADEEFHINNORSTTW find the answer to
ADEEFIIIJSSTTTU fides et justitia
ADEEFIILNNOOPST self-opinionated
ADEEFIILNOPQRSU qualified person
ADEEFIKLMOORSST for old time's sake
ADEEFMMNOORRTVW forward movement
ADEEFNNNOOPRSTU spend a fortune on
ADEEGGHINNOOOST going to one's head
ADEEGGHINOPSSSU pedagoguishness
ADEEGGILNNORSTY destroying angel
ADEEGGMMNORRTTU Götterdämmerung
ADEEGHHIILLNPRS Gillian Shepherd
ADEEGHHILNNOORT hen on a hot girdle
ADEEGHILNNORSTT on the danger list
ADEEGHJLNOPSTUY Stephen Jay Gould
ADEEGHNNORRTTUU get the runaround
ADEEGHNOORRTTUZ raze to the ground
ADEEGIILLMNRRTU ring-tailed lemur
ADEEGIILNNOQSTU leading question
ADEEGINNOPRSSSW spread one's wings
ADEEGJMNNOPSSTU pass judgement on
ADEEHHHHNOTTWWY the how and the why
ADEEHHHIMNNORSS Hamish Henderson
ADEEHHINOPSTTTU put into the shade
ADEEHHJNNNOORRV Johann von Herder
ADEEHIIILLMMRTW William Meredith
ADEEHIIMNNOORTT Dominion Theatre
ADEEHIKKNOOSSTT soaked to the skin
ADEEHILNNOORSTW let one's hair down
ADEEHILOOSTTTTV the devil's tattoo
ADEEHIMNNOOOSTT hand it to someone
ADEEHINNNPRRSTU Arthur Pendennis
ADEEHINNOPRTTTW paint the town red
ADEEHLMOORSSTTY the same old story
ADEEIIINNOSSTTZ desensitization
ADEEIIKRSSTTTTU strike attitudes
ADEEIILOPRRSSTV private soldiers
ADEEIIMMMNOOSSS Moses Maimonides
ADEEIIMNNORSTTU underestimation
ADEEIIMNNRRSSTU rudimentariness
ADEEIIMNOPRRSSU Monsieur de Paris
ADEEIINNNOOPSST opinionatedness
ADEEILMNORSTTVY demonstratively
ADEEIMMNNNNORSS mind one's manners
ADEEIMNNORSTTUV undemonstrative
ADEEIMNOORSTTTT it does not matter
ADEEKLLNNOOOPRV Leopold von Ranke
ADEEMNNNOOPSTUW put one's name down
ADEENNORSSSTUUV adventurousness
ADEFGHHIKNOORTT knight of the road
ADEFGHILMNOSSUW Flushing Meadows
ADEFGIIIKMNNRTY identifying mark
ADEFHIIILNORSTWW whistle for a wind
ADEFHIINORSTUVY a hive of industry
ADEFHIMNOPRSTUY Pyramid of the Sun
ADEFHKNOORRSSSU hours of darkness
ADEFHLMNOOORTWW woman of the world
ADEFHMMNNOPRSYY Manfred Symphony
ADEFIIIIKLLMNRW William Friedkin
ADEFIILLLLMMORR Millard Fillmore
ADEFIKMMMNNOSUU Museum of Mankind
ADEFILMNORRTUUU Our Mutual Friend
ADEFINNNOOOSTTU foundation stone
ADEFINNOOPRRRTU put in an order for
ADEGHHINNOPRRST right-hand person
ADEGHIILNPSSSTW pigs and whistles
ADEGHILNORRSTTW world-shattering
ADEGHIMNOPPRRSS grasshopper mind
ADEGIIILLLNOPRU Luigi Pirandello
ADEGIIILNNOOPST leading position
ADEGIIILNOORTTU Giulio Andreotti
ADEGIIIOPRRSTTT prestidigitator
ADEGILLNNOQRTUY grandiloquently
ADEGNNNOOSSSTTU stand to one's guns
ADEHHIIMMOPRRST hermaphroditism
ADEHHINNNOORSTW throw in one's hand
ADEHIIIKLLLLNOO in all likelihood
ADEHIIKNNRSSVYY Andrei Vyshinsky
ADEHIKNNOPRRSST Perth and Kinross
ADEHINNNOORRSSW draw in one's horns
ADEIIIILLMNORSW William Ironside
ADEIIJLNPRRSTUU jurisprudential
ADEIIKNNSSSTTTV St Kitts and Nevis
ADEIILNOPPRRSSS dispersal prison
ADEIIMMMOOOPTX Deo Optimo Maximo
ADEIKKLNNOOTTTY not take kindly to
ADEILNOOOSSSTWW sow one's wild oats
ADFGGHIILMNPSTY and pigs might fly
ADFGGHINNOOORTY good for anything
ADFGGIINOOORTTW Waiting For Godot
ADFGHIIKNNORRTW forward-thinking
ADFGIILNNOQRUUY qualifying round
ADFHHMMNOOORTTU from hand to mouth
ADGHIIILNPQSUUW washing-up liquid
ADGHIINNNOSTTTW notwithstanding
ADGHIMMNNOORRSU darning mushroom
ADHIMNNNOOSSTUU Hudson Mountains
ADHINOOOPRSTTTY Dorothy Pattison
ADIIMNNNOPSSTUU Pindus Mountains
ADINNNOOPPSSTTU stand upon points
AEEEEEEFHINQRTU The Faerie Queene
AEEEEEGHHLRSSTW grease the wheels

AEEEEEHKLRSSTVW	the weaker vessel
AEEEEEKLMMRSSTX	make less extreme
AEEEEEKORRRSTVV	reverse takeover
AEEEEFFKMORRTVY	make every effort
AEEEEFGHNOSSTTV	The Eve of St Agnes
AEEEEFHIKLNRRRT	Kathleen Ferrier
AEEEEFHNNORSSTT	feather one's nest
AEEEEGGILMORRST	Georges Lemaître
AEEEEGGLNORRTVY	George Trevelyan
AEEEEGIKLNPRSSU	pleasure-seeking
AEEEEGIPRRRSTTU	Pierre Trésaguet
AEEEEHHINNNSTVV	in seventh heaven
AEEEEHKLNOOSSTT	take to one's heels
AEEEEIILMNPRSTX	experimentalise
AEEEEIILMNPRTXZ	experimentalize
AEEEEILNNPRRRTU	entrepreneurial
AEEEEINNPRSSTTV	penetrativeness
AEEEEINPRRSSTTV	representatives
AEEEELNORSSTTTX	to a lesser extent
AEEEFFGGIIKMNOS	Siege of Mafeking
AEEEFFGHLOORSTV	the gloves are off
AEEEFFHHIKNOSTT	take the shine off
AEEEFFHIKLLLMOR	make life hell for
AEEEFFLLLNOORSV	fall over oneself
AEEEFFLNOORRSSW	forswear oneself
AEEEFGHHIKOTTTW	take the weight of
AEEEFGHIIINNPRT	a finger in the pie
AEEEFGHIILNNRTT	life-threatening
AEEEFGIILLNRSTV	everlasting life
AEEEFGIILNORSSV	give oneself airs
AEEEFGIIMNOTTUZ	time-zone fatigue
AEEEFGLNOOOSTUU	out of one's league
AEEEFHHILPRRSST	The Pearl Fishers
AEEEFHIIKNNNOSV	have one's knife in
AEEEFHIILLNNRST	Leni Riefenstahl
AEEEFHIKMORRTTT	take it from there
AEEEFHILMNNOOTV	In the Name of Love
AEEEFHINNRRTTUU	in the near future
AEEEFHINORRSTVY	Harvey Firestone
AEEEFHOORRRSTWW	the worse for wear
AEEEFHORRSSSTTW	stress of weather
AEEEFIKLLOOPPRW	keep a low profile
AEEEFILLNORSTUV	feel revulsion at
AEEEFILMMOPRSTT	Temple of Artemis
AEEEFKLLNNNOOSS	fall on one's knees
AEEEFKLLNNOOSST	fall to one's knees
AEEEFKLNNOOPSTU	take upon oneself
AEEEFLLLLORRTVW	fellow-traveller
AEEEGGINNOPPRSS	passenger pigeon
AEEEGGLNNOORRRV	governor-general
AEEEGGMNOOOSSTT	get someone's goat
AEEEGHHILNORTTT	in the altogether
AEEEGHHIMPRRTTU	high temperature
AEEEGHIIMNNRTTW	in agreement with
AEEEGHIMMMRSTUU	Hermitage Museum
AEEEGHIMNNRSTWY	Ernest Hemingway
AEEEGHINNOPRSST	parthenogenesis
AEEEGHMNRRSSTTU	measure strength
AEEEGIILMNNRRTV	trigeminal nerve
AEEEGIKLOOPPSTV	ask people to give
AEEEGILLMNNNSST	gentlemanliness
AEEEGILMNNNSSSS	meaninglessness
AEEEGILMPQRRSUU	square leg umpire
AEEEGILNNOPRTTY	potential energy
AEEEGILNNPPRRST	sleeping partner
AEEEGILNNRSSSTV	everlastingness
AEEEGIMNOPRSSST	spermatogenesis
AEEEGKNNOOSSSTT	get one's skates on
AEEEHHIKORSTTUW	Keith Waterhouse
AEEEHHMORRSTTTW	weather the storm
AEEEHIIKLLMORSW	Willie Shoemaker
AEEEHIIMMNORRST	immersion heater
AEEEHIIMNPPRSSV	misapprehensive
AEEEHILORSTTUXY	heterosexuality
AEEEHKMNOORSTTW	Smoke on the Water
AEEEHLNOOORSSTT	lose one's heart to
AEEEHMOPPPRRSTU	upper atmosphere
AEEEHORRRSSTTUW	wear the trousers
AEEEIIILMNORSSV	Olivier Messiaen
AEEEIIILMNPRSTX	experientialism
AEEEIIILNPRSTTX	experientialist
AEEEIILMMNPRSTX	experimentalism
AEEEIILMNPRSTTX	experimentalist
AEEEIIMNNOPRSST	in one's spare time
AEEEIIMNNOPRTTX	experimentation
AEEEIINNNSSTTTV	inattentiveness
AEEEIIPRRSSSSTV	passive resister
AEEEIKLMOQRRSTU	square kilometre
AEEEILMNPPRSSTU	supplementaries
AEEEILNQRRSTUWY	Squire Trelawney
AEEEIMNOPRRSSTX	extemporariness
AEEEINNRSSSSTUV	unassertiveness
AEEEKMNNOOOPSTU	take someone up on
AEEEKMOORRSTTUV	make overtures to
AEEELLLNNOOSTTW	tell one's own tale
AEEELMNOQRRSSSU	quarrelsomeness
AEEELMOPRRSSTUU	poulters' measure
AEEELNOPRSSSSTT	stateless person
AEEEMMOOPRRRTTU	room temperature
AEEEMNNRSTTTTUU	untrue statement
AEEEMNOPRRSSTUW	Weston-super-Mare
AEEFFHIORRSTTTW	of the first water
AEEFFHJMNOORSST	Thomas Jefferson
AEEFFMOPRSSTTTU	feast of trumpets
AEEFGGHIILNNRSS	sharing feelings
AEEFGGIILLLNSST	self-legislating
AEEFGHHNNOOOTUV	not have enough of
AEEFGHILLNNOOST	along the lines of
AEEFGHIMNNORRTT	the morning after
AEEFGHINORRSTTW	fearing the worst
AEEFGIILNNNORRS	infernal regions
AEEFGIKLNOPSSTY	style of speaking
AEEFGILNNNOORSY	lay one's finger on
AEEFGILNNRSSTUU	Augustin Fresnel
AEEFGIMNNRRSTTU	transfigurement
AEEFGINOPRSSWXY	way of expressing
AEEFHHLMOOOPRTT	Temple of Hathoor
AEEFHILLLLOTVYY	lily of the valley
	lily-of-the-valley
AEEFHILLMOSSTTU	Thales of Miletus
AEEFHNNOORRTTTW	On the Waterfront
AEEFIIKMNNOORST	seek information

AEEFIILLNOSSTWY Wassily Leontief
AEEFIILMNOPRSSS false impression
AEEFIILNNRSTTTU first-lieutenant
AEEFIILNOOPRSSS professionalise
AEEFIILNOOPRSSZ professionalize
AEEFIIMNORSSTTT Minister of State
AEEFILMNNSSSTTU self-sustainment
AEEFKKLOOOOPRTU keep a lookout for
AEEFLLLNOPRSSUW all-powerfulness
AEEFNOOOPRRTTWY power of attorney
AEEGGIILLMMORSW William Rees-Mogg
AEEGGIKMNOSSSTU make suggestions
AEEGGINNNORTUUY Annie Get Your Gun
AEEGHHIMORSTTTW go with the stream
AEEGHHLOOPPRTTY telephotography
AEEGHIINORSSSST raise one's sights
AEEGHIKLOPRRTTW tight-rope walker
AEEGHIKMNORSSTW make things worse
AEEGHINNNORSTTU sing another tune
AEEGHINOOSTTTWY easy to get on with
AEEGHLLMNOOSSTZ Thomson's gazelle
AEEGHMOORRRSTTU surrogate mother
AEEGHORRSSSTTUU Roget's Thesaurus
AEEGIIKLLMNPSST spelling mistake
AEEGIILNNPPRRSS springer spaniel
AEEGIILNORRTTVY interrogatively
AEEGIINORRSSTTT gastroenteritis
gastro-enteritis
AEEGIKMNNOPRSST on speaking terms
AEEGIMMNRSSSTUY measuring system
AEEGIMNOPRSSTTY operating system
AEEGIMNRRRTTUWZ Gewürztraminer
AEEGINNNORRSTUV turn in one's grave
AEEGLMNNNNOORTV non-governmental
AEEHHHIINRTTTWW whiter than white
AEEHHHILLMNORRT Herman Hollerith
AEEHHHILLNNOPPT phenolphthalein
AEEHHIILMNOPPST Mephistophelian
AEEHHIIMNNOTTWW The Woman in White
AEEHHIMNNOOSSTU the Mansion House
AEEHHJJNNOORSVY John Harvey-Jones
AEEHHJMNNNNORWY John Henry Newman
AEEHHKLOOORTTWY look the other way
AEEHIIKLLMNNSTW Kenneth Williams
AEEHIIKLMORSTTT that's more like it
AEEHIILNNOORSTT lie in one's throat
AEEHIIMNNOPPRSS misapprehension
AEEHIIMOPRSTTTW with time to spare
AEEHIKLNNOPRTUY phenylketonuria
AEEHILLLNOORTWW leather on willow
AEEHILMMNOOPRRY Holy Roman Empire
AEEHILNORRSSTTT in the last resort
AEEHIMNORRSTTTW remonstrate with
AEEHINNOOORSSTV have one's roots in
AEEHKLNOOPSTTUW slow on the uptake
AEEHMPPRSSSTXYY express sympathy
AEEIIINOORRTTXZ exteriorization
AEEIILLMMNNORRT Martin Niemöller
AEEIILMNOOPRSTT metropolitanise
AEEIILMNOOPRTTZ metropolitanize
AEEIILNNOPPRTTY plenipotentiary
AEEIILNOORRSTUV revolutionaries
AEEIILNRTTTTUXY intertextuality
AEEIIMNOOPRTTXZ extemporization
AEEIINOPRRSSTTV preservationist
AEEIKLNNOPRSSUV Nikolaus Pevsner
AEEIKMNOOSSSSSS kiss someone's ass
AEEILLMMNOOOPSS oil someone's palm
AEEILMNNNPRSTTU instrument panel
AEEILMNNOPPSTTU supplementation
AEEILMNOOPPRTTU perpetual motion
AEEILNNNOOPPRSS personal pension
AEEILNORRSSTTUU Russian roulette
AEEINNOPRSSTTTU unprotestantise
AEEINNOPRSTTTUZ unprotestantize
AEENNNOOOOPRSTT not open to reason
AEENNNOOPSSSSTU spontaneousness
AEFGGHJLOORRTUU go for the jugular
AEFGHHIILOQRTUY of higher quality
AEFGHHILLNOORRW harrowing of hell
AEFGHILNORRSTTT trial of strength
AEFGHIMOOORRSTT go for a short time
AEFGIIMNNOORRST resignation from
AEFHIILOOPSTTWY play footsie with
AEFHIJLOPSSSUUV Flavius Josephus
AEFHKKMOOORRSTW make short work of
AEFIIIILLMNNSTY infinitesimally
AEFIILLMNNOSTTU most influential
AEFIILLMNOSSTTU self-stimulation
AEFIILMNOOPRSSS professionalism
AEFIKNNSSSTWYYZ Stefan Wyszynski
AEFILNNNOOOPRSS non-professional
AEGGGIIILLNORTV give a grilling to
AEGGGLNNNOOOOVY Yvonne Goolagong
AEGGHHINNNOOTUV not having enough
AEGGHIIKLLOOTTU go out like a light
AEGGHILLNOORSTY shooting gallery
AEGGHINNNOORSST sing another song
AEGGIIKLMNOORVY Giorgiy Malenkov
AEGGINNNOOOSWWY going one's own way
AEGHHIIMNNORSTT Nottinghamshire
AEGHHIIOOPRRRST historiographer
AEGHHILNNNOSSTT nothing less than
AEGHIIIINNORSTV have its origin in
AEGHIIOORTTTUVY give authority to
AEGHINNNOOPRRST harp on one string
AEGIJKLMNNNNRSU Jurgen Klinsmann
AEGIKLNNOORTUWY now you're talking
AEGILNNOPPRRSTU learning support
AEGINNOPPPRSTTU Puppet on a String
AEHHIINOPPSSSTW wish happiness to
AEHHIIOPPRSSTTY physiotherapist
AEHHLLORSTTTTUW thrust to the wall
AEHIIILLLMRSSWY Shirley Williams
AEHKLOOORTTTTUW work out the total
AEHLLNNOOOPRTTY Anthony Trollope
AEHLLNOOPPRTTUY put on the payroll
AEIIIMMNPSSTUVY passive immunity
AEIILLNNNNOTTUY unintentionally
AEIILLNOOPPRSTY prepositionally
AEIILMNNRSSTTTU instrumentalist
AEIILMNNRSTTTUY instrumentality

AEIILMOPRSTTTWY military two-step
AEIILNOOPRSTTYZ proselytization
AEIIMNNNORSTTTU instrumentation
AEILMOOPPRRSTTY stop temporarily
AEILNOOOPPRRTTY proportionately
AEIMMNNNOORSTUU Mourne Mountains
AELNNNOOOPPRRSU personal pronoun
AFFHILLORSTUUYY yours faithfully
AFFIIIILLOPPPPR Fra Filippo Lippi
AFFILMOORRSSTTT from first to last
AFGIIKMNNNOOPRT non-profit-making
AFGINOOOOPRRRSW arrow-poison frog
AFHKLNOOORRTWWW Frank W Woolworth
AFMMNNOOOOPRTTU poor man of mutton
AGGHHHINORSSTTU sharing thoughts
AGGHIINOOSTTUWY go without saying
AGHHIILLLLNSSYY shilly-shallying
AGHHILLMOOOPSTT ophthalmologist
AGHIILNNNOPTTUW without planning
AGHIKKLLNOOOSTW look who's talking
AGHIKNNOOORTTWW know a thing or two
AGIIILLLMMNSTUU multilingualism
AGIIJKMNOORRTWY working majority
AGIIMMNNORTTTUY grant immunity to
AHHIIJLNOOPPSSU John Philip Sousa
AHHILLMOOOPPRSY moral philosophy
AHHINOOOPPRSSTT anthroposophist
AHIILMNOORRSTUY military honours
AHLLMNOOOPRRSTW Worrall Thompson
AIIIILLNOQRSTUY inquisitorially
AIIIJMMNNNOORTY join in matrimony
AIIIMNNOPRSTTTU it is unimportant
AIILLLMNOPSSUUY pusillanimously
AIILLNOOPPSSTUY suppositionally
AIKNNNNOQTTUUWY unknown quantity

B

BBBBEEFGIIILRTT flibbertigibbet
BBBDEEFLOOOOTUY blue-footed booby
BBCDDEEEEINOTVY not be deceived by
BBCDEEEGHLOORTT cobbled together
BBCEEILMNOSSSTU combustibleness
BBCHKKOOOOORRYY by hook or by crook
BBDDEEHHHLOOOOY hobbledehoyhood
BBDEEEGHINOSTTT send to the gibbet
BBDEEEHIILNORTT bite on the bridle
BBDEELLMMNOSSUY Summoned by Bells
BBEEEEINNNNOOST bee in one's bonnet
BBEEEHHILLOTTTW hit below the belt
BBEEEHILLNOTTTU bite on the bullet
BBEEFHLLMOORTTU bolt from the blue
BCCCEEEEIILRSXY exercise bicycle
BCCCEEEIIMNRTTU cubic centimetre
BCCEEEEHILNNOST the noble science
BCCEEEFHHIILTTY The Bicycle Thief
BCCEEEIILMNNOSU bioluminescence
BCCEGHIMNNNRRUU number-crunching
BCCEHINOORRSSTU cross the Rubicon
BCCEMMNNNOOOSTY by common consent
BCDDDEELLNOOOSS cold-bloodedness
BCDDEEEGIINNORS being considered
BCDDEEGHHIOSSTT the bitch goddess
BCDDEGIOOOPRRSS proscribed goods
BCDDGILLLNOORUY bloodcurdlingly
BCDEEEEFFIMNORT become different
BCDEEEEHHINNSST behind the scenes
BCDEEEILMMOOORS become more solid
BCDEGIIILNOSTUY building society
BCDEHIOORRSSSTT Scottish Borders
BCDEIIILRSTTTUY destructibility
BCEEEEEGNOORRSZ Ebenezer Scrooge
BCEEEEFGIKLORTW leg before wicket
BCEEEEGHILMRRSU limburger cheese
BCEEEEGKLLMOOPR Pembroke College
BCEEEEHLOPRRRST brothel-creepers
BCEEEEIMMMMORTT committee member
BCEEEELMNOORRTT Roberto Clemente
BCEEEEMOPRRSSSS Bessemer process
BCEEEFFGILNORTY benefit of clergy
BCEEEFGHIIOPRTT tip of the iceberg
BCEEEFGIMNRRTUU Recumbent Figure
BCEEEFIIKNNSSST sickness benefit
BCEEEGILLNNOORT longicorn beetle
BCEEEHILMOOOSTT become hostile to
BCEEEILMNNOOSTV become insolvent
BCEEEILNPSSSSTU susceptibleness
BCEEFFGHJOOSTTU go off the subject
BCEEFFGOOORTTYY Geoffrey Boycott
BCEEFHIKLNNRRUY Huckleberry Finn
BCEEGILLNNOOORS Robinson College
BCEEHIILLMNOTWW combine well with
BCEEIIILLNNNOVZ Vincenzo Bellini
BCEEIILMPRSSTUV visible spectrum
BCEEINORSSSTTUV obstructiveness
BCEHHIMNOORSSUY Hieronymus Bosch
BCEHIIIIINOSTTX exhibitionistic
BCEIIILMNOPTTTY contemptibility
BCEIIILMOPRSSTY compressibility
BCEIIKLNNOOOSSV block one's vision
BCEIKMNOOOPRSSY proboscis monkey
BCGIIIIILNORRTY incorrigibility
BCIIKNNOOORSTTU instruction book
BDDEEEFILRSSTUY Tess Durbeyfield
BDDEEEGHOORRSTV Theodor Svedberg
BDDEEIILMNNOTUY Double Indemnity
BDDEEIKLOORSTUW work double tides
BDDEGHIIOOOPRST prohibited goods
BDEEEELLNOOSSTV do one's level best
BDEEEFFHMOORTUY buy the freedom of
BDEEEFILNNPRSUW funnel-web spider
BDEEEGHILLMOSTT goldsmith beetle
BDEEFIIIILNNSTY indefensibility
BDEEGOOOOORTTTU too good to be true
BDEEHILLNOOPRSS hold responsible
BDEEHLMORRSTUUU shout blue murder
BDEEHMNOOPRSTUU Prometheus Bound
BDEFGILLNOOOORW Robin Goodfellow
BDEGIIIIILNSTTY indigestibility
BDEGIINNOORSTWZ bring down to size
BDEHHILLOOORRTT Theodor Billroth
BDEHHILNOOSTWWW how the wind blows
BDEHIIILNNNOTWW Blowin' in the Wind

BDIIIILLNOSSTUY indissolubility
BEEEEEEFNNORRSV never before seen
BEEEEFILNNNOOSS feel in one's bones
BEEEEGILNNSSSTU genteel business
BEEEEGILNPRSSTV Steven Spielberg
BEEEEHIILNNSTWW in between whiles
BEEEEHIILNPRRRS irreprehensible
BEEEEHLMNNOPRTU telephone number
BEEEFFFHINOORTT for the benefit of
BEEEFGHIIMNORTT for the time being
BEEEFIILLNNORSY fire in one's belly
BEEEGGHIIILLRTW whirligig beetle
BEEEGGNOOORRRST George Robertson
BEEEGHILNNOSTTT tighten one's belt
BEEEHILLNORRSTV Neville Brothers
BEEEHKMNNOOPSTU keep one's thumb on
BEEELMNOORSSSTU troublesomeness
BEEEMNOOPRSTTUU butter someone up
BEEFFGHHIORSTUV give the brush-off
BEEFHHINORSTTUV The Birth of Venus
BEEFIKNOOORTUWY before you know it
BEEFKLORRSTTTUY butterfly stroke
BEEGGIJLOORRSSU Jorge Luis Borges
BEEGHHIMPSTTUUV give the thumbs-up
BEEGHIILNNORSSU neighbourliness
BEEGHIILNOORRTZ Lorenzo Ghiberti
BEEGIILOOORSSUU Louise Bourgeois
BEEGIJLNORRSSUU Julius Rosenberg
BEEHIIINOPRSSTV prohibitiveness
BEEHIIMMRRSSTVY shiver my timbers
BEEHILNNOPPRRTU born in the purple
BEEHIMNOORRRRST Herbert Morrison
BEEHLLOORRSTTUW Robert Southwell
BEEIIIILRRRSTVY irreversibility
BEEINNORSSSTUUV unobtrusiveness
BEFGINOOOSSSTUU go out of business
BEFILLLOPRTUUWY powerfully built
BEGGHHHIILRSTTT the bright lights
BEGGHIINNOOOTTW to be going on with
BEGHILNOOORSTTU troubleshooting
BEGIIIIILLLNTTY intelligibility
BEGIIJLNOSSTUUV Justus von Liebig
BEHHIJKLNOOOSTW John Wilkes Booth
BEHILMNORSSTTUW twirl one's thumbs
BEHIMNNOORTTUWY with money to burn
BEHLNNNOOOORSWW blow one's own horn
BEIIIIILMRRSSTY irremissibility
BEIIIIILRRSSTTY irresistibility
BEIIILMNNOOSSTU Benito Mussolini
BEILLLOOORTTUUY I'll trouble you to
BELLLORSSTUUWYY slowly but surely
BENNNOOPRRTTTUU Burton-upon-Trent
BFGHIINNOORTTTU nothing for it but
BFMMOOOOOPRTTTT from top to bottom
BGGGHIIILNNORTT bringing to light

C

CCCDEEEIIMNOSST domestic science
CCCDEEFIIKNNORT confidence trick
CCCEEEHILNORSTT electrotechnics
CCCEEEILLOOPRST collector's piece
CCCEEEILNRRRTTU electric current
CCCEEEIMNNNOOSY conscience money
CCCEEEIMNOPRSTU computer science
CCCEEEINNOPRRST eccentric person
CCCEEFINNOOOPRS conscience-proof
CCCEEIILMNOORRT microelectronic
CCCEEIILMNORSTU electronic music
CCCEFIIKLLNOORT Frick Collection
CCCEGIIIKNNOQUV quick-conceiving
CCCEIILNORSTUUY Security Council
CCCIIIMNOPRRSTU circumscription
CCDDDEEEILNOORU Crocodile Dundee
CCDDDEHHILNOOOS second childhood
CCDDEEELNNNOOSS send condolences
CCDDEEGILNNNOSY condescendingly
CCDEEEEFHIIQRTU certified cheque
CCDEEEEFINNOORV videoconference
CCDEEEEILOPRRTW electric-powered
CCDEEEFINNNOOOV convenience food
CCDEEGHIMNNOOST The Second Coming
CCDEEHILNNORRRS Children's Corner
CCDEEINNOORRRTU under correction
CCDEEINOPRSTUUV superconductive
CCDEFGIILNORRTU correcting fluid
CCDEIINOOOPRTUV voice production
CCDEILNNORRRSUU run circles round
CCDIILMNOOOOPST cold composition
CCEEEEFFIINPPTY fifty pence piece
CCEEEEFGIMNOORU economic refugee
CCEEEEFILNRRSTT Fertile Crescent
CCEEEEFLNNOQSSU self-consequence
CCEEEEFNNOPRRSS press conference
CCEEEEGLLLORRTU college lecturer
CCEEEEHHINQRSSU Chinese chequers
CCEEEEILMMOSTTT select committee
CCEEEEINNOPRRTT reception centre
CCEEEELMNNOPSTX complex sentence
CCEEEENRRRRSUVY reserve currency
CCEEEFINNNOOQSU in consequence of
CCEEEFNNNOOOQSU of no consequence
CCEEEHHLOOSSTTT close to the chest
CCEEEHHNOOPPRSS phosphorescence
CCEEEHIIKPPPSTU pick up the pieces
CCEEEHILOOPRRTT electrophoretic
CCEEEIMNOQRSTUU musique concrète
CCEEEINNOSSSTUV consecutiveness
CCEEEMNOOOPRRRT Emperor Concerto
CCEEFFFIILNSSUY self-sufficiency
CCEEFHKLOORRTTU clerk of the court
CCEEFIIINOPRSTT perfectionistic
CCEEFILNOOOPRUU Council of Europe
CCEEGHIILOPSSTT telescopic sight
CCEEGIINNNNORTT interconnecting
CCEEGIMORRSSTUY cosmetic surgery
CCEEHHLNNOORUUV luncheon voucher
CCEEIIKNORSSTTT rocket scientist
CCEEIINNNNOORTT interconnection
CCEEIMMNNORTTUY community centre
CCEEIMNOORSSTUY consumer society
CCEFHKKKNOOOSST knock the socks of
CCEFILNNOOSSSUU unconscious self

	unselfconscious
CCEFMNOOOPRTTTU	contempt of court
CCEGHHIIKNOTTUW	without checking
CCEGHIIKNNNOPRS	no spring chicken
CCEGIILOOOOSTTX	ecotoxicologist
CCEIILLNOOORSSU	collision course
CCEIILNNOOSSTUY	conscientiously
CCEIIOORRSTTUUU	circuitous route
CCEINNNOOSSSSUU	unconsciousness
CCEINNOOPSSSSUU	conspicuousness
CCHIIILNNOOSTUV	Luchino Visconti
CCHILMMNOOOSTUY	community school
CCIILLNOOPRRUVY	Privy Councillor
CCIILNNOOPSSUUY	inconspicuously
CCIIMNNOORSSTTU	misconstruction
CCNNOORRRSSTUUY	cross-country run
CDDDFINOOORSSSU	discord of sounds
CDDEEEEEINNNPRT	interdependence
CDDEEEELNNPRTUY	unprecedentedly
CDDEEEFIIKLRRSU	Frederick Delius
CDDEEEHIIMNOTVY	The Divine Comedy
CDDEEEILNORSVWY	newly discovered
CDDEEFGIMOORRTV	get divorced from
CDDEEFIIILLNPSS	self-disciplined
CDDEEGIILLNOOSU	Golden Delicious
	golden delicious
CDDEEOOPPRRTTUX	exported product
CDDEFILLNOOSTTU	Sutton Coldfield
CDDEFINOOSSUUUX	Eudoxus of Cnidus
CDDEIIMMMNNOTUY	community-minded
CDDEIINNORSSSUU	under discussion
CDDEIMOOPPRRTTU	imported product
CDDFFFIIILNOTTU	difficult to find
CDDGIIINNNOOOOT	in good condition
CDDIILOORSSSUUU	Diodorus Siculus
CDEEEEEFLNNSSSS	defencelessness
CDEEEEEKNORSVWY	every second week
CDEEEEFIKRRRSTV	Frederick Treves
CDEEEEFLNNRSSST	self-centredness
CDEEEEGHIILNRSV	Received English
CDEEEEHILNNORRV	hold in reverence
CDEEEEHILPRSTTW	wield the sceptre
CDEEEEIIINNNPRX	inexperienced in
CDEEEEINNNORTTT	detention centre
CDEEEEINNNPRSTU	superintendence
CDEEEEKLNNOSTTY	keenly contested
CDEEEFFGILLLNOU	Nuffield College
CDEEEFFIIILLNOR	Federico Fellini
CDEEEFFIILORRVY	delivery officer
CDEEEFGHIILNRRS	Friedrich Engels
CDEEEFGHLLOORRT	Hertford College
CDEEEFIIMMNNOTT	definite comment
CDEEEFIIMNNOOPS	piece of one's mind
CDEEEFILNOSSSST	close-fistedness
CDEEEGHIMNNRUVY	needing very much
CDEEEGIIILNNSTV	listening device
CDEEEHHILPRSTUW	whited sepulchre
CDEEEHIIKLNRRSS	Erskine Childers
CDEEEHMMSSSTUUU	Deutsches Museum
CDEEEHNNORRTTUU	under the counter
	under-the-counter
CDEEEIINNPRRSWW	windscreen-wiper
CDEEEIINPRSSSTV	descriptiveness
CDEEEIKNOOPPRST	pocket one's pride
CDEEEILMOPSSTTU	complete studies
CDEEEINNNPRSTUY	superintendency
CDEEEINRSSSTTUV	destructiveness
CDEEELLOORSSSTT	settle old scores
CDEEENNPSSSSTUU	unsuspectedness
CDEEFGHIKMNOOTY	The King of Comedy
CDEEFHIMMNOOOTT	come to the mind of
CDEEFHINNOOORTW	one of the in-crowd
CDEEFIILNORSTYY	friendly society
CDEEFILLPRSSTUY	disrespectfully
CDEEFILNORSSTTU	self-destruction
CDEEFIOORSSSTUU	course of studies
CDEEGHIMNNNOPRU	uncomprehending
CDEEGIILNNOOTTV	declining to vote
CDEEGIILNORRTVV	revolving credit
CDEEGKLMMNNOOOW	common knowledge
CDEEIIILNNSSUVZ	uncivilizedness
CDEEIIINNSSSTTV	distinctiveness
CDEEIIKNQSSTTUW	quick-wittedness
CDEEIINRRSSTUVY	service industry
CDEEILNNORSSSUU	incredulousness
CDEEIMNNOOPSSSU	compendiousness
CDEFHIIILNORRST	Linford Christie
CDEFHIMNOOSSTUU	The Sound of Music
CDEFIIIINNNOSTT	fine distinction
CDEFIIMMOOOSSTT	soft commodities
CDEFIMNNNOOOSSU	focus one's mind on
CDEGHHLOOPPSTYY	depth psychology
CDEGHIKLLNOOUVW	Ludwig von Köchel
CDEGIIIMMNNOOSS	decommissioning
CDEGIIKLLMMNOOT	till kingdom come
CDEGIILNNOOORST	endocrinologist
CDEGILNNOOPRRSY	correspondingly
CDEGINNOOOPRRST	corresponding to
CDEHILNORSSTTUY	clothes industry
CDEIIIJNNOSSSUU	injudiciousness
CDEILMNNOOPRSUU	under compulsion
CDELOOPRRSSUWZZ	crossword puzzle
CDFFFIILOOTTUUY	out of difficulty
CDGIINOOPRSSSUU	discussion group
CDHIILNOPRSTUUU	pulchritudinous
CDHIOORRSSSSTWW	cross swords with
CDIIIINOSSSTUUV	vicissitudinous
CDIILNNOOSSTUUY	discontinuously
CEEEEEEJPPRRRSS	jeepers creepers
CEEEEEHINNPPRTY	threepenny piece
CEEEEEHLRRSSTTT	Chester-le-Street
CEEEEFFIINNSSTV	ineffectiveness
CEEEEFHINNOPRST	in the presence of
CEEEEFHINORRTTW	with reference to
CEEEEFINNNNORRT	non-interference
CEEEEGHINOORTVV	give the once-over
CEEEEGIIKLNPPRR	Peregrine Pickle
CEEEEHHHIRSTTTW	The Three Witches
CEEEEHHLNOOPPST	the chosen people
CEEEEIILLNOPRRR	Pierre Corneille
CEEEELNOOOSSSTY	close one's eyes to
CEEEFFGHNOOSSTT	get off one's chest

CEEEFIIOPPRSTVW prospective wife
CEEEFLLMNOSSSUX flex one's muscles
CEEEFLNORRSSSUU resourcefulness
CEEEGHILORRSSTU Gloucestershire
CEEEGHLLMNOOORT Homerton College
CEEEGHLLOORSTTY closely together
CEEEGHLNORSSSTT stretch one's legs
CEEEGILLLLRSTTY little grey cells
CEEEGINNNOOSSTV give one's consent
CEEEGLNOOPPRSSS People's Congress
CEEEHHIINPRSSSW Chinese whispers
CEEEHIIJNORSSTV join the services
CEEEHIILLNPRTTT The Little Prince
CEEEHIILNNRSTWZ Wiener schnitzel
CEEEHIIMNOPRSSV comprehensivise
CEEEHIIMNOPRSVZ comprehensivize
CEEEHIJLNNORTWW jewel in the crown
CEEEHIKKLNOPSSU kick up one's heels
CEEEHILMNOPRSVY comprehensively
CEEEHILOOPRRSST electrophoresis
CEEEHIMORRSSTTY stereochemistry
CEEEHINOPRRSSTT in other respects
CEEEHLMMNOOOPPT the common people
CEEEIIKMPQQRTUU emperick qutique
CEEEIILLNNOSUUV nouvelle cuisine
CEEEIIMNOPSSTTV competitiveness
CEEEIIMNORSTTUX excrementitious
CEEEIINORRRSSTU resurrectionise
CEEEIINORRRSTUZ resurrectionize
CEEEIKLNNOOPSST line one's pockets
CEEEILOPRRSTTVY retrospectively
CEEEIMNNOORSSSU ceremoniousness
CEEEINPQRSSSTUU picturesqueness
CEEFGGOOORRSSST Cross of St George
CEEFGHIIMOPSTTU get up to mischief
CEEFGHINNOORRST fight ones corner
CEEFGIIILMNNORS in foreign climes
CEEFGIILMNOORST to foreign climes
CEEFHIIIKMNNOTT in the nick of time
CEEFHKKLOORRSTW clerk of the works
CEEFINNOPRRSSTU perfunctoriness
CEEGHHIJLNNORSS John Schlesinger
CEEGHIILRSSTUVX exclusive rights
CEEGIIMMNOOOTTT go into committee
CEEHHHRRSTTTTTU stretch the truth
CEEHHIINOORRSTW white rhinoceros
CEEHHIMNORSTTUW not much the wiser
CEEHHINOPRRRSTW Christopher Wren
CEEHIIIMMNOOPST noisomemephitic
CEEHIIJLRRSSTUU Julius Streicher
CEEHIIMNNNOOPRS incomprehension
CEEHIIMNOSSSSUV mischievousness
CEEHIINPPRTTTUU put in the picture
CEEHIIORRRSSTTT Scottish terrier
CEEHIKLNNOPRTUY phenylketonuric
CEEHIKLORSSTTTU stick to the rules
CEEHIMMOORSTTTW come to terms with
CEEHIMNOORTTUWY without ceremony
CEEHINNOPRRSSTU puss in the corner
CEEHKMNOOPRSTTU put the mockers on
CEEHLLNNOPPSSUU pull one's punches
CEEHLMNNOORSSST Loch Ness monster
CEEHMMOOOOORSTT come home to roost
CEEIIINOPRSSSTX expressionistic
CEEIIKNNNOOSSST stick one's nose in
CEEIIMNNOPSSSUU impecuniousness
CEEIINNRSSSTTUV instructiveness
CEEIINOPPRSSSTU precipitousness
CEEIINORRRSSTTU resurrectionist
CEEIKNOPRRSTTVY poverty stricken
poverty-stricken
CEEILMNNOORSUUY unceremoniously
CEEIMNNNOOOOSTW come into one's own
CEEIMNNOOOPRTTY protection money
CEEIMNNOPSSSTUV consumptiveness
CEEIMOOPRRSSSTU osmotic pressure
CEEINNNOOSSSTTU contentiousness
CEEINOPPRSSSSUU perspicuousness
CEFGIIINNNOOORT in recognition of
CEFGILMMNOORTTY Montgomery Clift
CEFHHLLOOOOTTUW out of whole cloth
CEFHIIIINNOTTVY in the vicinity of
CEFHILLNOORSTTW with self-control
CEFHMNOOOPRSTTW show contempt for
CEFHNOOORTTTUUY out of the country
CEFIIILNPPRRSST first principles
CEGGHILNOOOORST geochronologist
CEGHHIINNQRSTTU thirst-quenching
CEGHIIILNNOSTTU ethnolinguistic
CEGHIIMOOPRSTTW come to grips with
CEGHILMNOOOSTUY ethnomusicology
CEGIIILNNORSTUU neurolinguistic
CEGIIKMNNNORSSS morning sickness
CEGIIMMMNOSSTUW swimming costume
CEGIKNNOOSSSTTU stick to one's guns
CEGILNOOPPSSSTY Synoptic Gospels
CEGINNNOORSSSUU incongruousness
CEHIILMMNNOOOST common in the soil
CEHINNOOPRSSSTY post-synchronise
CEHINNOOPRSSTYZ post-synchronize
CEIIIIMNOPRSSST impressionistic
CEIIINNORRSSTTU insurrectionist
CEIIKLMQRSSSTUY Mistress Quickly
CEIILNNOPSSSTUU punctiliousness
CEIINNOPSSSTTUU intussusception
CEIMMNNNOOOPSST non compos mentis
CEKLLNOOPPSSSUU pull up one's socks
CFGHHHLOOOOSTTU school of thought
CFGHIIIKNNRSSTY cry stinking fish
CFGIINNOOORRTUY country of origin
CFIIMMNOOOOSSTU out of commission
CGGHIIMNNNOOOTT coming to nothing
CGHMNOOOOOTTUUY Too Much Too Young
CGIIIMNNNOOOTTT not coming into it
CGIILMNOOPSSSTU gossip columnist
CHHHINNOORRSTUY ornithorhynchus
CINOOOPPRSTTTUY opportunity cost

D

DDDEHIIMOORSUXY sodium hydroxide
DDEEEEEFFGMOORR degree of freedom
DDEEEEFFGHNOOPT go off the deep end

DDEEEFHILMNOORW middle of nowhere
DDEEEGHHHOOPRST the Good Shepherd
DDEEEGHHILLOPVY highly-developed
DDEEEGHILOORSTV deliver the goods
DDEEEGIILNPRRUV underprivileged
DDEEEGIKNOOOPRR keep in good order
DDEEEHIKNORRRVW Hendrik Verwoerd
DDEEEIILNRSSTTY disinterestedly
DDEEFGINNOPQSUU queen of puddings
DDEEGGHIINOSSTU dodging the issue
DDEEGHIILMNNSST light-mindedness
DDEEGHIIMNNRSST right-mindedness
DDEEHHNNOORRSUU one hundred hours
DDEEHINNORSTUWW snowed under with
DDEEINOORRRSSUV nervous disorder
DDEFGHLNOOOPSSU slough of despond
DDEFIMNNNOOSSSU soundness of mind
DDEGHIIINNSSTUU undistinguished
DDEHHNOORRSTUUW two hundred hours
DDEHILNOORTTUWW world without end
DDEIILLMNNOOUWW mullioned window
DEEEEEFGILNPSST deepest feelings
DEEEEEGHILNOTTV give the needle to
DEEEEFGKLNOORTW tree of knowledge
DEEEEGHOPRRSSTT pressed together
DEEEEGIIMNNRSSV divine messenger
DEEEEGILNORRRTV golden retriever
DEEEEHHKOOORRTT Theodore Roethke
DEEEEHNOPRRSTUY superheterodyne
DEEEEIILMNNTTTY identity element
DEEEEILPRRSSVXY express delivery
DEEEELMNOOPRTVV overdevelopment
DEEEENNOOPRSTTT pretend not to see
DEEEFGHIILRRSTW Wilfred Thesiger
DEEEFGIILMNNRST self-determining
DEEEFGIMOPRRSTT Gottfried Semper
DEEEFHHIOPRSSTT ship of the desert
DEEEFHIJNORRTTU Return of the Jedi
DEEEFIINNOSSTTY sense of identity
DEEEFIINOPRSSXX fixed expression
DEEEFINPRSTTUUX put six feet under
DEEEGHNNOOOPRTT get the drop on one
DEEEGKLNNOOOSTW to one's knowledge
DEEEHHIMNNOPSST Stephen Sondheim
DEEEHIIRRSSSTTW the Weird Sisters
DEEEHLLLOPRSTUW well-upholstered
DEEEIILMMNRRSTU delirium tremens
DEEEIINOPSSSTUX expeditiousness
DEEEILMOPRRSTWY Lord Peter Wimsey
DEEELMMNNOPRTUY underemployment
DEEFFGGHNOORTTU get off the ground
DEEFGHIINSSSTTT tight-fistedness
DEEFGHILOORRTVW give the world for
DEEFGIIINNNRSTT find interesting
DEEFHHLMOORRSTU from the shoulder
DEEFIIINOOPRSVV deprive of vision
DEEFILMNNORRSTY on friendly terms
DEEFINOOORRSSSU odoriferousness
DEEFLMNOOOOPRRY money for old rope
DEEGGHHILNOORTT holding together
DEEGGIMOOOPPRSU Georges Pompidou
DEEGHHIILNNORST holding the reins
DEEGHHIINNOTTWW Gone With the Wind
Gone with the Wind
DEEGHIIMNPRSSTX Midnight Express
DEEGHILNNOORTTW get on in the world
DEEGHIMNOORSSTW Weedon Grossmith
DEEGIIKLLMNNOOW Willem De Kooning
DEEHHIIIMSTTTWW swim with the tide
DEEHHLNOORSSTTU shoulder-shotten
DEEHIINNNOORSST thorn in one's side
DEEIIIILNOPRSSTT stilpnosiderite
DEEIILNOPRSSSTW low-spiritedness
DEEIILNOPRSSTUY serendipitously
DEEIKKLLNORRSUW unskilled worker
DEEILNNPRRTTUUY uninterruptedly
DEEMNNOOOORSTUW drown someone out
DEFFIINOOOPRTTY proof of identity
DEFGGHIIKLNNORT forked lightning
DEFGHIIKLLNOSTY Idylls of the King
DEFGHIILNNOSTTW fling to the winds
DEFGHILOPRSSTTY softly-sprighted
DEFGHINNOORSSTU shift one's ground
DEFHHIINOOOPRTZ dip of the horizon
DEFHHIKLNOORTTW think the world of
DEFHIIMNNOORSTU fourth dimension
DEFHINOOORRTTTW not the word for it
DEFHLNOOOOPRTTW on top of the world
DEFIMMNNOOORSTT Simon de Montfort
DEFNNOOOOPSTTUW put one's foot down
DEGHHINNNOORTTU thin on the ground
DEGHIIIMNNNORST in one's right mind
DEGHIIIMNNSSTTU distinguishment
DEGHIILLMOORSTV Oliver Goldsmith
DEGIIIKNNORRSSU serious drinking
DEGIILNNOOPRSSU gird up one's loins
DEHHIIMOPRRSTYY hyperthyroidism
DEHHINOORSTTTWW throw to the winds
DEHINOOPRRSTTUW put in other words
DEIIILLMNNOSSTU disillusionment
DEIILLNOOOPPRRT ill-proportioned
DEIILOOOPPUVVXX vox populi vox Dei
DEIIMMNOOOOPPTV doppio movimento
DEIIMNOOOPPRRST misproportioned
DEIINNORSSSSTUU industriousness
DEIINNRRSSSTUUY sunrise industry
DEIKMNNNNOOOSWW know one's own mind
DFHIIKLNNOOTTUW I wouldn't think of
DFILMMNOOOOOSSW Wisdom of Solomon
DGHHIINNOOOTTTW with nothing to do
DGHIIILNOOPPRSW idol-worshipping
DGHIINNNOOORVYZ Nizhniy Novgorod
DIILLMNOSTTUUUY multitudinously

E

EEEEEHHIMNRSTTW the Three Wise Men
EEEEEHHIMRRSTTT three times three
EEEEEHIQRRSTTUV quite the reverse
EEEEEHNNNORRTVV on the never-never
EEEEFGIIMNOOSVV give someone five
EEEEGGGILLNORRV George Grenville
EEEEGGHNOORSVVY George von Hevesy

EEEEGGINNORTVWY	give new energy to
EEEEGHHINOORTTV	one over the eight
EEEEGHILLMNOOSV	give someone hell
EEEEGHIMNOORSST	see someone right
EEEEGHLNOORSTUY	heterogeneously
EEEEGHMOORTTUVY	you've got me there
EEEEGINNNPRRTTV	prevent entering
EEEEGNNNOORSSTV	get on one's nerves
EEEEHHIORRSUWWY	Wish You Were Here
EEEEHHIRRSSSTTT	The Three Sisters
EEEEHIILMRRSTWW	Meriwether Lewis
EEEEHILMMORRRTW	Mortimer Wheeler
EEEEHILMOORSTVW	somewhere to live
EEEEHILNNOPSSST	Elsie Stephenson
EEEEHIMNNOOSSTT	in someone's teeth
EEEEHKLLLNRTTWY	Henry Kettlewell
EEEEHMNOOOSSTTT	to someone's teeth
EEEEIINNNPSSSVX	inexpensiveness
EEEEIMOOPPRSTTX	opposite extreme
EEEEKNNOOPRSTUV	put over one's knee
EEEELMNORRSSSSS	remorselessness
EEEENNOORRSSUVY	run one's eyes over
EEEFFFHHILOORRT	for the life of her
EEEFFFILNOOPRSU	offer up one's life
EEEFFGHHILORRTT	right off the reel
EEEFFIINNNOSSSV	inoffensiveness
EEEFGGHINORTTTU	get the finger out
EEEFGIIKOOPRRSV	Sergei Prokofiev
EEEFGILNNOORSST	forget one's lines
EEEFGILNORSSTVY	self-sovereignty
EEEFHHHLNOOOSTT	hot on the heels of
EEEFHIINNORSTTT	in the interest of
EEEFHIKNNNOOSTT	think on one's feet
EEEFHILOOPSSTTV	Lives of the Poets
EEEFHLLNOTTTTUX	to the full extent
EEEFHNNOOORRSTW	none the worse for
EEEFHOOPSTTTUUY	put the eyes out of
EEEFNNOOOSSSSTU	out of one's senses
EEEGHHINOPRTTUV	give up the throne
EEEGHILLNNORSTT	there's no telling
EEEGIIMNNOPRRSV	evening primrose
EEEGIIMNOOOSTTV	give it to someone
EEEGILNNNNRSSTU	unrelentingness
EEEGILORRRSSTVY	retrogressively
EEEGINOPRRSSSSV	progressiveness
EEEGKMNNOOPSTUY	get one's monkey up
EEEGLLLMNOOPSSU	pull someone's leg
EEEHIILLMNNOTVW	Willem Einthoven
EEEHIINPPRRRSTT	interpretership
EEEHIJLMNNOORUV	juvenile hormone
EEEHIJLOPPRSSTY	Joseph Priestley
EEEHIKMNORSTTWY	The New York Times
EEEHIKNNOOPRSST	keep one's shirt on
EEEHLMNNOOSSSUW	unwholesomeness
EEEHMNOORRSSTVY	every mother's son
EEEIIMMOORRSSST	stereoisomerism
EEEIIMNOOPRSSST	permission to see
EEEIINOPRRSSTTX	trite expression
EEEIINOPRSSSTTU	repetitiousness
EEEILLLLNNRTTTT	Little Nell Trent
EEEILLNNNNOOOST	not on one's nellie
EEEIMNNOOOPRSSW	in someone's power
EEEINNNOSSSSTTU	sententiousness
EEEINNOPRSSSTTU	pretentiousness
EEELNOPPRSSSSSU	purposelessness
EEEMNOPSSSSTTUU	tempestuousness
EEFFFHHIILMOORT	for the life of him
EEFFFHILNOORSST	shift for oneself
EEFFGHIKNOORSTT	king of the forest
EEFFHHHIIORSSTT	I Shot the Sheriff
EEFFHHNOOORSTTU	front of the house
EEFFILLNORSSTWY	win effortlessly
EEFFILNOOORSSTY	story of one's life
EEFGGIIIMRSTWZZ	Mister Fezziwigg
EEFGHHIKNOORTTT	think of together
EEFGHHIOOPRSTTT	fight to the ropes
EEFGHHNNOORSTTT	on the strength of
EEFGHIINOPRRSTT	The Rite of Spring
EEFGHILNOOPSTTU	slip of the tongue
EEFGHIOORSTTTTW	get the worst of it
EEFGHNOORRSTTTW	tower of strength
EEFGILLMNOORSSS	smelling of roses
EEFGILMMOORRTUV	remove guilt from
EEFGILNNOOOOSST	lose one's footing
EEFGINNNOOPRSTU	put one's finger on
EEFHHHILNNORSTT	thorn in the flesh
EEFHIILNOORRTTW	throw into relief
EEFHMMNOOPRSTTU	spur of the moment
	spur-of-the-moment
EEFHNNOOPRSSTUU	push one's fortune
EEFIILMNOOPSTTU	put some life into
EEFILLLMNOSSSUU	mellifluousness
EEFILNNNNOORSTU	turn in on oneself
EEFLLMMNOOOOPST	Temple of Solomon
EEFLNOPRSSSSUUU	superfluousness
EEGGGHIMOORRSST	George Grossmith
EEGGGIINOSSSTUV	give suggestions
EEGGHIIMNNNNOOSS	eggs in moonshine
EEGGHIKNOORRTTW	working together
EEGGHINOPRTTTTU	putting together
EEGHHHILOOSTTTU	To the Lighthouse
EEGHHHINNOOORSS	on one's high horse
EEGHHLNOSSSSTTU	thoughtlessness
EEGHHOOPRRRRTUV	Hugh Trevor-Roper
EEGHIILLNNSSTVY	seventy shilling
EEGHIILMNNOPTTT	in the melting-pot
EEGHILMNNOOOPST	phenomenologist
EEGHINNOOSSSSTT	set one's sights on
EEGHINNOPSTTTTU	putting the stone
EEGHINNORSSSTUU	unrighteousness
EEGHINOORSSTTTU	get one's shirt out
EEGIIILNORRSSSU	irreligiousness
EEGIIINNNOOOPSV	give one's opinion
EEGIIINOPSTTTVV	positive vetting
EEGIILNNNRSTTUY	uninterestingly
EEGIIMNNNRSSTTU	unremittingness
EEGIINNORSSSTUV	vertiginousness
EEGINNOPPRSSSSU	unprepossessing
EEGINOOPPRSSTUV	give one's support
EEHHHILORSTTTWW	worth the whistle
EEHHIIKLMSSTTTY	the sky's the limit
EEHHILNOORTTTWW	throw in the towel

EEHIIILLMNSTTWZ Wilhelm Steinitz
EEHIIKOPPRRRRSY Yorkshire Ripper
EEHIINOOORSSSVW show one's ivories
EEHIJOOPPSSTTTU just the opposite
EEIIIINNQSSSTUV inquisitiveness
EEIIIMNNNORSTTV interventionism
EEIIINNNORSTTTV interventionist
EEIILNNOORRTTTU trinitrotoluene
EEIIMNNOSSTTTUW Women's Institute
EEIIMNOORRSSSTU meritoriousness
EEIINNNNNOORTTV non-intervention
EEIKLMNPRRSSSTY sprinkler system
EEILLMMNOOPRSSY promise solemnly
EEILNNOPRSTTUUY unpretentiously
EEIMNNRSSTTTTUV investment trust
EEINNNOOPPRSSTU inopportuneness
EFFHHIILNRSSTTU in the first flush
EFGGHIILNOPTTTY Flight into Egypt
EFGGIINNNORSSUV unforgivingness
EFGHHHIIKNOPTTW knight of the whip
EFGHHIKNOOPSTTT knight of the post
EFGHIIIKNNORSST finishing stroke
EFGHIIJLNORTUWY junior-flyweight
EFGHIILNOORTVWW overflowing with
EFGHIMNNNOOORTY Money for Nothing
EFGHINNNOORTTUU out of the running
EFGIIKLLLMNOSTY Killing Me Softly
EFHHHIMOOOPRSTT shoot from the hip
EFIIIIILNNPSTTV split infinitive
EFIILOOQRSSSTUU fossil turquoise
EFIINNOOOPSTTTU put one's foot in it
EFINNNOOOPRRTTU point of no return
EGGGHIIMNNOSTTV get things moving
EGGHHHHINORTTTU through the night
EGGHIIIKLNNRSTT lightning strike
EGGHIILMMNNRSTU summer lightning
EGGHILMOOOOPRST geomorphologist
EGGLNOOOSSSTTUU slog one's guts out
EGHHHHIIOPSSTTT hit the high spots
EGHHILNOOPRSTTT plight one's troth
EGHIIIKLNNORSTV shrinking violet
EGHIIJLLNOOPSTU Joseph Guillotin
EGHILLNOORRSSTT Rollright Stones
EGHIMMNNNOORRST the morn's morning
EGIILNNNOQSTUUY unquestioningly
EGKNOOORSSTTUUW work one's guts out
EHHHIJOOPRSTTWW Joseph Whitworth
EHHILNOOORSTTTW throw to the lions
EHIILLMOOPPRTTU photomultiplier
EHIINOOQSTTTUUW without question
EHIJMNOPPRSTUYY Jupiter Symphony
EHILLNNNOOPRSSU pull in one's horns
EHINORRSSSTTTUW trustworthiness
EIIIMNOOPPRSSTU superimposition
EIILLMMNNOOORTT montmorillonite
EIILLNORSSSSTUU illustriousness
EIILOPRRSSTTUUY surreptitiously
EIILOPRSSSTTUUY superstitiously
EJLLLLMNOOORRTY Jelly Roll Morton

F

FFGHIINNORSSSTU soft furnishings
FGGHHHHILOOTTUY thought highly of
FGHHIIIKLNNSTUW wishful thinking
FINOOOOOPPRRTTU out of proportion

G

GHHIIIINNNOTTTW with nothing in it
GHHIIIKNNOTTTUW without thinking

H

HHIMMNNNNOOOTTTU month in month out